Small Business Sourcebook

ISSN 0883-3397

Small Business Sourcebook

The Entrepreneur's Resource

THIRTIETH EDITION

Volume 3

Specific Small Business Profiles
General Small Business Topics

(Entries 18673-30407)

Sonya D. Hill
Project Editor

GALE
CENGAGE Learning

Detroit • New York • San Francisco • New Haven, Conn • Waterville, Maine • London

GALE
CENGAGE Learning®

Small Business Sourcebook, 30th edition

Project Editor: Sonya D. Hill

Editorial Support Services: Charles Beaumont

Composition and Electronic Prepress: Gary Leach

Manufacturing: Rita Wimberley

For product information and technology assistance, contact us at
Gale Customer Support, 1-800-877-4253.
For permission to use material from this text or product,
submit all requests online at **www.cengage.com/permissions.**
Further permissions questions can be emailed to
permissionrequest@cengage.com

Gale
27500 Drake Rd.
Farmington Hills, MI, 48331-3535

ISBN-13: 978-1-4144-7957-6 (set)
ISBN-10: 1-4144-7957-3 (set)
ISBN-13: 978-1-4144-7958-3 (vol. 1)
ISBN-10: 1-4144-7958-1 (vol. 1)
ISBN-13: 978-1-4144-7959-0 (vol. 2)
ISBN-10: 1-4144-7959-X (vol. 2)
ISBN-13: 978-1-4144-7960-6 (vol. 3)
ISBN-10: 1-4144-7960-3 (vol. 3)
ISBN-13: 978-1-4144-7961-3 (vol. 4)
ISBN-10: 1-4144-7961-1 (vol. 4)
ISBN-13: 978-1-4144-7962-0 (vol. 5)
ISBN-10: 1-4144-7962-X (vol. 5)
ISBN-13: 978-1-4144-7963-7 (vol. 6)
ISBN-10: 1-4144-7963-8 (vol. 6)

ISSN 0883-3397

Printed in the United States of America
1 2 3 4 5   17 16 15 14 13

Contents

The appeal of small business ownership remains perpetually entrenched in American culture as one of the most viable avenues for achieving the American Dream. To many entrepreneurs going into business for themselves represents financial independence, an increased sense of identity and self-worth, and the fulfillment of personal goals. Small business owners strive to make their mark in today's competitive marketplace by establishing healthy businesses that can, over time, become legacies handed down from one generation to the next. Entrepreneurs from each generation tackle the obstacles and adversities of the current business and economic climate to test their business savvy and generate opportunities. Today's entrepreneurs face many of the problems of their predecessors, as well as some distinctly new challenges.

With the rightsizing, downsizing, and reorganization of corporate America, many individuals have decided to confront the risks of developing and operating their own businesses. Small business ownership is rapidly becoming a viable alternative to what is perceived as an equally unstable corporate environment. These entrepreneurs, many of whom have firsthand experience with the problems and inefficiencies inherent in today's large corporations, seek to improve upon an archaic business model and to capitalize on their own ingenuity and strengths. Led by their zeal, many would-be entrepreneurs let their desire, drive, and determination overshadow the need for business knowledge and skill. Ironically, aids in obtaining these components of entrepreneurial success are widely available, easily accessible, and often free of charge.

Small Business Sourcebook (SBS) is a six-volume annotated guide to more than 21,310 listings of live and print sources of information designed to facilitate the start-up, development, and growth of specific small businesses, as well as over 26,280 similar listings on general small business topics. An additional 12,367 state-specific listings and over 2,220 U.S. federal government agencies and offices specializing in small business issues, programs, and assistance are also included. *SBS* covers 340 specific small business profiles and 99 general small business topics.

Features of This Edition

This edition of *Small Business Sourcebook* has been revised and updated, incorporating thousand of changes to names, addresses, contacts, and descriptions of listings from the previous edition.

Contents and Arrangement

The geographical scope of *SBS* encompasses the United States and Canada, with expanded coverage for resources pertaining to international trade and for resources that have a U.S. or Canadian distributor or contact. Internet sites that are maintained outside of the U.S. and Canada are also included if they contain relevant information for North American small businesses. Resources that do not relate specifically to small businesses are generally not included.

The information presented in *SBS* is grouped within four sections: Specific Small Business Profiles, General Small Business Topics, State Listings, and Federal Government Assistance. Detailed outlines of these sections may be found in the Users' Guide following this Introduction. Also included is a Master Index to Volumes 1 through 6.

Specific Small Business Profiles This section includes the following types of resources: start-up information, associations and other organizations, educational programs, directories of educational programs, reference works, sources of supply, statistical sources, trade periodicals, videocassettes/audiocassettes, trade shows and conventions, consultants, franchises and business opportunities, computerized databases, computer systems/software, Internet databases, libraries, and research centers-all arranged by business type. Entries range from Accounting Service to Word Processing Service, and include such businesses as Airbag Replacement Service Centers, Computer Consulting, Damage Restoration Service, and Web Site Design.

General Small Business Topics This section offers such resources as associations, books, periodicals, articles, pamphlets, educational programs, directories of educational programs, videocassettes/audiocassettes, trade shows and conventions, consultants, computerized databases, Internet databases, software, libraries, and research centers, arranged alphabetically by business topic.

State Listings Entries include government, academic, and commercial agencies and organizations, as well as select coverage of relevant state-specific publications; listings are arranged alphabetically by state, territory, and Canadian province. Some examples include small business development consultants, educational programs, financing and loan programs, better business bureaus, and chambers of commerce.

Federal Government Assistance Listings specializing in small business issues, programs, assistance, and polic-yare arranged alphabetically by U.S. government agency or office; regional or branch offices are listed alphabetically by state.

Master Index All entries in Volumes 1 through 6 are arranged in one alphabetic index for convenience.

Entries in *SBS* include (as appropriate andavailable):

- Organization, institution, or product name
- Contact information, including contact name, address and phone, toll-free, and fax numbers
- Author/editor, date(s), and frequency
- Availability, including price
- Brief description of purpose, services, or content
- Company and/or personal E-mail addresses
- Web site addresses

SBS also features the following:

Guide to Publishers—An alphabetic listing of 2,470 companies, associations, institutions, and individuals that publish the periodicals, directories, guidebooks, and other publications noted in the Small Business Profiles and General Topics sections. Users are provided with full contact information, including address, phone, fax,and e-mail and URL when available. The Guide to Publishers facilitates contact with publishers and provides a one- stop resource for valuable information.

Method of Compilation

SBS was compiled by consulting small business experts and entrepreneurs, as well as a variety of resources, including direct contact with the associations, organizations, and agencies through telephone surveys, Internet research, or through materials provided by those listees; government resources; and data obtained from other relevant Gale directories. *SBS* was reviewed by a team of small business advisors, all of whom have numerous years of expertise in small business counseling and identification of small business information resources. The last and perhaps most important resource we utilize is direct contact with our readers, who provide valuable comments and suggestions to improve our publication. *SBS* relies on these comprehensive market contacts to provide today's entrepreneurs with relevant, current, and accurate informationon all aspects of small business.

Available in Electronic Formats

Licensing. Small Business Sourcebook is available for licensing. The complete database is provided in a fielded format and is deliverable on such media as disk or CD-ROM. For more information, contact Gale's Business Development Group at1-800-877-GALE, or visit our website at www.gale.com/bizdev.

Comments and Suggestions Welcome

Associations, agencies, business firms, publishers, and other organizations that provide assistance and information to the small business community are encouraged to submit material about their programs, activities, services, or products. Comments and suggestions from users of this directory are also welcomed and appreciated. Please contact:

Project Editor
Small Business Sourcebook
Gale, Cengage Learning
27500 Drake Rd.
Farmington Hills, MI 48331-3535
Phone: (248) 699-4253
Fax: (248) 699-8070
E-mail: BusinessProductsgale.com
URL: www.gale.com

Small Business Sourcebook (*SBS*) provides information in a variety of forms and presentations for comprehensive coverage and ease of use. The directory contains four parts within two volumes:

- Specific Small Business Profiles
- General Small Business Topics
- State Listings
- Federal Government Assistance

Information on specific businesses is arranged by type of business; the many general topics that are of interest to the owners, operators, or managers of all small businesses are grouped in a separate section for added convenience. Users should consult the various sections to benefit fully from the information *SBS* offers. For example, an entrepreneur with a talent or interest in the culinary arts could peruse a number of specific small business profiles, such as Restaurant, Catering, Cooking School, Specialty Food/Wine Shop, Bakery/Doughnut Shop, Healthy Restaurant, or Candy/Chocolate Store. Secondly, the General Small Business Topics section could be consulted for any applicable subjects, such as Service Industry, Retailing, Franchising, and other relevant topics. Then, the appropriate state within the State Listings section would offer area programs and offices providing information and support to small businesses, including venture capital firms and small business development consultants. Finally, the Federal Government Assistance section could supply relevant government offices, such as procurement contacts.

Features Included in Volumes 1 through 3

List of Small Business Profiles. This list provides an alphabetic outline of the small businesses profiled, with cross-references for related profiles and for alternate names by which businesses may be identified. The page number for each profile is indicated.

Standard Industrial Classification (SIC) Codes for Profiled Small Businesses. This section lists four-digit SIC codes and corresponding classification descriptions for the small businesses profiled in this edition. The SIC system,

which organizes businesses by type, is a product of the Statistical Policy Division of the U.S. Office of Management and Budget. Statistical data produced by government, public, and private organizations is usually categorized according to SIC codes, thereby facilitating the collection, comparison, and analysis of data as well as providing a uniform method for presenting statistical information. Hence, knowing the SIC code for a particular small business increases access and the use of a variety of statistical data from many sources.

Guide to Publishers. This resource lists alphabetically the companies, associations, institutions, and individuals that publish the periodicals, directories, guidebooks, and other publications noted in the "Small Business Profiles" and "General Topics" sections. Users are provided with full contact information, including address, phone, fax, and e-mail and URL when available. The "Guide" facilitates contact with publishers and provides a one-stop resource for valuable information.

Glossary of Small Business Terms. This glossary defines nearly 400 small business terms, including financial, governmental, insurance, procurement, technical, and general business definitions. Cross-references and acronyms are also provided.

Small Business Profiles A-Z. A total of 340 small businesses is represented in volumes 1 through 3. Profiles are listed alphabetically by business name. Entries within each profile are arranged alphabetically by resource type, within up to 17 subheadings. These subheadings are detailed below:

- *Start-up Information*—Includes periodical articles, books, manuals, book excerpts, kits, and other sources of information. Entries offer title; publisher; address; phone, fax, toll-free numbers; company e-mail and URL addresses; and a description. Bibliographic data is provided for cited periodical articles whenever possible.

- *Associations and Other Oganizations*—Includes trade and professional associations whose members gather and disseminate information of interest to small business owners. Entries offer the association's name; address; phone, toll-free and fax numbers; company e-mail address; contact name; purpose and objective; a description of membership; telecommunication services; and a listing of its publications, including publishing frequency.

- **Educational Programs**—Includes university and college programs, schools, training opportunities, association seminars, correspondence courses, and other educational programs.Entries offer name of program or institution, sponsor name, address, phone, toll-free and fax numbers, e-mail and URL addresses; and description of program.

- **Directories of Educational Programs**—Includes directories and other publications that list educational programs. Entries offer name of publication; publisher name, address, and phone, toll-free and fax numbers; editor; frequency or date of publication; price; and description of contents, including directory arrangement and indexes.

- **Reference Works**—Includes handbooks, manuals, textbooks, guides, directories, dictionaries, encyclopedias, and other published reference materials. Entries offer name of publication; publisher name, address, and phone, toll-free and fax numbers; e-mail and URL addresses; and, when available, name of author or editor, publication year or frequency, and price. A brief description is often featured.

- **Sources of Supply**—Includes buyer's guides,directories, special issues of periodicals, and other publications that list sources of equipment, supplies, and services related to the operation of the profiled small business. Entries offer publication name; publisher name, address, and phone, toll-free and fax numbers; e-mail and URL addresses; and, when available, editor's name, frequency or publication year, and price. A brief description of the publication, including directory arrangement and indexes, is often provided.

- **Statistical Sources**—Includes books, reports, pamphlets, and other sources of statistical data of interest to an owner, operator or manager of the profiled small business, such as wage, salary, and compensation data; financial and operating ratios; prices and costs; demographics; and other statistical information. Entries offer publication/data source name; publisher (if applicable); address; phone, toll-free and fax numbers of data source; publication date or frequency; and price. A brief description of the publication/data source is often provided.

- **Trade Periodicals**—Includes trade journals, newsletters, magazines, and other serials that offer information about the management and operation of the profiled small business. Such periodicals often contain industry news; trends and developments; reviews; articles about new equipment and supplies;

and other information related to business operations. Entries offer publication name; publisher name, address, phone, toll-free and fax numbers, and e-mail and URL addresses; editor name; publication frequency; andprice. A brief description of the publication's content is also included, when known.

- **Videocassettes/Audiocassettes**—Includes videocassettes, audiocassettes, and other audiovisual media offering information on the profiled small business. Entries offer program title; distributor name, address, phone, toll-free and fax numbers, and e-mail and URL addresses; description of program; release date; price; and format(s).

- **Trade Shows and Conventions**—Includes tradeshows, exhibitions, expositions, conventions, and other industry meetings that provide prospective and existing business owners with the opportunity to meet and exchange information with their peers, review commercial exhibits, establish business or sales contacts, and attend educational programs. Entries offer event name; sponsor or management company name, address, phone, toll-free and fax numbers, and e-mail and URL addresses; a description of the event, including audience, frequency, principal exhibits, and dates and locations of event for as many years ahead as provided by the event's sponsor.

- **Consultants**—Includes consultants and consulting organizations that provide services specifically related to the profiled small business. Entries offer individual consultant or consulting organization name, address, and phone, toll-free and fax numbers; company and individual e-mail addresses; and a brief description of consulting services. (For e-mail and URL addresses, see the Small Business Development Consultants subheadings in the State Listings section in Volume 2.)

- **Franchises and Business Opportunities**—Includes companies granting franchise licenses for enterprises falling within the scope of the profiled small business, as well as other non-franchised business opportunities that operate within a given network or system. Entries offer franchise name, address, phone, toll-free and fax numbers, and e-mail and URL addresses, as well as a description of the franchise or business opportunity, which has been expanded whenever possible to include the number of existing franchises, the founding date of the franchise, franchise fees, equity capital requirements, royalty fees, any managerial assistance offered, and available training.

- **Computerized Databases**—Includes diskettes, magnetic tapes, CD-ROMs, online systems, and other computer-readable databases. Entries offer database name; producer name, address, phone, toll-free and fax numbers, e-mail and URL addresses; description; and available format(s), including vendor name.

(Many university and public libraries offer online information retrieval services that provide searches of databases, including those listed in this category.)

- **Computer Systems/Software**—Includes software and computerized business systems designed to assist in the operation of the profiled small business. Entries offer name of the software or system; publisher name, address, phone, toll-free and fax-numbers; price; and description.

- **Libraries**—Includes libraries and special collections that contain material especially applicable to the profiled small business. Entries offer library or collection name; parent organization (where applicable); address; phone, toll-free and fax numbers; e-mail and URL addresses; contact name and title; scope of collection; and description of holdings, subscriptions, and services.

- **Research Centers**—Includes university-related and independently operated research institutes and information centers that generate, through their research programs, data related to the operation of the profiled small business. Also listed are associations and other business-related organizations that conduct research programs. Entries offer name of organization; address; phone, toll-free and fax numbers; company web site address; contact name and personal e-mail; a description of principal fields of research or services; publications, including title and frequency; and related conferences.

Features Included in Volumes 2 through 6

General Small Business Topics. This section offers chapters on different topics in the operation of any small business, for example, venture capital and other funding, or compensation. Chapters are listed alphabetically by small business topic; entries within each chapter are arranged alphabetically, within up to 14 subheadings, by resource type:

- **Associations and Other Organizations**—Includes trade and professional associations that gather and disseminate information of interest to small business owners. Entries offer the association's name; address; phone, toll-free and fax numbers; organization e-mail and URL addresses; contact name; purpose and objectives; a description of membership; telecommunication services; and a listing of its publications, including publishing frequency.

- **Educational Programs**—Includes university and college programs, schools, training opportunities, association seminars, correspondence courses, and other educational programs. Entries offer name of program or institution, sponsor name, address, phone, toll-free and fax numbers, e-mail and URL addresses, and description of program.

- **Directories of Educational Programs**—Includes directories and other publications that list educational programs. Entries offer name of publication; publisher name, address, phone, toll-free and fax numbers, and e-mail and URL addresses; editor; frequency or date of publication; price; and description of contents, including arrangement and indexes.

- **Reference Works**—Includes articles, handbooks, manuals, textbooks, guides, directories, dictionaries, encyclopedias, and other published reference materials. Entries offer title of article, including bibliographic information; name of publication; publisher name, address, phone, toll-free and fax numbers, and e-mail and URL addresses; and, when available, name of author or editor, publication year or frequency, and price. A brief description is often featured.

- **Sources of Supply**—Includes buyer's guides, directories, special issues of periodicals, and other publications that list sources of equipment, supplies, and services. Entries offer publication name; publisher name, address, phone, toll-free and fax numbers, and e-mail and URL addresses; editor's name, frequency or publication year, price, and a brief description of the publication, when available.

- **Statistical Sources**—Includes books, reports, pamphlets, and other sources of statistical data of interest to an owner, operator, or manager of a small business, such as wage, salary, and compensation data; financial and operating ratios; prices and costs; demographics; and other statistical information. Entries offer publication/data source name; publisher (if applicable); address; phone, toll-free and fax numbers of data source; publication date or frequency; and price. A brief description is often provided.

- **Trade Periodicals**—Includes journals, newsletters, magazines, and other serials. Entries offer name of publication; publisher name, address, phone, toll-free and fax numbers, and e-mail and URL addresses; and name of editor, frequency, and price. A brief description of the periodical's content is included when known.

- **Videocassettes/Audiocassettes**—Includes videocassettes, audiocassettes, and other audiovisual media. Entries offer program title; distributor name, address, phone, toll-free and fax numbers, and e-mail and URL addresses; price; description of program; release date; and format(s).

- **Trade Shows and Conventions**—Includes trade shows, exhibitions, expositions, seminars, and conventions. Entries offer event name; sponsor or management company name, address, phone, toll-free and fax numbers, and e-mail and URL addresses; frequency of event; and dates and locations of the event for as many years ahead as known.

- **Consultants**—Includes consultants and consulting organizations. Entries offer individual consultant or-consulting organization name, address, and phone, toll-free and fax numbers; company and individual e-mail addresses; and a brief description of consulting services. (See also Consultants in the State Listings section.)

- **Computerized Databases**—Includes diskettes, CD-ROMs, magnetic tape, online systems and other computer-readable databases. Entries offer database name; producer, address, phone, toll-free and fax numbers, and e-mail and URL addresses; description; and available format(s), including vendor name. (Many university and public libraries offer online information retrieval services that provide searches of databases, including those listed in this category.)

- **Computer Systems/Software**—Includes software and computerized business systems. Entries offer name of the software or system; publisher name, ad-dress, phone, toll-free and fax numbers, and e-mail and URL addresses; price; and description.

- **Libraries**—Includes libraries and special collections that contain material applicable to the small business topic. Entries offer library or collection name, parent organization (where applicable), address, phone and fax numbers, e-mail and URL addresses, scope of collection, and description of holdings and services.

- **Research Centers**— Includes university-related and independently operated research institutes and information centers that generate, through their research programs, data related to specific small business topics. Entries offer name of organization, address, phone, toll-free and fax numbers, e-mail and URL addresses, a description of principal fields of research or services, and related conferences.

State Listings. This section lists various sources of information and assistance available within given states, ter-ritories, and Canadian provinces; entries include governmen-tal, academic, and commercial agencies, and are arranged alphabetically within up to 15 subheadings by resource type:

- **Small Business Development Center Lead Of-fice**— Includes the lead small business development center (SBDC) for each state.

- **Small Business Development Centers**—Includes any additional small business development centers (SBDC) in the state, territory, or province. SBDCs provide support services to small businesses, includ-ing individual counseling, seminars, conferences, and learning center activities.

- **Small Business Assistance Programs**—Includes state small business development offices and other programs offering assistance to small businesses.

- **SCORE Offices**—Includes SCORE office(s) for each state. The Service Corps of Retired Executives As-sociation (SCORE), a volunteer program sponsored by the Small Business Administration, offers counsel-ing, workshops, and seminars across the U.S. for small business entrepreneurs.

- **Better Business Bureaus**—Includes various better business bureaus within each state. By becoming a member of the local Better Business Bureau, a small business owner can increase the prestige and cred-ibility of his or her business within the community, as well as make valuable business contacts.

- **Chambers of Commerce**—Includes various chambers of commerce within each state. Chambers of Commerce are valuable sources of small business advice and information; often, local chambers sponsor SCORE counseling several times per month for a small fee, seminars, conferences, and other workshops to its members. Also, by becoming a member of the local Chamber of Commerce, a small business owner can increase the prestige and cred-ibility of his or herbusiness within the community, as well as make valuable business contacts.

- **Minority Business Assistance Programs**—Includes minority business development centers and other sources of assistance for minority-owned business.

- **Financing and Loan Programs**—Includes venture capital firms, small business investment companies (SBIC), minority enterprise small business investment companies (MESBIC), and other programs that provide funding to qualified small businesses.

- **Procurement Assistance Programs**—Includes state services such as counseling, set-asides, and sheltered-market bidding, which are designed to aid small businesses in bidding on government contracts.

- **Incubators/Research and Technology Parks**— Includes small business incubators, which provide newly established small business owners with work sites, business services, training, and consultation; also includes research and technology parks, which sponsor research and facilitate commercialization of new technologies.

- **Educational Programs**—Includes university and col-lege programs, as well as those sponsored by other organizations that offer degree, nondegree, certificate, and correspondence programs in entrepreneurship and in small business development.

- **Legislative Assistance**—Includes committees, subcommittees, and joint committees of each state's senate and house of representatives that are concerned with small business issues and regulations.

- **Consultants**—Includes consultants and consulting firms offering expertise in small business development.

- **Publications**—Includes publications related to small business operations within the profiled state.

- **Publishers**—Includes publishers operating in or for the small business arena within the profiled state.

Federal Government Assistance. This section lists federal government agencies and offices, many with additional listings for specific offices, as well as regional or district branches. Main agencies or offices are listed alphabetically; regional, branch, ordistrict offices are listed after each main office or agency.

Master Index. This index provides an alphabetic listing of all entries contained in Volumes 1 through 6. Citations are referenced by their entry numbers. Publication titles are rendered in italics.

Acknowledgements

The editors would like to extend sincere thanks to the following members of the Small Business Sourcebook advisory board for their expert guidance, recommendations, and suggestions for the ongoing development of this title:

Susan C. Awe
Assistant Director,
William J. Parish Memorial Business Library

Jill Clever
Business Technology Specialist,
Toledo-Lucas County Public Library

Jules Matsoff
District Manager,
Service Corps of Retired Executives (SCORE) Milwaukee
  Chapter

Ken MacKenzie
President,
Southeast Business Appraisal

The editors would also like to thank the individuals from associations and other organizations who provided information for the compilation of this directory.

List of Small Business Profiles

This list is an outline of the 341 small businesses profiled in this edition of Small Business Sourcebook. The beginning page number of each profile is provided. For convenience, this index also provides cross-references to small businesses known by alternate names, businesses contained within other small business profiles, and synonymous or related businesses.

Standard Industrial Classification (SIC) Codes for Profiled Small Businesses

Included here are the four-digit SIC codes and corresponding classification descriptions for the businesses profiled in this edition. The SIC system, which organizes businesses by type, is a product of the Statistical Policy Division of the U.S. Office of Management and Budget. Statistical data produced by government, public, and private organizations usually are categorized according to SIC codes, thereby facilitating the collection, comparison, and analysis of data as well as providing a uniform method for presenting statistical information. Hence, knowing the SIC code for a particular small business increases the access to, and the use of, a variety of statistical data from many sources. The following SIC codes were obtained from the 1987 edition of the Standard Industrial Classification Manual, the most recent version available. (The term "nec" stands for "not elsewhere classified.")

Accounting Service

7291   Tax return preparation services

8721   Accounting, auditing, and bookkeeping services

Adult Day Care Center

8322   Individual and family social services (includes adult day carecenters)

Advertising Service

7311   Advertising agencies (includes advertising consultants)

7312   Outdoor advertising agencies

7313   Radio, television, and publishers' advertising representatives

7319   Advertising, nec

7331   Direct mail advertising services

8999   Services, nec (includes advertising copywriters)

Airbag Replacement Service Centers

7538   General automotive repair shops

7539   Automotive repair shops, nec

Air Charter Service

4512   Air transportation, scheduled (includes air cargo and passenger carriers)

4513   Air courier services

4522   Air transportation, nonscheduled (includes charter service)

Air-conditioning/Heating and Cooling Contractor

1711   Plumbing, heating, and air-conditioning contractors

Air Purification/Cleaning Service

7699   Repair shops and related services, nec (includes furnace cleaning service)

Ambulance Service

4119   Local passenger transportation, nec (includes ambulance service, road)

4522   Air transportation, nonscheduled (includes ambulance service, air)

Amusement Arcade

7993   Coin-operated amusement devices

Amusement/Water Park

7996   Amusement parks

7999   Amusement and recreation services, nec (includes waterslides and wave pools)

Animal Breeder

0279   Animal specialties, nec (includes kennels, breeding and raising own stock)

0752   Animal specialty services, except veterinary (includes breeding of animals other than farm animals)

Animal Clinic

0742   Veterinary service for animal specialties (includes animal hospitals for pets and other animals)

Antique Shop

5932   Used merchandise stores (includes retail antique stores)

Air Purification/Cleaning Service

7641   Reupholstery and furniture repair (includes antique furniture repair and restoration)

7699   Repair shops and related services, nec (includes antique repair and restoration, except furniture)

Apartment Locating Service

6531   Real Estate Agents and Managers

Appliance Store

5722   Household appliance stores

Appraisal Service

7389   Business services, nec (includes appraisers, except real estate)

6531   Real estate agents and managers (includes appraisers, realestate)

Aquarium Maintenance/Leasing Service

7359   Equipment rental and leasing, nec

8999   Services, nec

Archery/Target/Shooting Range

7999   Amusement and recreation services, nec (includes archery ranges, shooting galleries, shooting ranges, and trap-shooting facilities, except membership)

Architectural Restoration/Conservation

8712   Architectural Services

Art Gallery

5932   Used merchandise stores (includes retailers of art objects)

| 5999 | Miscellaneous retail stores, nec (includes art dealers) |
| 8412 | Museums and art galleries (includes noncommercial art galleries) |

Art Supplies Store

| 5999 | Miscellaneous retail stores, nec (includes retail artists' supplies and materials stores) |

Assisted Living Facilities

8051	Skilled nursing care facilities (includes extended care facilities and skilled nursing homes)
8052	Intermediate care facilities (includes intermediate care nursing homes)
8059	Nursing and personal care facilities, nec (includes rest homeswith health care)

Association Management Service

8611	Business associations
8621	Professional membership organizations
8631	Labor unions and similar labor organizations
8641	Civic, social, and fraternal associations
8699	Membership organizations, nec
8741	Management services (does not include operating staff)

Auctioneer

5154	Livestock (includes wholesale livestock auctioning)
5999	Miscellaneous retail stores, nec (includes retail general merchandise auction rooms)
7389	Business services, nec (includes auctioneering services)

Auto Supply Store

| 5531 | Auto and home supply stores |

Automobile Detailing/Painting Service

| 7532 | Automotive paint shops |

| 7542 | Carwashes (includes detailing, cleaning and polishing, new autos on a contract or fee basis; washing and polishing, automotive; waxing and polishing, automotive) |

Automobile/Truck Leasing Service

7513	Truck rental and leasing, without drivers
7514	Passenger car rental, without drivers
7515	Passenger car leasing, without drivers

Baby Store

| 5999 | Miscellaneous retail stores, nec (includes retail baby) |

Bagel Shop

| 2051 | Bread and other bakery products, except cookies and crackers (includes bagels) |
| 5461 | Retail bakeries (includes retail bagel stores) |

Bait and Tackle Shop

| 5941 | Sporting goods stores and bicycle shops (includes bait and tackle shops and fishing equipment, retail) |

Bakery/Doughnut Shop

| 5461 | Retail bakeries |

Bar/Cocktail Lounge

| 5813 | Drinking places alcoholic beverages (includes bars, cocktail lounges, saloons, tap rooms, taverns, and like establishments) |

Beauty Supply Center

| 5087 | Service establishment equipment and supplies (includes wholesale barber shop and beauty parlor equipment and supplies) |

Bed and Breakfast Operation

| 7011 | Hotels and motels (includes bed and breakfast inns) |

Beekeeping

| 0279 | Animal specialties, nec (includes apiaries and bee farms) |

Beeper/Paging Service

| 4812 | Radiotelephone communications (includes beeper and paging services) |

Bicycle Shop

| 5941 | Sporting goods stores and bicycle shops |
| 7699 | Repair shops and related services, nec (includes bicycle repair shops) |

Billiards Hall

| 7999 | Amusement and recreation services, nec (includes billiard parlors) |

Blacktop Surfacing Business

| 1771 | Concrete work (includes blacktop work: private driveways and private parking areas contractors) |

Blind Cleaning/Installation

| 2431 | Millwork (includes wood blinds and shutters) |
| 2591 | Drapery hardware and window blinds and shades |

Body Care Shop

| 5999 | Miscellaneous retail stores, nec (includes cosmetics stores) |

Book Publishing

| 2731 | Books; publishing or publishing and printing |

Bookbinder

| 2789 | Bookbinding and related work |

Bookkeeping

| 8721 | Accounting, auditing, and bookkeeping services |

Bookstore

| 5932 | Used merchandise stores (includes used book retailers) |
| 5942 | Bookstores |

Bottled Water Service

| 5149 | Groceries and related products, nec (includes natural spring and mineral water bottling and distribution services) |

5499   Miscellaneous food stores (incluces mineral water, retail)

Bowling Alley

7933   Bowling centers

Brewery Operation

2082   Malt beverages

Bridal Shop/Bridal Consultant

5621   Women's clothing stores (includes retail bridal shops, exceptcustom designers)

Building/Home Inspection

7389   Business services, nec (includes safety inspection, except automotive)

Building Maintenance/Custodial Service

7349   Building cleaning and maintenance services, nec (includes interior building cleaning services, contract janitorial services, and like enterprises)

Bulletin Board Service

4822   Telegraph and other message communications (includes electronic mail services)

7379   Computer related services, nec

Business Broker Service

7389   Business services, nec (includes business brokers buying ardselling business enterprises)

Business Consulting Service

8748   Business consulting services, nec

Business Services Operation

8744   Facilities support management services (includesbasemaintenance, providing personnel on continuing basis)

Butcher Shop

5423   Meat and fish (seafood) markets, including freezer provisioners

---

5499   Miscellaneous food stores (includes retail poultry dealers)

Cable Network

1623   Water, Sewer, Pipeline, and Communications and Power Line Construction (includes cable television line construction-contractors)

1731   Electrical Work (includes cable television hookup-contractors)

4841   Cable and Other Pay Television Services

Calligraphy Service

7389   Business services, nec (includes lettering services)

Camera Shop

5946   Camera and photographic supply stores

7699   Repair shops and related services, nec (includes camera repair shops)

Campground Management

7033   Recreational vehicle parks and campsites

Candy/Chocolate Shop

5441   Candy, nut, and confectionery stores

Car Alarm and Stereo Store

5531   Auto and home supply stores (includes automobile accessorydealers, retail)

5731   Radio, television, and consumer electronics stores (includesautomotive stereo equipment, retail)

Car Inspection Service

7549   Automotive services, except repair services and car washes(includes inspection service, automotive)

Car Towing Service

7549   Automotive services, except repair services and car washes(includes automotive towing and wrecker services)

Car Wash

7542   Car washes

Career Counseling

7389   Business services, nec (includes career counseling service)

Carpentry Service

1751   Carpentry work

Catering Service

5812   Eating places (includes caterers)

CD-ROM Developer/Producer

7372   Prepackaged software (includes pre-packaged computer software publishers)

7379   Computer related services, nec (includes database developers)

Cellular Phone/Telephone Business

4812   Radiotelephone communications

5999   Miscellaneous retail stores, nec (includes telephone stores, retail)

Charter Boat Service

4499   Water transportation service, nec (includes boat rental, commercial)

Check Cashing Service

6099   Functions related to depository banking, nec (includes check cashing agencies)

Children's Apparel Shop

5611   Men's and boys' clothing stores

5641   Children's and infants' wear stores

5651   Family clothing stores

5699   Miscellaneous apparel and accessory stores (includes children's wear)

5932   Used merchandise stores (includes retail second hand clothing stores)

Children's Day Care Center

8351   Child day care services

Chimney Sweeping Business

7349   Building cleaning and maintenance services, nec (includeschimney cleaning service)

Christmas Decoration Store

5999   Miscellaneous retail stores, nec

Christmas Tree Farm

0811   Timber tracts (includes Christmas tree growing)

Clipping Service

7389   Business services, nec (includes press clipping service)

Clothing Designer

2311   Men's and boys' suits, coats, and overcoats

2325   Men's and boys' separate trousers and slacks

2329   Men's and boys' clothing, nec

2331   Women's, misses', and juniors' blouses and shirts

2335   Women's, misses', and juniors' dresses

2337   Women's, misses', and juniors' suits, skirts, and coats

2361   Girls', children's, and infants' dresses, blouses, and shirts

Clothing Store

5611   Men's and boys' clothing and accessory stores

5621   Women's clothing stores

5632   Women's accessory and specialty stores

5641   Children's and infants' wear stores

5651   Family clothing stores

5699   Miscellaneous apparel and accessory stores

5932   Used merchandise stores (includes retail secondhand clothing stores)

Coffee Service

5149   Groceries and related products, nec (includes coffee, wholesale)

Coin/Stamp Dealer

5961   Catalog and mail order houses (includes retail mail order coinand stamp businesses)

5999   Miscellaneous retail stores, nec

Comedy Club

5813   Drinking placesMalcoholic beverages (includes nightclubs)

Comic Book/Collectibles Store

5999   Miscellaneous retail stores, nec

Commercial/Graphic Art Business

7336   Commercial art and graphic design

Commercial Mail Receiving Agency

7389   Business services, nec (includes post office contract stations)

Compact Disc/Record Store

5735   Recorded and prerecorded tape stores

Computer Consulting

7379   Computer related services, nec (includes computer consultants

Computer Data Storage Company

3572   Computer storage devices

Computer Learning/Training Center

8243   Data processing schools

Computer Maintenance and Repair Service

7378   Computer maintenance and repair

Computer Programming and Data Processing Service

7374   Computer processing and data preparation services

Computer Store

5734   Computer and computer software stores

Computer System Integrators

7371   Computer programming services

Computer integrated systems design

7373   Computer integrated systems design

7379   Computer related services, nec (includes computer consultants and database developers)

Computerized Billing Service

7374   Computer processing and data preparation and processing services

Computerized Matching Service

7299   Miscellaneous personal services, nec (includes dating services)

7375   Information retrieval services

Concession Stand Business

5812   Eating places (includes concession stands in airports and sports arenas, and refreshment stands)

7999   Amusement and recreation services, nec (concession operators andamusement concessions)

Consignment Shop

5932   Used merchandise stores (includes clothing stores, secondhand retail; furniture stores, secondhand retail; home furnishing stores, secondhand retail)

Construction Company

1521   General contractors—single family houses

1522   General contractors—residential buildings other than single-family

Consumer Electronics Store

5731   Radio, television, and consumer electronics stores

Convenience Store

5411   Grocery stores (includes retail convenience food stores)

Cooking School

8299   Schools and educational services, nec (includes cooking schools)

Copy Shop

| 7334 | Photocopying and duplicating services |

Cosmetics Business

2844	Perfumes, cosmetics, and other to let preparations
5122	Drugs, drug proprietaries, and druggists' sundries (includes cosmetics—wholesale)
5963	Direct selling establishments (includes canvassers, headquarters for retail sale of merchandise, and direct selling organizations—retail)
5999	Miscellaneous retail stores, nec (includes cosmeticsstores—retail)

Costume Shop

| 7299 | Miscellaneous personal services, nec (includes costume rental) |
| 7922 | Theatrical producers and miscellaneous theatrical services (includes theatrical costume design) |

Craft Artisan

| 3269 | Pottery products, nec (includes art and ornamental ware; pottery; ceramic articles for craft shops; cookware; crockery; china, earthenware and stoneware figures; kitchen articles; coarse earthenware; lamp bases; and vases) |

Craft/Hobby Shop

| 5945 | Hobby, toy, and game shops (includes retail hobby stores and craft kit and supply retailers) |
| 5947 | Gift, novelty, and souvenir shops pottery; ceramic articles for craft shops; cookware; crockery; china, earthenware and stoneware figures; kitchen articles; coarse earthenware; lamp bases; and vases) |

Create Your Own...Store

| 3269 | Pottery Products, nec |

Credit Card Issuing Service

| 5947 | Gift, Novelty, and Souvenir Shops |
| 5999 | Micellaneous Retail Stores, nec |

Credit Card Issuing Service

| 6153 | Short-Term Business Credit Institutions, Except Agricultural (includes credit card service, collection by central agency) |
| 7389 | Business Services, nec (includes credit card service collection by individual firms) |

Credit Repair Service

| 7299 | Miscellaneous personal services, nec (includes debt counseling and adjustment services) |

Credit Reporting and Collection Service

| 7322 | Adjustment and collection services |
| 7323 | Credit reporting services |

Damage Restoration Service

| 1790 | Special trade contractors, nec (includes cleaning building exteriors, campproofing buildings, dewatering, fireproofing buildings, steam cleaning of building exteriors, and waterproofing) |

Dance School

| 7911 | Dance studios, schools, and halls |

Delicatessen/Sandwich Shop

| 5812 | Eating places (includes sandwich bars or shops and submarine sandwich shops) |

Desktop Publishing Company

2711	Publishing, or publishing and printing newspapers
2721	Publishing, or publishing and printing periodicals
2731	Publishing, or publishing and printing books
2741	Miscellaneous publishing

Dial-it Services

| 4813 | Telephone communications, except radio-telephone |

Diaper Service

| 7219 | Laundry and garment services, nec |

Disc Jockey Service

| 8999 | Services, nec |

Domestic Help/Maid Service

| 7349 | Building cleaning and maintenance services, nec (includes housekeeping and office cleaning services) |
| 8811 | Private households (includes private households employing cooks, maids, and other domestic help) |

Driving School

| 8249 | Vocational schools, nec (includes truck driving schools) |
| 8299 | Schools and educational services, nec (includes automobile driving instruction) |

Drug Store/Pharmacy

| 5912 | Drug stores and proprietary stores |

Dry Cleaning Service/Coin-Operated Laundry

| 7215 | Coin-operated laundries and dry cleaning services |
| 7216 | Dry cleaning plants, except rug cleaning |

Editorial/Freelance Writing Business

| 8999 | Services, nec (includes writing and ghostwriting services) |

Electrical Contractor

| 1731 | Electrical work (includes trade contractors engaged in on-site electrical work) |

Electrical Lighting Supply Store

| 5719 | Miscellaneous home furnishings stores (includes retail lamp and shade shops) |

Employee Leasing Service

| 7363 | Help supply services |

Employment Agency

| 361 | Employment agencies |

Engraving/Monogramming Service

3479   Coating, engraving, and allied services, nec (includes jewelryand silverware engraving)

7389   Business services, nec (includes advertising embroidery services, embossing services, and identification engraving services)

Environmental Consultant

8748   Business consulting services, nec

Environmental Store

5999   Miscellaneous retail stores, nec

Estate Planning

8811   Private Households

Estate Sales Business

6530   Real estate agents and managers

Executive Recruiting Agency

7361   Employment agencies (includes executive placement)

Fashion Accessories Business

3961   Costume jewelry and costume novelties, except precious metal

5137   Women's, children's, and infants' clothing and accessories

5632   Women's accessory and specialty stores

Fax Service

4822   Telegraph and other message communications (includes facsimile transmission services)

Film and Video Production Operation

7812   Motion picture and videotape production services

Financial Planning Service

282   Investment Advice

Fish and Seafood Store

5421   Meat and fish (seafood) markets, including freezer provisioners

Fish Farm

0273   Animal aquaculture (includes fish farms except hatcheries)

Floor Covering/Restoration Business

5713   Floor covering stores—retail

Florist

5992   Florists

Food Delivery Service

5812   Eating places

5963   Direct selling establishments (includes door-to-door selling organizations and mobile lunch wagons)

5999   Miscellaneous retail stores, nec

Formalwear Rental Business

7299   Miscellaneous personal services, nec (includes tuxedo rental)

Freight Forwarding Service

4731   Arrangement of transportation of freight and cargo (includes freight forwarding services)

Fund Raising Consultant

7389   Business services, nec (includes fund raising on a contract or fee basis)

Funeral Service

7261   Funeral services and crematories

Fur Farm

0271   Fur-bearing animals and rabbits

Fur Store

5632   Women's accessory and specialty stores (includes fur shops and furriers)

Furniture Restoration Service

7641   Reupholstery and furniture repair

Gambling Organizations/Service

7011   Hotels and Motels (includes casino hotels)

7993   Coin-Operated Amusement Devices

7999   Amusement and Recreation Services, nec (includes gambling establishments not primarily operating coin-operated machines and lotteries, operation of)

9311   Public Finance Taxation, and Monetary Policy (includes gambling control boards-government and lottery control boards-government)

Genealogy Service

7299   Miscellaneous personal services, nec (includes genealogical investigation service)

Gift Basket Service

5961   Catalog and mail-order houses

Gift/Card Shop

5943   Stationery stores

5947   Gift, novelty, and souvenir shops (includes card shops)

Glass Repair and Replacement Service

1751   Carpentry work (includes prefabricated window and door installation)

7536   Automotive glass replacement shops

Golf Shop

5941   Sporting goods stores and bicycle shops (includes retail golf goods and equipment stores)

Gourmet Coffee/Tea House

5499   Miscellaneous food stores (includes coffee stores, retail)

5812   Eating places (includes coffee shops)

Greenhouse/Garden Center/Nursery Business

0181   Ornamental floricultural and nursery products (includes greenhouses for floral products, growing of nursery stock, growing of potted plants)

5261   Retail nurseries, lawn and garden supply stores (includes nursery stock, seeds, and bulbs, retail)

Greeting Card Publishing

2771   Greeting card publishing and printing

8999   Services, nec (includes hand painting of greeting cards)

Grocery Store

5411   Grocery stores

Gunsmith/Gun Shop

5941   Sporting good stores and bicycle shops (includes firearms, retail)

7699   Repair shops and related services, nec (includes gunsmith shops)

Hair Replacement/Electrolysis Clinic

7299   Miscellaneous personal services, nec (includes depilatory salons, electrolysis, and hair weaving or replacement services)

Hair Salon/Barber Shop

7231   Beauty shops (includes beauty and barber shops combined)

7241   Barber shops

Handwriting Analysis Consultant

7389   Business services, nec (includes handwriting analysis)

Hardware Store

5251   Hardware stores

Hat Store

5611   Men's and boys' clothing and accessory stores (includes retail hat stores)

5621   Women's accessory and specialty stores (includes retail millinery stores)

Hazardous Waste Disposal Business

4953   Refuse systems (includes hazardous waste material disposal sites)

Healthy Restaurants

5812   Eating Places

Health Food Store

5499   Miscellaneous food stores (includes health food stores)

Hearing Aid Testing and Fitting Service

5999   Miscellaneous retail stores, nec (includes hearing aids, retail)

8099   Health and allied services, nec (includes hearing testing service)

Herb Farm

0191   General farms, primarily crop

2833   Medical chemicals and botanical products (includes herb grinding, grading, and milling)

5499   Miscellaneous food stores (includes spice and herb stores)

Home Accessory Store

5714   Drapery, curtain, and upholstery stores

5719   Miscellaneous home furnishings stores

Home Furnishings Store

5712   Furniture stores

5719   Miscellaneous home furnishings stores

5932   Used merchandise stores (including antique and secondhand retail furniture stores)

Home Health Care Service

8082   Home health care services

Horse Riding Academy

752   Animal specialty services, except veterinary (includes boarding and training horses)

Hotel/Motel/Resort Operation

7011   Hotels and motels (includes resort hotels)

Housesitting Service

8999   Services, nec

Ice Cream/Frozen Yogurt Shop

5451   Dairy products stores (includes retail packaged ice cream stores)

5812   Eating places (includes retail dairy bars)

563   Direct selling establishments (includes ice cream wagons)

Image Consultant

8299   Schools and educational services, nec (includes personal development schools)

8743   Public relations services

Import/Export Service

4731   Arrangement of the transportation of freight and cargo

Incubator

7389   Business services, nec

8748   Business consulting services, nec

Information Broker

7375   Information retrieval services

Insulation Contractor

1742   Plastering, dry wall, acoustical, and insulation work (includes insulation installation contractors)

Insurance Agency

6411   Insurance agents, brokers, and services

Interior Design Service

7389   Business services, nec (includes interior decoration consulting services and interior design services)

Internet/Online Service Provider

4822   Telegraph and other message communications (includes electronicmail services)

7379   Computer related services, nec

Investment/Securities Broker

6211   Security brokers, dealers, and flotation companies

Jewelry Store

5632   Women's accessory and specialty stores (includes costume jewelry stores)

5944	Jewelry stores
7631	Watch, clock, and jewelry repair

Job Training/Retraining

8331	Job training and vocational rehabilitation services (includesjob training)

Kiosk/Pushcart/Vendor Business

5812	Eating places (includes box lunch stands, concession stands,food bars, hamburger and hot dog stands, ice cream stands, refreshment stands, and soft drink stands)

Landscaping Service

0781	Landscape counseling and planning services
0782	Lawn and garden services
0783	Ornamental shrub and tree services

Lawn Maintenance Service

0782	Lawn and garden services
0783	Ornamental shrub and tree services

Limousine Service

4119	Local passenger transportation, nec (includes hearse and limousine rental, with drivers)
7514	Passenger car rental (includes limo rental, w/o drivers)

Lingerie Shop

5632	Lingerie storesMretail

Liquor Store

5921	Liquor stores

Literary Agency

7389	Business services, nec (includes agents and brokers for authors and non-performing artists)

Locksmith

7699	Repair shops and related services, nec (includes locksmith shops and made-to order lock parts)

Luggage and Leather Goods Business

5948	Luggage and leather goods stores

Lumberyard

5211	Lumber and other building materials dealers

Machine Shop/Metalorking Shop

3541	Machine tools, metal cutting types
3542	Machine tools, metal forming types
3544	Special dies and tools, die sets, jigs and fixtures, and industrial molds
3545	Cutting tools, machine tool accessories, and machinists' precision measuring devices
3549	Metalworking machinery, nec

Mail Order Business

5961	Catalog and mail order houses

Management Consulting Service

8742	Management consulting services

Manufacturer's Representative

7389	Business services, nec

Marine Shop

5551	Boat dealers (includes retail marine supply dealers)

Market Research and Analysis

8732	Commercial, economic, sociological, and educational research
8742	Management consulting services

Martial Arts Studio

7999	Amusement and recreation services, nec (includes Judo and Karate instruction)

Masonry, Stonework, and Plastering Contractors

1741	Masonry, stone setting, and other stonework
1742	Plastering, dry wall, acoustical, and insulation work

Massage Therapist

7299	Massage parlor 8049 Offices and clinics of health practitioners,nec

Mediation Service

7389	Business services, nec (includes arbitration and conciliationservices)

Medical and Dental Instrument Manufacturing

3841	Surgical and medical instruments and apparatus
3843	Dental equipment and supplies

Medical Claims Service

6411	Insurance agents, brokers, and service (includes processing ofmedical claims on a contract or fee basis)

Medical Laboratory Service

8071	Medical laboratories

Medical Supplies Store

5047	Medical, dental, and hospital equipment and supplies

Medical Transcription Service

7374	Computer processing and data preparation and processing services

Messenger/Delivery/Subpoena Service

4215	Courier services, except by air (includes letter, mail, package,and parcel delivery services)
4822	Telegraph and other message communication (includes cablegrams, mailgrams, electronic mail, and other message services)
7389	Business services, nec (includes process serving services)

Miniature Golf Course Operation

7999	Amusement and recreation services, nec (includes miniature golf course operations)

Modeling School/Agency

7363	Help supply services (includes modeling services)

8299	Schools and educational services, nec (includes modeling schools)

Mortgage Broker

6162	Mortgage bankers and loan correspondents (includes mortgage brokers using own money)
6163	Loan brokers (includes mortgage brokers arranging for loans but using money of others)
6211	Security brokers, dealers, and flotation companies (includes buying and selling mortgages)

Motorcycle/Moped Store

5571	Motorcycle dealers

Movie Theatre Operation

7832	Motion picture theatres, except drive-ins
7833	Drive-in motion picture theatres

Moving Service

4212	Local trucking, without storage (includes furniture and other moving services)
4214	Local trucking, with storage (includes furniture and household goods moving services)

Music School

8299	Schools and educational services, nec (includes music schools)

Music Shop

5736	Musical instrument stores
5932	Used merchandise stores (includes retailers of secondhand musical instruments)
7699	Repair shops and related services, nec (includes musical instrument repair shops)

Musical Instrument Repair/Piano Tuning Service

7699	Repair shops and related services, nec (includes musical instrument repair shops and piano tuning and repair)

Nail Salon

7231	Beauty shops (includes manicure and pedicure salons)

Nanny Service

7299	Miscellaneous personal services, nec (includes babysitting bureaus)

New Age Services and Supplies

5999	Miscellaneous retail stores, nec
8999	Services, nec

New and Used Car Dealer

5511	Motor vehicle dealers (new and used)
5521	Motor vehicle dealers (used only)

Newsletter Publishing

2721	Periodicals; publishing or publishing and printing
2741	Miscellaneous publishing (includes business service newsletters publishing and/or printing)

Novelty Items Business

2499	Wood products, nec (includes wood and wood fiber novelties)
2514	Metal household furniture (includes metal novelty furniture)
2679	Converted paper and paperboard products, nec (includes paper novelties)
3199	Leather goods, nec (includes leather novelties)
3229	Pressed and blown glass and glassware, nec (includes novelty glassware made in glassmaking plants)
3231	Glass products, made of purchased glass (includes glass novelties)
3499	Fabricated metal products, nec (includes metal novelties and specialties, except advertising novelties)
3961	Costume jewelry and costume novelties, except precious metal and gems

3999	Manufacturing industries, nec (includes bone, beaded and shell novelties)

Nursing Home/Long-Term Care Center

8051	Skilled nursing care facilities
8052	Intermediate care facilities (includes intermediate care nursing homes)
8059	Nursing and personal care facilities, nec (includes convalescent homes, rest homes, and like facilities)

Nutritional Consultant/Diet Planner

7299	Miscellaneous personal services, nec (includes diet workshops)
8049	Offices and clinics of health practitioners, nec (includes offices of nutritionists and offices of dietitians)

Office Design Service

7389	Business services, nec (includes interior decorating and design services)

Office Supply/Equipment Store

5943	Stationery stores (includes retail office forms and supplies stores)

Online Store

5734	Computer and computer software stores
7375	Information retrieval services

Paint/Wall Covering Center

5231	Paint, glass, and wallpaper stores

Painting Contractors

1721	Painting and paperhanging contractors

Party Entertainment Services

7929	Bands, orchestras, actors, and other entertainers and entertainment groups

Party/Reunion Planning Service

7359	Equipment rental and leasing, nec (includes party supplies rental and leasing)
8999	Services, nec

Pawnbroker

5932   Used merchandise stores (includes pawnshops)

Payroll Preparation Service

8721   Accounting, auditing, and bookkeeping services (includes payrollaccounting service)

Periodical/Newspaper Publishing

2721   Periodicals; publishing or publishing and printing

Personal Shopping Service

7299   Miscellaneous personal services, nec (includes shopping servicesfor individuals)

Pest Control Service

0851   Forestry services (includes forest pest control)

7342   Disinfecting and pest control services

Pet Boarding/Grooming Service

0279   Animal specialties, nec (includes breeding kennels)

0752   Animal specialty services (includes boarding kennels, doggrooming services, and related services)

Pet Cemetery

0782   Lawn and garden services (includes independent cemetery upkeep services)

6531   Real estate agents and managers (includes cemetery management services)

6553   Cemetery subdividers and developers (includes animal cemetery operations)

Pet Obedience School

0752   Animal specialty services, except veterinary (includes training of pets and other animal specialties)

Pet Shop

5999   Miscellaneous retail stores, nec (includes pet shops)

Pet Sitting Service

0752   Animal specialty services, except veterinary

Photo Finishing Center

7384   Photo finishing laboratories

7819   Services allied to motion picture production (includes motion picture film processing)

Photographer, Commercial

7335   Commercial photography

Photographic Studio

7221   Photographic studios, portrait

Physical Fitness Center

7991   Physical fitness facilities

Physical Therapy Clinic/Practice

8049   Offices and clinics of health practitioners, nec (includes offices of physical therapists)

Pizzeria

5812   Eating places (includes pizza parlors and pizzerias)

Plant Leasing Service

7359   Equipment rental and leasing, nec (includes plants)

Plumbing Service

1711   Plumbing, heating, and air-conditioning contractors

Porcelain Refinishing Service

1799   Special trade contractors, nec

Power Washing Service

1799   Special trade contractors, nec (includes cleaning of building exteriors)

7349   Building cleaning and maintenance services, nec (includes cleaning of building interiors)

7542   Car washes (includes automotive washing and polishing)

Prepaid Phone Card Business

4812   Radiotelephone communications

4813   Telephone communications, except radiotelephone

Print/Frame Shop

7699   Repair shops and related services, nec (includes custom picture framing services)

Printing Business

2752   Commercial printing, lithographic

2754   Commercial printing, gravure

2759   Commercial printing, nec

2761   Manifold business form printers

Private Investigation/Personal Security Service

7381   Detective, guard, and armored car services

Private Label Product Manufacturer/Retailer

3999   Manufacturing industries, nec

5399   Miscellaneous general merchandise stores

5499   Miscellaneous food stores 5699 Miscellaneous apparel and accessory stores

5999   Miscellaneous retail stores, nec

Professional Organizer

7299   Miscellaneous personal services, nec

7389   Business services, nec

Property Management

6531   Real estate agents and managers

Public Relations Consultant

8743   Public relations services

Public Warehousing/Ministorage Operation

4221   Farm product warehousing and storage

4222   Refrigerated warehousing and storage

4225   General warehousing and storage

4226   Special warehousing and storage, nec (includes fur storage, household goods warehousing and storage, whiskey warehousing, and like enterprises)

Quick Oil Change Service

5541　Gasoline service stations (includes automobile servicestations—retail)

7538　General automotive repair shops

Radio Station

4832　Radio broadcasting stations

Radon Testing Service

1799　Special trade contractors, nec

8734　Testing laboratories

Real Estate Agency

6531　Real estate agents and managers

Real Estate Investment Service

6798　Real estate investment trusts

Recording Studio

7399　Business services, nec (includes recording studios operating on a contract or fee basis)

Recreational Vehicle Dealer

5561　Recreational vehicle dealers

Recycling Business

5093　Scrap and waste materials

Rental Service

7299　Miscellaneous personal services, nec (includes clothing rental)

7352　Medical equipment rental and leasing

7353　Heavy construction equipment and leasing

7359　Equipment rental and leasing, nec

7377　Computer rental and leasing

7999　Amusement and recreation services, nec (includes pleasure boat rental, canoe and rowboat rental, bicycle, motorcycle and moped rental, and sporting goods rental)

Restaurant

5812　Eating places (includes sit-down, carry-out, and fast food)

Resume Service

7338　Secretarial anc court reporting services (includes resumewriting services)

Roofing Contractor

1761　Roofing, siding, and sheet metal work

Satellite Dish Service

4841　Cable and other pay television services (includes directbroadcast satellite services and satellite master antenna systems services)

Screen Printing Business

2261　Finishers of broadwoven fabrics of cotton (includes printing andfinishing of cotton broadwoven fabrics)

2262　Finishers of broadwoven fabrics of manmade fiber and silk(includes printing manmade fiber and silk broadwoven fabrics)

2759　Commercial printing, nec (includes screen printing on glass, plastics, paper, and metal, including highway signs)

Security Systems Service

7382　Security systems services

Seminar Planner/Lecturer

8999　Services, nec (including lecturers)

Service Station/Auto Repair and Service Shop

5541　Gasoline service stations

7532　Top, body, and upholstery repair shops and paint shops

7533　Automotive exhaust system repair shops

7534　Tire retreading and repair shops

7536　Automotive glass replacement shops

7537　Automotive transmission repair shops

7538　General automotive repair shops

7539　Automotive repair shops, nec

Sewer and Drain Cleaning Business

7699　Repair shops and related services, nec (includes sewer cleaning and rodding and septic tank cleaning) Sewing Center 5722 Household appliance stores (includes retail sewing machine stores)

5949　Sewing, needlework, and piece goods stores

7699　Repair shops and related services, nec (includes sewing machine repair shops)

Shoe Repair Shop

7251　Shoe repair shops and shoeshine parlors

Shoe Store

5661　Shoe stores

Sign Shop

3993　Signs and advertising specialties

7389　Business services, nec (includes sign painting shops)

Silk Plant Shop

5999　Miscellaneous retail stores, nec (includes artificial flowers—retail)

Skating Rink Operation

7999　Amusement and recreation services, nec (includes ice and rollerskating rink operations)

Ski Shop

5941　Sporting goods stores and bicycle shops

Software Publishing

7372　Packaged software

Solar Energy Design/Contracting Business

1711　Plumbing, heating, and air-conditioning contractors (includes solar heating apparatus contractors)

1742	Plastering, dry wall, acoustical, and insulation work (includes solar reflecting insulation film contractors)

Specialized Staffing

7361	Employment Agencies
7363	Help Supply Services

Specialty Foods/Wine Shop

5499	Miscellaneous food stores
5921	Liquor stores (includes packaged wine—retail)

Sports Promotional Services

7941	Professional Sports Clubs and Promoters

Sporting Goods Store

5941	Sporting goods stores and bicycle shops

Surveying Service

8713	Surveying services (includes surveying: land, water, and aerial)

Swimming Pool/Hot Tub Business

1799	Special trade contractors, nec (includes swimming pool construction contractors)
5999	Miscellaneous retail stores, nec (includes hot tubs, retail)
7389	Business services, nec (includes swimming pool cleaning and maintenance services)
7999	Amusement and recreation services, nec (includes swimming pooloperations)

Tailor Shop

5699	Miscellaneous apparel and accessory stores (includes customtailor shops) 7219 Laundry and garment services, nec (includes tailorshops, except custom or merchant tailors)

Talent Agency

7922	Theatrical producers and miscellaneous theatrical services (includes agents)

Tanning Parlor/Sauna

7299	Miscellaneous personal services (includes steam baths and tanning salons)

Tattoo Parlor

7299	Miscellaneous personal services, nec (includes tattoo parlors)

Tax Preparation Business

7291	Tax return preparation services
8721	Accounting, auditing, and bookkeeping services

Taxicab/Van Shuttle Service

4121	Taxicabs

Taxidermy Service

7699	Repair shops and related services, nec (includes taxidermy)

Teacher Supply Store

5999	Miscellaneous retail stores, nec

Telemarketing Service

7389	Business services, nec (includes telemarketing services operating on a contract or fee basis)

Telephone Answering Service

7389	Business services, nec (includes answering services)

Television/Radio Repair Service

7622	Radio and television repair shops

Television Station

4833	Television broadcasting stations

Temporary Employment Agency

7363	Help supply services (includes temporary help services

Tennis Court/Racquet Club Operation

7997	Membership sports and recreation clubs (includes racquetball and tennis clubs)
7999	Amusement and recreation services, nec (includes nonmembership racquetball and tennis court operations)

Tire Dealer

5531	Auto and home supply stores (includes retail tire dealers) 7534 Tire retreading and repair shops

Tobacco Shop

5993	Tobacco stores and stands

Tour Guide Operation/Adventure Service

4725	Tour operations
7999	Amusement and recreation services, nec (includes tour guides)

Toy Business

5945	Hobby, toy, and game shops

Trade Show/Conference Management Service

7389	Business services, nec (includes trade show arrangement)

Translating/Interpreting Service

7389	Business services, nec (includes translation service)

Travel Agency

4724	Travel agencies

Trucking Business

4212	Local trucking, without storage services
4213	Trucking, except local
4214	Local trucking, with storage services

Tutoring Service

8299	Schools and educational services, nec (includes tutoring services)

Typesetting Business

2791	Typesetting

Typing/Stenographic Service

7338	Secretarial and court reporting services (includes stenographic and typing services)

Upholstery/Carpet Services

1752	Floor laying and other floor work, nec (includes carpet laying and removing services)

5714   Drapery, curtain, and upholstery stores (includes upholstery materials stores)

7217   Carpet and upholstery cleaning

Vending Machine Merchandising and Service Business

5962   Automatic merchandising machine operators (includes retail sale of products through vending machines)

7359   Equipment rental and leasing services, nec (includes vending machine rental businesses)

Videocassette Rental Store

5735   Recorded and prerecorded tape stores (includes retail videotape stores)

7841   Videotape rental establishments

Vision Center

5995   Optical goods stores

Voice Mail Service

4813   Telephone communications, except radiotelephone (includes voice telephone communications)

Water Conditioning Service

7389   Business services, nec (includes water softener services)

Web Site Design

7371   Computer programming services (includes custom computer programs or systems software development and computer software systems analysis and design)

Weight Reduction/Control Center

7991   Physical fitness facilities (includes reducing facilities and slenderizing salons)

Welcome Service

7389   Business service, nec (includes welcoming service)

Window Dressing Business

3993   Signs and advertising specialties (includes advertising displays, except printed, and window and lobby cutouts and displays)

7319   Advertising, nec (includes display advertising services, exceptoutdoor)

Word Processing Service

7338   Secretarial and court reporting services (includes wordprocessing services)

List of General Small Business Topics

This section covers sources of assistance applicable to a variety of small businesses. Resources are arranged by topic and include associations, educational programs, directories of educational programs, reference works, sources of supply, statistical sources, periodicals, videocassettes/audiocassettes, trade shows and conventions, consultants, computerized databases, computer systems/software, Internet databases, libraries, and research centers.

ASSOCIATIONS AND OTHER ORGANIZATIONS

18673 ■ NASSCO
11521 Cronridge Dr., Ste. J
Owings Mills, MD 21117
Ph: (410)486-3500
Fax: (410)486-6838
Co. E-mail: john@visu-sewer.com
URL: http://www.nassco.org
Contact: John Nelson, President

Description: Companies providing services including sewer evaluation, cleaning, inspection, and rehabilitation; manufacturers and suppliers of sewer service equipment; consulting engineers and municipal government officials. Serves as a forum for discussion of needs, ideas and information among members. Works to: improve standards and procedures for sewer evaluation, maintenance, rehabilitation and worker safety; promote members' services and assist in marketing sewer service of equipment, materials and supplies; educate owners, engineers and inspectors about sewer rehabilitation methods and procedures. Conducts training seminars in maintenance and rehabilitation, inspection and safety. Provides referral services. **Founded:** 1976. **Publications:** *Manual of Practices.* **Awards:** Jeffrey D. Ralston Memorial Scholarship (Annual); The NASSCO Jeffrey D. Ralston Memorial Scholarships. **Telecommunication Services:** brad@ces-sses.com.

18674 ■ Sump and Sewage Pump Manufacturers Association (SSPMA)
PO Box 647
Northbrook, IL 60065-0647
Ph: (847)559-9233
Fax: (847)559-9235
Co. E-mail: hdqtrs@sspma.org
URL: http://www.sspma.org
Contact: Susan OGrady, President

Description: Manufacturers of residential sump pumps (cellar drainers) and sewage pumps. Seeks to: develop and promulgate quality standards implement a certification and labeling program for all products conforming to these standards; investigate market size and activity; promote improved provisions in building codes on the use of sump and sewage pumps. **Founded:** 1956.

REFERENCE WORKS

18675 ■ *"Acing the Test" in Contractor (Vol. 57, January 2010, No. 1, pp. 32)*
Pub: Penton Media, Inc.

Ed: Robert P. Mader. **Description:** A ward winning mechanical system retrofitting of a middle school in Ohio is discussed. The school now operates at 37,800 Btu/sq. ft and reduced a significant amount of pollutants from being emitted into the environment.

18676 ■ *"Are EO Programs Right for Your Business?" in Contractor (Vol. 56, October 2009, No. 10, pp. 49)*
Pub: Penton Media, Inc.

Ed: Susan Linden McGreevy. **Description:** Some of the laws regarding equal opportunity programs are discussed. Suggestions for mechanical contractors who are considering certification to qualify for these programs are presented.

18677 ■ *"Be Proactive - Closely Review Contracts" in Contractor (Vol. 56, July 2009, No. 7, pp. 19)*
Pub: Penton Media, Inc.

Ed: Al Schwartz. **Description:** Contract disputes can make subcontractors suffer big financial losses or even cause a new subcontractor to fail. Subcontractors should scour the plans and specifications for any references to work that might remotely come under their scope and to cross out any line in the contract that does not accurately reflect the work that they agreed to.

18678 ■ *"Be Wary of Dual-Flush Conversion Kits" in Contractor (Vol. 56, September 2009, No. 9, pp. 66)*
Pub: Penton Media, Inc.

Ed: John Koeller; Bill Gauley. **Description:** Recommendation of untested dual-flush conversion devices for tank-type toilets in the United States have been questioned. The products are being advertised as having the ability to convert single-flush to a dual-flush toilet. No evidence of water conservation from using such devices has been recorded.

18679 ■ *"BIM and You: Know Its Benefits and Risks" in Contractor (Vol. 57, January 2010, No. 1, pp. 46)*
Pub: Penton Media, Inc.

Ed: Susan Linder McGreevy. **Description:** Building Information Modeling is intended to be 'collaborative' and this could raise legal issues if a contractor sends an electronic bid and it is filtered out. Other legal issues that mechanical contractors need to consider before using this technology are discussed.

18680 ■ *"Climate Right Systems Provides Pre-Assembled Equipment Packages" in Contractor (Vol. 56, July 2009, No. 7, pp. 1)*
Pub: Penton Media, Inc.

Description: Climate Right Systems offers completely engineered, assembled, and tested equipment packages for hydronic heating and cooling. This package does away with the need to custom fabricate on-site and lets mechanical and plumbing contractors expand their offerings without added overhead and risk.

18681 ■ *"Commercial Water Efficiency Initiatives Announced" in Contractor (Vol. 56, November 2009, No. 11, pp. 5)*
Pub: Penton Media, Inc.

Ed: Robert P. Mader. **Description:** Plumbing engineers John Koeller and Bill Gauley are developing a testing protocol for commercial toilets. The team said commercial toilets should have a higher level of flush performance than residential toilets for certification.

The Environmental Protection Agency's WaterSense program wants to expand the program into the commercial/institutional sector.

18682 ■ *"Contractors Fret Over Credit, People, Government" in Contractor (Vol. 57, February 2010, No. 2, pp. 7)*
Pub: Penton Media, Inc.

Ed: Robert P. Mader. **Description:** Telephone interviews with 22 plumbing and HVAC contractors reveal that only two had sales increases for 2009 and that overall, contractors were down anywhere from seven to 25 percent. In the repair/service market, the residential sector was holding its own but the commercial portion was lagging behind.

18683 ■ *"Corporate Park Retrofits for Water Savings" in Contractor (Vol. 56, October 2009, No. 10, pp. 5)*
Pub: Penton Media, Inc.

Description: Merrit Corporate Park in Norwalk, Connecticut has been interested in improving building efficiency and one of their buildings has been retrofitted with water-efficient plumbing systems which will allow them to save as much as two million gallons of water. ADP Service Corp. helped the park upgrade their plumbing system.

18684 ■ *"The Customer Is Right Even If He's Wrong" in Contractor (Vol. 57, February 2010, No. 2, pp. 12)*
Pub: Penton Media, Inc.

Ed: Al Schwarz. **Description:** Mechanical contractors should note that customers will make a judgment based upon the impression that they form on their first meeting. Contractors can maintain a professional image by washing their trucks and having the personnel dress uniformly. Contractors have every right to demand that employees clean up and make a better impression on customers.

18685 ■ *"Got to be Smarter than the Average Bear" in Contractor (Vol. 56, September 2009, No. 9, pp. 82)*
Pub: Penton Media, Inc.

Ed: Bob Mader. **Description:** International Association of Plumbing and Mechanical Officials Green Technical Committee has debated the need for contractors to have certifications in installing green plumbing. Some have argued that qualifications would discourage homeowners from improving their properties. Comments from executives are also included.

18686 ■ *"Grainger Show Highlights Building Green, Economy" in Contractor (Vol. 57, February 2010, No. 2, pp. 3)*
Pub: Penton Media, Inc.

Ed: Candace Roulo. **Description:** chief U.S. economist told attendees of the Grainger's 2010 Total MRO Solutions National Customer Show that the economic recovery would be subdued. Mechanical contractors who attended the event also learned about building sustainable, green products, and technologies, and economic and business challenges.

18687 ■ *"Green Pipe Helps Miners Remove the Black"* in Contractor (Vol. 57, January 2010, No. 1, pp. 1)
Pub: Penton Media, Inc.
Description: Lyons Co. Mechanical Contractors and Engineers installed a piping system for the River View Coal Mine facility's shower rooms. Lyons used Aquatherm's polypropylene piping system which creates seamless connections in the piping.

18688 ■ *"Hansen Mechanical Performs Boiler Upgrade at Brookfield Zoo"* in Contractor (Vol. 57, February 2010, No. 2, pp. 7)
Pub: Penton Media, Inc.
Description: Hansen Mechanical installed a donated boiler in the Brookfield Zoo from Weil-McLain. The boilers were installed in the zoo's 'The Swamp' and 'The Living Coast' exhibits.

18689 ■ *"Homebuilders Continue to be Our Nemesis"* in Contractor (Vol. 56, July 2009, No. 7, pp. 50)
Ed: Bob Mader. **Description:** Homebuilders rank high on the greed scale along with Wall Street brokers. There is this one instance when a builder gave copies of another contractor's quotes that have just been blackened out and another instance when one builder let other bidders visit a site while the current mechanical contractor is working.

18690 ■ *"How to Detect and Prevent Employee Fraud"* in Contractor (Vol. 56, October 2009, No. 10, pp. 57)
Pub: Penton Media, Inc.
Ed: James R. Leichter. **Description:** Mechanical contractors can prevent employee fraud by handing out a detailed employment policy manual to their employees and making sure that their invoices are numbered. It is also highly advised to have bank statements reconciled by a third party.

18691 ■ *"IAPMO GTC Debates Supplement"* in Contractor (Vol. 56, September 2009, No. 9, pp. 3)
Pub: Penton Media, Inc.
Ed: Robert P. Mader. **Description:** Green Technical Committee of the International Association of Plumbing and Mechanical Officials is developing a Green Plumbing and Mechanical Supplement. The supplement provides for installation of systems by licensed contractors and installers. Comments from officials are also presented.

18692 ■ *"IAPMO GTC Finalizes Green Supplement"* in Contractor (Vol. 57, January 2010, No. 1, pp. 1)
Pub: Penton Media, Inc.
Description: International Association of Plumbing and Mechanical Officials' Green Technical Committee finalized the Green Plumbing & Mechanical Code Supplement. The supplement was created to provide a set of provisions that encourage sustainable practices and work towards the design and construction of plumbing and mechanical systems.

18693 ■ *"IAPMO GTC Votes to Limit Showers to 2.0-GPM"* in Contractor (Vol. 56, September 2009, No. 9, pp. 1)
Pub: Penton Media, Inc.
Ed: Robert P. Mader. **Description:** Green Technical Committee of the International Association of Plumbing and Mechanical Officials has voted to limit showers to 2.0 GPM. It is also developing a Green Plumbing and Mechanical Supplement. Comments from executives are also supplied.

18694 ■ *"IAPMO Seeks Group Participants"* in Contractor (Vol. 56, September 2009, No. 9, pp. 37)
Pub: Penton Media, Inc.
Description: International Association of Plumbing and Mechanical Officials is accepting applications for task groups that will develop its Uniform Plumbing Code and Uniform Mechanical Code. The codes are developed using American National Standards Institute accredited consensus process. Task groups are assigned to address a specific topic or problem.

18695 ■ *"Keep Customers Out of the Yellow Pages"* in Contractor (Vol. 56, November 2009, No. 11, pp. 47)
Pub: Penton Media, Inc.
Ed: Matt Michel. **Description:** Mechanical contractors should keep customers away from the Yellow Pages where they could find their competition by putting stickers on the water heater or the front of the directory. Giving out magnets to customers and putting the company name on sink rings and invoices are other suggestions.

18696 ■ *"LA Passes HET Ordinance, California Greens Code"* in Contractor (Vol. 56, September 2009, No. 9, pp. 1)
Pub: Penton Media, Inc.
Ed: Candace Ruolo. **Description:** Los Angeles City Council has passed a Water Efficiency Requirements ordinance. The law mandates lower low-flow plumbing requirements for plumbing fixtures installed in new buildings and retrofits. Under the ordinance, a toilet's maximum flush volume may not exceed 1.28-gpf.

18697 ■ *"The Latest on E-Verify"* in Contractor (Vol. 56, September 2009, No. 9, pp. 58)
Pub: Penton Media, Inc.
Ed: Susan McGreevy. **Description:** United States government has required federal contractors to use its E-Verify program to verify the eligibility of incoming and existent employees. The use of the program is seen to eliminate Social Security mismatches.

18698 ■ *"Major Advances in Heat Pump Technology"* in Contractor (Vol. 57, January 2010, No. 1, pp. 42)
Pub: Penton Media, Inc.
Ed: Mark Eatherton. **Description:** Tax credits make ground-source heat pump technology more economically feasible. Suggestions on how to choose the right ground-source heat pump technology to install in a house are discussed.

18699 ■ *"Most Popular Tools? The Survey Says"* in Contractor (Vol. 57, February 2010, No. 2, pp. 1)
Pub: Penton Media, Inc.
Ed: Robert P. Mader. **Description:** According to a survey of individuals in the field, mechanical contractors are purchasing more of their tools at home centers and they are also increasingly working in the service, repair, and retrofit markets. The survey also found that the reciprocating saw is the most used corded power tool. Additional purchasing habits of mechanical contractors are listed.

18700 ■ *"A Necessary Balancing Act: Bookkeeping"* in Contractor (Vol. 56, November 2009, No. 11, pp. 22)
Pub: Penton Media, Inc.
Ed: Al Schwartz. **Description:** Pros and cons of getting a bookkeeper or a certified public accountant for the subcontractor are discussed. A bookkeeper can help a subcontractor get new accounting software up and running while an accountant will more than likely keep after the books at regular intervals throughout the year.

18701 ■ *"Niche Markets, Green Will Be Okay in 2010"* in Contractor (Vol. 57, January 2010, No. 1, pp. 1)
Pub: Penton Media, Inc.
Ed: Robert P. Mader . **Description:** Mechanical contractors will see most of their work stemming from niche markets, such as green work, as well as service work in 2010. It is said that things will turn around for the industry in 2012 and 2013 and one forecast believes that anything outside of the institutional or more public sector work could be down 15 to 30 percent.

18702 ■ *"Papal Permit Trumps the Plumbing Codes"* in Contractor (Vol. 57, February 2010, No. 2, pp. 20)
Pub: Penton Media, Inc.
Ed: Dave Yates. **Description:** Despite the plumbing code, a plumbing contractor was able to convince the inspector to approve his application to install a sacristy sink which drains into the ground instead of the sewer system. Details of the church's system are presented.

18703 ■ *"PMA Launches Online Education Program"* in Contractor (Vol. 56, October 2009, No. 10, pp. 8)
Pub: Penton Media, Inc.
Description: Plumbing & Mechanical Association of Georgia launched an online program that covers technical and business management that will help contractors run their businesses. Future courses will include math for plumbers, graywater systems, and recession-proofing your business.

18704 ■ *"Pre-Certified LEED Hotel Prototype Reduces Energy Use, Conserves Water"* in Contractor (Vol. 57, January 2010, No. 1, pp. 3)
Pub: Penton Media, Inc.
Ed: Candace Roulo. **Description:** Marriott International Inc.'s LEED pre-certified prototype hotel will reduce a hotel's energy and water consumption by 25 percent and save owners approximately $100,000. Their Courtyard Settler's Ridge in Pittsburgh will be the first hotel built based on the prototype.

18705 ■ *"Public Bathroom Pressure Woes Resolved"* in Contractor (Vol. 56, September 2009, No. 9, pp. 44)
Pub: Penton Media, Inc.
Ed: Dave Yates. **Description:** Design and construction of a public bathroom's plumbing system in the United States are discussed. Installed plumbing fixtures with flush valves would not function properly. The installation of Grundfos SQE variable-speed pumps has resolved problems with the bathroom's water pressure.

18706 ■ *"Selling a Job When There's Buyer's Remorse"* in Contractor (Vol. 56, December 2009, No. 12, pp. 37)
Pub: Penton Media, Inc.
Ed: H. Kent Craig. **Description:** Advice on how contractors should manage low-profit jobs in the United States are presented. Efforts should be made to try and find at least one quality field foreman or superintendent. Contractors should also try to respectfully renegotiate the terms of the job.

18707 ■ *"Software Solutions Increase Productivity"* in Contractor (Vol. 57, February 2010, No. 2, pp. 26)
Pub: Penton Media, Inc.
Ed: William Feldman; Patti Feldman. **Description:** Singletouch is a real-time data capture solution for mechanical and other contractors that work in jobs that require materials and workload tracking. Contractors get information on extreme weather and sudden changes in the cost of materials. The OptimumHVAC optimization software by Optimum Energy is designed to optimize energy savings in commercial buildings.

18708 ■ *"Technology to the Rescue"* in Contractor (Vol. 56, July 2009, No. 7, pp. 22)
Pub: Penton Media, Inc.
Ed: Candace Ruolo. **Description:** Features of several products that will make the job of a mechanical contractor easier are discussed. These include Ridgid's line of drain and sewer inspection cameras and monitors, Motion Computing's Motion F5 tablet rugged tablet PC, the JobClock from Exaktime, and the TeleNav Track tool for mobile workforce management.

18709 ■ *"Tracking Your Fleet Can Increase Bottom Line"* in Contractor (Vol. 56, November 2009, No. 11, pp. 26)
Pub: Penton Media, Inc.
Ed: Candace Roulo. **Description:** GPS fleet management system can help boost a contractor's profits, employee productivity, and efficiency. These are available as a handheld device or a cell phone that employees carry around or as a piece of hardware installed in a vehicle. This lets managers track assets and communicate with employees about jobs.

18710 ■ *"Trade Craft: Take Pride in Your Trade, Demand Excellence"* in Contractor (Vol. 56, October 2009, No. 10, pp. 24)
Pub: Penton Media, Inc.
Ed: Al Schwartz. **Description:** There is a need for teaching, developing, and encouraging trade craft. An apprentice plumber is not only versed in the

mechanical aspects of the trade but he also has a working knowledge of algebra, trigonometry, chemistry, and thermal dynamics. Contractors should be demanding on their personnel regarding their trade craft and should only keep and train the very best people they can hire.

18711 ■ *"Train Now to Get the Competitive Edge" in Contractor (Vol. 56, October 2009, No. 10, pp. 58)*
Pub: Penton Media, Inc.
Ed: Merry Beth Hall. **Description:** Due to the harsh economic climate, mechanical contractors would be well-served to train their employees while they have time to take them out of the field. This will help ensure that they are not behind when the economic recovery happens. Suggestions on how to choose the best type of training are presented.

18712 ■ *"Use Social Media to Enhance Brand, Business" in Contractor (Vol. 56, December 2009, No. 12, pp. 14)*
Pub: Penton Media, Inc.
Ed: Elton Rivas. **Description:** Advice on how to plumbing contractors should use online social networks to increase sales is presented including such issues as clearly defining goals and target audience. An additional advantage to this medium is that advertisements can easily be shared with other users.

18713 ■ *"Water Efficiency Bill Move Through Congress" in Contractor (Vol. 56, July 2009, No. 7, pp. 20)*
Pub: Penton Media, Inc.
Ed: Kevin Schwalb. **Description:** National Association, a plumbing-heating-cooling contractor, was instrumental in drafting the Water Advanced Technologies for Efficient Resource Use Act of 2009 and they are also backing the Water Accountability Tax Efficiency Reinvestment Act. The first bill promotes WaterSense-labeled products while the other promotes water conservation through tax credits.

SOURCES OF SUPPLY

18714 ■ *Plumbing Engineer--Product Directory Issue: Engineered Plumbing Systems Directory*
Trend Publishing
URL(s): www.thewholesaler.com. **Released:** Monthly; 12 times a year. **Price:** $50, Individuals one year. **Covers:** Over 400 plumbing products from approximately 250 manufacturers. **Entries include:** Company name, phone, fax, website, and e-mail; name of engineering contact with the firm. **Database includes:** List of American Society of Plumbing Engineers (ASPE) national officers, industry associations.

TRADE PERIODICALS

18715 ■ *Indiana Contractor: Air Conditioning, Heating, Plumbing, Refrigeration, Sheet Metal*
Pub: Indiana Association of Plumbing Heating, Cooling Contractors
URL(s): www.iaphcc.com/Membership/IndianaContractorMagazine/tabid/75/Default. **Released:** Quarterly

FRANCHISES AND BUSINESS OPPORTUNITIES

18716 ■ **Rooter-Man**
A-Corp
268 Rangeway Rd.
N Billerica, MA 01862
Ph: (800)700-8062
Fax: (978)667-1144
Co. E-mail: info@rooterman.com
URL: http://www.rooterman.com

Description: A successful and proven system built around the exclusive use of the Rooter-Man Trademark territory. With your license you will have access to the management skills and know how of professionals who have had years of experience in the plumbing, and drain clearing industries. **No. of Franchise Units:** 445. **Founded:** 1970.. **Franchised:** 1981. **Equity Capital Needed:** $25,000. **Franchise Fee:** $7,950. **Financial Assistance:** Yes. **Training:** A complete 2 day training program devoted to advanced techniques in both practical and management training. Training will consist of 2 days at various locations across the country. Provides unlimited ongoing support by personal coach.

ASSOCIATIONS AND OTHER ORGANIZATIONS

18717 ■ American Needlepoint Guild (ANG)
2424 American Ln.
Madison, WI 53704-3102
Ph: (608)443-2476
Fax: (608)443-2474
Co. E-mail: membership@needlepoint.org
URL: http://www.needlepoint.org
Contact: Sue Haines, Vice President
Description: Males and females of all ages who enjoy needlepoint. Seeks to provide educational and cultural development through participation in and encouragement of interest in the art and history of needlepoint. Sponsors amateur and professional needlework exhibits; offers correspondence courses and teacher and judging certification programs; sponsors annual seminar. **Founded:** 1972. **Publications:** *Needle Pointers* (6/year). **Educational Activities:** American Needlepoint Guild Seminar (Annual); American Needlepoint Guild Show (Annual).

18718 ■ American Sewing Guild (ASG)
9660 Hillcroft, Ste. 510
Houston, TX 77096
Ph: (713)729-3000
Fax: (713)721-9230
Co. E-mail: ddias@asg.org
URL: http://www.asg.org
Contact: Margo Martin, Executive Director
Description: Home sewers and people interested in sewing. Provides current sewing information and advice through lectures, demonstrations, classes, seminars, and fashion shows. Seeks to improve communication between home sewers and sewing industry. Encourages the development of neighborhood workshop groups. **Founded:** 1978. **Awards:** Community Service Volunteer of the Year (Annual); Member of the Year (Annual).

18719 ■ The National Needle Arts Association (TNNA)
1100-H Brandywine Blvd.
Zanesville, OH 43701-7303
Ph: (740)455-6773
Free: 800-889-8662
Fax: (740)452-2552
Co. E-mail: tnna.info@offinger.com
URL: http://www.tnna.org
Contact: Joel Woodcock, President
Description: Manufacturers, retailers and distributors of upscale needle art products (needlepoint, embroidery, cross stitch, crochet, knitting, books and accessories). Advances its community of professional businesses by encouraging the passion for needle arts though education, industry knowledge exchange and a strong marketplace. **Founded:** 1975. **Publications:** *Directory of Exhibitors* (Semiannual); *TNNA Today*. **Awards:** Excellence in Needlework Award (Annual).

REFERENCE WORKS

18720 ■ *"35-Year-Old Downtown Fabric Store Closes Doors" in The Times and Democrat (September 29, 2009)*
Pub: The Times and Democrat
Description: Warren's Fashion Fabrics Inc., a 35-year-old retail fabric, decor and sewing store, officially closed its doors due, in part, to the changing tide of the industry in which fewer women sew and products from countries such as China are so cheap.

18721 ■ *Enterprising Women in Urban Zimbabwe: Gender, Microbusiness, and Globalization*
Pub: Indiana University Press
Contact: Janet Rabinowitch, Director
E-mail: jrabinow@indiana.edu
Ed: Mary Johnson Osirim. **Released:** April 1, 2009. **Price:** $39.95. **Description:** An investigation into the business and personal experiences of women entrepreneurs in the microenterprise sector in Zimbabwe. Many of these women work as market traders, crocheters, seamstresses, and hairdressers.

18722 ■ *"Fabric, Craft Store Opens in North Bibb" in Macon Telegraph (July 17, 2010)*
Pub: Macon Telegraph
Ed: Linda S. Morris. **Description:** Ohio-based Jo-Ann Fabrics and Craft Stores opened a new shop in Macon, Georgia. The store will feature items for crafters, hobbyists, needle artists and seamstresses.

18723 ■ *"Group Sewing for Area Charities" in Messenger-Inquirer (July 7, 2010)*
Pub: Messenger-Inquirer
Ed: Beth Wilberding. **Description:** Hobby Lobby in Owensboro, Kentucky features a weekly sewing group that made 656 pillowcases for area agencies.

18724 ■ *"How-To Workshops Teach Sewing, Styles" in St. Louis Post-Dispatch (September 14, 2010)*
Pub: St. Louis Post-Dispatch
Ed: Kalen Ponche. **Description:** Profile of DIY Style Workshop in St. Charles, Missouri, where sewing, designing and teaching is offered. The shop is home base for DIY Style, a Website created by mother and daughter to teach younger people how to sew.

18725 ■ *"Jo-Ann Fabric and Craft Stores Joins ArtFire.com to Offer Free Online Craft Marketplace" in Internet Wire (January 26, 2010)*
Pub: Comtex News Network, Inc.
Description: Jo-Ann Fabric and Craft Stores has entered into a partnership with ArtFire.com which will provide sewers and crafters all the tools they need in order to make and sell their products from an online venue.

18726 ■ *"Jo-Ann Launches Quilt Your Colors Contest to Celebrate National Sewing Month" in Internet Wire (September 10, 2010)*
Pub: Comtex
Description: Jo-Ann Fabric and Craft Stores featured a contest to create a quilt in order to promote National Sewing Month.

18727 ■ *"Liora Manne to Debut Fabric Line" in Home Textiles Today (Vol. 31, May 24, 2011, No. 13, pp. 4)*
Pub: Reed Business Information
Contact: Jeff Greisch, President
Description: Textile and product designer Liora Manne will debut her new decorative fabric collection at the Showtime in High Point, North Carolina in June 2011. More than 22 fabric patterns and solid colors using Manne's patented Lamontage textile design process will be featured and can be used for indoor/outdoor decorative fabrics, furniture, decorative pillows, upholstery and more.

18728 ■ *"Make It Yourself: Home Sewing, Gender, and Culture, 1890-1930" in Business History Review (Vol. 84, Autumn 2010, No. 3, pp. 602)*
Pub: Harvard Business School
Contact: Brian Kenny, Chief Marketing Officer
E-mail: bkenny@hbs.edu
Ed: Alexis McCrossen. **Description:** Review of the publication, 'Make It Yourself: Home Sewing, Gender, and Culture, 1890-1930, a nonfiction work.

18729 ■ *"Readers Share How Sewing Shaped the Fabric of Their Lives" in Virginian-Pilot (September 14, 2010)*
Pub: Virginian-Pilot
Ed: Jamesetta Walker. **Description:** People discuss the ways sewing has help enrich their lives, from public service projects and conventions centered on sewing.

18730 ■ *"Remodeled Stores Help Fabric Retailer Stitch Up Profit Growth" in Investor's Business Daily (January 7, 2010, pp. A06)*
Pub: Investor's Business Daily
Ed: Marilyn Much. **Description:** Overview of the successful plan implemented by Darrell Webb for Jo-Ann Fabric and Craft stores to stimulate growth and generate revenue; changes include better inventory controls and remodeling; statistical data included.

18731 ■ *"Sewing Is a Life Skill; Teaching To Sew Is An Art" in Virginia-Pilot (August 31, 2010)*
Pub: Virginia-Pilot
Ed: Jamesetta Walker. **Description:** In conjunction with National Sewing Month, the American Sewing Guild is sponsoring a two-day workshop featuring Stephanie Kimura.

18732 ■ *"Sewing Resurgence" in Northeast Mississippi Daily Journal (June 11, 2010)*
Pub: Northeast Mississippi Daily Journal
Ed: Ginna Parsons. **Description:** Information about the growing trend in sewing is discussed.

18733 ■ *"Sewing Shoppe Is All His" in News & Observer (October 8, 2010)*
Pub: News & Observer
Ed: Sue Stock. **Description:** Profile of My Sewing Shoppe, authorized sales and service dealers for Pfaff and Singer sewing machines, and also sells items for sewing, embroider and quilting. The store is located in Raleigh, North Carolina area.

18734 ■ *"S.M. Whitney Co. (1868-2010)" in Canadian Business (Vol. 83, October 12, 2010, No. 17, pp. 27)*

Pub: Rogers Media Ltd.

Ed: Angelina Chapin. **Description:** A history of S.M. Whitney Company is presented. The cotton company was opened in 1868. The cotton is sold to textile manufacturers after crops have been picked, ginned and baled. The company closed down in 2010 after chief executive officer Barry Whitney decided to sell his last bale of cotton.

18735 ■ *"Suddenly, Sewing Is Hip Again for Kids, Moms and Crafters" in Atlanta Journal-Constitution (August 29, 2010)*

Pub: Atlanta Journal-Constitution

Ed: Rosalind Bentley. **Description:** Across Atlanta, Georgia, along with the entire nation, sewing classes are increasing in popularity.

18736 ■ *"Sunbrella Engages Consumers Via Social Media" in Home Textiles Today (Vol. 31, May 24, 2011, No. 13, pp. 4)*

Pub: Reed Business Information

Contact: Jeff Greisch, President

Description: Performance fabric brand Sunbrella is marketing to social media, such as Facebook and Twitter, in order to boost consumer interest and retailer support.

18737 ■ *"Ultimate Business of the Week: McDougals Sewing Center" in Houston Chronicle (December 2, 2010)*

Pub: Houston Chronicle

Description: Profile of family owned, McDouglas Sewing Center located in Houston, Texas. The shop offers computerized sewing machines, supplies, classes and repairs.

TRADE PERIODICALS

18738 ■ *Sew News: Creating For You and Your Home*

Pub: Primedia Consumer Media and Magazine Group

URL(s): www.sewnews.com/index.html. **Ed:** Ellen March. **Released:** 6/yr. **Price:** $21.98, Individuals; $38.98, Two years; $27.98, Canada; $33.98, Other countries; $50.98, Two years; $62.98, Institutions 2 years.

VIDEOCASSETTES/ AUDIOCASSETTES

18739 ■ *Cotton Production*
CEV Multimedia
1020 SE Loop 289
Lubbock, TX 79404
Ph: (806)745-8820
Free: 877-610-5017
Fax: (800)243-6398
Co. E-mail: cev@cevmultimedia.com
URL: http://www.cevmultimedia.com
Contact: Jeff Lansdell, President
Released: 19??. **Price:** $59.95. **Description:** Outlines all areas of the cotton industry from planting to clothing production. **Availability:** VHS.

18740 ■ *How to Make Money in a Home-Based Sewing Business*
Nancy's Notions Ltd.
333 Beichl Ave.
P.O. Box 683
Beaver Dam, WI 53916-0683
Ph: (920)887-7321
Free: 800-725-0361
Fax: (800)255-8119
Co. E-mail: customerservice@nancysnotions.com
URL: http://www.nancysnotions.com
Released: 1989. **Description:** Turn your hobby into a money-making operation with these sew-for-profit tips. **Availability:** VHS.

TRADE SHOWS AND CONVENTIONS

18741 ■ **Industrial Fabrics Association International Expo**
Industrial Fabrics Association International
1801 County Rd. B W
Roseville, MN 55113-4061
Ph: (651)222-2508
Free: 800-225-4324
Fax: (651)631-9334
Co. E-mail: generalinfo@ifai.com
URL: http://www.ifai.com
Contact: Stephen M. Warner, Chief Executive Officer
E-mail: smwarner@ifai.com
URL(s): www.ifai.com. **Frequency:** Annual. **Principal Exhibits:** Industrial and commercial fabric equipment, supplies, and services. **Telecommunication Services:** generalinfo@ifai.com.

FRANCHISES AND BUSINESS OPPORTUNITIES

18742 ■ **Color-Glo International**
CGI International Inc.
7111-7115 Ohms Ln.
Minneapolis, MN 55439
Ph: (952)835-1338
Free: 800-333-8523
Fax: (952)835-1395
Co. E-mail: cgiinc@aol.com
URL: http://www.colorglo.com
Description: Fabric re-dyeing and restoration service franchises. **No. of Franchise Units:** 121. **No. of Company-Owned Units:** 1. **Founded:** 1978.. **Franchised:** 1984. **Equity Capital Needed:** $44,500-$49,300. **Franchise Fee:** $16,750-$25,000. **Financial Assistance:** None. **Training:** Yes.

18743 ■ **Hometown Threads**
209 Hudson Trace
Augusta, GA 30907
Ph: (706)737-7687
Fax: (706)737-7690
Co. E-mail: info@hometownthreads.com
URL: http://www.hometownthreads.com
Description: Retail embroidery store located within Wal-Mart encourage shoppers to create and buy custom designed gifts and products. **No. of Franchise Units:** 44. **No. of Company-Owned Units:** 4. **Founded:** 1998.. **Franchised:** 2001. **Equity Capital Needed:** Total investment $165,000. **Franchise Fee:** $29,000. **Royalty Fee:** 6%. **Financial Assistance:** Third party financing available. **Training:** Offers 3 weeks training at headquarters, 2 weeks at franchisees location with ongoing support.

LIBRARIES

18744 ■ **Center for the History of American Needlework Library**
1445 E. Cruikshank Rd.
Valencia, PA 16059-3709
Ph: (724)586-5325
Co. E-mail: charlottearn@hotmail.com
Contact: Mary Ann Geiger, Executive Director
Scope: Needlework, embroidery, lacemaking, textile fabrics, weaving, spinning, costume. **Services:** Library open to the public for reference use only. **Founded:** 1975. **Holdings:** 2000 books; 7000 leaflets/magazines; 3500 slides; textile collection.

ASSOCIATIONS AND OTHER ORGANIZATIONS

18745 ■ Shoe Service Institute of America (SSIA)
305 Huntsman Ct.
Bel Air, MD 21015
Ph: (410)569-3425
Fax: (410)569-8333
Co. E-mail: don@shoeglue.com
URL: http://www.ssia.info
Contact: Donald Rinaldi, President
Description: Finders (wholesalers) of shoe repair supplies and equipment. Supplier members are manufacturers, tanners and distributors. **Founded:** 1904. **Publications:** *Shoe Service Institute of America--Membership Directory* (Annual). **Awards:** Silver Cup (Annual).

FRANCHISES AND BUSINESS OPPORTUNITIES

18746 ■ Heel Quik! & Heel/Sew Quik!
Heel Quik!, Inc.
2359 Windy Hill Rd., Ste. 400
Marietta, GA 30067
Ph: (770)951-9440
Fax: (770)933-8268
Description: Instant shoe repair, clothing alterations and monogramming. **No. of Franchise Units:** 730. **No. of Company-Owned Units:** 2. **Founded:** 1984.. **Franchised:** 1985. **Equity Capital Needed:** $20,000-$85,000. **Franchise Fee:** $17,500. **Training:** Yes.

START-UP INFORMATION

18747 ■ *"Stepping Out' in Small Business Opportunities (Get Rich At Home 2010)*
Pub: Harris Publications Inc.
Description: Earn $1 million a year selling flip flops? A Flip Flop Shop franchise will help individuals start their own business.

18748 ■ *"Well-Heeled Startup" in Business Journal Portland (Vol. 27, November 12, 2010, No. 37, pp. 1)*
Pub: Portland Business Journal
Ed: Erik Siemers. **Description:** Oh! Shoes LLC expects to receive about $1.5 million in funding from angel investors, while marketing a new line of high heel shoes that are comfortable, healthy, and attractive. The new line of shoes will use the technology of athletic footwear while having the look of an Italian designer. Oh! Shoes hopes to generate $35 million in sales by 2014.

ASSOCIATIONS AND OTHER ORGANIZATIONS

18749 ■ **Footwear Distributors and Retailers of America (FDRA)**
1319 F St. NW, Ste. 700
Washington, DC 20004
Ph: (202)737-5660
Fax: (202)645-0789
Co. E-mail: info@fdra.org
URL: http://www.fdra.org
Contact: Peter Mangione, President
E-mail: ptmangione@fdra.org
Description: Volume shoe store chains. Conducts traffic, foreign sourcing, customs, leadership and employment relations' seminars. **Founded:** 1944. **Publications:** *Footwear Distributors and Retailers of America--Membership Listing Online.*

18750 ■ **National Shoe Retailers Association (NSRA)**
7386 N La Cholla Blvd.
Tucson, AZ 85741-2305
Ph: (520)209-1710
Free: 800-673-8446
URL: http://www.nsra.org
Contact: Mark Denkler, Chairman
Description: Proprietors of independent shoe stores and stores with major shoe departments. Provides business services and professional development programs including bankcard processing, shipping, freight discounts, free website listing, employee training; conducts research; monitors legislation. **Scope:** footwear, business start up employee relations, marketing. **Founded:** 1912. **Subscriptions:** 500 archival material business records clippings periodicals. **Publications:** *Business Performance Report* (Biennial). **Educational Activities:** National Shoe Retailers Association Conference (Semiannual); Leadership Conference (Biennial). **Awards:** Retail Excellence Awards (Annual).

18751 ■ **Pedorthic Footcare Association (PFA)**
8400 Westpark Dr., 2nd Fl.
McLean, VA 22102
Fax: (703)995-4456
Co. E-mail: info@pedorthics.org
URL: http://www.pedorthics.org
Contact: Brian Lagana, Executive Director
Description: Professionals involved in the field of pedorthics. (Pedorthics is the design, manufacture, fit and modification of shoes and foot orthoses to alleviate foot problems caused by disease, overuse, or injury). **Scope:** orthopedic footwear and conservative care of the foot. **Founded:** 1958. **Subscriptions:** 100 archival material books business records clippings periodicals. **Publications:** *When the Shoe Fits.* **Awards:** Aristotle Mirones (Annual); Seymour Lefton, Vendor of the Year (Annual).

REFERENCE WORKS

18752 ■ *"Adidas' Brand Ambitions" in Business Journal Portland (Vol. 27, December 10, 2010, No. 41, pp. 1)*
Pub: Portland Business Journal
Ed: Erik Siemers. **Description:** Adidas AG, the second-largest sporting goods brand in the world, hopes to increase global revenue by 50 percent by 2015. The German company, which reported $14.5 billion sales, plans to improve its U.S. market. The U.S. is Adidas' largest, but also the most underperforming market for the firm.

18753 ■ *"Apparel' in Retail Merchandiser (Vol. 51, July-August 2011, No. 4, pp. 14)*
Pub: Phoenix Media Corporation
Description: NPD Group Inc. released current sales statistics for the women's apparel market along with men's apparel. It also reported annual shoes sales for 2010. Statistical data included.

18754 ■ *"Design program in Athletic Footwear" in Occupational Outlook Quarterly (Vol. 55, Fall 2011, No. 3, pp. 21)*
Pub: U.S. Bureau of Labor Statistics
Description: The Fashion Institute of Technology offers the only certificate program in performance athletic footwear design in the U.S. The program focuses on conceptualizing and sketching shoe designs and covers ergonomic, anatomical, and material considerations for athletic footwear design.

18755 ■ *"EEOC Sues Charlotte-Based Lebo's" in Charlotte Observer (February 7, 2007)*
Pub: Knight-Ridder/Tribune Business News
Ed: Mike Drummond. **Description:** The U.S. Equal Employment Opportunity Commission filed a pregnancy discrimination lawsuit against Lebo's Shoe Stores, located in Charlotte, North Carolina. The suit alleges the store withdrew an offer to hire a woman after finding out she was pregnant.

18756 ■ *"Energy Outfitter Wings Into Houston" in Houston Business Journal (Vol. 40, December 4, 2009, No. 30, pp. 2A)*
Pub: American City Business Journals
Ed: Ford Gunter. **Description:** Red Wing Shoe Company Inc. has launched its personal protective equipment (PPE) line for oil and gas industry crewmen in North America by opening a 13,000 square foot distribution hub in Houston, Texas. The Houston facility was created to supply directly the oil and gas industry and to carry inventory for select distributors.

18757 ■ *"Hot Kicks, Cool Price" in Black Enterprise (Vol. 37, December 2006, No. 5, pp. 34)*
Pub: Earl G. Graves Publishing Co. Inc.
Ed: Topher Sanders. **Description:** Stephon Marbury of the New York Nicks introduced a new basketball shoe, the Starbury One, costing $14.98. The shoes are an addition to the Starbury clothing line and although the privately owned company would not disclose figures; stores sold out of a month's worth of inventory in merely three days.

18758 ■ *"How to Keep Your Cool and Your Friends in a Heat Wave" in Canadian Business (Vol. 83, August 17, 2010, No. 13-14, pp. 79)*
Pub: Rogers Media Ltd.
Ed: Angelina Chapin. **Description:** A buyer's guide of menswear clothing for businessmen is presented. The products include an antiperspirant and deodorant, men's dress shorts, shoes and bamboo fabric undershirt.

18759 ■ *"Laced Up and Ready to Run" in Barron's (Vol. 89, July 6, 2009, No. 27, pp. 12)*
Pub: Dow Jones & Co., Inc.
Ed: Christopher C. Williams. **Description:** Shares of Foot Locker could raise from $10 to about $15 a share with the improvement of the economy. The company has benefited from prudent management and merchandising as well as better cost cutting, allowing it to better survive in a recession.

18760 ■ *"Life's Work: Manolo Blahnik" in Harvard Business Review (Vol. 88, December 2010, No. 12, pp. 144)*
Pub: Harvard Business School Publishing
Ed: Alison Beard. **Description:** Shoe designer Manolo Blahnik recounts his beginnings in the shoe industry and the influence art has had on his work, as well as balancing art and commerce. He also discusses the importance of quality materials and craftsmanship and the benefits of managing an independent, family-owned business.

18761 ■ *"Portland Wooing Under Armour to West Coast Facility" in Baltimore Business Journal (Vol. 27, January 29, 2010, No. 39, pp. 1)*
Pub: American City Business Journals
Ed: Andy Giegerich. **Description:** Baltimore, Maryland sports apparel maker, Under Armour, is planning a west coast expansion with Portland, Oregon among the sites considered to house its apparel and footwear

design center. Portland officials counting on the concentration of nearly 10,000 activewear workers in the city will help lure the company to the city.

18762 ■ "Research Reports: How Analysts Size Up Companies" in Barron's (Vol. 88, July 14, 2008, No. 28, pp. M13)
Pub: Dow Jones & Co., Inc.
Ed: Anita Peltonen. **Description:** Shares of Bankrate and AutoZone both get a 'Buy' rating from analysts while Zions Bancorporation's shares are downgraded from 'Outperform' to 'Neutral'. The shares of Jet Blue Airline and Deckers Outdoor, a manufacturer of innovative footwear, are also rated and discussed. Statistical data included.

18763 ■ "Retail News: Children's Boutique Relocates to Conway" in Sun News (June 4, 2010)
Pub: The Sun News
Description: Little Angel's Children's Boutique and Big Oak Frame Shop have moved to downtown locations in Conway, South Carolina. Little Angel's will sell children's clothing and accessories, shoes and gifts, while the frame shop will offer custom framing along with the sale of stationary, invitations and local prints.

18764 ■ "Retail Woes: The Shoe Doesn't Fit for Gerald Loftin's Stock Picks" in Black Enterprise (Vol. 38, July 2008, No. 12, pp. 40)
Pub: Earl G. Graves Publishing Co. Inc.
Ed: Steve Garmhausen. **Description:** Each of the three stocks that Gerald Loftin picked in May 2007 have lost money; DSW, the designer shoe retailer, fell by 63.7 percent; paint and coatings retailer Sherwin-Williams Co. fell by 7.2 percent; and Verizon Communications Inc. fell by 1.4 percent. Statistical data included.

18765 ■ "Rough Q1 Begs Question: Is the Crocs Craze Over?" in Brandweek (Vol. 49, April 21, 2008, No. 16, pp. 16)
Pub: VNU Business Media, Inc.
Ed: Eric Newman. **Description:** Crocs, a rubber shoemaker, announced last week that it missed its expected first quarter revenues by 15 percent. The popular rubber sandals are suffering in sales due to a number of factors including a tougher economic environment, less expensive, knock-off brands, the cold weather delay of the spring season and fading consumer interest in plastic shoes.

18766 ■ Shoe Factory Buyer's Guide
Pub: Shoe Trades Publishing Co.
Contact: Inta Huns, Editor
E-mail: inta@shoetrades.com
URL(s): www.shoetrades.com/directories.php. **Released:** Annual; Latest edition 2008. **Price:** $59, Individuals. **Covers:** Over 600 suppliers and their representatives to the shoe manufacturing industries in the United States and Canada. **Entries include:** Company name, address, phone, fax, trade and brand names, list of products or services. **Arrangement:** Classified by type of product or service. **Indexes:** Product, trademark.

18767 ■ "Shop Around" in Houston Chronicle (December 7, 2010, pp. 3)
Pub: Houston Chronicle
Ed: Tara Dooley. **Description:** Profile of Diana Candida and Maria Martinez who partnered to open Beatniks, a shop carrying vintage clothing, art from various artists, dance shoes, and jewelry.

18768 ■ Sneaker Wars: The Enemy Brothers Who Founded Adidas and Puma and the Family Feud that Forever Changed the Business of Sport
Pub: Ecco
Ed: Barbara Smit. **Released:** 2009. **Price:** $26.95. **Description:** A history of Puma and Adidas shoes and the two German brothers who built the empires.

18769 ■ "Stepping Up" in Baltimore Business Journal (Vol. 28, October 22, 2010, No. 24, pp. 1)
Pub: Baltimore Business Journal
Ed: Erik Siemers. **Description:** Uner Armour Inc. will release its Micro G line of four basketball sneakers on October 23, 2010. The company's executives

mentioned that Under Armour's goal is to appeal to customers, and not to chip away at Nike Inc.'s supremacy in basketball shoes. The new sneakers will range from $80 to $110.

18770 ■ The Towering World of Jimmy Choo: A Story of Power, Profits, and the Pursuit of the Perfect Shoe
Pub: Bloomsbury USA
Ed: Lauren Goldstein Crowe, Sagra Maceira de Rosen. **Released:** 2009. **Description:** Profile of Jimmy Choo and his pursuit to manufacture the perfect shoe.

18771 ■ "Unpleasant Surprise" in Barron's (Vol. 88, March 24, 2008, No. 12, pp. 60)
Pub: Dow Jones & Company, Inc.
Ed: Shirley A. Lazo. **Description:** Discusses the $175 million that footwear company Genesco received in a settlement with Finish Line and UBS is considered as a stock distribution and is taxable as dividend income. Railroad company CSX raised its quarterly common payout from 15 cents to 18 cents.

18772 ■ "Walk This Way" in Barron's (Vol. 90, August 23, 2010, No. 34, pp. 13)
Pub: Barron's Editorial & Corporate Headquarters
Ed: Christopher C. Williams. **Description:** Crocs and Skechers are selling very popular shoes and sales show no signs of winding down. The shares of both companies are attractively prices.

18773 ■ "Zappo's CEO On Going to Extremes for Customers" in Harvard Business Review (Vol. 88, July-August 2010, No. 7-8, pp. 41)
Pub: Harvard Business School Publishing
Ed: Tony Hsieh. **Description:** Footwear firm Zappos. com Inc. improved corporate performance through enhanced customer service. Enhancements include highly visible phone numbers, avoidance of scripts, and viewing call centers as marketing departments.

STATISTICAL SOURCES

18774 ■ The Athletic Footwear Market
Pub: Rector Press, Ltd.
Contact: Lewis Sckolnick, President
Released: 2009. **Price:** Contact Rector Press.

18775 ■ Market Outlook for Footwear
Pub: Business Trend Analysts, Inc.
Released: 2005-2006. **Price:** $2995.00. **Description:** An in-depth investigation of the size and growth of the U.S. market for men's, women's, and children's footwear, including all types of dress shoes, casual footwear, boots, slippers, athletic shoes, work shoes, and more.

18776 ■ RMA Annual Statement Studies
Pub: Risk Management Association
Contact: Kevin M. Blakey, President
Released: Annual. **Price:** $175.00 2006-07 edition, $105.00. **Description:** Contains composite balance sheets and income statements for more than 360 industries, including the accounting, auditing, and bookkeeping industries. Also contains five years of comparative historical data for discerning trends. Includes 16 commonly used ratios, computed for most of the size groupings for nearly every industry.

TRADE PERIODICALS

18777 ■ Shoe Retailing Today
Pub: National Shoe Retailers Association
Ed: Nancy Hultquist, Editor. **Released:** Quarterly. **Price:** Included in membership; $35, individuals; $55, elsewhere. **Description:** Provides news of activities and developments in independent shoe retailing. Recurring features include member news, calendar of events, product reference guide and vendor profiles.

TRADE SHOWS AND CONVENTIONS

18778 ■ China International Footwear Fair
Neway International Trade Fairs Ltd.
9/F, Fortis Tower
77 Gloucester Rd.
Wan Chai, China

Ph: 852 2561 5566
Fax: 852 2811 9156
Co. E-mail: info@newayfairs.com
URL: http://www.newayfairs.com
URL(s): aplf.com. **Principal Exhibits:** Footwear and accessories, manufacturing, and manufacturing materials. **Telecommunication Services:** info@aplf. com.

FRANCHISES AND BUSINESS OPPORTUNITIES

18779 ■ The Athlete's Foot
Global Franchise Group
1346 Oakbrook Dr., Ste. 170
Norcross, GA 30093
Ph: (880)524-6444
Fax: (770)514-4903
URL: http://www.theathletesfoot.com
Description: Retailer specializing in athletic footwear. **No. of Franchise Units:** 95. **Founded:** 1972.. **Franchised:** 1973. **Equity Capital Needed:** $209,950-$495,250; $250,000 net worth, $100,000-$150,000 cash liquidity. **Franchise Fee:** $15,000-$30,000. **Royalty Fee:** 5%. **Financial Assistance:** Third party financing available. **Training:** Provides 5 days at headquarters, 5 days at opening with ongoing support.

18780 ■ Kiddie Kobbler Ltd.
PO Box 27038
Kingston, ON, Canada K7M 8W5
Ph: (613)592-5515
Fax: (613)592-5314
Co. E-mail: kiddiekobblerltd@rogers.com
URL: http://www.kiddiekobbler.com
Description: Children's shoe stores with brand name footwear for all seasons plus dance and athletic footwear, accessories, and apparel too. **No. of Franchise Units:** 13. **Founded:** 1946. **Franchised:** 1968. **Equity Capital Needed:** $175,000-$300,000. **Franchise Fee:** $35,000. **Training:** 3 weeks in an existing location.

18781 ■ Les Franchises Panda Ltee/Panda Franchises Ltd.
259 Labelle Blvd. Suite 201
Rosemere, QC, Canada J7A 2H3
Ph: (450)818-9741
Fax: (450)622-2939
URL: http://www.pandashoes.com
Description: Children's shoe specialist. **No. of Franchise Units:** 28. **No. of Company-Owned Units:** 3. **Founded:** 1972. **Franchised:** 1974. **Equity Capital Needed:** $125,000 start-up; $200,00-$350,000 total investment. **Franchise Fee:** $25,000. **Training:** Yes.

18782 ■ Shoes-n-Feet
The Toe Box
15015 Main St., Ste. 211
Bellevue, WA 98007
Ph: (425)830-1605
Free: 888-994-FEET
Fax: (425)562-5005
Co. E-mail: jb.smith@shoesnfeet.com
URL: http://www.shoesnfeet.com
Description: Education based healthy shoe store servicing the baby-boomer generation. **No. of Franchise Units:** 8. **No. of Company-Owned Units:** 1. **Founded:** 1998.. **Franchised:** 2002. **Equity Capital Needed:** $185,000-$226,500. **Franchise Fee:** $25,000. **Royalty Fee:** 5%. **Training:** Provides up to 160 hours training at headquarters and at franchisee's location as needed with ongoing support.

18783 ■ Z-Coil Pain Relief Footwear
Z-Tech Inc.
6932 4th St. NW
Albuquerque, NM 87107
Ph: (505)345-2222
Free: 800-268-6239
Fax: (505)938-5770
Co. E-mail: franchise@zcoil.com
URL: http://www.zcoil.com
Description: Retailing of revolutionary line of footwear specifically designed for foot, leg and back pain relief. **No. of Franchise Units:** 66. **No. of**

Company-Owned Units: 1. **Founded:** 1995.. **Franchised:** 2005. **Equity Capital Needed:** $88,150-$160,800. **Franchise Fee:** $15,000. **Financial Assistance:** Limited third party financing available. **Training:** Offers 5 day training program and ongoing support.

LIBRARIES

18784 ■ National Shoe Retailers Association Library
3037 W. Ina Rd.
Tucson, AZ 85741
Ph: (520)209-1710

Free: 800-673-8446
Co. E-mail: info@nsra.org
URL: http://www.nsra.org
Contact: Chuck Schuyler, President
Scope: Footwear, business start-up, employee relations, marketing. **Services:** Library not open to the public. **Holdings:** 500 periodicals, clippings, business records, and archival materials.

ASSOCIATIONS AND OTHER ORGANIZATIONS

18785 ■ **International Sign Association (ISA)**
1001 N Fairfax St., Ste. 301
Alexandria, VA 22314-1587
Ph: (703)836-4012
Fax: (703)836-8353
Co. E-mail: info@signs.org
URL: http://www.signs.org
Contact: Lori Anderson, President
E-mail: lori.anderson@signs.org

Description: Manufacturers, users, and suppliers of on-premise signs and sign products produced by more than 400,000 employees in all 50 states and 69 countries. Exists to support, promote and improve the $30 billion-a-year sign industry, which sustains the nation's nearly $3 trillion-a-year retail industry. **Founded:** 1944. **Publications:** *International Sign Association--Membership Directory* (Annual). **Educational Activities:** International Sign Association International Sign Expo (Annual); ISA Midwest Sign Show; ISA Northwest Sign Show; ISA Southern Sign Show; ISA Summer Sign Expo (Annual); ISA Western Sign Expo. **Awards:** Sign Design Award (Annual); Kirk L. Brimley Distinguished Service Award (Annual).

REFERENCE WORKS

18786 ■ *"Bright Lights, Big Impact: Why Digital Billboards are Growing in Popularity"* in *Inc. (March 2008, pp. 61-62)*
Pub: Gruner & Jahr USA Publishing

Ed: Sarah Goldstein. **Description:** Clear Channel provides high tech digital billboards which allow companies to change advertising as often as necessary during a contract period. The Outdoor Advertising Association of America predicts the growth of digital billboards at several hundred per year over the next few years. CEO of Magic Media believes all billboards will eventually go digital.

18787 ■ *"First the Merger: Then, The Culture Clash. How To Fix the Little Things That Can Tear a Company Apart"* in *Inc. (January 2008)*
Pub: Gruner & Jahr USA Publishing

Ed: Elaine Appleton Grant. **Description:** Ways three CEOs handled the culture classes that followed after company mergers; companies profiled include Fuel Outdoor, an outdoor advertising company; Nelson, an interior design and architecture firm; and Beber Silverstein, an ad agency.

18788 ■ *"Sign, Sign, Everywhere a Sign: How I Did It: Richard Schaps"* in *Inc. (October 2007, pp. 128)*
Pub: Gruner & Jahr USA Publishing

Ed: Stephanie Clifford. **Description:** Richard Schaps shares the story of selling his outdoor-advertising firm, Van Wagner for $170 million and sharing the wealth with his employees. Schaps then started another outdoor-sign company.

18789 ■ *Signs of the Times Magazine--Buyers' Guide Issue*
Pub: ST Media Group International Inc.
Contact: Tedd Swormstedt, President
URL(s): www.stmediagroup.comwww.stmediagroup.com/index.php3?d=pubs&p=st. **Ed:** Wade Swormstedt. **Released:** Annual; December. **Publication includes:** List of more than 600 manufacturers and distributors of equipment and supplies for the sign industry; trade associations, consultants, trade shows, and other related organizations. **Entries include:** For manufacturers and distributors--Company name, address, phone, name of sales contact; manufacturer listings also include product lines. For others--Organization name, address, phone; trade show listings include dates. **Arrangement:** Alphabetical. **Indexes:** Product, fax number, trade name.

18790 ■ *Signs of the Times Magazine--Sign Erection and Maintenance Directory Section*
Pub: ST Media Group International Inc.
Contact: Tedd Swormstedt, President
URL(s): www.stmediagroup.com/index.php3?d=pubs&p=st. **Released:** Monthly **Publication includes:** List of over 750 companies that erect or maintain electrical signs. **Entries include:** Company name, address, phone, services. **Arrangement:** Geographical. **Indexes:** Product.

18791 ■ *Signs of the Times Magazine--Sign Supply Distributors Directory Section*
Pub: ST Media Group International Inc.
Contact: Tedd Swormstedt, President
URL(s): www.stpubs.comwww.signweb.com, www.stmediagroup.com/index.php3?d=pubs&p=st. **Released:** Monthly **Price:** $39, per year -13 issues; $59, Canada Surface mail; $94, Canada 1st Class mail; $62, Other countries Surface mail; $60, Two years USA; $101, Two years Canada by surface mail; $171, Two years Canada by I class mail; $112, Two years Other countries by surface mail. **Publication includes:** List of more than 80 suppliers of products and services used by sign companies; all listings are paid. **Entries include:** Name of firm, address, phone, code indicating type of product. **Arrangement:** Geographical.

STATISTICAL SOURCES

18792 ■ *RMA Annual Statement Studies*
Pub: Risk Management Association
Contact: Kevin M. Blakey, President
Released: Annual. **Price:** $175.00 2006-07 edition, $105.00. **Description:** Contains composite balance sheets and income statements for more than 360 industries, including the accounting, auditing, and bookkeeping industries. Also contains five years of comparative historical data for discerning trends. Includes 16 commonly used ratios, computed for most of the size groupings for nearly every industry.

TRADE PERIODICALS

18793 ■ *SignCraft: The guide to profitable and creative sign production*
Pub: Signcraft Publishing Co.
Contact: Dennis McIltrot, Partner
URL(s): www.signcraft.com. **Released:** 7/yr. **Price:** $39, Individuals; $69, Two years; $49, Other countries; $91, Other countries 2 years.

18794 ■ *Signs of the Times*
Pub: ST Media Group International Inc.
Contact: Tedd Swormstedt, President
URL(s): www.stmediagroup.com/index.php3?d=pubs&p=stsignweb.com/. **Ed:** Wade Swormstedt. **Released:** 13/yr.

FRANCHISES AND BUSINESS OPPORTUNITIES

18795 ■ **FASTSIGNS International Inc.**
2542 Highlander Way
Carrollton, TX 75006-2333
Ph: (800)827-7446
Fax: (866)422-4927
Co. E-mail: customer.care@fastsigns.com
URL: http://www.fastsigns.com
Contact: Catherine Monson, Chief Executive Officer

Description: Sign and graphics solutions provider for businesses worldwide. **No. of Franchise Units:** 535. **Founded:** 1985. **Franchised:** 1986. **Equity Capital Needed:** $176,063-$292,511 total investment range; net worth, $250,000; liquidity, $75,000. **Franchise Fee:** $34,500. **Financial Assistance:** Yes. **Training:** 2 week new owner training program, 2 week on site support during store opening. Grand opening marketing campaign. Consultation is provided in every area of the business. **Telecommunication Services:** fran.sales@fastsigns.com.

18796 ■ **Signal Graphics Business Centers**
848 Broadway
Denver, CO 80203
Ph: (303)779-6789
Free: 800-852-6336
Fax: (303)779-8445
Co. E-mail: info@signalgraphics.com
URL: http://www.signalgraphics.com

Description: A high volume business without the heavy investment & the complexity associated with traditional printing shops. Expanded portfolio of products & services well beyond the scope of our competition, including printing, copying, packaging and shipping. A unique approach and a low franchise fee & royalty. **No. of Franchise Units:** 34. **No. of Company-Owned Units:** 3. **Founded:** 1974.. **Franchised:** 1982. **Equity Capital Needed:** $50,000 minimum cash. **Franchise Fee:** $25,000. **Financial Assistance:** Yes. **Training:** Yes.

18797 ■ **SIGNARAMA, Inc.**
2121 Vista Pky.
West Palm Beach, FL 33411
Ph: (561)640-5570
Co. E-mail: franchise@signarama.com
URL: http://www.signarama.com

Description: One of the largest Sign Franchise with over 650 stores in 25 countries. Rated 1 in industry past 5 years running by Entrepreneur Magazine's Franchise 500 issues. Our Full-Service Sign Centres utilize the latest in computerized sign making technology. Sign-A-Rama maintains support personnel in Toronto to handle growth in Canada. **No. of Franchise Units:** 900. **Founded:** 1986. **Franchised:** 1987. **Equity Capital Needed:** $45,000 initial investment. **Franchise Fee:** $42,500. **Financial Assistance:** Yes. **Training:** Offers 5 weeks training and ongoing support.

18798 ■ Signs First

Monotag Corp.
PO Box 11569
Memphis, TN 38111
Free: 800-852-2163

Description: Computer-aided design sign stores. **No. of Franchise Units:** 33. **Founded:** 1966. **Franchised:** 1987. **Equity Capital Needed:** $30,000-$118,000. **Franchise Fee:** $7,500-$17,500. **Royalty Fee:** 6%. **Training:** Offers 2 weeks training at headquarters, at franchisee's location, regional locations and ongoing support.

18799 ■ Signs Now

Allegra Network, LLC
47585 Galleon Dr.
Plymouth, MI 48170
Free: 800-726-9050
Fax: (248)596-8601
Co. E-mail: phill@signsnow.com
URL: http://www.signsnowfranchise.com

Description: Computerized 24-hour sign shop, offering signs and graphics for business and retail. **No. of Franchise Units:** 184. **Founded:** 1983.. **Franchised:** 1986. **Equity Capital Needed:** Total investment range $169,832-$333,322; $100,000 liquid. **Franchise Fee:** $45,000 MatchMaker, $35,000 startup & 20,000 resale. **Financial Assistance:** Yes. **Training:** Provides 3 week program at headquarters followed by onsite training.

18800 ■ Signs by Tomorrow

8681 Robert Fulton Dr.
Columbia, MD 21046
Ph: (800)765-7446
Co. E-mail: sales@signsbytomorrow.com
URL: http://www.signsbytomorrow.com

Description: Computerized sign shops offering signs and graphics for virtually all sizes of businesses. Franchisee's responsibility is to manage the sales and administrative areas in servicing a business-to-business clientele during regular working hours. **No. of Franchise Units:** 160. **No. of Company-Owned Units:** 1. **Founded:** 1986.. **Franchised:** 1987. **Equity Capital Needed:** Total investment range $114,000-$230,000; net worth $250,000, liquidity $50,000. **Franchise Fee:** $34,500. **Training:** Training includes 2 weeks at headquarters, 2 weeks of onsite, and assistance with the grand opening.

REFERENCE WORKS

18801 ■ *"Austin's GMP Growth Top in Nation"*
in Austin Business JournalInc. (Vol. 29,
January 8, 2010, No. 44, pp. 1)
Pub: American City Business Journals
Ed: Jacob Dirr. **Description:** Austin's gross metropolitan product (GMP) has grown by 2 percent, putting it
in the top 5 for GMP growth among the largest 100
American metropolitan areas. Insights into the area's
business and technology services are examined.

TRADE PERIODICALS

18802 ■ *Interior Design*
Pub: Reed Business Information
Contact: Jeff Greisch, President
URL(s): www.interiordesign.net/. **Released:** 15/yr.
Price: $59.95, Individuals; $87, Canada; $187, Other
countries.

18803 ■ *Paint & Decorating Retailer*
Magazine
Pub: Paint and Decorating Retailers Association
Contact: Jeff Baggaley, President
URL(s): www.pdra.org/pdr_magazine. **Released:**
Monthly

TRADE SHOWS AND CONVENTIONS

18804 ■ Charlotte Gift and Jewelry Show
Charlotte Gift and Jewelry Show
3710 Latrobe Dr., Ste. 110
Charlotte, NC 28211
Ph: (704)365-4152
Fax: (704)365-4154
Co. E-mail: michael@charlottegiftshow.com
URL(s): www.charlottegiftshow.com. **Frequency:**
Quarterly. **Audience:** Trade buyers. **Principal Exhib-
its:** Gifts, housewares, jewelry, crafts, silk plants and
flowers, tabletop, glassware, collectibles, acces-
sories, home decorating accessories, basketry, and
other related products. **Dates and Locations:**
Merchandise Mart. **Telecommunication Services:**
michael@charlottegiftshow.com.

LIBRARIES

**18805 ■ American Floral Art School - Floral
Library**
2519 W. Altgeld Ave., Ste. 100
Chicago, IL 60647-1910
Ph: (312)922-9328
Co. E-mail: americanfl@americanfloralartschool.com
URL: http://www.americanfloralartschool.com
Contact: James Moretz, Director
Scope: Flower arrangement and symbolism, floral
design, language of flowers. **Services:** Library is accessible on a restricted basis. **Founded:** 1965. **Holdings:** 6000 books; 500 uncataloged items; periodicals; photographs; videotapes. **Subscriptions:** 60
journals and other serials; 2 newspapers. **Telecommunication Services:** jamesflowerman@aol.com.

ASSOCIATIONS AND OTHER ORGANIZATIONS

18806 ▪ Ice Skating Institute (ISI)
6000 Custer Rd., Bldg. 9
Plano, TX 75023
Ph: (972)735-8800
Fax: (972)735-8815
Co. E-mail: isi@skateisi.org
URL: http://www.skateisi.org
Contact: Peter G. Martell, Executive Director
URL(s): www.skateisi.com. **Description:** Represents ice rink owners and managers; builders and suppliers for the industry; skaters; ice skating instructors. Seeks to educate ice arena owners, operators, and instructors and to increase public interest in ice skating. Provides information or building ice facilities. Provides recreational ice skater class programs, and a national test registration program to identify and record skating skill development in free-style, couple and pair skating, ice dancing, figures, hockey, and speed skating. Sponsors Ice Skating Hall of Fame, annual conference and trade show and annual recreational ice skating competitions. Offers professional certification courses through ISI's Ice Arena Institute of Management. **Founded:** 1959. **Publications:** *The ISI EDGE*; *ISI EDGE* (Bimonthly); *Recreational Ice Skating* (Quarterly); *Skaters and Coaches Handbook*; *Recreational Ice Skating* (Quarterly); *Ice Skating Institute--U.S./International Membership Directory* (Annual); *Recreational Ice Skater Team Competition Standards*. **Educational Activities:** Ice Skating Institute Annual Conference (Annual); Adult Championships (Annual); Synchronized Skating Championships (Annual). **Awards:** Ice Skating Institute of America Education Foundation Scholarships; ISIA Education Foundation Scholarship (Annual).

18807 ▪ Professional Skaters Association (PSA)
3006 Allegro Park SW
Rochester, MN 55902
Ph: (507)281-5122
Fax: (507)281-5491
Co. E-mail: office@skatepsa.com
URL: http://skatepsa.com
Contact: Angela Riviello-Steffano, President
Description: Professional ice skaters engaged in the teaching, coaching and performing of ice skating. Strives to form a cohesive body of all professional ice skaters for the benefit of the profession, to protect the interests of members' pupils, to advance all aspects of both ice figure skating and recreational skating, and to promote high ethical and professional standards in the field. Grades teachers on the basis of on-ice proficiency and oral examination. Operates placement service. **Founded:** 1938. **Publications:** *Coaches Manual*; *Professional Skater* (Bimonthly); *Professional Skaters Association–Membership Directory* (Annual); *Professional Skaters Association--Rating Systems Manual* (Periodic); *Skaters Handbook*. **Educational Activities:** U.S. Open Professional Figure Skating Championship (Annual). **Awards:** F. Ritter Shumway Award; Betty Berens Award; Coach of the Year (Annual).

18808 ▪ Roller Skating Association International (RSA)
6905 Corporate Dr.
Indianapolis, IN 46278
Ph: (317)347-2626
Fax: (317)347-2636
Co. E-mail: rsa@rollerskating.com
URL: http://www.rollerskating.org
Contact: Susan Melenchuk, Executive Director
Description: Independent roller skating rink operators; associate members are rink managers, teachers, and suppliers and manufacturers. Promotes the business and recreational sport of roller skating. Provides business and marketing information to skating center owners. **Scope:** roller skating. **Founded:** 1937. **Subscriptions:** 100 archival material artwork audiovisuals books clippings periodicals. **Publications:** *Roller Skating Business* (Bimonthly); *Roller Skating Manufacturer's Newsletter*. **Awards:** Rink Operator of the Year (Annual); Teacher/Coach of the Year (Annual).

STATISTICAL SOURCES

18809 ▪ *RMA Annual Statement Studies*
Pub: Risk Management Association
Contact: Kevin M. Blakey, President
Released: Annual. **Price:** $175.00 2006-07 edition, $105.00. **Description:** Contains composite balance sheets and income statements for more than 360 industries, including the accounting, auditing, and bookkeeping industries. Also contains five years of comparative historical data for discerning trends. Includes 16 commonly used ratios, computed for most of the size groupings for nearly every industry.

TRADE PERIODICALS

18810 ▪ *American Hockey Magazine*
Pub: Touchpoint Publishing
URL(s): www.usahockeymagazine.com. **Released:** 10/yr. **Price:** $15, Individuals.

18811 ▪ *The ISI EDGE*
Pub: Ice Skating Institute
Contact: Peter G. Martell, Executive Director
Ed: Carol Jackson Editor, cjackson@skateisi.org.
Released: Bimonthly. **Description:** Provides information of interest to member ice rinks; promotional ideas, management tips, energy saving suggestions, and instructional information.

18812 ▪ *Rinksider*
Pub: Target Publishing Company Inc.
URL(s): www.rinksider.com. **Released:** Bimonthly. **Price:** $20, Individuals; $35, Two years; $45, Individuals 3 years.

TRADE SHOWS AND CONVENTIONS

18813 ▪ FUN Expo
Reed Exhibitions North American Headquarters
383 Main Ave.
Norwalk, CT 06851
Ph: (203)840-4800
Fax: (203)840-5805
Co. E-mail: inquiry@reedexpo.com
URL: http://www.reedexpo.com
URL(s): www.funexpo.com. **Price:** $20, Pre-registered, members; $40, Pre-registered, non-members; $65, Onsite registered, members; $90, Onsite registered, non-members. **Frequency:** Annual. **Principal Exhibits:** Amusement and recreation products for family and location based entertainment centers, small amusement parks and family oriented businesses such as bowling centers, skating rinks, sports parks, miniature golf courses, golf driving ranges, family restaurants, resorts and other entertainment/recreation businesses.

18814 ▪ Roller Skating Association Convention and Trade Show
Roller Skating Association International
6905 Corporate Dr.
Indianapolis, IN 46278
Ph: (317)347-2626
Fax: (317)347-2636
Co. E-mail: rsa@rollerskating.com
URL: http://www.rollerskating.org
URL(s): www.rollerskating.com. **Price:** $100, Onsite. **Frequency:** Annual. **Audience:** Roller skating rink operators and managers; skating teachers. **Principal Exhibits:** Skate manufacturers, suppliers; novelty companies; snack bar items; sound and lighting; flooring; and arcade games.

LIBRARIES

18815 ▪ National Museum of Roller Skating Archives
4730 South St.
Lincoln, NE 68506
Ph: (402)483-7551
Fax: (402)483-1465
Co. E-mail: directorcurator@rollerskatingmuseum.com
URL: http://www.rollerskatingmuseum.com
Contact: James Vannurden
Scope: Roller skating, skating rules, roller skating history. **Services:** Library open to the public by appointment. **Founded:** 1980. **Holdings:** 1500 books; 8000 photographs; 125 periodical titles; papers of individuals prominent in roller skating; patents; prints; medals; trophies; films; costumes; archival materials; memorabilia. **Subscriptions:** 18 journals and other serials.

ASSOCIATIONS AND OTHER ORGANIZATIONS

18816 ■ Cross Country Ski Areas Association (CCSAA)
259 Bolton Rd.
Winchester, NH 03470
Ph: (603)239-4341
Free: 877-779-2754
Fax: (603)239-6387
Co. E-mail: ccsaa@xcski.org
URL: http://www.xcski.org
Contact: Chris Frado, Executive Director
Description: Owners and operators of cross country ski facilities; suppliers to the industry; individuals engaged in businesses related to cross-country skiing. Seeks to foster, stimulate, and promote cross country skiing in North America; to protect the legitimate interests of the cross-country ski area. Serves as a clearinghouse for cross-country ski areas of all sizes. Compiles and distributes information concerning ongoing developments in the cross country ski industry. Provides trail signs for ski areas to adequately inform or instruct the skier. Works with national groups such as the SnowSports Industries America, National Ski Patrol System, Professional Ski Instructors of America, and Canadian Ski Council. Compiles statistics on the ski industry. **Founded:** 1977. **Publications:** *Nordic Network* (Quarterly); *The Best of Cross Country Skiing--Membership Directory and Beginner's Guide* (Annual); *The Best of Cross Country Skiing and Snowshoeing: Membership Directory and Beginner's Guide* (Annual); *Cross Country Close to Home: A Ski Area Development Manual*; *The Best of Cross Country Skiing & Snowshoeing* (Annual). **Educational Activities:** Cross Country Ski Areas Association Annual Convention (Annual).

18817 ■ Eastern Winter Sports Representatives Association (EWSRA)
PO Box 88
White Haven, PA 18661
Ph: (570)443-7180
Fax: (570)443-0388
Co. E-mail: ewsra@uplink.net
URL: http://www.ewsra.org
Contact: Kent Fried, Board Member
E-mail: chris_bremer@yahoo.com
Description: Independent company sales representatives for firms associated with the snow-ski industry. Conducts preview showings of hard and soft goods for retailers. **Founded:** 1971.

18818 ■ Midwest Winter Sports Representatives Association (MWSRA)
c/o Gayle Snyder
PO Box 76
Hazelhurst, WI 54531
Ph: (715)358-6262
Fax: (866)623-6155
Co. E-mail: mwsragayle@aol.com
URL: http://www.midwestwinterreps.com
Contact: Gayle Snyder, Executive Director
Description: Manufacturers' representatives serving the Midwest ski industry. Coordinates buying shows.

Founded: 1966. **Publications:** *Buyers Guide* (Annual). **Educational Activities:** Buying Show.

18819 ■ National Brotherhood of Skiers (NBS)
1525 E 53rd St., Ste. 418
Chicago, IL 60615
Ph: (773)955-4100
URL: http://www.nbs.org
Contact: Diana C. Starks, President
Description: Minority ski clubs. Promotes winter sports among minorities, with emphasis on youth. Seeks to locate and develop talented ski racers through local, regional, and national competitions. Promotes the development of Olympic-quality minority skiers. Offers two-year athletic scholarships for qualified youth to attend Ski Academies. Encourages participation in United States Ski Association competitions. Supports Building Skills and Talents programs and community-based youth motivational improvement programs. **Founded:** 1973. **Publications:** *NBS Directory* (Annual); *Skiers Edge* (Quarterly).

18820 ■ National Ski Patrol System (NSP)
133 S Van Gordon St., Ste. 100
Lakewood, CO 80228
Ph: (303)988-1111
Fax: (303)988-3005
Co. E-mail: nsp@nsp.org
URL: http://www.nsp.org
Contact: Tim White, Executive Director
Description: Promotes ski safety and handling of injuries at ski areas. Assists municipal and federal agencies in cold weather disasters and in rescue attempts involving air crashes, mountain accidents, and blizzards; all members are trained in winter emergency care, receive special training in cold weather survival and rescue, must pass Ski Patrol proficiency and toboggan handling tests, and are trained in avalanche recognition and rescue. Maintains inventory of winter rescue equipment and patrol supplies. **Founded:** 1938. **Publications:** *Ski Patrol Magazine* (Quarterly); *Winter Catalog*.

18821 ■ National Ski and Snowboard Retailers Association (NSSRA)
1601 Feehanville Dr., Ste. 300
Mount Prospect, IL 60056-6035
Ph: (847)391-9825
Free: 888-257-1168
Fax: (847)391-9827
Co. E-mail: info@nssra.com
URL: http://www.nssra.com
Contact: Thomas B. Doyle, President
E-mail: tdoyle@nssra.com
Description: Ski & snowboard stores. Represents the interests of members and provides services beneficial to their businesses. Compiles statistics. **Founded:** 1987. **Publications:** *NSSRA Newsletter* (Quarterly); *NSSRA Newsletter*.

18822 ■ National Snow Industries Association (NSIA)—Association Nationale des Industries de la Neige
245 Victoria Ave., Ste. 810
Westmount, QC, Canada H3Z 2M6

Ph: (514)939-7370
Free: 800-263-6742
Fax: (514)939-7371
Co. E-mail: central.station@nsia.ca
URL: http://www.nsia.ca/P1/home.asp
Contact: Anna Di Meglio, President
Description: Manufacturers and distributors of snow sports equipment including skis, snowboards, and winter outdoor products. Promotes participation in winter sports; works to insure a healthy business climate for members. Sponsors research programs; compiles industry statistics and marketing. **Founded:** 1962. **Publications:** *Scoop* (Quarterly); *Show Directory* (Annual). **Educational Activities:** National Snow Industries Association Tradeshow (Annual).

18823 ■ National Sporting Goods Association (NSGA)
1601 Feehanville Dr., Ste. 300
Mount Prospect, IL 60056
Ph: (847)296-6742
Free: 800-815-5422
Fax: (847)391-9827
Co. E-mail: info@nsga.org
URL: http://www.nsga.org
Contact: Matt Carlson, President
E-mail: mcarlson@nsga.org
Description: Provides services, education and information to assist member to profit in a competitive marketplace. **Founded:** 1929. **Publications:** *NSGA Buying Guide* (Annual); *NSGA Buying Guide* (Annual); *Sports Participation-Series I & II* (Annual); *National Sporting Goods Association--Buying Guide* (Annual); *NSGA Sports Retailer--Store Equipment and Services Directory Issue*; *Cost of Doing Business Survey*; *The Team Line-Up*; *NSGA Retail Focus* (Bimonthly). **Educational Activities:** Management Conference and Team Dealer Summit (Annual). **Telecommunication Services:** nsga1699@aol.com.

18824 ■ Professional Ski Instructors of America (PSIA)
133 S Van Gordon St., Ste. 200
Lakewood, CO 80228
Ph: (303)987-9390
Fax: (303)988-9489
Co. E-mail: mist@thesnowpros.org
URL: http://www.psia.org
Contact: Mark Dorsey, Chief Executive Officer
Description: Professional-certified Alpine and Nordic ski teachers. Promotes ski instruction by professional teachers. Developed American Teaching Method (ATM), which has received international recognition. Sponsors and publishes results of educational research through the Professional Ski Instructors of America Educational Foundation; develops clinics and management seminars. Establishes a library of books and publications on ski technique, teaching, and ski history. **Founded:** 1961. **Publications:** *Convention Proceedings* (Annual); *PSIA Accessories Catalog*; *Ski School Management* (3/year).

18825 ■ Scoop
245 Victoria Ave., Ste. 810
Westmount, QC, Canada H3Z 2M6
Ph: (514)939-7370

Free: 800-263-6742
Fax: (514)939-7371
Co. E-mail: central.station@nsia.ca
URL: http://www.nsia.ca/P1/home.asp
Contact: Anna Di Meglio, President
Released: Quarterly

18826 ■ Show Directory
245 Victoria Ave., Ste. 810
Westmount, QC, Canada H3Z 2M6
Ph: (514)939-7370
Free: 800-263-6742
Fax: (514)939-7371
Co. E-mail: central.station@nsia.ca
URL: http://www.nsia.ca/F1/home.asp
Contact: Anna Di Meglio, President
Released: Annual

18827 ■ SnowSports Industries America (SIA)
8377-B Greensboro Dr.
McLean, VA 22102
Ph: (703)556-9020
Fax: (703)821-8276
Co. E-mail: siamail@snowsports.org
URL: http://www.snowsports.org
Contact: Bryan Ginn, Manager
E-mail: bginn@snowsports.org
URL(s): www.thesnowtrade.org. **Description:** Manufacturers, distributors, and suppliers of ski, snowboard, on-snow, and outdoor action sports apparel, equipment, footwear, and accessories. Monitors activities at the federal level to protect the interest of on-snow product manufacturers and distributors. Provides information on the on-snow industry to the media. Promotes snow sports through market development programs. Conducts research programs. Operates 14 committees. **Scope:** skiing, outdoor action sports. **Founded:** 1954. **Subscriptions:** archival material artwork books business records clippings periodicals. **Publications:** *SIA Member Update* (Quarterly); *SIA Snow Sports Book* (Annual); *Retailer/Rep Advisor* (Biennial); *SIA Member Update* (Semimonthly); *SIA Trade Show Directory* (Annual); *USIA Ski Area and Associate Membership Directory* (Annual); *USIA Ski and Outdoor Sports Show Directory* (Annual). **Educational Activities:** Snowsports Show (Annual); The SIA Snow Show (Annual).

18828 ■ Western Winter Sports Representatives Association (WWSRA)
726 Tenacity Dr., Unit B
Longmont, CO 80504
Ph: (303)532-4002
Free: 866-929-4572
Co. E-mail: info@wwsra.com
URL: http://www.wwsra.com
Contact: Morgan Turner, President
Description: Representatives in the ski industry. Sponsors buyers' shows in the Eastern U.S. Membership and activities are focused in the western part of the U.S. **Founded:** 1949. **Publications:** *Ski Show Directory-Sporting Goods Directory* (Semiannual).

REFERENCE WORKS

18829 ■ QuickBooks for the New Bean Counter: Business Owner's Guide 2006
Pub: Wheatmark
Ed: Joseph L. Catallini. **Released:** July 2006. **Price:** $21.95. **Description:** Profile of QuickBooks software, offering insight into using the software's accounting and bookkeeping functions.

18830 ■ SIA Snow Sports Book
Pub: SnowSports Industries America
Contact: Bryan Ginn, Manager
E-mail: bginn@snowsports.org
URL(s): www.snowlink.comwww.snowsports.org. **Released:** Annual; August. **Covers:** 1,000 manufacturers, distributors, and suppliers of ski, snowboard, on-snow, and in-line skate apparel, equipment, and accessories who are members of SIA and who exhibit at the SIA show. **Entries include:** Company name, address, phone, names of management, sales representatives, and products (including trade or brand names). **Arrangement:** Alphabetical. **Indexes:** Product by brand name, personnel.

18831 ■ "VC Boosts WorkForce; Livonia Software Company to Add Sales, Marketing Staff" in Crain's Detroit Business (March 24, 2008)
Pub: Crain Communications, Inc.
Ed: Tom Henderson. **Description:** WorkForce Software Inc., a company that provides software to manage payroll processes and oversee compliance with state and federal regulations and with union rules, plans to use an investment of $5.5 million in venture capital to hire more sales and marketing staff.

TRADE PERIODICALS

18832 ■ Cross Country Skier: The Journal of Nordic Skiing
Pub: Country Skier L.L.C.
URL(s): www.crosscountryskier.com. **Ed:** Ron Bergin. **Released:** Quarterly **Price:** $12.75, Individuals; $24.95, Two years.

18833 ■ Ski
Pub: Time4 Media
Contact: Thomas Beusse, President
URL(s): www.skinet.com/ski. **Released:** 8/yr, from September to May. **Price:** $10, Individuals.

18834 ■ Skiing: The Magazine of Winter Adventure
Pub: Time4 Media
Contact: Thomas Beusse, President
URL(s): www.skinet.com/skiing. **Released:** 7/yr (issued monthly Sept. thru April). **Price:** $19.97 Individuals.

18835 ■ Sporting Goods Dealer: The Voice of Team Dealers Since 1899
Pub: Bill Communications Inc.
URL(s): www.sgdealer.com/sportinggoodsdealer/index.jsp. **Released:** Bimonthly

VIDEOCASSETTES/ AUDIOCASSETTES

18836 ■ Old School
Tapeworm Video Distributors
25876 The Old Road #141
Stevenson Ranch, CA 91381
Ph: (661)257-4904
Fax: (661)257-4820
Co. E-mail: sales@tapeworm.com
URL: http://www.tapeworm.com
Released: 19??. **Price:** $14.95. **Description:** Presents the first snowboarding competition at Ski Cooper Colorado 1980. **Availability:** VHS.

18837 ■ Space Cowboys: Dysfunctional Superheroes II
Tapeworm Video Distributors
25876 The Old Road #141
Stevenson Ranch, CA 91381
Ph: (661)257-4904
Fax: (661)257-4820
Co. E-mail: sales@tapeworm.com
URL: http://www.tapeworm.com
Released: 1997. **Price:** $14.95. **Description:** Presents footage of snowboarders, skateboarders, and freestyle BMX riders. **Availability:** VHS.

18838 ■ Steep Snow
Keen Media
857 Pulpit Rock Circle N.
Colorado Springs, CO 80918
Ph: (719)593-2155
Free: 800-363-5336
Fax: (719)593-2888
Co. E-mail: jim@keenmedia.com
URL: http://www.keenmedia.com
Released: 19??. **Price:** $34.95. **Description:** Provides instruction on techniques, equipment, and weather and terrain for hunters, hikers, skiers, and others finding it necessary to cross steep snow. **Availability:** VHS.

TRADE SHOWS AND CONVENTIONS

18839 ■ The SIA Snow Show
SnowSports Industries America (SIA)
8377-B Greensboro Dr.
McLean, VA 22102
Ph: (703)556-9020
Fax: (703)821-8276
Co. E-mail: siamail@snowsports.org
URL: http://www.snowsports.org
Contact: Bryan Ginn, Manager
E-mail: bginn@snowsports.org
URL(s): www.thesnowtrade.org. **Frequency:** Annual. **Audience:** Members of SIA to exhibit or attend as a raw material or service providers, attendees are retail or corporate buyers only. **Principal Exhibits:** Ski, snowboard, outdoor sports, snowshoe companies with equipment, clothing, and accessories. **Dates and Locations:** , Convention Center.

18840 ■ Ski Dazzle - Los Angeles Ski Show and Snowboard Expo
Ski Dazzle, LLC.
1550 S. Coast Hwy.
Laguna Beach, CA 92651
Ph: (949)497-4977
Fax: (949)497-4123
Co. E-mail: support@skidazzle.com
URL: http://www.skidazzle.com
URL(s): www.skidazzle.com. **Price:** $12, Onsite; $3, Onsite children 6 through 12 years; children 5 and under free. **Frequency:** Annual. **Audience:** Snow skiing, snow boarding and winter sports enthusiasts/consumers. **Principal Exhibits:** Ski equipment and snow boarding, clothing, and accessories; travel-related products and services. **Dates and Locations:** , Convention Center.

18841 ■ Toronto Ski, Snowboard and Travel Show
Canadian National Sportsmen's Shows
703 Evans Ave., Ste. 202
Toronto, ON, Canada M9C 5E9
Ph: (416)695-0311
Fax: (416)695-0381
Contact: Harley Austin, Show Manager
E-mail: austin@sportshows.ca
URL(s): www.torontoskishow.ca. **Frequency:** Annual. **Audience:** General public. **Principal Exhibits:** Ski and snowboard manufacturers, retailers; ski resorts, tourist bureaus, travel agencies, hotels, ski clinics and demonstrations, associations, clubs, ski swap and sale.

LIBRARIES

18842 ■ Canadian Ski Museum Archives—Le Musee Canadien du Ski.
98 Powell Ave.
Ottawa, ON, Canada K1S 2A3
Ph: (613)234-0930
Fax: (613)722-2914
Co. E-mail: info@skimuseum.ca
URL: http://www.skimuseum.ca
Contact: Ryan Scranton
Scope: Skiing, snowboarding, ski history, Canadian winter sport. **Services:** Library open to the public with restrictions. **Founded:** 1971. **Holdings:** 2000 books; archival materials, photographs.

18843 ■ U.S. National Ski Hall of Fame and Museum - Roland Palmedo National Ski Library—National Ski Hall of Fame and Museum - Roland Palmedo National Ski Library.
PO Box 191
Ishpeming, MI 49849-0191
Ph: (906)485-6323
Fax: (906)486-4570
Co. E-mail: administrator@skihall.com
URL: http://www.skihall.com
Scope: Skiing. **Services:** Copying; library open to the public for reference use only. **Founded:** 1954. **Holdings:** 1300 volumes; 20 VF drawers of reports, pamphlets, clippings; 180 films. **Subscriptions:** 7 journals and other serials.

START-UP INFORMATION

18844 ■ *The 100 Best Businesses to Start When You Don't Want To Work Hard Anymore*

Pub: Career Press Inc.

Ed: Lisa Rogak. **Price:** $16.99. **Description:** Author helps burned-out workers envision a new future as a small business owner. Systems analysis, adventure travel outfitting, bookkeeping, food delivery, furniture making, and software development are among the industries examined.

18845 ■ *"Local Startup Hits Big Leagues" in Austin Business JournalInc. (Vol. 28, December 19, 2008, No. 40, pp. 1)*

Pub: American City Business Journals

Ed: Christopher Calnan. **Description:** Qcue LLC, an Austin, Texas-based company founded in 2007 is developing a software system that can be used by Major League Baseball teams to change the prices of their single-game tickets based on variables affecting demand. The company recently completed a trial with the San Francisco Giants in 2008.

18846 ■ *"OtherInbox Ready for Revenue: Software Startup Expects Profits in '09" in Austin Business JournalInc. (Vol. 28, January 2, 2009)*

Pub: American City Business Journals

Ed: Christopher Calnan. **Description:** Founder of Austin, Texas-based OtherBox Inc. expects the company to generate revenue through subscriptions and advertising and also reach profitability in 2009. The company's email management tool sends secondary mail to an alternate location thereby freeing up the work inbox for more urgent messages.

ASSOCIATIONS AND OTHER ORGANIZATIONS

18847 ■ **Business Software Alliance (BSA)**
1150 18th St. NW, Ste. 700
Washington, DC 20036
Ph: (202)872-5500
Fax: (202)872-5501
Co. E-mail: info@bsa.org
URL: http://www.bsa.org
Contact: Robert Holleyman, II, President

Description: Computer software publishers. Promotes the free world trade of business software by combating international software piracy, advancing intellectual property protection, and increasing market access. **Founded:** 1988. **Publications:** *Guide to Software Management* (Annual); *Software Review* (Quarterly).

18848 ■ **Entertainment Software Association (ESA)**
575 7th St. NW, Ste. 300
Washington, DC 20004

Ph: (202)223-2400
Co. E-mail: esa@theesa.com
URL: http://www.theesa.com
Contact: Michael D. Gallagher, President
URL(s): www.e3expo.com. **Description:** Represents the interactive entertainment software publishing industry. Established an autonomous rating board to rate interactive entertainment software. Established a program to combat piracy in the United States and around the world. Represents members on industry issues at the federal and state level. Provides market research and information. **Founded:** 1994. **Educational Activities:** Electronic Entertainment Expo (E3) (Annual); Electronic Entertainment Expo - E3 (Annual); E3 Media & Business Summit. **Awards:** ESA Foundation Computer and Video Game Scholarship Program. **Telecommunication Services:** dhewitt@theesa.com.

18849 ■ **Free Software Foundation (FSF)**
51 Franklin St., 5th Fl.
Boston, MA 02110-1301
Ph: (617)542-5942
Fax: (617)542-2652
Co. E-mail: info@fsf.org
URL: http://www.fsf.org
Contact: Richard M. Stallman, President
Description: Promotes computer users' right to use, study, copy, modify, and redistribute computer programs; development and use of free (as in freedom) software, particularly the GNU operating system and free (as in freedom) documentation; promotes ethical and political issues of freedom in the use of software. **Founded:** 1985. **Publications:** *GNU Service Directory* (Semiannual); *GNU Project*; *GNU's Bulletin* (Annual). **Awards:** Award for the Advancement of Free Software (Annual).

18850 ■ **International Computer Music Association (ICMA)**
1819 Polk St., Ste. 330
San Francisco, CA 94109
Fax: (734)878-3031
Co. E-mail: icma@umich.edu
URL: http://www.computermusic.org
Contact: Tae Hong Park, President
Description: Composers, computer software and hardware developers, researchers and musicians. Works to advance individuals and institutions involved in the technical, creative and performance aspects of computer music. Provides networking opportunities; sponsors research and projects; holds competitions. **Scope:** computer music. **Founded:** 1974. **Subscriptions:** archival material articles. **Awards:** Best Presentation Award; Eric Siday Musical Creativity Award (Annual); International Computer Music Commission Awards (Annual); Best Presentation Award; International Computer Music Commission Awards; Swets & Zeitlinger Distinguished Paper Award (Annual); Eric Siday Musical Creativity Award; Swets and Zeitlinger Distinguished Paper Award.

18851 ■ **Society for Software Quality (SSQ)**
PO Box 27634
San Diego, CA 92198
Co. E-mail: info@ssq.org
URL: http://www.ssq.org
Contact: Merle Kemble, President
Description: Software professionals. Seeks to advance the art, science, and technology of software

quality assurance. Promotes professional development of members and encourages high standards in the field. Fosters communication between the public and the industry. Assists colleges and universities in developing and implementing curricula in quality evaluation and methodologies. Operates speakers' bureau. **Founded:** 1984. **Educational Activities:** Achieving Quality Software. **Awards:** Dusty Rhodes Memorial Scholastic Grant (Annual).

18852 ■ **Software and Information Industry Association (SIIA)**
1090 Vermont Ave. NW, 6th Fl.
Washington, DC 20005-4095
Ph: (202)289-7442
Free: 800-388-7478
Fax: (202)289-7097
Co. E-mail: info@siia.net
URL: http://www.siia.net
Contact: Kenneth Wasch, President
URL(s): www.spa.org, www.siia.com. **Description:** Seeks to promote the interest of the software and information industries. Protects intellectual property and advocate a legal and regulatory environment that benefits the industry. Serves as a resource to members. **Founded:** 1984. **Publications:** *Information Times*; *eNewsletters*; *The Annual Directory of the Information Industry Association*; *Information Times: A Publication of the Information Industry Association* (Bimonthly); *Press Room*; *Information Sources: The IIA Annual Membership Directory* (Continuous). **Awards:** Codie Awards (Annual); CODiE Awards. **Telecommunication Services:** gjohnson@siia.net.

REFERENCE WORKS

18853 ■ *"Abacast, Citadel Strike Radio Ad Deal" in Business Journal Portland (Vol. 27, December 31, 2010, No. 44, pp. 3)*

Pub: Portland Business Journal

Ed: Erik Siemers. **Description:** Software firm Abacast Inc. has partnered with Citadel Media to aid the latter's advertising sales. Citadel provides radio networks and syndicated programs to 4,200 affiliate stations.

18854 ■ *"ACC Game Development Program Opens" in Austin Business JournalInc. (Vol. 28, October 31, 2008, No. 33, pp. 1)*

Pub: American City Business Journals

Ed: Sandra Zaragoza. **Description:** Austin, Texas-based Austin Community College has launched its Game Development Institute. The institute was created to meet the gaming industry's demand for skilled workers. One hundred students have enrolled with the institute.

18855 ■ *"All Those Applications, and Phone Users Just Want to Talk" in Advertising Age (Vol. 79, August 11, 2008, No. 31, pp. 18)*

Pub: Crain Communications, Inc.

Ed: Mike Vorhaus. **Description:** Although consumers are slowly coming to text messaging and other data applications, a majority of those Americans surveyed stated that they simply want to use their cell phones to talk and do not care about other activities. Statistical data included.

18856 ■ *"AMT's Partner Program Enables New Security Business Models" in Internet Wire (August 12, 2010)*
Pub: Comtex
Description: AMT, technical provider of physical access control Software as a Service (Saas) solutions, has developed a new Partner Program that allows partners to outsource any technical abilities lacking to AMT with no upfront fees.

18857 ■ *"Angel Investments Tripled in 2009" in Austin Business JournalInc. (Vol. 29, January 8, 2010, No. 44, pp. 1)*
Pub: American City Business Journals
Ed: Christopher Calnan. **Description:** Central Texas Angel Network (CTAN) has invested $3.5 million in 12 ventures, which include 10 in Austin, Texas in 2009 to triple the amount it invested during 2008. The largest recipient of CTAN's investments is life sciences, which attracted 20 percent of the capital, while software investments fell to 18 percent. The new screening process that helps startups secure CTAN capital is explored.

18858 ■ *"Apps For Anybody With an Idea" in Advertising Age (Vol. 79, October 20, 2008, No. 39, pp. 29)*
Pub: Crain Communications, Inc.
Ed: Beth Snyder Bulik. **Description:** Apple's new online App Store is open to anyone with an idea and the ability to write code and many of these developers are not only finding a sense of community through this venue but are also making money since the sales are split with Apple, 30/70 in the developer's favor.

18859 ■ *"Arctic IT Honored" in Alaska Business Monthly (Vol. 27, October 2011, No. 10, pp. 10)*
Pub: Alaska Business Publishing Company
Ed: Nancy Pounds. **Description:** Arctic Information Technology Inc. was named to Everything Channel's 2011 Computer Reseller News (CRN) Next-Generation 250 list. The firm provides business software and network infrastructure solutions.

18860 ■ *"Arizona Firms In Chicago Go For Gold With '08 Games" in The Business Journal - Serving Phoenix and the Valley of the Sun (Vol. 28, August 8, 2008, No. 49, pp. 1)*
Pub: American City Business Journals, Inc.
Ed: Patrick O'Grady. **Description:** More than 20 U.S. athletes will wear Arizona-based eSoles LLC's custom-made insoles to increase their performance at the 2008 Beijing Olympics making eSoles one of the beneficiaries of the commercialization of the games. Translation software maker Auralog Inc saw a 60 percent jump in sales from its Mandarin Chinese language applications.

18861 ■ *"Attivio Brings Order to Data" in Information Today (Vol. 26, February 2009, No. 2, pp. 14)*
Pub: Information Today, Inc.
Ed: Marji McClure. **Description:** Profile of Attivio, the high tech firm offering next-generation software that helps businesses to consolidate data and eliminate enterprise silos.

18862 ■ *"AVG Introduces Security Software Suite for SMBs 551179" in eWeek (October 12, 2010)*
Pub: Ziff Davis Enterprise
Description: AVG Technologies s offering its AVG Internet Security 2011 Business Edition and AVG Anti-Virus Business Edition designed to give Internet-active SMB owners protection. The system protects online transactions and email communications as well as sensitive customer data and AVG Anti-Virus 2011 Business edition offers real-time protection against the latest online threats.

18863 ■ *"BancVue to Expand" in Austin Business JournalInc. (Vol. 29, November 27, 2009, No. 38, pp. 1)*
Pub: American City Business Journals
Ed: Kate Harrington. **Description:** Significant growth of BancVue in the past six years has prompted the company to look for a site that could increase its office space from 25,000 square feet to 65,000 square feet. BancVue offers bank and credit union software solutions and is planning to lease or buy a property in Austin, Texas.

18864 ■ *"Bar Hopping: Your Numbers At a Glance" in Inc. (January 2008, pp. 44-45)*
Pub: Gruner & Jahr USA Publishing
Ed: Michael Fitzgerald. **Description:** Software that helps any company analyze data include Crystal Xcelsius, a program that takes data from Excel documents and turns them into animated gauges, charts and graphs; CashView, a Web-based application that tracks receivables and payables; iDashboards, a Web-based programs that produces animated gauges, maps, pie charts and graphs; Corda Human Capital Management, that transforms stats like head count, productivity, and attrition into graphs and dials; NetSuite, a Web-based application that tracks key indicators; and Cognos Now, that gauges, dials, and graphs data.

18865 ■ *"BayTSP, NTT Data Corp. Enter Into Reseller Pact to Market Online IP Monitoring" in Professional Services Close-Up (Sept. 11, 2009)*
Pub: Close-Up Media
Description: Due to incredible interest from distributors and content owners across Asia, NTT Data Corp. will resell BayTSP's online intellectual property monitoring, enforcement, business intelligence and monetization services in Japan.

18866 ■ *"Behind the Scenes: Companies At the Heart of Everyday Life" in Inc. (February 2008, pp. 26-27)*
Pub: Gruner & Jahr USA Publishing
Ed: Athena Schindelheim. **Description:** Profiles of companies providing services to airports, making the environment safer and more efficient, as well as more comfortable for passengers and workers. Centerpoint Manufacturing provides garbage bins that can safely contain explosions producing thousands of pounds of pressure; Infax, whose software displays arrival and departure information on 19-foot-wide screens; Lavi Industries, whose products include security barricades, hostess stands, and salad-bar sneeze guards; and SATech maker of rubber flooring that helps ease discomfort for workers having to stand for long periods of time.

18867 ■ *"Being all a-Twitter" in Canadian Business (Vol. 81, December 8, 2008, No. 21, pp. 22)*
Pub: Rogers Media Ltd.
Ed: Andrew Wahl. **Description:** Marketing experts suggest that advertising strategies have to change along with new online social media. Companies are advised to find ways to incorporate social software because workers and customers are expected to continue its use.

18868 ■ *"Best Managed Companies (Canada)" in Canadian Business (Vol. 82, Summer 2009, No. 8, pp. 38)*
Pub: Rogers Media
Ed: Calvin Leung. **Description:** Agrium Inc. and Barrick Gold Corporation are among those that are found to be the best managed companies in Canada. Best managed companies also include software firm Open Text Corporation, which has grown annual sales by 75 percent and annual profits by 160 percent since 1995. Open Text markets software that allow firms to manage word-based data, and has 46,000 customers in 114 countries.

18869 ■ *"Beyond Microsoft and Yahoo!: Some M&A Prospects" in Barron's (Vol. 88, March 17, 2008, No. 11, pp. 39)*
Pub: Dow Jones & Company, Inc.
Ed: Eric J. Savitz. **Description:** Weak quarterly earnings report for Yahoo! could pressure the company's board to cut a deal with Microsoft. Electronic Arts is expected to win its hostile $26-a-share bid for Take-Two Interactive Software. Potential targets and buyers for mergers and acquisitions are mentioned.

18870 ■ *"Beyond YouTube: New Uses for Video, Online and Off" in Inc. (October 2007, pp. 53-54)*
Pub: Gruner & Jahr USA Publishing
Ed: Leah Hoffmann. **Description:** Small companies are using video technology for embedding messages into email, broadcasting live interactive sales and training seminars, as well as marketing campaigns. Experts offer insight into producing and broadcasting business videos.

18871 ■ *The Big Switch*
Pub: W. W. Norton & Company, Inc.
Ed: Nicholas Carr. **Released:** January 19, 2009. **Price:** $16.95 paperback. **Description:** Today companies are dismantling private computer systems and tapping into services provided via the Internet. This shift is remaking the computer industry, bringing competitors such as Google to the forefront and threatening traditional companies like Microsoft and Dell. The book weaves together history, economics, and technology to explain why computing is changing and what it means for the future.

18872 ■ *"Blog Buzz Heralds Arrival of IPhone 2.0" in Advertising Age (Vol. 79, June 9, 2008, No. 40, pp. 8)*
Pub: Crain Communications, Inc.
Ed: Abbey Klaasen. **Description:** Predictions concerning the next version of the iPhone include a global-positioning-system technology as well as a configuration to run on a faster, 3G network.

18873 ■ *Business Feasibility Analysis Pro*
Pub: Prentice Hall PTR
Ed: Palo Alto Software. **Released:** August 2006. **Price:** $28.40. **Description:** Profile of software developed to support small business management and/or entrepreneurship text. Step-by-step instructions are provided.

18874 ■ *"BusinessOnLine Launches a New Web-Based Search Engine Optimization Tool" in Internet Wire (October 19, 2009)*
Pub: Comtex News Network, Inc.
Description: First Link Checker, a complimentary new search engine optimization tool that helps site owners optimize their on-page links by understanding which of those links are actually being counted in Google's relevancy algorithm, was developed by BusinessOnLine, a rapidly growing Internet marketing agency. This tool will make it easy for the average web master to ensure that their internal link structure is optimized.

18875 ■ *"CarBiz Inc. Speaking At NABD" in Canadian Corporate News (May 14, 2007)*
Pub: Comtex News Network Inc.
Description: CarBiz Inc., a leading provider of software, consulting, and training solutions to the United States' automotive industry, had two of its executive officers speak at the National Alliance of Buy Here - Pay Here Dealers (NABD), a conference that draws over 2,000 dealers, service providers, and experts from across the United States.

18876 ■ *"A Case Study: Real-Life Business Planning" in Entrepreneur (February 3, 2009)*
Pub: Entrepreneur Media Inc.
Ed: Tim Berry. **Description:** Provides a case study of a two-day planning meeting for Palo Alto Software in which the executives of the company met for their annual planning cycle and discussed ways in which the company needed to change in order to stay viable in today's tough economic climate.

18877 ■ *"Cerner Works the Business Circuit" in Business Journal-Serving Metropolitan Kansas City (Vol. 26, October 5, 2007, No. 4, pp. 1)*
Pub: American City Business Journals, Inc.
Ed: Rob Roberts. **Description:** Cerner Corporation is embracing the coming of the electronic medical record exchange by creating a regional health information organization (RHIO) called the CareEntrust. The RHIO convinced health insurers to share

claims data with patients and clinicians. At the Center Health Conference, held October 7 to 10, Cerner will demonstrate the software it developed for CareEntrust to the 40,000 healthcare and information technology professionals.

18878 ■ *"ChemSW Software Development Services Available for Outsourcing" in Information Today (Vol. 26, February 2009, No. 2, pp. 30)*
Pub: Information Today, Inc.
Description: ChemSW software development services include requirements analysis, specification development, design, development, testing, and system documentation as an IT outsourcing solution. The company can also develop software tracking systems for satellite stockrooms, provide asset management integration solutions and more.

18879 ■ *"ClickFuel Launches New Products to Help Small and Mid-Sized Businesses Bolster Their Brand Online" in Internet Wire (Dec. 3,2009)*
Pub: Comtex News Network, Inc.
Description: Boostability, a provider of Enterprise Search Engine Optimization (SEO) software technology, has partnered with ClickFuel, a firm that designs, tracks and manages Internet marketing campaigns in order to leverage Boostability's technology in order to deliver comprehensive SEO solutions to small and mid-size businesses; three new products will also become available for these business clients to help them manage all facets of their online presence.

18880 ■ *"ClickFuel Launches New Products to Help Small and Mid-Sized Businesses Bolster Their Brand Online" in Internet Wire (Dec. 3, 2009)*
Pub: Comtex News Network, Inc.
Description: Boostability, a provider of Enterprise Search Engine Optimization (SEO) software technology, has partnered with ClickFuel, a firm that designs, tracks and manages Internet marketing campaigns in order to leverage Boostability's technology in order to deliver comprehensive SEO solutions to small and mid-size businesses; three new products will also become available for these business clients to help them manage all facets of their online presence.

18881 ■ *"ClickFuel Unveils Internet Marketing Tools for Small Businesses" in Internet Wire (October 19, 2009)*
Pub: Comtex News Network, Inc.
Description: ClickFuel, a firm that manages, designs and tracks marketing campaigns has unveiled a full software suite of affordable services and technology solutions designed to empower small business owners and help them promote and grow their businesses through targeted Internet marketing campaigns.

18882 ■ *"Clouds in the Forecast" in Information Today (Vol. 28, September 2011, No. 8, pp. 10)*
Pub: Information Today, Inc.
Ed: Paula J. Hane. **Description:** Cloud computing is software, applications, and data stored remotely and accessed via the Internet with output displayed on a client device. Recent developments in cloud computing are explored.

18883 ■ *Computer Accounting Essentials with Microsoft Office Accounting 2010*
Pub: McGraw-Hill Higher Education
Ed: Carol Yacht, Susan Crosson. **Released:** March 10, 2010. **Description:** Step-by-step guide to using Microsoft's Office Professional 2007 Accounting program.

18884 ■ *"Contec Innovations Inc.: MovieSet.com First to Mobilize Content Using BUZmob" in Canadian Corporate News (May 16, 2007)*
Pub: Comtex News Network Inc.
Description: Contec Innovations Inc., a provider of mobile infrastructure software, announced that MovieSet.com is the first Internet portal to mobilize their content using BUZmob, the company's new mobile

publishing service that allows content publishers to enable mobile access to their feed-based content on any mobile device or network in real-time.

18885 ■ *"Cut Energy Waste" in Inc. (Vol. 31, January-February 2009, No. 1, pp. 42)*
Pub: Mansueto Ventures LLC
Description: Carbon Control, Edison, and Saver software programs help companies cut carbon emissions by reducing the amount of energy consumed by computers while they are idle.

18886 ■ *"Dear Customer: Managing E-Mail Campaigns" in Inc. (March 2008, pp. 58-59)*
Pub: Gruner & Jahr USA Publishing
Ed: Ryan Underwood. **Description:** Internet services that help firms manage their online business including email marketing, to manage subscriber lists, comply with spam regulations, monitor bouncebacks, and track potential customers are profiled. Constant Contact, MobileStorm Stun, Campaign Monitor, Pop Commerce, Emma, and StrongMail E-mail Server are among software and services highlighted.

18887 ■ *"Descartes Launches Ocean Shipment Management Suite" in Canadian Corporate News (May 16, 2007)*
Pub: Comtex News Network Inc.
Description: Descartes Systems Group, a global on-demand software-as-a-service (SaaS) logistics solutions provider, launched the latest release of its Descartes Ocean Shipment Management Suite. The release integrates customs compliance services with Descartes' Rate Builder solution, a central database for global shipment and rate information, and Descartes Global Logistics Network (GLN) messaging capabilities.

18888 ■ *"Design Programs for HVAC Sizing Solutions" in Contractor (Vol. 57, January 2010, No. 1, pp. 44)*
Pub: Penton Media, Inc.
Ed: William Feldman; Patti Feldman. **Description:** Rhvac 8 is an HVAC design program that lets users calculate peak heating and cooling load requirements for rooms, zones, systems, and entire buildings. The HVAC Pipe Sizer software for the iPhone enables quick sizing of a simple piping system.

18889 ■ *"A Dog-Day Pooch" in Canadian Business (Vol. 79, September 11, 2006, No. 18, pp. 19)*
Pub: Rogers Media
Ed: Andrew Wahl. **Description:** Acquisition deal of Hummingbird Ltd by Canadian software maker Open Text Corp., is discussed.

18890 ■ *"Don't Touch My Laptop, If You Please Mr. Customs Man" in Canadian Electronics (Vol. 23, June-July 2008, No. 4, pp. 6)*
Pub: Action Communication Inc.
Ed: Mark Borkowski. **Description:** Canadian businessmen bringing electronic devices to the US can protect the contents of their laptops by hiding their data from US border agents. They can also choose to clean up the contents of their laptop using file erasure programs.

18891 ■ *"DST Turns to Banks for Credit" in The Business Journal-Serving Metropolitan Kansas City (Vol. 27, October 3, 2008, No. 3, pp. 1)*
Pub: American City Business Journals, Inc.
Ed: Rob Roberts. **Description:** Kansas City, Missouri-based DST Systems Inc., a company that provides sophisticated information processing, computer software services and business solutions, has secured a new five-year, $120 million credit facility from Enterprise Bank and Bank of the West. The deal is seen to reflect that the region and community-banking model remain stable. Comments from executives are also provided.

18892 ■ *"Eagles Measure Suite Success" in Philadelphia Business Journal (Vol. 30, September 9, 2011, No. 30, pp. 1)*
Pub: American City Business Journals Inc.
Ed: John George. **Description:** Philadelphia Eagles have a new software program that helps suite holders keep track of how their suite is being used and

whether they are getting a return on their investment. The software allows suite holders to better utilize and distribute their tickets.

18893 ■ *"EBSCO Adds New Features to EBSCOhost Content Viewer" in Information Today (Vol. 26, February 2009, No. 2, pp. 31)*
Pub: Information Today, Inc.
Description: EBSCOhost Content Viewer historical digital archive collection provides a visual overview of a displayed document, highlighting search keywords on the page as well as providing a document map that shows the number of times a given keyword is mentioned in a periodical, monograph, article, or other document. For periodical content, the viewer lets users browse multiple issues in a volume without leaving the interface; features include zoom and pan technology similar to online maps.

18894 ■ *"Elastic Path Software Joins Canada in G20 Young Entrepreneur Summit" in Internet Wire (June 14, 2010)*
Pub: Comtex
Description: The Canadian Youth Business Foundation hosted the G20 Young Entrepreneur Summit and announced that Harry Chemko of British Columbia's Elastic Path Software will be a member of the Canadian delegation at the G20 Young Entrepreneur Summit. Details are included.

18895 ■ *"Elemental Nabs $5.5 Million" in The Business Journal-Portland (Vol. 25, July 18, 2008, No. 19, pp. 1)*
Pub: American City Business Journals, Inc.
Ed: Aliza Earnshaw. **Description:** Elemental Technologies Inc., a Portland, Oregon-based software company got $5.5 million in new funding, bringing its total invested capital to $7.1 million in nine months since October 2008. The company plans to launch Badaboom, software for converting video into various formats, later in 2008.

18896 ■ *"The Emergence of Governance In an Open Source Community" in Academy of Management Journal (Vol. 50, No. 5, October 2007, pp. 1079)*
Pub: Academy of Management
Contact: Ming-Jer Chen, President
Ed: Siiobhan O'Mahony, Fabrizio Ferraro. **Description:** Study examined the method of self-governance among small communities producing collective goods, focusing on an open source software community. Results revealed that a combination of bureaucratic and democratic practices helped its governance system.

18897 ■ *"Empire of Pixels" in Entrepreneur (Vol. 37, September 2009, No. 9, pp. 50)*
Pub: Entrepreneur Media, Inc.
Ed: Jason Daley. **Description:** Entrepreneur Jack Levin has successfully grown Imageshack, an image-hosting Web service. The Website currently gets 50 million unique visitors a month. Levin has launched Y-Frog, an application that uses Imageshack to allow Twitter users to add images to their posts.

18898 ■ *The Entrepreneurial Culture Network Advantage Within Chinese and Irish Software Firms*
Pub: Edward Elgar Publishing, Incorporated
Ed: Tsang. **Released:** October 2006. **Price:** $95.00. **Description:** Ways national cultural heritage influences entrepreneurial ventures are discussed.

18899 ■ *"Ex Libris Rosetta Hits the Market" in Information Today (Vol. 26, February 2009, No. 2, pp. 30)*
Pub: Information Today, Inc.
Description: Ex Libris Rosetta, the latest version of the Ex Libris Group's Digital Preservation System supports the acquisition, validation, ingest, storage, management, preservation, and dissemination of digital objects, allowing libraries the infrastructure and technology to preserve and facilitate access to digital collections. The firm's Ex Libris Rosseta Charter Program helps users develop strategic collaboration between Ex Libris and its customers to improve the product.

18900 ■ *"Fly Phishing" in Canadian Business (Vol. 80, October 22, 2007, No. 21, pp. 42)*
Pub: Rogers Media

Ed: Andy Holloway. **Description:** Symantec Corporation's report shows consumers and companies have effectively installed network defenses that prevent unwanted access. Phishing packages are readily available and are widely used. Other details of the Internet Security Threat Report are presented.

18901 ■ *"The Folly of Google's Latest Gambit" in Barron's (Vol. 89, July 13, 2009, No. 28, pp. 23)*
Pub: Dow Jones & Co., Inc.

Ed: Eric J. Savitz. **Description:** Google will enter the operating systems business with the introduction of the Google Chrome OS but its success is dubious because the project is still a year or so away while Microsoft will release an updated version of Windows by then; another problem is that Google already has another OS called Android which will overlap with the Chrome OS's market.

18902 ■ *"Forsys Metals Corporation Goes "Live" With Q4's On-Demand Disclosure Management Software" in Canadian Corporate News (May 16, 2007)*
Pub: Comtex News Network Inc.

Description: Forsys Metals Corp. selected Q4 Web Systems to automate its corporate website disclosure with Q4's software platform which also automates and simplifies many of the administrative tasks that Forsys was doing manually, allowing them to focus their internal resources on the business.

18903 ■ *"Game On" in Canadian Business (Vol. 80, February 12, 2007, No. 4, pp. 15)*
Pub: Rogers Media

Ed: Calvin Leung. **Description:** The plan of president of TransGaming Vikas Gupta to create innovative software programs for games that can be played in different operating systems is discussed.

18904 ■ *"Game On! African Americans Get a Shot at $17.9 Billion Video Game Industry" in Black Enterprise (Vol. 38, July 2008, No. 12, pp. 56)*
Pub: Earl G. Graves Publishing Co. Inc.

Ed: Carolyn M. Brown. **Description:** Despite the economic crisis, consumers are still purchasing the hottest video games and hardware. Tips for African American developers who want to become a part of this industry that lacks content targeting this demographic are offered.

18905 ■ *"Game Plan" in Canadian Business (Vol. 79, September 11, 2006, No. 18, pp. 50)*
Pub: Rogers Media

Ed: Joe Castaldo. **Description:** Strategies adopted by gaming companies to revitalize their business and give a stimulus to their falling resources are presented.

18906 ■ *"German Win Through Sharing" in Canadian Business (Vol. 83, September 14, 2010, No. 15, pp. 16)*
Pub: Rogers Media Ltd.

Ed: Jordan Timm. **Description:** German economic historian Eckhard Hoffner has a two-volume work showing how German's relaxed attitude toward copyright and intellectual property helped it catch up to industrialized United Kingdom. Hoffner's research was in response to his interest in the usefulness of software patents. Information on the debate regarding Canada's copyright laws is given.

18907 ■ *"Getting Rid of Global Glitches: Choosing Software For Trade Compliance" in Black Enterprise (Vol. 41, September 2010, No. 2, pp. 48)*
Pub: Earl G. Graves Publishing Co. Inc.

Ed: Marcia Wade Talbert. **Description:** Compliance software for trading with foreign companies must be compatible with the U.S. Census Bureau's Automated Export System (www.aesdirect.gov). It has to be current with regulatory requirements for any country in the world. Whether owners handle their own compli-

ance or hire a logistics company, they need to be familiar with this software in order to access reports and improve transparency and efficiency of theft supply chain.

18908 ■ *"Global: Put It on Autopilot" in Entrepreneur (Vol. 35, October 2007, No. 10, pp. 110)*
Pub: Entrepreneur Media Inc.

Ed: Laurel Delaney. **Description:** A business that aims to enter the global market must first streamline its global supply chain (GSC). A streamlined GSC can be achieved by laying out the company's processes and by automating it with supply chain management software. Advantages of GSC automation such as credibility are provided.

18909 ■ *"Google Edges into Wireless E-Mail" in Globe & Mail (February 19, 2007, pp. B5)*
Pub: CTVglobemedia Publishing Inc.

Ed: Simon Avery. **Description:** Google Inc. has introduced a free mobile e-mail service in Canada. The mobile users can read, send, and search messages using the new software.

18910 ■ *"Google Places a Call to Bargain Hunters" in Advertising Age (Vol. 79, September 29, 2008, No. 36, pp. 13)*
Pub: Crain Communications, Inc.

Ed: Abbey Klaassen. **Description:** Google highlighted application developers who have created tools for its Android mobile phone in the device's unveiling; applications such as ShopSavvy and CompareEverywhere help shoppers to find bargains by allowing them to compare prices in their local areas and across the web.

18911 ■ *Graduate Assistantship Directory in Computing*
Pub: Association for Computing Machinery
Contact: Wendy Hall, President

URL(s): www.acm.org/gad/credit_new.html. **Entries include:** Institution name, address, name and title of contact, degrees offered, area of expertise, financial aid offered, stipend amount, department facilities (hardware and software), school enrollment, required exams, admission deadlines. **Database covers:** Fellowships and assistantships in the computer sciences offered at U.S. and Canadian educational institutions. **Arrangement:** Geographical.

18912 ■ *"A Hacker in India Hijacked His Website Design and Was Making Good Money Selling It" in Inc. (December 2007, pp. 77-78, 80)*
Pub: Gruner & Jahr USA Publishing

Ed: Darren Dahl. **Description:** John Anton, owner of an online custom T-shirt business and how a company in India was selling software Website templates identical to his firm's Website.

18913 ■ *"His Banking Industry Software Never Caught On, so Bill Randle is Now Targeting the Health Care Market" in Inc. (March 2008)*
Pub: Gruner & Jahr USA Publishing

Ed: Alex Salkever. **Description:** Profile of Bill Randle, bank executive turned entrepreneur; Randle tells how he changed his focus for his company from banking software to healthcare software. The firm employs ten people who secure online billing and recordkeeping systems for hospitals and insurers. Randle discusses critical decisions that will impact his firm in the coming year. Three experts offer advice.

18914 ■ *"Holiday Sales Look Uncertain for Microsoft and PC Sellers" in Puget Sound Business Journal (Vol. 29, November 28, 2008, No. 32)*
Pub: American City Business Journals

Ed: Todd Bishop. **Description:** Personal computer makers face uncertain holiday sales for 2008 as a result of the weak U.S. economy and a shift toward low-cost computers. Personal computer shipments for the fourth quarter 2008 are forecast to drop 1 percent compared to the same quarter 2007.

18915 ■ *"How Hard Could It Be? Adventures In Software Demol'ling" in Inc. (December 2007, pp. 99-100)*
Pub: Gruner & Jahr USA Publishing

Ed: Joel Spolsky. **Description:** Founder and CEO of Fog Creek Software, a New York City software developer shares insight into his software demo tour used to promote his firm's products.

18916 ■ *"HR Tech on the Go" in Workforce Management (Vol. 88, November 16, 2009, No. 12, pp. 1)*
Pub: Crain Communications Inc.

Ed: Ed Frauenheim. **Description:** Examination of the necessity of mobile access of human resources software applications that allow managers to recruit, schedule and train employees via their mobile devices; some industry leaders believe that mobile HR applications are vital while others see this new technology as hype.

18917 ■ *"iControl Networks Powers Comcast's XFINITY (Reg) Home Security Service" in Benzinga.com (June 9, 2011)*
Pub: Benzinga.com

Ed: Benzinga Staff. **Description:** Comcast's XFINITY Home Security Service is powered by iControl Networks' OpenHome (TM) software platform. The service provides intrusion and fire protection along with interactive features such as home monitoring, home management, and energy management services with Web and mobile access.

18918 ■ *"Image Conscious" in Canadian Business (Vol. 81, March 17, 2008, No. 4, pp. 36)*
Pub: Rogers Media

Ed: Andrew Wahl. **Description:** Idee Inc. is testing an Internet search engine for images that does not rely on tags but compares its visual data to a database of other images. The company was founded and managed by Leila Boujnane as an off-shoot of their risk-management software firm. Their software has already been used by image companies to track copyrighted images and to find images within their own archives.

18919 ■ *"Ingrian and Channel Management International Sign Distribution Agreement" in Canadian Corporate News (May 16, 2007)*
Pub: Comtex News Network Inc.

Description: Channel Management International (CMI), a Canadian channel management and distribution company, and Ingrian Networks, Inc., the leading provider of data privacy solutions, announced a Canadian distribution agreement to resell Ingrian encryption solutions to the Canadian market.

18920 ■ *"Inside Intel's Effectiveness System for Web Marketing" in Advertising Age (Vol. 81, January 25, 2010, No. 4, pp. 4)*
Pub: Crain's Communications

Ed: Beth Snyder Bulik. **Description:** Overview of Intel's internally developed program called Value Point System in which the company is using in order to evaluate and measure online marketing effectiveness.

18921 ■ *"Intel to Buy McAfee Security Business for 768B" in eWeek (August 19, 2010)*
Pub: Ziff Davis Enterprise

Description: Intel will acquire security giant McAfee for approximately $7.68 billion, whereby McAfee would become a wholly owned subsidiary of Intel and would report to Intel's Software and Services Group.

18922 ■ *"iPhone Apps Big Business" in Austin Business JournalInc. (Vol. 28, November 14, 2008, No. 35, pp. 1)*
Pub: American City Business Journals

Ed: Christopher Calnan. **Description:** Members of the computer software industry in Austin, Texas have benefited from developing applications for Apple Inc.'s iPhone. Pangea Software Inc.'s revenues have grown by developing iPhone applications. Lexcycle LLC, on the other hand, has created an application that enables users to read books on the iPhone.

18923 ■ *"iPhone Apps In a Flash"* in *Entrepreneur (Vol. 37, October 2009, No. 10, pp. 38)*
Pub: Entrepreneur Media, Inc.
Description: Ansca is developing Corona, a software development kit for the Apple iPhone. The kit reduces development time and allows individuals with knowledge of software to develop iPhone applications.

18924 ■ *"Is It Time to Ban Swearing at Work?"* in *HR Specialist (Vol. 8, September 2010, No. 9, pp. 2)*
Pub: Capitol Information Group Inc.
Description: Screening software has been developed to identify profanity used in business correspondence.

18925 ■ *"iSymmetry's Technological Makeover Or, How a Tech Company Finally Grew Up and Discovered the World Wide Web"* in *Inc. (October 2007)*
Pub: Gruner & Jahr USA Publishing
Description: Profile of iSymmetry, an Atlanta, Georgia-based IT recruiting firm, covering the issues the company faces keeping its technology equipment up-to-date. The firm has devised a program that will replace its old server-based software systems with on-demand software delivered via the Internet, known as software-as-a-service. Statistical information included.

18926 ■ *"Johnny Royal of Luthier Society Unveils Archimedes 1.0 Trailer"* in *Internet Wire (October 22, 2009)*
Pub: Comtex News Network, Inc.
Description: Luthier Society, a social media and viral branding agency, has released the first viral video for the company's ROI weighted-value software platform named Archimedes 1.0; users of the software will be able to determine the depth of their outreach efforts, saturation rate, value of their Internet presence and the geo-spatial location of their audience; this will give a true, monetized value for ROI (Return on Investment) in social media marketing.

18927 ■ *"Keeping Up With the Joneses: Outfitting Your Company With Up-To-Date Technology is Vital"* in *Black Enterprise (November 2007)*
Pub: Earl G. Graves Publishing Co. Inc.
Ed: Sonya A. Donaldson. **Description:** Small businesses, whether home-based or not, need to keep up with new technological developments including hardware, software, and the Internet.

18928 ■ *"Lights, Camera, Action: Tools for Creating Video Blogs"* in *Inc. (Volume 32, December 2010, No. 10, pp. 57)*
Pub: Inc. Magazine
Ed: John Brandon. **Description:** A video blog is a good way to spread company news, talk about products, and stand out among traditional company blogs. New editing software can create two- to four-minute blogs using a webcam and either Windows Live Essentials, Apple iLife 2011, Powerdirector 9 Ultra, or Adobe Visual Communicator 3.

18929 ■ *"Make Relationships Count: CRM Software That Works"* in *Black Enterprise (Vol. 38, February 2008, No. 7, pp. 60)*
Pub: Earl G. Graves Publishing Co. Inc.
Ed: Fiona Haley. **Description:** Customer relationship management (CRM) software can help any small business keep track of clients. Descriptions of the latest CRM software offered are profiled, including Salesforce.com, Microsoft Dynamics, and Saga Software.

18930 ■ *"Media Software and Data Services"* in *MarketingMagazine (Vol. 115, September 27, 2010, No. 13, pp. 78)*
Pub: Rogers Publishing Ltd.
Description: Media software and data services information in Canada is presented.

18931 ■ *"Meetings Go Virtual"* in *HRMagazine (Vol. 54, January 2009, No. 1, pp. 74)*
Pub: Society for Human Resource Management
Contact: Henry G. Jackson, President
E-mail: hjackson@shrm.org
Ed: Elizabeth Agnvall. **Description:** Microsoft Office Live Meeting conferencing software allows companies to schedule meetings from various company locations, thus saving travel costs.

18932 ■ *"Microsoft Clicks Into High Speed"* in *Hispanic Business (Vol. 30, July-August 2008, No. 7-8, pp. 54)*
Pub: Hispanic Business, Inc.
Ed: Derek Reveron. **Description:** Microsoft's diversity hiring and vendor diversity program to capture more Hispanic consumer and business-to-business market is described. One of the main goals of these programs is to hire more Hispanic executives and managers who will help the company develop and market products and services that will appeal and benefit Hispanic consumers.

18933 ■ *"Microsoft Goes Macrosoft"* in *Barron's (Vol. 89, July 27, 2009, No. 30, pp. 25)*
Pub: Dow Jones & Co., Inc.
Ed: Mark Veverka. **Description:** Microsoft reported a weak quarter on the heels of a tech rally which suggests the economy has not turned around. Marc Andreesen describes his new venture-capital fund as focused on 'classic tech' and that historical reference places him in the annals of the last millennium.

18934 ■ *"Microsoft Releases Office Security Updates"* in *Mac World (Vol. 27, November 2010, No. 11, pp. 66)*
Pub: Mac Publishing
Ed: David Dahlquist. **Description:** Office for Mac and Mac Business Unit are Microsoft's pair of security- and stability-enhancing updates for Office 2008 and Office 2004. The software will improve the stability and compatibility and fixes vulnerabilities that would allow attackers to overwrite Mac's memory with malicious code.

18935 ■ *"Mimosa Systems Gains 150,000 New NearPoint Users"* in *Information Today (Vol. 26, February 2009, No. 2, pp. 31)*
Pub: Information Today, Inc.
Description: Mimosa System's NearPoint archive solution features email and file archiving, e-discovery, archive virtualization, and disaster recovery capabilities.

18936 ■ *"More Leading Retailers Using Omniture Conversion Solutions to Boost Sales and Ecommerce Performance"* in *Internet Wire (Sept. 22,2009)*
Pub: Comtex News Network, Inc.
Description: Many retailers are utilizing Omniture conversion solutions to improve the performance of their ecommerce businesses; recent enhancements to Omniture Merchandising and Omniture Recommendations help clients drive increased conversion to their Internet ventures.

18937 ■ *"More Leading Retailers Using Omniture Conversion Solutions to Boost Sales and Ecommerce Performance"* in *Internet Wire (Sept. 22,2009)*
Pub: Comtex News Network, Inc.
Description: Many retailers are utilizing Omniture conversion solutions to improve the performance of their ecommerce businesses; recent enhancements to Omniture Merchandising and Omniture Recommendations help clients drive increased conversion to their Internet ventures.

18938 ■ *"My Favorite Tool for Organizing Data"* in *Inc. (Vol. 33, November 2011, No. 9, pp. 46)*
Pub: Inc. Magazine
Ed: Abram Brown. **Description:** Intelligence software firm uses Roambi, a Web-based service that turns spreadsheet data into interactive files for iPhones and iPads.

18939 ■ *"New Database Brings Doctors Out of the Dark"* in *Business Courier (Vol. 26, October 23, 2009, No. 26, pp. 1)*
Pub: American City Business Journals, Inc.
Ed: James Ritchie. **Description:** A database created by managed care consulting firm Praesentia allows doctors in Cincinnati to compare average reimbursements from health insurance companies to doctors in different areas. Specialist doctors in the city are paid an average of $172.25 for every office consultation.

18940 ■ *"New IPhone Also Brings New Way of Mobile Marketing"* in *Advertising Age (Vol. 79, June 16, 2008, No. 24, pp. 23)*
Pub: Crain Communications, Inc.
Ed: Abbey Klaasen. **Description:** Currently there are two kinds of applications for the iPhone and other mobile devices: native applications that allow for richer experiences and take advantage of features that are built into a phone and web applications, those that allow access to the web through specific platforms. Marketers are interested in creating useful experiences for customers and opening up the platforms which will allow them to do this.

18941 ■ *"New Sprint Phone Whets Appetite for Applications"* in *The Business Journal-Serving Metropolitan Kansas City (Vol. 26, July 25, 2008)*
Pub: American City Business Journals, Inc.
Ed: Suzanna Stagemeyer. **Description:** Firms supporting the applications of the new Samsung Instinct, which was introduced by Sprint Nextel Corp. in June 2008, have reported usage rates increase for their products. Handmark, whose mobile services Pocket Express comes loaded with Instinct, has redirected employees to meet the rising demand for the services. Other views and information on Instinct, are presented.

18942 ■ *"New Wave of Business Security Products Ushers in the Kaspersky Anti-Malware Protection System"* in *Internet Wire (October 26, 2010)*
Pub: Comtex
Description: Kaspersky Anti-Malware System provides anti-malware protection that requires minimal in-house resources for small businesses. The system offers a full range of tightly integrated end-to-end protection solutions, ensuring unified protection across an entire network, from endpoint and mobile device protection to file server, mail server, network storage and gateway protection. It provides flexible centralized management, immediate threat visibility and a level of responsiveness not seen in other anti-malware approaches.

18943 ■ *"Nonprofit NAIC Acquires Software Developer as For-Profit Arm"* in *Crain's Detroit Business (Vol. 25, June 22, 2009, No. 25, pp. 10)*
Pub: Crain Communications Inc. - Detroit
Ed: Sherri Begin Welch. **Description:** Details of National Association of Investors Corporation's acquisition of a Massachusetts investment software developer in order to offer more products to investment clubs and individual investors nationwide.

18944 ■ *"Not Your Father's Whiteboard"* in *Inc. (Vol. 33, November 2011, No. 9, pp. 50)*
Pub: Inc. Magazine
Ed: Adam Baer. **Description:** Sharp's new interactive whiteboard is really a 70-inch touch screen monitor with software for importing presentations from any Windows 7 computer.

18945 ■ *"Nothing Like a Weak Team Or An Unrealistic Schedule To Start a Project Off Right"* in *Inc. (November 2007, pp. 85-87)*
Pub: Gruner & Jahr USA Publishing
Ed: Joel Spolsky. **Description:** Five easy ways to fail meeting a project deadline are discussed by the owner of a software development company: start with second-rate team of developers, set weekly milestones, negotiate a deadline, divide tasks equitably, and work until midnight.

18946 ■ *"OCE Boosts JetStream Productivity"* in *American Printer (Vol. 128, August 1, 2011, No. 8)*
Pub: Penton Media Inc.
Description: New Oce JetStream 1400 and 3000 digital full-color inkjet presses are profiled. The new models promise higher speed to grow print volume.

18947 ■ *"Oce Business Services: Discovery Made Easy" in Information Today (Vol. 26, February 2009, No. 2, pp. 31)*
Pub: Information Today, Inc.
Ed: Barbara Brynko. **Description:** Oce Business Services provides document process management and electronic discovery through its CaseData repertoire of legal management solutions.

18948 ■ *"Off the RIM' in Canadian Business (Vol. 80, January 15, 2007, No. 2, pp. 7)*
Pub: Rogers Media
Ed: John Gray. **Description:** The reasons for the rise and fall in stock prices of the software company, Research In Motion Ltd., from September 2006 to January 2007, are analyzed.

18949 ■ *"Office Retooled" in Canadian Business (Vol. 80, March 26, 2007, No. 7, pp. 67)*
Pub: Rogers Media
Ed: Andrew Wahl. **Description:** The merits and demerits of using new Google Apps Premier Edition are presented.

18950 ■ *"Office Tech: A Pretty Little Vista" in Canadian Business (Vol. 80, January 29, 2007, No. 3, pp. 61)*
Pub: Rogers Media
Ed: Andrew Wahl. **Description:** The features of the new version of Microsoft Windows Vista OS and Microsoft Office 2007 are described.

18951 ■ *"Omniture's Next Version of SearchCenter Delivers Landing Page Optimization" in Internet Wire (September 24, 2009)*
Pub: Comtex News Network, Inc.
Description: Omniture, Inc., a leading provider of online business optimization software, has announced a new release of Omniture SearchCenter; this latest version will allow search engine marketers to test landing pages across campaigns and ad groups.

18952 ■ *"On Beyond Powerpoint: Presentations Get a Wake-Up Call" in Inc. (November 2007, pp. 58-59)*
Pub: Gruner & Jahr USA Publishing
Ed: Michael Fitzgerald. **Description:** New software that allows business presentations to be shared online are profiled, including ProfCast, audio podcasts for sales, marketing, and training; SmartDraw2008, software that creates professional graphics; Dimdim, an open-Web conferencing tool; Empressr, a hosted Web service for creating, managing, and sharing multimedia presentations; Zentation, a free tool that allows users to watch slides and a videos of presenter; Spresent, a Web-based presentation tool for remote offices or conference calls.

18953 ■ *Open Source Solutions for Small Business Problems*
Pub: Charles River Media
Ed: John Locke. **Released:** May 2004. **Price:** $35.95. **Description:** Open source software provides solutions to many small business problems such as tracking electronic documents, scheduling, accounting functions, managing contact lists, and reducing spam.

18954 ■ *"Oracle and Tauri Group Honored by Homeland Security and Defense Business Council" in Wireless News (December 15, 2009)*
Pub: Close-Up Media
Description: Selected as members of the year by the Homeland Security and Defense Business Council were Oracle, a software company that has provided thought leadership and strategic insights as well as The Tauri Group, an analytical consultancy, that has demonstrated a unique understanding of the role of small business and its vital contribution to the success of the country's security.

18955 ■ *"Our Gadget of the Week" in Barron's (Vol. 88, March 24, 2008, No. 12, pp. 47)*
Pub: Dow Jones & Company, Inc.
Ed: Tiernan Ray. **Description:** Review of the $299 Apple Time Capsule, which is a 500-megabyte hard disk drive and a Wi-Fi router, rolled into one device. The device allows users to create backup files without the need for sophisticated file management software.

18956 ■ *"Owner of IT Firm MK2 Tying Future to Software" in Crain's Cleveland Business (Vol. 30, June 15, 2009, No. 23, pp. 3)*
Pub: Crain Communications, Inc.
Ed: Chuck Soder. **Description:** Donald Kasper, owner of MK2 Technologies LLC of Cleveland, Ohio discusses his recent acquisition of a portion of ProSource Solution. The move will help expand the two companies' custom software development plans.

18957 ■ *"Paging Dr. Phil' in Canadian Business (Vol. 79, September 25, 2006, No. 19, pp. 21)*
Pub: Rogers Media
Ed: John Gray. **Description:** Increasing corporate crimes in software industry is discussed by focusing on recent case of Hewlett and Packard.

18958 ■ *"Panda Security for Business 4.05" in SC Magazine (Vol. 21, July 2010, No. 7, pp. 50)*
Pub: Haymarket Media Inc.
Description: Profile of Panda Security for Business, software offering endpoint security protection for computer desktops and servers is presented.

18959 ■ *"The Paper Shredder" in Business Courier (Vol. 26, September 11, 2009, No. 20, pp. 1)*
Pub: American City Business Journals, Inc.
Ed: Dan Monk. **Description:** DotLoop Company, owned by entrepreneur Austin Allison, is developing the DotLoop software, which eliminates paperwork in the processing of real estate contracts. The software allows realtors to take control of the negotiation process and is adaptable to the rules of different US states.

18960 ■ *"Paperless Bookkeeping Program" in Fleet Owner Online (February 15, 2011)*
Pub: Penton Business Media Inc.
Description: TruckTax launched its new paperless bookkeeping system to help manage bookkeeping tasks, accounting and business tax information and filings for truckers.

18961 ■ *"PC Connection Acquires Cloud Software Provider" in New Hampshire Business Review (Vol. 33, March 25, 2011, No. 6, pp. 8)*
Pub: Business Publications Inc.
Description: Merrimack-based PC Connection Inc. acquired ValCom Technology, a provider of cloud-based IT service management software. Details of the deal are included.

18962 ■ *"PC Running Slowly? How to Rev Up Your Machine" in Inc. (Vol. 33, November 2011, No. 9, pp. 46)*
Pub: Inc. Magazine
Ed: John Brandon. **Description:** Software that keeps PCs tuned up and running smoothing are profiled: AUSLO6ICS BOOSTSPEED 5, $50; Tuneup Utilities 2011, $40; Slimware Slimcleaner 1.9, free; and IOBIT Advanced Systemcare Pro 4, $20 a year.

18963 ■ *"PopCap Games Achieves Significant Increase in Return on Ad Spend With Omniture SearchCenter" in Internet Wire (September 15, 2009)*
Pub: Comtex News Network, Inc.
Description: PopCap Games, a leading computer games provider, is using Omniture SearchCenter together with Omniture SiteCatalyst to increase revenue from its search engine marketing campaign. Omniture, Inc. is a leading provider of Internet business optimization software.

18964 ■ *"The Power of Negative Thinking" in Inc. (Volume 32, December 2010, No. 10, pp. 43)*
Pub: Inc. Magazine
Ed: Jason Fried. **Description:** A Website is software and most businesses have and need a good Website to generate business. Understanding for building a powerful Website is presented.

18965 ■ *"Power Ranger" in Inc. (November 2007, pp. 131)*
Pub: Gruner & Jahr USA Publishing
Ed: Nitasha Tiku. **Description:** Surveyor software is designed to power down computers when not in use, in order to save energy.

18966 ■ *Practical Tech for Your Business*
Pub: Kiplinger Books and Tapes
Ed: Michael J. Martinez. **Released:** 2002. **Description:** Advice is offered to help small business owners choose the right technology for their company. The guide tells how to get started, network via the Internet, create an office network, use database software, and conduct business using mobile technology.

18967 ■ *"Precision Crop Control with Valley Irrigation/CropMetrics Partnership" in Farm Industry News (January 6, 2011)*
Pub: Penton Business Media Inc.
Description: Irrigation systems have become a precision farming tool since partnering with agronomic software systems to apply products across the field by prescription. Valley Irrigation and CropMetrics have partnered in order to variably control water, fertilizer and other crop management products through a center pivot irrigation system.

18968 ■ *"Press Release: Trimble Introduces CFX-750 Display" in Farm Industry News (January 4, 2011)*
Pub: Penton Business Media Inc.
Description: Trimble is offering a touch screen display called the CFX-750. The new 8-inch full-color display allows farmers to choose the specific guidance, steering and precision agriculture capabilities that best fit their farm's particular needs. The display can be upgraded as business needs change, including the addition of GLONASS capabilities, or the addition of section and rate control for crop inputs such as seed, chemicals and fertilizer.

18969 ■ *"Programs Provide Education and Training" in Contractor (Vol. 56, September 2009, No. 9, pp. 56)*
Pub: Penton Media, Inc.
Ed: William Feldman; Patti Feldman. **Description:** Opportunity Interactive's Showroom v2 software provides uses computer graphics to provide education and training on HVAC equipment and systems. It can draw heat pump balance points for a specific home. Meanwhile, Simutech's HVAC Training Simulators provide trainees with 'hands-on' HVACR training.

18970 ■ *"Protection One Introduces Home and Business Security iPhone App" in Wireless News (November 13, 2009)*
Pub: Close-Up Media
Description: Protection One, Inc., a provider of security systems to business and residential customers, has developed an application that allows users to access their security panels and receive real-time updates from their iPhone or iPod touch devices.

18971 ■ *"Providers Ride First Wave of eHealth Dollars" in Boston Business Journal (Vol. 31, June 10, 2011, No. 20, pp. 1)*
Pub: Boston Business Journal
Ed: Julie M. Donnelly. **Description:** Health care providers in Massachusetts implementing electronic medical records technology started receiving federal stimulus funds. Beth Israel Deaconess Medical Center was the first hospital to qualify for the funds.

18972 ■ *Publishers, Distributors, and Wholesalers of the United States*
Pub: R.R. Bowker L.L.C.
URL(s): www.bowker.com. **Released:** Annual; latest edition 2010. **Price:** $500, Individuals in 2 volumes; hard cover. **Covers:** Over 196,066 publishers, distributors, and wholesalers; includes associations, museums, software producers and manufacturers, and others not included in 'Books in Print'. **Entries include:** Publisher name, editorial and ordering addresses, e-mail, websites, phone, Standard Address Numbers (SANs), International Standard Book Number prefix. **Arrangement:** Alphabetical; distributors and wholesalers are listed separately. **Indexes:** ISBN prefix, abbreviation, type of business, imprint

name, geographical, inactive and out of business company name, toll-free phone and fax, wholesaler and distributor.

18973 ■ *"Publishing Technology Introduces IngentaConnect Mobile" in Information Today (Vol. 26, February 2009, No. 2, pp. 33)*
Pub: Information Today, Inc.
Description: College undergraduates will find Publishing Technology's newest publisher product, IngentaConnect Mobile helpful. The product allows users to read articles and abstracts on mobile devices. According to a recent study, 73 percent of young adults with wireless hand-held devices use them to access non-voice data on any given day.

18974 ■ *"Putting the App in Apple" in Inc. (Vol. 30, November 2008, No. 11, pp.)*
Pub: Mansueto Ventures LLC
Ed: Nitasha Tiku. **Description:** Aftermarket companies are scrambling to develop games and widgets for Apple's iPhone. Apple launched a kit for developers interested in creating iPhone-specific software along with the App Store, and an iTunes spinoff. Profiles of various software programs that may be used on the iPhone are given.

18975 ■ *QuickBooks All-in-One Desk Reference for Dummies*
Pub: John Wiley & Sons, Incorporated
Ed: Stephen L. Nelson. **Released:** January 2007. **Price:** $29.99 (US), $42.99 (Canadian). **Description:** Compilation of nine self-contained minibooks to get the most from QuickBooks accounting software. Companion Web site with sample business plan workbook and downloadable profit-volume cost analysis workbook included.

18976 ■ *QuickBooks Simple Start for Dummies*
Pub: John Wiley and Sons, Inc.
Ed: Stephen L. Nelson. **Released:** October 2004. **Price:** $21.99. **Description:** Profile of Intuits new accounting software geared to micro businesses. Advice is offered on daily, monthly, and yearly accounting activities covering records, sales tax, and reports.

18977 ■ *QuickBooks X on Demand*
Pub: Que
Ed: Gail Perry. **Released:** December 2006. **Price:** $34.99. **Description:** Step-by-step training for using various small business financial software programs; includes illustrated, full color explanations.

18978 ■ *QuickBooks X for Dummies*
Pub: John Wiley & Sons, Incorporated
Ed: Stephen L. Nelson. **Released:** November 2006. **Price:** $21.99. **Description:** Key features of QuickBooks software for small business are introduced. Invoicing and credit memos, recoding sales receipts, accounting, budgeting, taxes, payroll, financial reports, job estimating, billing, tracking, data backup, are among the features.

18979 ■ *"Quickoffice's MobileFiles Pro App Enables Excel Editing On-the-Go" in Information Today (Vol. 26, February 2009, No. 2, pp. 31)*
Pub: Information Today, Inc.
Description: Quickoffice Inc. introduced MobileFiles Pro, which features editable Microsoft Office functionality for the iPone and iPod touch. The application allows users to edit and save Microsoft Excel files in .xls format, transfer files to and from PC and Mac desktops via Wi-Fi, and access and synchronize with Apple MobileMe accounts.

18980 ■ *"Remote Control: Working From Wherever" in Inc. (February 2008, pp. 46-47)*
Pub: Gruner & Jahr USA Publishing
Ed: Ryan Underwood. **Description:** New technology allows workers to perform tasks from anywhere via the Internet. Profiles of products to help connect to your office from afar include, LogMein Pro, a Web-based service that allowsaccess to a computer from anywhere; Xdrive, an online service that allows users to store and swap files; Basecamp, a Web-based tools that works like a secure version of MySpace; MojoPac Freedom, is software that allows users to copy their computer's desktop to a removable hard

drive and plug into any PC; WatchGuard Firebox X Core e-Series UTM Bundle, hardware that blocks hackers and viruses while allowing employees to work remotely; TightVNC, a free open-source software that lets you control another computer via the Internet.

18981 ■ *"RES Stakes Its Claim in Area" in Philadelphia Business Journal (Vol. 28, January 29, 2010, No. 50, pp. 1)*
Pub: American City Business Journals
Ed: Peter Key. **Description:** RES Software Company Inc. of Amsterdam, Netherlands appointed Jim Kirby as president for the Americas and Klaus Besier as chairman in an effort to boost the firm's presence in the US. Brief career profiles of Kirby and Besier are included. RES develops software that allows management of information flow between an organization and its employees regardless of location.

18982 ■ *"Route Optimization Impacts the Bottom Line" in Contractor (Vol. 56, November 2009, No. 11, pp. 48)*
Pub: Penton Media, Inc.
Ed: Dave Beaudry. **Description:** Plumbing and HVAC businesses can save a significant amount of money from route optimization. The process begins with gathering information on a fleet and a routing software tool can determine the effectiveness of current route configurations and identify preferable route plans.

18983 ■ *Salesforce.com Secrets of Success: Best Practices for Growth and Profitability*
Pub: Prentice Hall Business Publishing
Contact: Jerome Grant, President
Ed: David Taber. **Released:** May 15, 2009. **Price:** $34.99. **Description:** Guide for using Salesforce. com; it provides insight into navigating through user groups, management, sales, marketing and IT departments in order to achieve the best results.

18984 ■ *"Save the Date" in Barron's (Vol. 90, September 13, 2010, No. 37, pp. 35)*
Pub: Barron's Editorial & Corporate Headquarters
Ed: Mark Veverka. **Description:** Mark Hurd is the new Co-President of Oracle after being forced out at Hewlett-Packard where he faced a harassment complaint. HP fired Hurd due to expense account malfeasance. Hurd is also set to speak at an Oracle trade show in San Francisco on September 20, 2010.

18985 ■ *"Scitable Puts Nature Education on the Map" in Information Today (Vol. 26, February 2009, No. 2, pp. 29)*
Pub: Information Today, Inc.
Description: Nature Education, a division of the Nature Publishing Group, released its first product, Scitable, a free online resource for undergraduate biology students and educators. The service includes over 180 overviews of key genetics concepts as well as social networking features, including groups and functionality, that lets students work with classmates and others. Teachers can use the service to set up public or private groups for students.

18986 ■ *"Second Cup?' in Canadian Business (Vol. 81, July 21, 2008, No. 11, pp. 50)*
Pub: Rogers Media Ltd.
Ed: Calvin Leung. **Description:** Profile of James Gosling who is credited as the inventor of the Java programming language; however, the 53-year-old software developer feels ambivalent for being credited as inventor since many people contributed to the language. Netscape and Sun Microsystems incorporation of the programming language into Java is presented.

18987 ■ *"Sense of Discovery" in Business Journal Portland (Vol. 27, November 19, 2010, No. 38, pp. 1)*
Pub: Portland Business Journal
Ed: Erik Siemers. **Description:** Tigard, Oregon-based Exterro Inc. CEO Bobby Balachandran announced plans to go public without the help of an institutional investor. Balachandran believes Exterro could grow to a $100 million legal compliance

software company in the span of three years. Insights on Exterro's growth as market leader in the $1 billion legal governance software market are also given.

18988 ■ *"Serials Solutions Launches 360 Resource Manager Consortium Edition" in Information Today (Vol. 26, February 2009, No. 2, pp. 32)*
Pub: Information Today, Inc.
Description: Serials Solutions new Serials Solutions 360 Resource Manager Consortium Edition helps consortia, groups and member libraries with their e-resource management services. The products allows users to consolidate e-resource metadata and acquisition information into one place, which enables groups to manage holdings, subscriptions, licensing, contacts, and cost information and to streamline delivery of information to members.

18989 ■ *"A Side Project Threatens To Get Totally Out of Control and I Think, 'How Fun" in Inc. (October 2007, pp. 81-82)*
Pub: Gruner & Jahr USA Publishing
Ed: Joel Spolsky. **Description:** Profile of Fog Creek Software, makers of project-management software for other software developers. Fog Creek's owner discusses his idea to create a new product for his firm.

18990 ■ *"Skype on Steroids" in Inc. (Vol. 31, January-February 2009, No. 1, pp. 46)*
Pub: Mansueto Ventures LLC
Ed: Nitasha Tiku. **Description:** Free software called VoxOx allows users to make calls over the Internet and connects all email and IM accounts.

18991 ■ *"Slow but Steady into the Future" in Barron's (Vol. 88, July 7, 2008, No. 27, pp. M)*
Pub: Dow Jones & Co., Inc.
Ed: Mark Veverka. **Description:** Investors are advised to maintain their watch on the shares of business software company NetSuite. The company's chief executive officer, Zach Nelson, claims that the company has a 10-year lead on its competitors with the development of software-as-a service.

18992 ■ *"Small is Bountiful for Intuit" in Barron's (Vol. 90, September 13, 2010, No. 37, pp. 22)*
Pub: Barron's Editorial & Corporate Headquarters
Ed: Mark Veverka. **Description:** Finance software maker Intuit wants to tap the underserved small business market. One analyst sees Intuit's shares rising 25 percent to 55 percent in the next 12 months from September 2010.

18993 ■ *"A Software Company's Whimsical Widgets Were an Instant Hit. But Its Core Product Was Getting Overshadowed' in Inc. (Jan. 2008)*
Pub: Gruner & Jahr USA Publishing
Ed: Alex Salkever. **Description:** A widget designed as a marketing tool tuned into a hit on Facebook. Should ChipIn shift its focus?.

18994 ■ *The Software Encyclopedia: A Guide for Personal, Professional and Business Users*
Pub: R.R. Bowker L.L.C.
URL(s): www.bowker.com/catalog/000103.htm. **Ed:** D. Gravesande. **Released:** Annual; latest edition May, 2008. **Price:** $460, Individuals for set of 2 volumes; soft cover. **Description:** Contains listings of over 44,600 software programs from 4,646 publishers and distributors. **Database includes:** Includes listing of Best Software Applications and some of the most highly recommended products over the past few years. **Arrangement:** Two alphabetical sections for software, one by title, the other by system/application; also, one alphabetical section for publishers. **Indexes:** Title, system/application.

18995 ■ *"Software Solutions Increase Productivity" in Contractor (Vol. 57, February 2010, No. 2, pp. 26)*
Pub: Penton Media, Inc.
Ed: William Feldman; Patti Feldman. **Description:** Singletouch is a real-time data capture solution for mechanical and other contractors that work in jobs that require materials and workload tracking. Contrac-

tors get information on extreme weather and sudden changes in the cost of materials. The OptimumHVAC optimization software by Optimum Energy is designed to optimize energy savings in commercial buildings.

18996 ■ *"Software Solutions from Trane and Carrier"* in *Contractor (Vol. 56, July 2009, No. 7, pp. 38)*
Pub: Penton Media, Inc.
Ed: William Feldman; Patti Feldman. **Description:** Trane Trace 700 software helps HVAC contractors optimize the design of a building's HVAC system and aids in the evaluation of various key energy-saving concepts, including daylighting, high-performance glazing, and other optimization strategies. Carrier's E20-II family of software programs lets contractors increase the accuracy of an HVAC system estimate.

18997 ■ *"Software's Last Hurrah"* in *Canadian Business (Vol. 81, December 24, 2007, No. 1, pp. 27)*
Pub: Rogers Media
Ed: Andrew Wahl. **Description:** Canada's software industry could be facing a challenge with IBM's acquisition of Cognos, which was the country's last major independent business intelligence company and was also IBM's largest acquisition ever. Next in line to Cognos in terms of prominence is Open Text Corporation, which could also be a possible candidate for acquisition, as analysts predict.

18998 ■ *"Startup on Cusp of Trend"* in *Austin Business JournalInc. (Vol. 29, January 8, 2010, No. 44, pp. 1)*
Pub: American City Business Journals
Ed: Christopher Calnan. **Description:** Austin-based Socialware Inc. introduced a new business called social middleware, which is a software that is layered between the company network and social networking Website used by workers. The software was designed to give employers a measure of control over content while allowing workers to continue using online social networks.

18999 ■ *"The State of the Art in End-User Software Engineering"* in *ACM Computing Surveys (Vol. 43, Fall 2011, No. 3, pp. 21)*
Pub: Association for Computing Machinery
Description: Most programs today are not written by professional software developers but by people with expertise in other domains working towards goals for which they need computational support. A discussion of empirical research about end-user software engineering activities and the technologies designed to support them is presented. Several crosscutting issues in the design of EUSE tools, including the roles of risk, reward, and domain complexity, and self-efficacy in the design of EUSE tools and the potential of educating users about software engineering principles are also examined.

19000 ■ *"The Story of Diane Greene"* in *Barron's (Vol. 88, July 14, 2008, No. 28, pp. 31)*
Pub: Dow Jones & Co., Inc.
Ed: Mark Veverka. **Description:** Discusses the ousting of Diane Greene as a chief executive of VMWare, a developer of virtualization software, after the firm went public; in this case Greene, a brilliant engineer, should not be negatively impacted by the decision because it is common for companies to bring in new executive leadership that is more operations oriented after the company goes public.

19001 ■ *"A Survey of Combinatorial Testing"* in *ACM Computing Surveys (Vol. 43, Summer 2011, No. 2, pp. 11)*
Pub: Association for Computing Machinery
Ed: Changhai Nie, Hareton Leung. **Description:** Combinatorial Testing (CT) can detect failures triggered by interactions of parameters in the Software Under Test (SUT) with a covering array test suite generated by some sampling mechanisms. Basic concepts and notations of CT are covered.

19002 ■ *"A Survey of Comparison-Based System-Level Diagnosis"* in *ACM Computing Surveys (Vol. 43, Fall 2011, No. 3, pp. 22)*
Pub: Association for Computing Machinery
Ed: Elias P. Duarte Jr., Roverli P. Ziwich, Luiz C.P. Albini. **Description:** The growing complexity and dependability requirements of hardware, software, and networks demand efficient techniques for discovering disruptive behavior in those systems. Comparison-based diagnosis is a realistic approach to detect faulty units based on the outputs of tasks executed by system units. This survey integrates the vast amount of research efforts that have been produced in this field.

19003 ■ *"Taking the Steps Into the Clouds"* in *New Hampshire Business Review (Vol. 33, March 25, 2011, No. 6, pp. 19)*
Pub: Business Publications Inc.
Ed: Tim Wessels. **Description:** Cloud services include Internet and Web security, spam filtering, message archiving, work group collaboration, IT asset management, help desk and disaster recovery backup.

19004 ■ *"Tech Deal Couples Homegrown Firms"* in *The Business Journal-Serving Greater Tampa Bay (Vol. 28, July 4, 2008, No. 28, pp. 1)*
Pub: American City Business Journals, Inc.
Ed: Michael Hinman. **Description:** Tampa Bay, Florida-based Administrative Partners Inc. was acquired by Tribridge Inc. resulting in the strengthening of the delivery of Microsoft products to clients. Other details of the merger of the management consulting services companies are presented.

19005 ■ *"Technology to the Rescue"* in *Contractor (Vol. 56, July 2009, No. 7, pp. 22)*
Pub: Penton Media, Inc.
Ed: Candace Ruolo. **Description:** Features of several products that will make the job of a mechanical contractor easier are discussed. These include Ridgid's line of drain and sewer inspection cameras and monitors, Motion Computing's Motion F5 tablet rugged tablet PC, the JobClock from Exaktime, and the TeleNav Track tool for mobile workforce management.

19006 ■ *"Technology: What Seems To Be the Problem? Self Service Gets a Tune-Up"* in *Inc. (February 2008, pp. 43-44)*
Pub: Gruner & Jahr USA Publishing
Ed: Darren Dahl. **Description:** Self-service software can save companies money when responding to customer service phone calls, text or email messages. More companies are relying on alternatives such as automated Web-based self-service systems.

19007 ■ *"Ted Stahl: Executive Chairman"* in *Inside Business (Vol. 13, September-October 2011, No. 5, pp. NC6)*
Pub: Great Lakes Publishing Co.
Ed: Miranda S. Miller. **Description:** Profile of Ted Stahl, who started working in his family's business when he was ten years old is presented. The firm makes dies for numbers and letters used on team uniforms. Another of the family firms manufactures stock and custom heat-printing products, equipment and supplies. It also educates customers on ways to decorate garments with heat printing products and offers graphics and software for customers to create their own artwork.

19008 ■ *"Thinking Strategically About Technology"* in *Franchising World (Vol. 42, August 2010, No. 8, pp. 9)*
Pub: International Franchise Association
Ed: Bruce Franson. **Description:** Nearly 25 percent of companies waste money from their technology budget. Most of the budget is spent on non-strategic software. Ways to spend money on technology for any franchise are examined.

19009 ■ *"A Timely Boon for Small Investors"* in *Barron's (Vol. 88, March 24, 2008, No. 12, pp. 48)*
Pub: Dow Jones & Company, Inc.
Ed: Theresa W. Carey. **Description:** Nasdaq Data Store's new program called Market Replay allows investors to accurately track stock price movements. The replay can be as long as a day of market time and allows investors to determine whether they executed stock trades at the best possible price.

19010 ■ *"Touching the Future"* in *Canadian Business (Vol. 81, July 21, 2008, No. 11, pp. 41)*
Pub: Rogers Media Ltd.
Ed: Matt McClearn. **Description:** Microsoft Corp. has launched a multi-touch product which is both a software and hardware technology called Microsoft Surface. The innovative product allows people to use it at the same time, however touch-based computers are reported to be around $100,000. Other features and benefits of the product are presented.

19011 ■ *"Trust But Verify: FMLA Software Isn't Foolproof, So Apply a Human Touch"* in *HR Specialist (Vol. 8, September 2010, No. 9, pp. 3)*
Pub: Capitol Information Group Inc.
Description: Employers are using software to track FMLA information, however, it is important for employers to review reasons for eligibility requirements, particularly when an employee is reportedly overstepping the bounds within leave regulations due to software error.

19012 ■ *"Two Field Service Management Solutions"* in *Contractor (Vol. 56, November 2009, No. 11, pp. 37)*
Pub: Penton Media, Inc.
Ed: William Feldman; Patti Feldman. **Description:** Bella Solutions Field Service Software v. 4.2 is a web based solution for HVAC service contractors that enables scheduling of emergency, one-time, multi-visit or periodically recurring jobs with drag and drop appointments. VaZing is another web based solution that costs $99 per month for contractors. It can handle line-item discounting and invoices aside from scheduling.

19013 ■ *"Two Ways to Find New Customers"* in *Inc. (Vol. 31, January-February 2009, No. 1, pp. 41)*
Pub: Mansueto Ventures LLC
Description: Latest software programs that help sales staff connect to new leads are profiled. Salesconx provides online leads while Demandbase reports users on a particular Website.

19014 ■ *"Unbound ID Raises $2 Million"* in *Austin Business JournalInc. (Vol. 28, December 12, 2008, No. 39, pp. 1)*
Pub: American City Business Journals
Ed: Christopher Calnan. **Description:** Austin, Texas-based Unbound ID Corporation has secured $2 million in funding from venture capital firm Silverton Partners. The company has developed identity management software for network directories. The market for identity management technology is expected to grow to more than $12.3 billion by 2014.

19015 ■ *"Unbreakable"* in *Canadian Business (Vol. 79, October 9, 2006, No. 20, pp. 111)*
Pub: Rogers Media
Ed: Robert Hercz. **Description:** The features and functions of Neutrino, an embedded operating system developed by QNX Software Systems are discussed.

19016 ■ *"uTest Discusses the Evolution of Crowdsourcing Models at CrowdConf 2010"* in *Internet Wire (October 1, 2010)*
Pub: Comtex
Description: World's largest software testing marketplace, uTest, announces its first conference dedicated to the emerging field of crowdsourcing along with the future of distributed work. A panel of experts will discuss common misconceptions about crowdsourcing using real-world examples.

19017 ■ *"Video Surveillance Enters Digital Era, Makes Giant Strides"* in *Arkansas Business (Vol. 26, September 28, 2009, No. 39, pp. 1)*
Pub: Journal Publishing Inc.
Ed: Jamie Walden. **Description:** Arkansas business owners are finding that the newest technology in video surveillance is leading to swift apprehension of thieves due to the high-quality digital imagery now being captured on surveillance equipment. Motion detection software for these systems is enhancing

the capabilities of these systems and providing opportunities for businesses that would normally have problems integrating these systems.

19018 ■ *"A Virtual Jog Mode for CAM" in Modern Machine Shop (Vol. 84, November 2011, No. 6, pp. 22)*
Pub: Gardner Business Media, Inc.
Contact: Richard G. Kline, President
E-mail: rkline@gardnerweb.com
Ed: Edwin Gasparraj. **Description:** In many cases, CAM programming required a specific, user-defined path. Siemens PLMs Generic Motion Controller is an alternative that defines the tool path within CAM. The program is a virtual 'teach' mode that enables the user to capture cutter locations by jogging machines axes within CAM.

19019 ■ *"The Virtual Office" in Canadian Business (Vol. 80, April 9, 2007, No. 8, pp. 64)*
Pub: Rogers Media
Ed: Andrew Wahl. **Description:** The business operation of Eloqua which runs all its IT systems using its own online software is discussed.

19020 ■ *"What Has Sergey Wrought?" in Barron's (Vol. 89, July 13, 2009, No. 28, pp. 8)*
Pub: Dow Jones & Co., Inc.
Ed: Alan Abelson. **Description:** Sergey Aleynikov is a computer expert that once worked for Goldman Sachs but he was arrested after he left the company and charged with theft for bringing with him the code for the company's proprietary software for high-frequency trading. The stock market has been down for four straight weeks as of July 13, 2009 which reflects the reality of how the economy is still struggling.

19021 ■ *"Will the Force Be With Salesforce?" in Barron's (Vol. 88, March 24, 2008, No. 12, pp. 20)*
Pub: Dow Jones & Company, Inc.
Ed: Mark Veverka. **Description:** Shares of Salesforce.com are likely to drop from the $44.83-a-share level in the face of a deteriorating economy and financial sector and thus lower demand for business software. The company is unlikely to deliver on its ambitious earnings forecasts for 2008 especially with strengthening competition from Oracle.

19022 ■ *"Women Losing IT Ground" in Marketing to Women (Vol. 21, February 2008, No. 2, pp. 6)*
Pub: EPM Communications Inc.
Contact: Ira Mayer, President
E-mail: imayer@epmcom.com
Description: According to a study conducted by The National Center for Women & Information Technology, women in technology are losing ground. Statistical data included.

19023 ■ *"Yammer Gets Serious" in Inc. (Volume 32, December 2010, No. 10, pp. 58)*
Pub: Inc. Magazine
Ed: Eric Markowitz. **Description:** Yammer, an internal social network for companies, allows coworkers to share ideas and documents in real-time. Details of this service are included.

19024 ■ *"Yes, No, and Somewhat Likely: Survey the World with Web Polls" in Inc. (October 2007, pp. 58-59)*
Pub: Gruner & Jahr USA Publishing
Ed: Don Steinberg. **Description:** Online tools for surveying customers, employees and the general public include Zoomergan zPro and Zoomerang Sample, software designed to send surveys and allows viewing results; SurveyMonkey software creates, administers and allows viewing online surveys and results; Vizu software places a one-question poll on a particular Website; and Vovici EFM Feedback, a subscription service providing ongoing surveys to customers or employees.

19025 ■ *"Zeon Solutions Teams with Endeca for SaaS Version of Endeca InFront" in Entertainment Close-Up (October 25, 2011)*
Pub: Close-Up Media
Description: Zeon Solutions, an enterprise e-commerce and Website development firm announced a special licensing partnership with Endecca

Technologies. Endeca is an information management software company that provides small and mid-size retailers with high-performance Customer Experience Management technology.

STATISTICAL SOURCES

19026 ■ *RMA Annual Statement Studies*
Pub: Risk Management Association
Contact: Kevin M. Blakey, President
Released: Annual. **Price:** $175.00 2006-07 edition, $105.00. **Description:** Contains composite balance sheets and income statements for more than 360 industries, including the accounting, auditing, and bookkeeping industries. Also contains five years of comparative historical data for discerning trends. Includes 16 commonly used ratios, computed for most of the size groupings for nearly every industry.

19027 ■ *Standard & Poor's Industry Surveys*
Pub: Standard & Poor's Corp.
Released: Annual. **Price:** $3633.00. **Description:** Two-volume book that examines the prospects for specific industries, including trucking. Also provides analyses of trends and problems, statistical tables and charts, and comparative company analyses.

TRADE PERIODICALS

19028 ■ *Cutter IT Journal*
Pub: Cutter Information Corp.
Ed: Ed Yourdon, Editor. **Released:** Monthly. **Price:** Free. **Description:** Provides IT managers with practical and objective views on the latest technology and management trends.

19029 ■ *Datamation: The Emerging Technologies Magazine for Today's IS*
Pub: Reed Business Information
Contact: Jeff Greisch, President
URL(s): www.datamation.com. **Released:** Semimonthly

19030 ■ *DCLNews*
Pub: Data Conversion Laboratory
Contact: Mark Gross, President
Released: Monthly. **Price:** Included in membership;. **Description:** E-journal providing you insider information on XML and SGML, along with the latest technology and e-publishing news.

19031 ■ *Dr. Dobb's Journal: The World of Software Development*
Pub: UBM PLC
Contact: David Levin, Chief Executive Officer
URL(s): drdobbs.com. **Ed:** Michael Swaine. **Released:** Monthly **Price:** $25, Individuals; $99.95, Individuals CD-ROM library.

19032 ■ *ENT: The Independent Newspaper for Windows NT Enterprise Computing*
Pub: 101 Communications
Contact: Neil Vitale, President
URL(s): entmag.com/aboutus/aboutent.asp?editorialsid=17. **Released:** 18/yr. **Price:** Free U.S.; $54.95, Canada and Mexico; $64.95, Other countries.

19033 ■ *Journal of Software: Improvement and Practice*
Pub: John Wiley & Sons Inc.
Contact: Stephen M. Smith, President
URL(s): onlinelibrary.wiley.com/journal/10.1002/(-ISSN)2047-7481. **Released:** 7/yr. **Price:** £209, Individuals print; $363, Other countries print; $727, Institutions, other countries print; €469, Institutions, other countries print; £370, Institutions print.

19034 ■ *Maximum PC*
Pub: Future Network USA
URL(s): maximumpc.com. **Ed:** Michael Brown, Gordon Mah Ung. **Released:** Monthly **Price:** $14.95, Individuals; $24.95, Individuals 12 CDs; $29.95, Other countries; $49.95, Other countries two years; $1.95, Single issue.

19035 ■ *Media Computing*
Pub: Dreamscape Productions
Ed: Sheridan Tatsuno, Editor, statsuno@aol.com.
Released: Monthly. **Price:** $495, institutions in the U.S. and Canada; $550, institutions elsewhere. **Description:** Supplies analysis of multimedia, internet, intranet, and web computing issues. Recurring features include interviews and reports of meetings.

19036 ■ *Productivity Software*
Pub: Worldwide Videotex
Released: Monthly. **Price:** $150. **Description:** Provides information on computer software.

19037 ■ *Softletter*
Pub: Rick Chapman
Ed: Rick Chapman, Editor, jtarter@softletter.com.
Released: Semimonthly. **Price:** $399, individuals. **Description:** Analyzes market trends and company strategies in microcomputer software publishing and development. Recurring features include industry statistics and case studies.

19038 ■ *Software: Practice and Experience*
Pub: John Wiley & Sons Inc.
Contact: Stephen M. Smith, President
URL(s): onlinelibrary.wiley.com/journal/10.1002/(-ISSN)1097-024X. **Ed:** Prof. Andy J. Wellings, Prof. R.N. Horspool. **Released:** 12/yr. **Price:** $4988, Institutions print; $4988, Institutions, other countries print; €3219, Institutions, other countries print; £2546, Institutions print; $4988, Institutions, Canada and Mexico print.

19039 ■ *Software Tech News*
Pub: Data & Analysis Center for Software
Released: Quarterly. **Price:** Free. **Description:** Disseminates information and news about software technology and engineering, especially as required by the U.S. Department of Defense.

VIDEOCASSETTES/ AUDIOCASSETTES

19040 ■ *How to Keep Score in Baseball*
Tapeworm Video Distributors
25876 The Old Road #141
Stevenson Ranch, CA 91381
Ph: (661)257-4904
Fax: (661)257-4820
Co. E-mail: sales@tapeworm.com
URL: http://www.tapeworm.com
Released: 1995. **Description:** Explains how to use charts and formulas to record statistics and scores. **Availability:** VHS.

TRADE SHOWS AND CONVENTIONS

19041 ■ *COMDEX*
Ziff-Davis Inc.
28 E 28th St.
New York, NY 10016-7939
Ph: (212)503-3500
Fax: (212)503-4599
Co. E-mail: randy_zane@ziffdavis.com
URL: http://www.ziffdavis.com
Contact: Vivek Shah, Chief Executive Officer
URL(s): www.comdex.com/. **Frequency:** Annual. **Audience:** Volume resellers and value-adders of small computers and related items; only a virtual trade show since 2003. **Principal Exhibits:** Small computer systems, related peripherals, software, accessories, services, and supplies. **Dates and Locations:** , Sands Expo and Convention Center.

19042 ■ *Computer Game Developers' Conference*
UBM LLC
240 West 35th Street
New York, CA 94403
Ph: (650)513-4300
Free: 800-842-0798

Fax: (650)513-4618
URL: http://www.cmp.com
URL(s): www.gdconf.com. **Frequency:** Annual. **Principal Exhibits:** Equipment, supplies, and services for developers and producers of computer games. **Telecommunication Services:** pchapnick@cmp.com.

CONSULTANTS

19043 ■ Century Small Business Solutions
152 N El Camino Real
Encinitas, CA 92024-2849
Ph: (760)633-4725
Contact: John R. Todd, Principal
Scope: Focuses on improving the profitability of growth-oriented small businesses through business planning, controlling expenses, marketing to find new customers and tax planning to minimize taxes. **Founded:** 1993. **Seminars:** QuickBooks training and Budgeting for your Small Business.

19044 ■ CheckMark Software Inc.
724 Whalers Way, Bldg. H, Ste. 101
Fort Collins, CO 80525-7578
Ph: (970)225-0522
Free: 800-444-9922
Fax: (970)225-0611
Co. E-mail: info@checkmark.com
URL: http://www.checkmark.com
Contact: Jim Mathre, President
Scope: Developer of accounting software tools for small businesses and provides fast, easy to use, affordable accounting and payroll solutions to small and medium sized businesses. Provides payroll software and multiledger integrated accounting software. **Founded:** 1984. **Publications:** *Multi-Ledger, CheckMark Payroll for Macintosh; CheckMark Payroll for Windows.* **Special Services:** Multi-Ledger™; Payroll.

19045 ■ David Collison
2328 NE Smokey Hill Dr.
Lee's Summit, MO 64086-7018
Ph: (816)524-6099
Co. E-mail: dcollison@kc.rr.com
Contact: David E. Collison, Manager
Scope: Consultant in software development, robot integration, and user interfaces.

19046 ■ Creative Computer Resources Inc.
5001 Horizons Dr., Ste. 200
Columbus, OH 43220-5291
Ph: (614)384-7557
Free: 866-720-0209
Fax: (614)573-6331
Co. E-mail: team@planet-ccr.com
URL: http://www.planet-ccr.com
Contact: M. Erik Mueller, President
E-mail: merikm@planet-ccr.com
Scope: Offers information systems support, custom software development, website design, development and implementation. Provides information technology support and management services to small and mid-size businesses. **Founded:** 1996.

19047 ■ DacEasy Inc.—Sage Software Inc.
1715 N Brown Rd.
Lawrenceville, GA 30043
Free: 800-222-0505
Co. E-mail: sales@daceasy.com
URL: http://www.daceasy.com
Contact: Greg Hammermaster, President
URL(s): www.sagedaceasy.com. **Scope:** Develops an accounting system for small businesses that integrates accounting, invoicing, payroll, communications, and management software into a single package. **Founded:** 1981. **Seminars:** Tech Tuesday - Sage DacAccess Query and Publisher: Creating Basic Queries and Formatting, May, 2012; Tech Tuesday - Graphics Form Designer, Mar, 2012; Tech Tuesday - Year End Processes with Sage DacEasy; DacEasy Training.

19048 ■ On-Q Software Inc.
13764 SW 11 St.
Miami, FL 33184
Ph: (305)553-2400

Free: 800-553-2862
Fax: (305)220-2666
Co. E-mail: info@on-qsoftware.com
URL: http://www.on-qsoftware.com
Contact: Hermenegildo Cajigas, Treasurer
E-mail: hcajigas@on-qsoftware.com
Scope: Provider of the small business community with simple to use, feature rich software. Provides software solutions including time and fixed fee billing, due date tracking and practice manager. **Founded:** 1987.

19049 ■ Profit Associates Inc.
26 Hunters Forest Dr.
Charleston, SC 29414
Ph: (843)763-5718
Free: 800-688-6304
Fax: (843)763-5719
Co. E-mail: bobrog@profit-associates.com
URL: http://www.profit-associates.com
Contact: Bob Rogers, Managing Director
E-mail: bobrog@awod.com
Scope: A team of management and turnaround specialists providing consulting services. Focuses on the problems of small to medium-sized businesses in the manufacturing, distribution, construction, software. Specializes in employee productivity and incentives, management reengineering, profit and expense controls, production planning, strategic business planning, marketing and public relations, or ISO 9000 support. **Founded:** 1993. **Seminars:** Essential Elements of a Good Incentive Program; Why Look at Management Re-engineering; The Profit & Expense Control Process; The Executive Coaching Alternative.

19050 ■ Rothman Consulting Group Inc.
38 Bonad Rd.
Arlington, MA 02476
Ph: (781)641-4046
Fax: (781)641-2764
Co. E-mail: jr@jrothman.com
URL: http://www.jrothman.com
Contact: Johanna Rothman, President
E-mail: jr@jrothman.com
Scope: Works with software organizations to improve product development practices. Works with clients to find the leverage points that will increase their effectiveness as organizations and as managers, helping ship the right product at the right time, and recruit and retain the best people. **Founded:** 1994. **Publications:** "Manage Your Project Portfolio: Increase Your Capacity and Finish More Projects"; "Manage It! Your Guide to Modern, Pragmatic Project Management"; "Behind Closed Doors: Secrets of Great Management"; "Hiring the Best Knowledge Workers, Techies & Nerds"; "Corrective Action for the Software Industry". **Seminars:** Transitioning to Agile in Stockholm, May, 2012; PSL:Problem Solving Leadership, May, 2012; Working Effectively In Geographically Distributed Agile Project Teams, Apr, 2012.

19051 ■ RSA - The Security Division of EMC
174 Middlesex Tpke.
Bedford, MA 01720
Ph: (781)515-5000
Free: 877-772-4900
Fax: (781)515-5010
Co. E-mail: conferenceinfo@rsa.com
URL: http://www.rsa.com
Contact: Arthur W. Coviello, Jr., President
URL(s): www.rsasecurity.com. **Scope:** Firm develops and markets platform independent software developer's kits, end user products, and provides comprehensive consulting services in the cryptographic sciences. **Founded:** 2006. **Publications:** "Proofs for Two-Server Password Authentication," 2005; "On the security of RSA encryption in TLS," 2002; "Efficient finite field basis conversion involving dual bases," 1999; "Broadband Network and Device Security"; "Wireless Security"; "XmlSecurity". **Telecommunication Services:** pubs@rsasecurity.com; investor@rsasecurity.com; ajuels@rsasecurity.com; rhousley@rsasecurity.com; contact@rsasecurity.com. **Special Services:** BSAFE; TIPEM; RSA SecurID®; RSA®; RSA ClearTrust®.

19052 ■ SiteShapers
4070 Goldfinch St., Ste. D
San Diego, CA 92103
Ph: (619)231-6907
Fax: (619)231-7061
Co. E-mail: inquiry@siteshapers.com
URL: http://www.siteshapers.com
Contact: Irene Jernigan, Manager
Scope: Conducts needs assessment and marketing productivity workshops for high-technology manufacturers and service firms. Specializes in web site strategies and design, marketing strategies, planning, research and promotion. Serves electronics and software, instruments and health care industries. **Founded:** 1985.

19053 ■ S.V. Writing Services
4471 Park Bristol Pl.
San Jose, CA 95136-2510
Ph: (408)972-2476
Fax: (408)224-8496
Contact: Tarlochan S. Nahal, President
Scope: Firm specializes in computer hardware and software documentation; online documentation; wafer processing equipment manuals; desktop publishing and illustration. Uses in-house Macintosh Quadra and Pentium-based computers running Inter leaf, Frame Maker, Word Perfect, Microsoft Word, and Ventura. Serves the semiconductor, electronics, and computer hardware or software industries. **Founded:** 1985.

LIBRARIES

19054 ■ Boston University - Corporate Education Center Library
1 Executive Dr., Ste. 301
Chelmsford, MA 01824-2558
Ph: (978)649-8200
Free: 800-288-7246
Fax: (978)649-62145
Co. E-mail: info@corpedgroup.com
URL: http://www.corpedgroup.com/
Scope: Software engineering, business administration and management, computer programming languages, program methodology, project management, computer science, social work. **Services:** Interlibrary loan; copying; SDI; Library open to the public by appointment. **Founded:** 1980. **Holdings:** 5000 books. **Subscriptions:** 150 journals and other serials; 10 newspapers.

19055 ■ Follett Software Company Resource Center
1391 Corporate Dr.
McHenry, IL 60050-7041
Ph: (815)344-8700
Free: 800-323-3397
Fax: (815)344-8774
URL: http://www.follettsoftware.com
Contact: Simona Rollinson, President
Scope: Computers. **Services:** SDI; Library not open to the public. **Founded:** 1986. **Holdings:** 100 books; 50 reports. **Subscriptions:** 34 journals and other serials; 3 newspapers.

19056 ■ IBM Corporation - Burlington Technical Library
967-B, 1000 River St.
Essex Junction, VT 05452-4299
Ph: (802)769-6519
Fax: (802)769-6501
Co. E-mail: karenlyn@us.ibm.com
URL: http://www.ibm.com/us/en/
Contact: Karen Kromer Lynch, Director, Library Services
Scope: Semiconductor manufacturing, chemistry, computing, solid-state electronics, physics, business and professional, project management, programming, management science, mathematics. **Services:** Interlibrary loan; Center not open to the public. **Founded:** 1965. **Holdings:** 10,000 books; 100 reels of microfilm. **Subscriptions:** 160 journals and other serials.

**19057 ■ IBM Corporation - Library/
Information Resource Center**
Dept. LVUS, B/908 Z/9819
11400 Burnet Rd.
Austin, TX 78758
Ph: (512)823-0404
Co. E-mail: gillen@us.ibm.com
URL: http://www.ibm.com/us/en/
Contact: Bev Gerzcvske, Manager
Scope: Computer architecture, RISC, personal computing, telecommunications, management, human factors, communications. **Services:** Interlibrary loan; Library not open to the public. **Founded:** 1967. **Holdings:** 11,000 books; 500 bound periodical volumes; 400 videotapes; 200 audiocassettes; 2000 reels of microfilm. **Subscriptions:** 300 journals, newsletters, and other serials; 15 newspapers. **Telecommunication Services:** auslib@us.ibm.com; llevitan@us.ibm.com.

19058 ■ Mentor Graphics Corporation Library
8005 SW Boeckman Rd.
Wilsonville, OR 97070-9733
Ph: (503)685-7000
Free: 800-592-2210
URL: http://www.mentor.com
Contact: Rachel Berrington, Librarian
Scope: Software engineering, electronics manufacturing, EDA industry. **Services:** Interlibrary loan; copying; SDI; library not open to the public. **Founded:** 1995. **Holdings:** Figures not available.

**19059 ■ UNISYS Corporation - West Coast
Information Center**
25725 Jeronimo Rd., MS-260
Mission Viejo, CA 92691
Ph: (714)380-5061
Fax: (714)380-5138
URL: http://www.unisys.com/unisys
Contact: M. Patricia Feeney, Manager, Information Technology
Scope: Computer architecture, computer programming, software design, hardware engineering design,

data communications, management. **Services:** Interlibrary loan; center open to the public at librarian's discretion. **Founded:** 1974. **Holdings:** 5000 books; 3500 technical reports; 3000 other cataloged items. **Subscriptions:** 225 journals and other serials.

RESEARCH CENTERS

**19060 ■ Carnegie Mellon University -
Software Engineering Institute (SEI)**
4500 5th Ave.
Pittsburgh, PA 15213-2612
Ph: (412)268-5800
Free: 888-201-4479
Fax: (412)268-6257
Co. E-mail: info@sei.cmu.edu
URL: http://www.sei.cmu.edu
Contact: Paul D. Nielsen, Chief Executive Officer
Services: CERT Coordination Center. **Founded:** 1984. **Publications:** *news@sei; SEI Annual Report.* **Educational Activities:** SEI Conferences; Software Engineering Process Group Conference; Workshops, continuing education, and special training courses. **Awards:** IEEE Process Improvement Award, cosponsored with IEEE.

**19061 ■ Massachusetts Institute of
Technology - CADLAB**
MIT Rm. 3-458
77 Massachusetts Ave.
Cambridge, MA 02139
Ph: (617)258-6016
Fax: (617)452-2461
Co. E-mail: drwallac@mit.edu
URL: http://cadlab.mit.edu
Contact: Prof. David Wallace, Director
Founded: 1981.

**19062 ■ Montana State University, Bozeman -
Information Technology Center (ITC)**
Renne Library Basement
Bozeman, MT 59717-3240

Ph: (406)994-1010
Fax: (406)994-4600
Co. E-mail: gwen@cns.montana.edu
URL: http://www.montana.edu/itcenter/index.html
Services: Computer software consultation. **Educational Activities:** Computer seminar courses. **Telecommunication Services:** itcadmin@montana.edu.

**19063 ■ University of Illinois at Chicago -
Electronic Visualization Laboratory (EVL)**
SEO Rm. 1120, MC 152
Department of Computer Science
851 S Morgan St.
Chicago, IL 60607-7053
Ph: (312)996-3002
Fax: (312)413-7585
Co. E-mail: spiff@uic.edu
URL: http://www.evl.uic.edu
Contact: Jason Leigh, Director
Founded: 1973. **Telecommunication Services:** webdev@evl.uic.edu.

**19064 ■ University of North Florida - Institute
of Police Technology and Management (IPTM)**
12000 Alumni Dr.
Jacksonville, FL 32224-2678
Ph: (904)620-4786
Fax: (904)620-2453
Co. E-mail: info@iptm.org
URL: http://www.iptm.org
Contact: Leonard R. Jacob, Director
Services: Offers management and supervisory training, drug investigation and enforcement, and specialty courses; Trains in-service law enforcement officers in traffic safety, criminal investigation, and microcomputer training. **Founded:** 1980. **Publications:** *Traffic Accident Investigations and Traffic Accident Reconstruction.* **Telecommunication Services:** ljacob@unf.edu.

Solar Energy Design/Contracting Business

ASSOCIATIONS AND OTHER ORGANIZATIONS

19065 ■ Air-Conditioning Heating and Refrigeration Institute (AHRI)
2111 Wilson Blvd., Ste. 500
Arlington, VA 22201
Ph: (703)524-8800
Fax: (703)562-1942
Co. E-mail: ahri@ahrinet.org
URL: http://www.ahrinet.org
Contact: Stephen Yurek, President
Description: Manufacturers of air conditioning, refrigeration and heating products and components. Develops and establishes equipment and application standards and certifies performance of certain industry products; provides credit and statistical services to members. Provides representation and technical assistance to government entities in federal, state and local legislative matters; provides public relations, consumer education and promotional programs for the industry. **Founded:** 1953. **Publications:** *ARI Curriculum Guide; Minuteman* (Monthly).

19066 ■ Alternative Energy Resources Organization
432 N Last Chance Gulch St.
Helena, MT 59601
Ph: (406)443-7272
Fax: (406)442-9120
Co. E-mail: aero@aeromt.org
URL: http://www.aeromt.org
Contact: Jonda Crosby, Executive Director
Description: Promotes sustainable agriculture, resource conservation and transportation choices through community education and citizen representation. Provides current programs that focus on sustainable agriculture, farm improvement clubs, beginning and retiring farmers, smart growth, and a more localized food system for greater community self-reliance. **Scope:** sustainable agriculture, gardening, alternative energy, rural communities, transportation and planning. **Subscriptions:** 1500. **Publications:** *Abundant Montana* (Annual); *AERO Sun-Times* (Quarterly); *Big Sky or Big Sprawl Montana at the Crossroads*; *Montana's Sustainable Agriculture Farming with Foresight.* **Educational Activities:** Alternative Energy Resources Organization Meeting (Annual); Alternative Energy Resources Organization Meeting (Annual). **Awards:** Northern Rockies Sustainable Agriculture Award (Annual).

19067 ■ American Solar Energy Society (ASES)
4760 Walnut St., Ste. 106
Boulder, CO 80301-2843
Ph: (303)443-3130
Fax: (303)443-3212
Co. E-mail: info@solartoday.org
URL: http://www.ases.org
Contact: Chuck Kutscher, Director
Description: Professional energy society organized to promote a wide utilization of solar energy through the application of science and technology. Encourages basic and applied research and development. Conducts workshops; organizes forums inviting researchers, policymakers, practitioners and consumers for discussion, analysis, and debate. Promotes education by compiling and disseminating information to schools, universities, and the community. **Founded:** 1954. **Publications:** *Solar Today* (Bimonthly); *American Solar Energy Society-- Membership Directory*; *Advances in Solar Energy* (Annual). **Educational Activities:** National Passive Solar Conference (Annual); National Solar Conference (Annual). **Awards:** Charles Greeley Abott Award (Annual); Fellows of the Society (Annual); Hoyt Clarke Hottel Award (Annual); John and Barbara Yellott Award (Annual); Passive Pioneer Award (Annual); Rebecca Vories Award (Annual); Women in Solar Energy Award (Annual).

19068 ■ Renew the Earth (RTE)
1850 Centennial Park Dr., Ste. 105
Reston, VA 20191
Ph: (703)689-4670
Co. E-mail: steve@renew-the-earth.org
URL: http://www.renew-the-earth.org
Contact: Ms. Debbie Reed, Executive Director
Description: Individuals and groups working toward a sustainable future by promoting a safe and healthy environment. Coordinates National Awards for Environmental Sustainability program to recognize positive environmental programs. Operates the Environmental Success Index, a clearinghouse of more than 1600 working environmental projects available to community groups, the media, businesses, policy makers, and individuals dedicated to implementing and promoting positive environmental change. Moving toward developing an international program. **Scope:** community-based environmental success stories. **Founded:** 1989. **Subscriptions:** video recordings. **Publications:** *RTE Environmental Success Index* (Annual). **Awards:** National Award for Environmental Sustainability (Annual).

19069 ■ Solar Energy Industries Association (SEIA)
805 15th St. NW, Ste. 510
Washington, DC 20005
Ph: (202)682-0556
Fax: (202)682-0559
Co. E-mail: info@seia.org
URL: http://www.seia.org
Contact: Rhone Resch, President
E-mail: rresch@seia.org
Description: Manufacturers, installers, distributors, contractors, and engineers of solar energy systems and components. Aims to accelerate and foster commercialization of solar energy conversion for economic purposes. Maintains Solar Energy Research and Education Foundation. Compiles statistics; offers computerized services. **Founded:** 1974. **Publications:** *Solar Industry Journal* (Quarterly); *Solar Industry Journal* (Quarterly). **Educational Activities:** SOLTECH (Annual). **Awards:** Renewable Leadership Awards (Annual).

19070 ■ Solar Rating and Certification Corporation (SRCC)
400 High Point Dr., Ste. 400
Cocoa, FL 32926
Ph: (321)213-6037
Fax: (321)821-0910
Co. E-mail: srcc@solar-rating.org
URL: http://www.solar-rating.org
Contact: Eileen Prado, Executive Director
Description: Serves as a rating and certification board for domestic solar hot water and pool heating panels and systems. **Scope:** directory of certified solar equipment. **Founded:** 1980. **Publications:** *Directory of SRCC Certified Solar Collector and System Ratings* (Annual); *Directory of SRCC Certified Collectors and Solar Water Heating Systems Ratings* (Irregular); *Directory of SRCC Certified Solar Collector and Water Heating System Ratings* (Periodic).

REFERENCE WORKS

19071 ■ "$40M Fund Created for Big Energy Project" in Austin Business JournalInc. (Vol. 29, November 27, 2009, No. 38, pp. 1)
Pub: American City Business Journals
Ed: Christopher Calnan. **Description:** A group of Texas businessmen, called Republic Power Partners LP, is planning to raise $40 million in order to launch an alternative energy project. The 6,000-megawatt initiative would generate solar, biomass and wind power in West Texas and could cost as much as $10 billion.

19072 ■ "Acing the Test" in Contractor (Vol. 57, January 2010, No. 1, pp. 32)
Pub: Penton Media, Inc.
Ed: Robert P. Mader. **Description:** A ward winning mechanical system retrofitting of a middle school in Ohio is discussed. The school now operates at 37,800 Btu/sq. ft and reduced a significant amount of pollutants from being emitted into the environment.

19073 ■ "Adventures at Hydronicahh" in Contractor (Vol. 56, September 2009, No. 9, pp. 52)
Pub: Penton Media, Inc.
Ed: Mark Eatherton. **Description:** Installation of the heating system of a lakeview room are described. The room's radiant windows are powered by electricity from a solar PV array and a propane-powered hydrogen fuel cell. The system will be programmed to use the most energy available.

19074 ■ "Adventures at Hydronicahh" in Contractor (Vol. 56, November 2009, No. 11, pp. 36)
Pub: Penton Media, Inc.
Ed: Mark Eatherton. **Description:** Part 6 of the installation of a five stage ground-source heat pump for a hydronic heating system is discussed. The heat exchanger will be bidirectional in the plan described.

19075 ■ "Adventures at Hydronicahh" in Contractor (Vol. 56, October 2009, No. 10, pp. 42)
Pub: Penton Media, Inc.
Ed: Mark Eatherton. **Description:** Design and installation of a solar thermal system for a hydronic heating project is described. This portion has two 32-square feet of flat plate glazed solar collectors that are tied to a 120-gallon reverse indirect DHW heater.

19076 ■ "Alternative Energy Calls for Alternative Marketing" in Indoor Comfort Marketing (Vol. 70, June 2011, No. 6, pp. 8)
Pub: Industry Publications Inc.
Ed: Richard Rutigliano. Description: Advice for marketing solar energy products and services is given.

19077 ■ "Aquarium's Solar Demonstration Project Exceeds Expectations" in Contractor (Vol. 57, February 2010, No. 2, pp. 1)
Pub: Penton Media, Inc.
Ed: Candace Roulo. Description: Seattle Aquarium cafe installed flat-plate solar collectors to preheat water and data has shown that the system has allowed them to off-set almost double their expected consumption of natural gas. It is estimated that rthe solar panels will shrink the aquarium's carbon footprint by 2.5 tons of carbon dioxide each year.

19078 ■ "Big Energy Deals Power OptiSolar's Local Growth" in Sacramento Business Journal (Vol. 25, August 22, 2008, No. 25, pp. 1)
Pub: American City Business Journals, Inc.
Ed: Celia Lamb. Description: Solar energy projects are driving Sacramento, California-based OptiSolar's growth. The company is set to begin construction of its first photovoltaic project in Ontario. It also plans to build the world largest photovoltaic project in San Luis Obispo County.

19079 ■ "Bold Goals Will Require Time" in Contractor (Vol. 56, October 2009, No. 10, pp. S2)
Pub: Penton Media, Inc.
Ed: Ted Lower. Description: Offering a broad range of courses is the Radiant Panel Association (RPA), an organization that holds education as its top priority. The RPA must lead the industry by raising the educational bar for future installers.

19080 ■ "The Business of Activism" in Entrepreneur (Vol. 37, September 2009, No. 9, pp. 43)
Pub: Entrepreneur Media, Inc.
Ed: Mary Catherine O'Connor. Description: San Francisco, California-based business incubator Virgance has been promoting sustainable projects by partnering with businesses. The company has launched campaigns which include organizing homeowners in negotiating with solar installers. The company is also planning to expand its workforce.

19081 ■ "Can HOAs Stop You From Going Green?" in Contractor (Vol. 56, July 2009, No. 7, pp. 39)
Pub: Penton Media, Inc.
Ed: Susan Linden McGreevy. Description: There have been cases concerning homeowners' associations objections to the installation of wind turbines and solar panels. Precedence with the courts show that they will look at several factors when deciding to uphold restrictions on property use including whether the item encroaches on the rights of others, is likely to adversely affect property values, and also the state of enforcement.

19082 ■ "Chicago Botanic Garden Builds Green Research Facility" in Contractor (Vol. 56, December 2009, No. 12, pp. 5)
Pub: Penton Media, Inc.
Ed: Candace Roulo. Description: Chicago Botanic Garden has built a laboratory and research facility in Illinois. The facility is set to receive a United States Green Building Council LEED Gold certification. The building features a solar photovoltaic array, radiant flooring and water-conserving plumbing products.

19083 ■ "China's Transition to Green Energy Systems" in Energy Policy (Vol. 39, October 2011, No. 10, pp. 5909-5919)
Pub: Reed Elsevier Reference Publishing
Ed: Wei Li, Guojun Song, Melanie Beresford, Ben Ma. Description: The economics of home solar water heaters and their growing popularity in Dezhous City, China is discussed.

19084 ■ "Chinese Solar Panel Manufacturer Scopes Out Austin" in Austin Business JournalInc. (Vol. 29, October 30, 2009, No. 34, pp. 1)
Pub: American City Business Journals
Ed: Jacob Dirr. Description: China's Yingli Green Energy Holding Company Ltd. is looking for a site in order to construct a $20 million photovoltaic panel plant. Both Austin and San Antonio are vying to house the manufacturing hub. The project could create about 300 jobs and give Austin a chance to become a player in the solar energy market. Other solar companies are also considering Central Texas as an option to set up shop.

19085 ■ Directory of SRCC Certified Collectors and Solar Water Heating Systems Ratings
Pub: Solar Rating and Certification Corporation
Contact: Eileen Prado, Executive Director
URL(s): www.solar-rating.org/ratings/ratings.htm. Released: Irregular; Latest edition 2010. Price: Free. Covers: Nearly 20 manufacturers of solar collectors and water heaters certified by the organization. Entries include: Company name, address, system model and description, including technical specifications, thermal performance ratings, etc. , for one or more systems. Arrangement: Classified by type of system. Indexes: Company name.

19086 ■ "Doing the Right Thing" in Black Enterprise (Vol. 38, July 2008, No. 12, pp. 50)
Pub: Earl G. Graves Publishing Co. Inc.
Ed: Tamara E. Holmes. Description: More business owners are trying to become more environmentally friendly, either due to their belief in social responsibility or for financial incentives or for both reasons. Tips for making one's business more environmentally responsible are included as well as a listing of resources that may be available to help owners in their efforts.

19087 ■ "East Coast Solar" in Contractor (Vol. 57, February 2010, No. 2, pp. 17)
Pub: Penton Media, Inc.
Ed: Dave Yates. Description: U.S. Department of Energy's Solar Decathlon lets 20 college student-led teams from around the world compete to design and build a solar-powered home. A mechanical contractor discusses his work as an advisor during the competition.

19088 ■ "Eco Smart Home Will Showcase Green Technology" in Contractor (Vol. 56, September 2009, No. 9, pp. 3)
Pub: Penton Media, Inc.
Ed: Steve Spaulding. Description: Eco Smart World Wide is building the Eco Smart Demonstration House to promote the latest in sustainable, renewable and high-efficiency practices and products. The company will use insulated concrete forms in the construction of the building. Features and dimensions of the structure are also presented.

19089 ■ "Election Could Undo Renewable Energy Quotas" in The Business Journal - Serving Phoenix and the Valley of the Sun (Vol. 28, July 11, 2008, No. 45, pp. 1)
Pub: American City Business Journals, Inc.
Ed: Patrick O'Grady. Description: Competition for the three open seats in the Arizona Corporation Commission is intense, with 12 candidates contesting for the three slots. The commission's mandates for renewable energy and infrastructure investment will also be at stake.

19090 ■ "ESolar Partners With Penglai on Landmark Solar Thermal Agreement for China" in Business of Global Warming (January 25, 2010, pp. 8)
Pub: Investment Weekly News
Description: Penglai Electric, a privately-owned Chinese electrical power equipment manufacturer, and eSolar, a global provider of cost-effective and reliable solar power plants, announced a master licensing agreement in which eSolar will build at least 2 gigawatts of solar thermal power plants in China over the next 10 years.

19091 ■ "Everett Dowling" in Hawaii Business (Vol. 54, August 2008, No. 2, pp. 32)
Pub: Hawaii Business Publishing
Ed: Jason Ubay. Description: Real estate developer Everett Dowling, president of Dowling Company Inc., talks about the company's sustainable management and services. The company's office has been retrofitted to earn a Leadership in Energy and Environmental Design (LEED) certification. Dowling believes that real estate development can be part of the sustainable solution.

19092 ■ "Final State Budget Is a Mixed Bag of Key Industries" in The Business Journal - Serving Phoenix and the Valley of the Sun (Vol. 28, July 4, 2008, No. 44, pp. 3)
Pub: American City Business Journals, Inc.
Ed: Mike Sunnucks; Patrick O'Grady. Description: Approved by Governor Janet Napolitano and passed by the Arizona Legislature, the $9.9 billion state budget is beneficial to some industries in the business community. The tax cap for on Arizona Lottery has been removed which is beneficial to the industry, while the solar energy industry and real estate developers stand to lose from the spending bill. Other details of the finance budget are presented.

19093 ■ "Florida's Bright Upside" in Tampa Bay Business Journal (Vol. 29, November 6, 2009, No. 46, pp. 1)
Pub: American City Business Journals
Ed: Michael Hinman. Description: Florida's Public Service Commission (PSC) decision on a power purchase agreement that could add 25 megawatts of solar energy on Tampa Electric Company's offerings is presented. The decision could support the growing market for suppliers and marketers of renewable energy such as Jabil Circuit Inc., which manufactures photovoltaic modules. Details of the agreement are discussed.

19094 ■ "For Giving Us a Way To Say Yes To Solar: Lynn Jurich and Edward Fenster" in Inc. (Volume 32, December 2010, No. 10, pp. 110)
Pub: Inc. Magazine
Description: Profile of entrepreneurs Lynn Jurich and Edward Fenster, cofounders of SunRun. The firm installs solar panels at little or no cost and homeowners sign 20-year contracts to buy power at a fixed price.

19095 ■ "FSU's OGZEB Is Test Bed for Sustainable Technology" in Contractor (Vol. 56, October 2009, No. 10, pp. 1)
Pub: Penton Media, Inc.
Ed: Candace Roulo. Description: Florida State University has one of 14 off-grid zero emissions buildings (OGZEB) in the U.S.; it was built to research sustainable and alternative energy systems. The building produces electricity from 30 photovoltaic panels and it also has three AET water heating solar panels on the roof.

19096 ■ "Fuel for Thought; Canadian Business Leaders on Energy Policy" in Canadian Business (Vol. 81, September 15, 2008, No. 14-15, pp. 12)
Pub: Rogers Media Ltd.
Ed: Joe Castaldo. Description: Most Canadian business leaders worry about the unreliability of the oil supply but feel that Canada is in a better position to benefit from the energy supply crisis than other countries. Many respondents also highlighted the need to invest in renewable energy sources.

19097 ■ "Germans Win Solar Decathlon - Again" in Contractor (Vol. 56, November 2009, No. 11, pp. 1)
Pub: Penton Media, Inc.
Ed: Robert P. Mader. Description: Students from Technische Universtat Darmstadt won the U.S. Department of Energy's Solar Decathlon by designing and building the most attractive and efficient solar-powered home. The winner's design produced a surplus of power even during three days of rain and photovoltaic panels covered nearly every exterior surface.

19098 ■ *"Got to be Smarter than the Average Bear"* in Contractor (Vol. 56, September 2009, No. 9, pp. 82)

Pub: Penton Media, Inc.

Ed: Bob Mader. **Description:** International Association of Plumbing and Mechanical Officials Green Technical Committee has debated the need for contractors to have certifications in installing green plumbing. Some have argued that qualifications would discourage homeowners from improving their properties. Comments from executives are also included.

19099 ■ *"Green Light"* in The Business Journal-Portland (Vol. 25, July 11, 2008, No. 18, pp. 1)

Pub: American City Business Journals, Inc.

Ed: Erik Siemers. **Description:** Ecos Consulting, a sustainability consulting company based in Portland, Oregon, is seeing a boost in revenue as more businesses turn to sustainable practices. The company's revenue rose by 50 percent in 2007 and employees increased from 57 to 150. Other details about Ecos' growth are discussed.

19100 ■ *"Greenhouse Announces Merger With Custom Q, Inc."* in Investment Weekly (January 30, 2010, pp. 338)

Pub: Investment Weekly News

Description: In accordance with an Agreement and Plan of Share Exchange, GreenHouse Holdings, Inc., an innovative green solutions provider, has gone public via a reverse merger with Custom Q, Inc.

19101 ■ *"How Green Is The Valley?"* in Barron's (Vol. 88, July 4, 2008, No. 28, pp. 13)

Pub: Dow Jones & Co., Inc.

Description: San Jose, California has made a good start towards becoming a leader in alternative energy technology through the establishment of United Laboratories' own lab in the city. The certification process for photovoltaic cells will be dramatically shortened with this endeavor.

19102 ■ *"Hydronicahh - Everything in Modulation"* in Contractor (Vol. 56, December 2009, No. 12, pp. 24)

Pub: Penton Media, Inc.

Ed: Mark Eatherton. **Description:** Management and the environmental impact of a home hydronic system are discussed. Radiant windows have the potential to reduce energy consumption. A variable speed delta T pump is required for the construction of a hydronic wood pit.

19103 ■ *"It's Always 55 Degrees F"* in Contractor (Vol. 56, September 2009, No. 9, pp. 38)

Pub: Penton Media, Inc.

Ed: Carol Fey. **Description:** Geothermal-exchange heating and cooling systems can save businesses up to 60 percent on energy costs for heating and cooling. Geothermal systems get heat from the earth during winter. Design, features and installation of geothermal systems are also discussed.

19104 ■ *"Letting the Sunshine In"* in Barron's (Vol. 89, July 6, 2009, No. 27, pp. 11)

Pub: Dow Jones & Co., Inc.

Ed: Katherine Cheng. **Description:** Solar energy industry leaders believe the industry needs aid from the US government regarding the funding of its research efforts and lowering solar energy costs. The climate change bill passed by the US House of Representatives signifies the US government's desire to significantly reduce carbon dioxide emissions.

19105 ■ *"Magpower May Build Solar Panels Here"* in Austin Business Journal (Vol. 31, May 13, 2011, No. 10, pp. A1)

Pub: American City Business Journals Inc.

Ed: Christopher Calnan. **Description:** RRE Austin Solar LLC CEO Doven Mehta has revealed plans to partner with Portugal-based Magpower SA, only if Austin energy buys electricity from planned solar energy farm in Pflugerville. Austin Energy has received 100 bids from 35 companies to supply 200 megawatts of solar- and wind-generated electricity.

19106 ■ *"N.E.'s Largest Solar Site Set for Scituate Landfill"* in Boston Business Journal (Vol. 30, December 17, 2010, No. 47, pp. 1)

Pub: Boston Business Journal

Ed: Kyle Alspach. **Description:** A closed 12-acre landfill in Scituate, Massachusetts is the proposed site for a 2.4-megawatt solar power plant. The town government will buy the power at a discounted rate, saving it $200,000 annually.

19107 ■ *"On Growth Path of Rising Star"* in Boston Business Journal (Vol. 31, June 24, 2011, No. 22, pp. 3)

Pub: Boston Business Journal

Ed: Kyle Alspach. **Description:** 1366 Technologies Inc. of Lexington, Massachusetts is considered a rising solar power technology company. The firm secured $150 million loan guarantee from the US Department of Energy that could go to the construction of a 1,000 megawatt solar power plant.

19108 ■ *"One on One With SEIA's President, CEO"* in Contractor (Vol. 57, January 2010, No. 1, pp. 40)

Pub: Penton Media, Inc.

Ed: Dave Yates. **Description:** Solar Energy Industries Association President and CEO Rhone Resch says that the deployment of solar systems in the U.S. has exploded since 2005 and that there is a need to make inroads for shaping the U.S. energy policy. Resch says one of the hurdles they face is that there are no universal standards.

19109 ■ *"Proposal Ruffles Builders"* in Austin Business JournalInc. (Vol. 29, November 20, 2009, No. 37, pp. 1)

Pub: American City Business Journals

Ed: Jacob Dirr. **Description:** A proposal that requires heating, ventilation and cooling equipment checking for a new commercial building having an area of at least 10,000 square feet might cost 25 cents to 50 cents per square foot for the owners. This may lead to higher housing costs. Both the Building and Fire Code Board of Appeals and the Mechanical Plumbing and Solar Board have recommended the plan.

19110 ■ *"PSC Approves $130M TECO Solar Project"* in Tampa Bay Business Journal (Vol. 30, December 18, 2009, No. 52, pp. 1)

Pub: American City Business Journals

Ed: Michael Hinman. **Description:** Florida's Public Service Commission has endorsed Tampa Electric Company's plan to add 25 megawatts of solar energy to its portfolio. TECO's plan needed the approval by PSC to defray additional costs for the project through ratepayers.

19111 ■ *"San Diego Museum Receives LEED Certification"* in Contractor (Vol. 57, January 2010, No. 1, pp. 14)

Pub: Penton Media, Inc.

Description: San Diego Natural History Museum received an LEED certification for existing buildings. The certification process began when they committed to displaying the Dead Sea Scrolls in 2007 and they had to upgrade their buildings' air quality and to control for air moisture, temperature, and volume. They reduced their energy consumption by upwards of 20 percent.

19112 ■ *"Saudi Overtures"* in The Business Journal-Portland (Vol. 25, August 15, 2008, No. 23, pp. 1)

Pub: American City Business Journals, Inc.

Ed: Aliza Earnshaw. **Description:** Saudi Arabia's huge revenue from oil is creating opportunities for Oregon companies as the country develops new cities, industrial zones, and tourism centers. Oregon exported only $46.8 million worth of goods to Saudi Arabia in 2007 but the kingdom is interested in green building materials and methods, renewable energy and water quality control, and nanotechnology all of which Oregon has expertise in.

19113 ■ *"Seeing Green in Going Green"* in The Business Journal-Serving Greater Tampa Bay (Vol. 28, July 4, 2008, No. 28, pp. 1)

Pub: American City Business Journals, Inc.

Ed: Janet Leiser. **Description:** Atlanta, Georgia-based developer IDI Corp. is pushing for Leadership in Energy and Environmental Design certification for

the warehouse that is currently under construction at Madison Business Center along Port Sutton and U.S. 41. The industrial building is the first in Tampa Bay to seek certification for LEED as set by the U.S. Green Building Council.

19114 ■ *"Silicon Success: Solar Energy Shines for Dawn Alston Paige"* in Black Enterprise (Vol. 38, October 2007, No. 3, pp. 46)

Pub: Earl G. Graves Publishing Co. Inc.

Ed: Evan Mynatt. **Description:** Dawn Alson Paige, senior vice president and co-founder of Piedmont Investment Advisors predicted MBMC Electronic Materials to climb to $50 in 12 to 18 months, however the stock rose higher hitting $61 in early August, due to the international push for alternative energy.

19115 ■ *"Solar Choices"* in Contractor (Vol. 56, October 2009, No. 10, pp. 32)

Pub: Penton Media, Inc.

Ed: Tom Scheel. **Description:** Price, performance, and ease of installation of a flat plate versus an evacuated tube collector for a plumbing and heating job are compared. The better choice with regards to weight, aesthetics, efficiency in warm or cool climates, year round load, and space heating is discussed.

19116 ■ *"Solar Credit Lapse Spur Late Demand"* in The Business Journal - Serving Phoenix and the Valley of the Sun (Vol. 28, July 18, 2008)

Pub: American City Business Journals, Inc.

Ed: Patrick O'Grady. **Description:** Businesses looking to engage in the solar energy industry are facing the problems of taxation and limited solar panel supply. Solar panels manufacturers are focusing more on the European market. Political issues surrounding the federal tax credit policy on solar energy users are also discussed.

19117 ■ *"Solar Hot Water Sales Are Hot, Hot, Hot"* in Contractor (Vol. 56, December 2009, No. 12, pp. 22)

Pub: Penton Media, Inc.

Ed: Dave Yates. **Description:** Plumbing contractors in the United States can benefit from the increased sales of solar thermal water systems. Licensed plumbers have the base knowledge on the risks associated from heating and storing water. Safety issues associated with solar water heaters are also included.

19118 ■ *"Sustainability Is Top Priority for GreenTown Chicago"* in Contractor (Vol. 56, November 2009, No. 11, pp. 1)

Pub: Penton Media, Inc.

Ed: Candace Roulo. **Description:** GreenTown Chicago 2009 conference tackled energy-efficient practices and technologies, green design and building, and sustainable policies. Water conservation was also a topic at the conference and one mayor who made a presentation said that reducing the water loss in the system is a priority in the city's endeavor.

19119 ■ *"Top 50 Exporters"* in Hispanic Business (Vol. 30, July-August 2008, No. 7-8, pp. 42)

Pub: Hispanic Business, Inc.

Ed: Hildy Medina. **Description:** Increases in exports revenues reported by food exporters and green companies in a time of economic slowdown in the U.S are described. Food exporters have benefited from the growth of high-volume grocery stores in underdeveloped countries and the German governments' promotion of solar energy has benefited the U.S. solar heating equipment and solar panel manufactures.

19120 ■ *"UA Turns Ann Arbor Green"* in Contractor (Vol. 56, September 2009, No. 9, pp. 5)

Pub: Penton Media, Inc.

Ed: Robert P. Mader. **Description:** Instructors at the United Association of Plumbers and Steamfitters have studied the latest in green and sustainable construction and service at the Washtenaw Community College in Michigan. Classes included building information modeling, hydronic heating and cooling and advanced HVACR troubleshooting. The UA is currently focusing on green training.

19121 ■ *"University Data Center Goes Off-Grid, Is Test Bed" in Contractor (Vol. 57, February 2010, No. 2, pp. 1)*
Pub: Penton Media, Inc.
Ed: Candace Roulo. **Description:** Syracuse University's Green Data Center has gone off-grid through the use of natural gas fired turbines. It is expected to use 50 percent less energy than a typical computer center. The center's heating and cooling system setup is also discussed.

19122 ■ *"Warm Floors Make Warm Homes" in Contractor (Vol. 56, October 2009, No. 10, pp. S18)*
Pub: Penton Media, Inc.
Ed: Lisa Murton Beets. **Description:** Three award winning radiant floor-heating installations are presented. The design and the equipment used for these systems are discussed.

19123 ■ *"Was Mandating Solar Power Water Heaters For New Homes Good Policy?" in Hawaii Business (Vol. 54, August 2008, No. 2, pp. 28)*
Pub: Hawaii Business Publishing
Description: Senator Gary L. Kooser of District 7 Kauai-Niihau believes that the mandating of energy-efficient water heaters for new single-family homes starting in 2010 will help cut Hawaii's oil consumption. Ron Richmond of the Hawaii Solar Energy Association says that the content of SB 644 has negative consequences as it allows for choice of energy and not just solar, and it also eliminates tax credits for new homebuyers.

19124 ■ *"Water Conservation Helps GC's Building Attain LEED Gold Status" in Contractor (Vol. 56, September 2009, No. 9, pp. 5)*
Pub: Penton Media, Inc.
Description: Green contractor Marshall Erdman has built a new office building using green design. The facility is seen to become a prime Leadership in Energy and Environmental Design (LEED) building model. Details of the building's design and features are also provided.

19125 ■ *"Water Distiller" in Canadian Business (Vol. 81, September 29, 2008, No. 16, pp. 52)*
Pub: Rogers Media Ltd.
Ed: Matthew McClearn. **Description:** Les Fairn's invention of a water distiller called a Solarsphere was recognized in the Great Canadian Invention Competition. Fairn's invention resembles a buoy that uses the sun's energy to vaporize dirty water then leaves the impurities behind in a sump. The invention has an application for producing potable water in impoverished countries.

19126 ■ *"Yates Helps Turn Log Home Green" in Contractor (Vol. 56, December 2009, No. 12, pp. 40)*
Pub: Penton Media, Inc.
Description: Upgrading and greening of a log home's HVAC system in Pennsylvania is discussed. F. W. Behler Inc. president Dave Yates was chosen to manage the project. A large coil of R-flex was used to connect the buffer tank to the garage's radiant heat system.

19127 ■ *"Yates Turns Log Home Green - Part Three" in Contractor (Vol. 57, January 2010, No. 1, pp. 5)*
Pub: Penton Media, Inc.
Description: Dave Yates of F.W. Behler Inc. discusses remodeling a log home's HVAC system with geo-to-radiant heat and thermal-solar systems. The solar heater's installation is discussed.

19128 ■ *"Yudelson Challenges San Antonio Groups" in Contractor (Vol. 56, October 2009, No. 10, pp. 6)*
Pub: Penton Media, Inc.
Description: Green building consultant and author Jerry Yudelson made a presentation for the Central Texas Green Building Council and Leadership San Antonio where he discussed the European approach to sustainability and how it can be used for designing green buildings. Yudelson also discussed how to use sustainable practices for planning 25 years into the future.

TRADE PERIODICALS

19129 ■ *Wind Energy Weekly*
Pub: American Wind Energy Association
Ed: Thomas O. Gray, Editor, tom_gray@igc.org. **Released:** Weekly. **Price:** Included in membership; $595, nonmembers. **Description:** Provides wind energy trade news, plus covers energy and environmental policy. Recurring features include news of research, reports of meetings, job listings, and notices of publications available. Remarks: Available only via E-mail account.

TRADE SHOWS AND CONVENTIONS

19130 ■ **World Energy Engineering Congress**
Association of Energy Engineers
4025 Pleasantdale Rd., Ste. 420
Atlanta, GA 30340
Ph: (770)447-5083
Fax: (770)446-3969
Co. E-mail: info@aeecenter.org
URL: http://www.aeecenter.org
Contact: Larry Good, President
URL(s): www.energycongress.com. **Price:** $995, Members; $895, AEE members, government, and nonprofit orgs. **Frequency:** Fall. **Audience:** Energy engineers, managers, facility managers, and VPs of operations. **Principal Exhibits:** Energy equipment, supplies, and services. **Dates and Locations:** Georgia World Congress Center. **Telecommunication Services:** ted@aeecenter.org.

CONSULTANTS

19131 ■ **CPIX Risk Services**
1500, 727 - 7th Ave. SW
Calgary, AB, Canada T2P 0Z5
Ph: (403)261-6061
Fax: (403)261-6068
Co. E-mail: insurance@cpix.com
URL: http://www.cpix.com
Contact: Sam Jackson, President
E-mail: sam@cpix.com
Scope: Provider of Energy Insurance Reciprocal (EIR)-based insurance solutions to the energy industry. Offers risk services to reduce, manage and control the cost of risk in four specialized areas: safety and loss control, risk surveys, loss control program audits, facility inspections, hazard analysis, job observations, task analysis, impact forecasting; support, training, loss investigation, claims management, loss information sharing, on going audits and inspections; alternative risk financing; and mentoring offers periodic workshops, guest lectures, program structure evaluation and a forum for idea development and evaluation. **Founded:** 1993. **Telecommunication Services:** insurance@eigltd.com.

COMPUTERIZED DATABASES

19132 ■ *Energy Design Update*
76 9th Ave., 7 Fl.
New York, NY 10011-4962
Ph: (212)771-0786
Free: 800-234-1660
Fax: (212)771-0796
Co. E-mail: aspen-customerservice@wolterskluwer.com
URL: http://www.aspenpublishers.com
Contact: Mark Dorman, President
Availability: Online: Aspen Publishers Inc. **Type:** Full-text.

LIBRARIES

19133 ■ **Alternative Energy Resources Organization Library—AERO Library.**
432 N. Last Chance Gulch
Helena, MT 59601-5014
Ph: (406)443-7272
Fax: (406)442-9120
Co. E-mail: aero@aeromt.org
URL: http://www.aeromt.org
Contact: Bryan von Lossberg, Executive Director
Scope: Sustainable agriculture, renewable energy, community self-reliance. **Services:** Full library access to members (open to the public for reference use only). **Founded:** 1974. **Holdings:** 550 books; 120 bound periodical volumes; 3 VF drawers of topical resource material. **Subscriptions:** 15 journals and other serials.

19134 ■ **Arizona State University - Architectural and Environmental Design Library**
College of Architecture
Tempe, AZ 85287-1705
Ph: (480)965-6400
Co. E-mail: deborah.koshinsky@asu.edu
URL: http://www.asu.edu
Contact: Annmarie Leonard
URL(s): lib.asu.edu/architecture/. **Scope:** Architecture, city planning, landscape architecture, industrial design, interior design, graphic design. **Services:** Interlibrary loan; copying; Library open to the public; special collections open to the public by appointment. **Founded:** 1960. **Holdings:** 50,000 volumes; 150 cassette and tape recordings; 563 titles on microfilm; 125 films and videocassettes; archives; microfiche; CD-ROMs. **Subscriptions:** 140 journals and other serials.

19135 ■ **Arizona State University - Architectural and Environmental Design Library - Solar Energy Collection**
PO Box 871705
Tempe, AZ 85287-1705
Ph: (480)965-7422
Co. E-mail: deborah.koshinsky@asu.edu
URL: http://lib.asu.edu/architecture/collections/solar-energy
Contact: Deborah Koshinsky, Archivist Librarian
Scope: Photovoltaics, solar thermal, architectural design, wind power, tidal and wave power, thermo-electric conversion, energy conservation, other renewable energy. **Services:** Interlibrary loan; copying; library open to the public. **Founded:** 1954. **Holdings:** 18,000 archival items; technical papers and reports; pamphlets; brochures; clippings; reprints; product information.

19136 ■ **Ball State University - Center for Energy Research/Education/Service (CERES)**
Architecture Bldg., Rm. 018
2000 W. University Ave.
Muncie, IN 47306
Ph: (765)285-1135
Fax: (765)285-5622
Co. E-mail: ceres@bsu.edu
URL: http://cms.bsu.edu/Academics/CentersandInstitutes/CERES.aspx
Contact: Robert J. Koester, Director
Scope: Energy, solar energy, community planning, design, building performance analysis, computer simulation. **Services:** Copying; Center open to the public with restrictions. **Founded:** 1982. **Holdings:** 200 books; 200 technical reports. **Subscriptions:** 20 journals and other serials. **Telecommunication Services:** library@bsu.edu; rkoester@bsu.edu.

19137 ■ **Boston Architectural Center - Alfred Shaw and Edward Durell Stone Library**
320 Newbury St., 6th Fl.
Boston, MA 02115
Ph: (617)585-0155
Free: 877-585-0100
Fax: (617)585-0151
Co. E-mail: library@the-bac.edu
URL: http://the-bac.edu/resources/library
Contact: Susan Lewis, Director, Library Services
Scope: Architectural design and history, building technology, urban planning, urban design, landscape architecture, photography, interior design, solar energy. **Services:** Copying; library open to the public for reference only. **Founded:** 1966. **Holdings:** 44,000 books; 800 bound periodical volumes; 800 student theses; 40,000 slides; 500

other cataloged items; archives. **Subscriptions:** 120 journals and other serials. **Telecommunication Services:** susan.lewis@the-bac.edu.

19138 ■ Burt Hill Kosar Rittelmann Associates Library
400 Morgan Ctr.
101 E. Diamond St.
Butler, PA 16001-5977
Ph: (724)285-4761
Fax: (412)285-6815
Co. E-mail: dianne.sinz@burthill.com
URL: http://www.burthill.com
Contact: John Brock, Director
Scope: Energy use in buildings, solar energy, building products and design, architecture, engineering, interior design. **Services:** Library not open to the public. **Founded:** 1936. **Holdings:** 12,000 volumes. **Subscriptions:** 176 journals and other serials. **Telecommunication Services:** john.brock@burthill.com.

19139 ■ Florida Solar Energy Center Research Library
1679 Clearlake Rd.
Cocoa, FL 32922-5703
Ph: (321)638-1461
Fax: (321)638-1463
Co. E-mail: rickling@fsec.ucf.edu
URL: http://www.fsec.ucf.edu/en/about/facilities/library.htm
Contact: James Fenton, Director
Scope: Solar and other alternative sources of energy, science, technology. **Services:** Interlibrary loan; copying; Library open to the public with restrictions. **Founded:** 1975. **Holdings:** 13,000 books; 2364 bound periodical volumes; 12,477 technical documents; 7715 vertical files; 7572 slides; 56,522 microfiche; 10 films; 213 videotapes. **Subscriptions:** 212 journals and other serials. **Telecommunication Services:** info@fsec.ucf.edu.

19140 ■ Northeast Sustainable Energy Association Library
50 Miles St.
Greenfield, MA 01301-3212
Ph: (413)774-6051
Fax: (413)774-6053
Co. E-mail: nesea@nesea.org
URL: http://www.nesea.org
Contact: Jennifer Marrapese, Executive Director
Scope: Solar energy, alternative energy sources, sustainable transportation and building practices, solar electric vehicles, renewable energy, the environment. **Services:** Copying (5 cents per copy); library open to the public for reference use only. **Founded:** 1974. **Holdings:** 200 books. **Subscriptions:** 30 journals and other serials.

19141 ■ Sustainable Buildings Industries Council Library
1090 Vermont Ave. NW, Ste. 700
Washington, DC 20036
Ph: (202)289-7800
Fax: (202)289-1092
URL: http://www.nibs.org/?page=sbic
Scope: Passive solar energy - design, construction, technology, industry. **Services:** Library open to the public by appointment. **Founded:** 1980. **Holdings:** Documents from national laboratories, government contractors and agencies, and private programs.

19142 ■ U.S. Dept. of Energy - Energy Library
1000 Independent Ave., SW
Forrestal Bldg. Rm. GA-138
Washington, DC 20585
Ph: (202)586-5000
Fax: (212)586-0573
Co. E-mail: forrestal.library@hq.doe.gov
URL: http://energy.gov/oe/information-center/library
Contact: Robin Henderson
Scope: Energy resources and technologies: economic, environmental, and social aspects of energy; energy regulation; energy statistics; management. **Services:** Interlibrary loan; SDI; Library open to DOE Headquarters staff and authorized contractors **Founded:** 1947. **Holdings:** 500,000 million volumes of books, journals, technical reports, government documents. **Subscriptions:** 1600 journals and other serials. **Telecommunication Services:** robin.d.henderson@hq.doe.gov.

RESEARCH CENTERS

19143 ■ Ball State University - Center for Energy Research/Education/Service (CERES)
Architecture Bldg., Rm. 018
Muncie, IN 47306
Ph: (765)285-1135
Fax: (765)285-5622
Co. E-mail: ceres@bsu.edu
URL: http://www.bsu.edu/ceres
Contact: Prof. Robert J. Koester, Director
Founded: 1982. **Publications:** *CERES Annual Report.* **Educational Activities:** Workshops, energy awareness programs, periodic public lectures, and guest lecture program. **Telecommunication Services:** rkoester@bsu.edu.

19144 ■ California State Polytechnic University, Pomona - John T. Lyle Center for Regenerative Studies
4105 W University Dr.
Pomona, CA 91768
Ph: (909)869-5155
Fax: (909)869-5188
Co. E-mail: crs@csupomona.edu
URL: http://www.csupomona.edu/~crs
Contact: Kyle D. Brown, Director
Founded: 1994. **Awards:** Nathaniel Dwings Award, California Fish and Game Grant. **Telecommunication Services:** kdbrown@csupomona.edu.

19145 ■ U.S. Department of Energy - National Renewable Energy Laboratory (NREL)
1617 Cole Blvd.
Golden, CO 80401-3305
Ph: (303)275-3000
Fax: (303)275-3097
Co. E-mail: dan_arvizu@nrel.gov
URL: http://www.nrel.gov
Contact: Dan E. Arvizu, Chief Executive Officer
URL(s): www.energy.gov. **Description:** Description: Publishes reference materials, teachers lessons, and project ideas on renewable energy and energy efficiency topics. **Services:** Technology transfer. **Founded:** 1974. **Educational Activities:** Regional

and national renewable energy conferences. **Telecommunication Services:** public.affairs@nrel.gov; linda_lung@nrel.gov.

19146 ■ University of Central Florida - Florida Solar Energy Center (FSEC)
1679 Clearlake Rd.
Cocoa, FL 32922-5703
Ph: (321)638-1000
Fax: (321)638-1010
Co. E-mail: solarinfo@fsec.ucf.edu
URL: http://www.fsec.ucf.edu/en
Contact: Prof. James Fenton, Director
Services: Self-guided tours: open to the public. **Founded:** 1975. **Publications:** *Photocatalyst Report; FSEC Annual Report; Solar Collector Newsletter.* **Educational Activities:** Distance learning program; FSEC Short courses, on solar and energy efficiency.

19147 ■ University of Oregon - Solar Energy Center
Department of Physics
1274 University of Oregon
Eugene, OR 97403-1274
Ph: (541)346-4745
Fax: (541)346-5861
Co. E-mail: fev@uoregon.edu
URL: http://solardata.uoregon.edu
Contact: Frank Vignola, Director
Services: Monitoring performance of photovoltaic systems: in the field; Monitoring the solar resource: in the region; Solar Energy exhibits, films, lectures, and demonstrations (Occasionally). **Founded:** 1975. **Publications:** *Solar Newsletter* (Semiannual). **Educational Activities:** Workshops and Solar Seminars (Occasionally), on a wide range of topics associated with energy resources and architectural applications.

19148 ■ University of Tennessee at Knoxville - Energy, Environment and Resources Center (EERC)
311 Conference Ctr. Bldg.
Knoxville, TN 37996-4134
Ph: (865)974-4251
Fax: (865)974-1838
Co. E-mail: barkenbu@utk.edu
URL: http://eerc.ra.utk.edu
Contact: Jack N. Barkenbus, Executive Director
Services: Speakers' bureau. **Founded:** 1973. **Publications:** *The Review of Policy Research* (Quarterly); *Working paper series.* **Educational Activities:** Energy, Environment, and Resource Fields Seminars. **Awards:** EERC Fellowships; Waste Management Internships Program.

19149 ■ University of Wisconsin—Madison - Solar Energy Laboratory (SEL)
1343 Engineering Research Bldg.
1500 Engineering Dr.
Madison, WI 53706-1687
Ph: (608)263-5626
Fax: (608)262-8464
Co. E-mail: klein@engr.wisc.edu
URL: http://sel.me.wisc.edu
Contact: Prof. Sanford A. Klein, Director
Founded: 1954.

ASSOCIATIONS AND OTHER ORGANIZATIONS

19150 ■ **National Staff Development Council (NSDC)**
5995 Fairfield Rd. No. 4
Oxford, OH 45056
Ph: (513)523-6029
Free: 800-727-7288
Fax: (513)523-0638
Co. E-mail: nsdcoffice@aol.com
URL: http://www.nsdc.org
Contact: Stephanie Hirsh, Executive Director
URL(s): www.learningforward.org. **Description:** Provides assistance and support to local school district personnel whose primary responsibility is the administration, supervision, and coordination of staff development programs. Promotes public policy favorable to the development of comprehensive district-based staff development programs. Provides information on effective staff development programs, new models of staff development, theories of adult learning, planning and funding of district-based staff development programs, and relevant research. Sponsors regional workshops on topics such as conducting effective staff development programs. **Founded:** 1969. **Publications:** *Journal of Staff Development* (Quarterly); *The Learning Principal* (8/year); *Teachers Teaching Teachers* (8/year). **Awards:** Best Research Award; Best Evaluation of Staff Development Award; Staff Development Book of the Year; Susan Loucks-Horsley Award; Best Dissertation Research (Annual); Best Evaluation of Staff Development (Annual); Shirley Havens Support and Classified Staff Development (Annual); Staff Development Book of the Year (Annual); Susan Loucks-Horsley Award (Annual); Shirley Havens Support and Classified Staff Development Award. **Telecommunication Services:** nsdcoffice@nsdc.org.

19151 ■ **OAS Staff Association (OASSA)**
1889 F St. NW, Ste. 691
Washington, DC 20006
Ph: (202)458-6230
Fax: (202)458-3466
Co. E-mail: staffadmin@oas.org
URL: http://staff.oas.org/english/default.asp
Contact: Carla Sorani, President
Description: Staff members of the Organization of American States General Secretariat. Serves as a union to negotiate employment conditions and labor rights with the OAS administration. **Founded:** 1928. **Publications:** *Staff News.*

REFERENCE WORKS

19152 ■ *Alternative Travel Directory: The Complete Guide to Traveling, Studying, and Living Overseas*
Pub: Transitions Abroad Publishing
Contact: Dr. Joanna Hubbs, President
URL(s): www.transitionsabroad.com/publications/atd/index.shtml. **Ed:** Ron Mader. **Released:** Annual; January; latest edition 7th. **Price:** $19.95, Individuals.

Covers: Over 2,000 sources of information on international employment, education, and specialty travel opportunities. **Entries include:** Source name, address, phone, description, cost dates. **Arrangement:** Classified by subject and country. **Indexes:** Geographical.

19153 ■ *"Area Hurt By Doctor Deficiency" in The Business Journal-Serving Metropolitan Kansas City (Vol. 27, October 17, 2008, No. 5, pp. 1)*
Pub: American City Business Journals, Inc.
Ed: Rob Roberts. **Description:** Kansas City, Missouri may face a shortage of doctors, according to the Metropolitan Medical Society of Greater Kansas City. Over the next ten years the city needs to recruit more doctors in order to address the problem. Practicing physicians are having difficulties recruiting.

19154 ■ *"Bankruptcies" in Crain's Detroit Business (Vol. 24, September 29, 2008, No. 39, pp. 4)*
Pub: Crain Communications Inc.
Description: Current list of business that filed for Chapter 7 or 11 protection in U.S. Bankruptcy Court in Detroit include manufacturers, real estate companies, a printing company and a specialized staffing company.

19155 ■ *Complete Guide to Public Employment*
Pub: Impact Publications
Contact: Dr. Ronald L. Krannich, Chief Executive Officer
E-mail: ron@impactpublications.com
URL(s): www.impactpublications.com. **Ed:** Ron Krannich, Caryl Krannich. **Released:** Triennial; Latest edition 3rd. **Price:** $19.95, Individuals paper. **Publication includes:** List of federal, state, and local government agencies and departments, trade and professional associations, contracting and consulting firms, nonprofit organizations, foundations, research organizations, political support groups, and other organizations offering public service career opportunities. **Entries include:** Organization name, address, phone, name and title of contact. Complete title is "Complete Guide to Public Employment: Opportunities and Strategies with Federal, State, and Local Government;" Trade and Professional Associations; Contracting and Consulting Firms; Foundations; Research Organizations; and Political Support Groups. **Arrangement:** Classified by type of service. **Indexes:** Subject.

19156 ■ *Directory of Contract Staffing Firms*
Pub: C.E. Publications Inc.
URL(s): www.cjhunter.com/dcsf/overview.html. **Released:** Annual **Covers:** Nearly 1,300 contract firms actively engaged in the employment of engineering, IT/IS, and technical personnel for 'temporary' contract assignments throughout the world. **Entries include:** Company name, address, phone, name of contact, email, web address. **Arrangement:** Alphabetical. **Indexes:** Geographical.

19157 ■ *Federal Jobs Digest*
Pub: Federal Jobs Digest
URL(s): www.jobsfed.com. **Released:** 25x/yr. **Price:** $125, U.S.; $152.75, Canada; $183.75, Individuals Europe; $112.50, Libraries; $140.25, Libraries Canada; $171.25, Libraries Europe. **Covers:** Over 10,000 specific job openings in the federal government in each issue. Vacancies from over 300 Federal Agencies are covered. **Entries include:** Position name, title, General Schedule (GS) grade, and Wage Grade (WG), closing date for applications, announcement number, application address, phone, and name of contact. **Arrangement:** By federal department or agency, then geographical.

19158 ■ *INSIGHT Into Diversity*
Pub: INSIGHT Into Diversity
URL(s): www.aarjobs.com. **Ed:** Lucy Knapp-Yanni. **Released:** Monthly **Price:** $15, Individuals subscription per/year; $8, Individuals subscription for 1/2 year. **Covers:** In each issue, about 300 positions at a professional level (most requiring advanced study) available to women, minorities, veterans, and the handicapped; listings are advertisements placed by employers with affirmative action programs. **Entries include:** Company or organization name, address, contact name; description of position including title, requirements, duties, application procedure, salary, etc. **Arrangement:** Classified by profession.

19159 ■ *Journal of the American Medical Association--Physician Service Opportunities Overseas Section*
Pub: American Medical Association
Contact: Edward Hill, President
URL(s): jama.ama-assn.org/content/extract/289/1/34. **Released:** Irregular; latest edition August 2002. **Publication includes:** List of more than 60 organizations that provide assignments overseas for physicians from the United States. **Entries include:** Organization name, address, phone, contact person, countries served, and medical specialties sought. **Arrangement:** Alphabetical.

19160 ■ *"King of the Crib: How Good Samaritan Became Ohio's Baby HQ" in Business Courier (Vol. 27, June 18, 2010, No. 7, pp. 1)*
Pub: Business Courier
Ed: James Ritchie. **Description:** Cincinnati's Good Samaritan hospital had 6,875 live births in 2009, which is more than any other hospital in Ohio. They specialize in the highest-risk pregnancies and deliveries and other hospitals are trying to grab Good Samaritan's share in this niche.

19161 ■ *National Directory for Employment in Education*
Pub: American Association for Employment in Education
Contact: Jack Kronser, President
URL(s): www.aaee.org/. **Released:** Annual; winter; latest edition 2008-2009. **Price:** $20, Nonmembers Processing fee $2; $10, Members processing fee $2. **Covers:** about 600 placement offices maintained by teacher-training institutions and 300 school district

personnel officers and/or superintendents responsible for hiring profesional staff. **Entries include:** Institution name, address, phone, contact name, email address, and website. **Arrangement:** Geographical. **Indexes:** Personal name, subject-field of teacher training, institutions which provide vacancy bulletins and placement services to non-enrolled students.

19162 ■ "The People Puzzle; Re-Training America's Workers" in The Economist (Vol. 390, January 3, 2009, No. 8612, pp. 32)
Pub: The Economist Newspaper Inc.
Description: With thousands of workers losing their jobs, America is now facing the task of getting them back to work. With an overall unemployment rate of 6.7 percent, the federal government has three main ways for leading workers back to employment: training them for new jobs, providing unemployment insurance in order to replace lost wages during the period of job-hunting; and matching employers who desire a skill with workers who have that skill. Specialized staffing agencies provide employers and potential employees with the help necessary to find a job in some of the more niche markets.

19163 ■ "Q&A With Devin Ringling: Franchise's Services Go Beyond Elder Care" in Gazette (October 2, 2010)
Pub: The Gazette
Ed: Bill Radford. **Description:** Profile of franchise, Interim HealthCare, in Colorado Springs, Colorado; the company offers home care services that include wound care and specialized feedings to shopping and light housekeeping. It also runs a medical staffing company that provides nurses, therapists and other health care workers to hospitals, prisons, schools and other facilities.

19164 ■ SER Network Directory
Pub: SER-Jobs for Progress National
Contact: Ignacio Salazar, President
URL(s): www.ser-national.org. **Released:** Annual; Latest edition 2009. **Covers:** Approximately 130 affiliated agencies in 90 U.S. cities of SER ("Service, Employment, Redevelopment")-Jobs for Progress National, Inc., an organizat on of Hispanics that provides employment and training, services to disadvantaged youth and adults, especially Hispanics. **Entries include:** Organization name, address, phone, name of president, services provided, satellite offices, if any. **Arrangement:** Geographical.

19165 ■ "Sign of the Times: Temp-To-Perm Attorneys" in HRMagazine (Vol. 54, January 2009, No. 1, pp. 24)
Pub: Society for Human Resource Management
Contact: Henry G. Jackson, President
E-mail: hjackson@shrm.org
Ed: Bill Leonard. **Description:** A growing number of law firms are hiring professional staff on a temp-to-perm basis according to the president of Professional Placement Services in Florida. Firms can save money while testing potential employees on a temporary basis.

19166 ■ "Staffing Firm Grows by Following Own Advice-Hire a Headhunter" in Crain's Detroit Business (Vol. 24, October 6, 2008, No. 40, pp. 1)
Pub: Crain Communications, Inc.
Ed: Sherri Begin. **Description:** Profile of Venator Holdings L.L.C., a staffing firm that provides searches for companies in need of financial-accounting and technical employees; the firm's revenue has increased from $1.1 million in 2003 to a projected $11.5 million this year due to a climate in which more people are exiting the workforce than are coming in with those particular specialized skills and the need for a temporary, flexible workforce for contract placements at companies that do not want to take on the legacy costs associated with permanent employees. The hiring of an external headhunter to find the right out-of-state manager for Venator is also discussed.

19167 ■ "Work To Do" in Canadian Business (Vol. 81, July 22, 2008, No. 12-13, pp. 22)
Pub: Rogers Media Ltd.
Ed: Jane Bao. **Description:** Recruiting firm Manpower revealed that 36 percent of Canadian employers had trouble filling positions in 2007, highlighting

the labor shortage and the need to bring in more workers. Underemployment of immigrants costs up to $6 billion to Canada's economy every year. Other views regarding Canada's labor shortage and on its economic impact are presented.

SOURCES OF SUPPLY

19168 ■ Atlanta JobBank: The Job Hunter's Guide to Georgia
Adams Media Corporation
Contact: Gary Krebs, Director
E-mail: swatrous@adamsmedia.com
URL(s): www.adamsmedia.com. **Released:** latest edition 15th. **Price:** $17.95, Individuals Paperback. **Covers:** 3,900 employers in the state of Georgia, including Albany, Columbus, Macon, and Savannah. **Entries include:** Firm or organization name, address, local phone, toll-free phone, fax, description of organization, subsidiaries, other locations, recorded jobline, name and title of contact, typical titles for common positions, educational backgrounds desired, number of employees, benefits offered, training programs, internships, parent company, revenues, e-mail and URL address, projected number of hires. **Database includes:** Information on the basics of job winning and writing resumes and cover letters; electronic job search information; 330 industry associations; 90 online career resources; 235 employment services. **Arrangement:** Classified by industry. **Indexes:** Alphabetical.

19169 ■ Boston JobBank: The Job Hunter's Guide to the Bay State
Adams Media Corporation
Contact: Gary Krebs, Director
E-mail: swatrous@adamsmedia.com
URL(s): www.adamsmedia.com. **Released:** Annual; latest edition 20th. **Price:** $17.95, Individuals Paperback. **Covers:** Over 7,000 employers in Massachusetts. **Entries include:** Firm or organization name, address, local phone, toll-free phone, fax, e-mail, URL, recorded jobline, hours, names of management, name and title of contact, titles of common positions, entry-level positions, fringe benefits offered, stock exchange listing, description of organization, subsidiaries, location of headquarters, educational background desired, projected number of hires, training programs, internships, parent company, number of employees, revenues, other U.S. Locations, and international locations. **Database includes:** Information on the basics of job winning and writing resumes and cover letters; electronic job search information; 330 industry associations; 90 online career resources; 420 employment services. **Arrangement:** Classified by industry. **Indexes:** Alphabetical.

19170 ■ California Job Journal
California Job Journal
Contact: Rich Heintz, Editor
URL(s): www.jobjournal.com. **Ed:** Clayton Babcock. **Released:** Weekly. Latest edition 2011. **Price:** Free. **Covers:** Employment issues and job openings in California from entry-level to executive positions. **Entries include:** Company name, address, phone, type of business, name and title of contact; comprehensive description of position and required skills/background, salary and/or benefits offered. **Database includes:** Career guidance and job search advice. **Arrangement:** Classified by field of employment.

19171 ■ Carolina JobBank: The Job Hunter's Guide to North and South Carolina
Adams Media Corporation
Contact: Gary Krebs, Director
E-mail: swatrous@adamsmedia.com
URL(s): www.adamsmediastore.com/product/180/6. **Released:** latest edition 7th. **Price:** $12.21. Individuals Paperback. **Covers:** 4,600 employers in North Carolina and South Carolina. **Entries include:** Firm or organization name, address, local phone, toll-free phone, fax, e-mail, URL, recorded jobline, description of organization, subsidiaries, other locations, hours, names of management, name and title of contact, location of headquarters, typical titles for common positions, educational backgrounds desired, projected number of hires, company benefits, stock exchange listing, training programs and internships, parent

company, number of employees, revenues. **Database includes:** Information on the basics of getting a job and writing resumes and cover letters; regional employment outlook; 330 industry associations; 90 online career resources; 280 employment services. **Arrangement:** Classified by industry. **Indexes:** Alphabetical.

19172 ■ Chicago JobBank: The Job Hunter's Guide to Metro Chicago
Adams Media Corporation
Contact: Gary Krebs, Director
E-mail: swatrous@adamsmedia.com
URL(s): www.adamsmedia.com. **Released:** Annual; Latest edition 19th. **Price:** $17.95, Individuals Paperback; $9, Individuals sale price. **Covers:** About 5,500 major employers in northern and central Illinois including Aurora, Peoria, Rockford, and Springfield. **Entries include:** Firm or organization name, address, local phone, toll-free phone, fax, e-mail, URL, description of organization, hours, recorded jobline, subsidiaries, names of management, name and title of contact, names of management, headquarters locations, typical titles for entry-level and middle-level positions, educational backgrounds desired, company benefits, stock exchange listing, training programs, internships, parent company, number of employees, revenues, other U.S. Locations, international locations. **Database includes:** Information on the basics of job winning and writing resumes and cover letters; electronic job search information; 330 industry association; 90 online career resources, 480 employment services. **Arrangement:** Classified by industry. **Indexes:** Alphabetical.

19173 ■ Dallas/Ft. Worth JobBank: The Job Hunter's Guide to the Dallas-Fort Worth Metroplex
Adams Media Corporation
Contact: Gary Krebs, Director
E-mail: swatrous@adamsmedia.com
URL(s): www.adamsmediastore.com/product/732/6. **Released:** Annual; latest edition 14th. **Price:** $9, Individuals Paperback. **Covers:** 4,000 employers in the Dallas/Ft. Worth, Texas, area including Abilene, Amarillo, Arlington, Garland, Irving, Lubbock, Plano. **Entries include:** Firm or organization name, address, local phone, toll-free phone, fax, e-mail, URL, recorded jobline, hours, description of organization, subsidiaries, names of management, name and title of contact, location of headquarters, typical titles for common positions, educational backgrounds desired, company benefits, stock exchange listing, training programs, internships, parent company, number of employees, revenues, projected number of hires. **Database includes:** Information on the basics of getting a job and writing resumes and cover letters; electronic job search information. **Arrangement:** Classified by industry. **Indexes:** Alphabetical.

19174 ■ Denver JobBank: The Job Hunter's Guide to Colorado
Adams Media Corporation
Contact: Gary Krebs, Director
E-mail: swatrous@adamsmedia.com
URL(s): www.adamsmedia.com. **Ed:** Steven Graber. **Released:** latest edition 14th. **Price:** $17.95, Individuals 4 used & new. **Covers:** 3,500 employers in Denver and the rest of Colorado including Aurora, Boulder, Colorado Springs, Lakewood. **Entries include:** Firm or organization name, address, local phone, toll-free phone, fax, e-mail, URL, description of organization, subsidiaries, other locations, hours, recorded jobline, names of management, name and title of contact, headquarters location, projected number of hires; listings may also include typical titles for common positions, educational backgrounds desired, company benefits, stock exchange listing, training programs, internships, parent company, number of employees, revenues. **Database includes:** Information on the basics of job winning and writing resumes and cover letters; searching for a job online; regional employment outlook; 330 industry associations; 90 online career resources; 150 employment services. **Arrangement:** Classified by industry. **Indexes:** Alphabetical.

19175 ■ Federal Career Opportunities
Federal Research Service Inc.
Contact: Sandy Harris, President
URL(s): www.fedjobs.com/index.html. **Released:** Biweekly; Latest edition 2010. **Price:** $19.97, Mem-

bers per copy; $59.95, Members 6 issues; $99.95, Members 12 issues; $39.95, Members 26 issues. **Covers:** more than 3,000 current federal job vacancies in the United States and overseas; includes permanent, part-time, and temporary positions. **Entries include:** Position title, location, series and grade, job requirements, special forms, announcement number, closing date, application address. **Arrangement:** Classified by occupation.

19176 ■ Florida JobBank: The Job Hunter's Guide to the Sunshine State
Adams Media Corporation
Contact: Gary Krebs, Director
E-mail: swatrous@adamsmedia.com
URL(s): www.adamsmediastore.com. **Released:** latest edition 16th. **Price:** $17.95, Individuals payment with order; $9, Individuals sale price. **Covers:** 5,500 employers in Florida including Fort Lauderdale, Jacksonville, Miami, Orlando, Tampa. **Entries include:** Firm or organization name, address, local phone, toll-free phone, fax, e-mail addresses, web addresses, description of organization, subsidiaries, hours, recorded jobline, name and title of contact, headquarters location, typical titles for common positions, educational backgrounds desired, number of projected hires, company benefits, stock exchange listing, training programs, internships, parent company, number of employees, revenues, other U.S. Locations, international locations. **Database includes:** Information on the basics of job winning and writing resumes and cover letters; electronic job search information; 330 industry associations; 90 online career resources; 285 employment services. **Arrangement:** Classified by industry. **Indexes:** Alphabetical.

19177 ■ Houston JobBank: The Job Hunter's Guide to Houston
Adams Media Corporation
Contact: Gary Krebs, Director
E-mail: swatrous@adamsmedia.com
URL(s): www.adamsmedia.com. **Released:** Annual; latest edition 12th. **Price:** $17.95, Individuals 3 used & new. **Covers:** Over 4,000 employers in Houston, Texas and the surrounding areas including Bayton, Beaumont, Galveston, Pasadena. **Entries include:** Firm or organization name, address, local phone, toll-free phone, fax, recorded jobline, e-mail, URL, hours, name and title of contact; description of organization; headquarters location, subsidiaries, operations at the facility, names of management, typical titles for common positions, educational backgrounds desired, number of projected hires, fringe benefits offered, stock exchange listing, training programs, internships, parent company, number of employees, revenues, other U.S. locations, international locations. **Database includes:** Information on the basics of job winning and writing resumes and cover letters; electronic job search information; 330 industry associations; 90 online career resources; 145 employment services. **Arrangement:** Classified by industry. **Indexes:** Alphabetical.

19178 ■ International Employment Hotline
International Employment Hotline
URL(s): www.internationaljobs.org/monthly.html. **Released:** Monthly **Price:** $69, Individuals per 1 year; $21, Individuals per 3 months; $39, Individuals per 6 months; $129, Individuals per 2 years. **Covers:** Temporary and career job openings overseas and advice for international job hunters. **Entries include:** Company name, address, job title, description of job, requirements, geographic location of job. **Arrangement:** Geographical.

19179 ■ Los Angeles JobBank: The Job Hunter's Guide to Southern California
Adams Media Corporation
Contact: Gary Krebs, Director
E-mail: swatrous@adamsmedia.com
URL(s): www.adamsmedia.com. **Released:** Annual; latest edition 17th. **Price:** $16.95, Individuals Paperback. **Covers:** Over 7,900 southern California employers including Orange, Riverside, San Bernardino, San Diego, Santa Barbara and Ventura counties. **Entries include:** Firm or organization name, address, local phone, toll-free phone, fax, e-mail, URL, recorded jobline, hours, subsidiaries, other locations,

names of management, name and title of contact, description of organization, number of employees, headquarters location, typical titles for common positions, educational backgrounds desired, fringe benefits offered, stock exchange listing, training programs, internships, parent company, number of employees, revenues, corporate headquarters, and number of projected hires. Projected hires. **Database includes:** Information on the basics of job winning and writing resumes and cover letters; electronic job search information; 330 industry associations; 90 online career resources; 515 employment services. **Arrangement:** Classified by industry. **Indexes:** Alphabetical.

19180 ■ Metropolitan Washington DC JobBank: The Job Hunter's Guide to Washington DC
Adams Media Corporation
Contact: Gary Krebs, Director
E-mail: swatrous@adamsmedia.com
URL(s): www.adamsmedia.com. **Released:** Latest edition 17th. **Price:** $17.95, Individuals Paperback. **Covers:** 6,900 employers in Washington, D.C., Greater Baltimore, and Northern Virginia. **Entries include:** Firm or organization name, address, local phone, toll-free phone, fax, recorded jobline, name and title of contact, description of organization, subsidiaries, other locations, names of management, hours, titles for common positions, educational backgrounds desired, company benefits, stock exchange listing, location of headquarters, training programs, internships, parent company, number of employees, revenues, email and URL address, projected number of hires. **Database includes:** Information on the basics of job winning and writing resumes and cover letters; electronic job search information; 330 industry associations; 90 online career resources; 250 employment services. **Arrangement:** Classified by industry. **Indexes:** Alphabetical.

19181 ■ National JobBank
Adams Media Corporation
Contact: Gary Krebs, Director
E-mail: swatrous@adamsmedia.com
URL(s): www.adamsmediastore.com/product/national-jobbank-2010-with-cd/caree rs. **Released:** Annual; Latest edition 2010. **Price:** $475, Individuals payment with order. **Covers:** Over 20,000 employers nationwide. **Entries include:** Firm or organization name, address, local phone, toll-free phone, fax, contact name and title, description of organization, headquarters location, names of management, number of employees, other locations, subsidiaries, parent company, projected number of hires, training offered, internships, hours, recorded jobline, typical titles for common positions, educational backgrounds desired, stock exchange (if listed), fringe benefits offered. Several state and regional volumes are available and described separately. **Arrangement:** Geographical. **Indexes:** Geographical and classified by industry.

19182 ■ San Francisco Bay Area JobBank: The Job Hunter's Guide to Northern California
Adams Media Corporation
Contact: Gary Krebs, Director
E-mail: swatrous@adamsmedia.com
URL(s): www.adamsmedia.com. **Released:** Latest edition 18th. **Price:** $17.95, Individuals Paperback. **Covers:** About 5,600 employers in the San Francisco Bay area and the Northern half of California including Oakland, Sacramento, San Jose, and Silicon Valley. **Entries include:** Firm or organization name, address, local phone, toll-free phone, fax, e-mail, URL, recorded jobline, hours, description of organization, subsidiaries, other locations, number of employees, name and title of contact, headquarters location, typical titles for common positions, educational backgrounds desired, company benefits, stock exchange listing, training programs, internships, parent company, and number of employees, revenues, corporate headquarters, and number of projected hires. **Database includes:** Information on the basics of job winning and writing resumes and cover letters; electronic

job search information; 330 industry associations; 90 online career resources; 350 employment services. **Arrangement:** Classified by industry. **Indexes:** Alphabetical.

19183 ■ Seattle JobBank: The Job Hunter's Guide to Washington
Adams Media Corporation
Contact: Gary Krebs, Director
E-mail: swatrous@adamsmedia.com
URL(s): www.adamsmediastore.com/product/716/6. **Released:** latest edition 13th. **Price:** $17.95, Individuals Paperback. **Covers:** About 4,800 employers in Washington state, including Spokane, Tacoma, and Bellevue. **Entries include:** Firm or organization name, address, local phone, toll-free phone, fax, e-mail, URL, description of organization, subsidiaries, name and title of contact, headquarters location, recorded jobline, typical titles for common positions, educational backgrounds desired, projected number of hires, company benefits, stock exchange listing, training programs, internships, parent company, number of employees, revenues. **Database includes:** Information on the basics of job winning and writing resumes and cover letters; regional employment outlook; 330 industry associations; 90 online career resources; 135 employment services. **Arrangement:** Classified by industry. **Indexes:** Alphabetical.

TRADE PERIODICALS

19184 ■ Graduating Engineer & Computer Careers
Pub: Career Recruitment Media
Contact: Joseph Moore, President
E-mail: jmoore@alloyeducation.com
URL(s): www.graduatingengineer.com. **Released:** Quarterly **Price:** $16.95, Individuals.

19185 ■ Insight into Diversity: The EEO Recruitment Publication
Pub: INSIGHT Into Diversity
URL(s): www.insightintodiversity.com. **Ed:** Michael Rainey. **Released:** Monthly

19186 ■ Mobility: The total relocation magazine
Pub: Employee Relocation Council
Contact: Sarah Albus, Manager
E-mail: salbus@erc.org
URL(s): www.worldwideerc.org/MOBILITY/Pages/index.aspx. **Released:** Monthly **Price:** $48, Individuals.

19187 ■ NSBE Magazine: National Society of Black Engineers
Pub: NSBE Publications
Contact: Franklin Moore, Manager
URL(s): www.nsbe.org/News-Media/Magazines/About-NSBE-Magazine.aspx. **Released:** 3/yr. **Price:** $20, Individuals; $35, Other countries; $15, Students.

19188 ■ Public Personnel Management
Pub: International Personnel Management Association
Contact: Neil Reichenberg, Executive Director
E-mail: nreichenberg@ipma-hr.org
URL(s): www.ipma-hr.org/publications. **Released:** Quarterly **Price:** $130, Individuals print & online; $175, Other countries print & online; $100, Individuals online only.

19189 ■ Staffing Industry Analysts
Pub: Staffing Industry Analysts Inc.
Contact: Craig Johnson, Analyst
E-mail: basin@staffingindustry.com
Released: Bimonthly, 22/year. **Description:** Focuses on the temporary help and employment services industry. Provides information on economic forecasts, employment indicators, finance, labor and market trends, stocks, and statistics.

CONSULTANTS

19190 ■ Columbia Consultants Ltd.—Columbia Consultants.Net L.L.C.
8950 State Route 108, Ste. 226
Columbia, MD 21045

Ph: (410)992-4700
Free: 800-783-7574
Fax: (410)992-4518
Contact: Carol Price, President
Scope: A complete personnel service offering placement of both permanent and temporary employees. Provides professional services and integrated solutions. **Founded:** 1969.

19191 ■ The Purchasing Department (TPD)
34 Claremont Ave.
Maplewood, NJ 07040-2118
Fax: (973)275-0749
Co. E-mail: eostpd@aol.com
Contact: James T. Milway, Principal
E-mail: jtmtpd@aol.com
Scope: Provides state of the art procurement arrangements, process re-engineering and outsourcing assistance to any business wishing to achieve purchasing savings and efficiencies to improve bottom line results. Available to provide contract services to businesses requiring specialized supplemental assistance to back up own personnel on special projects. **Founded:** 1992. **Seminars:** Green Purchasing: Buying Recycled Products; Ethics; Measuring Purchasing Performance; Supplier Teaming and Quality; Preparing for ISO 9000 in the Purchasing Department.

19192 ■ SBR International—SBR Global
30 Adelaide St. E, Ste. 600
The Graeme Bldg.
Toronto, ON, Canada M5C 3G8
Ph: (416)962-7500
Fax: (416)962-7505
Co. E-mail: bizdev@sbr-global.com
URL: http://www.sbr-global.com
Contact: Kevin Gauci, Managing Director
Scope: Specializes in the leasing of multi-disciplinary, high-performance work teams at customer in-house cost, under a mixed military/general contracting model. Engagements include BPR, IE, SA, market and competitor intelligence, logistics, strategy, audit, workouts/turnarounds, M and A support/targeting, statistics and micro-economic modeling, PMO support. **Founded:** 1979. **Seminars:** Electronic counter measures; Strategic planning; Project management. **Telecommunication Services:** info@optimussbr.com.

FRANCHISES AND BUSINESS OPPORTUNITIES

19193 ■ AtWork Personnel Services
3215 John Sevier Hwy.
Knoxville, TN 37920
Free: 800-383-0804
Fax: (865)573-1171
URL: http://www.atworkpersonnel.com
Description: Customized staffing service. **No. of Franchise Units:** 36. **Founded:** 1990.. **Franchised:** 1992. **Equity Capital Needed:** $143,600-$226,800. **Franchise Fee:** $0-$25,000. **Royalty Fee:** 6.1-1.6%. **Training:** Training includes 5 days minimum at headquarters, 3-5 days onsite, 2 days of meeting and ongoing support.

19194 ■ Lloyd Staffing
445 Broadhollow Rd., Ste. 119
Melville, NY 11747
Ph: (631)777-7600
Free: 888-292-6678
Fax: (631)777-7626
Co. E-mail: info@lloydstaffing.com
URL: http://www.lloydstaffing.com
Contact: Keith Banks, President
E-mail: kbanks@lloydstaffing.com
Description: Specialized staffing services. **Scope:** Group of staffing-related divisions offering retained and contingency search and computer training. Areas of discipline include: bilingual/global services, accounting/finance. **Founded:** 1971. **Training:** Yes. **Special Services:** e-Procurement through Ringo.

19195 ■ Party Personnel Franchise Systems
11720 Hadley
Overland Park, KS 66210
Ph: (913)451-0218
Fax: (913)451-8941
Description: Hospitality & entertainment staffing. **No. of Franchise Units:** 1. **No. of Company-Owned Units:** 1. **Founded:** 1993. **Franchised:** 2003. **Equity Capital Needed:** $22,500-$40,000. **Franchise Fee:** $15,000. **Royalty Fee:** 3%. **Training:** Training includes 2 weeks at headquarters, 1 week/year at franchisee's location and ongoing support.

COMPUTERIZED DATABASES

19196 ■ *HireDiversity.com*
5385 Hollister Ave., Ste. 204
Santa Barbara, CA 93111
Ph: (805)964-4554
Fax: (805)964-5539
Co. E-mail: hd@hirediversity.com
URL: http://www.hispanicbusiness.com
Contact: Jesus Chavarria, President
URL(s): www.hirediversity.com. **Price:** Free to job seekers. **Entries include:** Name, address, phone, employment history, salary requirements, level of management experience, education, geographical preference, and language. **Database covers:** Over 95,000 resumes of multicultural professionals and recent college graduates who are seeking employment with Fortune 500 companies; job listings with a large variety of companies.

19197 ■ *Library Literature & Information Science Full Text™*
10 Estes St.
Ipswich, MA 01938-2106
Ph: (978)356-6500
Free: 800-653-2726
Fax: (978)356-6565
Co. E-mail: information@ebscohost.com
URL: http://www.ebscohost.com
Contact: Tim Collins, President
E-mail: tcollins@ebscohost.com
Availability: Online: EBSCO Publishng. **Type:** Bibliographic; Full-text.

LIBRARIES

19198 ■ Brandeis University - Center for Youth and Communities - Library
415 South St.
Waltham, MA 02453
Ph: (781)736-4835
Fax: (781)736-3773
Co. E-mail: melchior@brandeis.edu
URL: http://cyc.brandeis.edu
Contact: Alan Melchior, Deputy Director
Scope: Employment and income research, youth employment and education, employee benefits, welfare reform, public/private partnership, networking in social programs. **Services:** Library open to the public by appointment. **Holdings:** 3000 volumes. **Telecommunication Services:** cyc@brandeis.edu.

19199 ■ Colorado Department of Labor & Employment, Labor Market Information Library
633 17th St., Ste. 400
Denver, CO 80202-3660
Ph: (303)318-8851
Fax: (303)620-4988
URL: http://www.colorado.gov/cs/Satellite/CDLE-Main/CDLE/1249907618315#!mi
Scope: Labor market information. **Services:** Library open to the public for reference use only. **Holdings:** 100 books; 1000 unbound reports; 500 unbound periodicals; all official Colorado labor force estimates. **Subscriptions:** 20 journals and other serials.

19200 ■ District of Columbia Public Library - Business, Economics and Vocations Division
Martin Luther King Memorial Library
901 G St. NW, Rm. 107
Washington, DC 20001
Ph: (202)727-0321
Co. E-mail: mlkjrlibrary@dc.gov
URL: http://www.dclibrary.org/
Contact: David Robinson, Division Manager
Scope: Business; statistics, economics, vocations, investment, real estate, import, export, accounting, taxation, business report writing, organizational behavior, commerce, management, marketing, labor, transportation. **Services:** Interlibrary loan; copying; division open to the public. **Founded:** 1907. **Holdings:** 55,639 books; 1150 bound periodical volumes; 471 business directories; 6000 pamphlets; 508 telephone directories; 5521 reels of microfilm; 88 microcards; 7268 microfiche. **Subscriptions:** 428 journals and other serials; 35 newspapers and financial services. **Telecommunication Services:** david.robinson@dc.gov.

19201 ■ New York Department of Labor - Labor Research Library
W. Averell Harriman State Office Campus
Bldg. 12
Albany, NY 12240-0013
Ph: (518)457-9000
Free: 800-662-1220
Co. E-mail: ashley.hibbard@labor.state.ny.us
URL: http://www.labor.ny.gov
Contact: R. Ashley Hibbard, Senior Librarian
Scope: Employment, statistics, economic and business conditions, personnel management, unions, unemployment insurance, wages and hours, labor legislation, vocational education and guidance. **Services:** Interlibrary loan; copying; Library open to the public with restrictions. **Founded:** 1907. **Holdings:** 3000 titles (books and documents); 20 VF drawers. **Subscriptions:** 175 journals and other serials.

RESEARCH CENTERS

19202 ■ University of Texas at Arlington - Center for Research on Organizational and Managerial Excellence (CROME)
Management Department, Box 19467
Arlington, TX 76019
Ph: (817)272-3866
Fax: (817)272-3122
Co. E-mail: wheeler@uta.edu
URL: http://www.uta.edu/ra/real/editprofile.php?onlyview=1&pid=512
Contact: Kenneth G. Wheeler, Director
Founded: 1984. **Publications:** *CROME Working papers.*

START-UP INFORMATION

19203 ■ *"Local Flavor" in Entrepreneur (Vol. 35, November 2007, No. 11, pp. 110)*
Pub: Entrepreneur Media Inc.
Ed: Nichole L. Torres. **Description:** Local food products are growing in the market today as consumers are becoming interested in where their food comes; you can start a business by investigating the kinds of foods popular in your region.

ASSOCIATIONS AND OTHER ORGANIZATIONS

19204 ■ **American Cheese Society (ACS)**
2696 S Colorado Blvd., Ste. 570
Denver, CO 80222-5954
Ph: (720)328-2788
Fax: (720)328-2786
Co. E-mail: info@cheesesociety.org
URL: http://www.cheesesociety.org
Contact: Christine Hyatt, President
Description: Represents producers, manufacturers, retailers, distributors and others interested in the specialty and farmstead cheese industry. Aims to promote cheese appreciation and to provide useful information on cheese making in a farm, house, or a manufacturing plant environment. Includes activities such as annual conferences, cheese tasting and workshops on cheese making. Conducts discussions on the technical and economical aspects of cheese making. Sponsors competitions; maintains speakers' bureau. **Founded:** 1983. **Publications:** *American Cheese Society--Membership Directory.*

19205 ■ **Greek Food and Wine Institute (GFWI)**
34-80 48th St.
Long Island City, NY 11101
Ph: (718)729-5277
Co. E-mail: info@gfwi.org
URL: http://www.gfwi.org
Description: Food, wine and spirits producers, importers, and distributors from Greece and the U.S. Educates food and wine trade and consumers about the quality, variety, uses, and healthfulness of Greek foods, wines, and spirits. Conducts educational programs. **Founded:** 1992. **Publications:** *Gastronomia* (Semiannual); *Greek Wine Manual: Guide Sommeliers & Wine Professionals.* **Educational Activities:** Greek Food and Wine Institute Board meeting (Annual).

19206 ■ **International Dairy-Deli-Bakery Association (IDDBA)**
PO Box 5528
Madison, WI 53705-0528
Ph: (608)310-5000
Fax: (608)238-6330
Co. E-mail: iddba@iddba.org
URL: http://www.iddba.org
Contact: Steve Beekhuizen, President
Description: Companies and organizations engaged in the production, processing, packaging, marketing, promotion, and/or selling of cheese and cheese products, bakery, or delicatessen and delicatessen-related items. Aims to further the relationship between manufacturing, production, marketing and distribution channels utilized in the delivery of deli, dairy, and bakery foods to the marketplace. Develops and disseminates information concerning deli, dairy, and bakery foods. **Founded:** 1964. **Publications:** *Dairy-Deli-Bake Digest* (Monthly); *IDDBA and You* (Monthly); *Trainer's Tool Kit*; *Who's Who in Dairy-Deli-Bakery* (Periodic); *Dairy-Deli-Bake Digest*; *Who's Who in Dairy-Deli Bakery*; *WrapUp*; *IDDBA Legis-Letter.* **Educational Activities:** Dairy-Deli-Bake (Annual); Dairy-Deli-Bake Seminar and Expo (Annual). **Awards:** International Dairy-Deli-Bakery Association Undergraduate Scholarships; Undergraduate/Graduate Scholarships (Annual).

19207 ■ **National Association for the Specialty Food Trade (NASFT)**
136 Madison Ave., 12th Fl.
New York, NY 10016
Ph: (212)482-6440
Free: 800-627-3869
Fax: (212)482-6459
Co. E-mail: customerservice@nasft.org
URL: http://www.specialtyfood.com
Contact: Dennis Deschaine, Chairman
Description: Represents manufacturers, distributors, processors, importers, retailers, and brokers of specialty and gourmet foods. Aims to foster trade, commerce and interest in the specialty food industry. **Founded:** 1952. **Publications:** *Specialty Food Magazine* (10/year). **Awards:** Sofi Awards (Annual).

19208 ■ **Opimian, the Wine Society of Canada—La Societe Opimian**
5165 Sherbrooke St. W, Ste. 420
Montreal, QC, Canada H4A 1T6
Ph: (514)483-5551
Free: 800-361-9421
Fax: (514)481-9699
Co. E-mail: opim@opim.ca
URL: http://www.opim.ca
Contact: Pierre Chanzonkov, General Manager
Description: Individuals interested in wine. Promotes increased public appreciation of wine. Conducts educational programs. **Founded:** 1973.

DIRECTORIES OF EDUCATIONAL PROGRAMS

19209 ■ *Major Food & Drink Companies of the World*
Pub: Graham & Whiteside
URL(s): www.gale.cengage.com. **Ed:** Heather Brewin, Sandra James, Helen Porter, Chris Tapster. **Released:** Annual; Latest edition 16th; Published May, 2012. **Price:** $1460, Individuals. **Covers:** Over 9,200 worldwide companies involved in the food and drink industry. **Entries include:** Company name, address, phone and names and titles of key personnel. **Availability:** Online: Cengage Learning Inc. **Type:** Directory.

REFERENCE WORKS

19210 ■ *"At Wine Kiosk, Show ID, Face Camera, Swipe Card and Blow" in Pittsburgh Post-Gazette (November 28, 2010)*
Pub: Pittsburgh-Post Gazette
Ed: Dennis B. Roddy. **Description:** New technology installed on wine kiosks enables sellers to abide by the law. This technology tests blood alcohol levels and warns people if they have recently used a mouthwash before testing.

19211 ■ *"Bagging Profits; High-End Grocers Expand Despite Stale Economy" in Crain's Detroit Business (Vol. 24, March 24, 2008, No. 12, pp. 1)*
Pub: Crain Communications, Inc.
Ed: Nancy Kaffer. **Description:** Discusses the expansion plans of several high-end grocery stores in the Detroit area and the reasons why, despite the poor economy, these gourmet grocers are doing well. Statistical data included.

19212 ■ *"The Bear Arrives - With Bargain Hunters" in Barron's (Vol. 88, July 7, 2008, No. 27, pp. M3)*
Pub: Dow Jones & Co., Inc.
Ed: Kopin Tan. **Description:** US stock markets have dropped 20 percent below their highs, entering the bear market at the end of June 2008. It was also the worst performance of the stock markets during June. Wine maker Constellation Brands, however, reported a 50 percent rise in net income for the first quarter of 2008.

19213 ■ *"The Believer" in Inc. (December 2007, pp. 130-138)*
Pub: Gruner & Jahr USA Publishing
Ed: Leigh Buchanan. **Description:** Profile of Selena Cuffe, wine importer and socially conscious woman entrepreneur, who is focusing her talents on helping South Africa get wine products to America.

19214 ■ *Beverage Marketing Directory*
Pub: Beverage Marketing Corp.
Contact: Michael C. Bellas, Chief Executive Officer
E-mail: mbellas@beveragemarketing.com
URL(s): www.beveragemarketing.com/?service=publications&section=directory. **Released:** Annual; Latest edition 33rd; 2011. **Price:** $1435, Individuals softcover or in PDF format; $5495, Individuals database on CD-ROM; $5495, Canada database on CD-ROM. **Covers:** Over 25,500 beer wholesalers, wine and spirits wholesalers, soft drink bottlers and franchisors, breweries, wineries, distilleries, alcoholic beverage importers, bottled water companies; and trade associations, government agencies, micro breweries, juice, coffee, tea, milk companies, and others concerned with the beverage and bottling industries; coverage includes Canada. **Entries include:** Beverage and bottling company listings contain company name, address, phone, names of key executives, number of employees, brand names, and other information, including number of franchisees, number of delivery trucks, sales volume. Suppliers and related companies and

organizations listings include similar but less detailed information. **Arrangement:** Geographical. **Indexes:** Personnel, supplier's product, company name.

19215 ■ *"Booze Makers Battle Over Turkey Day"* in Advertising Age *(Vol. 78, October 29, 2007, No. 43, pp. 4)*

Pub: Crain Communications, Inc.

Ed: Jeremy Mullman. **Description:** Beer and wine marketers are jockeying for position in regards to the Thanksgiving holiday.

19216 ■ *"Cheap Thrills: Where to Look When You're Craving a Low-Price Wine"* in Chicago Tribune *(January 12, 2009)*

Pub: McClatchy-Tribune Information Services

Ed: Bill Daley. **Description:** Wines priced $15 and above are being hit the hardest by the economic downturn while cheaper wines, specifically those priced between $3 and $6, are seeing a growth in sales.

19217 ■ *"Closures Pop Cork on Wine Bar Sector Consolidation"* in Houston Business Journal *(Vol. 40, January 22, 2010, No. 37, pp. A2)*

Pub: American City Business Journals

Ed: Allison Wollam. **Description:** Wine bar market in Houston, Texas is in the midst of a major shift and heads toward further consolidation due to the closure of pioneering wine bars that opened in the past decade. The Corkscrew owner, Andrew Adams, has blamed the creation of competitive establishments to the closure which helped wear out his concept.

19218 ■ *"Construction Firms Support NAACP Plan"* in Business Courier *(Vol. 27, September 24, 2010, No. 21, pp. 1)*

Pub: Business Courier

Ed: Lucy May. **Description:** Executives of Turner Construction Company and Messer Construction Company expressed their support for the Cincinnati National Association for the Advancement of Colored People Construction Partnership Agreement. The agreement involves the setting of rules for the involvement of firms owned by African Americans in major projects in Cincinnati.

19219 ■ *"Dancing With Giants: Acquisition and Survival of the Family Firm"* in Family Business Review *(Vol. 19, December 2006, No. 4, pp. 289)*

Pub: Family Firm Institute

Contact: Judy L. Green, President

Ed: Adam Steen, Lawrence S. Welch. **Description:** Responses of family firms to mergers and acquisitions are analyzed taking the example of the takeover of an Australian wine producer and family firm.

19220 ■ *"Eagle's Wine Kiosk Is Area's 1st"* in Pittsburgh Post-Gazette *(October 28, 2010)*

Pub: Pittsburgh-Post Gazette

Ed: Bob Batz Jr. **Description:** Giant Eagle Market District store at Settlers Ridge opened the first self-serve wine kiosk in Western Pennsylvania. The kiosk will have a built-in breathalyzer panel to ensure safety.

19221 ■ *"Food & Wine Publisher Tries His Hand at Saber Rattling"* in Advertising Age *(Vol. 77, December 4, 2006, No. 49, pp. 16)*

Pub: Crain Communications, Inc.

Description: French vineyards are facing a massive overproduction crisis due to a falling number in the amount of wine the French are drinking per week.

19222 ■ *"Fromm Family Foods Converts Old Feed Mill Into Factory for Gourmet Pet Food"* in Wisconsin State Journal *(August 3, 2011)*

Pub: Capital Newspapers

Ed: Barry Adams. **Description:** Fromm Family Foods, a gourmet cat and dog food company spent $10 million to convert an old feed mill into a pet food manufacturing facility. The owner forecasts doubling or tripling its production of 600 tons of feed per week in about five years.

19223 ■ *"Gallo Family Vineyards to Raise Funds for Meals On Wheels"* in Food & Beverage Close-Up *(November 4, 2011)*

Pub: Close-Up Media

Description: Gallo family is committed to raising funds for Meals On Wheels Association of America and hosts a fundraiser annually.

19224 ■ *"Grape Expectations"* in Canadian Business *(Vol. 80, Winter 2007, No. 24, pp. 57)*

Pub: Rogers Media

Ed: Joe Castaldo. **Description:** Laura McCain-Jensen bought a 15-acre vineyard in the Niagara wine country after a trip to Ontario for her husband's hair transplant. The vineyard has since been renamed Creekside Estate Winery and now produces two celebrity-branded wines under the name of golfer Mike Weir and hockey player Wayne Gretsky.

19225 ■ *"Growing Pains"* in Canadian Business *(Vol. 81, July 22, 2008, No. 12-13, pp. 35)*

Pub: Rogers Media Ltd.

Ed: Alex Mylnek. **Description:** Laughing Stock Vineyards' Cynthia Enns and David Enns plan to target young buyers by using social media. The Enns however, are concerned that targeting younger buyers may affect Laughing Stock's image as a premium brand. Additional information regarding the company's future plans is presented.

19226 ■ *"Heat Brings Out Flavor, Not Visitors to Wineries"* in Saint Louis Business Journal *(Vol. 31, August 12, 2011, No. 51, pp. 1)*

Pub: Saint Louis Business Journal

Ed: Rick Desloge. **Description:** St. Louis, Missouri's wine industry seems to benefit from the heat wave. The hot weather is expected to give grapes more flavor.

19227 ■ *"Homes, Not Bars, Stay Well Tended"* in Advertising Age *(Vol. 79, January 28, 2008, No. 4, pp. 8)*

Pub: Crain Communications, Inc.

Ed: Jeremy Mullman. **Description:** Due to the downturn in the economy, consumers are drinking less at bars and restaurants; however, according to the Distilled Spirits Council of the United States, they are still purchasing expensive liquor to keep in their homes.

19228 ■ *"J&J Snack Rakes in Sales"* in Philadelphia Business Journal *(Vol. 28, September 25, 2009, No. 32, pp. 1)*

Pub: American City Business Journals

Ed: Peter van Allen. **Description:** Analysts expect J&J Snack Foods Corporation to boost earnings by 48 percent for fiscal year ending September 2009. Stable commodity prices have benefited the company.

19229 ■ *"Lawyers Cash In On Alcohol"* in Business Journal Portland *(Vol. 27, November 19, 2010, No. 38, pp. 1)*

Pub: Portland Business Journal

Ed: Andy Giegerich. **Description:** Oregon-based law firms have continued to corner big business on the state's growing alcohol industry as demand for their services increased. Lawyers, who represent wine, beer and liquor distillery interests, have seen their workload increased by 20 to 30 percent in 2009.

19230 ■ *"LCB Puts a Cork in Kiosk Wine Sales"* in Times Leader *(December 22, 2010)*

Pub: Wilkes-Barre Publishing Company

Ed: Andrew M. Seder. **Description:** The Pennsylvania Liquor Control Board closed down thirty Pronto Wine Kiosks located in supermarkets throughout the state. The Board cited mechanical and technological issues such as products not dispensing.

19231 ■ *"LCB Turning Off Wine Vending Machines"* in Pittsburgh Post-Gazette *(September 20, 2011)*

Pub: PG Publishing Company

Ed: Tracie Mauriello. **Description:** Grocery store shoppers will no longer be able to purchase a bottle of wine from wine kiosks in Pennsylvania.

19232 ■ *"Leinie's Charts National Craft Beer Rollout"* in The Business Journal-Milwaukee *(Vol. 25, August 29, 2008, No. 49, pp. A1)*

Pub: American City Business Journals, Inc.

Ed: Rich Rovito. **Description:** Jacob Leinenkugel Brewing Co. is expected to complete the national rollout of its craft beer brands, while the launch of a new beer is prepared for this fall. The rollout is will likely benefit MillerCoors LLC, and will leave Alaska as the only state without Leinenkugel beer. Other views and information on Leinenkugel's national rollout are presented.

19233 ■ *"Little Cheer in Holiday Forecast for Champagne"* in Advertising Age *(Vol. 88, November 17, 2008, No. 43, pp. 6)*

Pub: Crain Communications, Inc.

Ed: Jeremy Mullman. **Description:** Due to a weak economy that has forced consumers to trade down from the most expensive alcoholic beverages as well as a weak U.S. dollar that has driven already lofty Champagne prices higher, makers of the French sparkling wine are anticipating a brutally slow holiday season.

19234 ■ *"Millennials: The Great White Hope for Wine Industry"* in Advertising Age *(Vol. 81, December 6, 2010, No. 43, pp. 2)*

Pub: Crain Communications, Inc.

Ed: E.J. Shultz. **Description:** Generation offers category of most growth potential in 30 years and 7-Eleven and vintner are taking notice.

19235 ■ *"Moet, Rivals Pour More Ad Bucks Into Bubbly"* in Advertising Age *(Vol. 88, September 3, 2007, No. 35, pp. 4)*

Pub: Crain Communications, Inc.

Ed: Jeremy Mullman. **Description:** In an attempt to revive sluggish sales, champagne companies are raising their advertising budgets, transforming themselves from light-spending seasonal players to year-round heavyweights in the advertising world.

19236 ■ *"New Recipes Added to IAMS Naturals Pet Food Line"* in MMR *(Vol. 28, August 1, 2011, No. 11, pp. 17)*

Pub: Racher Press Inc.

Description: Procter & Gamble Company's IAMS brand has created a new pet food line called IAMS Naturals for pet owners wishing to feed their pets natural, wholesome food. IAMS Sensitive Naturals has ocean fish and its first ingredient for dogs with sensitivities. IAMS Simple & Natural features chicken with no fillers.

19237 ■ *"The Price Is Right: What You Can Learn From the Wine Industry"* in Advertising Age *(Vol. 88, February 11, 2008, No. 6, pp. 14)*

Pub: Crain Communications, Inc.

Ed: Lenore Skenazy. **Description:** In California a wine study was conducted in which participants' brains were hooked up to an MRI so researchers could watch what was happening in both the taste centers as well as the pleasure centers; the participants were given three different wines but were told that the samples were from a variety of wines that differed radically in price; surprisingly, the differences did not affect the taste centers of the brain, however, when the participants were told that a sample was more expensive, the pleasure centers were greatly affected.

19238 ■ *"Russian Renaissance"* in Chicago Tribune *(September 22, 2008)*

Pub: McClatchy-Tribune Information Services

Ed: Alex Rodriguez. **Description:** Winemakers from Russia are returning to the craft and quality of winemaking now that they are free from Soviet restraints.

19239 ■ *"Secaucus-Based Freshpet is Barking Up the Right Tree"* in Record *(September 8, 2011)*

Pub: North Jersey Media Group

Ed: Rebecca Olles. **Description:** Freshpet produces a variety of nutritious, refrigerated pet foods and treats for cats and dogs. The firm introduced five new recipes and treats to its grain-free line called Vital line. The Vital line mimics the ancestral diets of dogs and cats.

19240 ■ *"Seward Restaurant Garners Accolades"* in Alaska Business Monthly (Vol. 27, October 2011, No. 10, pp. 9)

Pub: Alaska Business Publishing Company

Ed: Nancy Pounds. **Description:** Resurrection Road House of Seward, Alaska won the Wine Spectator's Aware of Excellence in 2011. The award honors restaurants that handle at least 100 gourmet wines that are skillfully paired with the cuisine.

19241 ■ *"Silver Springs Creamery Opens Retail"* in Bellingham Business Journal (Vol. March 2010, pp. 3)

Pub: Sound Publishing Inc.

Description: Eric Sundstrom, owner of Silver Springs Creamery, announced the opening of its on-site retail store that will sell the farm's goat and cow cheese, yogurt, ice cream and flesh milk.

19242 ■ *"A Soggy Harvest"* in Business Journal-Portland (Vol. 24, October 5, 2007, No. 32, pp. 1)

Pub: American City Business Journals, Inc.

Ed: Robin J. Moody. **Description:** Vintners in Willamette Valley are facing a tough challenge with a rainy wine harvest season and a delay in the ripening of grapes due to a cool spring and August. Rain decreased the sugar content of grapes and poses a danger with molds. The economic impact of the rainy harvest season in wine making is discussed.

19243 ■ *"The Spirit of a Man: Kedar Massenburg's Intoxicating Style of Conducting Business"* in Black Enterprise (Vol. 38, March 2008)

Pub: Earl G. Graves Publishing Co. Inc.

Ed: Sonia Alleyne. **Description:** Profile of Kedar Massenburg, personal trainer at The Gym in Montvale, New Jersey. Massenburg also operates an independent record label and management company as well as Kedar Beverages LLC founded in 2005. His latest venture is winemaking.

19244 ■ *"Top 50 Exporters"* in Hispanic Business (Vol. 30, July-August 2008, No. 7-8, pp. 42)

Pub: Hispanic Business, Inc.

Ed: Hildy Medina. **Description:** Increases in exports revenues reported by food exporters and green companies in a time of economic slowdown in the U.S are described. Food exporters have benefited from the growth of high-volume grocery stores in underdeveloped countries and the German governments' promotion of solar energy has benefited the U.S. solar heating equipment and solar panel manufactures.

19245 ■ *"The Trouble With $150,000 Wine"* in Barron's (Vol. 88, July 7, 2008, No. 27, pp. 33)

Pub: Dow Jones & Co., Inc.

Ed: Orley Ashenfelter. **Description:** Review of the book, 'The Billionaire's Vinegar: The Mystery of the World's Most Expensive Bottle of Wine,' which discusses vintners along with the marketing and distribution of wine as well as the winemaking industry as a whole.

19246 ■ *"What'll You Have Tonight?"* in Barron's (Vol. 88, July 4, 2008, No. 28, pp. 22)

Pub: Dow Jones & Co., Inc.

Ed: Neil A. Martin. **Description:** Shares of Diageo could rise by 30 percent a year from June 2008 after it slipped due to U.S. sales worries. The company also benefits from the trend toward more premium alcoholic beverage brands worldwide especially in emerging markets.

19247 ■ *Wine Investment for Portfolio Diversification: How Investing in Wine Can Yield Greater Returns than Stocks and Bonds*

Pub: Wine Appreciation Guild

Contact: Donna Bottrell, President

E-mail: donna@wineappreciation.com

Ed: Mahesh Kumar. **Released:** October 2005. **Price:** $45.00. **Description:** Analysis of the performance of investments in fine wines, particularly Bordeaux, is presented. History verifies that wine has traditionally been a sound investment offering a higher expected return over the market relative to its overall contribution of risk. Wine can be used as an effective means of diversifying one's portfolio.

19248 ■ *"The Wine Spectator"* in Business Courier (Vol. 27, November 26, 2010, No. 30, pp. 1)

Pub: Business Courier

Ed: Dan Monk. **Description:** Vintner Select, a wine distributor, will introduce an internationally known portfolio of more than 50 German and Austrian wines. The company now distributes about 900 different wine labels from 220 producers in 10 countries to smaller, independent retailers in Indiana, Kentucky and Ohio.

19249 ■ *"Wirtz Partners With California Liquor Wholesaler To Expand Reach"* in Chicago Tribune (December 17, 2008)

Pub: McClatchy-Tribune Information Services

Ed: Mike Hughlett. **Description:** Young's Market Co. and Wirtz Beverage Group have tentatively agreed to a joint venture that will give both companies a larger reach in the wine and liquor distribution business.

19250 ■ *"Yao Ming Courts China's Wine Boom"* in Wall Street Journal Eastern Edition (November 28, 2011, pp. B4)

Pub: Dow Jones & Company Inc. Enterprise Media Group

Contact: Clare Hart, President

Ed: Jason Chow. **Description:** Yao Ming, the former NBA 7-foot 6-inch Chinese basketball star, is set to cash in on the market potential for wine in China. He has created his own winery in California, Yao Family Wines, which will produce wines solely for the Chinese market.

19251 ■ *"Your Turn in the Spotlight"* in Inc. (Volume 32, December 2010, No. 10, pp. 57)

Pub: Inc. Magazine

Ed: John Brandon. **Description:** Examples of three video blogs created by entrepreneurs to promote their businesses and products are used to show successful strategies. Wine Library TV promotes a family's wine business; SHAMA.TV offers marketing tips and company news; and Will It Blend? promotes sales of a household blender.

SOURCES OF SUPPLY

19252 ■ *Beverage Industry--Annual Manual Issue*

BNP Media

Contact: Al Reser, President

URL(s): directories.bevindustry.com/manual. **Released:** Annual; Latest edition 2010. **Publication includes:** List of over 1,700 companies supplying equipment and materials to the soft drink, beer, wine, bottled water, and juice industries; industry associations; bottling and supply franchise companies; beer importers distributors; manufacturers' representatives; soft drink distributors. **Entries include:** For suppliers--Company name, address, phone, code to indicate products. For associations--Name, address, phone, name of president; some association listings also include meeting date and location and names of other executives. For franchise companies--Name, address, phone, names and titles of executives, number of plants, number of franchised plants, products, foreign involvement. For beer importers and distributors--Name, address, phone, names and titles of key executives, brands handled. For manufacturers' representatives--Name, address, phone, names of contacts, market areas, products represented. **Database includes:** Statistics and industry surveys. **Arrangement:** State associations and supplier associations are geographical; other listings are alphabetical. **Indexes:** Trade name, product/service.

STATISTICAL SOURCES

19253 ■ *The Cheese Market*

Pub: Rector Press, Ltd.

Contact: Lewis Sckolnick, President

Released: 2009. **Price:** Contact Rector Press. **Description:** Examines the growth areas within Analyzes consumer attitudes and buying habits and identifies trends that will affect market growth. Focuses on the specialty cheese segment as well as on low-fat, low-sodium, and low-cholesterol varieties. Also covers distribution and marketing strategies, and provides profiles of major cheese marketers.

19254 ■ *The U.S. Pasta Market*

Pub: Business Trend Analysts, Inc.

Released: 2002. **Price:** $1,695.00. **Description:** Provides in-depth coverage of the markets for all types of pasta products, including dry pasta, shelf-stable pasta mixes and dinners, fresh pasta, frozen pasta, and canned pasta products.

TRADE PERIODICALS

19255 ■ *The Art of Eating*

Pub: The Art of Eating

URL(s): www.artofeating.com/. **Released:** Quarterly **Price:** $96, Two years; $52, Individuals; $67, Other countries; $13.50, Single issue.

19256 ■ *Bread Pudding Recipe Exchange*

Pub: Prosperity & Profits Unlimited, Distribution Services

Ed: A. Doyle, Editor. **Released:** Annual. **Price:** $2, U.S.; $3, Canada; $4, elsewhere. **Description:** Presents recipe possibilities for bread pudding, sample greetings, and more.

19257 ■ *The Cheese Reporter*

Pub: Cheese Reporter Publishing Company Inc.

Contact: Kevin Thome, Director

E-mail: kthome@cheesereporter.com

URL(s): www.cheesereporter.com/. **Ed:** Dick Groves. **Released:** Weekly **Price:** $130, Individuals yearly mailed subscription periodical mail; $185, Individuals yearly mailed subscription first class mail; $250, Other countries airmail; $355, Other countries 2 years (airmail); $195, Two years yearly mailed subscription periodical mail; $85, Individuals 26 weeks mailed subscription periodical mail; $35, Individuals 4 weeks mailed subscription periodical mail; $60, Individuals 12 weeks mailed subscription periodical mail.

19258 ■ *The Food & Beverage International*

Pub: Journal Publications Inc.

URL(s): www.fbworld.com. **Released:** Bimonthly

19259 ■ *Gourmet News*

Pub: United Publications Inc.

Contact: J.G. Taliaferro, Jr., President

URL(s): www.unitedpublications.comwww.gourmet-news.com/. **Ed:** Rocelle Aragon. **Released:** Monthly

19260 ■ *The National Culinary Review: Official Magazine of the American Culinary Federation*

Contact: Kay Orde, Editor

E-mail: korde@acfchefs.net

URL(s): www.acfchefs.org/Content/Navigation-Menu2/About/Media/Publications/de fault.htm. **Ed:** Kay Orde. **Released:** Monthly **Price:** $60, Individuals; $200, Other countries.

19261 ■ *Uncorked*

Pub: The California Wine Club

Ed: Bruce Boring, Editor. **Released:** Monthly. **Price:** Included in membership. **Description:** Profiles wineries and the wine industry. Recurring features include interviews, news of research, reports of meetings, book reviews, and columns titled Up Close & Personal, Fun Facts, To Your Health, Recipes, What They Say, Tasting Notes, Alumni Notes, and Questions & Answers.

19262 ■ *The Wine Advocate*

Pub: Robert M. Parker, Jr.

Contact: Robert M. Parker, Jr., Publisher

Released: Bimonthly, 6/year. **Price:** $75, individuals; $90, Canada; $100, other countries. **Description:** Serves as an independent guide to fine wines.

19263 ■ *Wine Enthusiast Magazine*

Pub: The Wine Enthusiast Inc.

Contact: Hank Rosen, President

URL(s): www.winemag.com. **Ed:** Adam Strum. **Price:** $29.95, Individuals; $49.95, Two years; $69.95, Individuals 3 years; $49.95, Canada; $79.95, Other countries.

19264 ■ *Wine News*
Pub: T.E. Smith Inc.
URL(s): www.thewinenews.com. **Released:** Bi-monthly **Price:** $25, Individuals; $60, Out of country.

19265 ■ *Wine & Spirits Magazine*
Pub: Wine & Spirits Magazine Inc.
URL(s): www.wineandspiritsmagazine.com. **Ed:** Joshua Greene. **Released:** Monthly; 8/yr. **Price:** $29.95, Individuals; $51.95, Two years; $15, Individuals first class mail; $10, Canada and Mexico.

19266 ■ *Wines & Vines*
Pub: Hiaring Co.
Contact: Chet Klingensmith, President
URL(s): www.winesandvines.com. **Ed:** Jim Gordon. **Released:** Monthly **Price:** $38, Individuals; $48, Canada and Mexico; $85, Other countries; $59, Two years USA.

VIDEOCASSETTES/ AUDIOCASSETTES

19267 ■ *Cheese 101*
International Dairy-Deli-Bakery Association (IDDBA)
PO Box 5528
Madison, WI 53705-0528
Ph: (608)310-5000
Fax: (608)238-6330
Co. E-mail: iddba@iddba.org
URL: http://www.iddba.org
Contact: Steve Beekhuizen, President
Released: 19??. **Price:** $50.00. **Description:** Discusses the high margin, high profit product, cheese and explains how they differ in taste and the qualities of 16 varieties. **Availability:** VHS.

19268 ■ *Cheese Classics of America*
International Dairy-Deli-Bakery Association (IDDBA)
PO Box 5528
Madison, WI 53705-0528
Ph: (608)310-5000
Fax: (608)238-6330
Co. E-mail: iddba@iddba.org
URL: http://www.iddba.org
Contact: Steve Beekhuizen, President
Released: 19??. **Price:** $100.00. **Description:** Merchandising and training video. **Availability:** VHS.

19269 ■ *International Cheese Classics*
International Dairy-Deli-Bakery Association (IDDBA)
PO Box 5528
Madison, WI 53705-0528
Ph: (608)310-5000
Fax: (608)238-6330
Co. E-mail: iddba@iddba.org
URL: http://www.iddba.org
Contact: Steve Beekhuizen, President
Released: 19??. **Price:** $100.00. **Description:** Merchandising and training video. **Availability:** VHS.

19270 ■ *Jancis Robinson's Wine Course*
Wellspring Media
A Division of Genius Products Inc.
25000 Ave. Stanford, Ste. 96
Valencia, CA 91355
Free: 800-514-1314
Fax: (800)861-3759
Co. E-mail: info@wellspring.com
URL: http://www.wellspring.com
Released: 1998. **Price:** $99.95. **Description:** Hosted by expert Jancis Robinson, editor of the Oxford Companion to Wine, this series gives the viewer a lighthearted introduction to the world of wine. Covers how wine is made, how to taste it and how to store it. Five hours on five videocassettes. **Availability:** DVD.

TRADE SHOWS AND CONVENTIONS

19271 ■ Dairy-Deli-Bake Seminar and Expo
International Dairy-Deli-Bakery Association (IDDBA)
PO Box 5528
Madison, WI 53705-0528
Ph: (608)310-5000

Fax: (608)238-6330
Co. E-mail: iddba@iddba.org
URL: http://www.iddba.org
Contact: Steve Beekhuizen, President
URL(s): www.iddba.org. **Frequency:** Annual. **Audience:** Retailers, wholesalers, distributors, and manufacturers of the dairy, deli, and bakery industry. **Principal Exhibits:** Dairy, deli, and bakery products, packaging, and equipment.

19272 ■ International Fancy Food and Confection Show/Winter
National Association for the Specialty Food Trade Inc.
8 W 40th St., 4th Fl.
New York, NY 10018-3901
Ph: (212)921-1690
Fax: (212)921-1898
URL(s): www.specialtyfood.com. **Frequency:** Annual. **Audience:** Retailers, brokers, importers, buyers, chefs, caterers and related personnel. **Principal Exhibits:** Pates, cheeses, specialty meats and seafood, condiments, sauces, mustards, vinegars, chocolates, fine candies, biscuits, cookies, cakes, jams, jellies, preserves, coffees, teas, fruits, nuts, special beverages, beer, wine, ice creams, desserts, and cooking accessories. **Dates and Locations:** Moscone Convention Center.

19273 ■ Ottawa Wine and Food Show
Player Expositions International
255 Clemow Ave.
Ottawa, ON, Canada K1S 2B5
Ph: (613)567-6408
Fax: (613)567-2718
URL: http://www.playerexpo.com
URL(s): www.playerexpo.com. **Frequency:** Annual. **Audience:** Restaurant, hotels, clubs, catering-fine food stores, specialty food stores, wine clubs, and the general public. **Principal Exhibits:** Fine wines and foods, and beer from around the world. **Dates and Locations:** Congress Centre. **Telecommunication Services:** wineshow@playerexpo.com.

FRANCHISES AND BUSINESS OPPORTUNITIES

19274 ■ Auntie Anne's Inc.
48-50 W Chestnut St., Ste. 200
Lancaster, PA 17603
Ph: (717)435-1479
Fax: (717)435-1471
Co. E-mail: LindaE@auntieannesinc.com
URL: http://www.auntieannesfranchising.com
Description: Serves fresh, hot hand-rolled soft pretzels. **No. of Franchise Units:** 1,150. **No. of Company-Owned Units:** 14. **Founded:** 1988.. **Franchised:** 1990. **Equity Capital Needed:** $197,875-$364,100. **Franchise Fee:** $30,000. **Training:** 2 week training program is provided for owners, including onsite training at time of store opening.

19275 ■ Blenz Coffee
535 Thurlow St., Ste. 300
Vancouver, BC, Canada V6E 3L2
Ph: (604)682-2995
Fax: (604)684-2542
Description: Coffee beverages and coffee beans. **No. of Franchise Units:** 25. **No. of Company-Owned Units:** 2. **Founded:** 1990.. **Franchised:** 1992. **Equity Capital Needed:** $30,000-$70,000 plus equity. **Training:** Yes.

19276 ■ Borvin Beverage
Borvin Beverage Franchise Corp.
1022 King St.
Alexandria, VA 22314
Fax: (703)836-6654
Description: Wine distribution and wholesale. **No. of Franchise Units:** 1. **No. of Company-Owned Units:** 1. **Founded:** 1992.. **Franchised:** 1994. **Equity Capital Needed:** $250,000 liquid assets; $50,000 net worth. **Franchise Fee:** $25,000-$75,000. **Training:** Yes.

19277 ■ Bulk Barn Foods Limited
55 Leek Crescent
Richmond Hill, ON, Canada L4B 3Y2

Ph: (905)886-6756
Fax: (905)886-3717
URL: http://www.bulkbarn.ca
Description: Specialized bulk retailer in Canada, offering bulk and packaged products, including a range of candy making, cake making and decorating, snacks, health foods, vitamins and supplements. **No. of Franchise Units:** 190. **Founded:** 1982.. **Franchised:** 1982. **Equity Capital Needed:** $600,000 minimum investment required; $150,000 plus start-up capital required. **Franchise Fee:** $35,000. **Training:** Start-up and onsite.

19278 ■ Cafe Fondue Franchise Systems Inc.
281 W 80th Pl.
Merrillville, IN 46410
Ph: (219)793-1511
Fax: (219)793-1511
Description: Fondue - specialty restaurant. **No. of Company-Owned Units:** 1. **Founded:** 1998.. **Franchised:** 2003. **Equity Capital Needed:** $136,000-$307,000. **Franchise Fee:** $35,000. **Royalty Fee:** 4%. **Training:** Provides 2 weeks training at headquarters and 2 weeks onsite.

19279 ■ Cena
12501 N Hwy. 395, Ste. 3
Spokane, WA 99218
Ph: (509)448-1725
Free: 888-667-2362
Fax: (509)448-9380
Description: Meal preparation/assembly center and wine shop. **No. of Franchise Units:** 10. **No. of Company-Owned Units:** 1. **Founded:** 2004.. **Franchised:** 2005. **Equity Capital Needed:** $148,400-$205,500; express/kiosk option available. **Franchise Fee:** $30,000. **Royalty Fee:** 5%. **Training:** Provides 4 days training at headquarters, 3 days onsite and ongoing support.

19280 ■ Crescent Wines
2255 King George Hwy., Ste. 108
Surrey, BC, Canada V4A 5A4
Ph: (604)542-0211
Co. E-mail: whiterock@crescentwines.com
URL: http://www.crescentwines.com
Description: Wine making. **No. of Franchise Units:** 2. **No. of Company-Owned Units:** 1. **Founded:** 1996.. **Equity Capital Needed:** $50,000-$75,000 liquid capital available. **Franchise Fee:** $20,000. **Training:** Offers full-training and ongoing support.

19281 ■ Desert Moon Fresh Mexican Grill
Desert Moon Franchise LLC
Description: Specializes in Mexican food delicacies. **No. of Franchise Units:** 15. **No. of Company-Owned Units:** 3. **Founded:** 1992.. **Franchised:** 1999. **Equity Capital Needed:** $350,000. **Franchise Fee:** $25,000. **Financial Assistance:** Yes. **Training:** Yes.

19282 ■ Entrees Made Easy
4858 E Baseline Rd., Ste. 104
Mesa, AZ 85206
Ph: (480)985-7900
Fax: (480)985-7909
Description: Meal preparation service. **No. of Franchise Units:** 21. **No. of Company-Owned Units:** 2. **Founded:** 2004.. **Franchised:** 2006. **Equity Capital Needed:** $172,800-$296,500. **Franchise Fee:** $30,000. **Royalty Fee:** 5%. **Training:** 1 week training at headquarters, 1 week onsite and ongoing support.

19283 ■ The Honeybaked Ham Co. and Cafe
The HBH Franchise Co. LLC
3875 Mansell Rd.
Alpharetta, GA 30022
Ph: (678)966-3254
Free: 866-968-7424
Fax: (678)966-3134
URL: http://www.honeybakedonline.com
Description: Specialty retailer of high quality spiral-sliced hams and turkeys. **No. of Franchise Units:** 183. **No. of Company-Owned Units:** 280. **Founded:** 1957.. **Franchised:** 1998. **Equity Capital Needed:**

$350,000 net worth with $100,000 available as equity contribution. **Franchise Fee:** $30,000. **Training:** Comprehensive 14 day program at corporate training store.

19284 ■ Pretzels Plus Inc.
639 Frederick St.
Hanover, PA 17331
Ph: (717)633-7927
Fax: (717)633-5078
Co. E-mail: beline@pretzelsplus.com
URL: http://www.pretzelsplus.com
Contact: Bradley L. Eline, President
Description: Soft pretzels. **No. of Franchise Units:** 24. **Founded:** 1991.. **Franchised:** 1992. **Equity Capital Needed:** $80,000. **Franchise Fee:** $12,000. **Training:** Yes.

19285 ■ Rosevine Winery
2424 N. Federal Hwy., Ste. 455
Boynton Beach, FL 33426
Ph: (561)416-9096
Fax: (561)416-9098
Description: Make-your-own-wine retail shops. **No. of Company-Owned Units:** 2. **Founded:** 2003.. **Franchised:** 2004. **Equity Capital Needed:** $246,000-$425,000. **Franchise Fee:** $35,000. **Royalty Fee:** 6%. **Training:** Offers 3-5 days training at franchisees location, 10 days at 1810 Winery and ongoing support.

19286 ■ Sushi Shop
MTY Group
3465 Thimens Blvd.
Montreal, QC, Canada H4R 1V5
Ph: (514)336-8885
Free: 866-891-6633
Fax: (514)336-9222
Co. E-mail: info@sushishop.com
URL: http://www.sushishop.com
Description: The franchise offers retail selling of products and by-products of Sushi. **No. of Franchise Units:** 117. **No. of Company-Owned Units:** 1. **Founded:** 2000.. **Franchised:** 2001. **Equity Capital Needed:** $175,000-$250,000 investment required; $75,000-$150,000 start-up capital required. **Franchise Fee:** $30,000. **Training:** Yes.

19287 ■ A Taste Above
120 Carlton St., Ste. 207
Toronto, ON, Canada M5A 4K2
Ph: (416)935-0050
Fax: (416)935-0463
Co. E-mail: info@atasteabove.com
URL: http://www.atasteabove.com
Description: Chef prepared gourmet cuisine prepared in our own kitchens vacuumed packed, cooler fresh in measured quantities of serving per pack for home and commercial use. **No. of Company-Owned Units:** 1. **Founded:** 2004.. **Franchised:** 2004. **Franchise Fee:** From $30,000. **Training:** Yes.

19288 ■ Vitner's Cellar Franchising International, Inc.
4020 Somers Dr.
Burton, MI 48529
Ph: (810)742-9463
Free: 800-480-7417
Fax: (810)743-9466
Co. E-mail: info@vintnerscellar.com
Description: Produce and sell wine onsite year round. **No. of Franchise Units:** 46. **No. of Company-Owned Units:** 1. **Founded:** 1993.. **Franchised:** 1994. **Equity Capital Needed:** $119,500-$191,000. **Franchise Fee:** $45,000. **Training:** Yes.

19289 ■ We're Rolling Pretzel Co.
WRPC Inc.
2500 W State St.
Alliance, OH 44601
Ph: (330)823-0575
Free: 888-549-7655
Fax: (330)821-9808
URL: http://www.wererolling.com
Description: Soft pretzel company. **No. of Franchise Units:** 27. **No. of Company-Owned Units:** 17. **Founded:** 1996.. **Franchised:** 2000. **Equity Capital Needed:** $74,000-$184,000. **Franchise Fee:**

$15,000. **Royalty Fee:** 5%. **Financial Assistance:** Third party financing available. **Training:** Offers 7 days at headquarters and 7 days onsite.

19290 ■ Wetzel's Pretzels
Wetzel's Pretzels, LLC
35 Hugus Alley, Ste. 300
Pasadena, CA 91103
Ph: (626)432-6900
Fax: (626)432-6904
Description: Pretzels. **No. of Franchise Units:** 253. **No. of Company-Owned Units:** 11. **Founded:** 1994.. **Franchised:** 1996. **Equity Capital Needed:** $156,300-$369,950. **Franchise Fee:** $35,000. **Royalty Fee:** 7%. **Training:** Offers 2 weeks at headquarters, 4 days at franchisee's location and ongoing support.

19291 ■ Wine Lovers, Inc.
387 Wellington Street
London, ON, Canada N6C 6A8
Ph: (519)913-2423
Fax: (519)471-1442
Co. E-mail: info@wineloversonline.com
URL: http://www.wineloversonline.com
Description: Wine Lovers has established a business model that allows potential franchise owners a 'Turn Key' operation that allows minimal investments with minimal risk. We have established suppliers, equipment and management training.

19292 ■ Wine Not Custom Wineries
380 Spring Gate Blvd.
Thornhill, ON, Canada L4J 4K6
Ph: (888)946-3668
Fax: (888)946-3668
Co. E-mail: sales@wineryfranchise.com
URL: http://www.winenotinternational.com
Description: Our wineries are full service, federally bonded wineries equipped with state of the art fermentation equipment, professional tasting bar & lounge areas. We also provide direct retail & wholesale sales, customized labeling & a unique customer participation experience. **No. of Franchise Units:** 9. **Founded:** 2002.. **Equity Capital Needed:** $125,000-$438,500; $200,000-$600,000 with bistro. **Franchise Fee:** $50,000. **Training:** Yes.

19293 ■ WineStyles Inc.
5100 W Copans Rd., Ste. 310
Margate, FL 33063
Ph: (954)984-0070
Fax: (954)984-0074
Description: Wine store. **No. of Franchise Units:** 180. **Founded:** 2002.. **Franchised:** 2002. **Equity Capital Needed:** $150,000. **Franchise Fee:** $25,000. **Training:** Yes.

19294 ■ ZamLows Sugarfree Low-Carb
ZamLows Franchising Company
222 Pitts Rd.
Friendship, TN 38034
Ph: (731)660-3045
Fax: (731)660-5612
Description: Low-carb grocery for diabetics and dieters. **No. of Company-Owned Units:** 1. **Founded:** 2001.. **Franchised:** 2004. **Equity Capital Needed:** $122,000-$247,000. **Franchise Fee:** $20,000. **Training:** Yes.

COMPUTERIZED DATABASES

19295 ■ Wine On Line
400 E 59th St., Ste. 9F
New York, NY 10022
Ph: (212)755-4363
Co. E-mail: info@punchin.com
URL: http://www.wineonline.net
Availability: Online: Wine On Line International; Punch In International Syndicate. **Type:** Directory; Transactional.

LIBRARIES

19296 ■ American Institute of Food Distribution, Inc. - Information and Research Center—The Food Institute.
1 Broadway Plaza, 2nd Fl.
Elmwood Park, NJ 07407

Ph: (201)791-5570
Fax: (201)791-5222
Co. E-mail: jkastrinsky@foodinstitute.com
URL: http://www.foodinstitute.com/
Contact: Brian Todd, President
Scope: Food industry. **Services:** Center open to the public on fee basis. **Founded:** 1928. **Subscriptions:** 400 journals and other serials. **Publications:** *Food Business Mergers and Acquisitions.* **Telecommunication Services:** food1@foodinstitute.com.

19297 ■ Napa Valley Wine Library Association Library
1492 Library Ln.
St. Helena, CA 94574-1143
Ph: (707)963-5244
Fax: (707)963-5264
Co. E-mail: director@shpl.org
URL: http://www.napawinelibrary.com/
Contact: Jennifer Baker, Director, Library Services
Scope: Grapes, viticulture, wine and winemaking. **Services:** Interlibrary loan; copying; Library open to the public. **Founded:** 1962. **Holdings:** 6000 books; 200 bound periodical volumes; 12 VF drawers; 99 reels of microfilm. **Subscriptions:** 55 journals and other serials. **Telecommunication Services:** allie@shpl.org; bobbie@shpl.org.

19298 ■ St. Joseph's University - Academy of Food Marketing - Campbell Library
157 Mandeville Hall
5600 City Ave.
Philadelphia, PA 19131
Ph: (610)PRF
Co. E-mail: sbennett@sju.edu
URL: http://www.sju.edu/int/academics/hsb/foodmarketing/academy/campbell.html
Contact: Sonia Bennett
Scope: Food marketing. **Services:** Interlibrary loan; copying; Library open to the public for reference use only (reciprocal privileges extended to food industry libraries and organizations). **Founded:** 1965. **Holdings:** 1500 books; 1650 bound periodical volumes; 200 items in corporation files; 256 reels of microfilm; journals and doctoral dissertations; 753 microfiche; 500 subject information files. **Subscriptions:** 320 journals and other serials.

19299 ■ University of California, Davis - University Libraries - Special Collections
100 NW Quad
Shields Library, 1st Fl.
Davis, CA 95616-5292
Ph: (530)752-1621
Fax: (916)754-5758
Co. E-mail: dmorrison@ucdavis.edu
URL: http://www.lib.ucdavis.edu/dept/specol/
Contact: Liz Phillips
Scope: Reference. **Services:** Copying; collections open to the public for reference use only. **Founded:** 1966. **Holdings:** 129,500 books; 18,700 lin.ft. of archives and manuscripts. **Subscriptions:** 40 journals and other serials; 2 newspapers. **Telecommunication Services:** speccoll@ucdavis.edu.

RESEARCH CENTERS

19300 ■ Texas Tech University - Texas Wine Marketing Research Institute (TWMRI)
PO Box 41162
Lubbock, TX 79409-1240
Ph: (806)742-3077
Fax: (806)742-3042
Co. E-mail: tim.dodd@ttu.edu
URL: http://www.depts.ttu.edu/hs/texaswine
Contact: Dr. Natalia Kolyesnikova, Associate Director
E-mail: n.kolyesnikova@ttu.edu
Founded: 1989. **Publications:** *Profile of the Texas Wine Industry* (Annual); *TWMRI Research articles; TWMRI Research reports.* **Awards:** TWMRI Assistantships (Annual), to students interested in wine marketing. **Telecommunication Services:** texaswine@ttu.edu.

**19301 ■ University of British Columbia -
Wine Research Centre (WRC)**
2205 E Mall
Faculty of Land & Food Systems
Vancouver, BC, Canada V6T 1Z4
Ph: (604)822-0005

Fax: (604)822-5143
Co. E-mail: hjjvv@interchange.ubc.ca
URL: http://www.landfood.ubc.ca/wine
Contact: Dr. Hennie J.J. van Vuuren, Director
Founded: 1999. **Awards:** WRC Postdoctoral fellowships, in molecular yeast genetics. **Telecommunication Services:** wine@interchange.ubc.ca.

START-UP INFORMATION

19302 ■ *The 100 Best Businesses to Start When You Don't Want To Work Hard Anymore*
Pub: Career Press Inc.
Ed: Lisa Rogak. **Price:** $16.99. **Description:** Author helps burned-out workers envision a new future as a small business owner. Systems analysis, adventure travel outfitting, bookkeeping, food delivery, furniture making, and software development are among the industries examined.

ASSOCIATIONS AND OTHER ORGANIZATIONS

19303 ■ **Association of Golf Merchandisers (AGM)**
PO Box 7247
Phoenix, AZ 85011-7247
Ph: (602)604-8250
Fax: (602)604-8251
Co. E-mail: info@agmgolf.org
URL: http://www.agmgolf.org
Contact: Desane Blaney, Executive Director
Description: Golf buyers and vendors. Dedicated to maximizing members' learning and earning capabilities. Conducts continuing educational programs; provides networking opportunities, scholarships and a forum for communication; compiles statistics. **Founded:** 1989. **Publications:** *AGM Merchandise Manual.* **Awards:** AGM Scholarship Fund (Annual).

19304 ■ **Athletic Equipment Managers Association (AEMA)**
460 Hunt Hill Rd.
Freeville, NY 13068
Ph: (607)539-6300
Fax: (607)539-6340
Co. E-mail: aema@frontiernet.net
URL: http://www.equipmentmanagers.org
Contact: Dorothy Cutting, Office Manager
Description: Athletic equipment managers and others who handle sports equipment for junior high and high schools, colleges, recreation centers, and professional sports; individuals involved in athletic management and coaching or the handling or purchasing of athletic, physical education, or recreational equipment. Aims to improve the profession of equipment management and promote a better working relationship among those interested in problems of management. Works collectively to facilitate equipment improvement for greater safety among participants in all sports. Conducts workshops and clinics. Maintains job placement service. **Founded:** 1974. **Publications:** *The Scoreboard* (3/year). **Awards:** Athletic Equipment Managers Association College Scholarships; College Scholarship; Glenn Sharp Award (Annual).

19305 ■ **Canadian Sporting Goods Association (CSGA)—Association Canadienne d'Articles de Sport**
300 rue du Sacrement St., Ste. 420
Montreal, QC, Canada H2Y 1X4
Ph: (514)393-1132
Free: 888-393-3002
Fax: (514)393-9513
Co. E-mail: csga@csga.ca
URL: http://csga.ca
Contact: Mr. Gord Cundell, President
Description: Sporting goods sales representatives, manufacturers, suppliers, distributors, retailers, and importers. Represents members' interests in international trade matters; functions as liaison between members and government agencies involved in the manufacture and trade of sporting goods. Conducts industry surveys; makes available discount programs and services to members. **Founded:** 1917. **Publications:** *CSGA Info-Bulletin Newsletter* (Weekly); *CSGA Sport-Trade Directory.* **Educational Activities:** Hockey and Sports Show (Annual). **Awards:** Jack Cooper Lifetime Achievement Award (Annual); Jack Cooper Lifetime Achievement Award.

19306 ■ *CSGA Info-Bulletin Newsletter*
300 rue du Saint-Sacrement St., Ste. 420
Montreal, QC, Canada H2Y 1X4
Ph: (514)393-1132
Free: 888-393-3002
Fax: (514)393-9513
Co. E-mail: csga@csga.ca
URL: http://csga.ca
Contact: Mr. Gord Cundell, President
Released: Weekly

19307 ■ *CSGA Sport-Trade Directory*
300 rue du Saint-Sacrement St., Ste. 420
Montreal, QC, Canada H2Y 1X4
Ph: (514)393-1132
Free: 888-393-3002
Fax: (514)393-9513
Co. E-mail: csga@csga.ca
URL: http://csga.ca
Contact: Mr. Gord Cundell, President

19308 ■ **National Ski and Snowboard Retailers Association (NSSRA)**
1601 Feehanville Dr., Ste. 300
Mount Prospect, IL 60056-6035
Ph: (847)391-9825
Free: 888-257-1168
Fax: (847)391-9827
Co. E-mail: info@nssra.com
URL: http://www.nssra.com
Contact: Thomas B. Doyle, President
E-mail: tdoyle@nssra.com
Description: Ski & snowboard stores. Represents the interests of members and provides services beneficial to their businesses. Compiles statistics. **Founded:** 1987. **Publications:** *NSSRA Newsletter* (Quarterly); *NSSRA Newsletter.*

19309 ■ **National Sporting Goods Association (NSGA)**
1601 Feehanville Dr., Ste. 300
Mount Prospect, IL 60056
Ph: (847)296-6742
Free: 800-815-5422
Fax: (847)391-9827
Co. E-mail: info@nsga.org
URL: http://www.nsga.org
Contact: Matt Carlson, President
E-mail: mcarlson@nsga.org
Description: Provides services, education and information to assist member to profit in a competitive marketplace. **Founded:** 1929. **Publications:** *NSGA Buying Guide* (Annual); *NSGA Buying Guide* (Annual); *Sports Participation-Series I & II* (Annual); *National Sporting Goods Association--Buying Guide* (Annual); *NSGA Sports Retailer--Store Equipment and Services Directory Issue*; *Cost of Doing Business Survey*; *The Team Line-Up*; *NSGA Retail Focus* (Bimonthly). **Educational Activities:** Management Conference and Team Dealer Summit (Annual). **Telecommunication Services:** nsga1699@aol.com.

19310 ■ **Professional Paddlesports Association (PPA)**
2700 Flat Creek Valley Road
Lake Toxaway, NC 28747-9552
Ph: (828)577-2484
Fax: (828)966-4716
Co. E-mail: dwhitmire@atspropaddle.com
URL: http://www.propaddle.com
Contact: Don Roberts, Chairman
Description: Renters and outfitters of canoes, kayaks, and rafts; manufacturers and distributors of equipment and products. Promotes safety in non-power watercraft; seeks to protect the nation's waterways and the rights of the public to use them. Provides members with legislative representation; on-water liability insurance; member service programs; certification courses; and professional development. **Founded:** 1978. **Educational Activities:** National Waterways (Annual). **Awards:** Environmental Excellence (Annual); Frank A. Jones Memorial (Annual).

19311 ■ **Soccer Industry Council of America (SICA)**
c/o Sporting Goods Manufacturers Association
8505 Fenton St., Ste. 211
Silver Spring, MD 20910
Ph: (301)495-6321
Fax: (301)495-6322
Co. E-mail: info@sgma.com
URL: http://www.sgma.com
Contact: Tom Cove, President
Description: Subsidiary organization of the Sporting Goods Manufacturers Association. Manufacturers, suppliers, and retailers of soccer apparel, footwear and equipment; others involved in the soccer industry. Promotes the growth of soccer in the U.S. Supports grassroots programs that offer playing opportunities to economically-disadvantaged youth, as well as the physically and mentally handicapped. Publishes statistical abstract and overview of the American soccer marketplace. **Founded:** 1985. **Publications:** *National Soccer Participation Survey* (Annual); *Retail Soccer USA*; *Soccer in the USA.* **Educational Activities:** Leadership Conference (Annual); Soccer Industry Council of America Seminar.

19312 ■ Sporting Goods Manufacturers Association (SGMA)
8505 Fenton St., Ste. 211
Silver Spring, MD 20910
Ph: (301)495-6321
Fax: (301)495-6322
Co. E-mail: info@sgma.com
URL: http://www.sgma.com
Contact: Tom Cove, President
Description: Manufacturers of athletic clothing, footwear, and sporting goods. Seeks to increase sports participation and create growth in the sporting goods industry. Owns and operates the largest sports products trade show in the world. **Founded:** 1906. **Publications:** SGMA Recreation Market Report (Periodic); Sports Edge NewsWire (Semiweekly); American Sports Data Analysis Participation Summary Report (Periodic). **Educational Activities:** Retail Summit (Annual); The Super Show.

19313 ■ Trade Association of Paddlesports (TAPS)
11781 A. Watertank Rd.
Burlington, WA 98233
Ph: (559)340-8277
Co. E-mail: info@gopaddle.org
URL: http://www.gopaddle.org
Contact: Mr. Tim Rosenhan, President
Description: Manufacturers, retailers, outfitters, importers and liveries of paddlesports equipment. Seeks to support, encourage and promote the paddlesports trade in North America. Provides information and referrals on sources of insurance for paddlesports businesses; undertakes research projects; develops and maintains safety, warning and product performance standards; conducts statistical surveys; co-organized the National River Cleanup Week; conducts educational programs; lobbies on behalf of the industry. **Founded:** 1998. **Educational Activities:** Paddlesports Symposia (Annual).

19314 ■ Water Sports Industry Association (WSIA)
PO Box 568512
Orlando, FL 32856-8512
Ph: (407)251-9039
Fax: (407)251-9039
Co. E-mail: info@wsia.net
URL: http://www.wsia.net
Contact: Jim Emmons, President
Description: Manufacturers and distributors of water sports equipment including skis, boats, wet suits, and towlines. Regular members are manufacturers and importers whose revenues are primarily derived from the water sports industry; associate members are firms with sales and manufacturing interests not primarily directed towards watersports. Monitors legislation affecting the water sports industry and keeps manufacturers and distributors informed of such action. Promotes the sports of water skiing, wakeboarding, kneeboarding, tubing and riding personal watercraft. **Founded:** 1986. **Awards:** Dealer of the Year (Annual).

REFERENCE WORKS

19315 ■ "Adidas' Brand Ambitions" in Business Journal Portland (Vol. 27, December 10, 2010, No. 41, pp. 1)
Pub: Portland Business Journal
Ed: Erik Siemers. **Description:** Adidas AG, the second-largest sporting goods brand in the world, hopes to increase global revenue by 50 percent by 2015. The German company, which reported $14.5 billion sales, plans to improve its U.S. market. The U.S. is Adidas' largest, but also the most underperforming market for the firm.

19316 ■ "Always Striving" in Women In Business (Vol. 61, December 2009, No. 6, pp. 28)
Pub: American Business Women's Association
Ed: Kathleen Leighton. **Description:** Jennifer Mull discusses her responsibilities and how she attained success as CEO of Backwoods, a gear and clothing store founded by her father in 1973. She places importance on being true to one's words and beliefs, while emphasizing the capacity to tolerate risks in

business. Mull defines success as an evolving concept and believes there must always be something to strive for.

19317 ■ "Arizona Firms In Chicago Go For Gold With '08 Games" in The Business Journal - Serving Phoenix and the Valley of the Sun (Vol. 28, August 8, 2008, No. 49, pp. 1)
Pub: American City Business Journals, Inc.
Ed: Patrick O'Grady. **Description:** More than 20 U.S. athletes will wear Arizona-based eSoles LLC's custom-made insoles to increase their performance at the 2008 Beijing Olympics making eSoles one of the beneficiaries of the commercialization of the games. Translation software maker Auralog Inc saw a 60 percent jump in sales from its Mandarin Chinese language applications.

19318 ■ "Athletes' Performance Building $10 Million Facility In ASU Park" in The Business Journal - Serving Phoenix and the Valley of the Sun (Vol. 28, August 8, 2008, No. 49, pp. 1)
Pub: American City Business Journals, Inc.
Ed: Jan Buchholz. **Description:** Athletes' Performance's planned facility at Arizona State University is scheduled to begin in November 2008 and expected to be completed by September 2009. The new building will almost double the company's training space as it will expand from around 19,000 square feet to 35,000 square feet.

19319 ■ "Buck-ing the Trend?" in Baltimore Business Journal (Vol. 28, August 13, 2010, No. 14, pp. 1)
Pub: Baltimore Business Journal
Ed: Gary Haber. **Description:** Baltimore Orioles' new manager Buck Showalter has managed to win games for fans. However, not all businesses around Camden Yards were boosted by the Orioles' surge as street vendors complained of worsening business.

19320 ■ "Cabela's Repays Incentives as Sales Lag" in Business Journal-Milwaukee (Vol. 28, November 19, 2010, No. 7, pp. A1)
Pub: Milwaukee Business Journal
Ed: Stacy Vogel Davis. **Description:** Cabela's has given back $266,000 to the government of Wisconsin owing to its failure to meet projected revenue goals for its Richfield, Wisconsin store. It has also failed to meet sales tax and hiring projection. The company received $4 million in incentives from Washington County.

19321 ■ "Can the State Afford a Big Time College Football Program?" in Hawaii Business (Vol. 53, March 2008, No. 9, pp. 26)
Pub: Hawaii Business Publishing
Description: Jill Nunokawa, civil rights at University of Hawaii, believes that athletics are extra-curricular and that the state needs to focus on priorities. State representative K. Mark Takai says that a football program brings pride and inspiration and can generate revenue and provide economic opportunities.

19322 ■ "Chiefs Hope Renovations Score Big With Sponsors" in The Business Journal-Serving Metropolitan Kansas City (Vol. 26, July 11, 2008)
Pub: American City Business Journals, Inc.
Ed: James Dornbrook. **Description:** Kansas City Chiefs officials expect to obtain 12 to 14 new major sponsors with the completion of the Arrowhead Stadium renovations. The new sponsorship opportunities will include naming rights for the stadium and practice facility. The team's marketing strategies are discussed.

19323 ■ "Design program in Athletic Footwear" in Occupational Outlook Quarterly (Vol. 55, Fall 2011, No. 3, pp. 21)
Pub: U.S. Bureau of Labor Statistics
Description: The Fashion Institute of Technology offers the only certificate program in performance athletic footwear design in the U.S. The program focuses on conceptualizing and sketching shoe designs and covers ergonomic, anatomical, and material considerations for athletic footwear design.

19324 ■ "Fight Against Fake" in The Business Journal-Portland (Vol. 25, July 18, 2008, No. 19, pp. 1)
Pub: American City Business Journals, Inc.
Ed: Erik Siemers. **Description:** Companies, such as Columbia Sportswear Co. and Nike Inc., are fighting the counterfeiting of their sportswear and footwear products through the legal process of coordinating with law enforcement agencies to raid factories. Most of the counterfeiting factories are in China and India. Other details on the issue are discussed.

19325 ■ "Fledgling Brands May Take the Fall With Steve & Barry's" in Advertising Age (Vol. 79, July 7, 2008, No. 26, pp. 6)
Pub: Crain Communications, Inc.
Ed: Natalie Zmuda. **Description:** Steve & Barry's, a retailer that holds licensing deals with a number of designers and celebrities, may have to declare bankruptcy; this leaves the fate of the retailer's hundreds of licensing deals and exclusive celebrity lines in question.

19326 ■ "Great Expectations" in Canadian Business (Vol. 81, April 14, 2008, No. 6, pp. 34)
Pub: Rogers Media
Ed: Andy Holloway. **Description:** Therma Blades Inc. says that the reports that say their Therma Blade ice skates were not working properly were inaccurate. The major mistake of the company was to fail to manage the public's expectation when they touted the blades as revolutionary. Therma Blades Inc. has since tested the product with the help of 120 players and physiological testing done on elite level players show that there was a 10 percent improvement in energy efficiency.

19327 ■ "Hitting the Green" in Canadian Business (Vol. 81, July 22, 2008, No. 12-13, pp. 34)
Pub: Rogers Media Ltd.
Ed: Andy Holloway. **Description:** RBC is sponsoring the Canadian Open golf tournament, which is the second-oldest event in the PGA Tour. RBC is expected to receive television exposure on CBS and the Golf Channel. Additional information relating to the sponsorship is presented.

19328 ■ "HOK Sport May Build Own Practice" in The Business Journal-Serving Metropolitan Kansas City (Vol. 26, August 29, 2008, No. 51, pp. 1)
Pub: American City Business Journals, Inc.
Ed: Rob Roberts. **Description:** HOK Sport Venue Event is considering a spin-off from its parent company, HOK Group Inc. HOK Sport spokeswoman Gina Leo confirms that the firm is exploring structures, including a management buyout. Some of HOK Sport Venue Event's Minnesota projects are discussed.

19329 ■ "An Ice Boost in Revenue; Wings Score With Expanded Corporate Sales" in Crain's Detroit Business (Vol. 25, June 1, 2009, No. 22)
Pub: Crain Communications Inc. - Detroit
Ed: Bill Shea. **Description:** Stanley Cup finals always boost business for the Detroit area, even during a recession. The Red Wings corporate office reported corporate sponsorship revenue luxury suite rentals, Legends Club seats and advertising were up 40 percent this year over 2008.

19330 ■ "Insider" in Canadian Business (Vol. 80, Winter 2007, No. 24, pp.)
Pub: Rogers Media
Ed: Zena Olijnyk. **Description:** Lululemon Athletica started in 1998 after Dennis Wilson takes a yoga class and notices a demand from women for breathable clothes. The company opened their first outlet in Vancouver in November 2000 then opened their first U.S. store in 2003 until finally going public July 27, 2007 where its stocks doubled in value within days of trading.

19331 ■ "It's a New Game: Killerspin Pushes Table Tennis to Extreme Heights" in Black

Enterprise (Vol. 37, October 2006, No. 3, pp. 73)
Pub: Earl G. Graves Publishing Co. Inc.
Ed: Bridget McCrea. **Description:** Profile of Robert Blackwell and his company Killerspin L.L.C., which is popularizing the sport of table tennis. Killerspin has hit $1 million in revenues due to product sales primarily generated through the company's website, magazines, DVDs, and event ticket sales.

19332 ■ *"Lawyers Sued Over Lapsed Lacrosse Patent" in Crain's Detroit Business (Vol. 25, June 8, 2009, No. 23, pp. 5)*
Pub: Crain Communications Inc. - Detroit
Ed: Chad Halcom. **Description:** Warrior Sports Inc., a manufacturer of lacrosse equipment located in Warren, Michigan is suing the law firm Dickinson Wright PLLC and two of its intellectual property lawyers over patent rights to lacrosse equipment.

19333 ■ *"Marathon Money" in Hawaii Business (Vol. 53, December 2007, No. 6, pp. 127)*
Pub: Hawaii Business Publishing
Ed: Jolyn Okimoto Rosa. **Description:** Discusses the effects of the Honolulu Marathon on small businesses' sales. The Running Room, for instance, experience growth in sales starting from the training season up to the end of the race, as a surge of Hawaiian residents and tourists come into the store for items such as running shoes and blister kits. The marathon's impact on Hawaii's tourism is examined as well.

19334 ■ *"NFL Labor, Legal Issues Hang Over Detroit Lions' Rebuilding Efforts" in Crain's Detroit Business (Vol. 26, January 11, 2010, No. 2)*
Pub: Crain Communications Inc.
Ed: Bill Shea. **Description:** Overview of the possible outcomes regarding labor talks with Detroit Lion's players as well as the outcome of a U.S. Supreme Court decision that could boost franchise values but at the expense of fans and corporate sponsors.

19335 ■ *"Nike's Next Splash" in The Business Journal-Portland (Vol. 25, August 22, 2008, No. 24, pp. 1)*
Pub: American City Business Journals, Inc.
Ed: Erik Siemers. **Description:** Business analysts expect Nike to bid for the endorsement services of swimmer Michael Phelps after the swimmer's contract with Speedo expires. The company, however, is a lightweight in the swimming apparel market and is not focusing on swimming as a growth sector.

19336 ■ *"One Paddle, Two Paddle" in Hawaii Business (Vol. 53, October 2007, No. 4, pp. 65)*
Pub: Hawaii Business Publishing
Ed: Kyle Galdeira. **Description:** Oiwi Ocean Gear's strategy may not give instant profits, but it works well for the company's goal of providing high-quality apparel for paddlers. The apparel company produces and markets swimwear, paddling jerseys and active wear. The company's strategy is compared with the selling of mass-produced clothes lower prices.

19337 ■ *"Packers Still Want Marketing Deal With Favre" in The Business Journal-Milwaukee (Vol. 25, August 15, 2008, No. 47, pp. A1)*
Pub: American City Business Journals, Inc.
Ed: Mark Kass. **Description:** The Green Bay Packers plan to offer a $20 million marketing agreement to quarterback Brett Favre, including a clothing, merchandise, and collectibles line. The team is pursuing the agreement despite trading Favre to the New York Jets on 6 August 2008.

19338 ■ *"Portland Wooing Under Armour to West Coast Facility" in Baltimore Business Journal (Vol. 27, January 29, 2010, No. 39, pp. 1)*
Pub: American City Business Journals
Ed: Andy Giegerich. **Description:** Baltimore, Maryland sports apparel maker, Under Armour, is planning a west coast expansion with Portland, Oregon among the sites considered to house its apparel and footwear

design center. Portland officials counting on the concentration of nearly 10,000 activewear workers in the city will help lure the company to the city.

19339 ■ *"Recovery on Tap for 2010?" in Orlando Business Journal (Vol. 26, January 1, 2010, No. 31, pp. 1)*
Pub: American City Business Journals
Ed: Melanie Stawicki Azam, Richard Bilbao, Christopher Boyd, Anjali Fluker. **Description:** Economic forecasts for Central Florida's leading business sectors in 2010 are presented. These sectors include housing, film and TV, sports business, law, restaurants, aviation, tourism and hospitality, banking and finance, commercial real estate, retail, health care, insurance, higher education, and manufacturing. According to some local executives, Central Florida's economy will slowly recover in 2010.

19340 ■ *"Retail Center Pitched" in Business Courier (Vol. 27, June 18, 2010, No. 7, pp. 1)*
Pub: Business Courier
Ed: Dan Monk. **Description:** Jeffrey R. Anderson Real Estate Inc.'s plan for a retail center in Butler County, Ohio could have three department stores in the 1.1 million-square-foot property. An outdoor sports retailer is also part of the plans.

19341 ■ *"Sabathia Deal Makes Dollars and Sense" in The Business Journal-Milwaukee (Vol. 25, July 11, 2008, No. 42, pp. A1)*
Pub: American City Business Journals, Inc.
Ed: Mark Kass. **Description:** It was reported that the Milwaukee Brewers' acquisition of CC Sabathia will mean that the team will pick up an estimated $5 million in salary that Sabathia is owed for the remainder of the season. Because of this, the team will not make a profit in 2008. The acquisition of Sabathia is expected to cause an increase in attendance and merchandise revenue over the remainder of the season.

19342 ■ *"Sheets Energy Strips Unveils New Vending Machines" in Food and Beverage Close-Up (August 12, 2011)*
Pub: Close-Up Media
Description: Sheets Energy Strips is installing vending machines in malls, office buildings, stadiums and arenas in New York, New Jersey, Connecticut and Florida. These machines will offer 4 packs, 10 packs and Sheets branded hats and T-shirts.

19343 ■ *Sporting Goods and Activewear Buyers*
Pub: Briefings Media Group
Contact: Alan M. Douglas, President
E-mail: adouglas@douglaspublications.com
URL(s): www.salesmansguide.comwww.douglaspublications.com. Ed: Patrick Snyder. **Released:** Annual; Latest edition 2004-2005 edition. **Price:** $1299, Individuals CD-ROM. **Covers:** 18,400 buyers and 10,700 stores in the sporting goods and activewear industry, covering the United States, Puerto Rico, the Virgin Islands, and Canada. **Entries include:** Store name, address, phone, fax; e-mail; URL; names and titles of key personnel; financial data; branch/subsidiary name and address; products and/or services provided; sales volume; type of store; number of stores; buying groups. **Arrangement:** Geographical. **Indexes:** Store name, new listings, mail order, buying group, online retailer.

19344 ■ *"Surfing's Next Safari" in Entrepreneur (Vol. 37, July 2009, No. 7, pp. 24)*
Pub: Entrepreneur Media, Inc.
Ed: Dennis Romero. **Description:** Profile of Firewire Surfboards, a San Diego-based maker of lightweight surfboards, aims to capture surfing enthusiasts' attention with its use of unusual and high-tech materials. Firewire's biggest challenge is the preference for old-school surfboards, but the company is determined to revolutionize how surfboards should be made. The company's various innovations and experiences are also discussed.

19345 ■ *"Tigers Put to Test; Can Team Win Back Fans, Advertisers?" in Crain's Detroit*

Business (Vol. 24, October 6, 2008, No. 40, pp. 1)
Pub: Crain Communications, Inc.
Ed: Bill Shea. **Description:** Despite the enormous amount of money the Detroit Tigers' owner Mike Ilitch spent on player salaries, a record $137.6 million this season, the team finished in last-place; ticket sales and advertising dollars for next season are expected to fall dramatically. Additional speculation regarding the future of the ball team is included.

19346 ■ *"To the Extreme" in Entrepreneur (Vol. 36, February 2008, No. 2, pp. 21)*
Pub: Entrepreneur Media Inc.
Ed: Lindsay Holloway. **Description:** Extreme sports are increasing in number, with companies seeing the market potential of these sports for the 10- to 30-year-old age group. Entrepreneurs are launching innovated products catering to extreme sports-related markets. Details on the opportunities provided by the growth of extreme sports are discussed.

19347 ■ *"Under Armour Wants to Equip Athletes, Too" in Boston Business Journal (Vol. 29, July 8, 2011, No. 9, pp. 1)*
Pub: American City Business Journals Inc.
Ed: Ryan Sharrow. **Description:** Baltimore sportswear maker Under Armour advances plans to enter into the equipment field, aiming to strengthen its hold on football, basketball and lacrosse markets where it already has a strong market share. The company is now cooking up licensing deals to bolster the firm's presence among athletes.

19348 ■ *"Viewing Ironman As Gold, R.I. Firm Buys Its Parent" in The Business Journal-Serving Greater Tampa Bay (Vol. 28, September 19, 2008)*
Pub: American City Business Journals, Inc.
Ed: Pete Williams. **Description:** Providence Equity Partners purchased World Triathlon Corp., parent company of the Ironman Triathlon, for an undisclosed sum. The acquisition means that the World Triathlon Headquarters will move to Tampa, Florida, and allows Providence Equity Partners to stage or license rights to Ironman and half-Ironman distance events.

19349 ■ *"What Players in the Midmarket Are Talking About" in Mergers & Acquisitions: The Dealmaker's Journal (March 1, 2008)*
Pub: SourceMedia, Inc.
Description: Sports Properties Acquisition Corp. went public at the end of January; according to the company's prospectus, it is not limiting its focus to just teams, it is also considering deals for stadium construction companies, sports leagues, facilities, sports-related advertising and licensing of products, in addition to other related segments.

STATISTICAL SOURCES

19350 ■ *RMA Annual Statement Studies*
Pub: Risk Management Association
Contact: Kevin M. Blakey, President
Released: Annual. **Price:** $175.00 2006-07 edition, $105.00. **Description:** Contains composite balance sheets and income statements for more than 360 industries, including the accounting, auditing, and bookkeeping industries. Also contains five years of comparative historical data for discerning trends. Includes 16 commonly used ratios, computed for most of the size groupings for nearly every industry.

TRADE PERIODICALS

19351 ■ *Mountainwest Golf*
Pub: Harris Publishing Inc.
URL(s): mountainwestgolf.com/. **Ed:** Steve Smeed. **Released:** Quarterly **Price:** $8.95, Individuals; $15.95, Two years; $21.95, Individuals 3 years; $28.95, Other countries; $55.95, Other countries 2 years; $81.95, Other countries 3 years; $23.95, Canada; $45.95, Canada 2 years; $66.95, Canada 3 years.

19352 ■ *NSSRA Newsletter*
Pub: National Ski and Snowboard Retailers Association
Contact: Thomas B. Doyle, President
E-mail: tdoyle@nssra.com
Released: Quarterly. **Price:** Included in membership. **Description:** Informs ski and snowboard retail stores

on critical industry issues such as guidelines and litigation exposure and marketing.

19353 ■ *Out Your Backdoor*
Pub: Out Your Backdoor
URL(s): www.outyourbackdoor.com. **Ed:** Jeff Potter.
Released: Monthly

19354 ■ *Sporting Goods Dealer: The Voice of Team Dealers Since 1899*
Pub: Bill Communications Inc.
URL(s): www.sgdealer.com/sportinggoodsdealer/index.jsp. **Released:** Bimonthly

19355 ■ *The Team Line-Up*
Pub: National Sporting Goods Association
Contact: Matt Carlson, President
E-mail: mcarlson@nsga.org
Ed: Thomas B. Doyle, Editor, tdoyle@nsga.org. **Released:** Quarterly. **Price:** Included in membership. **Description:** Intended for member athletic team distributors who specialize in supplying equipment to high schools, colleges, and organized teams. Monitors athletic rule-making bodies and carries articles on such topics as safety and sports equipment and the liability of sports equipment manufacturers in lawsuits concerning sports injuries. Recurring features include notices of rules changes and rules committee meetings.

19356 ■ *USA Table Tennis Magazine*
Pub: U.S.A. Table Tennis
Contact: Larry Hodges, Executive Director
E-mail: larry@larrytt.com
Released: Bimonthly. **Price:** $20, Included in membership. **Description:** Covers the sport of table tennis.

VIDEOCASSETTES/ AUDIOCASSETTES

19357 ■ *Air Raid*
Tapeworm Video Distributors
25876 The Old Road #141
Stevenson Ranch, CA 91381
Ph: (661)257-4904
Fax: (661)257-4820
Co. E-mail: sales@tapeworm.com
URL: http://www.tapeworm.com
Released: 19??. **Price:** $19.95. **Description:** Exciting aerial feats in motorcross, snowboarding, surfing, skateboarding, wakeboarding, and BMX racing. **Availability:** VHS.

19358 ■ *The Best of Golf in Paradise*
Tapeworm Video Distributors
25876 The Old Road #141
Stevenson Ranch, CA 91381
Ph: (661)257-4904
Fax: (661)257-4820
Co. E-mail: sales@tapeworm.com
URL: http://www.tapeworm.com
Released: 1996. **Price:** $19.95. **Description:** Johnny Bench presents resort destinations, celebrity bloopers, instruction, tips, and golf gadgets. **Availability:** VHS.

19359 ■ *Coach Curry's Quarterback Clinic: Developing the Quarterback*
Karol Media
Hanover Industrial Estates
375 Stewart Rd.
Wilkes Barre, PA 18773-7600
Ph: (570)822-8899
Free: 800-526-4773
Co. E-mail: sales@karolmedia.com
URL: http://www.karolmedia.com
Released: 1997. **Price:** $19.95. **Description:** Provides football drills and instruction **Availability:** VHS.

19360 ■ *The Coach's 10 Commandments of Positive Athletic Parenting*
Karol Media
Hanover Industrial Estates
375 Stewart Rd.
Wilkes Barre, PA 18773-7600
Ph: (570)822-8899

Free: 800-526-4773
Co. E-mail: sales@karolmedia.com
URL: http://www.karolmedia.com
Released: 1997. **Price:** $12.95. **Description:** Coach George Curry explains to parents how to give positive support to their kids, the team, and to coaches, and how to avoid negative behavior. **Availability:** VHS.

19361 ■ *How to Be the Kid with the Perfect Swing*
Tapeworm Video Distributors
25876 The Old Road #141
Stevenson Ranch, CA 91381
Ph: (661)257-4904
Fax: (661)257-4820
Co. E-mail: sales@tapeworm.com
URL: http://www.tapeworm.com
Released: 19??. **Price:** $19.95. **Description:** Dave Griffin's Baseball School presents basic techniques to "hit like a pro.". **Availability:** VHS.

19362 ■ *Playing and Coaching Winning Baseball and Softball*
Karol Media
Hanover Industrial Estates
375 Stewart Rd.
Wilkes Barre, PA 18773-7600
Ph: (570)822-8899
Free: 800-526-4773
Co. E-mail: sales@karolmedia.com
URL: http://www.karolmedia.com
Released: 1997. **Price:** $19.95. **Description:** Instruction and guidance for little league coaches. **Availability:** VHS.

19363 ■ *Space Cowboys: Dysfunctional Superheroes II*
Tapeworm Video Distributors
25876 The Old Road #141
Stevenson Ranch, CA 91381
Ph: (661)257-4904
Fax: (661)257-4820
Co. E-mail: sales@tapeworm.com
URL: http://www.tapeworm.com
Released: 1997. **Price:** $14.95. **Description:** Presents footage of snowboarders, skateboarders, and freestyle BMX riders. **Availability:** VHS.

19364 ■ *Steep Snow*
Keen Media
857 Pulpit Rock Circle N.
Colorado Springs, CO 80918
Ph: (719)593-2155
Free: 800-363-5336
Fax: (719)593-2888
Co. E-mail: jim@keenmedia.com
URL: http://www.keenmedia.com
Released: 19??. **Price:** $34.95. **Description:** Provides instruction on techniques, equipment, and weather and terrain for hunters, hikers, skiers, and others finding it necessary to cross steep snow. **Availability:** VHS.

TRADE SHOWS AND CONVENTIONS

19365 ■ **American Alliance for Health, Physical Education, Recreation, and Dance - National Conference and Exposition**
American Alliance for Health, Physical Education, Recreation and Dance (AAHPERD)
1900 Association Dr.
Reston, VA 20191-1598
Ph: (703)476-3400
Free: 800-213-7193
Fax: (703)476-9527
Co. E-mail: membership@aahperd.org
URL: http://www.aahperd.org
Contact: Ang Chen, President
URL(s): www.aahperd.org. **Frequency:** Annual. **Audience:** Health and physical education teachers, coaches, athletic directors, trainers, officials, dance teachers, and related professionals and students. **Principal Exhibits:** Physical educational sporting

goods, supplies, equipment, publishers, and service organization representatives. **Telecommunication Services:** conv@aahperd.org.

19366 ■ **Annual Allegheny Sport, Travel and Outdoor Show**
International Sport Show Producers Association (IS-SPA)
PO Box 480084
Denver, CO 80248-0084
Ph: (303)892-6800
Free: 800-457-2434
Fax: (303)892-6322
Co. E-mail: dseymour@iei-expos.com
URL: http://www.sportshow.org
Contact: Jeff Haughton, President
URL(s): www.sportandtravel.com/pittsburgh/. **Frequency:** Annual. **Principal Exhibits:** Sports, travel and outdoor show. **Dates and Locations:** Expomart. **Telecommunication Services:** expoinc@expoinc.com.

19367 ■ **Annual Reading Sport, Travel and Outdoor Show**
International Sport Show Producers Association (IS-SPA)
PO Box 480084
Denver, CO 80248-0084
Ph: (303)892-6800
Free: 800-457-2434
Fax: (303)892-6322
Co. E-mail: dseymour@iei-expos.com
URL: http://www.sportshow.org
Contact: Jeff Haughton, President
URL(s): www.phillysportshow.com. **Frequency:** Annual. **Audience:** Greater Washington DC area. **Principal Exhibits:** Sports, travel and outdoor show. **Telecommunication Services:** info@sportshows.com.

19368 ■ **Annual Rockford RV, Camping and Travel Show**
International Sport Show Producers Association (IS-SPA)
PO Box 480084
Denver, CO 80248-0084
Ph: (303)892-6800
Free: 800-457-2434
Fax: (303)892-6322
Co. E-mail: dseymour@iei-expos.com
URL: http://www.sportshow.org
Contact: Jeff Haughton, President
URL(s): www.showtimeproduction.net/rvshow/. **Frequency:** Annual. **Principal Exhibits:** RVs, camping and travel. **Telecommunication Services:** brenda@showtimeproduction.net.

19369 ■ **Asiafit**
Neway International Trade Fairs Ltd.
9/F, Fortis Tower
77 Gloucester Rd.
Wan Chai, China
Ph: 852 2561 5566
Fax: 852 2811 9156
Co. E-mail: info@newayfairs.com
URL: http://www.newayfairs.com
URL(s): www.newayfairs.com/asiafit. **Frequency:** Annual. **Principal Exhibits:** Asia fitness equipment, sporting goods & facilities.

19370 ■ **Cincinnati Travel, Sports, and Boat Show**
Hart Productions, Inc.
322 E. Main St.
Batavia, OH 45103
Ph: (513)797-7900
Free: 877-704-8190
Fax: (513)797-1013
URL: http://www.hartproductions.com
URL(s): www.hartproductions.com. **Price:** $11, Onsite. **Frequency:** Annual. **Audience:** General public. **Principal Exhibits:** Showcasing a world of travel and recreation featuring vacation travel exhibits, boats, sporting goods, fishing and hunting equipment and seminars. **Dates and Locations:** , Dr. Albert B. Sabin Convention Center. **Telecommunication Services:** chip@hartproductions.com.

19371 ■ Detroit Boat Show

Michigan Boating Industries Association
32398 5 Mile Rd.
Livonia, MI 48154-6109
Ph: (734)261-0123
Free: 800-932-2628
Fax: (734)261-0880
Co. E-mail: boatmichigan@mbia.org
URL: http://www.mbia.org
Contact: John J. Ropp, President
E-mail: jropp@mbia.org
URL(s): www.mbia.org. **Price:** $12, adult; children ages 12 & under. **Frequency:** Annual. **Audience:** Trade professionals and general public. **Principal Exhibits:** Boats, fishing equipment, boat-related accessories, charter rentals, nautical attire, trailer and outboard motors, and personal watercraft. **Dates and Locations:** , Cobo Conference and Exhibition Center.

19372 ■ Eastern Fishing and Outdoor Exposition

Eastern Fishing and Outdoor Exposition Inc.
750 Central Ave., Ste. R
Dover, NH 03820
Ph: (603)431-4315
Fax: (603)431-1971
Co. E-mail: info@sportshows.com
URL: http://www.sportshows.com
URL(s): www.sportshows.com/. **Price:** $9. **Frequency:** Annual. **Audience:** Metro Boston/Worcester Market. **Principal Exhibits:** Fishing and outdoor sports. **Telecommunication Services:** info@sportshows.com.

19373 ■ Eastern Sports & Outdoor Show

Reed Exhibitions North American Headquarters
383 Main Ave.
Norwalk, CT 06851
Ph: (203)840-4800
Fax: (203)840-5805
Co. E-mail: inquiry@reedexpo.com
URL: http://www.reedexpo.com
URL(s): www.easternsportshow.com. **Price:** $10, adult; $9, seniors; $4, children 6 - 12 years. **Frequency:** Annual. **Audience:** General public. **Principal Exhibits:** Recreational vehicles, boats, hunting and fishing equipment, clothing, and related outdoor products, resorts, SUVs, retailers and manufacturers, motorcycles, ATVs, travel and tourism. **Dates and Locations:** , Pennsylvania Farm Show Complex. **Telecommunication Services:** eseveral@reedexpo.com.

19374 ■ Fort Wayne Sports, Vacation, and Boat Show

Trio Enterprises, Inc.
3624 Maxim Dr.
Fort Wayne, IN 46815
Ph: (219)483-2638
Free: 800-446-2638
Fax: (219)484-0876
URL(s): www.boatsafloat.com. **Frequency:** Annual. **Audience:** General public. **Principal Exhibits:** Recreational vehicles, boats, and travel and vacation information. **Dates and Locations:** , Allen County War Memorial Coliseum. **Telecommunication Services:** data@boatsafloat.com.

19375 ■ FUN Expo

Reed Exhibitions North American Headquarters
383 Main Ave.
Norwalk, CT 06851
Ph: (203)840-4800
Fax: (203)840-5805
Co. E-mail: inquiry@reedexpo.com
URL: http://www.reedexpo.com
URL(s): www.funexpo.com. **Price:** $20, Pre-registered, members; $40, Pre-registered, non-members; $65, Onsite registered, members; $90, Onsite registered, non-members. **Frequency:** Annual. **Principal Exhibits:** Amusement and recreation products for family and location based entertainment centers, small amusement parks and family oriented businesses such as bowling centers, skating rinks, sports parks, miniature golf courses, golf driving ranges, family restaurants, resorts and other entertainment/recreation businesses.

19376 ■ H2X Canada Hardware & Home Improvement Expo & Conference

Messe Frankfurt Inc.
1600 Parkwood Cir., Ste. 515
Atlanta, GA 30339
Ph: (770)984-8016
Fax: (770)984-8023
Co. E-mail: info@usa.messefrankfurt.com
URL: http://www.usa.messefrankfurt.com
URL(s): meesefrankfurt.com/shows/northamerica/h2x/index.htm. **Frequency:** Annual. **Audience:** Volume buyers, including retailers and manufacturers' representatives. **Principal Exhibits:** Hardware, housewares, giftware, paint, wallcovering, and products for leisure living, and home improvement. **Dates and Locations:** , Coliseum Exhbition Place.

19377 ■ The Imprinted Sportswear Show, Long Beach

IMPRESSIONS magazine
1145 Sanctuary Pkwy., Ste. 350
Alpharetta, GA 30004-4756
Ph: (770)291-5574
Free: 800-241-9034
Fax: (770)777-8684
Co. E-mail: mderryberry@impressionsmag.com
URL: http://www.impressionsmag.com
URL(s): www.issshows.com. **Frequency:** Annual. **Audience:** Buyers of imprinted sportswear, screen printing/embroidery equipment, supplies and apparel. **Principal Exhibits:** T-shirts, pre-prints, and other apparel; design software; screen-printing supplies and equipment; transfers, lettering, embroidery equipment and supplies. **Dates and Locations:** , Convention Center. **Telecommunication Services:** nikkihouston@nielsen.com.

19378 ■ The Imprinted Sportswear Show, Orlando

IMPRESSIONS magazine
1145 Sanctuary Pkwy., Ste. 350
Alpharetta, GA 30004-4756
Ph: (770)291-5574
Free: 800-241-9034
Fax: (770)777-8684
Co. E-mail: mderryberry@impressionsmag.com
URL: http://www.impressionsmag.com
URL(s): www.issshows.com. **Frequency:** Annual. **Audience:** Buyers of imprinted sportswear, screen printing/embroidery equipment, supplies, and apparel. **Principal Exhibits:** T-shirts, pre-prints, apparel, design software, screen-printing supplies and equipment, transfers, lettering, and embroidery equipment and supplies.

19379 ■ JAGEN UND FISCHEN - International Exhibition for Hunters, Fishermen and Marksmen

Kallman Worldwide, Inc.
4 North St., Ste. 800
Waldwick, NJ 07463-1842
Ph: (201)251-2600
Fax: (201)251-2760
Co. E-mail: info@kallman.com
URL: http://www.kallman.com
URL(s): www.jagenundfischen.deComment2. **Principal Exhibits:** Equipment, supplies, and services for hunters, fishermen, and marksmen. **Telecommunication Services:** newsline@messe-muenchen.de.

19380 ■ Kansas City Boat & Sportshow

National Marine Manufacturers Association
231 S. LaSalle St., Ste. 2050
Chicago, IL 60604
Ph: (312)946-6200
Co. E-mail: info@generalsportshows.com
URL: http://www.generalsportshows.com
URL(s): www.kansascitysportshow.com. **Price:** $10, adults; youth 15 and younger. **Frequency:** Annual. **Principal Exhibits:** Sports.

19381 ■ Kansas Sports, Boat, & Travel Show

Industrial Expositions, Inc.
1675 Larimer St., No. 700
Denver, CO 80248-0084
Ph: (303)892-6800
Free: 800-457-2434

Fax: (303)892-6322
Co. E-mail: info@iei-expos.com
URL: http://www.iei-expos.com/
URL(s): www.agievents.com/shows/display.cfm?showid=74. **Frequency:** Annual. **Audience:** General public. **Principal Exhibits:** Recreational vehicles, boats, sports equipment, and travel destination information; fishing and hunting equipment, supplies, and services. **Dates and Locations:** , Coliseum. **Telecommunication Services:** rwhitacre-prp@ks.rr.com.

19382 ■ Louisville Boat, RV & Sportshow

Douglas Expositions Inc.
10000 Shelbyville Rd., No. 111
Anchorage, KY 40223-2950
Ph: (502)244-5660
URL(s): www.louisvilleboatshow.com. **Frequency:** Annual. **Principal Exhibits:** Sports, boating and vacations, hunting and fishing, recreational vehicles. **Telecommunication Services:** kmuncy@nmma.org.

19383 ■ Milwaukee Journal Sentinel Sports Show

Milwaukee Journal Sentinel
PO Box 371
Milwaukee, WI 53201
Ph: (414)224-2000
Fax: (414)225-5000
URL: http://www.journalsentinel.com
Contact: Elizabeth Brenner, President
E-mail: bbrenner@journalsentinel.com
URL(s): www2.jsonline.com/sportsshow/. **Frequency:** Annual. **Principal Exhibits:** Sports equipment, supplies, and services. **Telecommunication Services:** info@duckbaylodge.com.

19384 ■ Northwest Sportshow

National Marine Manufacturers Association
231 S. LaSalle St., Ste. 2050
Chicago, IL 60604
Ph: (312)946-6200
Co. E-mail: info@generalsportshows.com
URL: http://www.generalsportshows.com
URL(s): www.northwestsportshow.com. **Price:** $10, adults; $5, senior; children 15 & younger. **Frequency:** Annual. **Audience:** Sporting enthusiasts, sporting goods professionals. **Principal Exhibits:** Boating, fishing, hunting, camping, RVing.

19385 ■ Outdoor Retailer Summer Market

VNU Expo
310 Broadway
Laguna Beach, CA 92651
Ph: (946)376-6200
Free: 800-486-2701
Fax: (949)497-5290
Co. E-mail: interbike@wyoming.com
URL: http://www.vnuexpo.com
URL(s): www.outdoorretailer.com. **Price:** $30, Onsite late retailers; $375, Onsite industry affiliate. **Frequency:** Annual. **Audience:** Owners and managers of the specialty sports retail stores. **Principal Exhibits:** Human-powered outdoor sports goods. **Telecommunication Services:** kenji.haroutunian@nielsen.com.

19386 ■ Outdoor Retailer Winter Market

VNU Expo
310 Broadway
Laguna Beach, CA 92651
Ph: (946)376-6200
Free: 800-486-2701
Fax: (949)497-5290
Co. E-mail: interbike@wyoming.com
URL: http://www.vnuexpo.com
URL(s): www.outdoorretailer.com. **Price:** $30, Onsite late retailers; $375, industry affiliate. **Frequency:** Annual. **Audience:** Owners and managers of specialty sports retail stores. **Principal Exhibits:** Human-powered outdoor sports goods. **Telecommunication Services:** kenji.haroutunian@nielsen.com.

19387 ■ Rocky Mountain Snowmobile Expo

Industrial Expositions, Inc.
1675 Larimer St., No. 700
Denver, CO 80248-0084
Ph: (303)892-6800
Free: 800-457-2434

Fax: (303)892-6322
Co. E-mail: info@iei-expos.com
URL: http://www.iei-expos.com'
URL(s): www.gsevents.com/shows/display.
cfm?showID=57&action=exhibitors. Price: $6, On-
site. Frequency: Annual. Audience: Snowmobilers.
Principal Exhibits: Snowmobiles, clothing and accessories, recreational vehicles, travel and accommodations. Telecommunication Services: dsey-
mour@agievents.com.

19388 ■ Scuba ExtaSea Expo
Industrial Expositions, Inc.
1675 Larimer St., No. 700
Denver, CO 80248-0084
Ph: (303)892-6800
Free: 800-457-2434
Fax: (303)892-6322
Co. E-mail: info@iei-expos.com
URL: http://www.iei-expos.com/
URL(s): www.bigasalloutdoors.com/scuba. Price: $7,
Onsite. Frequency: Annual. Audience: General
public. Principal Exhibits: Scuba diving, snorkeling,
travel and accessories. Telecommunication Ser-
vices: info@iei-expos.com.

19389 ■ The Shooting, Hunting, and Outdoor Trade Show (SHOT SHOW)
Reed Exhibitions Contemporary Forums
6377 Clark Ave., Ste. 200
Dublin, CA 94568
Ph: (925)828-7100
Fax: (800)329-9923
Co. E-mail: info@cforums.com
URL: http://www.contemporaryforums.com
URL(s): www.shotshow.org. Audience: Federally
licensed firearms dealers and legitimate sporting
goods dealers. Principal Exhibits: Shooting and
hunting equipment and products; sports accessories,
clothing, and supplies. Telecommunication Ser-
vices: nbogdanski@reedexpo.com.

19390 ■ United States Professional Tennis Association Convention
United States Professional Tennis Association
(USPTA)
3535 Briarpark Dr., Ste. 1
Houston, TX 77042-5233

Ph: (713)978-7782
Free: 800-USP-TA4U
Fax: (713)978-7780
Co. E-mail: uspta@uspta.org
URL: http://www.uspta.com
Contact: Tim Heckler, Chief Executive Officer
E-mail: tim.heckler@uspta.org
URL(s): www.uspta.com. Frequency: Annual. Audi-
ence: Tennis-teaching professionals, industry del-
egates, and general public. Principal Exhibits: Ten-
nis equipment, supplies, and services.

19391 ■ Washington Sportsmen's Show
International Sport Show Producers Association (IS-
SPA)
PO Box 480084
Denver, CO 80248-0084
Ph: (303)892-6800
Free: 800-457-2434
Fax: (303)892-6322
Co. E-mail: dseymour@iei-expos.com
URL: http://www.sportshow.org
Contact: Jeff Haughton, President
URL(s): www.thesportshows.com/wss'. Price: $12,
Onsite adult; $5, Onsite juniors (6-16); children under
6 free. Frequency: Annual. Principal Exhibits:
Sportsmen's show.

19392 ■ World Fishing and Outdoor Exposition
Eastern Fishing and Outdoor Exposition Inc.
750 Central Ave., Ste. R
Dover, NH 03820
Ph: (603)431-4315
Fax: (603)431-1971
Co. E-mail: info@sportshows.com
URL: http://www.sportshows.com
URL(s): www.sportshows.com/suffern/index.html.
Frequency: Annual. Audience: Metro New York City
Market. Principal Exhibits: Fishing and outdoor
sports. Telecommunication Services: info@sports-
hows.com.

FRANCHISES AND BUSINESS OPPORTUNITIES

19393 ■ Golf Etc.
Golf Etc. of America Inc.
2201 Commercial Ln.
Granbury, TX 76048-5698
Free: 800-806-8633
Co. E-mail: sales@golfetc.com
URL: http://www.GolfEtc.com
Description: Sales of golf clubs and golf acces-
sories. No. of Franchise Units: 35. Founded: 1992..
Franchised: 1995. Equity Capital Needed:
$225,000-$450,000. Franchise Fee: $30,000. Train-
ing: Provides 5 days training at corporate office in
Granbury, TX, 3-4 days at franchisees location, 5
days plus optional advanced training and ongoing
support.

19394 ■ Play it Again Sports
Winmark Corp.
605 Hwy. 169 N, Ste. 400
Minneapolis, MN 55441-6536
Ph: (763)520-8500
Free: 800-433-2540
Fax: (763)520-8410
Co. E-mail: winmark.information@winmarkcorpora-
tion.com
URL: http://www.winmarkcorporation.com
Description: Sells new and used sports equipment
and clothing. Franchisees purchase discount inventory through closeouts and overruns and accept used
equipment in trade from customers, reducing retail
prices by 40-60%. No. of Franchise Units: 325.
Founded: 1983.. Franchised: 1988. Equity Capital
Needed: $244,800-$391,900; Approximately 30%
cash requirement. Franchise Fee: $25,000. Train-
ing: Training includes product acquisition, inventory
management, staff hiring and training, customer
service, advertising and marketing, and merchandising. Ongoing regional meetings and national training
conferences held annually.

ASSOCIATIONS AND OTHER ORGANIZATIONS

19395 ■ **International Gay Rodeo Association (IGRA)**
PO Box 460504
Aurora, CO 80046-0504
Co. E-mail: askigra@igra.com
URL: http://www.igra.com
Contact: Tommy Channel, Administrative Assistant
Description: Gay rodeo associations in the United States and Canada. Promotes public interest in rodeo events and seeks to increase participation in rodeo by gay people. Facilitates communication and cooperation among members; sponsors competitions. **Founded:** 1985. **Publications:** *Safety Video*; *2005 Rodeo Resource Guidebook*.

DIRECTORIES OF EDUCATIONAL PROGRAMS

19396 ■ *Encyclopedia of Sports Business Contacts*
Pub: Global Sports Productions Ltd.
Contact: Ed Kobak, President
E-mail: Ekobak@yahoo.com
URL(s): www.sportsbooksempire.com. **Ed:** Edward T. Kobak, Jr. **Released:** Biennial; latest edition 1st. **Price:** $79.95, Individuals perfect bound; plus shipping charges $13.50. **Covers:** Sports organizations, associations, clubs, leagues, teams, corporate sponsors, sports media, facilities, sports agents and lawyers, organizations for the physically challenged, and manufacturers and retailers of sporting goods. **Entries include:** Company name, address, phone, fax, email and web addresses, names and titles of key personnel.

19397 ■ *International Sports Directory*
Pub: Global Sports Productions Ltd.
Contact: Ed Kobak, President
E-mail: Ekobak@yahoo.com
URL(s): www.sportsbooksempire.com. **Ed:** Edward T. Kobak, Jr. **Released:** Latest edition 3rd. **Price:** $45, Individuals perfect bound; plus shipping charges $5.25. **Covers:** International men's and women's professional club sports, Olympic and multi-sport international games, sports federations, publications, Olympic committees, sports information centers, and IOC recognized sports federations. **Entries include:** Company name, address, phone, fax, e-mail and web addresses, names and titles of key personnel.

REFERENCE WORKS

19398 ■ *"10 Trends That Are Shaping Global Media Consumption" in Advertising Age (Vol. 81, December 6, 2010, No. 43, pp. 3)*
Pub: Crain Communications, Inc.
Ed: Ann Marie Kerwin. **Description:** Ad Age offers the statistics from the TV penetration rate in Kenya to the number of World Cup watchers and more.

19399 ■ *"Advertisers Hooked on Horns, their Playground" in Austin Business JournalInc. (Vol. 28, July 25, 2008, No. 19, pp. A1)*
Pub: American City Business Journals
Ed: Sandra Zaragoza. **Description:** Renovation of the D.K. Royal-Texas Memorial Stadium has increased its advertising revenue from $570,000 in 1993 to $10 in 2008. Sponsorship has grown in the past years due to the revenue-sharing agreement, a ten-year contract through 2015 between the University of Texas and IMG College Sports.

19400 ■ *"Arizona Firms In Chicago Go For Gold With '08 Games" in The Business Journal - Serving Phoenix and the Valley of the Sun (Vol. 28, August 8, 2008, No. 49, pp. 1)*
Pub: American City Business Journals, Inc.
Ed: Patrick O'Grady. **Description:** More than 20 U.S. athletes will wear Arizona-based eSoles LLC's custom-made insoles to increase their performance at the 2008 Beijing Olympics making eSoles one of the beneficiaries of the commercialization of the games. Translation software maker Auralog Inc saw a 60 percent jump in sales from its Mandarin Chinese language applications.

19401 ■ *"Athletes' Performance Building $10 Million Facility In ASU Park" in The Business Journal - Serving Phoenix and the Valley of the Sun (Vol. 28, August 8, 2008, No. 49, pp. 1)*
Pub: American City Business Journals, Inc.
Ed: Jan Buchholz. **Description:** Athletes' Performance's planned facility at Arizona State University is scheduled to begin in November 2008 and expected to be completed by September 2009. The new building will almost double the company's training space as it will expand from around 19,000 square feet to 35,000 square feet.

19402 ■ *Athletic Business--Professional Directory Section*
Pub: Athletic Business Publications Inc.
URL(s): www.athleticbusiness.com. **Ed:** Andrew Cohen. **Released:** Monthly; Latest edition 2010. **Price:** $8, per issue. **Publication includes:** List of architects, engineers, contractors, and consultants in athletic facility planning and construction; all listings are paid. **Entries include:** Company name, address, phone, fax and short description of company. **Arrangement:** Alphabetical.

19403 ■ *"Back to Business" in Retail Merchandiser (Vol. 51, September-October 2011, No. 5, pp. 18)*
Pub: Phoenix Media Corporation
Ed: Eric Slack. **Description:** National Football League owners and players have reached a labor agreement for the next ten years. America's football league can once again focus on providing fans with a great product both on and off the field.

19404 ■ *"Bars, Restaurants to Offer Prix Fixe Menus, Space to Race Patrons" in Boston*

19399 ■ *Business Journal (Vol. 29, July 22, 2011, No. 11, pp. 1)*
Pub: American City Business Journals Inc.
Ed: Alexander Jackson. **Description:** Restaurants and bar owners in Baltimore, Maryland have changed the way they do business as the Baltimore Grand Prix approaches. Owners have gone so far as to offering new services or renting out their entire restaurants to companies for the three-day event in September.

19405 ■ *The Blind Side*
Pub: W. W. Norton & Company, Inc.
Ed: Michael Lewis. **Released:** 2007. **Price:** $13.95. **Description:** The evolving business of football, viewed through the rise of the left tackle, Michael Oher.

19406 ■ *"Blues Asking Price Out of Their League" in Saint Louis Business Journal (Vol. 32, September 23, 2011, No. 4, pp. 1)*
Pub: Saint Louis Business Journal
Ed: Amy Kurtovic. **Description:** St. Louis Blues owner Dave Checketts wanted the hockey team sold before the start of the season and he believed the team could fetch $200 million or more. However, Hockey insiders believe the price was too high when considering the team's high debt ratio and several other National Hockey League teams on the market.

19407 ■ *"The Board Shorts Executive" in Hawaii Business (Vol. 53, January 2008, No. 7, pp. 33)*
Pub: Hawaii Business Publishing
Ed: Mike Markrich. **Description:** Vans Triple Crown of Surfing executive director Randy Rarick believes that the surfing business requires knowledge of the sport and integrity to the game's lifestyle and spirit. His organization manages surfing events, and has generated jobs for the locals. Plans for Vans Triple Crown are supplied.

19408 ■ *"Buck-ing the Trend?" in Baltimore Business Journal (Vol. 28, August 13, 2010, No. 14, pp. 1)*
Pub: Baltimore Business Journal
Ed: Gary Haber. **Description:** Baltimore Orioles' new manager Buck Showalter has managed to win games for fans. However, not all businesses around Camden Yards were boosted by the Orioles' surge as street vendors complained of worsening business.

19409 ■ *"Calling An Audible" in The Business Journal-Milwaukee (Vol. 25, August 1, 2008, No. 45, pp. A1)*
Pub: American City Business Journals, Inc.
Ed: David Dedge. **Description:** Tough economic conditions are forcing entertainment businesses in Milwaukee, Wisconsin, to try new business strategies to keep attracting customers. These strategies include keeping prices steady despite increasing costs and new sales promotions.

19410 ■ *"Can the State Afford a Big Time College Football Program?" in Hawaii*

Business (Vol. 53, March 2008, No. 9, pp. 26)
Pub: Hawaii Business Publishing

Description: Jill Nunokawa, civil rights at University of Hawaii, believes that athletics are extra-curricular and that the state needs to focus on priorities. State representative K. Mark Takai says that a football program brings pride and inspiration and can generate revenue and provide economic opportunities.

19411 ■ *"Chew On This: Soul Fans to 'Chew' Games' First Play" in Philadelphia Business Journal (Vol. 30, September 30, 2011, No. 33, pp. 3)*
Pub: American City Business Journals Inc.

Ed: John George. **Description:** Arena football team Philadelphia Soul extended its marketing partnership with Just Born Inc. The team's fans will enter a contest where the winner will be allowed to select the team's first play during a home game.

19412 ■ *"Chiefs Hope Renovations Score Big With Sponsors" in The Business Journal-Serving Metropolitan Kansas City (Vol. 26, July 11, 2008)*
Pub: American City Business Journals, Inc.

Ed: James Dornbrook. **Description:** Kansas City Chiefs officials expect to obtain 12 to 14 new major sponsors with the completion of the Arrowhead Stadium renovations. The new sponsorship opportunities will include naming rights for the stadium and practice facility. The team's marketing strategies are discussed.

19413 ■ *"City Eyeing Tax Breaks for Arena" in Boston Business Journal (Vol. 29, June 3, 2011, No. 4, pp. 1)*
Pub: American City Business Journals Inc.

Ed: Daniel J. Sernovitz. **Description:** Baltimore City is opting to give millions of dollars in tax breaks and construction loans to a group of private investors led by William Hackerman who is proposing to build a new arena and hotel at the Baltimore Convention Center. The project will cost $500 million with the state putting up another $400 million for the center's expansion.

19414 ■ *"The Colt Effect" in Hawaii Business (Vol. 53, January 2008, No. 7, pp. 30)*
Pub: Hawaii Business Publishing

Ed: David K. Choo. **Description:** Participation at the Bowl Championship Games can help the University of Hawaii financially. Playing at a prominent sports event could provoke donations from alumni and increase enrollment at the university. Examples of universities that earned generous income by becoming a part of prestigious sporting events are presented.

19415 ■ *"Contracting Firm Sees Timing Right for Expansion" in Tampa Bay Business Journal (Vol. 29, November 13, 2009, No. 47, pp. 1)*
Pub: American City Business Journals

Ed: Janet Leiser. **Description:** Construction management company Moss & Associates LLC of Fort Lauderdale, Florida has launched its expansion to Tampa Bay. Moss & Associates has started the construction of the Marlins stadium in Miami, Florida's Little Havana section. It also plans to diversify by embarking on other government development, such as health care facilities and airports.

19416 ■ *"Detroit Scores When Tigers Play; Studies Predict Winning Economy" in Crain's Detroit Business (Vol. 24, March 31, 2008, No. 13)*
Pub: Crain Communications, Inc

Ed: Bill Shea. **Description:** East Lansing-based Anderson Economic Group and the Detroit Regional Chamber predict that the economic impact of the Detroit Tigers will be very positive for the region due to an unexpected World Series trip two years ago followed by another strong season in 2007, player acquisitions and the popular Jim Leyland again managing the team. Statistical data included.

19417 ■ *"DHR Hires Carr for Sports Group" in Crain's Detroit Business (Vol. 25, June 8,*

2009, No. 23, pp. 5)
Pub: Crain Communications Inc. - Detroit

Ed: Sherri Begin Welch. **Description:** Lloyd Carr, former head football coach for University of Michigan, has taken a position with DHR International in order to expand its searches for collegiate and professional sports organizations, recruit athletic directors, head coaches and other executives.

19418 ■ *"Eagles Measure Suite Success" in Philadelphia Business Journal (Vol. 30, September 9, 2011, No. 30, pp. 1)*
Pub: American City Business Journals Inc.

Ed: John George. **Description:** Philadelphia Eagles have a new software program that helps suite holders keep track of how their suite is being used and whether they are getting a return on their investment. The software allows suite holders to better utilize and distribute their tickets.

19419 ■ *"Easy Answers? Hall No" in Charlotte Business Journal (Vol. 25, December 17, 2010, No. 39, pp. 1)*
Pub: Charlotte Business Journal

Ed: Erik Spanberg. **Description:** Charlotte, North Carolina-based NASCAR Hall of Fame has been trying to recover from its shaky start, but still bullish on the future as officials intensify promotions. Sports museums and halls of fame are mainly dependent on families and always search for new exhibits and great appearances to boost attendance.

19420 ■ *"Economics at Play When Allocating Seats to Series" in Boston Business Journal (Vol. 27, October 26, 2007, No. 39, pp. 1)*
Pub: American City Business Journals Inc.

Ed: Jesse Noyes, Naomi R. Kooker. **Description:** Business executives are trying to obtain as many baseball tickets to the World Series as possible. Allocating corporate seats to the Series is about maintaining tight relationships and influence clients. It is a key to business relationships.

19421 ■ *"Five-Ring Circus" in Entrepreneur (Vol. 35, November 2007, No. 11, pp. 76)*
Pub: Entrepreneur Media Inc.

Ed: Scott Bernard Nelson. **Description:** China's economy is growing and is expected to do well even after the 2008 Olympics, but growth could slow from eleven percent to eight or nine percent. Chinese portfolio concerns with regard to health and environmental records and bureaucratic fraud are discussed.

19422 ■ *"For DVD Company, No Extra Innings: Capturing a Season Takes Fast Work" in Boston Business Journal (Vol. 27, December 7, 2007)*
Pub: American City Business Journals Inc.

Ed: Terry Lefton. **Description:** Details of the development of MLB's annual World Series film by MLB Productions are discussed. The company is compelled to produce the film in a short period of time due to a promised November 27, 2007 delivery date. According to Elizabeth Scott, MLB vice president of programming and business affairs, she was concerned about the things that could directly affect sales.

19423 ■ *"Game On at Jordan's New Spot" in Crain's Chicago Business (Vol. 34, October 24, 2011, No. 42, pp. 34)*
Pub: Crain Communications Inc.

Ed: Laura Bianchi. **Description:** Michael Jordan partnered with Cornerstone Restaurant Group to launch Michael Jordan's Steakhouse in Chicago. Details are included.

19424 ■ *"Getting in the Game" in Baltimore Business Journal (Vol. 27, October 16, 2009, No. 23, pp. 1)*
Pub: American City Business Journals

Ed: Ryan Sharrow. **Description:** Crystal Palace FC USA is finalizing a deal with a North Carolina development team to build a 7,000 seat stadium by early 2012 in spite of efforts by Baltimore Mayor Sheila Dixon to bring in professional soccer's DC United. The planned stadium is in the Carroll Camden Industrial area near M&T Bank Stadium. Plans for the new stadium are included.

19425 ■ *"Goodbye, Locker Room: Hello, Boardroom" in Inc. (Vol. 33, October 2011, No. 8, pp. 30)*
Pub: Inc. Magazine

Ed: Issie Lapowsky, Kasey Wehrum. **Description:** In 2005, the National Football League started the NFL Business Management and Entrepreneurial Program. Since the onset of the program, 700 players have participated in the program which takes place at the business schools of Harvard, the University of Pennsylvania, Northwestern and Stanford.

19426 ■ *"Goodyear Extends Exclusive Deal to Supply NASCAR's Tires" in Charlotte Observer (February 4, 2007)*
Pub: Knight-Ridder/Tribune Business News

Ed: David Poole. **Description:** Goodyear tires will continue to be the exclusive tire provider at NASCAR's Nextel Cup, Busch and Truck series through the year 2012.

19427 ■ *"Grand Prix Didn't Fill Up City's Hotels" in Boston Business Journal (Vol. 29, September 16, 2011, No. 19, pp. 1)*
Pub: American City Business Journals Inc.

Ed: Alexander Jackson. **Description:** Baltimore Grand Prix inaugural race failed to fill the hotels in Baltimore, Maryland as hoteliers reported rooms to spare during the three-day event. City officials expected downtown hotels to nearly sell out Labor Day weekend.

19428 ■ *"Great Expectations" in Canadian Business (Vol. 81, April 14, 2008, No. 6, pp. 34)*
Pub: Rogers Media

Ed: Andy Holloway. **Description:** Therma Blades Inc. says that the reports that say their Therma Blade ice skates were not working properly were inaccurate. The major mistake of the company was to fail to manage the public's expectation when they touted the blades as revolutionary. Therma Blades Inc. has since tested the product with the help of 120 players and physiological testing done on elite level players show that there was a 10 percent improvement in energy efficiency.

19429 ■ *"Hedge-Fund Titan Cohen Plans Bid for Dodgers" in Wall Street Journal Eastern Edition (November 25 , 2011, pp. C3)*
Pub: Dow Jones & Company Inc. Enterprise Media Group

Contact: Clare Hart, President

Ed: Matthew Futterman, Gregory Zuckerman. **Description:** Steven A. Cohen, the founder and head of hedge-fund SAC Capital Advisors LLC is looking to make an offer at the bankruptcy auction for the financially-troubled Los Angeles Dodgers baseball team.

19430 ■ *"High-Tech, Niche Options Change Sports Marketing" in Crain's Detroit Business (Vol. 24, March 17, 2008, No. 11, pp. 14)*
Pub: Crain Communications, Inc.

Ed: Leah Boyd. **Description:** Sports advertisers have an ever-increasing menu of high-tech or niche marketing options such as interactive campaigns through cell phones and electronic banners which can span areas.

19431 ■ *"Hitting the Green" in Canadian Business (Vol. 81, July 22, 2008, No. 12-13, pp. 34)*
Pub: Rogers Media Ltd.

Ed: Andy Holloway. **Description:** RBC is sponsoring the Canadian Open golf tournament, which is the second-oldest event in the PGA Tour. RBC is expected to receive television exposure on CBS and the Golf Channel. Additional information relating to the sponsorship is presented.

19432 ■ *"HOK Sport May Build Own Practice" in The Business Journal-Serving Metropolitan Kansas City (Vol. 26, August 29, 2008, No. 51, pp. 1)*
Pub: American City Business Journals, Inc.

Ed: Rob Roberts. **Description:** HOK Sport Venue Event is considering a spin-off from its parent company, HOK Group Inc. HOK Sport spokeswoman

Gina Leo confirms that the firm is exploring structures, including a management buyout. Some of HOK Sport Venue Event's Minnesota projects are discussed.

19433 ■ "An Ice Boost in Revenue; Wings Score With Expanded Corporate Sales" in Crain's Detroit Business (Vol. 25, June 1, 2009, No. 22)
Pub: Crain Communications Inc. - Detroit
Ed: Bill Shea. **Description:** Stanley Cup finals always boost business for the Detroit area, even during a recession. The Red Wings corporate office reported corporate sponsorship revenue luxury suite rentals, Legends Club seats and advertising were up 40 percent this year over 2008.

19434 ■ "It's Back to Business for the Ravens" in Boston Business Journal (Vol. 29, July 29, 2011, No. 12, pp. 1)
Pub: American City Business Journals Inc.
Ed: Scott Dance. **Description:** The Baltimore Ravens football team has been marketing open sponsorship packages following the end of the National Football League lockout. Team officials are working to get corporate logos and slogans on radio and television commercials and online advertisements.

19435 ■ "LED Screen Technology Takes Centre Stage" in Canadian Electronics (Vol. 23, June-July 2008, No. 4, pp. 17)
Pub: Action Communication Inc.
Ed: Ed Whitaker. **Description:** Display technologies based on light emitting diodes are becoming more popular due to their flexibility, versatility and reproducibility of displays. These are being increasingly used in different applications, such as advertising and concerts.

19436 ■ "Local Startup Hits Big Leagues" in Austin Business JournalInc. (Vol. 28, December 19, 2008, No. 40, pp. 1)
Pub: American City Business Journals
Ed: Christopher Calnan. **Description:** Qcue LLC, an Austin, Texas-based company founded in 2007 is developing a software system that can be used by Major League Baseball teams to change the prices of their single-game tickets based on variables affecting demand. The company recently completed a trial with the San Francisco Giants in 2008.

19437 ■ "Looking for a Sales Tax Extension" in Milwaukee Business Journal (Vol. 27, January 29, 2010, No. 18, pp. A1)
Pub: American City Business Journals
Ed: Mark Kass. **Description:** Milwaukee, Wisconsin-area business executives believe the extension of the Miller Park 0.1 percent sales tax could help fund a new basketball arena to replace the 21-year-old Bradley Center in downtown Milwaukee. However, any sales tax expansion that includes the new basketball arena would need approval by Wisconsin's legislature.

19438 ■ "The Major Leagues: Have Front-Office Positions Opened Up for Blacks?" in Black Enterprise (Vol. 37, February 2007, No. 7, pp.)
Pub: Earl G. Graves Publishing Co. Inc.
Ed: Alexis McCombs. **Description:** Major leave sports teams are hiring more African Americans to manage and coach teams. Statistical data included.

19439 ■ Marketing Outrageously: How to Increase Your Revenue by Staggering Amounts
Pub: Bard Press
Ed: Jon Spoelstra. **Released:** July 25, 2001. **Price:** $24.95. **Description:** Creative marketing strategies are defined. The book shows how considering marketing problems as outrageously but consistently can benefit any small business. The author talks about his own experience when there were not adequate funds for marketing and advertising and the outrageous approach he created to promote sports teams.

19440 ■ "Minor-League Baseball's Sliders Plan Stock Offering" in Crain's Detroit Business (Vol. 25, June 15, 2009, No. 24, pp. 3)
Pub: Crain Communications Inc. - Detroit
Ed: Bill Shea. **Description:** New minor-league baseball team is raising funds to build a new stadium in Waterford Township, Michigan because banks are unwilling to provide loans for the project. Owners of the Midwest Sliders in Ypsilanti, Michigan are waiting for the federal Securities and Exchange Commission to approve a Regulation A public offering.

19441 ■ "Moms Dis Super Bowl Ads" in Marketing to Women (Vol. 21, March 2008, No. 3, pp. 6)
Pub: EPM Communications Inc.
Contact: Ira Mayer, President
E-mail: imayer@epmcom.com
Description: According to a survey by the Marketing to Moms Coalition, although 80 percent of moms tune into the Super Bowl most complain that the advertisements are not appropriate for a family sports viewing experience.

19442 ■ "Money Ball" in Canadian Business (Vol. 80, October 22, 2007, No. 21, pp. 40)
Pub: Rogers Media
Ed: Andy Holloway. **Description:** Rising Canadian dollar has a positive impact on the sports industry. Canadian team executives earn revenues in Canadian dollar, but pay expensive American dollar. Athletes who play in the Canadian Football Leagues benefit most from the increasing rate.

19443 ■ "Money and the Mayhem" in Canadian Business (Vol. 83, September 14, 2010, No. 15, pp. 52)
Pub: Rogers Media Ltd.
Ed: Greg Hudson. **Description:** Ultimate Fighting Championship (UFC) has hired Tom Wright as director of operations for Canada, who managed to get mixed martial arts sanctioned in Ontario. Canada is UFC's largest market after the US and accounting for about 15-20 percent in annual revenue.

19444 ■ "Nation of Islam Businessman Who Became Manager for Muhannmad Ali Dies" in Chicago Tribune (August 28, 2008)
Pub: McClatchy-Tribune Information Services
Ed: Trevor Jensen. **Description:** Profile of Jabir Herbert Muhammad who died on August 25, after heart surgery; Muhammad lived nearly all his life on Chicago's South Side and ran a number of small businesses including a bakery and a dry cleaners before becoming the manager to famed boxer Mohammad Ali.

19445 ■ "Newcomers Join Roster of Indoor Sports Venues" in Business Review, Albany New York (Vol. 34, October 12, 2007, No. 28, pp. 1)
Pub: American City Business Journals, Inc.
Ed: Adam Sichko. **Description:** Indoor sports scene in Albany, New York is growing, with several indoor training facilities with a special attention to baseball and softball being built. These facilities include the $2.2 million Extra Innings facility in Ballston Corporate Technology Park and the Warning Track facility on Route 9 in Malta. The market for indoor sports, which is seen as saturated, is analyzed.

19446 ■ "NFL Labor, Legal Issues Hang Over Detroit Lions' Rebuilding Efforts" in Crain's Detroit Business (Vol. 26, January 11, 2010, No. 2)
Pub: Crain Communications Inc.
Ed: Bill Shea. **Description:** Overview of the possible outcomes regarding labor talks with Detroit Lion's players as well as the outcome of a U.S. Supreme Court decision that could boost franchise values but at the expense of fans and corporate sponsors.

19447 ■ "Nike's Next Splash" in The Business Journal-Portland (Vol. 25, August 22, 2008, No. 24, pp. 1)
Pub: American City Business Journals, Inc.
Ed: Erik Siemers. **Description:** Business analysts expect Nike to bid for the endorsement services of swimmer Michael Phelps after the swimmer's contract

with Speedo expires. The company, however, is a lightweight in the swimming apparel market and is not focusing on swimming as a growth sector.

19448 ■ "Packers Still Want Marketing Deal With Favre" in The Business Journal-Milwaukee (Vol. 25, August 15, 2008, No. 47, pp. A1)
Pub: American City Business Journals, Inc.
Ed: Mark Kass. **Description:** The Green Bay Packers plan to offer a $20 million marketing agreement to quarterback Brett Favre, including a clothing, merchandise, and collectibles line. The team is pursuing the agreement despite trading Favre to the New York Jets on 6 August 2008.

19449 ■ "Palace Adds Marketing Arm; College Sponsorships First Step In New Effort" in Crain's Detroit Business (October 1, 2007)
Pub: Crain Communications Inc. - Detroit
Ed: Bill Shea. **Description:** Palace Sports and Entertainment is restructuring itself from operating the Detroit Piston's basketball team and concert venues into a marketing company that also runs sports teams and venues. The firm signed a deal to handle sponsorship sales for colleges and universities.

19450 ■ "Peter Bynoe Trades Up" in Black Enterprise (Vol. 38, July 2008, No. 12, pp. 30)
Pub: Earl G. Graves Publishing Co. Inc.
Ed: Alexis McCombs. **Description:** Chicago-based Loop Capital Markets L.L.C. has named Peter Bynoe managing director of corporate finance. Bynoe was previously a senior partner at the law firm DLA Piper U.S. L.L.P., where he worked on stadium deals.

19451 ■ "Pro Teams Shift Ad Budgets; Naming Rights Deals Near $1 Billion" in Brandweek (Vol. 49, April 21, 2008, No. 16, pp. 18)
Pub: VNU Business Media, Inc.
Ed: Barry Janoff. **Description:** More and more professional sports marketers are spending less of their advertising budgets on traditional media outlets such as television, print and radio; the growing trend in sports marketing is in utilizing new media venues such as the Internet in which innovative means are used to encourage interaction with fans.

19452 ■ "Race Benefits: Changes Afoot for Ironman" in Business Journal Serving Greater Tampa Bay (Vol. 30, October 29, 2010, No. 45, pp. 1)
Pub: Tampa Bay Business Journal
Ed: Margaret Cashill. **Description:** World Triatholon Corporation, organizer of the Ironman World Championship 70.3, will move the sports event from Florida to Nevada in 2011. A replacement event, the 5150 Triathlon Series, will be held in 2011 and the series finale will be staged in Florida's Clearwater Beach. How hotels and motels in the area will benefit from the 5150 Triathlon Series is discussed.

19453 ■ "Race-Week Schedule Filling Up With Galas, Nonprofit Fundraisers" in Boston Business Journal (Vol. 29, July 22, 2011, No. 11, pp. 1)
Pub: American City Business Journals Inc.
Ed: Alexander Jackson. **Description:** Baltimore, Maryland-based businesses and nonprofit groups have been planning their own events to coincide with the Baltimore Grand Prix during the Labor Day weekend. They also plan to partner with others in hopes of drumming up new business, raising money or to peddle their brands.

19454 ■ "Raptor Opens Consultancy" in Austin Business Journal (Vol. 31, July 8, 2011, No. 18, pp. 1)
Pub: American City Business Journals Inc.
Ed: Christopher Calnan. **Description:** Boston hedge fund operator Raptor Group launched Raptor Accelerator, a consulting business providing sales and advisory services to early-stage companies in Central Texas. Aside from getting involved with the startups

in which the Raptor Group invests, Raptor Accelerator will target firms operating in the sports, media, entertainment, and content technology sectors.

19455 ■ "The Reality of Fantasy Sports" in Entrepreneur (Vol. 37, September 2009, No. 9, pp. 52)
Pub: Entrepreneur Media, Inc.
Ed: Jason Ankeny. Description: United States fantasy sports business has grown into a $1 billion industry. Fantasy gaming in the country remains affordable and accessible despite the increase in the prices of tickets to sports games. Comments from analysts are also presented.

19456 ■ "Recovery on Tap for 2010?" in Orlando Business Journal (Vol. 26, January 1, 2010, No. 31, pp. 1)
Pub: American City Business Journals
Ed: Melanie Stawicki Azam, Richard Bilbao, Christopher Boyd, Anjali Fluker. Description: Economic forecasts for Central Florida's leading business sectors in 2010 are presented These sectors include housing, film and TV, sports business, law, restaurants, aviation, tourism and hospitality, banking and finance, commercial real estate, retail, health care, insurance, higher education, and manufacturing. According to some local executives, Central Florida's economy will slowly recover in 2010.

19457 ■ "Reds Hit Ratings Homer" in Business Courier (Vol. 27, July 30, 2010, No. 13, pp. 1)
Pub: Business Courier
Ed: Steve Watkins, James Ourand. Description: Cincinnati Reds fans have tuned in to their TVs and radios as their team made a hottest start to a season. The Reds TV ratings have increased 49 percent during the first six months of 2010 and continued to rise while the Reds' games broadcast on WLW-AM reported the highest average audience share per game of any Major League Baseball team.

19458 ■ "Rooting for Hispanic Dollars" in Hispanic Business (October 2007, pp. 76, 80)
Pub: Hispanic Business
Description: Sports franchises are working to gain and retain the Hispanic market.

19459 ■ "Sabathia Deal Makes Dollars and Sense" in The Business Journal-Milwaukee (Vol. 25, July 11, 2008, No. 42, pp. A1)
Pub: American City Business Journals, Inc.
Ed: Mark Kass. Description: It was reported that the Milwaukee Brewers' acquisition of CC Sabathia will mean that the team will pick up an estimated $5 million in salary that Sabathia is owed for the remainder of the season. Because of this, the team will not make a profit in 2008. The acquisition of Sabathia is expected to cause an increase in attendance and merchandise revenue over the remainder of the season.

19460 ■ Scorecasting
Pub: Crown Business Books
Ed: Tobias Moskowitz, L. Jon Wertheim. Released: January 25, 2011. Price: $26.00. Description: Behavioral economist and veteran writer partner to write about research and studies revealing the hidden forces that shape how basketball, baseball, football and hockey games are played, won and lost.

19461 ■ "Sheets Energy Strips Unveils New Vending Machines" in Food and Beverage Close-Up (August 12, 2011)
Pub: Close-Up Media
Description: Sheets Energy Strips is installing vending machines in malls, office buildings, stadiums and arenas in New York, New Jersey, Connecticut and Florida. These machines will offer 4 packs, 10 packs and Sheets branded hats and T-shirts.

19462 ■ "Sounders Kicking Ball to Fans" in Puget Sound Business Journal (Vol. 29, November 28, 2008, No. 32, pp. 1)
Pub: American City Business Journals
Ed: Greg Lamm. Description: Major League Soccer expansion team, Seattle Sounders FC, hopes to build fan support leading to its inaugural season 2009-

2010 by tapping online social networks. The club launched fan clubs with actual powers over its decision making and Websites similar to Facebook.

19463 ■ "Spillover Effects" in Crain's Detroit Business (Vol. 24, October 6, 2008, No. 40, pp. 29)
Pub: Crain Communications, Inc.
Description: Earlier this year, the Detroit Regional Chamber estimated that the Detroit Tiger's baseball team's 81 home games would have a $277 million positive economic impact on the region. Due to the poor performance of the team, fewer fans are spending money on tickets, which translates into fewer dollars coming into the region. Lower viewership on television has also been a result of the Tiger's losing season.

19464 ■ "Squeeze Play" in Baltimore Business Journal (Vol. 28, September 3, 2010, No. 17, pp. 1)
Pub: Baltimore Business Journal
Ed: Daniel J. Sernovitz. Description: The Baltimore Grand Prix is seen to benefit businesses in Baltimore, Maryland's Inner Harbor. It is also seen to create a rift between the city government and some office workers.

19465 ■ "Stadium Developers Seek a Win With the State" in The Business Journal-Serving Metropolitan Kansas City (Vol. 26, August 22, 2008)
Pub: American City Business Journals, Inc.
Ed: Rob Roberts. Description: Three Trails Redevelopment LLC is hoping to win $30 million in state tax credits from the Missouri Development Finance Board for the construction of an 18,500-seat Wizards stadium. The project is contingent on state tax incentives and the company remains optimistic about their goal.

19466 ■ "Still No Arena Financing Plan" in Sacramento Business Journal (Vol. 28, May 27, 2011, No. 13, pp. 1)
Pub: Sacramento Business Journal
Ed: Kelly Johnson. Description: The government of Sacramento, California has yet to devise a plan to finance the construction of a proposed stadium. The arena is estimated to cost $387 million. A brief description of the facility is also included.

19467 ■ "Study: Austin is Ready for a Pro Sports Team" in Austin Business JournalInc. (Vol. 29, December 25, 2009, No. 42, pp. 1)
Pub: American City Business Journals
Ed: Kate Harrington. Description: A study shows that Austin, Texas, with a total income of about $62 billion annually, is capable of hosting teams in the NBA, NHL, NFL and Major League Soccer. The capacity of 82 markets in the US and Canada was verified to assess their financial ability to support professional sports teams. Factors affecting Austin's ability to host a professional team are also presented.

19468 ■ "Super Bowl Events Get Tax Breaks" in Business Journal-Serving Phoenix and the Valley of the Sun (Vol. 7, October 12, 2007, No. 28)
Pub: American City Business Journals, Inc.
Ed: Mike Sunnucks. Description: Cities of Glendale and Phoenix, Arizona increased sales taxes in September 2007 and have issued tax exemptions for professional sporting events like the Super Bowl. Phoenix is planning to exempt events included in the 2009 NBA All-Star Game. National Football League's tax abatement requirement to cities hosting the Super Bowl is discussed.

19469 ■ "Teams Buy Into Screen Scene" in Business First Buffalo (October 5, 2007, pp. 1)
Pub: American City Business Journals, Inc.
Ed: James Fink. Description: Buffalo Bills, Buffalo Sabres, University of Buffalo, and Buffalo Bisons have all purchased new ribbon informational boards and video scoreboards to enhance their marketing strategies and improve the experience of sports fans. Vision boards of University of Buffalo and Sabres were installed by Daktronics, while Bills bought a Mit-

subishi Diamond Vision board. The features that make the new scoreboards good promotional tools are described.

19470 ■ "Ted Stahl: Executive Chairman" in Inside Business (Vol. 13, September-October 2011, No. 5, pp. NC6)
Pub: Great Lakes Publishing Co.
Ed: Miranda S. Miller. Description: Profile of Ted Stahl, who started working in his family's business when he was ten years old is presented. The firm makes dies for numbers and letters used on team uniforms. Another of the family firms manufactures stock and custom heat-printing products, equipment and supplies. It also educates customers on ways to decorate garments with heat printing products and offers graphics and software for customers to create their own artwork.

19471 ■ "Tigers Put to Test; Can Team Win Back Fans, Advertisers?" in Crain's Detroit Business (Vol. 24, October 6, 2008, No. 40, pp. 1)
Pub: Crain Communications, Inc.
Ed: Bill Shea. Description: Despite the enormous amount of money the Detroit Tigers' owner Mike Ilitch spent on player salaries, a record $137.6 million this season, the team finished in last-place; ticket sales and advertising dollars for next season are expected to fall dramatically. Additional speculation regarding the future of the ball team is included.

19472 ■ "Tim Tebow Foundation to Hold Pink 'Cleats for a Cure' Auction" in Travel & Leisure Close-Up (October 20, 2011)
Pub: Close-Up Media
Description: Tim Tebow Foundation partnered with XV Enterprises to hold the 'Cleats for a Cure' auction on eBay. Tebow is auctioning off a pair of pink cleans he wore during the Denver Broncos vs. Tennessee Titans game October 3, 2010. All funds will go toward finding a cure for breast cancer.

19473 ■ "To the Extreme" in Entrepreneur (Vol. 36, February 2008, No. 2, pp. 21)
Pub: Entrepreneur Media Inc.
Ed: Lindsay Holloway. Description: Extreme sports are increasing in number, with companies seeing the market potential of these sports for the 10- to 30-year-old age group. Entrepreneurs are launching innovated products catering to extreme sports-related markets. Details on the opportunities provided by the growth of extreme sports are discussed.

19474 ■ "Under Armour Wants to Equip Athletes, Too" in Boston Business Journal (Vol. 29, July 8, 2011, No. 9, pp. 1)
Pub: American City Business Journals Inc.
Ed: Ryan Sharrow. Description: Baltimore sportswear maker Under Armour advances plans to enter into the equipment field, aiming to strengthen its hold on football, basketball and lacrosse markets where it already has a strong market share. The company is now cooking up licensing deals to bolster the firm's presence among athletes.

19475 ■ "'Unknown' Muted Grand Prix Impact" in Boston Business Journal (Vol. 29, September 9, 2011, No. 18, pp. 3)
Pub: American City Business Journals Inc.
Ed: Alexander Jackson. Description: Baltimore Grand Prix caught restaurateurs, hoteliers and street vendors in Baltimore, Maryland unprepared for the thousands of race fans who attended the inaugural event over Labor Day weekend. The race popularity is relatively unknown to them and some felt they were not able to make as much money as they had hoped.

19476 ■ "Used to Being Courted" in Business Courier (Vol. 24, March 14, 2008, No. 49, pp. 1)
Pub: American City Business Journals, Inc.
Ed: Dan Monk. Description: College basketball coach Sean Miller is reported to be earning up to $900,000 a year. A look into the contract at regional universities show Thad Matta makes over $2 million in a year and that UK's Billy Gillispie makes over $2.7 million.

19477 ■ *"USF Plans $30M Sports Complex" in Tampa Bay Business Journal (Vol. 29, October 23, 2009, No. 44, pp. 1)*
Pub: American City Business Journals
Ed: Jane Meinhardt. **Description:** University of South Florida (USF) is going to build a new sports complex with the aid of a $30 million loan from BB&T. The project, which is also comprised of new and renovated athletic facilities on USF's Tampa campus, is projected to create more than $37 million in revenue in its first year. Revenues from the said facilities are expected to achieve an annual growth of at least four percent.

19478 ■ *"Vanity Plates" in Canadian Business (Vol. 82, April 27, 2009, No. 7, pp. 26)*
Pub: Rogers Media
Ed: Andy Holloway. **Description:** Politicians in the U.S. called for the review of firms that availed of the bailout money but are under deals for naming rights of sports stadiums. Angus Reid's Corporate Reputation and Sponsorship Index found for example, that there is little correlation between sponsoring arenas on having a better brand image. It is suggested that firms who enter these deals build closer to people's homes.

19479 ■ *"Viewing Ironman As Gold, R.I. Firm Buys Its Parent" in The Business Journal-Serving Greater Tampa Bay (Vol. 28, September 19, 2008)*
Pub: American City Business Journals, Inc.
Ed: Pete Williams. **Description:** Providence Equity Partners purchased World Triathlon Corp., parent company of the Ironman Triathlon, for an undisclosed sum. The acquisition means that the World Triathlon Headquarters will move to Tampa, Florida, and allows Providence Equity Partners to stage or license rights to Ironman and half-Ironman distance events.

19480 ■ *"Wells' Is Title Sponsor for Volleyball Championship" in Ice Cream Reporter (Vol. 22, August 20, 2008, No. 9, pp. 4)*
Pub: Ice Cream Reporter
Description: Wells' Dairy was chosen to sponsor the 29th Annual National Association of Intercollegiate Athletics (NAIA) Volleyball National Championship to be held in Sioux City, Iowa. Blue Bunny will sponsor the 2008 NAIA Women's Volleyball National Championship, also a Wells' brand.

19481 ■ *"What Players in the Midmarket Are Talking About" in Mergers & Acquisitions: The Dealmaker's Journal (March 1, 2008)*
Pub: SourceMedia, Inc.
Description: Sports Properties Acquisition Corp. went public at the end of January; according to the company's prospectus, it is not limiting its focus to just teams, it is also considering deals for stadium construction companies, sports leagues, facilities, sports-related advertising and licensing of products, in addition to other related segments.

19482 ■ *"What Women Watch on TV" in Marketing to Women (Vol. 21, February 2008, No. 2, pp. 6)*
Pub: EPM Communications Inc.
Contact: Ira Mayer, President
E-mail: imayer@epmcom.com
Description: According to BIGresearch, women are more likely to watch sports than they are soap operas. Statistical data included.

19483 ■ *"Winning Gold" in The Business Journal-Milwaukee (Vol. 25, August 8, 2008, No. 46, pp. A1)*
Pub: American City Business Journals, Inc.
Ed: Rich Rovito. **Description:** Johnson Controls Inc. of Milwaukee, Wisconsin is taking part in the 2008 Beijing Olympics with the installation of its sustainable control equipment and technology that monitor over 58,000 points in 18 Olympic venues. Details of Johnson Controls' green products and sustainable operations in China are discussed.

19484 ■ *"With Traffic Jam in Super Bowl, Can Any Auto Brand Really Win?" in Advertising*

Age (Vol. 81, December 6, 2010, No. 43, pp. 1)
Pub: Crain Communications, Inc.
Ed: Rupal Parekh, Brian Steinberg. **Description:** Car marketers are doubling down for Super Bowl XLV in Arlington, Texas and asking their ad agencies to craft commercials unique enough to break through the clutter and to capture viewers' attention.

TRADE PERIODICALS

19485 ■ *The American Quarter Horse Journal*
Pub: American Quarter Horse Association
URL(s): www.aqha.com/magazines. **Released:** 10/yr. **Price:** $25, Individuals; $50, Canada; $80, Other countries.

19486 ■ *Cutting Horse Chatter: Official Publication of the National Cutting Horse Assn*
Pub: National Cutting Horse Association
Contact: Chubby Turner, President
URL(s): www.chatteronline.comwww.nchacutting.com/ag/pubs/chatterhome.php. **Ed:** Stacy Pigott. **Released:** Monthly

19487 ■ *Deer and Turkey Show Previews*
Pub: Target Communications Corp.
Contact: Glenn Helgeland, President
E-mail: glenn@deerinfo.com
URL(s): www.deerinfo.com/. **Ed:** Glenn Helgeland. **Released:** 1/yr, 5 different states, 1 issue/state. **Price:** Free.

19488 ■ *The Quarter Racing Journal*
Pub: American Quarter Horse Association
URL(s): www.aqha.com/Racing.aspx. **Ed:** Andrea Caudill. **Released:** Monthly **Price:** $25, Individuals; $80, Other countries; $50, Canada; $60, Individuals 3 years; $135, Canada 3 years; $225, Other countries 3 years.

19489 ■ *South Carolina Wildlife*
Pub: South Carolina Department of Natural Resources
URL(s): www.scwildlife.com. **Ed:** David Lucas. **Released:** Bimonthly **Price:** $18, Individuals; $30, Two years.

TRADE SHOWS AND CONVENTIONS

19490 ■ International Sport Summit
E.J. Krause & Associates, Inc.
6550 Rock Spring Dr., Ste. 500
Bethesda, MD 20817
Ph: (301)493-5500
Fax: (301)493-5705
Co. E-mail: info@ejkrause.com
URL: http://www.ejkrause.com
Contact: Sharon Deutch, Director
E-mail: deutch@ejkrause.com
URL(s): www.ejkrause.com. **Frequency:** Annual. **Audience:** Trade professionals. **Principal Exhibits:** Equipment, supplies, and services for sports facilities and events. **Telecommunication Services:** lecker@ejkrause.com.

19491 ■ Michigan Interscholastic Athletic Administrators Mid-Winter Conference
Michigan Interscholastic Athletic Administrator Association
35445 Hathaway
Livonia, MI 48150-2513
Ph: (734)422-3569
Fax: (734)762-9957
URL: http://www.miaaa.com
Contact: Jack Johnson, Convention Manager
E-mail: jakdoljohn@aol.com
URL(s): www.miaaa.com. **Frequency:** Annual. **Audience:** Educators in the field of secondary interscholastic athletic administration. **Principal Exhibits:** Sports supplies, athletic equipment, clothing, publications, fund raisers, and athletic training supplies, and awards companies. **Dates and Locations:** , Grand Traverse Resort.

CONSULTANTS

19492 ■ Jim Castello Marketing Communications Consultants
711 Red Wing Dr.
Lake Mary, FL 32746
Ph: (407)321-6322
Fax: (407)321-8460
Contact: James E. Castello, Jr., President
Scope: Consultant develops creative ideas and marketing strategies, including collateral programs, public relations, advertising, and brochures. Industries served: All golf related industry/business, golf manufacturers, golf resorts, golf residential developments, golf professionals, golf clothing, golf accessories, golf associations, and golf travel. **Founded:** 1989. **Seminars:** How To Seminar for Family Fun Center Entrepreneurs; How To Seminar for Creativity in Golf Marketing; The Golf Business on the Internet.

FRANCHISES AND BUSINESS OPPORTUNITIES

19493 ■ Awards Express
United Trophy Company
2400 First Ave. North
Birmingham, AL 35203
Ph: (205)322-4999
Free: 800-874-5008
Fax: (205)322-4941
Description: Trophies, awards, and recognition and promotional products. **No. of Franchise Units:** 1. **Founded:** 1965.. **Franchised:** 2006. **Equity Capital Needed:** $25,000-$50,000. **Franchise Fee:** $12,500. **Financial Assistance:** Yes. **Training:** Yes.

19494 ■ i9 Sports
1723 S Kings Ave.
Brandon, FL 33511
Ph: (800)975-2937
Fax: (813)662-9114
Co. E-mail: franchisesales@i9sports.com
URL: http://www.i9sports.com
Description: They provide Amateur sports leagues, tournaments & events. **No. of Franchise Units:** 115. **No. of Company-Owned Units:** 1. **Founded:** 2002.. **Franchised:** 2003. **Equity Capital Needed:** $44,900-$72,900. **Franchise Fee:** $19,900. **Royalty Fee:** 7.5%. **Financial Assistance:** Third party financing available. **Training:** 1 week provided at headquarters, 2 days of onsite, and optional refresher training available.

19495 ■ Puckmasters International
2300-2850 Shaughnessy St.
Port Coquitlam, BC, Canada V3C 6K5
Ph: (604)552-4373
Free: 888-775-7825
Fax: (604)552-7709
Co. E-mail: info@puckmasters.com
URL: http://www.puckmasters.com
Description: Hockey training centers. **No. of Franchise Units:** 20. **No. of Company-Owned Units:** 1. **Founded:** 1993.. **Franchised:** 1996. **Equity Capital Needed:** $130,000-$695,000. **Franchise Fee:** $30,000. **Royalty Fee:** 6%. **Training:** 14 days at headquarters, 9 days at franchisees location and ongoing support.

19496 ■ Skyhawks
Skyhawks Sports Camps
6311 E Mt. Spokane Park Dr.
Mead, WA 99021
Free: 800-376-9142
Fax: (888)466-2318
Description: Youth sports programs. **No. of Franchise Units:** 68. **Founded:** 1979.. **Franchised:** 2007. **Equity Capital Needed:** $40,000-$68,000, including franchise fee. **Franchise Fee:** $15,000. **Training:** Yes.

19497 ■ Velocity Sports Performance
151 Kalmus Drive, Bldg. C, Suite-200
Costa Mesa, CA 92626
Ph: (714)640-3360

Fax: (866)269-7024

URL: http://www.velocitysp.com

Description: Training for Sports. **No. of Franchise Units:** 65. **No. of Company-Owned Units:** 5. **Founded:** 1999. **Franchised:** 2002. **Equity Capital Needed:** $554,800-$1,500,000. **Franchise Fee:** $54,000. **Royalty Fee:** 6%. **Training:** Includes 2 weeks training at corporate headquarters, 1 week at franchisee's location, and periodic conferences and quarterly sales training.

COMPUTERIZED DATABASES

19498 ■ *CSW Stats (CSW)*
c/o VegasInsider.com Inc.
5300 NW 33rd Ave., Ste. 119
Fort Lauderdale, FL 33309
Ph: (702)233-5738
Free: 800-321-5562
Fax: (702)294-1322
Co. E-mail: dandros@vegasinsider.com
URL: http://www.cswstats.com
Availability: Online: Computer Sports World; Computer Sports World. **Type:** Directory; Full-text.

19499 ■ *Sports CustomWire®*
625 N Washington St., Ste. 301
Alexandria, VA 22314
Ph: (703)820-2000
Free: 800-266-8399
Fax: (703)820-2005
Co. E-mail: cs@comtex.com
URL: http://www.comtex.com
Contact: Chip Brian, President

Availability: Online: Comtex News Network Inc.; Comtex News Network Inc. **Type:** Full-text.

ASSOCIATIONS AND OTHER ORGANIZATIONS

19500 ■ American Congress on Surveying and Mapping (ACSM)
5119 Pegasus Ct., Ste. Q
Frederick, MD 21704
Ph: (240)439-4615
Fax: (240)439-4952
Co. E-mail: curtis.sumner@acsm.net
URL: http://www.acsm.net
Contact: Curtis W. Sumner, Executive Director
URL(s): www.acsmcongress.org. **Description:** Professionals, technicians, and students in the field of surveying and mapping including surveying of all disciplines, land and geographic information systems, cartography, geodesy, photogrammetry, engineering, geophysics, geography, and computer graphics; American Association for Geodetic Surveying, American Cartographic Association, and National Society of Professional Surveyors. Objectives are to: advance the sciences of surveying and mapping; promote public understanding and use of surveying and mapping; speak on the national level as the collective voice of the profession; provide publications to serve the surveying and mapping community. Member organizations encourage improvement of university and college curricula for surveying and mapping. **Founded:** 1941. **Publications:** *Surveying and Land Information Science* (Quarterly); *Surveying and Land Information Systems: Devoted to the Advancement of the Sciences of Surveying and Mapping*; *Cartography and Geographic Information Science* (Quarterly); *Cartography and Geographic Information Science*. **Awards:** Honorary Member; Presidential Citations; Schonstedt Scholarship in Surveying; AAGS Graduate Fellowship Awards; Nettie Dracup Memorial Scholarships; The NSPS Scholarships; The Schonstedt Scholarships in Surveying; ACSM-CaGIS Map Design Competition Awards; Berntsen International Scholarship in Surveying; The Berntsen International Scholarships in Surveying Technology; AAGS Joseph F. Dracup Scholarship Awards; Kris M. Kunze Memorial Scholarships; The Lowell H. and Dorothy Loving Undergraduate Scholarships; The Cady McDonnell Memorial Scholarships; NSPS Board of Governors Scholarships. **Telecommunication Services:** info@acsm.net; ilse.genovese@acsm.net; csumner@acsm.net.

19501 ■ National Society of Professional Surveyors (NSPS)
5119 Pegasus Ct., Ste. Q
Frederick, MD 21704
Ph: (240)439-4615
Fax: (240)439-4956
Co. E-mail: curtis.sumner@nsps.us.com
URL: http://www.nspsmo.org
Contact: Curtis W. Sumner, Executive Director
Description: Consists of professional surveyors, pre-professionals, technicians, and students. Encourages members to adopt and adhere to standards of ethical and professional behavior and to provide a professional service to the public. Maintains liaison with other professional societies; promotes public confidence in services rendered by members; monitors laws and regulations affecting the profession; helps to develop curricula for teaching surveying. **Awards:** Excellence in Professional Journalism Award; Surveying Excellence Award; NSPS Scholarships; Surveying Excellence Award.

19502 ■ Professional Surveyors Canada—Geometres professionnels du Canada
303 - 1390 Prince of Wales Dr.
Ottawa, ON, Canada K2C 3N6
Ph: (613)695-8333
Free: 800-241-7200
Co. E-mail: info@psc-gpc.ca
URL: http://www.psc-gpc.ca
Contact: Sarah J. Cornett, Executive Director
Description: Represents the interests of professional surveyor in Canada. Aims to build and enable a strong multi-faced community of surveying professionals. Works on behalf of its members to encourage and enable an environment where their work is valued as underpinning the fabric of society for the safety and economic well being of Canadians. **Founded:** 1976. **Awards:** Champlain Award.

19503 ■ Surveyors Historical Society (SHS)
628 Ridge Ave.
Lawrenceburg, IN 47025-1912
Ph: (812)537-2000
Fax: (812)537-2000
Co. E-mail: surveyorshistoricalsociety@yahoo.com
URL: http://www.surveyhistory.org/surveyor's_historical_society.htm
Contact: Roger Woodfill, Administrator
URL(s): www.surveyorshistoricalsociety.com. **Description:** Persons interested in the history of surveying. Dedicated to the preservation of surveying instruments, records, memorabilia, and relics. Seeks to educate the public about the history of surveying. Organizes displays of surveying memorabilia and instruments. Conducts research projects. Operates speakers' bureau and museum; compiles statistics. **Scope:** land surveying, mapping. **Founded:** 1977. **Subscriptions:** 100 books. **Publications:** *Backsights* (Semiannual).

DIRECTORIES OF EDUCATIONAL PROGRAMS

19504 ■ *Directory of Private Accredited Career Schools and Colleges of Technology*
Pub: Accrediting Commission of Career Schools and Colleges of Technology
Contact: Michale S. McComis, Executive Director
Released: On web page. **Price:** Free. **Description:** Covers 3900 accredited post-secondary programs that provide training programs in business, trade, and technical fields, including various small business endeavors. Entries offer school name, address, phone, description of courses, job placement assistance, and requirements for admission. Arrangement is alphabetical.

REFERENCE WORKS

19505 ■ *"Ask Inc." in Inc. (October 2007, pp. 73-74)*
Pub: Gruner & Jahr USA Publishing
Description: An online marketing research firm investigates the use of online communities such as MySpace and Second life in order to recruit individuals to answer surveys.

19506 ■ *"Blacks Go Broadband: High Speed Internet Adoption Grows Among African Americans" in Black Enterprise (Vol. 38, February 2008)*
Pub: Earl G. Graves Publishing Co. Inc.
Ed: Cliff Hocker. **Description:** Number of black households using broadband Internet services tripled since 2005 according to a survey conducted by Pew Internet and American Life Project.

19507 ■ *"Broadband Reaches Access Limits in Europe" in Information Today (Vol. 26, February 2009, No. 2, pp. 22)*
Pub: Information Today, Inc.
Ed: Jim Ashling. **Description:** Eurostat (the Statistical Office of the European communities) reports results from is survey regarding Internet use by businesses throughout its 27-member states. Iceland, Finland and the Netherlands provide the most access at broadband speeds, followed by Belgium, Spain and France.

19508 ■ *"Crime and Punishment" in Canadian Business (Vol. 81, December 24, 2007, No. 1, pp. 21)*
Pub: Rogers Media
Ed: Joe Castaldo. **Description:** Cmpass Inc.'s survey of 137 Canadian chief executive officers showed that they want tougher imposition of sentences on white-collar criminals, as they believe that the weak enforcement of securities laws gives an impression that Canada is a country where it is easy to get away with fraud.

19509 ■ *"Currency: I'm Otta Here" in Entrepreneur (Vol. 35, October 2007, No. 10, pp. 72)*
Pub: Entrepreneur Media Inc.
Ed: C.J. Prince. **Description:** Liberum Research revealed that 193 chief financial officers (CFOs) at small companies have either resigned or retired during the first half of 2007. A survey conducted by Tatum found that unreasonable expectations from the management and compliance to regulations are the main reasons why CFOs are leaving small firms. The chief executive officer's role in making CFOs stay is also discussed.

19510 ■ *"The Duty of Wealth: Canadian Business Leaders on Nepotism and Philanthropy" in Canadian Business (Vol. 80, Winter 2007, No. 24)*
Pub: Rogers Media
Ed: Joe Castaldo. **Description:** Fifty-one percent of the respondents in a survey of business leaders say that the decision to allow adult children to join a fam-

ily firm should be based on the circumstances at the time. He CEOs that were surveyed also believed that billionaires should donate an average of forty percent of their estates and keep the rest for their family.

19511 ■ *"ForeSee Finds Satisfaction On Web Sites, Bottom Line" in Crain's Detroit Business (Vol. 24, February 25, 2008, No. 8, pp. 3)*

Pub: Crain Communications Inc. - Detroit

Ed: Tom Henderson. **Description:** Ann Arbor-based ForeSee Results Inc. evaluates user satisfaction on Web sites. The company expects to see an increase of 40 percent in revenue for 2008 with plans to expand to London, Germany, Italy and France by the end of 2009.

19512 ■ *"Hot Air: On Global Warming and Carbon Tax" in Canadian Business (Vol. 81, October 13, 2008, No. 17, pp. 12)*

Pub: Rogers Media Ltd.

Ed: Joe Castaldo. **Description:** Survey of Canadian business leaders revealed that the environment is a key issue in Canada's federal elections. Respondents believe that Prime Minister Stephen Harper's views on global warming and climate change are closer to their own views. Other key information on the survey is presented.

19513 ■ *"Keep Them Posted" in Entrepreneur (Vol. 35, October 2007, No. 10, pp. 39)*

Pub: Entrepreneur Media Inc.

Ed: Gwen Moran. **Description:** Survey by the Pew Internet and American Life Project found that 12 million American adults maintain blogs, which are created for personal and business reasons. Blogs are effective in giving a business a personal touch while informing the public about its operations and products. Tips on how to create an effective business blog are presented.

19514 ■ *"May I Handle That For You?" in Inc. (March 2008, pp. 40, 42)*

Pub: Gruner & Jahr USA Publishing

Ed: Taylor Mallory. **Description:** According to a recent survey, 53 percent of all companies outsource a portion of their human resources responsibilities. Ceridian, Administaff, Taleo, KnowledgeBank, and CheckPoint HR are among the companies profiled.

19515 ■ *"Merger Brings New Force to Hispanic Marketing Industry" in Hispanic Business (July-August 2007, pp. 60)*

Pub: Hispanic Business

Description: Merger between Latin Force LLC, a marketing strategy firm and Geoscape International Inc., a consumer intelligence and data analytics company is discussed.

19516 ■ *"More Businesses Will Shift Health Costs to Workers" in Business Review, Albany New York (Vol. 34, November 16, 2007, No. 33, pp. 1)*

Pub: American City Business Journals, Inc.

Ed: Barbara Pinckney. **Description:** Survey conducted by consulting firm Benetech Inc. showed that sixty percent of employers are planning to increase payroll deductions to pay for health insurance premiums. More than ninety percent of the employers prefer HMO plans, followed by Preferred Provider Organizations. Other details of the survey are discussed.

19517 ■ *"Nanotech Impact is Smaller Than Hoped For" in Boston Business Journal (Vol. 27, October 26, 2007, No. 39, pp. 1)*

Pub: American City Business Journals Inc.

Ed: Jackie Noblett. **Description:** Survey by the Massachusetts Technology Collaborative showed that nanotechnology firms are within the early stages of operations and need funding to make them profitable. Details on some nanotech companies and their operations and difficulties in developing or mass producing their products are discussed.

19518 ■ *"The Next Generation: African Americans Are Successfully Launching Businesses Earlier In Life" in Black*

Enterprise (January 2008)

Pub: Earl G. Graves Publishing Co. Inc.

Ed: Tennille M. Robinson. **Description:** According to a survey conducted by OPEN, a team dedicated small business at American Express, Generation Y individuals are three times more likely to start their own company. Three African American individuals who did just that are profiled.

19519 ■ *"Praise for Tax Cuts" in Canadian Business (Vol. 80, November 19, 2007, No. 23, pp. 16)*

Pub: Rogers Media

Ed: Joe Castaldo. **Description:** A Compas Inc. survey found that most of the 158 business leaders polled are in favor of federal tax cuts. The findings revealed that the respondents gave an average of 74 percent to the mini-budget, an unusual score for a government initiative. Other opinions on the government's tax relief are presented.

19520 ■ *"Reading the Public Mind" in Harvard Business Review (Vol. 88, October 2010, No. 10, pp. 27)*

Pub: Harvard Business School Publishing

Ed: Andrew O'Connell. **Description:** Examination of the various methods for obtaining public opinion and consumer preferences is provided; an outline of the disadvantages and benefits of both are also given.

19521 ■ *"Survey: Apartment Rents Continue to Climb as Home Market Slows" in Business Review, Albany New York (November 23, 2007)*

Pub: American City Business Journals, Inc.

Ed: Michael DeMasi. **Description:** Survey by Sunrise Management and Consulting shows that asking rents for apartments in the Capital Region increased for the thirteenth consecutive time. The survey, which was conducted between August and October 2007, also showed that Albany County, New York had the highest average asking rent, followed by Rensselaer County, Saratoga County, and Schenectady County.

19522 ■ *"Survey Profile" in Small Business Economic Trends (April 2008, pp. 19)*

Pub: National Federation of Independent Business

Ed: William C. Dunkelberg, Holly Wade. **Description:** Two graphs and a table presenting the profile of small businesses that participated in the National Federation of Independent Business (NFIB) survey are provided. The actual number of firms, their industry types, and the number of full and part-time employees are also given.

19523 ■ *"Survey Profile" in Small Business Economic Trends (March 2008, pp. 19)*

Pub: National Federation of Independent Business

Ed: William C. Dunkelberg, Holly Wade. **Description:** Two graphs and a table that present the profile of small businesses that participated in the National Federation of Independent Business (NFIB) survey are provided. The actual number of firms, their industry types, and the number of full and part-time employees are also given.

19524 ■ *"Survey Profile" in Small Business Economic Trends (February 2008, pp. 19)*

Pub: National Federation of Independent Business

Ed: William C. Dunkelberg, Holly Wade. **Description:** Two graphs and a table that present the profile of small businesses that participated in the National Federation of Independent Business (NFIB) survey are provided. The actual number of firms, their industry types, and the number of full and part-time employees are also given.

19525 ■ *"Survey Says Commercial Real Estate Headed for Turbulence" in Commercial Property News (March 17, 2008)*

Pub: Nielsen Company

Description: Commercial real estate sector is declining due to the sluggish U.S. economy. According to a recent survey, national office, retail and hospitality markets are also on the decline.

19526 ■ *"Tell Us What You Really Think Collecting Customer Feedback" in Inc. (Vol. 30, December 2008, No. 12, pp. 52)*

Pub: Mansueto Ventures LLC

Ed: Ryan Underwood. **Description:** According to a recent survey, nearly 77 percent of online shoppers review consumer-generated reviews of products before making a purchase.

19527 ■ *"To Offshore Or Not To Offshore?" in Converting (Vol. 25, October 1, 2007, No. 10, pp. 10)*

Pub: Reed Business Information Inc.

Ed: Mark Spaulding. **Description:** Offshore manufacturing and the issue of buying raw materials from foreign suppliers by American companies is discussed. Results of a study conducted by Cap Gemini and Pro Logis regarding offshore manufacturing, especially to China, are presented.

19528 ■ *"Yes, No, and Somewhat Likely: Survey the World with Web Polls" in Inc. (October 2007, pp. 58-59)*

Pub: Gruner & Jahr USA Publishing

Ed: Don Steinberg. **Description:** Online tools for surveying customers, employees and the general public include Zoomergan zPro and Zoomerang Sample, software designed to send surveys and allows viewing results; SurveyMonkey software creates, administers and allows viewing online surveys and results; Vizu software places a one-question poll on a particular Website; and Vovici EFM Feedback, a subscription service providing ongoing surveys to customers or employees.

TRADE PERIODICALS

19529 ■ *CE News*

Pub: Mercor Media

URL(s): www.cenews.com. **Ed:** Bob Drake. **Released:** Monthly

19530 ■ *Geomatica*

Pub: Canadian Institute of Geomatics

Contact: Anthony Sani, President

URL(s): www.cig-acsg.ca/english/geomatica/geomatica.php. **Ed:** Mike Pinch. **Released:** Quarterly **Price:** C$275, Canada.

19531 ■ *NAMS News Online*

Pub: National Association of Marine Surveyors

Contact: Steven P. Weiss, President

Ed: Chris LaBure, Editor. **Released:** Semiannual. **Description:** Provides news of interest to marine surveyors, underwriters, and adjusters. Covers developments at the International Maritime Bureau, government regulations affecting the field, the national marine conference, and regional meetings. Recurring features include news of research, news of members, information on publications available, and columns titled Cargo and Yachts.

19532 ■ *The Ontario Land Surveyor*

Pub: Association of Ontario Land Surveyors

URL(s): www.aols.org/contact.asp. **Released:** Quarterly

19533 ■ *Professional Surveyor*

Pub: Reed Business Geo, Inc.

URL(s): www.profsurv.com/. **Ed:** TJ Frazier. **Released:** Monthly **Price:** $20, Canada; $72, Other countries.

TRADE SHOWS AND CONVENTIONS

19534 ■ **California Land Surveyors Association Conference**

California Land Surveyors Association (CLSA)

526 S E St.

Santa Rosa, CA 95404

Ph: (707)578-6016

Fax: (707)578-4406

Co. E-mail: clsa@californiasurveyors.org

URL: http://www.californiasurveyors.org/index.asp

Contact: Bill Hofferber, President

E-mail: bhofferb@rcflood.org

URL(s): www.californiasurveyors.org/conference. html. **Price:** $125, Pre-registered; $150, Onsite. **Frequency:** Annual. **Audience:** Land surveyors and civil engineers. **Principal Exhibits:** Land surveying equipment, computers, vehicles, software, and two-way communication systems.

COMPUTER SYSTEMS/ SOFTWARE

19535 ■ *Land Survey Calculator*
4768 Rte. 89
Romulus, NY 14487
Ph: (315)257-9303
Free: 800-828-6772
Fax: (315)549-7118
Co. E-mail: info@dynacompsoftware.com
Price: $19.95. **Description:** Available for PC computers. Program for performing land survey calculations.

19536 ■ *Sight Survey Professional 2009*
PO Box 9646
Asheville, NC 28815
Ph: (828)338-2516
Free: 800-777-7978
Co. E-mail: support@carlsonsw.com
URL: http://www.carlsonsw.com/PL_Simplicity.html
Description: Available for Windows 95/98/NT/ 2000/XP compatibles. Coordinate geometry program for land surveyors. Integrates COGO and CAD.

LIBRARIES

19537 ■ Alberta Land Surveyor's Association Library
10020 - 101A Ave., Ste. 1000
Edmonton, AB, Canada T5J 3G2
Ph: (403)429-8805
Free: 800-665-2572
Fax: (403)429-3374
Co. E-mail: info@alsa.ab.ca
URL: http://www.ccls-ccag.ca
Contact: Brian E. Munday, Executive Director
URL(s): www.alsa.ab.ca. **Scope:** Surveying. **Services:** Copying; library open to the public at librarian's discretion. **Founded:** 1910. **Holdings:** Books and videos. **Telecommunication Services:** munday@ alsa.ab.ca.

19538 ■ British Columbia Land Surveyors Foundation - Anna Papove Memorial Library
2400 Bevan Ave., Ste. 301
Sidney, BC, Canada V8L 1W1
Ph: (250)655-7222
Fax: (250)655-7223
Co. E-mail: abcls@telus.net
URL: http://www.abcls.ca
Contact: Vicki Pettigrew
Scope: Surveying - land, water, air; boundaries. **Services:** Copying; library open to the public. **Founded:** 1905. **Holdings:** 900 books; 100 serials; 100 reports; 100 VF drawers; 5 videotapes; 50 other cataloged items; archival records. **Subscriptions:** 10 journals and other serials from land surveying associations. **Telecommunication Services:** crintoul@abcls.ca.

19539 ■ Washington State Department of Natural Resources - Public Land Survey Office
Natural Resources Bldg., 3rd Fl.
1111 Washington St., SE
Olympia, WA 98504
Ph: (360)902-1190
Fax: (360)902-1191
Co. E-mail: plso@dnr.wa.gov
URL: http://www.dnr.wa.gov/businesspermits/topics/ surveys/pages/eng_plso_overview.aspx
Contact: Mick Sprouffske, Supervisor
Scope: Cadastral and geodetic survey information. **Services:** Copying; office open to the public for a fee(appointment preferred). **Founded:** 1951. **Holdings:** 300,000 aperture cards of survey maps; 300 reels of microfilm of original government survey notes; 3500 field books from private surveyors; 500,000 scanned images of survey maps and historic survey documents.

RESEARCH CENTERS

19540 ■ Hope College - Carl Frost Center for Social Science Research
100 E 8th St., Ste. 220
Holland, MI 49422-9000
Ph: (616)395-7556
Fax: (616)395-7410
Co. E-mail: hill@hope.edu
URL: http://www.hope.edu/frostcenter
Contact: Dr. Martin Hill, Director
Founded: 1990. **Publications:** *Carl Frost Center for Social Science Research Reports.* **Awards:** Course-release research fellowships; Carl Frost Center for Social Science Research Student internship; Student faculty research grants. **Telecommunication Services:** frostcenter@hope.edu.

ASSOCIATIONS AND OTHER ORGANIZATIONS

19541 ■ Association of Pool and Spa Professionals (APSP)
2111 Eisenhower Ave., Ste. 500
Alexandria, VA 22314
Ph: (703)838-0083
Fax: (703)549-0493
Co. E-mail: memberservices@apsp.org
URL: http://www.apsp.org
Contact: Joe Amato, Chairman of the Board
Description: Builders, dealers, designers, service companies, retail stores, engineers, manufacturers, distributors, public officials, suppliers, and service persons concerned with public and residential swimming pools, spas, and hot tubs. Aims to raise spa and pool industry standards; expand interest and use of swimming pools, spas, and hot tubs; seeks to achieve uniformity in federal, state, and local regulations affecting swimming pool, spa, and hot tub operations. Promotes the industry to the consumer; protects interests of the industry through government relations and technical programs. Establishes voluntary standards for the design and construction of swimming pools and spas. Compiles cost of doing business data and other statistics. **Founded:** 1956. **Publications:** *AQ* (Quarterly). **Educational Activities:** International Expo (Annual). **Awards:** International Awards of Excellence; APSP International Awards of Excellence (Annual); Swimming Pool, Spa, and Hot Tub Awards of Excellence (Annual).

19542 ■ Diving Equipment and Marketing Association (DEMA)
3750 Convoy St., Ste. 310
San Diego, CA 92111-3741
Ph: (858)616-6408
Free: 800-862-3483
Fax: (858)616-6495
Co. E-mail: info@dema.org
URL: http://www.dema.org
Contact: Jeff Nadler, Vice President
Description: International recreational scuba diving and snorkeling organizations and associations promoting or reporting diving activities, individuals or organizations providing educational, retail, travel, media or other services in the field. Aims to promote advancement within the diving equipment industry, encourage the growth of diving activities, and enhance public enjoyment of recreational diving. Cooperates with domestic governmental and private agencies that develop standards or are involved in regulating activities affecting the diving industry and related products. Seeks to establish continuing education programs to instruct and assist industry members in business, quality control and the marketing of diving products. Organizes conferences dealing with topics such as governmental regulations, product standards, quality control, and standardized bookkeeping methods. **Scope:** scuba diving, snorkeling. **Founded:** 1972. **Publications:** *DEMA News & Industry Report* (Monthly). **Educational Activities:** Diving Equipment and Marketing Association Tradeshow (Annual).

19543 ■ IAPMO—IAPMO Research and Testing Inc.
5001 E Philadelphia St.
Ontario, CA 91761-2816
Ph: (909)472-4100
Free: 800-854-2766
Fax: (909)472-4150
Co. E-mail: iapmo@iapmo.org
URL: http://www.iapmo.org
Contact: Dan Daniels, President
Description: Government agencies, administrative officials, sales representatives, manufacturers, associations, and members of associations related to the plumbing field. Sponsors and writes Uniform Plumbing Codes; also sponsors Uniform Mechanical Code. Sponsors speakers' bureau. **Founded:** 1926. **Publications:** *Official Magazine* (Bimonthly); *Drinking Water & Backflow Prevention; Directory of Listed Plumbing Products* (Bimonthly); *Directory of Manufactured Housing/RV Research Recommendations* (Bimonthly); *Official* (Bimonthly); *Directory of Listed Plumbing Products for Mobile Homes and Recreational Vehicles* (Bimonthly); *Directory of Listed Plumbing Products* (Weekly); *Directory of Listed Plumbing Products for Mobile Homes and Recreational Vehicles* (Bimonthly); *Uniform Mechanical Illustrated Training Manual* (Periodic); *Uniform Plumbing Code Illustrated Training Manual.* **Awards:** American Flag Award (Annual); Government Person of the Year (Annual); Industry Person of the Year (Annual); George Kauffman Lifetime Achievement Award (Annual); Joseph Kneidinger Green Contractor of the Year (Annual).

19544 ■ National Swimming Pool Foundation (NSPF)
4775 Granby Cir.
Colorado Springs, CO 80919-3131
Ph: (719)540-9119
Fax: (719)540-2787
Co. E-mail: info@nspf.org
URL: http://www.nspf.org
Contact: John D. Puetz, President
Description: Aims to improve public health by creating a safer aquatic environment through education and research and to attract more people to aquatic exercise. Works toward its mission with educational products like the Aquatic Safety Compendium, Certified Pool/Spa Operator training, Certified Pool/Spa Inspector training and the World Aquatic Health Conference. Provides program for pool and spa operators and health officials, certifying over 200,000 from 45 countries. **Founded:** 1965. **Publications:** *Aquatic Risk Management* (Periodic); *Emergency Response Planning Book* (Periodic); *Pool Math Workbook* (Periodic). **Awards:** Board of Directors' Scholarship Award; Ray B. Essick Scholarship Award; Research Fellowship Grants; NSPF Ray B. Essick Scholarship Awards; National Swimming Pool Foundation Board of Directors' Scholarship Awards; National Swimming Pool Foundation Scholarship Awards.

REFERENCE WORKS

19545 ■ *"Everyone Out of the Pool' in Barron's (Vol. 89, July 20, 2009, No. 29, pp. 18)*
Pub: Dow Jones & Co., Inc.
Ed: Sandra Ward. **Description:** Shares of Pool Corp. could drop as continued weakness in the housing market weakens the market for swimming pool equipment. The company's shares are trading at $18.29, about 20 times projected 2009 earnings of $0.91 a share.

SOURCES OF SUPPLY

19546 ■ *AQUA--Buyers' Guide Issue*
Athletic Business Publications Inc.
URL(s): www.aquamagazine.com. **Ed:** Scott Webb. **Released:** Annual; Latest edition 2009. **Covers:** Swimming pool and spa product manufacturers, distributors, representatives, and trade shows. **Entries include:** Company name, address, phone, fax, E-mail, toll-free phone, website, name and title of contact, number of employees, geographical area served for distributors and representatives only, year established, products manufactured (or sold in the case of the distributors & representatives). **Arrangement:** Alphabetical; distributors and representatives also listed geographical by state. **Indexes:** Brand name; product manufactured; state covered (distributors & representatives).

STATISTICAL SOURCES

19547 ■ *RMA Annual Statement Studies*
Pub: Risk Management Association
Contact: Kevin M. Blakey, President
Released: Annual. **Price:** $175.00 2006-07 edition, $105.00. **Description:** Contains composite balance sheets and income statements for more than 360 industries, including the accounting, auditing, and bookkeeping industries. Also contains five years of comparative historical data for discerning trends. Includes 16 commonly used ratios, computed for most of the size groupings for nearly every industry.

TRADE PERIODICALS

19548 ■ *AQUA Magazine: The Business Magazine for Spa and Pool Professionals*
Pub: Athletic Business Publications Inc.
URL(s): www.aquamagazine.com/default.aspx. **Released:** Monthly

19549 ■ *Pool & Spa Marketing*
Pub: Kenilworth Media Inc.
URL(s): www.poolspamarketing.com/. **Released:** 6/yr. **Price:** $98, Other countries; $77, Individuals.

TRADE SHOWS AND CONVENTIONS

19550 ■ Atlantic City Pool and Spa Show
Northeast Spa & Pool Association
6B South Gold Dr.
Hamilton, NJ 08691

Ph: (732)972-9111
Fax: (609)689-9110
Co. E-mail: info@nespapool.org
URL: http://www.nespapool.org
Contact: Lawrence S. Caniglia, Executive Director
URL(s): www.nespapool.org/acshow. **Frequency:** Annual. **Audience:** Swimming pool and spa industry retailers, builders, installers, service companies, and pool operators. **Principal Exhibits:** Pools, spas, pumps, filters, heaters, chemicals, toys/games, outdoor furniture, enclosures, covers (pool, spa), parts, accessories, decks, pool tables, wood-burning stoves, Christmas products, saunas, tanning beds, computer software. **Dates and Locations:** , Atlantic City Convention Center.

19551 ■ IHS Adana
Tuyap Fairs and Exhibitions Organization Inc.
E-5 Karayolu Uzeri
Gurpinar Kavsagi
34500 Istanbul, Turkey
Ph: 90 212 8671100
Co. E-mail: sales@tuyap.com.tr
URL: http://www.tuyap.com.tr
URL(s): www.tuyap.com.tr/. **Frequency:** Biennial. **Audience:** Builders, architects, and other industry professionals. **Principal Exhibits:** Heating, cooling, air conditioning, natural gas, installation, insulation, latest technologies.

CONSULTANTS

19552 ■ Bucher, Willis and Ratliff Corp.—Bucher, Willis and Ratliff Consulting Engineers, Planners
903 E 104th St., Ste. 800
Kansas City, MO 64131-3451
Ph: (816)363-2696
Fax: (816)363-0027
URL: http://www.bwrcorp.com
Contact: Larry White, President
Scope: Professional consulting engineers, planners and architects offering engineering services in studying the feasibility, planning, design, specification writing and inspection of construction for bridges, highways, streets, dams, airports, industrial and domestic water and waste treatment facilities, environmental compliance, water and sewerage systems and cross country utilities. Also offers planning services in comprehensive planning, recreational planning, urban renewal planning, airport planning, transportation planning, off-street parking and zoning for statewide, regional and local governmental agencies, as well as architectural services in the design of governmental centers, group housing, schools, swimming pools and commercial and industrial buildings. **Founded:** 1957. **Seminars:** The New Normal: Development Trends in a Changing Economy, 2010; Quality of life, Oct, 2008; Transportation Workshop, Sep,

2008; Infrastructure workshop, Jun, 2008; Housing Workshop, May, 2008; Community development, Apr, 2008; Focus session, Mar, 2008.

19553 ■ Milton Costello, Consulting Engineer
4 Sandstone Ln.
Stony Brook, NY 11790-3102
Ph: (631)751-3030
Co. E-mail: poolengr@prodigy.net
Contact: Milton Costello, President
E-mail: poolengr07@gmail.com
Scope: Consulting engineer specializing in aquatic facilities, swimming pool projects, auditoriums, park complexes and open water recreation facilities and soil mechanics structures and related construction failures. Expert witness in swimming pool and related aquatic safety injury cases. **Founded:** 1951.

19554 ■ Short Elliott Hendrickson Inc. (SEH)
3535 Vadnais Center Dr.
Saint Paul, MN 55110-5196
Ph: (651)490-2000
Free: 800-325-2055
Fax: (651)490-2150
Co. E-mail: info@sehinc.com
URL: http://www.sehinc.com
Contact: Sam Claassen, President
E-mail: sclaassen@sehinc.com
Scope: Expertise in airport planning and design, architectural design, electrical or mechanical engineering, environmental engineering, heavy civil, municipal engineering, transportation, urban design, waste water engineering, water engineering. **Founded:** 1927. **Publications:** "Sending the Right Signals: Project Management for Telecommunication Sites on Water Tanks," Journal of Protective Coatings & Linings, May, 2008; "The Transportation Aspect of Disaster Planning," 2008; "Performance Or Preference? a Look at Selected Systems for Water Tank Interiors," Journal of Protective Coatings & Linings, May, 2007; "Old Tanks, Tight Budgets: How Does the Job Get Done," Journal of Protective Coatings & Linings, May, 2005; "Painting for Antenna Installations on Water Storage Facilities," Today Magazine, Feb, 2003; "Bioterrorism, Cyberterrorism and Water Supplies," Wisconsin Water Well Association Journal, Jan, 2003; "They're Water Storage Tanks," Today Magazine, Jul, 2002. **Telecommunication Services:** bphelps@sehinc.com. **Special Services:** SEH®.

19555 ■ Veenstra & Kimm Inc.
3000 Westown Pkwy.
West Des Moines, IA 50266-1320
Ph: (515)225-8000
Free: 800-241-8000
Fax: (515)225-7848
Co. E-mail: vk@v-k.net
URL: http://www.v-k.net
Contact: Robert H. Veenstra, President
E-mail: bveenstra@v-k.net
Scope: The practice includes a wide range of consulting services involving sewer systems and

wastewater treatment plants, water supply, distribution, storage and treatment, streets and highways, airports, bridges, land surveys and site planning, swimming pools, solid waste disposal systems, and expert testimony on engineering matters in litigations. **Founded:** 1961.

FRANCHISES AND BUSINESS OPPORTUNITIES

19556 ■ ASP-America's Swimming Pool Co.
ASP Franchising Inc.
Description: Swimming pool maintenance and repairs. **No. of Franchise Units:** 98. **No. of Company-Owned Units:** 1. **Founded:** 2001.. **Franchised:** 2005. **Equity Capital Needed:** $48,840-$89,960. **Franchise Fee:** $22,000-$37,000. **Royalty Fee:** 8-5%. **Financial Assistance:** Third party financing available. **Training:** Provides 12 days training at headquarters, 2 days onsite and ongoing support.

LIBRARIES

19557 ■ Chemtura Corporation Library
1801 U.S. Hwy. 52, W.
West Lafayette, IN 47906
Ph: (765)497-6275
Fax: (765)497-6680
Co. E-mail: annharmon@chemtura.com
URL: http://www.e1.greatlakes.com/corp/common/jsp/index.jsp
Contact: Ann Harmon, Librarian
URL(s): www.chemtura.com. **Scope:** Chemistry - bromine, organic, polymer; flame retardants; pool chemicals; business resources. **Services:** Copying; SDI; Library not open to the public. **Founded:** 1965. **Holdings:** 4000 books; 2000 bound periodical volumes; 10,000 reports; 5000 archival materials; 100 microfiche; 600 reels of microfilm. **Subscriptions:** 250 journals and other serials; 5 newspapers.

19558 ■ International Swimming Hall of Fame - Henning Library
One Hall of Fame Dr.
Fort Lauderdale, FL 33316
Ph: (954)462-6536
Fax: (954)525-4031
Co. E-mail: ischmid@ishof.org
URL: http://www.ishof.org/library.html
Contact: Bob Duenkel, Executive Director
Scope: Swimming history and instruction, sports medicine and psychology, pool care and management, diving and water polo, swim officiating, synchronized swimming. **Services:** Copying; research services; photo duplication; Library open to the public by appointment. **Founded:** 1968. **Holdings:** 7601 books; 130 bound periodical volumes; 307 scrapbooks; 110 theses and dissertations; 92 archives; guidebooks; swimmers' biographies; games, charts, tables for swimming officiating. **Subscriptions:** 20 journals and other serials. **Telecommunication Services:** bduenkel@ishof.org.

DIRECTORIES OF EDUCATIONAL PROGRAMS

19559 ■ *Directory of Private Accredited Career Schools and Colleges of Technology*
Pub: Accrediting Commission of Career Schools and Colleges of Technology
Contact: Michale S. McComis, Executive Director
Released: On web page. **Price:** Free. **Description:** Covers 3900 accredited post-secondary programs that provide training programs in business, trade, and technical fields, including various small business endeavors. Entries offer school name, address, phone, description of courses, job placement assistance, and requirements for admission. Arrangement is alphabetical.

REFERENCE WORKS

19560 ■ *"A Family's Fortune" in Canadian Business (Vol. 80, Winter 2007, No. 24, pp. 103)*
Pub: Rogers Media
Ed: Graham F. Scott. **Description:** James Richardson started as a tailor before moving into the grain business because his clients paid him in sacks of wheat and barley. The James Richardson and Sons Ltd. entered the radio business in 1927 but later sold it off in 1951.

TRADE PERIODICALS

19561 ■ *The Custom Tailor*
Pub: Custom Tailors and Designers Association of America
URL(s): www.ctda.com/. **Ed:** Suzanne Kilgore. **Released:** 3/yr. **Price:** $50, Individuals.

VIDEOCASSETTES/ AUDIOCASSETTES

19562 ■ *How to Make Money in a Home-Based Sewing Business*
Nancy's Notions Ltd.
333 Beichl Ave.
P.O. Box 683
Beaver Dam, WI 53916-0683
Ph: (920)887-7321
Free: 800-725-0361
Fax: (800)255-8119
Co. E-mail: customerservice@nancysnotions.com
URL: http://www.nancysnotions.com
Released: 1989. **Description:** Turn your hobby into a money-making operation with these sew-for-profit tips. **Availability:** VHS.

FRANCHISES AND BUSINESS OPPORTUNITIES

19563 ■ **Heel Quik! & Heel/Sew Quik!**
Heel Quik!, Inc.
2359 Windy Hill Rd., Ste. 400
Marietta, GA 30067
Ph: (770)951-9440
Fax: (770)933-8268
Description: Instant shoe repair, clothing alterations and monogramming. **No. of Franchise Units:** 730. **No. of Company-Owned Units:** 2. **Founded:** 1984.. **Franchised:** 1985. **Equity Capital Needed:** $20,000-$85,000. **Franchise Fee:** $17,500. **Training:** Yes.

ASSOCIATIONS AND OTHER ORGANIZATIONS

19564 ■ **Association of Talent Agents (ATA)**
9255 Sunset Blvd., Ste. 930
Los Angeles, CA 90069
Ph: (310)274-0628
Fax: (310)274-5063
Co. E-mail: rnoval@agentassociation.com
URL: http://www.agentassociation.com
Contact: Karen Stuart, Executive Director

Description: Talent agencies that have clients in the Screen Actors Guild, American Federation of Television and Radio Artists, Directors Guild of America, Writers Guild of America, East, and Writers Guild of America, West. Negotiates terms of franchise agreements with these guilds and maintains liaison with their representatives. Assists members with contract problems, interpretations, rulings, residual matters, and arbitrations. Employs legal counsel to prepare opinions upon request and to file briefs in arbitrations and labor commission hearings. Maintains liaison with labor commission representatives in San Francisco and Los Angeles, CA, and intervenes on behalf of individual members having special problems. Conducts seminars and symposia. **Scope:** law, arbitration, minority rights, legislative history. **Founded:** 1937. **Subscriptions:** books monographs periodicals. **Publications:** *Employment Law.* **Awards:** Distinguished Agent (Periodic).

19565 ■ **International Entertainment Buyers Association (IEBA)**
600 12th Ave. S, No. 513
Nashville, TN 37203-6615
Ph: (615)679-9601
Free: 888-999-4322
Fax: (615)463-0163
Co. E-mail: info@ieba.org
URL: http://www.ieba.org
Contact: Tiffany Davis, Executive Director

Description: Talent buyers and sellers, artists, managers, agents, venue operators and managers, and entertainment organizations; others with an interest in the entertainment industry, including advertisers, promoters, lighting, sound, and film technicians, and staging, production, and music businesses. Promotes professional advancement of members; seeks to ensure provision of high-quality entertainment purchasing services to customers. Serves as a clearinghouse on talent agencies and upcoming performances; facilitates exchange among members; represents members' commercial and professional interests. **Founded:** 1970. **Awards:** Several Industry Award (Annual).

REFERENCE WORKS

19566 ■ *Billboard's International Talent and Touring Guide*
Pub: Nielsen Co.
Contact: Greg Farrar, President

URL(s): www.orderbillboard.com/ProductDetails.aspx?ID=78194. **Released:** Annual; Latest edition 2012. **Price:** $179, Individuals. **Covers:** Over 30,000 artists, managers and agents from 68 countries worldwide, including the USA. and Canada; tour facilities and services; venues; entertainers, booking agents, hotels, and others in the entertainment industry; international coverage. **Entries include:** Company name, address, phone, fax, names and titles of key personnel. **Arrangement:** Classified by line of business; venues are then geographical. **Indexes:** Product/service.

19567 ■ *"A Digital Makeover for the Modeling Business" in Inc. (February 2008, pp. 82-86, 88-89)*
Pub: Gruner & Jahr USA Publishing
Ed: David H. Freedman. **Description:** Ways the Ford Modeling Agency is using the online You Tube to realign its business are presented. Products to help a firm grow its presence on the Internet are included.

19568 ■ *Hollywood Representation Directory*
Pub: Nielsen Co.
Contact: Greg Farrar, President

URL(s): www.hcdonline.com. **Released:** Latest edition 38th. **Price:** $64.95, Individuals. **Covers:** Over 2,000 agencies and management companies, and over 10,000 agents and personal managers within those companies. Majority of listings are located in Los Angeles and New York. **Entries include:** company name, staff names and titles, address, phone, fax, e-mail address, web site address, company type, types of clients, and guild and organization affiliations. **Arrangement:** Alphabetical by company. **Indexes:** Client category, affiliation, individual names.

19569 ■ *International Television and Video Almanac*
Pub: Quigley Publishing Co.
Contact: William J. Quigley, President

URL(s): quigleypublishing.com/. **Ed:** Eileen Quigley. **Released:** Annual; January; latest edition 2013. **Price:** $235, Individuals. **Covers:** "Who's Who in Motion Pictures and Television and Home Video," television networks, major program producers, major group station owners, cable television companies, distributors, firms serving the television and home video industry, equipment manufacturers, casting agencies, literary agencies, advertising and publicity representatives, television stations, associations, list of feature films produced for television; statistics, industry's year

in review, award winners, satellite and wireless cable provider, primetime programming, video producers, distributors, wholesalers. **Entries include:** Generally, company name, address, phone; manufacturer and service listings may include description of products and services and name of contact; producing, distributing, and station listings include additional detail, and contacts for cable and broadcast networks. **Arrangement:** Classified by service or activity. **Indexes:** Full.

19570 ■ *Talk Show Yearbook*
Pub: Broadcast Interview Source Inc.
Contact: Kevin Madden, Manager

URL(s): www.expertclick.com. **Ed:** Mitchell P. Davis. **Released:** Annual; winter. **Price:** $185, Individuals. **Covers:** more than 700 contacts at radio and television talk shows. **Entries include:** Name of contact, format, market, address, phone, fax, name of talk show, station call letters, ADI information. **Database includes:** Reports on the top 100 markets in the country. **Arrangement:** Geographical. **Indexes:** Station call letters or network name.

TRADE PERIODICALS

19571 ■ *Variety: The International Entertainment Weekly*
Pub: Reed Business Information
Contact: Jeff Greisch, President

URL(s): www.reedbusiness.com/us.html. **Ed:** Tim Gray. **Released:** Weekly; 50/yr. **Price:** $259, Individuals; $25, Individuals monthly.

TRADE SHOWS AND CONVENTIONS

19572 ■ **International Association of Fairs and Expositions Trade Show**
International Association of Fairs and Expositions (IAFE)
3043 E. Cairo St.
Springfield, MO 65802
Ph: (417)862-5771
Free: 800-516-0313
Fax: (417)862-0156
Co. E-mail: iafe@fairsandexpos.com
URL: http://www.fairsandexpos.com
Contact: Jim Tucker, Chief Executive Officer
E-mail: jimt@fairsandexpos.com

URL(s): www.fairsandexpos.com. **Frequency:** Annual. **Audience:** Fair managers, staffs, and board members; carnival owners and staffs; concessionaires; talent and other agencies related to the fair industry. **Principal Exhibits:** Talent agencies, concessionaires, novelties, amusement devices, insurance, ribbons, plaques, attractions, and equipment. Products and services for the fair industry. **Dates and Locations:** , Hilton Hotel. **Telecommunication Services:** iafe@fairsandexpos.com.

ASSOCIATIONS AND OTHER ORGANIZATIONS

19573 ■ Suntanning Association for Education (SAE)
PO Box 1181
Gulf Breeze, FL 32562
Ph: (850)939-3388
Free: 800-536-8255
Fax: (801)348-9571
Co. E-mail: suntanningedu@gmail.com
URL: http://www.suntanningedu.com
Description: Companies and individuals involved in the indoor tanning industry. Educates members and the public about indoor tanning. Conducts educational and training program for salon operators; sponsors research. **Founded:** 1986.

REFERENCE WORKS

19574 ■ "Looking Like a Million Bucks" in Entrepreneur (Vol. 37, August 2009, No. 8, pp. 102)
Pub: Entrepreneur Media, Inc.
Ed: Jason Daley. **Description:** Sunset Tan's Jeff Bozz says he and Devin Haman are executive producers of the show and that they want to stretch the truth a bit and make fun of it. Haman says the business is all about VIP service for everyone and that they want all their clients to feel like celebrities.

FRANCHISES AND BUSINESS OPPORTUNITIES

19575 ■ Aruba Tanning Franchise
Aruba Franchising Group, LLC
3456 Emmorton Rd.
Abingdon, MD 21009
Ph: (813)935-5087
Fax: (813)425-5799
Description: Tanning salon. **No. of Company-Owned Units:** 2. **Founded:** 2005.. **Franchised:** 2007. **Equity Capital Needed:** $242,000-$630,000. **Franchise Fee:** $29,500. **Training:** Yes.

19576 ■ Executive Tans
CSE International LLC
603 Park Point Dr., No. 224
Golden, CO 80401
Ph: (303)988-9999
Free: 877-393-2826
Fax: (303)988-5390
Description: Tanning salon. **No. of Franchise Units:** 35. **Founded:** 1991. **Franchised:** 1995. **Equity Capital Needed:** $258,000-$448,000. **Franchise**

Fee: $25,000. **Royalty Fee:** $795/month. **Training:** Includes 1 week training at headquarters, 1 week at franchisee's location and ongoing support.

19577 ■ Image Sun Tanning Centers
TC Franchising Inc.
5514 Metro Pky.
Sterling Heights, MI 48310
Free: 866-313-8266
Fax: (586)314-0516
Co. E-mail: franchise@ateimagesun.com
URL: http://www.imagesun.com
Description: Tanning salon. **No. of Franchise Units:** 31. **No. of Company-Owned Units:** 5. **Founded:** 1996.. **Franchised:** 2000. **Equity Capital Needed:** $187,000-$440,000. **Franchise Fee:** $25,000. **Financial Assistance:** Yes. **Training:** Up to 1 week and 5 days onsite with ongoing support.

19578 ■ Mama Mio Pregnancy Spa & Imaging Centre
Becoming Mom
5685 Deerfield Blvd.
Mason, OH 45040
Ph: (813)935-5087
Fax: (813)425-5799
Description: Maternity spa. **No. of Company-Owned Units:** 1. **Founded:** 2006.. **Franchised:** 2007. **Equity Capital Needed:** $250,000-$460,000. **Franchise Fee:** $37,500. **Training:** Yes.

19579 ■ Palm Beach Mega Tan
Palm Beach Franchise Corp.
1411 King St., E
Courtice, ON, Canada L1E 2J6
Ph: (905)434-8168
Free: 888-878-7882
Fax: (905)434-2579
Co. E-mail: info@palmbeachmegatan.com
URL: http://www.palmbeachmegatan.com
Description: Upscale and professional tanning salon franchise. Extensive in-house training with ongoing support. State of the art equipment, looks better and gets fast effective tanning results. Secure and successful operating system comes with extensive manuals. President nominated for Canadian Woman Entrepreneur of the Year 2003, Business Excellence Award 2002, Canadian Salon of the Year Award 1995 and 1997. **No. of Franchise Units:** 25. **No. of Company-Owned Units:** 3. **Founded:** 1992.. **Franchised:** 2001. **Equity Capital Needed:** $50,000 start-up capital; $270,000 total investment. **Franchise Fee:** $20,000. **Training:** Full salon and classroom training provided.

19580 ■ The Palms Tanning Resort
8577 E Arapahoe Rd., Ste. A
Greenwood Village, CO 80112

Ph: (720)488-6890
Fax: (303)688-3789
URL: http://www.thepalmstanningresort.com
Description: Tanning salon. **No. of Franchise Units:** 2. **No. of Company-Owned Units:** 3. **Founded:** 2003.. **Franchised:** 2003. **Equity Capital Needed:** $489,750-$517,000. **Franchise Fee:** $35,000. **Royalty Fee:** 6%. **Financial Assistance:** Limited third party financing available. **Training:** Offers 1 week training at headquarters, 1 week onsite and ongoing support.

19581 ■ Planet Beach Franchising Corporation
5161 Taravella rd.
Marrero, LA 70072
Ph: (504)361-5550
Fax: (504)361-5540
Description: Tanning spa franchise. **No. of Franchise Units:** 340. **No. of Company-Owned Units:** 1. **Founded:** 1995.. **Franchised:** 1996. **Equity Capital Needed:** Liquid capital $50,000 (market specific). **Franchise Fee:** $10,000 non-uv; $30,000 with uv. **Financial Assistance:** Yes. **Training:** Yes.

19582 ■ Sol'exotica Tanning Spa
Sol'exotica Franchising Inc.
1425 Cormorant Rd., Ste. 302
Ancaster, ON, Canada L9G 4V5
Ph: (905)529-3826
Free: 866-432-1826
Co. E-mail: franchising@solexotica.com
URL: http://www.solexotica.com
Description: Tanning salon. **No. of Franchise Units:** 25. **Founded:** 1994.. **Franchised:** 2007. **Equity Capital Needed:** $40,000 start-up capital required; $45,000-$200,000 investment required. **Franchise Fee:** $15,000. **Training:** Yes, from A to Z.

19583 ■ SunBanque Island Tanning
Sunbanque Corp.
2384 Yonge St., Ste. 1400
Toronto, ON, Canada M4P 3J4
Ph: (416)488-5838
Description: Offers sun tanning services. **No. of Franchise Units:** 10. **No. of Company-Owned Units:** 5. **Founded:** 1983. **Franchised:** 1983. **Equity Capital Needed:** $30,000-$40,000. **Franchise Fee:** $5,000. **Financial Assistance:** Yes. **Training:** Yes.

19584 ■ Tropi Tan
5152 Commerce Rd.
Flint, MI 48507
Ph: (810)230-6789
Fax: (810)230-1115
Description: Tanning services. **No. of Franchise Units:** 14. **No. of Company-Owned Units:** 5. **Founded:** 1979.. **Franchise Fee:** $25,000. **Training:** Yes.

ASSOCIATIONS AND OTHER ORGANIZATIONS

19585 ■ National Tattoo Association (NTA)
485 Business Park Ln.
Allentown, PA 18109-9120
Ph: (610)433-7261
Fax: (610)433-7294
Co. E-mail: curt@nationaltattoo.com
URL: http://www.nationaltattooassociation.com
Contact: Florence Makofske, Treasurer
Description: Tattoo artists and enthusiasts. Promotes tattooing as a viable contemporary art form; seeks to upgrade standards and practices of tattooing. Offers advice on selecting a tattoo artist and studio. Holds seminars for tattoo artists to improve skills and learn better hygienic practices. Operates museum and biographical archives. **Scope:** tattoo. **Founded:** 1976. **Subscriptions:** 6. **Awards:** Best Black/White Design Sheet; Best Cover-Up Tattoo; Best Portrait Tattoo; Best Sleeve; Best Tattooed Female; Best Tattooed Male; Best Tattooist; Best Traditional Tattoo; Best Unique Tattoo; Bob Shaw Golden Age Award; Enthusiast of the Year; Fine Art Award; Most Realistic Tattoo; Nicest Studio Award; Best Black and Gray Design Sheet (Annual); Best Black/Gray Back Piece (Annual); Best Cover-Up Tattoo (Annual); Best Large Tattoo (Annual); Best Portrait Tattoo (Annual); Best Tattooed Female (Annual); Best Tattooed Male (Annual); Best Tattooist (Annual); Best Traditional Style Tattoo (Annual); Best Unique Tattoo (Annual); Bob Show Golden Age Award (Annual); Elizabeth Weinzirl Award (Annual); Most Realistic Tattoo (Annual); Nicest Tattoo Studio (Annual).

REFERENCE WORKS

19586 ■ "King Ink" in Inc. (November 2007, pp. 98-102, 104, 106, 108)
Pub: Gruner & Jahr USA Publishing
Ed: Max Chafkin. **Description:** Profile of Mario Barth, whose goal is to build the Starbucks of tattoo parlors; the tattoo industry is worth $2.3 billion in the U.S.

19587 ■ "Verizon Small Business Awards Give Companies a Technology Edge" in Hispanic Business (July-August 2009, pp. 32)
Pub: Hispanic Business
Ed: Patricia Marroquin. **Description:** Verizon Wireless awards grants to twenty-four companies in California. The winning businesses ranged from barbershop to coffee shop, tattoo parlor to florist.

TRADE PERIODICALS

19588 ■ Tattoo: The Magazine of Dermagraphics
Pub: Paisano Publications L.L.C.
Contact: John Lagana, Chief Executive Officer
URL(s): www.easyriders.com. **Released:** Monthly **Price:** $29.95, Individuals; $54.95, Two years.

TRADE SHOWS AND CONVENTIONS

19589 ■ National Tattoo Association Convention
National Tattoo Association
485 Business Park Ln.
Allentown, PA 18109-9120
Ph: (610)433-7261
Co. E-mail: nattat2@fast.net
URL: http://www.nationaltattooassociation.com
URL(s): www.nationaltattooassociation.com/convention.html. **Price:** $40, Pre-registered; $50, Onsite. **Frequency:** Annual. **Audience:** Trade professionals and general public. **Principal Exhibits:** Tattooing, jewelry, books, t-shirts, and other tattoo related items.

LIBRARIES

19590 ■ Lyle Tuttle Tattooing - Tattoo Art Museum Library
837 Columbus Ave.
San Francisco, CA 94133
Ph: (707)462-4406
Fax: (707)462-4433
Co. E-mail: lyletutt@pacific.net
Contact: Lyle Tuttle, Director
Scope: Tattooing and related arts. **Services:** Copying; Library open to the public. **Founded:** 1974. **Holdings:** 200 books; drawings; tattoo equipment; memorabilia; art reproductions.

START-UP INFORMATION

19591 ■ *The 100 Best Businesses to Start When You Don't Want To Work Hard Anymore*
Pub: Career Press Inc.
Ed: Lisa Rogak. **Price:** $16.99. **Description:** Author helps burned-out workers envision a new future as a small business owner. Systems analysis, adventure travel outfitting, bookkeeping, food delivery, furniture making, and software development are among the industries examined.

ASSOCIATIONS AND OTHER ORGANIZATIONS

19592 ■ American Taxation Association (ATA)
9201 University City Blvd.
Charlotte, NC 28223
Ph: (704)687-7696
Co. E-mail: americantaxationassociation@aaahq.org
URL: http://aaahq.org/ata/index.htm
Contact: Sandy Callaghan, President
Description: Membership comprises primarily university professors teaching federal income tax, federal estate, and/or gift tax courses; other members are practitioners, including certified public accountants. Seeks to further taxation education. Researches the impact of the tax process, particularly tax code sections, on the social and economic structure of the U.S. Maintains speakers' bureau. **Founded:** 1974. **Awards:** Dissertation Award; Outstanding Service Award (Annual); Ray M. Sommerfeld Outstanding Tax Educator Award (Annual); Tax Manuscript Award; Teaching Innovation Award (Annual).

19593 ■ Canadian Institute of Chartered Accountants (CICA)—L'Institut Canadien des comptables agrees - Institut Canadien des Comptables Agrees
277 Wellington St. W
Toronto, ON, Canada M5V 3H2
Ph: (416)977-3222
Free: 800-268-3793
Fax: (416)977-8585
Co. E-mail: member.services@cica.ca
URL: http://www.cica.ca
Contact: Kevin J. Dancey, President
E-mail: kevin.dancey@cica.ca
Description: Sets national accounting, auditing, and financial reporting standards. Maintains an active professional development program for its members. Represents the profession's viewpoint on federal legislation issues and matters of national concern. Confers with other national organizations to achieve worldwide harmonization of accounting and auditing standards. **Founded:** 1902. **Publications:** *Directory of Canadian Chartered Accountants* (Periodic); *Directory of Canadian Chartered Accountants* (Periodic); *Directory of Canadian Chartered Accountants* (Biennial); *CA Magazine: For Canada's Chartered Accountants*. **Telecommunication Services:** jan.burns@cica.ca.

19594 ■ Canadian Tax Foundation (CTF)—L'Association Canadienne d'Études Fiscales (ACEF)
595 Bay St., Ste. 1200
Toronto, ON, Canada M5G 2N5
Ph: (416)599-0283
Free: 877-733-0283
Fax: (416)599-9283
Co. E-mail: admin@ctf.ca
URL: http://www.ctf.ca
Contact: Larry Chapman, Chief Executive Officer
E-mail: lchapman@ctf.ca
Description: Individuals and organizations with an interest in taxation. Promotes increased awareness of the Canadian Tax Code and the social ramifications of taxation. Serves as a clearinghouse on taxation; sponsors research and educational programs. **Services:** Information service: for members. **Founded:** 1945. **Publications:** *Annual Conference Report*; *CTF Annual Report* (Monthly); *Canadian Tax Highlights* (Monthly); *Canadian Tax Journal* (Bimonthly; Quarterly); *Canadian Tax Papers Series* (Occasionally); *Finances of the Nation* (Annual); *Tax Memos*; *Tax for the Owner Manager* (Quarterly); *Taxation of Private Corporations and Their Shareholders* (Occasionally). **Educational Activities:** National tax and corporate management tax conferences (Annual); Regional conferences (Annual). **Telecommunication Services:** srichardson@ctf.ca.

19595 ■ *Canadian Tax Journal*
595 Bay St., Ste. 1200
Toronto, ON, Canada M5G 2N5
Ph: (416)599-0283
Free: 877-733-0283
Fax: (416)599-9283
Co. E-mail: admin@ctf.ca
URL: http://www.ctf.ca
Contact: Larry Chapman, Chief Executive Officer
E-mail: lchapman@ctf.ca
URL(s): www.ctf.ca/ctfweb/en/. **Ed:** Brian R. Carr. **Released:** Bimonthly; Quarterly **Price:** C$55, Single issue mailing cost, outside Canada; $295, Individuals.

19596 ■ *Directory of Canadian Chartered Accountants*
277 Wellington St. W
Toronto, ON, Canada M5V 3H2
Ph: (416)977-3222
Free: 800-268-3793
Fax: (416)977-8585
Co. E-mail: member.services@cica.ca
URL: http://www.cica.ca
Contact: Kevin J. Dancey, President
E-mail: kevin.dancey@cica.ca
Released: Periodic

19597 ■ Institute of Tax Consultants (ITC)
7500 212th SW, Ste. 205
Edmonds, WA 98026-7617
Ph: (425)774-3521
Co. E-mail: kraemerc@juno.com
URL: http://www.taxprofessionals.homestead.com/welcome.html
Contact: Carol Kraemer, Registrar
Description: Aims to provide tax practitioners with the opportunity to upgrade their professionalism through certification. Conducts educational programs and certification examinations. **Founded:** 1981.

19598 ■ National Association of Tax Professionals (NATP)
PO Box 8002
Appleton, WI 54914-8002
Free: 800-558-3402
Co. E-mail: natp@natptax.com
URL: http://www.natptax.com
Contact: Jo Ann Schoen, President
Description: Serves professionals who work in all areas of tax practice, including individual practitioners, enrolled agents, certified public accountants, accountants, attorneys and certified financial planners. **Founded:** 1979. **Publications:** *TAXPRO Journal* (Quarterly); *TAXPRO Weekly E-Mail* (Weekly). **Awards:** Tax Professional of the Year (Annual).

19599 ■ National Society of Accountants (NSA)
1010 N Fairfax St.
Alexandria, VA 22314
Ph: (703)549-6400
Free: 800-966-6679
Fax: (703)549-2984
Co. E-mail: members@nsacct.org
URL: http://www.nsacct.org
Contact: Sharon E. Cook, President
Description: Professional organization and its affiliates represent 30,000 members who provide auditing, accounting, tax preparation, financial and estate planning, and management services to approximately 19 million individuals and business clients. Most members are sole practitioners or partners in small to mid-size accounting firms. **Founded:** 1945. **Publications:** *Income and Fees of Accountants in Public Practice*; *NSA Practice Advisor* (8/year); *NSAlert* (Biweekly); *National Public Accountant*; *NSPA Washington Reporter*; *National Society of Public Accountants - Yearbook*. **Awards:** National Society of Accountants Scholarship Program; The Stanley H. Stearman Awards; Accountant of the Year (Annual); ASO of the Year (Annual). **Telecommunication Services:** arichman@nsacct.org; arichman@nsacct.orgg.

19600 ■ National Tax Association (NTA)
725 15th St. NW, No. 600
Washington, DC 20005-2109
Ph: (202)737-3325
Fax: (202)737-7308
Co. E-mail: natltax@aol.com
URL: http://www.ntanet.org
Contact: Matthew N. Murray, President
Description: Government and corporate tax officials, accountants, consultants, economists, attorneys, and others interested in the field of taxation. Promotes nonpartisan academics, study of taxation; encour-

ages better understanding of the common interests of national, state, and local governments in matters of taxation and public finance; and disseminates higher quality research through publications and conferences. **Founded:** 1907. **Publications:** *National Tax Journal* (Quarterly). **Educational Activities:** Conference on Taxation; Spring Symposium (Annual). **Awards:** Daniel M. Holland Medal (Annual); Outstanding Doctoral Dissertation Award (Annual); Daniel M. Holland Medal; Jeanne S. Mattersdorf Memorial Fund Award; Outstanding Doctoral Dissertation Award; NTA-TIA Outstanding Doctoral Dissertation Honorable Mention Award (Annual).

19601 ■ Professional Accountant
250 Consumers Rd., Ste. 1007
Toronto, ON, Canada M2J 4V6
Ph: (416)350-8145
Free: 877-515-4447
Fax: (416)350-8146
Co. E-mail: president@professionalaccountant.org
URL: http://www.professionalaccountant.org
Contact: Mr. John Singer, Vice President
Released: Quarterly

19602 ■ Society of Professional Accountants of Canada (SPAC)—La societe des comptables professionnels du Canada
250 Consumers Rd., Ste. 1007
Toronto, ON, Canada M2J 4V6
Ph: (416)350-8145
Free: 877-515-4447
Fax: (416)350-8146
Co. E-mail: president@professionalaccountant.org
URL: http://www.professionalaccountant.org
Contact: Mr. John Singer, Vice President
Description: Professional accountants and individuals working to pass qualifying accountancy examinations. Promotes ongoing professional education among accountants; encourages students to enter the accounting field; works to advance the profession of accounting. Gathers and disseminates information on accounting; sponsors educational programs; conducts professional accountancy qualifying examinations. **Founded:** 1978. **Publications:** *Professional Accountant* (Quarterly).

19603 ■ Tax Executives Institute (TEI)
1200 G St. NW, Ste. 300
Washington, DC 20005-3814
Ph: (202)638-5601
Fax: (202)638-5607
URL: http://www.tei.org
Contact: Timothy J. McCormally, Executive Director
Description: Professional society of executives administering and directing tax affairs for corporations and businesses. Maintains TEI Education Fund. **Founded:** 1944. **Publications:** *The Tax Executive* (Bimonthly); *The Tax Executive*; *The Tax Executive* (Bimonthly); *Value-Added Taxes - A Comparative Analysis.* **Awards:** Distinguished Service Award (Annual).

REFERENCE WORKS

19604 ■ "2011 Tax Information of Interest" in Business Owner (Vol. 35, November-December 2011, No. 6, pp. 10)
Pub: DL Perkins Company
Description: Compilation of 2011 tax information to help small business take advantage of all tax incentives.

19605 ■ "Accrual vs. Cash Accounting, Explained" in Business Owner (Vol. 35, July-August 2011, No. 4, pp. 13)
Pub: DL Perkins Company
Description: Cash method versus accrual accounting methods are examined, using hypothetical situations.

19606 ■ "Adler Blanchard & Freeman Reports New SmartKeeper Bookkeeping Service" in Professional Services Close-Up (March 24, 2011)
Pub: Close-Up Media
Description: Profile of Adler Blanchard & Freeman (AB&F) accountants and business advisors. The firm

has expanded its client offerings to include their new SmartKeeper Business and Personal Bookkeeping Service for small to mid-sized companies and individuals.

19607 ■ Beat the Taxman 2006: Easy Ways to Save Tax in Your Small Business
Pub: John Wiley & Sons, Incorporated
Ed: Stephen Thompson. **Released:** May 2006. **Price:** $21.95. **Description:** Tax advice is given to help small businesses maximize returns for 2006.

19608 ■ Beat the Taxman 2007: Easy Ways to Save Tax in Your Small Business, 2007 Edition For the 2006 Tax Year
Pub: John Wiley & Sons, Incorporated
Ed: Stephen Thompson. **Released:** December 2006. **Price:** $26.99. **Description:** Year-round tax planner for entrepreneurs; the book is written in a question and answer format to help small business owners save money on annual taxes.

19609 ■ Beat the Taxman: Easy Ways to Tax Save in Your Small Business
Pub: John Wiley & Sons, Incorporated
Ed: Stephen Thompson. **Released:** May 2008. **Price:** $26.95. **Description:** Concise tax planner to help entrepreneurs take advantage of current tax laws.

19610 ■ "A Bigger Deal" in Crain's Cleveland Business (Vol. 28, November 12, 2007, No. 45, pp. 1)
Pub: Crain Communications, Inc.
Ed: Shawn A. Turner. **Description:** In an attempt to boost its revenue CBiz Inc., a provider of accounting and business services, is looking to balance its acquisitions of smaller companies with larger ones as part of its overall growth strategy.

19611 ■ "Bookkeeping Service Opens First Sacramento Franchise" in Sacramento Bee (April 13, 2011)
Pub: Sacramento Bee
Ed: Mark Glover. **Description:** Franchise bookkeeping service called BookKeeping Express opened its new office in Roseville, California; its first shop in the area.

19612 ■ "Businesses Balk at 1099 Provision in Health Reform Law" in Baltimore Business Journal (Vol. 28, August 13, 2010, No. 14, pp. 1)
Pub: Baltimore Business Journal
Ed: Scott Dance. **Description:** Small business advocates and accountants have criticized the Internal Revenue Service Form 1099 provision in the health care reform law as not worth the cost of time and money. Critics believe the policy would create a deluge of the documents that is too much for the companies or the IRS to handle. Details of the provision are also discussed.

19613 ■ "Changing the Rules of the Accounting Game" in Canadian Business (Vol. 81, December 8, 2008, No. 21, pp. 19)
Pub: Rogers Media Ltd.
Ed: Al Rosen. **Description:** Interference from world politicians in developing accounting standards is believed to have resulted in untested rules that are inferior to current standards. European lawmakers have recently asked to change International Financial Reporting Standards.

19614 ■ "Channeling for Growth" in The Business Journal-Serving Greater Tampa Bay (Vol. 28, July 11, 2008, No. 29, pp. 1)
Pub: American City Business Journals, Inc.
Ed: Margie Manning. **Description:** HSN Inc., one of the largest employers in Tampa Bay, Florida, is expected to spend an additional $9.7 million annually as it plans to hire more accounting, internal audit, legal, treasury and tax personnel after its spin-off to a public company. Details on the company's sales growth are provided.

19615 ■ "Convergence Collaboration: Revising Revenue Recognition" in Management Accounting Quarterly (Vol. 12,

Spring 2011, No. 3, pp. 18)
Pub: Management Accounting Quarterly
Ed: Jack T. Ciesielski, Thomas R. Weirich. **Description:** While revenue recognition is critical, regulations have been developed on an ad hoc basis until now. The joint FASB/IASB proposed accounting standard on revenue recognition is a meaningful convergence of standards that will require a major adjustment for financial statement preparers. The proposal is a radical departure from the way revenue has been recognized by the U.S. GAAP. For industries such as consulting, engineering, construction, and technology, it could dramatically change revenue recognition, impacting the top line. The new proposed standard, its potential impact, and the critical role that contracts play is examined thoroughly.

19616 ■ "Crash Pads" in Business Courier (Vol. 24, November 2, 2008, No. 29, pp. 1)
Pub: American City Business Journals, Inc.
Ed: Jon Newberry. **Description:** Francisca Webster accumulated $4 million in mortgage debt in about 2 months. She filed a lawsuit against her tax preparer and her mortgage broker contending that the defendants had breached their fiduciary duties to her and made fraudulent misrepresentations to her. The other details of the case are supplied.

19617 ■ Deduct It! Lower Your Small Business Taxes
Pub: NOLO
Ed: Stephen Fishman. **Released:** November 2006. **Price:** $34.99. **Description:** Information is provided to help small companies maximize taxable deductions.

19618 ■ Deduct It!: Lower Your Small Business Taxes
Pub: NOLO
Ed: Stephen Fishman. **Released:** November 2009. **Price:** $34.99. **Description:** Ways to make the most of tax deductions for any small business are covered. The book is organized into categories featuring common deductions, start-up expenses, health deductions, entertainment, travel, inventory, equipment and more. Current tax laws and numbers for 2008 are included.

19619 ■ "Defer Tax with Installment Sale Election" in Business Owner (Vol. 35, September-October 2011, No. 5, pp. 12)
Pub: DL Perkins Company
Description: It is critical to consult with a tax professional before selling any high-value asset in order to minimize taxes.

19620 ■ "DHS Finalizes Rules Allowing Electronic I-9s" in HR Specialist (Vol. 8, September 2010, No. 9, pp. 5)
Pub: Capitol Information Group Inc.
Description: U.S. Department of Homeland Security issued regulations that give employers more flexibility to electronically sing and store I-9 employee verification forms.

19621 ■ Directory of Global Professional Accounting and Business Certifications
Pub: John Wiley & Sons, Incorporated
Ed: Lal Balkaran. **Released:** February 9, 2007. **Price:** $35.00. **Description:** Resource for international accounting, auditing, and business professions.

19622 ■ "Do Fair Value Adjustments Influence Dividend Policy?" in Accounting and Business Research (Vol. 41, Spring 2011, No. 2, pp. 51)
Pub: American Institute of Certified Public Accountants
Contact: Barry C. Melancon, President
E-mail: bmelancon@aicpa.org
Ed: Igor Goncharov, Sander van Triest. **Description:** The impact of positive fair value adjustments on corporate distributions is examined using a Russian setting that requires disclosure of unrealized fair value adjustments in income. It was found that there is no rise in dividends due to positive fair value adjustments and that on the contrary, a negative relationship exists between adjustments and dividend changes.

19623 ■ *"Down to the Wire for Your Taxes"* in *Women In Business (Vol. 63, Spring 2011, No. 1, pp. 22)*

Pub: American Business Women's Association

Ed: Maureen Sullivan. Description: A look at a last-minute checklist to consult before filing annual corporate tax returns for a small business owner is presented. Enlisting professional help for small business taxes is always a good investment. However, small business owners have to make sure their records back up their filing when planning to go it alone.

19624 ■ *EBay Income: How ANYONE of Any Age, Location, and/or Background Can Build a Highly Profitable Online Business with eBay*

Pub: Atlantic Publishing Company

Released: December 1, 2010. Price: $24.95. Description: A complete overview of eBay is given and guides any small company through the entire process of creating the auction and auction strategies, photography, writing copy, text and formatting, multiple sales, programming tricks, PayPal, accounting, creating marketing, merchandising, managing email lists, advertising plans, taxes and sales tax, best time to list items and for how long, sniping programs, international customers, opening a storefront, electronic commerce, buy-it now pricing, keywords, Google marketing and eBay secrets.

19625 ■ *"Economic Crisis and Accounting Evolution"* in *Accounting and Business Research (Vol. 41, Summer 2011, No. 3, pp. 2159)*

Pub: American Institute of Certified Public Accountants

Contact: Barry C. Melancon, President

E-mail: bmelancon@aicpa.org

Ed: Gregory Waymire, Sudipta Basu. Description: Financial reporting changes at the face of economic crises are studied using a punctuated equilibrium evolution. Findings show that financial reporting has a minor impact but may amplify economic crises. Attempts to enhance accounting amid economic crises may not be as beneficial as planned.

19626 ■ *"Economic Crisis and Accounting Evolution"* in *Accounting and Business Research (Vol. 41, Summer 2011, No. 3, pp. 2159)*

Pub: Routledge

Ed: Gregory Waymire, Sudipta Basu. Description: Financial reporting changes at the face of economic crises are studied using a punctuated equilibrium evolution. Findings show that financial reporting has a minor impact but may amplify economic crises. Attempts to enhance accounting and economic crises may not be as beneficial as planned.

19627 ■ *Electronic Commerce: Technical, Business, and Legal Issues*

Pub: Prentice Hall PTR

Ed: Oktay Dogramaci; Aryya Gangopadhyay; Yelena Yesha; Nabil R. Adam. Released: August 1998. Description: Provides insight into the goals of using the Internet to grow a business in the areas of networking and telecommunication, security, and storage and retrieval; business areas such as marketing, procurement and purchasing, billing and payment, and supply chain management; and legal aspects such as privacy, intellectual property, taxation, contractual and legal settlements.

19628 ■ *Employer Legal Forms Simplified*

Pub: Nova Publishing Company

Ed: Daniel Sitarz. Released: August 2007. Price: $24.95. Description: Business reference containing the following forms needed to handle employees in any small business environment: application, notice, confidentiality, absence, federal employer forms and notices, and many payroll forms. All forms are included on a CD that comes in both PDF and text formats. Adobe Acrobat Reader software is also included on the CD. The forms are valid in all fifty states and Washington, DC.

19629 ■ *"Finally, Justice"* in *Canadian Business (Vol. 82, April 27, 2009, No. 7, pp. 12)*

Pub: Rogers Media

Ed: John Gray. Description: Former investment adviser Alex Winch feels that he was vindicated with the Canadian Court's ruling that Livent Inc. founders Garth Drabinsky and Myron Gottlieb were guilty of fraud. Drabinsky filed a libel case on Winch over Winch's letter that complained over Livent's accounting procedures. Winch also criticized the inconsistent accounting during Drabinsky's term as chief executive of another firm.

19630 ■ *"Foreign (In)Direct Investment and Corporate Taxation"* in *Canadian Journal of Economics (Vol. 44, November 2011, No. 4, pp. 1497)*

Pub: Blackwell Publishers Ltd.

Ed: Georg Wamser. Description: Foreign investments of multinational firms are often complex in that they involve conduit entities. In particular, a multinational can pursue either a direct or an indirect investment strategy, where the latter involves an intermediate corporate entity and is associated with enhanced opportunities for international tax planning. As a consequence, in the case of indirect investments, the role of corporate taxation in destination countries may change. An investigation into the effects of corporation taxation on foreign investment decisions of German multinationals, taking explicitly into account that firms choose in a first stage the investment regime. (direct vs. indirect) is provided.

19631 ■ *"Getting More Out of Retirement"* in *Agency Sales Magazine (Vol. 39, November 2009, No. 10, pp. 48)*

Pub: MANA

Ed: Joshua D. Mosshart. Description: Overview of the Tax Increase Prevention and Reconciliation Act, which lets employees convert to a Roth IRA in 2010. The benefits of conversion depend on age and wealth and it is best to consult a tax advisor to determine the best strategy for retirement planners.

19632 ■ *"Give Until It Works"* in *Hispanic Business (Vol. 30, March 2008, No. 3, pp. 26)*

Pub: Hispanic Business

Ed: Rick Munarriz. Description: Donating to qualified charities and non-profit organizations for maximizing tax advantage to be availed on the income tax bill is examined. The amount that can be deducted from the total taxable amount is usually less then the actual amount donated and must be made during that calendar year.

19633 ■ *Home Business Tax Deductions: Keep What You Earn*

Pub: NOLO

Ed: Stephen Fishman. Released: November 2006. Price: $34.99. Description: Home business tax deductions are outlined. Basic information on the ways various business structures are taxed and how deductions work is included.

19634 ■ *"How To: Manage Your Cash Better"* in *Inc. (Volume 32, December 2010, No. 10, pp. 69)*

Pub: Inc. Magazine

Description: A monthly guide to policies, procedures and practices for managing cash for a small business.

19635 ■ *"IFRS Monopoly: the Pied Piper of Financial Reporting"* in *Accounting and Business Research (Vol. 41, Summer 2011, No. 3, pp. 291)*

Pub: American Institute of Certified Public Accountants

Contact: Barry C. Melancon, President

E-mail: bmelancon@aicpa.org

Ed: Shyam Sunder. Description: The disadvantages of granting monopoly to the international financial reporting standards (IFRS) are examined. Results indicate that an IFRS monopoly removes the chances for comparing alternative practices and learning from

them. An IFRS monopoly also eliminates customization of financial reporting to fit local differences in governance, business, economic, and legal conditions.

19636 ■ *"Internal Auditor Wants Ethics Review of City's Casper Golf Contract"* in *Business Courier (Vol. 27, September 10, 2010, No. 19, pp. 1)*

Pub: Business Courier

Ed: Dan Monk. Description: Mark Ashworth, an internal auditor for Cincinnati, Ohio is pushing for an ethics review of management contract for seven city-owned golf courses. Ashworth wants the Ohio Ethics Commission to investigate family ties between a superintendent for the Cincinnati Recreation Commission and Billy Casper Golf.

19637 ■ *"IRS Announces New Standards for Tax Preparers"* in *Bellingham Business Journal (Vol. February 2010, pp. 9)*

Pub: Sound Publishing Inc.

Ed: Isaac Bonnell. Description: A new oversight plan was announced by the Internal Revenue Services (IRS) that will require tax professionals to pass a competency test and register with the government in order to ensure greater accountability in the industry.

19638 ■ *"It's Time to Take Full Responsibility"* in *Harvard Business Review (Vol. 88, October 2010, No. 10, pp. 42)*

Pub: Harvard Business School Publishing

Ed: Rosabeth Moss Kanter. Description: A case for corporate responsibility is cited, focusing on long-term impact and the effects of public accountability.

19639 ■ *JK Lasser's Small Business Taxes 2077: Your Complete Guide to a Better Bottom Line*

Pub: John Wiley & Sons, Incorporated

Ed: Barbara Weltman. Released: November 2006. Price: $17.95. Description: J.K. Lasser's guide that offers tax facts and strategies for small businesses. The book helps to maximize deductions while learning tax planning strategies.

19640 ■ *"Kaboom!"* in *Canadian Business (Vol. 81, November 10, 2008, No. 19, pp. 18)*

Pub: Rogers Media Ltd.

Ed: Al Rosen, Mark Rosen. Description: International Financial Reporting Standards (IFRS) is a good idea in theory but was implemented in a hurry and had poor quality standards from the beginning.

19641 ■ *"Know Your Numbers"* in *Inc. (Volume 32, December 2010, No. 10, pp. 39)*

Pub: Inc. Magazine

Ed: Norm Brodsky. Description: Ways to maximize profit and minimize tax burden are presented.

19642 ■ *"Lifesavers"* in *Black Enterprise (Vol. 41, December 2010, No. 5, pp. 38)*

Pub: Earl G. Graves Publishing Co. Inc.

Ed: Tamara E. Holmes. Description: Profile of Interventional Nephrology Specialists Access Center and founders Dr. Omar Davis and Dr. Natarsha Grant; the center generated $5.5 million in revenue for 2009. Details on how they run their successful center are included.

19643 ■ *"Living in a 'Goldfish Bowl"* in *WorkingUSA (Vol. 11, June 2008, No. 2, pp. 277)*

Pub: Blackwell Publishers Ltd.

Ed: John Lund. Description: Recent changes in laws, regulations and even the reporting format of labor organization annual financial reports in both the U.S. and Australia have received surprisingly little attention, yet they have significantly increased the amount of information available both to union members and the public in general, as reports in both countries are available via government Websites. While such financial reporting laws are extremely rare in European countries, with the exception of the UK and Ireland, the U.S. and Australian reporting systems have become among the most detailed in the world. After reviewing these changes in financial reporting and the availability of these reports, as well as comparing and contrasting the specific reporting requirements of each country, this paper then examines the cost-benefit impact of more detailed financial reporting.

19644 ■ Make Sure It's Deductible
Pub: McGraw-Hill Companies Inc.
Contact: Deven Sharma, President
Ed: Evelyn Jacks. **Released:** November 2006. **Price:** $22.95. **Description:** Tax planning, strategies are provided to help small businesses maximize deductions.

19645 ■ Make Your Life Tax Deductible: Easy Techniques to Reduce Your Taxes and Start Building Wealth Immediately
Pub: McGraw-Hill Companies Inc.
Contact: Deven Sharma, President
Ed: David Meier. **Released:** December 2005. **Price:** $16.95 (US), $22.95 (Canadian). **Description:** Over 150 tax deductions are listed to help small business owners lower taxes and boost profits.

19646 ■ "May I Handle That For You?" in Inc. (March 2008, pp. 40, 42)
Pub: Gruner & Jahr USA Publishing
Ed: Taylor Mallory. **Description:** According to a recent survey, 53 percent of all companies outsource a portion of their human resources responsibilities. Ceridian, Administaff, Taleo, KnowledgeBank, and CheckPoint HR are among the companies profiled.

19647 ■ MBA In a Day
Pub: John Wiley and Sons, Inc.
Ed: Steven Stralser, PhD. **Released:** 2004. **Price:** $34.95. **Description:** Management professor presents important concepts, business topics and strategies that can be used by anyone to manage a small business or professional practice. Topics covered include: human resources and personal interaction, ethics and leadership skills, fair negotiation tactics, basic business accounting practices, project management, and the fundamentals of economics and marketing.

19648 ■ "Merger Mania: Regional Snaps Up HVS" in The Business Journal-Serving Greater Tampa Bay (Vol. 28, September 26, 2008, No. 40, pp. 1)
Pub: American City Business Journals, Inc.
Ed: Alexis Muellner. **Description:** It was reported that Harper Van Scoik & Co. LLP has finalized a merger with Carr Riggs & Ingram LLC. The agreement, effective October 1, 2008, is a merger of HVS assets into CRI. Bill Carr, a managing partner, revealed that HVS' $5 million in revenue will take CRI from $78 million to $82 million in revenue.

19649 ■ "My Favorite Tool for Managing Expenses" in Inc. (Volume 32, December 2010, No. 10, pp. 60)
Pub: Inc. Magazine
Ed: J.J. McCorvey. **Description:** Web-based service called Expensify is outlined. The service allows companies to log expenses while away from the office using the service's iPhone application.

19650 ■ "New Century's Fall Has a New Culprit" in Barron's (Vol. 88, March 31, 2008, No. 13, pp. 20)
Pub: Dow Jones & Company, Inc.
Ed: Jonathan R. Laing. **Description:** Court examiner Michael Missal reports that New Century Financial's auditor contributed to New Century's demise by its negligence in permitting improper and imprudent practices related to New Century's accounting processes. New Century's bankruptcy filing is considered the start of the subprime-mortgage crisis.

19651 ■ "New Institutional Accounting and IFRS" in Accounting and Business Research (Vol. 41, Summer 2011, No. 3, pp. 309)
Pub: American Institute of Certified Public Accountants
Contact: Barry C. Melancon, President
E-mail: bmelancon@aicpa.org
Ed: Peter Wysocki. **Description:** A new framework for institutional accounting research is presented. It has five fundamental components — efficient versus inefficient results, interdependencies, causation, level

of analysis, and institutional structure. The use of the framework for evaluation accounting institutions such as the international financial reporting standards is discussed.

19652 ■ "New Institutional Accounting and IFRS" in Accounting and Business Research (Vol. 41, Summer 2011, No. 3, pp. 309)
Pub: Routledge
Ed: Peter Wysocki. **Description:** A new framework for institutional accounting research is presented. It has five fundamental components: efficient versus inefficient results, interdependencies, causation, level of analysis, and institutional structure. The use of the framework for evaluation accounting institutions such as the international financial reports standards (IFRS) is discussed.

19653 ■ "Olympus is Urged to Revise Board" in Wall Street Journal Eastern Edition (November 28, 2011, pp. B3)
Pub: Dow Jones & Company Inc. Enterprise Media Group
Contact: Clare Hart, President
Ed: Phred Dvorak. **Description:** Koji Miyata, once a director on the board of troubled Japanese photographic equipment company, is urging the company to reorganize its board, saying the present group should resign their board seats but keep their management positions. The company has come under scrutiny for its accounting practices and costly acquisitions.

19654 ■ "Paperless Bookkeeping Program" in Fleet Owner Online (February 15, 2011)
Pub: Penton Business Media Inc.
Description: TruckTax launched its new paperless bookkeeping system to help manage bookkeeping tasks, accounting and business tax information and filings for truckers.

19655 ■ "Pick and Save" in Entrepreneur (Vol. 36, April 2008, No. 4, pp. 66)
Pub: Entrepreneur Media, Inc.
Ed: C.J. Prince. **Description:** Business owners can purchase the needed big equipment to offset this year's expected profit. They can also switch to annualized computing of quarterly income and estimated tax payments to pay less estimated taxes for the first half of the year. Other tips on tax planning are provided.

19656 ■ "Privacy Concern: Are 'Group' Time Sheets Legal?" in HR Specialist (Vol. 8, September 2010, No. 9, pp. 4)
Pub: Capitol Information Group Inc.
Description: Under the Fair Labor Standards Act (FLSA) employers are required to maintain and preserve payroll or other records, including the number of hours worked, but it does not prescribe a particular order or form in which these records must be kept.

19657 ■ "Proposed Accounting Changes Could Complicate Tenant's Leases" in Baltimore Business Journal (Vol. 28, July 2, 2010, No. 8, pp. 1)
Pub: Baltimore Business Journal
Ed: Daniel J. Sernovitz. **Description:** The Financial Accounting Standards Board has proposed that companies must indicate the value of real estate leases as assets and liabilities on balance sheets instead of expenses. The proposals could cause some companies to document millions of dollars in charges on their books or find difficulty in getting loans.

19658 ■ QuickBooks All-in-One Desk Reference for Dummies
Pub: John Wiley & Sons, Incorporated
Ed: Stephen L. Nelson. **Released:** January 2007. **Price:** $29.99 (US), $42.99 (Canadian). **Description:** Compilation of nine self-contained minibooks to get the most from QuickBooks accounting software. Companion Web site with sample business plan workbook and downloadable profit-volume cost analysis workbook included.

19659 ■ QuickBooks Simple Start for Dummies
Pub: John Wiley and Sons, Inc.
Ed: Stephen L. Nelson. **Released:** October 2004. **Price:** $21.99. **Description:** Profile of Intuits new accounting software geared to micro businesses. Advice is offered on daily, monthly, and yearly accounting activities covering records, sales tax, and reports.

19660 ■ "Quicken Starter Edition 2008" in Black Enterprise (Vol. 38, March 2008, No. 8, pp. 54)
Pub: Earl G. Graves Publishing Co. Inc.
Ed: Sonya A. Donaldson. **Description:** Profile of Quicken Starter Edition 2008 offering programs that track spending; it will also categorize tax deductible expenses.

19661 ■ Reading Financial Reports for Dummies
Pub: John Wiley and Sons, Inc.
Ed: Lita Epstein. **Released:** January 2009. **Price:** $21.99. **Description:** This second edition contains more new and updated information, including new information on the separate accounting and financial reporting standards for private/small businesses versus public/large businesses; updated information reflecting 2007 laws on international financial reporting standards; new content to match SEC and other governmental regulatory changes over the last three years; new information about how the analyst-corporate connection has changed the playing field; the impact of corporate communications and new technologies; new examples that reflect the current trends; and updated Websites and resources.

19662 ■ "Reform or Perish" in Canadian Business (Vol. 82, April 27, 2009, No. 7, pp. 20)
Pub: Rogers Media
Ed: Al Rosen. **Description:** It is believed that Canada needs to fix its financial regulatory framework in order to provide more oversight on accounting procedures that is often left up to auditors. While the U.S. has constantly rebuilt its regulatory framework, Canada has not instituted reforms on its regulations. Canada entered the recession with a strong system but needs to build more substance into it.

19663 ■ Sarbanes-Oxley for Dummies, 2nd Ed.
Pub: John Wiley and Sons, Inc.
Ed: Jill Gilbert Welytok. **Released:** February 2008. **Price:** $21.99. **Description:** Provides the latest Sarbanes-Oxley (SOX) legislation with procedures to safely and effectively reduce compliance costs. Topics include way to: establish SOX standards for IT professionals, minimize compliances costs for every aspect of a business, survive a Section 404 audit, avoid litigation under SOX, anticipate future rules and trends, create a post-SOX paper trail, increase a company's standing and reputation, work with SOX in a small business, meet new SOX standards, build a board that can't be bought, and to comply with all SOX management mandates.

19664 ■ Sarbanes-Oxley for Small Businesses: Leveraging Compliance for Maximum Advantage
Pub: John Wiley & Sons, Incorporated
Ed: Peggy M. Jackson. **Released:** November 2006. **Price:** $39.95. **Description:** Book lists five ways the Sarbane Oxley Act helps small businesses.

19665 ■ Schaum's Outline Financial Management, Third Edition
Pub: McGraw-Hill
Ed: Jae K. Shim; Joel G. Siegel. **Released:** May 2007. **Price:** $22.95 (CND). **Description:** Rules and regulations governing corporate finance, including the Sarbanes-Oxley Act are discussed.

19666 ■ "SEC Extends Small Business Deadline for SOX Audit Requirement" in HRMagazine (Vol. 53, August 2008, No. 8, pp. 20)
Pub: Society for Human Resource Management
Contact: Henry G. Jackson, President
E-mail: hjackson@shrm.org
Description: Securities and Exchange Commission has approved a one-year extension of the compli-

ance date for smaller public companies to meet the Section 404(b) auditor attestation requirement of the Sarbanes-Oxley Act.

19667 ■ Self-Employed Tax Solutions: Quick, Simple, Money-Saving, Audit-Proof Tax and Recordkeeping Basics
Pub: The Globe Pequot Press
Ed: June Walker. **Released:** January 1, 2009. **Price:** $17.95. **Description:** A simple system for maintaining tax records and filing tax forms for any small business is explored.

19668 ■ Small Business Tax Deductions 2006
Pub: Continuing Education of the Bar-California
Ed: Stephen Fishman. **Released:** June 2006. **Price:** $99.00. **Description:** Allowable tax deductions for small business in 2006 are explained.

19669 ■ Smart Tax Write-Offs, 5th Ed.
Pub: Rayve Productions, Inc.
Ed: Norm Ray. **Released** February 2008. **Price:** $15.95. **Description:** Guidebook to help small business owners take advantage of legitimate tax deductions for home-based and other entrepreneurial businesses.

19670 ■ "Smart Year-End Tax Moves" in Business Owner (Vol. 35, November-December 2011, No. 6, pp. 8)
Pub: DL Perkins Company
Description: Managing small business and individual taxes is more important in a bad economy. It is imperative to seek all tax incentives that apply to your business.

19671 ■ "Spotlight on Principles-based Financial Reporting" in Business Horizons (September-October 2007, pp. 359)
Pub: Elsevier Technology Publications
Ed: Laureen A. Maines. **Description:** Employment of principles-based standards in order to generate reliable financial reporting and to reduce misrepresentations is discussed. Rules-based standards are distinguished from principles-based standards.

19672 ■ "Statistical Data of Interest" in Business Owner (Vol. 35, July-August 2011, No. 4, pp. 7)
Pub: DL Perkins Company
Description: Sources of federal tax revenue are presented; payroll taxes, 36 percent; corporate income tax, 12 percent, other 4 percent, excise taxes, 3 percent, individual income tax, 45 percent.

19673 ■ "Surviving an IRS Audit: Tips for Small Businesses" in Agency Sales Magazine (Vol. 39, July 2009, No. 7, pp. 52)
Pub: MANA
Ed: Joshua D. Mosshart. **Description:** It is a good idea to enlist the services of a tax professional even if an audit is expected to go smoothly since the IRS is likely to scrutinize the unreported income and personal as well as business expenses of a small business during an audit.

19674 ■ Tax Savvy for Small Business
Pub: NOLO
Ed: Frederick W. Daily. **Released:** November 2006. **Price:** $36.99. **Description:** Strategies to help small business owners claim all legitimate deductions and keep accurate records.

19675 ■ Tax Smarts for Small Business
Pub: Sourcebooks, Inc.
Contact: Len Vlahos, President
E-mail: dominique@sourcebooks.com
Ed: James O. Parker. **Released:** December 2006. **Price:** $27.95. **Description:** Tax guide for small businesses.

19676 ■ "Test Your Structural Integrity" in Entrepreneur (Vol. 37, August 2009, No. 8, pp. 60)
Pub: Entrepreneur Media, Inc.
Ed: Jennifer Lawler. **Description:** Tax considerations can be important when choosing a business structure. For example, profits are taxed to the corporation in a

C corp while profits are taxed only once at an S corp or a limited liability company. Meeting a tax professional should be done prior to switching to a different structure.

19677 ■ "Throughput Metrics Meet Six Sigma" in Management Accounting Quarterly (Vol. 12, Spring 2011, No. 3, pp. 12)
Pub: Management Accounting Quarterly
Ed: Shaun Aghili. **Description:** Throughput accounting (TA) metrics can be combined with six sigma's DMAIC methodology and various time-tested analysis and measurement tools for added effectiveness in resolving resource constraint issues. The goal is to optimize not only the output of a specific department but that of the entire system, by implementing a cost accounting system that is conducive to system optimization while increasing product quality, process integrity, or ideally, both.

19678 ■ Top Tax Savings Ideas: How to Survive in Today's Tough Tax Environment
Pub: Entrepreneur Press
Ed: Thomas J. Stemmy. **Released:** March 2004. **Price:** $18.95 (US), $26.95 (Canadian). **Description:** Tax deductions, fringe benefits, and tax deferrals for small businesses.

19679 ■ "ValienteHernandez Acquired" in The Business Journal-Serving Greater Tampa Bay (Vol. 28, September 12, 2008, No. 38, pp. 1)
Pub: American City Business Journals, Inc.
Ed: Alexis Muellner. **Description:** Minnesota accounting firm LarsonAllen LLP has acquired Florida-based ValienteHernandez PA, creating a company with 35 employees to be based in ValienteHernandez's newly built office in Tampa Bay Area. Other details about the merger are provided.

19680 ■ "Welcome Back" in Canadian Business (Vol. 82, April 27, 2009, No. 7, pp. 25)
Pub: Rogers Media
Ed: Sarka Halas. **Description:** Some Canadian companies such as Gennum Corporation have taken advantage of corporate sale-leasebacks to raise money at a time when credit is hard to acquire. Corporate sale-leasebacks allow companies to sell their property assets while remaining as tenants of the building. Sale-leasebacks allow firms to increase capital while avoiding the disruptions that may result with moving.

19681 ■ "Where Women Work" in Marketing to Women (Vol. 21, April 2008, No. 4, pp. 8)
Pub: EPM Communications Inc.
Contact: Ira Mayer, President
E-mail: imayer@epmcom.com
Description: According to the U.S. Census Bureau, 60 percent of America's professional tax preparers are women. Also features additional trends concerning women in the workplace. Statistical data included.

19682 ■ Working Papers, Chapters 1-14 for Needles/Powers/Crosson's Financial and Managerial Accounting
Pub: Cengage South-Western
Ed: Belverd E. Needles, Marian Powers, Susan V. Crosson. **Released:** May 10, 2010. **Price:** $62.95. **Description:** Appropriate accounting forms for completing all exercises, problems and cases in the text are provided for financial management of a small company.

19683 ■ "Year-End Tax Tips" in Hawaii Business (Vol. 53, December 2007, No. 6, pp. 136)
Pub: Hawaii Business Publishing
Ed: Kathleen Bryan. **Description:** Tax planning tips for the end of 2007, in relation to the tax breaks that are scheduled to expire, are presented. Among the tax breaks that will be expiring at the 2007 year-end are sales tax deduction in the state and local level, premiums on mortgage insurance, and deduction on tuition. The impacts of these changes are discussed.

TRADE PERIODICALS

19684 ■ Canadian MoneySaver
Pub: Dale Ennis
Ed: Dale Ennis, Editor. **Released:** 11/year. **Price:** $19.95, Canada U.S. $36 elsewhere. **Description:**

Examines taxes, investment, and financial planning in Canada. Recurring features include interviews, book reviews, and notices of publications available.

19685 ■ CPA Client Tax Letter
Pub: American Institute of Certified Public Accountants
Contact: Barry C. Melancon, President
E-mail: bmelancon@aicpa.org
Ed: Maria Luzarraga Albanese, Editor. **Released:** Quarterly. **Price:** $119, members; $148.75, nonmembers. **Description:** Covers tax planning, including laws and legislation.

19686 ■ The Exempt Organization Tax Review
Pub: Tax Analysts
Contact: Christopher Bergin, President
URL(s): www.taxanalysts.com/www/website.nsf/Web/ EOTR?OpenDocument. **Released:** Monthly

19687 ■ Farm Tax Saver
Pub: Sara Wyant
Released: Monthly. **Description:** Monitors changes in tax laws and analyzes how they affect farm families. Covers areas such as social security tax, tax shelters, tax on investments, and tax records required on transportation costs. Recurring features include editorials and news of research.

19688 ■ Financial and Estate Planning
Pub: CCH Inc.
Contact: Mike Sabbatis, President
URL(s): tax.cchgroup.com/FEP/default. **Ed:** Sidney Kess. **Released:** Monthly **Price:** $1479, Individuals CD-ROM; $1465, Individuals print.

19689 ■ The Insurance Tax Review
Pub: Tax Analysts
Contact: Christopher Bergin, President
URL(s): www.taxanalysts.com/www/website.nsf/Web/ ITR?OpenDocument. **Released:** Monthly **Price:** $699, Individuals.

19690 ■ International Tax and Public Finance
Pub: Springer Netherlands
Contact: Zachary Rolnik, Managing Director
E-mail: zrolnik@wkap.com
URL(s): www.springerlink.com/content/102915/. **Ed:** Ruud A. De Mooij. **Released:** Bimonthly **Price:** €1111, Institutions print or online; €1333, Institutions print & enchanced access.

19691 ■ Intertax
Pub: Kluwer Academic/Plenum Publishing Corp.
Contact: Martin E. Tash, President
URL(s): www.kluwerlawonline.com/productinfo. php?pubcode=TAXI. **Ed:** Otmar Thommes. **Released:** Monthly **Price:** €1031, Individuals print or online; $1376, Individuals print or online; £758, Individuals print or online.

19692 ■ Journal of the American Taxation Association (JATA)
Pub: American Accounting Association
Contact: Greg Waymire, President
URL(s): aaahq.org/ata/_ATAMenu/ATAPubJATA.html. **Ed:** John Phillips. **Released:** Semiannual; with a third conference supplement. **Price:** $120, Individuals print; $160, Individuals online from volume 21 to current issue; $175, Individuals online and print.

19693 ■ The Journal of Taxation
Pub: RIA Group
URL(s):   ria.thomson.com/estore/detail. aspx?ID=JTAX. **Ed:** Carol Conjura, Sheldon I. Banoff, Peter J. Connors, Michael J. Miller, Herbert H. Alpert, Lorence L. Bravenec, Joseph I. Graf. **Released:** Monthly **Price:** $410, Individuals print; $595, Individuals online/print bundle; $465, Individuals online.

19694 ■ Partnership Tax Planning & Practice
Pub: CCH Inc.
Contact: Mike Sabbatis, President
Ed: James Rooney, Editor. **Released:** Monthly. **Price:** $439. **Description:** Explanatory comments on partnership, taxation, full text of pertinent code and acquisition provisions, post 1954 revenue rulings, revenue procedures.

19695 ■ *The Practical Tax Lawyer*
Pub: American Law Institute-American Bar Association Continuing Professional Education
URL(s): www.ali-aba.org/index.cfm?fuseaction=publications.periodical&pub=PTL. **Released:** Quarterly **Price:** $75, Individuals; $59, Members special for ABA tax section members; $40, Individuals online; $99, Individuals print and online; $169, Two years print and online; $139, Two years special for ABA tax section; $89, Two years online only.

19696 ■ *The Tax Executive*
Pub: Tax Executives Institute
Contact: Timothy J. McCormally, Executive Director
URL(s): www.tei.org/. **Released:** Bimonthly **Price:** $22, Single issue; $120, Individuals regular; $110, Institutions; $145, Other countries; $135, Institutions, other countries; $110, government.

19697 ■ *Tax Notes Today*
Pub: Tax Analysts
Contact: Christopher Bergin, President
URL(s): www.tax.org/www/website.nsf/Web/Expert3?OpenDocument. **Ed:** Lee Sheppard, Martin A. Sullivan. **Released:** Weekly **Price:** $1999, Individuals.

19698 ■ *Tax Practice Bulletin*
Pub: Tax Management Inc.
Ed: Glenn B. Davis, Editor. **Released:** Biweekly. **Price:** $735 includes Tax Practice Series CD-ROM; $930 with state forms; $102. **Description:** Answers most of the common questions tax professionals face in daily practice. Provides analyses by expert practitioners.

19699 ■ *Tax Savings Report*
Pub: National Taxpayers Union
Contact: Duane Parde, President
Ed: Peter Sepp, Editor. **Released:** 10/year; 10/year. **Price:** $39.95, /year; $39, individuals. **Description:** Imparts tax savings tips and ideas on how to best use IRS regulations to the taxpayer's advantage. Discusses such topics as expense deductions, tax planning for senior citizens, job hunting expense deductions, and child care tax credit. Recurring features include columns titled Answers to Your Tax Questions and Tax Briefs.

19700 ■ *Taxes--The Tax Magazine*
Pub: CCH Inc.
Contact: Mike Sabbatis, President
URL(s): onlinestore.cch.com/productdetail.asp?productid=591. **Ed:** Shannon Jett Fischer. **Released:** Monthly **Price:** $349, Individuals.

19701 ■ *The TaxLetter*
Pub: MPL Communications Inc.
Contact: Barrie Martland, President
E-mail: bmartland@mplcomm.com
Released: Monthly. **Price:** $89. **Description:** Acts as a consumer newsletter that specializes in personal tax-planning, offering timely advice, information, and recommendations on personal and business tax-planning strategies. Features columns titled Shelter-Watch, RRSP Watch, Looking Out for No. 1, Managing Your Money, and Tax-Wise Investor.

19702 ■ *TAXPRO Monthly*
Pub: National Association of Tax Professionals
Ed: Char DeCoster, Editor, cdecosteratsnatptax.com. **Released:** Monthly. **Price:** Included in membership. **Description:** Helps to communicate the purposes of the Association, which are to foster high standards in the tax preparation profession and to promote and protect the interests of tax practitioners. Includes tax law and regulations, statistics, and news of members.

19703 ■ *Valuation Researcher*
Pub: Valuation Research Corp.
Ed: Theresa Miller, Editor, tmiller@valuationresearch.com. **Released:** 6/year. **Price:** Free. **Description:** Publishes valuation news and information for use in asset management, finance, and tax planning.

19704 ■ *Worldwide Tax Daily*
Pub: Tax Analysts
Contact: Christopher Bergin, President
URL(s): www.tax.org/www/website.nsf/Web/Expert3?OpenDocument. **Ed:** Lee Sheppard, Martin A. Sullivan. **Released:** Weekly **Price:** $999, Individuals.

VIDEOCASSETTES/AUDIOCASSETTES

19705 ■ *CPE Network: Tax & Accounting Report*
Bisk Education
9417 Princess Palm Ave.
Tampa, FL 33619
Free: 800-874-7877
Co. E-mail: info@bisk.com
URL: http://www.bisk.com
Released: 19??. **Price:** $1200.00. **Description:** Provides information on current tax regulations and current accounting and auditing changes. Video newsletter published 11 times per year. **Availability:** VHS.

TRADE SHOWS AND CONVENTIONS

19706 ■ Institute of Internal Auditors - USA International Conference
Institute of Internal Auditors
247 Maitland Ave.
Altamonte Springs, FL 32701
Ph: (407)937-1111
Fax: (407)937-1101
Co. E-mail: customerrelations@theiia.org
URL: http://na.theiia.org/Pages/IIAHome.aspx
Contact: Richard F. Chambers, President
Frequency: Annual. **Audience:** All levels of internal auditors from every industry. **Principal Exhibits:** Internal auditing equipment, supplies, and services, software, computer related equipment.

19707 ■ New Jersey Accounting, Business & Technology Show & Conference
Flagg Management, Inc.
353 Lexington Ave.
New York, NY 10016
Ph: (212)286-0333
Fax: (212)286-0086
Co. E-mail: flaggmgmt@msn.com
URL: http://www.flaggmgmt.com
URL(s): www.flaggmgmt.com/nj. **Frequency:** Annual. **Audience:** CPAs, accounting professionals, business and financial executives of New Jersey, Fortune 1000 corporations, business owners and managers, IT managers. **Principal Exhibits:** Information and technology, financial and business services, computer accounting systems, software, tax preparation, accounting, audit, practice management software - windows, and computer and business systems. Banking, insurance, financial and business software. Internet, online systems and middle market software and investment services. **Telecommunication Services:** flaggmgmt@msn.com.

CONSULTANTS

19708 ■ The Business Advisor
6 Main St.
Hamilton, ON, Canada L9S 1M8
Ph: (705)431-0511
Fax: (705)431-0522
Contact: Jacob M. Hoeppner, President
Scope: Assists in the preparation and implementation of efficient systems and procedures. Advises on business and management methods and procedures. Provides temporary interim management solutions for businesses requiring leadership to re-evaluate business direction and operations. Offers accounting and tax advice. Prepares for business succession. **Founded:** 2000.

19709 ■ John Alan Cohan
433 N Camden Dr., Ste. 600
Beverly Hills, CA 90210

Ph: (310)278-0203
Free: 800-255-1529
Fax: (310)859-8656
Co. E-mail: johnalancohan@aol.com
URL: http://www.johnalancohan.com
Contact: Cohan John Alan, Principal
Scope: Consultant assists in the development of business plans for startups in the fields of livestock, horses, farming, or aviation. Also provides tax consultations and tax opinion letters to support deductions. **Founded:** 1981.

19710 ■ Hollingsworth & Associates
395 Wellington Rd. S, Ste. 101
London, ON, Canada N6C 4P9
Ph: (519)649-2001
Fax: (519)649-7880
Co. E-mail: jack@hollingsworth.net
Contact: Jack Hollingsworth, President
E-mail: jack@hollingsworth.net
Scope: Acts as management accountants, tax and management consultants, and offsite controllers. Consulting services include software selection, and financial information systems. Accounting and tax preparation. **Founded:** 1993.

19711 ■ Mitchell and Titus L.L.P.—Mitchell/Titus
1 Battery Park Plz., 27th Fl.
New York, NY 10004-1405
Ph: (212)709-4500
Fax: (212)709-4680
URL: http://www.mitchelltitus.com
Contact: Bert N. Mitchell, Chief Executive Officer
Scope: Firm provides assurance, advisory business services, transaction support and tax services. Specializes in auditing and accounting services, tax planning and preparation services management and business advisory services. **Founded:** 1974. **Publications:** "ITEM Club Budget preview report," 2010; "Year end personal planning," 2010; "Steering towards the future using the Pre Budget Report to help the UK rebound," 2009; "Be careful what you wish for," 2009; "Year end personal planning," 2009. **Seminars:** Budget Seminar 2010, Mar, 2010.

FRANCHISES AND BUSINESS OPPORTUNITIES

19712 ■ Accountants, Inc.
Select Appointments
111 Anza Blvd., No. 400
Burlingame, CA 94010
Ph: (650)579-1111
Free: 800-491-9411
Description: Placement for accounting & finance candidates. **No. of Franchise Units:** 16. **No. of Company-Owned Units:** 22. **Founded:** 1986.. **Franchised:** 1994. **Equity Capital Needed:** $144,400-$193,700 + franchise fee. **Franchise Fee:** $30,000. **Financial Assistance:** Yes. **Training:** Yes.

19713 ■ Cash Plus
Cash Plus, Inc.
3002 Dow Ave., Ste, 120
Tustin, CA 92780
Ph: (714)731-2274
Free: 888-707-2274
Fax: (714)731-2099
Description: Check cashing service and related services, including money orders, wire transfers, cash advances, mailboxes, notary, UPS, fax, snacks, tax filing and other items. **No. of Franchise Units:** 91. **No. of Company-Owned Units:** 2. **Founded:** 1984.. **Franchised:** 1988. **Equity Capital Needed:** $190,200-$269,700. **Franchise Fee:** $35,000. **Financial Assistance:** Yes. **Training:** Provides training including easy-to-run computerized operating system, promotions and check verification and payday advance process.

19714 ■ CFO Today Inc.
545 E Tennessee St.
Tallahassee, FL 32308
Ph: (850)681-1941
Free: 888-643-1348

Fax: (850)561-1374
URL: http://www.cfotoday.com
Description: Offers regional franchise program through which a regional owner solicits local franchisees. Local franchisees operate an accounting and tax practice, utilizing special marketing techniques, in addition to operational and computer systems, to provide tax, record keeping and other services to clients. **No. of Franchise Units:** 103. **No. of Company-Owned Units:** 1. **Founded:** 1989.. **Franchised:** 1990. **Equity Capital Needed:** $24,400-$40,000. **Franchise Fee:** $24 000. **Royalty Fee:** 8%. **Training:** Provides 5 days training at corporate headquarters and 1 day onsite, with ongoing support.

19715 ■ Colbert/Ball Tax Service
2616 S Loop West, Ste. 110
Houston, TX 77054
Ph: (713)592-5555
Free: 888-288-8675
Fax: (713)395-1606
URL: http://www.colbertballtax.biz
Description: Full service tax preparation. **No. of Franchise Units:** 235. **No. of Company-Owned Units:** 1. **Founded:** 1995.. **Franchised:** 2000. **Equity Capital Needed:** $33,235-$50,735. **Franchise Fee:** $15,000. **Royalty Fee:** 15%. **Financial Assistance:** Third Party Financing Available. **Training:** Yes.

19716 ■ Electronic Tax Filers (ETF)
The St. Simons Corporation
PO Box 2077
Cary, NC 27512-2077
Ph: (919)469-0651
Free: 800-945-9277
Fax: (919)460-5935
Description: E-filing and refund loans. **No. of Franchise Units:** 44. **No. of Company-Owned Units:** 2. **Founded:** 1990.. **Franchised:** 1990. **Equity Capital Needed:** $25,000. **Franchise Fee:** $10,500. **Financial Assistance:** Yes. **Training:** Yes.

19717 ■ ExpressTax Service Inc.
Express Tax Service Inc.
3030 Hartley Rd., Ste. 320
Jacksonville, FL 32257-8209
Ph: (904)262-0031
Free: 888-417-4461
Fax: (904)262-2864
Co. E-mail: franchise@expresstaxservice.com
URL: http://www.expresstaxservice.com
Description: Tax preparation and electronic filing services. **No. of Franchise Units:** 404. **Founded:** 1997.. **Franchised:** 2002. **Equity Capital Needed:** $15,375-$40,100/Co-located $3,500-$8,000. **Franchise Fee:** $1,500$2,500. **Training:** Yes.

19718 ■ Instant Tax Service
ITS Financial, LLC
1 S Main St., Ste. 1400
Dayton, OH 45402
Ph: (888)870-1040
Fax: (888)297-2199
Co. E-mail: franchise@instanttaxservice.com
Description: Provides tax return preparation, electronic filing, refund options and financial services. **No. of Franchise Units:** 1,197. **No. of Company-Owned Units:** 16. **Founded:** 2000.. **Franchised:** 2004. **Equity Capital Needed:** $39,000-$89,000, total investment required. **Franchise Fee:** $34,000. **Financial Assistance:** Yes. **Training:** Yes.

19719 ■ Jackson Hewitt Tax Service
Cendant Corp.
3 Sylvan Way, 2nd Fl.
Parsippany, NJ 07054
Ph: (973)496-1040
Free: 800-475-2904
Fax: (973)496-2760
Description: Awards franchise territories to individuals who are dedicated to producing the highest-quality tax return possible. The Company utilizes a proprietary computerized tax interview system, designed to maximize deductions, reduce math errors and produce an accurate tax return for every customer. The Super fast Refund is the trademark for a refund anticipation loan, which allows customers their refund minus fees in 24 hours or less. cannot receive financing from banks. **No. of Franchise**

Units: 4,200. **Founded:** 1960.. **Franchised:** 1986. **Equity Capital Needed:** $47,430-$75,205. **Franchise Fee:** $25,000. **Financial Assistance:** Yes. **Training:** 5 day training program designed to teach business partners the skills necessary to launch a new franchise operation. This also includes workshops, seminars and group discussions. Extensive 2 days of training for electronic filing system.

19720 ■ Ledgerplus
259 E 7th Ave.
Tallahassee, FL 32303
Ph: (888)643-1348
Description: Accounting, tax & consultation. **No. of Franchise Units:** 156. **No. of Company-Owned Units:** 5. **Founded:** 1989.. **Franchised:** 1991. **Equity Capital Needed:** $29,000. **Franchise Fee:** $16,000. **Financial Assistance:** Yes. **Training:** Yes.

19721 ■ Ledgers Professional Services
17665 Leslie St., Ste. 39
Newmarket, ON, Canada L3Y 3E3
Ph: (905)953-1268
Co. E-mail: sales@ledgers.com
URL: http://www.ledgers.com
Description: Provides a comprehensive suite of services to small businesses, including bookkeeping, payroll and personal income taxes to corporate financial statement preparation and tax returns. **No. of Franchise Units:** 50. **No. of Company-Owned Units:** 1. **Founded:** 1994.. **Franchised:** 1996. **Equity Capital Needed:** $10,000. **Franchise Fee:** $20,000. **Training:** Provides 5 days training.

19722 ■ Liberty Tax Service
1716 Corporate Landing
Virginia Beach, VA 23454
Ph: (757)493-8855
Free: 800-790-3863
Fax: (800)880-6432
Co. E-mail: sales@libtax.com
URL: http://www.libertytaxfranchise.com
Description: Income tax preparation and electronic filing loan service. **No. of Franchise Units:** 3,800. **No. of Company-Owned Units:** 29. **Founded:** 1996.. **Franchised:** 1997. **Equity Capital Needed:** $56,800-$69,900; $50,000 liquid capital required. **Franchise Fee:** $40,000. **Financial Assistance:** Financing available for those who qualify. **Training:** 1 week operations training followed by 2 day update training and annual advanced trainings; year-round tax, technical, operational, and marketing support.

19723 ■ Liberty Tax Service
110 Riviera Dr., Ste. 16
Markham, ON. Canada L3R 5M1
Ph: (905)943-2640
Free: 800-790-3863
Fax: (866)902-1245
Co. E-mail: sales@ibtax.com
URL: http://www.libertytaxcanada.ca
Description: Tax preparation service. **No. of Franchise Units:** 252. **No. of Company-Owned Units:** 31. **Founded:** 1972.. **Franchised:** 1997. **Equity Capital Needed:** $33,350-$54,900. **Franchise Fee:** $25,000. **Training:** Provides 5 days training.

19724 ■ Padgett Business Services
400 Blue Hill Dr., Ste. 201
Westwood, MA 02090
Free: 877-729-8725 x225
Co. E-mail: padgett@smallbizpros.com
URL: http://www.smallbizpros.com
Description: Padgett provides an array of services to small businesses, such as consulting, financial reporting, government compliance, payroll and tax preparation services. Padgett also offers credit card processing, pension and 125 plan administration, equipment financing and workers' compensation payment service. **No. of Franchise Units:** 435. **Founded:** 1966. **Franchised:** 1975. **Equity Capital Needed:** Total investment and net worth $105,955; liquid or cash $78,750. **Franchise Fee:** $56,000. **Financial Assistance:** Third party financing up to $75,000. Also enrolled in the SBA registry. **Training:** Initial training 12 days field visits, covering marketing, operations, and software. Ongoing training and support is provided through regular seminars in market-

ing, operations, tax, etc. Support is delivered through toll-free telephone and a wide range of information and material is provided via the company's web site.

19725 ■ Tax Centers of America
1611 E Main St.
Russellville, AR 72801
Ph: (479)968-4796
Free: 800-364-2012
Fax: (479)968-8012
Co. E-mail: moreinfo@tcoa.net
URL: http://www.tcoa.net
Description: Tax centers. **No. of Franchise Units:** 117. **No. of Company-Owned Units:** 1. **Founded:** 1992.. **Franchised:** 1995. **Equity Capital Needed:** $20,300-$63,550. **Franchise Fee:** $10,000-$35,000. **Royalty Fee:** $30-55/return. **Training:** Offers 4 days of training and ongoing support.

COMPUTERIZED DATABASES

19726 ■ *Daily Tax Report*
1801 S Bell St.
Arlington, VA 22202
Free: 800-372-1033
Co. E-mail: customercare@bna.com
URL: http://www.bna.com
Availability: Online: Bloomberg LP-Bloomberg BNA; Thomson Reuters - Westlaw. **Type:** Full-text.

19727 ■ *e-JEP*
2014 Broadway, Ste. 305
Nashville, TN 37203
Ph: (615)322-2595
Fax: (615)343-7590
Co. E-mail: aeainfo@vanderbilt.edu
URL: http://www.vanderbilt.edu/AEA
Contact: Angus Deaton, President
Availability: Online: American Economic Association; Thomson Reuters - Westlaw. CD-ROM: American Economic Association. **Type:** Full-text.

19728 ■ *Federal Income Taxation of Corporations and Shareholders*
2395 Midway Rd.
Carrollton, TX 75006
Free: 800-431-9025
Co. E-mail: ria@thomson.com
URL: http://ria.thomsonreuters.com
Availability: Online: Thomson Reuters - RIA Tax & Accounting Unit. **Type:** Full-text.

19729 ■ *Federal Taxes Weekly Alert*
2395 Midway Rd.
Carrollton, TX 75006
Free: 800-431-9025
Co. E-mail: ria@thomson.com
URL: http://ria.thomsonreuters.com
Availability: Online: Thomson Reuters - RIA Tax & Accounting Unit. **Type:** Full-text.

19730 ■ *IRS Practice and Procedure*
2395 Midway Rd.
Carrollton, TX 75006
Free: 800-431-9025
Co. E-mail: ria@thomson.com
URL: http://ria.thomsonreuters.com
Availability: Online: Thomson Reuters - RIA Tax & Accounting Unit. **Type:** Full-text.

19731 ■ *ProQuest Accounting & Tax™*
789 E Eisenhower Pkwy.
Ann Arbor, MI 48106-1346
Ph: (734)761-4700
Free: 800-521-0600
Co. E-mail: info@il.proquest.com
URL: http://www.il.proquest.com
Contact: Matt Dunie, President
Availability: Online: ProQuest Co.; ProQuest LLC - Dialog; ProQuest LLC - Dialog. **Type:** Bibliographic.

19732 ■ *State Tax Notes®*
400 S Maple Ave., Ste. 400
Falls Church, VA 22046
Ph: (703)533-4400

Free: 800-955-2444
Co. E-mail: cservice@tax.org
URL: http://www.taxanalysts.com
Availability: Online: LexisNexis Group. **Type:** Full-text.

19733 ■ *State Tax Today®*
400 S Maple Ave., Ste. 400
Falls Church, VA 22046
Ph: (703)533-4400
Free: 800-955-2444
Co. E-mail: cservice@tax.org
URL: http://www.taxanalysts.com
Availability: Online: Tax Analysts. **Type:** Full-text.

19734 ■ *The Tax Directory®*
400 S Maple Ave., Ste. 400
Falls Church, VA 22046
Ph: (703)533-4400
Free: 800-955-2444
Co. E-mail: cservice@tax.org
URL: http://www.taxanalysts.com
Availability: Online: LexisNexis Group. CD-ROM: Tax Analysts. **Type:** Directory.

19735 ■ *Tax Management Memorandum*
1801 S Bell St.
Arlington, VA 22202
Free: 800-372-1033
Co. E-mail: customercare@bna.com
URL: http://www.bna.com/tax-accounting-t5000
Availability: Online: The Bureau of National Affairs Inc. - Tax and Accounting Division. **Type:** Full-text.

19736 ■ *Tax Notes® Today*
400 S Maple Ave., Ste. 400
Falls Church, VA 22046
Ph: (703)533-4400
Free: 800-955-2444
Co. E-mail: cservice@tax.org
URL: http://www.taxanalysts.com
Availability: Online: PricewaterhouseCoopers LLP; ProQuest LLC - Dialog; LexisNexis Group. **Type:** Full-text.

19737 ■ *Weekly Report*
1801 S Bell St.
Arlington, VA 22202
Free: 800-372-1033
Co. E-mail: customercare@bna.com
URL: http://www.bna.com/tax-accounting-t5000
Availability: Online: The Bureau of National Affairs Inc. - Tax and Accounting Division; Thomson Reuters - Westlaw. **Type:** Full-text.

COMPUTER SYSTEMS/ SOFTWARE

19738 ■ *Accountant's Relief*
140 Fell Ct.
Hauppauge, NY 11788
Ph: (888)999-1366
Free: 800-829-7354
Fax: (800)927-1283
Co. E-mail: contactus@accountantsworld.com
URL: http://www.accountantsworld.com
Description: Available for IBM computers and compatibles. System prepares 53 tax forms and schedules and calculates various personal and business taxes.

19739 ■ *BNA Estate and Gift Tax Planner*
1801 S Bell St.
Arlington, VA 22202
Ph: (800)424-2938
Free: 800-424-2938
Fax: (703)341-2938
Co. E-mail: software@bna.com
URL: http://www.bnasoftware.com
Price: Contact BNA. **Description:** Available for IBM computers. System calculates federal and state taxes for the estates of spouses.

19740 ■ *BNA Income Tax Planner*
1801 S Bell St.
Arlington, VA 20037
Ph: (800)424-2938
Free: 800-424-2938

Fax: (703)341-2938
Co. E-mail: software@bna.com
URL: http://www.bnasoftware.com
Price: Contact BNA. **Description:** Available for IBM computers and compatibles. Calculates federal and state individual income taxes.

19741 ■ *FAS Fixed Asset Programs / Sage Software SB, Inc.*
2325 Dulles Corner Blvd., Ste. 800
Herndon, VA 20171
Ph: (703)793-2700
Free: 800-368-2405
Fax: (703)793-2770
URL: http://www.sagenorthamerica.com
Description: Windows based. System calculates taxes and provides comparisons of tax liability over a certain number of years.

19742 ■ *TAX/PACK: Professional 1040*
Division of Analytical Processes Corp.
737 S Townsend Ave.
Montrose, CO 81401
Ph: (805)525-1040
Free: 800-525-1040
Fax: (970)249-8511
Co. E-mail: info@taxpack.com
URL: http://www.alpinedata.com
Price: $410 (with laser), $245 (without laser). **Description:** Available for IBM computers and compatibles. Provides tax form preparation.

19743 ■ *Tax Preparer*
7852 Ivanhoe Ave.
La Jolla, CA 92037
Ph: (858)454-0121
Fax: (858)454-7559
Co. E-mail: support@howardsoft.com
URL: http://www.howardsoft.com
Price: $229.00. **Description:** Available for IBM and Apple II computers and compatibles. System automating the preparation of tax returns. Handles IRS worksheets, recordkeeping, stocks, bonds, rental, accounts, and depreciated assets.

19744 ■ *Tax Preparer: California Supplement*
7852 Ivanhoe Ave.
La Jolla, CA 92037
Ph: (858)454-0121
Fax: (858)454-7559
Co. E-mail: support@howardsoft.com
URL: http://www.howardsoft.com
Price: $149.00. **Description:** Available for IBM and Apple II computers and compatibles. System providing automated tax preparation for California state income taxes.

19745 ■ *Tax$imple*
8 Emery Ave.
Randolph, NJ 07869
Ph: (973)989-8955
Free: 800-989-8955
Fax: (973)366-5877
Co. E-mail: support@taxsimple.com
URL: http://www.taxsimple.com/
Price: Contact Tax$imple for Pricing. **Description:** Available for IBM computers and compatibles. System for tax professionals offering tax form input, calculations, tables, schedules, and printing options.

LIBRARIES

19746 ■ **Baker & McKenzie - Library**
BCE Pl.
181 Bay St., Ste. 2100
Toronto, ON, Canada M5J 2T3
Ph: (416)863-1221
Fax: (416)863-6275
URL: http://www.bakernet.com/BakerNet/default.htm
Contact: Irene Batna, Librarian
Scope: Law - corporate, commercial, labor, tax. **Services:** Interlibrary loan; Library not open to the public. **Holdings:** Figures not available.

19747 ■ **Brooklyn Public Library - Business Library**
280 Cadman Plaza, W.
Tillary St.
Brooklyn, NY 11201
Ph: (718)623-7000
Co. E-mail: busref@brooklynpubliclibrary.org
URL: http://www.brooklynpubliclibrary.org/locations/business
Contact: Dionne Mack-Harvin, Executive Director
Scope: Accounting, advertising, business management, business procedure, career development and employment, finance, insurance, investment, public relations, small business, real estate. **Services:** Copying; Library open to the public. **Founded:** 1943. **Holdings:** 133,000 books; 730,000 microfiche; 22,000 reels of microfilm; 1000 directories; 120 videocassettes and DVDs; selective U.S. government documents depository. **Subscriptions:** 700 journals and other serials; 5 newspapers.

19748 ■ **Caixa Geral do Depositos SA - Mediateca e Centro de Informacao Europeia**
Edificio-Sede da CGD, Av Joao XXI, 63
P-1000 Lisbon, Portugal
Co. E-mail: ana.monteiro@cgd.pt
URL: http://www.cgd.pt
Scope: Finance. **Services:** Centre open to the public. **Founded:** 1994. **Holdings:** 40,000 volumes. **Subscriptions:** 1000 journals and other serials.

19749 ■ **CMA Ontario - Member Services Centre**
70 University Ave., Ste. 101
Toronto, ON, Canada M5J 2M4
Ph: (416)204-3142
Fax: (416)977-1365
Co. E-mail: msc@cma-ontario.org
Contact: Patricia Black, Manager, Member Services
Scope: Accounting, management, finance, strategy, taxation, investments. **Services:** Copying; SDI; Library not open to the public. **Founded:** 1990. **Holdings:** 2069 books; 267 videocassettes; 184 audiocassettes; 6 videodiscs. **Subscriptions:** 53 journals and other serials; 2 newspapers.

19750 ■ **Deloitte & Touche - Library**
350 S. Grand Ave.
Los Angeles, CA 90071-3462
Ph: (213)688-0800
Fax: (213)688-0100
URL: http://www.deloitte.com
Scope: Auditing, taxation, management consultation, actuarial services, employee benefits, valuation consultation. **Services:** Library not open to the public. **Holdings:** Figures not available.

19751 ■ **Deloitte & Touche - Toronto North Library**
5140 Yonge St., Ste. 1700
Toronto, ON, Canada M2N 6L7
Ph: (416)229-2100
Fax: (416)229-2524
URL: http://www.deloitte.com
Contact: Lynn Idnurm
Scope: Tax. **Services:** Library not open to the public. **Holdings:** Books; bound periodical volumes.

19752 ■ **Epstein, Becker, & Green, PC Law Library**
250 Park Ave.
New York, NY 10177-1211
Ph: (212)351-4500
Fax: (212)878-8600
URL: http://www.ebglaw.com
Scope: Law - labor and employment, litigation, health, corporate, elder law, taxation. **Services:** Interlibrary loan; Library not open to the public. **Holdings:** 1500 books. **Subscriptions:** 250 journals and other serials; 10 newspapers.

19753 ■ **Ernst & Young Center for Business Knowledge**
155 N. Wacker Dr.
Chicago, IL 60606
Ph: (312)879-2000

Fax: (312)879-4000
URL: http://www.ey.com
Scope: Accounting, taxation, consulting, healthcare.
Services: Interlibrary loan; library not open to the
public. Holdings: 3000 books. Subscriptions: 500
journals and other serials.

**19754 ■ Ernst & Young Center for Business
Knowledge**
1 Victory Pk., Ste. 2000
2323 Victory Ave.
Dallas, TX 75219
Ph: (214)969-8000
Fax: (214)969-8587
URL: http://www.ey.com
Scope: Consulting, accounting, tax accounting, audit-
ing. Services: Center open to the public at librarian's
discretion.

19755 ■ Ernst & Young Library
875 E. Wisconsin Ave.
Milwaukee, WI 53202
Ph: (414)273-5900
URL: http://www.ey.com
Scope: Taxation, tax law, accounting, auditing. Services: Performs searches on fee basis for clients
only. Holdings: 1200 books. Subscriptions: 35
journals and other serials.

**19756 ■ Ernst & Young LLP Center for
Business Knowledge**
5 Times Sq.
New York, NY 10019
Ph: (212)773-3000
Fax: (212)773-6350
URL: http://www.ey.com/PH/en/OurLocations
Scope: Accounting and auditing, taxation, finance.
Services: Interlibrary loan; copying; library open to
clients and SLA members. Founded: 1953. Hold-
ings: 3500 books. Subscriptions: 500 journals and
other serials.

19757 ■ Fenwick & West LLP Law Library
Silicon Valley Center
801 California St.
Mountain View, CA 94041-2008
Ph: (650)988-8500
Fax: (650)938-5200
Co. E-mail: library@fenwick.com
URL: http://www.fenwick.com
Contact: Sharon McNally Lahey, Director, Library
    Services
Scope: Securities, corporate, employment, Interna-
tional taxation, intellectual property, litigation. Ser-
vices: Interlibrary loan; copying; Library not open to
the public. Founded: 1973. Holdings: 2500 books.
Subscriptions: 86 journals and other serials; 2
newspapers.

**19758 ■ Greene Radovsky Maloney Share
Library**
4 Embarcadero Ctr., Ste. 4000
San Francisco, CA 94111
Ph: (415)981-1400
Fax: (415)777-4961
Co. E-mail: info@greeneradovsky.com
URL: http://www.greeneradovsky.com
Scope: Taxation. Services: Interlibrary loan; copy-
ing; library not open to the public. Founded: 1984.
Holdings: 1200 books; 75 bound periodical volumes.
Subscriptions: 150 journals and other serials; 10
newspapers.

19759 ■ Huddleston, Bolen LLP Law Library
611 3rd Ave.
Huntington, WV 25701
Ph: (304)529-6181
Fax: (304)522-4312
URL: http://www.huddlestonbolen.com/
Scope: Taxation/estate, corporate/securities/banking,
federal litigation, labor. Services: Library not open to
the public. Holdings: 35,000 books.

**19760 ■ Illinois CPA Society - Information &
Research Center**
550 W. Jackson, Ste. 900
Chicago, IL 60661-5716
Ph: (312)601-4613
Free: 800-993-0407

Fax: (312)906-8045
Co. E-mail: research@icpas.org
URL: http://www.icpas.org
Contact: Michele Courtney, Assistant Director
Scope: Accounting; auditing; taxation; business. Services: Research and book requests by phone or
email. Founded: 1981. Holdings: 5000 books; 50
bound periodical volumes. Subscriptions: 100
journals and other serials.

19761 ■ KPMG - Research Centre
777 Dunsmuir St.
Vancouver, BC, Canada V7Y 1K3
Ph: (604)691-3000
Fax: (604)691-3031
URL: http://www.kpmg.ca
Scope: Accounting, tax, general business, stocks.
Services: SDI; Library not open to the public.
Founded: 1982. Holdings: 1000 books; 70 bound
periodical volumes. Subscriptions: 50 journals and
other serials; 6 newspapers.

**19762 ■ Polsinelli Shalton Welte Suelthaus
PC Law Library**
700 W. 47th St., Ste. 1000
Kansas City, MO 64112
Ph: (816)753-1000
Fax: (816)753-1536
Co. E-mail: bfullerton@pswlaw.com
URL: http://www.pswlaw.com/
Contact: Karin L. Weaver
Scope: Law - tax, bankruptcy, real estate; litigation;
product liability. Services: Interlibrary loan; copying;
SDI; Library open to clients only. Holdings: 15,000
books. Subscriptions: 1500 journals and other seri-
als; 10 newspapers.

19763 ■ Power Budd LLP Law Library
First Canadian Place, Ste. 7210
Toronto, ON, Canada M5X 1C7
Ph: (416)642-8580
Fax: (416)640-2777
Co. E-mail: lrhodes@powerbudd.com
Contact: Lesley Rhodes, Librarian
Scope: Energy, environmental and corporate law.
Services: Library not open to the public. Holdings:
Figures not available.

**19764 ■ PricewaterhouseCoopers - Research
Centre**
1250 Boul Rene-Levesque O
Bureau 2800
Montreal, QC, Canada H3B 2G4
Ph: (514)205-5000
Fax: (514)938-5709
URL: http://www.pwc.com/ca
Scope: Accounting, tax, management, business,
finance. Founded: 1993. Subscriptions: 200 jour-
nals and other serials.

19765 ■ Protape, Inc. Library
1540 Broadway
New York, NY 10036
Contact: Richard Sobelsohn
Scope: Accounting, law, real estate, English, math,
insurance, travel, taxation, stock broker, medical billing, claims adjusting, private investigation, paralegal.
Services: Library not open to the public. Founded:
1970. Holdings: 25,000 books; 250 bound periodical
volumes. Subscriptions: 65 journals and other serials; 20 newspapers.

19766 ■ Reid and Riege, PC Library
1 Financial Plaza
Hartford, CT 06103
Ph: (860)278-1150
Fax: (860)240-1002
Co. E-mail: info@rrlawpc.com
URL: http://www.rrlawpc.com
Scope: Law - tax, corporate. Services: Interlibrary
loan; copying; Library not open to the public.
Founded: 1950. Holdings: 10,000 books; 100 bound
periodical volumes. Subscriptions: 30 journals and
other serials.

19767 ■ Tax Executives Institute Library
1200 G. St. NW, Ste. 300
Washington, DC 20005-3814
Ph: (202)638-5601

Fax: (202)638-5607
Co. E-mail: asktei@tei.org
URL: http://www.tei.org
Contact: Timothy J. McCormally, Executive Director
Scope: Taxation; tax - legislation, administration,
management. Services: Copying; library open to TEI
members upon written request. Founded: 1944.
Holdings: 500 books; 500 professional memoranda.
Subscriptions: 20 journals and other serials. Tele-
communication Services: tmccormally@tei.org.

**19768 ■ Trumbull County Law Library
Association Library**
120 High St., NW
Warren, OH 44481
Ph: (330)675-2525
Fax: (330)675-2527
Co. E-mail: director@trumbulllaw.org
URL: http://www.tclla.org
Contact: George W. Baker, Director
Scope: Law - Ohio, labor, tax. Services: Copying;
Library open to the public with restrictions. Founded:
1899. Holdings: 32,000 books; 67,000 microfiche.
Subscriptions: 7 newspapers.

**19769 ■ U.S. Dept. of the Treasury - Treasury
Library**
1500 Pennsylvania Ave. NW, Rm. 1428
Washington, DC 20220
Ph: (202)622-0990
Fax: (202)622-6415
Co. E-mail: library.reference@do.treas.gov
URL: http://www.ustreas.gov/offices/management/
    privacy-records
Scope: Taxation, public finance, law, domestic and
International economics, economic conditions and
management. Services: Interlibrary loan within D.C.;
copying; library open to the public by appointment for
reference use only. Founded: 1789. Holdings:
70,000 books and bound periodical volumes; 500,000
microforms. Subscriptions: 300 journals and other
serials; 6 newspapers.

19770 ■ U.S. Tax Court Library
400 2nd St., NW
Washington, DC 20217
Ph: (202)521-4585
Fax: (202)521-4574
Co. E-mail: tclib@ustaxcourt.gov
URL: http://www.ustaxcourt.gov
Contact: Elsa B. Silverman, Librarian
Scope: Federal tax law - income, estate, and gift.
Services: Interlibrary loan; library not open to the
public. Founded: 1924. Holdings: 60,000 books;
9000 bound periodical volumes; Congressional
Record, Federal Register, and federal tax legislation.
Subscriptions: 200 journals and other serials.

**19771 ■ Willamette Management Associates
Library**
8600 W. Bryn Mawr Ave., Ste. 950
Chicago, IL 60631
Ph: (773)399-4300
Fax: (773)399-4310
Co. E-mail: vaplatt@willamette.com
URL: http://www.willamette.com
Contact: Victoria A. Platt, Specialist
Scope: Business valuation, tax, gift and estate,
finance. Services: Interlibrary loan; copying. Library
not open to the public. Founded: 1969. Telecom-
munication Services: cmblalock@willamette.com.

RESEARCH CENTERS

**19772 ■ American Institute for Economic
Research (AIER)**
250 Division St.
Great Barrington, MA 01230
Ph: (413)528-1216
Free: 888-528-1216
Fax: (413)528-0103
Co. E-mail: info@aier.org
URL: http://www.aier.org
Contact: Charles Murray, President
Founded: 1933. Publications: *Economic Education
Bulletin* (Monthly); *AIER Research reports* (Semi-
monthly). Educational Activities: Conferences and
consultations with educators and economists; Sum-

mer program for graduate students, two available for 4-weeks. **Awards:** Grants for students in PhD programs, who have completed the 8-week program.

19773 ■ American Law Institute (ALI)
4025 Chestnut St.
Philadelphia, PA 19104
Ph: (215)243-1600
Fax: (215)243-1636
Co. E-mail: lliebman@law.columbia.edu
URL: http://www.ali.org
Contact: Prof. Lance Liebman, Director
Founded: 1923. **Publications:** *ALI Reporter; Annual meeting proceeding; ALI Annual report; Principles of the Law* (Occasionally); *Restatements of the Law* (Periodic); *Model Penal Code and the Uniform Commercial Code* (Occasionally). **Educational Activities:** ALI Annual Meeting, members only; Project meetings (Periodic). **Telecommunication Services:** ali@ali.org.

19774 ■ Auburn University - Center for Governmental Services (CGS)
2236 Haley Ctr.
Auburn University, AL 36849-5268
Ph: (334)844-4781
Free: 800-446-0376
Fax: (334)844-1919
Co. E-mail: vealdon@auburn.edu
URL: http://www.auburn.edu/outreach/cgs
Contact: Dr. Don-Terry Veal, Director
Services: Technical assistance: to municipalities, counties, and state agencies in solving specific problems. **Founded:** 1976. **Educational Activities:** Annual County Government Officials Conference, on management; Annual Public Personnel Administrators Conference.

19775 ■ Canadian Tax Foundation (CTF)—L'Association Canadienne d'Études Fiscales (ACEF)
595 Bay St., Ste. 1200
Toronto, ON, Canada M5G 2N5
Ph: (416)599-0283
Free: 877-733-0283
Fax: (416)599-9283
Co. E-mail: admin@ctf.ca
URL: http://www.ctf.ca
Contact: Larry Chapman, Chief Executive Officer
E-mail: lchapman@ctf.ca
Description: Individuals and organizations with an interest in taxation. Promotes increased awareness of the Canadian Tax Code and the social ramifications of taxation. Serves as a clearinghouse on taxation; sponsors research and educational programs. **Services:** Information service: for members. **Founded:** 1945. **Publications:** *Annual Conference Report; CTF Annual Report* (Monthly); *Canadian Tax Highlights* (Monthly); *Canadian Tax Journal* (Bimonthly; Quarterly); *Canadian Tax Papers Series* (Occasionally); *Finances of the Nation* (Annual); *Tax Memos; Tax for the Owner Manager* (Quarterly); *Taxation of Private Corporations and Their Shareholders* (Occasionally). **Educational Activities:** National tax and corporate management tax conferences (Annual); Regional conferences (Annual). **Telecommunication Services:** srichardson@ctf.ca.

19776 ■ Cascade Policy Institute
4850 SW Scholls Ferry Rd., Ste. 103
Portland, OR 97225
Ph: (503)242-0900
Fax: (503)242-3822
Co. E-mail: info@cascadepolicy.org
URL: http://www.cascadepolicy.org
Contact: John A. Charles, Jr., President
Founded: 1991. **Publications:** *Cascade Commentaries* (Weekly); *Cascade Quickpoints* (Weekly); *Cascade Update* (Semiannual). **Educational Activities:** Cascade Policy Institute Intern program, summer program for graduate students; Cascade Policy Institute Lecture series (Annual), features national experts. **Awards:** Children's Scholarship Fund, scholarships for K-8 low income students. **Telecommunication Services:** john@cascadepolicy.org.

19777 ■ Citizens for Tax Justice (CTJ)
1616 P St. NW, Ste. 200
Washington, DC 20036
Ph: (202)299-1066
Fax: (202)299-1065
Co. E-mail: ctj@tasctj.org
URL: http://www.ctj.org
Contact: Robert S. McIntyre, Director
Founded: 1979. **Publications:** *CTJ Update* (Quarterly); *Studies and analyses.*

19778 ■ Competitive Enterprise Institute (CEI)
1899 L St. NW, 12th Fl.
Washington, DC 20036
Ph: (202)331-1010
Fax: (202)331-0640
Co. E-mail: info@cei.org
URL: http://cei.org
Contact: Fred L. Smith, Jr., President
Founded: 1984. **Publications:** *CEI Planet* (Bimonthly). **Educational Activities:** Warren Brooks Memorial Dinner (Annual). **Awards:** Julian Simon Award (Annual); Warren Brookes Journalism Fellowship. **Telecommunication Services:** fsmith@cei.org.

19779 ■ Employee Benefit Research Institute (EBRI)
1100 13th St. NW, Ste. 878
Washington, DC 20005
Ph: (202)659-0670
Fax: (202)775-6312
Co. E-mail: info@ebri.org
URL: http://www.ebri.org
Contact: Dallas L. Salisbury, President
E-mail: salisbury@ebri.org
Description: Corporations, consulting firms, banks, insurance companies, unions, and others with an interest in the future of employee benefit programs. Purpose is to contribute to the development of effective and responsible public policy in the field of employee benefits through research, publications, educational programs, seminars, and direct communication. Sponsors a broad range of studies on retirement income, health, disability, and other benefit programs; disseminates study results. Maintains research library with information on employee benefit programs. **Scope:** A public policy research organization serving as an employee benefits information source on health, welfare and retirement issues. Services include: basic benefit program descriptions, legislation analysis, media coverage and interpretation and long-range planning. Specializes in research on pensions, social security, health care, Medicare, long-term care, and flexible benefits. Serves government, academic consumers, consultants, banks, insurance companies, investment managers, law and accounting firms, corporations, and individuals. **Services:** Congressional briefings. **Founded:** 1978. **Subscriptions:** 4000 audiovisuals books clippings monographs periodicals. **Publications:** "Retirement Security in the United States-Current Sources, Future Prospects, and Likely Outcomes of Current Trends," 2006; "Estimating the Value of Changes in OASI Benefits Under Social Security Reforms," Jun, 2006; "Will Wider Use of Evidence-Based Medicine Significantly Enhance Healthcare Quality and Affordability: Implications for Consumer-Driven Health Benefits," 2003; "Consumer Driven Health Benefits: A Continuing Evolution," 2002; "The Economic Costs of the Uninsured Implications for Business and Government," 2000; "The Future of Private Retirement Plans," 2000; "EBRI Issue Briefs"; "EBRI Notes"; "Pension Investment Report PIR"; "EBRI Data book on Employee Benefits"; "Fundamentals of Employee Benefits Programs". **Educational Activities:** American Savings Education Council; Choose to Save Education Program; Fellows program, for academics, media, retirees; Policy forums (Biennial). **Awards:** EBRI Lillywhite Award (Annual); The EBRI Lillywhite Award (Annual). **Seminars:** Policy Forums, Congressional Briefings. **Telecommunication Services:** salisbury@ebri.org.

19780 ■ Florida TaxWatch
PO Box 10209
Tallahassee, FL 32302
Ph: (850)222-5052
Fax: (850)222-7476
Co. E-mail: dcalabro@floridataxwatch.org
URL: http://www.floridataxwatch.org
Contact: Dominic M. Calabro, President
Founded: 1979. **Publications:** *Budget Watch Series; Florida TaxWatch Research reports* (Occasionally); *Report and Recommendations of the Government Cost Savings Task Force* (Annual). **Educational Activities:** Ideas in Action Forum; Government Cost Savings Task Force (5/year); Membership meeting (Annual). **Awards:** Prudential Financial-Davis Productivity Awards, providing cash awards and recognition to Florida's highly productive government workers; Florida TaxWatch Paid internships.

19781 ■ The Fraser Institute
1770 Burrard St., 4th Fl.
Vancouver, BC, Canada V6J 3G7
Ph: (604)688-0221
Free: 800-665-3558
Fax: (604)688-8539
Co. E-mail: brett.skinner@fraserinstitute.org
URL: http://www.fraserinstitute.org
Contact: Brett J. Skinner, President
Founded: 1974. **Publications:** *The Fraser Institute Annual Report; Fraser Forum* (Monthly); *Public Policy Sources and Economic Freedom of the World* (10/year). **Educational Activities:** Roundtables (Monthly); The Fraser Institute Seminars (Periodic); Annual General Meeting. **Telecommunication Services:** info@fraserinstitute.ca.

19782 ■ Free Market Foundation
2001 Plano Pky., Ste. 1600
Plano, TX 75075
Ph: (972)941-4444
Fax: (972)423-6162
Co. E-mail: info@libertyinstitute.org
URL: http://www.libertylegal.org
Contact: Kelly J. Shackelford, President
Services: Provides public service announcements for radio stations. **Founded:** 1972. **Publications:** *Legislative Bulletins; Lone Star Report; Voter's Guide.* **Educational Activities:** Sponsors briefings on issues affecting Texas.

19783 ■ Hoover Institution on War, Revolution and Peace—Hoover Institution
434 Galvez Mall
Stanford University
Stanford, CA 94305-6010
Ph: (650)723-1754
Free: 877-466-8374
Fax: (650)723-1687
URL: http://www.hoover.org
Contact: John Raisian, Director
Founded: 1919. **Publications:** *Hoover Digest; Hoover Institution Annual Report; Syndicated newspaper column; Viewpoints; Essays in Public Policy; Hoover Institution on War, Revolution and Peace Quarterly Newsletter.* **Educational Activities:** National Fellows Program; Seminars and individual lectures; Hoover Institution on War, Revolution and Peace Conferences.

19784 ■ Institute for Research on the Economics of Taxation (IRET)
1710 Rhode Island Ave. NW, 11th Fl.
Washington, DC 20036
Ph: (202)463-1400
Fax: (202)463-6199
Co. E-mail: sentin@iret.org
URL: http://www.iret.org
Contact: Stephen J. Entin, President
Founded: 1977. **Publications:** *Congressional Advisory; Economic Policy Bulletin; Papers, Bylines, and testimony.* **Educational Activities:** Policy meetings (Monthly); periodic congressional, business and media briefings on public policy issues and events; Congressional Staff Seminar Series (Annual), attended by congressional staff, academic and other lecturers.

19785 ■ International Association of Assessing Officers - Research and Technical Services Department
314 W 10th St.
Kansas City, MO 64105
Ph: (816)701-8100

Free: 800-616-4226
Fax: (816)701-8149
Co. E-mail: library@iaao.org
URL: http://www.iaao.org
Contact: Lisa Daniels, Executive Director
Founded: 1934. **Publications:** *Fair and Equitable* (Monthly); *Journal of Property Tax Assessment and Administration* (Quarterly). **Educational Activities:** Research and Technical Services Department Conference (Annual), September or October; Workshops, one-day courses. **Telecommunication Services:** daniels@iaao.org.

19786 ■ League of California Cities
1400 K St., Ste. 400
Sacramento, CA 95814
Ph: (916)658-8200
Fax: (916)658-8240
Co. E-mail: okabel@cacities.org
URL: http://www.cacities.org
Contact: Chris McKenzie, Executive Director
Services: Legal Service Program: provides legal inquiry, educational, and litigation-oriented service to city attorneys. **Founded:** 1898. **Publications:** *Priority Focus* (Weekly); *Special reports*; *Special interest newsletters*; *Western City Magazine* (Monthly). **Educational Activities:** Professional development and training for elected and appointed city officials and city staff. **Telecommunication Services:** cmckenzie@cacities.org.

19787 ■ National Bureau of Economic Research (NBER)
1050 Massachusetts Ave.
Cambridge, MA 02138
Ph: (617)868-3900
Fax: (617)868-2742
Co. E-mail: info@nber.org
URL: http://www.nber.org
Contact: Dr. James Poterba, President
Description: Conducts analyses of economic issues, including economic growth and fluctuations, productivity, financial institutions, money, international economic problems, taxation, government spending, labor studies, health, and American economic history. **Founded:** 1920. **Publications:** *Macroeconomics Annual*; *NBER Digest*; *NBER Reporter*; *Tax Policy and the Economy* (Annual). **Educational Activities:** Six-week summer institute for economists. **Telecommunication Services:** op@nber.org.

19788 ■ National Center for Policy Analysis (NCPA)
12770 Coit Rd., Ste. 800
Dallas, TX 75251-1339
Ph: (972)386-6272
Fax: (972)386-0924
Co. E-mail: media@ncpa.org
URL: http://www.ncpa.org
Contact: John C. Goodman, President
Founded: 1983. **Publications:** *Daily Policy Digest* (Daily); *Health Policy Digest* (Weekly); *NCPA Alert* (Bimonthly); *Today at the NCPA* (Daily); *What's New at the NCPA* (Weekly). **Educational Activities:** Public policy forums; Hatton Sumners Distinguished Lecture Series. **Awards:** NCPA Internships.

19789 ■ New York Public Interest Research Group (NYPIRG)
107 Washington Ave.
Albany, NY 12210
Ph: (518)436-0876

Fax: (518)432-6178
Co. E-mail: nyc@nypirg.org
URL: http://www.nypirg.org
Contact: Rebecca Weber, Executive Director
Founded: 1973. **Publications:** *NYPIRG AGENDA* (Quarterly); *Council Watch*. **Educational Activities:** NYPIRG Conferences (3/year), throughout the state.

19790 ■ Peter G. Peterson Institute for International Economics
1750 Massachusetts Ave. NW
Washington, DC 20036-1903
Ph: (202)328-9000
Fax: (202)659-3225
Co. E-mail: kstewart@piie.com
URL: http://www.iie.com
Contact: Dr. C. Fred Bergsten, Director
Founded: 1981. **Publications:** *Peter G. Peterson Institute for International Economics Books*; *Policy analyses*; *Policy briefs*; *Peter G. Peterson Institute for International Economics Working papers*. **Educational Activities:** Policy conferences; Press conferences; Peter G. Peterson Institute for International Economics Seminars; Briefings on leading international economic policy issues. **Telecommunication Services:** comments@piie.com.

19791 ■ Taxpayers' Federation of Illinois (TFI)
430 E Vine St., Ste. A
Springfield, IL 62703
Ph: (217)522-6818
Fax: (217)522-6823
Co. E-mail: tom@iltaxwatch.org
URL: http://www.taxpayfedil.org
Contact: J. Thomas Johnson, President
Services: Lobbying. **Founded:** 1940. **Publications:** *TFI Annual report*; *Illinois Tax Facts Newsletter* (Monthly). **Educational Activities:** Seminars and addresses, for civic groups and legislators; Annual Membership Meetings; TFI Fall meeting.

19792 ■ Texas Public Policy Foundation (TPPF)
900 Congress Ave., Ste. 400
Austin, TX 78701
Ph: (512)472-2700
Fax: (512)472-2728
Co. E-mail: brollins@texaspolicy.com
URL: http://www.texaspolicy.com
Contact: Brooke L. Rollins, President
Services: Offers information to the media, government officials, leaders in business, and the community. **Founded:** 1989. **Publications:** *TPPF Newsletters*; *Policy Issue Papers*; *TPPF Reports*; *Videos*. **Educational Activities:** Conferences, seminars, and policy forums; Policy Orientation for the Texas Legislature; Policy Primer Series. **Telecommunication Services:** info@texaspolicy.com.

19793 ■ University of Arkansas at Little Rock - Institute for Economic Advancement (IEA)
2801 S University Ave.
Little Rock, AR 72204-1099
Ph: (501)569-8519
Fax: (501)569-8538
Co. E-mail: jlyoungquist@ualr.edu
URL: http://www.aiea.ualr.edu/
Contact: Jim Youngquist, Executive Director
Founded: 1960.

19794 ■ University of Michigan - Office of Tax Policy Research (OTPR)
Stephen M. Ross School of Business
701 Tappan St., Rm. W7715
Ann Arbor, MI 48109-1234
Ph: (734)763-3068
Fax: (734)763-4032
Co. E-mail: jslemrod@umich.edu
URL: http://www.bus.umich.edu/OTPR/
Contact: Prof. Joel Slemrod, Director
Founded: 1987. **Publications:** *Tax Research News* (Semiannual). **Educational Activities:** Conference on relevant tax issues (Annual). **Telecommunication Services:** otpr@umich.edu.

19795 ■ University of Toronto - Institute for Policy Analysis (IPA)
Joseph L. Rotman School of Management
105 St. George St.
Toronto, ON, Canada M5S 3E6
Ph: (416)978-1888
Fax: (416)978-4629
Co. E-mail: ihorstmann@rotman.utoronto.ca
URL: http://www.rotman.utoronto.ca/riib/
Contact: Prof. Ig Horstmann, Director
Services: Advisory services: to decision makers within government and industry; Research training: both in quantitative analysis in social sciences. **Founded:** 1967. **Publications:** *IPA Annual Report*; *IPA Working Papers*. **Educational Activities:** Graduate instruction; IPA Seminars; Special conferences, all for participants in its policy and economic analysis program; IPA Workshops.

19796 ■ Utah Foundation
10 W Broadway, Ste. 307
Salt Lake City, UT 84101
Ph: (801)355-1400
Fax: (801)355-1470
Co. E-mail: steve@utahfoundation.org
URL: http://www.utahfoundation.org
Contact: Stephen J. Kroes, President
Founded: 1945. **Publications:** *Utah Foundation Research Reports* (5/year); *Special reports* (Occasionally); *Statistical Review of Government in Utah* (Biennial). **Telecommunication Services:** brooke@utahfoundation.org.

19797 ■ Washington Research Council (WRC)
16300 Christensen Rd., Ste. 207
Tukwila, WA 98188
Ph: (206)467-7088
Free: 800-294-7088
Fax: (206)467-6957
Co. E-mail: rsdavis@researchcouncil.org
URL: http://www.researchcouncil.org/mx/hm.asp?id=home
Contact: Richard S. Davis, President
Services: Specialty research: as requested by Council members or local organizations with interests in state governmental policies. **Founded:** 1932. **Publications:** *How Washington Compares*; *Special Reports*; *State Budget Trends*; *WRC Notebook* (Monthly). **Educational Activities:** WRC Annual meeting, in the spring for members and guests. **Awards:** Pathfinder.

ASSOCIATIONS AND OTHER ORGANIZATIONS

19798 ■ American Public Transportation Association (APTA)
1666 K St. NW, Ste. 1100
Washington, DC 20006
Ph: (202)496-4800
Fax: (202)496-4324
Co. E-mail: info@apta.com
URL: http://www.apta.com
Contact: William Millar, President
E-mail: wmillar@apta.com
Description: Motor bus and rapid transit systems; organizations responsible for planning, designing, constructing, financing and operating transit systems; business organizations which supply products and services to transit, academic institutions and state associations and departments of transportation. Represents the public interest in improving transit. Encourages cooperation among its members, their employees, the general public and compliance with the letter and spirit of equal opportunity principles. Seeks to: collect information relative to public transit; assist in the training, education and professional development of all persons involved in public transit; and engage in activities which promote public transit. Provides a medium for exchange of experiences, discussion, and a comparative study of public transit affairs; Promotes research. **Scope:** urban transportation and related fields. **Founded:** 1882. **Subscriptions:** 10000 archival material articles books papers periodicals reports. **Publications:** *Passenger Transport* (Biweekly); *Transit Fact Book*; *American Public Transportation Association--Membership Directory* (Annual); *Passenger Transport: The Weekly Newspaper of the Public Transportation Industry* (Weekly (Mon.)); *Transit Training Resources Directory*. **Educational Activities:** American Public Transportation Association Expo (Annual); International Public Transit Expo; EXPO (Triennial). **Awards:** Awards Program (Annual); Safety Awards (Annual).

19799 ■ Chartered Institute of Logistics and Transport in North America (CILTNA)—Institut agree de la logistique et des transports Amerique du Nord
275 Slater St., Ste. 900
Ottawa, ON, Canada K1P 5H9
Ph: (613)688-1438
Fax: (613)688-0966
Co. E-mail: cuylits@ciltna.com
URL: http://www.ciltna.com
Contact: Ed Cuylits, Executive Director
Description: Professionals in the transportation industries. Promotes high standards of ethics and practice among members; encourages study and interest in transportation and related fields. Makes available continuing professional education opportunities to members. **Founded:** 1919. **Publications:** *Pegasus* (Quarterly). **Educational Activities:** North American Transport (Annual). **Awards:** CSL Gold Medal (Annual); CSL Gold Medal.

19800 ■ National Bus Traffic Association (NBTA)
111 K St. NE, 9th Fl.
Washington, DC 20002
Ph: (202)898-2700
Fax: (202)842-0850
URL: http://www.bustraffic.org
Description: Establishes by the intercity regular route bus carriers. Serves as tariff publisher for its industry. **Founded:** 1933.

19801 ■ *Pegasus*
275 Slater St., Ste. 900
Ottawa, ON, Canada K1P 5H9
Ph: (613)688-1438
Fax: (613)688-0966
Co. E-mail: cuylits@ciltna.com
URL: http://www.ciltna.com
Contact: Ed Cuylits, Executive Director
Released: Quarterly

19802 ■ Taxicab, Limousine and Paratransit Association (TLPA)
3200 Tower Oaks Blvd., Ste. 220
Rockville, MD 20852
Ph: (301)984-5700
Fax: (301)984-5703
Co. E-mail: info@tlpa.org
URL: http://www.tlpa.org
Contact: Robert McBride, President
Description: Ground transportation fleet owners operating 108,000 passenger vehicles including taxicabs, limousines, sedans, airport shuttles, paratransit, and non-emergency medical. **Founded:** 1917. **Publications:** *Transportation Leader* (Quarterly); *Transportation Leader* (Quarterly); *The Transportation Leader--Buyer's Guide Issue* (Annual). **Educational Activities:** Taxicab, Limousine and Paratransit Association Conference (Annual). **Awards:** Driver of the Year (Annual); Operator of the Year (Annual).

19803 ■ Transportation Association of Canada (TAC)—Association des Transports du Canada
2323 St. Laurent Blvd.
Ottawa, ON, Canada K1G 4J8
Ph: (613)736-1350
Fax: (613)736-1395
Co. E-mail: secretariat@tac-atc.ca
URL: http://www.tac-atc.ca
Contact: Doug McNeill, President
Description: Government agencies and private organizations involved in transportation. Maintains technical information service; compiles statistics. **Scope:** all facets of transportation. **Founded:** 1914. **Subscriptions:** 18000 books periodicals video recordings.

19804 ■ United Motorcoach Association (UMA)
113 S West St., 4th Fl.
Alexandria, VA 22314-2824
Ph: (703)838-2929
Free: 800-424-8262
Fax: (703)838-2950
Co. E-mail: info@uma.org
URL: http://www.uma.org
Contact: Mr. William Allen, Chairman
Description: Represents bus and motorcoach companies. Concerns itself with issues related to buses such as safety standards and regulations. **Founded:** 1971. **Publications:** *Operating Ratio Study*; *Safety and Courtesy Video*.

REFERENCE WORKS

19805 ■ *"21st Century Filling Station"* in Austin Business JournalInc. (Vol. 29, December 11, 2009, No. 40, pp. 1)
Pub: American City Business Journals
Ed: Jacob Dirr. **Description:** Clean Energy Fuels Corporation announced plans for the construction of a $1 million, 17,000 square foot compressed natural gas fueling station at or near the Austin-Bergstrom International Airport (ABIA). Clean Energy Fuels hopes to encourage cab and shuttle companies in the ABIA to switch from gasoline to natural gas.

19806 ■ *"Business Start-Up a Learning Experience for Young Bellingham Entrepreneur"* in Bellingham Herald (July 18, 2010)
Pub: Bellingham Herald
Ed: Dave Gallagher. **Description:** Profile of 21-year-old entrepreneur, Chase Larabee, who developed an online program that helps airport fixed-based operators handle refueling, hotel and transportation reservations and other requests from private airplane pilots.

19807 ■ *"City's Streetcar Utility Estimate Way Off Mark"* in Business Courier (Vol27, November 19, 2010, No. 29. , pp. 1)
Pub: Business Courier
Ed: Dan Monk, Lucy May. **Description:** Duke Energy Corporation has released new estimates that show moving electric and gas lines alone for Cincinnati, Ohio's proposed streetcar project could cost more than $20 million. However, the city has only estimated the relocation to cost $5 million in federal grant applications.

19808 ■ *"Funkhouser Wants Region to Get On Board Light Rail"* in Business Journal-Serving Metropolitan Kansas City (November 30, 2007)
Pub: American City Business Journals, Inc.
Ed: Suzanna Stagemeyer. **Description:** Mark Funhouser, Mayor of Kansas City, is planning to construct a regional multimodal public transit system. A previous light rail plan was rescinded due to logistical, financial and legal problems. Details of the light transit plans are discussed.

19809 ■ *How to Start a Home-Based Senior Care Business: Check-in-Care, Transportation Services, Shopping and Cooking*
Pub: Globe Pequot Press
Ed: James L. Ferry. **Released:** January 1, 2010. **Price:** $18.95. **Description:** Information is provided to start a home-based senior care business.

19810 ■ *"MV Transportation Winds $133M Contract" in Black Enterprise (Vol. 38, November 2007, No. 4, pp. 30)*
Pub: Earl G. Graves Publishing Co. Inc.
Ed: Marcia A. Wade. **Description:** MV Transportation won a $133 million contract to operate 139 fixed-route buses in the San Gabriel and Pomona valley areas of California.

19811 ■ *"People; E-Commerce, Online Games, Mobile Apps" in Advertising Age (Vol. 80, October 19, 2009, No. 35, pp. 14)*
Pub: Crain's Communications
Ed: Nat Ives. **Description:** Profile of People Magazine and the ways in which the publisher is moving its magazine forward by exploring new concepts in a time of declining newsstand sales and advertising pages; among the strategies are e-commerce such as the brand People Style Watch in which consumers are able highlight clothing and jewelry and then connect to retailers' sites and a channel on Taxi TV, the network of video-touch screens in New Your City taxis.

19812 ■ *"People; E-Commerce, Online Games, Mobile Apps: This Isn't Your Mom's People" in Advertising Age (Vol. 80, October 19, 2009, No. 35)*
Pub: Crain's Communications
Ed: Nat Ives. **Description:** Profile of People Magazine and the ways in which the publisher is moving its magazine forward by exploring new concepts in a time of declining newsstand sales and advertising pages; among the strategies are e-commerce such as the brand People Style Watch in which consumers are able highlight clothing and jewelry and then connect to retailers' sites and a channel on Taxi TV, the network of video-touch screens in New Your City taxis.

19813 ■ *"Taxis Are Set to Go Hybrid" in Philadelphia Business Journal (Vol. 30, September 16, 2011, No. 31, pp. 1)*
Pub: American City Business Journals Inc.
Ed: Natalie Kostelni. **Description:** Taxis are going hybrid in several major states such as New York, California and Maryland where it is mandated, but it is yet to happen in Philadelphia, Pennsylvania with the exception of one taxi company. Freedom Taxi is awaiting Philadelphia Parking Authority's sign off.

19814 ■ *The Transportation Leader--Buyer's Guide Issue*
Pub: Taxicab, Limousine and Paratransit Association
Contact: Robert McBride, President
URL(s): www.tlpa.org. **Released:** Annual; Latest edition 2009. **Publication includes:** List of manufacturers of taxicabs, minibuses, vans, limousines, parts, service equipment, wheelchair lifts, communications systems; also includes consultants, insurance agencies, advertising services, propane or natural gas systems; dealers in used vehicles, two-way radios, and meters; and other companies servicing the for-hire vehicle fleet industry (taxicabs, limousines, vans, and minibuses). **Entries include:** Company name, address, phone, contact person, and brief description of product or service. **Arrangement:** Alphabetical. **Indexes:** Product or service, provided by vendor.

STATISTICAL SOURCES

19815 ■ *RMA Annual Statement Studies*
Pub: Risk Management Association
Contact: Kevin M. Blakey, President
Released: Annual. **Price:** $175.00 2006-07 edition, $105.00. **Description:** Contains composite balance sheets and income statements for more than 360 industries, including the accounting, auditing, and bookkeeping industries. Also contains five years of comparative historical data for discerning trends. Includes 16 commonly used ratios, computed for most of the size groupings for nearly every industry.

TRADE PERIODICALS

19816 ■ *Bus Ride*
Pub: Power Trade Media L.L.C.
Contact: Valerie Valtierra, Director
E-mail: vvaltierra@churchexecutive.com
URL(s): busride.com. **Ed:** David Hubbard, Steve Kane. **Released:** Monthly **Price:** $39, Individuals;

$64, Individuals; $42, Canada; $69, Two years Canada; $98, Canada 3 years; $75, Other countries; $125, Two years other countries; $175 Two years 3 years.

19817 ■ *Commercial Carrier Journal*
Pub: Randall-Reilly Publishing Co.
Contact: Michael Reilly, President
E-mail: mreilly@rrpub.com
URL(s): www.ccjdigital.com/. **Released:** Monthly **Price:** Free.

19818 ■ *In the Driver's Seat*
Pub: Ontario Safety League
Ed: Terry Thompson, Editor. **Released:** Monthly. **Price:** Included in membership. **Description:** Commercial driver safety newsletter.

19819 ■ *Transportation Leader*
Pub: Taxicab, Limousine and Paratransit Association
Contact: Robert McBride, President
URL(s): www.tlpa.org. **Released:** Quarterly **Price:** $16, Individuals; $26, U.S. via airmail.

LIBRARIES

19820 ■ Alabama Department of Transportation - Research & Development Bureau - Research Library
1409 Coliseum Blvd.
Montgomery, AL 36110
Ph: (334)253-6940
Fax: (334)264-2042
Co. E-mail: brownje@dot.state.al.us
URL: http://www.dot.state.al.us/rdweb/Index.htm
Contact: Jeffrey W. Brown
Scope: Transportation. **Services:** Interlibrary loan; Library not open to the public. **Founded:** 1953. **Holdings:** 1000 books; 5000 reports. **Subscriptions:** 8 journals and other serials.

19821 ■ California State Department of Motor Vehicles - Licensing Operations Division - Research and Development Branch - Traffic Safety Research Library
2415 1st Ave., MS F-126
Sacramento, CA 95818
Ph: (916)657-3079
Free: 800-368-4327
Fax: (916)657-8589
Co. E-mail: dluong@dvm.ca.gov
Contact: Douglas Luong, Analyst
Scope: Automobile transportation. **Services:** Copying; library not open to the public. **Holdings:** 500 books; 10,000 bound periodical volumes; reports; manuscripts. **Subscriptions:** 20 journals and other serials.

19822 ■ ConnDOT Library and Information Center
2800 Berlin Tpke.
Newington, CT 06111-4116
Ph: (860)594-2000
Fax: (860)594-3039
Co. E-mail: drew.coleman@ct.gov
URL: http://www.ct.gov/dot/site/default.asp
Contact: Betty Ambler, Librarian
Scope: Transportation. **Services:** Interlibrary loan; copying; library open to the public by appointment. **Founded:** 1983. **Holdings:** 10,000 books; 10,000 reports; videos.

19823 ■ Kansas Department of Transportation Library—KDOT Library.
700 SW Harrison St.
Eisenhower State Office Bldg., 4th Fl. W.
Topeka, KS 66603-3745
Ph: (785)291-3854
Fax: (785)291-3717
Co. E-mail: library@ksdot.org
Contact: Marie Manthe, Librarian
Scope: Transportation. **Services:** Interlibrary loan; Library open to the public. **Founded:** 1963. **Holdings:** 3000 books; 20,000 reports; 175 CD-ROMs; 100 videos. **Subscriptions:** 100 journals and other serials.

19824 ■ Kentucky Transportation Center Library
University of Kentucky
176 Raymond Bldg.
Lexington, KY 40506-0281
Ph: (859)257-2155
Free: 800-432-0719
Fax: (859)257-1815
Co. E-mail: lwhayne@engr.uky.edu
URL: http://www.kyt2.com/
Contact: Laura Whayne, Librarian
Scope: Transportation. **Services:** Interlibrary loan; copying; Library open to the public. **Founded:** 1980. **Holdings:** 6000 books; 9000 reports; 800 videotapes. **Subscriptions:** 300 journals and other serials. **Telecommunication Services:** vbrock@engr.uky.edu.

19825 ■ K.T. Analytics Library
885 Rosemount Rd.
Oakland, CA 94610
Ph: (510)839-7702
Fax: (510)839-9887
Scope: Parking management, transportation systems management, demand management, transit planning, congestion pricing, road tolling, fleet management, intelligent transportation systems, air quality. **Services:** Library not open to the public. **Holdings:** 500 reports; 200 manuscripts. **Subscriptions:** 10 journals and other serials.

19826 ■ Missouri Highway and Transportation Department - Division of Materials Library
105 W. Capitol Ave.
Jefferson City, MO 65102-0270
Ph: (573)751-6735
Free: 888-275 6636
Fax: (573)526-5636
Co. E-mail: michael.meyerhoff@mail.modot.state.mo.us
URL: http://www.modot.org/
Contact: Mona Scott
Scope: Transportation. **Services:** Library not open to the public. **Holdings:** Figures not available.

19827 ■ Montana Department of Transportation Library
2701 Prospect Ave.
Helena, MT 59620-1001
Ph: (406)444-6338
Free: 800-335-7592
Fax: (406)444-6204
Co. E-mail: ssillick@mt.gov
URL: http://www.mdt.mt.gov/research/unique/services.shtml
Contact: Susan Sillick
Scope: Transportation. **Services:** Interlibrary loan; copying. **Holdings:** 10,000 items; reports; CD-ROMs; video. **Subscriptions:** 10 journals and other serials. **Telecommunication Services:** mdtresearch@mt.gov.

19828 ■ New Jersey Department of Transportation Research Library
1035 Parkway Ave.
Trenton, NJ 08625-0600
Ph: (609)530-5289
Fax: (609)530-2052
Co. E-mail: library@dot.state.nj.us
URL: http://www.state.nj.us/transportation/refdata/library/
Contact: Carol Paszamant, Librarian
Scope: Transportation. **Services:** Interlibrary loan; copying; library open to the public by appointment. **Founded:** 1962. **Holdings:** 300 books; 11,000 reports. **Subscriptions:** 50 journals and other serials.

19829 ■ North Carolina Department of Transportation, Research and Development Library
PO Box 25201
Raleigh, NC 27611
Ph: (919)715-2463

Fax: (919)715-0137
Co. E-mail: rhhall@dot.state.nc.us
URL: http://www.ncdot.org/
Contact: Bob Hall
Scope: Transportation. **Services:** Interlibrary loan; copying; Library open to the public for reference use only. **Holdings:** 11,209 books; 20,021 reports; 132 videos. **Subscriptions:** 57 journals and other serials.

19830 ■ North Dakota Department of Transportation - Materials and Research Division Library
608 East Blvd.
Bismarck, ND 58505-0700
Ph: (701)328-2500
Free: 855-637-6237
Fax: (701)328-0310
Co. E-mail: gweisger@nd.gov
URL: http://www.dot.nd.gov
Contact: Gerri Weisgerber, Manager, Administration
Scope: Transportation. **Services:** Library not open to the public. **Founded:** 1970. **Holdings:** 6600 reports. **Subscriptions:** 5 journals and other serials.

19831 ■ South Carolina Department of Transportation Library
955 Park St., Rm. 110
Columbia, SC 29202
Ph: (803)737-9897
Free: 855-467-2368
Fax: (803)737-0824
Co. E-mail: adcockda@dot.state.sc.us
URL: http://www.dot.state.sc.us
Contact: Ann Adcock, Manager
Scope: Transportation, engineering, mass transit. **Services:** Interlibrary loan; transportation related research; library open to the public. **Founded:** 1998. **Holdings:** 5500 books; 90 bound periodical volumes; 1900 reports; 250 videos. **Subscriptions:** 41 journals and other serials; 10 newspapers. **Telecommunication Services:** SCDOT_contact@scdot.org.

19832 ■ Vermont Agency of Transportation, Policy and Planning Division Library
1 National Drive
c, VT 05633-0001
Ph: (802)828-3960

Fax: (802)828-3983
URL: http://www.aot.state.vt.us
Contact: Sandy Aja
Scope: Transportation. **Holdings:** Figures not available.

RESEARCH CENTERS

19833 ■ Southwest Region University Transportation Center (SWUTC)
Texas Transportation Institute
Texas A&M University System
3135 TAMU
College Station, TX 77843-3135
Ph: (979)845-5815
Fax: (979)845-9761
Co. E-mail: d-burke@tamu.edu
URL: http://swutc.tamu.edu
Contact: Dock Burke, Director
Founded: 1988. **Educational Activities:** Graduate instruction. **Telecommunication Services:** swutc@tamu.edu.

DIRECTORIES OF EDUCATIONAL PROGRAMS

19834 ■ *Directory of Private Accredited Career Schools and Colleges of Technology*
Pub: Accrediting Commission of Career Schools and Colleges of Technology
Contact: Michale S. McComis, Executive Director
Released: On web page. **Price:** Free. **Description:** Covers 3900 accredited post-secondary programs that provide training programs in business, trade, and technical fields, including various small business endeavors. Entries offer school name, address, phone, description of courses, job placement assistance, and requirements for admission. Arrangement is alphabetical.

VIDEOCASSETTES/ AUDIOCASSETTES

19835 ■ *Taxidermy by Video*
Allied Video Corp.
PO Box 702618
Tulsa, OK 74170
Free: 800-926-5892
Fax: (918)587-1550
URL: http://www.alliedvd.com
Released: 1987. **Description:** This series reveals the secret techniques of professional taxidermy, covering all its aspects, including mounting and finishing. Such popular animals as the Mallard Duck, White Tail Deer and Large Mouth Bass are fully examined. **Availability:** VHS.

REFERENCE WORKS

19836 ■ *"Commentary. On Federal Reserve's Cut of Interest Rates" in Small Business Economic Trends (January 2008, pp. 3)*
Pub: National Federation of Independent Business
Description: Federal Reserve cut interest rates and announced its economic outlook on September 18, 2007 to stimulate spending. The cut in interest rates, however, may not help in supporting consumer spending because savers may lose interest income. The expected economic impact of the interest rate cuts and the U.S. economic outlook are also discussed.

19837 ■ *"Commentary. Small Business Economic Trends" in Small Business Economic Trends (March 2008, pp. 3)*
Pub: National Federation of Independent Business
Ed: William C. Dunkelberg, Holly Wade. **Description:** Commentary on the economic trends for small businesses in the U.S. is presented. Analysis of the labor market and low interest rates is given. The effect of the Federal Reserve's policy announcement on small business owner optimism is also discussed.

19838 ■ *"Commentary. Small Business Economic Trends" in Small Business Economic Trends (February 2008, pp. 3)*
Pub: National Federation of Independent Business
Ed: William C. Dunkelberg, Holly Wade. **Description:** Commentary on the economic trends for small businesses in the U.S. is presented. Analysis of the U.S. Federal Reserve Board's efforts to prevent a recession is given. Reduction in business inventories is also discussed.

19839 ■ *Educational Dealer--Buyers' Guide Issue*
Pub: Fahy-Williams Publishing Inc.
Contact: Tina Manzer, Director
E-mail: tmanzer@fwpi.com
URL(s): www.eddealermagazine.com. **Released:** Annual; August. **Publication includes:** List of approximately 2,000 suppliers of educational materials

and equipment. **Entries include:** Company name, address, phone, products or services. **Arrangement:** Classified by product or service.

19840 ■ *"Going Dutch" in Canadian Business (Vol. 81, October 27, 2008, No. 18, pp. 40)*
Pub: Rogers Media Ltd.
Description: Experts like Philippe Bergevin suggest that current economic conditions in Canada are similar to those of the Netherlands in the 1970s. The Organisation for Economic Co-operation suggested that Canada should instead invest in sovereign wealth funds similar to Norway's policy.

19841 ■ *"Risk and Reward" in Canadian Business (Vol. 81, October 13, 2008, No. 17, pp. 21)*
Pub: Rogers Media Ltd.
Ed: Calvin Leung. **Description:** Macro-economist and currency analyst Mark Venezia believes that stable financial institutions, free-market reforms, and the role of central banks in keeping inflation and exchange rates stable could make emerging-market bonds strong performers for better future returns. Venezia's other views on emerging-market bonds are discussed.

19842 ■ *"Sense and Consensus" in Canadian Business (Vol. 81, October 13, 2008, No. 17, pp. 22)*
Pub: Rogers Media Ltd.
Ed: David Wolf. **Description:** Stock analysts' agree that earning estimates are seen to be optimistic in relation to their global economic outlook. Analysts are expected to cut earnings projections by fall because it may negatively affect the Canadian stock market. Other view on market analysis are presented.

TRADE PERIODICALS

19843 ■ *Educational Dealer: The Magazine for the School Supply Industry*
Pub: Fahy-Williams Publishing Inc.
Contact: Tina Manzer, Director
E-mail: tmanzer@fwpi.com
URL(s): www.eddealermagazine.com. **Released:** 5/yr. **Price:** Free.

19844 ■ *Teacher Magazine*
Pub: Editorial Projects in Education
Contact: Virginia B. Edwards, President
URL(s): www.teachermagazine.org/tm/index.html.
Ed: Virginia B. Edwards. **Released:** 9/yr. **Price:** $90, Individuals.

TRADE SHOWS AND CONVENTIONS

19845 ■ *Ed Expo*
National School Supply and Equipment Association (NSSEA)
8380 Colesville Rd., Ste. 250
Silver Spring, MD 20910
Ph: (301)495-0240
Free: 800-395-5550
Fax: (301)495-3330
Co. E-mail: customerservice@nssea.org
URL: http://www.nssea.org
Contact: Jim McGarry, President
E-mail: jmcgarry@nssea.org
URL(s): www.nssea.org/events/future.cfm. **Frequency:** Annual. **Audience:** Dealers and distributors of educational supplies. **Principal Exhibits:** Educational supplies and instructional materials. **Telecommunication Services:** nssea@nssea.org.

19846 ■ *The School Equipment Show*
National School Supply and Equipment Association (NSSEA)
8380 Colesville Rd., Ste. 250
Silver Spring, MD 20910
Ph: (301)495-0240
Free: 800-395-5550
Fax: (301)495-3330
Co. E-mail: customerservice@nssea.org
URL: http://www.nssea.org
Contact: Jim McGarry, President
E-mail: jmcgarry@nssea.org
URL(s): www.nssea.org. **Frequency:** Annual. **Audience:** School supply and equipment dealers. **Principal Exhibits:** Manufacturers of school products and school equipment (excluding textbooks). **Telecommunication Services:** nssea@nssea.org.

REFERENCE WORKS

19847 ■ *Customer Inter@ctions Buyer's Guide & Directory Issue*
Pub: Technology Marketing Corp.
URL(s): www.tmcnet.com. **Ed:** Linda Driscoll. **Released:** Annual; December. **Price:** $25. **Publication includes:** Over 1100 domestic and foreign suppliers of equipment, products, and services to the telecommunications/telemarketing industry. **Entries include:** Company name, address, phone, names of key sales personnel; type of firm, sales, products and services. **Arrangement:** Alphabetical and by product. **Indexes:** Service, product.

STATISTICAL SOURCES

19848 ■ *Successful Telemarketing*
Pub: McGraw-Hill
Ed: Bob Stone and John Wyman. **Released:** 1991. **Price:** 1992 - Hardcover $19.95. **Description:** Provides information on various uses of telemarketing, including advertising, sales promotions, and fundraising.

VIDEOCASSETTES/ AUDIOCASSETTES

19849 ■ *90 Telemarketing Selling Skills for the '90s*
American Media, Inc.
4621 121st St.
Urbandale, IA 50323-2311
Ph: (515)224-0919
Free: 888-776-8268
Fax: (515)327-2555
Co. E-mail: custsvc@ammedia.com
URL: http://www.ammedia.com
Released: 1990. **Price:** $1595.00. **Description:** Segments from various Billue seminars have been put together to provide this up-to-date course on telemarketing skills. **Availability:** VHS.

19850 ■ *Phoning for Profits*
1st Financial Training Services
1515 E. Woodfield Rd., Ste. 345
Schaumburg, IL 60173
Ph: (847)969-0900
Free: 800-442-8662
Fax: (847)969-0521
URL: http://www.1stfinancialtraining.com
Released: 1987. **Price:** $250.00. **Description:** Using the phone as a communication tool is a good way to increase sales. **Availability:** VHS; 3/4 U.

19851 ■ *Secrets of Telemarketing Scripts*
Instructional Video
2219 C St.
Lincoln, NE 68502
Ph: (402)475-6570
Free: 800-228-0164

Fax: (402)475-6500
Co. E-mail: feedback@insvideo.com
URL: http://www.insvideo.com
Released: 19??. **Price:** $75.00. **Description:** Consultant Judy Lanier demonstrates how to develop a workable telemarketing script. Shows a team of people developing a script and reveals the result. **Availability:** VHS.

19852 ■ *Selling on the Phone*
American Media, Inc.
4621 121st St.
Urbandale, IA 50323-2311
Ph: (515)224-0919
Free: 888-776-8268
Fax: (515)327-2555
Co. E-mail: custsvc@ammedia.com
URL: http://www.ammedia.com
Released: 1987. **Price:** $475.00. **Description:** A quick training film for telephone salespeople, from call planning to close. **Availability:** VHS; 3/4 U.

19853 ■ *Setting Up a Telemarketing Program*
Instructional Video
2219 C St.
Lincoln, NE 68502
Ph: (402)475-6570
Free: 800-228-0164
Fax: (402)475-6500
Co. E-mail: feedback@insvideo.com
URL: http://www.insvideo.com
Released: 19??. **Price:** $75.00. **Description:** Consultant Judy Lanier explains how to set up a business to business telemarketing operation, covering sales, marketing, operations, and customer base. **Availability:** VHS.

19854 ■ *Telemarketing Skills in Minutes*
American Media, Inc.
4621 121st St.
Urbandale, IA 50323-2311
Ph: (515)224-0919
Free: 888-776-8268
Fax: (515)327-2555
Co. E-mail: custsvc@ammedia.com
URL: http://www.ammedia.com
Released: 1987. **Description:** On four tapes, a thorough training program for telephone salespeople. **Availability:** VHS; 3/4 U.

19855 ■ *Telephone Manners*
Encyclopedia Britannica
331 N. LaSalle St.
Chicago, IL 60654
Ph: (312)347-7159
Free: 800-323-1229
Fax: (312)294-2104
URL: http://www.britannica.com
Released: 1989. **Description:** This valuable new program demonstrates every important step in telephone usage including identifying yourself and your organization, personalizing your calls, repeating all instructions given, taking notes of important messages, remembering calls on hold, listening to the

caller's mood as well as the message, using common courtesey word and conveying warmth. **Availability:** VHS; 3/4 U.

19856 ■ *Telephone Selling: A New Approach*
Video Arts, Inc.
c/o Aim Learning Group
8238-40 Lehigh
Morton Grove, IL 60053-2615
Free: 877-444-2230
Fax: (416)252-2155
Co. E-mail: service@aimlearninggroup.com
URL: http://www.aimlearninggroup.com
Released: 1991. **Price:** $790.00. **Description:** Keith Einstein shares his three-point approach to telephone sales. **Availability:** VHS; 8 mm; 3/4 U; Special order formats.

19857 ■ *What Is Telemarketing and How Do I Get Started?*
1st Financial Training Services
1515 E. Woodfield Rd., Ste. 345
Schaumburg, IL 60173
Ph: (847)969-0900
Free: 800-442-8662
Fax: (847)969-0521
URL: http://www.1stfinancialtraining.com
Released: 1987. **Price:** $425.00. **Description:** Starting a career in telemarketing is explained in this tape. **Availability:** VHS; 3/4 U.

TRADE SHOWS AND CONVENTIONS

19858 ■ Incoming Call Center Management (ICCM)
Advanstar Communications
641 Lexington Ave., 8th Fl.
New York, NY 10022
Ph: (212)951-6600
Free: 800-346-0085
Fax: (212)951-6793
Co. E-mail: info@advantstar.com
URL: http://www.advanstar.com
Contact: Robert Krakoff, President
URL(s): www.iccmchicago.com. **Frequency:** Annual. **Audience:** Call Center Managers. **Principal Exhibits:** Call center industry management. **Telecommunication Services:** btorrey@questex.com.

COMPUTERIZED DATABASES

19859 ■ *Big Yellow: Yellow Pages on the Web*
2200 W Airfield Dr.
Dallas, TX 75261
Ph: (972)453-7000
Free: 800-555-4833
Fax: (888)839-4480
Co. E-mail: info@supermedia.com
URL: http://www.supermedia.com
Contact: Peter Mcdonald, President
Availability: Online: SuperMedia LLC. **Type:** Directory.

19860 ■ *FONE*Data*
22382 Avenida Empresa
Rancho Santa Margarita, CA 92688-2112
Ph: (949)858-3000
Free: 800-MELISSA
Fax: (949)589-5211
URL: http://www.melissadata.com
Availability: Online: Melissa DATA Corp. CD-ROM: Melissa DATA Corp. **Type:** Directory; Statistical.

RESEARCH CENTERS

19861 ■ **Columbia University - Columbia Institute for Tele-Information (CITI)**
Uris Hall, Ste. 1A
Columbia Business School
3022 Broadway
New York, NY 10027
Ph: (212)854-4222
Fax: (212)854-1471
Co. E-mail: sr2132@columbia.edu
URL: http://www4.gsb.columbia.edu/citi/
Contact: Prof. Eli M. Noam, Director

Founded: 1983. **Publications:** *Information Exchange Newsletter* (Semiannual); *CITI Working Paper Series*. **Educational Activities:** CITI Seminars. **Telecommunication Services:** noam@columbia.edu.

ASSOCIATIONS AND OTHER ORGANIZATIONS

19862 ■ *Advisor*
24 Olive St., Unit 10
Grimsby, ON, Canada L3M 2B6
Ph: (905)309-0224
Free: 800-896-1054
Fax: (905)309-0225
Co. E-mail: info@camx.ca
URL: http://www.camx.ca/call-center/index_ang.cfm
Contact: Linda Osip, Executive Director
Released: Bimonthly

19863 ■ Association of TeleServices International (ATSI)
12 Academy Ave.
Atkinson, NH 03811
Ph: (703)234-4111
Free: 866-896-ATSI
Fax: (703)435-4390
Co. E-mail: admin@i.org
URL: http://www.atsi.org
Contact: Larry Goldenberg, President
Description: Telephone answering and voice message service providers. Seeks to foster growth and development in the industry. Represents the industry before Congress and regulatory agencies; negotiates with telephone companies. Holds seminars and workshops on the latest telecommunications technology; compiles statistics. Maintains hall of fame. **Founded:** 1942. **Publications:** *Connections* (Bimonthly); *TeleCommunicator* (Biweekly); *Association of Telemessaging Services International--Membership Directory* (Annual); *TeleCommunicator*. **Educational Activities:** Association of Teleservices International Conference (Annual). **Awards:** Award of Excellence (Annual). **Telecommunication Services:** admin@atsi.org.

19864 ■ Canadian Call Management Association (CAM-X)
24 Olive St., Unit 10
Grimsby, ON, Canada L3M 2B6
Ph: (905)309-0224
Free: 800-896-1054

Fax: (905)309-0225
Co. E-mail: info@camx.ca
URL: http://www.camx.ca/call-center/index_ang.cfm
Contact: Linda Osip, Executive Director
Description: Call centers and message exchanges. Promotes excellence in the handling of voice and electronic messages. Represents members' interests; facilitates technical advancement in the field of telecommunications. **Founded:** 1964. **Publications:** *Advisor* (Bimonthly). **Awards:** Award of Excellence; Call Centre Award of Distinction.

VIDEOCASSETTES/ AUDIOCASSETTES

19865 ■ *Telephone Manners*
Encyclopedia Britannica
331 N. LaSalle St.
Chicago, IL 60654
Ph: (312)347-7159
Free: 800-323-1229
Fax: (312)294-2104
URL: http://www.britannica.com
Released: 1989. **Description:** This valuable new program demonstrates every important step in telephone usage including identifying yourself and your organization, personalizing your calls, repeating all instructions given, taking notes of important messages, remembering calls on hold, listening to the caller's mood as well as the message, using common courtesey word and conveying warmth. **Availability:** VHS; 3/4 U.

TRADE SHOWS AND CONVENTIONS

19866 ■ Incoming Call Center Management (ICCM)
Advanstar Communications
641 Lexington Ave., 8th Fl.
New York, NY 10022
Ph: (212)951-6600
Free: 800-346-0085
Fax: (212)951-6793
Co. E-mail: info@advanstar.com
URL: http://www.advanstar.com
Contact: Robert Krakoff, President
URL(s): www.iccmchicago.com. **Frequency:** Annual. **Audience:** Call Center Managers. **Principal Exhib-**

its: Call center industry management. **Telecommunication Services:** btorrey@questex.com.

CONSULTANTS

19867 ■ Telecommunications Consultants of America
117 N Prospect Ave.
Bergenfield, NJ 07621
Ph: (201)384-0660
Fax: (847)806-7872
Contact: John C. Fuhrman, President
Scope: Produces telecommunications economies through increased efficiencies and/or alternate methods. Analyzes and audits phone services, files claims and negotiates orders with the communications carrier, and designs networks and station software. Active throughout the U.S., Canada, Puerto Rico, and Mexico. Clients from all types of organizations and industries, including government. **Founded:** 1968. **Publications:** "Telemanagement," Prentice Hall. **Seminars:** Introduction to Telecommunications Management, a 5-day seminar.

LIBRARIES

19868 ■ Museum of Independent Telephony - Archives Collection
412 S. Campbell
Abilene, KS 67410
Ph: (785)263-2681
Co. E-mail: heritagecenterdk@sbcglobal.net
URL: http://www.heritagecenterdk.com/museum_of_independent_telephony.html
Contact: Jeff Sheets
Scope: Telephone history and technology. **Services:** Copying; collection open to the public. **Founded:** 1973. **Holdings:** 1000 books; 1000 bound periodical volumes; 1000 other cataloged items; 500 manuscripts; 120 boxes of loose periodicals; 150 tapes. **Subscriptions:** 10 journals and other serials.

19869 ■ Ohio Bell - Corporate Information Resource Center
45 Erieview Plaza, Rm. 820
Cleveland, OH 44114-1813
Ph: (216)822-2740
Contact: John Jakovcic, Assistant Manager
Scope: Business, management, telecommunications, personnel, computers, marketing, Ohio Bell and Bell System history. **Services:** Interlibrary loan; copying; Library open to the public at librarian's discretion. **Founded:** 1951. **Holdings:** 5000 books. **Subscriptions:** 150 journals and other serials; 10 newspapers.

ASSOCIATIONS AND OTHER ORGANIZATIONS

19870 ■ Electronics Technicians Association International (ETA)
5 Depot St.
Greencastle, IN 46135-8024
Ph: (765)653-8262
Free: 800-288-3824
Fax: (765)653-4287
Co. E-mail: eta@eta-i.org
URL: http://www.eta-i.org
Contact: Stephen Fleeman, Vice Chairman
Description: Skilled electronics technicians. Provides placement service; offers certification examinations for electronics technicians and satellite, fiber optics, and data cabling installers. Compiles wage and manpower statistics. Administers FCC Commercial License examinations and certification of computer network systems technicians and web and internet specialists. **Scope:** technical, business training, employment, customer relations. **Founded:** 1978. **Subscriptions:** 300 audiovisuals monographs video recordings. **Publications:** The High-Tech News (Bimonthly). **Educational Activities:** Service Retail Convention (Annual); Electronics Technicians Association International Workshop (Annual). **Awards:** Technician of the Year; Educator of the Year (Annual); President's Award (Annual); Technician of the Year (Annual).

19871 ■ International Society of Certified Electronics Technicians (ISCET)
3608 Pershing Ave.
Fort Worth, TX 76107-4527
Ph: (817)921-9101
Free: 800-946-0201
Fax: (817)921-3741
Co. E-mail: info@iscet.org
URL: http://www.iscet.org
Contact: Dan Mundy, President
E-mail: dmundy@earthlink.net
Description: Technicians in 50 countries who have been certified by the society. Seeks to provide a fraternal bond among certified electronics technicians, raise their public image and improve the effectiveness of industry education programs for technicians. Offers training programs in new electronics information. Maintains library of service literature for consumer electronic equipment, including manuals and schematics for out-of-date equipment. Offers all FCC licenses. Sponsors testing program for certification of electronics technicians in the fields of audio, communications, computer, consumer, industrial, medical electronics, radar, radio-television and video. **Founded:** 1965. **Publications:** ISCET Update (Quarterly). **Educational Activities:** National Professional Service Convention and Trade Show (Annual). **Awards:** Technician of the Year; Technician of the Year Award.

DIRECTORIES OF EDUCATIONAL PROGRAMS

19872 ■ Directory of Private Accredited Career Schools and Colleges of Technology
Pub: Accrediting Commission of Career Schools and Colleges of Technology
Contact: Michale S. McComis, Executive Director
Released: On web page. **Price:** Free. **Description:** Covers 3900 accredited post-secondary programs that provide training programs in business, trade, and technical fields, including various small business endeavors. Entries offer school name, address, phone, description of courses, job placement assistance, and requirements for admission. Arrangement is alphabetical.

REFERENCE WORKS

19873 ■ "Don't' Hate the Cable Guy" in Saint Louis Business Journal (Vol. 31, August 5, 2011, No. 50, pp. 1)
Pub: Saint Louis Business Journal
Ed: Angela Mueller. **Description:** Charter Communications named John Birrer as senior vice president of customer experience. The company experienced problems with its customer services.

19874 ■ "For Apple, It's Showtime Again" in Barron's (Vol. 90, August 30, 2010, No. 35, pp. 29)
Pub: Barron's Editorial & Corporate Headquarters
Ed: Eric J. Savitz. **Description:** Speculations on what Apple Inc. will unveil at its product launch event are presented. These products include a possible new iPhone Nano, a new update to its Apple TV, and possibly a deal with the Beatles to distribute their songs over iTunes.

TRADE PERIODICALS

19875 ■ The High-Tech News
Pub: ETA International
Ed: Bryan Allen, Editor, bryan@eta-i.org. **Released:** Monthly. **Price:** Included in membership. **Description:** Serves member technicians with news of the Association and the electronics industry, including items on service, education, employment, management, and events. Contains information on membership, management, telecommunications, and business and technical training programs. Recurring features include editorials, news of research, letters to the editor, book reviews, and a calendar of events.

LIBRARIES

19876 ■ Antique Wireless Association Library/Museum
PO Box 421
Bloomfield, NY 14469
URL: http://www.antiquewireless.org
Scope: History of radio, television, telegraph; electricity; communication. **Services:** Library open to the public by appointment. **Founded:** 1952. **Holdings:** 2000 books; 5000 radio/electronic magazines. **Subscriptions:** 40 journals and other serials.

ASSOCIATIONS AND OTHER ORGANIZATIONS

19877 ■ **Alliance of Canadian Cinema, Television and Radio Artists (ACTRA)**
625 Church St., 3rd Fl.
Toronto, ON, Canada M4Y 2G1
Ph: (416)489-1311
Free: 800-387-3516
Fax: (416)489-8076
Co. E-mail: national@actra.ca
URL: http://www.actra.ca
Contact: Ferne Downey, President
Description: Performing artists in the television, radio, film, and other recorded media. Seeks to obtain equitable compensation and safe working conditions for members. Represents members in negotiations with employers; monitors workplace conditions in the film and broadcasting industries. **Founded:** 1943. **Publications:** *InterACTRA News* (Quarterly).

19878 ■ **Associated Press Broadcast (APB)**
AP Broadcast News Center
1100 13th St., Ste. 700
Washington, DC 20005
Ph: (202)641-9921
Free: 800-342-5127
Co. E-mail: lperryman@ap.org
URL: http://www.apbroadcast.com
Contact: Mary Junck, Chairwoman
Description: Broadcast stations in the United States that are members of the Associated Press. Advances journalism through radio and television. Cooperates with the AP in order to make available accurate and impartial news. Serves as a liaison between radio and television stations that are members of the AP and representatives of those stations. **Founded:** 1941. **Awards:** APB National Awards (Annual).

19879 ■ **Association for Interactive Marketing (AIM)**
1430 Broadway, 8th Fl.
New York, NY 10018
Ph: (212)790-1408
Free: 888-337-0008
Fax: (212)391-9233
URL: http://www.interactivehq.org/
Contact: Kevin M. Nooman, Executive Director
Description: Organizations, corporations, and individuals interested in the interactive television industry. Promotes the interests and image of the interactive television industry through political action and press releases. Provides reporters with research assistance, expert opinions, and contact information. Works to keep members updated on issues affecting the industry. Maintains speakers' bureau; conducts research and educational programs; offers placement service. Hosts networking events around the country, seminars, and conferences. **Scope:** interactive television, telecommunications. **Founded:** 1992. **Subscriptions:** archival material audiovisuals books clippings monographs periodicals. **Educational Activities:** Dinner and a Deal (Monthly).

19880 ■ **Association of Public Television Stations (APTS)**
2100 Crystal Dr., Ste. 700
Arlington, VA 22202
Ph: (202)654-4200
Fax: (202)654-4236
Co. E-mail: pbutler@apts.org
URL: http://www.apts.org
Contact: Patrick Butler, President
Description: Public television licensees whose goal is to organize efforts of public television stations in areas of planning and research and in representation before the government. Maintains current information on the public television system including such areas as licensee characteristics, financing and industry trends; makes projections on system growth and income. Monitors social, economic and demographic trends that have an impact on public television services. Prepares and disseminates general information about public television to policymaking agencies, the press, and the public. **Founded:** 1979. **Publications:** *Communique* (Quarterly); *Transitions* (Quarterly); *Update* (Quarterly). **Awards:** Grassroots Award (Annual); 21st Century (Annual).

19881 ■ **Broadcast Cable Credit Association (BCCA)**
550 W Frontage Rd., Ste. 3600
Northfield, IL 60093
Ph: (847)881-8757
Fax: (847)784-8059
Co. E-mail: info@bccacredit.com
URL: http://www.bccacredit.com
Contact: Richard Taub
Description: Enables members to efficiently manage credit risk and increase profitability. Provides industry specific credit reports on individual agencies, advertisers, or buying services (local or national). **Founded:** 1961. **Publications:** *BCCA Credit Handbook* (Annual); *Credit and Collection Survey; Update* (Monthly); *The Financial Manager for the Media Professional/ Credit Topics* (Bimonthly). **Educational Activities:** Broadcast Cable Credit Association Conference (Annual); Distance Learning (Monthly). **Awards:** Lifetime Achievement (Annual).

19882 ■ **Broadcast Education Association (BEA)**
1771 N St. NW
Washington, DC 20036-2800
Ph: (202)429-5355
Free: 888-380-7222
Fax: (202)775-2981
Co. E-mail: hbirks@nab.org
URL: http://www.beaweb.org
Contact: Heather Birks, Executive Director
E-mail: hbirks@nab.org
Description: Universities and colleges; faculty and students; promotes improvement of curriculum and teaching methods, broadcasting research, television and radio production, and programming teaching on the college level. **Founded:** 1955. **Publications:** *Journal of Broadcasting and Electronic Media; Journal of Broadcasting & Electronic Media* (Quarterly); *Feedback* (Quarterly); *Journal of Broadcasting and Electronic Media* (Quarterly). **Educational Activities:** Broadcast Education Association Convention (Annual); Broadcast Education Association Convention (Annual); Broadcast Education Association Annual Convention (Annual). **Awards:** Harold E. Fellows Scholarships; Walter S. Patterson Scholarships; Helen J. Sioussat/Fay Wells Scholarships; Alexander M. Tanger Scholarships; Two Year/Community Broadcast Education Association Scholarship Awards; Abe Voron Scholarships; Vincent T. Wasilewski Scholarships. **Telecommunication Services:** tbailey@nab.org; beainfo@beaweb.org; beamemberservices@nab.org.

19883 ■ **Cabletelevision Advertising Bureau (CAB)**
830 Third Ave., 2nd Fl.
New York, NY 10022
Ph: (212)508-1200
Fax: (212)832-3268
Co. E-mail: chuckt@cabletvadbureau.com
URL: http://www.thecab.tv
Contact: Mr. Sean Cunningham, President
Description: Ad-supported cable networks. Provides marketing and advertising support to members and promotes the use of cable by advertisers and ad agencies locally, regionally, and nationally. **Scope:** cable industry, cable advertising. **Founded:** 1981. **Subscriptions:** books periodicals. **Publications:** *Cable Network Profiles* (Annual); *TV Facts* (Annual). **Educational Activities:** Cable Advertising (Annual). **Awards:** Cable Advertising Awards (Annual); Creative Commercial Production Awards; Award for Local Sales Achievement; Sales Achievement Awards.

19884 ■ **Canadian Association of Broadcasters (CAB)—Association Canadienne des Radiodiffuseurs (ACR)**
PO Box 627, Sta. B
Ottawa, ON, Canada K1P 5S2
Ph: (613)233-4035
Fax: (613)233-6961
Co. E-mail: cab@cab-acr.ca
URL: http://www.cab-acr.ca
Contact: Mr. Elmer Hildebrand, Chairman
Description: Collective voice of the majority of Canada's private radio and television stations, networks, and specialty services. Develops industrywide strategic plans, works to improve the financial health of the industry, and promotes private broadcasting's role as Canada's leading programmer and local service provider. **Founded:** 1926. **Awards:** Gold Ribbon Award for Broadcast Excellence (Annual); Hall of Fame (Annual); BBM Canada Scholarships; Ruth Hancock Scholarships; Gold Ribbon for Community Service (Radio); Gold Ribbon for Promotion of Musical Canadian Talent (Radio); Gold Ribbon Award for Broadcast Excellence; Gold Ribbon for Community Service (Television); Gold Ribbon for Community Service (Specialty/Pay/PPV); Gold Ribbon for Outstanding Community Service by an Individual Broadcaster; Gold Ribbon Award for News, Documentary, and Information Programming (Annual). **Telecommunication Services:** cab@cab-acr.org.

19885 ■ CTAM - Cable and Telecommunications Association for Marketing
120 Waterfront St., Ste. 200
Oxon Hill, MD 20745
Ph: (301)485-8900
Fax: (301)560-4964
Co. E-mail: info@ctam.com
URL: http://www.ctam.com
Contact: Char Beales, President
Description: Network of cable and telecommunications professionals dedicated to the pursuit of marketing excellence. Provides its members with competitive marketing resources including education, research, networking and leadership opportunities. **Scope:** cable and telecommunications marketing. **Founded:** 1975. **Subscriptions:** 300. **Publications:** *CTAM Quarterly Journal* (Quarterly). **Awards:** Chairman's Award (Periodic); CTAM Hall of Fame (Annual); Grand TAM Award (Annual); Mark Awards (Annual); Rainmaker Award (Annual); TAMI Awards (Annual); One of a Kind Award (Periodic).

19886 ■ *InterACTRA News*
625 Church St., 3rd Fl.
Toronto, ON, Canada M4Y 2G1
Ph: (416)489-1311
Free: 800-387-3516
Fax: (416)489-8076
Co. E-mail: national@actra.ca
URL: http://www.actra.ca
Contact: Ferne Downey, President
Released: Quarterly

19887 ■ International Radio and Television Society Foundation (IRTS)
1697 Broadway, 10th Fl.
New York, NY 10019
Ph: (212)867-6650
Fax: (212)867-6653
URL: http://irtsfoundation.org
Contact: Joyce M. Tudryn, President
URL(s): www.irts.org. **Description:** Individuals interested in management, sales, or executive production in the radio, television, and cable industries and their allied fields. Seeks to educate members through seminars. Conducts summer internships for college students majoring in communications. **Founded:** 1939. **Publications:** *International Radio and Television Society Newsletter*; *International Radio and Television Society Foundation--Roster Yearbook* (Annual); *International Radio and Television Society Foundation--Roster Yearbook* (Annual). **Educational Activities:** International Radio and Television Society Foundation Luncheon. **Awards:** Barry Sherman Fellowship (Annual); Coltrin Case Study Award (Annual); IRTS Foundation Award (Annual); IRTS Gold Medal (Annual); IRTS Stanton Fellow Award (Annual); Foundation Award; Gold Medal Award; International Radio and Television Society Foundation Summer Fellowships Program; Coltrin Professor of the Year (Annual); Stephen K. Nenno Inspirational Fellow Award (Annual).

19888 ■ Jones NCTI
9697 E Mineral Ave.
Centennial, CO 80112
Ph: (303)797-9393
Free: 866-575-7206
Fax: (303)797-9394
Co. E-mail: customerservice@ncti.com
URL: http://www.ncti.com
Contact: Timothy J. Burke, President
URL(s): www.jonesncti.com. **Description:** Provides comprehensive broadband training for the cable television industry. Offers career training resources and courses in areas ranging from customer service procedures to optical fiber system design, installation, and maintenance. **Founded:** 1968. **Publications:** *Spanish/English CATV Dictionary*. **Telecommunication Services:** infouse@ncti.com; info@jonesncti.com; customercare@jonesncti.com.

19889 ■ National Association of Broadcasters (NAB)
1771 N St. NW
Washington, DC 20036
Ph: (202)429-5300

Fax: (202)429-4199
Co. E-mail: nab@nab.org
URL: http://www.nab.org
Contact: Steven W. Newberry, Chairman of the Board
Description: Serves as the voice for the nation's radio and television broadcasters. Advances the interests of members in federal government, industry and public affairs; improves the quality and profitability of broadcasting; encourages content and technology innovation; and spotlights the important and unique ways stations serve their communities. Delivers value to its members through advocacy, education and innovation. Relies on the grassroots strength of its television and radio members and state broadcast associations. Helps broadcasters seize opportunities in the digital age. Offers broadcasters a variety of programs to help them grow in their careers, promote diversity in the workplace and strengthen their businesses. **Scope:** broadcasting. **Founded:** 1922. **Subscriptions:** archival material books clippings monographs periodicals. **Awards:** Crystal Awards (Annual); Distinguished Service Award (Annual); Engineering Achievement in Radio Award (Annual); Engineering Achievement in Television Award (Annual); Mal Beville Award (Annual); Marconi Radio Award (Annual); National Radio Award (Annual); Service to America Awards (Annual); Engineering Achievement Awards; Marconi Radio Awards; Hugh Malcolm Beville, Jr. Award; Spirit of Broadcasting Award; International Broadcasting Excellence Award; Wally Jorgenson Award.

19890 ■ National Association of Television Program Executives (NATPE)
5757 Wilshire Blvd., Penthouse 10
Los Angeles, CA 90036-3681
Ph: (310)453-4440
Fax: (310)453-5258
Co. E-mail: info@natpe.org
URL: http://www.natpe.org
Contact: Jordan Levin, Co-Chairman
Description: Program directors of television stations, networks, and multiple station groups; persons engaged in television programming (including cable, DBS and multimedia) or production; representatives of related businesses, such as station representatives, advertising agencies, film and package show producers and distributors and research organizations. Seeks to contribute to the improvement of television programming by providing a forum for discussion of ideas and exchange of information concerning programming, production and related fields. Maintains NATPE Educational Foundation. Sponsors faculty development program, seminars and international exchange program. Sponsors six faculty internships. **Founded:** 1963. **Awards:** Faculty Development Grant (Annual); Brandon Tartikoff Legacy Awards (Annual); Brandon Tartikoff Legacy Awards.

19891 ■ National Cable and Telecommunications Association (NCTA)
25 Massachusetts Ave. NW, Ste. 100
Washington, DC 20001-1413
Ph: (202)222-2300
Fax: (202)222-2514
Co. E-mail: webmaster@ncta.com
URL: http://www.ncta.com
Contact: Michael K. Powell, President
Description: Franchised cable operators, programmers, and cable networks; associate members are cable hardware suppliers and distributors; affiliate members are brokerage and law firms and financial institutions; state and regional cable television associations cooperate, but are not affiliated, with the organization. Serves as national medium for exchange of experiences and opinions through research, study, discussion, and publications. Represents the cable industry before Congress, the Federal Communications Commission and various courts on issues of primary importance. Conducts research program in conjunction with National Academy of Cable Programming. Sponsors, in conjunction with Motion Picture Association of America, the Coalition Opposing Signal Theft, an organization designed to deter cable signal theft and to develop anti-piracy materials. Provides promotional aids and information on legal, legislative and regulatory matters. Compiles

statistics. **Founded:** 1952. **Publications:** *Cable Industry Overview* (Semiannual). **Educational Activities:** National Cable Show (Annual). **Awards:** Distinguished Vanguard Awards for Leadership; Vanguard Award for Cable Operations Management.

19892 ■ North American Broadcasters Association (NABA)
Canadian Broadcasting Ctre.
25 John St. W, Ste. 6C300
Toronto, ON, Canada M5V 3G7
Ph: (416)598-9877
Fax: (416)598-9774
Co. E-mail: contact@nabanet.com
URL: http://www.nabanet.com/nabaweb
Contact: Robert Briskman, President
Description: Network broadcasters in North America concerned with international matters that affect broadcasting. Seeks to identify, study and provide solutions to international questions concerning broadcasting. Creates opportunities for North American broadcasters to share information, identify common interests and reach on issues of an international nature. Works with other international broadcasters' associations and unions toward gaining an effective voice in international circles on matters that affect broadcasting. Organizes international conferences in conjunction with other broadcasting associations. **Founded:** 1972. **Educational Activities:** North American Broadcasters Association Meeting (Annual). **Awards:** NABA International Achievement Award; NABA International Achievement Award (Annual).

19893 ■ Public Media Business Association (PMBA)
1760 Old Meadow Rd., Ste. 500
McLean, VA 22102
Ph: (703)506-3292
Fax: (703)506-3266
Co. E-mail: aschwarz@pmbaonline.org
URL: http://www.pbma.org
Contact: Andy Schwarz, Executive Director
Description: Represents finance, human resources, information systems, and administrative managers in public broadcasting. **Founded:** 1981.

19894 ■ Radio-Television News Directors' Association (RTNDA)
2175 Sheppard Ave. E, Ste. 310
Toronto, ON, Canada M2J 1W8
Ph: (416)756-2213
Free: 877-257-8632
Fax: (416)491-1670
Co. E-mail: info@rtndacanada.com
URL: http://www.rtndacanada.com
Contact: Ian Koenigsfest, President
Description: Radio and television news executives and personnel. Promotes the professional development of broadcast journalists in Canada. Sponsors national scholarship program. **Founded:** 1962. **Awards:** Lifetime Achievement Award (Annual); President's Fellowship (Annual); RTNDA National Awards (Annual); RTNDA National Awards.

19895 ■ Television Bureau of Advertising (TVB)
3 E 54th St., 10th Fl.
New York, NY 10022-3108
Ph: (212)486-1111
Fax: (212)935-5631
Co. E-mail: info@tvb.org
URL: http://www.tvb.org
Contact: Steve Lanzano, President
Description: Television stations, station sales representatives, and program producers/syndicates. Strives to increase advertiser dollars to U.S. spot television. Represents television stations to the advertising community. **Scope:** broadcasting. **Founded:** 1954. **Subscriptions:** 200. **Educational Activities:** Television Bureau of Advertising Annual Conference (Annual). **Awards:** TVB Automotive Commercial Competition (Annual).

DIRECTORIES OF EDUCATIONAL PROGRAMS

19896 ■ *Directory of Private Accredited Career Schools and Colleges of Technology*
Pub: Accrediting Commission of Career Schools and Colleges of Technology
Contact: Michale S. McComis, Executive Director
Released: On web page. **Price:** Free. **Description:** Covers 3900 accredited post-secondary programs that provide training programs in business, trade, and technical fields, including various small business endeavors. Entries offer school name, address, phone, description of courses, job placement assistance, and requirements for admission. Arrangement is alphabetical.

REFERENCE WORKS

19897 ■ *"10 Trends That Are Shaping Global Media Consumption" in Advertising Age (Vol. 81, December 6, 2010, No. 43, pp. 3)*
Pub: Crain Communications, Inc.
Ed: Ann Marie Kerwin. **Description:** Ad Age offers the statistics from the TV penetration rate in Kenya to the number of World Cup watchers and more.

19898 ■ *"A&E Networks" in Brandweek (Vol. 49, April 21, 2008, No. 16, pp. SR9)*
Pub: VNU Business Media, Inc
Ed: Anthony Crupi. **Description:** Provides contact information for sales and marketing personnel for the A&E Networks as well as a listing of the station's top programming and an analysis of the current season and the target audience for those programs running in the current season. A&E has reinvented itself as a premium entertainment brand over the last five years and with its $2.5 million per episode acquisition of The Sopranos, the station signaled that it was serious about getting back into the scripted programming business. The acquisition also helped the network compete against other cable networks and led to a 20 percent increase in prime-time viewers.

19899 ■ *"ABC" in Brandweek (Vol. 49, April 21, 2008, No. 16, pp. SR6)*
Pub: VNU Business Media, Inc.
Ed: John Consoli. **Description:** Provides contact information for sales and marketing personnel for the ABC network as well as a listing of the station's top programming and an analysis of the current season and the target audience for those programs running in the current season.

19900 ■ *"ACTRA Phones It in" in Canadian Business (Vol. 80, January 15, 2007, No. 2, pp. 8)*
Pub: Rogers Media
Ed: Denis Seguin. **Description:** The strike held by the members of the ACTRA or Canadian Cinema, Television and Radio Artists from January 8 2007, due to the contract dispute with the trade association representing Canadian producers, is discussed.

19901 ■ *"Advertisers Don't Party With CBS's Swingers" in Advertising Age (Vol. 79, July 7, 2008, No. 26, pp. 1)*
Pub: Crain Communications, Inc.
Ed: Brian Steinberg. **Description:** Broadcast networks that are trying to air edgier programming such as CBS's 'Swingtown' but are running into problems with advertisers who are fearful of consumer complaints and backlash when running commercials during such fare.

19902 ■ *"Advertising May Take a Big Hit in Southwest/AirTran Merger" in Baltimore Business Journal (Vol. 28, October 1, 2010, No. 21, pp. 1)*
Pub: Baltimore Business Journal
Ed: Gary Haber. **Description:** Advertising on television stations and the publishing industry in Baltimore could drop as a result of the merger between rival discount airlines Southwest Airlines and AirTran Airways. Southwest is among the top advertisers in the U.S., spending $126 million in 2009. No local jobs are expected to be affected because neither airline uses a local advertising firm.

19903 ■ *"Alliance Atlantis Takes a Cheekier Attitude to Life" in Globe & Mail (March 5, 2007, pp. B5)*
Pub: CTVglobemedia Publishing Inc.
Ed: Keith McArthur. **Description:** Alliance Atlantis Communications Inc. is re-brancing its human life ministry Life Network specialty channel as Slice. The new channel is being promoted with an advertising campaign.

19904 ■ *"As Seen On TV" in Canadian Business (Vol. 80, November 5, 2007, No. 22, pp. 93)*
Pub: Rogers Media
Ed: Zena Olijnyk. **Description:** StarBrand Media Inc. is one of the companies providing fans with information on how and where to purchase the items that television characters are using. StarBrand created the style section found on different television shows' Websites, such as that of the Gossip Girl and Smallville. The benefits of using sites like StarBrand are evaluated.

19905 ■ *"Astral Media Set to Broadcast Coast to Coast" in Globe & Mail (February 24, 2007, pp. B5)*
Pub: CTVglobemedia Publishing Inc.
Ed: Grant Robertson. **Description:** The decision of Astral Media Inc. to acquire Standard Broadcasting Corp. Ltd. for $1.2 billion, with a view to increase its broadcast coverage, is discussed.

19906 ■ *"At 5-Year Mark, News 9 Makes Presence Felt in Competition for Ad Dollars" in Business Review, Albany New York (October 5, 2007)*
Pub: American City Business Journals, Inc.
Ed: Barbara Pinckney. **Description:** The 24-hour news channel Capital News 9 can be watched live by viewers on their cell phones beginning late 2007 or early 2008 as part of a deal between Time Warner Cable and Sprint Nextel Corporation to bring Sprint's Pivot technology. News 9 marked its fifth year and plans to continue expanding coverage and provide better services to viewers.

19907 ■ *"Autoline Goes West" in Michigan Vue (Vol. 13, July-August 2008, No. 4, pp. 6)*
Pub: Entrepreneur Media Inc.
Ed: Dave Gibbons. **Description:** Profile of Blue Sky Productions, a Detroit-based production company that produces the nationally syndicated television series 'Autoline', which traditionally probes inside the Detroit auto industry; the company recently decided to shoot in Southern California, an area that now has an immense auto industry but has been virtually ignored by the media. Blue Sky originally slated four shows but ended up producing eleven due to the immense amount of material they discovered concerning the state of California's auto market.

19908 ■ *Bacon's Radio/TV/Cable Directory, Volume 1*
Pub: Cision US Inc.
Contact: Joe Bernardo, President
URL(s): us.cision.com. **Released:** Annual; Latest edition 2012. **Price:** $650, Individuals. **Covers:** over 13,500 radio and television stations, including college radio and public television stations, and cable companies. **Entries include:** For radio and television stations--Call letters, address, phone, names and titles of key personnel, programs, times broadcast, name of contact, network affiliation, frequency or channel number, target audience data. For cable companies--Name, address, phone, description of activities. **Arrangement:** Geographical.

19909 ■ *"The Best Five-Month Run Since 1938" in Barron's (Vol. 89, August 3, 2009, No. 31, pp. M3)*
Pub: Dow Jones & Co., Inc.
Ed: Kopin Tan. **Description:** US stock markets ended July 2009 registering the highest five-month rise since 1938. The shares of Cablevision could rise as the company simplifies its structure and spins off its Madison Square Garden unit. The shares of Potash Corp. could fall as the company faces lower earnings due to falling potash purchases.

19910 ■ *"Betting on a Happy Ending" in Barron's (Vol. 88, July 7, 2008, No. 27, pp. 14)*
Pub: Dow Jones & Co., Inc.
Ed: Dimitra DeFotis. **Description:** Shares of Time Warner, priced at $14.69 each, appear under-priced as financial analysts discount the value of the company. The company should be worth more than $20 a share as the company is spinning off Time Warner Cable.

19911 ■ *"'Biggest Loser' Adds Bit of Muscle to Local Economy" in Crain's Detroit Business (Vol. 26, January 4, 2010, No. 1, pp. 1)*
Pub: Crain Communications Inc.
Ed: Chad Halcom. **Description:** NBC's weight-loss reality show, 'The Biggest Loser' has helped the local economy and generated a new crop of local startup businesses due to past contestants that were from the Detroit area.

19912 ■ *"Black Network Shifts Gears: Struggling Channel To Focus On Broadband TV" in Black Enterprise (Vol. 38, November 2007, No. 4, pp. 34)*
Pub: Earl G. Graves Publishing Co. Inc.
Ed: Wendy Isom. **Description:** Rick Newberger, president and CEO of Black Family Channel's television platform discusses its plans to switch to broadband format programming offering various channels simultaneously with fewer costs.

19913 ■ *"Branding Specialist" in Black Enterprise (Vol. 38, July 2008, No. 12, pp. 1)*
Pub: Earl G. Graves Publishing Co. Inc.
Ed: Faith Chukwudi. **Description:** Interview with Wonya Lucas who is the chief marketing officer for Discovery Communications and is known for building strong brands by understanding her audience and generating buy-in throughout the organization; Lucas discusses her role in the corporation, guerilla marketing techniques, and what companies tend to overlook in marketing their products or services.

19914 ■ *Broadcast Engineering--Equipment Reference Manual*
Pub: Penton
Contact: Raymond E. Maloney, President
URL(s): www.broadcastengineering.comwww.penton.com/Profile/BroadcastEngineering.aspx. **Released:** Annual; fall. **Publication includes:** List of more than 1,400 manufacturers and distributors of communications equipment for radio, television, and recording applications. **Entries include:** For manufacturers--Company name, address. For distributors and dealers--Company name, address, phone, product or service provided, geographic area covered. **Database includes:** Specifications for major brands of professional broadcast hardware. **Arrangement:** Manufacturers are alphabetical; dealers and distributors are geographical. **Indexes:** Product/service.

19915 ■ *Broadcasting & Cable Yearbook: A Broadcasting and R.R. Bowker Publication*
Pub: R.R. Bowker L.L.C.
URL(s): www.bowker.com. **Released:** Annual; latest edition 2010. **Price:** $395, Individuals softbound. **Covers:** Over 17,000 television and radio stations in the United States, its territories, and Canada; cable MSOs and their individual systems; television and radio networks, broadcast and cable group owners, station representatives, satellite networks and services, film companies, advertising agencies, government agencies, trade associations, schools, and suppliers of professional and technical services, including books, serials, and videos; communications lawyers. **Entries include:** Company name, address, phone, fax, names of executives. Station listings include broadcast power, other operating details. **Arrangement:** Stations and systems are geographical, others are alphabetical. **Indexes:** Alphabetical.

19916 ■ *"CBC Eyes Partners for TV Downloads" in Globe & Mail (February 9, 2006, pp. B1)*
Pub: CTVglobemedia Publishing Inc.
Ed: Grant Robertson. **Description:** The details on Canadian Broadcasting Corp.'s distribution agreement with Google Inc. and Apple Computer Inc. are presented.

19917 ■ "CBS" in Brandweek (Vol. 49, April 21, 2008, No. 16, pp. SR6)
Pub: VNU Business Media, Inc.
Ed: John Consoli. **Description:** Provides contact information for sales and marketing personnel for the CBS network as well as a listing of the station's top programming and an analysis of the current season and the target audience for those programs running in the current season.

19918 ■ "CBS Television Distribution" in Brandweek (Vol. 49, April 21, 2008, No. 16, pp. SR13)
Pub: VNU Business Media, Inc.
Ed: Marc Berman. **Description:** Provides contact information for sales and marketing personnel for CBS Television Distribution as well as a listing of the station's top programming and an analysis of the current season and the target audience for those programs running in the current season. Due to the unprecedented, decade-plus advantage of first-run leaders such as Wheel of Fortune, Oprah, Judge Judy and Entertainment Tonight, CBS is poised to remain a leader among the syndicates.

19919 ■ "Comcast Networks" in Brandweek (Vol. 49, April 21, 2008, No. 16, pp. SR9)
Pub: VNU Business Media, Inc.
Ed: Anthony Crupi. **Description:** Provides contact information for sales and marketing personnel for the Comcast networks as well as a listing of the station's top programming and an analysis of the current season and the target audience for those programs running in the current season. Experts believe Comcast will continue to acquire more stations into their portfolio.

19920 ■ "Commercials Make Us Like TV More" in Harvard Business Review (Vol. 88, October 2010, No. 10, pp. 36)
Pub: Harvard Business School Publishing
Ed: Leif Nelson. **Description:** Research indicates that people prefer commercial interruption over uninterrupted shows due to the break creating a reactivation of the initial pleasure when beginning a desirable activity.

19921 ■ CPB Public Broadcasting Directory
Pub: Corporation for Public Broadcasting
Contact: Patricia de Stacy Harrison, President
URL(s): www.cpb.org/stations/isis. **Released:** Annual **Covers:** Public television and radio stations, national and regional public broadcasting organizations and networks, state government agencies and commissions, and other related organizations. **Entries include:** For radio and television stations--Station call letters, frequency or channel, address, phone, licensee name, licensee type, date on air, antenna height, area covered, names and titles of key personnel. For organizations--Name, address, phone, name and title of key personnel. **Arrangement:** National and regional listings are alphabetical; state groups and the public radio and television stations are each geographical; other organizations and agencies are alphabetical. **Indexes:** Geographical, personnel, call letter, licensee type (all in separate indexes for radio and television).

19922 ■ "CRTC Signals CHUM Deal Will Get Nod" in Globe & Mail (May 2, 2007, pp. B3)
Pub: CTVglobemedia Publishing Inc.
Ed: Grant Robertson. **Description:** The likely approval of Canadian Radio-Television and Telecommunications Commission to the proposed acquisition of CHUM Ltd. by CTVglobemedia Inc. is discussed.

19923 ■ "CTV's CHUM Proposal Gets Chilly Reception" in Globe & Mail (May 1, 2007, pp. B1)
Pub: CTVglobemedia Publishing Inc.
Ed: Grant Robertson. **Description:** The possible violation of broadcast regulations in case of acquisition of CHUM Ltd. by CTV Inc. for $1.4 billion is discussed.

19924 ■ "The CW" in Brandweek (Vol. 49, April 21, 2008, No. 16, pp. SR8)
Pub: VNU Business Media, Inc.
Ed: John Consoli. **Description:** Provides contact information for sales and marketing personnel for the CW network as well as a listing of the station's top

programming and an analysis of the current season and the target audience for those programs running in the current season. Purchases of advertising feel that Warner Bros. and CBS made a mistake merging The WB and UPN into the new CW rather than folding UPN into the more-established WB; compared to last season ratings are down more than 20 percent across the board.

19925 ■ "Detroit Pawn Shop to be Reality TV Venue" in UPI NewsTrack (July 10, 2010)
Pub: United Press International-USA
Description: TruTV will present a new series called 'Hardcore Pawn' to compete with the History Channel's successful show 'Pawn Stars'. The show will feature American Jewelry and Loan in Detroit, Michigan and its owner Les Gold, who runs the store with his wife and children.

19926 ■ "Discovery Networks" in Brandweek (Vol. 49, April 21, 2008, No. 16, pp. SR9)
Pub: VNU Business Media, Inc.
Ed: Anthony Crupi. **Description:** Provides contact information for sales and marketing personnel for the Discovery networks as well as a listing of the station's top programming and an analysis of the current season and the target audience for those programs running in the current season. The networks flagship station returned to the top 10 in 2007, averaging 1.28 million viewers.

19927 ■ "Disney-ABC Domestic Television Distribution" in Brandweek (Vol. 49, April 21, 2008, No. 16, pp. SR13)
Pub: VNU Business Media, Inc.
Ed: Marc Berman. **Description:** Provides contact information for sales and marketing personnel for Disney-ABC Domestic Television Distribution as well a listing of the station's top programming and an analysis of the current season and the target audience for those programs running in the current season.

19928 ■ "Don't' Hate the Cable Guy" in Saint Louis Business Journal (Vol. 31, August 5, 2011, No. 50, pp. 1)
Pub: Saint Louis Business Journal
Ed: Angela Mueller. **Description:** Charter Communications named John Birrer as senior vice president of customer experience. The company experienced problems with its customer services.

19929 ■ "The Endless Flow of Russell Simmons" in Entrepreneur (Vol. 37, September 2009, No. 9, pp. 24)
Pub: Entrepreneur Media, Inc.
Ed: Josh Dean. **Description:** Entrepreneur Russell Simmons has successfully grown his businesses by focusing on underserved markets. Simons has never given up on any business strategy. He has also entered the music, clothing and television industries.

19930 ■ "Exiting Stage Left" in Baltimore Business Journal (Vol. 28, June 18, 2010, No. 6, pp. 1)
Pub: Baltimore Business Journal
Ed: Scott Dance. **Description:** Film professionals including crew members and actors have been leaving Maryland to find work in other states such as Michigan, Louisiana, and Georgia where bigger budgets and film production incentives are given. Other consequences of this trend in local TV and film production are discussed.

19931 ■ "Fox" in Brandweek (Vol. 49, April 21, 2008, No. 16, pp. SR3)
Pub: VNU Business Media, Inc.
Ed: John Consoli. **Description:** Provides contact information for sales and marketing personnel for the Fox network as well as a listing of the station's top programming and an analysis of the current season and the target audience for those programs running in the current season. In terms of upfront advertising dollars, it looks as if Fox will be competing against NBC for third place due to its success at courting the 18-49-year-old male demographic.

19932 ■ "Fox Cable Entertainment Networks" in Brandweek (Vol. 49, April 21, 2008, No. 16, pp. SR10)
Pub: VNU Business Media, Inc.
Ed: Anthony Crupi. **Description:** Provides contact information for sales and marketing personnel for the Fox Cable Entertainment networks as well as a listing of the station's top programming and an analysis of the current season and the target audience for those programs running in the current season.

19933 ■ Freelancing for Journalists
Pub: Routledge
Ed: Diana Harris. **Released:** January 1, 2010. **Price:** $110.00. **Description:** Comprehensive guide showing the specific skills required for those wishing to freelance in newspapers, magazines, radio, television, and as online journalists.

19934 ■ "Hitting the Green" in Canadian Business (Vol. 81, July 22, 2008, No. 12-13, pp. 34)
Pub: Rogers Media Ltd.
Ed: Andy Holloway. **Description:** RBC is sponsoring the Canadian Open golf tournament, which is the second-oldest event in the PGA Tour. RBC is expected to receive television exposure on CBS and the Golf Channel. Additional information relating to the sponsorship is presented.

19935 ■ "How to Boost Your Super Bowl ROI" in Advertising Age (Vol. 80, December 7, 2009, No. 41, pp. 3)
Pub: Crain's Communications
Ed: Abbey Klaassen. **Description:** Internet marketing is essential, even for the corporations that can afford to spend $3 million on a 30-second Super Bowl spot; last year, Super Bowl advertising reached an online viewership of 99.5 million while 98.7 million people watched the game on television validating the idea that public relations must go farther than a mere television ad campaign. Social media provides businesses with a longer shelf life for their ad campaigns. Advice is also given regarding ways in which to strategize a smart and well-thought plan for utilizing the online marketing options currently available.

19936 ■ "It Could Be Worse" in Barron's (Vol. 89, July 27, 2009, No. 30, pp. 5)
Pub: Dow Jones & Co., Inc.
Ed: Alan Abelson. **Description:** Media sources are being fooled by corporate America who is peddling an economic recovery rather than reality as shown by the report of a rise in existing home sales which boosted the stock market even if it was a seasonal phenomenon. The phrase 'things could be worse' sums up the reigning investment philosophy in the U.S. and this has been stirring up the market.

19937 ■ "Johnson Publishing Expands: Moving Into Television and Internet To Extend Brand" in Black Enterprise (October 2007)
Pub: Earl G. Graves Publishing Co. Inc.
Ed: Tamara E. Holmes. **Description:** Johnson Publishing Company has followed the lives of black families in both Ebony and Jet magazines. The media firm has expanded its coverage by developing entertainment content for television, the Internet and other digital arenas.

19938 ■ "KXAN Seeks Larger Studio, Office Space" in Austin Business Journal (Vol. 31, May 27, 2011, No. 12, pp. A1)
Pub: American City Business Journals Inc.
Ed: Cody Lyon. **Description:** Austin NBC affiliate KXAN Television is opting to sell its property north of downtown and relocate to another site. The station is now inspecting possible sites to house its broadcasting facility and employees totaling as many as 200 people. Estimated cost of the construction of the studios and offices is $13 million plus another million in moving the equipment.

19939 ■ "Lifetime Networks" in Brandweek (Vol. 49, April 21, 2008, No. 16, pp. SR10)
Pub: VNU Business Media, Inc.
Ed: Anthony Crupi. **Description:** Provides contact information for sales and marketing personnel for the ABC network as well as a listing of the station's top

programming and an analysis of the current season and the target audience for those programs running in the current season. Lifetime will still produce its original signature movies but will now focus its emphasis more clearly on series development in order to appeal to a younger, hipper female demographic.

19940 ▪ "Local TV Hits Media Radar Screen" in Business Courier (Vol. 27, July 2, 2010, No. 9, pp. 1)
Pub: Business Courier

Ed: Dan Monk. **Description:** Fort Wright, Kentucky-based broadcasting company Local TV LLC has acquired 18 television stations since its founding in 2007, potentially boosting its chances of becoming a media empire. In the last twelve months that ended in March 2010, Local TV LLC has posted total revenues of $415 million. How Local TV LLC has entered into cost-sharing deals with other stations is also discussed.

19941 ▪ "Looking Like a Million Bucks" in Entrepreneur (Vol. 37, August 2009, No. 8, pp. 102)
Pub: Entrepreneur Media, Inc.

Ed: Jason Daley. **Description:** Sunset Tan's Jeff Bozz says he and Devin Haman are executive producers of the show and that they want to stretch the truth a bit and make fun of it. Haman says the business is all about VIP service for everyone and that they want all their clients to feel like celebrities.

19942 ▪ "Marketing: You Are On the Air: Radio and TV Producers Are Looking For Shows Starring Smart CEOs" in Inc. (December 2007, pp. 67-69)
Pub: Gruner & Jahr USA Publishing

Ed: Sarah Goldstein. **Description:** Many successful entrepreneurs are being hired to host television and radio shows in order to share business expertise.

19943 ▪ Matthews Media Directory
Pub: Marketwire

URL(s): www.cdn-news.com www.marketwire.com. **Released:** Semiannual; Latest edition 50th. **Covers:** Daily newspapers, radio and television stations, trade magazines, networks and newswires and press galleries in Canada.

19944 ▪ "MEC, Churchill Downs Saddle Up in Racing Deal" in Globe & Mail (March 6, 2007, pp. B1)
Pub: CTVglobemedia Publishing Inc.

Ed: Greg Keenan. **Description:** The formation of a company called TrackNet Media Group LLC by Magna Entertainment Corp. and Churchill Downs Inc. for the broadcast of horse races on television is discussed. The efforts of the two companies to revive public interest in horse racing are described.

19945 ▪ Media, Organizations and Identity
Pub: Palgrave Macmillan

Ed: Lilie Chouliaraki, Mette Morsing. **Released:** January 19, 2010. **Price:** $90.00. **Description:** The mass media, press and television are a essential in the formation of corporate identity and the promotion of business image and reputation. This book offers a new perspective into the interrelationships between media and organizations over three dimensions: media as business, media in business and business in the media.

19946 ▪ "Mentoring Support" in Black Enterprise (Vol. 38, July 2008, No. 12, pp. 64)
Pub: Earl G. Graves Publishing Co. Inc.

Description: With his relocation from his multicultural team in New York to the less diverse Scripps Networks' headquarters in Knoxville, Earl Cokley has made it a top priority to push for more diversity and mentoring opportunities within the management of the media and marketing company.

19947 ▪ Mississippi News Media Directory
Pub: News Media Directories

Contact: Brian Highberger, Publisher

URL(s): www.newsmediadirectories.net/product-p/07msnmd.htm. **Released:** Annual; Latest edition 2011-2012. **Price:** $45, Individuals; $65, Individuals CD; $85, Individuals Combo-Directory and CD. **Cov-**

ers: Newspapers, periodicals, radio and television broadcasting stations, and press services operating in Mississippi. **Entries include:** Publisher or company name, address, phone, names and titles of key personnel, publication title, call letters, hours of operation, and frequency. **Arrangement:** Classified by type of media. **Indexes:** Title, call letters, county index.

19948 ▪ "Moms Dis Super Bowl Ads" in Marketing to Women (Vol. 21, March 2008, No. 3, pp. 6)
Pub: EPM Communications Inc.

Contact: Ira Mayer, President

E-mail: imayer@epmcom.com

Description: According to a survey by the Marketing to Moms Coalition, although 80 percent of moms tune into the Super Bowl most complain that the advertisements are not appropriate for a family sports viewing experience.

19949 ▪ "Moving Into the Digital Space: How New Media Create Opportunities for Minorities" in Black Enterprise (February 2008)
Pub: Earl G. Graves Publishing Co. Inc.

Ed: Sonia Alleyne. **Description:** The Internet is becoming an alternative to traditional sources of entertainment; nearly 16 percent of American households who use the Internet watch television online. One such Internet show features a variety of African American lifestyles.

19950 ▪ "MTV Networks" in Brandweek (Vol. 49, April 21, 2008, No. 16, pp. SR10)
Pub: VNU Business Media, Inc.

Ed: Anthony Crupi. **Description:** Provides contact information for sales and marketing personnel for the MTV networks as well as a listing of the station's top programming and an analysis of the current season and the target audience for those programs running in the current season. MTV networks include MTV, VH1, Nickelodeon and Comedy Central.

19951 ▪ "NBC" in Brandweek (Vol. 49, April 21, 2008, No. 16, pp. SR6)
Pub: VNU Business Media, Inc.

Ed: John Consoli. **Description:** Provides contact information for sales and marketing personnel for the NBC network as well as a listing of the station's top programming and an analysis of the current season and the target audience for those programs running in the current season. NBC also devised a new strategy of announcing its prime-time schedule 52 weeks in advance which was a hit for advertisers who felt this gave them a better opportunity to plan for product placement. Even with the station's creative sales programs, they could face a challenge from Fox in terms of upfront advertisement purchases.

19952 ▪ "NBC Universal Cable" in Brandweek (Vol. 49, April 21, 2008, No. 16, pp. SR11)
Pub: VNU Business Media, Inc.

Ed: Anthony Crupi. **Description:** Provides contact information for sales and marketing personnel for the NBC Universal Cable networks as well as a listing of the station's top programming and an analysis of the current season and the target audience for those programs running in the current season. The network's stations include USA, Sci Fi and Bravo. Ad revenue for the network grew 30 percent in the first quarter.

19953 ▪ "NBC Universal Domestic Television Distribution" in Brandweek (Vol. 49, April 21, 2008, No. 16, pp. SR13)
Pub: VNU Business Media, Inc.

Ed: Marc Berman. **Description:** Provides contact information for sales and marketing personnel for NBC Universal Domestic Television Distribution as well as a listing of the station's top programming and an analysis of the current season and the target audience for those programs running in the current season.

19954 ▪ "Network TV" in Canadian Business (Vol. 79, September 11, 2006, No. 18, pp. 136)
Pub: Rogers Media

Ed: Gerry Blackwell. **Description:** The functions and features of the new Mediasmart LCD TV offered by Hewlett-Packard are discussed.

19955 ▪ "New Sony HD Ads Tout Digital" in Brandweek (Vol. 49, April 21, 2008, No. 16, pp. 5)
Pub: VNU Business Media, Inc.

Description: Looking to promote Sony Electronics' digital imaging products, the company has launched another campaign effort known as HDNA, a play on the words high-definition and DNA; originally Sony focused the HDNA campaign on their televisions, the new ads will include still and video cameras as well and marketing efforts will consist of advertising in print, Online, television spots and publicity at various venues across the country.

19956 ▪ "Nortel Makes Customers Stars in New Campaign" in Brandweek (Vol. 49, April 21, 2008, No. 16, pp. 8)
Pub: VNU Business Media, Inc.

Ed: Mike Beirne. **Description:** Nortel has launched a new television advertising campaign in which the business-to-business communications technology provider cast senior executives in 30-second TV case studies that show how Nortel's technology helped their businesses innovate.

19957 ▪ "Not the Six O'Clock News" in Canadian Business (Vol. 80, January 15, 2007, No. 2, pp. 10)
Pub: Rogers Media

Ed: Marlene Rego. **Description:** The proposal by Paul Jay, the chief executive officer of Independent World Television, to launch The Real News Project, is discussed. The objective of the project is to establish an independent news and current affairs network solely through viewers.

19958 ▪ "Our World with Black Enterprise" in Black Enterprise (Vol. 37, February 2007, No. 7, pp. 145)
Pub: Earl G. Graves Publishing Co. Inc.

Description: Our World with Black Enterprise is a television broadcast that features roundtable discussions and interviews with important African American figures.

19959 ▪ "Political Ads Big Boost to Local Media" in Baltimore Business Journal (Vol. 28, October 22, 2010, No. 24, pp. 1)
Pub: Baltimore Business Journal

Ed: Scott Dance. **Description:** Information about the intense demand for advertising time from political campaigns in Baltimore, Maryland is provided. The surge in political advertisement spending would mean big money for local broadcasters, because they see a surging demand for local advertising time for virtually any time of day.

19960 ▪ "Prime-Time Exposure" in Inc. (March 2008, pp. 66, 68)
Pub: Gruner & Jahr USA Publishing

Ed: Adam Bluestein. **Description:** Product placement in television shows has increase sales for many companies. Tips for placing products or services into TV shows are explained: consider hiring an agency, target efforts, dream up a plot point, be ready to go on short notice, and work the niches.

19961 ▪ "Private TV Industry's Profit Climbs Four Percent" in Globe & Mail (March 29, 2006, pp. B6)
Pub: CTVglobemedia Publishing Inc.

Ed: Simon Tuck. **Description:** The private television industry in Canada is experiencing 4 percent increase in its profits, i.e. $242.2 millions. The revenues of CTV contributed more to this increase in profits.

19962 ▪ "Pro Teams Shift Ad Budgets; Naming Rights Deals Near $1 Billion" in Brandweek (Vol. 49, April 21, 2008, No. 16, pp. 18)
Pub: VNU Business Media, Inc.

Ed: Barry Janoff. **Description:** More and more professional sports marketers are spending less of their advertising budgets on traditional media outlets such as television, print and radio; the growing trend in sports marketing is in utilizing new media venues such as the Internet in which innovative means are used to encourage interaction with fans.

19963 ■ "Recovery on Tap for 2010?" in Orlando Business Journal (Vol. 26, January 1, 2010, No. 31, pp. 1)

Pub: American City Business Journals

Ed: Melanie Stawicki Azam, Richard Bilbao, Christopher Boyd, Anjali Fluker. Description: Economic forecasts for Central Florida's leading business sectors in 2010 are presented. These sectors include housing, film and TV, sports business, law, restaurants, aviation, tourism and hospitality, banking and finance, commercial real estate, retail, health care, insurance, higher education, and manufacturing. According to some local executives, Central Florida's economy will slowly recover in 2010.

19964 ■ "Reds Hit Ratings Homer" in Business Courier (Vol. 27, July 30, 2010, No. 13, pp. 1)

Pub: Business Courier

Ed: Steve Watkins, James Ourand. Description: Cincinnati Reds fans have tuned in to their TVs and radios as their team made a hottest start to a season. The Reds TV ratings have increased 49 percent during the first six months of 2010 and continued to rise while the Reds' games broadcast on WLW-AM reported the highest average audience share per game of any Major League Baseball team.

19965 ■ "Scripps' Dinner Bell" in Business Courier (Vol. 24, October 19, 2008, No. 27, pp. 1)

Pub: American City Business Journals, Inc.

Ed: Dan Monk. Description: Discusses the split of E.W. Scripps Co.'s Food Network into a separate publicly traded company Scripps Networks Interactive could produce expansion into Asia and Europe.

19966 ■ "Scripps Networks" in Brandweek (Vol. 49, April 21, 2008, No. 16, pp. SR12)

Pub: VNU Business Media, Inc.

Ed: Anthony Crupi. Description: Provides contact information for sales and marketing personnel for the Scripps networks as well as a listing of the station's top programming and an analysis of the current season and the target audience for those programs running in the current season. Scripps networks include HGTV and the Food Network. HGTV boasts on of the industry's best commercial-retention averages, keeping nearly 97 percent of its viewers during advertising breaks.

19967 ■ "Sony Pictures Television" in Brandweek (Vol. 49, April 21, 2008, No. 16, pp. SR13)

Pub: VNU Business Media, Inc.

Ed: Marc Berman. Description: Provides contact information for sales and marketing personnel for Sony Pictures Television Distribution as well as a listing of the station's top programming and an analysis of the current season and the target audience for those programs running in the current season.

19968 ■ "Spillover Effects" in Crain's Detroit Business (Vol. 24, October 6, 2008, No. 40, pp. 29)

Pub: Crain Communications, Inc.

Description: Earlier this year, the Detroit Regional Chamber estimated that the Detroit Tiger's baseball team's 81 home games would have a $277 million positive economic impact on the region. Due to the poor performance of the team, fewer fans are spending money on tickets, which translates into fewer dollars coming into the region. Lower viewership on television has also been a result of the Tiger's losing season.

19969 ■ "A Sports Extravaganza - To Go" in Canadian Business (Vol. 79, June 19, 2006, No. 13, pp. 21)

Pub: Rogers Media

Ed: Andy Holloway. Description: Television broadcasting industry in Canada utilizing advanced technologies like mobile television and internet protocol television in broadcasting major sports events. Large number of new technologies are being invented to support increasing demand.

19970 ■ "State Expects Increase of $50 Million from Film Bills; Come Back, Al Roker" in Crain's Detroit Business (March 24, 2008)

Pub: Crain Communications, Inc.

Ed: Bill Shea. Description: Overview of the new film initiative and its incentives designed to entice more film work to Michigan; the measures could bring $50 million to $100 million in movie production work for the rest of this year compared to the $4 million total the state saw last year. Also discusses the show 'DEA' which was filmed in Detroit and stars Al Roker.

19971 ■ "Storytelling Star of Show for Scripps" in Business Courier (Vol. 26, November 13, 2009, No. 29, pp. 1)

Pub: American City Business Journals, Inc.

Ed: Dan Monk. Description: Rich Boehne, CEO Of the EW Scripps Company in Cincinnati has authorized a new training program in storytelling for employees at Scripps' 10 television stations. He believes that the training will improve the quality of broadcasting content. His plans to improve quality of newspaper content are also discussed.

19972 ■ "Study: New Moms Build A Lot of Brand Buzz" in Brandweek (Vol. 49, April 21, 2008, No. 16, pp. 7)

Pub: VNU Business Media, Inc.

Description: According to a new survey which sampled 1,721 pregnant women and new moms, this demographic is having 109 word-of-mouth conversations per week concerning products, services and brands. Two-thirds of these conversations directly involve brand recommendations. The Internet is driving these word-of-mouth, or W-O-M, conversations among this segment, beating out magazines, television and other forms of media.

19973 ■ "Summit, Lions Gate are in Talks to Merge Studios" in Wall Street Journal Eastern Edition (November 29, 2011, pp. B2)

Pub: Dow Jones & Company Inc. Enterprise Media Group

Contact: Clare Hart, President

Ed: Erica Orden, Michelle Kung. Description: Movie studio Summit Entertainment LLC is in talks with television producer Lions Gate Entertainment Corporation about a possible merger. Previous talks have taken place, but no deal was ever reached. Such a deal would create a large, independent studio able to compete in the market with the big Hollywood giants.

19974 ■ "Survey: More Buyers Expect to Spend Less in Most Media" in Advertising Age (Vol. 79, July 7, 2008, No. 26, pp. 3)

Pub: Crain Communications, Inc.

Ed: Megan McIlroy. Description: Marketers are decreasing their budgets for advertising in television, radio, newspaper and outdoor due to the economic downturn. Statistical data concerning advertising agencies and marketers included.

19975 ■ "Telemundo" in Brandweek (Vol. 49, April 21, 2008, No. 16, pp. SR8)

Pub: VNU Business Media, Inc.

Ed: John Consoli. Description: Provides contact information for sales and marketing personnel for the Telemundo network as well as a listing of the station's top programming and an analysis of the current season and the target audience for those programs running in the current season.

19976 ■ "Television Broadcasting" in MarketingMagazine (Vol. 115, September 27, 2010, No. 13, pp. 16)

Pub: Rogers Publishing Ltd.

Description: Market statistics covering the Canadian television broadcasting industry are covered.

19977 ■ Television & Cable Factbook

Pub: Warren Communications News Inc.

Contact: Daniel Warren, President

E-mail: dwarren@warren-news.com

URL(s): www.warren-news.com/factbook.htm. Released: Annual; Latest edition 2012. Price: $945, Individuals first copy, print or online; $295, Individuals second copy, print or online; $195, Individuals third copy, print or online & subsequent seats; $995, Individuals full online data, additional per seat. Cov-

ers: Commercial and noncommercial television stations and networks, including educational, low-power and instructional TV stations, and translators; United States cable television systems; cable and television group owners; program and service suppliers; and brokerage and financing companies. Entries include: For stations--Call letters, licensee name and address, studio address and phone; identification of owners, sales and legal representatives and chief station personnel; rates, technical data, map of service area, and Nielsen circulation data. For cable systems-- Name, address, basic and pay subscribers, programming and fees, physical plant; names of personnel and ownership. Ownership. Arrangement: Geographical by state, province, city, county, or country. Indexes: Call letters, product/service, name, general subject.

19978 ■ "Telus Tunes in to the TV Revolution" in Globe & Mail (February 18, 2006, pp. B4)

Pub: CTVglobemedia Publishing Inc.

Ed: Eric Reguly. Description: The business growth plans of chief executive officer Darren Entwistle of Telus Corp. are presented.

19979 ■ "Top of the Food Chain" in Entrepreneur (Vol. 37, October 2009, No. 10, pp. 19)

Pub: Entrepreneur Media Inc.

Ed: Jennifer Wang. Description: Television producer Mark Burnett discusses his latest reality television production, Shark Tank. The show pits venture capitalists against entrepreneurs in a contest to obtain business funding.

19980 ■ "Transform Your Life" in Black Enterprise (Vol. 37, January 2007, No. 6, pp. 14)

Pub: Earl G. Graves Publishing Co. Inc.

Description: Through the magazine, television and radio programs, events, and the website, the various platforms of Black Enterprise will provide the tools necessary to achieve success in business ventures, career aspirations, and personal goals.

19981 ■ "Trib TV Station Switching to Fox" in Crain's Chicago Business (Vol. 31, March 31, 2008, No. 13, pp. 14)

Pub: Crain Communications, Inc.

Ed: Michelle Greppi. Description: Signaling the new Tribune owner Sam Zell's divergence from previous management is the company's shift of its KSWB-TV station in San Diego to News Corp.'s Fox from CW Television Network.

19982 ■ "Turner Broadcasting System" in Brandweek (Vol. 49, April 21, 2008, No. 16, pp. SR13)

Pub: VNU Business Media, Inc.

Ed: Anthony Crupi. Description: Provides contact information for sales and marketing personnel for the Turner Broadcasting System networks as well as a listing of the station's top programming and an analysis of the current season and the target audience for those programs running in the current season. Recent acquisitions are also discussed.

19983 ■ "TV Revenue Slide Hits CanWest Profit" in Globe & Mail (January 13, 2006, pp. B3)

Pub: CTVglobemedia Publishing Inc.

Ed: Grant Robertson. Description: CanWest Global Communications Corp. posted drop in profits by 14 percent for first quarter 2006. The downward trend in profits is attributed to low television revenues.

19984 ■ "Twentieth Television" in Brandweek (Vol. 49, April 21, 2008, No. 16, pp. SR16)

Pub: VNU Business Media, Inc.

Ed: Marc Berman. Description: Provides contact information for sales and marketing personnel for Twentieth Television as well as a listing of the station's top programming and an analysis of the current season and the target audience for those programs running in the current season.

19985 ■ "Univision" in Brandweek (Vol. 49, April 21, 2008, No. 16, pp. SR8)
Pub: VNU Business Media, Inc.

Ed: John Consoli. **Description:** Provides contact information for sales and marketing personnel for the Univision network as well as a listing of the station's top programming and an analysis of the current season and the target audience for those programs running in the current season. Univision is the No. 1 network on Friday nights in the 18-34 demographic, beating all English-language networks.

19986 ■ "Waco Pawn Shop Owners Say Reality Isn't Much Like 'Pawn Stars' TV Show" in Waco Tribune-Herald (August 15, 2010)
Pub: Waco Tribune-Herald

Ed: Mike Copeland. **Description:** Area pawn shop owners report that the television show on cable TV does not represent the true life operations of a pawn shop. The Las Vegas shop represented on TV boasts 30 employees and 21 on-call experts, which is not the case in reality.

19987 ■ "Warner Bros. Domestic Television Distribution" in Brandweek (Vol. 49, April 21, 2008, No. 16, pp. SR16)
Pub: VNU Business Media, Inc.

Ed: Marc Berman. **Description:** Provides contact information for sales and marketing personnel for Warner Bros. Domestic Television Distribution as well as a listing of the station's top programming and an analysis of the current season and the target audience for those programs running in the current season.

19988 ■ The Weather Channel
Pub: Harvard Business School Press

Ed: Frank Batten with Jeffrey L. Cruikshank. **Released:** 2002. **Price:** $29.95. **Description:** Frank Batten illustrates the power of a resourceful growth strategy along with details the journey he successfully took his small, private newspaper into the cable industry.

19989 ■ "What Women Watch on TV" in Marketing to Women (Vol. 21, February 2008, No. 2, pp. 6)
Pub: EPM Communications Inc.

Contact: Ira Mayer, President

E-mail: imayer@epmcom.com

Description: According to BIGresearch, women are more likely to watch sports than they are soap operas. Statistical data included.

19990 ■ "A Whiff of TV Reality" in Houston Business Journal (Vol. 40, January 22, 2010, No. 37, pp. A1)
Pub: American City Business Journals

Ed: Christine Hall. **Description:** Houston, Texas-based Waste Management Inc.'s president and chief operation officer, Larry O'Donnel shares some of his experience as CBS Television Network reality show 'Undercover Boss' participant. O'Donnell believes the show was a great way to show the customers how tough their jobs are and reveals that the most difficult job was being a sorter at the recycling center.

SOURCES OF SUPPLY

19991 ■ BIA's Television Yearbook
BIA Financial Network Inc.

Contact: Thomas J. Buono, Chief Executive Officer

E-mail: tbuono@bia.com

URL(s): www.bia.com. **Released:** Annual; Latest edition 2012. **Price:** $240, Individuals. **Covers:** U.S. Television markets and their inclusive stations, television equipment manufacturers, and related service providers and trade associations. **Entries include:** For stations--Call letters, address; name and phone of general manager, owner, and other key personnel; technical attributes, rep firm, network affiliation, last acquisition date and price and ratings for total day and prime time. For others--Company or organization name, address, phone, description. **Database includes:** Annual market data, including television

revenue, demographics, economic indicators, and viewing trends. **Arrangement:** Classified by market. **Indexes:** Numerical by market rank; call letters.

TRADE PERIODICALS

19992 ■ Broadcast Engineering: Journal of Digital Television
Pub: Penton

Contact: Raymond E. Maloney, President

URL(s): www.broadcastengineering.com. **Ed:** Brad Dick, David Austerberry. **Released:** Monthly; 24 regular issues US/CAN, 12 (World/Asia).

19993 ■ Broadcaster
Pub: Business Information Group

Contact: Bruce Creighton, President

URL(s): www.broadcastermagazine.com. **Released:** Monthly **Price:** $45.95, Canada plus taxes; $45.95, Individuals in U.S.; $59.95, Other countries.

19994 ■ Cable Yellow Pages
Pub: Teton Media Inc.

URL(s): www.cableyellowpages.com. **Released:** Annual **Price:** $42.95, Individuals.

19995 ■ TV International Daily
Pub: Informa Publishing Group

Released: Daily. **Price:** $1,995, U.S. via fax; $1,995, U.S. via e-mail; $2,495, U.S. via fax and. **Description:** Provides news on international television, cable, satellite, digital, and pay and pay-per-view. Remarks: Available via fax or e-mail.

VIDEOCASSETTES/ AUDIOCASSETTES

19996 ■ Community TV: A Portrait of DCTV
Downtown Community TV Center
87 Lafayette St.
New York, NY 10013-4435
Ph: (212)966-4510
Fax: (212)219-0248

Released: 1989. **Description:** The relationship between this progressive independent station and network TV, as well as the history of porta-pak journalism is examined. **Availability:** VHS; 3/4 U.

TRADE SHOWS AND CONVENTIONS

19997 ■ NAB Show
National Association of Broadcasters
1771 N. St., N.W.
Washington, DC 20036
Ph: (202)429-5300
Free: 800-342-2460
Fax: (202)429-4199
Co. E-mail: nab@nab.org
URL: http://www.nab.org
Contact: Steven W. Newberry, Chief Executive Officer

URL(s): www.nabshow.com. **Frequency:** Annual. **Audience:** Radio and television broadcasters and related broadcasting industry professionals. **Principal Exhibits:** Radio and television broadcasting equipment, supplies, and services; supplies and services for production, post-production, computing, multimedia, telecommunications and corporate communications. **Dates and Locations:** , Convention Center/Sands Expo Center/Hilton.

19998 ■ Radio-Television News Directors Association International Conference & Exhibition
Radio-Television News Directors Association
529 14th St., N.W., Ste. 425
Washington, DC 20045
Ph: (202)659-6510
Free: 800-807-8632

Fax: (202)223-4007
Co. E-mail: rtnda@rtnda.org
URL: http://www.rtnda.org
Contact: Jane Nassiri, Executive Director
E-mail: janen@rtnda.org

URL(s): www.rtnda.org. **Frequency:** Annual. **Audience:** Professionals from the television, radio and cable industries, along with representatives from government, publications and special interest groups. **Principal Exhibits:** Equipment, supplies, and services for the radio and television news industries, including cameras, recorders, weather equipment, computers, and software.

CONSULTANTS

19999 ■ A & A Research
690 Sunset Blvd.
Kalispell, MT 59901-3641
Ph: (406)752-7857
Fax: (406)752-0194
Contact: Judith Doonan, President
Scope: Offers marketing research services, specializing in newspaper readership and advertising studies. Also specializes in audience research and programming studies for radio and television stations, minority broadcasting, new business and retail marketing research, and advertising consulting and research. Also prepares public opinion polls. Serves private industries as well as government agencies. **Founded:** 1978. **Seminars:** Three R's of Advertising; Precision Advertising; Audience Research Workshop; Use of Research in Radio Programming.

20000 ■ Baker Scott & Co.
1259 Rte. 46
Parsippany, NJ 07054
Ph: (973)263-3355
Fax: (973)263-9255
Co. E-mail: exec.search@bakerscott.com
URL: http://www.bakerscott.com
Contact: Judith Bouer, President
E-mail: judy@bakerscott.com
Scope: Consulting services include executive recruiting, employment attitude surveys, and screening organization plans. Industries served: telecommunication, cable TV, broadcasting entertainment, and financial institutions. The firm is integrated horizontally across functional discipline such as accounting, administration, call center, data processing, engineering, finance, general operations, marketing and technical and plant operations. **Founded:** 1979. **Seminars:** Offers seminar programs on interview techniques, management skills, and customer service.

20001 ■ The Benchmark Co.—Benchmark Market Research
907 S Congress Ave., Ste. 7
Austin, TX 78704
Ph: (512)707-7500
Free: 800-688-7010
Fax: (512)707-7757
Co. E-mail: thebenc@earthlink.net
URL: http://www.thebenchmarkcompany.net
Contact: Dr. Robert E. Balon, Chief Executive Officer
E-mail: rob@diningoutwithrobbalon.com
Scope: Full service consultants to the communications industry, specializing in radio and television. Also serves newspapers and ad agencies with extensive market research. **Founded:** 1987. **Publications:** "Radio in the 90S; Audience, Promotion and Marketing Strategies". **Seminars:** The Rules of the Ratings Game Seminar.

20002 ■ Cable Ad Ventures Corp.
95 Mountainview Terr.
Hillsdale, NJ 07642-1023
Ph: (201)666-5131
Contact: Jay L. Campbell, President
E-mail: j@cavcorp.com
Scope: Specializes in the cable television field, working with programmers, advertisers and producers in developing original programming for cable television distribution. Company also produces television programming; works in representing companies in placing existing or new television programs in the cable marketplace. **Founded:** 1982.

20003 ■ D.E.M. Allen & Associates Ltd.
130 Cree Cres.
Winnipeg, MB, Canada R3J 3W1
Ph: (204)889-9202
Fax: (204)831-6650
Co. E-mail: gneilson@dema.mb.ca
URL: http://www.dema.mb.ca
Contact: G. R. Henke, President
E-mail: ghenke@dema.mb.ca

URL(s): www.dema.ca. **Scope:** Telecommunications consultants, experienced in AM, FM and television broadcasting, CATV systems, LF/HF, VHF/UHF and microwave systems and satellite earth stations; RF measurements and evaluations related to SCADA; LMCS in the millimeters portion of the spectrum as well as the 2.5Ghz MDS/MMDS field; electromagnetic compatibility and electromagnetic immunity including non-ionizing radiation evaluation and measurement. Services include planning, design, supervision and adjustment of broadcast transmitting facilities, including specifications, tender evaluation, preparation of reports, technical briefs for Federal Regulatory bodies, evaluation and measurements associated with RF propagation and electromagnetic energy throughout the radio frequency spectrum. Industries served: Broadcast, communications and national defense agencies. **Founded:** 1964. **Telecommunication Services:** ghenke@dema.mb.ca.

20004 ■ DeMers Programming Media Consultants
204 Exton Commons
Exton, PA 19341
Ph: (610)363-2636
Fax: (610)363-2198
Co. E-mail: info@demersprogramming.com
URL: http://www.demersprogramming.com
Contact: Alex Demers, President
E-mail: alex@demersprogramming.com

Scope: Programming and marketing consultants offering advice for broadcasters and broadcast related businesses. Services include: music and format controls, strategic planning, talent coaching and acquisition, research and promotional planning. Serves private and government sectors. **Founded:** 1986. **Publications:** "12 Steps To A One Share - Uncovering The Clutter," Feb, 2005; "Get Your Mind Out Of The Clutter - DeMers Dispatch Winter '05"; "See Spot Run...Over The Golden Goose"; "Radio's Attention Deficit Disorder"; "Program The Seller"; "At Issue: Staying Creative"; "Take A Hard Look At Your Special Programming"; "A Fresh Coat Of Paint"; "Guerrilla Radio". **Seminars:** Diary Keepers Plus Research; Marketing, Merchandising and Money.

20005 ■ Elder Engineering Inc.
35 Auckland Ln.
King City, ON, Canada L7B 1C1
Ph: (905)833-5141
Fax: (905)833-2101
Co. E-mail: eldeng@sympatico.ca
Contact: Stuart K. Hahn, Manager

Scope: Expertise regarding communications and broadcast transmitting systems encompasses feasibility study, frequency search, site selection, propagation tests, and protection analysis. Experienced with antenna design, contour predictions, equipment specification, technical brief, bid selection, tuning, testing, certification and proof of performance for newer improved transmitting facilities in LF to UHF bands; design studies for broadband multi station AM, FM, TV or DRB antenna and transmission systems at a common site, point-to-point STL, microwave distant learning, MDS, or teleconferencing systems. Industries served: radio, television, broadcasters and applicants, power utilities, government agencies, radio communications licensees, and manufacturers. **Founded:** 1961.

20006 ■ Financial Solutions Inc.
309 W Jefferson St.
La Grange, KY 40031
Ph: (502)225-9900
Free: 877-952-9766

Fax: (502)225-9997
Co. E-mail: robin@lawsonfinancial.net
URL: http://www.lawsonfinancial.net
Contact: Robin H. Lawson, Owner
E-mail: robin@lawsonfinancial.net

Scope: Offers financial brokerage services to the broadcasting industry in the Midwest United States. **Founded:** 1993. **Publications:** "Eighty percent of Americans agree they would benefit from having basic financial education and information," 2009; "Finra Investor Education Survey, 2007"; "How Are Mutual Funds Taxed". **Seminars:** Long Term Care, Estate Planning, Retirement, Financial Management.

20007 ■ Forsyth Consulting
9 Laurier Ave.
Toronto, ON, Canada M4X 1S2
Ph: (416)964-0812
Fax: (416)964-1304
Co. E-mail: ajforsyth9@rogers.com
Contact: Andrew J. Forsyth, President
E-mail: ajforsyth9@rogers.com

Scope: Specialized in regulatory affairs applicable to radio, television, cable, and satellite. Provides CRTC applications and interventions, compliance strategies and analysis, strategic planning and market positioning, creative programming, management sales, talent and formative development, acquisitions, benefit package strategies, and broadcast property sale representation. Industries served: Broadcasting. **Founded:** 1989.

20008 ■ Bentley Miller Lights Inc.
96 Glenmore Rd.
Toronto, ON, Canada M4L 3M3
Ph: (416)699-4786
Co. E-mail: bentley@bentleymiller.com
URL: http://www.bentleymiller.com
Contact: Bentley Miller, President
E-mail: bentley@bentleymiller.com

Scope: A lighting design/consulting company which offers lighting design and photography services for both private and government television production groups. Also offers systems design for television studios. This includes, client consultation, equipment specifying, supervising installation through system debugging and commissioning. Firm also offers lighting design services ranging from large scale spectaculars to news, drama and children's programs. Industries served: television producers, both private and public, government agencies, communications media, film and digital based media, performing arts, and education. **Founded:** 1993. **Publications:** "Ace lightning and the carnival of the doom". **Seminars:** Sony Professional Workshops; Ryerson Summer Workshops; Lightsource Creativity Clinics.

20009 ■ SEMO Communications Corp.
107 Semo Ln.
Sikeston, MO 63801
Ph: (573)471-6599
Free: 800-635-8230
Fax: (573)471-6878
Co. E-mail: cableme@semocommunications.com
URL: http://www.semocommunications.com
Contact: Tyrone Garrett, President

Scope: Consults on cable television systems and other communications services. **Founded:** 1976. **Telecommunication Services:** semosupport@cablerocket.com.

20010 ■ Stewart/Laurence Associates Inc.
118 Rte. 9 N
Englishtown, NJ 07726
Ph: (732)972-8000
Fax: (561)807-2557
Co. E-mail: info@stewartlaurence.com
URL: http://www.stewartlaurence.com
Contact: Mel Stewart Klein, President
E-mail: mel@stewartlaurence.com

Scope: An executive search firm assists corporations with the recruitment of top level management personnel. It recruits key executives (President, CEO, CFO, General Manager, VP Sales, VP Mktg, etc.) for start-up, high tech and venture capital companies internationally. Fields of expertise include: medical device and bio medical technology, Internet/Intranet, digital

and graphic imaging, software, networking, telecommunications, and wireless/WAP. **Founded:** 1969. **Telecommunication Services:** mel@stewartlaurence.com.

20011 ■ Technology Group Communications
8750 W Bryn Mawr Ave., Ste. 460
Chicago, IL 60631-3545
Ph: (773)695-9601
Fax: (773)675-2635
Contact: Alan G. Kraus, President

Scope: Established to provide in-depth engineering and integration services to the growing high performance enterprise network market. The firm has the ability to turnkey design, install, test and maintain large scale data communications networks of fiber, coax, twisted pair, and wireless media. Experience and expertise in all aspects of multi-product local area networking integration and installation. Projects have included the complete design, installation and certification of major facility networks for large manufacturing, educational and office facilities. **Founded:** 1983.

20012 ■ Victory Studios
2247 15th Ave. W
Seattle, WA 98119-2417
Ph: (206)282-1776
Fax: (206)282-3535
Co. E-mail: matt@victorystudios.com
URL: http://www.victorystudios.com
Contact: Mark MacDonald, President

Scope: Offers marketing, distribution, and syndication consultation regarding television programming for program producers. Also provides production services through an affiliate company, American Production Services. Work involves editing, audio narration, recording, computer graphics, NTSC-PAL, video and audio duplication, and camera equipment rental (stages and grip truck), and multimedia services. Industries served: Broadcast and industrial media, and government agencies. **Founded:** 1998.

20013 ■ Walter S. Wydro Consultants
57 Woodhill Rd.
Newtown, PA 18940-3013
Ph: (215)860-2288
Fax: (215)860-5502
Contact: Walter S. Wydro, President

Scope: Engineering consultants in telecommunications and cable television, offering research and development of new products, system growth analysis, financial and technical evaluation and planning for municipal services, and litigation testimony. **Founded:** 1967.

COMPUTERIZED DATABASES

20014 ■ *BaselineFT's In Production Database*
3415 S Sepulveda Blvd., Ste. 200
Los Angeles, CA 90034
Ph: (310)482-3400
Free: 800-858-3669
Fax: (310)393-7799
URL: http://www.baselineresearch.com
Availability: Online: Baseline LLC. **Type:** Full-text.

LIBRARIES

20015 ■ Alliance for Children and Television - Resource Library—L'Alliance pour L'Enfant et la Television.
1400 Rene-Levesque Blvd. E., Ste. 713
Montreal, QC, Canada H2L 2M2
Ph: (514)597-5417
Fax: (416)515-0467
Co. E-mail: cbowen@ymamj.org
URL: http://www.act-aet.tv
Contact: Chantal Bowen, Executive Director

Scope: Television and children, media, broadcasting. **Services:** Library open with permission only. **Founded:** 1974. **Holdings:** Figures not available.

20016 ■ CBC/Radio Canada Maritimes - Broadcast Materials, Halifax Centre
PO Box 3000
Halifax, NS, Canada B3J 3E9

Ph: (902)420-4160
Fax: (902)420-4281
Co. E-mail: doug.kirby@cbc.ca
URL: http://www.cbc.ca/archives
Contact: Doug Kirby, Media Specialist
Scope: Television news, children's television, television comedy, agriculture and resources television, performance and programming television. **Services:** Library open to the public by appointment. **Founded:** 1955. **Holdings:** 100,000 television archival items. **Subscriptions:** 13 newspapers.

20017 ■ National Press Club - Eric Friedheim Library & News Information Center
529 14th St. NW, 13th Fl.
Washington, DC 20045
Ph: (202)662-7523
Co. E-mail: bshankle@press.org
URL: http://press.org/library
Contact: Julie Schoo, Director, Library Services
Scope: Current events; journalism - craft, history; print and broadcast media. **Services:** Copying; audio cassette copying (fee); library open to members. **Founded:** 1984. **Holdings:** 2500 books; NPC luncheon audiocassettes & videotapes; newsletters; microfilm; CDs. **Subscriptions:** 250 newspapers, magazines, journals, and newsletters.

20018 ■ Right Management Consultants - Corporate Research Center
1818 Market St., 33rd Fl.
Philadelphia, PA 19103

20019 ■ TV Ontario Library
PO Box 200, Sta. Q
Toronto, ON, Canada M4T 2T1
Ph: (416)484-2600
Free: 800-613-0513
Co. E-mail: rvolpatti@tvo.org
URL: http://ww3.tvo.org
Contact: Robert Knowles
Scope: Educational television, television production, broadcasting, distance education, communications, multimedia, children and television. **Services:** Interlibrary loan; copying; library open to the public for reference use only. **Founded:** 1970. **Holdings:** 10,000 books; TV Ontario documents, program guides, and newspaper clippings. **Subscriptions:** 200 journals and other serials. **Telecommunication Services:** asktvo@tvo.org.

20020 ■ University of California, Los Angeles - UCLA Film and Television Archive - Research and Study Center
46 Powell Library
Los Angeles, CA 90095-1517
Ph: (310)206-5388
Fax: (310)206-5392
Co. E-mail: arsc@ucla.edu
URL: http://www.cinema.ucla.edu
Contact: Mark Quigley
Scope: U.S. theatrical films and broadcast television programs, theatrical newsreels, films of recognized importance in world film history, television news programs, animated films. **Services:** Archive open to the public for scholarly and project-oriented onsite

research only. **Founded:** 1965. **Holdings:** 220,000 motion picture prints and negatives; 95,000 television films and tapes.

RESEARCH CENTERS

20021 ■ Massachusetts Institute of Technology - Media Lab
Bldg. E14 & E15
77 Massachusetts Ave.
Cambridge, MA 02139-4307
Ph: (617)253-5960
Co. E-mail: hoffman@media.mit.edu
URL: http://www.media.mit.edu
Contact: Joi Ito, Director
E-mail: joi@media.mit.edu
Founded: 1985. **Telecommunication Services:** communications@media.mit.edu.

20022 ■ Texas Tech University - Center for Communications Research (CCR)
College of Mass Communications, Box 43082
Lubbock, TX 79409-3082
Ph: (806)742-3385
Fax: (806)742-1085
Co. E-mail: p.muhlberger@ttu.edu
URL: http://www.depts.ttu.edu/masscom/about/ccr.php
Contact: Prof. Peter Muhlberger, Director
Founded: 1972. **Publications:** *Journalism Educator; Journalism Quarterly; Journal of Broadcasting and Electronic Media; Journal of Media Economics; Public Opinion Quarterly.*

ASSOCIATIONS AND OTHER ORGANIZATIONS

20023 ■ American Staffing Association (ASA)
277 S Washington St., Ste. 200
Alexandria, VA 22314-3675
Ph: (703)253-2020
Fax: (703)253-2053
Co. E-mail: asa@americanstaffing.net
URL: http://www.americanstaffing.net
Contact: Mr. Richard Wahlquist, President
Description: Promotes and represents the staffing industry through legal and legislative advocacy, public relations, education, and the establishment of high standards of ethical conduct. **Founded:** 1966. **Publications:** Co-Employment Guide; ASA Membership and Resource Directory; Staffing Success (Bi-monthly); ASA Managers Guide to Employment Law. **Educational Activities:** Staffing World (Annual). **Awards:** Staffing VOICE Awards; Chapter Merit Awards; Leadership Hall of Fame Award; Care Award (Annual); Communications Awards (Annual); Employee of the Year (Annual); Leadership Hall of Fame (Annual).

20024 ■ Association of Manpower Franchise Owners (AMFO)
6737 W Washington St., Ste. 1300
Milwaukee, WI 53214
Ph: (414)276-2651
Fax: (414)276-7704
Co. E-mail: info@amfo.org
URL: http://www.amfo.org
Contact: Jane A. Svinicki, Executive Director
Description: Serves as a forum for exchange of ideas and information among members; acts as liaison between members and the parent company. Studies and critiques procedures and policies of Manpower International; solicits suggestions from members regarding smooth operation of a temporary employee service. Provides formalized procedure for resolution of grievances among members and between members and the parent company. **Founded:** 1971.

20025 ■ National Association of Personnel Services (NAPS)
6625 Hwy. 53 E, Ste. 410-201
Dawsonville, GA 30534
Ph: (706)531-0060
Fax: (866)739-4750
Co. E-mail: jsacerdote@recruitinglife.com
URL: http://www.recruitinglife.com
Contact: Conrad Taylor, President
Description: Private employment and temporary service firms. Compiles statistics on professional agency growth and development; conducts certification program and educational programs. Association is distinct from former name of National Association of Personnel Consultants. **Founded:** 1961. **Publications:** National Directory of Personnel Service Firms (Annual). **Telecommunication Services:** info@recruitinglife.com.

20026 ■ National Association of Professional Employer Organizations (NAPEO)
707 N St. Asaph St.
Alexandria, VA 22314
Ph: (703)836-0466
Fax: (703)836-0976
Co. E-mail: info@napeo.org
URL: http://www.napeo.org
Contact: Pat Cleary, President
Description: Professional employer organizations. Seeks to enhance professionalism in the professional employer industry. Sponsors educational and public information programs. Maintains speakers' bureau; compiles statistics. **Founded:** 1984. **Educational Activities:** Professional Employee Conference and Marketplace (Annual).

REFERENCE WORKS

20027 ■ "AT&T To Acquire Black Telecom Firm" in Black Enterprise (Vol. 38, January 2008, No. 6, pp. 24)
Pub: Earl G. Graves Publishing Co. Inc.
Ed: Alan Hughes. **Description:** Details of AT&T's acquisition of ChaseCom LP, a telecommunications company based in Houston, Texas, are covered.

20028 ■ "Calling All Recruiters: Agent HR Puts Staffing Agents In Charge" in Black Enterprise (Vol. 38, December 2007, No. 5, pp. 72)
Pub: Earl G. Graves Publishing Co. Inc.
Ed: Chana Garcia. **Description:** Recruiting and staffing agencies are seeing a drop in services due to slow economic growth. AgentHR partners with full-service recruiters who have three to five year's experience-specialists soliciting their own clients, provide staffing services, and manage their own accounts, thus combining the roles of recruiter and salesperson.

20029 ■ "Impressive Numbers: Companies Experience Substantial Increases in Dollars, Employment" in Hispanic Business (July-August 2007)
Pub: Hispanic Business
Ed: Derek Reveron. **Description:** Profiles of five fastest growing Hispanic companies reporting increases in revenue and employment include Brightstar, distributor of wireless products; Greenway Ford Inc., a car dealership; Fred Loya Insurance, auto insurance carrier; and Group O, packaging company; and Diverse Staffing, Inc., an employment and staffing firm.

20030 ■ "Matchmakers Anticipating Tech Valley Boom" in Business Review, Albany New York (Vol. 34, November 2, 2007, No. 31, pp. 1)
Pub: American City Business Journals, Inc.
Ed: Adam Sichko. **Description:** Qualified candidates are coming to permanent placement companies after being downsized elsewhere. The top five projected fastest-growing and top five projected fasted-decreasing jobs in the Capital Region are presented.

20031 ■ "Overseas Overtures" in Business Journal-Portland (Vol. 24, October 26, 2007, No. 35, pp. 1)
Pub: American City Business Journals, Inc.
Ed: Robin J. Moody. **Description:** Oregon has a workforce shortage, specifically for the health care industry. Recruiting agencies, such as the International Recruiting Network Inc., answers the high demand for workforce by recruiting foreign employees. The difficulties recruiting companies experience with regards to foreign labor laws are investigated.

20032 ■ "Priority: Business For Sale" in Inc. (January 2008, pp. 28)
Pub: Gruner & Jahr USA Publishing
Ed: Elaine Appleton Grant. **Description:** Profile of an employment agency providing registered nurses to hospitals and nursing homes. The company began as an temporary placement agency for IT professionals and is now for sale at the asking price of $4.2 million.

20033 ■ "Q&A With Devin Ringling: Franchise's Services Go Beyond Elder Care" in Gazette (October 2, 2010)
Pub: The Gazette
Ed: Bill Radford. **Description:** Profile of franchise, Interim HealthCare, in Colorado Springs, Colorado; the company offers home care services that include wound care and specialized feedings to shopping and light housekeeping. It also runs a medical staffing company that provides nurses, therapists and other health care workers to hospitals, prisons, schools and other facilities.

20034 ■ "Regional Talent Network Unveils Jobs Web Site" in Crain's Cleveland Business (Vol. 30, June 1, 2009, No. 21, pp. 11)
Pub: Crain Communications, Inc.
Description: Regional Talent Network launched WhereToFindHelp.org, a Website designed to act as a directory of all Northeast Ohio resources that can help employers recruit and job seekers look for positions. The site also lists organizations offering employment and training services.

20035 ■ "Sign of the Times: Temp-To-Perm Attorneys" in HRMagazine (Vol. 54, January 2009, No. 1, pp. 24)
Pub: Society for Human Resource Management
Contact: Henry G. Jackson, President
E-mail: hjackson@shrm.org
Ed: Bill Leonard. **Description:** A growing number of law firms are hiring professional staff on a temp-to-perm basis according to the president of Professional Placement Services in Florida. Firms can save money while testing potential employees on a temporary basis.

20036 ■ "Temporary Measures" in Occupational Outlook Quarterly (Vol. 54, Fall 2010, No. 3, pp. 36)
Pub: U.S. Bureau of Labor Statistics
Description: Data on temporary help services employment from the U.S. Bureau of Labor Statistics suggests good news for all nonfarm workers. The data had been rising steadily for most of 2009.

20037 ■ "Temporary Theory" in Canadian Business (Vol. 80, November 5, 2007, No. 22, pp. 33)
Pub: Rogers Media
Ed: Joe Castaldo. **Description:** Employing a temporary manager is ideal for companies working on a strict budget and limited time. The strategy will provide the company with the skills of an expert manager for a cost that is less than that of hiring a full-time manager. The usage of interim managers, specifically in short-term projects, is discussed.

20038 ■ "Work To Do" in Canadian Business (Vol. 81, July 22, 2008, No. 12-13, pp. 22)
Pub: Rogers Media Ltd.
Ed: Jane Bao. **Description:** Recruiting firm Manpower revealed that 36 percent of Canadian employers had trouble filling positions in 2007, highlighting the labor shortage and the need to bring in more workers. Underemployment of immigrants costs up to $6 billion to Canada's economy every year. Other views regarding Canada's labor shortage and on its economic impact are presented.

STATISTICAL SOURCES

20039 ■ RMA Annual Statement Studies
Pub: Risk Management Association
Contact: Kevin M. Blakey, President
Released: Annual. **Price:** $175.00 2006-07 edition, $105.00. **Description:** Contains composite balance sheets and income statements for more than 360 industries, including the accounting, auditing, and bookkeeping industries. Also contains five years of comparative historical data for discerning trends. Includes 16 commonly used ratios, computed for most of the size groupings for nearly every industry.

FRANCHISES AND BUSINESS OPPORTUNITIES

20040 ■ AHEAD Human Resources, Inc.
AHEAD Human Resources, Inc.
2209 Heather Ln.
Louisville, KY 40218
Free: 877-485-5858
Fax: (502)485-0801
Description: Temporary staffing. **No. of Franchise Units:** 7. **Founded:** 1995.. **Franchised:** 2000. **Equity Capital Needed:** Need working capital. **Franchise Fee:** $17,700-$23,700. **Training:** Yes.

20041 ■ AtWork Medical Services
3215 John Sevier Hwy.
Knoxville, TN 37290
Free: 800-383-0804
Fax: (865)573-1171
Description: Temporary & full-time medical staffing services. **No. of Franchise Units:** 14. **Founded:** 1990.. **Franchised:** 2003. **Equity Capital Needed:** $143,600-$226,800. **Franchise Fee:** $0-$25,000. **Royalty Fee:** 6.1.-1.6%. **Training:** Provides 5 days at headquarters, 2-5 days onsite and ongoing support.

20042 ■ CareersUSA Franchise
Careers Franchising Inc.
6501 Congress Ave., Ste. 200
Boca Raton, FL 33487
Ph: (561)995-7000
Free: 888-CAR-EERS
Fax: (561)995-7001
Co. E-mail: tfeldman@careerusa.com
URL: http://www.careerusa.com
Description: A temporary, temp-to-hire and direct hire placement staffing service specializing in clerical, administrative, accounting and light service personnel in varied industries and organizations. **No. of Franchise Units:** 3. **No. of Company-Owned Units:** 17. **Founded:** 1981.. **Franchised:** 1987. **Equity Capital Needed:** $63,625-$189,075. **Franchise Fee:** $22,500. **Financial Assistance:** Yes. **Training:** Yes.

20043 ■ Express Employment Professionals
8516 NW Expy.
Oklahoma City, OK 73162
Ph: (877)652-6400
Co. E-mail: franchising@expresspersonnel.com
URL: http://www.franchising.expresspersonnel.com
Description: Is an international fullservice staffing corporation with three distinct divisions available in one franchise agreement. The franchised offices provide clients with temporary help, full-time placements, and executive recruitment. **No. of Franchise Units:** 550. **Founded:** 1983.. **Franchised:** 1985. **Equity Capital Needed:** $153,750-$242,500. **Franchise Fee:** $35,000. **Financial Assistance:** Yes. **Training:** 2 week initial training at headquarters, 1 week in certified training office and ongoing field training and support. Followed by additional time in new office with assigned field representative.

20044 ■ Link Staffing Services
Personnel Concepts
1800 Bering Dr., Ste. 800
Houston, TX 77057
Ph: (713)784-4400
Free: 800-848-5465
Fax: (713)784-4454
Co. E-mail: franchise@linkstaffing.com
URL: http://www.linkstaffing.com
Description: Supplies light industrial and industrial personnel to a variety of retail, commercial and manufacturing businesses. **No. of Franchise Units:** 55. **No. of Company-Owned Units:** 10. **Founded:** 1980.. **Franchised:** 1994. **Equity Capital Needed:** $93,000-$171,000. **Franchise Fee:** $30,000. **Financial Assistance:** Yes. **Training:** Support center classes include operations, management, sales and computer applications and an ongoing program of advanced curriculum including field training

20045 ■ Pridestaff
7535 N Palm Ave., Ste. 101
Fresno, CA 93711-1393
Ph: (559)449-5804

Fax: (559)432-4371
Description: Recruiting Agency. **No. of Franchise Units:** 36. **No. of Company-Owned Units:** 3. **Founded:** 1978.. **Franchised:** 1995. **Equity Capital Needed:** $162,000-$237,000. **Franchise Fee:** $32,000. **Training:** Yes.

20046 ■ Protingent Staffing
16650 NE 79th St., Ste. 200
Redmond, WA 98052
Ph: (425)284-7777
Fax: (425)642-8001
Co. E-mail: franchiseinfo@protingent.com
URL: http://www.protingent.com
Description: Technical staffing firm. **No. of Franchise Units:** 2. **No. of Company-Owned Units:** 2. **Founded:** 2001.. **Franchised:** 2007. **Equity Capital Needed:** $90,000-$132,000. **Franchise Fee:** $25,000. **Training:** Offers 2 weeks training at Seattle headquarters covering account management, recruiting, back office and client/candidate tracking system training.

20047 ■ Remedy Intelligent Staffing
Koosharem Corp.
3820 State St.
Santa Barbara, CA 93105-3182
Ph: (800)753-0196
Fax: (805)617-1309
Description: Recruiting Services. **No. of Franchise Units:** 89. **No. of Company-Owned Units:** 255. **Founded:** 1974.. **Franchised:** 1987. **Equity Capital Needed:** $117,000-$200,000. **Franchise Fee:** $30,000. **Training:** Includes classroom training, field training and online web courses in the areas of strategic planning, sales support, operations and client retention.

20048 ■ Spherion
925 N Point Pkwy.
Alpharetta, GA 30005
Ph: (678)867-3702
Free: 800-903-0082
Fax: (678)867-3190
Description: Flexible staffing solutions. **No. of Franchise Units:** 89. **No. of Company-Owned Units:** 285. **Founded:** 1946.. **Franchised:** 1956. **Equity Capital Needed:** $57,500-$135,700; Franchise fee $121,800-$391,700. **Franchise Fee:** $15,000. **Training:** Yes.

20049 ■ TRC Staffing Services, Inc.
115 Perimeter Center Pl. NE, Ste. 850
Atlanta, GA 30346
Ph: (800)488-8008
Description: Provides office support, clerical, word processing, data processing, marketing and light industrial personnel to businesses. **No. of Franchise Units:** 30. **No. of Company-Owned Units:** 23. **Founded:** 1980.. **Equity Capital Needed:** $15,000. **Franchise Fee:** $75,000 minimum liquid. **Training:** Yes.

ASSOCIATIONS AND OTHER ORGANIZATIONS

20050 ■ American Sports Builders Association (ASBA)

8480 Baltimore National Pike, No. 307
Ellicott City, MD 21043
Ph: (410)730-9595
Free: 866-501-2722
Fax: (410)730-8833
Co. E-mail: info@sportsbuilders.org
URL: http://sportsbuilders.org
Contact: Mark Brogan, Chairman
Description: Contractors who install running tracks, synthetic turf fields, tennis courts and indoor sports surfaces; manufacturers who supply basic materials for construction; accessory suppliers, designers, architects, and consultants of facilities. Provides guidelines for tennis court construction, running track construction, fencing, synthetic turf field construction and lighting. Offers certification and awards programs. **Founded:** 1965. **Publications:** *Tennis and Track Construction Guidelines* (Periodic); *Buyers Guide for Tennis Court Construction* (Periodic); *Running Tracks: A Construction and Maintenance Manual* (Semiannual). **Awards:** Outstanding Indoor Tennis Facility Award (Annual); Outstanding Outdoor Tennis Facility Award (Annual); Outstanding Track/Facility Award (Annual); Outstanding Residential Tennis Court/Facility Award (Annual).

20051 ■ American Tennis Association (ATA)

9701 Apollo Dr., Ste. 301
Largo, MD 20774
Ph: (240)487-5953
Co. E-mail: fscott@americantennisassociation.org
URL: http://www.americantennisassociation.org
Contact: Dr. Franklyn Scott, Jr., President
Description: Persons interested in tennis. Promotes and develops tennis regardless of race. Supports training programs to develop Teaching Professionals. Sponsors training programs for young players; conducts 60 state and local tournaments. **Founded:** 1916. **Publications:** *ATA News* (Quarterly).

20052 ■ International Health, Racquet and Sportsclub Association (IHRSA)

Seaport Ctr.
70 Fargo St.
Boston, MA 02210
Ph: (617)951-0055
Free: 800-228-4772
Fax: (617)951-0056
Co. E-mail: info@ihrsa.org
URL: http://www.ihrsa.org
Contact: Joe Moore, President
Description: Health, racquet, and sport clubs; racquet sports manufacturers and suppliers. Promotes the continued growth of the health, racquet, and sports club industry in 70 countries. Aids member clubs in making educated business decisions. Sets standards for club management; offers group purchasing program. Organizes management training seminars. Compiles statistics; disseminates information. Conducts market research and educational programs; conducts sponsored membership promotion programs. Provides government relations and public relations services. **Scope:** government relations, club operations. **Founded:** 1981. **Publications:** *Profiles of Success; Club Business International* (Monthly). **Educational Activities:** International Health, Racquet and Sportsclub Association Convention (Annual).

20053 ■ International Tennis Hall of Fame (ITHOF)

194 Bellevue Ave.
Newport, RI 02840
Ph: (401)849-3990
Free: 800-457-1144
Co. E-mail: newport@tennisfame.com
URL: http://www.tennisfame.com
Contact: Tony Trabert, President
Description: Seeks to foster interest in tennis, its history, and its athletic heroes. Supports junior tennis training programs; conducts amateur and professional grass-court competitions; maintains a museum. Produces video programs. Inducts new Hall of Fame members annually, including administrators, coaches, players, and writers. **Founded:** 1954. **Publications:** *Hall of Fame News* (Quarterly). **Awards:** Golden Achievement Award (Annual); Great Tennis Nation (Biennial); International Tennis Hall of Fame; Samuel Hardy Award; Bill Talbert Junior Sportsmanship Awards (Annual); Davis Cup and Fed Cup Awards of Excellence (Annual); Tennis Educational Merit Award for Women; Tennis Educational Merit Award for Men.

20054 ■ Professional Tennis Registry (PTR)

PO Box 4739
Hilton Head Island, SC 29938
Ph: (843)785-7244
Free: 800-421-6289
Fax: (843)686-2033
Co. E-mail: ptr@ptrtennis.org
URL: http://www.ptrtennis.org
Contact: Jorge Andrew, President
Description: Tests, certifies, and registers international tennis teaching professionals; Certification requires successful completion of a written and on-court examinations. Sponsors workshops, tennis clinics, and charitable program. Holds competitions; compiles statistics; maintains placement service. **Founded:** 1976. **Publications:** *TennisPro* (Bimonthly); *USPTR Membership Directory* (Annual); *TennisPro: The International Magazine of PTR Tennis Teachers and Coaches* (Bimonthly).

20055 ■ Sony Ericsson WTA Tour

1 Progress Plz., Ste. 1500
St. Petersburg, FL 33701
Ph: (727)895-5000
Fax: (727)894-1982
Co. E-mail: webmaster@wtatour.com
URL: http://www.sonyericssonwtatour.com
Contact: Stacey Allaster, Chief Executive Officer
Purpose: Works to increase and strengthen the global popularity and stature of the women's professional tennis tour, and to further advance the game as the preeminent sport for women worldwide. **Founded:** 1975. **Awards:** Diamond Aces (Annual); Doubles Team of the Year (Annual); Most Impressive Newcomer (Annual); Most Improved Player (Annual); Player of the Year (Annual).

20056 ■ United States Professional Tennis Association (USPTA)

3535 Briarpark Dr., Ste. 1
Houston, TX 77042-5233
Ph: (713)978-7782
Free: 800-USP-TA4U
Fax: (713)978-7780
Co. E-mail: uspta@uspta.org
URL: http://www.uspta.com
Contact: Tim Heckler, Chief Executive Officer
E-mail: tim.heckler@uspta.org
Description: Professional tennis instructors, tennis-teaching professionals and college coaches. Seeks to improve tennis instruction in the United States; maintains placement bureau and library. Offers specialized education; sponsors competitions; administrates an adult tennis league and a nationwide program to introduce children ages 3-10 to tennis. Sponsors annual "Tennis Across America" program each spring. **Founded:** 1927. **Publications:** *ADDvantage* (Monthly); *USPTA Membership Directory: Of the Governing Body of Tennis-Teaching Professionals* (Annual); *ADDvantage: The magazine for men and women tennis-teaching professionals* (Monthly). **Educational Activities:** United States Professional Tennis Association Convention (Annual). **Awards:** Division of the Year; Newsletter of the Year; Player of the Year; Alex Gordon Award for Professional of the Year.

20057 ■ United States Racquet Stringers Association (USRSA)

PO Box 3392
Duluth, GA
Ph: (760)536-1177
Fax: (760)536-1171
Co. E-mail: usrsa@racquettech.com
URL: http://www.racquettech.com
Contact: David Bone, Executive Director
Description: Racquet stringers; individuals interested in learning about the stringing of racquets and new patterns on the market. Conducts experiments with new racquets and patterns. Provides free stringing business consulting service. Offers Certification Program. Offers instruction-workshops and video instruction. **Founded:** 1975. **Publications:** *Racquet Sports Industry* (10/year); *RacquetTECH.com; The Stringer's Digest* (Semiannual); *Total Racquet Service*.

20058 ■ United States Racquetball Association (USAR)—USA Racquetball

1685 W Uintah St.
Colorado Springs, CO 80904-2969
Ph: (719)635-5396
Fax: (719)635-0685
Co. E-mail: jhiser@usra.org
URL: http://www.usra.org
Contact: Cheryl Kirk, President
Description: Represents racquetball players and enthusiasts. Promotes racquetball as a sport; organizes racquetball to be a self-governing sport of, by,

and for the players; encourages building of facilities for the sport; conducts racquetball events including annual national and international tournaments. Maintains hall of fame, junior player programs, and charitable programs. **Founded:** 1969. **Publications:** *Racquetball Magazine* (Bimonthly). **Educational Activities:** United States Racquetball Association Competition (Annual); High Performance Camp (Annual). **Awards:** Athletes (Annual); Hall of Fame (Annual); Racquetball Hall of Fame; Joe Sobek Outstanding Contribution Award; John Halverson Fair Play Award.

20059 ■ United States Squash Racquets Association (USSRA)
555 8th Ave., Ste. 1102
New York, NY 10018-4311
Ph: (212)268-4090
Fax: (212)268-4091
Co. E-mail: office@ussquash.com
URL: http://www.ussquash.com
Contact: Mr. Kevin Klipstein, Chief Executive Officer
Description: Member of United States Olympic Committee. Aims to establish and enforce uniformity in the rules of the game, standardize court specifications and schedules, and conduct tournaments. **Founded:** 1904. **Publications:** *National Court Survey* (Triennial); *National Court Survey* (Triennial); *Squash Magazine* (10/year); *U.S. Squash Racquets Association--Official Yearbook*; *U.S. Squash Racquets Association--Official Yearbook.*

20060 ■ United States Tennis Association (USTA)
70 W Red Oak Ln.
White Plains, NY 10604
Ph: (914)696-7000
Free: 800-990-8782
Fax: (914)696-7167
Co. E-mail: memberservices@usta.com
URL: http://www.usta.com
Contact: Gordon Smith, Executive Director
URL(s): www.usopen.org. **Description:** Federation of local tennis clubs, educational institutions, recreation departments, and other groups and individuals interested in the promotion of tennis. Works to develop tennis as a means of healthful recreation and physical fitness and maintain high standards of fair play and sportsmanship. Sanctions thousands of tennis tournaments for all age groups throughout the U.S. each year. Sponsors Junior Program for boys and girls under 18 years of age; U.S. national tennis team; national championships for various age groups; National Circuit tournament for pro and amateur players; Davis Cup, Fed Cup, Olympics international matches; and adult recreational leagues. Compiles statistics on leading professional and amateur players. **Founded:** 1881. **Publications:** *Tennis Championships Magazine* (Periodic); *Tennis USA* (Annual). **Awards:** Maureen Connolly Brinker Award; Bobby

Kaplan Sportsmanship Award; John T. McGovern Umpires' Award; Member Organization of the Year Seniors' Service Award; Service Bowl Award; Jack Stahr Award; Super Seniors' Service Award; Outstanding Tennis Facility Awards; United States Open Tennis Championships; Bill Talbert Junior Sportsmanship Awards; Eve Kraft Community Service Award; Volunteer Service Award; Dr. Allen B. Stowe Sportsmanship Award; Ralph W. Westcott USTA Family of the Year Award; Girls' 18 National Championships Sportsmanship Award; NJTL Chapter of the Year Award.

20061 ■ WTA Tour Players Association (WTA)
100 2nd Ave. S
St. Petersburg, FL 33701
Ph: (727)895-5000
Fax: (727)894-1982
URL: http://www.wtatennis.com
Contact: Stacey Allaster, Chief Executive Officer
Description: Professional women tennis players. Purpose is to represent members with regard to professional tournaments. **Founded:** 1973. **Publications:** *Players Handbook* (Annual).

REFERENCE WORKS

20062 ■ *"Growing Strong" in Entrepreneur (Vol. 35, November 2007, No. 11, pp. 36)*
Pub: Entrepreneur Media Inc.
Ed: Nichole L. Torres. **Description:** Amy Langer founded Salo LL with partner John Folkestad. The company is growing fast since its 2002 launch, with over $40 million in projections for 2007. The finance and accounting staffing company tops the list of the fastest-growing women-led companies in North America.

TRADE PERIODICALS

20063 ■ *Black Tennis Magazine: Tennis*
Pub: Black Tennis Magazine
URL(s): www.btmag.com. **Released:** Quarterly **Price:** $15, Individuals; $28, Two years; $40, Individuals 3 years.

20064 ■ *Tennis Magazine*
Pub: Miller Publishing Group L.L.C.
URL(s): www.tennis.com/. **Ed:** Ed McGrogan. **Released:** Annual; September. **Price:** $20, Two years; $15, Individuals.

VIDEOCASSETTES/ AUDIOCASSETTES

20065 ■ *Consistent Tennis Wins*
Tapeworm Video Distributors
25876 The Old Road #141
Stevenson Ranch, CA 91381

Ph: (661)257-4904
Fax: (661)257-4820
Co. E-mail: sales@tapeworm.com
URL: http://www.tapeworm.com
Released: 1996. **Price:** $39.95. **Description:** Host Tom Avery discusses tennis techniques such as ground strokes, volleys, warm-up routines and breathing. **Availability:** VHS.

TRADE SHOWS AND CONVENTIONS

20066 ■ United States Professional Tennis Association Convention
United States Professional Tennis Association (USPTA)
3535 Briarpark Dr., Ste. 1
Houston, TX 77042-5233
Ph: (713)978-7782
Free: 800-USP-TA4U
Fax: (713)978-7780
Co. E-mail: uspta@uspta.org
URL: http://www.uspta.com
Contact: Tim Heckler, Chief Executive Officer
E-mail: tim.heckler@uspta.org
URL(s): www.uspta.com. **Frequency:** Annual. **Audience:** Tennis-teaching professionals, industry delegates, and general public. **Principal Exhibits:** Tennis equipment, supplies, and services.

LIBRARIES

20067 ■ International Tennis Hall of Fame and Tennis Museum Library
Newport Casino
194 Bellevue Ave.
Newport, RI 02840
Ph: (401)849-3990
Free: 800-457-1144
Fax: (401)849-8780
Co. E-mail: research@tennisfame.com
URL: http://www.tennisfame.com
Contact: Nicole Markham, Curator, Collections
Scope: Lawn tennis, court tennis, other racquet games. **Services:** Copying. **Founded:** 1954. **Holdings:** 5000 books; 300,000 photographs; periodicals; catalogs; Newport RI Social History. **Subscriptions:** 5 journals and other serials. **Telecommunication Services:** newport@tennisfame.com.

20068 ■ Racquet and Tennis Club Library
370 Park Ave.
New York, NY 10022-5968
Ph: (212)753-9700
Fax: (212)980-7180
Contact: Gerard J. Belliveau, Jr., Librarian
Scope: Sports, court and lawn tennis, early American sport. **Services:** Mail queries answered; copying; Library open to researchers by appointment. **Founded:** 1916. **Holdings:** 20,000 books. **Subscriptions:** 45 journals and other serials.

ASSOCIATIONS AND OTHER ORGANIZATIONS

20069 ■ Tire Industry Association (TIA)
1532 Pointer Ridge Pl., Ste. G
Bowie, MD 20716-1883
Ph: (301)430-7280
Free: 800-876-8372
Fax: (301)430-7283
Co. E-mail: info@tireindustry.org
URL: http://www.tireindustry.org
Contact: Gary Albright, President
Description: Corporations engaged in all sectors of the replacement tire industry. Seeks to advance members' interests. Serves as a clearinghouse on economic and regulatory issues affecting the replacement tire industry; conducts educational programs; sponsors lobbying activities. **Founded:** 1921. **Publications:** *Tire Retreading/Repair Journal* (Monthly). **Educational Activities:** Performance Tires & Wheels TIA; World Tire Conference and Exhibition (Annual). **Awards:** Hall of Fame (Annual).

20070 ■ Tire Retread and Repair Information Bureau (TRIB)
1013 Birch St.
Falls Church, VA 22046
Ph: (703)533-7677
Free: 877-394-6811
Fax: (703)533-7678
Co. E-mail: info@retread.org
URL: http://www.retread.org
Contact: Bob Majewski, President
Description: Retreaders, tire repair information, suppliers to the retread industry. Serves as information resource for the retread industry. Receives logistical support from industry associations, suppliers and retreaders. Operates speakers' bureau. **Scope:** retreaded tires/repair of tires/importance of proper tire inflation. **Founded:** 1973. **Subscriptions:** articles.

REFERENCE WORKS

20071 ■ *"Goodyear Extends Exclusive Deal to Supply NASCAR's Tires" in Charlotte Observer (February 4, 2007)*
Pub: Knight-Ridder/Tribune Business News
Ed: David Poole. **Description:** Goodyear tires will continue to be the exclusive tire provider at NASCAR's Nextel Cup, Busch and Truck series through the year 2012.

20072 ■ *"Miami's 'Big Wheels' Keep Latin America Rolling" in Hispanic Business (July-August 2007, pp. 46-47)*
Pub: Hispanic Business
Ed: Frank Nelson. **Description:** Four top Hispanic owned exporters of tires are discussed. All four companies are based in Miami, Florida.

20073 ■ *Modern Tire Dealer--Facts/Directory Issue*
Pub: Bobit Business Media
Contact: Ty Bobit, President
URL(s): www.moderntiredealer.com. **Ed:** Bob Ulrich. **Released:** Annual **Publication includes:** Directories of tire and car service suppliers, tire shop jobbers, and national and state associations. **Entries include:** Generally, listings show company or organization name, address, phone, names and titles of key personnel. Listings for manufacturers include products. **Arrangement:** Manufacturers and national associations are alphabetical; jobbers and state associations are geographical. **Indexes:** Product.

20074 ■ *Tire Review--Sourcebook & Directory Issue*
Pub: Babcox
URL(s): www.tirereview.com. **Ed:** Jim Smith. **Released:** Annual; latest edition 2007. **Publication includes:** About 850 suppliers of tires, repair equipment, and automotive service supplies and equipment to tire dealers and retreaders. **Entries include:** Company name, address, phone, name and title of contact, products, brand names, email and website addresses. **Arrangement:** Alphabetical. **Indexes:** Product, brand name.

20075 ■ *Who Makes It and Where Directory*
Pub: Tire Guides Inc.
Contact: Bennett Garfield, Owner
URL(s): tireguides.com. **Ed:** Alfred Snyder. **Released:** Annual; Latest edition 2011. **Price:** $8, Single issue up to 24 copies. **Covers:** Over 600 tire, wheel, and tube manufacturers; international, domestic, and worldwide coverage. **Entries include:** Company name, address, phone, website addresses, and toll free numbers. **Database includes:** List of antique and odd size tire dealers; manufacturer toll-free phone numbers. **Arrangement:** Classified by Department of Transportation identification code numbers. **Indexes:** Brand name.

STATISTICAL SOURCES

20076 ■ *World Markets for Tires and Rubber*
Pub: Business Trend Analysts, Inc.
Released: 2001-2002. **Price:** $2495.00. **Description:** Analyzes worldwide supply and demand for tires and natural and synthetic rubber. Competitor profiles provide insight to marketing strategies, R & D activities, financial performance, and more.

TRADE PERIODICALS

20077 ■ *Tire Business: Your Number One information resource*
Pub: Crain Communications Inc.
Contact: Rance Crain, President
E-mail: rcrain@crain.com
URL(s): www.tirebusiness.com. **Ed:** Dave Zielasko. **Released:** Semimonthly **Price:** $79, Individuals; $148, Two years; $107, Individuals Canada; $194, Two years Canada; $119, Other countries; $208, Two years all other countries; $99, Individuals web only.

20078 ■ *Tire Retreading/Repair Journal*
Pub: Tire Industry Association
Contact: Gary Albright, President
URL(s): www.tireindustry.org/publications.asp. **Ed:** Kevin Rohlwing. **Released:** Monthly **Price:** $60, U.S. and Canada; $70, Other countries.

20079 ■ *Tire Review: Dedicated to Building your Business*
Pub: Babcox
URL(s): www.tirereview.com/www.babcox.com/site/our-brands/tire-review. **Ed:** Jim Smith. **Released:** Monthly

TRADE SHOWS AND CONVENTIONS

20080 ■ World Tire Conference and Exhibition
Tire Industry Association (TIA)
1532 Pointer Ridge Pl., Ste. G
Bowie, MD 20716-1883
Ph: (301)430-7280
Free: 800-876-8372
Fax: (301)430-7283
Co. E-mail: info@tireindustry.org
URL: http://www.tireindustry.org
Contact: Gary Albright, President
URL(s): www.tireindustry.org. **Frequency:** Annual. **Audience:** Tire dealers, re-treaders and repairs; trucking industry personnel; government personnel; environmentalists; recyclers. **Principal Exhibits:** Tire re-treading and repairing equipment; tires; reduction and removal; computer systems; waste to energy systems; allied services, including: brake equipment, wheel alignment, tire balancers, tire drangers, and service trucks; rubber recycling technologies; recycled rubber products. **Dates and Locations:** , Fair & Expo Center. **Telecommunication Services:** info@tireindustry.org.

FRANCHISES AND BUSINESS OPPORTUNITIES

20081 ■ Big O Tires
TBC Retail Group
Description: Retail tire and under-car service centers. **No. of Franchise Units:** 392. **No. of Company-Owned Units:** 64. **Founded:** 1962.. **Franchised:** 1982. **Equity Capital Needed:** $100,000 minimum liquidity; $300,000 minimum net worth. **Franchise Fee:** 0-$30,000. **Financial Assistance:** Yes. **Training:** 7-week training program, including classroom and hands-on application in a fully operational retail training store and ongoing support through regional schools, seminars, and clinics.

20082 ■ Canadian Tire Corp., Ltd
2180 Yonge St.
Toronto, ON, Canada M4P 2V8
Ph: (416)480-3647
Fax: (416)480-3480
Co. E-mail: dealers@canadiantire.com
URL: http://corp.canadiantire.ca/EN/JoinOurTeam/RetailOwnership/Pages/AboutCT2.aspx
Description: Retailers of automotive, sports, leisure and home products. **No. of Franchise Units:** 485. **Founded:** 1922.. **Franchised:** 1934. **Equity Capital Needed:** $125,000. **Training:** 6 month Retail Leadership Development Program.

20083 ■ Rent-n-Roll Custom Wheels and Tires—RNR Custom Wheels & Tires
SPF Mgt. Co., LLC
14620 N Nebraska Ave., Bldg. B
Tampa, FL 33613

Ph: (813)977-9800
Fax: (813)978-0534
Description: Custom wheels and tires. **No. of Franchise Units:** 50. **No. of Company-Owned Units:** 8. **Founded:** 1999.. **Franchised:** 2003. **Equity**

Capital Needed: $288,795-$563,475. **Franchise Fee:** $25,000. **Royalty Fee:** 4%. **Financial Assistance:** Third party financing available. **Training:** Available 2 weeks at headquarters, 2 weeks at franchisee's location and ongoing support.

ASSOCIATIONS AND OTHER ORGANIZATIONS

20084 ■ **American Wholesale Marketers Association (AWMA)**
2750 Prosperity Ave., Ste. 530
Fairfax, VA 22031
Ph: (703)208-3358
Free: 800-482-2962
Fax: (703)573-5738
Co. E-mail: info@awmanet.org
URL: http://www.awmanet.org
Contact: Scott Ramminger, President
E-mail: scottr@awmanet.org
Description: Represents the interests of distributors of convenience-related products. Its members include wholesalers, retailers, manufacturers, brokers and allied organizations from across the U.S. and abroad. Programs include strong legislative representation in Washington and a broad spectrum of targeted education, business and information services. Sponsors the country's largest show for candy and convenience related products in conjunction with its semi-annual convention. **Founded:** 1991. **Publications:** *Buying Guide and Membership Directory* (Annual); *Convenience Distribution: AWMA's Magazine for Candy, Tobacco, Grocery, Foodservice and General Merchandiser Marketers*; *Quick Topics Newsletter*, *Convenience Distribution*; *Distribution Channels Buying Guide & AWMA Membership Directory* (Monthly). **Educational Activities:** Summit and Business Exchange (Annual); The Convenience Distributor Conference & Expo (Annual); Real Deal Expo (Annual); The AWMA Show - The Convenience Distributor Conference and Expo (Annual). **Awards:** Hall of Fame, Deans (Annual).

20085 ■ **International Premium Cigar and Pipe Retailers (IPCPR)**
No. 4 Bradley Park Ct., Ste. 2-H
Columbus, GA 31904-3637
Ph: (706)494-1143
Fax: (706)494-1893
Co. E-mail: info@ipcpr.org
URL: http://www.rtda.org
Description: Retailers of legal tobacco products and related items. Conducts marketing and merchandising programs. **Founded:** 1932. **Publications:** *Tobacco Retailers' Almanac* (Annual).

20086 ■ **Tobacco Merchants Association (TMA)**
PO Box 8019
Princeton, NJ 08543-8019
Ph: (609)275-4900
Fax: (609)275-8379
Co. E-mail: tma@tma.org
URL: http://www.tma.org
Contact: Farrell Delman, President
Description: Manufacturers of tobacco products, leaf dealers, suppliers, distributors, and others related to the tobacco industry. Maintains records of trademarks. **Founded:** 1915. **Publications:** *Executive Summary* (Weekly); *Issues Monitor* (Biennial); *Legis-*

lative Bulletin (Biweekly); *Tobacco Barometer* (Monthly); *Tobacco Trade Barometer* (Monthly); *Tobacco Weekly* (Weekly); *World Alert* (Weekly). **Educational Activities:** Tobacco International (Annual). **Awards:** TMA Award (Semiannual).

20087 ■ **Tobacconists' Association of America (TAA)**
PO Box 81152
Conyers, GA 30013-9152
Ph: (770)597-6264
Co. E-mail: t-a-a@t-a-a.us
URL: http://www.t-a-a.com
Description: Retail tobacco merchants, usually one firm to an area or city, selling quality pipes, lighters, cigars, smokers, requisites, and personally blended tobaccos. **Founded:** 1968.

REFERENCE WORKS

20088 ■ *"Roll Your Own" in Business North Carolina (Vol. 28, March 2008, No. 3, pp. 66)*
Pub: Business North Carolina
Ed: Amanda Parry. **Description:** Profile of U.S. Flue-Cured Tobacco Growers who process tobacco and make cigarettes. Details of the program are outlined.

20089 ■ *"San Marcos May Ban Smoking" in Austin Business Journal (Vol. 31, June 17, 2011, No. 15, pp. 1)*
Pub: American City Business Journals Inc.
Ed: Vicky Garza. **Description:** The City Council of San Marcos, Texas will hold a public hearing regarding a proposed citywide smoking ban. The city is moving towards the smoking ban because it appears a statewide ban may be enacted.

20090 ■ *"Smoke Signals: Johnny Drake On What To Expect In a Fine Cigar" in Black Enterprise (Vol. 38, December 2007, No. 5, pp. 195)*
Pub: Earl G. Graves Publishing Co. Inc.
Ed: Alan Hughes. **Description:** Profile of Johnny Drake, co-owner of the retail tobacco company Renaissance Cigar Emporium. According to the Retail Tobacco Dealers of America, 320 million handmade cigars are sold in the U.S. annually.

20091 ■ *"What's Working Now: In Providing Jobs for North Carolinians" in Business North Carolina (Vol. 28, February 2008, No. 2, pp. 16)*
Pub: Business North Carolina
Ed: Edward Martin, Frank Maley. **Description:** Individuals previously employed in the furniture, tobacco, or textile manufacturing sectors have gone back to school to be trained in new sectors in the area such as life sciences, finances and other emerging sectors.

TRADE PERIODICALS

20092 ■ *Cigar Aficionado*
Pub: M. Shanken Communications Inc.
Contact: Stephen Senatore, Director
E-mail: ssenatore@mshanken.com
URL(s): www.cigaraficionado.com/Cigar/Home. **Released:** Bimonthly **Price:** $19.95, Individuals; $35.95,

Two years; $38, Canada; $70, Canada two years; $56, Other countries; $102, Other countries 2 years.

20093 ■ *Convenience Distribution: AWMA's Magazine for Candy, Tobacco, Grocery, Foodservice and General Merchandiser Marketers*
Pub: American Wholesale Marketers Association
Contact: Scott Ramminger, President
E-mail: scottr@awmanet.org
URL(s): www.awmanet.org/dc_latest. **Ed:** Joan Fay. **Released:** 10/yr. **Price:** $36, Individuals domestic; $66, Other countries.

20094 ■ *TMA Issues Monitor*
Pub: Tobacco Merchants Association of the U.S. Inc.
Ed: Darryl Jayson, Editor. **Released:** Semiannual. **Price:** Included in membership. **Description:** Tracks issues and trends affecting the tobacco industry worldwide. Covers import and export news, related legislation, production and marketing information, and statistics.

20095 ■ *TMA Legislative Bulletin*
Pub: Tobacco Merchants Association of the U.S. Inc.
Ed: Kay Carmello, Editor. **Released:** Biweekly. **Price:** Included in membership. **Description:** Reports on federal and state legislation and regulations affecting the tobacco industry.

20096 ■ *TMA Tobacco Weekly*
Pub: Tobacco Merchants Association of the U.S. Inc.
Ed: David Goldstein, Editor. **Released:** Weekly. **Price:** Included in membership. **Description:** Summarizes key domestic tobacco industry issues as they develop at the federal, state, and local levels. Covers excise taxes, marketing and distribution, corporate finance, leaf and trade, health campaigns, and product liability.

20097 ■ *TMA Trademark Report*
Pub: Tobacco Merchants Association of the U.S. Inc.
Ed: Kathy McCormick, Editor. **Released:** Monthly. **Price:** Included in membership. **Description:** Tracks tobacco product and tobacco accessory trademarks and brand names from test markets through registration. Covers renewals and cancellations.

20098 ■ *TMA World Alert*
Pub: Tobacco Merchants Association of the U.S. Inc.
Ed: Marketa Stoy, Editor. **Released:** Weekly. **Price:** Included in membership. **Description:** Covers tobacco industry and corporate issues worldwide, on a country-by-country basis, including corporate finance, excise taxes, marketing and distribution developments, leaf and trade, and health campaigns.

20099 ■ *Tobacco Barometer: Cigarettes, Cigars, Smoking Tobacco, Chewing Tobacco and Snuff*
Pub: Tobacco Merchants Association of the U.S. Inc.
Ed: Mark Schoenfeld, Editor. **Released:** Quarterly. **Price:** Included in membership. **Description:** Lists statistics on quarterly and cumulative production and sales of smoking tobacco, chewing tobacco, and snuff. Makes comparisons with the same period of the previous year, and has an analysis of current

developments and trends. Recurring features include legislative and labor activities which affect the prices of these products.

20100 ■ Tobacco Industry Litigation Reporter
Pub: Thomson West
Contact: Kathryn M. Downing, President
Ed: Kenneth Bradley, Esq., Editor, tomh@andrews-pub.com. **Released:** Monthly. **Price:** $2088.96. **Description:** Monitors major litigation brought against the tobacco industry. Reports on discovery, protective orders, and cross-claims in asbestos cases and on the preemption provision of the Federal Cigarette Labeling and Advertising Act.

20101 ■ Tobacco International
Pub: Lockwood Publications Inc.
Contact: Robert M. Lockwood, President
E-mail: robertlockwoodsr@lockwoodpublications.com
URL(s): www.tobaccointernational.com/. **Ed:** Edward E. Ted Hoyt, III. **Released:** Monthly **Price:** $49, Individuals; $74, Two years; $129, Other countries air mail; $199, Other countries air mail, 2 years.

20102 ■ Tobacco Trade Barometer: Imports
Pub: Tobacco Merchants Association of the U.S. Inc.
Ed: Mark Schoenfeld, Editor. **Released:** Monthly. **Price:** Included in membership. **Description:** Carries statistics on imports of tobacco leaf and tobacco products. Gives tables on type, by country of origin, with quantities being brought in and their values. Quantity is given by weight and in pieces; value in U.S. dollars.

20103 ■ US Tobacco Trade Barometer: Exports
Pub: Tobacco Merchants Association of the U.S. Inc.
Ed: Mark Schoenfeld, Editor. **Released:** Monthly. **Price:** Included in membership. **Description:** Carries statistics on exports of tobacco and tobacco products. Gives listings by country of destination, with quantities and values exported in the current month, in the year to date, and in comparison with previous periods.

VIDEOCASSETTES/ AUDIOCASSETTES

20104 ■ All You Need to Know About Cigars!
Tapeworm Video Distributors
25876 The Old Road #141
Stevenson Ranch, CA 91381
Ph: (661)257-4904
Fax: (661)257-4820
Co. E-mail: sales@tapeworm.com
URL: http://www.tapeworm.com
Released: 19??. **Price:** $19.95. **Description:** Covers the history of cigars, the cigar lifestyle, and advice for both novices and connoisseurs. **Availability:** VHS.

20105 ■ But a Good Cigar Is a Smoke!
Tapeworm Video Distributors
25876 The Old Road #141
Stevenson Ranch, CA 91381
Ph: (661)257-4904
Fax: (661)257-4820
Co. E-mail: sales@tapeworm.com
URL: http://www.tapeworm.com
Released: 1997. **Price:** $14.95. **Description:** Presents an in depth look at every aspect of cigars. **Availability:** VHS.

20106 ■ Cigars 101
ELN Communications
155 North 35th St.
Seattle, WA 98103
Ph: (206)256-0420
Fax: (206)256-0419
Co. E-mail: eln@eln.com
URL: http://www.eln.com
Released: 19??. **Price:** $19.95. **Description:** Provides how-to instruction in cutting, selecting, storing, and smoking cigars. **Availability:** VHS.

20107 ■ The Havana: Cigar of Connoisseurs
Janson Media
88 Semmens Rd.
Harrington Park, NJ 07640

Ph: (201)784-8488
Free: 800-818-4066
Fax: (201)784-3993
Co. E-mail: betsy@janson.com
URL: http://www.janson.com
Contact: Stephen Janson, President
Released: 19??. **Price:** $24.95. **Description:** Documents the history and tradition of Cuban Havana cigars. **Availability:** VHS; DVD.

20108 ■ Smoke in Your Eyes
Tapeworm Video Distributors
25876 The Old Road #141
Stevenson Ranch, CA 91381
Ph: (661)257-4904
Fax: (661)257-4820
Co. E-mail: sales@tapeworm.com
URL: http://www.tapeworm.com
Released: 19??. **Price:** $24.95. **Description:** Presents Vuelto Abajo, a prosperous tobacco growing region, its cigar factories, and personal interviews with cigar rollers. **Availability:** VHS.

FRANCHISES AND BUSINESS OPPORTUNITIES

20109 ■ Shefield Gourmet
2265 W Railway St.
Abbotsford, BC, Canada V2S 2E3
Ph: (604)859-1014
Fax: (604)859-1711
Description: Tobacco products, coffees, and gifts. **No. of Franchise Units:** 13. **Founded:** 1996.. **Franchised:** 1996. **Equity Capital Needed:** $70,000-$180,000 inventory. **Franchise Fee:** $25,000. **Training:** Yes.

LIBRARIES

20110 ■ Imperial Tobacco Ltd. - Corporate Information Center
3711 St. Antoine St.
Montreal, QC, Canada H4C 3P6
Ph: (514)932-6161
Fax: (514)932-0363
Co. E-mail: rdumais@itl.ca
Contact: Robin Dumais, Associate
Scope: Tobacco, management, science. **Services:** Interlibrary loan. **Founded:** 1938. **Holdings:** 6000 books; 10,000 pamphlets; 20 VF drawers of photographs and patents. **Subscriptions:** 360 journals and other serials.

20111 ■ Lorillard Tobacco Company Library
Box 21688
Greensboro, NC 27420-1688
Ph: (336)335-6896
Fax: (336)335-6640
Co. E-mail: lsklandanowski@lortobco.com
Contact: Connie Childers
Scope: Tobacco products and manufacturing, tobacco chemistry. **Services:** Interlibrary loan; copying; Library open to the public by appointment. **Founded:** 1959. **Holdings:** 4200 books; 5700 bound periodical volumes; 1000 boxes of unbound periodicals. **Subscriptions:** 140 journals and other serials.

20112 ■ New York Public Library - The Research Libraries - Humanities and Social Sciences Library - Arents Tobacco Collection
Brooke Russell Astor Reading Room, 3rd Fl., Rm. 328
5th Ave. and 42nd St.
New York, NY 10018-2788
Ph: (212)642-0110
Fax: (212)302-4815
Co. E-mail: rarebook@nypl.org
URL: http://www.nypl.org/locations/schwarzman/arents-collection
Contact: Sarah Augusta Dickson, Curator
Scope: Tobacco, herbals, history, medicine, law, manufacture, marketing; smoking and health. **Services:** Open to qualified researchers by card of admission secured in Special Collections Office. **Founded:** 1944. **Holdings:** 13,000 books and manuscripts; 150,000 cards and pieces of ephemera. **Subscriptions:** 10 journals and other serials.

20113 ■ Philip Morris Corporate Library
100 Park Ave., 17th Fl.
New York, NY 10017
Ph: (917)663-3863
Fax: (917)663-5317
Co. E-mail: david.deschenes@us.pm.com
Contact: David Deschenes, Director
Scope: Business, marketing, finance, tobacco. **Services:** Library not open to the public. **Holdings:** 2000 books; microfiche; tobacco trade literature. **Subscriptions:** 160 journals and other serials; 20 newspapers.

20114 ■ PM USA Library—Philip Morris USA - Library.
6601 W. Broad St.
Richmond, VA 23261
Ph: (804)484-8897
Free: 800-343-0975
URL: http://www.philipmorrisusa.com/en/cms/Home/default.aspx
Contact: Cornita Winston, Manager
Scope: Tobacco, chemistry, biochemistry, botany, physics, plant physiology. **Services:** Interlibrary loan. **Founded:** 1959. **Holdings:** 30,000 books; 10,000 bound periodical volumes; 350 AV programs; 5000 microfiche; 40 VF drawers of clippings; 7500 reels of microfilm of periodicals. **Subscriptions:** 300 journals and other serials; 6 newspapers.

20115 ■ Tobacco Merchants Association of the U.S. - Howard S. Cullman Library
PO Box 8019
Princeton, NJ 08543-8019
Ph: (609)275-4900
Fax: (609)275-8379
Co. E-mail: judith@tma.org
URL: http://www.tma.org/tmalive/FrmMain
Contact: Farrell Delman, President
Scope: Tobacco industry and products. **Services:** Copying; Library open to the public for reference use only by appointment only. **Founded:** 1915. **Holdings:** 2000 books; 296 bound periodical volumes; 150 VF drawers of pamphlets, archives, and clippings; 18 shelves of government reports; 135 drawers of trademark file cards; 25 drawers of brand file cards. **Subscriptions:** 99 journals and other serials; 10 newspapers.

20116 ■ U.S. Bureau of Alcohol, Tobacco, Firearms and Explosives Reference Library
99 New York Ave., NE
Washington, DC 20226
Ph: (202)927-7890
Fax: (202)927-8883
Co. E-mail: atfmail@atf.gov
URL: http://www.atf.gov
Contact: Vicki R. Herrmann, Librarian
Scope: Alcohol, tobacco, firearms, explosives. **Services:** Interlibrary loan; copying; SDI; reading room open to the public by appointment; archives open to the public with written permission. **Founded:** 1979. **Holdings:** 750 books; 100 bound periodical volumes; 1000 lin.ft. of indexed hearings, projects, tasks, and correspondence; 25 drawers of microfiche of historical documents; CD-ROMs. **Subscriptions:** 50 journals and other serials. **Telecommunication Services:** atftips@atf.gov; webmaster@atf.gov.

20117 ■ U.S. Bureau of Alcohol, Tobacco and Firearms - National Laboratory Center Library
6000 Ammendale Rd.
Beltsville, MD 20705-1250
Ph: (202)648-6074
Fax: (301)315-0519
Co. E-mail: susan.barned@atf.gov
URL: http://www.atf.gov/
Contact: Sue Wright, Librarian
URL(s): www.atf.gov/contact/service-centers/. **Scope:** Alcohol, analytical techniques, forensic sciences, firearms, tobacco, explosives. **Services:** Library not open to the public. **Founded:** 1972. **Holdings:** 5700 books; 4000 bound periodical volumes; 200 total journal titles; government documents; archives. **Subscriptions:** 42 journals and other serials. **Telecommunication Services:** susan.barned@usdoj.gov.

START-UP INFORMATION

20118 ■ *The 100 Best Businesses to Start When You Don't Want To Work Hard Anymore*

Pub: Career Press Inc.

Ed: Lisa Rogak. **Price:** $16.99. **Description:** Author helps burned-out workers envision a new future as a small business owner. Systems analysis, adventure travel outfitting, bookkeeping, food delivery, furniture making, and software development are among the industries examined.

20119 ■ *"Business Start-Up a Learning Experience for Young Bellingham Entrepreneur" in Bellingham Herald (July 18, 2010)*

Pub: Bellingham Herald

Ed: Dave Gallagher. **Description:** Profile of 21-year-old entrepreneur, Chase Larabee, who developed an online program that helps airport fixed-based operators handle refueling, hotel and transportation reservations and other requests from private airplane pilots.

20120 ■ *Design and Launch an Online Travel Business in a Week*

Pub: Entrepreneur Press

Contact: Perlman Neil, President

Ed: Charlene Davis. **Released:** May 1, 2009. **Price:** $17.95. **Description:** Guide providing techniques and professional advice for starting an online travel business. Tips are given to build a Website, find qualified providers and to set up a payment system.

20121 ■ *Home-Based Travel Agent, 5th Edition*

Pub: The Intrepid Traveler

Ed: Kelly Monaghan. **Released:** March 2006. **Price:** $59.95. **Description:** Advice for starting and running a home-based travel agency is given.

20122 ■ *"Online Fortunes" in Small Business Opportunities (Fall 2008)*

Pub: Entrepreneur Media Inc.

Description: Fifty hot, e-commerce enterprises for the aspiring entrepreneur to consider are featured; virtual assistants, marketing services, party planning, travel services, researching, web design and development, importing as well as creating an online store are among the businesses featured.

ASSOCIATIONS AND OTHER ORGANIZATIONS

20123 ■ *ACTA Voyage*
Released: Quarterly

20124 ■ **Adventure Travel Trade Association (ATTA)**
601 Union St., 42nd Fl.
Seattle, WA 98101
Ph: (360)805-3131

Fax: (360)805-0649
Co. E-mail: info@adventuretravel.biz
URL: http://www.adventuretravel.biz
Contact: Mr. Shannon Stowell, President
Description: Serves the adventure travel industry. Aims to grow the adventure travel industry overall and to help build up its member organizations. Provides exposure, marketing expertise, education, research, and discount to its members. **Founded:** 1990. **Educational Activities:** Adventure Travel World Summit (Annual).

20125 ■ **Association of Canadian Travel Agencies (ACTA)—Association Canadienne des Agences de Voyages**
2560 Matheson Blvd. E, Ste. 328
Mississauga, ON, Canada L4W 4Y9
Ph: (905)282-9294
Free: 888-257-2282
Fax: (905)282-9826
Co. E-mail: actacan@acta.ca
URL: http://www.acta.ca
Contact: David McCaig, President
Description: Travel agents, tour operators, airlines, hotels, destination marketing organizations, cruise and rail lines, and automobile rental companies in Canada. Ensures consumers have professional and meaningful travel counseling by providing effective leadership in advocacy, public relations, research and education on behalf of the retail travel industry in Canada. **Founded:** 1977.

20126 ■ **Canadian Tourism Research Institute (CTRI)**
c/o The Conference Board of Canada
255 Smyth Rd.
Ottawa, ON, Canada K1H 8M7
Ph: (613)526-3280
Free: 866-711-2262
Fax: (613)526-4857
Co. E-mail: ctri@conferenceboard.ca
URL: http://www.conferenceboard.ca/topics/economics/CTRI/default.aspx
Contact: Daniel Muzyka, President
Description: Represents travel and tourism businesses. Seeks to increase understanding of the needs and interests of tourists. Serves as a clearinghouse on tourism in Canada. Sponsors commercial tourism research.

20127 ■ **International Association of Tour Managers - North American Region (IATM North America)**
24 Blevins Rd.
Kerhonkson, NY 12446-1302
Ph: (212)208-6800
Fax: (212)208-6800
Co. E-mail: chairman@tourmanager.org
URL: http://www.tourmanager.org
Contact: Scott McScott, Chairman
Description: Works to maintain the highest possible standards of tour management; guarantee excellence of performance; educate the travel world on the role of the tour manager (also referred to as tour director, tour escort, or tour leader) in the successful comple-

tion of the tour itinerary and in bringing business to related industries. Represents members in influencing legislation and advising on travel policy. Trains tour managers to plan, research, and lead tours to specific domestic and foreign destinations; operates Advisory Board in Professional Tour Management; offers placement service; conducts Professional travel agents, travel wholesalers, airlines, hotel associations, shipping lines, tourist organizations, restaurants, shops, and entertainment organizations Tour Management International Certificate Program. **Founded:** 1962. **Publications:** *The Professional Tour Manager* (Quarterly).

20128 ■ **The International Ecotourism Society (TIES)**
PO Box 96503
Washington, DC 20090-6503
Ph: (202)506-5033
Fax: (202)789-7279
Co. E-mail: info@ecotourism.org
URL: http://www.ecotourism.org
Contact: Dr. Kelly S. Bricker, Chairperson

Description: Works to generate and disseminate information about ecotourism. Represents members from academics, consultants, conservation professionals and organizations, governments, architects, tour operators, lodge owners and managers, general development experts, and ecotourists in more than 80 countries. Provides guidelines and standards, training, technical assistance, research and publications to foster sound ecotourism development. **Founded:** 1990. **Publications:** *TIES eNewsletter*; *Ecotourism: An Annotated Bibliography for Planners and Managers*; *The Environmental Tourist: An Ecotourism Revolution*; *Tourism, Ecotourism, and Protected Areas*. **Awards:** TIES Lifetime Achievement Award.

20129 ■ **International Galapagos Tour Operators Association (IGTOA)**
PO Box 1713
Lolo, MT 59847
Co. E-mail: exd@igtoa.org
URL: http://www.igtoa.org
Contact: Matt Kareus, Executive Director

Description: Individuals and corporations conducting tours to the Galapagos Islands; educational and scientific institutions with an interest in the Islands and their ecosystems. Promotes tourism with the lowest possible environmental impact; seeks to preserve the unique ecosystems and species indigenous to the Galapagos Islands. Raises funds to support environmental protection initiatives; serves as a clearinghouse on low-impact nature tourism; facilitates communication and cooperation among members. **Founded:** 1997. **Awards:** Becario (Annual).

20130 ■ **National Tour Association (NTA)**
101 Prosperous Pl., Ste. 350
Lexington, KY 40509
Ph: (859)226-4444
Free: 800-682-8886

Fax: (859)226-4414
Co. E-mail: questions@ntastaff.com
URL: http://www.ntaonline.com
Contact: Jim Reddekopp, Jr., Chief Executive Officer
Description: Operators of group tours and packaged travel; travel industry-related companies providing services/facilities to tour operators (hotels, attractions, restaurants); and destination marketing organizations such as convention and visitor bureaus, and state tourism departments. Seeks to: maintain a code of ethical standards within the tour industry; develop and increase public interest in packaged travel. Represents members before governmental bodies and agencies. Conducts research and educational programs. **Scope:** travel and tour. **Founded:** 1951. **Subscriptions:** archival material reports. **Publications:** *Courier* (Monthly); *NTA Tuesday* (Monthly). **Awards:** Bob Everidge Lifetime Achievement Award (Annual); Volunteer of the Year (Annual).

20131 ■ *RVC Directory*
116 Lisgar St., Ste. 600
Ottawa, ON, Canada K2P 0C2
Ph: (613)238-3883
Co. E-mail: info@tiac.travel
URL: http://www.tiac.travel
Contact: David F. Goldstein, President
Released: Annual **Price:** free for members.

20132 ■ *TIAC Talk*
116 Lisgar St., Ste. 600
Ottawa, ON, Canada K2P 0C2
Ph: (613)238-3883
Co. E-mail: info@tiac.travel
URL: http://www.tiac.travel
Contact: David F. Goldstein, President
Released: Weekly **Price:** included in membership dues.

20133 ■ *TIAC Talk Issue Focus*
116 Lisgar St., Ste. 600
Ottawa, ON, Canada K2P 0C2
Ph: (613)238-3883
Co. E-mail: info@tiac.travel
URL: http://www.tiac.travel
Contact: David F. Goldstein, President
Released: Periodic

20134 ■ **Tourism Industry Association of Canada (TIAC)—Association de L'Industrie Touristique du Canada**
116 Lisgar St., Ste. 600
Ottawa, ON, Canada K2P 0C2
Ph: (613)238-3883
Co. E-mail: info@tiac.travel
URL: http://www.tiac.travel
Contact: David F. Goldstein, President
Description: Promotes viability of Canada's tourism industries. Serves as a unified voice for the industry in communications with government agencies responsible for tourism and related matters; conducts lobbying activities. **Founded:** 1930. **Publications:** *RVC Directory* (Annual); *TIAC Talk* (Weekly); *TIAC Talk Issue Focus* (Periodic). **Educational Activities:** Canada's Tourism Leadership Summit (Annual). **Awards:** TIAC / Parks Canada Sustainable Tourism Scholarships.

20135 ■ **United States Tour Operators Association (USTOA)**
345 Seventh Ave., Ste. 1801
New York, NY 10001
Ph: (212)599-6599
Fax: (212)599-6744
Co. E-mail: information@ustoa.com
URL: http://www.ustoa.com
Description: Represents wholesale tour operators, common carriers, associations, government agencies, suppliers, purveyors of travel services, trade press, communications media, and public relations and advertising representatives. Encourages and supports professional and financial integrity in tourism. Protects the legitimate interests of the consumer and the retail agent from financial loss from business conducted with members. Provides tour operators with an opportunity to formulate and express an independent industry voice on matters of common interest and self-regulation. Strives to facilitate and

develop travel on a worldwide basis. **Founded:** 1972. **Educational Activities:** United States Tour Operators Association Conference (Annual).

DIRECTORIES OF EDUCATIONAL PROGRAMS

20136 ■ *Directory of Private Accredited Career Schools and Colleges of Technology*
Pub: Accrediting Commission of Career Schools and Colleges of Technology
Contact: Michale S. McComis, Executive Director
Released: On web page. **Price:** Free. **Description:** Covers 3900 accredited post-secondary programs that provide training programs in business, trade, and technical fields, including various small business endeavors. Entries offer school name, address, phone, description of courses, job placement assistance, and requirements for admission. Arrangement is alphabetical.

REFERENCE WORKS

20137 ■ *"2010 Book of Lists" in Business Courier (Vol. 26, December 26, 2009, No. 36, pp. 1)*
Pub: American City Business Journals, Inc.
Description: Rankings of companies and organizations within the business services, education, finance, health care, hospitality and tourism, real estate, and technology industries in the Cincinnati, Ohio-Northern Kentucky area are presented. Rankings are based on sales, business size, or other statistics.

20138 ■ *"B&B Hopes to Appeal to Fiat Execs" in Crain's Detroit Business (Vol. 25, June 15, 2009, No. 24, pp. 21)*
Pub: Crain Communications Inc. - Detroit
Ed: Daniel Duggan. **Description:** Cobblestone Manor, a ten-room bed and breakfast in Auburn Hills, Michigan is hoping to provide rooms for Fiat executives. The owners have been working with travel organizations to promote the castle-like bed and breakfast which appeals to European visitors.

20139 ■ *"Bill Kaneko" in Hawaii Business (Vol. 53, December 2007, No. 6, pp. 32)*
Pub: Hawaii Business Publishing
Ed: David K. Choo. **Description:** Hawaii Institute for Public Affairs chief executive officer and president Bill Kaneko believes that the Hawaiian economy is booming, however, he also asserts that the economy is too focused on tourism and real estate. Kaneko has also realized the that the will of the people is strong while he was helping with the Hawaiian 2050 Sustainability Plan. The difficulties of making a sustainable Hawaii are discussed.

20140 ■ *"The British Aren't Coming" in Crain's Chicago Business (Vol. 34, October 24, 2011, No. 42, pp. 3)*
Pub: Crain Communications Inc.
Ed: Brigid Sweeney. **Description:** In a move to attract tourists back to Chicago, its Convention and Tourism Bureau is marketing in London, England, Mexico, and Canada, but not Germany or France because of budget constraints.

20141 ■ *Cruise Travel--Cruise Calendar Section: The Worldwide Cruise Vacation Magazine*
Contact: Charles Doherty, Editor
URL(s): www.cruisetravelmag.com. **Ed:** Charles Doherty. **Released:** Bimonthly; Three times yearly: April, August, and December. **Price:** $19.97, Individuals per year. **Publication includes:** Listing of cruises by major cruise lines worldwide. **Entries include:** Cruise line company name, name of cruise ship, length of cruise, departure dates, destinations and ports-of-call, price range. **Arrangement:** Classified by cruising area, then port of departure.

20142 ■ *"Cruising In Choppy Water" in The Business Journal-Portland (Vol. 25, August 22, 2008, No. 24, pp. 1)*
Pub: American City Business Journals, Inc.
Ed: Erik Siemers. **Description:** Yacht builder Christensen Shipyards Inc. is experiencing robust business despite the slowing US economy, building four

yachts a year as of 2008. The company expects revenues to hit $90 million and is opening a 500,000-square-foot plant in Tennessee.

20143 ■ *"DePaul To Train Hotel Leaders" in Chicago Tribune (September 22, 2008)*
Pub: McClatchy-Tribune Information Services
Ed: Kathy Bergen. **Description:** With help from a $7.5 million grant from the Conrad N. Hilton Foundation, DePaul University will dramatically expand its role as a training ground for the tourism-industry with the opening of a School of Hospitality.

20144 ■ *"Destination Africa: A Look at How Tourism Could Change the Face and Economics of Africa" in Black Enterprise (February 2008)*
Pub: Earl G. Graves Publishing Co. Inc.
Ed: Sonia Alleyne. **Description:** Countries in Africa are experiencing high rates of growth in tourism than the worldwide average. Statistical data included.

20145 ■ *Double or Nothing: How Two Friends Risked It All to Buy One of Las Vegas' Legendary Casinos*
Pub: HarperBusiness
Ed: Tom Breitling, with Cal Fussman. **Released:** March 2008. **Price:** $24.95. **Description:** Founders of a successful Internet travel agency share their experience from startup to selling the company.

20146 ■ *"Doubletree Finds a Niche for Giving Back" in Hotel and Motel Management (Vol. 225, July 2010, No. 8, pp. 6)*
Pub: Questex Media Group Inc.
Ed: Paul J. Heney. **Description:** Profile of Doubletree Hotel's community outreach programs that help employee volunteers work to educate children and the public about issues important to the environment.

20147 ■ *Driving With No Brakes: How a Bunch of Hooligans Built the Best Travel Company in the World*
Pub: Grand Circle Corporation
Ed: Alan and Harriet Lewis. **Price:** $19.95. **Description:** Inspirational book about how two courageous leaders built a remarkable company that can thrive in change and succeed in an unpredictable world. Important lessons for any business leader trying to create value in the 21st Century are included.

20148 ■ *"Eco-Preneuring" in Small Business Opportunities (Jan. 2008)*
Pub: Harris Publications Inc.
Description: Iceland Naturally is a joint marketing effort among tourism and business interests hoping to increase demand for Icelandic products including frozen seafood, bottled water, agriculture, and tourism in North America.

20149 ■ *"Eco-Preneuring" in Small Business Opportunities (July 2008)*
Pub: Entrepreneur Media Inc.
Ed: Mary C. Pearl. **Description:** Profile of Wildlife Trust, a rapidly growing global organization dedicated to innovative conservation science linking health and ecology. With partners in nearly twenty countries, Wildlife Trust draws on global strengths in order to respond to well-defined local needs. In the Dominican Republic, they are working with the community and local biologists in order to restore fishing and create jobs in the field of ecotourism.

20150 ■ *"Get Wrecked" in Canadian Business (Vol. 80, November 19, 2007, No. 23, pp. S13)*
Pub: Rogers Media
Ed: Thomas Watson. **Description:** Key West economy has benefited from wrecks as salvaging lost items became a lucrative business. The USAFS General Hoyt S. Vanderberg is expected to be sunk and will provide a good opportunity for wreck dives. The trends in Key West tourism are evaluated.

20151 ■ *"Goldbelt Inc.: Targeting Shareholder Development" in Alaska Business Monthly (Vol. 27, October 2011, No. 10, pp. 108)*
Pub: Alaska Business Publishing Company
Ed: Tracy Kalytiak. **Description:** Profile of Goldbelt Inc., the company that has changed its original focus of timber to real estate to tourism and then to government contracting opportunities.

20152 ■ *"Gov. Kasich to Put DOD On Short Leash"* in Business Courier (Vol. 27, November 26, 2010, No. 30, pp. 1)
Pub: Business Courier
Ed: Dan Monk. **Description:** Ohio Governor-elect John Kasich proposed the privatization of the Ohio Department of Development in favor of a nonprofit corporation called JobsOhio. Kasich believes that the department has lost its focus by adding to its mission issues such as energy efficiency and tourism.

20153 ■ *A Guide to College Programs in Hospitality, Tourism, & Culinary Arts*
Pub: International Council on Hotel, Restaurant, and Institutional Education
Contact: Susan Fournier, President
E-mail: susan.fournier@ritz.edu
URL(s): www.chrie.org. **Released:** Biennial; latest edition 9th. **Price:** $29.95, Members CD-ROM; $59.95, Nonmembers CD-ROM; $149.95, Members hardbound; $199.95, Nonmembers hardbound. **Covers:** About 500 secondary and technical institutes, colleges, and universities; international coverage. **Entries include:** School name, address, areas of study, degrees offered, name and title of contact, program description, financial aid information, tuition and fees, admission and graduation requirements. **Arrangement:** Alphabetical, geographical, specialization.

20154 ■ *"Happy Trails: RV Franchiser Gives Road Traveling Enthusiasts a Lift"* in Black Enterprise (Vol. 38, July 2008, No. 12, pp. 47)
Pub: Earl G. Graves Publishing Co. Inc.
Ed: Tamara E. Holmes. **Description:** Overview of Bates International Motor Home Rental Systems Inc., a growing franchise that gives RV owners the chance to rent out their big-ticket purchases to others when they are not using them; Sandra Williams Bate launched the company as a franchise in July 1997 and now has a fleet of 30 franchises across the country. She expects the company to reach 2.2 million for 2008 due to a marketing initiative that will expand the company's presence.

20155 ■ *Heads in Beds*
Pub: Prentice Hall PTR
Ed: Ivo Raza. **Released:** May 28, 2004. **Description:** Advice is given to help build brands, generate sales and grow profits through marketing for any hospitality or tourism business.

20156 ■ *"Hola and Aloha"* in Hawaii Business (Vol. 53, December 2007, No. 6, pp. 131)
Pub: Hawaii Business Publishing
Ed: Jason Ubay. **Description:** Juan Carlos Bianchetti is the trilingual owner of Ole Tours Hawaii, a travel wholesaler that targets Portuguese and Spanish-speaking visitors. The competition for American and Japanese tourists is already tight, which is why Bianchetti opted to target a different segment of the Hawaii tourism market. Plans for the company's expansion in Kauai, Brazil, and Argentina, are mentioned.

20157 ■ *"Hotels Get a Fill-Up"* in Crain's Detroit Business (Vol. 25, June 1, 2009, No. 22, pp. 1)
Pub: Crain Communications Inc. - Detroit
Ed: Daniel Duggan. **Description:** Hot Rod Power Tour will have a $1 million economic impact on the area when it arrives in June 2009; the tour will bring 3,500 out-of-state custom vehicles to the event, whose owners will be needing hotel rooms.

20158 ■ *"Ill Winds; Cuba's Economy"* in The Economist (Vol. 390, January 3, 2009, No. 8612, pp. 20)
Pub: The Economist Newspaper Inc.
Description: Cuba's long-term economic prospects remain poor with the economy forecasted to grow only 4.3 percent for the year, about half of the original forecast, due in part to Hurricane Gustav which caused $10 billion in damage and disrupted the food-supply network and devastated farms across the region; President Raul Castro made raising agricultural production a national priority and the rise in global commodity prices hit the country hard. The only bright spot has been the rise in tourism which is up 9.3 percent over 2007.

20159 ■ *"Indigenous Tourism Operators"* in International Journal of Entrepreneurship and Small Business (Vol. 10, July 6, 2010, No. 4)
Pub: Publishers Communication Group
Ed: Andrews Cardow, Peter Wiltshier. **Description:** Emergent enthusiasm for tourism as a savior for economic development in the Chatham Islands of New Zealand is highlighted.

20160 ■ *JAX FAX--Travel Marketing Magazine*
Pub: Jet Airtransport Exchange Inc.
Contact: Chantal Guillou-Brennan, Manager
E-mail: chantal@jaxfax.com
URL(s): www.jaxfaxmagazine.com. **Released:** Monthly **Price:** $5, per copy; $15, per year; $12, per year group rate (5 or more); $3, back issues; $38, Canada and Mexico per year. **Covers:** over 6,000 specific scheduled and charter flights and tours to more than 80 destinations worldwide. **Entries include:** Date of flight or tour, city of departure, destination, minimum and maximum prices, operator or wholesaler identification; contact name, address, phone, telex, telefax, commission rates. **Database includes:** Interviews, promotion and special interest features, editorials, and news about cruises, car rentals, motorcoach touring, flight and tour operations, destinations, etc. **Arrangement:** Geographical by destination. **Indexes:** Destination.

20161 ■ *"Making Visitors Out Of Listeners"* in Hawaii Business (Vol. 54, July 2008, No. 1, pp. 18)
Pub: Hawaii Business Publishing
Ed: Casey Chin. **Description:** Japanese workers are subscribing to the Official Hawaii Podcast in iTunes, which offers a free 20-minute, Japanese-language audio content on different topics, such as dining reviews and music from local artists. The concept is a way to attract Japanese travelers to come to Hawaii.

20162 ■ *"Marathon Money"* in Hawaii Business (Vol. 53, December 2007, No. 6, pp. 127)
Pub: Hawaii Business Publishing
Ed: Jolyn Okimoto Rosa. **Description:** Discusses the effects of the Honolulu Marathon on small businesses' sales. The Running Room, for instance, experience growth in sales starting from the training season up to the end of the race, as a surge of Hawaiian residents and tourists come into the store for items such as running shoes and blister kits. The marathon's impact on Hawaii's tourism is examined as well.

20163 ■ *"The Next Waive"* in Hawaii Business (Vol. 53, January 2008, No. 7, pp. 27)
Pub: Hawaii Business Publishing
Ed: Cathy S. Cruz-George. **Description:** Only 40,000 Koreans took a visit to Hawaii in 2007, a decline from the pre-September averages of 123,000 visits. The number of Korean visitors in Hawaii could increase if the visa waiver proposal is passed. Efforts to improve Hawaiian tourism are presented.

20164 ■ *OAG Business Travel Planner: The Official Lodging Directory of the American Hotel & Motel Association*
Pub: Reed Travel Group OAG Travel Services Div.
URL(s): www.oag.com. **Released:** Quarterly **Covers:** 14,500 destination cities, military installations (U.S. only), and colleges and universities in North America; over 78,000 hotels and motels; calendar of events; city, state or province, and national tourist offices; tour operators; car rental agencies; airlines and charter air taxi firms, and airport limousine services; consulates and missions of foreign countries in North America; United States foreign service offices; hotel and motel systems, and toll free reservations services; airport club locations, frequent flyer and frequent guest information. **Entries include:** For destinations--Place name, airport name and code or note on nearest air service; entries for larger cities include convention facilities, hotel name, address, phone, rates, location, number of meeting rooms, fax; whether member of the American Hotel and Motel Association. For calendar of events--Date, name and location of event, and names, addresses, and phone numbers of state and local tourism agen-

cies. Separate toll-free section for hotel/motel systems and travel-related firms. Other listings include company or office name, address, phone. **Database includes:** Maps of city centers with hotel locations; airport diagrams, and metropolitan resort area maps; attractions; convention facilities. **Arrangement:** Primarily geographical.

20165 ■ *OAG Travel Planner European Edition*
Pub: Official Airline Guides
Contact: Alan Glass, Chief Executive Officer
URL(s): www.oag.com. **Released:** Quarterly **Price:** $632, Individuals Online; $705, Individuals CD. **Covers:** Over 14,000 destination cities in Europe; 16,923 hotels; hotel chains and reservations services; calendars of events; city, regional, and national tourist offices; airline reservation numbers; car rental agencies; ground transportation information; U.S. military installations; consulates and missions of foreign countries in the United States and Canada; airport, ground, and rail services. **Entries include:** Section for a country begins with climate, currency, documentary requirements, consulate, and other information; holiday and public event calendar for following six months; list of the country's tourist offices at home and abroad. For individual destinations--Place name, name and mileage from nearest airport, dialing code for each city; hotel name, address, phone, fax, telex, postal number, room rates, number of rooms, and quality rating, where applicable. **Database includes:** City and country maps; airport diagrams. **Arrangement:** Geographical.

20166 ■ *"Orbitz Adds Parent Panel"* in Marketing to Women (Vol. 21, March 2008, No. 3, pp. 5)
Pub: EPM Communications Inc.
Contact: Ira Mayer, President
E-mail: imayer@epmcom.com
Description: Orbitz introduces the Orbitz Parent Panel in an attempt to better connect with traveling families.

20167 ■ *"The Personal Touch: Entrepreneur Turns Good Taste, Love of Luxury Into Lucrative Venture"* in Black Enterprise (October 2007)
Pub: Earl G. Graves Publishing Co. Inc.
Ed: Tamara E. Holmes. **Description:** Profile of Chaka Fattah Jr. who turned his taste for luxurious things into a successful luxury travel and concierge service catering to business owners, corporate executives, athletes, and entertainers.

20168 ■ *"Plans for $160M Condo Resort in Wisconsin Dells Moves Forward"* in Commercial Property News (March 18, 2008)
Pub: Nielsen Company
Description: Plans for the Grand Cambrian Resort in the Wisconsin Dells is discussed. The luxury condominium resort will include condos, townhomes, and condo-hotel style residences, two water parks, meeting space and indoor entertainment space, as well as a spa, four restaurants and retail offerings.

20169 ■ *"Rock Hall Shifts Advertising to 'Significant Markets' in Region"* in Crain's Cleveland Business (Vol. 28, July 23, 2007, No. 29, pp. 6)
Pub: Crain Communications, Inc.
Ed: John Booth. **Description:** Cleveland's Rock and Roll Hall of Fame and Museum is attempting a different marketing strategy this year with aims of reaching a broader audience in the Midwest and Great Lakes regions.

20170 ■ *"Saudi Overtures"* in The Business Journal-Portland (Vol. 25, August 15, 2008, No. 23, pp. 1)
Pub: American City Business Journals, Inc.
Ed: Aliza Earnshaw. **Description:** Saudi Arabia's huge revenue from oil is creating opportunities for Oregon companies as the country develops new cities, industrial zones, and tourism centers. Oregon exported only $46.8 million worth of goods to Saudi Arabia in 2007 but the kingdom is interested in green

building materials and methods, renewable energy and water quality control, and nanotechnology all of which Oregon has expertise in.

20171 ■ Selling the Invisible: A Field Guide to Modern Marketing
Pub: Business Plus
Ed: Harry Beckwith. Price: $22.95. Description: Tips for marketing and selling intangibles such as health care, entertainment, tourism, legal services, and more are provided.

20172 ■ "Senate OKs Funds for Promoting Tourism" in Crain's Detroit Business (Vol. 24, March 31, 2008, No. 13, pp. 6)
Pub: Crain Communications, Inc.
Ed: Amy Lane. Description: Discusses the Senate proposal which allocates funds for Michigan tourism and business promotion as well as Michigan's No Worker Left Behind initiative a program that provides free tuition at community colleges and other venues to train displaced workers for high-demand occupations.

20173 ■ "Small Dutch Islands Saba, Statia Content With Low-Key Niche" in Travel Weekly (Vol. 69, August 16, 2010, No. 33, pp. 22)
Pub: NorthStar Travel Media LLC
Ed: Gay Nagle Myers. Description: Small Caribbean islands market and promote their region for tourism by never competing with the bigger destinations. Saba and Statia are the two smallest islands in the Caribbean and rely on repeat guests, word-of-mouth recommendations and travel agents willing to promote them.

20174 ■ "State Tourism Likely to Decline Two Percent this Year" in Crain's Detroit Business (Vol. 24, April 14, 2008, No. 15, pp. 6)
Pub: Crain Communications Inc.
Ed: Amy Lane. Description: Due to such national and state economic conditions such as unemployment, the housing crisis and rising gasoline and food prices, Michigan's tourism industry is likely to decline about 2 percent this year.

20175 ■ "Sunriver Venture Hits Snag" in The Business Journal-Portland (Vol. 25, August 1, 2008, No. 21, pp. 1)
Pub: American City Business Journals, Inc.
Ed: Robin J. Moody. Description: Portland, Oregon based-Sunwest Management Inc. has divided its Sunriver resort community to make way for a redevelopment plan. Sunwest owner Jon Harder and three partners formed SilverStar Destinations LLC to broker the purchase and redevelopment of the property. Details and description of the redevelopment project are also presented.

20176 ■ "The Superfluous Position" in Entrepreneur (Vol. 37, July 2009, No. 7, pp. 62)
Pub: Entrepreneur Media, Inc.
Description: Profile of an anonymous editor at a multimedia company that publishes tourism guides who shares his experiences in dealing with an officemate who was promoted as creative manager of content. Everyone was irritated by this person, who would constantly do something to justify his new title. The biggest problem was the fact that this person didn't have a clear job description.

20177 ■ "Tourism Bureau Seeks Hotel Tax Hike" in Baltimore Business Journal (Vol. 27, December 18, 2009, No. 32, pp. 1)
Pub: American City Business Journals
Ed: Rachel Bernstein. Description: Baltimore, Maryland's tourism agency, Visit Baltimore, has proposed a new hotel tax that could produce $2 million annually for its marketing budget, fund improvements to the city's 30-year-old convention center and help it compete for World Cup soccer games. Baltimore hotel leaders discuss the new tax.

20178 ■ Tourism and Entrepreneurship: International Perspectives
Pub: Elsevier Science & Technology Books
Ed: Stephen Page, Jovo Ateljevic. Released: June 1, 2009. Price: $69.95. Description: Trends in tourism development are explored, focusing on the impact of entrepreneurship in the context of regional and local tourism development.

20179 ■ "Tourism Push Rising in Fall" in Philadelphia Business Journal (Vol. 30, August 26, 2011, No. 28, pp. 1)
Pub: American City Business Journals Inc.
Ed: Peter Van Allen. Description: Philadelphia is offering events for tourists this fall despite massive cuts for tourism promotion. Governor Tim Corbet slashed $5.5 million in funding for the state's tourism-promotion agencies which received $32 million in 2009. The agencies were forced to cooperate and fend for themselves using the hotel taxes that sustain them.

20180 ■ The Travel Agent's Complete Desk Reference, 5th Edition
Pub: The Intrepid Traveler
Ed: Kelly Monaghan. Released: August 25, 2009. Price: $39.95. Description: Reference book that provides essential information to the home-based travel agent.

20181 ■ "Travel In Style, Or Not: Finding a Company Travel Service for Every Budget" in Inc. (January 2008, pp. 36-37)
Pub: Gruner & Jahr USA Publishing
Ed: Larry Olmsted. Description: Profiles of various travel services to help small businesses. Firms profiled include Cassis Travel Services, providing first class bookings; Open from American Express, specializing in business class travel; Travelocity business, providing travel agents with 24/7 services; Diners Club Corporate Card, with many features; and Expedia Corporate Travel, allowing users to compare prices for airline tickets, hotels, and car rentals.

20182 ■ "Travel Tears" in Crain's Chicago Business (Vol. 31, November 17, 2008, No. 46, pp. 3)
Pub: Crain Communications, Inc.
Ed: Bob Tita. Description: Hotels, restaurants and conventions are seeing a decline in profits due to corporate travel cutbacks and the sagging economy. City and state revenues derived from taxes on tourism-related industries are also suffering.

20183 ■ "Turbulent Times and Golden Opportunity" in Business Strategy Review (Vol. 21, Spring 2010, No. 1, pp. 34)
Pub: Wiley-Blackwell
Ed: Don Sull. Description: For those feeling storm-tossed by today's economy, the author believes there's much to learn from Carnival Cruise Lines, a company that discovered that turbulence often has an upside.

20184 ■ "TW Trade Shows to Offer Seminars On Niche Selling, Social Media" in Travel Weekly (Vol. 69, October 4, 2010, No. 40, pp. 9)
Pub: NorthStar Travel Media LLC
Description: Travel Weekly's Leisure World 2010 and Fall Home Based Travel Agent Show focused on niche selling, with emphasis on all-inclusives, young consumers, groups, incentives, culinary vacations, and honeymoon or romance travel.

20185 ■ "Tweaking On-Board Activities, Equipment Saves Fuel, Reduces CO2" in Canadian Sailings (June 30, 2008)
Pub: UBM Global Trade
Contact: Leonard J. Corallo, President
Description: Optimizing ship activities and equipment uses less fuel and therefore reduces greenhouse gas emissions. Ways in which companies are implementing research and development techniques in order to monitor ship performance and analyze data in an attempt to become more efficient are examined.

20186 ■ "Up In the Air" in The Business Journal-Serving Greater Tampa Bay (Vol. 28, July 18, 2008, No. 30, pp. 1)
Pub: American City Business Journals, Inc.
Ed: Margie Manning. Description: Views and information on Busch Gardens and on its future, are presented. The park's 3,769 employees worry for their future, after tourism industry experts have expressed concerns on possible tax cuts and other cost reductions. The future of the park, which ranks number 19 as the most visited park in the world, is expected to have a major impact on the tourism industry.

20187 ■ "The Visitor Rebound" in Canadian Business (Vol. 80, November 5, 2007, No. 22, pp. 23)
Pub: Rogers Media
Ed: Graham Silnicki. Description: Overnight visits to Canada are expected to fall by 5.3 percent in 2008, however spending is expected to drop by only 2 percent. Senior economist Alex Fritsche thinks that tourism from the U.S. will improve in 2009; the reasons for the expected growth in 2009 are examined.

20188 ■ "The Way I Work" in Inc. (March 2008, pp. 102-104, 106)
Pub: Gruner & Jahr USA Publishing
Ed: Hannah Clark Steiman. Description: Profile of Howard Lefkowitz, CEO of Vegas.com, a Website that allows visitors to book flights, reserve hotel rooms, buy show tickets, make spa appointments, and coordinate any and all aspects of a trip to Las Vegas. The firm also runs brick-and-mortar box offices and concierge desks at various cities.

20189 ■ "What's the Black Travel Market Worth?" in Black Enterprise (Vol. 38, January 2008, No. 6, pp. 54)
Pub: Earl G. Graves Publishing Co. Inc.
Ed: Aisha Sylvester. Description: African American travel market, both business and pleasure, is one of the top three fastest growing markets in the industry. Hugh Riley, director of marketing for the Caribbean Tourism Organization shares his ideas on the relationship between African American travelers and the Caribbean tourism industry.

20190 ■ "Where's the Lava" in Hawaii Business (Vol. 53, November 2007, No. 5, pp. 18)
Pub: Hawaii Business Publishing
Ed: Jason Ubay. Description: Hawaii Volcanoes National Park used to allow visitors to drive to the end of the paved coastal park road and view flowing lava that came from Kilauea until it reached the sea. On Father's Day morning in June 2007, Kilauea began erupting outside the park and the lava flows inland to Kahaualea and Wao Kele O Puna natural area reserves. In July 2007 321,217 visitors came to the park, a 14 percent increase compared to the same month in 2006.

20191 ■ "The World Is Your Hospital" in Canadian Business (Vol. 81, July 22, 2008, No. 12-13, pp. 62)
Pub: Rogers Media Ltd.
Ed: Sharda Prashad. Description: Medical tourism is seen as a booming industry around the world and is expected to grow to around $40 billion in 2010. Key information regarding medical tourism and services are presented. Views on the possible impact of medical tourism on Canada's health care industry, as well as medical tourism opportunities in Canada, are also given.

STATISTICAL SOURCES

20192 ■ Travel Agencies and Tour Operators Market
Pub: Rector Press, Ltd.
Contact: Lewis Skolnick, President
Released: 2009. Price: Contact Rector Press.

TRADE PERIODICALS

20193 ■ Bermuda Now
Pub: Bermuda Department of Tourism
Contact: Karin Darrell, Manager
Ed: Melanie Astwood, Editor. Released: 4/year.
Price: Free. Description: Offers promotional articles on Bermuda to encourage growth of the tourist industry and to keep the U.S. travel industry abreast of news about the island's visitors.

20194 ■ *Cruise Travel Magazine: The Number One Worldwide Cruise Vacation Magazine*
Pub: World Publishing Co.
URL(s): www.cruisetravelmag.com/. **Ed:** Charles Doherty. **Released:** Bimonthly **Price:** $24.94, Individuals; $50, Canada; $60, Other countries.

20195 ■ *Dude, Guest & Vacation Ranches*
Pub: Bibliotheca Press
Ed: A. Doyle, Editor. **Released:** Irregular. **Price:** $7.95, U.S.. **Description:** Lists dude, guest, and vacation ranches for tourists.

20196 ■ *Hideaways Newsletter*
Pub: Hideaways International
Contact: Michael F. Thiel, Founder
E-mail: mthiel@hideaways.com
Ed: Peg Aaronian, Editor, paaronian@hideaways.com. **Released:** Quarterly. **Price:** $129, Included in membership. **Description:** Features articles on issues of interest to villa vacationers and those seeking high quality, high service vacation options. Includes extensive reports on vacation accommodations; destination descriptions; members' ratings of villas, hotels, cruise ships, and yacht charters; travel tips; and news from recommended properties/cruise lines. Recurring features include compilations of quarterly travel surveys, and columns titled Members News, Members Forum, and Trade Winds. Occasional supplements focusing on one destination, i.e., the Caribbean, Paris, etc. Remarks: Subscription includes semiannual, full-color "Hideaways Guide.".

20197 ■ *Hot Springs, Mineral Waters*
Pub: Bibliotheca Press
Ed: A. Doyle, Editor. **Released:** Irregular. **Price:** $7.95, U.S.. **Description:** Lists hot springs and mineral water locations for tourists.

20198 ■ *Hotel & Travel Index--International Edition*
Pub: Hotel & Travel Index International Edition
Northstar Travel Group
URL(s): www.htihotelink.comwww.northstartravelmedia.com, www.travelweekly.com/. **Released:** Quarterly **Price:** $125, U.S. and other countries one year.

20199 ■ *Journeywoman Online Magazine: The Magazine for Women Who Love to Travel*
Pub: Journeywoman
URL(s): www.journeywoman.com/. **Ed:** Evelyn Hannon. **Released:** Irregular **Price:** Free.

20200 ■ *National Bus Trader: The Magazine of Bus Equipment for the United States and Canada*
Pub: National Bus Trader Inc.
URL(s): www.busmag.com/. **Ed:** Larry Plachno. **Released:** Monthly **Price:** $25, Individuals; $30, Other countries.

20201 ■ *OAG Flight-Finder Asia Pacific Plus*
Pub: Official Airline Guides
Contact: Alan Glass, Chief Executive Officer
URL(s): www.oag.com/graphics/travelplus.htm. **Released:** Monthly

20202 ■ *Southern Festivals: The South's Festival Newspaper*
Pub: Southern Festivals
URL(s): www.southfest.com/festival_list/georgia.html. **Released:** Bimonthly

20203 ■ *Spa Magazine*
Pub: Islands Publishing Co.
URL(s): www.spamagazine.com. **Released:** 7/yr. **Price:** $11.97, U.S.; $20.97, Canada; $36.97, Other countries.

20204 ■ *Travelweek*
Pub: Concepts Travel Media Ltd.
URL(s): www.travelweek.ca. **Ed:** Patrick Dineen. **Released:** Weekly (Thurs.)

20205 ■ *Tuesday*
Pub: National Tour Association
Ed: Julie Lawson, Editor. **Released:** Monthly. **Price:** Included in membership. **Description:** Promotes high standards in the tour industry and public interest in North American escorted tours. Provides information

for group tour operators and suppliers in the U.S. and Canada. Carries legislative updates. Recurring features include Association and member news.

20206 ■ *Woodall's Northeast Outdoors*
Pub: Woodall Publications Corp.
Contact: Mellissa Robinson, Manager
E-mail: mrobinson@affinityroup.com
URL(s): www.woodalls.biz/output.cfm?id=1017811. **Released:** Bimonthly **Price:** $20, Individuals.

TRADE SHOWS AND CONVENTIONS

20207 ■ Annual Allegheny Sport, Travel and Outdoor Show
International Sport Show Producers Association (IS-SPA)
PO Box 480084
Denver, CO 80248-0084
Ph: (303)892-6800
Free: 800-457-2434
Fax: (303)892-6322
Co. E-mail: dseymour@iei-expos.com
URL: http://www.sportshow.org
Contact: Jeff Haughton, President
URL(s): www.sportandtravel.com/pittsburgh/. **Frequency:** Annual. **Principal Exhibits:** Sports, travel and outdoor show. **Dates and Locations:** Expomart. **Telecommunication Services:** expoinc@expoinc.com.

20208 ■ Colorado RV Adventure Travel Show
Colorado Recreation Vehicle Association
PO Box 480084
Denver, CO 80248-0084
Ph: (303)892-6800
Free: 800-457-2434
URL: http://www.crva.org/
URL(s): www.gsevents.com. **Price:** $7, Onsite. **Frequency:** Annual. **Audience:** General Public. **Principal Exhibits:** Recreational vehicles, accessories and travel.

20209 ■ Eastern Sports & Outdoor Show
Reed Exhibitions North American Headquarters
383 Main Ave.
Norwalk, CT 06851
Ph: (203)840-4800
Fax: (203)840-5805
Co. E-mail: inquiry@reedexpo.com
URL: http://www.reedexpo.com
URL(s): www.easternsportshow.com. **Price:** $10, adult; $9, seniors; $4, children 6 - 12 years. **Frequency:** Annual. **Audience:** General public. **Principal Exhibits:** Recreational vehicles, boats, hunting and fishing equipment, clothing, and related outdoor products, resorts, SUVs, retailers and manufacturers, motorcycles, ATVs, travel and tourism. **Dates and Locations:** , Pennsylvania Farm Show Complex. **Telecommunication Services:** eseveral@reedexpo.com.

20210 ■ Fort Wayne Sports, Vacation, and Boat Show
Trio Enterprises, Inc.
3624 Maxim Dr.
Fort Wayne, IN 46815
Ph: (219)483-2638
Free: 800-446-2638
Fax: (219)484-0876
URL(s): www.boatsafloat.com. **Frequency:** Annual. **Audience:** General public. **Principal Exhibits:** Recreational vehicles, boats, and travel and vacation information. **Dates and Locations:** , Allen County War Memorial Coliseum. **Telecommunication Services:** data@boatsafloat.com.

20211 ■ Louisville Boat, RV & Sportshow
Douglas Expositions Inc.
10000 Shelbyville Rd., No. 111
Anchorage, KY 40223-2950
Ph: (502)244-5660
URL(s): www.louisvilleboatshow.com. **Frequency:** Annual. **Principal Exhibits:** Sports, boating and vacations, hunting and fishing, recreational vehicles. **Telecommunication Services:** kmuncy@nmma.org.

20212 ■ Travel Media Showcase
Atlantic City Convention & Visitors Authority
2314 Pacific Ave.
Atlantic City, NJ 08401
Ph: (609)348-7100
Fax: (609)348-7287
URL: http://www.atlanticcitynj.com/
URL(s): www.travelmediashowcase.com. **Price:** $2095, exhibitor (1 rep); $2595, exhibitor (2 reps). **Frequency:** Annual. **Audience:** Trade. **Principal Exhibits:** Tourism industry and travel media convention. **Telecommunication Services:** kerry@jveroassociates.com.

FRANCHISES AND BUSINESS OPPORTUNITIES

20213 ■ GolfAhoy Golf & Cruise Travel Bureau
GolfAhoy BVI Ltd.
5328 Calgary Tr., Ste. 1165
Edmonton, AB, Canada T6H 4J8
Free: 877-415-5442
Fax: (780)669-5667
Description: Golf tourism and cruise travel bureau. **No. of Franchise Units:** 54. **No. of Company-Owned Units:** 2. **Founded:** 1988.. **Franchised:** 2000. **Equity Capital Needed:** $16,040-$18,260 start-up. **Franchise Fee:** $9,600. **Financial Assistance:** Yes. **Training:** Yes.

20214 ■ Lantis Fireworks & Lasers
Lantis Franchising
PO Box 491
Draper, UT 84020
Free: 800-443-3040
Description: Provide pyrotechnical and laser displays. **No. of Franchise Units:** 1. **No. of Company-Owned Units:** 2. **Founded:** 1988.. **Franchised:** 2003. **Equity Capital Needed:** $172,400-$274,000. **Franchise Fee:** $50,000. **Royalty Fee:** 6%. **Training:** Available at headquarters 4-6 weeks.

20215 ■ Outdoor Connection
424 Neosho
Burlington, KS 66839
Ph: (620)364-5500
Free: 888-548-0636
Fax: (620)364-5563
Co. E-mail: info@outdoor-connectioion.com
URL: http://www.outdoor-connection.com
Description: Hunting and fishing travel service. **No. of Franchise Units:** 61. **No. of Company-Owned Units:** 2. **Founded:** 1988.. **Franchised:** 1990. **Equity Capital Needed:** $7,550-$12,250. **Franchise Fee:** $6,500. **Royalty Fee:** 4%. **Financial Assistance:** In-house assistance available with franchise fee. **Training:** 2 days at headquarters, 2-3 days annual convention and ongoing support.

LIBRARIES

20216 ■ Davenport University - Thomas F. Reed, Jr. Memorial Library
4123 W. Main St.
Kalamazoo, MI 49006
Ph: (616)382-2835
Free: 800-632-8928
Fax: (269)382-2657
Co. E-mail: kz_library@davenport.edu
URL: http://www.davenport.edu/
Contact: Judith J. Bosshart, Director
Scope: Business, data processing, administrative services, accounting, humanities, paralegal, medical records, healthcare administration, computer and information processing. **Services:** Interlibrary loan; copying; faxing; library open to the public for reference use only. **Founded:** 1981. **Holdings:** 14,200 books; 995 videotapes. **Subscriptions:** 12,000 journals and other serials; 6 newspapers. **Telecommunication Services:** judy.bosshart@davenport.edu; Library@Davenport.edu.

20217 ■ Pannell Kerr Forster Library
29 Broadway
New York, NY 10006-3201
Ph: (212)867-8000

Fax: (212)687-4346
Co. E-mail: dsu@pkfny.com
URL: http://www.pkfnewyork.com
Scope: Research on hospitality, tourism, accounting, auditing, real estate. **Services:** Library not open to the public. **Founded:** 1945. **Holdings:** 2000 volumes; pamphlets; clippings. **Subscriptions:** 50 journals and other serials. **Telecommunication Services:** info@pkfny.com.

20218 ■ Travel Industry Association of America Library
1100 New York Ave. NW, Ste. 450
Washington, DC 20005-3934
Ph: (202)408-8422
Fax: (202)408-1255
Co. E-mail: feedback@ustravel.org
URL: http://www.ustravel.org
Contact: Suzanne D. Cook, Senior Vice President, Research
Scope: Travel and tourism. **Services:** Library not open to the public. **Founded:** 1941. **Holdings:** 3000 research documents; 3800 government documents; 250 unpublished travel research reports; 15,000 clippings; 20 tapes. **Subscriptions:** 27 journals and other serials. **Telecommunication Services:** research@ustravel.org.

20219 ■ University of Wisconsin--Stout - Library Learning Center
315 10th Ave.
Menomonie, WI 54751
Ph: (715)232-1215
Free: 800-787-8688
Fax: (715)232-1783
Co. E-mail: library@uwstout.edu
URL: http://www.uwstout.edu/lib/
Contact: William Johnston, Director
Scope: Industrial technology; hospitality and tourism; human development and family life education; home economics; business; vocational rehabilitation; early childhood education; manufacturing engineering; technology education. **Services:** Interlibrary loan;

copying; document delivery; SDI; Center open to the public. **Founded:** 1908. **Holdings:** 226,551 books; 19,694 AV titles; 1,243,068 microforms; 1705 archives. **Subscriptions:** 1057 journals; 19 newspapers. **Telecommunication Services:** robertsp@uwstout.edu.

RESEARCH CENTERS

20220 ■ College of Forestry and Conservation - Institute for Tourism and Recreation Research
University of Montana
32 Campus Dr., No. 1234
Missoula, MT 59812-1234
Ph: (406)243-5686
Fax: (406)243-4845
Co. E-mail: request@forestry.umt.edu
URL: http://www.forestry.umt.edu/
Contact: Kate Cenis, Director
Description: Provides research data needed to support the state's tourism industry.

20221 ■ State University of New York at Buffalo - Center for Executive Development
108 Jacobs Management Ctr.
Buffalo, NY 14260
Ph: (716)645-3200
Fax: (716)645-3501
Co. E-mail: mgt-ced@buffalo.edu
URL: http://www.mgt.buffalo.edu/executive
Contact: Courtney Walsh, Executive Director
Founded: 1978. **Educational Activities:** Seminars and training programs for industry, including a continuing education program in accounting.

20222 ■ University of Calgary - World Tourism Education and Research Centre (WTERC)
Scurfield Hall
Haskayne School of Business
2500 University Dr. NW
Calgary, AB, Canada T2N 1N4

Ph: (403)220-3800
Fax: (403)282-0266
Co. E-mail: brent.ritchie@haskayne.ucalgary.ca
URL: http://haskayne.ucalgary.ca/research/research-centres/wterc
Contact: Dr. J.R. Brent Ritchie, Chairperson
Founded: 1989.

20223 ■ University of Central Florida - Dick Pope, Sr. Institute for Tourism Studies
Rosen College of Hospitality Management
9907 Universal Blvd.
Orlando, FL 32819
Ph: (407)903-8028
Fax: (407)903-8105
Co. E-mail: apizam@mail.ucf.edu
URL: http://www.hospitality.ucf.edu/dick_pope.html
Contact: Dr. Abraham Pizam, Director
Founded: 1979. **Publications:** *Proprietary Research Reports.* **Educational Activities:** Dick Pope, Sr. Institute for Tourism Studies Conferences; Faculty workshops; Industry seminars; Public and private research consultation opportunities; Research colloquiums (Monthly); Sponsorship opportunities. **Telecommunication Services:** dpi@mail.ucf.edu.

20224 ■ University of Colorado at Boulder - Business Research Division
420 UCB
Leeds School of Business
Boulder, CO 80309-0420
Ph: (303)492-8227
Fax: (303)492-3620
Co. E-mail: richard.wobbekind@colorado.edu
URL: http://leeds.colorado.edu/brd
Contact: Dr. Richard Wobbekind, Director
Services: Provides businesspersons, city managers, planners, association executives, and others with information useful in the operation of their organizations. **Founded:** 1915. **Educational Activities:** Annual Colorado Business Economic Outlook Forum, in December. **Telecommunication Services:** brdinfo@colorado.edu.

START-UP INFORMATION

20225 ■ *"Fun And Easy Gold Mines" in Small Business Opportunities (Fall 2008)*
Pub: Entrepreneur Media Inc.
Description: Twenty-five businesses that cater to the booming children's market are profiled; day care services, party planning, special events video-making, tutoring, personalized children's toys and products and other services geared toward the kids market are included.

20226 ■ *"Honoring Creativity" in Playthings (Vol. 107, January 1, 2009, No. 1, pp. 28)*
Pub: Reed Business Information
Contact: Jeff Greisch, President
Ed: Cliff Annicelli. **Description:** Toy & Game Inventors Expo is held annually in conjunction with the Chicago Toy & Game Fair. The event honors toy inventors in the categories of Game Design, Toy Design and Rising Stars, plus a lifetime achievement award. Profile of the company, Toying With Games, founded by Joyce Johnson and Colleen McCarthy-Evans are included in the article.

20227 ■ *The Specialty Shop: How to Create Your Own Unique and Profitable Retail Business*
Pub: AMACOM
Ed: Dorothy Finell. **Released:** February 27, 2007. **Price:** $21.95. **Description:** Advise to start retail businesses, including bakeries, gift shops, toy stores, book shops, tea houses, clothing boutiques, and other unique stores.

ASSOCIATIONS AND OTHER ORGANIZATIONS

20228 ■ **Strawberry Shortcake Chat Group**
138 E Main Cross St.
Greenville, KY 42345
Ph: (270)338-4318
Co. E-mail: jenniferbowles@bellsouth.net
URL: http://www.strawberrybonkers.com
Contact: Jennifer Bowles, Editor
Description: Owners and admirers of Strawberry Shortcake dolls. Promotes collection and preservation of Strawberry Shortcake dolls. Facilitates communication among members; serves as a clearinghouse on Strawberry Shortcake dolls. **Founded:** 1996.

20229 ■ **Toy Industry Association (TIA)**
1115 Broadway, Ste. 400
New York, NY 10010
Ph: (212)675-1141
Free: 888-884-TOYS
Fax: (212)633-1429
Co. E-mail: info@toyassociation.org
URL: http://www.toyassociation.org
Contact: Soren Torp Laursen, Chairman
URL(s): www.toy-tia.org. **Description:** Provides business services to U.S. manufacturers and importers of toys. Manages American International Toy Fair; represents the industry before Federal, State and Local government on issues of importance; provides legal and legislative counsel; conducts educational programs; compiles industry statistics. **Founded:** 1916. **Publications:** *ToyInfo.org*; *American International Toy Fair Official Directory* (Annual); *Toy Challenges and Opportunities* (Annual); *The Official American International Toy Fair Directory* (Annual). **Educational Activities:** Toy Fair '13 (Annual); American International Toy Fair (Annual). **Awards:** Toy of the Year (Annual).

20230 ■ **U.S.A. Toy Library Association (USA-TLA)**
2719 Broadway Ave.
Evanston, IL 60201
Ph: (847)612-6966
Fax: (847)864-8473
Co. E-mail: jqi@comcast.net
URL: http://usatla.org
Contact: Judith Q. Iacuzzi, Executive Director
Description: Child care professionals, parents, and others interested in the role of toys and play in child development. Promotes the importance of play and the development of toy libraries in public and school libraries, hospitals, day care centers, and mobile collections. Seeks to broaden understanding of how toys can educate, increase parent-child interaction, and aid in development and therapy of disabled children. **Founded:** 1984.

REFERENCE WORKS

20231 ■ *"The ABCs of a Good Show" in Playthings (Vol. 106, October 1, 2008, No. 9, pp. 18)*
Pub: Reed Business Information
Contact: Jeff Greisch, President
Ed: Karyn M. Peterson. **Description:** ABC Kids Expo 2008 made a strong showing with products for babies, kids and new/expecting parents. The new Naturally Kids section promoting eco-friendly products was the highlight of the show.

20232 ■ *"ACC Game Development Program Opens" in Austin Business JournalInc. (Vol. 28, October 31, 2008, No. 33, pp. 1)*
Pub: American City Business Journals
Ed: Sandra Zaragoza. **Description:** Austin, Texas-based Austin Community College has launched its Game Development Institute. The institute was created to meet the gaming industry's demand for skilled workers. One hundred students have enrolled with the institute.

20233 ■ *"Bakugan Battle Brawlers" in Advertising Age (Vol. 79, November 17, 2008, No. 43, pp. S2)*
Pub: Crain Communications, Inc.
Ed: Kate Fitzgerald. **Description:** Spin Master toys has a new hit, Bakugan Battle Brawlers, an interactive game board with 106 characters that battle with one another in tournaments. Bakugan tournaments are being held at Toys 'R' Us stores.

20234 ■ *"Blues at the Toy Fair: Industry Reeling From Recalls, Lower Sales Volumes" in Crain's New York Business (February 18, 2008)*
Pub: Crain Communications Inc.
Ed: Elisabeth Cordova. **Description:** Over 1,500 toy developers and vendors will attend the American International Toy Fair, expected to be low-key due to recent recalls of toys not meeting American safety standards. Toy retailers and manufacturers, as well as the Chinese government, are promoting product testing to prevent toxic metals in toys.

20235 ■ *"Cents and Sensibility" in Playthings (Vol. 107, January 1, 2009, No. 1, pp. 19)*
Pub: Reed Business Information
Contact: Jeff Greisch, President
Ed: Pamela Brill. **Description:** Recent concerns over safety, phthalate and lead paint and other toxic materials, as well as consumers going green, are issues discussed by toy manufacturers. Doll manufacturers also face increase labor and material costs and are working to design dolls that girls will love.

20236 ■ *"The China Tax" in Forbes (Vol. 180, October 1, 2007, No. 6, pp. 35)*
Pub: Forbes Inc.
Ed: Robyn Meredith. **Description:** U.S. consumers can see a rise in prices for goods made in China due to growing pressure from Congress to ensure safe products from that country. Taxing products imported from China could be levied in five different forms listed.

20237 ■ *"Consignment Shop Offers Children's Clothes, Products" in Frederick News-Post (August 19, 2010)*
Pub: Federick News-Post
Ed: Ed Waters Jr. **Description:** Sweet Pea Consignments for Children offers used items for newborns to pre-teens. The shop carries name brand clothing as well as toys, books and baby products.

20238 ■ *"Counting on Cornhole: Popular Bean Bag Game Brings Crowds to Bars" in Boston Business Journal (Vol. 29, July 15, 2011, No. 10, pp. 1)*
Pub: American City Business Journals Inc.
Ed: Alexander Jackson. **Description:** Cornhole game is being used by bars to spur business as the games hikes beer and food sales on slow weekdays. The game is played with two cornhole boards facing each other and is played with one or two people on one team who try to place a bag on the board.

20239 ■ *"A Curious Appeal (Market for Scientific Toys)" in Playthings (Vol. 106, October 1, 2008, No. 9, pp. 26)*
Pub: Reed Business Information
Contact: Jeff Greisch, President
Ed: Pamela Brill. **Description:** Science and nature toys are still popular with children. Kits allow kids to make candy, soap, grow miniature gardens, catch bugs and more. These hands-on kits have manufacturers watching trends to create more toys in this category.

20240 ■ *"Dealing With Dangers Abroad"* in *Financial Executive (Vol. 23, December 2007, No. 10, pp. 32)*

Pub: Financial Executives International

Ed: Jeffrey Marshall. **Description:** Clear processes and responsibilities for risk management for all companies going global are essential. U.S. toy manufacturer, Matel was put into crisis mode after its Chinese-made toys were recalled due to the use of lead-based paint or tiny magnets in its products.

20241 ■ *"Despite Hot Toys, Holiday Sales Predicted To Be Ho-Ho-Hum"* in *Drug Store News (Vol. 29, November 12, 2007, No. 14, pp. 78)*

Pub: Drug Store News

Ed: Doug Desjardins. **Description:** Summer toy recalls have retailers worried about holiday sales in 2007. Mattel was heavily impacted from the recall of millions of toys manufactured in China.

20242 ■ *"Disney Has High Hopes for Duffy"* in *Canadian Business (Vol. 83, October 12, 2010, No. 17, pp. 14)*

Pub: Rogers Media Ltd.

Ed: James Cowan. **Description:** The reintroduction of Duffy is expected to create a new, exclusive product line that distinguishes Disney's parks and stores from competitors. Duffy, a teddy bear, was first introduced at a Disney World store in Florida in 2002. The character was incorporated into the Disney mythology when its popularity grew in Japan.

20243 ■ *"A Doll That Looks Like You: Will Custom Toys Take Off?"* in *Inc. (Volume 32, December 2010, No. 10, pp. 144)*

Pub: Inc. Magazine

Ed: Shivani Vora. **Description:** Profiles of various companies that provide custom items that look like people.

20244 ■ *"Down on the Boardwalk"* in *Retail Merchandiser (Vol. 51, September-October 2011, No. 5, pp. 56)*

Pub: Phoenix Media Corporation

Ed: Eric Slack. **Description:** Classic board game, Monopoly, continues to be the most recognized game brand while staying fresh by entering new markets and gaming platforms for all walks of life. Monopoly is available in over 100 countries, translated into 43 languages and played by more than 1 billion people since its introduction, and the game is tailored to each geographic market it enters.

20245 ■ *"Earth Angels"* in *Playthings (Vol. 106, September 1, 2008, No. 8, pp. 10)*

Pub: Reed Business Information

Contact: Jeff Greisch, President

Ed: Karyn M. Peterson. **Description:** ImagiPlay toy company has partnered with Whole Foods Market to distribute the company's wooden playthings across the country. The company's Earth-friendly business model is outlined.

20246 ■ *"Enforcer In Fantasyland"* in *Crain's New York Business (Vol. 24, February 25, 2008, No. 8, pp. 10)*

Pub: Crain Communications Inc.

Ed: Hilary Potkewitz. **Description:** Patent law, particularly in the toy and game industry, is recession-proof according to Barry Negrin, partner at Pryor Cashman. Negrin co-founded his patent practice group. Despite massive recalls of toys and the concern over toxic toys, legal measures are in place in this industry.

20247 ■ *"Familiar Fun"* in *Crain's Cleveland Business (Vol. 28, October 22, 2007, No. 42, pp. 3)*

Pub: Crain Communications Inc.

Ed: John Booth. **Description:** Marketing for the 2007 holiday season has toy retailers focusing on American-made products because of recent recalls of toys produced in China that do not meet U.S. safety standards.

20248 ■ *"Fitness Made Fun"* in *Playthings (Vol. 106, September 1, 2008, No. 8, pp. 12)*

Pub: Reed Business Information

Contact: Jeff Greisch, President

Ed: Karyn M. Peterson. **Description:** Nintendo Wii has developed the Wii Fit game that allows gamers to engage in over forty physical activities through its Balance Board accessory, an engineered platform that senses weight and shifts in movement and balance. It also offers virtual trainers to talk participants through the activities and keeps track of the progress of multiple users.

20249 ■ *"Game Changer"* in *Canadian Business (Vol. 83, June 15, 2010, No. 10, pp. 52)*

Pub: Rogers Media Ltd.

Ed: Jordan Timm. **Description:** Ubisoft chose Ontario to be the site for its new development studio and it has appointed Jade Raymond as its managing director. Raymond was born in Montreal in 1975 and studied computer science at McGill. Raymond is said to possess the understanding of the game industry's technical, art, and business components.

20250 ■ *The Game Makers*

Pub: Harvard Business School Press

Ed: Philip E. Orbanes. **Released:** November 2003. **Price:** $29.95. **Description:** Profile of game expert and president of a specialty game company, author of books about games, Monopoly championship judge, senior vice president of research and development at Parker Brothers, and inventor of board and card games in highlighted.

20251 ■ *"Going Green, Going Slowly"* in *Playthings (Vol. 106, September 1, 2008, No. 8, pp. 17)*

Pub: Reed Business Information

Contact: Jeff Greisch, President

Ed: Nancy Zwiers. **Description:** Sustainability and greener materials for both product and packaging in the toy industry has become important for protecting our environment. However, in a recent survey nearly 60 percent of responders stated environmental issues did not play a part in purchasing a toy or game for their children.

20252 ■ *"Hobbies Hold Fast"* in *Playthings (Vol. 106, November 1, 2008, No. 1, pp. 6)*

Pub: Reed Business Information

Contact: Jeff Greisch, President

Ed: Karyn M. Peterson. **Description:** Profile of the 24th Annual iHobby Expo is presented. The event is a combined trade and consumer show offering a look at the latest releases in die-cast collectibles, model railroads and aircraft, slot cars, remote control vehicles, rocketry, robotics, military toys, wood/plastic model kits, games, etc.

20253 ■ *"Importers Share Safety Liability"* in *Feedstuffs (Vol. 80, January 21, 2008, No. 3, pp. 19)*

Pub: Miller Publishing Company, Inc.

Description: Pet food and toys containing lead paint are among products from China being recalled due to safety concerns. American Society for Quality's list of measures that outsourcing companies can take to help ensure safer products being imported to the U.S.

20254 ■ *"Inside Out"* in *Playthings (Vol. 107, January 1, 2009, No. 1, pp. 3)*

Pub: Reed Business Information

Contact: Jeff Greisch, President

Description: Mattel signed on as the global master toy licensee for Cartoon Network's The Secret Saturdays while Toy Island signed a deal for wooden toys based on several leading Nick Jr. properties.

20255 ■ *"The Last Ingredient?"* in *Canadian Business (Vol. 81, October 13, 2008, No. 17, pp. 88)*

Pub: Rogers Media Ltd.

Ed: Rachel Pulfer. **Description:** Views and information on Cookie Jar Group's plan to acquire rights for Strawberry Shortcake and the Care Bears are discussed. The move would make Cookie Jar a major

player in the global children's entertainment market. Cookie Jar chief executive, Michael Hirsh is believed to be securing funds for the planned $195 million acquisition.

20256 ■ *"Look, Leap, and License"* in *Retail Merchandiser (Vol. 51, July-August 2011, No. 4, pp. 16)*

Pub: Phoenix Media Corporation

Description: Toys highlighting the Licensing International Expo 2011 included a life-sized Cookie Monster, Papa Smurf, Power Rangers, Transformer, and margarita wrestlers. Taking licensed properties international was a common theme at this year's show.

20257 ■ *"Look Out, Barbie, Bratz are Back"* in *Canadian Business (Vol. 83, August 17, 2010, No. 13-14, pp. 18)*

Pub: Rogers Media Ltd.

Ed: Joe Castaldo. **Description:** California-based MGA Entertainment has wrestled back control over Bratz from Mattel after a six-year legal battle. However, MGA owner Isaac Larian could still face legal hurdles if Mattel pursues a retrial. He now has to revive the brand which virtually disappeared from stores when Mattel won the rights for Bratz.

20258 ■ *"Making Factory Tours Count"* in *Playthings (Vol. 107, January 1, 2009, No. 1, pp. 14)*

Pub: Reed Business Information

Contact: Jeff Greisch, President

Ed: Malcolm Denniss. **Description:** The importance of touring an overseas toy supplier's manufacturing facility is stressed. Strategies for general factory visits are outlined in order to determine safety-related quality assurance issues in production.

20259 ■ *"Mattel's Got a Monster Holiday Hit, But Will Franchise Have Staying Power?"* in *Advertising Age (Vol. 81, December 6, 2010, No. 43)*

Pub: Crain Communications, Inc.

Ed: Beth Snyder Bulik. **Description:** Monster High transmedia play expands beyond dolls to merchandise, apparel and entertainment.

20260 ■ *"Nat'l Instruments Connects with Lego"* in *Austin Business JournalInc. (Vol. 28, August 22, 2008, No. 23, pp. 1)*

Pub: American City Business Journals

Ed: Laura Hipp. **Description:** Austin-based National Instruments Corporation has teamed with Lego Group from Denmark to create a robot that can be built by children and can be used to perform tasks. Lego WeDo, their latest product, uses computer connection to power its movements. The educational benefits of the new product are discussed.

20261 ■ *The Official American International Toy Fair Directory*

Pub: Toy Industry Association

Contact: Soren Torp Laursen, Chairman

URL(s): www.toy-tia.org. **Released:** Annual; Latest edition 2009. **Covers:** About 1,500 toy, game, and holiday decoration manufacturers and their representatives. **Entries include:** Company name, address, phone, e-mail, fax, website, booth number or location at Toy Fair, products, name of representative. **Arrangement:** Classified by show site and booth/room number. **Indexes:** Company name, product, exhibit location, member exhibitors and trade names.

20262 ■ *"Paper Cache"* in *Playthings (Vol. 106, October 1, 2008, No. 9, pp. 9)*

Pub: Reed Business Information

Contact: Jeff Greisch, President

Ed: Karyn M. Peterson. **Description:** New toys in the paper play category are capturing children's imaginations with pirate ships and fairy houses and more they can build or design themselves. Hands-on paper and cardboard-based kits offer options for all ages.

20263 ■ *"Play It Safe"* in *Entrepreneur (Vol. 35, November 2007, No. 11, pp. 26)*

Pub: Entrepreneur Media Inc.

Ed: Gwen Moran. **Description:** U.S.-based toy manufacturers find opportunity from concerns regarding the recent recalls of toys that are made in China.

The situation can provide better probability of parents buying toys made in the U.S. or Europe, where manufacturing standards are stricter.

20264 ■ *The Race for a New Game Machine: Creating the Chips Inside the Xbox 360 and the PlayStation 3*
Pub: Citadel Press
Contact: Steven Zacharius, President
E-mail: szacharius@kensingtonbooks.com

Ed: David Shippy, Mickie Phipps. **Released:** 2009. **Price:** $21.95. **Description:** The story of Microsoft and Sony's race to deliver the goods for the Xbox 360 and Playstation 3 is explored.

20265 ■ *"Sign of Progress"* in Playthings (Vol. 106, October 1, 2008, No. 9, pp. 4)
Pub: Reed Business Information
Contact: Jeff Greisch, President

Ed: Cliff Annicelli. **Description:** The ramifications of the toy recalls in 2007 are discussed. Mandates for lead-free toys and other safety issues are having an impact on the American toy industry.

20266 ■ *"The State of the Stores"* in Playthings (Vol. 106, November 1, 2008, No. 10, pp. 8)
Pub: Reed Business Information
Contact: Jeff Greisch, President

Ed: Dana French. **Description:** Investigation into the top twenty-five toy and game retailers shows that video games and related handheld and console systems as well as computer games were number one with America's children in 2007.

20267 ■ *"This Year's Model"* in Playthings (Vol. 107, January 1, 2009, No. 1, pp. 23)
Pub: Reed Business Information
Contact: Jeff Greisch, President

Ed: Karyn M. Peterson. **Description:** Toy manufacturers, as well as retailers, address the need to exceed safety and quality demands by consumers when developing new toys and games for children.

20268 ■ *"Thomas and His Washington Friends"* in CFO (Vol. 23, October 2007, No. 10, pp. 18)
Pub: CFO Publishing Corporation

Ed: Alix Stuart. **Description:** Reliance on Chinese suppliers to America's toymakers may become quite costly as Congress considers legislation that would increase fines to as high as $50 million for companies selling tainted products. The legislation would also require independent mandatory testing for makers of products for children.

20269 ■ *"A 'To Do' List"* in Playthings (Vol. 107, January 1, 2009, No. 1, pp. 9)
Pub: Reed Business Information
Contact: Jeff Greisch, President

Ed: Richard Gottlieb. **Description:** Profile of the Building Our Future Toy Conference held in October 2008. Participants discussed the industry's future and is seeking ways to understand the toys children want in today's society.

20270 ■ *"Toy Scares Drive Business"* in Boston Business Journal (Vol. 27, November 23, 2007, No. 43, pp. 1)
Pub: American City Business Journals, Inc.

Ed: Joan Goodchild. **Description:** Several Boston businesses have tapped into the lead content scare in toys and other products manufactured in China. ConRoy Corporation LLC launched Toy Recall Alert!, an online tool to alert consumers about new recalls while Hybrivet Systems introduced screening test kit, LeadCheck. Other new products pertaining to toy safety are discussed.

20271 ■ *"Toy Story"* in Forbes (Vol. 180, October 15, 2007, No. 8, pp. 102)
Pub: Forbes Inc.

Description: Three voluntary recalls of Chinese-made toys were announced by American toymakers, sending Mattel stocks plummeting.

20272 ■ *"Toy Story: U.S.-Made a Hot Seller"* in Crain's Detroit Business (Vol. 23, December 17, 2007, No. 51, pp. 3)
Pub: Crain Communications Inc. - Detroit

Ed: Chad Halcom. **Description:** American Plastic Toys, located in Walled Lake, Michigan reports all its toys are made in the U.S. and have passed all U.S. safety standards. Revenue for American Plastic Toys reached nearly $33 million in 2005, and the company expects to exceed that because of recent toy safety recalls of products produced in China.

20273 ■ *"VTech Targets Tots With a Wee Wii"* in Advertising Age (Vol. 79, September 8, 2008, No. 33, pp. 14)
Pub: Crain Communications, Inc.

Ed: Beth Snyder Bulik. **Description:** V-Motion is a video-game console targeting 3-to-7-year-olds and is manufactured by educational toy company VTech. The company is marketing the product as a kind of Wii for preschoolers and hopes to build a formidable brand presence in the kids' electronics market.

20274 ■ *"Weathering the Economic Storm"* in Playthings (Vol. 107, January 1, 2009, No. 1, pp. 10)
Pub: Reed Business Information
Contact: Jeff Greisch, President

Ed: J. Tol Broome Jr. **Description:** Six steps for toy companies to survive the economic turndown are outlined: Outline your business model; seek professional input; meet with your banker; cut your costs; manage your inventory; and use your trade credit.

20275 ■ *"Wham-O's Wisdom"* in Playthings (Vol. 107, January 1, 2009, No. 1, pp. 13)
Pub: Reed Business Information
Contact: Jeff Greisch, President

Ed: Tim Walsh. **Description:** Toy historian Tim Walsh discusses the history of the toy industry and shares secrets to his success. Walsh is the creator of toys and board games.

20276 ■ *"Work for Play: Careers in Video Game Development"* in Occupational Outlook Quarterly (Vol. 55, Fall 2011, No. 3, pp. 2)
Pub: U.S. Bureau of Labor Statistics

Ed: Drew Liming, Dennis Vilorio. **Description:** Game developers make a living creating the games the public enjoys playing. The video gaming industry reported sales over $10 billion in 2009 and employed 32,000 people in 34 states. Career options in video game development are featured.

20277 ■ *"Xbox 360 Excels as a Media Hub"* in Hispanic Business (October 2009, pp. 40)
Pub: Hispanic Business

Ed: Jeremy Nisen. **Description:** Xbox 360 video game console from Microsoft offers games, amazing graphics and state-of-the-art accessories. The trend towards purchase of the Xbox includes more than teenagers.

20278 ■ *"Zakkamono Taps Growing Market for Collectibles"* in Hawaii Business (Vol. 54, September 2008, No. 3, pp. 68)
Pub: Hawaii Business Publishing

Ed: Casey Chin. **Description:** Profile of Zakkamono, a business that designs and sells designer toys, shirts and other collectibles; the first toys being Mousubi and Miao figurines. Owners Zakka and Rae Huo say that one of the business' challenges is finding manufacturing resources. Other details about Zakkamono are discussed.

STATISTICAL SOURCES

20279 ■ *RMA Annual Statement Studies*
Pub: Risk Management Association
Contact: Kevin M. Blakey, President

Released: Annual. **Price:** $175.00 2006-07 edition, $105.00. **Description:** Contains composite balance sheets and income statements for more than 360 industries, including the accounting, auditing, and bookkeeping industries. Also contains five years of comparative historical data for discerning trends. Includes 16 commonly used ratios, computed for most of the size groupings for nearly every industry.

20280 ■ *Standard & Poor's Industry Surveys*
Pub: Standard & Poor's Corp.

Released: Annual. **Price:** $3633.00. **Description:** Two-volume book that examines the prospects for specific industries, including trucking. Also provides analyses of trends and problems, statistical tables and charts, and comparative company analyses.

TRADE PERIODICALS

20281 ■ *The Toy Book*
Pub: Adventure Publishing Group Inc.

URL(s): www.adventurepublishinggroup.com/ap-toy-book.html. **Released:** Monthly **Price:** $48, Individuals; $200, Other countries airmail only; $80, Two years; $56, Canada and Mexico; $100, Individuals 3 years.

20282 ■ *Toys & Games: Canada's Toy Industry Magazine*
Pub: Playtonic Communications

URL(s): toysandgamesmagazine.ca. **Released:** Bimonthly **Price:** $21, Canada; $60, Other countries.

TRADE SHOWS AND CONVENTIONS

20283 ■ *Canadian Toy and Hobby Fair*
Canadian Toy Association
7777 Keele St., Ste. 212
Concord, ON, Canada L4K 1Y7
Ph: (905)660-5690
Fax: (905)660-6103
Co. E-mail: info@cdntoyassn.com
URL: http://www.cdntoyassn.com

URL(s): www.cdntoyassn.com. **Frequency:** Annual. **Audience:** Trade professionals. **Principal Exhibits:** Toys, games, books, and seasonal decorations and hobby products. **Dates and Locations:** , International Centre.

20284 ■ *CHA Winter Convention and Trade Show*
Craft and Hobby Association (CHA)
319 E 54th St.
Elmwood Park, NJ 07407
Ph: (201)835-1200
Free: 800-822-0494
Fax: (201)797-0657
Co. E-mail: info@craftandhobby.org
URL: http://www.craftandhobby.org
Contact: Steven Z. Berger, President
E-mail: sberger@craftandhobby.org

URL(s): www.chashow.org. **Price:** Pre-registered, members; $25. **Frequency:** Annual. **Audience:** Owners, corporate officers and buyers from craft, hobby, DIY stores, general merchandise stores, wholesalers, and professional crafters. **Principal Exhibits:** Crafts, ceramics, floral accessories, dollhouse miniatures, aromatics, art materials and frames, jewelry findings, fabrics, needlework and quilting supplies, home decor, rubber stamps, stencils and scrapbooking supplies.

20285 ■ *Just Kidstuff - A Division of the New York International Gift Fair*
George Little Management, LLC
1133 Westchester Ave., Ste. N136
White Plains, NY 10606
Ph: (914)421-3200
Free: 800-272-SHOW
Co. E-mail: cathy_steel@glmshows.com
URL: http://www.glmshows.com

URL(s): www.nyigf.com. **Frequency:** Semiannual. **Audience:** Buyers from specialty and department stores, giftshops, jewelry stores, interior designers, importers and distributors of home products, mail order catalogs. **Principal Exhibits:** Presents a wide variety of upscale products for children of all ages, including bedding, furniture, dolls, toys and games, gifts, clothes, books and educational products and accessories. **Telecommunication Services:** deborah_hilfman@glmshows.com.

20286 ■ Supermarket Promotion Show
Association of Retail Marketing Services
10 Drs. James Parker Blvd., Ste. 103
Red Bank, NJ 07701-1500
Ph: (732)842-5070
Fax: (732)219-1938
Co. E-mail: info@goarms.com
URL: http://www.goarms.com
Contact: Michael Levine, President
Price: $Free. **Frequency:** Annual. **Audience:** Buyers of retail, consumer incentives. **Principal Exhibits:** Dinnerware, glassware, housewares, books, videos, games, sweepstakes, dolls, and plush toys suppliers. **Dates and Locations:** , Ramada Congress Hotel. **Telecommunication Services:** info@goarms.com.

FRANCHISES AND BUSINESS OPPORTUNITIES

20287 ■ Compuchild
Compuchild Services of America
1800 Halifax St.
Camel, IN 46032
Ph: (317)817-9817
Free: 800-619-5437
Fax: (317)818-8184
Description: Computer education to children. **No. of Franchise Units:** 69. **No. of Company-Owned Units:** 1. **Founded:** 1994.. **Franchised:** 1995. **Equity Capital Needed:** $15,000. **Franchise Fee:** $12,500 or $17,500. **Financial Assistance:** Yes. **Training:** Yes.

20288 ■ Learning Express
29 Buena Vista St.
Devens, MA 01434
Ph: (800)436-8697
Fax: (978)889-1010
Description: Educational toy store. **No. of Franchise Units:** 160. **Founded:** 1987.. **Franchised:** 1987. **Equity Capital Needed:** $100,000 capital requirement. **Franchise Fee:** $35,000. **Training:** Yes.

20289 ■ Once Upon a Child
Winmark Corp.
605 Hwy. 169 N, Ste. 400
Minneapolis, MN 55441-6536
Ph: (763)520-8500
Free: 800-433-2540
Fax: (763)520-8410
Co. E-mail: winmark.information@winmarkcorporation.com
URL: http://www.winmarkcorporation.com
Description: Franchises consignment shops featuring children's products including toys, books, furniture, and apparel. **No. of Franchise Units:** 247. **Founded:** 1985. **Franchised:** 1993. **Equity Capital Needed:** $221,300-$312,600; approximately 30% cash requirement. **Franchise Fee:** $25,000. **Training:** Yes.

COMPUTERIZED DATABASES

20290 ■ *Gifts & Decorative Accessories*
3731 NW 8th Ave.
Boca Raton, FL 33431
Ph: (561)750-0151
Fax: (561)750-0152
Co. E-mail: sandowinfo@sandowmedia.com
URL: http://www.sandowmedia.com
Availability: Online: Sandow Media. **Type:** Full-text; Directory.

START-UP INFORMATION

20291 ■ *How to Start a Home-Based Event Planning Business*
Pub: Globe Pequot Press
Ed: Jill Moran. **Released:** July 2007. **Price:** $18.95.
Description: Guide to starting and growing a business planning events from a home-based firm.

20292 ■ *Mommy Millionaire: How I Turned My Kitchen Table Idea Into a Million Dollars and How You Can, Too!*
Pub: St. Martin's Press LLC
Ed: Kim Lavine. **Released:** February 19, 2008. **Price:** $14.95. **Description:** Advice, secrets and lessons for making a million dollars from a mom who turned her kitchen into a successful business; tools cover developing and patenting an idea, cold calling, trade shows, QVC, big retailers, manufacturing, and raising venture capital.

ASSOCIATIONS AND OTHER ORGANIZATIONS

20293 ■ **Canadian National Exhibition (CNE)—Exposition Nationale Canadienne**
Press Bldg.
Exhibition Pl.
210 Princes Blvd.
Toronto, ON, Canada M6K 3C3
Ph: (416)263-3800
Fax: (416)263-3838
Co. E-mail: info@theex.com
URL: http://www.theex.com
Contact: Brian Ashton, President
Description: Organizations sponsoring and participating in the Canadian National Exhibition. Promotes efficient and profitable operation of the exhibition. Facilitates cooperation among members; conducts promotional activities. **Founded:** 1879.

20294 ■ **Center for Exhibition Industry Research (CEIR)**
12700 Park Central Dr., Ste. 308
Dallas, TX 75251
Ph: (972)687-9242
Fax: (972)692-6020
Co. E-mail: info@ceir.org
URL: http://www.ceir.org
Contact: Carrie Freeman Parsons, Chairperson
Description: Promotes the growth, awareness and value of exhibitions and other face-to-face marketing events by producing and delivering research-based knowledge tools. Consists of exhibition organizers, service providers, exhibitors, CVBs and facilities. **Scope:** industry marketing, professional development, history, growth, trends. **Founded:** 1978. **Subscriptions:** 150 articles books clippings periodicals reports.

20295 ■ **Council of Protocol Executives (COPE)**
101 W 12th St., Ste. PH-H
New York, NY 10011

Ph: (212)633-6934
Fax: (212)633-6934
Co. E-mail: copeorg@aol.com
URL: http://www.councilofprotocolexecutives.org
Contact: Felice F Axelrod, President
Description: Persons who coordinate executive level meetings and special events for governments, corporations, and professional and nonprofit organizations; dedicated to increasing the level of professionalism in the field. Works to develop new ideas in all areas of meeting planning and identify trends in the industry. Reviews and recommends new and existing facilities and suppliers; conducts educational programs covering topics such as invitations, sports marketing, wines, entertainment of foreign guests, and speakers and entertainers; facilitates networking among members. **Founded:** 1988. **Publications:** *Protocol* (Annual).

20296 ■ **Event Service Professionals Association (ESPA)**
191 Clarksville Rd.
Princeton Junction, NJ 08550
Ph: (609)799-3712
Fax: (609)799-7032
Co. E-mail: info@acomonline.org
URL: http://www.acomonline.org
Contact: David Dvorak, President
Description: Convention service directors and managers of hotels, convention centers, and convention bureaus. Works to increase the effectiveness, productivity and quality of meetings, conventions and exhibitions. Works to establish high ethical standards, improve professional management techniques and increase awareness of client, employer and provider needs. Maintains speakers' bureau, resource center, and placement services; compiles statistics. Conducts research and educational programs. **Founded:** 1988. **Awards:** Executive Excellence Award (Annual); Convention Service Manager of the Year (Annual); Meeting Professional of the Year Award (Annual); Member of the Year Award (Annual).

20297 ■ **Exhibit Designers and Producers Association (EDPA)**
10 Norden Pl.
Norwalk, CT 06855
Ph: (203)852-5698
Fax: (203)854-6735
Co. E-mail: jprovost@edpa.com
URL: http://www.edpa.com
Contact: Cam Stevens, President
Description: Firms designing and building exhibits for trade shows and museums. Conducts educational and research programs. **Founded:** 1954. **Publications:** *EDP Action News* (Bimonthly); *EDPA.COM-munications* (Monthly); *EDPA Today* (Quarterly). **Educational Activities:** Exhibit Designers and Producers Association Convention (Annual). **Awards:** Hazel Hays Award; Ambassador Award; EDDIE Award; Designer of the Year Award; Ambassador Award (Annual); Chapter of the Year (Annual); Hazel Hays Award (Annual).

20298 ■ **Exposition Service Contractors Association (ESCA)**
5068 W Plano Pkwy., Ste. 300
Plano, TX 75093
Ph: (972)447-8212
Free: 877-792-3722
Fax: (972)447-8209
Co. E-mail: info@esca.org
URL: http://www.esca.org
Contact: Bruce Nable, President
Description: Engages in the provision of material and/or services normally furnished for trade shows, conventions, exhibitions and corporate meetings. Serves as a clearinghouse for the exchange of information among members and all other entities of the trade show and convention field. Seeks to promote and maintain progressive business and professional standards; advances better show techniques; improves the efficiency of material handling and on-site organization; enhances the use of manpower. **Founded:** 1970. **Publications:** *Guide to Exposition Service* (Annual). **Educational Activities:** Summer Educational Conference (Annual).

20299 ■ **International Association of Conference Center Administrators (IACCA)**
PO Box 298
Church Hill, MD 21623
Ph: (443)282-5858
Co. E-mail: admin@iacca.org
URL: http://www.iacca.org
Contact: Pam Harris, President
Description: Provides support to conference center administrators and furthers their professional development. Conducts educational programs; compiles statistics; offers information on legislative and legal trends. Offers professional certification. **Founded:** 1976. **Publications:** *IACCA Journal* (Periodic). **Educational Activities:** Journey of Leadership (Annual). **Awards:** Frank M. Washburn Award (Annual).

20300 ■ **International Association of Conference Centers (IACC)**
243 N Lindbergh Blvd.
St. Louis, MO 63141-7851
Ph: (314)993-8575
Fax: (314)993-8919
Co. E-mail: info@iacconline.org
URL: http://www.iacconline.org
Contact: Peter Stewart, President
Description: Executive, resort, corporate, college/university, and nonresidential conference centers in 13 countries; firms providing products and services to conference centers; conference center personnel. Promotes members' interests and disseminates marketing information. Provides educational programs, speakers, and trainers within the industry; conducts public relations campaign. Maintains Internet site with searchable database of all members. **Founded:** 1981. **Publications:** *Conference Center Concept.* **Awards:** Future Leaders Award (Annual).

20301 ■ **International Association of Exhibitions and Events (IAEE)**
12700 Park Central Dr., Ste. 308
Dallas, TX 75251

Ph: (972)458-8002
Fax: (972)458-8119
Co. E-mail: info@iaee.com
URL: http://www.iaee.com
Contact: David Dubois, President
Description: Managers and executives of shows, exhibits, and expositions; suppliers are associate members. Sponsors seminars to educate show managers. Conducts surveys, compiles statistics, and maintains placement service. Works to promote the exhibition industry throughout the world and to provide for the education and professional growth of its members. **Scope:** exposition management. **Founded:** 1928. **Subscriptions:** audio recordings books video recordings. **Publications:** E2: Exhibitions and Events (Monthly); IAEM Membership Directory and Buyer's Guide (Annual). **Educational Activities:** Expo! Expo! IAEE's Annual Meeting and Exhibition (Annual). **Awards:** Distinguished Service Merit (Annual). **Telecommunication Services:** news@iaee.com.

20302 ■ Professional Convention Management Association (PCMA)
35 E Wacker Dr., Ste. 500
Chicago, IL 60601-2105
Ph: (312)423-7262
Free: 877-827-7262
Fax: (312)423-7222
Co. E-mail: deborah.sexton@pcma.org
URL: http://www.pcma.org
Contact: Johnnie C. White, Chairman
Description: Represents the interests of meeting management executives from associations, non-profit organizations, corporations independent meeting planning companies, and multi-management firms who recognize the importance of meetings to their organization. Provides education, research and advocacy to advance the meetings and hospitality industry. Empowers members with the tools they need to succeed as meeting professionals and to promote the value of the industry to their organizations and the general public. **Founded:** 1957. **Publications:** Professional Convention Management Association--Membership Directory (Annual). **Awards:** Achievement Award (Annual); Distinguished Convention Service Manager Award (Annual); Distinguished Member Award (Annual); Educator of the Year Award (Annual); Spirit Award (Annual); Educator of the Year Award; Spirit Award; Distinguished Meeting Professional of the Year Award; Distinguished Convention Service Manager of the Year Award; Distinguished Member of the Year Award; Outstanding Service to a Chapter Award.

20303 ■ Trade Show Exhibitors Association (TSEA)
2301 S Lake Shore Dr., Ste. 1005
Chicago, IL 60616
Ph: (312)842-8732
Fax: (312)842-8744
Co. E-mail: tsea@tsea.org
URL: http://www.tsea.org
Contact: Margit B. Weisgal, President
Description: Exhibitors working to improve the effectiveness of trade shows as a marketing tool. Purposes are to promote the progress and development of trade show exhibiting; to collect and disseminate trade show information; conduct studies, surveys, and stated projects designed to improve trade shows; to foster good relations and communications with organizations representing others in the industry; to undertake other activities necessary to promote the welfare of member companies. Sponsors Exhibit Industry Education Foundation and professional exhibiting seminars; the forum series of educational programs on key issues affecting the industry. Maintains placement services; compiles statistics. **Publications:** Trade Show Ideas Magazine (Monthly); Trade Show Ideas; Trade Show Exhibitors Association--Membership Directory and Industry Buyer's Guide (Continuous). **Awards:** Focus Awards; President's Award (Annual); Chairman's Award (Annual); Distinguished Service Award (Annual).

DIRECTORIES OF EDUCATIONAL PROGRAMS

20304 ■ Meeting Planners International--Oregon Chapter--Annual

Membership Directory
Pub: LLM Publications Inc.
Contact: Linda L. Pope, President
E-mail: linda@llm.com
URL(s): www.llm.com/flippages.html. **Released:** Annual; Latest edition 2007-2008. **Covers:** Members of the Meeting Planners International in Oregon. **Entries include:** Name contact information, product/service provided.

REFERENCE WORKS

20305 ■ "$3 Million in Repairs Prep Cobo for Auto Show" in Crain's Detroit Business (Vol. 26, January 4, 2010, No. 1, pp. 1)
Pub: Crain Communications Inc.
Ed: Nancy Kaffer. **Description:** Overview of the six projects priced roughly at $3 million which were needed in order to host the North American International Auto Show; show organizers stated that the work was absolutely necessary to keep the show in the city of Detroit.

20306 ■ "2008 Woman of the Year Gala" in Hispanic Business (Vol. 30, July-August 2008, No. 7-8, pp. 58)
Pub: Hispanic Business, Inc.
Ed: Brynne Chappell. **Description:** Brief report on the sixth annual Women of the Year Awards gala which was held at JW Marriott Desert Ridge Resort and Spa is given: 20 women were honored with these awards for their professional contribution, commitment to the advancement of the Hispanic community and involvement with charitable organizations.

20307 ■ "ALA: Hot Topics for Librarianship" in Information Today (Vol. 28, September 2011, No. 8, pp. 17)
Pub: Information Today, Inc.
Ed: Barbara Brynko. **Description:** Highlights from the American Library Association Annual Conference and Exhibition are listed. Thousands of attendees sought out services, displays, demos, new product rollouts, and freebies. Emerging technology for librarians, staff development, gray literature, interlibrary loans, and next-generation interfaces were among the topics discussed.

20308 ■ "And In This Briefcase" in Mergers & Acquisitions: The Dealmaker's Journal (March 1, 2008)
Pub: SourceMedia, Inc.
Description: ACG San Diego decided to address the impact the changes in the economy will have on potential private equity transactions as well as what criteria private equity firms are looking for when assessing a company. At the opening of the chapter's 2008 breakfast meeting, real-world case studies were utilized with the audiences' participation in order to assess pre-deal risk scenarios.

20309 ■ Annual Trade Show Directory
Pub: Forum Publishing Co.
Contact: Justo Rey, President
URL(s): www.forum123.com/inc/sdetail/214. **Released:** Annual; Latest edition 2011. **Price:** $39.95, Individuals. **Covers:** over 2,400 merchandise trade shows throughout the United States and Canada. **Entries include:** Company name, address, phone, estimated attendance and number of exhibitors, show description. **Arrangement:** Classified by product, then chronological. **Indexes:** Product, type of show.

20310 ■ "AREE Meets in Atlantic City" in Indoor Comfort Marketing (Vol. 70, June 2011, No. 6, pp. 28)
Pub: Industry Publications Inc.
Description: Highlights of the Atlantic Region Energy Expo are provided.

20311 ■ "Around the World in a Day" in Agency Sales Magazine (Vol. 39, August 2009, No. 8, pp. 36)
Pub: MANA
Ed: Jack Foster. **Description:** Highlights of Manufacturer's Agents National Association (MANA) member Les Rapchak one-day visit to Basra, Iraq are presented. Rapchak completed the trip via Frankfurt,

Germany and Kuwait with a stop afterwards in Istanbul, Turkey. His purpose for the trip was to take part in a seminar at the State Company for Petrochemical Industries.

20312 ■ "Art Attack 2007 Comes to Minneapolis" in Art Business News (Vol. 34, November 2007, No. 11, pp. 11)
Pub: Pfingsten Publishing, LLC
Description: Overview of Art Attack 2007, an open studio and gallery crawl in the Northeast Minneapolis Arts District which featured artists working in glass, ceramics, jewelry, mosaics, mixed media, photography, painting, pottery, sculpture, textiles and wood.

20313 ■ "Art Miami Comes to Miami's Wynwood Art District" in Art Business News (Vol. 34, November 2007, No. 11, pp. 18)
Pub: Pfingsten Publishing, LLC
Description: In December, The Art Group will hold its Art Miami fair in the Wynwood Art District; the exhibitors range from painting, sculpture, video and works on paper.

20314 ■ "Artexpo Celebrates 30th Anniversary" in Art Business News (Vol. 34, November 2007, No. 11, pp. 18)
Pub: Pfingsten Publishing, LLC
Description: In honor of its 30th anniversary Artexpo New York 2008 will be an unforgettable show offering a collection of fine-art education courses for both trade and consumer attendees and featuring a variety of artists working in all mediums.

20315 ■ "An Artwork in Progress" in Hawaii Business (Vol. 53, March 2008, No. 9, pp. 45)
Pub: Hawaii Business Publishing
Ed: Jolyn Okimoto Rosa. **Description:** Art galleries in Honolulu, Hawaii holds the First Friday Gallery Walk and other special events, which draw crowd to and increase sales activities in the city's downtown. The district also advocates for the reintroduction of Honolulu's Chinatown to the people. Details regarding the art galleries' Chinatown revival and its local economic impact are discussed.

20316 ■ Association Management--Convention Center & Convention Bureau Directory
Pub: American Society of Association Executives
Contact: John H. Graham, IV, President
URL(s): www.asaecenter.org. **Ed:** Debra Popovich. **Released:** Annual; February. **Price:** Free Online version. **Publication includes:** List of convention halls, centers, auditoriums, arenas, and convention and visitors bureaus in the United States, Canada, and abroad. **Entries include:** Name of hall or CVB, phone, fax, and exhibit space available. **Arrangement:** Geographical. **Telecommunication Services:** Email: mhallin@asaenet.org .

20317 ■ "Attorney Panel Tackles Contract Questions" in Agency Sales Magazine (Vol. 39, September-October 2009, No. 9, pp. 8)
Pub: MANA
Ed: Jack Foster. **Description:** MANAfest conference tackled issues regarding a sales representative's contract. One attorney from the panel advised reps to go through proposed agreements with attorneys who are knowledgeable concerning rep laws. Another attorney advised reps to communicate with a company to ask about their responsibilities if that company is facing financial difficulty.

20318 ■ "Auto Show Aims to Electrify" in Crain's Detroit Business (Vol. 26, January 11, 2010, No. 2, pp. 1)
Pub: Crain Communications, Inc.
Ed: Ryan Beene. **Description:** Overview of the North American International Auto show include sixteen production and concept vehicles including eight from the Detroit 3. High-tech battery suppliers as well as hybrid and electric vehicles will highlight the show.

20319 ■ "Avanti Hosts Users Conference" in American Printer (Vol. 128, July 1, 2011, No. 7)
Pub: Penton Media Inc.
Description: Avanti Computer Systems Ltd. hosted its 19th annual users conference in Washington DC. In-plant and commercial printers were in attendance.

20320 ■ *"BBB Hires Marketing Firm to Attract More Businesses"* in Baltimore Business Journal (Vol. 27, January 1, 2010, No. 35, pp. 1)
Pub: American City Business Journals
Ed: Julekha Dash. **Description:** Better Business Bureau (BBB) of Greater Maryland hired Bystry Carson & Associates Ltd. to assist in its rebranding efforts in order to entice more businesses. Bystry Carson will promote BBB's new mission at lectures, seminars, and networking events, as well as educate businesses about the agency through blogs and Twitter. BBB's services are also outlined.

20321 ■ *"Biz Assesses 'Textgate' Fallout; Conventions, Smaller Deals Affected"* in Crain's Detroit Business (Vol. 24, March 31, 2008)
Pub: Crain Communications, Inc.
Ed: Tom Henderson. **Description:** Businesspeople who were trying to measure the amount of economic damage is likely to be caused due to Mayor Kwame Kilpatrick's indictment on eight charges and found that: automotive and other large global deals are less likely to be affected than location decisions by smaller companies and convention site decisions. Also being affected are negotiations in which Mexican startup companies were planning a partnership with the TechTown incubator to pursue opportunities in the auto sector; those plans are being put on hold while they look at other sites.

20322 ■ *"Bottom-Fishing and Speed-Dating in India"* in Barron's (Vol. 88, March 24, 2008, No. 12, pp. M12)
Pub: Dow Jones & Company, Inc.
Ed: Elliot Wilson. **Description:** Indian stocks have fallen hard in 2008, with Mumbai's Sensex 30 down 30 percent from its January 2008 peak of 21,000 to 14,995 in March. The India Private Equity Fair 2008 attracted 140 of the world's largest private equity firms and about 24 of India's fastest-growing corporations. Statistical data included.

20323 ■ *"The British Aren't Coming"* in Crain's Chicago Business (Vol. 34, October 24, 2011, No. 42, pp. 3)
Pub: Crain Communications Inc.
Ed: Brigid Sweeney. **Description:** In a move to attract tourists back to Chicago, its Convention and Tourism Bureau is marketing in London, England, Mexico, and Canada, but not Germany or France because of budget constraints.

20324 ■ *"Calendar"* in Crain's Detroit Business (Vol. 24, March 10, 2008, No. 10, pp. 21)
Pub: Crain Communications, Inc.
Description: Listing of events in the Detroit area include conferences addressing entrepreneurialism, economic development, and women business ownership.

20325 ■ *"Calendar"* in Crain's Detroit Business (Vol. 24, March 17, 2008, No. 11, pp. 20)
Pub: Crain Communications, Inc.
Description: Listing of events in the Detroit area include conferences addressing entrepreneurialism, economic development, and women business ownership.

20326 ■ *"Calendar"* in Crain's Detroit Business (Vol. 24, March 24, 2008, No. 12, pp. 25)
Pub: Crain Communications, Inc.
Description: Listing of events in the Detroit area include conferences addressing entrepreneurialism, economic development, and women business ownership.

20327 ■ *"Calendar"* in Crain's Detroit Business (Vol. 24, March 31, 2008, No. 13, pp. 1)
Pub: Crain Communications, Inc.
Description: Listing of events in the Detroit area include conferences addressing entrepreneurialism, economic development, and minority business ownership.

20328 ■ *"Calendar"* in Crain's Detroit Business (Vol. 24, April 7, 2008, No. 14, pp. 27)
Pub: Crain Communications, Inc.
Description: Listing of events in the Detroit area include conferences addressing entrepreneurialism, economic development, and minority business ownership.

20329 ■ *"Calendar"* in Crain's Detroit Business (Vol. 24, April 14, 2008, No. 15, pp. 25)
Pub: Crain Communications Inc.
Description: Listing of events in the Detroit area include conferences addressing entrepreneurialism, economic development, and ways in which to develop environmentally friendly buildings.

20330 ■ *"Calendar"* in Crain's Detroit Business (Vol. 24, September 22, 2008, No. 38, pp. 17)
Pub: Crain Communications Inc.
Description: Listing of events in the Detroit area include conferences addressing entrepreneurialism, economic development, and women business ownership.

20331 ■ *"Calendar"* in Crain's Detroit Business (Vol. 24, October 6, 2008, No. 40, pp. 22)
Pub: Crain Communications, Inc.
Description: Listing of events in the Detroit area include conferences addressing entrepreneurialism, economic development, manufacturing, marketing, the housing crisis and women business ownership.

20332 ■ *"Calendar"* in Crain's Detroit Business (Vol. 26, January 11, 2010, No. 2, pp. 16)
Pub: Crain Communications, Inc.
Description: Listing of events includes seminars sponsored by the Detroit Economic Club as well as conferences dealing with globalization and graphic design.

20333 ■ *"Calendar"* in Crain's Detroit Business (Vol. 26, January 18, 2010, No. 3, pp. 16)
Pub: Crain Communications, Inc.
Description: Listing of events includes seminars sponsored by the Detroit Economic Club as well as conferences dealing with globalization and marketing.

20334 ■ *"CarBiz Inc. Speaking At NABD"* in Canadian Corporate News (May 14, 2007)
Pub: Comtex News Network Inc.
Description: CarBiz Inc., a leading provider of software, consulting, and training solutions to the United States' automotive industry, had two of its executive officers speak at the National Alliance of Buy Here - Pay Here Dealers (NABD), a conference that draws over 2,000 dealers, service providers, and experts from across the United States.

20335 ■ *"Celebrate Success. Embrace Innovation"* in Black Enterprise (Vol. 37, February 2007, No. 7, pp. 145)
Pub: Earl G. Graves Publishing Co. Inc.
Description: 2007 Women of Power Summit provides networking opportunities, empowerment sessions, and nightly entertainment. More than 500 executive women of color are expected to attend this inspiring summit in Phoenix, February 7-10.

20336 ■ *"Change Is in the Air"* in Agency Sales Magazine (Vol. 39, August 2009, No. 8, pp. 30)
Pub: MANA
Ed: Jack Foster. **Description:** Highlights of the Power-Motion Technology Representatives Association (PTRA) 37th Annual Conference, which projected an economic upturn, are presented. Allan Bealulieu of the Institute for Trend Research gave the positive news while Manufacturer's Agents National Association (MANA) president Brain Shirley emphasized the need to take advantage of a turnaround.

20337 ■ *"Chattanooga at a Glance"* in Women In Business (Vol. 62, June 2010, No. 2, pp. 29)
Pub: American Business Women's Association
Ed: Jill Yates Bagby. **Description:** City of Chattanooga, Tennessee is the location of the 2010 American Business Women's Association (ABWA) National Women's Leadership Conference. The city offers historical sites, parks and tourist attractions, as well as dining options.

20338 ■ *"Clinic to Use Medical Summit to Pump Up Cardiology Center"* in Crain's Cleveland Business (Vol. 28, October 1, 2007, No. 39, pp. 6)
Pub: Crain Communications, Inc.
Ed: Chuck Soder. **Description:** Overview of the Medical Innovation Summit, sponsored by the Cleveland Clinic and regional business recruitment group Team NEO, whose theme was cardiology. The goal for this year's summit went beyond finding companies for the cardiovascular center, it also looked to market the region to other industries with growth potential.

20339 ■ *"Clusters Last Stand?"* in Canadian Electronics (Vol. 23, February 2008, No. 1, pp. 6)
Pub: CLB Media Inc.
Description: Survival of technology clusters was the focus of Strategic Microelectronics Council's conference entitled, 'The Power of Community: Building Technology Clusters in Canada'. Clusters can help foster growth in the microelectronics sector, and it was recognized that government intervention is needed to maintain these clusters.

20340 ■ *"Conference Calendar"* in Marketing to Women (Vol. 21, April 2008, No. 4, pp. 7)
Pub: EPM Communications Inc.
Contact: Ira Mayer, President
E-mail: imayer@epmcom.com
Description: Listing of current conferences and events concerning women, marketing and business.

20341 ■ *"Conference Calendar"* in Marketing to Women (Vol. 21, March 2008, No. 3, pp. 7)
Pub: EPM Communications Inc.
Contact: Ira Mayer, President
E-mail: imayer@epmcom.com
Description: Listing of current conferences and events aimed at women entrepreneurs and leaders.

20342 ■ *"Conference Calendar"* in Marketing to Women (Vol. 21, February 2008, No. 2, pp. 1)
Pub: EPM Communications Inc.
Contact: Ira Mayer, President
E-mail: imayer@epmcom.com
Description: Listing of current conferences and events concerning women, marketing and business.

20343 ■ *"Conference Calendar"* in Marketing to Women (Vol. 22, July 2009, No. 7, pp. 7)
Pub: EPM Communications Inc.
Contact: Ira Mayer, President
E-mail: imayer@epmcom.com
Description: Listing of conferences and seminars targeting female entrepreneurs.

20344 ■ *"Conference Calendar"* in Marketing to Women (Vol. 22, August 2009, No. 8, pp. 7)
Pub: EPM Communications Inc.
Contact: Ira Mayer, President
E-mail: imayer@epmcom.com
Description: Listing of conferences and seminars targeting female entrepreneurs.

20345 ■ *"Convention Budgeting Best Practice"* in Franchising World (Vol. 42, November 2010, No. 11, pp. 11)
Pub: International Franchise Association
Contact: Stephen J. Caldeira, Chief Executive Officer
E-mail: scaldeira@franchise.org
Ed: Steve Friedman. **Description:** Franchise conventions can offer benefits to both franchisor and franchisee in terms of culture-building, professional education and networking. However, these conventions can be costly. Tips for planning a successful franchising convention on a budget are outlined.

20346 ∎ *"Convention Calendar" in Black Enterprise (Vol. 37, February 2007, No. 7, pp. 68)*

Pub: Earl G. Graves Publishing Co. Inc.

Description: Listing of conventions and trade show of interest to minority and women business leaders.

20347 ∎ *"Convention Calendar" in Black Enterprise (Vol. 37, December 2006, No. 5, pp. 74)*

Pub: Earl G. Graves Publishing Co. Inc.

Description: Listing of conferences and summits targeting African American business owners and executives.

20348 ∎ *"Convention Calendar" in Black Enterprise (Vol. 37, November 2006, No. 4, pp. 76)*

Pub: Earl G. Graves Publishing Co. Inc.

Description: Listing of conferences targeted at African American executives and business owners.

20349 ∎ *"Datebook" in Crain's Chicago Business (Vol. 31, March 24, 2008, No. 12, pp. 18)*

Pub: Crain Communications, Inc.

Description: Listing of events in the Detroit area include conferences addressing entrepreneurialism, economic development, secrets of getting hired, and women business ownership.

20350 ∎ *"Datebook" in Crain's Chicago Business (Vol. 31, March 31, 2008, No. 13, pp. 1)*

Pub: Crain Communications, Inc.

Description: Listing of events in the Detroit area include conferences addressing entrepreneurialism, economic development, secrets of getting hired, and women business ownership.

20351 ∎ *"Datebook" in Crain's Chicago Business (Vol. 31, April 28, 2008, No. 17, pp. 18)*

Pub: Crain Communications, Inc.

Description: Listing of events in the Detroit area include conferences addressing entrepreneurialism, economic development, and women business ownership.

20352 ∎ *"Datran Media Executives to Lead Industry Debates Across Q1 Conferences" in Internet Wire (January 22, 2010)*

Pub: Comtex News Network, Inc.

Description: Datran Media, an industry-leading digital marketing technology company, will be sending members of its management team to several conferences in the early part of the first quarter of 2010; discussions will include Internet marketing innovations, e-commerce and media distribution.

20353 ∎ *"Designing Events Updates Online Suite" in Wireless News (October 25, 2009)*

Pub: Close-Up Media

Description: Designing Events, an outsourcing and consulting firm for conferences and meetings, announced the release of an update to its Designing Events Online suite of web-based management and marketing tools; features include enhanced versions of online registration and collaboration, content management, session development, social media and conference websites.

20354 ∎ *"Detroit Hosts Conferences on Green Building, IT, Finance" in Crain's Detroit Business (Vol. 25, June 1, 2009, No. 22, pp. 9)*

Pub: Crain Communications Inc. - Detroit

Ed: Tom Henderson. **Description:** Detroit will host three conferences in June 2009, one features green technology, one information technology and the third will gather black bankers and financial experts from across the nation.

20355 ∎ *"Developer Banks On East Submarket, Slowdown Not a Hinderance" in The Business Journal-Serving Greater Tampa Bay (August 1, 2008)*

Pub: American City Business Journals, Inc.

Ed: Janet Leiser. **Description:** CLW Industrial Group and Cobalt Industrial REIT II have teamed up to develop a 14-acre area in northeast Hillsborough County, Florida. The $15 million industrial park project includes the 175,000-square-foot New Tampa Commerce Center, scheduled for completion in the first quarter of 2009.

20356 ∎ *"Developers Await Hotel" in The Business Journal-Portland (Vol. 25, July 11, 2008, No. 18, pp. 1)*

Pub: American City Business Journals, Inc.

Ed: Wendy Culverwell. **Description:** Developers are eager to start the construction of a new hotel at the Oregon Convention Center in Portland, Oregon as hey say that the project will help boost the convention center neighborhood. The project, called The Westin Portland at the Convention Center, is partly handled by Ashforth Pacific Inc.

20357 ∎ *"The Display Group Is Super-Sized" in Michigan Vue (Vol. 13, July-August 2008, No. 4, pp. 34)*

Pub: Entrepreneur Media Inc.

Description: Profile of the Display Group, located in downtown Detroit, this company provides custom designed mobile marketing displays as well as special event production services for trade show displays. The rental house and design service is also beginning to see more business due to the film initiative, which provides incentives for films that are shooting in Michigan.

20358 ∎ *"Dow Champions Innovative Energy Solutions for Auto Industry at NAIAS" in Business of Global Warming (January 25, 2010, pp. 7)*

Pub: Investment Weekly News

Description: This year's North American International Auto Show in Detroit will host the 'Electric Avenue' exhibit sponsored by the Dow Chemical Company. The display will showcase the latest in innovative energy solutions from Dow as well as electric vehicles and the technology supporting them. This marks the first time a non-automotive manufacturer is part of the main floor of the show.

20359 ∎ *"Downtowns Must Court Young, CEOs for Cities President Says" in Crain's Detroit Business (Vol. 24, October 6, 2008, No. 40, pp. 18)*

Pub: Crain Communications, Inc.

Ed: Amy Lane. **Description:** It is important to produce more college graduates, and keep them in Michigan, according to CEOs for Cities President Carol Coletta when she spoke to a session at the West Michigan Regional Policy Conference which was held in September in Grand Rapids. Ways in which city leaders can connect students to communities, resulting in employees who have vested interest in the region, are also discussed.

20360 ∎ *"The Early Bird Gets the Worm" in Black Enterprise (Vol. 37, January 2007, No. 6, pp. 111)*

Pub: Earl G. Graves Publishing Co. Inc.

Ed: Tykisha N. Lundy. **Description:** General Motors hosts the Black Enterprise Conference And Expo: Where Deals Are Made at Walt Disney World's Swan and Dolphin Resort, May 9-12. The conference will offer great information to entrepreneurs.

20361 ∎ *"East-Side Real Estate Forum Detours To Grand Rapids" in Crain's Detroit Business (Vol. 24, October 6, 2008, No. 40, pp. 17)*

Pub: Crain Communications, Inc.

Ed: Daniel Duggan. **Description:** Tom Wackerman was elected chairman of the University of Michigan-Urban Land Institute Real Estate Forum and proposed that the annual conference be held in Grand Rapids due to the brisk economic activity he was finding there; although the idea was initially met with resistance, the plan to introduce East-siders to the West side began receiving more enthusiasm due to the revitalization of the area, which was once considered to have a bleak outlook. Many are hoping to learn the lessons of those who were able to change a negative economic climate into a positive one in which the cooperation of private business and government can work together to accomplish goals.

20362 ∎ *"Economy Forcing Meeting Planners to Think Fast" in Crain's Cleveland Business (Vol. 30, June 15, 2009, No. 23, pp. 15)*

Pub: Crain Communications, Inc.

Ed: Amy Ann Stoessel. **Description:** Meeting planners are working hard to meet lower corporate budgets when planning events.

20363 ∎ *"Entrepreneurs Conference" in Black Enterprise (Vol. 38, February 2008, No. 7, pp. 163)*

Pub: Earl G. Graves Publishing Co. Inc.

Description: Black Enterprise Entrepreneurs Conference and Expo will be held May 14-17, 2008 at the Charlotte Westin Hotel and Charlotte Convention Center in North Carolina. Entrepreneurs are given the opportunity to present their business ideas in the Bevator Pitch Competition for a chance to win products and services.

20364 ∎ *"Events Struggling with Fees" in Philadelphia Business Journal (Vol. 28, November 20, 2009, No. 40, pp. 1)*

Pub: American City Business Journals

Ed: Peter van Allen. **Description:** Dad Vail Regatta organizers told Philadelphia officials their plans to move the rowing event out of Philadelphia into Rumson, New Jersey was due to rising fees from the city and the loss of corporate sponsorship. Smaller events have been left out of funding or transferred to other locations due, in part, to higher fees also.

20365 ∎ *"Finding Room for Financing" in The Business Journal-Serving Metropolitan Kansas City (Vol. 26, August 1, 2008, No. 47, pp. 1)*

Pub: American City Business Journals, Inc.

Ed: Rob Roberts. **Description:** Kansas City officials are expecting to receive financing recommendations for a new 1,000-room convention headquarters hotel. The $300-million project could be financed either through private ownership with public subsidies, or through public ownership with tax-exempt bond financing. Other views and information on the project and its expected economic impact, are presented.

20366 ∎ *"Four Exhibition Considerations" in American Printer (Vol. 128, August 1, 2011, No. 8)*

Pub: Penton Media Inc.

Description: Four questions to ask at the Graph Expo will help printers improve their own business.

20367 ∎ *"Grainger Show Highlights Building Green, Economy" in Contractor (Vol. 57, February 2010, No. 2, pp. 3)*

Pub: Penton Media, Inc.

Ed: Candace Roulo. **Description:** chief U.S. economist told attendees of the Grainger's 2010 Total MRO Solutions National Customer Show that the economic recovery would be subdued. Mechanical contractors who attended the event also learned about building sustainable, green products, and technologies, and economic and business challenges.

20368 ∎ *"Grand Action Makes Grand Changes in Grand Rapids" in Crain's Detroit Business (Vol. 25, June 1, 2009, No. 22, pp. M012)*

Pub: Crain Communications Inc. - Detroit

Ed: Amy Lane. **Description:** Businessman Dick DeVos believes that governments are not always the best to lead certain initiatives. That's why, in 1991, he gathered 50 west Michigan community leaders and volunteers to look consider the construction of an arena and expanding or renovating local convention operations. Grand Action has undertaken four major projects in the city.

20369 ∎ *"Half a World Away" in Tampa Bay Business Journal (Vol. 30, December 4, 2009, No. 50, pp. 1)*

Pub: American City Business Journals

Ed: Jane Meinhardt. **Description:** Enterprise Florida has offered four trade grants for Florida's marine industry businesses to give them a chance to tap into the Middle East market at the Dubai International Boat Show on March 9 to 13, 2010. The grants pay for 50 percent of the exhibition costs for the qualifying business.

20370 ■ "Here's the Deal" in Crain's Cleveland Business (Vol. 30, June 15, 2009, No. 23, pp. 14)
Pub: Crain Communications, Inc.
Description: Incentives being offered by hotels, restaurants, golf courses and major chains in order to promote bookings for meetings or conferences in the Cleveland area are listed.

20371 ■ "Herrell's Launches New Corporate Identity at Fancy Food Show" in Ice Cream Reporter (Vol. 23, July 20, 2010, No. 8, pp. 3)
Pub: Ice Cream Reporter
Description: Herrell's ice cream introduced a new corporate branding at the Summer 2010 Fancy Food Show last summer. Slightly Mad Communications advertising agency developed the new brand to reflect the era of the early 1970s.

20372 ■ "Hotel Tax Eyed For Waukesha" in The Business Journal-Milwaukee (Vol. 25, August 29, 2008, No. 49, pp. A1)
Pub: American City Business Journals, Inc.
Ed: Rich Kirchen. **Description:** Midwest Airlines Center chairman Frank Gimbel wants Waukesha County to help in the funding of the $200-million expansion of the convention center through a hotel room tax. The Waukesha hotel industry is expected to oppose the new room tax. Other views and information on the planned new room tax in Waukesha are presented.

20373 ■ "How to Declutter Your Life Closet Cleanup: Putting a Lid on Clutter" in Atlanta Journal-Constitution (May 1, 2011)
Pub: Atlanta Journal-Constitution
Ed: Felicia Feaster. **Description:** The annual Closets and Home Organization Convention and Expo spotlights new products and services designed to help people get organized at home or the workplace. The organization sector is holding steady despite the recession and is expected to expand into garage organization.

20374 ■ IAEM Membership Directory and Buyer's Guide
Pub: National Association of Exposition Managers, Inc.
URL(s): www.iaee.com. **Released:** Annual; December. **Price:** Free to members. **Covers:** Over 1,600 show manager members and 1,700 associate members (including service suppliers, convention hall representatives, and others). **Entries include:** Individual's name, title, firm name, address, phone and fax number. **Arrangement:** Member lists are alphabetical by personal name; classified by company name and product/service. **Indexes:** Association or company affiliation.

20375 ■ "IFA-AAG Professional Athlete Franchise Summit Scores" in Franchising World (Vol. 42, August 2010, No. 8, pp. 56)
Pub: International Franchise Association
Ed: Miriam L. Brewer. **Description:** The first International Franchise Association-Allied Athlete Group Franchise summit spotlighted athletes turned business owners addressing peers on franchising. The summit is expected to become an annual event.

20376 ■ "Industry Events 2011" in American Printer (Vol. 128, August 1, 2011, No. 8)
Pub: Penton Media Inc.
Description: Listing of events of interest to graphic arts and printing businesses in presented.

20377 ■ "Industry/Events 2011" in American Printer (Vol. 128, July 1, 2011, No. 7)
Pub: Penton Media Inc.
Description: PMA, the Worldwide Community of Imaging Association launched its new CliQ with how-to tips, product reviews and monthly photo contests. PMA formed a partnership with the Consumer Electronics Association to make changes to this year's annual convention.

20378 ■ "IPEX Moves to London Venue" in American Printer (Vol. 128, July 1, 2011, No. 7)
Pub: Penton Media Inc.
Description: IPES 2014 is being relocated to London's ExCeL International Exhibition and Conference Centre from March 26 to April 2, 2014.

20379 ■ "Javo Beverage to Feature On-Demand Coffee System" in GlobeNewswire (October 20, 2009)
Pub: Comtex News Network, Inc.
Description: During the National Association of Convenience Store Show (NACS) at the Las Vegas Convention Center, Javo Beverage Company, Inc., a leading provider of premium dispensable coffee and tea-based beverages to the foodservice industry, will introduce its on-demand hot coffee system as well as a new line of products for the convenience store industry.

20380 ■ "Jay Berkowitz to Present Making Social Media Money Seminar at Affiliate Summit West" in Entertainment Close-Up (January 15, 2010)
Pub: Close-Up Media
Description: Highlights of Jay Berkowitz's conference, 'Making Social Media Make Money' include ways in which to develop Internet marketing strategies that will maximize Website traffic and convert that traffic to sales.

20381 ■ "Kent Officials Seek Further KSU, City Unity" in Crain's Cleveland Business (Vol. 28, December 3, 2007, No. 48, pp. 3)
Pub: Crain Communications, Inc.
Ed: Jay Miller. **Description:** Kent State University and Portage County are searching for a developer who will use a three-acre parcel to bring new life to the city's sagging downtown and create an area that will better link the town and the Kent State campus. The project will include a hotel and conference center as well as retail and restaurant space.

20382 ■ "Kuno Creative to Present B2B Social Media Campaign Webinar" in Entertainment Close-Up (August 25, 2011)
Pub: Close-Up Media
Description: Kuno Creative, an inbound marketing agency, will host Three Steps of a Successful B2B Social Media Campaign. The firm is a provider of Website development, branding, marketing strategy, public relations, Internet marketing, and inbound marketing.

20383 ■ "Let's Put On a Show" in Inc. (November 2007, pp. 127)
Pub: Gruner & Jahr USA Publishing
Ed: Elaine Appleton Grant. **Description:** Profile of Jeff Baker, CEO of Image 4, designer of trade show exhibits. Baker shares details of the firm's commitment to being green.

20384 ■ "Local Green Technology on Display" in Crain's Detroit Business (Vol. 26, January 18, 2010, No. 3, pp. 1)
Pub: Crain Communications Inc.
Ed: Ryan Beene. **Description:** Detroit's 2010 North American International Auto Show put the newest, most innovative green technologies on display showing that the Southeast Michigan automobile industry is gaining traction with its burgeoning e-vehicle infrastructure. Think, a Norwegian electric city-car manufacturer is eyeing sites in Southeast Michigan in which to locate its corporate headquarters and technical center for its North American branch.

20385 ■ "Look, Leap, and License" in Retail Merchandiser (Vol. 51, July-August 2011, No. 4, pp. 16)
Pub: Phoenix Media Corporation
Description: Toys highlighting the Licensing International Expo 2011 included a life-sized Cookie Monster, Papa Smurf, Power Rangers, Transformer, and margarita wrestlers. Taking licensed properties international was a common theme at this year's show.

20386 ■ Mail Order in the Internet Age
Pub: Morgan James Publishing, LLC
Ed: Ted Ciuba. **Released:** May 2004. **Price:** $19.95.
Description: Direct response market, or mail order, for marketing and selling a product or service is discussed, with emphasis on how direct marketing compares favorably to other methods in terms of speed, ease, profitability, and affordability. Advice is given for writing ads; seminars to attend; and newsletters, mailing lists and magazines in which to subscribe.

20387 ■ "Major Golf Retail Show in the Rough for 2010" in Orlando Business Journal (Vol. 26, January 15, 2010, No. 33, pp. 1)
Pub: American City Business Journals
Ed: Anjali Fluker. **Description:** The 57th Annual PGA Merchandise Show in Orlando, Florida is projected to attract 39,000 attendees in 2010, compared with 41,000 in 2009. According to the Orange County Convention Center, economic benefits that could be obtained from the 2010 edition of the golf retail show might reach only $77 million, compared with $78 million generated last year.

20388 ■ "MANAfest Provides Reps with Tools for the Future" in Agency Sales Magazine (Vol. 39, September-October 2009, No. 9, pp. 36)
Pub: MANA
Ed: Jack Foster. **Description:** Former Harley Davidson director of communications Ken Schmidt was the keynote speaker at the MANAfest conference; he discussed how the company delivered itself from bankruptcy. Selling Power magazine publisher Gerhard Gschwandtner also made a presentation; he believes that there will be opportunities for sales people involved in relationship selling.

20389 ■ "Minnesota ABC Event Looks at Government Contracting" in Finance and Commerce Daily Newspaper (November 23, 2010)
Pub: Dolan Media Newswires
Ed: Brian Johnson. **Description:** Minnesota Associated Builders and Contractors hosted an event focusing on doing business with government agencies. Topics included bidding work, awarding jobs, paperwork, guidelines, certifications and upcoming projects.

20390 ■ "More Than 1,000 Attend Second WaterSmart" in Contractor (Vol. 56, November 2009, No. 11, pp. 3)
Pub: Penton Media, Inc.
Description: Over 1,000 plumbing and water conservation professionals attended the second WaterSmart Innovations Conference and Exposition in Las Vegas. Plumbing industry personalities made presentations during the conference and several innovative products were displayed at the trade show.

20391 ■ "Nobody Knows What To Do" in Barron's (Vol. 88, March 17, 2008, No. 11, pp. 40)
Pub: Dow Jones & Company, Inc.
Ed: Mark Veverka. **Description:** Attendees of the South by Southwest Interactive conference failed to get an insight on how to make money on the Web from former Walt Disney CEO Michael Eisner when Eisner said there's no proven business model for financing projects. Eisner said he finances his projects with the help of his connections to get product-placement deals.

20392 ■ "Norvax University Health Insurance Sales Training and Online Marketing Conference" in Internet Wire (January 27, 2010)
Pub: Comtex News Network, Inc.
Description: Overview of the Norvax University Marketing and Sales Success Conference Tour which includes insurance sales training seminars, proven and innovative online marketing techniques and a host of additional information and networking opportunities.

20393 ■ "Not Enough Room" in Austin Business JournalInc. (Vol. 29, November 13,

2009, No. 36, pp. A1)
Pub: American City Business Journals
Ed: Jacob Dirr. **Description:** Hotel and convention business in downtown Austin, Texas lost nearly $5.3 million when Dell Inc. relocated its annual convention to Las Vegas. However, lack of capital caused the postponement of various hotel projects which need to be finished in order to attract well-attended conventions. Makeover projects on Austin's Waller Creek and Sixth Street are discussed.

20394 ■ *"Now See This" in Entrepreneur (Vol. 36, April 2008, No. 4, pp. 53)*
Pub: Entrepreneur Media, Inc.
Ed: Mike Hogan. **Description:** New high definition (HD) products are to be introduced in 2008 at the Consumer Electronics Show and the Macworld Conference & Expo. HD lineup from companies such as Dell Inc. and Hewlett-Packard Co. are discussed.

20395 ■ *"Nowspeed and OneSource to Conduct Webinar" in Internet Wire (December 14, 2009)*
Pub: Comtex News Network, Inc.
Description: OneSource, a leading provider of global business information, and Nowspeed, an Internet marketing agency, will conduct a webinar titled 'How to Develop Social Media Content That Gets Results' in order to provide marketers insight into how to develop and optimize effective social media content to get consumer results that translate into purchases and lead generation.

20396 ■ *"Nowspeed's David Reske to Speak at SolidWorks World 2010 in Anaheim" in Internet Wire (January 7, 2010)*
Pub: Comtex News Network, Inc.
Description: David Reske managing director at Nowspeed, an Internet marketing agency based in the Boston area, will be presenting at SolidWorks World 2010; the convention's presentation will focus on proven methodologies, practical tips and real-world case studies in order to help attendees leverage the powerful Internet marketing innovations that are proving effective for businesses.

20397 ■ *"O'Loughlin Cuts $6 Million for Chesterfield Doubletree" in Saint Louis Business Journal (Vol. 32, September 2, 2011, No. 1, pp. 1)*
Pub: Saint Louis Business Journal
Ed: Angela Mueller. **Description:** Lodging Hospitality Management (LHM) acquired the Doubletree Hotel and Conference Center in Chesterfield, Missouri and added it as the 18th hotel in its portfolio. LHM chairman and CEO Bob O'Loughlin plans to invest nearly $15 million in the hotel, including $9 for renovation.

20398 ■ *"One World" in American Printer (Vol. 128, August 1, 2011, No. 8)*
Pub: Penton Media Inc.
Description: Graph Expo will highlight entrepreneurs focused on the connection between content, technology and business models.

20399 ■ *"The Open Mobile Summit Opens in San Francisco Today: John Donahoe CEO eBay to Keynote" in Benzinga.com (November 2, 2011)*
Pub: Benzinga.com
Ed: Benzinga Staff. **Description:** eBay's CEO, John Donahoe was keynote speaker at the 4th Annual Open Mobile Summit held in San Francisco, California. eBay is one of the 130 companies participating as speakers at the event.

20400 ■ *"People/Calendar" in Brandweek (Vol. 49, April 21, 2008, No. 16, pp. 30)*
Pub: VNU Business Media, Inc.
Description: Listing of current conferences, tradeshows and events concerning the marketing industry.

20401 ■ *"People and Places" in Entrepreneur (Vol. 36, February 2008, No. 2, pp. 12)*
Pub: Entrepreneur Media Inc.
Ed: Rieva Lesonsky. **Description:** Websites of different organizations that can provide entrepreneurs with business help are presented. Business-related events such as the Women in Charge conference and Xerox Smart Business Symposium are mentioned.

20402 ■ *"PHCC Convention, Show Gets High Marks" in Contractor (Vol. 56, December 2009, No. 12, pp. 1)*
Pub: Penton Media, Inc.
Ed: Robert P. Mader. **Description:** Plumbing-Heating-Cooling Contractors National Association has held its first convention and trade show in New Orleans, Louisiana. Attendees were treated to a variety of seminars and exhibitors during the event. Comments from event organizers are also given.

20403 ■ *"Pipe Show Finds a Way for Smokers to Light Up" in Crain's Chicago Business (Vol. 31, April 28, 2008, No. 17, pp. 57)*
Pub: Crain Communications, Inc.
Ed: H. Lee Murphy. **Description:** With the help of attorneys within its local membership of 150 pipe collectors, the Chicagoland Pipe Collectors Club will be allowed to smoke at its 13th International Pipe & Tobacciana Show at Pheasant Run Resort. The event is expected to draw 4,000 pipe enthusiasts from as far as China and Russia.

20404 ■ *"Plan Your Next Event at Newport News Marriott at City Center" in Benzinga.com (July 29, 2011)*
Pub: Benzinga.com
Ed: Benzinga Staff. **Description:** Newport News Marriott at City Center is promoting itself as the premier venue for business meetings, conventions and weddings.

20405 ■ *"Plumbing, Heating Products Shine at Greenbuild" in Contractor (Vol. 57, January 2010, No. 1, pp. 3)*
Pub: Penton Media, Inc.
Ed: Robert P. Mader. **Description:** Among the many exhibitors at Greenbuild 2009 was T&S Brass which showcased their low-flow pre-rinse spray valves and Watts Water Technologies which showed off their hot water recirculating system. Aquatherm and Acorn Engineering were also at the show.

20406 ■ *"Plumbing, Heating Products Shine at Greenbuild Expo" in Contractor (Vol. 56, December 2009, No. 12, pp. 1)*
Pub: Penton Media, Inc.
Ed: Robert P. Mader. **Description:** Greenbuild Show held in Phoenix, Arizona has showcased the latest in plumbing and heating products. Zurn displayed its EcoVantage line of fixtures and valves during the event. Meanwhile, Sloan Valve offered its washdown 1-pint/flush Alphine urinal.

20407 ■ *"Polite Conversation" in Mergers & Acquisitions: The Dealmaker's Journal (March 1, 2008)*
Pub: SourceMedia, Inc.
Description: In January, industry leaders and dealmakers met at Davos to discuss topics ranging from the possibility of a recession to what lies ahead in the deal market.

20408 ■ *"Prepping for the Unpredictable" in Crain's Cleveland Business (Vol. 30, June 15, 2009, No. 23, pp. 16)*
Pub: Crain Communications, Inc.
Ed: Joel Hammond. **Description:** Michael Ferrara, event planner and designer for Executive Caterers discusses the many events he has planned.

20409 ■ *"Proposal for a Macomb County Visitors Bureau Draws Mixed Reaction" in Crain's Detroit Business (Vol. 24, March 31, 2008, No. 13)*
Pub: Crain Communications, Inc.
Ed: Chad Halcom. **Description:** Discusses the newly formed M-59 Corridor Business Association and its proposal to create a convention and visitors bureau dedicated to the county's interests.

20410 ■ *"Real-Life Coursework for Real-Life Business People" in Women In Business (Vol. 63, Summer 2011, No. 2, pp. 22)*
Pub: American Business Women's Association
Ed: Leigh Elmore. **Description:** American Business Women's Association National Women's Leadership Conference provides members with academic busi-

ness training courses. Members can take a variety of MBA-level courses that are taught by University of Kansas School of Business professors. Courses include marketing, management, leadership and communication and decision making.

20411 ■ *"Renren Partners With Recruit to Launch Social Wedding Services" in Benzinga.com (June 7, 2011)*
Pub: Benzinga.com
Ed: Benzinga Staff. **Description:** Renren Inc. and Recruit Company Ltd. partnered to build a wedding social media catering to engaged couples and newlyweds in China. The platform will integrate online wedding related social content and offline media such as magazine and wedding exhibitions.

20412 ■ *"Rock Festival: High Spirited Conventioneers Celebrate Their Good Fortune" in Canadian Business (Vol. 81, March 31, 2008, No. 5)*
Pub: Rogers Media
Ed: Jeff Sanford. **Description:** Soaring prices of commodities in the mining industry have been very good for the attendees of the 76th annual conference of the Prospectors & Developers Association of Canada. A speaker at the conference expects commodity prices to come off a bit but not fall dramatically as it did in the 1980's.

20413 ■ *"RPA Preps for Building Radiant Conference, Show" in Contractor (Vol. 57, January 2010, No. 1, pp. 5)*
Pub: Penton Media, Inc.
Description: Radiant Panel Association is accepting registrations for its Building Radiant 2010 Conference and Trade Show. The conference will discuss radiant heating as well as insurance and other legal matters for mechanical contractors.

20414 ■ *"A Safe Bet" in Entrepreneur (Vol. 35, October 2007, No. 10, pp. 26)*
Pub: Entrepreneur Media Inc.
Ed: Carol Tice. **Description:** U.S. Department of Defense has developed a program, called the Defense Venture Catalyst Initiative or DeVenCI, that will match defense officials to the products that they need. DeVenCI uses conferences to showcase the defense contractors and their technologies to defense managers. Details of how this program helps both contractors and defense officials are overviewed.

20415 ■ *"Save the Date" in Mergers & Acquisitions: The Dealmaker's Journal (March 1, 2008)*
Pub: SourceMedia, Inc.
Description: Listing of conferences and forums that deal with business and investing, particularly with mergers and acquisitions. Includes dates, locations and Internet addresses.

20416 ■ *"Save the Date" in Barron's (Vol. 90, September 13, 2010, No. 37, pp. 35)*
Pub: Barron's Editorial & Corporate Headquarters
Ed: Mark Veverka. **Description:** Mark Hurd is the new Co-President of Oracle after being forced out at Hewlett-Packard where he faced a harassment complaint. HP fired Hurd due to expense account malfeasance. Hurd is also set to speak at an Oracle trade show in San Francisco on September 20, 2010.

20417 ■ *"Secrets To Trade Show Success" in Women Entrepreneur (September 12, 2008)*
Pub: Entrepreneur Media Inc.
Ed: Lesley Spencer Pyle. **Description:** Trade shows require an enormous amount of work, but they are an investment that can pay off handsomely because they allow a business to get their product or service in front of their target market. Advice regarding trade shows is given including selecting the correct venue, researching the affair and following up on leads obtained at the event.

20418 ■ *"Sherwin-Williams Workers Forgo Travel for Virtual Trade Show" in Crain's Cleveland Business (Vol. 28, October 15,*

2007, No. 41)
Pub: Crain Communications, Inc.
Ed: John Booth. **Description:** Overview of Cyber-Coating 2007, a cutting-edge virtual three-dimensional trade show that exhibitors such as Sherwin-Williams Co.'s Chemical Coatings Division will take part in by chatting verbally or via text messages in order to exchange information and listen to pitches just like they would on an actual trade show floor.

20419 ■ *"Show Dates" in Art Business News (Vol. 34, November 2007, No. 11, pp. 18)*
Pub: Pfingsten Publishing, LLC
Description: Listing of conferences, trade shows and gallery openings for artists and those in the art industry.

20420 ■ *"Silverdome Bidders Bring New Proposals" in Crain's Detroit Business (Vol. 24, March 17, 2008, No. 11, pp. 23)*
Pub: Crain Communications, Inc.
Ed: Daniel Duggan. **Description:** Discusses the seven plans which have been proposed as part of the third round of bidding for the Pontiac Silverdome; proposals range from Global Baseball Inc., a baseball league that would pit a team from every country against one another, to an Indian casino, a musical 'hall of fame', a convention center, a horse track, a hotel and an indoor water park.

20421 ■ *"Six Tips To Maximize Networking Opportunities" in Women Entrepreneur (November 3, 2008)*
Pub: Entrepreneur Media Inc.
Ed: Tamara Monosoff. **Description:** Networking events fall into the realm of business development as opposed to immediate sales opportunities. It is important to remember that these events provide a chance to build relationships that may someday help one's business. Tips to help make the most out of networking events are provided.

20422 ■ *"Social Media Event Slated for March 25" in Bellingham Business Journal (Vol. February 2010, pp. 3)*
Pub: Sound Publishing Inc.
Description: Center for Economic Vitality (CEV) and the Technology Alliance Group (TAG) will host the 2010 Social Media Conference at the McIntyre Hall Performing Arts & Conference Center in Mt. Vernon, Washington. The event will provide networking opportunities for attendees.

20423 ■ *"Speak Better: Five Tips for Polished Presentations" in Women Entrepreneur (September 19, 2008)*
Pub: Entrepreneur Media Inc.
Ed: Suzannah Baum. **Description:** Successful entrepreneurs agree that exemplary public speaking skills are among the core techniques needed to propel their business forward. A well-delivered presentation can result in securing a new distribution channel, gaining new customers, locking into a new referral stream or receiving extra funding.

20424 ■ *"Sponsorship, Booths Available for Spring Business Showcase" in Bellingham Business Journal (Vol. February 2010, pp. 3)*
Pub: Sound Publishing Inc.
Description: Third Annual Spring Business Showcase still have space available for vendors and sponsors. The event gives local businesses the opportunity to increase their visibility and provides a means to increase sales and build relationships.

20425 ■ *"State of a Fair!" in Small Business Opportunities (March 2008)*
Pub: Harris Publications Inc.
Ed: Shelly Buss. **Description:** State fairs are money-making venues; one company made $2 million in 12 days at the Minnesota State Fair.

20426 ■ *"State Fairgrounds Adding Year-Round Attractions" in Crain's Detroit Business (Vol. 24, February 18, 2008, No. 7, pp. 17)*
Pub: Crain Communications Inc. - Detroit
Ed: Robert Ankeny. **Description:** Michigan State Fairgrounds and Exposition Center shares its plans to become a year-round recreation, entertainment and education center.

20427 ■ *"Success Products" in Black Enterprise (Vol. 37, February 2007, No. 7, pp. 135)*
Pub: Earl G. Graves Publishing Co. Inc.
Ed: Tanisha A. Sykes. **Description:** Using innovative resources that are already at your fingertips instead of trying to reach out to companies first is a great way to discover whether you have a viable idea or product. Be motivated to start an e-newsletter letting people know about your products and attend conferences like The Motivation Show, the world's largest exhibition of motivational products and services related to performance in business.

20428 ■ *"Tax-Free Zones Need Shows; Out-of-State Shoppers Are Key To Success" in Crain's Detroit Business (Vol. 24, January 28, 2008, No. 4)*
Pub: Crain Communications Inc. - Detroit
Ed: Daniel Duggan. **Description:** Sales tax-free zones are being considered by Michigan's legislators in order to promote the state as a conference destination.

20429 ■ *"Teachable Moments: Worth Every Penny" in Pet Product News (Vol. 64, December 2010, No. 12, pp. 34)*
Pub: BowTie Inc.
Ed: Cheryl Reeves. **Description:** Pet bird retailers can attain both outreach to customers and enhanced profitability by staging educational events such as the annual Parrot Palooza event of Burlington, New Jersey-based Bird Paradise. Aside from attracting a global audience, Parrot Palooza features seminars, workshops, classes, and bird-related contests.

20430 ■ *"Tic-Tac-Show" in American Printer (Vol. 128, August 1, 2011, No. 8)*
Pub: Penton Media Inc.
Description: Graph Expo has become the US print industry's main event. There will be as many as 500 exhibitors at this year's event and the Graphic Arts Show Company lists over 30 co-located events as well as 53 new sessions in the seminar program's 28 education categories.

20431 ■ *"Tool Time" in Entrepreneur (Vol. 36, March 2008, No. 3, pp. 90)*
Pub: Entrepreneur Media Inc.
Ed: Nichole A. Torres. **Description:** DaVinci Institute holds an annual event in Colorado to display new products and inventions. Innovative Design Engineering Animation is a consulting company that helps inventors develop product through various stages. NineSigma Inc. has an online marketplace where inventors can post ideas for clients needing new products.

20432 ■ *"Tourism Bureau Seeks Hotel Tax Hike" in Baltimore Business Journal (Vol. 27, December 18, 2009, No. 32, pp. 1)*
Pub: American City Business Journals
Ed: Rachel Bernstein. **Description:** Baltimore, Maryland's tourism agency, Visit Baltimore, has proposed a new hotel tax that could produce $2 million annually for its marketing budget, fund improvements to the city's 30-year-old convention center and help it compete for World Cup soccer games. Baltimore hotel leaders discuss the new tax.

20433 ■ *Trade Show Exhibitors Association--Membership Directory and Industry Buyer's Guide*
Pub: Trade Show Exhibitors Association
Contact: Margit B. Weisgal, President
URL(s): www.tsea.org. **Released:** Continuous; Updated every month. **Covers:** About 2,300 members of the Trade Show Exhibitors Association. **Entries include:** Name, address, phone, fax, e-mail, web site, name of contact. **Arrangement:** Classified by type of business or association. **Indexes:** Alphabetical by name.

20434 ■ *"Tradeshow Attendance Incentives Add Up" in Pet Product News (Vol. 64, December 2010, No. 12, pp. 14)*
Pub: BowTie Inc.
Ed: Mark E. Battersby. **Description:** Pointers on how pet specialty retailers can claim business travel tax and income tax deductions for expenses paid or

incurred in participation at tradeshows, conventions, and meetings are presented. Incentives in form of these deductions could allow pet specialty retailers to gain business benefits, aside from the education and enjoyment involved with the travel.

20435 ■ *Tradeshow Week Data Book*
Pub: Tradeshow Week Inc.
Contact: Maggie Moe, Manager
E-mail: maggie.moe@reedbusiness.com
URL(s): www.tradeshowweek.comwww.reedbusiness.com, databook.tradeshowweek.com/aspx/TradeshowSearch.aspx. **Released:** Annual; Latest edition 2010. **Price:** $305, Individuals plus $25 shipping and handling. **Covers:** Nearly 5,300 trade and public shows with at least 5,000 net square feet of exhibit space scheduled in the United States and Canada up to five years from publication date. **Entries include:** Show title, show management and sponsor, show description, location, dates, general contractor, estimated net square feet of exhibit space, number and profile of exhibitors and participants, fees, associated seminars, meetings and conferences, show history, future dates and sites. **Arrangement:** Classified by industry category. **Indexes:** Geographical, alphabetical, chronological, show management, show size, rotation pattern, new shows.

20436 ■ *Tradeshow Week Major Exhibit Hall Directory*
Pub: Tradeshow Week Inc.
Contact: Maggie Moe, Manager
E-mail: maggie.moe@reedbusiness.com
URL(s): www.tradeshowweek.com. **Released:** Annual; Latest edition 2009. **Price:** $250, Individuals full web access (plus $25 shipping & handling). **Covers:** Exhibition facilities with at least 25,000 square feet of prime exhibit space, including convention centers, hotels, auditoriums, arenas, and other facilities in the United States, Canada, and Mexico. **Entries include:** Hall name, address, facility manager name, title, and phone number, prime and total exhibit space size; utilities available; number of meeting rooms and capacity; parking sites; rates; new construction and expansions; recent openings. **Arrangement:** Geographical. **Indexes:** Hall size, floorplan.

20437 ■ *"Travel Tears" in Crain's Chicago Business (Vol. 31, November 17, 2008, No. 46, pp. 3)*
Pub: Crain Communications, Inc.
Ed: Bob Tita. **Description:** Hotels, restaurants and conventions are seeing a decline in profits due to corporate travel cutbacks and the sagging economy. City and state revenues derived from taxes on tourism-related industries are also suffering.

20438 ■ *"A Vegas Sensation Inaugural Artexpo Las Vegas" in Art Business News (Vol. 34, November 2007, No. 11, pp. 1)*
Pub: Pfingsten Publishing, LLC
Ed: Jennifer Dulin. **Description:** Overview of the first Artexpo Las Vegas which featured exhibitors, artists and buyers and was a wonderful place for networking.

20439 ■ *"Wal-Mart Doesn't Sell Council" in The Business Journal-Serving Metropolitan Kansas City (Vol. 26, July 4, 2008, No. 43, pp. 1)*
Pub: American City Business Journals, Inc.
Ed: Steve Vockrodt. **Description:** Wal-Mart Stores Inc. announced that it will move the location of its annual convention from Kansas City, Missouri to Orlando, Florida. The change of venue came after Rick Hughes, Kansas City Convention and Visitors Association president rejected Wal-Mart's proposal to subsidize a new hotel in the downtown area that is needed for the event.

20440 ■ *"The Weeks Ahead" in Crain's New York Business (Vol. 24, January 7, 2008, No. 1, pp. 26)*
Pub: Crain Communications, Inc.
Description: Listing of events in the Detroit area include conferences addressing entrepreneurialism, economic development, and women business ownership.

20441 ■ *"The Weeks Ahead" in Crain's New York Business (Vol. 24, January 14, 2008, No. 2, pp. 20)*
Pub: Crain Communications, Inc.
Description: Listing of events in the Detroit area include conferences addressing entrepreneurialism, economic development, and women business ownership.

20442 ■ *"Welcome to Babesland" in Women In Business (Vol. 62, June 2010, No. 2, pp. 33)*
Pub: American Business Women's Association
Ed: Leigh Elmore. **Description:** Music group, Four Bitchin' Babes will be performing at the 2010 American Business Women's Association's National Women's Leadership Conference. The group has been in the industry for 20 years and has released nine albums. The Four Bitchin' Babes consist of Sally Fingerett, Nancy Moran, Deirdre Flint, and Debi Smith.

20443 ■ *"Women of Power" in Black Enterprise (Vol. 41, November 2010, No. 4, pp. 94)*
Pub: Earl G. Graves Publishing Co. Inc.
Description: Black Enterprise Women of Power Summit will be held February 23-26, 2011 at the Ritz Carlton in Orlando, Florida. Speakers will offer insight into career, household, and life in general.

20444 ■ *"Women of Power Summit" in Black Enterprise (Vol. 38, February 2008, No. 7, pp. 163)*
Pub: Earl G. Graves Publishing Co. Inc.
Description: Third annual Women of Power Summit, hosted by State Farm, will host over 700 executive women of color offering empowerment sessions, tips for networking, along with entertainment.

20445 ■ *"Worry No. 1 at Auto Show" in Crain's Detroit Business (Vol. 24, January 21, 2008, No. 3, pp. 1)*
Pub: Crain Communications Inc. - Detroit
Ed: Brent Snavely. **Description:** Recession fears clouded activity at the 2008 Annual North American International Auto Show. Automakers are expecting to see a drop in sales due to slow holiday retail spending as well as fallout from the subprime lending crisis.

20446 ■ *"WQA's Leadership Conference Tackles Industry Issues" in Contractor (Vol. 56, October 2009, No. 10, pp. 3)*
Pub: Penton Media, Inc.
Ed: Candace Roulo. **Description:** Water Quality Association's Mid-Year Leadership Conference held in Bloomingdale, Illinois in September 2009 tackled lead regulation, water softeners, and product efficiency. The possibility of a WQA green seal was discussed by the Water Sciences Committee and the Government Relations Committee meeting.

20447 ■ *"Your Turn in the Spotlight" in Inc. (March 2008, pp. 30)*
Pub: Gruner & Jahr USA Publishing
Ed: Elaine Appleton Grant. **Description:** Profile of a Tennessee business that produces events and concerts. The company offers a complete package of services handling staging, lighting, video, musical instrument rentals, and audio support. The founder has decided to sell the business and details of the asking price, price rationale, the pros and cons of buying the firm and its bottom line are examined.

TRADE PERIODICALS

20448 ■ *Association Meetings: The Independent Voice of the Association Industry*
Pub: Primedia Business Magazines & Media
URL(s): meetingsnet.com/associationmeetings/. **Ed:** Sue Pelletier, Barbara Scofidio. **Released:** Bimonthly **Price:** $65, Canada; $98, Other countries.

20449 ■ *Corporate & Incentive Travel*
Pub: Coastal Communications Corp.
Contact: Andrew Shaw, Director
URL(s): www.themeetingmagazines.com/index/Default.aspx?tabid=197. **Released:** Monthly

20450 ■ *Facility Manager*
Pub: International Association of Venue Managers
Contact: Dexter King, President
URL(s): www.iaam.org/Facility_manager/Pages/Facility_Issues.htm. **Ed:** R.V. Baugus. **Released:** Bimonthly **Price:** $55, Free members; $85, Two years North America; $110, Out of state.

20451 ■ *Healthcare Convention & Exhibitors Association--AIP Alert*
Pub: Healthcare Convention and Exhibitors Association
Contact: Peggy Furuman, President
Released: 2/year. **Price:** Free. **Description:** Disseminates information to health care associations, exhibitors, and their Exhibitors Advisory Councils (EAC). Reports on innovative ideas and focuses on specific problems and solutions pertaining the effective display of health care products. Seeks to communicate the benefits of membership. Recurring features include news of research, reports of meetings and industry issues, news of educational opportunities, and notices of publications available.

20452 ■ *Meetings & Conventions: The Meeting & Incentive Planners Resource*
Pub: Northstar Travel Media L.L.C.
Contact: Thomas Kemp, Chief Executive Officer
E-mail: tkemp@ntmllc.com
URL(s): www.meetings-conventions.com. **Ed:** Loren G. Edelstein. **Released:** Monthly **Price:** $89, Individuals print; $119, Canada and Mexico print; $209, Other countries print; $41.50, Individuals online.

20453 ■ *Meetings & Incentive Travel*
Pub: Business Information Group
Contact: Bruce Creighton, President
URL(s): www.meetingscanada.com/. **Released:** 6/yr.

20454 ■ *Trade Show Ideas*
Pub: Trade Show Exhibitors Association
Contact: Margit B. Weisgal, President
Released: Monthly, combined (July/August). **Price:** Included in membership; $79 for subscription only. **Description:** Supplies news and information of interest to exhibit managers and their suppliers. Carries case studies, 'how-to' items, checklists, and industry data. Recurring features include interviews, news of research and of educational opportunities, and reports of meetings. Also includes columns titled Destinations, Thoughts from the Corner Office, Market-Wise, Profiles and Member Network Exchange.

VIDEOCASSETTES/AUDIOCASSETTES

20455 ■ *The Trade Show Advantage*
Creative Training Solutions
5 Timberline Dr.
Voorhees, NJ 08043
Ph: (856)784-3468
Free: 800-515-4114
Fax: (856)784-7087
Co. E-mail: mail@creativetraining.com
URL: http://www.creativetraining.com
Released: 19??. **Price:** $395.00. **Description:** Shows how to set up a booth at a trade show. Includes everything from personal comportment to information on the typical trade show environment. Includes planning guide, handout, and audiocassette. **Availability:** VHS.

20456 ■ *Working the Booth: Trade Show Success*
American Media, Inc.
4621 121st St.
Urbandale, IA 50323-2311
Ph: (515)224-0919
Free: 888-776-8268
Fax: (515)327-2555
Co. E-mail: custsvc@ammedia.com
URL: http://www.ammedia.com
Released: 1992. **Price:** $395.00. **Description:** Details techniques on successfully setting up and maintaining a booth at a trade show. Stresses etiquette, professionalism, positivity, correct prospect handling, and salesmanship. **Availability:** VHS; 3/4 U; 8 mm.

TRADE SHOWS AND CONVENTIONS

20457 ■ *Destinations Showcase*
International Association of Convention & Visitor Bureaus
2025 M St., NW, Ste. 500
Washington, DC 20036
Ph: (202)296-7888
Fax: (202)296-7889
Co. E-mail: info@destinationmarketing.org
URL: http://www.iacvb.org
URL(s): www.destinationsshowcase.com. **Frequency:** Annual. **Audience:** Convention, meeting, trade show, and travel planners. **Principal Exhibits:** Convention center and convention bureau information. **Telecommunication Services:** jduda@destinationmarketing.org.

20458 ■ *HSMAI Affordable Meetings Exposition and Conference*
Hospitality Sales and Marketing Association International (HSMAI)
1760 Old Meadow Rd., Ste. 500
McLean, VA 22102
Ph: (703)506-3280
Free: 877-643-3511
Fax: (703)506-3266
Co. E-mail: info@hsmai.org
URL: http://www.hsmai.org
Contact: Robert A. Gilbert, President
E-mail: bgilbert@hsmai.org
URL(s): www.affordablemeetings.com. **Frequency:** Annual. **Audience:** Planners, executives, and decision-makers from corporations and associations; religious, social, ethnic, sports, and educational groups. **Principal Exhibits:** Services for cost-conscious meeting planners. **Telecommunication Services:** affordablemeetings@jspargo.com.

20459 ■ *International Association of Fairs and Expositions Trade Show*
International Association of Fairs and Expositions (IAFE)
3043 E. Cairo St.
Springfield, MO 65802
Ph: (417)862-5771
Free: 800-516-0313
Fax: (417)862-0156
Co. E-mail: iafe@fairsandexpos.com
URL: http://www.fairsandexpos.com
Contact: Jim Tucker, Chief Executive Officer
E-mail: jimt@fairsandexpos.com
URL(s): www.fairsandexpos.com. **Frequency:** Annual. **Audience:** Fair managers, staffs, and board members; carnival owners and staffs; concessionaires; talent and other agencies related to the fair industry. **Principal Exhibits:** Talent agencies, concessionaires, novelties, amusement devices, insurance, ribbons, plaques, attractions, and equipment. Products and services for the fair industry. **Dates and Locations:** , Hilton Hotel. **Telecommunication Services:** iafe@fairsandexpos.com.

CONSULTANTS

20460 ■ *Intex Exhibit Systems L.L.C.*
1846 Sequoia Ave.
Orange, CA 92868
Ph: (714)940-0369
Free: 800-331-6633
Fax: (714)935-0223
Co. E-mail: info@intexexhibits.com
URL: http://www.intexexhibits.com
Contact: Matthias D. Kemeny, President
E-mail: mdk@intexexhibits.com
Scope: Specializes in the design and production of exhibits, displays and pavilions for world fairs, tradeshows and similar events. Services include product design, industrial and engineering design for educational exhibits, museum exhibits and science and technology museology. Serves private industry as well as government agencies. **Founded:** 1979. **Publications:** "Trade Show Marketing," Sep, 2000;

"Exhibitor Times," 1998. **Special Services:** Fast-pack™; Panelflo™; affordable-1™; thegraphic arm™; Expression™; TigerMark™.

START-UP INFORMATION

20461 ■ *"Can You Say $1 Million? A Language-Learning Start-Up Is Hoping That Investors Can" in Inc. (Vol. 33, November 2011, No. 9, pp. 116)*
Pub: Inc. Magazine
Ed: April Joyner. **Description:** Startup, Verbling is a video platform that links language learners and native speakers around the world. The firm is working to raise money to hire engineers in order to build the product and redesign their Website.

ASSOCIATIONS AND OTHER ORGANIZATIONS

20462 ■ *Action CTIC Action*
1 Nicholas St., Ste. 1202
Ottawa, ON, Canada K1N 7B7
Ph: (613)562-0379
Fax: (613)241-4098
Co. E-mail: info@cttic.org
URL: http://www.cttic.org
Contact: Kristel Blais, Director, Administration
Released: Periodic

20463 ■ **The American Association of Language Specialists (TAALS)**
PO Box 27306
Washington, DC 20038-7306
Co. E-mail: admissions@taals.net
URL: http://www.taals.net
Description: Professional association of conference interpreters, translators, revisers and precis-writers. **Founded:** 1957.

20464 ■ **American Translators Association (ATA)**
225 Reinekers Ln., Ste. 590
Alexandria, VA 22314
Ph: (703)683-6100
Fax: (703)683-6122
Co. E-mail: ata@atanet.org
URL: http://www.atanet.org
Contact: Ms. Dorothee Racette, President
Description: Fosters the professional development of translators and interpreters and promotes the translation and interpretation professions. **Founded:** 1959. **Publications:** *ATA Chronicle* (Monthly); *Translation and Interpretation Services Survey* (Biennial); *Translator and Interpreter Programs in North America*; *ATA Directory of Translators and Interpreters*; *American Translators Association--Membership Directory* (Annual). **Educational Activities:** American Translators Association Annual Conference (Annual); American Translators Association Conference (Annual). **Awards:** Lewis Galantiere Award; Alexander Gode Medal; Ungar German Translation Award; Student Translation Award; Alexander Gold Medal (Annual); Ungar German Translation Award (Biennial).

20465 ■ **Association of Legal Court Interpreters and Translators (ALCIT)—Association des Traducteurs et**

Interpretes Judiciaires
438 St. Antoine E
Montreal, QC, Canada H2Y 1A5
Ph: (514)845-3113
Fax: (514)845-3006
Co. E-mail: admin@atij.ca
URL: http://www.atij.ca
Description: Interpreters and translators working in courts of law. Promotes professional advancement of members; seeks to insure high standards of practice in the field of court translation. Conducts continuing professional education programs; facilitates exchange of information among members.

20466 ■ **Association of Visual Language Interpreters of Canada (AVLIC)**
110 - 39012 Discovery Way
Squamish, BC, Canada V8B 0E5
Ph: (604)617-8502
Fax: (604)567-8502
Co. E-mail: avlic@avlic.ca
URL: http://www.avlic.ca/index.php
Contact: Christie Reaume, President
Description: Sign language interpreters. Promotes standardization of sign language; seeks to insure excellence in the practice of visual language interpretation. Conducts continuing professional development courses for members. **Founded:** 1979. **Publications:** *AVLIC News* (3/year). **Awards:** AEIP Graduating Student Award (Annual); Edward C. Bealer Award of Merit (Biennial); Phyllis Joynt Mentorship Award (Biennial). **Telecommunication Services:** president@avlic.ca.

20467 ■ *AVLIC News*
110 - 39012 Discovery Way
Squamish, BC, Canada V8B 0E5
Ph: (604)617-8502
Fax: (604)567-8502
Co. E-mail: avlic@avlic.ca
URL: http://www.avlic.ca/index.php
Contact: Christie Reaume, President
Released: 3/year

20468 ■ **Canadian Translators, Terminologists and Interpreters Council (CTTIC)—Conseil des traducteurs, terminologues et interpretes du Canada**
1 Nicholas St., Ste. 1202
Ottawa, ON, Canada K1N 7B7
Ph: (613)562-0379
Fax: (613)241-4098
Co. E-mail: info@cttic.org
URL: http://www.cttic.org
Contact: Kristel Blais, Director, Administration
Description: Provincial societies representing 3,000 translators and interpreters. Promotes advancement of the professions of translation and interpretation. Formulates standards of knowledge and practice for translators and interpreters; conducts certification examinations. Coordinates members' activities; represents members in international professional organizations; sponsors educational and research programs. **Scope:** translation, interpretation. **Founded:** 1970. **Subscriptions:** archival material

audio recordings books clippings periodicals video recordings. **Publications:** *Meta* (Quarterly); *Action CTIC Action* (Periodic). **Awards:** CTIC Volunteer Award (Annual).

20469 ■ **Literary Translators' Association of Canada (LTAC)—Association des Traducteurs et Traductrices Literariness du Canada (ATTLC)**
LB 601 Concordia University
Montreal, QC, Canada H3G 1M8
Ph: (514)848-2424
Fax: (514)848-2621
Co. E-mail: communications@concordia.ca
URL: http://www.concordia.ca
Contact: Jean Simard, Board Member
Description: Literary translators. Promotes literary translation and the interests of literary translators in Canada. Networks with cultural associations and agencies worldwide; lobbies government and cultural agencies regarding funding and copyright. **Founded:** 1975. **Publications:** *Transmission* (Quarterly); *Literary Translators Association of Canada--Directory of Members' Works* (Periodic). **Educational Activities:** Literary Translators' Association of Canada Conference (Annual). **Awards:** John Glassco Translation Prize; John Glaces Translation Prize (Annual). **Telecommunication Services:** info@attlc-ltac.org.

20470 ■ *Meta*
1 Nicholas St., Ste. 1202
Ottawa, ON, Canada K1N 7B7
Ph: (613)562-0379
Fax: (613)241-4098
Co. E-mail: info@cttic.org
URL: http://www.cttic.org
Contact: Kristel Blais, Director, Administration
Released: Quarterly

20471 ■ *Transmission*
LB 601 Concordia University
Montreal, QC, Canada H3G 1M8
Ph: (514)848-2424
Fax: (514)848-2621
Co. E-mail: communications@concordia.ca
URL: http://www.concordia.ca
Contact: Jean Simard, Board Member
Released: Quarterly

REFERENCE WORKS

20472 ■ *American Translators Association--Membership Directory*
Pub: American Translators Association
Contact: Ms. Dorothee Racette, President
URL(s): atanet.org/local_bin/login.pl?redirect=/membership/membershipdirect o ry.php. **Released:** Annual; summer. **Description:** Includes more than 9,000 member translators, interpreters, and linguists in the United States and over 60 countries. **Entries include:** Name, address, phone, languages in which member has ATA certification. **Arrangement:** Alphabetical.

20473 ■ *"The Americans Are Coming"* in *The Economist (Vol. 390, January 3, 2009, No. 8612, pp. 44)*
Pub: The Economist Newspaper Inc.
Description: Student recruitment consultancies, which help place international students at universities in other countries and offer services such as interpreting or translating guidelines, are discussed; American universities who have shunned these agencies in the past; the result has been that America underperforms in relation to its size with a mere 3.5 percent of students on its campuses that are from abroad.

20474 ■ *"Arizona Firms In Chicago Go For Gold With '08 Games"* in *The Business Journal - Serving Phoenix and the Valley of the Sun (Vol. 28, August 8, 2008, No. 49, pp. 1)*
Pub: American City Business Journals, Inc.
Ed: Patrick O'Grady. **Description:** More than 20 U.S. athletes will wear Arizona-based eSoles LLC's custom-made insoles to increase their performance at the 2008 Beijing Olympics making eSoles one of the beneficiaries of the commercialization of the games. Translation software maker Auralog Inc saw a 60 percent jump in sales from its Mandarin Chinese language applications.

20475 ■ *ATA Directory of Translators and Interpreters*
Pub: American Translators Association
Contact: Ms. Dorothee Racette, President
URL(s): www.atanet.org. **Covers:** over 5,800 member translators and interpreters. **Entries include:** Name, address, languages in which proficient, subject competencies, professional background. **Arrangement:** Alphabetical, area of specialization, language. **Indexes:** Language-subject competency (with state).

20476 ■ *"Encouraging Study in Critical Languages"* in *Occupational Outlook Quarterly (Vol. 55, Summer 2011, No. 2, pp. 23)*
Pub: U.S. Bureau of Labor Statistics
Description: Proficiency in particular foreign languages is vital to the defense, diplomacy, and security of the United States. Several federal programs provide scholarships and other funding to encourage high school and college students to learn languages of the Middle East, China, and Russia.

20477 ■ *"The Future Is Another Country; Higher Education"* in *The Economist (Vol. 390, January 3, 2009, No. 8612, pp. 43)*
Pub: The Economist Newspaper Inc.
Description: Due to the growth of the global corporation, more ambitious students are studying at universities abroad; the impact of this trend is discussed.

20478 ■ *"Internet Translation Service Helps Burmese"* in *News-Sentinel (May 10, 2011)*
Pub: New-Sentinel
Ed: Ellie Bogue. **Description:** Catherine Kasper Place, Parkview Health Community Outreach, Allen County-Fort Wayne Department of Health and Advantage Health have partnered to help the Burmese Community in the area by providing an online service that links doctors' offices with translators in order to provide better healthcare.

20479 ■ *"Machine Transliteration Survey"* in *ACM Computing Surveys (Vol. 43, Fall 2011, No. 3, pp. 17)*
Pub: Association for Computing Machinery
Ed: Sarvnaz Karimi, Falk Scholer, Andrew Turpin. **Description:** Machine transliteration is the process of automatically transforming the script of a word from a source language to a target language, while preserving pronunciation. The development of algorithms specifically for machine transliteration began over a decade ago based on the phonetics of source and target languages, followed by approaches using statistical and language-specific methods. In this survey, the key methodologies introduced in transliteration literature are reviewed. The approaches are categorized based on the resources and algorithms used, and the effectiveness is compared.

20480 ■ *"Making Visitors Out Of Listeners"* in *Hawaii Business (Vol. 54, July 2008, No. 1, pp. 18)*
Pub: Hawaii Business Publishing
Ed: Casey Chin. **Description:** Japanese workers are subscribing to the Official Hawaii Podcast in iTunes, which offers a free 20-minute, Japanese-language audio content on different topics, such as dining reviews and music from local artists. The concept is a way to attract Japanese travelers to come to Hawaii.

20481 ■ *"Online Translation Service Aids Battlefield Troops"* in *Product News Network (August 30, 2011)*
Pub: Thomas Publishing Company
Description: Linquist online service, LinGo Link provides real-time interpreter support to military troops overseas. Interpreters skilled in multiple languages and dialects are used in various areas and in multiple instances without requiring physical presence. The service is available through commercial cellular or WiFi services or tactical communications network. The system accommodates exchange of audio, video, photos, and text during conversations via smartphones and mobile peripheral devices.

20482 ■ *"Speaking In Tongues: Rosetta Stone's TOTALE Adds 'Social' To Language Learning"* in *Black Enterprise (Vol. 41, September 2010, No. 2)*
Pub: Earl G. Graves Publishing Co. Inc.
Ed: Sonya A. Donaldson. **Description:** As small businesses become more globalized, it is necessary to learn new languages in order to compete. Rosetta Stone's TOTALe is profiled.

20483 ■ *"Web Translation Made Simple"* in *Inc. (Vol. 33, October 2011, No. 8, pp. 44)*
Pub: Inc. Magazine
Ed: Adam Baer. **Description:** Smartling is a Web-based service that translates sites into more than 50 foreign languages. The software will begin translation right after setting up the account.

TRADE PERIODICALS

20484 ■ *Views*
Pub: R I D Publications
Released: Monthly, except combined Aug./Setp. issue. **Price:** $36, U.S.; $36, elsewhere. **Description:** Newsletter for interpreters for the deaf.

TRADE SHOWS AND CONVENTIONS

20485 ■ **American Translators Association Annual Conference**
American Translators Association (ATA)
225 Reinekers Ln., Ste. 590
Alexandria, VA 22314
Ph: (703)683-6100
Fax: (703)683-6122
Co. E-mail: ata@atanet.org
URL: http://www.atanet.org
Contact: Ms. Dorothee Racette, President
URL(s): www.atanet.org. **Frequency:** Annual. **Audience:** Translators and interpreters. **Principal Exhibits:** Publications, software and services. **Telecommunication Services:** conference@atanet.org.

CONSULTANTS

20486 ■ **DTS Language Services Inc.—Duke Translation Services**
7780 Brier Creek Pky., Ste. 325
Raleigh, NC 27617
Ph: (919)942-0666
Free: 800-524-0722
Fax: (919)942-0686
Co. E-mail: contact@dtstrans.com
URL: http://www.dtstrans.com
Contact: Duncan Shaw, Manager, Information Technology
E-mail: dshaw@dtstrans.com
Scope: Offers a complete range of foreign language services, including translation of engineering and technical documentation, bids and proposals, instruction and training materials, correspondence, patents and legal documentation, advertising copy and brochures, and many other services. Maintains both English and foreign language word processing equipment to produce camera-ready copy of most materials in-house. Industries served: engineering, computer hardware, electronics industry, pharmaceuticals, telecommunications and software. **Founded:** 1972.

20487 ■ **ENLASO Corp.**
4888 Pearl East Cir., Ste. 300E
Boulder, CO 80301
Ph: (303)516-0857
Free: 866-415-6820
Fax: (303)516-1701
Co. E-mail: contact@translate.com
URL: http://www.translate.com
Contact: John Watkins, President
E-mail: jwatkins@translate.com
Scope: Services include translations from and into foreign languages. Specializes in technical and legal documents, patents, specifications and instruction manuals translation. Also active in advertising in foreign languages, including copy-writing, artwork, typesetting and video and audio. Serves private industries and government agencies. **Founded:** 1968. **Publications:** "Cross-Cultural Training and Localization," Feb, 2008; "Using Symbols and Icons in Localization"; "Marketing Communications, Culture, and Localization"; "Culture: Overlooked Web Globalization Ingredient"; "Documentation Localization Process Tune-Up"; "Multilingual Flash Production"; "How to Economize When Localizing Graphics"; "Xml Internationalization and Localization," Sams, Jun, 2001. **Seminars:** A growing market: Non-English speakers in the US. **Special Services:** Rainbow™; Album™; Horizon™; Lexikon™.

20488 ■ **Languages Inc.**
1010 Spring Mill Ave., Ste. 100
Conshohocken, PA 19428-2391
Ph: (215)763-7787
Free: 800-346-5071
Fax: (610)825-4430
Contact: Jeff Levin, Principal
Scope: Provides translations and narration services for corporate video and audiovisual products. In house capabilities include beta cam SP and AVID non linear editing, international video standards conversion, duplication and fulfillment. Also offers text translation in all fields and languages, as well as typesetting and mechanical production. Industries served: international corporations and production houses. **Founded:** 1966.

20489 ■ **Rosetta Stone Associates**
34 Franklin St., Ste. 200A
Nashua, NH 03064-2699
Ph: (603)883-9388
Free: 800-472-2896
Fax: (603)595-8673
Co. E-mail: info@mv.com
URL: http://www.mv.com/biz/rosetta
Contact: John Furey, President
E-mail: jfurey@rosettastoneinc.net
Scope: Technical and scientific translation and localization services offered inmost major languages of the world. Subject matter is highly diverse, covering such areas as advertising, patents, user manuals, financial statements, contracts, technical and scientific journals, proposals, and correspondence. Typesetting services is available as needed. Provides qualified interpreters to handle foreign visits, conferences, seminars, and training programs. Additionally, provides language instruction for either individuals and groups tailored to client's specific needs. Industries served manufacturing, academia, finance, legal, computer, High technology, airlines, research, and government agencies. **Founded:** 1972. **Publications:** "Rosetta Stone Bought By Eurotext Translations," Oct, 2002. "Partnership with Eurotext," Ireland, Jun, 2000. **Telecommunication Services:** support@mv.com; translate@rosettastoneinc.net.

20490 ■ **Thomas J. Snow**
27 Dennison Ave.
Binghamton, NY 13901-2106

Ph: (607)723-5702

Scope: Offers consulting in languages, information, and communication. Translation from and into any language of texts in any field of technology, including marketing literature and user documentation. **Founded:** 1970.

20491 ■ Suzuki, Myers & Associates Ltd.
46320 Ten Mile Rd.
Novi, MI 48376-0852
Ph: (248)344-0909
Fax: (248)344-0092
Co. E-mail: office@suzukimyers.com
URL: http://www.suzukimyers.com
Contact: Izumi Suzuki, President
E-mail: izumi.suzuki@suzukimyers.com

Scope: Offers marketing and sales assistance to firms approaching the Japan market, as well as cultural and communications training for staff who working in or with Japanese companies or subsidiaries, and public affairs assistance to firms approaching Japan. Assistance includes technical or promotional translating and interpreting. Industries served: Automotive OEM clients and their vendors, service firms, professionals, city and county development agencies, government agencies, and some retail operations. **Founded:** 1984. **Seminars:** Selling Goods and Services to the Japanese; Hosting Japanese; Education in Japan; Single in Japan; PR: The US/Japan Interface; Lawyers and the Japanese Client; A Japan Cultural Sampler.

20492 ■ Transimpex Translations Inc.
1 E 34th St., Ste. 301
Kansas City, MO 64111
Ph: (816)561-3777
Free: 888-877-4679

Fax: (816)561-5515
Co. E-mail: translations@transimpex.com
URL: http://www.transimpex.com
Contact: Doris Ganser, Chief Executive Officer
E-mail: doris@transimpex.com

Scope: Offers industrial, legal, technical and scientific translation, interpreting, foreign language typesetting, advertising, audio and video presentation, localization/internationalization, translator/interpreter training, and expertise on translation and international trade worldwide. **Founded:** 1974. **Seminars:** Legal and Technical Translation Workshop; Starting and Operating a Translation Business; Translator Ethics; Language Identification; Translation and Localization for International Trade; Culture Training; T and I Training.

FRANCHISES AND BUSINESS OPPORTUNITIES

20493 ■ Language Leaders Franchising LLC
Foreign Language Network, L.L.C.
401 W. State St.
Geneva, IL 60134
Ph: (630)377-8794

Description: Foreign language education and interpreting. **No. of Company-Owned Units:** 1. **Founded:** 1998.. **Franchised:** 2004. **Equity Capital Needed:** $18,700-$107,000. **Franchise Fee:** $10,000-$90,000. **Royalty Fee:** 15%. **Training:** 2 days training at headquarters.

LIBRARIES

20494 ■ New Brunswick Translation Bureau Library—Bureau de Traduction du Nouveau-Brunswick Bibliotheque.
Marysville Pl., 1st Fl.
20 McGloin St.
Fredericton, NB, Canada E3A 5T8

Ph: (506)453-2920
Fax: (506)459-7911
Co. E-mail: chrystiane.mallaley@gnb.ca
URL: http://www.gnb.ca/0099/Translation/index-e.asp
Contact: Jean-Marc Gionet, Library Technician

Scope: Communications, terminology, lexicography, interpretation, language arts. **Services:** Interlibrary loan; copying. **Founded:** 1967. **Holdings:** 6500 books. **Subscriptions:** 250 journals and other serials; 6 newspapers.

20495 ■ University of Texas at Dallas - Center for Translation Studies - Translation Library
School of Arts & Humanities, JO51
800 W. Campbell Rd.
Richardson, TX 75080-3021
Ph: (972)883-2092
Fax: (972)883-6303
Co. E-mail: schulte@utdallas.edu
URL: http://translation.utdallas.edu
Contact: Rainer Schulte, Director

Scope: Literary translations. **Services:** Library open to the public. **Founded:** 1984. **Holdings:** Literary works in translation; original source language texts.

RESEARCH CENTERS

20496 ■ University of Texas at Dallas - Center for Translation Studies
PO Box 830688
Richardson, TX 75083-0688
Ph: (972)883-2092
Fax: (972)883-6303
Co. E-mail: schulte@utdallas.edu
URL: http://www.utdallas.edu/research/cts
Contact: Prof. Rainer Schulte, Director

Founded: 1980. **Publications:** *Translation Review* (3/year). **Educational Activities:** Translation workshops. **Awards:** Center for Translation Studies Fellowships.

START-UP INFORMATION

20497 ■ *The 100 Best Businesses to Start When You Don't Want To Work Hard Anymore*

Pub: Career Press Inc.

Ed: Lisa Rogak. **Price:** $16.99. **Description:** Author helps burned-out workers envision a new future as a small business owner. Systems analysis, adventure travel outfitting, bookkeeping, food delivery, furniture making, and software development are among the industries examined.

20498 ■ *"Business Start-Up a Learning Experience for Young Bellingham Entrepreneur" in Bellingham Herald (July 18, 2010)*

Pub: Bellingham Herald

Ed: Dave Gallagher. **Description:** Profile of 21-year-old entrepreneur, Chase Larabee, who developed an online program that helps airport fixed-based operators handle refueling, hotel and transportation reservations and other requests from private airplane pilots.

20499 ■ *Design and Launch an Online Travel Business in a Week*

Pub: Entrepreneur Press

Contact: Perlman Neil, President

Ed: Charlene Davis. **Released:** May 1, 2009. **Price:** $17.95. **Description:** Guide providing techniques and professional advice for starting an online travel business. Tips are given to build a Website, find qualified providers and to set up a payment system.

20500 ■ *Home-Based Travel Agent, 5th Edition*

Pub: The Intrepid Traveler

Ed: Kelly Monaghan. **Released:** March 2006. **Price:** $59.95. **Description:** Advice for starting and running a home-based travel agency is given.

20501 ■ *"Online Fortunes" in Small Business Opportunities (Fall 2008)*

Pub: Entrepreneur Media Inc.

Description: Fifty hot, e-commerce enterprises for the aspiring entrepreneur to consider are featured; virtual assistants, marketing services, party planning, travel services, researching, web design and development, importing as well as creating an online store are among the businesses featured.

ASSOCIATIONS AND OTHER ORGANIZATIONS

20502 ■ *ACTA Voyage*
Released: Quarterly

20503 ■ **Adventure Travel Trade Association (ATTA)**
601 Union St., 42nd Fl.
Seattle, WA 98101
Ph: (360)805-3131

Fax: (360)805-0649
Co. E-mail: info@adventuretravel.biz
URL: http://www.adventuretravel.biz
Contact: Mr. Shannon Stowell, President
Description: Serves the adventure travel industry. Aims to grow the adventure travel industry overall and to help build up its member organizations. Provides exposure, marketing expertise, education, research, and discount to its members. **Founded:** 1990. **Educational Activities:** Adventure Travel World Summit (Annual).

20504 ■ **American Society of Travel Agents (ASTA)**
1101 King St., Ste. 200
Alexandria, VA 22314
Ph: (703)739-2782
Fax: (703)739-2782
Co. E-mail: askasta@asta.org
URL: http://www.astanet.com
Contact: Nina Meyer, President
URL(s): www.asta.org. **Description:** Travel agents; allied members are representatives of carriers, hotels, resorts, sightseeing and car rental companies, official tourist organizations, and other travel interests. Aims to: promote and encourage travel among people of all nations and the use of professional travel agents worldwide; serve as an information resource for the travel industry worldwide; promote and represent the views and interests of travel agents to all levels of government and industry; promote professional and ethical conduct in the travel agency industry worldwide; facilitate consumer protection and safety for the traveling public. Maintains biographical archives and travel hall of fame. Conducts research and education programs. **Founded:** 1931. **Publications:** *ASTA Officials Directory* (Annual); *Dateline ASTA* (Weekly); *American Society of Travel Agents--Membership Directory* (Annual). **Educational Activities:** ASTA World Travel Congress/American Society of Travel Agents (Annual); ASTA's CruiseFest/American Society of Travel Agents. **Awards:** Allied Member Award (Annual); Lifetime Achievement Award (Periodic); Travel Agent of the Year (Annual); Travel Hall of Fame Award (Annual); Young Professional Award (Annual); Alaska Airlines Scholarships; American Express Travel Scholarships; American Society of Travel Agents AVIS Scholarships; Arizona Chapter Gold Scholarships; Healy Graduate Scholarships; Pleasant Hawaiian Holidays Scholarships; Stan and Leone Pollard Scholarships; George Reinke Scholarships; Nancy Stewart Scholarships; Allied Member Award; Travel Agent of the Year Award; Travel Hall of Fame; David J. Hallissey Memorial Scholarships; Holland America Line-Westours Research Grants; Travel Journalist of the Year Award. **Telecommunication Services:** askasta@astahq.com.

20505 ■ **Association of Canadian Travel Agencies (ACTA)—Association Canadienne des Agences de Voyages**
2560 Matheson Blvd. E, Ste. 328
Mississauga, ON, Canada L4W 4Y9
Ph: (905)282-9294
Free: 888-257-2282

Fax: (905)282-9826
Co. E-mail: actacan@acta.ca
URL: http://www.acta.ca
Contact: David McCaig, President
Description: Travel agents, tour operators, airlines, hotels, destination marketing organizations, cruise and rail lines, and automobile rental companies in Canada. Ensures consumers have professional and meaningful travel counseling by providing effective leadership in advocacy, public relations, research and education on behalf of the retail travel industry in Canada. **Founded:** 1977.

20506 ■ **Association of Destination Management Executives (ADME)**
PO Box 2307
Dayton, OH 45401-2307
Ph: (937)586-3727
Fax: (937)586-3699
Co. E-mail: info@adme.org
URL: http://www.adme.org
Contact: Fran Rickenbach, Executive Vice President
Description: Works to increase the professionalism of owners, CEOs and employees of destination management companies. Conducts educational conferences and meetings. **Founded:** 1995. **Publications:** *ADME Xpressions* (Quarterly). **Educational Activities:** Association of Destination Management Executives Conference (Annual). **Awards:** Best Innovative Event (Annual); Best Logistics (Annual); Best Overall Program (Annual); Destination Management Professional of the Year (Annual); Destination Management Rising Star (Annual).

20507 ■ **Association of Retail Travel Agents (ARTA)**
4320 N Miller Rd.
Scottsdale, AZ 85251
Ph: (859)269-9739
Free: 866-369-8969
Fax: (866)743-2087
Co. E-mail: pat@artonline.com
URL: http://www.arta.travel
Contact: Pat Funk, Executive Director
Description: Represents retail travel agents and agencies in North America. Promotes the interests of retail travel agents through representation on industry councils, testimony before Congress and participation government proceedings. Conducts joint marketing and educational programs; sponsors work-study program. **Founded:** 1962. **Publications:** *ARTA E-News.*

20508 ■ **Association of Travel Marketing Executives (ATME)**
PO Box 3176
West Tisbury, MA 02575
Ph: (508)693-0550
Fax: (508)693-0115
Co. E-mail: admin@atme.org
URL: http://www.atme.org
Contact: Henry Harteveldt, Chairman
Description: Travel marketing executives working in an executive or managerial capacity related to marketing a travel product or service including airlines, cruise lines, hotels, and convention and visi-

tors' bureaus. Prepares special reports; conducts Certified Travel Marketing Executive educational program; honors travel marketing executives. **Founded:** 1980. **Publications:** *Directory of ATME Members* (Annual); *Travel Marketing Decisions* (Quarterly); *ATMES Travel Marketing Newsletter - Market Flash.* **Educational Activities:** Association of Travel Marketing Executives Seminar; Travel Marketing Conference (Annual). **Awards:** Atlas Awards.

20509 ■ The Buzz
505 Consumers Rd., Ste. 406
Toronto, ON, Canada M2J 4V8
Ph: (416)484-4450
Free: 800-589-5776
Fax: (416)484-4140
Co. E-mail: info@citc.ca
URL: http://www.citc.ca
Contact: Ed Bennington, Chairman
Released: Monthly

20510 ■ Canadian Institute of Travel Counsellors (CITC)—Institut Canadiens des Conseillers en Voyages
505 Consumers Rd., Ste. 406
Toronto, ON, Canada M2J 4V8
Ph: (416)484-4450
Free: 800-589-5776
Fax: (416)484-4140
Co. E-mail: info@citc.ca
URL: http://www.citc.ca
Contact: Ed Bennington, Chairman
Description: Represents individual travel professionals in Canada; promotes professional development through seminars, home study courses, conferences and workshops; offers professional certification programs leading to the Certified Travel Counsellor (CTC) and Certified Travel Manager (CTM) designations, and consumer awareness. **Founded:** 1968. **Publications:** *The Buzz* (Monthly).

20511 ■ Canadian Tourism Research Institute (CTRI)
c/o The Conference Board of Canada
255 Smyth Rd.
Ottawa, ON, Canada K1H 8M7
Ph: (613)526-3280
Free: 866-711-2262
Fax: (613)526-4857
Co. E-mail: ctri@conferenceboard.ca
URL: http://www.conferenceboard.ca/topics/economics/CTRI/default.aspx
Contact: Daniel Muzyka, President
Description: Represents travel and tourism businesses. Seeks to increase understanding of the needs and interests of tourists. Serves as a clearinghouse on tourism in Canada. Sponsors commercial tourism research.

20512 ■ European Travel Commission (ETC)
50 W 23rd St., 11th Fl.
New York, NY 10010
Co. E-mail: etc@spring-obrien.com
URL: http://www.VisitEurope.com/us
Contact: Robert K. Franklin, Executive Director
Description: Represents government tourism organizations cooperating to promote travel to Europe and further international goodwill and economic prosperity. **Founded:** 1948. **Publications:** *VisitEurope* (Monthly). **Educational Activities:** Trans-Atlantic Travel Marketing Conference (Annual). **Awards:** Europa Award (Annual).

20513 ■ Institute of Certified Travel Agents
148 Linden St.
Wellesley, MA 02182
Ph: (781)237-0280
Free: 800-542-4282
Fax: (781)237-3860
Co. E-mail: info@thetravelinstitue.com
URL: http://thetravelinstitute.com
Contact: Diane Petras, President
E-mail: dpetras@thetravelinstitute.com
Description: Individuals who have been accredited as Certified Travel Counselors (CTC) or Certified Travel Associates (CTA) must meet the institute's testing and experience requirements. Seeks to increase the level of competence in the travel industry. Provides continuing education and examina-

tion and certification programs; conducts workshops and professional management seminars. Operates Travel Career Development Program to increase professional skills and Destination Specialist Programs to enhance the geographical knowledge of sales agents. Organizes study groups of instruction with enrolled student bodies in most major cities. **Founded:** 1964. **Publications:** *Travel Counselor* (Bimonthly); *Institute of Certified Travel Agents--Directory* (Annual); *ICTA Travel Management Text Series.* **Telecommunication Services:** icta-info@icta.com.

20514 ■ International Association of Tour Managers - North American Region (IATM North America)
24 Blevins Rd.
Kerhonkson, NY 12446-1302
Ph: (212)208-6800
Fax: (212)208-6800
Co. E-mail: chairman@tourmanager.org
URL: http://www.tourmanager.org
Contact: Scott McScott, Chairman
Description: Works to maintain the highest possible standards of tour management; guarantee excellence of performance; educate the travel world on the role of the tour manager (also referred to as tour director, tour escort, or tour leader) in the successful completion of the tour itinerary and in bringing business to related industries. Represents members in influencing legislation and advising on travel policy. Trains tour managers to plan, research, and lead tours to specific domestic and foreign destinations; operates Advisory Board in Professional Tour Management; offers placement service; conducts Professional travel agents, travel wholesalers, airlines, hotel associations, shipping lines, tourist organizations, restaurants, shops, and entertainment organizations Tour Management International Certificate Program. **Founded:** 1962. **Publications:** *The Professional Tour Manager* (Quarterly).

20515 ■ International Galapagos Tour Operators Association (IGTOA)
PO Box 1713
Lolo, MT 59847
Co. E-mail: exd@igtoa.org
URL: http://www.igtoa.org
Contact: Matt Kareus, Executive Director
Description: Individuals and corporations conducting tours to the Galapagos Islands; educational and scientific institutions with an interest in the Islands and their ecosystems. Promotes tourism with the lowest possible environmental impact; seeks to preserve the unique ecosystems and species indigenous to the Galapagos Islands. Raises funds to support environmental protection initiatives; serves as a clearinghouse on low-impact nature tourism; facilitates communication and cooperation among members. **Founded:** 1997. **Awards:** Becario (Annual).

20516 ■ International Gay and Lesbian Travel Association (IGLTA)
1201 NE 26th St., Ste. 103
Fort Lauderdale, FL 33305
Ph: (954)630-1637
Fax: (954)630-1652
Co. E-mail: iglta@iglta.org
URL: http://www.iglta.org
Contact: John Tanzella, President
Description: Travel agents, tour operators, hoteliers, guesthouse and resort owners, travel clubs, and allied businesses interested in promoting travel services to the gay community. Works to: enhance member businesses; inform travel agents and consumers about properties, businesses, and destinations welcoming gay clientele; provide a networking opportunity for members. Offers familiarization trips to promote member businesses in locations of special appeal to gay travelers. Operates public awareness campaign. **Founded:** 1983. **Publications:** *IGLTA Connections* (Annual). **Educational Activities:** International Gay and Lesbian Travel Association Conference (Annual).

20517 ■ National Association of Cruise-Oriented Agencies (NACOA)
St. 7378 Atlantic Blvd., Ste. No. 115
Margate, FL 33063

Ph: (305)663-5626
Free: 866-816-7143
Co. E-mail: nacoafl@aol.com
URL: http://www.nacoaonline.com
Contact: Donna Kaye Esposito, President
Description: Professional association of travel agencies dedicated to the cruise vacation product. Provides educational and training programs, including Seminars-At-Sea, and Ship Inspection weekends. Offers Safe Sail insurances and Errors and Omissions insurance. **Founded:** 1985. **Publications:** *Now Sea This.*

20518 ■ National Tour Association (NTA)
101 Prosperous Pl., Ste. 350
Lexington, KY 40509
Ph: (859)226-4444
Free: 800-682-8886
Fax: (859)226-4414
Co. E-mail: questions@ntastaff.com
URL: http://www.ntaonline.com
Contact: Jim Reddekopp, Jr., Chief Executive Officer
Description: Operators of group tours and packaged travel; travel industry-related companies providing services/facilities to tour operators (hotels, attractions, restaurants); and destination marketing organizations such as convention and visitor bureaus, and state tourism departments. Seeks to: maintain a code of ethical standards within the tour industry; develop and increase public interest in packaged travel. Represents members before governmental bodies and agencies. Conducts research and educational programs. **Scope:** travel and tour. **Founded:** 1951. **Subscriptions:** archival material reports. **Publications:** *Courier* (Monthly); *NTA Tuesday* (Monthly). **Awards:** Bob Everidge Lifetime Achievement Award (Annual); Volunteer of the Year (Annual).

20519 ■ Opening Door
8049 Ormesby Ln.
Woodford, VA 22580-3211
Co. E-mail: contactus@accessiblevirginia.org
URL: http://www.travelguides.org
Description: Acts as clearinghouse and consultant to the travel and lodging industry for disabled travelers. Sponsors seminars on disability etiquette and the effect of the Americans with Disabilities Act on public accommodations. Maintains speakers' bureau. Conducts activities internationally. Publishes travel and access guides. **Founded:** 1987. **Publications:** *Virginia Travel Guide for Persons with Disabilities* (Biennial). **Awards:** Beverly Chapman Award (Annual).

20520 ■ Pacific Asia Travel Association (PATA)
Bryant and Tripptree Ltd.
164 Loop Pl.
Trinidad, CA 95570
Ph: (707)232-2102
Fax: (707)540-6259
Co. E-mail: communications@pata.org
URL: http://www.pata.org
Contact: Mr. Gregory Duffell, Chief Executive Officer
Description: Represents Government tourist bureaus; cruise companies, airlines, railroads, commercial travel bureaus, hotels, tour operators and hotel associations throughout the world. Conducts marketing program to promote travel to the countries and islands of the Greater Pacific region; works to facilitate and unify entry and exit procedures in members' countries; provides travel information service to the industry; disseminates travel news to the press and other media; coordinates market research to determine potential markets and the future impact of overseas travelers. Develops destination development task forces. Compiles statistics. **Scope:** tourism, Asia. **Founded:** 1951. **Subscriptions:** 2000 books films periodicals video recordings. **Publications:** *Pacific Asia Travel Association--Annual Report* (Annual); *PATA Quarterly Statistical Report* (Quarterly); *PATA Worldwide Chapter Directory* (Annual). **Awards:** Chapter Awards (Annual); Face of the Future Award (Annual); Honorary Life Membership (Annual); Merit of Award (Annual); PATA Gold Awards (Annual).

20521 ■ RVC Directory
116 Lisgar St., Ste. 600
Ottawa, ON, Canada K2P 0C2
Ph: (613)238-3883
Co. E-mail: info@tiac.travel
URL: http://www.tiac.travel
Contact: David F. Goldstein, President
Released: Annual **Price:** free for members.

20522 ■ TIAC Talk
116 Lisgar St., Ste. 600
Ottawa, ON, Canada K2P 0C2
Ph: (613)238-3883
Co. E-mail: info@tiac.travel
URL: http://www.tiac.travel
Contact: David F. Goldstein, President
Released: Weekly **Price:** included in membership dues.

20523 ■ TIAC Talk Issue Focus
116 Lisgar St., Ste. 600
Ottawa, ON, Canada K2P 0C2
Ph: (613)238-3883
Co. E-mail: info@tiac.travel
URL: http://www.tiac.travel
Contact: David F. Goldstein, President
Released: Periodic

20524 ■ Tourism Industry Association of Canada (TIAC)—Association de L'Industrie Touristique du Canada
116 Lisgar St., Ste. 600
Ottawa, ON, Canada K2P 0C2
Ph: (613)238-3883
Co. E-mail: info@tiac.travel
URL: http://www.tiac.travel
Contact: David F. Goldstein, President
Description: Promotes viability of Canada's tourism industries. Serves as a unified voice for the industry in communications with government agencies responsible for tourism and related matters; conducts lobbying activities. **Founded:** 1930. **Publications:** RVC Directory (Annual); TIAC Talk (Weekly); TIAC Talk Issue Focus (Periodic). **Educational Activities:** Canada's Tourism Leadership Summit (Annual). **Awards:** TIAC / Parks Canada Sustainable Tourism Scholarships.

20525 ■ United States Tour Operators Association (USTOA)
345 Seventh Ave., Ste. 1801
New York, NY 10001
Ph: (212)599-6599
Fax: (212)599-6744
Co. E-mail: information@ustoa.com
URL: http://www.ustoa.com
Description: Represents wholesale tour operators, common carriers, associations, government agencies, suppliers, purveyors of travel services, trade press, communications media, and public relations and advertising representatives. Encourages and supports professional and financial integrity in tourism. Protects the legitimate interests of the consumer and the retail agent from financial loss from business conducted with members. Provides tour operators with an opportunity to formulate and express an independent industry voice on matters of common interest and self-regulation. Strives to facilitate and develop travel on a worldwide basis. **Founded:** 1972. **Educational Activities:** United States Tour Operators Association Conference (Annual).

20526 ■ U.S. Travel Association (TIAA)
1100 New York Ave. NW, Ste. 450
Washington, DC 20005-3934
Ph: (202)408-8422
Fax: (202)408-1255
Co. E-mail: feedback@ustravel.org
URL: http://www.ustravel.org
Contact: Roger J. Dow, President
Description: Corporations engaged in the hospitality and travel industries. Promotes increased profitability within the travel industries. Serves as a clearinghouse on the hospitality, travel, and related industries; represents members' interests on the national level; conducts industry research and surveys. Facilitates communication and cooperation among members. **Founded:** 1941. **Awards:** Mercury Awards; Hall of Leaders; Travel Hall of Leaders (Annual).

20527 ■ U.S. Travel Data Center (USTDC)
c/o Travel Industry Association of America
1100 New York Ave. NW, Ste. 450
Washington, DC 20005-3934
Ph: (202)408-8422
Fax: (202)408-1255
Co. E-mail: feedback@ustravel.org
URL: http://www.tia.org
Description: Conducts statistical, economic, and market research concerning travel; encourages standardized travel research terminology and techniques. Monitors trends in travel activity and the travel industry. Measures the economic impact of travel on geographic areas and the cost of travel in the U.S. Evaluates the effect of government programs on travel and the travel industry. Forecasts travel activity and expenditures. **Founded:** 1973. **Publications:** Survey of State Travel Offices (Annual). **Educational Activities:** Travel Outlook Forum (Annual).

DIRECTORIES OF EDUCATIONAL PROGRAMS

20528 ■ Directory of Private Accredited Career Schools and Colleges of Technology
Pub: Accrediting Commission of Career Schools and Colleges of Technology
Contact: Michale S. McComis, Executive Director
Released: On web page. **Price:** Free. **Description:** Covers 3900 accredited post-secondary programs that provide training programs in business, trade, and technical fields, including various small business endeavors. Entries offer school name, address, phone, description of courses, job placement assistance, and requirements for admission. Arrangement is alphabetical.

REFERENCE WORKS

20529 ■ "2010 Book of Lists" in Austin Business JournalInc. (Vol. 29, December 25, 2009, No. 42, pp. 1)
Pub: American City Business Journals
Description: Rankings of companies and organizations within the business services, finance, healthcare, hospitality and travel, insurance, marketing and media, professional services, real estate, education and technology industries in Austin, Texas are presented. Rankings are based on sales, business size, and other statistics.

20530 ■ "2010 Book of Lists" in Business Courier (Vol. 26, December 26, 2009, No. 36, pp. 1)
Pub: American City Business Journals, Inc.
Description: Rankings of companies and organizations within the business services, education, finance, health care, hospitality and tourism, real estate, and technology industries in the Cincinnati, Ohio-Northern Kentucky area are presented. Rankings are based on sales, business size, or other statistics.

20531 ■ "2010 Book of Lists" in Tampa Bay Business Journal (Vol. 30, December 22, 2009, No. 53, pp. 1)
Pub: American City Business Journals
Description: Rankings of companies and organizations within the human resources, banking and finance, business services, healthcare, real estate, technology, hospitality and travel, and education industries in the Greater Tampa Bay area are presented. Rankings are based on sales, business size, and more.

20532 ■ "B&B Hopes to Appeal to Fiat Execs" in Crain's Detroit Business (Vol. 25, June 15, 2009, No. 24, pp. 21)
Pub: Crain Communications Inc. - Detroit
Ed: Daniel Duggan. **Description:** Cobblestone Manor, a ten-room bed and breakfast in Auburn Hills, Michigan is hoping to provide rooms for Fiat executives. The owners have been working with travel organizations to promote the castle-like bed and breakfast which appeals to European visitors.

20533 ■ "Bill Kaneko" in Hawaii Business (Vol. 53, December 2007, No. 6, pp. 32)
Pub: Hawaii Business Publishing
Ed: David K. Choo. **Description:** Hawaii Institute for Public Affairs chief executive officer and president Bill Kaneko believes that the Hawaiian economy is booming, however, he also asserts that the economy is too focused on tourism and real estate. Kaneko has also realized the that the will of the people is strong while he was helping with the Hawaiian 2050 Sustainability Plan. The difficulties of making a sustainable Hawaii are discussed.

20534 ■ Bottin Touristique du Quebec
Pub: Quebec Dans Le Monde
Contact: Alain Prujiner, President
URL(s): www.quebecmonde.com. **Released:** Annual; Latest edition 15th; 2009-2010. **Price:** $51.95, Individuals. **Covers:** Approximately 800 business, cultural and recreational travel agencies and agents in Quebec. **Entries include:** Company name, address, phone, fax, agent name, address, phone, fax, activities. **Arrangement:** Alphabetical. **Indexes:** Subject, geographical.

20535 ■ "The British Aren't Coming" in Crain's Chicago Business (Vol. 34, October 24, 2011, No. 42, pp. 3)
Pub: Crain Communications Inc.
Ed: Brigid Sweeney. **Description:** In a move to attract tourists back to Chicago, its Convention and Tourism Bureau is marketing in London, England, Mexico, and Canada, but not Germany or France because of budget constraints.

20536 ■ "Cruising In Choppy Water" in The Business Journal-Portland (Vol. 25, August 22, 2008, No. 24, pp. 1)
Pub: American City Business Journals, Inc.
Ed: Erik Siemers. **Description:** Yacht builder Christensen Shipyards Inc. is experiencing robust business despite the slowing US economy, building four yachts a year as of 2008. The company expects revenues to hit $90 million and is opening a 500,000-square-foot plant in Tennessee.

20537 ■ "DePaul To Train Hotel Leaders" in Chicago Tribune (September 22, 2008)
Pub: McClatchy-Tribune Information Services
Ed: Kathy Bergen. **Description:** With help from a $7.5 million grant from the Conrad N. Hilton Foundation, DePaul University will dramatically expand its role as a training ground for the tourism-industry with the opening of a School of Hospitality.

20538 ■ "Destination Africa: A Look at How Tourism Could Change the Face and Economics of Africa" in Black Enterprise (February 2008)
Pub: Earl G. Graves Publishing Co. Inc.
Ed: Sonia Alleyne. **Description:** Countries in Africa are experiencing high rates of growth in tourism than the worldwide average. Statistical data included.

20539 ■ Double or Nothing: How Two Friends Risked It All to Buy One of Las Vegas' Legendary Casinos
Pub: HarperBusiness
Ed: Tom Breitling, with Cal Fussman. **Released:** March 2008. **Price:** $24.95. **Description:** Founders of a successful Internet travel agency share their experience from startup to selling the company.

20540 ■ "Doubletree Finds a Niche for Giving Back" in Hotel and Motel Management (Vol. 225, July 2010, No. 8, pp. 6)
Pub: Questex Media Group Inc.
Ed: Paul J. Heney. **Description:** Profile of Doubletree Hotel's community outreach programs that help employee volunteers work to educate children and the public about issues important to the environment.

20541 ■ Driving With No Brakes: How a Bunch of Hooligans Built the Best Travel Company in the World
Pub: Grand Circle Corporation
Ed: Alan and Harriet Lewis. **Price:** $19.95. **Description:** Inspirational book about how two courageous leaders built a remarkable company that can thrive in

change and succeed in an unpredictable world. Important lessons for any business leader trying to create value in the 21st Century are included.

20542 ■ "Eco-Preneuring" in Small Business Opportunities (Jan. 2008)
Pub: Harris Publications Inc.

Description: Iceland Naturally is a joint marketing effort among tourism and business interests hoping to increase demand for Icelandic products including frozen seafood, bottled water, agriculture, and tourism in North America.

20543 ■ "Eco-Preneuring" in Small Business Opportunities (July 2008)
Pub: Entrepreneur Media Inc.

Ed: Mary C. Pearl. **Description:** Profile of Wildlife Trust, a rapidly growing global organization dedicated to innovative conservation science linking health and ecology. With partners in nearly twenty countries, Wildlife Trust draws on global strengths in order to respond to well-defined local needs. In the Dominican Republic, they are working with the community and local biologists in order to restore fishing and create jobs in the field of ecotourism.

20544 ■ "F1 Makes Room(s) for Aspiring Entrepreneur" in Austin Business Journal (Vol. 31, July 1, 2011, No. 17, pp. 1)
Pub: American City Business Journals Inc.

Ed: Vicky Garza. **Description:** Formula One fan and graphic designer Danielle Crespo cashes in on the June 17, 2012 racing event in Austin, Texas via hosting a Website that allows users to book hotel rooms. She invested less than $100 and long hours on this enterprise which now has 74,000-plus visitors.

20545 ■ "Get Wrecked" in Canadian Business (Vol. 80, November 19, 2007, No. 23, pp. S13)
Pub: Rogers Media

Ed: Thomas Watson. **Description:** Key West economy has benefited from wrecks as salvaging lost items became a lucrative business. The USAFS General Hoyt S. Vanderberg is expected to be sunk and will provide a good opportunity for wreck dives. The trends in Key West tourism are evaluated.

20546 ■ "Goldbelt Inc.: Targeting Shareholder Development" in Alaska Business Monthly (Vol. 27, October 2011, No. 10, pp. 108)
Pub: Alaska Business Publishing Company

Ed: Tracy Kalytiak. **Description:** Profile of Godbelt Inc., the company that has changed its original focus of timber to real estate to tourism and then to government contracting opportunities.

20547 ■ "Gov. Kasich to Put DOD On Short Leash" in Business Courier (Vol. 27, November 26, 2010, No. 30, pp. 1)
Pub: Business Courier

Ed: Dan Monk. **Description:** Ohio Governor-elect John Kasich proposed the privatization of the Ohio Department of Development in favor of a nonprofit corporation called JobsOhio. Kasich believes that the department has lost its focus by adding to its mission issues such as energy efficiency and tourism.

20548 ■ "Happy Trails: RV Franchiser Gives Road Traveling Enthusiasts a Lift" in Black Enterprise (Vol. 38, July 2008, No. 12, pp. 47)
Pub: Earl G. Graves Publishing Co. Inc.

Ed: Tamara E. Holmes. **Description:** Overview of Bates International Motor Home Rental Systems Inc., a growing franchise that gives RV owners the chance to rent out their big-ticket purchases to others when they are not using them; Sandra Williams Bate launched the company as a franchise in July 1997 and now has a fleet of 30 franchises across the country. She expects the company to reach 2.2 million for 2008 due to a marketing initiative that will expand the company's presence.

20549 ■ Heads in Beds
Pub: Prentice Hall PTR

Ed: Ivo Raza. **Released:** May 28, 2004. **Description:** Advice is given to help build brands, generate sales and grow profits through marketing for any hospitality or tourism business.

20550 ■ "Hola and Aloha" in Hawaii Business (Vol. 53, December 2007, No. 6, pp. 131)
Pub: Hawaii Business Publishing

Ed: Jason Ubay. **Description:** Juan Carlos Bianchetti is the trilingual owner of Ole Tours Hawaii, a travel wholesaler that targets Portuguese and Spanish-speaking visitors. The competition for American and Japanese tourists is already tight, which is why Bianchetti opted to target a different segment of the Hawaii tourism market. Plans for the company's expansion in Kauai, Brazil, and Argentina, are mentioned.

20551 ■ "An Ill Wind: Icelandic Bank Failures Chill Atlantic Canada" in Canadian Business (Vol. 81, November 10, 2008, No. 19, pp. 10)
Pub: Rogers Media Ltd.

Ed: Charles Mandel. **Description:** Bank failures in Iceland have put a stop to flights ferrying Icelanders to Newfoundland to purchase Christmas gifts, thereby threatening Newfoundland's tourism industry. The credit of Newfoundland's fisheries is also being squeezed since most of Atlantic Canadian seafood processors hold lines of credit from Icelandic banks.

20552 ■ "Ill Winds; Cuba's Economy" in The Economist (Vol. 390, January 3, 2009, No. 8612, pp. 20)
Pub: The Economist Newspaper Inc.

Description: Cuba's long-term economic prospects remain poor with the economy forecasted to grow only 4.3 percent for the year, about half of the original forecast, due in part to Hurricane Gustav which caused $10 billion in damage and disrupted the food-supply network and devastated farms across the region; President Raul Castro made raising agricultural production a national priority and the rise in global commodity prices hit the country hard. The only bright spot has been the rise in tourism which is up 9.3 percent over 2007.

20553 ■ "Indigenous Tourism Operators" in International Journal of Entrepreneurship and Small Business (Vol. 10, July 6, 2010, No. 4)
Pub: Publishers Communication Group

Ed: Andrews Cardow, Peter Wiltshier. **Description:** Emergent enthusiasm for tourism as a savior for economic development in the Chatham Islands of New Zealand is highlighted.

20554 ■ The Itty Bitty Guide to Business Travel
Pub: Chronicle Books LLC

Ed: Stacie Krachir, Carrie Rosten. **Released:** April 2004. **Description:** Advice on all aspects of business travel, including low-price airfare, packing and coping with stress.

20555 ■ "Luxe Hotels on a Budget" in Inc. (Volume 32, December 2010, No. 10, pp. 60)
Pub: Inc. Magazine

Ed: Adam Baer. **Description:** Off & Away Website allows users to vie for discounted hotel rooms at more than 100 luxury properties. To compete, users buy $1 bids and each time an individual bids the price of the room goes up by 10 cents.

20556 ■ "Making Visitors Out Of Listeners" in Hawaii Business (Vol. 54, July 2008, No. 1, pp. 18)
Pub: Hawaii Business Publishing

Ed: Casey Chin. **Description:** Japanese workers are subscribing to the Official Hawaii Podcast in iTunes, which offers a free 20-minute, Japanese-language audio content on different topics, such as dining reviews and music from local artists. The concept is a way to attract Japanese travelers to come to Hawaii.

20557 ■ "Marathon Money" in Hawaii Business (Vol. 53, December 2007, No. 6, pp. 127)
Pub: Hawaii Business Publishing

Ed: Jolyn Okimoto Rosa. **Description:** Discusses the effects of the Honolulu Marathon on small businesses' sales. The Running Room, for instance, experience growth in sales starting from the training season up to the end of the race, as a surge of

Hawaiian residents and tourists come into the store for items such as running shoes and blister kits. The marathon's impact on Hawaii's tourism is examined as well.

20558 ■ "The Next Waive" in Hawaii Business (Vol. 53, January 2008, No. 7, pp. 27)
Pub: Hawaii Business Publishing

Ed: Cathy S. Cruz-George. **Description:** Only 40,000 Koreans took a visit to Hawaii in 2007, a decline from the pre-September averages of 123,000 visits. The number of Korean visitors in Hawaii could increase if the visa waiver proposal is passed. Efforts to improve Hawaiian tourism are presented.

20559 ■ "Not Enough Room" in Austin Business JournalInc. (Vol. 29, November 13, 2009, No. 36, pp. A1)
Pub: American City Business Journals

Ed: Jacob Dirr. **Description:** Hotel and convention business in downtown Austin, Texas lost nearly $5.3 million when Dell Inc. relocated its annual convention to Las Vegas. However, lack of capital caused the postponement of various hotel projects which need to be finished in order to attract well-attended conventions. Makeover projects on Austin's Waller Creek and Sixth Street are discussed.

20560 ■ OAG Business Travel Planner: The Official Lodging Directory of the American Hotel & Motel Association
Pub: Reed Travel Group OAG Travel Services Div.

URL(s): www.oag.com. **Released:** Quarterly **Covers:** 14,500 destination cities, military installations (U.S. only), and colleges and universities in North America; over 78,000 hotels and motels; calendar of events; city, state or province, and national tourist offices; tour operators; car rental agencies; airlines and charter air taxi firms, and airport limousine services; consulates and missions of foreign countries in North America; United States foreign service offices; hotel and motel systems, and toll free reservations services; airport club locations, frequent flyer and frequent guest information. **Entries include:** For destinations--Place name, airport name and code or note on nearest air service; entries for larger cities include convention facilities, hotel name, address, phone, rates, location, number of meeting rooms, fax; whether member of the American Hotel and Motel Association. For calendar of events--Date, name and location of event, and names, addresses, and phone numbers of state and local tourism agencies. Separate toll-free section for hotel/motel systems and travel-related firms. Other listings include company or office name, address, phone. **Database includes:** Maps of city centers with hotel locations; airport diagrams; and metropolitan resort area maps; attractions; convention facilities. **Arrangement:** Primarily geographical.

20561 ■ OAG Travel Planner European Edition
Pub: Official Airline Guides

Contact: Alan Glass, Chief Executive Officer

URL(s): www.oag.com. **Released:** Quarterly **Price:** $632, Individuals Online; $705, Individuals CD. **Covers:** Over 14,000 destination cities in Europe; 16,923 hotels; hotel chains and reservations services; calendars of events; city, regional, and national tourist offices; airline reservation numbers; car rental agencies; ground transportation information; U.S. military installations; consulates and missions of foreign countries in the United States and Canada; airport, ground, and rail services. **Entries include:** Section for a country begins with climate, currency, documentary requirements, consulate, and other information; holiday and public event calendar for following six months; list of the country's tourist offices at home and abroad. For individual destinations--Place name, name and mileage from nearest airport, dialing code for each city; hotel name, address, phone, fax, telex, postal number, room rates, number of rooms, and quality rating, where applicable. **Database includes:** City and country maps; airport diagrams. **Arrangement:** Geographical.

20562 ■ Official Hotel Guide
Pub: Northstar Travel Media L.L.C.

Contact: Thomas Kemp, Chief Executive Officer

E-mail: tkemp@ntmllc.com

URL(s): www.northstartravelmedia.com/. **Released:** Annual **Covers:** in four volumes, 29,000 hotels, motels, and resorts worldwide. Volume 1 covers most of the U.S. ; Volume 2 covers the rest of the U.S. and the Western Hemisphere; Volume 3 covers Europe, the Middle East, Asia, and Africa. Volume 4 specialty travel guide includes listings of golf resorts and tennis resorts; health spas, dude ranches, bed and breakfasts, and casino & hotels in the United States; also includes lists of hotels in the Caribbean with golf, tennis, casinos, and all-inclusive. **Entries include:** Hotel/motel/resort name, address, phone, fax, CRS's, number of rooms or units, rates, brief description of facilities, ratings, codes indicating credit cards accepted, email and website addresses, and travel agent's commission, if any. **Arrangement:** Geographical.

20563 ■ "Orbitz Adds Parent Panel" in Marketing to Women (Vol. 21, March 2008, No. 3, pp. 5)
Pub: EPM Communications Inc.
Contact: Ira Mayer, President
E-mail: imayer@epmcom.com
Description: Orbitz introduces the Orbitz Parent Panel in an attempt to better connect with traveling families.

20564 ■ "The Personal Touch: Entrepreneur Turns Good Taste, Love of Luxury Into Lucrative Venture" in Black Enterprise (October 2007)
Pub: Earl G. Graves Publishing Co. Inc.
Ed: Tamara E. Holmes. **Description:** Profile of Chaka Fattah Jr. who turned his taste for luxurious things into a successful luxury travel and concierge service catering to business owners, corporate executives, athletes, and entertainers.

20565 ■ "Plans for $160M Condo Resort in Wisconsin Dells Moves Forward" in Commercial Property News (March 18, 2008)
Pub: Nielsen Company
Description: Plans for the Grand Cambrian Resort in the Wisconsin Dells is discussed. The luxury condominium resort will include condos, townhomes, and condo-hotel style residences, two water parts, meeting space and indoor entertainment space, as well as a spa, four restaurants and retail offerings.

20566 ■ "Recovery on Tap for 2010?" in Orlando Business Journal (Vol. 26, January 1, 2010, No. 31, pp. 1)
Pub: American City Business Journals
Ed: Melanie Stawicki Azam, Richard Bilbao, Christopher Boyd, Anjali Fluker. **Description:** Economic forecasts for Central Florida's leading business sectors in 2010 are presented. These sectors include housing, film and TV, sports business, law, restaurants, aviation, tourism and hospitality, banking and finance, commercial real estate, retail, health care, insurance, higher education, and manufacturing. According to some local executives, Central Florida's economy will slowly recover in 2010.

20567 ■ "Saudi Overtures" in The Business Journal-Portland (Vol. 25, August 15, 2008, No. 23, pp. 1)
Pub: American City Business Journals, Inc.
Ed: Aliza Earnshaw. **Description:** Saudi Arabia's huge revenue from oil is creating opportunities for Oregon companies as the country develops new cities, industrial zones, and tourism centers. Oregon exported only $46.8 million worth of goods to Saudi Arabia in 2007 but the kingdom is interested in green building materials and methods, renewable energy and water quality control, and nanotechnology all of which Oregon has expertise in.

20568 ■ "Save Money on Travel With These Websites for Frequent Fliers" in Inc. (Vol. 31, January-February 2009, No. 1, pp. 44)
Pub: Mansueto Ventures LLC
Description: Four Websites offering services to the business traveler are profiled: MissRefund.com will get the taxes and fuel surcharges back to any traveler canceling a flight; Vayama.com is a booking site focused on routes and destinations not generally available online; Airfarewatchdog.com searches for listing sites for best travel deals; and Yapta alerts users to good prices for particular flights.

20569 ■ Selling the Invisible: A Field Guide to Modern Marketing
Pub: Business Plus
Ed: Harry Beckwith. **Price:** $22.95. **Description:** Tips for marketing and selling intangibles such as health care, entertainment, tourism, legal services, and more are provided.

20570 ■ "Senate OKs Funds for Promoting Tourism" in Crain's Detroit Business (Vol. 24, March 31, 2008, No. 13, pp. 6)
Pub: Crain Communications, Inc.
Ed: Amy Lane. **Description:** Discusses the Senate proposal which allocates funds for Michigan tourism and business promotion as well as Michigan's No Worker Left Behind initiative, a program that provides free tuition at community colleges and other venues to train displaced workers for high-demand occupations.

20571 ■ "Small Dutch Islands Saba, Statia Content With Low-Key Niche" in Travel Weekly (Vol. 69, August 16, 2010, No. 33, pp. 22)
Pub: NorthStar Travel Media LLC
Ed: Gay Nagle Myers. **Description:** Small Caribbean islands market and promote their region for tourism by never competing with the bigger destinations. Saba and Statia are the two smallest islands in the Caribbean and rely on repeat guests, word-of-mouth recommendations and travel agents willing to promote them.

20572 ■ "State Tourism Likely to Decline Two Percent this Year" in Crain's Detroit Business (Vol. 24, April 14, 2008, No. 15, pp. 6)
Pub: Crain Communications Inc.
Ed: Amy Lane. **Description:** Due to such national and state economic conditions such as unemployment, the housing crisis and rising gasoline and food prices, Michigan's tourism industry is likely to decline about 2 percent this year.

20573 ■ "Tourism Bureau Seeks Hotel Tax Hike" in Baltimore Business Journal (Vol. 27, December 18, 2009, No. 32, pp. 1)
Pub: American City Business Journals
Ed: Rachel Bernstein. **Description:** Baltimore, Maryland's tourism agency, Visit Baltimore, has proposed a new hotel tax that could produce $2 million annually for its marketing budget, fund improvements to the city's 30-year-old convention center and help it compete for World Cup soccer games. Baltimore hotel leaders discuss the new tax.

20574 ■ Tourism and Entrepreneurship: International Perspectives
Pub: Elsevier Science & Technology Books
Ed: Stephen Page, Jovo Ateljevic. **Released:** June 1, 2009. **Price:** $69.95. **Description:** Trends in tourism development are explored, focusing on the impact of entrepreneurship in the context of regional and local tourism development.

20575 ■ "Tourism Push Rising in Fall" in Philadelphia Business Journal (Vol. 30, August 26, 2011, No. 28, pp. 1)
Pub: American City Business Journals Inc.
Ed: Peter Van Allen. **Description:** Philadelphia is offering events for tourists this fall despite massive cuts for tourism promotion. Governor Tim Corbet slashed $5.5 million in funding for the state's tourism-promotion agencies which received $32 million in 2009. The agencies were forced to cooperate and fend for themselves using the hotel taxes that sustain them.

20576 ■ The Travel Agent's Complete Desk Reference, 5th Edition
Pub: The Intrepid Traveler
Ed: Kelly Monaghan. **Released:** August 25, 2009. **Price:** $39.95. **Description:** Reference book that provides essential information to the home-based travel agent.

20577 ■ The Travel Book: Guide to the Travel Guides
Pub: Scarecrow Press Inc.
Contact: Patricia Zline, Manager
E-mail: pzline@rowman.com
URL(s): rowman.com/Scarecrow. **Released:** Latest edition 2nd. **Covers:** Travel guides from throughout the world. **Arrangement:** Geographical by country. **Indexes:** Alphabetical.

20578 ■ "Travel In Style, Or Not: Finding a Company Travel Service for Every Budget" in Inc. (January 2008, pp. 36-37)
Pub: Gruner & Jahr USA Publishing
Ed: Larry Olmsted. **Description:** Profiles of various travel services to help small businesses. Firms profiled include Cassis Travel Services, providing first class bookings; Open from American Express, specializing in business class travel; Travelocity business, providing travel agents with 24/7 services; Diners Club Corporate Card, with many features; and Expedia Corporate Travel, allowing users to compare prices for airline tickets, hotels, and car rentals.

20579 ■ "Travel Tears" in Crain's Chicago Business (Vol. 31, November 17, 2008, No. 46, pp. 3)
Pub: Crain Communications, Inc.
Ed: Bob Tita. **Description:** Hotels, restaurants and conventions are seeing a decline in profits due to corporate travel cutbacks and the sagging economy. City and state revenues derived from taxes on tourism-related industries are also suffering.

20580 ■ "Turbulent Times and Golden Opportunity" in Business Strategy Review (Vol. 21, Spring 2010, No. 1, pp. 34)
Pub: Wiley-Blackwell
Ed: Don Sull. **Description:** For those feeling storm-tossed by today's economy, the author believes there's much to learn from Carnival Cruise Lines, a company that discovered that turbulence often has an upside.

20581 ■ "TW Trade Shows to Offer Seminars On Niche Selling, Social Media" in Travel Weekly (Vol. 69, October 4, 2010, No. 40, pp. 9)
Pub: NorthStar Travel Media LLC
Description: Travel Weekly's Leisure World 2010 and Fall Home Based Travel Agent Show focused on niche selling, with emphasis on all-inclusives, young consumers, groups, incentives, culinary vacations, and honeymoon or romance travel.

20582 ■ "Tweaking On-Board Activities, Equipment Saves Fuel, Reduces CO2" in Canadian Sailings (June 30, 2008)
Pub: UBM Global Trade
Contact: Leonard J. Corallo, President
Description: Optimizing ship activities and equipment uses less fuel and therefore reduces greenhouse gas emissions. Ways in which companies are implementing research and development techniques in order to monitor ship performance and analyze data in an attempt to become more efficient are examined.

20583 ■ "Up In the Air" in The Business Journal-Serving Greater Tampa Bay (Vol. 28, July 18, 2008, No. 30, pp. 1)
Pub: American City Business Journals, Inc.
Ed: Margie Manning. **Description:** Views and information on Busch Gardens and on its future, are presented. The park's 3,769 employees worry for their future, after tourism industry experts have expressed concerns on possible tax cuts and other cost reductions. The future of the park, which ranks number 19 as the most visited park in the world, is expected to have a major impact on the tourism industry.

20584 ■ "The Visitor Rebound" in Canadian Business (Vol. 80, November 5, 2007, No. 22, pp. 23)
Pub: Rogers Media
Ed: Graham Silnicki. **Description:** Overnight visits to Canada are expected to fall by 5.3 percent in 2008, however spending is expected to drop by only 2 percent. Senior economist Alex Fritsche thinks that tourism from the U.S. will improve in 2009; the reasons for the expected growth in 2009 are examined.

20585 ■ *"The Way I Work" in Inc. (March 2008, pp. 102-104, 106)*
Pub: Gruner & Jahr USA Publishing
Ed: Hannah Clark Steiman. **Description:** Profile of Howard Lefkowitz, CEO of Vegas.com, a Website that allows visitors to book flights, reserve hotel rooms, buy show tickets, make spa appointments, and coordinate any and all aspects of a trip to Las Vegas. The firm also runs brick-and-mortar box offices and concierge desks at various cities.

20586 ■ *"Website for Women 50 Launches" in Marketing to Women (Vol. 21, April 2008, No. 4, pp. 5)*
Pub: EPM Communications Inc.
Contact: Ira Mayer, President
E-mail: imayer@epmcom.com
Description: Vibrantnation.com is an online community targeting women over age 50; members can share recommendations on a variety of topics such as vacation spots, retailers and financial issues.

20587 ■ *"What Moms Want" in Marketing to Women (Vol. 21, February 2008, No. 2, pp. 6)*
Pub: EPM Communications Inc.
Contact: Ira Mayer, President
E-mail: imayer@epmcom.com
Description: According to a survey conducted by Eureka's Spa, moms would rather have an experience gift than flowers or chocolate. The top five dream gifts include a spa day, a weekend getaway, maid service, a bathroom makeover or a getaway weekend with girlfriends.

20588 ■ *"What's the Black Travel Market Worth?" in Black Enterprise (Vol. 38, January 2008, No. 6, pp. 54)*
Pub: Earl G. Graves Publishing Co. Inc.
Ed: Aisha Sylvester. **Description:** African American travel market, both business and pleasure, is one of the top three fastest growing markets in the industry. Hugh Riley, director of marketing for the Caribbean Tourism Organization shares his ideas on the relationship between African American travelers and the Caribbean tourism industry.

20589 ■ *"Where's the Lava" in Hawaii Business (Vol. 53, November 2007, No. 5, pp. 18)*
Pub: Hawaii Business Publishing
Ed: Jason Ubay. **Description:** Hawaii Volcanoes National Park used to allow visitors to drive to the end of the paved coastal park road and view flowing lava that came from Kilauea until it reached the sea. On Father's Day morning in June 2007, Kilauea began erupting outside the park and the lava flows inland to Kahaualea and Wao Kele O Puna natural area reserves. In July 2007 321,217 visitors came to the park, a 14 percent increase compared to the same month in 2006.

20590 ■ *"The World Is Your Hospital" in Canadian Business (Vol. 81, July 22, 2008, No. 12-13, pp. 62)*
Pub: Rogers Media Ltd.
Ed: Sharda Prashad. **Description:** Medical tourism is seen as a booming industry around the world and is expected to grow to around $40 billion in 2010. Key information regarding medical tourism and services are presented. Views on the possible impact of medical tourism on Canada's health care industry, as well as medical tourism opportunities in Canada, are also given.

STATISTICAL SOURCES

20591 ■ *RMA Annual Statement Studies*
Pub: Risk Management Association
Contact: Kevin M. Blakey, President
Released: Annual. Price: $175.00 2006-07 edition, $105.00. **Description:** Contains composite balance sheets and income statements for more than 360 industries, including the accounting, auditing, and bookkeeping industries. Also contains five years of comparative historical data for discerning trends. Includes 16 commonly used ratios, computed for most of the size groupings for nearly every industry.

20592 ■ *Travel Agencies and Tour Operators Market*
Pub: Rector Press, Ltd.
Contact: Lewis Sckolnick, President
Released: 2009. Price: Contact Rector Press.

TRADE PERIODICALS

20593 ■ *Andrew Harper's Hideaway Report*
Pub: Harper Associates Inc.
Contact: Andrew Harper, Editor
Released: Monthly. Price: $135, U.S.; $165, elsewhere. **Description:** Reviews small and exclusive vacation resorts, executive retreats, and hotels for the sophisticated traveler.

20594 ■ *ARTAFAX*
Pub: Association of Retail Travel Agents
Ed: Nikole Williams, Editor, nikolew@grouptravelleader.com. Released: Daily. Price: Included in membership. **Description:** Reviews developments in the travel industry for retail travel agents. Covers topics such as ethics, tour operations, transportation services, educational opportunities, commissions, and political action in pertinent issues. Includes chapter and Association news.

20595 ■ *Austrian Information*
Pub: Austrian Press and Information Service
Contact: Ms. Alice Irvin, Director
Released: Bimonthly. Price: Free. **Description:** Publishes about all aspects of Austria, including its history, government, society, arts, and culture.

20596 ■ *Corporate & Incentive Travel*
Pub: Coastal Communications Corp.
Contact: Andrew Shaw, Director
URL(s): www.themeetingmagazines.com/index/Default.aspx?tabid=197. Released: Monthly

20597 ■ *Corporate Meetings & Incentives: The Senior Executives Guide to Decision Making*
Pub: Primedia Business Magazines & Media
URL(s): meetingsnet.com/corporatemeetingsincentives/. Ed: Barbara Scofidio. Released: Monthly Price: $97, Canada; $123, Free to qualified subscribers in USA; $123. Other countries.

20598 ■ *Cruise Connoisseur*
Pub: Traveling Times Inc.
Ed: Mirko A. Ilich, Editor. Released: 6/year. **Description:** Presents information on cruise destinations.

20599 ■ *DogGone*
Pub: Doggone
Contact: Robyn Peters, Publisher
E-mail: roblipete@earthlink.net
Released: Bimonthly. Price: $25, U.S.; $38, Canada; $48, elsewhere. **Description:** Highlights destinations and travel tips for people who vacation with their dogs. Also covers creative activities for pets and their owners to enjoy together, travel advice, and personal stories. Recurring features include columns titled Products for Pooches, Travel Pointers, Road Trip, From the Groomer's Table, The Trainers Territory, A Dog's Haus, and Dining With Dogs.

20600 ■ *Dude, Guest & Vacation Ranches*
Pub: Bibliotheca Press
Ed: A. Doyle, Editor. Released: Irregular. Price: $7.95, U.S.. **Description:** Lists dude, guest, and vacation ranches for tourists.

20601 ■ *El Planeta Platica*
Pub: Ron Mader
Contact: Ron Mader, Publisher
E-mail: ron@txinfinet.com; ronmader@aol.com
Released: Quarterly. Price: $25, U.S.. **Description:** Covers tourism in Latin America with an environmental slant. Features articles and a list of resources. Recurring features include book reviews.

20602 ■ *Entree*
Pub: Entree Travel
Ed: William Tomicki, Editor, wtomicki@aol.com. Released: Monthly. Price: $75, individuals U.S.. **Description:** Features an insider's look at luxury hotels, cruises, tours, spas, restaurants, and travel around

the world. Contains advice and tips on luxury travel, bargains, and services. Recurring features include book/wine reviews.

20603 ■ *Hideaways Newsletter*
Pub: Hideaways International
Contact: Michael F. Thiel, Founder
E-mail: mthiel@hideaways.com
Ed: Peg Aaronian, Editor, paaronian@hideaways.com. Released: Quarterly. Price: $129, Included in membership. **Description:** Features articles on issues of interest to villa vacationers and those seeking high quality, high service vacation options. Includes extensive reports on vacation accommodations; destination descriptions; members' ratings of villas, hotels, cruise ships, and yacht charters; travel tips; and news from recommended properties/cruise lines. Recurring features include compilations of quarterly travel surveys, and columns titled Members News, Members Forum, and Trade Winds. Occasional supplements focusing on one destination, i.e., the Caribbean, Paris, etc. Remarks: Subscription includes semiannual, full-color "Hideaways Guide.".

20604 ■ *International Journal of Tourism Research*
Pub: John Wiley & Sons Inc.
Contact: Stephen M. Smith, President
URL(s): onlinelibrary.wiley.com/journal/10.1002/(-ISSN)1522-1970. Ed: John Fletcher. Released: Bimonthly Price: $531, Other countries print only; £501, Institutions print only; €631, Institutions print only; $980, Institutions, other countries print only; €727, Institutions print with online; £576, Institutions print with online; $1127, Institutions, other countries print with online.

20605 ■ *Journeywoman Online Magazine: The Magazine for Women Who Love to Travel*
Pub: Journeywoman
URL(s): www.journeywoman.com/. Ed: Evelyn Hannon. Released: Irregular Price: Free.

20606 ■ *Meetings & Incentive Travel*
Pub: Business Information Group
Contact: Bruce Creighton, President
URL(s): www.meetingscanada.com/. Released: 6/yr.

20607 ■ *OAG Flight-Finder Asia Pacific Plus*
Pub: Official Airline Guides
Contact: Alan Glass, Chief Executive Officer
URL(s): www.oag.com/graphics/travelplus.htm. Released: Monthly

20608 ■ *Southern Festivals: The South's Festival Newspaper*
Pub: Southern Festivals
URL(s): www.southfest.com/festival_list/georgia.html. Released: Bimonthly

20609 ■ *Spa Magazine*
Pub: Islands Publishing Co.
URL(s): www.spamagazine.com. Released: 7/yr. Price: $11.97, U.S.; $20.97, Canada; $36.97, Other countries.

20610 ■ *Travel Weekly: The National Newspaper of the Travel Industry*
Pub: Northstar Travel Media L.L.C.
Contact: Thomas Kemp, Chief Executive Officer
E-mail: tkemp@ntmllc.com
URL(s): www.travelweekly.com. Ed: Joe Rosen, Rob Fixmer. Released: Weekly (Mon.)

20611 ■ *Travel World News Magazine: The Magazine for Destination Travel Specialists*
Pub: Travel Industry Network Inc.
URL(s): www.travelworldnews.com. Ed: Carol A. Petro. Released: Monthly Price: $25, By mail; $40, Canada; $60, Other countries.

20612 ■ *TravelAge West*
Pub: Northstar Travel Media L.L.C.
Contact: Thomas Kemp, Chief Executive Officer
E-mail: tkemp@ntmllc.com
URL(s): www.travelagewest.com. Ed: Christopher Batin. Released: Biweekly

20613 ■ *Traveling Times*
Pub: Traveling Times Inc.
Ed: Mirko A. Ilitch, Editor. **Released:** Quarterly. **Description:** Highlights popular vacation spots around the world.

20614 ■ *Travelweek*
Pub: Concepts Travel Media Ltd.
URL(s): www.travelweek.ca. **Ed:** Patrick Dineen. **Released:** Weekly (Thurs.)

20615 ■ *Woodall's Northeast Outdoors*
Pub: Woodall Publications Corp.
Contact: Mellissa Robinson, Manager
E-mail: mrobinson@affinityroup.com
URL(s): www.woodalls.biz/output.cfm?id=1017811.
Released: Bimonthly **Price:** $20, Individuals.

VIDEOCASSETTES/ AUDIOCASSETTES

20616 ■ *Going Places*
MPI Home Video
16101 S. 108th Ave.
Orland Park, IL 60467
Ph: (708)460-0555
Free: 800-323-0442
Fax: (708)873-3177
URL: http://www.mpihomevideo.com
Released: 19??. **Price:** $79.98. **Description:** Eight-volume set features NBC's Al Roker exploring the world's most popular vacation spots. **Availability:** VHS.

20617 ■ *I Can Do It! Judi Wineland*
Direct Cinema Ltd.
PO Box 10003
Santa Monica, CA 90410-1003
Ph: (310)636-8200
Free: 800-525-0000
Fax: (310)636-8228
Co. E-mail: orders@directcinemalimited.com
URL: http://www.directcinema.com
Released: 1985. **Description:** Wineland describes the tribulations, maneuvers and backroom strategies that resulted in her multi-million dollar travel company. **Availability:** VHS; 3/4 U; Special order formats.

20618 ■ *Inside Business Today*
GPN Educational Media
1550 Executive Drive
Elgin, IL 60123
Ph: (402)472-2007
Free: 800-228-4630
Fax: (800)306-2330
Co. E-mail: askgpn@smarterville.com
URL: http://www.shopgpn.com
Released: 1989. **Description:** Leaders in business and industry tell their success stories in this extensive series. **Availability:** VHS; 3/4 U.

TRADE SHOWS AND CONVENTIONS

20619 ■ Annual Reading Sport, Travel and Outdoor Show
International Sport Show Producers Association (IS-SPA)
PO Box 480084
Denver, CO 80248-0084
Ph: (303)892-6800
Free: 800-457-2434
Fax: (303)892-6322
Co. E-mail: dseymour@iei-expos.com
URL: http://www.sportshow.org
Contact: Jeff Haughton, President
URL(s): www.phillysportshow.com. **Frequency:** Annual. **Audience:** Greater Washington DC area. **Principal Exhibits:** Sports, travel and outdoor show. **Telecommunication Services:** info@sportshows.com.

20620 ■ Annual Rockford RV, Camping and Travel Show
International Sport Show Producers Association (IS-SPA)
PO Box 480084
Denver, CO 80248-0084

Ph: (303)892-6800
Free: 800-457-2434
Fax: (303)892-6322
Co. E-mail: dseymour@iei-expos.com
URL: http://www.sportshow.org
Contact: Jeff Haughton, President
URL(s): www.showtimeproduction.net/rvshow/. **Frequency:** Annual. **Principal Exhibits:** RVs, camping and travel. **Telecommunication Services:** brenda@ showtimeproduction.net.

20621 ■ Eastern Sports & Outdoor Show
Reed Exhibitions North American Headquarters
383 Main Ave.
Norwalk, CT 06851
Ph: (203)840-4800
Fax: (203)840-5805
Co. E-mail: inquiry@reedexpo.com
URL: http://www.reedexpo.com
URL(s): www.easternsportshow.com. **Price:** $10, adult; $9, seniors; $4, children 6 - 12 years. **Frequency:** Annual. **Audience:** General public. **Principal Exhibits:** Recreational vehicles, boats, hunting and fishing equipment, clothing, and related outdoor products, resorts, SUVs, retailers and manufacturers, motorcycles, ATVs, travel and tourism. **Dates and Locations:** , Pennsylvania Farm Show Complex. **Telecommunication Services:** eseveral@reedexpo. com.

20622 ■ Fort Wayne Sports, Vacation, and Boat Show
Trio Enterprises, Inc.
3624 Maxim Dr.
Fort Wayne, IN 46815
Ph: (219)483-2638
Free: 800-446-2638
Fax: (219)484-0876
URL(s): www.boatsafloat.com. **Frequency:** Annual. **Audience:** General public. **Principal Exhibits:** Recreational vehicles, boats, and travel and vacation information. **Dates and Locations:** , Allen County War Memorial Coliseum. **Telecommunication Services:** data@boatsafloat.com.

20623 ■ Kansas Sports, Boat, & Travel Show
Industrial Expositions, Inc.
1675 Larimer St., No. 700
Denver, CO 80248-0084
Ph: (303)892-6800
Free: 800-457-2434
Fax: (303)892-6322
Co. E-mail: info@iei-expos.com
URL: http://www.iei-expos.com/
URL(s): www.agievents.com/shows/display.cfm?showid=74. **Frequency:** Annual. **Audience:** General public. **Principal Exhibits:** Recreational vehicles, boats, sports equipment, and travel destination information; fishing and hunting equipment, supplies, and services. **Dates and Locations:** , Coliseum. **Telecommunication Services:** rwhitacre-prp@ks.rr. com.

20624 ■ Louisville Boat, RV & Sportshow
Douglas Expositions Inc.
10000 Shelbyville Rd., No. 111
Anchorage, KY 40223-2950
Ph: (502)244-5660
URL(s): www.louisvilleboatshow.com. **Frequency:** Annual. **Principal Exhibits:** Sports, boating and vacations, hunting and fishing, recreational vehicles. **Telecommunication Services:** kmuncy@nmma.org.

20625 ■ Quad City Boat and Vacation Show
International Sport Show Producers Association (IS-SPA)
PO Box 480084
Denver, CO 80248-0084
Ph: (303)892-6800
Free: 800-457-2434
Fax: (303)892-6322
Co. E-mail: dseymour@iei-expos.com
URL: http://www.sportshow.org
Contact: Jeff Haughton, President
URL(s): www.iowashows.com. **Price:** $6; kids ages 12 and under. **Frequency:** Annual. **Principal Exhibits:** Boats, fishing tackle, resorts, tourism associations, motorhomes. **Dates and Locations:** River Center.

20626 ■ Travel Media Showcase
Atlantic City Convention & Visitors Authority
2314 Pacific Ave.
Atlantic City, NJ 08401
Ph: (609)348-7100
Fax: (609)348-7287
URL: http://www.atlanticcitynj.com/
URL(s): www.travelmediashowcase.com. **Price:** $2095, exhibitor (1 rep); $2595, exhibitor (2 reps). **Frequency:** Annual. **Audience:** Trade. **Principal Exhibits:** Tourism industry and travel media convention. **Telecommunication Services:** kerry@jveroassociates.com.

CONSULTANTS

20627 ■ The Tactix Group
1619 N 102 St.
Omaha, NE 68114
Ph: (402)393-3800
Fax: (402)393-5151
Co. E-mail: info@thetactixgroup.com
URL: http://www.thetactixgroup.com
Contact: Douglas R. Little, President
E-mail: dlittle@tactixinc.com
Scope: Offers integrated marketing system design and implementation, for customer relationship management. Serves manufacturing, distributing, high-tech, banking, and executive benefit industries. **Founded:** 1987. **Special Services:** Saleslogix (Client Server) Sales Automation Software.

FRANCHISES AND BUSINESS OPPORTUNITIES

20628 ■ All About Honeymoons
All About Honeymoons Franchise Corporation
Description: Honeymoon resort, wedding and travel specialists. **No. of Franchise Units:** 101. **No. of Company-Owned Units:** 1. **Founded:** 1994.. **Franchised:** 2003. **Equity Capital Needed:** $32,900-$75,900. **Franchise Fee:** $9,500-$29,500. **Royalty Fee:** Varies. **Financial Assistance:** Limited third party financing available. **Training:** Initial 3-day training program at corporate headquarters, optional training at franchisee's location with ongoing support.

20629 ■ Cruise Holidays
Travel Leaders Leisure Group, LLC
3033 Campus Dr., Ste. W320
Minneapolis, MN 55441
Ph: (954)344-2576
Fax: (763)219-4182
URL: http://www.cruiseholidays.com
Description: Largest cruise-travel franchise in North America. Headquartered in Minneapolis with over 200 locations throughout North America. **No. of Franchise Units:** 134. **No. of Company-Owned Units:** 4. **No. of Operating Units:** 178. **Founded:** 1984. **Franchised:** 1984. **Equity Capital Needed:** $10,350-$160,350. **Franchise Fee:** $9,500-$30,000. **Royalty Fee:** to 3%. **Financial Assistance:** Limited third party financing available. **Training:** Provides 1 week at headquarters, at franchisee's location that varies, conference calls, 2 day annual mid-year meeting, 6-7 day annual convention, and 7 day annual group training seminar.

20630 ■ Cruise Planners /American Express
CP Franchising, LLC
3300 University Dr., Ste. 602
Coral Springs, FL 33065
Ph: (954)344-8060
Free: 888-582-2150
Fax: (954)755-5898
Co. E-mail: franchising@cruiseplanners.com
URL: http://www.beacruiseagent.com
Description: Cruise agency. **No. of Franchise Units:** 740. **Founded:** 1994.. **Franchised:** 1999. **Equity Capital Needed:** $9,995-$19,590, includes franchise fee, training, and airfare. **Franchise Fee:** 0-$9,995 depending on experience. **Financial Assistance:** Yes. **Training:** Pre-training commencement materials, 5 day training seminar (includes airfare, hotel, ground transportation, all meals, ship inspections, classroom seminars, materials). Advanced training seminars available.

20631 ■ CruiseOne
WTH
1201 W Cypress Creek Rd., Ste. 100
Ft. Lauderdale, FL 33309
Ph: (954)958-3701
Free: 800-892-3928
Fax: (954)958-3697
Co. E-mail: franchise@cruiseone.com
URL: http://www.cruiseone.com
Description: Complete turnkey, low onetime investment. No monthly sales quota. No experience
required. Complete training & support. Work from
home or office. Full or part-time. Earn the highest
commissions & bonuses. **No. of Franchise Units:**
775. **Founded:** 1992.. **Franchised:** 1993. **Franchise
Fee:** $9,800 plus discounts for veterans and minori-
ties. **Training:** Comprehensive 6 day training program
at corporate headquarters in Ft. Lauderdale and
ongoing support.

20632 ■ Expedia CruiseShipCenters
1055 West Hastings, Ste. 400
Vancouver, BC, Canada V6E 2E9
Ph: (888)783-0133
Fax: (604)685-1245
Co. E-mail: franchising@expediafranchise.com
URL: http://www.expediafranchise.com
Description: The center mainly deals with cruise
sales in Canada. They have centers all across
Canada and are a leading force worldwide. **No. of
Franchise Units:** 132. **No. of Company-Owned
Units:** 1. **Founded:** 1987.. **Franchised:** 1987. **Equity
Capital Needed:** $60,000-$90,000 start up capital
required; $125,000-$150,000 total investment. **Fran-
chise Fee:** $43,000. **Training:** Initial week long train-
ing and ongoing support.

20633 ■ Outdoor Connection
424 Neosho
Burlington, KS 66839
Ph: (620)364-5500
Free: 888-548-0636
Fax: (620)364-5563
Co. E-mail: info@outdoor-connectoion.com
URL: http://www.outdoor-connection.com
Description: Hunting and fishing travel service. **No.
of Franchise Units:** 61. **No. of Company-Owned
Units:** 2. **Founded:** 1988. **Franchised:** 1990. **Equity
Capital Needed:** $7,550-$12,250. **Franchise Fee:**
$6,500. **Royalty Fee:** 4%. **Financial Assistance:** In-
house assistance available with franchise fee. **Train-
ing:** 2 days at headquarters, 2-3 days annual conven-
tion and ongoing support.

20634 ■ Tix Travel and Ticket Agency Inc.
201 Main St.
Nyack-On-Hudson, NY 10960
Ph: (845)358-1007
Free: 800-20W-NTIX
Fax: (845)358-1266
URL: http://www.tixtravel.com
Description: A travel agency and concert and sport-
ing event tickets outlet. **No. of Franchise Units:** 400.
No. of Company-Owned Units: 1. **Founded:** 1982..
Franchised: 1989. **Equity Capital Needed:** From
$3,495. **Franchise Fee:** From $3,495. **Training:** Yes.

20635 ■ TPI Travel Services
Travel Pros Inc.
2901 W Busch Blvd., Ste. 408
Tampa, FL 33618-4566
Ph: (813)281-5670
Free: 800-393-7767
Co. E-mail: support@tpitravel.com
Description: Full service travel agency. **No. of
Franchise Units:** 460. **No. of Company-Owned
Units:** 1. **Founded:** 1987.. **Equity Capital Needed:**
$10,000. **Franchise Fee:** $4,995 **Training:** Yes.

**20636 ■ Travel Lines Express Franchise
Group**
9858 Glades Rd.
Boca Raton, FL 33434
Ph: (561)482-9557
Description: Full service home based travel agency.
No. of Franchise Units: 50. **No. of Company-
Owned Units:** 1. **Founded:** 1980.. **Franchised:**
2003. **Equity Capital Needed:** $1,000-$3,000. **Fran-
chise Fee:** $300. **Training:** Yes.

**20637 ■ Uniglobe Travel International Limited
Partnership**
1199 West Pender St., Ste. 900
Vancouver, BC, Canada V6E 2R1
Ph: (604)718-2614
Fax: (604)718-2678
URL: http://www.uniglobetravel.com
Description: International travel management system
that specializes in providing travel services to the
small to mid-size enterprise market. The travel
organization has over 700 franchise and Global
Partner locations in more than 30 countries in the
Americas, Europe, Asia, and Africa. Operating under
a well-recognized brand name, UNIGLOBE travel
agencies specialize in providing travel services to
corporate accounts and to leisure travelers. **No. of
Franchise Units:** 122. **Founded:** 1981.. **Franchised:**
1981. **Equity Capital Needed:** $10,000-$100,000.
Franchise Fee: $5,000-$20,000.

**20638 ■ Uniglobe Travel, LLC (Irvine,
California)**
18662 MacArthur Blvd., Ste. 100
Irvine, CA 92612
Ph: (949)623-9000
Free: 800-863-1606
Fax: (949)623-9008
Description: Travel franchisor. A National TV adver-
tising, consumer-recognized brand image, profitability
software programs one-on-one travel agency busi-
ness consultation, franchise operator and manager
forums, preferred supplier override programs and
unparalleled training in all facets of the travel industry.
Entrepreneur Magazine awarded Uniglobe 1 in Travel
Agency Franchising. **No. of Franchise Units:** 1,100.
Founded: 1980. **Franchised:** 1981. **Equity Capital
Needed:** $5,500-$20,200 conversion; $98,450-
$134,950 start-up; $3,600-$13,500 home based.
Franchise Fee: $3,000-$29,500. **Training:** Offers
the industry's most in-depth training courses international management academy, advanced international
management academy, Uniglobe orientation, commercial sales. vacation sales, group and incentive
sales, video-based training and financial management.

LIBRARIES

**20639 ■ American Hotel & Lodging
Association Information Center**
1201 New York Ave. N.W., Ste. 600
Houston, TX 77204-3028
Ph: (202)289-3100
Free: 888-743-2515
Fax: (202)289-3199
Co. E-mail: informationcenter@ahla.com
URL: http://www.ahla.com
Contact: Lydia Westbrook, Director, Research
Scope: Hotels and restaurants; travel and tourism.
Services: Library open to the public with restrictions
by appointment only. **Founded:** 1988. **Holdings:**
2500 volumes; microfilms; archives. **Subscriptions:**
100 journals and other serials.

**20640 ■ Davenport University - Thomas F.
Reed, Jr. Memorial Library**
4123 W. Main St.
Kalamazoo, MI 49006
Ph: (616)382-2835
Free: 800-632-8928
Fax: (269)382-2657
Co. E-mail: kz_library@davenport.edu
URL: http://www.davenport.edu/
Contact: Judith J. Bosshart, Director
Scope: Business, data processing, administrative
services, accounting. humanities, paralegal, medical
records, healthcare administration, computer and
information processing. **Services:** Interlibrary loan;
copying; faxing; library open to the public for reference use only. **Founded:** 1981. **Holdings:** 14,200
books; 995 videotapes. **Subscriptions:** 12,000
journals and other serials; 6 newspapers. **Telecommunication Services:** judy.bosshart@davenport.
edu; Library@Davenport.edu.

**20641 ■ Midstate College - Barbara Fields
Memorial Library - Special Collections**
R. Dale Bunch Student Ctr., Rm. 403
411 W. Northmoor Rd.
Peoria, IL 61614-3542
Ph: (309)692-4092
Fax: (309)692-3893
Co. E-mail: zbrown@midstate.edu
URL: http://www.midstate.edu/
Contact: Zachary M. Brown, Director, Library
Services
Scope: Travel and tourism; court reporting, paralegal
services; office assistant, office computer applications, business administration, business computer
accounting; medical assistant, medical transcription,
medical clinical office assistant; legal transcription,
administrative assistant; computer information specialist; business administration. **Services:** Interlibrary
loan; copying; faxing. **Founded:** 1976. **Holdings:**
8000 books; audiotapes; videotapes. **Subscriptions:**
100 journals and other serials; 4 newspapers.

20642 ■ Nadasdy Ferenc Museum Library
Varkerulet 1
H-9600 Sarvar, Hungary
Ph: 36 95 320158
Fax: 36 95 320158
Co. E-mail: nadasdy.sarvar@museum.hu
URL: http://www.museum.hu/museum/index_hu.ph-
p?ID=669
Contact: Takacs Zoltan, Director
Scope: Regional history. **Services:** Copying; library
open to the public with restrictions. **Founded:** 1951.
Holdings: 4000 volumes. **Telecommunication Ser-
vices:** muzeum.sarvar@mail.globonet.hu.

**20643 ■ Society for Accessible Travel and
Hospitality Library—S.A.T.H.**
347 5th Ave., Ste. 605
New York, NY 10016
Ph: (212)447-7284
Fax: (212)447-1928
Co. E-mail: sathtravel@aol.com
URL: http://www.sath.org
Contact: Jani Nayar, Coordinator
Scope: Travel advice on facilities for persons with
disabilities. **Services:** Library opens to members only.
Founded: 1976. **Holdings:** Travel guides for people
with disabilities and literature provided by tourist of-
fices, carriers, hotels, foreign organizations, destina-
tions, and car rental agencies; statistics. **Subscrip-
tions:** 5 journals and other serials; 3 newspapers.
Telecommunication Services: sathinfo@sath.org.

**20644 ■ Travel Industry Association of
America Library**
1100 New York Ave. NW, Ste. 450
Washington, DC 20005-3934
Ph: (202)408-8422
Fax: (202)408-1255
Co. E-mail: feedback@ustravel.org
URL: http://www.ustravel.org
Contact: Suzanne D. Cook, Senior Vice President,
Research
Scope: Travel and tourism. **Services:** Library not
open to the public. **Founded:** 1941. **Holdings:** 3000
research documents; 3800 government documents;
250 unpublished travel research reports; 15,000 clip-
pings; 20 tapes. **Subscriptions:** 27 journals and
other serials. **Telecommunication Services:** re-
search@ustravel.org.

RESEARCH CENTERS

**20645 ■ College of Forestry and
Conservation - Institute for Tourism and
Recreation Research**
University of Montana
32 Campus Dr., No. 1234
Missoula, MT 59812-1234
Ph: (406)243-5686
Fax: (406)243-4845
Co. E-mail: request@forestry.umt.edu
URL: http://www.forestry.umt.edu/
Contact: Kate Cenis, Director
Description: Provides research data needed to sup-
port the state's tourism industry.

20646 ■ Travel and Tourism Research Association (TTRA)
5300 Lakewood Rd.
Whitehall, MI 49461
Ph: (248)708-8872

Fax: (248)814-7150
Co. E-mail: mpalmer@ttra.com
URL: http://www.ttra.com
Contact: Michael Palmer, Chief Executive Officer
Services: Reference services: to assist the travel research and marketing industry in finding information sources and solving business problems.

Founded: 1971. **Publications:** *Annual conference proceedings*; *Journal of Travel Research* (Quarterly); *TTRA Newsletter* (Quarterly). **Educational Activities:** TTRA Annual conference. **Awards:** JTR Best Article Award; Student Research Award; Travel Research Grant; Travel Research Student Contest; Slattery Marketing Award for Students, Professionals. **Telecommunication Services:** info@ttra.com.

START-UP INFORMATION

20647 ■ *"Pump Up the Profits: Teaching Small Biz How to Handle Fuel and Reduce Costs!" in Small Business Opportunities (March 2008)*
Pub: Harris Publications Inc.
Description: Profile of 4Refuel, a company that delivers diesel and biodiesel fuel to customers individual fuelings.

20648 ■ *"Road Map To Riches" in Small Business Opportunities (September 2010)*
Pub: Harris Publications Inc.
Description: Profile of Philip Nenadov who launched The Transportation Network Group during the recession. This franchise is low cost and can earn six figures while working from home by becoming a trucking agent.

ASSOCIATIONS AND OTHER ORGANIZATIONS

20649 ■ **American Trucking Associations (ATA)—Transport Topics Online**
950 N Glebe Rd., Ste. 210
Arlington, VA 22203-4181
Ph: (703)838-1700
Free: 800-517-7370
Fax: (703)683-2292
Co. E-mail: media@trucking.org
URL: http://www.truckline.com
Contact: Walter B. McCormick, Jr., President
URL(s): www.ttnews.com. **Description:** Motor carriers, suppliers, state trucking associations, and national conferences of trucking companies. Works to influence the decisions of federal, state, and local government bodies; promotes increased efficiency, productivity, and competitiveness in the trucking industries; sponsors American Trucking Associations Foundation. Provides quarterly financial and operating statistics service. Offers comprehensive accounting service for all sizes of carriers. Promotes highway and driver safety; supports highway research projects; and studies technical and regulatory problems of the trucking industry. Sponsors competitions; compiles statistics. Maintains numerous programs and services including: Management Information Systems Directory; Compensation Survey; Electronic Data Interchange Standards. **Scope:** trucking, transportation. **Founded:** 1933. **Subscriptions:** 28000. **Publications:** *Truck Fleet Directory* (Annual); *Motor Carrier Technology Directory* (Annual); *North American Truck Fleet Directory* (Annual); *Transport Topics*; *Transport Topics* (Weekly); *Standard Trucking and Transportation Statistics*; *Trucksource: Sources of Trucking Industry Information* (Annual); *Motor Carrier Professional Services Directory* (Annual); *Utility Fleet Management: The Transport Topics Publishing Group Magazine for Utility and Public Works Fleet Professionals* (Monthly); *Executive and Ownership Report*; *How and Where to Check Driving Records and Report Accidents*. **Educational Activities:** Transportation Equipment Exhibition (Annual); Management

Conference and Exhibition (Annual). **Awards:** National Truck Safety Contest; Industrial Safety Contest; President's Trophy; National Truck Driving Championships; National Driver of the Year Award; Safety Director of the Year Award. **Telecommunication Services:** atamembership@trucking.org; orders@trucking.org; circulation@trucking.org.

20650 ■ **Canadian Trucking Alliance (CTA)—Alliance Canadienne du Camionnage**
555 Dixon Rd.
Toronto, ON, Canada M9W 1H8
Ph: (613)236-9426
Free: 866-823-4076
Co. E-mail: publicaffairs@cantruck.ca
URL: http://www.cantruck.ca
Contact: Don Streuber, Chairman
Description: Trucking companies. Seeks to advance the road transportation industries. Serves as a forum for the exchange of information among members; represents members' interests before labor and industrial organizations, government agencies, and the public. **Publications:** *Crossing International Borders: A Trucker's Guide.*

20651 ■ *The Counsellor*
1660 N Service Rd. E, Ste. 115
Oakville, ON, Canada L6H 7G3
Ph: (905)827-0587
Free: 877-501-PMTC
Fax: (905)827-8212
Co. E-mail: info@pmtc.ca
URL: http://www.pmtc.ca
Contact: Bruce J. Richards, President
Released: Quarterly

20652 ■ *Crossing International Borders: A Trucker's Guide*
555 Dixon Rd.
Toronto, ON, Canada M9W 1H8
Ph: (613)236-9426
Free: 866-823-4076
Co. E-mail: publicaffairs@cantruck.ca
URL: http://www.cantruck.ca
Contact: Don Streuber, Chairman

20653 ■ **Distribution and LTL Carriers Association (DLTLCA)**
c/o American Trucking Association
950 N Glebe Rd., Ste. 210
Arlington, VA 22203-4181
Ph: (703)838-7970
Free: 800-545-7091
Fax: (703)838-7994
Co. E-mail: bfarrell@trucking.org
URL: http://www.trucking.org
Contact: Robert Farrell, President
Description: Represents for-hire motor common carriers of general freight who specialize in less-than-truckload shipments throughout the U.S. Provides government relations, networking, business development programs, and publications. **Founded:** 1938. **Publications:** *Transportation Executive Update: A Publication of the Regular Common Carrier Conference* (Quarterly).

20654 ■ **Freight Carriers Association of Canada (FCA)**
427 Garrison Rd., Unit 3 and 4
Fort Erie, ON, Canada L2A 6E6
Free: 800-559-7421
Fax: (905)994-0117
Co. E-mail: info@fca-natc.org
URL: http://www.fca-natc.org
Contact: Dave Sirgey, President
Description: Canadian motor carriers involved in domestic transportation. Creates and provides statistical and operational information to all parties involved in motor carrier transportation. Offers statistical information. **Founded:** 1995. **Publications:** *Fuel Calculation Bulletin* (Weekly); *News* (Bimonthly).

20655 ■ *Fuel Calculation Bulletin*
427 Garrison Rd., Unit 3 and 4
Fort Erie, ON, Canada L2A 6E6
Free: 800-559-7421
Fax: (905)994-0117
Co. E-mail: info@fca-natc.org
URL: http://www.fca-natc.org
Contact: Dave Sirgey, President
Released: Weekly

20656 ■ **International Truck Parts Association (ITPA)**
1720-10 Ave. S, Ste. 4
PMB 199
Great Falls, MT 59405
Free: 866-346-5692
Fax: (800)895-4654
Co. E-mail: info@itpa.com
URL: http://www.itpa.com
Contact: Greg Mundy, Chairman
Description: Represents companies specializing in the purchase and sale of used and rebuilt heavy-duty truck components. **Founded:** 1974. **Awards:** Lifetime Achievement Award.

20657 ■ **Mid-West Truckers Association (MTA)**
2727 N Dirksen Pkwy.
Springfield, IL 62702
Ph: (217)525-0310
Fax: (217)525-0342
Co. E-mail: info@mid-westtruckers.com
URL: http://www.mid-westtruckers.com
Description: Owners and operators of trucking companies. Serves as a unified voice for truckers nationwide; conducts lobbying. Sponsors services to members including: mass purchasing program, whereby members may purchase parts at wholesale rates; drug and alcohol testing program; assistance with international registration; license plate procurement; group insurance programs self-funded worker's Compensation Program. Conducts seminars and educational programs; maintains speakers' bureau. **Scope:** safety, drugs, alcohol, truck and trailer maintenance. **Founded:** 1961. **Subscriptions:** 102 video recordings. **Publications:** *Keep on Truckin News*; *Cost Summary Booklet*; *Keep on Truckin' News* (Monthly). **Educational Activities:** Midwest

Truck Show (Annual); Mid-West Truck Show (Annual). **Awards:** Safe and Courteous Driver Award (Annual); Truck of the Year Award (Annual).

20658 ■ National Private Truck Council (NPTC)
950 N Glebe Rd., Ste. 530
Arlington, VA 22203-4183
Ph: (703)683-1300
Fax: (703)683-1217
Co. E-mail: info@nptc.org
URL: http://www.nptc.org
Contact: Gary F. Petty, President
E-mail: gpetty@nptc.org

Description: Represents private motor carrier truck fleets and their suppliers. **Scope:** fleet management, finance, safety, legal and regulatory, equipment. **Founded:** 1939. **Subscriptions:** 12. **Publications:** *Fleet Owner* (Bimonthly); *Private Fleet Directory/ FleetSeek*; *Weekly Update* (Weekly); *Business Trucking* (Monthly); *National Private Truck Council-- Membership Directory & Buyer's Guide* (Annual); *Membership Directory & Buyers' Guide* (Annual). **Educational Activities:** Education Management & Exhibition (Annual). **Awards:** CTP Scholarship; Driver Hall of Fame; Fleet Safety Awards; CTP Scholarship (Annual); Dodi Reagan Humanitarian Award (Annual); Driver Hall of Fame (Annual); Fleet Award (Annual); Fleet Safety Award (Annual); CTP Scholarship Program; Dodi Reagan Humanitarian Award; Private Fleet Executive of the Year. **Telecommunication Services:** tmoore@nptc.org.

20659 ■ National Tank Truck Carriers (NTTC)
950 N Glebe Rd., Ste. 520
Arlington, VA 22203
Ph: (703)838-1960
Free: 800-441-1414
Fax: (703)838-8860
Co. E-mail: nttcstaff@tanktruck.org
URL: http://www.tanktruck.org
Contact: Dan Furth, President
E-mail: dfurth@tanktruck.org

Description: Common or contract "for-hire" tank truck carriers transporting liquid and dry bulk commodities, chemicals, food processing commodities, petroleum, and related products; allied industry suppliers. Promotes federal standards of construction, design, operation and use of tank trucks and equipment. Coordinates truck transportation system for shippers of bulk commodities. Secures improvements in tank specifications. Sponsors annual schools; conducts research. **Founded:** 1945. **Publications:** *National Tank Truck Directory* (Annual); *Washington Newsletter* (Monthly); *National Tank Truck Carrier Directory* (Annual); *Cargo Tank Hazardous Materials Regulations* (Annual). **Educational Activities:** Cargo Tank Maintenance Seminar (Annual). **Awards:** Safety Award (Annual). **Telecommunication Services:** jconley@tanktruck.org.

20660 ■ National Truck Equipment Association (NTEA)
37400 Hills Tech Dr.
Farmington Hills, MI 48331-3414
Ph: (248)489-7090
Free: 800-441-6832
Fax: (248)489-8590
Co. E-mail: info@ntea.com
URL: http://www.ntea.com
Contact: Steven Sill, President
E-mail: ssill@aspeneq.com

Description: Serves as a trade group for commercial truck, truck body, truck equipment, trailer and accessory manufacturers and distributors. Advises members of current federal regulations affecting the manufacturing and installation of truck bodies and equipment; works to enhance the professionalism of management and improve profitability in the truck equipment business. **Scope:** commercial truck industry, fleet and utility, association industries. **Founded:** 1964. **Subscriptions:** periodicals. **Publications:** *Excise Tax Bulletin* (Periodic); *Membership Roster and Product Directory* (Annual); *NTEA News* (Monthly); *Truck Equipment Handbook*; *NTEA Technical Report* (Monthly); *Membership Roster and Product Directory* (Annual); *NTEA News* (Monthly); *National*

Truck Equipment Association--Market Resource Guide (Annual). **Educational Activities:** The Work Truck Show and Annual NTEA Convention (Annual).

20661 ■ News
427 Garrison Rd., Unit 3 and 4
Fort Erie, ON, Canada L2A 6E6
Free: 800-559-7421
Fax: (905)994-0117
Co. E-mail: info@fca-natc.org
URL: http://www.fca-natc.org
Contact: Dave Sirgey, President
Released: Bimonthly

20662 ■ Newsbriefs
1660 N Service Rd. E, Ste. 115
Oakville, ON, Canada L6H 7G3
Ph: (905)827-0587
Free: 877-501-PMTC
Fax: (905)827-8212
Co. E-mail: info@pmtc.ca
URL: http://www.pmtc.ca
Contact: Bruce J. Richards, President
Released: Monthly

20663 ■ Owner-Operator Independent Drivers Association (OOIDA)
1 NW OOIDA Dr.
Grain Valley, MO 64029-7903
Ph: (816)229-5791
Free: 800-444-5791
Fax: (816)229-0518
Co. E-mail: jim_johnston@ooida.com
URL: http://www.ooida.com
Contact: Jim Johnston, President
URL(s): www.landlinemag.com. **Description:** Truck owner-operators, small fleet operators, and drivers. Lobbying association seeking to improve owner-operator working conditions. Provides national recognition and a channel for members to voice interests and concerns on changes that affect the trucking business. Addresses issues including: freight rates commensurate with costs; rules guaranteeing prompt payment for owner-operators; flexible hours of operation; taxes; safety initiatives. Offers medical, truck, dental, and accident programs. Sponsors research programs; compiles statistics; maintains speakers' bureau. **Founded:** 1973. **Publications:** *Land Line* (10/year); *Owner-Operator News* (Quarterly); *Land Line: The Business Magazine for professional Truckers* (Monthly). **Awards:** OOIDA Scholarship (Annual); Safe Driving Award (Annual); OOIDA Mary Johnston Scholarships. **Telecommunication Services:** webmaster@ooida.com.

20664 ■ Private Motor Truck Council of Canada (PMTC)—Association Canadienne du Camionnage d'Entreprise
1660 N Service Rd. E, Ste. 115
Oakville, ON, Canada L6H 7G3
Ph: (905)827-0587
Free: 877-501-PMTC
Fax: (905)827-8212
Co. E-mail: info@pmtc.ca
URL: http://www.pmtc.ca
Contact: Bruce J. Richards, President
Description: Private truck fleet operators and others with an interest in the trucking industry. Represents members' interests before government and international regulatory bodies and the public. **Founded:** 1977. **Publications:** *The Counsellor* (Quarterly); *Newsbriefs* (Monthly).

20665 ■ Professional Truck Driver Institute (PTDI)
555 E Braddock Rd.
Alexandria, VA 22314-2182
Ph: (703)647-7015
Fax: (703)836-6610
Co. E-mail: ptdi@truckload.org
URL: http://www.ptdi.org
Contact: Terry Burnett, Chairman of the Board
Description: Stakeholders include carriers, schools, trade associations, manufacturers, insurance companies, regulatory bodies, funding organizations, and suppliers to the trucking industry. Develops skill and curriculum standards for truck driver training and standards for the certification of truck driver training courses; certifies commercial truck driver training

courses and driver finishing programs. **Founded:** 1986. **Publications:** *Certification Standards and Requirements for Entry-Level Tractor-Trailer Driver Courses*; *Certification Standards and Requirements for Tractor-Trailer Driver Finishing Programs*; *Curriculum Standard Guidelines for Entry-Level Tractor-Trailer Driver Courses*; *Skill Standards for Entry-Level Tractor-Trailer Drivers*; *Skill Standards for Professional Solo Tractor-Trailer Drivers*. **Awards:** Lee J. Crittenden Memorial Award (Annual).

20666 ■ Specialized Carriers and Rigging Association (SC&RA)
2750 Prosperity Ave., Ste. 620
Fairfax, VA 22031-4312
Ph: (703)698-0291
Fax: (571)722-1698
Co. E-mail: info@scranet.org
URL: http://www.scranet.org
Contact: Raynor Parker, President

Description: Common carriers, crane and rigging companies, and millwright contractors engaged in the transportation of heavy and specialized articles, machinery, iron and steel, construction, and military traffic. Operates Heavy and Specialized Carriers Tariff Bureau. Conducts Fleet Safety and Outstanding Hauling, Rigging, and Millwright Job of the Year contests. Compiles statistics. **Founded:** 1948. **Publications:** *Specialized Carriers and Rigging Association-Newsletter* (Weekly); *SC & RA Newsletter*; *Specialized Carriers & Rigging Association-- Membership Directory* (Annual); *Directory of Truck Escort Services*; *Moving the World*. **Educational Activities:** Specialized Transportation (Annual). **Awards:** Crane and Rigging Safety Awards (Annual); Driver of the Year (Annual); President's Award (Annual); SC&R Foundation Scholarship (Annual); Transportation Safety Awards (Annual); SC and R Foundation Scholarships; Transportation Safety Awards; Golden Achievement Award; Pinnacle Award; Million Miler Safety Award; Longevity Awards; Million Miler Award for Safety Excellence; SC&RA Hauling Job of the Year Awards (Annual); SC and R Foundation Grant Program; Hauling Job of the Year Award; Crane and Rigging Job of the Year Awards; Crane and Rigging Safety/Safety Improvement Awards; Transportation Fleet Safety/Safety Improvement Awards; Crane and Rigging Zero Accidents Award.

20667 ■ Trucking Management, Inc. (TMI)
PO Box 860725
Shawnee, KS 66286-0725
Ph: (913)568-5873
Co. E-mail: info@tmiweb.org
URL: http://www.tmiweb.org
Contact: David Smith, President

Description: Less-Than-Truckload (LTL) motor carriers. Promotes economic interests of unionized LTL motor carriers. Represents members' interests in public policy and economic issues. Works as the primary multi-employer bargaining arm of the unionized general freight trucking industry. **Founded:** 1963.

20668 ■ Truckload Carriers Association (TCA)
555 E Braddock Rd.
Alexandria, VA 22314-2182
Ph: (703)838-1950
Fax: (703)836-6610
Co. E-mail: tca@truckload.org
URL: http://www.truckload.org
Contact: Chris Burruss, President
E-mail: cburruss@truckload.org

Description: Engages in the truckload segment of the motor carrier industry. Represents dry van, refrigerated, flatbed and intermodel container carriers operating in the 48 contiguous states as well as Alaska, Mexico and Canada. Represents operators of over 200,000 trucks. **Founded:** 1938. **Educational Activities:** Truckload Carriers Association (Annual). **Awards:** Truckload Carriers Association Scholarships; Driver of the Year (Annual); TCA Scholarship (Annual).

DIRECTORIES OF EDUCATIONAL PROGRAMS

20669 ■ *Directory of Private Accredited Career Schools and Colleges of Technology*
Pub: Accrediting Commission of Career Schools and Colleges of Technology
Contact: Michale S. McComis, Executive Director
Released: On web page. **Price:** Free. **Description:** Covers 3900 accredited post-secondary programs that provide training programs in business, trade, and technical fields, including various small business endeavors. Entries offer school name, address, phone, description of courses, job placement assistance, and requirements for admission. Arrangement is alphabetical.

REFERENCE WORKS

20670 ■ *American Motor Carrier Directory*
Pub: UBM Global Trade
Contact: Leonard J. Corallo, President
URL(s): www.cbizmedia.com. **Released:** Annual; December. **Publication includes:** Lists of all licensed Less Than Truckload (LTL) general commodity carriers in the United States; includes specialized motor carriers and related services includes refrigerated carriers, heavy haulers, bulk haulers, riggers, and specified commodity carriers; state and federal regulatory bodies governing the trucking industry; tariff publishing bureaus; freight claim councils; industry associations, etc. **Entries include:** For carriers and services--Company name, address of headquarters and terminals, phones, tariffs followed, names of executives, insurance, and equipment information, services or commodities handled. Principal content of publication is listing of direct point-to-point services of LTL general commodity carriers throughout the United States and to Canada and Mexico. **Arrangement:** Alphabetical.

20671 ■ *Commercial Carrier Journal--Buyers' Guide Issue*
Pub: Reed Business Information
Contact: Tad Smith, Chief Executive Officer
URL(s): www.reedbusiness.com. **Released:** Annual; October. **Price:** $10. **Publication includes:** List of vehicles, components and accessories suppliers for the truck and bus fleet markets. **Entries include:** Company name, address, phone, fax, e-mail, internet address, trade names. **Arrangement:** Classified by product and alphabetical.

20672 ■ *"Compelling Opportunities" in Barron's (Vol. 88, March 10, 2008, No. 10, pp. 39)*
Pub: Dow Jones & Company, Inc.
Ed: Neil A. Martin. **Description:** Michael L. Reynal, portfolio manager of Principal International Emerging Markets Fund, is bullish on the growth prospects of stocks in emerging markets. He is investing big on energy, steel, and transportation companies.

20673 ■ *"Con-Way Project Back in High Gear" in Business Journal Portland (Vol. 27, November 5, 2010, No. 36, pp. 1)*
Pub: Portland Business Journal
Ed: Wendy Culverwell. **Description:** Trucking firm Con-Way Inc. intends to sell parcels of land from a property comprising 16 blocks and 20 prime acres west of the Pearl District in Portland, Oregon. In 2009, Con-Way abandoned plans to sell the property. As Con-Way reclaims control over design and usage of the property, it also expressed willingness to cooperate with a master developer on a related real estate project.

20674 ■ *"Credit Crunch Gives, Takes Away" in The Business Journal-Serving Metropolitan Kansas City (Vol. 27, October 17, 2008, No. 5, pp. 1)*
Pub: American City Business Journals, Inc.
Ed: Suzanna Stagemeyer. **Description:** Although many Kansas City business enterprises have been adversely affected by the U.S. credit crunch, others have remained relatively unscathed. Examples of how local businesses are being impacted by the crisis

are provided including: American Trailer & Storage Inc., which declared bankruptcy after failing to pay a long-term loan; and NetStandard, a technology firm who, on the other hand, is being pursued by prospective lenders.

20675 ■ *"CSX Transportation: Supplier Diversity on the Right Track" in Hispanic Business (July-August 2009, pp. 34)*
Pub: Hispanic Business
Description: CSX Transportation is a leader in delivering essential products, operating as many as 1,200 trains and a fleet of more than 100,000 freight cars. CSX attributes its success by valuing diversity in both hiring and supplier contracts.

20676 ■ *"Dealer Gets a Lift with Acquisitions at Year's End" in Crain's Detroit Business (Vol. 26, January 11, 2010, No. 2, pp. 3)*
Pub: Crain Communications, Inc.
Ed: Ryan Beene. **Description:** Alta Equipment Co., a forklift dealer, closed 2009 with a string of acquisitions expecting to double the firm's employee headcount and triple its annual revenue. Alta Lift Truck Services, Inc., as the company was known before the acquisitions, was founded in 1984 as Michigan's dealer for forklift manufacturer Yale Materials Handling Corp.

20677 ■ *"Family Throne" in Hawaii Business (Vol. 53, March 2008, No. 9, pp. 51)*
Pub: Hawaii Business Publishing
Ed: Cathy S. Cruz-George. **Description:** Jeanette and George Grace inherited Paradise Lua Inc., a portable toilet company founded by George's father. The toilets are rented by Aloha Stadium during football season and St. Patrick's Day block party among others. The company has 2,500 toilets and 20 pumping trucks and had earnings of $1.3 million in 2007.

20678 ■ *"Freeing the Wheels of Commerce" in Hispanic Business (July-August 2007, pp. 50, 52, 54)*
Pub: Hispanic Business
Ed: Keith Rosenblum. **Description:** SecureOrigins, a border-based partnership with high-tech innovators is working to move goods faster, more efficiently, and securely.

20679 ■ *Heavy Duty Representatives Profile Directory*
Pub: Heavy Duty Representatives Association
Contact: Larry Rosenthal, President
URL(s): www.hdra.org. **Ed:** Cara R. Giebner. **Released:** Annual; January. **Covers:** About 75 independent sales agencies which sell heavy-duty components to the trucking and aftermarket industries. **Entries include:** Name of company, address, phone, name and title of principal, experience in industry, sales territory, warehouse space, product lines, services. **Arrangement:** Alphabetical. **Indexes:** Geographical.

20680 ■ *Heavy Duty Trucking--Council of Fleet Specialists Equipment Buyer's Guide & Services Directory*
Pub: Newport Communications Div. HIC Corp.
URL(s): www.truckinginfo.com/hdt/archives/1996/01/index.asp. **Ed:** Doug Condra. **Released:** Annual; January. **Price:** $45, included in subscription; free to equipment and maintenance managers. **Covers:** 500 Council of Fleet Specialists member manufacturers and wholesalers specializing in heavy-duty truck parts and repairs. **Entries include:** Company name, address, phone, names of executives, parts or services manufactured or available; wholesaler listings also show area served. A special section of 'Heavy Duty Trucking' magazine prepared by the Council of Fleet Specialists, 315 Delaware, Kansas City, MO 64105 (816-421-2600). **Arrangement:** Wholesalers are geographical; manufacturers are alphabetical. **Indexes:** Wholesaler name.

20681 ■ *"Is 'Tsunami' of Freight in our Future?" in Business Courier (Vol. 26, November 27, 2009, No. 31, pp. 1)*
Pub: American City Business Journals, Inc.
Ed: Dan Monk. **Description:** Freight companies are planning for cargo-container shipping facilities on the riverfront of Cincinnati in light of the completion of the

$5 billion Panama Canal expansion in 2015. The city's capability to utilize the growth in freight has been under investigation by authorities.

20682 ■ *"iSymmetry's Technological Makeover Or, How a Tech Company Finally Grew Up and Discovered the World Wide Web" in Inc. (October 2007)*
Pub: Gruner & Jahr USA Publishing
Description: Profile of iSymmetry, an Atlanta, Georgia-based IT recruiting firm, covering the issues the company faces keeping its technology equipment up-to-date. The firm has devised a program that will replace its old server-based software systems with on-demand software delivered via the Internet, known as software-as-a-service. Statistical information included.

20683 ■ *"The Market's (Very) Tender Spring Shoots" in Barron's (Vol. 88, March 31, 2008, No. 13, pp. M3)*
Pub: Dow Jones & Company, Inc.
Ed: Kopin Tan. **Description:** Expansion in price-earnings multiples and a lower credit-default risk index has encouraged fans of the spring-awakening theory. Shares of industrial truckers have gone up 32 percent in 2008 and some shares are pushing five-year highs brought on by higher efficiency and earnings from more load carried. The prospects of the shares of Foot Locker are also discussed.

20684 ■ *National Highway and Airway Carriers Directory*
Pub: National Highway Carriers Directory Inc.
Contact: Pam William Ferreira, President
URL(s): www.national-highway.com/NHCD/index.jsp. **Released:** Semiannual; Latest edition 2010. **Price:** $295, Individuals one issue only; $345, Individuals for 2 issues per year, fall and spring, 1yr sub.; $395, Individuals online. **Covers:** Over 2,500 motor and airway carriers. LTL, TL, intermodal, refrigerated freight forwarders, warehousing, Canadian Carriers, Brokers, North American Railroads and Ocean Carriers. **Entries include:** Company name, address, phone, fax, names of key personnel, number of trucks, locations of terminals, terminal phone numbers, terminal fax numbers, kind of equipment insurance available, routes, tariffs, and points served direct in North America. **Arrangement:** Geographical, alphabetical.

20685 ■ *National Tank Truck Carrier Directory*
Pub: National Tank Truck Carriers
Contact: Dan Furth, President
E-mail: dfurth@tanktruck.org
URL(s): www.tanktruck.org/docs/default-document-library/2012_directory_order_form.pdf. **Released:** Annual; Latest edition 58th; 2012. **Price:** $54, Members; $80, Nonmembers. **Covers:** For-hire tank truck carriers serving petroleum, chemical, and other industries in the United States, Canada, Australia, England, Europe, Japan, Mexico, and South Africa. Also lists major shippers who use tank trucks, intermodal bulk facilities, industry suppliers, and state related associations affiliated with the American Trucking Associations. **Entries include:** Company name, address, phone, names of executives, list of products or services. **Database includes:** Names and addresses of the Department of Transportation field personnel. **Arrangement:** Separate geographical sections for carriers and associations; shippers and industry suppliers are alphabetical. **Indexes:** Personal name, company name.

20686 ■ *National Truck Equipment Association--Market Resource Guide*
Pub: National Truck Equipment Association
Contact: Steven Sill, President
E-mail: ssill@aspeneq.com
URL(s): www.ntea.com. **Released:** Annual; Latest edition 2011. **Price:** $50, Nonmembers; $10, Members. **Covers:** Over 1,500 distributors who install commercial truck bodies and related equipment on chassis-cabs, truck body and equipment manufacturers, and associates. **Entries include:** Company name, address, phone, fax, e-mail, web site, name and title of contact; membership type and year began membership, products or services. **Arrangement:**

Alphabetical. **Indexes:** Distributors are geographical; manufacturers and associates classified by product/service and geographical.

20687 ■ NATSO--Membership Directory
Pub: NATSO
Contact: Lisa J. Mullings, President
URL(s): www.natso.com. **Released:** Annual **Covers:** Over 1,300 North American travel plazas, truck stops, supplier firms, and corporate parent firms. **Entries include:** Truck stop name, street and mailing addresses, phone, names of key personnel, corporate affiliations. Similar detail given for suppliers and corporate parent firms. **Arrangement:** Geographical. **Indexes:** Member truck stops by U.S. and interstate highway; supplier, product/service.

20688 ■ "Paperless Bookkeeping Program" in Fleet Owner Online (February 15, 2011)
Pub: Penton Business Media Inc.
Description: TruckTax launched its new paperless bookkeeping system to help manage bookkeeping tasks, accounting and business tax information and filings for truckers.

20689 ■ "Presidential Address: Innovation in Retrospect and Prospect" in Canadian Journal of Electronics (Vol. 43, November 2010, No. 4)
Pub: Journal of the Canadian Economics Association
Ed: James A. Brander. **Description:** Has innovation slowed in recent decades? While there has been progress in information and communications technology, the recent record of innovation in agriculture, energy, transportation and healthcare sectors is cause for concern.

20690 ■ "Ryder's Shock Absorbers Are In Place" in Barron's (Vol. 88, March 24, 2008, No. 12, pp. 19)
Pub: Dow Jones & Company, Inc.
Ed: Christopher C. Williams. **Description:** Shares of Ryder System Inc. are expected to continue rising on the back of rising earnings, forecast at $5.20 a share for 2009. The shares of the truck freight company hit a 52-week high of $62.27 each and may reach $70 a share.

20691 ■ "Sedo Keeps Trucking in Good Times and Bad" in Crain's Chicago Business (Vol. 31, April 28, 2008, No. 17, pp. 35)
Pub: Crain Communications, Inc.
Ed: Samantha Stainburn. **Description:** Discusses Seko Worldwide Inc., an Itasca-based freight forwarder, and its complicated road to growth and expansion on a global scale.

20692 ■ "Staffing Firms are Picking Up the Pieces, Seeing Signs of Life" in Milwaukee Business Journal (Vol. 27, February 5, 2010, No. 19)
Pub: American City Business Journals
Ed: Rich Rovito. **Description:** Milwaukee, Wisconsin-based staffing firms are seeing signs of economic rebound as many businesses turned to temporary employees to fill the demands for goods and services. Economic observers believe the growth in temporary staffing is one of the early indicators of economic recovery.

20693 ■ Truck Frame & Axle Repair Association--Membership Directory
Pub: Truck-frame & Axle Repair Association
Contact: Paul Jones, President
E-mail: pjonesafa@aol.com
URL(s): www.taraassociation.com. **Released:** Biennial; August of odd years. **Price:** Free. **Covers:** About 150 regular and associate members that repair heavy-duty truck equipment or supply the industry. **Entries include:** Firm name, address, phone, key personnel, coding to indicate specialties. **Database includes:** Map showing locations of members. **Arrangement:** Geographical.

20694 ■ "Truckers Walk Strike Line" in Puget Sound Business Journal (Vol. 29, October 24, 2008, No. 27, pp. 1)
Pub: American City Business Journals
Ed: Steve Wilhelm. **Description:** Teamsters Local 174 went on strike against Oak Harbor Freight Lines Inc. over alleged company violations of federal labor

laws. The union also accuses the company of engaging directly with employees and holding mandatory meetings about contract negotiations.

STATISTICAL SOURCES

20695 ■ RMA Annual Statement Studies
Pub: Risk Management Association
Contact: Kevin M. Blakey, President
Released: Annual. **Price:** $175.00 2006-07 edition, $105.00. **Description:** Contains composite balance sheets and income statements for more than 360 industries, including the accounting, auditing, and bookkeeping industries. Also contains five years of comparative historical data for discerning trends. Includes 16 commonly used ratios, computed for most of the size groupings for nearly every industry.

20696 ■ Standard & Poor's Industry Surveys
Pub: Standard & Poor's Corp.
Released: Annual. **Price:** $3633.00. **Description:** Two-volume book that examines the prospects for specific industries, including trucking. Also provides analyses of trends and problems, statistical tables and charts, and comparative company analyses.

TRADE PERIODICALS

20697 ■ American Trucker--Badger Edition: Serving Upper Peninsula of Michigan, Wisconsin
Pub: Primedia Business
URL(s): www.trucker.com. **Released:** Monthly **Price:** $48, Individuals.

20698 ■ American Trucker--Buckeye Edition: Serving Ohio
Pub: Primedia Business
URL(s): www.trucker.com. **Released:** Monthly **Price:** $48, Individuals.

20699 ■ American Trucker--Central States Edition: Serving Iowa, Kansas, Nebraska, Western Missouri
Pub: Primedia Business
URL(s): www.trucker.com. **Released:** Monthly **Price:** $48, Individuals; $60, Other countries.

20700 ■ American Trucker--Illinois Edition: Serving Eastern Missouri, Illinois
Pub: Primedia Business
URL(s): www.trucker.com. **Released:** Monthly **Price:** $48, Individuals.

20701 ■ American Trucker--South Central Edition: Serving Arkansas, Louisiana, Oklahoma, Texas
Pub: Primedia Business
URL(s): www.trucker.com. **Released:** Monthly **Price:** $48, Individuals.

20702 ■ Bulk Transporter
Pub: Primedia Business Magazines
URL(s): bulktransporter.com/. **Ed:** Jay Russell Miller, Charles E. Wilson. **Released:** Monthly

20703 ■ CALTRUX
Pub: California Trucking Association
Ed: Michael Riley, Editor, mriley@caltrux.org. **Released:** Monthly. **Price:** Included in membership. **Description:** Provides news, commentary, announcements, and advertising of interest to California truck fleet owners and managers. Carries legislative updates, news of developments in the state regulatory agencies, and a calendar of events.

20704 ■ Commercial Carrier Journal
Pub: Randall-Reilly Publishing Co.
Contact: Michael Reilly, President
E-mail: mreilly@rrpub.com
URL(s): www.ccjdigital.com/. **Released:** Monthly **Price:** Free.

20705 ■ Fleet Equipment: The Leading Information Resource for Fleet Equipment Managers
Pub: Babcox
URL(s): www.fleetequipmentmag.com/www.babcox.com/site/our-brands/fleet-equipment. **Ed:** Seth Skydel, Carol Birkland. **Released:** Monthly **Price:** Free.

20706 ■ Heavy Duty Trucking: The Fleet Business Authority
Pub: H.I.C. Corp.
Contact: Doug Condra, Principal
URL(s): www.newportcommunicationsgroup.com/. **Ed:** Oliver Patton, Deborah Lockridge. **Released:** Monthly

20707 ■ In the Driver's Seat
Pub: Ontario Safety League
Ed: Terry Thompson, Editor. **Released:** Monthly. **Price:** Included in membership. **Description:** Commercial driver safety newsletter.

20708 ■ Keep on Truckin News
Pub: Mid-West Truckers Association
Ed: Don Schaefer, Editor, dhscubs@aol.com. **Released:** Monthly. **Price:** Included in membership. **Description:** Offers owners and operators of trucks information relating to the Association and the industry in general. Contains information on services available to members, including mass purchasing, international registration assistance, license plate procurement, drug testing, self-funded workers compensation, EPA Storm Water Permits, and group insurance plans. Reports on legislative and regulatory changes that affect the industry. Recurring features include news of members, news of research, and notices of Association activities.

20709 ■ Land Line: The Business Magazine for professional Truckers
Pub: Owner-Operator Independent Drivers Association
Contact: Jim Johnston, President
URL(s): www.landlinemag.com. **Released:** Monthly

20710 ■ National Truck Rate Report
Pub: U.S. Department of Agriculture
Ed: Alesia Swan, Editor, alesia.swan@usda.gov. **Released:** Weekly, always Wednesday. **Price:** $10, U.S. and Canada per month; $20, elsewhere per month mailed; $60. **Description:** Lists truck rates per load to selected markets throughout the U.S. Also reports on trucks available in relation to shippers' needs. Recurring features include statistics on the total reported domestic and import truck shipments of fresh fruit and vegetables.

20711 ■ SC & RA Newsletter
Pub: Specialized Carriers and Rigging Association
Contact: Raynor Parker, President
Ed: Jennifer Callahan, Editor, jcallahan@scranet.org. **Released:** Weekly. **Price:** Included in membership. **Description:** Reports on current regulatory, safety, and industrial relations developments. Offers news of business opportunities. Recurring features include news of research, news of members, book reviews, and a calendar of events.

20712 ■ Standard Trucking and Transportation Statistics
Pub: American Trucking Associations
Contact: Walter B. McCormick, Jr., President
Ed: Bob Costello, Editor, bcostell@trucking.org. **Released:** Quarterly. **Price:** $78.75, members; $105, nonmembers. **Description:** Source for up-to-date statistics in the industry.

20713 ■ Truck West
Pub: Business Information Group
Contact: Bruce Creighton, President
URL(s): www.trucknews.com. **Released:** Monthly **Price:** $37.95, Canada taxes applicable; $66.95, U.S.; $66.95, Out of country.

20714 ■ Trucker's Connection
Pub: Trucker's Connection Inc.
URL(s): www.truckersconnection.com. **Ed:** Megan Cullingford. **Released:** Monthly **Price:** $26.95, Individuals; $45, Canada; $90, Other countries.

TRADE SHOWS AND CONVENTIONS

20715 ■ American Trucking Association Management Conference & Exhibition
American Trucking Association
950 N. Glebe Rd., Ste. 210
Arlington, VA 22203-4181

Ph: (703)838-1700
Co. E-mail: meetingsteam@trucking.org
URL: http://www.trucking.org/Pages/Home.aspx
URL(s): www.trucking.org/mce/Pages/default.aspx.
Frequency: Annual. Audience: Chief executive officers and upper level management of motor carrier companies, as well as executives from suppliers to the trucking industry. Principal Exhibits: Equipment, supplies, and services related to the trucking industry. Telecommunication Services: meetingsteam@trucking.org.

20716 ■ Great American Trucking Show (GATS)

Sellers Expositions
222 Pearl St., Ste. 300
New Albany, IN 47150
Ph: (812)949-9200
Free: 800-558-8767
Fax: (812)949-9600
URL: http://www.sellersexpo.com
Contact: Warren Sellers, Chief Executive Officer
E-mail: wss315@aol.com
URL(s): www.gatsonline.com. Audience: Truck owners and operators, exempt haulers, company drivers and truck drivers for hire, aftermarket parts purchasers, purchasing agents, mechanics, fleet owner. Principal Exhibits: Trucks and related equipment, supplies, and services.

20717 ■ Mid-America Trucking Show

Exhibit Management Associates, Inc.
1404 Browns Ln., Ste. E
Louisville, KY 40207
Ph: (502)899-3892
Fax: (502)899-3952
Co. E-mail: clrockwell@truckingshow.com
URL: http://www.truckingshow.com
URL(s): www.truckingshow.com. Frequency: Annual. Audience: Owner-operators, fleet operators, sales managers, and maintenance personnel. Principal Exhibits: Equipment, trucks, supplies, and services for the trucking industry. Dates and Locations: , Kentucky Fair and Exposition Center.

20718 ■ Midwest Truck Show

Mid-West Truckers Association (MTA)
2727 N Dirksen Pkwy.
Springfield, IL 62702
Ph: (217)525-0310
Fax: (217)525-0342
Co. E-mail: info@mid-westtruckers.com
URL: http://www.mid-westtruckers.com
URL(s): www.mid-westtruckers.com/. Frequency: Annual. Audience: Owners of trucking companies (for hire and private). Principal Exhibits: Trucks, trailers, financing information, computers, communication and satellite equipment insurance information, and related equipment, supplies, and services. Dates and Locations: , Prairie Capital Convention Center. Telecommunication Services: info@mid-westtruckers.com.

20719 ■ Service Specialists Association Annual Convention

Service Specialists Association
c/o Wade & Partners
160 Symphony Way
Elgin, IL 60120
Ph: (330)725-7160
Free: 800-763-5717

Fax: (330)722-5638
Co. E-mail: trucksvc@aol.com
URL: http://www.truckservice.org
URL(s): truckservice.org. Frequency: Annual. Audience: Trade-Heavy Duty Aftermarket. Principal Exhibits: Exhibits related to truck repair operations rebuilding departments, individuals who have maintained shop equipment such as hydraulic press or heat treating furnace.

20720 ■ Truckload Carriers Association

Truckload Carriers Association (TCA)
555 E Braddock Rd.
Alexandria, VA 22314-2182
Ph: (703)838-1950
Fax: (703)836-6610
Co. E-mail: tca@truckload.org
URL: http://www.truckload.org
Contact: Chris Burruss, President
E-mail: cburruss@truckload.org
URL(s): www.truckload.org. Frequency: Annual. Principal Exhibits: Trucking equipment, supplies, and services. Telecommunication Services: tcameetings@truckload.org.

20721 ■ The Work Truck Show and Annual NTEA Convention

National Truck Equipment Association (NTEA)
37400 Hills Tech Dr.
Farmington Hills, MI 48331-3414
Ph: (248)489-7090
Free: 800-441-6832
Fax: (248)489-8590
Co. E-mail: info@ntea.com
URL: http://www.ntea.com
Contact: Steven Sill, President
E-mail: ssill@aspeneq.com
URL(s): www.ntea.com/. Frequency: Annual. Audience: Owners, commercial truck distributors, dealers, up fitters, manufacturers, buyers, users, sales, marketing, financial, administrative, engineers, and shop manag. Principal Exhibits: Chassis, commercial truck, bodies, mounted equipment, accessories, and supplies. Telecommunication Services: jim@ntea.com.

CONSULTANTS

20722 ■ Claude Travis & Associates

2550 Holtman Dr. NE
Grand Rapids, MI 49525-1815
Ph: (616)364-0869
Fax: (616)364-0869
Contact: Claude J. Travis, President
Scope: Fleet consultant offering truck and fleet maintenance studies, fleet fuel economy testing and expert witness work relating to truck safety, trucks and truck products and accidents. Serves trucking companies, manufacturers of trucks and parts, government and lawyers. Founded: 1978.

LIBRARIES

20723 ■ American Truck Historical Society - Zoe James Memorial Library

PO Box 901611
Kansas City, MO 64190-1611
Ph: (816)891-9900

Fax: (205)870-3069
Co. E-mail: info@aths.org
URL: http://www.aths.org
Contact: Lee Young, Librarian
Scope: Trucks, truck companies, people in trucking. Services: Copying; library open to the public. Founded: 1971. Holdings: 1100 books; 180 bound periodical volumes; 250 biographies; 700 company histories; 30,000 unbound periodicals; 500 slides; 100 videotapes; 100,000 photographs. Subscriptions: 45 journals and other serials. Telecommunication Services: bill@aths.org.

20724 ■ Manitoba Trucking Association Library

25 Bunting St.
Winnipeg, MB, Canada R2X 2P5
Ph: (204)632-6600
Fax: (204)694-7134
Co. E-mail: info@trucking.mb.ca
URL: http://www.trucking.mb.ca
Contact: Bob Dolyniuk, Executive Director
Scope: Transportation. Holdings: Figures not available.

RESEARCH CENTERS

20725 ■ American Transportation Research Institute (ATRI)

950 N Glebe Rd., Ste. 210
Arlington, VA 22203
Ph: (703)838-1966
Fax: (770)432-0638
Co. E-mail: rbrewster@trucking.org
URL: http://www.atri-online.org
Contact: Rebecca Brewster, President
Founded: 1986. Publications: Inventory of Truck Related Research (Annual). Educational Activities: Ad hoc meetings. Telecommunication Services: atri@trucking.org.

20726 ■ University of Michigan - Center for National Truck and Bus Statistics (CNTBS)

Transportation Research Institute
2901 Baxter Rd.
Ann Arbor, MI 48109-2150
Ph: (734)764-0248
Fax: (734)764-2640
Co. E-mail: dfblower@umich.edu
URL: http://www.umtri.umich.edu/divisionPage.php-?pageID=4
Contact: Dr. Daniel Blower, Director
Founded: 1988. Publications: Truck and Bus Accident Factbook (Annual). Educational Activities: Training opportunities, to graduate students. Telecommunication Services: cntbs@umich.edu.

20727 ■ University of New Brunswick - Transportation Group

Department of Civil Engineering
Fredericton, NB, Canada E3B 5A3
Ph: (506)453-5113
Fax: (506)453-3568
Co. E-mail: edh@unb.ca
URL: http://www.unb.ca/transpo
Contact: Dr. Eric D. Hildebrand, Coordinator
Founded: 1968. Educational Activities: Guest speakers from government and industry; Transportation Seminar.

START-UP INFORMATION

20728 ■ *"Advantage Tutoring Center" in Bellingham Business Journal (Vol. February 2010, pp. 16)*
Pub: Sound Publishing Inc.
Ed: Ashley Mitchell. **Description:** Profile of the newly opened Advantage Tutoring, owned by Mary and Peter Morrison. The center offers programs ranging from basic homework help to subject-specific enrichment.

20729 ■ *"Fun And Easy Gold Mines" in Small Business Opportunities (Fall 2008)*
Pub: Entrepreneur Media Inc.
Description: Twenty-five businesses that cater to the booming children's market are profiled; day care services, party planning, special events videomaking, tutoring, personalized children's toys and products and other services geared toward the kids market are included.

20730 ■ *Start Your Own Tutoring and Test Prep Business: Your Step-by-Step Guide to Success*
Pub: Entrepreneur Press
Contact: Perlman Neil, President
Ed: Rich Mintzer. **Released:** September 9, 2010. **Price:** $17.95. **Description:** Are you an advocate of higher learning? Do you enjoy teaching others? Are you interested in starting a business that makes money and a positive impact? Keys for starting a successful tutoring and test preparation small business are presented.

ASSOCIATIONS AND OTHER ORGANIZATIONS

20731 ■ **Independent Educational Consultants Association (IECA)**
3251 Old Lee Hwy., Ste. 510
Fairfax, VA 22030-1504
Ph: (703)591-4850
Free: 800-808-IECA
Fax: (703)591-4860
Co. E-mail: info@iecaonline.com
URL: http://www.iecaonline.com
Contact: Marilyn Emerson, President
Description: Represents the interests of established educational consultants. Brings family the knowledge and skills of an experienced professional. Gives advice to students with special circumstances such as learning or physical disabilities, emotional or behavioral issues. Helps members update knowledge and maintain skills through meetings, workshops, training programs, and information exchanges with colleges, schools, programs, and other consultants. Members are required to maintain the highest standards of ethical practice. **Founded:** 1976. **Publications:** *IECA Directory* (Annual). **Educational Activities:** Independent Educational Consultants Association Workshop; Independent Educational Consultants Association Conference (Semiannual).

REFERENCE WORKS

20732 ■ *"An Educated Play on China" in Barron's (Vol. 88, June 30, 2008, No. 26, pp. M6)*
Pub: Dow Jones & Co., Inc.
Ed: Mohammed Hadi. **Description:** New Oriental Education & Technology Group sells English-language courses to an increasingly competitive Chinese workforce that values education. The shares in this company have been weighed down by worries on the impact of the Beijing Olympics on enrollment and the Sichuan earthquake. These shares could be a great way to get exposure to the long-term growth in China.

20733 ■ *"The Future Is Another Country; Higher Education" in The Economist (Vol. 390, January 3, 2009, No. 8612, pp. 43)*
Pub: The Economist Newspaper Inc.
Description: Due to the growth of the global corporation, more ambitious students are studying at universities abroad; the impact of this trend is discussed.

20734 ■ *"Pre-K Pressure" in Hawaii Business (Vol. 53, October 2007, No. 4, pp. 32)*
Pub: Hawaii Business Publishing
Ed: David K. Choo. **Description:** Kindergarten admission in Hawaii is becoming more competitive. Parents, for example, prepare their children for the kindergarten admissions process by bringing them to the schools before the interview or by paying for tutorial services. The impacts of increased competition in school admissions on the life of Hawaiian children are discussed.

20735 ■ *"Trend: Tutors to Help You Pump Up the Staff" in Business Week (September 22, 2008, No. 4100, pp. 45)*
Pub: McGraw-Hill Companies, Inc.
Ed: Reena Janaj. **Description:** High-level managers are turning to innovation coaches in an attempt to obtain advice on how to better sell new concepts within their companies. Individuals as well as consulting firms are now offering this service.

TRADE PERIODICALS

20736 ■ *DETC News*
Pub: Distance Education and Training Council
Contact: Michael P. Lambert, Executive Director
Ed: Sally R. Welch, Editor, sally@detc.org. **Released:** 2/year. **Description:** Discusses issues pertaining to distance study education and reports activities of the Council. Recurring features include news of research, book reviews, news of members, and a calendar of events.

20737 ■ *Exceptional Children*
Pub: Council for Exceptional Children
Contact: Bruce Ramirez, Executive Director
URL(s): www.cec.sped.org/Content/NavigationMenu/ Publications2/ExceptionalCh ildren/. **Ed:** Margo Mastropieri, Thomas Scruggs. **Released:** Quarterly **Price:** $95, Individuals print & online; $105, Canada print &

online; $130, Other countries print and online; $86, U.S. and other countries online only; $196, Institutions print & online; $206, Institutions, Canada print & online; $231, Institutions, other countries print & online; $178, U.S. and other countries institution; online only.

20738 ■ *Teaching Exceptional Children*
Pub: Council for Exceptional Children
Contact: Bruce Ramirez, Executive Director
URL(s): www.cec.sped.org/Content/NavigationMenu/ Publications2/TEACHINGExcep tionalChildren/ default.htm. **Ed:** Barbara Ludlow. **Released:** 6/yr. **Price:** $99, Individuals print & online; $109, Canada print & online; $134, Other countries print & online; $90, U.S. and other countries online only; $215, Institutions print & online; $225, Institutions, Canada print & online; $250, Institutions, other countries print & online; $197, U.S. and other countries institution; online only.

FRANCHISES AND BUSINESS OPPORTUNITIES

20739 ■ **ABC Tutors In Home Tutoring**
7234 W 151st St.
Overland Park, KS 66223
Ph: (913)961-7800
Fax: (913)685-0533
Description: Academic tutoring. **No. of Franchise Units:** 4. **No. of Company-Owned Units:** 1. **Founded:** 2004.. **Franchised:** 2005. **Equity Capital Needed:** $29,500-$52,500. **Franchise Fee:** $19,500. **Royalty Fee:** 4-6%. **Financial Assistance:** In-house assistance available for franchise fee. **Training:** Provides 3 days of onsite training with ongoing support.

20740 ■ **Academy for Mathematics & English**
20 Wertheim Ct., Unit 12
Richmond Hill, ON, Canada L4B 3A8
Ph: (905)731-0404
Fax: (905)731-6178
Co. E-mail: balti@acadfor.com
URL: http://www.tutoringacademy.ca
Description: Math tutoring system. Tutoring is also offered for English, Physics and Chemistry. **No. of Franchise Units:** 35. **No. of Company-Owned Units:** 1. **Founded:** 1993.. **Franchised:** 1993. **Equity Capital Needed:** $120,000-$150,000. **Franchise Fee:** $35,000. **Training:** 3 week initial training, 1 week on-site and ongoing support.

20741 ■ **Chyten Educational Services**
1723 Massachusetts Ave.
Lexington, MA 02420
Ph: (508)720-9827
Description: Tutoring and test preparation. **No. of Franchise Units:** 36. **No. of Company-Owned Units:** 4. **Founded:** 1999.. **Franchised:** 2007. **Equity Capital Needed:** $113,900-$234,000. **Franchise Fee:** $37,500. **Royalty Fee:** 10%. **Financial Assistance:** Third party financing available. **Training:**

Offers training up to 10 days at corporate headquarters, up to 3 days at franchisee's location and ongoing support provided.

20742 ■ Club Z! In-Home Tutoring

Club Z! Inc.
15310 Aberly Dr., Ste. 185
Tampa, FL 33647
Ph: (813)931-5516
Fax: (813)932-2485
Co. E-mail: leads@clubztutoring.com
URL: http://www.clubztutoring.com

Description: In-home tutoring services. **No. of Franchise Units:** 412. **No. of Company-Owned Units:** 1. **Founded:** 1995.. **Franchised:** 1997. **Equity Capital Needed:** $32,500. **Franchise Fee:** $24,500. **Training:** Yes.

20743 ■ Huntington Center Services

Huntington Learning Centers, Inc.
496 Kinderkamack Rd.
Oradell, NJ 07649
Ph: (201)261-8400
Free: 800-653-8400
Co. E-mail: franchise@huntingtonlearningcenter.com
URL: http://www.huntingtonfranchise.com

Description: Provides individualized instruction to school-aged children and adults in remedial and speed reading, study skills, spelling, phonics, mathematics, and Scholastic Aptitude Test (SAT) preparation. **No. of Franchise Units:** 250. **No. of Company-Owned Units:** 30. **Founded:** 1977.. **Franchised:** 1985. **Equity Capital Needed:** Total investment range $162,000-$257,600. **Franchise Fee:** $24,000. **Financial Assistance:** Yes. **Training:** Training program, provides detailed demographic data for desired location, site selection and start-up assistance.

20744 ■ Kumon Math and Reading Centres

640 Applewood Crescent
Vaughan, ON, Canada L4K 4B4
Ph: (416)490-1434
Free: 800-266-6681
Fax: (905)738-1765
Co. E-mail: franchisecanada@kumon.com
URL: http://www.kumonfranchise.ca

Description: Provides an individualized after school math and reading program for students. **No. of Franchise Units:** 330. **No. of Company-Owned Units:** 4. **Founded:** 1988.. **Franchised:** 1958. **Equity Capital Needed:** $61,000-$152,000. **Franchise Fee:** $1,000. **Training:** Yes.

20745 ■ The Learning Experience

4855 N. Technology Way, Ste. 700
Boca Raton, FL 33431
Ph: (561)886-6400
Fax: (561)886-6433
Co. E-mail: franchise@tlecorp.com
URL: http://www.thelearningexperience.com

Description: The Learning Experience is one of the fastest growing childcare center operators in the Northeastern United States with current expansion in the Michigan and North Carolina markets. Through the development of detailed franchisee training, meticulous operational manuals and an unparalleled student curriculum, The Learning Experience remains on the cutting edge within the childcare industry. **No. of Franchise Units:** 96. **No. of Company-Owned Units:** 19. **Founded:** 2001.. **Franchised:** 2001. **Equity Capital Needed:** $150,000. **Franchise Fee:** $60,000. **Financial Assistance** Yes. **Training:** Provides an in-depth orientation on every aspect of the business, including a sophisticated but user-friendly computer system. Offers reinforcement and support systems throughout tenure as a franchisee.

20746 ■ Mathnasium Learning Centers

5120 W Goldleaf Cir., Ste. 300
Los Angeles, CA 90056
Ph: (877)531-6284
Fax: (310)943-2111
Co. E-mail: franchise@mathnasium.com
URL: http://www.mathnasium.com

Description: Mathnasium provides the most effective mathematics in education available to grade school children after school, in an attractive neighborhood learning center environment. The Mathnasium Method, developed over 30 years of hands-on experience, is engaging for students and builds confidence as it builds real understanding. Created to address a real need in the market by a team with unparalleled success in the industry, the business model is strong and the opportunity is now. **No. of Franchise Units:** 389. **No. of Company-Owned Units:** 2. **Founded:** 2002.. **Franchised:** 2003. **Equity Capital Needed:** $82,250-$136,000 initial investment range. **Franchise Fee:** $37,000. **Training:** Initial training 1 week online followed by 1 week in person at corporate headquarters. Support continues with ongoing training, in-the-field regional managers and monthly conference calls.

20747 ■ Scholars Education Centre

Scholars Canada
101 N Syndicate
Thunder Bay, ON, Canada P7C 3V4
Ph: (807)345-2661
Fax: (807)768-5226
Co. E-mail: parry@scholarscanada.com
URL: http://www.scholarscanada.com

Description: Offers Personalized Programs targeting the individual needs of students and their families. Credible, standardized Canadian assessments are used to obtain the information needed to personalize the student's program. **No. of Franchise Units:** 8. **No. of Company-Owned Units:** 3. **Founded:** 1998. **Franchised:** 2000. **Equity Capital Needed:** $50,000-$80,000 plus applicable taxes. **Franchise Fee:** $25,000 plus applicable taxes. **Training:** 2 weeks training provided.

20748 ■ Sylvan Learning Center

Sylvan Learning Inc.
1001 Fleet St.
Baltimore, MD 21202
Ph: (410)843-8880
Free: 800-284-8214
Fax: (410)843-6265
Co. E-mail: sylvanfranchise@Educate.com
URL: http://www.sylvanfranchise.com

Description: Offers services that supplements education programs in reading, mathematics, and other subjects for both children and adults. **No. of Franchise Units:** 890. **No. of Company-Owned Units:** 40. **Founded:** 1979.. **Franchised:** 1980. **Equity Capital Needed:** $188,000-$305,000. **Franchise Fee:** $42,000-$48,000. **Training:** Training at corporate headquarters and locally. Basic training, regional training, regional meetings, and annual conferences.

20749 ■ Tutoring Club

Tutoring Club, LLC
11241 Eastern Ave.
Henderson, NV 89052
Free: 888-674-6425

Description: Center providing individualized after-school instruction. **No. of Franchise Units:** 111. **No. of Company-Owned Units:** 1. **Founded:** 1991.. **Franchised:** 1999. **Equity Capital Needed:** $26,300-$127,300. **Franchise Fee:** $15,000-$34,500. **Royalty Fee:** 10-12%. **Financial Assistance:** Third party financing available. **Training:** Offers 2 weeks at headquarters, 1 day onsite with ongoing support.

LIBRARIES

20750 ■ American Federation of Teachers Library

555 New Jersey Ave., NW
Washington, DC 20001
Ph: (202)879-4400
Fax: (202)879-4406
Co. E-mail: online@aft.org
URL: http://www.aft.org
Contact: Bernadette Bailey

Scope: Labor, education. **Services:** Library open to members only. **Founded:** 1916. **Holdings:** 1400 books. **Subscriptions:** 300 journals and other serials; 11 newspapers.

20751 ■ Instructional Media Services, Inc.

PO Box 711
Merton, WI 53056
Ph: (262)369-9200
Fax: (262)538-1491
Co. E-mail: imsinfo@imseducates.com
URL: http://www.imseducates.com

Scope: Educational curriculum. **Services:** Center open to the public. **Founded:** 1990. **Holdings:** 20,000 16mm educational films; 10,000 video cassettes; 100 laser discs; 2500 museum specimens; miniature dioramas; Jonas miniature models; mounted plants and animals; museum artifacts. **Subscriptions:** 10 journals and other serials.

20752 ■ Oakland University - School of Education and Human Services - Educational Resources Laboratory

350 Pawley Hall
Rochester Hills, MI 48309-4494
Ph: (248)370-2485
Fax: (248)370-4226
Co. E-mail: amphelps@oakland.edu
URL: http://www.oakland.edu/erl
Contact: Barbara Antoinette Begin Campbell, Coordinator

Scope: Education - general, pre-school-12th grade, multi-cultural diversity, career; children's literature. **Services:** Wireless computer lab; presentation equipment; laminator; book binder; poster maker; guest memberships with borrowing privileges available for purchase. **Founded:** 1962. **Holdings:** 30,000 books, journals, videotapes, DVDs, digital cameras and camcorders, and desktop and laptop computers. **Subscriptions:** 20 journals and other serials. **Telecommunication Services:** begincam@oakland.edu.

20753 ■ Traverse City Regional Educational Media Center - REMC 2 Central

1101 Red Dr.
Traverse City, MI 49684-4465
Ph: (231)922-6200
Fax: (231)922-6270
Co. E-mail: mbacon@tbaisd.k12.mi.us
URL: http://www.tbaisd.k12.mi.us
Contact: Maggie Bacon, Coordinator

Scope: Educational curriculum; print and non-print media and materials. **Services:** Copying (with fee); center open to the public with restrictions. **Founded:** 1968. **Holdings:** 15,000 videocassettes.

20754 ■ Wisconsin Literacy Resource Network

310 Price Pl.
Madison, WI 53705-3209
Ph: (608)266-1207
Fax: (608)266-1690
Co. E-mail: muellej@board.tec.wi.us
URL: http://www.wtcsystem.edu/
Contact: Mark Johnson, Director, Education

Scope: Literacy, basic education. **Founded:** 1986. **Holdings:** Figures not available. **Telecommunication Services:** mark.johnson@wtcsystem.edu; debbie.parker@wtcsystem.edu.

Typesetting Business

ASSOCIATIONS AND OTHER ORGANIZATIONS

20755 ■ **Printing Brokerage/Buyers Association International (PB/BA)—PBBA International Inc.**
1530 Locust St., Mezanine 124
Philadelphia, PA 19102
Ph: (215)821-6581
Free: 877-585-7141
Fax: (215)359-1577
Co. E-mail: contactus@pbba.org
URL: http://www.pbba.org
Contact: Vincent Mallardi, President
E-mail: vince@pbba.org
Description: Printing buyers/brokers/distributors, printers, typographers, binders, envelope and book manufacturers, packagers, color separation houses, pre-press service organizations, and related companies in the graphic arts industry. Promotes understanding, cooperation, and interaction among members while obtaining the highest standard of professionalism in the graphic arts industry. Gathers information on current technology in the graphic communications industry. Sponsors seminars for members to learn how to work with buyers, brokers and printers; also conducts technical and management seminars. Maintains referral service; compiles statistics. Conducts charitable programs. **Scope:** Printing and publishing marketing and corporate development specialists, whose services include start ups, joint ventures, acquisitions, mergers, contract negotiation, international trade, seminars, workshops, facilities planning, and cost reduction programs. Serves private industries as well as government agencies. **Founded:** 1985. **Subscriptions:** 500 books. **Publications:** "Hot Markets for 2007-2008," Jan, 2005. **Awards:** Printing Broker of the Year (Annual); Vendor of the Year (Annual). **Seminars:** How to Sell Printing Effectively; Sales Compensation and Management; How to Buy Printing Effectively; Hot Markets; International Priority Commerce. **Special Services:** Findprint®; Salesort®.

20756 ■ **Type Directors Club (TDC)**
347 W 36th St., Ste. 603
New York, NY 10018
Ph: (212)633-8943
Fax: (212)633-8944
Co. E-mail: director@tdc.org
URL: http://tdc.org
Contact: Charles Nix, Chairman
Description: Serves as a professional society of typographic designers, type directors, and teachers of typography; sustaining members are individuals with interests in typographic education. Seeks to stimulate research and disseminate information. Provides speakers, classes and offers presentations on history and new developments in typography. **Scope:** typography. **Founded:** 1946. **Subscriptions:** 1800 books video recordings. **Publications:** *Typography 28*. **Awards:** Student Award (Annual); TDC Scholarship (Annual); Type Directors Club Medal (Periodic).

REFERENCE WORKS

20757 ■ *"Agfa: M-Press Leopard Debuts"* in *American Printer (Vol. 128, June 1, 2011, No. 6)*
Pub: Penton Media Inc.
Description: M-Press Leopard is a new version of the machine that offers advanced ink jet technology at a lower price point. Agfa Graphics introduced the new version that allows for new applications that require more manual handling.

20758 ■ *"Avanti Hosts Users Conference"* in *American Printer (Vol. 128, July 1, 2011, No. 7)*
Pub: Penton Media Inc.
Description: Avanti Computer Systems Ltd. hosted its 19th annual users conference in Washington DC. In-plant and commercial printers were in attendance.

20759 ■ *"Avoid a Tablet Generation Gap"* in *American Printer (Vol. 128, July 1, 2011, No. 7)*
Pub: Penton Media Inc.
Description: Individuals between the ages of 18-34 are the only generation that is more likely to own a laptop computer or netbook insead of a desktop computer. Statistical data included.

20760 ■ *"Boston Printer Celebrates 60th Anniversary"* in *American Printer (Vol. 128, August 1, 2011, No. 8)*
Pub: Penton Media Inc.
Description: Shawmut printing is celebrating its 60th anniversary. The family business plans to increase efficiency through automation, monitoring job progress online from start to finish.

20761 ■ *"Business is Unbelievable"* in *American Printer (Vol. 128, August 1, 2011, No. 8)*
Pub: Penton Media Inc.
Ed: Katherine O'Brien. **Description:** Most commercial printers have seen an increase in business over the last year.

20762 ■ *"ContiTech Celebrates 100 Years"* in *American Printer (Vol. 128, July 1, 2011, No. 7)*
Pub: Penton Media Inc.
Description: ContiTech celebrated 100 years in business. The firm started in 1911 after developing the first elastic printing blanket. Other milestones for the firm include its manufacturing process for compressible printing blankets, the Conti-Air brand and climate-neutral printing blankets.

20763 ■ *"Crouser Offers UV Coating Price Report"* in *American Printer (Vol. 128, June 1, 2011, No. 6)*
Pub: Penton Media Inc.
Description: Crouser and Associates will offer the 'Pricing Off-Line UV Coating' report that provides background information on all three types of protec-

tive printing coatings and price guidance. The report will also offer comparisons of four popular types of offline equipment.

20764 ■ *"Customer OKs on Press"* in *American Printer (Vol. 128, August 1, 2011, No. 8)*
Pub: Penton Media Inc.
Description: Printers discuss the value of having customers meet at the plant in order to okay print colors for projects.

20765 ■ *"Design Center Shows Quality of Digital Paper"* in *American Printer (Vol. 128, June 1, 2011, No. 6)*
Pub: Penton Media Inc.
Description: Digital Design Centers allows printers to customize marketing tools in order to promote their own digital printing capabilities.

20766 ■ *"Digital Printing Walks the Plank"* in *American Printer (Vol. 128, August 1, 2011, No. 8)*
Pub: Penton Media Inc.
Description: Digital print manufacturing is discussed.

20767 ■ *"Feeding the Elephants While Searching for Greener Pastures"* in *American Printer (Vol. 128, July 1, 2011, No. 7)*
Pub: Penton Media Inc.
Ed: Bob Rosen. **Description:** Three steps to help printers to build a new business while facing the challenges to the existing business are outlined.

20768 ■ *"First U.S. :M-Press Tiger with Inline Screen Printing"* in *American Printer (Vol. 128, June 1, 2011, No. 6)*
Pub: Penton Media Inc.
Description: Graphic Tech located in California bought :M-Press Tiger, the first in North America with an inline screen printing unit.

20769 ■ *"Flint Group Raises Prices"* in *American Printer (Vol. 128, August 1, 2011, No. 8)*
Pub: Penton Media Inc.
Description: Due to the rising cost for raw materials, Flint Group is raising their prices for inks and coatings in North American.

20770 ■ *"Four Exhibition Considerations"* in *American Printer (Vol. 128, August 1, 2011, No. 8)*
Pub: Penton Media Inc.
Description: Four questions to ask at the Graph Expo will help printers improve their own business.

20771 ■ *"Fujifilm Invites Printers to Take the 'Onset Challenge"* in *American Printer (Vol. 128, August 1, 2011, No. 8)*
Pub: Penton Media Inc.
Description: Fujifilm North American Corporation's Graphic Systems Division offers a new five-step product selection and return-on-investment calculator for the Onset family of wide-format printers.

20772 ■ *"Guide to Carbon Footprinting"* in *American Printer (Vol. 128, June 1, 2011, No. 6)*

Pub: Penton Media Inc.

Description: PrintCity Alliance published its new report, 'Carbon Footprint & Energy Reduction for Graphic Industry Value Chain.' The report aims to help improve the environmental performance of printers, converters, publishers, brand owners and their suppliers.

20773 ■ *"How to Save Money on Ink"* in *American Printer (Vol. 128, July 1, 2011, No. 7)*

Pub: Penton Media Inc.

Description: Tips are shared to help graphic arts and printing companies save money on raw materials. Factors to consider once the type of ink is decided are also outlined.

20774 ■ *"Improving the USPS"* in *American Printer (Vol. 128, July 1, 2011, No. 7)*

Pub: Penton Media Inc.

Description: National Postal Forum held in San Diego, California May 1-4, 2011 hosted 4,000 attendees. Highlights of the event are provided.

20775 ■ *"Industry Events 2011"* in *American Printer (Vol. 128, August 1, 2011, No. 8)*

Pub: Penton Media Inc.

Description: Listing of events of interest to graphic arts and printing businesses in presented.

20776 ■ *"Industry/Events 2011"* in *American Printer (Vol. 128, July 1, 2011, No. 7)*

Pub: Penton Media Inc.

Description: PMA, the Worldwide Community of Imaging Association launched its new CliQ with how-to tips, product reviews and monthly photo contests. PMA formed a partnership with the Consumer Electronics Association to make changes to this year's annual convention.

20777 ■ *"Interchangeable or Irreplaceable?"* in *American Printer (Vol. 128, August 1, 2011, No. 8)*

Pub: Penton Media Inc.

Description: Creating and maintaining customers is important for all graphic design and printing companies. Tips are shared to help maintain good customer satisfaction and repeat business.

20778 ■ *"IPEX Moves to London Venue"* in *American Printer (Vol. 128, July 1, 2011, No. 7)*

Pub: Penton Media Inc.

Description: IPES 2014 is being relocated to London's ExCeL International Exhibition and Conference Centre from March 26 to April 2, 2014.

20779 ■ *"JDF Integration: 3 Key Tips"* in *American Printer (Vol. 128, August 1, 2011, No. 8)*

Pub: Penton Media Inc.

Description: Three tips for implementing cross-vendor integrations are outlined.

20780 ■ *"KBA, Graphic Art System Partner on Cold Foil"* in *American Printer (Vol. 128, June 1, 2011, No. 6)*

Pub: Penton Media Inc.

Description: KBA North America has partnered with Graphic Art System to retrofit and equip presses with cold foil machines.

20781 ■ *"Kodak Offers Cloud-Based Operating Option"* in *American Printer (Vol. 128, June 1, 2011, No. 6)*

Pub: Penton Media Inc.

Description: Kodak partnered with VMware to offer its first Virtual Operating Environment option for Kodak Unified Workflow Solutions. The new feature enables cost savings, increased efficiency and failover protection.

20782 ■ *Literary Market Place: The Directory of the American Book Publishing Industry*

Pub: Information Today Inc.

Contact: Thomas H. Hogan, President

E-mail: ctuthill@infotoday.com

URL(s): books.infotoday.com. **Released:** Annual; Latest edition 2012. **Price:** $339, Individuals 2-volume set/softbound plus $25 shipping/handling; $305.10, Individuals first time standing order. **Covers:** Over 12,500 firms or organizations offering services related to the publishing industry, including book publishers in the United States and Canada who issued three or more books during the preceding year, plus a small press section of publishers who publish less than three titles per year or those who are self-published. Also included: book printers and binders; book clubs; book trade and literary associations; selected syndicates, newspapers, periodicals, and radio and TV programs that use book reviews or book publishing news; translators and literary agents. **Entries include:** For publishers--Company name, address, phone, address for orders, principal executives, editorial directors, and managers, date founded, number of titles in previous year, number of backlist titles in print, types of books published, ISBN prefixes, representatives, imprints, and affiliations. For suppliers, etc.--Listings usually show firm name, address, phone, executives, services, etc. **Arrangement:** Classified by line of business. **Indexes:** Principal index is 35,000-item combined index of publishers, publications, and personnel; several sections have geographical and/or subject indexes; translators are indexed by source and target language.

20783 ■ *"Metallics Education"* in *American Printer (Vol. 128, June 1, 2011, No. 6)*

Pub: Penton Media Inc.

Description: Guide 'Curious About Print: Your Guide to the World of Curious Metallics' provides hints and tips to help printers maximize selection and reproduction, advice on working with metallic and UV inks, and recommendations for gaining quantity without sacrificing quality.

20784 ■ *"MFSA Officially Endorses Five-Day USPS Delivery"* in *American Printer (Vol. 128, August 1, 2011, No. 8)*

Pub: Penton Media Inc.

Description: Board of Directors of the Mailing and Fulfillment Service Association (MFSA) voted to support the US Postal Service's move to five-day delivery service.

20785 ■ *"New Approach to Mechanical Binding"* in *American Printer (Vol. 128, July 1, 2011, No. 7)*

Pub: Penton Media Inc.

Description: EcoBinder coil binding system from Kugler-Womako eliminates traditional plastic combs or wire spiral with the use of 22-mm wide printable paper rings.

20786 ■ *"OCE Boosts JetStream Productivity"* in *American Printer (Vol. 128, August 1, 2011, No. 8)*

Pub: Penton Media Inc.

Description: New Oce JetStream 1400 and 3000 digital full-color inkjet presses are profiled. The new models promise higher speed to grow print volume.

20787 ■ *"One World"* in *American Printer (Vol. 128, August 1, 2011, No. 8)*

Pub: Penton Media Inc.

Description: Graph Expo will highlight entrepreneurs focused on the connection between content, technology and business models.

20788 ■ *"Paper a la Carte"* in *American Printer (Vol. 128, June 1, 2011, No. 6)*

Pub: Penton Media Inc.

Description: Blurb, the online publishing platform, launched ProLine which features Mohawk Superfine and Mohawk proPhoto papers. ProLine papers offer two finishes: Pearl Photo and Uncoated.

20789 ■ *"Paper Choices Made Simple"* in *American Printer (Vol. 128, June 1, 2011, No. 6)*

Pub: Penton Media Inc.

Description: Choices, a new initiative by Boise, provides professional guidance to help customers and consumers make informed, effective choices for using paper.

20790 ■ *"Paper Replaces PVC for Gift Cards"* in *American Printer (Vol. 128, June 1, 2011, No. 6)*

Pub: Penton Media Inc.

Description: Monadnock Envi Card Stock replaces paper for gift cards, loyalty cards, membership cards, hotel keys and durable signage. This renewable wood fiber alternative to PVC card materials comes from Monadock Paper Mills.

20791 ■ *"Prices Continue to Rise"* in *American Printer (Vol. 128, June 1, 2011, No. 6)*

Pub: Penton Media Inc.

Description: Prices were increased by both Flint Group and Ashland Performance Materials by 7-10 percent and 5-15 percent respectively.

20792 ■ *"Printers to the Trade"* in *American Printer (Vol. 128, July 1, 2011, No. 7)*

Pub: Penton Media Inc.

Description: Wholesale printing is discussed. Two wholesale printers share insight into their success, from business philosophies in general to practices that build strong relationships.

20793 ■ *"QR Codes: OK, I Get It Now"* in *American Printer (Vol. 128, July 1, 2011, No. 7)*

Pub: Penton Media Inc.

Description: QR Code technology is discussed. It is up to the user to enter the proper QR Code.

20794 ■ *"Reducing the Book's Carbon Footpring"* in *American Printer (Vol. 128, July 1, 2011, No. 7)*

Pub: Penton Media Inc.

Description: Green Press Initiative's Book Industry Environmental Council is working to achieve a 20 percent reduction in the book industry's carbon footprint by 2020. The Council is made up of publishers, printers, paper suppliers, and non-governmental organizations.

20795 ■ *"Root, Root, Root for the P.A. Hutchison Co."* in *American Printer (Vol. 128, August 1, 2011, No. 8)*

Pub: Penton Media Inc.

Description: The P.A. Hutchison Company celebrate 100 years in the printing business. President and CEO Chris Hutchison presented awards to employees, however employees also presented awards to Chris and his father as Employer of the Century.

20796 ■ *"Sappi Awards Gold NA Printers of the Year Winners"* in *American Printer (Vol. 128, July 1, 2011, No. 7)*

Pub: Penton Media Inc.

Description: Sappi Fine Paper North America honored ten gold winners of its 14th North American Printers of the Year awards. Each gold winning printer will receive $20,000 to support marketing and brand initiatives.

20797 ■ *"Seeing the Light"* in *American Printer (Vol. 128, July 1, 2011, No. 7)*

Pub: Penton Media Inc.

Description: Four printing demos on sheetfed, digital, label and pad printing equipment were highlighted at the Fifth UV Days held in Stuttgart, Germany in May 2011.

20798 ■ *"Seven Tips for Continuous Improvement"* in *American Printer (Vol. 128, July 1, 2011, No. 7)*

Pub: Penton Media Inc.

Description: Seven tips are given to help any graphic arts or printing company improve by integrating lean manufacturing into operations.

20799 ■ *"Something Old and Something New"* in *American Printer (Vol. 128, August 1, 2011, No. 8)*

Pub: Penton Media Inc.

Description: Trade journalists and industry analysts were invited to Fujifilm North America Corporation's Hanover Park, Illinois facility to view it's sheetfed inkjet press. The JPress 720 is the first and only of its kind in the world.

20800 ■ *"Successful First Year for Twin Rivers"* in American Printer (Vol. 128, June 1, 2011, No. 6)
Pub: Penton Media Inc.
Description: Profile of Twin Rivers located in Maine. The firm manufactured 380,000 tons of free sheet and hybrid-groundwood papers in its first year.

20801 ■ *"Tic-Tac-Show"* in American Printer (Vol. 128, August 1, 2011, No. 8)
Pub: Penton Media Inc.
Description: Graph Expo has become the US print industry's main event. There will be as many as 500 exhibitors at this year's event and the Graphic Arts Show Company lists over 30 co-located events as well as 53 new sessions in the seminar program's 28 education categories.

20802 ■ *"Transcontinental to Exchange Assets with Quad/Graphics"* in American Printer (Vol. 128, August 1, 2011, No. 8)
Pub: Penton Media Inc.
Description: Transcontinental Inc. and Quad/Graphics Inc. entered into an agreement where Transcontinental will indirectly acquire all shares of Quad Graphics Canada Inc.

20803 ■ *"Try a Little Social Media"* in American Printer (Vol. 128, June 1, 2011, No. 6)
Pub: Penton Media Inc.
Description: Social media helps keep Ussery Printing on customers radar. Jim David, VP of marketing for the firm, states that 350 people following them on Facebook are from the local area.

20804 ■ *"Use Ink Presets to Minimize Makeready"* in American Printer (Vol. 128, July 1, 2011, No. 7)
Pub: Penton Media Inc.
Description: Automatic registration systems enable most printers to be in register very quickly after press startup. If the paper, ink and press time wasted during makeready can be reduced, these savings will flow directly to the bottom line. Ink presetting as an economical solution to set color quickly is a trend that continues to gain momentum.

20805 ■ *"UV Suppliers Form Strategic Alliance"* in American Printer (Vol. 128, June 1, 2011, No. 6)
Pub: Penton Media Inc.
Description: British ultra-violent curing systems developer Integration Technology Ltd. formed a strategic alliance with UV technology provider IST Metz GmbH of Germany in order to offer a complete line of UV solutions for the printing industry.

20806 ■ *"Web to Print"* in American Printer (Vol. 128, August 1, 2011, No. 8)
Pub: Penton Media Inc.
Description: Jerry Kennelly, CEO and founder of Tweak.com believes that Web-to-Design is middleware with no content. His firm offers an easy to use interface that flows right into the printer's workflow with no additional costs.

STATISTICAL SOURCES

20807 ■ *RMA Annual Statement Studies*
Pub: Risk Management Association
Contact: Kevin M. Blakey, President
Released: Annual. Price: $175.00 2006-07 edition, $105.00. Description: Contains composite balance sheets and income statements for more than 360 industries, including the accounting, auditing, and bookkeeping industries. Also contains five years of comparative historical data for discerning trends. Includes 16 commonly used ratios, computed for most of the size groupings for nearly every industry.

TRADE PERIODICALS

20808 ■ *American Typecasting Fellowship Newsletter*
Pub: American Typecasting Fellowship
Ed: Richard L. Hopkins, Editor. Released: Periodic. Description: Devoted to conveying information on the preservation of equipment and technology related to metal typecasting. Covers type founding, type design, matrix making, and letterpress printing. Recurring features include letters to the editor and news of members.

20809 ■ *Imaging News: Guide*
Contact: Arthur S. Diamond, Editor
URL(s): www.imagingnews.com/imagingnews.html.
Ed: Arthur S. Diamond. Released: Monthly Price: $175, Individuals.

TRADE SHOWS AND CONVENTIONS

20810 ■ Graphics of the Americas
Printing Association of Florida, Inc.
6275 Hazeltine National Dr.
Orlando, FL 32822
Ph: (407)240-8009
Free: 800-749-4855
Fax: (407)240-8333
Co. E-mail: agaither@pafgraf.org
URL: http://www.pafgraf.org
URL(s): www.graphicsoftheamericas.com. Frequency: Annual. Audience: Graphics arts trade. Principal Exhibits: Graphic arts and specialty printing equipment, supplies, and services. Dates and Locations: , Convention Center. Telecommunication Services: spatt@pafgraf.org.

LIBRARIES

20811 ■ Carnegie-Mellon University - University Libraries - Special Collections
Hunt Library
4909 Frew St.
Pittsburgh, PA 15213-3890
Ph: (412)268-2444
Fax: (412)268-6945
Co. E-mail: mj0g@andrew.cmu.edu
URL: http://www.library.cmu.edu
Contact: Mary Kay Johnsen, Librarian, Special Collections
Scope: History of printing, 19th-century English literature, landmark books of science. Services: Library open to the public. Founded: 1960. Holdings: 12,000 books. Telecommunication Services: UL-huntref@andrew.cmu.edu.

20812 ■ Cleveland Public Library - Literature Department
Main Bldg., 2nd Fl.
325 Superior Ave.
Cleveland, OH 44114-1271
Ph: (216)623-2881
Co. E-mail: literature@cpl.org
URL: http://www.cpl.org/thelibrary/subjectscollections/literature.aspx
Contact: Amy Dawson, Manager
Scope: Fiction, drama and theater, film, radio, television, poetry, essays, humor, oratory and public speaking, craft of writing, literary criticism and biography, classical Greek and Latin, linguistics, journalism, book trade, printing, publishing, Library and information science. Services: Department open to the public. Founded: 1869. Holdings: 500,000 volumes; 11,368 bound periodical volumes; 23,000 theater programs and playbills; 16,000 titles of microform editions of plays and miscellanea; 190 vertical files. Subscriptions: 825 journals and other serials.

20813 ■ Free Library of Philadelphia - Social Science & History Department
1901 Vine St.
Philadelphia, PA 19103
Ph: (215)686-5396
Fax: (215)563-3628
URL: http://www.freelibrary.org
Contact: Jim DeWalt, Director
Scope: History, biography, social sciences, law, travels and geography, archeology, anthropology, sports and games. Services: Interlibrary loan. Founded: 1953. Holdings: 228,000 volumes; 53,900 pamphlets; 35 VF drawers of clippings. Subscriptions: 610 journals and other serials.

20814 ■ Grolier Club of New York Library
47 E. 60th St.
New York, NY 10022
Ph: (212)838-6690
Fax: (212)838-2445
Co. E-mail: ejh@grolierclub.org
URL: http://www.grolierclub.org
Contact: Eric Holzenberg, Director
Scope: Bibliography, history of printing, book-collecting, bookselling, arts of the book. Services: Library open to the public with restrictions. Founded: 1884. Holdings: 100,000 volumes; 5000 prints and portraits; bookplates. Subscriptions: 100 journals and other serials. Telecommunication Services: fpena@grolierclub.org; mconstantinou@grolierclub.org.

20815 ■ Rochester Institute of Technology - Melbert B. Cary, Jr. Graphic Arts Collection
Wallace Memorial Library
90 Lomb Memorial Dr.
Rochester, NY 14623-5604
Ph: (585)475-2408
Fax: (585)475-6900
Co. E-mail: ahfwml@rit.edu
URL: http://library.rit.edu/cary
Contact: Steven K. Galbraith, Curator
Scope: Printing history, type specimens, typography, book arts, press books, calligraphy, papermaking, graphic arts, bookbinding. Services: Copying (limited); collection open to the public. Founded: 1969. Holdings: 50,000 books; 20 VF drawers of clippings; ephemera; pamphlets; 50 boxes of posters, broadsides, drawings; 400 boxes of correspondence and manuscript material. Subscriptions: 20 journals and other serials. Telecommunication Services: skgtwc@rit.edu; circwml@rit.edu.

20816 ■ Yale University - Arts Library - Special Collections
Robert B. Haas Family Arts Library, Lower Level
180 York St.
New Haven, CT 06520-8318
Ph: (203)432-4439
Fax: (203)432-0549
Co. E-mail: jae.rossman@yale.edu
URL: http://www.library.yale.edu/arts/specialcollections
Contact: Jae Jennifer Rossman, Assistant Director
Scope: Typography, book illustration and design, bookbinding, papermaking, bookplates, private presses, artists' books, conceptual books, and fine printing. Services: Collection open to the public. Founded: 1967. Holdings: 20,000 books; prints and broadsides; type specimens; archive of student printing, including masters' theses from School of Graphic Design and School of Photography at Yale; 1 million bookplates; Japanese prints; stage and costume designs. Subscriptions: 20 journals and other serials.

ASSOCIATIONS AND OTHER ORGANIZATIONS

20817 ■ AFL-CIO - SEIU - District 925
1914 N 34th St., Ste. 100
Seattle, WA 98103
Ph: (206)322-3010
Free: 866-734-8925
Fax: (206)547-5581
Co. E-mail: khart@seiu925.org
URL: http://www.seiu925.org
Contact: Karen Hart, President
Description: National union of secretaries, stenographers, typists, clerks, and other office, technical, and professional workers in the U.S. Promotes collective bargaining for office workers and sponsors research and educational programs on pay equality, automation, and career advancement. Seeks to organize the nearly 20 million office workers in the U.S.; compiles statistics. **Founded:** 1981.

20818 ■ National Association of Legal Secretaries International
8159 E 41st St.
Tulsa, OK 74145-3313
Ph: (918)582-5188
Fax: (918)582-5907
Co. E-mail: info@nals.org
URL: http://www.nals.org
Contact: Helene L. Wood, President
Description: Legal secretaries and others employed in work of a legal nature in law offices, banks, and courts. Sponsors legal secretarial training courses and awards those passing a two-day examination the rating of Certified Professional Legal Secretary. **Founded:** 1929. **Publications:** *Career Legal Secretary*; *Manual for Lawyer's Assistant*. **Educational Activities:** National Forum and Education Conference (Annual).

20819 ■ National Court Reporters Association (NCRA)
8224 Old Courthouse Rd.
Vienna, VA 22182-3808
Ph: (703)556-6272
Free: 800-272-6272
Fax: (703)556-6291
Co. E-mail: president@ncrahq.org
URL: http://www.ncra.org
Contact: Suelynn Morgan, President
URL(s): www.ncraonline.org. **Description:** Represents independent state, regional, and local associations. Verbatim court reporters who work as official reporters for courts and government agencies, as freelance reporters for independent contractors, and as captioners for television programming; retired reporters, teachers of court reporting, and school officials; student court reporters. Conducts research; compiles statistics; offers several certification programs; and publishes journal. **Scope:** shorthand reporting and reporters. **Founded:** 1899. **Subscriptions:** 3000 books monographs periodicals. **Publications:** *National Court Reporters Association--Court Reporter Sourcebook* (Annual); *National Court Reporters Association--The Court Reporters Sourcebook* (Annual); *National Court Reporters Association--The Court Reporters Sourcebook* (Annual); *Journal of Court Reporting: Official Publication of National Court Reporters Assn.* **Educational Activities:** National Court Reporters Association Annual Convention & Exposition (Annual). **Awards:** Endorsers of the Year (Annual); Distinguished Service Award; Fellow of the Academy of Professional Reporters; CASE Award of Excellence; National Court Reporters Association Student Intern Scholarships; New Professional Reporter Grants; Frank Sarli Memorial Scholarships. **Telecommunication Services:** msic@ncrahq.org.

20820 ■ Society of Corporate Secretaries and Governance Professionals
240 W 35th St., Ste. 400
New York, NY 10001-2506
Ph: (212)681-2000
Fax: (212)681-2005
Co. E-mail: research@governanceprofessionals.org
URL: http://www.governanceprofessionals.org
Contact: John A. Seethoff, Chairman
Description: Corporate secretaries, assistant secretaries, officers and executives of corporations and others interested in corporate practices and procedures. Conducts surveys and research. Sponsors educational programs for members. Maintains a central information and reference service. **Founded:** 1946. **Publications:** *The Corporate Secretary* (Monthly).

DIRECTORIES OF EDUCATIONAL PROGRAMS

20821 ■ *Directory of Private Accredited Career Schools and Colleges of Technology*
Pub: Accrediting Commission of Career Schools and Colleges of Technology
Contact: Michale S. McComis, Executive Director
Released: On web page. **Price:** Free. **Description:** Covers 3900 accredited post-secondary programs that provide training programs in business, trade, and technical fields, including various small business endeavors. Entries offer school name, address, phone, description of courses, job placement assistance, and requirements for admission. Arrangement is alphabetical.

TRADE SHOWS AND CONVENTIONS

20822 ■ National Association of Executive Secretaries Annual Conference
Association of Executive and Administrative Professionals (AEAP)
900 S Washington St., Ste. G-13
Falls Church, VA 22046
Ph: (703)237-8616
Fax: (703)533-1153
Co. E-mail: headquarters@theaeap.com
URL: http://www.theaeap.com
URL(s): www.naesaa.com. **Price:** $139, Members; $149, Non-members. **Frequency:** Annual. **Principal Exhibits:** Business education products and services. **Telecommunication Services:** headquarters@naesaa.com.

ASSOCIATIONS AND OTHER ORGANIZATIONS

20823 ▪ Canadian Carpet Institute (CCI)—Institut Canadien du Tapis
200-435 St. Laurent Blvd.
Ottawa, ON, Canada K1K 2Z8
Ph: (613)749-3265
Fax: (613)745-8753
Co. E-mail: info@canadiancarpet.org
URL: http://www.canadiancarpet.org
Contact: Walter Eckhardt, President
Description: Carpet manufacturers and suppliers. Seeks to advance the carpet and related industries. Facilitates exchange of information among members; serves as a clearinghouse on technical, regulatory, and maintenance issues relevant to carpeting; represents members' commercial and regulatory interests. **Founded:** 1963.

20824 ▪ Society of Cleaning and Restoration Technicians (SCRT)
4402 S Danville Dr.
Abilene, TX 79605
Ph: (800)949-4728
Fax: (325)692-1823
Co. E-mail: info@scrt.org
URL: http://www.scrt.org
Contact: Gary Glenn, President
Description: Professional on-site carpet and upholstery cleaners, firms, and suppliers. Provides a forum for the exchange of technical and procedural information, including catastrophe restoration data, updates on new chemicals and processes, and technical, management, sales, and production materials. Monitors and reports on events affecting the carpet cleaning industry. Conducts workshops. **Scope:** fibers, fabrics, production, sales, marketing, janitorial, inspections. **Founded:** 1970. **Subscriptions:** 7. **Publications:** *The Monitor; Technical* (5/year).

DIRECTORIES OF EDUCATIONAL PROGRAMS

20825 ▪ *Directory of Private Accredited Career Schools and Colleges of Technology*
Pub: Accrediting Commission of Career Schools and Colleges of Technology
Contact: Michale S. McComis, Executive Director
Released: On web page. **Price:** Free. **Description:** Covers 3900 accredited post-secondary programs that provide training programs in business, trade, and technical fields, including various small business endeavors. Entries offer school name, address, phone, description of courses, job placement assistance, and requirements for admission. Arrangement is alphabetical.

REFERENCE WORKS

20826 ▪ *Carpet Cleaners Institute of the Northwest--Membership Roster*
Pub: Carpet Cleaners Institute of the Northwest
Contact: Dan Joner, President
URL(s): www.ccinw.org. **Released:** Annual; May. **Covers:** Approximately 330 member companies

involved in the carpet cleaning industry in Alberta, British Columbia, Idaho, Oregon, and Washington. **Entries include:** Company name, address, phone, owner name.

TRADE PERIODICALS

20827 ▪ *Cleaning & Restoration*
Pub: Restoration Industry Association
Contact: Frank L. Headen, President
E-mail: fheaden@firstrestoration.com
URL(s): www.restorationindustry.org/content/cr-magazine. **Released:** Monthly **Price:** $69, Nonmembers; $79, Nonmembers Canada; $99, Nonmembers international.

20828 ▪ *ICS Cleaning Specialist: Information for Today's Floor Care Professional*
Pub: Specialist Publications Inc.
URL(s): www.icsmag.com. **Ed:** Jeffrey Stouffer. **Released:** Monthly **Price:** Free.

20829 ▪ *National Floor Trends Magazine*
Pub: Specialist Publications Inc.
URL(s): www.ntlfloortrends.com/. **Ed:** Arpi Nalbandian, Jeff Golden. **Released:** Monthly **Price:** Free.

VIDEOCASSETTES/ AUDIOCASSETTES

20830 ▪ *Upholstering a Dining Room Chair*
RMI Media
1365 N. Winchester St.
Olathe, KS 66061-5880
Ph: (913)768-1696
Free: 800-745-5480
Fax: (800)755-6910
Co. E-mail: actmedia@act.org
URL: http://www.actmedia.com
Released: 1987. **Description:** Bonnie Enault demonstrates how to upholster two different types of dining room chairs. Specific instructions include how to remove old upholstering and how to measure, cut, and attach new fabric. **Availability:** VHS; 3/4 U.

CONSULTANTS

20831 ▪ Cleaning Consultant Services Inc. (CCS)
3693 E Marginal Way S
Seattle, WA 98134
Ph: (206)682-9748
Fax: (206)622-6876
Co. E-mail: wgriffin@cleaningconsultants.com
URL: http://www.cleaningbusiness.com
Contact: William R. Griffin, President
E-mail: wgriffin@cleaningconsultants.com
URL(s): www.cleaningbusiness.com. **Description:** Publishes books on floor care, carpet care, self-employment, window washing, custodial training and many other areas related to the cleaning industry. Reaches market through direct mail, reviews

and listings, telephone sales, ads, catalogs and trade shows. **Scope:** Provider of engineering and consulting services. It deals with claim and dispute resolution, program and material development, and cleaning services. **Founded:** 1973. **Publications:** "Raising the Bar with Science, Training and Upward Mobility," Jan, 2010; "Technology Revolutionizes the Cleaning Process "Cleaning for Health" is the New Mantra," Distribution Sales and Management Magazine, May, 2003; "Bill Griffin's Crystal Balls-Cleaning Trends in the Usa 2001," Floor Care is Hot in 2001," Mar, 2001; "Inclean Magazine (Australia), Feb, 2001; "Maintaining Swimming Pools, Spas, Whirlpool Tubs and Saunas," Executive House keeping, Feb, 2001; "Whats New with Floor Care," 2001. **Seminars:** Stone Maintenance Technician (SMT) IICRC Certification Course; Carpet Cleaning Technician; Apprentice/Basic Skills; Organizing Custodial Operations for Maximum Efficiency; How to Sell & Price Contract Cleaning; Starting a House cleaning Business; Rugs & Carpet Cleaning; How to Start and Operate a Successful Cleaning Business; Cleaning Schools in the 2000and Beyond; Bringing About and Working Through Change; Organizing Custodial Operations for Maximum Efficiency; Floor Care Technician (FCT)11 CPC Certified Course; Administering Cleaning Service Contracts. **Telecommunication Services:** ccs@cleaningconsultants.com; marketing@cleaningconsultants.com.

20832 ▪ Surface Technologies Inc. (STI)
18 Willotta Dr.
Suisun City, CA 94534-1446
Ph: (707)864-6313
Free: 800-241-2982
Contact: Richard E. Larson, President
Scope: Specializes in carpet, tile, wood, stone, and vinyl floor covering inspection and testing. Evaluates floor covering samples for durability, clean ability, and longevity of appearance. Trains hotel and other institutional personnel to maintain, clean, and repair floor coverings. Industries served include floor and wall covering and upholstery fabric manufacturers, as well as producers of all types of architectural surfaces. **Founded:** 1998. **Seminars:** Complaint Reduction Program; Selling Floor Covering Defensively; Turn Complaints into More Business; Presented to department stores and floor covering specialty stores.

FRANCHISES AND BUSINESS OPPORTUNITIES

20833 ▪ Chem-Dry Carpet Drapery & Upholstery Cleaning
Harris Research, Inc.
1530 N 1000 W
Logan, UT 84321
Ph: (435)890-1051
Free: 877-307-8233
Fax: (435)755-8490
Co. E-mail: sales@chemdry.com
URL: http://www.chemdry.com
Description: They offer carpet cleaning service. **No. of Franchise Units:** 2,150. **Founded:** 1977.. **Franchised:** 1978. **Equity Capital Needed:** $29,950-

$127,000. **Franchise Fee:** $15,000. **Royalty Fee:** $350/month. **Financial Assistance:** Limited in-house financing available. **Training:** Provides 5 days at headquarters, video training and ongoing support.

20834 ■ Chem-Dry Carpet and Upholstery Cleaning

Harris Research, Inc.
1530 N 1000 W
Logan, UT 84321
Ph: (435)890-1051
Free: 877-307-8233
Fax: (435)755-8490
Co. E-mail: sales@chemdry.com
URL: http://www.chemdry.com
Description: Specializes in the care of carpet, drapery, upholstery and most fabrics. **No. of Franchise Units:** 4,500. **Founded:** 1977.. **Franchised:** 1978. **Equity Capital Needed:** $25,000-$175,000, initial down payment $8,495. **Franchise Fee:** $12,950-$34,850. **Financial Assistance:** Yes. **Training:** 5 days in-house training, yearly National Convention, and ongoing operational support.

20835 ■ ChemDry Canada Ltd.

8472 Harvard Pl.
Chilliwack, BC, Canada V2P 7Z5
Free: 888-243-6379
Fax: (604)795-7071
Co. E-mail: franchisesales@chemdry.ca
URL: http://www.chemdry.ca
Description: Carpet and upholstery cleaning service. **No. of Franchise Units:** 77. **Franchised:** 1978. **Equity Capital Needed:** $20,000-$60,000 total investment; $20,000 startup capital required. **Franchise Fee:** $815/month. **Training:** Provides5 days training, including travel and accommodation.

20836 ■ Coit Cleaning and Restoration Services

897 Hinckley Rd.
Burlingame, CA 94010
Ph: (800)243-8797
Fax: (650)692-8397
Co. E-mail: franchise@coit.com
URL: http://www.coit.com
Description: Coit is a multi-service cleaning company, offering drapery cleaning, carpet cleaning, upholstery cleaning, area rug cleaning, air duct cleaning and more. **No. of Franchise Units:** 42. **No. of Company-Owned Units:** 8. **Founded:** 1950.. **Franchised:** 1962. **Equity Capital Needed:** $50,000-$145,000. **Franchise Fee:** $24,000-$40,000. **Financial Assistance:** Yes. **Training:** Includes 10 days in corporate office.

20837 ■ Creative Colors International

19015 S Jodi Rd., Ste. E
Mokena, IL 60448
Ph: (800)933-2656
Fax: (708)478-1636
Co. E-mail: campaign65@creativecolorsintl.com
URL: http://www.creativecolorsintl.com
Description: Specializes in providing services for the repair, coloring, cleaning, and restoration of leather, vinyl, cloth, velour, plastics and other upholstery surfaces and related services on a mobile basis primarily to commercial customers. These customers include auto dealerships, hotels, airports, and individuals. **No. of Franchise Units:** 72. **No. of Company-Owned Units:** 3. **Founded:** 1980.. **Franchised:** 1991. **Equity Capital Needed:** $50,000. **Franchise Fee:** $29,500. **Financial Assistance:** Yes. **Training:** An initial training course of 3 weeks is conducted at National Headquarters. In addition, a field representative will spend 1 week with franchise owner when business commences operation to establish accounts.

20838 ■ Duraclean International, Inc.

220 Campus Dr.
Arlington Heights, IL 60004
Ph: (800)251-7070
Fax: (847)704-7101
Co. E-mail: info@duraclean.com
URL: http://www.duraclean.com
Description: Carpet cleaning, ceiling & wall cleaning, water/fire/smoke damage restoration, janitorial, hard surface floor care, ventilation duct cleaning, high pressure washing, ultrasonic blind cleaning, mold remediation. **No. of Franchise Units:** 374. **No. of Company-Owned Units:** 20. **Founded:** 1930.. **Franchised:** 1945. **Equity Capital Needed:** $32,599-$88,999. **Franchise Fee:** $17,500. **Financial Assistance:** Yes. **Training:** Initial training provides training manuals, videotapes, schools, local hands-on assistance, magazines, bulletins, conventions and area meetings and ongoing support.

20839 ■ Heaven's Best Carpet & Upholstery Cleaning

M-CO Inc.
247 N 1st E
Rexburg, ID 83440
Ph: (208)359-1106
Fax: (208)359-1236
Description: Heaven's Best is a unique, low-moisture cleaning process which provides a great alternative to the traditional total saturation methods of cleaning. Our customers love our dry-in-one-hour process. All aspects of the business are covered during the training. All franchisee's must attend the training. **No. of Franchise Units:** 1,264. **Founded:** 1983. **Franchised:** 1983. **Equity Capital Needed:** $28,900-$65,000. **Franchise Fee:** $14,450. **Financial Assistance:** Yes. **Training:** Yes.

20840 ■ Interior Magic International, LLC

211 Cotton Grove Rd.
Lexington, NC 27292
Ph: (336)249-9976
Fax: (336)249-9978
Co. E-mail: info@myinteriormagic.com
URL: http://www.myinteriormagic.com
Description: Mobile business system that includes the most desirable combination of services available in the automotive reconditioning industry. We offer expert repair and re-dyeing of leather, vinyl, plastic, velour and carpet, as well as vapor steam clearing, permanent odor elimination, stain removal, and a specialized carpet protection system. Our customers include auto dealers, restaurants, hotels other commercial clients and individuals. **No. of Franchise Units:** 40. **Founded:** 2001.. **Franchised:** 2004. **Equity Capital Needed:** $17,800, includes start-up equipment and training. **Franchise Fee:** $14,900 and up. **Financial Assistance:** Yes. **Training:** Yes.

20841 ■ Langenwalter Carpet Dyeing

Lagenwalter Industries, Inc.
1111 Richfield Rd.
Placentia, CA 92670
Ph: (714)528-7610
Description: Complete carpet color correction, including bleach spots, sun fading, pet stains, food stains, punch and other discolorations. Also, complete color changes and full wall-to-wall carpet dyeing. **No. of Franchise Units:** 65. **No. of Company-Owned Units:** 2. **Founded:** 1972.. **Franchised:** 1980. **Equity Capital Needed:** $42,000 Minimum. **Franchise Fee:** $12,500. **Training:** Yes.

20842 ■ Modernistic Cleaning Services

Koppang Franchise Development Co.
1460 Rankin St.
Troy, MI 48083
Ph: (248)589-1700
Free: 877-567-7264
Fax: (248)589-2660
Description: Full service carpet and upholstery cleaning company. **No. of Franchise Units:** 4. **Founded:** 1972.. **Franchised:** 1999. **Equity Capital Needed:** $65,000. **Franchise Fee:** $30,000. **Financial Assistance:** Yes. **Training:** Yes.

20843 ■ Professional Carpet Systems, Inc.

4211 Atlantic Ave.
Raleigh, NC 27604
Ph: (919)875-8871
Free: 800-925-5055
Fax: (919)875-9855
Co. E-mail: info@procarpetssys.com
URL: http://www.professionalcarpetsystems.com
Description: Onsite carpet re-dyeing, servicing thousands of apartment complexes, hotels and motels worldwide. Other services include carpet cleaning, rejuvenation, repair, water and flood damage restoration and odor control. **No. of Franchise**

Units: 70. **Founded:** 1978.. **Franchised:** 1982. **Equity Capital Needed:** $20,000. **Franchise Fee:** $9,995. **Financial Assistance:** Yes. **Training:** 2 weeks in Raleigh, NC for initial training. Eleven 2 day sessions are held every year for additional training, most with industry certification available. In addition, we have periodic workshops and an annual convention. During the training program, franchisees gain hands-on experience.

20844 ■ Servpro

Servpro Industries, Inc.
801 Industrial Blvd.
Gallatin, TN 37066
Ph: (615)451-0600
Free: 800-826-9586
Fax: (615)451-1602
Co. E-mail: franchise@servpronet.com
URL: http://www.servpro.com
Description: A completely diversified cleaning and restoration business, with multiple income opportunities. The insurance restoration market (fire, smoke and water damage) is their main focus. Specialize in commercial & residential cleaning. **No. of Franchise Units:** 1,600. **Founded:** 1967.. **Franchised:** 1969. **Equity Capital Needed:** $133,050-$181,450. **Franchise Fee:** $42,000. **Training:** Intensive home study curriculum, manuals and videos. Provides 2 weeks training in state of the art national training facility, 1 week set up/opening assistance, and trainer assistance. Ongoing support, convention, regional and area meetings, formal business reviews, newsletters, bulletins, and more.

20845 ■ Sparkle Carpet Cleaning

Sparkle Development Co.
1222 S Main Ave.
Scranton, PA 18504
Ph: (570)344-4660
Free: 800-298-4660
Fax: (570)344-7076
Description: Cleaners of carpet and upholstery. **No. of Franchise Units:** 2. **No. of Company-Owned Units:** 5. **Founded:** 1981.. **Equity Capital Needed:** $10,000-$15,000. **Franchise Fee:** $5,000-$9,000. **Royalty Fee:** $75-150/month. **Training:** Yes.

20846 ■ Stanley Steemer Carpet Cleaner

Stanley Steemer International Inc.
5500 Stanley Steemer Pkwy.
Dublin, OH 43017
Ph: (614)764-2000
Free: 800-783-2637
Fax: (614)761-3176
URL: http://www.stanleysteemer.com
Description: Carpet and upholstery cleaning and other related services. **No. of Franchise Units:** 223. **No. of Company-Owned Units:** 73. **Equity Capital Needed:** $93,690-$221,175. **Franchise Fee:** $20,000-$100,000. **Royalty Fee:** 7%. **Financial Assistance:** Limited in-house and third party assistance available. **Training:** Provides 2 weeks training at headquarters, as well as various training offered throughout the year and ongoing support.

20847 ■ Steam Brothers Professional Cleaning and Restoration

Steam Brothers Inc.
P.O. Box 3036
Bismarck, ND 58502
Ph: (701)222-1263
Fax: (701)222-1372
Description: Offers services such as carpet, drapery and upholstery cleaning; fire, smoke and water damage restoration; furnace and air-duct cleaning; and acoustical ceiling cleaning. **No. of Franchise Units:** 23. **Founded:** 1977.. **Franchised:** 1984. **Equity Capital Needed:** $5,000 operating capital plus new or used van and truck mounted cleaning equipment. **Franchise Fee:** $16,000. **Training:** Offers training at headquarters in Bismarck, ND for 5 days. Training at franchisee's location is for 2 days.

Vending Machine Merchandising and Service Business

START-UP INFORMATION

20848 ■ *"A Self-Serving Opportunity" in Black Enterprise (Vol. 37, February 2007, No. 7, pp. 52)*
Pub: Earl G. Graves Publishing Co. Inc.
Ed: James C. Johnson. **Description:** Questions are answered regarding the startup of a vending machine business.

ASSOCIATIONS AND OTHER ORGANIZATIONS

20849 ■ **Canadian Automatic Merchandising Association (CAMA)—Association Canadienne d'Auto Distribution (ACAD)**
2233 Argentia Rd., Ste. 100
Mississauga, ON, Canada L5N 2X7
Ph: (905)826-7695
Free: 888-849-2262
Fax: (905)826-4873
Co. E-mail: info@vending-cama.com
URL: http://www.vending-cama.com
Contact: Amanda Curtis, Executive Director
Description: Corporations and individuals engaged in the vending industry. Promotes growth and development of the automatic merchandising market. Represents members' interests before industrial organizations, government agencies, and the public. **Telecommunication Services:** acurtis@vending-cama.com.

20850 ■ **National Automatic Merchandising Association (NAMA)**
20 N Wacker Dr., Ste. 3500
Chicago, IL 60606-3102
Ph: (312)346-0370
Fax: (312)704-4140
Co. E-mail: dgary@vending.org
URL: http://www.vending.org
Contact: Carla Balakgie, President
Description: Manufacturing and operating companies in the automatic vending machine industry; food service management firms; office coffee machine operators; suppliers of products and services. Compiles industry statistics. **Founded:** 1936. **Publications:** *National Automatic Merchandising Association-Directory of Members*; *National Automatic Merchandising Association-In Touch* (Quarterly); *National Automatic Merchandising Association--Directory of Members* (Annual). **Educational Activities:** OneShow (Annual); NAMA National Expo - National Automatic Merchandising Association (Annual); NAMA Spring Expo (Annual). **Awards:** Foundation Scholarship Program (Annual). **Telecommunication Services:** expo@vending.org.

20851 ■ **National Bulk Vendors Association (NBVA)**
1202 E Maryland Ave., Ste. 1K
Phoenix, AZ 85014-1342
Ph: (888)628-2872
Free: 888-NBV-AUSA

Fax: (480)302-5108
Co. E-mail: admin@nbva.org
URL: http://www.nbva.info
Contact: Steve Schechner, President
URL(s): www.nbva.org. **Description:** Manufacturers, distributors, and operators of bulk vending merchandise and equipment. **Founded:** 1950. **Educational Activities:** National Bulk Vendors Association Workshop (Annual).

REFERENCE WORKS

20852 ■ *Automatic Merchandiser--Blue Book Buyer's Guide Issue*
Pub: Cygnus Business Media
Contact: Rich Reiff, President
URL(s): www.vendingmarketwatch.comwww.cygnus.com. **Ed:** Elliot Maras. **Released:** Annual **Publication includes:** Suppliers of products, services, and equipment to the merchandise vending, contract foodservice, and office coffee service industries. **Entries include:** Company name, address, phone, names of executives, trade and brand names, and products or services offered. **Arrangement:** Classified by type of business. **Indexes:** Alphabetical, product.

20853 ■ *"AVT Featured on TD Waterhouse Market News Website and in Vending Times Magazine" in Benzinga.com (August 17, 2011)*
Pub: Benzinga.com
Ed: Benzinga Staff. **Description:** AVT Inc. was featured online and in an article reporting the firm's plan to install automated vending machines in high-profile areas including malls, office buildings, stadiums and arenas.

20854 ■ *"AVT Launches New ExpressPay Vending Systems" in Benzinga.com (July 13, 2011)*
Pub: Benzinga.com
Ed: Benzinga Staff. **Description:** AVT Inc. has developed a new high-tech vending system that features a touch screen interface and a cashless payment system so users can find what they want easily and pay using a credit card.

20855 ■ *"Buck-ing the Trend?' in Baltimore Business Journal (Vol. 28, August 13, 2010, No. 14, pp. 1)*
Pub: Baltimore Business Journal
Ed: Gary Haber. **Description:** Baltimore Orioles' new manager Buck Showalter has managed to win games for fans. However, not all businesses around Camden Yards were boosted by the Orioles' surge as street vendors complained of worsening business.

20856 ■ *"Cannabis Science Signs Exclusive and Non-Exclusive Agreement with Prescription Vending Machines" in Benzinga.com (October 29, 2011)*
Pub: Benzinga.com
Ed: Benzinga Staff. **Description:** Cannabis Science Inc., a biotech company developing pharmaceutical cannabis products has partnered with Prescription

Vending Machines Inc. and its principal Vincent Meddizadeh to provide industry specific consulting and advisory services to Cannabis Science.

20857 ■ *"Eagle's Wine Kiosk Is Area's 1st" in Pittsburgh Post-Gazette (October 28, 2010)*
Pub: Pittsburgh-Post Gazette
Ed: Bob Batz Jr. **Description:** Giant Eagle Market District store at Settlers Ridge opened the first self-serve wine kiosk in Western Pennsylvania. The kiosk will have a built-in breathalyzer panel to ensure safety.

20858 ■ *"Effort Is Growing to Offer Healthier Choices in Vending Machines" in Philadelphia Inquirer (July 29, 2011)*
Pub: Philadelphia Media Network Inc.
Ed: Don Sapatkin. **Description:** Since Boston's mayor announced a ban on the sale of all sugar sweetened beverages on city properties, it seems more cities, states, hospitals, businesses, and even park systems are following suit. Thus, vending machines are beginning to offer healthier snacks and drinks to consumers.

20859 ■ *"Essentially Organic Vending Takes Healthy Snacks to Ohio High School" in Entertainment Close-Up (September 13, 2011)*
Pub: Close-Up Media
Description: Essentially Organic Vending is offering students a healthy alternative for their snacking. The vending machines will be stocked with nutritious energy options.

20860 ■ *"EX3D to Launch In-Theater Vending Machines for Stylish RealD 3D Glasses" in Entertainment Close-Up (August 16, 2011)*
Pub: Close-Up Media
Description: Marchon3d has partnered with Cinemark and UltraStar Cinemas to install vending machines selling Marchon3D's line of patented, curved RealD 3D compatible eyeglasses.

20861 ■ *"H.I.G. Capital Announces Acquisition of Next Generation Vending" in Benzinga.com (October 29, 2011)*
Pub: Benzinga.com
Ed: Benzinga Staff. **Description:** H.I.G. Capital LLC, a leader in global private investments, acquired Next Generation Vending and Food Service Inc. Next Generation is a provider of vending services for corporate and institutional clients in Northeastern United States.

20862 ■ *"High-Tech Machines Show a New Age of Vending" in Wisconsin State Journal (October 14, 2011)*
Pub: Wisconsin State Journal
Ed: Barry Adams. **Description:** Vending machines are looking more like an iPad than the machines of the past. These high tech machines are seeing sharp rises in use.

20863 ■ *"IF Challenges Atlanta's Vending Monopoly" in Benzinga.com (July 28, 2011)*
Pub: Benzinga.com
Ed: Benzinga Staff. **Description:** A lawsuit was filed by The Institute for Justice to challenge Atlanta's

unconstitutional vending monopoly on behalf of two Atlanta street vendors.

20864 ■ "LCB Turning Off Wine Vending Machines" in Pittsburgh Post-Gazette (September 20, 2011)
Pub: PG Publishing Company
Ed: Tracie Mauriello. **Description:** Grocery store shoppers will no longer be able to purchase a bottle of wine from wine kiosks in Pennsylvania.

20865 ■ "Moooove Over, Sodas: Okaloosa to Get Dairy Vending Machines for Two Schools" in Northwest Florida Daily News (September 27, 2001)
Pub: Freedom Communications
Ed: Katie Tammen. **Description:** Two Okaloosa County high schools will be offering more lunch options by installing refrigerated vending machines featuring dairy-related food.

20866 ■ "National Automatic Merchandising Association Takes Vending on the Road" in Food and Beverage Close-Up (September 6, 2011)
Pub: Close-Up Media
Description: National Automatic Merchandising Association launched the new age of vending and is taking its machines, products and technology on the road to say thank you to loyal users of vending machines.

20867 ■ "A Parisian Vending Machine for Baguettes 24/7" in Benzinga.com ()
Pub: Benzinga.com
Ed: Benzinga Staff. **Description:** Jean-Louis Hecht has created a vending machine that offers fresh baguettes 24 hours a day, seven days a week.

20868 ■ "Research and Markets Adds Report: Vending Machines" in Travel and Leisure Close-Up (October 20, 2011)
Pub: Close-Up Media
Description: Research and Markets has added 'Vending Machines — Global Strategic Business Report' to its lineup. The report analyzes globally installed vending machines in US million dollars by the following product types: Beverage, Food, Cigarette, and Other Products (includes personal and health care products, contraceptives, books, magazines).

20869 ■ "Sheets Energy Strips Unveils New Vending Machines" in Food and Beverage Close-Up (August 12, 2011)
Pub: Close-Up Media
Description: Sheets Energy Strips is installing vending machines in malls, office buildings, stadiums and arenas in New York, New Jersey, Connecticut and Florida. These machines will offer 4 packs, 10 packs and Sheets branded hats and T-shirts.

20870 ■ "Sodexo Updates Healthy Vending Program" in Entertainment Close-Up (September 25, 2011)
Pub: Close-Up Media
Description: Sodexo launched its Your Health Your Way On-the-Go program for its vending machines across the nation.

20871 ■ "The Ultimate Vending Machine" in Benzinga.com (August 15, 2011)
Pub: Benzinga.com
Ed: Benzinga Staff. **Description:** Louis Hecht, a baker from Hombourg-Haut, France is selling fresh-baked bread in vending machines. Each machine holds 90 pre-cooked loaves which are warmed before being delivered to the customer.

20872 ■ Vending Times--Buyers Guide and Directory Issue
Pub: Vending Times Inc.
Contact: Alicia Lavay-Kertes, President
E-mail: alicia@vendingtimes.net
URL(s): www.vendingtimes.com. **Released:** Annual; Latest edition 2012. **Price:** $40, Individuals includes shipping and handling. **Publication includes:** Lists of manufacturers and suppliers of equipment and products used by vending machine industry operators, including product venders, juke boxes, pinball and other games; industry trade associations. **Entries include:** Company name, address, phone, names of key personnel, description of products. **Database includes:** Specifications of major vending machines. **Arrangement:** Classified by product or service.

20873 ■ "Vista-Based NCV Bought by Canteen Vending" in North County Times (October 18, 2011)
Pub: Lee Enterprises Inc.
Ed: Pat Maio. **Description:** Details of North Carolina-based Canteen Vending Services' acquisition of NCV Refreshment Services, are given.

20874 ■ "Working the Streets" in Baltimore Business Journal (Vol. 28, July 30, 2010, No. 12, pp. 1)
Pub: Baltimore Business Journal
Ed: Amanda Pino. **Description:** Reports show that street vendors are popping up on new corners in Baltimore, Maryland, with city-inspected stainless steel food carts in tow. Applications for street vending licenses shot up at the end of 2009 and into this summer. It is believed that pinning down the exact number of vendors operating at any one point is difficult.

STATISTICAL SOURCES

20875 ■ RMA Annual Statement Studies
Pub: Risk Management Association
Contact: Kevin M. Blakey, President
Released: Annual. **Price:** $175.00 2006-07 edition, $105.00. **Description:** Contains composite balance sheets and income statements for more than 360

industries, including the accounting, auditing, and bookkeeping industries. Also contains five years of comparative historical data for discerning trends. Includes 16 commonly used ratios, computed for most of the size groupings for nearly every industry.

20876 ■ The Vended Foods Market
Pub: Rector Press, Ltd.
Contact: Lewis Sckolnick, President
Released: 2009. **Price:** Contact Rector Press.

TRADE PERIODICALS

20877 ■ Automatic Merchandiser: The Monthly Management Magazine for Vending and OCS Professionals
Pub: Cygnus Business Media
Contact: Rich Reiff, President
URL(s): www.vendingmarketwatch.com/www.cygnusb2b.com/PropertyPub.cfm?PropertyID=100.
Released: Monthly **Price:** Free.

TRADE SHOWS AND CONVENTIONS

20878 ■ Atlantic Coast Exposition - Showcasing the Vending and Food Service Industry
South Carolina Automatic Merchandising Association
PO Box 3159
Durham, NC 27715-3159
Ph: (919)383-0044
Fax: (919)383-0035
URL(s): atlanticcoastexpo.com. **Frequency:** Annual. **Audience:** Vending, food service, and OCS personnel. **Principal Exhibits:** Vending machines, office coffee service equipment, food stuffs, and related goods and services. **Telecommunication Services:** info@atlanticcoastexpo.com.

FRANCHISES AND BUSINESS OPPORTUNITIES

20879 ■ Protocol, LLC.
2110 Cheshire Way, Ste. A
Greensboro, NC 27405
Ph: (336)553-0755
Free: 800-227-5336
Fax: (336)553-0756
Co. E-mail: customerservice@protocolvending.com
URL: http://www.protocolvending.com
Description: Business opportunity in vending machine distributorships. **No. of Franchise Units:** 40,000. **Founded:** 1987.. **Franchised:** 1996. **Equity Capital Needed:** $10,200-$22,000. **Franchise Fee:** $500. **Financial Assistance:** Limited in-house financing available. **Training:** 1 day at headquarters, periodically onsite, 3 day annual convention with ongoing support.

ASSOCIATIONS AND OTHER ORGANIZATIONS

20880 ■ **Entertainment Merchants Association (EMA)**
16530 Ventura Blvd., Ste. 400
Encino, CA 91436-4551
Ph: (818)385-1500
Fax: (818)933-0910
Co. E-mail: emaoffice@entmerch.org
URL: http://www.entmerch.org
Contact: Crossan Andersen, President

Description: Retailers and distributors of videocassettes and videodiscs; associate members are major studios or independent companies that produce video programming and manufacturers of video games, accessories, and other goods and services for the video software industry. Represents and acts as spokesperson for the video software merchandising industry. Conducts statistical survey of video retailing; offers legal counsel representing members' interests in Washington, DC. Offers seminars on management and inventory control. **Founded:** 1981. **Publications:** *VSDA Video Voice* (Monthly). **Educational Activities:** East Coast Video Show. **Awards:** DVD Certification Program; DVD Technical Awards (Annual); EMA Retailer of the Year (Annual); Home Entertainment Awards (Annual).

20881 ■ **InfoComm International**
11242 Waples Mill Rd., Ste. 200
Fairfax, VA 22030
Ph: (703)273-7200
Free: 800-659-7469
Co. E-mail: customerservice@infocomm.org
URL: http://www.infocomm.org
Contact: Greg Jeffreys, President

Description: Represents for-profit individuals and organizations that derive revenue from the commercialization or utilization of communications technology. Ensures the credibility and desirability of its members' products and services by representing the communications industry to the public, business, education, and governments. **Founded:** 1939. **Publications:** *ICIA Membership Directory* (Annual); *Info-Community News* (Quarterly). **Awards:** Distinguished Achievement Award; ICIA Achievement Awards (Annual).

REFERENCE WORKS

20882 ■ *"Are Movie Theaters Doomed?"* in *Business Horizons (November-December 2007, pp. 491)*
Pub: Elsevier Technology Publications

Ed: Jon Silver, John McDonnell. **Description:** Theater operators must embrace new technologies and more diverse target markets if they are to stem the decline in theatergoers. Movie theaters remain highly vulnerable to trends in the home entertainment industry.

20883 ■ *"Beyond YouTube: New Uses for Video, Online and Off"* in *Inc. (October 2007, pp. 53-54)*
Pub: Gruner & Jahr USA Publishing

Ed: Leah Hoffmann. **Description:** Small companies are using video technology for embedding messages into email, broadcasting live interactive sales and training seminars, as well as marketing campaigns. Experts offer insight into producing and broadcasting business videos.

20884 ■ *"Blockbuster Launches Internet Movie Downloads to Compete Against Netflix, Others"* in *Chicago Tribune (December 3, 2008)*
Pub: McClatchy-Tribune Information Services

Ed: Eric Benderoff. **Description:** Blockbuster Inc., the DVD rental giant, has launched a new service that delivers movies to their customer's homes via the Internet in an attempt to compete against Netflix and other competitors.

20885 ■ *Bowker's Complete Video Directory*
Pub: R.R. Bowker L.L.C.

URL(s): www.bowker.com. **Released:** Annual; Latest edition March, 2011. **Price:** $595, Individuals hardcover. **Covers:** In four volumes, over 250,000 theatrical and nontheatrical videocassette titles (Vols. 1 and 2: Entertainment, Vols. 3 and 4 educational special interest). **Entries include:** Video title, date released, supplier name, cast, producer/director name, suggested list price, description of contents. **Arrangement:** Alphabetical. **Indexes:** Volumes 1-3--Title; Volumes 1 and 2--Genre, series, laser or videodisc, 8mm, closed-caption video, international standards, manufacturers and distributors, services and suppliers, entertainment; Volume 1--Spanish-language video, award-winning video, cast/director; Volumes 3 and 4--Education/special interest.

20886 ■ *Exceptional Service, Exceptional Profit: The Secrets of Building a Five-Star Customer Service Organization*
Pub: AMACOM

Ed: Leonard Inghilleri, Micah Solomon. **Released:** April 1, 2010. **Price:** $21.95. **Description:** Team of insiders share exclusive knowledge of the loyalty-building techniques pioneered by the world's most successful service leaders, including brick-and-mortar stars such as The Ritz-Carlton and Lexus and online success stories such as Netflix and CD Baby.

20887 ■ *"For DVD Company, No Extra Innings: Capturing a Season Takes Fast Work"* in *Boston Business Journal (Vol. 27, December 7, 2007)*
Pub: American City Business Journals Inc.

Ed: Terry Lefton. **Description:** Details of the development of MLB's annual World Series film by MLB Productions are discussed. The company is compelled to produce the film in a short period of time due to a promised November 27, 2007 delivery date. According to Elizabeth Scott, MLB vice president of programming and business affairs, she was concerned about the things that could directly affect sales.

20888 ■ *"iMozi Integrates Esprida LiveControl for Advanced DVD Kiosk Hardware"* in *Wireless News (December 20, 2010)*
Pub: Close-Up Media Inc.

Description: Provider of self-service entertainment technology, iMozi Canada has partnered with Esprida to make its automated DVD Kiosk solutions Esprida-enabled. Esprida develops remote device management solutions and will offer enhanced capabilities and to improve customer experience for users.

20889 ■ *International Television and Video Almanac*
Pub: Quigley Publishing Co.

Contact: William J. Quigley, President
URL(s): quigleypublishing.com/. **Ed:** Eileen Quigley. **Released:** Annual; January; latest edition 2013. **Price:** $235, Individuals. **Covers:** "Who's Who in Motion Pictures and Television and Home Video," television networks, major program producers, major group station owners, cable television companies, distributors, firms serving the television and home video industry, equipment manufacturers, casting agencies, literary agencies, advertising and publicity representatives, television stations, associations, list of feature films produced for television; statistics, industry's year in review, award winners, satellite and wireless cable provider, primetime programming, video producers, distributors, wholesalers. **Entries include:** Generally, company name, address, phone; manufacturer and service listings may include description of products and services and name of contact; producing, distributing, and station listings include additional detail, and contacts for cable and broadcast networks. **Arrangement:** Classified by service or activity. **Indexes:** Full.

20890 ■ *"Netflix Gets No Respect"* in *Barron's (Vol. 89, July 27, 2009, No. 30, pp. 26)*
Pub: Dow Jones & Co., Inc.

Ed: Tiernan Ray. **Description:** Netflix met expectations when they announced their second quarter sales but their shares still fell by almost 10 percent. Analysts say their entry into the 'streaming video' business is a mixed bag since customers are increasingly buying the cheaper monthly plan and this is dragging the economics of the business.

20891 ■ *"Netflix vs. Blockbuster"* in *Inc. (October 2007, pp. 32)*
Pub: Gruner & Jahr USA Publishing

Description: Nexflix, the mail-order DVD rental service, is losing market share to Blockbuster, even after matching prices to that of its competitors. Entrepreneurs are asked how they would run Netflix to gain back market share.

20892 ■ *"Public Media Works to Launch DVD Kiosk Operations in Toronto, Canada"* in *Internet Wire (November 15, 2010)*
Pub: Comtex

Description: Public Media Works Inc. along with its EntertainmentXpress Inc., have partnered with Spot Venture Distribution Inc. and Signifi Solutions Inc., both headquartered in Toronto, Canada, to manage and expand the Spot DVD movie and game kiosk business in greater Toronto and other Canadian locations.

20893 ■ *Video Source Book*
Pub: Cengage Learning Inc.
Contact: Ronald Dunn, President
URL(s): www.gale.cengage.com. **Released:** Annual; Latest edition 48th; October, 2011. **Price:** $825, Individuals. **Covers:** Approximately 160,000 videos covering more than 130,000 complete programs available from more than 2,100 distributors. **Entries include:** Video title, release year, description, run time, format, audience, MPAA rating, credits, producer, awards, distributor, price. Distributor's address and phone are given in a separate list. **Arrangement:** Alphabetical. **Indexes:** Subject, cast, special formats, distributor, awards, alternate title.

STATISTICAL SOURCES

20894 ■ *RMA Annual Statement Studies*
Pub: Risk Management Association
Contact: Kevin M. Blakey, President
Released: Annual. **Price:** $175.00 2006-07 edition, $105.00. **Description:** Contains composite balance sheets and income statements for more than 360 industries, including the accounting, auditing, and bookkeeping industries. Also contains five years of comparative historical data for discerning trends. Includes 16 commonly used ratios, computed for most of the size groupings for nearly every industry.

TRADE PERIODICALS

20895 ■ *Home Media Retailing*
Contact: Thomas K. Arnold, Publisher
URL(s): www.homemediamagazine.com. **Released:** Weekly **Price:** $49.99, Individuals print; $79.99, Canada and Mexico print; $99.99, Elsewhere print.

20896 ■ *Variety: The International Entertainment Weekly*
Pub: Reed Business Information
Contact: Jeff Greisch, President
URL(s): www.reedbusiness.com/us.html. **Ed:** Tim Gray. **Released:** Weekly; 50/yr. **Price:** $259, Individuals; $25, Individuals monthly.

20897 ■ *Video Watchdog: The Perfectionist's Guide to Fantastic Video*
Pub: Video Watchdog
URL(s): www.videowatchdog.com. **Ed:** Tim Lucas.
Released: Monthly **Price:** $48, Individuals bulk mail - U.S.; $57, Individuals 1st class - U.S.; $69, Other countries economy; $78, Other countries airmail.

TRADE SHOWS AND CONVENTIONS

20898 ■ *VSDA's Home Entertainment*
Home Entertainment Events
201 Sandpointe Ave., Ste. 500
Santa Ana, CA 92707
Free: 800-854-3112
Fax: (714)513-8848
URL: http://www.homemediaexpo.com
URL(s): www.digmedia.org. **Frequency:** Annual **Audience:** Video/DVD retailers (trade only). **Principal Exhibits:** Re-recorded video software, computer software for video retailers, accessory products for retailers and manufacturers, and trade publications. **Telecommunication Services:** info@digmedia.org.

COMPUTERIZED DATABASES

20899 ■ *BaselineFT's In Production Database*
3415 S Sepulveda Blvd., Ste. 200
Los Angeles, CA 90034
Ph: (310)482-3400
Free: 800-858-3669
Fax: (310)393-7799
URL: http://www.baselineresearch.com
Availability: Online: Baseline LLC. **Type:** Full-text.

LIBRARIES

20900 ■ American Film Institute - Louis B. Mayer Library
2021 N. Western Ave.
Box 27999
Los Angeles, CA 90027-1657
Ph: (323)856-7654

Fax: (323)856-7803
Co. E-mail: library@afi.com
URL: http://www.afi.com/about/library.aspx
Contact: Caroline Sisneros, Librarian
Scope: Moving pictures, television, video, cable, satellite. **Services:** Copying; indexing (microfiche); library open to the public. **Founded:** 1969. **Holdings:** 14,000 books; 900 bound periodical volumes; 6000 motion picture and television scripts; 44 oral history transcripts; 535 seminar transcripts; 600 seminar audiotapes; 75 reels of microfilm. **Subscriptions:** 100 journals and other serials (approximately); 5 newspapers.

20901 ■ Jerome Hill Library
32 2nd Ave.
New York, NY 10003-8631
Ph: (212)505-5181
Fax: (212)477-2714
Co. E-mail: robert@anthologyfilmarchives.org
URL: http://anthologyfilmarchives.org
Contact: Robert Haller, Director, Collections
Scope: History of cinema, avant-garde film, video, performance art. **Services:** Copying; library open to the public by appointment. **Founded:** 1970. **Holdings:** 10,000 books; 250 bound periodical series; 650 magnetic tapes; 1100 stills files (arranged by director); 450 film and video vertical Organization files; 2600 individual vertical files; audiotapes of lectures; International publications and periodicals; manuscripts; letters; fil stills and audio recordings. **Subscriptions:** 300 journals and other serials.

20902 ■ Hollywood Film Archive Library
8391 Beverly Blvd. PMB 321
Hollywood, CA 90048
Ph: (323)655-4968
Co. E-mail: cabaret66@aol.com
URL: http://hfarchive.com
Contact: D. Richard Baer, Director
Scope: Motion pictures, television, video. **Services:** Library open to the public by appointment only. **Founded:** 1972. **Holdings:** 2400 volumes; 6000 motion picture stills; Monthly Film Bulletin, 1934 to present; Motion Picture Exhibitor, 1931-1972; Motion Picture Herald, 1944-1960; Boxoffice, 1960 to present.

ASSOCIATIONS AND OTHER ORGANIZATIONS

20903 ■ Accreditation Council on Optometric Education (ACOE)
c/o American Optometric Association
243 N Lindbergh Blvd., 1st Fl.
St. Louis, MO 63141-7851
Ph: (314)991-4100
Fax: (314)991-4101
Co. E-mail: accredit@aoa.org
URL: http://www.aoa.org/x5153.xml
Contact: J. Bart Campbell, Chairman
Description: Accrediting body for professional Optometric Degree (O.D.) programs (examination, diagnosis, and treatment and management of diseases and disorders of the vision system, the eyes and associated structures as well as diagnosis of related systemic conditions), paraoptometric educational programs, and optometric residency programs. Members are appointed by the president of the American Optometric Association. Works to ensure the quality of optometric education by establishing and applying valid educational standards and announces list of accredited programs. **Founded:** 1934. **Educational Activities:** Accreditation Council on Optometric Education Meeting (Annual); Accreditation Council on Optometric Education Meeting (Annual).

20904 ■ American Academy of Optometry (AAO)
6110 Executive Blvd., Ste. 506
Bethesda, MD 20852
Ph: (321)710-3937
Free: 800-368-6263
Fax: (407)893-9890
Co. E-mail: aof@aaoptom.org
URL: http://www.aaopt.org
Contact: Dr. Karla Zadnik, President
Description: Represents optometrists, educators, and scientists interested in optometric education, and standards of care in visual problems. Conducts continuing education for optometrists and visual scientists. Sponsors 4-day annual meeting. **Publications:** *Optometry & Vision Science; Geographic Directory of Members; Eye Mail Monthly* (Monthly); *Optometry and Vision Science* (Monthly); *Optometry and Vision Science--Geographical Directory, American Academy of Optometry Issue* (Biennial). **Educational Activities:** American Academy of Optometry (Annual); American Academy of Optometry Conference (Annual). **Awards:** Garland W. Clay Award; Eminent Service Award; William Feinbloom Award; Glenn A. Fry Lecture Award; Honorary and Life Fellowships; Charles F. Prentice Medal; Founder's Award; VISTAKON Research Grants; Carol C. Koch Award (Annual); Charles F. Prentice Medal (Annual); Founder's Award (Annual); Garland W. Clay Award (Annual); Glenn A. Fry Award (Annual); Julius Neumueller Award (Annual); William Feinbloom Award (Annual); The William C. Ezell Fellowships; Terrance Ingraham Pediatric Optometry Residency Awards; Antoinette M. Molinari Memorial Scholarships; VISTAKON Research Grants; VSP Research Grants; Carel

C. Koch Memorial Medal Award; Julius F. Neumueller Award in Optics; Terrance Ingraham Pediatric Optometry Residency Award; VISTAKON George Mertz and Sheldon Wechsler Residency Awards. **Telecommunication Services:** aaoptom@aaoptom.org.

20905 ■ American Board of Opticianry (ABO)
6506 Loisdale Rd., Ste. 209
Springfield, VA 22150
Ph: (703)719-5800
Free: 800-296-1379
Fax: (703)719-9144
Co. E-mail: mail@abo-ncle.org
URL: http://www.abo-ncle.org
Description: Provides uniform standards for dispensing opticians by administering the National Opticianry Competency Examination and by issuing the Certified Optician Certificate to those passing the exam. Administers the Master in Ophthalmic Optics Examination and issues certificates to opticians at the advanced level passing the exam. Maintains records of persons certified for competency in eyeglass dispensing. Adopts and enforces continuing education requirements; assists and encourages state licensing boards in the use of the National Opticianry Competency Examination for licensure purposes. **Founded:** 1979.

20906 ■ American Optometric Association (AOA)
243 N Lindbergh Blvd.
St. Louis, MO 63141
Ph: (314)991-4100
Free: 800-365-2219
Fax: (314)991-4101
Co. E-mail: rlhopping@aoa.org
URL: http://www.aoa.org
Contact: Dori M. Carlson, President
E-mail: dmcarlson@aoa.org
Description: Professional association of optometrists, students of optometry, and paraoptometric assistants and technicians. Purposes are: to improve the quality, availability, and accessibility of eye and vision care; to represent the optometric profession; to help members conduct their practices; to promote the highest standards of patient care. Monitors and promotes legislation concerning the scope of optometric practice, alternate health care delivery systems, health care cost containment, Medicare, and other issues relevant to eye/vision care. Supports the International Library, Archives and Museum of Optometry which includes references on ophthalmic and related sciences with emphasis on the history and socioeconomic aspects of optometry. Operates Vision U.S.A. program, which provides free eye care to the working poor, and the InfantSEE program, which provides free vision assessments for infants between six and twelve months of age. Conducts specialized education programs; operates placement service; compiles statistics. Maintains museum. Conducts Seal of Acceptance Program. **Scope:** vision, eye care, optometry. **Founded:** 1898. **Subscriptions:** 8500 archival material audiovisuals books clippings periodicals. **Publications:** *Optometry: Journal of the American Optometric Association* (Monthly). **Educational Activities:** American Optometric As-

sociation Congress (Annual). **Awards:** Apollo Award (Annual); Distinguished Service Award (Annual); National Optometrist of the Year Award (Annual); Paraoptometric of the Year Award (Annual); Young Optometrist of the Year Award (Annual); Apollo Award; Distinguished Service Award; Optometrist of the Year Award; Young Optometrist of the Year (Annual).

20907 ■ American Optometric Foundation (AOF)
2909 Fairgreen St.
Orlando, FL 32803
Ph: (321)710-3937
Fax: (407)893-9890
Co. E-mail: aof@aaoptom.org
URL: http://www.aaopt.org/aof/about/index.asp
Contact: Catherine S. Amos, President
Description: Optometrists, optometric organizations, corporations, and the public. Promotes research, education, literature, and professional advancement in the visual sciences. Supports fellowships in graduate research. **Founded:** 1947. **Publications:** *The Torch* (Quarterly). **Educational Activities:** American Academy of Optometry Meeting (Annual). **Awards:** Antoinette Molinari Memorial (Annual); Vincent Salierno Memorial Scholarship (Annual); Vistakon Research (Annual); William Ezell Fellowship (Annual); Antoinette Molinari Memorial Scholarship; Vincent Salierno Memorial Scholarship; Vistakon Research Grants.

20908 ■ American Optometric Student Association (AOSA)
243 N Lindbergh Blvd.
St. Louis, MO 63141
Ph: (314)983-4321
Fax: (314)991-4101
Co. E-mail: mburle@theaosa.org
URL: http://www.theaosa.org
Contact: Marlene Burle, Executive Director

URL(s): www.aoanet.org. **Description:** Optometric students, state optometric associations, and family members of optometric students. Collects updated information on progress in the optometry field. Provides members with opportunities to work in areas of health care need such as local community health projects, school curriculum changes, and health manpower legislation. Works to improve optometric education and health care for the general population. Maintains active liaison with other optometric associations. Conducts communications program. **Founded:** 1972. **Publications:** *AOSA Foresight: Optometry Looking Forward* (Semiannual); *Communicator* (9/year). **Educational Activities:** Optometry's Meeting (Annual). **Awards:** Raymond I. Myers Award (Annual); Student Award in Clinical Ethics (Annual).

20909 ■ Association of Regulatory Boards of Optometry (ARBO)
200 S College St., Ste. 2030
Charlotte, NC 28202
Ph: (704)970-2710

Fax: (704)970-2720
Co. E-mail: arbo@arbo.org
URL: http://www.arbo.org
Contact: Jerry Ritch, Chairman
Description: Represents the North American regulatory boards of optometry. Works to assist member licensing agencies in regulating the practice of optometry for the public welfare. **Founded:** 1919. **Publications:** *Directory of Boards of Optometry* (Annual). **Educational Activities:** Association of Regulatory Boards of Optometry Regional meeting.

20910 ■ Association of Schools and Colleges of Optometry (ASCO)
6110 Executive Blvd., Ste. 420
Rockville, MD 20852
Ph: (301)231-5944
Fax: (301)770-1828
Co. E-mail: carmstrong@optec.org
URL: http://www.opted.org/i4a/pages/index.
  cfm?pageid=1
Contact: Martin A. Wall, Executive Director
Description: Works to achieve excellence in optometric education and to helping its member schools/colleges prepare well-qualified graduates for entrance into the profession of optometry. Aims to serve the American public through the continued advancement and promotion of all aspects of academic optometry. **Founded:** 1941. **Publications:** *Faculty Directory; Faculty Survey Report* (Annual); *Optometric Education* (Quarterly); *Residency Online Directory; Student Survey Report* (Annual); *Optometric Education; Faculty Directory of the Schools and Colleges of Optometry.* **Educational Activities:** Association of Schools and Colleges of Optometry Meeting (Annual); Special Interest Groups Workshop/Business Meetings (Annual). **Awards:** Dr. Jack Bennett Award (Periodic); CIBA/ASCO Student Award in Clinical Ethics (Annual); CIBA Vision Guest Lecturer Program (Annual); Dr. Lester Janoff Award for Writing Excellence (Annual). **Telecommunication Services:** mwall@opted.org.

20911 ■ Association of Vision Science Librarians (AVSL)
University of Michigan
1000 Wall St.
Ann Arbor, MI 48105
Ph: (734)763-9468
Fax: (734)936-9050
Co. E-mail: djmatthews@scco.edu
URL: http://www.lhl.uab.edu/avsl
Contact: Ms. DJ Matthews, Chairperson
Description: Works to foster collective and individual acquisition and dissemination of vision science information. Improves services for persons seeking vision science information. Develops standards among member-affiliated libraries. **Founded:** 1968. **Publications:** *International Directory of Members* (3/year). **Educational Activities:** Association of Vision Science Librarians Meeting (Annual); MLA SIG Meeting (Annual).

20912 ■ Better Vision Institute (BVI)
c/o Vision Council of America
225 Reinekers Ln., Ste. 700
Alexandria, VA 22314
Ph: (703)548-4560
Fax: (703)548-4580
Co. E-mail: ezb@thevisioncouncil.org
URL: http://www.thevisioncouncil.org/bvi
Contact: Paul E. Michelson, Chairman
Description: Advisory council of the Vision Council of America. Carried out in consultation with a board of eye care professionals who inform the public of the need for more adequate vision care. **Founded:** 1929. **Publications:** *BVI Perspective.*

20913 ■ Canadian Association of Optometrists (CAO)—Association Canadienne des Optometristes
234 Argyle Ave.
Ottawa, ON, Canada K2P 1B9
Ph: (613)235-7924
Free: 888-263-4676

Fax: (613)235-2025
Co. E-mail: info@opto.ca
URL: http://opto.ca
Contact: Glenn Campbell, Executive Director
Description: The mission of the Canadian Association of Optometrists is to represent the profession of Optometry; to enhance the quality, availability, and accessibility of eye, vision, and related health care; to enhance and promote the independent, and ethical decision-making of its members; and to assist Doctors of Optometry in practicing successfully in accordance with the highest standards of patient care. **Scope:** eye care. **Founded:** 1941. **Publications:** *CJO* (Quarterly); *In Touch* (Monthly). **Awards:** CO-ETF (Annual).

20914 ■ *Canadian Journal of Ophthalmology*
610-1525 Carling Ave.
Ottawa, ON, Canada K1Z 8R9
Ph: (613)729-6779
Fax: (613)729-7209
Co. E-mail: cos@eyesite.ca
URL: http://www.eyesite.ca
Contact: Jennifer Brunet-Colvey, Chief Executive Officer
Released: Bimonthly **Price:** C$125, in Canada.

20915 ■ Canadian Ophthalmological Society (COS)—Societe Canadienne d'Ophthalmologie
610-1525 Carling Ave.
Ottawa, ON, Canada K1Z 8R9
Ph: (613)729-6779
Fax: (613)729-7209
Co. E-mail: cos@eyesite.ca
URL: http://www.eyesite.ca
Contact: Jennifer Brunet-Colvey, Chief Executive Officer
Description: Works to ensure the provision of optimal eye care to all Canadians by promoting excellence in ophthalmology and providing services to support its members in practice. **Founded:** 1937. **Publications:** *Canadian Journal of Ophthalmology* (Bimonthly).

20916 ■ *CJO*
234 Argyle Ave.
Ottawa, ON, Canada K2P 1B9
Ph: (613)235-7924
Free: 888-263-4676
Fax: (613)235-2025
Co. E-mail: info@opto.ca
URL: http://opto.ca
Contact: Glenn Campbell, Executive Director
Released: Quarterly

20917 ■ College of Optometrists in Vision Development
215 W Garfield Rd., Ste. 210
Aurora, OH 44202
Ph: (330)995-0718
Free: 888-268-3770
Fax: (330)995-0719
Co. E-mail: info@covd.org
URL: http://www.covd.org
Contact: Ms. Pamela R. Happ, Executive Director
Description: Optometrists involved in developmental vision care and vision therapy with emphasis on visual information processing in visually related learning problems. Seeks to establish a body of practitioners who are knowledgeable in functional and developmental concepts of vision, to insure that the public will receive continually improving vision care; to enable members to maintain the highest standards of professional knowledge and competency; to educate and encourage optometrists to qualify for membership and fellowship in the college; to certify optometrists skilled in this specialty. Conducts national educational programs and public information programs. **Publications:** *Optometry and Vision Development Journal* (Quarterly); *Visions Newsletter* (Bimonthly); *E-mail Newsletter Briefs* (Weekly); *Membership Directory and Desk Reference* (Annual); *College of Optometrists in Vision Development-- Membership Directory* (Annual). **Educational Activities:** College of Optometrists in Vision Development

Annual Meeting (Annual). **Awards:** A.M. Skeffington Award (Annual); G.N. Getman Award (Annual); Presidents Award (Annual).

20918 ■ Contact Lens Manufacturers Association (CLMA)
PO Box 29398
Lincoln, NE 68529
Ph: (402)465-4122
Free: 800-344-9060
Fax: (402)465-4187
Co. E-mail: clmassociation@aol.com
URL: http://www.clma.net
Contact: Mr. Al Vaske, President
Description: Represents contact lens laboratories, material, solution and equipment manufacturers in the United States and abroad. Aims to increase awareness and utilization of custom-manufactured contact lenses. **Founded:** 1961. **Publications:** *Contact Lens Manufacturers Association--Member Directory* (Annual). **Educational Activities:** Contact Lens Manufacturers Association Conference (Annual). **Awards:** Dr. Joseph Dallos Award; Honorary Recognition Award; Trailblazers Award; Leonardo da Vinci Award; Creative Design and Process Award (Periodic); Dr. Joseph Dallos Award (Annual); Honorary Recognition Award (Annual); Industry Enhancement Award (Annual); Lab Technician of the Year (Annual); Leonardo da Vinci Award (Periodic); Trailblazers Award (Annual); GP Lens Practitioner of the Year (Annual). **Telecommunication Services:** c_pantle@sbcglobal.net.

20919 ■ *In Touch*
234 Argyle Ave.
Ottawa, ON, Canada K2P 1B9
Ph: (613)235-7924
Free: 888-263-4676
Fax: (613)235-2025
Co. E-mail: info@opto.ca
URL: http://opto.ca
Contact: Glenn Campbell, Executive Director
Released: Monthly

20920 ■ National Academy of Opticianry (NAO)
8401 Corporate Dr., Ste. 605
Landover, MD 20785
Ph: (301)577-4828
Free: 800-229-4828
Fax: (301)577-3880
Co. E-mail: info@nao.org
URL: http://www.nao.org
Contact: Gaye Wilson, President
Description: Offers review courses for national certification and state licensure examinations to members. Maintains speakers' bureau and Career Progression Program. **Founded:** 1963. **Publications:** *Academy Newsletter* (Quarterly); *Ophthalmic Dispensing Review Book.* **Awards:** Beverly Myers Achievement Award (Annual); Hall of Fame (Annual).

20921 ■ National Association of Vision Professionals (NAVP)
c/o Michele D. Hartlove
1775 Church St. NW
Washington, DC 20036
Ph: (202)234-1010
Co. E-mail: mhartlove@usa.net
URL: http://visionpros.org
Contact: Jeff Robinson, President
Description: Individuals responsible for or connected with vision conservation and eye health programs in public or private agencies and institutions. Serves as a forum for ideas and programs, cooperates with other agencies, and promotes professional standards. Certifies vision screening personnel. **Founded:** 1978. **Publications:** *NAVP Newsletter.*

20922 ■ National Board of Examiners in Optometry (NBEO)
200 S College St., No. 2010
Charlotte, NC 28202
Ph: (704)332-9565
Free: 800-969-EXAM

Fax: (704)332-9568
Co. E-mail: nbeo@optometry.org
URL: http://www.optometry.org
Contact: Jack Terry, Executive Director
Description: Administers entry-level criterion-referenced credentialing examinations to students and graduates of accredited schools and colleges of optometry for use by individual state licensing boards. Provides other evaluation, assessment, and survey services to the profession. **Founded:** 1951. **Publications:** *Test Points* (3/year).

20923 ■ National Contact Lens Examiners (NCLE)
6506 Loisdale Rd., Ste. 209
Springfield, VA 22150
Ph: (703)719-5800
Fax: (703)719-9144
Co. E-mail: mail@abo-ncle.org
URL: http://www.abo.org
Description: Serves as National certifying agency promoting continued development of opticians and technicians as contact lens fitters by formulating standards and procedures for determination of entry-level competency. Assists in the continuation, development, administration, and monitoring of a national Contact Lens Registry Examination (CLRE), which verifies entry-level competency of contact lens fitters. Issues certificates. Activities include: maintaining records of those certified in contact lens fitting; encouraging state occupational licensing and credentialing agencies to use the CLRE for licensure purposes; identifying contact lens dispensing education needs as a result of findings of examination programs; disseminating information to sponsors of contact lens continuing education programs. **Founded:** 1979.

20924 ■ National Optometric Association (NOA)
5009 Beatties Ford Rd., Ste. 107, No. 278
Charlotte, NC 28216
Free: 877-394-2020
Co. E-mail: info@nationaloptometricassociation.com
URL: http://nationaloptometricassociation.com
Contact: Dr. Vicki L. Hughes, President
Description: Represents optometrists dedicated to increasing awareness of the status of eye/vision health in the minority community and the national community at-large. Strives to make known the impact of the eye/vision dysfunction on the effectiveness and productivity of citizens and the academic proficiency of students. Conducts national minority recruiting programs, job placement, assistance programs for graduates, practitioners, and optometric organizations, and the promotion of delivery of care. Maintains speakers' bureau. Offers specialized education program. **Founded:** 1969. **Educational Activities:** National Optometric Association Convention (Annual). **Awards:** Cave Award (Annual); Founder's Award (Annual); Optometrist of the Year (Annual).

20925 ■ Opticians Association of America (OAA)
4064 E Fir Hill Dr.
Lakeland, TN 38002
Ph: (901)388-2423
Free: 800-443-8997
Fax: (901)388-2348
Co. E-mail: oaa@oaa.org
URL: http://www.oaa.org
Contact: Christopher M. Allen, Executive Director
Description: Retail dispensing opticians who fill prescriptions for glasses or contact lenses written by a vision care specialist. Works to advance the science of ophthalmic optics. Conducts research and educational programs. Maintains museum and speakers' bureau. Compiles statistics. **Scope:** opticianry. **Founded:** 1926. **Subscriptions:** 1000. **Publications:** *American Optician* (Quarterly); *American Optician* (Quarterly). **Educational Activities:** National Opticians Convention (Annual). **Awards:** Russell Fritz Memorial Scholarship (Annual).

20926 ■ Opticians Association of Canada (OAC)—Association des Opticiens du Canada
2706-83 Garry St.
Winnipeg, MB, Canada R3C 4J9

Ph: (204)982-6060
Free: 800-847-3155
Fax: (204)947-2519
Co. E-mail: canada@opticians.ca
URL: http://www.opticians.ca
Contact: Robert Dalton, Executive Director
Description: Dispensing opticians. Promotes advancement of opticianry. Works to safeguard members' economic and professional interests. Conducts educational programs. **Scope:** opticianry. **Founded:** 1989. **Subscriptions:** audio recordings books video recordings. **Publications:** *Vision* (Bimonthly).

20927 ■ Vision
2706-83 Garry St.
Winnipeg, MB, Canada R3C 4J9
Ph: (204)982-6060
Free: 800-847-3155
Fax: (204)947-2519
Co. E-mail: canada@opticians.ca
URL: http://www.opticians.ca
Contact: Robert Dalton, Executive Director
Released: Bimonthly

20928 ■ Vision Council
225 Reinekers Ln., Ste. 700
Alexandria, VA 22314
Ph: (703)548-4560
Free: 866-826-0290
Fax: (703)548-4580
Co. E-mail: info@thevisioncouncil.org
URL: http://www.thevisioncouncil.org
Contact: Edward E. Greene, Chief Executive Officer
Description: Trade association of optical industry companies that sponsor exhibits at industry trade shows. Works to serve the collective interests of the ophthalmic community; encourages the public to visit eye care practitioners regularly. Seeks to produce top quality trade shows. Conducts public educational programs. **Founded:** 1985. **Publications:** *The Vision Council Report* (Annual). **Educational Activities:** International Vision Expo (Semiannual).

20929 ■ Vision Council, Optical Lab Division
11096 Lee Hwy., Ste. A-101
Fairfax, VA 22030-5039
Ph: (703)359-2830
Free: 800-477-5652
Fax: (703)359-2834
Co. E-mail: ola@ola-labs.org
URL: http://www.ola-labs.org
Description: Represents independent, wholesale ophthalmic laboratories and suppliers serving the ophthalmic field. **Founded:** 1894. **Educational Activities:** The OLA (Annual). **Awards:** OLA Awards of Excellence (Annual).

DIRECTORIES OF EDUCATIONAL PROGRAMS

20930 ■ *Directory of Private Accredited Career Schools and Colleges of Technology*
Pub: Accrediting Commission of Career Schools and Colleges of Technology
Contact: Michale S. McComis, Executive Director
Released: On web page. **Price:** Free. **Description:** Covers 3900 accredited post-secondary programs that provide training programs in business, trade, and technical fields, including various small business endeavors. Entries offer school name, address, phone, description of courses, job placement assistance, and requirements for admission. Arrangement is alphabetical.

REFERENCE WORKS

20931 ■ *Contact Lens Manufacturers Association--Member Directory*
Pub: Contact Lens Manufacturers Association
Contact: Mr. Al Vaske, President
URL(s): www.clma.net/. **Released:** Annual; Latest edition 2012. **No. of Listings:** 130. **Entries include:** Company name, address, phone, name and title of contact. **Arrangement:** Alphabetical within membership categories. **Indexes:** Geographical.

20932 ■ *"SEEing an Opportunity; Golden's Eyewear Chain Has a National Vision" in Crain's Detroit Business (Vol. 24, January 7, 2008, No. 1)*
Pub: Crain Communications Inc. - Detroit
Ed: Sheena Harrison. **Description:** Richard Golden, who recently sold D.O.C. Optics Corporation is planning to build a new national eyewear chain called SEE Inc., which stands for Selective Eyewear Elements. SEE will sell expensive-looking glasses at lower prices than designer styles.

20933 ■ *"Visionary Riches" in Small Business Opportunities (Winter 2009)*
Pub: Entrepreneur Press
Contact: Perlman Neil, President
Description: Profile of Sterling Optical, which was included in a recent listing of 25 franchise high performers in The Wall Street Journal and is poised for mega-growth due to its offerings of professional eye exams, impeccable customer service, convenient locations and a great selection of eyewear.

STATISTICAL SOURCES

20934 ■ *RMA Annual Statement Studies*
Pub: Risk Management Association
Contact: Kevin M. Blakey, President
Released: Annual. **Price:** $175.00 2006-07 edition, $105.00. **Description:** Contains composite balance sheets and income statements for more than 360 industries, including the accounting, auditing, and bookkeeping industries. Also contains five years of comparative historical data for discerning trends. Includes 16 commonly used ratios, computed for most of the size groupings for nearly every industry.

TRADE PERIODICALS

20935 ■ *AAO News*
Pub: Alberta Association of Optometrists
Released: Bimonthly. **Price:** Included in membership. **Description:** Covers news of interest in the field of optometry in Canada.

20936 ■ *AOA News*
Pub: American Optometric Association
URL(s): www.aoa.org/x4794.xml. **Released:** 18/yr.

20937 ■ *Eyecare Business: Retail Strategies for Profitable Dispensing*
Pub: Wolters Kluwer Pharma Solutions Inc.
Contact: Bob Boucher, Chief Executive Officer
URL(s): www.eyecarebusiness.com/. **Released:** Monthly

20938 ■ *Eyewitness*
Pub: Contact Lens Society of America
Contact: Vicky Sheppard, President
URL(s): www.clsa.info. **Ed:** Ledonna buckner, Editor. **Released:** Quarterly **Price:** Included in membership. **Description:** Informs members of developments in the contact lens industry. Also reports on related educational information and technical papers. Recurring features include news of research, calendar of events, reports of meetings, and associate member listing.

20939 ■ *Gleams*
Pub: Glaucoma Research Foundation
Contact: Thomas M. Brunner, President
Ed: Catalina San Agustin, Editor, catalinas@glaucoma.org. **Released:** Quarterly, 3/year. **Price:** Free. **Description:** Examines the results of clinical and basic research on glaucoma. Seeks to increase public knowledge of the eye disease and discusses prevention of blindness from the disease. Contains articles on glaucoma research, treatment updates and tips on living with glaucoma.

20940 ■ *National Glaucoma Research Report*
Pub: American Health Assistance Foundation
Contact: Stacy Pagos Haller, President
Released: 3/year. **Price:** Free. **Description:** Highlights the work of glaucoma researchers and provides tips for individuals with glaucoma. Recurring features include news of research and columns titled From the Presidents and Ask the Experts.

20941 ■ *Optometric Education*
Pub: Association of Schools and Colleges of Optometry
Contact: Martin A. Wall, Executive Director
URL(s): www.opted.org/i4a/pages/index. cfm?pageid=3367. **Ed:** Elizabeth Hoppe, Dominick M. Maino, Geoffrey W. Goodfellow. **Released:** 3/yr. **Price:** $30, Individuals; $40, Other countries.

TRADE SHOWS AND CONVENTIONS

20942 ■ Annual Meeting of the American Academy of Ophthalmology
American Academy of Ophthalmology (AAC)
PO Box 7424
San Francisco, CA 94120-7424
Ph: (415)561-8500
Fax: (415)561-8533
Co. E-mail: customer_service@aao.org
URL: http://www.aao.org
Contact: David W. Parke, II, Chief Executive Officer
URL(s): www.aao.org. **Frequency:** Annual. **Audience:** Ophthalmologists and related trade professionals. **Principal Exhibits:** Ophthalmic equipment and instruments.

20943 ■ California Optometric Association OptoWest
California Optometric Association
2415 K St.
Sacramento, CA 95816
Ph: (916)441-3990
Free: 800-877-5738
Fax: (916)448-1423
Co. E-mail: contact@coavision.org
URL: http://www.coavision.org
URL(s): www.optowest.com/. **Frequency:** Annual. **Principal Exhibits:** Optometric equipment, supplies, and services.

20944 ■ International Vision Expo and Conference/West
Reed Exhibitions Contemporary Forums
6377 Clark Ave., Ste. 200
Dublin, CA 94568
Ph: (925)828-7100
Fax: (800)329-9923
Co. E-mail: info@cforums.com
URL: http://www.contemporaryforums.com
URL(s): www.visionexpowest.com. **Frequency:** Annual. **Audience:** Industry buyers, opticians, and optometrists. **Principal Exhibits:** Contact lenses, solutions, and care kits; frames; glass and plastic ophthalmic lenses; plano sunglasses; specialty lenses; business and record management systems; computer systems; dispensing, display, and examination equipment; laboratory systems; office furniture and design services; training programs; vision aids. **Dates and Locations:** Convention Center. **Telecommunication Services:** inquiry@vision.reedexpo.com.

20945 ■ MOA Fall Seminar
Michigan Optometric Association
530 W. Ionia St.
Lansing, MI 48933
Ph: (517)482-0616
Fax: (517)482-1611
URL: http://michigan.aoa.org
Contact: Cindy Schnetzler, Executive Director
E-mail: cindy@themoa.org
URL(s): www.michigan.aoa.org. **Frequency:** Annual. **Audience:** Professional optometrists, optometric technicians and assistants, and ophthalmic suppliers. **Principal Exhibits:** Ophthalmic supplies and services. **Dates and Locations:** , Lansing Center.

FRANCHISES AND BUSINESS OPPORTUNITIES

20946 ■ Pearle Vision, Inc.
Cole National Corp.
4000 Luxottica Pl.
Mason, OH 45040
Ph: (513)765-3327
Free: 800-732-7531

Fax: (513)492-3462
Co. E-mail: opportunities@pearlevision.com
URL: http://www.pearlevision.com/fh.htm
Description: Eyewear and eye-care stores. **No. of Franchise Units:** 343. **No. of Company-Owned Units:** 289. **Founded:** 1961.. **Franchised:** 1980. **Equity Capital Needed:** $184,008-$528,353. **Franchise Fee:** None. **Royalty Fee:** 7%. **Training:** Offers 1 week at headquarters, 1 week at franchisee's location, at company-owned location (optional) 1 week and ongoing support.

20947 ■ Sterling Optical
Emerging Vision, Inc.
520 8th Ave., Rm. 2300
New York, NY 10018
Ph: (516)390-2133
Fax: (516)320-8073
URL: http://www.sterlingoptical.com
Description: Franchises optic centers. **No. of Franchise Units:** 180. **No. of Company-Owned Units:** 10. **Founded:** 1919.. **Franchised:** 1992. **Equity Capital Needed:** $100,000-$660,000. **Franchise Fee:** $20,000. **Training:** Ongoing training programs with initial focus on in-store operation and business operating systems. Continuing education through on-site visits.

LIBRARIES

20948 ■ American Academy of Optometry Library
6110 Executive Blvd., Ste. 506
Rockville, MD 20852
Ph: (301)984-1441
Fax: (301)984-4737
Co. E-mail: aaoptom@aaoptom.org
URL: http://www.aaopt.org
Contact: Lois Schoenbrun, Executive Director
Scope: Optometry, physiological optics, ocular pathology. **Services:** Library not open to the public. **Holdings:** Optometry & Vision Science (formerly the American Journal of Optometry & Physiological Optics). **Subscriptions:** 12 journals and other serials. **Telecommunication Services:** loiss@aaoptom. org.

20949 ■ American Optometric Association - International Library, Archives & Museum of Optometry—ILAMO.
243 N. Lindbergh Blvd.
St. Louis, MO 63141
Ph: (314)991-4100
Free: 800-365-2219
Fax: (314)991-4101
Co. E-mail: ilamo@aoa.org
URL: http://www.aoa.org/x11718.xml
Contact: Linda Draper, Librarian, Special Collections
Scope: Vision, optometry, ophthalmology, optics. **Services:** Interlibrary loan; copying; Library open to the public. **Founded:** 1902. **Holdings:** 10,000 books; 400 feet of archives. **Subscriptions:** 300 journals and other serials. **Telecommunication Services:** ljdraper@aoa.org.

20950 ■ Florida Ophthalmic Institute Library
7106 NW 11th Pl.
Gainesville, FL 32605-3140
Ph: (352)331-2020
Fax: (352)331-2019
URL: http://sites.google.com/site/flophthalmicinstitute
Contact: Norman S. Levy, Doctor
Scope: Ophthalmology, visual sciences. **Services:** Library not open to the public. **Founded:** 1977. **Holdings:** 104 books; 14 bound periodical volumes. **Subscriptions:** 14 journals and other serials.

20951 ■ National Eye Research Foundation Library
9461 Harrison St.
Des Plaines, IL 60016-1542
Ph: (800)621-2258
Fax: (847)564-0807
Co. E-mail: info@nerf.org
URL: http://www.nerf.org
Scope: Optometry. **Services:** Library open to the public for reference use only. **Founded:** 1955.

20952 ■ Pennsylvania College of Optometry - Gerard Cottet Library
8360 Old York Rd.
Elkins Park, PA 19027
Ph: (215)780-1260
Free: 800-824-6262
Co. E-mail: library@salus.edu
URL: http://www.salus.edu/facilities/library.html
Contact: Keith Lammers, Director
URL(s): ecampus.salus.edu/library. **Scope:** Optometry, ophthalmology, optics theory, ophthalmic optics, contact lenses, low vision rehabilitation. **Services:** Interlibrary loan; copying; library open to the public with restrictions. **Founded:** 1918. **Holdings:** 8000 books; 21,000 bound periodical volumes; 2 VF drawers of old instruments pamphlets; 125 videocassettes; 9650 audiocassettes; 100 slides; 160 CD-ROMs; 16 CD-ROM. **Subscriptions:** 280 journals and other serials.

20953 ■ Southern California College of Optometry - M.B. Ketchum Memorial Library
2575 Yorba Linda Blvd.
Fullerton, CA 92831-1699
Ph: (714)449-7440
Fax: (714)879-0481
Co. E-mail: library@scco.edu
URL: http://scco.ent.sirsi.net/client/default
Contact: D. J. Matthews, Director, Library Services
Scope: Optometry, optics, ophthalmology; vision. **Services:** Interlibrary loan; copying; Library open to the public with restrictions. **Founded:** 1948. **Holdings:** 10,000 books; 6000 bound periodical volumes; 450 theses; 500 AV programs. **Subscriptions:** 360 serials. **Telecommunication Services:** djmatthews@scco.edu.

RESEARCH CENTERS

20954 ■ Dry Eye and Tear Research Center
Regions Hospital
640 Jackson St.
Saint Paul, MN 55101
Ph: (651)254-1001
Fax: (651)254-1480
Co. E-mail: j.d.nelson@healthpartners.com
Contact: Dr. J. Daniel Nelson, Director
Founded: 1982.

20955 ■ Duke University - Eye Center
DUMC 3802
Durham, NC 27710
Ph: (919)684-6611
Free: 800-422-1575
Fax: (919)681-6343
Co. E-mail: info@dukeeye.org
URL: http://www.dukehealth.org/eye_center
Contact: Dr. David L. Epstein, Chairperson

20956 ■ University of Calgary - Vision and Aging Laboratory (VAL)
Department of Psychology
2500 University Dr. NW
Calgary, AB, Canada T2N 1N4
Ph: (403)220-5561
Fax: (403)282-8249
Co. E-mail: donkline@ucalgary.ca
URL: http://www.psych.ucalgary.ca/PACE/VA-Lab/
Contact: Prof. Donald Kline, Director
Services: Gerontological vision testing and correction. **Founded:** 1986. **Educational Activities:** Public presentations. **Awards:** Graduate awards; Teaching and research assistantships.

20957 ■ University of California, Los Angeles - Jules Stein Eye Institute (JSEI)
100 Stein Plz.
Los Angeles, CA 90095-7000
Ph: (310)206-7202
Fax: (310)794-7906
Co. E-mail: mondinopatients@jsei.ucla.edu
URL: http://www.jsei.org
Contact: Bartly J. Mondino, Director
Services: UCLA Mobile Eye Clinic. **Founded:** 1966. **Publications:** JSEI Annual report; Clinical Update (3/year); EYE (3/year). **Educational Activities:** Jules Stein Eye Institute Seminar; Grand Rounds (Weekly).

20958 ■ University of Texas—Houston Health Science Center - Cizik Eye Clinic
Memorial Hermann Medical Plz., 18th Fl.
6400 Fannin St.
Houston, TX 77030

Ph: (713)559-5200
Fax: (713)795-0733
Co. E-mail: richard.s.ruiz@uth.tms.edu
URL: http://www.cizikeye.org
Services: Hermann Eye Fund: provides help for indigent patients and funds for research and teach-ing. **Founded:** 1977. **Educational Activities:** Courses and seminars; Postdoctoral degree program.

ASSOCIATIONS AND OTHER ORGANIZATIONS

20959 ■ Advisor
24 Olive St., Unit 10
Grimsby, ON, Canada L3M 2E6
Ph: (905)309-0224
Free: 800-896-1054
Fax: (905)309-0225
Co. E-mail: info@camx.ca
URL: http://www.camx.ca/call-center/index_ang.cfm
Contact: Linda Osip, Executive Director
Released: Bimonthly

20960 ■ Association of TeleServices International (ATSI)
12 Academy Ave.
Atkinson, NH 03811
Ph: (703)234-4111
Free: 866-896-ATSI
Fax: (703)435-4390
Co. E-mail: admin@i.org
URL: http://www.atsi.org
Contact: Larry Goldenberg, President
Description: Telephone answering and voice message service providers. Seeks to foster growth and development in the industry. Represents the industry before Congress and regulatory agencies; negotiates with telephone companies. Holds seminars and workshops on the latest telecommunications technology; compiles statistics. Maintains hall of fame. **Founded:** 1942. **Publications:** *Connections* (Bimonthly); *TeleCommunicator* (Biweekly); *Association of Telemessaging Services International--Membership Directory* (Annual); *TeleCommunicator*. **Educational Activities:** Association of Teleservices International Conference (Annual). **Awards:** Award of Excellence (Annual). **Telecommunication Services:** admin@atsi.org.

20961 ■ Canadian Call Management Association (CAM-X)
24 Olive St., Unit 10
Grimsby, ON, Canada L3M 2B6
Ph: (905)309-0224
Free: 800-896-1054
Fax: (905)309-0225
Co. E-mail: info@camx.ca
URL: http://www.camx.ca/call-center/index_ang.cfm
Contact: Linda Osip, Executive Director
Description: Call centers and message exchanges. Promotes excellence in the handling of voice and electronic messages. Represents members' interests; facilitates technical advancement in the field of telecommunications. **Founded:** 1964. **Publications:** *Advisor* (Bimonthly). **Awards:** Award of Excellence; Call Centre Award of Distinction

20962 ■ Telecommunications Industry Association (TIA)
2500 Wilson Blvd., Ste. 300
Arlington, VA 22201
Ph: (703)907-7700
Free: 703-907-7776
Fax: (703)907-7727
Co. E-mail: tia@tiaonline.org
URL: http://www.tiaonline.org
Contact: Grant Seiffert, President
Description: Serves the communications and IT industry, with proven strengths in standards development, domestic and international public policy, and trade shows. Facilitates business development and opportunities and a competitive market environment; provides a forum for member companies, the manufacturers and suppliers of products and services used in global communications. Represents the communications sector of the Electronic Industries Alliance. **Founded:** 1988. **Publications:** *Industry Pulse*; *Channel Intelligence Report*; *Industry Beat* (Weekly); *PulseOnline* (Monthly); *TIA Network* (Weekly); *TIA Directory and Desk Reference*. **Educational Activities:** NXTcomm (Annual). **Telecommunication Services:** gseiffert@tiaonline.org; tia@tia.eia.org.

REFERENCE WORKS

20963 ■ Telecommunications Directory
Pub: Cengage Learning Inc.
Contact: Ronald Dunn, President
URL(s): www.gale.cengage.comhttp://www.gale.cengage.com/servlet/BrowseSeriesServlet?region=9&imprint=000&cf=es&titleCode=CSSG&edition=.
Released: Annual; Latest edition 23rd; April, 2012. **Price:** $993, Individuals. **Covers:** Two volumes-North America and International, Cover approximately 6,000 national and international voice and data communications networks, electronic mail services, teleconferencing facilities and services, facsimile services, Internet access providers, videotex and teletext operations, transactional services, local area networks, audiotex services, microwave systems/networkers, satellite facilities, and others involved in telecommunications, including related consultants, advertisers/marketers; associations, regulatory bodies, and publishers. **Entries include:** Company or organization name, address, phone, fax, year established, name and title of contact, executive officers and board of directors, function or type of service; geographical area served; NAICS and SIC codes; number of employees; general description, including telecommunications-related activities; product/service; specific applications; means of access and equipment required; publications; intended market and availability; pricing; stock exchanges traded and ticker symbols; financial figures. **Database includes:** Extensive glossary of terms, acronyms, and concepts. **Arrangement:** Alphabetical by company name; within geographic region. **Indexes:** Name of firm/acronym, personal name, geographical (with name, address, phone, and director), and function/type of service (with name, address, phone). Indexes are cumulative. **Availability:** Online: Cengage Learning Inc. **Type:** Directory.

TRADE PERIODICALS

20964 ■ Audiotex Update
Pub: Worldwide Videotex
Ed: Mark Wright, Editor, markedit@juno.com. **Released:** Monthly. **Price:** $165, U.S. and Canada; $180, elsewhere. **Description:** Provides the latest news and information on the audiotex industry. Discusses voice processing/information products, services, companies, marketing strategies, and research and development. Recurring features include news of research and book reviews.

CONSULTANTS

20965 ■ Network Consulting & Associates Inc.
1626 S Luther Ave.
Oakbrook Terrace, IL 60181-5254
Ph: (630)424-1600
Fax: (630)424-1650
Contact: Dave Keating, President
Scope: Project management specialists with expertise in design, development, installation and ongoing operation of telecommunications systems including private networks, corporate voice networks, telephone systems, videoconferencing, voice mail systems, bypass systems, fiber optics, microwave, facsimile and premise distribution systems. Specialty areas include requirements definitions, RFP's, proposal evaluations, feasibility studies and system cut-overs. **Founded:** 1986. **Seminars:** Getting Started - Your Own In-house Project; IBM Midrange AS400 Support; Network Evaluations.

20966 ■ Reston Consulting Group Inc.—RCG Inc.
462 Herndon Pky., Ste. 203
Herndon, VA 20170-5234
Ph: (703)834-1155
Fax: (703)834-3086
Co. E-mail: info@rcg.com
URL: http://www.rcg.com
Contact: Brij Bhushan, President
E-mail: brijb@rcg.com
Scope: Provider of consulting services for voice, data, video and integrated communication networks; develops plans for networks. Also provides network design, engineering and integration services. Serves private industries as well as government agencies. **Founded:** 1987. **Telecommunication Services:** information@rcg.com.

LIBRARIES

20967 ■ Alcatel Network Systems, Inc. - Library
2912 Wake Forest Rd.
Raleigh, NC 27609
Ph: (919)850-6414
Fax: (919)850-5131
Co. E-mail: joan.viscounty@usa.alcatel.com
URL: http://www.alcatel.com
Contact: Joan Viscounty, Librarian
Scope: Telecommunications, electronics, computers, business management. **Services:** Library open to the public by appointment. **Founded:** 1958. **Holdings:** 3000 books; 120 bound periodical volumes;

175 proceedings of conferences and symposia; 200 engineering reports. **Subscriptions:** 225 journals and other serials.

20968 ■ Pitney Bowes Information Center
1 Elmcroft Rd.
Stamford, CT 06926
Ph: (203)356-5000
Free: 800-522-0020
Fax: (203)924-3637
URL: http://www.pb.com
Scope: Computers, software engineering, printing technology, inks, adhesives, physics, postal service,

telecommunications. **Services:** Interlibrary loan; center not open to the public. **Founded:** 1953. **Holdings:** 3000 books. **Subscriptions:** 300 journals and other serials.

RESEARCH CENTERS

20969 ■ University of Louisville - Information Technology Resource Center (iTRC)
Shelby Campus
9001 Shelbyville Rd.
Louisville, KY 40222

Ph: (502)852-0900
Fax: (502)852-4701
Co. E-mail: graham@louisville.edu
Contact: James H. Graham, Jr., Director

Services: New technology testing; Support: to local and commonwealth economic agencies. **Founded:** 1990. **Educational Activities:** Seminars and product demonstrations. **Telecommunication Services:** info@theitrc.com.

ASSOCIATIONS AND OTHER ORGANIZATIONS

20970 ■ International Desalination Association (IDA)
PO Box 387
Topsfield, MA 01983
Ph: (978)887-0410
Fax: (978)887-0411
Co. E-mail: info@idadesal.org
URL: http://www.idadesal.org
Contact: Dr. Corrado Sommariva, President
Description: Users and suppliers of desalination equipment; water reuse and reclamation consultants. Seeks to develop and promote worldwide application of desalination and desalination technology in maintaining water supplies, controlling water pollution, and purifying, treating, and reusing water. Disseminates information on desalination-related subjects and water reuse. Encourages the establishment of standards, specifications, procedures, and the efficient use of water for energy. Conducts seminars and workshops. **Founded:** 1985. **Publications:** *IDA Membership Directory* (Annual); *IDA Newsletter* (Bimonthly); *IDA Desalination and Water Reuse Quarterly* (Quarterly). **Educational Activities:** World Congress on Desalination and Water Reuse (Biennial). **Awards:** Channabasappa Memorial Scholarships; IDA Fellowship Awards; Channabasappa Memorial Scholarship; IDA Fellowship Award (Biennial).

20971 ■ National Utility Contractors Association (CWC) - Clean Water Council (CWC)
3925 Chain Bridge Rd., Ste. 301
Fairfax, VA 22030
Ph: (703)358-9300
Fax: (703)358-9307
Co. E-mail: bill@nuca.com
URL: http://www.nuca.com
Contact: Bill Hillman, Chief Executive Officer
Description: Construction, engineering, manufacturing, distribution, labor, and general business associations. Promotes increased federal funding for water quality infrastructure. Conducts educational programs to raise public awareness of water quality issues; conducts lobbying activities. **Founded:** 1990.

20972 ■ Water Quality Association (WQA)
4151 Naperville Rd.
Lisle, IL 60532-3696
Ph: (630)505-0160
Fax: (630)505-9637
Co. E-mail: info@wqa.org
URL: http://www.wqa.org
Contact: Dave Haataja, Executive Director
Description: Individuals or firms engaged in the manufacture and/or assembly and distribution and/or retail selling of water treatment equipment, supplies, and services. Promotes the acceptance and use of industry equipment, products, and services. Provides activities, programs, and services designed to improve economy and efficiency within the industry. Conducts expositions and certification and equipment validation programs. Compiles statistics. **Scope:** water quality improvement. **Founded:** 1974. **Subscriptions:** books. **Publications:** *Water Quality Glossary*; *WQA NewsFax* (Bimonthly); *Water Professional Database*; *Validated Water Treatment Equipment Directory* (Updated continuously; printed on request); *Water Quality Association--Membership Directory* (Annual); *Directory of WQA Certified Personnel* (Annual); *Water Treatment Fundamentals*; *Water Treatment Fundamentals Seminar Audio Series*. **Educational Activities:** Water Quality Association Convention (Annual); Water Opportunity Show (Annual). **Awards:** Hall of Fame Award (Annual).

REFERENCE WORKS

20973 ■ *"Blackwater is LEED Golden for Port of Portland Building"* in Contractor (Vol. 56, October 2009, No. 10, pp. 3)
Pub: Penton Media, Inc.
Ed: Robert P. Mader. **Description:** Worrel Water Technologies' Tidal Wetlands Living Machine recycles blackwater from the toilets and sends it right back to flush the toilets. The Technology is being installed in the new headquarters of the Port of Portland which aims to get awarded a gold certificate from the Leadership in Energy and Environmental Design.

20974 ■ *"Corporate Park Retrofits for Water Savings"* in Contractor (Vol. 56, October 2009, No. 10, pp. 5)
Pub: Penton Media, Inc.
Description: Merrit Corporate Park in Norwalk, Connecticut has been interested in improving building efficiency and one of their buildings has been retrofitted with water-efficient plumbing systems which will allow them to save as much as two million gallons of water. ADP Service Corp. helped the park upgrade their plumbing system.

20975 ■ *"More Than 1,000 Attend Second WaterSmart"* in Contractor (Vol. 56, November 2009, No. 11, pp. 3)
Pub: Penton Media, Inc.
Description: Over 1,000 plumbing and water conservation professionals attended the second WaterSmart Innovations Conference and Exposition in Las Vegas. Plumbing industry personalities made presentations during the conference and several innovative products were displayed at the trade show.

20976 ■ *"Next Stage of Green Building will be Water Efficiency"* in Contractor (Vol. 56, July 2009, No. 7, pp. 41)
Pub: Penton Media, Inc.
Description: One market report says that water efficiency and conservation will become critical factors in green design, construction, and product selection in the next five years from 2009. The report outlines how critical it will be for the construction industry to address responsible water practices in the future.

20977 ■ *"Snow Melt Systems Offer Practical Solutions"* in Contractor (Vol. 56, October 2009, No. 10, pp. S6)
Pub: Penton Media, Inc.
Ed: Lisa Murton Beets. **Description:** Cases are discussed in which the installation of a snow melt system becomes a necessity. One example describes how limited space means there would be no place to put plowed snow; snow melt systems can also resolve problems that arise due to an excess of melting snow.

20978 ■ *"Water Company Eyeing Region for a New Plant"* in Charlotte Business Journal (Vol. 25, December 10, 2010, No. 38, pp. 1)
Pub: Charlotte Business Journal
Ed: Ken Elkins. **Description:** California-based Niagara Bottling Company is hoping to find a site in Charlotte, North Carolina where it can build a water bottling plant that would employ 70 workers. The investment is expected to cost about $25 million to $40 million.

20979 ■ *Water Conditioning & Purification--Buyers Guide Issue*
Pub: Publicom, Inc.
URL(s): www.wcponline.com/login. **Released:** Continuous **Price:** Free. **Publication includes:** List of about 800 manufacturers and suppliers in the water treatment and purification industry. **Entries include:** Company name, address, phone, name of contact, line of business. **Arrangement:** Classified by product/ service, then alphabetical. **Indexes:** Brand and trade names, product.

20980 ■ *Water Quality Association--Membership Directory*
Pub: Water Quality Association
Contact: Dave Haataja, Executive Director
URL(s): www.wqa.org. **Released:** Annual; July. **Covers:** About 1,860 retailer, individual, and allied members, and about 540 member manufacturers and suppliers and 450 international members. **Entries include:** For manufacturers and suppliers--Company name, address, phone, names and titles of key personnel, description of products and services. For retailers--Member name, company name, address, phone. For others--Member name, company name (if any), address. **Arrangement:** Manufacturers and suppliers are alphabetical; others are geographical in separate lists. **Indexes:** Member company listing.

20981 ■ *"WQA Develops Certification Program"* in Contractor (Vol. 57, January 2010, No. 1, pp. 56)
Pub: Penton Media, Inc.
Description: Water Quality Association is now offering a new certification program for companies that may be affected by California's law that prohibits any products intended to convey or dispense water for human consumption that is not lead-free. All pipe or plumbing fixtures must be certified by a third party certification body.

20982 ■ *"WQA's Leadership Conference Tackles Industry Issues"* in Contractor (Vol.

56, October 2009, No. 10, pp. 3)
Pub: Penton Media, Inc.
Ed: Candace Roulo. **Description:** Water Quality Association's Mid-Year Leadership Conference held in Bloomingdale, Illinois in September 2009 tackled lead regulation, water softeners, and product efficiency. The possibility of a WQA green seal was discussed by the Water Sciences Committee and the Government Relations Committee meeting.

STATISTICAL SOURCES

20983 ■ *The U.S. Market for Bottled, Enhanced and Flavored Water - 3rd Edition*
Pub: MarketResearch.com
Released: 2003. **Price:** $2250.00. **Description:** The U.S. Market for Bottled and Enhanced Edition Water is a brand-new report that offers a unique perspective on the changing market for bottled spring and fortified waters. No other market research report provides both the comprehensive analysis and extensive data that The U.S. Market for Bottled and Enhanced Water offers.

TRADE PERIODICALS

20984 ■ *Drinking Water & Backflow Prevention*
Pub: IAPMO
Contact: Dan Daniels, President
Ed: Krystal Renea Garza, Editor. **Released:** Monthly. **Price:** $45, U.S. year; $53 Canada and Mexico.; $59, elsewhere year. **Description:** Presents articles directed toward 'individuals, companies, organizations, agencies, and municipalities with an interest in drinking water protection and backflow prevention.' Contains information on safety standards, water system protection, training programs, cross-connection control, and all issues related to preventing the contamination of potable drinking water supplies with backflow prevention devices. Recurring features include case studies, letters to the editor, news of research, columns titled Test Your Investigative Skills and Backflow Prevention Device Repairs, and reports of meetings. Also carries news of educational opportunities, job listings, notices of publications available, and a calendar of events.

20985 ■ *MainStream / Streamline*
Pub: American Water Works Association
Contact: David B. LaFrance, Executive Director
Ed: Mary A. Parmelee, Editor, mparmele@awwa.org. **Released:** Biweekly, online; print issue is published quarterly. **Price:** Included in membership; $16, nonmembers U.S. and Canada; $22, nonmembers. **Description:** Carries news of the Association and features about the drinking water industry, including regulations, legislation, conservation, treatment, quality, distribution, management, and utility operations. Recurring features include letters to the editor, a calendar of events, reports of meetings, news of educational opportunities, notices of publications available, education and job opportunities in the industry and legislative news.

20986 ■ *Operations Forum*
Pub: Water Environment Federation
Contact: Jeff Eger, Executive Director
URL(s): www.wef.org. **Released:** Monthly **Price:** $79, Nonmembers.

20987 ■ *Water Conditioning & Purification*
Pub: Publicom, Inc.
URL(s): www.wcponline.com/. **Released:** Monthly **Price:** Free trial.

20988 ■ *Water Desalination Report*
Pub: Maria C. Smith
Ed: Tom Pankratz, Editor. **Released:** Weekly. **Price:** $500, U.S. **Description:** Concentrates on the activities of government and industry worldwide concerning the desalination of seawater and brackish water. Discusses such topics as problems with water supply and reuse, resource planning, and pollution control. Reports on federal budgets, regulation, new and future programs, opportunities in business, and research. Recurring features include book reviews and a schedule of activities.

20989 ■ *Water Policy Report*
Pub: Inside Washington Publishers
Contact: Korila Malecha, Manager
Released: Biweekly, every other Monday. **Price:** $650, U.S. and Canada; $700, elsewhere. **Description:** Reports on federal water quality programs and policies. Covers topics such as drinking water, toxics, enforcement, monitoring, and state/EPA relations.

20990 ■ *Water Technology*
Pub: National Trade Publications Inc.
Contact: Mike Perkins, Director
E-mail: mperkins@ntpinc.com
URL(s): www.watertechonline.com. **Released:** Monthly

VIDEOCASSETTES/ AUDIOCASSETTES

20991 ■ *Natural Waste Water Treatment*
Bullfrog Films, Inc.
PO Box 149
Oley, PA 19547
Ph: (610)779-8226
Free: 800-543-3764
Fax: (610)370-1978
Co. E-mail: video@bullfrogfilms.com
URL: http://bullfrogfilms.com
Released: 1987. **Description:** A look at small decentralized sewage treatment plants that use the natural purifying characteristics of marsh plants. **Availability:** VHS; 3/4 U.

TRADE SHOWS AND CONVENTIONS

20992 ■ Environmex/Watermex South China - International Environment & Water Management Technology, Equipment & Control Systems Exhibition
Hong Kong Exhibition Services Ltd.
Units 1203, 12/F
Harcourt House
39 Gloucester Rd.
Wanchai, China
Ph: 852 2804 1500
Fax: 852 2528 3103
Co. E-mail: exhibit@hkesallworld.com
URL: http://www.hkesallworld.com
URL(s): www.environmexasia.com. **Frequency:** Biennial. **Audience:** Trade professionals. **Principal Exhibits:** Environment and water management equipment, supplies, and services.

FRANCHISES AND BUSINESS OPPORTUNITIES

20993 ■ Culligan International Co.—Culligan InternationalCulligan Intnl;
9399 W Higgins Rd, Ste. 1100.
Rosemont, IL 60018-4940
Ph: (847)430-2800
Free: 877-386-0823
Fax: (847)430-1519
Co. E-mail: internationalinfo@culligan.com
URL: http://www.culligan.com
Contact: Mark Seals, Chief Executive Officer
Description: Water treatment devices, softeners, filters, drinking water units and bottled water. **Scope:** A water treatment company providing water filtration products including water softeners, water filtration systems, drinking water systems, and whole-house filtration systems. Offers reverse osmosis and deionization services, delivered bottled water, free basic water analysis and site surveys, engineering/design assistance, educational programs, variety of sales, rental and leasing plans. Industries served: manufacturing, new construction, restaurants, grocery, hospitality, education, healthcare, assisted living, car washes, government, laundries, and beauty salons/spas. **No. of Franchise Units:** 549. **No. of Company-Owned Units:** 71. **Founded:** 1921. **Equity Capital Needed:** $103,000-$342,000 investment. **Franchise Fee:** $25,000. **Training:** Yes.

COMPUTERIZED DATABASES

20994 ■ *WATERNET Bibliographic Database*
6666 W Quincy Ave.
Denver, CO 80235-3098
Ph: (303)794-7711
Free: 800-926-7337
Fax: (303)347-0804
URL: http://www.awwa.org
Contact: David B. LaFrance, Executive Director
Availability: CD-ROM: American Water Works Association. **Type:** Bibliographic.

LIBRARIES

20995 ■ Arizona Department of Environmental Quality Library
1110 W. Washington St.
Phoenix, AZ 85007
Ph: (602)771-2217
Free: 800-234-5677
Fax: (602)771-2399
URL: http://www.azdeq.gov
Contact: Lorraine Cona, Librarian
Scope: Water quality, hazardous waste, wastewater, water pollution, air quality, solid waste. **Services:** Library open to the public. **Founded:** 1988. **Holdings:** 1500 books.

20996 ■ CDM - Herman G. Dresser Library—Camp Dresser & McKee.
50 Hampshire St.
Cambridge, MA 02139
Ph: (617)452-6000
Fax: (617)452-8000
Co. E-mail: infocenter@cdm.com
URL: http://www.cdm.com
Contact: Stephen J. Hickox, Chief Executive Officer
Scope: Environmental engineering, waste disposal, wastewater and solid waste management, water supply, water resources, hazardous wastes, infrastructure management. **Services:** Interlibrary loan; library open to the public by appointment only. **Founded:** 1963. **Holdings:** 13000 books; 900 bound periodical volumes; 4000 reports; 5000 report data/computations; 2500 pamphlets; 4000 reprints of articles written by employees; 4000 microfiche. **Subscriptions:** 100 journals and other serials.

20997 ■ Clough Harbor & Associates Library
III Winners Circle
Albany, NY 12205-0269
Ph: (518)453-4500
Fax: (518)458-1735
Co. E-mail: info@chacompanies.com
URL: http://www.chacompanies.com
Contact: Raymond L. Rudolph, Jr., Chief Executive Officer
Scope: The environment, sewage, wastewater. **Services:** Library not open to the public. **Founded:** 1989. **Holdings:** 2000 books; 50 bound periodical volumes; 1000 reports; 1500 catalogs. **Subscriptions:** 35 journals and other serials; 3 newspapers. **Telecommunication Services:** rrudolph@chacompanies.com.

20998 ■ EIMCO Baker Process Equipment Company Technical Library
669 W. 200 S.
Salt Lake City, UT 84110-0300
Ph: (801)526-2000
Fax: (801)526-2435
Scope: Water treatment, waste management, solid/liquid separation technology. **Founded:** 1976. **Holdings:** 1550 books; 500 bound periodical volumes; 500 documents; 40 VF drawers of technical files.

20999 ■ Greeley and Hansen LLC Library
100 S. Wacker Dr., Ste. 1400
Chicago, IL 60606-4004
Ph: (312)558-9000

Fax: (312)558-1006
Co. E-mail: bgoeser@greeley-hansen.com
URL: http://www.greeley-hansen.com
Contact: Bonnie C. Goeser, Librarian
Scope: Wastewater and water treatment, solid waste disposal, sewerage, flood control, hydraulics. **Services:** Interlibrary loan; copying; Library open to the public with restrictions. **Founded:** 1914. **Holdings:** 2000 books; 14,000 internal reports and drawings; 30,000 microforms. **Subscriptions:** 10 journals and other serials. **Telecommunication Services:** jrobak@greeley-hansen.com.

21000 ■ Kentucky Department for Environmental Protection - EPIC Library
14 Reilly Rd.
Frankfort, KY 40601
Ph: (502)564-2150
Fax: (502)564-4245
Co. E-mail: lance.burk@mail.state.ky.us
URL: http://www.dep.ky.gov
Scope: Water quality, air quality, waste management, environmental law. **Services:** Interlibrary loan; copying. **Founded:** 1980. **Holdings:** 480 monographs; 7500 reports on paper and microfiche. **Subscriptions:** 150 journals and other serials.

21001 ■ Massachusetts Water Resources Authority Library
100 1st Ave., Bldg. 39
Boston, MA 02129
Ph: (617)305-5583
Fax: (617)788-4899
Co. E-mail: mwralib@mwra.state.ma.us
URL: http://www.mwra.com
Contact: Elizabeth Steele
Scope: Water, wastewater, law. **Services:** Interlibrary loan; copying; library open to the public by appointment. **Founded:** 1986. **Holdings:** 4000 books; 1300 reports; microfilm; videos; CDs. **Subscriptions:** 20 journals and other serials. **Telecommunication Services:** kristin.macdougall@mwra.state.ma.us.

21002 ■ Nalco Company Library
1601 W. Diehl Rd.
Naperville, IL 60563-1198
Ph: (630)305-1000
Free: 800-265-5059
Fax: (630)305-2900
URL: http://www.nalco.com
Contact: Maureen Livingston
Scope: Chemistry, water treatment, polymer science. **Services:** Interlibrary loan; services open to the public by appointment. **Founded:** 1928. **Holdings:** 25,000 books; 10,000 bound periodical volumes; 28 VF drawers of bulletins, reprints; 20 VF drawers of technical data; 4000 unbound journals; microfilm. **Subscriptions:** 400 journals and other serials.

21003 ■ Oklahoma State University - Ecotoxicology and Water Quality Research Laboratory Library
501 Life Sciences, W.
Stillwater, OK 74078
Ph: (405)744-5555
Fax: (405)744-7824
Co. E-mail: jbelden@okstate.edu
URL: http://zoology.okstate.edu/index.php/ecotox-a-water-quality-lab
Contact: Jason B. Belden, Professor
Scope: Water pollution. **Holdings:** 8000 volumes of reprints.

21004 ■ Malcolm Pirnie Virtual Library/LSSI
12850 Middlebrook Rd., Ste. 400
Germantown, MD 20874-5281
Free: 888-909-1020
Fax: (301)540-0903
Co. E-mail: lenore.grossinger@lssi.com
URL: http://www.lssi.com/pirnie/about.html
Contact: Lenore Grossinger, Librarian Project Manager
Scope: Environmental engineering, water, wastewater, air pollution, hazardous waste and solid waste management. **Services:** Interlibrary loan; copying; library not open to the public. **Founded:** 1970. **Holdings:** 7000 volumes; 1000 U.S. Environmental

Protection Agency reports. **Subscriptions:** 200 journals and other serials. **Telecommunication Services:** allyson.morrison@lssi.com.

21005 ■ University of the District of Columbia - D.C. Water Resources Research Center Library—Water Resources Research Institute (WRRI).
4340 Connecticut Ave. NW, Bldg. 52 R 416G
Washington, DC 20008
Ph: (202)274-7124
Co. E-mail: whare@udc.edu
URL: http://www.udc.edu/wrri
Contact: Dr. William W. Hare, Director
Scope: Water - quality, quantity, problems, planning and policy, conservation; groundwater. **Services:** Center open to faculty members and students. **Holdings:** 4000 volumes.

21006 ■ University of Hawaii at Manoa - Water Resources Research Center Library
Holmes Hall 285
2540 Dole St.
Honolulu, HI 96822
Ph: (808)956-7847
Fax: (808)956-5044
Co. E-mail: wrrc@hawaii.edu
URL: http://www.wrrc.hawaii.edu
Contact: Dr. Roger W. Babcock, Associate
Scope: Water - cycles, supply, quantity, quality, management, protection, planning. **Services:** Library open to the University community. **Holdings:** 6500 volumes; 400 reports. **Subscriptions:** 10 journals and other serials.

RESEARCH CENTERS

21007 ■ Central State University - International Center for Water Resources Management (ICWRM)
1400 Brush Row Rd.
Wilberforce, OH 45384-1004
Ph: (937)376-6212
Fax: (937)376-6257
Co. E-mail: sri@centralstate.edu
URL: http://www.centralstate.edu/academics/bus_ind/water_res/index.html
Contact: Nancy Bridgman, Executive Director
E-mail: nbridgman@centralstate.edu
Services: Advisory services (Occasionally). **Founded:** 1987. **Publications:** ICWRM Annual reports. **Educational Activities:** Short courses on Water Management Topics (Occasionally); Undergraduate programs, includes education and research in environmental engineering, water resources management, geology and earth science; ICWRM Workshops (Occasionally). **Awards:** Benjamin Bannker Scholarships (Annual), for high achieving U.S. students in the areas of environmental engineering, water resources management and geology; DO-STEM Scholarships (5/year), for students entering into environmental engineering, water resources management and geology from high schools or community colleges with high grade point average; Louis Strokes Scholarship for Water Resources Management Majors (Annual), two academic year Scholarships for students from Ohio in the field of Water Resources Management which includes an internship at the North Easter Ohio Region Sewer District; NNSA - Scholarships.

21008 ■ Cooling Technology Institute Inc.
2611 FM 1960 W, Ste. A-101
Houston, TX 77068-3730
Ph: (281)583-4087
Fax: (281)537-1721
Co. E-mail: vmanser@cti.org
URL: http://www.cti.org
Contact: Mike Thurston, President
Description: Seeks to improve the technology, design and performance of water conservation apparatus. Develops standard specifications for cooling towers; provides inspection services. Conducts research through technical subcommittees. Sponsors projects; maintains speakers' bureau. **Scope:** cooling towers. **Services:** Speakers' Bureau. **Founded:** 1950. **Subscriptions:** reports. **Publications:** CTI News (Quarterly); Journal of the Cooling Tower Insti-

tute (Semiannual); CTI Journal (Semiannual); CTI Manual; CTI News (Semiannual). **Educational Activities:** Summer Work Meetings (Annual); CTI Summer Workshop; CTI Workshops and seminars; CTI Annual Conference.

21009 ■ Environmental Research Foundation (ERF)
PO Box 160
New Brunswick, NJ 08903
Ph: (732)828-9995
Free: 888-272-2435
Fax: (732)791-4603
Co. E-mail: info@rachel.org
URL: http://www.rachel.org
Contact: Peter Montague, Executive Director
Description: Seeks to enhance public awareness of allergies, their symptoms, and remedies; fosters research in allergy. Produces and distributes teaching aids; participates in allergy teaching programs and seminars worldwide. Maintains speakers' bureau. **Founded:** 1980. **Publications:** Rachel's Environment & Health Weekly; Allergies and Your Family; Environmentally Sick Schools; The Impossible Child; Is This Your Child; Allergies Do Alter Activities and Behavior; Impossible Child or Allergic Child; Is This Your Child's World; Our Toxic World A Wake Up Call; Recognize and Manage Your Allergies; Why An Environmentally Clean Classroom; Why Some Children Can't Learn or Behave. **Telecommunication Services:** erf@rachel.org.

21010 ■ Grand Valley State University - Robert B. Annis Water Resources Institute
Lake Michigan Ctr.
740 W Shoreline Dr.
Muskegon, MI 49441
Ph: (616)331-3749
Fax: (616)331-3864
Co. E-mail: steinmaa@gvsu.edu
URL: http://www.gvsu.edu/wri
Contact: Alan D. Steinman, Director
Services: Information resource: for government units and consulting engineers. **Founded:** 1986. **Publications:** Water Resources Review (Semiannual). **Educational Activities:** Educational programs and cruises, for the public, K-12 students, and college students; Hazardous Waste Management Workshop, for government units and consulting engineers; Periodic workshops, on groundwater, surface water, and regional GIS systems; Project WET. **Awards:** Robert B. Annis Graduate and Undergraduate Internships; Ronald Ward Scholarship; Scientech Internships; Vander Mey Internship.

21011 ■ McGill University - Environmental Engineering Laboratory
Macdonald Engineering Bldg., Rm. 492
Department of Civil Engineering & Applied Mechanics
817 Sherbrooke St. W
Montreal, QC, Canada H3A 2K6
Ph: (514)398-6861
Fax: (514)398-7361
Co. E-mail: ronald.gehr@mcgill.ca
URL: http://www.mcgill.ca/civil/grad/areas/environmental
Contact: Prof. Ronald Gehr, Director
Educational Activities: Graduate research training in engineering.

21012 ■ Morehead State University - Water Testing Laboratory (WTL)
150 University Blvd.
Morehead, KY 40351
Ph: (606)783-2962
Fax: (606)783-5045
Co. E-mail: t.pass@moreheadstate.edu
URL: http://www2.moreheadstate.edu/wtl
Contact: Dr. Ted Pass, Director
Founded: 1979.

21013 ■ Ohio State University - Water Resources Center (WRC)
311 Hitchcock Hall
2070 Neil Ave.
Columbus, OH 43210
Ph: (614)292-2807

Fax: (614)292-3780
Co. E-mail: walker.455@osu.edu
URL: http://wrc.osu.edu
Contact: Dr. Harold Walker, Director

Founded: 1959. **Educational Activities:** WRC Seminars; WRC Symposium (Annual). **Telecommunication Services:** ohiowrc@osu.edu.

21014 ■ Oklahoma State University - Ecotoxicology and Water Quality Research Laboratory

430 Life Sciences W
Stillwater, OK 74078
Ph: (405)744-9691
Fax: (405)744-7824
Co. E-mail: bidwelj@okstate.edu
URL: http://zoology.okstate.edu/zoo_affl/ewqrl/ecotoxlb.htm
Contact: Dr. Joseph R. Bidwell, Director

Founded: 1967.

21015 ■ South Dakota State University - South Dakota Water Resources Research Institute (SDWRI)

SAE 211, Box 2120
Brookings, SD 57007
Ph: (605)688-4910

Fax: (605)688-4917
Co. E-mail: van.kelley@sdstate.edu
URL: http://wri.sdstate.edu
Contact: Dr. Van C. Kelley, Director
Services: Interpretation and Consultation Service: for use of waters analyzed through the Water Quality and Water Pesticide Lab. **Founded:** 1964. **Publications:** *Water News* (Quarterly). **Educational Activities:** Big Sioux Water Festival (Annual); Lake Water Quality Workshop (Annual), designed for teachers, extension educators and lake residents; Lakes are Cool Festival; Northern Prairie Water Festival (Annual). **Telecommunication Services:** jennifer.pickard@sdstate.edu.

21016 ■ Tennessee Technological University - Center for the Management, Utilization and Protection of Water Resources

PO Box 5033
Cookeville, TN 38505
Ph: (931)372-3507
Fax: (931)372-6346
Co. E-mail: dgeorge@tntech.edu
URL: http://www.tntech.edu/wrc/home
Contact: Dr. Dennis B. George, Director
Telecommunication Services: cmupwr@tntech.edu.

21017 ■ Texas State University-San Marcos - Edwards Aquifer Research and Data Center (EARDC)

Freeman Aquatic Science Bldg.
San Marcos, TX 78666

Ph: (512)245-2329
Fax: (512)245-2669
Co. E-mail: glennlongley@txstate.edu
URL: http://www.eardc.txstate.edu
Contact: Dr. Glenn Longley, Director
Services: Laboratory services. **Founded:** 1979. **Publications:** *Newsletter* (Semiannual). **Educational Activities:** Ten aquatic studies summer camps, aquatic studies field days, educational presentations, seminars and workshops. **Awards:** Graduate stipends.

21018 ■ University of Massachusetts at Amherst - Massachusetts Water Resources Research Center (WRRC)

Blaisdell House
310 Hicks Way
Amherst, MA 01003
Ph: (413)545-2842
Fax: (413)545-2304
Co. E-mail: rees@ecs.umass.edu
URL: http://www.umass.edu/tei/wrrc
Contact: Paula Rees, Director
Services: Coordination of lake and river citizen monitoring. **Founded:** 1965. **Publications:** *WRRC Technical reports*. **Educational Activities:** Water Resources Research Conference (Annual), in late October; WRRC Workshops (Occasionally), in Massachusetts and New England. **Awards:** USGS Small Grants; Water Resource Institute Program Grants. **Telecommunication Services:** wrrc@tei.umass.edu.

START-UP INFORMATION

21019 ■ *Design and Launch Your eCommerce Business in a Week*
Pub: Entrepreneur Press
Contact: Perlman Neil, President
Ed: Jason R. Rich. **Released:** July 2008. **Price:** $17.95. **Description:** Guide to help anyone start an online business in one week; included tips for Website design.

21020 ■ *E-Preneur*
Pub: Career Press, Inc.
Ed: Richard Goossen. **Released:** April 2008. **Price:** $15.99. **Description:** Entrepreneurs in the new virtual marketplace are examined. The book surveys and explains the field of Web 2.0 and entrepreneurs successfully using the virtual marketplace.

21021 ■ *"Five Low-Cost Home Based Startups" in Women Entrepreneur (December 16, 2008)*
Pub: Entrepreneur Media Inc.
Ed: Lesley Spencer Pyle. **Description:** During tough economic times, small businesses have an advantage over large companies because they can adjust to economic conditions more easily and without having to go through corporate red tape that can slow the implementation process. A budding entrepreneur may find success by taking inventory of his or her skills, experience, expertise and passions and utilizing those qualities to start a business. Five low-cost home-based startups are profiled. These include starting an online store, a virtual assistant service, web designer, sales representative and a home staging counselor.

21022 ■ *How to Start a Home-Based Web Design Business, 4th Edition*
Pub: Globe Pequot Press
Ed: Jim Smith. **Released:** July 1, 2010. **Price:** $18.95. **Description:** Comprehensive guide contains all the necessary tools and strategies required to successfully launch and grow a Web design business.

21023 ■ *"A Matter of Online Trust" in Entrepreneur (Vol. 37, August 2009, No. 8, pp. 35)*
Pub: Entrepreneur Media, Inc.
Ed: Mikal E. Belicove. **Description:** Startup websites should make their potential customers feel confident to do business with them. To build customer's trust, the website should have an attractive and professional design, clear and simple navigation, error-free copy, and physical address, telephone number, and e-mail address.

21024 ■ *"Online Fortunes" in Small Business Opportunities (Fall 2008)*
Pub: Entrepreneur Media Inc.
Description: Fifty hot, e-commerce enterprises for the aspiring entrepreneur to consider are featured; virtual assistants, marketing services, party planning, travel services, researching, web design and development, importing as well as creating an online store are among the businesses featured.

21025 ■ *Start Your Own Net Services Business*
Pub: Entrepreneur Press
Contact: Perlman Neil, President
Released: February 1, 2009. **Price:** $17.95. **Description:** Web design, search engine marketing, new-media online, and blogging, are currently the four most popular web services available. This book provides information to start a net service business.

21026 ■ *Starting an iPhone Application Business for Dummies*
Pub: Wiley Publishing Inc.
Contact: William J. Pesce, President
Ed: Aaron Nicholson, Joel Elad, Damien Stolarz. **Released:** October 26, 2009. **Price:** $24.99. **Description:** Ways to create a profitable, sustainable business developing and marketing iPhone applications are profiled.

21027 ■ *Starting a Yahoo! Business For Dummies*
Pub: John Wiley & Sons, Incorporated
Ed: Rob Snell. **Released:** May 27, 2006. **Price:** $24.99. **Description:** Advice helps turn Web browsers into buyers, boost online traffic, and information to launch a profitable online business.

21028 ■ *"Startup Aims to Cut Out Coupon Clipping" in The Business Journal-Serving Metropolitan Kansas City (Vol. 26, August 15, 2008, No. 49)*
Pub: American City Business Journals, Inc.
Ed: Suzanna Stagemeyer. **Description:** TDP Inc., who started operations 18 months ago, aims to transform stale coupon promotions using technology by digitizing the entire coupon process. The process is expected to enable consumers to hunt coupons online where they will be automatically linked to loyalty cards. Other views and information on TDP and its services are presented.

21029 ■ *"Truthfully Speaking" in Entrepreneur (Vol. 35, November 2007, No. 11, pp. 118)*
Pub: Entrepreneur Media Inc.
Ed: Amanda C. Kooser. **Description:** Internet startup guru Guy Kawasaki talks about his new Web venture Truemors and shares tips on creating a successful Web-based company.

21030 ■ *Web Design Business*
Pub: Globe Pequot Press
Ed: Jim Smith. **Released:** January 2007. **Price:** $18.95. **Description:** Information for starting a home-based Web design firm is given.

ASSOCIATIONS AND OTHER ORGANIZATIONS

21031 ■ IDEAlliance - International Digital Enterprise Alliance
1421 Prince St., Ste. 230
Alexandria, VA 22314-2805
Ph: (703)837-1070

Fax: (703)837-1072
Co. E-mail: dsteinhardt@idealliance.org
URL: http://www.idealliance.org
Contact: Chip Harding, Chairman
Description: Works to advance user-driven, cross-industry solutions for all publishing and content-related processes by developing standards fostering business alliances and identifying best practices.
Founded: 1966.

EDUCATIONAL PROGRAMS

21032 ■ Active Server Pages I
EEI Communications
8945 Guilford Rd., Ste. 145
Columbia, MD 21046
Ph: (410)309-8200
Free: 888-253-2762
Fax: (410)630-3980
Co. E-mail: train@eeicom.com
URL: http://www.eeicom.com/eei-training-services
Price: $745.00. **Description:** Covers Active Server Pages (ASP) basics and development, building an ASP dictionary object, utilizing text files, researching and installing third-party ASP components, and writing advanced database queries. **Dates and Locations:** Silver Spring, MD; Alexandria, VA; Hunt Valley, MD; and Columbia, MD.

21033 ■ Adobe ColdFusion I
EEI Communications
8945 Guilford Rd., Ste. 145
Columbia, MD 21046
Ph: (410)309-8200
Free: 888-253-2762
Fax: (410)630-3980
Co. E-mail: train@eeicom.com
URL: http://www.eeicom.com/eei-training-services
Price: $745.00. **Description:** Geared towards experienced Web designers, this seminar covers creating databases and Web sites utilizing ColdFusion. **Dates and Locations:** Alexandria, VA.

21034 ■ Adobe Dreamweaver I (Onsite)
EEI Communications
8945 Guilford Rd., Ste. 145
Columbia, MD 21046
Ph: (410)309-8200
Free: 888-253-2762
Fax: (410)630-3980
Co. E-mail: train@eeicom.com
URL: http://www.eeicom.com/eei-training-services
Price: $797.00. **Description:** Covers utilizing Dreamweaver's page-layout capabilities, site management tools, and support for dynamic HTML to create Web pages. **Dates and Locations:** Silver Spring, MD; Alexandria, VA; and Columbia, MD.

21035 ■ Adobe Dreamweaver II (Onsite)
EEI Communications
8945 Guilford Rd., Ste. 145
Columbia, MD 21046
Ph: (410)309-8200
Free: 888-253-2762

Fax: (410)630-3980
Co. E-mail: train@eeicom.com
URL: http://www.eeicom.com/eei-training-services
Price: $797.00. **Description:** This seminar covers advanced Web page development focusing on CSS Layout, advanced site building features, site management, behaviors, interactivity, and customization. **Dates and Locations:** Silver Spring, MD; Columbia, MD; and Alexandria, VA.

21036 ■ Adobe Dreamweaver III (Onsite)
EEI Communications
8945 Guilford Rd., Ste. 145
Columnia, MD 21046
Ph: (410)309-8200
Free: 888-253-2762
Fax: (410)630-3980
Co. E-mail: train@eeicom.com
URL: http://www.eeicom.com/eei-training-services
Price: $797.00. **Description:** Learn how to set up and use Dreamweaver to build serverside scripting (ASP, ColdFusion, or PHP) in order to manage database content on the Web. **Dates and Locations:** Silver Spring, MD.

21037 ■ Adobe Fireworks I
EEI Communications
8945 Guilford Rd., Ste. 145
Columbia, MD 21046
Ph: (410)309-8200
Free: 888-253-2762
Fax: (410)630-3980
Co. E-mail: train@eeicom.com
URL: http://www.eeicom.com/eei-training-services
Price: $745.00. **Description:** Covers utilizing Fireworks and drawing tools, photo editing tools, and optimization features to create Web graphics. **Dates and Locations:** Silver Spring, MD.

21038 ■ Adobe GoLive
EEI Communications
8945 Guilford Rd., Ste. 145
Columbia, MD 21046
Ph: (410)309-8200
Free: 888-253-2762
Fax: (410)630-3980
Co. E-mail: train@eeicom.com
URL: http://www.eeicom.com/eei-training-services
Price: $745.00. **Description:** Covers utilizing GoLive, a visual Web design program, to create complex Web pages. **Dates and Locations:** Silver Spring, MD; Alexandria, VA; Hunt Valley, MD; and Columbia, MD.

21039 ■ Cascading Style Sheets (CSS) I
EEI Communications
8945 Guilford Rd., Ste. 145
Columbia, MD 21046
Ph: (410)309-8200
Free: 888-253-2762
Fax: (410)630-3980
Co. E-mail: train@eeicom.com
URL: http://www.eeicom.com/eei-training-services
Price: $745.00. **Description:** Building upon Web Page Development I and II, this seminar covers the introduction of Document Object Module (DOM) and working with cascading style sheets. **Dates and Locations:** Alexandria, VA.

21040 ■ JavaScript for Non-Programmers
EEI Communications
8945 Guilford Rd., Ste. 145
Columbia, MD 21046
Ph: (410)309-8200
Free: 888-253-2762
Fax: (410)630-3980
Co. E-mail: train@eeicom.com
URL: http://www.eeicom.com/eei-training-services
Price: $1,065.00. **Description:** Covers creating and applying JavaScript to a Web site. **Dates and Locations:** Silver Spring, MD; Alexandria, VA; Hunt Valley, MD; and Columbia, MD.

REFERENCE WORKS

21041 ■ "The 40-Year-Old Intern" in Entrepreneur (Vol. 37, October 2009, No. 10, pp. 90)
Pub: Entrepreneur Media, Inc.
Ed: Kristin Ladd. **Description:** Brian Kurth's VocationVacation is an internship program aimed at helping people experience their dream job. The website, launched in January 2004, matches people with businesses that allow them to experience their fantasy jobs.

21042 ■ "352 Media Group Opens New Tampa Web Design and Digital Marketing Office" in Entertainment Close-Up (May 2, 2011)
Pub: Close-Up Media
Description: 352 Media Group opened its newest office in Tampa, Florida in May 2011. The firm is noted for its achievements in Web design and digital marketing.

21043 ■ "529.com Wins Outstanding Achievement in Web Development" in Investment Weekly (November 14, 2009, pp. 152)
Pub: Investment Weekly News
Description: Web Marketing Association's 2009 WebAward for Financial Services Standard of Excellence and Investment Standard of Excellence was won by 529.com, the website from Upromise Investments, Inc., the leading administrator of 529 college savings plans.

21044 ■ "Aiming at a Moving Web Target" in Entrepreneur (Vol. 37, August 2009, No. 8, pp. 30)
Pub: Entrepreneur Media, Inc.
Ed: Dan O'Shea. **Description:** Rapidly increasing numbers of businesspeople are web surfing on mobile phones. To make a website that is accessible to people on the move, the main page should be light on images and graphics and the most important information should be put near the top. A more intensive route is to create a separate mobile-specific website.

21045 ■ "Analyzing the Analytics" in Entrepreneur (Vol. 37, October 2009, No. 10, pp. 42)
Pub: Entrepreneur Media, Inc.
Ed: Mikal E. Belicove. **Description:** Startups can maximize Web analytics by using them to monitor traffic sources and identify obstacles to converting them into targeted behaviors . Startups should set trackable Web site goals and continuously track traffic and conversion rates.

21046 ■ "Apparel Apparatchic at Kmart" in Barron's (Vol. 88, March 17, 2008, No. 11, pp. 16)
Pub: Dow Jones & Company, Inc.
Description: Kmart began a nationwide search for women to represent the company in a national advertising campaign. Contestants need to upload their photos to Kmart's website and winners will be chosen by a panel of celebrity judges. The contest aims to reverse preconceived negative notions about the store's quality and service.

21047 ■ "Attention, Please" in Entrepreneur (Vol. 36, April 2008, No. 4, pp. 52)
Pub: Entrepreneur Media, Inc.
Ed: Andrea Cooper. **Description:** Gurbaksh Chahal created his own company ClickAgents at the age of 16, and sold it two years later for $40 million to ValueClick. He then founded BlueLithium, an online advertising network on behavioral targeting, which Yahoo! Inc. bought in 2007 for $300 million. Chahal, now 25, talks about his next plans and describes how BlueLithium caught Yahoo's attention.

21048 ■ "Attorney Internet Marketing Services Launched by SEO Advantage at SEOLegal.com" in Internet Wire (October 5, 2009)
Pub: Comtex News Network, Inc.
Description: SEO Advantage, an Internet marketing and website designer firm, has extended its services to the legal industry.

21049 ■ "Attract More Online Customers: Make Your Website Work Harder for You" in Black Enterprise (Vol. 37, November 2006, No. 4, pp. 66)
Pub: Earl G. Graves Publishing Co. Inc.
Description: Having an impressive presence on the Internet has become crucial. Detailed advice on making your website serve your business in the best way possible is included.

21050 ■ "Auctions and Bidding: a Guide for Computer Scientists" in ACM Computing Surveys (Vol. 43, Summer 2011, No. 2, pp. 10)
Pub: Association for Computing Machinery
Ed: Simon Parsons, Juan A. Rodriguez-Aguilar, Mark Klein. **Description:** There are various actions: single dimensional, multi-dimensional, single-sided, double-sided, first-price, second-price, English, Dutch, Japanese, sealed-bid, and these have been extensively discussed and analyzed in economics literature. This literature is surveyed from a computer science perspective, primarily from the viewpoint of computer scientists who are interested in learning about auction theory, and to provide pointers into the economics literature for those who want a deeper technical understanding. In addition, since auctions are an increasingly important topic in computer science, the article also looks at work on auctions from the computer science literature. The aim is to identify what both bodies of work tell us about creating electronic auctions.

21051 ■ "Auto Show Taps Moms" in Marketing to Women (Vol. 21, April 2008, No. 4, pp. 3)
Pub: EPM Communications Inc.
Contact: Ira Mayer, President
E-mail: imayer@epmcom.com
Description: Teamed with Mother Proof, an online site which features automotive content aimed at moms, the Chicago Auto Show will present a full day of programming with the emphasis on mom.

21052 ■ "avVaa World Health Care Products Rolls Out Internet Marketing Program" in Health and Beauty Close-Up (September 18, 2009)
Pub: Close-Up Media
Description: avVaa World Health Care Products, Inc., a biotechnology company, manufacturer and distributor of nationally branded therapeutic, natural health care and skin products, has signed an agreement with Online Performance Marketing to launch of an Internet marketing campaign in order to broaden its presence online. The impact of advertising on the Internet to generate an increase in sales is explored.

21053 ■ "The Bankrate Double Pay" in Barron's (Vol. 88, March 24, 2008, No. 12, pp. 27)
Pub: Dow Jones & Company, Inc.
Ed: Neil A. Martin. **Description:** Shares of Bankrate may rise as much as 25 percent from their level of $45.08 a share due to a strong cash flow and balance sheet. The company's Internet business remains strong despite weakness in the online advertising industry and is a potential takeover target.

21054 ■ "Banks Fall Short in Online Services for Savvy Traders" in Barron's (Vol. 88, March 17, 2008, No. 11, pp. 35)
Pub: Dow Jones & Company, Inc.
Ed: Theresa W. Carey. **Description:** Banc of America Investment Services, WellsTrade, and ShareBuilder are at the bottom of the list of online brokerages because they offer less trading technologies and product range. Financial shoppers miss out on a lot of customized tools and analytics when using these services.

21055 ■ "Be Wary of Legal Advice on Internet, Lawyers Warn" in Crain's Detroit Business (Vol. 24, September 22, 2008, No. 38, pp. 16)
Pub: Crain Communications Inc.
Ed: Harriet Tramer. **Description:** While some lawyers feel that the proliferation of legal information on the Internet can point people in the right direction, others

maintain that it simply results in giving false hope, may bring about confusion or worse yet, it sometimes makes their jobs even harder.

21056 ■ *"Boom has Tech Grads Mulling Their Options" in Globe & Mail (March 14, 2006, pp. B1)*
Pub: CTVglobemedia Publishing Inc.
Ed: Grant Robertson. **Description:** Internet giant Google Inc. has stepped up its efforts to hire the talented people, in Canada, at Waterloo University in southern Ontario, to expand its operations. The details of the job market and increasing salaries are analyzed.

21057 ■ *"Borders Previews New Web Site" in Crain's Detroit Business (Vol. 23, October 8, 2007, No. 41, pp. 4)*
Pub: Crain Communications Inc. - Detroit
Ed: Sheena Harrison. **Description:** Borders Group Inc. previewed its new Website that allows customers to buy items that include the Magic Shelf, a virtual bookcase that displays available recommended books, movies and music.

21058 ■ *"Bottoms Up!" in Entrepreneur (Vol. 36, April 2008, No. 4, pp. 128)*
Pub: Entrepreneur Media, Inc.
Ed: Amanda C. Kooser. **Description:** Jill Bernheimer launched her online alcohol business Domaine547 in 2007, and encountered challenges as legal issues over the licensing and launching of the business took about seven months to finish. Domain547 features blog and forum areas. Marketing strategy that connects to the social community is one of the ways to reach out to customers.

21059 ■ *"Building a Better Twitter Brand: My Foray Into Social Analytics" in Inc. (Vol. , pp.)*
Pub: Inc. Magazine
Ed: John Brandon. **Description:** A small business using Twitter to research and promote the firm decided to test some Web-based dashboards that allow you to manage and analyze accounts on multiple social media networks including Facebook, Twitter, and LinkedIn.

21060 ■ *"Building Your Business: A Strong Web Presence Is a Must" in Black Enterprise (Vol. 38, December 2007, No 5, pp. 74)*
Pub: Earl G. Graves Publishing Co. Inc.
Ed: Tennille M. Robinson. **Description:** Building a strong presence on the Internet is crucial to any growing business. Websites can provide information or sell merchandise, but the site must also make sure the customer knows how to use and navigate around within the site. Common mistakes to avoid when designing a small business Website are outlined.

21061 ■ *"BusinessOnLine Launches a New Web-Based Search Engine Optimization Tool" in Internet Wire (October 19, 2009)*
Pub: Comtex News Network, Inc.
Description: First Link Checker, a complimentary new search engine optimization tool that helps site owners optimize their on-page links by understanding which of those links are actually being counted in Google's relevancy algorithm, was developed by BusinessOnLine, a rapidly growing Internet marketing agency. This tool will make it easy for the average web master to ensure that their internal link structure is optimized.

21062 ■ *"Can You Say $1 Million? A Language-Learning Start-Up Is Hoping That Investors Can" in Inc. (Vol. 33, November 2011, No. 9, pp. 116)*
Pub: Inc. Magazine
Ed: April Joyner. **Description:** Startup, Verbling is a video platform that links language learners and native speakers around the world. The firm is working to raise money to hire engineers in order to build the product and redesign their Website.

21063 ■ *"CarTango Lauches Site for Women" in Marketing to Women (Vol. 21, April 2008,*

No. 4, pp. 5)
Pub: EPM Communications Inc.
Contact: Ira Mayer, President
E-mail: imayer@epmcom.com
Description: CarTango.com is an Internet site that seeks to overcome what women say are dismissive or pushy salespeople by allowing the shoppers the chance to decide what they want before inviting dealers to compete for their business.

21064 ■ *"Chamber Offers Seminar on Web Design" in Charlotte Observer (February 6, 2007)*
Pub: Knight-Ridder/Tribune Business News
Ed: Joe DePriest. **Description:** Belmont Chamber of Commerce and Gaston College Small Business Center will offer seminars on online Web design.

21065 ■ *"Chris Curtis Preaches the Gospel of Internet Success" in Black Enterprise (Vol. 38, March 2008, No. 8, pp. 56)*
Pub: Earl G. Graves Publishing Co. Inc.
Ed: Anthony Calypso. **Description:** Profile of the Web Business Ownership Series, a collection of 20 free seminars that help small businesses learn about the Web development process.

21066 ■ *"A Class Act" in Hawaii Business (Vol. 53, March 2008, No. 9, pp. 25)*
Pub: Hawaii Business Publishing
Ed: Cathy S. Cruz-George. **Description:** LBoost is a startup company that offers online content for the educational magazine 'Weekly Reader'. The website features quizzes and allows users to accumulate points and redeem rewards afterward. Other details about the company are discussed.

21067 ■ *"Click Here to Book" in Caterer & Hotelkeeper (October 28, 2011, No. 288)*
Pub: Reed Reference Publishing
Ed: Ross Bentley. **Description:** Customers expectations are determined by the quality of a Website when booking hotel rooms.

21068 ■ *"A Click In the Right Direction: Website Teaches Youth Financial Literacy" in Black Enterprise (Vol. 38, December 2007, No. 5)*
Pub: Earl G. Graves Publishing Co. Inc.
Ed: Nicole Norfleet. **Description:** Profile of Donald Lee Robinson who launched SkillsThatClick, a Website that teaches young individuals ages 12 to 15 about money management. Robinson shares how he used his Navy career as a model for designing the site.

21069 ■ *Clicking Through: A Survival Guide for Bringing Your Company Online*
Pub: Bloomberg Press
Ed: Jonathan I. Ezor. **Released:** October 1999. **Description:** Summary of legal compliance issues faced by small companies doing business on the Internet, including copyright and patent laws.

21070 ■ *"Clicks For Cash: Earning More From Your Website" in Inc. (December 2007, pp. 64-65)*
Pub: Gruner & Jahr USA Publishing
Ed: Michael Fitzgerald. **Description:** Ways to use a company's Website to generate revenue are discussed. Free services for placing ads include Google AdSense, AdBrite, AuctionAds, Chitkia eMiniMalls, Vizu Answers, and Value Click; profiles of each service are presented.

21071 ■ *The Complete Guide to Google Adwords: Secrets, Techniques, and Strategies You Can Learn to Make Millions*
Pub: Atlantic Publishing Company
Released: December 1, 2010. **Price:** $24.95. **Description:** Google AdWords, when it launched in 2002 signaled a fundamental shift in what the Internet was for so many individuals and companies. Learning and understanding how Google AdWords operates and how it can be optimized for maximum exposure, boosting click through rates, conversions, placement, and selection of the right keywords, can be the key to a successful online business.

21072 ■ *"Consumer Electronics: Brick and Mortar Vs. Online" in Retail Merchandiser (Vol. 51, September-October 2011, No. 5, pp. 15)*
Pub: Phoenix Media Corporation
Description: Brick and mortar retailers with Websites are discovering that the Internet is used more for research than purchasing when it comes to electronics products. According to a recent study conducted by The NPD Group shows that 56 percent of consumers research televisions online before purchasing, but only 19 percent actually buy them online.

21073 ■ *"Contec Innovations Inc.: MovieSet.com First to Mobilize Content Using BUZmob" in Canadian Corporate News (May 16, 2007)*
Pub: Comtex News Network Inc.
Description: Contec Innovations Inc., a provider of mobile infrastructure software, announced that MovieSet.com is the first Internet portal to mobilize their content using BUZmob, the company's new mobile publishing service that allows content publishers to enable mobile access to their feed-based content on any mobile device or network in real-time.

21074 ■ *Content Rich: Writing Your Way to Wealth on the Web*
Pub: 124 S Mercedes Rd.
Ed: Jon Wuebben. **Released:** April 2008. **Price:** $19. 95. **Description:** A definitive search engine optimization (SEO) copywriting guide for search engine rankings and sales conversion. It includes topics not covered in other books on the subject and targets the small to medium sized business looking for ways to maximize online marketing activities as well as designers and Web developers seeking to incorporate more SEO techniques into design and content.

21075 ■ *"Conversations with Customers" in Business Journal Serving Greater Tampa Bay (Vol. 31, December 31, 2010, No. 1, pp. 1)*
Pub: Tampa Bay Business Journal
Description: Tampa Bay, Florida-based businesses have been using social media to interact with customers. Forty percent of businesses have been found to have at least one social media platform to reach customers and prospects.

21076 ■ *"Coping with the Web" in Agency Sales Magazine (Vol. 39, December 2009, No. 11, pp. 52)*
Pub: MANA
Ed: Karen Saunders. **Description:** When branding your company on the Internet, strategy should first be discussed with the website designer and the target and niche audience should also be defined. Describing 'what' and 'how' the product or service is offering is also important. In addition, perception, the logo, and the tag line are some elements that are needed to create a brand.

21077 ■ *Crush It!*
Pub: HarperStudio/HarperCollins
Ed: Gary Vaynerchuk. **Released:** 2009. **Price:** $19. 99. **Description:** Ways the Internet can help entrepreneurs turn their passions into successful companies.

21078 ■ *"Cyber Thanksgiving Online Shopping a Growing Tradition" in Marketing Weekly News (December 12, 2009, pp. 137)*
Pub: Investment Weekly News
Description: According to e-commerce analysts, Thanksgiving day is becoming increasingly important to retailers in terms of online sales. Internet marketers are realizing that consumers are already searching for Black Friday sales and if they find deals on the products they are looking for, they are highly likely to make their purchase on Thanksgiving day instead of waiting.

21079 ■ *"DCAA-Compliant Accounting Solution Provider Intros Redesign of Website at sympaq.com" in Entertainment Close-Up (April 18, 2011)*
Pub: Close-Up Media
Description: Aldebaron Inc., developer of DCAA-compliant accounting solution SYMPAQ SQL, launched a new Website that will assist government contractors access information about their products and services.

21080 ■ Design and Launch an Online Travel Business in a Week
Pub: Entrepreneur Press
Contact: Perlman Neil, President
Ed: Charlene Davis. Released: May 1, 2009. Price: $17.95. Description: Guide providing techniques and professional advice for starting an online travel business. Tips are given to build a Website, find qualified providers and to set up a payment system.

21081 ■ "Designing Events Updates Online Suite" in Wireless News (October 25, 2009)
Pub: Close-Up Media
Description: Designing Events, an outsourcing and consulting firm for conferences and meetings, announced the release of an update to its Designing Events Online suite of web-based management and marketing tools; features include enhanced versions of online registration and collaboration, content management, session development, social media and conference websites.

21082 ■ Designing Websites for Every Audience
Pub: F & W Publications, Incorporated
Ed: Ilise Benun. Released: January 2003. Description: Twenty-five case studies targeting six difference audiences are used to help a business design, or make over, a Website.

21083 ■ "Do-It-Yourself Portfolio Management" in Barron's (Vol. 89, July 13, 2009, No. 28, pp. 25)
Pub: Dow Jones & Co., Inc.
Ed: Mike Hogan. Description: Services of several portfolio management web sites are presented. These web sites include MarketRiders E.Adviser, TD Ameritrade and E.

21084 ■ "Dots Sings To New Tune With Its Radio Station" in Crain's Cleveland Business (Vol. 30, June 15, 2009, No. 23, pp. 7)
Pub: Crain Communications, Inc.
Description: Dots LLC, a women's clothing retailer, has launched an online radio station on its Website. The station plays the in-store music to customers while they are shopping online.

21085 ■ "Drive Traffic To Your Blog" in Women Entrepreneur (January 13, 2009)
Pub: Entrepreneur Media Inc.
Ed: Lesley Spencer Pyle. Description: Internet social networking has become a vital component to marketing one's business. Tips are provided on how to establish a blog that will attract attention to one's business and keep one's customers coming back for more.

21086 ■ eBay Business the Smart Way
Pub: AMACOM
Ed: Joseph T. Sinclair. Released: June 6, 2007. Price: $17.95. Description: eBay commands ninety percent of all online auction business. Computer and software expert and online entrepreneur shares information to help online sellers get started and move merchandise on eBay. Tips include the best ways to build credibility, find products to sell, manage inventory, create a storefront Website, and more.

21087 ■ EBay Income: How ANYONE of Any Age, Location, and/or Background Can Build a Highly Profitable Online Business with eBay
Pub: Atlantic Publishing Company
Released: December 1, 2010. Price: $24.95. Description: A complete overview of eBay is given and guides any small company through the entire process of creating the auction and auction strategies, photography, writing copy, text and formatting, multiple sales, programming tricks, PayPal, accounting, creating marketing, merchandising, managing email lists, advertising plans, taxes and sales tax, best time to list items and for how long, sniping programs, international customers, opening a storefront, electronic commerce, buy-it now pricing, keywords, Google marketing and eBay secrets.

21088 ■ Effective Web Presence Solutions for Small Businesses: Strategies for Successful Implementation
Pub: IGI Global
Ed: Stephen Burgess,, Carmine Sellitto, Stergios Karanasio, Stan Karanasios. Released: March 1, 2009. Price: $165.00. Description: Business strategies to implement a Web presence for any small business, is examined, focusing on website development.

21089 ■ Electronic Commerce
Pub: Course Technology
Ed: Gary Schneider, Bryant Chrzan, Charles McCormick. Released: May 1, 2010. Price: $117.95. Description: E-commerce can open the door to more opportunities than ever before for small business. Packed with real-world examples and cases, the book delivers comprehensive coverage of emerging online technologies and trends and their influence on the electronic marketplace. It details how the landscape of online commerce is evolving, reflecting changes in the economy and how business and society are responding to those changes. Balancing technological issues with the strategic business aspects of successful e-commerce, the new edition includes expanded coverage of international issues, social networking, mobile commerce, Web 2.0 technologies, and updates on spam, phishing, and identity theft.

21090 ■ Emerging Business Online: Global Markets and the Power of B2B Internet Marketing
Pub: FT Press
Ed: Lara Fawzy, Lucas Dworksi. Released: October 1, 2010. Price: $49.99. Description: An introduction into ebocube (emerging business online), a comprehensive proven business model for Internet B2B marketing in emerging markets.

21091 ■ "Empire of Pixels" in Entrepreneur (Vol. 37, September 2009, No. 9, pp. 50)
Pub: Entrepreneur Media, Inc.
Ed: Jason Daley. Description: Entrepreneur Jack Levin has successfully grown Imageshack, an image-hosting Web service. The Website currently gets 50 million unique visitors a month. Levin has launched Y-Frog, an application that uses Imageshack to allow Twitter users to add images to their posts.

21092 ■ "Entrepreneur Column" in Entrepreneur (September 24, 2009)
Pub: Entrepreneur Media, Inc.
Ed: Allen Moon. Description: In an attempt to compete with Google, Microsoft and Yahoo have entered a partnership to merge their search services; advice on the best ways to get noticed on this new search engine entitled Bing, is provided.

21093 ■ The Essential Online Solution: The 5-Step Formula for Small Business Success
Pub: John Wiley & Sons, Incorporated
Ed: Rick Segel; Barbara Callan-Bogia. Released: October 2006. Price: $22.95. Description: Strategies to help any small business increase its online presence and compete with big retail chains. Tips for success Web design are included.

21094 ■ The Facebook Effect: The Inside Story of the Company That Is Connecting the World
Pub: Simon & Shuster
Ed: David Kirkpatrick. Released: June 8, 2010. Price: $26.00. Description: There's never been a Website like Facebook: more than 350 million people have accounts, and if the growth rate continues, by 2013 every Internet user worldwide will have his or her own page. No one's had more access to the inner workings of the phenomenon than Kirkpatrick, a senior tech writer at Fortune magazine. Written with the full cooperation of founder Mark Zuckerberg, the book follows the company from its genesis in a Harvard dorm room through its successes over Friendster and MySpace, the expansion of the user base, and Zuckerberg's refusal to sell.

21095 ■ The Facebook Era: Tapping Online Social Networks to Build Better Products, Reach New Audiences, and Sell More Stuff
Pub: Prentice Hall
Ed: Clara Shih. Price: $24.99. Description: The '90s were about the World Wide Web of information and the power of linking Web pages. Today it's about the World Wide Web of people and the power of the social graph. Online social networks are fundamentally changing the way we live, work, and interact. They offer businesses immense opportunities to transform customer relationships for profit: opportunities that touch virtually every business function, from sales and marketing to recruiting, collaboration to executive decision-making, product development to innovation.

21096 ■ "Fast Fact: Women's Online Habits" in Marketing to Women (Vol. 22, July 2009, No. 7, pp. 1)
Pub: EPM Communications Inc.
Contact: Ira Mayer, President
E-mail: imayer@epmcom.com
Description: Lists the Internet habits of women. Statistical data included.

21097 ■ "Financo Panel Lauds Product, Online Marketing" in Home Textiles Today (Vol. 31, January 25, 2010, No. 3, pp. 1)
Pub: Reed Business Information, Inc.
Ed: James Mammarella. Description: Overview of the Financo Annual Merchandising Industry Chief Executives Event during which there was much discussion on the merits of e-commerce, online marketing as well as the traditional methods of brand recognition and retailing.

21098 ■ "Fitter from Twitter" in Boston Business Journal (Vol. 30, December 17, 2010, No. 47, pp. 1)
Pub: Boston Business Journal
Ed: Lisa van der Pool. Description: Small businesses are increasing their use of the Twitter microblogging platform to attract and retain customers. Lisa Johnson, who owns Modern Pilates studios, managed to raise awareness of her personal brand nationally through the social media platform.

21099 ■ "For MySpace, A Redesign to Entice Generation Y" in The New York Times (October 27, 2010, pp. B3)
Pub: The New York Times Company
Ed: Miguel Helft. Description: MySpace is redesigning its Website in order to attract individuals from the Generation Y group.

21100 ■ "ForeSee Finds Satisfaction On Web Sites, Bottom Line" in Crain's Detroit Business (Vol. 24, February 25, 2008, No. 8, pp. 3)
Pub: Crain Communications Inc. - Detroit
Ed: Tom Henderson. Description: Ann Arbor-based ForeSee Results Inc. evaluates user satisfaction on Web sites. The company expects to see an increase of 40 percent in revenue for 2008 with plans to expand to London, Germany, Italy and France by the end of 2009.

21101 ■ "Forsys Metals Corporation Goes "Live" With Q4's On-Demand Disclosure Management Software" in Canadian Corporate News (May 16, 2007)
Pub: Comtex News Network Inc.
Description: Forsys Metals Corp. selected Q4 Web Systems to automate its corporate website disclosure with Q4's software platform which also automates and simplifies many of the administrative tasks that Forsys was doing manually, allowing them to focus their internal resources on the business.

21102 ■ "Fresh Direct's Crisis" in Crain's New York Business (Vol. 24, January 14, 2008, No. 2, pp. 3)
Pub: Crain Communications, Inc.
Ed: Lisa Fickenscher. Description: Freshdirect, an Internet grocery delivery service, finds itself under siege from federal immigration authorities, customers and labor organizations due to its employment practice of hiring illegals. At stake is the grocer's reputation as well as its ambitious growth plans, including an initial public offering of its stock.

21103 ■ *"The Frugal Billionaire"* in Canadian Business (Vol. 79, Winter 2006, No. 24, pp. 63)
Pub: Rogers Media
Ed: Joe Castaldo. Description: The achievements of David Cheriton are described, along with his investments in various firms, including Google Inc.

21104 ■ *"Funbrain Launches Preschool Content"* in Marketing to Women (Vol. 21, March 2008, No. 3, pp. 3)
Pub: EPM Communications Inc.
Contact: Ira Mayer, President
E-mail: imayer@epmcom.com
Description: Funbrain.com launches The Moms and Kids Playground, a section of the website devoted to activities and games for moms and kids aged 2 to 6; content aims at building early computer skills and to teach basic concepts such as counting and colors.

21105 ■ *"Get Online or Be Left Behind"* in Women In Business (Vol. 61, August-September 2009, No. 4, pp. 33)
Pub: American Business Women's Association
Ed: Diane Stafford. Description: Technology's significance for the connectivity purposes among business people is discussed. Details on the use of wireless tools and online social media to boost technology IQ are presented.

21106 ■ *"Get Online Quick in the Office Or in the Field"* in Contractor (Vol. 56, October 2009, No. 10, pp. 47)
Pub: Penton Media, Inc.
Ed: William Feldman; Patti Feldman. Description: Contractors can set up a web site in minutes using the www.1and1.com website. Verizon's Novatel MIFI 2372 HSPA personal hotspot device lets contractors go online in the field. The StarTech scalable business management system helps contractors manage daily operations.

21107 ■ Getting Clients and Keeping Clients for Your Service Business
Pub: Atlantic Publishing Company
Ed: Anne M. Miller; Gail Brett Levine. Released: August 28, 2008. Price: $24.95 paperback. Description: Tips are offered to help any small service business identify customers, brand and grow the business, as well as development of logos, brochures and Websites.

21108 ■ *"Google Edges into Wireless E-Mail"* in Globe & Mail (February 19, 2007, pp. B5)
Pub: CTVglobemedia Publishing Inc.
Ed: Simon Avery. Description: Google Inc. has introduced a free mobile e-mail service in Canada. The mobile users can read, send, and search messages using the new software.

21109 ■ *"Google's Next Stop: Below 350?"* in Barron's (Vol. 88, March 10, 2008, No. 10, pp. 17)
Pub: Dow Jones & Company, Inc.
Ed: Jacqueline Doherty. Description: Share prices of Google Inc. are expected to drop from their level of $433 each to below $350 per share. The company is expected to miss its earnings forecast for the first quarter of 2008, and its continued aggressive spending on non-core areas will eventually bring down earnings.

21110 ■ *"Graceful Landing"* in Entrepreneur (Vol. 37, November 2009, No. 11, pp. 59)
Pub: Entrepreneur Media, Inc.
Ed: Mikal E. Belicove. Description: Successful marketers regularly use Website landing pages to capture qualified leads and make sales. It is believed that an effective landing page devoted to a single product or service offering can significantly boost leads and conversion rates. Organizations can create a top-notch landing page by anticipating customer expectations and focusing on a clear call to action.

21111 ■ *"Growth of Free Dailies Dropping"* in Globe & Mail (March 24, 2007, pp. B7)
Pub: CTVglobemedia Publishing Inc.
Ed: Grant Robertson. Description: The decrease in the readership of free newspapers in Canada, in view of growing preference for online news, is discussed.

21112 ■ *"A Hacker in India Hijacked His Website Design and Was Making Good Money Selling It"* in Inc. (December 2007, pp. 77-78, 80)
Pub: Gruner & Jahr USA Publishing
Ed: Darren Dahl. Description: John Anton, owner of an online custom T-shirt business and how a company in India was selling software Website templates identical to his firm's Website.

21113 ■ *"Happy Blogging"* in Black Enterprise (Vol. 38, January 2008, No. 6, pp. 47)
Pub: Earl G. Graves Publishing Co. Inc.
Ed: Sonya A. Donaldson. Description: Individual seeks advice for setting up a Website and starting a blog; Squarespace and Weebly both offer Web design.

21114 ■ *"Harlequin Leads the Way"* in Marketing to Women (Vol. 22, July 2009, No. 7, pp. 1)
Pub: EPM Communications Inc.
Contact: Ira Mayer, President
E-mail: imayer@epmcom.com
Description: Although the publishing industry has been slow to embrace new media options, the Internet is now a primary source for reaching women readers. Harlequin has been eager to court their female consumers over the Internet and often uses women bloggers in their campaigns strategies.

21115 ■ *"Harley-Davidson Moves to Unconventional Marketing Plan"* in Business Journal-Milwaukee (Vol. 28, November 26, 2010, No. 8, pp. A1)
Pub: Milwaukee Business Journal
Ed: Rich Rovito. Description: Harley Davidson Inc. hired Boulder, Colorado-based Victors & Spoils, an agency that specializes in crowdsourcing, to implement a new creative marketing model. Under the plan, Harley Davidson will draw on the ideas of its brand enthusiasts to help guide the brand's marketing direction.

21116 ■ *"Harnessing the Wisdom of Crowds"* in Entrepreneur (Vol. 37, September 2009, No. 9, pp. 74)
Pub: Entrepreneur Media, Inc.
Ed: Mark Henricks. Description: Online customer service business Get Satisfaction has registered growth. The business enables customers to search for answers to common product questions. Customers use the service to post questions, complaints, and even product ideas.

21117 ■ *"Has Microsoft Found a Way to Get at Yahoo?"* in Advertising Age (Vol. 79, July 7, 2008, No. 26, pp. 4)
Pub: Crain Communications, Inc.
Ed: Abbey Klaassen. Description: Microsoft's attempt to acquire Yahoo's search business is discussed as is Yahoo's plans for the future at a time when the company's shares have fallen dangerously low.

21118 ■ *"A Home's Identity in Black and White"* in Crain's Chicago Business (Vol. 31, April 21, 2008, No. 16, pp. 35)
Pub: Crain Communications, Inc.
Ed: Lisa Bertagnoli. Description: Real estate agents are finding that showing customers a written floor plan is a trend that is growing since many buyers feel that Online virtual tours distort a room. Although floor plans cost up to $500 to have drawn up, they clearly show potential buyers the exact dimensions of rooms and how they connect.

21119 ■ How to Make Money with Social Media: Using New and Emerging Media to Grow Your Business
Pub: FT Press
Ed: Jamie Turner, Reshma Shah. Released: October 1, 2010. Price: $24.99. Description: Marketers, executives, entrepreneurs are shown more effective ways to utilize Internet social media to make money. This guide brings together both practical strategies and proven execution techniques for driving maximum value from social media marketing.

21120 ■ *"How to Make Your Website Really Sell"* in Entrepreneur (Vol. 37, September 2009, No. 9, pp. 79)
Pub: Entrepreneur Media, Inc.
Ed: David Port. Description: Advice on how to succeed in Internet marketing is presented. Offering visitors purchase incentives on the home page is encouraged. Delivery of customized landing pages and content is also recommended.

21121 ■ *"How Marketers Can Tap the Web"* in Sales and Marketing Management (November 12, 2009)
Pub: Nielsen Business Media, Inc.
Description: Internet marketing strategies require careful planning and tools in order to track success. Businesses are utilizing this trend to attract new clients as well as keep customers they already have satisfied. Advice on website development and design is provided.

21122 ■ *"How Not to Build a Website"* in Women Entrepreneur (December 24, 2008)
Pub: Entrepreneur Media Inc.
Ed: Erica Ruback; Joanie Reisen. Description: Tips for producing a unique and functional Website are given as well as a number of lessons a pair of entrepreneurs learned while trying to launch their networking website, MomSpace.com.

21123 ■ How to Open and Operate a Financially Successful Bookstore on Amazon and Other Web Sites: With Companion CD-ROM
Pub: Atlantic Publishing Company
Released: December 1, 2010. Price: $39.95. Description: This book was written for every used book aficionado and bookstore owner who currently wants to take advantage of the massive collection of online resources available to start and run your own online bookstore business.

21124 ■ How to Use the Internet to Advertise, Promote, and Market Your Business or Web Site: With Little or No Money
Pub: Atlantic Publishing Company
Released: December 1, 2010. Price: $24.95. Description: Information is given to help build, promote, and make money from your Website or brick and mortar store using the Internet, with minimal costs.

21125 ■ *"Hunter and the Hunted"* in Canadian Business (Vol. 81, Summer 2008, No. 9, pp. 12)
Pub: Rogers Media Ltd.
Ed: Thomas Watson. Description: Brian Hunter, a partner in oil and gas engineering firm Montane Resources, invested his life savings in Vancouver-based Canacord Capital Corp. Details of the asset-backed commercial paper fiasco and Hunter's use of Facebook to encourage other investors to participate in his claim against the mortgage company are presented.

21126 ■ I'm on LinkedIn - Now What? (Second Edition): A Guide to Getting the Most Out of LinkedIn
Pub: Happy About
Ed: Diane Danielson. Released: January 7, 2009. Price: $19.95. Description: Designed to help get the most out of LinkedIn, the popular business networking site and follows the first edition and includes the latest and great approaches using LinkedIn. With over 32 million members there is a lot of potential to find and develop relationships to help in your business and personal life, but many professionals find themselves wondering what to do once they sign up. This book explains the different benefits of the system and recommends best practices (including LinkedIn Groups) so that you get the most out of LinkedIn.

21127 ■ *"Image Conscious"* in Canadian Business (Vol. 81, March 17, 2008, No. 4, pp. 36)
Pub: Rogers Media
Ed: Andrew Wahl. Description: Idee Inc. is testing an Internet search engine for images that does not rely on tags but compares its visual data to a database of other images. The company was founded

and managed by Leila Boujnane as an off-shoot of their risk-management software firm. Their software has already been used by image companies to track copyrighted images and to find images within their own archives.

21128 ■ *"In Print and Online" in Marketing to Women (Vol. 22, August 2009, No. 8, pp. 3)*
Pub: EPM Communications Inc.
Contact: Ira Mayer, President
E-mail: imayer@epmcom.com

Description: Seventeen magazine is unifying its print and Online editions with complementary content, a strategy that seems to be working as every aspect of Seventeen drives the reader to another component.

21129 ■ *Information Industry Directory*
Pub: Cengage Learning Inc.
Contact: Ronald Dunn, President
URL(s): www.gale.cengage.com. **Released:** Annual; Latest edition 38th; April, 2013. **Price:** $1160, Individuals. **Covers:** Approximately 12,000 organizations, systems, and services involved in the production and distribution of information in electronic form: database producers and their products online host services, transactional services, library and information networks, bibliographic utilities, library management systems, information retrieval software, mailing list services, fee-based information on demand services, document delivery sources, data collection and analysis centers and firms, and related consultants, service companies, professional and trade associations, publishers, and research activities. **Entries include:** Name of parent organization, name of system of service, address, phone, toll-free phone, fax, telex, email address, year founded name of unit head, size of staff, names of any affiliated organizations, financial information. Internet access information, general description of electronic product, system, or service, subjects covered or areas of service offered, sources of data for the system, type and quantity of stored information in all forms, publications and microform products and services, computer-based products and services, other services, clientele served, availability and restrictions, name of contact. **Arrangement:** Alphabetical. **Indexes:** Master, database name, software name, publication/microform title, function/service, personal name, subject, geographical.

21130 ■ *"Inside Intel's Effectiveness System for Web Marketing" in Advertising Age (Vol. 81, January 25, 2010, No. 4, pp. 4)*
Pub: Crain's Communications
Ed: Beth Snyder Bulik. **Description:** Overview of Intel's internally developed program called Value Point System in which the company is using in order to evaluate and measure online marketing effectiveness.

21131 ■ *"Inside an Online Bazaar" in Entrepreneur (Vol. 37, September 2009, No. 9, pp. 38)*
Pub: Entrepreneur Media Inc.
Ed: Kara Ohngren. **Description:** Etsy.com is a website that provides a marketplace for handmade products. The site has attracted more than 250,000 sellers since its launch in 2005. Site features and services are also supplied.

21132 ■ *"Internet Marketing 2.0: Closing the Online Chat Gap" in Agent's Sales Journal (November 2009, pp. 14)*
Pub: Summit Business Media
Ed: Jeff Denenholz. **Description:** Advice regarding the implementation of an Internet marketing strategy for insurance agencies includes how and why to incorporate a chat feature in which a sales agent can communicate in real-time with potential or existing customers. It is important to understand if appropriate response mechanisms are in place to convert leads into actual sales.

21133 ■ *"Internet Marketing Agency .Com Marketing Wins National Awards for Web Design and SEO" in Marketing Weekly News (Jan. 2, 2010)*
Pub: Investment Weekly News
Description: Internet marketing agency .Com Marketing has won two bronze awards for its exceptional quality web services; the company is a full-service interactive marketing and advertising agency that specializes in a variety of online services including web design, social media marketing and press releases.

21134 ■ *"Internet Marketing Agency .Com Marketing Wins National Awards for Web Design and SEO" in Marketing Weekly News (January 2, 2010)*
Pub: Investment Weekly News
Description: Internet marketing agency .Com Marketing has won two bronze awards for its exceptional quality web services; the company is a full-service interactive marketing and advertising agency that specializes in a variety of online services including web design, social media marketing and press releases.

21135 ■ *"It's a Hit" in Entrepreneur (Vol. 36, March 2008, No. 3, pp. 110)*
Pub: Entrepreneur Media Inc.
Ed: John Jantsch. **Description:** Entrepreneurs use the Web to market business and keeping relevant content in the Website is important to address questions from customers. Other considerations in marketing businesses online include: interacting with site visitors, using Web applications for project collaboration and file storage, and encouraging customers to post reviews.

21136 ■ *"It's a New Game: Killerspin Pushes Table Tennis to Extreme Heights" in Black Enterprise (Vol. 37, October 2006, No. 3, pp. 73)*
Pub: Earl G. Graves Publishing Co. Inc.
Ed: Bridget McCrea. **Description:** Profile of Robert Blackwell and his company Killerspin L.L.C., which is popularizing the sport of table tennis. Killerspin has hit $1 million in revenues due to product sales primarily generated through the company's website, magazines, DVDs, and event ticket sales.

21137 ■ *"Johnson's Taps Online Animation" in Marketing to Women (Vol. 21, April 2008, No. 4, pp. 3)*
Pub: EPM Communications Inc.
Contact: Ira Mayer, President
E-mail: imayer@epmcom.com
Description: Johnson's has launched a new integrated campaign for its baby lotion in an effort to appeal to the growing number of moms online.

21138 ■ *"JumpTV to Hold Conference Call to Discuss Q1 Results and Annual General Meeting" in Canadian Corporate News (May 16, 2007)*
Pub: Comtex News Network Inc.
Description: Profile of JumpTv, the world's leading broadcaster of ethnic television over the Internet, and the results of a conference that discussed their first quarter 2007 financial report as well as the company's business goals. Statistical data included.

21139 ■ *"Kawasaki's New Top Gun" in Brandweek (Vol. 49, April 21, 2008, No. 16, pp. 18)*
Pub: VNU Business Media, Inc.
Description: Discusses Kawasaki's marketing plan which included designing an online brochure in which visitors could create a video by building their own test track on a grid and then selecting visual special effects and musical overlay. This engaging and innovative marketing technique generated more than 166,000 unique users within the first three months of being launched.

21140 ■ *"Keep Them Posted" in Entrepreneur (Vol. 35, October 2007, No. 10, pp. 39)*
Pub: Entrepreneur Media Inc.
Ed: Gwen Moran. **Description:** Survey by the Pew Internet and American Life Project found that 12 million American adults maintain blogs, which are created for personal and business reasons. Blogs are effective in giving a business a personal touch while informing the public about its operations and products. Tips on how to create an effective business blog are presented.

21141 ■ *"Kid-Friendly Business Sources" in Black Enterprise (Vol. 37, January 2007, No. 6, pp. 40)*
Pub: Earl G. Graves Publishing Co. Inc.
Ed: Carolyn M. Brown. **Description:** Financial or business camps are a great way to encourage a child who interested in starting his or her own business. A number of these camps are available each year including Kidpreneurs Conference and Bull and Bear Investment Camp. Other resources are available online. Resources included.

21142 ■ *"Kuno Creative to Present B2B Social Media Campaign Webinar" in Entertainment Close-Up (August 25, 2011)*
Pub: Close-Up Media
Description: Kuno Creative, an inbound marketing agency, will host Three Steps of a Successful B2B Social Media Campaign. The firm is a provider of Website development, branding, marketing strategy, public relations, Internet marketing, and inbound marketing.

21143 ■ *"Last Founder Standing" in Conde Nast Portfolio (Vol. 2, June 2008, No. 6, pp. 124)*
Pub: Conde Nast Publications
Contact: David Carey, President
Ed: Kevin Maney. **Description:** Interview with Amazon CEO Jeff Bezos in which he discusses the economy, the company's new distribution center and the hiring of employees for it, e-books, and the overall vision for the future of the firm.

21144 ■ *"Laterooms and Octopus Travel Top Greenlight's Integrated Search Report for the Hotel Sector" in Internet Wire (October 23, 2009)*
Pub: Comtex News Network, Inc.
Description: According to a research report conducted by Greenlight, the UK's leading independent Internet search marketing agency, the most visible hotel websites in natural search during June 2009 are premierinn.com, booking.com and laterooms.com; OctopusTravel.com generated the greatest share of the paid search section with 21 percent visibility. The report is focused on the hotel sector and covers the second quarter of 2009. Statistical data included.

21145 ■ *"Lavante, Inc. Joins Intersynthesis, Holistic Internet Marketing Company" in Internet Wire (November 5, 2009)*
Pub: Comtex News Network, Inc.
Description: Lavante, Inc., the leading provider of on-demand vendor information and profit recovery audit solutions for Fortune 1000 companies has chosen Intersynthesis, a new holistic Internet marketing firm, as a provider of pay for performance services. Lavante believes that Intersynthesis' expertise and knowledge combined with their ability to develop integrated strategies, will help them fuel more growth.

21146 ■ *"Legal Aid: Sample Legal Documents can Lower Your Attorney Fees" in Black Enterprise (Vol. 37, October 2006, No. 3, pp. 210)*
Pub: Earl G. Graves Publishing Co. Inc.
Ed: Tamara E. Holmes. **Description:** FreeLegalForms.net provides thousands of free legal forms. These forms are not a substitute for consultation with an attorney but the sample documents can help save you time and money.

21147 ■ *"Legislating the Cloud" in Information Today (Vol. 28, October 2011, No. 9, pp. 1)*
Pub: Information Today, Inc.
Description: Internet and telecommunications industry leaders are asking for legislation to address the emerging market in cloud computing. Existing communications laws do not adequately govern the modern Internet.

21148 ■ *"A Life of Spice" in Entrepreneur (Vol. 37, September 2009, No. 9, pp. 46)*
Pub: Entrepreneur Media, Inc.
Ed: Jason Daley. **Description:** Matt and Bryan Walls have successfully grown their Atlanta, Georgia-based Snorg Tees T-shirt company. The company has expanded its product offering and redesigned its Website to be more user-friendly. The company has registered between $5 and 10 million in 2008.

21149 ■ *"Lights, Camera, Action: Tools for Creating Video Blogs" in Inc. (Volume 32, December 2010, No. 10, pp. 57)*
Pub: Inc. Magazine
Ed: John Brandon. **Description:** A video blog is a good way to spread company news, talk about products, and stand out among traditional company blogs. New editing software can create two- to four-minute blogs using a webcam and either Windows Live Essentials, Apple iLife 2011, Powerdirector 9 Ultra, or Adobe Visual Communicator 3.

21150 ■ *"MaggieMoo's Ice Cream and Treatery" in Ice Cream Reporter (Vol. 23, September 20, 2010, No. 10, pp. 7)*
Pub: Ice Cream Reporter
Description: MaggieMoo's Ice Cream and Treatery has launched a new Website where visitors can learn about the brands newest ice cream innovations.

21151 ■ *"Make It Easy" in Entrepreneur (Vol. 36, May 2008, No. 5, pp. 49)*
Pub: Entrepreneur Media, Inc.
Ed: Mike Hogan. **Description:** Zoho has a Planner that keep contacts, notes and reminders and a DB & Reports feature for reports, data analysis and pricing comparisons. WebEx WebOffice Workgroup supports document management and templates for contacts lists, time sheets and sales tracking. Other online data manages are presented.

21152 ■ *"Marketing Management Analytics Announces MMA Digital" in Internet Wire (January 26, 2010)*
Pub: Comtex News Network, Inc.
Description: Innovator and pioneer in marketing effectiveness, Marketing Management Analytics, is offering a new service called MMA Digital; using this service companies will be able to more accurately measure the effects of digital media alongside other marketing tools in order to better understand and leverage the drivers of online marketing success.

21153 ■ *"McD's Warms Up For Olympics Performance" in Advertising Age (Vol. 79, July 7, 2008, No. 26, pp. 8)*
Pub: Crain Communications, Inc.
Description: Overview of McDonald's marketing plans for the company's sponsorship of the Olympics which includes a website, an alternate-reality game, names featured on U.S. athletes and on-the-ground activities.

21154 ■ *"Milk Producers Target Moms" in Marketing to Women (Vol. 21, January 2008, No. 1, pp. 3)*
Pub: EPM Communications Inc.
Contact: Ira Mayer, President
E-mail: imayer@epmcom.com
Description: In an attempt to encourage moms to serve milk with meals, the American Dairy Association partners with the New York State Dietetic Association to promote milk via a new logo, website and contest.

21155 ■ *"Million Dollar Website: Simple Steps to Help You Compete with the Big Boys-Even on a Small Business Budget*
Pub: Prentice Hall Press
Ed: Lori Culwell. **Released:** May 9, 2010. **Price:** $19.95. **Description:** Resource for any small business owner wishing to build a successful Website in order to compete with big box stores.

21156 ■ *"Mobile Presence, in a Flash: DIY Tools for Creating Smartphone-Friendly Websites" in Inc. (Vol. 33, November 2011,*
No. 9, pp. 50)
Pub: Inc. Magazine
Ed: John Brandon. **Description:** DudaMobile and FiddleFly convert regular Websites into mobile sites that work on most smartphones. Profiles of both apps services are included.

21157 ■ *"Most Viewed Stories, Videos on farmindustrynews.com in 2010" in Farm Industry News (January 4, 2011)*
Pub: Penton Business Media Inc.
Description: The top ten most popularly viewed stories and videos presented on farmindustrynews.com Website are listed.

21158 ■ *"The Neighborhood Watch" in Hawaii Business (Vol. 53, March 2008, No. 9, pp. 36)*
Pub: Hawaii Business Publishing
Ed: David K. Choo. **Description:** OahuRe.com offers information on Hawaii real estate market, with spreadsheets and comparative market analysis page, which shows properties that are active, sold, or in escrow. Other details about OahuRe.com are discussed. A list of other top real estate websites in Hawaii and in the U.S. in general is provided.

21159 ■ *"Net Connections" in Black Enterprise (Vol. 38, July 2008, No. 12, pp. 28)*
Pub: Earl G. Graves Publishing Co. Inc.
Ed: Anthony S. Calypso. **Description:** Marketers are making strategic partnerships with online social networks in an attempt to gain further market reach. The value of these networks appears to be on the rise forcing media companies to recalculate their strategies for delivering products to customers.

21160 ■ *"Networking Web Sites: a Two-Edged Sword" in Contractor (Vol. 56, October 2009, No. 10, pp. 52)*
Pub: Penton Media, Inc.
Ed: H. Kent Craig. **Description:** People need to be careful about the information that they share on social networking Web sites. They should realize that future bosses, coworkers, and those that might want to hire them might read those information. Posting on these sites can cost career opportunities and respect.

21161 ■ *"The New Basics of Marketing" in Inc. (February 2008, pp. 75-81)*
Pub: Gruner & Jahr USA Publishing
Ed: Leigh Buchanan. **Description:** New tools for marketing a business or service include updating or upgrading a Website, using email or texting, or advertising on a social Internet network.

21162 ■ *"New Recession-Proof Internet Marketing Package Allows Businesses to Ramp Up Web Traffic and Profits" in PR Newswire (Jan. 25, 2010)*
Pub: PR Newswire Association, LLC
Description: Profile of Reel Web Design, a leading marketing firm in New York City that caters to small to medium sized businesses with smaller budgets that need substantial return on investment; Reel Web Design offers video production and submission, web design and maintenance and press release writing among additional services.

21163 ■ *"New Recession-Proof Internet Marketing Package Allows Businesses to Ramp Up Web Traffic and Profits" in PR Newswire (Jan. 25, 2010)*
Pub: PR Newswire Association, LLC
Description: Profile of Reel Web Design, a leading marketing firm in New York City that caters to small to medium sized businesses with smaller budgets that need substantial return on investment; Reel Web Design offers video production and submission, web design and maintenance and press release writing among additional services.

21164 ■ *"New TurnHere Survey Reveals Online Video Trends" in Internet Wire (October 22, 2009)*
Pub: Comtex News Network, Inc.
Description: TurnHere, Inc., the leading online video marketing services company, released the findings of its recent survey regarding current and future trends in online video among marketing agencies and brand recognition; the report found that online video has
and will continue to play a prominent role in the realm of marketing edging out both search and email marketing campaigns. Additional highlights and statistical data included.

21165 ■ *"A New Way to Tell When to Fold" in Barron's (Vol. 88, July 7, 2008, No. 27, pp. 27)*
Pub: Dow Jones & Co., Inc.
Ed: Theresa W. Carey. **Description:** Overview of the Online trading company SmartStops, a firm that aims to tell investors when to sell the shares of a particular company. The company's Web site categorizes stocks as moving up, down, or sideways, and calculates exit points for individual stocks based on an overall market trend.

21166 ■ *"Norvax University Health Insurance Sales Training and Online Marketing Conference" in Internet Wire (January 27, 2010)*
Pub: Comtex News Network, Inc.
Description: Overview of the Norvax University Marketing and Sales Success Conference Tour which includes insurance sales training seminars, proven and innovative online marketing techniques and a host of additional information and networking opportunities.

21167 ■ *"Oh, Behave!" in Entrepreneur (Vol. 36, April 2008, No. 4, pp. 87)*
Pub: Entrepreneur Media, Inc.
Ed: Gwen Moran. **Description:** Online social networks can pose awkward situations for users. These include instances such as getting a link request from someone you do not know, having a contact post embarrassing information on your site, and a contact asking you to be refer him to one of your business contacts. Tips on how to deal with these situations are discussed.

21168 ■ *"Omniture's Next Version of SearchCenter Delivers Landing Page Optimization" in Internet Wire (September 24, 2009)*
Pub: Comtex News Network, Inc.
Description: Omniture, Inc., a leading provider of online business optimization software, has announced a new release of Omniture SearchCenter; this latest version will allow search engine marketers to test landing pages across campaigns and ad groups.

21169 ■ *"On Target" in Canadian Business (Vol. 81, July 22, 2008, No. 12-13, pp. 45)*
Pub: Rogers Media Ltd.
Ed: Calvin Leung. **Description:** Companies such as LavalifePRIME, a dating website devoted to singles 45 and older, discuss the value of marketing and services aimed at Canada's older consumers. One-third of Canada's 33 million people are 50-plus, controlling 77 percent of the countries wealth.

21170 ■ *"Online Forex Broker Tadawul FX Intros Arabic Website" in Entertainment Close-Up (June 23, 2011)*
Pub: Close-Up Media
Description: Online forex broker, Tadawul FX, launched its Arabic language Website, noting that the Middle East is a key market for the investment firm.

21171 ■ *"Online Marketing and Promotion of Canadian Films via Social Media Tools" in CNW Group (January 27, 2010)*
Pub: Comtex News Network, Inc.
Description: Telefilm Canada announced the launch of a pilot initiative aimed at encouraging the integration of online marketing and the use of social media tools into means of distribution ahead of a films' theatrical release. During this pilot phase Web-Cine 360 will target French-language feature films.

21172 ■ *"Online Postings Really Influence Older Women" in Marketing to Women (Vol. 22, July 2009, No. 7, pp. 8)*
Pub: EPM Communications Inc.
Contact: Ira Mayer, President
E-mail: imayer@epmcom.com
Description: Women over the age of 55 are more likely to be swayed to purchase a product by referrals from others, including Online postings by strangers. Another key influence is associated with the brand's ability to address their lifestyle needs.

21173 ■ *"Online Self-Publishing Services"* in *Black Enterprise (Vol. 37, November 2006, No. 4, pp. 90)*
Pub: Earl G. Graves Publishing Co. Inc.
Description: Profiles of five online self-publishing services.

21174 ■ *"Orbitz Adds Parent Panel"* in *Marketing to Women (Vol. 21, March 2008, No. 3, pp. 5)*
Pub: EPM Communications Inc.
Contact: Ira Mayer, President
E-mail: imayer@epmcom.com
Description: Orbitz introduces the Orbitz Parent Panel in an attempt to better connect with traveling families.

21175 ■ *"Ordering Pizza Hut From Your Facebook Page?"* in *Advertising Age (Vol. 79, November 10, 2008, No. 42, pp. 50)*
Pub: Crain Communications, Inc.
Ed: Emily Bryson York. **Description:** Fast-food chains are experimenting with delivery/takeout services via social networks such as Facebook and iPhone applications. This also allows the chains to build valuable databases of their customers.

21176 ■ *"Our Gadget of the Week: Mostly, I Liked It"* in *Barron's (Vol. 88, July 14, 2008, No. 28, pp. 31)*
Pub: Dow Jones & Co., Inc.
Ed: Jay Palmer. **Description:** Review of the Apple iPhone 3G, which costs $199, has better audio and is slightly thicker than its predecessor; using the 3G wireless connection makes going online faster but drains the battery faster too.

21177 ■ *"Our World with Black Enterprise"* in *Black Enterprise (Vol. 37, February 2007, No. 7, pp. 145)*
Pub: Earl G. Graves Publishing Co. Inc.
Description: Our World with Black Enterprise is a television broadcast that features roundtable discussions and interviews with important African American figures.

21178 ■ *"Pagetender LLC Releases Website Design Package for HubSpot Users"* in *Internet Wire (September 30, 2009)*
Pub: Comtex News Network, Inc.
Description: Profile of Pagetender LLC, a Certified HubSpot partner, who announced a Website Design Package marketed specifically for HubSpot Owner and Marketer users. This packaged was developed for small to medium sized businesses that want a website designed or their current site redesigned on HubSpot's Content Management System. Companies that would like a more robust site have the option of adding Flash development, ecommerce and photo galleries.

21179 ■ *"P&G to Mine E-Commerce Potential"* in *Business Courier (Vol. 26, September 18, 2009, No. 21, pp. 1)*
Pub: American City Business Journals, Inc.
Ed: Lisa Biank Fasig. **Description:** Procter & Gamble (P&G) is looking to turn the hits to the company's Websites into increased sales. The program will include a shop now option to track all emerging sales.

21180 ■ *"Paterson Plots Comeback With Internet IPO"* in *Globe & Mail (February 20, 2006, pp. B1)*
Pub: CTVglobemedia Publishing Inc.
Ed: Grant Robertson. **Description:** The initial public offering plans of chief executive officer Scott Paterson of JumpTV.com are presented.

21181 ■ *"Pet-Food Crisis a Boon to Organic Players"* in *Advertising Age (Vol. 78, April 9, 2007, No. 15, pp. 3)*
Pub: Crain Communications, Inc.
Ed: Jack Neff. **Description:** In the wake of the pet-food recall crisis, the natural-and-organic segment of the market is gaining recognition and sales; one such manufacturer, Blue Buffalo, has not only seen huge sale increases but also has witnessed a 50-60

percent increase in traffic to the brand's website which has led to the decision to move up the timetable for the brand's first national ad campaign.

21182 ■ *"Play By Play: These Video Products Can Add New Life to a Stagnant Website"* in *Black Enterprise (Vol. 41, December 2010, No. 5)*
Pub: Earl G. Graves Publishing Co. Inc.
Ed: Marcia Wade Talbert. **Description:** Web Visible, provider of online marketing products and services, cites video capability as the fastest-growing Website feature for small business advertisers. Profiles of various devices for adding video to a Website are included.

21183 ■ *"The Power of Negative Thinking"* in *Inc. (Volume 32, December 2010, No. 10, pp. 43)*
Pub: Inc. Magazine
Ed: Jason Fried. **Description:** A Website is software and most businesses have and need a good Website to generate business. Understanding for building a powerful Website is presented.

21184 ■ *"Pretentious and Loving It"* in *Entrepreneur (Vol. 37, August 2009, No. 8, pp. 34)*
Pub: Entrepreneur Media, Inc.
Ed: Eric Mahoney. **Description:** Pitchfork.com features reviews of albums from independent artists. Their most innovative section is Pitchfork.tv, featuring videos of bands, and Forkcast along with their Features section that contains articles about bands and their histories.

21185 ■ *"Pro Livestock Launches Most Comprehensive Virtual Sales Barn for Livestock and Breed Stock"* in *Benzinga.com (October 29, 2011)*
Pub: Benzinga.com
Ed: Benzinga Staff. **Description:** Pro Livestock Marketing launched the first online sales portal for livestock and breed stock. The firm has designed a virtual sales barn allowing individuals to purchase and sell cattle, swine, sheep, goats, horses, rodeo stock, show animals, specialty animals, semen and embryos globally. It is like an eBay for livestock and will help ranchers and farmers grow.

21186 ■ *"Recalls Cause Consumers to Put More Stock in Online Reviews"* in *Crain's Cleveland Business (Vol. 28, November 12, 2007, No. 45)*
Pub: Crain Communications, Inc.
Ed: Jack Neff. **Description:** Due to the string of product recalls over the last year, consumers are looking at online product reviews to help them make purchasing decisions which could reshape marketing for a wide range of products.

21187 ■ *"Recovery2.0: a Work in Progress"* in *Tampa Bay Business Journal (Vol. 30, December 18, 2009, No. 52, pp. 3)*
Pub: American City Business Journals
Ed: Margaret Cashill. **Description:** The debut of the Recovery.gov 2.0 version has raised questions regarding the Website's price tag, which will cost nearly $18 million. Tampa, Florida-based GSL Solutions Inc. president Michael Gaines believes the Websites created with existing technologies tend to cost less than custom development. The difference between Recovery.org and Recovery.gov are explained.

21188 ■ *"Reportlinker Adds Report: Social Networks: Five Consumer Trends for 2009"* in *Wireless News (October 23, 2009)*
Pub: Close-Up Media
Description: 'Social Networks: Five Consumer Trends for 2009,' a new market research report by Reportlinker.com found that in the countries of Italy and Spain lag behind their European neighbors in Internet development. Since large numbers of consumers in these two countries remain offline, only a minimal portion of total advertising spending goes into Internet marketing, and those advertising campaigns are directed at the relatively young, affluent users. Statistical data included.

21189 ■ *"Reportlinker.com Adds Report: GeoWeb and Local Internet Markets: 2008 Edition"* in *Entertainment Close-Up (September 11, 2009)*
Pub: Close-Up Media
Description: Reportlinker.com is adding a new market research report that is available in its catalogue: GeoWeb and Local Internet Markets - 2008 Edition; highlights include the outlook for consumer mapping services and an examination of monetizing services and an analysis the development outlook for geospacial Internet market, also referred to as the Geoweb.

21190 ■ *"Research Reports: How Analysts Size Up Companies"* in *Barron's (Vol. 88, March 17, 2008, No. 11, pp. M13)*
Pub: Dow Jones & Company, Inc.
Ed: Anita Peltonen. **Description:** Shares of Applied Industrial Technologies are ranked Market Perform while the shares of Google get a buy rating. Salix Pharmaceuticals gets a Sell/Above-Average risk rating. The shares of Dune Energy, Franklin Resources, Internet Brands, Piper Jaffray, and Texas Instruments are also rated.

21191 ■ *"Resource Line"* in *Black Enterprise (Vol. 37, January 2007, No. 6, pp. 6)*
Pub: Earl G. Graves Publishing Co. Inc.
Description: Interactive Media Editor, Philana Patterson, writes a column for blackenterprise.com that offers advice and provides resources for entrepreneurs, corporate executives, business owners, and budding investors.

21192 ■ *"Retail Franchises to Start Now"* in *Entrepreneur (Vol. 37, August 2009, No. 8, pp. 88)*
Pub: Entrepreneur Media, Inc.
Ed: Tracy Stapp. **Description:** Listing of retail franchises is presented and is categorized based on their products sold. The total cost of the franchise and the website are also included as well as additional statistical data.

21193 ■ *"The Right Time for REITs"* in *Barron's (Vol. 88, July 14, 2008, No. 28, pp. 32)*
Pub: Dow Jones & Co., Inc.
Ed: Mike Hogan. **Description:** Discusses the downturn in U.S. real estate investment trusts so these are worth considering for investment. Several Websites that are useful for learning about real estate investment trusts for investment purposes are presented.

21194 ■ *"Rise Interactive, Internet Marketing Agency, Now Offers Social Media Training and Advisory Services"* in *Internet Wire (Nov. 4, 2009)*
Pub: Comtex News Network, Inc.
Description: Profile of Rise Interactive, a full-service Internet marketing agency which has recently added social media to its list of offerings; the agency touts that its newest service gives their clients the power to have ongoing communication with current and potential customers on the sites they are most actively visiting.

21195 ■ *"ROIonline Announces Streaming Video Products"* in *Marketing Weekly News (December 5, 2009, pp. 155)*
Pub: Investment Weekly News
Description: ROIonline LLC, an Internet marketing firm serving business-to-business and the industrial marketplace, has added streaming video options to the Internet solutions it offers its clients; due to the huge increase of broadband connections, videos are now commonplace on the Internet and can often convey a company's message in a must more efficient, concise and effective way that will engage a website's visitor thus delivering a high return on a company's investment.

21196 ■ *"Rumor Has It"* in *Entrepreneur (Vol. 35, October 2007, No. 10, pp. 30)*
Pub: Entrepreneur Media Inc.
Ed: Chris Penttila. **Description:** Some entrepreneurs like Ren Moulton and Dan Scudder regard rumor sites and product blogs as great sources of market

research. However, there are legal issues that must be studied before using these Internet sites in marketing and product development. The use and limitations of rumor sites and product blogs are provided.

21197 ■ "Schipul Enhances Website Via Tendenci 5" in Entertainment Close-Up (March 30, 2011)
Pub: Close-Up Media
Description: Schipul, Website marketing and design firm, upgraded their Website using Tendenci 5 which features capabilities that cater to the interests of the user. Tendenci 5 also powers Websites for Houston Technology Center, Discovery Green, Tendenci and YMCA Houston.

21198 ■ The Search: How Google and Its Rival Rewrote the Rules of Business and Transformed Our Culture
Pub: Penguin Group Incorporated
Ed: John Battelle. Released: October 3, 2006. Price: $14.95. Description: Provides a history of Internet search technology.

21199 ■ The SEO Manifesto: A Practical and Ethical Guide to Internet Marketing and Search Engine Optimization
Pub: Cape Project Management Inc.
Ed: Dan Tousignant, Pamela Gobiel. Released: December 5, 2011. Price: $14.99. Description: Comprehensive guide for each phase of launching an online business; chapters include checklists, process descriptions, and examples.

21200 ■ "Sharing the Micro Wealth" in Entrepreneur (Vol. 37, July 2009, No. 7, pp. 46)
Pub: Entrepreneur Media, Inc.
Ed: Jennie Dorris. Description: Step-by-step guide is presented on how Kiva.org, a website which allows people to make microloans to entrepreneurs across the world, works. The website, founded by Matt Flannery, raises $1 million weekly and it will add U.S. entrepreneurs to its list of loan recipients in June 2010. Other features of Kiva.org are discussed.

21201 ■ "Shipping 2.0" in Entrepreneur (Vol. 36, April 2008, No. 4, pp. 54)
Pub: Entrepreneur Media, Inc.
Ed: Heather Clancy. Description: Doggypads.com contacted with Web 2.0 service provider Shipwire to handle its warehouse concerns. The service works by paying a rent to Shipwire and they will store the client's items. The client's customers can continue to order from the client's website and Shipwire will take care of delivery. Doggypads was able to save up on costs by using Shipwire.

21202 ■ "Shoestring-Budget Marketing" in Women Entrepreneur (January 5, 2009)
Pub: Entrepreneur Media Inc.
Ed: Maria Falconer. Description: Pay-per-click search engine advertising is the traditional type of e-marketing that may not only be too expensive for certain kinds of businesses but also may not attract the quality customer base a business looking to grow needs to find. Social networking websites have become a mandatory marketing tool for business owners who want to see growth in their sales; tips are provided for utilizing these networking websites in order to gain more visibility on the Internet which can, in turn, lead to the more sales.

21203 ■ "Siteworx Earns 4 Interactive Media Awards in Q1 of 2011" in Entertainment Close-Up (, 2011)
Pub: Close-Up Media
Description: Details of the four awards Siteworx earned for its achievements in Web development and design are outlined.

21204 ■ The Small Business Owner's Manual: Everything You Need to Know to Start Up and Run Your Business
Pub: Career Press, Incorporated
Ed: Joe Kennedy. Released: June 2005. Price: $19.99 (US), $26.95 (Canadian). Description: Comprehensive guide for starting a small business, focusing on twelve ways to obtain financing, business plans, selling and advertising products and

services, hiring and firing employees, setting up a Web site, business law, accounting issues, insurance equipment, computers, banks, financing, customer credit and collection, leasing, and more.

21205 ■ "Social Media: Communicate the Important Stuff" in Agency Sales Magazine (Vol. 39, November 2009, No. 10, pp. 52)
Pub: MANA
Ed: Jack Foster. Description: Social media such as Twitter or Facebook allows businesses to communicate with their customers over great distances but this technology can take away from the personal touch. For those that want to implement these tools in their marketing plans, they should first find out which social media networks their target audience use and give their customers reasons to become fans.

21206 ■ "Social Media, E-Mail Remain Challenging for Employees" in Workforce Management (Vol. 88, December 14, 2009, No. 13, pp. 4)
Pub: Crain Communications Inc.
Ed: Ed Frauenheim. Description: Examining the impact of Internet social networking and the workplace; due to the power of these new technologies, it is important that companies begin to set clear policies regarding Internet use and employee privacy.

21207 ■ "Social Networkers for Hire" in Black Enterprise (Vol. 40, December 2009, No. 5, pp. 56)
Pub: Earl G. Graves Publishing Co., Inc.
Ed: Brittany Hutson. Description: Companies are utilizing social networking sites in order to market their brand and personally connect with consumers and are increasingly looking to social media specialists to help with this task. Aliya S. King is one such web strategist, working for ICED Media by managing their Twitter, Facebook, YouTube and Flickr accounts for one of their publicly traded restaurant clients.

21208 ■ "Social Networking Butterfly" in Entrepreneur (Vol. 37, September 2009, No. 9, pp. 48)
Pub: Entrepreneur Media, Inc.
Ed: Jason Daley. Description: Entrepreneur Ashley Qualls has successfully grown Whateverlife.com. The site was originally created to share Qualls' custom MySpace.com templates with friends and family. Qualls is planning to redesign the site as a social network focused on Web design.

21209 ■ "Social Networking Site for Moms" in Marketing to Women (Vol. 21, March 2008, No. 3, pp. 3)
Pub: EPM Communications Inc.
Contact: Ira Mayer, President
E-mail: imayer@epmcom.com
Description: The Cradle is a social networking site devoted to pregnancy and new parenthood

21210 ■ "Sometimes, Second Impressions Count Most" in Canadian Business (Vol. 83, October 12, 2010, No. 17, pp. 11)
Pub: Rogers Media Ltd.
Ed: Richard Branson. Description: Developing a favorable impression at the first point of contact is imperative for businesses. Managers who want their organizations to make positive first and second impressions need to learn to balance the Web's labor-saving efficiencies with human assistants. The importance of considering the customer relations value in company Websites is also explained.

21211 ■ "Sticking to Stories; Havey Ovshinksy Changes Method, Keeps the Mission" in Crain's Detroit Business (Vol. 24, March 31, 2008)
Pub: Crain Communications, Inc.
Ed: Daniel Duggan. Description: Profile of Harvey Ovshinsky, an award-winning documentary filmmaker who has reinvented his work with corporations who want to market themselves with the transition to digital media. His company, HKO Media, takes

Ovshinsky's art of storytelling and enhances it through multimedia operations on the Internet through a joint venture with a man he once mentored, Bob Kernen.

21212 ■ "Stimulating Fare at the SBA" in Barron's (Vol. 89, July 20, 2009, No. 29, pp. 12)
Pub: Dow Jones & Co., Inc.
Ed: Jim McTague. Description: Internet access at the Small Business Administration slowed down on 7 July 2009, apparently caused by employees streaming videos of the Michael Jackson tribute. The agency claims that the event did not disrupt its operations.

21213 ■ "Success Products" in Black Enterprise (Vol. 37, February 2007, No. 7, pp. 135)
Pub: Earl G. Graves Publishing Co. Inc.
Ed: Tanisha A. Sykes. Description: Using innovative resources that are already at your fingertips instead of trying to reach out to companies first is a great way to discover whether you have a viable idea or product. Be motivated to start an e-newsletter letting people know about your products and attend conferences like The Motivation Show, the world's largest exhibition of motivational products and services related to performance in business.

21214 ■ Success Secrets of Social Media Marketing Superstars
Pub: Entrepreneur Press
Contact: Perlman Neil, President
Ed: Mitch Meyerson. Released: June 1, 2010. Price: $21.95. Description: Provides access to the playbooks of social media marketers who reveal their most valuable strategies and tactics for standing out in the new online media environment.

21215 ■ "Suncoast Pest Control Introduces New Website" in Entertainment Close-Up (March 16, 2011)
Pub: Close-Up Media
Description: Florida pest control company, Suncoast Pest Control, launched a new Website to better serve their customers. The new Website will allow users to reach local Florida pest control professionals 24 hours a day.

21216 ■ "A Taxing Proposition" in Black Enterprise (Vol. 37, January 2007, No. 6, pp. 6)
Pub: Earl G. Graves Publishing Co. Inc.
Description: Learn how to avoid tax problems on Black Enterprise's website, blackenterprise.com.

21217 ■ "Tee Off Online" in Black Enterprise (Vol. 37, January 2007, No. 6, pp. 52)
Pub: Earl G. Graves Publishing Co. Inc.
Ed: James C. Johnson. Description: The E-Com Resource Center is one of many resources that are available for those interested in starting an e-commerce business. One of the first steps is to create a business plan, of which there are free samples available at BPlans.com.

21218 ■ "Texas Fold 'Em" in Canadian Business (Vol. 79, October 9, 2006, No. 20, pp. 44)
Pub: Rogers Media
Ed: John Gray. Description: New policies of the United States law makers for the online casino industries that could force many of them out of business are discussed.

21219 ■ "Things Really Clicking for Macy's Online" in Business Courier (Vol. 24, November 30, 2008, No. 33, pp. 1)
Pub: American City Business Journals, Inc.
Ed: Lisa Biank Fasig. Description: Retailer Macy's online division Macys.com are projecting sales at $1billion in 2007, compared to $620 million in 2006. Macy's new online features and products and the growth of online retail sector are also discussed.

21220 ■ "Thomas Industrial Network Unveils Custom SPEC" in Entertainment Close-Up

(March 3, 2011)
Pub: Close-Up Media

Description: Thomas Industrial Network assists custom manufacturers and industrial service providers a complete online program called Custom SPEC which includes Website development and Internet exposure.

21221 ■ *"Tim Armstrong" in Canadian Business (Vol. 81, July 21, 2008, No. 11, pp. 10)*
Pub: Rogers Media Ltd.

Ed: Calvin Leung. **Description:** Interview with Tim Armstrong who is the president of advertising and commerce department of Google Inc. for North America; the information technology company executive talked about the emerging trends and changes to YouTube made by the company since its acquisition in 2006.

21222 ■ *"To Blog, Or Not To Blog" in Canadian Business (Vol. 80, December 25, 2006, No. 1, pp. 15)*
Pub: Rogers Media

Ed: Andy Holloway. **Description:** The growing use of weblogs for internet marketing by business enterprises is discussed.

21223 ■ *"The Top Mistakes of Social Media Marketing" in Agency Sales Magazine (Vol. 39, November 2009, No. 9, pp. 42)*
Pub: MANA

Ed: Pam Lontos; Maurice Ramirez. **Description:** One common mistake in social media marketing is having more than one image on the Internet because this ruins a business' credibility. Marketers need to put out messages that are useful to their readers and to keep messages consistent.

21224 ■ *"Traffic's Up: Website's Down Preventing Costly Crashes" in Inc. (March 2008, pp. 55-56)*
Pub: Gruner & Jahr USA Publishing

Ed: Darren Dahl. **Description:** Grid Web hosting protects a small company's Website when a sudden burst of Internet traffic hits enabling it to continue rather than be crippled. Options can vary in cost from $4 to $1,000 monthly and include using a shared server, grid server, virtual private server, or a dedicated server. The article explains each option.

21225 ■ *"Traits that Makes Blogs Attractive to Book Publishers" in Marketing to Women (Vol. 22, July 2009, No. 7, pp. 1)*
Pub: EPM Communications Inc.

Contact: Ira Mayer, President

E-mail: imayer@epmcom.com

Description: Book publishers are finding a beneficial relationship between themselves and women bloggers on the Internet. A high visitor count, frequent updates and active readership are criteria for identifying the blogs with the most clout and therefore providing the greatest benefit to publishers.

21226 ■ *"Transform Your Life" in Black Enterprise (Vol. 37, January 2007, No. 6, pp. 14)*
Pub: Earl G. Graves Publishing Co. Inc.

Description: Through the magazine, television and radio programs, events, and the website, the various platforms of Black Enterprise will provide the tools necessary to achieve success in business ventures, career aspirations, and personal goals.

21227 ■ *"The Twittering Class" in Entrepreneur (Vol. 37, September 2009, No. 9, pp. 40)*
Pub: Entrepreneur Media, Inc.

Ed: Mikal E. Belicove. **Description:** Advice on how entrepreneurs can use online social networks to promote their businesses is presented. Facebook offers applications and advertising solutions to promote Websites, products and services. Twitter, on the other hand, provides instant messaging, which can be done through computer or cell phone.

21228 ■ *"Twitterville: How Businesses Can Thrive in the New Global Neighborhoods*
Pub: Portfolio Hardcover

Ed: Shel Israel. **Price:** $23.95. **Description:** Twitter is the most rapidly adopted communication tool in history, going from zero to ten million users in just over two years. On Twitter, word can spread faster than wildfire. Companies no longer have the option of ignoring the conversation. Unlike other hot social media spaces, Twitterville is dominated by professionals, not students. And despite its size, it still feels like a small town. Twitter allows people to interact much the way they do face-to-face, honestly and authentically.

21229 ■ *"Unlimited Priorities Strengthens Executive Team" in Entertainment Close-Up (November 1, 2011)*
Pub: Close-Up Media

Description: Founder and president of Unlimited Priorities Corporation, Iris L. Hanney, added two executive level professionals to her team. The new employees will help increase the firm's capabilities in social media and information technology.

21230 ■ *"Up To Code? Website Eases Compliance Burden for Entrepreneurs" in Black Enterprise (Vol. 38, March 2008, No. 8, pp. 48)*
Pub: Earl G. Graves Publishing Co. Inc.

Ed: Robin White-Goode. **Description:** Business.gov is a presidential E-government project created to help small businesses easily find, understand, and comply with laws and regulations pertaining to a particular industry.

21231 ■ *"Utah Technology Council: Social Media Is Here to Stay; Embrace It" in Wireless News (December 14, 2009)*
Pub: Close-Up Media

Description: Social media outlets such as Facebook and Twitter are blurring the lines between advertising, public relations, branding and marketing; businesses must stop thinking in terms of traditional marketing versus Internet marketing if they want to succeed in today's marketing climate.

21232 ■ *"A View to a Killer Business Model" in Black Enterprise (Vol. 40, December 2009, No. 5, pp. 50)*
Pub: Earl G. Graves Publishing Co., Inc.

Ed: Sonya A. Donaldson. **Description:** Profile of Gen2Media Corp., a production, technology and Internet marketing firm based in Florida with offices in New York; Gen2Media is utilizing the advances in technology to now include video in its online marketing offerings.

21233 ■ *"Virtus.com Wins 'Best of Industry' WebAward for Excellence in Financial Services" in Investment Weekly News (October 24, 2009)*
Pub: Investment Weekly News

Description: Web Marketing Association honored Virtus.com, the Website of Virtus Investment Partners, Inc., for Outstanding Achievement in Web Development and Acsys Interactive was awarded the Financial Services Standard of Excellence Award for developing the site. The site was part of a rebranding effort and is a one-stop portal for both financial advisors and their investors.

21234 ■ *"Virtus.com Wins 'Best of Industry' WebAward for Excellence in Financial Services" in Investment Weekly News (Oct. 24, 2009, pp. 227)*
Pub: Investment Weekly News

Description: Web Marketing Association honored Virtus.com, the Website of Virtus Investment Partners, Inc., for Outstanding Achievement in Web Development and Acsys Interactive was awarded the Financial Services Standard of Excellence Award for developing the site. The site was part of a rebranding effort and is a one-stop portal for both financial advisors and their investors.

21235 ■ *"The Way I Work" in Inc. (March 2008, pp. 102-104, 106)*
Pub: Gruner & Jahr USA Publishing

Ed: Hannah Clark Steiman. **Description:** Profile of Howard Lefkowitz, CEO of Vegas.com, a Website that allows visitors to book flights, reserve hotel

rooms, buy show tickets, make spa appointments, and coordinate any and all aspects of a trip to Las Vegas. The firm also runs brick-and-mortar box offices and concierge desks at various cities.

21236 ■ *"Web-Based Solutions Streamline Operations" in Contractor (Vol. 56, December 2009, No. 12, pp. 28)*
Pub: Penton Media, Inc.

Ed: William Feldman; Patti Feldman. **Description:** Sage Project Lifecycle Management is a Web-based service platform for plumbing and HVAC contractors. It enables effective workflow and document management. Projectmates, on the other hand, is a Web-based enterprise-wide solution for managing both commercial plumbing and HVAC projects.

21237 ■ *"Web Biz Brulant Surfing for Acquisition Candidates" in Crain's Cleveland Business (Vol. 28, December 3, 2007, No. 48, pp. 6)*
Pub: Crain Communications, Inc.

Ed: Chuck Soder. **Description:** Brulant Inc., a provider of web development and marketing services, is looking to acquire other companies after growing for five years straight. The company is one of the largest technology firms in Northeast Ohio.

21238 ■ *"Web-Preneuring" in Small Business Opportunities (May 2008)*
Pub: Harris Publications Inc.

Description: 1&1 Internet provides known servers with more than 6.84 million customers through contracts with both consumer and business users. It operates five secure data centers housing 40,000 servers that process more than 5 billion monthly emails.

21239 ■ *"Web to Print" in American Printer (Vol. 128, August 1, 2011, No. 8)*
Pub: Penton Media Inc.

Description: Jerry Kennelly, CEO and founder of Tweak.com believes that Web-to-Design is middleware with no content. His firm offers an easy to use interface that flows right into the printer's workflow with no additional costs.

21240 ■ *"Web Sight: Do You See What I See?" in Entrepreneur (Vol. 35, October 2007, No. 10, pp. 58)*
Pub: Entrepreneur Media Inc.

Ed: Heather Clancy. **Description:** Owners of Trunkt, a boutique in New York that showcases independent designs, have created a new style of Website called Trunkt.org. The Website allows buyers to select the products they want to see and designers can choose anytime which of their items will be displayed on the site. An explanation of the strategy that helped bring Trunkt closer to its clients is presented.

21241 ■ *"Web Site Design, Content Can Boost Diversity" in HRMagazine (Vol. 53, August 2008, No. 8, pp. 20)*
Pub: Society for Human Resource Management
Contact: Henry G. Jackson, President
E-mail: hjackson@shrm.org

Description: Design and content of an employer's Website influences prospective young job candidates, especially young black job seekers, a new academic study has found. The findings appear in Black and White and Read All Over: Race Differences in Reactions To Recruitment Web Sites, published in the summer 2008 issue of the Human Resource Management Journal.

21242 ■ *"Web Site Focuses on Helping People Find Jobs, Internships with Area Businesses" in Crain's Detroit Business (Vol. 26, Jan. 4, 2010)*
Pub: Crain Communications Inc.

Ed: Dustin Walsh. **Description:** DetroitIntern.com, LLC is helping metro Detroit college students and young professionals find career-advancing internships or jobs with local businesses.

21243 ■ *"Web Traffic Numbers Facing Scrutiny" in Boston Business Journal (Vol. 27, November 2, 2007, No. 40, pp. 1)*
Pub: American City Business Journals Inc.

Ed: Jesse Noyes. **Description:** Interactive Advertising Bureau (IAB) held a summit meeting with major industry players in an effort to create more transparent standards for measuring Internet traffic. The terms at issue were registered users, unique visitors, time spent and retention.

21244 ■ *"Web Translation Made Simple" in Inc. (Vol. 33, October 2011, No. 8, pp. 44)*
Pub: Inc. Magazine
Ed: Adam Baer. **Description:** Smartling is a Web-based service that translates sites into more than 50 foreign languages. The software will begin translation right after setting up the account.

21245 ■ *"Webadvertising" in MarketingMagazine (Vol. 115, September 27, 2010, No. 13, pp. 70)*
Pub: Rogers Publishing Ltd.
Description: Website advertising in Canada is examined.

21246 ■ *"Website Backup Made Simple" in Inc. (Vol. 33, September 2011, No. 7, pp. 52)*
Pub: Inc. Magazine
Ed: John Brandon. **Description:** Tools to back up content on a Website are profiled. Vaultpress works only with sites that run on the WordPress publishing platform and CodeGuard works with a variety of publishing platforms and hosting services.

21247 ■ *"Website Triples Traffic in Three Weeks Using Press Releases" in PR Newswire (January 5, 2010)*
Pub: PR Newswire Association, LLC
Description: Irbtrax, an Internet marketing firm, concluded a comprehensive study revealing that online press release submission services offer measurable Website traffic-building results.

21248 ■ *"Website for Women 50 Launches" in Marketing to Women (Vol. 21, April 2008, No. 4, pp. 5)*
Pub: EPM Communications Inc.
Contact: Ira Mayer, President
E-mail: imayer@epmcom.com
Description: Vibrantnation.com is an online community targeting women over age 50; members can share recommendations on a variety of topics such as vacation spots, retailers and financial issues.

21249 ■ *"Wendy Turner; Vice-President and General Manager, Vocalo.org" in Crain's Chicago Business (Vol. 31, May 5, 2008, No. 18, pp. 22)*
Pub: Crain Communications, Inc.
Ed: Kevin McKeough. **Description:** Profile of Wendy Turner who is a leader at Vocalo, a combination of talk radio and Web site, where listeners can set up profile pages similar to those on Facebook.

21250 ■ *"What You Look Like Online" in Black Enterprise (Vol. 37, January 2007, No. 6, pp. 56)*
Pub: Earl G. Graves Publishing Co. Inc.
Ed: Marcia A. Reed-Woodard. **Description:** Of 100 executive recruiters 77 percent stated that they use search engines to check the backgrounds of potential job candidates, according to a survey conducted by ExecuNet. Of those surveyed 35 percent stated that they eliminate potential candidates based on information they find online so it is important to create a positive Web presence which highlights professional image qualities.

21251 ■ *"What's In Your Toolbox" in Women In Business (Vol. 61, August-September 2009, No. 4, pp. 7)*
Pub: American Business Women's Association
Ed: Mimi Kopulos. **Description:** Business owners are increasingly turning to using social networking websites, such as Facebook, LinkedIn and Twitter, to promote their companies. The number of adult social media users has increased from 8 percent in 2005 to 35 percent in 2009.

21252 ■ *"Why-Max?" in Canadian Business (Vol. 81, July 22, 2008, No. 12-13, pp. 19)*
Pub: Rogers Media Ltd.
Ed: Andrew Wahl. **Description:** Nascent technology known as LTE (Long Term Evolution) is expected to challenge Intel's WiMax wireless technology as the wireless broadband standard. LTE , which is believed

to be at least two years behind WiMax in development, is likely to be supported by wireless and mobile-phone carriers. Views and information on WiMax and LTE are presented.

21253 ■ *"Why Some Get Shaften By Google Pricing" in Advertising Age (Vol. 79, July 14, 2008, No. 7, pp. 3)*
Pub: Crain Communications, Inc.
Ed: Abbey Klaassen. **Description:** Google's search advertising is discussed as well as the company's pricing structure for these ads.

21254 ■ *"Why Women Blog and What They Read" in Marketing to Women (Vol. 22, July 2009, No. 7, pp. 8)*
Pub: EPM Communications Inc.
Contact: Ira Mayer, President
E-mail: imayer@epmcom.com
Description: Listing of topics that are visited the most by female Internet users. Statistical data included.

21255 ■ *"Will the Force Be With Salesforce?" in Barron's (Vol. 88, March 24, 2008, No. 12, pp. 20)*
Pub: Dow Jones & Company, Inc.
Ed: Mark Veverka. **Description:** Shares of Salesforce.com are likely to drop from the $44.83-a-share level in the face of a deteriorating economy and financial sector and thus lower demand for business software. The company is unlikely to deliver on its ambitious earnings forecasts for 2008 especially with strengthening competition from Oracle.

21256 ■ *"Winner: Private Company, Less Than $100M" in Crain's Detroit Business (Vol. 25, June 22, 2009, No. 25)*
Pub: Crain Communications Inc. - Detroit
Ed: Tom Henderson. **Description:** Profile of ForeSee Results, an Ann Arbor, Michigan-based firm that uses the University of Michigan American Consumer Satisfaction Index to help businesses measure satisfaction with their Websites.

21257 ■ *"Women Clicking to Earn Virtual Dollars" in Sales and Marketing Management (November 11, 2009)*
Pub: Nielsen Business Media, Inc.
Ed: Stacy Straczynski. **Description:** According to a new report from Internet marketing firm Q Interactive, women are increasingly playing social media games where they are able to click on an ad or sign up for a promotion to earn virtual currency. Research is showing that this kind of marketing may be a potent tool, especially for e-commerce and online stores.

21258 ■ *"WordStream Announces a Pair of Firsts for SEO and PPC Keyword Research Tools" in Internet Wire (November 10, 2009)*
Pub: Comtex News Network, Inc.
Description: WordSteam, Inc., a provider of pay-per-click (PPC) and search engine optimization (SEO) solutions for continuously expanding and optimizing search marketing efforts has released two new features in their flagship Keyword Management solution; these tools will allow marketers to analyze data from paid search, organic search and estimated totals from keyword suggestion tools side-by-side.

21259 ■ *"Work Smarter" in Entrepreneur (Vol. 36, April 2008, No. 4, pp. 70)*
Pub: Entrepreneur Media, Inc.
Ed: Amanda C. Kooser. **Description:** Online applications that address a business' particular needs are presented. These web applications offer email services, collaboration services of sharing and editing documents and presentations, and tie-ups with online social networking sites. Details on various web applications are provided.

21260 ■ *"The Yahoo Family Tree" in Conde Nast Portfolio (Vol. 2, June 2008, No. 6, pp. 34)*
Pub: Conde Nast Publications
Contact: David Carey, President
Ed: Blaise Zerega. **Description:** Yahoo, founded in 1994 by Stanford students Jerry Yang and David Filo, is still an Internet powerhouse. The company's history is also outlined as well as the reasons in which Microsoft desperately wants to acquire the firm.

21261 ■ *"You Are What They Click" in Entrepreneur (Vol. 37, July 2009, No. 7, pp. 43)*
Pub: Entrepreneur Media, Inc.
Ed: Mikal Belicove. **Description:** Hiring the right website design firm is the first stage in building an online business, and this involves various factors such as price, technical expertise, and talent. Writing a request for proposal (RFP) detailing the website's details, which include purpose, budget and audience, is the first step the process. Other tips in finding the right web designer are given.

21262 ■ *"Your Annual Business Tune-Up" in Business Week (December 28, 2006)*
Pub: McGraw-Hill Companies
Ed: Karen E. Klein. **Description:** Interview with entrepreneurial expert, Ty Freyvogel, founder of EntrpreneursLab.com. Freyvogel gives tips on how a thorough review of existing systems, vendors, customers, and employees could help keep an entrepreneur's business not only safe but highly successful in the upcoming year.

21263 ■ *"Your Turn in the Spotlight" in Inc. (Volume 32, December 2010, No. 10, pp. 57)*
Pub: Inc. Magazine
Ed: John Brandon. **Description:** Examples of three video blogs created by entrepreneurs to promote their businesses and products are used to show successful strategies. Wine Library TV promotes a family's wine business; SHAMA.TV offers marketing tips and company news; and Will It Blend? promotes sales of a household blender.

21264 ■ *"Zen and the Art of Twitter Maintenance" in Agency Sales Magazine (Vol. 39, September-October 2009, No. 9, pp. 48)*
Pub: MANA
Ed: Terry Brock. **Description:** Online social networks such as Twitter, LinkedIn, and Facebook should be used to stay in touch with business relationships, especially customers. There should be a focus on making customers happy and building the bottom-line when using these tools.

21265 ■ *"Zeon Solutions Teams with Endeca for SaaS Version of Endeca InFront" in Entertainment Close-Up (October 25, 2011)*
Pub: Close-Up Media
Description: Zeon Solutions, an enterprise e-commerce and Website development firm announced a special licensing partnership with Endecca Technologies. Endeca is an information management software company that provides small and mid-size retailers with high-performance Customer Experience Management technology.

TRADE PERIODICALS

21266 ■ *Digital Design Newsletter*
Pub: Dynamic Graphics Inc.
Contact: David Moffly, Owner
Ed: Sara Booth, Editor, booth@dgusa.com. **Released:** Monthly. **Price:** $48, U.S.; $83.46, Canada. **Description:** Contains how-to articles on electronic illustration, graphic design, and production via real-world projects.

21267 ■ *Mastering CorelDRAW Newsletter*
Pub: Kazak Communications
Ed: Chris Dickman, Editor. **Released:** 10/year. **Price:** $47. **Description:** Covers CorelDRAW graphics applications. Offers tips and tricks with a hands-on focus. Remarks: Also available on diskette.

21268 ■ *Online: The Leading Magazine for Information Professionals*
Pub: Online, A Division of Information Today Inc.
URL(s): www.infotoday.com/online/default.shtml. **Ed:** Marydee Ojala. **Released:** Bimonthly **Price:** $124.95, Individuals; $235, Two years; $141, Canada and Mexico; $167, Other countries.

CONSULTANTS

21269 ■ **Construction Computing Solutions Inc.—CCS Inc.**
40 Orchard Ct.
Brick, NJ 08724-4396

Ph: (732)899-4319

Fax: (732)899-1921

Co. E-mail: constructioncomputing@comcast.net

URL: http://www.ccspcs.com

Contact: Gerry Bierbrauer, President

E-mail: gerryb@ccswebservices.com

Scope: Links home and small business customers, contractors and engineers with their PC system's hardware and software to achieve the maximum productivity that the hardware and software allow. Offers individual and network PC consulting services for home users, small (0-10 user) to medium (10-50 user) businesses, and construction and engineering companies in the tri-state area in the following general areas: Evaluation of computer needs, hardware, software and training, sales and installation of hardware and software as needed, sales, set up and training on construction specific software, training for and/or administration of software and network functions, internet sales, set up, access, email, and web pages. **Founded:** 1997.

21270 ■ Creative Computer Resources Inc.

5001 Horizons Dr., Ste. 200

Columbus, OH 43220-5291

Ph: (614)384-7557

Free: 866-720-0209

Fax: (614)573-6331

Co. E-mail: team@planet-ccr.com

URL: http://www.planet-ccr.com

Contact: M. Erik Mueller, President

E-mail: merikm@planet-ccr.com

Scope: Offers information systems support, custom software development, website design, development and implementation. Provides information technology support and management services to small and mid-size businesses. **Founded:** 1996.

FRANCHISES AND BUSINESS OPPORTUNITIES

21271 ■ TruePresence

1401 Russell St.

Baltimore, MD 21230

Ph: (410)649-2160

Fax: (410)649-2166

Description: Web design/development & internet marketing. **No. of Franchise Units:** 17. **Founded:** 2003.. **Franchised:** 2005. **Equity Capital Needed:** $48,000. **Franchise Fee:** $35,000. **Royalty Fee:** 6%. **Training:** Offers 5 days at headquarters, 3 days at franchisees location with ongoing support.

LIBRARIES

21272 ■ District of Columbia Public Library - Technology and Science Division

Martin Luther King Memorial Library

901 G St., NW, Rm. 220

Washington, DC 20001

Ph: (202)727-1175

Fax: (202)727-1129

Co. E-mail: commentssuggestions.dcpl@dc.gov

URL: http://www.dclibrary.org

Contact: Diane Henry, Assistant Director

Scope: Automobile and appliance repair, botany, cookery, general science, geology, genetics, manufacturing, nutrition, paleontology, pet care, printing, zoology, mathematics, computer science, biology, domestic arts, earth science, chemistry and chemical technology, physics, engineering, agriculture, gardening, medicine, psychiatry, astronomy, consumer information, health, veterinary science, physical anthropology. **Services:** Interlibrary loan; copying; free Wi-Fi access; library open to the public. **Founded:** 1907. **Holdings:** 92,127 books; 2500 bound periodical volumes; 5755 microforms; 65 VF drawers. **Subscriptions:** 300 journals and other serials. **Telecommunication Services:** mlkjrlibrary@dc.gov.

21273 ■ NORTEL Information Resource Network

5945 Airport Rd., Ste. 360

Mississauga, ON, Canada L4V 1R9

Ph: (905)863-7000

Free: 800-466-7835

Fax: (613)763-4982

URL: http://www.nortel.com

Contact: John M. Doolittle, Senior Vice President, Corporate Services

URL(s): www.nortel-canada.com. **Scope:** Telecommunications, computer science, electronics, systems engineering. **Services:** Center not open to the public. **Founded:** 1971. **Holdings:** 12,000 books; 3000 bound periodical volumes; 8000 conferences; reports. **Subscriptions:** 800 journals and other serials; 15 newspapers.

RESEARCH CENTERS

21274 ■ Design Management Institute (DMI)

101 Tremont St., Ste. 300

Boston, MA 02108

Ph: (617)338-6380

Fax: (617)338-6570

Co. E-mail: jtobin@dmi.org

URL: http://www.dmi.org/dmi/html/index.htm

Contact: Karen Reuther, President

E-mail: kreuther@dmi.org

Services: Environmental information for design managers. **Founded:** 1975. **Publications:** *The Design Management Journal.* **Educational Activities:** Seminars and symposia, through its Center for Education; Conference on Design Management (Annual); Corporate Identity Conference. **Telecommunication Services:** dmistaff@dmi.org.

START-UP INFORMATION

21275 ■ *Becoming a Personal Trainer for Dummies*
Pub: John Wiley and Sons, Inc.
Ed: Melyssa Michael, Linda Formichelli. **Released:** October 2004. **Price:** $19.99 (US), $25.99 (Canadian). **Description:** Legal and tax issues involved in starting and running a personal trainer firm. The book offers suggestions for incorporating massage and nutritional services.

ASSOCIATIONS AND OTHER ORGANIZATIONS

21276 ■ American Society of Bariatric Physicians (ASBP)
2821 S Parker Rd., Ste. 625
Aurora, CO 80014
Ph: (303)770-2526
Fax: (303)779-4834
Co. E-mail: laurie@asbp.org
URL: http://www.asbp.org
Contact: Laurie Traetow, Executive Director
E-mail: laurie@asbp.org
Description: Physicians with a special interest in the study and treatment of obesity and associated conditions. Encourages excellence in the practice of bariatric medicine through exchange of information, research, and continuing education. Sponsors regional courses and clinical research programs. Offers a physician referral service. **Founded:** 1950. **Publications:** *The Bariatrician* (Quarterly); *News from ASBP* (Bimonthly); *American Society of Bariatric Physicians--Directory* (Annual); *American Journal of Bariatric Medicine: The Bariatrician* (Quarterly). **Educational Activities:** Obesity & Associated Conditions Symposium (Annual); Regional Obesity Course (Annual); Obesity and Associated Conditions Symposium of American Society of Bariatric Physicians (Annual). **Awards:** Bariatrician of the Year (Annual); Fellow (Annual); Dr. Raymond E. Dietz Meritorious Service Award (Annual). **Telecommunication Services:** info@asbp.org.

21277 ■ Overeaters Anonymous World Service Office (OA WSO)
PO Box 44020
Rio Rancho, NM 87174-4020
Ph: (505)891-2664
Fax: (505)891-4320
Co. E-mail: info@oa.org
URL: http://www.oa.org
Contact: Naomi Lippel, Managing Director
Description: Individuals who have a desire to stop eating compulsively. Program is a twelve-step self-help fellowship patterned after that of Alcoholics Anonymous. **Founded:** 1960. **Publications:** *Lifeline* (Monthly). **Educational Activities:** Overeaters Anonymous World Service Office Meeting; World Service Business Conference (Annual); World Service Convention (Triennial).

21278 ■ Take Off Pounds Sensibly (TOPS)
PO Box 070360
Milwaukee, WI 53207
Ph: (414)482-4620
Free: 800-932-8677
Co. E-mail: topsinteractive@tops.org
URL: http://www.tops.org/default.aspx
Contact: Barb Cady, President
Description: Weight control self-help association using group dynamics, competition, and recognition to help members lose weight. Advocates physician-approved individual programs, and physician-set weight goals. **Founded:** 1948. **Publications:** *TOPS News* (Monthly). **Educational Activities:** International Recognition Days (Annual).

REFERENCE WORKS

21279 ■ *Everything is Possible: Life and Business Lessons from a Self-Made Billionaire and the Founder of Slim-Fast*
Pub: Newmarket Press
Ed: S. Daniel Abraham. **Released:** February 10, 2010. **Price:** $24.95. **Description:** A profile of the founder of Slim-Fast nutritional diet drink used to help people lose weight.

TRADE PERIODICALS

21280 ■ *Calorie Control Commentary*
Pub: Calorie Control Council
Released: 2/year. **Price:** Free; $10 international subscriptions.. **Description:** Focuses on the scientific and regulatory status of diet sweeteners, fat substitutes, and low-calorie and reduced-fat foods and beverages. Includes articles and statistics concerning dieting in the U.S.

21281 ■ *Shape*
Pub: American Media, Inc.
URL(s): www.shape.com. **Released:** Monthly **Price:** $17.97, Individuals print; $32.97, Canada; $46.97, Other countries; $29.97, Individuals digital & print.

TRADE SHOWS AND CONVENTIONS

21282 ■ California Dietetic Association Meeting
California Dietetic Association
7740 Manchester Ave., Ste. 102
Playa Del Rey, CA 90293-8499
Ph: (310)822-0177
Fax: (310)823-0264
Co. E-mail: patsmith@dietitian.org
URL: http://www.dietitian.org
Contact: Nicole Quartuccio, President
E-mail: president@dietitian.org
Frequency: Annual. **Audience:** Nutrition and dietetic professionals. **Principal Exhibits:** Food and nutrition services.

CONSULTANTS

21283 ■ Center for Lifestyle Enhancement - Columbia Medical Center of Plano
3901 W 15th St.
Plano, TX 75075
Ph: (972)596-6800
Fax: (972)519-1299
Co. E-mail: mcp.cle@hcahealthcare.com
URL: http://www.medicalcenterofplano.com
Contact: Harvey Fishero, President
Scope: Provides professional health counseling in the areas of general nutrition for weight management, eating disorders, diabetic education, cholesterol reduction and adolescent weight management. Offers work site health promotion and preventive services. Also coordinates speaker's bureau, cooking classes and physician referrals. Industries served: education, insurance, healthcare, retail or wholesale, data processing and manufacturing throughout Texas. **Founded:** 1975. **Seminars:** Rx Diet and Exercise; Smoking Cessation; Stress Management; Health Fairs; Fitness Screenings; Body Composition; Nutrition Analysis; Exercise Classes; Prenatal Nutrition; SHAPEDOWN; Successfully Managing Diabetes; Gourmet Foods for Your Heart; The Aging Heart; Heart Smart Saturday featuring Day of Dance; Weight-Loss Management Seminars; The Right Stroke for Men; Peripheral Artery Disease Screening; Menstruation: The Cycle Begins; Boot Camp for New Dads; Grand parenting 101: Caring for Kids Today; Teddy Bear Camp; New Baby Day Camp; Safe Sitter Baby-Sitting Class.

FRANCHISES AND BUSINESS OPPORTUNITIES

21284 ■ Curves
Curves International
100 Ritchie Rd.
Waco, TX 76712
Free: 800-848-1096
Fax: (254)399-8004
Description: Fitness and weight loss center for women. **No. of Franchise Units:** 6,385. **Founded:** 1995.. **Franchised:** 1995. **Equity Capital Needed:** $29,900-$65,000. **Franchise Fee:** $29,900, including equipment. **Training:** Yes.

21285 ■ DIET CENTER
Health Management Group Co. (PWLC)
395 Springside Dr.
Akron, OH 44333-2434
Ph: (330)666-7952
Free: 800-440-7952
Fax: (330)666-2197
Co. E-mail: info@pwlc.com
URL: http://www.pwlc.com
Description: Diet Center counselors work one-on-one with clients, helping develop a personalized, low-fat eating style and a more active lifestyle. With the aid of a new behavior-management program, clients design their own practical solutions for losing and maintaining weight, learning to improve their health

and appearance by focusing on reducing body fat areas. **No. of Franchise Units:** 74. **Founded:** 1970.. **Franchised:** 1973. **Equity Capital Needed:** $50,000, liquidity. **Franchise Fee:** $25,000. **Training:** Training is provided both at the home office and in regional. Includes nutritional training.

21286 ■ Jenny Craig Weight Loss & Management Centres

Jenny Craig International, Inc.
5770 Fleet St.
Carlsbad, CA 92008
Ph: (760)696-4000
Free: 888-848-8885
Co. E-mail: franchising@jennycraig.com
URL: http://www.jennycraig.com
Description: Offers a weight loss program in the U.S. and Canada featuring personal counseling, low-calorie Jenny's Cuisine, and a supportive and motivating environment. **No. of Franchise Units:** 216. **No. of Company-Owned Units:** 431. **Founded:** 1983. **Franchised:** 1987. **Equity Capital Needed:** $165,600-$349,500. **Franchise Fee:** $25,000. **Training:** Yes.

21287 ■ L.A. Weight Loss Centers

420 Dresher Rd., Ste. 200
Horsham, PA 19044
Ph: (215)246-4302
Free: 888-258-7099
Fax: (215)346-8810
Description: Personalized weight management. **No. of Franchise Units:** 373. **No. of Company-Owned Units:** 437. **Founded:** 1989. **Franchised:** 1998. **Equity Capital Needed:** $84,600-$149,800. **Franchise Fee:** $20,000. **Royalty Fee:** 7%. **Training:** 4 weeks at headquarters, 3 weeks at franchisee's location and ongoing support.

21288 ■ Lite For Life

Lite for Life Franchise Corp., Inc.
398 Main St.
Los Altos, CA 94022
Ph: (650)941-3200

Fax: (650)559-3111
Description: Weight loss and nutritional consulting. **No. of Franchise Units:** 2. **No. of Company-Owned Units:** 4. **Founded:** 1978.. **Franchised:** 2003. **Equity Capital Needed:** $75,000+/-. **Franchise Fee:** $20,000. **Training:** Yes.

21289 ■ Lucille Roberts Fitness Express

Women's Fitness Franchising, LLC
Description: Women's fitness & weight-loss center. **No. of Franchise Units:** 5. **Founded:** 1970. **Franchised:** 2005. **Equity Capital Needed:** $271,850-$402,400. **Franchise Fee:** $25,000. **Royalty Fee:** 6%. **Financial Assistance:** Third party financing available. **Training:** Offers 1 week at headquarters with ongoing support.

21290 ■ SureSlim Wellness Clinic

Sure Slim Holdings Inc.
4632 Boulderwood Dr.
Victoria, BC, Canada V8Y 3G5
Ph: (250)995-0482
Free: 866-773-0177
Fax: (866)595-4003
Co. E-mail: Gerald@sureslim.ca
URL: http://www.sureslim.ca
Description: The franchise offers successful weight loss system. **No. of Franchise Units:** 14. **No. of Company-Owned Units:** 1. **Founded:** 2000.. **Franchised:** 2002. **Equity Capital Needed:** $135,000. **Franchise Fee:** $35,000. **Training:** Yes.

LIBRARIES

21291 ■ American Dietetic Association - Knowledge Center

120 S. Riverside Plaza, Ste. 20000
Chicago, IL 60606-6995
Ph: (312)877-1600, x4864
Free: 800-877-1600
Fax: (312)899-4739
Co. E-mail: knowledge@eatright.org
URL: http://www.eatright.org/
Scope: Nutrition, dietetics, food service. **Services:** Interlibrary loan; copying; Library open to the public

by appointment. **Founded:** 1990. **Holdings:** 3000 books. **Subscriptions:** 60 journals and other serials; 4 newspapers.

21292 ■ National Eating Disorder Information Centre

ES 7-421
200 Elizabeth St.
Toronto, ON, Canada M5G 2C4
Ph: (416)340-4156
Free: 866-633-4220
Fax: (416)340-4736
Co. E-mail: nedic@uhn.on.ca
URL: http://www.nedic.ca
Contact: Merryl Bear, Director
Scope: Eating disorders, food preoccupation, weight preoccupation, support groups. **Services:** Centre open to the public. **Founded:** 1985. **Holdings:** 50 books. **Subscriptions:** 250 journals and other serials.

RESEARCH CENTERS

21293 ■ Columbia University - New York Obesity Research Center—Columbia University - Centro de Investigacion sobre Obesidad

College of Physicians & Surgeons
St. Luke's-Roosevelt Hospital Ctr.
1111 Amsterdam Ave., Scrymser Basement
New York, NY 10025
Ph: (212)523-4196
Fax: (212)523-3416
Co. E-mail: fxp1@columbia.edu
URL: http://www.nyorc.org/
Contact: Dr. F. Xavier Pi-Sunyer, Director
Founded: 1980. **Educational Activities:** Postdoctoral training program; Predoctoral training, for PhD candidates of the university's Institute of Human Nutrition; New York Obesity Research Center Seminars (Weekly); New York Obesity Research Center Symposia (Semiannual). **Awards:** New York Obesity Research Center Research fellowships, for pre- and postdoctoral students; New York Obesity Research Center Research grants, for pilot and feasibility studies on obesity. **Telecommunication Services:** dg108@columbia.edu.

FRANCHISES AND BUSINESS OPPORTUNITIES

21294 ■ Housewarmers
6500 Greenville Ave.
Dallas, TX 75206
Ph: (214)534-5041
Free: 866-241-8065

Fax: (404)235-0702
Description: Neighborhood welcoming service. **No. of Franchise Units:** 50. **No. of Company-Owned Units:** 7. **Founded:** 1999. **Franchised:** 2002. **Equity Capital Needed:** $15,200-$55,900. **Franchise Fee:** $12,500-$50,000. **Royalty Fee:** 12%. **Training:** Offers 3-4 days training at headquarters, 2 visits at franchisee's location, and ongoing support.

21295 ■ Newcomers Welcome Service
900 Victors Way, Ste. 200
Ann Arbor, MI 48108

Ph: (734)994-9199
Fax: (734)994-9323
Description: Welcome service. **No. of Company-Owned Units:** 7. **Founded:** 1960.. **Franchised:** 2007. **Equity Capital Needed:** $15,000-$20,000. **Franchise Fee:** $25,000. **Royalty Fee:** $75/week.

SOURCES OF SUPPLY

21296 ■ *Visual Merchandising & Store Design--Buyers' Guide Issue*
ST Media Group International Inc.
Contact: Tedd Swormstedt, President
URL(s): stmediagroup.comvmsd.com, www.stmedia-group.com/index.php3?d=pubs&p=vm. **Released:** Annual; Latest edition 2009. **Publication includes:** Over 1,300 manufacturers and distributors of retail display equipment and products; nearly 600 store design, lighting, and visual merchandising firms; related trade and professional associations. **Entries include:** For manufacturers and service firms--Company name, address, phone, name and title of contact, number of employees, sales volume, products. Similar data given for associations. **Database includes:** Calendar of events. **Arrangement:** Alphabetical. **Indexes:** Product, fax number.

TRADE PERIODICALS

21297 ■ *Creative: The Magazine of Promotion and Marketing*
Pub: Magazines/Creative Inc.
URL(s): www.creativemag.com. **Released:** Bimonthly **Price:** $30, Individuals; $50, Other countries; $4, Single issue; $20, Individuals illustrated guide; $44, Two years.

21298 ■ *Stores: The Magazine for Retail Decision Makers*
Pub: NRF Enterprises Inc.
Contact: Ellen Davis, Director
E-mail: davise@nrf.com
URL(s): www.stores.org. **Ed:** Susan Reda. **Released:** Monthly **Price:** Free to retailers and to members of NRF; $120, Nonmembers.

21299 ■ *Visual Merchandising and Store Design*
Pub: ST Media Group International Inc.
Contact: Tedd Swormstedt, President
URL(s): www.stmediagroup.com/index.php3?d=pubs&p=vmvmsd.com/. **Ed:** Anne DiNardo. **Released:** Monthly **Price:** $42, Individuals U.S.; $66, Individuals 2 years, U.S.; $62, Individuals Canada (surface); $100, Individuals 2 years, Canada (surface); $65, Individuals Mexico/Foreign (surface); $105, Individuals 2 years, Mexico/Foreign (surface); $100, Individuals Mexico, 1st Class; $175, Individuals 2 years, Mexico 1st Class; $115, Individuals Central/South America; $205, Individuals 2 years, Central/South America.

VIDEOCASSETTES/ AUDIOCASSETTES

21300 ■ *Home Decorating Combo*
Nancy's Notions Ltd.
333 Beichl Ave.
P.O. Box 683
Beaver Dam, WI 53916-0683

Ph: (920)887-7321
Free: 800-725-0361
Fax: (800)255-8119
Co. E-mail: customerservice@nancysnotions.com
URL: http://www.nancysnotions.com
Released: 1987. **Description:** This video contains two programs on fabric-based home decoration: "Window Treatments" and "Instant Decorating.". **Availability:** VHS.

TRADE SHOWS AND CONVENTIONS

21301 ■ *Global Shop - Tradeshow and Seminars for Visual Merchandiser*
VNU Expositions
14685 Avion Pkwy., Ste. 400
Chantilly, VA 20151
Ph: (703)488-2700
Free: 800-765-7615
Fax: (703)488-2725
URL: http://www.vnuexpo.com
URL(s): www.globalshop.org. **Price:** $35. **Frequency:** Annual. **Audience:** Trade only; retailers, store designers, operations and construction professionals, brand marketers, visual merchandisers. **Principal Exhibits:** Retail display props and decorations.

FRANCHISES AND BUSINESS OPPORTUNITIES

21302 ■ *Blind Brokers Network*
23052 Alicia Pky., Ste. H202
Mission Viejo, CA 92692
Ph: (949)768-6695
Description: Discount blinds, shades and shutters. **No. of Franchise Units:** 301. **No. of Company-Owned Units:** 1. **Founded:** 1985.. **Franchised:** 2006. **Equity Capital Needed:** $1,495-$4,995. **Training:** Offers 3 days at headquarters, by phone and vendor training and ongoing support.

21303 ■ *Gotcha Covered*
1611 N Stemmons Fwy., Ste. 318
Carrollton, TX 75006
Ph: (972)466-2544
Fax: (972)446-6774
URL: http://www.gotchacoveredblinds.com
Description: Blinds, shades, shutters and draperies. **No. of Franchise Units:** 125. **Founded:** 1995.. **Franchised:** 1999. **Equity Capital Needed:** $50,100-$82,300 total investment; $65,000 cash liquidity. **Franchise Fee:** $39,900-$59,900. **Royalty Fee:** 4-8%. **Training:** Offers 2 weeks at headquarters, aditional week of training at headquarters after 4 months, and ongoing field training and support.

21304 ■ *The Screenmobile*
The Screenmobile Corp.
72050A Corporate Way
Thousand Palms, CA 92276
Free: 800-775-7795
Fax: (760)343-7543
Description: Window and door screening. **No. of Franchise Units:** 94. **No. of Company-Owned Units:** 1. **Founded:** 1980.. **Franchised:** 1982. **Equity Capital Needed:** $90,000. **Franchise Fee:** $35,500-$69,500. **Training:** Yes.

21305 ■ *Today's Window Fashions*
5519 S Mission Rd., No. E
Bonsall, CA 92003
Ph: (760)630-8119
Free: 877-998-6329
Fax: (760)923-7234
Co. E-mail: todaysblinds1@aol.com
URL: http://www.todaysblinds.com
Description: Custom window coverings. **No. of Franchise Units:** 32. **No. of Company-Owned Units:** 1. **Founded:** 1993.. **Franchised:** 1997. **Equity Capital Needed:** $52,000-$59,000. **Franchise Fee:** $49,000. **Royalty Fee:** 4%. **Financial Assistance:** Limited third party financing available. **Training:** Offers 5 days at corporate headquarters, 5 days of onsite, and ongoing support.

21306 ■ *V2K Window Decor & More*
7853 E Arapahoe Ct., Ste. 3100
Centennial, CO 80112
Ph: (800)200-0835
Fax: (303)202-5201
URL: http://www.franchiseV2k.com
Description: Window treatments/digital design services. **No. of Franchise Units:** 186. **Founded:** 1996.. **Franchised:** 1997. **Franchise Fee:** $59,900. **Training:** Offers 2 weeks training followed by 1 week advanced training after 4 months in the field.

LIBRARIES

21307 ■ *Art Institute of Philadelphia Library*
1610 Chestnut St.
Philadelphia, PA 19103
Ph: (215)405-6402
Co. E-mail: rschachter@aii.edu
URL: http://www.artinstitutes.edu/philadelphia
Contact: Ruth Schachter, Director
URL(s): www.artinstitutes.edu/philadelphia/student-life/library.aspx. **Scope:** Visual communications, interior design, industrial design, animation, fashion marketing, fashion design, visual merchandising, photography, website design, multimedia. **Services:** Interlibrary loan; copying; library not open to the public (circulation services provided for students and faculty). **Founded:** 1974. **Holdings:** 31,000 volumes; 2000 videocassettes; audiocassettes. **Subscriptions:** 180 print subscriptions and other serials.

ASSOCIATIONS AND OTHER ORGANIZATIONS

21308 ■ Business Technology Association (BTA)
12411 Wornall Rd., Ste. 200
Kansas City, MO 64145
Ph: (816)941-3100
Free: 800-325-7219
Fax: (816)941-4838
Co. E-mail: info@bta.org
URL: http://www.bta.org
Contact: Tom Ouellette, President
Description: Dealers and resellers of office equipment and networking products and services. Offers 60 seminars on management, service, technology, and business systems. Conducts research, provides business-supporting services and benefits, including insurance, and legal counsel. **Founded:** 1926 **Publi-**cations: *BTA Membership Directory* (Annual); *Business Owner* (Bimonthly). **Awards:** Channel Choice Awards; Manufacturer/Supplier Award; Reseller of the Year; Channel Choice Award (Annual); Manufacturer/Supplier Award (Annual); Reseller of the Year (Annual).

DIRECTORIES OF EDUCATIONAL PROGRAMS

21309 ■ *Directory of Private Accredited Career Schools and Colleges of Technology*
Pub: Accrediting Commission of Career Schools and Colleges of Technology
Contact: Michale S. McComis, Executive Director
Released: On web page. **Price:** Free. **Description:** Covers 3900 accredited post-secondary programs that provide training programs in business, trade, and technical fields, including various small business endeavors. Entries offer school name, address, phone, description of courses, job placement assistance, and requirements for admission. Arrangement is alphabetical.

TRADE PERIODICALS

21310 ■ *Scroll*
Pub: Wordstar Processing Users' Group Inc.

Ed: Dr. David M. Rafky, Editor. **Released:** Bimonthly. **Price:** Included in membership. **Description:** Provides news regarding various aspects of word processing with WordStar software, includes reviews of word processing software, computer tips, a glossary of terms used in each issue, and information for writers. Recurring features include letters to the editor, news of research, and book reviews. Regular columns titled Fade-In, In Response, and Computers and the Disabled.

Accounting

START-UP INFORMATION

21311 ■ *The Small Business Start-Up Kit*
Pub: NOLO
Ed: Peri Pakroo. **Released:** January 2008. **Price:**
$29.99. **Description:** Entrepreneurial advice for
launching a new business. Topics include compliance
with state regulations, sole proprietorships, partnerships, corporations, limited liability companies, as
well as accounting and tax information.

21312 ■ *Start and Run a Bookkeeping
Business*
Pub: Self-Counsel, Incorporated
Ed: Angie Mohr. **Released:** October 2005. **Price:**
$17.95 (US), $22.95 (Canadian). **Description:** Advice
for starting and running a bookkeeping service busi-
ness. Includes MS Word and PDF formats for use in
Windows-based PC.

ASSOCIATIONS AND OTHER ORGANIZATIONS

21313 ■ **Accountants Global Network (AGN)**
2851 S Parker Rd., Ste. 850
Aurora, CO 80014
Ph: (303)743-7880
Free: 800-782-2272
Fax: (303)743-7660
Co. E-mail: rhood@agn.org
URL: http://www.agn-na.org
Contact: Rita J. Hood, Executive Director
Description: Represents and promotes the fields of
separate and independent accounting and consulting
firms serving business organizations. **Founded:**
1978.

21314 ■ **Canadian Payroll Association
(CPA)—Association canadienne de la paie**
250 Bloor St. E, Ste. 1600
Toronto, ON, Canada M4W 1E6
Ph: (416)487-3380
Free: 800-387-4693
Fax: (416)487-3384
Co. E-mail: membership@payroll.ca
URL: http://www.payroll.ca
Contact: Patrick Culhane, President
Description: Represents the payroll community in
Canada; offers education programs, advocacy ef-
forts, products and services to help members en-
hance and adapt payroll operations, meet new
legislative requirements, address changing workplace
needs and take advantage of emerging technologies.
Scope: payroll, finance, employment standards, ac-
counting, monetary, fiscal legislation. **Founded:**
1978. **Subscriptions:** archival material books clippings periodicals. **Publications:** CPA E-Source
(Bimonthly); Dialogue Magazine (Bimonthly).
Awards: The Board of Directors Award (Annual); The
CPA Partner Award; The Diana Ferguson Award (Annual); Board of Directors Award; Certification Achievement Award; CPA Partner Award; Diana Ferguson
Award.

21315 ■ **Community Banking Advisory
Network (CBAN)**
624 Grassmere Park Dr., Ste. 15
Nashville, TN 37211
Ph: (615)377-3392
Free: 800-231-2524
Fax: (615)377-7092
Co. E-mail: info@bankingcpas.com
URL: http://www.bankingcpas.com
Contact: Patrick Pruett, Executive Director
Description: Certified Public Accounting (CPA) firms
providing financial and consulting services to com-
munity banks. Seeks to advance CPA services to the
community banking industry. Sponsors continuing
education and training courses; conducts industry
and member surveys; facilitates formation of joint
ventures; makes available marketing assistance;
facilitates resource sharing among members.
Founded: 1995. **Publications:** Community Banking
Advisor (Quarterly). **Educational Activities:** Community Banking Track at Super Conference (Annual);
Community Banking Advisory Network Conference
(Annual).

21316 ■ **Construction Industry CPAs/
Consultants Association (CICPAC)**
15011 E Twilight View Dr.
Fountain Hills, AZ 85268
Ph: (480)836-0300
Free: 800-864-0491
Fax: (480)836-0400
Co. E-mail: jcorcoran@cicpac.com
URL: http://www.cicpac.com
Contact: John J. Corcoran, Executive Director
Description: Certified Public Accounting (CPA) firms
providing financial and consulting services to con-
struction companies. Seeks to advance CPA services
to the construction industries. Sponsors continuing
education and training courses; conducts industry
and member surveys; facilitates formation of joint
ventures; makes available marketing assistance;
facilitates resource sharing among members. **Educational Activities:** Construction Industry CPAs/
Consultants Association Conference (Annual); CIC-
PAC Education Conference and Annual Meeting (Annual).

21317 ■ **CPA Auto Dealer Consultants
Association (CADCA)**
624 Grassmere Park Dr., Ste. 15
Nashville, TN 37211
Ph: (615)377-3392
Free: 800-231-2524
Fax: (615)377-7092
Co. E-mail: info@autodealercpas.net
URL: http://www.autodealercpas.net
Contact: Patrick Pruett, Executive Director
Description: Certified Public Accounting (CPA) firms
providing financial and consulting services to automo-
bile dealers. Seeks to advance CPA services to
automobile dealers. Sponsors continuing education
and training courses; conducts industry and member
surveys; facilitates formation of joint ventures; makes
available marketing assistance; facilitates resource

sharing among members. **Founded:** 1996. **Publications:** Auto Focus (Quarterly). **Educational Activities:** Education and Networking Conference (Semiannual).

21318 ■ *CPA E-Source*
250 Bloor St. E, Ste. 1600
Toronto, ON, Canada M4W 1E6
Ph: (416)487-3380
Free: 800-387-4693
Fax: (416)487-3384
Co. E-mail: membership@payroll.ca
URL: http://www.payroll.ca
Contact: Patrick Culhane, President
Released: Bimonthly

21319 ■ **CPA Manufacturing Services
Association (MSA)**
624 Grassmere Park Dr., Ste. 15
Nashville, TN 37211
Ph: (615)373-9880
Free: 800-231-2524
Fax: (615)377-7092
Co. E-mail: info@manufacturingcpas.com
URL: http://www.manufacturingcpas.com
Contact: Erik Horstmann, President
Description: Certified Public Accounting (CPA) firms
providing financial and consulting services to the
manufacturing industries. Seeks to advance CPA
services to manufacturers. Sponsors continuing
education and training courses; conducts industry
and member surveys; facilitates formation of joint
ventures; makes available marketing assistance;
facilitates resource sharing among members. **Publications:** Client (Periodic).

21320 ■ *Dialogue Magazine*
250 Bloor St. E, Ste. 1600
Toronto, ON, Canada M4W 1E6
Ph: (416)487-3380
Free: 800-387-4693
Fax: (416)487-3384
Co. E-mail: membership@payroll.ca
URL: http://www.payroll.ca
Contact: Patrick Culhane, President
Released: Bimonthly **Price:** C$95, /year.

21321 ■ **International Budget Partnership
(IBP)**
820 1st St. NE, Ste. 510
Washington, DC 20002
Ph: (202)408-1080
Fax: (202)408-8173
Co. E-mail: info@internationalbudget.org
URL: http://internationalbudget.org
Contact: Warren Krafchik, Director
Description: Works to assist civil society organiza-
tions globally to improve budget policies and decision-
making processes. **Founded:** 1997. **Publications:**
IBP Newsletter (Bimonthly); A Guide to Budget Work
for NGOs; Budgeting for the Future, Building another
Europe. **Educational Activities:** International Budget
Conference (Biennial).

21322 ■ PrimeGlobal
3235 Satellite Blvd., Bldg. 400, Ste. 300
Duluth, GA 30096
Ph: (678)417-7730
Fax: (678)999-3959
Co. E-mail: kmead@primeglobal.net
URL: http://www.primeglobal.net
Contact: Kevin Mead, President
Description: Works to ensure that the standard for accounting, auditing, and management services are maintained. **Founded:** 1977.

21323 ■ Society of Depreciation Professionals (SDP)
555 8th Ave., Ste. 1902
New York, NY 10018
Ph: (212)804-7178
Fax: (646)417-6378
Co. E-mail: admin@depr.org
URL: http://www.depr.org
Contact: John Spanos, President
Description: Accountants and other individuals with an interest in the depreciation of assets. Promotes "professionalism and ethics within the art of depreciation." Serves as a forum for the discussion of issues affecting depreciation; sponsors continuing professional development courses for members. **Founded:** 1987.

EDUCATIONAL PROGRAMS

21324 ■ Accounting's New Guidelines: From GAAP to IFRS (Onsite)
AMA
600 AMA Way
Saranac Lake, NY 12983-5534
Ph: (212)586-8100
Free: 877-566-9441
Fax: (518)891-0368
Co. E-mail: customerservice@amanet.org
URL: http://www.amaseminars.org
Price: $2,095.00 for non-members; $1,895.00 for AMA members and $1,623.00 for General Services Administration (GSA) members. **Description:** Understand the complexities of the coming GAAP-to-IFRS changeover in this two-day course.

21325 ■ AMA's Budgeting Workshop (Onsite)
American Management Association
600 AMA Way
Saranac Lake, NY 12983-5534
Ph: (212)586-8100
Free: 877-566-9441
Fax: (518)891-0368
Co. E-mail: customerservice@amanet.org
URL: http://www.amaseminars.org
Price: $2,345.00 for non-members; $2,095.00 for AMA members; and $1,794.00 for General Services Administration (GSA) members. **Description:** Two-day seminar covering the budgeting process from fundamentals through development and how to measure performance. **Dates and Locations:** New York, NY; Washington, DC; Arlington, VA; and Atlanta, GA.

21326 ■ AMA's Course on Financial Analysis (Onsite)
American Management Association
600 AMA Way
Saranac Lake, NY 12983-5534
Ph: (212)586-8100
Free: 877-566-9441
Fax: (518)891-0368
Co. E-mail: customerservice@amanet.org
URL: http://www.amaseminars.org
Price: $2,545.00 for non-members; $2,295.00 for AMA members; and $1,965.00 for General Services Administration (GSA) members. **Description:** Three-day seminar for managers with budget responsibilities; covers corporate planning, capital investments, cash flow, balance sheets, mergers and acquisitions, and other financial aspects of business. **Dates and Locations:** New York, NY; Atlanta, GA; Chicago, IL; Arlington, VA; Washington, DC; and San Francisco, CA.

21327 ■ Budgeting for Publications
EEI Communications
8945 Guilford Rd., Ste. 145
Columbia, MD 21046
Ph: (410)309-8200
Free: 888-253-2762
Fax: (410)630-3980
Co. E-mail: train@eeicom.com
URL: http://www.eeicom.com/eei-training-services
Price: $425.00. **Description:** Seminar that covers the basics of developing and monitoring budgets for the publications department, including types of publications departments, profit and cost centers, defining profit, margins, revenues, and analysis, budgeting traps, and what you can and cannot control. **Dates and Locations:** Alexandria, VA.

21328 ■ CMC's Course on Financial Analysis (Onsite) (Canada)
Canadian Management Centre (CMC)
150 York St., 5th Fl.
Toronto, ON, Canada M5H 3S5
Ph: (416)214-5678
Free: 877-262-2519
Fax: (416)313-4985
Co. E-mail: cmcinfo@cmctraining.org
URL: http://www.cmctraining.org
Contact: John Wright, President
Price: $2,195.00 Canadian for non-members; $2,395.00 Canadian for CMC members. **Description:** Two-day seminar for managers with budget responsibilities; covers corporate planning, capital investments, cash flow, balance sheets, mergers and acquisitions, and other financial aspects of business. **Dates and Locations:** Toronto, ON.

21329 ■ Debits and Credits: How Accounting Really Works
Canadian Management Centre (CMC)
150 York St., 5th Fl.
Toronto, ON, Canada M5H 3S5
Ph: (416)214-5678
Free: 877-262-2519
Fax: (416)313-4985
Co. E-mail: cmcinfo@cmctraining.org
URL: http://www.cmctraining.org
Contact: John Wright, President
Price: $2,195.00 for members; $2,395.00 for non-members. **Description:** Developed for business professional with no accounting skills. Master the essentials of accounting and put yourself in a position to succeed. **Dates and Locations:** Toronto, ON.

21330 ■ Fixed Asset Accounting (Onsite)
American Management Association
600 AMA Way
Saranac Lake, NY 12983-5534
Ph: (212)586-8100
Free: 877-566-9441
Fax: (518)891-0368
Co. E-mail: customerservice@amanet.org
URL: http://www.amaseminars.org
Price: $2,095.00 for non-members; $1,895.00 for AMA members; and $1,623.00 for General Services Administration (GSA) members. **Description:** Two-day seminar for accountants and managers with less than two years of experience in fixed asset accounting; covers tax benefits, transitioning to a computerized system, and getting started with paperwork. **Dates and Locations:** Arlington, VA; Atlanta, GA; and Washington, DC.

21331 ■ Fundamentals of Cost Accounting (Onsite)
American Management Association
600 AMA Way
Saranac Lake, NY 12983-5534
Ph: (212)586-8100
Free: 877-566-9441
Fax: (518)891-0368
Co. E-mail: customerservice@amanet.org
URL: http://www.amaseminars.org
Price: $2,195.00 for non-members; $1,995.00 for AMA members; and $1,708.00 for General Services Administration (GSA) members. **Description:** Covers the use of cost accounting, analyzing reports, choosing a cost system, and measuring results. **Dates and Locations:** Chicago, IL; and San Diego, CA.

21332 ■ Fundamentals of Finance and Accounting for Administrative Professionals (Onsite)
American Management Association
600 AMA Way
Saranac Lake, NY 12983-5534
Ph: (212)586-8100
Free: 877-566-9441
Fax: (518)891-0368
Co. E-mail: customerservice@amanet.org
URL: http://www.amaseminars.org
Price: $1,895.00; $1,695.00 for AMA members; and $1,451.00 for General Services Administration (GSA) members. **Description:** Covers basic accounting principles, cash flow accounting, and learning to understand various financial documents. **Dates and Locations:** New York, NY.

21333 ■ Government Contract Accounting (Onsite)
Seminar Information Service, Inc.
20 Executive Park, Ste. 120
Irvine, CA 92614
Ph: (949)261-9104
Free: 877-SEM-INFO
Fax: (949)261-1963
Co. E-mail: info@seminarinformation.com
URL: http://www.seminarinformation.com
Price: $1,025.00. **Description:** Accounting principles as they relate to procurement activities with the Federal Government, with focus on Government forms and formats, direct and indirect cost rate submissions, cost principles, dealing with Government auditors, changes and delay claims and terminations. **Dates and Locations:** Las Vegas, NV.

21334 ■ How to Develop and Administer a Budget (Onsite)
Fred Pryor Seminars & CareerTrack
5700 Broadmoor St., Ste. 300
Mission, KS 66202
Ph: (800)780-8476
Free: 800-944-8503
Fax: (913)967-8849
Co. E-mail: customerservice@pryor.com
URL: http://www.careertrack.com
Price: $179.00; $169.00 for groups of 5 or more. **Description:** Covers the benefits of budgeting, budgeting concepts, templates, and methods for evaluating budgets. **Dates and Locations:** Cities throughout the United States.

21335 ■ How to Use Crystal Reports (Onsite)
Fred Pryor Seminars & CareerTrack
5700 Broadmoor St., Ste. 300
Mission, KS 66202
Free: 800-780-8476
Fax: (913)967-8849
Co. E-mail: customerservice@pryor.com
URL: http://www.pryor.com
Price: $199.00; $189.00 for groups of 5 or more. **Description:** Learn effective data management, including financial, sales, and personal presentation and distribution. **Dates and Locations:** Cities throughout the United States.

21336 ■ How to Use QuickBooks (Onsite)
Fred Pryor Seminars & CareerTrack
5700 Broadmoor St., Ste. 300
Mission, KS 66202
Free: 800-780-8476
Fax: (913)967-8849
Co. E-mail: customerservice@pryor.com
URL: http://www.pryor.com
Price: $199.00; $189.00 for groups of 5 or more. **Description:** Learn how to manage your inventory, track costs of your business, generate professional invoices and purchase orders, manage accounts payables and receivables and more. **Dates and Locations:** Cities throughout the United States.

21337 ■ Organizing and Managing Accounts Payable (Onsite)
Seminar Information Service, Inc.
20 Executive Park, Ste. 120
Irvine, CA 92614
Ph: (949)261-9104
Free: 877-SEM-INFO

Fax: (949)261-1963
Co. E-mail: info@seminarinformation.com
URL: http://www.seminarinformation.com
Price: $199.00. **Description:** Comprehensive seminar where you'll learn the best practices guaranteed to improve your accuracy, as well as techniques, tips and shortcuts that will help you get more done in less time. **Dates and Locations:** Cities throughout the United States.

21338 ■ Organizing and Managing Accounts Payable (Onsite)
Padgett-Thompson Seminars
Rockhurst University CEC
14502 W. 105th St.
Lenexa, KS 66215
Free: 800-349-1935
URL: http://www.findaseminar.com/tpd/Padgett-Thompson-Seminars.asp
Price: $199.00. **Description:** Seminar promotes the latest proven techniques and best practices to improve accuracy and save money for your company. **Dates and Locations:** Cherry Hill, NJ; Arlington, VA.

21339 ■ Project Cost Management: Estimating, Budgeting and Earned Value Analysis (Onsite)
Canadian Management Centre (CMC)
150 York St., 5th Fl.
Toronto, ON, Canada M5H 3S5
Ph: (416)214-5678
Free: 877-262-2519
Fax: (416)313-4985
Co. E-mail: cmcinfo@cmctraining.org
URL: http://www.cmctraining.org
Contact: John Wright, President
Price: $1,845.00 for members; $1,995.00 for non-members. **Description:** Learn how to apply proven methods, tools, and techniques to prepare estimates, develop and monitor budgets, manage cash flow, and use earned value analysis. **Dates and Locations:** Toronto, ON.

21340 ■ The Sales And Use Tax Seminar (Onsite)
Seminar Information Service, Inc.
20 Executive Park, Ste. 120
Irvine, CA 92614
Ph: (949)261-9104
Free: 877-SEM-INFO
Fax: (949)261-1963
Co. E-mail: info@seminarinformation.com
URL: http://www.seminarinformation.com
Price: $199.00. **Description:** Learn how to determine which transactions are taxable, find exemptions you may not be aware of, and handle business partners who aren't in compliance with new tax laws. **Dates and Locations:** Cities throughout the United States.

21341 ■ Super-Effective Techniques for Collecting Accounts Receivable (Onsite)
Padgett-Thompson Seminars
Rockhurst University CEC
14502 W. 105th St.
Lenexa, KS 66215
Free: 800-349-1935
URL: http://www.findaseminar.com/tpd/Padgett-Thompson-Seminars.asp
Price: $179.00. **Description:** Designed to get participants up to speed on the basic issues involved with collecting overdue money. **Dates and Locations:** Boston, MA.

REFERENCE WORKS

21342 ■ "2011 Tax Information of Interest" in Business Owner (Vol. 35, November-December 2011, No. 6, pp. 10)
Pub: DL Perkins Company
Description: Compilation of 2011 tax information to help small business take advantage of all tax incentives.

21343 ■ "Accountants Get the Hook" in Canadian Business (Vol. 80, October 22, 2007, No. 21, pp. 19)
Pub: Rogers Media
Ed: John Gray. **Description:** Chartered Accountants of Ontario handed down the decision on Douglas Barrington, Anthony Power and Claudio Russo's professional misconduct case. The three accountants of Deloitte & Touche LLP must pay C$100,000 in fines and C$417,000 in costs. Details of the disciplinary case are presented.

21344 ■ Accounting and Finance for Your Small Business
Pub: John Wiley & Sons, Incorporated
Ed: Steven M. Bragg; E. James Burton. **Released:** April 2006. **Price:** $49.00. **Description:** Financial procedures and techniques for establishing and maintaining a profitable small company are outlined.

21345 ■ "Accrual vs. Cash Accounting, Explained" in Business Owner (Vol. 35, July-August 2011, No. 4, pp. 13)
Pub: DL Perkins Company
Description: Cash method versus accrual accounting methods are examined, using hypothetical situations.

21346 ■ "Adler Blanchard & Freeman Reports New SmartKeeper Bookkeeping Service" in Professional Services Close-Up (March 24, 2011)
Pub: Close-Up Media
Description: Profile of Adler Blanchard & Freeman (AB&F) accountants and business advisors. The firm has expanded its client offerings to include their new SmartKeeper Business and Personal Bookkeeping Service for small to mid-sized companies and individuals.

21347 ■ "Bar Hopping: Your Numbers At a Glance" in Inc. (January 2008, pp. 44-45)
Pub: Gruner & Jahr USA Publishing
Ed: Michael Fitzgerald. **Description:** Software that helps any company analyze data include Crystal Xcelsius, a program that takes data from Excel documents and turns them into animated gauges, charts and graphs; CashView, a Web-based application that tracks receivables and payables; iDashboards, a Web-based programs that produces animated gauges, maps, pie charts and graphs; Corda Human Capital Management, that transforms stats like head count, productivity, and attrition into graphs and dials; NetSuite, a Web-based application that tracks key indicators; and Cognos Now, that gauges, dials, and graphs data.

21348 ■ "Battling Back from Betrayal" in Harvard Business Review (Vol. 88, December 2010, No. 12, pp. 130)
Pub: Harvard Business School Publishing
Ed: Daniel McGinn. **Description:** Stephen Greer's scrap metal firm, Hartwell Pacific, lost several million dollars due to a lack of efficient and appropriate inventory audits, accounting procedures, and new-hire reference checks for his foreign operations. Greer believes that balancing growth with control is a key component of success.

21349 ■ Beat the Taxman: Easy Ways to Tax Save in Your Small Business
Pub: John Wiley & Sons, Incorporated
Ed: Stephen Thompson. **Released:** May 2008. **Price:** $26.95. **Description:** Concise tax planner to help entrepreneurs take advantage of current tax laws.

21350 ■ "A Bigger Deal" in Crain's Cleveland Business (Vol. 28, November 12, 2007, No. 45, pp. 1)
Pub: Crain Communications, Inc.
Ed: Shawn A. Turner. **Description:** In an attempt to boost its revenue CBiz Inc., a provider of accounting and business services, is looking to balance its acquisitions of smaller companies with larger ones as part of its overall growth strategy.

21351 ■ "Book of Lists 2010" in Philadelphia Business Journal (Vol. 28, December 25, 2009, No. 45, pp. 1)
Pub: American City Business Journals
Description: Rankings of companies and organizations within the banking, biotechnology, economic development, healthcare, hospitality, law and accounting, marketing and media, real estate, and technology industries in the Philadelphia, Pennsylvania area are presented. Rankings are based on sales, business size, and more.

21352 ■ "Bookkeeping Service Opens First Sacramento Franchise" in Sacramento Bee (April 13, 2011)
Pub: Sacramento Bee
Ed: Mark Glover. **Description:** Franchise bookkeeping service called BookKeeping Express opened its new office in Roseville, California; its first shop in the area.

21353 ■ "Businesses Balk at 1099 Provision in Health Reform Law" in Baltimore Business Journal (Vol. 28, August 13, 2010, No. 14, pp. 1)
Pub: Baltimore Business Journal
Ed: Scott Dance. **Description:** Small business advocates and accountants have criticized the Internal Revenue Service Form 1099 provision in the health care reform law as not worth the cost of time and money. Critics believe the policy would create a deluge of the documents that is too much for the companies or the IRS to handle. Details of the provision are also discussed.

21354 ■ "Cautions On Loans With Your Business" in Business Owner (Vol. 35, July-August 2011, No. 4, pp. 5)
Pub: DL Perkins Company
Description: Caution must be used when borrowing from or lending to any small business. Tax guidelines for the borrowing and lending practice are also included.

21355 ■ "Changing the Rules of the Accounting Game" in Canadian Business (Vol. 81, December 8, 2008, No. 21, pp. 19)
Pub: Rogers Media Ltd.
Ed: Al Rosen. **Description:** Interference from world politicians in developing accounting standards is believed to have resulted in untested rules that are inferior to current standards. European lawmakers have recently asked to change International Financial Reporting Standards.

21356 ■ Computer Accounting Essentials with Microsoft Office Accounting 2010
Pub: McGraw-Hill Higher Education
Ed: Carol Yacht, Susan Crosson. **Released:** March 10, 2010. **Description:** Step-by-step guide to using Microsoft's Office Professional 2007 Accounting program.

21357 ■ "Convergence Collaboration: Revising Revenue Recognition" in Management Accounting Quarterly (Vol. 12, Spring 2011, No. 3, pp. 18)
Pub: Management Accounting Quarterly
Ed: Jack T. Ciesielski; Thomas R. Weirich. **Description:** While revenue recognition is critical, regulations have been developed on an ad hoc basis until now. The joint FASB/IASB proposed accounting standard on revenue recognition is a meaningful convergence of standards that will require a major adjustment for financial statement preparers. The proposal is a radical departure from the way revenue has been recognized by the U.S. GAAP. For industries such as consulting, engineering, construction, and technology, it could dramatically change revenue recognition, impacting the top line. The new proposed standard, its potential impact, and the critical role that contracts play is examined thoroughly.

21358 ■ Deduct It!: Lower Your Small Business Taxes
Pub: NOLO
Ed: Stephen Fishman. **Released:** November 2009. **Price:** $34.99. **Description:** Ways to make the most of tax deductions for any small business are covered.

The book is organized into categories featuring common deductions, start-up expenses, health deductions, entertainment, travel, inventory, equipment and more. Current tax laws and numbers for 2008 are included.

21359 ■ *Directory of Global Professional Accounting and Business Certifications*
Pub: John Wiley & Sons, Incorporated
Ed: Lal Balkaran. **Released:** February 9, 2007. **Price:** $35.00. **Description:** Resource for international accounting, auditing, and business professions.

21360 ■ *"Do Fair Value Adjustments Influence Dividend Policy?" in Accounting and Business Research (Vol. 41, Spring 2011, No. 2, pp. 51)*
Pub: American Institute of Certified Public Accountants
Contact: Barry C. Melancon, President
E-mail: bmelancon@aicpa.org
Ed: Igor Goncharov, Sander van Triest. **Description:** The impact of positive fair value adjustments on corporate distributions is examined using a Russian setting that requires disclosure of unrealized fair value adjustments in income. It was found that there is no rise in dividends due to positive fair value adjustments and that on the contrary, a negative relationship exists between adjustments and dividend changes.

21361 ■ *EBay Income: How ANYONE of Any Age, Location, and/or Background Can Build a Highly Profitable Online Business with eBay*
Pub: Atlantic Publishing Company
Released: December 1, 2010. **Price:** $24.95. **Description:** A complete overview of eBay is given and guides any small company through the entire process of creating the auction and auction strategies, photography, writing copy, text and formatting, multiple sales, programming tricks, PayPal, accounting, creating marketing, merchandising, managing email lists, advertising plans taxes and sales tax, best time to list items and for how long, sniping programs, international customers, opening a storefront, electronic commerce buy-it now pricing, keywords, Google marketing and eBay secrets.

21362 ■ *"Economic Crisis and Accounting Evolution" in Accounting and Business Research (Vol. 41, Summer 2011, No. 3, pp. 2159)*
Pub: American Institute of Certified Public Accountants
Contact: Barry C. Melancon, President
E-mail: bmelancon@aicpa.org
Ed: Gregory Waymire, Sudipta Basu. **Description:** Financial reporting changes at the face of economic crises are studied using a punctuated equilibrium evolution. Findings show that financial reporting has a minor impact but may amplify economic crises. Attempts to enhance accounting amid economic crises may not be as beneficial as planned.

21363 ■ *"Economic Crisis and Accounting Evolution" in Accounting and Business Research (Vol. 41, Summer 2011, No. 3, pp. 2159)*
Pub: Routledge
Ed: Gregory Waymire, Sudipta Basu. **Description:** Financial reporting changes at the face of economic crises are studied using a punctuated equilibrium evolution. Findings show that financial reporting has a minor impact but may amplify economic crises. Attempts to enhance accounting and economic crises may not be as beneficial as planned.

21364 ■ *Electronic Commerce: Technical, Business, and Legal Issues*
Pub: Prentice Hall PTR
Ed: Oktay Dogramaci; Aryya Gangopadhyay; Yelena Yesha; Nabil R. Adam. **Released:** August 1998. **Description:** Provides insight into the goals of using the Internet to grow a business in the areas of networking and telecommunication, security, and storage and retrieval; business areas such as marketing, procurement and purchasing, billing and payment, and sup-

ply chain management; and legal aspects such as privacy, intellectual property, taxation, contractual and legal settlements.

21365 ■ *Employer Legal Forms Simplified*
Pub: Nova Publishing Company
Ed: Daniel Sitarz. **Released:** August 2007. **Price:** $24.95. **Description:** Business reference containing the following forms needed to handle employees in any small business environment: application, notice, confidentiality, absence, federal employer forms and notices, and many payroll forms. All forms are included on a CD that comes in both PDF and text formats. Adobe Acrobat Reader software is also included on the CD. The forms are valid in all fifty states and Washington, DC.

21366 ■ *"Ethics Commission May Hire Collection Agency" in Tulsa World (August 21, 2010)*
Pub: World Publishing
Ed: Barbara Hoberock. **Description:** Oklahoma Ethics Commission is considering a more to hire a collection agency or law firm in order to collect fees from candidates owing money for filing ate financial reports.

21367 ■ *"Final State Budget Is a Mixed Bag of Key Industries" in The Business Journal - Serving Phoenix and the Valley of the Sun (Vol. 28, July 4, 2008, No. 44, pp. 3)*
Pub: American City Business Journals, Inc.
Ed: Mike Sunnucks; Patrick O'Grady. **Description:** Approved by Governor Janet Napolitano and passed by the Arizona Legislature, the $9.9 billion state budget is beneficial to some industries in the business community. The tax cap for on Arizona Lottery has been removed which is beneficial to the industry, while the solar energy industry and real estate developers stand to lose from the spending bill. Other details of the finance budget are presented.

21368 ■ *"Finally, Justice" in Canadian Business (Vol. 82, April 27, 2009, No. 7, pp. 12)*
Pub: Rogers Media
Ed: John Gray. **Description:** Former investment adviser Alex Winch feels that he was vindicated with the Canadian Court's ruling that Livent Inc. founders Garth Drabinsky and Myron Gottlieb were guilty of fraud. Drabinsky filed a libel case on Winch over Winch's letter that complained over Livent's accounting procedures. Winch also criticized the inconsistent accounting during Drabinsky's term as chief executive of another firm.

21369 ■ *Finance & Accounting: How to Keep Your Books and Manage Your Finances with an MBA, a CPA, or a Ph.D*
Pub: Adams Media Corporation
Ed: Suzanne Caplan. **Price:** $19.95.

21370 ■ *"The Finance Function In A Global Corporation" in Harvard Business Review (Vol. 86, July-August 2008, No. 8, pp. 108)*
Pub: Harvard Business School Press
Ed: Mihir A. Desai. **Description:** Designing and implementing a successful finance function in a global setting is discussed. Additional topics include the internal capital market, managing risk and budgeting capital internationally.

21371 ■ *Financial Management 101: Get a Grip on Your Business Numbers*
Pub: Self-Counsel Press, Incorporated
Ed: Angie Mohr. **Released:** November 2007. **Price:** $16.95. **Description:** An overview of business planning, financial statements, budgeting and advertising for small businesses. s.

21372 ■ *Financial Times Guide to Business Start Up 2007*
Pub: Pearson Education, Limited
Contact: Steven A. Dowling, President
Ed: Sara Williams; Jonquil Lowe. **Released:** November 2006. **Price:** $52.50. **Description:** Guide for starting and running a new business is presented. Sections include ways to get started, direct marketing, customer relations, management and accounting.

21373 ■ *The Flaw of Averages: Why We Underestimate Risk in the Face of Uncertainty*
Pub: John Wiley & Sons, Inc.
Ed: Sam L. Savage. **Released:** June 3, 2009. **Price:** $22.95. **Description:** Personal and business plans are based on uncertainties on a daily basis. The common avoidable mistake individuals make in assessing risk in the face of uncertainty is defined. The explains why plans based on average assumptions are wrong, on average, in areas as diverse as finance, healthcare, accounting, the war on terror, and climate change.

21374 ■ *"Function Over Forms?" in Barron's (Vol. 88, June 30, 2008, No. 26, pp. 17)*
Pub: Dow Jones & Co., Inc.
Ed: Eric Savitz. **Description:** Securities and Exchange Commission (SEC) chairman Christopher Cox wants the SEC to consider an overhaul of the forms used to meet the agency's disclosure requirements. Cox also said that the U.S. Generally Accepted Accounting Standards has too many rules with exceptions and alternative interpretations.

21375 ■ *Getting Rich In Your Underwear: How To Start and Run a Profitable Home-Based Business*
Pub: HCM Publishing
Ed: Peter I. Hupalo. **Released:** April 1, 2005. **Price:** $17.95. **Description:** Book offers insight into starting a home-based business. Entrepreneurs will learn about business models and the home business; distribution and fulfillment of product or service; marketing and sales; how to overcome the fear of starting a business; personal success characteristics; naming a business; zoning and insurance; intellectual capital; copyrights, trademarks, and patents; limited liability companies and S-corporations; business expenses and accounting; taxes; fifteen basic steps for starting a home-based business, state resources for starting a home company; and seven home-based business ideas.

21376 ■ *"Give Until It Works" in Hispanic Business (Vol. 30, March 2008, No. 3, pp. 26)*
Pub: Hispanic Business
Ed: Rick Munarriz. **Description:** Donating to qualified charities and non-profit organizations for maximizing tax advantage to be availed on the income tax bill is examined. The amount that can be deducted from the total taxable amount is usually less then the actual amount donated and must be made during that calendar year.

21377 ■ *"Growing Strong" in Entrepreneur (Vol. 35, November 2007, No. 11, pp. 36)*
Pub: Entrepreneur Media Inc.
Ed: Nichole L. Torres. **Description:** Amy Langer founded Salo LL with partner John Folkestad. The company is growing fast since its 2002 launch, with over $40 million in projections for 2007. The finance and accounting staffing company tops the list of the fastest-growing women-led companies in North America.

21378 ■ *"Handle With Care" in Hawaii Business (Vol. 53, October 2007, No. 5, pp. 66)*
Pub: Hawaii Business Publishing
Ed: Kenneth Sheffield. **Description:** Discusses a fiduciary, who may be a board member, business owner, or a trustee, and is someone who supervises and manages the affairs and the resources of a principal. Fiduciary duties, which include accounting, cost review and risk management, must be served with the benefit of the principal as the priority. Ways of breaching fiduciary duties and how to avoid them are discussed.

21379 ■ *"The Hidden Tax" in Canadian Business (Vol. 81, April 14, 2008, No. 6, pp. 28)*
Pub: Rogers Media
Ed: Al Rosen. **Description:** Accounting fraud could take out a sizable sum from one's retirement fund when computed over a long period of time. The much bigger tax on savings is the collective impact of the smaller losses that do not attract the attention they

deserve. Ensuring that investors are not unnecessarily taxed 2 percent of their total investments every year outweighs the benefit of a 2 percent reduction in personal tax rates.

21380 ■ *How to Start an Internet Sales Business*
Pub: Lulu.com

Ed: Dan Davis. **Released:** August 2005. **Price:** $19.95. **Description:** Small business guide for launching an Internet sales company. Topics include business structure, licenses, and taxes.

21381 ■ *How to Start and Run a Small Book Publishing Company: A Small Business Guide to Self-Publishing and Independent Publishing*
Pub: HCM Publishing

Ed: Peter I. Hupalo. **Released:** August 30, 2002. **Price:** $18.95. **Description:** The book teaches all aspects of starting and running a small book publishing company. Topics covered include: inventory accounting in the book trade, just-in-time inventory management, turnkey fulfillment solutions, tax deductible costs, basics of sales and use tax, book pricing, standards in terms of the book industry, working with distributors and wholesalers, cover design and book layout, book promotion and marketing, how to select profitable authors to publish, printing process, printing on demand, the power of a strong backlist, and how to value copyright.

21382 ■ *"How To: Manage Your Cash Better"* in *Inc.* (Volume 32, December 2010, No. 10, pp. 69)
Pub: Inc. Magazine

Description: A monthly guide to policies, procedures and practices for managing cash for a small business.

21383 ■ *"IFRS Monopoly: the Pied Piper of Financial Reporting"* in *Accounting and Business Research* (Vol. 41, Summer 2011, No. 3, pp. 291)
Pub: American Institute of Certified Public Accountants

Contact: Barry C. Melancon, President

E-mail: bmelancon@aicpa.org

Ed: Shyam Sunder. **Description:** The disadvantages of granting monopoly to the international financial reporting standards (IFRS) are examined. Results indicate that an IFRS monopoly removes the chances for comparing alternative practices and learning from them. An IFRS monopoly also eliminates customization of financial reporting to fit local differences in governance, business, economic, and legal conditions.

21384 ■ *"Internal Auditor Wants Ethics Review of City's Casper Golf Contract"* in *Business Courier* (Vol. 27, September 10, 2010, No. 19, pp. 1)
Pub: Business Courier

Ed: Dan Monk. **Description:** Mark Ashworth, an internal auditor for Cincinnati, Ohio is pushing for an ethics review of management contract for seven city-owned golf courses. Ashworth wants the Ohio Ethics Commission to investigate family ties between a superintendent for the Cincinnati Recreation Commission and Billy Casper Golf.

21385 ■ *"IRS Announces New Standards for Tax Preparers"* in *Bellingham Business Journal* (Vol. February 2010, pp. 9)
Pub: Sound Publishing Inc.

Ed: Isaac Bonnell. **Description:** A new oversight plan was announced by the Internal Revenue Services (IRS) that will require tax professionals to pass a competency test and register with the government in order to ensure greater accountability in the industry.

21386 ■ *"Kaboom!"* in *Canadian Business* (Vol. 81, November 10, 2008, No. 19, pp. 18)
Pub: Rogers Media Ltd.

Ed: Al Rosen, Mark Rosen. **Description:** International Financial Reporting Standards (IFRS) is a good idea in theory but was implemented in a hurry and had poor quality standards from the beginning.

21387 ■ *"Know Your Numbers"* in *Inc.* (Volume 32, December 2010, No. 10, pp. 39)
Pub: Inc. Magazine

Ed: Norm Brodsky. **Description:** Ways to maximize profit and minimize tax burden are presented.

21388 ■ *"Lifesavers"* in *Black Enterprise* (Vol. 41, December 2010, No. 5, pp. 38)
Pub: Earl G. Graves Publishing Co. Inc.

Ed: Tamara E. Holmes. **Description:** Profile of Interventional Nephrology Specialists Access Center and founders Dr. Omar Davis and Dr. Natarsha Grant; the center generated $5.5 million in revenue for 2009. Details on how they run their successful center are included.

21389 ■ *"Living in a 'Goldfish Bowl"* in *WorkingUSA* (Vol. 11, June 2008, No. 2, pp. 277)
Pub: Blackwell Publishers Ltd.

Ed: John Lund. **Description:** Recent changes in laws, regulations and even the reporting format of labor organization annual financial reports in both the U.S. and Australia have received surprisingly little attention, yet they have significantly increased the amount of information available both to union members and the public in general, as reports in both countries are available via government Websites. While such financial reporting laws are extremely rare in European countries, with the exception of the UK and Ireland, the U.S. and Australian reporting systems have become among the most detailed in the world. After reviewing these changes in financial reporting and the availability of these reports, as well as comparing and contrasting the specific reporting requirements of each country, this paper then examines the cost-benefit impact of more detailed financial reporting.

21390 ■ *"Market Volatility and Your Retirement"* in *Agency Sales Magazine* (Vol. 39, August 2009, No. 8, pp. 48)
Pub: MANA

Ed: Joshua D. Mosshart. **Description:** Strategies for retirees in managing investments amid market volatility are presented. Retirees should keep their withdrawal assumptions conservative, maintain sensible asset allocation, review and rebalance their portfolio and allow a financial professional to guide them. Insights on market volatility are also given.

21391 ■ *"May I Handle That For You?"* in *Inc.* (March 2008, pp. 40, 42)
Pub: Gruner & Jahr USA Publishing

Ed: Taylor Mallory. **Description:** According to a recent survey, 53 percent of all companies outsource a portion of their human resources responsibilities. Ceridian, Administaff, Taleo, KnowledgeBank, and CheckPoint HR are among the companies profiled.

21392 ■ *MBA In a Day*
Pub: John Wiley and Sons, Inc.

Ed: Steven Stralser, PhD. **Released:** 2004. **Price:** $34.95. **Description:** Management professor presents important concepts, business topics and strategies that can be used by anyone to manage a small business or professional practice. Topics covered include: human resources and personal interaction, ethics and leadership skills, fair negotiation tactics, basic business accounting practices, project management, and the fundamentals of economics and marketing.

21393 ■ *"Merger Mania: Regional Snaps Up HVS"* in *The Business Journal-Serving Greater Tampa Bay* (Vol. 28, September 26, 2008, No. 40, pp. 1)
Pub: American City Business Journals, Inc.

Ed: Alexis Muellner. **Description:** It was reported that Harper Van Scoik & Co. LLP has finalized a merger with Carr Riggs & Ingram LLC. The agreement, effective October 1, 2008, is a merger of HVS assets into CRI. Bill Carr, a managing partner, revealed that HVS' $5 million in revenue will take CRI from $78 million to $82 million in revenue.

21394 ■ *Mergers and Acquisitions from A to Z*
Pub: Amacom

Ed: Andrew J. Sherman, Milledge A. Hart. **Released:** January 2006. **Price:** $35.00. **Description:** Guide for

the entire process of mergers and acquisitions, including taxes, accounting, laws, and projected financial gain.

21395 ■ *Microfinance*
Pub: Palgrave Macmillan

Ed: Mario La Torre; Gianfranco A. Vento; Philip Molyneux. **Released:** October 2006. **Price:** $80.00. **Description:** Microfinance involves the analysis of operational, managerial and financial aspects of a small business.

21396 ■ *Minding Her Own Business, 4th Ed.*
Pub: Sphinx Publishing

Ed: Jan Zobel. **Released:** January 1, 2005. **Price:** $16.95. **Description:** A guide to taxes and financial records for women entrepreneurs is presented.

21397 ■ *"My Favorite Tool for Managing Expenses"* in *Inc.* (Volume 32, December 2010, No. 10, pp. 60)
Pub: Inc. Magazine

Ed: J.J. McCorvey. **Description:** Web-based service called Expensify is outlined. The service allows companies to log expenses while away from the office using the service's iPhone application.

21398 ■ *"New Century's Fall Has a New Culprit"* in *Barron's* (Vol. 88, March 31, 2008, No. 13, pp. 20)
Pub: Dow Jones & Company, Inc.

Ed: Jonathan R. Laing. **Description:** Court examiner Michael Missal reports that New Century Financial's auditor contributed to New Century's demise by its negligence in permitting improper and imprudent practices related to New Century's accounting processes. New Century's bankruptcy filing is considered the start of the subprime-mortgage crisis.

21399 ■ *"New Institutional Accounting and IFRS"* in *Accounting and Business Research* (Vol. 41, Summer 2011, No. 3, pp. 309)
Pub: American Institute of Certified Public Accountants

Contact: Barry C. Melancon, President

E-mail: bmelancon@aicpa.org

Ed: Peter Wysocki. **Description:** A new framework for institutional accounting research is presented. It has five fundamental components — efficient versus inefficient results, interdependencies, causation, level of analysis, and institutional structure. The use of the framework for evaluation accounting institutions such as the international financial reporting standards is discussed.

21400 ■ *"New Institutional Accounting and IFRS"* in *Accounting and Business Research* (Vol. 41, Summer 2011, No. 3, pp. 309)
Pub: Routledge

Ed: Peter Wysocki. **Description:** A new framework for institutional accounting research is presented. It has five fundamental components: efficient versus inefficient results, interdependencies, causation, level of analysis, and institutional structure. The use of the framework for evaluation accounting institutions such as the international financial reports standards (IFRS) is discussed.

21401 ■ *"New Money"* in *Entrepreneur* (Vol. 36, February 2008, No. 2, pp. 62)
Pub: Entrepreneur Media Inc.

Ed: C.J. Prince. **Description:** Tips on how to handle business finance, with regard to the tightened credit standards imposed by leading institutions, are provided. These include: selling receivables, margining blue chips, and selling purchase orders.

21402 ■ *"Olympus is Urged to Revise Board"* in *Wall Street Journal Eastern Edition* (November 28, 2011, pp. B3)
Pub: Dow Jones & Company Inc. Enterprise Media Group

Contact: Clare Hart, President

Ed: Phred Dvorak. **Description:** Koji Miyata, once a director on the board of troubled Japanese photographic equipment company, is urging the company to reorganize its board, saying the present group should resign their board seats but keep their management positions. The company has come under scrutiny for its accounting practices and costly acquisitions.

21403 ■ *The One Minute Entrepreneur*
Pub: Doubleday

Ed: Ken Blanchard; assisted by Don Hutson and Ethan Willis. **Released:** 2008. **Price:** $19.95. **Description:** Four traditional business ideas are covered including: revenue needs to exceed expenses, bill collection, customer service, and employee motivation in order to be successful.

21404 ■ *Open Source Solutions for Small Business Problems*
Pub: Charles River Media

Ed: John Locke. **Released:** May 2004. **Price:** $35.95. **Description:** Open source software provides solutions to many small business problems such as tracking electronic documents, scheduling, accounting functions, managing contact lists, and reducing spam.

21405 ■ *Outfoxing the Small Business Owner*
Pub: Adams Media Corporation

Ed: Gene Marks. **Released:** January 2005. **Description:** Special skill sets are required to sell, service or deal with small business customers.

21406 ■ *"Paperless Bookkeeping Program" in Fleet Owner Online (February 15, 2011)*
Pub: Penton Business Media Inc.

Description: TruckTax launched its new paperless bookkeeping system to help manage bookkeeping tasks, accounting and business tax information and filings for truckers.

21407 ■ *"Pick and Save" in Entrepreneur (Vol. 36, April 2008, No. 4, pp. 66)*
Pub: Entrepreneur Media, Inc.

Ed: C.J. Prince. **Description:** Business owners can purchase the needed big equipment to offset this year's expected profit. They can also switch to annualized computing of quarterly income and estimated tax payments to pay less estimated taxes for the first half of the year. Other tips on tax planning are provided.

21408 ■ *"Piece of Health Law 'A Goner" in Baltimore Business Journal (Vol. 28, November 19, 2010, No. 28, pp. 1)*
Pub: Baltimore Business Journal

Ed: Kent Hoover. **Description:** Montana Senator Max Baucus, a Democrat who heads the Senate Finance Committee, has revealed his plan to push legislation that would repeal the 1099 IRS provision that was created by the health care reform law and will result in more paperwork for small businesses when it goes into effect in 2012.

21409 ■ *"Place Restrictions on Your Stock Shares" in Business Owner (Vol. 35, July-August 2011, No. 4, pp. 14)*
Pub: DL Perkins Company

Description: It is critical for any small business owner to be certain that the buyer or recipient of any part of the company represents that the stock is being acquired or given for investment purposes only.

21410 ■ *"Proposed Accounting Changes Could Complicate Tenant's Leases" in Baltimore Business Journal (Vol. 28, July 2, 2010, No. 8, pp. 1)*
Pub: Baltimore Business Journal

Ed: Daniel J. Sernovitz. **Description:** The Financial Accounting Standards Board has proposed that companies must indicate the value of real estate leases as assets and liabilities on balance sheets instead of expenses. The proposals could cause some companies to document millions of dollars in charges on their books or find difficulty in getting loans.

21411 ■ *"Prosecutors Dish Sordid AIPC Story" in The Business Journal-Serving Metropolitan Kansas City (Vol. 27, September 19, 2008, No. 1)*
Pub: American City Business Journals, Inc.

Ed: Suzanna Stagemeyer. **Description:** Prosecutors in the American Italian Pasta Co.'s accounting fraud case have revealed evidence on the schemes used by then-officers of the company to commit fraud. District attorney John Wood has dubbed the case as the largest corporate fraud lawsuit in the history of the district of Missouri. How AIPC fell from being an industry leader is also discussed.

21412 ■ *QuickBooks All-in-One Desk Reference for Dummies*
Pub: John Wiley & Sons, Incorporated

Ed: Stephen L. Nelson. **Released:** January 2007. **Price:** $29.99 (US), $42.99 (Canadian). **Description:** Compilation of nine self-contained minibooks to get the most from QuickBooks accounting software. Companion Web site with sample business plan workbook and downloadable profit-volume cost analysis workbook included.

21413 ■ *QuickBooks for the New Bean Counter: Business Owner's Guide 2006*
Pub: Wheatmark

Ed: Joseph L. Catallini. **Released:** July 2006. **Price:** $21.95. **Description:** Profile of QuickBooks software, offering insight into using the software's accounting and bookkeeping functions.

21414 ■ *QuickBooks Simple Start for Dummies*
Pub: John Wiley and Sons, Inc.

Ed: Stephen L. Nelson. **Released:** October 2004. **Price:** $21.99. **Description:** Profile of Intuit's new accounting software geared to micro businesses. Advice is offered on daily, monthly, and yearly accounting activities covering records, sales tax, and reports.

21415 ■ *QuickBooks X on Demand*
Pub: Que

Ed: Gail Perry. **Released:** December 2006. **Price:** $34.99. **Description:** Step-by-step training for using various small business financial software programs; includes illustrated, full color explanations.

21416 ■ *QuickBooks X for Dummies*
Pub: John Wiley & Sons, Incorporated

Ed: Stephen L. Nelson. **Released:** November 2006. **Price:** $21.99. **Description:** Key features of Quick-Books software for small business are introduced. Invoicing and credit memos, recoding sales receipts, accounting, budgeting, taxes, payroll, financial reports, job estimating, billing, tracking, data backup, are among the features.

21417 ■ *"Quicken Starter Edition 2008" in Black Enterprise (Vol. 38, March 2008, No. 8, pp. 54)*
Pub: Earl G. Graves Publishing Co. Inc.

Ed: Sonya A. Donaldson. **Description:** Profile of Quicken Starter Edition 2008 offering programs that track spending; it will also categorize tax deductible expenses.

21418 ■ *Reading Financial Reports for Dummies*
Pub: John Wiley and Sons, Inc.

Ed: Lita Epstein. **Released:** January 2009. **Price:** $21.99. **Description:** This second edition contains more new and updated information, including new information on the separate accounting and financial reporting standards for private/small businesses versus public/large businesses; updated information reflecting 2007 laws on international financial reporting standards; new content to match SEC and other governmental regulatory changes over the last three years; new information about how the analyst-corporate connection has changed the playing field; the impact of corporate communications and new technologies; new examples that reflect the current trends; and updated Websites and resources.

21419 ■ *"Reform or Perish" in Canadian Business (Vol. 82, April 27, 2009, No. 7, pp. 20)*
Pub: Rogers Media

Ed: Al Rosen. **Description:** It is believed that Canada needs to fix its financial regulatory framework in order to provide more oversight on accounting procedures that is often left up to auditors. While the U.S. has constantly rebuilt its regulatory framework, Canada has not instituted reforms on its regulations. Canada entered the recession with a strong system but needs to build more substance into it.

21420 ■ *Sarbanes-Oxley for Dummies, 2nd Ed.*
Pub: John Wiley and Sons, Inc.

Ed: Jill Gilbert Welytok. **Released:** February 2008. **Price:** $21.99. **Description:** Provides the latest Sarbanes-Oxley (SOX) legislation with procedures to safely and effectively reduce compliance costs. Topics include way to: establish SOX standards for IT professionals, minimize compliances costs for every aspect of a business, survive a Section 404 audit, avoid litigation under SOX, anticipate future rules and trends, create a post-SOX paper trail, increase a company's standing and reputation, work with SOX in a small business, meet new SOX standards, build a board that can't be bought, and to comply with all SOX management mandates.

21421 ■ *Schaum's Outline Financial Management, Third Edition*
Pub: McGraw-Hill

Ed: Jae K. Shim; Joel G. Siegel. **Released:** May 2007. **Price:** $22.95 (CND). **Description:** Rules and regulations governing corporate finance, including the Sarbanes-Oxley Act are discussed.

21422 ■ *"SEC Extends Small Business Deadline for SOX Audit Requirement" in HRMagazine (Vol. 53, August 2008, No. 8, pp. 20)*
Pub: Society for Human Resource Management
Contact: Henry G. Jackson, President
E-mail: hjackson@shrm.org

Description: Securities and Exchange Commission has approved a one-year extension of the compliance date for smaller public companies to meet the Section 404(b) auditor attestation requirement of the Sarbanes-Oxley Act.

21423 ■ *Self-Employed Tax Solutions: Quick, Simple, Money-Saving, Audit-Proof Tax and Recordkeeping Basics*
Pub: The Globe Pequot Press

Ed: June Walker. **Released:** January 1, 2009. **Price:** $17.95. **Description:** A simple system for maintaining tax records and filing tax forms for any small business is explored.

21424 ■ *Six SIGMA for Small Business*
Pub: Entrepreneur Press

Ed: Greg Brue. **Released:** October 2005. **Price:** $19.95 (US), $26.95 (Canadian). **Description:** Jack Welch's Six SIGMA approach to business covers accounting, finance, sales and marketing, buying a business, human resource development, and new product development.

21425 ■ *"Small is Bountiful for Intuit" in Barron's (Vol. 90, September 13, 2010, No. 37, pp. 22)*
Pub: Barron's Editorial & Corporate Headquarters

Ed: Mark Veverka. **Description:** Finance software maker Intuit wants to tap the underserved small business market. One analyst sees Intuit's shares rising 25 percent to 55 percent in the next 12 months from September 2010.

21426 ■ *The Small Business Bible: Everything You Need to Know to Succeed in Your Small Business*
Pub: John Wiley and Sons, Inc.

Ed: Steven D. Strauss. **Released:** September 2008. **Price:** $19.95 (US), $28.99 (Canadian). **Description:** Comprehensive guide to starting and running a successful small business. Topics include bookkeeping and financial management, marketing, publicity, and advertising.

21427 ■ *Small Business Desk Reference*
Pub: Penguin Books USA Inc.

Ed: Gene Marks. **Released:** December 2004. **Description:** Comprehensive guide for starting or running a successful small business, focusing on buying a business or franchise, writing a business plan, financial management, accounting, legal issues, human resources management, operations, marketing, sales, customer service, taxes, insurance, and ethics. Information for launching a restaurant, property management firm, retail outlet, consulting firm, and service business is included.

21428 ■ Small Business for Dummies, 3rd Ed.

Pub: John Wiley and Sons, Inc.
Ed: Eric Tyson; Jim Schell. Released: March 2008. Price: $21.99. Description: Guidebook for anyone wanting to start or grow a small business; topics include information financing, budgeting, marketing, management and more.

21429 ■ The Small Business Owner's Manual: Everything You Need to Know to Start Up and Run Your Business

Pub: Career Press, Incorporated
Ed: Joe Kennedy. Released: June 2005. Price: $19.99 (US), $26.95 (Canadian). Description: Comprehensive guide for starting a small business, focusing on twelve ways to obtain financing, business plans, selling and advertising products and services, hiring and firing employees, setting up a Web site, business law, accounting issues, insurance, equipment, computers, banks, financing, customer credit and collection, leasing, and more.

21430 ■ Small Business Survival Guide

Pub: Adams Media Corporation
Contact: Gary Krebs, Director
E-mail: swatrous@adamsmedia.com
Ed: Cliff Ennico. Price: $12.95. Description: Small business expert provides strategies to start a company and survive in the 21st Century. He shows small business owners how to succeed despite challenges that can defeat any firm. His advice covers suppliers; customers and contractors; competitors and creditors; spouses, family and friends; as well as the ways lawyers, accountants and other can steal an entrepreneur's success. Ennico also describes how startups can comply with local regulations.

21431 ■ Small Business Survival Guide: Starting, Protecting, and Securing Your Business for Long-Term Success

Pub: Adams Media Corporation
Ed: Cliff Ennico. Released: September 2005. Price: $12.95 (US), $17.95 (Canadian). Description: Entrepreneurship in the new millennium. Topics include creditors, taxes, competition, business law, and accounting.

21432 ■ Smart Tax Write-Offs, 5th Ed.

Pub: Rayve Productions, Inc.
Ed: Norm Ray. Released: February 2008. Price: $15.95. Description: Guidebook to help small business owners take advantage of legitimate tax deductions for home-based and other entrepreneurial businesses.

21433 ■ "Smart Year-End Tax Moves" in Business Owner (Vol. 35, November-December 2011, No. 6, pp. 8)

Pub: DL Perkins Company
Description: Managing small business and individual taxes is more important in a bad economy. It is imperative to seek all tax incentives that apply to your business.

21434 ■ "Spotlight on Pensions" in Business Horizons (Vol. 51, March-April 2008, No. 2, pp. 105)

Pub: Elsevier Advanced Technology Publications
Ed: Laureen A. Maines. Description: Perceptions of pension burden and risk among financial statement users is likely to increase with changes in pension accounting. These perceptions might affect decisions on pension commitments and investments.

21435 ■ "Spotlight on Principles-based Financial Reporting" in Business Horizons (September-October 2007, pp. 359)

Pub: Elsevier Technology Publications
Ed: Laureen A. Maines. Description: Employment of principles-based standards in order to generate reliable financial reporting and to reduce misrepresentations is discussed. Rules-based standards are distinguished from principles-based standards.

21436 ■ "Staffing Firm Grows by Following Own Advice-Hire a Headhunter" in Crain's Detroit Business (Vol. 24, October 6, 2008, No. 40, pp. 1)

Pub: Crain Communications, Inc.
Ed: Sherri Begin. Description: Profile of Venator Holdings L.L.C., a staffing firm that provides searches for companies in need of financial-accounting and technical employees; the firm's revenue has increased from $1.1 million in 2003 to a projected $11.5 million this year due to a climate in which more people are exiting the workforce than are coming in with those particular specialized skills and the need for a temporary, flexible workforce for contract placements at companies that do not want to take on the legacy costs associated with permanent employees. The hiring of an external headhunter to find the right out-of-state manager for Venator is also discussed.

21437 ■ "State Budget Woes Hurt Many Vendors, Senior Services" in Sacramento Business Journal (Vol. 25, August 15, 2008, No. 24, pp. 1)

Pub: American City Business Journals, Inc.
Ed: Melanie Turner. Description: Delays in the passage of the California state budget have adversely affected the health care industry. The Robertson Adult Day Health Care had taken out loans to keep the business afloat. The state Legislature has reduced Medi-Cal reimbursement to health care providers by 10 percent.

21438 ■ Streetwise Finance and Accounting for Entrepreneurs: Set Budgets, Manage Costs, Keep Your Business Profitable

Pub: Adams Media Corporation
Ed: Suzanne Caplan. Released: November 2006. Price: $25.95. Description: Book offers a basic understanding of accounting and finance for small businesses, including financial statements, credits and debits, as well as establishing a budget. Strategies for small companies in financial distress are included.

21439 ■ Streetwise Small Business Book of Lists: Hundreds of Lists to Help You Reduce Costs, Increase Revenues, and Boost Your Profits!

Pub: Adams Media Corporation
Contact: Gary Krebs, Director
E-mail: swatrous@adamsmedia.com
Ed: Gene Marks. Released: September 2006. Price: $25.95. Description: Strategies to help small business owners locate services, increase sales, and lower expenses.

21440 ■ Tactical Entrepreneur: The Entrepreneur's Game Plan

Pub: Sortis Publishing
Ed: Brian J. Hazelgren. Released: September 2005. Price: $14.95. Description: A smart, realistic business plan is essential for any successful entrepreneur. Besides offering products or services, small business owners must possess skills in accounting, planning, human resources management, marketing, and information technology.

21441 ■ "Take Control of Your Company's Finances" in Green Industry Pro (Vol. 23, March 2011, No. 3, pp. 24)

Pub: Cygnus Business Media
Ed: Gregg Wartgow. Description: Understanding that when certain leading indicators that affect the outcome of certain lagging indicators are aligned, companies will be able to take control of their firm's finances. Ways to improve the processes that drive financial performance for landscape firms are outlined.

21442 ■ "Technology and Returnable Asset Management" in Canadian Electronics (Vol. 23, February 2008, No. 1, pp. 6)

Pub: CLB Media Inc.
Ed: Mark Borkowski. Description: Peter Kastner, president of Vestigo Corporation, believes that public companies without an asset track, trace, and control system in place could face Sarbanes-Oakley liability if error-prone processes result to misstatements of

asset inventory positions. He also thinks that the system can improve return on assets by increasing the utilization of returnables.

21443 ■ "Test Your Structural Integrity" in Entrepreneur (Vol. 37, August 2009, No. 8, pp. 60)

Pub: Entrepreneur Media, Inc.
Ed: Jennifer Lawler. Description: Tax considerations can be important when choosing a business structure. For example, profits are taxed to the corporation in a C corp while profits are taxed only once at an S corp or a limited liability company. Meeting a tax professional should be done prior to switching to a different structure.

21444 ■ "Throughput Metrics Meet Six Sigma" in Management Accounting Quarterly (Vol. 12, Spring 2011, No. 3, pp. 12)

Pub: Management Accounting Quarterly
Ed: Shaun Aghili. Description: Throughput accounting (TA) metrics can be combined with six sigma's DMAIC methodology and various time-tested analysis and measurement tools for added effectiveness in resolving resource constraint issues. The goal is to optimize not only the output of a specific department but that of the entire system, by implementing a cost accounting system that is conducive to system optimization while increasing product quality, process integrity, or ideally, both.

21445 ■ "ValienteHernandez Acquired" in The Business Journal-Serving Greater Tampa Bay (Vol. 28, September 12, 2008, No. 38, pp. 1)

Pub: American City Business Journals, Inc.
Ed: Alexis Muellner. Description: Minnesota accounting firm LarsonAllen LLP has acquired Florida-based ValienteHernandez PA, creating a company with 35 employees to be based in ValienteHernandez's newly built office in Tampa Bay Area. Other details about the merger are provided.

21446 ■ "Welcome Back" in Canadian Business (Vol. 82, April 27, 2009, No. 7, pp. 25)

Pub: Rogers Media
Ed: Sarka Halas. Description: Some Canadian companies such as Gennum Corporation have taken advantage of corporate sale-leasebacks to raise money at a time when credit is hard to acquire. Corporate sale-leasebacks allow companies to sell their property assets while remaining as tenants of the building. Sale-leasebacks allow firms to increase capital while avoiding the disruptions that may result with moving.

21447 ■ "Where Women Work" in Marketing to Women (Vol. 21, April 2008, No. 4, pp. 8)

Pub: EPM Communications Inc.
Contact: Ira Mayer, President
E-mail: imayer@epmcom.com
Description: According to the U.S. Census Bureau, 60 percent of America's professional tax preparers are women. Also features additional trends concerning women in the workplace. Statistical data included.

21448 ■ Working Papers, Chapters 1-14 for Needles/Powers/Crosson's Financial and Managerial Accounting

Pub: Cengage South-Western
Ed: Belverd E. Needles, Marian Powers, Susan V. Crosson. Released: May 10, 2010. Price: $62.95. Description: Appropriate accounting forms for completing all exercises, problems and cases in the text are provided for financial management of a small company.

TRADE PERIODICALS

21449 ■ Keep Up to Date on Accounts Payable

Pub: Progressive Business Publications
Ed: Nathan Hall, Editor, nhall@pbp.com. Released: 23/year. Price: $230, individuals. Description: Supplies updates on state and local sales use taxes, plus IRS 1099 regulations and best practices in accounts payable. Recurring features include interviews, news of research, a calendar of events, and a column titled Sharpen Your Judgment.

VIDEOCASSETTES/ AUDIOCASSETTES

21450 ■ CPE Network: Accounting and Auditing Report
Bisk Education
9417 Princess Palm Ave.
Tampa, FL 33619
Free: 800-874-7877
Co. E-mail: info@bisk.com
URL: http://www.bisk.com
Released: 1994. **Price:** $799.00. **Description:** Outlines informaton on current industry issues, pronouncements, new standards, recent decisions, insider reports on exposure drafts, and other early indicators of upcoming changes in the accounting and auditing areas. Video newsletter published 11 times per year. **Availability:** VHS.

21451 ■ Small Business Accounting Systems
Instructional Video
2219 C St.
Lincoln, NE 68502
Ph: (402)475-6570
Free: 800-228-0164
Fax: (402)475-6500
Co. E-mail: feedback@insvideo.com
URL: http://www.insvideo.com
Released: 19??. **Price:** $19.95. **Description:** Illustrates basic small business accounting, providing instruction on recording transactions, the balance sheet, and the income statement. **Availability:** VHS.

CONSULTANTS

21452 ■ American Topical Association, Americana Unit (AU)
17 Peckham Rd.
Poughkeepsie, NY 12603
Ph: (845)452-2126
Fax: (781)459-0392
Co. E-mail: info@americanaunit.org
URL: http://www.americanaunit.org
Contact: Dennis M. Dengel, Treasurer
Description: A study unit of the American Topical Association and the American Philatelic Society. Works to collect stamps commemorating or picturing Americans or Americana; to research and publish philatelic information concerning the Americana topic; to encourage and support topical stamp exhibitions pertaining to Americana; to share this knowledge and experience with fellow collectors. **Scope:** Philatelic club devoted to the collecting of stamps, covers and other philatelic material related to the topic of Americana. **Founded:** 1951. **Publications:** *Americana Philatelic News* (Quarterly); *Index to Americana Philatelic News, 1970-85*. **Educational Activities:** National Topical Stamp Show (Annual). **Awards:** Merit Award (Annual).

21453 ■ Larry J. Anderson Insurance
1200 35th St., Ste. 206-4
West Des Moines, IA 50266-1953
Ph: (515)221-1973
Fax: (515)221-0074
Contact: Larry J. Anderson, Owner
E-mail: andy4021@aol.com
Scope: Offers business consulting services including temporary technical aid in accounting, turn around and cash management, and bail-out assistance. Also provides operations research, models, forecasting, project scheduling, and economic forecasting services. Provides assistance in group health insurance in both fully insured groups and self-funded groups. **Founded:** 1984.

21454 ■ Avery, Cooper & Co.
4918-50th St.
Yellowknife, NT, Canada X1A 2P2
Ph: (867)873-3441
Free: 800-661-0787

Fax: (867)873-2353
Co. E-mail: gerry@averyco.nt.ca
URL: http://www.averycooper.com
Contact: Bernie H. Bauhaus, Manager
E-mail: bernieb@averyco.nt.ca
Scope: Accounting and management consulting firm. **Founded:** 1969. **Seminars:** Sage Software Training. **Special Services:** ACCPAC Plus; Sage Accpac ERP.

21455 ■ Business Learning Center (BLC)
2206 SE Washington St.
Portland, OR 97222-7615
Ph: (503)653-7108
Fax: (503)786-6064
Co. E-mail: blcmay19@msn.com
Contact: Richard J. Wood, Owner
Scope: Provider of every type of business service for small businesses, including accounting and tax services, business forms and systems, and investment counseling. **Founded:** 1979.

21456 ■ CBIZ Inc.
6050 Oak Tree Blvd. S, Ste. 500
Cleveland, OH 44131-6951
Ph: (216)447-9000
Fax: (216)447-9007
URL: http://www.cbizinc.com
Contact: Jerome P. Grisko, President
URL(s): www.cbiz.com. **Scope:** A business consulting and tax services firm providing financial, consulting, tax and business services through seven groups: Financial management, tax advisory, construction and real estate, health-care, litigation support, capital resource and CEO outsource. **Founded:** 1996. **Publications:** "FAS 154: Changes in the Way We Report Changes," 2006; "Equity-Based Compensation: How Much Does it Really Cost Your Business," 2006; "Preventing Fraud - Tips for Nonprofit Organizations"; "Today's Workforce and Nonprofit Organizations: Meeting a Critical Need"; "IRS Highlights Top Seven Form 990 Errors". **Seminars:** Health Care - What the Future Holds; Consumer Driven Health Plans; Executive Plans; Health Savings Accounts; Healthy Wealthy and Wise; Legislative Update; Medicare Part D; Retirement Plans.

21457 ■ CheckMark Software Inc.
724 Whalers Way, Bldg. H, Ste. 101
Fort Collins, CO 80525-7578
Ph: (970)225-0522
Free: 800-444-9922
Fax: (970)225-0611
Co. E-mail: info@checkmark.com
URL: http://www.checkmark.com
Contact: Jim Mathre, President
Scope: Developer of accounting software tools for small businesses and provides fast, easy to use, affordable accounting and payroll solutions to small and medium sized businesses. Provides payroll software and multiledger integrated accounting software. **Founded:** 1984. **Publications:** *MultiLedger*; *CheckMark Payroll for Macintosh*; *CheckMark Payroll for Windows*. **Special Services:** MultiLedger™; Payroll.

21458 ■ Comprehensive Professional Management Inc.
222 E Dundee Rd.
Wheeling, IL 60090-3009
Ph: (847)520-1301
Fax: (847)520-0372
Co. E-mail: bob@cpmincfs.com
Contact: Kathy Rathunde, Principal
Scope: Services include accounting, financial planning, litigation support, pension profit sharing administration, practice surveys, professional corporation issues, retirement and estate planning and tax advice.

21459 ■ DacEasy Inc.—Sage Software Inc.
1715 N Brown Rd.
Lawrenceville, GA 30043
Free: 800-222-0505
Co. E-mail: sales@daceasy.com
URL: http://www.daceasy.com
Contact: Greg Hammermaster, President
URL(s): www.sagedaceasy.com. **Scope:** Develops an accounting system for small businesses that integrates accounting, invoicing, payroll, communica-

tions, and management software into a single package. **Founded:** 1981. **Seminars:** Tech Tuesday - Sage DacAccess Query and Publisher: Creating Basic Queries and Formatting, May, 2012; Tech Tuesday - Graphics Form Designer, Mar, 2012; Tech Tuesday - Year End Processes with Sage DacEasy; DacEasy Training.

21460 ■ Dorn & Associates Inc.
8506 Bass Lake Rd.
Minneapolis, MN 55428-5304
Ph: (763)533-7689
Fax: (763)533-1143
Contact: John L. Dorn, President
Scope: Services include accounting, marketing, employment partnership, new doctor agreements, personnel issues and human resources assessment, practice management, practice merger acquisition sale and liquidation, practice surveys and valuation, staff development and training. **Founded:** 2000.

21461 ■ Doyle & Dulaney
41 Sutter St., Ste. 1629
San Francisco, CA 94104-4903
Ph: (415)398-3140
Contact: Thomas Doyle, Director
Scope: Business and financial consultants specializing in manual and computer bookkeeping and accounting systems. Expertise in fund accounting, business methods and procedures, reports and other written communications such as manuals, handbooks, and procedure guides. Also skilled in forms design, records management, and instructional material development. Serving nonprofit organizations, the professions, and smaller service-oriented businesses. **Founded:** 1981.

21462 ■ Earl Rodney CPA
5787 W Sunrise Blvd.
Plantation, FL 33313-6269
Ph: (954)583-3635
Fax: (954)321-0532
Contact: Earl Rodney, Owner
Scope: Business and finance consultant serving all industries, nonprofit, and government in Florida. Activities include public accounting, auditing, taxation, expert witness, management advisory services, governmental audits, nonprofit audits, and financial statement disclosures. Also conducts peer reviews of CPA firms. **Founded:** 1980. **Publications:** "Depreciation in the Practical Accountant". **Seminars:** Off site Peer Reviews; Classes in accounting disclosures and in how to audit non profit organizations.

21463 ■ Frankel and Topche P.C.
1700 Galloping Hill Rd.
Kenilworth, NJ 07033
Ph: (908)298-7700
Fax: (908)298-7701
Co. E-mail: info@frankelandtopche.com
URL: http://www.frankelandtopche.com
Contact: Mark J. Tikkanen, Director
E-mail: mtikkanen@frankelandtopche.com
Scope: Offers financial consulting for closely held businesses. Assists in mergers and acquisitions, tax planning, strategic business planning, family succession planning, accounting, auditing, and obtaining financing. The firm serves small businesses in the service, retail, wholesale, and manufacturing industries. Specializes in real estate, lumber and building materials, and service businesses. **Founded:** 1990. **Seminars:** Annual Tax Seminar.

21464 ■ Arnold S. Goldin & Associates Inc.
5030 Champion Blvd., Ste. G-6231
Boca Raton, FL 33496
Ph: (561)994-5810
Fax: (561)994-5860
Co. E-mail: arnold@goldin.com
URL: http://www.goldin.com
Contact: Arnold S. Goldin, Principal
E-mail: arnold@goldin.com
Scope: An accounting and management consulting firm. Serves clients worldwide. Provides management services. Handles monthly write-ups and tax returns. **Founded:** 1978.

21465 ■ Horwath International Association—Crowe Horwath International
420 Lexington Ave., Ste. 526
New York, NY 10170-0526
Ph: (212)808-2000
Fax: (212)808-2020
Co. E-mail: contactus@horwath.com
URL: http://www.horwath.com
Contact: Mark Hildebrand, Chief Executive Officer
E-mail: mhildebrand@horwath.com
Scope: Services include: Accounting, auditing, tax and management consulting. Provides innovative business solutions in the area of assurance, business services, consulting, corporate finance, risk management, tax and technology. **Founded:** 1991. **Publications:** "Does Your Business Have an E-Commerce Strategy"; "Americas Tax Facts," 2007; "Caring Sharing Investing Growing: The Story of Horwath International," Nov, 2006; "How To Franchise Internationally"; "International Tax Planning Manual: Expatriates and Migrants"; "Americas Tax Facts 2007"; "European and Middle East Tax Facts 2008"; "International Offshore Financial Services"; "International Tax Planning Manual: Corporations"; "Asia or Pacific Tax News 2008: Issue 2"; "FOMB: A Quiz for Business Owners". **Seminars:** Demand Creation Training, Dec, 2006; Marketing, Dec, 2006.

21466 ■ Charles A. Krueger—Scheree L. Krueger
1908 Innsbrooke Dr.
Sun Prairie, WI 53590
Ph: (608)837-5247
Fax: (608)825-7538
Co. E-mail: ckrueger@bus.wisc.edu
Contact: Charles Krueger, Owner
Scope: Financial management consultant specializing in professional education programs for managers and executives. Programs include: Finance and accounting for nonfinancial executives, financial management for executives, and developing and using financial information for decision making. Major industries served include manufacturing, service, healthcare and insurance. **Founded:** 1982. **Publications:** "Monitoring Financial Results, chapter in Corporate Controllers Manual," Warren Gorham and Lamont. **Seminars:** Finance and Accounting for Nonfinancial Executives; Financial Management for Health Care Executives; Financial Management for Insurance Executives; Direct Costing; Flexible Budgeting; Contribution Reporting; Building Value and Driving Profits - A Business Simulation.

21467 ■ Mitchell and Titus L.L.P.—Mitchell/Titus
1 Battery Park Plz., 27th Fl.
New York, NY 10004-1405
Ph: (212)709-4500
Fax: (212)709-4680
URL: http://www.mitchelltitus.com
Contact: Bert N. Mitchell, Chief Executive Officer
Scope: Firm provides assurance, advisory business services, transaction support and tax services. Specializes in auditing and accounting services, tax planning and preparation services management and business advisory services. **Founded:** 1974. **Publications:** "ITEM Club Budget preview report," 2010; "Year end personal planning," 2010; "Steering towards the future using the Pre Budget Report to help the UK rebound," 2009; "Be careful what you wish for," 2009; "Year end personal planning," 2009. **Seminars:** Budget Seminar 2010, Mar, 2010.

21468 ■ Penny & Associates Inc.
2748 Bur Oak Ave., Unit 2
Markham, ON, Canada L6B 1K4
Ph: (905)985-0712
Free: 800-699-6190
Fax: (905)985-9461
Co. E-mail: mail@pennyinc.com
URL: http://www.pennyinc.com
Contact: Betty Penny, President
E-mail: betty@pennyinc.com
Scope: Accounting and management firm that offers accounting and business solutions. Assistance in preparation of financial reports, reconciliation of inter company accounts, foreign currency transactions, investment trades and auditor working paper files

and assistance in developing accounting policies and procedures. Provides part-time controllers to prepare financial statements, cash flow management, credit negotiations and give financial management advice or oversee accounting staff. **Founded:** 1994. **Seminars:** Quick Books, Aug, 2001; How to Stand Up to People Without Being a Jerk; How to Build Influence and Rapport With Almost Anyone; Dealing With Dissatisfied, Different and Difficult People; Effective Public Speaking; How to Incorporate Yourself; Company Perks: Attracting & Retaining Good People; FIRST AID. **Telecommunication Services:** info@pennyinc.com. **Special Services:** Quickbooks®.

21469 ■ PYA GatesMoore
33424 Peachtree Rd. NE, Monarch Twr., Ste. 700
Atlanta, GA 30326
Ph: (404)266-9876
Fax: (404)266-2669
Co. E-mail: info@pyagatesmoore.com
URL: http://www.pyagatesmoore.com
Contact: Ed Pershing, President
E-mail: epershing@pyapc.com
Scope: Firm provides management consulting and accounting services to medical practices, hospital owned practices, staff model managed care organizations, IPAs, MSOs, PO, and PHOs. Services include comprehensive operational assessments, managed care negotiations, practice start-ups and expansion, development of MSOs, strategic planning, mergers, cost accounting analysis, practice valuations, income division plans, medical record documentation and coding reviews, expert witness testimony, patient satisfaction surveys and corporate compliance planning. **Founded:** 1982. **Publications:** "Practicing Medicine in the 21st Century"; "Physicians, Dentists and Veterinarians"; "Insurance Portability and Accountability Act Privacy Manual"; "How To Guide for your Medical Practice and Health Insurance Portability and Accountability Act Security Manual"; "A How To Guide for your Medical Practice"; "Cost Analysis Made Simple: A Step by Step Guide to Using Cost Accounting to Ensure Practice Profitability"; "Cost Cutting Strategies for Medical Practices"; "Cost Cutting Strategies for Medical Practices"; "Getting the Jump on Year-End Tax Planning"; "New 401(k) Safe Harbor Option: Increased Opportunities for the Physician and Practice"; "Not All Tax News is Bad News"; "Shareholder Agreements: Identifying and Addressing Five Risk Areas"; "Surprise - Your Practice has a Deferred Income Tax Liability". **Seminars:** Documenting and Billing High Risk Codes, 2010; Current Challenges in Ob/Gyn Recruiting, 2010; Planning for Physician Wind-down & Retirement, 2010; HITECH "How To" - Opportunities & Risks, 2010; Pediatric Coding and Audits; Recruiting and Retaining Physicians; How to Prepare for the Recovery Audit Contractors - RAC, 2010; Meaningful Use Rule, 2010; The Revenue Stream in Practice, Apr, 2008; Improving Efficiencies in a Small Family Medicine Practice, Oct, 2007; Using Compensation Models to Improve Performance, Sep, 2007; The Financial Side of Personnel Management, Sep, 2007; Pay for Performance-Is it Really Contracting for Quality?, New York State Ophthalmological Society, Sep, 2007; Beyond the Class Action Settlement Payments-Looking Prospectively at Managed Care Companies Behavior, New York State Ophthalmological Society, Sep, 2007; Protecting your clients from Embezzlement, Jun, 2007; What P4P Means to Your Medical Practice, May, 2007; Finance for the Practicing Physician, May, 2007; Trashing, Dipping and Ghosts in Medical Practices: Protecting your clients from Embezzlement, Apr, 2006.

21470 ■ Marion S. Rice
5281 Pinnacle Rd.
Dayton, OH 45417-6442
Ph: (937)859-7763
Fax: (937)847-0046
Contact: Marion Rice, Owner
Scope: Provider of consultation to individuals and small businesses on tax management and bookkeeping activities.

21471 ■ The Stillwater Group—Stillwater Consulting Group Inc.
920 E Shore Dr.
Stillwater, NJ 07875

Ph: (973)579-7080
Fax: (973)579-7970
Co. E-mail: education@stillwater.com
URL: http://www.stillwater.com
Contact: David Woodward, Chief Operating Officer
Scope: Provides strategic planning, budget and financial management, process improvement, organizational design and assessment, and college student services operations. **Founded:** 1993. **Publications:** "Integrated Resource Planning (Irp)," Business Officer Magazine, 2005; "The Economic Risk Conundrum," University Business Magazine; "Revenue Analysis and Tuition Strategy"; "Managing Advancement Services: Processes and Paper".

21472 ■ Donald C. Wright CPA
3906 Lawndale Ln. N
Plymouth, MN 55446-2940
Ph: (763)478-6999
Co. E-mail: donaldwright@compuserve.com
URL: http://www.donaldwrightcpa.com
Contact: Donald C. Wright, President
E-mail: donaldwright@compuserve.com
Scope: Offers accounting, tax, and small business consulting services. Services include cash flow and budgeting analysis; financial forecast and projections; financial statements; reviews and compilations; tax planning, tax preparation; IRS and state/local representation; international taxation; estate, gift and trust tax return preparation; benefit plan services; business succession planning; estate planning; financial planning; management advisory services, pension and profit sharing plans, retirement planning, expert witness services and employee benefits plans. Serves individuals, corporations, partnerships, and non-profit organizations. **Founded:** 1968. **Seminars:** Qualified pension plans and employee welfare benefit plans.

21473 ■ Zolfo Cooper L.L.C.
Grace Bldg., 1114 Ave. of the Americas, 41st Fl.
New York, NY 10036
Ph: (212)561-4000
Fax: (212)213-1749
Co. E-mail: rrandall@zolfocooper.com
URL: http://www.zolfocooper.com
Contact: Mark Cervi, Director
Scope: Provider of accounting consulting services to businesses. Specializes in restructuring and turnaround consulting; interim and crisis management; performance improvement; creditor advisory; cross-border restructuring and corporate finance. **Founded:** 1985.

COMPUTERIZED DATABASES

21474 ■ e-JEP
2014 Broadway, Ste. 305
Nashville, TN 37203
Ph: (615)322-2595
Fax: (615)343-7590
Co. E-mail: aeainfo@vanderbilt.edu
URL: http://www.vanderbilt.edu/AEA
Contact: Angus Deaton, President
Availability: Online: American Economic Association; Thomson Reuters - Westlaw. CD-ROM: American Economic Association. **Type:** Full-text.

COMPUTER SYSTEMS/ SOFTWARE

21475 ■ Aatrix Top Pay
2100 Library Cir.
Grand Forks, ND 58201
Ph: (701)746-6017
Free: 800-426-0854
Fax: (701)787-0594
URL: http://www.aatrix.com
Price: Contact Aatrix. **Description:** Handles payroll calculations and tax deductions for both salaried and hourly employees.

21476 ■ Argos Software / ABECAS Insight
5737 N Fresno St.
Fresno, CA 93710
Ph: (559)227-1000

Fax: (559)227-9644
Co. E-mail: info@argosoftware.com
URL: http://www.argosoftware.com
Description: Available for MS-DOS operating system. Payroll system for agricultural employees.

LIBRARIES

21477 ■ Buffalo & Erie County Public Library - Business, Science & Technology
1 Lafayette Sq.
Buffalo, NY 14203
Ph: (716)858-8900
Fax: (716)858-6211
URL: http://www.buffalolib.org
Contact: Nancy Mueller, Division Manager
Scope: Investments, real estate, economics, marketing, engineering, computer science, technology, medical information for laymen, consumer information, automotive repair. **Services:** Interlibrary loan; copying; library open to the public. **Founded:** 1952. **Holdings:** 312,916 books; 60,516 bound periodical volumes; 600 periodical. **Subscriptions:** 2908 journals and other serials; 4 newspapers.

21478 ■ Carnegie Library of Pittsburgh - Downtown & Business
612 Smithfield St.
Pittsburgh, PA 15222-2506
Ph: (412)281-7141

Fax: (412)471-1724
Co. E-mail: downtown@carnegielibrary.org
URL: http://www.carnegielibrary.org/locations/
   downtown
Contact: Karen Rossi, Department Head
Scope: Investments, small business, entrepreneurship, management, marketing, insurance, advertising, personal finance, accounting, real estate, job and career, International business. **Services:** Library open to the public. **Founded:** 1924. **Holdings:** 13,000 business volumes; VF materials; microfilm; looseleaf services; AV materials.

21479 ■ Napier University - Craiglockhart Campus Library
219 Colinton Rd.
Edinburgh EH14 1DJ, United Kingdom
Ph: 44 131 4554260
Fax: 44 131 4554276
Co. E-mail: craiglockhartlc@napier.ac.uk
URL: http://staff.napier.ac.uk/services/library/about/
   Pages/default.aspx
Contact: Catherine Walker, Manager
Scope: Accounting, economics, finance, hospitality and tourism, languages, law, management, marketing, statistics. **Holdings:** Books; videos. **Telecommunication Services:** library@napier.ac.uk.

21480 ■ Nichols College - Conant Library
124 Center Rd.
Dudley, MA 01571
Ph: (508)213-2333

Free: 800-470-3379
Co. E-mail: reference@nichols.edu
URL: http://www.nichols.edu/academics/academics/
   Library
Contact: Jim Douglas, Director, Library Services
Scope: Management, advertising, finance and accounting, small business, marketing, taxation, economics, International trade, humanities. **Services:** Interlibrary loan; copying; information service to groups; document delivery; library open to Dudley and Webster residents. **Founded:** 1962. **Holdings:** 48,000 volumes; 1677 audio/visual titles; 3804 reels of microfilm. **Subscriptions:** 278 journals and electronic subscriptions. **Telecommunication Services:** jim.douglas@nichols.edu.

21481 ■ University of Kentucky - Business & Economics Information Center
B&E Info. Ctr., Rm. 116
335-BA Gatton College of Business & Economics
Lexington, KY 40506-0034
Ph: (859)257-8936
Fax: (859)257-1333
Co. E-mail: mrazeeq@pop.uk.edu
URL: http://www.uky.edu//Provost/academicpro-
   grams.html
Contact: Michael A. Razeeq, Librarian, Business
URL(s): gatton.uky.edu/. **Scope:** Business, economics, business management, marketing, finance, accounting. **Services:** Library open to the public for reference use only. **Founded:** 1993. **Telecommunication Services:** cber@uky.edu; klimar@pop.uky.edu; provost@email.uky.edu.

START-UP INFORMATION

21482 ■ *"Drink Up" in Black Enterprise (Vol. 38, March 2008, No. 8, pp. 50)*
Pub: Earl G. Graves Publishing Co. Inc.
Ed: Tennille H. Robinson. **Description:** Advice is given to an individual seeking to start a natural juice small business, along with information for finding a bottling company.

21483 ■ *"Fixing Up the Area: Leo Piatz Opens General Repair Business" in The Dickinson Press (November 16, 2010)*
Pub: Dickinson Press
Ed: Ashley Martin. **Description:** Profile of Leo Piatz, owner of Leo's Repair in Dickinson, North Dakota; Piatz provides welding and fabricating services to farmers and ranchers in the area.

21484 ■ *"Local Flavor" in Entrepreneur (Vol. 35, November 2007, No. 11, pp. 110)*
Pub: Entrepreneur Media Inc.
Ed: Nichole L. Torres. **Description:** Local food products are growing in the market today as consumers are becoming interested in where their food comes; you can start a business by investigating the kinds of foods popular in your region.

21485 ■ *Starting and Running Your Own Horse Business*
Pub: Storey Publishing, LLC
Ed: Mary Ashby McDonald. **Released:** November 1, 2009. **Price:** $19.95. **Description:** Insight into starting and running a successful equestrian business is given. The book covers safety, tips for operating a riding school or horse camp, strategies for launching a carriage business, along with tax and insurance advice.

ASSOCIATIONS AND OTHER ORGANIZATIONS

21486 ■ **ACDI/VOCA**
50 F St. NW, Ste. 1075
Washington, DC 20001
Ph: (202)469-6000
Free: 800-929-8622
Fax: (202)469-6257
Co. E-mail: av-ca@acdivoca.org
URL: http://www.acdivoca.org
Contact: Carl H. Leonard, President
Description: Agricultural cooperatives, agribusinesses, farmers' organizations, and farm credit banks in the United States. Assists in organizing and providing technical assistance for cooperatives and agribusinesses in developing countries, usually under contract with the Agency for International Development. Advises governmental and other agencies in agricultural marketing, supply, and credit; carries out feasibility studies for specific agribusiness ventures; arranges formal and on-the-job training in cooperative practices for government officials, cooperative functionaries, and rural leaders; conducts short- and long-term technical assistance programs. Conducts

extensive global volunteer programs that introduce American agricultural and financial know-how to developing economies, an exchange that furthers international cooperation and fellowship and promotes global business. Invites resumes of U.S. agriculture, business, and finance experts who are willing to serve overseas on short-term assignments. **Scope:** Organization's mission is to promote economic opportunities for cooperatives, enterprises and communities through the application of sound business practice. **Founded:** 1997. **Publications:** *ACDI/VOCA World Report* (Quarterly). **Awards:** Volunteer of the Year Award (Annual). **Telecommunication Services:** webmaster@acdivoca.org.

21487 ■ *AGCare Update*
100 Stone Rd. W, Ste. 106
Guelph, ON, Canada N1G 5L3
Ph: (519)837-1326
Fax: (519)837-3209
Co. E-mail: agcare@agcare.org
URL: http://www.agcare.org
Contact: Paul Wettlaufer, Chairman
Released: Quarterly

21488 ■ **Agri-Energy Roundtable (AER)**
PO Box 5565
Washington, DC 20016
Ph: (202)887-0528
Co. E-mail: agenergy@aol.com
URL: http://www.agribusinesscouncil.org/aer.htm
Contact: Nicholas E. Hollis, Executive Director
Description: International association that includes oil company executives and leaders of international agribusinesses. Serves as an information clearinghouse to improve dialogue on cooperative energy-agricultural development among the industrialized and developing nations. Attempts to bridge the gap on food and energy issues through cooperation between the oil exporting countries and western technology in the private sector. Sponsors trade missions. **Founded:** 1980. **Publications:** *Agri-Energy Report* (Quarterly); *Regional Africa Bulletin*; *Agri-Enterprise in Development: New Leadership and Technology for Food Security*; *Beyond Food and Energy Security: New Agribusiness Markets and Technologies*; *Food and Energy Security: Managing the New Technologies*; *Managing Agro-Economic Peacekeeping: Trade and Development Realities for Food Security*. **Awards:** World Food Policy Award.

21489 ■ **Agribusiness Council (ABC)**
PO Box 5565
Washington, DC 20016-1165
Ph: (202)296-4563
Co. E-mail: info@agribusinesscouncil.org
URL: http://agribusinesscouncil.org
Contact: Nicholas E. Hollis, President
Description: Business organizations, universities and foundations, and individuals interested in stimulating and encouraging agribusiness in cooperation with the public sector, both domestic and international. Seeks to aid in relieving the problems of world food supply. Supports coordinated agribusiness in the developing nations by identifying opportunities for investment of U.S. private-sector technology manage-

ment and financial resources. Advises agribusiness leaders about selected developing countries with good investment climates; brings potential investment opportunities to the attention of U.S. agribusiness firms; coordinates informal network of state agribusiness councils and grassroots organization; encourages companies to make investment feasibility studies in agribusiness; provides liaison and information exchange between agribusiness firms, governments, international organizations, universities, foundations, and other groups with the objective of identifying areas of cooperation and mutual interest; encourages projects geared to the conversion of subsistence farming to intensive, higher income agriculture in order to bring the world's rural populations, wherever feasible, into the market economy. **Founded:** 1967.

21490 ■ **Agricultural Groups Concerned About Resources and the Environment (AGCARE)**
100 Stone Rd. W, Ste. 106
Guelph, ON, Canada N1G 5L3
Ph: (519)837-1326
Fax: (519)837-3209
Co. E-mail: agcare@agcare.org
URL: http://www.agcare.org
Contact: Paul Wettlaufer, Chairman
Description: Farmers and agricultural industries. Promotes environmentally sustainable food production. Facilitates communication among members; serves as a clearinghouse on sustainable agriculture. **Founded:** 1987. **Publications:** *AGCare Update* (Quarterly); *Project Report* (Periodic).

21491 ■ **American Brahmousin Council (ABC)**
PO Box 88
Whitesboro, TX 76273
Ph: (903)564-3995
URL: http://www.brahmousin.org
Contact: Bob Cummins, Director (Interim)
Description: Breeders of Brahmousin cattle.

21492 ■ **American Society of Agricultural Consultants (ASAC)**
N78 W 14573 Appleton Ave., Ste. 287
Menomonee Falls, WI 53051
Ph: (262)253-6902
Fax: (262)253-6903
Co. E-mail: cmerry@countryside-marketing.com
URL: http://www.agconsultants.org
Contact: Paige Gilligan, President
E-mail: paige@agresticsolutions.com
Description: Members are independent, full-time consultants in many specialty areas serving agribusiness interests throughout the world. Strives to maintain high standards of ethics and competence in the consulting field. Provides referral service to agribusiness interests seeking consultants having specific knowledge, experience, and expertise. Maintains liaison with governmental agencies utilizing consultants and with legislative and administrative acts affecting consultants. **Scope:** Association of agricultural consultants serving its membership through ethics, networking, strong continuing education. Maintains

directory of members who provide a variety of agricultural consulting services. **Founded:** 1963. **Publications:** *American Society of Agricultural Consultants--Membership Directory* (Annual). **Seminars:** Leading Edge Consulting; Communications for Ag Professionals; Seven Habits of Highly Effective People; Ethics. **Telecommunication Services:** cmerry@agconsultants.org.

21493 ■ *Canadian Biosystems Engineering*
2028 Calico Crescent
Orleans, ON, Canada K4A 4L7
Ph: (613)590-0975
Fax: (519)836-5708
Co. E-mail: bioeng@bioeng.ca
URL: http://www.bioeng.ca
Contact: Ron MacDonald, President

21494 ■ Canadian Consulting Agrologists Association (CCAA)
510, 5920-1A St. SW
Calgary, AB, Canada T2H 0G3
Fax: (403)255-4592
Co. E-mail: terry.betker@mnp.ca
URL: http://www.ccaa.bz
Contact: Terry Betker, President
Description: Agrologists and other agricultural consultants. Seeks to advance the science and practice of agriculture; promotes professional development of members. Makes available support and services to farmers; conducts research and educational programs. **Founded:** 1973. **Awards:** CCAA Lifetime Achievement Award (Periodic); Distinguished Certified Agricultural Consultant (Annual).

21495 ■ Canadian Society for Bioengineering (CSBE)—La Societe Canadienne de Genie Agroalimentaire et de Bioingenierie
2028 Calico Crescent
Orleans, ON, Canada K4A 4L7
Ph: (613)590-0975
Fax: (519)836-5708
Co. E-mail: bioeng@bioeng.ca
URL: http://www.bioeng.ca
Contact: Ron MacDonald, President
Description: Individuals engaged in the practice of agricultural and biosystems engineering; agricultural and biosystems engineering educators and students. Seeks to advance the study and practice of agricultural engineering and bioengineering. Conducts research; makes available continuing professional development programs for members. **Founded:** 1958. **Publications:** *Canadian Biosystems Engineering*; *Perspectives* (Quarterly). **Awards:** Jim Beamish Award; Young Engineer of the Year Award; John Clark Award; John Turnbull Award; CSAE Fellow; Maple Leaf Award; Glenn Downing Award.

21496 ■ Communicating for America (CA)
PO Box 677
Fergus Falls, MN 56538-0677
Ph: (218)739-3241
Free: 800-432-3276
Fax: (218)739-3832
Co. E-mail: memberbenefits@cainc.org
URL: http://www.communicatingforamerica.org
Contact: Wayne Nelson, President
Description: Promotes the general health, well being and advancement of people in agriculture and agribusiness. Participates in federal and state issues that affect the quality of life in rural America and provides members with a variety of money-saving benefit programs. Conducts grants program, research on rural issues, and international exchange programs with an agricultural focus. **Founded:** 1972. **Publications:** *CA Highlights* (Monthly); *CAEP In Touch* (Quarterly); *Smart Choices* (Quarterly); *CA Highlights*.

21497 ■ National Council of Agricultural Employers (NCAE)
8233 Old Courthouse Rd., Ste. 200
Vienna, VA 22182
Ph: (703)790-9039

Fax: (703)790-0345
Co. E-mail: matt@ncaeonline.org
URL: http://www.ncaeonline.org
Contact: Luawanna Hallstrom, President
Description: Growers of agricultural commodities who employ hand labor for field crops; processors and handlers, farm and commodity organizations, and others whose business is related to labor-intensive farming in the U.S. Aims to improve the position and image of U.S. agriculture as an employer of labor and to facilitate and encourage the establishment and maintenance of an adequate force of agricultural employees. Serves as clearinghouse for exchange of information on labor supply, length of employment, and other conditions of work. Does not engage in recruitment, housing, supplying, or employment of agricultural workers, and does not represent its members or others in negotiating with labor unions or other organizations, or in agreeing to any contract relating to hours, wages, or working conditions. Keeps member abreast of national legislation affecting agricultural labor. **Founded:** 1964.

21498 ■ Organization for Competitive Markets (OCM)
PO Box 6486
Lincoln, NE 68506
Ph: (402)817-4443
URL: http://www.competitivemarkets.com
Contact: David Hutchins, Executive Director
Description: Works for increased competition and protection for the agricultural marketplace. Works against "abuse of corporate power and consolidation of the agricultural market". **Publications:** *OCM Newsletter*.

21499 ■ *Perspectives*
2028 Calico Crescent
Orleans, ON, Canada K4A 4L7
Ph: (613)590-0975
Fax: (519)836-5708
Co. E-mail: bioeng@bioeng.ca
URL: http://www.bioeng.ca
Contact: Ron MacDonald, President
Released: Quarterly

21500 ■ *Project Report*
100 Stone Rd. W, Ste. 106
Guelph, ON, Canada N1G 5L3
Ph: (519)837-1326
Fax: (519)837-3209
Co. E-mail: agcare@agcare.org
URL: http://www.agcare.org
Contact: Paul Wettlaufer, Chairman
Released: Periodic

21501 ■ United Agribusiness League (UAL)
54 Corporate Park
Irvine, CA 92606-5105
Ph: (949)975-1424
Free: 800-223-4590
Fax: (949)975-1573
Co. E-mail: info@aul.org
URL: http://www.ual.org
Contact: Richard Schmidt, President
Description: Agricultural industries and businesses. Promotes the development and common interest of the agricultural industry. Works to coordinate members' activities to advance agribusiness in general; provides services and benefits to enable members to realize greater productive efficiency. Serves as a clearinghouse on international agribusiness. Provides employee health care plans and other insurance to agribusinesses. **Founded:** 1980. **Publications:** *Ag Crime Prevention Brochures*; *Crime Prevention* (Quarterly); *Healthy Times* (Monthly). **Awards:** UAL/UABI Annual Scholarship Program (Annual); UAL/UABT Scholarship Program. **Telecommunication Services:** info@ual.org.

REFERENCE WORKS

21502 ■ *"14 Tips to Tune Up Your Self-Propelled Sprayer" in Farm Industry News (November 3, 2010)*
Pub: Penton Business Media Inc.
Description: Tips for maintaining a self-propelled sprayer used to apply farm chemicals and fertilizers are listed.

21503 ■ *"100-BU. Beans" in Farm Industry News (Vol. 42, January 1, 2009, No. 1)*
Pub: Penton Media Inc.
Contact: John French, President
Ed: Lynn Grooms. **Description:** Demand for soybeans has increased and growers are seeing an increase in yields as well due to breeders that are using molecular-assisted selection; other aspects of the soybean market are presented.

21504 ■ *"100 Percent Equipment Tax Deduction Deadline Nears" in Farm Industry News (December 1, 2010)*
Pub: Penton Business Media Inc.
Description: Farmers and small business owners are warned that the first deadline for taking advantage of the tax code provision that allows them to deduct the full purchase price of qualified capital expenditures up to $500,000 during the tax year is nearing.

21505 ■ *"$550 Cash Rent on 330 Acres in Iowa" in Farm Industry News (November 30, 2011)*
Pub: Penton Business Media Inc.
Ed: Karen McMahon. **Description:** A farmer in Iowa accepted a bid for $550/acre for his 330-acre farm for one year. The next closest bid was $350/acre. This rent will amount to more than the farmer paid for all of his land in the 1960s and 1970s. High rents are not alarming because of the high profitability farmers are currently receiving from crops.

21506 ■ *"2011 FinOvation Awards" in Farm Industry News (January 19, 2011)*
Pub: Penton Business Media Inc.
Ed: Jodie Wehrspann. **Description:** The 2011 FinOvation Award winners are announced, covering new products that growers need for corn and soybean crops. Winners range from small turbines and a fuel-efficient pickup to a Class 10 combine and drought-tolerant hybrids.

21507 ■ *Ag Equipment Power*
Pub: Clintron Publishers
Contact: Clint Withers, President
E-mail: craig@agpowermag.com
URL(s): www.agpowermag.com. **Ed:** Craig Withers. **Released:** Monthly; Latest edition 2010. **Price:** $12, Individuals. **Publication includes:** Featuring news agricultural equipment and technology for growers in Washington, Idaho, and Oregon. List of about 750 manufacturers, distributors, dealers, and suppliers of new and used farm machinery and chemicals; coverage limited to Washington, Oregon, and Idaho. **Entries include:** Company name, address, product lines. **Arrangement:** Classified by for subscribers.

21508 ■ *"Ag Firms Harvest Revenue Growth" in The Business Journal-Serving Metropolitan Kansas City (Vol. 26, July 18, 2008, No. 45, pp. 1)*
Pub: American City Business Journals, Inc.
Ed: Steve Vockrodt. **Description:** Five of the biggest agricultural companies in the Kansas City area, except one, reported multibillion-dollar revenue increases in 2007. The companies, which include Lansing Trade Group, posted a combined $9.5 billion revenue growth. The factors that affected the revenue increase in the area's agricultural companies, such as prices and high demand, are also examined.

21509 ■ *"Ag Officials Employ Preventive Pest Control" in Yakima Herald-Republic (June 24, 2011)*
Pub: Yakima Herald-Republic
Ed: Ross Courtney. **Description:** Washington State Department of Agriculture is placing vineyard traps for the European grapevine moth, an invasive species whose larvae eat grape buds and fruit clusters, thus exposing the vines to diseases that could destroy them.

21510 ■ *Agri Marketing--Marketing Services Guide Issue*
Pub: Doane Agricultural Services
Contact: Lynn Henderson, President
E-mail: lhenderson@doane.com
URL(s): www.doane.com. **Released:** Annual; latest edition 2009. **Publication includes:** Lists over 1400 top agricultural companies in the United States, lead-

ing agricultural advertisers (for past five years), marketing services firms (including public relations, photography, editorial, art and graphics, audiovisual, marketing research, marketing consultants), and United States and Canadian radio and television broadcasting stations, advertising and public relations agencies, network programming, and publications. Agriculture-related associations are included. **Entries include:** For leading companies--Logo, name, address, phone, names of key personnel, products, marketing area, fiscal year, name and city of advertising and/or public relations agency handling account. For leading print advertisers--Company name, address, phone, key personnel, publication unit, sales representative firm, full-page space and cost for advertising. For agencies--Company name, address, name and phone of contact, year established, total agency billings, breakdown of billings by type of activity fo. **Arrangement:** Alphabetical. **Indexes:** Service company's service, publication location.

21511 ■ Agri Marketing--The Top 50: Ag's Biggest Agencies Issue
Pub: Doane Agricultural Services
Contact: Lynn Henderson, President
E-mail: lhenderson@doane.com
URL(s): www.doane.com. **Released:** Annual; April or May. **Publication includes:** List of the top 50 U.S. and Canadian advertising agencies and public relations firms, chosen on the basis of agricultural business income. **Entries include:** Agency name, location, income for agricultural accounts in most recent year, branch offices, major clients served. **Arrangement:** Alphabetical.

21512 ■ "Agribusiness: How to Get Rich in Farming" in Canadian Business (Vol. 80, January 29, 2007, No. 3, pp. 42)
Pub: Rogers Media
Ed: Peter Shawn Taylor. **Description:** The trends pertaining to the income of Canadian farmers are examined. The methods of increasing the profits of Canadian agribusinesses are discussed.

21513 ■ "Agricharts Launches New Mobile App for Ag Market" in Farm Industry News (December 1, 2011)
Pub: Penton Business Media Inc.
Description: AgriCharts provides market data, agribusiness Website hosting and technology solutions for the agricultural industry. AgriCharts is a division of Barchart.com Inc. and announced the release of a new mobile applications that offers real-time or delayed platform for viewing quotes, charts and analysis of grains, livestock and other commodity markets.

21514 ■ "Allowing Ethanol Tax Incentive to Expire Would Risk Jobs, RFAas Dinneen Says" in Farm Industry News (November 3, 2010)
Pub: Penton Business Media Inc.
Description: Jobs would be at risk if the ethanol tax incentive expires.

21515 ■ "Alternative Energy is a Major Topic at Agritechnica 2011" in Farm Industry News (November 16, 2011)
Pub: Penton Business Media Inc.
Ed: Mark Moore. **Description:** Sustainable agricultural systems were a hot topic at this year's Agritechnia 2011, held in Germany. Germany is a leader in the development of on-farm biogas systems.

21516 ■ "Apples, Decoded: WSU Scientist Unraveling the Fruit's Genetics" in Puget Sound Business Journal (Vol. 29, September 5, 2008, No. 20)
Pub: American City Business Journals
Ed: Clay Holtzman. **Description:** Washington State University researcher is working to map the apple's genome in order to gain information about how the fruit grows, looks and tastes. His work, funded by a research grant from the US Department of Agriculture and the Washington Apple Commission is crucial to improving the state's position as an apple-producing region.

21517 ■ "Art of the Online Deal" in Farm Industry News (March 25, 2011)
Pub: Penton Business Media Inc.
Description: Farmers share advice for shopping online for machinery; photos, clean equipment, the price, equipment details, and online sources topped their list.

21518 ■ "Atlantis-Resistant Figures on the Up" in Farmer's Weekly (March 28, 2008, No. 320)
Pub: Reed Business Information
Contact: Jeff Greisch, President
Description: Researches are studying the number of cases in which blackgrass became resistant to Atlantis to determine if the resistance is due mainly to the ALS target-site mechanism or enhanced metabolism.

21519 ■ "Autumn Rat Control Essential for Poultry Units" in Poultry World (Vol. 165, September 2011, No. 9, pp. 32)
Pub: Reed Business Information Inc.
Description: Dr. Alan Buckle discusses the use of rodenticides control, focusing on poultry units.

21520 ■ "The Bear Arrives - With Bargain Hunters" in Barron's (Vol. 88, July 7, 2008, No. 27, pp. M3)
Pub: Dow Jones & Co., Inc.
Ed: Kopin Tan. **Description:** US stock markets have dropped 20 percent below their highs, entering the bear market at the end of June 2008. It was also the worst performance of the stock markets during June. Wine maker Constellation Brands, however, reported a 50 percent rise in net income for the first quarter of 2008.

21521 ■ "Because He Is Still Growing: Horst Rechelbacher: Intelligent Nutrients Minneapolis" in Inc. (Volume 32, December 2010, No. 10)
Pub: Inc. Magazine
Ed: Mike Hoffman. **Description:** Horst Rechelbacher, founder of hair care company Aveda, and after selling Aveda to Estee Lauder, he is expanding into a nutraceuticals company offering hair care products that are organically grown.

21522 ■ "The Believer" in Inc. (December 2007, pp. 130-138)
Pub: Gruner & Jahr USA Publishing
Ed: Leigh Buchanan. **Description:** Profile of Selena Cuffe, wine importer and socially conscious woman entrepreneur, who is focusing her talents on helping South Africa get wine products to America.

21523 ■ "Bertha's Birth Stirs Juice" in Barron's (Vol. 88, July 14, 2008, No. 28, pp. M11)
Pub: Dow Jones & Co., Inc.
Ed: Tom Sellen. **Description:** Price of frozen concentrated orange juice, which has risen to four-month highs of $1.3620 in July 2008 is due, in part, to the hurricane season that has come earlier than normal in the far eastern Atlantic thereby possibly harming the 2008-2009 Florida orange crop. Future tropical-storm development will affect the prices of this commodity.

21524 ■ "Best Turnaround Stocks" in Canadian Business (Vol. 82, Summer 2009, No. 8, pp. 32)
Pub: Rogers Media
Ed: Calvin Leung. **Description:** Canadian companies that are believed to have the potential for the best turnaround stocks are presented. Suggested stocks include those of Migao Corporation, which is rated by most research firms as a Buy. Migao produces potash-based fertilizers for the Chinese market.

21525 ■ "Beverage Brand Vies To Be the Latest Purple Prince" in Brandweek (Vol. 49, April 21, 2008, No. 16, pp. 20)
Pub: VNU Business Media, Inc.
Ed: Becky Ebenkamp. **Description:** Profile on the new beverage product Purple and its founder, Ted Farnsworth; Purple is a drink that blends seven antioxidant-rich juices to create what Mr. Farnsworth calls a 'Cascade Effect' that boosts antioxidants' ef-

fectiveness. Mr. Farnsworth is marketing the brand's Oxygen Radical Absorbance Capability (ORAC) which is a value of 7,600 compared with orange juice's 1,200.

21526 ■ "Biodiesel Poised to Regain Growth" in Farm Industry News (January 21, 2011)
Pub: Penton Business Media Inc.
Description: According to Gary Haer, vice president of sales and marketing for Renewable Energy Group, the biodiesel industry is positioned to regain growth in 2011 with the reinstatement of the biodiesel blendersa tax credt of $1 per gallon.

21527 ■ "Bottler Will Regain Its Pop" in Barron's (Vol. 88, March 17, 2008, No. 11, pp. 56)
Pub: Dow Jones & Company, Inc.
Ed: Alexander Eule. **Description:** Discusses he 30 percent drop in the share price of PepsiAmericas Inc. from their 2007 high which presents an opportunity to buy into the company's dependable U.S. market and fast growing Eastern European business. The bottler's Eastern European operating profits in 2007 grew to $101 million from $21 million in 2006.

21528 ■ "Brazil's New King of Food" in Barron's (Vol. 89, July 13, 2009, No. 28, pp. 28)
Pub: Dow Jones & Co., Inc.
Ed: Kenneth Rapoza. **Description:** Perdigao and Sadia's merger has resulted in the creation of Brasil Foods and the shares of Brasil Foods provides a play on both Brazil's newly energized consumer economy and its role as a major commodities exporter. Brasil Foods shares could climb as much as 36 percent.

21529 ■ "Brewing National Success" in Hawaii Business (Vol. 53, November 2007, No. 5, pp. 46)
Pub: Hawaii Business Publishing
Ed: Alex Salkever. **Description:** Kona Brewing Co. (KBC) is already selling its brews in four cities in Florida and 17 other states and Japan as well. KBC is currently forming a deal with Red Hook to produce Longboard Lager and other KBC brews at Red Hooks' brewery in New Hampshire. KBC's chief executive officer Mattson Davis shares KBC's practices for success.

21530 ■ "Buhler Versatile Launches Next Generation of Equipment" in Farm Industry News (November 23, 2011)
Pub: Penton Business Media Inc.
Ed: Jodie Wehrspann. **Description:** Canadian owned Versatile is expanding its four-wheel drive tractor division with sprayers, tillage, and seeding equipment.

21531 ■ "Building Portfolios for a World of 2.5 Percent Gains" in Barron's (Vol. 88, July 7, 2008, No. 27, pp. L9)
Pub: Dow Jones & Co., Inc.
Ed: Karen Hube. **Description:** Interview with Harold Evenski whom is a financial planner running a fee-only planning practice; he continues to caution investors against pursuing short-term gains and focusing on long-term trends. He advises investors against investing in commodity and real estate stocks and is concerned about the possible effects of high inflation.

21532 ■ Business Management for Tropical Dairy Farmers
Pub: CSIRO Publishing
Ed: John Moran. **Released:** August 1, 2009. **Price:** $33.95. **Description:** Business management skills required for dairy farmers are addressed, focusing on financial management and ways to improve cattle housing and feeding systems.

21533 ■ "Businessman Legend Passes: Charles H. James II Credited With Transforming Family Business" in Black Enterprise (December 2007)
Pub: Earl G. Graves Publishing Co. Inc.
Ed: Tara C. Walker. **Description:** Profile of Charles H. James II, president and chairman of The James Corporation, a family-owned multigenerational food distribution company that started as a produce firm.

21534 ■ *"A Busy Little Parasite" in Hawaii Business (Vol. 53, March 2008, No. 9, pp. 1)*
Pub: Hawaii Business Publishing
Ed: Jason Ubay. **Description:** Bee mites were first sighted in Hawaii by Michael Kliks on April 6, 2007 and have since been a cause of concern for the beekeeping industry and pollinated-dependent crop industry. Hawaii's agricultural industry estimates that the losses due to bee mites may amount to between $42 million and $62 million. Steps taken to address the issue are discussed.

21535 ■ *"Buying Seed by Weight or By Count" in Farm Industry News (October 20, 2010)*
Pub: Penton Business Media Inc.
Ed: Mark Moore. **Description:** Soybean producers have the option of buying seeds by count or by weight; tips for either method of purchase are outlined.

21536 ■ *"Buzz Kill" in Canadian Business (Vol. 83, August 17, 2010, No. 13-14, pp. 24)*
Pub: Rogers Media Ltd.
Ed: Rachel Mendleson. **Description:** Beekeeping industry has been plagued by a massive wave of honeybee deaths since 2006, which pushed upward the cost of per hive-rental. The death of honeybees has put the food supply at risk since it jeopardized the growth of pumpkins, as well as other crops in large acreage. Insights on the Colony Collapse Disorder are outlined.

21537 ■ *"Can Turfway Park Stay in the Race?" in Business Courier (Vol. 26, January 8, 2010, No. 38, pp. 1)*
Pub: American City Business Journals, Inc.
Ed: Jon Newberry. **Description:** Legalization of slot machine gambling in Kentucky could affect raceway Turfway Park and the state's thoroughbred industry. Thousands of farms and jobs in the industry could be lost if slot machine gambling is approved.

21538 ■ *"Careers in Organic Food Preparation" in Occupational Outlook Quarterly (Vol. 54, Fall 2010, No. 3, pp. 3)*
Pub: U.S. Bureau of Labor Statistics
Ed: Adam Bibler. **Description:** Organic methods of food production, including methods that combine science with traditional farming practices, are outlined. Facts regarding careers in organic food preparation are presented.

21539 ■ *"Case IH Announces Strategy to Meet 2014 Clean Air Standards" in Farm Industry News (September 15, 2011)*
Pub: Penton Business Media Inc.
Ed: Jodie Wehrspann. **Description:** Case IH will meet EPA's stringent engine emissions limits imposed in 2014, called Tier 4. The limits call for a 90 percent reduction in particulate matter and nitrogen oxides (NOx) over the Tier 3 requirements from a few years ago.

21540 ■ *"Cash Rents Reach Sky-High Levels" in Farm Industry News (November 23, 2011)*
Pub: Penton Business Media Inc.
Ed: Karen McMahon. **Description:** Strong commodity prices are driving land values creating a hot rental market for farm land. Highest rents occur when farmers compete head-to-head for land.

21541 ■ *"CGB Purchases Illinois Grain-Fertilizer Firm" in Farm Industry News (December 2, 2011)*
Pub: Penton Business Media Inc.
Description: CGB Enterprises Inc bought Twomey Company's grain and fertilizer assets. The purchase includes eight locations and a barge loading terminal near Gladstone, Illinois and storage capacity of 51 million bushels and 18,000 tons of liquid fertilizer.

21542 ■ *"Cheese Spread Whips Up a Brand New Bowl" in Brandweek (Vol. 49, April 21, 2008, No. 16, pp. 17)*
Pub: VNU Business Media, Inc.
Ed: Mike Beirne. **Description:** Mrs. Kinser's Pimento Cheese Spread is launching a new container for its product in order to attempt stronger brand marketing with a better bowl in order to win over the heads of

households as young as in their 30s. The company also intends to begin distribution in Texas and the West Coast. Mrs. Kinser's is hoping that the new packaging will provide a more distinct branding and will help consumers distinguish what flavor they are buying.

21543 ■ *"Chino Valley Ranches: a Family of Farmers" in Retail Merchandiser (Vol. 51, September-October 2011, No. 5, pp. 79)*
Pub: Phoenix Media Corporation
Ed: Angela Forsyth. **Description:** Charles B. Nichols and his wife Isabella purchased their ranch in Beaumont, California in the early 1950s. The family has been raising their chickens, producing eggs with quality, integrity and honesty the foundation of their business.

21544 ■ *"Chopping Option Added to Calmer Corn Head Kits" in Farm Industry News (January 16, 2011)*
Pub: Penton Business Media Inc.
Description: New equipment for combines, called the BT Chopper option for Calmer Corn Heads, will chop and crust BT corn stalks into confetti-sized pieces for easier decomposition in the field.

21545 ■ *"Coca-Cola Looks Ready to Pause" in Barron's (Vol. 88, March 10, 2008, No. 10, pp. 18)*
Pub: Dow Jones & Company, Inc.
Ed: Michael Santoli. **Description:** Shares of Coca-Cola are expected to turn sideways or experience a slight drop from $59.50 each to the mid-50 level. The company has seen its shares jump 40 percent since 2006, when it was in a series of measures to improve profitability.

21546 ■ *"Coming Soon: Electric Tractors" in Farm Industry News (November 21, 2011)*
Pub: Penton Business Media Inc.
Ed: Jodie Wehrspann. **Description:** The agricultural industry is taking another look at electric farm vehicles. John Deere Product Engineering Center said that farmers can expect to see more diesel-electric systems in farm tractors, sprayers, and implements.

21547 ■ *"Commodities: Who's Behind the Boom?" in Barron's (Vol. 88, March 31, 2008, No. 13, pp. 3)*
Pub: Dow Jones & Company, Inc.
Ed: Gene Epstein. **Description:** Proliferation of mutual funds and exchange traded funds tied to commodities indexes has helped speculative buying reach unusual levels. Index funds are estimated to account for 40 percent of all bullish bets on commodities. Commodities could drop by 30 percent as speculators retreat. Statistical data included.

21548 ■ *"Community Food Co-op Creates Revolving Loan Program for Local Farmers" in Bellingham Business Journal (Vol. February 2010, pp. 3)*
Pub: Sound Publishing Inc.
Description: Community Food Co-op's Farm Fund received a $12,000 matching grant from the Sustainable Whatcom Fund of the Whatcom Community Foundation. The Farm Fund will create a new revolving loan program for local farmers committed to using sustainable practices.

21549 ■ *"Company Severs Ties with Chiquita, Starts Own Brand" in Business Journal-Serving Phoenix and the Valley of the Sun (October 5, 2007)*
Pub: American City Business Journals, Inc.
Ed: Mike Sunnucks. **Description:** Melones International is ending a deal with Chiquita Brands International Inc. Melones will now distribute its produce in the U.S. under its own brand, called Plain Jane. Alejandro N. Canelos Jr., head of the firm, stated their relationship with Chiquita was good, but wants to promote the Plain Jane brand name.

21550 ■ *"Confidence High, But Lenders More Cautious" in Farmer's Weekly (March 28,*

2008, No. 320)
Pub: Reed Business Information
Contact: Jeff Greisch, President
Description: Discusses the effect of the global credit crunch on farmers as well as recent auctions which were timed to beat changes to capital gains tax.

21551 ■ *"Corn Belt Farmland Prices Hit Record Levels" in Farm Industry News (December 1, 2011)*
Pub: Penton Business Media Inc.
Ed: David Hest. **Description:** Farmland prices have set records over the last six months in Iowa. Farmland broker and auction company owner, Murray Wise, believes this is not a bubble, that the economics of this market are solid.

21552 ■ *"Corn May Get Shucked By Soy" in Barron's (Vol. 88, March 31, 2008, No. 13, pp. M12)*
Pub: Dow Jones & Company, Inc.
Ed: Angie Pointer. **Description:** Acreage allotted to soybeans could jump by 12 percent from 2007's 63.6 million as the price for soybeans reaches record highs. Corn acreage could drop by 6.7 percent as other crops expand and higher fertilizer prices shift farmers away from corn.

21553 ■ *"Count Out The Consumer" in Barron's (Vol. 88, July 7, 2008, No. 27, pp. 10)*
Pub: Dow Jones & Co., Inc.
Description: American consumers are not expected to give the US economy its much-needed boost as the rising food and energy prices are taking their toll. US consumers have cut spending on utilities and food and are increasing their use of credit cards.

21554 ■ *"Crop Insurance Harvest Prices in 2011" in Farm Industry News (November 9, 2011)*
Pub: Penton Business Media Inc.
Ed: Gary Schnitkey. **Description:** Risk Management Agency (RMA) reported harvest prices for corn and soybean grown in the Midwest with corn at $6.32 per bushel, 31 cents higher than the project $6.01; soybeans were at $12.14 per bushel, down $1.35 from the projected price of $13.49.

21555 ■ *"Dean Foods" in Ice Cream Reporter (Vol. 23, November 20, 2010, No. 12, pp. 8)*
Pub: Ice Cream Reporter
Description: The impact of higher commodity prices can be seen in the recent news from Dean Foods, the largest U.S. dairy company, which reported that rising butterfat and other dairy commodity costs have led to lower-than-expected quarterly profits after it cut prices to compete with private-label brands.

21556 ■ *"Deere to Open Technology Center in Germany" in Chicago Tribune (September 3, 2008)*
Pub: McClatchy-Tribune Information Services
Ed: James P. Miller. **Description:** Deere & Co. plans to open a technology and innovation center in Germany; details of the company's expansion plans are discussed.

21557 ■ *"Department of Agriculture" in Ice Cream Reporter (Vol. 23, November 20, 2010, No. 12, pp. 8)*
Pub: Ice Cream Reporter
Description: Department of Agriculture notes that food price inflation for 2010 will be at its lowest since 1992.

21558 ■ *"Dick Haskayne" in Canadian Business (Vol. 81, March 31, 2008, No. 5, pp. 72)*
Pub: Rogers Media
Ed: Andy Holloway. **Description:** Dick Haskayne says that he learned a lot about business from his dad who ran a butcher shop where they had to make a decision on buying cattle and getting credit. Haskayne says that family, friends, finances, career, health, and infrastructure are benchmarks that have to be balanced.

21559 ■ *Directory of American Agriculture*
Pub: Agricultural Resources & Communications Inc.
URL(s): foodandagnetwork.com/catalog/directory-american-agriculture. **Released:** Irregular; Latest edition 2005. **Price:** $64.95, Individuals hard copy. **Covers:** National and state agricultural organizations; federal and state agricultural departments, agencies, and programs; colleges of agriculture at land grant universities, state 4-H leaders, farm broadcasters and publications, farm credit councils, agricultural information services and other agricultural organizations, agencies and institutions. **Entries include:** Organization name, address, phone, fax, name and title of contact. National organization entries include additional information. **Arrangement:** Alphabetical. **Indexes:** Categorical, by type of organization.

21560 ■ *"Dividing to Conquer" in Barron's (Vol. 88, March 31, 2008, No. 13, pp. 22)*
Pub: Dow Jones & Company, Inc.

Ed: Andrew Bary. **Description:** Altria's spin off of Philip Morris International could unlock substantial value for both domestic and international cigarette concerns. The strong brands and ample payouts from both companies will most likely impress investors.

21561 ■ *"Don't Fall Foul of Farming's Workplace Killer" in Farmer's Weekly (March 28, 2008, No. 320)*
Pub: Reed Business Information
Contact: Jeff Greisch, President

Description: Discusses the Work at Height Regulations that were introduced to reduce the risk of injury and death caused by accidental falls in the workplace.

21562 ■ *"Dow AgroSciences Buys Wheat Breeding Firm in Pacific Northwest" in Farm Industry News (July 29, 2011)*
Pub: Penton Business Media Inc.

Description: Dow AgroSciences purchased Northwest Plant Breeding Company, a cereals breeding station in Washington in 2011. The acquisition will help Dow expand its Hyland Seeds certified wheat seed program foundation in the Pacific Northwest. Financial terms of the deal were not disclosed.

21563 ■ *"Drought Takes Toll on Farmers, Restaurants" in Saint Louis Business Journal (Vol. 31, August 12, 2011, No. 51, pp. 1)*
Pub: Saint Louis Business Journal

Ed: E.B. Solomont. **Description:** The drought in St. Louis, Missouri has adversely impacted farmers and restaurants in the areas. Diners can expect to lose some ingredients from their menus.

21564 ■ *"DuPontas Pioneer Hi-Bred, Evogene to Develop Rust-Resistant Soybean Varieties" in Farm Industry News (November 22, 2011)*
Pub: Penton Business Media Inc.

Ed: Karen McMahon. **Description:** DuPont and Evogene have signed a new contract to work together to develop resistance in soybeans to rust. Financial terms of the agreement were not disclosed.

21565 ■ *"Eco-Preneuring" in Small Business Opportunities (Jan. 2008)*
Pub: Harris Publications Inc.

Description: Iceland Naturally is a joint marketing effort among tourism and business interests hoping to increase demand for Icelandic products including frozen seafood, bottled water, agriculture, and tourism in North America.

21566 ■ *"Eco-Preneuring" in Small Business Opportunities (July 2008)*
Pub: Entrepreneur Media Inc.

Ed: Mary C. Pearl. **Description:** Profile of Wildlife Trust, a rapidly growing global organization dedicated to innovative conservation science linking health and ecology. With partners in nearly twenty countries, Wildlife Trust draws on global strengths in order to respond to well-defined local needs. In the Dominican Republic, they are working with the community and local biologists in order to restore fishing and create jobs in the field of ecotourism.

21567 ■ *"Egg Fight: The Yolk's on the Short" in Barron's (Vol. 88, July 7, 2008, No. 27, pp. 20)*
Pub: Dow Jones & Co., Inc.

Ed: Christopher C. Williams. **Description:** Shares of Cal-Maine Foods, the largest egg producer and distributor in the US, are due for a huge rise because of the increase in egg prices. Short sellers, however, continue betting that the stock, priced at $31.84 each, will eventually go down.

21568 ■ *"EPA Grants E15 Waiver for 2001-2006 Vehicles" in Farm Industry News (January 21, 2011)*
Pub: Penton Business Media Inc.

Description: U.S. Environmental Protection Agency waived a limitation on selling gasoline that contains more than 10 percent ethanol for model year 2001-2006 cars and light trucks, allowing fuel to contain up to 15 percent ethanol (E15) for these vehicles.

21569 ■ *Equipment Marketing and Distribution Association--Membership Directory*
Contact: Miller Hadskey, President
E-mail: miller@shortlinesales.com
URL(s): www.emda.net/directory.htm. **Released:** Annual **Covers:** 120 members; coverage includes Canada. **Entries include:** Company name, address, phone, name of principal executive, territory covered. **Arrangement:** Alphabetical.

21570 ■ *Ethnic Solidarity for Economic Survival: Korean Greengrocers in New York City*
Pub: Russell Sage Foundation Publications
Ed: Pyong Gap Min. **Released:** August 2008. **Price:** $32.50. **Description:** Investigations into the entrepreneurial traditions of Korean immigrant families in New York City running ethnic businesses, particularly small grocery stores and produce markets. Social, cultural and economic issues facing these retailers are discussed.

21571 ■ *"Every Year, Thousands of People Are Killed By Pathogens In Food. William Hanson Wants To Help" in Inc. (November 2007, pp. 46-47)*
Pub: Gruner & Jahr USA Publishing
Ed: Dalia Fahmy. **Description:** OmniFresh 1000 System tests produce for pathogens such as E.coli and salmonella. The firm is able to test for these pathogens in two hours compared to traditional tests that take as many as three days. Each year some 5,000 Americans die from food-borne diseases.

21572 ■ *"Experts Discuss New Tax Rules in Webinar to Help Farmers With Year-End Tax Planning" in Farm Industry News (November 22, 2011)*
Pub: Penton Business Media Inc.

Description: Section 179 deductions and Bonus Depreciation tax rules for years 2011 and 2012 and how they impact farming operations are available at TractorLife.com. The Website helps farmers maintain and extend the operating lives of their tractors.

21573 ■ *"Farm Aid" in Canadian Business (Vol. 80, November 5, 2007, No. 22, pp. 123)*
Pub: Rogers Media
Ed: Calvin Leung. **Description:** Canadian farmers experiencing difficulties with increasing their earning as the price of production is greater than the amount they earn from produce. Government assistance programs, including the Canadian Agricultural Income Stabilization, are aimed at helping farmers mitigate the impacts of the high prices of production. The effectiveness of Canadian farm policies are evaluated.

21574 ■ *"Farming Season Starts in December" in Farm Industry News (November 29, 2011)*
Pub: Penton Business Media Inc.
Ed: Kent Lock. **Description:** One farmer suggests the season starts in December because one third of his seed and fertilizer for the following year has already been bought and paid for and his cropping mix changes little from one year to another.

21575 ■ *"Fast-Release Calcium Could Help Control Club Root" in Farmer's Weekly (March 28, 2008, No. 320)*
Pub: Reed Business Information
Contact: Jeff Greisch, President
Description: According to initial observations from a new HGCA club root research study, applications of fertilizers that rapidly release calcium may help improve performance of both susceptible and resistant oilseed rape varieties.

21576 ■ *"Feedback From Payers Will Be Vital For Future Developments" in Farmer's Weekly (March 28, 2008, No. 320)*
Pub: Reed Business Information
Contact: Jeff Greisch, President
Description: Potato Council staff will carry on working with levy payers to retain the same high caliber of marketing, research and other activities.

21577 ■ *"Fertilizer for Growth" in Canadian Business (Vol. 83, September 14, 2010, No. 15, pp. 76)*
Pub: Rogers Media Ltd.
Ed: Bryan Borzykowski. **Description:** Australian-based BHP Billiton launches a C$38.5 billion hostile takeover bid for Saskatchewan-based Potash Corporation and some investors immediately bought Potash stock at C$130. However, Potash has resisted BHP's offer and announced a plan to try to stop the deal.

21578 ■ *"A Few Points of Contention" in Barron's (Vol. 88, July 14, 2008, No. 28, pp. 3)*
Pub: Dow Jones & Co., Inc.
Ed: Michael Santoli. **Description:** Headline inflation tends to revert to the lower core inflation, which excludes food and energy in its calculation over long periods. Prominent private equity figures believe that regulators should allow more than the de facto 10 percent to 25 percent limit of commercial banks to hasten the refunding of the financial sector.

21579 ■ *"The Final Frontier" in Canadian Business (Vol. 80, October 8, 2007, No. 20, pp. 127)*
Pub: Rogers Media
Ed: Andy Holloway. **Description:** Effects of economic development in Northern Canada's natural environment are discussed. The caribou, which are still a primary source of food and clothing in the region, are dying. It is assumed that mining and petroleum projects are affecting the migration patterns of the animals inhabiting the region. The need to maintain a balance between the needs of resource companies and traditional businesses is also discussed.

21580 ■ *"FinOvation 2009" in Farm Industry News (Vol. 42, January 1, 2009, No. 1)*
Pub: Penton Media Inc.
Contact: John French, President
Ed: Karen McMahon; David Hest; Mark Moore. **Description:** New and innovative products and technologies are presented.

21581 ■ *"First Impression of Robotic Farming Systems" in Farm Industry News (September 30, 2011)*
Pub: Penton Business Media Inc.
Ed: Jodie Wehrspann. **Description:** Farm Science Review featured tillage tools and land rollers, including John Deere's GPS system where a cart tractor is automatically controlled as well as a new line of Kinze's carts and a video of their robotic system for a driver-less cart tractor.

21582 ■ *"Five Ways to Make RTK Pay" in Farm Industry News (March 25, 2011)*
Pub: Penton Business Media Inc.
Ed: David Hest. **Description:** It is important for farmers to decide whether they are seeking greater accuracy or faster payback when upgrading navigation systems. The trend towards higher accuracy continues to grow.

21583 ■ *"Food & Wine Publisher Tries His Hand at Saber Rattling" in Advertising Age (Vol. 77, December 4, 2006, No. 49, pp. 16)*
Pub: Crain Communications, Inc.
Description: French vineyards are facing a massive overproduction crisis due to a falling number in the amount of wine the French are drinking per week.

21584 ■ *"For Going All Out to Transform the Way Our Food Is Grown: Chuck Lacy" in Inc. (Volume 32, December 2010, No. 10, pp. 94)*
Pub: Inc. Magazine
Ed: Adam Bluestein. **Description:** Profile of Rotokawa Cattle Company and its mission to transform the business of beef and grow their herd of beef cattle.

21585 ■ *"For Putting Down Roots in Business: Amy Norquist: Greensulate, New York City" in Inc. (Volume 32, December 2010, No. 10, pp. 106)*
Pub: Inc. Magazine
Ed: Christine Lagorio. **Description:** Profile of Amy Norquist who left her position at an environmental nonprofit organization to found Greensulate. Her firm insulates rooftops with lavender, native grasses and succulents called sedum in order to eliminate carbon from the atmosphere.

21586 ■ *"Fossil Fuel, Renewable Fuel Shares Expected to Flip Flop" in Farm Industry News (April 29, 2011)*
Pub: Penton Business Media Inc.
Description: Total energy use of fossil fuels is predicted to fall 5 percent by the year 2035, with renewable fuel picking it up.

21587 ■ *"Fries With That?" in Canadian Business (Vol. 81, September 29, 2008, No. 16, pp. 33)*
Pub: Rogers Media Ltd.
Ed: Calvin Leung. **Description:** Profile of Toronto-based New York Fries, which has four stores in South Korea, is planning to expand further as well as into Hong Kong and Macau; the company also has a licensee in the United Arab Emirates whom is also planning to expand.

21588 ■ *"Frosted Flakes Goes For Gold" in Marketing to Women (Vol. 21, April 2008, No. 4, pp. 3)*
Pub: EPM Communications Inc.
Contact: Ira Mayer, President
E-mail: imayer@epmcom.com
Description: Kellogg is appealing to health-conscious moms with its new product Frosted Flakes Gold.

21589 ■ *"Fuel King: The Most Fuel-Efficient Tractor of the Decade is the John Deere 8295R" in Farm Industry News (November 10, 2011)*
Pub: Penton Business Media Inc.
Description: Farm Industry News compiled a list of the most fuel-efficient tractors with help from the Nebraska Tractor Test Lab, with the John Deere 8295R PTO winner of the most fuel-efficient tractor of the decade.

21590 ■ *Fugitive Denim: A Moving Story of People and Pants in the Borderless World of Global Trade*
Pub: W.W. Norton & Company
Ed: Rachel Snyder. **Released:** April 2009. **Price:** $16.95. **Description:** In-depth study of the global production and processes of how jeans are designed, sewn, and transported as well as how the cotton for denim is grown, regulated, purchased and processed.

21591 ■ *"Game On: The Hunt Is On for Nation's Top Keeper" in Farmer's Weekly (March 28, 2008, No. 320)*
Pub: Reed Business Information
Contact: Jeff Greisch, President
Description: Gamekeepers must strike the natural balance that encourages wildlife and protects game. CLA Game Fair and Farmer's Weekly are holding a competition for Gamekeeper of the Year 2008.

21592 ■ *"General Clark Stresses Ethanols Role In National Security At Ag Connect" in Farm Industry News (January 11, 2011)*
Pub: Penton Business Media Inc.
Description: General Clark stressed the role of ethanols in national security at the AgConnect.

21593 ■ *"GL Homes Buys 1,000 Acres in Former Agricultural Reserve" in Miami Daily Business Review (March 26, 2008)*
Pub: ALM Media Inc.
Ed: Polyana da Costa. **Description:** One of the nation's largest home builders, GL Homes, purchased over 1,000 acres of agricultural land in Southern Palm Beach County, Florida. Plans for 554 residential units are detailed.

21594 ■ *"Good Things Happen When We Buy Local" in Crain's Detroit Business (Vol. 24, October 6, 2008, No. 40, pp. 7)*
Pub: Crain Communications, Inc.
Description: Michigan is facing incredibly difficult economic times. One way in which each one of us can help the state and the businesses located here is by purchasing our goods and services from local vendors. The state Agriculture Department projected that if Michigan households earmarked $10 per week in their grocery purchases to made-in-Michigan products, this would generate $30 million a week in economic impact.

21595 ■ *"Grape Expectations" in Canadian Business (Vol. 80, March 12, 2007, No. 6, pp. 55)*
Pub: Rogers Media
Ed: Andrea Jezvovit. **Description:** The emergence of Nova Scotia as one of the leading wine-making places in Canada, in view of its favorable climate for growing grapes, is discussed.

21596 ■ *"The Great Cleanup" in Canadian Business (Vol. 81, April 14, 2008, No. 6, pp. 50)*
Pub: Rogers Media
Ed: Graham Silnicki. **Description:** China's rectification program includes the licensing of 100 percent of food producers and monitoring of 100 percent of raw materials for exports between August and December, 2007. There is a lot of money to be made for those who are willing to help China win its quality battle. PharmEng International Inc. is one of the companies that helps Chinese companies meet international quality standards.

21597 ■ *"Grow-Ops" in Canadian Business (Vol. 81, October 27, 2008, No. 18, pp. 112)*
Pub: Rogers Media Ltd.
Ed: Calvin Leung. **Description:** Canada's agriculture and agri-food industry is ripe for expansion and to meet global demand that is expected to double by 2050. Better water management and biotechnology are among the strategies that could help increase output of Canada's agricultural industry.

21598 ■ *"Growers Urged to Allow for Soil Nutrients" in Farmer's Weekly (March 28, 2008, No. 320)*
Pub: Reed Business Information
Contact: Jeff Greisch, President
Ed: Andrew Blake. **Description:** Discusses the importance of taking in account soil nitrogen supplies when planning their remaining fertilizer applications.

21599 ■ *"Growing Pains" in Canadian Business (Vol. 81, July 22, 2008, No. 12-13, pp. 35)*
Pub: Rogers Media Ltd.
Ed: Alex Mylnek. **Description:** Laughing Stock Vineyards' Cynthia Enns and David Enns plan to target young buyers by using social media. The Enns however, are concerned that targeting younger buyers may affect Laughing Stock's image as a premium brand. Additional information regarding the company's future plans is presented.

21600 ■ *"Half Empty or Half Full" in Crain's Chicago Business (Vol. 31, March 24, 2008, No. 12, pp. 4)*
Pub: Crain Communications, Inc.
Ed: Meghan Streit. **Description:** Lifeway Foods Inc., the health food company which manufactures a yogurt-like drink called kefir, is being negatively affected by the soaring price of milk; however, the fact that probiotics are picking up in the market may mean that Lifeway stands a good chance of bouncing back and the company's lower share price could be an opportunity for long-term investors who have a tolerance for risk.

21601 ■ *"Head of Horse Farmers and Owners Jockey for Saratoga Pastures, Breeder Awards" in Business Review, Albany New York (Nov. 23, 2007)*
Pub: American City Business Journals, Inc.
Ed: Robin K. Cooper. **Description:** Trends in Saratoga County's equine industry are discussed. More than fifty horse farms and 11,000 horses are in Saratoga, which is more than any other county in New York. Joe McMahon, a horse breeder and also the vice president of New York Breeders Sales Company, plans to expand his business by tapping into a new market. He plans to build his stable of top registered New York stallions.

21602 ■ *"Hello, Old Friends" in Business Courier (Vol. 24, October 12, 2008, No. 26, pp. 1)*
Pub: American City Business Journals, Inc.
Ed: Jon Newberry. **Description:** Pittsburgh-based Iron City Brewing Co., a company born out of Pittsburgh Brewing Co.'s reorganization, is resuming the production of Wiedemann Bohemian Style Special Beer. Cincinnati-based Christian Moerlein Brewing Co. is also bringing back its famous Burger beer, which hasn't been available locally for a couple of years. The two companies' plans regarding the reintroduction of their beer products are discussed.

21603 ■ *A History of Small Business in America*
Pub: University of North Carolina Press
Contact: Kate Douglas Torrey, Director
E-mail: kate_torrey@unc.edu
Ed: Mansel G. Blackford. **Released:** May 2003. **Price:** $22.95. **Description:** History of American small business from the colonial era to present, showing how it has played a role in the nation's economic, political, and cultural development across manufacturing, sales, services and farming.

21604 ■ *"Hopes Grow for Milk Price Increase From Tesco" in Farmer's Weekly (March 28, 2008, No. 320)*
Pub: Reed Business Information
Contact: Jeff Greisch, President
Description: Farmers will see an increase in the price supermarket Tesco will pay for their milk.

21605 ■ *"How Growers Buy" in Farm Industry News (Vol. 42, January 1, 2009, No. 1)*
Pub: Penton Media Inc.
Contact: John French, President
Ed: Karen McMahon. **Description:** According to a survey regarding the buying habits among large commercial growers, most prefer to purchase from local retailers, customer service is important concerning their decision on who to buy products from, and price and convenience seem to be more important then brand.

21606 ■ *"How High Can Soybeans Fly?" in Barron's (Vol. 88, March 10, 2008, No. 10, pp. M14)*
Pub: Dow Jones & Company, Inc.
Ed: Kenneth Rapoza. **Description:** Prices of soybeans have risen to $14.0875 a bushel, up 8.3 percent for the week. Increased demand, such as in China and in other developing economies, and the investment-driven commodities boom are boosting prices.

21607 ■ *"How Sweet It Will Be" in Barron's (Vol. 89, July 13, 2009, No. 28, pp. M13)*
Pub: Dow Jones & Co., Inc.
Ed: Debbie Carlson. **Description:** Raw sugar experienced a rally in the first half of 2009 and the long term outlook for sugar prices is still good. However, there is a likely near-term correction due to the onset of Brazilian harvest that could be 20.7 percent higher for 2009 as compared to the previous year and October contracts could fall to 15.61 cents per pound.

21608 ■ "An Ill Wind: Icelandic Bank Failures Chill Atlantic Canada" in Canadian Business (Vol. 81, November 10, 2008, No. 19, pp. 10)
Pub: Rogers Media Ltd.
Ed: Charles Mandel. **Description:** Bank failures in Iceland have put a stop to flights ferrying Icelanders to Newfoundland to purchase Christmas gifts, thereby threatening Newfoundland's tourism industry. The credit of Newfoundland's fisheries is also being squeezed since most of Atlantic Canadian seafood processors hold lines of credit from Icelandic banks.

21609 ■ "Ill Winds; Cuba's Economy" in The Economist (Vol. 390, January 3, 2009, No. 8612, pp. 20)
Pub: The Economist Newspaper Inc.
Description: Cuba's long-term economic prospects remain poor with the economy forecasted to grow only 4.3 percent for the year, about half of the original forecast, due in part to Hurricane Gustav which caused $10 billion in damage and disrupted the food-supply network and devastated farms across the region; President Raul Castro made raising agricultural production a national priority and the rise in global commodity prices hit the country hard. The only bright spot has been the rise in tourism which is up 9.3 percent over 2007.

21610 ■ "Illinois Farmland Tops $11,000 Per Acre" in Farm Industry News (June 27, 2011)
Pub: Penton Business Media Inc.
Ed: Karen McMahon. **Description:** Farmland property in Illinois continues to grow in value, selling for $11,000 per acre. Statistical data included.

21611 ■ "Importers Share Safety Liability" in Feedstuffs (Vol. 80, January 21, 2008, No. 3, pp. 19)
Pub: Miller Publishing Company, Inc.
Description: Pet food and toys containing lead paint are among products from China being recalled due to safety concerns. American Society for Quality's list of measures that outsourcing companies can take to help ensure safer products being imported to the U.S.

21612 ■ "Investment Bank Predicts Shakeup in Farm Equipment Industry" in Farm Industry News (November 16, 2011)
Pub: Penton Business Media Inc.
Ed: Jodie Wehrspann. **Description:** Farming can expect to see more mergers and acquisitions in the agricultural equipment industry, as it appears to be in the early stages of growth over the next few years.

21613 ■ "Irene Rosenfeld; Chairman and CEO, Kraft Foods Inc." in Crain's Chicago Business (Vol. 31, May 5, 2008, No. 18, pp. 31)
Pub: Crain Communications, Inc.
Ed: David Sterrett. **Description:** Profile of Irene Rosenfeld who is the chairman and CEO of Kraft Foods Inc. and is entering the second year of a three-year plan to boost sales of well-known brands such as Oreo, Velveeta and Oscar Mayer while facing soaring commodity costs and a declining market-share. Ms. Rosenfeld's turnaround strategy also entails spending more on advertising and giving managers more control over their budgets and product development.

21614 ■ "Kraft Taps Cheese Head; Jordan Charged With Fixing Foodmaker's Signature Product" in Crain's Chicago Business (April 14, 2008)
Pub: Crain Communications, Inc.
Ed: David Sterrett. **Description:** Kraft Foods Inc. has assigned Rhonda Jordan, a company veteran, to take charge of the cheese and dairy division which has been losing market shares to cheaper store-brand cheese among cost-sensitive shoppers as Kraft and its competitors raise prices to offset soaring dairy costs.

21615 ■ "Land Agent Taken Over" in Farmer's Weekly (March 28, 2008, No. 320)
Pub: Reed Business Information
Contact: Jeff Greisch, President
Description: Property business Smiths Gore will take over Cluttons' rural division, one of the oldest names in land agency. Cluttons said it had decided to sell its rural business as part of a strategic repositioning that would refocus the business on commercial, residential and overseas opportunities.

21616 ■ "The Latin Beat Goes On" in Barron's (Vol. 88, July 7, 2008, No. 27, pp. L5)
Pub: Dow Jones & Co., Inc.
Ed: Tom Sullivan. **Description:** Latin American stocks have outperformed other regional markets due to rising commodities prices and favorable economic climate. Countries such as Brazil, Mexico, Chile, and Peru provide investment opportunities, while Argentina and Venezuela are tougher places to invest.

21617 ■ "Leapin' Lizards, Does SoBe Have Some Work To Do On Life Water" in Brandweek (Vol. 49, April 21, 2008, No. 16, pp. 32)
Pub: VNU Business Media, Inc.
Ed: Amy Shea. **Description:** Discusses the competing marketing campaigns of both Vitaminwater, now owned by Coca-Cola, and SoBe Life Water which is owned by Pepsi; also looks at the repositioning of Life Water as a thirst-quencher, rather than a green product as well as the company's newest advertising campaign.

21618 ■ "Leica Beefs Up Steering Options, Steering Display Features" in Farm Industry News (January 10, 2011)
Pub: Penton Business Media Inc.
Description: Leica Geosystems is offering a new hydraulic steering kit for older tractors, along with new steering patterns and other features on its Leica mojo3C and mojoMINI displays.

21619 ■ "Leinie's Charts National Craft Beer Rollout" in The Business Journal-Milwaukee (Vol. 25, August 29, 2008, No. 49, pp. A1)
Pub: American City Business Journals, Inc.
Ed: Rich Rovito. **Description:** Jacob Leinenkugel Brewing Co. is expected to complete the national rollout of its craft beer brands, while the launch of a new beer is prepared for this fall. The rollout is will likely benefit MillerCoors LLC, and will leave Alaska as the only state without Leinenkugel beer. Other views and information on Leinenkugel's national rollout are presented.

21620 ■ "Levy Boards: From Unity Comes Farming's Strength" in Farmer's Weekly (March 28, 2008, No. 320)
Pub: Reed Business Information
Contact: Jeff Greisch, President
Description: Discusses the amalgamation of five farming levy boards to create the Agriculture and Horticulture Development Board.

21621 ■ "Li'l Guy Rolls Up Into Bigger Company" in The Business Journal-Serving Metropolitan Kansas City (Vol. 26, September 12, 2008)
Pub: American City Business Journals, Inc.
Ed: Suzanna Stagemeyer. **Description:** Li'l Guy Foods, a Mexican food company in Kansas City, Missouri, has merged with Tortilla King Inc. Li'l Guy's revenue in 2007 was $3.3 million, while a newspaper report said that Tortilla King's revenue in 2001 was $7.5 million. Growth opportunities for the combined companies and Li'l Guy's testing of the Wichita market are discussed.

21622 ■ "Lords Should Get Real About Food" in Farmer's Weekly (March 28, 2008, No. 320)
Pub: Reed Business Information
Contact: Jeff Greisch, President
Description: Discusses the reasons why farming needs subsidies and suggests that the House of Lords should look at the way that grocery stores are operating.

21623 ■ "Making the Most of Milk to Revive a Falling Market" in Farmer's Weekly (March 28, 2008, No. 320)
Pub: Reed Business Information
Contact: Jeff Greisch, President
Description: DairyCo, eight of whom are working dairy farmers, aim to promote a feeding campaign for better herd health, provide research into efficient labor use, and sponsor discussion groups to enhance business skills.

21624 ■ "Marketer Bets Big on U.S.'s Growing Canine Obsession" in Advertising Age (Vol. 79, April 14, 2008, No. 15, pp. 14)
Pub: Crain Communications, Inc.
Ed: Emily Bryson York. **Description:** Overview of FreshPet, a New Jersey company that began marketing two brands of refrigerated dog food-Deli Fresh and FreshPet Select-which are made from fresh ingredients such as beef, rice and carrots. The company projects continued success due to the amount of money consumers spend on their pets as well as fears derived from the 2007 recalls that inspired consumers to look for smaller, independent manufacturers that are less likely to source ingredients from China.

21625 ■ "Markets Defy the Doomsayers" in Barron's (Vol. 88, March 24, 2008, No. 12, pp. M5)
Pub: Dow Jones & Company, Inc.
Ed: Leslie P. Norton. **Description:** US stock markets registered strong gains, with the Dow Jones Industrial Average rising 3.43 percent on the week to close at 12,361.32, in a rally that may be seen as short-covering. Shares of Hansen Natural are poised for further drops with a slowdown in the energy drink market.

21626 ■ "Maternity Wear Goes Green" in Marketing to Women (Vol. 21, March 2008, No. 3, pp. 3)
Pub: EPM Communications Inc.
Contact: Ira Mayer, President
E-mail: imayer@epmcom.com
Description: Mother's Work Inc. has launched a series of environmentally-friendly products made from such sustainable fibers as organic cotton and bamboo.

21627 ■ "McCormick Focuses on Customer, Dealer Service" in Farm Industry News (September 17, 2010)
Pub: Penton Business Media Inc.
Description: McCormick has developed a new plan that focuses on fast and complete service to both customers and dealers.

21628 ■ "Melamine Analytical Methods Released" in Feedstuffs (Vol. 80, October 6, 2008, No. 41, pp. 2)
Pub: Miller Publishing Company
Description: Romer Labs has released new validations for its AgraQuant Melamine enzyme-linked immunosorbent assay. The test kit screens for melamine in feed and diary products, including pet foods, milk and milk powder. Melamine by itself is nontoxic in low doses, but when combined with cyanuric acid it can cause fatal kidney stones. The Chinese dairy industry is in the midst of a huge melamine crisis; melamine-contaminated dairy and food products from China have been found in more than 20 countries.

21629 ■ "Milk Producers Target Moms" in Marketing to Women (Vol. 21, January 2008, No. 1, pp. 3)
Pub: EPM Communications Inc.
Contact: Ira Mayer, President
E-mail: imayer@epmcom.com
Description: In an attempt to encourage moms to serve milk with meals, the American Dairy Association partners with the New York State Dietetic Association to promote milk via a new logo, website and contest.

21630 ■ "Minimizing Import Risks" in Canadian Sailings (July 7, 2008)
Pub: UBM Global Trade
Contact: Leonard J. Corallo, President
Ed: Jack Kohane. **Description:** New food and product safety laws may be enacted by Canada's Parliament; importers, retailers and manufacturers could face huge fines if the new laws are passed.

21631 ■ "Minnesota Farms' Net Worth Grows 10 Percent Each Year for 15 Years" in Farm Industry News (August 22, 2011)
Pub: Penton Business Media Inc.
Ed: Dale Nordquist. **Description:** The average value of farms in Minnesota is growing at a fast pace. Total

assets per farm have increased by more than $1.1 million over the past 15 years. Statistical data included.

21632 ■ *"Monsanto's Next Single-Bag Refuge Product Approved" in Farm Industry News (December 5, 2011)*

Pub: Penton Business Media Inc.

Description: Monsanto's refuge-in-a-bag (RIB) product was approved for commercialization in 2012. The Genuity VT Double Pro RIB Complete is a blend of 95 percent Genuity VT Double Pro and 5 percent refuge (non-Bt) seed and provides above-ground pest control and not corn rootworm protection.

21633 ■ *"The Mood of a Nation" in Canadian Business (Vol. 81, April 14, 2008, No. 6, pp. 56)*

Pub: Rogers Media

Ed: Joe Castaldo. **Description:** Independent Fish Harvesters Inc. processes more kilograms a year and has had to hire more workers but its managers worry about how a slowdown in the U.S. economy will affect his business. A planned shopping complex in Mirabel Quebec, the manufacturing industry in Kitchener, Ontario, and a cattle farming business in Sarnia, Ontario are discussed to provide a snapshot of the challenges that business in Canada are facing as recession looms.

21634 ■ *"More Cuts On the Way At Ag School" in Business First-Columbus (December 14, 2007, pp. A1)*

Pub: American City Business Journals, Inc.

Ed: Carrie Ghose. **Description:** Program cuts at Ohio State University's Agriculture School are discussed. A voluntary retirement incentive to reduce staff was approved by the University's trustees. Since 2000, the College of Food, Agricultural and Environmental Sciences' staff have decreased by 21 percent, while the faculty experienced a 25 percent reduction. According to Bobby Moser, the college's dean, the institution is looking for other ways to generate income.

21635 ■ *"Most Viewed Stories, Videos on farmindustrynews.com in 2010" in Farm Industry News (January 4, 2011)*

Pub: Penton Business Media Inc.

Description: The top ten most popularly viewed stories and videos presented on farmindustrynews.com Website are listed.

21636 ■ *National Agri-Marketing Association--Directory of Members*

Pub: National Agri-Marketing Association

Contact: Vicki Henrickson, President

URL(s): www.nama.org. **Released:** Annual; January. **Price:** $150. **Covers:** 2,500 persons active in agricultural advertising and marketing for manufacturers, advertising agencies, and media. Published as part of the Agri-Marketing Marketing Services Guide. **Entries include:** Member name and position, company name, address, phone. **Arrangement:** Geographical, alphabetical.

21637 ■ *"National Cattlemen's Beef Association" in Retail Merchandiser (Vol. 51, September-October 2011, No. 5, pp. 77)*

Pub: Phoenix Media Corporation

Description: National Cattlemen's Beef Association offers a wide range of tools and information to keep its members informed regarding the state of the beef industry. Their Website provides tools to help cattle producers improve operations.

21638 ■ *"The New Alchemists" in Canadian Business (Vol. 81, October 27, 2008, No. 18, pp. 22)*

Pub: Rogers Media Ltd.

Ed: Joe Castaldo. **Description:** Ethanol industry expects second-generation ethanol or cellulosic biofuels to provide ecologically friendly technologies than the ethanol made from food crops. Government and industries are investing on producing cellulosic biofuels.

21639 ■ *"New Crop Protection Products from Monsanto, Valent, DuPont, FMC, BASF" in Farm Industry News (December 17, 2010)*

Pub: Penton Business Media Inc.

Ed: Mark Moore. **Description:** Glyphosate-dominated herbicides are declining because a more diversified market for corn and soybeans is available. New crop care includes old chemistries, new formulations and unique combinations of both giving farmers more choices to protect the yield potential of their corn and soybean crops. Profiles of new products are included.

21640 ■ *"New Ethanol Plant Planned In Iowa to Use Corn Stover" in Farm Industry News (June 27, 2011)*

Pub: Penton Business Media Inc.

Ed: Lynn Grooms. **Description:** DuPont Danisco Cellulosic Ethanol (DDCE) will buy land next to the Lincolnway Energy corn-based ethanol plant in Nevada, Iowa in order to produce ethanol from corn stover at the location.

21641 ■ *"New Life for Old Chemistries" in Farm Industry News (Vol. 42, January 1, 2009, No. 1)*

Pub: Penton Media Inc.

Contact: John French, President

Ed: Mark Moore. **Description:** To expand the uses of familiar crop protection products, chemical companies are utilizing biotechnology research and development tools; many off-patent products are being rejuvenated with small changes to make the product even better than it was when originally conceived.

21642 ■ *"New Yetter Stubble Solution Prevents Tire, Track Damage" in Farm Industry News (November 21, 2011)*

Pub: Penton Business Media Inc.

Description: The new Yetter 5000 Stalk Devastator helps prevent premature tire and track wear and damage caused by crop stubble.

21643 ■ *"The Next Big Thing" in Farm Industry News (Vol. 42, January 1, 2009, No. 1)*

Pub: Penton Media Inc.

Contact: John French, President

Ed: David Hest. **Description:** Communication technology that allows farmers to detect equipment location, travel speed and real-time fuel and sprayer/combine tank levels will pay off with better machine use efficiency, improved maintenance and reduced downtime. These telemetry systems will be widely available in the next few years.

21644 ■ *"Nonstop Round Baler Earns Top International Award for Krone" in Farm Industry News (November 18, 2011)*

Pub: Penton Business Media Inc.

Ed: Karen McMahon. **Description:** The new Ultima baler from Krone can make and net a bale in 40 seconds without stopping, thus producing 90 bales an hour. The new baler, still in test stage, won top honors at the Agritechnica farm equipment show in Hannover, Germany.

21645 ■ *"Numerous Changes Made to Crop Production and Consumption Forecasts" in Farm Industry News (November 9, 2011)*

Pub: Penton Business Media Inc.

Ed: Darrel Good. **Description:** USDA November Crop Production and WASDE reports contained various changes in production and consumption forecasts for corn, soybeans, and wheat for the current marketing year. A brief summary for each crop is included.

21646 ■ *"Ocean of Opportunity" in Hawaii Business (Vol. 53, October 2007, No. 4, pp. 61)*

Pub: Hawaii Business Publishing

Ed: Mike Markrich. **Description:** Brew Moon owner Marcus Bender and former Coca-Cola Enterprises Inc. executive Jim Stevens have introduced Kai Vodka in June 2007. The new drink is being marketed to professional women, the number of which is increasing based on a research by the Queens College Department of Sociology. The development process of the new product is also discussed.

21647 ■ *"One-Pass Tillage" in Farm Industry News (Vol. 42, January 1, 2009, No. 1)*

Pub: Penton Media Inc.

Contact: John French, President

Description: Bigham Brothers Inc.'s One Pass Terr-Till, a tool that breaks up compacted soil while cutting heavy residue, is reviewed.

21648 ■ *"OPEC Exposed" in Hawaii Business (Vol. 54, September 2008, No. 3, pp. 2)*

Pub: Hawaii Business Publishing

Ed: Serena Lim. **Description:** Organization of the Petroleum Exporting Countries (OPEC) has said that their effort in developing an alternative energy source has driven prices up. The biofuel sector is criticizing the statement, saying that a research study found that biofuels push petroleum prices down by 15 percent. Details on the effect of rising petroleum prices are discussed.

21649 ■ *"Org to Moms: Eat Your Veggies" in Marketing to Women (Vol. 21, April 2008, No. 4, pp. 3)*

Pub: EPM Communications Inc.

Contact: Ira Mayer, President

E-mail: imayer@epmcom.com

Description: In order to increase the purchase and consumption of fruit and vegetables to moms, the non profit Produce for Better Health Foundation is launching a series of initiatives.

21650 ■ *"Outlook for Montana Agriculture" in Montana Business Quarterly (Vol. 49, Spring 2011, No. 1, pp. 26)*

Pub: Bureau of Business & Economic Research

Ed: George Haynes. **Description:** Montana farmers and ranchers are rebounding from lower prices and production to higher prices and record production in 2010. The state has limited dairy and hog production, but farm income is still likely rise between 15 to 25 percent in 2010 over previous year.

21651 ■ *"Perry's Goes Organic" in Ice Cream Reporter (Vol. 22, December 20, 2008, No. 1, pp. 1)*

Pub: Ice Cream Reporter

Description: Family-owned Perry's Ice Cream is starting a new line of organic ice cream in both vanilla and chocolate flavors. All Perry's products are made with milk and cream from local dairy farmers.

21652 ■ *"Pet-Food Industry Too Slow" in Advertising Age (Vol. 78, March 26, 2007, No. 13, pp. 29)*

Pub: Crain Communications, Inc.

Description: Many crisis-communications experts believe that the pet-food industry mishandled the problem by waiting almost a month to recall the 60 million 'wet-food' products after numerous consumer complaints. Experts site that the first 24 to 49 hours are the most important in dealing with a crisis of this nature.

21653 ■ *"Pioneer Unveils Drought-Tolerant Hybrids" in Farm Industry News (January 6, 2011)*

Pub: Penton Business Media Inc.

Description: Eight new drought-tolerant hybrids are now available across five genetic platforms from Pioneer. The new hybrids, marketed under the Optimum AQUAmax brand name (previously announced as Drought Tolerant 1 Hybrids), contain a collection of native corn traits that improve water access and utilization.

21654 ■ *"Playing Defense" in Crain's Chicago Business (Vol. 31, November 10, 2008, No. 45, pp. 4)*

Pub: Crain Communications, Inc.

Ed: Monee Fields-White. **Description:** Chicago's money managers are increasingly investing in local companies such as Caterpillar Inc., a maker of construction and mining equipment, Kraft Foods Inc. and Baxter International Inc., a manufacturer of medical products, in an attempt to bolster their portfolios. These companies have a history of surviving tough economic times.

21655 ■ *"Potash Sale Must Be Blocked" in Canadian Business (Vol. 83, October 12, 2010, No. 17, pp. 24)*
Pub: Rogers Media Ltd.
Ed: Kasey Coholan. **Description:** Chief executive officers (CEOs) and corporate leaders in Canada are concerned about the possible sale of Potash Corporation to foreign buyers. A Compas Inc. poll recently asked CEOs whether the Canadian Government should step in to block the sale of the country's largest fertilizer firm.

21656 ■ *"Precision Crop Control with Valley Irrigation/CropMetrics Partnership" in Farm Industry News (January 6, 2011)*
Pub: Penton Business Media Inc.
Description: Irrigation systems have become a precision farming tool since partnering with agronomic software systems to apply products across the field by prescription. Valley Irrigation and CropMetrics have partnered in order to variably control water, fertilizer and other crop management products through a center pivot irrigation system.

21657 ■ *"Precision Fertilizer Spreading Shown at Agritechnica" in Farm Industry News (November 23, 2011)*
Pub: Penton Business Media Inc.
Ed: Karen McMahon. **Description:** Rauch, the German firm, introduced a new system that precisely spreads fertilizer on crops. The new product was shown at Agritechnica.

21658 ■ *"Preparing for Weed Control" in Farmer's Weekly (March 28, 2008, No. 320)*
Pub: Reed Business Information
Contact: Jeff Greisch, President
Description: Profile of Richard Beachell who farms in a joint venture with his neighbor. Beachell discusses nitrogen applications, fungicides and the reduction of pesticides.

21659 ■ *"Presidential Address: Innovation in Retrospect and Prospect" in Canadian Journal of Electronics (Vol. 43, November 2010, No. 4)*
Pub: Journal of the Canadian Economics Association
Ed: James A. Brander. **Description:** Has innovation slowed in recent decades? While there has been progress in information and communications technology, the recent record of innovation in agriculture, energy, transportation and healthcare sectors is cause for concern.

21660 ■ *"Press Release: New Corn Hybrid from Seed Consultants" in Farm Industry News (January 6, 2011)*
Pub: Penton Business Media Inc.
Description: Seed Consultants Inc. is releasing its first proprietary corn line called SC 1101. The product was developed, bred, and tested for the eastern Corn Belt diseases, soils, and growing conditions.

21661 ■ *"Press Release: New Trough Drinker From Pride of the Farm" in Farm Industry News (January 5, 2011)*
Pub: Penton Business Media Inc.
Description: Model WPO70 is a 90-inch long trough drinker designed for high-capacity feedyard applications and features foam-filly poly construction and a rib-reinforced trough. A description of this new offering from Pride of the Farm is included.

21662 ■ *"Press Release: Revolver Grain Auger End from Mauer Manufacturing" in Farm Industry News (December 17, 2010)*
Pub: Penton Business Media Inc.
Description: Profile of the Revolver Grain Auger End from Mauer Manufacturing is presented. The new design eliminates grain loss/dribble, reduces grain in the next year's crop, and has a greater clearance for combine unloading auger.

21663 ■ *"Press Release: Trimble Introduces CFX-750 Display" in Farm Industry News (January 4, 2011)*
Pub: Penton Business Media Inc.
Description: Trimble is offering a touch screen display called the CFX-750. The new 8-inch full-color display allows farmers to choose the specific guidance, steering and precision agriculture capabilities that best fit their farm's particular needs. The display can be upgraded as business needs change, including the addition of GLONASS capabilities, or the addition of section and rate control for crop inputs such as seed, chemicals and fertilizer.

21664 ■ *"Pressure Growing on Processors" in Farmer's Weekly (March 28, 2008, No. 320)*
Pub: Reed Business Information
Contact: Jeff Greisch, President
Description: Increasing milk prices may be inevitable in order to stop more farmers from leaving the industry and encourage them to produce more milk.

21665 ■ *"Prison Farms are Closing, but the Manure Remains" in Canadian Business (Vol. 83, August 17, 2010, No. 13-14, pp. 9)*
Pub: Rogers Media Ltd.
Ed: Steve Maich. **Description:** The explanation given by Canada's government ministers on planned closure of the prison farms and scrapping of the long form census are designed by mixing of spin, argument and transparent justification. The defense should have been plausible but the ministers could not handle the simple questions about statistics and prison job training with pretense.

21666 ■ *"Pro Livestock Launches Most Comprehensive Virtual Sales Barn for Livestock and Breed Stock" in Benzinga.com (October 29, 2011)*
Pub: Benzinga.com
Ed: Benzinga Staff. **Description:** Pro Livestock Marketing launched the first online sales portal for livestock and breed stock. The firm has designed a virtual sales barn allowing individuals to purchase and sell cattle, swine, sheep, goats, horses, rodeo stock, show animals, specialty animals, semen and embryos globally. It is like an eBay for livestock and will help ranchers and farmers grow.

21667 ■ *"Prosecutors Dish Sordid AIPC Story" in The Business Journal-Serving Metropolitan Kansas City (Vol. 27, September 19, 2008, No. 1)*
Pub: American City Business Journals, Inc.
Ed: Suzanna Stagemeyer. **Description:** Prosecutors in the American Italian Pasta Co.'s accounting fraud case have revealed evidence on the schemes used by then-officers of the company to commit fraud. District attorney John Wood has dubbed the case as the largest corporate fraud lawsuit in the history of the district of Missouri. How AIPC fell from being an industry leader is also discussed.

21668 ■ *"Purdue Agronomist: Consider Costs Before Tilling" in Farm Industry News (November 8, 2011)*
Pub: Penton Business Media Inc.
Ed: Lisa Schluttenhofer. **Description:** Farmers consider soil drainage, fertilizer and planting needs as well as economic thresholds before making tillage decisions, according to a Purdue extension agronomist.

21669 ■ *"The Quality Revolution" in Canadian Business (Vol. 81, November 10, 2008, No. 19, pp. 128)*
Pub: Rogers Media Ltd.
Ed: Andrew Nikiforuk. **Description:** John Volpe believes that the pursuit of quantity of food choices leads to tasteless meals, expanding waistlines, and food poisoning and stresses emphasis on food quality and food security.

21670 ■ *"R&D Will Remain a Key Priority" in Farmer's Weekly (March 28, 2008, No. 320)*
Pub: Reed Business Information
Contact: Jeff Greisch, President
Description: Executives as well as the board of the new Horticultural Development Company (HDC) remain committed to the efficient delivery of research and development, a promotional drive and communications over the coming year.

21671 ■ *"Recipe for Disaster?" in Sacramento Business Journal (Vol. 25, July 4, 2008, No. 18, pp. 1)*
Pub: American City Business Journals, Inc.
Ed: Mark Anderson. **Description:** Restaurateurs are challenged with balancing rising operating costs and what customers are willing to pay for their services. Flour prices in 2008 have increased by 46 percent from April 2007. Other views on the situation, as well as trends, forecasts and statistics on sales, outlook on economic conditions, consumer price index, and the typical split of restaurant revenue, are presented.

21672 ■ *"Red Diesel Cost Sparks a Move to Home-Grown Fuel" in Farmer's Weekly (March 28, 2008, No. 320)*
Pub: Reed Business Information
Contact: Jeff Greisch, President
Description: Due to the rising cost of red diesel, the idea of growing one's own tractor fuel has an undeniable attraction for many farmers. A growing pressure is weighing on engine manufacturers to produce designs that can run on both SVO as well as biodiesel.

21673 ■ *"Red, Pink and More: Cause Marketing Surges as a Prime Tactic to Reach Female Customers" in Marketing to Women (April 2008)*
Pub: EPM Communications Inc.
Contact: Ira Mayer, President
E-mail: imayer@epmcom.com
Description: According to the American Marketing Association, forty percent of women say they are more likely to purchase a product or service if they know a certain amount of the price is being donated directly to a cause or campaign that they believe in supporting.

21674 ■ *"Report: McD's Pepsi Score Best With Young Hispanics" in Brandweek (Vol. 49, April 21, 2008, No. 16, pp. 8)*
Pub: VNU Business Media, Inc.
Ed: Della de Lafuente. **Description:** According to a new report, in order to reach Hispanic Gen Yers, marketing strategists need to understand this demographic's 'bi-dentity,' something which has proved an elusive task to many marketers. Another trend is the emergence of Latinas who have careers, as opposed to just jobs. There is an opportunity to tap this new, young and empowered female market with innovative messaging. Statistical data included.

21675 ■ *"Roll Your Own" in Business North Carolina (Vol. 28, March 2008, No. 3, pp. 66)*
Pub: Business North Carolina
Ed: Amanda Parry. **Description:** Profile of U.S. Flue-Cured Tobacco Growers who process tobacco and make cigarettes. Details of the program are outlined.

21676 ■ *"Roseville Investing Big in Downtown" in Sacramento Business Journal (Vol. 28, September 2, 2011, No. 27, pp. 1)*
Pub: Sacramento Business Journal
Ed: Michael Shaw. **Description:** The city of Roseville, California is planning to invest in downtown development projects. The plan includes a new town square, a venue for a farmers market and an interactive water fountain.

21677 ■ *"Russian Renaissance" in Chicago Tribune (September 22, 2008)*
Pub: McClatchy-Tribune Information Services
Ed: Alex Rodriguez. **Description:** Winemakers from Russia are returning to the craft and quality of winemaking now that they are free from Soviet restraints.

21678 ■ *"Safer Ammonium-Nitrate-Based Fertilizer" in Farm Industry News (Vol. 42, January 1, 2009, No. 1)*
Pub: Penton Media Inc.
Contact: John French, President
Description: Honeywell has patented a new technology which it will use to develop a highly effective, safer ammonium-nitrate-based fertilizer that has a significantly lower potential for explosion.

21679 ■ *"Salary Hike for Managers Reflects Demand"* in *Farmer's Weekly* (March 28, 2008, No. 320)
Pub: Reed Business Information
Contact: Jeff Greisch, President
Description: Discusses the Institute of Agricultural Management and its survey of farm managers' pay and conditions; farm managers are getting paid 25 percent more than in 2003.

21680 ■ *"SCPA Members Seek Senate Support for H.R. 872"* in *Farm Industry News* (May 26, 2011)
Pub: Penton Business Media Inc.
Ed: Forrest Laws. Description: U.S. House of Representatives passed legislation, H.R. 372 the Reducing Regulatory Burdens Act that frees pesticide applicators from having to obtain NPDES permits for applications over or near water.

21681 ■ *"The Second Most Fuel-Efficient Tractor of the Decade: John Deere 8320R"* in *Farm Industry News* (November 10, 2011)
Pub: Penton Business Media Inc.
Description: John Deere's 8320R Tractor was ranked second in the Farm Industry News listing of the top 40 most fuel-efficient tractors of the decade, following the winner, John Deere's 8295R PTO tractor.

21682 ■ *"Seed-Count Labeling"* in *Farm Industry News* (October 20, 2010)
Pub: Penton Business Media Inc.
Ed: Mark Moore. Description: National Conference on Weights and Measures voted to standardize testing methods and procedures that will verify seed-count labeling.

21683 ■ *"Self-Employment in the United States"* in *Montly Labor Review* (Vol. 133, September 2010, No. 9, pp. 17)
Pub: Bureau of Labor Statistics
Description: Self employment in 2009 in the U.S. continued to be more common among men, Whites, Asians, and older workers and in the agriculture, construction, and services industries.

21684 ■ *"Shear Profit"* in *Crain's Cleveland Business* (Vol. 28, October 29, 2007, No. 43, pp. 3)
Pub: Crain Communications, Inc.
Ed: David Bennett. Description: Alpaca farms are becoming a very profitable business for a number of Northeast Ohio entrepreneurs due to the high return on initial investments, tax incentives and the rise in demand for the animals. Ohio leads the country in the number of alpaca farms with roughly one-third located in Northeast Ohio.

21685 ■ *"A Simple Old Reg that Needs Dusting Off"* in *Barron's* (Vol. 88, June 30, 2008, No. 26, pp. 35)
Pub: Dow Jones & Co., Inc.
Ed: Gene Epstein. Description: Senator Joe Lieberman has a point when he accused speculators of inflating the prices of food and fuel futures but introducing legislation to address speculation has an alternative. The senator's committee should instead demand that the Commodity Futures Trading Commission enforce position limits on the maximum number of contracts in a given market per speculative entity.

21686 ■ *"Sleep It Off In a Silo B & B"* in *Chicago Tribune* (December 14, 2008)
Pub: McClatchy-Tribune Information Services
Ed: Bill Daley. Description: Profile of Oregon's Abbey Road Farm bed-and-breakfast which is located on an 82-acre working farm; guests stay in shiny metal farm silos which have been converted into luxury rooms with views of the farm.

21687 ■ *"A Soggy Harvest"* in *Business Journal-Portland* (Vol. 24, October 5, 2007, No. 32, pp. 1)
Pub: American City Business Journals, Inc.
Ed: Robin J. Moody. Description: Vintners in Willamette Valley are facing a tough challenge with a rainy wine harvest season and a delay in the ripening of grapes due to a cool spring and August. Rain decreased the sugar content of grapes and poses a danger with molds. The economic impact of the rainy harvest season in wine making is discussed.

21688 ■ *"Sole Proprietorship Returns, 2008 Part 2"* in *SOI Bulletin* (Vol. 30, Summer 2010, No. 1, pp. 27)
Pub: Government Printing Office
Description: Table of Nonfarm Sole Proprietorships is presented. Statistics are broken down by sector reporting all nonfarm industries as well as agriculture, forestry, hunting and fishing.

21689 ■ *"Spend Wisely on Managing Your Hedgerows"* in *Farmer's Weekly* (March 28, 2008, No. 320)
Pub: Reed Business Information
Contact: Jeff Greisch, President
Ed: Richard Winspear. Description: Discusses the importance of a well-managed hedge which should gradually grow upwards and outwards where eventually it would reach the point when rejuvenation by coppicing or laying was needed to restart the cycle.

21690 ■ *"State Investment Goes Sour"* in *Business Journal Portland* (Vol. 26, December 4, 2009, No. 39, pp. 1)
Pub: American City Business Journals Inc.
Ed: Erik Siemers. Description: Oregon might recoup only $500,000 of a $20 million loan to Vancouver-based Cascade Grain Products LLC. Cascace Grain's ethanol plant in Clatskanie, OR will be put into auction under the supervision of a bankruptcy court.

21691 ■ *"Stone to Run Hickory Farmer's Market"* in *Charlotte Observer* (January 31, 2007)
Pub: Knight-Ridder/Tribune Business News
Ed: Jen Aronoff. Description: Betty Stone has been hired to manage the Downtown Hickory Farmers Market. The market will run from May 5 through October 6, 2007.

21692 ■ *"Stronger Corn? Take It Off Steroids, Make It All Female"* in *Farm Industry News* (December 5, 2011)
Pub: Penton Business Media Inc.
Ed: Brian Wallheimer. Description: Purdue University researcher found that higher improvements in corn crops, and possibly other crops, were yielded when steroids were discontinued.

21693 ■ *"Taking the 'Comprehensive' Out of Immigration Reform"* in *Hispanic Business* (September 2007, pp. 8)
Pub: Hispanic Business
Ed: Patricia Guadalupe. Description: Information about the AgJOBS bill, legislation that would grant legal residency to migrant agricultural workers is discussed.

21694 ■ *"Temporary Measures"* in *Occupational Outlook Quarterly* (Vol. 54, Fall 2010, No. 3, pp. 36)
Pub: U.S. Bureau of Labor Statistics
Description: Data on temporary help services employment from the U.S. Bureau of Labor Statistics suggests good news for all nonfarm workers. The data had been rising steadily for most of 2009.

21695 ■ *"Time to Leave the Party?"* in *Barron's* (Vol. 88, March 24, 2008, No. 12, pp. M16)
Pub: Dow Jones & Company, Inc.
Ed: Andrea Hotter. Description: Prices of commodities such as gold, copper, crude oil, sugar, cocoa, and wheat have fallen from their all-time highs set in the middle of March 2008. Analysts, however, caution that this decline in prices may be temporary, and that a banking crisis may trigger new price rises in commodities.

21696 ■ *"Too Much Precaution About Biotech Corn"* in *Barron's* (Vol. 88, March 17, 2008, No. 11, pp. 54)
Pub: Dow Jones & Company, Inc.
Ed: Mark I. Schwartz. Description: In the U.S., 90 percent of cultivated soybeans are biotech varietals as well as 60 percent of the corn. Farmers have significantly reduced their reliance on pesticides in the growing of biotech corn. Biotech cotton cultivation has brought hundreds of millions of dollars in net financial gains to farmers. The European Union has precluded the cultivation or sale of biotech crops within its border.

21697 ■ *"Top 50 Exporters"* in *Hispanic Business* (Vol. 30, July-August 2008, No. 7-8, pp. 42)
Pub: Hispanic Business, Inc.
Ed: Hildy Medina. Description: Increases in exports revenues reported by food exporters and green companies in a time of economic slowdown in the U.S are described. Food exporters have benefited from the growth of high-volume grocery stores in underdeveloped countries and the German governments' promotion of solar energy has benefited the U.S. solar heating equipment and solar panel manufactures.

21698 ■ *"Top Design Award for Massey Ferguson 7624 Dyna-VT"* in *Farm Industry News* (November 14, 2011)
Pub: Penton Business Media Inc.
Description: Massey Ferguson won top honors for its MF 7624 Dyna-VT as the Golden Tractor for Design award in the 2012 Tractor of the Year competition. The award is presented annually by journalists from 22 leading farming magazines in Europe and manufacturers have to be nominated to enter.

21699 ■ *"Top Worst Weeds in Corn"* in *Farm Industry News* (November 29, 2011)
Pub: Penton Business Media Inc.
Ed: John Pocock. Description: Effective weed control for profitable crops is discussed with information from leading weed scientists from the University of Illinois Extension. It is important for farmers to know what their worst weed is in order to choose the best product, or mix of products, to control them.

21700 ■ *"Trading Down at the Supermarket"* in *Barron's* (Vol. 88, July 14, 2008, No. 28, pp. 36)
Pub: Dow Jones & Co., Inc.
Ed: Alexander Eule. Description: Shares of Ralcorp Holdings are cheap at around $49.95 after slipping 20 percent prior to their acquisition of Post cereals from Kraft. Some analysts believe its shares could climb over 60 percent to $80 as value-seeking consumers buy more private label products.

21701 ■ *"Tri-State to Get New Headquarters"* in *Business Courier* (Vol. 27, October 22, 2010, No. 25, pp. 1)
Pub: Business Courier
Ed: James Ritchie. Description: Hong Kong-based corn processing firm Global Bio-Chem Technology is set to choose Greater Cincinnati, Ohio as a location of its North American headquarters. The interstate access, central location, and low labor and property costs might have enticed Global Bio-Chem to invest in the region. Statistics on Chinese direct investment in U.S. are also presented.

21702 ■ *"The Trouble With $150,000 Wine"* in *Barron's* (Vol. 88, July 7, 2008, No. 27, pp. 33)
Pub: Dow Jones & Co., Inc.
Ed: Orley Ashenfelter. Description: Review of the book, 'The Billionaire's Vinegar: The Mystery of the World's Most Expensive Bottle of Wine,' which discusses vintners along with the marketing and distribution of wine as well as the winemaking industry as a whole.

21703 ■ *"Trouble With Transport"* in *Farmer's Weekly* (March 28, 2008, No. 320)
Pub: Reed Business Information
Contact: Jeff Greisch, President
Description: Profile of Richard Crewe and his wife Jane who farm alongside a main trans-Canadian railway line but keep getting pushed back on their delivery of malt barley.

21704 ■ *"Truffled Ahead: Farms for Rare Delicacy Gain Ground In State"* in *Puget Sound Business Journal* (Vol. 29, December

26, 2008, No. 36)

Pub: American City Business Journals

Ed: Steve Wilhelm. Description: Twenty farmers in Washington started small plots for truffles, which are irregular fungi growing around tree roots and are considered restaurant delicacies. These truffles could generate $35,000 per acre, although they need a decade to mature.

21705 ■ "Turfway Slowing its Gait" in Business Courier (Vol. 26, November 6, 2009, No. 28, pp. 1)

Pub: American City Business Journals, Inc.

Ed: Jon Newberry. Description: Kentucky's Turfway Park will be decreasing its weekly race schedule from five days to three days in the first two months of 2010, and to four days in March 2010. The decision to make reductions in the schedule is attributed to the relocation of thoroughbred racing to states that allow casino gambling. As a result, Turfway Park's resources and purse money would be focused on less days.

21706 ■ "Up on the Farm" in Canadian Business (Vol. 81, October 27, 2008, No. 18, pp. 119)

Pub: Rogers Media Ltd.

Ed: Sean Silcoff. Description: Investing in Saskatchewan's agricultural land is explored. Calvert government's lifting of restrictions on ownership of land have enabled Doug Emsley and Brad Farquhar to invest in farmlands in the area. Emsley and Farquhar lease the farmlands they own, enabling farmers to buy equipment and improve crop yields.

21707 ■ "Up On The Farm" in Canadian Business (Vol. 81, March 31, 2008, No. 5, pp. 23)

Pub: Rogers Media

Ed: John Gray. Description: Agricultural products have outperformed both energy and metal and even the prospect of a global economic slowdown does not seem to hinder its prospects. The Organization for Economic Cooperation and Development sees prices above historic equilibrium levels during the next ten years given that fuel and fertilizers remain high and greater demand from India and China remain steady.

21708 ■ "Versatile's Back" in Farm Industry News (Vol. 42, January 1, 2009, No. 1)

Pub: Penton Media Inc.

Contact: John French, President

Ed: Jodie Wehrspann. Description: Overview of Winnipeg, Manitoba's tractor manufacturer Versatile's strategy to rebrand its tractor segment; the strategy comes a year after Russian Combine Factory Rost-selmash Ltd. bought the majority share of common stock from the Canadian business.

21709 ■ "A Very Good Year for Beer" in Entrepreneur (Vol. 37, October 2009, No. 10, pp. 18)

Pub: Entrepreneur Media Inc.

Ed: Jennie Dorris. Description: Americans are shifting to craft beers, as shown by the almost 6 percent rise in craft beer sales in 2008. Mass-market domestic brand beer grew 0.6 percent while imported beer sales declined by 3.4 percent.

21710 ■ "Virus Threatens WNY Peach Industry" in Business First Buffalo (October 12, 2007, pp. 1)

Pub: American City Business Journals, Inc.

Ed: Thomas Hartley. Description: Plum pox virus, which first appeared in Niagara County, Buffalo, New York in 2005, attacks peaches and there is no known cure to date. The $2 million peach industry in West New York can be destroyed by this virus, which is safe for humans, but makes peaches unmarketable. Other information about plum pox virus and the potential economic damage it can cause is discussed.

21711 ■ "We All Scream for Ice Cream" in Crain's Chicago Business (Vol. 31, April 28, 2008, No. 17, pp. 48)

Pub: Crain Communications, Inc.

Ed: Phuong Ly. Description: Profile of Oberweis' ice cream shops which has expanded its business by delivering dairy products to grocery stores.

21712 ■ "Welch's Uses Taste Strips in Ads" in Marketing to Women (Vol. 21, April 2008, No. 4, pp. 3)

Pub: EPM Communications Inc.

Contact: Ira Mayer, President

E-mail: imayer@epmcom.com

Description: Welch's is positioning its 139-year-old brand in a new and inventive way with a new marketing campaign in which print ads will feature a tamper-evident flavor pouch that contains a dissolving taste strip flavored with Welch's grape juice.

21713 ■ "Welsh Meat Sales on the Rise" in Farmer's Weekly (March 28, 2008, No. 320)

Pub: Reed Business Information

Contact: Jeff Greisch, President

Description: Due, in part, to marketing efforts, retail sales of Welsh lamb and beef rose significantly in the first two months of 2008.

21714 ■ "What'll You Have Tonight?" in Barron's (Vol. 88, July 4, 2008, No. 28, pp. 22)

Pub: Dow Jones & Co., Inc.

Ed: Neil A. Martin. Description: Shares of Diageo could rise by 30 percent a year from June 2008 after it slipped due to U.S. sales worries. The company also benefits from the trend toward more premium alcoholic beverage brands worldwide especially in emerging markets.

21715 ■ "What's In a Name?" in Barron's (Vol. 88, March 17, 2008, No. 11, pp. 7)

Pub: Dow Jones & Company, Inc.

Ed: Alan Abelson. Description: Eliot Spitzer's resignation incidentally caused the stock market to go up by 400 points. The Federal Reserve Board's new Term Securities Lending Facility provides liquidity to the big lenders by funneling $200 billion in the form of 28-day loans of Treasuries. The analysis of Paul Brodsky and Lee Quaintance of QB Partners on the demand for commodities is also discussed.

21716 ■ "Where Canada Meets the World" in Canadian Business (Vol. 80, October 8, 2007, No. 20, pp. 86)

Pub: Rogers Media

Ed: Zena Olijnyk. Description: An overview of facilities within Canada's borders that contributes to the country's economy is presented. The facilities include fishing vessels and seaports. Agencies that regulate the borders such as the Canada Border Services Agency and the Department of Fisheries and Oceans are also presented.

21717 ■ "Which Direction are Herbicides Heading?" in Farm Industry News (October 11, 2011)

Pub: Penton Business Media Inc.

Ed: Jennifer Shike. Description: Currently, one of the best solutions for growers fighting weed resistance may be 2,4-D or other auxin herbicides.

21718 ■ "The Whole Package" in Entrepreneur (Vol. 36, February 2008, No. 2, pp. 24)

Pub: Entrepreneur Media Inc.

Description: Holy Bohn, owner of The Honest Statute, developed an environmentally-friendly packaging for her pet food products. The company hired a packaging consultant and spent $175,000. Big corporations also spend money and plunge into the latest trends in packaging ranging from lighter and flexible to temperature-sensitive labels.

21719 ■ "Why Nestle Should Sell Alcon" in Barron's (Vol. 88, March 17, 2008, No. 11, pp. M12)

Pub: Dow Jones & Company, Inc.

Ed: Sean Walters. Description: Nestle should sell Alcon because Nestle can't afford to be complacent as its peers have made changes to their portfolios to boost competitiveness. Nestle's stake in Alcon and L'Oreal have been ignored by investors and Nestle could realize better value by strengthening its nutrition division through acquisitions.

21720 ■ "The Worm Lady" in Hawaii Business (Vol. 53, October 2007, No. 4, pp. 57)

Pub: Hawaii Business Publishing

Ed: Jolyn Okimoto Rosa. Description: Mindy Jaffe, also known as the worm lady, founded the Waikiki Worm Company in 2004 and sells composting worms. The company, which received much attention from the media, has earned $54,000 in revenue in 2004, and $92,000 and $120,000 in 2005 and 2006, respectively. Jaffe's past ventures and the challenges she is facing with her new company are discussed.

21721 ■ "Wrigley's a Rich Meal for Mars" in Crain's Chicago Business (Vol. 31, May 5, 2008, No. 18, pp. 2)

Pub: Crain Communications, Inc.

Ed: Steven R. Strahler. Description: Mars Inc. will have to manage wisely in order to make their acquisition of Wm. Wrigley Jr. Co. profitable due to the high selling price of Wrigley which far exceeds the industry norm. Statistical data included.

TRADE PERIODICALS

21722 ■ Agri Marketing

Pub: Doane Agricultural Services

Contact: Lynn Henderson, President

E-mail: lhenderson@doane.com

URL(s): www.agrimarketing.com. Released: Monthly Price: $42, U.S. and Canada; $72, U.S. and Canada two years; $70, Other countries; $120, Other countries two years.

21723 ■ Agribusiness: An International Journal

Pub: John Wiley & Sons Inc.

Contact: Stephen M. Smith, President

URL(s): onlinelibrary.wiley.com/journal/10.1002/(-ISSN)1520-6297. Ed: Ronald W. Cotterill. Released: Quarterly Price: $1966, Institutions print only; $2022, Institutions, Canada print only; $2050, Institutions rest of world, print only; $2261, Institutions print with online; $2317, Institutions, Canada print with online; $2345, Institutions rest of world, print with online.

21724 ■ American Journal of Agricultural Economics

Pub: Oxford University Press

URL(s): ajae.oxfordjournals.org/. Ed: Erick Lichtenberg, Jeffrey H. Dorfman. Released: 5/yr. Price: $530, Institutions print & online; $486, Institutions print; $442, Institutions online; €629, Institutions print & online; €576, Institutions print; €524, Institutions online; £511, Institutions, other countries print & online; £469, Institutions, other countries print; £426, Institutions, other countries online.

21725 ■ Arizona Farm Bureau News

Pub: Arizona Farm Bureau Federation

Released: Semimonthly. Price: $25, U.S.. Description: Covers the agricultural industry with an emphasis on Arizona. Specializes in issue specific and regulatory news.

21726 ■ Canola Digest

Pub: Canola Council of Canada

Contact: Kelly Funke, Associate Editor

E-mail: funkek@canola-council.org

Ed: Dave Wilkins, Editor, wilkinsd@canola-council. org. Released: 4x/yr. Price: $35, U.S. and Canada. Description: Provides information on canola and related interests. Recurring features include on farm articles, market reports analysis, news of research, a calendar of events, reports of meetings, and news of educational opportunities, industry news and issues.

21727 ■ Composting News

Pub: McEntee Media Corp.

Ed: Ken McEntee, Editor, ken@recycle.cc. Released: Monthly. Price: $83, individuals; $93, Canada and Mexico; $105, other countries. Description: Covers news and trends in the composting industry. Also reports on compost product prices. Recurring features include letters to the editor, interviews, news of research, a calendar of events, reports of meetings, and notices of publications available.

21728 ■ *The Davlin Report*
Pub: The Davlin Report Inc.
Ed: Andrew Davlin, Jr., Editor, aquaandy@aol.com.
Released: Periodic. **Price:** $39.95, U.S. 4 issues; $59.95, U.S. 8 issues. **Description:** Reports on the aquaculture industry & companies, oil & gas companies & attractive common stocks.

21729 ■ *Farm Bureau News*
Pub: American Farm Bureau Federation
Contact: Bob Stallman, President
Ed: Lynne Finnerty, Editor, lynnef@fb.org. **Released:** Bimonthly, except monthly in August & December. **Price:** $10, individuals $10/year; $30, individuals first class delivery; $48. **Description:** Discusses current legislation, court decisions, trade issues, and the use of innovative production methods. Recurring features include editorials, commentaries and the President's Column.

21730 ■ *Farm Industry News*
Pub: Southwest Farm Press Agribusiness Div.
URL(s): www.farmindustrynews.com/. **Released:** 12/yr.

21731 ■ *Farm and Ranch News*
Pub: Farm & Ranch News
URL(s): www.farmandranchnews.com. **Ed:** George Parker, Jr. **Released:** Monthly **Price:** $12.50, Individuals in Florida; $15, Out of state.

21732 ■ *Fastline--Illinois Farm Edition*
Pub: Fastline
URL(s): www.fastline.com/v100/index.aspx. **Released:** 13/yr. **Price:** $20, Individuals; $35, Two years; $45, Canada and Mexico; $95, Other countries.

21733 ■ *Fastline--Indiana Farm Edition*
Pub: Fastline
URL(s): www.fastline.com/v100/index.aspx. **Released:** 13/yr. **Price:** $40, Individuals 3 years; $35, Two years; $20, Individuals; $45, Canada and Mexico; $95, Other countries.

21734 ■ *Fastline--Iowa Farm Edition*
Pub: Fastline
URL(s): www.fastline.com/v100/index.aspx. **Released:** 13/yr. **Price:** $40, Individuals 3 years; $35, Two years; $20, Individuals; $45, Canada and Mexico; $95, Other countries.

21735 ■ *Fastline--Kansas Farm Edition*
Pub: Fastline
URL(s): www.fastline.com/v100/index.aspx. **Released:** 13/yr. **Price:** $20, Individuals; $35, Two years; $45, Canada and Mexico; $95, Other countries; $40, Individuals 3 years.

21736 ■ *Fastline--Kentucky Farm Edition*
Pub: Fastline
URL(s): www.fastline.com/v100/index.aspx. **Released:** 13/yr. **Price:** $20, Individuals; $35, Two years; C$45, Canada and Mexico; $95, Other countries; $40, Individuals 3 years.

21737 ■ *Fastline--Mid-Atlantic Farm Edition*
Pub: Fastline
URL(s): www.fastline.com/v100/index.aspx. **Released:** 13/yr. **Price:** $20, Individuals; $35, Two years; $45, Canada and Mexico; $95, Other countries; $40, Individuals 3 years.

21738 ■ *Fastline--Mid-South Farm Edition*
Pub: Fastline
URL(s): www.fastline.com/v100/index.aspx. **Released:** 13/yr. **Price:** $20, Individuals; $35, Two years; $45, Canada and Mexico; $95, Other countries; $40, Individuals 3 years.

21739 ■ *Fastline--Minnesota Farm Edition*
Pub: Fastline
URL(s): www.fastline.com/v100/index.aspx. **Released:** 13/yr. **Price:** $20, Individuals; $35, Two years; $45, Canada and Mexico; $95, Other countries.

21740 ■ *Fastline--Missouri Farm Edition*
Pub: Fastline
URL(s): www.fastline.com/v100/index.aspx. **Released:** 13/yr. **Price:** $20, Individuals; $35, Two years; $45, Canada and Mexico; $95, Other countries.

21741 ■ *Fastline--Nebraska Farm Edition*
Pub: Fastline
URL(s): www.fastline.com/v100/index.aspx. **Released:** 13/yr. **Price:** $20, Individuals; $35, Two years; $45, Canada and Mexico; $95, Other countries; $40, Individuals 3 years.

21742 ■ *Fastline--Northeast Farm Edition*
Pub: Fastline
URL(s): www.fastline.com/v100/index.aspx. **Released:** 13/yr. **Price:** $40, Individuals 3 years; $35, Two years; $20, Individuals; $45, Canada and Mexico; $95, Other countries.

21743 ■ *Fastline--Ohio Farm Edition*
Pub: Fastline
URL(s): www.fastline.com/v100/index.aspx. **Released:** 13/yr. **Price:** $20, Individuals; $35, Two years; $45, Canada and Mexico; $95, Other countries; $40, Individuals 3 years.

21744 ■ *Fastline--Oklahoma Farm Edition*
Pub: Fastline
URL(s): www.fastline.com. **Released:** 13/yr. **Price:** $20, Individuals; $35, Two years; $45, Canada and Mexico; $95, Other countries; $40, Individuals 3 years.

21745 ■ *Fastline--Rocky Mountain Farm Edition*
Pub: Fastline
URL(s): www.fastline.com/v100/index.aspx. **Released:** 13/yr. **Price:** $40, Individuals 3 years; $35, Two years; $20, Individuals; $45, Canada and Mexico; $95, Other countries.

21746 ■ *Fastline--Southeast Farm Edition*
Pub: Fastline
URL(s): www.fastline.com/v100/index.aspx. **Released:** 13/yr. **Price:** $20, Individuals; $35, Two years; $45, Canada and Mexico; $95, Other countries.

21747 ■ *Fastline--Tennessee Farm Edition*
Pub: Fastline
URL(s): www.fastline.com/v100/index.aspx. **Released:** 13/yr. **Price:** $40, Individuals 3 years; $35, Two years; $45, Canada and Mexico; $95, Other countries; $20, Individuals.

21748 ■ *Fastline--Texas Farm Edition*
Pub: Fastline
URL(s): www.fastline.com/v100/index.aspx. **Released:** 13/yr. **Price:** $20, Individuals; $35, Two years; $45, Canada and Mexico; $95, Other countries.

21749 ■ *Fastline--Wisconsin Farm Edition*
Pub: Fastline
URL(s): www.fastline.com/. **Released:** 13/yr. **Price:** $40, Individuals 3 years; $35, Two years; $20, Individuals; $45, Canada and Mexico; $95, Other countries.

21750 ■ *Grainews*
Pub: Agricore United
URL(s): www.grainews.ca/. **Ed:** Lyndsey Smith, Dave Bedard. **Released:** 17/yr (plus specials). **Price:** C$41.10, Canada; C$67.27, Two years.

21751 ■ *Journal of International Food and Agribusiness Marketing*
Pub: Routledge Journals Taylor & Francis Group
URL(s): www.tandf.co.uk/journals/WIFA. **Ed:** Erdener Kaynak. **Released:** Quarterly **Price:** $125, Individuals online only; $134, Individuals print + online; $523, Institutions online only; $581, Institutions print + online.

21752 ■ *The Leader for Agriculture*
Pub: NYFEA--The Association for Educating Agricultural Leaders
Ed: Gordon Stone, Editor, gordonstone@nyfea.org. **Released:** Semiannual. **Price:** $15, individuals. **Description:** Serves as a communications link between state associations. Provides information on state and national educational programs, activities, and meetings. Recurring features include interviews, reports of meetings, and news of educational opportunities.

21753 ■ *Pulse Newsletter*
Pub: Saskatchewan Pulse Corp.
Contact: Donald Jaques, Administrator
Released: Bimonthly. **Price:** $10.70, U.S. and Canada. **Description:** Provides information on the Saskatchewan pulse crop development board, as well as research and marketing of pulses. Recurring features include news of research, a calendar of events, and reports of meetings.

TRADE SHOWS AND CONVENTIONS

21754 ■ Mid-South Farm and Gin Supply Exhibit
Southern Cotton Ginners Association
874 Cotton Gin Pl.
Memphis, TN 38106
Ph: (901)947-3104
Fax: (901)947-3103
Co. E-mail: mary.stice@southerncottonginners.org
URL: http://www.southerncottonginners.org
Frequency: Annual. **Audience:** Agribusiness professionals. **Principal Exhibits:** Agricultural equipment, supplies and services. **Dates and Locations:** , Memphis Cook Convention Center.

21755 ■ Spokane Ag Expo
Spokane Regional Chamber of Commerce
AG Bureau
801 W. Riverside, Ste. 100
Spokane, WA 99201
Ph: (509)624-1393
Free: 800-776-5263
Fax: (509)747-0077
Co. E-mail: info@chamber.spokane.net
URL: http://www.spokanechamber.org
Contact: Rich Hadley, Chief Executive Officer
E-mail: rhadley@greaterspokane.org
URL(s): www.agshow.org. **Price:** $12, adult; $8, youth 12-18 years old; children under 12. **Frequency:** Annual. **Audience:** Farmers, ranchers, agribusiness professionals, and general public. **Principal Exhibits:** Farm machinery, technology, and services. **Telecommunication Services:** moleary@chamber.spokane.net.

21756 ■ VIV Poultry Yutav
FGS Fuarcilik As.
Celiktepe 4.
80650 Istanbul, Turkey
Ph 90 212 2828808
Fax 90 212 2812713
Co. E-mail: fgsfair@fgsfair.com.tr
URL(s): www.hkf-fairs.com. **Frequency:** Annual. **Principal Exhibits:** Poultry farming, breeding, feed, and processing.

21757 ■ World AgExpo
International Agri-Center, Inc.
4450 S. Laspina St.
Tulare, CA 93274-9539
Ph: (559)688-1751
Free: 800-999-9186
Fax: (559)686-5065
Co. E-mail: info@farmshow.org
URL: http://www.farmshow.org
Contact: Jerry Sinift, Chief Executive Officer
E-mail: jerry@farmshow.org
URL(s): www.worldagexpo.com. **Frequency:** Annual. **Audience:** Farmers, dairymen and international buyers. **Principal Exhibits:** Agricultural equipment, supplies and services. **Telecommunication Services:** info@farmshow.org.

CONSULTANTS

21758 ■ Adayana Healthcare Group
3905 Vincennes Rd., Ste. 402
Indianapolis, IN 46268
Ph: (317)415-0500
Free: 800-285-8859
Fax: (317)415-0501
Co. E-mail: editor@adayana.com
URL: http://www.adayana.com
Contact: Tim Penny, President
Scope: Provider of custom designed training programs in the following areas: sales, sales management, coaching, market research, strategic planning, and mergers and acquisition consulting. Also provides technical training and product launch support in the areas of agricultural inputs, equipment, distribution and technology. **Founded:** 2001. **Seminars:** Strategies for Meeting the Expectations of Tomorrow's Workforce, Feb, 2010; Fundamentals of Agriculture; Managing Target Marketing Strategies; Developing a Marketing Mindset; Building a Value Proposition; Defining, Delivering, and Capturing Value; Handling Objections and Closing the Sale; Territory Management and Key Account Planning; Motivation and Performance Management. **Telecommunication Services:** rkim@adayana.com.

21759 ■ Agland Investment Services Inc.
900 Larkspur Landing Cir., Ste. 205
Larkspur, CA 94939
Ph: (415)461-5820
Fax: (415)461-5821
Co. E-mail: agland@aglandinvest.com
URL: http://www.aglandinvest.com
Contact: William P. Mott, President
E-mail: wmott@aglandinvest.com
Scope: An agribusiness consulting and investment company which provides a wide range of economic, marketing, technical and investment consultation to agricultural producers, agribusiness companies and government agencies in the Western United States and in many countries around the world. The firm tends to concentrate on high-value specialty crops, including fruits, vegetables and cut flowers. **Founded:** 1976. **Seminars:** Agribusiness Training Programs; Financial Analysis Training.

21760 ■ Agpro Inc.
859 Airport Rd.
Paris, TX 75462-7151
Ph: (903)785-5531
Free: 800-527-1030
Fax: (903)784-7895
Co. E-mail: info@agprousa.com
URL: http://www.agprousa.com
Contact: Joann Gribble, President
Scope: Offers agricultural engineering design consultation for animal raising facilities including dairies, beef feedlots, swine operations and embryo transplant facilities. Services include land utilization, plot plans, building design, equipment selection, integration with other farm and commercial activities, pollution control systems, genetic engineering systems and computer applications. Also offers computer control and automation consultation, as well as consultation on waste management and control for food processing plants. Expertise in dairy, swine manure handling and their processing needs. **Founded:** 1962. **Publications:** "PD Exclusive: Progressivedairy.com," Jul, 2008; "ANM: Industry Insights," Mar, 2007.

21761 ■ Agri-Business Consultants Inc.
911 Edison Ave.
Lansing, MI 48910-3339
Ph: (517)482-7506
Fax: (517)482-7506
Contact: Mark A. Otto, President
E-mail: maotto@ameritech.net
Scope: Agricultural consultants providing fertilizer recommendations, crop protection recommendations, soil fertility and crop protection consulting, irrigation scheduling, educational sessions, contract research and expert witness services. Industries served: Farmers and ag chemical companies. **Founded:** 1983.

21762 ■ AgriCapital Corp.—William Goodbar
Agricapital
1410 Broadway, Ste. 1802
New York, NY 10018-5018
Ph: (212)944-9500
Fax: (212)944-9525
Co. E-mail: info@agricapital.com
URL: http://www.agricapital.com
Contact: David J. Repking, Vice President
E-mail: repking@agricapital.com
Scope: Provider of investment banking services for agribusiness clients in the United States and abroad, including financial consulting, debt and equity placements and joint ventures, and mergers and acquisitions. Industries served: Agribusiness and food companies. **Founded:** 1983. **Publications:** "The New Geogolitics of food," 2012; "What formers Can Teach Harvard Business School," 2012; "Seed world"; "Strategic Agribusiness Review," Dec, 2003; "Yield," Jun, 2003; "Feed Management," May, 2002. **Seminars:** Thoughts on Private Equity and Agribusiness, Sep, 2009; Capital Markets and the Crop Input Sector, Oct, 2006; Views on the Crop Protection Industry, Sep, 2005; Mergers and Acquisitions in the US Food and Agribusiness Industry, Sep, 2002.

21763 ■ Agricultural Consulting Services Inc.
1634 Monroe Ave.
Rochester, NY 14618-9769
Ph: (585)473-1100
Free: 877-310-1100
Fax: (877)245-2200
Co. E-mail: acs@acsoffice.com
URL: http://www.acsoffice.com
Contact: Richard F. Wildman, President
E-mail: rwildman@acsoffice.com
Scope: Provider of farm business management services including business and economic analysis, computer hardware and software installation and training, and enterprise budgets and analysis. Also offers crop production management, monitoring, and advises in the areas of crop nutrition, pest management, weed control, tillage practices, and irrigation scheduling. Environmental work includes complete analytical and monitoring services for soil, wastewater, sludge, and groundwater. Serves farms and agribusiness. **Founded:** 1983. **Publications:** "Forage - Timing of First Cutting," May, 2009.

21764 ■ Agricultural Engineering Associates (AEA)
1000 Promontory Dr.
Uniontown, KS 66779
Ph: (620)756-1000
Free: 800-499-5893
Fax: (620)756-4600
Co. E-mail: johng@agengineering.com
URL: http://www.agengineering.com
Contact: John A. George, President
E-mail: johng@agengineering.com
Scope: Agricultural engineering consultants offering guidance on the design of swine production facilities, beef feedlots, dairy facilities, waste management systems, soil and water conservation design and resource development including watershed planning, dam design and irrigation supply dam design, grain and feed storage, drying and processing facilities, irrigation system evaluation and design, rural water district system design, land leveling design for irrigation and drainage and land surveying. Industries served: production and commercial agriculture, research, demonstration and test facilities, government agencies and in-house materials testing laboratories. **Founded:** 1974.

21765 ■ Agricultural Investment Associates Inc.
1000 Skokie Blvd., Ste. 358
Wilmette, IL 60091
Ph: (847)251-8822
Fax: (847)251-8876
Co. E-mail: johncottingham@att.net
Contact: William B. Sayre, President
Scope: Investment consultant to domestic and foreign institutions, corporations and individuals covering investments in farms, ranches and agri businesses. Services include feasibility studies, appraisals, management, analysis and negotiations. **Founded:** 1982.

21766 ■ Agrisoft - CMC—CMC Inc.
9130 Anaheim Pl., Ste. 120
Rancho Cucamonga, CA 91730
Ph: (909)980-5338
Fax: (909)987-3154
Co. E-mail: info@agrisoftsolutions.com
URL: http://www.agrisoftcmc.com
Contact: Anthony Barton, President
Scope: Provider of turnkey software and hardware solutions for the animal agricultural industry. Other software solutions include business process consulting, custom application development, software installation and maintenance and equipment configuration. Industries served: chicken, egg, turkey and swine industries. **Founded:** 1985. **Publications:** *C.M.C. Feed Mill Interface; C.M.C. General Accounting; Poultry and Egg Production and Accounting System; CMC Pullet Flock Records; CMC Layer Flock Records; CMC Flock Cost Sheets System; CMC Flock Projection System; CMC Flock Modeling System; Unprocessed Egg Inventory System; CMC Egg Gradeout System; CMC Integrated Poultry Accounting; CMC Integrated Egg Industry Accounting; CMC Perishable Distribution System; CMC Purchase Order System; CMC Inventory/Processing System; CMC Order Entry/Pricing System; CMC Accounts Receivable System; CMC Dispatch; CMC Trucking System; CMC EDI Interface System; CMC Payroll; CMC Accounts Payable System; CMC General Ledger; CMC Fixed Asset Depreciation Systems; CMC Commodity Purchase System; CMC Growout Flock Records; CMC Breeder Flock Records; C.M.C. Poultry and Egg Distribution/Processing System.* **Seminars:** AgriSoft CMCs Client Seminar, Oct, 2008. **Special Services:** Agrisoft ERP; Agrisoft AIM.

21767 ■ AgriSolutions Inc.—Apogee Solutions Corp.
31832 Delhi Rd.
Brighton, IL 62012
Ph: (618)372-3000
Free: 888-486-2208
Fax: (618)372-4000
Co. E-mail: internetmail@agrisolutions.com
URL: http://www.agrisolutions.com
Contact: Allen Lash, President
E-mail: alash@agrisolutions.com
Scope: Offers agricultural consulting services including business planning and growth, historical performance analysis, strategic planning assistance, planning for financial success, CFO financial assistance, project consulting, entity consolidation, credit sourcing, budgeting, business succession, and estate and retirement planning. Other services provided are benchmarking comparisons, accounting and tax services and education and training to manage businesses. Serves the agricultural sector including farmers, non-farm entrepreneurs, financial institutions and agribusinesses. Clients range from local farmers to multinational agribusinesses. **Founded:** 1967. **Telecommunication Services:** info@agrisolutions.com. **Special Services:** AgManager,AgriSolutions.

21768 ■ Agvise Laboratories Inc.
PO Box 510
Northwood, ND 58267-0510
Ph: (701)587-6010
Fax: (701)587-6013
Co. E-mail: agvise@polarcomm.com
URL: http://www.agvise.com
Contact: Robert Deutsch, President
E-mail: agvise@polarcomm.com
URL(s): www.agviselabs.com. **Scope:** Provides agriculture testing services such as soil testing and plant analysis including, GLP and Non-GLP analysis to crop consultants, fertilizer retailers, producers, engineering firms and pesticide registration companies. **Founded:** 1976. **Publications:** "Manure and Nematode Test Results on the Internet"; "Sampling and Submitting Livestock Waste for Analysis"; "Precision Ag Helpers"; "New Minnesota Corn Nitrogen Fertilizer Guidelines"; "Zone Nutrient Management in Sugar beet Production"; "Reducing Soybean Cyst Nematode with Crop Rotation"; "Fall Strip Tillage: More and More Each Year"; "High Soil Nitrates Fol-

lowing Drought!"; "High Soil pH-Can we Fix this Problem?". **Seminars:** Precision Ag-Update 2009, 2009; Rock Rolling-Is It For You?, 2009; Seed Placed Fertilizer Limits, 2009; Precision Soil Testing, 2008; Soil Fertility Seminars; Tornado Tale; Compaction Update; Delta Yield; Phosphorus for Soybean; Soil Amendments; Strip Tillage Update; Sulfur for Corn.

21769 ■ Ascheman Associates Inc.
2921 Beverly Dr.
Urbandale, IA 50322-4255
Ph: (515)276-7371
Contact: Robert E. Ascheman, President
E-mail: rascheman@aol.com
Scope: Provides consulting, expert witness and related agribusiness services to agricultural-oriented businesses including: producers; agrochemical; fertilizer, seed and equipment companies; the insurance industry; the legal profession and government agencies. **Founded:** 1979. **Seminars:** Value of Grid Soil Sampling; Liming by the Grid System; Integrated Crop Management Services.

21770 ■ Buzz Me
5206 Pear Butte Dr.
Yakima, WA 98901-1667
Ph: (509)452-6555
Fax: (509)452-6555
Contact: Dr. Daniel F. Mayer, Owner
Scope: Provider of consulting services dealing with entomology (insects). Provides pest control recommendations, research with new pesticides and chemical testing and expert witness services. **Founded:** 1980. **Publications:** "Pollinator Protection: A Bee and Pesticide Handbook," Wicwas Press.

21771 ■ The Canada Co.—C.C. Canada-B.I.C.
819 Mill St.
Camden, SC 29020-4416
Ph: (803)432-9780
Fax: (803)432-0232
Co. E-mail: cclandman@aol.com
URL: http://www.carolinalandandfarms.com
Contact: Clarence C. Canada, President
E-mail: cclandman@bellsouth.net
Scope: Provider of consulting services in forest management and appraisal. Services include financial counsel especially in the agricultural field and timberland; and aid in securing loans with major insurance companies for agricultural and agribusiness loans. Also advises large corporations, as well as individuals, on real estate investments and acquisitions. Works with government agencies. **Founded:** 1957. **Telecommunication Services:** cclandman@bellsouth.net.

21772 ■ Clark Consulting International Inc.—CCI Marketing
435 Root St.
Park Ridge, IL 60068-0068
Ph: (847)836-5100
Fax: (847)589-8889
Co. E-mail: warren.clark@ccimarketing.com
URL: http://www.ccimarketing.com
Contact: Warren E. Clark, Chief Executive Officer
E-mail: warren.clark@ccimarketing.com
Scope: Multipurpose agri marketing communications consulting firm including public relations; market research; advertising and direct mail expertise. Serves the seed; chemical; machinery; computer and agricultural futures industries. Internet promotion and product marketing in agriculture. **Founded:** 1986. **Seminars:** Managing Your Consulting Practice Using Computers; Winning Ag PR Programs That Produce Results; Ag Targeted Direct Mail Niche Marketing. **Special Services:** AgPR online.

21773 ■ Custom Forestry Inc.
16798 Claridon Troy Rd.
Burton, OH 44021-9606
Ph: (440)834-1680
Fax: (440)834-1680
Co. E-mail: lynneebel@hotmail.com
Contact: Ralph Hershberger, Owner
Scope: Offers forestry consulting services that include forest management, timber sales, valuations, timber trespass valuations and litigation, advice on federal assistance programs, Christmas tree planta-

tion management, multiple use land management, shelter-belts, silviculture, and insect management. **Founded:** 1986.

21774 ■ DPRA Inc.
200 Research Dr.
Manhattan, KS 66503
Ph: (785)539-3565
Fax: (785)539-5353
Co. E-mail: info@dpra.com
URL: http://www.dpra.com
Contact: Dr. Jim Micak, President
Scope: Consultants on a variety of environmental problems and situations. Experience includes agriculture, agribusiness, water pollution control, and hazardous and municipal waste management. Activities emphasize litigation support, data management, and information services, as well as international programs. Serves private industries as well as government agencies. **Founded:** 1961. **Telecommunication Services:** mary.carter@dpra.com; joe.pittari@dpra.com. **Special Services:** TALIRA®.

21775 ■ Eastern Laboratory Service Associates
517 N George St.
York, PA 17404-2765
Ph: (717)846-4953
Fax: (717)846-4986
Contact: T. F. Lagattuta, Director
Scope: Provider of technical counsel on chemical and microbiological testing, evaluation and quality control services primarily for environmental, agribusiness, feed industry and food manufacturing. Offers consultation, advisory services, research and development on technical problems, new product formulation, and product or process improvement. Also performs general testing of refrigerants, food products, solid waste, water and waste water for compliance with EPA, DER, FDA and other governmental agencies. **Founded:** 1959.

21776 ■ Trenna R. Grabowski CPA Ltd.
15 N 12th St.
DuBois, IL 62831
Ph: (618)787-4430
Fax: (618)787-4460
Co. E-mail: trenna@agcpa.net
Contact: Trenna R. Grabowski, Owner
E-mail: grabeau@midwest.net
URL(s): www.theagcpa.net. **Scope:** Offers financial management, strategic planning, and budgeting for agribusiness and small and family-owned firms. Heavily involved in tax planning and research. Consulting on choosing hardware and software for agribusiness. Related experience in personal financial planning, tax planning, and projections. Speaking and teaching a specialty, seminars, workshops, and conference presentations available. **Founded:** 1985. **Publications:** "Refund Anticipation Loans-Do They Make Sense," Jan, 2010; "Employee Turnover and Corporate Culture," Jan, 2010; "Stock Market: A New Year Sparks Optimism," Jan, 2010; "Tax Organizers-Friend or Foe," Jan, 2010. **Seminars:** Agribusiness Tax Seminar; Tax Planning; Incorporating the Farm; Alternative Forms of Business Organization: Estate and Financial Planning; The Farm Business Plan.

21777 ■ J.H. Hare & Associates Ltd.—HYPER-EGG
270 Roslyn Rd., Ste. 1
Winnipeg, MB, Canada R3L 0H3
Ph: (204)477-0066
Free: 800-661-4273
Fax: (204)488-0051
URL: http://www.hyper-egg.com
Contact: Marina Bondareva, Controller
Scope: Agribusiness management consultants with extensive experience in Animal nutrition and feed formulation, agri marketing, technical services to agribusiness, agricultural promotion, and sales and sales training. Serves the agriculture and food and beverage industries, as well as government agencies. **Founded:** 1970. **Special Services:** X-CEL; X-Change; X-Change Plus.

21778 ■ Indiana Design Consortium Inc. (IDC)
416 Main St.
Lafayette, IN 47902
Ph: (765)423-5469
Fax: (765)423-4440
Co. E-mail: idc@idc-marketing.com
URL: http://www.idc-marketing.com
Contact: Robert J. Kennedy, President
E-mail: robert@idc-marketing.com
Scope: Provider of marketing and marketing communications services for industrial, service oriented, and agribusiness clients. Also involved in industrial product design for industry and agribusiness. **Founded:** 1972.

21779 ■ INTRANCO Inc.
1825 I St. NW, Ste. 400
Washington, DC 20006-5403
Ph: (202)429-6820
Contact: William Lake, President
Scope: Provider of management consulting for agribusinesses, primarily enterprises in the Third World. Works with private entrepreneurs and government-sponsored institutions. Has experience with livestock, fruits, vegetables, field crops, small animals, fisheries and poultry. Engages in the international trade of agricultural equipment, machinery and raw products. Industries served: Food and feed industries and government agencies. **Founded:** 1985. **Seminars:** Mold Inhibitors in the 1990 Decade; Agribusiness in West Africa - Is It Possible?; Poultry in Nigeria - The Challenge.

21780 ■ McKinnon, Allen & Associates Western Ltd.
1115-46th Ave. SE
Calgary, AB, Canada T2G 2A5
Ph: (403)243-4345
Contact: S. Douglas Allen, President
Scope: The firms multidisciplinary work team provides independent opinions and practical solutions to a variety of problems in the areas of agribusiness, farm and ranch management, agricultural environmental consulting and rural land use. Specific areas of expertise are as follows: Financial advisory consulting, agricultural environmental monitoring, general agricultural management consulting, economic evaluation, land use planning, land valuation, surface rights disputes and expropriations, farm management for absentee owners, and damage claims. **Founded:** 1960. **Publications:** "Observations of pH in field soils near a sour gas plant in Alberta," Springer Netherlands, 1983.

21781 ■ Micro-Macro International Inc. (MMI)
183 Paradise Blvd., Ste. 108
Athens, GA 30607
Ph: (706)548-4557
Free: 800-837-8664
Fax: (706)548-4891
Co. E-mail: pamaaron@mmilabs.com
URL: http://www.mmilabs.com
Contact: Harry A. Mills, President
E-mail: harrymills@mmilabs.com
Scope: Offers consultation on agricultural production field, container, greenhouse and hydroponic systems. Provides analytical services for the analysis of water, waste water, soil, plant tissue and other biological substances for their element content. Industries served: Agricultural producers, research institutes and individuals, fertilizer manufacturers and government agencies. **Founded:** 1988. **Publications:** "Plant Analysis Handbook," 1991; "Diagnosis and Recommendation Integrated Systems (Dris)"; "Kjeldahl Method for Nitrogen Determination"; "Plant Nutrition Manual". **Seminars:** Techniques of soil testing and plant analysis; Laboratory instruction on methods of analysis. **Telecommunication Services:** ara@mmilabs.com; lara@mmilabs.com.

21782 ■ Miller Agricultural Consulting Services
10967 County Road 19
Lawton, ND 58345-9661

Ph: (701)655-3591
Contact: Judith Miller, Principal
Scope: Agricultural consultant working with clients in the area of machine design and safety as it pertains to machines used in the production of agricultural crops. Crops include wheat, barley, corn, sunflowers, sugar beets, and potatoes. Special emphasis on farm safety issues, crop drying systems, and forensic evaluation. **Founded:** 1976.

21783 ■ J. Stewart Murray Agency—Murray J Stewart Agency
639 Borebank St.
Winnipeg, MB, Canada R3N 1G1
Ph: (204)488-3885
Co. E-mail: smurray6@shaw.ca
Contact: Stewart J. Murray, President
E-mail: smurray6@shaw.ca
Scope: Marketing and sales consultants for agri-industrial automotive. Industries served: Agriculture-agribusiness, industrial supply trades and government agencies in Canada. **Founded:** 1989.

21784 ■ G.V. Olsen Associates
123 Picketts Ridge Rd.
Redding, CT 06896
Ph: (203)770-3433
Fax: (203)938-4186
Contact: Gustav Olsen, President
E-mail: gusolsen@hotmail.com
Scope: Provides agribusiness research, analysis and report writing services, focusing on farm input products such as seed, fertilizer, chemicals, and machinery, as well as production, storage, transportation, and marketing of food and fiber products. Also identifies and evaluates new market and product opportunities. Industries served: Agribusiness, biotechnology, food and agriculture. **Founded:** 1979.

21785 ■ Pest Pros Inc.—Data Associates
10086 1st St.
Plainfield, WI 54966
Ph: (715)335-4046
Fax: (715)335-4746
Co. E-mail: pestpros@uniontel.net
URL: http://www.pestprosinc.com
Contact: Randy M. Van Haren, President
Scope: Offers agricultural consulting involving fertility and pesticide recommendations, soil microbe assay and contract research. **Founded:** 1984. **Telecommunication Services:** pestpros@wrc.coop.

21786 ■ SEA-ARM Consulting Associates—Sea-Arm Co.
640 Line St.
Hollister, CA 95023
Ph: (831)637-1468
Contact: Samuel Armstrong, President
Scope: Offers expertise regarding financial restructuring (including start-ups and spin-offs) and technology transfer, relating to agriculture production, processing and marketing. Special emphasis on cooperatives. Industries served: Agriculture, agribusiness, cooperatives and government. **Founded:** 1980. **Seminars:** Starting a New Business; Strawberry Production, Organic farm productions, Marketing.

21787 ■ Sobek Engineering
51492 Sobek Rd. E
Edwall, WA 99008-9703
Ph: (509)236-2371
Fax: (509)236-2426
Co. E-mail: sobekeng@aol.com
Contact: Irvin G. Sobek, President
Scope: Provider of consulting engineering service in the food processing field and associated agribusiness areas. Has served in the frozen food, flour milling, and freeze-drying areas, as well as agricultural and industrial accident investigation. Also conducts noise surveys and noise abatement engineering. **Founded:** 1977.

21788 ■ Southern Plantations Group Inc.
2410 Westgate Dr., Ste. 101
Albany, GA 31708
Ph: (229)439-0012

Fax: (229)883-8881
Co. E-mail: spg@splantations.com
URL: http://www.splantations.com
Contact: Joseph H. Marshall, President
E-mail: jmarshall@splantations.com
Scope: Provider of appraisal and counseling services for investors and lenders in farm land, timberland and agribusiness projects across the Southern U.S.; and farm planning, budgeting, management, and accounting services for farmers near its area of activity. Specific services include establishing and reviewing investment criteria, investment selection and negotiation, alternative investment analysis and review, management and operations audits, appraisals, problem investments, and management of property investment and divestment. Industries served: investors, lenders, government agencies, agribusinesses in production, agriculture, input, and marketing sectors. U.S., southeast Asia and Latin America. **Founded:** 1978.

21789 ■ Sterling Executive Counselors Inc.
516 S Pokegama Ave.
Grand Rapids, MN 55744-3838
Ph: (218)326-4421
Free: 888-326-4421
Fax: (218)326-4430
Contact: Marsha Kelly, President
Scope: Public affairs and management consultants offering reputation and issue management, public relations, and government relations counsel. Industries served: agribusiness, pet, gaming, forest products, natural resources and energy. **Founded:** 1999.

21790 ■ Ralph E. Williams & Associates
c/o Purdue University, 901 W State St.
West Lafayette, IN 47907
Ph: (765)494-4560
Fax: (765)494-2152
Co. E-mail: rew@purdue.edu
Contact: Dr. Ralph E. Williams, President
E-mail: ralph_williams@entm.purdue.edu
Scope: Offers services in forensic entomology, use of insects in crime scene investigations. Serves prosecuting attorneys, law enforcement agencies, state and local coroners and medical examiners. Also provides training and consulting services in livestock and poultry pest control and public health pest control. Serves agribusiness, local and state public health agencies and individuals. **Founded:** 1984. **Publications:** "Modern Gas Processing Methods," Artech House Publishers, Jul, 1990. **Seminars:** Forensic Entomology Training Session; Livestock and Poultry Pest Management.

COMPUTERIZED DATABASES

21791 ■ *AGRICOLA Database*
Abraham Lincoln Bldg.
10301 Baltimore Ave.
Beltsville, MD 20705
Ph: (301)504-5755
Fax: (301)504-6927
Co. E-mail: webmaster@nal.usda.gov
URL: http://www.nalusda.gov
Availability: Online: ProQuest LLC - Dialog; U.S. Department of Agriculture - National Agricultural Library; EBSCO Publishing; STN International; ProQuest LLC - RefWorks-COS; Wolters Kluwer Health - Ovid. CD-ROM: Wolters Kluwer Health - Ovid. **Type:** Bibliographic.

LIBRARIES

21792 ■ Albany Historical Society, Inc. - Library/Special Collections
c/o Doyle Bechtelheimer
415 Grant
Sabetha, KS 66534
Ph: (913)284-3446
URL: http://www.albanydays.org
Contact: Daryl Bechtelheimer, President
Scope: Agricultural equipment, railroads one-room schools. **Services:** Library open to the public. **Founded:** 1965. **Holdings:** 200 books.

21793 ■ Alberta Agriculture and Food - Crop Diversification Centre South - Branch Library
301 Horticultural Station Road East
Brooks, AB, Canada T1R 1E6
Ph: (403)362-1308
Fax: (403)362-1306
Co. E-mail: shelley.barkley@gov.ab.ca
URL: http://www1.agric.gov.ab.ca/$department/deptdocs.nsf/all/opp4386
Contact: Shelley Barkley, Coordinator, Information
Scope: Plants, pathology, horticulture, entomology, special crops. **Services:** Interlibrary loan; copying; library open to the public. **Holdings:** Figures not available.

21794 ■ Alberta Agriculture, Food and Rural Development - Business Management Innovations Branch Library
201 Provincial Bldg.
5030-50 St.
Olds, AB, Canada T4H 1S1
Ph: (403)556-4328
Fax: (403)556-7545
URL: http://www.agric.gov.ab.ca/app21/rtw/index.jsp
Scope: Agriculture, economics, technology, agricultural economics, farm management, finance, computer. **Services:** Interlibrary loan; copying; library open to public for reference use. **Holdings:** Figures not available.

21795 ■ Booz Allen Hamilton - Research Services and Information Center
225 W. Wacker Dr., Ste. 2270
Chicago, IL 60606
Ph: (312)419-8100
Fax: (312)578-4667
URL: http://www.boozallen.com
Contact: Dr. Ralph Shrader, Chairman
Scope: Management, agribusiness, finance, marketing, manufacturing, retailing, information management, consumer products, healthcare, telecommunications, food retailing, consulting, electronic commerce. **Services:** Interlibrary loan; Center not open to the public. **Founded:** 1965. **Holdings:** 5000 books; client reports; company Annual reports. **Subscriptions:** 300 serials.

21796 ■ Canada Agriculture and Agri-Food - Dairy and Swine Research and Development Centre Lennoxville - Canadian Agriculture Library—Bibliotheque Canadienne de l'Agriculture - Lennoxville.
2000 College St.
Sherbrooke, QC, Canada J1M 0C8
Ph: (819)780-7202
Fax: (819)564-4974
Co. E-mail: francine.bernard@agr.gc.ca
URL: http://www4.agr.gc.ca
Contact: Josee Toulouse, Section Chief
Scope: Dairy cattle, pigs. **Services:** Interlibrary loan; copying; library provides limited on-site consultation to the public. **Holdings:** 5000 books; 6000 e-books. **Subscriptions:** 3750 journals and other serials. **Telecommunication Services:** jacques.surprenant@agr.gc.ca.

21797 ■ Canadian Grain Commission Library—Commission canadienne des graines.
303 Main St., Rm. 801
Winnipeg, MB, Canada R3C 3G8
Ph: (204)983-2770
Free: 1 866 317 4289
Fax: (204)983-2751
Co. E-mail: library-bibliotheque@grainscanada.gc.ca
URL: http://www.grainscanada.gc.ca
Contact: Dawn Bassett, Director, Library Services
Scope: Cereal chemistry, cereals, oilseeds, grain industry and trade, baking, brewing, milling. **Services:** Interlibrary loan; copying; SDI; Library open to the public for reference use only. **Founded:** 1972. **Holdings:** 5000 books; 10,000 bound periodical volumes; 1000 pamphlets; 1500 reports. **Subscriptions:** 200 journals and other serials; 10 newspapers. **Telecommunication Services:** contact@grainscanada.gc.ca.

21798 ■ Cargill, Incorporated Information Center—Cargill Infocenter.
PO Box 9300
Minneapolis, MN 55440-9300
Ph: (952)742-6498
Free: 800-227-4455
Fax: (952)742-6062
Co. E-mail: peter_sidney@cargill.com
URL: http://www.cargill.com
Contact: Peter Sidney, Assistant Vice President
Scope: Food ingredients and systems, grain storage and handling, commodity trading, agribusiness, finance, marketing, biochemistry, hybrid corn breeding and genetics, animal feeding and nutrition, vegetable oil processing and chemistry, agricultural and food products, market research, food retailing and food service, consumers. **Services:** Center not open to the public. **Founded:** 1946. **Holdings:** 4500 books; 1100 market research reports (total collection is 70 percent electronic). **Subscriptions:** 650 journals and other serials and newspapers (and over 50 percent online).

21799 ■ Delaware Valley College of Science and Agriculture - Joseph Krauskopf Memorial Library
700 E. Butler Ave.
Doylestown, PA 18901-2697
Ph: (215)489-2953
Co. E-mail: library@delval.edu
URL: http://www.delval.edu/library
Contact: Peter Kupersmith, Director, Library Services
Scope: Agribusiness, agronomy, large animal science, biology, communication, computer and business information systems, criminal justice administration, dairy science, English literature, equine science, food industry, horticulture, ornamental horticulture, chemistry, business administration, small animal science, turf management, wildlife conservation, zoo biology. **Services:** Interlibrary loan; copying; Library open to the public for reference use only. **Founded:** 1896. **Holdings:** 55,000 volumes; 4520 bound periodical volumes; 1525 reels of microfilm; 50,650 microfiche. **Subscriptions:** 13,000 journals. **Telecommunication Services:** peter.kupersmith@delval.edu.

21800 ■ Illinois Agricultural Association - Illinois Farm Bureau Information Research Center
1701 Towanda Ave.
Box 2901
Bloomington, IL 61701
Ph: (309)557-2534
Fax: (309)557-3185
Co. E-mail: eculver@iflb.org
URL: http://www.ilfb.org/
Contact: Ellen Culver, Director
Scope: Agriculture - economics, marketing, cooperatives, management, insurance, the environment. **Services:** Interlibrary loan; copying; subscriptions; Internet training; abstracting; library open to the public for reference use only. **Founded:** 1957. **Holdings:** 5000 volumes; 100 microforms; 500 aud o/visual materials. **Subscriptions:** 500 journals and other serials; 7 newspapers.

21801 ■ International Fertilizer Development Center - Travis P. Hignett Memorial Library
PO Box 2040
Muscle Shoals, AL 35662
Ph: (256)381-6600
Fax: (256)381-7408
Co. E-mail: cbennett@ifdc.org
URL: http://www.ifdc.org/About/Library
Contact: Cheryl Bennett, Librarian
Scope: Fertilizers, agricultural economics, nutrient management, agribusiness, training. **Services:** Interlibrary loan; literature searching Library not open to the public; document delivery. **Founded:** 1977. **Holdings:** 20,000 books; 4365 bound periodical volumes; 468 pamphlets; 337 AV programs; 20,000 patents. **Subscriptions:** 200 journals and other serials. **Telecommunication Services:** general@ifdc.org.

21802 ■ International Food Policy Research Institute Library
2033 K St., NW
Washington, DC 20006
Ph: (202)862-5600
Fax: (202)467-4439
Co. E-mail: ifpri-library@cgiar.org
URL: http://www.ifpri.org/resources
Contact: Luz Marina Alvare, Director
Scope: Food policy and research, developmental economics, International trade, food security, agricultural economics and statistics, food safety. **Services:** Interlibrary loan; copying; Library open to the public by appointment. **Founded:** 1977. **Holdings:** 1600 books; 230 research reports. **Subscriptions:** 200 journals and other serials. **Telecommunication Services:** l.alvare@cgiar.org.

21803 ■ Mississippi State University - Agricultural & Forestry Experiment Station - Delta Research and Extension Center
PO Box 197
Stoneville, MS 38776-0197
Ph: (662)686-9311
Fax: (662)686-7336
Co. E-mail: rhwatson@drec.msstate.edu
URL: http://msucares.com/drec
Contact: Rhonda H. Watson, Librarian
URL(s): mafes.msstate.edu/branches/delta.asp.
Scope: Agriculture, botany, agricultural economics, mathematics, agricultural engineering, meteorology. **Services:** Interlibrary loan; copying; library open to the public. **Founded:** 1966. **Holdings:** 14,500 books; 6000 bound periodical volumes; 348 reels of microfilm; 50,000 pamphlets. **Subscriptions:** 225 journals and other serials; 10 newspapers.

21804 ■ Pioneer Hi-Bred International, Inc. - Library Resources Group
7300 NW 62nd Ave.
Johnston, IA 50131-1004
Ph: (515)535-4199
Fax: (515)535-2184
Co. E-mail: dana.smith@pioneer.com
URL: http://www.pioneer.com
Contact: Dana Smith, Librarian
Scope: Plant genetics, agriculture, agribusiness, law, taxation, business. **Services:** Interlibrary loan; library not open to the public. **Founded:** 1983. **Holdings:** 1480 books. **Subscriptions:** 180 journals and other serials.

21805 ■ Purdue University Libraries--KRAN - Management and Economics Library—MEL.
Hicks Undergraduate, Ground Fl.
504 W. State St.
West Lafayette, IN 47907-2058
Ph: (765)494-2920
Co. E-mail: kranlib@purdue.edu
URL: http://www.lib.purdue.edu/mel
Contact: Hal Kirkwood, Associate
Scope: Business Organization and management; economics - applied, history, principles, theory, systems; industrial relations; agricultural economics; business statistics and mathematics; marketing; taxation; real estate; finance; accounting. **Services:** Interlibrary loan; copying; library open to the public. **Founded:** 1959. **Holdings:** 115,485 volumes; 5067 bound Annual reports to stockholders; 112,953 microforms; newspaper clippings. **Subscriptions:** 1028 journals and other serials. **Telecommunication Services:** kirkwood@purdue.edu; parrlib@purdue.edu.

21806 ■ Sandoz Agro Corporate Library
1100 E Woodfield Rd., No. 500
Schaumburg, IL 60173-5116
Ph: (847)390-3600
Fax: (847)390-3945
Contact: Candy J. Ortman, Archivist Librarian
Scope: Pesticides, herbicides, organic chemistry, entomology, botany, agribusiness. **Services:** Interlibrary loan. **Founded:** 1940. **Holdings:** 7500 books; 7000 bound periodical volumes; 7000 reels of microfilm. **Subscriptions:** 180 journals and other serials.

21807 ■ Tennessee Valley Authority - TVA Environmental Research Center - TVA Research Library—TVA National Fertilizer Library; TVA Chemical Engineering Library.
PO Box 1010
Muscle Shoals, AL 35662-1010
Ph: (256)386-2601
Free: 800-831-5744
Co. E-mail: tvainfo@tva.com
URL: http://www.tva.gov
Scope: Environmental sciences, biomass, chemistry, chemical engineering, competitive business marketing, environmental sciences, waste management. **Services:** Interlibrary loan. **Founded:** 1935. **Holdings:** 600 volumes; government documents. **Subscriptions:** 6 journals and other serials.

21808 ■ U.S.D.A. Economic Research Service - ERS Reference Center
1800 M St., NW
Washington, DC 20036-5831
Ph: (202)694-5058
Fax: (202)694-5757
Co. E-mail: mgraham@ers.usda.gov
URL: http://www.ers.usda.gov
Contact: Marilynn Graham, Specialist, Technical Services
Scope: Agricultural economics. **Services:** Interlibrary loan; copying (limited); Center open to the public by appointment. **Founded:** 1982. **Holdings:** 16,000 monographs; 10,000 microforms; microfiche; archives. **Subscriptions:** 318 journals and other serials.

21809 ■ University of California, Berkeley - Giannini Foundation of Agricultural Economics - Research Library
248 Giannini Hall, No. 3310
Berkeley, CA 94720-3310
Ph: (510)642-7121
Fax: (510)643-8911
Co. E-mail: gflibrary@berkeley.edu
URL: http://are.berkeley.edu/library/
Contact: Jeffrey Cole
Scope: Agriculture - economics, labor, land utilization, valuation and tenure, marketing and transportation problems, cost of production and marketing studies; agricultural economic developments in Lesser Developed Countries; environmental economics; water resources economics; conservation of natural resources. **Services:** Interlibrary loan; copying; Library open to qualified researchers for reference use only. **Founded:** 1930. **Holdings:** 21,000 volumes; 153,000 pamphlets; 3900 microforms; 150 maps; 540 microfiche titles, 3400 reels of microfilm. **Subscriptions:** 3000 journals and other serials.

21810 ■ University of California, Davis - Agricultural and Resource Economics Library
Social Sciences & Humanities Bldg., Rm. 4101
One Shields Ave.
Davis, CA 95616-8512
Ph: (530)752-1540
Fax: (530)752-5614
Co. E-mail: arel@primal.ucdavis.edu
URL: http://arelibrary.ucdavis.edu
Contact: Barbara Hegenbart, Librarian
Scope: Agricultural economics; agricultural business; land, resource, environmental and consumer economics. **Services:** Interlibrary loan; document delivery; copying; Library open to the public for reference use only. **Founded:** 1951. **Holdings:** 7000 volumes; 150,000 pamphlets; 2600 serials. **Subscriptions:** 8580 journals and other serials.

21811 ■ University of Illinois at Urbana-Champaign - Isaac Funk Family Library of Agricultural, Consumer and Environmental Sciences Library
200 ACES Library, Information and Alumni Ctr.
1101 S. Goodwin, MC-633
Urbana, IL 61801
Ph: (217)333-2416

Fax: (217)333-0558
Co. E-mail: allen2@uiuc.edu
URL: http://www.library.illinois.edu/agx/
Contact: Robert S. Allen, Librarian
Scope: Agricultural economics, animal science, agricultural engineering, crops, biotechnology, family and consumer economics, foods and nutrition, human development and family ecology, textiles, horticulture, food science and technology, environmental science, agricultural history, forestry, soils. **Services:** Interlibrary loan; copying; Library open to the public. **Founded:** 1915. **Holdings:** 200,000 volumes; 12,000 microforms; CD-ROMs; reports; patents; microfiche. **Subscriptions:** 3200 journals and other serials. **Telecommunication Services:** jzumalt@illinois.edu.

21812 ■ University of Minnesota, St. Paul - Magrath Library
1984 Buford Ave.
St. Paul, MN 55108
Ph: (612)624-2233
Fax: (612)626-7585
Co. E-mail: magrath@umn.edu
URL: http://lib.umn.edu/magrath
Contact: JoAnn DeVries
Scope: Agricultural and applied economics; agricultural engineering; agricultural education; home economics; agronomy and plant genetics; animal science; horticultural sciences; biological sciences; food science and nutrition; plant pathology; soil science; biochemistry; family social science; adult education; social work; Vo-Tech education; design; housing; apparel. **Services:** Interlibrary loan; copying; document delivery; Library open to the public for reference use only. **Founded:** 1890. **Holdings:** 441,420 volumes; 437,283 documents; 208 AV programs; 977 CD-ROMs; 55,367 microfiche; 1937 microfilm; 3111 maps. **Subscriptions:** 3208 journals and other serials. **Telecommunication Services:** stpcirc@umn. edu; wlougee@tc.umn.edu.

21813 ■ University of Wisconsin--Madison - Land Tenure Center Collection
550 N. Park St.
Madison, WI 53706
Ph: (608)262-6416
Co. E-mail: sventura@wisc.edu
URL: http://nelson.wisc.edu/ltc
Contact: Stephen Ventura, Director
Scope: Land tenure, agrarian reform, agricultural economics, Latin America, Asia, Africa, Eastern Europe, rural development, developing countries. **Services:** Interlibrary loan; copying; Library open to the public. **Founded:** 1962. **Holdings:** 30,000 books; 1200 bound periodical volumes; 36,000 unbound reports, manuscripts, clippings, pamphlets, documents; 8 VF drawers of microfilm and microfiche; 100 titles of Economic Development Plans; 250 titles of dissertations. **Subscriptions:** 350 journals and other serials.

21814 ■ University of Wisconsin--Madison - Steenbock Memorial Library
550 Babcock Dr.
Madison, WI 53706-1293
Ph: (608)262-9635
Fax: (608)263-3221
URL: http://steenbock.library.wisc.edu
Contact: Jeanne Eloranta
Scope: Life sciences, agriculture, veterinary medicine, biotechnology, food and dairy science, family studies, consumer science, agricultural economics. **Services:** Interlibrary loan; copying; document delivery; Library open to the public. **Founded:** 1904. **Holdings:** 124,000 books; 121,582 monographs; 73,607 bound periodical volumes; 493,000 government documents; 90,221 microforms; 765 AV programs. **Subscriptions:** 2503 journals and other serials.

21815 ■ Vermont Community and Technical Colleges Library
Hartness Library System
Main St.
Randolph Center, VT 05061
Ph: (802)728-1237
Free: 800-431-0025

Fax: (802)728-1506
Co. E-mail: library@vtc.edu
URL: http://hartness.vsc.edu
Contact: David Sturges, Director, Library Services
Scope: Engineering technologies architectural, civil, computer, electrical, electronics, mechanical; architecture and building technology; automotive technology; business technology; construction management; landscape development; semi-conductor processing; veterinary technology; nursing; science fiction; dairy management; agribusiness. **Services:** Copying; workstations; library open to the public with restrictions. **Founded:** 1964. **Holdings:** 56,000 books; 5000 e-books. **Subscriptions:** 200 journals and other serials; 8 newspapers. **Telecommunication Services:** library@ccv.edu; dsturges@vtc.edu.

21816 ■ Western Maryland Public Libraries - Regional Library
100 S. Potomac St.
Hagerstown, MD 21740
Ph: (301)739-3250
Fax: (301)739-5839
Co. E-mail: jthompson@washcolibrary.org
URL: http://www.westmdlib.info
Contact: Joe Thompson, Associate Director
Scope: Small business; antiques and collectibles; Civil Service and vocational tests; small scale farming. **Services:** Interlibrary loan; copying; library open to the public with restrictions. **Founded:** 1968. **Holdings:** 62,000 books; 2500 audiovisuals. **Subscriptions:** 3 newspapers.

RESEARCH CENTERS

21817 ■ Agricultural Utilization Research Institute (AURI)
PO Box 599
Crookston, MN 56716-0599
Ph: (218)281-7600
Free: 800-279-5010
Fax: (218)281-3759
Co. E-mail: tspaeth@auri.org
URL: http://www.auri.org
Contact: Teresa Spaeth, Executive Director
Services: Technical assistance to farmers, agribusinesses, and producer groups: New product development, feasibility testing, technology development (Daily). **Founded:** 1989. **Publications:** *Ag Innovation News* (Quarterly).

21818 ■ American Seed Research Foundation (ASRF)
1701 Duke St., Ste. 275
Alexandria, VA 22314
Ph: (703)837-8140
Fax: (703)837-9365
Co. E-mail: ajorss@amseed.org
URL: http://www.seedresearch.org
Founded: 1959.

21819 ■ Arizona State University - Center for Environmental Economics and Sustainability Policy
W.P. Carey School of Business
Department of Economics
Tempe, AZ 85287-9801
Ph: (480)965-0352
Fax: (480)965-0748
Co. E-mail: ceesp@asu.edu
URL: http://wpcarey.asu.edu/CEESP/index.cfm
Contact: Natalie J. Cardita, Assistant
Publications: *Center for Environmental Economics and Sustainability Policy Working Papers.* **Educational Activities:** Pre-doctoral Program.

21820 ■ California Institute for Rural Studies (CIRS)
221 G St., Ste. 204
Davis, CA 95616
Ph: (530)756-6555
Co. E-mail: info@cirsinc.org
URL: http://www.cirsinc.org
Contact: Gail Wadsworth, Executive Director
Services: Consulting: on a contract basis. **Founded:** 1977. **Publications:** *Reports and Working Papers; Rural California Report* (Quarterly). **Educational Ac-**

tivities: Leadership and liaison training; CIRS Conferences. **Telecommunication Services:** gwadsworth@cirsinc.org.

21821 ■ California State University, Fresno - Center for Agricultural Business (CAB)
2910 E Barstow Ave.
Fresno, CA 93740-0115
Ph: (559)278-4405
Fax: (559)278-6032
Co. E-mail: mpaggi@csufresno.edu
URL: http://cab.cati.csufresno.edu
Contact: Mechel Paggi, Director
Founded: 1985. **Publications:** *CAB Conference proceedings* (Annual). **Educational Activities:** Seminars in personnel management and labor laws, in English and Spanish; Seminars in business planning and agricultural trade.

21822 ■ Indiana Agricultural Leadership Institute (IALI)
72 W Main St.
Danville, IN 46122
Ph: (317)745-0947
Fax: (317)745-0956
Co. E-mail: beth@agriinstitute.org
URL: http://www.agriinstitute.org
Contact: Beth Archer, Executive Director
Services: Agricultural Leadership Development Program; Resource for Developing Community Leadership Program. **Founded:** 1982. **Publications:** *IALI Newsletter* (Bimonthly). **Educational Activities:** Indiana Agricultural Forum; Indiana Agricultural Leadership Program; Annual meetings and focus forums. **Telecommunication Services:** cultivate@ agriinstitute.org.

21823 ■ Institute for Agriculture and Trade Policy (IATP)
2105 1st Ave. S
Minneapolis, MN 55404
Ph: (612)870-0453
Fax: (612)870-4846
Co. E-mail: iatp@iatp.org
URL: http://www.iatp.org
Contact: Jim Harkness, President
E-mail: jharkness@iatp.org
Description: Individuals concerned with the current plight of the small farm in the U.S. Seeks to educate voters about federal farm legislation and efforts to expand sustainable and local food systems. Conducts research and disseminates information on government farm policies. Provides funds for lobbying farm issues. Promotes adoption of U.S. farm policies that will benefit the international farming community as well as domestic farmers. Maintains speakers' bureau. **Founded:** 1971. **Publications:** *Food Safety and Health* (Monthly); *Global Food Watch* (Biweekly); *IATP News* (Monthly); *Intellectual Property and Biodiversity News* (Weekly). **Telecommunication Services:** jharkness@iatp.org.

21824 ■ Iowa State University of Science and Technology - Midwest Agribusiness Trade Research and Information Center (MATRIC)
578 Heady Hall
Ames, IA 50011-1070
Ph: (515)294-1183
Fax: (515)294-6336
Co. E-mail: babcock@iastate.edu
URL: http://www.matric.iastate.edu
Contact: Prof. Bruce A. Babcock, Executive Director
Services: Consulting with non-university organizations and agribusinesses to discover and fulfill research and informational needs. **Founded:** 1987. **Publications:** *Working papers and research papers.* **Educational Activities:** MATRIC Conferences, seminars, on policy and trade issues for agricultural products. **Telecommunication Services:** matric@ iastate.edu.

21825 ■ George Morris Centre
225-150 Research Ln.
Guelph, ON, Canada N1G 4T2
Ph: (519)822-3929

Fax: (519)837-8721
Co. E-mail: info@georgemorris.org
URL: http://www.georgemorris.org
Contact: Robert (Bob) Seguin, Executive Director
Founded: 1990. **Publications:** *Market reports*; *George Morris Centre Newsletter*; *George Morris Centre Research reports*. **Educational Activities:** Canadian Agri-Food Executive Development Program; George Morris Centre Courses, on futures and options trading; Canadian Total Excellence in Agricultural Management Program.

21826 ■ New Mexico State University - Agricultural Experiment Station (AES)
PO Box 30003, MSC 3BF
Las Cruces, NM 88003-8003
Ph: (575)646-3125
Fax: (575)646-5975
Co. E-mail: sloring@nmsu.edu
URL: http://aces.nmsu.edu/aes
Contact: Dr. Steven Loring, Associate Director
Services: Science-based information service: to citizens of New Mexico, via the Cooperative Extension Service; Technology transfer: for producers, consumers, and environmentalists of the state (Annual). **Founded:** 1889. **Publications:** *Agricultural Experiment Station Research Bulletins* (Occasionally). **Educational Activities:** Conferences, workshops, short courses, field days (Annual), for farmers, cattlemen, conservationists, and homemakers of the state. **Awards:** AES Undergraduate internships, at off-campus science centers.

21827 ■ North Carolina State University - Research Stations Division
1001 Mail Service Ctr.
Raleigh, NC 27699-1001
Ph: (919)733-3236
Fax: (919)733-1754
Co. E-mail: sandy.stewart@ncagr.gov
URL: http://www.ncagr.com/research/
Contact: Alexander M. Stewart, Director

21828 ■ Prairie Agricultural Machinery Institute (PAMI)
Hwy. 5 W, Box 1150
Humboldt, SK, Canada S0K 2A0
Ph: (306)682-2555
Free: 800-567-7264
Fax: (306)682-5080
Co. E-mail: humboldt@pami.ca
URL: http://www.pami.ca
Contact: David Gullacher, President
E-mail: dgullacher@pami.ca
Founded: 1974. **Publications:** *PAMI Research reports* (Occasionally).

21829 ■ Purdue University - Center for Food and Agricultural Business
Krannert Bldg., Rm. 781
403 W State St.
West Lafayette, IN 47907-2056
Ph: (765)494-4247
Fax: (765)494-4333
Co. E-mail: gray@purdue.edu
URL: http://www.agecon.purdue.edu/cab
Contact: Dr. Allan Gray, Director
Founded: 1936. **Publications:** *Center for Food and Agricultural Business Articles*. **Educational Activities:** Food and agribusiness management education programs, including programs that focus on specific functional management areas such as marketing, finance, personnel management, sales management, and relationship marketing. **Telecommunication Services:** agbusinessinfo@purdue.edu.

21830 ■ University of Delaware - Halophyte Biotechnology Center
College of Earth, Ocean, & Environment
700 Pilottown Rd.
Lewes, DE 19958
Ph: (302)645-4264
Fax: (302)645-4028
Co. E-mail: jackg@udel.edu
URL: http://www.ceoe.udel.edu/halophyte
Contact: Prof. John L. Gallagher, Director
Publications: *Halophyte Biotechnology Center Newsletter*. **Educational Activities:** Degree and non-degree programs, in halophyte agronomy and biology, comparative wetland ecology, plant nutrition in saline soils, and salt tolerance mechanisms.

21831 ■ University of Florida - Institute of Food and Agricultural Sciences (IFAS)
1008 McCarty Hall
Gainesville, FL 32611-0180
Ph: (352)392-1971
Fax: (352)265-6932
Co. E-mail: jackpayne@ufl.edu
URL: http://www.ifas.ufl.edu
Contact: Dr. Jack Payne, Senior Vice President
Founded: 1964. **Publications:** *Faculty Directory* (Semiannual); *Impact Magazine* (Semiannual); *Inside IFAS Newsletter* (Monthly); *Newsline Newsletter* (Quarterly).

ASSOCIATIONS AND OTHER ORGANIZATIONS

21832 ■ **International Reciprocal Trade Association (IRTA)**
524 Middle St.
Portsmouth, VA 23704
Ph: (757)393-2292
Fax: (757)257-4014
Co. E-mail: ron@irta.com
URL: http://www.irta.com/
Contact: Michael Mercier, President
Description: Individuals, partnerships, corporations, and firms that engage in the commercial barter industry worldwide, including local trade exchanges which act as clearinghouses, and corporate trade companies which arrange domestic and international barter transactions. Works to foster and promote the interests of the commercial barter industry through the establishment of ethical standards and self-regulation; to represent members before government agencies in matters affecting the industry; to introduce firms engaged in bartering activities; to resolve disputes between members; influence public laws and regulations affecting the industry; disseminate information and conduct public relations programs. Serves as a clearinghouse for industry and public inquiries. Compiles statistics on the segment of commercial barter accounted for by organized trade exchanges and corporate trade companies. Conducts consumer protection, educational, and training programs. Operates Corporate Barter Council as a self-governing body for the corporate trade sector. Awards professional accreditation; operates referral and placement services; maintains speakers' bureau; supports charitable programs. **Scope:** commercial barter. **Founded:** 1979. **Subscriptions:** clippings papers. **Educational Activities:** Barter Congress (Annual); Barter Congress (Annual). **Awards:** IRTA Hall of Fame (Annual).

21833 ■ **Waterfront Center**
3844 Beecher St. NW
Washington, DC 20009
Ph: (202)337-0356
Fax: (202)986-0448
Co. E-mail: mail@waterfrontcenter.org
URL: http://www.waterfrontcenter.org
Contact: Dick Rigby, Director
Description: State and local governments; architectural, engineering, and design firms; developers; educational institutions; persons in the boating industry; interested others. Helps communities develop waterfronts that facilitate economic growth while providing for public access and recreation. Conducts forums that address problems and opportunities in a particular community; provides on-site analyses and consulting; offers slide presentations; conducts research. **Founded:** 1981. **Publications:** *Urban Waterfront Resource List* (Periodic); *Waterfront World Spotlight* (Quarterly); *Caution: Working Waterfront: The Impact of Change on Marine Businesses*; *The Waterfront: A Worldwide Urban Success Story*

(Annual); *Waterfronts: Cities Reclaim Their Edge*. **Awards:** Excellence on the Waterfront Award (Annual).

REFERENCE WORKS

21834 ■ *"Age-Old System of Bartering Is Being Revolutionized by Phoenix Company, Premier Barter"* in *Internet Wire (July 12, 2010)*
Pub: Comtex
Description: Premier Barter is helping entrepreneurs rediscover the system of bartering as a method of exchanging goods and services without cash or credit.

21835 ■ *"Area Small Businesses Enjoy Benefits of Bartering Group"* in *News-Herald (August 22, 2010)*
Pub: The News-Herald
Ed: Brandon C. Baker. **Description:** ITEX is a publicly traded firm that spurs cashless, business-to-business transactions within its own marketplace. Details of the bartering of goods and services within the company are outlined.

21836 ■ *"Bartering, Browsing, Borrowing to Save"* in *Reading Eagle (July 20, 2010)*
Pub: Reading Eagle/Reading Times
Ed: Jessica Bakeman. **Description:** Various forms of bartering are outlined to help small companies as well as individuals.

21837 ■ *"Bartering is Local Club's Stock in Trade"* in *Pueblo Chieftain (September 6, 2010)*
Pub: The Pueblo Chieftain
Ed: Loretta Sword. **Description:** As the economy waivers, a barter club in Pueblo, Colorado thrives. An examination of the club and the way it operates is included.

21838 ■ *"Bartering Makes a Return in Hard Times"* in *Atlanta Journal-Constitution (October 2, 2010, pp. A15)*
Pub: Atlanta Journal-Constitution
Ed: Bill York. **Description:** The advantages of bartering are explored.

21839 ■ *"Bartering Takes Businesses Back to Basics: Broker's Exchange Helps Members to Reach New Customers"* in *Buffalo News (July 9, 2010)*
Pub: The Buffalo News
Ed: Dino Grandoni. **Description:** Bartering clubs can help small businesses reach new customers and to expand their business.

21840 ■ *"Bartering Trades on Talents"* in *Reading Eagle (June 20, 2010)*
Pub: Reading Eagle/Reading Times
Ed: Tony Lucia. **Description:** Bartering is not just a way of trading goods and services, it can be an essential tool for small business to survive in a bad economy.

21841 ■ *"Beat the Buck: Bartering Tips from In-The-Know Authors"* in *(June 23, 2010)*
Pub: The Telegraph
Ed: Jill Moon. **Description:** The Art of Barter is a new book to help small businesses learn this art form in order to expand customer base and reserve cash flow.

21842 ■ *"Benefits of Bartering"* in *Mail Tribune (November 22, 2010)*
Pub: Mail Tribune
Ed: Damian Mann. **Description:** Various people discuss the use of bartering for their small companies in order to improve business.

21843 ■ *"Businesses Band Together in Destin Bartering to Keep Heads Above Water"* in *Destin Log (July 24, 2010)*
Pub: The Destin Log
Ed: Andrew Metz. **Description:** Profile of The Barter Company located in Destin, Florida, whose owner believes that bartering for goods and services can help small companies in a down economy.

21844 ■ *"Fair Exchange"* in *Food and Drink (Winter 2010, pp. 84)*
Pub: Schofield Media Group
Ed: Don Mardak. **Description:** Bartering can assist firms in the food and beverage industry to attract new customers, maximize resources, and reduce cash expenses.

21845 ■ *"A Family's Fortune"* in *Canadian Business (Vol. 80, Winter 2007, No. 24, pp. 103)*
Pub: Rogers Media
Ed: Graham F. Scott. **Description:** James Richardson started as a tailor before moving into the grain business because his clients paid him in sacks of wheat and barley. The James Richardson and Sons Ltd. entered the radio business in 1927 but later sold it off in 1951.

21846 ■ *"International Monetary Barter Helps Discretionary Industry"* in *Benzinga.com (January 24, 2011)*
Pub: Benzinga.com
Ed: Benzinga Staff. **Description:** International Monetary Systems Limited, a business-to-business bartering firm, is helping wedding and event planners close deals with customers with bartering solutions.

21847 ■ *"Poor Economy Inspires Rich Alternatives In a Modern and Tax-Free, Twist on Bartering"* in *Houston Chronicle (June 7, 2010)*
Pub: Houston Chronicle Publishing Company
Ed: Michael Rubinkam. **Description:** Time banking helps individuals and firms receive goods or services by depositing time dollars into a bank reserved for receipt of goods and services.

21848 ■ *"Will Work for Equity"* in *Inc. (March 2008, pp. 50, 52)*
Pub: Gruner & Jahr USA Publishing
Ed: Ryan McCarthy. **Description:** Profile of Dave Graham and his information technology company;

Graham built his business by taking equity in client firms rather than charging fees. Four tips to consider before signing a work-for-equity business deal are outlined.

ASSOCIATIONS AND OTHER ORGANIZATIONS

21849 ■ American Mutual Life Association (AMLA)
19424 S Waterloo Rd.
Cleveland, OH 44119-3250
Ph: (216)531-1900
Fax: (216)531-8123
Co. E-mail: amla@americanmutual.org
URL: http://americanmutual.org
Description: Fraternal benefit life insurance society. Maintains recreation center. **Founded:** 1910. **Publications:** *Our Voice* (Biweekly).

21850 ■ American Society of Pension Professionals and Actuaries (ASPPA)
4245 N Fairfax Dr., Ste. 750
Arlington, VA 22203-1648
Ph: (703)516-9300
Fax: (703)516-9308
Co. E-mail: asppa@asppa.org
URL: http://www.asppa.org
Contact: Robert M. Richter, President

URL(s): www.aspa.org. **Description:** Aims to educate pension actuaries, consultants, administrators, and other benefits professionals. Seeks to preserve and enhance the private pension system as part of the development of a cohesive and coherent national retirement income policy. **Founded:** 1966. **Publications:** *ASPPA Yearbook* (Annual). **Awards:** Presidential Scholarship; Educator's Award (Annual); Presidential Scholarship (Annual); Educator's Award; Harry T. Eidson Founder's Award; Martin Rosenberg Academic Achievement Award; Harry T. Eidson Founder's Award (Annual); Martin Rosenberg Academic Achievement Award (Semiannual).

21851 ■ Council on Employee Benefits (CEB)
1311 King St.
Alexandria, VA 22314
Ph: (703)549-6025
Fax: (703)549-6027
Co. E-mail: scanfield@ceb.org
URL: http://www.ceb.org
Contact: Robert B. Arthur, President

Description: Employers seeking informal exchange of experiences and information on the design, financing, and administration of employee benefit programs, both domestic and international. Provides a medium for the exchange of ideas, information, and statistics; sponsors or conducts research projects on benefits; makes known its views on legislative matters affecting employee benefits. Conducts research. **Founded:** 1946.

21852 ■ Employee Benefit Research Institute (EBRI)
1100 13th St. NW, Ste. 878
Washington, DC 20005
Ph: (202)659-0670
Fax: (202)775-6312
Co. E-mail: info@ebri.org
URL: http://www.ebri.org
Contact: Dallas L. Salisbury, President
E-mail: salisbury@ebri.org
Description: Corporations, consulting firms, banks, insurance companies, unions, and others with an interest in the future of employee benefit programs. Purpose is to contribute to the development of effective and responsible public policy in the field of employee benefits through research, publications, educational programs, seminars, and direct communication. Sponsors a broad range of studies on retirement income, health, disability, and other benefit programs; disseminates study results. Maintains research library with information on employee benefit programs. **Scope:** A public policy research organization serving as an employee benefits information source on health, welfare and retirement issues. Services include: basic benefit program descriptions, legislation analysis, media coverage and interpretation and long-range planning. Specializes in research on pensions, social security, health care, Medicare, long-term care, and flexible benefits. Serves government, academic consumers, consultants, banks, insurance companies, investment managers, law and accounting firms, corporations, and individuals. **Services:** Congressional briefings. **Founded:** 1978. **Subscriptions:** 4000 audiovisuals books clippings monographs periodicals. **Publications:** "Retirement Security in the United States-Current Sources, Future Prospects, and Likely Outcomes of Current Trends," 2006; "Estimating the Value of Changes in OASI Benefits Under Social Security Reforms," Jun, 2006; "Will Wider Use of Evidence-Based Medicine Significantly Enhance Healthcare Quality and Affordability: Implications for Consumer-Driven Health Benefits," 2003; "Consumer Driven Health Benefits: A Continuing Evolution," 2002; "The Economic Costs of the Uninsured Implications for Business and Government," 2000; "The Future of Private Retirement Plans," 2000; "EBRI Issue Briefs"; "EBRI Notes"; "Pension Investment Report PIR"; "EBRI Data book on Employee Benefits"; "Fundamentals of Employee Benefits Programs". **Educational Activities:** American Savings Education Council; Choose to Save Education Program; Fellows program, for academics, media, retirees; Policy forums (Biennial). **Awards:** EBRI Lillywhite Award (Annual); The EBRI Lillywhite Award (Annual). **Seminars:** Policy Forums, Congressional Briefings. **Telecommunication Services:** salisbury@ebri.org.

21853 ■ Employers Council on Flexible Compensation (ECFC)
1444 I St. NW, Ste. 700
Washington, DC 20005-6542
Ph: (202)659-4300
Free: 877-747-3539
Fax: (202)216-9646
Co. E-mail: nrankin@ecfc.org
URL: http://www.ecfc.org
Contact: Natasha Rankin, Executive Director
Description: Represents employers and service providers who have implemented or are interested in flexible compensation plans allowing employees to choose from a variety of benefits packages. Promotes flexible compensation plans including cafeteria plans, health reimbursement arrangements, cash-or-deferred plans and other defined contribution plans. Monitors legislation and represents members' interests before Congress. Lobbies to preserve and simplify the flexible compensation provisions of the Internal Revenue Code. **Founded:** 1981. **Educational Activities:** Flexible Benefit Administrator's Symposium (Annual). **Telecommunication Services:** info@ecfc.org.

21854 ■ ERISA Industry Committee (ERIC)
1400 L St. NW, Ste. 350
Washington, DC 20005
Ph: (202)789-1400
Fax: (202)789-1120
Co. E-mail: smacey@eric.org
URL: http://www.eric.org
Contact: Scott Macey, President
Description: Large corporations that sponsor employee pension, health, and other benefit programs. Represents the concerns of major employers regarding policy, legislative, judicial, and regulatory matters involving the administration of private retirement, health, and other employee benefit plans. Issues briefings to members' congressional representatives. Operates speakers' bureau. (ERISA is an acronym for the Employee Retirement Income Security Act of 1974). **Founded:** 1976.

21855 ■ International Foundation of Employee Benefit Plans (IFEBP)
18700 W Bluemound Rd.
Brookfield, WI 53045
Ph: (262)786-6700
Free: 888-334-3327
Fax: (262)364-1818
Co. E-mail: membership@ifebp.org
URL: http://www.ifebp.org
Contact: Richard Lyall, President
Description: Provides sources for employee benefits and compensation information and education, including seminars and conferences, books and an information center, CEBS and Certificate Series. Conducts more than 100 educational programs. Provides Internet job and resume posting service. **Scope:** employee benefits, human resources, compensation. **Founded:** 1954. **Holdings:** The computer-readable EMPLOYEE BENEFITS INFOSOURCE database contains more than 75,000 records dating from 1986 to the present; it is updated monthly with approximately 400 records. **Subscriptions:** 12000 books periodicals. **Publications:** *Employee Benefits Journal*; *Employee Benefits Infosource*; *Benefits & Compensation Digest*; *Legal-Legislative Reporter*; *Employee Benefits Infosource*; *Benefits & Compensation Digest* (Monthly); *Employee Benefits Infosource*™; *Employee Benefits Journal* (Quarterly). **Educational Activities:** Annual Employee Benefits Conference (Annual). **Telecommunication Services:** cebs@ifebp.org; ebinfo@ifebp.org.

21856 ■ International Society of Certified Employee Benefit Specialists (ISCEBS)
PO Box 209
Brookfield, WI 53008-0209

Ph: (262)786-8771
Fax: (262)786-8650
Co. E-mail: iscebs@iscebs.org
URL: http://www.iscebs.org
Contact: Sandra Wood, President
Description: Graduates of the Certified Employee Benefit Specialist Program, co-sponsored by the International Foundation of Employee Benefit Plans and the Wharton School of the University of Pennsylvania. Promotes continuing education and professional development of employee benefit practitioners through courses and seminars **Founded:** 1981. **Publications:** *International Society of Certified Employee Benefit Specialists--Membership Directory* (Annual); *International Society of Certified Employee Benefit Specialists--Membership Directory* (Annual); *Benefits Quarterly* (Quarterly).

21857 ■ National Coordinating Committee for Multi-employer Plans (NCCMP)
815 16th St. NW
Washington, DC 20006
Ph: (202)737-5315
Fax: (202)737-1308
Co. E-mail: nccmp@nccmp.org
URL: http://www.nccmp.org
Contact: Randy G. DeFrehn, Executive Director
Description: International trade unions and jointly administered employee benefit trust funds. Promotes the interests of organizations that provide retirement security, health, and other welfare benefits to individuals working in industries that, due to their structure, would not otherwise provide sufficient pension and welfare benefits. Lobbies before Congress and federal regulatory agencies and participates in judicial proceedings affecting multiemployer plans and participants. **Founded:** 1974. **Awards:** John L. Lewis Award (Annual).

21858 ■ National Institute of Pension Administrators (NIPA)
401 N Michigan Ave., Ste. 2200
Chicago, IL 60611
Free: 800-999-6472
Fax: (312)673-6609
Co. E-mail: nipa@nipa.org
URL: http://www.nipa.org
Contact: James Eberhardt, President
Description: Individuals with at least a year of experience in pension administration, full-time pension administration employees, and interested individuals. Sponsors educational program for the accreditation of pension administrators and a series of regional programs relative to pension/profit-sharing programs and administration. **Founded:** 1983. **Publications:** *PLAN Horizons* (Quarterly). **Educational Activities:** Business Management Conference (Annual).

21859 ■ Woman's Life Insurance Society
PO Box 5020
Port Huron, MI 48061-5020
Ph: (810)985-5191
Free: 800-521-9292
Fax: (810)985-6970
Co. E-mail: website@womanslife.org
URL: http://www.womanslife.org
Contact: Christopher J. Martin, President
Description: Fraternal benefit life insurance society focusing on the needs of women. Each review or local club engages in local charitable community projects. **Founded:** 1892. **Publications:** *Woman's Life* (Quarterly); *Woman's Life* (Quarterly). **Awards:** Woman of Distinction (Annual). **Telecommunication Services:** wkrabach@womanslifeins.com.

21860 ■ Workmen's Benefit Fund of the U.S.A. (WBF)
399 Conklin St., Ste. 310
Farmingdale, NY 11735-2614
Ph: (516)938-6060
Fax: (516)938-9020
Co. E-mail: info@wbfusa.org
URL: http://www.wbfusa.org
Description: Serves as a fraternal benefit life insurance society. **Founded:** 1884. **Publications:** *WBF in Action* (Quarterly). **Awards:** WBF Community Service Scholarship Award (Annual).

REFERENCE WORKS

21861 ■ *"16 Creative and Cheap Ways to Say 'Thank You'" in HR Specialist (Vol. 8, September 2010, No. 9, pp. 8)*
Pub: Capitol Information Group Inc.

Description: Tips for starting an employee appreciation program for a small company are presented.

21862 ■ *101 Businesses You Can Start with Less Than One Thousand Dollars: for Retirees*
Pub: Atlantic Publishing Company

Ed: Heather Lee Shepherd. **Released:** October 2007. **Price:** $21.95. **Description:** According to a study by the U.S. Department of Health and Human Resources, people starting their work careers will face the following situation when they retire at the age of 65: they will have annual incomes between $4,000 and $26,000. According to the Social Security Administration, today's retirees can count on corporate pensions and Social Security for 61 percent of their retirement income. The remainder must come from other sources. Therefore, if this holds true for the future, today's workers need to accumulate enough in personal savings to make up the 39 percent shortfall in retirement income. The solution for many will be to start a small part-time business.

21863 ■ *"401(k) Keys to Stable Value" in Barron's (Vol. 88, March 10, 2008, No. 10, pp. 40)*
Pub: Dow Jones & Company, Inc.

Ed: Tom Sullivan. **Description:** Stable-value funds offer investors stability in a period of volatility in financial markets, attracting $888 million in funds The Securities and Exchange Commission approved the launch of actively managed exchange-traded funds.

21864 ■ *"Amount Md. Pays to Unemployed Dips to Lowest Level Since '08" in Baltimore Business Journal (Vol. 28, November 12, 2010, No. 27)*
Pub: Baltimore Business Journal

Ed: Scott Dance. **Description:** Maryland paid out $50 million for unemployment benefits in September 2010 for its lowest payout since 2008. The drop in unemployment payout could mean lower taxes for employers who pay for the benefits. The unemployment rate in Maryland, however, increased to 7.5 percent.

21865 ■ *"The Annual Entitlement Lecture: Trustees of Medicare and Social Security Issue Another Dismal Report" in Barron's (March 31, 2008)*
Pub: Dow Jones & Company, Inc.

Ed: Thomas G. Donlan. **Description:** Expenditures on Medicare hospital insurance and the revenues available to pay for it have led to a gap of capital valued at $38.6 trillion. Slashing the benefits or raising taxes will not solve the gap which exists unless the government saves the money and invests it in private markets.

21866 ■ *"An Apple a Day" in Entrepreneur (Vol. 36, February 2008, No. 2, pp. 19)*
Pub: Entrepreneur Media Inc.

Ed: Mark Henricks. **Description:** Businesses are handling rising health coverage costs by providing employees with wellness programs, which include smoking-cessation programs, consumer-directed plans for savings on premiums, and limited medical care plans. Details on the growing trend regarding employee health coverage are discussed.

21867 ■ *"Are Prepaid Legal Services Worthwhile?" in Contractor (Vol. 56, December 2009, No. 12, pp. 31)*
Pub: Penton Media, Inc.

Ed: Susan Linden McGreevy. **Description:** Companies' provision of legal insurance as an employee benefit in the United States is discussed. Stoppage of premium payment halts employee coverage. It also does not cover all kinds of personal issues.

21868 ■ *"At Your Service: Corporate Concierges Come in Three Varieties" in Incentive (August 25, 2008)*
Pub: Nielson Business Media

Ed: Nathan Adkisson. **Description:** Companies are offering corporate concierge services to handle tasks for new employees as a sign-on benefit. Concierge of Boston has six employees that focus on fulfilling the needs of individuals.

21869 ■ *"Bank on It" in Hawaii Business (Vol. 53, November 2007, No. 5, pp. 60)*
Pub: Hawaii Business Publishing

Ed: Kathleen Bryan. **Description:** Many Baby Boomers that are preparing to retire would like to give back and make a difference. One way is to make gifts of Individual Retirement Assets (IRA). During 2007 people over 70 years can make withdrawals from an IRA and donate it without realizing the income as taxable.

21870 ■ *"Banks Fret About Gist Of Bailout" in The Business Journal-Serving Metropolitan Kansas City (Vol. 27, September 26, 2008, No. 2)*
Pub: American City Business Journals, Inc.

Ed: James Dornbrook. **Description:** Banks from the Kansas City area hope that the proposed $700 billion bailout will not send the wrong message. UMB Financial Corp. chairman says that he hopes that the bailout would benefit companies that were more risk restrained and punish those that took outsized risk. Other bank executives' perceptions on the planned bailout are given.

21871 ■ *"The Best Option for All" in American Executive (Vol. 7, September 2009, No. 5, pp. 170)*
Pub: RedCoat Publishing, Inc.

Ed: Ashley McGown. **Description:** Plaza Associates, a collections agency that conducts business primarily in the accounts receivable management sector, is the first in the industry to purchase 100 percent of the company from the founders through the formation of a leveraged Employee Stock Ownership Plan (ESOP).

21872 ■ *"Best Practices: Developing a Rewards Program" in Franchising World (Vol. 42, September 2010, No. 9, pp. 13)*
Pub: International Franchise Association

Ed: Leah Templeton. **Description:** Rewards for a job well done are examined in order to recognize franchisees for outstanding performance. Ways to customize a rewards program are outlined.

21873 ■ *"Bills Raise Blues Debate; An Unfair Edge or Level Playing Field?" in Crain's Detroit Business (Vol. 24, January 21, 2008, No. 3)*
Pub: Crain Communications Inc. - Detroit

Ed: Sherri Begin. **Description:** Changes in Michigan state law would change the way health insurance can be sold to individuals. Michigan Blue Cross Blue Shield is working to keep its tax-exempt status while staying competitive against for-profit insurers and nonprofit HMOs.

21874 ■ *"Boosting Corporate Entrepreneurship Through HRM Practices" in Human Resource Management (Vol. 49, July-August 2010, No. 4)*
Pub: John Wiley

Ed Ralf Schmelter, Rene Mauer, Christiane Borsch, Malte Brettel. **Description:** A study was conducted to determine which human resource management (HRM) practices promote corporate entrepreneurship (CE) in small and medium-sized enterprises (SMEs). Findings indicate that staff selection, staff development, training, and staff rewards on CE have a strong impact on SMEs.

21875 ■ *"Both Eyes on the Prize" in Canadian Business (Vol. 83, September 14, 2010, No. 15, pp. 42)*
Pub: Rogers Media Ltd.

Ed: Jacqueline Nelson. **Description:** North American executive compensation has fundamentally shifted partly due to pressure from the US government and recent adjustments in the way CEO pay packages are structured. The changes have also become common practice in Canada and helped in scrutinizing the executive pay.

21876 ■ "Build a Better Bonus" in Canadian Business (Vol. 80, January 15, 2007, No. 2, pp. 65)
Pub: Rogers Media
Ed: John Gray. **Description:** The use of employee performance incentives to enhance employee productivity is discussed. Tips for employers, on how to creative an effective bonus plan, are presented.

21877 ■ "Builders, Unions Aim to Cut Costs; Pushing Changes to Regain Share of Residential Market; Seek Council's Help" in Crain's New York Business
Pub: Crain Communications, Inc.
Ed: Erik Engquist. **Description:** Union contractors and workers are worried about a decline in their market share for housing so they intend to ask the City Council to impose new safety and benefit standards on all contractors to avoid being undercut by nonunion competitors.

21878 ■ Business Owner's Toolkit Tax Guide
Pub: Toolkit Media Group
Released: January 2009. **Price:** $17.95. **Description:** Resource addresses the tax-filing process while helping to minimize bills. Discussions are focused on important issues pertaining to the small business owner. Topics cover include: personal and business expenses and how they are differentiated, how employee benefit plans are handled on tax returns, and what the IRS looks for when conducting audits. Free online information and support is also included.

21879 ■ "Businesses Keep a Watchful Eye on Worker's Comp" in The Business Journal-Serving Greater Tampa Bay (September 5, 2008)
Pub: American City Business Journals, Inc.
Ed: Jane Meinhardt. **Description:** Pending a ruling from the Florida Supreme Court that could uphold the 2003 changes on workers' compensation law, the outcome would include restrictions on claimant attorneys' fees and allow the competitive workers' compensation insurance rates to remain low. However, insurance rates are expected to go up if the court overturns the changes.

21880 ■ "CEO Pay: Best Bang for Buck" in Philadelphia Business Journal (Vol. 30, September 30, 2011, No. 33, pp. 1)
Pub: American City Business Journals Inc.
Ed: Jeff Blumenthal. **Description:** A study by Strategic Research Solutions on the compensation of chief executive officers in Philadelphia, Pennsylvania-based public companies reveals that only a few of them performed according to expectations. These include Brian Roberts of Comcast, John Conway of Crown Holdings, and Frank Hermance of Ametek Inc.

21881 ■ "CEO Pay: The Details" in Crain's Detroit Business (Vol. 25, June 22, 2009, No. 25, pp.)
Pub: Crain Communications Inc. - Detroit
Description: Total compensation packages for CEOs at area companies our outlined. These packages include salary, bonuses, stock awards, and options.

21882 ■ "Change of Plans" in Entrepreneur (Vol. 35, November 2007, No. 11, pp. 74)
Pub: Entrepreneur Media Inc.
Ed: C.J. Prince. **Description:** Companies should provide 401K plans that meet employee needs and demographics, with new technology allowing providers to lower their own costs. Details on finding a plans that appeal to employees are examined.

21883 ■ "Connecting the Dots Between Wellness and Elder Care" in Benefits and Compensation Digest (Vol. 47, August 2010, No. 8, pp. 18)
Pub: International Foundation of Employee Benefit Plans
Contact: Richard Lyall, President
Ed: Sandra Timmermann. **Description:** Employees caring for aged and infirm parents deal with time and financial issues and other stresses. The connection

between health status of caregivers and employers' health care costs could be aided by linking programs and benefits with wellness and caregiving.

21884 ■ "Consulting Firm Goes Shopping" in Crain's Chicago Business (Vol. 31, April 28, 2008, No. 17, pp. 45)
Pub: Crain Communications, Inc.
Ed: Phuong Ly. **Description:** Clark & Wamberg LLC was created last year after the merger of Clark Inc. to a Dutch insurance conglomerate. Clark Inc. was a life insurance and benefits consultancy which had been on a downslide, returning just 5.6 percent a year to shareholders. In contrast Clark & Wamberg posted first-year revenue of $106.8 million, fueled by business from its executive compensation and health care clients.

21885 ■ "Corporate Canada Eyes Retiree Benefit Cuts" in Globe & Mail (March 8, 2006, pp. B3)
Pub: CTVglobemedia Publishing Inc.
Ed: Virginia Galt. **Description:** A survey on Canadian companies reveals that due to rising health care costs and increasing number of baby boomer retirements, these companies are to cut down on health benefits they are providing to these retired employees.

21886 ■ Create Your Own Employee Handbook: A Legal and Practical Guide
Pub: NOLO
Ed: Amy DelPo, Lisa Guerin. **Released:** June 2009. **Price:** $49.99. **Description:** Information for business owners to develop an employee handbook that covers company benefits, policies, procedures, and more.

21887 ■ "CreFirst To Reward Doctors for Reducing Costs, Improving Care" in Baltimore Business Journal (Vol. 28, June 4, 2010, No. 4, pp. 1)
Pub: Baltimore Business Journal
Ed: Scott Graham. **Description:** CareFirst Blue Cross Blue Shield plans to introduce a program that dangles big financial rewards to physicians who change the way they deliver primary care by improving the health of their sickest patients while reducing costs. The company will soon begin recruiting primary care physicians in Maryland, Washington DC, and Northern Virginia.

21888 ■ "Crouching Tigers Spring to Life" in Globe & Mail (April 14, 2007, pp. B1)
Pub: CTVglobemedia Publishing Inc.
Ed: Grant Robertson. **Description:** The prospects of the acquisition of BCE Inc, by Canadian pension funds are discussed. The effect of the growth of these pension funds on the Canadian economy is described.

21889 ■ "Cutting Health Care Costs: the 3-Legged Stool" in HR Specialist (Vol. 8, September 2010, No. 9, pp. 1)
Pub: Capitol Information Group Inc.
Description: Employer spending on health insurance benefits to employees is investigated.

21890 ■ "Desk-Bound No More" in Charlotte Business Journal (Vol. 25, August 13, 2010, No. 21, pp. 1)
Pub: Charlotte Business Journal
Ed: Adam O' Daniel. **Description:** Bank of America has launched a program that encourages employees to work on their own schedules. The program encourages productivity and health work-life balance. A survey has also revealed that employees feel more productive under the program.

21891 ■ "Discount Shopping: Holiday Shopping Meets Social Media" in Employee Benefit News (Vol. 25, December 1, 2011, No. 15)
Pub: SourceMedia Inc.
Ed: Rob J. Thurston. **Description:** Offering employees access to discount shopping using social media sites for Christmas bonuses, could be the gift that keeps on giving.

21892 ■ "Discovery Communications" in Workforce Management (Vol. 88, December 14, 2009, No. 13, pp. 17)
Pub: Crain Communications Inc.
Ed: Jeremy Smerd. **Description:** Discovery Communications provides its employees a wealth of free health services via a comprehensive work-site medical clinic that is available to its employees and their dependents. Overview of the company's innovative approach to healthcare is presented.??.

21893 ■ "Do You Have A Retirement Parachute?" in Barron's (Vol. 88, July 7, 2008, No. 27, pp. 32)
Pub: Dow Jones & Co., Inc.
Ed: Jane White. **Description:** The idea that American companies should emulate the Australian retirement system which implements a forced contribution rate for all employers regarding an adequate retirement plan for their employees is discussed.

21894 ■ "DoEs and DonEts" in Canadian Business (Vol. 79, July 17, 2006, No. 14-15, pp. 29)
Pub: Rogers Media
Ed: Andy Holloway; Erin Pooley; Thomas Watson. **Description:** Strategic tips for planning systematic investments, in order to make life more enjoyable after retirement, are elucidated.

21895 ■ "Doing the Right Thing" in Black Enterprise (Vol. 38, July 2008, No. 12, pp. 50)
Pub: Earl G. Graves Publishing Co. Inc.
Ed: Tamara E. Holmes. **Description:** More business owners are trying to become more environmentally friendly, either due to their belief in social responsibility or for financial incentives or for both reasons. Tips for making one's business more environmentally responsible are included as well as a listing of resources that may be available to help owners in their efforts.

21896 ■ "Doing Without" in Baltimore Business Journal (Vol. 28, June 11, 2010, No. 5, pp. 1)
Pub: Baltimore Business Journal
Ed: Scott Graham. **Description:** Maryland Health Care Commission report figures have shown only 47,661 small businesses provided some level of health coverage to 381,517 employees in 2009. These numbers are down from 51,283 employers who offered benefits to 407,983 employees in 2008 to highlight a disturbing trend in Maryland's small-group insurance market. Reasons for the drop are discussed.

21897 ■ "Don't Try This Offshore" in Harvard Business Review (Vol. 86, September 2008, No. 9, pp. 39)
Pub: Harvard Business School Press
Description: Fictitious outsourcing scenario is presented, with contributors offering advice. The suggestions address the ease or complexity of offshoring business creativity, along with challenges and benefits.

21898 ■ "Elder Care At Work" in HRMagazine (Vol. 53, September 2008, No. 9, pp. 111)
Pub: Society for Human Resource Management
Contact: Henry G. Jackson, President
E-mail: hjackson@shrm.org
Ed: Pamela Babcock. **Description:** Many employers are helping workers who face sudden, short-term elder care needs.

21899 ■ "Employee Motivation: A Powerful New Model" in Harvard Business Review (Vol. 86, July-August 2008, No. 8, pp. 78)
Pub: Harvard Business School Press
Ed: Nitin Nohria; Boris Groysbert; Linda Eling Lee. **Description:** Four drives underlying employee motivation are discussed as well as processes for leveraging these drives through corporate culture, job design, reward systems, and resource-allocation priorities.

21900 ■ *"Expert Sees No Radical Reform of 401(K) System" in Workforce Management (Vol. 88, November 16, 2009, No. 12, pp. 12)*
Pub: Crain Communications Inc.

Ed: Ed Frauenheim. **Description:** Although many would like to see an overhaul of the 401(k) retirement system, it is unlikely to occur anytime soon; however, the drastic stock market drop of 2008 has raised pointed questions about the 401(k) system and if it enables a secure retirement for American workers.

21901 ■ *"Experts Take the Temp of Obama Plan" in The Business Journal-Serving Metropolitan Kansas City (Vol. 27, November 14, 2008, No. 10)*
Pub: American City Business Journals, Inc.

Ed: Rob Roberts. **Description:** Kansas City, Missouri-based employee benefits experts say president-elect Barack Obama's health care reform plan is on track. Insurance for children and capitalization for health information technology are seen as priority areas. The plan is aimed at reducing the number of uninsured people in the United States.

21902 ■ *"Exposed?" in Mergers & Acquisitions: The Dealmaker's Journal (March 1, 2008)*
Pub: SourceMedia, Inc.

Ed: Jerry Abejo. **Description:** State-run pension plans' contributions are declining due to a loss of tax revenue from plummeting home values.

21903 ■ *"Facilitating and Rewarding Creativity During New Product Development" in Journal of Marketing (Vol. 75, July 2011, No. 4, pp. 53)*
Pub: American Marketing Association

Ed: James E. Burroughs, Darren W. Dahl, C. Page Moreau, Amitava Chattopadhay, Gerald J. Gorn. **Description:** A study to determine the effects of rewards to creativity in the process of new product development is presented. The findings show that the effect of rewards can be made positive if combined with appropriate creativity training.

21904 ■ *"Falling Local Executive Pay Could Suggest a Trend" in Tampa Bay Business Journal (Vol. 30, January 15, 2010, No. 4, pp. 1)*
Pub: American City Business Journals

Ed: Margie Manning. **Description:** Tampa Bay, Florida-based Raymond James Financial Inc. and MarineMax Inc.'s proxy statements have shown the decreasing compensation of the companies' highest paid executives. The falling trend in executive compensation was a result of intensified shareholder scrutiny and the economy.

21905 ■ *"The Final Say" in Hispanic Business (Vol. 30, March 2008, No. 3, pp. 52)*
Pub: Hispanic Business

Ed: Hildy Medina. **Description:** Vice-Chairwoman of the pensions and investments committee and Illinois State Senator Iris Martinez is the first Hispanic woman to be elected Senator and is advocating for pension funds to include Hispanic money managers and minority- and female-owned businesses in the investment plans.

21906 ■ *"Financial Education: Boomer's Spending Hurts Retirement" in Employee Benefit News (Vol. 25, November 1, 2011, No. 14, pp. 18)*
Pub: SourceMedia Inc.

Ed: Ann Marsh. **Description:** Financial planners and employers need to educate clients and employees about retirement planning. Boomers are spending money that should be saved for their retirement.

21907 ■ *"Get More Time Off" in Canadian Business (Vol. 80, March 12, 2007, No. 6, pp. 32)*
Pub: Rogers Media

Ed: June Morrow. **Description:** Expert advice to employees to make use of leaves of absence to improve their career instead of working continuously for a long period is presented.

21908 ■ *"Give a Little Back" in Canadian Business (Vol. 79, November 20, 2006, No. 23, pp. 17)*
Pub: Rogers Media

Ed: Jack Mintz. **Description:** The plans of Jim Flaherty, Canada's minister of finance, to remove the corporate tax bias on income paid to pension plans are discussed.

21909 ■ *"Glossary of Health Benefit Terms" in HRMagazine (Vol. 53, August 2008, No. 8, pp. 78)*
Pub: Society for Human Resource Management
Contact: Henry G. Jackson, President
E-mail: hjackson@shrm.org

Description: Glossary of health benefit terms is presented to help when choosing a health benefits package.

21910 ■ *"A Golden Retirement?" in Canadian Business (Vol. 81, December 8, 2008, No. 21, pp. 7)*
Pub: Rogers Media Ltd.

Ed: Paul Webster. **Description:** Canada Pension Plan Investment Board (CPPIB) is believed to have suffered heavy losses in global stock markets. CPPIB has moved aggressively into stock markets after independent managers started handling the funds in 2000.

21911 ■ *"Good Decisions. Bad Outcomes" in Harvard Business Review (Vol. 88, December 2010, No. 12, pp. 40)*
Pub: Harvard Business School Publishing

Ed: Dan Ariely. **Description:** Suggestions are provided for developing and implementing improved reward systems that in turn produce better decision-making processes. These include documenting critical assumptions and changing mind sets.

21912 ■ *Greening Your Small Business: How to Improve Your Bottom Line, Grow Your Brand, Satisfy Your Customers and Save the Planet*
Pub: Prentice Hall Press
Contact: Dame Marjorie M. Scardino, Chief Executive Officer

Ed: Jennifer Kaplan. **Released:** November 3, 2009. **Price:** $19.95. **Description:** A definitive resource for anyone who wants their small business to be cutting-edge, competitive, profitable, and eco-conscious. Stories from small business owners address every aspect of going green, from basics such as recycling waste, energy efficiency, and reducing information technology footprint, to more in-depth concerns such as green marketing and communications, green business travel, and green employee benefits.

21913 ■ *"Healthcare: How To Get a Better Deal" in Inc. (November 2007, pp. 34)*
Pub: Gruner & Jahr USA Publishing

Ed: Sarah Goldstein. **Description:** Things to consider when choosing an insurance carrier for your employees are explored.

21914 ■ *"Help Employees Give Away Some Of That Bonus" in Harvard Business Review (Vol. 86, July-August 2008, No. 8, pp. 1)*
Pub: Harvard Business School Press

Ed: Michael I. Norton; Elizabeth W. Dunn. **Description:** Research indicates that how employees spend their bonuses is key to their resultant happiness, rather than simply receiving the bonus itself. Firms that offer donation options can thereby increase employee satisfaction.

21915 ■ *"Hire Power" in Entrepreneur (Vol. 35, November 2007, No. 11, pp. 105)*
Pub: Entrepreneur Media Inc.

Ed: Mark Henricks. **Description:** Companies with big resources may hire human resource (HR) consultants to help with writing manuals, drafting policies and designing benefits for employees. HR consultants may also be hired to assist with specific functions or other strategic aspects.

21916 ■ *"How to Avoid the Three Big Mistakes" in Barron's (Vol. 88, March 10, 2008, No. 10, pp. 30)*
Pub: Dow Jones & Company, Inc.

Ed: Karen Hube. **Description:** Investors, particularly those having retirement investments, are advised to diversify their investments, refrain from market timing, and minimize payments to maximize investment gains. An investor committing these mistakes could lose as much as $375,000 dollars over ten years.

21917 ■ *"How Much is Too Much?" in Canadian Business (Vol. 79, July 17, 2006, No. 14-15, pp. 55)*
Pub: Rogers Media

Ed: John Gray. **Description:** Elucidates the emphasis on the need for companies to analyze the executive pay packages designed by compensation consultants.

21918 ■ *How to Start and Run Your Own Corporation: S-Corporations For Small Business Owners*
Pub: HCM Publishing

Ed: Peter I. Hupalo. **Released:** March 6, 2003. **Price:** $22.95. **Description:** Basics of corporate business structure are explained. Topics include discovering the best business structure for your company; how to decided between an S-Corporation and LLC; choosing the state in which to incorporate, how to form a corporation, angel investing, special issues for one-person corporations, the role of bylaws and corporate minutes, board of directors, taxes, workers' compensation issues, retirement plans, and more.

21919 ■ *"Inch by Inch, Employees Lose Ground" in Business Courier (Vol. 26, November 13, 2009, No. 29, pp. 1)*
Pub: American City Business Journals, Inc.

Ed: James Ritchie. **Description:** Employees in Ohio who retained their jobs have suffered losses in salary and other benefits, as companies exert efforts to save money. Thirty-four percent of employees experienced pay cuts. Statistical data included.

21920 ■ *"Insurers Warn Brokers" in Sacramento Business Journal (Vol. 25, August 22, 2008, No. 25, pp. 1)*
Pub: American City Business Journals, Inc.

Ed: Kathy Robertson. **Description:** Sacramento, California-based health plans have warned insurance brokers not to combine two different kinds of insurance products or they will be stricken from the sales network. The health plans also asked employers to promise not to combine plans with self-insurance. Such schemes are seen to destroy lower-premium health products.

21921 ■ *"International Benefits Roundup" in Employee Benefit News (Vol. 25, December 1, 2011, No. 15)*
Pub: SourceMedia Inc.

Description: Employee contributions to an employer-sponsored defined contribution plan in Japan will allowed on a tax-deductible basis; however, currently employee contributions are not allowed. The defined contribution plan is outlined for better understanding.

21922 ■ *"Investigation Hints at Workers' Comp Trouble" in Sacramento Business Journal (Vol. 25, July 4, 2008, No. 18, pp. 1)*
Pub: American City Business Journals, Inc.

Ed: Kelly Johnson. **Description:** In 500 California firms, a survey of worker compensation revealed that 38 percent of the companies had problems with required coverage. Government investigators are bothered that 107 companies did not respond to the official inquiry. Other views and information on the survey and on the expected economic implications of the findings are presented.

21923 ■ *"Is Raising CPP Premiums a Good Idea?" in Canadian Business (Vol. 83, July 20, 2010, No. 11-12, pp. 37)*
Pub: Rogers Media Ltd.

Description: Big labor is pushing for an increase in Canada Pension Plan premiums but pension consultants believe this system is not broken and that the government needs to focus on addressing the low rate of personal retirement savings. If the premiums go up, even those with high savings will be forced to pay more and it could block other plans that really address the real issue.

21924 ■ *"Is There a Doctor In the House?"* in *Black Enterprise (Vol. 41, December 2010, No. 5, pp. 42)*
Pub: Earl G. Graves Publishing Co. Inc.
Ed: Renita Burns. **Description:** Health insurance premiums have increased between 15 percent and 20 percent for small business owners, making it one of the most expensive costs. Ways to evaluate a health plan's costs and effectiveness are examined.

21925 ■ *"Kids in Crisis"* in *Employee Benefit News (Vol. 25, November 1, 2011, No. 14, pp. 26)*
Pub: SourceMedia Inc.
Ed: Lisa V. Gillespie. **Description:** Employers and vendor are taking more aggressive steps to help battle childhood obesity.

21926 ■ *"Labor Pains"* in *Canadian Business (Vol. 79, August 14, 2006, No. 16-17, pp. 80)*
Pub: Rogers Media
Description: Canada's employment insurance is analyzed in view of the growing shortage of labor.

21927 ■ *"Leave Policies: How to Avoid Leave-Related Lawsuits"* in *Employee Benefit News (Vol. 25, December 1, 2011, No. 15, pp. 12)*
Pub: SourceMedia Inc.
Ed: John F. Galvin. **Description:** Tips for employers when adding disability and maternity leave benefits to workers are outlined, with focus on ways to avoid leave-related lawsuits.

21928 ■ *"Legg's Compensation Committee Chair Defends CEO Fetting's Pay"* in *Boston Business Journal (Vol. 29, July 22, 2011, No. 11, pp. 1)*
Pub: American City Business Journals Inc.
Ed: Gary Haber. **Description:** Legg Mason Inc. CEO Mark R. Fetting has been awarded $5.9 million pay package and he expects to receive questions regarding it in the coming shareholders meeting. However, Baltimore, Maryland-based RKTL Associates chairman emeritus Harold R. Adams believes Fetting has done a tremendous job in bringing Legg's through a tough market.

21929 ■ *"Legislators Must Cut Cost of Government"* in *Crain's Detroit Business (Vol. 24, October 6, 2008, No. 40, pp. 6)*
Pub: Crain Communications, Inc.
Description: Southeast and West Michigan business leaders are setting aside their differences and have proposed clear agendas, ranging from eliminating the Michigan Business Tax to overhauling public employee and retiree benefits and pensions. Lawmakers must also come together to find solutions for the state's economy and discover an entirely new vision for the future of Michigan business.

21930 ■ *"Like Mom and Apple Pie"* in *Canadian Business (Vol. 79, October 9, 2006, No. 20, pp. 19)*
Pub: Rogers Media
Ed: Peter Shawn Taylor. **Description:** Impact of paying huge tax bills on the social benefits of family income is discussed. Income splitting as an effective way to lower household's overall tax bill is presented.

21931 ■ *"Looking For Financing?"* in *Hispanic Business (Vol. 30, July-August 2008, No. 7-8, pp. 16)*
Pub: Hispanic Business, Inc.
Ed: Frank Nelson. **Description:** Investment firms want to know about businesses that need funding for either expansion or acquisition; companies fitting this profile are interviewed and their perceptions are discussed. Investment firms need businesses to be realistic in their expectations and business plans which show spending of funds and expected benefits, long term goals, track record and strong management teams.

21932 ■ *"Managing Health Benefits in Small and Mid-Sized Organizations"*
Pub: Amacom
Ed: Patricia Halo. **Released:** July 1999. **Description:** Comprehensive guide for developing health care plans for companies employing between 50 and 5,000 employees in order to provide employees with better health care at lower prices.

21933 ■ *"M&I Execs May Get Golden Parachutes"* in *Business Journal-Milwaukee (Vol. 28, December 31, 2010, No. 14, pp. A3)*
Pub: Milwaukee Business Journal
Ed: Rich Kirchen. **Description:** Marshall and Isley Corporation's top executives have a chance to receive golden-parachute payments it its buyer, BMO Financial Group, repays the Troubled Asset Relief Program (TARP) loan on behalf of the company. One TARP rule prevents golden-parachute payments to them and the next five most highly paid employees of TARP recipients.

21934 ■ *"The Massachusetts Mess: Good Health Care Is Expensive"* in *Barron's (Vol. 89, July 27, 2009, No. 30, pp. 39)*
Pub: Dow Jones & Co., Inc.
Ed: Thomas G. Donlan. **Description:** Massachusetts' mandatory health insurance has produced the highest rate of insurance coverage among the states but the state is now unable to afford its dream of universal coverage just three years after they enacted it. This supposed model for federal health-care reform is turning out to be a joke.

21935 ■ *"Md. Tries to Recoup $73M from Actuary"* in *Baltimore Business Journal (Vol. 28, June 11, 2010, No. 5, pp. 1)*
Pub: Baltimore Business Journal
Ed: Gary Haber. **Description:** Maryland State Retirement and Pension System has won nearly $73 million in administrative ruling against Milliman Inc. over pension loss miscalculations. However, Milliman filed two court cases seeking to reverse the decision and to recoup to the state any money a court orders.

21936 ■ *"Medicare Plans Step Up Battle for Subscribers"* in *Sacramento Business Journal (Vol. 28, October 21, 2011, No. 34, pp. 1)*
Pub: Sacramento Business Journal
Ed: Kathy Robertson. **Description:** California's market for health plans have become increasingly competitive as more than 313,000 seniors try to figure out the best plans to meet their needs for 2012. Health plans are rated on Medicare materials to help consumers distinguish among the Medicare health maintenance organizations (HMOs).

21937 ■ *"Mettle Detector"* in *Canadian Business (Vol. 79, July 17, 2006, No. 14-15, pp. 63)*
Pub: Rogers Media
Ed: Calvin Leung. **Description:** The difficulties faced in completing the Certified Financial Analyst course, and the rewards one can expect after its completion, are discussed.

21938 ■ *"Monaco Pay Cut Draws Attention"* in *The Business Journal-Portland (Vol. 25, August 8, 2008, No. 22, pp. 1)*
Pub: American City Business Journals, Inc.
Ed: Erik Siemers. **Description:** Monaco Coach Corp. cut the salaries of five top executives in an effort to reduce the company's $178 million worth of inventory. The executives can earn the lost salary back if the inventory is reduced by $58 million a year after August 2008.

21939 ■ *"The Moody Blues"* in *Entrepreneur (Vol. 36, April 2008, No. 4, pp. 87)*
Pub: Entrepreneur Media, Inc.
Ed: Mark Henricks. **Description:** Depression among employees can affect their productivity and cost the company. Businesses with a workforce that is likely to have depression should inform their employees about the health benefits covered by insurance. Other details on how to address depression concerns among employees are discussed.

21940 ■ *"More Businesses Will Shift Health Costs to Workers"* in *Business Review, Albany New York (Vol. 34, November 16, 2007, No. 33, pp. 1)*
Pub: American City Business Journals, Inc.
Ed: Barbara Pinckney. **Description:** Survey conducted by consulting firm Benetech Inc. showed that sixty percent of employers are planning to increase payroll deductions to pay for health insurance premiums. More than ninety percent of the employers prefer HMO plans, followed by Preferred Provider Organizations. Other details of the survey are discussed.

21941 ■ *"More Small Businesses Willing to Fund Employees' Benefits"* in *Baltimore Business Journal (Vol. 28, June 18, 2010, No. 6, pp. 1)*
Pub: Baltimore Business Journal
Ed: Scott Graham. **Description:** An increasing number of small businesses in Maryland are tapping into potentially cheaper self-funded health plans instead of providing fully insured benefits to employees through traditional health plans. Self-funded health plans charge employers for health care up to a specified level. Economic implications of self-funded plans to small businesses are discussed.

21942 ■ *"New Year, New Estate Plan"* in *Hawaii Business (Vol. 53, February 2008, No. 8, pp. 54)*
Pub: Hawaii Business Publishing
Ed: Antony M. Orme. **Description:** Discusses the start of the new year which can be a time to revise wills and estate plans as failure to do so may create problems of unequal inheritance and increase in estate tax exemption, which could disinherit beneficiaries. Other circumstances that can prompt changes in wills and estate plans are presented.

21943 ■ *"Nobel Winners Provide Insight on Outsourcing, Contract Work"* in *Workforce Management (Vol. 88, November 16, 2009, No. 12, pp. 11)*
Pub: Crain Communications Inc.
Ed: Jeremy Smerd. **Description:** Insights into such workforce management issues as bonuses, employee contracts and outsourcing has been recognized by the Nobel Prize winners in economics whose research sheds a light on the way economic decisions are made outside markets.

21944 ■ *"OMERS Labors With Troubles at the Top"* in *Globe & Mail (February 26, 2007, pp. B3)*
Pub: CTVglobemedia Publishing Inc.
Ed: Elizabeth Church. **Description:** The trouble over fund management and leadership change in the Ontario Municipal Employees Retirement System is discussed.

21945 ■ *"Open Enrollment: Staying Healthy During Enrollment Season"* in *Employee Benefit News (Vol. 25, November 1, 2011, No. 14, pp. 41)*
Pub: SourceMedia Inc.
Ed: Shana Sweeney. **Description:** Tips for staying healthy during your benefit open enrollment period are outlined.

21946 ■ *Overcoming Barriers to Entrepreneurship in the United States*
Pub: Lexington Books
Ed: Diana Furchtgott-Roth. **Released:** March 28, 2008. **Price:** $24.95. **Description:** Real and perceived barriers to the founding and running of small businesses in America are discussed. Each chapter outlines how policy and economic environments can hinder business owners and offers tips to overcome these obstacles. Starting with venture capital access in Silicon Valley during the Internet bubble, the book goes on to question the link between personal wealth and entrepreneurship, examines how federal tax rates affect small business creation and destruction, explains the low rate of self-employment among Mexican immigrants, and suggests ways pension coverage can be increased in small businesses.

21947 ■ *"Paychecks of Some Bank CEOs Have a Pre-Recession Look"* in *Boston Business Journal (Vol. 29, May 13, 2011, No. 1, pp. 1)*
Pub: American City Business Journals Inc.
Ed: Gary Haber. **Description:** The salaries of United States-based bank chief executive officers have increased to pre-recession levels. Wells Fargo and Company's John G. Stumpf received $17.6 million in 2010. Community bank executives, on the other hand, have seen minimal increases.

21948 ■ *"Penny Chief Shops For Shares"* in *Barron's (Vol. 88, July 7, 2008, No. 27, pp. 29)*
Pub: Dow Jones & Co., Inc.
Ed: Teresa Rivas. **Description:** Myron Ullman III, chairman and chief executive officer of J.C. Penney, purchased $1 million worth of shares of the company. He now owns 393,140 shares of the company and an additional 1,282 on his 401(k) plan.

21949 ■ *"The People Puzzle; Re-Training America's Workers"* in *The Economist (Vol. 390, January 3, 2009, No. 8612, pp. 32)*
Pub: The Economist Newspaper Inc.
Description: With thousands of workers losing their jobs, America is now facing the task of getting them back to work. With an overall unemployment rate of 6.7 percent, the federal government has three main ways for leading workers back to employment: training them for new jobs, providing unemployment insurance in order to replace lost wages during the period of job-hunting; and matching employers who desire a skill with workers who have that skill. Specialized staffing agencies provide employers and potential employees with the help necessary to find a job in some of the more niche markets.

21950 ■ *"Perks Still Popular: Jets May be Out, but CEO Benefits Abound"* in *Crain's Detroit Business (Vol. 25, June 22, 2009)*
Pub: Crain Communications Inc. - Detroit
Ed: Ryan Beene. **Description:** Benefits packages of local CEOs are outlined. Statistical data included.

21951 ■ *"Picking a 529 College Savings Plan"* in *Black Enterprise (Vol. 37, February 2007, No. 7, pp. 46)*
Pub: Earl G. Graves Publishing Co. Inc.
Ed: Carolyn M. Brown. **Description:** Advice is given to help choose the right college savings plan.

21952 ■ *"A Piece of the Action"* in *Black Enterprise (Vol. 38, January 2008, No. 6, pp. 42)*
Pub: Earl G. Graves Publishing Co. Inc.
Ed: Alan Hughes. **Description:** Andre Williams, owner of Kaze Sushi restaurant, offered generous incentive plan-equity in the business in order to acquire Chef Kaze Chan and Chef Hari Chan. Williams' entrepreneurial pursuits are discussed.

21953 ■ *PPC's Guide to Choosing Retirement Plans for Small Businesses*
Pub: Practitioners Publishing Company
Released: June 2004. **Price:** $119.00. **Description:** Guide to evaluate and select retirement plans for small business.

21954 ■ *PPC's Guide to Compensation Planning for Small Business*
Pub: Practitioners Publishing Company
Released: September 2004. **Price:** $119.00. **Description:** Technical guide for developing a compensation system for small business. Forms and letters included.

21955 ■ *"Prescription for Health: Choosing the Best Healthcare Plan"* in *Black Enterprise (Vol. 38, July 2008, No. 12, pp. 48)*
Pub: Earl G. Graves Publishing Co. Inc.
Ed: Tamara E. Holmes. **Description:** According to a survey of small-business owners conducted by Sure-Payroll Inc., 20 percent of respondents have had a prospective employee refuse a job offer because healthcare benefits did not come with it. Cost is not the only reason many small-business owners do not offer these benefits. Guidelines to help take some of

the confusion out of the guesswork that comes with trying to find the proper fit concerning healthcare benefits are outlined.

21956 ■ *"The Price of Citizenship"* in *Canadian Business (Vol. 79, August 14, 2006, No. 16-17, pp. 13)*
Pub: Rogers Media
Ed: Jack Mintz. **Description:** Safety and insurance benefits provided by the Canadian government to Canadian passport holders returning from Lebanon, is discussed.

21957 ■ *"Recession Drags Down CEO Pay; Full Impact May Not Have Played Out"* in *Crain's Detroit Business (Vol. 25, June 22, 2009, No. 25)*
Pub: Crain Communications Inc. - Detroit
Ed: Ryan Beene. **Description:** Median overall compensation package for Detroit's top-compensated 50 CEOs was down 10.67 percent from $2.3 million in 2007 to $2.06 million in 2008. Statistical data included.

21958 ■ *Retire Dollar Smart*
Pub: Trafford Publishing
Ed: Jim Miller. **Released:** July 2006. **Price:** $25.99. **Description:** The difference between savings and investments and their importance is examined, along with four rules for converting good investments into even greater ones. Contingency plans for healthcare costs as well as ways to manage taxes on investments are discussed. Five methods to control the costs of investing and saving include the use of smart strategies; getting independent, accurate, complete information; investing passively; asking for a discount; and taking off your blinders. Ten steps for designing a foolproof retirement investment portfolio are also provided.

21959 ■ *"Retirement Barriers: Lowering Retirement System Barriers for Women"* in *Employee Benefit News (Vol. 25, December 1, 2011, No. 15)*
Pub: SourceMedia Inc.
Ed: Mary Nell Billings. **Description:** Challenges faced by small business for lowering retirement benefits barriers for women and minorities, which is difficult to put into practice, is discussed.

21960 ■ *"Retirement Plan Disclosures: Prepare Now for Fiduciary Rules"* in *Employee Benefit News (Vol. 25, November 1, 2011, No. 14, pp. 24)*
Pub: SourceMedia Inc.
Ed: Brian M. Pinheiro, Kurt R. Anderson. **Description:** Department of Labor has delayed the deadlines on new affirmative obligations for fiduciaries of retirement plans subject to the Employee Retirement Income Security Act. Details included.

21961 ■ *"RIM Rocks Out: Billionaire Bosses Sponsor a Free Concert for Deserving Staff"* in *Canadian Business (Vol. 80, Winter 2007, No. 24)*
Pub: Rogers Media
Ed: Joe Castaldo. **Description:** Jim Balsillie and Mike Lazaridis of Research in Motion Ltd. (RIM) rented out the Air Canada Centre in Toronto to give their employees a free concert that features performances by the Tragically Hip and Van Halen on November 15, 2007. RIM has sponsored concerts by Aerosmith, Tom Cochrane, and the Barenaked Ladies in past parties that only shows how far the company goes in terms of employee appreciation.

21962 ■ *"Running On Empty"* in *The Business Journal-Milwaukee (Vol. 25, July 4, 2008, No. 41, pp. A1)*
Pub: American City Business Journals, Inc.
Ed: David Doege. **Description:** Employers are more engaged in offering incentives designed to offset commuting costs. Among the incentives offered are gas cards, parking reimbursement and midyear wage increases. The other efforts to help employees with the costs of going to work are discussed.

21963 ■ *"A Safety Net in Need of Repair"* in *The Economist (Vol. 390, January 3, 2009, No. 8612, pp. 33)*
Pub: The Economist Newspaper Inc.
Description: America's unemployment-insurance scheme is outdated and skimpy compared to other industrialized countries despite the fact that Americans tend to work harder at returning to the job market; the benefits are lower and available for a smaller amount of time and less unemployed workers are even able to collect these benefits. Statistical data included.

21964 ■ *"Sales of Pension Income Targeted by Senator"* in *Wall Street Journal Eastern Edition (November 21 , 2011, pp. C7)*
Pub: Dow Jones & Company Inc.
Ed: Leslie Scism. **Description:** Senator Tom Harkin is concerned about a widening business in which retirees and veterans sell pension income to investors in the secondary market. The business provides major profits for middlemen. Harkin wants those who are considering such a sale to have adequate information provided and knowledge in order to avoid unscrupulous dealings.

21965 ■ *"A Say on Pay"* in *Canadian Business (Vol. 82, April 27, 2009, No. 7, pp. 14)*
Pub: Rogers Media
Ed: Joe Castaldo. **Description:** A COMPAS Inc. survey of 134 Canadian chief executive officers found that 44 percent agree that CEO compensation should be subject to a non-binding vote. The respondents were also divided on whether to allow shareholders to exercise retroactive clawbacks on executive compensation if firm performance turns out to be worse than projected.

21966 ■ *"Shopping Around for New Ideas"* in *Canadian Business (Vol. 79, July 17, 2006, No. 14-15, pp. 76)*
Pub: Rogers Media
Description: Pensions should be a win-win situation for both the employer and the employee. The perspective of both parties concerning pension plans is explored as well as the need to amend laws in order to make sure that one class of merchant does not suffer at the cost of another.

21967 ■ *"Small Biz Owners Are Tapping Into Health Savings Plans"* in *Small Business Opportunities (Fall 2007)*
Pub: Harris Publications Inc.
Ed: Michael L. Corne. **Description:** Health savings accounts were developed by Golden Rule, a United Healthcare company. Today, more than 40 percent of the company's customers are covered by health savings account plans.

21968 ■ *"Small Business Compensation"* in *Small Business Economic Trends (April 2008, pp. 10)*
Pub: National Federation of Independent Business
Ed: William C. Dunkelberg, Holly Wade. **Description:** Graphs and tables that present compensation plans and compensation changes of small businesses in the U.S. are provided. The figures include data from 1986 to 2008.

21969 ■ *"Small Business Compensation"* in *Small Business Economic Trends (March 2008, pp. 10)*
Pub: National Federation of Independent Business
Ed: William C. Dunkelberg, Holly Wade. **Description:** Graphs and tables that present compensation plans and compensation changes of small businesses in the U.S. are provided. The figures include data from 1968 to 2008.

21970 ■ *"Small Business Compensation"* in *Small Business Economic Trends (February 2008, pp. 10)*
Pub: National Federation of Independent Business
Ed: William C. Dunkelberg, Holly Wade. **Description:** Graphs and tables that present compensation plans and compensation changes of small businesses in the U.S. are provided. The figures include data from 1974 to 2008.

21971 ■ *"Small Business Compensation" in Small Business Economic Trends (January 2008, pp. 10)*
Pub: National Federation of Independent Business
Description: Graph from a survey of small businesses in the U.S. is given, representing small business compensation from January 1986 to December 2007. Tables showing actual compensation changes and compensation plans are also presented. A graph comparing small business prices and labor compensation is supplied.

21972 ■ *"Small Business Compensation" in Small Business Economic Trends (July 2010, pp. 10)*
Pub: National Federation of Independent Business
Description: A graph from a survey of small businesses in the U.S. is given representing small business compensation from January 1986 to June 2010. Tables showing actual compensation changes and compensation plans are also presented. A graph comparing small business prices and labor compensation is supplied.

21973 ■ *"Small Businesses Changing Their Health Plan Preferences" in Boston Business Journal (Vol. 29, June 24, 2011, No. 7, pp. 1)*
Pub: American City Business Journals Inc.
Ed: Scott Dance. **Description:** Small businesses in Maryland are shifting from traditional health plans to the consumer-oriented health savings accounts or HSAs. Health insurance industry experts say the change is indicative of the insurance buyers' desire to be more thrifty and discerning in their health care purchases.

21974 ■ *"Small Businesses Get Creative to Retain Workers" in Crain's Detroit Business (Vol. 24, March 17, 2008, No. 11, pp. 21)*
Pub: Crain Communications, Inc.
Ed: Nancy Kaffer. **Description:** Small businesses are often unable to compete with larger firms when it comes to offering employees fringe benefits and such perks as a company gym or an in-house chef; however, many smaller companies have found that the key to gaining employee loyalty lies in creating an atmosphere in which employees feel job satisfaction. Also provides tips on how to keep employees.

21975 ■ *"Small, But Mighty" in Employee Benefit News (Vol. 25, November 1, 2011, No. 14, pp. 32)*
Pub: SourceMedia Inc.
Ed: Andrea Davis. **Description:** Three consulting firms are facing the challenge of helping clients understand the new health care reform in a tight economy.

21976 ■ *"Something Different in the Air? The Collapse of the Schwarzenegger Health Plan in California" in WorkingUSA (June 2008)*
Pub: Blackwell Publishers Ltd.
Ed: Daniel J.B. Mitchell. **Description:** In January 2007, California Governor Arnold Schwarzenegger proposed a state universal health care plan modeled after the Massachusetts individual mandate program. A year later, the plan was dead. Although some key interest groups eventually backed the plan, it was overwhelmed by a looming state budget crisis and a lack of gubernatorial focus. Although much acclaimed for his stance on greenhouse gases, stem cells, hydrogen highways, and other Big Ideas, diffused gubernatorial priorities and a failure to resolve California's chronic fiscal difficulties let the clock run out on universal health care.

21977 ■ *"Spotlight on Pensions" in Business Horizons (Vol. 51, March-April 2008, No. 2, pp. 105)*
Pub: Elsevier Advanced Technology Publications
Ed: Laureen A. Maines. **Description:** Perceptions of pension burden and risk among financial statement users is likely to increase with changes in pension accounting. These perceptions might affect decisions on pension commitments and investments.

21978 ■ *"Spread Your Wings" in Canadian Business (Vol. 81, March 17, 2008, No. 4, pp. 31)*
Pub: Rogers Media
Ed: Megan Harman. **Description:** Financing from angel investors is one avenue that should be explored by startups. Angel investors are typically affluent individuals who invest their own money. Angel investors usually want at least 10 times their initial investment within eight years but they benefit the businesses through their help in decision-making and the industry expertise they provide.

21979 ■ *"State Expects Increase of $50 Million from Film Bills; Come Back, Al Roker" in Crain's Detroit Business (March 24, 2008)*
Pub: Crain Communications, Inc.
Ed: Bill Shea. **Description:** Overview of the new film initiative and its incentives designed to entice more film work to Michigan; the measures could bring $50 million to $100 million in movie production work for the rest of this year compared to the $4 million total the state saw last year. Also discusses the show 'DEA' which was filmed in Detroit and stars Al Roker.

21980 ■ *"Steeling for Battle" in Crain's Chicago Business (Vol. 31, April 21, 2008, No. 16, pp. 3)*
Pub: Crain Communications, Inc.
Ed: Bob Tita. **Description:** Discusses contract negotiations between the United Steelworkers union and ArcelorMittal USA Inc., the nation's largest steelmaker, and U.S. Steel Corp., the third-largest; the union sees these negotiations as the best chance in two decades to regain lost ground but industry experts predict the companies will try to reduce benefits, demand a separate, lower wage scale for new hires and look for relief from the rising costs for retirees' health insurance coverage.

21981 ■ *"Surprise Package" in Business Courier (Vol. 27, June 25, 2010, No. 8, pp. 1)*
Pub: Business Courier
Ed: Dan Monk, Jon Newberry, Steve Watkins. **Description:** More than 60 percent of the chief executive officers (CEOs) in Greater Cincinnati's 35 public companies took a salary cut in 2009, but stock grants resulted in large paper gains for the CEOs. The salary cuts show efforts of boards of directors to observe austerity. Statistics on increased values of stock awards for CEOs, median pay for CEOs, and median shareholder return are also presented.

21982 ■ *"Survey Finds State Execs Cool On Climate Change" in The Business Journal-Milwaukee (Vol. 25, August 8, 2008, No. 46, pp. A1)*
Pub: American City Business Journals, Inc.
Ed: David Doege. **Description:** According to a survey of business executives in Wisconsin, business leaders do not see climate change as a pressing concern, but businesses are moving toward more energy-efficient operations. The survey also revealed that executives believe that financial incentives can promote energy conservation. Other survey results are provided.

21983 ■ *"Survivorship Policies: Planning a Policy for Two" in Employee Benefit News (Vol. 25, November 1, 2011, No. 14, pp. 20)*
Pub: SourceMedia Inc.
Ed: Marli D. Riggs. **Description:** Survivorship insurance is becoming an added benefit high net worth individuals and executives should consider when evaluating life insurance policies.

21984 ■ *"Swinging For the Fences" in Academy of Management Journal (October 2007, pp. 1055)*
Pub: Academy of Management
Contact: Ming-Jer Chen, President
Ed: William Gerard Sanders, Donald C. Hambrick.
Description: Study examines managerial risk-taking vis-a-vis stock options of the company; results reveal that stock options instigate CEOs to take unwise risks that could bring huge losses to the company.

21985 ■ *"Take the Wheel: the Pension Protection Act Doesn't Mean You Can Sit Back and Relax" in Black Enterprise (October 2007)*
Pub: Earl G. Graves Publishing Co. Inc.
Ed: Mellody Hobson. **Description:** Pension Protection Act provides multiple benefits and tax advantages for retirement, however the investment options and contribution rates are very conservative.

21986 ■ *"Taking Full Advantage: What You Need To Know During Open-Enrollment Season" in Black Enterprise (Vol. 38, November 2007, No. 4)*
Pub: Earl G. Graves Publishing Co. Inc.
Ed: Donald Jay Korn. **Description:** Employees can change or enroll in new insurance benefits during the fall season. It is important to assess each plan offered and to determine your deductible. Statistical data included.

21987 ■ *"Tax Reform Analysis: Reforms Equal Smaller 401(k)s" in Employee Benefit News (Vol. 25, December 1, 2011, No. 15, pp. 19)*
Pub: SourceMedia Inc.
Ed: Lisa V. Gillespie. **Description:** According to a new analysis by the Employee Benefit Research Institute, two recent proposals to change existing tax treatment of 401(k) retirement plans could cost workers because they would lower their account balances towards retirement.

21988 ■ *"Teachers, U.S. Fund Providence Made Moves On BCE Buyout" in Globe & Mail (April 10, 2007, pp. B17)*
Pub: CTVglobemedia Publishing Inc.
Ed: Boyd Erman; Sinclair Stewart; Jacquie McNish. **Description:** The Ontario Teachers Pension Plan, the largest shareholder of telecommunications firm BCE Inc., has called for a partnership with buyout firm Providence Equity Partners Inc. in order to acquire BCE Inc.

21989 ■ *This Is Not Your Parents' Retirement: A Revolutionary Guide for a Revolutionary Generation*
Pub: Entrepreneur Press
Ed: Patrick P. Astre. **Released:** July 2005. **Price:** $19.95 (US), $26.95 (Canadian). **Description:** Mutual funds, stocks, bonds, insurance products, and tax strategies for retirement planning.

21990 ■ *"Tied to Home: Female Owned Businesses Export Less, And It's Not Just Because They're Smaller" in Canadian Business (April 14, 2008)*
Pub: Rogers Media
Ed: Lauren McKeon. **Description:** Only 12 percent of small and midsized enterprises that are run by women export their products and services. Government agencies can be more proactive in promoting the benefits of exporting by including women in case studies and recruiting women as mentors. Exporting provides great growth potential especially for the service sector where women have an advantage.

21991 ■ *"To Thine Own Self" in Entrepreneur (Vol. 35, November 2007, No. 11, pp. 50)*
Pub: Entrepreneur Media Inc.
Ed: Torabi Farnoosh. **Description:** Self-directed individual retirement account (IRA) provides more investment options as payoff from this can be higher than an average mutual fund. Details on how to manage self-directed IRAs are discussed.

21992 ■ *"Tradeshow Attendance Incentives Add Up" in Pet Product News (Vol. 64, December 2010, No. 12, pp. 14)*
Pub: BowTie Inc.
Ed: Mark E. Battersby. **Description:** Pointers on how pet specialty retailers can claim business travel tax and income tax deductions for expenses paid or incurred in participation at tradeshows, conventions, and meetings are presented. Incentives in form of these deductions could allow pet specialty retailers to gain business benefits, aside from the education and enjoyment involved with the travel.

21993 ■ *"Trust But Verify: FMLA Software Isn't Foolproof, So Apply a Human Touch" in HR Specialist (Vol. 8, September 2010, No. 9, pp. 3)*
Pub: Capitol Information Group Inc.
Description: Employers are using software to track FMLA information, however, it is important for employers to review reasons for eligibility require-

ments, particularly when an employee is reportedly overstepping the bounds within leave regulations due to software error.

21994 ■ "Types of Health Plans" in HRMagazine (Vol. 53, August 2008, No. 9, pp. 72)

Pub: Society for Human Resource Management
Contact: Henry G. Jackson, President
E-mail: hjackson@shrm.org
Description: Definitions are given for various types of health care coverage available. Fee-for-service (FFS), health maintenance organization (HMO), preferred provider organization (PPO), point of service (POS) and consumer-directed health plan (CDHP) are outlined.

21995 ■ "Uncashed Checks: Retirement Plans in a Quandry" in Employee Benefit News (Vol. 25, December 1, 2011, No. 15, pp. 18)

Pub: SourceMedia Inc.
Ed: Terry Dunne. **Description:** Complex issues arise when employees don't cash their 401(k) balance checks. The US Department of Labor permits plans to cash out accounts of former employees with less than $1,000 to reduce the cost and time required to manage them.

21996 ■ Understanding Workers Compensation: A Guide for Safety and Health Professionals

Pub: Government Institutes
Contact: Judith Rothman, Director
URL(s): www.govinstpress.com. **Price:** $72, Individuals Paperback; £44.95, Individuals Paperback. **Publication includes:** Listing of state and provincial workers compensation administrators. **Entries include:** Name, address, phone. Principal content of publication is explanation of the Workers Compensation System. **Database includes:** Sample forms, checklists, U.S. Chamber of Commerce analysis.

21997 ■ "Unions and Upward Mobility for Low-Wage Workers" in WorkingUSA (Vol. 11, September 2008, No. 3, pp. 337)

Pub: Blackwell Publishers Ltd.
Ed: John Schmitt, Margy Waller, Shawn Fremstad, Ben Zipperer. **Description:** Examination of the impact of unionization on the pay and benefits in fifteen important low-wage occupations is outlined. Even after controlling for important differences between union and nonunion workers, including such factors as age and education level, unionization improves the pay and benefits offered in what are otherwise low-paying occupations.

21998 ■ "Use a Benefits Checklist to Ease New-Hire Onboarding" in HR Specialist (Vol. 8, September 2010, No. 9, pp. 4)

Pub: Capitol Information Group Inc.
Description: Checklist to help employees enroll in a company's benefit offerings is provided, courtesy of Wayne State University in Detroit, Michigan.

21999 ■ "Wal-Mart Expansion Plans Hit Roadblock" in Crain's Chicago Business (Vol. 31, March 24, 2008, No. 12, pp. 2)

Pub: Crain Communications, Inc.
Ed: Monee Fields-White. **Description:** Wal-Mart Stores Inc.'s expansion plans in Chicago have suffered a series of setbacks due to a shifting political landscape in which may require the company to pay higher wages. Wal-Mart claims that its hourly pay and benefits are fair; however, the labor force does not agree.

22000 ■ "W&S to Trim Rich Retirement Plan" in Business Courier (Vol. 27, October 15, 2010, No. 24, pp. 1)

Pub: Business Courier
Ed: Dan Monk. **Description:** Insurance firm Western & Southern Financial Group announced that it will reduce the pension benefits of its 4,000 associates by more than 30 percent starting January 1, 2011. The move is expected to reduce annual retirement payments by several thousand dollars per associate. Western is a Fortune 500 company and has $34 billion in total assets.

22001 ■ "We Have a Budget, Too" in Entrepreneur (Vol. 37, October 2009, No. 10, pp. 89)

Pub: Entrepreneur Media, Inc.
Ed: Craig Matsuda. **Description:** One human resources executive at a financial services company claims that health care issues are as costly and irritating for companies as they are for the employees. Health care vendors and insurers try as much as possible to maximize profits, while companies exert much effort to maximize benefits for their workers.

22002 ■ "What Choice Did I Have?" in Entrepreneur (Vol. 37, October 2009, No. 10, pp. 88)

Pub: Entrepreneur Media, Inc.
Ed: Craig Matsuda. **Description:** Profile of a worker at a financial services company who acquired first hand knowledge concerning the relationship between health insurance costs and coverage. The worker's son got severely ill, forcing the worker to spend above what is covered by health insurance.

22003 ■ "What You Should Know About Signing Bonuses" in Black Enterprise (Vol. 38, October 2007, No. 3, pp. 70)

Pub: Earl G. Graves Publishing Co. Inc.
Ed: Marcia Reed-Woodard. **Description:** High-level corporate executives are receiving sign-on bonuses. According to a study conducted by World@Work, nearly 70 percent of employers signing bonuses attract key employees.

22004 ■ "Winners and Losers" in Crain's Detroit Business (Vol. 25, June 22, 2009, No. 25, pp. 18)

Pub: Crain Communications Inc. - Detroit
Description: Rankings for Detroit's 50 top-compensated CEOs has changed due to the economic recession. The biggest changes are discussed.

22005 ■ "Women Draw Less Pension Income" in Marketing to Women (Vol. 21, March 2008, No. 3, pp. 6)

Pub: EPM Communications Inc.
Contact: Ira Mayer, President
E-mail: imayer@epmcom.com
Description: According to a study by the Employee Benefit Research Institute, women over the age of 50 are much less likely to receive annuity and/or pension income. Statistical data included.

22006 ■ "Work At It!" in Hawaii Business (Vol. 53, October 2007, No. 4, pp. 44)

Pub: Hawaii Business Publishing
Ed: Cathy S. Cruz-George. **Description:** Employers in Hawaii are mitigating the effects of rising healthcare costs by giving their employees health insurance and offering wellness programs. Employer-based health insurance has increases by 87 percent in the United States over the 2000-2006 period. Wellness programs that address different aspects of employees' health, such as food consumption, drug compliance and smoking habits, are discussed.

TRADE PERIODICALS

22007 ■ Benefits Law Journal

Pub: Aspen Publishers Inc.
Contact: Mark Dorman, President
URL(s): www.aspenpublishers.com/Product. asp?catalog_name=Aspen&product_id=9 9 00038000. **Released:** Quarterly **Price:** $509, Individuals.

22008 ■ Benefits Quarterly

Pub: International Society of Certified Employee Benefit Specialists
Contact: Sandra Wood, President
URL(s): www.iscebs.org/Resources/BQ/Pages/BenefitsQuarterly.aspx. **Ed:** Jack L. VanDerhei. **Released:** Quarterly **Price:** $125, Individuals; $95, Students.

22009 ■ BNA Pension & Benefits Reporter

Pub: Bureau of National Affairs Inc.
Ed: David A. Sayre, Editor. **Price:** $1811, individual; online two users $2730. **Description:** Covers pension developments stemming from the passage of the Employee Retirement Income Security Act of 1974 (ERISA) and its amendments. Discusses pension and welfare benefit regulations, standards, enforcement actions, court decisions, legislative and administrative actions, agency options, and employee benefit trust fund requirements.

22010 ■ EBRI Issue Brief

Ed: Dallas Salisbury, Editor, salisbury@ebri.org. **Released:** Monthly. **Price:** Included in membership; $224, nonmembers; $25, single issue. **Description:** Examines, analyzes, and interprets key issues and trends in the employee benefits field. Covers one topic in-depth in each issue. Remarks: Price includes subscription to the newsletter Employee Benefit Notes.

22011 ■ EBRI Notes

Ed: Dallas Salisbury, Editor, salisbury@ebri.org. **Released:** Monthly. **Price:** Included in membership; $199, nonmembers. **Description:** 'Analyzes and discusses newly released employee benefits data and reviews a wide range of policy issues, research and publications.' Recurring features include news of research, legal analysis, legislative updates. Remarks: Subscription includes EBRI Issue Brief.

22012 ■ Employee Benefit Plan Review

Pub: Aspen Publishers, Inc.
Contact: Robert Becker, President
URL(s): www.aspenpublishers.com/product. asp?catalog_name=Aspen&product_id=SS 00136808. **Released:** Monthly **Price:** $315, Individuals.

22013 ■ Employee Benefits Cases

Pub: Bureau of National Affairs Inc.
Contact: David A. Sayre, Managing Editor
Released: Weekly, 50/year. **Price:** $1,141. **Description:** Reports full text of federal and state court opinions and selected decisions of arbitrators and the National Labor Relations Board on employee benefits issues. Recurring features include a cumulative index, digest, tables of cases, a topical index, and a classification guide.

22014 ■ Employee Benefits Management Directions

Pub: CCH Inc.
Contact: Mike Sabbatis, President
Released: Biweekly. **Price:** $299. **Description:** Considers new trends in employee benefits management, including 401k plans, family leave programs, health insurance, retirement plans, and relocation assistance. Provides tax information and news of legislation and court cases. Recurring features include news of educational opportunities and conferences. Remarks: Included with subscription to Employee Benefits Management.

22015 ■ Employee Relations Law Journal

Pub: Aspen Publishers Inc.
Contact: Mark Dorman, President
URL(s): www.aspenpublishers.com/Product. asp?catalog_name=Aspen&product_id=9 9 00036000. **Released:** Quarterly **Price:** $499, Single issue.

22016 ■ Employee Services Management

Pub: Employee Morale and Recreation Association
Contact: Randy Schools, President
E-mail: schoolsr@ors.od.nih.gov
URL(s): www.esmassn.org/Default.aspx?pageId=437339. **Ed:** Renee M. Mula. **Released:** Quarterly **Price:** $52, Individuals; $74, Two years; $67 Other countries; $6, Single issue.

22017 ■ Employment Relations Today

Pub: John Wiley & Sons Inc.
Contact: Stephen M. Smith, President
URL(s): onlinelibrary.wiley.com/journal/10.1002/(-ISSN)1520-6459. **Ed:** Carol DiPaolo. **Released:** Quarterly **Price:** $864, Individuals print; $864, Institutions, Canada and Mexico print, for Canada add 5% GST $888, Other countries print; $864, Institutions print; $864, Institutions, Canada and Mexico print, for Canada add 5% GST; $888, Institutions, other countries print.

22018 ■ Flexible Benefits
Pub: Aspen Publishers Inc.
Contact: Mark Dorman, President
Ed: Gregory E. Matthews, Editor. **Released:** Monthly.
Price: $290, individuals. **Description:** Features news and research of interest to benefit managers and consultants. Focus is on employee benefits that involve choice. Recurring features include news of research, reports of meetings, news of educational opportunities, and original analysis of regulations affecting benefits.

22019 ■ Journal of Compensation and Benefits
Pub: RIA Group
URL(s): west.thomson.com/store/product.aspx?product_id=17414579. **Ed:** Jeffrey D. Mamorsky. **Released:** Bimonthly **Price:** $567.48, Individuals.

22020 ■ Journal of Deferred Compensation: Nonqualified Plans and Executive Compensation
Pub: Aspen Publishers Inc.
Contact: Mark Dorman, President
URL(s): www.aspenpublishers.com/Product. asp?catalog_name=Aspen&product_id=S S 10836276. **Released:** 4/yr. **Price:** $389, Individuals.

22021 ■ Journal of Pension Benefits
Pub: Aspen Publishers Inc.
Contact: Mark Dorman, President
URL(s): www.aspenpublishers.com/Product. asp?catalog_name=Aspen&product_id=S S 10694064. **Ed:** Ilene Ferenczy, Adam Pozek. **Released:** Quarterly **Price:** $329, Individuals.

22022 ■ Journal of Pension Planning and Compliance
Pub: Aspen Publishers Inc.
Contact: Mark Dorman, President
URL(s): www.aspenpublishers.com/Product. asp?catalog_name=Aspen&product_id=S S 01482181. **Released:** 4/yr. **Price:** $419, Individuals.

22023 ■ Medical Benefits
Pub: Aspen Publishers Inc.
Contact: Mark Dorman, President
Ed: Margaret Mucklo, Editor. **Released:** Semimonthly. **Price:** $385. **Description:** Focuses on key developments, statistics, and studies relating to the health care system. Covers eight major topic areas: cost containment, employee benefits, employee health/wellness, quality of care, delivery systems, government in health care, legal issues, and health care expenditure data.

22024 ■ Pension Plan Guide
Pub: CCH Inc.
Contact: Mike Sabbatis, President
URL(s): hr.cch.com/products/productid-148.asp. **Released:** Weekly **Price:** $2175, Individuals print and CD-ROM.

22025 ■ Pension Plan Guide--Summary
Pub: CCH Inc.
Contact: Mike Sabbatis, President
Ed: Theodore Simons, Editor. **Released:** Weekly. **Price:** $139. **Description:** Focuses on pension nondiscrimination rules, benefit trends, court decisions, IRS and ERISA regulation and releases, withdrawal liability, and Supreme Court actions regarding pension plans.

22026 ■ What's New in Benefits & Compensation
Pub: Progressive Business Publications
Contact: Ron McRae, Editor-in-Chief
Ed: John T. Hiatt, Editor. **Released:** Semimonthly. **Price:** $299, individuals. **Description:** Communicates the latest legal, tax and policy developments that help benefits executives address cost concerns while meeting complex needs of employees. Recurring features include interviews, news of research, and a column titled Sharpen Your Judgment.

22027 ■ Work/Life Today
Pub: National Institute of Business Management
Ed: Sharon O'Malley, Editor. **Released:** Monthly. **Price:** $355, individuals. **Description:** Provides information on family-friendly benefit programs.

22028 ■ Work Span
Pub: WorldatWork
Contact: Anne C. Ruddy, President
E-mail: aruddy@worlatwork.org
Ed: Jean Christ-Offerson, Editor, jchristofferson@worldatwork.org. **Released:** 10/year. **Description:** Concentrates on issues in the fields of compensation and benefits and human resource management. Includes legislative updates, resources, and case studies.

22029 ■ WorldatWork Journal
Pub: WorldatWork
Contact: Anne C. Ruddy, President
E-mail: aruddy@worlatwork.org
Ed: Dan Cafaro, Editor, dcafaro@worldatwork.org. **Released:** 4/year. **Price:** $210, Included in membership; $85, nonmembers U.S. and U.S. territories;. **Description:** Offers strategic-focused articles dealing with topics such as compensation, benefits, and human resources management.

CONSULTANTS

22030 ■ A Friend of the Family—Friend of the Family Home Services Inc.
1Huntington Rd., Ste. 702
Athens, GA 30606
Ph: (770)725-2748
Fax: (706)725-1650
Co. E-mail: info@afriend.com
URL: http://www.afriend.com
Contact: Judith L. Merlin, President
E-mail: judim@afriend.com
Scope: Human resource development consultants for personal care services as part of employee benefit programs. Programs include: Childcare, elder care, home secretaries, shopping and errand services. Serves private industries as well as government agencies. **Founded:** 1984.

22031 ■ Abacus Benefit Consultants Inc.
55 Stamp Farm Rd.
Cranston, RI 02921-3401
Ph: (401)942-4900
Fax: (401)942-8989
Co. E-mail: info@abacusbci.com
URL: http://www.abacusbci.com
Contact: Robert Y. Chin, Principal
E-mail: rychin@abacusbci.com
Scope: Administrators and consultants for employee benefit plans. Offers clients a menu of services in the traditional full service approach and coordinate with insurance companies and/or mutual fund companies with unbundled service package for 401(k) plans. **Founded:** 1991.

22032 ■ Advanced Benefits & Human Resources
9350-F Snowden River Pkwy., Ste. 222
Columbia, MD 21045
Ph: (410)290-9037
Fax: (410)740-2568
Co. E-mail: hrb@abhr.com
Contact: Linda Polacek, President
Scope: Provides human resource consulting to high technology businesses. Offers services in the areas of human resources, benefits, and training. Creates, maintains, or updates current human resource functions. **Founded:** 1996.

22033 ■ A.E. Roberts Co.
11490 Xeon St. NW, Ste. 200
Coon Rapids, MN 55448-3111
Ph: (763)757-5119
Free: 800-486-4585
Fax: (413)215-6877
Scope: Specializes in compliance training, focusing on regulatory compliance and human resource management issues. **Founded:** 1989. **Seminars:** ADA Seminar; COBRA Seminar; FMLA Seminar; HIPAA Privacy Seminar; HIPAA Portability Seminar; Section 125 Cafeteria Plans Seminar.

22034 ■ Aldrich & Cox Inc. (A & C)
3075 Southwestern Blvd., Ste. 202
Orchard Park, NY 14127-1287
Ph: (716)675-6300
Fax: (716)675-2098
Co. E-mail: consult@aldrichandcox.com
URL: http://www.aldrichandcox.com
Contact: Charles H. Cox, President
E-mail: cox@aldrichandcox.com
Scope: Offers insurance and risk management counseling for all lines of insurance and self insurance to business, industry, institutions, political subdivisions, and utilities. Serves on a continuing basis but is also available for special projects, such as risk management audits in the Eastern United States and Canada. **Founded:** 1951.

22035 ■ AmeriFlex Financial Services
3700 State St., Ste. 310
Santa Barbara, CA 93105
Ph: (805)898-0893
Free: 800-425-1522
Fax: (805)898-0759
Co. E-mail: ameriflex@ameriflex.com
URL: http://www.ameriflex.com
Contact: Troy Hammond, President
E-mail: troy.hammond@ameriflex.com
Scope: Develops and markets retirement and employee benefit programs to businesses, schools districts, hospitals, non-profit organizations and individual investors. **Founded:** 1988. **Publications:** "Women and Retirement Planning," Jul, 2006; "Top Ten Financial Planning Tips for Women," Coastal Woman Magazine, 2005. **Special Services:** AmeriFlex®; CFP®.

22036 ■ Aon Hewitt—Hewitt AssocHewitt Associates;
100 Half Day Rd.
Lincolnshire, IL 60069-3342
Ph: (847)295-5000
Fax: (847)295-7634
Co. E-mail: info@aonhewitt.com
URL: http://www.aonhewitt.com
Contact: Julie Gordon, President
URL(s): www.aon.com. **Scope:** Offers services covering human resources, employee benefits, compensation, financial management, administration, consulting and outsourcing. **Founded:** 1940. **Publications:** "Lessons Uncovered: it Makes a Difference: Change Management and Hr Bpo"; "What Makes a Sourcing Advisor a Good Sourcing Advisor?". **Seminars:** How Do You Prepare and Educate Plan Participants, Nov, 2006. **Special Services:** Rapid eMerge™; M&A Management Center™.

22037 ■ Franklin F. Beach & Co.
5478 N Rolling Oaks Dr.
Memphis, TN 38119-4957
Ph: (901)763-4082
Fax: (901)767-1533
Contact: Franklin F. Beach, President
Scope: The firm offers counseling, estate planning and employee benefit planning including pension planning, profit sharing, executive compensation, health and welfare plans, business organization and management expertise. **Founded:** 1975.

22038 ■ Benefit Communications Inc. (BCI)
2126 21st Ave. S
Nashville, TN 37212-4318
Ph: (615)292-3786
Free: 800-489-3786
Fax: (615)383-7917
Co. E-mail: info@benefitcommunications.com
URL: http://www.benefitcommunications.com
Contact: Stu Brandt, Director
Scope: An employee benefit communications and servicing company that specializes in three areas voluntary products, employee communications and open enrollment outsourcing. **Founded:** 1981.

22039 ■ Benefit Partners Inc.
2140 Regent St., Ste. 1
Sudbury, ON, Canada P3E 5S8
Ph: (705)524-1559
Free: 800-461-6326

Fax: (705)524-5553
Co. E-mail: info@benefitpartners.com
URL: http://www.benefitpartners.com
Contact: Bruce Frick, Managing Director
E-mail: bruce.frick@benefitpartners.com
Scope: Services include employee benefits, pension, executive compensation, human resources and financial management. Industries served: Corporate and personal insurance planning and private wealth management. **Telecommunication Services:** denise.marshall@benefitpartners.com.

22040 ■ Benefit Sources & Solutions (BSS)—Rappoport, Scott Clu Chfc Inc.
1952 US Hwy. 22
Bound Brook, NJ 08805
Ph: (732)560-1010
Fax: (732)560-1049
Co. E-mail: srappoport@benefitsource.com
URL: http://www.benefitsource.com
Contact: Scott Rappoport, Chief Executive Officer
E-mail: srappoport@benefitsource.com
Scope: Provider of business leaders and human resource professionals at emerging companies and established global corporations with a personalized multi-faceted approach to manage their employee benefit programs. Designs, implements and administers employee benefit plans that are integrated in an employer's compensation package. **Founded:** 1989.

22041 ■ Benefits Dynamics Inc. (BDI)
89 N Haddon Ave., Ste. D
Haddonfield, NJ 08033-2473
Ph: (856)616-1400
Fax: (856)616-1401
Co. E-mail: benefit@benefitdynamics.com
Contact: JoAnn Massanova, President
E-mail: joannm@benefitdynamics.com
Scope: A full service employee benefit, record keeping consultant and outsourcing organization. Provides pension consulting, administration and actuarial services, cafeteria and flexible benefit plans, human resource systems outsourcing, interactive voice-response systems, electronic employee benefit enrollment and transportation plans. **Founded:** 1979.

22042 ■ Benetech Inc.
3947 Lennane Dr., Ste. 250
Sacramento, CA 95834
Ph: (916)484-6811
Free: 800-285-7526
Fax: (916)488-1743
Co. E-mail: db@benetechinc.com
URL: http://www.benetechinc.com
Contact: Robert L. Brandon, President
E-mail: robb@benetechinc.com
Scope: An actuarial consulting and administration firm specializing in retirement plans for small and medium-size businesses. Offers plan design, record keeping and consulting services. Consulting services in plan design options for Profit Sharing, 401k, and Defined Benefit Plans. **Founded:** 1974.

22043 ■ Larry W. Buck & Associates Inc.
710 N Post Oak Rd., Ste. 101
Houston, TX 77024
Ph: (713)278-0200
Fax: (713)278-0202
Co. E-mail: lbuck@lbuckassociates.com
Contact: N. Richard Magel, Vice President of Operations
Scope: Consulting firm active in risk management and employee benefit planning. **Founded:** 1977.

22044 ■ C F Services Group Inc.
9083 Shady Grove Ct.
Gaithersburg, MD 20877
Ph: (301)963-8820
Fax: (301)963-3733
Co. E-mail: jill@cfservicesgroup.com
URL: http://www.cfservicesgroup.com
Contact: Lenard S. Cohen, Owner
E-mail: len@cfservicesgroup.com
Scope: Provider of advice, information and comparisons regarding life insurance, mutual funds, limited partnerships, and other securities. Emphasis is on employee benefit planning and financial advice for businesses and key executives. Industries served: small businesses and professional practices.

Founded: 1981. **Publications:** "Leading Economic Index Is Designed To Assess The U.S Economic Outlook"; "Whole Life Insurance"; "Term Life Insurance"; "Universal Life Insurance"; "Variable Life Insurance"; "Auto Insurance"; "Insurance Claims"; "Maximizing Insurance Benefits"; "Insuring Your Future"; "Assessing Disability Insurance"; "Types of Health Care"; "Protecting Your Home"; "Additional Liability Coverage"; "Planning Options"; "Future of Social Security"; "Social Security Income"; "Keogh Plans"; "Equity-Indexed Annuities"; "Retirement Plan Distributions"; "Cash Management Basics". **Seminars:** Hanging the Help Wanted Sign, 2011; Where The Jobs Are, How To Spruce Up Your Skills And Ready Your, Finances For The Change.

22045 ■ Chernoff Diamond & Company L.L.C.
990 Stewart Ave., Ste. 520
Garden City, NY 11530-4869
Ph: (516)683-6100
Fax: (516)683-6163
Co. E-mail: mail@chernoffdiamond.com
URL: http://www.chernoffdiamond.com
Contact: Alexander Chernoff, Owner
Scope: Provider of comprehensive services and design; implementation and administration of employee benefit plans, pension, profit sharing and 401(k) plans; programs of executive and deferred compensation and sophisticated life insurance plans. Provides specialized advisory support in the areas of health and welfare, retirement and estate trust planning. **Founded:** 1975.

22046 ■ John Chute & Associates
150 Consumers Rd., Ste. 508
Toronto, ON, Canada M2J 1P9
Ph: (416)250-8600
Free: 800-565-2488
Fax: (416)250-8605
Co. E-mail: postmaster@jchute.com
URL: http://www.jchute.com
Contact: Jack Chute, President
E-mail: jack.chute@jchute.com
Scope: Provider of counsel in the design, costing and communication of all forms of employee benefit plans. Human resource consulting skills, training, team building, job evaluation, performance appraisal, labor relations. Also provides professional advice in corporate human resource and organizational development matters. **Founded:** 1982.

22047 ■ Compliance Consulting Corp. (CCC)
406 Marquis St.
Jackson, MS 39236
Ph: (601)982-1219
Free: 800-435-1266
Fax: (601)982-1220
Co. E-mail: admin@cobracompliance.com
URL: http://www.cobracompliance.com
Contact: Cecil Muse, Principal
E-mail: cmuse@cobracompliance.com
Scope: Provide clients with administration that meets all of the COBRA regulatory requirements. Offers critical functions necessary for a comprehensive COBRA and HIPAA administration program. **Founded:** 1986. **Telecommunication Services:** khughes@cobracompliance.com.

22048 ■ Comprehensive Professional Management Inc.
222 E Dundee Rd.
Wheeling, IL 60090-3009
Ph: (847)520-1301
Fax: (847)520-0372
Co. E-mail: bob@cpmincfs.com
Contact: Kathy Rathunde, Principal
Scope: Services include accounting, financial planning, litigation support, pension profit sharing administration, practice surveys, professional corporation issues, retirement and estate planning and tax advice.

22049 ■ CONEXIS Benefits Administrators L.P.
6191 N State Highway 161, Ste. 400
Irving, TX 75038
Ph: (214)596-6919
Free: 877-266-3947

Fax: (877)353-2948
Co. E-mail: sales@conexis.org
URL: http://www.conexis.org
Contact: Michael Close, President
Scope: Provider of web based COBRA HIPAA FSA direct bill compliance and administration services. Texas based outsourcing solution offers automated benefit administration for all-sized type of business. **Founded:** 1986. **Seminars:** COBRA/HPAA Compliance; FSA - What's new; Comparing FSA, HRA and HSA Programs.

22050 ■ Counts Benefit Services Inc.
102 Alessandra Ct., Ste. 181
Frederick, MD 21701
Ph: (301)694-3009
Fax: (301)694-3066
Co. E-mail: jcounts@countsbenefits.us
URL: http://www.countsfinancial.com
Contact: James E. Counts, Owner
E-mail: jcounts@countsbenefits.us
Scope: Consulting services include evaluation of employer's benefit plans as to cost vs. benefits, self insured benefits as well as fully insured welfare plans, and defined contribution/defined benefit plans. Also designs executive compensation programs and salary continuation benefits. Active with wide variety of industries. **Founded:** 1984. **Publications:** "Eighty percent of Americans agree they would benefit from having basic financial education and information". **Seminars:** The Financial Alternative to Success Seminar.

22051 ■ Aaron Deitsch, F.S.A.
107-23 71st Rd., Ste. 231
Forest Hills, NY 11375-0366
Ph: (718)793-9885
Fax: (718)793-9888
Co. E-mail: ad2@pensionconsultant.com
URL: http://www.pensionconsultant.com
Contact: Aaron Deitsch, Owner
Scope: Pension consultant and actuary providing consulting services in the employee benefits field, specializing in retirement plans. **Founded:** 1978. **Publications:** "Retirement Plan Basics"; "Retirement Plan Tips, Retirement Plan Traps"; "Profit Sharing Plan Tips, Profit Sharing Plan Traps"; "Defined Benefit Pension Plan Tips, Defined Benefit Pension Plan Traps"; "401(K) Plan Tips, 401(K) Plan Traps"; "401(K) Plans-Tips on Controlling 401(K) Plan Costs". **Seminars:** Pension Plan Library; Pension Plan Tools/Applications; Pension Plan and Retirement Plan Assistance.

22052 ■ Dorn & Associates Inc.
8506 Bass Lake Rd.
Minneapolis, MN 55428-5304
Ph: (763)533-7689
Fax: (763)533-1143
Contact: John L. Dorn, President
Scope: Services include accounting, marketing, employment partnership, new doctor agreements, personnel issues and human resources assessment, practice management, practice merger acquisition sale and liquidation, practice surveys and valuation, staff development and training. **Founded:** 2000.

22053 ■ Employee Benefit Research Institute (EBRI)
1100 13th St. NW, Ste. 878
Washington, DC 20005
Ph: (202)659-0670
Fax: (202)775-6312
Co. E-mail: info@ebri.org
URL: http://www.ebri.org
Contact: Dallas L. Salisbury, President
E-mail: salisbury@ebri.org
Description: Corporations, consulting firms, banks, insurance companies, unions, and others with an interest in the future of employee benefit programs. Purpose is to contribute to the development of effective and responsible public policy in the field of employee benefits through research, publications, educational programs, seminars, and direct communication. Sponsors a broad range of studies on retirement income, health, disability, and other benefit programs; disseminates study results. Maintains research library with information on employee benefit programs. **Scope:** A public policy research organiza-

tion serving as an employee benefits information source on health, welfare and retirement issues. Services include: basic benefit program descriptions, legislation analysis, media coverage and interpretation and long-range planning. Specializes in research on pensions, social security, health care, Medicare, long-term care, and flexible benefits. Serves government, academic consumers, consultants, banks, insurance companies, investment managers, law and accounting firms, corporations, and individuals. **Services:** Congressional briefings. **Founded:** 1978. **Subscriptions:** 4000 audiovisuals books clippings monographs periodicals. **Publications:** "Retirement Security in the United States-Current Sources, Future Prospects, and Likely Outcomes of Current Trends," 2006; "Estimating the Value of Changes in OASI Benefits Under Social Security Reforms," Jun, 2006; "Will Wider Use of Evidence-Based Medicine Significantly Enhance Healthcare Quality and Affordability: Implications for Consumer-Driven Health Benefits," 2003; "Consumer Driven Health Benefits: A Continuing Evolution," 2002; "The Economic Costs of the Uninsured Implications for Business and Government," 2000; "The Future of Private Retirement Plans," 2000; "EBRI Issue Briefs"; "EBRI Notes"; "Pension Investment Report PIR"; "EBRI Data book on Employee Benefits"; "Fundamentals of Employee Benefits Programs". **Educational Activities:** American Savings Education Council; Choose to Save Education Program; Fellows program, for academics, media, retirees; Policy forums (Biennial). **Awards:** EBRI Lillywhite Award (Annual); The EBRI Lillywhite Award (Annual). **Seminars:** Policy Forums, Congressional Briefings. **Telecommunication Services:** salisbury@ebri.org.

22054 ■ Employee Benefits of St. Cloud Inc.
400 Austin Ave., Ste. 1200
Waco, TX 76701
Ph: (320)251-0034
Free: 888-333-5859
Fax: (320)251-0340
Co. E-mail: serviceteam@julyservices.com
URL: http://www.ebsc-online.org
Contact: Jim Hudson, President
Scope: It is a national retirement plan services firm providing independent, high quality services and solutions to investment advisors, employers, and plan participants. They provide following services Web Access, Quarterly Statements, Technical Support. **Founded:** 1987.

22055 ■ Employee Services Management Association (ESM)—ESM Association
568 Spring Rd., Ste. D
Elmhurst, IL 60126-3896
Ph: (630)559-0020
Fax: (630)559-0025
Co. E-mail: esmahq@esmassn.org
URL: http://www.esmassn.org
Contact: Marci Kinnin, President
E-mail: marci.kinnin@cigna.com
Description: Corporations and governmental agencies that sponsor recreation, fitness, and service programs for their employees; associate members are manufacturers and suppliers in the employee recreation market and distributors of consumer products and services. Serves as an information resource network for members nationwide. Implements and maintains a diverse range of employee services; believes that employee services, as practical solutions to work/life issues, are essential to sound business management. Conducts programs that improves relations between employees and management, increases overall productivity, boosts morale, and reduces absenteeism and turnover. Covers the 10 Components of a Well-Rounded Employee Services Program such as employee stores, convenience services, recognition programs, recreation programs, travel services, and special events. **Scope:** Offers counsel on employee recreation/leisure activities and services for industry, business and government agencies. It provides an information and communication center for persons responsible for administering employee services, recreation and fitness programs. **Founded:** 1941. **Publications:** "Employee Services Management"; "A Strategic Component of Business". **Seminars:** Leadership Workshop.

22056 ■ The Epler Co.
450 B St., Ste. 750
San Diego, CA 92101
Ph: (619)239-0831
Fax: (619)239-0807
Co. E-mail: consultants@eplercompany.com
URL: http://www.eplercompany.com
Contact: Jane Barry, President
E-mail: jbarry@eplercompany.com
Scope: Offers actuarial and consulting services for employee benefits specializing in retirement plans, health, life, accidental death and dismemberment, long-term disability insurance plans, and executive compensation. Administers retiree health studies, AB1200 studies for schools, and merger studies on benefits. Conducts base pay, bonus and benefit surveys. Designs total compensation programs. **Founded:** 1971.

22057 ■ First Health
2610 Decker Lake Ln.
Salt Lake City, UT 84119
Ph: (801)954-6550
Fax: (801)954-4517
URL: http://firsthealth.coventryhealthcare.com
Contact: David A. Kreager, Vice President
Scope: Consultants active in the areas of retirement and savings plan design and administration, welfare plan design, and employee benefit communication. **Founded:** 1960.

22058 ■ Flex-Plan Services Inc. (FPS)
11400 SE 6th St., Ste. 125
Bellevue, WA 98004
Ph: (425)452-3500
Free: 800-669-3539
Fax: (425)451-7002
Co. E-mail: flexplan@flex-plan.com
URL: http://www.flex-plan.com
Contact: John Yochum, President
E-mail: jyochum@flex-plan.com
Scope: Flexible benefit plan design and administration for cafeteria-type plans, form 5500 preparation and employee benefit statements. Also assists with the design and administration of retirement plans. Offers customized Windows-based software systems that allow employers to communicate with and to enroll employees electronically for all employee benefit plans. Provides employee self service via internet and/or intranet. Industries served: All. **Founded:** 1989. **Telecommunication Services:** sales@flex-plan.com.

22059 ■ Gallagher Benefit Services Inc.
2 Pierce Pl.
Itasca, IL 60143-1203
Ph: (630)773-3800
Fax: (630)285-4000
Co. E-mail: Jim_Durkin@ajg.com
URL: http://www.ajg.com
Contact: James W. Durkin, Jr., President
URL(s): www.gallagherbenefits.com. **Scope:** Offers consultation in areas of benefits planning, delivery, and administration. Services include executive benefits programs, health and welfare schemes, healthcare analytics, human resource services, international benefits services, retirement plan services and voluntary benefits services. Industries served: healthcare, higher education, hospitality and restaurant, transportation and non profit organizations. **Publications:** "Final HIPAA Nondiscrimination and Wellness Plan Rules Issued," 2007; "Using Electronic Media For Employee Benefit Elections and Notices," 2006. **Seminars:** Safety By Design, Marina Center, South Sioux City, NE, Nov, 2008; Hospitality Loss Prevention, DFW Radisson South Hotel, Irving, TX, Mar, 2006.

22060 ■ Health Insurance Specialists Inc. (HISI)
17620-B Redland Rd.
Rockville, MD 20855
Ph: (301)590-0006

Fax: (301)590-0661
Co. E-mail: info@his-inc.com
URL: http://www.his-inc.com
Contact: Jon S. Belinkie, President
E-mail: jbelinkie@his-inc.com
Scope: Serves a wide variety of businesses and individuals by designing comprehensive insurance packages and benefit plans, full service insurance and financial services firm, third party administration, human resources outsourcing. **Founded:** 1982.

22061 ■ HealthChoice
583 D'Onofrio Dr., Ste. 101
Madison, WI 53719
Ph: (608)833-7988
Free: 800-334-7988
Fax: (608)833-7540
Co. E-mail: info@healthchoice.com
URL: http://www.healthchoice.com
Contact: Clifford Morris, President
Scope: Firm provides employee assistance program which concentrates on to reduce employer productivity loses. **Founded:** 1985. **Publications:** "Graduating From Child Care to Elder Care".

22062 ■ Healy & Associates Inc.
3033 W Jefferson St., Ste. 205
Joliet, IL 60435-6449
Ph: (815)741-0102
Fax: (815)744-5412
Contact: Richard Kelling, President
Scope: Personal development consultant with experience in alcoholism and family treatment; employee assistance program consultation and implementation; health promotion programming on stress, smoking cessation, weight control; alcohol and drug related prevention and educational programming; and individual, group and family counseling. Serves private industries as wells government agencies. **Founded:** 1982. **Seminars:** Assertive Communication; Alcohol and Drug Problems in the Workplace; Chemical Dependency: Enabling vs. Intervention; Stress Management; Employee Assistance Programs; Smoking Cessation in the Workplace; Eating and Weight Issues; Cultural Diversity Training; Adapting to Change in the Workplace; Adapting to Shift Work.

22063 ■ Hooker & Holcombe Inc.—H&H Investment Solutions
65 LaSalle Rd., Ste. 402
West Hartford, CT 06107-2397
Ph: (860)521-8400
Free: 800-457-1245
Fax: (860)521-3742
Co. E-mail: info@hhconsultants.com
URL: http://www.hhconsultants.com/HH
Contact: Arthur J. Assantes, President
E-mail: ajassantes@hhconsultants.com
Scope: Offers employee benefit services in the areas of pension plans, 401(k) plans, profit sharing, ESOP, thrift and savings plans, retirement plan outsourcing services and actuarial consulting. **Founded:** 1956.

22064 ■ In Plain English—R.H. Wohl & Associates Inc.
14501 Antigone Dr.
Gaithersburg, MD 20885-3300
Ph: (301)340-2821
Free: 800-274-9645
Fax: (301)279-0115
Co. E-mail: rwohl@inplainenglish.com
URL: http://www.inplainenglish.com
Contact: Ronald H. Wohl, President
E-mail: rwohl@inplainenglish.com
Scope: Management consultants helping government and businesses research, design, write and produce user oriented management information for human resources, employee benefits, business process, corporate and marketing needs. Services include: GSA mob is schedule for consulting to the government; employee benefit communications, plain English business writing workshops for print and electronic media; communicating strategy and tactics; marketing research, business planning and communications; readability testing; usability testing and monitoring strategy. **Founded:** 1977. **Publications:** "The Benefits Communication"; "The Employee Benefits Communication ToolKit," Commerce Clear-

inghouse; "Benefits Communication," Business and Legal Reports. **Seminars:** Plain English Writing Training; Summary Plan Description Compliance workshops; Re-Humanizing the Corporation, Human Resources and Employee Benefits Communication Workshop; 21 Writing Tips for the 21st Century; Make the Write Impression; Writing to Inform and Instruct; The Dreaded Nuts and Bolts; Writing to Persuade; Writing Policy and Procedure Manuals In Plain English; Writing for Accountants and Auditors In Plain English. **Special Services:** In Plain English®.

22065 ■ Infinisource
5210 N Main
Dayton, OH 45415
Ph: (937)275-6280
Free: 800-779-6384
Fax: (888)773-4209
Contact: Nancy L. Lee, President
E-mail: nlee@aurorasolutions.com
Scope: Provider of employee benefit administrative services to the outsourcing marketplace. Concentrates resources on the administration and compliance of employee benefit plans. Concentrate resources on the administration and compliance of employee benefit plans. Provides services no matter where medical claims are paid, where trustee services are located, or where record keeping is originated. **Founded:** 1997.

22066 ■ JPMorgan Compensation and Benefit Strategies
216 S Jefferson St., Ste. 600
Chicago, IL 60661
Ph: (312)454-3222
Fax: (312)454-1213
Co. E-mail: support@jpmorgan.com
URL: http://www.jpmorgan.com
Contact: Tom Terry, President
Scope: Provider of compensation, retirement plan and health care consulting services. Areas of expertise include: Compliance, employee communication, executive compensation, financial modeling, health and welfare, health improvement programs and retirement plans. **Founded:** 1991. **Publications:** "2012 Distribution Policy: Dividend and share repurchase facts and trends," Feb, 2012; "Time to Rethink Hurdle Rates: Understanding political risk premia in a new financial environment," Jan, 2012; "Light at the end of the tunnel: Getting ready for the return of the U.S. consumer," Nov, 2011; "Action speaks louder than words: Investors reward proactive strategies," Sep, 2011; "Navigating through another "pension storm": Prudent pension management in an uncertain market environment," Aug, 2011; "Beyond growth: Valuation and financial policy in the maturing tech sector," Jun, 2011; "It's deja vu all over again: How to be ready when the cheap capital environment ends," Jun, 2011; "The New Face of M&A: How a trillion dollars will change the strategic landscape," Apr, 2011; "Understanding the new growth paradigm: Opportunities to create value in an anemic growth environment," Nov, 2010. **Seminars:** Computershare The Source 2006: Inspiration and Insight; The PDP Advantage for Public Sector plans; National Municipal OPEB Liabilities Conference; Fourth Annual New England Public Finance Conference. Computershare The Source 2006: Inspiration and Insight; The PDP Advantage for Public Sector plans; National Municipal OPEB Liabilities Conference; Fourth Annual New England Public Finance Conference. **Telecommunication Services:** info@jpmorgan.com; jpm.actuaries@jpmorgan.com.

22067 ■ Managing Work and Family Inc.
1625 Sheridan Rd.
Wilmette, IL 60091
Ph: (847)308-0919
Fax: (661)885-7865
Co. E-mail: mwfam@aol.com
URL: http://www.mwfam.com
Contact: Bonnie Michaels, President
E-mail: Mwfam@aol.com
Scope: The firm was designed for employers interested in creating a culture and work environment conducive to loyalty and productivity from employees with family responsibilities. The firm offers consulting, organizational assessments, flexible work option design, training for managers and employees, child

and elder care services, videos, books and family days. Representative client industries include: Advertising, banking and finance, electronic communications, data processing, education, government, health care, hospitality, manufacturing, pharmaceutical and service industries. **Founded:** 1987. **Publications:** "Upside"; "Living Well, Tuning Out the Every Day Stresses on Vacation," Aug, 2006; "A Journey of Work-Life Renewal: The Power to Recharge & Rekindle Passion in Your Life," 2003; "Managing Work and Family Kopy kit"; "Solving the Work/Family Puzzle". **Seminars:** Building Resilience During Turbulent Times; Managing Employees During Stressful Times; WHAT'S YOUR RQ; Leadership Renewal for Work-Life Professionals; Leadership Renewal for Work-Life Professionals; Beyond Sensitivity and Diversity Training; Beyond balance For individuals newly displaced; Employee Information & Training; Beyond balance for individuals in stressful work life situations.

22068 ■ Money Source Financial Services Inc.
1328 S Main St.
Ann Arbor, MI 48104
Ph: (734)213-0300
Fax: (734)213-5900
Co. E-mail: info@msfs.com
URL: http://www.msfs.com
Contact: Thomas McLinden, President
E-mail: tommc@msfs.com
Scope: Provides clients with access to employee benefit programs. Offers access to nearly any investment or insurance products. Provides experience in the design, implementation, and funding of 401k plans, Simplified Employee Pension Plan SEP, profit sharing plans, money purchase plans, and IRA's and rollover plans. **Founded:** 1994.

22069 ■ New England Human Resource Group
36 Cedar Pond Dr.
Warwick, RI 02886
Ph: (401)826-2137
Contact: Ronald G. Snyder, President
Scope: Firm specializes in compensation systems, benefits, legal compliance, personnel policies, resources, employee relations law, safety and risk management, training and development, continuous improvement, career management, organizational change, strategic planning, human resource audits, ISO 9000 and QS 9000, professional development, financial planning, staffing, and executive development. **Founded:** 1985.

22070 ■ New Ways to Work Inc.
The Thoreau Ctr., 1016 Lincoln Blvd., Ste. 5
San Francisco, CA 94129
Ph: (415)995-9860
Fax: (707)824-4410
Co. E-mail: sgtrippe@nww.org
URL: http://www.newwaystowork.org
Contact: Steve Trippe, President
E-mail: sgtrippe@newwaystowork.org
Description: Helps communities build systems that connect schools, community organizations and businesses, and improve the services, educational programs and support the community provides for its youth. Engages and supports local communities in the invention and renewal of connected, comprehensive youth-serving systems. **Scope:** Focuses on improving the lives of the nations youth. helps communities build systems that connect schools, community organizations and businesses, and improve the services, educational programs and support the community provides for its youth. creates the environment and guides a process that brings the right people together with customized tools for powerful learning and dramatic change. **Founded:** 1972. **Publications:** "A Guide to Career Development Opportunities in California's High Schools". **Seminars:** Career pathways; building local intermediary organizations; strengthening youth councils; increasing youth involvement; creating quality work-based learning systems; All Youth-One Systems.

22071 ■ PAR Enterprises Inc.
1845 Summer St., Dept. It97
Stamford, CT 06905-5034

Ph: (203)973-0366
Free: 888-333-5727
Fax: (203)973-0366
Co. E-mail: par@par-ent.com
URL: http://www.par-ent.com
Contact: Dr. Paul A. Rivera, President
Scope: Assists in design, implementation and communication of healthcare, retirement, other welfare benefit programs, real estate needs, insurance and pension plans. **Publications:** "Official Compendium Of Inner City Street Games".

22072 ■ Princeton Health Systems Inc. (PHS)
9 Mercer St.
Princeton, NJ 08540
Ph: (609)924-7799
Free: 800-437-6668
Fax: (609)497-0739
URL: http://www.princetonhealthsystems.com
Contact: Beth Young, President
E-mail: byoung23@aol.com
Scope: Offers consulting services in the evaluation, planning, implementation and assessment of medical care services to employees, including cost containment strategies and health and fitness programs. **Founded:** 1981. **Publications:** "Certain Solutions Administrator's Guide," Johnson & Johnson Health Management Inc., 1992; "Sports Medicine Up-Date," New Jersey Medicine, 1991; "The Wrestlers' Nutrition Manual," Bucknell University, 1990.

22073 ■ Ralph Moss Ltd. (RML)
200 Town Centre Blvd., Ste. 102
Markham, ON, Canada L3R 8G5
Ph: (905)513-9868
Free: 888-667-7583
Fax: (905)513-9893
Co. E-mail: info@ralphmossltd.on.ca
URL: http://www.ralphmoss.ca
Contact: Jeanne Foot, President
E-mail: jeannef@ralphmossltd.on.ca
Scope: Acts as benefit consultants on projects, reviewing and making recommendations, not only on existing benefit programs, but also commenting on the taxability of benefits, legal issues and industry standards, as well as financial underwriting arrangements and other various cost factors. **Founded:** 1952. **Publications:** "Financial Planning Report".

22074 ■ Segal Co.
333 W 34th St.
New York, NY 10001-2402
Ph: (212)251-5000
Fax: (212)251-5490
Co. E-mail: contact@segalco.com
URL: http://www.segalco.com
Contact: Joseph A. LoCicero, President
Scope: A leading, independent firm of benefit, compensation and human resources consultants. In January 2002, Segal acquired Sibson Consulting, a human capital consulting firm. The combined organization, with more than 1, 000 employees is headquartered in Mew York and has offices throughout the United States, in Canada and the United Kingdom. Clients include corporations, non-profit organizations, professional service firms, state and local governments and joint boards of trustees administering pension, health and welfare plans under the Taft-Hartley Act. **Founded:** 1939. **Publications:** "Save Money and Improve Coverage with Global Health-Care Benefits", Mar, 2012; "Are You Prepared for Major Changes in Pension Accounting Standards?," Dec, 2011; "Time to Redesign? Comparing Public Sector DB and DC Retirement Plans," Aug, 2011; "Genetic Testing: An Ever-Evolving Health Field Raises Complex Coverage Issues," 2011; "Three Strategies for Controlling Pharmacy Benefit Costs," Feb, 2011; "Economy Spurs Examination of Public Sector Retirement Plans," Feb, 2011; "Using All the Tools: Communications as a "Do-It-Yourself" Project," Jan, 2011; "How to Plan a Successful RIF to Meet Restructured Services," 2010; "Proposed GASB Standards Would Alter the Meaning of Pension Expense," Jul, 2010; "Health Care Provider Reimbursement: A Better Way to Determine What's Fair?," Apr, 2010. **Seminars:** Annual Fund Administrators' Seminar, Jun, 2012.

22075 ■ Siebrand-Wilton Associates Inc.
PO Box 369
Marlboro, NJ 07746-0369
Ph: (732)917-0239
Fax: (732)972-0214
Co. E-mail: clientsvcs@s-wa.com
URL: http://www.s-wa.com
Contact: John S. Sturges, President
E-mail: bencomp@s-wa.com
Scope: Assesses, plans and implements human resources aspects of mergers and acquisitions. Offers human resources consulting in compensation and benefit plan design, mergers and acquisitions (HR aspects), business ethics assessment and development, editing, writing and association management services, and contract professionals and interim executives. **Founded:** 1986. **Publications:** "Should Government or Business Try to Save Medicare," HR News; "Executive Temping," HR Horizons; "When is an Employee Truly an Employee," HR Magazine; "Examining Your Insurance Carrier," HR Magazine.

22076 ■ The Stoller Co.
190 N Wiget Ln., Ste. 110
Walnut Creek, CA 94598
Ph: (925)932-1800
Fax: (925)932-1869
Co. E-mail: info@stollerco.com
URL: http://www.stollerco.com
Contact: J. Curtis Stoller, President
E-mail: curtstoller@stollerco.com
Scope: Specializes in retirement and 401K plans, human resources, compensation, systems consulting, and workplace compliance. **Founded:** 1976.

22077 ■ Swartzbaugh-Farber & Associates Inc.
1015 N 98th St., Westroads Pointe, Ste. 221
Omaha, NE 68114-2357
Ph: (402)397-5800
Fax: (402)397-5424
Co. E-mail: securefuture@swartzbaugh.com
URL: http://www.swartzbaugh.com
Contact: Robert Swartzbaugh, President
E-mail: bob.swartzbaugh@swartzbaugh.com
Scope: Specializes in group employee benefits and executive benefits compensation. **Founded:** 1993. **Seminars:** Health care Boot Camp, Aug, 2007; Benchmarking Seminar, 2007; Understanding HIPAA Seminar, Mar, 2006; HR - Developing a Profit Center, Nov, 2005.

22078 ■ TRI-AD Actuaries Inc.
221 W Crest St., Ste. 300
Escondido, CA 92025-1737
Ph: (760)743-7555
Free: 800-733-7555
Fax: (760)489-9343
Co. E-mail: info@tri-ad.com
URL: http://www.tri-ad.com
Contact: Curtis D. Hamilton, President
E-mail: chamilton@tri-ad.com
Scope: A full service human resources consulting and administration firm. Specializes in outsourcing benefit administration, designing comprehensive compensation and benefit programs, automating the HR department, reshaping your corporate culture and employee communication. Services include 401k Choice daily record keeping, actuarial services, COBRA Administration, Flexible spending, account administration, health and welfare benefit consulting, human resources effectiveness, organization effectiveness and retirement plans. **Founded:** 1974. **Publications:** "A Complete Chart of the 2008 Cost of Living Adjustments," Oct, 2007; "Check the Rollover Chart to See Which Types of Plans Will Accept Your Rollover," Aug, 2006; "A Complete Chart of the 2006 Cost of Living Adjustments," Jan, 2006; "Valerie Gieseke in Compensation and Benefits Review: Automating Benefits Administration," Nov, 2005. **Seminars:** Beyond COBRA: Offering More Comprehensive Post-Employment Benefits, Aug, 2009; Primer on Providers: Who Does What for Your 401(k) Plan, Jul, 2009; Refresher Course on the Basics of FSA Plan Administration, Jun, 2009; Found Money in Your 401(k) Plans, May, 2009; Found Money in Your Health & Welfare Benefit Plans, Apr, 2009; 401(k)

Loans: Deal or No Deal?, Apr, 2008; COBRA 101: What You Need to Know About COBRA, Apr, 2007; An Update on Automatic Enrollment, Mar, 2007; Preparing for COBRA Open Enrollment, Oct, 2006.

22079 ■ Donald C. Wright CPA
3906 Lawndale Ln. N
Plymouth, MN 55446-2940
Ph: (763)478-6999
Co. E-mail: donaldwright@compuserve.com
URL: http://www.donaldwrightcpa.com
Contact: Donald C. Wright, President
E-mail: donaldwright@compuserve.com
Scope: Offers accounting, tax, and small business consulting services. Services include cash flow and budgeting analysis; financial forecast and projections; financial statements; reviews and compilations; tax planning, tax preparation; IRS and state/local representation; international taxation; estate, gift and trust tax return preparation; benefit plan services; business succession planning; estate planning; financial planning; management advisory services, pension and profit sharing plans, retirement planning, expert witness services and employee benefits plans. Serves individuals, corporations, partnerships, and non-profit organizations. **Founded:** 1968. **Seminars:** Qualified pension plans and employee welfare benefit plans.

COMPUTERIZED DATABASES

22080 ■ *ABI/INFORM®*
789 E Eisenhower Pkwy.
Ann Arbor, MI 48106-1346
Ph: (734)761-4700
Free: 800-521-0600
Co. E-mail: info@il.proquest.com
URL: http://www.il.proquest.com
Contact: Matt Dunie, President
Availability: Online: ProQuest Co.; ProQuest LLC-Dialog; ProQuest LLC - Dialog; LexisNexis Group; STN International; Wolters Kluwer Health - Ovid. **Type:** Full-text; Bibliographic; Image.

22081 ■ *Business Insurance*
1155 Gratiot Ave.
Detroit, MI 48207
Ph: (313)446-6000
Free: 800-678-2427
Fax: (313)446-1616
Co. E-mail: info@crain.com
URL: http://www.crain.com
Availability: Online: ProQuest LLC - Dialog; LexisNexis Group; Crain Communications Inc. **Type:** Full-text.

22082 ■ *Compliance Guide for Plan Administrators*
2700 Lake Cook Rd.
Riverwoods, IL 60015
Ph: (847)267-7000
Free: 888-224-7377
Fax: (847)267-2873
Co. E-mail: info@cch.com
URL: http://www.cch.com
Contact: Mike Sabbatis, President
Availability: Online: CCH Inc. **Type:** Full-text.

22083 ■ *Employee Benefits Cases*
1801 S Bell St.
Arlington, VA 22202
Free: 800-372-1033
Co. E-mail: customercare@bna.com
URL: http://www.bna.com
Availability: Online: Thomson Reuters - Westlaw. **Type:** Full-text.

22084 ■ *Employee Benefits Infosource™*
18700 W Bluemound Rd.
Brookfield, WI 53045
Ph: (262)786-6700
Free: 888-334-3327

Fax: (262)364-1818
Co. E-mail: membership@ifebp.org
URL: http://www.ifebp.org
Contact: Richard Lyall, President
Availability: Online: ProQuest LLC - Dialog; International Foundation of Employee Benefit Plans. **Type:** Bibliographic.

22085 ■ *Pension & Benefits Daily™*
1801 S Bell St.
Arlington, VA 22202
Free: 800-372-1033
Co. E-mail: customercare@bna.com
URL: http://www.bna.com
Availability: Online: Bloomberg LP-Bloomberg BNA; Thomson Reuters - Westlaw. **Type:** Full-text.

22086 ■ *Pension & Benefits Reporter™*
1801 S Bell St.
Arlington, VA 22202
Free: 800-372-1033
Co. E-mail: customercare@bna.com
URL: http://www.bna.com
Availability: Online: Bloomberg LP-Bloomberg BNA; Thomson Reuters - Westlaw. **Type:** Full-text.

LIBRARIES

22087 ■ AIAS, Inc. - Library
PO Box 521
Logandale, NV 89021
Ph: (702)398-3701
Fax: (702)398-3700
Contact: D.K. Smith, Librarian
Scope: Employee stock ownership plans. **Services:** Library open to members only. **Founded:** 1970. **Holdings:** 2955 books; 2006 reports; 54 manuscripts. **Subscriptions:** 205 journals and other serials; 13 newspapers.

22088 ■ Employee Services Management Association Information Center
568 Spring Rd., Ste. D
Elmhurst, IL 60126-3896
Ph: (630)559-0020
Fax: (630)559-0025
Co. E-mail: esmahq@esmassn.org
URL: http://www.esmassn.org
Contact: Renee M. Mula, Executive Director
Scope: Employees - activities, sports, recreation, facilities, travel, fitness, wellness, pre-retirement planning, assistance programs, productivity, day care, eldercare. **Services:** Center open to the public for reference use only. **Founded:** 1941. **Holdings:** 50 volumes; archives. **Telecommunication Services:** reneemula@esmassn.org.

22089 ■ Ivins, Phillips, Barker Library
1700 Pennsylvania Ave. NW, Ste. 600
Washington, DC 20006
Ph: (202)393-7600
Fax: (202)393-7601
Co. E-mail: jefff@ipbtax.com
URL: http://ipbtax.com
Contact: Jeffrey T. Freilich, Librarian
Scope: Pensions, taxation. **Services:** Interlibrary loan; copying; library not open to the public. **Holdings:** 1000 volumes; technical reports; CD-ROMs.

22090 ■ Towers Perrin - Western Canada Information Centre
3700, 150 - 6 Ave., SW
Calgary, AB, Canada T2P 3Y7
Ph: (403)261-1432
Fax: (403)237-6733
Co. E-mail: val.ward@towers.com
Contact: Val Ward
Scope: Human resource management, total rewards, pensions, employee benefits, executive compensation, employee communications, pension and benefits administration services, pension fund asset management. **Services:** Interlibrary loan. **Founded:** 1984. **Holdings:** 1000 books. **Subscriptions:** 100 journals and other serials; 4 newspapers.

22091 ■ Towers Watson Information Centre
1100 Melville St., Ste. 1600
Vancouver, BC, Canada V6E 4A6

Ph: (604)691-1000
Fax: (604)691-1062
URL: http://www.towerswatson.com/
Scope: Actuarial science, employee benefits, compensation, human resources. **Holdings:** Figures not available.

RESEARCH CENTERS

22092 ■ Pennsylvania State University - Risk Management Research Center (RMRC)
310F Smeal College of Business
University Park, PA 16802
Ph: (814)865-3961
Fax: (814)865-6284
Co. E-mail: afs1@psu.edu
URL: http://www.smeal.psu.edu/rmrc
Contact: Prof. Arnold F. Shapiro, Director
Founded: 1985.

22093 ■ University of North Carolina at Chapel Hill - Cecil G. Sheps Center for Health Services Research
CB No. 7590
725 Martin Luther King Jr. Blvd.
Chapel Hill, NC 27599

Ph: (919)966-5011
Fax: (919)966-5764
Co. E-mail: timothy_carey@med.unc.edu
URL: http://www.shepscenter.unc.edu
Contact: Timothy S. Carey, Director
Services: Technical assistance: for a number of state agencies. **Founded:** 1968. **Publications:** *Consensus in DHHS Region IV: Women and Infant Health Indicators for Planning and Evaluation; North Carolina Health Professions Data Book; North Carolina Health Professions Fact Sheet.* **Educational Activities:** Annual DHHS Region IV Conference on Maternal and Child Health, Family Planning, and Services for Children With Special Health Needs; Annual DHHS Region IV Workshop on the Collection and Use of Data for MCH and Women's Health Planning and Evaluation; Seminars and training programs. **Awards:** Cecil G. Sheps Center for Health Services Research Postdoctoral fellowships, in mental health services research; Pre- and postdoctoral fellowships, in general health services research.

22094 ■ University of Pennsylvania - Pension Research Council (PRC)
3000 Steinberg Hall - Dietrich Hall
The Wharton School
3620 Locust Walk
Philadelphia, PA 19104-6302

Ph: (215)898-7620
Fax: (215)573-3418
Co. E-mail: mitchelo@wharton.upenn.edu
URL: http://www.pensionresearchcouncil.org
Contact: Prof. Olivia S. Mitchell, Executive Director

Founded: 1952. **Publications:** *PRC Newsletter; Working paper series.* **Educational Activities:** PRC Symposium (Annual). **Telecommunication Services:** prc@wharton.upenn.edu.

22095 ■ West Virginia University - Institute for Labor Studies and Research (ILSR)
Knapp Hall, Rm. 709
Ext. Service
Morgantown, WV 26506-6031
Ph: (304)293-3323
Fax: (304)293-3395
Co. E-mail: tony.michael@mail.wvu.edu
URL: http://laborstudiesandresearch.ext.wvu.edu
Contact: David Anthony (Tony) Michael, Program Director

Founded: 1959. **Educational Activities:** Residential programs and conferences.

Budgets/Budgeting

ASSOCIATIONS AND OTHER ORGANIZATIONS

22096 ■ American Association for Budget and Program Analysis (AABPA)
PO Box 1157
Falls Church, VA 22041
Ph: (703)941-4300
Fax: (703)941-1535
Co. E-mail: aabpa@aol.com
URL: http://www.aabpa.org
Contact: Jon Stehle, President
Description: Professionals in budgeting, policy analysis, and program & management analysis evaluation who are employed by the federal government, state and local agencies, private companies, and academic institutions. Seeks to advance knowledge in budgeting management and program analysis. Promotes the exchange of ideas and information. Conducts monthly program with guest speakers from government agencies, congress, and institutions. **Founded:** 1976. **Publications:** *Public Budgeting and Finance* (Quarterly); *Journal of Public Budgeting and Finance* (Quarterly). **Awards:** Distinguished Service Award (Annual). **Telecommunication Services:** aabpa@aabpa.org.

22097 ■ International Budget Partnership (IBP)
820 1st St. NE, Ste. 510
Washington, DC 20002
Ph: (202)408-1080
Fax: (202)408-8173
Co. E-mail: info@internationalbudget.org
URL: http://internationalbudget.org
Contact: Warren Krafchik, Director
Description: Works to assist civil society organizations globally to improve budget policies and decision-making processes. **Founded:** 1997. **Publications:** *IBP Newsletter* (Bimonthly); *A Guide to Budget Work for NGOs*; *Budgeting for the Future, Building another Europe*. **Educational Activities:** International Budget Conference (Biennial).

EDUCATIONAL PROGRAMS

22098 ■ Project Scheduling and Budgeting - Achieving Cost-Effective and Timely Delivery (Onsite)
Seminar Information Service, Inc.
20 Executive Park, Ste. 120
Irvine, CA 92614
Ph: (949)261-9104
Free: 877-SEM-INFO
Fax: (949)261-1963
Co. E-mail: info@seminarinformation.com
URL: http://www.seminarinformation.com
Price: $2,490.00. **Description:** Learn how to: Build schedules and budgets that transform project constraints into project success; Construct Work Breakdown Structures (WBS) and network diagrams and estimate task durations; Calculate Critical Path and optimize your project plan; Allocate costs and chart expected cash flow; Assign resources effectively and respond to end-date changes; Perform Earned Value Analysis (EVA) to keep the project on track.

REFERENCE WORKS

22099 ■ "2009: A Call For Vision" in Women Entrepreneur (January 28, 2009)
Pub: Entrepreneur Media Inc.
Ed: Elinor Robin. **Description:** Providing exemplary customer service, reducing expenses and creating an out-of-the-box niche are three key factors that will help business survive during this economic crisis. Business owners must see potential where others see failure in order to create new opportunities that may not only allow their business to survive during these times but may actually cause some businesses to thrive despite this economic downturn.

22100 ■ "Another Baby Step" in Canadian Business (Vol. 81, March 31, 2008, No. 5, pp. 32)
Pub: Rogers Media
Ed: Andrew Wahl. **Description:** Discusses the Canadian government's federal budget which makes it easier to tap into tax credits for corporate research and development. However, these steps do not really go far enough to boost industrial research levels in Canada. Making these incentives at least partially refundable could help during tough economic times.

22101 ■ "Budget Strategically to Stay on Course" in Entrepreneur (August 28, 2008)
Pub: Entrepreneur Media Inc.
Ed: Tim Berry. **Description:** Budgeting is one of the most valuable tools in a manager's arsenal. The importance of budgeting is discussed and tips for surviving an economic recession are provided.

22102 ■ "Business Must Stand Up And Be Counted" in Crain's Detroit Business (Vol. 24, October 6, 2008, No. 40, pp. 6)
Pub: Crain Communications, Inc.
Description: Discusses the challenges that the new mayor of Detroit faces concerning business, the state of the economy and the exceptionally tight budget the city is running on, which includes a lot of red ink. It is very likely that the city is going to see tax revenues fall substantially in the next few months and business leaders may find it in their favor to lend their support to the new mayor as well as provide him with the executive talent necessary to overcome some of these crucial issues.

22103 ■ "Business Stands Firm for Reform" in Crain's Detroit Business (Vol. 26, January 4, 2010, No. 1, pp. 3)
Pub: Crain Communications, Inc.
Ed: Amy Lane. **Description:** As Michigan faces a new year of budgetary problems, many business groups are preparing to hold firm against tax increases and instead push for enacting spending reforms.

22104 ■ "Different Aspects of Project Management" in Contractor (Vol. 57, February 2010, No. 2, pp. 30)
Pub: Penton Media, Inc.
Ed: H. Kent Craig. **Description:** There are differences when managing a two-man crew as a foreman and a 2,000 employee company as a corporate president. A project manager should have good skills in human psychology, accounting, and the knowledge of a mechanical engineer, architect, civil engineer, and also the meditative skills of a Zen master.

22105 ■ "Dream On: California's Budget Fix may not Last for Long." in Barron's (Vol. 89, July 27, 2009, No. 30, pp. 21)
Pub: Dow Jones & Co., Inc.
Ed: Jonathan R. Laing. **Description:** California's budget agreement which purports to eliminate a $26 billion deficit is discussed. The frequent budgetary dustups in the state calls for several reforms including a rainy day fund of 15 percent of any budget and a constitutional convention. Other reform suggestions are discussed.

22106 ■ "Efficient Cash Management Essential To Be Competitive" in Crain's Cleveland Business (Vol. 28, November 12, 2007, No. 45, pp. 25)
Pub: Crain Communications, Inc.
Ed: Ken Moultrie. **Description:** In order to sustain a business it is important to organize cash-management efforts around three core areas: cash in, static cash and cash out. Tips for the successful management of these areas are provided.

22107 ■ Entrepreneurial Finance
Pub: Pearson Education, Limited
Contact: Steven A. Dowling, President
Ed: Philip J. Adelman; Alan M. Marks. **Released:** July 2006. **Price:** $87.35. **Description:** Financial aspects of running a small business are covered; topics include sole proprietorships, partnerships, limited liability companies, and private corporations.

22108 ■ "Exit Strategy" in Barron's (Vol. 89, July 6, 2009, No. 27, pp. 3)
Pub: Dow Jones & Co., Inc.
Ed: Alan Abelson. **Description:** US Federal Reserve is not likely to change its easy-money strategy in the short term. States such as California are suffering from spiraling costs and declining revenues and are struggling to balance their budgets. The US unemployment rate climbed to 9.5 percent in June 2009.

22109 ■ "Facebook: A Promotional Budget's Best Friend" in Women Entrepreneur (February 1, 2009)
Pub: Entrepreneur Media Inc.
Ed: Tamara Monosoff. **Description:** Facebook began as a social networking website but has become a valuable marketing tool for all types of businesses, organizations and causes. Tips are provided for creating a Facebook account and growing one's network on Facebook.

22110 ■ *Financial Management 101: Get a Grip on Your Business Numbers*

Pub: Self-Counsel Press, Incorporated

Ed: Angie Mohr. **Released:** November 2007. **Price:** $16.95. **Description:** An overview of business planning, financial statements, budgeting and advertising for small businesses. s.

22111 ■ *"Get Back To Business Planning Fundamentals" in Entrepreneur (October 24, 2008)*

Pub: Entrepreneur Media Inc.

Ed: Tim Berry. **Description:** During a recession it is important to know what adjustment to make to your business plan. Some fundamentals to remember include: watching things more closely by tracking progress on cash, sales, new projects, customer satisfaction, ad spending and expenses; looking for built-in indicators such as what drives sales or expenses; watching what drives cash flow; and do not make mistakes such as laying off experienced employees too soon.

22112 ■ *"Handle With Care" in Hawaii Business (Vol. 53, October 2007, No. 5, pp. 66)*

Pub: Hawaii Business Publishing

Ed: Kenneth Sheffield. **Description:** Discusses a fiduciary, who may be a board member, business owner, or a trustee, and is someone who supervises and manages the affairs and the resources of a principal. Fiduciary duties, which include accounting, cost review and risk management, must be served with the benefit of the principal as the priority. Ways of breaching fiduciary duties and how to avoid them are discussed.

22113 ■ *"Inch by Inch, Employees Lose Ground" in Business Courier (Vol. 26, November 13, 2009, No. 29, pp. 1)*

Pub: American City Business Journals, Inc.

Ed: James Ritchie. **Description:** Employees in Ohio who retained their jobs have suffered losses in salary and other benefits, as companies exert efforts to save money. Thirty-four percent of employees experienced pay cuts. Statistical data included

22114 ■ *"Insurers No Longer Paying Premium for Advertising" in Brandweek (Vol. 49, April 21, 2008, No. 16, pp. SR3)*

Pub: VNU Business Media, Inc.

Ed: Eric Newman. **Description:** Insurance companies are cutting their advertising budgets after years of accelerated double-digit growth in spending due to the economic downturn, five years of record-breaking ad spend and a need to cut expenditures as claims costs rise and a competitive market keeps premiums in place. Statistical data included.

22115 ■ *"Irene Rosenfeld; Chairman and CEO, Kraft Foods Inc." in Crain's Chicago Business (Vol. 31, May 5, 2008, No. 18, pp. 31)*

Pub: Crain Communications, Inc.

Ed: David Sterrett. **Description:** Profile of Irene Rosenfeld who is the chairman and CEO of Kraft Foods Inc. and is entering the second year of a three-year plan to boost sales of well-known brands such as Oreo, Velveeta and Oscar Mayer while facing soaring commodity costs and a declining market-share. Ms. Rosenfeld's turnaround strategy also entails spending more on advertising and giving managers more control over their budgets and product development.

22116 ■ *"Key Budgeting Tips: For Your Management Team" in Agency Sales Magazine (Vol. 39, December 2009, No. 11, pp. 49)*

Pub: MANA

Ed: Gene Siciliano. **Description:** Constructing a budget must be the result of coordinated input and effort. Practice is also important in creating a budget and accurately predicting actual results is not the objective but giving the company a direction for course correction.

22117 ■ *"Life's Work: Oliver Sacks" in Harvard Business Review (Vol. 88, November 2010, No. 11, pp. 152)*

Pub: Harvard Business School Publishing

Ed: Lisa Burrell. **Description:** Neurologist and author Oliver Sacks discusses whether different types of minds tend toward certain skills, physician-patient communication, and his own perspectives from being a patient himself.

22118 ■ *"Local Hotels Brace for Downturn" in Crain's Chicago Business (Vol. 31, March 31, 2008, No. 13, pp. 3)*

Pub: Crain Communications, Inc.

Ed: Bob Tita. **Description:** Chicago hotels are seeing a noticeable drop in business-related guests so far this year due to a slumping national economy, tighter corporate expense budgets and higher airfares.

22119 ■ *Million Dollar Website: Simple Steps to Help You Compete with the Big Boys-Even on a Small Business Budget*

Pub: Prentice Hall Press

Ed: Lori Culwell. **Released:** May 9, 2010. **Price:** $19.95. **Description:** Resource for any small business owner wishing to build a successful Website in order to compete with big box stores.

22120 ■ *"Pick and Save" in Entrepreneur (Vol. 36, April 2008, No. 4, pp. 66)*

Pub: Entrepreneur Media, Inc.

Ed: C.J. Prince. **Description:** Business owners can purchase the needed big equipment to offset this year's expected profit. They can also switch to annualized computing of quarterly income and estimated tax payments to pay less estimated taxes for the first half of the year. Other tips on tax planning are provided.

22121 ■ *"Pro Teams Shift Ad Budgets; Naming Rights Deals Near $1 Billion" in Brandweek (Vol. 49, April 21, 2008, No. 16, pp. 18)*

Pub: VNU Business Media, Inc.

Ed: Barry Janoff. **Description:** More and more professional sports marketers are spending less of their advertising budgets on traditional media outlets such as television, print and radio; the growing trend in sports marketing is in utilizing new media venues such as the Internet in which innovative means are used to encourage interaction with fans.

22122 ■ *QuickBooks X for Dummies*

Pub: John Wiley & Sons, Incorporated

Ed: Stephen L. Nelson. **Released:** November 2006. **Price:** $21.99. **Description:** Key features of Quick-Books software for small business are introduced. Invoicing and credit memos, recoding sales receipts, accounting, budgeting, taxes, payroll, financial reports, job estimating, billing, tracking, data backup, are among the features.

22123 ■ *Small Business Cash Flow: Strategies for Making Your Business a Financial Success*

Pub: John Wiley & Sons, Incorporated

Ed: Denise O'Berry. **Released:** October 2006. **Price:** $19.95. **Description:** Tips to help small businesses manage money are given.

22124 ■ *Small Business Clustering Technology: Applications in Marketing, Management, Finance, and IT*

Pub: Idea Group Publishing

Ed: Robert C. MacGregor; Ann Hodgkinson. **Released:** June 2006. **Description:** An overview of the development and role of small business clusters in disciplines that include economics, marketing, management and information systems.

22125 ■ *Small Business for Dummies, 3rd Ed.*

Pub: John Wiley and Sons, Inc.

Ed: Eric Tyson; Jim Schell. **Released:** March 2008. **Price:** $21.99. **Description:** Guidebook for anyone wanting to start or grow a small business; topics include information financing, budgeting, marketing, management and more.

22126 ■ *Small Business Management*

Pub: John Wiley & Sons, Incorporated

Ed: Margaret Burlingame. **Released:** March 2007. **Price:** $44.95. **Description:** Advice for starting and running a small business as well as information on the value and appeal of small businesses, is given. Topics include budgets, taxes, inventory, ethics, e-commerce, and current laws.

22127 ■ *The Small Business Savings Plan: 101 Tactics for Controlling Costs and Boosting the Bottom Line*

Pub: Kaplan Books

Ed: Timothy R. Gase. **Released:** May 2007. **Price:** $28.00. **Description:** Strategies for small business owners to develop a savings plan and increase profits are outlined.

22128 ■ *Streetwise Finance and Accounting for Entrepreneurs: Set Budgets, Manage Costs, Keep Your Business Profitable*

Pub: Adams Media Corporation

Ed: Suzanne Caplan. **Released:** November 2006. **Price:** $25.95. **Description:** Book offers a basic understanding of accounting and finance for small businesses, including financial statements, credits and debits, as well as establishing a budget. Strategies for small companies in financial distress are included.

22129 ■ *Streetwise Small Business Book of Lists: Hundreds of Lists to Help You Reduce Costs, Increase Revenues, and Boost Your Profits!*

Pub: Adams Media Corporation

Contact: Gary Krebs, Director

E-mail: swatrous@adamsmedia.com

Ed: Gene Marks. **Released:** September 2006. **Price:** $25.95. **Description:** Strategies to help small business owners locate services, increase sales, and lower expenses.

22130 ■ *"Stretch Your Advertising Dollars" in Women Entrepreneur (January 27, 2009)*

Pub: Entrepreneur Media Inc.

Ed: Rosalind Resnick. **Description:** During such poor economic times, most businesses are having to cut their advertising budgets; tips for targeting your advertising dollars toward the customer base most likely to buy your product are given.

22131 ■ *"Taking a Pounding; Recession Fears Weigh Down Steakhouse Operator Morton's" in Crain's Chicago Business (March 31, 2008)*

Pub: Crain Communications, Inc.

Ed: Monee Fields-White. **Description:** Morton's Restaurant Group Inc. has seen a 50 percent drop in shares in the past six months due to the economy and cutbacks in corporate expense accounts; business customers provide the restaurant about 80 percent of its revenue.

22132 ■ *"Ten Ways to Save on Business Travel" in Women Entrepreneur (November 21, 2008)*

Pub: Entrepreneur Media Inc.

Ed: Julie Moline. **Description:** Advice regarding ways in which to save money when traveling for business is given.

22133 ■ *"Travel Leery" in Crain's Chicago Business (Vol. 31, March 31, 2008, No. 13, pp. 3)*

Pub: Crain Communications, Inc.

Description: Due to the rise in airline prices and a possible recession, many companies are starting to change their travel policies and limit travel spending.

22134 ■ *Valuing the Closely Held Firm*

Pub: Oxford University Press

Ed: Michael S. Long; Thomas A. Bryant. **Released:** March 2007. **Price:** $65.00. **Description:** The differences between a large and small firm and their ability to generate future cash flow are discussed.

22135 ■ *"Watchful Eye: Entrepreneur Protects Clients and His Bottom Line" in Black Enterprise (Vol. 38, March 2008, No. 8, pp. 46)*
Pub: Earl G. Graves Publishing Co. Inc.
Ed: Tennille M. Robinson. **Description:** Profile of Elijah Shaw, founder of Icon Services Corporation, a full service security and investigative service; Shaw shares his plans to protect clients while growing his business.

22136 ■ *"What Are You, A Bank? You Probably Lend Your Customers More Money Than You Realize." in Inc. (November 2007, pp. 81)*
Pub: Gruner & Jahr USA Publishing
Ed: Norm Brodsky. **Description:** Small business owners don't realize when that when customers do not pay on time, it is the same as lending them money. Tips to get customers to pay on time are listed.

22137 ■ *"Your Bottom Line: How To Bring In Dollars When Times Are Tough" in Small Business Opportunities (November 2007)*
Pub: Harris Publications Inc.
Description: Adding a new product or promoting a product in a new way can help any small business during hard economic times.

TRADE PERIODICALS

22138 ■ *OMB Watcher*
Pub: OMB Watch
Contact: Katherine McFate, President
Ed: . **Released:** Bimonthly. **Price:** individuals. **Description:** Summarizes initiatives and other administrative issues of the White House Office of Management and Budget (OMB). Frequently includes short analyses of the federal budget and regulatory processes as well as related issues.

22139 ■ *Public Budgeting and Finance*
Pub: North-South Center Press at the University of Miami
Contact: Mary M. Mapes, Manager
URL(s): www.wiley.com/bw/journal.asp?ref=0275-1100. **Released:** Quarterly **Price:** $93, Individuals print & online; €138, Individuals Europe, print & online; £91, Out of country print & online; $74, Members Americas, print & online; €110, Members Europe, print & online; £74, Members other countries, print & online; $446, Institutions print + online; £687, Institutions, other countries print + online; €446, Institutions Europe, print + online.

VIDEOCASSETTES/ AUDIOCASSETTES

22140 ■ *Budgeting*
Video Arts, Inc.
c/o Aim Learning Group
8238-40 Lehigh
Morton Grove, IL 60053-2615
Free: 877-444-2230

Fax: (416)252-2155
Co. E-mail: service@aimlearninggroup.com
URL: http://www.aimlearninggroup.com
Released: 1986. **Price:** $790.00. **Description:** An illustrative program for the business owner in how to balance the company's budget so as to move onto an upward course. **Availability:** VHS; 8 mm; 3/4 U; Special order formats.

22141 ■ *FASB 95: Statement of Cash Flows*
Bisk Education
9417 Princess Palm Ave.
Tampa, FL 33619
Free: 800-874-7877
Co. E-mail: info@bisk.com
URL: http://www.bisk.com
Released: 19??. **Price:** $199.00. **Description:** Profiles accounting techniques centering on the assessment of current and future cash inflows, outflows, and cash flow problems that lead to business failure. Includes workbook and quizzer. **Availability:** VHS.

CONSULTANTS

22142 ■ Larry J. Anderson Insurance
1200 35th St., Ste. 206-4
West Des Moines, IA 50266-1958
Ph: (515)221-1973
Fax: (515)221-0074
Contact: Larry J. Anderson, Owner
E-mail: andy4021@aol.com
Scope: Offers business consulting services including temporary technical aid in accounting, turn around and cash management, and bail-out assistance. Also provides operations research, models, forecasting, project scheduling, and economic forecasting services. Provides assistance in group health insurance in both fully insured groups and self-funded groups. **Founded:** 1984.

22143 ■ Business Methods Corp. (BMC)
503 Rte. 10 E
Randolph, NJ 07869
Ph: (973)703-2022
Fax: (973)328-4584
Co. E-mail: businessmethods@aol.com
URL: http://www.bmclogo.com
Contact: Dr. Kevin Chen, President
E-mail: kchenbmc@aol.com
Scope: Specialty advertising business which includes custom imprinted promotional product promotions. **Founded:** 1989.

22144 ■ Expenses Limited Inc.
2204 Morris Ave., Ste. 104
Union, NJ 07083-5914
Ph: (908)688-9080
Fax: (908)688-5045
Contact: Robert J. Giardina, Chief Executive Officer
Scope: Provides expense reduction services for general and administrative expense areas. Focuses on all type of industries. **Founded:** 1992.

22145 ■ Harvey C. Skoog
7151 E Addis Ave.
Prescott Valley, AZ 86314

Ph: (928)772-1448
Scope: Firm has expertise in taxes, payroll, financial planning, budgeting, buy/sell planning, business start-up, fraud detection, troubled business consulting, acquisition, and marketing. Serves the manufacturing, construction, and retailing industries in Arizona. **Founded:** 1977.

22146 ■ Mark Vanderstelt
9831 Gulfstream Ct.
Fishers, IN 46037
Ph: (317)576-9328
Fax: (317)576-9328
Contact: Mark Vanderstelt, Owner
Scope: Consulting services include financial planning and analysis, inventory control, cash management, return on investment, budgeting, pricing, system design and analysis, mergers and acquisitions, feasibility studies, data processing, cost systems and controls, and performance measurement. Also performs operational and financial reviews. **Founded:** 1985.

FRANCHISES AND BUSINESS OPPORTUNITIES

22147 ■ Leadership Management, Inc.
4567 Lake Shore Dr.
Waco, TX 76710
Ph: (800)568-1241
Fax: (254)772-9588
Description: The franchise provides business aids and services. **No. of Franchise Units:** 195. **Founded:** 1965.. **Franchised:** 1965. **Equity Capital Needed:** $35,000-$42,500. **Franchise Fee:** $30,000. **Royalty Fee:** 6%. **Financial Assistance:** Limited in-house financing available. **Training:** Includes 2 days training at headquarters, 2 days at franchisee's location and ongoing support.

COMPUTER SYSTEMS/ SOFTWARE

22148 ■ Aatrix Top Pay
2100 Library Cir.
Grand Forks, ND 58201
Ph: (701)746-6017
Free: 800-426-0854
Fax: (701)787-0594
URL: http://www.aatrix.com
Price: Contact Aatrix. **Description:** Handles payroll calculations and tax deductions for both salaried and hourly employees.

22149 ■ Argos Software / ABECAS Insight
5737 N Fresno St.
Fresno, CA 93710
Ph: (559)227-1000
Fax: (559)227-9644
Co. E-mail: info@argosoftware.com
URL: http://www.argosoftware.com
Description: Available for MS-DOS operating system. Payroll system for agricultural employees.

ASSOCIATIONS AND OTHER ORGANIZATIONS

22150 ■ Association for Business Communication (ABC)
PO Box 6143
Nacogdoches, TX 75962-0001
Ph: (540)231-8460
Fax: (646)349-5297
Co. E-mail: abcoffice@businesscommunication.org
URL: http://www.businesscommunication.org
Contact: Jim Dubinsky, Executive Director
Description: College teachers of business communication; management consultants in business communications; training directors and correspondence supervisors of business firms, direct mail copywriters, public relations writers, and others interested in communication for business. **Founded:** 1935. **Publications:** *Business Communication Quarterly* (Quarterly); *The Journal of Business Communication* (Quarterly); *Journal of Business Communication* (Quarterly); *Making Communication Requirements More Explicit in the AACSB Standards for MBA Programs.* **Educational Activities:** Association for Business Communication Annual Convention (Annual); Association for Business Communication Convention (Annual). **Awards:** Distinguished Publication on Business Communication; Outstanding Article in Business Communication Quarterly; Distinguished Publication on Business Communication (Annual); Kitty O. Locker Outstanding Researcher Award (Annual); Meada Gibbs Outstanding Teacher Award (Annual); Outstanding Article in Business Communication Quarterly (Annual); Outstanding Article in the Journal of Business Communication (Annual); Outstanding Doctoral Dissertation Award (Annual); Outstanding Article in the Journal of Business Communication. **Telecommunication Services:** abc-johnson@sfasu.edu.

22151 ■ International Association of Business Communicators (IABC)
601 Montgomery St., Ste. 1900
San Francisco, CA 94111
Ph: (415)544-4700
Free: 800-776-4222
Fax: (415)544-4747
Co. E-mail: member_relations@iabc.com
URL: http://www.iabc.com
Contact: Paulo H. Soares, Director
E-mail: paulo.henrique.soares@vale.com
Description: Represents Communication managers, public relations directors, writers, editors, audiovisual specialists, and others in the public relations and organizational communication field that use a variety of media to communicate with internal audiences (employees, management, association members, and leaders) and external audiences (media, customers, dealers, investors, and government). Conducts research in the communication field and encourages establishment of college-level programs in organizational communication. Offers accreditation program; conducts surveys on employee communication effectiveness and media trends. **Scope:** organizational communication. **Founded:** 1970. **Publications:** *Communication World: The Magazine for Communication Professionals; World Book of IABC Communicators; World Book of IABC Communicators; The Human Element.* **Educational Activities:** International Association of Business Communicators World Conference (Annual). **Awards:** Chairman's Award; IABC Fellow; Chairman's Award (Annual); Chapter Management Award (Annual); Excellence in Communication Leadership (Annual); Fellow Designation (Annual); Gold Quill (Annual); Lifetime Foundation Friend Award (Annual); Excellence in Communication Leadership (EXCEL) Award. **Telecommunication Services:** service_centre@iabc.com; service_center@iabc.com.

22152 ■ Society for Technical Communication (STC)
9401 Lee Hwy., Ste. 300
Fairfax, VA 22031
Ph: (703)522-4114
Fax: (703)522-2075
URL: http://www.stc.org
Contact: Dr. Hillary Hart, President
Description: Writers, editors, educators, scientists, engineers, artists, publishers, and others professionally engaged in or interested in the field of technical communication; companies, corporations, organizations, and agencies interested in the aims of the society. Seeks to advance the theory and practice of technical communication in all media. Sponsors high school writing contests. **Scope:** An individual membership organization dedicated to advancing the arts and sciences of technical communication. Members include technical writers and editors, content developers, documentation specialists, technical illustrators, instructional designers, academics, information architects, usability and human factors professionals, visual designers, web designers and developers, and translators. Provides support to teachers and students of technical communication through programs, scholarships, grants and loans, annual conferences, and seminars. Also provides information about events and courses related to technical communication. **Founded:** 1957. **Publications:** "Managing Writers: A Real World Guide to Managing Technical Documentation," 2009; "Advertising Rates," 2009; "The Current Economy: What's a Technical Communicator to Do," Oct, 2008; "Breaking Through the Glass Ceiling," May, 2008; "The Tipping Point Theory," Mar, 2008; "Recession Obsession," Feb, 2008; "English Technical Writing Guide," 2008; "Publishing Fundamentals: Unstructured Frame Maker 8," 2008; "Hello, My Name is Doug and I'm a Workaholic," Oct, 2007; "Results of original research"; "Original contributions to technical communication theory". **Educational Activities:** Society for Technical Communication Conference (Annual). **Awards:** International Technical Art Competition; International Technical Publications Competition; International Online Communication Competition; Marian Norby Scholarships STC Scholarships. **Seminars:** Web-Telephone; Salary Database.

EDUCATIONAL PROGRAMS

22153 ■ Adobe Captivate 3
EEI Communications
66 Canal Ctr. Plz., Ste. 200
Alexandria, VA 22314-5507
Ph: (703)683-7453
Free: 888-253-2762
Fax: (703)683-7310
Co. E-mail: train@eeicom.com
URL: http://www.eeicom.com/training
Price: $745.00. **Description:** Seminar that teaches how to create professional quality, interactive simulations and software demonstrations without any programming or multimedia knowledge, including basics, captions and timelines, images, pointer paths, buttons, and highlight boxes, movies, rollover captions and rollover images, slide labels and notes, audio, animation, and question slides. **Dates and Locations:** Alexandria, VA.

22154 ■ Advanced Editing
EEI Communications
8945 Guilford Rd., Ste. 145
Columbia, MD 21046
Ph: (410)309-8200
Free: 888-253-2762
Fax: (410)630-3980
Co. E-mail: train@eeicom.com
URL: http://www.eeicom.com/eei-training-services
Price: $745.00. **Description:** Covers advanced editing techniques, including copyediting, substantive editing, style sheets, English grammar, and query lists. **Dates and Locations:** Alexandria, VA.

22155 ■ Advanced Leadership Communication Strategies (Onsite)
American Management Association
600 AMA Way
Saranac Lake, NY 12983-5534
Ph: (212)586-8100
Free: 877-566-9441
Fax: (518)891-0368
Co. E-mail: customerservice@amanet.org
URL: http://www.amaseminars.org
Price: $2,645.00 for non-members; $2,395.00 for AMA members; and $2,051.00 for General Services Administration (GSA) members. **Description:** Three-day seminar to build on current strong leadership skills and influence across the board. **Dates and Locations:** Atlanta, GA; Chicago, IL; and New York, NY.

22156 ■ Assertive Communication - Essential Skills for Successful Women (Onsite)
Padgett-Thompson Seminars
Rockhurst University CEC
14502 W. 105th St.
Lenexa, KS 66215
Free: 800-349-1935
URL: http://www.findaseminar.com/tpd/Padgett-Thompson-Seminars.asp
Price: $199.00. **Description:** Assertiveness training for today's business woman. **Dates and Locations:** Appleton, WI.

22157 ■ Assertiveness Skills: Communicating With Authority and Impact (Onsite)
Learning Tree International Inc.
1805 Library St.
Reston, VA 20190-5660

Ph: (703)709-9119
Free: 800-843-8733
Fax: (703)709-6405
Co. E-mail: uscourses@learningtree.com
URL: http://www.learningtree.com
Contact: Nick Schacht, President
Price: $1,890.00. **Description:** Develop a positive, assertive style and build a skill set that will enable you to react positively in demanding situations. **Dates and Locations:** Reston, VA; Toronto, ON; Ottawa, ON; New York, NY; and Rockville, MD.

22158 ■ Assertiveness Training for Managers (Onsite) (Canada)
Canadian Management Centre (CMC)
150 York St., 5th Fl.
Toronto, ON, Canada M5H 3S5
Ph: (416)214-5678
Free: 877-262-2519
Fax: (416)313-4985
Co. E-mail: cmcinfo@cmctraining.org
URL: http://www.cmctraining.org
Contact: John Wright, President
Price: $2,295.00 Canadian for non-members; $2,095.00 Canadian for CMC members. **Description:** Covers using assertive behavior professionally, requesting change, managing conflict, and defining objectives. **Dates and Locations:** Toronto and Ottawa, ON.

22159 ■ Assertiveness Training for Women in Business (Canada)
Canadian Management Centre (CMC)
150 York St., 5th Fl.
Toronto, ON, Canada M5H 3S5
Ph: (416)214-5678
Free: 877-262-2519
Fax: (416)313-4985
Co. E-mail: cmcinfo@cmctraining.org
URL: http://www.cmctraining.org
Contact: John Wright, President
Price: $2,295.00 Canadian for non-members; $2,095.00 Canadian for CMC members. **Description:** Covers self-image, stress management, various communication techniques for assertiveness, and male and female workplace attitudes. **Dates and Locations:** Toronto, ON.

22160 ■ Assertiveness Training for Women in Business (Onsite)
American Management Association
600 AMA Way
Saranac Lake, NY 12983-5534
Ph: (212)586-8100
Free: 877-566-9441
Fax: (518)891-0368
Co. E-mail: customerservice@amanet.org
URL: http://www.amaseminars.org
Price: $2,345.00 for non-members; $2,095.00 for AMA members; and $1,794.00 for General Services Administration (GSA) members. **Description:** Covers self-image, stress management, various communication techniques for assertiveness, and male and female workplace attitudes. **Dates and Locations:** Cities throughout the United States.

22161 ■ Bargaining With Vendors and Suppliers (Onsite)
Padgett-Thompson Seminars
Rockhurst University CEC
14502 W. 105th St.
Lenexa, KS 66215
Free: 800-349-1935
URL: http://www.findaseminar.com/tpd/Padgett-Thompson-Seminars.asp
Price: $249.00. **Description:** A one-day seminar that teaches practical bargaining skills that will help a company come out of every negotiation a winner. **Dates and Locations:** Cities throughout the United States.

22162 ■ Business Conversation for Sales and Service (Onsite)
Seminar Information Service, Inc.
20 Executive Park, Ste. 120
Irvine, CA 92614
Ph: (949)261-9104
Free: 877-SEM-INFO

Fax: (949)261-1963
Co. E-mail: info@seminarinformation.com
URL: http://www.seminarinformation.com
Price: $225.00 for non-members; $165.00 for The Management Association, Inc. **Description:** Participants will learn practical tips and practice conversation. Build common ground with colleagues, customers, and senior managers, including methods to develop a repertoire of topics, make skillful transitions, develop confidence and draw people to you. **Dates and Locations:** Waukesha, WI.

22163 ■ Business Conversation Skills for the Multilingual Professional (Onsite)
American Management Association
600 AMA Way
Saranac Lake, NY 12983-5534
Ph: (212)586-8100
Free: 877-566-9441
Fax: (518)891-0368
Co. E-mail: customerservice@amanet.org
URL: http://www.amaseminars.org
Price: $1,995.00 for non-members; $1,795.00 for AMA members; and $1,537.00 for General Services Administration (GSA) members. **Description:** Comprehensive two-day workshop will improve your conversation skills on all levels to achieve your professional and organizational goals. **Dates and Locations:** New York, NY; and Chicago, IL.

22164 ■ Communicating Change
Canadian Management Centre (CMC)
150 York St., 5th Fl.
Toronto, ON, Canada M5H 3S5
Ph: (416)214-5678
Free: 877-262-2519
Fax: (416)313-4985
Co. E-mail: cmcinfo@cmctraining.org
URL: http://www.cmctraining.org
Contact: John Wright, President
Price: $945.00 for members; $1,095.00 for non-members. **Description:** Learn how to leverage communication as a critical vehicle for enabling change in an organization. **Dates and Locations:** Toronto, ON.

22165 ■ Communicating Effectively in Your Corporate Culture (Onsite)
Seminar Information Service, Inc.
20 Executive Park, Ste. 120
Irvine, CA 92614
Ph: (949)261-9104
Free: 877-SEM-INFO
Fax: (949)261-1963
Co. E-mail: info@seminarinformation.com
URL: http://www.seminarinformation.com
Price: Contact for fees. **Description:** Gives participants a sound understanding of the principles of effective communication and the skill to recognize and resolve communication breakdowns in the workplace. Attendees learn the objectives of communication, gain active listening skills and how to give directions that get results.

22166 ■ Communication Boot Camp (Onsite)
American Management Association
600 AMA Way
Saranac Lake, NY 12983-5534
Ph: (212)586-8100
Free: 877-566-9441
Fax: (518)891-0368
Co. E-mail: customerservice@amanet.org
URL: http://www.amaseminars.org
Price: $2,195.00 for non-members; $1,995.00 for AMA members; and $1,708.00 for General Services Administration (GSA) members. **Description:** Three-day seminar to assess your communication skills, develop listening competencies, increase cognitive skills, and roadmap for clearer communication. **Dates and Locations:** Washington, DC; Arlington, VA; and San Francisco, CA.

22167 ■ Communication and Interpersonal Skills: A Seminar for IT and Technical Professionals (Onsite)
American Management Association
600 AMA Way
Saranac Lake, NY 12983-5534
Ph: (212)586-8100

Free: 877-566-9441
Fax: (518)891-0368
Co. E-mail: customerservice@amanet.org
URL: http://www.amaseminars.org
Price: $2,095.00 for non-members; $1,895.00 for AMA members; and $1,623.00 for General Services Administration (GSA) members. **Description:** Learn how to combine your interpersonal communication skills effectively with your technical skills to get results. **Dates and Locations:** New York, NY; San Diego, CA; Dallas, TX, Chicago, IL; and San Francisco, CA.

22168 ■ Communication and Interpersonal Skills for IT & Technical Professionals (Onsite) (Canada)
Canadian Management Centre (CMC)
150 York St., 5th Fl.
Toronto, ON, Canada M5H 3S5
Ph: (416)214-5678
Free: 877-262-2519
Fax: (416)313-4985
Co. E-mail: cmcinfo@cmctraining.org
URL: http://www.cmctraining.org
Contact: John Wright, President
Price: $1,995.00 Canadian for non-members; $1,845.00 Canadian for CMC members. **Description:** Covers effective communication skills, prioritizing, and dealing with various types of communication styles. **Dates and Locations:** Toronto, ON.

22169 ■ Communication Skills: Results Through Collaboration (Onsite)
Seminar Information Service, Inc.
20 Executive Park, Ste. 120
Irvine, CA 92614
Ph: (949)261-9104
Free: 877-SEM-INFO
Fax: (949)261-1963
Co. E-mail: info@seminarinformation.com
URL: http://www.seminarinformation.com
Price: $2,490.00. **Description:** Learn how to: Achieve results in your communications with others; Build collaborative relationships that emphasize trust and respect; Communicate effectively using simple, concise and direct language; Enhance your active listening skills; Foster cross-cultural understanding in your workplace; Eliminate the roadblocks that undermine your ability to communicate effectively. **Dates and Locations:** Cities throughout the United States.

22170 ■ Communication Skills: Results Through Collaboration (Onsite)
Learning Tree International Inc.
1805 Library St.
Reston, VA 20190-5660
Ph: (703)709-9119
Free: 800-843-8733
Fax: (703)709-6405
Co. E-mail: uscourses@learningtree.com
URL: http://www.learningtree.com
Contact: Nick Schacht, President
Price: $2,490.00. **Description:** Learn to achieve results in your communications with others and build collaborative relationships. **Dates and Locations:** Cities throughout the United States and Canada.

22171 ■ Communication Skills for Women (Onsite)
Fred Pryor Seminars & CareerTrack
5700 Broadmoor St., Ste. 300
Mission, KS 66202
Free: 800-780-8476
Fax: (913)967-8849
Co. E-mail: customerservice@pryor.com
URL: http://www.pryor.com
Price: $99.00; $89.00 for groups of 5 or more. **Description:** Covers valuable insights women can use to enhance their communication style while earning the respect and cooperation of others, including how to control your emotions and stay composed and effective while under pressure. **Dates and Locations:** Cities throughout the United States.

22172 ■ Communication Techniques That Get Results: A Course for Administrative Professionals (Onsite)
AMA
600 AMA Way
Saranac Lake, NY 12983-5534
Ph: (212)586-8100
Free: 877-566-9441
Fax: (518)891-0368
Co. E-mail: customerservice@amanet.org
URL: http://www.amaseminars.org
Price: $1,545.00 for non-members; $1,395.00 for AMA members. **Description:** Meet changing job demands and deliver optimum results through better communication in this two-day course.

22173 ■ Comprehensive Proofreading (Onsite)
EEI Communications
8945 Guilford Rd., Ste. 145
Columbia, MD 21046
Ph: (410)309-8200
Free: 888-253-2762
Fax: (410)630-3980
Co. E-mail: train@eeicom.com
URL: http://www.eeicom.com/eei-training-services
Price: $797.00. **Description:** Covers creating proofreading checklists, using style guides, and proofreading electronic documents. **Dates and Locations:** Silver Spring, MD; and Alexandria, VA.

22174 ■ Conflict Communications
EEI Communications
8945 Guilford Rd., Ste. 145
Columbia, MD 21046
Ph: (410)309-8200
Free: 888-253-2762
Fax: (703)630-3980
Co. E-mail: train@eeicom.com
URL: http://www.eeicom.com/eei-training-services
Price: $425.00. **Description:** Learn to coach people through conflict, identify different levels and forms of conflict and why people react differently to conflict. **Dates and Locations:** Silver Spring, MD; Hunt Valley, MD; Columbia, MD; and Alexandria, VA.

22175 ■ Conflict Management Skills for Women (Onsite)
Seminar Information Service, Inc.
20 Executive Park, Ste. 120
Irvine, CA 92614
Ph: (949)261-9104
Free: 877-SEM-INFO
Fax: (949)261-1963
Co. E-mail: info@seminarinformation.com
URL: http://www.seminarinformation.com
Price: $99.00; $89.00 for four or more. **Description:** Learn how to keep unmanaged conflicts, disagreements and out-of-control emotions from harming your important working and personal relationships. **Dates and Locations:** Cities throughout the United States.

22176 ■ Critical Business Communication Skills
Padgett-Thompson Seminars
Rockhurst University CEC
14502 W. 105th St.
Lenexa, KS 66215
Free: 800-349-1935
URL: http://www.findaseminar.com/tpd/Padgett-Thompson-Seminars.asp
Price: $249.00. **Description:** A one-day seminar to help participants gain the critical skills needed to deliver engaging presentations. **Dates and Locations:** Mission, KS.

22177 ■ Critical Thinking and Out-of-the-Box Problem Solving (Onsite)
Seminar Information Service, Inc.
20 Executive Park, Ste. 120
Irvine, CA 92614
Ph: (949)261-9104
Free: 877-SEM-INFO

Fax: (949)261-1963
Co. E-mail: info@seminarinformation.com
URL: http://www.seminarinformation.com
Price: $2,490.00. **Description:** Learn how to: Make better decisions through critical thinking and creative problem solving; Adapt to different thinking styles in group and team environments; Foster an innovative environment in your workplace; Recognize and remove barriers to individual and group creativity; Systematically analyze a target problem; Present your ideas clearly and concisely for maximum stakeholder buy-in; Transform your creativity into practical business solutions. **Dates and Locations:** Rockville, MD; Reston, VA; Toronto, CN; Ottawa, CN; New York, NY; and Alexandria, VA.

22178 ■ Customer Focused Telephone Techniques (Onsite)
Seminar Information Service, Inc.
20 Executive Park, Ste. 120
Irvine, CA 92614
Ph: (949)261-9104
Free: 877-SEM-INFO
Fax: (949)261-1963
Co. E-mail: info@seminarinformation.com
URL: http://www.seminarinformation.com
Price: $370.00. **Description:** Participants learn the importance of telephone and acquire professional skills for better business practice, including calming angry clients and projecting a confident business image. **Dates and Locations:** Palatine, IL; and Waukesha, WI.

22179 ■ Designing for Diversity
EEI Communications
8945 Guilford Rd., Ste. 145
Columbia, MD 21046
Ph: (410)309-8200
Free: 888-253-2762
Fax: (410)630-3980
Co. E-mail: train@eeicom.com
URL: http://www.eeicom.com/eei-training-services
Price: $425.00. **Description:** Workshop to help you connect with all your audiences utilizing the appropriate visual imagery and words, including when not to send ethnically targeted messages, and designing 'one size fits all' publications when your budget won't permit targeted publications, and the effects of visual imagery on attitudes and behavior. **Dates and Locations:** Alexandria, VA.

22180 ■ Developing Diversity Communication and Messaging (Onsite)
Seminar Information Service, Inc.
20 Executive Park, Ste. 120
Irvine, CA 92614
Ph: (949)261-9104
Free: 877-SEM-INFO
Fax: (949)261-1963
Co. E-mail: info@seminarinformation.com
URL: http://www.seminarinformation.com
Price: $795.00. **Description:** Covers basic concepts of developing a diversity communication strategy and key techniques for communicating a diversity crisis.

22181 ■ Developing Dynamic Presentation Skills
Seminar Information Service, Inc.
20 Executive Park, Ste. 120
Irvine, CA 92614
Ph: (949)261-9104
Free: 877-SEM-INFO
Fax: (949)261-1963
Co. E-mail: info@seminarinformation.com
URL: http://www.seminarinformation.com
Price: $1,890.00. **Description:** Learn how to prepare an effective presentation by organizing key points into a coherent story; Capture and maintain audience interest and attention using interactive techniques. **Dates and Locations:** Reston, VA; Toronto, CN; and New York, NY.

22182 ■ Developing Effective Business Conversation Skills (Onsite)
American Management Association
600 AMA Way
Saranac Lake, NY 12983-5534
Ph: (212)586-8100
Free: 877-566-9441

Fax: (518)891-0368
Co. E-mail: customerservice@amanet.org
URL: http://www.amaseminars.org
Price: $2,095.00 for non-members; $1,895.00 for AMA members; and $1,623.00 for General Services Administration (GSA) members. **Description:** Learn effective business communication skills. **Dates and Locations:** Arlington, VA; Washington, DC; Chicago, IL; New York, NY; Atlanta, GA; and San Francisco, CA.

22183 ■ Developing Effective Communications Skills (Onsite)
Seminar Information Service, Inc.
20 Executive Park, Ste. 120
Irvine, CA 92614
Ph: (949)261-9104
Free: 877-SEM-INFO
Fax: (949)261-1963
Co. E-mail: info@seminarinformation.com
URL: http://www.seminarinformation.com
Price: $1,495.00. **Description:** learn skills for communicating powerfully, sending clear messages, and conducting challenging conversations while maintaining effective working relationships with supervisors and co-workers. **Dates and Locations:** New York, NY.

22184 ■ Dynamic Listening Skills for Successful Communication (Onsite)
American Management Association
600 AMA Way
Saranac Lake, NY 12983-5534
Ph: (212)586-8100
Free: 877-566-9441
Fax: (518)891-0368
Co. E-mail: customerservice@amanet.org
URL: http://www.amaseminars.org
Price: $1,995.00 for non-members; $1,795.00 for AMA members; and $1,537.00 for General Services Administration (GSA) members. **Description:** Develop listening skills that encourage productive interactions. **Dates and Locations:** New York, NY; Chicago, IL; Atlanta, GA; and San Francisco, CA.

22185 ■ Editorial Skills for Non-Editors (Onsite)
EEI Communications
8945 Guilford Rd., Ste. 145
Columbia, MD 21046
Ph: (410)309-8200
Free: 888-253-2762
Fax: (410)630-3980
Co. E-mail: train@eeicom.com
URL: http://www.eeicom.com/eei-training-services
Price: $497.00. **Description:** Covers punctuation and grammar, usage, and proofreading marks. **Dates and Locations:** Silver Spring, MD; and Alexandria, VA.

22186 ■ Effective Briefings
EEI Communications
8945 Guilford Rd., Ste. 145
Columbia, MD 22314
Ph: (410)309-8200
Free: 888-253-2762
Fax: (410)630-3980
Co. E-mail: train@eeicom.com
URL: http://www.eeicom.com/eei-training-services
Price: $425.00. **Description:** Hands-on course where you explore elements, principles, and guidelines of effective briefings, including how to deliver vocally, verbally, and visually, find the focus and the right tone, organize your message, create slides and handouts that support your message, and customize the message and delivery for your various audiences. **Dates and Locations:** Alexandria, VA.

22187 ■ Effective Business Writing (Onsite)
EEI Communications
8945 Guilford Rd., Ste. 145
Columbia, MD 21046
Ph: (410)309-8200
Free: 888-253-2762

Fax: (410)630-3980
Co. E-mail: train@eeicom.com
URL: http://www.eeicom.com/eei-training-services
Price: $497.00. **Description:** Covers the basic elements of writing effective business letters, e-mails, and memos, including grammar, audience analysis, persuasion, and usage problems. **Dates and Locations:** Silver Spring, MD; and Columbia, MD.

22188 ■ Effective Communication and Motivation (Onsite)
Seminar Information Service, Inc.
20 Executive Park, Ste. 120
Irvine, CA 92614
Ph: (949)261-9104
Free: 877-SEM-INFO
Fax: (949)261-1963
Co. E-mail: info@seminarinformation.com
URL: http://www.seminarinformation.com
Price: $580.00 for non-members; $435.00 for MRA members. **Description:** Gives managerial personnel a sound understanding of the principles of effective communication and the skill to recognize and to resolve communication breakdowns in the workplace. Participants learn to apply communication skills to problem solving, employee relations and performance appraisal. **Dates and Locations:** Waukesha, WI; and Palatine, IL.

22189 ■ Effective Executive Speaking (Onsite)
American Management Association
600 AMA Way
Saranac Lake, NY 12983-5534
Ph: (212)586-8100
Free: 877-566-9441
Fax: (518)891-0368
Co. E-mail: customerservice@amanet.org
URL: http://www.amaseminars.org
Price: $2,345.00 for non-members; $2,095.00 for AMA members; and $1,794.00 for General Services Administration (GSA) members. **Description:** Learn to speak, present, and communicate effectively. **Dates and Locations:** New York, NY; Chicago, IL; Washington, DC; Arlington, VA; Atlanta, GA; and San Francisco, CA.

22190 ■ Effective Presentation Techniques: Public Speaking
EEI Communications
8945 Guilford Rd., Ste. 145
Columbia, MD 21046
Ph: (410)309-8200
Free: 888-253-2762
Fax: (410)630-3980
Co. E-mail: train@eeicom.com
URL: http://www.eeicom.com/eei-training-services
Price: $425.00. **Description:** Covers assessing the audience, organizational skills, and effective delivery styles. **Dates and Locations:** Alexandria, VA.

22191 ■ Effective Technical Writing (Onsite)
American Management Association
600 AMA Way
Saranac Lake, NY 12983-5534
Ph: (212)586-8100
Free: 877-566-9441
Fax: (518)891-0368
Co. E-mail: customerservice@amanet.org
URL: http://www.amaseminars.org
Price: $2,195.00 for non-members; $1,995.00 for AMA members; and $1,708.00 for General Services Administration (GSA) members. **Description:** Covers the basics of writing technical documents such as reports, manuals, specifications, proposals, and instructions. **Dates and Locations:** New York, NY; San Francisco, CA; Chicago, IL; Arlington, VA; Washington, DC; and Houston, TX .

22192 ■ Enhancing Your People Skills
Seminar Information Service, Inc.
20 Executive Park, Ste. 120
Irvine, CA 92614
Ph: (949)261-9104
Free: 877-SEM-INFO

Fax: (949)261-1963
Co. E-mail: info@seminarinformation.com
URL: http://www.seminarinformation.com
Price: $1,495.00. **Description:** Build awareness and skill in the areas of team dynamics, group problem solving, and group decision making. The critical structural and behavioral dimensions of building and leading an effective work team or task force are fully explored. You will develop leadership skills applicable to many areas, but especially suited to self-directed work teams, employee participation teams, interdepartmental task groups, and other group situations where combined efforts are needed to reach optimal performance levels. **Dates and Locations:** New York, NY.

22193 ■ Essential Skills of Dynamic Public Speaking (Onsite)
Padgett-Thompson Seminars
Rockhurst University CEC
14502 W. 105th St.
Lenexa, KS 66215
Free: 800-349-1935
URL: http://www.findaseminar.com/tpd/Padgett-Thompson-Seminars.asp
Price: $249.00. **Description:** Workshop provides face-saving techniques that will make any business presentation easier. **Dates and Locations:** Davenport, IA.

22194 ■ The Essentials of Communicating With Diplomacy and Professionalism (Onsite)
Seminar Information Service, Inc.
20 Executive Park, Ste. 120
Irvine, CA 92614
Ph: (949)261-9104
Free: 877-SEM-INFO
Fax: (949)261-1963
Co. E-mail: info@seminarinformation.com
URL: http://www.seminarinformation.com
Price: $299.00; $269.00 for 4 or more. **Description:** Learn techniques to handle even the most difficult situations and difficult people with confidence. **Dates and Locations:** Cities throughout the United States.

22195 ■ The Essentials of Communication and Collaboration (Onsite)
Padgett-Thompson Seminars
Rockhurst University CEC
14502 W. 105th St.
Lenexa, KS 66215
Free: 800-349-1935
URL: http://www.findaseminar.com/tpd/Padgett-Thompson-Seminars.asp
Price: $149.00. **Description:** Seminar teaches the essential communication techniques that facilitate cooperation and collaboration at work. **Dates and Locations:** Cities throughout the United States.

22196 ■ Exceptional Presentation Training (Onsite)
Baker Communications Inc. (BCI)
10101 SW Fwy., Ste. 630
Houston, TX 77074
Ph: (713)627-7700
Fax: (713)587-2051
Co. E-mail: information@bakercommunications.com
URL: http://www.bakercommunications.com
Contact: Walter Rogers, President
Price: $1,700.00. **Description:** This workshop will aid all participants in helping to deliver their intended message to both internal and external clients. **Dates and Locations:** Cities throughout the United States and Canada.

22197 ■ Facilitation Skills (Onsite)
Learning Tree International Inc.
1805 Library St.
Reston, VA 20190-5660
Ph: (703)709-9119
Free: 800-843-8733
Fax: (703)709-6405
Co. E-mail: uscourses@learningtree.com
URL: http://www.learningtree.com
Contact: Nick Schacht, President
Price: $2,490.00. **Description:** For managers, supervisors, project managers, business analysts, and others who want to improve team performance and solve business problems. **Dates and Locations:** Toronto, CN; and Ottawa, CN.

22198 ■ Geometric Dimensioning and Tolerancing, Level 1 (Onsite)
Seminar Information Service, Inc.
20 Executive Park, Ste. 120
Irvine, CA 92614
Ph: (949)261-9104
Free: 877-SEM-INFO
Fax: (949)261-1963
Co. E-mail: info@seminarinformation.com
URL: http://www.seminarinformation.com
Price: $1,695.00. **Description:** Learn how to improve your effectiveness at communicating and interpreting specifications on engineering drawings.

22199 ■ Getting Better Results Through Conversations
Canadian Management Centre (CMC)
150 York St., 5th Fl.
Toronto, ON, Canada M5H 3S5
Ph: (416)214-5678
Free: 877-262-2519
Fax: (416)313-4985
Co. E-mail: cmcinfo@cmctraining.org
URL: http://www.cmctraining.org
Contact: John Wright, President
Price: $495.00 for members; $545.00 for non-members. **Description:** A half-day business communication workshop offering a concentrated blast of practical knowledge. **Dates and Locations:** Toronto, ON.

22200 ■ High Performance Business Writing (Onsite) (Canada)
Canadian Management Centre (CMC)
150 York St., 5th Fl.
Toronto, ON, Canada M5H 3S5
Ph: (416)214-5678
Free: 877-262-2519
Fax: (416)313-4985
Co. E-mail: cmcinfo@cmctraining.org
URL: http://www.cmctraining.org
Contact: John Wright, President
Price: $1,995.00 Canadian for non-members; $1,845.00 Canadian for CMC members. **Description:** Covers improving business writing skills, focusing on documents, letters, e-mails, reports, and memos. **Dates and Locations:** Toronto, ON; Montreal, PQ; Ottawa, ON; and Edmonton, AB.

22201 ■ How to Be an Outstanding Communicator (Onsite)
Padgett-Thompson Seminars
Rockhurst University CEC
14502 W. 105th St.
Lenexa, KS 66215
Free: 800-349-1935
URL: http://www.findaseminar.com/tpd/Padgett-Thompson-Seminars.asp
Price: $179.00. **Description:** One-day seminar that teaches how to get support from employees and co-workers, project a confident image, and master the key communication skills that you will need to succeed in the workplace. **Dates and Locations:** Cities throughout the United States.

22202 ■ How to Build Strategic Thinking Skills (Onsite)
Seminar Information Service, Inc.
20 Executive Park, Ste. 120
Irvine, CA 92614
Ph: (949)261-9104
Free: 877-SEM-INFO
Fax: (949)261-1963
Co. E-mail: info@seminarinformation.com
URL: http://www.seminarinformation.com
Price: $199.00. **Description:** Learn an effective strategy and execution to get positive results. **Dates and Locations:** Cities throughout the United States.

22203 ■ How to Communicate with Tact & Professionalism (Onsite)
Fred Pryor Seminars & CareerTrack
5700 Broadmoor St., Ste. 300
Mission, KS 66202
Free: 800-780-8476

Fax: (913)967-8849
Co. E-mail: customerservice@pryor.com
URL: http://www.pryor.com
Price: $299.00; $279.00 for groups of 3 or more. **Description:** Learn to become a polished, persuasive communicator and express your thoughts and ideas with clarity and diplomacy, including how to decode body language to understand what people are really saying. **Dates and Locations:** Cities throughout the United States.

22204 ■ How to Deliver Presentations with Ease & Confidence (Onsite)
Fred Pryor Seminars & CareerTrack
5700 Broadmoor St., Ste. 300
Mission, KS 66202
Free: 800-780-8476
Fax: (913)967-8849
Co. E-mail: customerservice@pryor.com
URL: http://www.pryor.com
Price: $179.00; $169.00 for groups of 5 or more. **Description:** Improve and enhance your effectiveness in every speaking situation without fear and anxiety. **Dates and Locations:** Cities throughout the United States.

22205 ■ How to Design Eye-Catching Brochures, Newspapers, Ads, Reports
Fred Pryor Seminars & CareerTrack
5700 Broadmoor St., Ste. 300
Mission, KS 66202
Ph: (800)780-8476
Free: 800-944-8503
Fax: (913)967-8849
Co. E-mail: customerservice@pryor.com
URL: http://www.careertrack.com
Price: $99.00; $89.00 for groups of 5 or more. **Description:** Covers basic design and layout skills for headlines, text, and graphics for printed documents. **Dates and Locations:** Cities throughout the United States.

22206 ■ How to Manage Conflict and Confrontation (Onsite)
Fred Pryor Seminars & CareerTrack
5700 Broadmoor St., Ste. 300
Mission, KS 66202
Free: 800-780-8476
Fax: (913)967-8849
Co. E-mail: customerservice@pryor.com
URL: http://www.pryor.com
Price: $99.00; $89.00 for groups of 5 or more. **Description:** Learn practical and proven techniques for managing workplace conflict. **Dates and Locations:** Cities throughout the United States.

22207 ■ How to Present Online: A Skills-Based Workshop (Onsite) (Live Online)
American Management Association
600 AMA Way
Saranac Lake, NY 12983-5534
Ph: (212)586-8100
Free: 877-566-9441
Fax: (518)891-0368
Co. E-mail: customerservice@amanet.org
URL: http://www.amaseminars.org
Price: $2,345.00 for non-members; $2,095.00 for AMA members; and $1,794.00 for General Services Administration (GSA) members. **Description:** Learn how to conduct presentations to online audiences with successful techniques.

22208 ■ How to Work Most Effectively with Your Boss (Onsite)
American Management Association
600 AMA Way
Saranac Lake, NY 12983-5534
Ph: (212)586-8100
Free: 877-566-9441
Fax: (518)891-0368
Co. E-mail: customerservice@amanet.org
URL: http://www.amaseminars.org
Price: $1,695.00 for non-members; $1,495.00 for AMA members. **Description:** Covers effective communication and problem solving teamwork skills. **Dates and Locations:** Atlanta, GA; and San Francisco, CA.

22209 ■ How to Work With Difficult, Demanding, and Inconsiderate People (Onsite)
Padgett-Thompson Seminars
Rockhurst University CEC
14502 W. 105th St.
Lenexa, KS 66215
Free: 800-349-1935
URL: http://www.findaseminar.com/tpd/Padgett-Thompson-Seminars.asp
Price: $249.00. **Description:** Learn what it takes to defuse angry coworkers and how to keep emotions in check. **Dates and Locations:** Edison, NJ; New York, NY; Melville, NY; Parsippany, NJ; Freehold, NJ; King of Prussia, PA; Mt. Laurel, NJ.

22210 ■ Improving Your Communication Skills for Success (Onsite)
Seminar Information Service, Inc.
20 Executive Park, Ste. 120
Irvine, CA 92614
Ph: (949)261-9104
Free: 877-SEM-INFO
Fax: (949)261-1963
Co. E-mail: info@seminarinformation.com
URL: http://www.seminarinformation.com
Price: $249.00. **Description:** Learn the essential communication skills you need to handle any situation that arises with confidence. **Dates and Locations:** Cities throughout the United States.

22211 ■ Indexing I (Onsite)
EEI Communications
66 Canal Center Plz., Ste. 200
Alexandria, VA 22314
Ph: (703)683-7453
Free: 888-253-2762
Fax: (703)683-7310
Co. E-mail: train@eeicom.com
URL: http://www.eeicom.com/training
Price: $745.00. **Description:** Covers indexing for websites and books, including determining key words, categorizing information, and using cross-references. **Dates and Locations:** Silver Spring, MD; Alexandria, VA; Hunt Valley, MD; and Columbia, MD.

22212 ■ Indexing II (Onsite)
EEI Communications
66 Canal Center Plz., Ste. 200
Alexandria, VA 22314
Ph: (703)683-7453
Free: 888-253-2762
Fax: (703)683-7310
Co. E-mail: train@eeicom.com
URL: http://www.eeicom.com/training
Price: $425.00. **Description:** Covers editing and evaluating indices. **Dates and Locations:** Silver Spring, MD; Alexandria, VA; Hunt Valley, MD; and Columbia, MD.

22213 ■ Influence Skills: Getting Results Without Direct Authority (Onsite)
Seminar Information Service, Inc.
20 Executive Park, Ste. 120
Irvine, CA 92614
Ph: (949)261-9104
Free: 877-SEM-INFO
Fax: (949)261-1963
Co. E-mail: info@seminarinformation.com
URL: http://www.seminarinformation.com
Price: $2,890.00. **Description:** Learn how to: Apply influence strategies to gain commitment from others and foster collaboration; Define desired outcomes for win-win results; Dynamically adjust your approach to others to gain buy-in; Achieve goals by enhancing trust and cooperation; Deal effectively with challenging behaviors to overcome resistance and inertia in others; Use knowledge and competence rather than position and status to influence others. **Dates and Locations:** Cities throughout the United States Ottawa and Toronto, CN.

22214 ■ Influence Strategies
Seminar Information Service, Inc.
20 Executive Park, Ste. 120
Irvine, CA 92614
Ph: (949)261-9104
Free: 877-SEM-INFO

Fax: (949)261-1963
Co. E-mail: info@seminarinformation.com
URL: http://www.seminarinformation.com
Price: $795.00. **Description:** Provides you with a greater understanding of your personal motive preferences, the preferences of others, and application of this dynamic toward becoming more effective in specific work situations. **Dates and Locations:** New York, NY.

22215 ■ Interactive Training Techniques for the Classroom (Onsite)
Seminar Information Service, Inc.
20 Executive Park, Ste. 120
Irvine, CA 92614
Ph: (949)261-9104
Free: 877-SEM-INFO
Fax: (949)261-1963
Co. E-mail: info@seminarinformation.com
URL: http://www.seminarinformation.com
Price: $370.00. **Description:** Participants prepare themselves to be both presenter and discussion leader. **Dates and Locations:** Waukesha, WI.

22216 ■ Interpersonal Skills for Managers (Onsite) (Canada)
Canadian Management Centre (CMC)
150 York St., 5th Fl.
Toronto, ON, Canada M5H 3S5
Ph: (416)214-5678
Free: 877-262-2519
Fax: (416)313-4985
Co. E-mail: cmcinfo@cmctraining.org
URL: http://www.cmctraining.org
Contact: John Wright, President
Price: $2,195.00 Canadian for non-members; $1,995.00 Canadian for CMC members. **Description:** Covers problem solving, negotiation, motivating and creating enthusiasm, dealing with conflict, and tactics for working with difficult employees. **Dates and Locations:** Toronto, ON; and Calgary, AB.

22217 ■ Introduction to Information Design
EEI Communications
8945 Guilford Rd., Ste. 145
Columbia, MD 21046
Ph: (410)309-8200
Free: 888-253-2762
Fax: (410)630-3980
Co. E-mail: train@eeicom.com
URL: http://www.eeicom.com/eei-training-services
Price: $745.00. **Description:** Topics include defining information design, understanding how users process information, techniques for information design, information graphics, and presenting Web information. **Dates and Locations:** Alexandria, VA.

22218 ■ Keeping the Team on Track (Onsite)
Seminar Information Service, Inc.
20 Executive Park, Ste. 120
Irvine, CA 92614
Ph: (949)261-9104
Free: 877-SEM-INFO
Fax: (949)261-1963
Co. E-mail: info@seminarinformation.com
URL: http://www.seminarinformation.com
Price: $370.00 for non-members; $275.00 for The Management Association, Inc. **Description:** Learn to recognize the signs of ineffective meetings and learn the formal tools to accomplish expected results with particular focus on managing the meeting process and techniques to keep the team on track. **Dates and Locations:** Waukesha, WI.

22219 ■ Managing Difficult and Sensitive Conversations (Onsite)
Canadian Management Centre (CMC)
150 York St., 5th Fl.
Toronto, ON, Canada M5H 3S5
Ph: (416)214-5678
Free: 877-262-2519

Fax: (416)313-4985
Co. E-mail: cmcinfo@cmctraining.org
URL: http://www.cmctraining.org
Contact: John Wright, President
Price: $495.00 for members; $545.00 for non-members. **Description:** Learn to confront others who are not performing and get them to change. **Dates and Locations:** Toronto, ON.

22220 ■ Managing Emotions under Pressure (Onsite)
Fred Pryor Seminars & CareerTrack
5700 Broadmoor St., Ste. 300
Mission, KS 66202
Free: 800-780-8476
Fax: (913)967-8849
Co. E-mail: customerservice@pryor.com
URL: http://www.pryor.com
Price: $149.00; $139.00 for groups of 5 or more. **Description:** Learn to develop self-discipline and manage your emotions in the workplace. **Dates and Locations:** Cities throughout the United States.

22221 ■ Managing Emotions and Thriving Under Pressure (Onsite)
Seminar Information Service, Inc.
20 Executive Park, Ste. 120
Irvine, CA 92614
Ph: (949)261-9104
Free: 877-SEM-INFO
Fax: (949)261-1963
Co. E-mail: info@seminarinformation.com
URL: http://www.seminarinformation.com
Price: $149.00. **Description:** Learn self-discipline skills and rid yourself of unproductive behaviors. **Dates and Locations:** Cities throughout the United States.

22222 ■ Managing Emotions in the Workplace: Strategies for Success (Onsite)
American Management Association
600 AMA Way
Saranac Lake, NY 12983-5534
Ph: (212)586-8100
Free: 877-566-9441
Fax: (518)891-0368
Co. E-mail: customerservice@amanet.org
URL: http://www.amaseminars.org
Price: $2,095.00 for non-members; $1,895.00 for AMA members; and $1,623.00 for General Services Administration (GSA) members. **Description:** Covers methods for effectively and professionally communicating emotion, creating positive work environments, and emotional control. **Dates and Locations:** Anaheim, CA; New York, NY; Atlanta, GA; Chicago, IL; Arlington, VA; and Washington, DC.

22223 ■ Managing Successful Negotiations (Onsite)
Seminar Information Service, Inc.
20 Executive Park, Ste. 120
Irvine, CA 92614
Ph: (949)261-9104
Free: 877-SEM-INFO
Fax: (949)261-1963
Co. E-mail: info@seminarinformation.com
URL: http://www.seminarinformation.com
Price: $1,595.00. **Description:** Designed to help you acquire the necessary concept, skills, and techniques to prepare for and to conduct successful negotiations. **Dates and Locations:** Chelmsford, MA.

22224 ■ Mistake-Free Grammar & Proofreading (Onsite)
Fred Pryor Seminars
5700 Broadmoor St., Ste. 300
Mission, KS 66202
Ph: (800)780-8476
Free: 800-944-8503
Fax: (913)967-8849
Co. E-mail: customerservice@pryor.com
URL: http://www.careertrack.com
Price: $149.00; $139.00 for groups of 5 or more. **Description:** Covers grammar and usage in business writing, including punctuation, capitalization, quotations, spelling, sentence structure, and related topics. **Dates and Locations:** Cities throughout the United States.

22225 ■ Negotiating Effectively (Onsite)
Seminar Information Service, Inc.
20 Executive Park, Ste. 120
Irvine, CA 92614
Ph: (949)261-9104
Free: 877-SEM-INFO
Fax: (949)261-1963
Co. E-mail: info@seminarinformation.com
URL: http://www.seminarinformation.com
Price: $1,150.00. **Description:** Learn basic negotiation techniques by focusing on the dynamics of interpersonal and group conflict; differing styles and approaches to negotiation; the negotiation process; and negotiating to achieve mutual benefit. **Dates and Locations:** New York, NY.

22226 ■ Negotiating to Win (Onsite)
American Management Association
600 AMA Way
Saranac Lake, NY 12983-5534
Ph: (212)586-8100
Free: 877-566-9441
Fax: (518)891-0368
Co. E-mail: customerservice@amanet.org
URL: http://www.amaseminars.org
Price: $2,345.00 for non-members; $2,095.00 for AMA members; and $1,794.00 for General Services Administration (GSA) members. **Description:** Covers appropriate scenarios for negotiation, persuasion skills, and strategies for oral and written negotiations. **Dates and Locations:** Cities throughout the Unite States.

22227 ■ Negotiating to Win (Onsite) (Canada)
Canadian Management Centre (CMC)
150 York St., 5th Fl.
Toronto, ON, Canada M5H 3S5
Ph: (416)214-5678
Free: 877-262-2519
Fax: (416)313-4985
Co. E-mail: cmcinfo@cmctraining.org
URL: http://www.cmctraining.org
Contact: John Wright, President
Price: $2,195.00 Canadian for non-members; $1,995.00 Canadian for CMC members. **Description:** Covers techniques for successful negotiations, in every industry and at every level; includes the negotiation process, overcoming people problems, and improving negotiation strategies. **Dates and Locations:** Calgary, AB; Ottawa, ON; Mississauga, ON; Vancouver, BC; and Toronto, ON.

22228 ■ Negotiation Skills: Achieving Successful Outcomes (Onsite)
Seminar Information Service, Inc.
20 Executive Park, Ste. 120
Irvine, CA 92614
Ph: (949)261-9104
Free: 877-SEM-INFO
Fax: (949)261-1963
Co. E-mail: info@seminarinformation.com
URL: http://www.seminarinformation.com
Price: $2,490.00. **Description:** Learn how to: Conduct principled negotiations that result in wise agreements; Incorporate a process approach into your negotiation skill set; Formulate principled communication strategies and styles to deflect 'hardball' tactics; Apply psychology principles to negotiate effectively; Enhance your negotiation skills by applying best practices in a real-world setting.

22229 ■ The Outstanding Receptionist (Onsite)
Fred Pryor Seminars & CareerTrack
5700 Broadmoor St., Ste. 300
Mission, KS 66202
Free: 800-780-8476
Fax: (913)967-8849
Co. E-mail: customerservice@pryor.com
URL: http://www.pryor.com
Price: $79.00; $74.00 for groups of 5 or more. **Description:** Learn how to improve your skills and better support everyone in your organization. **Dates and Locations:** Cities throughout the United States.

22230 ■ Perfecting Your Presentation Skills
Seminar Information Service, Inc.
20 Executive Park, Ste. 120
Irvine, CA 92614
Ph: (949)261-9104
Free: 877-SEM-INFO
Fax: (949)261-1963
Co. E-mail: info@seminarinformation.com
URL: http://www.seminarinformation.com
Price: $1,495.00. **Description:** Learn how to manage anxiety; develop dynamic delivery skills; connect with/focus on listeners; and how to gain confidence and comfort when presenting. **Dates and Locations:** New York, NY.

22231 ■ Performance Measurement Analysis (Onsite)
EEI Communications
8945 Guilford Rd., Ste. 145
Columbia, MD 21046
Ph: (410)309-8200
Free: 888-253-2762
Fax: (410)630-3980
Co. E-mail: train@eeicom.com
URL: http://www.eeicom.com/eei-training-services
Price: $1,065.00. **Description:** Through communication, integration, and alignment with objectives, Performance Measurement can help employees realize the value of their contributions to the organization. **Dates and Locations:** Silver Spring, MD; Hunt Valley, MD; Columbia, MD; and Alexandria, VA.

22232 ■ Persuasive Communications in Marketing and Public Relations
EEI Communications
8945 Guilford Rd., Ste. 145
Columbia, MD 21046
Ph: (410)309-8200
Free: 888-253-2762
Fax: (410)630-3980
Co. E-mail: train@eeicom.com
URL: http://www.eeicom.com/eei-training-service
Price: $1,065.00. **Description:** Course designed for department heads and project managers, as well as mid-level communications professionals who want to expand their public relations and marketing skills. **Dates and Locations:** Alexandria, VA.

22233 ■ Persuasive Leadership: Storytelling that Inspires (Onsite)
Seminar Information Service, Inc.
20 Executive Park, Ste. 120
Irvine, CA 92614
Ph: (949)261-9104
Free: 877-SEM-INFO
Fax: (949)261-1963
Co. E-mail: info@seminarinformation.com
URL: http://www.seminarinformation.com
Price: $1,499.00. **Description:** Participants develop their storytelling abilities and learn how to use humor to persuade and motivate others, as well as polish their existing speaking skills and develop powerful new ones.

22234 ■ The Power of Listening: Unlocking Your Communication Potential
Seminar Information Service, Inc.
20 Executive Park, Ste. 120
Irvine, CA 92614
Ph: (949)261-9104
Free: 877-SEM-INFO
Fax: (949)261-1963
Co. E-mail: info@seminarinformation.com
URL: http://www.seminarinformation.com
Price: $1,495.00. **Description:** Examine the listening process and assess your listening strengths and needs to develop effective listening techniques and strategies. **Dates and Locations:** New York, NY.

22235 ■ Powerful Communication Skills for Women (Onsite)
Padgett-Thompson Seminars
Rockhurst University CEC
14502 W. 105th St.
Lenexa, KS 66215

Free: 800-349-1935
URL: http://www.findaseminar.com/tpd/Padgett-Thompson-Seminars.asp
Price: $139.00. **Description:** A workshop designed specifically for professional women. **Dates and Locations:** Cities throughout the United States.

22236 ■ Professional Communication: What Message Are You Sending? (Onsite)
Fred Pryor Seminars & CareerTrack
5700 Broadmoor St., Ste. 300
Mission, KS 66202
Free: 800-780-8476
Fax: (913)967-8849
Co. E-mail: customerservice@pryor.com
URL: http://www.pryor.com
Price: $149.00; $139.00 for groups of 5 or more.
Description: Learn to communicate with confidence and credibility. **Dates and Locations:** Cities throughout the United States.

22237 ■ Resolving Conflict (Onsite)
Seminar Information Service, Inc
20 Executive Park, Ste. 120
Irvine, CA 92614
Ph: (949)261-9104
Free: 877-SEM-INFO
Fax: (949)261-1963
Co. E-mail: info@seminarinformation.com
URL: http://www.seminarinformation.com
Price: $1,495.00. **Description:** Provide you with an understanding of the nature of conflict in organizations, key approaches to managing conflict, and an insight into your style of handling conflict and ways to enhance your conflict resolution effectiveness. **Dates and Locations:** New York, NY.

22238 ■ Responding to Conflict: Strategies for Improved Communication (Onsite)
American Management Association
600 AMA Way
Saranac Lake, NY 12983-5534
Ph: (212)586-8100
Free: 877-566-9441
Fax: (518)891-0368
Co. E-mail: customerservice@amanet.org
URL: http://www.amaseminars.org
Price: $2,345.00 for non-members; $2,095.00 for AMA members; and $1,794.00 for General Services Administration (GSA) members. **Description:** Covers effective communication, diffusing misunderstanding, creating open and honest work environments, dealing with conflict, and improving listening skills. **Dates and Locations:** Arlington, VA; Chicago, IL; Atlanta, GA; San Francisco, CA; and New York, NY.

22239 ■ Responding to Conflict: Strategies for Improved Communication (Onsite) (Canada)
Canadian Management Centre (CMC)
150 York St., 5th Fl.
Toronto, ON, Canada M5H 3S5
Ph: (416)214-5678
Free: 877-262-2519
Fax: (416)313-4985
Co. E-mail: cmcinfo@cmctraining.org
URL: http://www.cmctraining.org
Contact: John Wright, President
Price: $2,395.00 Canadian for non-members; $2,195.00 Canadian for CMC members. **Description:** Covers effective communication, diffusing misunderstanding, creating open and honest work environments, dealing with conflict, and improving listening skills. **Dates and Locations:** Toronto, ON.

22240 ■ Sensitivity Skills in Working with Others (Onsite)
Seminar Information Service, Inc.
20 Executive Park, Ste. 120
Irvine, CA 92614
Ph: (949)261-9104
Free: 877-SEM-INFO
Fax: (949)261-1963
Co. E-mail: info@seminarinformation.com
URL: http://www.seminarinformation.com
Price: $275.00 for MRA members; $370.00 for non-members. **Description:** Learn the difference between behaviors that are appropriate, inappropriate, and

perhaps illegal, and improve skills in communicating across cultures. **Dates and Locations:** Waukesha, WI; and Palatine, IL.

22241 ■ Speak! Present! Influence! (Onsite)
Seminar Information Service, Inc.
20 Executive Park, Ste. 120
Irvine, CA 92614
Ph: (949)261-9104
Free: 877-SEM-INFO
Fax: (949)261-1963
Co. E-mail: info@seminarinformation.com
URL: http://www.seminarinformation.com
Price: $1,399.00. **Description:** Participants learn to overcome fear and relax under pressure; to become more dynamic and persuasive; to improve voice quality and speak without strain; to organize material for clear, effective delivery; and to make a personal connection with the audience. **Dates and Locations:** Cleveland, OH.

22242 ■ Speaking Skills for Professionals (Onsite)
Seminar Information Service, Inc.
20 Executive Park, Ste. 120
Irvine, CA 92614
Ph: (949)261-9104
Free: 877-SEM-INFO
Fax: (949)261-1963
Co. E-mail: info@seminarinformation.com
URL: http://www.seminarinformation.com
Price: $580.00 for non-members; $435.00 for The Management Association, Inc. **Description:** Learn the techniques and practices of expert speakers. Participants will learn how to gain people's attention, how to project an image of authority and competence, and how to speak with confidence. **Dates and Locations:** Waukesha, WI.

22243 ■ Strategies for Developing Effective Presentation Skills (Onsite)
American Management Association
600 AMA Way
Saranac Lake, NY 12983-5534
Ph: (212)586-8100
Free: 877-566-9441
Fax: (518)891-0368
Co. E-mail: customerservice@amanet.org
URL: http://www.amaseminars.org
Price: $2,195.00 for non-members; $1,995.00 for AMA members; and $1,708.00 for General Services Administration (GSA) members. **Description:** Covers overcoming stage fright, various types of presentations, developing a full presentation, and techniques for delivering a presentation, including answering questions and interacting with the audience. **Dates and Locations:** San Francisco, CA; Washington, DC; Arlington, VA; Chicago, IL; New York, NY; Atlanta, GA.

22244 ■ Strategies of Effective Writing (Onsite)
EEI Communications
8945 Guilford Rd., Ste. 145
Columbia, MD 21046
Ph: (410)309-8200
Free: 888-253-2762
Fax: (410)630-3980
Co. E-mail: train@eeicom.com
URL: http://www.eeicom.com/eei-training-services
Price: $797.00. **Description:** Covers basic writing skills, including effective planning as a means of saving time, generating ideas, organizing ideas, writing concisely and clearly, and attracting and holding readers' interest. **Dates and Locations:** Columbia, MD; Silver Spring, MD; and Alexandria, VA.

22245 ■ Strengthening Your People Skills in the Workplace (Onsite)
Padgett-Thompson Seminars
Rockhurst University CEC
14502 W. 105th St.
Lenexa, KS 66215

Free: 800-349-1935
URL: http://www.findaseminar.com/tpd/Padgett-Thompson-Seminars.asp
Price: $229.00. **Description:** A one-day workshop to gain the essential people skills needed to push your career ahead. **Dates and Locations:** San Jose, CA; Sacramento, CA; Oakland, CA.

22246 ■ Substantive Editing I (Onsite)
EEI Communications
8945 Guilford Rd., Ste. 145
Columbia, MD 21046
Ph: (410)309-8200
Free: 888-253-2762
Fax: (410)630-3980
Co. E-mail: train@eeicom.com
URL: http://www.eeicom.com/eei-training-services
Price: $797.00. **Description:** Covers editing for clarity and meaning, including reworking vague or inappropriate phrases, untangling muddled language, posing effective questions to the author, and revising with a purpose. **Dates and Locations:** Silver Spring, MD; and Alexandria, VA.

22247 ■ Successful Meeting Planning (Onsite)
American Management Association
600 AMA Way
Saranac Lake, NY 12983-5534
Ph: (212)586-8100
Free: 877-566-9441
Fax: (518)891-0368
Co. E-mail: customerservice@amanet.org
URL: http://www.amaseminars.org
Price: $1,545.00 for non-members; $1,395.00 for AMA members; and $1,195.00 for. **Description:** Covers all aspects of successfully planning a meeting, including objectives, budget, site selection, and working with vendors.

22248 ■ TechConnect (Onsite)
Seminar Information Service, Inc.
20 Executive Park, Ste. 120
Irvine, CA 92614
Ph: (949)261-9104
Free: 877-SEM-INFO
Fax: (949)261-1963
Co. E-mail: info@seminarinformation.com
URL: http://www.seminarinformation.com
Price: $1,399.00. **Description:** Learn how to put technical information into language a lay audience can understand, including how to organize information so it flows smoothly and leads to action and how to deliver information at the appropriate level of audience understanding and to be concise, to the point, and eliminate data dump. **Dates and Locations:** Cleveland, OH.

22249 ■ Technical Writing (Onsite)
EEI Communications
8945 Guilford Rd., Ste. 145
Columbia, MD 21046
Ph: (410)309-8200
Free: 888-253-2762
Fax: (410)630-3980
Co. E-mail: train@eeicom.com
URL: http://www.eeicom.com/eei-training-services
Price: $797.00. **Description:** Covers the technical writing process from analyzing an audience and developing a purpose to laying out a document with both text and graphics. **Dates and Locations:** Alexandria, VA.

22250 ■ Training Difficult Issues in Diversity (Onsite)
Seminar Information Service, Inc.
20 Executive Park, Ste. 120
Irvine, CA 92614
Ph: (949)261-9104
Free: 877-SEM-INFO
Fax: (949)261-1963
Co. E-mail: info@seminarinformation.com
URL: http://www.seminarinformation.com
Price: $1,395.00. **Description:** Provides trainers with a step-by-step curriculum for delivering training and education on the tougher issues, including racism, privilege, religion, sexual orientation, gender identity,

and oppression. Explore training techniques and models that get diversity messages across. **Dates and Locations:** New York, NY.

22251 ■ Webinars with a WOW Factor: Creating Memorable Meeting Across the Globe (Onsite)
Seminar Information Service, Inc.
20 Executive Park, Ste. 120
Irvine, CA 92614
Ph: (949)261-9104
Free: 877-SEM-INFO
Fax: (949)261-1963
Co. E-mail: info@seminarinformation.com
URL: http://www.seminarinformation.com
Price: $1,595.00. **Description:** Discover techniques that will make your material come to life on the screen and over the phone. **Dates and Locations:** Minneapolis, MN.

22252 ■ Writing Statements of Work: The Heart of Any Contract (Onsite)
Seminar Information Service, Inc.
20 Executive Park, Ste. 120
Irvine, CA 92614
Ph: (949)261-9104
Free: 877-SEM-INFO
Fax: (949)261-1963
Co. E-mail: info@seminarinformation.com
URL: http://www.seminarinformation.com
Price: $1,995.00. **Description:** Provides the essential information you'll need, including basic contract management concepts, to consistently develop and administer effective Statements of Work.

22253 ■ Writing for the Web II (Onsite)
EEI Communications
66 Canal Ctr. Plz., Ste. 200
Alexandria, VA 22314-5507
Ph: (703)683-7453
Free: 888-253-2762
Fax: (703)683-7310
Co. E-mail: train@eeicom.com
URL: http://www.eeicom.com/training
Price: $797.00. **Description:** Seminar for persons with 3-5 years' experience as a Web writer or editor, or have completed Writing for the Web I, covering how to define your genre and audience, develop a structure for your Web content, working with subject matter experts who aren't writers, making the most of your writing project, giving and getting feedback, writing links that work for your client, how to write menus so clients can use them, and recasting a print article for the Web. **Dates and Locations:** Columbia, MD.

22254 ■ XML Web Services (Onsite)
EEI Communications
8945 Guilford Rd., Ste. 145
Columbia, MD 22314
Ph: (410)309-8200
Free: 888-253-2762
Fax: (410)630-3980
Co. E-mail: train@eeicom.com
URL: http://www.eeicom.com/eei-training-services
Price: $1,065.00. **Description:** Learn how Web services can enhance your Web site and communication with other companies. **Dates and Locations:** Alexandria, VA.

REFERENCE WORKS

22255 ■ *10 Make-or-Break Career Moments: Navigate, Negotiate, and Communicate for Success*
Pub: Crown Business Books
Ed: Casey Hawley. **Released:** May 4, 2010. **Price:** $13.99. **Description:** Communication consultant, Casey Hawley, provides a guide to smart communication for any business setting.

22256 ■ *10 Steps to Successful Social Networking for Business*
Pub: ASTD
Contact: Tony Bingham, President
E-mail: tbingham@astd.org
Ed: Darin Hartley. **Released:** July 1, 2010. **Price:** $19.95. **Description:** Designed for today's fast-paced, need-it-yesterday business environment and

for the thousands of workers who find themselves faced with new assignments, responsibilities, and requirements and too little time to learn what they must know.

22257 ■ *The 29 Percent Solution*
Pub: Greenleaf Book Group Press
Ed: Ivan Misner, Michele Donovan. **Released:** 2008. **Price:** $21.95. **Description:** It is true that some people are better connected than others. That means that connecting is a skill that can be acquired. Networking skills used to increase business connections are highlighted.

22258 ■ *"The 40-Year-Old Intern" in Entrepreneur (Vol. 37, October 2009, No. 10, pp. 90)*
Pub: Entrepreneur Media, Inc.
Ed: Kristin Ladd. **Description:** Brian Kurth's VocationVacation is an internship program aimed at helping people experience their dream job. The website, launched in January 2004, matches people with businesses that allow them to experience their fantasy jobs.

22259 ■ *"2010 American Business Woman of ABWA" in Women In Business (Vol. 61, October-November 2009, No. 5, pp. 22)*
Pub: American Business Women's Association
Ed: Doris Brown. **Description:** Achievements of Doris Brown are presented in light of her being named as the 2010 American Business Woman of American Business Women's Association (ABWA). She specializes in the field of client and customer satisfaction for Avue Technologies. Brown believes that her involvement in the ABWA has helped her to see the importance of being a resource for other people.

22260 ■ *"Ace Every Introduction" in Women Entrepreneur (September 10, 2008)*
Pub: Entrepreneur Media Inc.
Ed: Cynthia McKay. **Description:** Making a powerful first impression is one of the most important marketing tools a business owner can possess. Advice about meeting new business contacts is given.

22261 ■ *"All In Good Fun" in Entrepreneur (Vol. 36, May 2008, No. 5, pp. 22)*
Pub: Entrepreneur Media, Inc.
Ed: Christopher Percy Collier. **Description:** According to a study conducted in 2007, humor in the workplace helps people communicate effectively and improves camaraderie. Company leaders and entrepreneurs can also tell humorous stories about themselves, but must also set lines that should not be crossed. The humorous atmosphere in the company YouSendIt is presented.

22262 ■ *"All Those Applications, and Phone Users Just Want to Talk" in Advertising Age (Vol. 79, August 11, 2008, No. 31, pp. 18)*
Pub: Crain Communications, Inc.
Ed: Mike Vorhaus. **Description:** Although consumers are slowly coming to text messaging and other data applications, a majority of those Americans surveyed stated that they simply want to use their cell phones to talk and do not care about other activities. Statistical data included.

22263 ■ *"The Americans Are Coming" in The Economist (Vol. 390, January 3, 2009, No. 8612, pp. 44)*
Pub: The Economist Newspaper Inc.
Description: Student recruitment consultancies, which help place international students at universities in other countries and offer services such as interpreting or translating guidelines, are discussed; American universities who have shunned these agencies in the past; the result has been that America underperforms in relation to its size with a mere 3.5 percent of students on its campuses that are from abroad.

22264 ■ *"Anytime Access" in Crain's Cleveland Business (Vol. 28, October 22, 2007, No. 42, pp. 17)*
Pub: Crain Communications, Inc.
Ed: Brad Dicken. **Description:** Technology continues to evolve in the competitive world of mobile communications in which the phone has become a sleek multitool that can take a call, send and e-mail, calculate the tip after dinner and snap a photograph.

22265 ■ *"The Art and Business of Motivation Speaking: Your Guide" in Inc. (Volume 32, December 2010, No. 10, pp. 124)*
Pub: Inc. Magazine
Ed: Leigh Buchanan. **Description:** Profile of Josh Shipp that discusses his career as a motivational speaker.

22266 ■ *"The Art of Persuasion: How You Can Get the Edge You Need To Reach Every Goal" in Small Business Opportunities (November 2007)*
Pub: Harris Publications Inc.
Ed: Paul Endress. **Description:** Expert in the field of psychology to business in the areas of communication, hiring and retention discusses a unique approach to solving business problems.

22267 ■ *"Attorney Internet Marketing Services Launched by SEO Advantage at SEOLegal.com" in Internet Wire (October 5, 2009)*
Pub: Comtex News Network, Inc.
Description: SEO Advantage, an Internet marketing and website designer firm, has extended its services to the legal industry.

22268 ■ *Awesomely Simple: Essential Business Strategies for Turning Ideas Into Action*
Pub: Jossey-Bass
Ed: John Spence. **Released:** September 8, 2009. **Price:** $24.95. **Description:** Six key strategies that create a foundation for achieving business excellence include: vivid vision, best people, a performance-oriented culture, robust communication, a sense of urgency, and extreme customer focus.

22269 ■ *Be a Brilliant Business Writer: Write Well, Write Fast, and Whip the Competition*
Pub: Crown Business Books
Ed: Jane Curry, Diana Young. **Released:** October 5, 2010. **Price:** $13.99. **Description:** Tools for mastering the art of persuasive writing in every document created, from email and client letters to reports and presentations, this book will help any writer convey their message with clarity and power, increase productivity by reducing rewrites, and provide the correct tone for navigating office politics.

22270 ■ *"Blog Buzz Heralds Arrival of IPhone 2.0" in Advertising Age (Vol. 79, June 9, 2008, No. 40, pp. 8)*
Pub: Crain Communications, Inc.
Ed: Abbey Klaasen. **Description:** Predictions concerning the next version of the iPhone include a global-positioning-system technology as well as a configuration to run on a faster, 3G network.

22271 ■ *"Book Smart" in Hawaii Business (Vol. 53, December 2007, No. 6, pp. 39)*
Pub: Hawaii Business Publishing
Ed: David K. Choo. **Description:** Different parts of a biography entry in the Black Book are examined in relation to their usage in starting a conversation with an executive. The second part, which is the educational background, is considered the most significant of all, due to the amount of information given. The importance of making connections in Hawaii is discussed.

22272 ■ *"Bridging the Gap: Contextualing Professional Ethics in Collaborative Writing Projects" in Business Communication Quarterly (Dec.2007)*
Pub: SAGE Publications USA
Contact: Blaise R. Simqu, President
Ed: J.A. Rice. **Description:** A classroom activity for business management students integrates ethical concepts with business writing strategies, while increasing understanding of writing ethics by emphasizing its rhetorical, contingent, and public nature.

22273 ■ *"The Business Value of Social Networks" in Agency Sales Magazine (Vol. 39, July 2009, No. 7, pp. 44)*
Pub: MANA
Ed: Daniel Burrus. **Description:** Personal and business uses of several Web 2.0 tools for salespeople are discussed. Leading questions which will guide salespeople in finding out if one particular tool will benefit them are presented.

22274 ■ "Can We Talk?" in Canadian Business (Vol. 79, September 11, 2006, No. 18, pp. 131)
Pub: Rogers Media
Ed: Sarah B. Hood. **Description:** The importance of informal communications and steps to build strong social networks within the organizations are discussed.

22275 ■ "Can You Hear Me Now?" in Harvard Business Review (Vol. 86, July-August 2008, No. 8, pp. 23)
Pub: Harvard Business School Press
Ed: Katharina Pick. **Description:** Tips for improving communication among boardroom members are presented. These include encouraging frankness via in-meeting leaders, and the ability of directors to meet without managers.

22276 ■ "Canadians Keep Memories in 'Inboxes' Instead of Shoe Boxes; MSN Canada" in Canadian Corporate News (May 14, 2007)
Pub: Comtex News Network Inc.
Description: According to an MSN Canada online poll, 76 percent of Canadians are creating 'virtual shoeboxes' with their email inboxes and archiving important messages, photos, and documents.

22277 ■ "Charlotte Pipe Launches Satirical Campaign" in Contractor (Vol. 57, January 2010, No. 1, pp. 6)
Pub: Penton Media, Inc.
Description: Charlotte Pipe and Foundry Co. launched an advertising campaign that uses social media and humor to make a point about how it can be nearly impossible to determine if imported cast iron pipes and fittings meet the same quality standards as what is made in the U.S. The campaign features 'pipe whisperers' and also spoofs pipe sniffing dogs.

22278 ■ Common Sense Purchasing: Hard Knock Lessons Learned from a Purchasing Pro
Pub: Booksurge, LLC
Ed: Tom DePaoli. **Released:** February 2004. **Price:** $9.99. **Description:** Guide to purchasing and negotiating deals.

22279 ■ "Competing for Jobs" in Women In Business (Vol. 63, Summer 2011, No. 2, pp. 37)
Pub: American Business Women's Association
Ed: Leigh Elmore. **Description:** Job hunting tips for women in the US in relation to generation demographic groups are presented. Effective communications and positive interactions are essential to career development. Generation groups' strengths and weaknesses as job seekers are also given.

22280 ■ "Conferencing Takes on High-Tech Futuristic Feel" in Crain's Cleveland Business (Vol. 28, October 29, 2007, No. 43, pp. 17)
Pub: Crain Communications, Inc.
Ed: Chuck Soder. **Description:** Overview of the newest technologies which are making local company's meetings more effective including: tele-presence, a videoconferencing technology, as well as virtual flip charts.

22281 ■ "Conversations with Customers" in Business Journal Serving Greater Tampa Bay (Vol. 31, December 31, 2010, No. 1, pp. 1)
Pub: Tampa Bay Business Journal
Description: Tampa Bay, Florida-based businesses have been using social media to interact with customers. Forty percent of businesses have been found to have at least one social media platform to reach customers and prospects.

22282 ■ "The Copyright Evolution" in Information Today (Vol. 28, November 2011, No. 10, pp. 1)
Pub: Information Today, Inc.
Ed: Nancy Davis Kho. **Description:** For information professionals, issues surrounding copyright compliance have traditionally been on the consumption side. However, today, content consumption is only half the

program because blogging, tweeting, and commenting is a vital part of more standard duties for workers as corporations aim to create authentic communications with customers.

22283 ■ "Creative Marketing: How to Cultivate a Network of Endless Referrals" in Agency Sales Magazine (Vol. 39, July 2009, No. 7, pp. 38)
Pub: MANA
Ed: Bob Burg. **Description:** Tips on how a salesperson can build a network of people that will bring them referrals are presented. Asking a person about their business and re-introducing one's self to an earlier acquaintance while remembering their names are some elements in the process of building this network.

22284 ■ "Deals Still Get Done at Drake's Coq d'Or" in Crain's Chicago Business (Vol. 31, November 17, 2008, No. 46, pp. 35)
Pub: Crain Communications, Inc.
Ed: Shia Kapos. **Description:** Chicago's infamous Coq d'Or, a restaurant and lounge located at the Drake Hotel, is still a favorite establishment for noted executives but the eatery is now trying to cater to younger professionals through marketing and offering new beverages that appeal to that demographic. Many find it the perfect environment in which to close deals, relax or network.

22285 ■ "Does Rudeness Really Matter?" in Academy of Management Journal (October 2007, pp. 1181)
Pub: Academy of Management
Contact: Ming-Jer Chen, President
Ed: Christine L. Porath, Amir Erez. **Description:** Study assessing the effect of impoliteness on performance and helpfulness showed rude behavior lowered performance levels and also decreased attitude of helpfulness.

22286 ■ "The Don't Do Lists" in Inc. (Vol. 33, October 2011, No. 8, pp. 65)
Pub: Inc. Magazine
Ed: Jennifer Alsever, Adam Bluestein. **Description:** Ten business leaders and experts share their don't do lists, the things that should be avoided when going on sales calls, planning business lunches, motivating employees and more are presented.

22287 ■ "Don't Leave Employees on the Outside Looking In" in Canadian Business (Vol. 83, July 20, 2010, No. 11-12, pp. 13)
Pub: Rogers Media Ltd.
Ed: Richard Branson. **Description:** Managers should be careful with employee's tendencies to use the word 'they' when problems occur since this shows that employees are not associating themselves with their company. Employees should be involved in the development of the company and improving the flow of information is important in overcoming this communication challenge.

22288 ■ "Drive Traffic To Your Blog" in Women Entrepreneur (January 13, 2009)
Pub: Entrepreneur Media Inc.
Ed: Lesley Spencer Pyle. **Description:** Internet social networking has become a vital component to marketing one's business. Tips are provided on how to establish a blog that will attract attention to one's business and keep one's customers coming back for more.

22289 ■ e-Riches 2.0: Next-Generation Marketing Strategies for Making Million Online
Pub: AMACOM
Ed: Scott Fox. **Released:** May 27, 2009. **Price:** $25.00. **Description:** Beginner's guide to using the Internet to help grow business, including the best ways to use email lists and newsletters, RSS feeds, online viral marketing, social networking, microblogging, online video and radio/podcasts, tele-seminars and webinars, search engine keyword advertising and affiliate program advertising.

22290 ■ Electronic Commerce
Pub: Course Technology
Ed: Gary Schneider, Bryant Chrzan, Charles McCormick. **Released:** May 1, 2010. **Price:** $117.95. **Description:** E-commerce can open the door to more opportunities than ever before for small business. Packed with real-world examples and cases, the book delivers comprehensive coverage of emerging online technologies and trends and their influence on the electronic marketplace. It details how the landscape of online commerce is evolving, reflecting changes in the economy and how business and society are responding to those changes. Balancing technological issues with the strategic business aspects of successful e-commerce, the new edition includes expanded coverage of international issues, social networking, mobile commerce, Web 2.0 technologies, and updates on spam, phishing, and identity theft.

22291 ■ "Elemental Nabs $5.5 Million" in The Business Journal-Portland (Vol. 25, July 18, 2008, No. 19, pp. 1)
Pub: American City Business Journals, Inc.
Ed: Aliza Earnshaw. **Description:** Elemental Technologies Inc., a Portland, Oregon-based software company got $5.5 million in new funding, bringing its total invested capital to $7.1 million in nine months since October 2008. The company plans to launch Badaboom, software for converting video into various formats, later in 2008.

22292 ■ Emerging Business Online: Global Markets and the Power of B2B Internet Marketing
Pub: FT Press
Ed: Lara Fawzy, Lucas Dworksi. **Released:** October 1, 2010. **Price:** $49.99. **Description:** An introduction into ebocube (emerging business online), a comprehensive proven business model for Internet B2B marketing in emerging markets.

22293 ■ "Empire of Pixels" in Entrepreneur (Vol. 37, September 2009, No. 9, pp. 50)
Pub: Entrepreneur Media, Inc.
Ed: Jason Daley. **Description:** Entrepreneur Jack Levin has successfully grown Imageshack, an image-hosting Web service. The Website currently gets 50 million unique visitors a month. Levin has launched Y-Frog, an application that uses Imageshack to allow Twitter users to add images to their posts.

22294 ■ "Entrepreneur Column" in Entrepreneur (September 24, 2009)
Pub: Entrepreneur Media, Inc.
Ed: Allen Moon. **Description:** In an attempt to compete with Google, Microsoft and Yahoo have entered a partnership to merge their search services; advice on the best ways to get noticed on this new search engine entitled Bing, is provided.

22295 ■ "Etiquette, Common Sense Often Lag Behind Smarter Devices" in Crain's Cleveland Business (Vol. 28, October 22, 2007, No. 42, pp. 21)
Pub: Crain Communications, Inc.
Ed: Chrissy Kadleck. **Description:** Discusses the importance of good etiquette in regards to electronic communication both within as well as outside the business world.

22296 ■ "Extreme Negotiations" in Harvard Business Review (Vol. 88, November 2010, No. 11, pp. 66)
Pub: Harvard Business School Publishing
Ed: Jeff Weiss, Aram Donigian, Jonathan Hughes. **Description:** Examination of military negotiation skills that are applicable in business situations. Skills include soliciting others' perspectives, developing and proposing multiple solutions, and inviting others to assess them.

22297 ■ "Facebook: A Promotional Budget's Best Friend" in Women Entrepreneur (February 1, 2009)
Pub: Entrepreneur Media Inc.
Ed: Tamara Monosoff. **Description:** Facebook began as a social networking website but has become a valuable marketing tool for all types of businesses,

organizations and causes. Tips are provided for creating a Facebook account and growing one's network on Facebook.

22298 ■ The Facebook Effect: The Inside Story of the Company That Is Connecting the World
Pub: Simon & Shuster

Ed: David Kirkpatrick. **Released:** June 8, 2010. **Price:** $26.00. **Description:** There's never been a Website like Facebook: more than 350 million people have accounts, and if the growth rate continues, by 2013 every Internet user worldwide will have his or her own page. No one's had more access to the inner workings of the phenomenon than Kirkpatrick, a senior tech writer at Fortune magazine. Written with the full cooperation of founder Mark Zuckerberg, the book follows the company from its genesis in a Harvard dorm room through its successes over Friendster and MySpace, the expansion of the user base, and Zuckerberg's refusal to sell.

22299 ■ The Facebook Era: Tapping Online Social Networks to Build Better Products, Reach New Audiences, and Sell More Stuff
Pub: Prentice Hall

Ed: Clara Shih. **Price:** $24.99. **Description:** The '90s were about the World Wide Web of information and the power of linking Web pages. Today it's about the World Wide Web of people and the power of the social graph. Online social networks are fundamentally changing the way we live, work, and interact. They offer businesses immense opportunities to transform customer relationships for profit: opportunities that touch virtually every business function, from sales and marketing to recruiting, collaboration to executive decision-making, product development to innovation.

22300 ■ "Fast Fact: Women's Online Habits" in Marketing to Women (Vol. 22, July 2009, No. 7, pp. 1)
Pub: EPM Communications Inc.

Contact: Ira Mayer, President

E-mail: imayer@epmcom.com

Description: Lists the Internet habits of women. Statistical data included.

22301 ■ "Faster and Shorter" in Canadian Business (Vol. 81, October 13, 2008, No. 17, pp. 25)
Pub: Rogers Media Ltd.

Ed: Terri Goveia. **Description:** Study revealed that instant messaging (IM) technologies are slowly becoming legitimate in the corporate world. IM is traditionally considered as a distraction, but it was found to let workers make targeted inquiries that gives them what they need in an instant. Other views and information about IMs is included.

22302 ■ Fierce Conversations
Pub: Berkley Trade

Ed: Susan Scott. **Released:** January 6, 2004. **Price:** $15.00. **Description:** Seven Principles of Fierce Conversations are addressed to help readers become effective conversationalists in both business and social settings.

22303 ■ "The File On..Jenne Distributors" in Crain's Cleveland Business (Vol. 28, October 8, 2007, No. 40, pp. 26)
Pub: Crain Communications, Inc.

Ed: Kimberly Bonvissuto. **Description:** Overview of the telecommunications equipment company, Jenne Distributors, a firm that is projecting more than $125 million in revenue for 2007.

22304 ■ "Five Steps to an Effective Business Call" in Hawaii Business (Vol. 53, October 2007, No. 4, pp. 64)
Pub: Hawaii Business Publishing

Ed: Matthew K. Ing. **Description:** University of Hawaii professor Libda Patrylak believes that communication skills are integral to business success, which is why businesses should know how to properly handle phone conversations. Presented are five ways of achieving effective business phone calls, such as setting rules for employees to follow with regards to answering calls and providing undivided attention to the other speaker.

22305 ■ "Five Things" in Hawaii Business (Vol. 53, November 2007, No. 5, pp. 20)
Pub: Hawaii Business Publishing

Ed: Jason Ubay. **Description:** Discusses products that are allowed to be carried on board airplane flights by business travelers.

22306 ■ "Five Tips for New Managers" in Hawaii Business (Vol. 53, November 2007, No. 5, pp. 59)
Pub: Hawaii Business Publishing

Ed: Jason Ubay. **Description:** New managers should remember to know what their roles are, learn from others, build an infrastructure according to the customer's needs, communicate professionally and have consideration.

22307 ■ The Game-Changer: How Every Leader Can Drive Everyday Innovation
Pub: Crown Business

Ed: A.G. Lafley, Ram Charan. **Price:** $27.50. **Description:** Management guru Charan and Proctor & Gamble CEO Lafley provide lessons to encourage innovation at all levels, including how to hire for and encourage an environment of communication and tangible work processes.

22308 ■ "Get on the Green" in Entrepreneur (Vol. 35, November 2007, No. 11, pp. 44)
Pub: Entrepreneur Media Inc.

Ed: James Park. **Description:** Golf is a sport where business people are provided with a casual atmosphere where they can open a conversation regarding business topics. Details on how spending time on the course provides a good environment for business discussions.

22309 ■ "Get Online or Be Left Behind" in Women In Business (Vol. 61, August-September 2009, No. 4, pp. 33)
Pub: American Business Women's Association

Ed: Diane Stafford. **Description:** Technology's significance for the connectivity purposes among business people is discussed. Details on the use of wireless tools and online social media to boost technology IQ are presented.

22310 ■ "Get Personal" in Entrepreneur (Vol. 36, April 2008, No. 4)
Pub: Entrepreneur Media, Inc.

Ed: Romanus Wolter. **Description:** Customers appreciate personal contact, and communicating with them can help business owners' customer relations. Some ways on how to keep a personal touch with customers and improve business dealings include blending technology with personal interaction and knowing what the customers want. Other tips are provided.

22311 ■ "Getting Drowned Out by the Brainstorm" in Canadian Business (Vol. 83, June 15, 2010, No. 10, pp. 91)
Pub: Rogers Media Ltd.

Ed: Joe Castaldo. **Description:** A study reveals that people generate more ideas when they do it alone rather than as part of a brainstorming group. The limited range of ideas is due to the fixation of group members on the first idea that gets offered.

22312 ■ "Getting Inventive With..Richard Brindisi and Gregory Vittardi" in Crain's Cleveland Business (Vol. 28, October 22, 2007, No. 42)
Pub: Crain Communications, Inc.

Ed: Kimberly Bonvissuto. **Description:** Profile of the SmartShopper, a handheld, voice-recognition device for dictating shopping and errand lists, and its creators, Richard G. Brindisi and Gregory Vittardi.

22313 ■ Getting More: How to Negotiate to Achieve Your Goals in the Real World
Pub: Crown Business Books

Ed: Stuart Diamond. **Released:** December 28, 2010. **Price:** $26.00. **Description:** When negotiating, people fail to meet their goals due to focusing on power and the 'win-win' instead of on relationships and perceptions, thus not finding enough things to trade. They think others should be rational when they are dealing with emotions and they get distracted from the real goal.

22314 ■ Getting to Yes: Negotiating Agreement Without Giving In
Pub: Penguin Books USA Inc.

Ed: Roger Fisher, William L. Ury, Bruce Patton. **Released:** December 1991. **Price:** $15.00. **Description:** Strategies for negotiating mutually acceptable agreements in all types of conflict.

22315 ■ The Golden 120 Seconds of Every Sales Call: A Fresh Innovative Look at the Sales Process
Pub: NorlightsPress.com

Ed: Peter G. Dennis. **Released:** October 28, 2009. **Price:** $15.95. **Description:** Salespeople who want to find their personal style, gain confidence, and avoid deal-killing mistakes must read this book. It will show both new and experienced sales professionals how to use key fundamentals with every call, every selling interaction, and every opportunity to make something happen. Anyone who sells for a living has experienced the magic moments that can make or break a sales. Advice is given to help recognize, and learn to cultivate, this vital part of the sales process.

22316 ■ "Grooming Your Online Persona" in Women In Business (Vol. 62, June 2010, No. 2, pp. 36)
Pub: American Business Women's Association

Ed: Diane Stafford. **Description:** Employees' use of online social networks could become a basis on how their employers, clients, or business partners would judge them. Personal details, pictures and other online data should be filtered to avoid inappropriate or uncomfortable situations and distinguish personal from professional or work life.

22317 ■ Groundswell: Winning in a World Transformed by Social Technologies
Pub: Harvard Business School Press

Ed: Charlene Li, Josh Bernoff. **Released:** 2008. **Price:** $29.95. **Description:** Corporate executives are struggling with a new trend: people using online social technologies (blogs, social networking sites, YouTube, podcasts) to discuss products and companies, write their own news, and find their own deals.

22318 ■ Groups in Context: Leadership and Participation in Small Groups
Pub: McGraw-Hill Companies Inc.

Contact: Deven Sharma, President

Ed: Gerald L. Wilson. **Released:** June 2004. **Price:** $62.98. **Description:** Small group communication skills for the workplace, in churches, social groups, or civic organizations.

22319 ■ Guide to Business Information on Central and Eastern Europe
Pub: Taylor and Francis Group Ltd

URL(s): www.taylorandfrancis.com. **Released:** Latest edition June, 2000. **Price:** $80, Individuals Hardback; $48, Individuals Paperback. **Covers:** Twelve countries of Central and Eastern Europe. **Entries include:** Country overview; current developments; company name, address, phone, fax; names and titles of key personnel; industries and services; legislation; and organizations.

22320 ■ Guide to Business Information on Russia, the NIS, and the Baltic States
Pub: Taylor and Francis Group Ltd

URL(s): www.taylorandfrancis.com. **Released:** Latest edition November, 2000. **Price:** £48, Individuals Paperback. **Covers:** Fifteen countries of Russia, the NIS, and the Baltic States. **Entries include:** Current developments; company name, address, phone, fax; industries and services; legislation; and organizations.

22321 ■ "Harlequin Leads the Way" in Marketing to Women (Vol. 22, July 2009, No. 7, pp. 1)
Pub: EPM Communications Inc.

Contact: Ira Mayer, President

E-mail: imayer@epmcom.com

Description: Although the publishing industry has been slow to embrace new media options, the Internet is now a primary source for reaching women readers. Harlequin has been eager to court their female consumers over the Internet and often uses women bloggers in their campaigns strategies.

22322 ■ "Help for Job Seekers" in Crain's Detroit Business (Vol. 26, January 18, 2010, No. 3, pp. 14)
Pub: Crain Communications Inc.
Description: CareerWorks is aimed at helping those who are in career transition or are looking for new jobs; this weekly collection of news, advertising and information includes weekly stories, events and the highlighting of a person who has successfully made the transition from one profession to another. On the Website, readers are welcome to post an anonymous resume in order to attract employers.

22323 ■ High Trust Selling: Make More Money, in Less Time, with Less Stress
Pub: Nelson Business
Ed: Todd Duncan. **Released:** April 2007. **Price:** $14.99. **Description:** Laws governing salesmanship are divided into two sections. The first deals with attitudes, aptitudes, and abilities required for successful selling; the second with communication, courtship, camaraderie and commitments between salespeople and their clients.

22324 ■ "Holidays Should Foster Mutual Respect" in Women In Business (Vol. 61, October-November 2009, No. 5, pp. 33)
Pub: American Business Women's Association
Ed: Diane Stafford. **Description:** Workplaces have modified the way year-end holiday celebrations are held in an effort to promote mutual respect. The workers' varying religious beliefs, political affiliations, and other differences have brought about the modifications. The importance of developing mutual understanding is emphasized as a mechanism to stimulate successful business ties.

22325 ■ "How Anger Poisons Decision Making" in Harvard Business Review (Vol. 88, September 2010, No. 9, pp. 26)
Pub: Harvard Business School Publishing
Ed: Jennifer S. Lerner, Katherine Shonk. **Description:** Importance of accountability in mitigating the negative effects of anger on the decision making process is stressed.

22326 ■ "How to Do the Business Dinner" in Business Owner (Vol. 35, March-April 2011, No. 2, pp. 7)
Pub: DL Perkins Company
Description: Dining with others, whether client of employee, it is important to use this as an opportunity to develop relationships. Tips are given to help make the best of a dining experience are provided.

22327 ■ "How the Generation Gap Can Hurt Your Business" in Agency Sales Magazine (Vol. 39, November 2009, No. 10, pp. 16)
Pub: MANA
Ed: Jack Foster. **Description:** Now that there are four generations of people in the workplace, there is a need to add flexibility to communications for independent manufacturers representatives. Managers can encourage the younger generations to do the research and the boomers to process information and let each side report to the other.

22328 ■ How to Make Money with Social Media: Using New and Emerging Media to Grow Your Business
Pub: FT Press
Ed: Jamie Turner, Reshma Shah. **Released:** October 1, 2010. **Price:** $24.99. **Description:** Marketers, executives, entrepreneurs are shown more effective ways to utilize Internet social media to make money. This guide brings together both practical strategies and proven execution techniques for driving maximum value from social media marketing.

22329 ■ "How to Make Your Website Really Sell" in Entrepreneur (Vol. 37, September 2009, No. 9, pp. 79)
Pub: Entrepreneur Media, Inc.
Ed: David Port. **Description:** Advice on how to succeed in Internet marketing is presented. Offering visitors purchase incentives on the home page is encouraged. Delivery of customized landing pages and content is also recommended.

22330 ■ "How Not to Build a Website" in Women Entrepreneur (December 24, 2008)
Pub: Entrepreneur Media Inc.
Ed: Erica Ruback; Joanie Reisen. **Description:** Tips for producing a unique and functional Website are given as well as a number of lessons a pair of entrepreneurs learned while trying to launch their networking website, MomSpace.com.

22331 ■ "How Pixar Fosters Collective Creativity" in Harvard Business Review (Vol. 86, September 2008, No. 9, pp. 64)
Pub: Harvard Business School Press
Ed: Ed Catmull. **Description:** Pixar Animation Studios illustrates peer-culture methods for fostering product development. These include allowing any employee to communicate with any other employee, providing a safe environment for new ideas, and watching the academic community closely for innovations.

22332 ■ "How to Plan and Execute Effective Sales Meetings" in Agency Sales Magazine (Vol. 39, August 2009, No. 8, pp. 8)
Pub: MANA
Ed: Jack Foster. **Description:** Basic guide to successful representative-manufacturer sales meetings based on effective planning is presented. The representative and the manufacturer will reap the benefits of a productive meeting only when they both focus on what's going to transpire before, during and after the event. Insights from industry players are also presented.

22333 ■ "HR Tech on the Go" in Workforce Management (Vol. 88, November 16, 2009, No. 12, pp. 1)
Pub: Crain Communications Inc.
Ed: Ed Frauenheim. **Description:** Examination of the necessity of mobile access of human resources software applications that allow managers to recruit, schedule and train employees via their mobile devices; some industry leaders believe that mobile HR applications are vital while others see this new technology as hype.

22334 ■ "Hunter and the Hunted" in Canadian Business (Vol. 81, Summer 2008, No. 9, pp. 12)
Pub: Rogers Media Ltd.
Ed: Thomas Watson. **Description:** Brian Hunter, a partner in oil and gas engineering firm Montane Resources, invested his life savings in Vancouver-based Canacord Capital Corp. Details of the asset-backed commercial paper fiasco and Hunter's use of Facebook to encourage other investors to participate in his claim against the mortgage company are presented.

22335 ■ "I Can Make Your Brain Look Like Mine" in Harvard Business Review (Vol. 88, December 2010, No. 12, pp. 32)
Pub: Harvard Business School Publishing
Description: Psychology professor Uri Hasson discusses findings that the brain waves of a speaker and a listener become similar as the listener's comprehension increases.

22336 ■ "Ideas at Work: Total Communicator" in Business Strategy Review (Vol. 21, Autumn 2010, No. 3, pp. 10)
Pub: Blackwell Publishers Ltd.
Ed: Stuart Crainer. **Description:** Vittorio Colao has been chief executive of Vodafone Group for two years. Prior to the company special experience as CEO of RCS MediaGroup in Milan, which publishes newspapers, magazines and books in Italy, Spain and France. Prior to RCS, he held other positions within Vodaphone. Colao shares his views on business, the global economy and leading Vodafone.

22337 ■ "Ideas at Work: Total Communicator" in Business Strategy Review (Vol. 21, Autumn 2010, No. 3, pp. 10)
Pub: Wiley-Blackwell
Ed: Stuart Crainer. **Description:** Vittorio Colao has been chief executive of Vodafone Group for two years. He brings to the company some special experience: from 2004-2006 he was CEO of RCS Media-

Group in Milan, which publishes newspapers, magazines and books in Italy, Spain and France. Colao shares his views on business, the global economy and leading Vodafone.

22338 ■ If You Have to Cry, Go Outside: And Other Things Your Mother Never Told You
Pub: HarperOne
Ed: Kelly Cutrone. **Released:** February 2, 2010. **Price:** $22.99. **Description:** Women's mentor advices on how to make it in one of the most competitive industries in the world, fashion. She has kicked people out of fashion shows, forced some of reality television's shiny start to fire their friends, and built her own company which is one of the most powerful public relations firms in the fashion business.

22339 ■ I'm on LinkedIn - Now What? (Second Edition): A Guide to Getting the Most Out of LinkedIn
Pub: Happy About
Ed: Diane Danielson. **Released:** January 7, 2009. **Price:** $19.95. **Description:** Designed to help get the most out of LinkedIn, the popular business networking site and follows the first edition and includes the latest and great approaches using LinkedIn. With over 32 million members there is a lot of potential to find and develop relationships to help in your business and personal life, but many professionals find themselves wondering what to do once they sign up. This book explains the different benefits of the system and recommends best practices (including LinkedIn Groups) so that you get the most out of LinkedIn.

22340 ■ "The 'In-Crowd' Online: Professionals Take Networking To New Levels" in Black Enterprise (Vol. 38, January 2008, No. 6, pp. 47)
Pub: Earl G. Graves Publishing Co. Inc.
Ed: Alwin A.D. Jones. **Description:** The Internet is providing new ways for professionals to network with others. New sites like LinkedIn.com provide entrepreneurs with access to others with a business life similar to theirs.

22341 ■ "In the Know?" in Entrepreneur (Vol. 37, July 2009, No. 7, pp. 30)
Pub: Entrepreneur Media, Inc.
Ed: Brad Feld. **Description:** Tips on what entrepreneurs should and should not share with their venture capitalists (VCs) are given. Entrepreneurs must be transparent with their VCs, but they should not bombard VCs with too many details. The aspect of a business that a VC is concerned with varies from one VC to another, and it is important that entrepreneurs understand the best way to communicate with their VC.

22342 ■ Information Technology for the Small Business: How to Make IT Work For Your Company
Pub: TAB Computer Systems, Incorporated
Ed: T.J. Benoit. **Released:** June 2006. **Price:** $17.95. **Description:** Basics of information technology to help small companies maximize benefits are covered. Topics include pitfalls to avoid, email and Internet use, data backup, recovery and overall IT organization.

22343 ■ "Integrating Business Core Knowledge through Upper Division Report Composition" in Business Communication Quarterly (December 2007)
Pub: SAGE Publications USA
Contact: Blaise R. Simqu, President
Ed: Joy Roach, Daniel Tracy, Kay Durden. **Description:** An assignment that integrates subjects and encourages the use of business communication report-writing skills is presented. This assignment is designed to complement business school curricula and help develop critical thinking and organizational skills.

22344 ■ "Internet Marketing 2.0: Closing the Online Chat Gap" in Agent's Sales Journal (November 2009, pp. 14)
Pub: Summit Business Media
Ed: Jeff Denenholz. **Description:** Advice regarding the implementation of an Internet marketing strategy for insurance agencies includes how and why to

incorporate a chat feature in which a sales agent can communicate in real-time with potential or existing customers. It is important to understand if appropriate response mechanisms are in place to convert leads into actual sales.

22345 ■ "An Introvert's Guide to Schmoozing" in Canadian Business (Vol. 83, July 20, 2010, No. 11-12, pp. 73)
Pub: Rogers Media Ltd.
Ed: Jasmine Budak. **Description:** Writer Nancy Ankowitz says that introverts seem to get grouped with social misfits but introverts are people who recharge by spending time alone. Ankowitz advises introverts to use their strengths in quiet strengths such as writing and listening as well as learning to speak in public.

22346 ■ "IPhone 3G" in Advertising Age (Vol. 79, November 17, 2008, No. 43, pp. 15)
Pub: Crain Communications, Inc.
Ed: Beth Snyder Bulik. **Description:** Review of Apple's new iPhone 3G which includes the addition of smart-phone applications as well as a price drop; the new functionalities as well as the lower price seems to be paying off for Apple who reported sales of 6.9 million iPhones in its most recent quarter, in which the 3G hit store shelves.

22347 ■ "Is It Time to Ban Swearing at Work?" in HR Specialist (Vol. 8, September 2010, No. 9, pp. 2)
Pub: Capitol Information Group Inc.
Description: Screening software has been developed to identify profanity used in business correspondence.

22348 ■ "Israeli Spam Law May Have Global Impact" in Information Today (Vol. 26, February 2009, No. 2, pp. 28)
Pub: Information Today, Inc.
Ed: David Mirchin. **Description:** Israels new law, called Amendment 40 of the Communications Law, will regulate commercial solicitations including those sent without permission via email, fax, automatic phone dialing systems, or short messaging technologies.

22349 ■ "It's Not About You" in Entrepreneur (Vol. 35, November 2007, No. 11, pp. 102)
Pub: Entrepreneur Media Inc.
Ed: Barry Farber. **Description:** Companies should focus on the customers' need and show them that they care about them. Listening to and learning about your customers can make selling easier; tips on how to stay focused on the customers' needs are outlined.

22350 ■ It's Not Just Who You Know: Transform Your Life (and Your Organization) by Turning Colleagues and Contacts into Lasting Relationships
Pub: Crown Business Books
Ed: Tommy Spaulding. **Released:** August 10, 2010. **Price:** $23.00. **Description:** Tommy Spaulding teaches the reader how to reach out to others in order to create lasting relationships that go beyond superficial contacts.

22351 ■ It's Not Who You Know - It's Who Knows You!: The Small Business Guide to Raising Your Profits by Raising Your Profile
Pub: John Wiley & Sons, Inc.
Ed: David Avrin. **Released:** November 9, 2010. **Price:** $24.95. **Description:** When it comes to promoting a small business or a brand, it is essential to know how valuable high-profile attention can be. But for most small companies, the cost of hiring an outside firm to increase attention can be too expensive.

22352 ■ "Jay Berkowitz to Present Making Social Media Money Seminar at Affiliate Summit West" in Entertainment Close-Up (January 15, 2010)
Pub: Close-Up Media
Description: Highlights of Jay Berkowitz's conference, 'Making Social Media Make Money' include ways in which to develop Internet marketing strategies that will maximize Website traffic and convert that traffic to sales.

22353 ■ "Just Shut The Hell Up" in Canadian Business (Vol. 81, July 22, 2008, No. 12-13, pp. 33)
Pub: Rogers Media Ltd.
Ed: Jane Bao. **Description:** Employees desire better communication as opposed to more communication from their managers. Advice regarding managing communication in the workplace is given including ways in which speakers can say more with fewer words.

22354 ■ "Keep Them Posted" in Entrepreneur (Vol. 35, October 2007, No. 10, pp. 39)
Pub: Entrepreneur Media Inc.
Ed: Gwen Moran. **Description:** Survey by the Pew Internet and American Life Project found that 12 million American adults maintain blogs, which are created for personal and business reasons. Blogs are effective in giving a business a personal touch while informing the public about its operations and products. Tips on how to create an effective business blog are presented.

22355 ■ "Keys to Overcome Fear of Follow-Up" in Agency Sales Magazine (Vol. 39, December 2009, No. 11, pp. 26)
Pub: MANA
Ed: Judy Garmaise. **Description:** In order to be more successful at making follow-up calls, salespeople should not take rejection personally and never assume that they are going to annoy prospects if they follow-up. Those that follow-up with prospects stand out among others since few salespeople do this.

22356 ■ The Language of Success: Business Writing That Informs, Persuades, and Gets Results
Pub: AMACOM
Ed: Tom Sant. **Released:** January 2008. **Price:** $15.00. **Description:** The damage that can be done when words are used ineffectively and the power to be gained when they are used well in business.

22357 ■ "Learning by Doing: Engaging Students through Learner-Centered Activities" in Business Communication Quarterly (Dec. 2007, pp. 451)
Pub: SAGE Publications USA
Contact: Blaise R. Simqu, President
Ed: Karl L. Smart, Nancy Csapo. **Description:** Active learning techniques, such as the Puzzle Brain Spark activity, allow students to engage in learning activities that allow deeper thinking, critical thinking, and problem solving ability that develop business management skills.

22358 ■ "Lessons Learned from Instructional Design Theory" in Business Communication Quarterly (December 2007, pp. 414)
Pub: SAGE Publications USA
Contact: Blaise R. Simqu, President
Ed: Lisa A. Burke. **Description:** Instructors should present course information to business students in a way that enhances understanding and should use presentation techniques that students may eventually use; course materials should be kept relevant and simple.

22359 ■ Liespotting: Proven Techniques to Detect Deception
Pub: St. Martins Press/Macmillan
Ed: Pamela Meyer. **Released:** July 20, 2010. **Price:** $24.99. **Description:** Liespotting links three disciplines: facial recognition training, interrogation training, and a comprehensive survey of research in the field - into a specialized body of information developed specifically to help business leaders detect deception and get the information they need to successfully conduct their most important interactions and transactions.

22360 ■ Life's a Game So Fix the Odds: How to Be More Persuasive and Influential in Your Personal and Business
Pub: John Wiley & Sons, Incorporated
Ed: Philip Hesketh. **Released:** September 2005. **Price:** $24.95 (US), $31.00 (Canadian). **Description:** Seven psychological reasons behind why and how people are persuaded and how to use these reasons to your advantage in both your personal and business life.

22361 ■ "Like Being There" in Canadian Business (Vol. 79, August 14, 2006, No. 16-17, pp. 77)
Pub: Rogers Media
Ed: Gerry Blackwell. **Description:** Latest video conferencing facilities at the Halo Collaboration Studio, are discussed.

22362 ■ "Lines of Communication" in Entrepreneur (Vol. 37, October 2009, No. 10, pp. 80)
Pub: Entrepreneur Media, Inc.
Ed: Brad Feld. **Description:** Entrepreneurial companies should establish a clear and open communication culture between their management teams and their venture capital backers. Chief executive officers should trust their leadership teams when it comes to communicating with venture capitalists.

22363 ■ "Listen Up: There's a Revolution in the Cubicle" in Barron's (Vol. 89, July 27, 2009, No. 30, pp. 18)
Pub: Dow Jones & Co., Inc.
Ed: Jay Palmer. **Description:** Plantronics will be among the first beneficiaries when the unified communications revolution arrives in the office. Plantronics' shares could rise to around 30 in 2009 from the 20s as of July 2009. Unified communications could create a huge new multimillion-dollar market for Plantronics.

22364 ■ "Local Knowledge" in Hawaii Business (Vol. 53, December 2007, No. 6, pp. 40)
Pub: Hawaii Business Publishing
Ed: David K. Choo. **Description:** Rules and facts business professionals need to know about the local life in Hawaii are presented. The important components in island life include knowledge Hawaiian high schools' histories and image, the local sports scene, special events, potluck ethics, and locals' favorite destination, which is Las Vegas.

22365 ■ "Looking Out for the Little Guys" in Black Enterprise (Vol. 38, October 2007, No. 3, pp. 58)
Pub: Earl G. Graves Publishing Co. Inc.
Ed: Kaylyn Kendall Dines. **Description:** Biz Tech-Connect is a Web portal that offers free online and social networking, along with four modules that help small businesses with marketing and advertising, communications and mobility, financial management, and customer relationship management.

22366 ■ Made to Stick: Why Some Ideas Survive and Others Die
Pub: Doubleday Broadway Publishing Group
Ed: Chip Heath; Dan Heath. **Released:** January 2, 2007. **Price:** $26.00. **Description:** Entertaining, practical guide to effective business communication; information is derived form psychosocial studies on memory, emotion and motivation.

22367 ■ "Making Diverse Teams Click" in Harvard Business Review (Vol. 86, July-August 2008, No. 8, pp. 20)
Pub: Harvard Business School Press
Ed: Jeffrey T. Polzer. **Description:** 360-degree feedback to increase the efficacy of diverse-member workplace teams, which involves each member providing feedback to the others on the team is discussed.

22368 ■ "Managing Corporate Social Networks" in Harvard Business Review (Vol. 86, July-August 2008, No. 8, pp. 26)
Pub: Harvard Business School Press
Ed: Adam M. Kleinbaum; Michael L. Tushman. **Description:** Tips on how to promote business creativity and foster knowledge building through business social networks are given.

22369 ■ "Managing the Facebookers; Business" in The Economist (Vol. 390, January 3, 2009, No. 8612, pp. 10)
Pub: Economist Newspaper Ltd.
Description: According to a report from PricewaterhouseCoopers, a business consultancy, workers from Generation Y, also known as the Net Generation, are

more difficult to recruit and integrate into companies that practice traditional business acumen. 61 percent of chief executive managers say that they have trouble with younger employees who tend to be more narcissistic and more interested in personal fulfillment with a need for frequent feedback and an overprecise set of objectives on the path to promotion which can be hard for managers who are used to a different relationship with their subordinates. Older bosses should prepare to make some concessions to their younger talent since some of the issues that make them happy include cheaper online ways to communicate and additional coaching, both of which are good for business.

22370 ■ *"Marketers Push for Mobile Tuesday as the New Black Friday' in Advertising Age (Vol. 79, December 1, 2008, No. 44, pp. 21)*
Pub: Crain Communications, Inc.

Ed: Natalie Zmuda. **Description:** Marketers are using an innovative approach in an attempt to stimulate business on the Tuesday following Thanksgiving by utilizing consumer's cell phones to alert them of sales or present them with coupons for this typically slow retail business day; with this campaign both advertisers and retailers are hoping to start Mobile Tuesday, another profitable shopping day in line with Black Friday and Cyber Monday.

22371 ■ *Marketing 2.0: Bridging the Gap between Seller and Buyer through Social Media Marketing*
Pub: Wheatmark

Ed: Bernie Borges. **Released:** July 14, 2009. **Price:** $22.95. **Description:** Winning strategies to attract people to your company and your employees using social media site on the Internet are outlined.

22372 ■ *"Marketing Scholarship 2.0' in Journal of Marketing (Vol. 75, July 2011, No. 4, pp. 225)*
Pub: American Marketing Association

Ed: Richard J. Lutz. **Description:** A study of the implications of changing environment and newer collaborative models for marketing knowledge production and dissemination is presented. Crowdsourcing has become a frequently employed strategy in industry. Academic researchers should collaborate more as well as the academe and industry, to make sure that important problems are being investigated.

22373 ■ *Mastering Business Negotiation*
Pub: Jossey Bass

Ed: Roy J. Lewicki; Alexander Hiam. **Released:** July 21, 2006. **Price:** $24.95. **Description:** Resource guide for any manager requiring practical strategies and ideas for negotiating in business; the book shows how to understand the game to better control the situation, predict the sequence of negotiations, identify tactics of others, and to apply the rules of the game.

22374 ■ *Mastering Business Negotiation: A Working Guide to Making Deals and Resolving Conflict*
Pub: Jossey-Bass Publishers

Ed: Roy J. Lewicki; Alexander Hiam. **Released:** July 21, 2006. **Price:** $24.95. **Description:** Provides extensive insight into practical strategies and ideas for conducting business negotiations.

22375 ■ *Masters of Sales: Secrets from Top Sales Professionals That Will Transform You Into a World Class Salesman*
Pub: Entrepreneur Press

Ed: Ivan R. Misner; Don Morgan. **Released:** August 15, 2007. **Price:** $19.95. **Description:** Eighty successful salespeople share insight into selling.

22376 ■ *MBA In a Day*
Pub: John Wiley and Sons, Inc.

Ed: Steven Stralser, PhD. **Released:** 2004. **Price:** $34.95. **Description:** Management professor presents important concepts, business topics and strategies that can be used by anyone to manage a small business or professional practice. Topics covered include: human resources and personal interaction,

ethics and leadership skills, fair negotiation tactics, basic business accounting practices, project management, and the fundamentals of economics and marketing.

22377 ■ *"Meetings Go Virtual' in HRMagazine (Vol. 54, January 2009, No. 1, pp. 74)*
Pub: Society for Human Resource Management
Contact: Henry G. Jackson, President
E-mail: hjackson@shrm.org

Ed: Elizabeth Agnvall. **Description:** Microsoft Office Live Meeting conferencing software allows companies to schedule meetings from various company locations, thus saving travel costs.

22378 ■ *"Mobile Security for Business V5' in SC Magazine (Vol. 20, August 2009, No. 8, pp. 55)*
Pub: Haymarket Media, Inc.

Description: Review of F-Secure's Mobile Security for Business v5 which offers protection for business smartphones that can be centralized for protection monitoring by IT administrators.

22379 ■ *"The Mobile Workforce Revolution' in Canadian Business (Vol. 81, March 31, 2008, No. 5, pp. 28)*
Pub: Rogers Media

Ed: Diane Horton. **Description:** Diane Horton explains how a mobile workforce helps companies cut costs, increase productivity, and boost employee motivation. Horton says that employees believe they usually become more productive by 15 to 30 percent after their companies go mobile.

22380 ■ *"More Power to Your Presentation' in Business Strategy Review (Vol. 21, Spring 2010, No. 1, pp. 50)*
Pub: Wiley-Blackwell

Ed: Roly Grimshaw. **Description:** You might wonder what similarities there can be between a Russian oligarch and an entrepreneur. When it comes to persuading people to invest, there are plenty.

22381 ■ *"Mosaid Grants First Wireless Parent License To Matsushita' in Canadian Electronics (Vol. 23, June-July 2008, No. 5, pp. 1)*
Pub: Action Communication Inc.

Description: Matsushita Electric Industrial Co. Ltd. has been granted a six-and-a-half-year license by Mosaid Technologies Inc. to manufacture the latter's products. The patent portfolio license agreement covers Mosaid's Wi-Fi, Wi-Max, CDMA-enabled notebook computers and other products.

22382 ■ *"'Mr. CEO, Please Do Elaborate On Your Firm's Metrics" in Business Courier (Vol. 24, February 29, 2008, No. 47, pp. 1)*
Pub: American City Business Journals, Inc.

Ed: Jon Newberry. **Description:** Discusses a rogue caller who goes by the name of Joe Herrick, Steven Nissan and Joe Harris has joined in over a dozen conference calls, asking chief executive officers on their plans and commenting on the companies' operations. The mystery caller attempts to pass himself off as a financial analyst. Transcripts of some conference calls, in which the rogue caller is involved, are provided.

22383 ■ *"Negotiating Muscle" in Black Enterprise (Vol. 38, February 2008, No. 7, pp. 70)*
Pub: Earl G. Graves Publishing Co. Inc.

Ed: Sonia Alleyne. **Description:** Negotiating historically has been a barrier for women in business, the book, 'Ask For It: How Women Can Use the Power of Negotiation to Get What They Really Want' helps professional females identify and create great business opportunities.

22384 ■ *"Net Profits: Get a Social Life" in Entrepreneur (Vol. 35, October 2007, No. 10, pp. 140)*
Pub: Entrepreneur Media Inc.

Ed: Amanda C. Kooser. **Description:** Social networking sites such as Facebook and MySpace have millions of users, a sign that social networking is a growing industry. One way to enter this industry is target

marketing, like Med3Q, a site for health-conscious individuals had done. How Med3q is earning through online advertising and sponsors is explained.

22385 ■ *"Networking Web Sites: a Two-Edged Sword' in Contractor (Vol. 56, October 2009, No. 10, pp. 52)*
Pub: Penton Media, Inc.

Ed: H. Kent Craig. **Description:** People need to be careful about the information that they share on social networking Web sites. They should realize that future bosses, coworkers, and those that might want to hire them might read those information. Posting on these sites can cost career opportunities and respect.

22386 ■ *"The New Guard' in Entrepreneur (Vol. 36, February 2008, No. 2, pp. 46)*
Pub: Entrepreneur Media Inc.

Ed: Amanda C. Kooser. **Description:** A natural language search engine is being developed by Powerset for better online searching. Zannel Inc. offers Instant Media Messaging platform, which allows for social networking using phones. Ning is an online platform that allows users to customize and control their social networks.

22387 ■ *"New Sprint Phone Whets Appetite for Applications" in The Business Journal-Serving Metropolitan Kansas City (Vol. 26, July 25, 2008)*
Pub: American City Business Journals, Inc.

Ed: Suzanna Stagemeyer. **Description:** Firms supporting the applications of the new Samsung Instinct, which was introduced by Sprint Nextel Corp. in June 2008, have reported usage rates increase for their products. Handmark, whose mobile services Pocket Express comes loaded with Instinct, has redirected employees to meet the rising demand for the services. Other views and information on Instinct, are presented.

22388 ■ *"The Next Big Thing' in Farm Industry News (Vol. 42, January 1, 2009, No. 1)*
Pub: Penton Media Inc.
Contact: John French, President

Ed: David Hest. **Description:** Communication technology that allows farmers to detect equipment location, travel speed and real-time fuel and sprayer/combine tank levels will pay off with better machine use efficiency, improved maintenance and reduced downtime. These telemetry systems will be widely available in the next few years.

22389 ■ *"The Next Generation of Bluetooth Headsets" in Inc. (Vol. 31, January-February 2009, No. 1, pp. 41)*
Pub: Mansueto Ventures LLC

Ed: Mark Spoonauer. **Description:** Information on the latest Bluetooth headsets that allow users to talk hands-free and the new technology that blocks ambient sounds is given. Aliph Jawbone, Plantronics Voyager Jabra BT530, and Motorola Motopure H15 are profiled.

22390 ■ *"'No Snitch' Culture in American Business" in Business Owner (Vol. 35, September-October 2011, No. 5, pp. 7)*
Pub: DL Perkins Company

Description: It is important to make known the fact that a businessman is performing unethical or illegal activities in his firm.

22391 ■ *"Nortel Makes Customers Stars in New Campaign" in Brandweek (Vol. 49, April 21, 2008, No. 16, pp. 8)*
Pub: VNU Business Media, Inc.

Ed: Mike Beirne. **Description:** Nortel has launched a new television advertising campaign in which the business-to-business communications technology provider cast senior executives in 30-second TV case studies that show how Nortel's technology helped their businesses innovate.

22392 ■ *"Not Your Dad's Business Card' in Small Business Opportunities (July 2008)*
Pub: Entrepreneur Press
Contact: Perlman Neil, President

Ed: Rob Schlacter. **Description:** Provides tips on how to effectively design and use business cards.

22393 ■ *"Office Party Attire" in Women In Business (Vol. 61, October-November 2009, No. 5, pp. 27)*
Pub: American Business Women's Association
Ed: Leigh Elmore. **Description:** Office holiday party attire should conform to factors such as time, location, scheduled events, and other company-furnished details. Observing this guideline can help in upholding the business nature of the party. Party attendees are also encouraged to network with other attendees, while tips on how to behave during the party are also presented.

22394 ■ *"Oh, Behave!" in Entrepreneur (Vol. 36, April 2008, No. 4, pp. 87)*
Pub: Entrepreneur Media, Inc.
Ed: Gwen Moran. **Description:** Online social networks can pose awkward situations for users. These include instances such as getting a link request from someone you do not know, having a contact post embarrassing information on your site, and a contact asking you to be refer him to one of your business contacts. Tips on how to deal with these situations are discussed.

22395 ■ *"On Beyond Powerpoint: Presentations Get a Wake-Up Call" in Inc. (November 2007, pp. 58-59)*
Pub: Gruner & Jahr USA Publishing
Ed: Michael Fitzgerald. **Description:** New software that allows business presentations to be shared online are profiled, including ProfCast, audio podcasts for sales, marketing, and training; SmartDraw2008, software that creates professional graphics; Dimdim, an open-Web conferencing tool; Empressr, a hosted Web service for creating, managing, and sharing multimedia presentations; Zentation, a free tool that allows users to watch slides and a videos of presenter; Spresent, a Web-based presentation tool for remote offices or conference calls.

22396 ■ *"The One Thing You Must Get Right When Building a Brand" in Harvard Business Review (Vol. 88, December 2010, No. 12, pp. 80)*
Pub: Harvard Business School Publishing
Ed: Patrick Barwise, Sean Meehan. **Description:** Four uses for new media include: communicating a clearly defined customer promise, creating trust via delivering on the promise, regularly improving on the promise, and innovating past what is familiar.

22397 ■ *"Online Postings Really Influence Older Women" in Marketing to Women (Vol. 22, July 2009, No. 7, pp. 8)*
Pub: EPM Communications Inc.
Contact: Ira Mayer, President
E-mail: imayer@epmcom.com
Description: Women over the age of 55 are more likely to be swayed to purchase a product by referrals from others, including Online postings by strangers. Another key influence is associated with the brand's ability to address their lifestyle needs.

22398 ■ *Open Source Solutions for Small Business Problems*
Pub: Charles River Media
Ed: John Locke. **Released:** May 2004. **Price:** $35.95. **Description:** Open source software provides solutions to many small business problems such as tracking electronic documents, scheduling, accounting functions, managing contact lists, and reducing spam.

22399 ■ *The Orange Revolution*
Pub: Free Press
Ed: Adrian Gostick, Chester Elton. **Released:** September 21, 2010. **Price:** $25.00. **Description:** Based on a 350,000-person study by the Best Companies Group, as well as research into exceptional teams at leading companies, including Zappos.com, Pepsi Beverages Company, and Madison Square Garden, the authors have determined a key set of characteristics displayed by members of breakthrough teams, and have identified a set of rules great teams live by, which generate a culture of positive teamwork and led to extraordinary results. Using specific stories from the teams they studied, they reveal in detail how these teams operate and how managers can

transform their own teams into such high performers by fostering: stronger clarity of goals, greater trust among team members, more open and honest dialogue, stronger accountability for all team members, and purpose-based recognition of team member contributions.

22400 ■ *"Ordering Pizza Hut From Your Facebook Page?" in Advertising Age (Vol. 79, November 10, 2008, No. 42, pp. 50)*
Pub: Crain Communications, Inc.
Ed: Emily Bryson York. **Description:** Fast-food chains are experimenting with delivery/takeout services via social networks such as Facebook and iPhone applications. This also allows the chains to build valuable databases of their customers.

22401 ■ *"OtherInbox Ready for Revenue: Software Startup Expects Profits in '09" in Austin Business JournalInc. (Vol. 28, January 2, 2009)*
Pub: American City Business Journals
Ed: Christopher Calnan. **Description:** Founder of Austin, Texas-based OtherBox Inc. expects the company to generate revenue through subscriptions and advertising and also reach profitability in 2009. The company's email management tool sends secondary mail to an alternate location thereby freeing up the work inbox for more urgent messages.

22402 ■ *"Our Gadget of the Week: Business Buddy" in Barron's (Vol. 88, July 7, 2008, No. 27, pp. 26)*
Pub: Dow Jones & Co., Inc.
Ed: Jay Palmer. **Description:** Review and evaluation of the Lenovo X300 laptop computer which offers executives a variety of features despite its smaller size and weight. The laptop is about 0.73 inch thick, comes with a 64-gigabyte solid-state drive from Samsung, and weighs less than three pounds.

22403 ■ *"Our Gadget of the Week: Mostly, I Liked It" in Barron's (Vol. 88, July 14, 2008, No. 28, pp. 31)*
Pub: Dow Jones & Co., Inc.
Ed: Jay Palmer. **Description:** Review of the Apple iPhone 3G, which costs $199, has better audio and is slightly thicker than its predecessor; using the 3G wireless connection makes going online faster but drains the battery faster too.

22404 ■ *Outsourcing: Information Technology, Original Equipment Manufacturer, Leo, Oursourcing, Offshoring Research Network, Crowdsourcing*
Pub: General Books LLC
Released: May 1, 2010. **Price:** $14.14. **Description:** Chapters include information for outsourcing firms and how to maintain an outsourcing business.

22405 ■ *The Owners Manual for Small Business*
Pub: Planning Shop
Ed: Rhonda Abrams. **Released:** December 2005. **Price:** $19.95. **Description:** Reference book offering tips for starting a small business, low-cost marketing, and communicating effectively.

22406 ■ *"PDAs Are Great - As Long As You Can Find Them" in Crain's Chicago Business (Vol. 31, May 5, 2008, No. 18, pp. 41)*
Pub: Crain Communications, Inc.
Ed: Jennifer Olvera. **Description:** Discusses a new service from Global Lost & Found Inc. in which after paying a one-time fee, customers receive a label with an identification number and a toll free phone number so if they lose a gadget such as a cell phone, PDA or laptop the finder can return the device and are rewarded with a gift card.

22407 ■ *"People Often Trust Eloquence More Than Honesty" in Harvard Business Review (Vol. 88, November 2010, No. 11, pp. 36)*
Pub: Harvard Business School Publishing
Ed: Todd Rogers, Michael I. Norton. **Description:** The article shows how deftly side-stepping a question in an eloquent manner generates a more posi-

tive response in an audience than does a direct answer that is ineffectively delivered. Implications for both politics and business are discussed.

22408 ■ *Persuasive Business Proposals*
Pub: AMACOM
Ed: Tom Sant. **Released:** December 2003. **Price:** $17.95. **Description:** Writing to win more customers, clients, and contracts.

22409 ■ *"Pet-Food Industry Too Slow" in Advertising Age (Vol. 78, March 26, 2007, No. 13, pp. 29)*
Pub: Crain Communications, Inc.
Description: Many crisis-communications experts believe that the pet-food industry mishandled the problem by waiting almost a month to recall the 60 million 'wet-food' products after numerous consumer complaints. Experts site that the first 24 to 49 hours are the most important in dealing with a crisis of this nature.

22410 ■ *"Pioneering Strategies for Entrepreneurial Success" in Business Horizons (Vol. 51, January-February 2008, No. 1, pp. 21)*
Pub: Elsevier Advanced Technology Publications
Ed: Candida G. Brush. **Description:** Entrepreneurs are known for new products, services, processes, markets and industries. In order to achieve success, they have to develop a clear vision, creatively manage finances, and use social skills to persuade others to commit to the venture. Pioneering strategies and their implementation are examined.

22411 ■ *The Power of Body Language*
Pub: Simon and Schuster Inc.
Contact: Carolyn Reidy, President
E-mail: carolyn.reidy@simonandschuster.com
Ed: Tonya Reiman. **Released:** 2008. **Price:** $15.00. **Description:** Body language expert describes the hidden meaning behind specific gestures, facial cues, stances, and body movements to help anyone communicate in business.

22412 ■ *The Power of Nice: How to Conquer the Business World with Kindness*
Pub: Doubleday
Ed: Linda Kaplan Thaler; Robin Koval. **Released:** September 19, 2006. **Price:** $17.95. **Description:** The key principles to running a business through thoughtfulness and kindness are exhibited with the use of success stories.

22413 ■ *The Power of a Positive No: How to Say No and Still Get to Yes*
Pub: Random Housing Publishing Group
Ed: William Ury. **Released:** December 2007. **Price:** $16.00. **Description:** According to the author, a positive no begins with yes and ends with yes.

22414 ■ *PPC's Guide to Small Business Consulting Engagements*
Pub: Practitioners Publishing Company
Released: March 2004. **Price:** $226.00. **Description:** Technical guide for conducting consulting engagements for small business.

22415 ■ *"Pressed for Time" in Marketing to Women (Vol. 21, March 2008, No. 3, pp. 1)*
Pub: EPM Communications Inc.
Contact: Ira Mayer, President
E-mail: imayer@epmcom.com
Description: Statistical data concerning the tools women use for time management which include gadgets as well as traditional media such as calendars.

22416 ■ *"Rapport Overhaul" in Small Business Opportunities (Winter 2009)*
Pub: Entrepreneur Press
Contact: Perlman Neil, President
Ed: Laurie Brown. **Description:** Advice concerning ways in which to build customer rapport is provided.

22417 ■ *Reading Financial Reports for Dummies*

Pub: John Wiley and Sons, Inc.

Ed: Lita Epstein. **Released:** January 2009. **Price:** $21.99. **Description:** This second edition contains more new and updated information, including new information on the separate accounting and financial reporting standards for private/small businesses versus public/large businesses; updated information reflecting 2007 laws on international financial reporting standards; new content to match SEC and other governmental regulatory changes over the last three years; new information about how the analyst-corporate connection has changed the playing field; the impact of corporate communications and new technologies; new examples that reflect the current trends; and updated Websites and resources.

22418 ■ *"Real-Time Computer-Mediated Communication" in Business Communication Quarterly (December 2007, pp. 466)*

Pub: SAGE Publications USA

Contact: Blaise R. Simqu, President

Ed: Amy Newman. **Description:** Technology-based simulation for business students to respond to emails and instant messages is presented. The simulation allows students to handle volume business correspondence at work with organizational context and under real-word business situations.

22419 ■ *"Reinventing Your Rep Training Program" in Agency Sales Magazine (Vol. 39, August 2009, No. 8, pp. 40)*

Pub: MANA

Description: Tips on how to encourage manufacturer's representatives to attend scheduled training sessions are given. Manufacturers should learn the value of keeping the training program up-to-date and communicate with the sales team to know what needs to be revamped. Problems faced by representatives with inside sales staff should also be addressed by the manufacturer.

22420 ■ *"Relationship "Farming" Tools" in Agency Sales Magazine (Vol. 39, August 2009, No. 8, pp. 46)*

Pub: MANA

Ed: Terry L. Brock. **Description:** Manufacturer's representatives should spend time, money and effort in establishing and maintaining relationships; one tool to help is the new Fujitsu S1500 scanner. The scanner can accomplish critical tasks, quickly, easily and at low cost. Other suggestions to help build better business relationships are given.

22421 ■ *"Research and Markets Adds Report: The U.S. Mobile Web Market" in Entertainment Close-Up (December 10, 2009)*

Pub: Close-Up Media

Description: Highlights of the new Research and Markets report 'The U.S. Mobile Web Market: Taking Advantage of the iPhone Phenomenon' include: mobile Internet marketing strategies; the growth of mobile web usage; the growth of revenue in the mobile web market; and a look at Internet business communications, social media and networking.

22422 ■ *"Rethinking the Organization" in Strategy & Leadership (Vol. 38, September-October 2010, No. 5, pp. 13-19)*

Pub: Emerald Inc.

Ed: Stephen Denning. **Description:** A study identifies the changes needed to be adopted by top managers to achieve game-changing innovation at an organization-wide level. Findings indicate that CEOs should practice pull management in order to nurture fruitful communication between employees and customers and achieve organizational involvement of customers.

22423 ■ *"Rise Interactive, Internet Marketing Agency, Now Offers Social Media Training and Advisory Services" in Internet Wire (Nov. 4, 2009)*

Pub: Comtex News Network, Inc.

Description: Profile of Rise Interactive, a full-service Internet marketing agency which has recently added social media to its list of offerings; the agency touts that its newest service gives their clients the power to have ongoing communication with current and potential customers on the sites they are most actively visiting.

22424 ■ *"The Rise of Pompei" in Retail Merchandiser (Vol. 51, September-October 2011, No. 5, pp. 13)*

Pub: Phoenix Media Corporation

Description: Soho creative consulting group follows its C3 philosophy to create an invigorated brand experience that transforms customers from consumers to empowered buyers. Pompei AD is a leading creative consultancy that specializes in design and branding for retail, museum, hospitality, and other sectors.

22425 ■ *"Rule of Thumb" in Entrepreneur (Vol. 36, May 2008, No. 5, pp. 44)*

Pub: Entrepreneur Media, Inc.

Ed: Guy Kawasaki. **Description:** Business presentations using PowerPoint are recommended to have no more than 10 slides, last no longer than 20 minutes and have font no smaller than 30 points. Topics covered should include problem, solution, business model, underlying technology, and projections among others.

22426 ■ *"Rumor Has It" in Entrepreneur (Vol. 35, October 2007, No. 10, pp. 30)*

Pub: Entrepreneur Media Inc.

Ed: Chris Penttila. **Description:** Some entrepreneurs like Ren Moulton and Dan Scudder regard rumor sites and product blogs as great sources of market research. However, there are legal issues that must be studied before using these Internet sites in marketing and product development. The use and limitations of rumor sites and product blogs are provided.

22427 ■ *"The Rypple Effect; Performance Management" in The Economist (Vol. 390, January 3, 2009, No. 8612, pp. 48)*

Pub: The Economist Newspaper Inc.

Description: New companies such as Rypple, a new, web-based service, claim that they can satisfy the Net Generation's need for frequent assessments while easing the burden this creates for management.

22428 ■ *"Sales Communications in a Mobile World" in Business Communication Quarterly (December 2007, pp. 492)*

Pub: SAGE Publications USA

Contact: Blaise R. Simqu, President

Ed: Daniel T. Norris. **Description:** Salespeople can take advantage of the latest mobile technologies while maintaining a personal touch with clients and customers through innovation, formality in interactions, client interactions, and protection and security of mobile data.

22429 ■ *"Saving Face Time" in Canadian Business (Vol. 81, December 8, 2008, No. 21, pp. 21)*

Pub: Rogers Media Ltd.

Ed: Calvin Leung. **Description:** Landing business deals in China requires fostering informal relationships as well as avoiding offensive gestures. Canadians planning to do business in China should be aware of the Chinese concept of 'face'. Other tips for doing business in China are listed.

22430 ■ *The Savvy Gal's Guide to Online Networking*

Pub: Booklocker.com Inc.

Ed: Diane K. Danielson, Lindsey Pollak. **Released:** August 10, 2007. **Price:** $14.95. **Description:** It is a truth universally acknowledged that a woman in search of a fabulous career must be in want of networking opportunities. Or so Jane Austen would say if she were writing, or more likely, blogging today. So begins the must-read guide to networking in the 21st Century. Authors and networking experts share the nuts, bolts and savvy secrets that businesswomen need in order to use technology to build professional relationships.

22431 ■ *The Savvy Girl's Guide to Online Networking*

Pub: Booklocker.com Inc.

Ed: Diane K. Danielson; Lindsey Pollak. **Released:** August 10, 2007. **Price:** $14.95. **Description:** The book offers tips, tactics and etiquette for business-women wishing to build professional relationships via email, online networks, blogs, and message boards.

22432 ■ *Say Everything: How Blogging Began, What It's Becoming, and Why It Matters*

Pub: Crown Business

Ed: Scott Rosenberg. **Released:** 2009. **Price:** $26.00. **Description:** A history of Internet blogs that explains how they started and why they matter to any small business.

22433 ■ *"Say Goodbye to Shy" in Canadian Business (Vol. 79, September 11, 2006, No. 18, pp. 125)*

Pub: Rogers Media

Ed: Alex Mlynek. **Description:** Tips and practices for effective communications at workplaces are presented.

22434 ■ *"Say Goodbye to Voicemail" in Agency Sales Magazine (Vol. 39, November 2009, No. 10, pp. 3)*

Pub: MANA

Description: Salespeople should think twice before leaving a voicemail. The emerging modern etiquette is to send a text message or to e-mail the customer or client. Communication suggestions for both salespeople and their principals are presented.

22435 ■ *"Scientific American Builds Novel Blog Network" in Information Today (Vol. 28, September 2011, No. 8, pp. 12)*

Pub: Information Today, Inc.

Ed: Kurt Schiller. **Description:** Scientific American launched a new blog network that joins a diverse lineup of bloggers cover various scientific topics under one banner. The blog network includes 60 bloggers providing insights into the ever-changing world of science and technology.

22436 ■ *"The Secret Strategy for Meaningful Sales Meetings" in Agency Sales Magazine (Vol. 39, December 2009, No. 11, pp. 40)*

Pub: MANA

Ed: Dave Kahle. **Description:** Sales meetings can be made more meaningful by focusing on the end results that the meeting seeks to achieve. Describing the changed behavior that is sought from the sales force and working backwards from there also help make a sales meeting more meaningful.

22437 ■ *"Secrets To Trade Show Success" in Women Entrepreneur (September 12, 2008)*

Pub: Entrepreneur Media Inc.

Ed: Lesley Spencer Pyle. **Description:** Trade shows require an enormous amount of work, but they are an investment that can pay off handsomely because they allow a business to get their product or service in front of their target market. Advice regarding trade shows is given including selecting the correct venue, researching the affair and following up on leads obtained at the event.

22438 ■ *"Shoestring-Budget Marketing" in Women Entrepreneur (January 5, 2009)*

Pub: Entrepreneur Media Inc.

Ed: Maria Falconer. **Description:** Pay-per-click search engine advertising is the traditional type of e-marketing that may not only be too expensive for certain kinds of businesses but also may not attract the quality customer base a business looking to grow needs to find. Social networking websites have become a mandatory marketing tool for business owners who want to see growth in their sales; tips are provided for utilizing these networking websites in order to gain more visibility on the Internet which can, in turn, lead to the more sales.

22439 ■ *"The Simon Cowell of Sales" in Inc. (March 2008, pp. 81-82)*

Pub: Gruner & Jahr USA Publishing

Ed: Norm Brodsky. **Description:** Successful selling tips to help anyone trying to close a deal are examined.

22440 ■ *"Six Tips To Maximize Networking Opportunities"* in *Women Entrepreneur (November 3, 2008)*
Pub: Entrepreneur Media Inc.
Ed: Tamara Monosoff. **Description:** Networking events fall into the realm of business development as opposed to immediate sales opportunities. It is important to remember that these events provide a chance to build relationships that may someday help one's business. Tips to help make the most out of networking events are provided.

22441 ■ *"Size Matters"* in *Entrepreneur (Vol. 36, April 2008, No. 4, pp. 44)*
Pub: Entrepreneur Media, Inc.
Ed: Robert Kiyosaki. **Description:** Entrepreneurs planning to expand their business face challenges when it comes to employing more people and addressing internal relationships, communications and procedures. People skills, organizational skills and leadership skills are some of the things to consider before adding employees.

22442 ■ *"Slow but Steady into the Future"* in *Barron's (Vol. 88, July 7, 2008, No. 27, pp. M)*
Pub: Dow Jones & Co., Inc.
Ed: Mark Veverka. **Description:** Investors are advised to maintain their watch on the shares of business software company NetSuite. The company's chief executive officer, Zach Nelson, claims that the company has a 10-year lead on its competitors with the development of software-as-a service.

22443 ■ *The Social Media Bible: Tactics, Tools, and Strategies for Business Success*
Pub: John Wiley & Sons, Inc.
Ed: Lon Safko, David Brake. **Released:** June 17, 2009. **Price:** $29.95. **Description:** Information is given to build or transform a business into social media, where customers, employees, and prospects connect, collaborate, and champion products and services in order to increase sales and to beat the competition.

22444 ■ *"Social Media: Communicate the Important Stuff"* in *Agency Sales Magazine (Vol. 39, November 2009, No. 10, pp. 52)*
Pub: MANA
Ed: Jack Foster. **Description:** Social media such as Twitter or Facebook allows businesses to communicate with their customers over great distances but this technology can take away from the personal touch. For those that want to implement these tools in their marketing plans, they should first find out which social media networks their target audience use and give their customers reasons to become fans.

22445 ■ *"Social Media, E-Mail Remain Challenging for Employees"* in *Workforce Management (Vol. 88, December 14, 2009, No. 13, pp. 4)*
Pub: Crain Communications Inc.
Ed: Ed Frauenheim. **Description:** Examining the impact of Internet social networking and the workplace; due to the power of these new technologies, it is important that companies begin to set clear policies regarding Internet use and employee privacy.

22446 ■ *"Social Networkers for Hire"* in *Black Enterprise (Vol. 40, December 2009, No. 5, pp. 56)*
Pub: Earl G. Graves Publishing Co., Inc.
Ed: Brittany Hutson. **Description:** Companies are utilizing social networking sites in order to market their brand and personally connect with consumers and are increasingly looking to social media specialists to help with this task. Aliya S. King is one such web strategist, working for ICED Media by managing their Twitter, Facebook, YouTube and Flickr accounts for one of their publicly traded restaurant clients.

22447 ■ *"Social Networking Butterfly"* in *Entrepreneur (Vol. 37, September 2009, No. 9, pp. 48)*
Pub: Entrepreneur Media, Inc.
Ed: Jason Daley. **Description:** Entrepreneur Ashley Qualls has successfully grown Whateverlife.com. The site was originally created to share Qualls' custom MySpace.com templates with friends and family. Qualls is planning to redesign the site as a social network focused on Web design.

22448 ■ *"Social Networking Site for Moms"* in *Marketing to Women (Vol. 21, March 2008, No. 3, pp. 3)*
Pub: EPM Communications Inc.
Contact: Ira Mayer, President
E-mail: imayer@epmcom.com
Description: The Cradle is a social networking site devoted to pregnancy and new parenthood.

22449 ■ *"Social Networks in the Workplace"* in *Strategy & Leadership (Vol. 38, July-August 2010, No. 4, pp. 50-53)*
Pub: Emerald Inc.
Ed: Daniel Burrus. **Description:** The opinions of futurist Daniel Burrus on a novel trend called 'Business 2.0', which involves the use of social networking applications as business tools, are presented. His suggestion that personal social networking technology can be used by businesses to improve collaboration, problem solving, and leadership communications to achieve continuous value innovation is discussed.

22450 ■ *"Sometimes, Second Impressions Count Most"* in *Canadian Business (Vol. 83, October 12, 2010, No. 17, pp. 11)*
Pub: Rogers Media Ltd.
Ed: Richard Branson. **Description:** Developing a favorable impression at the first point of contact is imperative for businesses. Managers who want their organizations to make positive first and second impressions need to learn to balance the Web's labor-saving efficiencies with human assistants. The importance of considering the customer relations value in company Websites is also explained.

22451 ■ *"Sound Check"* in *Agency Sales Magazine (Vol. 39, August 2009, No. 8, pp. 14)*
Pub: MANA
Ed: Dave Kahle. **Description:** Most customers believe salespersons are unable to do well in terms of listening, which is one of the four fundamental competencies of a sales person. Listening is the primary tool to uncover deeper and more powerful needs and motivations of the customer. A guide on how to listen better and improve listening effectiveness is presented.

22452 ■ *"Speak Better: Five Tips for Polished Presentations"* in *Women Entrepreneur (September 19, 2008)*
Pub: Entrepreneur Media Inc.
Ed: Suzannah Baum. **Description:** Successful entrepreneurs agree that exemplary public speaking skills are among the core techniques needed to propel their business forward. A well-delivered presentation can result in securing a new distribution channel, gaining new customers, locking into a new referral stream or receiving extra funding.

22453 ■ *The Speed of Trust*
Pub: Simon and Schuster Inc.
Contact: Carolyn Reidy, President
E-mail: carolyn.reidy@simonandschuster.com
Ed: Stephen M.R. Covey with Rebecca R. Merrill. **Description:** Advice is given to help cultivate trust in business, politics and personal relationships.

22454 ■ *"Spell It Out"* in *Entrepreneur (Vol. 36, April 2008, No. 4, pp. 123)*
Pub: Entrepreneur Media, Inc.
Ed: Emily Weisberg. **Description:** IM:It is an apparel and accessories company that markets products with instant messaging (IM) acronyms and emoticons. Examples of these are 'LOL' and 'GTG'. Other details on IM:It products are discussed.

22455 ■ *Start Your Own Blogging Business, Second Edition*
Pub: Entrepreneur Press
Contact: Perlman Neil, President
Released: July 1, 2010. **Price:** $17.95. **Description:** Interviews with professional bloggers from some of the most popular blogs on the Internet will help anyone interested in starting their own blogging business.

22456 ■ *"Staying Engaged"* in *Black Enterprise (Vol. 38, February 2008, No. 7, pp. 64)*
Pub: Earl G. Graves Publishing Co. Inc.
Ed: Sonia Alleyne. **Description:** Rules to help business leaders construct networking contacts in order to maximize professional success are outlined.

22457 ■ *"Study: Instant Messaging Can Benefit Workplaces"* in *HRMagazine (Vol. 53, August 2008, No. 8, pp. 20)*
Pub: Society for Human Resource Management
Contact: Henry G. Jackson, President
E-mail: hjackson@shrm.org
Description: Using text messaging at work is less, not more disruptive, even as it promotes more frequent communication, according to a study published in the Journal of Compute-Mediated Communication.

22458 ■ *"Stylish Successes"* in *Women In Business (Vol. 61, October-November 2009, No. 5, pp. 12)*
Pub: American Business Women's Association
Ed: Leigh Elmore; Megan L. Reese. **Description:** Amanda Horan Kennedy, Angela Samuels, Barbara Nast Saletan, and Patty Nast Canton are career women who ventured into entrepreneurship. They are deemed to possess networking and teamwork skills that ensured their success in the garment industry.

22459 ■ *"Sunbrella Engages Consumers Via Social Media"* in *Home Textiles Today (Vol. 31, May 24, 2011, No. 13, pp. 4)*
Pub: Reed Business Information
Contact: Jeff Greisch, President
Description: Performance fabric brand Sunbrella is marketing to social media, such as Facebook and Twitter, in order to boost consumer interest and retailer support.

22460 ■ *Table Talk: The Savvy Girl's Alternative to Networking*
Pub: AuthorHouse
Ed: Diane Danielson. **Released:** April 1, 2003. **Price:** $17.50. **Description:** Let's face it. Women and men are different. So why should we all have to network in the same way? And, why should women have to 'network' at all? Between family and work responsibilities, the idea of pressing flesh at some not-very-festive cocktail party is right up there in appeal with a root canal. But what if women could find a way to make career boosting connections that are actually fun? Enter 'table talk', a new way to network for time-pressed, professional women.

22461 ■ *"Team Bonding for Fun and Profit"* in *Women Entrepreneur (December 3, 2008)*
Pub: Entrepreneur Media Inc.
Ed: Eve Gumpel. **Description:** Discusses the benefits that competitions such as the 2008 BG U.S. Challenge in Lake Placid, New York, can offer in terms of team building and employee motivation as well as networking and the development of a positive working relationship with partners and competitors alike.

22462 ■ *"Tired of PowerPoint? Try This Instead"* in *Harvard Business Review (Vol. 88, September 2010, No. 9, pp. 30)*
Pub: Harvard Business School Publishing
Ed: Daniel McGinn, Stephanie Crowley. **Description:** Usefulness of graphic recording, also known as storyboarding or visual facilitation, during client meetings is illustrated.

22463 ■ *"Top IPhone Apps"* in *Advertising Age (Vol. 79, December 15, 2008, No. 46, pp. 17)*
Pub: Crain Communications, Inc.
Ed: Marissa Miley. **Description:** Free and low cost applications for the iPhone are described including Evernote, an application that allows users to outsource their memory to keep track of events, notes, ides and more; Handshake, a way for users to exchange business cards and pictures across Wi-Fi and 3G; CityTransit, an interactive map of the New York subway system that uses GPS technology to

find nearby stations and also tells the user if a train is out of commission that day; and Stage Hand which allows users to deliver a presentation, control timing and slide order on the spot.

22464 ■ *"The Top Mistakes of Social Media Marketing" in Agency Sales Magazine (Vol. 39, November 2009, No. 9, pp. 42)*
Pub: MANA
Ed: Pam Lontos; Maurice Ramirez. **Description:** One common mistake in social media marketing is having more than one image on the Internet because this ruins a business' credibility. Marketers need to put out messages that are useful to their readers and to keep messages consistent.

22465 ■ *"Tracking Your Fleet Can Increase Bottom Line" in Contractor (Vol. 56, November 2009, No. 11, pp. 26)*
Pub: Penton Media, Inc.
Ed: Candace Roulo. **Description:** GPS fleet management system can help boost a contractor's profits, employee productivity, and efficiency. These are available as a handheld device or a cell phone that employees carry around or as a piece of hardware installed in a vehicle. These lets managers track assets and communicate with employees about jobs.

22466 ■ *"Traits that Makes Blogs Attractive to Book Publishers" in Marketing to Women (Vol. 22, July 2009, No. 7, pp. 1)*
Pub: EPM Communications Inc.
Contact: Ira Mayer, President
E-mail: imayer@epmcom.com
Description: Book publishers are finding a beneficial relationship between themselves and women bloggers on the Internet. A high visitor count, frequent updates and active readership are criteria for identifying the blogs with the most clout and therefore providing the greatest benefit to publishers.

22467 ■ *"The Twittering Class" in Entrepreneur (Vol. 37, September 2009, No. 9, pp. 40)*
Pub: Entrepreneur Media, Inc.
Ed: Mikal E. Belicove. **Description:** Advice on how entrepreneurs can use online social networks to promote their businesses is presented. Facebook offers applications and advertising solutions to promote Websites, products and services. Twitter, on the other hand, provides instant messaging, which can be done through computer or cell phone.

22468 ■ *Twitterville: How Businesses Can Thrive in the New Global Neighborhoods*
Pub: Portfolio Hardcover
Ed: Shel Israel. **Price:** $23.95. **Description:** Twitter is the most rapidly adopted communication tool in history, going from zero to ten million users in just over two years. On Twitter, word can spread faster than wildfire. Companies no longer have the option of ignoring the conversation. Unlike other hot social media spaces, Twitterville is dominated by professionals, not students. And despite its size, it still feels like a small town. Twitter allows people to interact much the way they do face-to-face, honestly and authentically.

22469 ■ *"Understanding Persuasive Online Sales Messages from eBay Auctions" in Business Communication Quarterly (December 2007, pp. 482)*
Pub: SAGE Publications USA
Contact: Blaise R. Simqu, President
Ed: Barbara Jo White, Daniel Clapper, Rita Noel, Jenny Fortier, Pierre Grabolosa. **Description:** eBay product listings were studied to determine the requirements of persuasive sales writing. Potential sellers should use the proper keywords and make an authentic description with authentic photographs of the item being auctioned.

22470 ■ *"Urban Tree Service" in New Hampshire Business Review (Vol. 33, March 25, 2011, No. 6, pp. 35)*
Pub: Business Publications Inc.
Description: Urban Tree Service received the Professional Communications Award from the Tree Care Industry Association for excellence in marketing and communications.

22471 ■ *"Use Common Sense in Office Gift-Giving" in Women In Business (Vol. 61, October-November 2009, No. 5, pp. 32)*
Pub: American Business Women's Association
Ed: Maureen Sullivan. **Description:** Tips on office gift-giving during the Christmas season are discussed. Aside from ensuring appropriateness of the gift with respect to the recipient, a fixed giving budget must be adhered to. Gifts that can be used by anyone may be selected and those with religious overtones must be avoided.

22472 ■ *"Use Social Media to Enhance Brand, Business" in Contractor (Vol. 56, December 2009, No. 12, pp. 14)*
Pub: Penton Media, Inc.
Ed: Elton Rivas. **Description:** Advice on how plumbing contractors should use online social networks to increase sales is presented including such issues as clearly defining goals and target audience. An additional advantage to this medium is that advertisements can easily be shared with other users.

22473 ■ *"Using Teaching Teams to Encourage Active Learning" in Business Communication Quarterly (December 2007, pp. 457)*
Pub: SAGE Publications USA
Contact: Blaise R. Simqu, President
Ed: Lisa E. Gueldenzoph. **Description:** The practice of dividing classes into teaching teams to encourage active learning is studied. Students in business management courses become more involved in the learning process with this technique and collaborate to enhance better understanding of course content.

22474 ■ *"The Value of Conversations With Employees; Talk Isn't Cheap" in Gallup Management Journal (June 30, 2011)*
Pub: Gallup
Ed: Jessica Tyler. **Description:** When managers have meaningful exchanges with their employees, they don't only show they care, they also add value to their organization's bottom line.

22475 ■ *"Vistaprint Survey Indicates that Online Marketing Taking Hold Among Small Businesses" in Internet Wire (December 10, 2009)*
Pub: Comtex News Network, Inc.
Description: According to a comprehensive survey from Vistaprint N.V., small businesses are very likely to increase their use of Internet marketing strategies such as paid and organic search, email marketing, social media networking and custom websites over the next year. Trends continue to show that more small businesses are indeed adapting to the changing marketplace and are more willing to diversify their marketing strategies than ever before.

22476 ■ *"Wait a Minute!" in Entrepreneur (Vol. 37, September 2009, No. 9, pp. 76)*
Pub: Entrepreneur Media, Inc.
Ed: Jennifer Wang. **Description:** Advice on how entrepreneurs in the United States should secure funding in view of the economic crisis is presented. Enough interest should be stimulated so as to secure a follow-up meeting. Investors should be asked questions that would encourage them to tell stories related to the downturn.

22477 ■ *"We Move Forward as a Team" in Women In Business (Vol. 61, December 2009, No. 6, pp. 6)*
Pub: American Business Women's Association
Ed: Rene Street. **Description:** Based on her experiences in ABWA's National Board of Directors retreat, an executive director of the American Business Women's Association, shares her belief that interaction is necessary for a successful business enterprise. She believes that the problems presented in the retreat's team-building exercises are similar to challenges which are faced in ABWA, in the workplace, and in the marketplace.

22478 ■ *"The Web Gets Real" in Canadian Business (Vol. 79, July 17, 2006, No. 14-15, pp. 19)*
Pub: Rogers Media
Ed: Andrew Wahl. **Description:** Ron Lake's efforts of bringing the virtual and physical worlds more closely

together by using Geographic Markup Language (GML) are presented.

22479 ■ *What Men Don't Tell Woman about Business: Opening Up the Heavily Guarded Alpha Male Playbook*
Pub: John Wiley and Sons, Inc.
Ed: Christopher V. Fleet. **Released:** October 26, 2007. **Description:** Valuable guide for any woman in business, this book helps reveal everything a woman needs to know in order to understand, communicate, and compete with men in business.

22480 ■ *"What's In Your Toolbox" in Women In Business (Vol. 61, August-September 2009, No. 4, pp. 7)*
Pub: American Business Women's Association
Ed: Mimi Kopulos. **Description:** Business owners are increasingly turning to using social networking websites, such as Facebook, LinkedIn and Twitter, to promote their companies. The number of adult social media users has increased from 8 percent in 2005 to 35 percent in 2009.

22481 ■ *"What's Your Social Media Strategy?" in Black Enterprise (Vol. 41, November 2010, No. 4, pp. 75)*
Pub: Earl G. Graves Publishing Co. Inc.
Ed: Denise Campbell. **Description:** Advice for using social media sites such as Twitter, Facebook and LinkedIn as a professional networking tool is given.

22482 ■ *When Family Businesses are Best*
Pub: Palgrave Macmillan
Ed: Randel S. Carlock, John L. Ward. **Released:** March 1, 2010. **Price:** $45.00. **Description:** An exploration into effective planning and communication to help small businesses grow into multi-generation family enterprises.

22483 ■ *"When Good Deals Go Bad: How to Renegotiate a Contract" in Inc. (November 2007, pp. 33-34)*
Pub: Gruner & Jahr USA Publishing
Ed: Dee Gill. **Description:** Ways to renegotiate contracts are discussed. Robb Corwin of Gorilla Fuel discusses how he was able to renegotiate contracts in order to save his business.

22484 ■ *"Why LinkedIn is the Social Network that Will Never Die" in Advertising Age (Vol. 81, December 6, 2010, No. 43, pp. 2)*
Pub: Crain Communications, Inc.
Ed: Irina Slutsky. **Description:** Despite the popularity of Facebook, LinkIn in will always be a source for professionals who wish to network.

22485 ■ *"Why Mumbai at 1PM is the Center of the Business World" in Harvard Business Review (Vol. 88, October 2010, No. 10, pp. 38)*
Pub: Harvard Business School Publishing
Ed: Michael Segalla. **Description:** A time zone chart is presented for assisting in the planning of international conference calls.

22486 ■ *"Why Women Blog and What They Read" in Marketing to Women (Vol. 22, July 2009, No. 7, pp. 8)*
Pub: EPM Communications Inc.
Contact: Ira Mayer, President
E-mail: imayer@epmcom.com
Description: Listing of topics that are visited the most by female Internet users. Statistical data included.

22487 ■ *"Wi-Fi Finds Its Way Despite Nixed Plan for Free System" in Crain's Cleveland Business (Vol. 28, November 12, 2007, No. 45, pp. 3)*
Pub: Crain Communications, Inc.
Ed: Jay Miller. **Description:** Discusses the issues facing Cleveland and Northeast Ohio concerning their proposal to offer citizens wireless Internet services for free or a small fee.

22488 ■ *"The Wiki-Powered Workplace" in Workforce Management (Vol. 88, November 16, 2009, No. 12, pp. 8)*
Pub: Crain Communications Inc.
Description: Many organizations are successfully using wikis inside the corporate structure for business communications and knowledge sharing. Wikis can be a very powerful tool due to the inherent transparency that comes with allowing everything to be edited with the accountability of seeing who is doing the editing. A brilliant employee may be noticed sooner because they are doing work in the wiki and the work is being judged on its own merit.

22489 ■ *"Windstream Expands Business Service Into Monroe" in Marketing Weekly News (January 23, 2010, pp. 77)*
Pub: Investment Weekly News
Description: Windstream Corp. announces the expansion of its data and voice services into Monroe, N.C., which will give local businesses a new choice for advanced communication services and network security.

22490 ■ *"Wise Guy: Get In Good" in Entrepreneur (Vol. 35, October 2007, No. 10, pp. 46)*
Pub: Entrepreneur Media Inc.
Ed: Guy Kawasaki. **Description:** Good public relations are a requirement for business entrepreneurs, and it can be achieved through proper communication. Giving of and asking for favors are some of the ways to build relationships in the business world. Other tips on how to build good business relationships are provided.

22491 ■ *"Words at Work" in Information Today (Vol. 26, February 2009, No. 2, pp. 25)*
Pub: Information Today, Inc.
Description: Current new buzzwords include the following: digital amnesia, or overload by availability, speed and volume of digital information; maternal profiling, a form a discrimination against women; recipe malpractice, a reminder that just because you can turn on a stove it doesn't make you a chef; ringxiety, the act when everyone reaches for their cell phone when one rings; verbing, the practice of turning good nouns into verbs.

22492 ■ *"Work Smarter" in Entrepreneur (Vol. 36, April 2008, No. 4, pp. 70)*
Pub: Entrepreneur Media, Inc.
Ed: Amanda C. Kooser. **Description:** Online applications that address a business' particular needs are presented. These web applications offer email services, collaboration services of sharing and editing documents and presentations, and tie-ups with online social networking sites. Details on various web applications are provided.

22493 ■ *"The Workplace Generation Gaps" in Women In Business (Vol. 62, June 2010, No. 2, pp. 8)*
Pub: American Business Women's Association
Ed: Leigh Elmore. **Description:** Generation gaps among baby boomers, Generation X and Generation Y in the workplace are attributed to technological divides and differences in opinions. These factors could lead to workplace misunderstandings, employee turnover and communication difficulties. Details on managing such workplace gaps are discussed.

22494 ■ *"Yammer Gets Serious" in Inc. (Volume 32, December 2010, No. 10, pp. 58)*
Pub: Inc. Magazine
Ed: Eric Markowitz. **Description:** Yammer, an internal social network for companies, allows coworkers to share ideas and documents in real-time. Details of this service are included.

22495 ■ *"Your First 100 Days on Your New Job" in Women In Business (Vol. 63, Spring 2011, No. 1, pp. 28)*
Pub: American Business Women's Association
Ed: Diane Stafford. **Description:** The first 100 days on the job are crucial if the person's permanent hiring is conditional on surviving a probationary period. The new hire must do more than just master the job's technical details to maximize the chance of success. Details of some basic tips to fit into the corporate culture and get along with coworkers are also discussed.

TRADE PERIODICALS

22496 ■ *Corporate Writer and Editor*
Pub: Lawrence Ragan Communications Inc.
Released: Monthly. **Price:** $209, U.S.; $239, other countries. **Description:** Presents information designed to help corporate writers and editors create successful company publications. Topics include writing, design, finding the right outside designers and freelancers, and others.

22497 ■ *The Facilitator*
Pub: Nurre Ink
Contact: Susan M. Nurre, Editor
E-mail: snurre@thefacilitator.com
Released: Quarterly. **Price:** $35, U.S.; $35, institutions; $40, out of country. **Description:** Provides articles written by facilitators that are designed to link facilitators from around the world in a forum of sharing, networking, and communicating. Includes updates on training, automated meeting tools, and resources. Recurring features include tips and techniques, a calendar of events, reports of meetings, news of educational opportunities, book reviews, and notices of publications available.

22498 ■ *The Gauge*
Pub: Delahaye Medialink
Contact: Katharine Delahaye Paine, Publisher
E-mail: kpaine@delahaye.com
Ed: William Teunis Paarlberg, Editor, wpaarlberg@aol.com. **Released:** Bimonthly. **Price:** $75. **Description:** Provides information on and evaluates marketing communications activities of companies. Recurring features include interviews, news of research, and a calendar of events.

22499 ■ *Harvard Management Communication Letter*
Pub: Harvard Business School Publishing
Ed: Nick Morgan, Editor, nmorgan@hbsp.harvard.edu. **Released:** Monthly. **Price:** $99, U.S.; $119, Canada and Mexico; $139, elsewhere; $169, two years in. **Description:** Provides information and techniques for managers on effective communication.

22500 ■ *Journal of Employee Communication Management / Reagan Report*
Pub: Lawrence Ragan Communications Inc.
Ed: David Murray, Editor, dmurrayil@earthlink.net. **Released:** Bimonthly. **Price:** $249, U.S.; $279, other countries. **Description:** Covers corporate communications issues, such as increasing retention, developing measurement tools, and addressing issues such as mergers, downsizing, and branding.

22501 ■ *The Nash & Cibinic Report*
Pub: West Group
Ed: Ralph Nash, Editor. **Released:** Monthly. **Price:** $1,706.88. **Description:** Discusses government contracts analysis and reporting. Topics include procurement management, contractor claims, and competition and awards.

22502 ■ *The Retort*
Pub: The Chemists' Club Library
Released: Bimonthly. **Description:** Highlights the Club's services and resources about chemistry and the chemical business, as well as membership news and events. Recurring features include a collection and a column titled President's Message.

22503 ■ *Women Chemists*
Pub: American Chemical Society
Contact: Thomas H. Lane, President
Ed: Teri Quinn Gray, Editor. **Released:** Semiannual. **Description:** Aims "to be leaders in attracting, developing, and promoting women in the chemical sciences." Reports on women's achievements in the chemical sciences, as well as grants available, symposiums, and current events.

VIDEOCASSETTES/ AUDIOCASSETTES

22504 ■ *Communicate!*
Axzo Press
Thomson Course Technology
25 Thomson Pl.
Boston, MA 02210
Free: 888-534-5556
Fax: (888)715-0220
Co. E-mail: customerservice@axzopress.com
URL: http://www.axzopress.com
Released: 19??. **Price:** $98. **Description:** This video helps you and your associates learn what good communication is, analyze your own communication skills, and add to your existing skills. **Availability:** VHS.

22505 ■ *Communication*
American Media, Inc.
4621 121st St.
Urbandale, IA 50323-2311
Ph: (515)224-0919
Free: 888-776-8268
Fax: (515)327-2555
Co. E-mail: custsvc@ammedia.com
URL: http://www.ammedia.com
Released: 1989. **Price:** $1485.00. **Description:** Communication, in the form of memos, phone calls, and presentations are essential to business success. **Availability:** VHS; 3/4 U.

22506 ■ *Effective Presentations: How to Make Powerhouse Presentations That Get the Results You Want*
Instructional Video
2219 C St.
Lincoln, NE 68502
Ph: (402)475-6570
Free: 800-228-0164
Fax: (402)475-6500
Co. E-mail: feedback@insvideo.com
URL: http://www.insvideo.com
Released: 19??. **Price:** $69.95. **Description:** Describes effective presentation methods, including how to understand and evaluate your listeners' expectations, how to organize your ideas and make them interesting, and how to create your own style. Includes guidebook. **Availability:** VHS.

22507 ■ *How to Deal with the Foreign Accent: Diversity on the Phone*
Excellence in Training Corp.
c/o ICON Training
804 Roosevelt St.
Polk City, IA 50226
Free: 800-609-0479
Co. E-mail: info@icontraining.com
URL: http://www.icontraining.com
Released: 1991. **Price:** $375.00. **Description:** A guide to communicating with people whose first language is other than English. **Availability:** VHS; 3/4 U; Special order formats.

22508 ■ *Introduction to Technical and Business Communication*
GPN Educational Media
1550 Executive Drive
Elgin, IL 60123
Ph: (402)472-2007
Free: 800-228-4630
Fax: (800)306-2330
Co. E-mail: askgpn@smarterville.com
URL: http://www.shopgpn.com
Released: 1983. **Price:** $300.00. **Description:** This course teaches businessmen the fundamentals of technical writing and business communication. **Availability:** VHS; 3/4 U; Special order formats.

22509 ■ *Listening Skills*
Video Arts, Inc.
c/o Aim Learning Group
8238-40 Lehigh
Morton Grove, IL 60053-2615
Free: 877-444-2230

Fax: (416)252-2155
Co. E-mail: service@aimlearninggroup.com
URL: http://www.aimlearninggroup.com
Released: 1991. **Price:** $200.00. **Description:** The skill of listening is demonstrated using clips that show how people feel when they are not listened to. **Availability:** VHS; 8 mm; 3/4 U; Special order formats.

22510 ■ *Manners at Work*
American Media, Inc.
4621 121st St.
Urbandale, IA 50323-2311
Ph: (515)224-0919
Free: 888-776-8268
Fax: (515)327-2555
Co. E-mail: custsvc@ammedia.com
URL: http://www.ammedia.com
Released: 1990. **Price:** $395.00. **Description:** The basics of corporate etiquette, including introductions, handshakes, and professional conduct, are covered. **Availability:** VHS; 3/4 U; 8 mm.

TRADE SHOWS AND CONVENTIONS

22511 ■ Alliance Texas
Showorks Inc.
1205 N. Napa St.
Spokane, WA 99202
Ph: (509)838-8755
Fax: (509)838-2838
Co. E-mail: showorks@showorksinc.com
URL: http://www.showorksinc.com
URL(s): www.allianceforbiz.com. **Price:** $140, registered before early bird date; $165, registered through early bird date; $195, Onsite. **Audience:** Buyers and contracting officers from military bases. **Principal Exhibits:** Small business procurement opportunities.

22512 ■ Association for Business Communication Annual Convention
Association for Business Communication (ABC)
PO Box 6143
Nacogdoches, TX 75962-0001
Ph: (540)231-8460
Fax: (646)349-5297
Co. E-mail: abcoffice@businesscommunication.org
URL: http://www.businesscommunication.org
Contact: Jim Dubinsky, Executive Director
URL(s): www.businesscommunication.org. **Price:** $180, Members; $220, Non-members. **Frequency:** Annual. **Audience:** College business communication teachers. **Principal Exhibits:** Books and communication technology products.

22513 ■ Texas Press Association Annual Midwinter Conference and Trade Show
Texas Press Association (TPA)
718 W 5th St.
Austin, TX 78701-2783
Ph: (512)477-6755
Fax: (512)477-6759
Co. E-mail: mikehodges@texaspress.com
URL: http://www.texaspress.com/
Contact: Michael Hodges, Executive Director
E-mail: mikehodges@texaspress.com
URL(s): www.texaspress.com. **Frequency:** Annual. **Audience:** Newspaper publishers, editors, and members of corporate communications departments. **Principal Exhibits:** Equipment, supplies, and services for newspapers and corporate communication departments.

CONSULTANTS

22514 ■ American English Academy (AEA)—American English College
111 N Atlantic Blvd., Ste. 112
Monterey Park, CA 91754
Ph: (626)457-2800

Fax: (626)457-2808
Co. E-mail: admission@aea-usa.com
URL: http://www.aea-usa.com
Contact: Charles Policky, President
Scope: Specializes in providing on-site English language and communication development for corporations and individuals. Also develops and delivers training in speaking, writing, pronunciation, grammar, and idioms with an emphasis on business communication. Offers individual, small group, intensive, and long-distance learning. Programs tailor-made for each client. **Founded:** 1983. **Telecommunication Services:** info@aec.edu.

22515 ■ Ann Welsh Communications Inc.
2510 Yonge St., Ste. 325
Toronto, ON, Canada M4H 2P7
Ph: (416)972-1930
Fax: (416)972-6494
Co. E-mail: ann@annwelsh.com
URL: http://www.annwelsh.com
Contact: Ann Welsh, President
E-mail: ann@annwelsh.com
Scope: The helping organizations and communities make and communicate wise decisions that are good for business and good for people. Our combination of change management, marketing and public relations expertise helps our clients to achieve rapid, significant and lasting change - on an individual, organizational and community level. **Founded:** 1990.

22516 ■ Beeline Learning Solutions (BLS)
14911 Quorum Dr., Ste. 120
Dallas, TX 75254
Ph: (972)813-0465
Fax: (972)386-8667
Co. E-mail: info@consultingpartners.com
URL: http://www.beeline.com
Contact: Dominic Nagy, Manager
E-mail: dominic.nagy@consultingpartners.com
Scope: Consulting firm offering technology, content, and services addressing recruitment and sourcing, talent management, and learning and performance optimization. Solutions offered include contingent workforce solutions, vendor management software, talent management solutions, recruitment process outsourcing, performance management, applicant tracking, learning management and eLearning. **Founded:** 1990. **Special Services:** Beeline®.

22517 ■ BeeWall Diversity—Beewall & Company L.L.C.
22136 Westheimer Pkwy., Ste. 313
Katy, TX 77450-8296
Ph: (281)500-6000
Fax: (281)395-6095
Co. E-mail: info@beewalldiversity.com
Contact: Stephanie Thibeaux, President
E-mail: sthibeaux@beewalldiversity.com
Scope: A diversity, organizational development, and human resource consulting and training firm. Provides services in change management, conflict resolution, emotional intelligence, and organizational development. **Founded:** 2006.

22518 ■ Blackmon Roberts Group Inc.
902 S S Florida Ave., Ste. 205
Lakeland, FL 33803
Ph: (863)802-1280
Free: 877-450-3237
Fax: (863)802-1290
Co. E-mail: dbeinformation@blackmonroberts.com
URL: http://www.blackmonroberts.com
Contact: Sylvia Blackmon Roberts, President
E-mail: sylvia@blackmonroberts.com
Scope: Technical support consultant in technical writing, planning, research, needs analysis, marketing and training, offers training programs from cultural sensitivity issues to effective listening skills. **Founded:** 1992.

22519 ■ The Bosley Group—Bosley & AssociatesThe Plain Language Group;
824 Heather Ln.
Charlotte, NC 28209-2428
Ph: (704)641-1334

Fax: (704)523-1282
Co. E-mail: info@theplainlanguagegroup.com
Contact: Deborah S. Bosley, Owner
E-mail: deborah@theplainlanguagegroup.com
Scope: Writing consultant delivering simplified communication training and documentation to corporations. Services include communication audits, document design, and business and technical writing and training.

22520 ■ Kay Britten Communications Inc.
6057 Waterview Ct.
West Bloomfield, MI 48322
Ph: (248)592-0507
Contact: A. Britten Kay, Owner
Scope: Business communication master coach and motivator. Provides marketing and public relations consulting. **Founded:** 1984.

22521 ■ Casino, Hotel & Resort Consultants L.L.C.
4825 Quality Ct., Ste. B
Las Vegas, NV 89103
Ph: (702)528-9537
Co. E-mail: info@hraba.com
URL: http://www.hraba.com
Contact: John S. Hraba, President
E-mail: jshraba@aol.com
Scope: Casino and hospitality industry consultants. Firm specializes in developing and implementing customized forecast and labor management control systems that deliver immediate, positive impact to the company's bottom line. Involved in production planning, employ surveys and communication, inventory management, business process reviews, audits, development and implementation of key management reports. **Founded:** 1989. **Seminars:** Payroll Cost Control; Effective Staff Scheduling. **Telecommunication Services:** john.hraba@hraba.com.

22522 ■ Charismedia
610 W End Ave., Ste. B1
New York, NY 10001
Ph: (212)362-6808
Fax: (212)362-6809
Co. E-mail: charismedia@earthlink.net
URL: http://www.charismedia.net
Contact: Dr. Doe Lang, President
E-mail: charismedia@earthlink.net
Scope: Offers speech and image training as well as speech writing services for effective presentation skills. Conducts workshops like anti-stage fright breathing, psychophysical exercises, transformational success imagery, face reading and body language, EMDR (Eye Movement Desensitization Re-Processing) for Permanent Trauma and Fear Removal, Bach Flower remedies, thought field therapy, cross-cultural communication, speech, voice and diction; regional and foreign accent elimination and acquisition, Positive Perception Management (P.P.M.), Ad-libbing, humor and spontaneity training, fast creative speech preparation, Neuro-Linguistic Programming and Hypnosis. **Founded:** 1974. **Publications:** "Flaunt It"; "Improve Your Sex Life"; "Phone Power"; "Train Your Voice"; "Turning Tinny, Tiny Tones To Gold"; "The New Secrets of Charisma: How to Discover and Unleash your Hidden Powers," McGraw-Hill, Jul, 1999. **Seminars:** Services for Comfortable Effective Speaking.

22523 ■ Communispond
5 Lauras Ln.
East Hampton, NY 11937-5916
Ph: (631)907-8010
Free: 800-529-5925
Fax: (631)907-8011
URL: http://www.communispond.com
Contact: Bill Rosenthal, President
Scope: Provider of comprehensive communications and sales training resources. It partners with its clients to help them reach their strategic goals. The business communication curriculum includes executive presentation skills, senior executive, speaking on paper, communicating for improved performance, interviewing skills and media skills. The Socratic sales curriculum includes Socratic selling skills, sales presentation skills, Socratic negotiating skills, communicating for improved sales performance, selling on paper, hiring the right sales person and strategic

account management. Special techniques include methods for handling confrontational situations, conferences, meetings, news briefings, media interviews, sales proposals and speaker's bureaus. **Founded:** 1969. **Publications:** "Socratic Selling Skills: The Discipline of Customer-Centered Sales"; "It's Not What You Say, But How It Sounds"; "Butt Heads With the Boss Without Getting Fired"; "Five Critical Aspects to Getting More Return from Employee Training"; "Building Your Case: Five Forms of Evidence Reps Should Use to Persuade the Doctor"; "The Full Force of Your Ideas: Mastering the Science of Persuasion". **Seminars:** Executive Presentation Skills; Persuasive Dialogue, Aug, 2008; Sales Presentation Skills; Selling by Phone; Senior Executive Presentation Skills; Write up Front on the Web; Mastering Interpersonal Communication; Call Centers: Solving Customers Problems.

22524 ■ COMsciences Inc.
4712 Admiralty Way, Ste. 870
Marina del Rey, CA 90292
Ph: (310)823-5257
Fax: (323)937-0160
Co. E-mail: info@comsciences.com
URL: http://www.comsciences.com
Contact: Dr. Jack Torobin, Chief Executive Officer
E-mail: jtorobin@comsciences.com
Scope: Offers research services to support public relations, corporate advertising, impact of new communications media, communication entertainment, and internet/web development. Also provides strategic management consulting on communications, marketing, opinion surveys, and organizational development and assessment. The company specializes in media campaigns and evaluation tools. Also conducts government sponsored and media sponsored surveys. Serves all industry sectors, especially. com, wireless telecommunications, interactive media, and consumer electronics. **Founded:** 1989. **Publications:** "Wanted: Radical Thinking," Pmg World Magazine, Mar, 2003. **Telecommunication Services:** info@imovio.com. **Special Services:** iKIT®; imovio®.

22525 ■ DDL OMNI—DDL OMNI Engineering
8260 Greensboro Dr., Ste. 600
McLean, VA 22102
Ph: (703)903-9777
Fax: (703)903-9745
Co. E-mail: info@ddlomni.com
URL: http://www.ddlomni.com
Contact: James E. Schaeffer, President
Scope: Provider of technical services. It offers defense reinvestment and technology transfer, evaluation engineering, analysis support, and software test solutions. **Founded:** 1982. **Publications:** "Configuration Management Reports"; "Functional Requirement Documents"; "Groom Reports"; "Maintenance Requirement Cards"; "Operation and Maintenance Manuals"; "Pre-Mission Check Out Procedures"; "Shipping Reports"; "TempAlt Documents"; "Training Publications". **Seminars:** Small Business Development Program; Mentor Protege Program.

22526 ■ Development Resource Consultants (DRC)
PO Box 118
Rancho Cucamonga, CA 91729
Ph: (909)902-7655
Fax: (909)476-6942
Co. E-mail: drc@gotodrc.com
URL: http://www.gotodrc.com
Contact: Jerry R. Frey, Business Manager
E-mail: jfrey@gotodrc.com
Scope: Specializes in office re-organization, employee training in office organization, communication skills, sales training and career counseling. **Founded:** 1985. **Publications:** "Institute of Management Consultants Southern California Chapter," Jan, 2006.

22527 ■ Full Voice
3217 Broadway Ave., Ste. 300
Kansas City, MO 64111
Ph: (816)941-0011
Free: 800-684-8764

Fax: (816)931-8887
Co. E-mail: info@infullvoice.com
URL: http://www.fullvoice.us
Contact: Michienne Dixon, Principal
Scope: Vocal performance training firm offering consulting services and personal training sessions in the implementation of effective vocal communication techniques for the development of business relationships and career enhancement. Formalizes a program of proven techniques into a practical method of helping individuals improve their ability to better present themselves when speaking in a professional situation. Industries served: All. **Founded:** 1992. **Publications:** "You Can Sound Like You Know What You're Saying". **Seminars:** You Can Sound Like You Know What You're Saying; The Psychology of Vocal Performance; Security. . .the Ability to Accept Change; Knowing. . .the Key to Relaxed Public Communication; The Effective Voice for Customer Service Enhancement; You Can Speak With Conviction; How To Make Yours a Championship Team; Functional English For Foreign Trade. **Special Services:** FULL VOICE™.

22528 ■ Great Western Association Management Inc.
7995 E Prentice Ave., Ste. 100
Greenwood Village, CO 80111
Ph: (303)770-2220
Fax: (303)770-1614
Co. E-mail: info83@gwami.com
URL: http://www.gwami.com
Contact: Karen M. Wojdyla, President
E-mail: kwojdyla@gwami.com
Scope: Provider of clients with products and services to effectively manage existing and startup, for- and not-for-profit organizations. Clients select from a menu of services including association development and public relations, conferences and seminars, financial management, membership communications, and governance. Expertise also includes association strategic planning, compliance, lobbying, meeting planning, fundraising, marketing and communications. Serves national, regional and state organizations. **Founded:** 1983. **Seminars:** Site selection; Creative program development; Contract negotiations; On-site conference management; Trade show management; Travel and logistics.

22529 ■ The Handler Group Inc.
425 W End Ave., Apt. 3A
New York, NY 10024-5718
Ph: (212)873-1899
Contact: Mark Lambert Handler, President
E-mail: mlhandler@aol.com
Scope: Provider of marketing, communication planning, and design services, specializing in development of internal and external business communications. Develops corporate identity, corporate literature, employee communications, sales promotion materials, consumer product packaging and information, brochures, annual reports, and presentation materials. Industries served: Cable/television, technology software, business information, hospitality, and banking. **Founded:** 1976.

22530 ■ Herrick International: Partners for Performance
1834 Ridge Ave.
Evanston, IL 60201
Ph: (847)274-9206
Contact: Dr. Penny Hirsch, Principal
Scope: Firm partners with organizations to leverage employee performance. Areas of expertise include inter cultural communication, diversity, document design, leadership development and conflict resolution. **Publications:** "And Then She Said"; "How to Make Effective Business Presentation"; "Planning for Successful Interviews"; "It's Not What You Say"; "Cross-cultural issues with International LLM Students".

22531 ■ Beverly Hyman Ph.D. & Associates (BHA)—Beverly Hyman and Associates
23 E 10 St., Ste. 212
New York, NY 10003
Ph: (212)983-6250

Fax: (212)983-6342
Co. E-mail: bevhyman@aol.com
URL: http://www.beverlyhyman.com
Contact: Beverly Hyman, President
E-mail: bevhyman@aol.com
Scope: Communication and training consultants offering such programs as training the trainer, communications skills, business (or technical) writing, public speaking, management skills or supervisory skills, negotiations, direct communication (assertiveness training), women in management, time management, and sales training. Serves private industries as well as government agencies. **Founded:** 1979. **Publications:** "Training for Productivity"; "How Successful Women Manage"; "The Trainers Handbook The AMA Guide to Effective Training"; "The Heart of the Sale Making the Customers Need to Buy the Key to Successful Selling"; "How to Market by Telephone, How to Interview Effectively, Total Time Management and How to Motivate for Superior Performance". **Seminars:** Training the Trainer; Advanced Training the Trainer; Coaching and Counseling; Constructive Feedback; Supervisory Skills; Writing Skills; Interpersonal Communications; Leadership Skills; Presentation Skills; Customer Service; Communication Skills; Public Speaking; Negotiating Skills Women in Management; Time Management; Sales Training Skills; Assertiveness Skills; Executive Coaching. **Telecommunication Services:** info@beverlyhyman.com.

22532 ■ In Plain English—R.H. Wohl & Associates Inc.
14501 Antigone Dr.
Gaithersburg, MD 20885-3300
Ph: (301)340-2821
Free: 800-274-9645
Fax: (301)279-0115
Co. E-mail: rwohl@inplainenglish.com
URL: http://www.inplainenglish.com
Contact: Ronald H. Wohl, President
E-mail: rwohl@inplainenglish.com
Scope: Management consultants helping government and businesses research, design, write and produce user oriented management information for human resources, employee benefits, business process, corporate and marketing needs. Services include: GSA mob is schedule for consulting to the government; employee benefit communications, plain English business writing workshops for print and electronic media; communicating strategy and tactics; marketing research, business planning and communications; readability testing; usability testing and monitoring strategy. **Founded:** 1977. **Publications:** "The Benefits Communication"; "The Employee Benefits Communication ToolKit," Commerce Clearinghouse; "Benefits Communication," Business and Legal Reports. **Seminars:** Plain English Writing Training; Summary Plan Description Compliance workshops; Re-Humanizing the Corporation, Human Resources and Employee Benefits Communication Workshop; 21 Writing Tips for the 21st Century; Make the Write Impression; Writing to Inform and Instruct; The Dreaded Nuts and Bolts; Writing to Persuade; Writing Policy and Procedure Manuals In Plain English; Writing for Accountants and Auditors In Plain English. **Special Services:** In Plain English®.

22533 ■ Komei Inc.—Manage Your Writing
1800 Western Hills Rd. SE
Rio Rancho, NM 87124
Ph: (317)616-1810
Fax: (317)616-1811
Co. E-mail: solutions@komei.com
URL: http://www.komei.com
Contact: Kenneth W. Davis, President
E-mail: ken@komei.com
Scope: Global corporation dedicated to helping people and organizations change together, and reach their goals, through better communication. Offers customized in-house seminars, workshops, and coaching in writing, presentation skills, international and intercultural communication, and team and community building. **Founded:** 1995. **Publications:** "Written Communication Profiler"; "The McGraw-Hill 36-Hour Course in Business Writing and Communication"; "Mihaly Csikszentmihalyi: Good Business: Leadership, Flow, and the Making of Meaning"; "Richard Saul Wurman: Information Anxiety 2"; "The

Brand You 50"; "The Cluetrain Manifesto: The End of Business"; "What to Say to Get What You Want". **Seminars:** Writing; Presentation Skills; International and Intercultural Communication.

22534 ■ Miller, Hellwig Associates

150 W End Ave.
New York, NY 10023-5713
Ph: (212)799-0471
Fax: (212)877-0186
Co. E-mail: millerhelwig@earthlink.net
Contact: Ernest C. Miller, President
Scope: Consulting services in the areas of start-up businesses; small business management; employee surveys and communication; performance appraisals; executive searches; team building; personnel policies and procedures; market research. Also involved in improving cross-cultural and multi-cultural relationships, particularly with Japanese clients. **Founded:** 1984. **Seminars:** Objectives and standards/recruiting for boards of directors.

22535 ■ Roger S. Peterson Marketing & Communications

3090 Union St.
Rocklin, CA 95677-1837
Fax: (916)624-3069
Co. E-mail: peterson@sacramentowriters.com
URL: http://www.sacramentowriters.com/market_communication.asp
Contact: Roger S. Peterson, President
E-mail: peterson@sacramentowriters.com
Scope: Specializes in business-to-business marketing communications, marketing diagnostics and marketing strategy for small to mid sized firms. **Founded:** 1995. **Publications:** "The Secret to Incentive Program Success: Incentive ROI that makes bean counters smile!"; "The Magic Megaphone"; "Ama Handbook For: Managing Business-To-Business Marketing Communications," McGraw-Hill, Apr, 1997. **Seminars:** Essentials of Marketing; The Communications Audit; Survival Training for Product Managers; Marketing Positioning & Promotion; Marketing Tools and How to Use Them; Marketing for Small Business, various American Management Association Courses.

22536 ■ ProActive English

4355 SE 29th Ave.
Portland, OR 97202
Ph: (503)231-2906
Co. E-mail: infopae@proactive-english.com
URL: http://www.proactive-english.com
Contact: Margaret Lyman, Manager
E-mail: mlyman@proactive-english.com
Scope: Offers on-site individual and small group language and communication training. Sets up learning plans tailored to the needs and schedules of managers and executives who are non-native English speakers. Serves all industries. **Founded:** 1997. **Seminars:** Communicating in Business Situations; Presentations and Pronunciation; Tailored Curriculum; One-on-One Programs.

22537 ■ Reynolds Communication—Reynolds, Oksanna

184 Columbia Hts.
Brooklyn, NY 11201-2105
Ph: (718)625-6797
Co. E-mail: sreynold@stern.nyu.edu
Contact: Sana O. Reynolds, Principal
Scope: Consultant specializing in cross cultural and organizational communication. Areas of expertise include inter cultural communication, business and technical writing, presentation coaching, document

design and plain language consulting. **Founded:** 2006. **Publications:** "Composing effective e-mail messages," Communication World, Jul, 1997; "Selling to another language," Communication World, Dec, 1996.

22538 ■ Tom Shillock Consulting

5545 SW Windsor Ct.
Portland, OR 97221-2150
Ph: (503)291-7928
Fax: (503)221-2052
Co. E-mail: tomsh@qwest.net
Contact: Tom Shillock, Principal
E-mail: tomsh@qwest.net
Scope: Offers consulting services in marketing and communications including public relations and advertising. Industries served: high technology. **Founded:** 1988.

22539 ■ Syntaxis Inc.

2109 Broadway, Ste. 16-159
New York, NY 10023-2106
Ph: (212)799-3000
Fax: (212)799-3021
Co. E-mail: info@syntaxis.com
URL: http://www.syntaxis.com
Contact: Arnold Gross, Director
Scope: Firm trains business professionals to speak and write more powerfully. Areas include presentation skills, business writing, grammar, and e-mail etiquette. **Founded:** 1999. **Publications:** "Presentation Skills for Business Professionals"; "A Writing Guide for Business Professionals"; "E-Mail Etiquette for Business Professionals".

22540 ■ Tim W. Hrastar Associates

184 Abbey Dr.
Springboro, OH 45066
Ph: (937)886-0186
Fax: (937)886-0186
Contact: Tim W. Hrastar, Owner
E-mail: twh@rapportmarketing.com
Scope: Specializes in helping the accounting and legal professions improve their communications and client relations. Offers communications expertise with emphasis on interpersonal and organizational communications. Experienced in presentation skills coaching, meeting dynamics, counseling in marketing, and client relations communications for professional services field. Clients include Fortune 500 companies as well as small businesses, government agencies, and other organizations in such diverse fields as food service, finance, health care, travel, and consumer and industrial products. **Founded:** 1976. **Publications:** "A Plan to Increase Your Market Share hot," Sep, 2009; "Ask Your Client These Questions hot," Feb, 2009; "An Idea to Better Serve Your Small Business Client," 2009; "Ask Your Client These Questions," 2009; "Capturing Your Audience in Five Seconds," 2009; "Business Development in a Down Market," 2009; "Asking for the Business," 2009; "How Do You Look at the World," Jan, 2008; "Business Development Takes Patience, Persistence and a Plan," 2007; "How to Make Persuasive Presentations with Confidence"; "Returning Phone Calls, Why Its Important"; "Five Tips on Thinking Ahead of Your Clients"; "Rapport"; "Five Tips on Thinking Ahead of Your Clients"; "Returning Phone Calls, Why It's Important"; "The Eyes Have It!"; "Reducing Client Apprehension"; "How Would Your Clients Rate You in the Following Areas? Part I". **Seminars:** Business Development for Lawyers; Persuasive Communications in the Courtroom; How to Create and Deliver Persuasive Presentations; How to Create and Deliver Persuasive Presentations; Meeting Dynamics for

Lawyers: Conducting and Participating in Effective Meetings; Cool Tools to Improve Client Communications. **Special Services:** Rapport Marketing®.

22541 ■ Trendzitions Inc.

25691 Atlantic Ocean, Ste. B13
Lake Forest, CA 92630-8842
Ph: (949)727-9100
Free: 800-266-2767
Fax: (949)727-3444
Co. E-mail: ctooker@trendzitions.com
URL: http://www.trendzitions.com
Contact: Christian Tooker, President
E-mail: ctooker@trendzitions.com
Scope: Provider of services in the areas of communications consulting, project management, construction management, and furniture procurement. Offers information on spatial uses, building codes, ADA compliance and city ordinances. Also offers budget projections. **Founded:** 1986.

22542 ■ The Watts Corp.

22117 161st Ave. SE
Monroe, WA 98272-9171
Ph: (425)941-6781
Fax: (360)805-5873
Contact: Jeffrey H. Watts, Chief Executive Officer
E-mail: jeffrey@wattslink.com
Scope: A profit coach with expertise in sales and profitability, general operations. Available as seminar presenter and venture turn-around. **Founded:** 1984. **Seminars:** Customized programs to address specific needs of your company.

22543 ■ Write Wise Communications L.L.C.

488 W 19th St., Ste. 359
Houston, TX 77008
Ph: (713)863-9140
Fax: (713)863-9140
Co. E-mail: contact@writewisecommunications.com
URL: http://www.writewisecommunications.com
Contact: Alise Isbell, Owner
E-mail: alise@writewisecommunications.com
Scope: Firm specializes in needs assessment, strategic planning, training, communication effectiveness surveys, instructional design, course development, writing, organizational development, business planning, virtual teaming, process improvement, online education planning and implementation, and performance improvement. **Seminars:** Grammar Refresher for Adults; Business Writing for Business Professionals; Technical Writing; Writing Effective Proposals; Service Spotlight! Effective Written Presentations; Service Spotlight! Effective Verbal Presentations; Service Spotlight! Effective Distance Presentations; Effective Teamwork over Distance; Time Management; More Productive Meetings; Managing the Strategic Planning Process.

FRANCHISES AND BUSINESS OPPORTUNITIES

22544 ■ Allegra Marketing

Allegra Network
47585 Galleon Dr.
Plymouth, MI 48170
Ph: (800)726-9050
Fax: (248)596-8601
Co. E-mail: contact@2.allegranetwork.com
URL: http://www.allegranetwork.com
Description: Full service printing centers. **No. of Franchise Units:** 300. **Founded:** 1976.. **Franchised:** 1977. **Equity Capital Needed:** $162,464-$516,949 investment. **Franchise Fee:** $35,000 Start-up Model, $45,000 MatchMaker Model, $15,000 resale. **Training:** Yes.

ASSOCIATIONS AND OTHER ORGANIZATIONS

22545 ■ Association for Business Communication (ABC)
PO Box 6143
Nacogdoches, TX 75962-0001
Ph: (540)231-8460
Fax: (646)349-5297
Co. E-mail: abcoffice@businesscommunication.org
URL: http://www.businesscommunication.org
Contact: Jim Dubinsky, Executive Director
Description: College teachers of business communication; management consultants in business communications; training directors and correspondence supervisors of business firms, direct mail copywriters, public relations writers, and others interested in communication for business. **Founded:** 1935. **Publications:** *Business Communication Quarterly* (Quarterly); *The Journal of Business Communication* (Quarterly); *Journal of Business Communication* (Quarterly); *Making Communication Requirements More Explicit in the AACSB Standards for MBA Programs.* **Educational Activities:** Association for Business Communication Annual Convention (Annual); Association for Business Communication Convention (Annual). **Awards:** Distinguished Publication on Business Communication; Outstanding Article in Business Communication Quarterly; Distinguished Publication on Business Communication (Annual); Kitty O. Locker Outstanding Researcher Award (Annual); Meada Gibbs Outstanding Teacher Award (Annual); Outstanding Article in Business Communication Quarterly (Annual); Outstanding Article in the Journal of Business Communication (Annual); Outstanding Doctoral Dissertation Award (Annual); Outstanding Article in the Journal of Business Communication. **Telecommunication Services:** abcjohnson@sfasu.edu.

22546 ■ International Association of Business Communicators (IABC)
601 Montgomery St., Ste. 1900
San Francisco, CA 94111
Ph: (415)544-4700
Free: 800-776-4222
Fax: (415)544-4747
Co. E-mail: member_relations@iabc.com
URL: http://www.iabc.com
Contact: Paulo H. Soares, Director
E-mail: paulo.henrique.soares@vale.com
Description: Represents Communication managers, public relations directors, writers, editors, audiovisual specialists, and others in the public relations and organizational communication field that use a variety of media to communicate with internal audiences (employees, management, association members, and leaders) and external audiences (media, customers, dealers, investors, and government). Conducts research in the communication field and encourages establishment of college-level programs in organizational communication. Offers accreditation program; conducts surveys on employee communication effectiveness and media trends. **Scope:** organizational

communication. **Founded:** 1970. **Publications:** *Communication World: The Magazine for Communication Professionals*; *World Book of IABC Communicators*; *World Book of IABC Communicators*; *The Human Element.* **Educational Activities:** International Association of Business Communicators World Conference (Annual). **Awards:** Chairman's Award; IABC Fellow; Chairman's Award (Annual); Chapter Management Award (Annual); Excellence in Communication Leadership (Annual); Fellow Designation (Annual); Gold Quill (Annual); Lifetime Foundation Friend Award (Annual); Excellence in Communication Leadership (EXCEL) Award. **Telecommunication Services:** service_centre@iabc.com; service_center@iabc.com.

EDUCATIONAL PROGRAMS

22547 ■ Advanced Copyediting (Onsite)
EEI Communications
8945 Guilford Rd., Ste. 145
Columbia, MD 21046
Ph: (410)309-8200
Free: 888-253-2762
Fax: (410)630-3980
Co. E-mail: train@eeicom.com
URL: http://www.eeicom.com/eei-training-services
Price: $797.00. **Description:** This course will help you develop and enhance both knowledge and skills in the editing and production process. **Dates and Locations:** Alexandria, VA; Columbia, MD; and Silver Spring, MD.

22548 ■ Advanced Writing and Editing for Government Proposals
EEI Communications
8945 Guilford Rd., Ste. 145
Columbia, MD 21046
Ph: (410)309-8200
Free: 888-253-2762
Fax: (410)630-3980
Co. E-mail: train@eeicom.com
URL: http://www.eeicom.com/eei-training-services
Price: $745.00. **Description:** Developed for anyone who regularly writes, edits, or manages government proposals to explore proposal-specific writing and editing challenges, including how to ensure consistent voice no matter how many writers are involved. **Dates and Locations:** Alexandria, VA.

22549 ■ AMA's 2-Day Business Writing Workshop (Live Online)
American Management Association
600 AMA Way
Saranac Lake, NY 12983-5534
Ph: (212)586-8100
Free: 877-566-9441
Fax: (518)891-0368
Co. E-mail: customerservice@amanet.org
URL: http://www.amaseminars.org
Price: $1,995.00 for non-members; $1,795.00 for AMA members; and $1,537.00 for General Services Administration (GSA) members. **Description:** Learn

basic formats and formulas to compose documents and communicate what your readers need to know. **Dates and Locations:** Cities throughout the United States.

22550 ■ Basics of Government Contract Administration (Onsite)
Seminar Information Service, Inc.
20 Executive Park, Ste. 120
Irvine, CA 92614
Ph: (949)261-9104
Free: 877-SEM-INFO
Fax: (949)261-1963
Co. E-mail: info@seminarinformation.com
URL: http://www.seminarinformation.com
Price: $1,025.00. **Description:** Designed to show you how to fill out the most common standard forms, where the forms are found, and how proper forms preparation avoids administration pitfalls. **Dates and Locations:** Arlington, VA; and Norfolk, VA.

22551 ■ Business English and Grammar Review (Onsite)
Arizona Government Training Center
530 E McDowell Rd., Ste. 107-483
Phoenix, AZ 85004
Ph: (480)967-7544
Free: 800-970-1270
Fax: (480)966-6325
Co. E-mail: help@agts.com
URL: http://www.agts.com
Price: $229.00 for non-members; $189.00 for AGTS members. **Description:** Covers grammatical errors, punctuation, sentence structure, spelling, and plurals and possessives. **Dates and Locations:** Phoenix, AZ.

22552 ■ Business Grammar & Proofreading (Onsite)
Seminar Information Service, Inc.
20 Executive Park, Ste. 120
Irvine, CA 92614
Ph: (949)261-9104
Free: 877-SEM-INFO
Fax: (949)261-1963
Co. E-mail: info@seminarinformation.com
URL: http://www.seminarinformation.com
Price: $199.00. **Description:** Designed for busy professionals who want to brush up on grammar, spelling, proofreading and business usage. **Dates and Locations:** Cities throughout the United States.

22553 ■ Business Grammar and Proofreading (Onsite)
Padgett-Thompson Seminars
Rockhurst University CEC
14502 W. 105th St.
Lenexa, KS 66215
Free: 800-349-1935
URL: http://www.findaseminar.com/tpd/Padgett-Thompson-Seminars.asp
Price: $199.00. **Description:** A one-day workshop that features a 'no-fear' approach to dealing with spelling and grammar. **Dates and Locations:** Washington, DC; Edison, NJ.

22554 ■ Business Writing for Administrative Professionals

American Management Associat on
600 AMA Way
Saranac Lake, NY 12983-5534
Ph: (212)586-8100
Free: 877-566-9441
Fax: (518)891-0368
Co. E-mail: customerservice@amanet.org
URL: http://www.amaseminars.org
Price: $1,895.00 for non-members; $1,695.00 for AMA members; and $1,451.00 for General Services Administration (GSA) members. **Description:** Learn the skills and techniques you need to write and edit various documents. **Dates and Locations:** New York, NY; and Atlanta, GA.

22555 ■ Business Writing and Grammar Skills Made Easy and Fun! (Onsite)

Seminar Information Service, Inc.
20 Executive Park, Ste. 120
Irvine, CA 92614
Ph: (949)261-9104
Free: 877-SEM-INFO
Fax: (949)261-1963
Co. E-mail: info@seminarinformation.com
URL: http://www.seminarinformation.com
Price: $299.00; $269.00 for 4 or more. **Description:** Learn how to project your ideas effectively and clearly through proven techniques. **Dates and Locations:** Cities throughout the United States.

22556 ■ Business Writing & Grammar Skills (Onsite)

Seminar Information Service, Inc.
20 Executive Park, Ste. 120
Irvine, CA 92614
Ph: (949)261-9104
Free: 877-SEM-INFO
Fax: (949)261-1963
Co. E-mail: info@seminarinformation.com
URL: http://www.seminarinformation.com
Price: $299.00. **Description:** Two-day workshop where you'll learn techniques and shortcuts for getting your thoughts organized fast and your words flowing freely even if writing does not come naturally to you. **Dates and Locations:** Denver, CO; and Farmington Hills, MI.

22557 ■ Business Writing and Grammar Skills (Onsite)

Padgett-Thompson Seminars
Rockhurst University CEC
14502 W. 105th St.
Lenexa, KS 66215
Free: 800-349-1935
URL: http://www.findaseminar.com/tpd/Padgett-Thompson-Seminars.asp
Price: $299.00. **Description:** Developed exclusively for business professionals, this two-day workshop delivers tools and techniques that will add clarity and power to business documents. **Dates and Locations:** Cities throughout the United States.

22558 ■ Business Writing for the Multilingual Professional

American Management Association
600 AMA Way
Saranac Lake, NY 12983-5534
Ph: (212)586-8100
Free: 877-566-9441
Fax: (518)891-0368
Co. E-mail: customerservice@amanet.org
URL: http://www.amaseminars.org
Price: $2,195.00 for non-members; $1,995.00 for AMA members; and $1,708.00 for General Services Administration (GSA) members. **Description:** Learn practical techniques for creating effective business documents, with focus on correct English grammar and usage. **Dates and Locations:** New York, NY; Washington, DC; Arlington, VA; and San Francisco, CA.

22559 ■ Business Writing for Results (Onsite)

Fred Pryor Seminars & CareerTrack
5700 Broadmoor St., Ste. 300
Mission, KS 66202
Free: 800-780-8476
Fax: (913)967-8849
Co. E-mail: customerservice@pryor.com
URL: http://www.pryor.com
Price: $179.00; $169.00 for groups of 5 or more. **Description:** Learn to write powerful letters, memos, reports, and proposals that get results. **Dates and Locations:** Cities throughout the United States.

22560 ■ Clear Business, Technical, and E-mail Writing

Seminar Information Service, Inc.
20 Executive Park, Ste. 120
Irvine, CA 92614
Ph: (949)261-9104
Free: 877-SEM-INFO
Fax: (949)261-1963
Co. E-mail: info@seminarinformation.com
URL: http://www.seminarinformation.com
Price: $500.00. **Description:** This workshop provides a step-by-step process for designing and writing a clear document, e-mail message, or report with the use of writing, revising, and editing exercises. **Dates and Locations:** Redwood City, CA.

22561 ■ Communicating Up, Down and Across the Organization (Onsite) (Canada)

Canadian Management Centre (CMC)
150 York St., 5th Fl.
Toronto, ON, Canada M5H 3S5
Ph: (416)214-5678
Free: 877-262-2519
Fax: (416)313-4985
Co. E-mail: cmcinfo@cmctraining.org
URL: http://www.cmctraining.org
Contact: John Wright, President
Price: $1,995.00 Canadian for non-members; $1,845.00 Canadian for CMC members. **Description:** Seminar that encourages dialogue throughout the organization and between different departments, including gaining self-esteem, targeting your message by knowing your audience, building team commitment, develop interpersonal techniques for influencing, build persuasive business cases, and constructing an informative, attention getting project update. **Dates and Locations:** Toronto, ON; Calgary, AB; and Ottawa, CN.

22562 ■ Developing Procedures, Policies and Documentation (Onsite)

Seminar Information Service, Inc.
20 Executive Park, Ste. 120
Irvine, CA 92614
Ph: (949)261-9104
Free: 877-SEM-INFO
Fax: (949)261-1963
Co. E-mail: info@seminarinformation.com
URL: http://www.seminarinformation.com
Price: $1,555.00. **Description:** Learn how to define audience information needs and requirements and how to design information that meets user needs, including how to develop information that is user-friendly and accessible and how to organized information in modular and flexible units for later re-use.

22563 ■ E-mail and Business Writing (Onsite)

Fred Pryor Seminars & CareerTrack
5700 Broadmoor St., Ste. 300
Mission, KS 66202
Free: 800-780-8476
Fax: (913)967-8849
Co. E-mail: customerservice@pryor.com
URL: http://www.pryor.com
Price: $99.00; $89.00 for groups of 5 or more. **Description:** Learn how to craft e-mail messages that are grammatically correct, concise, and to the point. **Dates and Locations:** Cities throughout the United States.

22564 ■ The E-Mail and Business Writing Workshop (Onsite)

Padgett-Thompson Seminars
Rockhurst University CEC
14502 W. 105th St.
Lenexa, KS 66215
Free: 800-349-1935
URL: http://www.findaseminar.com/tpd/Padgett-Thompson-Seminars.asp
Price: $199.00. **Description:** A one-day seminar that offers tips and techniques to guarantee that every message written will be polished and on target. **Dates and Locations:** Cities throughout the United States.

22565 ■ Effective Business Writing (Onsite)

Baker Communications Inc. (BCI)
10101 SW Fwy., Ste. 630
Houston, TX 77074
Ph: (713)627-7700
Fax: (713)587-2051
Co. E-mail: information@bakercommunications.com
URL: http://www.bakercommunications.com
Contact: Walter Rogers, President
Price: $695.00. **Description:** Participants learn to convey ideas and information with clarity and precision in memos, letters, reports, and other business correspondence. **Dates and Locations:** Cities throughout the United States and Canads.

22566 ■ Effective Technical Writing (Onsite)

American Management Association (AMA)
1601 Broadway
New York, NY 10019-7420
Ph: (212)586-8100
Free: 877-566-9441
Fax: (212)903-8168
Co. E-mail: customerservice@amanet.org
URL: http://www.amanet.org
Contact: Charles R. Craig, Chairman
Price: $2,195.00 for non-members; $1,995.00 for AMA members. **Description:** Covers the basics of writing technical documents such as reports, manuals, specifications, proposals, and instructions. **Dates and Locations:** San Francisco, CA; Arlington, VA; and New York, NY.

22567 ■ Exceptional Business Writing and Goof-Proof Grammar

Fred Pryor Seminars & CareerTrack
5700 Broadmoor St., Ste. 300
Mission, KS 66202
Free: 800-780-8476
Fax: (913)967-8849
Co. E-mail: customerservice@pryor.com
URL: http://www.pryor.com
Price: $299.00; $279.00 for groups of 3 or more. **Description:** Learn how to communicate clearly and effectively so others view you as confident and capable. **Dates and Locations:** Cities throughout the United States.

22568 ■ Government Proposal Writing Basics

EEI Communications
8945 Guilford Rd., Ste. 145
Columbia, MD 21046
Ph: (410)309-8200
Free: 888-253-2762
Fax: (410)630-3980
Co. E-mail: train@eeicom.com
URL: http://www.eeicom.com/eei-training-services
Price: $745.00. **Description:** Designed for proposal novices at any level of writing ability, this course explains the unique features of government proposals and the government procurement process. **Dates and Locations:** Alexandria, VA.

22569 ■ Hands-On Business and Report Writing: The Art of Persuasion (Onsite)

Seminar Information Service, Inc.
20 Executive Park, Ste. 120
Irvine, CA 92614
Ph: (949)261-9104
Free: 877-SEM-INFO
Fax: (949)261-1963
Co. E-mail: info@seminarinformation.com
URL: http://www.seminarinformation.com
Price: $2,490.00. **Description:** Learn how to: Write compelling documents that focus your message; Compose targeted messages using a standard writing process; Improve document comprehension with polished grammar and punctuation; Produce winning proposals, recommendation reports and executive summaries; Create effective written communications

that drive your business; Develop a clear, persuasive writing style. **Dates and Locations:** New York, NY; Rockville, MD; Reston, VA; Ottawa, CN; and Toronto, CN.

22570 ■ How to Communicate with Diplomacy, Tact and Credibility (Onsite) (Canada)

Canadian Management Centre (CMC)
150 York St., 5th Fl.
Toronto, ON, Canada M5H 3S5
Ph: (416)214-5678
Free: 877-262-2519
Fax: (416)313-4985
Co. E-mail: cmcinfo@cmctraining.org
URL: http://www.cmctraining.org
Contact: John Wright, President
Price: $1,995.00 Canadian for non-members; $1,845.00 Canadian for CMC members. **Description:** Seminar covering how to mold your communication style to meet the needs of individual situations, develop active listening and questioning strategies, gain cooperation and respect by promoting and modeling tolerance with politically correct attitudes and communication, break through communication gridlock, expand the communication network, and turn communication conflicts into opportunities for cooperation and growth. **Dates and Locations:** Edmonton, AB; Mississauga, ON; Vaughan, ON; Calgary, AB; Toronto, ON; and Ottawa, ON.

22571 ■ How to Sharpen Your Business Writing Skills (Onsite)

American Management Association
600 AMA Way
Saranac Lake, NY 12983-5534
Ph: (212)586-8100
Free: 877-566-9441
Fax: (518)891-0368
Co. E-mail: customerservice@amanet.org
URL: http://www.amaseminars.org
Price: $2,445.00 for non-members; $2,195.00 for AMA members; and $1,880.00 for General Services Administration (GSA) members. **Description:** Covers how to solve common writing problems, various writing concepts, and how to write effective letters, memos, reports, and business proposals. **Dates and Locations:** San Francisco, CA; Arlington, VA; Washington, DC; and New York, NY.

22572 ■ How to Write Effective Policies and Procedures (Onsite)

Seminar Information Service, Inc.
20 Executive Park, Ste. 120
Irvine, CA 92614
Ph: (949)261-9104
Free: 877-SEM-INFO
Fax: (949)261-1963
Co. E-mail: info@seminarinformation.com
URL: http://www.seminarinformation.com
Price: $249.00. **Description:** Covers rules, strategies, guidelines and shortcuts that will make your job easier and ensure you get the results of a well-written policies and procedures that are read and understood by all. **Dates and Locations:** Cities throughout the United States.

22573 ■ Mapping Business Communications (Onsite)

Seminar Information Service, Inc.
20 Executive Park, Ste. 120
Irvine, CA 92614
Ph: (949)261-9104
Free: 877-SEM-INFO
Fax: (949)261-1963
Co. E-mail: info@seminarinformation.com
URL: http://www.seminarinformation.com
Price: $995.00. **Description:** Learn to identify the purpose of each communication define the specific action required from the reader customize the message for different audiences to achieve greater results organize communications to make information quick and easy to find, and present information in the way that best suits the target audience.

22574 ■ Mistake-Free Grammar & Proofreading (Onsite)

Fred Pryor Seminars & CareerTrack
5700 Broadmoor St., Ste. 300
Mission, KS 66202
Free: 800-780-8476
Fax: (913)967-8849
Co. E-mail: customerservice@pryor.com
URL: http://www.pryor.com
Price: $149.00; $139.00 for groups of 5 or more. **Description:** Learn grammar rules and to proofread with perfection. **Dates and Locations:** Cities throughout the United States.

22575 ■ Records Retention and Destruction (Onsite)

Fred Pryor Seminars & CareerTrack
5700 Broadmoor St., Ste. 300
Mission, KS 66202
Free: 800-780-8476
Fax: (913)967-8849
Co. E-mail: customerservice@pryor.com
URL: http://www.pryor.com
Price: $149.00; $139.00 for groups of 5 or more. **Description:** Gain valuable information for successfully organizing, storing, archiving and destroying your organization's critical business documents while eliminating risk and ensuring compliance with the latest legal requirements. **Dates and Locations:** Cities throughout the United States.

22576 ■ Substantive Editing III

EEI Communications
8945 Guilford Rd., Ste. 145
Columbia, MD 21046
Ph: (410)309-8200
Free: 888-253-2762
Fax: (410)630-3980
Co. E-mail: train@eeicom.com
URL: http://www.eeicom.com/eei-training-services
Price: $425.00. **Description:** Evaluate your editing style, fine tune your ability to differentiate levels of edit, review documents at the appropriate level, learn to set clear expectations, find new ways to give constructive feedback to writers, and learn to coach, rather than edit, to encourage better writing. **Dates and Locations:** Alexandria, VA.

22577 ■ Technical Writing: A Comprehensive Hands-On Introduction (Onsite)

Seminar Information Service, Inc.
20 Executive Park, Ste. 120
Irvine, CA 92614
Ph: (949)261-9104
Free: 877-SEM-INFO
Fax: (949)261-1963
Co. E-mail: info@seminarinformation.com
URL: http://www.seminarinformation.com
Price: $2,890.00. **Description:** Learn how to: Write clear, effective technical = documents, including user manuals and technical reports; Assess your target audience and develop documents to meet their needs; Choose the appropriate writing style to communicate to specialized audiences; Build effective sentences, paragraphs and sections that explain information clearly; Employ diagrams, tables, charts and other graphical tools effectively; Create informative and interesting content that your readers will comprehend and utilize. **Dates and Locations:** Reston, VA; Toronto, CN; Ottawa, CN; Rockville, MD; New York, NY; and Alexandria, VA.

22578 ■ Writing the Perfect Business E-Mail (Onsite)

EEI Communications
66 Canal Ctr. Plz., Ste. 200
Alexandria, VA 22314-5507
Ph: (703)683-7453
Free: 888-253-2762
Fax: (703)683-7310
Co. E-mail: train@eeicom.com
URL: http://www.eeicom.com/training
Price: $425.00. **Description:** Seminar that covers e-mails that get read and are understood, including keeping it short and simple, make it useful, spelling, grammar, and other problems, controlling emotion, writing attachments that get read, progress reports,

instructions, and evaluations and recommendations. **Dates and Locations:** Silver Spring, MD; Alexandria, VA; Hunt Valley, MD; and Columbia, MD.

22579 ■ Writing for the Web (Onsite)

AMA
600 AMA Way
Saranac Lake, NY 12983-5534
Ph: (212)586-8100
Free: 877-566-9441
Fax: (518)891-0368
Co. E-mail: customerservice@amanet.org
URL: http://www.amaseminars.org
Price: $1,995.00 for non-members; $1,795.00 for AMA members; $1,537.00 for General Services Administration (GSA) members. **Description:** Create online content that connects with readers to achieve better results in this two-day course. **Dates and Locations:** Atlanta, GA; San Francisco, CA; and New York, NY.

REFERENCE WORKS

22580 ■ "Ask Inc." in Inc. (January 2008, pp. 60)

Pub: Gruner & Jahr USA Publishing
Description: Ways to manage high volumes of email are examined.

22581 ■ Be a Brilliant Business Writer: Write Well, Write Fast, and Whip the Competition

Pub: Crown Business Books
Ed: Jane Curry, Diana Young. **Released:** October 5, 2010. **Price:** $13.99. **Description:** Tools for mastering the art of persuasive writing in every document created, from email and client letters to reports and presentations, this book will help any writer convey their message with clarity and power, increase productivity by reducing rewrites, and provide the correct tone for navigating office politics.

22582 ■ "Before You Hit Send: Crafting Workplace E-Mails to Avoid Mishaps" in Black Enterprise (Vol. 38, January 2008, No. 6, pp. 85)

Pub: Earl G. Graves Publishing Co. Inc.
Ed: Tennille M. Robinson. **Description:** Tips to use before sending an office email our presented. It is important to keep emails looking professional.

22583 ■ "Bridging the Gap: Contextualing Professional Ethics in Collaborative Writing Projects" in Business Communication Quarterly (Dec.2007)

Pub: SAGE Publications USA
Contact: Blaise R. Simqu, President
Ed: J.A. Rice. **Description:** A classroom activity for business management students integrates ethical concepts with business writing strategies, while increasing understanding of writing ethics by emphasizing its rhetorical, contingent, and public nature.

22584 ■ "Campaigner Survey: 46 Percent of Small Businesses Use Email Marketing" in Wireless News (November 21, 2009)

Pub: Close-Up Media
Description: Almost half (46 percent) of small businesses surveyed by Campaigner's 2009 State of Small Business Online Marketing, say that they rely on email marketing to help them find new customers, keep existing ones and grow their businesses. The survey also found that 36 percent of small businesses plan to begin using email marketing over the next year. The trend to utilize Internet marketing tools is allowing small businesses to grow faster and generate higher revenues than those that are not using these mediums.

22585 ■ "Canadians Keep Memories in 'Inboxes' Instead of Shoe Boxes; MSN Canada" in Canadian Corporate News (May 14, 2007)

Pub: Comtex News Network Inc.
Description: According to an MSN Canada online poll, 76 percent of Canadians are creating 'virtual shoeboxes' with their email inboxes and archiving important messages, photos, and documents.

22586 ■ *"Conferencing Takes on High-Tech Futuristic Feel" in Crain's Cleveland Business (Vol. 28, October 29, 2007, No. 43, pp. 17)*
Pub: Crain Communications, Inc.
Ed: Chuck Soder. **Description:** Overview of the newest technologies which are making local company's meetings more effective including: tele-presence, a videoconferencing technology, as well as virtual flip charts.

22587 ■ *"Creative Marketing: How to Cultivate a Network of Endless Referrals" in Agency Sales Magazine (Vol. 39, July 2009, No. 7, pp. 38)*
Pub: MANA
Ed: Bob Burg. **Description:** Tips on how a salesperson can build a network of people that will bring them referrals are presented. Asking a person about their business and re-introducing one's self to an earlier acquaintance while remembering their names are some elements in the process of building this network.

22588 ■ *"Etiquette, Common Sense Often Lag Behind Smarter Devices" in Crain's Cleveland Business (Vol. 28, October 22, 2007, No. 42, pp. 21)*
Pub: Crain Communications, Inc.
Ed: Chrissy Kadleck. **Description:** Discusses the importance of good etiquette in regards to electronic communication both within as well as outside the business world.

22589 ■ *"Extreme Negotiations" in Harvard Business Review (Vol. 88, November 2010, No. 11, pp. 66)*
Pub: Harvard Business School Publishing
Ed: Jeff Weiss, Aram Donigian, Jonathan Hughes. **Description:** Examination of military negotiation skills that are applicable in business situations. Skills include soliciting others' perspectives, developing and proposing multiple solutions, and inviting others to assess them.

22590 ■ *"Facebook: A Promotional Budget's Best Friend" in Women Entrepreneur (February 1, 2009)*
Pub: Entrepreneur Media Inc.
Ed: Tamara Monosoff. **Description:** Facebook began as a social networking website but has become a valuable marketing tool for all types of businesses, organizations and causes. Tips are provided for creating a Facebook account and growing one's network on Facebook.

22591 ■ *"Faster and Shorter" in Canadian Business (Vol. 81, October 13, 2008, No. 17, pp. 25)*
Pub: Rogers Media Ltd.
Ed: Terri Goveia. **Description:** Study revealed that instant messaging (IM) technologies are slowly becoming legitimate in the corporate world. IM is traditionally considered as a distraction, but it was found to let workers make targeted inquiries that gives them what they need in an instant. Other views and information about IMs is included.

22592 ■ *"Five Steps to an Effective Business Call" in Hawaii Business (Vol. 53, October 2007, No. 4, pp. 64)*
Pub: Hawaii Business Publishing
Ed: Matthew K. Ing. **Description:** University of Hawaii professor Libda Patrylak believes that communication skills are integral to business success, which is why businesses should know how to properly handle phone conversations. Presented are five ways of achieving effective business phone calls, such as setting rules for employees to follow with regards to answering calls and providing undivided attention to the other speaker.

22593 ■ *"Five Things..For Photo Fun" in Hawaii Business (Vol. 53, October 2007, No. 4, pp. 20)*
Pub: Hawaii Business Publishing
Ed: Cathy S. Cruz-George. **Description:** Featured is a buyers guide of products used for capturing or displaying digital photos; products featured include the Digital Photo Wallet and Light Affection.

22594 ■ *"Get Personal" in Entrepreneur (Vol. 36, April 2008, No. 4)*
Pub: Entrepreneur Media, Inc.
Ed: Romanus Wolter. **Description:** Customers appreciate personal contact, and communicating with them can help business owners' customer relations. Some ways on how to keep a personal touch with customers and improve business dealings include blending technology with personal interaction and knowing what the customers want. Other tips are provided.

22595 ■ *"Grooming Your Online Persona" in Women In Business (Vol. 62, June 2010, No. 2, pp. 36)*
Pub: American Business Women's Association
Ed: Diane Stafford. **Description:** Employees' use of online social networks could become a basis on how their employers, clients, or business partners would judge them. Personal details, pictures and other online data should be filtered to avoid inappropriate or uncomfortable situations and distinguish personal from professional or work life.

22596 ■ *"How to Boost Your Super Bowl ROI" in Advertising Age (Vol. 80, December 7, 2009, No. 41, pp. 3)*
Pub: Crain's Communications
Ed: Abbey Klaassen. **Description:** Internet marketing is essential, even for the corporations that can afford to spend $3 million on a 30-second Super Bowl spot; last year, Super Bowl advertising reached an online viewership of 99.5 million while 98.7 million people watched the game on television validating the idea that public relations must go farther than a mere television ad campaign. Social media provides businesses with a longer shelf life for their ad campaigns. Advice is also given regarding ways in which to strategize a smart and well-thought plan for utilizing the online marketing options currently available.

22597 ■ *"How Pixar Fosters Collective Creativity" in Harvard Business Review (Vol. 86, September 2008, No. 9, pp. 64)*
Pub: Harvard Business School Press
Ed: Ed Catmull. **Description:** Pixar Animation Studios illustrates peer-culture methods for fostering product development. These include allowing any employee to communicate with any other employee, providing a safe environment for new ideas, and watching the academic community closely for innovations.

22598 ■ *"How to Write a Report" in Canadian Business (Vol. 80, November 5, 2007, No. 22, pp. 41)*
Pub: Rogers Media
Ed: Gabriel Fuchs. **Description:** Basic rule in writing a report is the so-called USNA, which stands for Use Synonyms, No Acronyms. Synonyms make the report seem more interesting while acronyms increase the chance of being misunderstood. Details of how to write an impressive business report are given.

22599 ■ *"Hunter and the Hunted" in Canadian Business (Vol. 81, Summer 2008, No. 9, pp. 12)*
Pub: Rogers Media Ltd.
Ed: Thomas Watson. **Description:** Brian Hunter, a partner in oil and gas engineering firm Montana Resources, invested his life savings in Vancouver-based Canacord Capital Corp. Details of the asset-backed commercial paper fiasco and Hunter's use of Facebook to encourage other investors to participate in his claim against the mortgage company are presented.

22600 ■ *"I Can Make Your Brain Look Like Mine" in Harvard Business Review (Vol. 88, December 2010, No. 12, pp. 32)*
Pub: Harvard Business School Publishing
Description: Psychology professor Uri Hasson discusses findings that the brain waves of a speaker and a listener become similar as the listener's comprehension increases.

22601 ■ *Information Technology for the Small Business: How to Make IT Work For Your Company*
Pub: TAB Computer Systems, Incorporated
Ed: T.J. Benoit. **Released:** June 2006. **Price:** $17.95. **Description:** Basics of information technology to help small companies maximize benefits are covered. Topics include pitfalls to avoid, email and Internet use, data backup, recovery and overall IT organization.

22602 ■ *"Integrating Business Core Knowledge through Upper Division Report Composition" in Business Communication Quarterly (December 2007)*
Pub: SAGE Publications USA
Contact: Blaise R. Simqu, President
Ed: Joy Roach, Daniel Tracy, Kay Durden. **Description:** An assignment that integrates subjects and encourages the use of business communication report-writing skills is presented. This assignment is designed to complement business school curricula and help develop critical thinking and organizational skills.

22603 ■ *"An Introvert's Guide to Schmoozing" in Canadian Business (Vol. 83, July 20, 2010, No. 11-12, pp. 73)*
Pub: Rogers Media Ltd.
Ed: Jasmine Budak. **Description:** Writer Nancy Ankowitz says that introverts seem to get grouped with social misfits but introverts are people who recharge by spending time alone. Ankowitz advises introverts to use their strengths in quiet strengths such as writing and listening as well as learning to speak in public.

22604 ■ *"Is It Time to Ban Swearing at Work?" in HR Specialist (Vol. 8, September 2010, No. 9, pp. 2)*
Pub: Capitol Information Group Inc.
Description: Screening software has been developed to identify profanity used in business correspondence.

22605 ■ *"Israeli Spam Law May Have Global Impact" in Information Today (Vol. 26, February 2009, No. 2, pp. 28)*
Pub: Information Today, Inc.
Ed: David Mirchin. **Description:** Israels new law, called Amendment 40 of the Communications Law, will regulate commercial solicitations including those sent without permission via email, fax, automatic phone dialing systems, or short messaging technologies.

22606 ■ *The Language of Success: Business Writing That Informs, Persuades, and Gets Results*
Pub: AMACOM
Ed: Tom Sant. **Released:** January 2008. **Price:** $15.00. **Description:** The damage that can be done when words are used ineffectively and the power to be gained when they are used well in business.

22607 ■ *"Life's Work: Oliver Sacks" in Harvard Business Review (Vol. 88, November 2010, No. 11, pp. 152)*
Pub: Harvard Business School Publishing
Ed: Lisa Burrell. **Description:** Neurologist and author Oliver Sacks discusses whether different types of minds tend toward certain skills, physician-patient communication, and his own perspectives from being a patient himself.

22608 ■ *"Managing Corporate Social Networks" in Harvard Business Review (Vol. 86, July-August 2008, No. 8, pp. 26)*
Pub: Harvard Business School Press
Ed: Adam M. Kleinbaum; Michael L. Tushman. **Description:** Tips on how to promote business creativity and foster knowledge building through business social networks are given.

22609 ■ *"Meetings Go Virtual" in HRMagazine (Vol. 54, January 2009, No. 1, pp. 74)*
Pub: Society for Human Resource Management
Contact: Henry G. Jackson, President
E-mail: hjackson@shrm.org
Ed: Elizabeth Agnvall. **Description:** Microsoft Office Live Meeting conferencing software allows companies to schedule meetings from various company locations, thus saving travel costs.

22610 ■ *"Mosaid Grants First Wireless Parent License To Matsushita"* in *Canadian Electronics* (Vol. 23, June-July 2008, No. 5, pp. 1)*
Pub: Action Communication Inc.

Description: Matsushita Electric Industrial Co. Ltd. has been granted a six-and-a-half-year license by Mosaid Technologies Inc. to manufacture the latter's products. The patent portfolio license agreement covers Mosaid's Wi-Fi, Wi-Max, CDMA-enabled notebook computers and other products.

22611 ■ *"'Mr. CEO, Please Do Elaborate On Your Firm's Metrics'"* in *Business Courier* (Vol. 24, February 29, 2008, No. 47, pp. 1)*
Pub: American City Business Journals, Inc.

Ed: Jon Newberry. **Description:** Discusses a rogue caller who goes by the name of Joe Herrick, Steven Nissan and Joe Harris has joined in over a dozen conference calls, asking chief executive officers on their plans and commenting on the companies' operations. The mystery caller attempts to pass himself off as a financial analyst. Transcripts of some conference calls, in which the rogue caller is involved, are provided.

22612 ■ *"New Sprint Phone Whets Appetite for Applications"* in *The Business Journal-Serving Metropolitan Kansas City* (Vol. 26, July 25, 2008)*
Pub: American City Business Journals, Inc.

Ed: Suzanna Stagemeyer. **Description:** Firms supporting the applications of the new Samsung Instinct, which was introduced by Sprint Nextel Corp. in June 2008, have reported usage rates increase for their products. Handmark, whose mobile services Pocket Express comes loaded with Instinct, has redirected employees to meet the rising demand for the services. Other views and information on Instinct, are presented.

22613 ■ *"Not Your Dad's Business Card"* in *Small Business Opportunities* (July 2008)*
Pub: Entrepreneur Press
Contact: Perlman Neil, President

Ed: Rob Schlacter. **Description:** Provides tips on how to effectively design and use business cards.

22614 ■ *"Oh, Behave!"* in *Entrepreneur* (Vol. 36, April 2008, No. 4, pp. 87)*
Pub: Entrepreneur Media, Inc.

Ed: Gwen Moran. **Description:** Online social networks can pose awkward situations for users. These include instances such as getting a link request from someone you do not know, having a contact post embarrassing information on your site, and a contact asking you to be refer him to one of your business contacts. Tips on how to deal with these situations are discussed.

22615 ■ *"OtherInbox Ready for Revenue: Software Startup Expects Profits in '09"* in *Austin Business JournalInc.* (Vol. 28, January 2, 2009)*
Pub: American City Business Journals

Ed: Christopher Calnan. **Description:** Founder of Austin, Texas-based OtherBox Inc. expects the company to generate revenue through subscriptions and advertising and also reach profitability in 2009. The company's email management tool sends secondary mail to an alternate location thereby freeing up the work inbox for more urgent messages.

22616 ■ *"Our Gadget of the Week: Business Buddy"* in *Barron's* (Vol. 88, July 7, 2008, No. 27, pp. 26)*
Pub: Dow Jones & Co., Inc.

Ed: Jay Palmer. **Description:** Review and evaluation of the Lenovo X300 laptop computer which offers executives a variety of features despite its smaller size and weight. The laptop is about 0.73 inch thick, comes with a 64-gigabyte solid-state drive from Samsung, and weighs less than three pounds.

22617 ■ *"Our Gadget of the Week: Mostly, I Liked It"* in *Barron's* (Vol. 88, July 14, 2008,

No. 28, pp. 31)*
Pub: Dow Jones & Co., Inc.
Ed: Jay Palmer. **Description:** Review of the Apple iPhone 3G, which costs $199, has better audio and is slightly thicker than its predecessor; using the 3G wireless connection makes going online faster but drains the battery faster too.

22618 ■ *"Partnering for Success"* in *Art Business News* (Vol. 36, October 2009, No. 10, pp. 4)*
Pub: Summit Business Media
Ed: Jennifer Dulin Wiley. **Description:** In such a volatile economy many savvy artists and gallery owners are turning to out-of-the-box partnerships for continued success; these partnerships are also pervading the Internet, especially with such social media networks as Facebook and Twitter where artists and businesses can develop a loyal following.

22619 ■ *"People Often Trust Eloquence More Than Honesty"* in *Harvard Business Review* (Vol. 88, November 2010, No. 11, pp. 36)*
Pub: Harvard Business School Publishing
Ed: Todd Rogers, Michael I. Norton. **Description:** The article shows how deftly side-stepping a question in an eloquent manner generates a more positive response in an audience than does a direct answer that is ineffectively delivered. Implications for both politics and business are discussed.

22620 ■ *Persuasive Business Proposals*
Pub: AMACOM
Ed: Tom Sant. **Released:** December 2003. **Price:** $17.95. **Description:** Writing to win more customers, clients, and contracts.

22621 ■ *"Pressed for Time"* in *Marketing to Women* (Vol. 21, March 2008, No. 3, pp. 1)*
Pub: EPM Communications Inc.
Contact: Ira Mayer, President
E-mail: imayer@epmcom.com
Description: Statistical data concerning the tools women use for time management which include gadgets as well as traditional media such as calendars.

22622 ■ *"A Proper Welcome"* in *Canadian Business* (Vol. 79, July 17, 2006, No. 14-15, pp. 67)*
Pub: Rogers Media
Ed: Graham Lowe. **Description:** New-employee orientation programs of various companies are highlighted. Useful practices to create a comfortable ambiance for new recruits are elucidated as well.

22623 ■ *"Real-Time Computer-Mediated Communication"* in *Business Communication Quarterly* (December 2007, pp. 466)*
Pub: SAGE Publications USA
Contact: Blaise R. Simqu, President
Ed: Amy Newman. **Description:** Technology-based simulation for business students to respond to emails and instant messages is presented. The simulation allows students to handle volume business correspondence at work with organizational context and under real-word business situations.

22624 ■ *"Research and Markets Adds Report: The U.S. Mobile Web Market"* in *Entertainment Close-Up* (December 10, 2009)*
Pub: Close-Up Media
Description: Highlights of the new Research and Markets report 'The U.S. Mobile Web Market: Taking Advantage of the iPhone Phenomenon' include: mobile Internet marketing strategies; the growth of mobile web usage; the growth of revenue in the mobile web market; and a look at Internet business communications, social media and networking.

22625 ■ *"The Rypple Effect; Performance Management"* in *The Economist* (Vol. 390, January 3, 2009, No. 8612, pp. 48)*
Pub: The Economist Newspaper Inc.
Description: New companies such as Rypple, a new, web-based service, claim that they can satisfy the Net Generation's need for frequent assessments while easing the burden this creates for management.

22626 ■ *"Say Goodbye to Voicemail"* in *Agency Sales Magazine* (Vol. 39, November 2009, No. 10, pp. 3)*
Pub: MANA

Description: Salespeople should think twice before leaving a voicemail. The emerging modern etiquette is to send a text message or to e-mail the customer or client. Communication suggestions for both salespeople and their principals are presented.

22627 ■ *"Shoestring-Budget Marketing"* in *Women Entrepreneur* (January 5, 2009)*
Pub: Entrepreneur Media Inc.

Ed: Maria Falconer. **Description:** Pay-per-click search engine advertising is the traditional type of e-marketing that may not only be too expensive for certain kinds of businesses but also may not attract the quality customer base a business looking to grow needs to find. Social networking websites have become a mandatory marketing tool for business owners who want to see growth in their sales; tips are provided for utilizing these networking websites in order to gain more visibility on the Internet which can, in turn, lead to the more sales.

22628 ■ *"Social Media: Communicate the Important Stuff"* in *Agency Sales Magazine* (Vol. 39, November 2009, No. 10, pp. 52)*
Pub: MANA

Ed: Jack Foster. **Description:** Social media such as Twitter or Facebook allows businesses to communicate with their customers over great distances but this technology can take away from the personal touch. For those that want to implement these tools in their marketing plans, they should first find out which social media networks their target audience use and give their customers reasons to become fans.

22629 ■ *"Social Networking Site for Moms"* in *Marketing to Women* (Vol. 21, March 2008, No. 3, pp. 3)*
Pub: EPM Communications Inc.
Contact: Ira Mayer, President
E-mail: imayer@epmcom.com

Description: The Cradle is a social networking site devoted to pregnancy and new parenthood.

22630 ■ *"Spell It Out"* in *Entrepreneur* (Vol. 36, April 2008, No. 4, pp. 123)*
Pub: Entrepreneur Media, Inc.

Ed: Emily Weisberg. **Description:** IM:It is an apparel and accessories company that markets products with instant messaging (IM) acronyms and emoticons. Examples of these are 'LOL' and 'GTG'. Other details on IM:It products are discussed.

22631 ■ *Table Talk: The Savvy Girl's Alternative to Networking*
Pub: AuthorHouse

Ed: Diane Danielson. **Released:** April 1, 2003. **Price:** $17.50. **Description:** Let's face it. Women and men are different. So why should we all have to network in the same way? And, why should women have to 'network' at all? Between family and work responsibilities, the idea of pressing flesh at some not-very-festive cocktail party is right up there in appeal with a root canal. But what if women could find a way to make career boosting connections that are actually fun? Enter 'table talk', a new way to network for time-pressed, professional women.

22632 ■ *"Understanding Persuasive Online Sales Messages from eBay Auctions"* in *Business Communication Quarterly* (December 2007, pp. 482)*
Pub: SAGE Publications USA
Contact: Blaise R. Simqu, President

Ed: Barbara Jo White, Daniel Clapper, Rita Noel, Jenny Fortier, Pierre Grabolosa. **Description:** eBay product listings were studied to determine the requirements of persuasive sales writing. Potential sellers should use the proper keywords and make an authentic description with authentic photographs of the item being auctioned.

22633 ■ *"Vistaprint Survey Indicates that Online Marketing Taking Hold Among Small Businesses" in Internet Wire (December 10, 2009)*
Pub: Comtex News Network, Inc.
Description: According to a comprehensive survey from Vistaprint N.V., small businesses are very likely to increase their use of Internet marketing strategies such as paid and organic search, email marketing, social media networking and custom websites over the next year. Trends continue to show that more small businesses are indeed adapting to the changing marketplace and are more willing to diversify their marketing strategies than ever before.

22634 ■ *"Why Mumbai at 1PM is the Center of the Business World" in Harvard Business Review (Vol. 88, October 2010, No. 10, pp. 38)*
Pub: Harvard Business School Publishing
Ed: Michael Segalla. **Description:** A time zone chart is presented for assisting in the planning of international conference calls.

22635 ■ *"Wi-Fi Finds Its Way Despite Nixed Plan for Free System" in Crain's Cleveland Business (Vol. 28, November 12, 2007, No. 45, pp. 3)*
Pub: Crain Communications, Inc.
Ed: Jay Miller. **Description:** Discusses the issues facing Cleveland and Northeast Ohio concerning their proposal to offer citizens wireless Internet services for free or a small fee.

22636 ■ *"Words at Work" in Information Today (Vol. 26, February 2009, No. 2, pp. 25)*
Pub: Information Today, Inc.
Description: Current new buzzwords include the following: digital amnesia, or overload by availability, speed and volume of digital information; maternal profiling, a form a discrimination against women; recipe malpractice, a reminder that just because you can turn on a stove it doesn't make you a chef; ringxiety, the act when everyone reaches for their cell phone when one rings; verbing, the practice of turning good nouns into verbs.

22637 ■ *"Work Smarter" in Entrepreneur (Vol. 36, April 2008, No. 4, pp. 70)*
Pub: Entrepreneur Media, Inc.
Ed: Amanda C. Kooser. **Description:** Online applications that address a business' particular needs are presented. These web applications offer email services, collaboration services of sharing and editing documents and presentations and tie-ups with online social networking sites. Details on various web applications are provided.

22638 ■ *"The Workplace Generation Gaps" in Women In Business (Vol. 62, June 2010, No. 2, pp. 8)*
Pub: American Business Women's Association
Ed: Leigh Elmore. **Description:** Generation gaps among baby boomers, Generation X and Generation Y in the workplace are attributed to technological divides and differences in opinions. These factors could lead to workplace misunderstandings, employee turnover and communication difficulties. Details on managing such workplace gaps are discussed.

TRADE PERIODICALS

22639 ■ *Copy Editor*
Pub: Barbara Wallraff
Ed: Barbara Wallraff, Editor, barbaraw@copyeditor. com. **Released:** Bimonthly. **Price:** $39; $74, Canada and Mexico; $128, two years; $138, Canada and Mexico 2. **Description:** Covers new words, changes in usage, and reference books for editors.

22640 ■ *Writing That Works*
Pub: Communications Concepts Inc.
Contact: John De Lellis, Editor
Released: Monthly. **Price:** $119 U.S., Canada and Mexico. **Description:** Advises corporate, nonprofit, agency and independent communicators on business writing and publishing. Also covers writing techniques,

style matters, publication management, and online publishing. Publisher also sponsors annual APEX Awards for Publication Excellence.

VIDEOCASSETTES/ AUDIOCASSETTES

22641 ■ *Basic Steps for Better Business Writing*
Encyclopedia Britannica
331 N. LaSalle St.
Chicago, IL 60654
Ph: (312)347-7159
Free: 800-323-1229
Fax: (312)294-2104
URL: http://www.britannica.com
Released: 1988. **Price:** $1995.00. **Description:** This package of five video-cassettes, including a Leader's Guide, shows employees how to cut their writing time in half while generating written communications that sell ideas, stimulate action and reduce confusion.
Availability: VHS; 3/4 U.

22642 ■ *Better Business Grammar*
Briefings Publishing Group
2807 N. Parham Rd., Ste. 200
Richmond, VA 23294
Free: 800-791-8699
Fax: (570)320-2079
Co. E-mail: briefingsweborders@publishersservice-associates.com
URL: http://www.briefings.com
Released: 1991. **Price:** $79.00. **Description:** Basic tips for managers on how to get over common stumbling blocks of the English language when writing. **Availability:** VHS.

22643 ■ *Business Writing: Quick, Clear, Concise*
American Media, Inc.
4621 121st St.
Urbandale, IA 50323-2311
Ph: (515)224-0919
Free: 888-776-8268
Fax: (515)327-2555
Co. E-mail: custsvc@ammedia.com
URL: http://www.ammedia.com
Released: 1992. **Price:** $695.00. **Description:** Features tips on reducing writing time, improving clarity, and organizing ideas using a five-step method. Includes an instructor's guide, participant workbooks, an erase-board, and overhead transparencies. **Availability:** VHS; 3/4 U; 8 mm.

22644 ■ *Business Writing Skills Series*
Cambridge Educational
c/o Films Media Group
132 West 31st Street, 17th Floor
Ste. 124
New York, NY 10001
Free: 800-257-5126
Fax: (609)671-0266
Co. E-mail: custserve@films.com
URL: http://www.cambridgeol.com
Released: 199?. **Price:** $149.95. **Description:** Two tape series offers practical tips for organizing your thoughts effectively for written business communication. Includes advice on breaking writer's block, creating a strong opening and closing, choosing a formal versus an informal style, and more. **Availability:** VHS.

22645 ■ *Communication*
American Media, Inc.
4621 121st St.
Urbandale, IA 50323-2311
Ph: (515)224-0919
Free: 888-776-8268
Fax: (515)327-2555
Co. E-mail: custsvc@ammedia.com
URL: http://www.ammedia.com
Released: 1989. **Price:** $1485.00. **Description:** Communication, in the form of memos, phone calls, and presentations are essential to business success.
Availability: VHS; 3/4 U.

22646 ■ *Techniques to Improve Your Writing: Practical G/T Business Writing*
Instructional Video
2219 C St.
Lincoln, NE 68502
Ph: (402)475-6570
Free: 800-228-0164
Fax: (402)475-6500
Co. E-mail: feedback@insvideo.com
URL: http://www.insvideo.com
Released: 19??. **Price:** $79.95. **Description:** Outlines techniques on how to write reports, memos, and letters more clearly. Also covers tough punctuation and grammar questions. Includes handbook.
Availability: VHS.

CONSULTANTS

22647 ■ *Alliance Management International Ltd.*
PO Box 470691
Cleveland, OH 44147-0691
Ph: (440)838-1922
Co. E-mail: bob@bgruss.com
Contact: Ashok Vasudevan, Director
Scope: A consulting company that helps to form national and international strategic alliances. Handles alliances between companies forming joint ventures. Staff specialized in small company-large company alliance, alliance assessment and analysis, and alliance strategic planning. **Seminars:** Joint Business Planning; Developing a Shared Vision; Current and New/Prospective Partner Assessment; Customer Service; Sales Training; Leader and Management Skills.

22648 ■ *American English Academy (AEA)—American English College*
111 N Atlantic Blvd., Ste. 112
Monterey Park, CA 91754
Ph: (626)457-2800
Fax: (626)457-2808
Co. E-mail: admission@aea-usa.com
URL: http://www.aea-usa.com
Contact: Charles Policky, President
Scope: Specializes in providing on-site English language and communication development for corporations and individuals. Also develops and delivers training in speaking, writing, pronunciation, grammar, and idioms with an emphasis on business communication. Offers individual, small group, intensive, and long-distance learning. Programs tailor-made for each client. **Founded:** 1983. **Telecommunication Services:** info@aec.edu.

22649 ■ *Beeline Learning Solutions (BLS)*
14911 Quorum Dr., Ste. 120
Dallas, TX 75254
Ph: (972)813-0465
Fax: (972)386-8667
Co. E-mail: info@consultingpartners.com
URL: http://www.beeline.com
Contact: Dominic Nagy, Manager
E-mail: dominic.nagy@consultingpartners.com
Scope: Consulting firm offering technology, content, and services addressing recruitment and sourcing, talent management, and learning and performance optimization. Solutions offered include contingent workforce solutions, vendor management software, talent management solutions, recruitment process outsourcing, performance management, applicant tracking, learning management and eLearning. **Founded:** 1990. **Special Services:** Beeline®.

22650 ■ *The Handler Group Inc.*
425 W End Ave., Apt. 3A
New York, NY 10024-5718
Ph: (212)873-1899
Contact: Mark Lambert Handler, President
E-mail: mlhandler@aol.com
Scope: Provider of marketing, communication planning, and design services, specializing in development of internal and external business communications. Develops corporate identity, corporate literature, employee communications, sales promotion materials, consumer product packaging and information, brochures, annual reports, and presenta-

tion materials. Industries served: Cable/television, technology software, business information, hospitality, and banking. **Founded:** 1976.

22651 ■ Navarro, Kim & Associates
529 N Charles St., Ste. 202
Baltimore, MD 21201-5043
Ph: (410)837-6317
Fax: (410)837-6294
Co. E-mail: bnavarro@sprynet.com
Contact: Beltran Navarro, Director
E-mail: bnavarro@sprynet.com
Scope: Specializes in bridging the gap between firms and non-traditional ethnic communities, especially in community development and institutional building. **Founded:** 1984.

22652 ■ Turn of Phrase
2529 Meade Ct.
Ann Arbor, MI 48105
Ph: (734)995-1579
Fax: (734)995-1321
Contact: Sally Hanna, Agent
E-mail: sadlyhanne@aol.com
Scope: Offers professional writing and editing on business topics. For example, prepares reference manuals, user guides, learning guides, Microsoft Windows help systems, reports, white papers, and other types of documents. Specializes in writing about computer software, especially for non-technical readers. Industries served: engineering, computer, manufacturing. **Founded:** 1989.

22653 ■ Write It Well (WIW)
5626 Estates Dr.
Oakland, CA 94618
Ph: (510)655-6477
Fax: (510)291-9744
Co. E-mail: info@writeitwell.com
URL: http://www.writeitwell.com
Contact: Melanie Wise, Director
E-mail: melaniewise@writeitwell.com
Scope: Develops training programs, instructional materials, and procedures manuals; conduct customized in house classes in communications skills and performance management. Offers Training for Letter Communication. **Founded:** 1980. **Publications:** "Professional Writing Skills: A Self-Paced Training Program"; "Grammar for Grown ups A Self-Paced Training Program"; "Writing Performance Documentation A Self-Paced Training Program"; "Report and Proposal Writing for Environmental Professionals A Self-Paced Training Program"; "How to Write Reports and Proposals A Self-Paced Training Program"; "Just Commas 9 Basic Rules to Master Comma Usage"; "E-Mail - a Write it a Well Guide". **Seminars:** Business Writing; Effective E-Mail; Grammar Fundamentals; Technical Writing.

COMPUTER SYSTEMS/ SOFTWARE

22654 ■ *Better Business Writing*
Chris Learning
PO Box 25690
Rochester, NY 14625
Ph: (888)534-5556
Free: 800-442-7477
Fax: (888)715-0220
Co. E-mail: courseiltcrisp@thomaslearning.com
URL: http://www.axzopress.com
Contact: John Winder, President
Price: $13.95 (VCI CD-ROM). **Description:** Based on the Better Business Writing video and book. Includes book and user's guide.

RESEARCH CENTERS

22655 ■ Colorado State University - Center for Research on Communication and Technology
C-229 Clark Bldg.
Fort Collins, CO 80523-1785
Ph: (970)491-5674
Fax: (970)491-2908
Co. E-mail: don.zimmerman@colostate.edu
URL: http://www.colostate.edu/Depts/CROWACT
Founded: 1991.

22656 ■ University of Notre Dame - Fanning Center for Business Communication
Mendoza College of Business
Notre Dame, IN 46556
Ph: (574)631-8397
Fax: (574)631-5255
Co. E-mail: james.s.orourke.2@nd.edu
URL: http://business.nd.edu/Fanning_Center_for_ Business_Communication
Contact: Prof. James S. O'Rourke, IV, Director
Services: Instruction, counseling, and guidance: in management and corporate communication. **Founded:** 1990. **Publications:** *Management and Corporate Communication Case Studies* (Semiannual). **Educational Activities:** Conference on Corporate Communication (Annual); Management Development Seminars; Fanning Center for Business Communication Workshops. **Awards:** E.D. Fanning Award; L.B. Pilkinton Award.

START-UP INFORMATION

22657 ■ Entrepreneurship Strategy: Changing Patterns in New Venture Creation, Growth, and Reinvention
Pub: SAGE Publications USA
Contact: Blaise R. Simqu, President
Ed: Lisa K. Gundry; Jill R. Kickul. **Released:** August 2006. **Price:** $69.95. **Description:** Entrepreneurial strategies that incorporate new venture emergence, early growth, and reinvention and innovation are examined.

22658 ■ Going Solo: Developing a Home-Based Consulting Business from the Ground Up
Pub: McGraw-Hill Companies Inc.
Contact: Deven Sharma, President
Ed: William J. Bond. **Released:** January 1997. **Description:** Ways to turn specialized knowledge into a home-based successful consulting firm, focusing on targeting client needs, business plans, and growth.

ASSOCIATIONS AND OTHER ORGANIZATIONS

22659 ■ Association for Corporate Growth - Toronto Chapter (ACG)—Canadian Angus Association
720 Spadina Ave., Ste. 202
Toronto, ON, Canada M5S 2T9
Ph: (416)868-1881
Fax: (416)391-3633
Co. E-mail: acgtoronto@acg.org
URL: http://www.acg.org/toronto/default.aspx
Contact: Stephen B. Smith, President
Description: Professionals with a leadership role in strategic corporate growth. Seeks to facilitate the professional advancement of members, and the practice of corporate growth management. Fosters communication and cooperation among members; conducts continuing professional education programs. **Founded:** 1973. **Publications:** Mergers & Acquisitions - The Dealmaker's Journal (Monthly). **Educational Activities:** Association for Corporate Growth - Toronto Chapter Board meeting (Monthly); Capital Connection (Annual). **Awards:** Toronto Chapter Leadership Award (Annual).

22660 ■ Mergers & Acquisitions - The Dealmaker's Journal
720 Spadina Ave., Ste. 202
Toronto, ON, Canada M5S 2T9
Ph: (416)868-1881
Fax: (416)391-3633
Co. E-mail: acgtoronto@acg.org
URL: http://www.acg.org/toronto/default.aspx
Contact: Stephen B. Smith, President
Released: Monthly **Price:** included in membership dues.

EDUCATIONAL PROGRAMS

22661 ■ Total Productive Maintenance (TPM) & 5S (Onsite)
American Trainco
9785 S Maroon Cir., Ste. 300
Englewood, CO 80112
Ph: (303)531-4560
Free: 877-978-7246
Fax: (303)531-4565
Co. E-mail: Sales@AmericanTrainco.com
URL: http://www.americantrainco.com
Price: $990.00. **Description:** Two-day seminar that focuses on getting managers, maintenance personnel and equipment users all working together to prevent equipment problems and reduce expenditures. **Dates and Locations:** Cities throughout the United States.

REFERENCE WORKS

22662 ■ "3CDC's Biggest Year" in Business Courier (Vol. 26, December 18, 2009, No. 34, pp. 1)
Pub: American City Business Journals, Inc.
Ed: Lucy May. **Description:** Cincinnati Center City Development Corporation (3CDC) will make 2010 its biggest year with nearly $164 million projects in the works. Historic tax credits and continued help from the city have allowed the private nonprofit organization to finance mega projects such as the $43 million renovation and expansion of Washington Park. Other projects that 3CDC will start or complete in 2010 are presented.

22663 ■ The 7 Irrefutable Rules of Small Business Growth
Pub: John Wiley & Sons, Incorporated
Ed: Steven S. Little. **Released:** February 2005. **Price:** $18.95. **Description:** Proven strategies to maintain small business growth are outlined, covering topics such as technology, business plans, hiring, and more.

22664 ■ 10 Steps to Successful Social Networking for Business
Pub: ASTD
Contact: Tony Bingham, President
E-mail: tbingham@astd.org
Ed: Darin Hartley. **Released:** July 1, 2010. **Price:** $19.95. **Description:** Designed for today's fast-paced, need-it-yesterday business environment and for the thousands of workers who find themselves faced with new assignments, responsibilities, and requirements and too little time to learn what they must know.

22665 ■ The 29 Percent Solution
Pub: Greenleaf Book Group Press
Ed: Ivan Misner, Michele Donovan. **Released:** 2008. **Price:** $21.95. **Description:** It is true that some people are better connected than others. That means that connecting is a skill that can be acquired. Networking skills used to increase business connections are highlighted.

22666 ■ "$49M Defense Contracts Hits Austin" in Austin Business JournalInc. (Vol. 28, August 8, 2008, No. 21, pp. A1)
Pub: American City Business Journals
Ed: Laura Hipp. **Description:** BAE Systems PLC has landed a $49 million contract to build thermal cameras, which are expected to be installed on tanks in 2009 and 2010. BAE is expected to land other defense contracts and is likely to add employees in order to meet production demands.

22667 ■ "100-BU. Beans" in Farm Industry News (Vol. 42, January 1, 2009, No. 1)
Pub: Penton Media Inc.
Contact: John French, President
Ed: Lynn Grooms. **Description:** Demand for soybeans has increased and growers are seeing an increase in yields as well due to breeders that are using molecular-assisted selection; other aspects of the soybean market are presented.

22668 ■ "The 100 Fastest-Growing Companies" in Hispanic Business (Vol. 30, July-August 2008, No. 7-8, pp. 22)
Pub: Hispanic Business, Inc.
Ed: Michael Bowker. **Description:** CEO's of the five fastest growing Hispanic-owned companies discuss the success of their companies; most of them attribute their success to proper investment and diversification, effective innovations and seeing growth opportunities where others see roadblocks.

22669 ■ "The 100 Most Bullish Stocks" in Canadian Business (Vol. 81, Summer 2008, No. 9, pp. 81)
Pub: Rogers Media Ltd.
Ed: Megan Harman; Lauren McKeon. **Description:** 100 of the most bullish stocks are taken from the list of the 500 best-performing stocks. The idea is to narrow the list help investors in their investment decisions since it is difficult to choose from a large list. Analysts rate the companies with 5 being the most bullish and 1 the least. Other details of the roster are presented.

22670 ■ 101 Secrets to Building a Winning Business
Pub: Allen & Unwin
Ed: Andrew Griffiths. **Released:** September 1, 2009. **Price:** $14.95. **Description:** Provides expert information for running and growing a small business.

22671 ■ "352 Media Group Opens New Tampa Web Design and Digital Marketing Office" in Entertainment Close-Up (May 2, 2011)
Pub: Close-Up Media
Description: 352 Media Group opened its newest office in Tampa, Florida in May 2011. The firm is noted for its achievements in Web design and digital marketing.

22672 ■ "2009: A Call For Vision" in Women Entrepreneur (January 28, 2009)
Pub: Entrepreneur Media Inc.
Ed: Elinor Robin. **Description:** Providing exemplary customer service, reducing expenses and creating an out-of-the-box niche are three key factors that will

help business survive during this economic crisis. Business owners must see potential where others see failure in order to create new opportunities that may not only allow their business to survive during these times but may actually cause some businesses to thrive despite this economic downturn.

22673 ■ "2011 a Record Year for New Wind Energy Installations in Canada" in CNW Group (September 26, 2011)
Pub: CNW Group
Contact: Carolyn McGill-Davidson, President
Description: Canada reports a record for new wind energy projects in 2011 with about 1,338 MW of newly installed wind energy capacity expected to come on line, compared to 690 MW installed in 2010. Statistical data included.

22674 ■ "ABB Could Still Engineer an Upside" in Barron's (Vol. 89, July 20, 2009, No. 29, pp. M6)
Pub: Dow Jones & Co., Inc.
Ed: Goran Mijuk. **Description:** Swiss engineering company ABB can remain profitable as its power transmission and distribution activities continue to generate earnings. The company is also benefiting from increased exposure in emerging markets.

22675 ■ "ACE Back in Unfriendly Skies" in Globe & Mail (February 14, 2006, pp. B17)
Pub: CTVglobemedia Publishing Inc.
Ed: Brent Jang. **Description:** ACE Aviation Holdings Inc. reported $258 million profit for 2005. The opinions of analysts on the share price of the company for 2006 are presented.

22676 ■ "Achieving Greatness" in Black Enterprise (Vol. 38, January 2008, No. 6, pp. 50)
Pub: Earl G. Graves Publishing Co. Inc.
Description: Randall Pinkett, winner of a reality show on television and chairman of BCT Partners, insists that a business cannot survive by doing just enough or more of the same. Pinkett's New Jersey company provides management, technology and consulting to other firms.

22677 ■ "Actions to Implement Three Potent Post-Crisis Strategies" in Strategy & Leadership (Vol. 38, September-October 2010, No. 5)
Pub: Emerald Inc.
Ed: Saul J. Berman, Richard Christner, Ragna Bell. **Description:** The need for organizations to design and implement strategies to cope with the possible situations in the post-economic crisis environment is emphasized. The plans that organizations should implement to successfully manage uncertainty and complexity and to foster their eventual growth are discussed.

22678 ■ "Add Aquatics to Boost Business" in Pet Product News (Vol. 64, December 2010, No. 12, pp. 20)
Pub: BowTie Inc.
Ed: David Lass. **Description:** Pet stores are encouraged to add aquatics departments to increase profitability through repeat sales. This goal can be realized by sourcing, displaying, and maintaining high quality live fish. Other tips regarding the challenges associated with setting up an aquatics department are presented.

22679 ■ "Adidas' Brand Ambitions" in Business Journal Portland (Vol. 27, December 10, 2010, No. 41, pp. 1)
Pub: Portland Business Journal
Ed: Erik Siemers. **Description:** Adidas AG, the second-largest sporting goods brand in the world, hopes to increase global revenue by 50 percent by 2015. The German company, which reported $14.5 billion sales, plans to improve its U.S. market. The U.S. is Adidas' largest, but also the most underperforming market for the firm.

22680 ■ "AdvacePierre Heats Up" in Business Courier (Vol. 27, October 29, 2010, No. 26, pp. 1)
Pub: Business Courier
Ed: John Newberry. **Description:** Bill Toler, chief executive officer of AdvancePierre Foods, is aiming for more growth and more jobs. The company was formed after the merger of Pierre Foods with two Oklahoma-based food processing companies. Toler wants to expand production and is set to start adding employees in the next 6-12 months.

22681 ■ "Advancing the Ball" in Inside Healthcare (Vol. 6, December 2010, No. 7, pp. 31)
Pub: RedCoat Publishing Inc.
Ed: Michelle McNickle. **Description:** Profile of Medicalodges an elder-care specialty company that provides both patient care and technology development. President and CEO of the firm believes that hiring good employees is key to growth for any small business.

22682 ■ Advancing Research on Minority Entrepreneurship
Pub: SAGE Publications USA
Contact: Blaise R. Simqu, President
Ed: James H. Johnson Jr.; Timothy Bates; William E. Jackson III; James H. Johnson; William E. Jackson. **Released:** September 2007. **Price:** $34.00. **Description:** Although minorities are more likely to engage in start-up businesses than others, minority entrepreneurs are less likely to get their enterprises off the ground or succeed in growing their businesses. The higher failure rates, lower sales and profits and less employment are among topics discussed.

22683 ■ "Ag Firms Harvest Revenue Growth" in The Business Journal-Serving Metropolitan Kansas City (Vol. 26, July 18, 2008, No. 45, pp. 1)
Pub: American City Business Journals, Inc.
Ed: Steve Vockrodt. **Description:** Five of the biggest agricultural companies in the Kansas City area, except one, reported multibillion-dollar revenue increases in 2007. The companies, which include Lansing Trade Group, posted a combined $9.5 billion revenue growth. The factors that affected the revenue increase in the area's agricultural companies, such as prices and high demand, are also examined.

22684 ■ "Agribusiness: How to Get Rich in Farming" in Canadian Business (Vol. 80, January 29, 2007, No. 3, pp. 42)
Pub: Rogers Media
Ed: Peter Shawn Taylor. **Description:** The trends pertaining to the income of Canadian farmers are examined. The methods of increasing the profits of Canadian agribusinesses are discussed.

22685 ■ "AIC To Buy $350M of Real Estate" in Austin Business JournalInc. (Vol. 28, November 14, 2008, No. 35, pp. 1)
Pub: American City Business Journals
Ed: Kate Harrington. **Description:** Austin-based AIC Ventures LP is planning to buy $350 million worth of commercial real estate. The company's move will double its acquisitions. It is also planning to acquire 30 assets for its eight fun in 2009 from middle-market companies.

22686 ■ "Air Canada, WestJet Fill More Seats" in Globe & Mail (January 6, 2006, pp. B3)
Pub: CTVglobemedia Publishing Inc.
Ed: Brent Jang. **Description:** The reasons behind the increase in passenger for Air Canada and West-Jet Airlines Ltd. are presented.

22687 ■ "Airing It Out" in The Business Journal-Serving Greater Tampa Bay (Vol. 28, July 11, 2008, No. 29, pp. 1)
Pub: American City Business Journals, Inc.
Ed: Jane Meinhardt. **Description:** Flanders Corp. is planning to expand its business in Europe and Southeast Asia. The St. Petersburg, Florida-based company has about 2,800 employees and manufactures air filtration products for industrial and residential applications.

22688 ■ "Akerman Senterfitt Merger Deal Close" in The Business Journal-Serving Greater Tampa Bay (Vol. 28, July 18, 2008,
No. 30, pp. 1)
Pub: American City Business Journals, Inc.
Ed: Jeff Blumenthal. **Description:** Sources familiar to the negotiations of Akerman Senterfitt's planned merger with Wolf Block has disclosed that executive committees of both firms have approved the deal. They expect to create an 800-lawyer firm with a significant presence in the U.S. East Coast. Other views and information on the deal and its expected impact on law practice in Florida are presented.

22689 ■ "Alberta's Runaway Train" in Canadian Business (Vol. 80, December 25, 2006, No. 1, pp. 17)
Pub: Rogers Media
Ed: Andrew Nikiforuk. **Description:** The high revenue brought about by the growth in the number of oil sand plants in Canada and the simultaneous burden on infrastructure and housing is discussed.

22690 ■ "Algoma Shares Soar on Growing Sale Rumors" in Globe & Mail (February 13, 2007, pp. B1)
Pub: CTVglobemedia Publishing Inc.
Ed: Andrew Willis; Greg Keenan. **Description:** The stock prices of Algoma Steel Inc. have touched record high of $40 on the Toronto Stock Exchange. The growing rumors about the possible takeover bid is the major reason for the stock price growth.

22691 ■ "All In The Family" in Canadian Business (Vol. 79, September 25, 2006, No. 19, pp. 75)
Pub: Rogers Media
Ed: Zena Olijnyk. **Description:** Continuing ownership of Weston dynasty on Canada's largest chain Loblaw Co. is discussed.

22692 ■ "All Indicators in Michigan Innovation Index Drop in 4Q" in Crain's Detroit Business (Vol. 25, June 22, 2009, No. 25, pp. 9)
Pub: Crain Communications Inc. - Detroit
Ed: Ryan Beene. **Description:** Economic indicators that rate Michigan's innovation fell in the fourth quarter of 2008. The index of trademark applications, SBA loans, venture capital funding, new incorporations and other indicators traced dropped 12.6 points.

22693 ■ "All Revved Up" in Barron's (Vol. 90, September 13, 2010, No. 37, pp. 18)
Pub: Barron's Editorial & Corporate Headquarters
Ed: Christopher C. Williams. **Description:** Shares of Advance Auto Parts has returned 55 percent in a span of three years and the stock could still reach the mid-60s by 2011 from its price of 46.07 in the second week of September 2010. The shares are trading at just 13 times the 2011 earnings.

22694 ■ "Allen Tate Expanding to Research Triangle Park: Firm Expects Raleigh Market to Grow Faster" in Charlotte Observer (January 31, 2007)
Pub: Knight-Ridder/Tribune Business News
Ed: Doug Smith; Dudley Price. **Description:** Allen Tate Realtors expanded its operations to the Research Triangle area. The firm is predicting a strong market and growth in Charlotte, North Carolina.

22695 ■ "AllHipHop.com's Founders Thought a Weeklong Event Would Raise the Company" in Inc. (February 2008, pp. 48-51)
Pub: Gruner & Jahr USA Publishing
Ed: Kermit Pattison. **Description:** Co-founders Greg Watkins and Chuck Creekmur, planned a weeklong festival to promote their company, AllHipHop.com; the event nearly ruined the firm. The online firm provides news about hip hop artists and the industry and is updated daily.

22696 ■ "Amcon Distributing Co." in Arkansas Business (Vol. 26, November 9, 2009, No. 45, pp. 13)
Pub: Journal Publishing Inc.
Description: Amcon Distributing Co., a consumer products company, has bought the convenience store distribution assets of Discount Distributors from its parent, Harps Food Stores Inc., significantly increas-

ing its wholesale distribution presence in the northwest Arkansas market. The acquisition will be funded through Amcon's existing credit facilities.

22697 ■ *"Americhem to Shutter Maryland Operation"* in *Crain's Cleveland Business (Vol. 28, October 29, 2007, No. 43, pp. 14)*
Pub: Crain Communications, Inc.
Description: Americhem Inc., a manufacturer of colors and additives for polymer products has announced plans to expand two plants in Cuyahoga Falls while phasing out its operations in Salisbury, Maryland.

22698 ■ *"Analyzing the Analytics"* in *Entrepreneur (Vol. 37, October 2009, No. 10, pp. 42)*
Pub: Entrepreneur Media, Inc.
Ed: Mikal E. Belicove. **Description:** Startups can maximize Web analytics by using them to monitor traffic sources and identify obstacles to converting them into targeted behaviors . Startups should set trackable Web site goals and continuously track traffic and conversion rates.

22699 ■ *"Ann Arbor Google's Growth Dips"* in *Crain's Detroit Business (Vol. 25, June 8, 2009, No. 23, pp. 3)*
Pub: Crain Communications Inc. - Detroit
Ed: Bill Shea. **Description:** Global recession has slowed the growth of Google Inc. Three years ago, when Google moved to Ann Arbor, Michigan it estimated it would provide 1,000 new jobs within five years, so far the firm employs 250.

22700 ■ *"Are You Ignoring Trends That Could Shake Up Your Business?"* in *Harvard Business Review (Vol. 88, July-August 2010, No. 7-8, pp. 124)*
Pub: Harvard Business School Publishing
Ed: Elie Ofek, Luc Wathieu. **Description:** Ways for firms to capitalize on trends that might otherwise negatively affect their business are spotlighted. These include using certain aspects of the trend to augment traditional product/service offerings, and combining the trend with the offerings to transcend its traditional category.

22701 ■ *"Arizona Firms In Chicago Go For Gold With '08 Games"* in *The Business Journal - Serving Phoenix and the Valley of the Sun (Vol. 28, August 8, 2008, No. 49, pp. 1)*
Pub: American City Business Journals, Inc.
Ed: Patrick O'Grady. **Description:** More than 20 U.S. athletes will wear Arizona-based eSoles LLC's custom-made insoles to increase their performance at the 2008 Beijing Olympics making eSoles one of the beneficiaries of the commercialization of the games. Translation software maker Auralog Inc saw a 60 percent jump in sales from its Mandarin Chinese language applications.

22702 ■ *"Art Institute of Chicago Goes Green"* in *Contractor (Vol. 56, July 2009, No. 7, pp. 1)*
Pub: Penton Media, Inc.
Ed: Candace Roulo. **Description:** Art Institute of Chicago's Modern Wing museum addition will receive a certification that makes them one of the most environmentally sound museum expansions in the U.S. A modified variable-air-volume system is being used to meet temperature and humidity requirements in the building and it also has a double curtain wall to capture summer heat.

22703 ■ *"At 5-Year Mark, News 9 Makes Presence Felt in Competition for Ad Dollars"* in *Business Review, Albany New York (October 5, 2007)*
Pub: American City Business Journals Inc.
Ed: Barbara Pinckney. **Description:** The 24-hour news channel Capital News 9 can be watched live by viewers on their cell phones beginning late 2007 or early 2008 as part of a deal between Time Warner Cable and Sprint Nextel Corporation to bring Sprint's Pivot technology. News 9 marked its fifth year and plans to continue expanding coverage and provide better services to viewers.

22704 ■ *"Athletes' Performance Building $10 Million Facility In ASU Park"* in *The Business Journal - Serving Phoenix and the Valley of the Sun (Vol. 28, August 8, 2008, No. 49, pp. 1)*
Pub: American City Business Journals, Inc.
Ed: Jan Buchholz. **Description:** Athletes Performance's planned facility at Arizona State University is scheduled to begin in November 2008 and expected to be completed by September 2009. The new building will almost double the company's training space as it will expand from around 19,000 square feet to 35,000 square feet.

22705 ■ *"ATI Now Ready to Pounce on Biotech"* in *Austin Business JournalInc. (Vol. 28, August 22, 2008, No. 23, pp. 1)*
Pub: American City Business Journals
Ed: Laura Hipp. **Description:** Austin Technology Incubator has entered the biotechnology sector through a program of the University of Texas incubator. The company's bioscience program was set off by a grant from the City of Austin worth $125,000. The growth of Austin's biotechnology sector is examined.

22706 ■ *"ATS Secures Investment From Goldman Sachs"* in *The Business Journal - Serving Phoenix and the Valley of the Sun (Vol. 29, September 26, 2008, No. 4, pp. 1)*
Pub: American City Business Journals, Inc.
Ed: Patrick O'Grady. **Description:** Goldman Sachs made an investment to American Traffic Solutions Inc. (ATS) which will allow it to gain two seats on the board of the red-light and speed cameras maker. The investment will help ATS maintain its rapid growth which is at 83 percent over the past 18 months leading up to September 2008.

22707 ■ *"Auction Company Grows with Much Smaller Sites"* in *Automotive News (Vol. 86, October 31, 2011, No. 6488, pp. 23)*
Pub: Crain Communications Inc.
Ed: Arlena Sawyers. **Description:** Auction Broadcasting Company has launched auction sites and is expanding into new areas. The family-owned business will provide auctions half the size traditionally used. The firm reports that 40 percent of the General Motors factory-owned vehicles sold on consignment were purchased by online buyers, up 30 percent over 2010.

22708 ■ *"Austin's GMP Growth Top in Nation"* in *Austin Business JournalInc. (Vol. 29, January 8, 2010, No. 44, pp. 1)*
Pub: American City Business Journals
Ed: Jacob Dirr. **Description:** Austin's gross metropolitan product (GMP) has grown by 2 percent, putting it in the top 5 for GMP growth among the largest 100 American metropolitan areas. Insights into the area's business and technology services are examined.

22709 ■ *"Australian Firm Buys Off Sands Engineering Company for $1 Billion"* in *Globe & Mail (February 8, 2007, pp. B3)*
Pub: CTVglobemedia Publishing Inc.
Ed: David Ebner. **Description:** Australia's Worley-Parson Ltd. acquires Colt Engineering Corp., a private petroleum company, for $1 billion. The acquisition will provide WorleyParson an opportunity to expand its operations in Australia.

22710 ■ *"Avnet Inc.'s Expansion Fueled By Mergers and Acquisitions"* in *The Business Journal - Serving Phoenix and the Valley of the Sun (Vol. 28, September 12, 2008, No. 53, pp. 1)*
Pub: American City Business Journals, Inc.
Ed: Patrick O'Grady. **Description:** Avnet Inc. has grown and has nearly tripled its revenue in the past ten years through the company's acquisitions and consolidation. The company's revenue in 2008 is $17.9 billion. Other details about the company's growth are discussed.

22711 ■ *"Awaiting a Call from Deutsche Telekom"* in *Barron's (Vol. 90, September 6,*

2010, No. 36, pp. M5)
Pub: Barron's Editorial & Corporate Headquarters
Ed: Vito J. Racanelli. **Description:** Deutsche Telekom's (DT) T-Mobile USA Unit has settled in the number four position in the market and the parent company will need to decide if it will hold onto the company in the next 12-18 months from September 2010. T-Mobile's rivals will make critical improvements during this time and DT has the option to upgrade T-Mobile at the cost of improvements to its other units.

22712 ■ *Awesomely Simple: Essential Business Strategies for Turning Ideas Into Action*
Pub: Jossey-Bass
Ed: John Spence. **Released:** September 8, 2009. **Price:** $24.95. **Description:** Six key strategies that create a foundation for achieving business excellence include: vivid vision, best people, a performance-oriented culture, robust communication, a sense of urgency, and extreme customer focus.

22713 ■ *"Back to Business for Bishop Museum"* in *Hawaii Business (Vol. 54, August 2008, No. 2, pp. 53)*
Pub: Hawaii Business Publishing
Ed: Shara Enay. **Description:** Bishop Museum, ranked 224 in Hawaii Business' top 250 companies for 2008, had $29.5 million in gross sales for 2007, up 52.8 percent from the $19.3 million gross sales in 2006. The company has cut 24 positions in a restructuring effort for the museum's sustainability. Grants, artifacts and plans for sustainable operations are discussed.

22714 ■ *"Bagging Profits; High-End Grocers Expand Despite Stale Economy"* in *Crain's Detroit Business (Vol. 24, March 24, 2008, No. 12, pp. 1)*
Pub: Crain Communications, Inc.
Ed: Nancy Kaffer. **Description:** Discusses the expansion plans of several high-end grocery stores in the Detroit area and the reasons why, despite the poor economy, these gourmet grocers are doing well. Statistical data included.

22715 ■ *"The Balancing Act: How Busy Executives Make Their Lives Work"* in *Black Enterprise (Vol. 37, February 2007, No. 7, pp. 118)*
Pub: Earl G. Graves Publishing Co. Inc.
Ed: Marcia A. Reed-Woodard. **Description:** More than 70 percent of women with children work outside the home, according to a 2005 survey conducted by the U.S. Department of Labor Bureau. One of the biggest struggles these women face is balancing family with career aspirations and climbing the corporate ranks.

22716 ■ *"Baldwin Connelly Partnership Splits"* in *Business Journal Serving Greater Tampa Bay (Vol. 30, November 19, 2010, No. 48, pp. 1)*
Pub: Tampa Bay Business Journal
Ed: Alexis Muellner. **Description:** The fast-growing insurance brokerage Baldwin Connelly is now breaking up after five years. Two different entrepreneurial visions have developed within the organization and founders Lowry Baldwin and John Connell will not take separate tracks. Staffing levels in the firm are expected to remain the same.

22717 ■ *"BancVue to Expand"* in *Austin Business JournalInc. (Vol. 29, November 27, 2009, No. 38, pp. 1)*
Pub: American City Business Journals
Ed: Kate Harrington. **Description:** Significant growth of BancVue in the past six years has prompted the company to look for a site that could increase its office space from 25,000 square feet to 65,000 square feet. BancVue offers bank and credit union software solutions and is planning to lease or buy a property in Austin, Texas.

22718 ■ *"Bank Bullish on Austin"* in *Austin Business JournalInc. (Vol. 29, November 13, 2009, No. 36, pp. A1)*
Pub: American City Business Journals
Ed: Kate Harrington. **Description:** American Bank's presence in Austin, Texas has been boosted by new management and a new 20,000 square foot building.

This community bank intends to focus on building relationship with commercial banking customers. American Bank also plans to extend investment banking, treasury management, and commercial lending services.

22719 ■ "A Banking Play Without Banking Plagues" in Barron's (Vol. 88, March 31, 2008, No. 13, pp. 26)
Pub: Dow Jones & Company, Inc.
Ed: Jack Willoughby. **Description:** Fiserv's shares have been dragged down by about 20 percent which presents an appealing entry point since the shares could rise by 30 percent or more by 2009. The company enables banks to post and open new checks and keeps track of loans which are not discretionary processes of banks.

22720 ■ "Bargain Hunting In Vietnam" in Barron's (Vol. 88, July 14, 2008, No. 28, pp. M6)
Pub: Dow Jones & Co., Inc.
Ed: Elliot Wilson. **Description:** Vietnam's economy grew by just 6.5 percent for the first half of 2008 and its balance of payments ballooned to $14.4 billion. The falling stock prices in the country is a boon for bargain hunters and investing in the numerous domestic funds is one way of investing in the country. Some shares that investors are taking an interest in are also discussed.

22721 ■ "Bark Up The Right Tree" in Small Business Opportunities (Winter 2009)
Pub: Entrepreneur Press
Contact: Perlman Neil, President
Description: Profile of Central Bark, a daycare company catering to pets that offers franchise opportunities and is expanding rapidly despite the economic downturn; the company's growth strategy is also discussed.

22722 ■ "Bartering Takes Businesses Back to Basics: Broker's Exchange Helps Members to Reach New Customers" in Buffalo News (July 9, 2010)
Pub: The Buffalo News
Ed: Dino Grandoni. **Description:** Bartering clubs can help small businesses reach new customers and to expand their business.

22723 ■ "Bartering Trades on Talents" in Reading Eagle (June 20, 2010)
Pub: Reading Eagle/Reading Times
Ed: Tony Lucia. **Description:** Bartering is not just a way of trading goods and services, it can be an essential tool for small business to survive in a bad economy.

22724 ■ "Basel3 Quick Fix Actually Neither" in Canadian Business (Vol. 83, October 12, 2010, No. 17, pp. 19)
Pub: Rogers Media Ltd.
Ed: Thomas Watson. **Description:** Information about the so-called Basel 3 standards, which will require banks to hold top-quality capital totaling at least 7 percent of their risk-bearing assets is provided. The rules' supporters believe that a good balance has been reached between improving the Basel 2 framework and maintaining enough lending capital to stimulate an economic growth.

22725 ■ "Baskin-Robbins Expanding in China and U.S." in Ice Cream Reporter (Vol. 21, August 20, 2008, No. 9, pp. 1)
Pub: Ice Cream Reporter
Description: Baskin-Robbins will open its first store in Shanghai, China along with plans for 100 more shops in that country. They will also be expanding their market in the Dallas/Fort Worth, Texas area as well as Greater Cincinnati/Northern Kentucky regions.

22726 ■ "Baskin-Robbins Expanding to South Texas" in Ice Cream Reporter (Vol. 23, July 20, 2010, No. 8, pp. 4)
Pub: Ice Cream Reporter
Description: Baskin-Robbins will develop six new shops in south Texas after signing agreements with two franchisees.

22727 ■ "Baskin-Robbins: New in U.S., Old in Japan" in Ice Cream Reporter (Vol. 23, August 20, 2010, No. 9, pp. 2)
Pub: Ice Cream Reporter
Description: Baskin-Robbins is celebrating its first franchise in Japan.

22728 ■ "Baskin-Robbins Reopens in New Orleans" in Ice Cream Reporter (Vol. 23, September 20, 2010, No. 10, pp. 3)
Pub: Ice Cream Reporter
Description: Baskin-Robbins will open its first shop in New Orleans, Louisiana after Hurricane Katrina in 2005. The shop stands in the exact location of a Baskin-Robbins shop destroyed by Katrina.

22729 ■ "Baskin-Robbins Tests New Upscale Concept" in Ice Cream Reporter (Vol. 21, September 20, 2008, No. 10, pp. 1)
Pub: Ice Cream Reporter
Description: Baskin-Robbins is opening its new upscale store, Cafe 31 in an effort to invigorate its brand. The shop will serve fondues, cakes and other treats prepared by an in-store chef.

22730 ■ "Battling Back from Betrayal" in Harvard Business Review (Vol. 88, December 2010, No. 12, pp. 130)
Pub: Harvard Business School Publishing
Ed: Daniel McGinn. **Description:** Stephen Greer's scrap metal firm, Hartwell Pacific, lost several million dollars due to a lack of efficient and appropriate inventory audits, accounting procedures, and new-hire reference checks for his foreign operations. Greer believes that balancing growth with control is a key component of success.

22731 ■ "BCE Mulls Radical Changes With Industry Under Pressure" in Globe & Mail (March 30, 2007, pp. B1)
Pub: CTVglobemedia Publishing Inc.
Ed: Andrew Willis; Jacquie McNish; Catherine McLean. **Description:** An account on the expansion plans of BCE Inc., which plans to acquire TELUS Corp., is presented.

22732 ■ "BCE Wireless Growth Flags in Fourth Quarter" in Globe & Mail (February 8, 2007, pp. B5)
Pub: CTVglobemedia Publishing Inc.
Ed: Catherine McLean. **Description:** BCE Inc., the largest telecommunications provider in Canada, reported $699 million profit in the final quarter of 2006. The company signed up 169,000 wireless customers in the important holiday season.

22733 ■ Be the Elephant: Build a Bigger, Better Business
Pub: Workman Publishing Company
Ed: Steve Kaplan. **Price:** $19.95. **Description:** Entrepreneur and author sets out an accessible, no-frills plan for business owners, managers, and other industrialists to grow their businesses into elephants: big and strong but also smart. Advice is given on fostering a growth mind-set, assessing risk, and creating unique selling propositions.

22734 ■ Beans: Four Principles for Running a Business in Good Times or Bad
Pub: John Wiley & Sons, Incorporated
Ed: Leslie Yerkes, Charles Decker, Bob Nelson. **Released:** June 2003. **Price:** $19.95. **Description:** Profile of Monorail Espresso, the popular Seattle coffee company that has become prosperous by intentionally staying small and building a strong customer service program.

22735 ■ "The Bear Arrives - With Bargain Hunters" in Barron's (Vol. 88, July 7, 2008, No. 27, pp. M3)
Pub: Dow Jones & Co., Inc.
Ed: Kopin Tan. **Description:** US stock markets have dropped 20 percent below their highs, entering the bear market at the end of June 2008. It was also the worst performance of the stock markets during June. Wine maker Constellation Brands, however, reported a 50 percent rise in net income for the first quarter of 2008.

22736 ■ "Become A Brand" in Women Entrepreneur (September 14, 2008)
Pub: Entrepreneur Media Inc.
Ed: Suzy Girard-Ruttenberg. **Description:** Powerful brands are effective, innovative, exclusive or even socially conscious; it is important for small businesses to understand the power of becoming a brand since it is one of the best ways in which to position one's company and drive its growth.

22737 ■ "Bedding a Leader in Kohl's Q1 Gains" in Home Textiles Today (Vol. 31, May 24, 2011, No. 13, pp. 1)
Pub: Reed Business Information
Contact: Jeff Greisch, President
Description: Kohl's credited home furnishings, particularly bedding, as the leading source of its first-quarter sales and profit gains in 2011. Statistical data included.

22738 ■ "Beer Drinkers Wanted More. The Brewer Had No Room to Expand. How Could It Keep the Taps Flowing?" in Inc. (October 2007, pp. 65-66)
Pub: Gruner & Jahr USA Publishing
Ed: Alex Salkever. **Description:** Profile of John McDonald, founder of Boulevard, the second-largest beer company located in Kansas City, Missouri. McDonald tells how he was able to expand his turn-of-the-century brick building he had imported from Bavaria by developing a 70,000-square-foot building on four acres adjacent to his existing location rather move to a suburb.

22739 ■ "Beer Stocks Rally on Anheuser, InBev Report" in Globe & Mail (February 16, 2007, pp. B3)
Pub: CTVglobemedia Publishing Inc.
Ed: Keith McArthur. **Description:** The stock prices of beer manufacturing industries have increased considerably after impressive profit reports from Anheuser Busch Cos Inc. and InBev SA. Complete analysis in this context is presented.

22740 ■ The Beermat Entrepreneur: Turn Your Good Idea Into a Great Business
Pub: Pearson Education Ltd.
Contact: Rod Bristow, President
Ed: Mike Southon, Andrew Leigh, Chris West. **Released:** March 1, 2009. **Price:** $39.50. **Description:** Information to help start, maintain and grow a small business is given, along with suggestions for working with a bank.

22741 ■ "Behind the Numbers: When It Comes to Earnings, Look for Quality, Not Just Quantity" in Black Enterprise (July 2008, pp. 35)
Pub: Earl G. Graves Publishing Co. Inc.
Ed: Chris Keenan. **Description:** It is important for investors to examine the quality of a company's earnings rather than fixate on the quantity of those earnings. Advice is given regarding issues investors can look at when trying to determine the potential growth of a firm.

22742 ■ "Being Big By Design" in Canadian Business (Vol. 82, April 27, 2009, No. 7, pp. 39)
Pub: Rogers Media
Ed: Andrew Wahl. **Description:** Gennum expects that its planned acquisition of Tundra Semiconductor will expand its market presence and leverage its research and development better than working alone. The proposed friendly acquisition could challenge Zarlink Semiconductor as the largest Canadian semiconductor firm in terms of revenue. The merger could expand Gennum's addressable market to about $2 billion.

22743 ■ "Benchmark Makes Granduca Entrance" in Houston Business Journal (Vol. 40, January 8, 2010, No. 35, pp. 2)
Pub: American City Business Journals
Ed: Jennifer Dawson. **Description:** Houston, Texas-based Interfin Company, owner of the Hotel Granduca, has tapped the services of Benchmark Hospitality International to manage the property. The

hiring of Benchmark is part of Interfin's efforts to develop Granduca hotels in other markets. Statistical data included.

22744 ■ *"Best Cash Flow Generators"* in *Canadian Business (Vol. 81, Summer 2008, No. 9, pp. 73)*
Pub: Rogers Media Ltd.
Ed: Calvin Leung. **Description:** Table showing the five-year annualized growth rate and one-year stock performance of companies that have grown their cash flow per share at an annualized rate of 15 percent or more over the past five years. Analysts project that the cash flow trend will continue. Other details of the stock performance index are presented.

22745 ■ *"Best Defensive Stocks"* in *Canadian Business (Vol. 81, Summer 2008, No. 9, pp. 67)*
Pub: Rogers Media Ltd.
Ed: Calvin Leung. **Description:** Stocks of the companies presented have market capitalization of greater than $1 billion and dividend gains of at least 2 percent. A table showing the average one-year total return of the stocks is provided.

22746 ■ *"Best Growth Stocks"* in *Canadian Business (Vol. 81, Summer 2008, No. 9, pp. 61)*
Pub: Rogers Media Ltd.
Ed: Calvin Leung. **Description:** Table showing the one-year performance of growth stocks is presented. Edmonton-based Stantec Inc. expects to advance its sales and profits by 15 percent to 20 percent per year through tapping international markets and acquisitions. Analysts forecast a 17.1 percent growth rate annually over the next 3 to 5 years.

22747 ■ *"Best Growth Stocks"* in *Canadian Business (Vol. 82, Summer 2009, No. 8, pp. 28)*
Pub: Rogers Media
Ed: Calvin Leung. **Description:** Canadian stocks that are considered as the best growth stocks, and whose price-earnings ratio is less than their earnings growth rate, are suggested. Suggestions include pharmaceutical firm Paladin Labs, which was found to have 13 consecutive years of revenue growth. Paladin Labs acquires or licenses niche drugs and markets them in Canada.

22748 ■ *"Best Income Trust"* in *Canadian Business (Vol. 81, Summer 2008, No. 9, pp. 69)*
Pub: Rogers Media Ltd.
Ed: Calvin Leung. **Description:** Table showing five-year annualized growth rate and one-year stock performance of real estate investment trusts firms in Canada is presented. Calgary-based Boardwalk REIT is projected to grow the fastest among North American REITs over the next two years. Other details on the stock performance analysis are presented.

22749 ■ *"Best Managed Companies"* in *Canadian Business (Vol. 81, Summer 2008, No. 9, pp. 71)*
Pub: Rogers Media Ltd.
Ed: Calvin Leung. **Description:** Table showing the five-year annualized growth rate and one-year stock performance of companies that have grown their cash flow per share at an annualized rate of 15 percent or more over the past five years. Analysts project that the cash flow trend will continue. Other details of the stock performance index are presented.

22750 ■ *"Best Managed Companies (Canada)"* in *Canadian Business (Vol. 82, Summer 2009, No. 8, pp. 38)*
Pub: Rogers Media
Ed: Calvin Leung. **Description:** Agrium Inc. and Barrick Gold Corporation are among those that are found to be the best managed companies in Canada. Best managed companies also include software firm Open Text Corporation, which has grown annual sales by 75 percent and annual profits by 160 percent since 1995. Open Text markets software that allow firms to manage word-based data, and has 46,000 customers in 114 countries.

22751 ■ *"Best Turnaround Stocks"* in *Canadian Business (Vol. 81, Summer 2008, No. 9, pp. 65)*
Pub: Rogers Media Ltd.
Ed: Calvin Leung. **Description:** Share prices of Sierra Wireless Inc. and EXFO Electro Optical Engineering Inc. have fallen over the past year but have good chance at a rebound considering that the companies have free cash flow and no long-term debt. One-year stock performance analysis of the two companies is presented.

22752 ■ *"Best Value Stocks"* in *Canadian Business (Vol. 81, Summer 2008, No. 9, pp. 63)*
Pub: Rogers Media Ltd.
Ed: Calvin Leung. **Description:** Table showing the one-year performance of bargain or best-value stocks is presented. These stocks are undervalued compared to their North American peers, but it is projected that their five-year average return on equity is greater.

22753 ■ *"Better Card Collecting"* in *Canadian Business (Vol. 80, January 15, 2007, No. 2, pp. 66)*
Pub: Rogers Media
Ed: Sarah B. Hood. **Description:** Tips on how to collect business cards and use them for enhancing one's business performance are presented. Targeting specific people, taking notes and giving follow ups are some suggestions.

22754 ■ *"Better Made's Better Idea: Diversify Despite Rising Costs"* in *Crain's Detroit Business (Vol. 24, September 22, 2008, No. 38, pp. 18)*
Pub: Crain Communications Inc.
Ed: Nathan Skid. **Description:** Better Made Snack Foods Inc. is planning to expand its product lines and market reach as well as boost manufacturing capability during a time in which the company is being buffeted by rising commodity and fuel costs. The company feels that diversification is the key to maintain sales and growth.

22755 ■ *"Betting on the Glitz"* in *Canadian Business (Vol. 79, October 9, 2006, No. 20, pp. 104)*
Pub: Rogers Media
Ed: Zena Olijnyk. **Description:** Holt, Renfrew & Comany's expansion plans to cash on the booming demand for high end retail luxury markets are discussed.

22756 ■ *"Beyond Auto; Staffing Firm Malace Grabs Revenue Jump"* in *Crain's Detroit Business (Vol. 26, January 18, 2010, No. 3, pp. 3)*
Pub: Crain Communications Inc.
Ed: Sherri Welch. **Description:** Malace & Associates Inc., the Troy-based human resources management company, expects its diversification into nonautomotive industries to help double its revenues this year. Due to the automotive downturn, between October 2008 and March 2009 the company lost approximately 48 percent of its business.

22757 ■ *Beyond Booked Solid: Your Business, Your Life, Your Way-It's All Inside*
Pub: John Wiley and Sons, Inc.
Ed: Michael Port. **Released:** April 2008. **Price:** $24.95. **Description:** Professional service providers and small business owners will discover tactics and strategies for growing and expanding their companies while allowing them to find time to relax and enjoy their lives. Owners will learn to attract new clients and grow profits.

22758 ■ *"The Big 50"* in *Canadian Business (Vol. 81, Summer 2008, No. 9, pp. 125)*
Pub: Rogers Media Ltd.
Description: Large publicly held corporations are ranked based on market capitalization and stock performance. Potash Corp. of Saskatchewan topped the roster with 169.3 percent of return and even surpassing its 2007 result of 107 percent. A table showing the 2008 rankings of the companies is presented.

22759 ■ *"Big Energy Deals Power OptiSolar's Local Growth"* in *Sacramento Business Journal (Vol. 25, August 22, 2008, No. 25, pp. 1)*
Pub: American City Business Journals, Inc.
Ed: Celia Lamb. **Description:** Solar energy projects are driving Sacramento, California-based OptiSolar's growth. The company is set to begin construction of its first photovoltaic project in Ontario. It also plans to build the world largest photovoltaic project in San Luis Obispo County.

22760 ■ *"A Bigger Deal"* in *Crain's Cleveland Business (Vol. 28, November 12, 2007, No. 45, pp. 1)*
Pub: Crain Communications, Inc.
Ed: Shawn A. Turner. **Description:** In an attempt to boost its revenue CBiz Inc., a provider of accounting and business services, is looking to balance its acquisitions of smaller companies with larger ones as part of its overall growth strategy.

22761 ■ *Bigger Isn't Always Better*
Pub: AMACOM
Ed: Robert M. Tomasko. **Price:** $24.95.

22762 ■ *"Bigger TIF Makes Development Inroads"* in *The Business Journal-Serving Metropolitan Kansas City (Vol. 26, July 11, 2008, No. 44)*
Pub: American City Business Journals, Inc.
Ed: Rob Roberts. **Description:** On July 9, 2008 the Tax Increment Financing Commission voted to expand a TIF district to Tiffany Springs Road. The plan for the TIF district close to Kansas City International Airport is to include a-half mile of the road. The impacts of the expansion on construction projects and on the road network are analyzed.

22763 ■ *"Biodiesel Poised to Regain Growth"* in *Farm Industry News (January 21, 2011)*
Pub: Penton Business Media Inc.
Description: According to Gary Haer, vice president of sales and marketing for Renewable Energy Group, the biodiesel industry is positioned to regain growth in 2011 with the reinstatement of the biodiesel blendersa tax credt of $1 per gallon.

22764 ■ *"BK Menu Gives Casual Dining Reason to Worry"* in *Advertising Age (Vol. 79, November 17, 2008, No. 43, pp. 12)*
Pub: Crain Communications, Inc.
Ed: Emily Bryson York. **Description:** Burger King is beginning to compete with such casual dining restaurants as Applebees and the Cheesecake Factory with new premium menu items, including thicker burgers and ribs; statistical data regarding the casual dining segment which continues to fall and Burger King, whose sales continue to rise is included.

22765 ■ *"Black On Black Business: Moorehead Buys Hank Aaron's Toyota Dealership"* in *Black Enterprise (Vol. 38, February 2008, No. 7, pp. 28)*
Pub: Earl G. Graves Publishing Co. Inc.
Ed: Brenda Porter. **Description:** In a move to expand his automotive business, Thomas A. Moorehead, CEO of BMW/MINI of Sterling, Georgia bought Hank Aaron's Toyota automobile dealership in McDonough, Georgia. Moorehead stated that he will call the new store Toyota of McDonough.

22766 ■ *"Blacks Go Broadband: High Speed Internet Adoption Grows Among African Americans"* in *Black Enterprise (Vol. 38, February 2008)*
Pub: Earl G. Graves Publishing Co. Inc.
Ed: Cliff Hocker. **Description:** Number of black households using broadband Internet services tripled since 2005 according to a survey conducted by Pew Internet and American Life Project.

22767 ■ *"A Bleak Earnings View"* in *Barron's (Vol. 88, March 10, 2008, No. 10, pp. 15)*
Pub: Dow Jones & Company, Inc.
Description: Analysts expect consumer discretionary profits in the S&P 500 to drop 8.4 percent in the first quarter of 2008. A less confident consumer is expected to pull profits down, putting forecasts of earnings growth in the S&P 500 at risk. Statistical data included.

22768 ■ *"Blockbuster Launches Internet Movie Downloads to Compete Against Netflix, Others" in Chicago Tribune (December 3, 2008)*
Pub: McClatchy-Tribune Information Services
Ed: Eric Benderoff. **Description:** Blockbuster Inc., the DVD rental giant, has launched a new service that delivers movies to their customer's homes via the Internet in an attempt to compete against Netflix and other competitors.

22769 ■ *"Blue Bell Breaks Ground in South Carolina" in Ice Cream Reporter (Vol. 23, August 20, 2010, No. 9, pp. 3)*
Pub: Ice Cream Reporter
Description: Texas-based Blue Bell Creameries will open a new 2,000 square foot transfer facility in North Charleston, South Carolina. The facility will expand Blue Bell's distribution efforts in the state.

22770 ■ *"BofA Cutting 70 Charlotte Tech Jobs" in Charlotte Observer (January 31, 2007)*
Pub: Knight-Ridder/Tribune Business News
Ed: Rick Rothacker. **Description:** Bank of America announced the elimination of 70 technology positions at their Charlotte, North Carolina facility. The move is part of the company's effort to increase efficiency.

22771 ■ *"The Book On Indigo" in Canadian Business (Vol. 81, July 22, 2008, No. 12-13, pp. 29)*
Pub: Rogers Media Ltd.
Ed: Thomas Watson. **Description:** Indigo Books & Music Inc. reported record sales of $922 million resulting in a record net profit of $52.8 million for the 2008 fiscal year ended March 29, 2008. Earnings per share were $2.13, greater than Standard & Poor's expected $1.70 per share. Additional information concerning Indigo Books is presented.

22772 ■ *"Book Publishing is Growing" in Information Today (Vol. 28, October 2011, No. 9, pp. 10)*
Pub: Information Today, Inc.
Ed: Paula J. Hane. **Description:** U.S. book publishing industry is reporting growth in its sector, despite the poor economy. BookStats, a comprehensive statistical survey conducted on the modern publishing industry in the U.S. reported Americans are reading in all print and digital formats. In 2011, 114 million ebooks were sold and now account for 13.6 percent of revenue from adult fiction. In contrast, 603 million trade hardcover books (fiction and nonfiction) were sold in 2011, a 5.8 percent increase over 2008.

22773 ■ *"Boom has Tech Grads Mulling Their Options" in Globe & Mail (March 14, 2006, pp. B1)*
Pub: CTVglobemedia Publishing Inc.
Ed: Grant Robertson. **Description:** Internet giant Google Inc. has stepped up its efforts to hire the talented people, in Canada, at Waterloo University in southern Ontario, to expand its operations. The details of the job market and increasing salaries are analyzed.

22774 ■ *"Bottler Will Regain Its Pop" in Barron's (Vol. 88, March 17, 2008, No. 11, pp. 56)*
Pub: Dow Jones & Company, Inc.
Ed: Alexander Eule. **Description:** Discusses he 30 percent drop in the share price of PepsiAmericas Inc. from their 2007 high which presents an opportunity to buy into the company's dependable U.S. market and fast growing Eastern European business. The bottler's Eastern European operating profits in 2007 grew to $101 million from $21 million in 2006.

22775 ■ *"Bottom-Fishing and Speed-Dating in India" in Barron's (Vol. 88, March 24, 2008, No. 12, pp. M12)*
Pub: Dow Jones & Company, Inc.
Ed: Elliot Wilson. **Description:** Indian stocks have fallen hard in 2008, with Mumbai's Sensex 30 down 30 percent from its January 2008 peak of 21,000 to 14,995 in March. The India Private Equity Fair 2008

attracted 140 of the world's largest private equity firms and about 24 of India's fastest-growing corporations. Statistical data included.

22776 ■ *"Bountiful Barrels: Where to Find $140 Trillion" in Barron's (Vol. 88, July 14, 2008, No. 28, pp. 40)*
Pub: Dow Jones & Co., Inc.
Ed: Andrew Bary. **Description:** Surge in oil prices has caused a large transfer of wealth to oil-producing countries thereby reshaping the global economy. Oil reserves of oil exporting countries are now valued at $140 trillion. Economist Stephen Jen believes that this wealth will be transformed into paper assets as these countries invest in global stocks and bonds.

22777 ■ *"Brad Wall" in Canadian Business (Vol. 82, April 27, 2009, No. 7, pp. 9)*
Pub: Rogers Media
Ed: Joe Castaldo. **Description:** Saskatchewan Premier Brad Wall believes that the mood in the province is positive, as its economy is one of the few that is expected to post growth in 2009. Wall actively promotes the province in job fairs, offering $20,000 in tuition for recent college and university graduates that relocate in the province for seven years. Wall's views on the province's economy and challenges are presented.

22778 ■ *"Branching Out" in Canadian Business (Vol. 79, July 17, 2006, No. 14-15, pp. 41)*
Pub: Rogers Media
Description: Visa selected this narrative in an attempt to show the company's usefulness.

22779 ■ *"Breaking Through" in Inc. (January 2008, pp. 90-93)*
Pub: Gruner & Jahr USA Publishing
Ed: Mike Hofman. **Description:** Entrepreneur Keith R. McFarland, shares insight into why most successful companies eventually plateau, while others keep on growing.

22780 ■ *The Breakthrough Company*
Pub: Crown Publishing/Random House
Ed: Keith McFarland. **Released:** September 1, 2009. **Price:** $16.00 paperback. **Description:** Traits of high-growth players that actually make it in business.

22781 ■ *The Breakthrough Company: How Everyday Companies Become Extraordinary Performers*
Pub: Crown Publishing Company
Ed: Keith R. McFarland. **Released:** September 2009. **Price:** $16.00 paperback. **Description:** Author shares five years of building and analyzing the world's largest growth companies performance database and interviews with over 1,500 growth-company executives to help identify the secrets of breakthrough. This book will help any small business learn ways to avoid potential hazards along with way.

22782 ■ *"Brewed to Succeed; Mokarbia Perks Up Sales for King Coffee" in Crain's Detroit Business (Vol. 24, March 17, 2008, No. 11, pp. 3)*
Pub: Crain Communications, Inc.
Ed: Brent Snavely. **Description:** Profile of King Coffee Tea Services, Royal Oak-based company, whose distributing deal with Mokarabia coffee has generated an increase in sales.

22783 ■ *"Brewing National Success" in Hawaii Business (Vol. 53, November 2007, No. 5, pp. 46)*
Pub: Hawaii Business Publishing
Ed: Alex Salkever. **Description:** Kona Brewing Co. (KBC) is already selling its brews in four cities in Florida and 17 other states and Japan as well. KBC is currently forming a deal with Red Hook to produce Longboard Lager and other KBC brews at Red Hooks' brewery in New Hampshire. KBC's chief executive officer Mattson Davis shares KBC's practices for success.

22784 ■ *"Briarcliff Office Building Fills Up Fast" in The Business Journal-Serving Metropolitan Kansas City (Vol. 26, Sept. 5,*

2008, pp. 1)
Pub: American City Business Journals, Inc.
Ed: Rob Roberts. **Description:** Prior to its opening the Hilltop Office Building in Kansas City Missouri has attained 80 percent occupancy. FCStone Group Inc.'s plan to move to the building has boosted the facility's occupancy. Description and dimensions of the office building are also provided.

22785 ■ *Bridging the Equity Gap for Innovative SMEs*
Pub: Palgrave Macmillan
Ed: Elisabetta Gualandri. **Released:** December 1, 2009. **Price:** $85.00. **Description:** This book addresses the evaluation of financial constraints faced by innovative and startup companies and explores ways for bridging the financing and equity gap faced by small to medium business enterprises.

22786 ■ *"Broadband Reaches Access Limits in Europe" in Information Today (Vol. 26, February 2009, No. 2, pp. 22)*
Pub: Information Today, Inc.
Ed: Jim Ashling. **Description:** Eurostat (the Statistical Office of the European communities) reports results from a survey regarding Internet use by businesses throughout its 27-member states. Iceland, Finland and the Netherlands provide the most access at broadband speeds, followed by Belgium, Spain and France.

22787 ■ *"Building His Dream" in Business Courier (Vol. 24, January 25, 2008, No. 42, pp. 1)*
Pub: American City Business Journals, Inc.
Ed: Laura Baverman. **Description:** Technology entrepreneur Mahendra Vora plans to build a more than $100 million local IT headquarters for VTech Holdings Ltd by 2010. Acquisition of four $5 million companies within 2008 are part of the owner's plan to expand the office equipment company. Other plans for the IT company are discussed.

22788 ■ *"Building Your Business: A Strong Web Presence Is a Must" in Black Enterprise (Vol. 38, December 2007, No. 5, pp. 74)*
Pub: Earl G. Graves Publishing Co. Inc.
Ed: Tennille M. Robinson. **Description:** Building a strong presence on the Internet is crucial to any growing business. Websites can provide information or sell merchandise, but the site must also make sure the customer knows how to use and navigate around within the site. Common mistakes to avoid when designing a small business Website are outlined.

22789 ■ *"Burger Market Sizzling with Newcomers" in Boston Business Journal (Vol. 29, June 10, 2011, No. 5, pp. 1)*
Pub: American City Business Journals Inc.
Ed: Ryan Sharrow. **Description:** The burger trend in Maryland is on the rise with burger joints either opening up or expanding into several branches. Startup costs for this kind of business range between $250,000 to $400,000. With a growth rate of roughly 17 percent in 2009, this so-called better burger segment of the burger categories is expected to dominate the market for quite some time.

22790 ■ *"Business Diary" in Crain's Detroit Business (Vol. 24, October 6, 2008, No. 40, pp. 23)*
Pub: Crain Communications, Inc.
Description: Detailed listing of acquisitions, expansions, new products, new services, business contracts and startups from the Detroit area is provided.

22791 ■ *"Business Diary" in Crain's Detroit Business (Vol. 26, January 11, 2010, No. 2, pp. 16)*
Pub: Crain Communications Inc.
Description: Listing of local businesses involved in acquisitions, contracts, expansions, new products and services as well as startups in the region.

22792 ■ *Business Plans to Game Plans*
Pub: John Wiley and Sons, Inc.
Ed: Jan B. King. **Released:** 2003. **Price:** $27.50. **Description:** Information for running a small business are examined, focusing on action plans and ways to avoid the pitfalls of strategic planning. The

book describes how entrepreneurs should set standards, lead by example, look to the future, focus on important details, face reality, grow profitability, and take action.

22793 ■ *"Business Still Expected to Take Hit in 2008' in Business Journal-Serving Phoenix and the Valley of the Sun (December 28, 2007)*
Pub: American City Business Journals, Inc.
Ed: Ty Young. **Description:** Semiconductor industry is forecasting a slow first quarter for 2008 and industry analysts believe there will be decreased growth for the rest of the year. The impending recession in the U.S. will lead to a fall n consumer spending, which will in turn drive down the demand for electronics. The semiconductor revenue forecast for 2010 is also discussed.

22794 ■ *Business Vision: Beyond the Horizon, 2nd Ed.*
Pub: Business Vision Group
Ed: Dennis Wengert. **Released:** January 2009. **Description:** Challenges small business owners face when running their companies are addressed in order to position themselves for the future. The book teaches how to envision future direction and measure personal and business activities that provide an indication of personal progress in achieving visionary business leadership.

22795 ■ *"Businesses Owned by Minorities Proliferate" in MMR (Vol. 27, November 29, 2010, No. 18, pp. 33)*
Pub: Mass Market Retailers
Description: Ethnic minorities are launching new businesses faster than the general population of the U.S. Statistical data included.

22796 ■ *"Buying Power of Hispanics Growing" in Austin Business JournalInc. (Vol. 29, November 27, 2009, No. 38, pp. 1)*
Pub: American City Business Journals
Ed: Sandra Zaragoza. **Description:** Hispanic Marketing Symposium presented a report stating that the buying power of Hispanics of Austin, Texas has grown by 54 percent in last five years to $9.4 billion in 2009. Details on the projected growth of the Hispanic market in the are is covered.

22797 ■ *"Cadillac Tower Largest to Start in a Decade" in Globe & Mail (March 28, 2006, pp. B5)*
Pub: CTVglobemedia Publishing Inc
Ed: Elizabeth Church. **Description:** The plans of Cadillac Fairview Corporation Ltd. to build office towers, in downtown Canada, are presented

22798 ■ *"Campaigner Survey: 46 Percent of Small Businesses Use Email Marketing" in Wireless News (November 21, 2009)*
Pub: Close-Up Media
Description: Almost half (46 percent) of small businesses surveyed by Campaigner's 2009 State of Small Business Online Marketing, say that they rely on email marketing to help them find new customers, keep existing ones and grow their businesses. The survey also found that 36 percent of small businesses plan to begin using email marketing over the next year. The trend to utilize Internet marketing tools is allowing small businesses to grow faster and generate higher revenues than those that are not using these mediums.

22799 ■ *"Can America Invent Its Way Back?' in Business Week (September 22, 2008, No. 4100, pp. 52)*
Pub: McGraw-Hill Companies, Inc.
Description: Business leaders as well as economists agree that innovative new products. services and ways of doing business may be the only way in which America can survive the downward spiral of the economy; innovation economics may be the answer and may even provide enough growth to enable Americans to prosper in the years to come.

22800 ■ *"Can a Brazilian SUV Take On the Jeep Wrangler?' in Business Week*

(September 22, 2008, No. 4100, pp. 50)
Pub: McGraw-Hill Companies, Inc.
Ed: Helen Walters. **Description:** Profile of the Brazilian company TAC as well as the flourishing Brazilian car market; TAC has launched a new urban vehicle, the Stark, which has won prizes for innovation; the company uses local technology and manufacturing expertise.

22801 ■ *"Can Brewer Make Cheap Seats Pay?' in Globe & Mail (January 7, 2006, pp. B4)*
Pub: CTVglobemedia Publishing Inc.
Ed: Brent Jang. **Description:** The plans of chief executive officer Montie Brewer of Air Canada to upgrade airplanes are presented.

22802 ■ *"Can This Duo be Saved? Renovating 2 Tallest Edifices Downtown Will Be Costly, Owner Says" in Charlotte Observer (February 4, 2007)*
Pub: Knight-Ridder/Tribune Business News
Ed: Jefferson George. **Description:** Gastonia, North Carolina city leaders are making plans to renovate the Lawyers Building and the Commercial Building in an effort to revitalize the downtown area.

22803 ■ *"Can You Hear Them Now?' in Hawaii Business (Vol. 54, August 2008, No. 2, pp. 48)*
Pub: Hawaii Business Publishing
Ed: Jason Ubay. **Description:** Coral Wireless LLC (dba Mobi PCS) is ranked 237 in Hawaii Business' list of the state's top 250 companies for 2008. The company is a local wireless phone provider, which has expanded its market to Oahu, Maui and the Big Island since opening in 2006, offering 13 phones and unlimited texts and calls. Details on the company's sales are provided.

22804 ■ *"Canada, Not China, Is Partner In Our Economic Prosperity" in Crain's Chicago Business (Vol. 31, April 14, 2008, No. 15, pp. 14)*
Pub: Crain Communications, Inc.
Ed: Paul O'Connor. **Description:** In 2005 more than $500 billion in two-way trade crossed the friendly border between the Great Lakes states and Canadian provinces and for decades Canada is every Great Lakes State's number one and growing export market.

22805 ■ *"Canada's Oil Rush" in Canadian Business (Vol. 81, October 13, 2008, No. 17, pp. 58)*
Pub: Rogers Media Ltd.
Description: Excerpt from Andrew Nikiforuk's 'Tar Sands' details the exploration and development of oil sands in Alberta, Canada and its significance to the U.S. Canada has been the United State's largest supplier of oil since 2002, accounting for 18 percent of U.S. oil imports. Details regarding Canada's oil sand are examined.

22806 ■ *"Canadian Patients Give Detroit Hospitals a Boost' in Crain's Detroit Business (Vol. 24, April 14, 2008, No. 15, pp. 10)*
Pub: Crain Communications Inc.
Ed: Jay Greene. **Description:** Each year thousands of Canadians travel to Detroit area hospitals seeking quicker solutions to medical problems or access to services that are limited or unavailable in Canada.

22807 ■ *"Canadian Research Generates Innovation and Prosperity" in Canadian Business (Vol. 81, October 27, 2008, No. 18, pp. 87)*
Pub: Rogers Media Ltd.
Description: Universities play a key role in helping Canadians achieve prosperity, competitiveness, and quality of life by conducting more than a third of Canada's research. Research in universities help train graduates to apply sophisticated knowledge to real problems.

22808 ■ *"CanWEA Unveils WindVision for BC: 5,250 MW of Wind Energy by 2025" in CNW Group (October 4, 2011)*
Pub: CNW Group
Contact: Carolyn McGill-Davidson, President
Description: Wind industry leaders are asking British Columbia, Canada policy makers to created conditions to further develop and integrate wind energy in accordance with greenhouse gas emission targets and projected economic growth. Statistical data included.

22809 ■ *"Cash-Heavy Biovail on the Prowl for Deals" in Globe & Mail (March 24, 2006, pp. B1)*
Pub: CTVglobemedia Publishing Inc.
Ed: Leonard Zehr. **Description:** Biovail Corp. posted 48 percent rise in profits for 2005. The business growth plans of the company through acquisitions are presented.

22810 ■ *Cash In a Flash*
Pub: Crown Business Books
Ed: Robert G. Allen, Mark Victor Hansen. **Released:** December 28, 2010. **Price:** $15.00. **Description:** Proven, practical advice and techniques are given to help entrepreneurs make money quickly using skills and resources known to generate permanent and recurring income.

22811 ■ *"Caterpillar to Expand Research, Production in China" in Chicago Tribune (August 27, 2008)*
Pub: McClatchy-Tribune Information Services
Ed: James P. Miller. **Description:** Caterpillar Inc., the Peoria-based heavy-equipment manufacturer, plans to establish a new research-and-development center at the site of its rapidly growing campus in Wuxi.

22812 ■ *"A Cautionary Tale for Emerging Market Giants" in Harvard Business Review (Vol. 88, September 2010, No. 9, pp. 99)*
Pub: Harvard Business School Publishing
Ed: J. Stewart Black, Allen J. Morrison. **Description:** Key factors that negatively affected Japan corporate growth and organizational effectiveness include: devotion to established path, isolated domestic markets, homogenous executive teams, and a non-contentious labor force. Solutions include leadership development programs, multicultural input, and cross-cultural training.

22813 ■ *"Cemex Paves a Global Road to Solid Growth" in Barron's (Vol. 88, March 10, 2008, No. 10, pp. 24)*
Pub: Dow Jones & Company, Inc.
Ed: Sandra Ward. **Description:** Shares of Cemex are expected to perform well with the company's expected strong performance despite fears of a US recession. The company has a diverse geographical reach and benefits from a strong worldwide demand for cement.

22814 ■ *"Centrue Sets Down New Roots in St. Louis; Bank Looks to Expand in Exurbs of Chicago" in Crain's Chicago Business (May 5, 2008)*
Pub: Crain Communications, Inc.
Ed: H. Lee Murphy. **Description:** Centrue Financial Corp. has moved its headquarters from Ottawa to suburban St. Louis in search of higher-growth markets. The banks acquisitions and expansion plans are also discussed.

22815 ■ *"The Challenges of Commercial Work" in Indoor Comfort Marketing (Vol. 70, May 2011, No. 5, pp. 14)*
Pub: Industry Publications Inc.
Ed: Matt Spink. **Description:** The challenges faced by heating, ventilation, cooling small businesses expanding into commercial accounts are discussed.

22816 ■ *"Champion Enterprises Buys UK Company" in Crain's Detroit Business (Vol. 24, March 17, 2008, No. 11, pp. 4)*
Pub: Crain Communications, Inc.
Ed: Daniel Duggan. **Description:** With the acquisition of ModularUK Building Systems Ltd., a steel-frame modular manufacturer, Champion Enterprises has continued its expansion outside the United States.

22817 ■ *"The Changing Face of the U.S. Consumer"* in *Advertising Age (Vol. 79, July 7, 2008, No. 26, pp. 1)*
Pub: Crain Communications, Inc.
Ed: Peter Francese. **Description:** It is essential for marketers to examine demographic shifts when looking at ways in which to market brands. The average head-of-households is aging and marketers must not continue to ignore them. Statistical data included.

22818 ■ *"Channeling for Growth"* in *The Business Journal-Serving Greater Tampa Bay (Vol. 28, July 11, 2008, No. 29, pp. 1)*
Pub: American City Business Journals, Inc.
Ed: Margie Manning. **Description:** HSN Inc., one of the largest employers in Tampa Bay, Florida, is expected to spend an additional $9.7 million annually as it plans to hire more accounting, internal audit, legal, treasury and tax personnel after its spin-off to a public company. Details on the company's sales growth are provided.

22819 ■ *"Cheap Thrills: Where to Look When You're Craving a Low-Price Wine"* in *Chicago Tribune (January 12, 2009)*
Pub: McClatchy-Tribune Information Services
Ed: Bill Daley. **Description:** Wines priced $15 and above are being hit the hardest by the economic downturn while cheaper wines, specifically those priced between $3 and $6, are seeing a growth in sales.

22820 ■ *"Chiefs Hope Renovations Score Big With Sponsors"* in *The Business Journal-Serving Metropolitan Kansas City (Vol. 26, July 11, 2008)*
Pub: American City Business Journals, Inc.
Ed: James Dornbrook. **Description:** Kansas City Chiefs officials expect to obtain 12 to 14 new major sponsors with the completion of the Arrowhead Stadium renovations. The new sponsorship opportunities will include naming rights for the stadium and practice facility. The team's marketing strategies are discussed.

22821 ■ *"Children's Hospital to Grow"* in *Austin Business Journal (Vol. 31, July 22, 2011, No. 20, pp. A1)*
Pub: American City Business Journals Inc.
Ed: Sandra Zaragoza. **Description:** Austin, Texas-based Dell Children's Medical Center is set to embark on a tower expansion. The plan will accommodate more patients and make room for the hospital's growing specialty program.

22822 ■ *"Children's Products Maker Not the New Kid on the Block"* in *Crain's Cleveland Business (Vol. 28, November 26, 2007, No. 47, pp. 3)*
Pub: Crain Communications, Inc.
Ed: David Bennett. **Description:** Discusses the business model employed by Shamrock Industries Inc., a rising star in the competitive world of children's products; the company, which does business as Foundations Quality Children's Products, has expanded into a 63,000-square-foot distribution center which has boosted its local profile significantly.

22823 ■ *"The China Syndrome"* in *Canadian Business (Vol. 79, July 17, 2006, No. 14-15, pp. 25)*
Pub: Rogers Media
Ed: Peter Diekmeyer. **Description:** Contrasting pace of growth in China and India are presented. Reasons for the slow pace of growth of Canadian companies like CAE Inc. and Magna in India are also discussed.

22824 ■ *"China's ZTE in Hunt for Partners"* in *Globe & Mail (February 27, 2006, pp. B1)*
Pub: CTVglobemedia Publishing Inc.
Ed: Gordon Pitts. **Description:** The business growth plans of ZTE Corp. in Canada, through partnership, are presented.

22825 ■ *"Chris Curtis Preaches the Gospel of Internet Success"* in *Black Enterprise (Vol. 38, March 2008, No. 8, pp. 56)*
Pub: Earl G. Graves Publishing Co. Inc.
Ed: Anthony Calypso. **Description:** Profile of the Web Business Ownership Series, a collection of 20 free seminars that help small businesses learn about the Web development process.

22826 ■ *"Christ Hospital to Expand"* in *Business Courier (Vol. 27, June 25, 2010, No. 8, pp. 3)*
Pub: Business Courier
Ed: Dan Monk, James Ritchie. **Description:** Christ Hospital intends to invest more than $300 million and generate 200 jobs in an expansion of its Mount Auburn campus in Cincinnati, Ohio. About $22 million in retail activity can be created by the hospital expansion, which will also include a replacement garage and new surgery facilities.

22827 ■ *"Chuy's Gears Up to Serve Atlants, Other Untapped Cities"* in *Austin Business Journal (Vol. 31, June 17, 2011, No. 15, pp. 1)*
Pub: American City Business Journals Inc.
Ed: Cody Lyon. **Description:** Chuy's Holdings Inc. plans to expand into the Southeastern United States, particularly in Atlanta, Georgia. The restaurant, which secured $67.5 million in debt financing in May 2011, added 20 stores in five years and plans to open eight locations in 2011.

22828 ■ *"CIBC Spends $1.1 Billion on Caribbean Expansion"* in *Globe & Mail (March 14, 2006, pp. B1)*
Pub: CTVglobemedia Publishing Inc.
Ed: Sinclair Stewart. **Description:** Canadian Imperial Bank of Commerce (CIBC), the fifth-largest bank of Canada, is planning to spend $1.1billion to buy major share of Barbados-based First Caribbean International Bank. The details of the acquisition plan are presented.

22829 ■ *"Cineplex Sees Past the Big Picture"* in *Globe & Mail (February 8, 2007, pp. B9)*
Pub: CTVglobemedia Publishing Inc.
Ed: Shirley Won. **Description:** Cineplex Entertainment LP reported $4.6 million profit in the final quarter of 2006. The movie chain is introducing video-game tournaments and live rock concerts to improve sales.

22830 ■ *"Clean Bathrooms Are Big Key to Convenience Store's Success"* in *Marketing to Women (Vol. 23, January 2010, No. 1, pp. 3)*
Pub: EPM Communications Inc.
Contact: Ira Mayer, President
E-mail: imayer@epmcom.com
Description: Buc-ee's, a Texas-based convenience store chain, is attributing its large female consumer base to the cleanliness of its bathrooms. The chain actually markets itself specifically to female consumers.

22831 ■ *"Clean-Tech Focus Sparks Growth"* in *Philadelphia Business Journal (Vol. 28, January 15, 2010, No. 48, pp. 1)*
Pub: American City Business Journals
Ed: Peter Key. **Description:** Keystone Redevelopment Group and economic development organization Ben Franklin Technology Partners of Southeastern Pennsylvania have partnered in supporting the growth of new alternative energy and clean technology companies. Keystone has also been developing the Bridge Business Center.

22832 ■ *"ClearEdge Hums Along"* in *Business Journal Portland (Vol. 26, December 18, 2009, No. 41, pp. 1)*
Pub: American City Business Journals Inc.
Ed: Erik Siemers. **Description:** Hillsboro-based ClearEdge Power Inc. expanded its workforce and facilities with $15M capital from investors. Since May 2009, the number of employees increased from 40 to 150 and headquarters expanded from 5,000 to 80,000 square feet.

22833 ■ *"ClickFuel Unveils Internet Marketing Tools for Small Businesses"* in *Internet Wire (October 19, 2009)*
Pub: Comtex News Network, Inc.
Description: ClickFuel, a firm that manages, designs and tracks marketing campaigns has unveiled a full software suite of affordable services and technology solutions designed to empower small business owners and help them promote and grow their businesses through targeted Internet marketing campaigns.

22834 ■ *"Clicks From Round the World: Simplifying International E-Commerce"* in *Inc. (Volume 32, December 2010, No. 10, pp. 146)*
Pub: Inc. Magazine
Ed: Ryan Underwood. **Description:** By 2014, global e-commerce spending is expected to increase more than 90 percent, with much of that growth coming from Latin America.

22835 ■ *"Climate Right Systems Provides Pre-Assembled Equipment Packages"* in *Contractor (Vol. 56, July 2009, No. 7, pp. 1)*
Pub: Penton Media, Inc.
Description: Climate Right Systems offers completely engineered, assembled, and tested equipment packages for hydronic heating and cooling. This package does away with the need to custom fabricate on-site and lets mechanical and plumbing contractors expand their offerings without added overhead and risk.

22836 ■ *"CN Profit a Boon for Top Brass"* in *Globe & Mail (March 23, 2007, pp. B5)*
Pub: CTVglobemedia Publishing Inc.
Ed: Brent Jang. **Description:** Canadian National Railway Co., Montreal-based freight carrier, paid $7.3 million in compensation to its top five executives. The company has posted a record $2.1 billion profits in 2006.

22837 ■ *"CNinsure Offers Safety in Numbers"* in *Barron's (Vol. 90, September 13, 2010, No. 37, pp. 29)*
Pub: Barron's Editorial & Corporate Headquarters
Ed: Teresa Rivas. **Description:** China's insurance holding company CNinsure has a long growth future due to the nascent insurance market in the country. It has also been diversifying its offerings and it has a broad network in the nation. The shares of the company are trading cheaply at nearly 14 times its 2011 earnings, and is considered a good point for investors.

22838 ■ *"Coca-Cola Looks Ready to Pause"* in *Barron's (Vol. 88, March 10, 2008, No. 10, pp. 18)*
Pub: Dow Jones & Company, Inc.
Ed: Michael Santoli. **Description:** Shares of Coca-Cola are expected to turn sideways or experience a slight drop from $59.50 each to the mid-50 level. The company has seen its shares jump 40 percent since 2006, when it was in a series of measures to improve profitability.

22839 ■ *"Cogeco Profit Jumps 47 Percent in First Quarter"* in *Globe & Mail (January 13, 2006, pp. B3)*
Pub: CTVglobemedia Publishing Inc.
Ed: Catherine McLean. **Description:** The reasons behind 47 percent increase in first quarter 2006 profits for Cogeco Inc. are presented.

22840 ■ *"Coherent Laying Off 144 As It Prepares To Shut Auburn Plant"* in *Sacramento Business Journal (Vol. 25, August 1, 2008, No. 22, pp. 1)*
Pub: American City Business Journals, Inc.
Ed: Melanie Turner. **Description:** Sacramento, California-based Coherent Inc. is planning to lay off 144 workers at its Auburn facility. Coherent has been cutting payroll and its real estate holdings. Statistics on the company's earnings are also provided.

22841 ■ *"Cold Stone Creamery"* in *Ice Cream Reporter (Vol. 22, January 20, 2009, No. 2, pp. 8)*
Pub: Ice Cream Reporter
Description: Franchise News reports that Cold Stone Creamery is looking for master franchisees to support its expansion into the North German market. The report notes that following its successful launch in Denmark, the firm is also preparing for expansion into France.

22842 ■ *"Collection Agencies Industry Rankings"* in *Collections and Credit Risk (Vol. 14, September 1, 2009, No. 8, pp. 18)*
Pub: SourceMedia, Inc.
Description: Ranking of the top collection agencies in the United States in terms of the revenue generated in 2007 and 2088; statistical data included.

22843 ■ *"Collection Agencies Industry Rankings"* in *Collections and Credit Risk (Vol. 14, September 1, 2009, No. 8, pp. 18)*
Pub: SourceMedia, Inc.

Description: Ranking of the top collection agencies in the United States in terms of the revenue generated in 2007 and 2088; statistical data included.

22844 ■ *"Commensurate with Experience"* in *Entrepreneur (Vol. 37, October 2009, No. 10, pp. 84)*
Pub: Entrepreneur Media, Inc.

Ed: Carol Tice. **Description:** RingRevenue, a firm that specializes in pay-per-call technology that allows affiliate networks and advertising agencies to track purchases, began a funding round in June 2009 which it closed quickly after obtaining $3.5 million in venture capital. The round was closed earlier than the projections of its owners due to their track record.

22845 ■ *"Commentary: US Economic Recovery and Policy"* in *Small Business Economic Trends (July 2010, pp. 3)*
Pub: National Federation of Independent Business

Description: U.S. Government is making economic recovery difficult, with one of the largest tax increases in history arriving in six months. Meanwhile, Congress is looking into taxing successful businesses, which will potentially hamper growth and real investment. Other insights on the government's role in the country's economic growth are presented.

22846 ■ *"Commercial Water Efficiency Initiatives Announced"* in *Contractor (Vol. 56, November 2009, No. 11, pp. 5)*
Pub: Penton Media, Inc.

Ed: Robert P. Mader. **Description:** Plumbing engineers John Koeller and Bill Gauley are developing a testing protocol for commercial toilets. The team said commercial toilets should have a higher level of flush performance than residential toilets for certification. The Environmental Protection Agency's WaterSense program wants to expand the program into the commercial/institutional sector.

22847 ■ *"Companies Must Innovate, Regardless of Economy"* in *Crain's Detroit Business (Vol. 25, June 1, 2009, No. 22, pp. M007)*
Pub: Crain Communications Inc. - Detroit

Ed: Sherri Begin Welch. **Description:** Despite the economy, leaders of Michigan's successful companies stress that small businesses must innovate in order to grow.

22848 ■ *"Company Hopes To Pack Profits With Self-Storage"* in *Crain's Detroit Business (Vol. 24, February 18, 2008, No. 7, pp. 15)*
Pub: Crain Communications Inc. - Detroit

Ed: Daniel Duggan. **Description:** Storage Opportunity Partners has purchased a vacant building to convert into a self-storage facility.

22849 ■ *"Competitors' Resource-Oriented Strategies"* in *Academy of Management Review (January 2008, pp. 97)*
Pub: ScholarOne, Inc.

Ed: Laurence Capron, Olivier Chatain. **Description:** Firms can maintain a competitive advantage by implementing competitors' resource-oriented strategies to combat the resources of rivals in factor markets as well as political markets.

22850 ■ *The Complete Idiot's Guide to Starting and Running a Thrift Store*
Pub: Alpha Publishing House

Ed: Ravel Buckley, Carol Costa. **Released:** January 5, 2010. **Price:** $18.95. **Description:** Thrift stores saw a 35 percent increase in sales during the falling economy in 2008. Despite the low startup costs, launching and running a thrift store is complicated. Two experts cover the entire process, including setting up a store on a nonprofit basis, choosing a location, funding, donations for saleable items, recruiting and managing staff, sorting items, pricing, and recycling donations.

22851 ■ *"Computer Forensics Firms Get Boost From New Evidence Rules"* in *Crain's Detroit Business (Vol. 24, March 24, 2008, No. 12, pp. 28)*
Pub: Crain Communications, Inc.

Ed: Chad Halcom. **Description:** Computer forensics is a growing niche for firms such as the Center for Computer Forensics in Southfield; driving some of the growth are new amendments to the Federal Rules of Civil Procedure, which took effect about a year ago and address standards of evidence for electronic records, or 'e-discovery,' that are admissible for civil cases in federal courts.

22852 ■ *The Connection Key: Seven Ways the World's Most Successful Entrepreneurs Trounce the Competition and How You Can, Too*
Pub: John Wiley & Sons, Inc.

Ed: Maribeth Kuzmeski. **Released:** September 22, 2009. **Price:** $22.95. **Description:** The book is written under the premise that getting ahead in business does not come down to smarts, guts, rare talent, or plain old luck. While those things are helpful, the real missing ingredient is the ability to meaningfully connect with others.

22853 ■ *"Contracting Firm Sees Timing Right for Expansion"* in *Tampa Bay Business Journal (Vol. 29, November 13, 2009, No. 47, pp. 1)*
Pub: American City Business Journals

Ed: Janet Leiser. **Description:** Construction management company Moss & Associates LLC of Fort Lauderdale, Florida has launched its expansion to Tampa Bay. Moss & Associates has started the construction of the Marlins stadium in Miami, Florida's Little Havana section. It also plans to diversify by embarking on other government development, such as health care facilities and airports.

22854 ■ *"Conversation"* in *Harvard Business Review (Vol. 86, September 2008, No. 9, pp. 32)*
Pub: Harvard Business School Press

Ed: Susan Donovan. **Description:** Danish software entrepreneur Thorkil Sonne has helped improve employment for individuals with autism after discovering the perception of detail and remarkable memory skills in his own son, who has autism. His company, Specialisterne, was built via focusing on these strengths.

22855 ■ *"Coping With a Shrinking Planet"* in *Agency Sales Magazine (Vol. 39, December 2009, No. 11, pp. 46)*
Pub: MANA

Ed: Mark Young. **Description:** China and India are forcing big changes in the world and are posing a huge threat to U.S. manufacturers and their sales representatives. Reps may want to consider expanding into these territories. Helping sell American products out of the country presents an opportunity for economic expansion.

22856 ■ *Corporate Entrepreneurship: Top Managers and New Business Creation*
Pub: Cambridge University Press
Contact: Richard Ziemacki, President
E-mail: rziemacki@cambridge.org

Ed: Vijay Sathe. **Released:** February 2007. **Price:** $35.00. **Description:** Studies covering entrepreneurship and business growth are examined.

22857 ■ *"Cost Cuts Lead Dealers to Record Profits"* in *Globe & Mail (March 24, 2006, pp. B3)*
Pub: CTVglobemedia Publishing Inc.

Ed: Omar El Akkad. **Description:** The reasons behind posting of $4.3 billion profit by Canadian securities sector, for 2005, are presented.

22858 ■ *"Counting on Engagement at Ernst and Young"* in *Workforce Management (Vol. 88, November 16, 2009, No. 12, pp. 25)*
Pub: Crain Communications Inc.

Ed: Ed Frauenheim. **Description:** Employee engagement has been difficult to maintain through the recession but firms such as Ernst & Young have found that the effort to keep their employees loyal has paid off.

22859 ■ *"Courier 250 Companies Hope to Rebound From 2009"* in *Business Courier (Vol. 27, July 16, 2010, No. 11, pp. 1)*
Pub: Business Courier

Ed: Dan Monk, Jon Newberry. **Description:** Private companies that are featured in the Courier 250 publication have lost almost $4 billion in revenue, while combined sales dropped by 11 percent to 32 billion in 2009. Courier 250 is a guide to public companies, large nonprofits, private firms, and other related entities in Ohio's Cincinnati region.

22860 ■ *"Craig Muhlhauser"* in *Canadian Business (Vol. 81, September 15, 2008, No. 14-15, pp. 6)*
Pub: Rogers Media Ltd.

Ed: Andrew Wahl. **Description:** Interview with Craig Muhlhauser who is the CEO of Celestica, a manufacturing company that provides services for the electronics sector; Muhlhauser discusses the company's restructuring program, which he feels was the secret to their surprising first-quarter results. Muhlhauser states that the company is operating with more forward visibility and that understanding the opportunities during the current economic situation presents the biggest challenge.

22861 ■ *"Creativity: A Key Link to Entrepreneurial Behavior"* in *Business Horizons (September-October 2007, pp. 365)*
Pub: Elsevier Technology Publications

Ed: Stephen Ko, John E. Butler. **Description:** Importance of creativity and its link to entrepreneurial behavior is examined. In a study of various entrepreneurs, studies concluded that a solid knowledge base, a well-developed social network, and a strong focus on identifying opportunities are relevant to entrepreneurial behavior.

22862 ■ *Creativity and Innovation: Breaking New Ground..Without Breaking the Bank*
Pub: A. & C. Black

Ed: Janice Armstrong. **Released:** March 1, 2009. **Price:** $12.95. **Description:** Advice is given to help small business owners be creative in order to compete in their sector.

22863 ■ *"Criticare Sees Rapid Expansion"* in *Business Journal-Milwaukee (Vol. 28, December 31, 2010, No. 14, pp. A1)*
Pub: Milwaukee Business Journal

Ed: Rich Rovito. **Description:** Criticare Systems Inc. expanded its distribution network, added customers, launched two new products and transferred into a new building in Pewaukee, Wisconsin at the start of their fiscal year. Criticare expanded its workforce and now has nearly 140 full time employees.

22864 ■ *"A Crowd for the Cloud"* in *CIO (Vol. 24, October 2, 2010, No. 1, pp. 16)*
Pub: CIO

Ed: Stephanie Overby. **Description:** Information about a project which aimed to implement a cloud-based crowdsourcing platform and innovation-management process is provided. Chubb Group of Insurance Companies wanted to mine revenue-generating ideas from its 10,400 employees and hundreds of thousands of external agents. The company hosted its first innovation event using its new system in October 2008.

22865 ■ *"Cruising In Choppy Water"* in *The Business Journal-Portland (Vol. 25, August 22, 2008, No. 24, pp. 1)*
Pub: American City Business Journals, Inc.

Ed: Erik Siemers. **Description:** Yacht builder Christensen Shipyards Inc. is experiencing robust business despite the slowing US economy, building four yachts a year as of 2008. The company expects revenues to hit $90 million and is opening a 500,000-square-foot plant in Tennessee.

22866 ■ *"Cupcake Maker Grabs Outpost"* in *Crain's New York Business (Vol. 27, August 15, 2011, No. 33, pp. 16)*
Pub: Crain Communications, Inc.

Ed: Jermaine Taylor. **Description:** Family-owned miniature cupcake maker, Baked by Melissa, singed a ten-year lease, expanding their stores to five. The business was started three years ago by advertising executive Melissa Bushell.

22867 ■ *"Customer Loyalty: Making Your Program Excel' in Franchising World (Vol. 42, August 2010, No. 8, pp. 47)*

Pub: International Franchise Association

Ed: Steve Baxter. **Description:** Customer loyalty is key to any franchise operation's growth. Tips for identifying preferred customers are outlined.

22868 ■ *"Customers Turned Off? Not at Best Buy" in Barron's (Vol. 88, March 24, 2008, No. 12, pp. 29)*

Pub: Dow Jones & Company, Inc.

Ed: Sandra Ward. **Description:** Shares of Best Buy, trading at $42.41 each, are expected to rise to an average of $52 a share due to the company's solid fundamentals. The company's shares have fallen 20 percent from their 52-week high and are attractive given the company's bright prospects in the video game sector and high-definition video.

22869 ■ *Cute Little Store: Between the Entrepreneurial Dream and Business Reality*

Pub: Outskirts Press, Incorporated

Ed: Adeena Mignogna. **Released:** May 2006. **Price:** $11.95. **Description:** Challenges of starting and growing a retail business are profiled.

22870 ■ *"Cutting Credit Card Processing Costs" in Hawaii Business (Vol. 53, March 2008, No. 9, pp. 56)*

Pub: Hawaii Business Publishing

Ed: Robert K.O. Lum. **Description:** Accepting credit card payments offers businesses with profits from the discount rate. The discount rate includes processing fee, VISA & MasterCard assessment and interchange. Details regarding merchant service cost and discount rate portions are discussed. Statistical data included.

22871 ■ *"Data Center Plan Bearing Fruit From Apple, Spec Center" in Charlotte Business Journal (Vol. 25, October 15, 2010, No. 30, pp. 1)*

Pub: Charlotte Business Journal

Ed: Ken Elkins. **Description:** Apple Inc. is planning to expand its server farm at the North Carolina Data Center Corridor in Catawba County. T5 Partners, on the other hand, will build a shell building to house a server on the site. Infocrossing Inc. will also build an open data center in the area.

22872 ■ *"Data Firm Growth 'Opportunistic" in Tampa Bay Business Journal (Vol. 30, January 29, 2010, No. 6, pp. 1)*

Pub: American City Business Journals

Ed: Michael Hinman. **Description:** E Solutions Corporation is experiencing growth amid the economic downturn, with its Park Tower data center occupancy in Tampa Florida expanding from 14,000 square feet to 20,000 square feet. Details on the increased operations fueled by demand for information storage and management services offered by the company are discussed.

22873 ■ *"Daycare Dollars" in Small Business Opportunities (Winter 2009)*

Pub: Entrepreneur Media Inc.

Description: Profile of Maui Playcare, a franchise that provides parents drop-in daycare for their children without having to purchase a membership, make reservations or pay costly dues; the company is expanding beyond its Hawaiian roots onto the mainland and is expected to have between 40 and 50 locations signed by the end of 2010.

22874 ■ *"Deal Braces Cramer for Growth Run" in The Business Journal-Serving Metropolitan Kansas City (Vol. 26, July 4, 2008, No. 43, pp. 1)*

Pub: American City Business Journals, Inc.

Ed: James Dornbook. **Description:** Gardner, Kansas-based Cramer Products Inc. bought 100 percent of the stocks of Louisville, Kentucky-based Active Ankle Inc. from 26 private investors increasing its revenue by 20 percent. The latter is the second largest vendor of Cramer. Other details of the merger are presented.

22875 ■ *"Dealer Gets a Lift with Acquisitions at Year's End' in Crain's Detroit Business (Vol. 26, January 11, 2010, No. 2, pp. 3)*

Pub: Crain Communications, Inc.

Ed: Ryan Beene. **Description:** Alta Equipment Co., a forklift dealer, closed 2009 with a string of acquisitions expecting to double the firm's employee headcount and triple its annual revenue. Alta Lift Truck Services, Inc., as the company was known before the acquisitions, was founded in 1984 as Michigan's dealer for forklift manufacturer Yale Materials Handling Corp.

22876 ■ *"Debt Buyers Industry Rankings" in Collections and Credit Risk (Vol. 14, September 1, 2009, No. 8, pp. 19)*

Pub: SourceMedia, Inc.

Description: Ranking of the top debt buyers in the United States in terms of the revenue generated in 2007 and 2088; statistical data included.

22877 ■ *"Debutante NYSE Soars 20 Percent' in Globe & Mail (March 9, 2006, pp. B1)*

Pub: CTVglobemedia Publishing Inc.

Ed: John Partridge. **Description:** The debutant share trading of NYSE Group Inc. is discussed. The prices rose by 20 percent before closing.

22878 ■ *"December 19 Is a Great Day to be Terrible" in Internet Wire (December 15, 2009)*

Pub: Comtex News Network, Inc.

Description: Overview of the plans to market the grand opening of the newest Terrible Herbst location in Las Vegas, Nevada. Terrible Herbst is a complete convenience destination offering a gas station, convenience store, car wash and lube center.

22879 ■ *"A Decent Proposal' in Hawaii Business (Vol. 53, March 2008, No. 9, pp. 52)*

Pub: Hawaii Business Publishing

Ed: Jacy L. Youn. **Description:** Bonnie Cooper and Brian Joy own Big Rock Manufacturing Inc., a stone manufacturing company, which sells carved rocks and bowls, lava benches, waterfalls, and Buddhas. Details about the company's growth are discussed.

22880 ■ *"Deere to Open Technology Center in Germany" in Chicago Tribune (September 3, 2008)*

Pub: McClatchy-Tribune Information Services

Ed: James P. Miller. **Description:** Deere & Co. plans to open a technology and innovation center in Germany; details of the company's expansion plans are discussed.

22881 ■ *"Defense Contractor May Expand Locally; BAE Systems Ramps Up Vehicle Prototypes" in Crain's Detroit Business (March 24, 2008)*

Pub: Crain Communications, Inc.

Ed: Chad Halcom. **Description:** Profile of BAE Systems, a defense contractor, that has built a prototype in the highly competitive Joint Light Tactical Vehicle project; the company has also completed its prototype RG33L Mine Resistant Recovery Maintenance Vehicle and has plans for expansion.

22882 ■ *"Detroit Residential Market Slows; Bright Spots Emerge" in Crain's Detroit Business (Vol. 24, October 6, 2008, No. 40, pp. 11)*

Pub: Crain Communications, Inc.

Ed: Daniel Duggan. **Description:** Discusses the state of the residential real estate market in Detroit; although condominium projects receive the most attention, deals for single-family homes are taking place in greater numbers due to financing issues. Buyers can purchase a single family home with a 3.5 percent down payment compared to 20 percent for some condo deals because of the number of first-time homebuyer programs under the Federal Housing Administration.

22883 ■ *"Deutsche Bank Joins the Club" in Barron's (Vol. 88, March 31, 2008, No. 13, pp. M6)*

Pub: Dow Jones & Company, Inc.

Ed: Arindam Nag. **Description:** Deutsche Bank's tangible leverage has worsened sharply in the past year from 2.1 percent to 2.3 percent during 2002-

2006 to only 1.6 percent. The bank has also been accumulating a lot of illiquid assets and its Level-3 assets are three times its tangible equity.

22884 ■ *"Developers Await Hotel' in The Business Journal-Portland (Vol. 25, July 11, 2008, No. 18, pp. 1)*

Pub: American City Business Journals, Inc.

Ed: Wendy Culverwell. **Description:** Developers are eager to start the construction of a new hotel at the Oregon Convention Center in Portland, Oregon as hey say that the project will help boost the convention center neighborhood. The project, called The Westin Portland at the Convention Center, is partly handled by Ashforth Pacific Inc.

22885 ■ *"Developers Poised to Pull Trigers" in Boston Business Journal (Vol. 30, November 12, 2010, No. 42, pp. 1)*

Pub: Boston Business Journal

Ed: Craig M. Douglas. **Description:** Large residential projects are expected to break ground in Boston, Massachusetts in 2011, as real estate developers expect growth for the industry. Real estate experts expect more than 2,000 rental units to be available by 2011. Information on key real estate projects in Boston is presented.

22886 ■ *"Diamond in the Rough" in Canadian Business (Vol. 79, October 23, 2006, No. 21, pp. 71)*

Pub: Rogers Media

Ed: Mark Brown. **Description:** The opening of a new mine 420 kilometers northeast of Yellowknife in Northwest Territories by Tahera Diamond Corp. is discussed.

22887 ■ *"Digital Duplication" in Crain's Cleveland Business (Vol. 28, October 1, 2007, No. 39, pp. 3)*

Pub: Crain Communications, Inc.

Ed: David Bennett. **Description:** Profile of the business plan of eBlueprint Holdings LLC, a reprographics company that found success by converting customers' paper blueprints to an electronic format; the company plans to expand into other geographic markets by acquiring solid reprographics companies and converting their computer systems so that customers' blueprints can be managed electronically.

22888 ■ *"A Direct Approach' in Business Journal-Portland (Vol. 24, November 9, 2007, No. 36, pp. 1)*

Pub: American City Business Journals, Inc.

Ed: Matthew Kish. **Description:** Respond 2 LLC's annual revenue has increased from $14.2 million in 2004 to almost $50 million in 2007. The growth is attributed to a $100 million contract with Vonage. The role of the popularity of infomercials on the success of the Portland-based marketing company is evaluated.

22889 ■ *"Discovery Networks" in Brandweek (Vol. 49, April 21, 2008, No. 16, pp. SR9)*

Pub: VNU Business Media, Inc.

Ed: Anthony Crupi. **Description:** Provides contact information for sales and marketing personnel for the Discovery networks as well as a listing of the station's top programming and an analysis of the current season and the target audience for those programs running in the current season. The networks flagship station returned to the top 10 in 2007, averaging 1.28 million viewers.

22890 ■ *"The Display Group Is Super-Sized' in Michigan Vue (Vol. 13, July-August 2008, No. 4, pp. 34)*

Pub: Entrepreneur Media Inc.

Description: Profile of the Display Group, located in downtown Detroit, this company provides custom designed mobile marketing displays as well as special event production services for trade show displays. The rental house and design service is also beginning to see more business due to the film initiative, which provides incentives for films that are shooting in Michigan.

22891 ■ *"Dodge Frets Over Flood of Fast Money"* in Globe & Mail (May 2, 2007, pp. B1)
Pub: CTVglobemedia Publishing Inc.
Ed: Heather Scoffield. **Description:** The concern of governor of Bank of Canada, David Dodge, over the increase in global liquidity due to growth in the business of private equity, is discussed.

22892 ■ *"The Dogs of TSX"* in Canadian Business (Vol. 81, Summer 2008, No. 9, pp. 77)
Pub: Rogers Media Ltd.
Ed: Calvin Leung. **Description:** Table showing the one-year stock performance of the ten highest dividend-yielding stocks on the S&P/TSX 60 Composite Index is presented. This technique is similar to the 'Dogs of the Dow' approach. The idea in this investment strategy is to buy equal amounts of stocks from these companies and selling them a year later, and then repeat the process.

22893 ■ *"The Dogs of the TSX"* in Canadian Business (Vol. 82, Summer 2009, No. 8, pp. 42)
Pub: Rogers Media
Ed: Calvin Leung. **Description:** David Stanley revealed in an analysis of the ten companies on the S&P/TSX 60 index with the highest dividend yields, known as the Dogs of TSX, the dogs delivered an annual return of 13 percent between 1987 to 2005. The Dogs is a stock-picking method that involves buying the ten companies on the S&P/TSX 60 index with the highest dividend yields, and then selling them a year later.

22894 ■ *"Dollar Tree Store To Open Mid-July in Shelby Mall"* in La Crosse Tribune (June 20, 2010)
Pub: La Crosse Tribune
Ed: Steve Cahalan. **Description:** Dollar Tree Inc. plans to open a new store in the location formerly occupied by Family Dollar.

22895 ■ *Don't Bitch, Just Get Rich*
Pub: Simon and Schuster Inc.
Contact: Carolyn Reidy, President
E-mail: carolyn.reidy@simonandschuster.com
Ed: Toney Fitzgerald. **Released:** June 2006. **Price:** $16.00. **Description:** Advice is given to business leaders to help them shift from the position whereby money has power over you to taking responsibility for life choices in order to meet new challenges.

22896 ■ *"Down by the Bay"* in Canadian Business (Vol. 81, December 8, 2008, No. 21, pp. 15)
Pub: Rogers Media Ltd.
Ed: Calvin Leung. **Description:** Hudsons Bay Company chief executive Jeffrey Sherman believes that his vast experience in retail will help him find the company's customer base. Sales are estimated to increase 3.6 percent in 2009 after posting average annual retail sales increases of 5 percent between 2006 and 2008.

22897 ■ *"Dreyer's Grand Ice Cream"* in Ice Cream Reporter (Vol. 23, September 20, 2010, No. 10, pp. 8)
Pub: Ice Cream Reporter
Description: Dreyer's Grand Ice Cream will add one hundred new manufacturing jobs at its plant in Laurel, Maryland and another 65 new hires before the end of 2010 and another 35 in 2011.

22898 ■ *"Drilling Deep and Flying High"* in Barron's (Vol. 88, June 30, 2008, No. 26, pp. 34)
Pub: Dow Jones & Co., Inc.
Ed: Kenneth Rapoza. **Description:** Shares of Petrobras could rise another 25 percent if the three deepwater wells that the company has found proves as lucrative as some expect. Petrobras will become an oil giant if the reserves are proven.

22899 ■ *Duct Tape Marketing: The World's Most Practical Small Business Marketing Guide*
Pub: Thomas Nelson Inc.
Ed: John Jantsch. **Released:** May 2008. **Price:** $14.99. **Description:** Small business owners are provided the tools and tactics necessary to market and grow a business.

22900 ■ *"Dunkin' Donuts Franchise Looking Possible for 2011"* in Messenger-Inquirer (January 2, 2010)
Pub: Messenger-Inquirer
Ed: Joy Campbell. **Description:** Dunkin' Donuts has approved expansion of their franchises in the Owensboro, Kentucky region.

22901 ■ *"Duro Bag to Expand, Add 130 Jobs"* in Business Courier (Vol. 27, August 6, 2010, No. 14, pp. 1)
Pub: Business Courier
Ed: Jon Newberry. **Description:** Duro Bag Manufacturing Company will expand capacity at its Florence, Kentucky plant and will add around 130 jobs over the next few years. The state of Kentucky has given preliminary approval for up to $1 million in tax incentives over 10 years, tied to the creation of new jobs. The company's investment will include new production and packaging equipment and building improvements.

22902 ■ *"Dynamic Duo"* in Barron's (Vol. 88, March 10, 2008, No. 10, pp. 45)
Pub: Dow Jones & Company, Inc.
Ed: Shirley A. Lazo. **Description:** General Dynamics, the world's sixth-largest military contractor, raised its dividend payout by 20.7 percent from 29 cents to 35 cents a share. Steel Dynamics, producer of structural steel and steel bar products, declared a 2-for-1 stock split and raised its quarterly dividend by 33 percent to a split-adjusted 10 cents a share.

22903 ■ *E-Commerce in Regional Small to Medium Enterprises*
Pub: Idea Group Publishing
Ed: Robert MacGregor. **Released:** July 2007. **Price:** $99.95. **Description:** Strategies small to medium enterprises (SMEs) need to implement in order to compete with larger, global businesses and the role electronic commerce plays in this process are outlined. Studies of e-commerce in multiple regional areas, focusing on the role of business size, business sector, market focus, gender of CEO, and education level of the CEO are discussed.

22904 ■ *E-Myth Mastery: The Seven Essential Disciplines for Building a World Class Company*
Pub: HarperCollins Publishers Inc.
Ed: Michael E. Gerber. **Released:** March 2007. **Price:** $16.95. **Description:** Leadership, marketing, money, management, lead conversion, lead generation, client fulfillment are the seven keys to successful entrepreneurship.

22905 ■ *The E Myth Revisited: Why Most Small Businesses Don't Work and What to Do*
Pub: HarperCollins Publishers
Ed: Michael E. Gerber. **Released:** January 18, 2010. **Price:** $11.10. **Description:** The book dispels the myths surrounding starting a business and shows how traditional assumptions can get in the way of running a small company. Topics cover entrepreneurship from infancy to growth and covers franchising.

22906 ■ *The E-Myth Revisited: Why Most Small Businesses Don't Work and What to Do About It*
Pub: HarperInformation
Ed: Michael E. Gerber. **Released:** November 2005. **Price:** $39.00. **Description:** Keys for developing a prosperous small business is presented in an updated version of the author's best-seller published in the nineties.

22907 ■ *"Eastland Future Unclear: Local Merchants Say They're OK Amid Closings of 4 More Stores"* in Charlotte Observer (February 8, 2007)
Pub: Knight-Ridder/Tribune Business News
Ed: Nichole Monroe Bell. **Description:** Retailers in the Eastland Mall that market goods to shoppers looking for the urban, hip-hop look are most successful.

22908 ■ *"Eckert Sales Spell Relief for Coutu"* in Globe & Mail (January 18, 2006, pp. B4)
Pub: CTVglobemedia Publishing Inc.
Ed: Bertrand Marotte. **Description:** The details on Eckerd Corp., which posted rise in sales by 2.7 percent in December 2005, are presented. Eckerd Corp. is a unit of Jean Coutu Group (PJC) Inc.

22909 ■ *"Eclipse to Hire 50 for Airport Hangar"* in Business Review, Albany New York (Vol. 34, November 9, 2007, No. 32, pp. 3)
Pub: American City Business Journals, Inc.
Ed: Robin K. Cooper. **Description:** Eclipse Aviation, a jet manufacturer will hire fifty workers who will operate its new maintenance hangar at Albany International Airport. The company was expected to hire around twenty-five employees after it announced its plan to open one of the seven U.S. Factory Service Centers in 2005. Denise Zieske, the airport Economic Development Manager, expects the hangar construction to be completed by December 2007.

22910 ■ *"Eco-Preneuring"* in Small Business Opportunities (July 2008)
Pub: Entrepreneur Media Inc.
Ed: Mary C. Pearl. **Description:** Profile of Wildlife Trust, a rapidly growing global organization dedicated to innovative conservation science linking health and ecology. With partners in nearly twenty countries, Wildlife Trust draws on global strengths in order to respond to well-defined local needs. In the Dominican Republic, they are working with the community and local biologists in order to restore fishing and create jobs in the field of ecotourism.

22911 ■ *"Economy Peddles Rent In This Cycle"* in The Business Journal-Serving Metropolitan Kansas City (Vol. 26, August 8, 2008, No. 48)
Pub: American City Business Journals, Inc.
Ed: Ashlee Kieler. **Description:** Rental demand for apartment units in downtown Kansas City, Missouri, is increasing due to the housing crisis, lack of real estate development, and increasing popularity of the downtown area. The downtown area has 7,378 multifamily units as of June 2008, of which 4,114 are rentals.

22912 ■ *"An Educated Play on China"* in Barron's (Vol. 88, June 30, 2008, No. 26, pp. M5)
Pub: Dow Jones & Co., Inc.
Ed: Mohammed Hadi. **Description:** New Oriental Education & Technology Group sells English-language courses to an increasingly competitive Chinese workforce that values education. The shares in this company have been weighed down by worries on the impact of the Beijing Olympics on enrollment and the Sichuan earthquake. These shares could be a great way to get exposure to the long-term growth in China.

22913 ■ *Effective Small Business Management: An Entrepreneurial Approach*
Pub: Prentice Hall Higher Education
Ed: Norman M. Scarborough; Thomas W. Zimmerer; Douglas L. Wilson. **Released:** March 2006. **Price:** $178.33. **Description:** Provides undergraduate and graduate entrepreneurship and/or small business management courses with information to successfully launch a new company. The books offers entrepreneurs the tools required to develop staying power to succeed and grow their new business.

22914 ■ *"Efficient Cash Management Essential To Be Competitive"* in Crain's Cleveland Business (Vol. 28, November 12, 2007, No. 45, pp. 25)
Pub: Crain Communications, Inc.
Ed: Ken Moultrie. **Description:** In order to sustain a business it is important to organize cash-management efforts around three core areas: cash in, static cash and cash out. Tips for the successful management of these areas are provided.

22915 ■ *"El Paso Firm Rides Boom to the Top"* in Hispanic Business (Vol. 30,

July-August 2008, No. 7-8, pp. 28)
Pub: Hispanic Business, Inc.
Ed: Jeremy Nisen. **Description:** VEMAC, a commercial construction management and general contracting firm that is experiencing success despite the plummeting construction market is discussed. VEMAC's success is attributed to the Pentagons' $5 billion investment in construction for the benefit of new personnel and their families to be transferred to Fort Bliss, a U.S. army base adjacent to El Paso.

22916 ■ *"Elements For Success" in Small Business Opportunities (November 2008)*
Pub: Entrepreneur Press
Contact: Perlman Neil, President
Description: Profile of Elements, a physical fitness club that approach a healthy lifestyle for women, which includes the components of body, beauty and mind; the network of upscale, boutique style health clubs differ from other providers in its 'balanced lifestyle' approach to a healthy lifestyle. This unique niche is gaining in popularity despite the faltering economy.

22917 ■ *"Elevated Status" in Business Courier (Vol. 24, March 21, 2008, No. 50, pp. 1)*
Pub: American City Business Journals, Inc.
Ed: James Ritchie. **Description:** Overview of Tri-Health Inc.'s growth is presented. Currently, the company's revenue is estimated to be around $1 billion. Since 2004, the company was able to build patient towers, an outpatient facility in Lebanon, and was able to acquire the Group Health Associates physician practice. TriHealth recently hired 500 nurses in order to meet its needs.

22918 ■ *Email Marketing by the Numbers: How to Use the World's Greatest Marketing Tool to Take Any Organization to the Next Level*
Pub: John Wiley and Sons Inc.
Ed: Chris Baggott. **Released:** April 2007. **Price:** $29.99 (CND). **Description:** Tips for using email to market small business products and services are provided.

22919 ■ *The Emerging Markets Century: How a New Breed of World-Class Companies is Overtaking the World*
Pub: Free Press/Simon & Schuster Inc.
Ed: Antoine van Agtmael. **Released:** 2007. **Price:** $29.00. **Description:** An exploration of how companies like Lenovo and Haier who are presently in emerging economies are already competing with household name brands like Ford and Sony, thus proving globalization is here to stay.

22920 ■ *"Emerging Tech Fund Strong in 2009" in Austin Business JournalInc. (Vol. 29, December 25, 2009, No. 42, pp. 1)*
Pub: American City Business Journals
Ed: Christopher Calnan. **Description:** Texas' Emerging Technology Fund (ETF) has seen an increase in applications from the state's technology companies in 2009. ETF received 87 applications in 2009 from Central Texas companies versus 50 during 2008 while $10.5 million was given to seven Texas companies compared with $10.6 million to ten companies in 2008.

22921 ■ *"The Emperor Strikes Back" in Canadian Business (Vol. 80, March 26, 2007, No. 7, pp. 48)*
Pub: Rogers Media
Ed: Rachel Pulfer. **Description:** The financial performance of Fairfax Financial Holdings Ltd. in 2006 is presented. The efforts of chief executive Prem Watsa to lead the company towards growth track are also presented.

22922 ■ *"Employers Plan to Fill Jobs" in Philadelphia Business Journal (Vol. 28, February 5, 2010, No. 51, pp. 1)*
Pub: American City Business Journals
Ed: Peter van Allen. **Description:** Philadelphia, Pennsylvania's largest employers have openings for at least 6,000 jobs. But businesses remain cautious and are selective in hiring or waiting to see what happens to federal policy changes.

22923 ■ *"EnCana Surpasses All Canadian Profit Records" in Globe & Mail (February 16, 2007, pp. B5)*
Pub: CTVglobemedia Publishing Inc.
Ed: David Ebner. **Description:** Canada-based energy giant EnCana Corp. has reported $5.65 billion profits for the fiscal year 2006. The company has outpaced expectations by this impressive figure.

22924 ■ *"The End of the Line for Line Extensions?" in Advertising Age (Vol. 79, July 7, 2008, No. 26, pp. 3)*
Pub: Crain Communications, Inc.
Description: After years of double-digit growth, some of the most heavily extended personal-care products have slowed substantially or even declined in the U.S. Unilever's Dove and P&G's Pantene and Olay are two such brands that have been affected. Statistical data included.

22925 ■ *"Endeca Gears Up for Likely IPO Bid" in Boston Business Journal (Vol. 31, July 1, 2011, No. 23, pp. 1)*
Pub: Boston Business Journal
Ed: Kyle Alspach. **Description:** Endeca Inc. is readying itself for its plans to register as a public company. The search engine technology leader is enjoying continued growth with revenue up by 30 percent in 2010 while its expansion trend makes it an unlikely candidate for an acquisition.

22926 ■ *"The Endless Flow of Russell Simmons" in Entrepreneur (Vol. 37, September 2009, No. 9, pp. 24)*
Pub: Entrepreneur Media, Inc.
Ed: Josh Dean. **Description:** Entrepreneur Russell Simmons has successfully grown his businesses by focusing on underserved markets. Simons has never given up on any business strategy. He has also entered the music, clothing and television industries.

22927 ■ *"Energy Consulting Company to Expand" in Austin Business JournalInc. (Vol. 28, November 7, 2008, No. 34, pp. A1)*
Pub: American City Business Journals
Ed: Kate Harrington. **Description:** CLEAResult Consulting Inc. is planning to increase its workforce and move its headquarters to a larger office. The company has posted 1,000 percent increase in revenues. The company's adoption of best practices and setting of benchmark goals are seen as the reason for its growth.

22928 ■ *"Energy Sparks Job Growth" in The Business Journal-Serving Greater Tampa Bay (Vol. 28, August 8, 2008, No. 33, pp. 1)*
Pub: American City Business Journals, Inc.
Ed: Margie Manning. **Description:** Energy infrastructure projects in Tampa Bay, Florida, are increasing the demand for labor in the area. Energy projects requiring an increase in labor include TECO Energy Inc.'s plan for a natural gas pipeline in the area and the installation of energy management system in Bank of America's branches in the area.

22929 ■ *The Engine of America: The Secrets to Small Business Success from Entrepreneurs Who Have Made It!*
Pub: John Wiley and Sons, Inc.
Ed: Hector Barreto; Robert J. Wagman (As told to). **Released:** September 2007. **Price:** $24.95. **Description:** Successful business strategies from CEOs of fifty small businesses (some of which are now large corporations) are shared to help entrepreneurs start or grow an existing company.

22930 ■ *"Engine of Growth: U.S. Industry Funk hasn't Hurt Cummins or Its Investors" in Barron's (Vol. 88, July 14, 2008, No. 28, pp. 43)*
Pub: Dow Jones & Co., Inc.
Ed: Shirley A. Lazo. **Description:** Engine maker Cummins increased its quarterly common dividend by 40 percent to 17.5 cents per share from 12.5 cents. CVS Caremark's dividend saw a hike of 18.4 percent from 9.5 cents to 11.25 cents per share while its competitor Walgreen is continuing its 75th straight year of dividend distribution and its 33rd straight year of dividend hikes.

22931 ■ *Enterprise, Entrepreneurship and Innovation: Concepts, Context and Commercialization*
Pub: Elsevier Science and Technology Books
Ed: Robin Lowe, Sue Marriott. **Released:** June 2006. **Price:** $39.95. **Description:** Application of enterprise, innovation and entrepreneurship are discussed to help companies grow.

22932 ■ *Entrepreneurial Strategies: New Technologies and Emerging Markets*
Pub: Blackwell Publishing Inc.
Contact: Gordon Tibbitts, President
Ed: Arnold Cooper; Sharon Alvarez; Alejandro Carrera; Luiz Mesquita; Robert Vassolo. **Released:** August 2006. **Price:** $69.95. **Description:** Ideas to help a small business expand into emerging market economies (EMEs) are discussed. Despite the high failure rate, this book helps a small firm develop a successful plan.

22933 ■ *Entrepreneurial Strategy Emerging Businesses in Declining Industries*
Pub: Edward Elgar Publishing, Incorporated
Ed: Cassia. **Released:** July 2006. **Price:** $110.00. **Description:** Role of entrepreneurship in context of older and declining industries is explored. The book offers insight into entrepreneurial dynamics behind emerging businesses in declining industries, especially the roles of resources processes and people.

22934 ■ *The Entrepreneur's Guide to Managing Growth and Handling Crisis*
Pub: Greenwood Publishing Group, Inc.
Ed: Theo J. Van Dijk. **Released:** December 2007. **Price:** $39.95. **Description:** The author explains how entrepreneurs can overcome crisis by changing the way they handle customers, by putting new processes and procedures in place, and managing employees in a professional manner. The book includes appendices with tips for hiring consultants, creating job descriptions, and setting up systems to chart cash flow as well as worksheets, tables and figures and a listing of resources.

22935 ■ *Entrepreneurship: A Process Perspective*
Pub: Thomson South-Western
Ed: Robert A. Baron; Scott A. Shane. **Released:** February 2007. **Price:** $137.95. **Description:** Entrepreneurial process covering team building, finances, business plan, legal issues, marketing, growth and exit strategies.

22936 ■ *"Entrepreneurship: As Cool As It Gets" in Canadian Business (Vol. 80, January 29, 2007, No. 3, pp. 10)*
Pub: Rogers Media
Ed: Norman de Bono. **Description:** The proposed construction of a restaurant with ice in Dubai by the Canadian firm Iceculture Inc. for the Sharaf Group is discussed. The growth of the clientele of Iceculture Inc. is described.

22937 ■ *Entrepreneurship and Economic Growth*
Pub: Edward Elgar Publishing, Incorporated
Ed: Carree. **Released:** October 2006. **Price:** $195.00. **Description:** Historic and country-specific studies and articles regarding entrepreneurship and innovation, growth models, competition and productivity, and empirical evidence.

22938 ■ *Entrepreneurship and the Financial Community Starting Up and Growing New Businesses*
Pub: Edward Elgar Publishing, Incorporated
Ed: Clarysse. **Released:** November 2006. **Price:** $75.00. **Description:** Understanding the role of private equity providers in the development and growth processes of small business.

22939 ■ *Entrepreneurship and the Growth of Firms*
Pub: Edward Elgar Publishing, Incorporated
Ed: Davidsson. **Released:** December 2006. **Price:** $100.00. **Description:** Relationships between entrepreneurial skills and small business growth are explored.

22940 ■ Entrepreneurship, Innovation and Economic Growth
Pub: Edward Elgar Publishing, Incorporated
Ed: David B. Audretsch. Released: July 2006. Price: $145.00. Description: Links between entrepreneurship, innovation and economic growth are examined.

22941 ■ Entrepreneurship, Innovation and the Growth Mechanism of the Free-Enterprise Economies
Pub: Princeton University Press
Ed: Eytan Sheshinski; William J. Baumol. Released: January 2007. Price: $65.00. Description: Scholars address the free-enterprise Western economies.

22942 ■ Entrepreneurship: The Engine of Growth
Pub: Greenwood Publishing Group Inc.
Contact: Janann Sherman, Manager
Ed: Maria Minniti; Andrew Zacharakis; Stephen Spinelli; Mark P. Rice; Timothy G. Habbershon. Released: November 2006. Price: $300.00. Description: Dynamics of entrepreneurship are examined.

22943 ■ Entrepreneurship in the U.S.: The 2005 Assessment
Pub: Springer
Ed: Paul Reynolds. Released: March 2007. Price: $79.95. Description: Entrepreneurship and its role in the U.S. economy is discussed, examining new business creation and its impact on job growth, productivity enhancements, innovation, and social mobility.

22944 ■ "eResearch Issues Initiating Report on Aldershot Resources Ltd." in Canadian Corporate News (May 14, 2007)
Pub: Comtex News Network Inc.
Description: Overview of Bob Weir and Michael Wood's Initiating Report on Aldershot Resources Ltd., a junior Canadian-based uranium exploration company with prospective projects in Canada, Zambia, Australia, and a base metals project in Chile.

22945 ■ "Essential Releases Record First Quarter Results" in Canadian Corporate News (May 14, 2007)
Pub: Comtex News Network Inc.
Description: The first quarter of 2007 saw record financial performance despite numerous challenges for Essential Energy Services Trust. Statistical data included.

22946 ■ Exceptional Service, Exceptional Profit: The Secrets of Building a Five-Star Customer Service Organization
Pub: AMACOM
Ed: Leonard Inghilleri, Micah Solomon. Released: April 1, 2010. Price: $21.95. Description: Team of insiders share exclusive knowledge of the loyalty-building techniques pioneered by the world's most successful service leaders, including brick-and-mortar stars such as The Ritz-Carlton and Lexus and online success stories such as Netflix and CD Baby.

22947 ■ "Executive Decision: Lead a Double Life for Geac's Sake" in Globe & Mail (January 21, 2006, pp. B4)
Pub: CTVglobemedia Publishing Inc.
Ed: Simon Avery. Description: The details of growth of Geac Computer Corporation Ltd., under chief executive officer Charles Jones, are presented.

22948 ■ "Executive Decision: To Make Inroads Against RIM, Palm Steals Its Strategy" in Globe & Mail (March 25, 2006, pp. B3)
Pub: CTVglobemedia Publishing Inc.
Ed: Simon Avery. Description: The Palm Inc., global leader in portable device manufacturing, is looking forward to improve its sales of Palm Treos, a wireless portable device that connects to internet and email. Palm is also planning to build partnerships, under the efficient management of Michael Moskowitz, general manager and vice-president of Palm Inc., with the other companies to increase the sales of its wireless devices.

22949 ■ "Executive Interview: Arturo Elias" in Canadian Business (Vol. 80, January 29, 2007, No. 3, pp. 16)
Pub: Rogers Media
Ed: Thomas Watson. Description: The views of Arturo Elias, the president of General Motors Canada Limited, on the prospects of the growth of the company revenues during the year 2007 are presented.

22950 ■ "Expanding Middleby's Food Processing Biz" in Crain's Chicago Business (Vol. 31, April 21, 2008, No. 16, pp. 6)
Pub: Crain Communications, Inc.
Ed: David Sterrett. Description: Profile of the executive vice-president of the food processing company, Middleby Corp, whose business plan is to develop new products, begin looking for acquisitions and simplify operations in order to expand the firm.

22951 ■ "Expansions Signal Growing Interest in Waste-to-Energy Plants" in Crain's Cleveland Business (Vol. 28, November 5, 2007, No. 44)
Pub: Crain Communications, Inc.
Ed: Bruce Geiselman. Description: According to industry insiders, concerns about greenhouse gas emissions as well as escalating energy and waste disposal prices are fueling increased interest in waste-to-energy plants. Many plants are expanding and considering building new trash-burning plants; this marks the first growth in capacity in more than a decade.

22952 ■ "Explore New Avenues to Success..Boldly!" in Indoor Comfort Marketing (Vol. 70, May 2011, No. 5, pp. 18)
Pub: Industry Publications Inc.
Ed: Rich Rutigliano. Description: Strategies to help fuel companies succeed in today's market are explored.

22953 ■ "Exxon Braving the Danger Zones" in Globe & Mail (March 8, 2007, pp. B1)
Pub: CTVglobemedia Publishing Inc.
Ed: Shawn McCarthy. Description: The plans of Exxon Mobil Corp. to increase its revenues through the expansion of its operations in Asia, Africa, and the Middle East are discussed.

22954 ■ "Eyes to the Sky" in Canadian Business (Vol. 80, March 26, 2007, No. 7, pp. 33)
Pub: Rogers Media
Ed: Joe Castaldo. Description: The growth and prices of condominium market in the Canada are analyzed.

22955 ■ "Face Values: Going for Global Growth" in Business Strategy Review (Vol. 21, Autumn 2010, No. 3, pp. 60)
Pub: Wiley-Blackwell
Ed: Laura Tyson. Description: Global economic issues are discussed with Laura Tyson, former Dean of the London Business School, professor at University of California Berkeley, and current advisor to President Obama.

22956 ■ "Face Values: Responsibility Inc" in Business Strategy Review (Vol. 21, Summer 2010, No. 2, pp. 66)
Pub: Wiley-Blackwell
Ed: John Connolly. Description: Investment and growth in emerging markets will bring new opportunities, but with them added responsibility. Will companies be able to rise to meet the new responsibility agenda?.

22957 ■ "Face Values: Responsibility Inc." in Business Strategy Review (Vol. 21, Summer 2010, No. 2, pp. 66)
Pub: Blackwell Publishers Ltd.
Ed: John Connolly. Description: Investment and growth in emerging markets will bring new opportunities, but added responsibility comes with it. Will companies be able to rise to meet the new responsibility agenda?.

22958 ■ The Facebook Effect: The Inside Story of the Company That Is Connecting the World
Pub: Simon & Shuster
Ed: David Kirkpatrick. Released: June 8, 2010. Price: $26.00. Description: There's never been a Website like Facebook: more than 350 million people have accounts, and if the growth rate continues, by 2013 every Internet user worldwide will have his or her own page. No one's had more access to the inner workings of the phenomenon than Kirkpatrick, a senior tech writer at Fortune magazine. Written with the full cooperation of founder Mark Zuckerberg, the book follows the company from its genesis in a Harvard dorm room through its successes over Friendster and MySpace, the expansion of the user base, and Zuckerberg's refusal to sell.

22959 ■ "Familiar Fun" in Crain's Cleveland Business (Vol. 28, October 22, 2007, No. 42, pp. 3)
Pub: Crain Communications Inc.
Ed: John Booth. Description: Marketing for the 2007 holiday season has toy retailers focusing on American-made products because of recent recalls of toys produced in China that do not meet U.S. safety standards.

22960 ■ "Family Throne" in Hawaii Business (Vol. 53, March 2008, No. 9, pp. 51)
Pub: Hawaii Business Publishing
Ed: Cathy S. Cruz-George. Description: Jeanette and George Grace inherited Paradise Lua Inc., a portable toilet company founded by George's father. The toilets are rented by Aloha Stadium during football season and St. Patrick's Day block party among others. The company has 2,500 toilets and 20 pumping trucks and had earnings of $1.3 million in 2007.

22961 ■ "Fashion Forward - Frugally" in Entrepreneur (Vol. 37, July 2009, No. 7, pp. 18)
Pub: Entrepreneur Media, Inc.
Ed: Jason Daley. Description: Staci Deal, a Fayetteville-based franchisee of fashion brand Plato's Closet, shares her experiences on the company's growth. Deal believes that the economy, and the fact that Fayetteville is a college town, played a vital role in boosting the used clothing store's popularity. Her thoughts on being a young business owner, and the advantages of running a franchise are also given.

22962 ■ Faster Cheaper Better
Pub: Crown Business Books
Ed: Michael Hammer. Released: December 28, 2010. Price: $27.50. Description: Nine levels for transforming work in order to achieve business growth are outlined. The book helps small business compete against the low-wage countries.

22963 ■ "Female Hispanic Professionals by the Number" in Hispanic Business (Vol. 30, April 2008, No. 4, pp. 8)
Pub: Hispanic Business
Description: More executive opportunities are presenting themselves for future generations of Hispanic women who are more frequently being found in high-level positions. Statistical data included.

22964 ■ "Fewer People Dying At Work" in Sacramento Business Journal (Vol. 25, August 29, 2008, No. 26, pp. 1)
Pub: American City Business Journals, Inc.
Ed: Kathy Robertson. Description: Statistics show that workplace deaths in California dropped by 24 percent in 2007 compared with the previous year. Much of the decline was observed in the construction industry, where a slowing economy affected employment and dangerous work. The number of workplace deaths in the state also declined in all major categories except fires and explosions.

22965 ■ "Fifth Third CEO Kabat: A World of Difference" in Business Courier (Vol. 26, January 1, 2010, No. 37, pp. 1)
Pub: American City Business Journals, Inc.
Ed: Steve Watkins. Description: CEO Kevin Kabat of Cincinnati-based Fifth Third Bancorp believes that the bank's assets of $111 billion and stock value of

more than $10 indicate the recovery from the low stock prices posted in February 2009. He attributes the recovery from the federal government's stress test finding in May 2009 that Fifth Third needs to generate $1.1 billion.

22966 ■ "Fifth Third Spinoff" in Business Courier (Vol. 27, July 16, 2010, No. 11, pp. 1)
Pub: Business Courier
Ed: Dan Monk, Steve Watkins. **Description:** Electronic-funds transfer company Fifth Third Solutions (FTPS), a spinoff of Fifth Third Bancorp, is seeking as much as 200,000 square feet of new office space in Ohio. The bank's sale of 51 percent ownership stake to Boston-based Advent International Corporation has paved the way for the growth of FTPS. How real estate brokers' plans have responded to FTPS' growth mode is discussed.

22967 ■ "The File On..Jenne Distributors" in Crain's Cleveland Business (Vol. 28, October 8, 2007, No. 40, pp. 26)
Pub: Crain Communications, Inc.
Ed: Kimberly Bonvissuto. **Description:** Overview of the telecommunications equipment company, Jenne Distributors, a firm that is projecting more than $125 million in revenue for 2007.

22968 ■ "The File On..Skoda Minotti" in Crain's Cleveland Business (Vol. 28, October 8, 2007, No. 40, pp. 26)
Pub: Crain Communications, Inc.
Ed: Kimberly Bonvissuto. **Description:** Overview of Skoda Minotti, the accounting and financial services firm located in Mayfield Village; the company has 140 employees and an expanded slate of services.

22969 ■ "Filling the Gap" in Canadian Business (Vol. 80, March 12, 2007, No. 6, pp. 62)
Pub: Rogers Media
Ed: Andrew Wahl. **Description:** The chief executive officer of GAP, Bruce Poon Tip, shares his experience and efforts in the growth of the company to a leading position in Canada.

22970 ■ "Finalist: Private Company, Less Than $100M" in Crain's Detroit Business (Vol. 25, June 22, 2009, No. 25)
Pub: Crain Communications Inc. - Detroit
Ed: Nancy Kaffer. **Description:** Profile of W3R Consulting and CFO Patrick Tom= ina. The company offers information technology consulting. Tomina discusses the company's 505 strategy: to grow its annual revenue to $50 million in five years.

22971 ■ Financing Growth: Strategies, Capital Structure, and M and A Transactions
Pub: John Wiley and Sons, Inc.
Ed: Kenneth H. Marks, Larry E. Robbins, Gonzalo Fernandez, John P. Funkhouser, D.L. Williams. **Released:** September 1, 2009. **Price:** $95.00. **Description:** Guide for emerging growth and middle market companies includes information to help understand and apply the basics of corporate finance using empirical data and actual company cases to illustrate capital structures and financing approaches.

22972 ■ "Finding A Higher Gear" in Harvard Business Review (Vol. 86, July-August 2008, No. 8, pp. 68)
Pub: Harvard Business School Press
Ed: Thomas A. Stewart; Anand P. Raman. **Description:** Anand G. Mahindra, the chief executive officer of Mahindra and Mahindra Ltd., discusses how his company fosters innovation, drawn from customer centricity, and how this will grow the company beyond India's domestic market.

22973 ■ "Finding a Way to Continue Growing" in Green Industry Pro (Vol. 23, March 2011, No. 3, pp. 31)
Pub: Cygnus Business Media
Description: Profile of Brett Lemcke, VP of R.M. Landscape located in Rochester, New York. Lemcke tells how his Landscape Industry Certified credentials helped him to grow his business and beat out his competition.

22974 ■ "FirstMerit's Top Executive Turns Around Credit Quality" in Crain's Cleveland Business (Vol. 28, October 15, 2007, No. 41, pp. 3)
Pub: Crain Communications, Inc.
Ed: Shawn A. Turner. **Description:** Discusses the ways in which chairman and CEO Paul Greig has been able to improve FirstMerit Corp.'s credit quality and profit margin. Strategies included selling more than $70 million in bad loans, hiring a new chief credit officer and redirecting its focus on cross-selling its wealth and investment services to its commercial customers. Statistical data included.

22975 ■ "Fiscally Fit" in Entrepreneur (Vol. 37, October 2009, No. 10, pp. 130)
Pub: Entrepreneur Media, Inc.
Ed: Jason Daley. **Description:** Landrie Peterman, owner of an Anytime Fitness franchise in Oregon, describes how she turned her business around. The franchise, located in an industrial park, saw growth after six months with the help of corporate clients.

22976 ■ "Five-Ring Circus" in Entrepreneur (Vol. 35, November 2007, No. 11, pp. 76)
Pub: Entrepreneur Media Inc.
Ed: Scott Bernard Nelson. **Description:** China's economy is growing and is expected to do well even after the 2008 Olympics, but growth could slow from eleven percent to eight or nine percent. Chinese portfolio concerns with regard to health and environmental records and bureaucratic fraud are discussed.

22977 ■ "Food Fight" in Canadian Business (Vol. 79, November 6, 2006, No. 22, pp. 18)
Pub: Rogers Media
Ed: Zena Olijnyk. **Description:** The war between Canadian grocers and Wal-Mart due to its plans for opening new stores is analyzed.

22978 ■ "For Gilead, Growth Beyond AIDS" in Barron's (Vol. 88, June 30, 2008, No. 26, pp. 18)
Pub: Dow Jones & Co., Inc.
Ed: Jay Palmer. **Description:** First-quarter 2008 revenue for Gilead Sciences grew by 22 percent and an earnings gain of 19 percent thanks to their HIV-treatment drugs that comprised over two-thirds of the company's sales in 2007. An analyst has a 12-month target from June, 2008 of 65 per share. The factors behind the company's prospects are also discussed.

22979 ■ "Ford, Chrysler Dinged as Little Cars Rule Road" in Globe & Mail (March 2, 2007, pp. B3)
Pub: CTVglobemedia Publishing Inc.
Ed: Greg Keenan. **Description:** The Ford Motor Co. and the Chrysler Group posted a decline in automobile sales in the first two months of 2007. The sales statistics of other automobile companies in Canada are also presented.

22980 ■ "ForeSee Finds Satisfaction On Web Sites, Bottom Line" in Crain's Detroit Business (Vol. 24, February 25, 2008, No. 8, pp. 3)
Pub: Crain Communications Inc. - Detroit
Ed: Tom Henderson. **Description:** Ann Arbor-based ForeSee Results Inc. evaluates user satisfaction on Web sites. The company expects to see an increase of 40 percent in revenue for 2008 with plans to expand to London, Germany, Italy and France by the end of 2009.

22981 ■ "Formulating Policy With a Parallel Organization" in Strategy & Leadership (Vol. 38, September-October 2010, No. 5, pp. 33-38)
Pub: Emerald Inc.
Ed: Dale E. Zand, Thomas F. Hawk. **Description:** A study analyzes a case to examine the parallel organization concept and its successful implementation by a CEO to integrate independent divisions of a firm. Findings reveal that the implementation of the parallel organization improved the policy formulation, strategic planning profitability of the firm while also better integrating its independent divisions.

22982 ■ "Franchising Lures Boomers" in Business Journal-Portland (Vol. 24, November 9, 2007, No. 36, pp. 1)
Pub: American City Business Journals, Inc.
Ed: Wendy Culverwell. **Description:** Popularity of franchising has increased, and investors belonging to the baby boom generation contribute largely to this growth. The number of aging baby boomers is also increasing, particularly in Oregon, which means further growth of franchises can be expected. Reasons why franchising is a good investment for aging baby boomers are given.

22983 ■ "Free Fall" in Canadian Business (Vol. 79, September 11, 2006, No. 18, pp. 28)
Pub: Rogers Media
Ed: Zena Olijnyk. **Description:** Second quarter results of Imax Corp are reviewed. The company's performance and its future prospects are also presented.

22984 ■ "Fresh Direct's Crisis" in Crain's New York Business (Vol. 24, January 14, 2008, No. 2, pp. 3)
Pub: Crain Communications, Inc.
Ed: Lisa Fickenscher. **Description:** Freshdirect, an Internet grocery delivery service, finds itself under siege from federal immigration authorities, customers and labor organizations due to its employment practice of hiring illegals. At stake is the grocer's reputation as well as its ambitious growth plans, including an initial public offering of its stock.

22985 ■ "Fries With That?" in Canadian Business (Vol. 81, September 29, 2008, No. 16, pp. 33)
Pub: Rogers Media Ltd.
Ed: Calvin Leung. **Description:** Profile of Toronto-based New York Fries, which has four stores in South Korea, is planning to expand further as well as into Hong Kong and Macau; the company also has a licensee in the United Arab Emirates whom is also planning to expand.

22986 ■ "From Craft Biz To Wholesale Giant" in Women Entrepreneur (January 19, 2009)
Pub: Entrepreneur Media Inc.
Ed: Maria Falconer. **Description:** Advice is given on how to turn a small craft business into a full-time venture; tips to help one transition from a part-time designer to a full-time wholesaler and brand are also included.

22987 ■ "From Fat to Fit" in Canadian Business (Vol. 79, September 25, 2006, No. 19, pp. 100)
Pub: Rogers Media
Ed: Graham Scott. **Description:** The increase in physical fitness clubs across Canada is discussed.

22988 ■ "From Malls to Steel Plants" in Crain's Chicago Business (Vol. 31, April 28, 2008, No. 17, pp. 30)
Pub: Crain Communications, Inc.
Ed: Samantha Stainburn. **Description:** Profile of the company Graycor Inc. which started out as a sand-blasting and concrete-breaking firm but has grown into four businesses due to innovation and acquisitions. Graycor's businesses include: Graycor Industrial Constructors Inc., which builds and renovates power plants and steel mills; Graycor Construction Co., which erects stores, medical centers and office buildings; Graycor Blasting Co., which uses explosives and blasts tunnels for industrial cleaning, and Graycor International Inc., which provides construction services in Mexico.

22989 ■ "From OTC Sellers to Surgeons, Healthcare Marketers Target Women to Achieve Growth" in Marketing to Women (February 2008)
Pub: EPM Communications Inc.
Contact: Ira Mayer, President
E-mail: imayer@epmcom.com
Description: Healthcare companies are targeting women with ad campaigns, new product development and new technology in order to reach and develop brand loyalty.

22990 ■ *"Fromm Family Foods Converts Old Feed Mill Into Factory for Gourmet Pet Food" in Wisconsin State Journal (August 3, 2011)*
Pub: Capital Newspapers
Ed: Barry Adams. Description: Fromm Family Foods, a gourmet cat and dog food company spent $10 million to convert an old feed mill into a pet food manufacturing facility. The owner forecasts doubling or tripling its production of 600 tons of feed per week in about five years.

22991 ■ *"Frozen Dessert Year in Review.." in Ice Cream Reporter (Vol. 22, January 20, 2009, No. 2, pp. 1)*
Pub: Ice Cream Reporter
Description: Falling economy caused the closing of several ice cream plants across the U.S. in 2008. Top stories of interest to the industry are presented.

22992 ■ *"Frozen Yogurt Market Heats Up Again" in Houston Business Journal (Vol. 40, November 27, 2009, No. 29, pp. 1)*
Pub: American City Business Journals
Ed: Allison Wollam. Description: Frozen yogurt stores are being reestablished or expanding in new sites throughout Houston, Texas due to presumed oversupply of ice cream stores in the market. Among these stores are Berripop, BlueBerryHill, Fruitzzy, and Tasti D-Lite. Suggestions for these stores to focus on frozen yogurts in order to distinguish them from stores offering other products such as specialty drink items and sandwiches are outlined.

22993 ■ *"Funeral Directors Get Creative As Boomers Near Great Beyond" in Advertising Age (Vol. 79, October 13, 2008, No. 38, pp. 30)*
Pub: Crain Communications, Inc.
Ed: Lenore Skenazy. Description: Despite the downturn in the economy, the funeral business is thriving due to the number of baby boomers who realize the importance of making preparations for their death. Marketers are getting creative in their approach and many companies have taken into consideration the need for a more environmental friendly way to dispose of bodies and thus have created innovative businesses that reflect this need.

22994 ■ *"Gail Lissner; Vice-President, Appraisal Research Counselors" in Crain's Chicago Business (Vol. 31, May 5, 2008, No. 18, pp. 28)*
Pub: Crain Communications, Inc.
Ed: Phuong Ly. Description: Profile of Gail Lissner who is the vice-president of the Appraisal Research Counselors, a company that puts out the quarterly 'Residential Benchmark Report,' in which Ms. Lissner co-authors and is considered a must-read in the industry. Ms. Lissner has risen to become one of the most sought-after experts on the Chicago market considering real estate.

22995 ■ *"Gallery Street Launches ArtCandy" in Art Business News (Vol. 34, November 2007, No. 11, pp. 8)*
Pub: Pfingsten Publishing, LLC
Description: Fine-art reproduction house Gallery Street recently launched its new division, ArtCandy Editions; the division was created in order to help a network of artists expand the distribution of their work.

22996 ■ *The Game-Changer: How You Can Drive Revenue and Profit Growth with Innovation*
Pub: Crown Business
Ed: A.G. Lafley, Ram Charan. Released: 2009. Price: $27.50. Description: Former Proctor and Gamble CEO A.G. Lafley outlines principles of innovation that turned the company around and shows how that strategy can work for any business.

22997 ■ *"The Game of Operation" in Crain's Chicago Business (Vol. 31, April 28, 2008, No. 17, pp. 26)*
Pub: Crain Communications, Inc.
Ed: Samantha Stainburn. Description: Revenue at Medline Industries Inc., a manufacturer of medical products, has risen 12 percent a year since 1976, reaching $2.81 billion last year. Growth at the

company is due to new and increasingly sophisticated operations by surgeons which brings about the need for more specialized tools.

22998 ■ *"Games Gone Wild: City's Newest Public Company Aims for the Sky" in Business Courier (Vol. 27, September 24, 2010, No. 21, pp. 1)*
Pub: Business Courier
Ed: Dan Monk. Description: Video game company Zoo Entertainment Inc., which is based in Norwood near Cincinnati, Ohio aims to build a strong company and to position itself for future growth. The company reported $27.6 million in revenue for the first half of 2010 and analysts project $100 million in sales for 2011.

22999 ■ *"GE Looking to Extend Hot Streak" in Business Courier (Vol. 24, January 25, 2008, No. 42, pp. 1)*
Pub: American City Business Journals, Inc.
Ed: John Newberry. Description: GE Aviation has enjoyed strong revenues and sales due to increase aircraft engine orders. It has an engine backlog order of $19 million as of the end of 2007. Data on the aviation company's revenues, operating profit and total engine orders for the year 2004 to 2007 are presented.

23000 ■ *"GE Milestone: 1,000th Wind Turbine Installed in Canada" in CNW Group (October 4, 2011)*
Pub: CNW Group
Contact: Carolyn McGill-Davidson, President
Description: GE installed its 1,000th wind turbine in Canada at Cartier Wind Energy's Gros Morne project in the Gaspesie Region of Quebec, Canada. As Canada continues to expand its use of wind energy, GE plans to have over 1,100 wind turbines installed in the nation by the end of 2011.

23001 ■ *"Generational Savvy" in Hawaii Business (Vol. 54, August 2008, No. 2, pp. 135)*
Pub: Hawaii Business Publishing
Ed: Jolyn Okimoto Rosa. Description: Lawrence Takeo Kagawa founded Security Insurance Agency, later renamed Occidental Underwriters of Hawaii Ltd., in 1933 to provide insurance to Asian-Americans in Hawaii at lower premiums. Details on the company's history, growth investment products and Transamerica Life products and 75 years of family-run business are discussed.

23002 ■ *"Genzyme: Underrated Oversold" in Barron's (Vol. 88, March 24, 2008, No. 12, pp. 58)*
Pub: Dow Jones & Company, Inc.
Ed: Johanna Bennett. Description: Shares of biotechnology company Genzyme appear oversold and underrated at their $71.86 level. The company's finances are on a solid foundation, with revenues over $3.8 billion in 2007 and forecasts of $4.5-4.7 billion in revenue for 2008.

23003 ■ *Get Your Business to Work!: 7 Steps to Earning More, Working Less and Living the Life You Want*
Pub: BenBella Books
Contact: Glen Yeffeth, President
Ed: George Hedley. Released: June 9, 2010. Price: $24.95. Description: Complete step-by-step guide for the small business owner to realize profits, wealth and freedom.

23004 ■ *Getting to Scale: Growing Your Business Without Selling Out*
Pub: Berrett-Koehler Publishers, Incorporated
Ed: Jill Bamburg. Released: July 2006. Price: $14.95. Description: Ways for entrepreneurs to preserve the value of their company while maintaining growth and competitiveness.

23005 ■ *"Getting in Shape" in Crain's Cleveland Business (Vol. 28, December 3, 2007, No. 48, pp. 13)*
Pub: Crain Communications, Inc.
Ed: Chrissy Kadleck. Description: According to the Medical Fitness Association, the number of medically integrated health and fitness centers has grown from

79 centers in 1985 to 875 in 2006. Summa Wellness Institute, the 65,000-square-foot health-and-fitness facility which opened next to Summa Health Systems's outpatient medical center is discussed.

23006 ■ *"Giants Now Admit They Roam Planet Earth; Time To Buy?" in Barron's (Vol. 38, March 31, 2008, No. 13, pp. 39)*
Pub: Dow Jones & Company, Inc.
Ed: Eric J. Savitz. Description: Oracle's third-quarter results showed that top-line growth fell short of expectations but the company is expected to fare better than most applications companies in the downturn. Google had a flat growth in the number of people who click their online ads. The time for investors in the tech sector with a long-term horizon has arrived.

23007 ■ *The Girl's Guide to Building a Million-Dollar Business*
Pub: AMACOM
Ed: Susan Wilson Solovic. Released: 2008. Price: $21.95. Description: Success plan for women business owners; the book includes tips for determination, managing changing relationships, keeping employees and customers happy, getting and maintaining credit, overcoming gender bias, and creating a good business plan and solid brand.

23008 ■ *"The Global Economy, the Labor Force and Franchising's Future" in Franchising World (Vol. 42, September 2010, No. 9, pp. 35)*
Pub: International Franchise Association
Ed: Jeffrey A. Rosensweig. Description: Point forecasting and the methodology called scenario analysis are presented looking at the global economy and future of franchising in the U.S. and abroad.

23009 ■ *"Golden Spoon Accelerates Expansion Here and Abroad" in Ice Cream Reporter (Vol. 22, December 20, 2008, No. 1, pp. 2)*
Pub: Ice Cream Reporter
Description: Golden Spoon frozen yogurt franchise chain is developing 35 more locations in the Phoenix, Arizona area along with plans to open a store in Japan.

23010 ■ *Good Capitalism, Bad Capitalism, and the Economics of Growth and Prosperity*
Pub: Yale University Press
Ed: William J. Baumol, Robert E. Litan, Carl J. Schramm. Released: October 1, 2009. Price: $22.00. Description: The book identifies the conditions that characterize good capitalism and discusses capitalist economies.

23011 ■ *Good to Great: Why Some Companies Make the Leap..and Others Don't*
Pub: HarperInformation
Ed: Jim Collins. Released: October 2001. Price: $29.99. Description: Management styles for growing a modern business.

23012 ■ *"A Good Sign for Commercial Real Estate" in Austin Business JournalInc. (Vol. 29, December 18, 2009, No. 41, pp. 1)*
Pub: American City Business Journals
Ed: Kate Harrington. Description: Factors that could contribute to the reemergence of the commercial mortgage-backed securities market in Texas are discussed. These securities can potentially boost the commercial real estate market statewide as well as nationwide. Commercial mortgage-backed securities origination in 2009 is worth less that $1 billion, compared with $238 billion in 2008.

23013 ■ *The Google Story: Inside the Hottest Business, Media, and Technology Success of Our Time*
Pub: Random Housing Publishing Group
Ed: David A. Vise; Mark Malseed. Price: $26.00.

23014 ■ *"Graduates to the TSX in 2008" in Canadian Business (Vol. 81, Summer 2008, No. 9, pp. 79)*
Pub: Rogers Media Ltd.
Ed: Calvin Leung. Description: Table showing the market capitalization and stock performance of the companies that jumped to the TSX Venture Exchange

is presented. The 17 companies that made the leap to the list will have an easier time raising capital, although leeway must be made in investing since they are still new businesses.

23015 ■ *"Grand Action Makes Grand Changes in Grand Rapids" in Crain's Detroit Business (Vol. 25, June 1, 2009, No. 22, pp. M012)*
Pub: Crain Communications Inc. - Detroit
Ed: Amy Lane. **Description:** Businessman Dick De-Vos believes that governments are not always the best to lead certain initiatives. That's why, in 1991, he gathered 50 west Michigan community leaders and volunteers to look consider the construction of an arena and expanding or renovating local convention operations. Grand Action has undertaken four major projects in the city.

23016 ■ *"Green Clean Machine" in Small Business Opportunities (Winter 2010)*
Pub: Harris Publications Inc.
Description: Eco-friendly maid franchise plans to grow its $62 million sales base. Profile of Maid Brigade, a green-cleaning franchise is planning to expand across the country.

23017 ■ *"Green Light" in The Business Journal-Portland (Vol. 25, July 11, 2008, No. 18, pp. 1)*
Pub: American City Business Journals, Inc.
Ed: Erik Siemers. **Description:** Ecos Consulting, a sustainability consulting company based in Portland, Oregon, is seeing a boost in revenue as more businesses turn to sustainable practices. The company's revenue rose by 50 percent in 2007 and employees increased from 57 to 150. Other details about Ecos' growth are discussed.

23018 ■ *Greening Your Small Business: How to Improve Your Bottom Line, Grow Your Brand, Satisfy Your Customers and Save the Planet*
Pub: Prentice Hall Press
Contact: Dame Marjorie M. Scardino, Chief Executive Officer
Ed: Jennifer Kaplan. **Released:** November 3, 2009. **Price:** $19.95. **Description:** A definitive resource for anyone who wants their small business to be cutting-edge, competitive, profitable, and eco-conscious. Stories from small business owners address every aspect of going green, from basics such as recycling waste, energy efficiency, and reducing information technology footprint, to more in-depth concerns such as green marketing and communications, green business travel, and green employee benefits.

23019 ■ *"Groomers Eye Profit Growth Through Services" in Pet Product News (Vol. 64, December 2010, No. 12, pp. 26)*
Pub: BowTie Inc.
Ed: Kathleen M. Mangan. **Description:** Pet groomers can successfully offer add-on services by taking into account insider customer knowledge, store image, and financial analysis in the decision-making process. Many pet groomers have decided to add services such as spa treatments and training due to a slump in the bathing and grooming business. How some pet groomers gained profitability through add-on services is explored.

23020 ■ *"Ground Floor Opportunity" in Small Business Opportunities (July 2008)*
Pub: Entrepreneur Press
Contact: Perlman Neil, President
Description: Profile of Doug Disney, the founder of the booming franchise Tile Outlet Always in Stock, which sells ceramic and porcelain tile and stone products at wholesale prices; Disney found inspiration in a book he read in two days and that motivated him to expand his venture into a huge franchise opportunity.

23021 ■ *"Grow-Ops" in Canadian Business (Vol. 81, October 27, 2008, No. 18, pp. 112)*
Pub: Rogers Media Ltd.
Ed: Calvin Leung. **Description:** Canada's agriculture and agri-food industry is ripe for expansion and to meet global demand that is expected to double by

2050. Better water management and biotechnology are among the strategies that could help increase output of Canada's agricultural industry.

23022 ■ *Growing Business Handbook: Inspirational Advice from Successful Entrepreneurs and Fast-Growing UK Companies*
Pub: Kogan Page, Limited
Contact: Ben Glover, Director of Marketing
Ed: Adam Jolly. **Released:** February 2007. **Price:** $49.95. **Description:** Tips for growing and running a successful business are covered, focusing on senior managers in middle market and SME companies.

23023 ■ *"A Growing Concern" in Canadian Business (Vol. 79, October 9, 2006, No. 20, pp. 90)*
Pub: Rogers Media
Ed: Jeff Sanford. **Description:** With rich dividends being harvested by companies producing ethanol, after ethanol became a petrol additive, is discussed.

23024 ■ *"A Growing Dilemma" in Crain's Cleveland Business (Vol. 28, October 8, 2007, No. 40, pp. 19)*
Pub: Crain Communications, Inc.
Ed: Kimberly Bonvissuto. **Description:** Discusses small business owners who often have to grapple with the decision on whether or not to expand their operations and the importance of a business plan which may help owners with that decision.

23025 ■ *"Growing Field" in Crain's Detroit Business (Vol. 26, January 11, 2010, No. 2, pp. 3)*
Pub: Crain Communications Inc.
Description: Detroit's TechTown was awarded a combination loan and grant of $4.1 million from the U.S. Department of Housing and Urban Development to build a 15,000-square-foot stem cell center, a collection of laboratories that will be available to both for-profit companies and university researchers.

23026 ■ *Growing and Managing a Small Business: An Entrepreneurial Perspective*
Pub: Houghton Mifflin College Division
Ed: Kathleen R. Allen. **Released:** July 2006. **Price:** $105.27. **Description:** Introduction to business ownership and management from startup through growth.

23027 ■ *"Growing at the Margins" in Business Journal Serving Greater Tampa Bay (Vol. 30, November 5, 2010, No. 46, pp. 1)*
Pub: Tampa Bay Business Journal
Ed: Margie Manning. **Description:** Jabil Circuit Inc. has reported an increase in revenues from its smart phones and medical devices. The company has been focusing on its core services such as making smart phone parts and medical devices.

23028 ■ *"Growing Subscriber Base Fuels Roger's Rosy Outlook for 2007" in Globe & Mail (February 16, 2007, pp. B3)*
Pub: CTVglobemedia Publishing Inc.
Ed: Catherine McLean. **Description:** Canada-based Rogers Communications Inc. has projected increased profits for the 2007 fiscal year. The company has increased its market share by 14 percent with fourth quarter revenues of $176 million.

23029 ■ *Growing Your Business*
Pub: Routledge Inc.
Ed: Burke. **Released:** December 2006. **Price:** $150. 00. **Description:** Growth strategies for small businesses are presented.

23030 ■ *"Growing Your Business Through BPI Certification" in Indoor Comfort Marketing (Vol. 70, May 2011, No. 5, pp. 12)*
Pub: Industry Publications Inc.
Ed: Scott Vadino. **Description:** Profile of the Building Performance Institute and the ways BPI certification will help grow a heating, ventilation, cooling firm.

23031 ■ *"Growth Back on CIBC's Agenda" in Globe & Mail (March 3, 2006, pp. B1)*
Pub: CTVglobemedia Publishing Inc.
Ed: Sinclair Stewart. **Description:** The details on business growth of Canadian Imperial Bank of Commerce, which posted $547 million profit for first quarter 2006, are presented.

23032 ■ *Guerrilla Marketing, 4th Edition: Easy and Inexpensive Strategies for Making Big Profits from Your Small Business*
Pub: Houghton Mifflin Company
Ed: Jay Conrad Levinson. **Released:** May 2007. **Price:** $19.95. **Description:** Marketing strategies for small businesses is designed to revolutionize, expand and grow businesses. .

23033 ■ *"Habitat, Home Depot Expand Building Programs" in Contractor (Vol. 56, September 2009, No. 9, pp. 16)*
Pub: Penton Media, Inc.
Description: Habitat for Humanity International and The Home Depot Foundation are planning to expand their Partners in Sustainable Building program. The program will provide funds to help Habitat affiliates build 5,000 homes. Comments from executives are also included.

23034 ■ *"Halls Give Hospital Drive $11 Million Infusion" in The Business Journal-Serving Metropolitan Kansas City (Vol. 26, July 18, 2008)*
Pub: American City Business Journals, Inc.
Ed: Rob Roberts. **Description:** Don Hall, chairman of Hallmark Cards Inc., and eight family members have announced that they will give $11 million to Children's Mercy Hospitals and Clinics for its $800 million expansion plan. Hall Family Foundation president Bill Hall that contributions such as that for Children's Mercy reflect the charitable interests of the foundation's board and founders. The possible impacts of the Hall's donation are analyzed.

23035 ■ *The Handbook of Financing Growth: Strategies and Capital Structure*
Pub: John Wiley & Sons, Incorporated
Ed: Kenneth H. Marks, John P. Funkhouser, Larry E. Robbins. **Released:** March 2005. **Price:** $85.00 (US), $123.95 (Canadian). **Description:** Using empirical data and actual case studies, strategies are presented to illustrate capital structures and fund raising techniques for emerging growth and middle-market companies.

23036 ■ *"Happy Trails: RV Franchiser Gives Road Traveling Enthusiasts a Lift" in Black Enterprise (Vol. 38, July 2008, No. 12, pp. 47)*
Pub: Earl G. Graves Publishing Co. Inc.
Ed: Tamara E. Holmes. **Description:** Overview of Bates International Motor Home Rental Systems Inc., a growing franchise that gives RV owners the chance to rent out their big-ticket purchases to others when they are not using them; Sandra Williams Bate launched the company as a franchise in July 1997 and now has a fleet of 30 franchises across the country. She expects the company to reach 2.2 million for 2008 due to a marketing initiative that will expand the company's presence.

23037 ■ *"Harleysville Eyes Growth After Nationwide Deal" in Philadelphia Business Journal (Vol. 30, October 7, 2011, No. 34, pp. 1)*
Pub: American City Business Journals Inc.
Ed: Jeff Blumenthal. **Description:** Harleysville Group announced growth plans after the company was sold to Columbus, Ohio-based Nationwide Mutual Insurance Company for about $1.63 billion. Nationwide gained an independent agency platform in 32 states with the Harleysville deal.

23038 ■ *"Harnessing the Wisdom of Crowds" in Entrepreneur (Vol. 37, September 2009, No. 9, pp. 74)*
Pub: Entrepreneur Media, Inc.
Ed: Mark Henricks. **Description:** Online customer service business Get Satisfaction has registered growth. The business enables customers to search

for answers to common product questions. Customers use the service to post questions, complaints, and even product ideas.

23039 ■ *"Haute Flyers" in Canadian Business (Vol. 80, November 19, 2007, No. 23, pp. 68)*
Pub: Rogers Media

Ed: Rachel Pulfer. **Description:** Duckie Brown has been nominated by the Council of Fashion Designers of America as best menswear designer in the U.S. for 2007, along with leaders Calvin Klein and Ralph Lauren. The New York-based company was formed the day after September 11, 2001, but the timing did not hamper its growth. The works and plans of owners Steven Cox and Daniel Silver are described.

23040 ■ *"Have I Got a Deal For You" in Canadian Business (Vol. 83, October 12, 2010, No. 17, pp. 65)*
Pub: Rogers Media Ltd.

Ed: Bryan Borzykowski. **Description:** U.S. automobile market currently has more than three players, providing investors with a number of investment options. The sector is still mired in uncertainty, but people believe that these companies can only grow from this point forward. However, investors should use due diligence before jumping into the market.

23041 ■ *"Hawaii Business 2008 SB Success Awards" in Hawaii Business (Vol. 53, February 2008, No. 8, pp. 43)*
Pub: Hawaii Business Publishing

Description: Winners in the Hawaii Business 2008 SB Success Awards are presented; the awards give recognition for Hawaii small businesses with less than 100 employees and are based on four criteria, namely: unique service or product; rapid expansion or sales growth; longevity; and competency in overcoming challenges.

23042 ■ *"Hayes Lemmerz Reports Some Good News Despite Losses" in Crain's Detroit Business (Vol. 24, April 14, 2008, No. 15, pp. 4)*
Pub: Crain Communications Inc.

Ed: Nancy Kaffer. **Description:** Hayes Lemmerz International Inc., a wheel manufacturer from Northville that has reported a positive free cash flow for the first time in years, a narrowed net loss in the fourth quarter and significant restructuring of the company's debt.

23043 ■ *"Head of Horse Farmers and Owners Jockey for Saratoga Pastures, Breeder Awards" in Business Review, Albany New York (Nov. 23, 2007)*
Pub: American City Business Journals, Inc.

Ed: Robin K. Cooper. **Description:** Trends in Saratoga County's equine industry are discussed. More than fifty horse farms and 11,000 horses are in Saratoga, which is more than any other county in New York. Joe McMahon, a horse breeder and also the vice president of New York Breeders Sales Company, plans to expand his business by tapping into a new market. He plans to build his stable of top registered New York stallions.

23044 ■ *Heads in Beds*
Pub: Prentice Hall PTR

Ed: Ivo Raza. **Released:** May 28, 2004. **Description:** Advice is given to help build brands, generate sales and grow profits through marketing for any hospitality or tourism business.

23045 ■ *"Health Care Leads Sectors Attracting Capital" in Hispanic Business (Vol. 30, March 2008, No. 3, pp. 14)*
Pub: Hispanic Business

Ed: Scott Williams. **Description:** Discusses the capital gains of Hispanic-owned companies and other Hispanic leaders in the investment and retail fields in the year 2007. Sectors like health care, media, food and technology saw a healthy flow of capital due to successful mergers, acquisitions and increased private equity investments.

23046 ■ *"Health Centers Plan Expansion" in Crain's Detroit Business (Vol. 25, June 15,*

2009, No. 24, pp. 3)
Pub: Crain Communications Inc. - Detroit

Ed: Jay Greene. **Description:** Detroit has five federally qualified health centers that plan to receive over $3 million in federal stimulus money that will be used to expand projects that will care for uninsured patients.

23047 ■ *"Healthy Dose of Vitality" in Business Courier (Vol. 24, February 29, 2008, No. 47, pp. 1)*
Pub: American City Business Journals, Inc.

Ed: Dan Monk. **Description:** Healthy Advice plans to become a leading consumer brand and expand to pharmacies and hospitals. The growth opportunities for healthy Advice are discussed.

23048 ■ *"Helping Customers Fight Pet Waste" in Pet Product News (Vol. 64, November 2010, No. 11, pp. 52)*
Pub: BowTie Inc.

Ed: Sandy Robins. **Description:** Pet cleaning products manufacturers have been enjoying high sales figures by paying attention to changing pet ownership trends and environmental awareness. Meanwhile, the inclusion of user-friendly features in these products has also been boosted by the social role of pets and the media attention to pet waste. How manufacturers have been responding to this demand is explored.

23049 ■ *"Helping Women Grow Their Businesses One Entrepreneur at a Time" in Hispanic Business (July-August 2007, pp. 56-57)*
Pub: Hispanic Business

Ed: Hildy Medina. **Description:** American Express OPEN is a program focusing on women business owners whose companies report revenues of $200,000 or more. The program offers the chance to win a free year of mentoring, marketing and technology assistance along with a $50,000 line of credit.

23050 ■ *"High Energy: Gaurdie Banister Joins Aera As President and CEO" in Black Enterprise (Vol. 38, July 2008, No. 12, pp. 30)*
Pub: Earl G. Graves Publishing Co. Inc.

Ed: Brenda Porter. **Description:** Gaurdie Banister Jr. has been appointed president and CEO of Aera Energy L.L.C., becoming one of the first African Americans in the nation to run a major energy corporation. His plans for the firm include utilizing new, sophisticated technologies in order to unlock the 3-1/2 billion barrels of resources the company has on their books in a safe and environmentally friendly way. He also hopes to increase production and maintain cost leadership.

23051 ■ *"High Hopes: Ralph Mitchell's Picks Have Growth Potential" in Black Enterprise (Vol. 37, February 2007, No. 7, pp. 42)*
Pub: Earl G. Graves Publishing Co. Inc.

Ed: Carolyn M. Brown. **Description:** Ralph Mitchell, president and senior financial advisor of Braintree-Carthage Financial Group, offers three recommendations: Toll Brothers, Home Depot, and Lowe's.

23052 ■ *"The High-Intensity Entrepreneur" in Harvard Business Review (Vol. 88, September 2010, No. 9, pp. 74)*
Pub: Harvard Business School Publishing

Ed: Anne S. Habiby, Deirdre M. Coyle Jr. **Description:** Examination of the role of small companies in promoting global economic growth is presented. Discussion includes identifying entrepreneurial capability.

23053 ■ *"High Marks: Parker Hannifin's Stock Lauded by Wall Street Journal" in Crain's Cleveland Business (Vol. 28, November 5, 2007, No. 44)*
Pub: Crain Communications, Inc.

Description: According to The Wall Street Journal, Parker Hannifin Corp., a manufacturer of motion and control equipment, is one of eight stocks that are attractively priced and continuously showing growth.

23054 ■ *"His Place in the Sun" in Canadian Business (Vol. 79, October 23, 2006, No. 21, pp. 77)*
Pub: Rogers Media

Ed: Zena Olijnyk. **Description:** The business interests of Canadian real estate developer Derek Elliott in the Dominican Republic, is discussed.

23055 ■ *"Hispanic Business 100 Fastest-Growing Companies" in Hispanic Business (July-August 2007, pp. 28, 30, 32, 36)*
Pub: Hispanic Business

Description: Top 100 Hispanic businesses are ranked by sales growth 2002-2006, gross sales, profit ranges, number of employees, and year the firm was founded.

23056 ■ *"Hispanic Business 100 Fastest-Growing Companies" in Hispanic Business (July-August 2009, pp. 16-18)*
Pub: Hispanic Business

Ed: Joshua Molina. **Description:** Despite the recession, the 100 fastest growing companies profiled are able to maintain their competitive edge; federal contracts are key to their success. Service companies are at the top of the list and Texas and Florida are the states in which the top are located.

23057 ■ *"Hispanic Business 100 Fastest-Growing Companies" in Hispanic Business (July-August 2009, pp. 24-26, 28)*
Pub: Hispanic Business

Description: Comprehensive list of the top 100 Hispanic businesses for 2009; data includes company location and description, sales growth, revenues, profits and number of employees from 2004-2208.

23058 ■ *"Hispanic Executives Continue Their Rise to Prominence Amid a Shaky Economy" in Hispanic Business (January-February 2009, pp. 12-14)*
Pub: Hispanic Business

Ed: Michael Bowker. **Description:** Hispanic Business's 2009 Corporate Elite winners defied expectations and a tough economy and rose to the top of their industries; innovation being cited as key to growth of Hispanic-owned companies.

23059 ■ *"Hispantelligence Report" in Hispanic Business (January-February 2008, pp. 8)*
Pub: Hispanic Business

Description: Presentation of the Hispanic Business Stock Index shows the current value of fifteen Hispanic companies through December 2007. Forecasts showing increased growth for Hispanic-owned companies are also included.

23060 ■ *History of Canadian Business 1867-1914*
Pub: University of Toronto Press

Ed: R.T. Naylor. **Released:** 1975. **Description:** Covers the growth of business in Canada.

23061 ■ *"Hola and Aloha" in Hawaii Business (Vol. 53, December 2007, No. 6, pp. 131)*
Pub: Hawaii Business Publishing

Ed: Jason Ubay. **Description:** Juan Carlos Bianchetti is the trilingual owner of Ole Tours Hawaii, a travel wholesaler that targets Portuguese and Spanish-speaking visitors. The competition for American and Japanese tourists is already tight, which is why Bianchetti opted to target a different segment of the Hawaii tourism market. Plans for the company's expansion in Kauai, Brazil, and Argentina, are mentioned.

23062 ■ *"Hollander 95 Project Getting Bigger" in Boston Business Journal (Vol. 29, September 23, 2011, No. 20, pp. 1)*
Pub: American City Business Journals Inc.

Ed: Gary Haber. **Description:** Hollander 95 Business Park is in for a huge change as its new owners plan a $50 million expansion which calls for building as many as eight more buildings or a total of more than 500,000 square feed. FRP Development bought the site for $4.35 million at a foreclosure sale in July 2010 and is now seeking city approval for an Industrial Planned Unit Development designation.

23063 ■ *"Home Depot Eyes Wholesale Spinoff" in Globe & Mail (February 13, 2007, pp. B13)*
Pub: CTVglobemedia Publishing Inc.
Description: Home Depot Inc. is planning to sell or spinoff its professional supply business to focus on retail stores. The weakening sales and profits are the main driving force behind the company's decision.

23064 ■ *"A Home of Her Own" in Hawaii Business (Vol. 53, October 2007, No. 4, pp. 51)*
Pub: Hawaii Business Publishing
Ed: Maria Torres-Kitamura. **Description:** It was observed that the number of single women in Hawaii purchasing their own home has increased, as that in the whole United States where the percentage has increased from 14 percent in 1995 to 22 percent in 2006. However, First Hawaiian Bank's Wendy Lum thinks that the trend will not continue in Hawaii due to lending restrictions. The factors that women consider in buying a home of their own are presented.

23065 ■ *"Homelessness, Hair Care and 12,000 Bottles of Tequila" in Entrepreneur (Vol. 37, July 2009, No. 7, pp. 5)*
Pub: Entrepreneur Media, Inc.
Ed: Dennis Romero. **Description:** John Paul DeJoria believes that the biggest hurdle he has faced in business is rejection, and that the successful people will do whatever is required in order to succeed. DeJoria is the man behind Paul Mitchell Systems and Patron Tequila. He was recently included in Forbes magazine's list of global billionaires.

23066 ■ *"Hospital Errors Made Public" in Sacramento Business Journal (Vol. 25, August 8, 2008, No. 23, pp. 1)*
Pub: American City Business Journals, Inc.
Ed: Kathy Robertson. **Description:** California hospitals reported 1,224 serious and preventable errors for the fiscal year ended June 30, 2008. Consumer groups have expressed concerns at the number and level of violations. Views and information on the errors, as well as a table detailing the number of hospital errors classified by error type, are presented.

23067 ■ *"Hospital Revenue Healthier in 2009" in Orlando Business Journal (Vol. 26, February 5, 2010, No. 36, pp. 1)*
Pub: American City Business Journals
Ed: Melanie Stawicki Azam. **Description:** Orlando Health, Health Central and Adventist Health System are Florida-based hospital systems that generated the most profits in 2009. Orlando Health had the highest profit in 2009 at $73.3 million, contrary to about $31 million in losses in 2008. The increased profits are attributed to stock market recovery, cost-cutting initiatives, and rising patient volumes.

23068 ■ *"Hospitals See Major Shift To Outpatient Care" in The Business Journal-Milwaukee (Vol. 25, September 12, 2008, No. 51, pp. A1)*
Pub: American City Business Journals, Inc.
Ed: Corrinne Hess. **Description:** Statistics show that the revenue of Wisconsin hospitals from outpatient medical care is about to surpass revenue from hospital patients who stay overnight. This revenue increase is attributed to new technology and less-invasive surgery. Trends show that the shift toward outpatient care actually started in the late 1980s and early 1990s.

23069 ■ *"Hotels Seeking Room Downtown" in Crain's New York Business (Vol. 24, January 14, 2008, No. 2, pp. 32)*
Pub: Crain Communications, Inc.
Ed: Laura Koss-Feder. **Description:** In a rush to expand capacity in New York City, particularly lower Manhattan, the hotel industry plans to more than double the existing rooms in the area.

23070 ■ *"How Exports Could Save America" in Barron's (Vol. 89, July 20, 2009, No. 29, pp. 15)*
Pub: Dow Jones & Co., Inc.
Ed: Jonathan R. Laing. **Description:** Increase in US exports should help drive up the nation's economic growth, according to Wells Capital Management strategist Jim Paulsen. He believes US gross domestic product could grow by 3-3.5 percent annually starting in 2010 due to a more favorable trade balance.

23071 ■ *"How Hard Could It Be? The Four Pillars of Organic Growth" in Inc. (January 2008, pp. 69-70)*
Pub: Gruner & Jahr USA Publishing
Ed: Joel Spolsky. **Description:** Revenue, head count, public relations, and quality are the four most important aspects of any growing business.

23072 ■ *"How High Can Soybeans Fly?" in Barron's (Vol. 88, March 10, 2008, No. 10, pp. M14)*
Pub: Dow Jones & Company, Inc.
Ed: Kenneth Rapoza. **Description:** Prices of soybeans have risen to $14.0875 a bushel, up 8.3 percent for the week. Increased demand, such as in China and in other developing economies, and the investment-driven commodities boom are boosting prices.

23073 ■ *How to Make Big Money in Your Own Small Business: Unexpected Rules Every Small Business Owner Needs to Know*
Pub: Hyperion Press
Ed: Jeffrey J. Fox. **Released:** May 2004. **Price:** $16.95. **Description:** Former sales and marketing pro offers advice on growing a small business.

23074 ■ *How to Make Money with Social Media: Using New and Emerging Media to Grow Your Business*
Pub: FT Press
Ed: Jamie Turner, Reshma Shah. **Released:** October 1, 2010. **Price:** $24.99. **Description:** Marketers, executives, entrepreneurs are shown more effective ways to utilize Internet social media to make money. This guide brings together both practical strategies and proven execution techniques for driving maximum value from social media marketing.

23075 ■ *How to Open and Operate a Financially Successful Construction Company*
Pub: Atlantic Publishing Group, Inc.
Ed: Tanya R. Davis. **Released:** April 2008. **Price:** $39.95 paperback. **Description:** Construction businesses are predicted to be one of the fastest growing industries in the U.S. economy, according to the U.S. Bureau of Labor Statistics. A comprehensive guide is offered detailing the practical side of starting and growing a construction firm. The step-by-step guide provides sample business forms, leases, contracts, worksheets and checklists for planning and running the day-to-day operations.

23076 ■ *How to Open and Operate a Financially Successful Private Investigation Business: With Companion CD-ROM*
Pub: Atlantic Publishing Company
Released: December 1, 2010. **Price:** $39.95. **Description:** With a massive upside and potential for growth the private investigation sector is growing. The book will teach everything needed to know about working in the private investigation field, starting with the basics of what you can expect and what preconceptions that may just be Hollywood. Information is given to help choose a niche of investigation and hot to start thinking in the abstract, questioning everything but recognizing facts for what they are, as well as the differences between a private investigator and a police officer.

23077 ■ *"How to Secure U.S. Jobs" in Gallup Management Journal (October 27, 2011)*
Pub: Gallup
Ed: Jim Clifton. **Description:** If America doubled its number of engaged customers globally, it could triple exports, which would create more good jobs and put the US economy back on track.

23078 ■ *"How To Live To Be 100; John E. Green Co. Grows Through Diversification" in Crain's Detroit Business (February 18, 2008)*
Pub: Crain Communications Inc. - Detroit
Ed: Chad Halcom. **Description:** Continuity, name recognition, and inventiveness are keys to continuing growth for Highland Park, Michigan's John E. Green Company, designer of pipe systems and mechanical contractor.

23079 ■ *"How Two Flourishing Exporters Did It" in Hispanic Business (Vol. 30, July-August 2008, No. 7-8, pp. 46)*
Pub: Hispanic Business, Inc.
Ed: Richard Kaplan. **Description:** Vigorous growth in export revenues posted by two Hispanic-owned export companies Compasa LLC and Ametza LLC is discussed; both firms have benefited from their closer locations to major Mexican markets, superior quality of their products, market knowledge and the relationships of trust developed with key business partners.

23080 ■ *"HP Eats Into Rival Dell Sales as Profits Soar" in Globe & Mail (February 21, 2007, pp. B15)*
Pub: CTVglobemedia Publishing Inc.
Ed: Connie Guglielmo. **Description:** The world's largest personal computer maker Hewlett Packard Co. has reported increased profits by 26 percent to $1.55 billion during the first quarter. The company has outpaced its competitor Dell Inc. by offering low priced personal computers during this period.

23081 ■ *"HSBC Canada Posts 8.8 Percent Profit Gain in 2006" in Globe & Mail (February 20, 2007, pp. B14)*
Pub: CTVglobemedia Publishing Inc.
Ed: Andrew Willis. **Description:** HSBC Bank Canada reported profits of $497 million in 2006. The financial results of the company for 2006 are presented.

23082 ■ *"Huntington's Future At a Crossroads" in Crain's Cleveland Business (Vol. 30, June 22, 2009, No. 24, pp. 1)*
Pub: Crain Communications, Inc.
Ed: Arielle Kass. **Description:** Despite Huntington Bancshares plans to expand in the Cleveland, Ohio area, experts wonder if the bank will be able to take advantage of the area's growth in the long run. Statistical data included.

23083 ■ *"Husky Proceeds on Heavy-Oil Expansion" in Globe & Mail (March 21, 2006, pp. B1)*
Pub: CTVglobemedia Publishing Inc.
Ed: Patrick Brethour. **Description:** Canadian energy giant Husky Energy Inc. has started its $90 million engineering effort to determine the cost of the $2.3 billion heavy-oil up gradation expansion plan. Details of the project are elaborated upon.

23084 ■ *"Hyde Park Hungry for Expansion at Cap" in Business First-Columbus (October 12, 2007, pp. A1)*
Pub: American City Business Journals, Inc.
Ed: Dan Eaton. **Description:** The Cap, an area developed for the retail and restaurant industry, is experiencing major changes such as Hyde Park Restaurant System's planned expansion, and the expected departure of other tenants. The expansion of Hyde Park will lead to the relocation of Schakolad Chocolate Factory.

23085 ■ *"Hyundai's Hitting Its Stride" in Barron's (Vol. 89, July 20, 2009, No. 29, pp. M7)*
Pub: Dow Jones & Co., Inc.
Ed: Assif Shameen. **Description:** Hyundai Motors has kept growing by producing better products, enabling it to increase its sales and market share despite the weaker automotive market. The shares of Hyundai and Kia are poised to rise due to their improved finances.

23086 ■ *"IBM's Best-Kept Secret" in Canadian Business (Vol. 79, September 25, 2006, No. 19, pp. 19)*
Pub: Rogers Media
Ed: Andrew Wahl. **Description:** The contribution of IBM vice-president Steve Mills in company's development is discussed.

23087 ■ *"An Ice Boost in Revenue; Wings Score With Expanded Corporate Sales" in Crain's Detroit Business (Vol. 25, June 1, 2009, No. 22)*
Pub: Crain Communications Inc. - Detroit
Ed: Bill Shea. **Description:** Stanley Cup finals always boost business for the Detroit area, even during a recession. The Red Wings corporate office reported corporate sponsorship revenue luxury suite rentals, Legends Club seats and advertising were up 40 percent this year over 2008.

23088 ■ *"Ideas at Work: The Reality of Costs" in Business Strategy Review (Vol. 21, Summer 2010, No. 2, pp. 40)*
Pub: Wiley-Blackwell
Ed: Jules Goddard. **Description:** If you think that cost cutting is the surest way to business success, the author wants to challenge every assumption you hold. Costs are an outcome of sound strategy, never the goal of strategy. He offers a new perspective on what counts when it comes to costs.

23089 ■ *"Identify and Conquer" in Black Enterprise (Vol. 38, December 2007, No. 5, pp. 76)*
Pub: Earl G. Graves Publishing Co. Inc.
Ed: Tennille M. Robinson. **Description:** Twenty-two-year-old entrepreneur wants to expand her wholesale body oil and skincare products business.

23090 ■ *"Illinois Bets On Recycling Program" in Chicago Tribune (November 29, 2008)*
Pub: McClatchy-Tribune Information Services
Ed: Joel Hood. **Description:** Traditionally the holiday gift-giving season is one of the most wasteful times of year and the state of Illinois is granting $760,000 to small businesses and cities in an attempt to expand curbside recycling programs and hire additional workers to address electronic waste.

23091 ■ *"Illinois Farmland Tops $11,000 Per Acre" in Farm Industry News (June 27, 2011)*
Pub: Penton Business Media Inc.
Ed: Karen McMahon. **Description:** Farmland property in Illinois continues to grow in value, selling for $11,000 per acre. Statistical data included.

23092 ■ *"Imax Becomes Toast of Movie Industry" in Globe & Mail (January 10, 2006, pp. B2)*
Pub: CTVglobemedia Publishing Inc.
Ed: Grant Robertson. **Description:** The United States-based mainstream theatres company Imax Corp., has reported a 35 percent rise in its ticket sales, showing the growing interest of the American audience in the Imax formatted films. A complete focus on this trend is presented.

23093 ■ *Import/Export for Dummies*
Pub: John Wiley and Sons, Inc.
Ed: John J. Capela. **Released:** June 2008. **Price:** $19.99. **Description:** Provides entrepreneurs and small- to medium-size businesses with information required to start exporting products globally and importing goods to the U.S. Topics covered include the ins and outs of developing or expanding operations to gain market share, with details on the top ten countries in which America trades, from Canada to Germany to China.

23094 ■ *"Impressive Numbers: Companies Experience Substantial Increases in Dollars, Employment" in Hispanic Business (July-August 2007)*
Pub: Hispanic Business
Ed: Derek Reveron. **Description:** Profiles of five fastest growing Hispanic companies reporting increases in revenue and employment include Brightstar, distributor of wireless products; Greenway Ford Inc., a car dealership; Fred Loya Insurance, auto insurance carrier; and Group O, packaging company; and Diverse Staffing, Inc., an employment and staffing firm.

23095 ■ *"IMRA's Ultrafast Lasers Bring Precision, profits; Ann Arbor Company Eyes Expansion" in Crain's Detroit Business (March 10, 2008)*
Pub: Crain Communications, Inc.
Ed: Tom Henderson. **Description:** IMRA America Inc. plans to expand its headquarters and has applied for permits to build a fourth building that will house research and development facilities and allow the company more room for manufacturing; the company plans to add about 20 more employees that would include research scientists, manufacturing and assembly workers, engineers and salespeople. The growth is due mainly to a new technology of ultrafast fiber lasers that reduce side effects for those getting eye surgeries and help manufacturers of computer chips to reduce their size and cost.

23096 ■ *"In Addition, Pinkberry Reports It Is Opening a New Shop in Sunnyvale, CA" in Ice Cream Reporter (Vol. 23, October 20, 2010)*
Pub: Ice Cream Reporter
Description: Pinkberry opened a new shop in Sunnyvale, California, its fourth opening in the South Bay and its 101st location worldwide.

23097 ■ *"Inc. 500: the Class of 2011" in Inc. (Vol. 33, September 2011, No. 7, pp. 71)*
Pub: Inc. Magazine
Description: A listing of the Inc. 500 businesses that are rebuilding the economy and changing the world is presented.

23098 ■ *"Incubator Cooking Up Expansion Plans" in Business First Columbus (Vol. 25, December 5, 2008, No. 15, pp.)*
Pub: American City Business Journals
Ed: Kevin Kemper. **Description:** United States-based Science and Technology Campus Corporation is planning to build additional office space in Columbus, Ohio. The site is designed to accommodate three large tenants. Comment from company executives are presented.

23099 ■ *"Indian Buyer Gives Life to Algoma Expansion" in Globe & Mail (April 17, 2007, pp. B1)*
Pub: CTVglobemedia Publishing Inc.
Ed: Greg Keenan. **Description:** The proposed capacity expansion of Algoma Steel Inc. after its acquisition by Essar Global Ltd. is discussed.

23100 ■ *"Industrial Evolution" in Entrepreneur (Vol. 35, November 2007, No. 11, pp. 142)*
Pub: Entrepreneur Press
Contact: Perlman Neil, President
Ed: Nichole L. Torres. **Description:** Businesses often target specific customer bases, but it is possible that your business does not fit a particular industry as your services may also be needed in other fields. Details with regard to expanding businesses into other industries are discussed.

23101 ■ *"Industrial RE Market Shows Signs of Health" in Business Courier (Vol. 27, August 20, 2010, No. 16, pp. 1)*
Pub: Business Courier
Ed: Jon Newberry. **Description:** Cincinnati, Ohio's industrial real estate sector has experienced growth during the first half of 2010. The industry has seen a large net loss of occupied space in 2009.

23102 ■ *"Inn at Saratoga Owners Buy Caribbean Hotel" in Business Review, Albany New York (Vol. 34, November 2, 2007, No. 31, pp. 3)*
Pub: American City Business Journals, Inc.
Ed: Robin K. Cooper. **Description:** Bob Israel, owner of the Inn at Saratoga in Saratoga Springs, New York, made a $3 million to $4 million acquisition of the 22-room Mafolie Hotel and Restaurant in the Island of St. Thomas in the Caribbean. This is Israel's first real estate venture out of Saratoga Springs.

23103 ■ *"Innovating Globally" in Business Strategy Review (Vol. 21, Spring 2010, No. 1, pp. 24)*
Pub: Wiley-Blackwell
Ed: Costas Markides, Stuart Crainer. **Description:** Costas Markides has spent over two decades studying business strategy and innovation. Recently, he has been focusing on the bigger picture of how people can address major social problems. Can the techniques used by managers to create innovation inside organizations work with global change?.

23104 ■ *Innovative Approaches to Global Sustainability*
Pub: Palgrave Macmillan
Ed: Charles Wankel, James A.F. Stoner. **Released:** April 13, 2010. **Price:** $30.00. **Description:** Examples are given to help businesses become sustainable as we move towards a sustainable world.

23105 ■ *"Innovative Growth" in Small Business Opportunities (March 2008)*
Pub: Harris Publications Inc.
Ed: Peter Erickson. **Description:** Nine tips are outlined to help small companies and entrepreneurs to partner with larger companies.

23106 ■ *"Insider" in Canadian Business (Vol. 81, March 31, 2008, No. 5, pp. 76)*
Pub: Rogers Media
Ed: John Gray. **Description:** Discusses a comparison of an average Canadian family's finances in 1990 with the data from 2007. The average family in 2007 has over $80,000 in debt compared to just under $52,000 in 1990. However, Canadians have also been accumulating solid assets such as homes and stocks. This means that Canadian debt load has fallen from 22 percent in 1990 to 20 percent in 2007 when taken as a percentage of total net worth.

23107 ■ *Instant Cashflow: Hundreds of Proven Strategies to Win Customers, Boost Margins and Take More Money Home*
Pub: McGraw-Hill Companies Inc.
Contact: Deven Sharma, President
Ed: Bradley J. Sugars. **Released:** December 2005. **Price:** $17.95 (US), $22.95 (Canadian). **Description:** Nearly 300 proven marketing and sales strategies are shared by the author, a self-made millionaire. Advice on creating the proper mindset, generating new leads, boosting the conversion rate of leads to sales, maximizing the value of the average sale, and measuring results is included.

23108 ■ *Instant Profit: Successful Strategies to Boost Your Margin and Increase the Profitability of Your Business*
Pub: McGraw-Hill Companies Inc.
Contact: Deven Sharma, President
Ed: Bradley J. Sugars. **Released:** December 2005. **Price:** $16.95 (US), $22.95 (Canadian). **Description:** Advice on management, money, marketing, and merchandising a successful small business is offered.

23109 ■ *"Insuraprise Growing Fast" in Austin Business Journal (Vol. 31, April 22, 2011, No. 7, pp. 3)*
Pub: American City Business Journals Inc.
Ed: Sandra Zaragoza. **Description:** Austin, Texas-based Insuraprise Inc. is finalizing the purchase of a 24,000-square-foot office at 12116 Jekel Circle. The firm, with 23 salespeople and sales that are growing nearly 300 percent over the past 18 months, will now have room to grow. Insuraprise plans to hire 35 new salespersons for its call center.

23110 ■ *"Insurers No Longer Paying Premium for Advertising" in Brandweek (Vol. 49, April 21, 2008, No. 16, pp. SR3)*
Pub: VNU Business Media, Inc.
Ed: Eric Newman. **Description:** Insurance companies are cutting their advertising budgets after years of accelerated double-digit growth in spending due to the economic downturn, five years of record-breaking ad spend and a need to cut expenditures as claims costs rise and a competitive market keeps premiums in place. Statistical data included.

23111 ■ *"Intangible Assets" in Canadian Business (Vol. 79, July 17, 2006, No. 14-15, pp. 17)*
Pub: Rogers Media
Ed: Al Rosen. **Description:** Need for investors to check the actual worth of a company and not to get carried away by the inflated claims made by the company is emphasized.

23112 ■ *"International Dairy Queen" in Ice Cream Reporter (Vol. 23, October 20, 2010, No. 11, pp. 7)*
Pub: Ice Cream Reporter
Description: International Dairy Queen will open more than 100 new outlets in China in 2011, adding to the current level of more than 300 outlets in that country.

23113 ■ *International Entrepreneurship in Small and Medium Size Enterprises: Orientation, Environment and Strategy*
Pub: Edward Elgar Publishing, Incorporated
Ed: Hamid Etemad. **Released:** October 2004. **Price:** $130.00. **Description:** Issues involved in internationalizing small and medium sized (SME) businesses. Topics include an investigation into the emerging patterns of SME growth and international expansion in response to the changing competitive environment, dynamics of competitive behavior, entrepreneurial processes and a formulation of strategy.

23114 ■ *International Growth of Small and Medium Enterprises*
Pub: Routledge
Ed: Nina Nummela. **Released:** February 10, 2010. **Price:** $110.00. **Description:** This volume focuses on how companies expand their operations across borders through opportunity exploration and exploitation, and identification and development of innovations.

23115 ■ *"Internationalization of Australian Family Businesses" in Family Business Review (Vol. 19, September 2006)*
Pub: Family Firm Institute
Contact: Judy L. Green, President
Ed: Chris Graves, Jill Thomas. **Description:** Concept that managerial capabilities of family firms lag behind those of non-family counterparts as they expand is discussed.

23116 ■ *"Invacare Plans '08 Release for Portable Oxygen Product" in Crain's Cleveland Business (Vol. 28, October 22, 2007, No. 42, pp. 5)*
Pub: Crain Communications, Inc.
Ed: Chuck Soder. **Description:** Invacare Corp., an Elyria-based maker of home health care equipment, plans the release of a new 'extremely portable' oxygen concentration machine in 2008. The XP02 is expected to increase sales due to the popularity of portable oxygen concentrators.

23117 ■ *"Investors Finding Bay Area Deals" in Tampa Bay Business Journal (Vol. 29, November 6, 2009, No. 46, pp. 1)*
Pub: American City Business Journals
Ed: Margie Manning. **Description:** Private equity investors have found dozens of privately held companies in Tampa Bay area in Florida in which to invest $84 million fresh equity. Revenue generation, growth, solid management teams are some of the factors found by the investors on these companies which span a range of sizes and industries.

23118 ■ *"An Investor's Guide to This Year's Inc. 500" in Inc. (October 2007, pp. 34)*
Pub: Gruner & Jahr USA Publishing
Description: Three investment firms specializing in growth companies provide insight into today's market.

23119 ■ *"IPhone 3G" in Advertising Age (Vol. 79, November 17, 2008, No. 43, pp. 15)*
Pub: Crain Communications, Inc.
Ed: Beth Snyder Bulik. **Description:** Review of Apple's new iPhone 3G which includes the addition of smart-phone applications as well as a price drop; the new functionalities as well as the lower price seems to be paying off for Apple who reported sales of 6.9 million iPhones in its most recent quarter, in which the 3G hit store shelves.

23120 ■ *"Is 'Tsunami' of Freight in our Future?" in Business Courier (Vol. 26, November 27, 2009, No. 31, pp. 1)*
Pub: American City Business Journals, Inc.
Ed: Dan Monk. **Description:** Freight companies are planning for cargo-container shipping facilities on the riverfront of Cincinnati in light of the completion of the

$5 billion Panama Canal expansion in 2015. The city's capability to utilize the growth in freight has been under investigation by authorities.

23121 ■ *"Is Your Company Ready to Succeed?" in Business Strategy Review (Vol. 21, Spring 2010, No. 1, pp. 68)*
Pub: Wiley-Blackwell
Ed: Srikumar Rao. **Description:** The author asked thousands of students about the ideal company of the future, the kind of place where they would want to spend their lives.

23122 ■ *Island of Profit in a Sea of Red Ink Why 40 Percent of Your Business Is Unprofitable and How to Fix It*
Pub: Portfolio
Ed: Jonathan L.S. Byrnes. **Released:** October 14, 2010. **Price:** $27.95. **Description:** Top companies from around the world turn to Jonathan Byrnes to figure out where to find profit for their companies. He shows which parts of a business are worth expanding, and which are just a drain on resources. He has found that roughly 40 percent of any new client's business is unprofitable, and that profit increases of thirty percent or more are within reach.

23123 ■ *"It's In the Bag" in Entrepreneur (Vol. 36, April 2008, No. 4, pp. 122)*
Pub: Entrepreneur Media, Inc.
Ed: Celeste Hoang. **Description:** Sandy Stein launched Alexx Inc in 2004, which markets keychains, called Finders Key Purse, with unique designs to help find keys easier inside the purse. Some of the key ring designs are hearts, sandals, and crowns. The company has approximately $6 million worth of sales in 2007.

23124 ■ *"It's Not Perfect; But Illinois a Good Home for Business" in Crain's Chicago Business (Vol. 34, October 24, 2011, No. 42, pp. 18)*
Pub: Crain Communications Inc.
Description: Focusing on all factors that encompass Illinois' business environment, findings show that Illinois is a good place to start and grow a business. The study focused on corporate income tax rates and the fact that talent, access to capital and customers along with transportation connections are among the important factors the state has for small businesses.

23125 ■ *It's Not Who You Know - It's Who Knows You!: The Small Business Guide to Raising Your Profits by Raising Your Profile*
Pub: John Wiley & Sons, Inc.
Ed: David Avrin. **Released:** November 9, 2010. **Price:** $24.95. **Description:** When it comes to promoting a small business or a brand, it is essential to know how valuable high-profile attention can be. But for most small companies, the cost of hiring an outside firm to increase attention can be too expensive.

23126 ■ *"It's What You Know. It's Who You Know. It's China" in Inc. (Vol. 33, October 2011, No. 8, pp. 80)*
Pub: Inc. Magazine
Ed: David H. Freedman. **Description:** Michael Lee will be the first American entrepreneur to build big in China. The company is piloting two large commercial real estate developments, one in New York City the other in Nanjing, China.

23127 ■ *"ITT Places Its Bet With Defense Buy; Selling Equipment to Army Pays Off" in Crain's New York Business (Vol. 24, January 7, 2008)*
Pub: Crain Communications, Inc.
Description: ITT Corp.'s revenue has jumped by 20 percent in each of the past three years due to demand for the company's radio sets and night-vision goggles. The firm has acquired EDO Corp., which specializes in battlefield communications systems, in an attempt to expand its defense-industry division.

23128 ■ *"Ivorydale Looks to Clean Up" in Business Courier (Vol. 26, January 15, 2010,*

No. 39, pp. 1)
Pub: American City Business Journals, Inc.
Ed: Jon Newberry. **Description:** Cincinnati-based St. Bernard Soap Company plans to focus on new services such as product development and logistics and to continue growth and put excess capacity to work. The unit of Ontario, Canada-based Trillium Health Care Products Inc. is the largest contract manufacturer of bar soap in North America.

23129 ■ *"Jacksonville-based Interline Expanding in Janitorial-Sanitation Market" in Florida Times-Union (May 10, 2011)*
Pub: Florida Times-Union
Ed: Mark Basch. **Description:** Interline Brands Inc., located in Jacksonville, Florida, aims to grow its business with two recent acquisitions of firms that distribute janitorial and sanitation products. Interline markets and distributes maintenance, repair and operations products.

23130 ■ *Jan and Jeannie Levinson's Startup Guide to Guerilla Marketing: A Simple Battle Plan for Boosting Profits*
Pub: Entrepreneur Press
Ed: Jay Conrad Levinson; Jeannie Levinson. **Released:** January 2008. **Price:** $21.95. **Description:** Primer for marketing a new or existing business.

23131 ■ *"J&J Snack Rakes in Sales" in Philadelphia Business Journal (Vol. 28, September 25, 2009, No. 32, pp. 1)*
Pub: American City Business Journals
Ed: Peter van Allen. **Description:** Analysts expect J&J Snack Foods Corporation to boost earnings by 48 percent for fiscal year ending September 2009. Stable commodity prices have benefited the company.

23132 ■ *"Janitorial Equipment and Supplies US Market" in PR Newswire (October 24, 2011)*
Pub: PR Newswire
Description: United States demand for janitorial equipment and supplies (excluding chemical products) is predicted to rise 2.4 percent per year to $7.6 billion in 2013. New product development will lead to increased sales of higher-value goods in the industry.

23133 ■ *"J.C. Watts First Black John Deere Dealer" in Black Enterprise (Vol. 37, November 2006, No. 4, pp. 36)*
Pub: Earl G. Graves Publishing Co. Inc.
Ed: Kiara Ashanti. **Description:** Profile of former Congressman J.C. Watts Jr., a man who grew up in rural America and is the first African American to own a John Deere Dealership.

23134 ■ *"Jean Coutu Resuscitates Bottom Line" in Globe & Mail (January 11, 2006, pp. B5)*
Pub: CTVglobemedia Publishing Inc.
Ed: Bertrand Marotte. **Description:** The details on Jean Coutu Group (PJC) Inc., which posted $30.8 million profits for second quarter 2005, are presented.

23135 ■ *"Jet Sales Put Bombardier Back in Black" in Globe & Mail (March 30, 2006, pp. B1)*
Pub: CTVglobemedia Publishing Inc.
Ed: Bertrand Marotte. **Description:** The details on Bombardier Inc., which posted 20 percent rise in shares following $86 million profit for fourth quarter 2005, are presented.

23136 ■ *"Jobs Data Show A Slow Leak" in Barron's (Vol. 88, July 7, 2008, No. 27, pp. 34)*
Pub: Dow Jones & Co., Inc.
Ed: Gene Epstein. **Description:** In June 2008, the United States manufacturing sector showed an expansion, with the purchasing managers' index rising to 50.2 from 49.6; the unemployment rate in the US, which stayed steady at 5.5 percent in June 2008 is also discussed. Statistical data included.

23137 ■ *"Johnson Publishing Expands: Moving Into Television and Internet To Extend Brand" in Black Enterprise (October 2007)*
Pub: Earl G. Graves Publishing Co. Inc.
Ed: Tamara E. Holmes. **Description:** Johnson Publishing Company has followed the lives of black families in both Ebony and Jet magazines. The media

firm has expanded its coverage by developing entertainment content for television, the Internet and other digital arenas.

23138 ■ *Jump Start Your Business Brain*
Pub: Brain Brew Books

Ed: Doug Hall, Tom Peters. **Released:** 2005. **Price:** $16.99 paperback. **Description:** Author focuses on helping small business owners to become more successful using simple tools that help them discover, develop, and identify great ideas.

23139 ■ *Jump Start Your Business Brain: Ideas, Advice and Insights for Immediate Marketing and Innovation Success*
Pub: Emmis Books

Contact: Richard Hunt, President

E-mail: rhunt@emmis.com

Ed: Doug Hall. **Released:** April 2005. **Price:** $23.99. **Description:** Strategies to improve sales, marketing, and business development.

23140 ■ *"JumpTV to Hold Conference Call to Discuss Q1 Results and Annual General Meeting" in Canadian Corporate News (May 16, 2007)*
Pub: Comtex News Network Inc.

Description: Profile of JumpTv the world's leading broadcaster of ethnic television over the Internet, and the results of a conference that discussed their first quarter 2007 financial report as well as the company's business goals. Statistical data included.

23141 ■ *"KC Presents Healthy Market for Medical REIT" in Business Journal-Serving Metropolitan Kansas City (Vol. 26, November 30, 2007)*
Pub: American City Business Journals, Inc.

Ed: Rob Roberts. **Description:** Medical Properties Trust, the only real estate investment trust that specializes in buying hospitals, is planning to invest in Kansas City due to its fast growing hospital market. The company owns 29 properties nationwide and is still planning to increase its portfolio.

23142 ■ *"Keep On Truckin" in Boston Business Journal (Vol. 31, August 5, 2011, No. 28, pp. 3)*
Pub: Boston Business Journal

Ed: Lisa van der Pool. **Description:** Food truck business is booming in Boston with more than 25 trucks dotting the area including 15 new truck locations approved by the city in July 2011. The business is rather costly to start because it requires more than $100,000 capital and the food truck can run between $50,000 to $100,000.

23143 ■ *"Keeping Tabs" in Entrepreneur (Vol. 36, February 2008, No. 2, pp. 38)*
Pub: Entrepreneur Media Inc.

Ed: Robert Kiyosaki. **Description:** Measuring and reporting the number of customers being served by a business can help in the company's growth. Details on this idea are discussed.

23144 ■ *"Kid Rock" in Canadian Business (Vol. 81, Summer 2008, No. 9, pp. 54)*
Pub: Rogers Media Ltd.

Ed: John Gray. **Description:** Damien Reynolds is the founder, chairman and chief executive officer of Vancouver-based Longview Capital Partners. The investment bank, founded in 2005, is one of the fastest-growing companies in British Columbia. The recent economic downturn has battered the stocks of the company and its portfolio of junior miners.

23145 ■ *"Kinetico Exec Going Global to Increase Growth Flow" in Crain's Cleveland Business (Vol. 28, October 1, 2007, No. 39, pp. 5)*
Pub: Crain Communications, Inc.

Ed: David Bennett. **Description:** Shamus Hurley, the new CEO and president of Kinetico Inc., a manufacturer of water filtering and softening equipment for residential, commercial and municipal use, plans to expand the company to target markets overseas.

23146 ■ *"King of the Crib: How Good Samaritan Became Ohio's Baby HQ" in Business Courier (Vol. 27, June 18, 2010, No. 7, pp. 1)*
Pub: Business Courier

Ed: James Ritchie. **Description:** Cincinnati's Good Samaritan hospital had 6,875 live births in 2009, which is more than any other hospital in Ohio. They specialize in the highest-risk pregnancies and deliveries and other hospitals are trying to grab Good Samaritan's share in this niche.

23147 ■ *"Knowing Is Growing: Five Strategies To Develop You and Your Business" in Black Enterprise (Vol. 38, November 2007, No. 4, pp. 106)*
Pub: Earl G. Graves Publishing Co. Inc.

Ed: Erinn R. Johnson. **Description:** Five strategies for growing a small business are listed by Andrew Morrison, founder of the Small Business Camp. The camp provides training, coaching, and marketing services to entrepreneurs.

23148 ■ *"Kodiak Bucks Bear Market" in Austin Business JournalInc. (Vol. 29, December 18, 2009, No. 41, pp. 1)*
Pub: American City Business Journals

Ed: Kate Harrington. **Description:** Austin, Texas-based Kodiak Assembly Solutions LLC, a company that installs components into printed circuit boards for product or evaluation tool kit prototyping purposes, will expand despite the recession. It will relocate from a 28,000 square foot space to a 42,000 square foot space in North Austin. The firm will also increase its workforce by 20 employees.

23149 ■ *"Labor of Love" in Green Industry Pro (Vol. 23, March 2011, No. 3, pp. 14)*
Pub: Cygnus Business Media

Ed: Gregg Wartgow. **Description:** Profile of CLS Landscape Management in Chino, California and its owner who started the company when he was 21 years old. Kevin Davis built his landscape firm into a $20 million a year business without using any dedicated salesperson.

23150 ■ *"LaSalle Street Firms Cherry-Pick Talent As Wall Street Tanks" in Crain's Chicago Business (Vol. 31, November 17, 2008, No. 46)*
Pub: Crain Communications, Inc.

Ed: H. Lee Murphy. **Description:** Many local businesses are taking advantage of the lay offs that many major Wall Street firms are undergoing in their workforces; these companies see the opportunity to woo talent and expand their staff with quality executives.

23151 ■ *"Last Founder Standing" in Conde Nast Portfolio (Vol. 2, June 2008, No. 6, pp. 124)*
Pub: Conde Nast Publications

Contact: David Carey, President

Ed: Kevin Maney. **Description:** Interview with Amazon CEO Jeff Bezos in which he discusses the economy, the company's new distribution center and the hiring of employees for it, e-books, and the overall vision for the future of the firm.

23152 ■ *"Lathrop Finds Partner In LA" in The Business Journal-Serving Metropolitan Kansas City (Vol. 27, November 21, 2008, No. 11, pp. 1)*
Pub: American City Business Journals, Inc.

Ed: Steve Vockrodt. **Description:** Kansas, Missouri-based Lathrop and Gage LLP is planning to merge with Spillane Shaeffer Aronoff Bandlow LLP. The merging of the business law firms will add entertainment clients to Lathrop's fold. Comments from executives are also presented.

23153 ■ *"Lavante, Inc. Joins Intersynthesis, Holistic Internet Marketing Company" in Internet Wire (November 5, 2009)*
Pub: Comtex News Network, Inc.

Description: Lavante, Inc., the leading provider of on-demand vendor information and profit recovery audit solutions for Fortune 1000 companies has chosen Intersynthesis, a new holistic Internet marketing firm, as a provider of pay for performance

services. Lavante believes that Intersynthesis' expertise and knowledge combined with their ability to develop integrated strategies, will help them fuel more growth.

23154 ■ *"Law Firms Troll for Complaints Among Disgruntled Workers" in The Business Journal-Serving Greater Tampa Bay (Vol. 28, July 11, 2008)*
Pub: American City Business Journals, Inc.

Ed: Jane Meinhardt. **Description:** Economic slowdown has affected businesses as they downsize, seeing an increase in wage and hour complaints using loopholes in the Fair Labor Standards Act, from which several law firms are recently generating revenue. Federal judges notice the increase in lawsuits and ordered that law firms show cause for non-compliance.

23155 ■ *Law for the Small and Growing Business*
Pub: Jordans Publishing Limited

Ed: P. Bohm. **Released:** February 2007. **Price:** $59.98. **Description:** Legal and regulatory issues facing small businesses, including employment law, health and safety, commercial property, company law and finance are covered.

23156 ■ *"Leading Ohio Internet Marketing Firm Announces Growth in September" in Marketing Weekly News (September 26, 2009, pp. 24)*
Pub: Investment Weekly News

Description: Despite a poor economy, Webbed Marketing, a leading social media marketing and search engine optimization firm in the Midwest, has added five additional professionals to its fast-growing team. The company continues to win new business, provide more services and hire talented employees.

23157 ■ *Leap! 101 Ways to Grow Your Business*
Pub: Career Press, Inc.

Ed: Stephanie Chandler. **Released:** August 8, 2010. **Price:** $15.99. **Description:** Business growth requires more than a business plan and a dream. Tools and techniques to take a small company to the next level are outlined.

23158 ■ *"Leaps and Bounds: Liberty Power, Force 3 Ride Rapid Expansion to the Top" in Hispanic Business (July-August 2007, pp. 20-22, 24)*
Pub: Hispanic Business

Ed: Derek Reveron. **Description:** Profiles of Liberty Power Corporation, a Florida supplier of retail electricity and Force 3 Inc. of Maryland, network infrastructure developer are two of the 100 fastest growing Hispanic businesses recognized in 2007.

23159 ■ *"Lenders" in The Business Journal - Serving Phoenix and the Valley of the Sun (Vol. 28, July 25, 2008, No. 47, pp. 1)*
Pub: American City Business Journals, Inc.

Ed: Jan Buchholz. **Description:** Private equity lender Investor Mortgage Holdings Inc. has continued growing despite the crisis surrounding the real estate and financial industries and has accumulated a $700 million loan portfolio. Private lending has become increasingly important in financing real estate deals as commercial credit has dried up.

23160 ■ *Let's Buy a Company: How to Accelerate Growth Through Acquisitions*
Pub: Career Press, Incorporated

Ed: H. Lee Rust. **Released:** January 2006. **Price:** $18.99 (US), $25.95 (Canadian). **Description:** Advice for negotiating terms and pricing as well as other aspects of mergers and acquisitions in small companies.

23161 ■ *"Life Sciences Become State's Growth Powerhouse" in Crain's Detroit Business (Vol. 25, June 1, 2009, No. 22, pp. M008)*
Pub: Crain Communications Inc. - Detroit

Ed: Amy Lane. **Description:** According to a study conducted by Anderson Economic Group, Michigan's University Research Corridor has helped grow the life sciences industry. Statistical details included.

23162 ■ *"A Life of Spice" in Entrepreneur (Vol. 37, September 2009, No. 9, pp. 46)*
Pub: Entrepreneur Media, Inc.
Ed: Jason Daley. **Description:** Matt and Bryan Walls have successfully grown their Atlanta, Georgia-based Snorg Tees T-shirt company. The company has expanded its product offering and redesigned its Website to be more user-friendly. The company has registered between $5 and 10 million in 2008.

23163 ■ *"Life's Work: Ben Bradlee" in Harvard Business Review (Vol. 88, September 2010, No. 9, pp. 128)*
Pub: Harvard Business School Publishing
Ed: Alison Beard. **Description:** Newspaper publisher Ben Bradlee discusses factors that lead to success, including visible supervisors, enthusiasm, appropriate expansion, and the importance in truth in reporting.

23164 ■ *"Li'l Guy Rolls Up Into Bigger Company" in The Business Journal-Serving Metropolitan Kansas City (Vol. 26, September 12, 2008)*
Pub: American City Business Journals, Inc.
Ed: Suzanna Stagemeyer. **Description:** Li'l Guy Foods, a Mexican food company in Kansas City, Missouri, has merged with Tortilla King Inc. Li'l Guy's revenue in 2007 was $3.3 million, while a newspaper report said that Tortilla King's revenue in 2001 was $7.5 million. Growth opportunities for the combined companies and Li'l Guy's testing of the Wichita market are discussed.

23165 ■ *"Liquor Stores Sips on Growth Cocktail" in Globe & Mail (February 6, 2006, pp. B5)*
Pub: CTVglobemedia Publishing Inc.
Ed: Omar El Akkad. **Description:** The business growth plans of Liquor Stores Income Fund are presented.

23166 ■ *"The Little Biotech that Could" in Barron's (Vol. 89, July 27, 2009, No. 30, pp. 19)*
Pub: Dow Jones & Co., Inc.
Ed: Christopher C. Williams. **Description:** OSI Pharmaceuticals' shares is a compelling investment bet among small biotech firms due to its Tarceva anticancer drug which has a 23 percent market share as well as their strong balance sheet. OSI is planning to expand the use of Tarceva which could re-ignite sales and one analyst expects the shares to trade in the 40s one year from July 2009.

23167 ■ *"Live and Learn: Lionel Hurtubise" in Canadian Business (Vol. 80, January 29, 2007, No. 3, pp. 64)*
Pub: Rogers Media
Ed: Andy Holloway. **Description:** The views of Lionel Hurtubise, the chairman of SR Telecom, PolarSat, and STP, on his life and the growth of the Canadian telecommunications industry are presented.

23168 ■ *"Local Auto Suppliers Upbeat as Detroit 3's Prospects Trend Up" in Crain's Cleveland Business (Vol. 30, June 8, 2009, No. 22, pp. 1)*
Pub: Crain Communications, Inc.
Ed: Dan Shingler. **Description:** According to the Center for Automotive Research located in Ann Arbor, Michigan, if Detroit automakers can hold their market share, they will end up producing more vehicles as the market recovers.

23169 ■ *Local Enterprises in the Global Economy: Issues of Governance and Upgrading*
Pub: Edward Elgar Publishing, Incorporated
Ed: Hubert Schmitz. **Released:** November 2004. **Price:** $35.00 (soft cover), $110.00 (hard bound). **Description:** Examination of the relationships between globalization, corporate governance, and the economic performance of small businesses and local enterprises.

23170 ■ *"Local Outlook: Stronger Growth Ahead" in Montana Business Quarterly (Vol. 49, Spring 2011, No. 1, pp. 10)*
Pub: Bureau of Business & Economic Research
Ed: Paul E. Polzin. **Description:** Local economic growth is broken down into three areas: fastest growing in Richland, Gallatin and Flathead Counties; the second growth group consists of Yellowstone, Silver Bow, and Lewis and Clark Counties, which all grew at rates higher than the statewide average; slowest growth was seen in Missoula, Ravalli, Cascade, and Custer Counties. Statistical data included.

23171 ■ *"Locally Based Stocks Escape Worst of Market's Turmoil" in Crain's Detroit Business (Vol. 24, September 22, 2008, No. 38, pp. 4)*
Pub: Crain Communications Inc.
Ed: Daniel Duggan. **Description:** Locally-based companies did not take as big a hit as might be expected with the shock to the financial markets last week; this is due mainly to the fact that the region does not have heavy exposure to energy or capital markets.

23172 ■ *"Lombard Leaves Starbucks" in Black Enterprise (Vol. 38, July 2008, No. 12, pp. 28)*
Pub: Earl G. Graves Publishing Co. Inc.
Ed: Tamara E. Holmes. **Description:** Ken Lombard stepped down from his position as head of Starbuck's entertainment division; the company is restructuring its entertainment unit in an attempt to revitalize sales and reduce costs.

23173 ■ *"Long - And Leery" in Barron's (Vol. 88, March 31, 2008, No. 13, pp. 47)*
Pub: Dow Jones & Company, Inc.
Ed: Jack Willoughby. **Description:** Tom Claugus' Bay Resource Partners hedge fund has returned 20 percent annually since it started in 1993. Claugus says that he is as aggressively long as he has ever been despite the dangers of the U.S. market. Claugus' stock picks include Canadian Natural Resources, NII Holdings, and Discover Financial.

23174 ■ *"Looking For Financing?" in Hispanic Business (Vol. 30, July-August 2008, No. 7-8, pp. 16)*
Pub: Hispanic Business, Inc.
Ed: Frank Nelson. **Description:** Investment firms want to know about businesses that need funding for either expansion or acquisition; companies fitting this profile are interviewed and their perceptions are discussed. Investment firms need businesses to be realistic in their expectations and business plans which show spending of funds and expected benefits, long term goals, track record and strong management teams.

23175 ■ *"Loop Hotel Plan Locks Up Funding" in Crain's Chicago Business (Vol. 31, March 24, 2008, No. 12, pp. 2)*
Pub: Crain Communications, Inc.
Ed: Eddie Baeb. **Description:** Signaling further expansion in the downtown hotel market, the secured $395 million in financing will fund a 610-room luxury hotel operated by J.W. Marriott, a more upscale brand in the Marriott line.

23176 ■ *"Lots More Mr. Nice Guy" in Canadian Business (Vol. 80, October 22, 2007, No. 21, pp. 58)*
Pub: Rogers Media
Ed: Zena Olijnyk. **Description:** Galen Weston Jr., executive chairman of Loblaw and heir to the Weston family business, has his hands full running the company. Details of his turnaround strategies and ambitious plans to increase profitability of the business are discussed.

23177 ■ *Low Risk, High Reward*
Pub: R & R Publishing
Ed: Bob Reiss with Jeffrey L. Cruikshank. **Released:** 2000. **Price:** $19.95. **Description:** Successful entrepreneur teaches others about creating, growing and maintaining a successful business venture. The book offers a step-by-step approach to helping entrepreneurs minimize the risk involved in a new business while examining the skills and resources needed to succeed.

23178 ■ *"Loyalty Cards Score Points" in Crain's Cleveland Business (Vol. 30, June 8, 2009, No. 22, pp. 1)*
Pub: Crain Communications, Inc.
Ed: Chuck Soder. **Description:** Northeast Ohio retailers are promoting loyalty and rewards programs in order to attract and maintain loyal customers.

23179 ■ *"Lumber Rebounds" in Business Journal Portland (Vol. 26, December 11, 2009, No. 40, pp. 1)*
Pub: American City Business Journals Inc.
Ed: Erik Siemers. **Description:** Oregon's lumber industry could be boosted as wood consumption across the country is expected to increase by 11 percent or 34.5 billion board feet in 2010.

23180 ■ *"The Macomb Group: Bigger Can Be Better" in Crain's Detroit Business (Vol. 24, September 29, 2008, No. 39, pp. 34)*
Pub: Crain Communications Inc.
Ed: Chad Halcom. **Description:** Overview of the plan of The Macomb Group includes a strategy of growing from a small supplier to a medium-sized regional distributor of valves, pipes and fittings.

23181 ■ *Macrowikinomics: Rebooting Business and the World*
Pub: Portfolio Hardcover
Ed: Don Tapscott, Anthony D. Williams. **Released:** September 28, 2010. **Price:** $27.95. **Description:** Wikinomics Don Tapscott and Anthony Williams showed how mass collaboration was changing the way businesses communicate, create value,, and compete in the new global marketplace in 2007. Now, in the wake of the global financial crisis, the principles of wikinomics have become more powerful than ever.

23182 ■ *"Made In Canada" in Canadian Business (Vol. 80, March 12, 2007, No. 6, pp. 11)*
Pub: Rogers Media
Ed: Ian Harvey. **Description:** The devision of Christie Digital Systems Canada Inc. to increase production of its DLP projectors, in view of high demand from the United States, is discussed.

23183 ■ *"Magna Nears Top of Auto Parts Heap" in Globe & Mail (May 1, 2007, pp. B4)*
Pub: CTVglobemedia Publishing Inc.
Ed: Greg Keenan. **Description:** Magna International Inc. is poised to become the largest automobile parts supplier in North America. The state of the automobile parts industry in Canada is also discussed.

23184 ■ *"The Main Event" in Canadian Business (Vol. 80, November 19, 2007, No. 23, pp. 28)*
Pub: Rogers Media
Ed: Zena Olijnyk. **Description:** U.S.-based Lowe's Companies, Inc. will be opening three stores in Canada in December 2007 and another three in 2008. The housing market crisis in the U.S. is the reason behind the home improvement store's Canadian expansion. The impacts of the expansion on Canadian home care stores and on the market competition are evaluated.

23185 ■ *Make Your Business Survive and Thrive! 100+ Proven Marketing Methods to Help You Beat the Odds*
Pub: John Wiley & Sons, Incorporated
Ed: Priscilla Y. Huff. **Released:** December 2006. **Price:** $19.95. **Description:** Small business and entrepreneurial expert gives information to help small and home-based businesses grow.

23186 ■ *"Making the Cut; Osprey Takes Undervalued Courses to the Leader Board" in Crain's Detroit Business (Vol. 24, April 7, 2008, No. 14)*
Pub: Crain Communications, Inc.
Ed: Jason Deegan. **Description:** Profile of Osprey Management Co., a diverse real estate company that continues to expand its golf portfolio through the company's recreation division; although many developers are getting out of the field due to Michigan's sluggish golf industry, Osprey has found success by purchasing properties in turmoil for more affordable prices.

23187 ■ *"The Man Behind Brascan" in Canadian Business (Vol. 79, Winter 2006, No. 24, pp. 64)*
Pub: Rogers Media
Ed: Andy Holloway. **Description:** The role of Jack Cockwell in the growth of Brookfield Asset Management Inc., is described.

23188 ■ *"Management Matters with Mike Myatt: Are You Creating Growth in a Down Economy?' in Commercial Property News (March 17, 2008)*
Pub: Nielsen Company

Ed: Mike Myatt. **Description:** Senior executives are expected to create growth for their company regardless of recession, economic slowdown, inflation, or tight credit and capital markets.

23189 ■ *Managing Business Growth: Get a Grip on the Numbers That Count*
Pub: Self-Counsel Press, Incorporated

Ed: Angie Mohr. **Released:** October 2004. **Price:** $14.95. **Description:** Fourth book in the Numbers 101 for Small Business Series, teaches how small company owners can expand their businesses using sound financial planning.

23190 ■ *Managing Economies, Trade and International Business*
Pub: Palgrave Macmillan

Ed: Aidan O'Connor. **Released:** January 19, 2010. **Price:** $90.00. **Description:** An in-depth look at the areas that affect and influence international business, exploring specific issues businesses face in terms of economic development, trade law, and international marketing and management.

23191 ■ *Managing for Results*
Pub: HarperCollins Publishers, Inc.

Ed: Peter F. Drucker. **Released:** October 2006. **Price:** $16.95. **Description:** Entrepreneurs running successful small companies focus on opportunity rather than problems.

23192 ■ *"M&T On the March?' in Baltimore Business Journal (Vol. 28, November 12, 2010, No. 27, pp. 1)*
Pub: Baltimore Business Journal

Ed: Gary Haber. **Description:** Information on the growth of M&T Bank, as well as its expansion plans are presented. M&T recently acquired Wilmington Trust and took over $500 million in deposits from the failed K Bank. Analysts believe that M&T would continue its expansion through Washington DC and Richmond, Virginia, especially after a bank executive acknowledged that the markets in those areas are attractive.

23193 ■ *"A Manufacturing Revival' in Boston Business Journal (Vol. 31, May 27, 2011, No. 18, pp. 1)*
Pub: Boston Business Journal

Ed: Kyle Alspach. **Description:** Massachusetts' manufacturing sector has grown despite the high cost of labor, real estate and electricity. Manufacturing jobs in the state have increased to 2,800 in April 2011.

23194 ■ *"Manulife Posts Billion-Dollar Profit' in Globe & Mail (February 14, 2007, pp. B7)*
Pub: CTVglobemedia Publishing Inc.

Ed: Andrew Willis. **Description:** Manulife Financial Corp., Canada's largest insurer, reported $1.1 billion profit in the fourth quarter of 2006. The financial results of Manulife reflected a 39 percent rise in quarterly profit at the nation's wealth management division.

23195 ■ *"Marathon Money' in Hawaii Business (Vol. 53, December 2007, No. 6, pp. 127)*
Pub: Hawaii Business Publishing

Ed: Jolyn Okimoto Rosa. **Description:** Discusses the effects of the Honolulu Marathon on small businesses' sales. The Running Room, for instance, experience growth in sales starting from the training season up to the end of the race, as a surge of Hawaiian residents and tourists come into the store for items such as running shoes and blister kits. The marathon's impact on Hawaii's tourism is examined as well.

23196 ■ *"Marine Act Amendments Gain Parliamentary Approval' in Canadian Sailings*

(July 7, 2008)
Pub: UBM Global Trade
Contact: Leonard J. Corallo, President

Ed: Alex Binkley. **Description:** Changes to the Canada Marine Act provides better borrowing deals as well as an ability to tap into federal infrastructure funding for environmental protection measures, security improvements and other site enhancements.

23197 ■ *"Marketer Bets Big on U.S.'s Growing Canine Obsession" in Advertising Age (Vol. 79, April 14, 2008, No. 15, pp. 14)*
Pub: Crain Communications, Inc.

Ed: Emily Bryson York. **Description:** Overview of FreshPet, a New Jersey company that began marketing two brands of refrigerated dog food-Deli Fresh and FreshPet Select-which are made from fresh ingredients such as beef, rice and carrots. The company projects continued success due to the amount of money consumers spend on their pets as well as fears derived from the 2007 recalls that inspired consumers to look for smaller, independent manufacturers that are less likely to source ingredients from China.

23198 ■ *"The Market's (Very) Tender Spring Shoots" in Barron's (Vol. 88, March 31, 2008, No. 13, pp. M3)*
Pub: Dow Jones & Company, Inc.

Ed: Kopin Tan. **Description:** Expansion in price-earnings multiples and a lower credit-default risk index has encouraged fans of the spring-awakening theory. Shares of industrial truckers have gone up 32 percent in 2008 and some shares are pushing five-year highs brought on by higher efficiency and earnings from more load carried. The prospects of the shares of Foot Locker are also discussed.

23199 ■ *"Martin Marietta Expands Rock Solid Port Manatee Presence" in Tampa Bay Business Journal (Vol. 30, January 8, 2010, No. 3, pp. 1)*
Pub: American City Business Journals

Ed: Jane Meinhardt. **Description:** Raleigh, North Carolina-based Martin Marietta Materials Inc. has been granted by Florida's Manatee County Port Authority with a 30-year, $42 million contract. Through the contract, an aggregate terminal will be built by Martin Marietta at the port. Construction work is anticipated to start in earl 2010 with terminal operations commencing by late summer 2010.

23200 ■ *Mastering Business Growth and Change Made Easy*
Pub: Entrepreneur Press

Ed: Jeffrey A. Hansen. **Released:** October 2005. **Price:** $19.95 (US), $26.95 (Canadian). **Description:** Tips for growing a small business, regardless of state or environment.

23201 ■ *"Mattel's Got a Monster Holiday Hit, But Will Franchise Have Staying Power?' in Advertising Age (Vol. 81, December 6, 2010, No. 43)*
Pub: Crain Communications, Inc.

Ed: Beth Snyder Bulik. **Description:** Monster High transmedia play expands beyond dolls to merchandise, apparel and entertainment.

23202 ■ *"A Matter of Interest' in Canadian Business (Vol. 79, July 17, 2006, No. 14-15, pp. 21)*
Pub: Rogers Media

Ed: Jeff Sanford. **Description:** With the steady decrease in savings, the need for growth in Canada's payloan industry is discussed. Also emphasized are the challenges faced by payloan operators.

23203 ■ *"Maximizing the Success of New Products" in Black Enterprise (Vol. 38, October 2007, No. 3, pp. 70)*
Pub: Earl G. Graves Publishing Co. Inc.

Description: New product development drives business growth and profitability. University of Chicago offers a weeklong New Product Development in Innovation class for executive training.

23204 ■ *Maximum Marketing, Minimum Dollars: The Top 50 Ways to Grow Your Small Business*
Pub: Kaplan Books

Ed: Kim Gordon. **Released:** April 2006. **Price:** $24.00. **Description:** Marketing tips to increase sales are presented. Small business owners will learn to maximize marketing with 50 innovative and affordable methods, including online marketing.

23205 ■ *"MBA Project Turns on Tastebuds" in The Business Journal - Serving Phoenix and the Valley of the Sun (Vol. 28, August 15, 2008, No. 50)*
Pub: American City Business Journals, Inc.

Ed: Angela Gonzales. **Description:** Amol Khade, Venkat Nallapati and Govind Arora, master of businesss administration graduates from Thunderbird School of Global Management, have opened an Indian restaurant, called The Daba, in Tempe, Arizona. The Indian name of the restaurant means 'a place for travelers to stop for rest and food'. Franchise plans for the restaurant are discussed.

23206 ■ *"MBAs Plus Designers Equals New Life for Business" in Globe & Mail (April 24, 2007, pp. B1)*
Pub: CTVglobemedia Publishing Inc.

Ed: Gordon Pitts. **Description:** The need for Canadian companies to combine the skills of management graduates and designers to achieve corporate growth is discussed.

23207 ■ *"Meadowbrook CEO Sees 20 Percent Growth With New Acquisition" in Crain's Detroit Business (Vol. 24, March 10, 2008, No. 10, pp. 4)*
Pub: Crain Communications, Inc.

Ed: Jay Greene. **Description:** Discusses the major turnaround of Meadowbrook Insurance Group after Robert Cubbin became CEO and implemented a new business strategy.

23208 ■ *"Meadowbrook To Acquire ProCentury in $272.6 Million Deal" in Crain's Detroit Business (Vol. 24, February 25, 2008, No. 8, pp. 4)*
Pub: Crain Communications Inc. - Detroit

Description: Meadowbrook Insurance Group, based in Southfield, Michigan reports its proposed acquisition of ProCentury Corporation based in Columbus, Ohio. Meadowbrook provides risk-management to agencies, professional and trade associations and small-to-midsize businesses.

23209 ■ *"Medicaid Insurers See Growth in Small Business Market" in Boston Business Journal (Vol. 31, July 15, 2011, No. 25, pp. 1)*
Pub: Boston Business Journal

Ed: Julie M. Donnelly. **Description:** BMC HealthNet Plan announced plans to launch small business products to serve small businesses that are priced out of rising premium rates at large Massachusetts insurers. BMC joined competitors CeltiCare Health Plan and Neighborhood Health Plan in augmenting its core business.

23210 ■ *"The Medium 150' in Canadian Business (Vol. 81, Summer 2008, No. 9, pp. 129)*
Pub: Rogers Media Ltd.

Description: Medium-sized companies are ranked based on market capitalization and stock performance. Timminco Ltd. topped the roster with 1,294.2 percent returns, while Petrominerales Ltd. ranked second with 325.4 percent. A table showing the 2008 rankings of the companies is presented.

23211 ■ *Medium Sized Firms and Economics Growth*
Pub: Nova Science Publishers, Incorporated

Ed: Janez Prasniker. **Released:** April 2005. **Price:** $130.00. **Description:** Medium sized companies should have a more definitive presence in modern microeconomic theory, the theory of entrepreneurship, and the theory of financial markets.

23212 ■ *"Meet Joe Fresh" in Canadian Business (Vol. 79, November 6, 2006, No. 22, pp. 49)*
Pub: Rogers Media
Ed: Calvin Leung. **Description:** The efforts of Joseph Mimran, a fashion designer, in improving the business of Joe Fresh style products are analyzed.

23213 ■ *"Members Make Sacrifices for a World-Class Course" in Crain's Detroit Business (Vol. 24, April 7, 2008, No. 14, pp. 21)*
Pub: Crain Communications, Inc.
Ed: Jason Deegan. **Description:** Rees Jones Inc. completed a $1.8 million redesign of the Oakland Hills Country Club golf course last year. By all indications, the redesign has been a success since it is among the handful of courses good enough to host future majors which is beneficial for the local economy.

23214 ■ *Memos to the Prime Minister: What Canada Could Be in the 21st Century*
Pub: John Wiley & Sons, Incorporated
Ed: Harvey Schacter. **Released:** April 11, 2003. **Price:** $16.95. **Description:** A look into the business future of Canada. Topics include business, healthcare, think tanks, policy groups, education, the arts, economy, and social issues.

23215 ■ *"Menchie's Tops Restaurant Business' Future 50 List" in Ice Cream Reporter (Vol. 23, August 20, 2010, No. 9, pp. 4)*
Pub: Ice Cream Reporter
Description: Menchie's, frozen yogurt shop, announced it placed first in the Restaurant Business Magazine's Future 50, ranking the franchise the fastest-growing in the food industry.

23216 ■ *"Mercy Parent Nets Almost $1B in 2011" in Sacramento Business Journal (Vol. 28, September 30, 2011, No. 31, pp. 1)*
Pub: Sacramento Business Journal
Ed: Kathy Robertson. **Description:** Catholic Healthcare West has reported almost $1 billion in profits for 2010. The company has reported a profit margin of 8.7 percent. It also absorbed more than $1 billion in costs from charity care and government programs.

23217 ■ *"Merger Mania: Regional Snaps Up HVS" in The Business Journal-Serving Greater Tampa Bay (Vol. 28, September 26, 2008, No. 40, pp. 1)*
Pub: American City Business Journals, Inc.
Ed: Alexis Muellner. **Description:** It was reported that Harper Van Scoik & Co. LLP has finalized a merger with Carr Riggs & Ingram LLC. The agreement, effective October 1, 2008, is a merger of HVS assets into CRI. Bill Carr, a managing partner, revealed that HVS' $5 million in revenue will take CRI from $78 million to $82 million in revenue.

23218 ■ *"Mexican Companies to Rent Space in TechTown, Chinese Negotiating" in Crain's Detroit Business (Vol. 24, September 29, 2008, No. 39)*
Pub: Crain Communications Inc.
Ed: Tom Henderson. **Description:** Wayne State University's TechTown, the business incubator and research park, has signed an agreement with the Mexican government that will provide temporary office space to 25 Mexican companies looking to find customers or establish partnerships in Michigan. TechTown's executive director is negotiating with economic development officials from China. To accommodate foreign visitors the incubator is equipping offices with additional equipment and resources.

23219 ■ *"Michigan Institute of Urology Grows in Expertise, Services" in Crain's Detroit Business (Vol. 24, April 7, 2008, No. 14, pp. 13)*
Pub: Crain Communications, Inc.
Ed: Jay Greene. **Description:** One of the nation's largest urology groups, the Michigan Institute of Urology, plans to continue its growth by adding doctors and offering new treatment options. The growth is financially beneficial to the group, but it also cuts down on health care costs since the group can perform procedures for a lesser rate than at a hospital.

23220 ■ *"Micro-Cap Companies" in Canadian Business (Vol. 81, Summer 2008, No. 9, pp. 157)*
Pub: Rogers Media Ltd.
Description: Micro-cap companies have lower than $221 million in terms of market capitalization. Burnaby, British Columbia-based Fancamp Exploration Ltd. topped the roster with 1,116.7 percent in return. A table showing the 2008 rankings of the companies is presented.

23221 ■ *"MicroTech: No. 1 Fastest-Growing Company" in Hispanic Business (July-August 2009, pp. 20, 22)*
Pub: Hispanic Business
Ed: Suzanne Heibel. **Description:** Profile of Tony Jimenez, former lieutenant colonel in the Army and CEO and founder of Virginia-based information technology firm, Micro Tech LLC. Jimenez was named Latinos in Information Science and Technology Association's CEO of the Year for 2008.

23222 ■ *"Millennials: The Great White Hope for Wine Industry" in Advertising Age (Vol. 81, December 6, 2010, No. 43, pp. 2)*
Pub: Crain Communications, Inc.
Ed: E.J. Shultz. **Description:** Generation offers category of most growth potential in 30 years and 7-Eleven and vintner are taking notice.

23223 ■ *"Million-Dollar Babies" in Black Enterprise (Vol. 38, January 2008, No. 6, pp. 64)*
Pub: Earl G. Graves Publishing Co. Inc.
Ed: Tennille M. Robinson. **Description:** Books and programs to help any small business grow to the $1 million mark are outlined.

23224 ■ *"Mimosa Systems Gains 150,000 New NearPoint Users" in Information Today (Vol. 26, February 2009, No. 2, pp. 31)*
Pub: Information Today, Inc.
Description: Mimosa System's NearPoint archive solution features email and file archiving, e-discovery, archive virtualization, and disaster recovery capabilities.

23225 ■ *"Minnesota Farms' Net Worth Grows 10 Percent Each Year for 15 Years" in Farm Industry News (August 22, 2011)*
Pub: Penton Business Media Inc.
Ed: Dale Nordquist. **Description:** The average value of farms in Minnesota is growing at a fast pace. Total assets per farm have increased by more than $1.1 million over the past 15 years. Statistical data included.

23226 ■ *"MIR Growing With Help From Former Pfizer Workers" in Crain's Detroit Business (Vol. 24, January 28, 2008, No. 4, pp. 33)*
Pub: Crain Communications Inc. - Detroit
Ed: Tom Henderson. **Description:** Molecular Imaging Research Inc. helps fund research at its parent firm, Molecular Therapeutics Inc. The company provides imaging services and other in vivo and in vitro services to help pharmaceutical companies test new compounds.

23227 ■ *The Mirror Test: How to Breathe New Life Into Your Business*
Pub: Grand Central Publishing
Ed: Jeffrey W. Hayzlett. **Released:** May 10, 2010. **Price:** $24.99. **Description:** Consultant and author, Jeffrey Hayzlett, explains why a business is not doing well and asks the questions that most business managers are afraid to ask.

23228 ■ *"Mission: Poach California" in Business Journal Portland (Vol. 26, December 11, 2009, No. 40, pp. 1)*
Pub: American City Business Journals Inc.
Ed: Andy Giegerich. **Description:** Leaders of Greenlight Greater Portland, a privately funded economic development organization, will visit California five times in 2010 in an attempt to lure California businesses to expand or relocate in Oregon.

23229 ■ *"A Mixed-Bag Quarter" in Barron's (Vol. 88, July 7, 2008, No. 27, pp. 19)*
Pub: Dow Jones & Co., Inc.
Ed: Shirley A. Lazo. **Description:** Seven component companies of the Dow Jones Industrial Average increased their dividend payouts in the second quarter of 2008 despite the weak performance of the index. Five companies in the Dow Jones Transportation index and three in the Dow Jones Utilities also increased their dividends.

23230 ■ *"Mobile: Juanes Fans Sing for Sprint" in Advertising Age (Vol. 79, November 3, 2008, No. 41, pp. 22)*
Pub: Crain Communications, Inc.
Ed: Laurel Wentz. **Description:** Marketers are appealing to the Hispanic market since they are more prone to use their cell phones to respond to contests, download videos, ringtones, or other data activity. Sprint recently sponsored a contest inviting people to sing like Colombian megastar Juanes; the participants filmed and sent their videos using their cell phones rather than laptops or camcorders illustrating the Hispanic overindex on mobile-phone technology. The contest generated hundreds of thousands of dollars in additional fee revenue, as monthly downloads increased 63 percent.

23231 ■ *"Mobile Marketing Grows With Size of Cell Phone Screens" in Crain's Detroit Business (Vol. 24, January 14, 2008, No. 2, pp. 13)*
Pub: Crain Communications Inc. - Detroit
Ed: Bill Shea. **Description:** Experts are predicting increased marketing for cell phones with the inception of larger screens and improved technology.

23232 ■ *"The Mobile Workforce Revolution" in Canadian Business (Vol. 81, March 31, 2008, No. 5, pp. 28)*
Pub: Rogers Media
Ed: Diane Horton. **Description:** Diane Horton explains how a mobile workforce helps companies cut costs, increase productivity, and boost employee motivation. Horton says that employees believe they usually become more productive by 15 to 30 percent after their companies go mobile.

23233 ■ *"The Molson Way" in Canadian Business (Vol. 80, April 9, 2007, No. 8, pp. 36)*
Pub: Rogers Media
Ed: Andy Holloway. **Description:** The success of the seventh generation of Molson family in running the Molson Coors Brewing Co. since it was established 221 years ago by John Molson is discussed.

23234 ■ *"Money and the Mayhem" in Canadian Business (Vol. 83, September 14, 2010, No. 15, pp. 52)*
Pub: Rogers Media Ltd.
Ed: Greg Hudson. **Description:** Ultimate Fighting Championship (UFC) has hired Tom Wright as director of operations for Canada, who finally managed to get mixed martial arts sanctioned in Ontario. Canada is UFC's largest market after the US and accounting for about 15-20 percent in annual revenue.

23235 ■ *"Montana Outlook: Stronger Growth Ahead" in Montana Business Quarterly (Vol. 49, Spring 2011, No. 1, pp. 7)*
Pub: Bureau of Business & Economic Research
Ed: Patrick M. Barkey. **Description:** A look at Montana's economy and future growth is given. Experts are predicting that the state will experience new growth in 2011, with 2012 showing its best growth since 2006. Statistical data included.

23236 ■ *"Montana's Manufacturing Industry" in Montana Business Quarterly (Vol. 49, Spring 2011, No. 1, pp. 29)*
Pub: Bureau of Business & Economic Research
Ed: Todd A. Morgan, Charles E. Keegan III, Colin B. Sorenson. **Description:** Manufacturing remains a vital part of Montana's economy despite the recession and decline in the production of wood products. Statistical data included.

23237 ■ *"MooBella Adds Two Airports"* in *Ice Cream Reporter (Vol. 23, November 20, 2010, No. 12, pp. 5)*
Pub: Ice Cream Reporter
Description: MooBella Inc. has placed MooBella Ice Creamery machines in New England's Logan International Airport in Boston and in New Hampshire's Manchester-Boston Regional Airport.

23238 ■ *"More Jobs Heading to Suburb"* in *Austin Business JournalInc. (Vol. 29, November 20, 2009, No. 37, pp. 1)*
Pub: American City Business Journals
Ed: Kate Harrington. Description: Site of Advanced Integration Technologies (AIT) in Pflugerville, Texas might increase its workforce to 80 employees in the next six months due to the creation of an incentive package. Funds from the Pflugerville Community Development Corporation have been helping AIT's initiative to hire more workers. The firm receives $2,000 from the plan for every new employee it hires.

23239 ■ *"More Sales Leads, Please: Or, What Happened When Frontline Selling Started Practicing What It Preaches"* in *Inc. (November 2007)*
Pub: Gruner & Jahr USA Publishing
Description: Frontline Selling located in Oakland, New Jersey helps train sales teams to generate and convert sales leads. The consulting firm doubled their marketing budget to increase their own sales.

23240 ■ *"More SouthPark Shopping"* in *Charlotte Business Journal (Vol. 25, July 16, 2010, No. 17, pp. 1)*
Pub: Charlotte Business Journal
Ed: Will Boye. Description: Charlotte, North Carolina-based Bissel Companies has announced plans to expand its retail presence at the Siskey and Sharon properties in SouthPark. Bissel Companies has requested a rezoning to a mixed-use development classification so that it can utilize the entire ground floor of the Siskey building for restaurant and retail uses.

23241 ■ *More Than a Pink Cadillac*
Pub: McGraw-Hill
Ed: Jim Underwood. Released: 2002. Price: $23.95. Description: Profile of Mary Kay Ash who turned her $5,000 investment into a billion-dollar corporation. Ash's nine principles that form the foundation of her company's global success are outlined. Stories from her sales force leaders share ideas for motivating employees, impressing customers and building a successful company. The book emphasizes the leadership skills required to drive performance in any successful enterprise.

23242 ■ *"MPI Expansion Goes Back to Family Roots"* in *Crain's Detroit Business (Vol. 25, June 1, 2009, No. 22, pp. M007)*
Pub: Crain Communications Inc. - Detroit
Ed: Sherri Begin Welch. Description: William Parfet, grandson of Upjohn Company founder, is expanding MPI Research's clinical and early clinical research operations into two buildings in Kalamazoo, land which was once part of his grandfather's farm.

23243 ■ *The Multinational Enterprise Revisited: The Essential Buckley and Casson*
Pub: Palgrave Macmillan
Ed: Peter J. Buckley, Mark Casson. Released: January 5, 2010. Price: $95.00. Description: A compilation of essays gathered from over thirty years discussing the future of the multinational enterprise, and includes a new introduction and conclusion to bond the pieces together in a comprehensive overview of the theory of the multinational enterprise.

23244 ■ *"MV Transportation Winds $133M Contract"* in *Black Enterprise (Vol. 38, November 2007, No. 4, pp. 30)*
Pub: Earl G. Graves Publishing Co. Inc.
Ed: Marcia A. Wade. Description: MV Transportation won a $133 million contract to operate 139 fixed-route buses in the San Gabriel and Pomona valley areas of California.

23245 ■ *"Myths of Deleveraging"* in *Barron's (Vol. 90, August 23, 2010, No. 34, pp. M14)*
Pub: Barron's Editorial & Corporate Headquarters
Ed: Gene Epstein. Description: The opposite is true against reports about deleveraging or the decrease in credit since inflation-adjusted-investment factories and equipment rose 7.8 percent in the first quarter of 2010. On consumer deleveraging, sales of homes through credit is weak but there is a trend towards more realistic homeownership and consumer spending on durable goods rose 8.8 percent.

23246 ■ *"NBC Universal Cable"* in *Brandweek (Vol. 49, April 21, 2008, No. 16, pp. SR11)*
Pub: VNU Business Media, Inc.
Ed: Anthony Crupi. Description: Provides contact information for sales and marketing personnel for the NBC Universal Cable networks as well as a listing of the station's top programming and an analysis of the current season and the target audience for those programs running in the current season. The network's stations include USA, Sci Fi and Bravo. Ad revenue for the network grew 30 percent in the first quarter.

23247 ■ *"Neurosciences, Orthopedics Push Mease Dunedin Plan"* in *Tampa Bay Business Journal (Vol. 29, October 30, 2009, No. 45, pp. 1)*
Pub: American City Business Journals
Ed: Margie Manning. Description: Mease Dunedin Hospital has pushed with a $19 million renovation and expansion plan that would triple the space in its operating suites, in line with its effort to become a center of excellence focused on neurosciences, orthopedics and the spine. The hospital expects these kinds of specialties will help offset the cost of less profitable services.

23248 ■ *"Never Boring: Ad Agencies' Big Changes"* in *Business Courier (Vol. 24, February 8, 2008, No. 44, pp. 1)*
Pub: American City Business Journals, Inc.
Ed: Dan Monk. Description: Many changes are occurring in Cincinnati's advertising industry, including new clients, acquisitions, and market leaders, and an increase in employment. Bridge Worldwide passed Northlich LLC as the city's largest advertising agency.

23249 ■ *"New Beginnings for VIBE"* in *Black Enterprise (Vol. 37, November 2006, No. 4, pp. 34)*
Pub: Earl G. Graves Publishing Co. Inc.
Ed: Mashaun D. Simon. Description: Danyel Smith replaced Mimi Valdes as editor-in-chief of VIBE magazine after the Wicks Group, private equity firm focused on selected segments of the media, communications, and information industries, purchased the magazine.

23250 ■ *"New Drug Could Revitalize Amgen"* in *Barron's (Vol. 88, July 7, 2008, No. 27, pp. 23)*
Pub: Dow Jones & Co., Inc.
Ed: Johanna Bennett. Description: Shares of the biotechnology company Amgen could receive a boost from the release of the anti-osteoporosis drug cenosumab. The shares, priced at $48.84 each, are trading at 11 times expected earnings for 2008 and could also be boosted by cost cutting measures.

23251 ■ *"New Health Care Sector"* in *Hispanic Business (July-August 2009, pp. 10-12)*
Pub: Hispanic Business
Ed: Rob Kuznia. Description: Despite the recession and reform, the health care sector continues to grow at a fast rate. The top ten health care organizations are outlined.

23252 ■ *"New-Home Sales Grab a Foothold With Q2 Boost"* in *Sacramento Business Journal (Vol. 25, July 11, 2008, No. 19, pp. 1)*
Pub: American City Business Journals, Inc.
Ed: Michael Shaw. Description: Statistics show that homebuilders in Sacramento, California experienced an increase in new-home sales during the second quarter of 2008. It was also reported that builders moved more homes without slashing prices signifi-

cantly. Barry Grant, president of KB Home's Sacramento division, believes that the improvement is caused by the stability in the supply of resale homes.

23253 ■ *"New King Top the Charts"* in *The Business Journal-Portland (Vol. 25, August 8, 2008, No. 22, pp. 1)*
Pub: American City Business Journals, Inc.
Ed: Andy Giegerich. Description: Spanish-language KRYP-FM station's spring 2008 ratings soared to 6.4 from 2.8 for the previous year. The station timing is flawless given the fact that one of every three new Portland-area residents between 2002 and 2007 were Latino.

23254 ■ *"New Kittinger Showroom Twice the Size of the Last One"* in *Business First Buffalo (December 7, 2007, pp. 4)*
Pub: American City Business Journals, Inc.
Ed: Tracey Drury. Description: Kittinger Furniture Company, an upscale furniture maker, has opened a 6,000 square foot retail outlet at the Transit Road, New York. The company's moved to attract suburban and affluent customers for its high-end furniture products.

23255 ■ *"New Leadership Panel Has Advice for Collins"* in *Business First Buffalo (November 23, 2007, pp. 1)*
Pub: American City Business Journals, Inc.
Ed: David Bertola. Description: Business First and Leadership Buffalo sponsored a meeting that convened business and civic leaders to discuss issues important to the economic growth and development of Western New York. The panel made recommendations to the County Executive-elect Christopher Collins. Details of the forum are included.

23256 ■ *"New Life for Old Chemistries"* in *Farm Industry News (Vol. 42, January 1, 2009, No. 1)*
Pub: Penton Media Inc.
Contact: John French, President
Ed: Mark Moore. Description: To expand the uses of familiar crop protection products, chemical companies are utilizing biotechnology research and development tools; many off-patent products are being rejuvenated with small changes to make the product even better than it was when originally conceived.

23257 ■ *"A New Reality; There are Some Signs of Hope Amid 2009's Darkness"* in *Crain's Cleveland Business (Vol. 30, June 29, 2009, No. 25)*
Pub: Crain Communications, Inc.
Ed: John Booth. Description: Despite all the pessimism, there are some signs that the economy is slowly stabilizing.

23258 ■ *The New Role of Regional Management*
Pub: Palgrave Macmillan
Ed: Bjorn Ambos, Bodo B. Schlegelmilch. Released: January 19, 2010. Price: $95.00. Description: Regional management is becoming more important to companies as they expand globally. This book explores the challenges of European, United States and Asian companies and outlines how regional headquarters can develop into Dynamic Competence Relay centers to master these issues.

23259 ■ *"New Sprint Phone Whets Appetite for Applications"* in *The Business Journal-Serving Metropolitan Kansas City (Vol. 26, July 25, 2008)*
Pub: American City Business Journals, Inc.
Ed: Suzanna Stagemeyer. Description: Firms supporting the applications of the new Samsung Instinct, which was introduced by Sprint Nextel Corp. in June 2008, have reported usage rates increase for their products. Handmark, whose mobile services Pocket Express comes loaded with Instinct, has redirected employees to meet the rising demand for the services. Other views and information on Instinct, are presented.

23260 ■ *"New Stores, New Headquarters in Schenectady for Golub Corporation"* in *Business Review, Albany New York*

(November 23, 2007)
Pub: American City Business Journals, Inc.
Ed: Michael DeMasi. **Description:** Details of Golub Corporation's expansion plan are presented. The supermarket chain, which has 116 stores in six northeastern states, plans to open thirty more stores within the next three or four years. The company will also build 524,000 square feet of warehouse space which will help in supplying new stores. Its corporate headquarters will also move to a vacant lot in Schenectady, New York.

23261 ■ *New Technology-Based Firms in the New Millennium, Volume 5*
Pub: Elsevier Science and Technology Books
Ed: Ray Oakey; Saleema Kauser; Aard Groen; Peter van der Sijde. **Released:** November 2006. **Price:** $145.00. **Description:** Papers from the Annual High Technology Smal Firms conference are presented. Experts address strategic growth for these small firms.

23262 ■ *"New Technology, Growing Fan Base Fuel Truck Trend"* in *Nation's Restaurant News* (Vol. 45, June 13, 2001, No. 12, pp. 16)
Pub: Penton Media Inc.
Contact: John French, President
Ed: Ron Ruggless. **Description:** Food trucks drove more interest at this year's National Restaurant Association Restaurant Hotel-Motel Show in Chicago. The trend continues to show long-term growth.

23263 ■ *"New Year's Resolutions: How Three Companies Came Up With Their 2008 Growth Strategies"* in *Inc.* (January 2008, pp. 47-49)
Pub: Gruner & Jahr USA Publishing
Ed: Martha C. White. **Description:** Three companies share 2008 growth strategies; companies include a candle company, a voice mail and text messaging marketer, and hotel supplier of soap and shampoo.

23264 ■ *"Newcomers Join Roster of Indoor Sports Venues"* in *Business Review, Albany New York* (Vol. 34, October 12, 2007, No. 28, pp. 1)
Pub: American City Business Journals, Inc.
Ed: Adam Sichko. **Description:** Indoor sports scene in Albany, New York is growing, with several indoor training facilities with a special attention to baseball and softball being built. These facilities include the $2.2 million Extra Innings facility in Ballston Corporate Technology Park and the Warning Track facility on Route 9 in Malta. The market for indoor sports, which is seen as saturated, is analyzed.

23265 ■ *"The Next 20 Years: How Customer and Workforce Attitudes Will Evolve"* in *Harvard Business Review* (Vol. 85, July-August 2007, No. 7-8)
Pub: Harvard Business School Publishing
Ed: Neil Howe, William Strauss. **Description:** Identification of social categories inhabited by age groups is used to calculate how consumer and employee opinions and behavior will change, and how this will impact economic development and corporate growth.

23266 ■ *"Nine Sectors to Watch: Biotech"* in *Canadian Business* (Vol. 81, December 24, 2007, No. 1, pp. 48)
Pub: Rogers Media
Ed: Calvin Leung. **Description:** Forecasts on the Canadian biotechnology sector for 2008 are presented. Details on the increase in the number of biotechnology companies and prediction on the government's plan for business incentives are discussed.

23267 ■ *"Nine Sectors to Watch: Construction"* in *Canadian Business* (Vol. 81, December 24, 2007, No. 1, pp. 48)
Pub: Rogers Media
Ed: Jeff Sanford. **Description:** Infrastructure deficit of C$123 billion, and still growing, was recently reported by the Federation of Canadian Municipalities. Details on plans for infrastructure projects and forecasts on the construction sector for 2008 are discussed.

23268 ■ *"Nine Sectors to Watch: Energy"* in *Canadian Business* (Vol. 81, December 24, 2007, No. 1, pp. 54)
Pub: Rogers Media
Ed: Jeff Sanford. **Description:** One of the concerns in the petroleum industry is the fear of decline in production in many oilfields, as analysts predict the world will be pumping 17 percent less by 2025. Details on the continuing rise in demand and increase in prices are discussed.

23269 ■ *"Nine Sectors to Watch: Gold"* in *Canadian Business* (Vol. 81, December 24, 2007, No. 1, pp. 53)
Pub: Rogers Media
Ed: John Gray. **Description:** Turmoil in the financial markets, triggered by the meltdown in subprime mortgages, has pushed the price of gold to more than $840 an ounce in November 2007. Details on investor interest in gold and prediction on price trends in trade are discussed.

23270 ■ *"Nine Sectors to Watch: Metals"* in *Canadian Business* (Vol. 81, December 24, 2007, No. 1, pp. 46)
Pub: Rogers Media
Ed: John Gray. **Description:** Forecasts on the Canadian metal industries for 2008 are discussed. Details on mine production and the rise in prices are also presented.

23271 ■ *"Nine Sectors to Watch: Retail"* in *Canadian Business* (Vol. 81, December 24, 2007, No. 1, pp. 56)
Pub: Rogers Media
Ed: Zena Olijnyk. **Description:** Canadian consumers are expected to spend more in 2008 as the Canadian dollar hit par with the U.S. greenback after the slowdown in the U.S. economy. Forecasts on retail sales growth are discussed.

23272 ■ *"Nine Sectors to Watch: Telecom"* in *Canadian Business* (Vol. 81, December 24, 2007, No. 1, pp. 44)
Pub: Rogers Media
Ed: Andrew Wahl. **Description:** Forecasts on the Canadian telecommunications industry for 2008 are presented. Details on consumer spending growth, the popularity of broadband, and activities in the wireless sector are also discussed.

23273 ■ *"No Frills - And No Dodge"* in *Crain's Detroit Business* (Vol. 24, September 22, 2008, No. 38, pp. 3)
Pub: Crain Communications Inc.
Ed: Bradford Wernle. **Description:** Chrysler LLC is in the middle of a business plan known as Project Genesis, a five-year strategy in which the company will reduce the dealer count by combining its Jeep, Chrysler and Dodge brands under one rooftop wherever possible. Not every dealer will be able to arrange this deal because of the investment required to expand stores in which have low-overhead; many of these stores feel that low-overhead structures are more likely to survive difficult times than the larger stores in which the Genesis consolidation plan intends to implement.

23274 ■ *"No Lines, No Waiting"* in *The Business Journal-Serving Greater Tampa Bay* (Vol. 28, August 15, 2008, No. 34, pp. 1)
Pub: American City Business Journals, Inc.
Ed: Jane Meinhardt. **Description:** Voda LLC, which was founded to commercialize developments by David Fries, develops outdoor sensor networks used for environmental monitoring by markets like research, the security industry, and the government. Fries already licensed 12 technologies for clients for about $130,000 per technology. Other information on Voda LLC is presented.

23275 ■ *No Man's Land: What to Do When Your Company Is Too Big to Be Small but Too Small to Be Big*
Pub: Portfolio Publishing
Ed: Doug Tatum. **Released:** September 13, 2007. **Price:** $24.95. **Description:** Insight to help fast-growing companies navigate the fatal trap of no-man's land, a perilous zone where they have out-

grown the habits and practices that fueled their early growth but have not yet adopted new practices and resources in order to cope with new situations and challenges.

23276 ■ *"No Rooms for the Inn In This High-Rise"* in *Chicago Tribune* (October 4, 2008)
Pub: McClatchy-Tribune Information Services
Ed: Ameet Sachdev; Jim Kirk. **Description:** Construction has stalled for several hotel expansion projects due to the economy which has caused a decline in occupancy and little growth in average daily room rates in downtown Chicago because consumers and businesses are becoming more cautious in the amount of money they spend on travel.

23277 ■ *"No Surprises"* in *Canadian Business* (Vol. 79, September 25, 2006, No. 19, pp. 49)
Pub: Rogers Media
Ed: Jeff Sanford. **Description:** The increasing income trust sector in Canada is discussed.

23278 ■ *"Nonprofit to Grow"* in *Austin Business JournalInc.* (Vol. 29, January 22, 2010, No. 46, pp. 1)
Pub: American City Business Journals
Ed: Sandra Zaragoza. **Description:** Southwest Key Programs Inc. received a $2.1 million grant from the U.S. Economic Development Administration to help finance the building of a $3.6 million 'Social Enterprise Complex'. The complex is expected to create at least 100 jobs in East Austin, Texas. Details of the plan for the complex are presented.

23279 ■ *"Northern Kentucky Adds 1,355 Jobs in '07"* in *Business Courier* (Vol. 24, February 15, 2008, No. 45, pp. 3)
Pub: American City Business Journals, Inc.
Ed: Lucy May. **Description:** Jobs generated by new and expanding businesses in Northern Kentucky in 2007 totaled to 1,355, which boosted total business sales to $410 million. The ripple effects of the businesses are expected to create 5,432 new jobs and increase business sales to more than $888 million.

23280 ■ *"The Numbers Speak For Themselves"* in *Barron's* (Vol. 88, July 14, 2008, No. 28, pp. 16)
Pub: Dow Jones & Co., Inc.
Ed: Bill Alpert. **Description:** Discusses quant fund managers versus traditional long-short equity funds after quants outperformed traditional funds in the year 2000. Causes for the underperformance are outlined and statistical data is included.

23281 ■ *"Office Leasing Gains Ground"* in *Sacramento Business Journal* (Vol. 25, July 18, 2008, No. 20, pp. 1)
Pub: American City Business Journals, Inc.
Ed: Michael Shaw. **Description:** There were at least 84,000 square feet leased to companies in the Sacramento area in the three months prior to August 2008. This development is good news considering that overall vacant leases were around 247,000 square feet for the previous quarter.

23282 ■ *"Oh, Grow Up!"* in *Entrepreneur* (Vol. 35, October 2007, No. 10, pp. 120)
Pub: Entrepreneur Media Inc.
Ed: Mark Henricks. **Description:** Most entrepreneurs are overwhelmed with the idea of expanding their business, forgetting to strategically plan the process of business growth. However, there are certain steps entrepreneurs must take in turning a startup business into a bigger venture. Eight steps to growing a business, such as asking for advice and deciding on a focus are presented.

23283 ■ *"Ohio Commerce Draws Closer to Profitability"* in *Crain's Cleveland Business* (Vol. 28, October 29, 2007, No. 43, pp. 14)
Pub: Crain Communications, Inc.
Ed: Shawn A. Turner. **Description:** Overview of the business plan of Ohio Commerce Bank, a de novo, or startup bank that is close to turning the corner to profitability. The bank opened in November 2006 and focuses on dealing with small businesses totaling $5 million or less in annual revenues.

23284 ■ *"Ohio Franchise Buys 21 Jacksonville Area Papa John's"* in *Florida Times-Union (December 20, 2010)*

Pub: Florida Times-Union

Ed: Mark Basch. **Description:** Ohio-based Papa John's pizza franchise acquired 21 of the restaurants in Duval, Clay and St. Johns counties in Jacksonville, Florida.

23285 ■ *"Oil Patch Expects Richer Shell Offer"* in *Globe & Mail (January 3, 2006, pp. B1)*

Pub: CTVglobemedia Publishing Inc.

Ed: Andrew Willis; Patrick Brethour. **Description:** The concerns investors over the feasibility of Royal Dutch Shell PLC's acquisition of Shell Canada Ltd., for $7.6 billion, are presented. Shell Canada Ltd. reports rise in shares by ten percent.

23286 ■ *"OK, Bring in the Lawyers"* in *Crain's Chicago Business (Vol. 31, November 17, 2008, No. 46, pp. 26)*

Pub: Crain Communications, Inc.

Ed: Daniel Rome Levine. **Description:** Bankruptcy attorneys are finding the economic and credit crisis a benefit for their businesses due to the high number of business owners and mortgage holders that are need of their services. One Chicago firm is handling ten times the number of cases they did the previous year and of that about 80 percent of their new clients are related to the real estate sector.

23287 ■ *"On Growth Path of Rising Star"* in *Boston Business Journal (Vol. 31, June 24, 2011, No. 22, pp. 3)*

Pub: Boston Business Journal

Ed: Kyle Alspach. **Description:** 1366 Technologies Inc. of Lexington, Massachusetts is considered a rising solar power technology company. The firm secured $150 million loan guarantee from the US Department of Energy that could go to the construction of a 1,000 megawatt solar power plant.

23288 ■ *"On the High Road"* in *Crain's Cleveland Business (Vol. 28, October 8, 2007, No. 40, pp. 2)*

Pub: Crain Communications, Inc.

Description: According to the American Public Transportation Association, the Greater Cleveland Regional Transit Authority is the best public transit system in North America. Ridership has increased steadily in the last few years. Statistical data included.

23289 ■ *"On Hire Ground"* in *Entrepreneur (Vol. 36, February 2008, No. 2, pp. 19)*

Pub: Entrepreneur Media Inc.

Description: ADP Small Business Services, an economic consulting firm, showed that small businesses had increased employment rates in 2007 and added 77,000 jobs in November 2007. Entrepreneurial employment and data showing the contribution of small businesses to job growth are presented.

23290 ■ *"On a Roll"* in *Canadian Business (Vol. 79, Winter 2006, No. 24, pp. 49)*

Pub: Rogers Media

Ed: Thomas Watson. **Description:** The efforts of the Canadian automobile spare parts manufacturer, Magna International Inc., to expand into the the Russian market, are described.

23291 ■ *"One on One With SEIA's President, CEO"* in *Contractor (Vol. 57, January 2010, No. 1, pp. 40)*

Pub: Penton Media, Inc.

Ed: Dave Yates. **Description:** Solar Energy Industries Association President and CEO Rhone Resch says that the deployment of solar systems in the U.S. has exploded since 2005 and that there is a need to make inroads for shaping the U.S. energy policy. Resch says one of the hurdles they face is that there are no universal standards.

23292 ■ *"Online All the Time"* in *Retail Merchandiser (Vol. 51, July-August 2011, No. 4, pp. 18)*

Pub: Phoenix Media Corporation

Description: Ecommerce sales are rising at a steady pace and for cross-channel retailers it is boosting sales in the weak economy. Online sales are expected to reach $188 billion in 2011, boasting a 13.7 rate of growth.

23293 ■ *"Optimism Index"* in *Black Enterprise (Vol. 41, September 2010, No. 2, pp. 24)*

Pub: Earl G. Graves Publishing Co. Inc.

Description: According to a Pew Research Center report, 81 percent of African Americans expect to improve their finances in 2011. Blacks have carried a disproportionate share of job losses and housing foreclosures in the recession that began in 2007.

23294 ■ *"Oracle: No Profit of Doom"* in *Barron's (Vol. 88, March 31, 2008, No. 13, pp. 40)*

Pub: Dow Jones & Company, Inc.

Ed: Mark Veverka. **Description:** Oracle's revenues grew by 21 percent but fell short of expectation and their profits came in at the low-end of expectations. The company's shares dropped 8 percent but investors are advised to pay more attention to the company's earnings expansion rather than revenue growth in a slow economy. Nokia's Rick Simonson points out that their markets in Asia and particularly India is growing so they are not as affected by the U.S. economic conditions.

23295 ■ *"O'Reilly Will Soup Up KC Warehouse"* in *The Business Journal-Serving Metropolitan Kansas City (Vol. 26, August 15, 2008, No. 49)*

Pub: American City Business Journals, Inc.

Ed: Rob Roberts. **Description:** O'Reilly Automotive Inc. plans to construct a 215,000-square foot warehouse in Kansas City. The move is expected to triple the size of the company's distribution center. Other views and information on the planned warehouse construction, are presented.

23296 ■ *"Organic Dairy Farmers Wanted"* in *Canadian Business (Vol. 80, April 23, 2007, No. 9, pp. 11)*

Pub: Rogers Media

Ed: Wendy Glauser. **Description:** The growth of the Harmony Organic due to demand for organic dairy products is presented.

23297 ■ *Organizations Alive!: Six Things That Challenge - Seven That Bring Success*

Pub: Yuill & Associates

Ed: Jan Yuill. **Released:** January 2005. **Price:** $35.12 for book and guide. **Description:** New insight into understanding how organizations function as individuals is presented by an international consultant. Customer service, resource management, outsourcing, and management are among the issues covered.

23298 ■ *"Out to Draw Work, Talent"* in *Crain's Detroit Business (Vol. 24, April 14, 2008, No. 15, pp. 3)*

Pub: Crain Communications, Inc.

Ed: Bill Shea. **Description:** Profile of Southfield-based Kinetic Post Inc., a growing post-production house that offers video, audio, animation, print, online and related services to corporations and advertising agencies.

23299 ■ *"Out of Fashion"* in *Barron's (Vol. 88, March 17, 2008, No. 11, pp. 48)*

Pub: Dow Jones & Company, Inc.

Ed: Robin Goldwyn Blumenthal. **Description:** Shares of Perry Ellis International and G-III Apparel Group have taken some beating in the market despite good growth earnings prospects. Perry Ellis sees earnings growth of 8 to 11 percent for fiscal 2009, while G-III Apparel expects earnings growth of 25 percent.

23300 ■ *"The Outcome of an Organization Overhaul"* in *Black Enterprise (Vol. 41, December 2010, No. 5)*

Pub: Earl G. Graves Publishing Co. Inc.

Ed: Tamara E. Holmes. **Description:** Savvy business owners understand the need for change in order to stay competitive and be successful. This article examines how to manage change as well as what strategies can help employees to get with the program faster.

23301 ■ *"Outlook for Montana Agriculture"* in *Montana Business Quarterly (Vol. 49, Spring 2011, No. 1, pp. 26)*

Pub: Bureau of Business & Economic Research

Ed: George Haynes. **Description:** Montana farmers and ranchers are rebounding from lower prices and production to higher prices and record production in 2010. The state has limited dairy and hog production, but farm income is still likely rise between 15 to 25 percent in 2010 over previous year.

23302 ■ *Outsmart! How to Do What Your Competitors Can't*

Pub: FT Press

Ed: Jim Champy. **Released:** March 7, 2008. **Price:** $22.99. **Description:** Small business growth can be achieved through outsmarting your competition. The author identifies eight powerful ways to compete in the toughest marketplace.

23303 ■ *"Overview - Small Business Optimism"* in *Small Business Economic Trends (July 2009, pp. 4)*

Pub: National Federation of Independent Business

Description: Small businesses surveyed in the United States regarding their optimism index from 1986 to 2009 shows a marked difference as is presented in a graph. A small business optimism index from January 2004 to June 2009 is also given in tabular form. The index value was seasonally adjusted at 1986=100.

23304 ■ *"Overview - Small Business Optimism"* in *Small Business Economic Trends (September 2010, pp. 4)*

Pub: National Federation of Independent Business

Ed: William C. Dunkelberg, Holly Wade. **Description:** An optimism index among small businesses surveyed in the U.S. from 1986 to 2010 is presented in a graph. A small business optimism index from 2005 to 2010 is also given in tabular form.

23305 ■ *"Overview - Small Business Optimism"* in *Small Business Economic Trends (July 2010, pp. 4)*

Pub: National Federation of Independent Business

Description: An optimism index among small businesses surveyed in the U.S. from 1986 to 2010 is presented in graph form. A small business optimism index from January 2005 to June 2010 is also given in tabular form. The index value was seasonally adjusted at 1986=100.

23306 ■ *The Oz Principle*

Pub: Prentice Hall Press

Contact: Dame Marjorie M. Scardino, Chief Executive Officer

Ed: Roger Connors. **Released:** 1994. **Price:** $24.95. **Description:** The role of personal and organizational accountability in getting business results is profiled.

23307 ■ *The Pampered Chef*

Pub: Doubleday Broadway Publishing Group

Ed: Doris Christopher. **Description:** The Pampered Chef has been selling high quality kitchen tools through in-home cooking demonstration for twenty-five years. CEO and founder explains how she turned her one woman company into a to a business with sales approaching $1 billion. Christopher shares her story by providing the foundation, strategies for entrepreneurs, setting priorities, knowing when to expand and when to slow growth, and dealing with adversity.

23308 ■ *"P&G's Iams Finds Itself in a Pet-Food Dogfight"* in *Advertising Age (Vol. 78, March 5, 2007, No. 10, pp. 6)*

Pub: Crain Communications, Inc.

Ed: Jack Neff. **Description:** Proctor & Gamble Co.'s Iams has been slow to embrace the trend toward foods for pets that appear fit for human consumption. Competitors such as Nestle Purina have made big gains with its colorful premium Beneful brand and dry nuggets that look like chunks of vegetables and meat. Statistical data included.

23309 ■ *"Parent Firm's Global Reach, Stricter Air Quality Rules Have Stock Smiling"* in

Crain's Cleveland Business (October 15, 2007)
Pub: Crain Communications, Inc.
Ed: David Bennett. **Description:** Since Stock Equipment Co., a firm that makes industrial pollution control equipment, was acquired by Schenck Process Group, a diversified global manufacturer based in Germany, the company's orders from abroad have been on the rise. The purchase has opened the doors to regions such as Eastern and Central Europe, Latin America and Australia.

23310 ■ *"PD Targeting Audience Growth with Web Initiatives"* in Crain's Cleveland Business (Vol. 30, June 29, 2009, No. 25, pp. 1)
Pub: Crain Communications, Inc.
Ed: Kathy Ames Carr. **Description:** Plain Dealer's publisher C.Z. Egger has his news organization focusing on online offerings in order to build circulation of its newspaper. The 167-year-old paper boasts 1,305,203 readers in print and online weekly.

23311 ■ *"PDX Bucks National Trend"* in The Business Journal-Portland (Vol. 25, August 1, 2008, No. 21, pp. 1)
Pub: American City Business Journals, Inc.
Ed: Erik Siemers. **Description:** Portland International Airport could face problems as air carriers are planning to reduce capacity at the airport. The airport is showing signs of growth despite the slowdown in the airline industry. Other airlines that are planning to reduce seating capacity at the airport are also presented.

23312 ■ *"Peak Show"* in Canadian Business (Vol. 81, December 24, 2007, No. 1, pp. 28)
Pub: Rogers Media
Ed: Thomas Watson. **Description:** Factors affecting oil prices could include political instability and economic slowdown, but peak oil is not one of them as it is believed there is still plenty of oil in supply. Details on the oil supply and demand, trend for higher prices, and peak oil expert Matthew Simmons' prediction on the issue are discussed.

23313 ■ *"Penney's Buys Wal-Mart Site"* in Crain's Chicago Business (Vol. 31, March 31, 2008, No. 13, pp. 13)
Pub: Crain Communications, Inc.
Ed: Eddie Baeb. **Description:** J.C. Penny Co. bought the closed Wal-Mart location in Crystal Lake and plans to open a store next year in its push to become more prominent in non-mall locations; Penney plans to expand and renovate the store.

23314 ■ *"Penske Opens Its First Smart Car Dealership In Bloomfield Hills"* in Crain's Detroit Business (Vol. 24, January 21, 2008, No. 3)
Pub: Crain Communications Inc. - Detroit
Ed: Sheena Harrison. **Description:** Information about Penske Automotive Group's Smart Car addition to its dealership lineup. Smart Car pricing starts at $11,590, with more than 30,000 individuals reserving vehicles.

23315 ■ *"Perfecting the Process: Creating a Move Efficient Organization On Your Terms"* in Black Enterprise (Vol. 41, October 2010, No. 3)
Pub: Earl G. Graves Publishing Co. Inc.
Ed: Tamara E. Holmes. **Description:** More than ever, entrepreneurs need to identify new ways of doing business in a cost-effective manner in order to expand their companies, while remaining true to their customer demands.

23316 ■ *"Pet-Food Crisis a Boon to Organic Players"* in Advertising Age (Vol. 78, April 9, 2007, No. 15, pp. 3)
Pub: Crain Communications, Inc.
Ed: Jack Neff. **Description:** In the wake of the pet-food recall crisis, the natural-and-organic segment of the market is gaining recognition and sales; one such manufacturer, Blue Buffalo, has not only seen huge sale increases but also has witnessed a 50-60 percent increase in traffic to the brand's website which has led to the decision to move up the timetable for the brand's first national ad campaign.

23317 ■ *"PetSmart: A Barking Buy"* in Barron's (Vol. 89, July 6, 2009, No. 27, pp. 15)
Pub: Dow Jones & Co., Inc.
Ed: Jay Palmer. **Description:** Shares of PetSmart could climb from $21.70 to about $28 due to the company's improving profits, cash flow, and product portfolio. The company's shares are trading at 14 times projected 2010 earnings of $1.64 a share.

23318 ■ *"PGA Tourney Drives Area Economy, Image"* in Crain's Detroit Business (Vol. 24, April 7, 2008, No. 14, pp. 22)
Pub: Crain Communications, Inc.
Ed: Jason Deegan. **Description:** Discusses the major economic impact the 2008 PGA Championship will have when it visits the south course at Oakland Hills Country Club August 4-10.

23319 ■ *"Phoenix Company Realizing Dream of Global Growth"* in The Business Journal - Serving Phoenix and the Valley of the Sun (Vol. 28, July 18, 2008, No. 46, pp. 1)
Pub: American City Business Journals, Inc.
Ed: Chris Casacchia. **Description:** Phoenix, Arizona-based lubricant maker DreamBrands Inc. is realizing global growth. The company, which has been generating interest from institutional investors, is seeking a second round of funding. Details of the company's products and marketing plans are also discussed.

23320 ■ *"Pinellas Leaders Want First Leg of Light Rail"* in The Business Journal-Serving Greater Tampa Bay (Vol. 28, August 8, 2008, No. 33)
Pub: American City Business Journals, Inc.
Ed: Larry Halstead. **Description:** Proposed routes for the first leg of the planned light railway system in the Tampa Bay, Florida area are being presented as the Tampa Bay Area Regional Transportation Authority is about to make its master plan for the project. A sales tax for transit is being proposed to fund the project, as well as an expansion of the accompanying bus system.

23321 ■ *"Pioneer Bank Ready to Expand"* in Austin Business JournalInc. (Vol. 28, December 19, 2008, No. 40, pp. 1)
Pub: American City Business Journals
Ed: Christopher Calnan. **Description:** Pioneer Bank, an 18-month old community bank based in Dripping Springs, Texas is planning to raise $6 million to open branches in the Austin area, including Hays County locations such as San Marcos, Buda, and Kyle. Pioneer's deposits have growing from $2.2 million to $54 million in 18 months.

23322 ■ *"A Pioneer of Paying With Plastic"* in Crain's Chicago Business (Vol. 31, April 28, 2008, No. 17, pp. 39)
Pub: Crain Communications, Inc.
Ed: Phuong Ly. **Description:** Profile of Perfect Plastic Printing Corp., a family-owned company which manufactures credit cards, bank cards and gift cards and whose sales hit $50.1 million last year, a 16 percent jump from 2006.

23323 ■ *"Pitch for SPX Expansion was Full of Energy"* in Charlotte Business Journal (Vol. 25, November 19, 2010, No. 35, pp. 1)
Pub: Charlotte Business Journal
Ed: John Downey. **Description:** SPX Corporation announced that it will expand their headquarters in Ballantyne after Charlotte and North Carolina leaders made an aggressive push to retain the company. SPX Corporation is expected to invest $70 million for the expansion, which would mean 180 new jobs in Charlotte.

23324 ■ *"Playboy to Target Lucrative India Market With No-Nudes Version"* in Globe & Mail (January 2, 2006, pp. B2)
Pub: CTVglobemedia Publishing Inc.
Ed: Anand Giridharadas. **Description:** The planning of Chicago based Playboy Enterprises Inc. to target lucrative India market with no nudes version, in order to increase its market shares is discussed.

23325 ■ *"Playing Citigroup's Woes"* in Barron's (Vol. 88, March 31, 2008, No. 13, pp. M7)
Pub: Dow Jones & Company, Inc.
Ed: Steven M. Sears. **Description:** Citigroup's first-quarter earnings estimate was slashed to a $1.15-per-share-loss from 28 cents. A strategist recommends buying the company's shares at Sept. 20, 2008 put and selling a Sept. 17.50 put with a maximum profit of $166 if the shares is at or below $17.50 at expiration.

23326 ■ *"Playing to Win"* in Entrepreneur (Vol. 36, May 2008, No. 5, pp. 40)
Pub: Entrepreneur Media, Inc.
Ed: Robert Kiyosaki. **Description:** Four personality types needed by entrepreneurs to drive their leadership in business are given. 'I must be liked' are social directors and go-betweens; 'I must be comfortable' are those who seek job security and are not at ease with deadlines; I must be right are those strong in opinion; and 'I must win' are people in charge.

23327 ■ *"Point, Click, Buy"* in Barron's (Vol. 90, September 6, 2010, No. 36, pp. 11)
Pub: Barron's Editorial & Corporate Headquarters
Ed: Vito J. Racanelli. **Description:** Non-travel online retail sales from January to July 2010 increased nine percent which indicates that online shopping for the coming holidays will be good. Online sales are outpacing traditional shopping, but pricing is still critical.

23328 ■ *"PopCap Games Achieves Significant Increase in Return on Ad Spend With Omniture SearchCenter"* in Internet Wire (September 15, 2009)
Pub: Comtex News Network, Inc.
Description: PopCap Games, a leading computer games provider, is using Omniture SearchCenter together with Omniture SiteCatalyst to increase revenue from its search engine marketing campaign. Omniture, Inc. is a leading provider of Internet business optimization software.

23329 ■ *"Port Metro Vancouver Unveiled"* in Canadian Sailings (July 7, 2008)
Pub: UBM Global Trade
Contact: Leonard J. Corallo, President
Description: Vancouver Fraser Port Authority is marketing the port as Port Metro Vancouver; Along with the new name the port has announced additional strategies for continued growth and launched a new logo.

23330 ■ *"Portfolio Recovery Associates Expands Its Hampton Call Center"* in Internet Wire (January 20, 2010)
Pub: Comtex News Network, Inc.
Description: Entering into a lease amendment in order to expand its Hampton, Virginia call center and extend its lease agreement, Portfolio Recovery Associates, Inc., a company that collects, purchases and manages defaulted consumer debt, plans to upgrade the existing space enabling them to draw on local talent.

23331 ■ *"Portland Wooing Under Armour to West Coast Facility"* in Baltimore Business Journal (Vol. 27, January 29, 2010, No. 39, pp. 1)
Pub: American City Business Journals
Ed: Andy Giegerich. **Description:** Baltimore, Maryland sports apparel maker, Under Armour, is planning a west coast expansion with Portland, Oregon among the sites considered to house its apparel and footwear design center. Portland officials counting on the concentration of nearly 10,000 activewear workers in the city will help lure the company to the city.

23332 ■ *"The Power Brokers"* in Crain's Chicago Business (Vol. 31, April 28, 2008, No. 17, pp. 41)
Pub: Crain Communications, Inc.
Ed: Samantha Stainburn. **Description:** Profile of BlueStar Energy Services Inc., one of the first suppliers to cash in on the deregulation f the electricity

market by the Illinois Legislature; last year BlueStar's revenue was $171.1 million, up from $600,000 in 2002, the year the company was founded.

23333 ■ "Power Partnerships" in Business Courier (Vol. 27, October 22, 2010, No. 25, pp. 1)

Pub: Business Courier

Ed: Lucy May. **Description:** The $400 million Harrah's casino and the $47 million redevelopment and expansion of Washington Park are project aimed at boosting the economy in downtown Cincinnati, Ohio. These projects will be done in cooperation with the National Association for the Advancement of Colored People. Insights into the role of minority-owned businesses in regional economic development are explored.

23334 ■ The Power of Social Networking: Using the Whuffie Factor to Build Your Business

Pub: Crown Business Books

Ed: Tara Hunt. **Released:** May 4, 2010. **Price:** $15.00. **Description:** This book shows how any small business can harness its power by increasing whuffie, the store of social capital that is the currency of the digital world. Blogs and social networks such as Facebook and Twitter are used to help grow any small firm.

23335 ■ "Price War: Managerial Salaries Are Beating the National Average, But Maybe Not for Long" in Canadian Business (March 31, 2008)

Pub: Rogers Media

Ed: Megan Harman. **Description:** Real average hourly earnings of managers increase by 20 percent in ten years as companies increase wages to avoid the risk of losing key managers to the competition and in preparation for the retirement of baby boomers. Tough market conditions affect management more since their incentives are tied to individual and corporate performance.

23336 ■ Principled Profit: Marketing that Puts People First

Pub: Accurate Writing & More

Ed: Shel Horowitz. **Price:** $17.50. **Description:** The importance for companies to market ethically and honestly is stressed. Quality marketing will build customer loyalty and that will translate into new customers and repeat business. A customer-retention strategy is outlined along with ideas to increase profits of any small business.

23337 ■ "Principles for Creating Growth in Challenging Times" in Agency Sales Magazine (Vol. 39, September-October 2009, No. 9, pp. 35)

Pub: MANA

Ed: Robert Goshen. **Description:** Creating a productive environment is one vital key for businesses to utilize during the challenging times that arise due to a weak economy; other important factors include maintaining a good relationship with the staff, responding appropriately to challenges and keeping a sense of humor.

23338 ■ "Priority: Recessionade" in Inc. (February 2008, pp. 19-20)

Pub: Gruner & Jahr USA Publishing

Ed: Amy Feldman. **Description:** Despite signs of inflation, entrepreneurs see these tough economic times as an opportunity to start or grow their businesses. Five entrepreneurs share insight into ways this economic downturn can work to grow their businesses.

23339 ■ "Private Label Manufacturers Association" in Ice Cream Reporter (Vol. 23, July 20, 2010, No. 8, pp. 7)

Pub: Ice Cream Reporter

Description: Branded frozen dessert manufacturers sold more frozen desserts in terms of sales volume and revenue and market share in 2009. Statistical details included.

23340 ■ "Procter & Gamble Boosts Bet on Exclusive Brands" in Business Courier (Vol. 27, July 9, 2010, No. 10, pp. 1)

Pub: Business Courier

Ed: Jon Newberry. **Description:** Procter & Gamble is creating more special versions of its brands such as Pringles and Pampers exclusively for retail partners such as Tesco in the U.K. The greater push towards this direction is seen as a way to regain market share.

23341 ■ "Profit Predictions Look Too Plump" in Barron's (Vol. 88, March 31, 2008, No. 13, pp. 37)

Pub: Dow Jones & Company, Inc.

Ed: Johanna Bennett. **Description:** Full-year forecast points to a 14 percent gain for 2008 but the second-half profit increases would have to grow at a fast rate and peak at 61 percent in the fourth quarter to achieve this. Trends in the U.S. economic conditions are also discussed.

23342 ■ "Profit Strong Rona to Maintain Acquisition Strategy" in Globe & Mail (February 22, 2007, pp. B14)

Pub: CTVglobemedia Publishing Inc.

Description: Canada-based Rona Inc., home improvement retailer that reported record annual profit in 2006, will continue its strategy of acquisitions. The company has reported profits of $190.6 million in 2006.

23343 ■ "The Profitability of Mobility" in Entrepreneur (Vol. 37, September 2009, No. 9, pp. 98)

Pub: Entrepreneur Media, Inc.

Ed: John Daley. **Description:** Wireless Zone franchisee Jonah Engler says he manages the business by hiring managers that could do the job. He has given his employees small equity ownership in the company. He also says great service and referrals have contributed to his business' growth.

23344 ■ Profits Aren't Everything. They're the Only Thing: No-Nonsense Rules from the Ultimate Contrarian and Small Business Guru

Pub: HarperCollins Publishers

Ed: George Cloutier. **Released:** September 9, 2010. **Price:** $24.99. **Description:** In difficult economic times, the only way for small businesses to survive is to maximize profits. Thirteen steps to maximize profits in a slow economy are outlined.

23345 ■ "Project Could Forge Path to Jobs, Growth" in Business Courier (Vol. 26, September 11, 2009, No. 20, pp. 1)

Pub: American City Business Journals, Inc.

Ed: Lucy May. **Description:** The planned 13.5 mile Mill Creek Greenway Trail extension could create 445 jobs and bring $52 million to the economy of Cincinnati, Ohio. The trail extension would cost $24 million and would be used for recreational purposes.

23346 ■ "PRWT Service Acquires Pharmaceutical Plant: Firm Wins Multimillion-Dollar Contract with Merck" in Black Enterprise (March 2008)

Pub: Earl G. Graves Publishing Co. Inc.

Ed: Tamara E. Holmes. **Description:** PRWT Services Inc. expanded through its acquisition of a chemical manufacturing plant in New Jersey. The Whitehouse Station, part of Merck & Co. Inc. produces active pharmaceutical ingredients for antibiotics, making PRWT the first minority-owned company in the U.S. to manufacture active pharmaceutical ingredients.

23347 ■ "Public Media Works to Launch DVD Kiosk Operations in Toronto, Canada" in Internet Wire (November 15, 2010)

Pub: Comtex

Description: Public Media Works Inc. along with its EntertainmentXpress Inc., have partnered with Spot Venture Distribution Inc. and Signifi Solutions Inc., both headquartered in Toronto, Canada, to manage and expand the Spot DVD movie and game kiosk business in greater Toronto and other Canadian locations.

23348 ■ "Public Opinion" in Entrepreneur (Vol. 36, April 2008, No. 4, pp. 28)

Pub: Entrepreneur Media, Inc.

Ed: Aliza Sherman. **Description:** According to a 2007 report from Group and Organization Management, women in top positions can lead publicly traded companies to stock price and earnings growth. Some women business owners say that going public has provided them with the capital to grow. Details on the potential of women-managed publicly traded companies are discussed.

23349 ■ "Pumping in Africa" in Canadian Business (Vol. 79, October 23, 2006, No. 21, pp. 162)

Pub: Rogers Media

Ed: Jeff Sanford. **Description:** EastCoast Energy Corp.'s business venture of opening a natural gas company based in Tanzania and marketing of natural gas to expanding markets in East Africa is discussed.

23350 ■ "Putting 'Extra' in Extra-Silky Shampoo" in Crain's Chicago Business (Vol. 31, April 28, 2008, No. 17, pp. 37)

Pub: Crain Communications, Inc.

Ed: Phuong Ly. **Description:** Profile of HallStar Co., a Chicago-based company which develops and manufactures specialty chemicals to upgrade existing products such as hair dye, lotion and deodorant. HallStar has seen its annual earnings rise more than 30 percent since 2002.

23351 ■ "Putting 'Great' Back Into A&P" in Crain's New York Business (Vol. 24, January 7, 2008, No. 1, pp. 3)

Pub: Crain Communications, Inc.

Description: After five straight years ending in 2005, A&P Grocery lost revenue; due to a sweeping plan to freshen up its supermarkets the company returned to growth mode and was able to acquire longtime competitor Pathmark Stores.

23352 ■ "Putting the Service-Profit Chain to Work" in Harvard Business Review (Vol. 86, July-August 2008, No. 8, pp. 118)

Pub: Harvard Business School Press

Ed: James L. Heskett; Thomas O. Jones; Gary W. Loveman; W. Earl Sasser Jr.; Leonard A. Schlesinger. **Description:** Advice is given on how to foster profitability in service businesses. Topics include the link between employee satisfaction and customer satisfaction, internal service quality, external service value, and revenue growth.

23353 ■ "The Puzzle of Our Productivity" in Canadian Business (Vol. 83, September 14, 2010, No. 15, pp. 22)

Pub: Rogers Media Ltd.

Ed: Rachel Madison. **Description:** Industry Canada economist Annette Ryan revealed in a presentation to the Canadian Association for Business Economics that growth in Canadian labor productivity has steadily declined since the 1980s. Ryan believes that business decisions have played an important role in the poor productivity results. Other details of the findings are presented.

23354 ■ "Qualcomm Could Win Big as the IPhone 3G Calls" in Barron's (Vol. 88, July 4, 2008, No. 28, pp. 30)

Pub: Dow Jones & Co., Inc.

Ed: Eric J. Savitz. **Description:** Apple iPhone 3G's introduction could widen the smartphone market thereby benefiting handset chipmaker Qualcomm in the process. Qualcomm Senior V.P., Bill Davidson sees huge potential for his company's future beyond phones with their Snapdragon processor. The prospects of Sun Microsystems' shares are also discussed.

23355 ■ "Quantivo Empowers Online Media Companies to Immediately Expand Audiences and Grow Online Profits" in Internet Wire (Nov. 18, 2009)

Pub: Comtex News Network, Inc.

Description: Quantivo, the leader in on-demand Behavioral Analytics, has launched a new solution that includes 22 of the most critical Internet audience behavior insights as out-of-the-box reports; Internet marketers need to understand their audience, what they want and how often to offer it to them in order to gain successful branding and campaigns online.

23356 ■ *Raising Capital*
Pub: Kiplinger Books and Tapes
Ed: Andrew J. Sherman. Price: $34.95. Description: Corporate attorney provides a comprehensive guide using in-depth, practical advice on raising money to start and grow a business. A 115-page appendix contains samples of financing agreements, forms and questionnaires.

23357 ■ *"R&R Ice Cream" in Ice Cream Reporter (Vol. 23, November 20, 2010, No. 12, pp. 8)*
Pub: Ice Cream Reporter
Description: R&R Ice Cream, the United Kingdom's largest ice cream manufacturer, has completed a private offering of senior secured notes that has raised 298 million (pounds sterling) to fund expansion and acquisitions.

23358 ■ *"R&R Launches Upscale Spoony's and Low Fat Dragon's Den" in Ice Cream Reporter (Vol. 23, August 20, 2010, No. 9, pp. 3)*
Pub: Ice Cream Reporter
Description: European ice cream manufacturer R&R has acquired French ice cream maker Rolland and will position itself as an upscale challenger to brands like Ben & Jerry's.

23359 ■ *"The RBC Dynasty Continues" in Globe & Mail (January 30, 2006, pp. B1)*
Pub: CTVglobemedia Publishing Inc.
Ed: Gordon Pitts. Description: The details on business growth of Royal Bank of Canada, under chief executive officer Gordon Nixon, are presented.

23360 ■ *"RBC's Hot Foreign Operations Contribute to Record Profit" in Globe & Mail (March 3, 2007, pp. B3)*
Pub: CTVglobemedia Publishing Inc.
Ed: Andrew Willis. Description: Royal Bank of Canada posted 27.6 percent growth in the final quarter of 2006. The bank posted $1.49 billion in profits.

23361 ■ *"Ready To Take Your Business Global?" in Black Enterprise (Vol. 41, August 2010, No. 1, pp. 89)*
Pub: Earl G. Graves Publishing Co. Inc.
Ed: Alan Hughes. Description: The 2010 Black Enterprise Entrepreneurs Conference held in May stressed the need for all small firms to promote a global agenda in order to stay competitive.

23362 ■ *"Real Estate Wheeling and Dealing Picks Up" in Business Journal Portland (Vol. 27, October 29, 2010, No. 35, pp. 1)*
Pub: Portland Business Journal
Ed: Wendy Culverwell. Description: LoopNet has listed 33 prominent commercial properties for sale in Portland, Oregon's real estate market. However, reasons for the sales rush are not totally clear, but speculations point to the end of the Bush tax cuts in 2010 that prompted real estate investors to close the deals and avoid the increase in capital gains taxes.

23363 ■ *"Recent Deals Signal an M&A Resurgence" in Austin Business JournalInc. (Vol. 29, January 22, 2010, No. 46, pp. 1)*
Pub: American City Business Journals
Ed: Jacob Dirr. Description: The acquisition of at least six Austin, Texas technology companies reflects the growing acquisition activity in the US. Corporations have bought 86 companies and spent $7.3 billion during the fourth quarter of 2009. Insights into the impact of the acquisition activity to Austin's entrepreneurial energy are also given.

23364 ■ *"Red Mango Set to Grow in Florida" in Ice Cream Reporter (Vol. 23, September 20, 2010, No. 10, pp. 2)*
Pub: Ice Cream Reporter
Description: Red Mango will add 12 new locations throughout Florida. The stores offer healthy, nutritious frozen yogurt, smoothies and parfaits.

23365 ■ *"Rediscovering the Land of Opportunity" in Green Industry Pro (July 2011)*
Pub: Cygnus Business Media
Ed: Gregg Wartgow. Description: Landscape contractors need to discover new strategies that will generate leads and convert those leads into sales.

23366 ■ *"Remodeled Stores Help Fabric Retailer Stitch Up Profit Growth" in Investor's Business Daily (January 7, 2010, pp. A06)*
Pub: Investor's Business Daily
Ed: Marilyn Much. Description: Overview of the successful plan implemented by Darrell Webb for Jo-Ann Fabric and Craft stores to stimulate growth and generate revenue; changes include better inventory controls and remodeling; statistical data included.

23367 ■ *"A Renewal in Rentals" in Barron's (Vol. 88, March 17, 2008, No. 11, pp. 17)*
Pub: Dow Jones & Company, Inc.
Description: Discusses the projected entry of the estimated 82 million echo-boomers into the rentals market and the influx of immigrants and displaced homeowners which could turn apartments into lucrative investments again. While apartment-building completions rose slowly since 2003, demand is expected to increase steeply until 2015.

23368 ■ *"Renewed Vision" in Hawaii Business (Vol. 54, August 2008, No. 2, pp. 49)*
Pub: Hawaii Business Publishing
Ed: Jason Ubay. Description: Saint Francis Healthcare System of Hawaii, ranked 81 in Hawaii's top 250 companies for 2008, has been rebranding to focus on senior community healthcare and sold some of its operations, which explains the decline in gross sales from $219.5M in 2006 to $122.7M in 2007. The system's senior services and home hospice service expansion are provided.

23369 ■ *Renovate Before You Innovate: Why Doing the New Thing Might Not Be the Right Thing*
Pub: Portfolio Publishing
Ed: Sergio Zyman, with Armin A Brott. Released: Octobr 4, 2004. Description: The author uses his experience as the manager behind the introduction to the New Coke as an example of a lazy business growth strategy. He offers insight into successful growth strategies for any small business owner.

23370 ■ *"Rental Demand Boosts Revenue for Sun Communities Inc." in Crain's Detroit Business (Vol. 24, March 24, 2008, No. 12, pp. 4)*
Pub: Crain Communications, Inc.
Ed: Daniel Duggan. Description: Despite the decline in sales of manufactured homes, demand for rental units and rent-to-own programs have brought Sun Communities Inc. increased revenue. The real estate investment trust, based in Southfield, owns, operates, finances and develops manufactured home communities in the Midwest and Southeast. Statistical data included.

23371 ■ *"Reply! Grows at Unprecedented Rate, Rips Beta Off Its Marketplace" in Marketing Weekly News (September 19, 2009, pp. 149)*
Pub: Investment Weekly News
Description: Profile of Reply.com, a leader in locally-targeted Internet marketing, announced significant growth in terms of revenue, enhanced features and services and new categories since launching its beta Reply! Marketplace platform. Even in the face of an economic downturn, the company has posted over 50 percent revenue growth in the Real Estate and Automotive categories.

23372 ■ *"Retail in Austin Strong, Will Continue to Be" in Austin Business JournalInc. (Vol. 29, January 22, 2010, No. 46, pp. 1)*
Pub: American City Business Journals
Ed: Jacob Dirr. Description: Retail sector in Austin, Texas has outpaced the national average in value, mid-tier, high-end and drugs retail sectors, according to a report by Pitney Bowes. The national consulting

firm's report has projected growth in every sector until the end of fiscal 2012. Data regarding other sectors is also included.

23373 ■ *"Retail Franchises to Start Now" in Entrepreneur (Vol. 37, August 2009, No. 8, pp. 88)*
Pub: Entrepreneur Media, Inc.
Ed: Tracy Stapp. Description: Listing of retail franchises is presented and is categorized based on their products sold. The total cost of the franchise and the website are also included as well as additional statistical data.

23374 ■ *"Retail Slump Deflates Local Development" in Business Courier (Vol. 24, February 29, 2008, No. 47, pp. 1)*
Pub: American City Business Journals, Inc.
Ed: Lisa Biank Fasig. Description: 2007 sales of the retail industry are the slowest since the year 2003, driving retail stores to reconsider their expansion plans for 2008. A number of retail projects have been delayed, cancelled or altered, including Newport Pavilion, Rivers Crossing, Wal-Mart Supercenters, Legacy Place and Millworks. The impacts of retail slowdown on development projects are analyzed further.

23375 ■ *"Ric Elis/Dan Feldstein" in Charlotte Business Journal (Vol. 25, December 31, 2010, No. 41, pp. 6)*
Pub: Charlotte Business Journal
Ed: Ken Elkins. Description: Charlotte, North Carolina-based Internet marketing firm Red Ventures has grown significantly. General Atlantic has purchased stakes in Red Ventures.

23376 ■ *Riches in Niches: How to Make It Big in a Small Market*
Pub: Career Press, Inc.
Ed: Susan Friedmann. Released: May 10, 2007. Price: $21.99. Description: The multiple factors that separate the experts from the service professionals who may actually have betters skills, but are never heard about, are discussed. The seven secrets every entrepreneur should know are listed.

23377 ■ *"Riding High" in Small Business Opportunities (November 2008)*
Pub: Entrepreneur Press
Contact: Perlman Neil, President
Ed: Stan Roberts. Description: Profile of David Sanborn who found a way to turn his passion for biking into a moneymaking opportunity by opening his own bicycle shops; Sanborn's goal is to become the largest independent bike retailer in the United States.

23378 ■ *"Right From the Start" in Small Business Opportunities (July 2010)*
Pub: Harris Publications Inc.
Ed: Ed Krug. Description: Ed Krug from Pitch Blue provides sales support services by partnering with small and mid-sized companies to set and reach new revenue targets.

23379 ■ *"RIM's Test of Faith" in Canadian Business (Vol. 80, April 9, 2007, No. 8, pp. 29)*
Pub: Rogers Media
Ed: Joe Castaldo. Description: The growth of Research In Motion Ltd. in terms of its sales and profits despite a patent suit on it and competition of rivals is discussed.

23380 ■ *"Rise in Occupancy Rate Fuels Area Hotel Building Boom" in Crain's Detroit Business (Vol. 24, March 10, 2008, No. 10, pp. 14)*
Pub: Crain Communications, Inc.
Ed: Jonathan Eppley. Description: Due to a rise in the region's yearly occupancy rate, a number of new hotel construction and renovation projects are slated for the Detroit area.

23381 ■ *"Rising in the East; Research and Development" in The Economist (Vol. 390, January 3, 2009, No. 8612, pp. 47)*
Pub: The Economist Newspaper Inc.
Description: Impressive growth of the technological research and development in Asian countries is discussed. Statistical data included.

23382 ■ *Risk Takers and Innovators, Great Canadian Business Ventures Since 1950*
Pub: Altitude Publishing
Ed: Sandra Phinney. **Released:** June 15, 2004. **Price:** $7.95. **Description:** Successful business leaders share their creativity, technology skills, and entrepreneurship.

23383 ■ *"The Road Map for Scotiabank's Asian Expansion" in Globe & Mail (April 7, 2007, pp. B3)*
Pub: CTVglobemedia Publishing Inc.
Ed: Tara Perkins. **Description:** Executive vice-president of Bank of Nova Scotia, Rob Pitfield shares his plan to expand the bank's Asian market.

23384 ■ *"Roger Rechler Played Major Role in Long Island's Evolution" in Commercial Property News (March 17, 2008)*
Pub: Nielsen Company
Description: Profile of Roger Rechler, real estate developer on Long Island, New York, is presented. Rechler, who died in March 2008, was instrumental in the development, ownership and operations of the largest commercial real estate portfolio on Long Island.

23385 ■ *"The Role of Human and Financial Capital in the Profitability and Growth of Women-Owned Small Firms" in Journal of Small Business Management*
Pub: Blackwell Publishing Inc.
Contact: Gordon Tibbitts, President
Ed: Susan Coleman. **Description:** Examines the relationship between the human and financial capital in both men and women-owned businesses and firm performance in the service and retail sectors.

23386 ■ *"Roseville Ob-Gyn Group Grows With Patient Focus, Diverse Services" in Crain's Detroit Business (Vol. 24, April 7, 2008, No. 14)*
Pub: Crain Communications, Inc.
Ed: Christine Snyder. **Description:** According to the American Medical Association, the number of medical groups of 10 or more physicians has been growing. Eastside Gynecology Obstetrics is one such group which has seen its yearly revenue grow due to a good business plan and a diversity of services and doctors.

23387 ■ *"Roundy' Pushing Chicago Expansion" in Milwaukee Business Journal (Vol. 27, February 12, 2010, No. 20, pp. A1)*
Pub: American City Business Journals
Ed: Rich Kirchen. **Description:** Roundy Supermarkets Inc. is expanding in Chicago, Illinois as the Milwaukee-based company is set to open one store in downtown Chicago and another in the Arlington suburb. The store openings have been pushed back to spring and early summer in 2010 due to the economic downturn.

23388 ■ *"Rule of the Masses: Reinventing Fashion Via Crowdsourcing" in WWD (Vol. 200, July 26, 2010, No. 17, pp. 1)*
Pub: Conde Nast Publications
Contact: David Carey, President
Ed: Cate T. Corcoran. **Description:** Large apparel brands and retailers are crowdsourcing as a way to increase customer loyalty and to build their businesses.

23389 ■ *"S2C Global Installs Its First Mass Production Aquaduct Unit in North America" in Canadian Corporate News (May 16, 2007)*
Pub: Comtex News Network Inc.
Description: S2C Global Systems, a leader of distributing 5-gallon bottled water units to the consumer, has announced the installation of its first mass production Aquaduct in Surrey, British Columbia.

23390 ■ *"Sabathia Deal Makes Dollars and Sense" in The Business Journal-Milwaukee (Vol. 25, July 11, 2008, No. 42, pp. A1)*
Pub: American City Business Journals, Inc.
Ed: Mark Kass. **Description:** It was reported that the Milwaukee Brewers' acquisition of CC Sabathia will mean that the team will pick up an estimated $5 mil-

lion in salary that Sabathia is owed for the remainder of the season. Because of this, the team will not make a profit in 2008. The acquisition of Sabathia is expected to cause an increase in attendance and merchandise revenue over the remainder of the season.

23391 ■ *"Salad Creations To Open 2nd Location" in Crain's Detroit Business (Vol. 24, March 3, 2008, No. 9, pp. 26)*
Pub: Crain Communications Inc. - Detroit
Ed: Brent Snavely. **Description:** Salad Creations, a franchise restaurant that allows customers to create their own salads and also offers soups and sandwiches; Salad Creations plans to open a total of five locations by the end of 2008.

23392 ■ *"Sales Gave W&S Record '07" in Business Courier (Vol. 24, March 14, 2008, No. 49, pp. 1)*
Pub: American City Business Journals, Inc.
Ed: Jon Newberry. **Description:** Western & Southern Financial Group was able to achieve a record $365 million in net income thanks in large part to the double-digit increases in profits by its W&S Agency Group field offices and non-insurance businesses. The sale of their Integrated Investment Services Subsidiary and shares in several Marriot hotels also added to the record profit.

23393 ■ *Salesforce.com Secrets of Success: Best Practices for Growth and Profitability*
Pub: Prentice Hall Business Publishing
Contact: Jerome Grant, President
Ed: David Taber. **Released:** May 15, 2009. **Price:** $34.99. **Description:** Guide for using Salesforce. com; it provides insight into navigating through user groups, management, sales, marketing and IT departments in order to achieve the best results.

23394 ■ *"Samsung's Metamorphosis" in Austin Business Journal (Vol. 31, May 20, 2011, No. 11, pp. 1)*
Pub: American City Business Journals Inc.
Ed: Christopher Calnan. **Description:** Samsung Austin Semiconductor LP, a developer of semiconductors for smartphones and tablet computers, plans to diversify its offerings to include niche products: flash memory devices and microprocessing devices. In light of this strategy, Samsung Austin will be hiring 300 engineers as part of a $3.6 billion expansion of its plant.

23395 ■ *"Saratoga Eagle Project Quenches Thirst To Grow" in Business Review, Albany New York (Vol. 34, November 30, 2007, No. 35, pp. 3)*
Pub: American City Business Journals, Inc.
Ed: Robin K. Cooper. **Description:** Saratoga Eagle Sales and Service will be searching for contractors for the construction of its new beverage distribution center at the WJ Grande Industrial Park in Saratoga Springs, New York. The $8 million, 107,000 square foot facility is part of Saratoga Eagle's expansion plan. The company's growth in the Capital Region market and $1.3 million tax break are discussed.

23396 ■ *"Saudi Overtures" in The Business Journal-Portland (Vol. 25, August 15, 2008, No. 23, pp. 1)*
Pub: American City Business Journals, Inc.
Ed: Aliza Earnshaw. **Description:** Saudi Arabia's huge revenue from oil is creating opportunities for Oregon companies as the country develops new cities, industrial zones, and tourism centers. Oregon exported only $46.8 million worth of goods to Saudi Arabia in 2007 but the kingdom is interested in green building materials and methods, renewable energy and water quality control, and nanotechnology all of which Oregon has expertise in.

23397 ■ *"Scotiabank Targets More Baby Boomers" in Globe & Mail (March 4, 2006, pp. B5)*
Pub: CTVglobemedia Publishing Inc.
Ed: Elizabeth Church. **Description:** Bank of Nova Scotia posted $844 million profit for first quarter 2006. The plans of the bank to achieve baby boomer client base are presented.

23398 ■ *"Scripps' Dinner Bell" in Business Courier (Vol. 24, October 19, 2008, No. 27, pp. 1)*
Pub: American City Business Journals, Inc.
Ed: Dan Monk. **Description:** Discusses the split of E.W. Scripps Co.'s Food Network into a separate publicly traded company Scripps Networks Interactive could produce expansion into Asia and Europe.

23399 ■ *"Sean Durfy" in Canadian Business (Vol. 80, April 23, 2007, No. 9, pp. 14)*
Pub: Rogers Media
Ed: Michelle Magnan. **Description:** Sean Durfy, president of WestJet Airlines Ltd., feels that marketing is essential factor for growth of airline industry.

23400 ■ *"Sears' Profit Result Puts Ball in Parent's Court" in Globe & Mail (February 3, 2006, pp. B4)*
Pub: CTVglobemedia Publishing Inc.
Ed: Marina Strauss. **Description:** Sears Canada Inc. achieved $783.4 million in profits for fourth quarter 2005. The financial performance of the company paves way for the acquisition of Sears Holdings Corp.

23401 ■ *"Second to None" in Crain's Detroit Business (Vol. 26, January 18, 2010, No. 3, pp. 9)*
Pub: Crain Communications Inc.
Ed: Nancy Kaffer. **Description:** Second-stage companies are beginning to attract more attention from government entities and the business community alike, due in part to their ability to create jobs more rapidly than their counterparts both smaller and larger. Second-stage companies have between 10-99 employees and consistently have supplied the most jobs, despite overall job declines in recent years.

23402 ■ *"Secret Ingredient" in Entrepreneur (Vol. 35, November 2007, No. 11, pp. 172)*
Pub: Entrepreneur Media Inc.
Ed: Sara Wilson. **Description:** Ojon Corporation in Burlington, Ontario, Canada has developed a natural hair- and skin-care line from ojon oil. The oil, which has very good restorative effects on hair, is extracted from nuts found in ojon trees in the rainforests of Honduras. Details on how Ojon Corporation started and its growing venture in the market are outlined.

23403 ■ *"Secrets To Trade Show Success" in Women Entrepreneur (September 12, 2008)*
Pub: Entrepreneur Media Inc.
Ed: Lesley Spencer Pyle. **Description:** Trade shows require an enormous amount of work, but they are an investment that can pay off handsomely because they allow a business to get their product or service in front of their target market. Advice regarding trade shows is given including selecting the correct venue, researching the affair and following up on leads obtained at the event.

23404 ■ *"Sedo Keeps Trucking in Good Times and Bad" in Crain's Chicago Business (Vol. 31, April 28, 2008, No. 17, pp. 35)*
Pub: Crain Communications, Inc.
Ed: Samantha Stainburn. **Description:** Discusses Seko Worldwide Inc., an Itasca-based freight forwarder, and its complicated road to growth and expansion on a global scale.

23405 ■ *"SEEing an Opportunity; Golden's Eyewear Chain Has a National Vision" in Crain's Detroit Business (Vol. 24, January 7, 2008, No. 1)*
Pub: Crain Communications Inc. - Detroit
Ed: Sheena Harrison. **Description:** Richard Golden, who recently sold D.O.C. Optics Corporation is planning to build a new national eyewear chain called SEE Inc., which stands for Selective Eyewear Elements. SEE will sell expensive-looking glasses at lower prices than designer styles.

23406 ■ *"Seeking Local SBA Loan?" in Business Courier (Vol. 26, October 16, 2009, No. 25, pp. 1)*
Pub: American City Business Journals, Inc.
Ed: Steve Watkins. **Description:** The largest banks in Greater Cincinnati reduced Small Business Administration (SBA) lending by 41 percent for the fiscal

year ended September 2009. For the year, local SBA loans from all banks in the area declined 25 percent. The importance of SBA loans for growth of small business is examined.

23407 ■ *"Sense of Discovery"* in Business Journal Portland (Vol. 27, November 19, 2010, No. 38, pp. 1)
Pub: Portland Business Journal
Ed: Erik Siemers. **Description:** Tigard, Oregon-based Exterro Inc. CEO Bobby Balachandran announced plans to go public without the help of an institutional investor. Balachandran believes Exterro could grow to a $100 million legal compliance software company in the span of three years. Insights on Exterro's growth as market leader in the $1 billion legal governance software market are also given.

23408 ■ *"Seton Grows Heart Institute"* in Austin Business Journal (Vol. 31, July 15, 2011, No. 19, pp. A1)
Pub: American City Business Journals Inc.
Ed: Sandra Zaragoza. **Description:** Seton Heart Institute experienced significant growth in the last six months. The organization added physicians, specialists and outreach offices across Central Texas.

23409 ■ *"A Shallow Pool"* in Canadian Business (Vol. 81, Summer 2008, No. 9, pp. 44)
Pub: Rogers Media Ltd.
Ed: Joe Castaldo. **Description:** Bank of Canada projected in its 'Monetary Policy Report' a growth rate of 1.4 percent in 2008 and does not expect the economy to fully recover until mid-2010. The Canadian stock market has been recovering although slowly with just a 1.6 percent gain by April 30. Other details on the Canadian equity market are presented.

23410 ■ *"Shear Profit"* in Crain's Cleveland Business (Vol. 28, October 29, 2007, No. 43, pp. 3)
Pub: Crain Communications, Inc.
Ed: David Bennett. **Description:** Alpaca farms are becoming a very profitable business for a number of Northeast Ohio entrepreneurs due to the high return on initial investments, tax incentives and the rise in demand for the animals. Ohio leads the country in the number of alpaca farms with roughly one-third located in Northeast Ohio.

23411 ■ *"Shell Profit Top $2 Billion as Oil Sands Output Surges"* in Globe & Mail (January 26, 2006, pp. B6)
Pub: CTVglobemedia Publishing Inc.
Ed: Patrick Brethour. **Description:** The reasons behind posting of $2 billion profits for 2005, by Shell Canada Ltd. are presented.

23412 ■ *"Shoestring-Budget Marketing"* in Women Entrepreneur (January 5, 2009)
Pub: Entrepreneur Media Inc.
Ed: Maria Falconer. **Description:** Pay-per-click search engine advertising is the traditional type of e-marketing that may not only be too expensive for certain kinds of businesses but also may not attract the quality customer base a business looking to grow needs to find. Social networking websites have become a mandatory marketing tool for business owners who want to see growth in their sales; tips are provided for utilizing these networking websites in order to gain more visibility on the Internet which can, in turn, lead to the more sales.

23413 ■ *"Shopped Out; Retailing Gloom"* in The Economist (Vol. 390, January 3, 2009, No. 8612, pp. 26)
Pub: The Economist Newspaper Inc.
Description: Economic volatility in the retail sector is having an impact on a number of countries around the globe. Europe is experiencing hard economic times as well and unless businesses have a strong business plan banks feel unable to lend the money necessary to tide the retailers over. The falling pound has increased the cost of imported goods and small to midsize retail chains may not be able to weather such an unforgiving economic climate.

23414 ■ *"Should You Invest in the Long Tail?"* in Harvard Business Review (Vol. 86, July-August 2008, No. 8, pp. 88)
Pub: Harvard Business School Press
Ed: Anita Elberse. **Description:** Relevance of the long tail, or the sustainability of sales after a given product's launch is examined. It is posited that niche sales are not as sustainable as those for products with broader appeal.

23415 ■ *"Show Me the Love"* in Canadian Business (Vol. 79, November 6, 2006, No. 22, pp. 77)
Pub: Rogers Media
Ed: Jeannette Hanna. **Description:** The strategies to improve brand image with relation to success of Tim Horton's brand are presented.

23416 ■ *"Sign Up To Grow Your Business, Generate Jobs"* in Women Entrepreneur (November 25, 2008)
Pub: Entrepreneur Media Inc.
Ed: Eve Gumpel. **Description:** Nell Merlino has announced the new Make Mine A Million-Dollar Race, which aims to encourage hundreds of thousands of women entrepreneurs to grow their business to revenue goals of $250,00, $500,000 or $1 million and more as well as create 800,000 new jobs in an attempt to stimulate the nation's economy.

23417 ■ *"The Silvery Moon Moves to Larger Space"* in Bellingham Business Journal (Vol. March 2010, pp. 5)
Pub: Sound Publishing Inc.
Description: Jewelry store, the Silvery Moon, moved to a larger location in order to expand its business. The new location was chosen because it offers the firm more visibility. The store offers find silver and gold pieces and specializes in Pacific Northwest native jewelry.

23418 ■ *"Six Leading Economists on What to Expect in the Year Ahead: Glen Hodgson; Canada in Depth"* in Canadian Business (December 24, 2007)
Pub: Rogers Media
Ed: Glen Hodgson. **Description:** Western Canada is expected to have the best economic performance for 2008 among all of the country's regions with a growth rate of 3.6 percent for Alberta and three percent for British Columbia. Details on the country's growth in real income, trends in the labor market, and the effect of Canadian dollar's parity with the U.S. dollar on exports are discussed.

23419 ■ *"Six Leading Economists on What to Expect in the Year Ahead: Peter Buchanan"* in Canadian Business (December 24, 2007)
Pub: Rogers Media
Ed: Peter Buchanan. **Description:** The world economy is expected to grow by five percent in 2008, which is below the pace of the previous two years. Details on the U.S. credit crunch, the U.S. dollar's depreciation, and the economic expansion of developing economies are discussed.

23420 ■ *"Size Matters"* in Entrepreneur (Vol. 36, April 2008, No. 4, pp. 44)
Pub: Entrepreneur Media, Inc.
Ed: Robert Kiyosaki. **Description:** Entrepreneurs planning to expand their business face challenges when it comes to employing more people and addressing internal relationships, communications and procedures. People skills, organizational skills and leadership skills are some of the things to consider before adding employees.

23421 ■ *"Skinner's No Drive-Thru CEO"* in Crain's Chicago Business (Vol. 31, April 28, 2008, No. 17, pp. 1)
Pub: Crain Communications, Inc.
Ed: David Sterrett. **Description:** Profile of James Skinner who was named CEO for McDonald's Corp. in November 2004 and has proved to be a successful leader despite the number of investors who doubted him when he came to the position. Mr. Skinner has overseen three years of unprecedented sales growth and launched the biggest menu expansion in 30 years.

23422 ■ *"The Skype's the Limit"* in Canadian Business (Vol. 80, February 12, 2007, No. 4, pp. 70)
Pub: Rogers Media
Ed: Gerry Blackwell. **Description:** The increase in the market share of Skype Technologies S.A.'s Internet phone service to 171 million users is discussed.

23423 ■ *"The Small 300"* in Canadian Business (Vol. 81, Summer 2008, No. 9, pp. 137)
Pub: Rogers Media Ltd.
Description: Small cap-companies are ranked based on market capitalization and stock performance. Calgary-based Grande Cache Coal Corp. topped the roster with 1,000 percent of return resulting from strong sales. A table showing the 2008 rankings of the companies is presented.

23424 ■ *"Small Business Capital Outlays"* in Small Business Economic Trends (April 2008, pp. 16)
Pub: National Federation of Independent Business
Ed: William C. Dunkelberg, Holly Wade. **Description:** Graphs and tables that present the capital outlays of small businesses in the U.S. are provided. The tables include figures on planned and actual capital expenditures, and type and amount of capital expenditures.

23425 ■ *"Small Business Capital Outlays"* in Small Business Economic Trends (March 2008, pp. 16)
Pub: National Federation of Independent Business
Ed: William C. Dunkelberg, Holly Wade. **Description:** Graphs and tables that present the capital outlays of small businesses in the U.S. are provided. The tables include figures on planned and actual capital expenditures, and type and amount of capital expenditures.

23426 ■ *"Small Business Capital Outlays"* in Small Business Economic Trends (February 2008, pp. 16)
Pub: National Federation of Independent Business
Ed: William C. Dunkelberg, Holly Wade. **Description:** Graphs and tables that present the capital outlays of small businesses in the U.S. are provided. The tables include figures on planned and actual capital expenditures, and type and amount of capital expenditures.

23427 ■ *"Small Business Capital Outlays"* in Small Business Economic Trends (January 2008, pp. 16)
Pub: National Federation of Independent Business
Description: Graph representing actual and planned capital expenditures among small businesses surveyed in the U.S. from January 1986 to December 2007 is given. Tables showing actual capital expenditures, type of capital expenditures made, amount of capital expenditures made, and capital expenditure plans are also presented.

23428 ■ *Small Business Cash Flow: Strategies for Making Your Business a Financial Success*
Pub: John Wiley & Sons, Incorporated
Ed: Denise O'Berry. **Released:** October 2006. **Price:** $19.95. **Description:** Tips to help small businesses manage money are given.

23429 ■ *Small Business for Dummies, 3rd Ed.*
Pub: John Wiley and Sons, Inc.
Ed: Eric Tyson; Jim Schell. **Released:** March 2008. **Price:** $21.99. **Description:** Guidebook for anyone wanting to start or grow a small business; topics include information financing, budgeting, marketing, management and more.

23430 ■ *"Small Business Earnings"* in Small Business Economic Trends (April 2008, pp. 6)
Pub: National Federation of Independent Business
Ed: William C. Dunkelberg, Holly Wade. **Description:** Two tables and a graph presenting the earnings of small businesses in the U.S. are provided. Statistics for actual earnings changes are provided. The figures in the graph include data from 1986 to 2008.

23431 ■ "Small Business Earnings" in Small Business Economic Trends (March 2008, pp. 6)
Pub: National Federation of Independent Business
Ed: William C. Dunkelberg, Holly Wade. Description: Two tables and a graph representing the earnings of small businesses in the U.S. are presented. Statistics for actual earnings changes are provided. The figures in the graph include data from 1986 to 2008.

23432 ■ "Small Business Earnings" in Small Business Economic Trends (February 2008, pp. 6)
Pub: National Federation of Independent Business
Ed: William C. Dunkelberg, Holly Wade. Description: Two tables and a graph representing the earnings of small businesses in the U.S. are presented. Statistics for actual earnings changes are provided. The figures in the graph include data from 1974 to 2008.

23433 ■ "Small Business Earnings" in Small Business Economic Trends (January 2008, pp. 6)
Pub: National Federation of Independent Business
Description: Graph from a survey of small businesses in the U.S. is given, representing actual small business earnings from January 1986 to December 2007. Tables showing actual earnings changes and most important reason for lower earnings are also presented.

23434 ■ "Small Business Earnings" in Small Business Economic Trends (September 2010, pp. 6)
Pub: National Federation of Independent Business
Ed: William C. Dunkelberg, Holly Wade. Description: A graph from a survey of small businesses in the U.S. is given, representing actual small business earnings from January 1986 to August 2010. Tables showing actual earnings changes and most important reason for lower earnings are also presented.

23435 ■ "Small Business Earnings" in Small Business Economic Trends (July 2010, pp. 6)
Pub: National Federation of Independent Business
Description: A graph from a survey of small businesses in the U.S. is given representing actual small business earnings from January 1986 to June 2010. Tables showing actual earnings changes and most important reason for lower earnings are also presented.

23436 ■ Small Business: Innovation, Problems and Strategies
Pub: Nova Science Publishers, Inc.
Ed: John E. Michaels, Leonardo F. Piraro. Released: April 1, 2009. Price: $89.00. Description: Innovation is a fundamental determinant of value creation in businesses and can also be a key to successful economic growth. The innovative process and innovative effort of small companies are examined and evaluated, along with alternative strategies.

23437 ■ "Small Business Outlook" in Small Business Economic Trends (April 2008, pp. 4)
Pub: National Federation of Independent Business
Ed: William C. Dunkelberg, Holly Wade. Description: Three tables and a graph presenting forecasts in business expansions of small businesses in the U.S. are presented. The figures presented in the graph include data from 1986 to 2008.

23438 ■ "Small Business Outlook" in Small Business Economic Trends (March 2008, pp. 4)
Pub: National Federation of Independent Business
Ed: William C. Dunkelberg, Holly Wade. Description: Three tables and a graph representing forecasts in business expansions of small businesses in the U.S. are presented. The figures presented in the graph include data from 1986 to 2008.

23439 ■ "Small Business Outlook" in Small Business Economic Trends (February 2008, pp. 4)
Pub: National Federation of Independent Business
Ed: William C. Dunkelberg, Holly Wade. Description: Three tables and a graph representing forecasts

in business expansions of small businesses in the U.S. are presented. The figures presented in the graph include data from 1974 to 2008.

23440 ■ "Small Business Outlook" in Small Business Economic Trends (January 2008, pp. 4)
Pub: National Federation of Independent Business
Description: Graph representing outlook among small businesses surveyed in the U.S. from January 1986 to December 2007 is presented. Tables showing small business outlook for expansion and outlook for general business conditions from January 2002 to December 2007 and the most important reasons for expansion outlook are also given.

23441 ■ "Small Business Outlook" in Small Business Economic Trends (July 2009, pp. 4)
Pub: National Federation of Independent Business
Description: Outlook among small businesses surveyed in the United States from January 1986 to June 2009 is presented. Tables showing small business outlook for expansion and outlook for general business conditions from January 2004 to June 2009 and the most important reasons for expansion outlook are also given.

23442 ■ "Small Business Outlook" in Small Business Economic Trends (September 2010, pp. 4)
Pub: National Federation of Independent Business
Ed: William C. Dunkelberg, Holly Wade. Description: A graph representing outlook among small businesses surveyed in the U.S. from January 1986 to August 2010 is presented. Tables showing small business outlook for expansion and outlook for general business conditions from January 2005 to August 2010, and most important reasons for expansion outlook are also given.

23443 ■ "Small Business Outlook" in Small Business Economic Trends (July 2010, pp. 4)
Pub: National Federation of Independent Business
Description: A graph representing outlook among small businesses surveyed in the U.S. from January 1986 to June 2010. Tables showing small business outlook for expansion and outlook for general business conditions from January 2005 to June 2010, and most important reasons for expansion outlook are also given.

23444 ■ "Small Business Prices" in Small Business Economic Trends (July 2010, pp. 8)
Pub: National Federation of Independent Business
Description: A graph from a survey of small businesses in the U.S. is given representing business prices from January 1986 to June 2010. Actual prices (last three months) and planned prices (next three months) were compared in the graph. Tables of actual price changes and price plans from January 2005 to June 2010 are also supplied.

23445 ■ "Small Business Sales" in Small Business Economic Trends (September 2010, pp. 7)
Pub: National Federation of Independent Business
Ed: William C. Dunkelberg, Holly Wade. Description: A graph from a survey of small businesses in the U.S. is given, representing sales from January 1986 to August 2010. Actual sales (prior three months) and expected sales (next three months) were compared in the graph. Tables of actual sales changes and sales expectations from January 2005 to August 2010 are also given.

23446 ■ "Small Business Sales" in Small Business Economic Trends (July 2010, pp. 7)
Pub: National Federation of Independent Business
Description: A graph from a survey of small businesses in the U.S. is given representing sales from January 1986 to June 2010. Actual sales (prior three months) and expected sales (next three months) were compared in the graph. Tables of actual sales changes and sales expectations from January 2005 to June 2010 are also given.

23447 ■ Small Business Savvy
Pub: Adams Media Corporation
Contact: Gary Krebs, Director
E-mail: swatrous@adamsmedia.com
Ed: Norma J. Rist; Katina Z. Jones. Released: 2002. Description: Advice is given to women wishing to start their own companies using guidance and real-

world examples to help position themselves for future growth. Tips to survive through a bad economic environment, breaking into a market, working with less money, accepting change, and ways to balance success with personal life are explored.

23448 ■ Small Business Sourcebook
Pub: Cengage Gale
Released: July 2009. Price: $578.00. Description: Two-volume guide to more than 27,300 listings of live and print sources for small business startups as well as small business growth and development. Over 30,500 topics are included.

23449 ■ Small Business Turnaround
Pub: Adams Media Corporation
Ed: Marc Kramer. Price: $17.95 paperback.

23450 ■ Small Giants: Companies That Choose to Be Great Instead of Big
Pub: Penguin Group
Ed: Bo Burlingame. Released: March 27, 2007. Price: $16.00. Description: Profiles of privately held companies that have become huge in their field without becoming large corporations.

23451 ■ "Small Wind Power Market to Double by 2015 at $634 Million" in Western Farm Press (September 30, 2011)
Pub: Penton Media, Inc.
Description: Small wind power provides cost-effective electricity on a highly localized level, in both remote settings as well as in conjunction with power from the utility grid. Government incentives are spurring new growth in the industry.

23452 ■ "Smith Fuels BNE Drive to Grow Job Market" in Business First Buffalo (November 2, 2007, pp. 1)
Pub: American City Business Journals, Inc.
Ed: James Fink. Description: David Smith is taking on the role as the new chairman of Buffalo Niagara Enterprise. He aims to market the Buffalo Niagara region to attract new businesses and help existing companies retain workers.

23453 ■ "Solar Credit Lapse Spur Late Demand" in The Business Journal - Serving Phoenix and the Valley of the Sun (Vol. 28, July 18, 2008)
Pub: American City Business Journals, Inc.
Ed: Patrick O'Grady. Description: Businesses looking to engage in the solar energy industry are facing the problems of taxation and limited solar panel supply. Solar panels manufacturers are focusing more on the European market. Political issues surrounding the federal tax credit policy on solar energy users are also discussed.

23454 ■ "Sophia Siskel; CEO, Chicago Botanic Garden" in Crain's Chicago Business (Vol. 31, May 5, 2008, No. 18, pp. 36)
Pub: Crain Communications, Inc.
Ed: John Rosenthal. Description: Profile of Sophia Siskel who is the CEO of the Chicago Botanic Garden and is overseeing the $100 million expansion which will put the Botanic Garden at the forefront of plant conservation science; Ms. Siskel is also an efficient marketer and researcher.

23455 ■ "A Sound Setup" in Black Enterprise (Vol. 38, November 2007, No. 4, pp. 100)
Pub: Earl G. Graves Publishing Co. Inc.
Ed: Anthony Calypso. Description: Choosing the right corporate identity can ensure that a business has the right foundation on which to build and grow.

23456 ■ "The Spark's Back in Sanyo" in Barron's (Vol. 88, March 31, 2008, No. 13, pp. M9)
Pub: Dow Jones & Company, Inc.
Ed: Jay Alabaster. Description: Things are looking up for Sanyo Electric after its string of calamities that range from major losses brought on by earthquake damage to its semiconductor operations and its near collapse and bailout. The company looks poised for a rebound as they are on track for their first net profit since 2003 and could beat its earnings forecast for 2008.

23457 ■ *"Speak Better: Five Tips for Polished Presentations"* in Women Entrepreneur (September 19, 2008)
Pub: Entrepreneur Media Inc.
Ed: Suzannah Baum. **Description:** Successful entrepreneurs agree that exemplary public speaking skills are among the core techniques needed to propel their business forward. A well-delivered presentation can result in securing a new distribution channel, gaining new customers, locking into a new referral stream or receiving extra funding.

23458 ■ *"A Sports Extravaganza - To Go"* in Canadian Business (Vol. 79, June 19, 2006, No. 13, pp. 21)
Pub: Rogers Media
Ed: Andy Holloway. **Description:** Television broadcasting industry in Canada utilizing advanced technologies like mobile television and internet protocol television in broadcasting major sports events. Large number of new technologies are being invented to support increasing demand.

23459 ■ *"Sprint Tries to Wring Out Positives"* in The Business Journal-Serving Metropolitan Kansas City (Vol. 26, August 8, 2008, No. 48)
Pub: American City Business Journals, Inc.
Ed: Suzanna Stagemeyer. **Description:** Sprint Nextel Corp. reported that 901,000 subscribers left the company in the quarter ending June 30, 2008; fewer than the nearly 1.1 million it lost in the previous quarter. Customer turnover also dropped to just less than 2 percent, compared to 2.45 percent in the first quarter of 2008.

23460 ■ *"Staffing Firm Grows by Following Own Advice-Hire a Headhunter"* in Crain's Detroit Business (Vol. 24, October 6, 2008, No. 40, pp. 1)
Pub: Crain Communications, Inc.
Ed: Sherri Begin. **Description:** Profile of Venator Holdings L.L.C., a staffing firm that provides searches for companies in need of financial-accounting and technical employees; the firm's revenue has increased from $1.1 million in 2003 to a projected $11.5 million this year due to a climate in which more people are exiting the workforce than are coming in with those particular specialized skills and the need for a temporary, flexible workforce for contract placements at companies that do not want to take on the legacy costs associated with permanent employees. The hiring of an external headhunter to find the right out-of-state manager for Venator is also discussed.

23461 ■ *"STAR TEC Incubator's Latest Resident Shows Promise"* in The Business Journal-Serving Greater Tampa Bay (August 8, 2008)
Pub: American City Business Journals, Inc.
Ed: Jane Meinhardt. **Description:** Field Forensics Inc., a resident of the STAR Technology Enterprise Center, has grown after being admitted into the business accelerator. The producer of defense and security devices and equipment has doubled 2007 sales as of 2008.

23462 ■ *"Starbucks Drive-Throughs: Can the Cafe Keep Its Cool?"* in Globe & Mail (January 6, 2006, pp. B7)
Pub: CTVglobemedia Publishing Inc.
Ed: Steven Gray. **Description:** The feasibility of Starbucks Corp.'s plans to introduce drive-through cafes is discussed.

23463 ■ *The Starbucks Experience*
Pub: McGraw-Hill
Ed: Joseph A. Michelli. **Released:** September 14, 2006. **Price:** $24.95. **Description:** Boardroom strategies, employee motivation tips, community involvement, and customer satisfaction are issues addressed, using Starbucks as a model.

23464 ■ *The Starbucks Experience: 5 Principles for Turing Ordinary into Extraordinary*
Pub: McGraw-Hill
Ed: Joseph A. Michelli. **Released:** November 2006.

23465 ■ *Start, Run, and Grow a Successful Small Business, 2nd Edition*
Pub: CCH Inc.
Contact: Mike Sabbatis, President
Ed: Susan M. Jacksack. **Price:** $24.95.

23466 ■ *Start Small, Finish Big*
Pub: Warner Business Books
Ed: Fred DeLuca. **Price:** $14.95.

23467 ■ *"State Film Business Tops $1.3 Billion"* in The Business Journal-Portland (Vol. 25, August 22, 2008, No. 24, pp. 1)
Pub: American City Business Journals, Inc.
Ed: Andy Giegerich. **Description:** Oregon's film industry has generated $1.39 billion in direct and indirect economic impact in 2007, a 55 percent rise from 2005 levels. The growth of the industry is attributed to tax incentives issued in 2007, which attracted film production companies from other states.

23468 ■ *"State of Play"* in Canadian Business (Vol. 79, June 19, 2006, No. 13, pp. 25)
Pub: Rogers Media
Ed: Andrew Wahl; Zena Olijnyk; Jeff Sanford. **Description:** Top 100 information technology companies in Canada are ranked by their market capitalization as of June 1. The statistics that show the revenues of these companies are also presented.

23469 ■ *"State Shock Prices Take Large Tumble"* in The Business Journal-Milwaukee (Vol. 25, September 12, 2008, No. 51, pp. A1)
Pub: American City Business Journals, Inc.
Ed: Rich Rovito. **Description:** Weak economic times have caused the stocks of most publicly traded companies in Wisconsin to dip in 2008. Companies that appeared on the worst performing stocks list also experienced drops in share price to as much as 70 percent. Information about the companies that experienced increases in stock prices is also presented. Statistical data included.

23470 ■ *"Steady Spending in Retail"* in Business Week (September 22, 2008, No. 4100, pp. 13)
Pub: McGraw-Hill Companies, Inc.
Ed: Tara Kalwarski. **Description:** Retail jobs have begun to decline on the national level despite the two percent growth in the industry over the last year; much of the growth has been attributed to the sales of higher-priced oil products.

23471 ■ *The Sticking Point Solution: 9 Ways to Move Your Business from Stagnation to Stunning Growth in Tough Economic Times*
Pub: Vanguard Press
Contact: Bill Smith, Director
E-mail: bill.smith@perseusbooks.com
Ed: Jay Abraham. **Released:** May 10, 2010. **Price:** $25.95. **Description:** Renowned business consultant, Jay Abraham, reveals the nine ways even successful businesses get stuck, hit plateaus, and fail to achieve their dreams and he explains how to get unstuck and create exponential growth.

23472 ■ *"Still Looking Good"* in Canadian Business (Vol. 80, March 26, 2007, No. 7, pp. 29)
Pub: Rogers Media
Ed: Andy Holloway. **Description:** The real estate prices in various parts of Canada are analyzed. The future growth potential of the industry is forecasted.

23473 ■ *"Still Stretching"* in Business Courier (Vol. 24, December 28, 2008, No. 37, pp. 1)
Pub: American City Business Journals, Inc.
Ed: Lucy May. **Description:** Minority-owned businesses have experienced growth in 2007 as Cincinnati and Hamilton County used a workforce development and economic inclusion policy. Kroger Co., for example, has been inducted to the Billion Dollar Roundtable in 2007 for attaining $1 billion in annual spending with suppliers that are minority- owned. The need for more progress within the minority-owned enterprises is discussed.

23474 ■ *"Stone Company Slated to Expand Here"* in Austin Business JournalInc. (Vol. 28, September 12, 2008, No. 26, pp. 1)
Pub: American City Business Journals
Ed: Jean Kwon. **Description:** Architectural Granite & Marble Inc. has a $6 million investment that moved the company from 2,500 square feet of space to a 10,000 square foot office in Southwest Austin, Texas. The investment will also provide for the company's expansion in Nashville, Tennessee and San Antonio, Texas.

23475 ■ *"Stop the Innovation Wars"* in Harvard Business Review (Vol. 88, July-August 2010, No. 7-8, pp. 76)
Pub: Harvard Business School Publishing
Ed: Vijay Govindarajan, Chris Trimble. **Description:** Methods for managing conflicts between partners during the innovation initiative process are highlighted. These include dividing the labor, assembling a dedicated team, and mitigating likelihood for any potential conflict.

23476 ■ *Straight Talk About Small Business Success in New Jersey: How to Maximize the Growth, Cash Flow and Profitability of Your Small Business*
Pub: Business Success Systems, Incorporated
Ed: Salim Omar. **Released:** April 2004. **Description:** Small business information geared to new and existing small businesses in New Jersey.

23477 ■ *Strategies for Growth in SMEs: The Role of Information and Information Systems*
Pub: Elsevier Science & Technology Books
Ed: Margi Levy, Philip Powell. **Released:** December 2004. **Price:** $62.95. **Description:** Role of information and information systems in the growth of small and medium-sized enterprises in the U.S.

23478 ■ *Streetwise Small Business Book of Lists: Hundreds of Lists to Help You Reduce Costs, Increase Revenues, and Boost Your Profits!*
Pub: Adams Media Corporation
Contact: Gary Krebs, Director
E-mail: swatrous@adamsmedia.com
Ed: Gene Marks. **Released:** September 2006. **Price:** $25.95. **Description:** Strategies to help small business owners locate services, increase sales, and lower expenses.

23479 ■ *Streetwise Small Business Turnaround: Revitalizing Your Struggling or Stagnant Enterprise*
Pub: Adams Media Corporation
Contact: Gary Krebs, Director
E-mail: swatrous@adamsmedia.com
Ed: Marc Kramer. **Released:** November 1999. **Description:** Practical tips and advice are provided for rejuvenating an existing small business.

23480 ■ *"Substantial Deal Expected to Create Jobs, Help Industrial Market"* in Tampa Bay Business Journal (Vol. 30, January 8, 2010, No. 3)
Pub: American City Business Journals
Ed: Janet Leiser. **Description:** Food distribution firm Gordon Food Service (GFS) is on the brink of purchasing Albertson's million-square-foot warehouse along with 158 acres of space. The deal between GFS and Albertson's could expand GFS' presence in west Central Florida. A history of GFS' growth is included.

23481 ■ *"Success Coach: Dare to Dream"* in Entrepreneur (Vol. 35, October 2007, No. 10, pp. 146)
Pub: Entrepreneur Media Inc.
Ed: Romaus Wolter. **Description:** Business goals that are seemingly impossible to reach can actually be achieved through careful planning. Making the goals clear is the first step toward achievement. Details for setting goals and how to attain them are presented.

23482 ■ *Success Secrets to Maximize Business in Canada*
Pub: Graphic Arts Center Publishing Company
Ed: Ken Coates. **Released:** October 5, 2000. **Description:** Part of the Culture Shock! Series that helps companies maximize business opportunities in Canada.

23483 ■ *A Successful Family Business*
Pub: Penguin Group USA Inc.
Ed: Neil Pahel, Janis Raye. **Released:** August 1, 2009. **Price:** $18.95. **Description:** Guide to running a family business includes information for expanding beyond the original family firm and family versus hired management.

23484 ■ *"SunBank Plans Expansion Via Wall-Mart" in Business Journal-Serving Phoenix and the Valley of the Sun (Vol. 10, November 9, 2007)*
Pub: American City Business Journals, Inc.
Ed: Chris Casacchia. **Description:** SunBank plans to install 12 to 14 branches in Wal-Mart stores in Arizona and hire 100 bankers by the end of 2008. Wal-Mart also offers financial products at other stores through partnerships with other banks.

23485 ■ *"Super Success" in Small Business Opportunities (November 2008)*
Pub: Entrepreneur Press
Contact: Perlman Neil, President
Description: Profile of PromoWorks LLC, a company founded by Michael Kent, that distributes samples of food at grocery stores for clients like Kraft Foods, Inc. and Kellogg Co. and also handles the logistics, provides the employees and tracks the products' sales.

23486 ■ *SuperCorp: How Vanguard Companies Create Innovation, Profits, Growth, and Social Good*
Pub: Crown Business
Ed: Rosabeth Moss Kanter. **Released:** 2009. **Price:** $27.50. **Description:** Harvard professor makes a persuasive case showing how social good is good for any company's bottom line.

23487 ■ *"Suppliers Look to Rack Up Big Sales to Distributors" in The Business Journal-Serving Metropolitan Kansas City (August 15, 2008)*
Pub: American City Business Journals, Inc.
Ed: James Dornbrook. **Description:** Suppliers of shelving units, conveyor systems and other equipment used in distribution facilities are expecting new business opportunities along with the planned intermodal projects in the Kansas City area. Suppliers have already observed that small distributors have started to relocate to the city because of the intermodal projects. Demand for shelves and lifts have also increased.

23488 ■ *"The Sure Thing That Flopped" in Harvard Business Review (Vol. 86, July-August 2008, No. 8, pp. 29)*
Pub: Harvard Business School Press
Ed: Gerald Zaltman; Lindsay Zaltman. **Description:** Fictitious brand extension scenario is presented, with contributors providing suggestions and advice. The company's struggles with expanding the brand may be alleviated by improving consumer research, focusing on emotional responses to products and services.

23489 ■ *"Survey: More Buyers Expect to Spend Less in Most Media" in Advertising Age (Vol. 79, July 7, 2008, No. 26, pp. 3)*
Pub: Crain Communications, Inc.
Ed: Megan McIlroy. **Description:** Marketers are decreasing their budgets for advertising in television, radio, newspaper and outdoor due to the economic downturn. Statistical data concerning advertising agencies and marketers included.

23490 ■ *"The Survey Says" in Collections and Credit Risk (Vol. 14, September 1, 2009, No. 8, pp. 16)*
Pub: SourceMedia, Inc.
Ed: Bill Grabarek; Darren Waggoner. **Description:** Revenue for the top accounts receivable management firms rose nearly 20 percent in 2008 despite

lower liquidation rates, a poor economy and riskier, albeit cheaper debt portfolios; the trend may continue this year as collection agencies expect revenue, on average, to increase 5.8 percent. Debt buyers, however, found that their revenue fell nearly 7 percent in 2008 and expect it to fall another 12 percent this year.

23491 ■ *"Survive the Small-to-Big Transition" in Entrepreneur (November 4, 2008)*
Pub: Entrepreneur Media Inc.
Ed: Elizabeth Wilson. **Description:** Transitioning a small company to a large company can be a challenge, especially during the time when it is too big to be considered small and too small to be considered big. Common pitfalls during this time are discussed as well as techniques business owners should implement when dealing with this transitional period.

23492 ■ *"Susan Leger Ferraro Built a $7.2 Million Day Care Business. Now She Wants To Expand-And Cash Out" in Inc. (January 2008, pp. 50-53)*
Pub: Gruner & Jahr USA Publishing
Ed: Dalia Fahmy. **Description:** Profile of Susan Leger Ferraro who wants to expand her chain of day care centers into Florida and California and sell part of her 87 percent stake to reduce financial risk.

23493 ■ *"Swedes Swoop In To Save Time" in Advertising Age (Vol. 78, January 29, 2007, No. 5, pp. 4)*
Pub: Crain Communications, Inc.
Ed: Nat Ives. **Description:** Overview of Stockholm's Bonnier Group, a family-owned publisher that is looking to expand its U.S. presence; Bonnier recently acquired a number of Time Inc. magazines.

23494 ■ *"Sweet Tea; Neil Golden" in Advertising Age (Vol. 79, November 17, 2008, No. 43, pp. 4)*
Pub: Crain Communications, Inc.
Ed: Emily Bryson York. **Description:** McDonald's launch of iced coffee and sweat tea, which were promoted via price cuts over the summer, helped to boost sales at the fast-food chain.

23495 ■ *"Sykes Group Targets GunnAllen" in The Business Journal-Serving Greater Tampa Bay (Vol. 28, September 5, 2008, No. 37, pp. 1)*
Pub: American City Business Journals, Inc.
Ed: Margie Manning. **Description:** GAH Holdings LLC, a newly formed investment company by John H. Sykes of Sykes Enterprises Inc., will add capital to Tampa Bay Area investment banking firm GunnAllen Holdings Inc. The capital infusion is to aid GunnAllen Holdings in expanding and diversifying as GAH becomes its largest shareholder.

23496 ■ *"Table Games Get a Leg Up" in Philadelphia Business Journal (Vol. 28, January 15, 2010, No. 48, pp. 1)*
Pub: American City Business Journals
Ed: Athena Merritt, Peter Van Allen. **Description:** Casino operators expect the addition of live table games such as poker and blackjack at existing and planned casinos in Philadelphia will generate 1,000 new jobs. Most of the jobs will be dealers and floor supervisors.

23497 ■ *"Taco Bell; David Ovens" in Advertising Age (Vol. 79, November 17, 2008, No. 43, pp. S2)*
Pub: Crain Communications, Inc.
Ed: Emily Bryson York. **Description:** Due to the addition of new products such as a low-calorie, low-fat Fresco menu; a fruity iced beverage; and a value initiative, Taco Bell now accounts for half of Yum Brands' profits. The chain has also benefited from a new chief marketing officer, David Ovens, who oversees ad support.

23498 ■ *"Taiwan Technology Initiatives Foster Growth" in Canadian Electronics (Vol. 23, February 2008, No. 1, pp. 28)*
Pub: CLB Media Inc.
Description: A study conducted by the Market Intelligence Center shows that currently, Taiwan is the world's larges producer of information technology

products such as motherboards, servers, and LCD monitors. In 2006, Taiwan's LED industry reached a production value of NTD 21 billion. This push into the LED sector shows the Ministry of Economic Affairs' plan to target industries that are environmentally friendly.

23499 ■ *"Taking a Chance" in Baltimore Business Journal (Vol. 28, July 16, 2010, No. 10, pp. 1)*
Pub: Baltimore Business Journal
Ed: Scott Dance. **Description:** North Avenue in Baltimore, Maryland is considered a rough neighborhood due to the dangers of prostitution and drug dealing. However, some entrepreneurs have taken the risk of building their businesses on North Avenue as revitalization efforts grow. One of the challenges for businesses in rough neighborhoods is bringing customers to their stores or offices.

23500 ■ *"Taking Collections" in Investment Dealers' Digest (Vol. 75, October 9, 2009, No. 38, pp. 19)*
Pub: SourceMedia, Inc.
Ed: Aleksandrs Rozens. **Description:** Although the nation's debt-collection industry has grown with increased reliance by consumers on credit, valuations of these firms have lessened due to the economy which has hurt some of the success of these firms in obtaining the debt back from consumers who are experiencing trying economic times.

23501 ■ *"Taking the Right Road" in Entrepreneur (Vol. 37, October 2009, No. 10, pp. 104)*
Pub: Entrepreneur Media Inc.
Ed: Jason Daley. **Description:** Joe Grubb's franchise of BrightStar Healthcare, a home health care provider, in Knoxville, Tennessee has grown into a $1 million business. Grubb, a former sales agent, experienced slow growth for his franchise and had to deal with cash flow issues during its first few months.

23502 ■ *"Tanganyika Announces First Quarter 2007 Results" in Canadian Corporate News (May 14, 2007)*
Pub: Comtex News Network Inc.
Description: Tanganyika Oil Company Ltd., announced the interim operating and financial results for the first quarter ending March 31, 2007. Statistical data included.

23503 ■ *"Tax Deal Yields Polaris Offices" in Business First-Columbus (October 26, 2007, pp A1)*
Pub: American City Business Journals, Inc.
Ed: Brian R. Ball. **Description:** Speculation on a possible office building construction is increasing with the expansion of tax incentives to build at the Polaris Centers of Commerce. Details of community reinvestment in the Columbus, Ohio area along with possible 15-year 100 percent tax abatements for Polaris office buildings are discussed.

23504 ■ *"Tea for 33 Million" in Canadian Business (Vol. 80, March 12, 2007, No. 6, pp. 10)*
Pub: Rogers Media
Ed: Wendy Glauser. **Description:** The plan of owner of Cargo & James Tea, Tim Grover, to expand his business in North America to reach about 33 million, is discussed.

23505 ■ *"The Tea Bag Test" in Canadian Business (Vol. 79, October 23, 2006, No. 21, pp. 93)*
Pub: Rogers Media
Ed: Clive Mather. **Description:** Tips for business executives, on how to manage leadership skills to attain optimal business growth, are presented.

23506 ■ *"A Team Sport" in Business Courier (Vol. 26, October 2, 2009, No. 23, pp. 1)*
Pub: American City Business Journals, Inc.
Ed: Lisa Biank Fasig. **Description:** Procter & Gamble (P&G) revised the way it works with marketing, design and public relations firms. Creative discussions will be managed by only two representatives,

the franchise leader and the brand agency leader in order for P&G to simplify operations as it grows larger and more global.

23507 ■ *"The Tech 100" in Canadian Business (Vol. 81, July 21, 2008, No. 11, pp. 48)*
Pub: Rogers Media Ltd.

Ed: Calvin Leung. **Description:** Absolute Software Corp. Day4 Energy Inc., Sandvine Corp., Norsat International Inc. and Call Genie Inc. are the five technology firms included in the annual ranking of top companies in Canada by market capitalization. The services and the one-year total return potential of the companies are presented.

23508 ■ *"Teeling and Gallagher: A Textbook for Success" in Agency Sales Magazine (Vol. 39, September-October 2009, No. 9, pp. 20)*
Pub: MANA

Ed: Jack Foster. **Description:** Profile of Teeling & Gallagher, a manufacturing firm that was founded in 1946 as the D.G. Teeling Company and continued as a one-person agency until 1960 when Tom Gallagher joined the company. Tom Gallagher talks about how things have changed and his work with his son Bob in the agency.

23509 ■ *"TELUS Drawing More Power From Its Wireless Operations" in Globe & Mail (February 17, 2007, pp. B3)*
Pub: CTVglobemedia Publishing Inc.

Ed: Catherine McLean. **Description:** TELUS Corp., the fast-growing wireless business company, posted tripled profits in the fourth quarter of 2006. The revenues of the company increased 8 percent in the same period.

23510 ■ *"Telus Tunes in to the TV Revolution" in Globe & Mail (February 18, 2006, pp. B4)*
Pub: CTVglobemedia Publishing Inc.

Ed: Eric Reguly. **Description:** The business growth plans of chief executive officer Darren Entwistle of Telus Corp. are presented.

23511 ■ *"Tempel Steel To Expand Its Chicago Plant" in Chicago Tribune (August 22, 2008)*
Pub: McClatchy-Tribune Information Services

Ed: James P. Miller. **Description:** Tempel Steel Co. is no longer considering transferring a Libertyville factory's production to Mexico; the company has responded to government incentives and will instead shift that work to its plant on Chicago's North Side.

23512 ■ *"Testing Firm to Add Jobs" in Business Courier (Vol. 26, December 11, 2009, No. 33, pp. 1)*
Pub: American City Business Journals, Inc.

Ed: Dan Monk. **Description:** Cincinnati-based Q Laboratories announced plans to add dozens of jobs with the $1.6 million stimulus assisted expansion. The company hired Michael Lichtenberg & Sons Construction Co. to build a new 9,000 square foot laboratory building.

23513 ■ *"Texas State Poised for Boom" in Austin Business JournalInc. (Vol. 29, January 29, 2010, No. 47, pp. 1)*
Pub: American City Business Journals

Ed: Sandra Zaragoza. **Description:** Texas State University, San Marcos has seen its student population grow to 30,800 and the university is set for $633 million in construction projects to address demand for student housing and building expansions and renovations. Details on the buildings and student housing plans for the projects are provided.

23514 ■ *"Thai Ice Cream Cremo Expanding to Middle East" in Ice Cream Reporter (Vol. 23, September 20, 2010, No. 10, pp. 3)*
Pub: Ice Cream Reporter

Description: Thai-based frozen dessert manufacturer Chomthana, maker of Cremo brand ice cream, is expanding into the Middle East.

23515 ■ *There's a Business In Every Woman: A 7-Step Guide to Discovering, Starting, and Building the Business of Your Dreams*
Pub: Ballantine/Random House

Ed: Ann M. Holmes. **Released:** 2008. **Price:** $15.00 paperback. **Description:** Economist and workplace expert provides a no-nonsense guide detailing seven steps to creating a successful business, based on her own experiences and on those of her employees. She highlights the importance of understanding and using your core competencies, building an organized infrastructure from the start, and planning for and managing your growth.

23516 ■ *The Thin Book of Naming Elephants: How to Surface Undiscussables for Greater Organizational Success*
Pub: Thin Book Publishing Co.
Contact: Sue Annis Hammond, Owner
E-mail: sue@thinbook.com

Ed: Sue Annis Hammond; Andrea B. Mayfield. **Released:** January 2004. **Price:** $10.95. **Description:** Organizational success is of upmost importance to today's entrepreneurs and organizations. The hierarchal system in which people are afraid to speak up in organizations is discussed. The points of view and inability to see things from an overall perspective can cause insecurity among employees. The three elephants present in every organization include: arrogance, hubris, and screamers and the damage caused by these elephants in any organization is examined.

23517 ■ *"Thirsty Lion on the Prowl" in Business Journal Portland (Vol. 27, November 5, 2010, No. 36, pp. 1)*
Pub: Portland Business Journal

Ed: Wendy Culverwell. **Description:** Concept Entertainment Inc.'s impending launch of the Thirsty Lion Pub and Grill at the Washington Square in downtown Portland, Oregon is part of its West Coast expansion plan. A discussion of the planning involved in realizing Thirsty Lion is discussed, along with pub offerings that are expected to be enjoyed by customers.

23518 ■ *"Thomas Morley; President, The Lube Stop Inc., 37" in Crain's Cleveland Business (Vol. 28, November 19, 2007, No. 46, pp. F-12)*
Pub: Crain Communications, Inc.

Ed: David Bennett. **Description:** Profile of Thomas Morley, president of The Lube Stop Inc., who is dedicated to promoting the company's strong environmental record as an effective way to differentiate Lube Stop from its competition. Since Mr. Morley came to the company in 2004, Lube Stop has increased sales by 10 percent and has boosted its operating profits by 30 percent.

23519 ■ *"Thomson Eyes Asia for Expansion" in Globe & Mail (February 10, 2006, pp. B4)*
Pub: CTVglobemedia Publishing Inc.

Ed: Grant Robertson. **Description:** The business growth plans of Thomson Corp., in Asia, are presented.

23520 ■ *"Time for a Little Pruning" in Barron's (Vol. 89, July 6, 2009, No. 27, pp. 13)*
Pub: Dow Jones & Co., Inc.

Ed: Dimitra DeFotis. **Description:** Investors are advised to avoid the shares of Whole Foods, American Tower, T. Rowe Price, Iron Mountain, Intuitive Surgical, Salesforce.com, and Juniper Networks due to their high price to earnings ratios. The shares of Amazon.com, Broadcom, and Expeditors International of Washington remain attractive to investors despite their high price to earnings ratios due to their strong growth.

23521 ■ *"Timken's Bearings Rolling in China, India" in Crain's Cleveland Business (Vol. 28, October 29, 2007, No. 43, pp. 14)*
Pub: Crain Communications, Inc.

Ed: David Bennett. **Description:** Canton-based Timken Co., a manufacturer of bearings and specialty metals, is seeing growing demand for its line of tapered roller bearings, which allow rail users to carry heavy car loads. The company is finding significant growth in China and India due to their rapidly growing rail markets.

23522 ■ *"Tips From a Turnaround Expert" in Business Owner (Vol. 35, July-August 2011, No. 4, pp. 8)*
Pub: DL Perkins Company

Description: The book, 'The Six Month Fix: Adventures in Rescuing Failing Companies' by Gary Sutton is summarized. It provides lessons for finding and building profits in failing firms.

23523 ■ *"TiVo, Domino's Team to Offer Pizza Ordering by DVR" in Advertising Age (Vol. 79, November 17, 2008, No. 43, pp. 48)*
Pub: Crain Communications, Inc.

Ed: Brian Steinberg. **Description:** Domino's Pizza and TiVo are teaming up to make it possible for customers to order from the restaurant straight from their DVR. The companies see that this kind of interactive television and consumer experience will only serve to generate more sales as the customer can be exposed to a fuller range of menu selections and will not have to interrupt their viewing, while workers can spend more time making the product.

23524 ■ *"TMC Development Closes $1.1 Million Real Estate Purchase" in Internet Wire (September 17, 2009)*
Pub: Comtex News Network, Inc.

Description: TMC Development announced the closing of a $1.1 million real estate purchase for Mansa, LLC dba Kwikee Mart, a Napa-based convenience store; TMC helped the company secure a Small Business Administration 504 loan in order to purchase the acquisition of a 3,464 square foot building. SBA created the 504 loan program to provide financing for growing small and medium-sized businesses.

23525 ■ *"Toes for Business" in Hispanic Business (October 2007, pp. 10, 12)*
Pub: Hispanic Business

Ed: Gabriel Rodriguez. **Description:** Prima ballerinas, Lorena and Lorna Feijoo, have increased box office sales by at least 30 to 40 percent. A discussion with Pedro Pablo Pena, artistic director of the Miami Hispanic Ballet Corps and founder of the first Choreographic Workshop of Havana is included.

23526 ■ *"Tofutti Brands" in Ice Cream Reporter (Vol. 23, September 20, 2010, No. 10, pp. 6)*
Pub: Ice Cream Reporter

Description: Tofutti Brands announced net sales at $4.5 million for second quarter 2010.

23527 ■ *"Top 49ers Alphabetical Listing with Five Years Rank and Revenue" in Alaska Business Monthly (Vol. 27, October 2011, No. 10, pp. 100)*
Pub: Alaska Business Publishing Company

Description: A listing of Alaska's top 49 performing companies ranked by revenue for years 2010 and 2011.

23528 ■ *"Top 50" in Entrepreneur (Vol. 35, November 2007, No. 11, pp. 38)*
Pub: Entrepreneur Media Inc.

Description: List of the 50 fastest-growing women-led businesses in North America is presented.

23529 ■ *"Top 50 By 1-Year Return" in Canadian Business (Vol. 81, Summer 2008, No. 9, pp. 121)*
Pub: Rogers Media Ltd.

Description: Table showing the top 50 Canadian companies ranked in terms of one-year return is presented. Toronto, Canada-based Timminco Ltd. topped the roster with a 1,294.2 percent in one-year return. However, the share prices of the company were affected by the recent controversy in its silicon purification process.

23530 ■ *"Top 50 By 5-Year Return" in Canadian Business (Vol. 81, Summer 2008, No. 9, pp. 123)*
Pub: Rogers Media Ltd.

Description: Table showing the rankings of the top 50 Canadian companies in terms of five-year return is presented. Silver Wheaton Corp. topped the roster with a 178.5 percent in five-year return. The company's share prices have skyrocketed despite increasing silver prices.

23531 ■ *"Top 50 in the Capital Market"* in *Canadian Business (Vol. 81, Summer 2008, No. 9, pp. 117)*
Pub: Rogers Media Ltd.
Description: Research in Motion Ltd. topped the list of companies in Canada in terms of market capitalization. The company's share prices surge to 119.8 percent in the year ended April 4. A table showing the top 50 Canadian companies in terms of market capitalization is presented.

23532 ■ *"Top 50 Exporters"* in *Hispanic Business (Vol. 30, July-August 2008, No. 7-8, pp. 42)*
Pub: Hispanic Business, Inc.
Ed: Hildy Medina. **Description:** Increases in exports revenues reported by food exporters and green companies in a time of economic slowdown in the U.S are described. Food exporters have benefited from the growth of high-volume grocery stores in underdeveloped countries and the German governments' promotion of solar energy has benefited the U.S. solar heating equipment and solar panel manufactures.

23533 ■ *"Top 50 In Profits"* in *Canadian Business (Vol. 81, Summer 2008, No. 9, pp. 116)*
Pub: Rogers Media Ltd.
Description: Royal Bank of Canada topped the Investor 500 by profits list despite the slower economic growth in Canada and the U.S. The bank was in the runner-up position in the 2007. RBC's growth strategy is through hefty acquisitions in the U.S. A table ranking the top 50 companies in Canada in terms of profits is presented.

23534 ■ *"Top 50 In Total Revenue"* in *Canadian Business (Vol. 81, Summer 2008, No. 9, pp. 119)*
Pub: Rogers Media Ltd.
Description: Table showing the top 50 Canadian companies in terms of total revenue is presented. Manulife Financial Corp. topped the list with revenue of 34.5 billion. The financial services firm is the 6th largest provider of life insurance in the world and the second largest in North America.

23535 ■ *"Top 100 Consolidate Gains"* in *Hispanic Business (Vol. 30, July-August 2008, No. 7-8, pp. 30)*
Pub: Hispanic Business, Inc.
Ed: Richard Kaplan. **Description:** Data developed by HispanTelligence on the increase in revenue posted by the top 100 fastest-growing U.S. Hispanic firms over the last five years is reported. Despite the economic downturn, the service sector, IT and health suppliers showed an increase in revenue whereas construction companies showed a marginal slump in revenue growth.

23536 ■ *"Top Private Companies"* in *Baltimore Business Journal (Vol. 28, August 27, 2010, No. 16, pp. 1)*
Pub: Baltimore Business Journal
Ed: Gary Haber. **Description:** The combined revenue of the 100 largest private firms in Maryland's Baltimore region dropped from about $22.7 billion in 2008 to $21 billion in 2009, an annual decrease of more than 7 percent. To survive the recession's impact, these firms resorted to strategies such as government contracting and overseas expansion. How these strategies affected the revenue of some firms is described.

23537 ■ *"Top Twenty Wealthiest Landowners"* in *Hawaii Business (Vol. 53, November 2007, No. 5, pp. 34)*
Pub: Hawaii Business Publishing
Description: Provided is a table of the wealthiest landowners in Hawaii. Their assessed value, total acres owned, prominent holdings, other notable holdings and years of presence in Hawaii are also provided. Statistical data included.

23538 ■ *"A Torch in the Darkness"* in *Canadian Business (Vol. 83, August 17, 2010, No. 13-14, pp. 66)*
Pub: Rogers Media Ltd.
Ed: Joe Castaldo. **Description:** Research In Motion (RIM) unveiled the BlackBerry Touch, featuring a touch screen as well as a physical keyboard, in an attempt to repel competitors and expand share in the consumer smart phone market. RIM shares have fallen 43 percent from its peak in 2009.

23539 ■ *"Tough-Love Boss at BMO Demands Retail Turnaround"* in *Globe & Mail (March 2, 2007, pp. B13)*
Pub: CTVglobemedia Publishing Inc.
Ed: Andrew Willis. **Description:** William Downe, the newly appointed chief executive of Bank of Montreal (BMO), discusses strategies to improve the number of retail customers. The BMO reported $292 million profits in the first quarter of 2007.

23540 ■ *"Toyota Expected to Construct Two N.A. Plants"* in *Globe & Mail (February 14, 2007, pp. B4)*
Pub: CTVglobemedia Publishing Inc.
Description: Toyota Motor Corp. is planning to construct two vehicle assembly plants in North America and one more plant in Canada. The company is also planning to sell 208,000 vehicles in 2007.

23541 ■ *"Toyota Marks Record Profit Sales"* in *Globe & Mail (February 7, 2007, pp. B10)*
Pub: CTVglobemedia Publishing Inc.
Ed: Martin Fackler. **Description:** The record quarterly sales and earnings reported by Japanese automaker Toyota Motor Corp. are discussed. The company sold 2.16 million vehicles during the quarter while registering 426.8 billion yen in profits.

23542 ■ *"Toyota Tops GM in Global Sales"* in *Globe & Mail (April 25, 2007, pp. B1)*
Pub: CTVglobemedia Publishing Inc.
Ed: Greg Keenan. **Description:** The success of Toyota Motor Corp. in surpassing General Motors Corp. in its global sales is discussed.

23543 ■ *Trading Places: SMEs in the Global Economy, A Critical Research Handbook*
Pub: Edward Elgar Publishing, Incorporated
Ed: Lloyd-Reason. **Released:** September 2006. **Price:** $110.00. **Description:** An overview of international research for small and medium-sized companies wishing to expand in the global economy.

23544 ■ *"Traffic Slows at O'Hare; As Airlines Cut Flights, City Tries to Push Expansion Forward"* in *Crain's Chicago Business (April 28, 2008)*
Pub: Crain Communications, Inc.
Ed: Paul Merrion; John Pletz. **Description:** O'Hare International Airport is seeing a decline in passenger traffic just as the city of Chicago presses cash-strapped airlines to fund the second phase of the airport's expansion which would include the extension of one runway, the relocation of two others and the construction of a new western terminal.

23545 ■ *"Tragedies Add Demand for Inspiron's Alert System"* in *Crain's Cleveland Business (Vol. 28, October 29, 2007, No. 43, pp. 5)*
Pub: Crain Communications, Inc.
Ed: Chuck Soder. **Description:** Inspiron Logistics Corp. has seen huge growth over the past months for its Wireless Emergency Notification System which colleges and universities have rushed to buy since the April 16 shootings at Virginia Tech. The company now makes more than half of its revenue by selling the systems to colleges whereas previous to the shootings the academic market accounted for just 20 percent of the company's sales.

23546 ■ *"Training Essential For Growth; It Doesn't Have To Cost Much"* in *Crain's Detroit Business (Vol. 24, January 21, 2008,*

No. 3, pp. 14)
Pub: Crain Communications Inc. - Detroit
Ed: Sheena Harrison. **Description:** Employee training is essential for small companies to achieve growth.

23547 ■ *"Training the Troops: Battlefield Simulations Bring Growth to UNITECH"* in *Black Enterprise (Vol. 38, February 2008, No. 7, pp. 30)*
Pub: Earl G. Graves Publishing Co. Inc.
Ed: Cliff Hocker. **Description:** Universal Systems and Technology (UNITECH) received a total of over $45 million U.S. Department of Defense orders during September and October 2007. UNITECH designs and manufactures battlefield simulation devices used to train troops in the Army and Marine Corps.

23548 ■ *"Transportation: Laidlaw's Chief Driver"* in *Canadian Business (Vol. 80, January 29, 2007, No. 3, pp. 14)*
Pub: Rogers Media
Ed: Michelle Magnan. **Description:** The role of Kevin Benson in the restructuring and growth of the bankrupt transportation company Laidlaw Inc. is described. The increase in the revenues of the restructures company is discussed.

23549 ■ *"Trisun Healthcare Eager to Add Centers"* in *Austin Business JournalInc. (Vol. 28, August 22, 2008, No. 23, pp. 1)*
Pub: American City Business Journals
Ed: Kate Harrington. **Description:** Austin-based nursing and rehabilitation centers operator Trisun Healthcare plans to build more facilities as part of a growth strategy that can expand beyond Texas. Trisun has 16 facilities along the corridor from San Antonio to Temple, and projects to have three more in Texas in 2008.

23550 ■ *"Troy Brewer Opens Own Bottling Operation"* in *Business Review, Albany New York (Vol. 34, November 16, 2007, No. 33, pp. 3)*
Pub: American City Business Journals, Inc.
Ed: Michael DeMasi. **Description:** Brown Brewing Company's owner Peter Martin invested in $100,000 worth of bottling equipment and has now doubled his production capacity to 3,000 barrels. Davidson Brothers, another brewery that bottles its own beer, sells 3,000 to 5,000 cases of beer annually. Industry sales of draft breweries are presented.

23551 ■ *True to Yourself: Leading a Values-Based Business*
Pub: Berrett-Koehler Publishers, Incorporated
Ed: Mark S. Albion. **Released:** June 2006. **Price:** $14.95. **Description:** Pressures faced by entrepreneurs running small companies are discussed. Advice is offered to help grow and maintain a profitable business.

23552 ■ *"Tulsa-Based Dollar Thrifty Adds Franchises"* in *Journal Record (December 7, 2010)*
Pub: Dolan Media Newswires
Ed: D. Ray Tuttle. **Description:** Dollar Thrifty Automotive Group Inc. opened 31 franchise locations in 2010 as part of its expansion plan in the U.S.

23553 ■ *"Turfway Slowing its Gait"* in *Business Courier (Vol. 26, November 6, 2009, No. 28, pp. 1)*
Pub: American City Business Journals, Inc.
Ed: Jon Newberry. **Description:** Kentucky's Turfway Park will be decreasing its weekly race schedule from five days to three days in the first two months of 2010, and to four days in March 2010. The decision to make reductions in the schedule is attributed to the relocation of thoroughbred racing to states that allow casino gambling. As a result, Turfway Park's resources and purse money would be focused on less days.

23554 ■ *"A Turn in the South"* in *The Economist (Vol. 390, January 3, 2009, No. 8612, pp. 34)*
Pub: The Economist Newspaper Inc.
Description: Overview of Charleston, South Carolina, a region that lost its navy base in 1996, which had provided work for more than 22,000 people; the

city developed a plan called Noisette in order to redevelop the area and today the economy is healthier and more diversified than it was a decade ago. Charleston was described as among the best cities for doing business by Inc. Magazine and seems to be handling the downturn of the economy fairly well. Statistical data regarding growth, business and population is included.

23555 ■ *"Twenty Years of Advocacy and Education" in Women Entrepreneur (January 18, 2009)*
Pub: Entrepreneur Media Inc.
Ed: Eve Gumpel. **Description:** Profile of Sharon Hadary who served as executive director of the Center for Women's Business Research for two decades; Hadary discusses what she has learned about women business owners, their impact on the economy and what successful business owners share in common.

23556 ■ *Twitterville: How Businesses Can Thrive in the New Global Neighborhoods*
Pub: Portfolio Hardcover
Ed: Shel Israel. **Price:** $23.95. **Description:** Twitter is the most rapidly adopted communication tool in history, going from zero to ten million users in just over two years. On Twitter, word can spread faster than wildfire. Companies no longer have the option of ignoring the conversation. Unlike other hot social media spaces, Twitterville is dominated by professionals, not students. And despite its size, it still feels like a small town. Twitter allows people to interact much the way they do face-to-face, honestly and authentically.

23557 ■ *"Two Local Firms Make Inc. List: Minority Business" in Indianapolis Business Journal (Vol. 31, August 30, 2010, No. 26, pp. 13A)*
Pub: Indianapolis Business Journal Corporation
Description: Smart IT staffing agency and Entap Inc., an IT outsourcing firm were among the top ten fastest growing black-owned businesses in the U.S. by Inc. magazine.

23558 ■ *"U-Swirl To Open in Salt Lake City Metro Market" in Ice Cream Reporter (Vol. 23, November 20, 2010, No. 12, pp. 4)*
Pub: Ice Cream Reporter
Description: Healthy Fast Food Inc., parent company to U-SWIRL International Inc., the owner and franchisor of U-SWIRL Frozen Yogurt cafes signed a franchising area development agreement for the Salt Lake City metropolitan area with Regents Management and will open 5 cafes over a five year period.

23559 ■ *"UC's Goering Center to Get New Director" in Business Courier (Vol. 24, February 15, 2008, No. 45, pp. 3)*
Pub: American City Business Journals, Inc.
Ed: Dan Monk. **Description:** Kent Lutz, director of University of Cincinnati Goering (UC) Center for Family & Private Business is to leave the resource center in June 2008 after nine years of service. Changes in the UC-affiliated institute include the expansion of the board from three to seven members and developing new programs related to family businesses.

23560 ■ *"The Ultimate Business Tune-Up: For Times Like These" in Inc. (Vol. 31, January-February 2009, No. 1, pp. 70)*
Pub: Mansueto Ventures LLC
Description: Twenty-three things do energize a small business in tough economic times are outlined with insight from successful entrepreneurs.

23561 ■ *"The Ultimate Cure" in Conde Nast Portfolio (Vol. 2, June 2008, No. 6, pp. 110)*
Pub: Conde Nast Publications
Contact: David Carey, President
Ed: David Ewing Duncan. **Description:** Small up-starts as well as pharmaceutical giants are developing drugs for the neurotechnology industry; these firms are attempting to adapt groundbreaking research into the basic workings of the brain to new drugs for ailments ranging from multiple sclerosis to dementia to insomnia.

23562 ■ *Ultimate Homebased Business Handbook: How to Start, Run, and Grow Your Own Profitable Business*
Pub: Entrepreneur Press
Ed: James Stephenson. **Released:** June 2008. **Price:** $29.95 (US), $34.95 (Canadian). **Description:** Detailed information for anyone wanting to start a home-based business. Topics include how-to tips, ideas, tools, and print and online resources.

23563 ■ *"UMKC, Hospital Drill Down on Deal" in The Business Journal-Serving Metropolitan Kansas City (Vol. 26, July 18, 2008, No. 45, pp. 1)*
Pub: American City Business Journals, Inc.
Ed: Rob Roberts. **Description:** University of Missouri Kansas City and Children's Mercy Hospital are negotiating the hospital's potential acquisition of the university's School of Dentistry building. The deal would transfer the 240,000-square foot dental school building to Children's Mercy. Plans for a new dental school building for the UMKC are also presented.

23564 ■ *"An Unfair Knock on Nokia" in Barron's (Vol. 88, March 10, 2008, No. 10, pp. 36)*
Pub: Dow Jones & Company, Inc.
Ed: Mark Veverka. **Description:** Discusses the decision by the brokerage house Exane to recommend a Sell on Nokia shares, presumably due to higher inventories, which is unfounded. The news that the company's inventories are rising is not an indicator of falling demand for its products. The company is also benefiting from solid management and rising market share.

23565 ■ *"Unify Corp. Back in the Black, Poised to Grow" in Sacramento Business Journal (Vol. 25, August 29, 2008, No. 26, pp. 1)*
Pub: American City Business Journals, Inc.
Ed: Melanie Turner. **Description:** It was reported that Unify Corp. returned to profitability in the fiscal year ended April 30, 2008 with a net income of $1.6 million, under the guidance of Todd Wille. Wille, who took over as the company's chief executive officer in October 2000, was named as Turnaround CEO of the Year in June 2008 for his efforts.

23566 ■ *"United Insurance To Grow St. Pete's Corporate Base" in The Business Journal-Serving Greater Tampa Bay (August 29, 2008)*
Pub: American City Business Journals, Inc.
Ed: Margie Manning. **Description:** United Insurance Holdings LC is on its way to becoming a public company by agreeing in a reverse merger with FMG Acquisition Corp. The $104.3 million agreement will provide the company's St. Petersburg operations the opportunity to grow. The other impacts of the proposed reverse merger are examined.

23567 ■ *"U.S. Retailer Eyes 'Tween' Market" in Globe & Mail (January 30, 2007, pp. B1)*
Pub: CTVglobemedia Publishing Inc.
Ed: Marina Strauss. **Description:** The decision of Tween Brands Inc. (Too Incorporated) to open 100 new stores in Canada as part of its expansion is discussed. The company's focus on targeting girls for its products is detailed.

23568 ■ *"U.S. Savvy Helps Fuel TD's Fortunes" in Globe & Mail (February 23, 2007, pp. B1)*
Pub: CTVglobemedia Publishing Inc.
Ed: Andrew Willis; Tavia Grant. **Description:** The rise in the revenues of Toronto-Dominion Bank due to its acquisition of American financial service providers and the rise in its domestic retail banking revenues are disussed.

23569 ■ *"Universal Energy Group Releases March 31, 2007 Financial Statements" in Canadian Corporate News (May 14, 2007)*
Pub: Comtex News Network Inc.
Description: Universal Energy Group Ltd., a company that sells electricity and natural gas to small to mid-size commercial and small industrial customers as well as residential customers, announced the release of its March 31, 2007 financial statements. Management's analysis and discussion of the company's financial condition and results of operations are listed. Statistical data included.

23570 ■ *"Uptick in Clicks: Nordstrom's Online Sales Surging" in Puget Sound Business Journal (Vol. 29, August 22, 2008, No. 18, pp. 1)*
Pub: American City Business Journals
Ed: Gregg Lamm. **Description:** Nordstrom Inc.'s on-line division grew its sales by 15 percent in the second quarter of 2008, compared to 2007's 4.3 percent in overall decline. The company expects their online net sales to reach $700 million in 2008 capturing eight percent of overall sales.

23571 ■ *"USAmeriBank Deals for Growth" in The Business Journal-Serving Greater Tampa Bay (Vol. 28, September 26, 2008, No. 40, pp. 1)*
Pub: American City Business Journals, Inc.
Ed: Margie Manning. **Description:** It is believed that the pending $14.9 million purchase of Liberty Bank by USAmeriBank could be at the forefront of a trend. Executives of both companies expect the deal to close by the end of 2008. USAmeriBank will have $430 million in assets and five offices in Pinellas, Florida once the deal is completed.

23572 ■ *"Utilities Report Lower Customer Growth Rate, Power Use" in The Business Journal - Serving Phoenix and the Valley of the Sun (Vol. 28, August 8, 2008, No. 49, pp. 1)*
Pub: American City Business Journals, Inc.
Ed: Patrick O'Grady. **Description:** Arizona Public Service Co. and Salt River Project are experiencing sharp decrease in customer growth rates due to less movement of people to the Valley. Arizona Public Service Co. expects a further decline of just 1 percent customer growth by the end of 2008 while Salt River Project expects this to grow between 1 to 2 percent for the two years ahead of 2008.

23573 ■ *"V&J Scores Partnership with Shaq" in Business Journal-Milwaukee (Vol. 25, October 12, 2007, No. 2, pp. A1)*
Pub: American City Business Journals, Inc.
Ed: Rich Kirchen. **Description:** O'Neal Franchise Group has agreed to a partnership with V&J Foods of Milwaukee to handle Auntie Anne's shops in New York, South Africa, Michigan, and the Caribbean. V&J O'Neal Enterprises will open six Auntie Anne's soft pretzel shops in Detroit towards the end of 2007. Planned international ventures of the partnership are presented.

23574 ■ *"VC Boosts WorkForce; Livonia Software Company to Add Sales, Marketing Staff" in Crain's Detroit Business (March 24, 2008)*
Pub: Crain Communications, Inc.
Ed: Tom Henderson. **Description:** WorkForce Software Inc., a company that provides software to manage payroll processes and oversee compliance with state and federal regulations and with union rules, plans to use an investment of $5.5 million in venture capital to hire more sales and marketing staff.

23575 ■ *"The VC Shakeout" in Harvard Business Review (Vol. 88, July-August 2010, No. 7-8, pp. 21)*
Pub: Harvard Business School Publishing
Ed: Joseph Ghalbouni, Dominique Rouzies. **Description:** Authors argue that in order to be successful, venture capital needs to focus less on how to sell a newly acquired investment and more on ways to grow a good company.

23576 ■ *The Venture Cafe*
Pub: Business Plus
Ed: Teresa Esser. **Released:** 2002. **Description:** Research covering the types of entrepreneurs who build new, high-technology ventures from the ground up. Author interviewed over 150 high-tech professionals in order to gather information to help others start high-tech companies.

23577 ■ *"VeriFone Announces Global Security Solutions Business" in Marketing Weekly News (October 3, 2009)*
Pub: Investment Weekly News
Description: Focused on delivering innovative security solutions, VeriFone Holdings, Inc. announced the formation of its Global Security Solutions Business Unit, including VeriShield Protect, an end-to-end encryption to protect cardholder data throughout the merchant and processor systems. The business will focus on consulting, sales and implementation of these new products in order to help retailers and processors protect customer data.

23578 ■ *"Verizon Comes Calling With 500 Jobs" in Business First Columbus (Vol. 25, September 15, 2008, No. 4, pp. 1)*
Pub: American City Business Journals
Ed: Brian R. Ball. **Description:** Hilliard, Ohio offered Verizon Wireless a 15-year incentive package worth $3.4 million for the company to move 300 customer financial services jobs to the city in addition to the 200 jobs from their facility in Dublin, Ohio. The incentives include a return of 15 percent of the income tax generated by the jobs.

23579 ■ *"Vernon Revamp" in Business Courier (Vol. 26, October 9, 2009, No. 24, pp. 1)*
Pub: American City Business Journals, Inc.
Ed: Dan Monk. **Description:** Al Neyer Inc. will redevelop the Vernon Manor Hotel as an office building for the Cincinnati Children's Hospital Medical Center. The project will cost $35 million and would generate a new investment vehicle for black investors who plan to raise $2.7 million in private offerings to claim majority ownership of the property after its renovations.

23580 ■ *"Virgin Mobile has Big Plans for Year Two" in Globe & Mail (March 6, 2006, pp. B5)*
Pub: CTVglobemedia Publishing Inc.
Ed: Catherine McLean. **Description:** The business growth plans of Virgin Mobile Canada are presented.

23581 ■ *"VISA: Canadians Spend $97 Million on Mom This Mother's Day" in Canadian Corporate News (May 16, 2007)*
Pub: Comtex News Network Inc.
Description: Visa Canada finds that Canadians are spending more on Mother's Day in recent years. Since 2002, sales of jewelry, flowers, and cards have climbed steadily in the week before Mother's Day weekend.

23582 ■ *"Vision for Camden in Better Focus" in Philadelphia Business Journal (Vol. 30, September 30, 2011, No. 33, pp. 1)*
Pub: American City Business Journals Inc.
Ed: Natalie Kostelni. **Description:** More than $500 million worth of projects aimed at redeveloping the downtown and waterfront areas of Camden, New Jersey are being planned. These include the construction of residential, commercial, and education buildings.

23583 ■ *"Visionary Riches" in Small Business Opportunities (Winter 2009)*
Pub: Entrepreneur Press
Contact: Perlman Neil, President
Description: Profile of Sterling Optical, which was included in a recent listing of 25 franchise high performers in The Wall Street Journal and is poised for mega-growth due to its offerings of professional eye exams, impeccable customer service, convenient locations and a great selection of eyewear.

23584 ■ *"Wachovia Gears Up for Major Arizona Expansion" in Business Journal-Serving Phoenix and the Valley of the Sun (Vol. 5, Oct. 5, 2007)*
Pub: American City Business Journals, Inc.
Ed: Chris Casacchia. **Description:** Wachovia, America's fourth-largest bank is finalizing a deal to build its Arizona headquarters in downtown Phoenix. The bank plans to add an additional 100 employees by June 2008 and double its financial network to 30 offices in four years. Wachovia will also convert fifteen World Savings Bank branches it acquired in 2006 through Golden West Financial Corporation.

23585 ■ *Wake Up and Smell the Zeitgeist*
Pub: Basic Books
Ed: Grand McCracken. **Released:** 2010. **Price:** $26.95. **Description:** Insight is given into an element of corporate success that's often overlooked and valuable suggestions are offered for any small business to pursue.

23586 ■ *"'Wal-Mart Effect' Feeds Grocer Price Wars" in Globe & Mail (March 15, 2007, pp. B14)*
Pub: CTVglobemedia Publishing Inc.
Ed: Marina Strauss. **Description:** The decrease in profit reports by Canadian grocery giants amidst high expansion plans by Wal-Mart Stores Inc. are discussed. This industry is witnessing the most severe pricing competitions in recent times.

23587 ■ *"Wal-Mart Expansion Plans Hit Roadblock" in Crain's Chicago Business (Vol. 31, March 24, 2008, No. 12, pp. 2)*
Pub: Crain Communications, Inc.
Ed: Monee Fields-White. **Description:** Wal-Mart Stores Inc.'s expansion plans in Chicago have suffered a series of setbacks due to a shifting political landscape in which may require the company to pay higher wages. Wal-Mart claims that its hourly pay and benefits are fair; however, the labor force does not agree.

23588 ■ *"Wal-Mart Proposed for Timmerman Plaza" in Business Journal-Milwaukee (Vol. 28, December 31, 2010, No. 14, pp. A1)*
Pub: Milwaukee Business Journal
Ed: Sean Ryan. **Description:** Dickson, Tennessee-based Gatlin Development Company Inc. owner Franklin C. Gatlin III revealed plans for a new Wal-Mart store in Timmerman Plaza in Milwaukee, Wisconsin. Wal-Mart plans to open up approximately 18 new stores in southeast Wisconsin in 2012 and the Timmerman project is the first of four that Gatlin will submit for city approval.

23589 ■ *"Wal-Mart Takes Expansion Up a Notch" in Globe & Mail (March 21, 2007, pp. B8)*
Pub: CTVglobemedia Publishing Inc.
Ed: Shirley Won. **Description:** Retail giant Wal-Mart Canada Corp. is planning to invest $500 million for expanding its business in Ontario region. It will open 21 new outlets by the end of 2007.

23590 ■ *"Walgreen Takes Up Doctoring" in Crain's Chicago Business (Vol. 31, March 31, 2008, No. 13, pp. 18)*
Pub: Crain Communications, Inc.
Ed: Mark Bruno. **Description:** Walgreen Co. has agreed to acquire two firms that provide on-site medical and pharmaceutical services to large companies. Walgreen feels that these facilities mark the future of health care for a number of large corporations.

23591 ■ *"Walk This Way" in Barron's (Vol. 90, August 23, 2010, No. 34, pp. 13)*
Pub: Barron's Editorial & Corporate Headquarters
Ed: Christopher C. Williams. **Description:** Crocs and Skechers are selling very popular shoes and sales show no signs of winding down. The shares of both companies are attractively prices.

23592 ■ *The Wall Street Journal. Complete Small Business Guidebook*
Pub: Three Rivers Press
Ed: Colleen DeBaise. **Released:** December 29, 2009. **Price:** $15.00. **Description:** The mechanics of building, running and growing a profitable business are outlined, teaching how to write a business plan, ways to finding money during lean years, how to keep stress in check, time management, investment in technology, hiring, marketing, management basics, angel investing and venture capital, as well as an exit strategy.

23593 ■ *"Walmart, Target Moving to Convenience Store Near You" in Hardware Retailing (Vol. 199, November 2010, No. 5, pp. 60)*
Pub: North American Retail Hardware Association
Contact: Mike O'Hara, President
Description: Walmart has plans to move into small convenience stores in Chicago, Detroit, San Francisco, and Los Angeles.

23594 ■ *"The War for Good Jobs; The World Will Be Led with Economic Force" in Gallup Management Journal (September 7, 2011)*
Pub: Gallup
Ed: Jim Clifton. **Description:** Gallup's chairman believes the next world war will be for good jobs and the winner will triumph with economic force, driven primarily by job creation and quality GDP growth.

23595 ■ *"Watchful Eye: Entrepreneur Protects Clients and His Bottom Line" in Black Enterprise (Vol. 38, March 2008, No. 8, pp. 46)*
Pub: Earl G. Graves Publishing Co. Inc.
Ed: Tennille M. Robinson. **Description:** Profile of Elijah Shaw, founder of Icon Services Corporation, a full service security and investigative service; Shaw shares his plans to protect clients while growing his business.

23596 ■ *"Wattles Plugs Back Into State" in Business Journal Portland (Vol. 27, November 19, 2010, No. 38, pp. 1)*
Pub: Portland Business Journal
Ed: Wendy Culverwell. **Description:** Denver, Colorado-based Ultimate Electronics Inc.'s first store in Oregon was opened in Portland and the 46th store in the chain of electronic superstores is expected to employ 70-80 workers. The venture is the latest for Mark Wattles, one of Oregon's most successful entrepreneurs, who acquired Ultimate from bankruptcy.

23597 ■ *"We All Scream for Ice Cream" in Crain's Chicago Business (Vol. 31, April 28, 2008, No. 17, pp. 48)*
Pub: Crain Communications, Inc.
Ed: Phuong Ly. **Description:** Profile of Oberweis' ice cream shops which has expanded its business by delivering dairy products to grocery stores.

23598 ■ *We Are Smarter Than Me: How to Unleash the Power of Crowds in Your Business*
Pub: Wharton School Publishing
Ed: Barry Libert; Jon Spector; Don Tapscott. **Released:** October 5, 2007. **Price:** $21.99. **Description:** Ways to use social networking and community in order to make decisions and plan your business, with a focus on product development, manufacturing, marketing, customer service, finance, management, and more.

23599 ■ *"Wear More Hats" in Canadian Business (Vol. 80, March 12, 2007, No. 6, pp. 39)*
Pub: Rogers Media
Ed: Michael Stern. **Description:** The need on the part of managers to volunteer to accept more responsibilities for their growth as well as that of company's is discussed.

23600 ■ *"Web Biz Brulant Surfing for Acquisition Candidates" in Crain's Cleveland Business (Vol. 28, December 3, 2007, No. 48, pp. 6)*
Pub: Crain Communications, Inc.
Ed: Chuck Soder. **Description:** Brulant Inc., a provider of web development and marketing services, is looking to acquire other companies after growing for five years straight. The company is one of the largest technology firms in Northeast Ohio.

23601 ■ *"Welcome to the Neighborhood" in Hawaii Business (Vol. 53, October 2007, No. 4, pp. 48)*
Pub: Hawaii Business Publishing
Ed: Jolyn Okimoto Rosa. **Description:** Finance Factors is planning to build branches in Manoa, and Liliha, as part of its strategy to position itself in high-

yield areas. The company chose Manoa and Liliha due to thee sites' rich deposits. Its strategy with regards to the branches' location and to the building design is discussed.

23602 ■ *"Wells Fargo Will Soon Lead Local Banks in Deposits"* in *Austin Business JournalInc. (Vol. 28, December 5, 2008, No. 38, pp. A1)*
Pub: American City Business Journals
Ed: Christopher Calnan. Description: Acquisition of Wachovia Corporation by Wells Fargo and Company will leave the latter as the top bank for deposits in Austin, Texas. The merged bank will have deposits of more than $ billion, more than the $3.9 billion deposits Bank of America maintains in the area.

23603 ■ *"Welsh Meat Sales on the Rise"* in *Farmer's Weekly (March 28, 2008, No. 320)*
Pub: Reed Business Information
Contact: Jeff Greisch, President
Description: Due, in part, to marketing efforts, retail sales of Welsh lamb and beef rose significantly in the first two months of 2008.

23604 ■ *"Wendy's Mulls Total Hortons Selloff"* in *Globe & Mail (January 7, 2006, pp. B5)*
Pub: CTVglobemedia Publishing Inc.
Ed: Sinclair Stewart; Omar El Akkad. Description: The plans of Wendy's International Inc. to spin off Tim Hortons are presented.

23605 ■ *"WestJet Ponders Growth Plan Following Record Profit"* in *Globe & Mail (February 15, 2007, pp. B15)*
Pub: CTVglobemedia Publishing Inc.
Ed: Brent Jang. Description: The Calgary-based WestJet Airlines Ltd., which reported a record $114.7 million profit last year, is planning to expand its operations by 2010. The airline is planning new services and carriers.

23606 ■ *What Works: Success in Stressful Times*
Pub: Harper Press
Ed: Hamish McRae. Released: January 21, 2010. Price: $30.12. Description: Exploration of success stories from across the glove, and what Michelle Obama referred to as 'the flimsy difference between success and failure.' Why do some initiatives take off while others flounder? How have communities managed to achieve so much while others struggle? What distinguishes the good companies from the bad? What lessons can be learned from the well-ordered Mumbai community made famous by 'Slumdog Millionaire'? Why have Canadian manners helped Whistler become the most popular ski resort in North America?.

23607 ■ *"What'll You Have Tonight?"* in *Barron's (Vol. 88, July 4, 2008, No. 28, pp. 22)*
Pub: Dow Jones & Co., Inc.
Ed: Neil A. Martin. Description: Shares of Diageo could rise by 30 percent a year from June 2008 after it slipped due to U.S. sales worries. The company also benefits from the trend toward more premium alcoholic beverage brands worldwide especially in emerging markets.

23608 ■ *"What's Holding Down Small Business?"* in *Business Owner (Vol. 35, November-December 2011, No. 6, pp. 3)*
Pub: DL Perkins Company
Description: According to a recent survey conducted by the National Federation of Independent Business, demand is the number one reason for slow growth to any small business in today's economy.

23609 ■ *"What's Next, Pup Tents in Bryant Park?"* in *Advertising Age (Vol. 78, January 29, 2007, No. 5, pp. 4)*
Pub: Crain Communications, Inc.
Ed: Stephanie Thompson. Description: Designers such as Ralph Lauren, Juicy Couture, Burberry and Kiehl's have been expanding their businesses with new clothing lines for pets. Packaged Facts, a division of MarketResearch.com, predicts that pet expenditures will continue to grow in the years to come.

23610 ■ *When Family Businesses are Best*
Pub: Palgrave Macmillan
Ed: Randel S. Carlock, John L. Ward. Released: March 1, 2010. Price: $45.00. Description: An exploration into effective planning and communication to help small businesses grow into multi-generation family enterprises.

23611 ■ *When Growth Stalls: How It Happens, Why You're Stuck, and what To Do About It*
Pub: John Wiley & Sons, Inc.
Ed: Steve McKee. Released: March 1, 2009. Price: $27.95. Description: Marketing expert presents evidence that demonstrates that slow growth experienced by a firm is usually not the cause of mismanagement or blundering, but by natural market forces and destructive internal dynamics that are often unrecognized.

23612 ■ *"When Success Isn't Enough"* in *Entrepreneur (Vol. 35, November 2007, No. 11, pp. 78)*
Pub: Entrepreneur Media Inc.
Ed: Chris Penttila. Description: Companies that achieve success can often times continue to push for more growth. Details on planning expansion and boosting sales of several companies are explored.

23613 ■ *"Where Next?"* in *Business Strategy Review (Vol. 21, Summer 2010, No. 2, pp. 20)*
Pub: Wiley-Blackwell
Description: The emergence of large, vibrant and seemingly unstoppable new markets has been the good news story of the past decade. Brazil, Russia, India and China (BRIC) are among those who have emerged blinking into the new economy.

23614 ■ *"Where's the Lava"* in *Hawaii Business (Vol. 53, November 2007, No. 5, pp. 18)*
Pub: Hawaii Business Publishing
Ed: Jason Ubay. Description: Hawaii Volcanoes National Park used to allow visitors to drive to the end of the paved coastal park road and view flowing lava that came from Kilauea until it reached the sea. On Father's Day morning in June 2007, Kilauea began erupting outside the park and the lava flows inland to Kahaualea and Wao Kele O Puna natural area reserves. In July 2007 321,217 visitors came to the park, a 14 percent increase compared to the same month in 2006.

23615 ■ *"While Competitors Shut Doors, Subway Is Still Growing"* in *Advertising Age (Vol. 79, July 21, 2008, No. 28, pp. 4)*
Pub: Crain Communications, Inc.
Ed: Emily Bryson York. Description: Subway, the largest fast-food chain, with 22,000 U.S. locations, is adding 800 this year, despite the economic downturn that has caused competitors such as Starbucks to close stores and McDonald's to focus its expansion abroad.

23616 ■ *"Whopper; Russ Klein"* in *Advertising Age (Vol. 79, November 17, 2008, No. 43, pp. S10)*
Pub: Crain Communications, Inc.
Ed: Emily Bryson York. Description: Burger King has seen a double digit increase in the sales of its Whopper hamburger despite the economic recession that has hit many in the restaurant industry particularly hard. For most of the spring, U.S. same-store-sales gains beat McDonald's.

23617 ■ *"Why the Rout in Financials Isn't Over"* in *Barron's (Vol. 88, June 30, 2008, No. 26, pp. 23)*
Pub: Dow Jones & Co., Inc.
Ed: Robin Goldwyn Blumenthal. Description: Top market technician Louise Yamada warns that the retreat in the shares of financial services is not yet over based on her analysis of stock charts. Yamada's analysis of the charts of Citigroup, Fifth Third Bancorp and Merrill Lynch are discussed together with the graphs for these shares. Statistical data included.

23618 ■ *"Why We'll Never Escape Facebook"* in *Canadian Business (Vol. 83, June 15, 2010, No. 10, pp. 28)*
Pub: Rogers Media Ltd.
Ed: James Cowan, Tamara Shopsin, Jason Fulford. Description: Facebook users are growing in numbers despite criticism of the site's privacy policies that have put the onus of keeping anonymous to the user. Facebook's business model and its growing influence on the Internet are discussed.

23619 ■ *"William Barr III; President, Co-Founder, Universal Windows Direct, 33"* in *Crain's Cleveland Business (November 19, 2007)*
Pub: Crain Communications, Inc.
Ed: David Bennett. Description: Profile of William Barr III, the president and co-founder of Universal Windows Direct, a manufacturer of vinyl windows and siding, whose successful salesmanship and leadership has propelled his company forward.

23620 ■ *"Winburn's Big Idea"* in *Business Courier (Vol. 27, October 8, 2010, No. 23, pp. 1)*
Pub: Business Courier
Ed: Dan Monk, Lucy May. Description: Cincinnati Councilman Charlie Winburn proposed the creation of Cincinnati Competitive Edge Division and to remake a small-business division of the city in order to start a job-creation program. The new division will monitor compliance to the city's small business inclusion regulations, as well as to help small business owners grow.

23621 ■ *"Windstream Expands Business Service Into Monroe"* in *Marketing Weekly News (January 23, 2010, pp. 77)*
Pub: Investment Weekly News
Description: Windstream Corp. announces the expansion of its data and voice services into Monroe, N.C., which will give local businesses a new choice for advanced communication services and network security.

23622 ■ *"Winner: Nonprofit, Human Services"* in *Crain's Detroit Business (Vol. 25, June 22, 2009, No. 25, pp. E002)*
Pub: Crain Communications Inc. - Detroit
Ed: Sherri Begin Welch. Description: Profile of Lighthouse of Oakland County, located in Pontiac, Michigan. The nonprofit and its three subsidiaries are operating on a consolidated 2009 budget of $8.5 million.

23623 ■ *"The Winner's Circle"* in *Hispanic Business (Vol. 30, April 2008, No. 4, pp. 20)*
Pub: Hispanic Business
Ed: Hildy Medina. Description: Although there has been progress concerning Hispanic women professionals who are growing in numbers in the upper echelons of the corporate arena, many still find that they face discrimination when it comes to pay and promotions. Statistical data included.

23624 ■ *"Wireless Provider's Star Grows $283 Million Brighter"* in *Hispanic Business (July-August 2007, pp. 60)*
Pub: Hispanic Business
Description: Profile of Brightstar Corporation, the world's largest wireless phone distribution and supply chain reported record growth in 2007.

23625 ■ *"Wirtz Partners With California Liquor Wholesaler To Expand Reach"* in *Chicago Tribune (December 17, 2008)*
Pub: McClatchy-Tribune Information Services
Ed: Mike Hughlett. Description: Young's Market Co. and Wirtz Beverage Group have tentatively agreed to a joint venture that will give both companies a larger reach in the wine and liquor distribution business.

23626 ■ *"WNY Casing In On Loonie's Climb"* in *Business First Buffalo (November 23, 2007, pp. 1)*
Pub: American City Business Journals, Inc.
Ed: Scott Thomas. Description: Economy of Western New York has rebounded since the 9/11 recession and the rise of the Canadian dollar, which has

contributed to the areas economic growth. Canadian shoppers are frequenting markets in the area due to the parity of the U.S. and Canadian dollar. Details of the cross-border shopping and its impact in WNY are discussed.

23627 ■ *"Women Clicking to Earn Virtual Dollars" in Sales and Marketing Management (November 11, 2009)*
Pub: Nielsen Business Media, Inc.

Ed: Stacy Straczynski. **Description:** According to a new report from Internet marketing firm Q Interactive, women are increasingly playing social media games where they are able to click on an ad or sign up for a promotion to earn virtual currency. Research is showing that this kind of marketing may be a potent tool, especially for e-commerce and online stores.

23628 ■ *"Women Inch Forward on Corporate Boards" in Marketing to Women (Vol. 21, April 2008, No. 4, pp. 6)*
Pub: EPM Communications Inc.
Contact: Ira Mayer, President
E-mail: imayer@epmcom.com

Description: According to the latest study by Inter-Organization Network, few huge leaps of progress and in some cases backsliding has taken place in regards to gender diversity on corporate boards. Statistical data included.

23629 ■ *"Work/Family Balance Boosts Business" in Marketing to Women (Vol. 21, February 2008, No. 2, pp. 8)*
Pub: EPM Communications Inc.
Contact: Ira Mayer, President
E-mail: imayer@epmcom.com

Description: Flexibility in the workplace is becoming a more important issue to both women and men. Statistical data included.

23630 ■ *"The World Is Your Hospital" in Canadian Business (Vol. 81, July 22, 2008, No. 12-13, pp. 62)*
Pub: Rogers Media Ltd.

Ed: Sharda Prashad. **Description:** Medical tourism is seen as a booming industry around the world and is expected to grow to around $40 billion in 2010. Key information regarding medical tourism and services are presented. Views on the possible impact of medical tourism on Canada's health care industry, as well as medical tourism opportunities in Canada, are also given.

23631 ■ *"A World of Opportunity: Foreign Markets Offer Diversity to Keen Investors" in Canadian Business (Vol. 81, Summer 2008, No. 9)*
Pub: Rogers Media Ltd.

Ed: Andrew Wahl. **Description:** International Monetary Fund projected in its 'World Economy Outlook' that there is a 25 percent chance that a global recession will occur in 2008 and 2009. Global growth rate is forecasted at 3.7 percent in 2008. Inflation in Asia emerging markets and forecasts on stock price indexes are presented.

23632 ■ *"The World Tomorrow" in Canadian Business (Vol. 81, December 24, 2007, No. 1, pp. 35)*
Pub: Rogers Media

Ed: Zena Olijnyk. **Description:** Global economy is predicted to be in a difficult period as analysts expect a slowdown in economic growth. Germany's Deutsche Bank wrote in a report about 'growth recession' that the chances of the world growth falling below two percent being one in three. Forecasts on other global economic aspects are explored.

23633 ■ *"World Wide Technology Expands" in Black Enterprise (Vol. 37, December 2006, No. 5, pp. 34)*
Pub: Earl G. Graves Publishing Co. Inc.

Ed: Marcia A. Wade. **Description:** World Wide Technology Inc. opened a streamlined, higher capacity 12,000-square-foot Integration Technology Center near its corporate headquarters in St. Louis. The new venture will transfer lower costs to customers.

23634 ■ *"Wowing Her Customers" in Women In Business (Vol. 61, August-September 2009, No. 4, pp. 34)*
Pub: American Business Women's Association

Ed: Kathleen Leighton. **Description:** Gail Worth, together with her brother, bought her parents' Harley-Davidson motorcycle dealership in Grandview, Missouri. She eventually had the dealership to herself when her brother broke out of the partnership. Gail says she is comfortable in a man's world kind of business and has expanded the business with a 10-acre site.

23635 ■ *"Wrigley's Newest Taste: Wolfberry" in Crain's Chicago Business (Vol. 31, March 31, 2008, No. 13, pp. 1)*
Pub: Crain Communications, Inc.

Ed: David Sterrett. **Description:** Wm. Wrigley Jr. Co. has introduced a gum line in China that touts the medicinal advantages of aloe vera to improve skin and wolfberry to boost energy in an attempt to keep the company positioned as the top candy firm in China.

23636 ■ *"The Wrong Tune" in The Business Journal-Portland (Vol. 25, July 25, 2008, No. 20, pp. 1)*
Pub: American City Business Journals, Inc.

Ed: Robin J. Moody. **Description:** Views and information on turnaround management and recovery plans of the Oregon Symphony, are presented. The nonprofit organization has lost a total of $5.1 million between 2002 and 2008, and $400,000 annual interest payments for a $7 million bank loan. Increased ticket sales, as well as cost cutting measures, are helping improve the finance of the organization.

23637 ■ *"Yamana's Golden Boy" in Canadian Business (Vol. 80, November 19, 2007, No. 23, pp. 49)*
Pub: Rogers Media

Ed: John Gray. **Description:** Profile of Peter Marrone, founder of the gold-producing company Yamana Gold Inc. in 2003. Yamana has grown since its 2003 launch, with $110 million reported earnings for the first three quarters in 2007. Marrone's career and how he built Yamana are discussed.

23638 ■ *"A Year After Fiorina's Exit, Hurd Makes His Mark" in Globe & Mail (February 8, 2006, pp. B9)*
Pub: CTVglobemedia Publishing Inc.

Ed: Shawn McCarthy. **Description:** The business growth strategies of chief executive officer Mark Hurd of Hewlett-Packard Co. are presented.

23639 ■ *"YoCream" in Ice Cream Reporter (Vol. 23, September 20, 2010, No. 10, pp. 6)*
Pub: Ice Cream Reporter

Description: YoCream reported a sales increase for third quarter 2010 at 15.6 percent and net income increasing 25 percent to $2,141,000 for that quarter.

23640 ■ *"Yogun Fruz Adds First Location in Southern New York State" in Ice Cream Reporter (Vol. 23, September 20, 2010, No. 10, pp. 2)*
Pub: Ice Cream Reporter

Description: Yogen Fruz signed a master franchise agreement to expand into the southern counties of New York State. The firm offers a healthy and beneficial option to fast food and typical dessert choices.

23641 ■ *"Yogurtini" in Ice Cream Reporter (Vol. 23, September 20, 2010, No. 10, pp. 7)*
Pub: Ice Cream Reporter

Description: Self-serve frozen yogurt chain, Yogurtini has opened its second store in Kansas City, Missouri.

23642 ■ *"You Won't Go Broke Filling Up On These Stocks" in Barron's (Vol. 88, July 14, 2008, No. 28, pp. 38)*
Pub: Dow Jones & Co., Inc.

Ed: Assif Shameen. **Description:** Due to high economic growth, pro-business policies and a consumption boom, the Middle East is a good place to look for equities. The best ways in which to gain

exposure to this market include investing in the real estate industry and telecommunications markets as well as large banks that serve corporations and consumers.

23643 ■ *"Your Big Give" in Small Business Opportunities (September 2008)*
Pub: Entrepreneur Press
Contact: Perlman Neil, President

Ed: Michael Guld. **Description:** Cause related marketing is beneficial to businesses as well as the communities they inhabit; three small businesses that are elevating their standing in the community while at the same time increasing their customer base are profiled.

23644 ■ *"Your Booming Business: How You Can Align Sales and Marketing for Dynamic Growth" in Small Business Opportunities (Spring 2008)*
Pub: Harris Publications Inc.

Ed: Voss W. Graham. **Description:** Voss Graham, founder and CEO of Inneractive Consulting Group Inc., works with companies to develop and hire successful sales teams. A checklist from the American Bankers Association to help write a business plan is included.

23645 ■ *"Your Business, Your Future: How to Predict and Harness Growth*
Pub: Allen and Unwin Pty., Limited

Ed: Linda Hailey. **Released:** January 2007. **Price:** $16.95. **Description:** Four distinct phases every small companies faces during growth are profiled.

23646 ■ *"Your First Business Plan: A Simple Question-and-Answer Format Designed to Help You Write Your Own Plan*
Pub: Sourcebooks, Inc.
Contact: Len Vlahos, President
E-mail: dominique@sourcebooks.com

Ed: Joseph A. Covello. **Released:** May 2005. **Price:** $14.95. **Description:** Writing a good first business plan outlines successful business growth.

23647 ■ *"Zakkamono Taps Growing Market for Collectibles" in Hawaii Business (Vol. 54, September 2008, No. 3, pp. 68)*
Pub: Hawaii Business Publishing

Ed: Casey Chin. **Description:** Profile of Zakkamono, a business that designs and designs designer toys, shirts and other collectibles; the first toys being Mousubi and Miao figurines. Owners Zakka and Rae Huo say that one of the business' challenges is finding manufacturing resources. Other details about Zakkamono are discussed.

23648 ■ *"Zebra's Changing Stripes" in Crain's Chicago Business (Vol. 31, November 17, 2008, No. 46, pp. 4)*
Pub: Crain Communications, Inc.

Ed: John Pletz. **Description:** Zebra Technologies Corp., the world's largest manufacturer of bar-code printers is profiled; the company's stock has plunged with shares declining 40 percent in the past three months grinding the firm's growth to a halt. Zebra's plans to regain revenue growth are also discussed.

23649 ■ *"ZF Revving Up Jobs, Growth" in Business Courier (Vol. 26, November 6, 2009, No. 28, pp. 1)*
Pub: American City Business Journals, Inc.

Ed: Jon Newberry. **Description:** Proposed $96 million expansion of German-owned automotive supplier ZF Steering systems LLC is anticipated to generate 299 jobs in Boone County, Kentucky. ZF might invest $90 million in equipment, while the rest will go to building and improvements.

TRADE PERIODICALS

23650 ■ *Expansion Management: Growth Strategies for Companies on the Move*
Pub: Penton Media Inc.

URL(s): www.expansionmanagement.com. **Released:** 6/yr.

23651 ■ *NACOMEX Insider*
Pub: NACOMEX USA Inc.
Ed: Robert Zises, Editor, zises@nacomex.com. **Released:** Quarterly. **Price:** $199, U.S.. **Description:** Provides information on historical values, current tactics, and residual value forecasting for ad valorem tax, bankruptcy, loss compensation, and related purposes. Recurring features include news of research and a column titled Industry Round-up.

VIDEOCASSETTES/ AUDIOCASSETTES

23652 ■ *Growing Your Company*
Instructional Video
2219 C St.
Lincoln, NE 68502
Ph: (402)475-6570
Free: 800-228-0164
Fax: (402)475-6500
Co. E-mail: feedback@insvideo.com
URL: http://www.insvideo.com
Released: 19??. **Price:** $99.00. **Description:** Offers advise on issues affecting business owners and managers, such as financial strategy, employee motivation, outselling the competition, and quality. **Availability:** VHS.

CONSULTANTS

23653 ■ BPT Consulting Associates Ltd.
12 Parmenter Rd., Ste. B-6
Londonderry, NH 03053
Ph: (603)437-8484
Free: 888-278-0030
Fax: (603)434-5388
Contact: John Kuczynski, Managing Director
Scope: Provides management consulting expertise and resources to cross-industry clients with services for: Business Management consulting, People/Human Resources Transition and Training programs, and a full cadre of multi-disciplined Technology Computer experts. Virtual consultants with expertise in e-commerce, supply chain management, organizational development, and business application development consulting. **Founded:** 1991.

23654 ■ Flor & Associates
179 Schan Dr.
Churchville, PA 18966-1619
Ph: (215)355-7466
Fax: (215)355-7464
Co. E-mail: fredflor@msn.com
Contact: Frederick Flor, President
Scope: Offers business development consulting helping companies increase the value of their businesses. Services include: market development for technologies sand products; product positioning strategies; technology assessment; competitive intelligence and analysis; team augmentation and facilitation; business growth strategies including acquisitions, licensing, and partnerships.

23655 ■ Herpers Gowling L.L.P.—310 DEBT Herpers Chagani Gowling Inc.
4 Hughson St. S, Ste. 300
Hamilton, ON, Canada L8N 3Z1
Ph: (905)529-3328
Free: 888-735-9909
Fax: (905)529-3980
Contact: Alex Herpers, President
Scope: Provides services to small and medium size businesses in the areas of financial management, strategic planning, mergers and acquisitions and re-

engineering/restructuring. **Founded:** 1996. **Special Services:** 310 DEBT®.

23656 ■ McMann & Ransford
1 Sugar Creek Center Blvd., Ste. 300
Sugar Land, TX 77478
Free: 866-267-0299
Co. E-mail: contact@mcmannransford.com
URL: http://www.mcmannransford.com
Contact: Dean E. McMann, Chief Executive Officer
E-mail: dmcmann@mcmannransford.com
Scope: Provides of management consulting, training, executive recruiting and market research services specializing in the professional services industry. **Founded:** 1990.

23657 ■ Plans and Solutions Inc.
7823 Mistic View Ct.
Derwood, MD 20855
Ph: (301)947-8150
Fax: (240)525-5601
Co. E-mail: info@plansandsolutions.com
URL: http://www.plansandsolutions.com
Contact: Kenneth D. Weiss, President
E-mail: kw@plansandsolutions.com
Scope: Market research and competitive analysis; marketing and promotion planning, and executing promotion plans. Specializes in registration and problem solving services that include food canning establishment and process registration, registration under the terrorism act, assistance in case of detention of shipments, and on-site inspection of processing plants and records. Most clients are minority-owned businesses in the USA and companies overseas that want to begin or increase exports to the United States and Canada. **Founded:** 1996. **Publications:** "Building an Import/Export Business," John Wiley & Sons, 2002; "How to Conquer the U.S. Market"; "Going Global (Getting Started in International Trade)". **Seminars:** U.S. Import Regulations on Food Products.

23658 ■ Norman A. Robins Consulting
5127 S Cornell Ave.
Chicago, IL 60615-4215
Ph: (773)667-6463
Contact: Norman A. Robins, President
Scope: Helps companies develop strategic plans that will improve profits, reduce costs, and accelerate growth. **Founded:** 1991.

23659 ■ The Sanderson Group Inc.
515 E 85 St., Ste. 4E
New York, NY 10028
Ph: (212)249-2556
Fax: (212)249-2557
URL: http://www.thesandersongroup.com
Contact: Robin Sanderson, President
E-mail: robin@thesandersongroup.com
Scope: Offers marketing consulting; communications and event/promotion marketing; develops objectives, establishes strategies and tactics to capitalize on the opportunities, and executes programs. Services provided include: strategic and marketing planning, target marketing with expertise in college or teen markets, integrated marketing programs, sampling, event marketing, new product development, corporate communications, strategic alliance formation, website strategic partnerships, website development and marketing, new business development, market research, sales and field force creation and management and customer acquisition. **Founded:** 1998.

23660 ■ Stillman H. Publishers Inc.
21405 Woodchuck Ln.
Boca Raton, FL 33428

Ph: (561)482-6343
Contact: Herbert Stillman, President
Scope: Offers consulting services in the following areas: management, start ups, profit maximization, world wide negotiating, interim management, corporate debt resolution. **Founded:** 1984.

LIBRARIES

23661 ■ Buffalo & Erie County Public Library - Business, Science & Technology
1 Lafayette Sq.
Buffalo, NY 14203
Ph: (716)858-8900
Fax: (716)858-6211
URL: http://www.buffalolib.org
Contact: Nancy Mueller, Division Manager
Scope: Investments, real estate, economics, marketing, engineering, computer science, technology, medical information for laymen, consumer information, automotive repair. **Services:** Interlibrary loan; copying; library open to the public. **Founded:** 1952. **Holdings:** 312,916 books; 60,516 bound periodical volumes; 600 periodical. **Subscriptions:** 2908 journals and other serials; 4 newspapers.

23662 ■ U.S. Dept. of Commerce Library and Information Center
1401 Constitution Ave., NW
Washington, DC 20230
Ph: (202)482-1154
Co. E-mail: lawlibrary@doc.gov
URL: http://library.doc.gov/client/default
Scope: Economics, export-import, foreign trade, business, economic theory, economic conditions, statistics, marketing, industry, finance, management, telecommunications. **Services:** Interlibrary loan; copying; Library open to the public for reference use only. **Founded:** 1913. **Holdings:** 45,000 books and bound periodical volumes; 4300 reels of microfilm; 250,000 volumes of microfiche; CD-ROMs. **Subscriptions:** 625 journals and other serials.

23663 ■ University of South Carolina - The Moore School of Business - Elliot White Springs Business Library
Francis M. Hipp Bldg., 2nd Fl.
1705 College St.
Columbia, SC 29208
Ph: (803)777-6032
Fax: (803)777-6876
Co. E-mail: gardnerd@mailbox.sc.edu
URL: http://library.sc.edu/business/index.html
Contact: Kathy Snediker
Scope: Corporations. **Services:** Interlibrary loan; copying; Library open to the public with restrictions. **Founded:** 1973. **Holdings:** 30,000 books; 4000 bound periodical volumes. **Subscriptions:** 350 journals and other serials; 5 newspapers. **Telecommunication Services:** busref@mailbox.sc.edu.

RESEARCH CENTERS

23664 ■ Minnesota Labor and Industry Department - Policy Development, Research and Statistics Unit
443 Lafayette Rd. N
Saint Paul, MN 55155
Ph: (651)284-5025
Free: 800-342-5354
Fax: (651)284-5726
Co. E-mail: dli.research@state.mn.us
URL: http://www.dli.mn.gov/Research.asp
Founded: 1985. **Publications:** *Minnesota Minimum Wage Report* (Annual); *Minnesota Worker's Compensation System Report* (Annual); *Minnesota Workplace Safety Report* (Annual).

START-UP INFORMATION

23665 ■ *Becoming a Personal Trainer for Dummies*
Pub: John Wiley and Sons, Inc.
Ed: Melyssa Michael, Linda Formichelli. **Released:** October 2004. **Price:** $19.99 (US), $25.99 (Canadian). **Description:** Legal and tax issues involved in starting and running a personal trainer firm. The book offers suggestions for incorporating massage and nutritional services.

23666 ■ *Enterprise Planning and Development: Small Business and Enterprise Start-Up Survival and Growth*
Pub: Elsevier Science and Technology Books
Ed: David Butler. **Released:** August 2006. **Price:** $42.95. **Description:** Innovation, intellectual property, and exit strategies are among the issues discussed in this book involving current entrepreneurship.

23667 ■ *How to Start, Operate and Market a Freelance Notary Signing Agent Business*
Pub: Gom Publishing, LLC
Ed: Victoria Ring. **Released:** September 2004. **Price:** $8.18. **Description:** Due to the changes in the 2001 Uniform Commercial Code allowing notary public agents to serve as a witness to mortgage loan closings (eliminating the 2-witness requirement under the old code), notaries are working directly for mortgage, title and signing companies as mobile notaries.

23668 ■ *Legal Guide for Starting and Running a Small Business*
Pub: NOLO
Ed: Fred S. Steingold. **Released:** August 2006. **Price:** $34.99. **Description:** Legal issues any small business owner needs to know for starting and running a successful business are outlined.

23669 ■ *Partnership: Small Business Start-Up Kit*
Pub: Nova Publishing Company
Ed: Daniel Sitarz. **Released:** November 2005. **Price:** $29.95. **Description:** Guidebook detailing partnership law by state covering the formation and use of partnerships as a business form. Information on filing requirements, property laws, legal liability, standards, and the new Revised Uniform Partnership Act is covered.

23670 ■ *Raising Capital*
Pub: Kiplinger Books and Tapes
Ed: Andrew J. Sherman. **Price:** $34.95. **Description:** Corporate attorney provides a comprehensive guide using in-depth, practical advice on raising money to start and grow a business. A 115-page appendix contains samples of financing agreements, forms and questionnaires.

23671 ■ *Small Business Legal Tool Kit*
Pub: Entrepreneur Press
Ed: Ira Nottonson; Theresa A. Pickner. **Released:** May 2007. **Price:** $36.95. **Description:** Legal expertise is provided by two leading entrepreneurial at-
torneys. Issues covered include forming and operating a business: taxes, contracts, leases, bylaws, trademarks, small claims court, etc.

23672 ■ *The Small Business Owner's Manual: Everything You Need to Know to Start Up and Run Your Business*
Pub: Career Press, Incorporated
Ed: Joe Kennedy. **Released:** June 2005. **Price:** $19.99 (US), $26.95 (Canadian). **Description:** Comprehensive guide for starting a small business, focusing on twelve ways to obtain financing, business plans, selling and advertising products and services, hiring and firing employees, setting up a Web site, business law, accounting issues, insurance, equipment, computers, banks, financing, customer credit and collection, leasing, and more.

23673 ■ *Working for Yourself: An Entrepreneur's Guide to the Basics*
Pub: Kogan Page, Limited
Contact: Ben Glover, Director of Marketing
Ed: Jonathan Reuvid. **Released:** September 2006. **Description:** Guide for starting a new business venture, focusing on raising financing, legal and tax issues, marketing, information technology, and site location.

23674 ■ *Your First Business Plan: A Simple Question-and-Answer Format Designed to Help You Write Your Own Plan*
Pub: Sourcebooks, Inc.
Contact: Len Vlahos, President
E-mail: dominique@sourcebooks.com
Ed: Joseph A. Covello. **Released:** May 2005. **Price:** $14.95. **Description:** Writing a good first business plan outlines successful business growth.

EDUCATIONAL PROGRAMS

23675 ■ Advanced Section 1031 Exchanges (Onsite)
Seminar Information Service, Inc.
20 Executive Park, Ste. 120
Irvine, CA 92614
Ph: (949)261-9104
Free: 877-SEM-INFO
Fax: (949)261-1963
Co. E-mail: info@seminarinformation.com
URL: http://www.seminarinformation.com
Price: $379.00. **Description:** This advanced seminar will provide you with practical tools and strategies you can use when participating in more complicated exchanges.

23676 ■ The Basics of Human Resource Law (Onsite)
Padgett-Thompson Seminars
Rockhurst University CEC
14502 W. 105th St.
Lenexa, KS 66215
Free: 800-349-1935
URL: http://www.findaseminar.com/tpd/Padgett-Thompson-Seminars.asp
Price: $249.00. **Description:** A one-day seminar covering the basics of human resources law. **Dates and Locations:** Worcester, MA; Providence, RI; Boston, MA.

23677 ■ Collections Laws (Onsite)
Fred Pryor Seminars & CareerTrack
5700 Broadmoor St., Ste. 300
Mission, KS 66202
Free: 800-780-8476
Fax: (913)967-8849
Co. E-mail: customerservice@pryor.com
URL: http://www.pryor.com
Price: $149.00; $139.00 for groups of 5 or more. **Description:** Learn to collect money effectively and legally with an understanding of the Fair Debt Collection Practices Act (FDCPA). **Dates and Locations:** Cities throughout the United States.

23678 ■ Commercial and Real Estate Loan Documents: More than Just Papers
Seminar Information Service, Inc.
20 Executive Park, Ste. 120
Irvine, CA 92614
Ph: (949)261-9104
Free: 877-SEM-INFO
Fax: (949)261-1963
Co. E-mail: info@seminarinformation.com
URL: http://www.seminarinformation.com
Price: $429.00. **Description:** Seminar designed to provide you with the key information you need to increase your working knowledge and understanding of the key legal and non-legal issues related to commercial loan documentation, including the meaning of loan documents, common documentation mistakes, more effective methods to replace existing lenders and deal with third parties, and collateral. **Dates and Locations:** Fayetteville, AR.

23679 ■ Concentrated Course in Construction Contracts (Onsite)
Seminar Information Service, Inc.
20 Executive Park, Ste. 120
Irvine, CA 92614
Ph: (949)261-9104
Free: 877-SEM-INFO
Fax: (949)261-1963
Co. E-mail: info@seminarinformation.com
URL: http://www.seminarinformation.com
Price: $1,195.00. **Description:** Four-day practical education in construction operations and construction law, including job set-up, claims avoidance, bonds, liens and insurance, specifications and bidding, labor relations, subcontracting, and more. **Dates and Locations:** Las Vegas, NV.

23680 ■ Data Analysis for EEO Professionals (Onsite)
Seminar Information Service, Inc.
20 Executive Park, Ste. 120
Irvine, CA 92614
Ph: (949)261-9104
Free: 877-SEM-INFO

Fax: (949)261-1963
Co. E-mail: info@seminarinformation.com
URL: http://www.seminarinformation.com
Price: $1,395.00. **Description:** Provides a solid understanding of the effective use of statistical analysis in EEO management and legal proceedings. Topics covered include: the legal basis for the use of statistics in EEO; which analytical tools are appropriate; how to interpret the results; when to conduct additional investigation; and strategies for presenting findings to management, agencies, and the courts. **Dates and Locations:** New York, NY.

23681 ■ Employment Discrimination Law Update (Onsite)
Seminar Information Service, Inc.
20 Executive Park, Ste. 120
Irvine, CA 92614
Ph: (949)261-9104
Free: 877-SEM-INFO
Fax: (949)261-1963
Co. E-mail: info@seminarinformation.com
URL: http://www.seminarinformation.com
Price: $895.00. **Description:** Covers changes in EEO law and enforcement, sexual harassment, resolving claims and implementing ADA, and the FMLA. **Dates and Locations:** San Francisco, CA; Chicago, IL; and Washington, DC.

23682 ■ The Essentials of Collections Law (Onsite)
Padgett-Thompson Seminars
Rockhurst University CEC
14502 W. 105th St.
Lenexa, KS 66215
Free: 800-349-1935
URL: http://www.findaseminar.com/tpd/Padgett-Thompson-Seminars.asp
Price: $179.00. **Description:** A one-day training session for accounts receivable professionals at all levels. **Dates and Locations:** Cities throughout the United States.

23683 ■ Harassment Prevention and Appropriate Behaviors in the Workplace (Onsite)
Seminar Information Service, Inc.
20 Executive Park, Ste. 120
Irvine, CA 92614
Ph: (949)261-9104
Free: 877-SEM-INFO
Fax: (949)261-1963
Co. E-mail: info@seminarinformation.com
URL: http://www.seminarinformation.com
Price: $895.00. **Description:** Explore the legal and policy concerns related to this complex workplace issue, including review and explore the guidelines for identifying inappropriate behavior; the laws, agency interpretations and court cases; and the key elements necessary for writing and implementing policies and procedures. **Dates and Locations:** New York, NY.

23684 ■ How to Legally Terminate Employees With Attitude Problems (Onsite)
Padgett-Thompson Seminars
Rockhurst University CEC
14502 W. 105th St.
Lenexa, KS 66215
Free: 800-349-1935
URL: http://www.findaseminar.com/tpd/Padgett-Thompson-Seminars.asp
Price: $199.00. **Description:** Learn how to act with confidence as you terminate problem employees who are damaging productivity and the company's effectiveness. **Dates and Locations:** Cities throughout the United States.

23685 ■ How to Manage an Information Security Program (Onsite)
Seminar Information Service, Inc.
20 Executive Park, Ste. 120
Irvine, CA 92614
Ph: (949)261-9104
Free: 877-SEM-INFO

Fax: (949)261-1963
Co. E-mail: info@seminarinformation.com
URL: http://www.seminarinformation.com
Price: $2,050.00. **Description:** Learn the components of a comprehensive plan, covering access control software applications; telecom/network security measures; physical protection of the computer facility; and the legal and regulatory aspects of information security.

23686 ■ Human Resources and the Law (Onsite)
Seminar Information Service, Inc.
20 Executive Park, Ste. 120
Irvine, CA 92614
Ph: (949)261-9104
Free: 877-SEM-INFO
Fax: (949)261-1963
Co. E-mail: info@seminarinformation.com
URL: http://www.seminarinformation.com
Price: $1,995.00. **Description:** Provides the human resources professional with an understanding of the laws that obligate employers, recent legislation and court cases defining employer/employee rights and obligations, legal and business considerations bearing on employer decisions, practical implications of the laws in day-to-day human resources operations, impact of the laws on the development of policies and procedures, and alternatives for minimizing the company's exposure to employee lawsuits and administrative charges. **Dates and Locations:** New York, NY.

23687 ■ Introduction to Human Resources Law
Seminar Information Service, Inc.
20 Executive Park, Ste. 120
Irvine, CA 92614
Ph: (949)261-9104
Free: 877-SEM-INFO
Fax: (949)261-1963
Co. E-mail: info@seminarinformation.com
URL: http://www.seminarinformation.com
Price: $995.00. **Description:** Overview of the legal issues associated with day-to-day employment-related decisions and actions. **Dates and Locations:** New York, NY.

23688 ■ Legal Issues in Real Estate Foreclosure (Onsite)
Seminar Information Service, Inc.
20 Executive Park, Ste. 120
Irvine, CA 92614
Ph: (949)261-9104
Free: 877-SEM-INFO
Fax: (949)261-1963
Co. E-mail: info@seminarinformation.com
URL: http://www.seminarinformation.com
Price: $369.00. **Description:** Gain practical procedural pointers on how to assertively protect your clients' financial interests through an in-depth understanding of the foreclosure process. **Dates and Locations:** Grand Rapids, MI; and Southfield, MI.

23689 ■ Payroll Law 2012 (Onsite)
Fred Pryor Seminars & CareerTrack
5700 Broadmoor St., Ste. 300
Mission, KS 66202
Free: 800-780-8476
Fax: (913)967-8849
Co. E-mail: customerservice@pryor.com
URL: http://www.pryor.com
Price: $199.00; $189.00 for groups of 5 or more. **Description:** Learn to handle payroll accurately, legally, and with confidence. **Dates and Locations:** Cities throughout the United States.

23690 ■ Payroll Law (Onsite)
Seminar Information Service, Inc.
20 Executive Park, Ste. 120
Irvine, CA 92614
Ph: (949)261-9104
Free: 877-SEM-INFO

Fax: (949)261-1963
Co. E-mail: info@seminarinformation.com
URL: http://www.seminarinformation.com
Price: $199.00. **Description:** Learn exactly where you're vulnerable in complying with complex FLSA mandates, identify common mistakes that get most companies hauled into court, and ensure 100 percent accuracy and compliance, as well as examine special payroll situations like garnishments and levies and involuntary deductions. **Dates and Locations:** Cities throughout the United States.

23691 ■ Payroll Law (Onsite)
Padgett-Thompson Seminars
Rockhurst University CEC
14502 W. 105th St.
Lenexa, KS 66215
Free: 800-349-1935
URL: http://www.findaseminar.com/tpd/Padgett-Thompson-Seminars.asp
Price: $199.00. **Description:** A one-day workshop that shows the vulnerabilities in your organization and how to fix the problems. **Dates and Locations:** Cities throughout the United States.

23692 ■ Practical Construction Law (Onsite)
Seminar Information Service, Inc.
20 Executive Park, Ste. 120
Irvine, CA 92614
Ph: (949)261-9104
Free: 877-SEM-INFO
Fax: (949)261-1963
Co. E-mail: info@seminarinformation.com
URL: http://www.seminarinformation.com
Price: $995.00. **Description:** Covers factors that must be considered at every stage of the construction process, including contracts, bidding for private and public work and Uniform Commercial Code. **Dates and Locations:** Las Vegas, NV.

23693 ■ A Practical Guide to the Davis-Bacon Act (Onsite)
Seminar Information Service, Inc.
20 Executive Park, Ste. 120
Irvine, CA 92614
Ph: (949)261-9104
Free: 877-SEM-INFO
Fax: (949)261-1963
Co. E-mail: info@seminarinformation.com
URL: http://www.seminarinformation.com
Price: $595.00. **Description:** Discussions of what the Act requires of contractors, special problem areas, overtime matters and calculations, sanctions for violations, how to develop on-going compliance procedures and more. **Dates and Locations:** Las Vegas, NV.

23694 ■ Property Condition Assessments Featuring E2018 Standard Guide (Onsite)
Seminar Information Service, Inc.
20 Executive Park, Ste. 120
Irvine, CA 92614
Ph: (949)261-9104
Free: 877-SEM-INFO
Fax: (949)261-1963
Co. E-mail: info@seminarinformation.com
URL: http://www.seminarinformation.com
Price: $895.00. **Description:** Two-day course with focus of the ASTM Property Condition Assessment standard and explains why it was developed. **Dates and Locations:** Dallas, TX; and Phoenix, AZ.

23695 ■ Property Taking Through Eminent Domain: What You Need to Know (Onsite)
Seminar Information Service, Inc.
20 Executive Park, Ste. 120
Irvine, CA 92614
Ph: (949)261-9104
Free: 877-SEM-INFO
Fax: (949)261-1963
Co. E-mail: info@seminarinformation.com
URL: http://www.seminarinformation.com
Price: $365.00. **Description:** Get the knowledge you need to exert the municipality's rights and achieve the best outcome possible, including how the Kelo ruling will affect your organization when considering a taking and get clear explanations of the parameters guiding the action.

23696 ■ **Real Estate Law: Advanced Issues and Answers (Onsite)**

Seminar Information Service, Inc.
20 Executive Park, Ste. 120
Irvine, CA 92614
Ph: (949)261-9104
Free: 877-SEM-INFO
Fax: (949)261-1963
Co. E-mail: info@seminarinformation.com
URL: http://www.seminarinformation.com

Price: $399.00. **Description:** Go beyond the basics for an advanced look at complicated real estate concerns like resolving title defects, finding practical solutions to environmental conflicts, clearing difficult liens from titles, and dealing properly with property affected by a bankruptcy. **Dates and Locations:** Baltimore, MD; Scranton, PA; Manchester, NH; and Atlanta, GA.

23697 ■ **Resolving Real Estate Title Defects (Onsite)**

Seminar Information Service, Inc.
20 Executive Park, Ste. 120
Irvine, CA 92614
Ph: (949)261-9104
Free: 877-SEM-INFO
Fax: (949)261-1963
Co. E-mail: info@seminarinformation.com
URL: http://www.seminarinformation.com

Price: $369.00. **Description:** Learn to recognize and resolve title problems that may arise during real estate transactions; Apply the standards of title examination effectively to uncover problems and prevent them whenever possible Confidently take the next step when you recognize a defect and ensure the transaction goes smoothly.

23698 ■ **Writing Effective EEO Investigative Reports**

Seminar Information Service, Inc.
20 Executive Park, Ste. 120
Irvine, CA 92614
Ph: (949)261-9104
Free: 877-SEM-INFO
Fax: (949)261-1963
Co. E-mail: info@seminarinformation.com
URL: http://www.seminarinformation.com

Price: $1,195.00. **Description:** Focuses exclusively on the written product of an effective investigation. Topics include understanding the Faragher-Ellert Affirmative Defense and addressing credibility. **Dates and Locations:** New York, NY.

DIRECTORIES OF EDUCATIONAL PROGRAMS

23699 ■ *Bond's Franchise Guide 2009*

Pub: Source Book Publications
Contact: Stephanie Woo, Editor

Ed: Robert E. Bond, Michelle Yang. **Released:** April 7, 2009. **Description:** Comprehensive directory offering prospective franchise owners a current and detailed profile of 1,000 franchises, as well as supplemental profiles of franchise attorneys and consultants; companies are divided into 45 categories for easy comparison.

23700 ■ *Neal-Schuman Guide to Finding Legal and Regulatory Information on the Internet*

Pub: Neal-Schuman Publishers Inc.
Contact: Patricia Glass Schuman, President
E-mail: pgs@neal-schuman.com

URL(s): www.neal-schuman.com. **Ed:** Yvonne J. Chandler. **Released:** new edition expected 2005. **Price:** $135, Individuals. **Covers:** 900 Internet sites offering local, state, and federal legal and government information. **Entries include:** Title, publishing agency, URL, brief description of the site.

REFERENCE WORKS

23701 ■ *"11th Circuit: Don't Break the Law to Comply with It" in Miami Daily Business*

Review (October 21, 2009)

Pub: Incisive Media
Contact: Lee Feldman, Manager
E-mail: lee.feldman@incisivemedia.com

Ed: Janet L. Conley. **Description:** Niagara Credit Solutions argued with a three-judge panel that the company broke the rule saying debt collectors must identify themselves so that they could comply with a rule barring debt collectors from communicating about a debt with third parties.

23702 ■ *"13D Filings" in Barron's (Vol. 88, March 24, 2008, No. 12, pp. M13)*

Pub: Dow Jones & Company, Inc.

Description: HealthCor Management called as problematic the plan of Magellan Health Services to use its high cash balances for acquisitions. Carlson Capital discussed with Energy Partners possible changes in the latter's board. Investor Carl Icahn suggested that Enzon Pharmaceuticals consider selling itself or divest some of its assets.

23703 ■ *"13D Filings" in Barron's (Vol. 88, March 10, 2008, No. 10, pp. M11)*

Pub: Dow Jones & Company, Inc.

Description: Barington Capital and Clinton Group sent a letter to Dillard's demanding a list of the company's stockholders. Elliott Associates announced that it is prepared to take over Packeteer for $5.50 a share. Strongbow capital suggested a change in leadership in Duckwall-ALCO Stores.

23704 ■ *"13D Filings: Investors Report to the SEC" in Barron's (Vol. 88, March 31, 2008, No. 13, pp. M10)*

Pub: Dow Jones & Company, Inc.

Description: Obrem Capital Management wants Micrel to rescind Micrel's shareholder-rights plan and to boost its board to six members from five. Patricia L. Childress plans to nominate herself to the board of Sierra Bancorp, and Luther King Capital Management may consider a competing acquisition proposal for Industrial Distribution Group.

23705 ■ *"13D Filings: Investors Report to the SEC" in Barron's (Vol. 88, July 4, 2008, No. 28, pp. M10)*

Pub: Dow Jones & Co., Inc.

Description: Robino Stortini Holdings will seek control of Investors Capital Holdings either alone or with members of the company's management. Discovery Group I will withhold its votes at the nomination of directors for TESSCO Technologies while JMB Capital Partners Master Fund plans to nominate a slate of candidates to the board of Maguire Properties.

23706 ■ *"13D Filings: Investors Report to the SEC" in Barron's (Vol. 89, July 13, 2009, No. 28, pp. M9)*

Pub: Dow Jones & Co., Inc.

Description: Bulldog Investors wants Hicks Acquisition Co. to liquidate and return money to shareholders and they believe that the acquisition of Graham Packaging by Hicks will not be completed in a timely manner. Discovery Group raised their holdings to 5.2 percent of Nobel Learning Communities.

23707 ■ *The 30-Second Commute*

Pub: McGraw-Hill

Ed: Beverley Williams; Don Cooper. **Released:** 2004. **Price:** $19.95. **Description:** Home-based business owners explain how entrepreneurs can avoid long commutes and high costs of working outside the home by starting a home-based company. Essential steps for launching a successful home-based business are covered, including type of business, legal issues, and writing a business plan.

23708 ■ *"$3.5 Million Lawsuit Points Finger at Black Firm" in Black Enterprise (Vol. 38, March 2008, No. 8)*

Pub: Earl G. Graves Publishing Co. Inc.

Ed: Cliff Hocker. **Description:** World Wide Technology, the world's largest black-owned company is being sued by a former employee for racial discrimination and retaliation. Details of the lawsuit are outlined.

23709 ■ *365 Answers about Human Resources for the Small Business Owner: What Every Manager Needs to Know about Work Place Law*

Pub: Atlantic Publishing Company

Ed: Mary Holihan. **Released:** June 2006. **Price:** $21.95. **Description:** Common questions employers ask about employees and the law are answered.

23710 ■ *"Accountants Get the Hook" in Canadian Business (Vol. 80, October 22, 2007, No. 21, pp. 19)*

Pub: Rogers Media

Ed: John Gray. **Description:** Chartered Accountants of Ontario handed down the decision on Douglas Barrington, Anthony Power and Claudio Russo's professional misconduct case. The three accountants of Deloitte & Touche LLP must pay C$100,000 in fines and C$417,000 in costs. Details of the disciplinary case are presented.

23711 ■ *"After the Storm: Following a Tragic Loss, the Chambers Family Is Starting To See the Light" in Black Enterprise (November 2007)*

Pub: Earl G. Graves Publishing Co. Inc.

Ed: Sheryl Nance Nash. **Description:** A family law firm filed bankruptcy after the death of a daughter.

23712 ■ *"AG Warns Slots MBE Plan Risky" in Boston Business Journal (Vol. 29, May 27, 2011, No. 3, pp. 1)*

Pub: American City Business Journals Inc.

Ed: Scott Dance. **Description:** Attorney General Doug Gansler states that the law extending the minority business program on slots parlors contracting through 2018 could be open to lawsuits. He recommended that the state should conduct a study proving that minority- and women-owned businesses do not get a fair share in the gaming industry before it signs the bill to avoid lawsuits from majority-owned firms.

23713 ■ *"Akerman Senterfitt Merger Deal Close" in The Business Journal-Serving Greater Tampa Bay (Vol. 28, July 18, 2008, No. 30, pp. 1)*

Pub: American City Business Journals, Inc.

Ed: Jeff Blumenthal. **Description:** Sources familiar to the negotiations of Akerman Senterfitt's planned merger with Wolf Block has disclosed that executive committees of both firms have approved the deal. They expect to create an 800-lawyer firm with a significant presence in the U.S. East Coast. Other views and information on the deal and its expected impact on law practice in Florida are presented.

23714 ■ *"All About The Benjamins" in Canadian Business (Vol. 81, September 29, 2008, No. 16, pp. 92)*

Pub: Rogers Media Ltd.

Ed: David Baines. **Description:** Discusses real estate developer Royal Indian Raj International Corp., a company that planned to build a $3 billion 'smart city' near the Bangalore airport; to this day nothing has ever been built. The company was incorporated in 1999 by Manoj C. Benjamin one investor, Bill Zack, has been sued by the developer for libel due to his website that calls the company a scam. Benjamin has had a previous case of fraud issued against him as well as a string of liabilities and lawsuits.

23715 ■ *"American Axle Sues to Force Steelmaker to Resume Suspended Parts Shipment" in Crain's Detroit Business (Vol. 25, June 15, 2009)*

Pub: Crain Communications Inc. - Detroit

Ed: Robert Sherefkin. **Description:** American Axle & Manufacturing Holdings Inc. is facing a shutdown if a Michigan court does not force Republic Engineered Products Inc., a specialty steelmaker, to ship parts. If the parts are not shipped, it could cause assembly plants to shutdown.

23716 ■ *American Bar Association Legal Guide for Small Business: Everything You*

Need to Know About Small Business
Pub: Random House Information Group
Contact: Markus Dohle, Accountant
Ed: American Bar Association. **Released:** June 10, 2010. **Description:** The American Bar Association provides insight into financial, health and family issues affecting small business, including start up issues, employment laws, financing a business, and selling a business.

23717 ■ *"Ann Alexander; Senior Attorney, Natural Resources Defense Council" in Crain's Chicago Business (Vol. 31, May 5, 2008, No. 18)*
Pub: Crain Communications, Inc.
Ed: Emily Stone. **Description:** Profile of Ann Alexander who is the senior attorney at the Natural Resources Defense Council and is known for her dedication to the environment and a career spent battling oil companies, steelmakers and the government to change federal regulations. One recent project aims to improve the Bush administration's fuel economy standards for SUVs. Past battles include her work to prevent permits from slipping through the cracks such as the proposal by London-based BP PLC to dump 54 percent more ammonia and 35 percent more suspended solids from its Whiting, Indiana refinery into Lake Michigan-the source of drinking water for Chicago and its surrounding communities.

23718 ■ *Antitrust Law: Economic Theory and Common Law Evolution*
Pub: Cambridge University Press
Contact: Richard Ziemacki, President
E-mail: rziemacki@cambridge.org
Ed: Keith N. Hylton. **Released:** January 22, 2010. **Price:** $39.99. **Description:** A consolidation of various perspectives on antitrust law and its evolution.

23719 ■ *"Antwerpen Takes on Chrysler Financial Over Foreclosure Sales" in Baltimore Business Journal (Vol. 28, July 30, 2010, No. 12, pp. 1)*
Pub: Baltimore Business Journal
Ed: Gary Haber. **Description:** Antwerpen Motorcars Ltd. aims to fight the scheduled foreclosure sale of real estate it leases in Baltimore County, including the showroom for its Hyundai dealership on Baltimore National Pike in Catonsville, Maryland. The company is planning to file papers in court to stop the scheduled August 11, 2010 auction sought by Chrysler Financial Services Americas LLC.

23720 ■ *Are Government Purchasing Policies Failing Small Business?: Congressional Hearing*
Pub: DIANE Publishing Company
Ed: John F. Kerry. **Released:** September 2002. **Price:** Paperback $35.00. **Description:** Covers Congressional hearing: Steven App, Treasury Department; Fred Armendariz and Major Clark, Small Business Administration; Susan Allen, Pan Asian American Chamber of Commerce; Stephen Denlinger, Latin American Management Association; Charles Henry, National Veteran's Business Development Corporation; Morris Hudson, MO Procurement Technology Assistance Centers; Bar Kasoff, Women Impact, Public Policy; Pam Mazza, Piliero, Massa and Pargament; Ron Newlan, HubZone Contract National Council; Pat Parker, Native American Management Service; Joann Payne, Women First National Legislative Commission; Mike Robinson, MA Small Business Development Centers; Ramon Rodriguez, Hispanic Chamber of Commerce; Angela Styles, Office of Management and Budget; Ralph Thomas, NASA; John Turner, MN Business Enterprise Legal Defense Fund; James Turpin, American Subcontractor's Association, Inc.; and Henry Wilfong, National Association of Small Disadvantaged Business.

23721 ■ *Atiyah's Accidents, Compensation and the Law*
Pub: Cambridge University Press
Contact: Richard Ziemacki, President
E-mail: rziemacki@cambridge.org
Ed: Peter Cane, Patrick Atiyah. **Released:** January 22, 2010. **Price:** $56.00. **Description:** Leading authority on the law of personal injuries compensation and the social, political and economic issues surrounding it.

23722 ■ *"Attend To Your Corporate Housekeeping" in Women Entrepreneur (December 4, 2008)*
Pub: Entrepreneur Media Inc.
Ed: Nina Kaufman. **Description:** Business owners can lose all the benefits and privileges of the corporate form if they do not follow proper corporate formalities such as holding an annual meeting, electing officers and directors and adopting or passing corporate resolutions. Creditors are able to take from one's personal assets if such formalities have not been followed.

23723 ■ *"Attorney Covers Climate in Copenhagen" in Houston Business Journal (Vol. 40, December 25, 2009, No. 33, pp. 1)*
Pub: American City Business Journals
Ed: Ford Gunter. **Description:** Houston environmental attorney Richard Faulk talks to the United Nations Climate Change Conference in Copenhagen, Denmark. Faulk believes the conference failed due to political differences between countries like US and China. Faulk believed the discussion of developed and developing countries on verification and limits on carbon emissions is something good that came from the conference.

23724 ■ *"Attorney Guides Biotech Company in $6 Million Initial Public Offering" in Miami Daily Business Review (March 26, 2008)*
Pub: ALM Media Inc.
Description: In order to raise capital to engage in a full-scale trial of MyoCell to receive clinical approval, Bioheart Inc., launched an initial public offering. Bioheart researches and develops cell therapies to treat heart damage.

23725 ■ *"Attorney Internet Marketing Services Launched by SEO Advantage at SEOLegal.com" in Internet Wire (October 5, 2009)*
Pub: Comtex News Network, Inc.
Description: SEO Advantage, an Internet marketing and website designer firm, has extended its services to the legal industry.

23726 ■ *"Attorney Panel Tackles Contract Questions" in Agency Sales Magazine (Vol. 39, September-October 2009, No. 9, pp. 8)*
Pub: MANA
Ed: Jack Foster. **Description:** MANAfest conference tackled issues regarding a sales representative's contract. One attorney from the panel advised reps to go through proposed agreements with attorneys who are knowledgeable concerning rep laws. Another attorney advised reps to communicate with a company to ask about their responsibilities if that company is facing financial difficulty.

23727 ■ *"Auto Repair Business Owner Sentenced" in Ventura County Star (November 20, 2010)*
Pub: Ventura County Star
Ed: Raul Hernandez. **Description:** Oxnard, California auto repair business owner was sentenced to jail for grand theft and falsification of smog certificate information.

23728 ■ *"Balancing Freedom of Speech with the Right To Privacy" in Pace Law Review (Fall 2007)*
Pub: American Society on Aging
Contact: Robert Stein, President
Ed: Anna Zwierz Messa. **Description:** Information is offered to help authorities and funeral directors cope with protests occurring during a funeral.

23729 ■ *"Banking on Twitter" in Baltimore Business Journal (Vol. 27, February 6, 2010, No. 40, pp. 1)*
Pub: American City Business Journals
Ed: Gary Haber. **Description:** Ways that banks are using Twitter, Facebook and other social networking sites to provide customer services is discussed. First Mariner Bank is one of those banks that are finding the social media platform as a great way to reach customers. Privacy issues regarding this marketing trend are examined.

23730 ■ *"Bankruptcies" in Crain's Detroit Business (Vol. 24, March 24, 2008, No. 12, pp. 6)*
Pub: Crain Communications, Inc.
Description: Current list of business that filed for Chapter 7 or 11 protection in U.S. Bankruptcy Court in Detroit include a construction company, a medical care company, a physical therapy firm and a communications firm.

23731 ■ *"Bankruptcies" in Crain's Detroit Business (Vol. 24, September 29, 2008, No. 39, pp. 4)*
Pub: Crain Communications Inc.
Description: Current list of business that filed for Chapter 7 or 11 protection in U.S. Bankruptcy Court in Detroit include manufacturers, real estate companies, a printing company and a specialized staffing company.

23732 ■ *"Bankruptcies" in Crain's Detroit Business (Vol. 24, October 6, 2008, No. 40, pp. 26)*
Pub: Crain Communications, Inc.
Description: Current businesses that have filed for Chapter 7 or 11 protection in U.S. Bankruptcy Court include an auto dealership, a gun range and a grocery service.

23733 ■ *"Bankruptcies" in Crain's Detroit Business (Vol. 26, January 4, 2010, No. 1, pp. 5)*
Pub: Crain Communications, Inc.
Ed: Dustin Walsh. **Description:** Listing of local businesses that filed for Chapter 7 or 11 protection in U.S. Bankruptcy Court in Detroit December 11-28. Under Chapter 11, a company files for reorganization. Chapter 7 involves total liquidation.

23734 ■ *"Bankruptcies" in Crain's Detroit Business (Vol. 26, January 11, 2010, No. 2, pp. 7)*
Pub: Crain Communications, Inc.
Ed: Dustin Walsh. **Description:** Listing of local businesses that filed for Chapter 7 or 11 protection in U.S. Bankruptcy Court in Detroit December 11-28. Under Chapter 11, a company files for reorganization. Chapter 7 involves total liquidation.

23735 ■ *"Bankruptcies Shoot Up 68 Percent" in Sacramento Business Journal (Vol. 25, July 18, 2008, No. 20, pp. 1)*
Pub: American City Business Journals, Inc.
Ed: Kathy Robertson. **Description:** Personal bankruptcy in the Sacramento area rose by 88 percent for the first half of 2008 while business bankruptcies rose by 50 percent for the same period. The numbers of consumer bankruptcy reflects the effect of high debt, rising mortgage costs, and declining home values on U.S. households.

23736 ■ *"Bankruptcies Soar As Market Takes a Tumble" in The Business Journal - Serving Phoenix and the Valley of the Sun (Vol. 28, August 22, 2008, No. 51, pp. 1)*
Pub: American City Business Journals, Inc.
Ed: Chris Casacchia. **Description:** Chapter 7 and Chapter 13 bankruptcy filings have increased 112 percent in July 2008, for a total of 1,225 filings in Phoenix. Chapter 11 business reorganizations also increased by 86 percent compared to 2007 figures because of the challenging national economy. Other views and information on the rise in bankruptcy filings in Phoenix are presented.

23737 ■ *"Bankruptcies Swell" in The Business Journal-Portland (Vol. 25, July 4, 2008, No. 17, pp. 1)*
Pub: American City Business Journals, Inc.
Ed: Andy Giegerich. **Description:** Individual and business bankruptcy filings in Portland, Oregon had increased. The rising gas and food prices, mortgage crisis and tightening lending standards are seen as causes of bankruptcies. Statistics on bankruptcy filings are also provided.

23738 ■ *"Bankruptcy Blowback" in Business Week (September 22, 2008, No. 4100, pp. 36)*
Pub: McGraw-Hill Companies, Inc.
Ed: Jessica Silver-Greenberg. **Description:** Changes to bankruptcy laws which were enacted in 2005 after banks and other financial institutions lobbied hard for them are now suffering the consequences of the laws which force more troubled borrowers to let their homes go into foreclosure; lenders suffer financially every time they have to take on a foreclosure and the laws in which they lobbied so hard to see enacted are now becoming a problem for these lending institutions. Details of the changes in the laws are outlined as are the affects on the consumer, the economy and the lenders.

23739 ■ *"Bankruptcy Claims Brooke, Gives Franchisees Hope" in The Business Journal-Serving Metropolitan Kansas City (October 31, 2008)*
Pub: American City Business Journals, Inc.
Ed: James Dornbrook; Steve Vockrodt. **Description:** Insurer Brooke Corp. was required to file for Chapter 11 bankruptcy for a deal to sell all of its assets to businessmen Terry Nelson and Lysle Davidson. The new Brooke plans to share contingency fees with franchisees. The impacts of the bankruptcy case on Brooke franchisees are discussed.

23740 ■ *Bankruptcy for Small Business*
Pub: Sphinx Publishing
Ed: Wendell Schollander. **Released:** July 1, 2008. **Price:** $22.95 paperback. **Description:** Bankruptcy laws can be used to save a small business, homes or other property. The book provides general information for small business owners regarding the reasons for money problems, types of bankruptcy available and their alternatives, myths about bankruptcy, and the do's and don'ts for filing for bankruptcy.

23741 ■ *Bankruptcy for Small Business, 2E: Know Your Legal Rights and Recover from Mistakes and Start Over Successfully*
Pub: Sourcebooks, Inc.
Contact: Len Vlahos, President
E-mail: dominique@sourcebooks.com
Ed: Wendell Schollander; Wes Schollander. **Released:** July 2008. **Price:** $22.95. **Description:** Bankruptcy laws can actually help small business owners save their companies, homes and other property. This book offers general information regarding reasons for money problems, types of bankruptcy available to small business owners as well as alternatives to bankruptcy and more.

23742 ■ *"Barred Collection Agency Sued by Colorado AG" in Collections & Credit Risk (Vol. 15, August 1, 2010, No. 7, pp. 7)*
Pub: SourceMedia Inc.
Description: Collection agency run by Chad Lee received notice that it is barred from collecting in the State of Colorado by Attorney General John Suther's office. A ruling cited that the firm engages in harassment or abuse and/or threats of violence, made false representations as to its legal status of debts, made false and misleading representations of nonpayment of debts that would result in arrest, and that Lee failed to disclose his previous felony conviction.

23743 ■ *"Battling Back from Betrayal" in Harvard Business Review (Vol. 88, December 2010, No. 12, pp. 130)*
Pub: Harvard Business School Publishing
Ed: Daniel McGinn. **Description:** Stephen Greer's scrap metal firm, Hartwell Pacific, lost several million dollars due to a lack of efficient and appropriate inventory audits, accounting procedures, and new-hire reference checks for his foreign operations. Greer believes that balancing growth with control is a key component of success.

23744 ■ *"Be Proactive - Closely Review Contracts" in Contractor (Vol. 56, July 2009, No. 7, pp. 19)*
Pub: Penton Media, Inc.
Ed: Al Schwartz. **Description:** Contract disputes can make subcontractors suffer big financial losses or even cause a new subcontractor to fail. Subcontractors should scour the plans and specifications for any

references to work that might remotely come under their scope and to cross out any line in the contract that does not accurately reflect the work that they agreed to.

23745 ■ *"Be Wary of Legal Advice on Internet, Lawyers Warn" in Crain's Detroit Business (Vol. 24, September 22, 2008, No. 38, pp. 16)*
Pub: Crain Communications Inc.
Ed: Harriet Tramer. **Description:** While some lawyers feel that the proliferation of legal information on the Internet can point people in the right direction, others maintain that it simply results in giving false hope, may bring about confusion or worse yet, it sometimes makes their jobs even harder.

23746 ■ *"Beer Sales 'Foament' a Dispute" in Philadelphia Business Journal (Vol. 28, October 9, 2009, No. 34, pp. 1)*
Pub: American City Business Journals
Ed: Peter van Allen. **Description:** Malt Beverages Distributors Association of Pennsylvania filed a case against the Liquor Control Board (LCB) at the Pennsylvania Supreme Court in order to further restrict store sales. The dispute stems from the supermarket chains circumventing the liquor law with the blessings of LCB.

23747 ■ *The Big Squeeze: Tough Times for the American Workers*
Pub: Pantheon Books
Ed: Steven Greenhouse. **Released:** 2009. **Price:** $25.95. **Description:** Labor correspondent for the New York Times reports on the bleak condition of the current workplace environment, citing violations of child labor laws and forced slave labor conditions in third world countries and robber baron era occurring often here in America that are expanding the number of working poor.

23748 ■ *"Bills Would Regulate Mortgage Loan Officers" in Crain's Detroit Business (Vol. 24, February 25, 2008, No. 8, pp. 9)*
Pub: Crain Communications Inc. - Detroit
Ed: Amy Lane. **Description:** New legislation in Michigan, if passed, would create a registration process for mortgage loan officers in the state in order to address the mortgage loan crisis.

23749 ■ *"BIM: The Risks You Need to Watch Out For" in Contractor (Vol. 57, February 2010, No. 2, pp. 28)*
Pub: Penton Media, Inc.
Ed: Susan Linden McGreevy. **Description:** Legal and risk management issues surrounding Building Information Modeling (BIM) can be divided into three categories namely; intellectual property, liability for content, and the responsibility for the inputs into the model. The agreement should be done in a way that protects the intellectual rights of the authors when using BIM.

23750 ■ *"BIM and You: Know Its Benefits and Risks" in Contractor (Vol. 57, January 2010, No. 1, pp. 46)*
Pub: Penton Media, Inc.
Ed: Susan Linden McGreevy. **Description:** Building Information Modeling is intended to be 'collaborative' and this could raise legal issues if a contractor sends an electronic bid and it is filtered out. Other legal issues that mechanical contractors need to consider before using this technology are discussed.

23751 ■ *"Biovail Hits SAC With $4.6 Billion Suit" in Globe & Mail (February 23, 2006, pp. B1)*
Pub: CTVglobemedia Publishing Inc.
Ed: Shawn McCarthy. **Description:** The details of Biovail Corp.'s securities fraud case against SAC Management LLC are presented.

23752 ■ *"BK Franchisees Lose Sleep Over Late-Night Rule" in Advertising Age (Vol. 79, August 11, 2008, No. 31, pp. 1)*
Pub: Crain Communications, Inc.
Ed: Emily Bryson York. **Description:** Burger King's corporate headquarters mandates that franchisees remain open until at least 2 a.m. Three Miami opera-

tors have filed a lawsuit that alleges the extended hours can be dangerous, do not make money and overtax the workforce.

23753 ■ *"Black's Truth: Will a Prison Stay Change the Way Conrad Black Operates?" in Canadian Business (Vol. 81, March 31, 2008, No. 5)*
Pub: Rogers Media
Ed: Matthew McClearn. **Description:** Conrad Black will serve a 6 and a half years in prison but he asserts that his successors at Hollinger International and Hollinger Inc. grossly mismanaged and unjustly enriched themselves. Black also asserts that International violated the so-called November Agreement and that he is the aggrieved party. Black's assertions show a character flaw that cannot be corrected in prison.

23754 ■ *"Blast Blame" in The Business Journal-Milwaukee (Vol. 25, September 5, 2008, No. 50, pp. 1)*
Pub: American City Business Journals, Inc.
Description: Rexnord Industries LLC and J.M. Brennan Inc.'s property damage trial in connection with the explosion at the Falk Corp. plant in Menomonee Valley, Wisconsin is set to begin. Lawyers for the two companies have failed to reach a settlement. A leaking propane line was seen as the cause of the blast.

23755 ■ *"Blood Diamonds are Forever" in Canadian Business (Vol. 83, August 17, 2010, No. 13-14, pp. 59)*
Pub: Rogers Media Ltd.
Ed: Matthew McClearn. **Description:** The failed case against Donald McKay who was found in possession of rough diamonds in a raid by Royal Canadian Mounted Police has raised doubts about Kimberley Process (KP) attempts to stop the illicit global trade in diamonds. KP has managed to reduce total global trade of blood diamonds by 1 percent in mid-2000.

23756 ■ *"Bloomberg Law Upgraded Its Online Legal Research Platform" in Information Today (Vol. 28, September 2011, No. 8, pp. 28)*
Pub: Information Today, Inc.
Description: Bloomberg Law upgraded its online legal research platform for law practices. The new services includes a redesigned interface, improved search capabilities, and expanded collaboration and workflow features, while maintaining it comprehensive law resources such as mergers and acquisitions, antitrust, and securities.

23757 ■ *"Boeing's Next Flight May Well Be to the South" in Puget Sound Business Journal (Vol. 29, November 21, 2008, No. 31, pp.)*
Pub: American City Business Journals
Ed: Steve Wilhelm. **Description:** Southern states in the U.S. are luring Boeing Company to locate a new plant in their region which is experiencing a growing industrial base while offering permissive labor laws as selling points.

23758 ■ *"Book of Lists 2010" in Philadelphia Business Journal (Vol. 28, December 25, 2009, No. 45, pp. 1)*
Pub: American City Business Journals
Description: Rankings of companies and organizations within the banking, biotechnology, economic development, healthcare, hospitality, law and accounting, marketing and media, real estate, and technology industries in the Philadelphia, Pennsylvania area are presented. Rankings are based on sales, business size, and more.

23759 ■ *"Border Boletin: UA to Take Lie-Detector Kiosk to Poland" in Arizona Daily Star (September 14, 2010)*
Pub: Arizona Daily Star
Ed: Brady McCombs. **Description:** University of Arizona's National Center for Border Security and Immigration Research will send a team to Warsaw, Poland to show border guards from 27 European Union countries the center's Avatar Kiosk. The Avatar technology is designed for use at border ports and airports to assist Customs officers detect individuals who are lying.

23760 ■ *"Bottoms Up!" in Entrepreneur (Vol. 36, April 2008, No. 4, pp. 128)*

Pub: Entrepreneur Media, Inc.

Ed: Amanda C. Kooser. Description: Jill Bernheimer launched her online alcohol business Domaine547 in 2007, and encountered challenges as legal issues over the licensing and launching of the business took about seven months to finish. Domain547 features blog and forum areas. Marketing strategy that connects to the social community is one of the ways to reach out to customers.

23761 ■ *"Bountiful Exterminator Indicted for Unlawful Pesticide Use" in Standard-Examiner (February 3, 2011)*

Pub: Standard-Examiner

Contact: Bart Wade, Director

E-mail: bwade@standard.net

Ed: Bryon Saxton. Description: Bugman Pest and Lawn Inc. indicted Coleman Nocks and his business, Bugman Pest and Lawn Inc. for three counts of unlawful use of the pesticide Fumitoxin, resulting in the death of two little girls.

23762 ■ *"Breaking Up" in Canadian Business (Vol. 80, March 12, 2007, No. 6, pp. 34)*

Pub: Rogers Media

Ed: John Gray. Description: The need for business partners to draft a shareholder agreement in the beginning of their business to make it easier to break their relationship in case of disputes later is discussed.

23763 ■ *"Brief: Janitorial Company Must Pay Back Wages" in Buffalo News (September 24, 2011)*

Pub: The Buffalo News

Ed: Jonathan D. Epstein. Description: Knights Facilities Management, located in Michigan, provides grounds maintenance and janitorial services at the Ralph Wilson Stadium in Buffalo, New York. The US Department of Labor ordered the firm to pay $22,000 in back wages and damages to 26 employees for overtime and minimum wage compensation. Details of the company's violation of the Fair Labor Standards Act are included.

23764 ■ *"Bristol-Myers Close to Settling Lawsuit" in Globe & Mail (January 23, 2006, pp. B6)*

Pub: CTVglobemedia Publishing Inc.

Ed: Barbara Martinez. Description: The details of shareholder case against Bristol-Myers Squibb Co. are presented. The dispute is over the company's claim on the efficiency of Vanlev drug.

23765 ■ *"Brooke Agents Claim Mistreatment" in The Business Journal-Serving Metropolitan Kansas City (Vol. 27, October 24, 2008, No. 7, pp. 1)*

Pub: American City Business Journals, Inc.

Ed: James Dornbrook. Description: Franchisees of Brooke Corp., an insurance franchise, face uncertainty as their bills remain unpaid and banks threaten to destroy their credit. The company bundled and sold franchisee loans to different banks, but the credit crunch left the company with massive debts and legal disputes.

23766 ■ *"Burger Heirs' Long-Bottled Fight Plays Out" in Business Courier (Vol. 24, January 11, 2008, No. 40, pp. 1)*

Pub: American City Business Journals, Inc.

Ed: Dan Monk. Description: Discussion of an heir to the Burger Brewing Co. Michael Cundall who has filed for permission to pursue efforts to question the legality of a 1984 transaction in which the Cundall family sold its share of the Central Investment Corp. (CIC). The court ruled that Cundall may continue fighting for his claim that his uncle, John Koons, breached fiduciary duties by pressuring the family to sell its CIC stake. Details of the court rulings are given.

23767 ■ *"Burned Investors Fire Back" in Canadian Business (Vol. 80, April 23, 2007, No. 9, pp. 12)*

Pub: Rogers Media

Ed: Geoff Kirbyson; Dan Lett. Description: The details of the oppression remedy suit filed by investors on Maple Leaf Distillers Inc. and Protos International are presented.

23768 ■ *"Business Diary" in Crain's Detroit Business (Vol. 24, October 6, 2008, No. 40, pp. 23)*

Pub: Crain Communications, Inc.

Description: Detailed listing of acquisitions, expansions, new products, new services, business contracts and startups from the Detroit area is provided.

23769 ■ *"Business Diary" in Crain's Detroit Business (Vol. 26, January 11, 2010, No. 2, pp. 16)*

Pub: Crain Communications Inc.

Description: Listing of local businesses involved in acquisitions, contracts, expansions, new products and services as well as startups in the region.

23770 ■ *"Business Looks for Results in Congress" in Baltimore Business Journal (Vol. 28, November 5, 2010, No. 26, pp. 1)*

Pub: Baltimore Business Journal

Ed: Kent Hoover. Description: Republican candidates in the 2010 Congressional elections were overwhelmingly supported by the business community. Republican John Boehner, who will be the next Speaker of the House, says that the party's victory would end economic uncertainty and would assist small businesses to rehire workers.

23771 ■ *"Business Owners Lien Trinity Project" in The Business Journal-Serving Greater Tampa Bay (Vol. 28, July 25, 2008, No. 31, pp. 1)*

Pub: American City Business Journals, Inc.

Ed: Janet Leiser. Description: The Internal Revenue Service is trying to collect $2.9 million from the developer of the Trinity Town Center, William Plaines, due to the delays in the project. This is in addition to a $5.2 million lien by the project's subcontractors.

23772 ■ *"Business Put Cash Behind Bernstein" in Baltimore Business Journal (Vol. 28, August 20, 2010, No. 15, pp. 1)*

Pub: Baltimore Business Journal

Ed: Scott Dance. Description: Baltimore, Maryland-based businesses have invested $40,000 to support lawyer Gregg L. Bernstein in the 2010 State Attorney election. The election campaign is being fueled by fear of a crime surge. Many businesses have been dealing with crimes such as muggings, shootings, and car break-ins.

23773 ■ *"Business as Usual at RIM, Balsillie Says" in Globe & Mail (March 6, 2007, pp. B1)*

Pub: CTVglobemedia Publishing Inc.

Ed: Simon Avery. Description: The continuation of normal business at Research In Motion Ltd., after the resignation of Jim Balsillie from the chairman's post, is described. The investigation of securities fraud at Research In Motion Ltd., and the continuation of Jim Balsillie as the co-chief executive officer of the company is discussed.

23774 ■ *"Businesses Keep a Watchful Eye on Worker's Comp" in The Business Journal-Serving Greater Tampa Bay (September 5, 2008)*

Pub: American City Business Journals, Inc.

Ed: Jane Meinhardt. Description: Pending a ruling from the Florida Supreme Court that could uphold the 2003 changes on workers' compensation law, the outcome would include restrictions on claimant attorneys' fees and allow the competitive workers' compensation insurance rates to remain low. However, insurance rates are expected to go up if the court overturns the changes.

23775 ■ *"Businesses Need to Know State, Federal Laws for Employing Minors" in Crain's Detroit Business (Vol. 25, June 15, 2009, No. 24)*

Pub: Crain Communications Inc. - Detroit

Ed: Nancy Kaffer. Description: Small business owners must know the law before employing minors. According to Steven Fishman, partner with Bodman LLP, who practices workplace law, most small business owners are not aware of laws regarding employment of minors.

23776 ■ *"California Company Suing City's Lupin Over its Generic Diabetes Drug" in Baltimore Business Journal (Vol. 27, January 1, 2010)*

Pub: American City Business Journals

Ed: Gary Haber. Description: California-based Depomed Inc. is suing Baltimore, Maryland-based Lupin Pharmaceuticals Inc. and its parent company in India over the patents to a diabetes drug. Lupin allegedly infringed on Depomed's four patents for Glumetza when it filed for permission to sell its own version of the drug with the US Food and Drug Administration. Details on generic pharmaceutical manufacturer tactics are discussed.

23777 ■ *"Can He Win the Patent Game?" in Globe & Mail (February 20, 2006, pp. B1)*

Pub: CTVglobemedia Publishing Inc.

Ed: Simon Avery; Paul Waldie. Description: A profile on managerial abilities of chief executive officer Jim Balsillie of Research In Motion Ltd., who will face the patent case with NTP Inc., is presented.

23778 ■ *Canadian Small Business Kit for Dummies*

Pub: John Wiley & Sons, Incorporated

Ed: Margaret Kerr; JoAnn Kurtz. Released: May 2006. Price: $28.99. Description: Resources include information on changes to laws and taxes for small businesses in Canada.

23779 ■ *"Canadian Wind Farm Sued Due to Negative Health Effects" in PC Magazine Online (September 22, 2011)*

Pub: PC Magazine

Description: Suncor Energy is being sued by a family in Ontario, Canada. The family claims that Suncor's wind turbines have created health problems for them, ranging from vertigo and sleep disturbance to depression and suicidal thoughts. The family's home is over 1,000 meters from the eight wind turbines, and according to Ontario officials, wind turbines must be a minimum of 550 meters from existing homes.

23780 ■ *"Carvel" in Ice Cream Reporter (Vol. 23, September 20, 2010, No. 10, pp. 7)*

Pub: Ice Cream Reporter

Description: Pamela Carvel, niece of Carvel founding soft serve has been barred from bringing any more lawsuits against her uncle's estate.

23781 ■ *"The Case for Treating the Sex Trade as an Industry" in Canadian Business (Vol. 83, October 12, 2010, No. 17, pp. 9)*

Pub: Rogers Media Ltd.

Ed: Steve Maich. Description: It is believed that the worst aspects of prostitution in Canada are exacerbated by the fact that it must take place in secret. The laws that deal with the market for sex have led to an unsafe working environment. Prostitutes believe their industry needs to be sanctioned and regulated rather than ignored and reviled.

23782 ■ *"Catch the Wind Announces Filing of Injunction Against Air Data Systems LLC and Philip Rogers" in CNW Group (September 30, 2011)*

Pub: CNW Group

Contact: Carolyn McGill-Davidson, President

Description: Catch the Wind, providers of laser-based wind sensor products and technology, filed an injunction against Optical Air Data Systems (OADS) LLC and its former President and CEO Philip L. Rogers. The complaint seeks to have OADS and Rogers return tangible and intangible property owned by Catch the Wind, which the firm believes to be critical to the operations of their business.

23783 ■ *"Cautions on Negotiating Business and Personal Contracts" in Business Owner (Vol. 35, March-April 2011, No. 2, pp. 12)*

Pub: DL Perkins Company

Description: Information is provided to help small business owners protect themselves during contract discussions, whether business or personal. A negotiating checklist is provided.

23784 ■ *"Centerpoint Funding In Limbo" in The Business Journal - Serving Phoenix and the Valley of the Sun (Vol. 28, August 1, 2008, No. 48)*

Pub: American City Business Journals, Inc.

Ed: Jan Buchholz. **Description:** Avenue Communities LLC has threatened to file a case against Mortgages Ltd. over the finance of the Centerpoint development project in Tempe, Arizona. Avenue Communities want Mortgages Ltd. to file a motion with the U.S. Bankruptcy Court so that it can secure financing for the project. Other views and information on the finance of Centerpoint, are presented.

23785 ■ *"CEOs Divided About Census" in Canadian Business (Vol. 83, August 17, 2010, No. 13-14, pp. 20)*

Pub: Rogers Media Ltd.

Ed: Jacqueline Nelson. **Description:** A Compass poll of Canadian CEOs on what the government should do with controversial long-form census is presented. The poll results show that 30 percent believe the government should remove any threat of punishment for failure to complete the survey. The CEOs also believe the law must be enforced by the government to encourage participation.

23786 ■ *"The CEO's New Armor" in Conde Nast Portfolio (Vol. 2, June 2008, No. 6, pp. 56)*

Pub: Conde Nast Publications

Contact: David Carey, President

Ed: John Cassidy. **Description:** Due to a new breed in C.E.O.'s contracts it is nearly impossible to fire them regardless of their performance. Despite the Sarbanes-Oxley Act in which attempted to codify C.E.O. responsibilities, corporate bosses responded by quietly demanding individual contracts, which, in many cases, were drawn up by their own lawyers and accepted by company boards with no outside oversight or review.

23787 ■ *"Changes Sought to Health Law" in Baltimore Business Journal (Vol. 28, July 30, 2010, No. 12, pp. 1)*

Pub: Baltimore Business Journal

Ed: Kent Hoover. **Description:** Business groups that opposed health care reform are working to undo parts of the new laws even before they go into effect. Business groups are gaining support for one legislative fix, which is repealing the law's provision that requires all businesses to file 1099 forms with the IRS any time they pay more than $600 a year to another business.

23788 ■ *"Channelside On the Blocks" in The Business Journal-Serving Greater Tampa Bay (Vol. 28, August 29, 2008, No. 36, pp. 1)*

Pub: American City Business Journals, Inc.

Ed: Michael Hinman. **Description:** In a bankruptcy auction for The Place, one of the more visible condominium projects at Channelside, the lowest bid is just below $73 a square foot. KeyBank National Association, the Key Developers Group LLC's lender, leads the auction planned for October 15, 2008. The reason behind the low minimum bid required to participate in the said action is discussed.

23789 ■ *"Chesley Fighting Ky. Disbarment" in Business Courier (Vol. 27, September 10, 2010, No. 19, pp. 1)*

Pub: Business Courier

Ed: Jon Newberry. **Description:** Stan Chesley, a Cincinnati attorney, has been accused of making false statements to the courts and bar officials, self-dealing in violation of the bar's conflict of interest rules, and failing to adequately inform clients. Kentucky Bar Association officials will seek to have Chesley permanently disbarred.

23790 ■ *"Child-Care Policy and the Labor Supply of Mothers with Young Children" in University of Chicago Press (Vol. 26, July 2008, No. 3)*

Pub: University of Chicago Press

Contact: Garrett P. Kiely, Director

E-mail: gkiely@press.uchicago.edu

Ed: Pierre Lefebvre, Philip Merrigan. **Description:** In 1997, the provincial government of Quebec, the second most populous province in Canada, initiated

a new childcare policy. Licensed childcare service providers began offering day care spaces at the reduced fee of $5 per day per child for children aged four. By 2000, the policy applied to all children not in kindergarten. Using annual data (1993-2002) drawn from Statistics Canada's Survey of Labour and Income Dynamics, the results show that the policy had a large and statistically significant impact on the labor supply of mothers with preschool children.

23791 ■ *"China Vs. the World: Whose Technology Is It?" in Harvard Business Review (Vol. 88, December 2010, No. 12, pp. 94)*

Pub: Harvard Business School Publishing

Ed: Thomas M Hout, Pankaj Ghemawat. **Description:** Examination of the regulation the Chinese government is implementing that require foreign corporations wishing to do business in the country to give up their new technologies. These regulations avoid World Trade Organization technology transfer provisions and complicate the convergence of socialism and capitalism.

23792 ■ *Choosing the Right Legal Form of Business: The Complete Guide to Becoming a Sole Proprietor, Partnership, LLC, or Corporation*

Pub: Atlantic Publishing Company

Ed: Pat Mitchell. **Released:** January 1, 2009. **Price:** $24.95. **Description:** According to the U.S. Small Business Administration, nearly 250,000 new businesses start up annually; currently there are over nine million small companies in the nation. The importance of choosing the proper legal form of business is stressed.

23793 ■ *"Citi Ruling Could Chill SEC, Street Legal Pacts" in Wall Street Journal Eastern Edition (November 29, 2011, pp. C1)*

Pub: Dow Jones & Company Inc. Enterprise Media Group

Contact: Clare Hart, President

Ed: Jean Eaglesham, Chad Bray. **Description:** A $285 million settlement was reached between the Securities and Exchange Commission and Citigroup Inc. over allegations the bank misled investors over a mortgage-bond deal. Now, Judge Jed S. Rakoff has ruled against the settlement, a decision that will affect the future of such attempts to prosecute Wall Street fraud. Rakoff said that the settlement was 'neither fair, nor reasonable, nor adequate, nor in the public interest.'.

23794 ■ *"CityLink Project On Hold" in Business Courier (Vol. 24, November 9, 2008, No. 30, pp. 3)*

Pub: American City Business Journals, Inc.

Ed: Dan Monk. **Description:** Developers of the CityLink project have indicated that it will be at least a year before they start the planned social services mall at 800 Bank West End. According to Tim Senff, Citylink CEO, the company wants to build bridges before constructing the buildings. The project's critics are still considering whether to appeal a court ruling regarding the facility's compliance with the city's zoning code.

23795 ■ *Clicking Through: A Survival Guide for Bringing Your Company Online*

Pub: Bloomberg Press

Ed: Jonathan I. Ezor. **Released:** October 1999. **Description:** Summary of legal compliance issues faced by small companies doing business on the Internet, including copyright and patent laws.

23796 ■ *"Climate Law Could Dig into our Coal-Dusted Pockets" in Business Courier (Vol. 26, November 20, 2009, No. 30, pp. 1)*

Pub: American City Business Journals, Inc.

Ed: Lucy May. **Description:** Passage of federal climate legislation into law is set to increase household cost for Greater Cincinnati, according to the calculation by the Brookings Institute. The increase for residents of the area will amount to $244 in 2020 and the city was ranked the sixth-highest rate in the nation, behind Indianapolis.

23797 ■ *"Collateral Damage" in Business Courier (Vol. 26, October 16, 2009, No. 25, pp. 1)*

Pub: American City Business Journals, Inc.

Ed: Jon Newberry. **Description:** Non-union construction firms representing Ohio Valley Associated Builders and Contractors Inc. have filed cases against unionized shops claiming violations of wage law in Ohio. Defendants say the violations are minor, however, they believe they are caught in the middle of the group's campaign to change the state's wage law.

23798 ■ *"Collection Agency Issues Whitepaper on Legal and Ethical Methods of Collecting on Overdue Accounts" in Internet Wire (July 20, 2009)*

Pub: Comtex News Network, Inc.

Description: American Profit Recovery, a collection agency based in Massachusetts and Michigan, has updated and reissued a whitepaper on what businesses can and cannot do regarding conversing with their customers in an attempt to collect on overdue accounts and payments. A detailed summary on the federal laws associated with collecting on overdue accounts is outlined in such a way that any business owner, manager, or responsible party can easily understand.

23799 ■ *"Combat Mission: Rebuffed, BAE Systems Fights Army Contract Decision" in Business Courier (Vol. 26, September 25, 2009)*

Pub: American City Business Journals, Inc.

Ed: Jon Newberry. **Description:** BAE Systems filed a complaint with the US Government Accountability Office after the US Army issued an order to BAE's competitor for armoured trucks which is potentially worth over $3 billion. Hundreds of jobs in Butler County, Ohio hinge on the success of the contract protest.

23800 ■ *Complete Employee Handbook: A Step-by-Step Guide to Create a Custom Handbook That Protects Both the Employer and the Employee*

Pub: Moyer Bell

Ed: Michael A. Holzschu. **Released:** August 2007. **Price:** $39.95. **Description:** Comprehensive guide for employers deal with personnel issues; CD-ROM contains sample employee handbooks, federal regulations and laws, forms for complying with government programs and worksheets for assessing personnel needs and goals.

23801 ■ *The Complete Guide to Buying a Business*

Pub: NOLO

Ed: Fred S. Steingold. **Released:** November 2007. **Price:** $24.99. **Description:** Key steps in buying a business are highlighted, focusing on legal issues, tax considerations, approaches for valuing a business, financing, structuring the deal, along with forms and documents for taking ownership are included.

23802 ■ *"Computer Forensics Firms Get Boost From New Evidence Rules" in Crain's Detroit Business (Vol. 24, March 24, 2008, No. 12, pp. 28)*

Pub: Crain Communications, Inc.

Ed: Chad Halcom. **Description:** Computer forensics is a growing niche for firms such as the Center for Computer Forensics in Southfield; driving some of the growth are new amendments to the Federal Rules of Civil Procedure, which took effect about a year ago and address standards of evidence for electronic records, or 'e-discovery,' that are admissible for civil cases in federal courts.

23803 ■ *"Contract Design as a Firm Capability" in Academy of Management Review (October 2007, pp. 1060)*

Pub: ScholarOne, Inc.

Ed: Nicholas Argyres, Kyle J. Mayer. **Description:** A firm's capabilities for designing detailed contracts and the role of managers, engineers, and lawyers in the design of such contracts is highlighted.

23804 ■ *"Contract Reveals Details of ACE Jet Deals" in Globe & Mail (January 24, 2006, pp. B3)*
Pub: CTVglobemedia Publishing Inc.
Ed: Brent Jang. **Description:** The details of contract between Boeing Co. and Air Canada are presented.

23805 ■ *"Contracts" in Agency Sales Magazine (Vol. 39, September-October 2009, No. 9, pp. 7)*
Pub: MANA
Description: One session at the MANAfest conference provided suggestions to sales representatives when negotiating a contract with their principals. New sales representatives need to stand their ground and to negotiate a fair and balanced contract with every principal that they sign on with.

23806 ■ *"A Conversation With Steven Hilfinger, Foley & Lardner L.L.P." in Crain's Detroit Business (Vol. 24, March 24, 2008, No. 12, pp. 1)*
Pub: Crain Communications, Inc.
Description: Interview with Steven Hilfinger who is a member of Foley & Lardner L.L.P.'s mergers and acquisitions practice and is co-chair of its automotive industry team. Hilfinger discusses such issues as the role a board of directors can play in the M&A process and the future of the auto market.

23807 ■ *"Corporex in Battle With Hedge Fund" in Business Courier (Vol. 24, December 21, 2008, No. 36, pp. 1)*
Pub: American City Business Journals, Inc.
Ed: Jon Newberry. **Description:** Discusses a breach of contract complaint that was filed by Apollo Real Estate Advisors against Corporex Companies Inc. but Corporex said that the lawsuit was intended to counter an arbitration complaint filed by Corporex against Apollo, which seeks $11 million in termination fees. The issue is in relation to the acquisition of Eagle Hospitality by Apollo earlier in 2007.

23808 ■ *"Crash Pads" in Business Courier (Vol. 24, November 2, 2008, No. 29, pp. 1)*
Pub: American City Business Journals, Inc.
Ed: Jon Newberry. **Description:** Francisca Webster accumulated $4 million in mortgage debt in about 2 months. She filed a lawsuit against her tax preparer and her mortgage broker contending that the defendants had breached their fiduciary duties to her and made fraudulent misrepresentations to her. The other details of the case are supplied.

23809 ■ *"Credit Crunch Gives, Takes Away" in The Business Journal-Serving Metropolitan Kansas City (Vol. 27, October 17, 2008, No. 5, pp. 1)*
Pub: American City Business Journals, Inc.
Ed: Suzanna Stagemeyer. **Description:** Although many Kansas City business enterprises have been adversely affected by the U.S. credit crunch, others have remained relatively unscathed. Examples of how local businesses are being impacted by the crisis are provided including: American Trailer & Storage Inc., which declared bankruptcy after failing to pay a long-term loan; and NetStandard, a technology firm who, on the other hand, is being pursued by prospective lenders.

23810 ■ *"Crime and Punishment" in Canadian Business (Vol. 81, December 24, 2007, No. 1, pp. 21)*
Pub: Rogers Media
Ed: Joe Castaldo. **Description:** Cmpass Inc.'s survey of 137 Canadian chief executive officers showed that they want tougher imposition of sentences on white-collar criminals, as they believe that the weak enforcement of securities laws gives an impression that Canada is a country where it is easy to get away with fraud.

23811 ■ *"Critics Target Bribery Law" in Wall Street Journal Eastern Edition (November 28, 2011, pp. B1)*
Pub: Dow Jones & Company Inc. Enterprise Media Group
Contact: Clare Hart, President
Ed: Joe Palazzuolo. **Description:** Concern about how the Foreign Corrupt Practices Act, the United States' anti-bribery law, is enforced has drawn the focus of corporate lobbyists. Corporations have paid some $4 billion in penalties in cases involving the law, which prohibits companies from paying foreign officials bribes. The US Chamber of Commerce believes amending the act should be a priority.

23812 ■ *"Crowdsourcing the Law" in LJN's Legal Tech Newsletter (October 1, 2010)*
Pub: Incisive Media
Contact: Lee Feldman, Manager
E-mail: lee.feldman@incisivemedia.com
Ed: Robert J. Ambrogi. **Description:** Spindle Law strives to make legal research faster and smarter using crowdsourcing as one means to reach users.

23813 ■ *"Currency: I'm Otta Here" in Entrepreneur (Vol. 35, October 2007, No. 10, pp. 72)*
Pub: Entrepreneur Media Inc.
Ed: C.J. Prince. **Description:** Liberum Research revealed that 193 chief financial officers (CFOs) at small companies have either resigned or retired during the first half of 2007. A survey conducted by Tatum found that unreasonable expectations from the management and compliance to regulations are the main reasons why CFOs are leaving small firms. The chief executive officer's role in making CFOs stay is also discussed.

23814 ■ *"D.A.G. Sues to Stay on Job" in Business Courier (Vol. 24, November 9, 2008, No. 30, pp. 4)*
Pub: American City Business Journals, Inc.
Ed: Jon Newberry. **Description:** D.A.G. Construction Co. filed a breach of contract lawsuit against the Cincinnati Metropolitan Housing Authority. The company asked the Hamilton County Pleas Court to stop the housing authority from taking over a $10 million senior housing project. According to the company, the agency displaced D.A.G. and its subcontractors without warning.

23815 ■ *"Dairy Queen Aims to Blitz Blizzberry" in Ice Cream Reporter (Vol. 23, August 20, 2010, No. 9, pp. 1)*
Pub: Ice Cream Reporter
Description: International Diary Queens has filed a lawsuit to stop Yogubliz Inc. from using Blizzberry and Blizz Frozen Yogurt as the name of its shops because the name is so close to Dairy Queen's Blizzard frozen dessert.

23816 ■ *"Day-Care Center Owner to Argue Against Liquor Store Opening Nearby" in Chicago Tribune (March 13, 2008)*
Pub: McClatchy-Tribune Information Services
Ed: Matthew Walberg. **Description:** NDLC's owner feels that Greenwood Liquors should not be granted its liquor license due to the claim that the NDLC is not only a day-care center but also a school that employs state-certified teachers.

23817 ■ *"Deal With Tribes Revives Revenue Stream" in Crain's Detroit Business (Vol. 24, March 24, 2008, No. 12, pp. 6)*
Pub: Crain Communications, Inc.
Ed: Amy Lane. **Description:** Michigan Bureau of State Lottery's 2003 launch of its Club Keno game caused the Little River Band of Ottawa Indians and the Little Traverse Bay Bands of Odawa Indians to halt payments of shared casino revenue with the state. The federal lawsuit that resulted has now been settled and tribal revenue-sharing will resume as well as $26 million in previous payments to the state of Michigan that the tribes had put into escrow.

23818 ■ *"Decorated Marine Sues Contractor" in Wall Street Journal Eastern Edition (November 29, 2011, pp. A4)*
Pub: Dow Jones & Company Inc. Enterprise Media Group
Contact: Clare Hart, President
Ed: Julian E. Barnes. **Description:** Marine Devon Maylie, who was awarded the Congressional Medal of Honor for bravery, has filed a lawsuit against defense contractor BAE Systems PLC claiming that the company prevented his hiring by another firm by saying he has a mental condition and a drinking problem. Maylie says that this was in retaliation for his objections to the company's plan to sell the Pakistani military high-tech sniper scopes.

23819 ■ *"Defensive Training" in Crain's Detroit Business (Vol. 24, September 22, 2008, No. 38, pp. 11)*
Pub: Crain Communications Inc.
Ed: Robert Ankeny. **Description:** Rising retaliation claims in regards to discrimination complaints are creating an atmosphere in which managers must learn how to avoid or deal with these lawsuits as well as the retaliation that often follows. Examples of cases are given as well as advice for dealing with such problems that may arise in the workplace.

23820 ■ *"Developer Wins Bout with Bank in Roundabout Way" in Tampa Bay Business Journal (Vol. 30, January 29, 2010, No. 6, pp. 1)*
Pub: American City Business Journals
Ed: Janet Leiser. **Description:** Developer Donald E. Phillips of Phillips Development and Realty LLC won against the foreclosure filed by First Horizon National Corporation, which is demanding the company to fully pay its $2.9 million loan. Phillips requested that his company pay monthly mortgage and extend the loan's maturity date.

23821 ■ *"Developers Compete for APG Project" in Baltimore Business Journal (Vol. 27, October 16, 2009, No. 23, pp. 1)*
Pub: American City Business Journals
Ed: Daniel J. Sernovitz. **Description:** Corporate Office Properties Trust has lost the case in Delaware bankruptcy court to prevent rival St. John Properties Inc. from going ahead with its plans to develop the 400 acres at Aberdeen Proving Ground (APG) in Maryland. Both developers have competed for the right to develop the two million square foot business park in APG.

23822 ■ *"DHS Finalizes Rules Allowing Electronic I-9s" in HR Specialist (Vol. 8, September 2010, No. 9, pp. 5)*
Pub: Capitol Information Group Inc.
Description: U.S. Department of Homeland Security issued regulations that give employers more flexibility to electronically sing and store I-9 employee verification forms.

23823 ■ *Dictionary of Real Estate Terms*
Pub: Barron's Educational Series Inc.
Contact: Alex Holtz, President
E-mail: aholtz@berronseduc.com
Ed: Jack P. Friedman, Jack C. Harris, J. Bruce Lindeman. **Released:** October 2008. **Price:** $13.99. **Description:** More than 2,500 real estate terms relating to mortgages and financing, brokerage law, architecture, rentals and leases, property insurance, and more.

23824 ■ *"Direct Recovery Associates Debt Collection Agency Beats Industry Record" in Internet Wire (June 24, 2010)*
Pub: Comtex
Description: Direct Recovery Associates Inc. was named as one of the highest collection records in the industry, which has consistently improved over 18 years. The firm is an international attorney-based debt collection agency.

23825 ■ *The Diversity Code: Unlocking the Secrets to Making Differences Work in the Real World*
Pub: AMACOM
Ed: Michelle T. Johnson. **Released:** September 8, 2010. **Price:** $19.95. **Description:** The most diligent compliance with laws and regulations can't foster true work place diversity. The best organizations have become genuine cross-cultural communities that believe equality in reconciling difference and valuing them. The book promotes understanding by answering many of the toughest questions that professionals and their employers are afraid to ask.

23826 ■ *"DOL Sets Stiff New Child Labor Penalties"* in *HR Specialist (Vol. 8, September 2010, No. 9, pp. 2)*

Pub: Capitol Information Group Inc.

Description: U.S. Department of Labor (DOL) will impose new penalties for employers that violate U.S. child labor laws. Details of the new law are included.

23827 ■ *"easyhome Ltd. Discovers Employee Fraud at an Easyfinancial Kiosk Company"* in *Internet Wire (October 14, 2010)*

Pub: Comtex

Description: Canada's leading merchandise leasing company and provider of financial services, easyhome Ltd., reported employee fraud totaling $3.4 million that was perpetrated against the firm's easyfinancial services business.

23828 ■ *"The Economic Loss Rule and Franchise Attorneys"* in *Franchise Law Journal (Vol. 27, Winter 2008, No. 3, pp. 192)*

Pub: American Bar Association

Contact: Carolyn Lamm, President

Ed: Christian C. Burden, Sean Trende. **Description:** Economic loss rule prohibits recovery of damages in tort when the subject injury is unaccompanied by either property damage or personal injury.

23829 ■ *"EEOC Sues Charlotte-Based Lebo's"* in *Charlotte Observer (February 7, 2007)*

Pub: Knight-Ridder/Tribune Business News

Ed: Mike Drummond. **Description:** The U.S. Equal Employment Opportunity Commission filed a pregnancy discrimination lawsuit against Lebo's Shoe Stores, located in Charlotte, North Carolina. The suit alleges the store withdrew an offer to hire a woman after finding out she was pregnant.

23830 ■ *Effect of the Overvalued Dollar on Small Exporters: Congressional Hearing*

Pub: DIANE Publishing Company

Ed: Donald Manzullo. **Released:** September 2002. **Price:** $30.00. **Description:** Congressional hearing: Witnesses: Dr. Lawrence Chimerine, Economist; Tony Raimondo, President and CEO, Behlen Manufacturing Company; Robert J. Weskamp, President, Wes-Tech, Inc.; Wayne Dollar, President, Georgia Farm Bureau; and Vargese George, President and CEO, Westex International, Inc. Appendix includes correspondence sent to committee on the overvalued dollar.

23831 ■ *Electronic Commerce: Technical, Business, and Legal Issues*

Pub: Prentice Hall PTR

Ed: Oktay Dogramaci; Aryya Gangopadhyay; Yelena Yesha; Nabil R. Adam. **Released:** August 1998. **Description:** Provides insight into the goals of using the Internet to grow a business in the areas of networking and telecommunication, security, and storage and retrieval; business areas such as marketing, procurement and purchasing, billing and payment, and supply chain management; and legal aspects such as privacy, intellectual property, taxation, contractual and legal settlements.

23832 ■ *"Eminent Domain Fight Looks Imminent"* in *The Business Journal-Serving Metropolitan Kansas City (Vol. 26, August 1, 2008, No. 47)*

Pub: American City Business Journals, Inc.

Ed: Rob Roberts. **Description:** Views and information on the proposed constitutional amendments that will limit the use of eminent domain in Missouri, are presented. The proposals are expected to largely ban the taking of private property for private development. It may be included in a November 4,2008 statewide vote for approval.

23833 ■ *"Employee Called for Jury Duty"* in *Business Owner (Vol. 35, March-April 2011, No. 2, pp. 14)*

Pub: DL Perkins Company

Description: State laws govern small business rights and obligations regarding employee jury duty obligations. All states do require that employers allow

employees to fulfill their jury duty obligations and retaliation, demotion, discipline or termination resulting from jury duty is illegal.

23834 ■ *"Employees Can't Be Punished for Refusing to Work Due to Safety Concerns"* in *HR Specialist (Vol. 8, September 2010, No. 9, pp. 1)*

Pub: Capitol Information Group Inc.

Description: Whistle-blower provisions in several federal laws make it illegal for employers to retaliate against employees who raise safety concerns to their employer or the government.

23835 ■ *"Employees Change Clothes at Work? Heed New Pay Rules"* in *HR Specialist (Vol. 8, September 2010, No. 9, pp. 1)*

Pub: Capitol Information Group Inc.

Description: U.S. Department of Labor issued a new interpretation letter that states times spent changing in and out of 'protective clothing' (e.g., helmets, smocks, aprons, gloves, etc.) is considered paid time. It also says time spent changing 'ordinary clothes' (i. e., uniform) may not be compensable itself, but could start the clock on the workday, meaning all activities after - such as walking to the workstation - would be paid time. More details and a link to the DOL are included.

23836 ■ *Employer Legal Forms Simplified*

Pub: Nova Publishing Company

Ed: Daniel Sitarz. **Released:** August 2007. **Price:** $24.95. **Description:** Business reference containing the following forms needed to handle employees in any small business environment: application, notice, confidentiality, absence, federal employer forms and notices, and many payroll forms. All forms are included on a CD that comes in both PDF and text formats. Adobe Acrobat Reader software is also included on the CD. The forms are valid in all fifty states and Washington, DC.

23837 ■ *The Employer's Legal Advisor*

Pub: AMACOM

Ed: Thomas M. Hanna. **Released:** April 30, 2007. **Price:** $24.00. **Description:** Attorney provides tips for reducing the possibility of a lawsuit and winning a case if one does go to court.

23838 ■ *"Employers See Workers' Comp Rates Rising"* in *Sacramento Business Journal (Vol. 28, April 8, 2011, No. 6, pp. 1)*

Pub: Sacramento Business Journal

Ed: Kelly Johnson. **Description:** Employers in California are facing higher workers compensation costs. Increased medical costs and litigation are seen to drive the trend.

23839 ■ *Enabling Environments for Jobs and Entrepreneurship: The Role of Policy and Law in Small Enterprise Employment*

Pub: International Labour Office

Ed: Gerhard Reinecke. **Released:** February 2004. **Price:** $83.25. **Description:** National policies, laws and regulations governing workplace safety.

23840 ■ *"Enforcer In Fantasyland"* in *Crain's New York Business (Vol. 24, February 25, 2008, No. 8, pp. 10)*

Pub: Crain Communications Inc.

Ed: Hilary Potkewitz. **Description:** Patent law, particularly in the toy and game industry, is recession-proof according to Barry Negrin, partner at Pryor Cashman. Negrin co-founded his patent practice group. Despite massive recalls of toys and the concern over toxic toys, legal measures are in place in this industry.

23841 ■ *Entrepreneurship: A Process Perspective*

Pub: Thomson South-Western

Ed: Robert A. Baron; Scott A. Shane. **Released:** February 2007. **Price:** $137.95. **Description:** Entrepreneurial process covering team building, finances, business plan, legal issues, marketing, growth and exit strategies.

23842 ■ *"Estate Tax Problems may Soon Disappear"* in *Contractor (Vol. 56, September 2009, No. 9, pp. 60)*

Pub: Penton Media, Inc.

Ed: Irv Blackman. **Description:** Advice on how to effectively plan estate tax in the United States. Pending changes to US estate tax laws are seen to resolve inheritance problems. Captive insurance firms can lower property and casualty insurance costs to transfer businesses to children.

23843 ■ *"Ethics Commission May Hire Collection Agency"* in *Tulsa World (August 21, 2010)*

Pub: World Publishing

Ed: Barbara Hoberock. **Description:** Oklahoma Ethics Commission is considering a more to hire a collection agency or law firm in order to collect fees from candidates owing money for filing late financial reports.

23844 ■ *"Exxon Braving the Danger Zones"* in *Globe & Mail (March 8, 2007, pp. B1)*

Pub: CTVglobemedia Publishing Inc.

Ed: Shawn McCarthy. **Description:** The plans of Exxon Mobil Corp. to increase its revenues through the expansion of its operations in Asia, Africa, and the Middle East are discussed.

23845 ■ *"Fair Play? China Cheats, Carney Talks and Rankin Walks; Here's the Latest"* in *Canadian Business (Vol. 81, March 17, 2008, No. 4)*

Pub: Rogers Media

Description: Discusses the World Trade Organization which says that China is breaking trade rules by taxing imports of auto parts at the same rate as foreign-made finished cars. Mark Carney first speech as the governor of the Bank of Canada made economists suspect a rate cut on overnight loans. Andre Rankin was ordered by the Ontario Securities Commission to pay $250,000 in investigation costs.

23846 ■ *Family Limited Partnership Deskbook*

Pub: American Bar Association

Contact: Carolyn Lamm, President

Ed: David T. Lewis; Andrea C. Chomakos. **Released:** March 25, 2008. **Price:** $169.95. **Description:** Forming and funding a family limited partnership or limited liability company is complicated. In-depth analysis of all facets of this business entity are examined using detailed guidance on the basic principles of drafting, forming, funding, and valuing an FLP or LLC and also covers tax concerns. Examples and extensive sample forms are included on a CD-ROM included with the book.

23847 ■ *"Family Takes Wind Turbine Companies to Court Over Gag Clauses on Health Effects of Turbines"* in *CNW Group (September 12, 2011)*

Pub: CNW Group

Contact: Carolyn McGill-Davidson, President

Description: Shawn and Trisha Drennan are concerned about the negative experiences other have had with wind turbines close to their homes, including adverse health effects. The couple's home will be approximately 650 meters from the Kingsbridge II wind farm project in Ontario, Canada.

23848 ■ *"FBI Initiates Fraud Inquiry Into Mortgage Lenders"* in *Miami Daily Business Review (March 26, 2008)*

Pub: ALM Media Inc.

Description: FBI has launched investigations into Countrywide Financial, the nation's largest mortgage lender, along with sixteen other firms, tied to the subprime mortgage crisis.

23849 ■ *"Fed May Ban Amphibian Trade"* in *Pet Product News (Vol. 64, November 2010, No. 11, pp. 13)*

Pub: BowTie Inc.

Description: U.S. Fish and Wildlife Service is seeking public input on a petition submitted by the conservation activist group Defenders of Wildlife. The petition involves possible classification of chytrid fungus-infected amphibians and amphibian eggs as 'injurious wildlife' under the Lacey Act. Interstate trading or importation of injurious wildlife into the U.S. is not allowed.

23850 ■ *"Federal Fund Valuable Tool For Small-Biz Innovators"* **in Crain's Detroit Business (Vol. 24, September 29, 2008, No. 39, pp. 42)**
Pub: Crain Communications Inc.

Ed: Nancy Kaffer. **Description:** Grants from the Small Business Innovation Research Program, or SBIR grants, are federal funds that are set aside for 11 federal agencies to allocate to tech-oriented small-business owners. Firms such as Biotechnology Business Consultants help these companies apply for SBIR grants.

23851 ■ *"Feds to Pay University $20M"* **in Business Courier (Vol. 27, July 23, 2010, No. 12, pp. 3)**
Pub: Business Courier

Ed: James Ritchie. **Description:** The U.S. government is set to pay University Hospital and medical residents who trained there $20 million as part of a tax dispute settlement. Around 1,000 former residents are to receive tax refunds. But the hospital must provide the U.S. Internal Revenue Service with extensive documentation.

23852 ■ *"The Fences of a Patent"* **in Information Today (Vol. 26, February 2009, No. 2, pp. 13)**
Pub: Information Today, Inc.

Ed: George H. Pike. **Description:** Patent law is examined using the Blackboard course management software used by many colleges and universities as its example.

23853 ■ *"Fight Against Fake"* **in The Business Journal-Portland (Vol. 25, July 18, 2008, No. 19, pp. 1)**
Pub: American City Business Journals, Inc.

Ed: Erik Siemers. **Description:** Companies, such as Columbia Sportswear Co. and Nike Inc., are fighting the counterfeiting of their sportswear and footwear products through the legal process of coordinating with law enforcement agencies to raid factories. Most of the counterfeiting factories are in China and India. Other details on the issue are discussed.

23854 ■ *"Fight Ensues Over Irreplaceable Gowns"* **in Tampa Bay Business Journal (Vol. 30, January 15, 2010, No. 4, pp. 1)**
Pub: American City Business Journals

Ed: Janet Leiser. **Description:** People's Princess Charitable Foundation Inc. founder Maureen Rorech Dunkel has sought Chapter 11 bankruptcy protection before a state court decides on the fate of the five of 13 Princess Diana Gowns. Dunkel and the nonprofit were sued by Patricia Sullivan of HRH Venture LLC who claimed they defaulted on $1.5 million in loans.

23855 ■ *"Fighting Detroit"* **in Baltimore Business Journal (Vol. 27, January 22, 2010, No. 38, pp. 1)**
Pub: American City Business Journals

Ed: Daniel J. Sernovitz. **Description:** Baltimore, Maryland-based car dealers could retrieve their franchises from car manufacturers, Chrysler LLC and General Motors Corporation, through a forced arbitration. A provision in a federal budget mandates the arbitration. The revoking of franchises has been attributed to the car manufacturers' filing of bankruptcy protection.

23856 ■ *"Final Player In Big Mortgage Fraud Operation Gets Jail Time"* **in Boston Business Journal (Vol. 31, May 27, 2011, No. 18, pp. 3)**
Pub: Boston Business Journal

Ed: Galen Moore. **Description:** Real estate broker Ralp Appolon has been sentenced to 70 months in prison for wire fraud. Appolon was part of a group that falsified information about property purchase prices. A total of ten mortgage lenders have become victims of the group.

23857 ■ *"Finally, Justice"* **in Canadian Business (Vol. 82, April 27, 2009, No. 7, pp. 12)**
Pub: Rogers Media

Ed: John Gray. **Description:** Former investment adviser Alex Winch feels that he was vindicated with the Canadian Court's ruling that Livent Inc. founders Garth Drabinsky and Myron Gottlieb were guilty of fraud. Drabinsky filed a libel case on Winch over Winch's letter that complained over Livent's accounting procedures. Winch also criticized the inconsistent accounting during Drabinsky's term as chief executive of another firm.

23858 ■ *"Firms Sue Doracon to Recoup More Than $1M in Unpaid Bills"* **in Baltimore Business Journal (Vol. 28, July 9, 2010, No. 9, pp. 1)**
Pub: Baltimore Business Journal

Ed: Scott Dance. **Description:** Concrete supplier Paul J. Rach Inc., Selective Insurance Company, and equipment leasing firm Colonial Pacific Leasing Corporation intend to sue Baltimore, Maryland-based Doracon Contracting Inc. for $1 million in unpaid bills. Doracon owed Colonial Pacific $794,000 and the equipment is still in Doracon's possession. Selective Insurance and Paul J. Rach respectively seek $132,000 and $88,000.

23859 ■ *"Five-Ring Circus"* **in Entrepreneur (Vol. 35, November 2007, No. 11, pp. 76)**
Pub: Entrepreneur Media Inc.

Ed: Scott Bernard Nelson. **Description:** China's economy is growing and is expected to do well even after the 2008 Olympics, but growth could slow from eleven percent to eight or nine percent. Chinese portfolio concerns with regard to health and environmental records and bureaucratic fraud are discussed.

23860 ■ *"Follow the ABCs of Buying a Business"* **in Women Entrepreneur (September 10, 2008)**
Pub: Entrepreneur Media Inc.

Ed: Nina Kaufman. **Description:** Buying a business will likely result in the largest single asset one will ever own. A list of steps one can take in order to educate and protect themselves is provided.

23861 ■ *"For Baxter, A Lingering PR Problem; Ongoing Focus On Heparin Deaths Ups Heat On CEO"* **in Crain's Chicago Business (April 21, 2008)**
Pub: Crain Communications, Inc.

Ed: Mike Colias. **Description:** Baxter International Inc.'s recall of the blood-thinning medication heparin has exposed the company to costly litigation and put the perils of overseas drug manufacturing in the spotlight. Wall Street investors predict that an indefinite halt in production of the drug should not hurt the company's bottom line since heparin represents a tiny sliver of the business. Since Baxter began recalling the drug in January its shares have continued to outpace most other medical stocks.

23862 ■ *"Former Synthes Officers Receive Prison Sentences"* **in Wall Street Journal Eastern Edition (November 22 , 2011, pp. B4)**
Pub: Dow Jones & Company Inc.

Ed: Peter Loftus. **Description:** Michael D. Huggins, formerly chief operating officer of medical-device maker Synthes Ltd., and Thomas B. Higgins, formerly the president of Synthes spine unit, were given prison sentences of nine months while a third executive, John J. Walsh, formerly director of regulatory and clinical affairs in the spine division, was given a five-month sentence for their involvement in the promotion of the unauthorized use of a bone cement produced by the company.

23863 ■ *"Franchise Law in China: Law, Regulations, and Guidelines"* **in Franchise Law Journal (Vol. 27, Summer 2007, No. 1, pp. 57)**
Pub: American Bar Association
Contact: Carolyn Lamm, President

Ed: Paul Jones, Erik Wulff. **Description:** Issues faced by foreign franchising are discussed, with a focus on China.

23864 ■ *"Franchisees Lose Battle Against BK"* **in Advertising Age (Vol. 79, June 2, 2008, No. 22, pp. 46)**
Pub: Crain Communications, Inc.

Ed: Emily Bryson York. **Description:** Burger King has had continuing litigation with former franchisees from New York, Luan and Elizabeth Sadik, who claim that Burger King's double cheeseburger, along with additional problems, created the environment for their eventual insolvency. Burger King has since terminated its test of selling the double cheeseburger for $1, although the company declined to comment on the reason for this decision.

23865 ■ *"Fraud Alleged at Norshield; Investors Out $215 Million"* **in Globe & Mail (March 8, 2007, pp. B1)**
Pub: CTVglobemedia Publishing Inc.

Ed: Paul Waldie. **Description:** The investigation of the diversion of $215 million in investors' money by the management of Norshield Asset Management (Canada) Ltd. is described.

23866 ■ *"Free Speech Vs. Privacy in Data Mining"* **in Information Today (Vol. 28, September 2011, No. 8, pp. 22)**
Pub: Information Today, Inc.

Ed: George H. Pike. **Description:** The U.S. Constitution does not explicitly guarantee the right of privacy. Organizations and businesses that require obtaining and disseminating information can be caught in the middle of privacy rights. The long-term impact on data mining, Internet marketing, and Internet privacy issues are examined.

23867 ■ *"From Buyout to Busted"* **in Business Week (September 22, 2008, No. 4100, pp. 18)**
Pub: McGraw-Hill Companies, Inc.

Ed: Emily Thornton; Deborah Stead. **Description:** Bankruptcy filings by private equity-backed companies are at a record high with 134 American firms taken private (or invested in) by buyout firms that have filed for protection this year under Chapter 11; this is 91 percent higher than the previous year, which had set a record when 70 of such companies filed for protection under Chapter 11.

23868 ■ *"FTC Takes Aim At Foreclosure 'Rescue' Firm"* **in The Business Journal-Serving Greater Tampa Bay (Vol. 28, September 19, 2008, No. 39)**
Pub: American City Business Journals, Inc.

Ed: Michael Hinman. **Description:** United Home Savers LLP has been ordered to halt its mortgage foreclosure rescue services after the Federal Trade Commission accused it of deceptive advertising. The company is alleged to have charged customers $1,200 in exchange for unfulfilled promises to keep them in their homes.

23869 ■ *"Full-Court Press for Apple"* **in Barron's (Vol. 88, March 24, 2008, No. 12, pp. 47)**
Pub: Dow Jones & Company, Inc.

Ed: Mark Veverka. **Description:** Apple Inc. is facing more intellectual property lawsuits in 2008, with 30 patent lawsuits filed compared to 15 in 2007 and nine in 2006. The lawsuits, which involve products such as the iPod and the iPhone, present some concern for Apple's shareholders.

23870 ■ *"Funeral Picketing Laws and Free Speech"* **in Kansas Law Review (Vol. 55, April 2007, No. 3, pp. 575-627)**
Pub: American Society on Aging
Contact: Robert Stein, President

Ed: Stephen R. McAllister. **Description:** In-depth information covering laws governing protests and freedom of speech during funerals is presented.

23871 ■ *"Get Fit On a Dine: Resolve To Be Healthy-and Wealthy-This New Year"* **in Black Enterprise (Vol. 38, January 2008, No. 6, pp. 86)**
Pub: Earl G. Graves Publishing Co. Inc.

Ed: Angela P. Moore-Thorpe. **Description:** According to International Health, Racquet, and Sportsclub Association, nearly 43 million people are members of health clubs in the U.S. Corporate wellness programs as well as laws and your rights as a club member are explained.

23872 ■ "Get Prepared for New Employee Free Choice Act" in HRMagazine (Vol. 53, December 2008, No. 12, pp. 22)
Pub: Society for Human Resource Management
Contact: Henry G. Jackson, President
E-mail: hjackson@shrm.org
Ed: Allen Smith. Description: According to the director of global labor and employee relations with Ingersoll Rand Company, unions may have started having employees signing authorization cards in anticipation of the Employee Free Choice Act. Once signed, the cards are good for one year and employers would have only ten days in which to prepare for bargaining with unions over the first labor contract. The Act also requires these negotiations be subject to mandatory arbitration if a contract is not reached within 120 days of negotiations with unions, resulting in employers' wage rates, health insurance, retirement benefits and key language about flexibility would be determined by an arbitrator with no vested interest in the success of the company.

23873 ■ "Getting Out of an IRS Mess" in Black Enterprise (Vol. 37, December 2006, No. 5, pp. 53)
Pub: Earl G. Graves Publishing Co. Inc.
Ed: Carolyn M. Brown. Description: Owing back taxes to the IRS can lead to huge penalties and interest. Here are some tips on how to handle paying the IRS what you owe them.

23874 ■ "The GHG Quandary: Whose Problem Is It Anyway?" in Canadian Business (Vol. 81, September 15, 2008, No. 14-15, pp. 72)
Pub: Rogers Media Ltd.
Ed: Matthew McClearn. Description: Nongovernmental organizations were able to revoke the permit for Imperial Oil Ltd's Kearl oilsands project on the grounds of its expected greenhouse gas emission but the court's ruling was rendered irrelevant by bureaucratic paper-shuffling shortly after. The idea of an environmental impact assessment as a guide to identify the consequences of a project is also discussed.

23875 ■ "Green Shift Sees Red" in Canadian Business (Vol. 81, September 29, 2008, No. 16)
Pub: Rogers Media Ltd.
Ed: Jeff Sanford. Description: Green Shift Inc. is suing the Liberal Party of Canada in an $8.5 million lawsuit for using the phrase 'green shift' when they rolled out their carbon tax and climate change policy. The company has come to be recognized as a consultant and provider of green products such as non-toxic, biodegradable cups, plates, and utensils for events.

23876 ■ Green Your Small Business: Profitable Ways to Become an Ecopreneur
Pub: McGraw-Hill
Ed: Scott Cooney. Released: November 7, 2008. Price: $19.95 paperback. Description: Advice and guidance is given to help any entrepreneur start, build or grow a green business, focusing on green business basics, market research and financing, as well as handling legal and insurance issues.

23877 ■ "Greenberg Sues U.S. Over AIG Rescue" in Wall Street Journal Eastern Edition (November 22 , 2011, pp. C3)
Pub: Dow Jones & Company Inc.
Ed: Liam Pleven, Serena Ng. Description: Former Chief Executive Officer of American International Group Inc., Maurice R. 'Hank' Greenberg, has filed a lawsuit against the United States and the Federal Reserve Bank of New York on behalf of shareholders and his company, Starr International Company Inc., claiming that the government was wrong in taking control of the insurance giant and used it to move tens of millions of dollars to the trading partners of AIG.

23878 ■ "Hard Times for Hard Money" in Sacramento Business Journal (Vol. 25, July 18, 2008, No. 20, pp. 1)
Pub: American City Business Journals, Inc.
Ed: Michael Shaw. Description: Three private lenders who supplied $1 million sued VLD Realty, its associated companies and owners Volodymyr and Leonid Dubinsky accusing them of default after a plan to build two subdivisions fell through. Investigators are finding that borrowers and lenders ignored most rules on private investments on real estate.

23879 ■ "Hearing Damage Leads to Settlement" in Register-Guard (August 13, 2011)
Pub: The Register-Guard
Ed: Karen McCowan. Description: Cynergy Pest Control lost a court battle when a rural Cottage Grove man was granted a $37,000 settlement after his hearing was damaged by the pest control companies method to eradicate gophers, using blasts in his neighbor's yard.

23880 ■ Here Come the Regulars: How to Run a Record Label on a Shoestring Budget
Pub: Faber & Faber, Inc.
Ed: Ian Anderson. Released: October 1, 2009. Price: $15.00. Description: Author, Ian Anderson launched his own successful record label, Afternoon Records when he was 18 years old. Anderson shares insight into starting a record label, focusing on label image, budget, blogging, potential artists, as well as legal aspects.

23881 ■ "Hike in Md.'s Alcohol Tax May Be Hard For Lawmakers to Swallow" in Baltimore Business Journal (Vol. 28, November 19, 2010, No. 28)
Pub: Baltimore Business Journal
Ed: Emily Mullin. Description: Maryland's General Assembly has been reluctant to support a dime-per-drink increase in alcohol tax that was drafted in the 2009 bill if the tax revenue goes into a separate fund. The alcohol tax increase is considered unnecessary by some lawmakers and business leaders due to impending federal spending boosts.

23882 ■ "Hispanic Businesses Try to Drum Up Cash to Battle Crime Spree" in Baltimore Business Journal (Vol. 28, September 3, 2010, No. 17)
Pub: Baltimore Business Journal
Ed: Scott Dance. Description: Hispanic businesses in Baltimore, Maryland have been raising funds to pay off-duty police officers to patrol a few blocks of Broadway in Fells Point to help curb crime. Efforts to make the area a Latin Town have failed owing to muggings, prostitution and drug dealing. Comments from small business owners are also given.

23883 ■ "Home Builder, Four Others, Face Sentencing" in Business Courier (Vol. 27, November 26, 2010, No. 30, pp. 1)
Pub: Business Courier
Ed: Jon Newberry. Description: Home builder Eernie Kurlemann was convicted on November 10, 2010 on six felony counts and faces up to 65 years in prison due to his part in a 2006 Warren County mortgage fraud scheme. Four other business people have pleaded guilty to related charges, and all are awaiting sentencing in early 2011.

23884 ■ House of Cards: A Tale of Hubris and Wretched Excess on Wall Street
Pub: Anchor Press
Ed: William D. Cohan. Released: February 9, 2010. Price: $16.95. Description: A historical account of the events leading up to the Bear Stearns implosion.

23885 ■ How to Form Your Own Corporation without a Lawyer for Under $75.00
Pub: Dearborn Trade Publishing Inc.
Contact: Roy Lipner, President
Ed: Ted Nicholas; Sean P. Melvin. Price: $19.95

23886 ■ How to Start a Bankruptcy Forms Processing Service
Pub: Graphico Publishing Company
Ed: Victoria Ring. Released: September 2004. Price: $39.00. Description: Due to the increase in bankruptcy filings, attorneys are outsourcing related jobs in order to reduce overhead.

23887 ■ How to Start and Run Your Own Corporation: S-Corporations For Small Business Owners
Pub: HCM Publishing
Ed: Peter I. Hupalo. Released: March 6, 2003. Price: $22.95. Description: Basics of corporate business structure are explained. Topics include discovering the best business structure for your company; how to decided between an S-Corporation and LLC; choosing the state in which to incorporate, how to form a corporation, angel investing, special issues for one-person corporations, the role of bylaws and corporate minutes, board of directors, taxes, workers' compensation issues, retirement plans, and more.

23888 ■ "Human Capital: When Change Means Terminating an Employee" in Black Enterprise (Vol. 41, November 2010, No. 4, pp. 40)
Pub: Earl G. Graves Publishing Co. Inc.
Ed: Tamara E. Holmes. Description: Covering successful business change strategies, this article focuses on how the law and nondiscrimination policies can affect this aspect of the workplace.

23889 ■ "Hunter and the Hunted" in Canadian Business (Vol. 81, Summer 2008, No. 9, pp. 12)
Pub: Rogers Media Ltd.
Ed: Thomas Watson. Description: Brian Hunter, a partner in oil and gas engineering firm Montane Resources, invested his life savings in Vancouver-based Canacord Capital Corp. Details of the asset-backed commercial paper fiasco and Hunter's use of Facebook to encourage other investors to participate in his claim against the mortgage company are presented.

23890 ■ "Identity Thieves Hit a New Low" in Information Today (Vol. 26, February 2009, No. 2, pp. 1)
Pub: Information Today, Inc.
Ed: Phillip Britt. Description: Identity thieves are opening credit lines after reading obituaries. Actual identity theft cases are examined.

23891 ■ "IF Challenges Atlanta's Vending Monopoly" in Benzinga.com (July 28, 2011)
Pub: Benzinga.com
Ed: Benzinga Staff. Description: A lawsuit was filed by The Institute for Justice to challenge Atlanta's unconstitutional vending monopoly on behalf of two Atlanta street vendors.

23892 ■ "If Just One Person Applies, Are You Required to Hire Him?" in HR Specialist (Vol. 8, September 2010, No. 9, pp. 7)
Pub: Capitol Information Group Inc.
Description: It is legal to decline hiring an applicant, or even promoting a current employee, if they are the only applicant for a particular position. It may be good choice to wait for more applicants or to change recruiting strategy.

23893 ■ "IFRS Monopoly: the Pied Piper of Financial Reporting" in Accounting and Business Research (Vol. 41, Summer 2011, No. 3, pp. 291)
Pub: American Institute of Certified Public Accountants
Contact: Barry C. Melancon, President
E-mail: bmelancon@aicpa.org
Ed: Shyam Sunder. Description: The disadvantages of granting monopoly to the international financial reporting standards (IFRS) are examined. Results indicate that an IFRS monopoly removes the chances for comparing alternative practices and learning from them. An IFRS monopoly also eliminates customization of financial reporting to fit local differences in governance, business, economic, and legal conditions.

23894 ■ "Illinois Regulators Revoke Collection Agency's License" in Collections & Credit Risk (Vol. 15, August 1, 2010, No. 7, pp. 13)
Pub: SourceMedia Inc.
Description: Creditors Service Bureau of Springfield, Illinois had its license revoked by a state regulatory

agency and was fined $55,000 because the owner and president, Craig W. Lewis, did not turn over portions of collected funds to clients.

23895 ■ *"Immigrants Trapped in Forex Mess"* in Boston Business Journal (Vol. 27, October 5, 2007, No. 36, pp. 1)
Pub: American City Business Journals Inc.
Ed: Jackie Noblett. **Description:** U. S. Commodity Futures Trading Commission and Swiss Federal Banking Commission are jointly working on the case of Tradex Swiss AG. Investors have filed lawsuits to recover their money. Details of the illegal operation of the Forex company are discussed.

23896 ■ *"Immigration Issues Frustrate Owners From Overseas"* in The Business Journal-Serving Greater Tampa Bay (Vol. 28, August 15, 2008)
Pub: American City Business Journals, Inc.
Ed: Margie Manning. **Description:** Investors who availed the E-2 visa program believe that the tightened restrictions on the visa program has trapped them in the United States. The E-2 investor visa program was designed to attract investors into the U.S., but restrictions were tightened after the September 11, 2001 attacks. Other views and information on E-2 and its impact on investors are presented.

23897 ■ *Incorporate Your Business: A 50 State Legal Guide to Forming a Corporation*
Pub: Nolo
Ed: Anthony Mancuso. **Released:** January 2004. **Description:** Legal guide to incorporating a business in the U.S., covering all 50 states.

23898 ■ *"An Insurance Roll-Up In Danger of Unraveling"* in Barron's (Vol. 88, March 17, 2008, No. 11, pp. 51)
Pub: Dow Jones & Company, Inc.
Ed: Bill Alpert. **Description:** Shares of National Financial Partners have fallen below their initial offering price as sputtering sales and management turnover leave many investors wondering. One of the company's star brokers is being sued for their 'life settlement' contracts while another broker is being pursued by the IRS for unpaid taxes.

23899 ■ *"An Integrative Model of Experiencing and Responding to Mistreatment at Work"* in Academy of Management Review (January 2008, pp. 76)
Pub: ScholarOne, Inc.
Ed: Julie B. Olson-Buchanan, Wendy R. Boswell. **Description:** Integrative model with theoretical framework is presented to increase understanding of the effects of an individual's perceived experience of workplace mistreatment in dispute resolutions and the person's response to it.

23900 ■ *"The Interview"* in Crain's Cleveland Business (Vol. 30, June 22, 2009, No. 24, pp. 9)
Pub: Crain Communications, Inc.
Description: In an interview with Mary K. Whitmer, partner at Kohrman Jackson & Krantz, she addresses issues facing the Northeast Ohio legal community. Ms. Whitmer is the new president of the Cleveland Metropolitan Bar Association.

23901 ■ *"Investment Firms Unite: Coalition Fights New Tax Law"* in Black Enterprise (Vol. 38, December 2007, No. 5, pp. 52)
Pub: Earl G. Graves Publishing Co. Inc.
Ed: Joyce Jones. **Description:** Minorities working in private equity, real estate and investment management firms have united to form the Access to Capital Coalition to oppose legislation that they feel would adversely affect their ability to attract investments and executives. Details of the group are included.

23902 ■ *"Investment Manager Disciplined"* in Sacramento Business Journal (Vol. 25, July 4, 2008, No. 18, pp. 1)
Pub: American City Business Journals, Inc.
Ed: Mark Anderson. **Description:** Community Capital Management's David A. Zwick is permanently barred by the Securities and Exchange Commission (SEC) from associating with any broker or dealer, after

investigations revealed that he took part in paying kickbacks to a bond trader. Other views and information on Community Capital, and on the SEC investigation on Zwick, are presented.

23903 ■ *"Investors Sue Jackson Properties for Fraud, Breach of Contract"* in The Business Journal - Serving Phoenix and the Valley of the Sun (Vol. 28, July 18, 2008, No. 46, pp. 1)
Pub: American City Business Journals, Inc.
Ed: Jan Buchholz. **Description:** Investors sued Jackson Properties EVB Inc. and Jackson Properties EVB LLC for fraud and breach of contract over a botched housing development deal. The investors also filed a complaint before the Arizona Corporation Commission. The investors stand to lose $8 million from the halted development deal.

23904 ■ *"Israeli Spam Law May Have Global Impact"* in Information Today (Vol. 26, February 2009, No. 2, pp. 28)
Pub: Information Today, Inc.
Ed: David Mirchin. **Description:** Israels new law, called Amendment 40 of the Communications Law, will regulate commercial solicitations including those sent without permission via email, fax, automatic phone dialing systems, or short messaging technologies.

23905 ■ *"Jennifer Hernandez Helps Developers Transform Contaminated Properties"* in Hispanic Business (Vol. 30, April 2008, No. 4, pp. 32)
Pub: Hispanic Business
Ed: Hildy Medina. **Description:** Jennifer Hernandez is a partner and head of the law firm of Holland & Knight's environmental practice which specializes in the restoration of polluted land where former industrial and commercial buildings once stood, known as brownfields. Brownfield redevelopment can be lucrative but costly due to the cleaning up of contaminated land and challenging because of federal and state environmental laws.

23906 ■ *"Judge Gives RIM One Last Chance"* in Globe & Mail (February 25, 2006, pp. B5)
Pub: CTVglobemedia Publishing Inc.
Ed: Barrie McKenna; Paul Waldie. **Description:** United States District Court Judge James Spencer offers more time for Research In Motion Ltd. (RIM) to settle the patent infringement dispute with NTP Inc. RIM's shares increase by 6.2 percent following the decision.

23907 ■ *"Judgment Day"* in Canadian Business (Vol. 79, September 11, 2006, No. 18, pp. 27)
Pub: Rogers Media
Ed: John Gray. **Description:** The long, drawn out legal proceedings carried out by Bre-X Minerals Ltd. whose case against its former vice chairman and chief geolist, John Felderhof are presented.

23908 ■ *"Juicy Feud; Deal Caps Years of Rancor in Wrigley Gum Dynasty"* in Crain's Chicago Business (Vol. 31, May 5, 2008, No. 18, pp. 1)
Pub: Crain Communications, Inc.
Ed: David Sterrett. **Description:** Discusses the sale of Wm. Wrigley Jr. Co. to Mars Inc. and Warren Buffett for $23 billion as well as the intra-family feuding which has existed for nearly a decade since William Wrigley Jr. took over as CEO of the company following his father's death.

23909 ■ *"Kimball Hill Files for Chapter 11"* in Crain's Chicago Business (Vol. 31, April 28, 2008, No. 17, pp. 12)
Pub: Crain Communications, Inc.
Description: Homebuilder Kimball Hill filed for Chapter 11 bankruptcy protection after months of negotiations with lenders. The firm plans to continue operations as it restructures its debt.

23910 ■ *"Lathrop Finds Partner In LA"* in The Business Journal-Serving Metropolitan

Kansas City (Vol. 27, November 21, 2008, No. 11, pp. 1)
Pub: American City Business Journals, Inc.
Ed: Steve Vockrodt. **Description:** Kansas, Missouri-based Lathrop and Gage LLP is planning to merge with Spillane Shaeffer Aronoff Bandlow LLP. The merging of the business law firms will add entertainment clients to Lathrop's fold. Comments from executives are also presented.

23911 ■ *"Law Firm Jones Day Coming to Boston"* in Boston Business Journal (Vol. 30, November 19, 2010, No. 43, pp. 1)
Pub: Boston Business Journal
Ed: Lisa van der Pool. **Description:** Jones Day is set to open an office in Boston, Massachusetts. The company will be the largest law firm to enter Boston since 2007. The firm will open with at least three partners.

23912 ■ *"Law Firms Plan Rate Bumps"* in Houston Business Journal (Vol. 40, December 25, 2009, No. 33, pp. 1)
Pub: American City Business Journals
Ed: Ford Gunter. **Description:** Survey shows that Houston, Texas-based law firms were in line with a 3.2 percent average rate hike projected for 2010. The big firms were ready to offset some losses with a rate bump of 4 percent while smaller firms have been expecting an increase of about 3 percent.

23913 ■ *"Law Firms See Improvement in Financing Climate"* in Sacramento Business Journal (Vol. 28, October 14, 2011, No. 33, pp. 1)
Pub: Sacramento Business Journal
Ed: Kathy Robertson. **Description:** Sacramento, California-based Weintraub Genshlea Chediak Law Corporation has helped close 26 financing deals worth more than $1.6 billion in 2010, providing indication of improvement in Sacramento's economy. Lawyers have taken advantage of low interest rates to make refinancing agreements and help clients get new funds.

23914 ■ *"Law Firms Troll for Complaints Among Disgruntled Workers"* in The Business Journal-Serving Greater Tampa Bay (Vol. 28, July 11, 2008)
Pub: American City Business Journals, Inc.
Ed: Jane Meinhardt. **Description:** Economic slowdown has affected businesses as they downsize, seeing an increase in wage and hour complaints using loopholes in the Fair Labor Standards Act, from which several law firms are recently generating revenue. Federal judges notice the increase in lawsuits and ordered that law firms show cause for non-compliance.

23915 ■ *Law (in Plain English) for Small Business*
Pub: Sourcebooks, Inc.
Contact: Len Vlahos, President
E-mail: dominique@sourcebooks.com
Ed: Leonard D. DuBoff. **Released:** November 2006. **Description:** Small business law is described in easy to read format.

23916 ■ *"Law Reform, Collective Bargaining, and the Balance of Power: Results of an Empirical Study"* in WorkingUSA (June 2008)
Pub: Blackwell Publishers Ltd.
Ed: Ellen Dannin, Michelle Dean, Gangaram Singh. **Description:** Despite Congress' having made clear policy statements in the National Labor Relations Act that the law was intended to promote equality of bargaining power between employers and employees, to promote the practice and procedure of collective bargaining as the method of setting workplace terms and conditions of employment, and forbidding construing the law 'so as to either interfere with or impede or diminish in any way the right to strike,' by early 1940, the courts had given employers the right to permanently replace strikers and implement their final offer at impasse. Judges have often justified these doctrines as promoting balance in bargaining. Critics contend that the doctrines have the capacity to destroy the right to strike, unbalance bargaining power, and divert parties from the process of bargain-

ing collectively. Some have proposed allowing temporary but not permanent striker replacement. The article uses a bargaining simulation followed by a survey and debriefing comments to test these opposing claims.

23917 ■ *Law for the Small and Growing Business*
Pub: Jordans Publishing Limited
Ed: P. Bohm. **Released:** February 2007. **Price:** $59. 98. **Description:** Legal and regulatory issues facing small businesses, including employment law, health and safety, commercial property, company law and finance are covered.

23918 ■ *"Lawyers Cash In On Alcohol" in Business Journal Portland (Vol. 27, November 19, 2010, No. 38, pp. 1)*
Pub: Portland Business Journal
Ed: Andy Giegerich. **Description:** Oregon-based law firms have continued to corner big business on the state's growing alcohol industry as demand for their services increased. Lawyers, who represent wine, beer and liquor distillery interests, have seen their workload increased by 20 to 30 percent in 2009.

23919 ■ *"Lawyers Lock Up Cops as Clients" in Sacramento Business Journal (Vol. 28, April 8, 2011, No. 6, pp. 1)*
Pub: Sacramento Business Journal
Ed: Kathy Robertson. **Description:** Sacramento-based law firm Mastagni, Holstedt and Chiurazzi has grown its client base by specializing in law enforcement labor issues. The firm represents 80,000 public sector correctional officers in the US. The firm has been experiencing an increase in new business as public sector employers face huge budget deficits.

23920 ■ *"Lawyers Sued Over Lapsed Lacrosse Patent" in Crain's Detroit Business (Vol. 25, June 8, 2009, No. 23, pp. 5)*
Pub: Crain Communications Inc. - Detroit
Ed: Chad Halcom. **Description:** Warrior Sports Inc., a manufacturer of lacrosse equipment located in Warren, Michigan is suing the law firm Dickinson Wright PLLC and two of its intellectual property lawyers over patent rights to lacrosse equipment.

23921 ■ *"Leaning Tower" in Business Courier (Vol. 27, June 4, 2010, No. 5, pp. 1)*
Pub: Business Courier
Ed: Jon Newberry. **Description:** New York-based developer Armand Lasky, owner of Tower Place Mall in downtown Cincinnati, Ohio has sued Birmingham, Alabama-based Regions Bank to prevent the bank's foreclosure on the property. Regions Bank claims Lasky was in default on an $18 million loan agreement. Details on the mall's leasing plan is also discussed.

23922 ■ *"Leave Policies: How to Avoid Leave-Related Lawsuits" in Employee Benefit News (Vol. 25, December 1, 2011, No. 15, pp. 12)*
Pub: SourceMedia Inc.
Ed: John F. Galvin. **Description:** Tips for employers when adding disability and maternity leave benefits to workers are outlined, with focus on ways to avoid leave-related lawsuits.

23923 ■ *"Legal Aid: Sample Legal Documents can Lower Your Attorney Fees" in Black Enterprise (Vol. 37, October 2006, No. 3, pp. 210)*
Pub: Earl G. Graves Publishing Co. Inc.
Ed: Tamara E. Holmes. **Description:** FreeLegal-Forms.net provides thousands of free legal forms. These forms are not a substitute for consultation with an attorney but the sample documents can help save you time and money.

23924 ■ *"Legalities of Diversity" in Hispanic Business (September 2007, pp. 26)*
Pub: Hispanic Business
Ed: Francisco Ramos Jr., Bill Krutzer. **Description:** Most companies in America have diversity programs, however, critics believe diversity can be used as reverse discrimination because minorities are getting preferential treatment in hiring, promotion, and admissions.

23925 ■ *"Legislating the Cloud" in Information Today (Vol. 28, October 2011, No. 9, pp. 1)*
Pub: Information Today, Inc.
Description: Internet and telecommunications industry leaders are asking for legislation to address the emerging market in cloud computing. Existing communications laws do not adequately govern the modern Internet.

23926 ■ *"The Letter of the Law" in Collections and Credit Risk (Vol. 14, November 1, 2009, No. 9, pp. 40)*
Pub: SourceMedia, Inc.
Ed: Michelle Dunn. **Description:** Analyzes the regulatory landscape regarding debt collection and the ways in which those in the field are dealing with a tough economy, unclear laws and the newest regulations.

23927 ■ *"Linens 'N Things, Dyson in Dust-Up" in Crain's Chicago Business (Vol. 31, March 24, 2008, No. 12, pp. 12)*
Pub: Crain Communications, Inc.
Description: Linens 'N Things is being sued by vacuum-cleaner manufacturer Dyson who is alleging that it hasn't been paid some of the $1.3 million it says it is owed for merchandise.

23928 ■ *"Local Manufacturers See Tax Proposal Hurting Global Operations" in Crain's Cleveland Business (Vol. 30, May 18, 2009, No. 20)*
Pub: Crain Communications, Inc.
Ed: Dan Shingler. **Description:** New tax laws proposed by the Obama Administration could hinder the efforts of some Northeast Ohio industrial companies from expanding their overseas markets. The law is designed to prevent companies from moving jobs overseas.

23929 ■ *"Look Before You Lease" in Women Entrepreneur (February 3, 2009)*
Pub: Entrepreneur Media Inc.
Ed: Nina L. Kaufman. **Description:** Top issues to consider before leasing an office space are discussed including: additional charges that may be expected on top of the basic rental price; determining both short- and long-term goals; the cost of improvements to the space; the cost of upkeep; and the conditions of the lease.

23930 ■ *"Look Out, Barbie, Bratz are Back" in Canadian Business (Vol. 83, August 17, 2010, No. 13-14, pp. 18)*
Pub: Rogers Media Ltd.
Ed: Joe Castaldo. **Description:** California-based MGA Entertainment has wrestled back control over Bratz from Mattel after a six-year legal battle. However, MGA owner Isaac Larian could still face legal hurdles if Mattel pursues a retrial. He now has to revive the brand which virtually disappeared from stores when Mattel won the rights for Bratz.

23931 ■ *"Making Factory Tours Count" in Playthings (Vol. 107, January 1, 2009, No. 1, pp. 14)*
Pub: Reed Business Information
Contact: Jeff Greisch, President
Ed: Malcolm Denniss. **Description:** The importance of touring an overseas toy supplier's manufacturing facility is stressed. Strategies for general factory visits are outlined in order to determine safety-related quality assurance issues in production.

23932 ■ *Managing Economies, Trade and International Business*
Pub: Palgrave Macmillan
Ed: Aidan O'Connor. **Released:** January 19, 2010. **Price:** $90.00. **Description:** An in-depth look at the areas that affect and influence international business, exploring specific issues businesses face in terms of economic development, trade law, and international marketing and management.

23933 ■ *"Market Recoups Its Losses - And Its Optimism" in Barron's (Vol. 89, July 20, 2009, No. 29, pp. M3)*
Pub: Dow Jones & Co., Inc.
Ed: Kopin Tan. **Description:** US stock markets gained heavily in the third week of July 2009, rising by about 7 percent during the week. The shares of

human resource management companies could be overpriced as they are trading at very high price-earnings multiples. Baxter International faces a class-action suit due to its alleged conspiracy with CSL to fix blood-plasma product prices.

23934 ■ *"Market Squeezes Some Lawyers" in Austin Business JournalInc. (Vol. 28, December 12, 2008, No. 39, pp. 1)*
Pub: American City Business Journals
Ed: Jean Kwon. **Description:** Austin, Texas-based lawyers have been adversely affected by the economic downtown. Fewer works for lawyers in mergers and acquisitions and other activities are being offered. Lawyers are refinancing debts and offering other services.

23935 ■ *"Maryland Ready to Defend Slots Minority Policy" in Boston Business Journal (Vol. 29, July 8, 2011, No. 9, pp. 3)*
Pub: American City Business Journals Inc.
Ed: Scott Dance. **Description:** The legality of Maryland's minority inclusion policy may be put under scrutiny once the lawsuit filed by rejected slots developer Baltimore City Entertainment Group on July 5, 2011 is heard in court. The lawsuit aims to stop the bidding process on a proposed casino in Baltimore because the minority policy amounts to reverse discrimination.

23936 ■ *McMafia: A Journey Through the Global Criminal Underworld*
Pub: Pantheon Books
Ed: Misha Glenny. **Released:** 2009. **Price:** $27.95. **Description:** Criminal entrepreneurs are using well-organized cosmopolitan networks to capitalize on globalization. Money from wars and illegal activities are being used to raise venture capital to finance criminal enterprises.

23937 ■ *"Md. Tries to Recoup $73M from Actuary" in Baltimore Business Journal (Vol. 28, June 11, 2010, No. 5, pp. 1)*
Pub: Baltimore Business Journal
Ed: Gary Haber. **Description:** Maryland State Retirement and Pension System has won nearly $73 million in administrative ruling against Milliman Inc. over pension loss miscalculations. However, Milliman filed two court cases seeking to reverse the decision and to recoup to the state any money a court orders.

23938 ■ *"Meet Rebecca. She's Here to Fire You" in Inc. (November 2007, pp. 25-26)*
Pub: Gruner & Jahr USA Publishing
Ed: Max Chafkin. **Description:** Amid liability concerns as well as CEO guilt, more and more firms are using consulting companies to fire workers. These outsourced firms help small companies structure severance and document information in order to limit legal liability when firing an employee.

23939 ■ *"Melnyk Loses Round in Battle for Hemosol" in Globe & Mail (January 24, 2007, pp. B3)*
Pub: CTVglobemedia Publishing Inc.
Ed: Leonard Zehr. **Description:** Biovail Corp. chairman Eugene Melnyk's loosing of the case against Catalyst Capital Group Inc. over the acquisition of Hemosol Corp. is discussed.

23940 ■ *Mergers and Acquisitions from A to Z*
Pub: Amacom
Ed: Andrew J. Sherman, Milledge A. Hart. **Released:** January 2006. **Price:** $35.00. **Description:** Guide for the entire process of mergers and acquisitions, including taxes, accounting, laws, and projected financial gain.

23941 ■ *"MF Global Moved Clients' Funds to BNY Mellon" in Wall Street Journal Eastern Edition (November 19 , 2011, pp. B2)*
Pub: Dow Jones & Company Inc.
Ed: Aaron Lucchetti. **Description:** Since the collapse of securities brokerage MF Global Holdings Ltd., one question has remained: where did the hundreds of millions of dollars in customers' accounts go? It has been revealed that MF Global moved those millions

from its own brokerage unit to Bank of New York Mellon Corporation in August of this year, just two months before filing for bankruptcy protection.

23942 ■ *"Midwest Looks 'Back to the Future"* *in The Business Journal-Milwaukee (Vol. 25, July 18, 2008, No. 43, pp. A1)*
Pub: American City Business Journals, Inc.
Ed: Rich Rovito. **Description:** Midwest Air Group Inc. announced plans to reduce their work force by 40 percent or 1,200 employees after an earlier announcement of a drastic fleet reduction. These steps are being taken by the company in an effort to avoid filing bankruptcy since this would cost the airline millions of dollars in legal and other professional fees.

23943 ■ *"Millions of Senior Citizens Swindled by Financial Fraud"* *in Black Enterprise (Vol. 41, September 2010, No. 2, pp. 24)*
Pub: Earl G. Graves Publishing Co. Inc.
Description: One of every five citizens over the age of 65 have been victims of financial fraud. Statistical data included.

23944 ■ *"Missing MF Global Funds Could Top $1.2 Billion"* *in Wall Street Journal Eastern Edition (November 22 , 2011, pp. A1)*
Pub: Dow Jones & Company Inc.
Ed: Aaron Lucchetti, Dan Strumpf. **Description:** As the investigation into the collapse of securities brokerage MF Global Holdings Ltd. continues, the question of what happened to customers' funds has to be answered. Now, it is believed that the actual amount of missing funds is much more than the $600 million originally thought, and could be well over $1.2 billion.

23945 ■ *"Monopoly Money Madness"* *in Canadian Business (Vol. 81, March 17, 2008, No. 4, pp. 9)*
Pub: Rogers Media
Description: Enbridge was given permission by the Ontario Energy Board to collect $22 million it spent on an out-of-court settlement for charging unfair fees from 1994 to 2002. Customers are essentially being gouged twice in this scenario. The monopoly of Enbridge should end and the consumers should not have to pay for the system's faults.

23946 ■ *"More Law Partners Jumping Ship"* *in Boston Business Journal (Vol. 27, October 5, 2007, No. 36, pp. 1)*
Pub: American City Business Journals Inc.
Ed: Lisa van der Pool. **Description:** Boston lawyers are moving from one law firm to another, a practice becoming more prevalent than in recent times. Loss of revenue, clients and poor partner morale are some of the reasons for these actions. Details of this profound trend are discussed.

23947 ■ *"Mosaid Grants First Wireless Parent License To Matsushita"* *in Canadian Electronics (Vol. 23, June-July 2008, No. 5, pp. 1)*
Pub: Action Communication Inc.
Description: Matsushita Electric Industrial Co. Ltd. has been granted a six-and-a-half-year license by Mosaid Technologies Inc. to manufacture the latter's products. The patent portfolio license agreement covers Mosaid's Wi-Fi, Wi-Max, CDMA-enabled notebook computers and other products.

23948 ■ *"Mulroney on the Record"* *in Canadian Business (Vol. 79, September 11, 2006, No. 18, pp. 43)*
Pub: Rogers Media
Description: Canada's former prime minister and senior partner at the law firm Ogilvy Renault, Brain Mulroney speaks about the major policies and initiatives of the current government and its impact on the country's economy.

23949 ■ *"A Nasty Russian Tale"* *in Canadian Business (Vol. 81, March 3, 2008, No. 3, pp. 85)*
Pub: Rogers Media
Ed: Andrew Nikiforuk. **Description:** Billionaires Alex Shnaider and Michael Shtaif entered a partnership for an oil venture which ended in a slew of litigations. Cases of breach of contract, injurious falsehood and

other related lawsuits were filed against Shnaider. Details of the lawsuits and the other parties involved in the disputes are presented.

23950 ■ *"Natalie Peterson; Corporate Counsel, Steris Corp., 39"* *in Crain's Cleveland Business (Vol. 28, November 19, 2007, No. 46, pp. F-14)*
Pub: Crain Communications, Inc.
Ed: Chuck Soder. **Description:** Profile of Natalie Peterson, corporate counsel for Steris Corp., a manufacturer of sterilization products; Peterson's blue-collar background did not detour her from her collegiate goals although she hardly knew how to fill out a college application. After graduating from Stanford Law School in 1997, she opted to return to Cleveland in lieu of more lucrative job offers in San Francisco. She has joined the school board and has participated in the 3Rs program, in which lawyers visit public schools in Cleveland to get students thinking about career choices and talk about constitutional law.

23951 ■ *"New Century's Fall Has a New Culprit"* *in Barron's (Vol. 88, March 31, 2008, No. 13, pp. 20)*
Pub: Dow Jones & Company, Inc.
Ed: Jonathan R. Laing. **Description:** Court examiner Michael Missal reports that New Century Financial's auditor contributed to New Century's demise by its negligence in permitting improper and imprudent practices related to New Century's accounting processes. New Century's bankruptcy filing is considered the start of the subprime-mortgage crisis.

23952 ■ *"New Health Law, Lack of Docs Collide on Cape Cod"* *in Boston Business Journal (Vol. 27, October 12, 2007, No. 37, pp. 1)*
Pub: American City Business Journals Inc.
Ed: Mark Hollmer. **Description:** There is a shortage of primary care providers at Outer Cape Health Services in Massachusetts, with the isolation of the area and as physicians look for higher paying careers in specialty positions. The Commonwealth Health Insurance Connector Authority is pushing for a new health insurance law and is working with Cape Cod Chamber of Commerce to conduct outreach programs.

23953 ■ *"New ICA, Ex-Builder Tangle Over Construction"* *in Boston Business Journal (Vol. 27, October 12, 2007, No. 37, pp. 1)*
Pub: American City Business Journals Inc.
Ed: Michelle Hillman. **Description:** Now-defunct George B.H. Macomber Company is suing the Institute of Contemporary Art (ICA) in Boston, Massachusetts as it believes that it has done extra work worth more than $6.6 million that was not included in the original contract with the construction of the museum. A series of setbacks and minor repairs has caused delays in the opening of the ICA, which was further complicated when Macomber began having financial difficulties.

23954 ■ *"New Law Lets Shareholders Play Hardball With Firms"* *in Globe & Mail (January 2, 2006, pp. B1)*
Pub: CTVglobemedia Publishing Inc.
Ed: Janet McFarland. **Description:** Business lawyer Wes Voorheis discusses about the launching of Bill 198 by plaintiffs' lawyers on behalf of ordinary retail investors.

23955 ■ *"New Race Suit at Local Coke Plant"* *in Business Courier (Vol. 24, February 1, 2008, No. 43, pp. 1)*
Pub: American City Business Journals, Inc.
Ed: Jon Newberry. **Description:** Another racial harassment lawsuit has been filed against the Coca-Cola Enterprises Inc. plant in Madisonville by its 23 black workers. The lawsuit alleges that the working environment at the plant continues to be offensive, abusive, intimidating and hostile. Details of the class-action suit are provided.

23956 ■ *"New Rule Rankles In Jersey"* *in Philadelphia Business Journal (Vol. 30,*

September 16, 2011, No. 31, pp. 1)
Pub: American City Business Journals Inc.
Ed: Jeff Blumenthal. **Description:** A new rule in New Jersey which taxes out-of-state companies that conduct business in the state earned the ire of several banks, mortgage lenders and credit card companies and prompted opponents to threaten to file lawsuits. The new rule is an amendment to New Jersey Division of Taxation's corporate business tax regulation and is retroactive to 2002. Details are given.

23957 ■ *"New Technology-Based Firms in the New Millennium, Volume 6*
Pub: Elsevier Science & Technology Books
Ed: Ray Oakey, R. Oakey. **Released:** May 2008. **Price:** $149.00. **Description:** Collection of papers from the Annual International High Technology Firms (HTSFs) Conference cover issues of importance to governments as they develop technological program. Papers are grouped into three sections: theory, strategy and clustering, and spin-off firms.

23958 ■ *"New York Collection Agency's Bribery Case Resolved"* *in Collections & Credit Risk (Vol. 15, August 1, 2010, No. 7, pp. 19)*
Pub: SourceMedia Inc.
Description: Criminal conviction and civil settlement in a bribery case and Medicaid scam involving H.I.S. Holdings Inc. and owner Deborah Kantor is examined.

23959 ■ *"The Next Step in Patent Reform"* *in Information Today (Vol. 28, November 2011, No. 10, pp. 1)*
Pub: Information Today, Inc.
Ed: George H. Pike. **Description:** The Leahy-Smith America Invents Act was signed into law in September 2011. The new act reformed the previous US patent system. Information involving the new patent law process is discussed.

23960 ■ *"No Matter the Workplace Size, Handbooks Can Play a Vital Role"* *in Crain's Cleveland Business (Vol. 28, November 12, 2007, No. 45)*
Pub: Crain Communications, Inc.
Ed: David Prizinsky. **Description:** Employee handbooks are important for even small businesses that wish to remain relatively informal since that documentation can help a company with a defense when confronted by employee or government lawsuits; they also demonstrate a consistency in policy which is a vital way in which employees, managers and owners remain focused on the company's prime goals.

23961 ■ *"Nobel Winners Provide Insight on Outsourcing, Contract Work"* *in Workforce Management (Vol. 88, November 16, 2009, No. 12, pp. 11)*
Pub: Crain Communications Inc.
Ed: Jeremy Smerd. **Description:** Insights into such workforce management issues as bonuses, employee contracts and outsourcing has been recognized by the Nobel Prize winners in economics whose research sheds a light on the way economic decisions are made outside markets.

23962 ■ *"Nortel Plays Big to Settle Lawsuits"* *in Globe & Mail (February 9, 2006, pp. B1)*
Pub: CTVglobemedia Publishing Inc.
Ed: Catherine McLean. **Description:** The details on Nortel Networks Corp.'s settlement of cases with shareholders are presented.

23963 ■ *"Not All Contracts a Good Fit for Fashion Reps"* *in Agency Sales Magazine (Vol. 39, September-October 2009, No. 9, pp. 10)*
Pub: MANA
Ed: Jack Foster. **Description:** Difficult situations regarding the relationship between sales representatives and their principals in the fashion industry are presented and suggestions on how to create contracts that seek to prevent potential problems are provided. Sales reps should make sure that manufacturer has a viable business that is well thought-out and adequately financed.

23964 ■ *"Not Enough To Go Around"* in The Business Journal-Milwaukee *(Vol. 25, August 15, 2008, No. 47, pp. A1)*
Pub: American City Business Journals, Inc.
Ed: David Doege. Description: Most of the creditors of bankrupt real estate developer Scott Fergus are likely to remain unpaid as he only has an estimated $30,000 available for paying debts. Creditors, as of the 13 August 2008 deadline for filing claims, have filed a total of $79.1 million in claims.

23965 ■ *"Not In Our Backyard"* in Canadian Business *(Vol. 80, October 22, 2007, No. 21, pp. 76)*
Pub: Rogers Media
Ed: Anrew Nikiforuk. Description: Alberta Energy and Utilities Board's proposed construction of electric transmission line has let to protests by landowners. The electric utility was also accused of spying on ordinary citizens and violating impartiality rules. Details of the case between Lavesta Area Group and the Board are discussed.

23966 ■ *"Oce Business Services: Discovery Made Easy"* in Information Today *(Vol. 26, February 2009, No. 2, pp. 31)*
Pub: Information Today, Inc.
Ed: Barbara Brynko. Description: Oce Business Services provides document process management and electronic discovery through its CaseData repertoire of legal management solutions.

23967 ■ *"Of Marks and Men"* in Canadian Business *(Vol. 80, March 12, 2007, No. 6, pp. 59)*
Pub: Rogers Media
Ed: Andy Holloway. Description: The importance on the part of business enterprises to register for trademarks to avoid any threat of litigation in future is discussed.

23968 ■ *"Ohio Collection Agency Settles Second Lawsuit"* in Collections & Credit Risk *(Vol. 15, July 1, 2010, No. 6, pp. 9)*
Pub: SourceMedia Inc.
Description: National Enterprise Systems, will pay $75,000 for illegal and abusive collection charged in a lawsuit filed by West Virginia's Attorney General's office. Money will be used to reimburse students and consumers who paid the illegal fees to the company.

23969 ■ *"OK, Bring in the Lawyers"* in Crain's Chicago Business *(Vol. 31, November 17, 2008, No. 46, pp. 26)*
Pub: Crain Communications, Inc.
Ed: Daniel Rome Levine. Description: Bankruptcy attorneys are finding the economic and credit crisis a benefit for their businesses due to the high number of business owners and mortgage holders that are need of their services. One Chicago firm is handling ten times the number of cases they did the previous year and of that about 80 percent of their new clients are related to the real estate sector.

23970 ■ *"Only in Canada, Eh?"* in Canadian Business *(Vol. 79, November 6, 2006, No. 22, pp. 17)*
Pub: Rogers Media
Ed: Al Rosen. Description: The ethics of corporate spying with relation to competitive information leakage are analyzed.

23971 ■ *"Open Price Agreements: Good Faith Pricing in the Franchise Relationship"* in Franchise Law Journal *(Vol. 27, Summer 2007, No. 1)*
Pub: American Bar Association
Contact: Carolyn Lamm, President
Ed: Douglas C. Berry, David M. Eyers, Daniel J. Oates. Description: Open price term contracts are important to franchise businesses. Details of open price contracts are examined.

23972 ■ *"OSC Eyes New Tack on Litigation"* in Globe & Mail *(April 9, 2007, pp. B1)*
Pub: CTVglobemedia Publishing Inc.
Ed: Janet McFarland. Description: The efforts of the Ontario Securities Commission to set up a tribunal for the investigation and control of securities fraud are described. The rate of the conviction of corporate officials in cases heard by the courts is discussed.

23973 ■ *"Others' Economic Woes Bring Business to Bankruptcy Attorney"* in The Business Journal - Serving Phoenix and the Valley of the Sun *(Vol. 28, July 4, 2008, No. 44, pp. 7)*
Pub: American City Business Journals, Inc.
Ed: Mike Sunnucks. Description: Economic slowdown has increased the demand for the services offered by law firms and bankruptcy attorneys. The number of small business and consumer bankruptcies has surged in 2005. Attorney Dan Gukeisen of Gukeisen Law Group PC has shifted his focus to handling bankruptcy filings and foreclosure matters.

23974 ■ *"Paging Dr. Phil"* in Canadian Business *(Vol. 79, September 25, 2006, No. 19, pp. 21)*
Pub: Rogers Media
Ed: John Gray. Description: Increasing corporate crimes in software industry is discussed by focusing on recent case of Hewlett and Packard.

23975 ■ *"P&G vs. IRS: Split Decision"* in Business Courier *(Vol. 27, July 16, 2010, No. 11, pp. 1)*
Pub: Business Courier
Ed: Jon Newberry. Description: Implications of a court ruling in a $435 million legal dispute between Procter & Gamble Company (P&G) and the Internal Revenue Service (IRS) are discussed. A $21 million win has been realized for P&G for its interpretation of research and development tax credits. However, the said case might involve more than $700 million in P&G tax deductions from 2001 through 2004 that the IRS had disallowed.

23976 ■ *"Patently Absurd"* in Globe & Mail *(January 28, 2006, pp. B4)*
Pub: CTVglobemedia Publishing Inc.
Ed: Barrie McKenna; Paul Waldie; Simon Avery. Description: An overview of facts about patent dispute between Research In Motion Ltd. and NTP Inc. is presented.

23977 ■ *"PBSJ Launches Internal Probe"* in Tampa Bay Business Journal *(Vol. 30, January 8, 2010, No. 3, pp. 1)*
Pub: American City Business Journals
Ed: Margie Manning. Description: Florida-based engineering firm PBSJ Corporation has started an internal investigation into possible violations of any laws, including the Foreign Corrupt Practices Act. Projects handled by subsidiary PBS&J International in foreign countries are the focus of the investigation.

23978 ■ *"Perspective: Borderline Issues"* in Entrepreneur *(Vol. 35, October 2007, No. 10, pp. 48)*
Pub: Entrepreneur Media Inc.
Ed: Joshua Kurlantzick. Description: Failure of the immigration reform bill is expected to result in increased difficulty in finding workers that would take on the dirty and perilous jobs, which are usually taken by immigrants. Regularizing immigration on the other hand will cost business owners money by making them spend for the legality of their employees' stay in the U.S. Other effects of immigration laws on entrepreneurs are discussed.

23979 ■ *"Pet Food Insider Sold Shares Before Recall"* in Globe & Mail *(April 10, 2007, pp. B1)*
Pub: CTVglobemedia Publishing Inc.
Ed: Keith McArthur. Description: The issue related the selling of share units by Mark Weins, chief financial officer of pet food firm Menu Foods Income Fund, just before the recall of contaminated pet food is discussed.

23980 ■ *"Piece of Health Law 'A Goner'"* in Baltimore Business Journal *(Vol. 28, November 19, 2010, No. 28, pp. 1)*
Pub: Baltimore Business Journal
Ed: Kent Hoover. Description: Montana Senator Max Baucus, a Democrat who heads the Senate Finance Committee, has revealed his plan to push legislation that would repeal the 1099 IRS provision

that was created by the health care reform law and will result in more paperwork for small businesses when it goes into effect in 2012.

23981 ■ *"Pioneers Get All The Perks"* in Canadian Business *(Vol. 81, March 3, 2008, No. 3, pp. 18)*
Pub: Rogers Media
Description: Suncor Energy Inc. will face royalty payments from 25% to 30% of net profits as it signs a new deal with Alberta. Biovail Corp., meanwhile, is under a U.S. grand jury investigation for supposed improprieties in Cardizem LA heart drug launch. The Conference Board of Canada's proposal to impose taxes on greenhouse gas emissions and other developments in the business community are discussed.

23982 ■ *"Pipe Show Finds a Way for Smokers to Light Up"* in Crain's Chicago Business *(Vol. 31, April 28, 2008, No. 17, pp. 57)*
Pub: Crain Communications, Inc.
Ed: H. Lee Murphy. Description: With the help of attorneys within its local membership of 150 pipe collectors, the Chicagoland Pipe Collectors Club will be allowed to smoke at its 13th International Pipe & Tobacciana Show at Pheasant Run Resort. The event is expected to draw 4,000 pipe enthusiasts from as far as China and Russia.

23983 ■ *"Plans for Coal-Fired Electricity Could Go Up in Smoke"* in Globe & Mail *(March 5, 2007, pp. B7)*
Pub: CTVglobemedia Publishing Inc.
Ed: Steve James. Description: The coal-fired power project initiated by Texas-based utility company TXU Corp. is receiving legal challenges from green groups. The possible disasters caused by the coal-fired plant are presented.

23984 ■ *"Play It Safe"* in Entrepreneur *(Vol. 35, November 2007, No. 11, pp. 26)*
Pub: Entrepreneur Media Inc.
Ed: Gwen Moran. Description: U.S.-based toy manufacturers find opportunity from concerns regarding the recent recalls of toys that are made in China. The situation can provide better probability of parents buying toys made in the U.S. or Europe, where manufacturing standards are stricter.

23985 ■ *"Porsche Raises VW Stake, Makes Bid for Firm"* in Globe & Mail *(March 26, 2007, pp. B5)*
Pub: CTVglobemedia Publishing Inc.
Ed: Chad Thomas. Jeremy Van Logan. Description: Automobile giant Porsche AG has increased its stake in Volkswagen AG to $54 billion recently. The company is planning a merger by claiming 30% stake under German law.

23986 ■ PPC's Small Business Tax Guide
Pub: Practitioners Publishing Company
Ed: Douglas L. Weinbrenner, Virginia R. Bergman, Toni M. Greenwall, James A. Keller, Scott Mayfield, Linda A. Markwood. Released: January 2005. Price: $189.00. Description: Business tax laws are covered in an easy to understand format.

23987 ■ PPC's Small Business Tax Guide, Vol. 2
Pub: Practitioners Publishing Company
Ed: Douglas L. Weinbrenner, Virginia R. Bergman, Toni M. Greenwall, James A. Keller, Scott Mayfield, Linda A. Markwood. Released: January 2005. Price: $189.00. Description: Second volume containing technical guide covering business tax laws.

23988 ■ *"A Practical Approach to Addressing Holdover Ex-Franchisee Trademark Issues"* in Franchise Law Journal *(Vol. 27, Summer 2007, No. 1)*
Pub: American Bar Association
Contact: Carolyn Lamm, President
Ed: Christopher P. Bussert, William M. Bryner. Description: Franchisor-franchisee relationships can become legally complicated when they are terminated. Laws governing trademarks and other proprietary materials are examined.

23989 ■ *"Practice Problems"* in *Crain's Cleveland Business (Vol. 30, June 22, 2009, No. 24, pp. 9)*
Pub: Crain Communications, Inc.
Ed: Arielle Kass. **Description:** Many laid off attorneys are finding few options in the down economy and some are setting up their own practices.

23990 ■ *"Prepaid Cards and State Unclaimed Property Laws"* in *Franchise Law Journal (Vol. 27, Summer 2007, No. 1, pp. 23)*
Pub: American Bar Association
Contact: Carolyn Lamm, President
Ed: Phillip W. Bohl, Kathryn J. Bergstrom, Kevin J. Moran. **Description:** Unredeemed value of electronic prepaid stored-value credit cards for retail purchases is known as breakage. Laws governing unclaimed property as it relates to these gift cards is covered.

23991 ■ *Prepare to Be a Teen Millionaire*
Pub: Health Communications, Inc.
Contact: Peter Vegso, President
Ed: Robyn Collins; Kimberly Spinks Burleson. **Released:** April 1, 2008. **Price:** $16.95. **Description:** Business reference for any teenager wishing to become a successful entrepreneur; advice is given from successful teenage millionaires. Topics covered include: choosing a business name, type, and location; use of the Internet; legal issues; branding, sales, and marketing; funding and financial management; return on investment; retirement; development of a sound business plan; and certification for minority or women-owned companies.

23992 ■ *"Prichard the Third"* in *Canadian Business (Vol. 83, October 12, 2010, No. 17, pp. 34)*
Pub: Rogers Media Ltd.
Ed: Thomas Watson. **Description:** Robert Prichard, the new chair of international business law firm Torys, talks about his current role; his job involved advising clients, representing the firm, being part of the leadership team, and recruiting talent. He considers 'Seven Days in Tibet' as the first book to have an influence on his world view.

23993 ■ *"Privacy Concern: Are 'Group' Time Sheets Legal?"* in *HR Specialist (Vol. 8, September 2010, No. 9, pp. 4)*
Pub: Capitol Information Group Inc.
Description: Under the Fair Labor Standards Act (FLSA) employers are required to maintain and preserve payroll or other records, including the number of hours worked, but it does not prescribe a particular order or form in which these records must be kept.

23994 ■ *"Prosecutors Dish Sordid AIPC Story"* in *The Business Journal-Serving Metropolitan Kansas City (Vol. 27, September 19, 2008, No. 1)*
Pub: American City Business Journals, Inc.
Ed: Suzanna Stagemeyer. **Description:** Prosecutors in the American Italian Pasta Co.'s accounting fraud case have revealed evidence on the schemes used by then-officers of the company to commit fraud. District attorney John Wood has dubbed the case as the largest corporate fraud lawsuit in the history of the district of Missouri. How AIPC fell from being an industry leader is also discussed.

23995 ■ *"Protection, Flexibility Make Single-Member LLCs Attractive"* in *Crain's Cleveland Business (Vol. 28, November 12, 2007, No. 45)*
Pub: Crain Communications, Inc.
Ed: Peter DeMarco. **Description:** Discusses the reasons why single-member limited liability companies are gaining popularity; LLC structure allows a great deal of flexibility and protects the owner from liability.

23996 ■ *"Quicksilver Resources Receives Favorable Judgement"* in *Canadian Corporate News (May 16, 2007)*
Pub: Comtex News Network Inc.
Description: The 236th Judicial District Court of Texas ruled in favor of Quicksilver Resources Inc., a crude oil and natural gas exploration and production

company, in the litigation between Quicksilver and CMS Marketing Services and Trading Company regarding the sale and purchase of 10,000 million British thermal units of natural gas per day at a minimum price of $2.47 per MMbtu, with the condition that the parties share any upside equally. The Court has rescinded the contract, rendering it void.

23997 ■ *"The Rage Offstage at Marvel"* in *Barron's (Vol. 88, June 30, 2008, No. 26, pp. 19)*
Pub: Dow Jones & Co., Inc.
Ed: Bill Alpert. **Description:** Lawsuits against Marvel Entertainment and Stan Lee are pushing the claims from Peter F. Paul that Stan Lee Media was undone by the actions of the accused. Paul's associates argue that Stan Lee Media owns rights to Marvel characters and that they want half the profits that Marvel is making.

23998 ■ *"Ralcorp Investigated for Rejecting ConAgra Bid"* in *Saint Louis Business Journal (Vol. 32, September 16, 2011, No. 3, pp. 1)*
Pub: Saint Louis Business Journal
Ed: Evan Binns. **Description:** New York-based Levi & Korsinsky started investigating Ralcorp Holidngs Inc. after it rejected ConAgra Foods Inc.'s third and latest takeover bid of $5.17 billion. The investigation would determine whether Ralcorp's directors had acted on behalf of shareholders' best interest.

23999 ■ *"Recovery on Tap for 2010?"* in *Orlando Business Journal (Vol. 26, January 1, 2010, No. 31, pp. 1)*
Pub: American City Business Journals
Ed: Melanie Stawicki Azam, Richard Bilbao, Christopher Boyd, Anjali Fluker. **Description:** Economic forecasts for Central Florida's leading business sectors in 2010 are presented. These sectors include housing, film and TV, sports business, law, restaurants, aviation, tourism and hospitality, banking and finance, commercial real estate, retail, health care, insurance, higher education, and manufacturing. According to some local executives, Central Florida's economy will slowly recover in 2010.

24000 ■ *"Reform Law Spares Community Banks from FDIC Fee Hike"* in *Baltimore Business Journal (Vol. 28, July 23, 2010, No. 11, pp. 1)*
Pub: Baltimore Business Journal
Ed: Gary Haber. **Description:** A new financial regulator bill has exempted community banks from increased Federal Insurance Deposit Corporation fees. Large banks with assets of $10 billion and above will be required to pay the higher fee in 2010. Small banks are seen to hold bank fees at bay owing to the exemption.

24001 ■ *"Regulation Papered Over"* in *Charlotte Business Journal (Vol. 25, November 5, 2010, No. 33, pp.)*
Pub: Charlotte Business Journal
Ed: Adam O'Daniel. **Description:** County courts in North Carolina are having challenges coping with its oversight and regulation duties as it becomes too busy with foreclosure cases. Clerks in some county courts have presided over foreclosure hearings because of the flooding of foreclosure cases.

24002 ■ *"Regulators Revoke Mann Bracken's Collection Agency Licenses"* in *Collections & Credit Risk (Vol. 15, September 1, 2010, No. 8, pp. 19)*
Pub: SourceMedia Inc.
Description: Maryland regulators have revoked the collections licenses of defunct law firm Mann Bracken LLP.

24003 ■ *"Retailers, Your Will, and More"* in *Agency Sales Magazine (Vol. 39, July 2009, No. 7, pp. 46)*
Pub: MANA
Ed: Melvin H. Daskal. **Description:** IRS audit guide for small retail businesses is presented. Tips on how to make a will with multiple beneficiaries are discussed together with medical expenses that can not be deducted.

24004 ■ *"Revocable, Irrevocable and Living Trusts"* in *Business Owner (Vol. 35, September-October 2011, No. 5, pp. 5)*
Pub: DL Perkins Company
Description: Comprehensive guide is offered to provide information on all forms of trusts.

24005 ■ *"RIM Allegedly Caused 'Substantial Harm"* in *Globe & Mail (January 18, 2006, pp. B6)*
Pub: CTVglobemedia Publishing Inc.
Ed: Simon Avery. **Description:** The details of dispute between Research In Motion Ltd. and NTP Inc. are presented.

24006 ■ *"RIM Says It's Willing to Cut a Check"* in *Globe & Mail (February 24, 2006, pp. B1)*
Pub: CTVglobemedia Publishing Inc.
Ed: Simon Avery. **Description:** The settlement terms proposed by Research In Motion Ltd. in a patent infringement case with NTP Inc. are presented.

24007 ■ *"RIM's Options Story Under Fire"* in *Globe & Mail (March 16, 2007, pp. B1)*
Pub: CTVglobemedia Publishing Inc.
Ed: Janet McFarland. **Description:** The investigation of the backdating of options by Research In Motion Ltd. is discussed. The analysis of the backdating of company's options issues by Professor Erik Lie from the University of Iowa is presented.

24008 ■ *"A Road Map to the New FTC Franchise Rule"* in *Franchise Law Journal (Vol. 27, Fall 2007, No. 2, pp. 105)*
Pub: American Bar Association
Contact: Carolyn Lamm, President
Ed: Gerald C. Wells, Dennis E. Wieczorek. **Description:** Information about the Federal Trade Commission's revised Franchise Rule (16 C.F.R. Part 436 Disclosure Requirements and Prohibitions Concerning Franchising) (the New Rule) which replaces the original 1978 Franchise Rule (the Old Rule) is given; a comprehensive overview of the New Rule and its implications for the franchise industry is included.

24009 ■ *"'Rocket Docket' Leaves Memphis Debtors Behind"* in *Commercial Appeal (November 28, 2009)*
Pub: Commercial Appeal
Ed: Bartholomew Sullivan. **Description:** According to an investigation by the Scripps Howard News Service, Memphians lodged 807 formal complaints about debt-collection practices to the Federal Trade Commission in a 2 1/2 -year period ending in July; Nearly 1/3 of the complaints involved some type of error with the debt in question. The majority of the complaints were leveled at NCO Group, which also generated the most complaints around the country.

24010 ■ *"RPA Preps for Building Radiant Conference, Show"* in *Contractor (Vol. 57, January 2010, No. 1, pp. 5)*
Pub: Penton Media, Inc.
Description: Radiant Panel Association is accepting registrations for its Building Radiant 2010 Conference and Trade Show. The conference will discuss radiant heating as well as insurance and other legal matters for mechanical contractors.

24011 ■ *"Rumor Has It"* in *Entrepreneur (Vol. 35, October 2007, No. 10, pp. 30)*
Pub: Entrepreneur Media Inc.
Ed: Chris Penttila. **Description:** Some entrepreneurs like Ren Moulton and Dan Scudder regard rumor sites and product blogs as great sources of market research. However, there are legal issues that must be studied before using these Internet sites in marketing and product development. The use and limitations of rumor sites and product blogs are provided.

24012 ■ *"Sabia Signals a Bold, New Course for BCE"* in *Globe & Mail (February 2, 2006, pp. B1)*
Pub: CTVglobemedia Publishing Inc.
Ed: Catherine McLean. **Description:** The reasons behind the decision of chief executive officer Michael Sabia to streamline operations of BCE Inc. are presented.

**24013 ■ "SEC Doesn't Buy Biovail's Claims"
in Barron's (Vol. 88, March 31, 2008, No. 13,
pp. 20)**

Pub: Dow Jones & Company, Inc.

Ed: Bill Alpert. Description: Overstatement of earnings and chronic fraudulent conduct has led the SEC
to file a stock fraud suit against Biovail, Eugene Melnyk and three others present or former employees of
Biovail. Melnyk had the firm file suit in 2006 that
blames short-sellers and stock researchers for the
company's drop in share price.

**24014 ■ Selling the Invisible: A Field Guide
to Modern Marketing**

Pub: Business Plus

Ed: Harry Beckwith. Price: $22.95. Description: Tips
for marketing and selling intangibles such as health
care, entertainment, tourism, legal services, and more
are provided.

**24015 ■ "Senators Predict Online School
Changes" in Puget Sound Business Journal
(Vol. 29, September 19, 2008, No. 22, pp. 1)**

Pub: American City Business Journals

Ed: Clay Holtzman. Description: State senators
promise to create new legislation that would tighten
the monitoring and oversight of online public schools.
The officials are concerned about the lack of oversight
of the programs as well as lack of knowledge about
content of the lessons.

**24016 ■ "Sense of Discovery" in Business
Journal Portland (Vol. 27, November 19, 2010,
No. 38, pp. 1)**

Pub: Portland Business Journal

Ed: Erik Siemers. Description: Tigard, Oregon-
based Exterro Inc. CEO Bobby Balachandran announced plans to go public without the help of an
institutional investor. Balachandran believes Exterro
could grow to a $100 million legal compliance
software company in the span of three years. Insights
on Exterro's growth as market leader in the $1 billion
legal governance software market are also given.

**24017 ■ "Shaky on Free Trade" in Canadian
Business (Vol. 81, December 24, 2007, No. 1,
pp. 29)**

Pub: Rogers Media

Ed: Rachel Pulfer. Description: Rhetoric at the U.S.
presidential elections seems to be pointing toward a
weaker free trade consensus, with Democratic
candidates being against the renewal of free trade
deals, while Republican candidates seem to be for
free trade.

**24018 ■ "Shopping Around for New Ideas" in
Canadian Business (Vol. 79, July 17, 2006,
No. 14-15, pp. 76)**

Pub: Rogers Media

Description: Pensions should be a win-win situation
for both the employer and the employee. The perspective of both parties concerning pension plans is
explored as well as the need to amend laws in order
to make sure that one class of merchant does not
suffer at the cost of another.

**24019 ■ "Sign of Progress" in Playthings
(Vol. 106, October 1, 2008, No. 9, pp. 4)**

Pub: Reed Business Information

Contact: Jeff Greisch, President

Ed: Cliff Annicelli. Description: The ramifications of
the toy recalls in 2007 are discussed. Mandates for
lead-free toys and other safety issues are having an
impact on the American toy industry.

**24020 ■ "Sign of the Times: Temp-To-Perm
Attorneys" in HRMagazine (Vol. 54, January
2009, No. 1, pp. 24)**

Pub: Society for Human Resource Management

Contact: Henry G. Jackson, President

E-mail: hjackson@shrm.org

Ed: Bill Leonard. Description: A growing number of
law firms are hiring professional staff on a temp-to-
perm basis according to the president of Professional
Placement Services in Florida. Firms can save money
while testing potential employees or a temporary
basis.

**24021 ■ "A Simple Old Reg that Needs
Dusting Off" in Barron's (Vol. 88, June 30,
2008, No. 26, pp. 35)**

Pub: Dow Jones & Co., Inc.

Ed: Gene Epstein. Description: Senator Joe Lieberman has a point when he accused speculators of
inflating the prices of food and fuel futures but
introducing legislation to address speculation has an
alternative. The senator's committee should instead
demand that the Commodity Futures Trading Commission enforce position limits on the maximum
number of contracts in a given market per speculative entity.

**24022 ■ "Six Leading Economists on What to
Expect in the Year Ahead: Derek Holt;
Housing" in Canadian Business (December
24, 2007)**

Pub: Rogers Media

Ed: Derek Holt. Description: The Canadian subprime
mortgage market could take a different turn from that
of the U.S. as laws governing Canada's mortgage
market indirectly limit the probability of a slowdown.
Details on how Canada avoided the slowdown in the
housing market and forecasts of new homes for 2008
are discussed.

**24023 ■ Small Business Access to Health
Care: Congressional Hearing**

Pub: DIANE Publishing Company

Ed: Donald A. Manzullo. Released: 2001. Price: $20.
00. Description: Congressional hearing held at
Crystal Lake, Illinois. Witnesses: Mary Blankenbaker,
Co-Owner, Benjamin's Restaurant; Ryan Brauns,
Senior Vice President, Rockford Consulting and
Brokerage; Scott Shalek, RHU, Shalek Financial
Services; Brad Close, National Federation of Indepen-
dent Businesses; Ken Koehler, Flowerwood, Inc.;
Brad Buxton, Vice President of Networks and Medi-
cal Management, Blue Cross and Blue Shield of Il-
linois; Isabella Wilson, Chief Financial Office, Illinois
Blower, Inc.; and James Milam, Illinois State Medical
Society.

24024 ■ Small Business Desk Reference

Pub: Penguin Books USA Inc.

Ed: Gene Marks. Released: December 2004. Description: Comprehensive guide for starting or running a successful small business, focusing on buying
a business or franchise, writing a business plan,
financial management, accounting, legal issues, human resources management, operations, marketing,
sales, customer service, taxes, insurance, and ethics. Information for launching a restaurant, property
management firm, retail outlet, consulting firm, and
service business is included.

24025 ■ Small Business Legal Strategies

Pub: Aspatore Books, Incorporated

Released: July 2004. Price: $37.95. Description:
Corporate Chairs and Partners from top firms in the
U.S. offering insight into selecting, engaging, employing, and benefiting from external corporate counsel
for the small business owner or executive.

24026 ■ Small Business Management

Pub: John Wiley & Sons, Incorporated

Ed: Margaret Burlingame. Released: March 2007.
Price: $44.95. Description: Advice for starting and
running a small business as well as information on
the value and appeal of small businesses, is given.
Topics include budgets, taxes, inventory, ethics,
e-commerce, and current laws.

24027 ■ Small Business Management

Pub: John Wiley and Sons Inc.

Ed: Margaret Burlingame; Don Gulbrandsen; Richard
M. Hodgetts; Donald F. Kuratko. Released: March
2007. Price: $44.95. Description: Tips for starting
and running a successful small business are given,
including advice on writing a business plan, financing, and the law.

24028 ■ Small Business Survival Guide

Pub: Adams Media Corporation

Contact: Gary Krebs, Director

E-mail: swatrous@adamsmedia.com

Ed: Cliff Ennico. Price: $12.95. Description: Small
business expert provides strategies to start a company and survive in the 21st Century. He shows small

business owners how to succeed despite challenges
that can defeat any firm. His advice covers suppliers;
customers and contractors; competitors and creditors; spouses, family and friends; as well as the ways
lawyers, accountants and other can steal an entrepreneur's success. Ennico also describes how startups
can comply with local regulations.

**24029 ■ Small Business Survival Guide:
Starting, Protecting, and Securing Your
Business for Long-Term Success**

Pub: Adams Media Corporation

Ed: Cliff Ennico. Released: September 2005. Price:
$12.95 (US), $17.95 (Canadian). Description:
Entrepreneurship in the new millennium. Topics
include creditors, taxes, competition, business law,
and accounting.

**24030 ■ Small Time Operator: How to Start
Your Own Business, Keep Your Books, Pay
Your Taxes, and Stay Out of Trouble**

Pub: Bell Springs Publishing

Ed: Bernard B. Kamoroff. Released: January 2008.
Price: $18.95. Description: Comprehensive guide
for starting any kind of business.

**24031 ■ "Snatching Talent: Local Law Firms
Quietly Boost Poaching" in Boston Business
Journal (Vol. 31, July 29, 2011, No. 27, pp. 3)**

Pub: Boston Business Journal

Ed: Lisa van der Pool. Description: National law
firms Jones Day and Latham & Watkins LLP set up
offices in Boston, Massachusetts. Their move also
created an upswing on confidential conversation as
both firms are aggressively poaching lawyers from
Boston's other top firms.

**24032 ■ "Soldiering On to Remake the SBA"
in Inc. (February 2008, pp. 21)**

Pub: Gruner & Jahr USA Publishing

Description: Steven Preston discusses efforts to
improve the Small Business Administration's processes to improve services to small businesses. Topics covered include customer service issues, loans,
and fraud.

**24033 ■ "Sorry: Good Defense for Mal
Offense" in The Business Journal-Serving
Metropolitan Kansas City (Vol. 26, July 4,
2008, No. 43, pp. 1)**

Pub: American City Business Journals, Inc.

Ed: Rob Roberts. Description: According to a survey
conducted by the Kansas City Business Journal, ten
hospitals in Kansas City showed that they have
adopted disclosure policies that include prompt apologies and settlement offers. The policy is effective in
minimizing medical malpractice lawsuits. Other
details of the survey are presented.

**24034 ■ "Soured Relationship Plays Out in
Courts" in The Business Journal-Serving
Greater Tampa Bay (Vol. 28, September 19,
2008, No. 39)**

Pub: American City Business Journals, Inc.

Ed: Janet Leiser. Description: Heirs of developer
Julian Hawthorne Lifset won a court battle to end a
50-year lease with Specialty Restaurants Corp. in
Rocky Point. The decision opens the Tampa Bay
prime waterfront property for new development.

**24035 ■ "Speedway Explored Sale" in
Business Courier (Vol. 24, October 12, 2008,
No. 26, pp. 1)**

Pub: American City Business Journals, Inc.

Ed: Jon Newberry. Description: Court records
revealed that Kentucky Speedway discussed a possible sale of its Gallatin County track to International
Speedway Corp. (ISC) before it sued NASCAR and
ISC in 2005 for monopolizing bigtime racing. Kentucky Speedway chairman Jerry Carroll explained in
a sworn statement that ISC was only interested in
the sale if it can buy the track for a cheap price. The
court proceedings and the sale allegations are
discussed.

**24036 ■ "State Democrats Push for Changes
to Plant Security Law" in Chemical Week (Vol.**

172, July 19, 2010, No. 17, pp. 8)
Pub: Access Intelligence L.L.C.
Contact: Donald Pazour, President
Ed: Kara Sissell. **Description:** Legislation has been introduced to revise the existing U.S. Chemical Facility Anti-Terrorism Standards (CFATS) that would include a requirement for facilities to use inherently safer technology (IST). The bill would eliminate the current law's exemption of water treatment plants and certain port facilities and preserve the states' authority to establish stronger security standards.

24037 ■ *"State Reaps $440M with Small-Biz Tax Crackdown" in Boston Business Journal (Vol. 27, October 19, 2007, No. 38, pp. 1)*
Pub: American City Business Journals Inc.
Ed: Lisa van der Pool. **Description:** Massachusetts Department of Revenue has generated $440 million from businesses who have not filed or paid enough taxes. Discover Tax is a database program that targets tax evaders. Small businesses are impacted by this system most.

24038 ■ *"State Unemployment Fraud Rising Sharply" in Sacramento Business Journal (Vol. 28, October 21, 2011, No. 34, pp. 1)*
Pub: Sacramento Business Journal
Ed: Michael Shaw. **Description:** California's Employment Development Department has reported that overpayments, especially due to fraud or misrepresentation, have increased from $88 million in 2008 to more than $250 million in 2010. However, criminal prosecutions in 2010 were fewer than in 2008 as the agency struggles to recover the money.

24039 ■ *Stay Out of Court: The Small Business Owners Guide to Prevent and Resolve Disputes and Avoid Lawsuit Hell*
Pub: Entrepreneur Press
Ed: Andrew A. Caffey. **Released:** January 24, 2005. **Price:** $17.95. **Description:** Business law attorney offers tools to help small company owners to solve disputes without going to court.

24040 ■ *"Stelco Investors Told Their Stock Now Worthless" in Globe & Mail (January 23, 2006, pp. B4)*
Pub: CTVglobemedia Publishing Inc.
Ed: Greg Keenan. **Description:** The reasons behind Ontario Superior Court's approval of Stelco Inc.'s restructuring proposal are presented.

24041 ■ *"Stikemans' Ascent, Its Legacy, and Its Future" in Globe & Mail (January 29, 2007, pp. B2)*
Pub: CTVglobemedia Publishing Inc.
Ed: Jacquie McNish. **Description:** Pierre Raymond, chairman of legal firm Stikeman Elliott LLP, talks about his strategies to handle competition, his challenges, and about Canada's present mergers and acquisition scenario. Stikeman achieved the first place in 2006 M&A legal rankings.

24042 ■ *"Stock Car Racing" in Canadian Business (Vol. 81, September 15, 2008, No. 14-15, pp. 29)*
Pub: Rogers Media Ltd.
Ed: Thomas Watson. **Description:** Some analysts predict a Chapter 11-style tune-up making GM and Ford a speculative turnaround stock. However, the price of oil could make or break the shares of the Big Three U.S. automobile manufacturers and if oil goes up too high then a speculative stock to watch is an electric car company called Zenn Motor Co.

24043 ■ *"Success Fees" in Canadian Business (Vol. 80, March 12, 2007, No. 6, pp.)*
Pub: Rogers Media
Ed: David Baines. **Description:** Legal issues regarding payment of lawyer fees termed 'fair fee' in Canada are discussed with an instance of Inmet Mining Corp.'s dealing with lawyer Irwin Nathanson.

24044 ■ *"Suits Keep Flying in Wireless Service Marketing Wars" in Globe & Mail (March 22, 2007, pp. B3)*
Pub: CTVglobemedia Publishing Inc.
Ed: Catherine McLean. **Description:** The suit filed by Telus Corp. against BCE Mobile Communications Inc. over the latter's alleged misleading advertisement in the press is discussed.

24045 ■ *"The Suits Look Better Than the Shares" in Barron's (Vol. 88, March 31, 2008, No. 13, pp. 25)*
Pub: Dow Jones & Company, Inc.
Ed: Bill Alpert. **Description:** Jos. A. Bank's inventory has increased sharply raising questions about the company's growth prospects. The company's shares have already dropped significantly from 46 to 23 and could still continue its slide. The company is also battling a class action suit where plaintiffs allege that the Bank inventories were bloated.

24046 ■ *"Sundt, DPR Score $470 Million Biotech Project" in The Business Journal - Serving Phoenix and the Valley of the Sun (Vol. 29, September 19, 2008, No. 3, pp. 1)*
Pub: American City Business Journals, Inc.
Ed: Jan Buchholz. **Description:** Sundt Inc. and DPR Construction Inc. were awarded the winning joint-venture contract to develop the second phase of the Arizona Biomedical Collaborative on the Phoenix Biomedical Campus. Both firms declined to comment, but an employee of the Arizona Board of Regents confirmed that the firms won the bidding. Views and information on the development project are presented.

24047 ■ *"Sunwest Vies To Stave Off Bankruptcy" in The Business Journal-Portland (Vol. 25, August 15, 2008, No. 23, pp. 1)*
Pub: American City Business Journals, Inc.
Ed: Robin J. Moody. **Description:** Sunwest Management Inc. is teetering on the edge of bankruptcy as creditors start foreclosure on nine of their properties. This could potentially displace residents of the assisted living operator. Sunwest is trying to sell smaller packages of properties to get a $100 million bridge loan to maintain operations.

24048 ■ *"Sutter, CHW Reject Blue Cross Deal" in Sacramento Business Journal (Vol. 25, August 15, 2008, No. 24, pp. 1)*
Pub: American City Business Journals, Inc.
Ed: Kathy Robertson. **Description:** California-based Sutter Health and Catholic Healthcare West have rejected the $11.8 million class action settlement in connection with contract rescissions between California hospitals and Anthem Blue Cross. Blue Cross can halt the settlement if not enough hospitals accept it. The deal covers all hospitals that owe money due to rescinded Blue Cross coverage.

24049 ■ *"Take on an Elephant Without Getting Trampled" in Globe & Mail (March 17, 2007, pp. B3)*
Pub: CTVglobemedia Publishing Inc.
Ed: Grant Robertson. **Description:** The plan of chief executive officer of Canpages Inc. Olivier Vincent to beat the profit margin and market share of Yellow Pages Group is discussed.

24050 ■ *Tax Savvy for Small Business: Year-Round Tax Strategies to Save You Money*
Pub: NOLO
Ed: Frederick W. Daily, Bethany K. Laurence. **Released:** September 2005. **Price:** $36.99. **Description:** Tax strategies for small business. Includes the latest tax numbers and laws as well as current Internal Revenue Service forms and publications.

24051 ■ *"The Ten Commandments of Legal Risk Management" in Business Horizons (Vol. 51, January-February 2008, No. 1, pp. 13)*
Pub: Elsevier Advanced Technology Publications
Ed: Michael B. Metzger. **Description:** Effective legal risk management is tightly linked with ethical and good management, and managers' behaviors have to be professional and based on ethically defensible principles of action. Basic human tendencies cannot be used in justifying questionable decisions in court. Guidelines for legal risk management are presented.

24052 ■ *"This Just In" in Crain's Detroit Business (Vol. 25, June 22, 2009, No. 25, pp. 1)*
Pub: Crain Communications Inc. - Detroit
Description: Yamasaki Associates, an architectural firm has been sued for non payment of wages to four

employees. Yamasaki spokesperson stated the economy has affected the company and it is focusing marketing efforts on areas encouraged by recovery funding.

24053 ■ *"Thousands Balk at Health Law Sign-Up Mandate" in Boston Business Journal (Vol. 27, November 9, 2007, No. 41, pp. 1)*
Pub: American City Business Journals Inc.
Ed: Mark Hollmer. **Description:** About 100,000 Massachusetts residents have not signed up for insurance plans created as part of the state's health care reform law. Insurers have underestimated the number of new customers signing up for insurance and come close to risking penalties if they do not get insurance by the end of 2007. The Commonwealth Health Insurance Connector Authority's deadline to buy insurance before penalties kick in is November 15, 2007.

24054 ■ *"TIA Wrestles with Procurement Issues" in Business Journal Serving Greater Tampa Bay (Vol. 30, November 12, 2010, No. 47, pp. 1)*
Pub: Tampa Bay Business Journal
Ed: Mark Holan. **Description:** Tampa International Airport (TIA) has been caught in conflict of interest and procurement policy issues after the Hillsborough County Aviation Authority learned of the spousal relationship of an employee with his wife's firm, Gresham Smith and Partners. Gresham already won contracts with TIA and was ahead of other firms in a new contract.

24055 ■ *"A 'To Do' List" in Playthings (Vol. 107, January 1, 2009, No. 1, pp. 9)*
Pub: Reed Business Information
Contact: Jeff Greisch, President
Ed: Richard Gottlieb. **Description:** Profile of the Building Our Future Toy Conference held in October 2008. Participants discussed the industry's future and is seeking ways to understand the toys children want in today's society.

24056 ■ *"'Tone-Deaf' Suitor or True Harasser: How to Tell" in HR Specialist (Vol. 8, September 2010, No. 9, pp. 1)*
Pub: Capitol Information Group Inc.
Description: Details are critical to any harassment charge in the workplace. Courts now list factors employers should consider when trying to determine whether an employee has been sexually harassed at work.

24057 ■ *"Top Law Firms Join Forces" in Business Journal Portland (Vol. 27, December 3, 2010, No. 40, pp. 1)*
Pub: Portland Business Journal
Ed: Andy Giegerich. **Description:** Law Firms Powell PC and Roberts Kaplan LLP will forge a collaboration, whereby 17 Roberts Kaplan attorneys will join the Portland, Oregon-based office of Lane Powell. The partnership is expected to strengthen the law firms' grip on Portland's banking clients.

24058 ■ *"Trial of Enron Ex-Bosses to Begin Today" in Globe & Mail (January 30, 2006, pp. B1)*
Pub: CTVglobemedia Publishing Inc.
Ed: Shawn McCarthy. **Description:** The details of the case against former executives Kenneth L. Lay and Jeffrey Skilling of Enron Corp. are presented.

24059 ■ *"The Trials of Brian Hunter" in Canadian Business (Vol. 81, March 3, 2008, No. 3, pp. 64)*
Pub: Rogers Media
Ed: Thomas Watson. **Description:** Brian Hunter was a considered a brilliant trader in Wall Street before he was blamed for the fall of the Amaranth hedge fund. Some people blame Hunter for placing bets based on unpredictable weather when he was a trader for Amaranth Advisors LLC. The accusation against Hunter that he conspired to manipulate natural gas prices is also discussed.

24060 ■ *"Tripped by Trump?"* in *The Business Journal-Serving Greater Tampa Bay (Vol. 28, July 25, 2008, No. 31, pp. 1)*
Pub: American City Business Journals, Inc.
Ed: Michael Hinman. **Description:** Jean Shahnasarian, a buyer of the Trump Tower Tampa, filed cases against Donald Trump, The Trump Organization Inc., and Trump Tower Tampa for giving misleading information about Trump's involvement in the project. She wants a return of her $278,000 deposit and does not want to take part in the sale of the project.

24061 ■ *"Troubled Project In Court"* in *The Business Journal-Portland (Vol. 25, July 25, 2008, No. 20, pp. 1)*
Pub: American City Business Journals, Inc.
Ed: Wendy Culverwell. **Description:** Views and information on Salpare Bay's Hayden Island project, as well as on financing problems and cases associated with the project, are presented. Construction of luxurious waterside condominiums stopped last fall, after the discovery of financing problems and subcontractors and other parties started filing claims and counterclaims.

24062 ■ *"Troy Patent Law Firm Launches Rent-Free Tech Incubator"* in *Crain's Detroit Business (Vol. 25, June 8, 2009, No. 23, pp. 4)*
Pub: Crain Communications Inc. - Detroit
Ed: Tom Henderson. **Description:** Young Basile Hanlon MacFarlane & Helmholdt PC, a patent law firm located in Troy, Michigan has created a small, rent-free technology incubator on site. The incubator will be called North Woodward Tech Incubator and has room for four or five startups. The incubator is for the earliest or pre-seed stage for entrepreneurs who have not yet gotten significant investment capital.

24063 ■ *"Truckers Walk Strike Line"* in *Puget Sound Business Journal (Vol. 29, October 24, 2008, No. 27, pp. 1)*
Pub: American City Business Journals
Ed: Steve Wilhelm. **Description:** Teamsters Local 174 went on strike against Oak Harbor Freight Lines Inc. over alleged company violations of federal labor laws. The union also accuses the company of engaging directly with employees and holding mandatory meetings about contract negotiations.

24064 ■ *"Trust But Verify: FMLA Software Isn't Foolproof, So Apply a Human Touch"* in *HR Specialist (Vol. 8, September 2010, No. 9, pp. 3)*
Pub: Capitol Information Group Inc.
Description: Employers are using software to track FMLA information, however, it is important for employers to review reasons for eligibility requirements, particularly when an employee is reportedly overstepping the bounds within leave regulations due to software error.

24065 ■ *"Trust Distrust"* in *Canadian Business (Vol. 79, July 17, 2006, No. 14-15, pp. 61)*
Pub: Rogers Media
Ed: John Gray. **Description:** The need to frame better trust deeds in order to protect the investor's money as well as their returns is examined.

24066 ■ *Ultimate Guide to Project Management*
Pub: Entrepreneurial Press
Ed: Sid Kemp. **Released:** October 2005. **Price:** $29.95 (US), $39.95 (Canadian). **Description:** Project management strategies including writing a business plan and developing a good advertising campaign.

24067 ■ *Ultimate Small Business Advisor*
Pub: Entrepreneur Press
Ed: Andi Axman. **Released:** May 2007. **Price:** $30.95. **Description:** Tip for starting and running a small business, including new tax rulings and laws affecting small business, are shared.

24068 ■ *Ultimate Startup Directory: Expert Advice and 1,500 Great Startup Ideas*
Pub: Entrepreneur Press
Ed: James Stephenson. **Released:** February 2007. **Price:** $30.95 (CND). **Description:** Startup op-

portunities in over 30 industries are given, along with information on investment, earning potential, skills, legal requirements and more.

24069 ■ *"Under Fire, Sabia Triggers Battle for BCE"* in *Globe & Mail (April 14, 2007, pp. B1)*
Pub: CTVglobemedia Publishing Inc.
Ed: Boyd Erman. **Description:** The announcement of negotiations for the sale of BCE Inc. by its chief executive officer Michael Sabia is discussed. The efforts of Ontario Teachers Pension Plan to submit its proposal for the sale are described.

24070 ■ *Understanding Small Business*
Pub: Tate Publishing and Enterprises, LLC
Ed: Edward McMahon. **Released:** May 2006. **Price:** $20.95. **Description:** Three step process to help an entrepreneur build a basic business plan and an effective cash flow statement to minimize risk.

24071 ■ *"Unfair Distraction of Employees"* in *Business Owner (Vol. 35, March-April 2011, No. 2, pp. 8)*
Pub: DL Perkins Company
Description: Fair Credit Collection Practices Act makes it illegal for collectors to contact a debtor at his or her place of employment if the collector is made aware that it is against personnel policy of the employer for the worker to take such a call.

24072 ■ *"Union, Heal Thyself"* in *Canadian Business (Vol. 81, July 21, 2008, No. 11, pp. 9)*
Pub: Rogers Media Ltd.
Description: General Motors Corp. was offered by the federal government a $250 million fund after the company declared plans to close its facility in Ontario. The government move is geared towards supporting the workers who have refused to support the automotive company. Details of the labor contract between General Motors and the Canadian Auto Workers are presented

24073 ■ *"Union Questions Patrick Cudahy Layoffs"* in *Business Journal-Milwaukee (Vol. 28, December 3, 2010, No. 9, pp. A1)*
Pub: Milwaukee Business Journal
Ed: Rich Ravito. **Description:** United Food and Commercial Workers Local 1473 is investigating Patrick Cudahy Inc.'s termination of 340 jobs. The union said the company has violated the law for failing to issue proper notice of a mass layoff.

24074 ■ *"U.S. Attorney Post the Latest Twist"* in *The Business Journal-Serving Greater Tampa Bay (Vol. 28, July 25, 2008, No. 31, pp. 1)*
Pub: American City Business Journals, Inc.
Ed: Jane Meinhardt. **Description:** Tampa, Florida-based lawyer A. Brian Albritton has been nominated to be the U.S. Attorney for the Middle District of Florida. He is an expert in cases involving white-collar crime, secret theft, noncompete agreements and other agreements.

24075 ■ *"U.S. Trade Body Clears Apple in Patent Case"* in *Wall Street Journal Eastern Edition (November 23 , 2011, pp. C1)*
Pub: Dow Jones & Company Inc. Enterprise Media Group
Contact: Clare Hart, President
Ed: Matt Jarzemsky, Paul Mozur. **Description:** HTC Corporation alleged in its patent-infringement case against Apple Inc. that Apple violated patents of S3 Graphics Inc., a company which was acquired by HTC Corporation. Now the International Trade Commission has issued a ruling saying that Apple did not violate the patents.

24076 ■ *"Universal Music Sues Grooveshark's Parent"* in *Wall Street Journal Eastern Edition (November 22 , 2011, pp. B5)*
Pub: Dow Jones & Company Inc.
Ed: Ethan Smith. **Description:** Escape Media Group Inc., the parent company of online-music service Grooveshark, and seven of its executives have been sued by Universal Music Group, which alleges patent infringement involving its sound recordings. The executives are alleged to have uploaded thousands of songs onto Grooveshark.

24077 ■ *"Unlicensed Utah Collection Agency Settles with Idaho Department of Finance"* in *Idaho Business Review, Boise (July 15, 2010)*
Pub: Idaho Business Review
Description: Federal Recovery Acceptance Inc., doing business as Paramount Acceptance in Utah, agreed to pay penalties and expenses after the firm was investigated by the state for improprieties. The firm was charged with conducting unlicensed collection activity.

24078 ■ *"Unpleasant Surprise"* in *Barron's (Vol. 88, March 24, 2008, No. 12, pp. 60)*
Pub: Dow Jones & Company, Inc.
Ed: Shirley A. Lazo. **Description:** Discusses the $175 million that footwear company Genesco received in a settlement with Finish Line and UBS is considered as a stock distribution and is taxable as dividend income. Railroad company CSX raised its quarterly common payout from 15 cents to 18 cents.

24079 ■ *"Unwanted News for Hospitals"* in *Business Courier (Vol. 24, October 26, 2008, No. 28, pp. 1)*
Pub: American City Business Journals, Inc.
Description: Christ and St. Luke Hospital might be sharing responsibility costs on the $207 million hospital being built by Health Alliance, the group they are parting with. Christ and St. Lu ke hospitals will be paying $60 million and $25 million for partial liability res pectively because the plans for the said project were already underway before they decided to withdraw. Christ Hospital is involved in a whistle-blower case that might cause $424 million in liability across the group.

24080 ■ *"Up To Code? Website Eases Compliance Burden for Entrepreneurs"* in *Black Enterprise (Vol. 38, March 2008, No. 8, pp. 48)*
Pub: Earl G. Graves Publishing Co. Inc.
Ed: Robin White-Goode. **Description:** Business.gov is a presidential E-government project created to help small businesses easily find, understand, and comply with laws and regulations pertaining to a particular industry.

24081 ■ *"Valuation of Intangible Assets in Franchise Companies and Multinational Groups"* in *Franchise Law Journal (Winter 2008)*
Pub: American Bar Association
Contact: Carolyn Lamm, President
Ed: Bruce S. Schaeffer, Susan J. Robins. **Description:** Intangible assets, also known as intellectual properties are the most valuable assets for companies today. Legal intellectual property issues faced by franchises firms are discussed.

24082 ■ *"Verdict: Few Legal Jobs"* in *Boston Business Journal (Vol. 31, June 17, 2011, No. 21 pp. 1)*
Pub: Boston Business Journal
Ed: Lisa van der Pool. **Description:** Law school graduates in Massachusetts are finding it harder to find work as the legal job market remains weak. The national employment rate for the 2010 law school class fell to 87.6 percent, while only 68.4 percent held jobs that require passing the bar examination.

24083 ■ *"Voices: Breaking the Corruption Habit"* in *Business Strategy Review (Vol. 21, Autumn 2010, No. 3, pp. 67)*
Pub: Wiley-Blackwell
Ed: David De Cremer. **Description:** In times of crisis, it seems natural that people will work together for the common good. David De Cremer cautions that, on the contrary, both economic and social research prove otherwise. He proposes steps for organizations to take to prevent corrupt behaviors.

24084 ■ *"VPA to Pay $9.5 Million to Settle Whistle-Blower Lawsuits"* in *Crain's Detroit Business (Vol. 26, January 11, 2010, No. 2, pp. 13)*
Pub: Crain Communications Inc.
Ed: Jay Greene. **Description:** According to Terrence Berg, first assistant with the U.S. Attorney's Office in Detroit, Voluntary Physicians Association, a local

home health care company, has agreed to pay $9.5 million to settle four whistle-blower lawsuits; the agreement settles allegations that VPA submitted claims to TriCare, the Michigan Medicaid program and Medicare for unnecessary home visits, tests and procedures.

24085 ■ "What Enforcement?" in Canadian Business (Vol. 81, December 24, 2007, No. 1, pp. 26)
Pub: Rogers Media
Ed: Al Rosen. **Description:** Securities enforcement in Canada needs to be improved in order to tackle white collar crimes that influence investors' opinion of the country. There have been high-profile cases where investigations have not been initiated. Details on the responsibilities of the securities commissions and the need for enforcement mandate in a separate agency are discussed.

24086 ■ "What's Good Faith Got to Do With Contracts?" in Contractor (Vol. 56, November 2009, No. 11, pp. 41)
Pub: Penton Media, Inc.
Ed: Susan Linden McGreevy. **Description:** Uniform Commercial Code makes the obligation to act in good faith a term of every commercial transaction. The code generally applies to the sale of goods and not to construction contracts but parties to a construction contract have the right to expect people to act in good faith and forego actions not related to the contract itself.

24087 ■ "When Are Sales Representatives Also Franchisees?" in Franchise Law Journal (Vol. 27, Winter 2008, No. 3, pp. 151)
Pub: American Bar Association
Contact: Carolyn Lamm, President
Ed: John R.F. Baer, David A. Beyer, Scott P. Weber. **Description:** Review of the traditional definitions of sales representatives along with information on how these distribution models could fit into various legal tests for a franchise.

24088 ■ "When Worlds Collide: The Enforceability of Arbitration Agreements in Bankruptcy" in Franchise Law Journal (Summer 2007)
Pub: American Bar Association
Contact: Carolyn Lamm, President
Ed: Mark A. Salzberg, Gary M. Zinkgraf. **Description:** Most franchise agreements carry broad arbitration clauses requiring arbitration of nearly all disputes between franchisor and franchisee; how these clauses govern issues of bankruptcy are explored.

24089 ■ "Whistleblower or Manipulator?" in Canadian Business (Vol. 81, July 22, 2008, No. 12-13, pp. 11)
Pub: Rogers Media Ltd.
Ed: John Gray. **Description:** Discusses Maria Messina who is portrayed by prosecutors of the Livent Inc. trial as a whistleblower, while defense lawyers insist that she is a manipulator. Defense lawyers allege that Messina, who was Livent's chief financial officer, is a character assassin that made money out of Livent's bankruptcy. Other views on Messina, as well as information on the case, are presented.

24090 ■ "Who's Next?" in Boston Business Journal (Vol. 27, November 16, 2007, No. 42, pp. 1)
Pub: American City Business Journals Inc.
Ed: Lisa van der Pool. **Description:** Boston, Massachusetts' burgeoning technology and biotech industries along with rising billing rates make it a unique legal market. Law firms cross the threshold either by merging with or acquiring a smaller law firm. Boston as a unique legal market is discussed.

24091 ■ "Why Copyright Isn't Property" in Information Today (Vol. 26, February 2009, No. 2, pp. 18)
Pub: Information Today, Inc.
Ed: K. Matthew Dames. **Description:** An overview of intellectual property is presented. Intellectual property refers to 'creations of the mind: inventions, literary and artistic works, and symbols, names, and designs used in commerce', according to the World Intel-

lectual Property Organization (WIPO). WIPO divides intellectual property into two categories: industrial property consisting of patents, trademarks, and industrial designs; and copyright: literary, artistic, creative, and aesthetic works.

24092 ■ "Will Focus on Business Continue?" in Baltimore Business Journal (Vol. 28, November 5, 2010, No. 26, pp. 1)
Pub: Baltimore Business Journal
Ed: Scott Dance. **Description:** The 2010 election may call for new efforts to teach new lawmakers to assure that the viewpoints of businesses are considered and accurately delivered. The Greater Baltimore Committee and similar groups have gathered reports on the competitiveness of Maryland and are planning to use them to make a case of keeping business a top priority.

24093 ■ Work at Home Now
Pub: Career Press, Inc.
Ed: Christine Durst, Michael Haaren. **Released:** October 9, 2010. **Price:** $14.99. **Description:** There are legitimate home-based jobs and projects that can be found on the Internet, but trustworthy guidance is scarce. There is a 58 to 1 scam ratio in work at-home advertising filled with fraud.

24094 ■ "Workers' Comp System Cuts Through Paper" in Sacramento Business Journal (Vol. 25, July 11, 2008, No. 19, pp. 1)
Pub: American City Business Journals, Inc.
Ed: Kelly Johnson. **Description:** California has started testing a new paperless system for handling disputed workers' compensation claims. It is believed that the shift will affect people both inside and outside of the state Division of Workers' Compensation and the state Workers' Compensation Appeals Board. The other details of the planned system are also presented.

24095 ■ "Working His Magic at Home" in Business Courier (Vol. 24, February 22, 2008, No. 46, pp. 1)
Pub: American City Business Journals, Inc.
Ed: Lucy May. **Description:** Rob Portman has left his position at the White House as budget director and decided to practice law at Squire, Sanders & Dempsey in Cincinnati. However, analysts believe that Portman's political career is not finished yet, as some expect him to become a gubernatorial or senatorial candidate in 2010. Portman's impacts on Cincinnati's business community are also evaluated.

24096 ■ Working for Yourself: Law and Taxes for Independent Contractors, Freelancers and Consultants
Pub: NOLO Publications
Ed: Stephen Fishman. **Released:** March 2008. **Price:** $39.99 paperback. **Description:** In-depth information is shared for contractors, freelancers and consultants involving business law and small business taxes.

24097 ■ Your Lawyer: An Owner's Manual
Pub: Agate Publishing, Incorporated
Ed: Henry C. Krasnow. **Released:** November 2005. **Price:** $14.00. **Description:** Small business guide that assists owners and managers to find, work with, and inspire attorneys. Includes an overview of the legal processes involved in running a small company.

24098 ■ Your Lawyer: An Owner's Manual
Pub: Agate Publishing
Ed: Henry C. Krasnow. **Price:** $14.00.

24099 ■ "Your Lawyer: An Owner's Manual, a Business Owner's Guide to Managing Your Lawyer" in Family Business Review (June 2006)
Pub: Family Firm Institute
Contact: Judy L. Green, President
Ed: Jane Hilburt-Davis. **Description:** Profile of the guide for managing a lawyer for a family-owned small business.

TRADE PERIODICALS

24100 ■ Association Law and Policy
Pub: American Society of Association Executives
Contact: John H. Graham, IV, President
Price: Included in membership. **Description:** Internet newsletter providing information on antitrust, tax,

employment, and other legal issue affecting associations and association executives.

24101 ■ The Business Torts Reporter
Pub: Aspen Publishers Inc.
Contact: Mark Dorman, President
URL(s): www.aspenpublishers.com/Product.asp?catalog_name=Aspen&category_name =&product_id=9900051000. **Ed:** Richard E. Kaye. **Released:** Monthly; 12/yr. **Price:** $605, Individuals with free standard shipping on U.S prepaid orders.

24102 ■ California Labor and Employment ALERT Newsletter
Pub: Castle Publications Ltd.
Contact: Richard Simmons, President
Released: Bimonthly. **Price:** $90; $105 includes 3-ring binder. **Description:** Reports on current developments in California and federal laws concerning personnel and employment issues. Recurring features include notices of publications available.

24103 ■ Insights: The Corporate & Securities Law Advisor
Pub: Aspen Publishers Inc.
Contact: Mark Dorman, President
URL(s): www.aspenpublishers.com/product.asp?catalog_name=Aspen&product_id=SS 08943524. **Released:** Monthly **Price:** $780, Individuals with free standard shipping on U.S prepaid orders.

24104 ■ Laborwatch
Pub: Berens & Tate, P.C.
Released: Monthly. **Price:** $167; $277, two years. **Description:** Monthly report on the developments in labor relations, employment litigation, and human resource management.

24105 ■ Legislative Watch
Pub: American Tort Reform Association
Contact: Sherman Joyce, President
Released: Weekly. **Price:** Included in membership. **Description:** Membership newsletter of the American Tort Reform Association.

VIDEOCASSETTES/ AUDIOCASSETTES

24106 ■ Business Litigation
National Institute for Trial Advocacy
361 Centennial Pkwy., Ste. 220
Louisville, CO 80027-1281
Ph: (720)890-4860
Free: 800-225-6482
Fax: (720)890-7069
Co. E-mail: customerservice@nita.org
URL: http://www.nita.org/
Released: 1987. **Price:** $1995.00. **Description:** Provides a practical primer to business litigation with an emphasis on the prevention of disputes, the effect they have on the client's business, and alternatives to going to court. Since many disputes do end up in civil court, the series covers pretrial and trial strategies, the examining of friendly and hostile witnesses, and closing statements. **Availability:** VHS; 3/4 U.

CONSULTANTS

24107 ■ Law Offices of David Bow Woo
700 S Flower St., Ste. 1100
Los Angeles, CA 90017-4113
Ph: (213)892-6309
Fax: (213)892-2215
Contact: David Bow Woo, Owner
E-mail: david.woo@azbar.org
Scope: Attorney specializing in business litigation and transactions. Emphasis is on financial motivation and import and export trade financing. **Founded:** 1990.

24108 ■ Comprehensive Professional Management Inc.
222 E Dundee Rd.
Wheeling, IL 60090-3009
Ph: (847)520-1301

Fax: (847)520-0372
Co. E-mail: bob@cpmincfs.com
Contact: Kathy Rathunde, Principal
Scope: Services include accounting, financial planning, litigation support, pension profit sharing administration, practice surveys, professional corporation issues, retirement and estate planning and tax advice.

24109 ■ donphin.com Inc.
1001 B Ave., Ste. 200
Coronado, CA 92118
Ph: (619)550-3533
Free: 800-234-3304
Fax: (619)600-0096
Co. E-mail: inquiry@donphin.com
URL: http://www.donphin.com
Contact: Vito Tanzi, President
Scope: Offers a comprehensive approach to understanding and applying a broad range of business principles: legal compliance issues, management concerns, health and safety, customer service, marketing, information management. Industries served: All developing small businesses. **Publications:** "Doing Business Right!"; "HR That Works!"; "Lawsuit Free! How to Prevent Employee Lawsuits"; "Building Powerful Employment Relationships!'; "Victims, Villains and Heroes: Managing Emotions in The Workplace". **Seminars:** Doing Business Right!; HR That Works!; Building Powerful Employment Relationships; Lawsuit Free!.

24110 ■ Invent Resources Inc. (IRI)
PO Box 548
Lexington, MA 02420-0005
Ph: (781)862-0200
Fax: (781)721-2300
Co. E-mail: pavelle@comcast.net
URL: http://www.weinvent.com
Contact: Dr. Richard Pavelle, President
E-mail: pavelle@comcast.net
Scope: Provider of consultancy services to provide support in developing and prototyping new, proprietary products. Offer inventory services on demand. Assist clients who need innovations in product lines. have hit technical bottlenecks, or need improvements in manufacturing processes. Provide assistance to individuals and clients in obtaining, reviewing, and strengthening patents. **Founded:** 1991. **Telecommunication Services:** rp@theworld.com.

24111 ■ Juroviesky and Ricci L.L.P.—Juroviesky L.L.P.
4950 Yonge St., Ste. 904
Toronto, ON, Canada M2N 6K1
Ph: (416)481-0718
Free: 877-578-7529
Fax: (416)481-1792
Co. E-mail: hjuroviesky@jruslaw.com
URL: http://www.jruslaw.com
Contact: Aaron Hershtal, Manager
Scope: A law firm providing legal services on both sides of the United States/Canadian border. Practice areas include international business and corporate law, corporate governance, U.S./Canadian litigation, U.S. and Canadian corporate tax planning; state, provincial, and local tax planning; and international tax planning. **Publications:** "The New Energy Consumer Protection Act- New Protection For Consumers?," Jan, 2011; "Is the United States the Next Great Tax Haven," Feb, 2005; "Under What Circumstances may Canadian Citizens Enter the United States as a Business Visitor," Feb, 2005; "Massachusetts Unsuccessful in its Sales and Use Tax Revenue Grab Against Drop Shippers," Feb, 2005; "Tax and Legal Hiccups in the Course of a US Acquisition," Feb, 2005; "Do I Need To Worry About Collecting and Remitting Sales/Use Tax When I Sell to US Customers," Jan, 2005.

24112 ■ Nixon Peabody L.L.P.
100 Summer St.
Boston, MA 02110-2106
Ph: (617)345-1000

Fax: (617)345-1300
URL: http://www.nixonpeabody.com
Contact: Andrew I. Glincher, President
Scope: Multi-practice law firm serving business, industry and individuals. Practice areas include antitrust, class actions, corporate governance and regulatory, corporate transactions, corporate trust, environmental, equipment finance, FDA regulatory, financial restructuring and bankruptcy, franchise and distribution, global finance, government contracts, government investigations and white collar defense, immigration, intellectual property, international, international arbitration, labor and employment, litigation and dispute resolution, private clients, private equity, products liability, mass and complex tort, project finance, public finance, real estate, securities, syndication, and tax. **Founded:** 1999. **Publications:** "Q&A with Deborah VanAmerongen: Direct Purchase Bonds (One on One: Industry Insight)," Mar, 2012; "Patient-Centered medical homes may reduce health care costs and improve patient health," Feb, 2012; "FDA's Draft Guidance on Social Media and Off-Label Communications," Jan, 2012; "The Investor Guide: Are Chinese Companies Still Worth Investing In?," Jan, 2012; "Passage to India: Ensuring 'safe travels' in business," Dec, 2008; "The Deputization of State AGs Under CPSIA," Dec, 2008; "New Rules Mandating the Disclosure of Consumer Complaints," Dec, 2008.

24113 ■ Ruf & Associates L.L.C.
510 East 770 North
Orem, UT 84097
Ph: (801)764-9100
Free: 866-589-8871
Fax: (866)589-8871
Co. E-mail: info@rufassociates.com
URL: http://www.rufassociates.com
Contact: Harold B. Ruf, Chief Executive Officer
E-mail: hruf@rufassociates.com
Scope: Provides consulting services for construction claims, cost segregation studies, litigation support, insurance claims, insurance claim appraisals, construction management and financial management. **Founded:** 1993. **Publications:** "The Cash Benefits of Cost Segregation." Jul, 2007.

FRANCHISES AND BUSINESS OPPORTUNITIES

24114 ■ AAA Franchise Legal Help Hotline
Franchise Foundations
4157 23rd St.
San Francisco, CA 94114
Free: 800-942-4402
Description: Advice on franchise legal issues. **Founded:** 1980..

24115 ■ Angiuli Katkin & Gentile, LLP
60 Bay St., PH Ste.
Staten Island, NY 10301
Ph: (718)816-0005
Fax: (718)816-4660
Description: Provide legal services for franchise operation. **Founded:** 1985..

24116 ■ Carter & Tani
402 E Roosevelt Rd., Ste. 206
Wheaton, IL 60187
Ph: (630)668-2135
Description: Assist start-up franchisees and franchisors. **Founded:** 1977..

24117 ■ Dickinson & Wheelock P.C.
7660 Woodway Dr., Ste. 460
Houston, TX 77063
Ph: (800)727-3458
Fax: (713)722-9688
Description: Franchise and business attorneys.

24118 ■ Franchise Law Team
30021 Tomas, Ste. 260
Rancho Santa Margarita, CA 92688
Ph: (949)459-7474
Free: 888-276-2976
Fax: (949)459-7772
Description: Registration, advice, and dispute resolution. **Founded:** 1985..

24119 ■ Friedman, Rosenwasser & Goldbaum, P.A.
The Plaza
5355 Town Center Rd., Ste. 801
Boca Raton, FL 33486
Ph: (561)395-5511
Fax: (561)395-2648
Description: International and domestic franchise services. **Founded:** 1986..

24120 ■ Gowling Lafleur Henderson LLP
550 Burrard St., Ste. 2300
Vancouver, BC, Canada V6C 2B5
Ph: (604)683-6498
Fax: (604)683-3558
Description: Full service law firm for franchisors. **Founded:** 1877..

24121 ■ Harold L. Kestenbaum, Esq.
90 Merrick Ave., Ste. 601
East Meadow, NY 11559
Ph: (516)745-0099
Fax: (516)745-0293
Description: Franchise attorney and consultant. **Founded:** 1977..

24122 ■ iFranchise Group
905 W 175th St., 2nd Fl.
Homewood, IL 60430
Ph: (708)957-2300
Fax: (708)957-2395
Co. E-mail: info@ifranchise.net
URL: http://www.ifranchise.com
Description: Offers services on strategic planning, franchise law, operations documentation, marketing and sales, and executive recruiting for franchisors.

24123 ■ James B. Sheets, Attorney at Law
101 Summit Ave., Ste. 304
Fort Worth, TX 76102
Ph: (817)335-6040
Fax: (817)335-2503
Description: Legal services.

24124 ■ Joseph J. Walczak, P.C.
12628 S Harlem Ave.
Palos Heights, IL 60463
Ph: (708)349-6908
Fax: (708)349-2438
Description: Franchise and trademark law. **Founded:** 1988..

24125 ■ Kanouse & Walker, P.A.
2255 Glades Rd., Ste. 324
Boca Raton, FL 33431
Ph: (561)451-8090
Fax: (561)451-8089
Description: Represents franchisees in buying a franchise. **Founded:** 1974..

24126 ■ Law Offices of Suzanne C. Cummings & Associates, P.C.
Two Main St., Ste. 300
Stoneham, MA 02180
Ph: (781)481-9090
Fax: (781)481-9191
Description: Franchise law and business advisors.

24127 ■ Marks & Klein, LLP, Attorneys-at-Law
63 Riverside Ave.
Red Bank, NJ 07701
Ph: (732)747-7100
Fax: (732)219-0625
Description: Franchisee and franchisor representation. **Founded:** 1971..

24128 ■ Mitchell J. Kassoff, Esq., Attorney
2 Foster Ct.
South Orange, NJ 07079-1002
Ph: (973)762-1776
Description: Nationwide legal representation. **Founded:** 1979..

24129 ■ Peter C. Lagarias, Esq.
The Legal Solutions Group, L.L.P.
1629 Fifth Ave.
San Rafael, CA 94901-1828
Ph: (415)460-0100

Fax: (415)460-1099
Description: Franchise litigation and service.

24130 ■ Zarco Einhorn Salkowski & Brito, P.A.
International Pl.
100 SE 2nd St., 27th Fl.
Miami, FL 33131
Ph: (305)374-5418
Fax: (305)374-5428
Description: Franchise and commercial litigation.
Founded: 1992..

COMPUTERIZED DATABASES

24131 ■ *ABA/BNA Lawyers' Manual on Professional Conduct™*
1801 S Bell St.
Arlington, VA 22202
Free: 800-372-1033
Co. E-mail: customercare@bna.com
URL: http://www.bna.com
Availability: Online: Bloomberg LP-Bloomberg BNA; Bloomberg LP-Bloomberg BNA; Thomson Reuters - Westlaw. **Type:** Full-text.

24132 ■ *Atlantic Provinces Reports (APR)*
PO Box 302
Fredericton, NB, Canada E3B 4Y9
Ph: (506)453-9921
Free: 800-561-0220
Fax: (506)453-9525
Co. E-mail: service@mlb.nb.ca
URL: http://www.mlb.nb.ca
Availability: Online: LexisNexis Canada Inc. **Type:** Bibliographic.

24133 ■ *Bankruptcy Law Reporter™*
1801 S Bell St.
Arlington, VA 22202
Free: 800-372-1033
Co. E-mail: customercare@bna.com
URL: http://www.bna.com
Availability: Online: Bloomberg LP-Bloomberg BNA; Thomson Reuters - Westlaw. **Type:** Full-text.

24134 ■ *The Bar Register of Preeminent Lawyers™*
121 Chanlon Rd.
New Providence, NJ 07974
Ph: (908)771-8704
Free: 800-526-4902
Fax: (908)771-8704
Co. E-mail: info@martindale.com
URL: http://www.martindale.com
Availability: Online: LexisNexis Martindale-Hubbell. **Type:** Directory.

24135 ■ *Canadian Law List*
1 Corporate Plz.
2075 Kennedy Rd.
Toronto, ON, Canada M1T 3V4
Ph: (416)609-3800
Free: 800-387-5351
Fax: (416)298-5082
URL: http://www.canadalawbook.ca
URL(s): www.canadianlawlist.com. **Availability:** Online: Thomson Reuters Canada Ltd.-Carswell-Canada Law Book. **Type:** Directory.

24136 ■ *CCH Tax Protos™*
90 Sheppard Ave. E, Ste. 300
Toronto, ON, Canada M2N 6X1
Ph: (416)224-2224
Free: 800-268-4522
Fax: (416)224-2243
Co. E-mail: cservice@cch.ca
URL: http://www.cch.ca
Availability: Online: Wolters Kluwer - CCH Canadian Ltd. **Type:** Bulletin board.

24137 ■ *Class Action Litigation Report®*
1801 S Bell St.
Arlington, VA 22202

Free: 800-372-1033
Co. E-mail: customercare@bna.com
URL: http://www.bna.com
Availability: Online: Bloomberg LP-Bloomberg BNA; Thomson Reuters - Westlaw. **Type:** Full-text.

24138 ■ *Computer Technology Law Report®*
1801 S Bell St.
Arlington, VA 22202
Free: 800-372-1033
Co. E-mail: customercare@bna.com
URL: http://www.bna.com
Availability: Online: Bloomberg LP-Bloomberg BNA; Thomson Reuters - Westlaw. **Type:** Full-text.

24139 ■ *Corporate Law Daily™*
1801 S Bell St.
Arlington, VA 22202
Free: 800-372-1033
Co. E-mail: customercare@bna.com
URL: http://www.bna.com
Availability: Online: Bloomberg LP-Bloomberg BNA; Thomson Reuters - Westlaw. **Type:** Full-text.

24140 ■ *Criminal Law Reporter™*
1801 S Bell St.
Arlington, VA 22202
Free: 800-372-1033
Co. E-mail: customercare@bna.com
URL: http://www.bna.com
Availability: Online: Bloomberg LP-Bloomberg BNA; Thomson Reuters - Westlaw. **Type:** Full-text.

24141 ■ *DART: British Columbia Statute Service*
1 Corporate Plz.
2075 Kennedy Rd.
Toronto, ON, Canada M1T 3V4
Ph: (416)609-3800
Free: 800-387-5351
Fax: (416)298-5082
URL: http://www.canadalawbook.ca
Availability: Online: Thomson Reuters Canada Ltd.-Carswell-Canada Law Book. **Type:** Full-text.

24142 ■ *DART: Western Decisions*
1 Corporate Plz.
2075 Kennedy Rd.
Toronto, ON, Canada M1T 3V4
Ph: (416)609-3800
Free: 800-387-5351
Fax: (416)298-5082
URL: http://www.canadalawbook.ca
Availability: Online: Thomson Reuters Canada Ltd.-Carswell-Canada Law Book. CD-ROM: Thomson Reuters Canada Ltd.-Carswell-Canada Law Book. **Type:** Full-text.

24143 ■ *EIU ViewsWire*
26 Red Lion Sq.
London WC1R 4HQ, United Kingdom
Ph: 20 7576 8181
Fax: 20 7576 8476
Co. E-mail: london@eiu.com
URL: http://www.eiu.com
Availability: Online: LexisNexis Group; Financial Times Ltd.; The Economist Group - Economist Intelligence Unit Ltd. **Type:** Full-text; Numeric.

24144 ■ *Electronic Commerce & Law Report™*
1801 S Bell St.
Arlington, VA 22202
Free: 800-372-1033
Co. E-mail: customercare@bna.com
URL: http://www.bna.com
Availability: Online: Bloomberg LP-Bloomberg BNA; Thomson Reuters - Westlaw. **Type:** Full-text.

24145 ■ *Family Law Reporter®*
1801 S Bell St.
Arlington, VA 22202
Free: 800-372-1033
Co. E-mail: customercare@bna.com
URL: http://www.bna.com
Availability: Online: Bloomberg LP-Bloomberg BNA; Thomson Reuters - Westlaw. **Type:** Full-text.

24146 ■ *Florida Jurisprudence on Westlaw®*
610 Opperman Dr.
Eagan, MN 55123
Ph: (651)687-7000
Free: 800-344-5008
Fax: (651)687-5827
Co. E-mail: west.customer.service@thomsonreuters.com
URL: http://www.westlaw.com
Availability: Online: Thomson Reuters - Westlaw. **Type:** Full-text.

24147 ■ *A Guide to Federal Sector Equal Employment Opportunity (EEO) Law and Practice*
1840 Wilson Blvd., Ste. 203
Arlington, VA 22201
Ph: (703)524-1355
Fax: (703)524-1463
Co. E-mail: deweypublications@gmail.com
URL: http://www.deweypub.com
Availability: CD-ROM: Dewey Publications Inc. **Type:** Full-text.

24148 ■ *A Guide to Merit Systems Protection Board (MSPB) Law and Practice*
1840 Wilson Blvd., Ste. 203
Arlington, VA 22201
Ph: (703)524-1355
Fax: (703)524-1463
Co. E-mail: deweypublications@gmail.com
URL: http://www.deweypub.com
Availability: CD-ROM: Dewey Publications Inc. **Type:** Full-text.

24149 ■ *Industrial Patent Activity in the United States Parts 1 and 2, 1974-1998 (IPA)*
Madison Bldgs. (East & West)
600 Dulany St.
Alexandria, VA 22314
Ph: (703)308-4357
Free: 800-786-9199
Fax: (703)306-2737
Co. E-mail: usptoinfo@uspto.gov
URL: http://www.uspto.gov
Availability: CD-ROM: U.S. Department of Commerce - Technology Administration - National Technical Information Service. **Type:** Patents/Trademarks.

24150 ■ *KeyCite®*
610 Opperman Dr.
Eagan, MN 55123
Ph: (651)687-7000
Free: 800-344-5008
Fax: (651)687-5827
Co. E-mail: west.customer.service@thomsonreuters.com
URL: http://www.westlaw.com
Availability: Online: Thomson Reuters - Westlaw. **Type:** Bibliographic; Full-text.

24151 ■ *The Law Digest*
121 Chanlon Rd.
New Providence, NJ 07974
Ph: (908)771-8704
Free: 800-526-4902
Fax: (908)771-8704
Co. E-mail: info@martindale.com
URL: http://www.martindale.com
Availability: Online: LexisNexis Martindale-Hubbell. **Type:** Full-text.

24152 ■ *Lawyer Locator*
121 Chanlon Rd.
New Providence, NJ 07974
Ph: (908)771-8704
Free: 800-526-4902
Fax: (908)771-8704
Co. E-mail: info@martindale.com
URL: http://www.martindale.com
Availability: Online: LexisNexis Martindale-Hubbell. **Type:** Directory.

24153 ■ *Mergers Unleashed People Database*
1 State St. Plz., 27th Fl.
New York, NY 10004
Ph: (212)803-8200

Free: 800-221-1809
Co. E-mail: custserv@sourcemedia.com
URL: http://www.sourcemedia.com
Availability: Online: Investcorp International Inc. -
SourceMedia Inc. **Type:** Directory.

24154 ■ *The National Law Journal*
120 Broadway, 5th Fl.
New York, NY 10271-1100
Ph: (212)457-9400
Fax: (646)417-7705
Co. E-mail: customercare@alm.com
URL: http://www.alm.com
Contact: William L. Pollak, President
Availability: Online: LexisNexis Group; ALM Properties Inc.; Thomson Reuters - Westlaw. **Type:** Full-text.

24155 ■ *New York Jurisprudence, 2d, LawDesk® CD-ROM ed.*
610 Opperman Dr.
Eagan, MN 55123
Ph: (651)687-7000
Free: 800-344-5008
Fax: (800)340-9378
Co. E-mail: west.customer.service@thomsonreuters.com
URL: http://west.thomson.com
Availability: CD-ROM: Thomson Reuters-Westlaw.
Type: Full-text.

24156 ■ *Ohio Jurisprudence on Westlaw®*
610 Opperman Dr.
Eagan, MN 55123
Ph: (651)687-7000
Free: 800-344-5008
Co. E-mail: west.customer.service@thomson.com
URL: http://west.thomson.com
Availability: Online: Thomson Reuters-Westlaw.
Type: Full-text.

24157 ■ *Pharmaceutical Law & Industry Report®*
1801 S Bell St.
Arlington, VA 22202
Free: 800-372-1033
Co. E-mail: customercare@bna.com
URL: http://www.bna.com
Availability: Online: Bloomberg LP-Bloomberg BNA.
Type: Full-text.

24158 ■ *State Tax Notes®*
400 S Maple Ave., Ste. 400
Falls Church, VA 22046
Ph: (703)533-4400
Free: 800-955-2444
Co. E-mail: cservice@tax.org
URL: http://www.taxanalysts.com
Availability: Online: LexisNexis Group. **Type:** Full-text.

24159 ■ *State Tax Today®*
400 S Maple Ave., Ste. 400
Falls Church, VA 22046
Ph: (703)533-4400
Free: 800-955-2444
Co. E-mail: cservice@tax.org
URL: http://www.taxanalysts.com
Availability: Online: Tax Analysts. **Type:** Full-text.

24160 ■ *The Tax Directory®*
400 S Maple Ave., Ste. 400
Falls Church, VA 22046
Ph: (703)533-4400
Free: 800-955-2444
Co. E-mail: cservice@tax.org
URL: http://www.taxanalysts.com
Availability: Online: LexisNexis Group. CD-ROM: Tax Analysts. **Type:** Directory.

24161 ■ *Texas Jurisprudence®, 3d, LawDesk® CD-ROM*
610 Opperman Dr.
Eagan, MN 55123
Ph: (651)687-7000
Free: 800-344-5008

Fax: (800)340-9378
Co. E-mail: west.customer.service@thomsonreuters.com
URL: http://west.thomson.com
Availability: CD-ROM: Thomson Reuters - Westlaw.
Type: Full-text.

24162 ■ *TOMES Plus® System*
777 E Eisenhower Pky.
Ann Arbor, MI 48108
Co. E-mail: info@truvenhealth.com
URL: http://www.truvenhealth.com
Availability: Online: Truven Health Analytics Inc.
Type: Bibliographic; Full-text; Numeric.

24163 ■ *Toxics Law Reporter™*
1801 S Bell St.
Arlington, VA 22202
Free: 800-372-1033
Co. E-mail: customercare@bna.com
URL: http://www.bna.com
Availability: Online: Bloomberg LP-Bloomberg BNA; Thomson Reuters - Westlaw. **Type:** Full-text.

LIBRARIES

24164 ■ **Alberta Securities Commission Library**
250-5th St. SW, Ste. 600
Calgary, AB, Canada T2P 0R4
Ph: (403)297-6454
Free: 877-355-0585
Fax: (403)297-6156
Co. E-mail: inquiries@asc.ca
URL: http://www.albertasecurities.com
Contact: Yanming Fei, Librarian
Scope: Securities legislation, corporate law. **Services:** Library not open to the public. **Holdings:** Figures not available.

24165 ■ **Arnold & Porter LLP Library**
399 Park Ave.
New York, NY 10022-4690
Ph: (212)715-1000
Fax: (212)715-1399
Co. E-mail: kim.fenty@aporter.com
URL: http://www.arnoldporter.com
Contact: Kim R. Fenty, Director, Library Services
Scope: Litigation; law - tax, corporate, and environmental. **Services:** Interlibrary loan; Library not open to the public. **Founded:** 1988. **Holdings:** 20,000 books; 400 bound periodical volumes. **Subscriptions:** 205 journals and other serials; 15 newspapers. **Telecommunication Services:** angel.cancela@aporter.com.

24166 ■ **Bryan Cave LLP Law Library**
1155 F St., NW
Washington, DC 20004
Ph: (202)508-6000
Fax: (202)508-6200
Co. E-mail: john.peirce@bryancave.com
URL: http://www.bryancave.com
Contact: John Peirce
Scope: Government and politics; law - commercial, corporate, environmental, intellectual property, taxation. **Services:** Interlibrary loan; copying; faxing; library open to the public with restrictions. **Founded:** 1978. **Holdings:** 11,000 volumes. **Subscriptions:** 200 journals and other serials.

24167 ■ **Hewlett-Packard Company - Legal/Tax Library**
3000 Hanover St.
M/S 1069
Palo Alto, CA 94304-1112
Ph: (650)857-1501
Fax: (650)857-5518
URL: http://www.hp.com
Contact: Emily Morris, Analyst
Scope: Legal topics, intellectual property, taxation. **Services:** Library not open to the public. **Holdings:** 2000 books. **Subscriptions:** 160 journals and other serials; 6 newspapers.

24168 ■ **Lang Michener LLP Library**
1500 Royal Centre
1055 W. Georgia St.
Vancouver, BC, Canada V6E 4N7
Ph: (604)689-9111
Fax: (604)685-7084
Co. E-mail: info@mcmillan.ca
URL: http://www.langmichener.ca/
Scope: Law - tax, mining; litigation; corporate securities. **Services:** Library not open to the public. **Holdings:** Figures not available.

24169 ■ **LECG, LLC Library**
2000 Powell St., Ste. 600
Emeryville, CA 94608
Ph: (510)985-6700
Fax: (510)653-9898
Co. E-mail: nadams@lecg.com
URL: http://www.lecg.com
Contact: Nancy Adams, Librarian
Scope: Economics, business, antitrust. **Services:** Library open to the public by appointment only. **Founded:** 1991. **Holdings:** 2500 books. **Subscriptions:** 50 journals and other serials; 4 newspapers.

24170 ■ **Long & Levit Library**
465 California St., 5th Fl.
San Francisco, CA 94104
Ph: (415)397-2222
Fax: (415)397-6392
Co. E-mail: info@longlevit.com
URL: http://www.longlevit.com
Scope: Insurance, environmental, professional liability, construction. **Services:** Interlibrary loan; copying; library open to the public at librarian's discretion. **Founded:** 1927. **Holdings:** 10,000 books. **Subscriptions:** 75 journals and other serials; 4 newspapers.

24171 ■ **McCarthy Tetrault Library**
777 Dunsmuir St., Ste. 1300
Vancouver, BC, Canada V7Y 1K2
Ph: (604)643-7100
Free: 877-244-7711
Fax: (604)643-7900
Co. E-mail: jlecky@mccarthy.ca
URL: http://www.mccarthy.ca
Contact: Joanne Lecky, Director, Library Services
Scope: Law, corporate law, securities. **Services:** Library not open to the public. **Holdings:** Figures not available. **Telecommunication Services:** scaird@mccarthy.ca; info@mccarthy.ca.

24172 ■ **Miller Thomson LLP Library**
Scotia Plaza
40 King St. W., Ste. 5800
Toronto, ON, Canada M5H 3S1
Ph: (416)595-8500
Free: 888-762-5559
Fax: (416)595-8695
Co. E-mail: toronto@millerthomson.com
URL: http://www.millerthomson.com
Contact: Ines Freeman, Librarian
Scope: Law - labor, estate, tax, corporate, commercial, environmental. **Services:** Interlibrary loan; copying; library not open to the public. **Holdings:** 2000 books. **Subscriptions:** 20 journals and other serials; 6 newspapers. **Telecommunication Services:** gbaranieski@millerthomson.com.

24173 ■ **University of Hawaii at West O'ahu - Center for Labor Education and Research - CLEAR Labor Law Library**
96-043 Ala Ike, Bldg. 400, Rm. 402
Pearl City, HI 96782
Ph: (808)454-4774
Co. E-mail: clear@hawaii.edu
URL: http://clear.uhwo.hawaii.edu/library.html
Contact: Dr. William Puette, Director
Scope: Labor law. **Services:** Library open to the public by appointment. **Holdings:** Law manuals, reports, and materials; article files.

RESEARCH CENTERS

24174 ■ Boston University - Center for Law, Business and Technology
School of Law, 8th Fl.
765 Commonwealth Ave.
Boston, MA 02215

Ph: (617)353-3112
Fax: (617)353-3077
Co. E-mail: meurer@bu.edu
URL: http://www.bu.edu/law
Contact: Prof. Michael Meurer, Director
Founded: 1987. **Educational Activities:** Seminars, symposia, conferences and speakers.

START-UP INFORMATION

24175 ■ *Become Your Own Boss in 12 Months: A Month-by-Month Guide to a Business that Works*
Pub: Adams Media Corporation
Contact: Gary Krebs, Director
E-mail: swatrous@adamsmedia.com
Ed: Melinda F. Emerson. **Released:** March 10, 2010. **Price:** $14.95. **Description:** Realistic planning guide to help would-be entrepreneurs transition from working for someone else to working for themselves is given. The key to successfully starting a new company lies in thoughtful preparation at least a year and a half before quitting a job.

24176 ■ *Becoming a Personal Trainer for Dummies*
Pub: John Wiley and Sons, Inc.
Ed: Melyssa Michael, Linda Formichelli. **Released:** October 2004. **Price:** $19.99 (US). $25.99 (Canadian). **Description:** Legal and tax issues involved in starting and running a personal trainer firm. The book offers suggestions for incorporating massage and nutritional services.

24177 ■ *Building a Dream: A Canadian Guide to Starting Your Own Business*
Pub: McGraw-Hill Ryerson Ltd.
Ed: Walter S. Good. **Released:** 2005. **Description:** Topics covered include evaluating business potential, new business ideas, starting or buying a business, franchise opportunities, business organization, protecting an idea, arranging financing, and developing a business plan.

24178 ■ *EBay Income: How ANYONE of Any Age, Location, and/or Background Can Build a Highly Profitable Online Business with eBay*
Pub: Atlantic Publishing Company
Released: December 1, 2010. **Price:** $24.95. **Description:** A complete overview of eBay is given and guides any small company through the entire process of creating the auction and auction strategies, photography, writing copy, text and software, multiple sales, programming tricks, PayPal, accounting, creating marketing, merchandising, managing email lists, advertising plans, taxes and sales tax, best time to list items and for how long, sniping programs, international customers, opening a storefront, electronic commerce, buy-it now pricing, keywords, Google marketing and eBay secrets.

24179 ■ *The Elements of Small Business*
Pub: Silver Lake Publishing
Ed: John Thaler. **Released:** October 2004. **Price:** $12.95. **Description:** Concepts, markets, worksheets, letters, business plans, and sample legal forms for starting and running a small business are included.

24180 ■ *Entrepreneurial Itch: What No One Tells You About Starting Your Own Business*
Pub: Self-Counsel Press Inc.
Ed: David Trahair. **Released:** December 2006. **Price:** $13.95. **Description:** Small business accountant shares a plan for starting a business.

24181 ■ *Entrepreneurship*
Pub: John Wiley and Sons Inc.
Ed: William D. Bygrave; Andrew Zacharakis. **Released:** March 2007. **Price:** $115.95. **Description:** Information for starting a new business is shared, focusing on marketing and financing a product or service.

24182 ■ *Entrepreneurship Strategy: Changing Patterns in New Venture Creation, Growth, and Reinvention*
Pub: SAGE Publications USA
Contact: Blaise R. Simqu, President
Ed: Lisa K. Gundry; Jill R. Kickul. **Released:** August 2006. **Price:** $69.95. **Description:** Entrepreneurial strategies that incorporate new venture emergence, early growth, and reinvention and innovation are examined.

24183 ■ *"Follow the Numbers: It's the Best Way To Spot Problems Before They Become Life-Threatening" in Inc. (January 2008, pp. 63-64)*
Pub: Gruner & Jahr USA Publishing
Ed: Norm Brodsky. **Description:** It is important for any small business to track monthly sales and gross margins by hand for the first year or two. When writing the numbers, be sure to break them out by product category or service type and by customer.

24184 ■ *"Getting Others To Take Your Startup Seriously" in Women Entrepreneur (August 1, 2008)*
Pub: Entrepreneur Media Inc.
Ed: Tamara Monosoff. **Description:** Writing a serious business plan is essential if you want others to take your startup endeavor seriously. As friends, family and acquaintances see you taking positive steps toward your goal they will begin to lend their support and may even help get the business off the ground.

24185 ■ *Getting Rich In Your Underwear: How To Start and Run a Profitable Home-Based Business*
Pub: HCM Publishing
Ed: Peter I. Hupalo. **Released:** April 1, 2005. **Price:** $17.95. **Description:** Book offers insight into starting a home-based business. Entrepreneurs will learn about business models and the home business; distribution and fulfillment of product or service; marketing and sales; how to overcome the fear of starting a business; personal success characteristics; naming a business; zoning and insurance; intellectual capital; copyrights, trademarks, and patents; limited liability companies and S-corporations; business expenses and accounting; taxes; fifteen basic steps for starting a home-based business; state resources for starting a home company; and seven home-based business ideas.

24186 ■ *Going Solo: Developing a Home-Based Consulting Business from the Ground Up*
Pub: McGraw-Hill Companies Inc.
Contact: Deven Sharma, President
Ed: William J. Bond. **Released:** January 1997. **Description:** Ways to turn specialized knowledge into a home-based successful consulting firm, focusing on targeting client needs, business plans, and growth.

24187 ■ *How to Get the Financing for Your New Small Business: Innovative Solutions from the Experts Who Do It Every Day*
Pub: Atlantic Publishing Company
Ed: Sharon L. Fullen. **Released:** May 2006. **Price:** $39.95, includes companion CD-Rom. **Description:** Ready capital is essential for starting and expanding a small business. Topics include traditional financing methods, financial statements, and a good business plan.

24188 ■ *How to Open and Operate a Financially Successful Private Investigation Business: With Companion CD-ROM*
Pub: Atlantic Publishing Company
Released: December 1, 2010. **Price:** $39.95. **Description:** With a massive upside and potential for growth the private investigation sector is growing. The book will teach everything needed to know about working in the private investigation field, starting with the basics of what you can expect and what preconceptions that may just be Hollywood. Information is given to help choose a niche of investigation and hot to start thinking in the abstract, questioning everything but recognizing facts for what they are, as well as the differences between a private investigator and a police officer.

24189 ■ *"Oh, Grow Up!" in Entrepreneur (Vol. 35, October 2007, No. 10, pp. 120)*
Pub: Entrepreneur Media Inc.
Ed: Mark Henricks. **Description:** Most entrepreneurs are overwhelmed with the idea of expanding their business, forgetting to strategically plan the process of business growth. However, there are certain steps entrepreneurs must take in turning a startup business into a bigger venture. Eight steps to growing a business, such as asking for advice and deciding on a focus are presented.

24190 ■ *"Rehab Will Turn Hospital Into Incubator" in The Business Journal-Serving Metropolitan Kansas City (Vol. 26, September 12, 2008)*
Pub: American City Business Journals, Inc.
Ed: Rob Roberts. **Description:** Independence Regional Health Center will be purchased by CEAH Realtors and be converted into the Independence Regional Entrepreneurial Center, a business incubator that will house startups and other tenants. Other details about the planned entrepreneurial center are provided.

24191 ■ *The Small Business Owner's Manual: Everything You Need to Know to Start Up and Run Your Business*
Pub: Career Press, Incorporated
Ed: Joe Kennedy. **Released:** June 2005. **Price:** $19.99 (US), $26.95 (Canadian). **Description:** Comprehensive guide for starting a small business, focusing on twelve ways to obtain financing, business plans, selling and advertising products and services, hiring and firing employees, setting up a

Web site, business law, accounting issues, insurance, equipment, computers, banks, financing, customer credit and collection, leasing, and more.

24192 ■ Start and Run a Delicatessen: Small Business Starters Series
Pub: How To Books
Ed: Deborah Penrith. **Released:** November 9, 2010. **Price:** $30.00. **Description:** Information for starting and running a successful delicatessen is provided. Insight is offered into selecting a location, researching the market, writing a business plan and more.

24193 ■ Starting Green: An Ecopreneur's Guide to Starting a Green Business from Business Plans to Profits
Pub: Entrepreneur Press
Contact: Perlman Neil, President
Ed: Glenn E. Croston. **Released:** September 9, 2010. **Price:** $21.95. **Description:** Entrepreneur and scientist outlines green business essentials and helps uncover eco-friendly business opportunities, build a sustainable business plan, and gain the competitive advantage.

24194 ■ "Startup Aims to Cut Out Coupon Clipping" in The Business Journal-Serving Metropolitan Kansas City (Vol. 26, August 15, 2008, No. 49)
Pub: American City Business Journals, Inc.
Ed: Suzanna Stagemeyer. **Description:** TDP Inc., who started operations 18 months ago, aims to transform stale coupon promotions using technology by digitizing the entire coupon process. The process is expected to enable consumers to hunt coupons online where they will be automatically linked to loyalty cards. Other views and information on TDP and its services are presented.

24195 ■ Swimming Against the Stream: Launching Your Business and Making Your Life
Pub: Macmillan Publishers Limited
Ed: Tim Waterstone. **Released:** March 2007. **Price:** $17.99. **Description:** Ten rules for launching a new business are outlined using real-life experiences.

24196 ■ "Three Weeks To Startup" in Entrepreneur (December 19, 2008)
Pub: Entrepreneur Media Inc.
Ed: Tim Berry; Sabrina Parsons. **Description:** Breakdown for realistically starting a business in three weeks is provided in detail.

24197 ■ The Toilet Paper Entrepreneur: The Tell-It-Like-It-Is Guide to Cleaning Up In Business, Even If You Are At the End of Your Roll
Pub: Obsidian Launch LLC
Ed: Mike Michalowicz. **Price:** $24.95. **Description:** The founder of three multimillion-dollar companies, including Obsidian Launch, a company that partners with first-time entrepreneurs to grow their concepts into industry leaders.

24198 ■ The Unofficial Guide to Starting a Small Business
Pub: John Wiley & Sons, Incorporated
Ed: Marcia Layton Turner. **Released:** October 2004. **Price:** $16.99. **Description:** Information and tools for starting a small business, covering the start-up process, from market research, to business plans, to marketing programs.

24199 ■ What No One Ever Tells You About Starting Your Own Business: Real-Life Start-Up Advice from 101 Successful Entrepreneurs
Pub: Kaplan Publishing
Ed: Jan Norman. **Released:** July 2004. **Price:** $18.95 (US), $28.95 (Canadian). **Description:** From planning to marketing, advice is given to entrepreneurs starting new companies. s.

ASSOCIATIONS AND OTHER ORGANIZATIONS

24200 ■ Auto Suppliers Benchmarking Association (ASBA)
4606 FM 1960 W, Ste. 250
Houston, TX 77069-9949
Ph: (281)440-5044
Fax: (281)440-6677
URL: http://www.asbabenchmarking.com
Description: Automotive supplier firms with an interest in benchmarking. Promotes the use of benchmarking, wherein businesses compare their processes with those of their competitors, as a means of improving corporate efficiency and profitability. Facilitates exchange of information among members; conducts target operations, procurement, development, and maintenance studies; identifies model business practices. **Founded:** 1996.

EDUCATIONAL PROGRAMS

24201 ■ Design Reviews for Effective Product Development (Onsite)
Seminar Information Service, Inc.
20 Executive Park, Ste. 120
Irvine, CA 92614
Ph: (949)261-9104
Free: 877-SEM-INFO
Fax: (949)261-1963
Co. E-mail: info@seminarinformation.com
URL: http://www.seminarinformation.com
Price: $725.00. **Description:** Seminar covering how formal design reviews can improve products by uncovering potential problems before they are discovered at a latter stage of development when the costs of correction are much higher, as well as the requirements for successful reviews. **Dates and Locations:** Troy, MI.

24202 ■ Disaster Recovery Planning: Ensuring Business Continuity (Onsite)
Learning Tree International Inc.
1805 Library St.
Reston, VA 20190-5660
Ph: (703)709-9119
Free: 800-843-8733
Fax: (703)709-6405
Co. E-mail: uscourses@learningtree.com
URL: http://www.learningtree.com
Contact: Nick Schacht, President
Price: $2,810.00. **Description:** Create, document, and test continuity arrangements for the organization. This course is valuable for those managing and maintaining the continuity of an organization's critical processes. **Dates and Locations:** Cities throughout the United States.

24203 ■ Maintenance Planning & Scheduling (Onsite)
American Trainco
9785 S Maroon Cir., Ste. 300
Englewood, CO 80112
Ph: (303)531-4560
Free: 877-978-7246
Fax: (303)531-4565
Co. E-mail: Sales@AmericanTrainco.com
URL: http://www.americantrainco.com
Price: $990.00. **Description:** Learn to reduce maintenance costs by better planning with your existing workforce. **Dates and Locations:** Cities throughout the United States.

24204 ■ Project Management: Skills for Success (Onsite)
Seminar Information Service, Inc.
20 Executive Park, Ste. 120
Irvine, CA 92614
Ph: (949)261-9104
Free: 877-SEM-INFO
Fax: (949)261-1963
Co. E-mail: info@seminarinformation.com
URL: http://www.seminarinformation.com
Price: $2,890.00. **Description:** Learn how to: Produce a project plan for successful delivery; Plan and run projects using best practices in a 6-step project management process; Implement risk management techniques and mitigation strategies; Estimate and schedule task work and duration with confidence; Implement monitoring tools and controls to keep you fully in command of the project; Recognize and practice the leadership skills needed to run a motivated team. **Dates and Locations:** Cities throughout the United States and Toronto and Ottawa, CN.

24205 ■ Project Quality Management for Project Managers - Delivering Consistent Quality (Onsite)
Seminar Information Service, Inc.
20 Executive Park, Ste. 120
Irvine, CA 92614
Ph: (949)261-9104
Free: 877-SEM-INFO
Fax: (949)261-1963
Co. E-mail: info@seminarinformation.com
URL: http://www.seminarinformation.com
Price: $2,490.00. **Description:** Learn how to: Implement effective project quality management best practices; Apply a proven analysis method to identify stakeholder quality expectations and refine project scope; Leverage an industry standard template to create a project Quality Management Plan (QMP); Generate a quality assurance task list that incorporates project, product and process; Transform quality assurance recommendations into corrective and improvement actions; Design and implement quality control gates throughout the project and product life cycles.

24206 ■ Strategic Marketing: Concepts and Strategies (Onsite)
Seminar Information Service, Inc.
20 Executive Park, Ste. 120
Irvine, CA 92614
Ph: (949)261-9104
Free: 877-SEM-INFO
Fax: (949)261-1963
Co. E-mail: info@seminarinformation.com
URL: http://www.seminarinformation.com
Price: $1,595.00. **Description:** Topics include the marketing process, defining the competition, and the marketing mix. **Dates and Locations:** Chelmsford, MA.

24207 ■ Strategic Planning for Organizational Success (Onsite)
Learning Tree International Inc.
1805 Library St.
Reston, VA 20190-5660
Ph: (703)709-9119
Free: 800-843-8733
Fax: (703)709-6405
Co. E-mail: uscourses@learningtree.com
URL: http://www.learningtree.com
Contact: Nick Schacht, President
Price: $2,490.00. **Description:** Learn to formulate strategic plans to help the organization advance and grow. **Dates and Locations:** Toronto, ON; Reston, VA.

REFERENCE WORKS

24208 ■ The 7 Irrefutable Rules of Small Business Growth
Pub: John Wiley & Sons, Incorporated
Ed: Steven S. Little. **Released:** February 2005. **Price:** $18.95. **Description:** Proven strategies to maintain small business growth are outlined, covering topics such as technology, business plans, hiring, and more.

24209 ■ "13D Filings" in Barron's (Vol. 88, March 24, 2008, No. 12, pp. M13)
Pub: Dow Jones & Company, Inc.
Description: HealthCor Management called as problematic the plan of Magellan Health Services to use its high cash balances for acquisitions. Carlson Capital discussed with Energy Partners possible changes in the latter's board. Investor Carl Icahn suggested that Enzon Pharmaceuticals consider selling itself or divest some of its assets.

24210 ■ "13D Filings" in Barron's (Vol. 88, March 10, 2008, No. 10, pp. M11)
Pub: Dow Jones & Company, Inc.
Description: Barington Capital and Clinton Group sent a letter to Dillard's demanding a list of the company's stockholders. Elliott Associates announced that it is prepared to take over Packeteer for $5.50 a share. Strongbow capital suggested a change in leadership in Duckwall-ALCO Stores.

24211 ■ *"13D Filings: Investors Report to the SEC"* in Barron's (Vol. 88, March 31, 2008, No. 13, pp. M10)
Pub: Dow Jones & Company, Inc.
Description: Obrem Capital Management wants Micrel to rescind Micrel's shareholder-rights plan and to boost its board to six members from five. Patricia L. Childress plans to nominate herself to the board of Sierra Bancorp, and Luther King Capital Management may consider a competing acquisition proposal for Industrial Distribution Group.

24212 ■ *"13D Filings: Investors Report to the SEC"* in Barron's (Vol. 88, July 4, 2008, No. 28, pp. M10)
Pub: Dow Jones & Co., Inc.
Description: Robino Stortini Holdings will seek control of Investors Capital Holdings either alone or with members of the company's management. Discovery Group I will withhold its votes on the nomination of directors for TESSCO Technologies while JMB Capital Partners Master Fund plans to nominate a slate of candidates to the board of Maguire Properties.

24213 ■ *The 30-Second Commute*
Pub: McGraw-Hill
Ed: Beverley Williams; Don Cooper. **Released:** 2004. **Price:** $19.95. **Description:** Home-based business owners explain how entrepreneurs can avoid long commutes and high costs of working outside the home by starting a home-based company. Essential steps for launching a successful home-based business are covered, including type of business, legal issues, and writing a business plan.

24214 ■ *"$50 Million Project for West Chester"* in Business Courier (Vol. 24, December 14, 2008, No. 35, pp. 1)
Pub: American City Business Journals, Inc.
Ed: Laura Baverman. **Description:** Commercial developer Scott Street Partners is planning to invest $50 million for the development of a site south of the Streets of West Chester retail center. The 31-acre project will generate 1,200 jobs, and will bring in offices, restaurants and a hotel. The development plans and the features of the site are discussed as well.

24215 ■ *101 Internet Businesses You Can Start from Home: How to Choose and Build Your Own Successful E-Business*
Pub: Maximum Press
Ed: Susan Sweeney. **Released:** June 2006. **Price:** $29.95. **Description:** Guide for starting and growing an Internet business; information for developing a business plan, risk levels, and promotional techniques are included.

24216 ■ *"Adapt or Die"* in Black Enterprise (Vol. 38, July 2008, No. 12, pp. 27)
Pub: Earl G. Graves Publishing Co. Inc.
Ed: Oguntoyinbo Lekan. **Description:** Turbulence in the domestic auto industry is hitting auto suppliers hard and black suppliers, the majority of whom contract with the Big Three, are just beginning to establish relationships with import car manufacturers. The more savvy CEOs are adopting new technologies in order to weather the downturn in the economy and in the industry as a whole.

24217 ■ *"Aeronautics Seeking New HQ Site"* in The Business Journal-Milwaukee (Vol. 25, September 5, 2008, No. 50, pp. 1)
Pub: American City Business Journals, Inc.
Ed: Rich Kirchen. **Description:** Milwaukee, Wisconsin-based Aeronautics Corp. of America is planning to move its headquarters to a new site. The company has started to search for a new site. It also plans to consolidate its operations under one roof.

24218 ■ *"The Agency Model Is Bent But Not Broken"* in Advertising Age (Vol. 79, July 7, 2008, No. 26, pp. 17)
Pub: Crain Communications, Inc.
Ed: Stephen Fajen. **Description:** In the new-media environment, advertising agencies must change the way in which they do business and receive payment.

24219 ■ *"The Agency-Selection Process Needs Fixing Now"* in Advertising Age (Vol. 79, July 7, 2008, No. 26, pp. 18)
Pub: Crain Communications, Inc.
Ed: Avi Dan. **Description:** Marketers are facing increased challenges in this sagging economic climate and must realize the importance of choosing the correct advertising agency for their company in order to benefit from a more-stable relationship that yields better business results. Advice for marketers regarding the best way to choose an agency is included.

24220 ■ *"Air Canada to Slash 600 Non-Union Jobs"* in Globe & Mail (February 11, 2006, pp. B3)
Pub: CTVglobemedia Publishing Inc.
Ed: Brent Jang. **Description:** The reasons behind workforce reduction by ACE Aviation Holdings Inc. at Air Canada are presented.

24221 ■ *"Airlines Mount PR Push to Win Public Support Against Big Oil"* in Advertising Age (Vol. 79, July 14, 2008, No. 7, pp. 1)
Pub: Crain Communications, Inc.
Ed: Michael Bush. **Description:** Top airline executives from competing companies have banded together in a public relations plan in which they are sending e-mails to their frequent fliers asking for aid in lobbying legislators to put a restriction on oil speculation.

24222 ■ *"All Fired Up!"* in Small Business Opportunities (November 2008)
Pub: Entrepreneur Media Inc.
Ed: Stan Roberts. **Description:** Profile of Brixx Wood Fired Pizza, which has launched a franchising program due to the amount of interest the company's founders received over the years; franchisees do not need experience in the food industry or pizza restaurant service business in order to open a franchise of their own because all franchisees receive comprehensive training in which they are educated on all of the necessary tools to effectively run the business.

24223 ■ *"All Options Open On Chrysler: Magna"* in Globe & Mail (February 28, 2007, pp. B3)
Pub: CTVglobemedia Publishing Inc.
Ed: Greg Keenan. **Description:** The 65 percent drop in the profits of Magna International Inc. and the plans of its chief executive officer Don Walker to make the company more competitive are discussed.

24224 ■ *"An Amazing Race"* in Canadian Business (Vol. 81, March 3, 2008, No. 3, pp. 25)
Pub: Rogers Media
Ed: Rachel Pulfer. **Description:** U.S. presidential candidates Barack Obama and Hilary Clinton lead the Democratic Part primaries while John McCain is a frontrunner at the Republican Party. These leading candidates have different plans for the U.S. economy which will affect Canada's own economy particularly concerning trade policies. The presidential candidates' proposals and the impacts of U.S. economic downturn on Canada are examined.

24225 ■ *"Americhem to Shutter Maryland Operation"* in Crain's Cleveland Business (Vol. 28, October 29, 2007, No. 43, pp. 14)
Pub: Crain Communications, Inc.
Description: Americhem Inc., a manufacturer of colors and additives for polymer products has announced plans to expand two plants in Cuyahoga Falls while phasing out its operations in Salisbury, Maryland.

24226 ■ *"Analyst Questions CanWest Papers' Viability"* in Globe & Mail (January 14, 2006, pp. B3)
Pub: CTVglobemedia Publishing Inc.
Ed: Grant Robertson. **Description:** The opinions of analyst Tim Casey of BMO Nesbitt Burns Inc. over the prospects of two newspapers Dose and National Post of CanWest Global Communications Corp., which planned cost restructuring efforts, are presented.

24227 ■ *"Are You Ready for a Transformation?"* in Women Entrepreneur (November 28, 2008)
Pub: Entrepreneur Media Inc.
Ed: Aliza Sherman. **Description:** Marlene J. Waldock, an expert in women's empowerment and reinvention, discusses brand modification and what a business owner should consider before attempting to change or modify their brand.

24228 ■ *"Are Your Goals Hitting the Right Target?"* in Business Strategy Review (Vol. 21, Autumn 2010, No. 3, pp. 46)
Pub: Wiley-Blackwell
Ed: Alan Meekings, Steve Briault, Andy Neely. **Description:** Setting targets is normal in most organizations. The authors think such a practice can cause more ham than good. They offer a better plan.

24229 ■ *The Art of the Start*
Pub: Portfolio Publishing
Ed: Guy Kawasaki. **Price:** $26.95. **Description:** Apple's Guy Kawasaki offers information to help would-be entrepreneurs create new enterprises. As founder and CEO of Garage Technology Ventures, he has field-tested his ideas with newly hatched companies and he takes readers through every phase of creating a business, from the very basics of raising money and designing a business model through the many stages that eventually lead to success and thus giving back to society.

24230 ■ *"Attend To Your Corporate Housekeeping"* in Women Entrepreneur (December 4, 2008)
Pub: Entrepreneur Media Inc.
Ed: Nina Kaufman. **Description:** Business owners can lose all the benefits and privileges of the corporate form if they do not follow proper corporate formalities such as holding an annual meeting, electing officers and directors and adopting or passing corporate resolutions. Creditors are able to take from one's personal assets if such formalities have not been followed.

24231 ■ *"Auction-Rate Cash Frees Up"* in The Business Journal-Portland (Vol. 25, August 15, 2008, No. 23, pp. 1)
Pub: American City Business Journals, Inc.
Ed: Aliza Earnshaw. **Description:** FEI Co. and RadiSys Corp. have received notices that UBS AG will buy back the auction-rate securities that were sold to them in around two years from 2008. FEI had $110.1 million invested in auction-rate securities while RadiSys holds $62.8 million of these securities.

24232 ■ *"Automaker Foundations Run Leaner"* in Crain's Detroit Business (Vol. 26, January 11, 2010, No. 2, pp. 1)
Pub: Crain Communications Inc.
Ed: Sherri Welch. **Description:** Overview of the Detroit automobile industry includes restoring profitability, smarter marketing strategies and philanthropy. Each company comprising the Big 3 is examined, as is their vision for the future.

24233 ■ *"Avnet Inc.'s Expansion Fueled By Mergers and Acquisitions"* in The Business Journal - Serving Phoenix and the Valley of the Sun (Vol. 28, September 12, 2008, No. 53, pp. 1)
Pub: American City Business Journals, Inc.
Ed: Patrick O'Grady. **Description:** Avnet Inc. has grown and has nearly tripled its revenue in the past ten years through the company's acquisitions and consolidation. The company's revenue in 2008 is $17.9 billion. Other details about the company's growth are discussed.

24234 ■ *"Back to Business for Bishop Museum"* in Hawaii Business (Vol. 54, August 2008, No. 2, pp. 53)
Pub: Hawaii Business Publishing
Ed: Shara Enay. **Description:** Bishop Museum, ranked 224 in Hawaii Business' top 250 companies for 2008, had $29.5 million in gross sales for 2007, up 52.8 percent from the $19.3 million gross sales in

2006. The company has cut 24 positions in a restructuring effort for the museum's sustainability. Grants, artifacts and plans for sustainable operations are discussed.

24235 ■ *"Back in the Race" in Barron's (Vol. 88, March 17, 2008, No. 11, pp. 43)*
Pub: Dow Jones & Company, Inc.
Ed: Leslie P. Norton. **Description:** Katherine Schapiro was able to get Sentinel International Equity's Morningstar classification to blended fund from a value fund rating after joining Sentinel from her former jobs at Strong Overseas Fund. Schapiro aims to benefit from the global rebalancing as the U.S.'s share of the world economy shrinks.

24236 ■ *"The Balanced Business" in Women In Business (Vol. 63, Spring 2011, No. 1, pp. 14)*
Pub: American Business Women's Association
Ed: Leigh Elmore. **Description:** The balance scoreboard has developed to a full strategic planning and management system from its early use as a simple performance measurement network. Executives are able to execute their strategies by using information from the balance scoreboard. Insights on Mayer Group Inc. executive Ken Mayer's view of the balance scorecard are also shared.

24237 ■ *"Bankruptcy Claims Brooke, Gives Franchisees Hope" in The Business Journal-Serving Metropolitan Kansas City (October 31, 2008)*
Pub: American City Business Journals, Inc.
Ed: James Dornbrook; Steve Vockrodt. **Description:** Insurer Brooke Corp. was required to file for Chapter 11 bankruptcy for a deal to sell all of its assets to businessmen Terry Nelson and Lysle Davidson. The new Brooke plans to share contingency fees with franchisees. The impacts of the bankruptcy case on Brooke franchisees are discussed.

24238 ■ *"Bark Up The Right Tree" in Small Business Opportunities (Winter 2009)*
Pub: Entrepreneur Press
Contact: Perlman Neil, President
Description: Profile of Central Bark, a daycare company catering to pets that offers franchise opportunities and is expanding rapidly despite the economic downturn; the company's growth strategy is also discussed.

24239 ■ *"Barnes Shakes Up Sara Lee Exec Suite" in Crain's Chicago Business (Vol. 31, April 21, 2008, No. 16, pp. 1)*
Pub: Crain Communications, Inc.
Ed: David Sterrett. **Description:** In an attempt to cut costs and boost profits, Sara Lee Corp.'s CEO Brenda Barnes is restructuring the company's management team.

24240 ■ *"BASF Launches $4.9 Billion Bid for Rival Engelhard" in Globe & Mail (January 4, 2006, pp. B7)*
Pub: CTVglobemedia Publishing Inc.
Ed: Mike Esterl; Steve Levine. **Description:** The plans of BASF AG, to acquire Engelhard Corp. for $4.9 billion, are presented.

24241 ■ *"Bayer Job Cuts to Hit Canada" in Globe & Mail (March 3, 2007, pp. B7)*
Pub: CTVglobemedia Publishing Inc.
Description: Bayer AG, German drug maker, planned cut of 6,100 jobs as a part of their cost-cutting strategies. The company, which plans to save 700 million euros by the end of 2007, may eliminate some positions in Canadian branches.

24242 ■ *"BCE Mulls Radical Changes With Industry Under Pressure" in Globe & Mail (March 30, 2007, pp. B1)*
Pub: CTVglobemedia Publishing Inc.
Ed: Andrew Willis; Jacquie McNish; Catherine McLean. **Description:** An account on the expansion plans of BCE Inc., which plans to acquire TELUS Corp., is presented.

24243 ■ *"Best Growth Stocks" in Canadian Business (Vol. 81, Summer 2008, No. 9, pp. 61)*
Pub: Rogers Media Ltd.
Ed: Calvin Leung. **Description:** Table showing the one-year performance of growth stocks is presented. Edmonton-based Stantec Inc. expects to advance its sales and profits by 15 percent to 20 percent per year through tapping international markets and acquisitions. Analysts forecast a 17.1 percent growth rate annually over the next 3 to 5 years.

24244 ■ *"The Best Option for All" in American Executive (Vol. 7, September 2009, No. 5, pp. 170)*
Pub: RedCoat Publishing, Inc.
Ed: Ashley McGown. **Description:** Plaza Associates, a collections agency that conducts business primarily in the accounts receivable management sector, is the first in the industry to purchase 100 percent of the company from the founders through the formation of a leveraged Employee Stock Ownership Plan (ESOP).

24245 ■ *"Better Made's Better Idea: Diversify Despite Rising Costs" in Crain's Detroit Business (Vol. 24, September 22, 2008, No. 38, pp. 18)*
Pub: Crain Communications Inc.
Ed: Nathan Skid. **Description:** Better Made Snack Foods Inc. is planning to expand its product lines and market reach as well as boost manufacturing capability during a time in which the company is being buffeted by rising commodity and fuel costs. The company feels that diversification is the key to maintain sales and growth.

24246 ■ *"Beyond Auto; Staffing Firm Malace Grabs Revenue Jump" in Crain's Detroit Business (Vol. 26, January 18, 2010, No. 3, pp. 3)*
Pub: Crain Communications Inc.
Ed: Sherri Welch. **Description:** Malace & Associates Inc., the Troy-based human resources management company, expects its diversification into nonautomotive industries to help double its revenues this year. Due to the automotive downturn, between October 2008 and March 2009 the company lost approximately 48 percent of its business.

24247 ■ *"A Big Dream That 'Was Going Nowhere" in Globe & Mail (February 4, 2006, pp. B4)*
Pub: CTVglobemedia Publishing Inc.
Ed: Konrad Yakabuski. **Description:** The reasons behind the decision of Bombardier Inc. to terminate its plans to develop jet airplanes are presented.

24248 ■ *"Big Sell-Off At Sunwest" in The Business Journal-Portland (Vol. 25, July 25, 2008, No. 20, pp. 1)*
Pub: American City Business Journals, Inc.
Ed: Robin J. Moody. **Description:** Oregon's largest operator of assisted living facilities Sunwest Management Inc. is expected to sell 132 of its properties. The planned sale, which is believed to be worth more than $1 billion, will help Sunwest pay creditors and investors. Other views and information on the planned sale, as well as on Sunwest's services which include adult day care, are presented.

24249 ■ *"Big Vision, Small Business*
Pub: Ivy Sea, Inc.
Ed: Jamie S. Walters. **Released:** October 10, 2002. **Price:** $17.95. **Description:** The power of the small enterprise is examined. The author shares her expertise as an entrepreneur and founder of a business consulting firm to help small business owners successfully run their companies. Interviews with more than seventy small business owners provide insight into visioning, planning, and establishing a small company, as well as strategies for good employee and customer relationships.

24250 ■ *"A Bigger Deal" in Crain's Cleveland Business (Vol. 28, November 12, 2007, No. 45, pp. 1)*
Pub: Crain Communications, Inc.
Ed: Shawn A. Turner. **Description:** In an attempt to boost its revenue CBiz Inc., a provider of accounting

and business services, is looking to balance its acquisitions of smaller companies with larger ones as part of its overall growth strategy.

24251 ■ *"Blackstone Set to Sell Stake" in Globe & Mail (March 17, 2007, pp. B6)*
Pub: CTVglobemedia Publishing Inc.
Ed: Tennille Tracy. **Description:** The plan of Blackstone Group to sell 10 percent of its stake to raise $4 billion and its proposal to go for initial public offering is discussed.

24252 ■ *"Block Plans Office Park Along K-10 Corridor" in The Business Journal-Serving Metropolitan Kansas City (Vol. 27, October 3, 2008)*
Pub: American City Business Journals, Inc.
Ed: Rob Roberts. **Description:** Kansas City, Missouri-based Block and Co. is planning to build four office buildings at the corner of College Boulevard and Ridgeview Road in Olathe. Features of the planned development are provided. Comments from executives are also presented.

24253 ■ *"Blood Bank" in Canadian Business (Vol. 80, February 12, 2007, No. 4, pp. 36)*
Pub: Rogers Media
Ed: Erin Pooley. **Description:** The plan of Insception Biosciences to popularize stem cell banks, which can store stem cells, is discussed.

24254 ■ *Blue Ocean Strategy: How to Create Uncontested Market Space and Make Competition Irrelevant*
Pub: Harvard Business School Publishing
Ed: W. Chan Kim. **Released:** January 2005. **Price:** $29.95.

24255 ■ *"The Board Shorts Executive" in Hawaii Business (Vol. 53, January 2008, No. 7, pp. 33)*
Pub: Hawaii Business Publishing
Ed: Mike Markrich. **Description:** Vans Triple Crown of Surfing executive director Randy Rarick believes that the surfing business requires knowledge of the sport and integity to the game's lifestyle and spirit. His organization manages surfing events, and has generated jobs for the locals. Plans for Vans Triple Crown are supplied.

24256 ■ *"Bovie Medical Makes Electrosurgical Strike" in The Business Journal-Serving Greater Tampa Bay (Vol. 28, August 22, 2008, No. 35)*
Pub: American City Business Journals, Inc.
Ed: Margie Manning. **Description:** Bovie Medical Group, which manufactures electrosurgical products, is planning to sell its manufacturing plant in the Tyrone Industrial Park and to purchase the former Harland Clarke facility. The moves are expected to boost the efficiency and the development of new products. Other information on Bovie Medical Group is presented.

24257 ■ *"Bracing for Impact" in Playthings (Vol. 106, September 1, 2008, No. 8, pp. 15)*
Pub: Reed Business Information
Contact: Jeff Greisch, President
Ed: J. Tol Broome Jr. **Description:** A good risk management plan for any company consists of making correct decisions in the following six key areas: operational, reputation, regulatory, legal, liquidity, and disaster.

24258 ■ *"Brewing National Success" in Hawaii Business (Vol. 53, November 2007, No. 5, pp. 46)*
Pub: Hawaii Business Publishing
Ed: Alex Salkever. **Description:** Kona Brewing Co. (KBC) is already selling its brews in four cities in Florida and 17 other states and Japan as well. KBC is currently forming a deal with Red Hook to produce Longboard Lager and other KBC brews at Red Hooks' brewery in New Hampshire. KBC's chief executive officer Mattson Davis shares KBC's practices for success.

24259 ■ *"Briarcliff Office Building Fills Up Fast" in The Business Journal-Serving Metropolitan Kansas City (Vol. 26, Sept. 5,*

2008, pp. 1)
Pub: American City Business Journals, Inc.

Ed: Rob Roberts. **Description:** Prior to its opening the Hilltop Office Building in Kansas City Missouri has attained 80 percent occupancy. FCStone Group Inc.'s plan to move to the building has boosted the facility's occupancy. Description and dimensions of the office building are also provided.

24260 ■ *"Bringing Big Guns" in Business Courier (Vol. 24, January 18, 2008, No. 41, pp. 1)*
Pub: American City Business Journals, Inc.

Ed: Lucy May. **Description:** Chief executive officer of Nidland Co. John Hayden was assigend as Cincinnati USA Partnership chairman. Hayden will bring his expertise to help the partnership drive economic development in the Greater Cincinnati area. Details of the parntership's plans are suplied.

24261 ■ *"Budget Strategically to Stay on Course" in Entrepreneur (August 28, 2008)*
Pub: Entrepreneur Media Inc.

Ed: Tim Berry. **Description:** Budgeting is one of the most valuable tools in a manager's arsenal. The importance of budgeting is discussed and tips for surviving an economic recession are provided.

24262 ■ *"Building Alexian Brothers' Clinical Reputation" in Crain's Chicago Business (Vol. 31, May 5, 2008, No. 18, pp. 6)*
Pub: Crain Communications, Inc.

Ed: Mike Colias. **Description:** Profile of the CEO of Alexian Brothers Medical Center in Elk Grove Village who plans to stabilize Alexian Brothers' financial performance in part by eliminating $20 million in annual costs.

24263 ■ *"Building His Dream" in Business Courier (Vol. 24, January 25, 2008, No. 42, pp. 1)*
Pub: American City Business Journals, Inc.

Ed: Laura Baverman. **Description:** Technology entrepreneur Mahendra Vora plans to build a more than $100 million local IT headquarters for VTech Holdings Ltd by 2010. Acquisition of four $5 million companies within 2008 are part of the owner's plan to expand the office equipment company. Other plans for the IT company are discussed.

24264 ■ *"Bumpy Ride Ahead for United" in Crain's Chicago Business (Vol. 31, May 5, 2008, No. 18, pp. 3)*
Pub: Crain Communications, Inc.

Ed: John Pletz. **Description:** Continental Airlines Inc. walked away from merger talks with United Airlines last week. Now the choices facing United boil down to going it alone in an increasingly stormy airline business or a less-desirable merger with US Airways Group Inc. Analysts expect United to lose $977 million this year due, mainly, to the high price of fuel.

24265 ■ *"Burdened by Debt, Borders Group Suspends Dividends, May Be Sold" in Crain's Detroit Business (Vol. 24, March 24, 2008, No. 12)*
Pub: Crain Communications, Inc.

Ed: Nancy Kaffer. **Description:** Ann Arbor-based Borders Group Inc. is exploring its options and may put itself up for sale due to its declining stock price and mounting debt. The company's fiscal year was capped by poor holiday sales and Borders does not have the cash on hand to meet the 2009 goals set in its strategic plan.

24266 ■ *A Business of My Own? 21 Steps to Successfully Starting and Running a Small Business*
Pub: Enfield Publishing

Ed: Marjorie Cleveland Fisher. **Released:** January 2005. **Description:** New ideas to start or grow a small business, including ideas for writing business plans with examples, adopting a business structure, and setting goals and objectives.

24267 ■ *"Business Plan Refines Focus" in Business Journal Portland (Vol. 27, December 10, 2010, No. 41, pp. 1)*
Pub: Portland Business Journal

Ed: Wendy Culverwell. **Description:** Organizers of the Oregon Business Plan's Leadership Summit 2010 seek the opinions of nearly 1,000 business, education, political, and civic leaders in an effort to address how to rehabilitate Oregon's economy. The opinion-seeking actions recognize the organizers' belief that the economic fate of the state depends on rural Oregon.

24268 ■ *Business Plans to Game Plans*
Pub: John Wiley and Sons, Inc.

Ed: Jan B. King. **Released:** 2003. **Price:** $27.50. **Description:** Information for running a small business are examined, focusing on action plans and ways to avoid the pitfalls of strategic planning. The book describes how entrepreneurs should set standards, lead by example, look to the future, focus on important details, face reality, grow profitability, and take action.

24269 ■ *Business Plans Handbook*
Pub: Cengage Learning Inc.
Contact: Ronald Dunn, President
URL(s): www.gale.cengage.com. **Released:** Annual; Latest edition 9th; Published May, 2002. **Price:** $231, Individuals. **Publication includes:** 24 actual business plans, including executive summaries, market profiles and analyses, product and production information, and management, personnel, and financial data. Appendix includes a sample business plan template; two fictional plans; listings of small business associations, consultants, venture capital/finance companies; SBA and SBDC offices; SCORE offices; small business term glossary; and a cumulative index. **Indexes:** Alphabetical by company type.

24270 ■ *Business Plans Kit for Dummies, 2nd Edition*
Pub: John Wiley and Sons Inc.
Released: September 2005.

24271 ■ *Business Plans That Work: A Guide for Small Business*
Pub: McGraw-Hill Companies Inc.
Contact: Deven Sharma, President
Ed: Jeffry A. Timmons, Stephen Spinelli, Andrew Zacharakis. **Released:** April 2004. **Price:** $12.89 (US), $24.95 (Canadian). **Description:** Guide for preparing a small business plan along with an analysis of potential business opportunities.

24272 ■ *"Business Succession Planning" in New Jersey Law Review (December 7, 2007)*
Pub: New Jersey Law Journal
Ed: Robert W. Cockren, Elga A. Goodman. **Description:** Ninety percent of American businesses are family-owned. The importance of estate planning for family-owned or controlled firms is covered.

24273 ■ *Business Vision: Beyond the Horizon, 2nd Ed.*
Pub: Business Vision Group
Ed: Dennis Wengert. **Released:** January 2009. **Description:** Challenges small business owners face when running their companies are addressed in order to position themselves for the future. The book teaches how to envision future direction and measure personal and business activities that provide an indication of personal progress in achieving visionary business leadership.

24274 ■ *"Businesses Still on the Mend" in Boston Business Journal (Vol. 29, September 9, 2011, No. 18, pp. 1)*
Pub: American City Business Journals Inc.
Ed: Scott Dance. **Description:** The 9/11 terrorist attacks have caused many companies in the US to dramatically shift course in response to changes in the economy. The concern that the cost of being unprepared for future disasters could be larger has remained among many companies.

24275 ■ *"Cadillac Tower Largest to Start in a Decade" in Globe & Mail (March 28, 2006, pp. B5)*
Pub: CTVglobemedia Publishing Inc.
Ed: Elizabeth Church. **Description:** The plans of Cadillac Fairview Corporation Ltd. to build office towers, in downtown Canada, are presented.

24276 ■ *"Calming Customers" in The Business Journal-Portland (Vol. 25, August 29, 2008, No. 25, pp. 1)*
Pub: American City Business Journals, Inc.
Ed: Kirsten Grind; Rob Smith. **Description:** Credit unions and banks in the Portland area are reaching out to clients in an effort to reassure them on the security of their money and the firms' financial stability. Roy Whitehead of Washington Federal Savings, for instance, wrote 41,000 customers of the bank to reassure them. The strategies of different banks and credit unions to answer their client's worries are discussed.

24277 ■ *"Can Brewer Make Cheap Seats Pay?" in Globe & Mail (January 7, 2006, pp. B4)*
Pub: CTVglobemedia Publishing Inc.
Ed: Brent Jang. **Description:** The plans of chief executive officer Montie Brewer of Air Canada to upgrade airplanes are presented.

24278 ■ *"Carveouts Back in Vogue" in Mergers & Acquisitions: The Dealmaker's Journal (March 1, 2008)*
Pub: SourceMedia, Inc.
Ed: Ken MacFadyen. **Description:** Discusses ways in which companies look for hidden assets that they can exploit in worsening economic times; oftentimes firms try to sell off assets or in other instances they will look to unlock value through public spinoffs or through internal reorganizations.

24279 ■ *"A Case Study: Real-Life Business Planning" in Entrepreneur (February 3, 2009)*
Pub: Entrepreneur Media Inc.
Ed: Tim Berry. **Description:** Provides a case study of a two-day planning meeting for Palo Alto Software in which the executives of the company met for their annual planning cycle and discussed ways in which the company needed to change in order to stay viable in today's tough economic climate.

24280 ■ *"Casinos See College as Job Jackpot" in The Business Journal-Serving Metropolitan Kansas City (Vol. 26, August 1, 2008, No. 47)*
Pub: American City Business Journals, Inc.
Ed: Suzanna Stagemeyer. **Description:** Wyandotte County casino managers revealed plans to develop partnerships with Kansas City Kansas Community College. The planned partnership is expected to include curriculum development and degree programs that would help train employees for the planned casinos. Other views and information on the project are presented.

24281 ■ *"The Caterer and Hotelkeeper Interview Patrick Harbour and Nathan Jones" in Caterer & Hotelkeeper (October 28, 2011, No. 288)*
Pub: Reed Reference Publishing
Description: Profiles of Patrick Harbour and Nathan Jones who quit their jobs to start their own catering business. The partners discuss their business strategy when launching their boutique catering firm and ways they are adapting to the slow economy in order to remain successful.

24282 ■ *"CAW Boss Troubled Over 'Vulnerable' Ford Plants" in Globe & Mail (January 19, 2006, pp. B6)*
Pub: CTVglobemedia Publishing Inc.
Ed: Greg Keenan. **Description:** The concerns of president Buzz Hargrove of Canadian Auto Workers on the impact of Ford Motor Co.'s restructuring efforts on closure of automotive plants in Canada, are presented.

24283 ■ "Centerra Caught in Kyrgyzstan Dispute" in Globe & Mail (April 19, 2007, pp. B5)
Pub: CTVglobemedia Publishing Inc.
Ed: Andy Hoffman. Description: The details of the demonstrations carried against government proposal to nationalize Centerra Gold Inc.'s assets are presented.

24284 ■ The Checklist Manifesto: How to Get Things Right
Pub: Metropolitan Books
Ed: Dr. Atul Gawande. Price: $24.50. Description: How tragic errors can be sharply reduced with a piece of paper, hand-drawn boxes, and a pencil.

24285 ■ "Chelsea Community Hospital to Merge with St. Joseph Mercy Health" in Crain's Detroit Business (Vol. 24, March 24, 2008, No. 12)
Pub: Crain Communications, Inc.
Ed: Jay Greene. Description: Chelsea Community Hospital has signed a letter of intent to merge with St. Joseph Mercy Health System and will negotiate merger terms, including a plan to fund an unspecified amount of facility improvements and equipment purchases at Chelsea.

24286 ■ "Children's Products Maker Not the New Kid on the Block" in Crain's Cleveland Business (Vol. 28, November 26, 2007, No. 47, pp. 3)
Pub: Crain Communications, Inc.
Ed: David Bennett. Description: Discusses the business model employed by Shamrock Industries Inc., a rising star in the competitive world of children's products; the company, which does business as Foundations Quality Children's Products, has expanded into a 63,000-square-foot distribution center which has boosted its local profile significantly.

24287 ■ "China's ZTE in Hunt for Partners" in Globe & Mail (February 27, 2006, pp. B1)
Pub: CTVglobemedia Publishing Inc.
Ed: Gordon Pitts. Description: The business growth plans of ZTE Corp. in Canada, through partnership, are presented.

24288 ■ "Choosing Strategies For Change" in Harvard Business Review (Vol. 86, July-August 2008, No. 8, pp. 130)
Pub: Harvard Business School Press
Ed: John P. Kotter; Leonard A. Schlesinger. Description: Methods for implementing organizational change include identifying potential areas of resistance, providing the necessary skills and information to counteract resistance, and assessing situational factors that may influence results.

24289 ■ "CIBC Spends $1.1 Billion on Caribbean Expansion" in Globe & Mail (March 14, 2006, pp. B1)
Pub: CTVglobemedia Publishing Inc.
Ed: Sinclair Stewart. Description: Canadian Imperial Bank of Commerce (CIBC), the fifth-largest bank of Canada, is planning to spend $1.1billion to buy major share of Barbados-based First Caribbean International Bank. The details of the acquisition plan are presented.

24290 ■ "Citadel Hires Three Lehman Execs" in Chicago Tribune (October 2, 2008)
Pub: McClatchy-Tribune Information Services
Ed: James P. Miller. Description: Citadel Investment Group LLC, Chicago hedge-fund operator, has hired three former senior executives of bankrupt investment banker Lehman Brothers Holding Inc. Citadel believes that the company's hiring spree will help them to further expand the firm's capabilities in the global fixed income business.

24291 ■ "City Struggles to Iron Out Tangled Transportation" in Crain's New York Business (Vol. 24, January 14, 2008, No. 2, pp. 33)
Pub: Crain Communications, Inc.
Ed: Judith Messina. Description: Discusses the possible solutions to improve lower Manhattan's transportation infrastructure including the construction of three new transit centers, an expansion in ferry service and the plan to get parked buses off the street.

24292 ■ "CityLink Project On Hold" in Business Courier (Vol. 24, November 9, 2008, No. 30, pp. 3)
Pub: American City Business Journals, Inc.
Ed: Dan Monk. Description: Developers of the CityLink project have indicated that it will be at least a year before they start the planned social services mall at 800 Bank West End. According to Tim Senff, Citylink CEO, the company wants to build bridges before constructing the buildings. The project's critics are still considering whether to appeal a court ruling regarding the facility's compliance with the city's zoning code.

24293 ■ "Civil Council Almost On Board With Light Rail Plan" in The Business Journal-Serving Metropolitan Kansas City (September 5, 2008)
Pub: American City Business Journals, Inc.
Ed: Steve Vockrodt. Description: Civic Council of Greater Kansas City has taken back its demand for the city to show a 10-year financial plan to win its endorsement of a light rail plan. The council said it will accept a five-year financial plan for the project. Details of the light rail plan are also presented.

24294 ■ "Cleanup to Polish Plating Company's Bottom Line" in Crain's Cleveland Business (Vol. 28, October 29, 2007, No. 43, pp. 4)
Pub: Crain Communications, Inc.
Ed: Jay Miller. Description: Barker Products Co, a manufacturer of nuts and bolts, is upgrading its aging facility which will allow them to operate at capacity and will save the company several hundred thousand dollars a year in operating costs. The new owners secured a construction loan from the county's new Commercial Redevelopment Fund which will allow them to upgrade the building which was hampered by years of neglect.

24295 ■ "Clothier Delays Opening" in The Business Journal-Serving Metropolitan Kansas City (Vol. 27, November 14, 2008, No. 10, pp. 1)
Pub: American City Business Journals, Inc.
Ed: Suzanna Stagemeyer. Description: Jos A. Bank Clothiers Inc. has delayed the opening of its store at the Kansas City Power and Light District in Missouri for the first quarter of 2009. The company is still waiting for other tenants to open shop in the district. Comments from officials concerning the retail sector are also presented.

24296 ■ "Comcast Networks" in Brandweek (Vol. 49, April 21, 2008, No. 16, pp. SR9)
Pub: VNU Business Media, Inc.
Ed: Anthony Crupi. Description: Provides contact information for sales and marketing personnel for the Comcast networks as well as a listing of the station's top programming and an analysis of the current season and the target audience for those programs running in the current season. Experts believe Comcast will continue to acquire more stations into their portfolio.

24297 ■ "Companies Must Set Goals for Diversity" in Crain's Detroit Business (Vol. 24, April 14, 2008, No. 15, pp. 16)
Pub: Crain Communications Inc.
Ed: Laura Weiner. Description: Diversity programs should start with a plan that takes into account exactly what the company wants to accomplish; this may include wanting to increase the bottom line with new contracts or wanting a staff that is more innovative in their ideas due to their varied backgrounds.

24298 ■ The Company We Keep: Reinventing Small Business for People, Community, and Place
Pub: Chelsea Green Publishing
Ed: John Abrams, William Grieder. Released: June 2006. Price: $18.00. Description: The new business trend in social entrepreneurship as a business plan enables small business owners to meet the triple bottom line of profits for people (employees and owners), community, and the environment.

24299 ■ Contingency Planning and Disaster Recovery: A Small Business Guide
Pub: John Wiley & Sons, Incorporated
Ed: Donna R. Childs, Stefan Dietrich. Released: October 2002. Description: Four keys issues to help a business plan for disasters include: preparation, response, recovery, and sample IT solutions in order to secure property and confidential data files and covers the six types of disasters: human errors, equipment failures, third-party failures, environmental hazards, fires and other structural catastrophes, and terrorism and sabotage.

24300 ■ "Continuously Monitoring Workers' Comp Can Limit Costs" in Crain's Cleveland Business (Vol. 28, October 8, 2007, No. 40, pp. 21)
Pub: Crain Communications, Inc.
Ed: Michael Lagnoni. Description: When operating without a plan for managing its workers' compensation program, a company risks losing money. For most companies workers' compensation insurance premiums are often reduced to an annual budget entry but employers who are actively involved in the management of their programs are more likely to experience reductions in premiums and limit indirect costs associated with claims.

24301 ■ "Copper Giant to Spin Off Silver Assets" in Globe & Mail (February 27, 2006, pp. B1)
Pub: CTVglobemedia Publishing Inc.
Ed: Sinclair Stewart; Andrew Willis. Description: The reasons behind the sale of silver mining assets by Codelco are presented.

24302 ■ "Copycat" in Canadian Business (Vol. 79, October 23, 2006, No. 21, pp. 53)
Pub: Rogers Media
Ed: Andrew Wahl. Description: The conversion of BCE Inc. into an income trust for tax advantages, soon after the transition of its business rival Telus Corp. into an income trust, is discussed.

24303 ■ "CP Rail Cuts Jobs to Keep Pace With CN" in Globe & Mail (January 16, 2006, pp. B1)
Pub: CTVglobemedia Publishing Inc.
Ed: Brent Jang. Description: Canadian Pacific Railway Ltd. (CPR) reduces workforce in order to remain competitive with Canadian National Railway Co. The details of CPR's proposal are presented.

24304 ■ "CPR Signals a Switch in Strategy to Narrow Competitive Gap With CN" in Globe & Mail (January 20, 2006, pp. B3)
Pub: CTVglobemedia Publishing Inc.
Ed: Brent Jang. Description: The reasons behind the restructuring efforts of Canadian Pacific Railway Ltd. are presented.

24305 ■ Craft, Inc.
Pub: Chronicle Books LLC
Ed: Meg Mateo Ilasco. Released: August 2007. Price: $16.95. Description: Business primer for entrepreneurial crafters wishing to turn their hobbies into a small business, including tips for developing products, naming the company, writing a business plan, applying for licenses, and paying taxes.

24306 ■ "Craig Muhlhauser" in Canadian Business (Vol. 81, September 15, 2008, No. 14-15, pp. 6)
Pub: Rogers Media Ltd.
Ed: Andrew Wahl. Description: Interview with Craig Muhlhauser who is the CEO of Celestica, a manufacturing company that provides services for the electronics sector; Muhlhauser discusses the company's restructuring program, which he feels was the secret to their surprising first-quarter results. Muhlhauser states that the company is operating with more forward visibility and that understanding the opportunities during the current economic situation presents the biggest challenge.

24307 ■ "Creativity: A Key Link to Entrepreneurial Behavior" in Business Horizons (September-October 2007, pp. 365)
Pub: Elsevier Technology Publications
Ed: Stephen Ko, John E. Butler. Description: Importance of creativity and its link to entrepreneurial behavior is examined. In a study of various entrepre-

neurs, studies concluded that a solid knowledge base, a well-developed social network, and a strong focus on identifying opportunities are relevant to entrepreneurial behavior.

24308 ■ "Credit Unions Cast Wary Eye at Paulson Plan, But Not Panicking Yet" in The Business Review Albany (Vol. 35, April 11, 2008, No. 1)
Pub: The Business Review
Ed: Barbara Pinckney. Description: Credit unions are suspicious of US Treasury Secretary Henry Paulson's plan to establish a single federally insured depository institution charter for all institutions covered by federal deposit insurance. The charter would replace national banks, federal savings associations, and federal credit union charters.

24309 ■ "Cruising In Choppy Water" in The Business Journal-Portland (Vol. 25, August 22, 2008, No. 24, pp. 1)
Pub: American City Business Journals, Inc.
Ed: Erik Siemers. Description: Yacht builder Christensen Shipyards Inc. is experiencing robust business despite the slowing US economy, building four yachts a year as of 2008. The company expects revenues to hit $90 million and is opening a 500,000-square-foot plant in Tennessee.

24310 ■ "DaimlerChrysler Bears Down on Smart" in Globe & Mail (March 27, 2006, pp. B11)
Pub: CTVglobemedia Publishing Inc.
Ed: Oliver Suess. Description: DaimlerChrysler AG, German automobile industry giant, is planning to cut down its workforce its Smart division. The Chrysler is also planning to stop the production of its four-seater models, to end losses at Smart division.

24311 ■ "Danger, Will Robinson!" in Business Owner (Vol. 35, July-August 2011, No. 4, pp. 3)
Pub: DL Perkins Company
Description: Critical measures each small business owner must take to ensure the success of their company are outlined.

24312 ■ Dare to Prepare - How to Win Before You Begin
Pub: Crown Publishing/Random House
Ed: Ronald M. Shapiro; Gregory Jordan. Released: February 24, 2009. Price: $14.95 paperback. Description: Shapiro uses his experience as one of America's top negotiators and lawyers to show how meticulous planning can raise the odds of success in business as well as in life.

24313 ■ "Deals Still Get Done at Drake's Coq d'Or" in Crain's Chicago Business (Vol. 31, November 17, 2008, No. 46, pp. 35)
Pub: Crain Communications, Inc.
Ed: Shia Kapos. Description: Chicago's infamous Coq d'Or, a restaurant and lounge located at the Drake Hotel, is still a favorite establishment for noted executives but the eatery is now trying to cater to younger professionals through marketing and offering new beverages that appeal to that demographic. Many find it the perfect environment in which to close deals, relax or network.

24314 ■ "December 19 Is a Great Day to be Terrible" in Internet Wire (December 15, 2009)
Pub: Comtex News Network, Inc.
Description: Overview of the plans to market the grand opening of the newest Terrible Herbst location in Las Vegas, Nevada. Terrible Herbst is a complete convenience destination offering a gas station, convenience store, car wash and lube center.

24315 ■ "Decline in Assets Is Costly for Advisers" in The Business Journal-Serving Metropolitan Kansas City (Vol. 27, October 24, 2008)
Pub: American City Business Journals, Inc.
Ed: James Dornbrook. Description: Financial advisers in the Kansas City, Missouri area are forced to cut costs as their assets have decreased sharply due to the huge drop in stock prices. American Century Investments was forced to diversify into foreign assets and cut 90 jobs as its assets dropped to $84 bil-

lion. Diversification has softened the impact of the steep decline in stock prices for Waddell & Reed Financial Inc.

24316 ■ "Deere to Open Technology Center in Germany" in Chicago Tribune (September 3, 2008)
Pub: McClatchy-Tribune Information Services
Ed: James P. Miller. Description: Deere & Co. plans to open a technology and innovation center in Germany; details of the company's expansion plans are discussed.

24317 ■ "Digital Duplication" in Crain's Cleveland Business (Vol. 28, October 1, 2007, No. 39, pp. 3)
Pub: Crain Communications, Inc.
Ed: David Bennett. Description: Profile of the business plan of eBlueprint Holdings LLC, a reprographics company that found success by converting customers' paper blueprints to an electronic format; the company plans to expand into other geographic markets by acquiring solid reprographics companies and converting their computer systems so that customers' blueprints can be managed electronically.

24318 ■ "Dividing to Conquer" in Barron's (Vol. 88, March 31, 2008, No. 13, pp. 22)
Pub: Dow Jones & Company, Inc.
Ed: Andrew Bary. Description: Altria's spin off of Philip Morris International could unlock substantial value for both domestic and international cigarette concerns. The strong brands and ample payouts from both companies will most likely impress investors.

24319 ■ "Diving for the Next Big Gold Rush" in Canadian Business (Vol. 80, February 12, 2007, No. 4, pp. 28)
Pub: Rogers Media
Ed: Thomas Watson. Description: The interest of Canadian mining companies led by Nautilus Minerals to invest in mining for deep sea-floor massive sulphide deposits, which have several minerals, is discussed.

24320 ■ "Do You Have A Retirement Parachute?" in Barron's (Vol. 88, July 7, 2008, No. 27, pp. 32)
Pub: Dow Jones & Co. Inc.
Ed: Jane White. Description: The idea that American companies should emulate the Australian retirement system which implements a forced contribution rate for all employers regarding an adequate retirement plan for their employees is discussed.

24321 ■ "Doctors Eye Rating Plan With Caution" in The Business Journal-Portland (Vol. 25, July 4, 2008, No. 17, pp. 1)
Pub: American City Business Journals, Inc.
Ed: Robin J. Moody. Description: Doctors in Portland, Oregon are wary of a new Providence Health Plan system that rates their performance on patients with certain medical conditions. The system is expected to discourage wasteful procedures, thereby, saving employers' money. Other mechanics of the rating system are also discussed.

24322 ■ "The Dogs of TSX" in Canadian Business (Vol. 81, Summer 2008, No. 9, pp. 77)
Pub: Rogers Media Ltd.
Ed: Calvin Leung. Description: Table showing the one-year stock performance of the ten highest dividend-yielding stocks on the S&P/TSX 60 Composite Index is presented. This technique is similar to the 'Dogs of the Dow' approach. The idea in this investment strategy is to buy equal amounts of stocks from these companies and selling them a year later, and then repeat the process.

24323 ■ Doing Business Anywhere: The Essential Guide to Going Global
Pub: John Wiley and Sons, Inc.
Ed: Tom Travis. Released: 2007. Price: $24.95. Description: Plans are given for new or existing businesses to organize, plan, operate and execute a business on a global basis. Trade agreements, brand protection and patents, ethics, security as well as cultural issues are among the issues addressed.

24324 ■ "Don't Quit When The Road Gets Bumpy" in Women Entrepreneur (November 25, 2008)
Pub: Entrepreneur Media Inc.
Ed: Bonnie Price. Description: Discusses techniques four women entrepreneurs are utilizing to keep their businesses successful despite the credit crunch and the economic downturn.

24325 ■ "Don't Try This Offshore" in Harvard Business Review (Vol. 86, September 2008, No. 9, pp. 39)
Pub: Harvard Business School Press
Description: Fictitious outsourcing scenario is presented, with contributors offering advice. The suggestions address the ease or complexity of offshoring business creativity, along with challenges and benefits.

24326 ■ "Doyle: Domino's New Pizza Seasoned with Straight Talk" in Crain's Detroit Business (Vol. 26, January 11, 2010, No. 2, pp. 1)
Pub: Crain Communications Inc.
Ed: Nathan Skid. Description: Interview with J. Patrick Doyle, the CEO of Domino's Pizza, Inc.; the company has launched a new marketing campaign that focuses on its bold new vision.

24327 ■ Dreams with a Deadline: How to Turn a Strategy for Tomorrow Into a Plan for Today
Pub: Pearson Education, Limited
Contact: Steven A. Dowling, President
Ed: Jacques Horovitz; Anne-Valerie Ohlsson-Corboz. Released: November 2006. Price: $54.00. Description: Tips for successful entrepreneurship are covered.

24328 ■ "Economic Crises Calls For Better Marketing Plans" in Entrepreneur (October 1, 2008)
Pub: Entrepreneur Media Inc.
Ed: Tim Berry. Description: Revising one's business plan is essential, especially during times of economic crisis; sales and marketing plans should be reviewed, analyzed and changed in an attempt to survive the economic downturn.

24329 ■ "Economic Outlook 2009" in Hispanic Business (January-February 2009, pp. 30, 32)
Pub: Hispanic Business
Ed: Dr. Juan Solana. Description: Successful business policies of the past no longer work in this economic climate. New tools and initiatives regarding monetary policy, fiscal policy and a higher multiplier are required to survive the crisis.

24330 ■ "Economic Stimulus Plan Needs Scrutiny" in Crain's Detroit Business (Vol. 24, April 7, 2008, No. 14, pp. 8)
Pub: Crain Communications, Inc.
Description: Overview of Mayor Kwame Kilpatrick's economic stimulus package which many believe needs to be scrutinized closely since the true financial status of Detroit is unclear.

24331 ■ "Efficient Cash Management Essential To Be Competitive" in Crain's Cleveland Business (Vol. 28, November 12, 2007, No. 45, pp. 25)
Pub: Crain Communications, Inc.
Ed: Ken Moultrie. Description: In order to sustain a business it is important to organize cash-management efforts around three core areas: cash in, static cash and cash out. Tips for the successful management of these areas are provided.

24332 ■ "The Emperor Strikes Back" in Canadian Business (Vol. 80, March 26, 2007, No. 7, pp. 48)
Pub: Rogers Media
Ed: Rachel Pulfer. Description: The financial performance of Fairfax Financial Holdings Ltd. in 2006 is presented. The efforts of chief executive Prem Watsa to lead the company towards growth track are also presented.

24333 ■ "EnCana Axes Spending on Gas Wells" in Globe & Mail (February 16, 2006, pp. B1)

Pub: CTVglobemedia Publishing Inc.

Ed: Dave Ebner. **Description:** The reasons behind EnCana Corp.'s cost spending measures by $300 million on natural gas wells are presented. The company projects 2 percent cut in gas and oil sales for 2006.

24334 ■ "Energy Sparks Job Growth" in The Business Journal-Serving Greater Tampa Bay (Vol. 28, August 8, 2008, No. 33, pp. 1)

Pub: American City Business Journals, Inc.

Ed: Margie Manning. **Description:** Energy infrastructure projects in Tampa Bay, Florida, are increasing the demand for labor in the area. Energy projects requiring an increase in labor include TECO Energy Inc.'s plan for a natural gas pipeline in the area and the installation of energy management system in Bank of America's branches in the area.

24335 ■ Entrepreneurial Management

Pub: McGraw-Hill

Ed: Robert J. Calvin. **Description:** Starting a new business takes careful consideration, determined preparation and a well-developed plan president of an international company that helps startups offers strategies, tools, techniques, models and methodologies for starting a new business. This guidebook covers all aspects of launching a new company as well as hands-on business skills and the motivation to keep new business owners moving towards success while conquering the entrepreneurial challenges along with way.

24336 ■ "Entrepreneurial Orientation and Firm Performance" in Journal of Small Business and Entrepreneurship (Vol. 23, Winter 2010, No. 1)

Pub: Canadian Council for Small Business and Entrepreneurship

Description: The article develops a theoretical model of the relationship between firm-level entrepreneurship and firm performance. This model is intended to further clarify the consequences of an 'entrepreneurial orientation', paying particular attention to the differential relationship that exists between the three sub-dimensions of entrepreneurial orientation and firm performance. Included in the theoretical model are other important variables (such as organizational structure and environmental characteristics) that may impact the EO-performance relationship. Propositions are developed regarding the various configurations of the sub-dimensions of EO and organizational structure that would be most appropriate in a given environmental context. Future research may also benefit from considering the important role that organizational strategy and life cycle stage play in this model. The implications of this model for both researchers and managers are discussed.

24337 ■ The Entrepreneur's Strategy Guide: Ten Keys for Achieving Marketplace Leadership

Pub: Greenwood Publishing Group Inc.

Contact: Janann Sherman, Manager

Ed: Tom Cannon. **Released:** September 2006. **Price:** $44.95. **Description:** Ten principles of marketplace leadership are explored. The book provides a plan for small businesses, including diagnostics, checklists, and other interactive exercises to study both external and internal principles.

24338 ■ Entrepreneurship

Pub: McGraw-Hill Higher Education

Ed: Robert D. Hisrich; Michael P. Peters; Dean A. Shepherd. **Released:** October 2006. **Price:** $106.50. **Description:** Advice is offered to entrepreneurs in formulating, planning, and implementing a business plan.

24339 ■ Entrepreneurship: A Process Perspective

Pub: Thomson South-Western

Ed: Robert A. Baron; Scott A. Shane. **Released:** February 2007. **Price:** $137.95. **Description:** Entrepreneurial process covering team building, finances, business plan, legal issues, marketing, growth and exit strategies.

24340 ■ Essentials of Entrepreneurship and Small Business Management

Pub: Prentice Hall PTR

Ed: Thomas W. Zimmerer; Norman M. Scarborough; Doug Wilson. **Released:** February 2007. **Price:** $106. 67. **Description:** New venture creation and the knowledge required to start a new business are shared. The challenges of entrepreneurship, business plans, marketing, e-commerce, and financial considerations are explored.

24341 ■ Everything I Know About Business I Learned at McDonald's: The 7 Leadership Principles that Drive Break Out Success

Pub: The McGraw-Hill Companies

Ed: Paul Facella. **Released:** 2009. **Price:** $24.95. **Description:** McDonald's management philosophy is as simple as its menu, but don't underestimate the effectiveness of founder Ray Kroc's business plan.

24342 ■ "Executive Decision: Damn the Profit Margins, Sleeman Declares War on Buck-a-Beer Foes" in Globe & Mail (January 28, 2006, pp. B3)

Pub: CTVglobemedia Publishing Inc.

Ed: Andy Hoffman. **Description:** The cost savings plans of chief executive officer John Sleeman of Sleeman Breweries Ltd. are presented.

24343 ■ "Executive Decision: Lead a Double Life for Geac's Sake" in Globe & Mail (January 21, 2006, pp. B4)

Pub: CTVglobemedia Publishing Inc.

Ed: Simon Avery. **Description:** The details of growth of Geac Computer Corporation Ltd., under chief executive officer Charles Jones, are presented.

24344 ■ "Executive Decision: To Make Inroads Against RIM, Palm Steals Its Strategy" in Globe & Mail (March 25, 2006, pp. B3)

Pub: CTVglobemedia Publishing Inc.

Ed: Simon Avery. **Description:** The Palm Inc., global leader in portable device manufacturing, is looking forward to improve its sales of Palm Treos, a wireless portable device that connects to internet and email. Palm is also planning to build partnerships, under the efficient management of Michael Moskowitz, general manager and vice-president of Palm Inc., with the other companies to increase the sales of its wireless devices.

24345 ■ "Executive Training" in Black Enterprise (Vol. 37, December 2006, No. 5, pp. 70)

Pub: Earl G. Graves Publishing Co. Inc.

Ed: Marcia A. Reed-Woodard. **Description:** Roy N. Gundy Jr. was preparing to introduce a new strategic plan within his division and understood that his plan may fail if not executed properly. He discusses his experience in the Wharton School's executive education workshop Implementing Strategy, at the University of Pennsylvania and gives tips on putting strategy into action.

24346 ■ "Expanding Middleby's Food Processing Biz" in Crain's Chicago Business (Vol. 31, April 21, 2008, No. 16, pp. 6)

Pub: Crain Communications, Inc.

Ed: David Sterrett. **Description:** Profile of the executive vice-president of the food processing company, Middleby Corp, whose business plan is to develop new products, begin looking for acquisitions and simplify operations in order to expand the firm.

24347 ■ "Experts Take the Temp of Obama Plan" in The Business Journal-Serving Metropolitan Kansas City (Vol. 27, November 14, 2008, No. 10)

Pub: American City Business Journals, Inc.

Ed: Rob Roberts. **Description:** Kansas City, Missouri-based employee benefits experts say president-elect Barack Obama's health care reform plan is on track. Insurance for children and capitalization for health information technology are seen as priority areas. The plan is aimed at reducing the number of uninsured people in the United States.

24348 ■ "Familiar Face Aims to Rebuild Distributor's Once-Strong Local Ties" in Crain's Cleveland Business (December 3, 2007)

Pub: Crain Communications, Inc.

Ed: David Bennett. **Description:** Phillips Contractors Supply, a tool distributor, has a new president and co-owner, James Beckett. Beckett was once vice president of operations so he knows the company well and has plans to re-establish the firm's presence in the region.

24349 ■ "Family Feud: Pawn Shop Empire Stalls with Transition to Second Generation" in Billings Gazette (December 19, 2010)

Pub: Billings Gazette

Ed: Jan Falstad. **Description:** Profile of Ben L. Brown Sr. and his pawn shop located in Billings, Montana is presented. Brown discusses his plan to transition his business to his children.

24350 ■ Family Limited Partnership Deskbook

Pub: American Bar Association

Contact: Carolyn Lamm, President

Ed: David T. Lewis; Andrea C. Chomakos. **Released:** March 25, 2008. **Price:** $169.95. **Description:** Forming and funding a family limited partnership or limited liability company is complicated. In-depth analysis of all facets of this business entity are examined using detailed guidance on the basic principles of drafting, forming, funding, and valuing an FLP or LLC and also covers tax concerns. Examples and extensive sample forms are included on a CD-ROM included with the book.

24351 ■ "The Family-Run Business" in Small Business Opportunities (Get Rich At Home 2010)

Pub: Harris Publications Inc.

Ed: Gene Siciliano. **Description:** The good, the bad and the ugly of succession planning for any small business is spotlighted.

24352 ■ "Film Giants Disney, Pixar Talk Marriage" in Globe & Mail (January 19, 2006, pp. B1)

Pub: CTVglobemedia Publishing Inc.

Ed: Merissa Marr; Nick Wingfield. **Description:** The plans of Walt Disney Co. to acquire Pixar Animation Studios are presented.

24353 ■ "Finalist: Private Company, Less Than $100M" in Crain's Detroit Business (Vol. 25, June 22, 2009, No. 25)

Pub: Crain Communications Inc. - Detroit

Ed: Nancy Kaffer. **Description:** Profile of W3R Consulting and CFO Patrick Tom= ina. The company offers information technology consulting. Tomina discusses the company's 505 strategy: to grow its annual revenue to $50 million in five years.

24354 ■ Financing Growth: Strategies, Capital Structure, and M and A Transactions

Pub: John Wiley and Sons, Inc.

Ed: Kenneth H. Marks, Larry E. Robbins, Gonzalo Fernandez, John P. Funkhouser, D.L. Williams. **Released:** September 1, 2009. **Price:** $95.00. **Description:** Guide for emerging growth and middle market companies includes information to help understand and apply the basics of corporate finance using empirical data and actual company cases to illustrate capital structures and financing approaches.

24355 ■ "Financing for NNSA Plant Is a Work in Progress" in The Business Journal-Serving Metropolitan Kansas City (October 24, 2008)

Pub: American City Business Journals, Inc.

Ed: Rob Roberts. **Description:** The Kansas City Council approved a development plan for a $500 million nuclear weapons parts plant in south Kansas City. The US Congress approved a $59 million annual lease payment to the plant's developer. Financing for the construction of the plant remains in question as the plant's developers have to shoulder construction costs.

24356 ■ *"Finding the Voice of the Marketplace" in Mergers & Acquisitions: The Dealmaker's Journal (March 1, 2008)*
Pub: SourceMedia, Inc.
Description: Companies oftentimes are unable to achieve their strategic goals through acquisition due, in part, to not understanding the target's market and its position in the marketplace.

24357 ■ *"Five Steps to Killer Business Ideas" in Hawaii Business (Vol. 53, December 2007, No. 6, pp. 135)*
Pub: Hawaii Business Publishing
Ed: Jason Ubay. **Description:** Five ways to formulating good business concepts are presented. The importance of keeping an open mind and analyzing the market is discussed.

24358 ■ *"Follow the ABCs of Buying a Business" in Women Entrepreneur (September 10, 2008)*
Pub: Entrepreneur Media Inc.
Ed: Nina Kaufman. **Description:** Buying a business will likely result in the largest single asset one will ever own. A list of steps one can take in order to educate and protect themselves is provided.

24359 ■ *"For Going All Out to Transform the Way Our Food Is Grown: Chuck Lacy" in Inc. (Volume 32, December 2010, No. 10, pp. 94)*
Pub: Inc. Magazine
Ed: Adam Bluestein. **Description:** Profile of Rotokawa Cattle Company and its mission to transform the business of beef and grow their herd of beef cattle.

24360 ■ *"Ford Fix Requires 'Painful' Remedy" in Globe & Mail (January 9, 2006, pp. B1)*
Pub: CTVglobemedia Publishing Inc.
Ed: Greg Keenan. **Description:** The plans of Ford Motor Co. to streamline Canadian operations are presented.

24361 ■ *"Forget the Elaborate Business Plans, Kids With Passion Are Our Next Great Entrepreneurs" in Inc. (October 2007, pp. 87-88)*
Pub: Gruner & Jahr USA Publishing
Description: George Gendron, founder and executive director of the Innovation and Entrepreneurship Program at Clark University, stresses the importance of encouraging business students in his entrepreneurial program to follow their passion. The program is dedicated to real-world entrepreneurship by creating businesses rather than business plans.

24362 ■ *"Former Chrysler Dealers Build New Business Model" in Crain's Detroit Business (Vol. 25, June 22, 2009, No. 25, pp. 3)*
Pub: Crain Communications Inc. - Detroit
Ed: Daniel Duggan. **Description:** Joe Ricci is one of 14 Detroit area dealerships whose franchises have been terminated. Ricci and other Chrysler dealers in the area are starting new businesses or switching to new franchises.= Ricci's All American Buyer's Service will be located in Dearborn and will sell only used cars.

24363 ■ *"Formulating Policy With a Parallel Organization" in Strategy & Leadership (Vol. 38, September-October 2010, No. 5, pp. 33-38)*
Pub: Emerald Inc.
Ed: Dale E. Zand, Thomas F. Hawk. **Description:** A study analyzes a case to examine the parallel organization concept and its successful implementation by a CEO to integrate independent divisions of a firm. Findings reveal that the implementation of the parallel organization improved the policy formulation, strategic planning profitability of the firm while also better integrating its independent divisions.

24364 ■ *"Founding Family Acquires Airport Marriott" in Crain's Cleveland Business (Vol. 28, November 5, 2007, No. 44, pp. 3)*
Pub: Crain Communications, Inc.
Ed: Stan Bullard. **Description:** Big River Real Estate LLC, part of the Marriott family's investment fund, is the new owner of the Cleveland Airport Marriott; renovations estimated at about $11 million will ensure that the hotel meets Marriott's standards.

24365 ■ *"Four Big Fat Business Plan Lies" in Entrepreneur (December 11, 2008)*
Pub: Entrepreneur Media Inc.
Ed: Tim Berry. **Description:** Business plans are essential for every business and do not necessarily have to be a complex document containing a full list of components. Other misconceptions concerning business plans are also discussed.

24366 ■ *"Franchisees Lose Battle Against BK" in Advertising Age (Vol. 79, June 2, 2008, No. 22, pp. 46)*
Pub: Crain Communications, Inc.
Ed: Emily Bryson York. **Description:** Burger King has had continuing litigation with former franchisees from New York, Luan and Elizabeth Sadik, who claim that Burger King's double cheeseburger, along with additional problems, created the environment for their eventual insolvency. Burger King has since terminated its test of selling the double cheeseburger for $1, although the company declined to comment on the reason for this decision.

24367 ■ *"Fries With That?" in Canadian Business (Vol. 81, September 29, 2008, No. 16, pp. 33)*
Pub: Rogers Media Ltd.
Ed: Calvin Leung. **Description:** Profile of Toronto-based New York Fries, which has four stores in South Korea, is planning to expand further as well as into Hong Kong and Macau; the company also has a licensee in the United Arab Emirates whom is also planning to expand.

24368 ■ *"From Craft Biz To Wholesale Giant" in Women Entrepreneur (January 19, 2009)*
Pub: Entrepreneur Media Inc.
Ed: Maria Falconer. **Description:** Advice is given on how to turn a small craft business into a full-time venture; tips to help one transition from a part-time designer to a full-time wholesaler and brand are also included.

24369 ■ *"From War Zone to Franchise Zone" in Entrepreneur (Vol. 37, August 2009, No. 8, pp. 104)*
Pub: Entrepreneur Media, Inc.
Ed: Jason Daley. **Description:** Ross Paterson says that he realized that the material he used in the Growth Coach franchise could give the people of Afghanistan the systematic model they need. Paterson says that the Afghans are very business-oriented people but that they work in a different system than Americans.

24370 ■ *"Gail Mukaihata Hannemann" in Hawaii Business (Vol. 53, January 2008, No. 7, pp. 24)*
Pub: Hawaii Business Publishing
Ed: Cathy S. Cruz-George. **Description:** Discusses the Girl Scouts of Hawaii which has altered its business model to become more appealing to young girls in the 21st century. Gail Mukaihata Hanneman, the chief executive officer of the nonprofit organization, states that the Girl Scouts has consolidated some of its operations to increase efficiency. Her views on what employers must learn about the youth and on the adults' roles in developing the younger generation are given.

24371 ■ *"Game On" in Canadian Business (Vol. 80, February 12, 2007, No. 4, pp. 15)*
Pub: Rogers Media
Ed: Calvin Leung. **Description:** The plan of president of TransGaming Vikas Gupta to create innovative software programs for games that can be played in different operating systems is discussed.

24372 ■ *"Game Plan" in Canadian Business (Vol. 79, September 11, 2006, No. 18, pp. 50)*
Pub: Rogers Media
Ed: Joe Castaldo. **Description:** Strategies adopted by gaming companies to revitalize their business and give a stimulus to their falling resources are presented.

24373 ■ *"Get Back To Business Planning Fundamentals" in Entrepreneur (October 24, 2008)*
Pub: Entrepreneur Media Inc.
Ed: Tim Berry. **Description:** During a recession it is important to know what adjustment to make to your business plan. Some fundamentals to remember include: watching things more closely by tracking progress on cash, sales, new projects, customer satisfaction, ad spending and expenses; looking for built-in indicators such as what drives sales or expenses; watching what drives cash flow; and do not make mistakes such as laying off experienced employees too soon.

24374 ■ *"Get Off The Rollercoaster" in Michigan Vue (Vol. 13, July-August 2008, No. 4, pp. 19)*
Pub: Entrepreneur Media Inc.
Ed: Donald N. Hobley Jr. **Description:** Benefits of creating and implementing a solid financial plan during these rocky economic times are examined. Things to keep in mind before meeting with a financial planner include risk assessment, investment goals, the length of time required to meet those goals and the amount of money one has available to invest.

24375 ■ *"Get Over Your Fear of Change" in Canadian Business (Vol. 83, June 15, 2010, No. 10, pp. 38)*
Pub: Rogers Media Ltd.
Ed: Michelle Magnan. **Description:** Organizational behavior professor Chip Heath says that resistance to change is based on the conflict between our analytical, rational side and our emotional side that is in love with comfort. Heath states that businesses tend to focus on the negatives during an economic crisis while they should be focusing on what is working and ways to do more of that.

24376 ■ *The Girl's Guide to Building a Million-Dollar Business*
Pub: AMACOM
Ed: Susan Wilson Solovic. **Released:** 2008. **Price:** $21.95. **Description:** Success plan for women business owners; the book includes tips for determination, managing changing relationships, keeping employees and customers happy, getting and maintaining credit, overcoming gender bias, and creating a good business plan and solid brand.

24377 ■ *"GM Axing Prices; Kerkorian Calls for Crisis Plan" in Globe & Mail (January 11, 2006, pp. B1)*
Pub: CTVglobemedia Publishing Inc.
Ed: Greg Keenan. **Description:** The financial restructuring proposal of investor Kirk Kerkorian for General Motors Corp. is presented.

24378 ■ *"Gold Medal" in Canadian Business (Vol. 79, October 9, 2006, No. 20, pp. 57)*
Pub: Rogers Media
Ed: Andrew Wahl. **Description:** Creativity skills and management strategies of Rob McEwen, founder and chief executive officer of Goldcorp Inc., are presented.

24379 ■ *"Grace Puma; Senior Vice-President of Strategic Sourcing, United Airlines" in Crain's Chicago Business (May 5, 2008)*
Pub: Crain Communications, Inc.
Ed: John Rosenthal. **Description:** Profile of Grace Puma who is the senior vice-president of strategic sourcing at United Airlines and is responsible for cutting costs at the company in a number of ways including scheduling safety inspections at the same time as routine maintenance, thereby reducing the downtime of each aircraft by five days as well as replacing a third of her staff with outside talent.

24380 ■ *"A Graceful (and Lucrative) Exit" in Black Enterprise (Vol. 38, November 2007, No. 4, pp. 108)*
Pub: Earl G. Graves Publishing Co. Inc.
Ed: Tamara E. Holmes. **Description:** BlueKey Business Brokerage helps clients buy, grow or sell a business. Four key points are examined in order to successfully exit a business.

24381 ■ "Grave Concerns" in Canadian Business (Vol. 81, July 21 2008, No. 11, pp. 25)

Pub: Rogers Media Ltd.

Ed: Andrew Nikiforuk. Description: Air pollution control regulations to reduce greenhouse gasses have been implemented by the Canadian government. The federal government is planning to construct a carbon funeral industry that will store the global warming gases, however the expenditure for the project will be shifted to the taxpayers. Details of the Bruce Peachy's initiative on how to reduce GHGs are presented.

24382 ■ "Great Canadian's President Folds His Cards" in Globe & Mail (February 21, 2006, pp. B4)

Pub: CTVglobemedia Publishing Inc.

Ed: Peter Kennedy. Description: The reasons behind the resignation of Anthony Martin as president of Great Canadian Gaming Corp. are presented.

24383 ■ "Green Acres" in Hawaii Business (Vol. 54, September 2008, No. 3, pp. 48)

Pub: Hawaii Business Publishing

Ed: Jan Tenbruggencate. Description: Bill Cowern's Hawaiian Mahogany is a forestry business that processes low-value trees to be sold as wood chips, which can be burned to create biodiesel. Cowern is planning to obtain certification to market carbon credits and is also working with Green Energy Hawaii for the permit of a biomass-fueled power plant. Other details about Cowern's business are discussed.

24384 ■ "The Green Conversation" in Harvard Business Review (Vol. 86, September 2008, No. 9, pp. 58)

Pub: Harvard Business School Press

Description: Six guidelines are presented for addressing and benefiting from environmentally conscious corporate decision making and practices. Topics covered include marketing, supply chain, and leadership.

24385 ■ "'Groundhog Day' B & B Likely Will Be Converted Into One In Real Life" in Chicago Tribune (October 21, 2008)

Pub: McClatchy-Tribune Information Services

Ed: Carolyn Starks. Description: Everton Martin and Karla Stewart Martin have purchased the Victorian house that was featured as a bed-and-breakfast in the 1993 hit move 'Groundhog Day'; the couple was initially unaware of the structure's celebrity status when they purchased it with the hope of fulfilling their dream of owning a bed-and-breakfast.

24386 ■ "Growers Urged to Allow for Soil Nutrients" in Farmer's Weekly (March 28, 2008, No. 320)

Pub: Reed Business Information

Contact: Jeff Greisch, President

Ed: Andrew Blake. Description: Discusses the importance of taking in account soil nitrogen supplies when planning their remaining fertilizer applications.

24387 ■ "A Growing Dilemma" in Crain's Cleveland Business (Vol. 28, October 8, 2007, No. 40, pp. 19)

Pub: Crain Communications, Inc.

Ed: Kimberly Bonvissuto. Description: Discusses small business owners who often have to grapple with the decision on whether or not to expand their operations and the importance of a business plan which may help owners with that decision.

24388 ■ "Growing Pains" in Canadian Business (Vol. 81, July 22, 2008, No. 12-13, pp. 35)

Pub: Rogers Media Ltd.

Ed: Alex Mylnek. Description: Laughing Stock Vineyards' Cynthia Enns and David Enns plan to target young buyers by using social media. The Enns however, are concerned that targeting younger buyers may affect Laughing Stock's image as a premium brand. Additional information regarding the company's future plans is presented.

24389 ■ "Handleman Liquidation Leaves Questions For Shareholders" in Crain's Detroit Business (Vol. 24, October 6, 2008, No. 40, pp. 4)

Pub: Crain Communications, Inc.

Ed: Nancy Kaffer. Description: Discusses Handleman Co., a Troy-based music distribution company, and their plan of liquidation and dissolution as well as how shareholders will be affected by the company's plan. Handleman filed its plan to liquidate and dissolve assets with the Securities and Exchange Commission in mid-August, following several quarters of dismal earnings.

24390 ■ "Has Microsoft Found a Way to Get at Yahoo?' in Advertising Age (Vol. 79, July 7, 2008, No. 26, pp. 4)

Pub: Crain Communications, Inc.

Ed: Abbey Klaassen. Description: Microsoft's attempt to acquire Yahoo's search business is discussed as is Yahoo's plans for the future at a time when the company's shares have fallen dangerously low.

24391 ■ "HBC Sets Friday as Deadline to Trump Zucker Takeover Bid' in Globe & Mail (January 18, 2006, pp. B1)

Pub: CTVglobemedia Publishing Inc.

Ed: Marina Strauss. Description: The reasons behind Hudson's Bay Co.'s decision to seek alternative bids on the company are presented. Investor Jerry Zucker earlier offered $1.1 billion for the company.

24392 ■ "Hello, Old Friends" in Business Courier (Vol. 24, October 12, 2008, No. 26, pp. 1)

Pub: American City Business Journals, Inc.

Ed: Jon Newberry. Description: Pittsburgh-based Iron City Brewing Co., a company born out of Pittsburgh Brewing Co.'s reorganization, is resuming the production of Wiedemann Bohemian Style Special Beer. Cincinnati-based Christian Moerlein Brewing Co. is also bringing back its famous Burger beer, which hasn't been available locally for a couple of years. The two companies' plans regarding the reintroduction of their beer products are discussed.

24393 ■ "High Energy: Gaurdie Banister Joins Aera As President and CEO' in Black Enterprise (Vol. 38, July 2008, No. 12, pp. 30)

Pub: Earl G. Graves Publishing Co. Inc.

Ed: Brenda Porter. Description: Gaurdie Banister Jr. has been appointed president and CEO of Aera Energy L.L.C., becoming one of the first African Americans in the nation to run a major energy corporation. His plans for the firm include utilizing new, sophisticated technologies in order to unlock the 3-1/2 billion barrels of resources the company has on their books in a safe and environmentally friendly way. He also hopes to increase production and maintain cost leadership.

24394 ■ "Higher Freight Rates Keep CPR Rolling in Profit' in Globe & Mail (February 1, 2006, pp. B3)

Pub: CTVglobemedia Publishing Inc.

Ed: Brent Jang. Description: Canadian Pacific Railway Ltd. posted $135.4 million in revenues for fourth quarter 2005. The company's earnings projections for 2006 and workforce reduction plans are presented.

24395 ■ "His Place in the Sun" in Canadian Business (Vol. 79, October 23, 2006, No. 21, pp. 77)

Pub: Rogers Media

Ed: Zena Olijnyk. Description: The business interests of Canadian real estate developer Derek Elliott in the Dominican Republic, is discussed.

24396 ■ "Historic Glenview Homes Could Be Torn Down" in Chicago Tribune (September 25, 2008)

Pub: McClatchy-Tribune Information Services

Ed: Courtney Flynn. Description: Leaders of the Glenview New Church would like to see a buyer emerge who would move and restore two historic homes sitting on the church's property. If a buyer

does not come forward the church plans to demolish the homes to make room for condominiums and the expansion of their school.

24397 ■ "Hit the Green" in Canadian Business (Vol. 79, August 14, 2006, No. 16-17, pp. 73)

Pub: Rogers Media

Ed: Andrew Wahl. Description: Reorganization of the bankrupt 4everSports golf company in the United States is discussed.

24398 ■ "HOK Sport May Build Own Practice" in The Business Journal-Serving Metropolitan Kansas City (Vol. 26, August 29, 2008, No. 51, pp. 1)

Pub: American City Business Journals, Inc.

Ed: Rob Roberts. Description: HOK Sport Venue Event is considering a spin-off from its parent company, HOK Group Inc. HOK Sport spokeswoman Gina Leo confirms that the firm is exploring structures, including a management buyout. Some of HOK Sport Venue Event's Minnesota projects are discussed.

24399 ■ "How I Did It: Laurel Touby Mediabistro" in Inc. (March 2008, pp. 124-126)

Pub: Gruner & Jahr USA Publishing

Ed: Eric Schine. Description: Profile of Laurel Touby and her business plan; Touby started Mediabistro as a series of parties that turned into an influential job listing and training Website for journalists. Last year she sold it for $23 million.

24400 ■ "How to Keep Your Sales from Running Out of Gas" in Agency Sales Magazine (Vol. 39, July 2009, No. 7, pp. 30)

Pub: MANA

Ed: John Graham. Description: Salespeople can let the good times deceive them into thinking that success will go on forever. Salespeople and businesses should see prospecting as a strategy for creating a continuing flow of business.

24401 ■ How to Make Big Money

Pub: Hyperion Books

Ed: Jeffrey J. Fox. Released: May 19, 2004. Price: $16.95. Description: Entrepreneur and consultant offers advice to help others create successful startups and prosper. Fox directs new business owners with a counterintuitive style and describes essential methods that beat the competition. Tips include: setting priorities, getting a personal driver, creating a contingency plan for employees, pricing to value, saving money, and getting an office outside of the home.

24402 ■ "How Not to Build a Website" in Women Entrepreneur (December 24, 2008)

Pub: Entrepreneur Media Inc.

Ed: Erica Ruback; Joanie Reisen. Description: Tips for producing a unique and functional Website are given as well as a number of lessons a pair of entrepreneurs learned while trying to launch their networking website, MomSpace.com.

24403 ■ How to Start a Home-Based Craft Business, 5th Edition

Pub: Globe Pequot Press

Ed: Kenn Oberrecht. Released: July 2007. Price: $18.95. Description: Advice for starting a home-based craft business is given, including sources for finding supplies on the Internet, writing a business plan, publicity, zoning ordinances, and more.

24404 ■ How to Start and Run Your Own Corporation: S-Corporations For Small Business Owners

Pub: HCM Publishing

Ed: Peter I. Hupalo. Released: March 6, 2003. Price: $22.95. Description: Basics of corporate business structure are explained. Topics include discovering the best business structure for your company; how to decided between an S-Corporation and LLC; choosing the state in which to incorporate, how to form a corporation, angel investing, special issues for one-person corporations, the role of bylaws and corporate minutes, board of directors, taxes, workers' compensation issues, retirement plans, and more.

24405 ■ *"How Will You Ever Replace Yourself?" in Canadian Business (Vol. 83, August 17, 2010, No. 13-14, pp. 77)*
Pub: Rogers Media Ltd.

Ed: Jacqueline Nelson. **Description:** SoftBank founder and CEO masayoshi Son created his very own school called SoftBank Academia in order to pick a successor that will follow his footprint. Son's strategy is extreme but other corporate leaders should pay attention to succession planning.

24406 ■ *How to Write a Business Plan*
Pub: NOLO

Ed: Mike McKeever. **Released:** January 2007. **Price:** $34.99. **Description:** Author, teacher and financial manager shows how to write an effective business plan. Examples and worksheets are included.

24407 ■ *How to Write a Business Plan*
Pub: Kogan Page, Limited
Contact: Ben Glover, Director of Marketing

Ed: Brian Finch. **Released:** February 10, 2010. **Price:** $17.95. **Description:** Starting with the premise that there's only one chance to make a good impression, this book covers all the issues involved in producing a successful business plan, from profiling competitors to forecasting marketing development.

24408 ■ *How to Write a Great Business Plan for Your Small Business in 60 Minutes or Less*
Pub: Atlantic Publishing

Ed: Sharon L. Fullen. **Released:** January 2006. **Price:** $39.95 includes CD-Rom **Description:** A good business plan outlines goals and works as a company's resume to obtain funding, credit from suppliers, management of the operations and finances, promotion and marketing, and more.

24409 ■ *"Husky Proceeds on Heavy-Oil Expansion" in Globe & Mail (March 21, 2006, pp. B1)*
Pub: CTVglobemedia Publishing Inc.

Ed: Patrick Brethour. **Description:** Canadian energy giant Husky Energy Inc. has started its $90 million engineering effort to determine the cost of the $2.3 billion heavy-oil up gradation expansion plan. Details of the project are elaborated upon.

24410 ■ *"Ian Gordon" in Canadian Business (Vol. 81, Summer 2008, No. 9, pp. 10)*
Pub: Rogers Media Ltd.

Ed: Matthew McClearn. **Description:** Bolder Investment Partners' Ian Gordon discussed the economic theory promulgated by Russian economist Nikolai Kondratieff. The cycle begins with a rising economy then followed by deflationary depression. Details of his views on the Kondratieff cycle and its application to the current economy are presented.

24411 ■ *"Ideas at Work: The Reality of Costs" in Business Strategy Review (Vol. 21, Summer 2010, No. 2, pp. 40)*
Pub: Wiley-Blackwell

Ed: Jules Goddard. **Description:** If you think that cost cutting is the surest way to business success, the author wants to challenge every assumption you hold. Costs are an outcome of sound strategy, never the goal of strategy. He offers a new perspective on what counts when it comes to costs.

24412 ■ *"Ill Winds; Cuba's Economy" in The Economist (Vol. 390, January 3, 2009, No. 8612, pp. 20)*
Pub: The Economist Newspaper Inc.

Description: Cuba's long-term economic prospects remain poor with the economy forecasted to grow only 4.3 percent for the year, about half of the original forecast, due in part to Hurricane Gustav which caused $10 billion in damage and disrupted the food-supply network and devastated farms across the region; President Raul Castro made raising agricultural production a national priority and the rise in global commodity prices hit the country hard. The only bright spot has been the rise in tourism which is up 9.3 percent over 2007.

24413 ■ *"In Puerto Rico, Slow and Steady Wins Race" in Globe & Mail (February 24, 2007, pp. B3)*
Pub: CTVglobemedia Publishing Inc.

Ed: Andrew Willis. **Description:** The plan of Scotiabank de Puerto Rico's chief executive officer Richard Waugh to improve its market presence using its international banking relations is discussed.

24414 ■ *"Inland Snaps Up Rival REITs" in Crain's Chicago Business (Vol. 31, November 17, 2008, No. 46, pp. 3)*
Pub: Crain Communications, Inc.

Ed: Alby Gallun. **Description:** Discusses Inland American Real Estate Trust Inc., a real estate investment trust that is napping up depressed shares of publicly traded competitors, a possible first step toward taking over these companies; however, with hotel and retail properties accounting for approximately 70 percent of its portfolio, the company could soon face its own difficulties.

24415 ■ *"Innovating Globally" in Business Strategy Review (Vol. 21, Spring 2010, No. 1, pp. 24)*
Pub: Wiley-Blackwell

Ed: Costas Markides, Stuart Crainer. **Description:** Costas Markides has spent over two decades studying business strategy and innovation. Recently, he has been focusing on the bigger picture of how people can address major social problems. Can the techniques used by managers to create innovation inside organizations work with global change?.

24416 ■ *"Inside the New Nortel" in Canadian Business (Vol. 79, November 6, 2006, No. 22, pp. 93)*
Pub: Rogers Media

Ed: Andrew Wahl. **Description:** The team plans of Nortel Networks to improve its technology market by appointing new team are analyzed.

24417 ■ *Instinct: Tapping Your Entrepreneurial DNA to Achieve Your Business Goals*
Pub: Warner Books, Incorporated

Ed: Mary H. Frakes; Thomas L. Harrison. **Released:** September 2006. **Price:** $15.99. **Description:** Research shows that entrepreneurs may attribute their success to genetics.

24418 ■ *"Insurers No Longer Paying Premium for Advertising" in Brandweek (Vol. 49, April 21, 2008, No. 16, pp. SR3)*
Pub: VNU Business Media, Inc.

Ed: Eric Newman. **Description:** Insurance companies are cutting their advertising budgets after years of accelerated double-digit growth in spending due to the economic downturn, five years of record-breaking ad spend and a need to cut expenditures as claims costs rise and a competitive market keeps premiums in place. Statistical data included.

24419 ■ *"Integrating Your Compliance Program" in Franchising World (Vol. 42, November 2010, No. 11, pp. 49)*
Pub: International Franchise Association

Ed: Melanie Bergeron. **Description:** Compliance is integral to every part of any business operation and it is necessary for a company to make standards and compliance to those standards a priority.

24420 ■ *"The Intrawest Empire" in Canadian Business (Vol. 79, October 9, 2006, No. 20, pp. 27)*
Pub: Rogers Media

Ed: Erik Heinrich. **Description:** The future development plans of Intrawest Corp., are discussed. Strategic plans of Joe Houssian, the chairman, president and chief executive officer of Intrawest Corp., are also presented.

24421 ■ *"Intrawest Puts Itself on Market" in Globe & Mail (March 1, 2006, pp. B1)*
Pub: CTVglobemedia Publishing Inc.

Ed: Elizabeth Church. **Description:** The reasons behind the decision of Intrawest Corp. to go for sale or seek partnerships are presented. The company appointed Goldman Sachs & Co. to meet the purpose.

24422 ■ *"Investing in the IT that Makes a Competitive Difference" in Harvard Business Review (Vol. 86, July-August 2008, No. 8, pp. 98)*
Pub: Harvard Business School Press

Ed: Andrew McAfee; Erik Brynjolfsson. **Description:** Components of a successful information technology management strategy are examined. These techniques are broad in spectrum, produce immediate results, are consistent and precise, facilitate monitoring, and promote enforceability.

24423 ■ *"Iogen, VW Look to Build Ethanol Plant" in Globe & Mail (January 9, 2006, pp. B3)*
Pub: CTVglobemedia Publishing Inc.

Ed: Simon Tuck. **Description:** Iogen Corp. and Volkswagen AG plan cellulose ethanol plant in Germany. The details of the project are presented.

24424 ■ *"Irene Rosenfeld; Chairman and CEO, Kraft Foods Inc." in Crain's Chicago Business (Vol. 31, May 5, 2008, No. 18, pp. 31)*
Pub: Crain Communications, Inc.

Ed: David Sterrett. **Description:** Profile of Irene Rosenfeld who is the chairman and CEO of Kraft Foods Inc. and is entering the second year of a three-year plan to boost sales of well-known brands such as Oreo, Velveeta and Oscar Mayer while facing soaring commodity costs and a declining marketshare. Ms. Rosenfeld's turnaround strategy also entails spending more on advertising and giving managers more control over their budgets and product development.

24425 ■ *"Jamieson Eyes $175 Million Trust IPO" in Globe & Mail (March 7, 2006, pp. B1)*
Pub: CTVglobemedia Publishing Inc.

Ed: Sinclair Stewart; Leonard Zehr. **Description:** The reasons behind $175 million initial public offering plans of Jamieson Laboratories Ltd. are presented.

24426 ■ *"Just Add Water and Lily Pads" in Crain's Chicago Business (Vol. 31, April 28, 2008, No. 17, pp. 50)*
Pub: Crain Communications, Inc.

Ed: Phuong Ly. **Description:** Aquascape Inc., a major manufacturer of pond-building supplies, is using the recent drought in the South which hurt its business significantly to create a new product: an upscale, decorative version of the rain barrel which will collect rainwater to circulate through a pond or a fountain.

24427 ■ *"Just Hang Up" in Barron's (Vol. 88, March 10, 2008, No. 10, pp. 45)*
Pub: Dow Jones & Company, Inc.

Ed: Tiernan Ray. **Description:** Sprint's shares are expected to continue falling while the company attempts to attract subscribers by cutting prices, cutting earnings in the process. The company faces tougher competition from better-financed AT&T and Verizon Communications.

24428 ■ *"Kawasaki's New Top Gun" in Brandweek (Vol. 49, April 21, 2008, No. 16, pp. 18)*
Pub: VNU Business Media, Inc.

Description: Discusses Kawasaki's marketing plan which included designing an online brochure in which visitors could create a video by building their own test track on a grid and then selecting visual special effects and musical overlay. This engaging and innovative marketing technique generated more than 166,000 unique users within the first three months of being launched.

24429 ■ *"Keeping Railcars 'Busy At All Times' At TTX" in Crain's Chicago Business (Vol. 31, April 28, 2008, No. 17, pp. 6)*
Pub: Crain Communications, Inc.

Ed: Bob Tita. **Description:** Profile of the president of Chicago railcar pool operator TTX Co. and his business plan for the company which includes improving fleet management and car purchasing through better use of data on railroad demand.

24430 ■ *"Kinetico Exec Going Global to Increase Growth Flow"* in Crain's Cleveland Business (Vol. 28, October 1, 2007, No. 39, pp. 5)

Pub: Crain Communications, Inc.

Ed: David Bennett. **Description:** Shamus Hurley, the new CEO and president of Kinetico Inc., a manufacturer of water filtering and softening equipment for residential, commercial and municipal use, plans to expand the company to target markets overseas.

24431 ■ *"Kroger Girds for Invasion of U.K. Chain"* in Business Courier (Vol. 24, November 2, 2008, No. 29, pp. 1)

Pub: American City Business Journals, Inc.

Ed: Jon Newberry. **Description:** Tesco PLC will be opening its first Fresh & Easy Neighborhood Markets in Southern California. The company has committed $500 million per year to get a share of the $500 billion US food retailing market and will be opening more stores in quick succession. Tesco's arrival can be difficult for Kroger because Kroger had obtained much of its success by using Tesco's UK model.

24432 ■ *"Lafley Gives Look At His Game Plan"* in Business Courier (Vol. 24, March 21, 2008, No. 50, pp. 1)

Pub: American City Business Journals, Inc.

Ed: Lisa Biank Fasig. **Description:** Overview of A.G. Lafley's book entitled 'The Game-Changer', is presented. Lafley, Procter & Gamble Co.'s chief executive officer, documented his philosophy and strategy in his book. His work also includes Procter & Gamble's hands-on initiatives such as mock-up grocery stores and personal interviews with homeowners.

24433 ■ *"Land Agent Taken Over"* in Farmer's Weekly (March 28, 2008, No. 320)

Pub: Reed Business Information

Contact: Jeff Greisch, President

Description: Property business Smiths Gore will take over Cluttons' rural division, one of the oldest names in land agency. Cluttons said it had decided to sell its rural business as part of a strategic repositioning that would refocus the business on commercial, residential and overseas opportunities.

24434 ■ *"Land on Boardwalk"* in Canadian Business (Vol. 82, April 27, 2009, No. 7, pp. 19)

Pub: Rogers Media

Ed: Calvin Leung. **Description:** Boardwalk REIT remains as one of the most attractive real estate investment trusts in Canada, with 73 percent of analysts rating the firm a Buy. Analyst Neil Downey believes that good management, as well as a good business model, makes Boardwalk a good investment. Downey is concerned however, that a worsening of Alberta's economy could significantly impact Boardwalk.

24435 ■ *"Last Founder Standing"* in Conde Nast Portfolio (Vol. 2, June 2008, No. 6, pp. 124)

Pub: Conde Nast Publications

Contact: David Carey, President

Ed: Kevin Maney. **Description:** Interview with Amazon CEO Jeff Bezos in which he discusses the economy, the company's new distribution center and the hiring of employees for it, e-books, and the overall vision for the future of the firm.

24436 ■ *"Lathrop Finds Partner In LA"* in The Business Journal-Serving Metropolitan Kansas City (Vol. 27, November 21, 2008, No. 11, pp. 1)

Pub: American City Business Journals, Inc.

Ed: Steve Vockrodt. **Description:** Kansas, Missouri-based Lathrop and Gage LLP is planning to merge with Spillane Shaeffer Aronoff Bandlow LLP. The merging of the business law firms will add entertainment clients to Lathrop's fold. Comments from executives are also presented.

24437 ■ *Leap! 101 Ways to Grow Your Business*

Pub: Career Press, Inc.

Ed: Stephanie Chandler. **Released:** August 8, 2010. **Price:** $15.99. **Description:** Business growth requires more than a business plan and a dream. Tools and techniques to take a small company to the next level are outlined.

24438 ■ *"Leaving a Legacy: Patricia Latimore and Bourdi Apreala Build a Comprehensive Estate Plan"* in Black Enterprise (January 2008)

Pub: Earl G. Graves Publishing Co. Inc.

Ed: Cliff Hocker. **Description:** Estate planning is critical for anyone, especially small business owners.

24439 ■ *"Lehman's Hail Mary Pass"* in Business Week (September 22, 2008, No. 4100, pp. 28)

Pub: McGraw-Hill Companies, Inc.

Ed: Matthew Goldstein; David Henry; Ben Levison. **Description:** Overview of Lehman Brothers' CEO Richard Fuld's plan to keep the firm afloat and end the stock's plunge downward; Fuld's strategy calls for selling off a piece of the firm's investment management business.

24440 ■ *"Like Father?"* in Canadian Business (Vol. 79, Winter 2006, No. 24, pp. 38)

Pub: Rogers Media

Ed: Zena Olijnyk. **Description:** The achievements of the chairman of Thomson Corp., David Thomson, are discussed. The plans of David Thomson to diversify into different areas of business are discussed.

24441 ■ *"Listen to Bond Market on Tembec"* in Globe & Mail (January 25, 2006, pp. B1)

Pub: CTVglobemedia Publishing Inc.

Ed: Derek DeCloet. **Description:** The feasibility of Tembec Inc.'s restructuring efforts is discussed.

24442 ■ *"Lombard Leaves Starbucks"* in Black Enterprise (Vol. 38, July 2008, No. 12, pp. 28)

Pub: Earl G. Graves Publishing Co. Inc.

Ed: Tamara E. Holmes. **Description:** Ken Lombard stepped down from his position as head of Starbuck's entertainment division; the company is restructuring its entertainment unit in an attempt to revitalize sales and reduce costs.

24443 ■ *"Looking Back"* in Entrepreneur (Vol. 36, March 2008, No. 3, pp. 118)

Pub: Entrepreneur Media Inc.

Ed: Romanus Wolter. **Description:** Entrepreneurs can learn from their mistakes and improve current operations by documenting new strategies and ideas from them, evaluating information and its possible effects, and integrating what has been learned with future plans.

24444 ■ *"Looking For Financing?"* in Hispanic Business (Vol. 30, July-August 2008, No. 7-8, pp. 16)

Pub: Hispanic Business, Inc.

Ed: Frank Nelson. **Description:** Investment firms want to know about businesses that need funding for either expansion or acquisition; companies fitting this profile are interviewed and their perceptions are discussed. Investment firms need businesses to be realistic in their expectations and business plans which show spending of funds and expected benefits, long term goals, track record and strong management teams.

24445 ■ *"Losses Threaten Comp Care's Future Viability"* in The Business Journal-Serving Greater Tampa Bay (Vol. 28, August 15, 2008, No. 34)

Pub: American City Business Journals, Inc.

Ed: Margie Manning. **Description:** Comprehensive Care Corp. expressed that it may have to cease or drastically curtail its operations if it won't be able to raise additional funding in the next two or three months. The firm, which provides managed behavioral health care services, is also believed to be exploring a sale. Other views and information on Comprehensive Care's finances and plans are presented.

24446 ■ *"Lotus Starts Slowly, Dodges Subprime Woes"* in Crain's Detroit Business (Vol. 24, April 14, 2008, No. 15, pp. 3)

Pub: Crain Communications, Inc.

Ed: Tom Henderson. **Description:** Discusses Lotus Bancorp Inc. and their business plan, which although is not right on target due to the subprime mortgage meltdown, is in a much better position than its competitors due to the quality of their loans.

24447 ■ *"Loyalty Pays"* in Entrepreneur (Vol. 36, February 2008, No. 2, pp. 63)

Pub: Entrepreneur Media Inc.

Ed: David Worrell. **Description:** Michael Vadini, chief executive officer of Titan Technology Partners looks after his stockholders and investors by making sure that they are protected from risk. Having been affected by the downturn in the technology industry between 2001 and 2004, Vadini granted his investors a liquidity preference. Details regarding his actions to retain investor loyalty are discussed.

24448 ■ *"The Macomb Group: Bigger Can Be Better"* in Crain's Detroit Business (Vol. 24, September 29, 2008, No. 39, pp. 34)

Pub: Crain Communications Inc.

Ed: Chad Halcom. **Description:** Overview of the plan of The Macomb Group includes a strategy of growing from a small supplier to a medium-sized regional distributor of valves, pipes and fittings.

24449 ■ *"Magna Stalwart to Push for Product Coups"* in Globe & Mail (April 9, 2007, pp. B1)

Pub: CTVglobemedia Publishing Inc.

Ed: Greg Keenan. **Description:** The resignation of Fred Gingl from the vice-chairmanship of the board of directors of Magna International Inc. is described. Mr. Gingl's plans to create wealth for Magna International Inc. through the development of new products are discussed.

24450 ■ *"Magna in Talks on Building Cars for DaimlerChrysler"* in Globe & Mail (February 27, 2007, pp. B1)

Pub: CTVglobemedia Publishing Inc.

Ed: Greg Keenan. **Description:** The plans of Magna International Inc. to purchase securities of Chrysler Corp. are discussed. The possibility of the manufacture of cars by Magna International Inc. for Daimler-Chrysler AG is discussed.

24451 ■ *"Magna Wants to Help Chrysler, but a Takeover's Not on the Cards"* in Globe & Mail (March 1, 2007, pp. B1)

Pub: CTVglobemedia Publishing Inc.

Ed: Greg Keenan. **Description:** The plans of Magna International Inc. to help Chrysler Corp. to overcome its financial problems are discussed. The appointment of Michael Neuman as the chief executive officer of Magna International Inc. is described.

24452 ■ *"Major Tech Employers Pulling Out"* in Sacramento Business Journal (Vol. 25, August 1, 2008, No. 22, pp. 1)

Pub: American City Business Journals, Inc.

Ed: Celia Lamb. **Description:** Biotechnology company Affymetrix Inc. is planning to close its West Sacramento, California plant and lay off 110 employees. The company said it will expand a corporate restructuring plan. Affymetrix also plans to lease out or sell its building at Riverside Parkway.

24453 ■ *"Managers as Visionaries: a Skill That Can Be Learned"* in Strategy and Leadership (Vol. 39, September-October 2011, No. 5, pp. 56-58)

Pub: Emerald Group Publishing Inc.

Ed: Stephen M. Millett. **Description:** A study uses research findings to examine whether visionary management can be learned. Results conclude that managers can learn visionary management through intuitive pattern recognition of trends and by using scenarios for anticipating and planning for likely future occurrences.

24454 ■ *"Managing the Facebookers; Business"* in The Economist (Vol. 390, January 3, 2009, No. 8612, pp. 10)

Pub: Economist Newspaper Ltd.

Description: According to a report from PricewaterhouseCoopers, a business consultancy, workers from Generation Y, also known as the Net Generation, are more difficult to recruit and integrate into companies that practice traditional business acumen. 61 percent of chief executive managers say that they have trouble with younger employees who tend to be more narcissistic and more interested in personal fulfillment with a need for frequent feedback and an overprecise set of objectives on the path to promotion which can be hard for managers who are used to a different relationship with their subordinates. Older bosses should prepare to make some concessions to their younger talent since some of the issues that make them happy include cheaper online ways to communicate and additional coaching, both of which are good for business.

24455 ■ "Mandel Site Favored For UWM Hall" in The Business Journal-Milwaukee (Vol. 25, September 19, 2008, No. 52, pp. A1)

Pub: American City Business Journals, Inc.

Description: University of Wisconsin-Milwaukee student residence hall's leading location is a site pushed by Mandel Group Inc. Real estate sources say that the developer's proposal offers the best opportunity for business development and the least conflict with nearby neighborhoods. Plans for the Mandel site are presented.

24456 ■ "Many Roads Lead to Value" in Barron's (Vol. 88, March 10, 2008, No. 10, pp. 46)

Pub: Dow Jones & Company, Inc.

Ed: Lawrence C. Strauss. **Description:** David J. Williams, lead manager of Excelsior Value & Restructuring Fund, invests in struggling companies and those companies whose turnarounds show promise. Morgan Stanley, Lehman Brothers, and Petroleo Brasileiro are some of the companies he holds shares in, while he has unloaded shares of Citigroup, Freddie Mac, and Sallie Mae.

24457 ■ "Marriott Checks Out Hotel Prospect" in The Business Journal-Serving Metropolitan Kansas City (Vol. 27, November 14, 2008, No. 10)

Pub: American City Business Journals, Inc.

Description: Marriott International Inc. is planning to operate a hotel in Kansas City, Missouri and may take over the Kansas City Marriott Downtown although other hotel operators are interested in bidding on the project.

24458 ■ "Massive Ford Restructuring to Cut 1,200 More Canadian Jobs" in Globe & Mail (January 24, 2006, pp. B1)

Pub: CTVglobemedia Publishing Inc.

Ed: Greg Keenan. **Description:** The details on streamlining of operations of Ford Motor Co., in Canada, are presented.

24459 ■ "Mayfair Considers Moving Boston Store" in The Business Journal-Milwaukee (Vol. 25, September 5, 2008, No. 50, pp. 1)

Pub: American City Business Journals, Inc.

Ed: Rich Kirchen. **Description:** Milwaukee, Wisconsin-based Bon-Ton Stores is planning to relocate its Boston Store at the Mayfair Mall. The existing store is to be redeveloped into smaller specialty shops. Details of the new facility are also presented.

24460 ■ "MBA Project Turns on Tastebuds" in The Business Journal - Serving Phoenix and the Valley of the Sun (Vol. 28, August 15, 2008, No. 50)

Pub: American City Business Journals, Inc.

Ed: Angela Gonzales. **Description:** Amol Khade, Venkat Nallapati and Govind Arora, master of businesss administration graduates from Thunderbird School of Global Management, have opened an Indian restaurant, called The Daba, in Tempe, Arizona. The Indian name of the restaurant means 'a place for travelers to stop for rest and food'. Franchise plans for the restaurant are discussed.

24461 ■ "McCormick Focuses on Customer, Dealer Service" in Farm Industry News (September 17, 2010)

Pub: Penton Business Media Inc.

Description: McCormick has developed a new plan that focuses on fast and complete service to both customers and dealers.

24462 ■ "Meadowbrook CEO Sees 20 Percent Growth With New Acquisition" in Crain's Detroit Business (Vol. 24, March 10, 2008, No. 10, pp. 4)

Pub: Crain Communications, Inc.

Ed: Jay Greene. **Description:** Discusses the major turnaround of Meadowbrook Insurance Group after Robert Cubbin became CEO and implemented a new business strategy.

24463 ■ "Measure Your Business Plan Results" in Entrepreneur (January 6, 2009)

Pub: Entrepreneur Media Inc.

Ed: Tim Berry. **Description:** Although no business plan is ever right on target, it is still essential for every business owner to create one; the way in which to analyze the actual results compared to the plan are discussed.

24464 ■ "Microsoft's Big Gamble" in Canadian Business (Vol. 81, March 3, 2008, No. 3, pp. 13)

Pub: Rogers Media

Ed: Andrew Wahl. **Description:** Microsoft Corp. is taking a big risk in buying Yahoo, as it is expected to pay more than $31 a share to finalize the acquisition. The deal would be seven and a half times bigger than any other that Microsoft has entered before, an execution of such deal is also anticipated to become a challenge for Microsoft. Recommendations or how Microsoft should handle the integration of the two businesses are given.

24465 ■ "Midtown Tampa Bay Taking Shape" in The Business Journal-Serving Greater Tampa Bay (Vol. 28, September 12, 2008, No. 38, pp. 1)

Pub: American City Business Journals, Inc.

Ed: Janet Leiser. **Description:** Midtown Tampa Bay's 610,000 square foot shopping and entertainment center is being planned in Florida and is to replace the Tampa Bay One project proposed years earlier. The retail center is to be developed by Bromley Cos. and Opus South Corp. and is expected to have five buildings. Other details about the plan are discussed.

24466 ■ "Midwest Looks 'Back to the Future" in The Business Journal-Milwaukee (Vol. 25, July 18, 2008, No. 43, pp. A1)

Pub: American City Business Journals, Inc.

Ed: Rich Rovito. **Description:** Midwest Air Group Inc. announced plans to reduce their work force by 40 percent or 1,200 employees after an earlier announcement of a drastic fleet reduction. These steps are being taken by the company in an effort to avoid filing bankruptcy since this would cost the airline millions of dollars in legal and other professional fees.

24467 ■ "Midwest Seeks Concessions From Creditors" in The Business Journal-Milwaukee (Vol. 25, July 25, 2008, No. 44, pp. A1)

Pub: American City Business Journals, Inc.

Ed: Rich Rovito. **Description:** Midwest Airlines Inc. is turning to creditors and lease holders for the financial aspect of its restructuring, which involves going back to serving popular business destinations. Chief executive officer Timothy believes that the company can survive in a niche market as long as it provides quality service. He discusses Midwest's restructuring plan.

24468 ■ "Million-Dollar Babies" in Black Enterprise (Vol. 38, January 2008, No. 6, pp. 64)

Pub: Earl G. Graves Publishing Co. Inc.

Ed: Tennille M. Robinson. **Description:** Books and programs to help any small business grow to the $1 million mark are outlined.

24469 ■ "Modern-Day Midas Hasn't Lost Touch" in Globe & Mail (January 19, 2006, pp. B4)

Pub: CTVglobemedia Publishing Inc.

Ed: Shirley Won. **Description:** The investment plans of chief executive officer Rob McEwen of U.S. Gold Corp. are presented.

24470 ■ "Monaco Pay Cut Draws Attention" in The Business Journal-Portland (Vol. 25, August 8, 2008, No. 22, pp. 1)

Pub: American City Business Journals, Inc.

Ed: Erik Siemers. **Description:** Monaco Coach Corp. cut the salaries of five top executives in an effort to reduce the company's $178 million worth of inventory. The executives can earn the lost salary back if the inventory is reduced by $58 million a year after August 2008.

24471 ■ "More Manufacturers Scout Military Contracts As Auto Industry Lags" in Crain's Detroit Business (Vol. 24, September 29, 2008, No. 39)

Pub: Crain Communications Inc.

Ed: Chad Halcom. **Description:** Many Michigan manufacturers are looking to grow with new military contracts now that the reality of the auto industry is becoming more clear; these companies see that the government contracts may be the only way in which they will be able to stay in business through these rough economic times.

24472 ■ "A Motorola Spinoff Is No Panacea" in Barron's (Vol. 88, March 31, 2008, No. 13, pp. 19)

Pub: Dow Jones & Company, Inc.

Ed: Mark Veverka. **Description:** Motorola's plan to try and spinoff their handset division is bereft of details as to how or specifically when in 2009 the spinoff would occur. There's no reason to buy the shares since there's a lot of execution risk to the plan. Motorola needs to hire a proven cellphone executive and develop a compelling new cellphone platform.

24473 ■ "'Mr. CEO, Please Do Elaborate On Your Firm's Metrics" in Business Courier (Vol. 24, February 29, 2008, No. 47, pp. 1)

Pub: American City Business Journals, Inc.

Ed: Jon Newberry. **Description:** Discusses a rogue caller who goes by the name of Joe Herrick, Steven Nissan and Joe Harris has joined in over a dozen conference calls, asking chief executive officers on their plans and commenting on the companies' operations. The mystery caller attempts to pass himself off as a financial analyst. Transcripts of some conference calls, in which the rogue caller is involved, are provided.

24474 ■ "Mr. Deeds" in Canadian Business (Vol. 81, March 31, 2008, No. 5, pp. 24)

Pub: Rogers Media

Ed: Thomas Watson. **Description:** Ron Sandler has the right experience to save Northern Rock PLC get through its liquidity problems. Sandler is known for saving Lloyd's of London in the mid-90's and he is not afraid to make enemies. Ron Sandler's assignment to help Northern Rock comes at a time when the health of the U.K. housing is not great.

24475 ■ "Muddy Portfolio Raises a Question: Just What Is National City Worth?" in Crain's Detroit Business (Vol. 24, April 7, 2008, No. 14)

Pub: Crain Communications, Inc.

Ed: Jay Miller. **Description:** National City Bank is looking at strategies to help it deal with its credit and loan problems which are reflected in its falling stock price. One possible solution is a merger with another bank, however most national banks are facing their own home-loan portfolio issues and may be unable to tackle another company's unresolved problems. Statistical data included.

24476 ■ "Museum Center to Exhibit New Look" in Business Courier (Vol. 24, February 22, 2008, No. 46, pp. 1)

Pub American City Business Journals, Inc.

Ed: Dan Monk. **Description:** Discusses a $120 million renovation is being planned for the Cincinnati Museum Center complex at Union Terminal. The project aims to build a 14-acre park and office spaces in the area. Details of the Museum Center's renovation plans are given.

24477 ■ "NBC" in Brandweek (Vol. 49, April 21, 2008, No. 16, pp. SR6)
Pub: VNU Business Media, Inc.
Ed: John Consoli. Description: Provides contact information for sales and marketing personnel for the NBC network as well as a listing of the station's top programming and an analysis of the current season and the target audience for those programs running in the current season. NBC also devised a new strategy of announcing its prime-time schedule 52 weeks in advance which was a hit for advertisers who felt this gave them a better opportunity to plan for product placement. Even with the station's creative sales programs, they could face a challenge from Fox in terms of upfront advertisement purchases.

24478 ■ "Needed: A Strategy; Banking In China" in The Economist (Vol. 390, January 3, 2009, No. 8612, pp. 54)
Pub: The Economist Newspaper Inc.
Description: International banks are competing for a role in China but are finding obstacles in their paths such as a reduction in the credit their operations may receive from Chinese banks and the role they can play in the public capital markets which remain limited.

24479 ■ "Net Connections" in Black Enterprise (Vol. 38, July 2008, No. 12, pp. 28)
Pub: Earl G. Graves Publishing Co. Inc.
Ed: Anthony S. Calypso. Description: Marketers are making strategic partnerships with online social networks in an attempt to gain further market reach. The value of these networks appears to be on the rise forcing media companies to recalculate their strategies for delivering products to customers.

24480 ■ Never Bet the Farm: How Entrepreneurs Take Risks, Make Decisions and How You Can, Too
Pub: Jossey Bass
Ed: Anthony Iaquinto; Stephen Spinelli Jr. Released: March 17, 2006. Price: $19.95. Description: Two successful entrepreneurs offer advice for others launching new businesses. The authors show that preparing for setbacks and using a framework to reduce risks and simplify decision making can increase chances for success.

24481 ■ "The New Arsenal of Risk Management" in Harvard Business Review (Vol. 86, September 2008, No. 9, pp. 92)
Pub: Harvard Business School Press
Ed: Kevin Bueler; Andrew Freeman; Ron Hulme. Description: Goldman Sachs Group Inc. is used to illustrate methods for successful risk management. The investment bank's business principles, partnerships, and oversight practices are discussed.

24482 ■ "A New Perspective On the Development Model for Family Business" in Family Business Review (Vol. 19, December 2006, No. 4, pp. 317)
Pub: Family Firm Institute
Contact: Judy L. Green, President
Ed: Matthew W. Rutherford, Lori A. Muse, Sharon L. Oswald. Description: Empirical test model of the developmental model for family business is proposed and owner, firm and family characteristics which have an impact on the development model are examined.

24483 ■ "A New Will to Win" in Harvard Business Review (Vol. 88, September 2010, No. 9, pp. 110)
Pub: Harvard Business School Publishing
Ed: Daniel McGinn. Description: Importance of succession and contingency planning are emphasized in this account of Rick Hendrick's response to business loss coupled with personal tragedy. Focus and determination in leadership are also discussed.

24484 ■ "New Year, New Estate Plan" in Hawaii Business (Vol. 53, February 2008, No. 8, pp. 54)
Pub: Hawaii Business Publishing
Ed: Antony M. Orme. Description: Discusses the start of the new year which can be a time to revise wills and estate plans as failure to do so may create

problems of unequal inheritance and increase in estate tax exemption, which could disinherit beneficiaries. Other circumstances that can prompt changes in wills and estate plans are presented.

24485 ■ "Nexen, OPTI Boost Oil Sands Spending" in Globe & Mail (February 18, 2006, pp. B5)
Pub: CTVglobemedia Publishing Inc.
Ed: Dave Ebner. Description: The reasons behind the decision of Nexen Inc. and OPTI Canada Inc., to allocate 10 percent more funding on oil sands, are presented.

24486 ■ "Nike's Next Splash" in The Business Journal-Portland (Vol. 25, August 22, 2008, No. 24, pp. 1)
Pub: American City Business Journals, Inc.
Ed: Erik Siemers. Description: Business analysts expect Nike to bid for the endorsement services of swimmer Michael Phelps after the swimmer's contract with Speedo expires. The company, however, is a lightweight in the swimming apparel market and is not focusing on swimming as a growth sector.

24487 ■ "No Frills - And No Dodge" in Crain's Detroit Business (Vol. 24, September 22, 2008, No. 38, pp. 3)
Pub: Crain Communications Inc.
Ed: Bradford Wernie. Description: Chrysler LLC is in the middle of a business plan known as Project Genesis, a five-year strategy in which the company will reduce the dealer count by combining its Jeep, Chrysler and Dodge brands under one rooftop wherever possible. Not every dealer will be able to arrange this deal because of the investment required to expand stores in which have low-overhead; many of these stores feel that low-overhead structures are more likely to survive difficult times than the larger stores in which the Genesis consolidation plan intends to implement.

24488 ■ "No Risk? No Reward" in Canadian Business (Vol. 79, September 11, 2006, No. 18, pp. 65)
Pub: Rogers Media
Ed: Dennis Seguin. Description: Box office performances of the Canadian films are presented. Strategies to revitalize the film businesses in Canada are suggested.

24489 ■ "Nobody Knows What To Do" in Barron's (Vol. 88, March 17, 2008, No. 11, pp. 40)
Pub: Dow Jones & Company, Inc.
Ed: Mark Veverka. Description: Attendees of the South by Southwest Interactive conference failed to get an insight on how to make money on the Web from former Walt Disney CEO Michael Eisner when Eisner said there's no proven business model for financing projects. Eisner said he finances his projects with the help of his connections to get product-placement deals.

24490 ■ "Nortel Starting From Scratch" in Globe & Mail (February 24, 2006, pp. B3)
Pub: CTVglobemedia Publishing Inc.
Ed: Catherine McLean. Description: The restructuring efforts of chief executive officer Mike Zafirovski of Nortel Networks Corp. are presented.

24491 ■ "Not the Six O'Clock News" in Canadian Business (Vol. 80, January 15, 2007, No. 2, pp. 10)
Pub: Rogers Media
Ed: Marlene Rego. Description: The proposal by Paul Jay, the chief executive officer of Independent World Television, to launch The Real News Project, is discussed. The objective of the project is to establish an independent news and current affairs network solely through viewers.

24492 ■ "Nursing Home Group Put on the Block" in Globe & Mail (February 23, 2006, pp. B1)
Pub: CTVglobemedia Publishing Inc.
Ed: Elizabeth Church. Description: The reasons behind the decision of Exetendicare Inc. to go for sale are presented.

24493 ■ "N.Y. Investors Reject AnorMed Board Proposal" in Globe & Mail (February 21, 2006, pp. B11)
Pub: CTVglobemedia Publishing Inc.
Ed: Leonard Zehr. Description: The reasons behind the denial of investors over the restructuring plans of AnorMed are presented.

24494 ■ "Ohio Commerce Draws Closer to Profitability" in Crain's Cleveland Business (Vol. 28, October 29, 2007, No. 43, pp. 14)
Pub: Crain Communications, Inc.
Ed: Shawn A. Turner. Description: Overview of the business plan of Ohio Commerce Bank, a de novo, or startup bank that is close to turning the corner to profitability. The bank opened in November 2006 and focuses on dealing with small businesses totaling $5 million or less in annual revenues.

24495 ■ "Olympus is Urged to Revise Board" in Wall Street Journal Eastern Edition (November 28, 2011, pp. B3)
Pub: Dow Jones & Company Inc. Enterprise Media Group
Contact: Clare Hart, President
Ed: Phred Dvorak. Description: Koji Miyata, once a director on the board of troubled Japanese photographic equipment company, is urging the company to reorganize its board, saying the present group should resign their board seats but keep their management positions. The company has come under scrutiny for its accounting practices and costly acquisitions.

24496 ■ "OMERS Joins Bid for U.K. Port Giant" in Globe & Mail (March 28, 2006, pp. B1)
Pub: CTVglobemedia Publishing Inc.
Ed: Paul Waldie. Description: The plans of Ontario Municipal Employees Retirement Board to partner with Goldman Sachs Group Inc., in order to acquire Associated British Ports PLC, are presented.

24497 ■ "On a Mission: Ginch Gonch Wants You to Get Rid of Your Tighty Whities" in Canadian Business (Vol. 81, September 29, 2008, No. 16)
Pub: Rogers Media Ltd.
Ed: Michelle Magnan. Description: New Equity Capital acquired underwear maker Ginch Gonch in July 2008; founder Jason Sutherland kept his position as creative director of the company and will retain his title as 'director of stitches and inches'. The company is known for its products, which are reminiscent of the days when people wore underwear covered in cowboys and stars as kids. The company also claims that Nelly, Justin Timberlake, and Hilary Duff have worn their products.

24498 ■ "On a Roll" in Canadian Business (Vol. 79, Winter 2006, No. 24, pp. 49)
Pub: Rogers Media
Ed: Thomas Watson. Description: The efforts of the Canadian automobile spare parts manufacturer, Magna International Inc., to expand into the the Russian market, are described.

24499 ■ "On a Roll" in Canadian Business (Vol. 79, October 9, 2006, No. 20, pp. 51)
Pub: Rogers Media
Ed: Joe Castaldo. Description: Corporate management strategies of Denis Turcotte, chief executive officer of Algoma Steel Inc., are presented.

24500 ■ "One Paddle, Two Paddle" in Hawaii Business (Vol. 53, October 2007, No. 4, pp. 65)
Pub: Hawaii Business Publishing
Ed: Kyle Galdeira. Description: Oiwi Ocean Gear's strategy may not give instant profits, but it works well for the company's goal of providing high-quality apparel for paddlers. The apparel company produces and markets swimwear, paddling jerseys and active wear. The company's strategy is compared with the selling of mass-produced clothes lower prices.

24501 ▪ *"Open Skies: Opportunity, Challenge for Airlines"* in *Crain's Chicago Business (April 21, 2008)*
Pub: Crain Communications, Inc.
Ed: Paul Merrion. Description: Discusses the new aviation agreement between Europe and the United States known as Open Skies; the pact creates opportunities for U.S. carriers to fly to new destinations in Europe from more U.S. cities; it also allows carriers to fly between European cities, something they have not been able to do until now.

24502 ▪ *"O'Reilly Will Soup Up KC Warehouse"* in *The Business Journal-Serving Metropolitan Kansas City (Vol. 26, August 15, 2008, No. 49)*
Pub: American City Business Journals, Inc.
Ed: Rob Roberts. Description: O'Reilly Automotive Inc. plans to construct a 215,000-square foot warehouse in Kansas City. The move is expected to triple the size of the company's distribution center. Other views and information on the planned warehouse construction, are presented.

24503 ▪ *"Organization Redesign and Innovative HRM"* in *Human Resource Management (Vol. 49, July-August 2010, No. 4, pp. 809-811)*
Pub: John Wiley
Ed: Pat Lynch. Description: An overview of the book, 'Organization Redesign and Innovative HRM' is presented.

24504 ▪ *"Organizing for Disaster: Lessons from the Military"* in *Business Horizons (November-December 2007, pp. 479)*
Pub: Elsevier Technology Publications
Ed: Michael R. Weeks. Description: Design of resilient and robust organizational structures for disaster management is discussed. These structures must be planned before disasters in order to be more effective and efficient.

24505 ▪ *"The Outcome of an Organization Overhaul"* in *Black Enterprise (Vol. 41, December 2010, No. 5)*
Pub: Earl G. Graves Publishing Co. Inc.
Ed: Tamara E. Holmes. Description: Savvy business owners understand the need for change in order to stay competitive and be successful. This article examines how to manage change as well as what strategies can help employees to get with the program faster.

24506 ▪ *"Paramount Said to be Working on Sale of Oil Sands Assets"* in *Globe & Mail (April 24, 2007, pp. B1)*
Pub: CTVglobemedia Publishing Inc.
Ed: Norval Scott. Description: The proposed sale of oil sands in Surmont and the shares of North American Oil Sands Corp. by Paramount Resources Ltd. is discussed.

24507 ▪ *"Patricia Hemingway Hall; President, Chief Operating Officer, Health Care Service Corp."* in *Crain's Chicago Business (May 5, 2008)*
Pub: Crain Communications, Inc.
Ed: Mike Colias. Description: Profile of Patricia Hemingway Hall who is the president and chief operating officer of Health Care Service Corp., a new strategy launched by Blue Cross & Blue Shield of Illinois; the new endeavor will emphasize wellness rather than just treatment across its four health plans.

24508 ▪ *"Pavilions Poised for Image Overhaul"* in *The Business Journal - Serving Phoenix and the Valley of the Sun (Vol. 28, August 22, 2008)*
Pub: American City Business Journals, Inc.
Ed: Jan Buchholz. Description: DeRitto Partners Inc. is expected to push through with plans for a major renovation of the 1.1 million-square foot Scottsdale Pavilions in Scottsdale, Arizona. An aggressive marketing campaign is planned to be included in the renovation, which aims to address high vacancy rates and competition. Views and information on the planned renovation are presented.

24509 ▪ *"PDX Bucks National Trend"* in *The Business Journal-Portland (Vol. 25, August 1, 2008, No. 21, pp. 1)*
Pub: American City Business Journals, Inc.
Ed: Erik Siemers. Description: Portland International Airport could face problems as air carriers are planning to reduce capacity at the airport. The airport is showing signs of growth despite the slowdown in the airline industry. Other airlines that are planning to reduce seating capacity at the airport are also presented.

24510 ▪ *"People; E-Commerce, Online Games, Mobile Apps"* in *Advertising Age (Vol. 80, October 19, 2009, No. 35, pp. 14)*
Pub: Crain's Communications
Ed: Nat Ives. Description: Profile of People Magazine and the ways in which the publisher is moving its magazine forward by exploring new concepts in a time of declining newsstand sales and advertising pages; among the strategies are e-commerce such as the brand People Style Watch in which consumers are able highlight clothing and jewelry and then connect to retailers' sites and a channel on Taxi TV, the network of video-touch screens in New Your City taxis.

24511 ▪ *"People; E-Commerce, Online Games, Mobile Apps: This Isn't Your Mom's People"* in *Advertising Age (Vol. 80, October 19, 2009, No. 35)*
Pub: Crain's Communications
Ed: Nat Ives. Description: Profile of People Magazine and the ways in which the publisher is moving its magazine forward by exploring new concepts in a time of declining newsstand sales and advertising pages; among the strategies are e-commerce such as the brand People Style Watch in which consumers are able highlight clothing and jewelry and then connect to retailers' sites and a channel on Taxi TV, the network of video-touch screens in New Your City taxis.

24512 ▪ *"Perfecting the Process: Creating a Move Efficient Organization On Your Terms"* in *Black Enterprise (Vol. 41, October 2010, No. 3)*
Pub: Earl G. Graves Publishing Co. Inc.
Ed: Tamara E. Holmes. Description: More than ever, entrepreneurs need to identify new ways of doing business in a cost-effective manner in order to expand their companies while remaining true to their customer demands.

24513 ▪ *"Peter Gilgan"* in *Canadian Business (Vol. 82, April 27, 2009, No. 7, pp. 58)*
Pub: Rogers Media
Ed: Calvin Leung. Description: Mattamy Homes Ltd. president and chief executive officer Peter Gilgan believes that their business model of building communities in an organized way brings advantages to the firm and for their customers. He also believes in adopting their product prices to new market realities. Gilgan considers the approvals regime in Ontario his biggest challenge in the last 20 years.

24514 ▪ *"Pinellas Leaders Want First Leg of Light Rail"* in *The Business Journal-Serving Greater Tampa Bay (Vol. 28, August 8, 2008, No. 33)*
Pub: American City Business Journals, Inc.
Ed: Larry Halstead. Description: Proposed routes for the first leg of the planned light railway system in the Tampa Bay, Florida area are being presented as the Tampa Bay Area Regional Transportation Authority is about to make its master plan for the project. A sales tax for transit is being proposed to fund the project, as well as an expansion of the accompanying bus system.

24515 ▪ *Planet Google: One Company's Audacious Plan to Organize Everything We Know*
Pub: Free Press
Ed: Randall Stross. Released: 2009. Price: $26.00. Description: The book examines Google, the leader in Internet search engines.

24516 ▪ *"The Play's the Thing"* in *Business Strategy Review (Vol. 21, Summer 2010, No. 2, pp. 58)*
Pub: Blackwell Publishers Ltd.
Ed: Michael G. Jacobides. Description: Those who study and plan strategies risk falling into the traps that maps, graphs, charts and matrices present. A better strategy might be using a playscript that can reveal the unfolding plots of business far better than traditional strategic tools as the landscapes shifts.

24517 ▪ *"The Play's the Thing"* in *Business Strategy Review (Vol. 21, Summer 2010, No. 2, pp. 58)*
Pub: Wiley-Blackwell
Ed: Michael G. Jacobides. Description: Those who study and plan strategies risk falling into the traps that maps, graphs, charts and matrices present. The author feels that strategy might best be cast as a dramatic playscript that can reveal the unfolding plots of business far better than traditional strategic tools, as the landscape shifts around us.

24518 ▪ *"Portfolio Recovery Associates Expands Its Hampton Call Center"* in *Internet Wire (January 20, 2010)*
Pub: Comtex News Network, Inc.
Description: Entering into a lease amendment in order to expand its Hampton, Virginia call center and extend its lease agreement, Portfolio Recovery Associates, Inc., a company that collects, purchases and manages defaulted consumer debt, plans to upgrade the existing space enabling them to draw on local talent.

24519 ▪ *The Power of Pull: How Small Moves, Smartly Made, Can Set Big Things in Motion*
Pub: Basic Books
Ed: John Hagel III, Seely Brown, Lang Divison. Released: April 13, 2010. Description: Examination of how we can effectively address the most pressing challenges in a rapidly changing and increasingly interdependent world is addressed. New ways in which passionate thinking, creative solutions, and committed action can and will make it possible for small businesses owners to seize opportunities and remain in step with change.

24520 ▪ *Prepare to Be a Teen Millionaire*
Pub: Health Communications, Inc.
Contact: Peter Vegso, President
Ed: Robyn Collins; Kimberly Spinks Burleson. Released: April 1, 2008. Price: $16.95. Description: Business reference for any teenager wishing to become a successful entrepreneur; advice is given from successful teenage millionaires. Topics covered include: choosing a business name, type, and location; use of the Internet; legal issues; branding, sales, and marketing; funding and financial management; return on investment; retirement; development of a sound business plan; and certification for minority or women-owned companies.

24521 ▪ *"Profico Takes Itself Off the Market"* in *Globe & Mail (March 14, 2006, pp. B1)*
Pub: CTVglobemedia Publishing Inc.
Ed: Deborah Yedlin; Dave Ebner. Description: Profico Energy Management Ltd., Canada's largest junior energy explorer, has backed off its potential acquisition plans. The decreased prices of the natural gas are the main reasons that caused Profico to back off from the acquisition plan.

24522 ▪ *"Purdue Agronomist: Consider Costs Before Tilling"* in *Farm Industry News (November 8, 2011)*
Pub: Penton Business Media Inc.
Ed: Lisa Schluttenhofer. Description: Farmers consider soil drainage, fertilizer and planting needs as well as economic thresholds before making tillage decisions, according to a Purdue extension agronomist

24523 ▪ *"Q&A: Joseph Ribkoff"* in *Canadian Business (Vol. 81, March 31, 2008, No. 5, pp. 4)*
Pub: Rogers Media
Ed: Zena Olijnyk. Description: Joseph Ribkoff started his career in the garment trade by sweeping floors and running deliveries for a dress manufacturer

called Town & Country and earned $16 a week. Ribkoff says that the key to controlling costs in Canada is to invest in the latest equipment and technology to stay competitive.

24524 ■ "Quarreling Parties Keep Schenectady Redevelopment Plan In Limbo" in The Business Review Albany (Vol. 35, April 4, 2008, No. 53)
Pub: The Business Review

Ed: Michael DeMasi. **Description:** First National Bank of Scotia chairman Louis H. Buhrmaster opposes the Erie Boulevard design project. as it could negatively affect access to the bank. Buhrmaster, aslo a vice president for Schenectady Industrial Corp, prohibits environmental assessment at the former American Locomotive property. The issues affecting the progress of the planned redevelopment at Schenectady are analyzed.

24525 ■ "Ready for the Worst? How to Disaster-Proof Your Business" in Inc. (Vol. 33, September 2011, No. 7, pp. 38)
Pub: Inc. Magazine

Ed: J.J. McCorvey, Dave Smith. **Description:** Twelve products to and services designed to help small businesses run smoothly in the event of a disaster are outlined.

24526 ■ "Realities May Blur Vision" in The Business Journal-Serving Metropolitan Kansas City (Vol. 27, September 19, 2008, No. 1, pp. 1)
Pub: American City Business Journals, Inc.

Ed: Rob Roberts. **Description:** Vision Metcalf is a study by Kansas City that depicts how Metcalf Avenue could look like if redeveloped. Redevelopment plans for the Metcalf corridor include a 20-story mixed-use building on a vacant car dealership. The challenges that the redevelopment plans will face are also analyzed.

24527 ■ "The Rebranding Game: If at First You Pick the Wrong Name, You Can Always Try, Try Again" in Inc. (Vol. 30, December 2008, No. 12)
Pub: Mansueto Ventures LLC

Ed: Ryan McCarthy. **Description:** Many entrepreneurs discover their firm's name can be too limiting or outdated. The process for rebranding a company is outlined.

24528 ■ "Recession-Proof Your Startup" in Crain's Chicago Business (Vol. 31, November 10, 2008, No. 45, pp. 24)
Pub: Crain Communications, Inc.

Description: Detailed information concerning ways in which to start a business during an economic crisis is provided. Ways in which to find financing, the importance of a solid business plan, customer service, problem-solving and finding the right niche for the region are also discussed.

24529 ■ "Recession Survival Tip: Less Is More" in Women Entrepreneur (December 31, 2008)
Pub: Entrepreneur Media Inc.

Ed: Suzy Girard-Ruttenberg. **Description:** These trying economic times can be an opportunity to make bold changes in one's business that may yield lasting results, not just short-term survival; simplification, accountability and shoring up one's margins are things to look at when determining the goals of the company.

24530 ■ "Red Tape Ties Detroit Housing Rehab Plan" in Crain's Detroit Business (Vol. 24, September 22, 2008, No. 38, pp. 1)
Pub: Crain Communications Inc.

Ed: Ryan Beene. **Description:** Venture-capital firm Wilherst Oxford LLC is a Florida-based company that has purchased 300 inner-city homes which were in foreclosure in Detroit. Wilherst Oxford is asking the city to forgive the existing tax and utility liens so the firm can utilize the money for home improvements. The city, however, is reluctant but has stated that they are willing to negotiate.

24531 ■ "Refreshing" in Canadian Business (Vol. 79, September 11, 2006, No. 18, pp. 22)
Pub: Rogers Media

Ed: Joe Castaldo. **Description:** Turnaround strategies and initiatives adopted by Canadian Beverage Corp. to boost its declining sales are presented.

24532 ■ "The Relationship Between Boards and Planning In Family Businesses" in Family Business Review (Vol. 19, March 2006, No. 1, pp. 65)
Pub: Family Firm Institute
Contact: Judy L. Green, President

Ed: Timothy Blumentritt. **Description:** Study determining the extent of control exercised by board of directors and advisory boards on business planning within family-owned businesses is covered.

24533 ■ "Renewed Vision" in Hawaii Business (Vol. 54, August 2008, No. 2, pp. 49)
Pub: Hawaii Business Publishing

Ed: Jason Ubay. **Description:** Saint Francis Healthcare System of Hawaii, ranked 81 in Hawaii's top 250 companies for 2008, has been rebranding to focus on senior community healthcare and sold some of its operations, which explains the decline in gross sales from $219.5M in 2006 to $122.7M in 2007. The system's senior services and home hospice service expansion are provided.

24534 ■ "Retail: Loblaw Goes for Broke" in Canadian Business (Vol. 80, January 29, 2007, No. 3, pp. 7)
Pub: Rogers Media

Ed: Zena Oiljnyk. **Description:** The efforts of Loblaw Companies Limited to reduce its operational expenses are described. The company's decision to reduce the number of employees at its national and regional offices, besides closing some of its facilities, is discussed.

24535 ■ "Retiring Baby Boomers and Dissatisfied Gen-Xers Cause..Brain Drain" in Agency Sales Magazine (Vol. 39, November 2009, No. 10)
Pub: MANA

Ed: Denise Kelly. **Description:** Due to the impending retirement of the baby boomers a critical loss of knowledge and experience in businesses will result. Creating a plan to address this loss of talent centered on the development of the younger generation is discussed.

24536 ■ "Return to Wealth; Bank Strategy" in The Economist (Vol. 390, January 3, 2009, No. 8612, pp. 56)
Pub: The Economist Newspaper Inc.

Description: UBS' strategy to survive these trying economic times is presented. Statistical data included. UBS has a stronger balance-sheet than most of its investment-banking peers and has reduced its portfolio.

24537 ■ Rework
Pub: Crown Business

Ed: Jason Fried, David Heinemeier Hansson. **Released:** March 9, 2010. **Price:** $22.00. **Description:** Works to help entrepreneurs and business owners to rethink strategy, customers, and getting things accomplished.

24538 ■ "The Road Map for Scotiabank's Asian Expansion" in Globe & Mail (April 7, 2007, pp. B3)
Pub: CTVglobemedia Publishing Inc.

Ed: Tara Perkins. **Description:** Executive vice-president of Bank of Nova Scotia, Rob Pitfield shares his plan to expand the bank's Asian market.

24539 ■ "Roadside Attraction" in Hawaii Business (Vol. 53, January 2008, No. 7, pp. 39)
Pub: Hawaii Business Publishing

Ed: Jason Ubay. **Description:** Businesses beside the Kamehameha Highway find ways to survive in a rural community. Sunshine Arts Hawaii, for instance,

uses a bright-colored and huge mural to attract tourists who drive along the highway. Other techniques employed by businesses in the aforementioned are des cribed.

24540 ■ "Rock Hall Shifts Advertising to 'Significant Markets' in Region" in Crain's Cleveland Business (Vol. 28, July 23, 2007, No. 29, pp. 6)
Pub: Crain Communications, Inc.

Ed: John Booth. **Description:** Cleveland's Rock and Roll Hall of Fame and Museum is attempting a different marketing strategy this year with aims of reaching a broader audience in the Midwest and Great Lakes regions.

24541 ■ "'Rocket Docket' Leaves Memphis Debtors Behind" in Commercial Appeal (November 28, 2009)
Pub: Commercial Appeal

Ed: Bartholomew Sullivan. **Description:** According to an investigation by the Scripps Howard News Service, Memphians lodged 807 formal complaints about debt-collection practices to the Federal Trade Commission in a 2 1/2 -year period ending in July; Nearly 1/3 of the complaints involved some type of error with the debt in question. The majority of the complaints were leveled at NCO Group, which also generated the most complaints around the country.

24542 ■ "Roseville Ob-Gyn Group Grows With Patient Focus, Diverse Services" in Crain's Detroit Business (Vol. 24, April 7, 2008, No. 14)
Pub: Crain Communications, Inc.

Ed: Christine Snyder. **Description:** According to the American Medical Association, the number of medical groups of 10 or more physicians has been growing. Eastside Gynecology Obstetrics is one such group which has seen its yearly revenue grow due to a good business plan and a diversity of services and doctors.

24543 ■ "Rule of Thumb" in Entrepreneur (Vol. 36, May 2008, No. 5, pp. 44)
Pub: Entrepreneur Media, Inc.

Ed: Guy Kawasaki. **Description:** Business presentations using PowerPoint are recommended to have no more than 10 slides, last no longer than 20 minutes and have font no smaller than 30 points. Topics covered should include problem, solution, business model, underlying technology, and projections among others.

24544 ■ "St. Rose Professor Builds Contractors and Micro-Doctors" in Business Review, Albany New York (Vol. 34, December 28, 2007, No. 39)
Pub: American City Business Journals, Inc.

Ed: Robin K. Cooper. **Description:** Mike Mathews is an associate professor at the College of Saint Rose School of Business and one of the founders of the Center for Micro Enterprises Development, which provides training programs on business planning and management. Details of the business school's curricula and foundations are discussed.

24545 ■ "Sandi Jackson; Alderman, 7th Ward, City of Chicago" in Crain's Chicago Business (Vol. 31, May 5, 2008, No. 18, pp. 31)
Pub: Crain Communications, Inc.

Ed: Sarah A. Klein. **Description:** Profile of Sandi Jackson who is an alderman of the 7th ward of the city of Chicago and is addressing issues such as poverty and crime as well as counting on a plan to develop the former USX Corp. steel mill to revitalize the area's economic climate.

24546 ■ "Satellite Down, Stock Up: Raytheon Is On Target With Ten Percent Dividend Increase" in Barron's (Vol. 88, March 31, 2008, No. 13)
Pub: Dow Jones & Company, Inc.

Ed: Shirley A. Lazo. **Description:** Raytheon hiked their quarterly dividend to 28 cents per share from 25.5 cents. Aircastle slashed their quarterly common dividend by 64 percent for them to retain additional capital that can be used to increase their liquidity position.

24547 ■ *Save Your Small Business: 10 Crucial Strategies to Survive Hard Times or Close Down and Move On*
Pub: NOLO
Contact: Ralph Warner, Chief Executive Officer
Ed: Ralph Warner, Bethany Laurence. **Released:** August 1, 2009. **Price:** $29.99. **Description:** According to a study among 500 businesses, 44 percent used credit cards in order to meet their firm's needs in the previous six months. Written by a business owner, this book provides twelve strategies to protect personal assets from creditors and survive the current recession.

24548 ■ *"Savvas Chamberlain" in Canadian Business (Vol. 81, March 17, 2008, No. 4, pp. 92)*
Pub: Rogers Media
Ed: Andrew Wahl. **Description:** Savvas Chamberlain says he feels cheated during his teenage years because life was not normal for him growing up in Cyprus with all the uprisings against Britain. Chamberlain says he runs Dalsa like he plays chess because all his positions are shown all the time but he keeps his strategy to himself.

24549 ■ *"Scanning Dell's Shopping List" in Barron's (Vol. 89, July 13, 2009, No. 28, pp. 24)*
Pub: Dow Jones & Co., Inc.
Ed: Mark Veverka. **Description:** It is believed that Dell will be looking for companies to acquire since they poached an experienced mergers-and-acquisitions executive. In addition Dell's CEO is reportedly telling people he plans to go shopping. Dell executives have also stated an interest in data storage.

24550 ■ *"Scotiabank Targets More Baby Boomers" in Globe & Mail (March 4, 2006, pp. B5)*
Pub: CTVglobemedia Publishing Inc.
Ed: Elizabeth Church. **Description:** Bank of Nova Scotia posted $844 million profit for first quarter 2006. The plans of the bank to achieve baby boomer client base are presented.

24551 ■ *"The Search for Big Oil" in Canadian Business (Vol. 80, April 9, 2007, No. 8, pp. 10)*
Pub: Rogers Media
Ed: Joe Castaldo. **Description:** The continuing effort of Canmex Minerals Corp. to explore for oil in Somalia despite the failure of several other companies is discussed.

24552 ■ *"The Seat-Of-The-Pants School of Marketing" in Brandweek (Vol. 49, April 21, 2008, No. 16, pp. 24)*
Pub: VNU Business Media, Inc.
Ed: David Vinjamuri. **Description:** Excerpt from the book 'Accidental Branding: How Ordinary People Build Extraordinary Brands,' by David Vinjamuri, discusses six shared principles for creating a brand that is unique and will be successful over the long-term.

24553 ■ *"A Security Risk?" in Canadian Business (Vol. 80, October 22, 2007, No. 21, pp. 36)*
Pub: Rogers Media
Ed: Joe Castaldo. **Description:** Garda World Security Corporation declared a C$1.5 million loss in the second quarter of 2007. The company's securities have been falling since June and hit a 52-week low of $15.90 in September. Details of the physical and cash-handling firm's strategy to integrate its acquisitions are discussed.

24554 ■ *"Shell Venture Aims at 'Oil Rocks'" in Globe & Mail (March 22, 2006, pp. B1)*
Pub: CTVglobemedia Publishing Inc.
Ed: Patrick Brethour. **Description:** Royal Dutch Shell PLC is all set to launch its Alberta's operations in bitumen deposits trapped in limestone. Details of the new venture are analyzed.

24555 ■ *"Shermag Plans Two Shutdowns, 300 More Layoffs" in Globe & Mail (February 13, 2007, pp. B5)*
Pub: CTVglobemedia Publishing Inc.
Ed: Bertrand Marotte. **Description:** Shermag Inc., Canada's largest publicly traded furniture company, is permanently closing two plants and eliminating 300 jobs. The mounting losses and deteriorating stock prices are stated as main reasons for plant shutdowns.

24556 ■ *"Shermag Says Refinishing Not Complete" in Globe & Mail (February 14, 2006, pp. B3)*
Pub: CTVglobemedia Publishing Inc.
Ed: Bertrand Marotte. **Description:** The details on restructuring efforts of Shermag Inc. are presented.

24557 ■ *"Shorts Story" in Barron's (Vol. 89, July 6, 2009, No. 27, pp. 16)*
Pub: Dow Jones & Co., Inc.
Ed: Gene Epstein. **Description:** Shares of Compass Minerals, J2 Global Communications, K12, Middleby, and Pactiv should be shorted by investors. These companies suffer from weaknesses in their business models, making them vulnerable to a share price decline.

24558 ■ *"Shorts Story" in Barron's (Vol. 89, July 6, 2009, No. 27, pp. 16)*
Pub: Dow Jones & Co., Inc.
Ed: Gene Epstein. **Description:** Shares of Compass Minerals, J2 Global Communications, K12, Middleby, and Pactiv should be shorted by investors. These companies suffer from weaknesses in their business models, making them vulnerable to a share price decline.

24559 ■ *"Should You Go Into Business With Your Spouse?" in Women Entrepreneur (September 1, 2008)*
Pub: Entrepreneur Media Inc.
Ed: Tamara Monosoff. **Description:** Things to consider before starting a business with one's spouse are discussed. Compatible work ethics, clear expectations of one another, long-term goals for the company and the status of the relationship are among the things to consider before starting a business endeavor with a spouse.

24560 ■ *"Sixty-Acre Vision for North Suburbs" in Business Courier (Vol. 24, April 4, 2008, No. 52, pp. 1)*
Pub: American City Business Journals, Inc.
Ed: Laura Baverman. **Description:** Al Neyer Inc. plans for a mixed-use development at the 60-acre site it has recently purchased. The mixed-use project could cost up to $100 million, and will include medical offices, residential buildings, and corporate offices. Details of Al Neyer's plans for the site are given.

24561 ■ *"Skinner's No Drive-Thru CEO" in Crain's Chicago Business (Vol. 31, April 28, 2008, No. 17, pp. 1)*
Pub: Crain Communications, Inc.
Ed: David Sterrett. **Description:** Profile of James Skinner who was named CEO for McDonald's Corp. in November 2004 and has proved to be a successful leader despite the number of investors who doubted him when he came to the position. Mr. Skinner has overseen three years of unprecedented sales growth and launched the biggest menu expansion in 30 years.

24562 ■ *"Sleeman Cuts Again as Cheap Suds Bite" in Globe & Mail (March 3, 2006, pp. B3)*
Pub: CTVglobemedia Publishing Inc.
Ed: Andy Hoffman. **Description:** The details on 5 percent employee reduction at Sleeman Breweries Ltd., which posted 86 percent decline in profits for fourth quarter 2005, are presented.

24563 ■ *"Slimmed-Down Supplier TI Automotive Relaunches" in Crain's Detroit Business (Vol. 26, January 11, 2010, No. 2, pp. 14)*
Pub: Crain Communications Inc.
Ed: Robert Sherefkin. **Description:** TI Automotive Ltd., one of the world's largest suppliers of fuel storage and delivery systems, has reorganized the

company by splitting it into five global divisions and is relaunching its brand which is now more focused on new technology.

24564 ■ *Small Business: An Entrepreneur's Business Plan*
Pub: South-Western
Ed: J.D Ryan, Gail P. Hiduke. **Released:** October 2008. **Price:** $119.95. **Description:** Assistance in preparing a business plan that identifies opportunities and ways to target a customer market.

24565 ■ *Small Business Desk Reference*
Pub: Penguin Books USA Inc.
Ed: Gene Marks. **Released:** December 2004. **Description:** Comprehensive guide for starting or running a successful small business, focusing on buying a business or franchise, writing a business plan, financial management, accounting, legal issues, human resources management, operations, marketing, sales, customer service, taxes, insurance, and ethics. Information for launching a restaurant, property management firm, retail outlet, consulting firm, and service business is included.

24566 ■ *Small Business Management*
Pub: John Wiley and Sons Inc.
Ed: Margaret Burlingame; Don Gulbrandsen; Richard M. Hodgetts; Donald F. Kuratko. **Released:** March 2007. **Price:** $44.95. **Description:** Tips for starting and running a successful small business are given, including advice on writing a business plan, financing, and the law.

24567 ■ *"Small is the New Big in Autos" in Globe & Mail (February 16, 2006, pp. B3)*
Pub: CTVglobemedia Publishing Inc.
Ed: Greg Keenan. **Description:** The reasons behind the introduction of subcompact cars by companies such as Ford Motor Co. are presented. The automobiles were unveiled at Canadian International Auto Show in Toronto.

24568 ■ *"So You Want to Start a Business?" in Women Entrepreneur (August 5, 2008)*
Pub: Entrepreneur Media Inc.
Ed: Cynthia McKay. **Description:** Advice for taking an idea and turning it into a legitimate business is given.

24569 ■ *"A Socko Payout Menu: Rural Phone Carrier Plots to Supercharge Its Shares" in Barron's (Vol. 88, June 30, 2008, No. 26, pp. M5)*
Pub Dow Jones & Co., Inc.
Ed: Shirley A. Lazo. **Description:** CenturyTel boosted its quarterly common payout to 70 cents from 6.75 cents per share die to its strong cash flows and solid balance sheet. Eastman Kodak's plan for a buyback will be partially funded by its $581 million tax refund. CME Group will buyback stocks through 2009 worth $1.1 billion.

24570 ■ *"Somanetics to Buy Back Up to $15 Million of Common Shares" in Crain's Detroit Business (Vol. 24, April 7, 2008, No. 14, pp. 4)*
Pub: Crain Communications, Inc.
Ed: Tom Henderson. **Description:** Somanetics Corp., a company that manufactures and markets noninvasive devices for monitoring blood oxygen levels in the brain and elsewhere in the body during surgery, plans to buy back up to $15 million worth of its common shares. Statistical data included on the company's current and past earnings and stock prices as well as its plans to increase revenue.

24571 ■ *"Sorrell Digs Deep to Snag TNS" in Advertising Age (Vol. 79, July 14, 2008, No. 7, pp. 1)*
Pub: Crain Communications, Inc.
Ed: Michael Bush. **Description:** Martin Sorrell's strategic vision for expansion in order to become the largest ad-agency holding company in the world is discussed.

24572 ■ *"Sorry: Good Defense for Mal Offense" in The Business Journal-Serving Metropolitan Kansas City (Vol. 26, July 4,*

2008, No. 43, pp. 1)
Pub: American City Business Journals, Inc.

Ed: Rob Roberts. Description: According to a survey conducted by the Kansas City Business Journal, ten hospitals in Kansas City showed that they have adopted disclosure policies that include prompt apologies and settlement offers. The policy is effective in minimizing medical malpractice lawsuits. Other details of the survey are presented.

24573 ■ *"A Sound Setup" in Black Enterprise (Vol. 38, November 2007, No. 4, pp. 100)*
Pub: Earl G. Graves Publishing Co. Inc.

Ed: Anthony Calypso. Description: Choosing the right corporate identity can ensure that a business has the right foundation on which to build and grow.

24574 ■ *"Special Sector" in Crain's Cleveland Business (Vol. 28, November 5, 2007, No. 44, pp. 3)*
Pub: Crain Communications, Inc.

Ed: David Bennett. Description: Specialty Metals Processing Inc. is investing more than $6 million to amp up productions; the company believes this big investment will pay off due to the company's ability to process complex metal alloys, such as titanium, in a region where there is a small number of competitors.

24575 ■ *"Spend Wisely on Managing Your Hedgerows" in Farmer's Weekly (March 28, 2008, No. 320)*
Pub: Reed Business Information
Contact: Jeff Greisch, President

Ed: Richard Winspear. Description: Discusses the importance of a well-managed hedge which should gradually grow upwards and outwards where eventually it would reach the point when rejuvenation by coppicing or laying was needed to restart the cycle.

24576 ■ *"Stadium Developers Seek a Win With the State" in The Business Journal-Serving Metropolitan Kansas City (Vol. 26, August 22, 2008)*
Pub: American City Business Journals, Inc.

Ed: Rob Roberts. Description: Three Trails Redevelopment LLC is hoping to win $30 million in state tax credits from the Missouri Development Finance Board for the construction of an 18,500-seat Wizards stadium. The project is contingent on state tax incentives and the company remains optimistic about their goal.

24577 ■ *"Staffing Firm Grows by Following Own Advice-Hire a Headhunter" in Crain's Detroit Business (Vol. 24, October 6, 2008, No. 40, pp. 1)*
Pub: Crain Communications, Inc.

Ed: Sherri Begin. Description: Profile of Venator Holdings L.L.C., a staffing firm that provides searches for companies in need of financial-accounting and technical employees; the firm's revenue has increased from $1.1 million in 2003 to a projected $11.5 million this year due to a climate in which more people are exiting the workforce than are coming in with those particular specialized skills and the need for a temporary, flexible workforce for contract placements at companies that do not want to take on the legacy costs associated with permanent employees. The hiring of an external headhunter to find the right out-of-state manager for Venator is also discussed.

24578 ■ *"Starbucks Drive-Throughs: Can the Cafe Keep Its Cool?" in Globe & Mail (January 6, 2006, pp. B7)*
Pub: CTVglobemedia Publishing Inc.

Ed: Steven Gray. Description: The feasibility of Starbucks Corp.'s plans to introduce drive-through cafes is discussed.

24579 ■ *"Starbucks' Wheel Strategy" in Puget Sound Business Journal (Vol. 29, October 3, 2008, No. 24, pp. 1)*
Pub: American City Business Journals

Ed: Greg Lamm. Description: Starbuck Corporation has placed drive-through windows in nearly 50 percent of its locations. Dorothy Kim, executive vice president of global strategy, revealed that the firm's

transformation strategy includes the addition of even more drive-through windows since people want the car-friendly conveniences.

24580 ■ *"Stelco Investors Told Their Stock Now Worthless" in Globe & Mail (January 23, 2006, pp. B4)*
Pub: CTVglobemedia Publishing Inc.

Ed: Greg Keenan. Description: The reasons behind Ontario Superior Court's approval of Stelco Inc.'s restructuring proposal are presented.

24581 ■ *"Stelco Seeks to Shave Its Fixed Costs" in Globe & Mail (March 8, 2007, pp. B1)*
Pub: CTVglobemedia Publishing Inc.

Ed: Greg Keenan. Description: The plans of Stelco Inc. to control its fixed costs in order to protect itself from economic downturns are discussed.

24582 ■ *"Still Unprepared For Natural Disasters" in Black Enterprise (Vol. 38, January 2008, No. 6, pp. 28)*
Pub: Earl G. Graves Publishing Co. Inc.

Ed: Alexis McCombs. Description: According to a study conducted by the American Red Cross, 19 percent of African Americans are not prepared for a natural disaster, compared to 10 percent of white Americans.

24583 ■ *"Stock Car Racing" in Canadian Business (Vol. 81, September 15, 2008, No. 14-15, pp. 29)*
Pub: Rogers Media Ltd.

Ed: Thomas Watson. Description: Some analysts predict a Chapter 11-style tune-up making GM and Ford a speculative turnaround stock. However, the price of oil could make or break the shares of the Big Three U.S. automobile manufacturers and if oil goes up too high then a speculative stock to watch is an electric car company called Zenn Motor Co.

24584 ■ *"Strategic Issue Management as Change Catalyst" in Strategy and Leadership (Vol. 39, September-October 2011, No. 5, pp. 20-29)*
Pub: Emerald Group Publishing Inc.

Ed: Bruce E. Perrott. Description: A study analyzes the case of a well-known Australian healthcare organization to examine how a company's periodic planning cycle is supplemented with a dynamic, real-time, strategic-issue-management system under high turbulence conditions. Findings highlight the eight steps that a company's management can use in its strategic issue management (SIM) process to track, monitor and manage strategic issues so as to ensure that the corporate, strategy, and capability are aligned with one another in turbulent times.

24585 ■ *Strategizing, Disequilibrium, and Profit*
Pub: Stanford University Press

Ed: John A. Mathews. Released: June 2006. Price: $24.95. Description: Author proposes the use of a conceptual framework that is consistent with real economies instead of equilibrium-based foundations when creating a business strategy.

24586 ■ *"Strategy: Hurry Up and Wait" in Business Courier (Vol. 24, February 1, 2008, No. 43, pp. 50)*
Pub: American City Business Journals, Inc.

Ed: Dan Monk. Description: It has taken years for Enerfab Inc. chairman Dave Herche to develop new product lines, form an expert management group and come up with a strategic-planning approach. However, his patience has paid off since Enerfab's revenue has grown by 93 percent since 2005. Herche's strategy for Enerfab and its impacts on the company are analyzed further.

24587 ■ *"Stung by Recession, Hemmer Regroups with New Strategy" in Business Courier (Vol. 27, June 4, 2010, No. 5, pp. 1)*
Pub: Business Courier

Ed: Lucy May. Description: Paul Hemmer Companies reduced its work force and outsourced operations such as marketing and architecture, in order for the commercial and construction firm to survive the

recession. Hammer's total core revenue in 2009 dropped to less than $30 million forcing the closure of its Chicago office.

24588 ■ *"Success Coach: Dare to Dream" in Entrepreneur (Vol. 35, October 2007, No. 10, pp. 146)*
Pub: Entrepreneur Media Inc.

Ed: Romaus Wolter. Description: Business goals that are seemingly impossible to reach can actually be achieved through careful planning. Making the goals clear is the first step toward achievement. Details for setting goals and how to attain them are presented.

24589 ■ *"Suitors Circling Chrysler as Sale Likely" in Globe & Mail (February 19, 2007, pp. B1)*
Pub: CTVglobemedia Publishing Inc.

Ed: Jason Singer. Description: DaimlerChrysler AG is planning to sell or spin-off the Chrysler Group, as a cost cutting strategy. Chrysler reported a 40 percent drop in fourth quarter profit because of the $1.5 billion operating loss.

24590 ■ *"Sunriver Venture Hits Snag" in The Business Journal-Portland (Vol. 25, August 1, 2008, No. 21, pp. 1)*
Pub: American City Business Journals, Inc.

Ed: Robin J. Moody. Description: Portland, Oregon based-Sunwest Management Inc. has divided its Sunriver resort community to make way for a redevelopment plan. Sunwest owner Jon Harder and three partners formed SilverStar Destinations LLC to broker the purchase and redevelopment of the property. Details and description of the redevelopment project are also presented.

24591 ■ *"Sunwest Vies To Stave Off Bankruptcy" in The Business Journal-Portland (Vol. 25, August 15, 2008, No. 23, pp. 1)*
Pub: American City Business Journals, Inc.

Ed: Robin J. Moody. Description: Sunwest Management Inc. is teetering on the edge of bankruptcy as creditors start foreclosure on nine of their properties. This could potentially displace residents of the assisted living operator. Sunwest is trying to sell smaller packages of properties to get a $100 million bridge loan to maintain operations.

24592 ■ *"Suppliers Look to Rack Up Big Sales to Distributors" in The Business Journal-Serving Metropolitan Kansas City (August 15, 2008)*
Pub: American City Business Journals, Inc.

Ed: James Dornbrook. Description: Suppliers of shelving units, conveyor systems and other equipment used in distribution facilities are expecting new business opportunities along with the planned intermodal projects in the Kansas City area. Suppliers have already observed that small distributors have started to relocate to the city because of the intermodal projects. Demand for shelves and lifts have also increased.

24593 ■ *"Survive the Small-to-Big Transition" in Entrepreneur (November 4, 2008)*
Pub: Entrepreneur Media Inc.

Ed: Elizabeth Wilson. Description: Transitioning a small company to a large company can be a challenge, especially during the time when it is too big to be considered small and too small to be considered big. Common pitfalls during this time are discussed as well as techniques business owners should implement when dealing with this transitional period.

24594 ■ *Tactical Entrepreneur: The Entrepreneur's Game Plan*
Pub: Sortis Publishing

Ed: Brian J. Hazelgren. Released: September 2005. Price: $14.95. Description: A smart, realistic business plan is essential for any successful entrepreneur. Besides offering products or services, small business owners must possess skills in accounting, planning, human resources management, marketing, and information technology.

24595 ■ *"Take 'Em Out of the Ball Game"* in *Canadian Business (Vol. 79, November 20, 2006, No. 23, pp. 19)*
Pub: Rogers Media
Ed: Andy Holloway. **Description:** Strategies adopted by retailers to retain profitable customers are discussed.

24596 ■ *"Talisman CEO Touts Benefits of Going It Alone"* in *Globe & Mail (March 22, 2006, pp. B1)*
Pub: CTVglobemedia Publishing Inc.
Ed: Dave Ebner. **Description:** The opinions of chief executive officer Jim Buckee of Talisman Energy Inc. on the benefits for the company to remain autonomous are presented.

24597 ■ *"Tea for 33 Million"* in *Canadian Business (Vol. 80, March 12, 2007, No. 6, pp. 10)*
Pub: Rogers Media
Ed: Wendy Glauser. **Description:** The plan of owner of Cargo & James Tea, Tim Grover, to expand his business in North America to reach about 33 million, is discussed.

24598 ■ *Technology Ventures: From Idea to Enterprise*
Pub: McGraw-Hill Higher Education
Ed: Thomas Byers, Richard Dorf, Andrew Nelson. **Released:** January 10, 2010. **Description:** An action-approached through the use of examples, exercises, cases, sample business plans, and recommended sources helps entrepreneurs start and run a technology-base small business.

24599 ■ *"Tee Off Online"* in *Black Enterprise (Vol. 37, January 2007, No. 6, pp. 52)*
Pub: Earl G. Graves Publishing Co. Inc.
Ed: James C. Johnson. **Description:** The E-Com Resource Center is one of many resources that are available for those interested in starting an e-commerce business. One of the first steps is to create a business plan, of which there are free samples available at BPlans.com.

24600 ■ *"Telesat's New Rocket Man"* in *Canadian Business (Vol. 80, January 29, 2007, No. 3, pp. 21)*
Pub: Rogers Media
Ed: Andrew Wahl. **Description:** The plans of Dan Goldberg, the chief executive officer of Telesat Canada, for the enhancement of the company's services are discussed.

24601 ■ *"Test Your Structural Integrity"* in *Entrepreneur (Vol. 37, August 2009, No. 8, pp. 60)*
Pub: Entrepreneur Media, Inc.
Ed: Jennifer Lawler. **Description:** Tax considerations can be important when choosing a business structure. For example, profits are taxed to the corporation in a C corp while profits are taxed only once at an S corp or a limited liability company. Meeting a tax professional should be done prior to switching to a different structure.

24602 ■ *There's a Business In Every Woman: A 7-Step Guide to Discovering, Starting, and Building the Business of Your Dreams*
Pub: Ballantine/Random House
Ed: Ann M. Holmes. **Released:** 2008. **Price:** $15.00 paperback. **Description:** Economist and workplace expert provides a no-nonsense guide detailing seven steps to creating a successful business, based on her own experiences and on those of her employees. She highlights the importance of understanding and using your core competencies, building an organized infrastructure from the start, and planning for and managing your growth.

24603 ■ *"Thirsty Lion on the Prowl"* in *Business Journal Portland (Vol. 27, November 5, 2010, No. 36, pp. 1)*
Pub: Portland Business Journal
Ed: Wendy Culverwell. **Description:** Concept Entertainment Inc.'s impending launch of the Thirsty Lion Pub and Grill at the Washington Square in downtown Portland, Oregon is part of its West Coast expansion

plan. A discussion of the planning involved in realizing Thirsty Lion is discussed, along with pub offerings that are expected to be enjoyed by customers.

24604 ■ *"Thomson Eyes Asia for Expansion"* in *Globe & Mail (February 10, 2006, pp. B4)*
Pub: CTVglobemedia Publishing Inc.
Ed: Grant Robertson. **Description:** The business growth plans of Thomson Corp., in Asia, are presented.

24605 ■ *"A Timely Matter"* in *Canadian Business (Vol. 81, March 31, 2008, No. 5, pp. 12)*
Pub: Rogers Media
Description: Discusses the committee responsible for restructuring $33 billion of asset-backed commercial paper which has moved back their implementation plan by a month citing complexities. British Columbia has surpassed the $1 billion mark in fiscal '07-'08 from their oil and gas rights. Biovail Corp. founder Eugene Melnyk said he had lost confidence in the management of the company.

24606 ■ *"Tom Gaglardi"* in *Canadian Business (Vol. 82, April 27, 2009, No. 7, pp. 56)*
Pub: Rogers Media
Ed: Calvin Leung. **Description:** Northland Properties Corporation president Tom Gaglardi believes that their business model of keeping much of operations in-house allows the firm to crate assets at a lesser price while commanding higher margins than their competitors. He believes that it is an ideal time to invest in the hospitality industry because of opportunities to purchase properties at low prices.

24607 ■ *"Top 50 In Profits"* in *Canadian Business (Vol. 81, Summer 2008, No. 9, pp. 116)*
Pub: Rogers Media Ltd.
Description: Royal Bank of Canada topped the Investor 500 by profits list despite the slower economic growth in Canada and the U.S. The bank was in the runner-up position in the 2007. RBC's growth strategy is through hefty acquisitions in the U.S. A table ranking the top 50 companies in Canada in terms of profits is presented.

24608 ■ *"Transportation Enterprise"* in *Advertising Age (Vol. 79, June 9, 2008, No. 23, pp. S10)*
Pub: Crain Communications, Inc.
Ed: Jean Halliday. **Description:** Overview of Enterprise rent-a-car's plan to become a more environmentally-friendly company. The family-owned business has spent $1 million a year to plant trees since 2006 and has added more fuel-efficient cars, hybrids and flex-fuel models.

24609 ■ *"Transportation: Laidlaw's Chief Driver"* in *Canadian Business (Vol. 80, January 29, 2007, No. 3, pp. 14)*
Pub: Rogers Media
Ed: Michelle Magnan. **Description:** The role of Kevin Benson in the restructuring and growth of the bankrupt transportation company Laidlaw Inc. is described. The increase in the revenues of the restructures company is discussed.

24610 ■ *"Turmoil Means Changes For Retailers"* in *The Business Journal-Serving Metropolitan Kansas City (Vol. 27, October 10, 2008, No. 4)*
Pub: American City Business Journals, Inc.
Ed: Suzanna Stagemeyer. **Description:** Impacts of the financial crisis on Kansas Metropolitan Area retailers are varied. Rob Dalzell, for instance, found it difficult to secure a loan for his new self-serve yogurt store Yummo. The trends in retailing in the area are examined further as well as ways in which local businesses are changing in an attempt to stay solvent during the economic downturn.

24611 ■ *The Ultimate Competitive Advantage*
Pub: Berrett-Koehler Publishers
Ed: Donald Mitchell; Carol Coles; B. Thomas Golisano. **Released:** March 12, 2003. **Price:** $36.95. **Description:** Results of a ten year study of companies that experienced fast growth over a three year

period shows that while unsuccessful companies apply outdated business models, the successful ones improve their business models every two to four years.

24612 ■ *Ultimate Guide to Buying or Selling Your Business*
Pub: Entrepreneur Press
Ed: Ira N. Nottonson. **Released:** September 2004. **Price:** $24.95 (US), $35.95 (Canadian). **Description:** Proven strategies to evaluate, negotiate, and buy or sell a small business. Franchise and family business succession planning is included.

24613 ■ *"UMKC, Hospital Drill Down on Deal"* in *The Business Journal-Serving Metropolitan Kansas City (Vol. 26, July 18, 2008, No. 45, pp. 1)*
Pub: American City Business Journals, Inc.
Ed: Rob Roberts. **Description:** University of Missouri Kansas City and Children's Mercy Hospital are negotiating the hospital's potential acquisition of the university's School of Dentistry building. The deal would transfer the 240,000-square foot dental school building to Children's Mercy. Plans for a new dental school building for the UMKC are also presented.

24614 ■ *"Unilever's CMO Finally Gets Down To Business"* in *Advertising Age (Vol. 79, July 7, 2008, No. 26, pp. 11)*
Pub: Crain Communications, Inc.
Ed: Jack Neff. **Description:** Overview of Unilever's chief marketing officer Simon Clift's strategy for promoting its products; now that the company has restructured, Clift is able to focus all of his energy on the challenges of the new-media climate that marketers are having to face.

24615 ■ *"Union, Heal Thyself"* in *Canadian Business (Vol. 81, July 21, 2008, No. 11, pp. 9)*
Pub: Rogers Media Ltd.
Description: General Motors Corp. was offered by the federal government a $250 million fund after the company declared plans to close its facility in Ontario. The government move is geared towards supporting the workers who have refused to support the automotive company. Details of the labor contract between General Motors and the Canadian Auto Workers are presented.

24616 ■ *"United Insurance To Grow St. Pete's Corporate Base"* in *The Business Journal-Serving Greater Tampa Bay (August 29, 2008)*
Pub: American City Business Journals, Inc.
Ed: Margie Manning. **Description:** United Insurance Holdings LC is on its way to becoming a public company by agreeing in a reverse merger with FMG Acquisition Corp. The $104.3 million agreement will provide the company's St. Petersburg operations the opportunity to grow. The other impacts of the proposed reverse merger are examined.

24617 ■ *"U.S. Playing Card Might Shuffle HQ"* in *Business Courier (Vol. 24, March 21, 2008, No. 50, pp. 1)*
Pub: American City Business Journals, Inc.
Ed: Jon Newberry. **Description:** United States Playing Card Co. is considering the possibility of relocating. It is expected that the company will finalize its decision by June 2008. According to Phil Dolci, the company's president, the firm is looking at certain locations in Ohio, Kentucky, and Indiana. He also revealed that the plan to relocate was prompted by the desire to improve the company's manufacturing facilities.

24618 ■ *"The Urge to Converge"* in *Canadian Business (Vol. 79, October 9, 2006, No. 20, pp. 41)*
Pub: Rogers Media
Ed: Andy Holloway. **Description:** Arthur Griffiths, chief executive officer of Infotec Business Systems Inc., decision to diversify into broad brand business is discussed.

24619 ■ *"The Value of Human Resource Management for Organizational Performance"* in *Business Horizons (November-December*

2007, pp. 503)
Pub: Elsevier Technology Publications
Ed: Yongmei Liu, James G. Combs, David J. Ketchen, R. Duane Ireland. **Description:** Benefits of human resource management for business are studied using date from 19,000 organizations. Human resource management adds value to business, especially when it is integrated with business strategy and when human resource systems are emphasized.

24620 ■ *"Versatile's Back" in Farm Industry News (Vol. 42, January 1, 2009, No. 1)*
Pub: Penton Media Inc.
Contact: John French, President
Ed: Jodie Wehrspann. **Description:** Overview of Winnipeg, Manitoba's tractor manufacturer Versatile's strategy to rebrand its tractor segment; the strategy comes a year after Russian Combine Factory Rostselmash Ltd. bought the majority share of common stock from the Canadian business.

24621 ■ *"Virgin Mobile has Big Plans for Year Two" in Globe & Mail (March 6, 2006, pp. B5)*
Pub: CTVglobemedia Publishing Inc.
Ed: Catherine McLean. **Description:** The business growth plans of Virgin Mobile Canada are presented.

24622 ■ *"Wal-Mart Relaunches Private Brand, Reimagines Stores Layout" in Marketing to Women (Vol. 22, July 2009, No. 7, pp. 5)*
Pub: EPM Communications Inc.
Contact: Ira Mayer, President
E-mail: imayer@epmcom.com
Description: Wal-Mart is focusing its strategies by centering on new store layouts that they believe will match their new branding of 'fast, friendly, and clean' and enable mothers to 'just get on with what they need to do.'.

24623 ■ *"Walker Seeks More Business Participation" in Business Journal-Milwaukee (Vol. 28, December 10, 2010, No. 10, pp. A1)*
Pub: Milwaukee Business Journal
Ed: Rich Kirchen. **Description:** Wisconsin governor Scott Walker is seeking the aid of Milwaukee business leaders to participate in resolving the challenges posed by the economic crisis. Walker is aiming to create 250,000 jobs. He is also planning to call a special session of the legislature to enact strategies to jumpstart the economy.

24624 ■ *The Wall Street Journal. Complete Small Business Guidebook*
Pub: Three Rivers Press
Ed: Colleen DeBaise. **Released:** December 29, 2009. **Price:** $15.00. **Description:** The mechanics of building, running and growing a profitable business are outlined, teaching how to write a business plan, ways to finding money during lean years, how to keep stress in check, time management, investment in technology, hiring, marketing, management basics, angel investing and venture capital, as well as an exit strategy.

24625 ■ *We Are Smarter Than Me: How to Unleash the Power of Crowds in Your Business*
Pub: Wharton School Publishing
Ed: Barry Libert; Jon Spector; Don Tapscott. **Released:** October 5, 2007. **Price:** $21.99. **Description:** Ways to use social networking and community in order to make decisions and plan your business, with a focus on product development, manufacturing, marketing, customer service, finance, management, and more.

24626 ■ *"Weathering the Economic Storm" in Playthings (Vol. 107, January 1, 2009, No. 1, pp. 10)*
Pub: Reed Business Information
Contact: Jeff Greisch, President
Ed: J. Tol Broome Jr. **Description:** Six steps for toy companies to survive the economic turndown are outlined: Outline your business model; seek professional input; meet with your banker; cut your costs; manage your inventory; and use your trade credit.

24627 ■ *"Welcome to the Neighborhood" in Hawaii Business (Vol. 53, October 2007, No. 4, pp. 48)*
Pub: Hawaii Business Publishing
Ed: Jolyn Okimoto Rosa. **Description:** Finance Factors is planning to build branches in Manoa, and Liliha, as part of its strategy to position itself in high-yield areas. The company chose Manoa and Liliha due to thee sites' rich deposits. Its strategy with regards to the branches' location and to the building design is discussed.

24628 ■ *"Wendy's Mulls Total Hortons Selloff" in Globe & Mail (January 7, 2006, pp. B5)*
Pub: CTVglobemedia Publishing Inc.
Ed: Sinclair Stewart; Omar El Akkad. **Description:** The plans of Wendy's International Inc. to spin off Tim Hortons are presented.

24629 ■ *"Weyerhaeuser's REIT Decision Shouldn't Scare Investors Away" in Barron's (Vol. 88, June 30, 2008, No. 26, pp. 18)*
Pub: Dow Jones & Co., Inc.
Ed: Christopher Williams. **Description:** Weyerhaeuser Co.'s management said that a conversion to a real estate investment trust was not likely in 2009 since the move is not tax-efficient as of the moment and would overload its non-timber assets with debt. The company's shares have fallen by 19.5 percent. However, the company remains an asset-rich outfit and its activist shareholder is pushing for change.

24630 ■ *"What Are You Doing Differently?" in Agency Sales Magazine (Vol. 39, December 2009, No. 11, pp. 3)*
Pub: MANA
Ed: Bryan C. Shirley. **Description:** Strategies that sales representatives can do to plan for a good year include professional development, networking with other reps, and making more sales calls and seeing more people. The end of the year is the perfect time for reps to write or re-write their mission statement and to conduct line profitability.

24631 ■ *"What Are Your Party's Legislative Priorities for 2008?" in Hawaii Business (Vol. 53, January 2008, No. 7, pp. 22)*
Pub: Hawaii Business Publishing
Description: Discusses the Democratic Party of Hawaii which will prioritize giving more opportunities to earn a living a wage in 2008, according to the party chairwoman Jeani Withington. The Republican Party chairman Willes K. Lee, meanwhile, states that his party will seek to enhance the local business climate. The political parties' plans for Hawaii for the year 2008 are presented in detail.

24632 ■ *"What Homes Do Retirees Want?" in Canadian Business (Vol. 79, July 17, 2006, No. 14-15, pp.)*
Pub: Rogers Media
Ed: Joe Cataldo. **Description:** The obstacles and challenges faced by homebuilders in Canada as well as the approach adopted by them to appeal to the mature homebuilders segment, is discussed.

24633 ■ *"What Players in the Midmarket Are Talking About" in Mergers & Acquisitions: The Dealmaker's Journal (March 1, 2008)*
Pub: SourceMedia, Inc.
Description: Sports Properties Acquisition Corp. went public at the end of January; according to the company's prospectus, it is not limiting its focus to just teams, it is also considering deals for stadium construction companies, sports leagues, facilities, sports-related advertising and licensing of products, in addition to other related segments.

24634 ■ *What Self-Made Millionaires Really Think, Know and Do: A Straight-Talking Guide to Business Success and Personal Riches*
Pub: John Wiley & Sons, Incorporated
Ed: Richard Dobbins; Barrie Pettman. **Released:** September 2006. **Price:** $24.95. **Description:** Guide for understanding the concepts of entrepreneurial

success; the book offers insight into bringing an idea into reality, marketing, time management, leadership skills, and setting clear goals.

24635 ■ *"What's Cooking?" in Entrepreneur (Vol. 36, April 2008, No. 4, pp. 98)*
Pub: Entrepreneur Media, Inc.
Ed: Eileen Figure Sandlin. **Description:** Unique and unusual restaurants have the potential to attract customers and provide them with fresh menu options. Outlining goals, strategies and details on proposed concept and target market can also help in restaurant planning. Other tips on how to plan launching your own restaurant are provided.

24636 ■ *When Family Businesses are Best*
Pub: Palgrave Macmillan
Ed: Randel S. Carlock, John L. Ward. **Released:** March 1, 2010. **Price:** $45.00. **Description:** An exploration into effective planning and communication to help small businesses grow into multigeneration family enterprises.

24637 ■ *"Why Intel Should Dump Its Flash-Memory Business" in Barron's (Vol. 88, March 10, 2008, No. 10, pp. 35)*
Pub: Dow Jones & Company, Inc.
Ed: Eric J. Savitz. **Description:** Intel Corp. must sell its NAND flash-memory business as soon as it possibly can to the highest bidder to focus on its PC processor business and take advantage of other business opportunities. Apple should consider a buyback of 10 percent of the company's shares to lift its stock.

24638 ■ *"Worth His Salt" in Hawaii Business (Vol. 53, January 2008, No. 7, pp. 45)*
Pub: Hawaii Business Publishing
Ed: Jolyn Okimoto Rosa. **Description:** Bryan Zada owns three PretzelMaker franchises, whose total loss amounted to $40,000 in 2003. Zada believes that listening to employees was one of the key steps in turning the business around. The efforts made to improve the franchises' products are also given.

24639 ■ *"The Wrong Tune" in The Business Journal-Portland (Vol. 25, July 25, 2008, No. 20, pp. 1)*
Pub: American City Business Journals, Inc.
Ed: Robin J. Moody. **Description:** Views and information on turnaround management and recovery plans of the Oregon Symphony, are presented. The non-profit organization has lost a total of $5.1 million between 2002 and 2008, and $400,000 annual interest payments for a $7 million bank loan. Increased ticket sales, as well as cost cutting measures, are helping improve the finance of the organization.

24640 ■ *"Xerox's Former CEO On Why Succession Shouldn't Be a Horse Race" in Harvard Business Review (Vol. 88, October 2010, No. 10, pp. 47)*
Pub: Harvard Business School Publishing
Ed: Anne Mulcahy. **Description:** The importance of beginning talks between chief executive officers and boards of directors as early as possible to ensure a smooth transition is stressed. This can also prevent turning successions into competitions, with the resultant loss of talent when other candidates 'lose'.

24641 ■ *"A Year After Fiorina's Exit, Hurd Makes His Mark" in Globe & Mail (February 8, 2006, pp. B9)*
Pub: CTVglobemedia Publishing Inc.
Ed: Shawn McCarthy. **Description:** The business growth strategies of chief executive officer Mark Hurd of Hewlett-Packard Co. are presented.

24642 ■ *"Young Entrepreneur's Business Plan? An Ice Cream Boat? Really Floats: Maine at Work" in Portland Press Herald (August 9, 2010)*
Pub: Portland Press Herald
Ed: Ray Routhier. **Description:** Profile of Jake Viola, founder of and ice cream boat located near Portland, Maine. Viola is a sophomore at Yale University and sells ice cream from his pontoon boat on Little Sebago lake.

24643 ■ *"Young Millionaires" in Entrepreneur (Vol. 35, October 2007, No. 10, pp. 76)*
Pub: Entrepreneur Media Inc.
Ed: Jessica Chen, Lindsay Hollway, Amanda C. Kooser, Kim Orr, James Park, Nichole L. Torres, and Sarah Wilson. **Description:** Young successful entrepreneurs of 2007 were chosen to talk about their success story and their business strategies in the past and those for the future. Among those featured are Kelly Flatley, Brendan Synnott, Herman Flores, Myles Kovacs, Haythem Haddad, Jim Wetzel, Lance Lawson, Jacob DeHart, Jake Nickell, Tim Vanderhook, Chris Vanderhook, Russell Vanderhook, Megan Duckett, Brad Sugars, John Vechey, Brian Fiete, Jason Kapalka, Nathan Jones, Devon Rifkin, Ryan Black, Ed Nichols, Jeremy Black, Amy Smilovic, Bob Shallenberger, and John Cavanagh.

24644 ■ *"Your Booming Business: How You Can Align Sales and Marketing for Dynamic Growth" in Small Business Opportunities (Spring 2008)*
Pub: Harris Publications Inc.
Ed: Voss W. Graham. **Description:** Voss Graham, founder and CEO of Inneractive Consulting Group Inc., works with companies to develop and hire successful sales teams. A checklist from the American Bankers Association to help write a business plan is included.

24645 ■ *Your Guide to Preparing a Plan to Raise Money for Your Own Business*
Pub: Productive Publications
Ed: Iain Williamson. **Released:** June 1991. **Description:** A good business plan is essential for raising money for any small business.

24646 ■ *"Zebra's Changing Stripes" in Crain's Chicago Business (Vol. 31, November 17, 2008, No. 46, pp. 4)*
Pub: Crain Communications, Inc.
Ed: John Pletz. **Description:** Zebra Technologies Corp., the world's largest manufacturer of bar-code printers is profiled; the company's stock has plunged with shares declining 40 percent in the past three months grinding the firm's growth to a halt. Zebra's plans to regain revenue growth are also discussed.

24647 ■ *"Zell Takes a Gamble on Tribune" in Globe & Mail (April 3, 2007, pp. B1)*
Pub: CTVglobemedia Publishing Inc.
Ed: Sinclair Stewart. **Description:** The purchase of the majority share in Tribune Co. by Samuel Zell is described. Samuel Zell's plans to keep the company's assets intact are discussed.

24648 ■ *"Zucker's HBC Shakeup Imminent" in Globe & Mail (February 20, 2006, pp. B3)*
Pub: CTVglobemedia Publishing Inc.
Ed: Marina Strauss. **Description:** The plans of investor Jerry Zucker to revamp Hudson's Bay Co., upon its acquisition, are presented.

TRADE PERIODICALS

24649 ■ *Enrich!*
Pub: National Chamber of Commerce for Women
Contact: Jay Orson, Manager, Advertising
Ed: R. Wright, Editor. **Released:** Bimonthly. **Price:** $96. **Description:** Strives to assist readers on business-plan, career-path, and pay-comparison goals.

VIDEOCASSETTES/ AUDIOCASSETTES

24650 ■ *Managing the Emerging Company*
Leslie T. McClure
PO Box 1223
Pebble Beach, CA 93953
Ph: (831)656-0553
Fax: (831)656-0555
Co. E-mail: leslie@411videoinfo.com
URL: http://www.411videoinfo.com
Released: 1997. **Price:** $990.00. **Description:** Ten-volume set deals with the functions of developing and running a business. **Availability:** VHS.

24651 ■ *Product Strategy: All the Right Moves*
RMI Media
1365 N. Winchester St.
Olathe, KS 66061-5880
Ph: (913)768-1696
Free: 800-745-5480
Fax: (800)755-6910
Co. E-mail: actmedia@act.org
URL: http://www.actmedia.com
Released: 1991. **Price:** $89.95. **Description:** Presents a case study of Carushka, a dance and exercise wear manufacturer, to demonstrate successful methods for increasing product use and customers; finding new uses for existing products; and broadening the product appeal to old and new markets. **Availability:** VHS.

CONSULTANTS

24652 ■ Ameriwest Business Consultants Inc. (ABCI)
3725 E Wade Ln.
Colorado Springs, CO 80917-5852
Ph: (719)380-7096
Fax: (719)380-7096
Co. E-mail: email@abchelp.com
URL: http://www.abchelp.com
Contact: Rodd Brechtl, President
E-mail: rodb@abchelp.com
Scope: Specializes in assisting start up businesses and those with sales of 5million dollars or less and those who have 50 employees or less. Services and products offered include written business plans; do it yourself business plan kits; business valuations; do it yourself business start up kits; written loan packages; do it yourself loan packaging guides; business analysis; do it yourself financial projections software; do it yourself complete financial analysis; website development assistance; general consulting. **Founded:** 1991.

24653 ■ Beacon Management - Management Consultants
1000 W McNab Rd.
Pompano Beach, FL 33069
Ph: (954)782-1119
Free: 800-771-8721
Fax: (954)969-2566
Co. E-mail: md@beaconmgmt.com
URL: http://www.beaconmgmt.com
Contact: Joyce Slencak, Manager
Scope: Specializes in change management, organized workplaces, multicultural negotiations and dispute resolutions and internet based decision making. **Founded:** 1985. **Publications:** "Sun-Sentinel Article," Oct, 2012.

24654 ■ Biomedical Management Resources (BMR)
PO Box 521125
Salt Lake City, UT 84152-1125
Ph: (801)272-4668
Fax: (801)277-3290
Co. E-mail: SeniorManagement@BiomedicalManagement.com
URL: http://www.biomedicalmanagement.com
Contact: Ping Fong, Jr., President
E-mail: pingfong@biomedicalmanagement.com
Scope: Provides business development, interim management, and executive search services. Assists companies in strategic alliances, corporate partnering, business acquisition. Demonstrated success in identifying recruiting, and placing key managers in difficult hire positions. **Founded:** 1993.

24655 ■ BPT Consulting Associates Ltd.
12 Parmenter Rd., Ste. B-6
Londonderry, NH 03053
Ph: (603)437-8484
Free: 888-278-0030
Fax: (603)434-5388
Contact: John Kuczynski, Managing Director
Scope: Provides management consulting expertise and resources to cross-industry clients with services for: Business Management consulting, People/Human Resources Transition and Training programs,

and a full cadre of multi-disciplined Technology Computer experts. Virtual consultants with expertise in e-commerce, supply chain management, organizational development, and business application development consulting. **Founded:** 1991.

24656 ■ Business Development Group Inc. (BDG)
29255 Laurel Woods Dr., Ste. 202
Southfield, MI 48034
Ph: (248)358-0121
Fax: (248)350-3025
Co. E-mail: info@busdevgroup.com
URL: http://www.busdevgroup.com
Contact: Neil J. Simon, President
E-mail: njsimon@aol.com
Scope: Consulting firm expertise in leadership development; strategic thinking; organizational transformation; team-based work systems; organizational learning; rapid change; knowledge management; competitive intelligence; crisis management; merger and acquisition integration; product integration and new product development. **Founded:** 1985. **Publications:** "Navigating in the Sea of Change," Competitive Intelligence Review Journal; "The Influence of Cultural Aspects of Strategic Information, Analysis and Delivery"; "What Leadership Needs From Competitive Intelligence Professionals," Journal of Association for Global and Strategic Information. **Seminars:** Process of Self-Design for the Evolving Organization; Large System Change Intervention; Self Assessment and the Transformational Process; The Knowledge Exchange - Shared Practices Workshop.

24657 ■ Business Resource Software Inc.
1779 Wells Branch Pky
Austin, TX 78728-7090
Ph: (512)251-7541
Free: 800-423-1228
Fax: (512)251-4401
URL: http://www.brs-inc.com
Contact: Kylon Gustin, President
Scope: Provides marketing and business planning software. Provides an evaluation of business conditions and advises the users about situations in their specific business. **Founded:** 1989. **Publications:** *Plan Write for Marketing; Quick Insight; Plan Write for Business; Business Insight; Insight for Sales Strategy; Plan Write Expert Edition.* **Special Services:** Plan Write?; Quick Insight?; Business Insight?.

24658 ■ BusinessPlanWorld.com
PO Box 1322, Sta. B
Mississauga, ON, Canada L4Y 4B6
Ph: (709)643-8544
Co. E-mail: theboss@businessplanworld.com
URL: http://www.businessplanworld.com
Contact: Kevin G. Brake, Chief Executive Officer
E-mail: theboss@businessplanworld.com
Scope: Services include business plan creation, complete website development services and educational software development. **Founded:** 1989. **Publications:** "How to open a Bed and Breakfast"; "How to open a Bookstore"; "How to open a Restaurant"; "How to open a Youth Center"; "How to open a Rough Collie Kennel"; "How to open a Video Store"; "How to open a Confectionery Store"; "How to open a Night Club/Bar".

24659 ■ Elizabeth Capen
27 E 95th St., Apt. 5E
New York, NY 10128-0824
Ph: (212)427-7654
Fax: (212)876-3190
Scope: Focuses on strategic marketing planning and positioning. Identifies effective marketing tools; plans and reviews advertising and collateral materials; writes business plans; and performs secondary research and competitive analysis. Industries served: services, small businesses, and entrepreneurial ventures in northeastern and middle Atlantic regions. **Founded:** 1985. **Seminars:** Handling Issues of Growth; Using Published Information as a Marketing Tool.

24660 ■ CAST Management Consultants Inc.
700 S Flower St., Ste. 1900
Los Angeles, CA 90017

Ph: (213)614-8066
Fax: (213)614-0760
Co. E-mail: info@castconsultants.com
URL: http://www.castconsultants.com
Contact: Steven C. McCollum, President

Scope: Management consultants active in the following areas: business strategy formulation, market analysis, business plan formulation, competitive advantage analysis, information technology development, organizational development, financial analysis and planning, strategic planning, entry strategies into new markets, implementation of strategy, international strategic planning, international marketing, and international joint venture. Serves private industries as well as government agencies. **Founded:** 1986.

24661 ■ CEA Investments Corp.
301-2210 W 40th Ave.
Vancouver, BC, Canada V6M 1W6
Ph: (604)689-5547
Co. E-mail: info@ceainvestment.com
Contact: Emmanuel B. Nicolas, Principal

Scope: Specializes in strategic planning, mergers and acquisitions, and operations consulting, to mid-sized corporations. Areas of expertise include corporate planning, financial engineering, joint venture structuring, international corporate networking, identifying acquisition opportunities, locating investment partners, corporate evaluations, negotiating buy/sell agreements, business planning, markets studies and products evaluation, and outsourcing. **Founded:** 1988.

24662 ■ Chamberlain & Cansler Inc.
2251 Perimeter Park Dr.
Atlanta, GA 30341
Ph: (770)457-5699
Contact: Charles L. Cansler, Owner

Scope: Firm specializes in strategic planning; profit enhancement; small business management; interim management; crisis management; turnarounds. **Founded:** 1986.

24663 ■ Clayton/Curtis/Cottrell
1722 Madison Ct.
Louisville, CO 80027-1121
Ph: (303)665-2005
Contact: Robert Cottrell, President

Scope: Market research firm specializes in providing consultations for packaged goods, telecommunications, direct marketing and printing, and packaging industries. Services include strategic planning; profit enhancement; startup businesses; mergers and acquisitions; joint ventures; divestitures; interim management; crisis management; turnarounds; market size, segmentation and rates of growth; competitor intelligence; image and reputation, and competitive analysis. **Founded:** 1981. **Publications:** "Turn an attitude into a purchase," Jul, 1995; "Mixed results for private label; price assaults by the national brands are getting heavy, but there's still a place for private label," Jun, 1995; "In-store promotion goes high-tech: is the conventional coupon destined for obsolescence?," Jun, 1995.

24664 ■ John Alan Cohan
433 N Camden Dr., Ste. 600
Beverly Hills, CA 90210
Ph: (310)278-0203
Free: 800-255-1529
Fax: (310)859-8656
Co. E-mail: johnalancohan@aol.com
URL: http://www.johnalancohan.com
Contact: Cohan John Alan, Principal

Scope: Consultant assists in the development of business plans for startups in the fields of livestock, horses, farming, or aviation. Also provides tax consultations and tax opinion letters to support deductions. **Founded:** 1981.

24665 ■ Comprehensive Business Services
3201 Lucas Cir.
Lafayette, CA 94549
Ph: (925)283-8272

Fax: (925)283-8272
Contact: Walter H. Diebold, President

Scope: Business/financial consultants with related experience in marketing, finance, organization, business planning, and profit development. Industries served include construction, manufacturing, and wholesale. **Founded:** 1985.

24666 ■ CRO Engineering Ltd.—Contract Research Organization
1895 William Hodgins Ln.
Carp, ON, Canada K0A 1L0
Ph: (613)839-1108
Fax: (305)832-8232
Contact: John Grefford, Principal
E-mail: grefford@ieee.org

Scope: Specializes in management services, contract R and D, risk analysis, business services, technology assessment, independent engineering verification and validation, audit services, project or program management, engineering cost analysis, technology research. Engineering review, business plan analysis and development. **Founded:** 1997.

24667 ■ DRI Consulting (DRIC)
2 Otter Ln.
Saint Paul, MN 55127-6436
Ph: (651)415-1400
Free: 866-276-4600
Fax: (651)415-9968
Co. E-mail: dric@dric.com
URL: http://www.dric.com
Contact: Megan Brogger, Principal
E-mail: meganbrogger@dric.com

Scope: Provides high-quality, research-based services and training in leadership, team processes, supervision, and management, and organizational development, clients with direct and substantial impact on individual and team performance and on organizational success through proven processes for selecting, developing and deploying leaders. **Founded:** 1991.

24668 ■ Entrepreneurial Strategies
107 S Yellowstone Ave., Ste. C
Bozeman, MT 59715
Ph: (406)587-5664
Fax: (406)586-0396
Co. E-mail: nfkrueger@rocketmail.com
Contact: Norris F. Krueger, Jr., Principal
E-mail: nfkrueger@hotmail.com

Scope: Academic consultants helping organizations become more entrepreneurial; helping communities become more entrepreneurial; providing market assessments for 'really new' products and technologies; offering strategic planning and marketing planning.

24669 ■ FCP Consulting
500 Sutter St., Ste. 507
San Francisco, CA 94102-1114
Ph: (415)956-5558
Fax: (415)956-5722
Contact: Cox Ferrall, President

Scope: Management consulting in Business-To-Business sales. **Founded:** 1986.

24670 ■ Fogg Management Consulting—C Davis Fogg Management Consulting Inc.
80 Shadow Farm Way
Wakefield, RI 02879-3635
Ph: (401)789-9511
Fax: (401)789-8544
Contact: C. Davis Fogg, President
E-mail: davis.fogg@foggmgt.com

Scope: Provides strategic planning and implementation services. Serves all industries, coaches CEO' s and senior executives. **Founded:** 1981. **Publications:** "Implementing Your Strategic Plan"; "Team Based Strategic Planning".

24671 ■ Frankel and Topche P.C.
1700 Galloping Hill Rd.
Kenilworth, NJ 07033
Ph: (908)298-7700

Fax: (908)298-7701
Co. E-mail: info@frankelandtopche.com
URL: http://www.frankelandtopche.com
Contact: Mark J. Tikkanen, Director
E-mail: mtikkanen@frankelandtopche.com

Scope: Offers financial consulting for closely held businesses. Assists in mergers and acquisitions, tax planning, strategic business planning, family succession planning, accounting, auditing, and obtaining financing. The firm serves small businesses in the service, retail, wholesale, and manufacturing industries. Specializes in real estate, lumber and building materials, and service businesses. **Founded:** 1990. **Seminars:** Annual Tax Seminar.

24672 ■ Gerson Goodson Inc. (GGI)
2451 McMullen Booth Rd., Ste. 201
Clearwater, FL 33759
Ph: (727)726-7619
Free: 888-237-7424
Fax: (727)726-2406
Co. E-mail: getrich@richgerson.com
URL: http://www.richgerson.com
Contact: Dr. Richard F. Gerson, President
E-mail: richard.gerson@richgerson.com

Scope: Independent consulting firm provides performance management solutions to improve performance and maximize productivity in organizations. Provides assistance to organizations in talent and performance management, leadership development, selection and hiring practices, employee and customer retention, and customer service. Conducts a systematic needs analysis of the entire marketing, sales and customer service operations of the company. Identifies hidden, neglected and underutilized marketing, sales and customer service assets. **Founded:** 1979. **Publications:** "Winning The Inner Game Of Selling," 1999; "Marketing Strategies for Small Businesses," 1994; "Measuring Customer Satisfaction," 1993; "Beyond Customer Service," 1992; "Achieving High Performance"; "Guaranteeing Performance Improvement"; "The Executive Athlete"; "Positive Performance Improvement". **Seminars:** Marketing Real Estate Services Management Development, Oct, 2007; Presentation Skills, Oct, 2007; From Member Service to Sales, Sep, 2007; Leadership Development, Sep, 2007; The Marketing Difference That Makes The Difference: How To Position Your Company For Rapid Growth Regardless Of The Economy Or The Competition; Growing Your Business With What You Already Have: How To Identify And Profit From The Hidden Marketing Assets That Are Currently Costing You Money; The R Factor In Customer Service: 5 Ways To Grow Your Business For Little Or No Cost.

24673 ■ Great Lakes Consulting Group Inc.
54722 Little Flower Trl.
Mishawaka, IN 46545
Ph: (574)287-4500
Fax: (574)233-2688
Contact: James E. Schrager, President
Scope: Provides consulting services in the areas of strategic planning; feasibility studies; start-up businesses; small business management; mergers and acquisitions; joint ventures; divestitures; interim management; crisis management; turnarounds; business process re-engineering; venture capital; and international trade. **Founded:** 1989.

24674 ■ Grimmick Consulting Services (GCS)
455 Donner Way
San Ramon, CA 94582
Ph: (925)735-1036
Fax: (925)735-1100
Co. E-mail: hank@grimmickconsulting.com
URL: http://www.grimmickconsulting.com
Contact: Henry Grimmick, President
E-mail: hank@grimmickconsulting.com

Scope: Provider of consulting services in the areas of strategic planning; organizational assessment; organizational development; leadership and management development Baldrige criteria, process improvement and balanced scorecards and team dynamics. **Founded:** 1993.

24675 ■ Health Strategy Group Inc.
46 River Rd.
Chatham, NY 12037

Ph: (518)392-6770
Contact: Cameron Battley, President
Scope: Provides consulting services in the areas of strategic planning, feasibility studies, start-up businesses, organizational development, market research, customer service audits, new product development, marketing, public relations. **Founded:** 1981. **Publications:** "Online Consumer Surveys as a Methodology for Assessing the Quality of the United States Health Care System," 2004.

24676 ■ Healthscope Inc.
400 Lancaster Ave.
Devon, PA 19333
Ph: (610)687-6199
Fax: (610)687-6376
Co. E-mail: health@voicenet.com
Contact: Brian King, President
E-mail: dmking47@hotmail.com
Scope: An independent health care management and consulting firm. Provides business planning, decision making and implementation support. Specialties include strategic business consulting, business plan development focused on bottom line improvement, revenue enhancement expense reduction planning and implementation, practice expansion consolidation, feasibility studies and decision making, new site service start-up planning and implementation practice valuation and transition, physician group mergers and affiliations, joint ventures, MSO planning, start up and management, IPA PO development support, physician network reengineering, medical practice management, baseline operational and financial assessment, managed care contracting support, personnel management, physician compensation planning, fee schedule development, day-to-day operations management supervision, financial management, clinical protocols development, customized management report development, physician and staff education; performance monitoring, billing system evaluation, planning and selection, interim or ongoing management support, practice reorganization, patient accounts management, practice marketing. **Founded:** 1986.

24677 ■ Hewitt Development Enterprises (HDE)
1717 N Bayshore Dr., Ste. 2154
Miami, FL 33132
Ph: (305)372-0941
Fax: (305)372-0941
Co. E-mail: info@hewittdevelopment.com
URL: http://www.hewittdevelopment.com
Contact: Robert G. Hewitt, Principal
E-mail: bob@hewittdevelopment.com
Scope: Specializes in strategic planning; profit enhancement; start-up businesses; interim management; crisis management; turnarounds; production planning; just-in-time inventory management; and project management. Serves senior management (CEOs, CFOs, division presidents, etc.) and acquirers of distressed businesses. **Founded:** 1985.

24678 ■ Horizon Consulting Services
1315 Garthwick Dr.
Los Altos, CA 94024-6147
Ph: (650)967-0906
Fax: (650)967-0906
Contact: Wendy Marshall Grossman, President
Scope: Assists start-up to mid-sized businesses to grow and increase profits through effective business plans and operational programs. Areas of expertise include business plans and strategies; market evaluations; competitive analysis; pricing financial plans and budgets; financial management; marketing strategies; product positioning and introduction, forecasting and analysis; and business policies and procedures. Concentrates on providing practical results, customized to the needs and budget of its clients. Industries served: high-technology industries including computers, software, communications, other electronic products and components, and other manufacturing and service industries. **Founded:** 1992.

24679 ■ K & T Training—K & T Consulting
103 Greenville St.
Newnan, GA 30263
Ph: (770)253-5870

Fax: (770)253-8866
Contact: J. R. Tumperi, President
Scope: Specializes in strategic planning; profit enhancement; organizational development; start-up businesses; interim management; crisis management; turnarounds; business process re-engineering; team building; cost controls. **Founded:** 1983.

24680 ■ Keiei Senryaku Corp.
19191 S Vermont Ave., Ste. 530
Torrance, CA 90502-1049
Ph: (310)366-3331
Free: 800-951-8780
Fax: (310)366-3330
Co. E-mail: takenakaes@earthlink.net
Contact: Kurt Miyamoto, President
Scope: Offers consulting services in the areas of strategic planning; feasibility studies; profit enhancement; organizational development; start-up businesses; mergers and acquisitions; joint ventures; divestitures; executive searches; sales management; and competitive analysis. **Founded:** 1989.

24681 ■ Management Strategies
1000 S Old Woodward Ave., Ste. 105
Birmingham, MI 48009
Ph: (248)258-2756
Fax: (248)258-3407
Co. E-mail: bob@hois.com
Contact: Robert E. Hoisington, President
E-mail: bob@hois.com
Scope: Firm specializes in strategic planning; feasibility studies; profit enhancement; organizational studies; start up businesses; turnarounds; business process re engineering; industrial engineering; marketing; ecommerce. **Founded:** 1985.

24682 ■ Market Focus
12 Maryland Rd.
Maplewood, NJ 07040
Ph: (973)378-2470
Fax: (973)378-2470
Co. E-mail: mcss66@marketfocus.com
Contact: Daniel A. Zaslow, President
E-mail: dakaslow@comcast.net
Scope: Offers advisory services to executives of corporate business units and mid-sized companies in the development and implementation of corporate and market strategies. Studies relate to business planning, new market/product entry, acquisitions and industry/competitive profiles for firms in advanced technology, business and financial services and basic industry. Projects focus on practical, effective approaches to maximizing the potential of existing operations and exploiting future growth opportunities. Practice philosophy emphasizes close client relationships, active management participation and senior consultant involvement. **Founded:** 1980. **Publications:** "Surviving in Hard Times," NJ Contractor. **Seminars:** Charting a Course for Future Company Growth; Marketing Planning; Construction Marketing in the 90's; Marketing and The CFO.

24683 ■ Marketing Leverage Inc.
2022 Laurel Oak Ln.
Palm City, FL 34990
Ph: (772)878-6495
Free: 800-633-1422
Fax: (772)659-8664
Co. E-mail: lkelly@marketingleverage.com
Contact: Lynn C. Kelly, President
E-mail: lkelly@marketingleverage.com
Scope: Consulting and research firm focusing on the targeting, retention and satisfaction of customers. Consulting is offered for due diligence; marketing and customer retention strategy; program design and implementation. Research services offered help clients determine service improvements that increase customer loyalty; boosting sales through better understanding buyer motivations; increasing the odds of product acceptance through new product concept testing; and improving the effectiveness of advertising, collateral, publications through audience evaluation. Clients include top financial services, insurance, health care, technology and management services organizations. **Founded:** 1987. **Publications:** "Creating Strategic Leverage"; "Exploring Corporate Strategy"; "Competitive Advantage"; "Breakpoint and Beyond "; "Competitive Strategy ". **Seminars:** Best

Practices in Brainstorming; Getting Results in the Real World; Finding the Leverage in Your Customer Strategy; The Role of Communications in Building Customer Loyalty; Building a Customer Centered Relationship and Making it Pay. **Special Services:** The Marketing Leverage Win/Loss Tracking System™.

24684 ■ McCreight & Company Inc.
36 Grove St.
New Canaan, CT 06840
Ph: (203)801-5000
Fax: (866)646-8339
Co. E-mail: roc@implementstrategy.com
URL: http://www.implementstrategy.com
Contact: John A. McCreight, President
E-mail: jmc@implementstrategy.com
Scope: Assist the global clients with strategy implementation involving large scale change, including mergers, divestitures, alliances and new business launches. **Founded:** 1983. **Publications:** "The Board's Role in Strengthening M and A Success," Boardroom Briefing, 2008; "Creating the Future," Ask Magazine, 2007; "Strategy Implementation Insights," Mccreight and Company Inc, Oct, 2007; "Sustaining Growth," Deloitte and Ct Technology Council, Jul, 2006; "A Four Phase Approach to Succession Planning," Southern Connecticut Newspapers Inc, 2005. **Seminars:** Successful Mergers and Acquisitions-An Implementation Guide; Global 100One-Face-to-the-Customer; Implementation of Strategic Change.

24685 ■ McDonald Consulting Group Inc.
1900 W Park Dr., Ste. 280
Westborough, MA 01581
Co. E-mail: info@mcdonaldconsultinggroup.com
URL: http://www.mcdonaldconsultinggroup.com
Contact: Ron A. McDonald, President
E-mail: rmcdonald@mcdonaldconsultinggroup.com
Scope: A management consulting firm specializing in assisting insurance companies improve operations. Provides services in the areas of strategic planning; profit enhancement; organizational development; interim management; crisis management; turnarounds; business process re-engineering; benefits and compensation planning and total quality management. **Founded:** 1993. **Publications:** "Improving Customer Focus through Organizational Structure," AASCIF News; "Changing Strategies in Hard Markets," The National Underwriter; "Moving Beyond Management 101: Postgraduate Time Management for Executives," The National Underwriter; "A New Attitude: 3 Clients Improved Results Through Our Fundamental Change Process," Bests Review; "How to Organize Your Company Around Your Customers," Bests Review. **Seminars:** How to establish "expense allowable"; How to design an incentive compensation plan around a units core success measures.

24686 ■ Jerome W. McGee & Associates—Bruce W. McGee & Associates
7826 Eastern Ave. NW, Ste. 300
Washington, DC 20012
Ph (202)726-7272
Fax: (202)726-2946
Contact: Bruce W. McGee, President
Scope: Business consultants experienced in office automation, small business management, invention and patent counseling, technology commercialization, loan packaging and business plan development. **Founded:** 1985. **Seminars:** Marketing Research for the High-Technology Business; Introduction to Microcomputers; Marketing Technological Products to Industry; How to Evaluate Your Technical Idea; Patenting Your Own Invention.

24687 ■ McShane Group Inc.
2345 York Rd., Ste. 102
Timonium, MD 21093
Ph: (410)560-0077
Fax: (410)560-2718
Co. E-mail: tmcshane@mcshanegroup.com
URL: http://www.mcshanegroup.com
Contact: Thomas P. McShane, President
E-mail: tmcshane@mcshanegroup.com
Scope: Turnaround consulting and crisis management firm. Specializes in due diligence services, interim management, strategic business realignments, business sale and asset depositions and debt

restructuring. Industries served: technology, financial, retail, distribution, medical, educational, manufacturing, contracting, environmental and health care. **Founded:** 1987.

24688 ■ Mefford, Knutson & Associates Inc. (MK)

6437 Lyndale Ave. S, Ste. 103
Richfield, MN 55423-1465
Ph: (612)869-8011
Free: 800-831-0228
Fax: (612)869-8004
Co. E-mail: info@mkaonline.net
URL: http://www.mkaonline.net
Contact: Jeanette Mefford, Director
E-mail: jmefford@mkaonline.com
Scope: A consulting and licensed business brokerage firm specializing in start-up businesses; strategic planning; mergers and acquisitions; joint ventures; divestitures; business process re-engineering; personnel policies and procedures; market research; new product development and cost controls. **Founded:** 1990.

24689 ■ Milestone Inc.—Blue SuitMilestone Consulting;

PO Box 630
Dedham, MA 02027
Ph: (781)467-1200
Fax: (781)467-0299
Co. E-mail: bob@milestoneideas.com
URL: http://www.milestoneideas.com
Contact: Robert J. Taraschi, President
E-mail: bob@milestoneideas.com
Scope: Facilitates 100 business creativity and innovation growth sessions per year. Assists to: Discover new growth strategies and planning options; create new ideas, new promises, value propositions, products and programs; identify and integrate customer passions in new and surprising ways; realize higher returns on involvement, interest and investment; refine processes, accelerate innovative growth and build better teams. **Founded:** 1980. **Publications:** "Can your brand tell a bigger story?" **Seminars:** Ideas in Action; Double-Gesturing; Growth in a period of no growth; Strike while the iron is cold; Natural Creative Strategies; The Enduring Power of Open Ended Creativity; Ideation Techniques to Drive Brand Value. **Special Services:** Milestone®; IMMERgENT®; SmartAlec.

24690 ■ MoneySoft Inc.

1 E Camelback Rd., Ste. 550
Phoenix, AZ 85012-1650
Ph: (602)266-7710
Free: 800-966-7797
URL: http://www.moneysoft.com
Contact: Bob Machiz, President
Scope: Specializes in the publication of software for the corporate acquisition and development communities. **Founded:** 1991. **Publications:** "The Price is Right? Or is It?"; "Preparing Financial Projections and Valuations"; "Negotiating Business Acquisitions"; "Managing the Process of Buying a Business"; "The Overpayment Trap"; "Strategies to Avoid the Overpayment Trap"; "The Value, Price and Cost of an Acquisition"; "The Trouble with EBITDA". **Special Services:** Corporate Valuation Professional?; DealSense?; BuyOutPlan?; Corporate Valuation?; Lightning Deal Reviewer?; Fixed Asset Pro?; Benchmark Pro 2006?; DealSense Plus; Mergerstat?.

24691 ■ New Commons

545 Pawtucket Ave., Studio 106A
Pawtucket, RI 02860
Ph: (401)351-7110
Fax: (401)351-7158
Co. E-mail: info@newcommons.com
URL: http://www.newcommons.com
Contact: Robert Leaver, Chief Executive Officer
E-mail: rleaver@newcommons.com
Scope: Builder of agile human networks to champion innovation and mobilize change; to pursue business opportunities; to custom design agile organizations and communities, to foster civic engagement. Clients include organizations on-profits, corporations, government agencies, educational institutions; networks-Trade/professional groups, IT services collaborations, service-sharing collectives; and communities- munici-

palities, states and statewide agencies, regional collaborations. **Founded:** 1982. **Publications:** "Plexus Imperative," Sep, 2005; "Creating 21st Century Capable Innovation Systems," Aug, 2004; "Call to Action: Building Providences Creative and Innovative Economy"; "Getting Results from Meetings"; "The Entrepreneur as Artist," Commonwealth Publications; "Leader and Agent of Change," Commonwealth Publications; "Achieving our Providence: Lessons of City-Building," Commonwealth Publications. **Seminars:** Introduction to Social Computing (Web 2.0), Jan, 2009; Every Company Counts, Jun, 2009; Facilitating for Results; Story-Making and Story-Telling. **Telecommunication Services:** inquiries@newcommons.com.

24692 ■ Nightingale Associates

7445 Setting Sun Way
Columbia, MD 21046
Ph: (410)381-4280
Fax: (410)381-4280
Co. E-mail: fredericknightingale@nightingaleassociates.net
URL: http://www.nightingaleassociates.net
Contact: Frederick C. Nightingale, Managing Director
E-mail: fredericknightingale@nightingaleAssociates.net
Scope: Management training and consulting firm offering the following skills: productivity and accomplishment; leadership skills for the experienced manager; management skills for the new manager; leadership and teambuilding; supervisory development; creative problem solving; real strategic planning; providing superior customer service; international purchasing and supply chain management; negotiation skills development and fundamentals of purchasing. **Founded:** 1984. **Seminars:** Productivity and Accomplishment Management Skills for the New Manager; Leadership and Team building; Advanced Management; Business Process Re engineering; Strategic Thinking; Creative Problem Solving; Customer Service; International Purchasing and Materials Management; Fundamentals of Purchasing; Negotiation Skills Development; Providing superior customer service; Leadership skills for the experienced manager.

24693 ■ P2C2 Group Inc.

4101 Denfeld Ave.
Kensington, MD 20895-1514
Ph: (301)942-7985
Fax: (301)942-7986
Co. E-mail: info@p2c2group.com
URL: http://www.p2c2group.com
Contact: James E. Kendrick, President
E-mail: kendrick@p2c2group.com
Scope: Works with clients on the business side of federal program and project management. Services include program/project planning and optimization; acquisition strategy and work statements; IT Capital Planning and Investment Control (CPIC); business cases - new, revisions, critiques; budget analysis - cost benefits- alternatives; CPIC, SELC, and security documentation; research, metrics, analysis, and case studies. Consulting support helping to: Define or redefine programs; strengthen portfolio management; identify alternatives for lean budgets; improve capital planning and investment; develop better plans and documentation, and evaluate performance of existing program investments. **Founded:** 1994. **Publications:** "OMB 300s Go Online," Federal Sector Report, Mar, 2007; "Using Risk-Adjusted Costs for Projects," Federal Sector Report, Feb, 2007; "Make Better Decisions Using Case Studies," Federal Sector Report, Jan, 2007; "PMO Performance Measurement & Metrics"; "Executive Sponsors for Projects"; "ABCs of the Presidential Transition"; "Financial Systems and Enterprise Portfolio Management"; "The Future of CPIC"; "Critical Factors for Program and Project Success"; "Using Risk-Adjusted Costs for Projects"; "Tactics for a Successful Year of CPIC"; "Operational Analysis Reviews"; "Successful IT Strategic Planning"; "Information Technology Investment Management". **Seminars:** Requests For Information; Pre Solicitation Marketing; Qualifications Statement Support For The Capital Planning And Investment Control (cpic) Process; How To Hire A Management Consultant And Get The Results You Expect.

24694 ■ Performance Consulting Associates Inc. (PCA)

3700 Crestwood Pky., Ste. 100
Duluth, GA 30096
Ph: (770)717-2737
Fax: (770)717-7014
Co. E-mail: info@pcaconsulting.com
URL: http://www.pcaconsulting.com
Contact: Richard A. Defazio, President
E-mail: defazio@pcaconsulting.com
Scope: Maintenance consulting and engineering firm specializing in production planning, project management, team building, and re-engineering maintenance. **Founded:** 1976. **Publications:** "Does Planning Pay," Plant Services, Nov, 2000; "Asset Reliability Coordinator," Maintenance Technology, Oct, 2000; "Know What it is You Have to Maintain," Maintenance Technology, May, 2000; "Does Maintenance Planning Pay," Maintenance Technology, Nov, 2000.; "What is Asset Management?"; "Implementing Best Business Practices".

24695 ■ Performance Consulting Group Inc.

8031 SW 35th Terr.
Miami, FL 33155-3443
Ph: (305)264-5577
Fax: (305)264-9079
Contact: Patrick J. O'Brien, President
Scope: Firm provides consulting services in the areas of strategic planning; profit enhancement; product development; and production planning. **Founded:** 1980.

24696 ■ Pioneer Business Consultants

9042 Garfield Ave., Ste. 211
Huntington Beach, CA 92646
Ph: (714)964-7600
Fax: (714)962-6585
Contact: John J. Collins, President
Scope: Offers general management consulting specializing in business acquisitions, tax and business planning, cash flow analyses, business valuations and business sales and expert witness court testimony regarding business sales, valuations and accounting. **Founded:** 1980.

24697 ■ Plans and Solutions Inc.

7823 Mistic View Ct.
Derwood, MD 20855
Ph: (301)947-8150
Fax: (240)525-5601
Co. E-mail: info@plansandsolutions.com
URL: http://www.plansandsolutions.com
Contact: Kenneth D. Weiss, President
E-mail: kw@plansandsolutions.com
Scope: Market research and competitive analysis; marketing and promotion planning, and executing promotion plans. Specializes in registration and problem solving services that include food canning establishment and process registration, registration under the terrorism act, assistance in case of detention of shipments, and on-site inspection of processing plants and records. Most clients are minority-owned businesses in the USA and companies overseas that want to begin or increase exports to the United States and Canada. **Founded:** 1996. **Publications:** "Building an Import/Export Business," John Wiley & Sons, 2002; "How to Conquer the U.S. Market"; "Going Global (Getting Started in International Trade)". **Seminars:** U.S. Import Regulations on Food Products.

24698 ■ Rothschild Strategies Unlimited L.L.C.

19 Thistle Rd.
Norwalk, CT 06851-1909
Ph: (203)846-6898
Fax: (203)847-1426
Co. E-mail: bill@strategyleader.com
URL: http://www.strategyleader.com
Contact: Stephen M. Rothschild, President
Scope: Consults with senior management and business level strategy teams to develop overall strategic direction, set priorities and creates sustainable competitive advantages and differentiators. Enables organizations to enhance their own strategic thinking and leadership skills so that they can continue to develop and implement profitable growth strategies. **Founded:** 1983. **Publications:** "Putting It All

Together-a guide to strategic thinking"; "Competitive Advantage"; "Ristaker, Caretaker, Surgeon & Undertaker four faces of strategic leadership"; "The Secret to GE's Success"; "Having the Right Strategic Leader and Team".

24699 ■ Sklar and Associates Inc.
242 Laurel Bay Dr.
Murrells Inlet, SC 29576
Ph: (843)798-0412
Fax: (843)651-3090
Co. E-mail: sklarincdc@aol.com
URL: http://www.sklarinc.com
Contact: Tim Sklar, President
Scope: Provider of consulting services for business acquisitions, business development and project finance. Provides audit oversight services to listed corporations on Sarbanes-Oxley compliance. Services include: Due diligence analyses and corporate governance. Industries served: transportation sectors, energy sector and commercial real estate industries. **Seminars:** Financial Analysis in MBA; Emerging Company Finance; Due Diligence in Business Acquisition; Business Valuation.

24700 ■ Staubs Business Services (SBS)
23320 S Vermont Ave.
Torrance, CA 90502-2940
Ph: (310)830-9128
Fax: (310)830-9128
Co. E-mail: harry_l_staubs@lamg.com
Contact: Harry L. Staubs, Principal
Scope: Provides business consulting support to new product development and business plans. **Founded:** 1994.

24701 ■ Tamayo Consulting Inc
169 Saxony Rd., Ste. 112
Encinitas, CA 92024-6779
Ph: (760)479-1352
Fax: (760)479-1465
Co. E-mail: info@tamayoconsulting.com
URL: http://www.tamayoconsulting.com
Contact: Jennifer Dreyer, President
E-mail: jdreyer@earthlink.net
Scope: It Provides training and consulting services. And also it specializes in leadership and team development. Industries served: private, non-profit, government, educational. **Founded:** 1986. **Seminars:** Presentation AdvantEdge Program; Lead point Development Program; Supervisor Development Programs.Identify Presentation Objectives; Implement 360-degree presentation assessment; conduct baseline-coaching session; Develop coaching plan; Staying connected.

24702 ■ ValueNomics Value Specialists
50 W San Fernando St., Ste. 600
San Jose, CA 95113
Fax: (408)200-6401
Co. E-mail: info@amllp.com
Contact: Gary E. Jones, Chief Executive Officer
Scope: Consulting is offered in the areas of financial management, process re-engineering, growth business services; governance, risk/compliance, SOX readiness and compliance, SAS 70, enterprise risk management, system security, operational and

internal audit; business advisory services; valuation services; CORE assessment; contract assurance; transaction advisory services, IT solutions and litigation support services. **Founded:** 1993. **Publications:** "Dueling Appraisers: How Differences in Input and Assumptions May Control the Value," Apr, 2005; "The Business of Business Valuation and the CPA as an expert witness"; "The Business of Business Valuation," McGraw-Hill Professional Publishers Inc.

24703 ■ VenturEdge Corp.
4711 Yonge St., Ste. 1105
Toronto, ON, Canada M2N 6K8
Ph: (416)224-2000
Fax: (416)224-2376
Co. E-mail: info@venturedge.com
URL: http://www.venturedge.com
Contact: Morris Langer, President
E-mail: langer@venturedge.com
Scope: Provides services including strategy formulation; business planning; financial management; business coaching; performance improvement; information management; merger, acquisitions and divestitures; family succession planning; competitive intelligence. **Founded:** 1972. **Publications:** "Reputation," Harvard Business School Press, 1996; "Competing for the Future," Harvard Business School Press, 1994; "The Fifth Discipline," 1990.

24704 ■ Vision Management
149 Meadows Rd.
Lafayette, NJ 07848-3120
Ph: (973)702-1116
Fax: (973)702-8311
Contact: Norman L. Naidish, President
Scope: Firm specializes in profit enhancement; strategic planning; business process reengineering; industrial engineering; facilities planning; team building; inventory management; and total quality management (TQM). **Founded:** 1984. **Publications:** "To increase profits, improve quality," Manufacturing Engineering, May, 2000.

24705 ■ Weich & Bilotti Inc.
600 Worcester Rd., 4th Fl.
Framingham, MA 01702
Ph: (508)663-1600
Fax: (508)663-1682
Co. E-mail: info@weich-bilotti.com
Contact: Mervyn D. Weich, Director
E-mail: mweich@weich-bilotti.com
Scope: Specializes in business plans, venture capital, computer information systems, turnaround/interim management, retail consulting, start-up process, college recruiting and IS and IT personnel. **Founded:** 1995.

24706 ■ Western Capital Holdings Inc.
10050 E Applewood Dr.
Parker, CO 80138
Ph: (303)841-1022
Contact: Patrick T. Frasco, President
Scope: Specialists in all phases of financial and management consulting. Provide strong emphasis in strategic planning and corporate development, financial analysis, acquisitions, investment banking and corporate finance. Projects range in size and

duration to fit clients needs. Services can be applied to many diverse financial projects that may include the following: Business plan development, budgeting and forecasting, strategic planning, cash flow analysis, cash flow management, corporate development, banking relations, asset management, and financial analysis. Industries served: Food industry, manufacturing, distribution, retailing, computer services, agribusiness, financial services, insurance, and government agencies. **Founded:** 1986. **Seminars:** Buy Low, Sell High, Collect Early and Pay Late; Preparing Your Company for Sale; Venture Capital - Finding an Angel.

COMPUTER SYSTEMS/ SOFTWARE

24707 ■ *Automate Your Business Plan 2009*
13381 White Sand Dr.
Tustin, CA 92780-4565
Ph: (714)544-0248
Free: 800-419-1513
Fax: (714)730-1414
Co. E-mail: lpinson@business-plan.com
URL: http://www.business-plan.com
Price: $95.00. **Description:** A computer program designed to help prepare a business plan.

RESEARCH CENTERS

24708 ■ Chadron State College - Nebraska Business Development Center (NBDC)
Burkhiser Technology Complex, Rm. 120
1000 Main St.
Chadron, NE 69337
Ph: (308)432-6282
Fax: (308)432-6430
Co. E-mail: jkoehn@csc.edu
URL: http://www.csc.edu/business/nbdc/about.csc
Contact: James Koehn, Assistant Director
Services: Consulting. **Founded:** 1977. **Publications:** *NBDC Business Calendar* (Annual). **Educational Activities:** Continuing education programs. **Awards:** Graduate assistantship in business & development.

24709 ■ University of Nebraska—Omaha - Nebraska Business Development Center (NBDC)
Mammel Hall, Ste. 200
College of Business Administration
Omaha, NE 68182-0248
Ph: (402)554-2521
Fax: (402)554-3473
Co. E-mail: rbernier@unomaha.edu
URL: http://nbdc.unomaha.edu
Contact: Robert E. (Bob) Bernier, Director
Services: Business consulting; Government procurement assistance; Manufacturing assistance. **Founded:** 1977. **Publications:** *Keys to Successful Business Start-Up in Nebraska*; *NBDC Business Calendar* (Annual). **Educational Activities:** Professional and Organizational Development (Weekly), by contract with corporations and organizations. **Awards:** NBDC Paid internships.

START-UP INFORMATION

24710 ■ *"Head West, Young Startup?'" in Boston Business Journal (Vol. 30, October 22, 2010, No. 39, pp. 1)*
Pub: Boston Business Journal
Ed: Galen Moore. **Description:** Startup companies Lark Technologies, Baydin and E la Cart Inc. are planning to leave Boston, Massachusetts for Silicon Valley. Lark has developed a vibrating wrist strap that syncs with a mobile phone's alarm clock.

REFERENCE WORKS

24711 ■ *"1Q Office Vacancies Mainly Up; Class A Space Bucks Trend, Falls'" in Crain's Detroit Business (Vol. 24, April 14, 2008, No. 15)*
Pub: Crain Communications, Inc.
Ed: Daniel Duggan. **Description:** Although more office space became vacant in the first quarter, Class A space went in the opposite direction with several local businesses are moving from less-desirable to more desirable areas.

24712 ■ *"Aeronautics Seeking New HQ Site'" in The Business Journal-Milwaukee (Vol. 25, September 5, 2008, No. 50, pp. 1)*
Pub: American City Business Journals, Inc.
Ed: Rich Kirchen. **Description:** Milwaukee, Wisconsin-based Aeronautics Corp. of America is planning to move its headquarters to a new site. The company has started to search for a new site. It also plans to consolidate its operations under one roof.

24713 ■ *"Affordable Again'" in The Business Journal-Serving Greater Tampa Bay (Vol. 28, July 18, 2008, No. 30, pp. 1)*
Pub: American City Business Journals, Inc.
Ed: Janet Leiser. **Description:** Rental rates for office space in the Tampa Bay area has dropped to $21.68 a foot, after demand for the second quarter of 2008 has remained low. Commercial real estate experts say that the industry can easily rebound from what is believed to be the weakest demand in 20 years. Other views, information and statistics on real estate demand and prices in Tampa Bay are, are presented.

24714 ■ *"Aircraft Maker May Land Here'" in Austin Business Journal (Vol. 31, April 15, 2011, No. 6, pp. 1)*
Pub: American City Business Journals Inc.
Ed: Jacob Dirr. **Description:** Icon Aircraft Inc. is planning to build a manufacturing facility in Austin, Texas. The company needs 100,000 square feet of space in a new or renovated plant. Executive comments are included.

24715 ■ *"Airmall Mulls I-95 Travel Plazas Bid'" in Boston Business Journal (Vol. 29, September 2, 2011, No. 17, pp. 3)*
Pub: American City Business Journals Inc.
Ed: Alexander Jackson. **Description:** Airmall USA is planning to move its food courts from the Baltimore/Washington International Thurgood Marshall Airport to the new travel plazas on Interstate 95. The plazas are up for bid.

24716 ■ *"Another California Firm On Way'" in Austin Business Journal (Vol. 31, May 6, 2011, No. 9, pp. 1)*
Pub: American City Business Journals Inc.
Ed: Christopher Calnan. **Description:** Main Street Hub Inc. is planning to build a facility in Austin, Texas. The company helps businesses manage their online reputations. Main Street has selected Aquila Commercial LLC as its real estate broker.

24717 ■ *"BancVue to Expand'" in Austin Business JournalInc. (Vol. 29, November 27, 2009, No. 38, pp. 1)*
Pub: American City Business Journals
Ed: Kate Harrington. **Description:** Significant growth of BancVue in the past six years has prompted the company to look for a site that could increase its office space from 25,000 square feet to 65,000 square feet. BancVue offers bank and credit union software solutions and is planning to lease or buy a property in Austin, Texas.

24718 ■ *"Bank Bullish on Austin'" in Austin Business JournalInc. (Vol. 29, November 13, 2009, No. 36, pp. A1)*
Pub: American City Business Journals
Ed: Kate Harrington. **Description:** American Bank's presence in Austin, Texas has been boosted by new management and a new 20,000 square foot building. This community bank intends to focus on building relationship with commercial banking customers. American Bank also plans to extend investment banking, treasury management, and commercial lending services.

24719 ■ *"Bellingham Boatbuilder Norstar Yachts Maintains Family Tradition'" in Bellingham Business Journal (Vol. February 2010, pp. 12)*
Pub: Sound Publishing Inc.
Ed: Isaac Bonnell. **Description:** Profile of Norstar Yachts and brothers Gary and Steve Nordtvedt who started the company in 1994. The company recently moved its operations to a 12,000 square foot space in the Fairhaven Marine Industrial Park.

24720 ■ *"Boeing's Next Flight May Well Be to the South'" in Puget Sound Business Journal (Vol. 29, November 21, 2008, No. 31, pp.)*
Pub: American City Business Journals
Ed: Steve Wilhelm. **Description:** Southern states in the U.S. are luring Boeing Company to locate a new plant in their region which is experiencing a growing industrial base while offering permissive labor laws as selling points.

24721 ■ *"Bond Hill Cinema Site To See New Life'" in Business Courier (Vol. 27, October 29, 2010, No. 26, pp. 1)*
Pub: Business Courier
Ed: Dan Monk. **Description:** Avondale, Ohio's Corinthian Baptist Church will redevelop the 30-acre former Showcase Cinema property to a mixed-use site that could feature a college, senior home, and retail.

Corinthian Baptist, which is one of the largest African-American churches in the region, is also planning to relocate the church.

24722 ■ *"Bovie Medical Makes Electrosurgical Strike'" in The Business Journal-Serving Greater Tampa Bay (Vol. 28, August 22, 2008, No. 35)*
Pub: American City Business Journals, Inc.
Ed: Margie Manning. **Description:** Bovie Medical Group, which manufactures electrosurgical products, is planning to sell its manufacturing plant in the Tyrone Industrial Park and to purchase the former Harland Clarke facility. The moves are expected to boost the efficiency and the development of new products. Other information on Bovie Medical Group is presented.

24723 ■ *"Cal-ISO Plans $125 Million Facility'" in Sacramento Business Journal (Vol. 25, August 1, 2008, No. 22, pp. 1)*
Pub: American City Business Journals, Inc.
Ed: Celia Lamb; Michael Shaw. **Description:** Sacramento, California-based nonprofit organization California Independent System Operator (ISO) is planning to build a new headquarters in Folsom. The new building would double its current leased space to 227,000 square feet. The ISO will seek tax-exempt bond financing for the project.

24724 ■ *Catawba County Chamber of Commerce--Membership Directory/Relocation Guide*
Pub: Catawba County Chamber of Commerce
Contact: Danny Hearn, President
E-mail: dhearn@catawbachamber.org
URL(s): www.catawbachamber.org. **Covers:** Chamber members. **Entries include:** Contact details.

24725 ■ *"Centrue Sets Down New Roots in St. Louis; Bank Looks to Expand in Exurbs of Chicago'" in Crain's Chicago Business (May 5, 2008)*
Pub: Crain Communications, Inc.
Ed: H. Lee Murphy. **Description:** Centrue Financial Corp. has moved its headquarters from Ottawa to suburban St. Louis in search of higher-growth markets. The banks acquisitions and expansion plans are also discussed.

24726 ■ *"Chuy's Gears Up to Serve Atlants, Other Untapped Cities'" in Austin Business Journal (Vol. 31, June 17, 2011, No. 15, pp. 1)*
Pub: American City Business Journals Inc.
Ed: Cody Lyon. **Description:** Chuy's Holdings Inc. plans to expand into the Southeastern United States, particularly in Atlanta, Georgia. The restaurant, which secured $67.5 million in debt financing in May 2011, added 20 stores in five years and plans to open eight locations in 2011.

24727 ■ *"Cities Work to Attract Small Biz'" in Crain's Detroit Business (Vol. 25, June 8, 2009, No. 23, pp. 20)*
Pub: Crain Communications Inc. - Detroit
Ed: Nancy Kaffer. **Description:** Royal Oak and other metropolitan cities are trying to attract small companies to their towns.

24728 ■ *"City, County May Kill VC Tax" in Business Journal-Portland (Vol. 24, October 12, 2007, No. 33, pp. 1)*
Pub: American City Business Journals, Inc.

Ed: Aliza Earnshaw. **Description:** City of Portland and Multnomah County in Oregon may soon kill taxes levied on venture capital (VC) firms, which is expected to take place in late October 2007. Capitalists have long been saying that taxation is driving them out of town, but this change is expected to generate more investments and persuade VC firms to relocate within city limits.

24729 ■ *"City Wooing Red Roof Inn for Return of Corporate HQ" in Business First-Columbus (October 19, 2007, pp. A1)*
Pub: American City Business Journals, Inc.

Description: Department of Development of Columbus, Ohio offered Red Roof Inns Inc. a four-year, 40 percent jobs growth initiative to entice the company to move its corporate headquarters into the city from Dallas, Texas. The Watermark Island office building off Dublin Road and Grandview Avenue will be the headquarters of the company if it accepts the offer.

24730 ■ *"Clinic to Use Medical Summit to Pump Up Cardiology Center" in Crain's Cleveland Business (Vol. 28, October 1, 2007, No. 39, pp. 6)*
Pub: Crain Communications, Inc.

Ed: Chuck Soder. **Description:** Overview of the Medical Innovation Summit, sponsored by the Cleveland Clinic and regional business recruitment group Team NEO, whose theme was cardiology. The goal for this year's summit went beyond finding companies for the cardiovascular center, it also looked to market the region to other industries with growth potential.

24731 ■ *"Creativity is Essential in Sagging Relocation Market" in Crain's Cleveland Business (Vol. 28, November 5, 2007, No. 44, pp. 19)*
Pub: Crain Communications, Inc.

Ed: Christine Gordillo. **Description** Since Northeast Ohio was headquarters to a number of Fortune 500 companies, residential real estate builders and brokers could count on corporate relocation clients for a steady stream of business. Today, corporations have become more cautious when relocating talent due to the costs involved which has forced industry experts to be more patient and more creative in the ways they attract out-of-town buyers who are likely to be a sure sell.

24732 ■ *"Criticare Sees Rapid Expansion" in Business Journal-Milwaukee (Vol. 28, December 31, 2010, No. 14, pp. A1)*
Pub: Milwaukee Business Journal

Ed: Rich Rovito. **Description:** Criticare Systems Inc. expanded its distribution network, added customers, launched two new products and transferred into a new building in Pewaukee, Wisconsin at the start of their fiscal year. Criticare expanded its workforce and now has nearly 140 full time employees.

24733 ■ *"Delaware Diaper Maker Wanting To Expand Less Than a Year After Move" in Business First-Columbus (December 7, 2007, pp. A6)*
Pub: American City Business Journals, Inc.

Ed: Dan Eaton. **Description:** Duluth, Georgia-based Associated Hygienic Products LLC is planning to expand its production operations by 20 percent and hire new workers. The diaper maker was awarded state incentives to facilitate its transfer from Marion to Delaware. Details are included.

24734 ■ *"Delta Looks at Downtown Departure" in Business Courier (Vol. 27, October 1, 2010, No. 22, pp. 1)*
Pub: Business Courier

Ed: Dan Monk. **Description:** Delta Air Lines Inc. has been looking for a smaller office for its reservations center in downtown Cincinnati, Ohio. Delta has informed the city of its plan to seek proposals on office space alternatives in advance of the 2011 lease expiration. Insights on the current employment status at the reservations center are also given.

24735 ■ *"Dollar Doldrums; How American Companies are Beating the Currency Crunch" in Inc. (March 2008, pp. 45-46)*
Pub: Gruner & Jahr USA Publishing

Ed: Sarah Goldstein. **Description:** Despite the low American dollar, some exporters are seeing a growth in their businesses, while other have had to relocate operations and switch to U.S. supplier. Four business owners tell how they are dealing with the current economic conditions.

24736 ■ *"Downtown Evens Tenant Ledger" in The Business Journal-Serving Metropolitan Kansas City (Vol. 26, July 11, 2008, No. 44, pp. 1)*
Pub: American City Business Journals, Inc.

Ed: Rob Roberts. **Description:** Financial services company PricewaterhouseCoopers will relocate its office from the Broadway Square building, but it will not leave downtown as it signs a long-term lease for a 27,000 square feet of space in Town Pavilion. Town Pavilion is the biggest multitenant office building in downtown. Downtown's market competitiveness is also examined.

24737 ■ *"Exxon Mobil Campus 'Clearly Happening" in Houston Business Journal (Vol. 40, January 15, 2010, No. 36, pp. 1)*
Pub: American City Business Journals

Ed: Jennifer Dawson. **Description:** Oil and gas company Exxon Mobil intends to relocate its employees from Houston, Texas and Fairfax, Virginia into a 400-acre site near the town of Spring, Texas. Meanwhile, Exxon Mobil has refused to disclose further details of the relocation plan. Insights from real estate professionals on this relocation plan are examined.

24738 ■ *"FIS-Metavante Deal Paying Off for Many" in Business Journal-Milwaukee (Vol. 28, December 17, 2010, No. 11, pp. A1)*
Pub: Milwaukee Business Journal

Ed: Rich Kirchen. **Description:** Jacksonville, Florida-based Fidelity National Information Services Inc., also known as FIS, has remained committed to Milwaukee, Wisconsin more than a year after purchasing Metavante Technologies Inc. FIS has transferred several operations into Metropolitan Milwaukee and has continued its contribution to charitable organizations in the area.

24739 ■ *"Formaspace Finds a Bigger Home" in Austin Business JournalInc. (Vol. 29, December 4, 2009, No. 39, pp. 1)*
Pub: American City Business Journals

Ed: Kate Harrington. **Description:** Formaspace Technical Furniture has signed a lease for 56,700 square feet in Harris Ridge Business Center at Northeast Austin, Texas. which represents one of the area's largest leases for 2009. The new lease enables Formaspace to hire new employees, invest in new equipment, and take advantage of a taxing designation created for manufacturers.

24740 ■ *"Good for Business: Houston is a Hot Spot for Economic Growth" in Black Enterprise (Vol. 37, October 2006, No. 3, pp. 216)*
Pub: Earl G. Graves Publishing Co. Inc.

Ed: Jeanette Valentine. **Description:** Fast-growing sectors in the biotechnology and healthcare industries are among the driving forces of Houston's economic growth. More than 76,000 small businesses in the area employ about one in four area workers, according to the Small Business Administration. Housing and business costs are 26 and 11 percent below the national average, respectively, garnering the attention of corporate giants.

24741 ■ *"Hyde Park Hungry for Expansion at Cap" in Business First-Columbus (October 12, 2007, pp. A1)*
Pub: American City Business Journals, Inc.

Ed: Dan Eaton. **Description:** The Cap, an area developed for the retail and restaurant industry, is experiencing major changes such as Hyde Park Restaurant System's planned expansion, and the expected departure of other tenants. The expansion of Hyde Park will lead to the relocation of Schakolad Chocolate Factory.

24742 ■ *"Insurance Firm Consolidates Offices; Integro Finds the Right Price Downtown" in Crain's New York Business (January 14, 2008)*
Pub: Crain Communications, Inc.

Description: Integro insurance brokers is relocating its headquarters to 1 State Street Plaza, where it will consolidate its operations in March. The firm feels that the upscale design will provide an appropriate setting for entertaining clients and an engaging work environment for employees.

24743 ■ *"Insurer Buys Foundation's Uptown HQ" in Charlotte Business Journal (Vol. 25, December 17, 2010, No. 39, pp. 1)*
Pub: Charlotte Business Journal

Ed: Will Boye. **Description:** Charlotte, North Carolina-based Synergy Coverage Solutions has purchased the three-story building owned by Foundations For the Carolinas for slightly more than $3 million. Synergy plans to relocate its operation in the uptown building by August 2011.

24744 ■ *"Is It Time to Move to a Real Office?' in Women Entrepreneur (December 30, 2008)*
Pub: Entrepreneur Media Inc.

Ed: Aliza Sherman. **Description:** Before moving a company from a home-office to a real office is important to make sure that the additional overhead that will be incurred by the move is comfortably covered and that the move is being done for the right reasons. Several women entrepreneurs who have moved their businesses from their homes to an actual rental space are profiled.

24745 ■ *"Kodiak Bucks Bear Market" in Austin Business JournalInc. (Vol. 29, December 18, 2009, No. 41, pp. 1)*
Pub: American City Business Journals

Ed: Kate Harrington. **Description:** Austin, Texas-based Kodiak Assembly Solutions LLC, a company that installs components into printed circuit boards for product or evaluation tool kit prototyping purposes, will expand despite the recession. It will relocate from a 28,000 square foot space to a 42,000 square foot space in North Austin. The firm will also increase its workforce by 20 employees.

24746 ■ *"KXAN Seeks Larger Studio, Office Space" in Austin Business Journal (Vol. 31, May 27, 2011, No. 12, pp. A1)*
Pub: American City Business Journals Inc.

Ed: Cody Lyon. **Description:** Austin NBC affiliate KXAN Television is opting to sell its property north of downtown and relocate to another site. The station is now inspecting possible sites to house its broadcasting facility and employees totaling as many as 200 people. Estimated cost of the construction of the studios and offices is $13 million plus another million in moving the equipment.

24747 ■ *"Lack of Support Drives Scientists Away from Valley" in The Business Journal - Serving Phoenix and the Valley of the Sun (Vol. 28, August 1, 2008, No. 48, pp. 1)*
Pub: American City Business Journals, Inc.

Ed: Angela Gonzales. **Description:** Lack of support for scientists has caused scientists like Dietrich Stephan to depart from the city. Stephan is expected to relocate to California where he has found funding for his company Navigenics. Other views and information on the rising rate of the departure of scientists are presented.

24748 ■ *"LatinWorks Cozies Up to Chevy in Detroit" in Austin Business Journal (Vol. 31, August 12, 2011, No. 23, pp. A1)*
Pub: American City Business Journals Inc.

Ed: Sandra Zaragoza. **Description:** Hispanic marketing agency LatinWorks opened an office in Detroit to better serve its client Chevrolet and to potentially secure more contracts from its parent company General Motors, whose offices are located nearby.

24749 ■ *"Law Firm Jones Day Coming to Boston" in Boston Business Journal (Vol. 30,*

November 19, 2010, No. 43, pp. 1)
Pub: Boston Business Journal
Ed: Lisa van der Pool. **Description:** Jones Day is set to open an office in Boston, Massachusetts. The company will be the largest law firm to enter Boston since 2007. The firm will open with at least three partners.

24750 ■ "Look Before You Lease" in Women Entrepreneur (February 3, 2009)
Pub: Entrepreneur Media Inc.
Ed: Nina L. Kaufman. **Description:** Top issues to consider before leasing an office space are discussed including: additional charges that may be expected on top of the basic rental price; determining both short- and long-term goals; the cost of improvements to the space; the cost of upkeep; and the conditions of the lease.

24751 ■ "Mayfair Considers Moving Boston Store" in The Business Journal-Milwaukee (Vol. 25, September 5, 2008, No. 50, pp. 1)
Pub: American City Business Journals, Inc.
Ed: Rich Kirchen. **Description:** Milwaukee, Wisconsin-based Bon-Ton Stores is planning to relocate its Boston Store at the Mayfair Mall. The existing store is to be redeveloped into smaller specialty shops. Details of the new facility are also presented.

24752 ■ "MBT Add On: Gone by 2012?" in Crain's Detroit Business (Vol. 24, October 6, 2008, No. 40, pp. 1)
Pub: Crain Communications, Inc.
Ed: Amy Lane. **Description:** Discusses the Michigan Business Tax (MBT), which has angered many businesses in the state due to the addition of a 21.99 percent surcharge. Although the tax policy will cut taxes on 63 percent of businesses in the state and represent no tax liability change for another nine percent of firms, other businesses will see increases of 100 percent or more. This increase means that many business owners will be forced to relocate or close their establishment and others will have to eliminate jobs. Lawmakers are attempting to find a solution to this problem.

24753 ■ "Mission: Poach California" in Business Journal Portland (Vol. 26, December 11, 2009, No. 40, pp. 1)
Pub: American City Business Journals Inc.
Ed: Andy Giegerich. **Description:** Leaders of Greenlight Greater Portland, a privately funded economic development organization, will visit California five times in 2010 in an attempt to lure California businesses to expand or relocate in Oregon.

24754 ■ "More Jobs Moving Out of City" in Business Courier (Vol. 24, March 14, 2008, No. 49, pp. 1)
Pub: American City Business Journals, Inc.
Ed: Steve Watkins; Laura Baverman. **Description:** UBS Financial Services Inc. is moving Gradison to Kenwood Town Place in Sycamore Township a year after UBS acquired Gradison. The township does not have a tax on earnings so the move will save Gradison's employees the 2.1 percent Cincinnati tax.

24755 ■ "Move South Could Bring Big Benefits" in Business Journal-Portland (Vol. 24, November 9, 2007, No. 36, pp. 1)
Pub: American City Business Journals, Inc.
Ed: Matthew Kish. **Description:** Freightliner LLC has announced that it would move around one-tenth of its jobs to Fort Mill, South Carolina, but stated that immediate plans for headquarters relocation have not been made. The relocation of its headquarters is expected to earn $100 million in economic incentives. The benefits of moving to the area, aside from the economic incentives, are discussed.

24756 ■ "Moving On: What's It Worth?" in Entrepreneur (Vol. 36, February 2008, No. 2, pp. 32)
Pub: Entrepreneur Media Inc.
Ed: Jacquelyn Lynn. **Description:** An area's cost of living should be considered by business owners when relocating, as it can affect operating costs and salary

expenses, among other issues. Details on how to decide on business relocation with regard to cost of living concerns are examined.

24757 ■ "NEMRA Announces Headquarters Move" in Agency Sales Magazine (Vol. 39, September-October 2009, No. 9, pp. 53)
Pub: MANA
Description: NEMRA, the National Electrical Manufacturers' Representatives Association is moving their headquarters to 28 Deer Street, Suite 302, Portsmouth, New Hampshire. The association has also added Michelle Rivers-Jameson as their manager of operations and Kirsty Stebbins as their manager of marketing and member services.

24758 ■ "A New Mix of Tenants Settles In" in Crain's New York Business (Vol. 24, January 14, 2008, No. 2, pp. 26)
Pub: Crain Communications, Inc.
Ed: Andrew Marks. **Description:** More and more nonfinancial firms are relocating downtown due to the new retailers and restaurants that are reshaping the look and feel of lower Manhattan.

24759 ■ "Office Leasing Gains Ground" in Sacramento Business Journal (Vol. 25, July 18, 2008, No. 20, pp. 1)
Pub: American City Business Journals, Inc.
Ed: Michael Shaw. **Description:** There were at least 84,000 square feet leased to companies in the Sacramento area in the three months prior to August 2008. This development is good news considering that overall vacant leases were around 247,000 square feet for the previous quarter.

24760 ■ "Opportunity Knocks" in Small Business Opportunities (September 2008)
Pub: Entrepreneur Media Inc.
Description: Profile of YourOffice USA, a franchise that provides home-based and small businesses cost-effective and efficient support through 'virtual' offices that are available as much or as little as the client needs it; they also supply necessary tools such as a professional business address, private mailbox service, personalized telephone answering and more that supports clients who want to look, act and operate with an advanced business image.

24761 ■ "Penney's Buys Wal-Mart Site" in Crain's Chicago Business (Vol. 31, March 31, 2008, No. 13, pp. 13)
Pub: Crain Communications, Inc.
Ed: Eddie Baeb. **Description:** J.C. Penny Co. bought the closed Wal-Mart location in Crystal Lake and plans to open a store next year in its push to become more prominent in non-mall locations; Penney plans to expand and renovate the store.

24762 ■ "Portland Wooing Under Armour to West Coast Facility" in Baltimore Business Journal (Vol. 27, January 29, 2010, No. 39, pp. 1)
Pub: American City Business Journals
Ed: Andy Giegerich. **Description:** Baltimore, Maryland sports apparel maker, Under Armour, is planning a west coast expansion with Portland, Oregon among the sites considered to house its apparel and footwear design center. Portland officials counting on the concentration of nearly 10,000 activewear workers in the city will help lure the company to the city.

24763 ■ "Race Benefits: Changes Afoot for Ironman" in Business Journal Serving Greater Tampa Bay (Vol. 30, October 29, 2010, No. 45, pp. 1)
Pub: Tampa Bay Business Journal
Ed: Margaret Cashill. **Description:** World Triatholon Corporation, organizer of the Ironman World Championship 70.3, will move the sports event from Florida to Nevada in 2011. A replacement event, the 5150 Triathlon Series, will be held in 2011 and the series finale will be staged in Florida's Clearwater Beach. How hotels and motels in the area will benefit from the 5150 Triathlon Series is discussed.

24764 ■ "RES Stakes Its Claim in Area" in Philadelphia Business Journal (Vol. 28,

January 29, 2010, No. 50, pp. 1)
Pub: American City Business Journals
Ed: Peter Key. **Description:** RES Software Company Inc. of Amsterdam, Netherlands appointed Jim Kirby as president for the Americas and Klaus Besier as chairman in an effort to boost the firm's presence in the US. Brief career profiles of Kirby and Besier are included. RES develops software that allows management of information flow between an organization and its employees regardless of location.

24765 ■ "Retail News: Children's Boutique Relocates to Conway" in Sun News (June 4, 2010)
Pub: The Sun News
Description: Little Angel's Children's Boutique and Big Oak Frame Shop have moved to downtown locations in Conway, South Carolina. Little Angel's will sell children's clothing and accessories, shoes and gifts, while the frame shop will offer custom framing along with the sale of stationary, invitations and local prints.

24766 ■ "Search Engine: GE Looks Around" in Business Courier (Vol. 24, March 7, 2008, No. 48, pp. 1)
Pub: American City Business Journals, Inc.
Ed: Laura Baverman. **Description:** GE Aviation, an aircraft engine company, could move about 1,500 Tri-employees to its new office in West Chester, Liberty Township, Northern Kentucky, as its leases are set to expire in 2009 and 2010. The company revealed that developers are prompting the firm to send out a request-for-proposal to choose development companies in 2008.

24767 ■ "Shire Seeking New Digs for Headquarters" in Philadelphia Business Journal (Vol. 30, September 2, 2011, No. 29, pp. 1)
Pub: American City Business Journals Inc.
Ed: Natalie Kostelni. **Description:** Dublin, Ireland-based Shire PLC announced plans to relocate its North American headquarters from Chesterbrook Corporate Center in Wayne, Pennsylvania and currently evaluating their options. The specialty biopharmaceutical firm is also considering a move to New Jersey or Delaware.

24768 ■ "The Silvery Moon Moves to Larger Space" in Bellingham Business Journal (Vol. March 2010, pp. 5)
Pub: Sound Publishing Inc.
Description: Jewelry store, the Silvery Moon, moved to a larger location in order to expand its business. The new location was chosen because it offers the firm more visibility. The store offers find silver and gold pieces and specializes in Pacific Northwest native jewelry.

24769 ■ "Sobering Consequences" in The Business Journal-Milwaukee (Vol. 25, July 11, 2008, No. 42, pp. A1)
Pub: American City Business Journals, Inc.
Ed: Rich Rovito. **Description:** Milwaukee Mayor Tom Barrett and Wisconsin Governor Jim Doyle met with MillerCoors management in an effort to convince the company to locate its corporate headquarters in the city. The company is expected to announce its decision by mid-July 2008. It was revealed that the decision-making process is focusing on determining an optimal location for the headquarters.

24770 ■ "State Printing Plant on the Move" in Sacramento Business Journal (Vol. 25, August 29, 2008, No. 26, pp. 1)
Pub: American City Business Journals, Inc.
Ed: Michael Shaw; Celia Lamb. **Description:** California is planning to replace its printing plant on Richards Boulevard and 7th Street with a newly built or leased facility in the Sacramento area. It was revealed that the project will meet the state's standards for new buildings. It is believed that the new site will require 15 acres or more depending on requirements.

24771 ■ "Suppliers Look to Rack Up Big Sales to Distributors" in The Business Journal-Serving Metropolitan Kansas City

(August 15, 2008)
Pub: American City Business Journals, Inc.

Ed: James Dornbrook. **Description:** Suppliers of shelving units, conveyor systems and other equipment used in distribution facilities are expecting new business opportunities along with the planned intermodal projects in the Kansas City area. Suppliers have already observed that small distributors have started to relocate to the city because of the intermodal projects. Demand for shelves and lifts have also increased.

24772 ■ *"Sykes Shift from GunnAllen to New Venture" in Tampa Bay Business Journal (Vol. 30, December 18, 2009, No. 52, pp. 1)*
Pub: American City Business Journals

Ed: Margie Manning. **Description:** Tampa, Florida's entrepreneur John H. Sykes acquired Pointe Capital Inc., a GunnAllen Holdings Inc. subsidiary, through his JHS Capital Holdings Inc. and changed the name to JHS Capital Advisors Inc. Sykes will become president and CEO of JHS Capital Advisors and will relocate its corporate headquarters to Tampa, Florida.

24773 ■ *"Taking the Over-the-Counter Route to US" in Barron's (Vol. 88, July 7, 2008, No. 27, pp. 24)*
Pub: Dow Jones & Co., Inc.

Ed: Eric Uhlfelder. **Description:** Many multinational companies have left the New York Stock Exchange and allowed their shares to trade over-the-counter. The companies have taken advantage of a 2007 SEC rule allowing publicly listed foreign companies to change trading venues if less than 5 percent of global trading volume in the past 12 months occurred in the US.

24774 ■ *"Tecumseh Products to Begin Moving HQ" in Crain's Detroit Business (Vol. 24, March 31, 2008, No. 13, pp. 35)*
Pub: Crain Communications, Inc.

Ed: Chad Halcom. **Description:** Tecumseh Products Co., a manufacturer of compressor products, will transfer its headquarters to Pittsfield Township near Ann Arbor.

24775 ■ *"Tri-State to Get New Headquarters" in Business Courier (Vol. 27, October 22, 2010, No. 25, pp. 1)*
Pub: Business Courier

Ed: James Ritchie. **Description:** Hong Kong-based corn processing firm Global Bio-Chem Technology is set to choose Greater Cincinnati, Ohio as a location of its North American headquarters. The interstate access, central location, and low labor and property costs might have enticed Global Bio-Chem to invest in the region. Statistics on Chinese direct investment in U.S. are also presented.

24776 ■ *"UC May Expand into Old Ford Plant" in Business Courier (Vol. 26, December 25, 2009, No. 35, pp. 1)*
Pub: American City Business Journals, Inc.

Ed: Dan Monk. **Description:** Developer Stuart Lichter is planning to acquire University of Cincinnati (UC) as a tenant at a two-story office building on a 132-acre site where a vacant Ford transmission plant is located. Details of the transaction are outlined.

24777 ■ *"U.S. Playing Card Might Shuffle HQ" in Business Courier (Vol. 24, March 21, 2008, No. 50, pp. 1)*
Pub: American City Business Journals, Inc.

Ed: Jon Newberry. **Description:** United States Playing Card Co. is considering the possibility of relocating. It is expected that the company will finalize its decision by June 2008. According to Phil Dolci, the company's president, the firm is looking at certain locations in Ohio, Kentucky, and Indiana. He also revealed that the plan to relocate was prompted by the desire to improve the company's manufacturing facilities.

24778 ■ *"Viewing Ironman As Gold, R.I. Firm Buys Its Parent" in The Business Journal-Serving Greater Tampa Bay (Vol. 28,*

September 19, 2008)
Pub: American City Business Journals, Inc.

Ed: Pete Williams. **Description:** Providence Equity Partners purchased World Triathlon Corp., parent company of the Ironman Triathlon, for an undisclosed sum. The acquisition means that the World Triathlon Headquarters will move to Tampa, Florida, and allows Providence Equity Partners to stage or license rights to Ironman and half-Ironman distance events.

24779 ■ *"'We Are Not a Marketing Company" in Boston Business Journal (Vol. 31, June 10, 2011, No. 20, pp. 1)*
Pub: Boston Business Journal

Ed: Julie M. Donnelly. **Description:** Vertex Pharmaceuticals Inc. is marketing its new Hepatitis C treatment, Incivek. The company hired people to connect patients to the drug. Vertex is also set to move to a new facility in Boston, Massachusetts.

24780 ■ *"Welcome: From the Chamber of Commerce" in Inside Business (Vol. 13, September-October 2011, No. 5, pp. SS5)*
Pub: Great Lakes Publishing Co.

Ed: Diane Helbig. **Description:** Diane Helbig, Chairperson for the Lakewood Chamber of Commerce in Ohio touts the areas as the best place to start and run a small company. Two colleges, real estate, and culture are among the reasons cited.

24781 ■ *"What City is the No. 1 Destination for Residents Moving From WNY?" in Business First Buffalo (October 26, 2007, pp. 1)*
Pub: American City Business Journals, Inc.

Ed: G. Scott Thomas. **Description:** IRS records reveal that 2,639 people moved from the Buffalo County Region of New York to the Rochester area from 2005 to 2006. Family considerations and career opportunities are the main factors for the almost reciprocal migration of people from Rochester to Buffalo, New York.

TRADE PERIODICALS

24782 ■ **Expansion Management: Growth Strategies for Companies on the Move**
Pub: Penton Media Inc.

URL(s): www.expansionmanagement.com. **Released:** 6/yr.

CONSULTANTS

24783 ■ Daniel Bloom and Associates Inc. (DBAI)
11517 128th Ave. N
Largo, FL 33778
Ph: (727)581-6216
Fax: (727)216-8532
Co. E-mail: dan@dbaiconsulting.com
URL: http://www.dbaiconsulting.com
Contact: Sharon Megiel, Consultant

Scope: Human resources management consultant with a specialization in corporate relocation. Offers clients a turn key service aimed at meeting the unique relocation needs of their employees. Develops and implements training programs within the relocation industry. **Founded:** 1980. **Publications:** "Where Have All the Elders Gone," Aug, 2002; "Recoup Your Hiring Investment," Brainbuzz.com, Aug, 2000; "Managing Your Lump Sum Program," Brainbuzz. com, Jun, 2000; "Buyer Value Options," Brainbuzz. com, Apr, 2000; "Just Get Me There". **Seminars:** Chaos in the Workplace: Multiple Generational Interactions; Training Effectiveness: Is the Cost Justified?; Human Capital Resource Management: A Six-Sigma Based Approach to Paving Your Way to the Table; Welcome to My World.

24784 ■ The Boyd Company Inc.
301 N Harrison St., Ste. 415
Princeton, NJ 08540-3512
Ph: (609)890-0726
Free: 800-974-2693

Fax: (609)920-0266
Co. E-mail: contact@theboydcompany.com
URL: http://www.theboydcompany.com
Contact: John H. Boyd, President
E-mail: jhb@theboydcompany.com
Scope: Provider of site selection services to corporate clients expanding or relocating manufacturing, office, and distribution warehousing facilities. Provides corporate management with objective and authoritative analyzes of all geographically variable costs and other quantitative and qualitative location factors affecting optimum site selection. Firm works throughout the 50 states on behalf of leading United States corporations and overseas companies planning direct investment in the United States. **Founded:** 1975. **Special Services:** BizCosts®.

24785 ■ C.D.S. Building Movers
8 Sweetnam Dr.
Ottawa, ON, Canada K2S 1G2
Ph: (613)836-1215
Free: 800-267-5516
Fax: (613)831-0240
Co. E-mail: info@cdsmovers.com
URL: http://www.cdsmovers.com
Contact: Doris Sweetnam, President
Scope: Structural engineering and building relocation consultants providing appraisals and feasibility studies for the relocation of large buildings and structures. Specializing in historic and heritage masonry buildings. **Founded:** 1987.

24786 ■ The Foster Group
13321 Purple Sage Rd.
Dallas, TX 75240
Ph: (972)690-4041
Fax: (972)692-7042
Contact: Mary Sue Foster, President
E-mail: marysue@earthlink.net
Scope: Provider of services including leadership development, team building, appreciative inquiry, conflict solution for managers and executive. Involves in fund raising, grant uniting for non-profits. **Founded:** 1992. **Publications:** "Move It! Relocating Your Business with No Downtime".

24787 ■ Hartford Despatch International—Hartford Despatch
225 Prospect St.
East Hartford, CT 06128-1654
Ph: (860)578-2600
Free: 800-678-9000
Fax: (860)282-1224
Co. E-mail: custsvc@hartforddespatch.com
URL: http://www.hartforddespatch.com
Contact: Anson B. Mooney, President
E-mail: amooney@hartforddespatch.com
Scope: Domestic and international relocation services company. An independent provider of worldwide moving and storage services. **Founded:** 1906.

24788 ■ NRI Relocation Inc. (NRI)
195 Arlington Heights Rd., Ste. 101
Buffalo Grove, IL 60089
Ph: (847)215-5000
Free: 800-598-8887
Fax: (847)215-7633
Co. E-mail: nri@nrirelocation.com
URL: http://www.nrirelocation.com
Contact: Susan L. Bender, Chief Executive Officer
E-mail: sbender@nrirelocation.com
Scope: A full service relocation management company. Assists corporations in the creation and execution of relocation programs. Services include developing, updating and implementing relocation policies for employees, new hires and special group moves; design and implementation of in-house or modified in-house relocation management; appraisal, marketing and acquisition of residential property; home finding temporary living; household goods transportation; policy counseling and spouse assistance. International services include language and cultural training; freight forwarding; destination services; Visa; repatriation and spouse assistance. **Founded:** 1985.

24789 ■ Overland, Pacific & Cutler Inc.
3750 Schaufele Ave., Ste. 150
Long Beach, CA 90808
Ph: (562)304-2000

Free: 800-400-7356
Fax: (562)304-2020
URL: http://www.opcservices.com
Contact: David A. Stadler, President

Scope: Provider of real estate development services. It offers on-site project administration, replacement, rehabilitation, and relocation services. **Founded:** 1980. **Seminars:** Right of Way Acquisition for Engineers, 2008; Commercial Relocations, 2008; Relax, It's Only Business Relocation, Dec, 2007; Relocation Nightmares, Aug, 2007; Relax. . . It's Only Residential Relocation, Mar, 2007.

24790 ■ Renal Center
12 Chelsea Ct.
Hillsdale, NJ 07642-1227
Ph: (201)664-4451

Fax: (201)664-1267
Contact: Christopher N. Carson, Principal
Scope: Construction Consulting, Construction Management, Building Management Consulting, Provide Expert Witness Testimony in Dispute Matters. Arbitrator for Alternate Dispute Resolution cases. **Founded:** 1984.

24791 ■ Wadley-Donovan GrowthTech L.L.C. (WDGT)
150 Morris Ave., Ste. 203
Springfield, NJ 07081-1315
Ph: (973)379-7700
Fax: (973)379-7771
Co. E-mail: info@wadley-donovan.com
URL: http://www.wdgtech.com
Contact: William A. Fredrick, President
E-mail: wfredrick@wadley-donovan.com
Scope: Business location/relocation specialists, from strategic planning through decision and implementa-

tion. Services include: Definition of strategic issues for the geographic deployment of people and facilities; delineating alternatives to the current geographic configuration; relocation feasibility analyses; identification and evaluation of locations for new facilities, or relocating operations; site identification and evaluation; economic development incentive negotiations; and relocation implementation services. Services extend to detailed planning, employee surveys, attrition management, and recruitment and training strategies at the new location. **Founded:** 1975. **Publications:** "Benefits from Economic and Workforce Development Collaboration"; "Finger lakes WiB transformation and integration of Workforce and Economic Development". **Seminars:** Corporate Location Trends in the Mid 1990s; Labor Challenges Facing Corporate America; Labor Quality Challenges and Employment Growth Opportunities for Center Cities.

ASSOCIATIONS AND OTHER ORGANIZATIONS

24792 ■ Better Business Bureau Wise Giving Alliance
4200 Wilson Blvd., Ste. 800
Arlington, VA 22203-1838
Ph: (703)276-0100
Fax: (703)525-8277
Co. E-mail: give@council.bbb.org
URL: http://www.bbb.org/us/charity
Contact: H. Art Taylor, President
URL(s): www.give.org, www.bbb.org/us/Wise-Giving.
Description: Supported by companies and local Better Business Bureaus operated autonomously in the United States and Puerto Rico, which are in turn supported by 270,000 local business members. Seeks to promote and foster the highest ethical relationship between businesses and the public through voluntary self-regulation, consumer and business education, and service excellence. Provides support to local Better Business Bureaus. Administers the advertising industry's self-regulatory program that monitors and investigates the truth and accuracy of national advertising claims; monitors and pre-screens advertising directed towards children. Develops information on national charitable organizations and whether they meet voluntary ethical standards for soliciting organizations. Provides information to help consumers and businesses make informed purchasing decisions and avoid costly scams and frauds; and settles consumer complaints through arbitration and other means. Operates BBB AUTO LINE, a national mediation and arbitration service providing an independent forum to resolve consumer complaints involving 32 participating auto manufacturers; Local Better Business Bureaus respond to more than 23 million requests for service annually, fielding 20 million pre-purchase inquiries and 3 million complaints. **Founded:** 2001. **Publications:** *Wise Giving Guide.* **Awards:** BBB National Torch Award for Marketplace Ethics (Annual). **Telecommunication Services:** info@bbb.org.

REFERENCE WORKS

24793 ■ "All About The Benjamins" in *Canadian Business* (Vol. 81, September 29, 2008, No. 16, pp. 92).
Pub: Rogers Media Ltd.
Ed: David Baines. **Description:** Discusses real estate developer Royal Indian Raj International Corp., a company that planned to build a $3 billion 'smart city' near the Bangalore airport; to this day nothing has ever been built. The company was incorporated in 1999 by Manoj C. Benjamin one investor, Bill Zack, has been sued by the developer for libel due to his website that calls the company a scam. Benjamin has had a previous case of fraud issued against him as well as a string of liabilities and lawsuits.

24794 ■ "Avoiding Invention Scams" in *Black Enterprise* (Vol. 37, January 2007, No. 6, pp. 46)
Pub: Earl G. Graves Publishing Co. Inc.
Ed: James C. Johnson. **Description:** Invention promotion firms provide inventors assistance in developing a prototype for product development. It is important to research these companies before making a commitment to work with them because there are a number of these firms that are not legitimate and have caused independent inventors to lose thousands of dollars by making false claims as to the market potential of the inventions.

24795 ■ "Black's Truth: Will a Prison Stay Change the Way Conrad Black Operates?" in *Canadian Business* (Vol. 81, March 31, 2008, No. 5)
Pub: Rogers Media
Ed: Matthew McClearn. **Description:** Conrad Black will serve a 6 and a half years in prison but he asserts that his successors at Hollinger International and Hollinger Inc. grossly mismanaged and unjustly enriched themselves. Black also asserts that International violated the so-called November Agreement and that he is the aggrieved party. Black's assertions show a character flaw that cannot be corrected in prison.

24796 ■ "Dating Games" in *Canadian Business* (Vol. 79, September 25, 2006, No. 19, pp. 23)
Pub: Rogers Media
Ed: John Gray. **Description:** Increasing stock option scandals in Canada and American companies is discussed.

24797 ■ "Do the Math" in *Canadian Business* (Vol. 79, October 9, 2006, No. 20, pp. 17)
Pub: Rogers Media
Ed: Al Rosen. **Description:** Faulty practices followed by regulators in Canadian stock market are discussed. The need for authorities to protect investors against these frauds are emphasized.

24798 ■ "FTC Takes Aim At Foreclosure 'Rescue' Firm" in *The Business Journal-Serving Greater Tampa Bay* (Vol. 28, September 19, 2008, No. 39)
Pub: American City Business Journals, Inc.
Ed: Michael Hinman. **Description:** United Home Savers LLP has been ordered to halt its mortgage foreclosure rescue services after the Federal Trade Commission accused it of deceptive advertising. The company is alleged to have charged customers $1,200 in exchange for unfulfilled promises to keep them in their homes.

24799 ■ "The Hidden Tax" in *Canadian Business* (Vol. 81, April 14, 2008, No. 6, pp. 28)
Pub: Rogers Media
Ed: Al Rosen. **Description:** Accounting fraud could take out a sizable sum from one's retirement fund when computed over a long period of time. The much bigger tax on savings is the collective impact of the smaller losses that do not attract the attention they deserve. Ensuring that investors are not unnecessarily taxed 2 percent of their total investments every year outweighs the benefit of a 2 percent reduction in personal tax rates.

24800 ■ "A History of Neglect" in *Canadian Business* (Vol. 79, September 11, 2006, No. 18, pp. 21)
Pub: Rogers Media
Ed: Al Rosen. **Description:** Faulty practices being followed by auditors and regulators of Canada are discussed. The need for appropriate steps to protect investors against these frauds are emphasized.

24801 ■ "Identity Crisis: The Battle For Your Data" in *Canadian Business* (Vol. 81, March 17, 2008, No. 4, pp. 12)
Pub: Rogers Media
Description: Nigel Brown explains that businesses must protect their data through encryption and tightening up access to data. Brown also points out that banks and merchants bear most of the costs for identity fraud and leaves individuals with a lot of pain and heartache in clearing their name.

24802 ■ "'Mr. CEO, Please Do Elaborate On Your Firm's Metrics" in *Business Courier* (Vol. 24, February 29, 2008, No. 47, pp. 1)
Pub: American City Business Journals, Inc.
Ed: Jon Newberry. **Description:** Discusses a rogue caller who goes by the name of Joe Herrick, Steven Nissan and Joe Harris has joined in over a dozen conference calls, asking chief executive officers on their plans and commenting on the companies' operations. The mystery caller attempts to pass himself off as a financial analyst. Transcripts of some conference calls, in which the rogue caller is involved, are provided.

24803 ■ "A Nasty Russian Tale" in *Canadian Business* (Vol. 81, March 3, 2008, No. 3, pp. 85)
Pub: Rogers Media
Ed: Andrew Nikiforuk. **Description:** Billionaires Alex Shnaider and Michael Shtaif entered a partnership for an oil venture which ended in a slew of litigations. Cases of breach of contract, injurious falsehood and other related lawsuits were filed against Shnaider. Details of the lawsuits and the other parties involved in the disputes are presented.

24804 ■ "New Ways to Catch a Thief" in *Barron's* (Vol. 88, March 10, 2008, No. 10, pp. 37)
Pub: Dow Jones & Company, Inc.
Ed: Theresa W. Carey. **Description:** Online brokerage firms employ different methods to protect the accounts of their customers from theft. These methods include secure Internet connections, momentary passwords, and proprietary algorithms.

24805 ■ "One-Time Area Trust Executive Finds Trouble in N.H." in *The Business Journal-Serving Metropolitan Kansas City* (September 12, 2008)
Pub: American City Business Journals, Inc.
Ed: Steve Vockrodt. **Description:** About 200 investors, some from Missouri's Kansas City area, claim that they had conducted business with Noble Trust Co. The trust company was placed under New Hampshire Banking Department's conservatorship

after $15 million was discovered to be missing from its account. It is alleged that the money was lost in a Colorado Ponzi scheme.

24806 ■ *"Prosecutors Dish Sordid AIPC Story" in The Business Journal-Serving Metropolitan Kansas City (Vol. 27, September 19, 2008, No. 1)*
Pub: American City Business Journals, Inc.
Ed: Suzanna Stagemeyer. **Description:** Prosecutors in the American Italian Pasta Co.'s accounting fraud case have revealed evidence on the schemes used by then-officers of the company to commit fraud. District attorney John Wood has dubbed the case as the largest corporate fraud lawsuit in the history of the district of Missouri. How AIPC fell from being an industry leader is also discussed.

24807 ■ *"Retailers Report 'Shrinkage' of Inventory on the Rise" in Arkansas Business (Vol. 26, September 28, 2009, No. 39, pp. 17)*
Pub: Journal Publishing Inc.
Ed: Mark Friedman. **Description:** According to a National Retail Security Survey report released last June, retailers across the country have lost about $36.5 billion in shrinkage, most of it at the hands of employees and shoplifters alike. Statistical data included.

24808 ■ *"The Trials of Brian Hunter" in Canadian Business (Vol. 81, March 3, 2008, No. 3, pp. 64)*
Pub: Rogers Media
Ed: Thomas Watson. **Description:** Brian Hunter was a considered a brilliant trader in Wall Street before he was blamed for the fall of the Amaranth hedge fund.

Some people blame Hunter for placing bets based on unpredictable weather when he was a trader for Amaranth Advisors LLC. The accusation against Hunter that he conspired to manipulate natural gas prices is also discussed.

24809 ■ *"U.S. Attorney Post the Latest Twist" in The Business Journal-Serving Greater Tampa Bay (Vol. 28, July 25, 2008, No. 31, pp. 1)*
Pub: American City Business Journals, Inc.
Ed: Jane Meinhardt. **Description:** Tampa, Florida-based lawyer A. Brian Albritton has been nominated to be the U.S. Attorney for the Middle District of Florida. He is an expert in cases involving white-collar crime, secret theft, noncompete agreements, and other agreements.

TRADE PERIODICALS

24810 ■ *Consumer Protection Report*
Pub: National Association of Attorneys General
Contact: Rob McKenna, President
Ed: Sarah Reznek, Editor, sreznek@naag.org. **Released:** Bimonthly. **Description:** Seeks to protect citizens from consumer frauds. Reports on legislation, regulations, the Federal Trade Commission, and on state activities such as consumer information and complaint programs. Examines consumer fraud lawsuits throughout the country, covering cases involving such matters as false advertising, fraudulent billing, and regulation of charitable trusts and organizations. Recurring features include announcements and news of publications.

24811 ■ *Homecare Administrative HORIZONS*
Pub: Beacon Health Corp.
Contact: Diane J. Omdahl, Editor-in-Chief
Released: Monthly. **Price:** $347, individuals. **Description:** Provides homecare agency management information on all kinds of business and personnel topics. Incorporates comprehensive how-to information, current regulatory requirements, and documentation strategies. Runs a series of articles, including how to move into managed care, how to manage and measure outcomes, how to survive scrutiny by medicare's fraud squad, strengthening agency/physician relationships, and personnel issues. Recurring features include columns titled Peaks & Valleys, Fine-tuning the Fundamentals, Clearing the Fog, and Higher Ground.

VIDEOCASSETTES/ AUDIOCASSETTES

24812 ■ *LBOs and Fraudulent Conveyances*
Practising Law Institute (PLI)
810 7th Ave., 21st Fl.
New York, NY 10019-5818
Ph: (212)824-5700
Free: 800-260-4754
Co. E-mail: info@pli.edu
URL: http://www.pli.edu
Contact: Victor J. Rubino, President
E-mail: vrubino@pli.edu
Released: 1988. **Price:** $24.95. **Description:** Defines state and federal laws regarding fradulent conveyances following a leverage buy-out. **Availability:** VHS.

ASSOCIATIONS AND OTHER ORGANIZATIONS

24813 ■ **Caribbean - Central American Action (CCAA)**
1300 Pennsylvania Ave., NW Ste. 700
Washington, DC 20004
Ph: (202)204-3050
Fax: (202)789-7349
Co. E-mail: info@c-caa.org
URL: http://www.c-caa.org
Contact: Anton E. Edmunds, President
Description: Promotes private-sector-led economic development in the Caribbean Basin and throughout the hemisphere; facilitates trade and investment in the region by stimulating a constructive dialogue between the private and public sectors to improve the policy and regulatory environments for business on both international and local levels; conducts policy-oriented programs in sectors such as financial services, transportation, energy, agriculture, textiles, intellectual property rights, tourism, telecommunications, and information technology. **Founded:** 1980. **Publications:** *CCAA Quarterly* (Quarterly); *Caribbean Region Profile* (Annual). **Educational Activities:** Miami Conference on the Caribbean Basin (Annual).

24814 ■ **European Travel Commission (ETC)**
50 W 23rd St., 11th Fl.
New York, NY 10010
Co. E-mail: etc@spring-obrien.com
URL: http://www.VisitEurope.com/us
Contact: Robert K. Franklin, Executive Director
Description: Represents government tourism organizations cooperating to promote travel to Europe and further international goodwill and economic prosperity. **Founded:** 1948. **Publications:** *VisitEurope* (Monthly). **Educational Activities:** Trans-Atlantic Travel Marketing Conference (Annual). **Awards:** Europa Award (Annual).

24815 ■ **Global Business Travel Association (GBTA)**
110 N Royal St., 4th Fl.
Alexandria, VA 22314
Ph: (703)684-0836
Fax: (703)342-4324
Co. E-mail: info@gbta.org
URL: http://www.gbta.org/usa/Pages/default.aspx
Contact: Craig Banikowski, President
Description: Travel managers and providers. Works to enhance the educational advancement and image of the profession and membership; enhance the value of the travel manager in meeting corporate travel needs and financial goals; provide education to members about industry matters, issues and technology; cultivate a positive public image of the corporate travel industry; advocate and protect the interests of members and their corporations on legislative and regulatory matters; promote safety, security, efficiency and quality travel; and enhance professionalism and recognition of the industry and individual members. Provides a forum for the constructive exchange of information and ideas among members. **Founded:**

1968. **Publications:** *Global Business Travel Association--Membership Directory* (Annual). **Awards:** Appreciation for Services (Annual); Mike Kabo Scholarship (Annual); GLP Program Scholarships; Mike Kabo Global Scholarships.

24816 ■ **IBAC Update**
999 Rue University, Ste. 16-33
Montreal, QC, Canada H3C 5J9
Ph: (514)954-8054
Fax: (514)954-6161
Co. E-mail: info@ibac.org
URL: http://www.ibac.org
Contact: Donald D. Spruston, Director General
Released: Quarterly

24817 ■ **International Business Aviation Council**
999 Rue University, Ste. 16-33
Montreal, QC, Canada H3C 5J9
Ph: (514)954-8054
Fax: (514)954-6161
Co. E-mail: info@ibac.org
URL: http://www.ibac.org
Contact: Donald D. Spruston, Director General
Description: International business aircraft associations; national and regional business aviation organizations or subgroups. Aims to provide information on all aspects of international business aircraft operations; ensure that the interests of international business aviation are brought to the attention of and understood by authorities; improve the safety, efficiency and economic use of business aircraft operating internationally. Stresses the importance of business aviation to the economy and to the well-being of all nations. Maintains liaison with international aviation organizations to ensure safe and orderly growth of international business aviation throughout the world. Compiles statistics. **Publications:** *IBAC Update* (Quarterly).

REFERENCE WORKS

24818 ■ *"Advertising May Take a Big Hit in Southwest/AirTran Merger"* in Baltimore Business Journal (Vol. 28, October 1, 2010, No. 21, pp. 1)
Pub: Baltimore Business Journal
Ed: Gary Haber. **Description:** Advertising on television stations and the publishing industry in Baltimore could drop as a result of the merger between rival discount airlines Southwest Airlines and AirTran Airways. Southwest is among the top advertisers in the U.S., spending $126 million in 2009. No local jobs are expected to be affected because neither airline uses a local advertising firm.

24819 ■ *"Airlines Mount PR Push to Win Public Support Against Big Oil"* in Advertising Age (Vol. 79, July 14, 2008, No. 7, pp. 1)
Pub: Crain Communications, Inc.
Ed: Michael Bush. **Description:** Top airline executives from competing companies have banded together in a public relations plan in which they are

sending e-mails to their frequent fliers asking for aid in lobbying legislators to put a restriction on oil speculation.

24820 ■ *"Airmall Mulls I-95 Travel Plazas Bid"* in Boston Business Journal (Vol. 29, September 2, 2011, No. 17, pp. 3)
Pub: American City Business Journals Inc.
Ed: Alexander Jackson. **Description:** Airmall USA is planning to move its food courts from the Baltimore/Washington International Thurgood Marshall Airport to the new travel plazas on Interstate 95. The plazas are up for bid.

24821 ■ *"Are Your Goals Hitting the Right Target?"* in Business Strategy Review (Vol. 21, Autumn 2010, No. 3, pp. 46)
Pub: Wiley-Blackwell
Ed: Alan Meekings, Steve Briault, Andy Neely. **Description:** Setting targets is normal in most organizations. The authors think such a practice can cause more harm than good. They offer a better plan.

24822 ■ *"Around the World in a Day"* in Agency Sales Magazine (Vol. 39, August 2009, No. 8, pp. 36)
Pub: MANA
Ed: Jack Foster. **Description:** Highlights of Manufacturer's Agents National Association (MANA) member Les Rapchak one-day visit to Basra, Iraq are presented. Rapchak completed the trip via Frankfurt, Germany and Kuwait with a stop afterwards in Istanbul, Turkey. His purpose for the trip was to take part in a seminar at the State Company for Petrochemical Industries.

24823 ■ *"Behind the Scenes: Companies At the Heart of Everyday Life"* in Inc. (February 2008, pp. 26-27)
Pub: Gruner & Jahr USA Publishing
Ed: Athena Schindelheim. **Description:** Profiles of companies providing services to airports, making the environment safer and more efficient, as well as more comfortable for passengers and workers. Centerpoint Manufacturing provides garbage bins that can safely contain explosions producing thousands of pounds of pressure; Infax, whose software displays arrival and departure information on 19-foot-wide screens; Lavi Industries, whose products include security barricades, hostess stands, and salad-bar sneeze guards; and SATech maker of rubber flooring that helps ease discomfort for workers having to stand for long periods of time.

24824 ■ *Being Self-Employed: How to Run a Business Out of Your Home, Claim Travel and Depreciation and Earn a Good Income Well into Your 70s or 80s*
Pub: Allyear Tax Guides
Ed: Holmes F. Crouch, Irma Jean Crouch, Barbara J. MacRae. **Released:** September 2004. **Price:** $24.95 (US), $37.95 (Canadian). **Description:** Guide for small business to keep accurate tax records.

24825 ■ *"Best Cash Flow Generators"* in Canadian Business (Vol. 82, Summer 2009,

No. 8, pp. 40)
Pub: Rogers Media
Ed: Calvin Leung. **Description:** Agrium Inc. and FirstService Corporation are in the list of firms that are found to have the potential to be the best cash flow generators in Canada. The list also includes WestJet Airlines Ltd., which accounts for 385 flights each day. More than 80 percent of analysts rate the airline stocks a Buy.

24826 ■ *"Bigger TIF Makes Development Inroads" in The Business Journal-Serving Metropolitan Kansas City (Vol. 26, July 11, 2008, No. 44)*
Pub: American City Business Journals, Inc.
Ed: Rob Roberts. **Description:** On July 9, 2008 the Tax Increment Financing Commission voted to expand a TIF district to Tiffany Springs Road. The plan for the TIF district close to Kansas City International Airport is to include a-half mile of the road. The impacts of the expansion on construction projects and on the road network are analyzed.

24827 ■ *"Boeing Scores $21.7 Billion Order in Indonesia" in Wall Street Journal Eastern Edition (November 18 , 2011, pp. B6)*
Pub: Dow Jones & Company Inc.
Ed: David Kesmodel, Laura Meckler. **Description:** Boeing has garnered a large contract to deliver Boeing 737 jets to Indonesia's Lion Air. There are those who are lobbying against the US government's practice of subsidizing foreign companies that make contracts with American aerospace companies.

24828 ■ *"Border Boletin: UA to Take Lie-Detector Kiosk to Poland" in Arizona Daily Star (September 14, 2010)*
Pub: Arizona Daily Star
Ed: Brady McCombs. **Description:** University of Arizona's National Center for Border Security and Immigration Research will send a team to Warsaw, Poland to show border guards from 27 European Union countries the center's Avatar Kiosk. The Avatar technology is designed for use at border ports and airports to assist Customs officers detect individuals who are lying.

24829 ■ *"The Business Owner's Flight Plan" in Entrepreneur (Vol. 37, July 2009, No. 7, pp. 22)*
Pub: Entrepreneur Media, Inc.
Description: Greg Rosner, author of 'The Road Warrior Survival Guide: Practical Tips for the Business Traveler,' shares insights on the stages of a typical business trip. Delegating a trusted colleague who can assume certain tasks that you cannot deal with remotely, expecting that the trip is not a vacation, and taking a Thursday night flight are some of the tips given to business travelers.

24830 ■ *"Business Start-Up a Learning Experience for Young Bellingham Entrepreneur" in Bellingham Herald (July 18, 2010)*
Pub: Bellingham Herald
Ed: Dave Gallagher. **Description:** Profile of 21-year-old entrepreneur, Chase Larabee, who developed an online program that helps airport fixed-based operators handle refueling, hotel and transportation reservations and other requests from private airplane pilots.

24831 ■ *"Business Travel Can be a Trip if Structured Right" in Globe & Mail (February 3, 2007, pp. B11)*
Pub: CTVglobemedia Publishing Inc.
Ed: Roma Luciw. **Description:** The importance of arranging a proper business trip for executives by employers, in order to achieve good benefits for the company, is discussed.

24832 ■ *"By Land, Air, and Sea: New Passport Rules in Effect" in Black Enterprise (Vol. 37, January 2007, No. 6., pp. 101)*
Pub: Earl G. Graves Publishing Co. Inc.
Ed: Stephanie Young. **Description:** As part of a new security measure by the Western Hemisphere Travel Initiative, a passport will now be required for U.S. citizens traveling by air between Mexico, Canada,

South and Central America, and the Caribbean. This initiative, designed to easily identify travelers and enforce border security, will most likely extend to land or sea travel no later than January 1, 2008.

24833 ■ *"Cell Phone the Ticket on American Airlines" in Chicago Tribune (November 14, 2008)*
Pub: McClatchy-Tribune Information Services
Ed: Julie Johnsson. **Description:** American Airlines is testing a new mobile boarding pass at O'Hare International Airport. Travelers on American can board flights and get through security checkpoints by flashing a bar code on their phones. Passengers must have an Internet-enabled mobile device and an active e-mail address in order to utilize this service.

24834 ■ *"City a Pawn in Airlines' Chess Game" in Business Courier (Vol. 24, January 18, 2008, No. 41, pp. 1)*
Pub: American City Business Journals, Inc.
Ed: Lisa Biank Fasig. **Description:** Delta Air Lines is under negotitaions with Northwest Airlines and UAL Corp. for a proposed merger. The deal will have a negative impact on Cincinnati as a hub regardless whether it goes to UAL or Northwest. The impacts of the planned merger on Cincinnati's labor market and airport traffic are discussed.

24835 ■ *"City Plans Downtown Congestion Fees" in Crain's Chicago Business (Vol. 31, May 5, 2008, No. 18, pp. 12)*
Pub: Crain Communications, Inc.
Description: By penalizing downtown drivers and rewarding public-transit users, Chicago officials plan to unclog Loop streets. The $153 million federal grant would establish a pilot network of express bus routes and set up a peak-period pricing system for city, street and private garage parking and for building loading zones.

24836 ■ *"City Struggles to Iron Out Tangled Transportation" in Crain's New York Business (Vol. 24, January 14, 2008, No. 2, pp. 33)*
Pub: Crain Communications, Inc.
Ed: Judith Messina. **Description:** Discusses the possible solutions to improve lower Manhattan's transportation infrastructure including the construction of three new transit centers, an expansion in ferry service and the plan to get parked buses off the street.

24837 ■ *"Civil Council Almost On Board With Light Rail Plan" in The Business Journal-Serving Metropolitan Kansas City (September 5, 2008)*
Pub: American City Business Journals, Inc.
Ed: Steve Vockrodt. **Description:** Civic Council of Greater Kansas City has taken back its demand for the city to show a 10-year financial plan to win its endorsement of a light rail plan. The council said it will accept a five-year financial plan for the project. Details of the light rail plan are presented.

24838 ■ *"Columbia Sale Narrowed To Two Developers" in The Business Journal-Milwaukee (Vol. 25, July 18, 2008, No. 43, pp. A1)*
Pub: American City Business Journals, Inc.
Ed: Corrinne Hess. **Description:** Officials of Columbia St. Mary's Inc plan to pick one of two real-estate developers who will buy the 8-acre property of the Columbia Hospital which the company will move away from when their new hospital has been constructed. The hospital on Newport Ave. has been on the market since 2001.

24839 ■ *"Congestion Relief" in Canadian Business (Vol. 80, February 12, 2007, No. 4, pp. 31)*
Pub: Rogers Media
Ed: Andrea Jezovit. **Description:** The development of a satellite-based system for traffic management including paying for parking fees by Skymeter Corp. is discussed.

24840 ■ *"Daley's Efforts to Ease Traffic Woes Fall Short" in Crain's Chicago Business (Vol. 31, May 5, 2008, No. 18, pp. 18)*
Pub: Crain Communications, Inc.
Description: Discusses some of the inherent problems of Mayor Daley's plan to reduce traffic congestion by creating a tax on drivers who park their cars

downtown during peak traffic periods and putting articulated buses on new bus-only lanes on major arterial streets leading into the Loop.

24841 ■ *"Debut Year Brings Success for Bike-Trail Boosters" in Business Courier (Vol. 24, January 4, 2008, No. 39, pp. 4)*
Pub: American City Business Journals, Inc.
Ed: Dan Monk. **Description:** Discusses the first year of Cincinnati's Trail Yeah has brought in success as five local government boards approve the bike-trail enthusiast group's endorsement of a cycling path that would connect the city's downtown to the Loveland Bike Trail. The group is planning to raise $3 million to $5 million for the trails first phase.

24842 ■ *"Defying Gravity?" in Canadian Business (Vol. 81, October 13, 2008, No. 17, pp. 17)*
Pub: Rogers Media Ltd.
Ed: Joe Castaldo. **Description:** Airlines around the world are expected to lose $4.1 billion in 2009, but experts believe Canadian airlines will be able to survive the economic challenges. Lower demand for air travel and uncertainty on oil prices are also expected to make the conditions more challenging. Views and key information on airlines in Canada and around the world are cited.

24843 ■ *"Delta Looks at Downtown Departure" in Business Courier (Vol. 27, October 1, 2010, No. 22, pp. 1)*
Pub: Business Courier
Ed: Dan Monk. **Description:** Delta Air Lines Inc. has been looking for a smaller office for its reservations center in downtown Cincinnati, Ohio. Delta has informed the city of its plan to seek proposals on office space alternatives in advance of the 2011 lease expiration. Insights on the current employment status at the reservations center are also given.

24844 ■ *"Developers Await Hotel" in The Business Journal-Portland (Vol. 25, July 11, 2008, No. 18, pp. 1)*
Pub: American City Business Journals, Inc.
Ed: Wendy Culverwell. **Description:** Developers are eager to start the construction of a new hotel at the Oregon Convention Center in Portland, Oregon as hey say that the project will help boost the convention center neighborhood. The project, called The Westin Portland at the Convention Center, is partly handled by Ashforth Pacific Inc.

24845 ■ *"Doctor On the Go: Concessions International Founder Opens Airport Clinic" in Black Enterprise (Vol. 38, October 2007, No. 3, pp. 34)*
Pub: Earl G. Graves Publishing Co. Inc.
Ed: Tara C. Walker. **Description:** Aero Clinic is an onsite healthcare facility designed to care for travelers. Located at Atlanta's Hartsfield-Jackson International Airport, the clinic is the first of its kind.

24846 ■ *"Don Bell" in Canadian Business (Vol. 80, November 5, 2007, No. 22, pp. 164)*
Pub: Rogers Media
Ed: Michelle Magnan. **Description:** Don Bell was not able to finish his degree at University of Calgary, however, he managed to build companies such as WestJet. Bell hates bureaucracy and believes in the importance of a good corporate culture. Details on his life as a father and a pilot along with his advice for entrepreneurs are given.

24847 ■ *"Don't Touch My Laptop, If You Please Mr. Customs Man" in Canadian Electronics (Vol. 23, June-July 2008, No. 4, pp. 6)*
Pub: Action Communication Inc.
Ed: Mark Borkowski. **Description:** Canadian businessmen bringing electronic devices to the US can protect the contents of their laptops by hiding their data from US border agents. They can also choose to clean up the contents of their laptop using file erasure programs.

24848 ■ *"Doubletree Finds a Niche for Giving Back" in Hotel and Motel Management (Vol.*

225, July 2010, No. 8, pp. 6)
Pub: Questex Media Group Inc.
Ed: Paul J. Heney. Description: Profile of Double-tree Hotel's community outreach programs that help employee volunteers work to educate children and the public about issues important to the environment.

24849 ■ *"Empowered" in Harvard Business Review (Vol. 88, July-August 2010, No. 7-8, pp. 94)*
Pub: Harvard Business School Publishing
Ed: Josh Bernoff, Ted Schadler. Description: HERO concept (highly empowered and resourceful operative) which builds a connection between employees, managers, and IT is outlined. The resultant additional experience and knowledge gained by employees improves customer relationship management.

24850 ■ *"Entrepreneurs: Search Party" in Business Strategy Review (Vol. 21, Autumn 2010, No. 3, pp. 30)*
Pub: Wiley-Blackwell
Ed: Georgina Peters. Description: Entrepreneurs tend to be fixated on coming up with a foolproof idea for a new business and then raising money to start it. Raising startup funds is difficult, but it doesn't have to be that way. Search funds offers an innovative alternative, and the results are often impressive.

24851 ■ *"First Airport Location for Paciugo Gelato" in Ice Cream Reporter (Vol. 23, October 20, 2010, No. 11, pp. 2)*
Pub: Ice Cream Reporter
Description: Paciugo Gelato and Caffee has part-nered with airport concessions developer Airmail to open a shop in the Cleveland Hopkins International Airport. The firm will create a wide variety of choices for travelers.

24852 ■ *"Five Things" in Hawaii Business (Vol. 53, November 2007, No. 5, pp. 20)*
Pub: Hawaii Business Publishing
Ed: Jason Ubay. Description: Discusses products that are allowed to be carried on board airplane flights by business travelers.

24853 ■ *"Flights of Fancy" in Crain's Chicago Business (Vol. 31, April 21, 2008, No. 16, pp. 27)*
Pub: Crain Communications, Inc.
Ed: Sarah A. Klein. Description: Due to the competi-tion for business travelers, who account for 30 percent of airline revenue, airlines are offering a number of luxury amenities, especially on long-haul routes.

24854 ■ *"Flying High Down Under" in Entrepreneur (Vol. 37, August 2009, No. 8, pp. 16)*
Pub: Entrepreneur Media, Inc.
Ed: Dan Oko. Description: V Australia offers direct flights from Los Angeles International Airport to Bris-bane, Melbourne, and Sydney in Australia. Their Boeing 777-300ER aircrafts has a fully stocked sit-down bar in the business class, touch screens with audio and video on demand and passengers get to perk up with Bulgari toiletries kits.

24855 ■ *"Flying the Unfriendly Skies" in Crain's Chicago Business (Vol. 31, April 21, 2008, No. 16, pp. 26)*
Pub: Crain Communications, Inc.
Ed: Sarah A. Klein. Description: Due to the number of Chicago companies and entrepreneurs who are traveling overseas more frequently in order to strengthen ties with customers, companies and of-tentimes even business partners, the number of flights leaving O'Hare International Airport for destina-tions abroad has surged; In 2007, international pas-sengers departing O'Hare totaled 5.7 million, up from 2.4 million in 1990.

24856 ■ *"For Going All Out to Transform the Way Our Food Is Grown: Chuck Lacy" in Inc. (Volume 32, December 2010, No. 10, pp. 94)*
Pub: Inc. Magazine
Ed: Adam Bluestein. Description: Profile of Ro-tokawa Cattle Company and its mission to transform the business of beef and grow their herd of beef cattle.

24857 ■ *"Fuel for Thought" in Canadian Business (Vol. 81, April 14, 2008, No. 6, pp. 18)*
Pub: Rogers Media
Ed: John Gray. Description: Discusses a web poll of 133 CEOs and other business leaders that shows that they predict oil prices to increase to US $113 per barrel over the 2008 to 2010 timeframe. Most of the respondents did not favor cutting gas taxes but this group wants the government to cut taxes on fuel-efficient vehicles and increase subsidies to local transit systems.

24858 ■ *"Full Speed Ahead: How to Get the Most Out of Your Company Vehicles" in Entrepreneur (Vol. 37, October 2009, No. 10, pp. 78)*
Pub: Entrepreneur Media, Inc.
Ed: Jill Amadio. Description: Methods of saving costs on purchasing and maintaining vehicles are described. Tips include shopping online, choosing hybrid vehicles, and choosing cars with incentives and lower insurance costs.

24859 ■ *"Glendale Pumping $29 Million Into Redevelopment" in The Business Journal - Serving Phoenix and the Valley of the Sun (Vol. 28, August 1, 2008, No. 48, pp. 1)*
Pub: American City Business Journals, Inc.
Ed: Mike Sunnucks. Description: Glendale City is planning to invest $29 million to improve city infra-structure like roadways and water and sewer lines over the next five years. Glendale's city council is also planning to hold a workshop on the redevelop-ment projects in September 2008. Other views and information on the redevelopment project, are pre-sented.

24860 ■ *Greening Your Small Business: How to Improve Your Bottom Line, Grow Your Brand, Satisfy Your Customers and Save the Planet*
Pub: Prentice Hall Press
Contact: Dame Marjorie M. Scardino, Chief Execu-tive Officer
Ed: Jennifer Kaplan. Released: November 3, 2009. Price: $19.95. Description: A definitive resource for anyone who wants their small business to be cutting-edge, competitive, profitable, and eco-conscious. Stories from small business owners address every aspect of going green, from basics such as recycling waste, energy efficiency, and reducing information technology footprint, to more in-depth concerns such as green marketing and communications, green busi-ness travel, and green employee benefits.

24861 ■ *"'Groundhog Day' B & B Likely Will Be Converted Into One In Real Life" in Chicago Tribune (October 21, 2008)*
Pub: McClatchy-Tribune Information Services
Ed: Carolyn Starks. Description: Everton Martin and Karla Stewart Martin have purchased the Victorian house that was featured as a bed-and-breakfast in the 1993 hit move 'Groundhog Day'; the couple was initially unaware of the structure's celebrity status when they purchased it with the hope of fulfilling their dream of owning a bed-and-breakfast.

24862 ■ *"Have Tag, Will Travel" in Inc. (Vol. 33, November 2011, No. 9, pp. 48)*
Pub: Inc. Magazine
Ed: Abram Brown. Description: Truleytag and Boo-merangit are provide services to protect luggage while traveling. Turlytag provides brightly colored ID tags and stickers that attach to any item and feature words Return Me along with the company's contact information. Boomerangit's ID tags and labels feature the words Return for Reward along with their informa-tion.

24863 ■ *"Heavy Duty: The Case Against Packing Lightly" in Crain's Chicago Business (Vol. 31, April 21, 2008, No. 16, pp. 29)*
Pub: Crain Communications, Inc.
Ed: Sarah A. Klein. Description: Penelope Biggs, a Northern Trust executive who manages sales teams in North America, Europe and Asia gives advice on traveling abroad for business including time manage-ment skills, handling time-zone hops and avoiding jet-lag.

24864 ■ *"Honest Harry" in Hawaii Business (Vol. 53, November 2007, No. 5, pp. 39)*
Pub: Hawaii Business Publishing
Ed: David K. Choo. Description: Mayor Harry Kim testified in support of the Superferry controversial in Hawaii last September 2007. Kim says that the Su-perferry would allow local business and families to have more opportunities for commerce and recre-ation. Kim's testimony was not persuasive enough for Maui Circuit Judge Joseph Cardoza who ruled that the Superferry may not operate while an environmen-tal assessment is being completed.

24865 ■ *"Hotel Tax Eyed For Waukesha" in The Business Journal-Milwaukee (Vol. 25, August 29, 2008, No. 49, pp. A1)*
Pub: American City Business Journals, Inc.
Ed: Rich Kirchen. Description: Midwest Airlines Center chairman Frank Gimbel wants Waukesha County to help in the funding of the $200-million expansion of the convention center through a hotel room tax. The Waukesha hotel industry is expected to oppose the new room tax. Other views and information on the planned new room tax in Wauke-sha are presented.

24866 ■ *"Hotels Get a Fill-Up" in Crain's Detroit Business (Vol. 25, June 1, 2009, No. 22, pp. 1)*
Pub: Crain Communications Inc. - Detroit
Ed: Daniel Duggan. Description: Hot Rod Power Tour will have a $1 million economic impact on the area when it arrives in June 2009; the tour will bring 3 500 out-of-state custom vehicles to the event, whose owners will be needing hotel rooms.

24867 ■ *"Hotels' Healthy Finish in '07" in Crain's Chicago Business (Vol. 31, March 24, 2008, No. 12, pp. 16)*
Pub: Crain Communications, Inc.
Ed: Alby Gallun. Description: Chicago's hotel market saw mostly rising occupancies and room rates in the fourth quarter of 2007, reflecting continued strong demand from leisure and business travelers; however, due to the current state of the economy hoteliers face an increasingly uncertain outlook.

24868 ■ *"How Hierarchy Can Hurt Strategy Execution" in Harvard Business Review (Vol. 88, July-August 2010, No. 7-8, pp. 74)*
Pub: Harvard Business School Publishing
Description: A series of charts illustrate Harvard Business Review's Advisory Council survey results regarding perceptions of strategy development and execution identifying obstacles and key factors af-fecting implementation.

24869 ■ *"Huberman Failing to Keep CTA on Track" in Crain's Chicago Business (Vol. 31, April 21, 2008, No. 16, pp. 22)*
Pub: Crain Communications, Inc.
Description: Discusses the deplorable service of CTA, the Chicago Transit Authority, as well as CTA President Ron Huberman who, up until last week had riders hoping he had the management skills neces-sary to fix the system's problems; Tuesday's event left hundreds of riders trapped for hours and thou-sands standing on train platforms along the Blue Line waiting for trains that never came.

24370 ■ *"I-5 Bridge Funding Unclear" in The Business Journal-Portland (Vol. 25, July 11, 2008, No. 18, pp. 1)*
Pub: American City Business Journals, Inc.
Ed: Andy Giegerich. Description: Financing for a new Interstate 5 bridge is unclear as Washington lawmakers identify two priority projects other than the planned bridge, which is shared with Oregon. An estimate says that the two states could pay between $487.6 million and $1.5 billion for the new bridge. Other details on the financing of the project are discussed.

24871 ■ *"Ideas at Work: The Reality of Costs" in Business Strategy Review (Vol. 21, Summer 2010, No. 2, pp. 40)*
Pub: Wiley-Blackwell
Ed: Jules Goddard. Description: If you think that cost cutting is the surest way to business success, the author wants to challenge every assumption you

hold. Costs are an outcome of sound strategy, never the goal of strategy. He offers a new perspective on what counts when it comes to costs.

24872 ■ *"Immigration Issues Frustrate Owners From Overseas"* in The Business Journal-Serving Greater Tampa Bay (Vol. 28, August 15, 2008)
Pub: American City Business Journals, Inc.
Ed: Margie Manning. **Description:** Investors who availed the E-2 visa program believe that the tightened restrictions on the visa program has trapped them in the United States. The E-2 investor visa program was designed to attract investors into the U.S., but restrictions were tightened after the September 11, 2001 attacks. Other views and information on E-2 and its impact on investors are presented.

24873 ■ *"In China, Railways to Riches"* in Barron's (Vol. 88, July 7, 2008, No. 27, pp. M9)
Pub: Dow Jones & Co., Inc.
Ed: Assif Shameen. **Description:** Shares of Chinese railway companies look to benefit from multimillion-dollar investments aimed at upgrading the Chinese railway network. Investment in the sector is expected to reach $210 billion for the 2006-2010 period.

24874 ■ *"Innovating Globally"* in Business Strategy Review (Vol. 21, Spring 2010, No. 1, pp. 24)
Pub: Wiley-Blackwell
Ed: Costas Markides, Stuart Crainer. **Description:** Costas Markides has spent over two decades studying business strategy and innovation. Recently, he has been focusing on the bigger picture of how people can address major social problems. Can the techniques used by managers to create innovation inside organizations work with global change?.

24875 ■ *"Innovation's Holy Grail"* in Harvard Business Review (Vol. 88, July-August 2010, No. 7-8, pp. 132)
Pub: Harvard Business School Publishing
Ed: C.K. Prahalad, R.A. Mashelkar. **Description:** Three forms of business innovation are presented, inspired by the tenets of Mahatma Gandhi. They are: changing organizational capabilities, sourcing or creating new capabilities, and disrupting conventional business models. Illustrations for these methods are also included.

24876 ■ *The Itty Bitty Guide to Business Travel*
Pub: Chronicle Books LLC
Ed: Stacie Krajchir, Carrie Rosten. **Released:** April 2004. **Description:** Advice on all aspects of business travel, including low-price airfare, packing and coping with stress.

24877 ■ *"Just Following Directions"* in Entrepreneur (Vol. 36, February 2008, No. 2, pp. 56)
Pub: Entrepreneur Media Inc.
Ed: Amanda C. Kooser. **Description:** Buyer's guide for purchasing Global Positioning System units is presented.

24878 ■ *"Keeping Railcars 'Busy At All Times' At TTX"* in Crain's Chicago Business (Vol. 31, April 28, 2008, No. 17, pp. 6)
Pub: Crain Communications, Inc.
Ed: Bob Tita. **Description:** Profile of the president of Chicago railcar pool operator TTX Co. and his business plan for the company which includes improving fleet management and car purchasing through better use of data on railroad demand.

24879 ■ *"Leave It Behind; Novel Packing Strategy"* in Crain's Chicago Business (Vol. 31, April 21, 2008, No. 16, pp. 32)
Pub: Crain Communications, Inc.
Ed: Sarah A. Klein. **Description:** Patrick Brady who investigates possible violations of the Foreign Corrupt Practices Act has a novel approach when traveling to frequent destinations which allows him to travel with only a carry-on piece of luggage: he leaves suits at dry cleaners in the places he visits most often and

since he mainly stays at the same hotels, he also leaves sets of workout clothes and running shoes with hotel staff.

24880 ■ *"Lightening the Load"* in Crain's Cleveland Business (Vol. 28, October 8, 2007, No. 40, pp. 3)
Pub: Crain Communications, Inc.
Ed: Jay Miller. **Description:** Companies reliant on barge deliveries are running well below capacity due to both the building up of silt at the bottom of the Cuyahoga River as well as the lower water levels which are causing a number of problems for the barges and big boats that deliver goods to the region.

24881 ■ *"Local Hotels Brace for Downturn"* in Crain's Chicago Business (Vol. 31, March 31, 2008, No. 13, pp. 3)
Pub: Crain Communications, Inc.
Ed: Bob Tita. **Description:** Chicago hotels are seeing a noticeable drop in business-related guests so far this year due to a slumping national economy, tighter corporate expense budgets and higher airfares.

24882 ■ *"Location, Location"* in Black Enterprise (Vol. 38, February 2008, No. 7, pp. 64)
Pub: Earl G. Graves Publishing Co. Inc.
Ed: Marcia Reed-Woodard. **Description:** Overseas work assignments are increasing, especially for workers in the U.S., Canada and Latin America.

24883 ■ *"The Long Game"* in Business Strategy Review (Vol. 21, Summer 2010, No. 2, pp. 36)
Pub: Wiley-Blackwell
Ed: Stuart Crainer. **Description:** Profile of Alibab.com and its CEO David Wei.

24884 ■ *"The Lords of Ideas"* in Business Strategy Review (Vol. 21, Autumn 2010, No. 3, pp. 57)
Pub: Wiley-Blackwell
Ed: Stuart Crainer. **Description:** True originators of modern business strategy are interviewed.

24885 ■ *"Luxe Hotels on a Budget"* in Inc. (Volume 32, December 2010, No. 10, pp. 60)
Pub: Inc. Magazine
Ed: Adam Baer. **Description:** Off & Away Website allows users to vie for discounted hotel rooms at more than 100 luxury properties. To compete, uses buy $1 bids and each time an individual bids the price of the room goes up by 10 cents.

24886 ■ *"Making Visitors Out Of Listeners"* in Hawaii Business (Vol. 54, July 2008, No. 1, pp. 18)
Pub: Hawaii Business Publishing
Ed: Casey Chin. **Description:** Japanese workers are subscribing to the Official Hawaii Podcast in iTunes, which offers a free 20-minute, Japanese-language audio content on different topics, such as dining reviews and music from local artists. The concept is a way to attract Japanese travelers to come to Hawaii.

24887 ■ *"Mass-Transit Backers: Change in State Funding Needed"* in Crain's Detroit Business (Vol. 24, October 6, 2008, No. 40, pp. 19)
Pub: Crain Communications, Inc.
Ed: Bill Shea. **Description:** Options to reform transportation and infrastructure funding in the state of Michigan are examined. Transit revitalization investment zones are also discussed.

24888 ■ *"Meetings Go Virtual"* in HRMagazine (Vol. 54, January 2009, No. 1, pp. 74)
Pub: Society for Human Resource Management
Contact: Henry G. Jackson, President
E-mail: hjackson@shrm.org
Ed: Elizabeth Agnvall. **Description:** Microsoft Office Live Meeting conferencing software allows companies to schedule meetings from various company locations, thus saving travel costs.

24889 ■ *"Mergers Mean Woe for Fliers; Airline Hookups Boost Fares, Diminish Service"* in Crain's Chicago Business (April 21, 2008)
Pub: Crain Communications, Inc.
Ed: John Pletz. **Description:** Discusses the impact airline mergers will have on customer service, pricing and business travel, particularly at Chicago's O'Hare International Airport.

24890 ■ *"Military Center a Go"* in Austin Business JournalInc. (Vol. 29, December 11, 2009, No. 40, pp. 1)
Pub: American City Business Journals
Ed: Kate Harrington. **Description:** The $40 million Armed Forces Guard and Reserve Center project at Austin-Bergstrom International Airport has resumed work after a delay of several years. The project is in both the House and Senate versions of the fiscal 2010 Military Construction and Veterans Appropriations Bill that would earmark $16.5 million for the center and $5.7 million for the maintenance facility. Details of construction plans are covered.

24891 ■ *"The Money Train: How Public Projects Shape Our Economic Future"* in Hawaii Business (Vol. 54, September 2008, No. 3, pp. 31)
Pub: Hawaii Business Publishing
Ed: Jason Ubay. **Description:** Public projects impact the construction industry as such projects create jobs and new infrastructure that can lead to private developments. Details on the government contracts and construction projects in Hawaii and their rising costs and impact on the state's economy are discussed.

24892 ■ *"MooBella Adds Two Airports"* in Ice Cream Reporter (Vol. 23, November 20, 2010, No. 12, pp. 5)
Pub: Ice Cream Reporter
Description: MooBella Inc. has placed MooBella Ice Creamery machines in New England's Logan International Airport in Boston and in New Hampshire's Manchester-Boston Regional Airport.

24893 ■ *"Muirhead Farmhouse B & B Owners Get Hospitality Right"* in Chicago Tribune (July 31, 2008)
Pub: McClatchy-Tribune Information Services
Ed: Glenn Jeffers. **Description:** Profile of the Muirhead Farmhouse, a bed-and-breakfast owned by Mike Petersdorf and Sarah Muirhead Petersdorf; Frank Lloyd Wright designed the historic farmhouse which blends farm life and history into a unique experience that is enhanced by the couple's hospitality.

24894 ■ *"Nighttime Shuttle to Connect Detroit, Ferndale, Royal Oak"* in Crain's Detroit Business (Vol. 24, October 6, 2008, No. 40, pp. 24)
Pub: Crain Communications, Inc.
Ed: Nancy Kaffer. **Description:** With hopes of bridging the social gap between the cities and suburbs, Chris Ramos has launched The Night Move, a new shuttle service that will ferry passengers between Royal Oak, Ferndale and downtown Detroit. The cost for a round trip ticket is $12.

24895 ■ *"No Rooms for the Inn In This High-Rise"* in Chicago Tribune (October 4, 2008)
Pub: McClatchy-Tribune Information Services
Ed: Ameet Sachdev; Jim Kirk. **Description:** Construction has stalled for several hotel expansion projects due to the economy which has caused a decline in occupancy and little growth in average daily room rates in downtown Chicago because consumers and businesses are becoming more cautious in the amount of money they spend on travel.

24896 ■ *"On the Go: a Busy Executive Is Always Well-Equipped for Travel"* in Black Enterprise (Vol. 40, July 2010, No. 12, pp. 106)
Pub: Earl G. Graves Publishing Co. Inc.
Ed: Sonia Alleyne. **Description:** Successful sales executive, Henry Watkins, shares tips on business travel.

24897 ■ *"On the High Road" in Crain's Cleveland Business (Vol. 28, October 8, 2007, No. 40, pp. 2)*

Pub: Crain Communications, Inc.

Description: According to the American Public Transportation Association, the Greater Cleveland Regional Transit Authority is the best public transit system in North America. Ridership has increased steadily in the last few years. Statistical data included.

24898 ■ *"Orbitz Adds Parent Panel" in Marketing to Women (Vol. 21, March 2008, No. 3, pp. 5)*

Pub: EPM Communications Inc.

Contact: Ira Mayer, President

E-mail: imayer@epmcom.com

Description: Orbitz introduces the Orbitz Parent Panel in an attempt to better connect with traveling families.

24899 ■ *"Our Gadget of the Week: Business Buddy" in Barron's (Vol. 88, July 7, 2008, No. 27, pp. 26)*

Pub: Dow Jones & Co., Inc.

Ed: Jay Palmer. **Description:** Review and evaluation of the Lenovo X300 laptop computer which offers executives a variety of features despite its smaller size and weight. The laptop is about 0.73 inch thick, comes with a 64-gigabyte solid-state drive from Samsung, and weighs less than three pounds.

24900 ■ *"Pack Mentality" in Crain's Chicago Business (Vol. 31, April 21, 2008, No. 16, pp. 31)*

Pub: Crain Communications, Inc.

Ed: Sarah A. Klein. **Description:** Jill Smart, the head of human resources for a company with 170,000 employees worldwide, frequently travels to India, London and Singapore; Ms. Smart provides advice concerning efficiency, time management and avoiding jet-lag.

24901 ■ *"Packing Chic" in Black Enterprise (Vol. 38, February 2008, No. 7, pp. 154)*

Pub: Earl G. Graves Publishing Co. Inc.

Ed: Sonai Alleyne. **Description:** Profile of Angela Theodora's leather overnight bags that offer a variety of smart compartments for the business traveler.

24902 ■ *"PDX Bucks National Trend" in The Business Journal-Portland (Vol. 25, August 1, 2008, No. 21, pp. 1)*

Pub: American City Business Journals, Inc.

Ed: Erik Siemers. **Description:** Portland International Airport could face problems as air carriers are planning to reduce capacity at the airport. The airport is showing signs of growth despite the slowdown in the airline industry. Other airlines that are planning to reduce seating capacity at the airport are also presented.

24903 ■ *"Pinellas Leaders Want First Leg of Light Rail" in The Business Journal-Serving Greater Tampa Bay (Vol. 28, August 8, 2008, No. 33)*

Pub: American City Business Journals, Inc.

Ed: Larry Halstead. **Description:** Proposed routes for the first leg of the planned light railway system in the Tampa Bay, Florida area are being presented as the Tampa Bay Area Regional Transportation Authority is about to make its master plan for the project. A sales tax for transit is being proposed to fund the project, as well as an expansion of the accompanying bus system.

24904 ■ *"The Play's the Thing" in Business Strategy Review (Vol. 21, Summer 2010, No. 2, pp. 58)*

Pub: Wiley-Blackwell

Ed: Michael G. Jacobides. **Description:** Those who study and plan strategies risk falling into the traps that maps, graphs, charts and matrices present. The author feels that strategy might best be cast as a dramatic playscript that can reveal the unfolding plots of business far better than traditional strategic tools, as the landscape shifts around us.

24905 ■ *"Portion of Silver Line Will Run By Year's End" in Crain's Cleveland Business (Vol. 28, November 5, 2007, No. 44, pp. 6)*

Pub: Crain Communications, Inc.

Ed: Jay Miller. **Description:** Cleveland's new Silver Line rapid transit will board its first passengers before the end of the year. The project is expected to spur economic development in the area and will speed transportation along Euclid Avenue.

24906 ■ *"Possible Green Light On Transit" in The Business Journal-Milwaukee (Vol. 25, July 25, 2008, No. 44, pp. A1)*

Pub: American City Business Journals, Inc.

Ed: David Doege. **Description:** $50 million in federal funding is being sought by Wisconsin's Milwaukee County Executive Scott Walker for the creation of two bus rapid transit lines, and is to be added to the unspent Milwaukee area federal funds worth $91.5 million. The new transit line will have new higher-speed buses and fewer stops than the traditional line.

24907 ■ *"Power Play" in Harvard Business Review (Vol. 88, July-August 2010, No. 7-8, pp. 84)*

Pub: Harvard Business School Publishing

Ed: Jeffrey Pfeffer. **Description:** Guidelines include in-depth understanding of resources at one's disposal, relentlessness that still provides opponents with opportunities to save face, and a determination not to be put off by the processes of politics.

24908 ■ *"Pride Lands Janitorial Work at New Terminal" in Sacramento Business Journal (Vol. 28, June 10, 2011, No. 15, pp. 1)*

Pub: Sacramento Business Journal

Ed: Kelly Johnson. **Description:** Pride Industries Inc. won the five-year $9.4 million contract to clean the Sacramento International Airport's new Terminal B, which will open in fall 2011. The nonprofit organization posts a revenue of $191 million for 2011 and currently employs more than 2,400 people with disabilities. The contract is expected to provide savings of over $3 million a year to the airport.

24909 ■ *"Proposed Transit Legislation" in Crain's Detroit Business (Vol. 24, October 6, 2008, No. 40, pp. 19)*

Pub: Crain Communications, Inc.

Description: Breakdown of state Representative Marie Donigan's proposed transit legislation includes tax increment financing. Other pieces of the proposed legislation are examined.

24910 ■ *"Put It In Drive" in Entrepreneur (Vol. 36, April 2008, No. 4, pp. 31)*

Pub: Entrepreneur Media, Inc.

Ed: Jill Amadio. **Description:** Commercial vehicle models for 2008 are presented. These new models are more user- and environment-friendly. Features and prices of car models and tips to consider before purchasing are presented.

24911 ■ *"Road Warriors: How To Survive Business Travel" in Crain's Detroit Business (Vol. 24, February 4, 2008, No. 5, pp. 11)*

Pub: Crain Communications Inc. - Detroit

Description: Entrepreneurs share tips that help save time and energy at airports when traveling for business.

24912 ■ *"Route Optimization Impacts the Bottom Line" in Contractor (Vol. 56, November 2009, No. 11, pp. 48)*

Pub: Penton Media, Inc.

Ed: Dave Beaudry. **Description:** Plumbing and HVAC businesses can save a significant amount of money from route optimization. The process begins with gathering information on a fleet and a routing software tool can determine the effectiveness of current route configurations and identify preferable route plans.

24913 ■ *"RT Seeking Ways to Finance Expansion" in Sacramento Business Journal (Vol. 28, July 29, 2011, No. 22, pp. 1)*

Pub: Sacramento Business Journal

Ed: Melanie Turner. **Description:** Sacramento Regional Transit District is considering ways to finance all its capital projects outlined in a 30-year transit master plan which would cost more than $7 billion to complete. Current funding sources include developer fees and state and federal assistance and fares. Part of the master plan is a light-rail line to Sacramento International Airport.

24914 ■ *"Running On Empty" in The Business Journal-Milwaukee (Vol. 25, July 4, 2008, No. 41, pp. A1)*

Pub: American City Business Journals, Inc.

Ed: David Doege. **Description:** Employers are more engaged in offering incentives designed to offset commuting costs. Among the incentives offered are gas cards, parking reimbursement and midyear wage increases. The other efforts to help employees with the costs of going to work are discussed.

24915 ■ *"Save Money on Travel With These Websites for Frequent Fliers" in Inc. (Vol. 31, January-February 2009, No. 1, pp. 44)*

Pub: Mansueto Ventures LLC

Description: Four Websites offering services to the business traveler are profiled: MissRefund.com will get the taxes and fuel surcharges back to any traveler canceling a flight; Vayama.com is a booking site focused on routes and destinations not generally available online; Airfarewatchdog.com searches for listing sites for best travel deals; and Yapta alerts users to good prices for particular flights.

24916 ■ *"Scanning the Field" in Business Courier (Vol. 26, January 8, 2010, No. 38, pp. 1)*

Pub: American City Business Journals, Inc.

Ed: Jon Newberry. **Description:** Anti-terror detection systems developer Valley Force Composite Technologies Inc. of Kentucky plans to enter the market with its high-resolution ODIN and Thor-LVX screening systems. These systems are expected to meet the increasing demand for airport security equipment.

24917 ■ *"Singapore Airlines' Balancing Act" in Harvard Business Review (Vol. 88, July-August 2010, No. 7-8, pp. 145)*

Pub: Harvard Business School Publishing

Ed: Loizos Heracleous, Jochen Wirtz. **Description:** Singapore Airlines is used as an illustration of organizational effectiveness. The article includes the firm's 4-3-3 rule of spending, its promotion of centralized as well as decentralized innovation, use of technology, and strategic planning.

24918 ■ *"Sleep It Off In a Silo B & B" in Chicago Tribune (December 14, 2008)*

Pub McClatchy-Tribune Information Services

Ed: Bill Daley. **Description:** Profile of Oregon's Abbey Road Farm bed-and-breakfast which is located on an 82-acre working farm; guests stay in shiny metal farm silos which have been converted into luxury rooms with views of the farm.

24919 ■ *"Small Dutch Islands Saba, Statia Content With Low-Key Niche" in Travel Weekly (Vol. 69, August 16, 2010, No. 33, pp. 22)*

Pub: NorthStar Travel Media LLC

Ed: Gay Nagle Myers. **Description:** Small Caribbean islands market and promote their region for tourism by never competing with the bigger destinations. Saba and Statia are the two smallest islands in the Caribbean and rely on repeat guests, word-of-mouth recommendations and travel agents willing to promote them.

24920 ■ *"The Solution" in Entrepreneur (Vol. 37, October 2009, No. 10, pp. 71)*

Pub: Entrepreneur Media, Inc.

Ed: Jennifer Wang. **Description:** Ford's 2010 Transit Connect is a compact commercial van developed specifically for small business owners. The compact van offers an integrated in-dash computer system providing a cellular broadband connection.

24921 ■ *"Sometimes You Have to Ignore the Rule Book" in Canadian Business (Vol. 83, September 14, 2010, No. 15, pp. 13)*

Pub: Rogers Media Ltd.

Ed: Richard Branson. **Description:** The rule book has provided a clear framework for employees particularly when cash and accounting are at issue.

However, sometimes rules were made to be broken and the rule book should not become an excuse for poor customer service or hinder great service. How Virgin Atlantic practices this type of corporate culture is discussed.

24922 ■ "Sound Advice From Dr. Sleep" in Crain's Chicago Business (Vol. 31, April 21, 2008, No. 16, pp. 30)
Pub: Crain Communications, Inc.
Ed: Sarah A. Klein. **Description:** James K. Wyatt, the director of the Sleep Disorders Centers at Rush University Medical Center in Chicago, gives advice to business executives concerning what to eat, how to nap and which drugs to take or avoid in order to ease the strain of air travel, particularly on overseas flights.

24923 ■ "South Lake Tahoe B & B Blocks Out Neveda's Neon" in Chicago Tribune (May 18, 2008)
Pub: McClatchy-Tribune Information Services
Ed: Randall Weissman. **Description:** Profile of the Black Bear Inn, a small bed-and-breakfast in South Lake Tahoe owned by Jerry Birdwell and Kevin Chandler; the welcoming ambience is a delightful departure from ski resort hotel rooms. Pricing and further details of the various rooms are described.

24924 ■ "State Aviation Fuel Tax Proposal Runs Into Turbulence" in Crain's Detroit Business (Vol. 25, June 15, 2009, No. 24, pp. 5)
Pub: Crain Communications Inc. - Detroit
Ed: Amy Lane. **Description:** Delta Airlines Inc. is concerned about a proposal that would change the way Michigan taxes aviation fuel. The plan would go from the current cents-per-gallon tax to a percentage tax on the wholesale price of fuel, which would raise the taxes significantly.

24925 ■ "State Weighs Tearing Down Hoan" in The Business Journal-Milwaukee (Vol. 25, August 22, 2008, No. 48, pp. A1)
Pub: American City Business Journals, Inc.
Ed: Pete Millard. **Description:** Department of Transportation of Wisconsin is studying the feasibility of tearing the Daniel Hoan Memorial Bridge down because rehabilitating the bridge is costly. Rebuilding the Interstate 794 at street level could be less expensive. The potential plans for the bridge are discussed further.

24926 ■ "Stay in Touch, Wherever You Roam: Smartphones for Overseas Travel" in Inc. (Volume 32, December 2010, No. 10, pp. 60)
Pub: Inc. Magazine
Description: International cell phones services are profiled, including HTC Aria, Nokia E73 Mode, Samsung Captivate, and Blackberry Bold 9650.

24927 ■ "Still in the Jet Set" in Barron's (Vol. 89, July 13, 2009, No. 28, pp. 13)
Pub: Dow Jones & Co., Inc.
Ed: Brad Davis. **Description:** Coastal Jet Service will be offering coast-to-coast flights and a one way ride on their Cessna Citation X will cost $4,600 plus tax. The service is a compromise between a corporate jet and a first-class seat on a commercial flight and the jets fly out of Westchester County, New York and land in Burbank, California.

24928 ■ "Strictly Business" in Black Enterprise (Vol. 38, October 2007, No. 3, pp. 62)
Pub: Earl G. Graves Publishing Co. Inc.
Description: Profile of the HP iPAQ hw6925 smartphone suited to small business use. The phone offers mobile word processing and messaging features great for the tech-savvy business traveler.

24929 ■ "Ten Ways to Save on Business Travel" in Women Entrepreneur (November 21, 2008)
Pub: Entrepreneur Media Inc.
Ed: Julie Moline. **Description:** Advice regarding ways in which to save money when traveling for business is given.

24930 ■ "TIA Wrestles with Procurement Issues" in Business Journal Serving Greater Tampa Bay (Vol. 30, November 12, 2010, No. 47, pp. 1)
Pub: Tampa Bay Business Journal
Ed: Mark Holan. **Description:** Tampa International Airport (TIA) has been caught in conflict of interest and procurement policy issues after the Hillsborough County Aviation Authority learned of the spousal relationship of an employee with his wife's firm, Gresham Smith and Partners. Gresham already won contracts with TIA and was ahead of other firms in a new contract.

24931 ■ "Tightening Economy Squeezes Business Travel" in HRMagazine (Vol. 53, August 2008, No. 8, pp. 19)
Pub: Society for Human Resource Management
Contact: Henry G. Jackson, President
E-mail: hjackson@shrm.org
Ed: Kathy Gurchiek. **Description:** New surveys show that some companies are not cutting out business travel, they are using cheaper hotels and cutting back on trade shows and conference travel. Statistical data included.

24932 ■ "To Build for the Future, Reach Beyond the Skies" in Canadian Business (Vol. 83, June 15, 2010, No. 10, pp. 11)
Pub: Rogers Media Ltd.
Ed: Richard Branson. **Description:** Richard Branson says that tackling an engineering challenge or a scientific venture is a real adventure for an entrepreneur. Branson discusses Virgin's foray into the aviation business and states that at Virgin, they build for the future.

24933 ■ "TomTom GO910: On the Road Again" in Black Enterprise (Vol. 37, January 2007, No. 6, pp. 52)
Pub: Earl G. Graves Publishing Co. Inc.
Ed: Stephanie Young. **Description:** TomTom GO 910 is a GPS navigator that offers detailed maps of the U.S., Canada, and Europe. Consumers view their routes by a customizable LCD screen showing everything from the quickest to the shortest routes available or how to avoid toll roads. Business travelers may find this product invaluable as it also functions as a cell phone and connects to a variety of other multi-media devices.

24934 ■ "Top IPhone Apps" in Advertising Age (Vol. 79, December 15, 2008, No. 46, pp. 17)
Pub: Crain Communications, Inc.
Ed: Marissa Miley. **Description:** Free and low cost applications for the iPhone are described including Evernote, an application that allows users to outsource their memory to keep track of events, notes, ides and more; Handshake, a way for users to exchange business cards and pictures across Wi-Fi and 3G; CityTransit, an interactive map of the New York subway system that uses GPS technology to find nearby stations and also tells the user if a train is out of commission that day; and Stage Hand which allows users to deliver a presentation, control timing and slide order on the spot.

24935 ■ "Tradeshow Attendance Incentives Add Up" in Pet Product News (Vol. 64, December 2010, No. 12, pp. 14)
Pub: BowTie Inc.
Ed: Mark E. Battersby. **Description:** Pointers on how pet specialty retailers can claim business travel tax and income tax deductions for expenses paid or incurred in participation at tradeshows, conventions, and meetings are presented. Incentives in form of these deductions could allow pet specialty retailers to gain business benefits, aside from the education and enjoyment involved with the travel.

24936 ■ "Traffic Slows at O'Hare; As Airlines Cut Flights, City Tries to Push Expansion Forward" in Crain's Chicago Business (April 28, 2008)
Pub: Crain Communications, Inc.
Ed: Paul Merrion; John Pletz. **Description:** O'Hare International Airport is seeing a decline in passenger traffic just as the city of Chicago presses cash-strapped airlines to fund the second phase of the airport's expansion which would include the extension of one runway, the relocation of two others and the construction of a new western terminal.

24937 ■ "A Train of Our Own" in Canadian Business (Vol. 79, July 17, 2006, No. 14-15, pp. 71)
Pub: Rogers Media
Ed: Victor Dwyer. **Description:** The luxuries and pleasure of traveling in private rail road cars are discussed.

24938 ■ "Travel In Style, Or Not: Finding a Company Travel Service for Every Budget" in Inc. (January 2008, pp. 36-37)
Pub: Gruner & Jahr USA Publishing
Ed: Larry Olmsted. **Description:** Profiles of various travel services to help small businesses. Firms profiled include Cassis Travel Services, providing first class bookings; Open from American Express, specializing in business class travel; Travelocity business, providing travel agents with 24/7 services; Diners Club Corporate Card, with many features; and Expedia Corporate Travel, allowing users to compare prices for airline tickets, hotels, and car rentals.

24939 ■ "Travel Leery" in Crain's Chicago Business (Vol. 31, March 31, 2008, No. 13, pp. 3)
Pub: Crain Communications, Inc.
Description: Due to the rise in airline prices and a possible recession, many companies are starting to change their travel policies and limit travel spending.

24940 ■ "Travel Rewards Take Off" in Inc. (Vol. 33, October 2011, No. 8, pp. 46)
Pub: Inc. Magazine
Ed: Matthew DeLuca. **Description:** Credit card companies are offering travel reward cards with special perks, including sign-up bonuses; three such cards are described.

24941 ■ "Travel Tears" in Crain's Chicago Business (Vol. 31, November 17, 2008, No. 46, pp. 3)
Pub: Crain Communications, Inc.
Ed: Bob Tita. **Description:** Hotels, restaurants and conventions are seeing a decline in profits due to corporate travel cutbacks and the sagging economy. City and state revenues derived from taxes on tourism-related industries are also suffering.

24942 ■ "The Traveler's Traveler" in Entrepreneur (Vol. 37, September 2009, No. 9, pp. 22)
Pub: Entrepreneur Media, Inc.
Ed: Kim Orr. **Description:** Business travel columnist Joe Sharkey says technology may someday replace business travel. Airlines are realizing that a part of the business travel market has disappeared. Sharkey also says airlines can never get those customers back.

24943 ■ "Turbulent Times and Golden Opportunity" in Business Strategy Review (Vol. 21, Spring 2010, No. 1, pp. 34)
Pub: Wiley-Blackwell
Ed: Don Sull. **Description:** For those feeling storm-tossed by today's economy, the author believes there's much to learn from Carnival Cruise Lines, a company that discovered that turbulence often has an upside.

24944 ■ "TW Trade Shows to Offer Seminars On Niche Selling, Social Media" in Travel Weekly (Vol. 69, October 4, 2010, No. 40, pp. 9)
Pub: NorthStar Travel Media LLC
Description: Travel Weekly's Leisure World 2010 and Fall Home Based Travel Agent Show focused on niche selling, with emphasis on all-inclusives, young consumers, groups, incentives, culinary vacations, and honeymoon or romance travel.

24945 ■ "Vacation, What Vacation?" in Black Enterprise (Vol. 41, August 2010, No. 1, pp. 36)
Pub: Earl G. Graves Publishing Co. Inc.
Description: Nearly 50 percent of employers expect employees to check in with the office while they are away on vacation.

24946 ■ *"Virgin America Flies with V&S on Web"* in *ADWEEK (Vol. 51, July 12 2010, No. 27, pp. 31)*
Pub: Nielsen Business Media Inc.
Description: Victors & Spoils, a crowdsourcing agency is examined.

24947 ■ *"Vonage V-Phone: Use Your Laptop to Make Calls Via the Internet"* in *Black Enterprise (Vol. 37, January 2007, No. 6, pp. 52)*
Pub: Earl G. Graves Publishing Co. Inc.
Ed: James C. Johnson. **Description:** Overview of the Vonage V-Phone, which is small flash drive device that lets you make phone calls through a high-speed Internet connection and plugs into any computer's USB port. Business travels may find this product to be a wonderful solution as it includes 250MB of memory and can store files, digital photos, MP3s, and more.

24948 ■ *"'We Had to Won the Mistakes"* in *Harvard Business Review (Vol. 88, July-August 2010, No. 7-8, pp. 108)*
Pub: Harvard Business School Publishing
Ed: Adi Ignatius. **Description:** Interview with Howard Schultz, CEO of Starbucks, covers topics that include investment in retraining, the impact of competition, premium quality, authenticity, customer services, strategy development, work-and-life issues, and international presence.

24949 ■ *"What's the Black Travel Market Worth?"* in *Black Enterprise (Vol. 38, January 2008, No. 6, pp. 54)*
Pub: Earl G. Graves Publishing Co. Inc.
Ed: Aisha Sylvester. **Description:** African American travel market, both business and pleasure, is one of the top three fastest growing markets in the industry. Hugh Riley, director of marketing for the Caribbean Tourism Organization shares his ideas on the relationship between African American travelers and the Caribbean tourism industry.

24950 ■ *"Wisdom from the Mountaintops"* in *Canadian Business (Vol. 83, October 12, 2010, No. 17, pp. 91)*
Pub: Rogers Media Ltd.
Ed: Matthew McClearn. **Description:** Techniques used to save lives on the world's highest mountains could make companies more creative. Mountaineers have time to talk to one another, and the resulting flow of ideas help climbers reach the summit. Organizations are expected to foster communication both internally and externally.

TRADE PERIODICALS

24951 ■ *Better Business Traveling*
Pub: Traveling Times Inc.
Ed: Mirko A. Ilich, Editor. **Released:** Monthly. **Description:** Provides news and information of interest to business travelers.

24952 ■ *Business Travel News*
Contact: David Meyer, Editor-in-Chief
E-mail: dmeyer@btnonline.com
URL(s): www.btnmag.com/businesstravelnews/index.jsp. **Released:** Weekly **Price:** Free.

24953 ■ *Corporate Meetings & Incentives: The Senior Executives Guide to Decision Making*
Pub: Primedia Business Magazines & Media
URL(s): meetingsnet.com/corporatemeetingsincentives/. **Ed:** Barbara Scofidio. **Released:** Monthly **Price:** $97, Canada; $123, Free to qualified subscribers in USA; $123, Other countries.

24954 ■ *Runzheimer Reports on Travel Management*
Pub: Runzheimer International
Contact: Rex A. Runzheimer, President
E-mail: rar@runzheimer.com
Ed: Phyllis Schumann, Sr., Editor, ps@runzheimer.com. **Released:** Quarterly. **Price:** Free Web Service. **Description:** Intended to help control business travel costs. Covers travel budgets, corporate arrangements with travel agencies, in-house travel departments, and travel policies for business firms. Also discusses negotiation of special rates/services with travel suppliers. Recurring features include a profile of a major city, with information on car rentals, hotels, and special attractions. Remarks: Also available via e-mail.

24955 ■ *Southern Festivals: The South's Festival Newspaper*
Pub: Southern Festivals
URL(s): www.southfest.com/festival_list/georgia.html. **Released:** Bimonthly

CONSULTANTS

24956 ■ **Off the Beaten Path L.L.C.**
7 E Beall St.
Bozeman, MT 59715
Ph: (406)586-1311
Free: 800-445-2995
Fax: (406)587-4147
Co. E-mail: travel@offthebeatenpath.com
URL: http://www.offthebeatenpath.com
Contact: Cory Lawrence, Chief Executive Officer
E-mail: coryl@offthebeatenpath.com
Scope: A travel planning services consultancy and consulting on ecotourism; positioning of one's lodge and business in the marketplace, pricing, marketing plans and strategic planning. **Founded:** 1986. **Seminars:** Soil to Bottle.

24957 ■ **CM Uberman Enterprises Inc.**
1370 Piccard Dr., Ste. 200
Rockville, MD 20850
Ph: (301)417-0030
Fax: (301)417-0507
Co. E-mail: reuberman@aol.com
Contact: Rudy Uberman, Vice President
E-mail: reuberman@aol.com
Scope: Conference and meeting management assistance offered to nonprofit institutions and agencies. Maintains a discount travel network covering hotels, airline flights, and care rentals. Serves all travelers: Corporate, nonprofit and personal. **Founded:** 1989.

LIBRARIES

24958 ■ **Maritz Travel Company Resource Center**
1375 N. Highway Dr.
Fenton, MO 63099
Ph: (636)827-4000
Free: 877-462-7489
URL: http://www.maritz.com
Contact: Steve Maritz, Chief Executive Officer
Scope: Travel data - hotels, restaurants, sightseeing, steamships, countries and cities. **Services:** Interlibrary loan; Library not open to the public. **Founded:** 1969. **Holdings:** 300 books; 177 bound periodical volumes; 95 VF drawers of travel-related brochures and reports; 2200 videotapes. **Subscriptions:** 35 journals and other serials.

24959 ■ **Nadasdy Ferenc Museum Library**
Varkerulet 1
H-9600 Sarvar, Hungary
Ph: 36 95 320158
Fax: 36 95 320158
Co. E-mail: nadasdy.sarvar@museum.hu
URL: http://www.museum.hu/museum/index_hu.php?ID=669
Contact: Takacs Zoltan, Director
Scope: Regional history. **Services:** Copying; library open to the public with restrictions. **Founded:** 1951. **Holdings:** 4000 volumes. **Telecommunication Services:** muzeum.sarvar@mail.globonet.hu.

24960 ■ **Travel Industry Association of America Library**
1100 New York Ave. NW, Ste. 450
Washington, DC 20005-3934
Ph: (202)408-8422
Fax: (202)408-1255
Co. E-mail: feedback@ustravel.org
URL: http://www.ustravel.org
Contact: Suzanne D. Cook, Senior Vice President, Research
Scope: Travel and tourism. **Services:** Library not open to the public. **Founded:** 1941. **Holdings:** 3000 research documents; 3800 government documents; 250 unpublished travel research reports; 15,000 clippings; 20 tapes. **Subscriptions:** 27 journals and other serials. **Telecommunication Services:** research@ustravel.org.

START-UP INFORMATION

24961 ■ *A Business of My Own? 21 Steps to Successfully Starting and Running a Small Business*
Pub: Enfield Publishing
Ed: Marjorie Cleveland Fisher. **Released:** January 2005. **Description:** New ideas to start or grow a small business, including ideas for writing business plans with examples, adopting a business structure, and setting goals and objectives.

24962 ■ *"Rehab Will Turn Hospital Into Incubator" in The Business Journal-Serving Metropolitan Kansas City (Vol. 26, September 12, 2008)*
Pub: American City Business Journals, Inc.
Ed: Rob Roberts. **Description:** Independence Regional Health Center will be purchased by CEAH Realtors and be converted into the Independence Regional Entrepreneurial Center, a business incubator that will house startups and other tenants. Other details about the planned entrepreneurial center are provided.

24963 ■ *"Startup Aims to Cut Out Coupon Clipping" in The Business Journal-Serving Metropolitan Kansas City (Vol. 26, August 15, 2008, No. 49)*
Pub: American City Business Journals, Inc.
Ed: Suzanna Stagemeyer. **Description:** TDP Inc., who started operations 18 months ago, aims to transform stale coupon promotions using technology by digitizing the entire coupon process. The process is expected to enable consumers to hunt coupons online where they will be automatically linked to loyalty cards. Other views and information on TDP and its services are presented.

24964 ■ *"Three Weeks To Startup" in Entrepreneur (December 19, 2008)*
Pub: Entrepreneur Media Inc.
Ed: Tim Berry; Sabrina Parsons. **Description:** Breakdown for realistically starting a business in three weeks is provided in detail.

EDUCATIONAL PROGRAMS

24965 ■ 2011 National Electrical Code (Onsite) (NEC)
American Trainco
9785 S Maroon Cir., Ste. 300
Englewood, CO 80112
Ph: (303)531-4560
Free: 877-978-7246
Fax: (303)531-4565
Co. E-mail: Sales@AmericanTrainco.com
URL: http://www.americantrainco.com
Price: $990.00. **Description:** Provides anyone working with electricity the most up-to-date, best practices for safe installation and maintenance of electrical systems and equipment, including the new 2011 Code changes. **Dates and Locations:** Cities throughout the United States.

24966 ■ Advanced Critical Thinking Applications Workshop (Onsite)
American Management Association
600 AMA Way
Saranac Lake, NY 12983-5534
Ph: (212)586-8100
Free: 877-566-9441
Fax: (518)891-0368
Co. E-mail: customerservice@amanet.org
URL: http://www.amaseminars.org
Price: $2,445.00 for non-members; $2,195.00 for AMA members; and $1,880.00 for General Services Administration (GSA) members. **Description:** Two-day seminar applying critical thinking skills and how they influence challenges in the work environment. **Dates and Locations:** San Francisco, CA; and New York, NY.

24967 ■ Air Conditioning & Refrigeration (Onsite)
American Trainco
9785 S Maroon Cir., Ste. 300
Englewood, CO 80112
Ph: (303)531-4560
Free: 877-978-7246
Fax: (303)531-4565
Co. E-mail: Sales@AmericanTrainco.com
URL: http://www.americantrainco.com
Price: $990.00. **Description:** Course designed for anyone who needs to understand basic operation, maintenance, and troubleshooting of air conditioning and refrigeration systems in order to improve efficiencies and uptime at their industrial plants and large building facilities. **Dates and Locations:** Cities throughout the United States.

24968 ■ AMA's Financial Modeling and Forecasting Workshop (Onsite)
American Management Association
600 AMA Way
Saranac Lake, NY 12983-5534
Ph: (212)586-8100
Free: 877-566-9441
Fax: (518)891-0368
Co. E-mail: customerservice@amanet.org
URL: http://www.amaseminars.org
Price: $2,545.00 for non-members; $2,295.00 for AMA members; and $1,965.00 for General Services Administration (GSA) members. **Description:** Three-day seminar that covers advanced Excel modeling techniques, creating your own model from real-world examples, and analyzing and applying findings to confirm your forecast. **Dates and Locations:** New York, NY; Dallas, TX; Washington, DC; Arlington, VA; and San Diego, CA.

24969 ■ Arc Flash Protection & Electrical Safety 70E
American Trainco
9785 S Maroon Cir., Ste. 300
Englewood, CO 80112
Ph: (303)531-4560
Free: 877-978-7246
Fax: (303)531-4565
Co. E-mail: Sales@AmericanTrainco.com
URL: http://www.americantrainco.com
Price: $990.00. **Description:** Training course designed to save lives, prevent disabling injuries, and prevent damage to plants, buildings and equipment. Participants learn about personal safety for working on or around electrical systems and equipment, how to use proper materials and procedures for doing electrical work, and the potential consequences for themselves and others if they don't. **Dates and Locations:** Cities throughout the United States.

24970 ■ Auditing the Manufacturing Process (Onsite)
Seminar Information Service, Inc.
20 Executive Park, Ste. 120
Irvine, CA 92614
Ph: (949)261-9104
Free: 877-SEM-INFO
Fax: (949)261-1963
Co. E-mail: info@seminarinformation.com
URL: http://www.seminarinformation.com
Price: $2,050.00. **Description:** Learn how to identify key manufacturing data to help objectively perform risk assessment of the conversion cycle, while discovering how to analyze the impact of shop floor activities on the balance sheet and income statement, and review the audit concerns in implementing new technologies. **Dates and Locations:** Boston, MA.

24971 ■ Basic Electricity for the Non Electrician (Onsite)
American Trainco
9785 S Maroon Cir., Ste. 300
Englewood, CO 80112
Ph: (303)531-4560
Free: 877-978-7246
Fax: (303)531-4565
Co. E-mail: Sales@AmericanTrainco.com
URL: http://www.americantrainco.com
Price: $990.00. **Description:** Understanding and working with industrial electricity. **Dates and Locations:** Cities throughout the United States.

24972 ■ Boiler Operation, Maintenance & Safety (Onsite)
American Trainco
9785 S Maroon Cir., Ste. 300
Englewood, CO 80112
Ph: (303)531-4560
Free: 877-978-7246
Fax: (303)531-4565
Co. E-mail: Sales@AmericanTrainco.com
URL: http://www.americantrainco.com
Price: $990.00. **Description:** Seminar designed to teach building and facility maintenance personnel how to service their own boiler safely reducing the need for outside service contractors, while at the same time increases your confidence and comfort level in operating and maintaining your own broilers. **Dates and Locations:** Cities throughout the United States.

24973 ■ Building a Strategy Focused Organization (Onsite)
EEI Communications
8945 Guilford., Ste. 145
Columbia, MD 21046
Ph: (410)309-8200
Free: 888-253-2762
Fax: (410)630-3980
Co. E-mail: train@eeicom.com
URL: http://www.eeicom.com/eei-training-services
Price: $1,625.00. **Description:** Identifies strategies that can help your organization meet the challenges of the competitive environment and improve overall effectiveness across organizational boundaries. **Dates and Locations:** Silver Spring, MD; Hunt Valley, MD; Columbia, MD; and Alexandria, VA.

24974 ■ Chilled Water Systems (Onsite)
American Trainco
9785 S Maroon Cir., Ste. 300
Englewood, CO 80112
Ph: (303)531-4560
Free: 877-978-7246
Fax: (303)531-4565
Co. E-mail: Sales@AmericanTrainco.com
URL: http://www.americantrainco.com
Price: $990.00. **Description:** Learn to control your systems and properly maintain them, getting the most out of them. **Dates and Locations:** Cities throughout the United States.

24975 ■ The Conference on Social Media (Onsite)
Seminar Information Service, Inc.
20 Executive Park, Ste. 120
Irvine, CA 92614
Ph: (949)261-9104
Free: 877-SEM-INFO
Fax: (949)261-1963
Co. E-mail: info@seminarinformation.com
URL: http://www.seminarinformation.com
Price: $199.00. **Description:** Learn how to make social media link your organization, including new tools and ways to grow your business, and how to define your strategy and create your plan prior to taking the leap into social media. **Dates and Locations:** Cities throughout the United States.

24976 ■ Developing a Balanced Scorecard for Business & Government
EEI Communications
8945 Guilford Rd., Ste. 145
Columbia, MD 21046
Ph: (410)309-8200
Free: 888-253-2762
Fax: (410)630-3980
Co. E-mail: train@eeicom.com
URL: http://www.eeicom.com/eei-training-services
Price: $1,065.00. **Description:** The Balanced Score-Card evaluates performance from four basic perspectives, Customer, Financial, Internal Processes and Learning and Growth. By utilizing Key Performance Indicators (KPIs) to reflect the performance of the organization at a variety of levels, the Balanced ScoreCard allows organizations to better understand, communicate and improve on organizational performance. **Dates and Locations:** Silver Spring, MD; Hunt Valley, MD; Columbia, MD; and Alexandria, VA.

24977 ■ Electrical Ladder Drawings, Schematics & Design (Onsite)
American Trainco
9785 S Maroon Cir., Ste. 300
Englewood, CO 80112
Ph: (303)531-4560
Free: 877-978-7246
Fax: (303)531-4565
Co. E-mail: Sales@AmericanTrainco.com
URL: http://www.americantrainco.com
Price: $990.00. **Description:** Training will include exercises where participants create schematic diagrams based on circuit descriptions, as well as interpreting schematic drawings so that they can provide verbal or written circuit descriptions and an understanding of several types of drawings and diagrams including Block, Pictorial, One-line, Wiring, Terminal, and Schematic. **Dates and Locations:** Cities throughout the United States.

24978 ■ Generators & Emergency Power (Onsite)
American Trainco
9785 S Maroon Cir., Ste. 300
Englewood, CO 80112
Ph: (303)531-4560
Free: 877-978-7246
Fax: (303)531-4565
Co. E-mail: Sales@AmericanTrainco.com
URL: http://www.americantrainco.com
Price: $990.00. **Description:** Learn what you can do, and should do with generators, to make sure your facility will keep running even when the electricity to your facility doesn't. **Dates and Locations:** Cities throughout the United States.

24979 ■ How to Conduct Your Own Energy Audit (Onsite)
American Trainco
9785 S Maroon Cir., Ste. 300
Englewood, CO 80112
Ph: (303)531-4560
Free: 877-978-7246
Fax: (303)531-4565
Co. E-mail: Sales@AmericanTrainco.com
URL: http://www.americantrainco.com
Price: $990.00. **Description:** Two-day hands-on seminar shows you how to find quick and inexpensive ways to immediately cut energy costs at your plant or facility. **Dates and Locations:** Orlando, FL.

24980 ■ HVAC Controls & Air Distribution (Onsite)
American Trainco
9785 S Maroon Cir., Ste. 300
Englewood, CO 80112
Ph: (303)531-4560
Free: 877-978-7246
Fax: (303)531-4565
Co. E-mail: Sales@AmericanTrainco.com
URL: http://www.americantrainco.com
Price: $990.00. **Description:** Learn how to 'control' their controls, and how to use fundamental air distribution principles for achieving consistent HVAC comfort and efficiency in buildings, plants and facilities. **Dates and Locations:** Cities throughout the United States.

24981 ■ Improve Your Analytical Skills: Making Information Work for You (Onsite)
American Management Association
600 AMA Way
Saranac Lake, NY 12983-5534
Ph: (212)586-8100
Free: 877-566-9441
Fax: (518)891-0368
Co. E-mail: customerservice@amanet.org
URL: http://www.amaseminars.org
Price: $1,995.00 for non-members; $1,795.00 for AMA members; and $1,537.00 for General Services Administration (GSA) members. **Description:** Learn how to assimilate, assess, organize, and analyze information. **Dates and Locations:** Cities throughout the United States.

24982 ■ Instrumentation, Process Measurement & Control (Onsite)
American Trainco
9785 S Maroon Cir., Ste. 300
Englewood, CO 80112
Ph: (303)531-4560
Free: 877-978-7246
Fax: (303)531-4565
Co. E-mail: Sales@AmericanTrainco.com
URL: http://www.americantrainco.com
Price: $990.00. **Description:** Learn why it is necessary to measure what is going on with your systems and equipment, how to measure it, and what those measurements may mean in terms of action that should be taken to eliminate future downtime and unnecessary expense. **Dates and Locations:** Phoenix, AZ; Denver, CO; Norcross, GA; Baltimore, MD; Harrisburg, PA; Arlington, TX; Salt Lake City, UT; Richmond, VA; and Everett, WA.

24983 ■ Inventory Control for Maintenance (Onsite)
American Trainco
9785 S Maroon Cir., Ste. 300
Englewood, CO 80112
Ph: (303)531-4560
Free: 877-978-7246
Fax: (303)531-4565
Co. E-mail: Sales@AmericanTrainco.com
URL: http://www.americantrainco.com
Price: $990.00. **Description:** Focus on building an inventory management system that will lead to better control through optimization of inventory quantities, organization of inventory and access to inventory. **Dates and Locations:** Phoenix, AZ; Salt Lake, UT; Orange County, CA; and Orlando, FL.

24984 ■ Maintenance Planning & Scheduling (Onsite)
American Trainco
9785 S Maroon Cir., Ste. 300
Englewood, CO 80112
Ph: (303)531-4560
Free: 877-978-7246
Fax: (303)531-4565
Co. E-mail: Sales@AmericanTrainco.com
URL: http://www.americantrainco.com
Price: $990.00. **Description:** Learn to reduce maintenance costs by better planning with your existing workforce. **Dates and Locations:** Cities throughout the United States.

24985 ■ Maintenance Welding (Onsite)
American Trainco
9785 S Maroon Cir., Ste. 300
Englewood, CO 80112
Ph: (303)531-4560
Free: 877-978-7246
Fax (303)531-4565
Co. E-mail: Sales@AmericanTrainco.com
URL: http://www.americantrainco.com
Price: $990.00. **Description:** Learn welding techniques, welding processes, metal and filler selection, cutting processes, new fabrications, troubleshooting defects, welding repair, personal safety, managing costs, record keeping and more. **Dates and Locations:** Cities throughout the United States.

24986 ■ Motor Selection, Maintenance, Testing & Replacement
American Trainco
9785 S Maroon Cir., Ste. 300
Englewood, CO 80112
Ph: (303)531-4560
Free: 877-978-7246
Fax: (303)531-4565
Co. E-mail: Sales@AmericanTrainco.com
URL http://www.americantrainco.com
Price: $495.00. **Description:** Seminar designed for anyone whose work is affected by motors at their facility, whether they are mechanics doing the work, a supervisor in charge of fixing problems, or purchasing agents responsible for saving money. **Dates and Locations:** Anchorage, AK; and Honolulu, HI.

24987 ■ PLC Programming & Applications (Onsite)
American Trainco
9785 S Maroon Cir., Ste. 300
Englewood, CO 80112
Ph: (303)531-4560
Free: 877-978-7246
Fax: 303)531-4565
Co. E-mail: Sales@AmericanTrainco.com
URL: http://www.americantrainco.com
Price: $990.00. **Description:** Provides skills needed to organize, plan, write, enter, test, and document SLC500 programs using the basic programming instructions and RSLogix software. **Dates and Locations** Cities throughout the United States.

24988 ■ PLCs for Non-Programmers (Onsite)
American Trainco
9785 S Maroon Cir., Ste. 300
Englewood, CO 80112
Ph: (303)531-4560
Free: 877-978-7246

Fax: (303)531-4565
Co. E-mail: Sales@AmericanTrainco.com
URL: http://www.americantrainco.com
Price: $990.00. **Description:** Seminar designed for maintenance technicians, electricians, or other non-programmers who need a general understanding of automation and Programmable Logic Controllers. **Dates and Locations:** Cities throughout the United States.

24989 ■ Plumbing & Pipefitting for Plants & Buildings (Onsite)
American Trainco
9785 S Maroon Cir., Ste. 300
Englewood, CO 80112
Ph: (303)531-4560
Free: 877-978-7246
Fax: (303)531-4565
Co. E-mail: Sales@AmericanTrainco.com
URL: http://www.americantrainco.com
Price: $990.00. **Description:** Covers the necessary requirements to follow code and safety regulations while providing the student with a practical foundation to quickly identify problems and solve them on their own, whether it's a low-pressure water supply line problem, drippy valve or a clogged drain trap. **Dates and Locations:** Orlando, FL; and Atlanta, GA.

24990 ■ Predictive Maintenance and Condition Monitoring (Onsite)
American Trainco
9785 S Maroon Cir., Ste. 300
Englewood, CO 80112
Ph: (303)531-4560
Free: 877-978-7246
Fax: (303)531-4565
Co. E-mail: Sales@AmericanTrainco.com
URL: http://www.americantrainco.com
Price: $990.00. **Description:** Provides the fundamentals of PdM and condition monitoring applicable to plants, facilities, and manufacturing lines. **Dates and Locations:** Orange County, CA; Los Angeles, CA; Denver, CO; Hartford, CT; Orlando, FL; Baltimore, MD; Las Vegas, NV; and Norfolk, VA.

24991 ■ The Proactive Leader I: Develop an Effective Agenda, Build Support, and Gain Traction
Seminar Information Service, Inc.
20 Executive Park, Ste. 120
Irvine, CA 92614
Ph: (949)261-9104
Free: 877-SEM-INFO
Fax: (949)261-1963
Co. E-mail: info@seminarinformation.com
URL: http://www.seminarinformation.com
Price: $1,495.00. **Description:** Learn to identify and prioritize arenas where you can effect change in your organization, including the skills of political competence to take the next steps toward building support and gaining traction for your idea. **Dates and Locations:** New York, NY.

24992 ■ Project Initiation and Planning (Onsite)
EEI Communications
8945 Guilford Rd., Ste. 145
Columbia, MD 21046
Ph: (410)309-8200
Free: 888-253-2762
Fax: (410)630-3980
Co. E-mail: train@eeicom.com
URL: http://www.eeicom.com/eei-training-services
Price: $1,065.00. **Description:** Learn how to incorporate project charter, work breakdown structure, a risk and change management plan, communications plan, schedule and budget to guarantee a successful project. **Dates and Locations:** Silver Spring, MD; Hunt Valley, MD; Columbia, MD; and Alexandria, VA.

24993 ■ Project Quality Management for Project Managers - Delivering Consistent Quality (Onsite)
Seminar Information Service, Inc.
20 Executive Park, Ste. 120
Irvine, CA 92614
Ph: (949)261-9104
Free: 877-SEM-INFO

Fax: (949)261-1963
Co. E-mail: info@seminarinformation.com
URL: http://www.seminarinformation.com
Price: $2,490.00. **Description:** Learn how to: Implement effective project quality management best practices; Apply a proven analysis method to identify stakeholder quality expectations and refine project scope; Leverage an industry standard template to create a project Quality Management Plan (QMP); Generate a quality assurance task list that incorporates project, product and process; Transform quality assurance recommendations into corrective and improvement actions; Design and implement quality control gates throughout the project and product life cycles.

24994 ■ Project Scheduling and Budgeting - Achieving Cost-Effective and Timely Delivery (Onsite)
Seminar Information Service, Inc.
20 Executive Park, Ste. 120
Irvine, CA 92614
Ph: (949)261-9104
Free: 877-SEM-INFO
Fax: (949)261-1963
Co. E-mail: info@seminarinformation.com
URL: http://www.seminarinformation.com
Price: $2,490.00. **Description:** Learn how to: Build schedules and budgets that transform project constraints into project success; Construct Work Breakdown Structures (WBS) and network diagrams and estimate task durations; Calculate Critical Path and optimize your project plan; Allocate costs and chart expected cash flow; Assign resources effectively and respond to end-date changes; Perform Earned Value Analysis (EVA) to keep the project on track.

24995 ■ Pump Repair & Maintenance (Onsite)
American Trainco
9785 S Maroon Cir., Ste. 300
Englewood, CO 80112
Ph: (303)531-4560
Free: 877-978-7246
Fax: (303)531-4565
Co. E-mail: Sales@AmericanTrainco.com
URL: http://www.americantrainco.com
Price: $990.00. **Description:** Learn common sense pump maintenance and repair techniques to keep facilities and equipment up and running. **Dates and Locations:** Cities throughout the United States.

24996 ■ Pumps & Pump Systems: Specification, Installation & Operation (Onsite)
American Trainco
9785 S Maroon Cir., Ste. 300
Englewood, CO 80112
Ph: (303)531-4560
Free: 877-978-7246
Fax: (303)531-4565
Co. E-mail: Sales@AmericanTrainco.com
URL: http://www.americantrainco.com
Price: $990.00. **Description:** From the pump and pump system, to the people who operate, maintain and design the pump system, this seminar will teach students how to identify the real problems causing pump failure, and how to avoid repeating those problems in the future. **Dates and Locations:** Cities throughout the United States.

24997 ■ Steam Systems Maintenance, Safety & Optimization (Onsite)
American Trainco
9785 S Maroon Cir., Ste. 300
Englewood, CO 80112
Ph: (303)531-4560
Free: 877-978-7246
Fax: (303)531-4565
Co. E-mail: Sales@AmericanTrainco.com
URL: http://www.americantrainco.com
Price: $990.00. **Description:** This course will teach you how to keep your steam system working efficiently and how to fix common problems and work safely reducing energy loss. **Dates and Locations:** Cities throughout the United States.

24998 ■ Strategic Planning for Organizational Success (Onsite)
Seminar Information Service, Inc.
20 Executive Park, Ste. 120
Irvine, CA 92614
Ph: (949)261-9104
Free: 877-SEM-INFO
Fax: (949)261-1963
Co. E-mail: info@seminarinformation.com
URL: http://www.seminarinformation.com
Price: $2,490.00. **Description:** Learn how to: Formulate strategic plans to help your organization advance and grow; Detect the strengths, weaknesses, opportunities and threats (SWOT) that drive strategy; Identify strategies to better position your organization for long-term competitive advantage; Translate strategy into action; Execute strategy and deliver results through people and processes; Establish strategic planning, monitoring and controlling mechanisms that ensure positive results. **Dates and Locations:** Toronto, CN; and Reston, VA.

24999 ■ Troubleshooting Mechanical Drive Systems & Rotating Equipment (Onsite)
American Trainco
9785 S Maroon Cir., Ste. 300
Englewood, CO 80112
Ph: (303)531-4560
Free: 877-978-7246
Fax: (303)531-4565
Co. E-mail: Sales@AmericanTrainco.com
URL: http://www.americantrainco.com
Price: $990.00. **Description:** Provide a new perspective on troubleshooting mechanical and rotating equipment and learn about basic mechanical applications, failures, life expectancy and maintenance shafts, bearings, couplings, chains, sprockets, bushings, gears, belts, sheaves and other mechanical components. You'll learn what data to measure, track and trend so that when equipment fails you can get quick answers to what is wrong, as well as fix the real problems with your equipment and not just the symptoms. **Dates and Locations:** Cities throughout the United States.

25000 ■ Understanding & Troubleshooting Hydraulics (Onsite)
American Trainco
9785 S Maroon Cir., Ste. 300
Englewood, CO 80112
Ph: (303)531-4560
Free: 877-978-7246
Fax: (303)531-4565
Co. E-mail: Sales@AmericanTrainco.com
URL: http://www.americantrainco.com
Price: $990.00. **Description:** Provides the basic building blocks and information you need to become proficient in working with industrial hydraulics and fluid power, whether a small mobile unit or large industrial installation. **Dates and Locations:** Cities throughout the United States.

25001 ■ Uninterruptable Power Supply (UPS) Maintenance and Readiness (Onsite)
American Trainco
9785 S Maroon Cir., Ste. 300
Englewood, CO 80112
Ph: (303)531-4560
Free: 877-978-7246
Fax: (303)531-4565
Co. E-mail: Sales@AmericanTrainco.com
URL: http://www.americantrainco.com
Price: $495.00. **Description:** Seminar designed for personnel responsible for the UPS systems in industrial plants, public facilities, and commercial buildings. **Dates and Locations:** Sacramento, CA.

25002 ■ Variable Frequency Drives (Onsite)
American Trainco
9785 S Maroon Cir., Ste. 300
Englewood, CO 80112
Ph: (303)531-4560
Free: 877-978-7246

Fax: (303)531-4565

Co. E-mail: Sales@AmericanTrainco.com

URL: http://www.americantrainco.com

Price: $990.00. **Description:** Learn how to troubleshoot common VFD problems, take care of your own equipment, and avoid costly repairs or service repairs, including how to identify hazards associated with working on VFDs, an understanding of the importance of safe work practices, recognition of the main components of a VFD system, and the different methods of controlling a VFD. **Dates and Locations:** Cities throughout the United States.

25003 ■ Water Treatment for Boilers, Chillers & Cooling Towers (Onsite)

American Trainco

9785 S Maroon Cir., Ste. 300

Englewood, CO 80112

Ph: (303)531-4560

Free: 877-978-7246

Fax: (303)531-4565

Co. E-mail: Sales@AmericanTrainco.com

URL: http://www.americantrainco.com

Price: $495.00. **Description:** One-day seminar to take the mystery out of creating, and stabilizing high water quality for your HVAC systems. **Dates and Locations:** Cities throughout the United States.

REFERENCE WORKS

25004 ■ "13D Filings" in Barron's (Vol. 88, March 24, 2008, No. 12, pp. M13)

Pub: Dow Jones & Company, Inc.

Description: HealthCor Management called as problematic the plan of Magellan Health Services to use its high cash balances for acquisitions. Carlson Capital discussed with Energy Partners possible changes in the latter's board. Investor Carl Icahn suggested that Enzon Pharmaceuticals consider selling itself or divest some of its assets.

25005 ■ "13D Filings: Investors Report to the SEC" in Barron's (Vol. 88, July 4, 2008, No. 28, pp. M10)

Pub: Dow Jones & Co., Inc.

Description: Robino Stortini Holdings will seek control of Investors Capital Holdings either alone or with members of the company's management. Discovery Group I will withhold its votes at the nomination of directors for TESSCO Technologies while JMB Capital Partners Master Fund plans to nominate a slate of candidates to the board of Maguire Properties.

25006 ■ The 100 Best Businesses to Start When You Don't Want To Work Hard Anymore

Pub: Career Press Inc.

Ed: Lisa Rogak. **Price:** $16.99. **Description:** Author helps burned-out workers envision a new future as a small business owner. Systems analysis, adventure travel outfitting, bookkeeping, food delivery, furniture making, and software development are among the industries examined.

25007 ■ "ACE Aims High With Spinoff of Repair Unit" in Globe & Mail (January 31, 2007, pp. B15)

Pub: CTVglobemedia Publishing Inc.

Ed: Brent Jang. **Description:** The decision of ACE Aviation Holdings Inc. to sell its aircraft maintenance division and add workforce at its El Salvador plant is discussed.

25008 ■ "Acquisition of a Uranium Exploration Project, Laguiche Basin, Opinaca Area, Quebec" in Canadian Corporate News (May 16, 2007)

Pub: Comtex News Network Inc.

Description: Dios Exploration Inc. negotiated an option agreement with Sirios Resources Inc. to explore the Opinaca Nord Property with a project that comprises one main anomaly cluster for gold in association with arsenic and two detailed uranium anomaly clusters.

25009 ■ "The Agency Model Is Bent But Not Broken" in Advertising Age (Vol. 79, July 7, 2008, No. 26, pp. 17)

Pub: Crain Communications, Inc.

Ed: Stephen Fajen. **Description:** In the new-media environment, advertising agencies must change the way in which they do business and receive payment.

25010 ■ "The Agency-Selection Process Needs Fixing Now" in Advertising Age (Vol. 79, July 7, 2008, No. 26, pp. 18)

Pub: Crain Communications, Inc.

Ed: Avi Dan. **Description:** Marketers are facing increased challenges in this sagging economic climate and must realize the importance of choosing the correct advertising agency for their company in order to benefit from a more-stable relationship that yields better business results. Advice for marketers regarding the best way to choose an agency is included.

25011 ■ "Air Canada to Slash 600 Non-Union Jobs" in Globe & Mail (February 11, 2006, pp. B3)

Pub: CTVglobemedia Publishing Inc.

Ed: Brent Jang. **Description:** The reasons behind workforce reduction by ACE Aviation Holdings Inc. at Air Canada are presented.

25012 ■ "Air Canada's Flight Plan for 777s Excludes India" in Globe & Mail (March 28, 2007, pp. B5)

Pub: CTVglobemedia Publishing Inc.

Ed: Brent Jang. **Description:** The decision of Air Canada to exclude India and to fly its Boeing 777s due to poor economic returns is discussed.

25013 ■ "All Eyes On Iris" in Canadian Business (Vol. 81, July 22, 2008, No. 12-13, pp. 20)

Pub: Rogers Media Ltd.

Ed: Jack Mintz. **Description:** Provincial governments in Canada are believed to be awaiting Alberta Finance Minister Iris Evans' financial and investment policies as well as Evans' development of a new saving strategy. Alberta is the only Canadian province that is in position to invest in sovereign wealth funds after it eliminated its debt in 2005.

25014 ■ "All Fired Up!" in Small Business Opportunities (November 2008)

Pub: Entrepreneur Media Inc.

Ed: Stan Roberts. **Description:** Profile of Brixx Wood Fired Pizza, which has launched a franchising program due to the amount of interest the company's founders received over the years; franchisees do not need experience in the food industry or pizza restaurant service business in order to open a franchise of their own because all franchisees receive comprehensive training in which they are educated on all of the necessary tools to effectively run the business.

25015 ■ "All In Good Fun" in Entrepreneur (Vol. 36, May 2008, No. 5, pp. 22)

Pub: Entrepreneur Media, Inc.

Ed: Christopher Percy Collier. **Description:** According to a study conducted in 2007, humor in the workplace helps people communicate effectively and improves camaraderie. Company leaders and entrepreneurs can also tell humorous stories about themselves, but must also set lines that should not be crossed. The humorous atmosphere in the company YouSendIt is presented.

25016 ■ "All Options Open On Chrysler: Magna" in Globe & Mail (February 28, 2007, pp. B3)

Pub: CTVglobemedia Publishing Inc.

Ed: Greg Keenan. **Description:** The 65 percent drop in the profits of Magna International Inc. and the plans of its chief executive officer Don Walker to make the company more competitive are discussed.

25017 ■ "Analyst Questions CanWest Papers' Viability" in Globe & Mail (January 14, 2006, pp. B3)

Pub: CTVglobemedia Publishing Inc.

Ed: Grant Robertson. **Description:** The opinions of analyst Tim Casey of BMO Nesbitt Burns Inc. over

the prospects of two newspapers Dose and National Post of CanWest Global Communications Corp., which planned cost restructuring efforts, are presented.

25018 ■ "Analysts Not Fazed By Constellation's Halt to New Nuclear Plants" in Baltimore Business Journal (Vol. 28, October 22, 2010, No. 24)

Pub: Baltimore Business Journal

Ed: Scott Dance. **Description:** Wall Street analysts believe that Constellation Energy Group Inc.'s decision to pull out of the nuclear construction business would not change their outlook on the company. New nuclear power had been one of Constellation's long-term goals, but the company pulled the plug on the project. It is believed that most investors were not expecting any payoff from the venture.

25019 ■ "Are You Ready for a Transformation?" in Women Entrepreneur (November 28, 2008)

Pub: Entrepreneur Media Inc.

Ed: Aliza Sherman. **Description:** Marlene J. Waldock, an expert in women's empowerment and reinvention, discusses brand modification and what a business owner should consider before attempting to change or modify their brand.

25020 ■ "Are Your Goals Hitting the Right Target?" in Business Strategy Review (Vol. 21, Autumn 2010, No. 3, pp. 46)

Pub: Blackwell Publishers Ltd.

Ed: Alan Meekings, Steve Briault, Andy Neely. **Description:** Setting targets is normal in most organizations. The authors think such a practice can cause more harm than good and offer a better strategy.

25021 ■ "Australian Firm Buys Off Sands Engineering Company for $1 Billion" in Globe & Mail (February 8, 2007, pp. B3)

Pub: CTVglobemedia Publishing Inc.

Ed: David Ebner. **Description:** Australia's Worley-Parson Ltd. acquires Colt Engineering Corp., a private petroleum company, for $1 billion. The acquisition will provide WorleyParson an opportunity to expand its operations in Australia.

25022 ■ "Automaker Foundations Run Leaner" in Crain's Detroit Business (Vol. 26, January 11, 2010, No. 2, pp. 1)

Pub: Crain Communications Inc.

Ed: Sherri Welch. **Description:** Overview of the Detroit automobile industry includes restoring profitability, smarter marketing strategies and philanthropy. Each company comprising the Big 3 is examined, as is their vision for the future.

25023 ■ "Avnet Inc.'s Expansion Fueled By Mergers and Acquisitions" in The Business Journal - Serving Phoenix and the Valley of the Sun (Vol. 28, September 12, 2008, No. 53, pp. 1)

Pub: American City Business Journals, Inc.

Ed: Patrick O'Grady. **Description:** Avnet Inc. has grown and has nearly tripled its revenue in the past ten years through the company's acquisitions and consolidation. The company's revenue in 2008 is $17.9 billion. Other details about the company's growth are discussed.

25024 ■ Awesomely Simple: Essential Business Strategies for Turning Ideas Into Action

Pub: Jossey-Bass

Ed: John Spence. **Released:** September 8, 2009. **Price:** $24.95. **Description:** Six key strategies that create a foundation for achieving business excellence include: vivid vision, best people, a performance-oriented culture, robust communication, a sense of urgency, and extreme customer focus.

25025 ■ "Back to Business for Bishop Museum" in Hawaii Business (Vol. 54, August 2009, No. 2, pp. 53)

Pub: Hawaii Business Publishing

Ed: Shara Enay. **Description:** Bishop Museum, ranked 224 in Hawaii Business' top 250 companies for 2008, had $29.5 million in gross sales for 2007, up 52.8 percent from the $19.3 million gross sales in 2006. The company has cut 24 positions in a restructuring effort for the museum's sustainability. Grants, artifacts and plans for sustainable operations are discussed.

25026 ■ "The Balanced Business" in Women In Business (Vol. 63, Spring 2011, No. 1, pp. 14)
Pub: American Business Women's Association
Ed: Leigh Elmore. **Description:** The balance scoreboard has developed to a full strategic planning and management system from its early use as a simple performance measurement network. Executives are able to execute their strategies by using information from the balance scoreboard. Insights on Mayer Group Inc. executive Ken Mayer's view of the balance scorecard are also shared.

25027 ■ "Baldwin Connelly Partnership Splits" in Business Journal Serving Greater Tampa Bay (Vol. 30, November 19, 2010, No. 48, pp. 1)
Pub: Tampa Bay Business Journal
Ed: Alexis Muellner. **Description:** The fast-growing insurance brokerage Baldwin Connelly is now breaking up after five years. Two different entrepreneurial visions have developed within the organization and founders Lowry Baldwin and John Connell will not take separate tracks. Staffing levels in the firm are expected to remain the same.

25028 ■ "Bark Up The Right Tree" in Small Business Opportunities (Winter 2009)
Pub: Entrepreneur Press
Contact: Perlman Neil, President
Description: Profile of Central Bark, a daycare company catering to pets that offers franchise opportunities and is expanding rapidly despite the economic downturn; the company's growth strategy is also discussed.

25029 ■ "Battered Loblaw Makes Deep Job Cuts" in Globe & Mail (January 23, 2007)
Pub: CTVglobemedia Publishing Inc.
Description: Loblaw Companies Ltd., supermarket giant, is eliminating up to 1,000 administrative jobs and shifting more buying responsibilities to its suppliers. The grocer will also introduce a national inventory strategy called 'category management'.

25030 ■ Battling Big Box: How Nimble Niche Companies Can Outmaneuver Giant Companies
Pub: Career Press, Inc.
Ed: Henry Dubroff, Susan J. Marks. **Released:** January 1, 2009. **Price:** $15.99. **Description:** Small companies can compete with larger firms through agility, adaptability, customer service, and credibility. Topics include information to help empower employees, build a powerful brand, manage cash flow, and maintaining a business vision.

25031 ■ "BCE Mulls Radical Changes With Industry Under Pressure" in Globe & Mail (March 30, 2007, pp. B1)
Pub: CTVglobemedia Publishing Inc.
Ed: Andrew Willis; Jacquie McNish; Catherine McLean. **Description:** An account on the expansion plans of BCE Inc., which plans to acquire TELUS Corp., is presented.

25032 ■ "Best Growth Stocks" in Canadian Business (Vol. 81, Summer 2008, No. 9, pp. 61)
Pub: Rogers Media Ltd.
Ed: Calvin Leung. **Description:** Table showing the one-year performance of growth stocks is presented. Edmonton-based Stantec Inc. expects to advance its sales and profits by 15 percent to 20 percent per year through tapping international markets and acquisitions. Analysts forecast a 17.1 percent growth rate annually over the next 3 to 5 years.

25033 ■ "Better Made's Better Idea: Diversify Despite Rising Costs" in Crain's Detroit Business (Vol. 24, September 22, 2008, No. 38, pp. 18)
Pub: Crain Communications Inc.
Ed: Nathan Skid. **Description:** Better Made Snack Foods Inc. is planning to expand its product lines and market reach as well as boost manufacturing capabil-

ity during a time in which the company is being buffeted by rising commodity and fuel costs. The company feels that diversification is the key to maintain sales and growth.

25034 ■ "Betting on the Glitz" in Canadian Business (Vol. 79, October 9, 2006, No. 20, pp. 104)
Pub: Rogers Media
Ed: Zena Olijnyk. **Description:** Holt, Renfrew & Comany's expansion plans to cash on the booming demand for high end retail luxury markets are discussed.

25035 ■ "A Big Dream That 'Was Going Nowhere" in Globe & Mail (February 4, 2006, pp. B4)
Pub: CTVglobemedia Publishing Inc.
Ed: Konrad Yakabuski. **Description:** The reasons behind the decision of Bombardier Inc. to terminate its plans to develop jet airplanes are presented.

25036 ■ Big Vision, Small Business
Pub: Ivy Sea, Inc.
Ed: Jamie S. Walters. **Released:** October 10, 2002. **Price:** $17.95. **Description:** The power of the small enterprise is examined. The author shares her expertise as an entrepreneur and founder of a business consulting firm to help small business owners successfully run their companies. Interviews with more than seventy small business owners provide insight into visioning, planning, and establishing a small company, as well as strategies for good employee and customer relationships.

25037 ■ "A Bigger Deal" in Crain's Cleveland Business (Vol. 28, November 12, 2007, No. 45, pp. 1)
Pub: Crain Communications, Inc.
Ed: Shawn A. Turner. **Description:** In an attempt to boost its revenue CBiz Inc., a provider of accounting and business services, is looking to balance its acquisitions of smaller companies with larger ones as part of its overall growth strategy.

25038 ■ "Blackstone Set to Sell Stake" in Globe & Mail (March 17, 2007, pp. B6)
Pub: CTVglobemedia Publishing Inc.
Ed: Tennille Tracy. **Description:** The plan of Blackstone Group to sell 10 percent of its stake to raise $4 billion and its proposal to go for initial public offering is discussed.

25039 ■ "Brewing National Success" in Hawaii Business (Vol. 53, November 2007, No. 5, pp. 46)
Pub: Hawaii Business Publishing
Ed: Alex Salkever. **Description:** Kona Brewing Co. (KBC) is already selling its brews in four cities in Florida and 17 other states and Japan as well. KBC is currently forming a deal with Red Hook to produce Longboard Lager and other KBC brews at Red Hooks' brewery in New Hampshire. KBC's chief executive officer Mattson Davis shares KBC's practices for success.

25040 ■ "Budget Strategically to Stay on Course" in Entrepreneur (August 28, 2008)
Pub: Entrepreneur Media Inc.
Ed: Tim Berry. **Description:** Budgeting is one of the most valuable tools in a manager's arsenal. The importance of budgeting is discussed and tips for surviving an economic recession are provided.

25041 ■ Building a Business the Buddhist Way
Pub: Celestial Arts Publishing Company
Ed: Geri Larkin. **Released:** September 2004. **Price:** $11.67 (Canadian). **Description:** Principles of entrepreneurship for starting and growing a business while maintaining a balance between business goals and spiritual goals.

25042 ■ "Calming Customers" in The Business Journal-Portland (Vol. 25, August 29, 2008, No. 25, pp. 1)
Pub: American City Business Journals, Inc.
Ed: Kirsten Grind; Rob Smith. **Description:** Credit unions and banks in the Portland area are reaching out to clients in an effort to reassure them on the

security of their money and the firms' financial stability. Roy Whitehead of Washington Federal Savings, for instance, wrote 41,000 customers of the bank to reassure them. The strategies of different banks and credit unions to answer their client's worries are discussed.

25043 ■ "Can Brewer Make Cheap Seats Pay?" in Globe & Mail (January 7, 2006, pp. B4)
Pub: CTVglobemedia Publishing Inc.
Ed: Brent Jang. **Description:** The plans of chief executive officer Montie Brewer of Air Canada to upgrade airplanes are presented.

25044 ■ "CanWest Plotting Buyback of Newspaper Income Trust" in Globe & Mail (February 7, 2007, pp. B1)
Pub: CTVglobemedia Publishing Inc.
Ed: Sinclair Stewart; Boyd Erman; Grant Robertson. **Description:** The CanWest Global Communications Corp.'s decision to sell its media assets in Australia and New Zealand in order to finance its plans of repurchasing its newspaper income trust CanWest MediaWorks Income Fund is discussed.

25045 ■ "Carveouts Back in Vogue" in Mergers & Acquisitions: The Dealmaker's Journal (March 1, 2008)
Pub: SourceMedia, Inc.
Ed: Ken MacFadyen. **Description:** Discusses ways in which companies look for hidden assets that they can exploit in worsening economic times; oftentimes firms try to sell off assets or in other instances they will look to unlock value through public spinoffs or through internal reorganizations.

25046 ■ "A Case Study: Real-Life Business Planning" in Entrepreneur (February 3, 2009)
Pub: Entrepreneur Media Inc.
Ed: Tim Berry. **Description:** Provides a case study of a two-day planning meeting for Palo Alto Software in which the executives of the company met for their annual planning cycle and discussed ways in which the company needed to change in order to stay viable in today's tough economic climate.

25047 ■ "CAW Boss Troubled Over 'Vulnerable' Ford Plants" in Globe & Mail (January 19, 2006, pp. B6)
Pub: CTVglobemedia Publishing Inc.
Ed: Greg Keenan. **Description:** The concerns of president Buzz Hargrove of Canadian Auto Workers on the impact of Ford Motor Co.'s restructuring efforts on closure of automotive plants in Canada, are presented.

25048 ■ "Children's Products Maker Not the New Kid on the Block" in Crain's Cleveland Business (Vol. 28, November 26, 2007, No. 47, pp. 3)
Pub: Crain Communications, Inc.
Ed: David Bennett. **Description:** Discusses the business model employed by Shamrock Industries Inc., a rising star in the competitive world of children's products; the company, which does business as Foundations Quality Children's Products, has expanded into a 63,000-square-foot distribution center which has boosted its local profile significantly.

25049 ■ "Choosing Strategies For Change" in Harvard Business Review (Vol. 86, July-August 2008, No. 8, pp. 130)
Pub: Harvard Business School Press
Ed: John P. Kotter; Leonard A. Schlesinger. **Description:** Methods for implementing organizational change include identifying potential areas of resistance, providing the necessary skills and information to counteract resistance, and assessing situational factors that may influence results.

25050 ■ "Cineplex Sees Past the Big Picture" in Globe & Mail (February 8, 2007, pp. B9)
Pub: CTVglobemedia Publishing Inc.
Ed: Shirley Won. **Description:** Cineplex Entertainment LP reported $4.6 million profit in the final quarter of 2006. The movie chain is introducing video-game tournaments and live rock concerts to improve sales.

25051 ■ *"Citadel Hires Three Lehman Execs"*
in Chicago Tribune (October 2, 2008)
Pub: McClatchy-Tribune Information Services

Ed: James P. Miller. **Description:** Citadel Investment Group LLC, Chicago hedge-fund operator, has hired three former senior executives of bankrupt investment banker Lehman Brothers Holding Inc. Citadel believes that the company's hiring spree will help them to further expand the firm's capabilities in the global fixed income business.

25052 ■ *"Civil Council Almost On Board With*
Light Rail Plan" in The Business
Journal-Serving Metropolitan Kansas City
(September 5, 2008)
Pub: American City Business Journals, Inc.

Ed: Steve Vockrodt. **Description:** Civic Council of Greater Kansas City has taken back its demand for the city to show a 10-year financial plan to win its endorsement of a light rail plan. The council said it will accept a five-year financial plan for the project. Details of the light rail plan are also presented.

25053 ■ *"Clothier Delays Opening" in The*
Business Journal-Serving Metropolitan
Kansas City (Vol. 27, November 14, 2008, No.
10, pp. 1)
Pub: American City Business Journals, Inc.

Ed: Suzanna Stagemeyer. **Description:** Jos A. Bank Clothiers Inc. has delayed the opening of its store at the Kansas City Power and Light District in Missouri for the first quarter of 2009. The company is still waiting for other tenants to open shop in the district. Comments from officials concerning the retail sector are also presented.

25054 ■ *"CN to Webcast 2007 Analyst*
Meeting in Toronto May 23-24" in Canadian
Corporate News (May 16, 2007)
Pub: Comtex News Network Inc.

Description: Canadian National Railway Company (CN) broadcast its analyst meeting in Toronto with a webcast which focused on CN's opportunities, strategies, and financial outlook through the year 2010.

25055 ■ *"Connie Ozan; Founder, Design*
Director, Twist Creative, 37" in Crain's
Cleveland Business (Vol. 28, November 19,
2007, No. 46)
Pub: Crain Communications, Inc.

Ed: John Booth. **Description:** Profile of Connie Ozan, design director and founder of Twist Creative, an advertising agency that she runs with her husband, Michael; Ms. Ozan credits her husband's business sense in bringing a more strategic side to the company in which to complement her art direction.

25056 ■ *"Copper Giant to Spin Off Silver*
Assets" in Globe & Mail (February 27, 2006,
pp. B1)
Pub: CTVglobemedia Publishing Inc.

Ed: Sinclair Stewart; Andrew Willis. **Description:** The reasons behind the sale of silver mining assets by Codelco are presented.

25057 ■ *"Copycat" in Canadian Business*
(Vol. 79, October 23, 2006, No. 21, pp. 53)
Pub: Rogers Media

Ed: Andrew Wahl. **Description:** The conversion of BCE Inc. into an income trust for tax advantages, soon after the transition of its business rival Telus Corp. into an income trust, is discussed.

25058 ■ *"Corporate Diversity Driving Profits"*
in Hispanic Business (Vol. 30, September
2008, No. 9, pp. 12)
Pub: Hispanic Business, Inc.

Ed: Michael Bowker. **Description:** U.S. businesses are beginning to appreciate the importance of diversity and are developing strategies to introduce a diverse workforce that reflects the cultural composition of their customers. The realization that diversity increases profits and the use of professional networks to recruit and retain skilled minority employees are two other new trends impacting corporate diversity in the U.S.

25059 ■ *"CP Rail Cuts Jobs to Keep Pace*
With CN" in Globe & Mail (January 16, 2006,
pp. B1)
Pub: CTVglobemedia Publishing Inc.

Ed: Brent Jang. **Description:** Canadian Pacific Railway Ltd. (CPR) reduces workforce in order to remain competitive with Canadian National Railway Co. The details of CPR's proposal are presented.

25060 ■ *"CPR Signals a Switch in Strategy to*
Narrow Competitive Gap With CN" in Globe &
Mail (January 20, 2006, pp. B3)
Pub: CTVglobemedia Publishing Inc.

Ed: Brent Jang. **Description:** The reasons behind the restructuring efforts of Canadian Pacific Railway Ltd. are presented.

25061 ■ *"Craig Muhlhauser" in Canadian*
Business (Vol. 81, September 15, 2008, No.
14-15, pp. 6)
Pub: Rogers Media Ltd.

Ed: Andrew Wahl. **Description:** Interview with Craig Muhlhauser who is the CEO of Celestica, a manufacturing company that provides services for the electronics sector; Muhlhauser discusses the company's restructuring program, which he feels was the secret to their surprising first-quarter results. Muhlhauser states that the company is operating with more forward visibility and that understanding the opportunities during the current economic situation presents the biggest challenge.

25062 ■ *"The Data Drivers" in Canadian*
Business (Vol. 81, September 15, 2008, No.
14-15, pp. 1)
Pub: Rogers Media Ltd.

Ed: Andrew Wahl. **Description:** Canadian regulators hope that an auction of telecommunications companies will inject more competition into the industry; however, newcomers may not be able to rely on lower prices in order to gain market share from the three major telecommunications companies that already have a stronghold on the market. Analysts feel that providing additional data service is the key to surviving market disruptions.

25063 ■ *"Deals Still Get Done at Drake's Coq*
d'Or" in Crain's Chicago Business (Vol. 31,
November 17, 2008, No. 46, pp. 35)
Pub: Crain Communications, Inc.

Ed: Shia Kapos. **Description:** Chicago's infamous Coq d'Or, a restaurant and lounge located at the Drake Hotel, is still a favorite establishment for noted executives but the eatery is now trying to cater to younger professionals through marketing and offering new beverages that appeal to that demographic. Many find it the perfect environment in which to close deals, relax or network.

25064 ■ *"Decline in Assets Is Costly for*
Advisers" in The Business Journal-Serving
Metropolitan Kansas City (Vol. 27, October
24, 2008)
Pub: American City Business Journals, Inc.

Ed: James Dornbrook. **Description:** Financial advisers in the Kansas City, Missouri area are forced to cut costs as their assets have decreased sharply due to the huge drop in stock prices. American Century Investments was forced to diversify into foreign assets and cut 90 jobs as its assets dropped to $84 billion. Diversification has softened the impact of the steep decline in stock prices for Waddell & Reed Financial Inc.

25065 ■ *"Deep Thoughts: Getting Employees*
to Think Better Requires a Bit of Creative
Thinking Itself" in Canadian Business (March
17, 2008)
Pub: Rogers Media

Ed: Lauren McKeon. **Description:** Discusses the reason a company needs to make their employees understand that ideas are the stuff of life. For employees to be more creative, they need to cultivate spark moments, play with possibilities, and venture into the unknown.

25066 ■ *"Deja Vu" in Canadian Business (Vol.*
81, July 22, 2008, No. 12-13, pp. 38)
Pub: Rogers Media Ltd.

Ed: Joe Castaldo. **Description:** Laurent Beaudoin has retired as chief executive officer for Bombardier Inc.'s, a manufacturer of regional and business

aircraft, but kept a role in the firm as a non-executive chairman. Beaudoin first resigned from the company in 1999, but had to return in 2004 to address challenging situations faced by the company. Beaudoin's views on management and the company are presented.

25067 ■ *"Desmarais Makes Move into U.S." in*
Globe & Mail (February 2, 2007, pp. B1)
Pub: CTVglobemedia Publishing Inc.

Ed: Andrew Willis. **Description:** The decision of Desmarais family, which runs Great-West Lifeco Inc., to acquire Putnam Investment Trust for $4.6 billion to enter the United States market, is discussed.

25068 ■ *"Dividing to Conquer" in Barron's*
(Vol. 88, March 31, 2008, No. 13, pp. 22)
Pub: Dow Jones & Company, Inc.

Ed: Andrew Bary. **Description:** Altria's spin off of Philip Morris International could unlock substantial value for both domestic and international cigarette concerns. The strong brands and ample payouts from both companies will most likely impress investors.

25069 ■ *"Diving for the Next Big Gold Rush"*
in Canadian Business (Vol. 80, February 12,
2007, No. 4, pp. 28)
Pub: Rogers Media

Ed: Thomas Watson. **Description:** The interest of Canadian mining companies led by Nautilus Minerals to invest in mining for deep sea-floor massive sulphide deposits, which have several minerals, is discussed.

25070 ■ *"Don't Quit When The Road Gets*
Bumpy" in Women Entrepreneur (November
25, 2008)
Pub: Entrepreneur Media Inc.

Ed: Bonnie Price. **Description:** Discusses techniques four women entrepreneurs are utilizing to keep their businesses successful despite the credit crunch and the economic downturn.

25071 ■ *"Don't Try This Offshore" in Harvard*
Business Review (Vol. 86, September 2008,
No. 9, pp. 39)
Pub: Harvard Business School Press

Description: Fictitious outsourcing scenario is presented, with contributors offering advice. The suggestions address the ease or complexity of offshoring business creativity, along with challenges and benefits.

25072 ■ *"Doyle: Domino's New Pizza*
Seasoned with Straight Talk" in Crain's
Detroit Business (Vol. 26, January 11, 2010,
No. 2, pp. 1)
Pub: Crain Communications Inc.

Ed: Nathan Skid. **Description:** Interview with J. Patrick Doyle, the CEO of Domino's Pizza, Inc.; the company has launched a new marketing campaign that focuses on its bold new vision.

25073 ■ *"Economic Crises Calls For Better*
Marketing Plans" in Entrepreneur (October 1,
2008)
Pub: Entrepreneur Media Inc.

Ed: Tim Berry. **Description:** Revising one's business plan is essential, especially during times of economic crisis; sales and marketing plans should be reviewed, analyzed and changed in an attempt to survive the economic downturn.

25074 ■ *"EnCana Axes Spending on Gas*
Wells" in Globe & Mail (February 16, 2006, pp.
B1)
Pub: CTVglobemedia Publishing Inc.

Ed: Dave Ebner. **Description:** The reasons behind EnCana Corp.'s cost spending measures by $300 million on natural gas wells are presented. The company projects 2 percent cut in gas and oil sales for 2006.

25075 ■ *"Entrepreneurial Orientation and*
Firm Performance" in Journal of Small
Business and Entrepreneurship (Vol. 23,

Winter 2010, No. 1)
Pub: Canadian Council for Small Business and Entrepreneurship

Description: The article develops a theoretical model of the relationship between firm-level entrepreneurship and firm performance. This model is intended to further clarify the consequences of an 'entrepreneurial orientation', paying particular attention to the differential relationship that exists between the three sub-dimensions of entrepreneurial orientation and firm performance. Included in the theoretical model are other important variables (such as organizational structure and environmental characteristics) that may impact the EO-performance relationship. Propositions are developed regarding the various configurations of the sub-dimensions of EO and organizational structure that would be most appropriate in a given environmental context. Future research may also benefit from considering the important role that organizational strategy and life cycle stage play in this model. The implications of this model for both researchers and managers are discussed.

25076 ■ *"Executive Decision: Damn the Profit Margins, Sleeman Declares War on Buck-a-Beer Foes"* *in Globe & Mail (January 28, 2006, pp. B3)*
Pub: CTVglobemedia Publishing Inc.

Ed: Andy Hoffman. **Description:** The cost savings plans of chief executive officer John Sleeman of Sleeman Breweries Ltd. are presented.

25077 ■ *"Executive Decision: Lead a Double Life for Geac's Sake"* *in Globe & Mail (January 21, 2006, pp. B4)*
Pub: CTVglobemedia Publishing Inc.

Ed: Simon Avery. **Description:** The details of growth of Geac Computer Corporation Ltd., under chief executive officer Charles Jones, are presented.

25078 ■ *"Expanding Middleby's Food Processing Biz"* *in Crain's Chicago Business (Vol. 31, April 21, 2008, No. 16, pp. 6)*
Pub: Crain Communications, Inc.

Ed: David Sterrett. **Description:** Profile of the executive vice-president of the food processing company, Middleby Corp, whose business plan is to develop new products, begin looking for acquisitions and simplify operations in order to expand the firm.

25079 ■ *"Exxon Braving the Danger Zones"* *in Globe & Mail (March 8, 2007, pp. B1)*
Pub: CTVglobemedia Publishing Inc.

Ed: Shawn McCarthy. **Description:** The plans of Exxon Mobil Corp. to increase its revenues through the expansion of its operations in Asia, Africa, and the Middle East are discussed.

25080 ■ *"Film Giants Disney, Pixar Talk Marriage"* *in Globe & Mail (January 19, 2006, pp. B1)*
Pub: CTVglobemedia Publishing Inc.

Ed: Merissa Marr; Nick Wingfield. **Description:** The plans of Walt Disney Co. to acquire Pixar Animation Studios are presented.

25081 ■ *"Find Your Marketing Mojo"* *in Business Owner (Vol. 35, July-August 2011, No. 4, pp. 14)*
Pub: DL Perkins Company

Description: Marketing and branding a small business can be learned and implemented by following a process that begins with setting and creating the vision that every successful venture requires: a crystal-clear vision for who you are, what you stand for, and why customers will come to you rather than competitors.

25082 ■ *"Finding the Voice of the Marketplace"* *in Mergers & Acquisitions: The Dealmaker's Journal (March 1, 2008)*
Pub: SourceMedia, Inc.

Description: Companies oftentimes are unable to achieve their strategic goals through acquisition due, in part, to not understanding the target's market and its position in the marketplace.

25083 ■ *"FirstMerit's Top Executive Turns Around Credit Quality"* *in Crain's Cleveland Business (Vol. 28, October 15, 2007, No. 41, pp. 3)*
Pub: Crain Communications, Inc.

Ed: Shawn A. Turner. **Description:** Discusses the ways in which chairman and CEO Paul Greig has been able to improve FirstMerit Corp.'s credit quality and profit margin. Strategies included selling more than $70 million in bad loans, hiring a new chief credit officer and redirecting its focus on cross-selling its wealth and investment services to its commercial customers. Statistical data included.

25084 ■ *"Five Steps to Killer Business Ideas"* *in Hawaii Business (Vol. 53, December 2007, No. 6, pp. 135)*
Pub: Hawaii Business Publishing

Ed: Jason Ubay. **Description:** Five ways to formulating good business concepts are presented. The importance of keeping an open mind and analyzing the market is discussed.

25085 ■ *"Flat or Slight Decline Seen for Nortel 2007 Revenue"* *in Globe & Mail (March 17, 2007, pp. B3)*
Pub: CTVglobemedia Publishing Inc.

Ed: Catherine McLean. **Description:** The forecast about Nortel Network Corp's decrease in the 2007 revenue and its restructuring to reduce costs is discussed.

25086 ■ *"Follow the ABCs of Buying a Business"* *in Women Entrepreneur (September 10, 2008)*
Pub: Entrepreneur Media Inc.

Ed: Nina Kaufman. **Description:** Buying a business will likely result in the largest single asset one will ever own. A list of steps one can take in order to educate and protect themselves is provided.

25087 ■ *"Ford Fix Requires 'Painful' Remedy"* *in Globe & Mail (January 9, 2006, pp. B1)*
Pub: CTVglobemedia Publishing Inc.

Ed: Greg Keenan. **Description:** The plans of Ford Motor Co. to streamline Canadian operations are presented.

25088 ■ *"Ford's $12.7 Billion Loss Signals End of an Era"* *in Globe & Mail (January 26, 2007, pp. B1)*
Pub: CTVglobemedia Publishing Inc.

Ed: Greg Keenan. **Description:** The loss of $12.7 billion incurred by Ford Motors Co., and its decision to close down several of its plants, cut thousands of jobs and focus on passenger cars, is discussed.

25089 ■ *"Founding Family Acquires Airport Marriott"* *in Crain's Cleveland Business (Vol. 28, November 5, 2007, No. 44, pp. 3)*
Pub: Crain Communications, Inc.

Ed: Stan Bullard. **Description:** Big River Real Estate LLC, part of the Marriott family's investment fund, is the new owner of the Cleveland Airport Marriott; renovations estimated at about $11 million will ensure that the hotel meets Marriott's standards.

25090 ■ *"Four Big Fat Business Plan Lies"* *in Entrepreneur (December 11, 2008)*
Pub: Entrepreneur Media Inc.

Ed: Tim Berry. **Description:** Business plans are essential for every business and do not necessarily have to be a complex document containing a full list of components. Other misconceptions concerning business plans are also discussed.

25091 ■ *"Franchisees Lose Battle Against BK"* *in Advertising Age (Vol. 79, June 2, 2008, No. 22, pp. 46)*
Pub: Crain Communications, Inc.

Ed: Emily Bryson York. **Description:** Burger King has had continuing litigation with former franchisees from New York, Luan and Elizabeth Sadik, who claim that Burger King's double cheeseburger, along with additional problems, created the environment for their eventual insolvency. Burger King has since terminated its test of selling the double cheeseburger for $1, although the company declined to comment on the reason for this decision.

25092 ■ *"Free Fall" in Canadian Business (Vol. 79, September 11, 2006, No. 18, pp. 28)*
Pub: Rogers Media

Ed: Zena Olijnyk. **Description:** Second quarter results of Imax Corp are reviewed. The company's performance and its future prospects are also presented.

25093 ■ *"Fries With That?" in Canadian Business (Vol. 81, September 29, 2008, No. 16, pp. 33)*
Pub: Rogers Media Ltd.

Ed: Calvin Leung. **Description:** Profile of Toronto-based New York Fries, which has four stores in South Korea, is planning to expand further as well as into Hong Kong and Macau; the company also has a licensee in the United Arab Emirates whom is also planning to expand.

25094 ■ *"From Craft Biz To Wholesale Giant" in Women Entrepreneur (January 19, 2009)*
Pub: Entrepreneur Media Inc.

Ed: Maria Falconer. **Description:** Advice is given on how to turn a small craft business into a full-time venture; tips to help one transition from a part-time designer to a full-time wholesaler and brand are also included.

25095 ■ *"From War Zone to Franchise Zone" in Entrepreneur (Vol. 37, August 2009, No. 8, pp. 104)*
Pub: Entrepreneur Media, Inc.

Ed: Jason Daley. **Description:** Ross Paterson says that he realized that the material he used in the Growth Coach franchise could give the people of Afghanistan the systematic model they need. Paterson says that the Afghans are very business-oriented people but that they work in a different system than Americans.

25096 ■ *"Gail Mukaihata Hannemann" in Hawaii Business (Vol. 53, January 2008, No. 7, pp. 24)*
Pub: Hawaii Business Publishing

Ed: Cathy S. Cruz-George. **Description:** Discusses the Girl Scouts of Hawaii which has altered its business model to become more appealing to young girls in the 21st century. Gail Mukaihata Hanneman, the chief executive officer of the nonprofit organization, states that the Girl Scouts has consolidated some of its operations to increase efficiency. Her views on what employers must learn about the youth and on the adults' roles in developing the younger generation are given.

25097 ■ *Get Your Business to Work!: 7 Steps to Earning More, Working Less and Living the Life You Want*
Pub: BenBella Books
Contact: Glen Yeffeth, President

Ed: George Hedley. **Released:** June 9, 2010. **Price:** $24.95. **Description:** Complete step-by-step guide for the small business owner to realize profits, wealth and freedom.

25098 ■ *"GM Axing Prices; Kerkorian Calls for Crisis Plan" in Globe & Mail (January 11, 2006, pp. B1)*
Pub: CTVglobemedia Publishing Inc.

Ed: Greg Keenan. **Description:** The financial restructuring proposal of investor Kirk Kerkorian for General Motors Corp. is presented.

25099 ■ *"Gold Medal" in Canadian Business (Vol. 79, October 9, 2006, No. 20, pp. 57)*
Pub: Rogers Media

Ed: Andrew Wahl. **Description:** Creativity skills and management strategies of Rob McEwen, founder and chief executive officer of Goldcorp Inc., are presented.

25100 ■ *Grace Puma; Senior Vice-President of Strategic Sourcing, United Airlines" in Crain's Chicago Business (May 5, 2008)*
Pub: Crain Communications, Inc.

Ed: John Rosenthal. **Description:** Profile of Grace Puma who is the senior vice-president of strategic sourcing at United Airlines and is responsible for cutting costs at the company in a number of ways including scheduling safety inspections at the same time as routine maintenance, thereby reducing the down-time of each aircraft by five days as well as replacing a third of her staff with outside talent.

25101 ■ *"The Grass is Greener" in Canadian Business (Vol. 79, August 14, 2006, No. 16-17, pp. 43)*
Pub: Rogers Media
Ed: Thomas Watson. **Description:** Owner of New Image Plans LLC, Joe White, shares his views on the Canadian market for the marijuana drug.

25102 ■ *"Green Acres" in Hawaii Business (Vol. 54, September 2008, No. 3, pp. 48)*
Pub: Hawaii Business Publishing
Ed: Jan Tenbruggencate. **Description:** Bill Cowern's Hawaiian Mahogany is a forestry business that processes low-value trees to be sold as wood chips, which can be burned to create biodiesel. Cowern is planning to obtain certification to market carbon credits and is also working with Green Energy Hawaii for the permit of a biomass-fueled power plant. Other details about Cowern's business are discussed.

25103 ■ *"The Green Conversation" in Harvard Business Review (Vol. 86, September 2008, No. 9, pp. 58)*
Pub: Harvard Business School Press
Description: Six guidelines are presented for addressing and benefiting from environmentally conscious corporate decision making and practices. Topics covered include marketing, supply chain, and leadership.

25104 ■ *"'Groundhog Day' B & B Likely Will Be Converted Into One In Real Life" in Chicago Tribune (October 21, 2008)*
Pub: McClatchy-Tribune Information Services
Ed: Carolyn Starks. **Description:** Everton Martin and Karla Stewart Martin have purchased the Victorian house that was featured as a bed-and-breakfast in the 1993 hit move 'Groundhog Day'; the couple was initially unaware of the structure's celebrity status when they purchased it with the hope of fulfilling their dream of owning a bed-and-breakfast.

25105 ■ *"Growing Pains" in Canadian Business (Vol. 81, July 22, 2008, No. 12-13, pp. 35)*
Pub: Rogers Media Ltd.
Ed: Alex Mylnek. **Description:** Laughing Stock Vineyards' Cynthia Enns and David Enns plan to target young buyers by using social media. The Enns however, are concerned that targeting younger buyers may affect Laughing Stock's image as a premium brand. Additional information regarding the company's future plans is presented.

25106 ■ *"Handleman Liquidation Leaves Questions For Shareholders" in Crain's Detroit Business (Vol. 24, October 6, 2008, No. 40, pp. 4)*
Pub: Crain Communications, Inc.
Ed: Nancy Kaffer. **Description:** Discusses Handleman Co., a Troy-based music distribution company, and their plan of liquidation and dissolution as well as how shareholders will be affected by the company's plan. Handleman filed its plan to liquidate and dissolve assets with the Securities and Exchange Commission in mid-August, following several quarters of dismal earnings.

25107 ■ *"Hartco Income Fund Announces the Completion of the CompuSmart Strategic Review" in Canadian Corporate News (May 14, 2007)*
Pub: Comtex News Network Inc.
Description: Hartco Income Fund announced that it has completed the process of exploring strategic options for CompuSmart and found that it should implement a plan to sell select stores and assets while consolidating remaining CompuSmart locations over the next sixty days.

25108 ■ *"Hawaii Business 2008 SB Success Awards" in Hawaii Business (Vol. 53, February 2008, No. 8, pp. 43)*
Pub: Hawaii Business Publishing
Description: Winners in the Hawaii Business 2008 SB Success Awards are presented; the awards give recognition for Hawaii small businesses with less than

100 employees and are based on four criteria, namely: unique service or product; rapid expansion or sales growth; longevity; and competency in overcoming challenges.

25109 ■ *"HBC Sets Friday as Deadline to Trump Zucker Takeover Bid" in Globe & Mail (January 18, 2006, pp. B1)*
Pub: CTVglobemedia Publishing Inc.
Ed: Marina Strauss. **Description:** The reasons behind Hudson's Bay Co.'s decision to seek alternative bids on the company are presented. Investor Jerry Zucker earlier offered $1.1 billion for the company.

25110 ■ *"High Energy: Gaurdie Banister Joins Aera As President and CEO" in Black Enterprise (Vol. 38, July 2008, No. 12, pp. 30)*
Pub: Earl G. Graves Publishing Co. Inc.
Ed: Brenda Porter. **Description:** Gaurdie Banister Jr. has been appointed president and CEO of Aera Energy L.L.C., becoming one of the first African Americans in the nation to run a major energy corporation. His plans for the firm include utilizing new, sophisticated technologies in order to unlock the 3-1/2 billion barrels of resources the company has on their books in a safe and environmentally friendly way. He also hopes to increase production and maintain cost leadership.

25111 ■ *"Hit the Green" in Canadian Business (Vol. 79, August 14, 2006, No. 16-17, pp. 73)*
Pub: Rogers Media
Ed: Andrew Wahl. **Description:** Reorganization of the bankrupt 4everSports golf company in the United States is discussed.

25112 ■ *"HOK Sport May Build Own Practice" in The Business Journal-Serving Metropolitan Kansas City (Vol. 26, August 29, 2008, No. 51, pp. 1)*
Pub: American City Business Journals, Inc.
Ed: Rob Roberts. **Description:** HOK Sport Venue Event is considering a spin-off from its parent company, HOK Group Inc. HOK Sport spokeswoman Gina Leo confirms that the firm is exploring structures, including a management buyout. Some of HOK Sport Venue Event's Minnesota projects are discussed.

25113 ■ *"Home Depot Eyes Wholesale Spinoff" in Globe & Mail (February 13, 2007, pp. B13)*
Pub: CTVglobemedia Publishing Inc.
Description: Home Depot Inc. is planning to sell or spinoff its professional supply business to focus on retail stores. The weakening sales and profits are the main driving force behind the company's decision.

25114 ■ *Hoover's Vision*
Pub: Cengage Learning Inc.
Contact: Michael Hansen, Chief Executive Officer
Ed: Gary Hoover. **Description:** Founder of Bookstop Inc. and Hoover's Inc. provides a plan to turn an enterprise into a success by showing entrepreneurs how to address inputs with an open mind in order to see more than what other's envision. Hoover pushes business owners to create and feed a clear and consistent vision by recognizing the importance of history and trends, then helps them find the essential qualities of entrepreneurial leadership.

25115 ■ *Hoover's Vision: Original Thinking for Business Success*
Pub: Thomson South-Western/Texere
Ed: Gary Hoover. **Released:** October 15, 2001. **Description:** Three keys to business success are to observe and understand other people, serve others while making their lives better, and develop a business style that expresses your5 own passions while serving others.

25116 ■ *"How to Keep Your Sales from Running Out of Gas" in Agency Sales Magazine (Vol. 39, July 2009, No. 7, pp. 30)*
Pub: MANA
Ed: John Graham. **Description:** Salespeople can let the good times deceive them into thinking that success will go on forever. Salespeople and businesses should see prospecting as a strategy for creating a continuing flow of business.

25117 ■ *"Husky Proceeds on Heavy-Oil Expansion" in Globe & Mail (March 21, 2006, pp. B1)*
Pub: CTVglobemedia Publishing Inc.
Ed: Patrick Brethour. **Description:** Canadian energy giant Husky Energy Inc. has started its $90 million engineering effort to determine the cost of the $2.3 billion heavy-oil up gradation expansion plan. Details of the project are elaborated upon.

25118 ■ *"In Puerto Rico, Slow and Steady Wins Race" in Globe & Mail (February 24, 2007, pp. B3)*
Pub: CTVglobemedia Publishing Inc.
Ed: Andrew Willis. **Description:** The plan of Scotiabank de Puerto Rico's chief executive officer Richard Waugh to improve its market presence using its international banking relations is discussed.

25119 ■ *"Inland Snaps Up Rival REITs" in Crain's Chicago Business (Vol. 31, November 17, 2008, No. 46, pp. 3)*
Pub: Crain Communications, Inc.
Ed: Alby Gallun. **Description:** Discusses Inland American Real Estate Trust Inc., a real estate investment trust that is napping up depressed shares of publicly traded competitors, a possible first step toward taking over these companies; however, with hotel and retail properties accounting for approximately 70 percent of its portfolio, the company could soon face its own difficulties.

25120 ■ *"Inside the New Nortel" in Canadian Business (Vol. 79, November 6, 2006, No. 22, pp. 93)*
Pub: Rogers Media
Ed: Andrew Wahl. **Description:** The team plans of Nortel Networks to improve its technology market by appointing new team are analyzed.

25121 ■ *"Intangible Assets" in Canadian Business (Vol. 79, July 17, 2006, No. 14-15, pp. 17)*
Pub: Rogers Media
Ed: Al Rosen. **Description:** Need for investors to check the actual worth of a company and not to get carried away by the inflated claims made by the company is emphasized.

25122 ■ *"International Nickel Ventures Corporation Reports Results for the First Quarter 2007" in Canadian Corporate News (May 16, 2007)*
Pub: Comtex News Network Inc.
Description: Profile of International Nickel Ventures Corporation (INV) including its financial report for the first quarter of fiscal 2007, its partnership and possible acquisition of Teck Cominco Limited, and its plans for the future. Statistical data included.

25123 ■ *"The Intrawest Empire" in Canadian Business (Vol. 79, October 9, 2006, No. 20, pp. 27)*
Pub: Rogers Media
Ed: Erik Heinrich. **Description:** The future development plans of Intrawest Corp., are discussed. Strategic plans of Joe Houssian, the chairman, president and chief executive officer of Intrawest Corp., are also presented.

25124 ■ *"Intrawest Puts Itself on Market" in Globe & Mail (March 1, 2006, pp. B1)*
Pub: CTVglobemedia Publishing Inc.
Ed: Elizabeth Church. **Description:** The reasons behind the decision of Intrawest Corp. to go for sale or seek partnerships are presented. The company appointed Goldman Sachs & Co. to meet the purpose.

25125 ■ *"Iogen, VW Look to Build Ethanol Plant" in Globe & Mail (January 9, 2006, pp. B3)*
Pub: CTVglobemedia Publishing Inc.
Ed: Simon Tuck. **Description:** Iogen Corp. and Volkswagen AG plan cellulose ethanol plant in Germany. The details of the project are presented.

25126 ■ *"It's Not About the G1; Google Just Wants You to Use the Mobile Web" in Advertising Age (Vol. 79, September 29, 2008,*

No. 36, pp. 32)
Pub: Crain Communications, Inc.
Ed: Abbey Klaassen. **Description:** Google's Android is the first serious competitor to Apple's iPhone; the company says that its goal is to simplify the mobile market and get wireless subscribers to use the mobile Internet and purchase smartphones.

25127 ■ *"J.C. Watts First Black John Deere Dealer"* in Black Enterprise (Vol. 37, November 2006, No. 4, pp. 36)
Pub: Earl G. Graves Publishing Co. Inc.
Ed: Kiara Ashanti. **Description:** Profile of former Congressman J.C. Watts Jr., a man who grew up in rural America and is the first African American to own a John Deere Dealership.

25128 ■ *"Just Be Nice"* in Canadian Business (Vol. 79, October 9, 2006, No. 20, pp. 141)
Pub: Rogers Media
Ed: Joe Castaldo. **Description:** The customer relationship management strategies on customer retention and satisfaction adopted by WestJet are discussed.

25129 ■ *"KC Plants Downshift"* in The Business Journal-Serving Metropolitan Kansas City (Vol. 27, November 7, 2008, No. 9, pp. 1)
Pub: American City Business Journals, Inc.
Ed: James Dornbrook. **Description:** Discusses Ford Motor Co. and General Motors' factories in the region; Ford Motor Co. removed the second shift on the F-150 line at the Kansas City Assembly Plant but added a shift to the production of the Ford Escape and Mercury Mariner in an attempt to avoid layoffs. One spokesman for General Motors, however, states that they cannot guarantee that they won't make any production cuts and layoffs in the future.

25130 ■ *"Kodak Cuts Deep in Effort to Change Focus"* in Globe & Mail (February 9, 2007, pp. B8)
Pub: CTVglobemedia Publishing Inc.
Ed: Gillian Wee. **Description:** Eastman Kodak Co., the world's largest photography company, is eliminating 5,000 more jobs than the originally planned 28,000 jobs. The job cuts are being driven by the sale of Kodak's health-imaging unit.

25131 ■ *"Labatt to Swallow Lakeport"* in Globe & Mail (February 2, 2007, pp. B1)
Pub: CTVglobemedia Publishing Inc.
Ed: Keith McArthur. **Description:** The decision of Labatt Brewing Company Ltd. to acquire Lakeport Brewing Income Fund for $201.4 million is discussed.

25132 ■ *"Lafley Gives Look At His Game Plan"* in Business Courier (Vol. 24, March 21, 2008, No. 50, pp. 1)
Pub: American City Business Journals, Inc.
Ed: Lisa Biank Fasig. **Description:** Overview of A.G. Lafley's book entitled 'The Game-Changer', is presented. Lafley, Procter & Gamble Co.'s chief executive officer, documented his philosophy and strategy in his book. His work also includes Procter & Gamble's hands-on initiatives such as mock-up grocery stores and personal interviews with homeowners.

25133 ■ *"Land Agent Taken Over"* in Farmer's Weekly (March 28, 2008, No. 320)
Pub: Reed Business Information
Contact: Jeff Greisch, President
Description: Property business Smiths Gore will take over Cluttons' rural division, one of the oldest names in land agency. Cluttons said it had decided to sell its rural business as part of a strategic repositioning that would refocus the business on commercial, residential and overseas opportunities.

25134 ■ *"Last Founder Standing"* in Conde Nast Portfolio (Vol. 2, June 2008, No. 6, pp. 124)
Pub: Conde Nast Publications
Contact: David Carey, President
Ed: Kevin Maney. **Description:** Interview with Amazon CEO Jeff Bezos in which he discusses the economy, the company's new distribution center and the hiring of employees for it, e-books, and the overall vision for the future of the firm.

25135 ■ *"Lathrop Finds Partner In LA"* in The Business Journal-Serving Metropolitan Kansas City (Vol. 27, November 21, 2008, No. 11, pp. 1)
Pub: American City Business Journals, Inc.
Ed: Steve Vockrodt. **Description:** Kansas, Missouri-based Lathrop and Gage LLP is planning to merge with Spillane Shaeffer Aronoff Bandlow LLP. The merging of the business law firms will add entertainment clients to Lathrop's fold. Comments from executives are also presented.

25136 ■ *The Leader of the Future 2*
Pub: Jossey Bass
Ed: Frances Hesselbein; Marshall Goldsmith. **Released:** September 18, 2006. **Price:** $27.95. **Description:** Wisdom is lent to any small business owner or leader of a nonprofit organization.

25137 ■ *Leadership 101: What Every Leader Needs to Know*
Pub: Nelson Business
Ed: John C. Maxwell. **Released:** September 2002. **Price:** $9.99. **Description:** Ways to enhance leadership skills focusing on following a vision and bringing others along.

25138 ■ *Leap! 101 Ways to Grow Your Business*
Pub: Career Press, Inc.
Ed: Stephanie Chandler. **Released:** August 8, 2010. **Price:** $15.99. **Description:** Business growth requires more than a business plan and a dream. Tools and techniques to take a small company to the next level are outlined.

25139 ■ *"Lehman's Hail Mary Pass"* in Business Week (September 22, 2008, No. 4100, pp. 28)
Pub: McGraw-Hill Companies, Inc.
Ed: Matthew Goldstein; David Henry; Ben Levison. **Description:** Overview of Lehman Brothers' CEO Richard Fuld's plan to keep the firm afloat and end the stock's plunge downward; Fuld's strategy calls for selling off a piece of the firm's investment management business.

25140 ■ *"Loblaw Posts 40 Percent Profit Drop as it Scrambles to Lower Costs"* in Globe & Mail (February 9, 2006, pp. B1)
Pub: CTVglobemedia Publishing Inc.
Ed: Marina Strauss. **Description:** The reasons behind 40 percent decline in profits for Lobalaw Companies Ltd., for fourth quarter 2005, are presented.

25141 ■ *"Lombard Leaves Starbucks"* in Black Enterprise (Vol. 38, July 2008, No. 12, pp. 28)
Pub: Earl G. Graves Publishing Co. Inc.
Ed: Tamara E. Holmes. **Description:** Ken Lombard stepped down from his position as head of Starbuck's entertainment division; the company is restructuring its entertainment unit in an attempt to revitalize sales and reduce costs.

25142 ■ *"Looking For Financing?"* in Hispanic Business (Vol. 30, July-August 2008, No. 7-8, pp. 16)
Pub: Hispanic Business, Inc.
Ed: Frank Nelson. **Description:** Investment firms want to know about businesses that need funding for either expansion or acquisition; companies fitting this profile are interviewed and their perceptions are discussed. Investment firms need businesses to be realistic in their expectations and business plans which show spending of funds and expected benefits, long term goals, track record and strong management teams.

25143 ■ *"The Lords of Ideas"* in Business Strategy Review (Vol. 21, Autumn 2010, No. 3, pp. 57)
Pub: Blackwell Publishers Ltd.
Ed: Stuart Crainer. **Description:** True originators of modern strategy are profiled.

25144 ■ *"Losses Threaten Comp Care's Future Viability"* in The Business Journal-Serving Greater Tampa Bay (Vol. 28,

August 15, 2008, No. 34)
Pub: American City Business Journals, Inc.
Ed: Margie Manning. **Description:** Comprehensive Care Corp. expressed that it may have to cease or drastically curtail its operations if it won't be able to raise additional funding in the next two or three months. The firm, which provides managed behavioral health care services, is also believed to be exploring a sale. Other views and information on Comprehensive Care's finances and plans are presented.

25145 ■ *"The Macomb Group: Bigger Can Be Better"* in Crain's Detroit Business (Vol. 24, September 29, 2008, No. 39, pp. 34)
Pub: Crain Communications Inc.
Ed: Chad Halcom. **Description:** Overview of the plan of The Macomb Group includes a strategy of growing from a small supplier to a medium-sized regional distributor of valves, pipes and fittings.

25146 ■ *"Magna Stalwart to Push for Product Coups"* in Globe & Mail (April 9, 2007, pp. B1)
Pub: CTVglobemedia Publishing Inc.
Ed: Greg Keenan. **Description:** The resignation of Fred Gingl from the vice-chairmanship of the board of directors of Magna International Inc. is described. Mr. Gingl's plans to create wealth for Magna International Inc. through the development of new products are discussed.

25147 ■ *"Magna in Talks on Building Cars for DaimlerChrysler"* in Globe & Mail (February 27, 2007, pp. B1)
Pub: CTVglobemedia Publishing Inc.
Ed: Greg Keenan. **Description:** The plans of Magna International Inc. to purchase securities of Chrysler Corp. are discussed. The possibility of the manufacture of cars by Magna International Inc. for Daimler-Chrysler AG is discussed.

25148 ■ *"Magna Wants to Help Chrysler, but a Takeover's Not on the Cards"* in Globe & Mail (March 1, 2007, pp. B1)
Pub: CTVglobemedia Publishing Inc.
Ed: Greg Keenan. **Description:** The plans of Magna International Inc. to help Chrysler Corp. to overcome its financial problems are discussed. The appointment of Michael Neuman as the chief executive officer of Magna International Inc. is described.

25149 ■ *"Major Tech Employers Pulling Out"* in Sacramento Business Journal (Vol. 25, August 1, 2008, No. 22, pp. 1)
Pub: American City Business Journals, Inc.
Ed: Celia Lamb. **Description:** Biotechnology company Affymetrix Inc. is planning to close its West Sacramento, California plant and lay off 110 employees. The company said it will expand a corporate restructuring plan. Affymetrix also plans to lease out or sell its building at Riverside Parkway.

25150 ■ *"Marriott Checks Out Hotel Prospect"* in The Business Journal-Serving Metropolitan Kansas City (Vol. 27, November 14, 2008, No. 10)
Pub: American City Business Journals, Inc.
Description: Marriott International Inc. is planning to operate a hotel in Kansas City, Missouri and may take over the Kansas City Marriot Downtown although other hotel operators are interested in bidding on the project.

25151 ■ *"MBA Essentials: Real-Life Instruction"* in Women In Business (Vol. 61, October-November 2009, No. 5, pp. 28)
Pub: American Business Women's Association
Ed: Leigh Elmore. **Description:** University of Kansas School of Business allied itself with the American Business Women's Association (ABWA) which led to the formation of the ABWA-KU MBA essentials program. With this program, ABWA members are exposed to graduate-level coursework that delves on business topics, such as strategy and operations.

25152 ■ *"MBA Project Turns on Tastebuds"* in The Business Journal - Serving Phoenix and the Valley of the Sun (Vol. 28, August 15,

2008, No. 50)
Pub: American City Business Journals, Inc.

Ed: Angela Gonzales. **Description:** Amol Khade, Venkat Nallapati and Govind Arora, master of businesss administration graduates from Thunderbird School of Global Management, have opened an Indian restaurant, called The Daba, in Tempe, Arizona. The Indian name of the restaurant means 'a place for travelers to stop for rest and food'. Franchise plans for the restaurant are discussed.

25153 ■ *"Measure Your Business Plan Results" in Entrepreneur (January 6, 2009)*
Pub: Entrepreneur Media Inc.

Ed: Tim Berry. **Description:** Although no business plan is ever right on target, it is still essential for every business owner to create one; the way in which to analyze the actual results compared to the plan are discussed.

25154 ■ *"Meet Joe Fresh" in Canadian Business (Vol. 79, November 6, 2006, No. 22, pp. 49)*
Pub: Rogers Media

Ed: Calvin Leung. **Description:** The efforts of Joseph Mimran, a fashion designer, in improving the business of Joe Fresh style products are analyzed.

25155 ■ *"Mentoring Support" in Black Enterprise (Vol. 38, July 2008, No. 12, pp. 64)*
Pub: Earl G. Graves Publishing Co. Inc.

Description: With his relocation from his multicultural team in New York to the less diverse Scripps Networks' headquarters in Knoxville, Earl Cokley has made it a top priority to push for more diversity and mentoring opportunities within the management of the media and marketing company.

25156 ■ *"Mettle Detector" in Canadian Business (Vol. 79, July 17, 2006, No. 14-15, pp. 63)*
Pub: Rogers Media

Ed: Calvin Leung. **Description:** The difficulties faced in completing the Certified Financial Analyst course, and the rewards one can expect after its completion, are discussed.

25157 ■ *"Microsoft Clicks Into High Speed" in Hispanic Business (Vol. 30, July-August 2008, No. 7-8, pp. 54)*
Pub: Hispanic Business, Inc.

Ed: Derek Reveron. **Description:** Microsoft's diversity hiring and vendor diversity program to capture more Hispanic consumer and business-to-business market is described. One of the main goals of these programs is to hire more Hispanic executives and managers who will help the company develop and market products and services that will appeal and benefit Hispanic consumers.

25158 ■ *"Microsoft's Big Gamble" in Canadian Business (Vol. 81, March 3, 2008, No. 3, pp. 13)*
Pub: Rogers Media

Ed: Andrew Wahl. **Description:** Microsoft Corp. is taking a big risk in buying Yahoo, as it is expected to pay more than $31 a share to finalize the acquisition. The deal would be seven and a half times bigger than any other that Microsoft has entered before, an execution of such deal is also anticipated to become a challenge for Microsoft. Recommendations on how Microsoft should handle the integration of the two businesses are given.

25159 ■ *"Midtown Tampa Bay Taking Shape" in The Business Journal-Serving Greater Tampa Bay (Vol. 28, September 12, 2008, No. 38, pp. 1)*
Pub: American City Business Journals, Inc.

Ed: Janet Leiser. **Description:** Midtown Tampa Bay's 610,000 square foot shopping and entertainment center is being planned in Florida and is to replace the Tampa Bay One project proposed years earlier. The retail center is to be developed by Bromley Cos. and Opus South Corp. and is expected to have five buildings. Other details about the plan are discussed.

25160 ■ *"Midwest Looks 'Back to the Future" in The Business Journal-Milwaukee (Vol. 25, July 18, 2008, No. 43, pp. A1)*
Pub: American City Business Journals, Inc.

Ed: Rich Rovito. **Description:** Midwest Air Group Inc. announced plans to reduce their work force by 40 percent or 1,200 employees after an earlier announcement of a drastic fleet reduction. These steps are being taken by the company in an effort to avoid filing bankruptcy since this would cost the airline millions of dollars in legal and other professional fees.

25161 ■ *"Midwest Seeks Concessions From Creditors" in The Business Journal-Milwaukee (Vol. 25, July 25, 2008, No. 44, pp. A1)*
Pub: American City Business Journals, Inc.

Ed: Rich Rovito. **Description:** Midwest Airlines Inc. is turning to creditors and lease holders for the financial aspect of its restructuring, which involves going back to serving popular business destinations. Chief executive officer Timothy believes that the company can survive in a niche market as long as it provides quality service. He discusses Midwest's restructuring plan.

25162 ■ *"Milton Touts ACE Unit to Would-Be Buyers" in Globe & Mail (February 10, 2007, pp. B6)*
Pub: CTVglobemedia Publishing Inc.

Ed: Brent Jang. **Description:** The decision of Air Canada chairman Robert Milton to sell Air Canada Technical Services unit is presented. ACE Aviation Holdings Inc. is the parent company of Air Canada.

25163 ■ *"Modern-Day Midas Hasn't Lost Touch" in Globe & Mail (January 19, 2006, pp. B4)*
Pub: CTVglobemedia Publishing Inc.

Ed: Shirley Won. **Description:** The investment plans of chief executive officer Rob McEwen of U.S. Gold Corp. are presented.

25164 ■ *"More Manufacturers Scout Military Contracts As Auto Industry Lags" in Crain's Detroit Business (Vol. 24, September 29, 2008, No. 39)*
Pub: Crain Communications Inc.

Ed: Chad Halcom. **Description:** Many Michigan manufacturers are looking to grow with new military contracts now that the reality of the auto industry is becoming more clear; these companies see that the government contracts may be the only way in which they will be able to stay in business through these rough economic times.

25165 ■ *More Than a Pink Cadillac*
Pub: McGraw-Hill

Ed: Jim Underwood. **Released:** 2002. **Price:** $23.95. **Description:** Profile of Mary Kay Ash who turned her $5,000 investment into a billion-dollar corporation. Ash's nine principles that form the foundation of her company's global success are outlined. Stories from her sales force leaders share ideas for motivating employees, impressing customers and building a successful company. The book emphasizes the leadership skills required to drive performance in any successful enterprise.

25166 ■ *Navigating Your Way to Business Success: An Entrepreneur's Journey*
Pub: FreeBridge Publishing, Inc.

Ed: Kathryn B. Freeland. **Released:** January 10, 2010. **Price:** $24.95. **Description:** Learn first-hand from a successful entrepreneur about assessing skills and talent, envisioning your company, planning a path to success, and then tapping into available government agencies to make your business become a reality.

25167 ■ *"NBC" in Brandweek (Vol. 49, April 21, 2008, No. 16, pp. SR6)*
Pub: VNU Business Media, Inc.

Ed: John Consoli. **Description:** Provides contact information for sales and marketing personnel for the NBC network as well as a listing of the station's top programming and an analysis of the current season and the target audience for those programs running in the current season. NBC also devised a new

strategy of announcing its prime-time schedule 52 weeks in advance which was a hit for advertisers who felt this gave them a better opportunity to plan for product placement. Even with the station's creative sales programs, they could face a challenge from Fox in terms of upfront advertisement purchases.

25168 ■ *"Needed: A Strategy; Banking In China" in The Economist (Vol. 390, January 3, 2009, No. 8612, pp. 54)*
Pub: The Economist Newspaper Inc.

Description: International banks are competing for a role in China but are finding obstacles in their paths such as a reduction in the credit their operations may receive from Chinese banks and the role they can play in the public capital markets which remain limited.

25169 ■ *"Net Connections" in Black Enterprise (Vol. 38, July 2008, No. 12, pp. 28)*
Pub: Earl G. Graves Publishing Co. Inc.

Ed: Anthony S. Calypso. **Description:** Marketers are making strategic partnerships with online social networks in an attempt to gain further market reach. The value of these networks appears to be on the rise forcing media companies to recalculate their strategies for delivering products to customers.

25170 ■ *"New Beginnings for VIBE" in Black Enterprise (Vol. 37, November 2006, No. 4, pp. 34)*
Pub: Earl G. Graves Publishing Co. Inc.

Ed: Mashaun D. Simon. **Description:** Danyel Smith replaced Mimi Valdes as editor-in-chief of VIBE magazine after the Wicks Group, private equity firm focused on selected segments of the media, communications, and information industries, purchased the magazine.

25171 ■ *"New BMO Boss Set to Cut 1,000 Jobs" in Globe & Mail (February 1, 2007, pp. B3)*
Pub: CTVglobemedia Publishing Inc.

Ed: Andrew Willis. **Description:** The decision of the new chief executive officer of the Bank of Montreal, Bill Downe, to cut down 1,000 jobs, to boost the company's performance is discussed.

25172 ■ *"Nexen, OPTI Boost Oil Sands Spending" in Globe & Mail (February 18, 2006, pp. B5)*
Pub: CTVglobemedia Publishing Inc.

Ed: Dave Ebner. **Description:** The reasons behind the decision of Nexen Inc. and OPTI Canada Inc., to allocate 10 percent more funding on oil sands, are presented.

25173 ■ *"No Frills - And No Dodge" in Crain's Detroit Business (Vol. 24, September 22, 2008, No. 38, pp. 3)*
Pub: Crain Communications Inc.

Ed: Bradford Wernie. **Description:** Chrysler LLC is in the middle of a business plan known as Project Genesis, a five-year strategy in which the company will reduce the dealer count by combining its Jeep, Chrysler and Dodge brands under one rooftop wherever possible. Not every dealer will be able to arrange this deal because of the investment required to expand stores in which have low-overhead; many of these stores feel that low-overhead structures are more likely to survive difficult times than the larger stores in which the Genesis consolidation plan intends to implement.

25174 ■ *"No Secrets; Businesses Find It Pays to Open Books to Employees" in Crain's Detroit Business (Vol. 26, January 18, 2010, No. 3)*
Pub: Crain Communications Inc.

Ed: Dustin Walsh. **Description:** Many businesses are finding that practicing an open-book management wherein employees share financial and decision-making duties that are usually left up to executives of firms creates a transparency within a company that eliminates the us versus them mentality between management and employees. Another benefit to this business model is that employees get to really participate in the business, learning to manage money and run a business entity.

25175 ■ *"Nortel Starting From Scratch"* in *Globe & Mail (February 24, 2006, pp. B3)*
Pub: CTVglobemedia Publishing Inc.
Ed: Catherine McLean. **Description:** The restructuring efforts of chief executive officer Mike Zafirovski of Nortel Networks Corp. are presented.

25176 ■ *"Not Just for Kids: ADHD can be Debilitating for an Employee, and Frustrating for Bosses"* in *Canadian Business (April 14, 2008)*
Pub: Rogers Media
Ed: Andy Holloway. **Description:** Up to four percent of North American adults continue to feel the effects of Attention Deficit Hyperactivity Disorder or Attention Deficit Disorder. Explaining the value of the task at hand to people who are afflicted with these conditions is one way to keep them engaged in the workplace. Giving them opportunities to create their own working structure is another strategy to manage these people.

25177 ■ *"Not the Six O'Clock News"* in *Canadian Business (Vol. 80, January 15, 2007, No. 2, pp. 10)*
Pub: Rogers Media
Ed: Marlene Rego. **Description:** The proposal by Paul Jay, the chief executive officer of Independent World Television, to launch The Real News Project, is discussed. The objective of the project is to establish an independent news and current affairs network solely through viewers.

25178 ■ *"Numerous Changes Made to Crop Production and Consumption Forecasts"* in *Farm Industry News (November 9, 2011)*
Pub: Penton Business Media Inc.
Ed: Darrel Good. **Description:** USDA November Crop Production and WASDE reports contained various changes in production and consumption forecasts for corn, soybeans, and what for the current marketing year. A brief summary for each crop is included.

25179 ■ *"On a Mission: Ginch Gonch Wants You to Get Rid of Your Tighty Whities"* in *Canadian Business (Vol. 81, September 29, 2008, No. 16)*
Pub: Rogers Media Ltd.
Ed: Michelle Magnan. **Description:** New Equity Capital acquired underwear maker Ginch Gonch in July 2008; founder Jason Sutherland kept his position as creative director of the company and will retain his title as 'director of stitches and inches'. The company is known for its products, which are reminiscent of the days when people wore underwear covered in cowboys and stars as kids. The company also claims that Nelly, Justin Timberlake, and Hilary Duff have worn their products.

25180 ■ *"On a Roll"* in *Canadian Business (Vol. 79, October 9, 2006, No. 20, pp. 51)*
Pub: Rogers Media
Ed: Joe Castaldo. **Description:** Corporate management strategies of Denis Turcotte, chief executive officer of Algoma Steel Inc., are presented.

25181 ■ *"One Paddle, Two Paddle"* in *Hawaii Business (Vol. 53, October 2007, No. 4, pp. 65)*
Pub: Hawaii Business Publishing
Ed: Kyle Galdeira. **Description:** Oiwi Ocean Gear's strategy may not give instant profits, but it works well for the company's goal of providing high-quality apparel for paddlers. The apparel company produces and markets swimwear, paddling jerseys and active wear. The company's strategy is compared with the selling of mass-produced clothes lower prices.

25182 ■ *"Ontario Keeps Bleeding Jobs as Michelin Closes Tire Plant"* in *Globe & Mail (February 3, 2006, pp. B1)*
Pub: CTVglobemedia Publishing Inc.
Ed: Greg Keenan; Heather Scoffield. **Description:** The reasons behind facility shutdown and workforce reduction by Michelin SA, in Ontario, are presented.

25183 ■ *"Open Skies: Opportunity, Challenge for Airlines"* in *Crain's Chicago Business (April 21, 2008)*
Pub: Crain Communications, Inc.
Ed: Paul Merrion. **Description:** Discusses the new aviation agreement between Europe and the United States known as Open Skies; the pact creates opportunities for U.S. carriers to fly to new destinations in Europe from more U.S. cities; it also allows carriers to fly between European cities, something they have not been able to do until now.

25184 ■ *"Paramount Said to be Working on Sale of Oil Sands Assets"* in *Globe & Mail (April 24, 2007, pp. B1)*
Pub: CTVglobemedia Publishing Inc.
Ed: Norval Scott. **Description:** The proposed sale of oil sands in Surmont and the shares of North American Oil Sands Corp. by Paramount Resources Ltd. is discussed.

25185 ■ *"Patricia Hemingway Hall; President, Chief Operating Officer, Health Care Service Corp."* in *Crain's Chicago Business (May 5, 2008)*
Pub: Crain Communications, Inc.
Ed: Mike Colias. **Description:** Profile of Patricia Hemingway Hall who is the president and chief operating officer of Health Care Service Corp., a new strategy launched by Blue Cross & Blue Shield of Illinois; the new endeavor will emphasize wellness rather than just treatment across its four health plans.

25186 ■ *"People; E-Commerce, Online Games, Mobile Apps"* in *Advertising Age (Vol. 80, October 19, 2009, No. 35, pp. 14)*
Pub: Crain's Communications
Ed: Nat Ives. **Description:** Profile of People Magazine and the ways in which the publisher is moving its magazine forward by exploring new concepts in a time of declining newsstand sales and advertising pages; among the strategies are e-commerce such as the brand People Style Watch in which consumers are able highlight clothing and jewelry and then connect to retailers' sites and a channel on Taxi TV, the network of video-touch screens in New Your City taxis.

25187 ■ *"People; E-Commerce, Online Games, Mobile Apps: This Isn't Your Mom's People"* in *Advertising Age (Vol. 80, October 19, 2009, No. 35)*
Pub: Crain's Communications
Ed: Nat Ives. **Description:** Profile of People Magazine and the ways in which the publisher is moving its magazine forward by exploring new concepts in a time of declining newsstand sales and advertising pages; among the strategies are e-commerce such as the brand People Style Watch in which consumers are able highlight clothing and jewelry and then connect to retailers' sites and a channel on Taxi TV, the network of video-touch screens in New Your City taxis.

25188 ■ *"Perfecting the Process: Creating a Move Efficient Organization On Your Terms"* in *Black Enterprise (Vol. 41, October 2010, No. 3)*
Pub: Earl G. Graves Publishing Co. Inc.
Ed: Tamara E. Holmes. **Description:** More than ever, entrepreneurs need to identify new ways of doing business in a cost-effective manner in order to expand their companies, while remaining true to their customer demands.

25189 ■ *"Playboy to Target Lucrative India Market With No-Nudes Version"* in *Globe & Mail (January 2, 2006, pp. B2)*
Pub: CTVglobemedia Publishing Inc.
Ed: Anand Giridharadas. **Description:** The planning of Chicago based Playboy Enterprises Inc. to target lucrative India market with no nudes version, in order to increase its market shares is discussed.

25190 ■ *"The Play's the Thing"* in *Business Strategy Review (Vol. 21, Summer 2010, No. 2, pp. 58)*
Pub: Blackwell Publishers Ltd.
Ed: Michael G. Jacobides. **Description:** Those who study and plan strategies risk falling into the traps that maps, graphs, charts and matrices present. A better strategy might be using a playscript that can reveal the unfolding plots of business far better than traditional strategic tools as the landscapes shifts.

25191 ■ *"Profit Strong Rona to Maintain Acquisition Strategy"* in *Globe & Mail (February 22, 2007, pp. B14)*
Pub: CTVglobemedia Publishing Inc.
Description: Canada-based Rona Inc., home improvement retailer that reported record annual profit in 2006, will continue its strategy of acquisitions. The company has reported profits of $190.6 million in 2006.

25192 ■ *"Ratio-Cination"* in *Canadian Business (Vol. 79, October 23, 2006, No. 21, pp. 164)*
Pub: Rogers Media
Ed: Ian McGugan. **Description:** Tips for investors, on how to make market observations before selecting companies for purchasing stocks, are presented.

25193 ■ *"Realities May Blur Vision"* in *The Business Journal-Serving Metropolitan Kansas City (Vol. 27, September 19, 2008, No. 1, pp. 1)*
Pub: American City Business Journals, Inc.
Ed: Rob Roberts. **Description:** Vision Metcalf is a study by Kansas City that depicts how Metcalf Avenue could look like if redeveloped. Redevelopment plans for the Metcalf corridor include a 20-story mixed-use building on a vacant car dealership. The challenges that the redevelopment plans will face are also analyzed.

25194 ■ *"Recession Survival Tip: Less Is More"* in *Women Entrepreneur (December 31, 2008)*
Pub: Entrepreneur Media Inc.
Ed: Suzy Girard-Ruttenberg. **Description:** These trying economic times can be an opportunity to make bold changes in one's business that may yield lasting results, not just short-term survival; simplification, accountability and shoring up one's margins are things to look at when determining the goals of the company.

25195 ■ *"Refreshing"* in *Canadian Business (Vol. 79, September 11, 2006, No. 18, pp. 22)*
Pub: Rogers Media
Ed: Joe Castaldo. **Description:** Turnaround strategies and initiatives adopted by Canadian Beverage Corp. to boost its declining sales are presented.

25196 ■ *"The Reinvention of Management"* in *Strategy and Leadership (Vol. 39, March-April 2011, No. 2, pp. 9)*
Pub: Emerald Group Publishing Inc.
Ed: Stephen Denning. **Description:** An examination found that critical changes in management practice involves five shifts. These shifts involve the firm's goals, model of coordination, the role of managers and values practiced. Other findings of the study are discussed.

25197 ■ *"Retail: Loblaw Goes for Broke"* in *Canadian Business (Vol. 80, January 29, 2007, No. 3, pp. 7)*
Pub: Rogers Media
Ed: Zena Oiljnyk. **Description:** The efforts of Loblaw Companies Limited to reduce its operational expenses are described. The company's decision to reduce the number of employees at its national and regional offices, besides closing some of its facilities, is discussed.

25198 ■ *"Return to Wealth; Bank Strategy"* in *The Economist (Vol. 390, January 3, 2009, No. 8612, pp. 56)*
Pub: The Economist Newspaper Inc.
Description: UBS' strategy to survive these trying economic times is presented. Statistical data included. UBS has a stronger balance-sheet than most of its investment-banking peers and has reduced its portfolio.

25199 ■ *Rework*
Pub: Crown Business
Ed: Jason Fried, David Heinemeier Hansson. **Released:** March 9, 2010. **Price:** $22.00. **Description:** Works to help entrepreneurs and business owners to rethink strategy, customers, and getting things accomplished.

25200 ■ "Right From the Start" in Small Business Opportunities (July 2010)
Pub: Harris Publications Inc.
Ed: Ed Krug. Description: Ed Krug from Pitch Blue provides sales support services by partnering with small and mid-sized companies to set and reach new revenue targets.

25201 ■ "The Road Map for Scotiabank's Asian Expansion" in Globe & Mail (April 7, 2007, pp. B3)
Pub: CTVglobemedia Publishing Inc.
Ed: Tara Perkins. Description: Executive vice-president of Bank of Nova Scotia, Rob Pitfield shares his plan to expand the bank's Asian market.

25202 ■ "Roadside Attraction" in Hawaii Business (Vol. 53, January 2008, No. 7, pp. 39)
Pub: Hawaii Business Publishing
Ed: Jason Ubay. Description: Businesses beside the Kamehameha Highway find ways to survive in a rural community. Sunshine Arts Hawaii, for instance, uses a bright-colored and huge mural to attract tourists who drive along the highway. Other techniques employed by businesses in the aforementioned are described.

25203 ■ "Rule of Thumb" in Entrepreneur (Vol. 36, May 2008, No. 5, pp. 44)
Pub: Entrepreneur Media, Inc.
Ed: Guy Kawasaki. Description: Business presentations using PowerPoint are recommended to have no more than 10 slides, last no longer than 20 minutes and have font no smaller than 30 points. Topics covered should include problem, solution, business model, underlying technology, and projections among others.

25204 ■ "Sabia Signals a Bold, New Course for BCE" in Globe & Mail (February 2, 2006, pp. B1)
Pub: CTVglobemedia Publishing Inc.
Ed: Catherine McLean. Description: The reasons behind the decision of chief executive officer Michael Sabia to streamline operations of BCE Inc. are presented.

25205 ■ "Samsung's Metamorphosis" in Austin Business Journal (Vol. 31, May 20, 2011, No. 11, pp. 1)
Pub: American City Business Journals Inc.
Ed: Christopher Calnan. Description: Samsung Austin Semiconductor LP, a developer of semiconductors for smartphones and tablet computers, plans to diversify its offerings to include niche products: flash memory devices and microprocessing devices. In light of this strategy, Samsung Austin will be hiring 300 engineers as part of a $3.6 billion expansion of its plant.

25206 ■ "Savvas Chamberlain" in Canadian Business (Vol. 81, March 17, 2008, No. 4, pp. 92)
Pub: Rogers Media
Ed: Andrew Wahl. Description: Savvas Chamberlain says he feels cheated during his teenage years because life was not normal for him growing up in Cyprus with all the uprisings against Britain. Chamberlain says he runs Dalsa like he plays chess because all his positions are shown all the time but he keeps his strategy to himself.

25207 ■ "Scouting and Keeping Good Talent in the Workplace" in Hawaii Business (Vol. 53, January 2008, No. 7, pp. 50)
Pub: Hawaii Business Publishing
Ed: Christie Dermegian. Description: Tips on improving employee selection and retention are presented. The strategies in choosing and keeping the right employees include identifying which type of people the company needs and improving the workplace environment.

25208 ■ "The Seat-Of-The-Pants School of Marketing" in Brandweek (Vol. 49, April 21, 2008, No. 16, pp. 24)
Pub: VNU Business Media, Inc.
Ed: David Vinjamuri. Description: Excerpt from the book 'Accidental Branding: How Ordinary People Build Extraordinary Brands,' by David Vinjamuri, discusses six shared principles for creating a brand that is unique and will be successful over the long-term.

25209 ■ "Shermag Plans Two Shutdowns, 300 More Layoffs" in Globe & Mail (February 13, 2007, pp. B5)
Pub: CTVglobemedia Publishing Inc.
Ed: Bertrand Marotte. Description: Shermag Inc., Canada's largest publicly traded furniture company, is permanently closing two plants and eliminating 300 jobs. The mounting losses and deteriorating stock prices are stated as main reasons for plant shutdowns.

25210 ■ "Shermag Says Refinishing Not Complete" in Globe & Mail (February 14, 2006, pp. B3)
Pub: CTVglobemedia Publishing Inc.
Ed: Bertrand Marotte. Description: The details on restructuring efforts of Shermag Inc. are presented.

25211 ■ "Shoppers Targets an Upscale Move" in Globe & Mail (January 19, 2007, pp. B4)
Pub: CTVglobemedia Publishing Inc.
Ed: Marina Strauss. Description: Shoppers Drug Mart Corp.'s plan to boost sales of cosmetics and take up global sourcing to offer new products is discussed.

25212 ■ "Should You Go Into Business With Your Spouse?" in Women Entrepreneur (September 1, 2008)
Pub: Entrepreneur Media Inc.
Ed: Tamara Monosoff. Description: Things to consider before starting a business with one's spouse are discussed. Compatible work ethics, clear expectations of one another, long-term goals for the company and the status of the relationship are among the things to consider before starting a business endeavor with a spouse.

25213 ■ "Sign Up To Grow Your Business, Generate Jobs" in Women Entrepreneur (November 25, 2008)
Pub: Entrepreneur Media Inc.
Ed: Eve Gumpel. Description: Nell Merlino has announced the new Make Mine A Million-Dollar Race, which aims to encourage hundreds of thousands of women entrepreneurs to grow their business to revenue goals of $250,00, $500,000 or $1 million and more as well as create 800,000 new jobs in an attempt to stimulate the nation's economy.

25214 ■ "Sleeman Cuts Again as Cheap Suds Bite" in Globe & Mail (March 3, 2006, pp. B3)
Pub: CTVglobemedia Publishing Inc.
Ed: Andy Hoffman. Description: The details on 5 percent employee reduction at Sleeman Breweries Ltd., which posted 86 percent decline in profits for fourth quarter 2005, are presented.

25215 ■ "Slimmed-Down Supplier TI Automotive Relaunches" in Crain's Detroit Business (Vol. 26, January 11, 2010, No. 2, pp. 14)
Pub: Crain Communications Inc.
Ed: Robert Sherefkin. Description: TI Automotive Ltd., one of the world's largest suppliers of fuel storage and delivery systems, has reorganized the company by splitting it into five global divisions and is relaunching its brand which is now more focused on new technology.

25216 ■ Small Business, Big Life: Five Steps to Creating a Great Life with Your Own Small Business
Pub: Thomas Nelson Inc.
Ed: Louis Barajas. Price: $22.99. Description: Barajas describes his and his father's independent entrepreneurial paths and suggests an inspirational approach to business that relies on four personal greatness cornerstones: truth, responsibility, aware-

ness, and courage, and on keeping in mind your vision and your team's needs. The book provides a new look at achieving a work/life balance.

25217 ■ "Small is the New Big in Autos" in Globe & Mail (February 16, 2006, pp. B3)
Pub: CTVglobemedia Publishing Inc.
Ed: Greg Keenan. Description: The reasons behind the introduction of subcompact cars by companies such as Ford Motor Co. are presented. The automobiles were unveiled at Canadian International Auto Show in Toronto.

25218 ■ "So You Want to Start a Business?" in Women Entrepreneur (August 5, 2008)
Pub: Entrepreneur Media Inc.
Ed: Cynthia McKay. Description: Advice for taking an idea and turning it into a legitimate business is given.

25219 ■ "Sorrell Digs Deep to Snag TNS" in Advertising Age (Vol. 79, July 14, 2008, No. 7, pp. 1)
Pub: Crain Communications, Inc.
Ed: Michael Bush. Description: Martin Sorrell's strategic vision for expansion in order to become the largest ad-agency holding company in the world is discussed.

25220 ■ "Stadium Developers Seek a Win With the State" in The Business Journal-Serving Metropolitan Kansas City (Vol. 26, August 22, 2008)
Pub: American City Business Journals, Inc.
Ed: Rob Roberts. Description: Three Trails Redevelopment LLC is hoping to win $30 million in state tax credits from the Missouri Development Finance Board for the construction of an 18,500-seat Wizards stadium. The project is contingent on state tax incentives and the company remains optimistic about their goal.

25221 ■ "Starbucks Drive-Throughs: Can the Cafe Keep Its Cool?" in Globe & Mail (January 6, 2006, pp. B7)
Pub: CTVglobemedia Publishing Inc.
Ed: Steven Gray. Description: The feasibility of Starbucks Corp.'s plans to introduce drive-through cafes is discussed.

25222 ■ "Stelco Investors Told Their Stock Now Worthless" in Globe & Mail (January 23, 2006, pp. B4)
Pub: CTVglobemedia Publishing Inc.
Ed: Greg Keenan. Description: The reasons behind Ontario Superior Court's approval of Stelco Inc.'s restructuring proposal are presented.

25223 ■ "Stelco Seeks to Shave Its Fixed Costs" in Globe & Mail (March 8, 2007, pp. B1)
Pub: CTVglobemedia Publishing Inc.
Ed: Greg Keenan. Description: The plans of Stelco Inc. to control its fixed costs in order to protect itself from economic downturns are discussed.

25224 ■ "Stepping Up" in Baltimore Business Journal (Vol. 28, October 22, 2010, No. 24, pp. 1)
Pub: Baltimore Business Journal
Ed: Erik Siemers. Description: Uner Armour Inc. will release its Micro G line of four basketball sneakers on October 23, 2010. The company's executives mentioned that Under Armour's goal is to appeal to customers, and not to chip away at Nike Inc.'s supremacy in basketball shoes. The new sneakers will range from $80 to $110.

25225 ■ "Stikemans' Ascent, Its Legacy, and Its Future" in Globe & Mail (January 29, 2007, pp. B2)
Pub: CTVglobemedia Publishing Inc.
Ed: Jacquie McNish. Description: Pierre Raymond, chairman of legal firm Stikeman Elliott LLP, talks about his strategies to handle competition, his challenges, and about Canada's present mergers and acquisition scenario. Stikeman achieved the first place in 2006 M&A legal rankings.

25226 ■ *"Stock Car Racing" in Canadian Business (Vol. 81, September 15, 2008, No. 14-15, pp. 29)*
Pub: Rogers Media Ltd.
Ed: Thomas Watson. **Description:** Some analysts predict a Chapter 11-style tune-up making GM and Ford a speculative turnaround stock. However, the price of oil could make or break the shares of the Big Three U.S. automobile manufacturers and if oil goes up too high then a speculative stock to watch is an electric car company called Zenn Motor Co.

25227 ■ *"Stockgroup Completes US $4.5 Million Financing" in Canadian Corporate News (May 16, 2007)*
Pub: Comtex News Network Inc.
Description: Stockgroup, a financial media company focused on collaborative technologies and user-generated content, will use the proceeds of the private placement for acquisitions and general working capital.

25228 ■ *"Stoneham Drilling Trust Announces Cash Distribution for May 2007" in Canadian Corporate News (May 16, 2007)*
Pub: Comtex News Network Inc.
Description: Stoneham Drilling Trust, an income trust that provides contract drilling services to natural gas and oil exploration and production companies operating in western Canada, announced that its cash distribution for the period from May 1, 2007 to May 31, 2007 will be $0.15 per trust unit ($1.80 per annum).

25229 ■ *"Strategy: Hurry Up and Wait" in Business Courier (Vol. 24, February 1, 2008, No. 43, pp. 50)*
Pub: American City Business Journals, Inc.
Ed: Dan Monk. **Description:** It has taken years for Enerfab Inc. chairman Dave Herche to develop new product lines, form an expert management group and come up with a strategic-planning approach. However, his patience has paid off since Enerfab's revenue has grown by 93 percent since 2005. Herche's strategy for Enerfab and its impacts on the company are analyzed further.

25230 ■ *Streetwise Small Business Turnaround: Revitalizing Your Struggling or Stagnant Enterprise*
Pub: Adams Media Corporation
Contact: Gary Krebs, Director
E-mail: swatrous@adamsmedia.com
Ed: Marc Kramer. **Released:** November 1999. **Description:** Practical tips and advice are provided for rejuvenating an existing small business.

25231 ■ *"Success Coach: Dare to Dream" in Entrepreneur (Vol. 35, October 2007, No. 10, pp. 146)*
Pub: Entrepreneur Media Inc.
Ed: Romaus Wolter. **Description:** Business goals that are seemingly impossible to reach can actually be achieved through careful planning. Making the goals clear is the first step toward achievement. Details for setting goals and how to attain them are presented.

25232 ■ *"Suitors Circling Chrysler as Sale Likely" in Globe & Mail (February 19, 2007, pp. B1)*
Pub: CTVglobemedia Publishing Inc.
Ed: Jason Singer. **Description:** DaimlerChrysler AG is planning to sell or spin-off the Chrysler Group, as a cost cutting strategy. Chrysler reported a 40 percent drop in fourth quarter profit because of the $1.5 billion operating loss.

25233 ■ *"Sunriver Venture Hits Snag" in The Business Journal-Portland (Vol. 25, August 1, 2008, No. 21, pp. 1)*
Pub: American City Business Journals, Inc.
Ed: Robin J. Moody. **Description:** Portland, Oregon based-Sunwest Management Inc. has divided its Sunriver resort community to make way for a redevelopment plan. Sunwest owner Jon Harder and three partners formed SilverStar Destinations LLC to broker

the purchase and redevelopment of the property. Details and description of the redevelopment project are also presented.

25234 ■ *"Suppliers Look to Rack Up Big Sales to Distributors" in The Business Journal-Serving Metropolitan Kansas City (August 15, 2008)*
Pub: American City Business Journals, Inc.
Ed: James Dornbrook. **Description:** Suppliers of shelving units, conveyor systems and other equipment used in distribution facilities are expecting new business opportunities along with the planned intermodal projects in the Kansas City area. Suppliers have already observed that small distributors have started to relocate to the city because of the intermodal projects. Demand for shelves and lifts have also increased.

25235 ■ *"Survive the Small-to-Big Transition" in Entrepreneur (November 4, 2008)*
Pub: Entrepreneur Media Inc.
Ed: Elizabeth Wilson. **Description:** Transitioning a small company to a large company can be a challenge, especially during the time when it is too big to be considered small and too small to be considered big. Common pitfalls during this time are discussed as well as techniques business owners should implement when dealing with this transitional period.

25236 ■ *"Take on an Elephant Without Getting Trampled" in Globe & Mail (March 17, 2007, pp. B3)*
Pub: CTVglobemedia Publishing Inc.
Ed: Grant Robertson. **Description:** The plan of chief executive officer of Canpages Inc. Olivier Vincent to beat the profit margin and market share of Yellow Pages Group is discussed.

25237 ■ *"Talisman CEO Touts Benefits of Going It Alone" in Globe & Mail (March 22, 2006, pp. B1)*
Pub: CTVglobemedia Publishing Inc.
Ed: Dave Ebner. **Description:** The opinions of chief executive officer Jim Buckee of Talisman Energy Inc. on the benefits for the company to remain autonomous are presented.

25238 ■ *"Tate & Lyle to Sell Redpath Division to American Sugar" in Globe & Mail (February 15, 2007, pp. B15)*
Pub: CTVglobemedia Publishing Inc.
Description: American Sugar Refining has agreed to acquire the Canadian sugar unit of Tate & Lyle PLC for $301.9 million. Tate & Lyle PLC has been selling off businesses and closing plants in order to focus on starches and Splenda.

25239 ■ *"TD Pares in U.S., Still Aims for Growth" in Globe & Mail (March 24, 2007, pp. B6)*
Pub: CTVglobemedia Publishing Inc.
Ed: Tara Perkins. **Description:** The decision of TD Banknorth Inc. to close some of its branches and remove 400 jobs, with a view to cutting down operational expenses, is discussed.

25240 ■ *"Tea for 33 Million" in Canadian Business (Vol. 80, March 12, 2007, No. 6, pp. 10)*
Pub: Rogers Media
Ed: Wendy Glauser. **Description:** The plan of owner of Cargo & James Tea, Tim Grover, to expand his business in North America to reach about 33 million, is discussed.

25241 ■ *"Telus Tunes in to the TV Revolution" in Globe & Mail (February 18, 2006, pp. B4)*
Pub: CTVglobemedia Publishing Inc.
Ed: Eric Reguly. **Description:** The business growth plans of chief executive officer Darren Entwistle of Telus Corp. are presented.

25242 ■ *"Thomson Eyes Asia for Expansion" in Globe & Mail (February 10, 2006, pp. B4)*
Pub: CTVglobemedia Publishing Inc.
Ed: Grant Robertson. **Description:** The business growth plans of Thomson Corp., in Asia, are presented.

25243 ■ *"Top 50 In Profits" in Canadian Business (Vol. 81, Summer 2008, No. 9, pp. 116)*
Pub: Rogers Media Ltd.
Description: Royal Bank of Canada topped the Investor 500 by profits list despite the slower economic growth in Canada and the U.S. The bank was in the runner-up position in the 2007. RBC's growth strategy is through hefty acquisitions in the U.S. A table ranking the top 50 companies in Canada in terms of profits is presented.

25244 ■ *"Tough-Love Boss at BMO Demands Retail Turnaround" in Globe & Mail (March 2, 2007, pp. B13)*
Pub: CTVglobemedia Publishing Inc.
Ed: Andrew Willis. **Description:** William Downe, the newly appointed chief executive of Bank of Montreal (BMO), discusses strategies to improve the number of retail customers. The BMO reported $292 million profits in the first quarter of 2007.

25245 ■ *"Toyota Expected to Construct Two N.A. Plants" in Globe & Mail (February 14, 2007, pp. B4)*
Pub: CTVglobemedia Publishing Inc.
Description: Toyota Motor Corp. is planning to construct two vehicle assembly plants in North America and one more plant in Canada. The company is also planning to sell 208,000 vehicles in 2007.

25246 ■ *"Transportation Enterprise" in Advertising Age (Vol. 79, June 9, 2008, No. 23, pp. S10)*
Pub: Crain Communications, Inc.
Ed: Jean Halliday. **Description:** Overview of Enterprise rent-a-car's plan to become a more environmentally-friendly company. The family-owned business has spent $1 million a year to plant trees since 2006 and has added more fuel-efficient cars, hybrids and flex-fuel models.

25247 ■ *"Transportation: Laidlaw's Chief Driver" in Canadian Business (Vol. 80, January 29, 2007, No. 3, pp. 14)*
Pub: Rogers Media
Ed: Michelle Magnan. **Description:** The role of Kevin Benson in the restructuring and growth of the bankrupt transportation company Laidlaw Inc. is described. The increase in the revenues of the restructures company is discussed.

25248 ■ *"Tri-State Lags Peer Cities in Jobs, Human Capital, Study Says" in Business Courier (Vol. 27, September 24, 2010, No. 21, pp. 1)*
Pub: Business Courier
Ed: Dan Monk, Lucy May. **Description:** Greater Cincinnati, Ohio has ranked tenth overall in the 'Agenda 360/Vision 2015 Regional Indicators Project' report. The study ranked 12-city-peer groups in categories such as job indicators standing and people indicators standing. The ranking of jobs and human capital study is topped by Minneapolis, followed by Denver, Raleigh, and Austin.

25249 ■ *"Trilogy Metals Inc.: Private Placement" in Canadian Corporate News (May 16, 2007)*
Pub: Comtex News Network Inc.
Description: Trilogy Metals Inc. announces a private placement of 10,000,000 units at $0.08 per unit in an effort to raise total gross proceeds of $800,000 which will be allocated to working capital, new acquisitions, and to service existing debt.

25250 ■ *"Turmoil Means Changes For Retailers" in The Business Journal-Serving Metropolitan Kansas City (Vol. 27, October 10, 2008, No. 4)*
Pub: American City Business Journals, Inc.
Ed: Suzanna Stagemeyer. **Description:** Impacts of the financial crisis on Kansas Metropolitan Area retailers are varied. Rob Dalzell, for instance, found it difficult to secure a loan for his new self-serve yogurt store Yummo. The trends in retailing in the area are examined further as well as ways in which local businesses are changing in an attempt to stay solvent during the economic downturn.

25251 ■ *"UMKC, Hospital Drill Down on Deal"*
in The Business Journal-Serving Metropolitan
Kansas City (Vol. 26, July 18, 2008, No. 45,
pp. 1)
Pub: American City Business Journals, Inc.

Ed: Rob Roberts. **Description:** University of Missouri Kansas City and Children's Mercy Hospital are negotiating the hospital's potential acquisition of the university's School of Dentistry building. The deal would transfer the 240,000-square foot dental school building to Children's Mercy. Plans for a new dental school building for the UMKC are also presented.

25252 ■ *"Under Fire, Sabia Triggers Battle for*
BCE" in Globe & Mail (April 14, 2007, pp. B1)
Pub: CTVglobemedia Publishing Inc.

Ed: Boyd Erman. **Description:** The announcement of negotiations for the sale of BCE Inc. by its chief executive officer Michael Sabia is discussed. The efforts of Ontario Teachers Pension Plan to submit its proposal for the sale are described.

25253 ■ *"Unify Corp. Back in the Black,*
Poised to Grow" in Sacramento Business
Journal (Vol. 25, August 29, 2008, No. 26, pp.
1)
Pub: American City Business Journals, Inc.

Ed: Melanie Turner. **Description:** It was reported that Unify Corp. returned to profitability in the fiscal year ended April 30, 2008 with a net income of $1.6 million, under the guidance of Todd Wille. Wille, who took over as the company's chief executive officer in October 2000, was named as Turnaround CEO of the Year in June 2008 for his efforts.

25254 ■ *"Unilever's CMO Finally Gets Down*
To Business" in Advertising Age (Vol. 79, July
7, 2008, No. 26, pp. 11)
Pub: Crain Communications, Inc.

Ed: Jack Neff. **Description:** Overview of Unilever's chief marketing officer Simon Clift's strategy for promoting its products; now that the company has restructured, Clift is able to focus all of his energy on the challenges of the new-media climate that marketers are having to face.

25255 ■ *"United Insurance To Grow St. Pete's*
Corporate Base" in The Business
Journal-Serving Greater Tampa Bay (August
29, 2008)
Pub: American City Business Journals, Inc.

Ed: Margie Manning. **Description:** United Insurance Holdings LC is on its way to becoming a public company by agreeing in a reverse merger with FMG Acquisition Corp. The $104.3 million agreement will provide the company's St. Petersburg operations the opportunity to grow. The other impacts of the proposed reverse merger are examined.

25256 ■ *"U.S. Retailer Eyes 'Tween' Market"*
in Globe & Mail (January 30, 2007, pp. B1)
Pub: CTVglobemedia Publishing Inc.

Ed: Marina Strauss. **Description:** The decision of Tween Brands Inc. (Too Incorporated) to open 100 new stores in Canada as part of its expansion is discussed. The company's focus on targeting girls for its products is detailed.

25257 ■ *"The Urge to Converge" in Canadian*
Business (Vol. 79, October 9, 2006, No. 20,
pp. 41)
Pub: Rogers Media

Ed: Andy Holloway. **Description:** Arthur Griffiths, chief executive officer of Infotec Business Systems Inc., decision to diversify into broad brand business is discussed.

25258 ■ *"Virgin Mobile has Big Plans for Year*
Two" in Globe & Mail (March 6, 2006, pp. B5)
Pub: CTVglobemedia Publishing Inc.

Ed: Catherine McLean. **Description:** The business growth plans of Virgin Mobile Canada are presented.

25259 ■ *"Wal-Mart Relaunches Private Brand,*
Reimagines Stores Layout" in Marketing to

Women (Vol. 22, July 2009, No. 7, pp. 5)
Pub: EPM Communications Inc.
Contact: Ira Mayer, President
E-mail: imayer@epmcom.com

Description: Wal-Mart is focusing its strategies by centering on new store layouts that they believe will match their new branding of 'fast, friendly, and clean' and enable mothers to 'just get on with what they need to do.'.

25260 ■ *"Walker Seeks More Business*
Participation" in Business Journal-Milwaukee
(Vol. 28, December 10, 2010, No. 10, pp. A1)
Pub: Milwaukee Business Journal

Ed: Rich Kirchen. **Description:** Wisconsin governor Scott Walker is seeking the aid of Milwaukee business leaders to participate in resolving the challenges posed by the economic crisis. Walker is aiming to create 250,000 jobs. He is also planning to call a special session of the legislature to enact strategies to jumpstart the economy.

25261 ■ *"Welcome to the Neighborhood" in*
Hawaii Business (Vol. 53, October 2007, No.
4, pp. 48)
Pub: Hawaii Business Publishing

Ed: Jolyn Okimoto Rosa. **Description:** Finance Factors is planning to build branches in Manoa, and Liliha, as part of its strategy to position itself in high-yield areas. The company chose Manoa and Liliha due to thee sites' rich deposits. Its strategy with regards to the branches' location and to the building design is discussed.

25262 ■ *"Wendy's Mulls Total Hortons*
Selloff" in Globe & Mail (January 7, 2006, pp.
B5)
Pub: CTVglobemedia Publishing Inc.

Ed: Sinclair Stewart; Omar El Akkad. **Description:** The plans of Wendy's International Inc. to spin off Tim Hortons are presented.

25263 ■ *"WestJet Ponders Growth Plan*
Following Record Profit" in Globe & Mail
(February 15, 2007, pp. B15)
Pub: CTVglobemedia Publishing Inc.

Ed: Brent Jang. **Description:** The Calgary-based WestJet Airlines Ltd., which reported a record $114.7 million profit last year, is planning to expand its operations by 2010. The airline is planning new services and carriers.

25264 ■ *"Weyerhaeuser's REIT Decision*
Shouldn't Scare Investors Away" in Barron's
(Vol. 88, June 30, 2008, No. 26, pp. 18)
Pub: Dow Jones & Co., Inc.

Ed: Christopher Williams. **Description:** Weyerhaeuser Co.'s management said that a conversion to a real estate investment trust was not likely in 2009 since the move is not tax-efficient as of the moment and would overload its non-timber assets with debt. The company's shares have fallen by 19.5 percent. However, the company remains an asset-rich outfit and its activist shareholder is pushing for change.

25265 ■ *"What Are You Doing Differently?" in*
Agency Sales Magazine (Vol. 39, December
2009, No. 11, pp. 3)
Pub: MANA

Ed: Bryan C. Shirley. **Description:** Strategies that sales representatives can do to plan for a good year include professional development, networking with other reps, and making more sales calls and seeing more people. The end of the year is the perfect time for reps to write or re-write their mission statement and to conduct line profitability.

25266 ■ *"What Players in the Midmarket Are*
Talking About" in Mergers & Acquisitions:
The Dealmaker's Journal (March 1, 2008)
Pub: SourceMedia, Inc.

Description: Sports Properties Acquisition Corp. went public at the end of January; according to the company's prospectus, it is not limiting its focus to just teams, it is also considering deals for stadium construction companies, sports leagues, facilities, sports-related advertising and licensing of products, in addition to other related segments.

25267 ■ *"What's Cooking?" in Entrepreneur*
(Vol. 36, April 2008, No. 4, pp. 98)
Pub: Entrepreneur Media, Inc.

Ed: Eileen Figure Sandlin. **Description:** Unique and unusual restaurants have the potential to attract customers and provide them with fresh menu options. Outlining goals, strategies and details on proposed concept and target market can also help in restaurant planning. Other tips on how to plan launching your own restaurant are provided.

25268 ■ *"Why Intel Should Dump Its*
Flash-Memory Business" in Barron's (Vol. 88,
March 10, 2008, No. 10, pp. 35)
Pub: Dow Jones & Company, Inc.

Ed: Eric J. Savitz. **Description:** Intel Corp. must sell its NAND flash-memory business as soon as it possibly can to the highest bidder to focus on its PC processor business and take advantage of other business opportunities. Apple should consider a buyback of 10 percent of the company's shares to lift its stock.

25269 ■ *"Winning Gold" in The Business*
Journal-Milwaukee (Vol. 25, August 8, 2008,
No. 46, pp. A1)
Pub: American City Business Journals, Inc.

Ed: Rich Rovito. **Description:** Johnson Controls Inc. of Milwaukee, Wisconsin is taking part in the 2008 Beijing Olympics with the installation of its sustainable control equipment and technology that monitor over 58,000 points in 18 Olympic venues. Details of Johnson Controls' green products and sustainable operations in China are discussed.

25270 ■ *"Worth His Salt" in Hawaii Business*
(Vol. 53, January 2008, No. 7, pp. 45)
Pub: Hawaii Business Publishing

Ed: Jolyn Okimoto Rosa. **Description:** Bryan Zada owns three PretzelMaker franchises, whose total loss amounted to $40,000 in 2003. Zada believes that listening to employees was one of the key steps in turning the business around. The efforts made to improve the franchises' products are also given.

25271 ■ *"A Year After Fiorina's Exit, Hurd*
Makes His Mark" in Globe & Mail (February 8,
2006, pp. B9)
Pub CTVglobemedia Publishing Inc.

Ed: Shawn McCarthy. **Description:** The business growth strategies of chief executive officer Mark Hurd of Hewlett-Packard Co. are presented.

25272 ■ *"Your Annual Business Tune-Up" in*
Business Week (December 28, 2006)
Pub McGraw-Hill Companies

Ed: Karen E. Klein. **Description:** Interview with entrepreneurial expert, Ty Freyvogel, founder of EntrpreneursLab.com. Freyvogel gives tips on how a thorough review of existing systems, vendors, customers, and employees could help keep an entrepreneur's business not only safe but highly successful in the upcoming year.

25273 ■ *"Zell Takes a Gamble on Tribune" in*
Globe & Mail (April 3, 2007, pp. B1)
Pub: CTVglobemedia Publishing Inc.

Ed: Sinclair Stewart. **Description:** The purchase of the majority share in Tribune Co. by Samuel Zell is described. Samuel Zell's plans to keep the company's assets intact are discussed.

25274 ■ *"Zucker's HBC Shakeup Imminent" in*
Globe & Mail (February 20, 2006, pp. B3)
Pub: CTVglobemedia Publishing Inc.

Ed: Marina Strauss. **Description:** The plans of investor Jerry Zucker to revamp Hudson's Bay Co., upon its acquisition, are presented.

VIDEOCASSETTES/ AUDIOCASSETTES

25275 ■ *Goal Setting*
1st Financial Training Services
1515 E. Woodfield Rd., Ste. 345
Schaumburg, IL 60173
Ph: (847)969-0900
Free 800-442-8662

Fax: (847)969-0521
URL: http://www.1stfinancialtraining.com
Released: 1987. **Price:** $150.00. **Description:** The importance of goals is discussed as well as types of goals, and characteristics of effective goals. **Availability:** VHS; 3/4 U.

25276 ■ Goals and Objectives
1st Financial Training Services
1515 E. Woodfield Rd., Ste. 345
Schaumburg, IL 60173
Ph: (847)969-0900
Free: 800-442-8662
Fax: (847)969-0521
URL: http://www.1stfinancialtraining.com
Released: 1987. **Price:** $150.00. **Description:** Supervisors are the ones who have to tell the workers just what it is exactly that the top brass wants from them. **Availability:** VHS; 3/4 U.

25277 ■ Goals: Setting and Achieving Them on Schedule
Cambridge Educational
c/o Films Media Group
132 West 31st Street, 17th Floor
Ste. 124
New York, NY 10001
Free: 800-257-5126
Fax: (609)671-0266
Co. E-mail: custserve@films.com
URL: http://www.cambridgeol.com
Released: 1986. **Price:** $49.95. **Description:** Setting realistic goals is one way for a person to get ahead, in either business or school. Ziglar shows you how. **Availability:** VHS.

25278 ■ Make More Money by Setting Goals/Rick Barrera
Instructional Video
2219 C St.
Lincoln, NE 68502
Ph: (402)475-6570
Free: 800-228-0164
Fax: (402)475-6500
Co. E-mail: feedback@insvideo.com
URL: http://www.insvideo.com
Released: 19??. **Price:** $95.00. **Description:** Rick Barrera offers his program developing the proper goals to increase business and income. Available only in the U.S. **Availability:** VHS.

CONSULTANTS

25279 ■ Adventure Learning Associates Inc.
567 Hale Rd.
Brattleboro, VT 05302
Ph: (802)254-6160
Free: 800-551-3210
Fax: (802)254-3852
Co. E-mail: info@alrna.com
URL: http://www.alrna.com
Contact: Paul A. Kidder, Owner Founder
E-mail: paul@alrna.com
Scope: Provider of consulting services and training in experiential training and development. Specifically provides team building, communications skills and empowerment skill sessions. Also focuses on needs analysis, strategic planning and visioning for newly developing groups. Firm specializes in training trainers in experiential outdoor programming. Industries served: all including government and can work with intact groups at all levels from line staff to boards and executive committees. **Founded:** 1990. **Seminars:** Train the Adventure Trainer.

25280 ■ Persephone C. Agrafiotis
302 N Bay St.
Manchester, NH 03104-2324
Ph: (603)625-8446
Fax: (603)625-8446
Co. E-mail: pagrafiotis@comcast.net
Contact: Persephone C. Agrafiotis, Manager
Scope: Provider of Record Review and Medical Expert Witness for Medical Legal cases in Medical Case Review, Nursing, Health Administration, Gerontology, Pediatrics and other clinical areas. Offers Health Care Management Consultation in Home Care, Long Term Care and General Management.

Provides expertise in Preferred Provider Contracting Negotiations, Accrediting Processed to include JCAHO, Operations Review, Operations Auditing, Strategic Planning, Business Ethics Review and Implementation. Policy and Procedure, Strategies for the Future Planning, Review/Revision/Implementation, and Educational Programming. Industries Served: health care, human services, government and educational institutions. **Founded:** 1979. **Publications:** "In service Education and Training"; "The American Journal of Nursing"; "An Analysis of the Curriculum of Moral Education of Baccalaureate Nursing Students in New England". **Seminars:** Organizational Development; Group Dynamics; Leadership; Motivation; Assertiveness and Change; Performance Appraisals; Principles of Management; Marketing Educational Programs; Rag Quilt Technique; Quilting 101; Sewing 101; Sampler Quilt Hand Pieced; UFO (Unfinished Object) Finishing; Individualized Project; Learn to Knit and/or Crochet.

25281 ■ Ameriwest Business Consultants Inc. (ABCI)
3725 E Wade Ln.
Colorado Springs, CO 80917-5852
Ph: (719)380-7096
Fax: (719)380-7096
Co. E-mail: email@abchelp.com
URL: http://www.abchelp.com
Contact: Rodd Brechtl, President
E-mail: rodb@abchelp.com
Scope: Specializes in assisting start up businesses and those with sales of 5million dollars or less and those who have 50 employees or less. Services and products offered include written business plans; do it yourself business plan kits; business valuations; do it yourself business start up kits; written loan packages; do it yourself loan packaging guides; business analysis; do it yourself financial projections software; do it yourself complete financial analysis; website development assistance; general consulting. **Founded:** 1991.

25282 ■ Blue Garnet Associates L.L.C.
8055 W Manchester Ave., Ste. 430
Los Angeles, CA 90293
Ph: (310)439-1930
Fax: (310)388-1657
URL: http://www.bluegarnet.net
Contact: Amanda Green, Principal
Scope: Provides expertise in organizational visioning, strategic and business planning, market opportunity and growth strategy, impact assessment, and leadership and governance. **Founded:** 2002.

25283 ■ BroadVision Inc.
1600 Seaport Blvd., Ste. 550, North Bldg.
Redwood City, CA 94063-5589
Ph: (650)295-0716
Free: 866-287-6669
Fax: (650)364-3425
Co. E-mail: info@broadvision.com
URL: http://www.broadvision.com
Contact: Dr. Pehong Chen, President
Scope: Firm delivers a combination of technologies and services in to the global market that enable its customers to power mission-critical web initiatives that ultimately deliver high-value to their bottom line. Areas of expertise include strategic services, interactive services, content and creative services and client services. Services include business planning, application strategy, ROI analysis, organization and business process consulting, building and deploying applications, content management, sourcing and workflow processes. **Founded:** 1993. **Publications:** *One-to-One Enterprise*; *One-to-One Knowledge*; *One-to-One Financial*; *One-to-One Retail Commerce*; *One-to-One Business Commerce*; *One-To-One Command Center*; *One-To-One Publishing Center*; *One-To-One Design Center*; *Onte-To-One Instant Publisher*; *One-To-One Billing*; *Retail Commerce Suite*; *MarketMaker*.

25284 ■ Flor & Associates
179 Schan Dr.
Churchville, PA 18966-1619
Ph: (215)355-7466

Fax: (215)355-7464
Co. E-mail: fredflor@msn.com
Contact: Frederick Flor, President
Scope: Offers business development consulting helping companies increase the value of their businesses. Services include: market development for technologies sand products; product positioning strategies; technology assessment; competitive intelligence and analysis; team augmentation and facilitation; business growth strategies including acquisitions, licensing, and partnerships.

25285 ■ Claude Hayes & Associates
9259 Hunterboro Dr.
Brentwood, TN 37027-6118
Ph: (615)370-8106
Fax: (615)370-8106
Contact: Claude W. Hayes, Jr., Owner
Scope: Provides services in the areas of turnarounds, reengineering, restructuring, reorganization, startups, high profile growth, acquisitions, divestitures, due diligence, strategic/business (marketing/sales) plans, inventory control and management, cost pricing and control, market management, demand forecasting. **Founded:** 1994.

25286 ■ Jarlett Consulting
3634 Tierra De Dios
Escondido, CA 92025
Ph: (760)745-1090
Contact: Frank E. Jarlett, President
Scope: Offers a comprehensive, integrated approach to successfully managing the future by understanding trends, setting goals, evaluating options, planning and managing. Includes analysis of global, national, state and local trends on technological, social, political and management issues. Provides products and services that meet future business goals, management of research and development, evaluating customers and competition, and writing winning proposals. **Founded:** 1984. **Publications:** "Making the Right Choices of Future Change and Growth".

25287 ■ J.B. Geller Consulting Inc.
9 Ridgedale Ln.
West Dennis, MA 02670-2545
Ph: (508)760-0044
Fax: (508)943-4122
Co. E-mail: jbgeller@capecod.net
Contact: Judith B. Geller, President
E-mail: jbgeller@attbi.com
Scope: A full service human resources consulting firm whose purpose is to empower leaders, managers and employees to welcome changes created by internal and external forces such as employment laws, mergers, acquisition, re-engineering, change in management, etc. Specific services include: management development, organizational development, visioning, personnel policy development and communication, recruitment, employee relations, team building, and career development. Industries served: Financial services, manufacturing, high-tech, health care, retail services, and government agencies. **Founded:** 1988. **Publications:** "Making Diversity Work"; "A Managers Guide to Human Behavior," American Management Association, 1994; "How to Comply with the Americans with Disabilities Act," American Management Association, 1992. **Seminars:** Visioning for Leaders: How to create and communicate a vision, purpose admission; Training Needs Assessment; How to Conduct Focus Groups; Interviewing Skills for Supervisors; Employment Laws for Supervisors; Disability Awareness Training; Prevention of Sexual Harassment; How to Comply with the Americans with Disabilities Act; Fearless Firing; Performance Management; How to Write Effective Job Descriptions; Diversity in the Workplace; Disability Awareness.

25288 ■ Lippert/Heilshorn and Associates Inc.
800 3rd Ave., 17th Fl.
New York, NY 10022-7649
Ph: (212)838-3777
Fax: (212)838-4568
Co. E-mail: keith@lhai.com
Contact: Jeffrey S. Hart, Director
Scope: An independent investor relations firm creating and supporting practices investor and media relations programs. Focuses on the development of

public company identity and the communication of strategic vision. Strategic investor relations counsel provides companies with a tactical plan that integrates finance, communication, marketing, and securities law compliance. Corporate communications capabilities include handling situations; develops and executing media programs specially tailored to clients' needs, opportunities, and corporate objectives. Message positioning, counsel and press outreach are designed to help attain strategic IR goals. **Founded:** 1984. **Seminars:** CME-accredited, UDMNJ Robert Wood Johnson School of Medicine May, 2011.

25289 ■ ReCourses Inc.
6101 Stillmeadow Dr.
Nashville, TN 37211-6518
Ph: (615)831-2277
Free: 888-476-5884
Fax: (615)831-2212
Co. E-mail: info@recourses.com
URL: http://www.recourses.com
Contact: Julie Warren, Manager
Scope: A management consulting firm that works exclusively with small service providers in the communications industry, including public relations firms, advertising agencies, interactive companies and design studios. Services include Total Business Review, a complete examination of your business starting with an on site examination or discussion, followed by written recommendations and then supplemented with six months of implementation guidance. Areas reviewed include positioning, marketing, management, personnel, structure, finance, retirement, technology and specific growth issues. **Founded:** 1994. **Publications:** "Managing (Right) for the First Time"; "Financial Management of a Marketing Firm". **Seminars:** 10th Annual New Business Summit , Jan, 2013; Event - TEDx Nashville: Success from the Inside Out--Alignment & Engagement , Apr, 20163; Event - AIGA Brand Academy (Emory Executive Education @ Goizueta Business School) , Apr, 2013; Measuring Economic Performance Measuring and Enhancing Performance in a Marketing Firm, Dec, 2012; Managing Client Relationships: Being Indispensable, Growing the Account, Making Money, Nov, 2012; The Business of Design Oct, 2012; Getting a Good Start in Your Creative Career, Nov, 2011; Research and Insights, Nov, 2011; Managing Client Relationships; Research and Strategy; Financial Management: Measuring and Enhancing Performance in a Marketing Firm, Sep, 2009; Building and Leading a Staff: The When, How, and What of Growth and Culture, Sep, 2009; Doing Effective Work: Adding Significance to the Strategic Portion of Your Work for Clients, Sep, 2009; Resourcing the Creative Process: Managing Pricing, Deadlines, Budgets, Quality, and Capacity, Apr, 2009. **Special Services:** ReCourses®.

LIBRARIES

25290 ■ University of South Carolina - The Moore School of Business - Elliot White Springs Business Library
Francis M. Hipp Bldg., 2nd Fl.
1705 College St.
Columbia, SC 29208
Ph: (803)777-6032
Fax: (803)777-6876
Co. E-mail: gardnerd@mailbox.sc.edu
URL: http://library.sc.edu/business/index.html
Contact: Kathy Snediker
Scope: Corporations. **Services:** Interlibrary loan; copying; Library open to the public with restrictions. **Founded:** 1973. **Holdings:** 30,000 books; 4000 bound periodical volumes. **Subscriptions:** 350 journals and other serials; 5 newspapers. **Telecommunication Services:** busref@mailbox.sc.edu.

ASSOCIATIONS AND OTHER ORGANIZATIONS

25291 ■ **Institute of Certified Business Counselors (ICBC)**
18831 Willamette Dr.
West Linn, OR 97068
Free: 877-422-2674
Fax: (503)635-1340
Co. E-mail: membership@i-cbc.org
URL: http://www.i-cbc.org
Description: Bankers, consultants, accountants, attorneys, appraisers, merger and acquisition specialists, estate planners, financial consultants and business brokers active in the continuation, evaluation, financing, or marketing of privately-held businesses. Offers training and advice on how to buy or sell a business, including information on what to look for in a prospective deal. Maintains speakers' bureau. **Founded:** 1975. **Publications:** *Directory of Certified Business Counselors* (Irregular); *The Certified Business Counselor* (Bimonthly); *CBC Roster* (Annual).

REFERENCE WORKS

25292 ■ *"Analysts: More Mergers for the Region's Hospitals" in Boston Business Journal (Vol. 30, October 15, 2010, No. 36, pp. 1)*
Pub: Boston Business Journal
Ed: Julie M. Donnelly. **Description:** A number of hospitals in Boston, Massachusetts are engaging in mergers and acquisitions. Caritas Christi Health Care is set to be purchased by Cerberus Capital Management. The U.S. healthcare reform law is seen to drive the development.

25293 ■ *"Are You Looking for an Environmentally Friendly Dry Cleaner?" in Inc. (Vol. 30, December 2008, No. 12, pp. 34)*
Pub: Mansueto Ventures LLC
Ed: Shivani Vora. **Description:** Greenopia rates the greenness of 52 various kinds of businesses, including restaurants, nail salons, dry cleaners, and clothing stores. The guidebooks are sold through various retailers including Barnes & Noble and Amazon.com.

25294 ■ *"Ask Inc." in Inc. (November 2007, pp. 70)*
Pub: Gruner & Jahr USA Publishing
Description: Advice is given for any entrepreneur considering the sale of a company.

25295 ■ *"Austin Energy May Build $2.3B Biomass Plant" in Austin Business JournalInc. (Vol. 28, July 25, 2008, No. 19, pp. A1)*
Pub: American City Business Journals
Ed: Kate Harrington. **Description:** An approval from the Austin City Council is being sought by Austin Energy for a 20-year supply contract with Nacogdoches Power LLC to build a $2.3 billion biomass plant

in East Texas. The 100-megawatt biomass plant, which is to run on waste wood, will have Austin Energy as its sole buyer.

25296 ■ *"Black On Black Business: Moorehead Buys Hank Aaron's Toyota Dealership" in Black Enterprise (Vol. 38, February 2008, No. 7, pp. 28)*
Pub: Earl G. Graves Publishing Co. Inc.
Ed: Brenda Porter. **Description:** In a move to expand his automotive business, Thomas A. Moorehead, CEO of BMW/MINI of Sterling, Georgia bought Hank Aaron's Toyota automobile dealership in McDonough, Georgia. Moorehead stated that he will call the new store Toyota of McDonough.

25297 ■ *Building a Dream: A Canadian Guide to Starting Your Own Business*
Pub: McGraw-Hill Ryerson Ltd.
Ed: Walter S. Good. **Released:** 2005. **Description:** Topics covered include evaluating business potential, new business ideas, starting or buying a business, franchise opportunities, business organization, protecting an idea, arranging financing, and developing a business plan.

25298 ■ *Buying and Selling a Business*
Pub: Entrepreneur Press
Ed: Ira Nottonson. **Released:** April 2008. **Price:** $32.95. **Description:** Tips for negotiating sales are presented. Attorney, Ira Nottonson presents both sides of negotiations by presenting the both buyer's and seller's perspectives. Critical steps in the sale process, including presentation, negotiation and documentations are discussed. The book teaches how to gain the upper hand, minimize financial risk and be a winner regardless of side.

25299 ■ *"Calista Sells Rural Newspapers" in Alaska Business Monthly (Vol. 27, October 2011, No. 10, pp. 8)*
Pub: Alaska Business Publishing Company
Ed: Nancy Pounds. **Description:** Calista sold its six newspapers, a magazine, shoppers and its printing house. Details of the sales are given.

25300 ■ *"CanWest Plotting Buyback of Newspaper Income Trust" in Globe & Mail (February 7, 2007, pp. B1)*
Pub: CTVglobemedia Publishing Inc.
Ed: Sinclair Stewart; Boyd Erman; Grant Robertson. **Description:** The CanWest Global Communications Corp.'s decision to sell its media assets in Australia and New Zealand in order to finance its plans of repurchasing its newspaper income trust CanWest MediaWorks Income Fund is discussed.

25301 ■ *"Capital Position" in Business Journal-Milwaukee (Vol. 28, December 24, 2010, No. 12, pp. A1)*
Pub: Milwaukee Business Journal
Ed: Rich Kirchen. **Description:** Canada-based BMO Financial Group has purchased Marshall and Isley Corporation (M and I), which dominated lending among Wisconsin businesses for decades. The sale

of M and I will enable other banks to recruit M and I's customers but BMO Financial remains a stronger competitor since it possesses a more potent capital position.

25302 ■ *"CGB Purchases Illinois Grain-Fertilizer Firm" in Farm Industry News (December 2, 2011)*
Pub: Penton Business Media Inc.
Description: CGB Enterprises Inc. bought Twomey Company's grain and fertilizer assets. The purchase includes eight locations and a barge loading terminal near Gladstone, Illinois and storage capacity of 51 million bushels and 18,000 tons of liquid fertilizer.

25303 ■ *"Competitive Restaurant Scene Lures Buyers to Saratoga Springs" in Business Review, Albany New York (Vol. 34, October 26, 2007)*
Pub: American City Business Journals, Inc.
Ed: Robin K. Cooper. **Description:** Restaurant industry in Saratoga Springs, New York, a competitive market, with the city having 102 licensed restaurants and 28,499 residents in 2006. Buyers tend to acquire restaurants in Saratoga Springs, New York due to its good market condition. Examples of restaurant acquisitions in Saratoga Springs are given.

25304 ■ *The Complete Guide to Buying a Business*
Pub: NOLO
Ed: Fred S. Steingold. **Released:** November 2007. **Price:** $24.99. **Description:** Key steps in buying a business are highlighted, focusing on legal issues, tax considerations, approaches for valuing a business, financing, structuring the deal, along with forms and documents for taking ownership are included.

25305 ■ *The Complete Guide to Selling a Business*
Pub: NOLO
Ed: Fred S. Steingold. **Released:** November 2007. **Price:** $34.99. **Description:** When selling a business it is critical that a sales agreement covers all key concerns from price and payment terms to liability protection and restrictions on future competition.

25306 ■ *"A Counter Offer" in Inc. (February 2008, pp.)*
Pub: Gruner & Jahr USA Publishing
Ed: Elaine Appleton Grant. **Description:** Online retailer offering a line of kitchen and home products has upgraded its Website in order to make the business more attractive to possible buyers of the company. The firm is asking $9.9 million and reported gross revenue of $12.7 in 2007. The owner suggests that a buyer add product lines geared towards more rooms of the home than currently offer on the retail site.

25307 ■ *"The Data Drivers" in Canadian Business (Vol. 81, September 15, 2008, No. 14-15, pp. 1)*
Pub: Rogers Media Ltd.
Ed: Andrew Wahl. **Description:** Canadian regulators hope that an auction of telecommunications companies will inject more competition into the industry;

however, newcomers may not be able to rely on lower prices in order to gain market share from the three major telecommunications companies that already have a stronghold on the market. Analysts feel that providing additional data service is the key to surviving market disruptions.

25308 ■ "Dow AgroSciences Buys Wheat Breeding Firm in Pacific Northwest" in Farm Industry News (July 29, 2011)
Pub: Penton Business Media Inc.

Description: Dow AgroSciences purchased Northwest Plant Breeding Company, a cereals breeding station in Washington in 2011. The acquisition will help Dow expand its Hyland Seeds certified wheat seed program foundation in the Pacific Northwest. Financial terms of the deal were not disclosed.

25309 ■ "Downtown Bank Got High Marks for Irwin Purchase, Is Looking For More" in Business Courier (Vol. 27, September 3, 2010, No. 18, pp. 1)
Pub: Business Courier

Ed: Steve Watkins. Description: First Financial Bancorp is looking to acquire more troubled banks following its purchase of Irwin Union Bank. The bank has reported a $383 million bargain purchase gain during the third quarter of 2009.

25310 ■ "Facebook Purchased Push Pop Press" in Information Today (Vol. 28, October 2011, No. 9, pp. 12)
Pub: Information Today, Inc.

Description: Facebook purchased Push Pop Press, a digital publishing company that developed a multi-touch interface for ebook publishing on the iPad.

25311 ■ "First Financial Aiming for Banking Big Leagues" in Business Courier (Vol. 26, December 4, 2009, No. 32, pp. 1)
Pub: American City Business Journals, Inc.

Ed: Steve Watkins. Description: First Financial Bancorp could dominate the community banking market of Greater Cincinnati after buying failed banks with the supervision of the FDIC. Details of the transactions are presented.

25312 ■ "First U.S. :M-Press Tiger with Inline Screen Printing" in American Printer (Vol. 128, June 1, 2011, No. 6)
Pub: Penton Media Inc.

Description: Graphic Tech located in California bought :M-Press Tiger, the first in North America with an inline screen printing unit.

25313 ■ "FIS-Metavante Deal Paying Off for Many" in Business Journal-Milwaukee (Vol. 28, December 17, 2010, No. 11, pp. A1)
Pub: Milwaukee Business Journal

Ed: Rich Kirchen. Description: Jacksonville, Florida-based Fidelity National Information Services Inc., also known as FIS, has remained committed to Milwaukee, Wisconsin more than a year after purchasing Metavante Technologies Inc. FIS has transferred several operations into metropolitan Milwaukee and has continued its contribution to charitable organizations in the area.

25314 ■ "Follow the ABCs of Buying a Business" in Women Entrepreneur (September 10, 2008)
Pub: Entrepreneur Media Inc.

Ed: Nina Kaufman. Description: Buying a business will likely result in the largest single asset one will ever own. A list of steps one can take in order to educate and protect themselves is provided.

25315 ■ "For Hospitals, a Dating Game" in Business Courier (Vol. 26, December 4, 2009, No. 32, pp. 1)
Pub: American City Business Journals, Inc.

Ed: James Ritchie. Description: Drake Center, Fort Hamilton Hospital, and West Chester Medical Center are among the members of Cincinnati's Health Alliance looking for potential buyers or partners. Meanwhile, Jewish Hospital, another member of the Alliance, will be bought by Mercy Health Partners by January 7, 2010.

25316 ■ "For the Seasoned Buyer" in Inc. (Vol. 30, November 2008, No. 11, pp. 32)
Pub: Mansueto Ventures LLC

Ed: Darren Dahl. Description: Dominick Fimiano shares his plans to sell his ten-year-old business that manufactures and sells frozen pizza dough and crusts as well as a variety of topped pizzas. Products are purchased by schools, hospitals, bowling alleys and amusement parks. The business sale includes the buyer's taking on Fimiano's son the firm's most senior employee.

25317 ■ "Former Gov. Fletcher Starts Blue Ash Firm" in Business Courier (Vol. 26, October 9, 2009, No. 24, pp. 1)
Pub: American City Business Journals, Inc.

Ed: Lucy May. Description: Former Kentucky Governor Ernie Fletcher partnered with Belcan Corporation founder Ralph Anderson to purchase Blue Ash, Ohio-based Virtual Medical Network and form Alton Healthcare LLC. The company's goal is to increase practice revenues by adapting technology to reinvent clinical practices and deliver best possible care to more patients.

25318 ■ "The Furniture Company Wanted to Sell Him Its Buildings-And Close Down. Should He Buy the Company, Too?" in Inc. (November 2007)
Pub: Gruner & Jahr USA Publishing

Ed: Alex Salkever. Description: Rick Detkowski, real estate investor, discusses his decision to purchase the furniture company housed in the buildings he was interested in buying. The property would have cost him between $500,000 to $1 million, he was able to purchase the property and business with its entire inventory of furniture, vehicles, and machinery for $1.8 million.

25319 ■ "'Green' Cleaner Buys Local Firm" in Puget Sound Business Journal (Vol. 29, December 19, 2008, No. 35, pp. 3)
Pub: American City Business Journals

Ed: Greg Lamm. Description: Washington-based Blue Sky Cleaners has purchased Four Seasons Cleaners. The green company also purchased Queen Anne store and Four Seasons' routes fro Snohomish County through Seattle.

25320 ■ "Harleysville Eyes Growth After Nationwide Deal" in Philadelphia Business Journal (Vol. 30, October 7, 2011, No. 34, pp. 1)
Pub: American City Business Journals Inc.

Ed: Jeff Blumenthal. Description: Harleysville Group announced growth plans after the company was sold to Columbus, Ohio-based Nationwide Mutual Insurance Company for about $1.63 billion. Nationwide gained an independent agency platform in 32 states with the Harleysville deal.

25321 ■ "Hedge-Fund Titan Cohen Plans Bid for Dodgers" in Wall Street Journal Eastern Edition (November 25 , 2011, pp. C3)
Pub: Dow Jones & Company Inc. Enterprise Media Group

Contact: Clare Hart, President

Ed: Matthew Futterman, Gregory Zuckerman. Description: Steven A. Cohen, the founder and head of hedge-fund SAC Capital Advisors LLC is looking to make an offer at the bankruptcy auction for the financially-troubled Los Angeles Dodgers baseball team.

25322 ■ "Higher Thread Count for Metropole" in Business Courier (Vol. 26, September 25, 2009, No. 22, pp. 1)
Pub: American City Business Journals, Inc.

Ed: Lisa Biank Fasig, Lucy May. Description: Cincinnati Center City Development Corporation is under contract to buy the 225-unit apartment building called Metropole Apartments and 21c Museum Hotel is the lead candidate for the space. Advocates of some residents of the low-income rental complex complain that this move could leave them homeless.

25323 ■ How to Buy and/or Sell a Small Business for Maximum Profit: A Step-by-Step Guide
Pub: Atlantic Publishing Company

Ed: Rene V. Richards. Released: January 2006. Price: $24.95. Description: Suggestions, insights and techniques for buying and selling small businesses, includes advice on when to buy or sell, how to market the business, explanation of legal and financial documents involved in the sale and closing of a deal.

25324 ■ "Intel to Buy McAfee Security Business for 768B" in eWeek (August 19, 2010)
Pub: Ziff Davis Enterprise

Description: Intel will acquire security giant McAfee for approximately $7.68 billion, whereby McAfee would become a wholly owned subsidiary of Intel and would report to Intel's Software and Services Group.

25325 ■ Let's Buy a Company: How to Accelerate Growth Through Acquisitions
Pub: Career Press, Incorporated

Ed: H. Lee Rust. Released: January 2006. Price: $13.99 (US), $25.95 (Canadian). Description: Advice for negotiating terms and pricing as well as other aspects of mergers and acquisitions in small companies.

25326 ■ "Local Firm Snaps up 91 Area Pizza Huts" in Orlando Business Journal (Vol. 26, January 8, 2010, No. 32, pp. 1)
Pub: American City Business Journals

Ed: Alexis Muellner, Anjali Fluker. Description: Orlando, Florida-based CFL Pizza LLC bought the 91 Orlando-area Pizza Hut restaurants for $35 million from parent company Yum! Brands Inc. CFL Pizza plans to distribute parts of the business to Central Florida vendors and the first business up for grabs is the advertising budget.

25327 ■ "M&I Execs May Get Golden Parachutes" in Business Journal-Milwaukee (Vol. 28, December 31, 2010, No. 14, pp. A3)
Pub: Milwaukee Business Journal

Ed: Rich Kirchen. Description: Marshall and Isley Corporation's top executives have a chance to receive golden-parachute payments it its buyer, BMO Financial Group, repays the Troubled Asset Relief Program (TARP) loan on behalf of the company. One TARP rule prevents golden-parachute payments to them and the next five most highly paid employees of TARP recipients.

25328 ■ Mergers and Acquisitions from A to Z
Pub: Amacom

Ed Andrew J. Sherman, Milledge A. Hart. Released: January 2006. Price: $35.00. Description: Guide for the entire process of mergers and acquisitions, including taxes, accounting, laws, and projected financial gain.

25329 ■ "Monsanto Acquires Targeted-Pest Control Technology Start-Up; Terms Not Disclosed" in Benzinga.com (, 2011)
Pub: Benzinga.com

Ed: Benzinga Staff. Description: Monsanto Company acquired Beelogics, a firm that researches and develops biological tools that control pests and diseases. Research includes a product that will help protect bee health.

25330 ■ "Murdock Carrousel Sold" in Charlotte Observer (January 31, 2007)
Pub: Knight-Ridder/Tribune Business News

Ed: Bob Fliss. Description: Details on the sale of the Murdock Carrousel shopping center are highlighted. The deal was reported at $281 million.

25331 ■ "The Next Chapter" in Business Courier (Vol. 26, November 20, 2009, No. 30, pp. 1)
Pub: American City Business Journals, Inc.

Ed: Lucy May. Description: Eric Browne and Mel Gravely purchased controlling interest in TriVersity Construction Group from CM-GC CEO Schuyler Murdoch and MBJ Consultants President Monroe Barnes. One third of the company was still owned by Cincinnati-based Messer and TriVersity and will continue to be a certified minority business enterprise.

25332 ■ *"P/Kaufmann Sells Bennettsville" in Home Textiles Today (Vol. 31, May 24, 2011, No. 13, pp. 6)*

Pub: Reed Business Information

Contact: Jeff Greisch, President

Description: Decorative Screen Printers purchased the printing and finishing facility of P/Kaufmann in Bennettsville, South Carolina. However, the firm will continue its focus on its core business, a vat printing facility for home furnishings fabrics.

25333 ■ *"Points of Light Sells MissionFish to eBay" in Non-Profit Times (Vol. 25, May 15, 2011, No. 7, pp. May 15, 2011)*

Pub: NPT Publishing Group Inc.

Contact: John McIlquham, President

Description: eBay purchased MissionFish, a subsidiary of Points of Light Institute for $4.5 million. MissionFish allows eBay sellers to give proceeds from sales to their favorite nonprofit organization and helps nonprofits raise funds by selling on eBay.

25334 ■ *"Portland's Hilton For Sale" in Business Journal Portland (Vol. 27, October 22, 2010, No. 34, pp. 1)*

Pub: Portland Business Journal

Ed: Wendy Culverwell. **Description:** Hilton Portland & Executive Tower, Portland's biggest hotel, is being sold by Cornerstone Real Estate Advisers LLC. Cornerstone hopes to close the deal for the 782-room complex by the end of 2010. Cornerstone contracted Jones Lang LaSalle to manage the sale, but terms to the deal are not available.

25335 ■ *"Ric Elis/Dan Feldstein" in Charlotte Business Journal (Vol. 25, December 31, 2010, No. 41, pp. 6)*

Pub: Charlotte Business Journal

Ed: Ken Elkins. **Description:** Charlotte, North Carolina-based Internet marketing firm Red Ventures has grown significantly. General Atlantic has purchased stakes in Red Ventures.

25336 ■ *"Rosewood Site Faces Big Cleanup" in Baltimore Business Journal (Vol. 27, February 6, 2010, No. 40, pp. 1)*

Pub: American City Business Journals

Ed: Daniel J. Sernovitz. **Description:** Environmental assessment report states that Maryland's Rosewood Center for the Developmentally Disabled has significant amounts of toxic chemicals, which could impact Stevenson University's decision to purchase the property. Senator Robert A. Zirkin believes that the state should pay for the cleanup, which is expected to cost millions.

25337 ■ *"RS Information Systems Signs Buyout Deal" in Black Enterprise (February 2008)*

Pub: Earl G. Graves Publishing Co. Inc.

Ed: Alan Hughes. **Description:** Details of the RS Information Systems buyout by Wyle, a privately held provider of high-tech aerospace engineering, testing, and research services.

25338 ■ *"Sale of Solo Cup Plant Pending" in Boston Business Journal (Vol. 29, June 17, 2011, No. 6, pp. 1)*

Pub: American City Business Journals Inc.

Ed: Daniel J. Sernovitz. **Description:** Baltimore developers Vanguard Equities Inc. and Greenberg Gibbons Commercial have contracted to buy the Solo Cup Company facility in Owing Mills and are now considering several plans for the property. Sale should be completed by September 2011 but no proposed sale terms are disclosed.

25339 ■ *"A Second Chance to Make a Living" in The Business Journal-Milwaukee (Vol. 25, September 19, 2008, No. 52, pp. A1)*

Pub: American City Business Journals, Inc.

Description: Unemployed workers and baby boomers are driving interest in purchasing small businesses. BizBuySell general manager Mike Handels-

man reveals that the supply of small businesses for sale is decreasing due to the increased demand. The trends in the small business market are analyzed.

25340 ■ *The Secret of Exiting Your Business Under Your Terms!*

Pub: Outskirts Press, Incorporated

Ed: Gene H. Irwin. **Released:** August 2005. **Price:** $29.95. **Description:** Topics include how to sell a business for the highest value, tax laws governing the sale of a business, finding the right buyer, mergers and acquisitions, negotiating the sale, and using a limited auction to increase future value of a business.

25341 ■ *Six SIGMA for Small Business*

Pub: Entrepreneur Press

Ed: Greg Brue. **Released:** October 2005. **Price:** $19.95 (US), $26.95 (Canadian). **Description:** Jack Welch's Six SIGMA approach to business covers accounting, finance, sales and marketing, buying a business, human resource development, and new product development.

25342 ■ *"Skype Ltd. Acquired GroupMe" in Information Today (Vol. 28, October 2011, No. 9, pp. 12)*

Pub: Information Today, Inc.

Description: Skype Ltd. acquired GroupMe, a group messaging company that allows users to form impromptu groups where they can text message, share data, and make conference calls for free and is supported on Android, iPhone, BlackBerry, and Windows phones.

25343 ■ *Small Business Desk Reference*

Pub: Penguin Books USA Inc.

Ed: Gene Marks. **Released:** December 2004. **Description:** Comprehensive guide for starting or running a successful small business, focusing on buying a business or franchise, writing a business plan, financial management, accounting, legal issues, human resources management, operations, marketing, sales, customer service, taxes, insurance, and ethics. Information for launching a restaurant, property management firm, retail outlet, consulting firm, and service business is included.

25344 ■ *"Start or Buy? It's a Tough Question for Eager Entrepreneurs" in Crain's Cleveland Business (Vol. 28, October 8, 2007, No. 40)*

Pub: Crain Communications, Inc.

Ed: David Prizinsky. **Description:** Discusses different approaches to becoming a small business owner.

25345 ■ *"Symantic Completes Acquisition of VeriSign's Security Business" in Internet Wire (August 9, 2010)*

Pub: Comtex

Description: Symantec Corporation acquired VeriSign's identity and authentication business, which includes Secure Sockets Layer (SSL) and Code Signing Certificate Services, the Managed Public Key Infrastructure (MPKI) Services, the VeriSign Trust Seal, the VeriSign Identity Protection (VIP) Authentication Service and the VIP Fraud Protection Service (FDS). The agreement also included a majority stake in VeriSign Japan.

25346 ■ *"Tektronix Buys Arbor Networks for Security Business" in eWeek (August 9, 2010)*

Pub: Ziff Davis Enterprise

Description: Tektronix Communications, provider of communications test and network intelligence solutions will acquire Arbor Networks. The deal will help Tektronix build a brand in security. Details of the transaction are included.

25347 ■ *"Today's Business Sale Climate" in Business Owner (Vol. 35, September-October 2011, No. 5, pp. 10)*

Pub: DL Perkins Company

Description: Despite the weak economy, there is a surplus of individuals wanting to purchase a small business. The Small Business Administration loan guarantees program helps with its loans for purchase/sale of business assistance.

25348 ■ *Ultimate Guide to Buying or Selling Your Business*

Pub: Entrepreneur Press

Ed: Ira N. Nottonson. **Released:** September 2004. **Price:** $24.95 (US), $35.95 (Canadian). **Description:** Proven strategies to evaluate, negotiate, and buy or sell a small business. Franchise and family business succession planning is included.

25349 ■ *"Unexpected Guest" in Business Journal-Milwaukee (Vol. 28, November 19, 2010, No. 7, pp. A1)*

Pub: Milwaukee Business Journal

Ed: Rich Rovito. **Description:** Caterpillar has agreed to purchase Bucyrus for $92 per share. The deal, which is subjected to a $200 million termination fee, is expected to close in mid-2011.

25350 ■ *"Vista-Based NCV Bought by Canteen Vending" in North County Times (October 18, 2011)*

Pub: Lee Enterprises Inc.

Ed: Pat Maio. **Description:** Details of North Carolina-based Canteen Vending Services' acquisition of NCV Refreshment Services, are given.

25351 ■ *"Welcome Back" in Canadian Business (Vol. 82, April 27, 2009, No. 7, pp. 25)*

Pub: Rogers Media

Ed: Sarka Halas. **Description:** Some Canadian companies such as Gennum Corporation have taken advantage of corporate sale-leasebacks to raise money at a time when credit is hard to acquire. Corporate sale-leasebacks allow companies to sell their property assets while remaining as tenants of the building. Sale-leasebacks allow firms to increase capital while avoiding the disruptions that may result with moving.

25352 ■ *"With New Listings, Business Brokers See Hope" in Business Courier (Vol. 27, September 3, 2010, No. 18, pp. 1)*

Pub: Business Courier

Ed: Lucy May. **Description:** Business brokers in Cincinnati, Ohio are expecting better prices in view of the strengthening economy.

25353 ■ *"Your Turn in the Spotlight" in Inc. (March 2008, pp. 30)*

Pub: Gruner & Jahr USA Publishing

Ed: Elaine Appleton Grant. **Description:** Profile of a Tennessee business that produces events and concerts. The company offers a complete package of services handling staging, lighting, video, musical instrument rentals, and audio support. The founder has decided to sell the business and details of the asking price, price rationale, the pros and cons of buying the firm and its bottom line are examined.

TRADE PERIODICALS

25354 ■ *Venture Capital Journal*

Pub: Venture Economics Inc.

Contact: Kathleen Devlin, Editor-in-Chief

E-mail: Lawrence.Aragon@thomson.com

Released: Monthly. **Price:** $960, U.S. first year; $1650, elsewhere for combination of print and. **Description:** Hard news, analysis and data on the North American private equity market.

VIDEOCASSETTES/ AUDIOCASSETTES

25355 ■ *How to Buy a Good Business with No Cash*

Cambridge Educational

c/o Films Media Group

132 West 31st Street, 17th Floor

Ste. 124

New York, NY 10001

Free: 800-257-5126

Fax: (609)671-0266
Co. E-mail: custserve@films.com
URL: http://www.cambridgeol.com
Released: 1987. **Price:** $39.95. **Description:** Successful venture capitalist Lionel Haines shows how someone can purchase a business without any cash. **Availability:** VHS; 3/4 U.

25356 ■ *New or Used? Buying a Firm or Starting Your Own*
Instructional Video
2219 C St.
Lincoln, NE 68502
Ph: (402)475-6570
Free: 800-228-0164
Fax: (402)475-6500
Co. E-mail: feedback@insvideo.com
URL: http://www.insvideo.com
Released: 19??. **Price:** $99.00. **Description:** Details the different options open to anyone wanting to start or obtain their own business. Discusses the various factors to be considered when putting a value on a company, negotiating price and terms, and closing the deal. **Availability:** VHS.

25357 ■ *Understanding Business Valuation*
Chesney Communications
2302 Martin St., Ste. 125
Irvine, CA 92612
Ph: (949)263-5500
Free: 800-223-8878
Fax: (949)263-5506
Co. E-mail: videocc@aol.com
URL: http://www.videocc.com
Released: 1987. **Description:** A look for the small businessman at how to plan the future of his company-growth, reinvestment and possible sale. **Availability:** VHS; 3/4 U.

CONSULTANTS

25358 ■ BPT Consulting Associates Ltd.
12 Parmenter Rd., Ste. B-6
Londonderry, NH 03053
Ph: (603)437-8484
Free: 888-278-0030
Fax: (603)434-5388
Contact: John Kuczynski, Managing Director
Scope: Provides management consulting expertise and resources to cross-industry clients with services for: Business Management consulting, People/Human Resources Transition and Training programs, and a full cadre of multi-disciplined Technology Computer experts. Virtual consultants with expertise in e-commerce, supply chain management, organizational development, and business application development consulting. **Founded:** 1991.

25359 ■ Business Team
1901 S Bascom Ave., Ste. 400
Campbell, CA 95008
Ph: (408)246-1102
Fax: (408)246-2219
Co. E-mail: sanjose@business-team.com
URL: http://www.business-team.com
Contact: William L. Kramer, Vice President
Scope: Business consulting services offered to companies looking for buyers. Specializes in mergers and acquisitions, business brokerage, and valuations. **Founded:** 1980. **Seminars:** Business Valuation Enhancing the Value of Your Company.

25360 ■ Country Squire Inc.
10400 Griffin Rd., Ste. 303B
Fort Lauderdale, FL 33328
Ph: (954)473-6009
Free: 800-887-4857
Fax: (954)434-0200
Co. E-mail: mike@thelandpro.com
URL: http://www.thelandpro.com
Contact: Michael G. Wietor, President
E-mail: mike@thelandpro.com
Scope: Provider of real estate service. Offers services in locating, pricing, and purchasing of real property as well as representation of both buyers and/or sellers in real estate transactions and the negotiation of sales or acquisitions of businesses. **Founded:** 1987. **Seminars:** Competitor Intelligence: How to Get It/How to Use It. **Telecommunication Services:** homes4ufla@aol.com.

25361 ■ Hampton Group
7172 Regional St., Ste. 290
Dublin, CA 94568
Ph: (925)830-3447
Free: 800-820-6424
Fax: (925)831-8194
Co. E-mail: dataforpeter@hotmail.com
Contact: Peter Siegel, Owner
E-mail: dataforpeter@hotmail.com
Scope: Consults on the buying and selling of small and medium-sized businesses. **Founded:** 1991.

25362 ■ Pundmann & Company Inc.
PO Box 446
Saint Charles, MO 63302
Ph: (636)940-1111
Fax: (636)925-0000
Co. E-mail: pundmann@aol.com
URL: http://www.pundmann.com
Contact: William R. Pundmann, President
E-mail: will@pundmann.com
Scope: Merchant banking firm providing advice to companies concerning mergers and acquisitions, private financing and business strategy. Offers clients expert assistance in a wide range of financial activities, such as asset redeployments, private placements, recapitalizations, strategic financial counseling and venture capital investments. Also provides in-house venture capital to clients. Industries served: general. **Founded:** 1984. **Telecommunication Services:** will@pundmann.com.

25363 ■ Harvey C. Skoog
7151 E Addis Ave.
Prescott Valley, AZ 86314
Ph: (928)772-1448
Scope: Firm has expertise in taxes, payroll, financial planning, budgeting, buy/sell planning, business start-up, fraud detection, troubled business consulting, acquisition, and marketing. Serves the manufacturing, construction, and retailing industries in Arizona. **Founded:** 1977.

25364 ■ Thomson Venture Economics Inc.—Thomson Financial Inc.Thomson Financial Services Inc.;
395 Hudson St., Ste. 3
New York, NY 10014
Ph: (212)807-5000
Fax: (212)807-5122
Contact: Ted Weissberg, President
E-mail: edward.weissberg@tfn.com
Scope: Venture capital and business development specialists providing customized research for industrial and financial corporations. Services include: identification of high-potential companies for investment, alliance or acquisition; assistance in establishing venture capital or strategic alliance programs; and assistance with specific acquisition searches. Services for institutional investors in venture capital include: Basic education and due diligence evaluation of venture capital as an investment; development of venture capital investment strategy; and identification of investment opportunities, portfolio monitoring, analysis, performance; and benchmarking for the venture capital asset class. Serves private industries as well as government agencies. **Founded:** 1961. **Seminars:** Performance Monitoring Workshop.

ASSOCIATIONS AND OTHER ORGANIZATIONS

25365 ■ Council on Employee Benefits (CEB)
1311 King St.
Alexandria, VA 22314
Ph: (703)549-6025
Fax: (703)549-6027
Co. E-mail: scanfield@ceb.org
URL: http://www.ceb.org
Contact: Robert B. Arthur, President
Description: Employers seeking informal exchange of experiences and information on the design, financing, and administration of employee benefit programs, both domestic and international. Provides a medium for the exchange of ideas, information, and statistics; sponsors or conducts research projects on benefits; makes known its views on legislative matters affecting employee benefits. Conducts research. **Founded:** 1946.

25366 ■ Employee Benefit Research Institute (EBRI)
1100 13th St. NW, Ste. 878
Washington, DC 20005
Ph: (202)659-0670
Fax: (202)775-6312
Co. E-mail: info@ebri.org
URL: http://www.ebri.org
Contact: Dallas L. Salisbury, President
E-mail: salisbury@ebri.org
Description: Corporations, consulting firms, banks, insurance companies, unions, and others with an interest in the future of employee benefit programs. Purpose is to contribute to the development of effective and responsible public policy in the field of employee benefits through research, publications, educational programs, seminars, and direct communication. Sponsors a broad range of studies on retirement income, health, disability, and other benefit programs; disseminates study results. Maintains research library with information on employee benefit programs. **Scope:** A public policy research organization serving as an employee benefits information source on health, welfare and retirement issues. Services include: basic benefit program descriptions, legislation analysis, media coverage and interpretation and long-range planning. Specializes in research on pensions, social security, health care, Medicare, long-term care, and flexible benefits. Serves government, academic consumers, consultants, banks, insurance companies, investment managers, law and accounting firms, corporations, and individuals. **Services:** Congressional briefings. **Founded:** 1978. **Subscriptions:** 4000 audiovisuals books clippings monographs periodicals. **Publications:** "Retirement Security in the United States-Current Sources, Future Prospects, and Likely Outcomes of Current Trends," 2006; "Estimating the Value of Changes in OASI Benefits Under Social Security Reforms," Jun, 2006; "Will Wider Use of Evidence-Based Medicine Significantly Enhance Healthcare Quality and Affordability: Implications for Consumer-Driven Health Benefits," 2003; "Consumer Driven Health Benefits: A Continuing Evolution," 2002; "The Economic Costs of the

Uninsured Implications for Business and Government," 2000; "The Future of Private Retirement Plans," 2000; "EBRI Issue Briefs"; "EBRI Notes"; "Pension Investment Report PIR"; "EBRI Data book on Employee Benefits"; "Fundamentals of Employee Benefits Programs". **Educational Activities:** American Savings Education Council; Choose to Save Education Program; Fellows program, for academics, media, retirees; Policy forums (Biennial). **Awards:** EBRI Lillywhite Award (Annual); The EBRI Lillywhite Award (Annual). **Seminars:** Policy Forums, Congressional Briefings. **Telecommunication Services:** salisbury@ebri.org.

25367 ■ Employers Council on Flexible Compensation (ECFC)
1444 I St. NW, Ste. 700
Washington, DC 20005-6542
Ph: (202)659-4300
Free: 877-747-3539
Fax: (202)216-9646
Co. E-mail: nrankin@ecfc.org
URL: http://www.ecfc.org
Contact: Natasha Rankin, Executive Director
Description: Represents employers and service providers who have implemented or are interested in flexible compensation plans allowing employees to choose from a variety of benefits packages. Promotes flexible compensation plans including cafeteria plans, health reimbursement arrangements, cash-or-deferred plans and other defined contribution plans. Monitors legislation and represents members' interests before Congress. Lobbies to preserve and simplify the flexible compensation provisions of the Internal Revenue Code. **Founded:** 1981. **Educational Activities:** Flexible Benefit Administrator's Symposium (Annual). **Telecommunication Services:** info@ecfc.org.

25368 ■ International Foundation of Employee Benefit Plans (IFEBP)
18700 W Bluemound Rd.
Brookfield, WI 53045
Ph: (262)786-6700
Free: 888-334-3327
Fax: (262)364-1818
Co. E-mail: membership@ifebp.org
URL: http://www.ifebp.org
Contact: Richard Lyall, President
Description: Provides sources for employee benefits and compensation information and education, including seminars and conferences, books and an information center, CEBS and Certificate Series. Conducts more than 100 educational programs. Provides Internet job and resume posting service. **Scope:** employee benefits, human resources, compensation. **Founded:** 1954. **Holdings:** The computer-readable EMPLOYEE BENEFITS INFOSOURCE database contains more than 75,000 records dating from 1986 to the present; it is updated monthly with approximately 400 records. **Subscriptions:** 12000 books periodicals. **Publications:** *Employee Benefits Journal*; *Employee Benefits Infosource*; *Benefits & Compensation Digest*; *Legal-Legislative Reporter*; *Employee Benefits Infosource*; *Benefits & Compensation Digest* (Monthly); *Employee Benefits Infosource™*;

Employee Benefits Journal (Quarterly). **Educational Activities:** Annual Employee Benefits Conference (Annual). **Telecommunication Services:** cebs@ifebp.org; ebinfo@ifebp.org.

25369 ■ UWC: Strategic Services on Unemployment and Workers' Compensation (UWC)
910 17th St. NW, Ste. 315
Washington, DC 20006
Ph: (202)223-8902
Fax: (202)783-1616
Co. E-mail: info@uwcstrategy.org
URL: http://www.uwcstrategy.org
Contact: Douglas J. Holmes, President
Description: Works to serve the business community by promoting Unemployment Insurance (UI) and Workers' Compensation (WC) programs that provide fair benefits to workers at affordable cost to employers and the community. **Founded:** 1933. **Publications:** *Highlights of State Unemployment Compensation Laws* (Annual). **Educational Activities:** Fall Forum for Staff Association Executives (Annual); National Unemployment Insurance Issues Conference (Annual). **Awards:** Unemployment Insurance Awards (Annual).

25370 ■ WorldatWork
14040 N Northsight Blvd.
Scottsdale, AZ 85260
Ph: (480)922-2020
Free: 866-816-2962
Fax: (480)483-8352
Co. E-mail: customerrelations@worldatwork.org
URL: http://www.worldatwork.org
Contact: Anne C. Ruddy, President
E-mail: aruddy@worlatwork.org
Description: Dedicated to knowledge leadership in compensation, benefits and total rewards, focusing on disciplines associated with attracting, retaining and motivating employees. Offers CCP, CBP, and GRP certification and education programs, conducts surveys, research and provides networking opportunities. **Scope:** Specializes in the design, implementation, and management of employee compensation, benefits and total rewards programs. Also promotes and sponsors research activities, conducts education and certification programs, and publishes a variety of educational and informational publications. **Founded:** 1955. **Publications:** "Telework A Critical Component of Your Total Rewards Strategy," World at Work Press. **Awards:** Keystone Award (Annual). **Seminars:** Consumerism in Practice: It's More than Account-Based Plans, It's Changing Behaviors; Competitive Market Pay: Pricing Critical Skills and Unique Positions; How-to: Employee Benefits Basics; Sales Compensation Design: Five Action Steps to Success; Regulatory Environments for Compensation Programs; Job Analysis, Documentation and Evaluation. **Special Services:** WorldatWork®; workspan®; WorldatWork Society of Certified Professionals®; Alliance for Work-Life Progress®.

REFERENCE WORKS

25371 ■ *"Both Eyes on the Prize"* in Canadian Business (Vol. 83, September 14, 2010, No. 15, pp. 42)
Pub: Rogers Media Ltd.
Ed: Jacqueline Nelson. **Description:** North American executive compensation has fundamentally shifted partly due to pressure from the US government and recent adjustments in the way CEO pay packages are structured. The changes have also become common practice in Canada and helped in scrutinizing the executive pay.

25372 ■ *"CEOs With Headsets"* in Harvard Business Review (Vol. 88, September 2010, No. 9, pp. 21)
Pub: Harvard Business School Publishing
Ed: Andrew Zimbalist. **Description:** Placing a salary cap on college coaches' compensation would not significantly affect coaching quality or an institution's ability to obtain talent. A salary growth rate comparison between coaches, university presidents, and full professors for the period 1986 to 2007 is also presented.

25373 ■ *"Fairness First"* in Canadian Business (Vol. 80, April 23, 2007. No. 9, pp. 45)
Pub: Rogers Media
Ed: Erin Pooley. **Description:** The need for the fair treatment of employees from the perspective of employee compensation is discussed

25374 ■ *"How Much is Too Much?"* in Canadian Business (Vol. 79, July 17, 2006, No. 14-15, pp. 55)
Pub: Rogers Media
Ed: John Gray. **Description:** Elucidates the emphasis on the need for companies to analyze the executive pay packages designed by compensation consultants.

25375 ■ *"Is Raising CPP Premiums a Good Idea?"* in Canadian Business (Vol. 83, July 20, 2010, No. 11-12, pp. 37)
Pub: Rogers Media Ltd.
Description: Big labor is pushing for an increase in Canada Pension Plan premiums but pension consultants believe this system is not broken and that the government needs to focus on addressing the low rate of personal retirement savings. If the premiums go up, even those with high savings will be forced to pay more and it could block other plans that really address the real issue.

25376 ■ *"Labor Compensation and Collective Bargaining Data"* in Montly Labor Review (Vol. 133, September 2010, No. 9, pp. 116)
Pub: Bureau of Labor Statistics
Description: Employment cost index is presented, citing compensation by occupation and industry group.

25377 ■ *"Mismanaging Pay and Performance"* in Business Strategy Review (Vol. 21, Summer 2010, No. 2, pp. 54)
Pub: Wiley-Blackwell
Ed: Rupert Merson. **Description:** Understanding the relationship between performance measurement and desired behaviors is an important element of a company's talent management.

25378 ■ *"New Work Order"* in Black Enterprise (Vol. 38, March 2008, No. 8, pp. 60)
Pub: Earl G. Graves Publishing Co. Inc.
Description: Today's management challenges includes issues of more competition, globalization, outsourcing and technological advances. Suggestions to help create progressive leadership in small business that sustains a competitive edge are listed.

25379 ■ *"Notes on Current Labor Statistics"* in Montly Labor Review (Vol. 133, September 2010, No. 9, pp. 75)
Pub: Bureau of Labor Statistics
Description: Principal statistics and calculated by the Bureau of Labor Statistics are presented. The series includes statistics on labor force; employment; unemployment; labor compensation; consumer, producer, and international prices; productivity; international comparisons; and injury and illness statistics.

25380 ■ *"Pay Fell for Many Local Execs in '09"* in Baltimore Business Journal (Vol. 28, July 2, 2010, No. 8, pp. 1)
Pub: Baltimore Business Journal
Ed: Gary Haber. **Description:** Compensation for the 100 highest-paid executives in the Baltimore, Maryland area decreased in 2009, compared with 2008. At least $1 million were received by 59 out of 100 executives in 2009, while 75 earned the said amount in 2008. Factors that contributed to the executives' decisions to take pay cuts are discussed.

25381 ■ *"Productivity Data"* in Montly Labor Review (Vol. 133, September 2010, No. 9, pp. 137)
Pub: Bureau of Labor Statistics
Description: Productivity data is presented through indexes of productivity, hourly compensation and unit costs in 2007.

25382 ■ *"Small Business Compensation"* in Small Business Economic Trends (September 2010, pp. 10)
Pub: National Federation of Independent Business
Ed: William C. Dunkelberg, Holly Wade. **Description:** A graph from a survey of small businesses in the U.S. is given, representing small business compensation from January 1986 to August 2010. Tables showing actual compensation changes and compensation plans are also presented. A graph comparing small business prices and labor compensation is supplied.

25383 ■ *"Small Business Compensation"* in Small Business Economic Trends (July 2010, pp. 10)
Pub: National Federation of Independent Business
Description: A graph from a survey of small businesses in the U.S. is given representing small business compensation from January 1986 to June 2010. Tables showing actual compensation changes and compensation plans are also presented. A graph comparing small business prices and labor compensation is supplied.

TRADE PERIODICALS

25384 ■ Benefits & Compensation Digest
Pub: International Foundation of Employee Benefit Plans
Contact: Richard Lyall, President
Released: Monthly. **Price:** $100. **Description:** Covers the field of employee benefits. Recurring features include notices of publications and educational opportunities, news and announcements for members, and a review of current literature. Formerly Employee Benefits Digest.

25385 ■ BNA Pension & Benefits Reporter
Pub: Bureau of National Affairs Inc.
Ed: David A. Sayre, Editor. **Price:** $1811, individual; online two users $2730. **Description:** Covers pension developments stemming from the passage of the Employee Retirement Income Security Act of 1974 (ERISA) and its amendments. Discusses pension and welfare benefit regulations, standards, enforcement actions, court decisions, legislative and administrative actions, agency options, and employee benefit trust fund requirements.

25386 ■ EBRI Issue Brief
Ed: Dallas Salisbury, Editor, salisbury@ebri.org. **Released:** Monthly. **Price:** Included in membership; $224, nonmembers; $25, single issue. **Description:** Examines, analyzes, and interprets key issues and trends in the employee benefits field. Covers one topic in-depth in each issue. Remarks: Price includes subscription to the newsletter Employee Benefit Notes.

25387 ■ EBRI Notes
Ed: Dallas Salisbury, Editor, salisbury@ebri.org. **Released:** Monthly. **Price:** Included in membership; $199, nonmembers. **Description:** 'Analyzes and discusses newly released employee benefits data and reviews a wide range of policy issues, research and publications.' Recurring features include news of research, legal analysis, legislative updates. Remarks: Subscription includes EBRI Issue Brief.

25388 ■ Employee Benefits Cases
Pub: Bureau of National Affairs Inc.
Contact: David A. Sayre, Managing Editor
Released: Weekly, 50/year. **Price:** $1,141. **Description:** Reports full text of federal and state court opinions and selected decisions of arbitrators and the National Labor Relations Board on employee benefits issues. Recurring features include a cumulative index digest, tables of cases, a topical index, and a classification guide.

25389 ■ Employee Benefits Review
Pub: S. Harman & Associates Inc.
Ed: Saundra K. Harman, Editor. **Released:** Monthly, 12/year. **Description:** Covers labor, personnel, and technical issues in the federal personnel area. Lists upcoming conferences, workshops, and training seminars. Remarks: Also available via e-mail.

25390 ■ Legal-Legislative Reporter
Pub: International Foundation of Employee Benefit Plans
Contact: Richard Lyall, President
Ed: Harry W. Burton, Editor. **Released:** Monthly. **Price:** $110 as part of publication package. **Description:** Presents news of court and legislative actions pertinent to employee benefit plans.

25391 ■ Retirement Plans Report
Pub: Western League of Savings Institutions
Ed: Gloria Sewell-Hacko, Editor. **Released:** Quarterly. **Description:** Reports on tax reform laws affecting retirement plan benefits. Covers IRAs (Individual Retirement Accounts) as well as the Basic Plan. Includes a question-and-answer column.

25392 ■ Wages and Hours
Pub: Bureau of National Affairs Inc.
Contact: Nancy J. Sedmak, Managing Editor
Released: Weekly. **Price:** $611. **Description:** Provides a guide to compliance with federal and state regulation of wages, hours, and child labor. Covers such topics as hours of work; minimum wage and overtime pay; equal pay; notice posting, reporting, and recordkeeping; enforcement and administration; exemptions; home work rules; public contracts; and industry and occupation checklists. Part of the BNA Policy and Practice Series, Wages and Hours can be purchased separately or in any combination with other binder publications entitled Compensation, Fair Employment Practices, Labor Relations, or Personnel Management.

25393 ■ Work Span
Pub: WorldatWork
Contact: Anne C. Ruddy, President
E-mail: aruddy@worlatwork.org
Ed: Jean Christ-Offerson, Editor, jchristofferson@worldatwork.org. **Released:** 10/year. **Description:** Concentrates on issues in the fields of compensation and benefits and human resource management. Includes legislative updates, resources, and case studies.

CONSULTANTS

25394 ■ The Epler Co.
450 B St., Ste. 750
San Diego, CA 92101
Ph: (619)239-0831
Fax: (619)239-0807
Co. E-mail: consultants@eplercompany.com
URL: http://www.eplercompany.com
Contact: Jane Barry, President
E-mail: jbarry@eplercompany.com
Scope: Offers actuarial and consulting services for employee benefits specializing in retirement plans, health, life, accidental death and dismemberment, long-term disability insurance plans, and executive compensation. Administers retiree health studies, AB1200 studies for schools, and merger studies on

benefits. Conducts base pay, bonus and benefit surveys. Designs total compensation programs. **Founded:** 1971.

25395 ■ Fox Lawson & Associates L.L.C.
1335 County Road D, Cir. E
Saint Paul, MN 55109-5260
Ph: (651)635-0976
Free: 800-383-0976
Fax: (651)635-0980
Co. E-mail: jfox@foxlawson.com
URL: http://www.foxlawson.com
Contact: James C. Fox, Partner
E-mail: jfox@foxlawson.com
Scope: A compensation and human resources consulting firm, provides services to businesses of all sizes including finance, manufacturing, high tech, software development, food, retail, wholesale trade, communications, transportation, service, not-for-profit and education. **Founded:** 1995. **Seminars:** Compensation Strategies - Not Having a Plan Could Break the Bank.

25396 ■ Harvey C. Skoog
7151 E Addis Ave.
Prescott Valley, AZ 86314

Ph: (928)772-1448
Scope: Firm has expertise in taxes, payroll, financial planning, budgeting, buy/sell planning, business start-up, fraud detection, troubled business consulting, acquisition, and marketing. Serves the manufacturing, construction, and retailing industries in Arizona. **Founded:** 1977.

COMPUTERIZED DATABASES

25397 ■ *Compensation Planning Journal*
1801 S Bell St.
Arlington, VA 22202
Free: 800-372-1033
Co. E-mail: customercare@bna.com
URL: http://www.bna.com/tax-accounting-t5000
Availability: Online: The Bureau of National Affairs Inc. - Tax and Accounting Division. **Type:** Full-text.

25398 ■ *Pension & Benefits Reporter*™
1801 S Bell St.
Arlington, VA 22202
Free: 800-372-1033
Co. E-mail: customercare@bna.com
URL: http://www.bna.com
Availability: Online: Bloomberg LP-Bloomberg BNA; Thomson Reuters - Westlaw. **Type:** Full-text.

25399 ■ *State Health Care Regulatory Developments*™
1801 S Bell St.
Arlington, VA 22202
Free: 800-372-1033
Co. E-mail: customercare@bna.com
URL: http://www.bna.com
Availability: Online: Bloomberg LP-Bloomberg BNA; Thomson Reuters - Westlaw. **Type:** Full-text.

LIBRARIES

25400 ■ Towers Watson Information Centre
1100 Melville St., Ste. 1600
Vancouver, BC, Canada V6E 4A6
Ph: (604)691-1000
Fax: (604)691-1062
URL: http://www.towerswatson.com/
Scope: Actuarial science, employee benefits, compensation, human resources. **Holdings:** Figures not available.

START-UP INFORMATION

25401 ■ *The Art of the Start: The Time-Tested, Battle-Hardened Guide for Anyone Starting Anything*
Pub: Penguin Books USA Inc.
Ed: Guy Kawasaki. **Released:** September 2004. **Price:** $26.95. **Description:** Advice for someone starting a new business covering topics such as hiring employees, building a brand, business competition, and management.

25402 ■ *Small Business Survival Guide*
Pub: Adams Media Corporation
Contact: Gary Krebs, Director
E-mail: swatrous@adamsmedia.com
Ed: Cliff Ennico. **Price:** $12.95. **Description:** Small business expert provides strategies to start a company and survive in the 21st Century. He shows small business owners how to succeed despite challenges that can defeat any firm. His advice covers suppliers; customers and contractors; competitors and creditors; spouses, family and friends; as well as the ways lawyers, accountants and other can steal an entrepreneur's success. Ennico also describes how startups can comply with local regulations.

REFERENCE WORKS

25403 ■ *"3Par: Storing Up Value" in Barron's (Vol. 90, August 30, 2010, No. 35, pp. 30)*
Pub: Barron's Editorial & Corporate Headquarters
Ed: Mark Veverka. **Description:** Dell and Hewlett Packard are both bidding for data storage company 3Par. The acquisition would help Dell and Hewlett Packard provide customers with a one-stop shop as customers move to a private cloud in the Internet.

25404 ■ *"13D Filings: Investors Report to the SEC" in Barron's (Vol. 88, March 31, 2008, No. 13, pp. M10)*
Pub: Dow Jones & Company, Inc.
Description: Obrem Capital Management wants Micrel to rescind Micrel's shareholder-rights plan and to boost its board to six members from five. Patricia L. Childress plans to nominate herself to the board of Sierra Bancorp, and Luther King Capital Management may consider a competing acquisition proposal for Industrial Distribution Group.

25405 ■ *"The 490 Made Chevy a Bargain Player" in Automotive News (Vol. 86, October 31, 2011, No. 6488, pp. S22)*
Pub: Crain Communications Inc.
Ed: David Phillips. **Description:** The first Chevrolet with the 490 engine was sold in 1913, but it was too expensive for masses. In 1914 the carmaker launched a lower-priced H-series of cars competitively priced. Nameplates such as Corvette, Bel Air, Camaro and Silverado have defined Chevrolet through the years.

25406 ■ *"2007 Fittest CEOs" in Hawaii Business (Vol. 53, October 2007, No. 4, pp. 40)*
Pub: Hawaii Business Publishing
Description: Discusses the outcome of the fittest chief executive officers in Hawaii competition for 2007. Hawaii Capital Management's David Low leads the list while Group Pacific (Hawaii) Inc.'s Chip Doyle and Greater Good Inc.s Kari Leong placed second and third, respectively. The CEO's routines, eating habits, and inspirations for staying fit are provided.

25407 ■ *"A&E Networks" in Brandweek (Vol. 49, April 21, 2008, No. 16, pp. SR9)*
Pub: VNU Business Media, Inc.
Ed: Anthony Crupi. **Description:** Provides contact information for sales and marketing personnel for the A&E Networks as well as a listing of the station's top programming and an analysis of the current season and the target audience for those programs running in the current season. A&E has reinvented itself as a premium entertainment brand over the last five years and with its $2.5 million per episode acquisition of The Sopranos, the station signaled that it was serious about getting back into the scripted programming business. The acquisition also helped the network compete against other cable networks and led to a 20 percent increase in prime-time viewers.

25408 ■ *"Achieving Sustained Competitive Advantage: A Family Capital Theory" in Family Business Review (Vol. 19, June 2006, No. 2, pp. 135)*
Pub: Family Firm Institute
Contact: Judy L. Green, President
Ed: James Hoffman, Mark Hoelscher, Ritch Sorenson. **Description:** Impact of capital assets on performance of family businesses is discussed.

25409 ■ *"After Price Cuts, Competition GPS Makers Lose Direction" in Brandweek (Vol. 49, April 21, 2008, No. 16, pp. 16)*
Pub: VNU Business Media, Inc.
Ed: Steve Miller. **Description:** Garmin and TomTom, two of the leaders in portable navigation devices, have seen lowering revenues due to dramatic price cuts and unexpected competition from the broadening availability of personal navigation on mobile phones. TomTom has trimmed its sales outlook for its first quarter while Garmin's stock dropped 40 percent since February.

25410 ■ *"The AHA Moment" in Hispanic Business (December 2010)*
Pub: Hispanic Business
Ed: Rebecca Vallaneda. **Description:** An interview with Gisela Girard on how competitive market conditions push buttons. Girard stepped down from her 18-month position as chairwoman the Association of Hispanic Advertising Agencies. She has more than 20 years of experience in advertising and research marketing.

25411 ■ *"Airlines Mount PR Push to Win Public Support Against Big Oil" in Advertising Age (Vol. 79, July 14, 2008, No. 7, pp.)*
Pub: Crain Communications, Inc.
Ed: Michael Bush. **Description:** Top airline executives from competing companies have banded together in a public relations plan in which they are sending e-mails to their frequent fliers asking for aid in lobbying legislators to put a restriction on oil speculation.

25412 ■ *"All For One, None for All?" in Canadian Business (Vol. 83, October 12, 2010, No. 17, pp. 60)*
Pub: Rogers Media Ltd.
Ed: Michael McCullogh. **Description:** The effect of the growth of Canada's overseas provincial trade offices on Canadian trade is discussed. Economic development commissions in the country have devised a single 'Consider Canada' campaign to pitch foreign investors. It is hoped that large cities will gain from banding together rather than competing against one another.

25413 ■ *"All Options Open On Chrysler: Magna" in Globe & Mail (February 28, 2007, pp. B3)*
Pub: CTVglobemedia Publishing Inc.
Ed: Greg Keenan. **Description:** The 65 percent drop in the profits of Magna International Inc. and the plans of its chief executive officer Don Walker to make the company more competitive are discussed.

25414 ■ *"Alpha Dogs: How Your Small Business Can Become a Leader of the Pack*
Pub: HarperInformation
Ed: Donna Fenn. **Released:** May 2007. **Price:** $14.95. **Description:** Ways for an entrepreneur to outsmart competitors in the marketplace, to generate higher sales, and earn lasting customer and employee loyalty.

25415 ■ *"Alpha Dogs: How Your Small Business Can Become a Leader of the Pack*
Pub: HarperCollins Publishers, Inc.
Ed: Donna Fenn. **Released:** May 2007. **Price:** $14.95. **Description:** Profiles of eight successful entrepreneurs along with information for developing customer service, technology and competition.

25416 ■ *"American Chemistry Council Launches Flagship Blog" in Ecology,Environment & Conservation Business (October 29, 2011, pp. 5)*
Pub: HighBeam Research
Description: American Chemistry Council (ACC) launched its blog, American Chemistry Matters, where interactive space allows bloggers to respond to news coverage and to discuss policy issues and their impact on innovation, competitiveness, job creation and safety.

25417 ■ *"The Anatomy of a High Potential" in Business Strategy Review (Vol. 21, Autumn 2010, No. 3, pp. 52)*
Pub: Blackwell Publishers Ltd.
Ed: Doug Ready, Jay Conger, Linda Hill, Emily Stecker. **Description:** Companies have long been interested in identifying high potential employees, but few firms know how to convert top talent into game changers, or people who can shape the future of the business. The authors have found the 'x factors' that can make a high-potential list into a strong competitive advantage.

25418 ■ *"The Anatomy of a High Potential' in Business Strategy Review (Vol. 21, Autumn 2010, No. 3, pp. 52)*
Pub: Wiley-Blackwell

Ed: Doug Ready, Jay Conger, Linda Hill, Emily Stecker. **Description:** Companies have long been interested in identifying high-potential employees, but few firms know how to convert top talent into game changers - people who can shape the future of the business. The authors have found the x-factors that can make the high-potential list into a strong competitive advantage.

25419 ■ *"Anytime Access" in Crain's Cleveland Business (Vol. 28, October 22, 2007, No. 42, pp. 17)*
Pub: Crain Communications, Inc.

Ed: Brad Dicken. **Description:** Technology continues to evolve in the competitive world of mobile communications in which the phone has become a sleek multitool that can take a call, send and e-mail, calculate the tip after dinner and snap a photograph.

25420 ■ *"Are Movie Theaters Doomed?' in Business Horizons (November-December 2007, pp. 491)*
Pub: Elsevier Technology Publications

Ed: Jon Silver, John McDonnell. **Description:** Theater operators must embrace new technologies and more diverse target markets if they are to stem the decline in theatergoers. Movie theaters remain highly vulnerable to trends in the home entertainment industry.

25421 ■ *"As Technology Changes, So Must African American Business" in Black Enterprise (Vol. 41, August 2010, No. 1, pp. 61)*
Pub: Earl G. Graves Publishing Co. Inc.

Ed: Sonya A. Donaldson. **Description:** Social media is essential to compete in today's business environment, especially for African American firms.

25422 ■ *"At the Drugstore, the Nurse Will See You Now" in Globe & Mail (April 13, 2007, pp. B1)*
Pub: CTVglobemedia Publishing Inc.

Ed: Marina Strauss. **Description:** The appointment of several health professionals including nurse, podiatrists, etc. by Rexall Co. at its drugstores to face competition from rivals, is discussed.

25423 ■ *"Awaiting a Call from Deutsche Telekom' in Barron's (Vol. 90, September 6, 2010, No. 36, pp. M5)*
Pub: Barron's Editorial & Corporate Headquarters

Ed: Vito J. Racanelli. **Description:** Deutsche Telekom's (DT) T-Mobile USA Unit has settled in the number four position in the market and the parent company will need to decide if it will hold onto the company in the next 12-18 months from September 2010. T-Mobile's rivals will make critical improvements during this time and DT has the option to upgrade T-Mobile at the cost of improvements to its other units.

25424 ■ *Balls!: 6 Rules for Winning Today's Business Game*
Pub: John Wiley & Sons, Incorporated

Ed: Alexi Venneri. **Released:** January 2005. **Price:** $29.95. **Description:** In order to be successful business leaders must be brave, authentic, loud, lovable, and spunky and they need to lead their competition.

25425 ■ *"Bark and Bite" in Canadian Business (Vol. 81, March 31, 2008, No. 5, pp. 20)*
Pub: Rogers Media

Ed: Rachel Pulfer. **Description:** Hillary Clinton and Barack Obama both want to renegotiate NAFTA but the most job losses in the American manufacturing industry is caused by technological change and Asian competition than with NAFTA. The risk of protectionist trade policies has increased given the political atmosphere.

25426 ■ *"BASF Launches $4.9 Billion Bid for Rival Engelhard' in Globe & Mail (January 4, 2006, pp. B7)*
Pub: CTVglobemedia Publishing Inc.

Ed: Mike Esterl; Steve Levine. **Description:** The plans of BASF AG, to acquire Engelhard Corp. for $4.9 billion, are presented.

25427 ■ *"Battle of the Titans" in Canadian Business (Vol. 81, March 17, 2008, No. 4, pp. 15)*
Pub: Rogers Media

Ed: Rachel Pulfer. **Description:** Regulatory authorities in Canada gave Thomson Corp and Reuters Group PLC the permission to go ahead with their merger. The merged companies could eclipse Bloomberg LP's market share of 33 percent. Authorities also required Thomson and Reuters to sell some of their databases to competitors.

25428 ■ *Battling Big Box: How Nimble Niche Companies Can Outmaneuver Giant Companies*
Pub: Career Press, Inc.

Ed: Henry Dubroff, Susan J. Marks. **Released:** January 1, 2009. **Price:** $15.99. **Description:** Small companies can compete with larger firms through agility, adaptability, customer service, and credibility. Topics include information to help empower employees, build a powerful brand, manage cash flow, and maintaining a business vision.

25429 ■ *Be a Brilliant Business Writer: Write Well, Write Fast, and Whip the Competition*
Pub: Crown Business Books

Ed: Jane Curry, Diana Young. **Released:** October 5, 2010. **Price:** $13.99. **Description:** Tools for mastering the art of persuasive writing in every document created, from email and client letters to reports and presentations, this book will help any writer convey their message with clarity and power, increase productivity by reducing rewrites, and provide the correct tone for navigating office politics.

25430 ■ *"Being Big By Design" in Canadian Business (Vol. 82, April 27, 2009, No. 7, pp. 39)*
Pub: Rogers Media

Ed: Andrew Wahl. **Description:** Gennum expects that its planned acquisition of Tundra Semiconductor will expand its market presence and leverage its research and development better than working alone. The proposed friendly acquisition could challenge Zarlink Semiconductor as the largest Canadian semiconductor firm in terms of revenue. The merger could expand Gennum's addressable market to about $2 billion.

25431 ■ *The Big Switch*
Pub: W. W. Norton & Company, Inc.

Ed: Nicholas Carr. **Released:** January 19, 2009. **Price:** $16.95 paperback. **Description:** Today companies are dismantling private computer systems and tapping into services provided via the Internet. This shift is remaking the computer industry, bringing competitors such as Google to the forefront ant threatening traditional companies like Microsoft and Dell. The book weaves together history, economics, and technology to explain why computing is changing and what it means for the future.

25432 ■ *"BK Menu Gives Casual Dining Reason to Worry" in Advertising Age (Vol. 79, November 17, 2008, No. 43, pp. 12)*
Pub: Crain Communications, Inc.

Ed: Emily Bryson York. **Description:** Burger King is beginning to compete with such casual dining restaurants as Applebees and the Cheesecake Factory with new premium menu items, including thicker burgers and ribs; statistical data regarding the casual dining segment which continues to fall and Burger King, whose sales continue to rise is included.

25433 ■ *"Blockbuster Launches Internet Movie Downloads to Compete Against Netflix, Others" in Chicago Tribune (December 3, 2008)*
Pub: McClatchy-Tribune Information Services

Ed: Eric Benderoff. **Description:** Blockbuster Inc., the DVD rental giant, has launched a new service

that delivers movies to their customer's homes via the Internet in an attempt to compete against Netflix and other competitors.

25434 ■ *Blue Ocean Strategy: How to Create Uncontested Market Space and Make Competition Irrelevant*
Pub: Harvard Business School Publishing

Ed: W. Chan Kim. **Released:** January 2005. **Price:** $29.95.

25435 ■ *"Blueprint for Profit: Family-Run Lumberyard Sets Sites On Sales of $100 Million a Year" in Small Business Opportunities (Jan. 2008)*
Pub: Harris Publications Inc.

Ed: Stan Roberts. **Description:** Profile of family-run lumberyard whose owner shares insight into the challenges of competing with big box operations like Home Depot and Lowe's.

25436 ■ *"Boston Scientific Makes Formal Offer for Guidant, Possibly Thwarting J&J" in Globe & Mail (January 9, 2006, pp. B6)*
Pub: CTVglobemedia Publishing Inc.

Ed: Silvia Pagan Westphal; Thomas M. Burton; Dennis Berman. **Description:** The details on Boston Scientific Corp.'s $25 billion bid on Guidant Corp. are presented. The company makes the move to outbid Johnson & Johnson.

25437 ■ *"Bring It On" in Entrepreneur (Vol. 35, November 2007, No. 11, pp. 52)*
Pub: Entrepreneur Media Inc.

Ed: Guy Kawasaki. **Description:** Tips on managing corporate competition in order to drive a company to success are presented.

25438 ■ *"Builders, Unions Aim to Cut Costs; Pushing Changes to Regain Share of Residential Market; Seek Council's Help" in Crain's New York Business*
Pub: Crain Communications, Inc.

Ed: Erik Engquist. **Description:** Union contractors and workers are worried about a decline in their market share for housing so they intend to ask the City Council to impose new safety and benefit standards on all contractors to avoid being undercut by nonunion competitors.

25439 ■ *Building Buzz to Beat the Big Boys*
Pub: Greenwood Publishing Group, Inc.

Ed: Steve O'Leary; Kim Sheehan. **Released:** March 30, 2008. **Price:** $39.95. **Description:** Seventy to eighty percent of small retail stores fail within the first five years of opening due to competition from big-box retailers and online stores. Service providers and small retailers should capitalize on the fact that they are local and can connect on a personal level with customers in a way the big stores cannot. Word of mouth marketing methods are very critical to any small retail or service company. This book is designed to help any small business compete against large competitors.

25440 ■ *Building Buzz to Beat the Big Boys*
Pub: Greenwood Publishing Group Inc.

Contact: Janann Sherman, Manager

Ed: Steve O'Leary. **Released:** March 2008. **Price:** $39.95. **Description:** Marketing methods to help small retailers compete against big box stores are examined. It is important for local stores to create a strong customer base.

25441 ■ *Business Warrior: Strategy for Entrepreneurs*
Pub: Clearbridge Publishing

Ed: Sun Tzu. **Released:** September 2006. **Price:** $19.95. **Description:** Advice to help entrepreneurs understand competitive strategies in order to succeed, focusing on sales, marketing, and personnel management.

25442 ■ *"Businesses Keep a Watchful Eye on Worker's Comp" in The Business Journal-Serving Greater Tampa Bay*

(September 5, 2008)
Pub: American City Business Journals, Inc.
Ed: Jane Meinhardt. **Description:** Pending a ruling from the Florida Supreme Court that could uphold the 2003 changes on workers' compensation law, the outcome would include restrictions on claimant attorneys' fees and allow the competitive workers' compensation insurance rates to remain low. However, insurance rates are expected to go up if the court overturns the changes.

25443 ■ *Busting the Myth of the Heroic CEO*
Pub: Cornell University Press
Contact: John G. Ackerman, Director
E-mail: jga4@cornell.edu
Ed: Michel Villette, Catherine Vuillermot. **Released:** 2010. **Price:** $24.95. **Description:** According to the authors, corporate leaders do not get ahead through productive risk-taking and innovation, but through ruthless exploitation of market imperfections and rivals.

25444 ■ *"Can a Brazilian SUV Take On the Jeep Wrangler?"* in *Business Week* (September 22, 2008, No. 4100, pp. 50)
Pub: McGraw-Hill Companies, Inc.
Ed: Helen Walters. **Description:** Profile of the Brazilian company TAC as well as the flourishing Brazilian car market; TAC has launched a new urban vehicle, the Stark, which has won prizes for innovation; the company uses local technology and manufacturing expertise.

25445 ■ *"Canadian Research Generates Innovation and Prosperity"* in *Canadian Business* (Vol. 81, October 27, 2008, No. 18, pp. 87)
Pub: Rogers Media Ltd.
Description: Universities play a key role in helping Canadians achieve prosperity, competitiveness, and quality of life by conducting more than a third of Canada's research. Research in universities help train graduates to apply sophisticated knowledge to real problems.

25446 ■ *"Capital Position"* in *Business Journal-Milwaukee* (Vol. 28, December 24, 2010, No. 12, pp. A1)
Pub: Milwaukee Business Journal
Ed: Rich Kirchen. **Description:** Canada-based BMO Financial Group has purchased Marshall and Isley Corporation (M and I), which dominated lending among Wisconsin businesses for decades. The sale of M and I will enable other banks to recruit M and I's customers but BMO Financial remains a stronger competitor since it possesses a more potent capital position.

25447 ■ *"Car Trouble"* in *Canadian Business* (Vol. 80, October 22, 2007, No. 21, pp. 27)
Pub: Rogers Media
Ed: Thomas Watson. **Description:** Contract between General Motors Corporation and the United Auto Workers Union has created a competitive arm for the U.S. Big Three automakers. Data on the market and production data of car companies are presented.

25448 ■ *"CarTango Lauches Site for Women"* in *Marketing to Women* (Vol. 21, April 2008, No. 4, pp. 5)
Pub: EPM Communications Inc.
Contact: Ira Mayer, President
E-mail: imayer@epmcom.com
Description: CarTango.com is an Internet site that seeks to overcome what women say are dismissive or pushy salespeople by allowing the shoppers the chance to decide what they want before inviting dealers to compete for their business.

25449 ■ *"CBC Chief: Future is Now"* in *Business Courier* (Vol. 27, August 13, 2010, No. 15, pp. 1)
Pub: Business Courier
Ed: Lucy May. **Description:** Tom Williams, chairman of the Cincinnati Business Committee (CBC), maintains that politicians and business leaders must cooperate to ensure the competitiveness of the city for the 21st Century. Under Williams' leadership, the CBC has put emphasis on initiatives related to

government efficiency, economic development, and public education. Williams' views on a proposed inland port are given.

25450 ■ *"Challenges Await Quad in Going Public"* in *Milwaukee Business Journal* (Vol. 27, January 29, 2010, No. 18, pp. A1)
Pub: American City Business Journals
Ed: Rich Rovito. **Description:** Sussex, Wisconsin-based Quad/Graphics Inc.'s impending acquisition of rival Canadian World Color Press Inc. will transform it into a publicly held entity for the first time. Quad has operated as a private company for nearly 40 years and will need to adjust to changes, such as the way management shares information with Quad/Graphics' employees. Details of the merger are included.

25451 ■ *Change in SMEs: The New European Capitalism*
Pub: Palgrave Macmillan
Ed: Katharina Bluhm; Rudi Schmidt. **Released:** October 2008. **Price:** $95.00. **Description:** Effects of global change on corporate governance, management, competitive strategies and labor relations in small-to-medium sized enterprises in various European countries are discussed.

25452 ■ *"Characteristics of Great Salespeople"* in *Agency Sales Magazine* (Vol. 39, November 2009, No. 10, pp. 40)
Pub: MANA
Ed: Paul Pease. **Description:** Tips for managers in order to maximize the performance of their sales personnel are presented through several vignettes. Using performance based commission that rewards success, having business systems that support sales activity, and having an organizational culture that embraces sales as a competitive edge are some suggestions.

25453 ■ *"Cheese Spread Whips Up a Brand New Bowl"* in *Brandweek* (Vol. 49, April 21, 2008, No. 16, pp. 17)
Pub: VNU Business Media, Inc.
Ed: Mike Beirne. **Description:** Mrs. Kinser's Pimento Cheese Spread is launching a new container for its product in order to attempt stronger brand marketing with a better bowl in order to win over the heads of households as young as in their 30s. The company also intends to begin distribution in Texas and the West Coast. Mrs. Kinser's is hoping that the new packaging will provide a more distinct branding and will help consumers distinguish what flavor they are buying.

25454 ■ *"Children's Products Maker Not the New Kid on the Block"* in *Crain's Cleveland Business* (Vol. 28, November 26, 2007, No. 47, pp. 3)
Pub: Crain Communications, Inc.
Ed: David Bennett. **Description:** Discusses the business model employed by Shamrock Industries Inc., a rising star in the competitive world of children's products; the company, which does business as Foundations Quality Children's Products, has expanded into a 63,000-square-foot distribution center which has boosted its local profile significantly.

25455 ■ *"Chinese Solar Panel Manufacturer Scopes Out Austin"* in *Austin Business JournalInc.* (Vol. 29, October 30, 2009, No. 34, pp. 1)
Pub: American City Business Journals
Ed: Jacob Dirr. **Description:** China's Yingli Green Energy Holding Company Ltd. is looking for a site in order to construct a $20 million photovoltaic panel plant. Both Austin and San Antonio are vying to house the manufacturing hub. The project could create about 300 jobs and give Austin a chance to become a player in the solar energy market. Other solar companies are also considering Central Texas as an option to set up shop.

25456 ■ *"Citadel Hires Three Lehman Execs"* in *Chicago Tribune* (October 2, 2008)
Pub: McClatchy-Tribune Information Services
Ed: James P. Miller. **Description:** Citadel Investment Group LLC, Chicago hedge-fund operator, has hired three former senior executives of bankrupt invest-

ment banker Lehman Brothers Holding Inc. Citadel believes that the company's hiring spree will help them to further expand the firm's capabilities in the global fixed income business.

25457 ■ *"Clash of the Titans"* in *Canadian Business* (Vol. 80, March 12, 2007, No. 6, pp. 27)
Pub: Rogers Media
Ed: Andrew Wahl. **Description:** The frequent allegations of Google Inc. and Microsoft Corp. against each other over copyright and other legal issues, with a view to taking away other's market share, is discussed.

25458 ■ *"Closures Pop Cork on Wine Bar Sector Consolidation"* in *Houston Business Journal* (Vol. 40, January 22, 2010, No. 37, pp. A2)
Pub: American City Business Journals
Ed: Allison Wollam. **Description:** Wine bar market in Houston, Texas is in the midst of a major shift and heads toward further consolidation due to the closure of pioneering wine bars that opened in the past decade. The Corkscrew owner, Andrew Adams, has blamed the creation of competitive establishments to the closure which helped wear out his concept.

25459 ■ *"Cloudy Future for VMware?"* in *Barron's* (Vol. 90, September 13, 2010, No. 37, pp. 21)
Pub: Barron's Editorial & Corporate Headquarters
Ed: Jonathan R. Laing. **Description:** VMWare dominated the virtualization market for years, but it may be ending as it faces more competition from rivals that offer cloud computing services. The company's stocks are also expensive and are vulnerable to the smallest mishap.

25460 ■ *"Coca-Cola Bottler Up for Sale: CEO J. Bruce Llewellyn Seeks Retirement"* in *Black Enterprise* (Vol. 37, December 2006, No. 5, pp. 31)
Pub: Earl G. Graves Publishing Co. Inc.
Ed: Marcia A. Wade. **Description:** J. Bruce Llewellyn of Brucephil Inc., the parent company of the Philadelphia Coca-Cola Bottling Co. has agreed to sell its remaining shares to Coca-Cola Co., which previously owned 31 percent of Philly Coke. Analysts believe that Coca-Cola will eventually sell its shares to another bottler.

25461 ■ *"Columbia Sale Narrowed To Two Developers"* in *The Business Journal-Milwaukee* (Vol. 25, July 18, 2008, No. 43, pp. A1)
Pub: American City Business Journals, Inc.
Ed: Corrinne Hess. **Description:** Officials of Columbia St. Mary's Inc plan to pick one of two real-estate developers who will buy the 8-acre property of the Columbia Hospital which the company will move away from when their new hospital has been constructed. The hospital on Newport Ave. has been on the market since 2001.

25462 ■ *"Combat Mission: Rebuffed, BAE Systems Fights Army Contract Decision"* in *Business Courier* (Vol. 26, September 25, 2009)
Pub: American City Business Journals, Inc.
Ed: Jon Newberry. **Description:** BAE Systems filed a complaint with the US Government Accountability Office after the US Army issued an order to BAE's competitor for armoured trucks which is potentially worth over $3 billion. Hundreds of jobs in Butler County, Ohio hinge on the success of the contract protest.

25463 ■ *"Companies Urged to Take Steps to Replenish Work Force"* in *Crain's Cleveland Business* (Vol. 28, October 29, 2007, No. 43, pp. 9)
Pub: Crain Communications, Inc.
Ed: Mike Verespej. **Description:** If America wants to stay competitive in the global marketplace, experts say that the education system will need serious improvements. According to Thomas J. Donahue,

president and CEO of the U.S. Chamber of Commerce, one-third of the K-through-12 students in the United States don't graduate from high school.

25464 ■ Competing in Emerging Markets
Pub: Taylor & Francis Group
Contact: Peter Rigby, Chief Executive Officer
Ed: Hemant Merchant. **Released:** October 2007. **Price:** $62.95. **Description:** Understanding the perils and promises of emerging markets to the growth of companies is discussed. Readings and case studies focus on the strategic and operational challenges companies face while competing in emerging markets.

25465 ■ "Competing On Resources" in Harvard Business Review (Vol. 86, July-August 2008, No. 8, pp. 140)
Pub: Harvard Business School Press
Ed: David J. Collis; Cynthia A. Montgomery. **Description:** Guidelines regarding assessing the value of resources, such as slow depreciation and superiority to competitors' similar resources are discussed.

25466 ■ "Competing on Talent Analytics" in Harvard Business Review (Vol. 88, October 2010, No. 10, pp. 52)
Pub: Harvard Business School Publishing
Ed: Thomas H. Davenport, Jeanne Harris, Jeremy Shapiro. **Description:** Six ways to use talent analytics to obtain the highest level of value from employees are listed. These include human-capital investment analysis, talent value models, workforce forecasts, and talent supply chains.

25467 ■ "Competition At Last?" in Canadian Business (Vol. 81, July 22, 2008, No. 12-13, pp. 7)
Pub: Rogers Media Ltd.
Description: Competition Policy Review Panel's 'Compete to Win' report revealed that Canada is being 'hollowed-out' by foreign acquisitions. The panel investigated competition and foreign investment policies in Canada. Key information on the report, as well as views on the Investment Canada Act and the Competition Act, is presented.

25468 ■ "Competition Qualms Overblown: Inco" in Globe & Mail (February 15, 2006, pp. B1)
Pub: CTVglobemedia Publishing Inc.
Ed: Wendy Stueck. **Description:** Inco Ltd. plans the acquisition of Falconbridge Ltd., for $12.5 billion. The advantages of the acquisition for Inco Ltd. are presented.

25469 ■ "Competition To Provide Liquidity on the New York Stock Exchange" in Business Horizons (November-December 2007, pp. 513)
Pub: Elsevier Technology Publications
Ed: Robert Battalio, Robert Jennings. **Description:** Provision of liquidity at the New York Stock Exchange is studied. On-floor traders enjoy some advantages in providing liquidity compared to off-floor traders. The NYSE is justified in implementing measures designed to level the playing field between on- and off-floor traders.

25470 ■ "The Competitive Imperative Of Learning" in Harvard Business Review (Vol. 86, July-August 2008, No. 8, pp. 60)
Pub: Harvard Business School Press
Ed: Amy C. Edmondson. **Description:** Experimentation and reflection are important components for maintaining success in the business world and are the kind of character traits that can help one keep his or her competitive edge.

25471 ■ "Competitive Restaurant Scene Lures Buyers to Saratoga Springs" in Business Review, Albany New York (Vol. 34, October 26, 2007)
Pub: American City Business Journals, Inc.
Ed: Robin K. Cooper. **Description:** Restaurant industry in Saratoga Springs, New York, a competitive market, with the city having 102 licensed restaurants and 28,499 residents in 2006. Buyers tend to acquire restaurants in Saratoga Springs, New York due to its good market condition. Examples of restaurant acquisitions in Saratoga Springs are given.

25472 ■ "Competitors Line Up to Save Failing Banks" in The Business Journal - Serving Phoenix and the Valley of the Sun (Vol. 28, July 25, 2008, No. 47, pp. 1)
Pub: American City Business Journals, Inc.
Ed: Chris Casacchia. **Description:** Financial institutions in Arizona are positioning themselves as possible buyers in the event of failure of one of their competitors. These banks have already approached the Federal Deposit Insurance Corp. about their ability to take over their more troubled competitors.

25473 ■ "Competitors' Resource-Oriented Strategies" in Academy of Management Review (January 2008, pp. 97)
Pub: ScholarOne, Inc.
Ed: Laurence Capron, Olivier Chatain. **Description:** Firms can maintain a competitive advantage by implementing competitor's' resource-oriented strategies to combat the resources of rivals in factor markets as well as political markets.

25474 ■ The Complete Guide to Selling a Business
Pub: NOLO
Ed: Fred S. Steingold. **Released:** November 2007. **Price:** $34.99. **Description:** When selling a business it is critical that a sales agreement covers all key concerns from price and payment terms to liability protection and restrictions on future competition.

25475 ■ The Connection Key: Seven Ways the World's Most Successful Entrepreneurs Trounce the Competition and How You Can, Too
Pub: John Wiley & Sons, Inc.
Ed: Maribeth Kuzmeski. **Released:** September 22, 2009. **Price:** $22.95. **Description:** The book is written under the premise that getting ahead in business does not come down to smarts, guts, rare talent, or plain old luck. While those things are helpful, the real missing ingredient is the ability to meaningfully connect with others.

25476 ■ "Construction Companies Think Smaller, Find Niches as Projects Become Fewer" in Crain's Detroit Business (March 10, 2008)
Pub: Crain Communications, Inc.
Ed: Daniel Duggan. **Description:** Due to the decline in development projects, construction firms are facing stronger competition for bids and are relying on their good track records or developing expertise in specific niches to get the job.

25477 ■ "Contractors Should Expand Their Services" in Contractor (Vol. 56, July 2009, No. 7, pp. 34)
Pub: Penton Media, Inc.
Ed: Steven Scandaliato. **Description:** All single family homes will be required to have fire sprinkler systems installed when the 2009 International Residential Code arrives. This presents an opportunity for plumbing contractors and they can be competitively priced against a fire protection contractor if they train their workforce to install sprinklers.

25478 ■ Corporate Entrepreneurship & Innovation
Pub: Thomson South-Western
Ed: Michael H. Morris; Donald F. Kuratko. **Released:** January 2007. **Price:** $104.95. **Description:** Innovation is the key to running a successful small business. The book helps entrepreneurs to develop the skills and business savvy to sustain a competitive edge.

25479 ■ "Cost of Md. Health Plan Not Known" in Baltimore Business Journal (Vol. 28, September 3, 2010, No. 17, pp. 1)
Pub: Baltimore Business Journal
Ed: Emily Mullin. **Description:** United States health reform is seen to result in increased health insurance prices in Maryland. However, health care reform advocates claim a new marketplace and increased competition will help keep costs down.

25480 ■ "CP Rail Cuts Jobs to Keep Pace With CN" in Globe & Mail (January 16, 2006, pp. B1)
Pub: CTVglobemedia Publishing Inc.
Ed: Brent Jang. **Description:** Canadian Pacific Railway Ltd. (CPR) reduces workforce in order to remain competitive with Canadian National Railway Co. The details of CPR's proposal are presented.

25481 ■ "CPR Signals a Switch in Strategy to Narrow Competitive Gap With CN" in Globe & Mail (January 20, 2006, pp. B3)
Pub: CTVglobemedia Publishing Inc.
Ed: Brent Jang. **Description:** The reasons behind the restructuring efforts of Canadian Pacific Railway Ltd. are presented.

25482 ■ "Crain's Nabs 15 Press Club Awards" in Crain's Cleveland Business (Vol. 30, June 29, 2009, No. 25, pp. 6)
Pub: Crain Communications, Inc.
Description: Crain's Cleveland Business was honored with 15 awards at the Ohio Excellence in Journalism competition conducted by the Press Club of Cleveland.

25483 ■ Creativity and Innovation: Breaking New Ground..Without Breaking the Bank
Pub: A. & C. Black
Ed: Janice Armstrong. **Released:** March 1, 2009. **Price:** $12.95. **Description:** Advice is given to help small business owners be creative in order to compete in their sector.

25484 ■ "Cupcake Eating Contest Draws World-Class Competitors" in Waterloo Courier (April 14, 2011)
Pub: Lee Enterprises
Ed: Amie Steffen. **Description:** World Cupcake Eating Championships were held at the Isle Casino Hotel Waterloo, Iowa, April 23, 2011. Major League Eating reports this to be the first time they've held a cupcake eating contest.

25485 ■ "Dairy Queen Ends Effort Against Yogubliz" in Ice Cream Reporter (Vol. 23, November 20, 2010, No. 12, pp. 1)
Pub: Ice Cream Reporter
Description: Dairy Queen has stopped demands that Yogubliz Inc. change its Blizzberry and Blizz Frozen Yogurt shops because they sound too much like Dairy Queen's Blizzard frozen dessert treat. Dairy Queen feared consumers would confuse the two brands.

25486 ■ "The Data Drivers" in Canadian Business (Vol. 81, September 15, 2008, No. 14-15, pp. 1)
Pub: Rogers Media Ltd.
Ed: Andrew Wahl. **Description:** Canadian regulators hope that an auction of telecommunications companies will inject more competition into the industry; however, newcomers may not be able to rely on lower prices in order to gain market share from the three major telecommunications companies that already have a stronghold on the market. Analysts feel that providing additional data service is the key to surviving market disruptions.

25487 ■ "David Low" in Hawaii Business (Vol. 53, October 2007, No. 4, pp. 38)
Pub: Hawaii Business Publishing
Ed: Cathy S. Cruz-George. **Description:** Hawaii Capital Management managing director David Low ranked first in the 2007 competition for fittest male executives in Hawaii. This 5-foot-9 executive, who weighed 225 lbs. in 2003, weighs 150 lbs. in 2007. The activities that improved Low's fitness, such as weight training, swimming, biking, and running, are discussed.

25488 ■ "The Dean of Design" in Canadian Business (Vol. 79, November 6, 2006, No. 22, pp. 42)
Pub: Rogers Media
Ed: Erin Pooley. **Description:** The need of a good business design to increase the business in saturated markets with relation to customer satisfaction is emphasized.

25489 ■ "Dean Foods" in Ice Cream Reporter (Vol. 23, November 20, 2010, No. 12, pp. 8)
Pub: Ice Cream Reporter
Description: The impact of higher commodity prices can be seen in the recent news from Dean Foods, the largest U.S. dairy company, which reported that rising butterfat and other dairy commodity costs have led to lower-than-expected quarterly profits after it cut prices to compete with private-label brands.

25490 ■ "Death of the PC" in Canadian Business (Vol. 83, October 12, 2010, No. 17, pp. 44)
Pub: Rogers Media Ltd.
Ed: Joe Castaldo. **Description:** The future of the personal computer (PC) is looking bleak as consumers are relying more on new mobile devices instead of their PC. A 'Wall Street Journal' article published in September 2010 reported that the iPad had cannibalized sales of laptops by as much as 50 percent. The emergence of tablet computers running alternative operating systems is also explained.

25491 ■ "Defense Contractor May Expand Locally; BAE Systems Ramps Up Vehicle Prototypes" in Crain's Detroit Business (March 24, 2008)
Pub: Crain Communications, Inc.
Ed: Chad Halcom. **Description:** Profile of BAE Systems, a defense contractor, that has built a prototype in the highly competitive Joint Light Tactical Vehicle project; the company has also completed its prototype RG33L Mine Resistant Recovery Maintenance Vehicle and has plans for expansion.

25492 ■ "Detroit Pawn Shop to be Reality TV Venue" in UPI NewsTrack (July 10, 2010)
Pub: United Press International-USA
Description: TruTV will present a new series called 'Hardcore Pawn' to compete with the History Channel's successful show 'Pawn Stars'. The show will feature American Jewelry and Loan in Detroit, Michigan and its owner Les Gold, who runs the store with his wife and children.

25493 ■ "Developers Compete for APG Project" in Baltimore Business Journal (Vol. 27, October 16, 2009, No. 23, pp. 1)
Pub: American City Business Journals
Ed: Daniel J. Sernovitz. **Description:** Corporate Office Properties Trust has lost the case in Delaware bankruptcy court to prevent rival St. John Properties Inc. from going ahead with its plans to develop the 400 acres at Aberdeen Proving Ground (APG) in Maryland. Both developers have competed for the right to develop the two million square foot business park in APG.

25494 ■ "Developers Vie for UWM Dorm" in The Business Journal-Milwaukee (Vol. 25, July 11, 2008, No. 42, pp. A1)
Pub: American City Business Journals, Inc.
Ed: Rich Kirchen. **Description:** Eight developers are competing to build a 500- to 700-student residence hall for the University of Wisconsin-Milwaukee. The residence hall will probably be developed within two miles of the main campus. It was revealed that the university's real estate foundation will select the successful bidder on July 25, 2008, and construction will begin by January 2009.

25495 ■ "The Digital Revolution is Over. Long Live the Digital Revolution!" in Business Strategy Review (Vol. 21, Spring 2010, No. 1, pp. 74)
Pub: Wiley-Blackwell
Ed: Gianvito Lanzolla, Jamie Anderson. **Description:** Many businesses are now involved in the digital marketplace. The authors argue that the new reality of numerous companies offering overlapping products means that it is critical for managers to understand digital convergence and to observe the imperatives for remaining competitive.

25496 ■ "Disney Has High Hopes for Duffy" in Canadian Business (Vol. 83, October 12, 2010, No. 17, pp. 14)
Pub: Rogers Media Ltd.
Ed: James Cowan. **Description:** The reintroduction of Duffy is expected to create a new, exclusive product line that distinguishes Disney's parks and stores from competitors. Duffy, a teddy bear, was first introduced at a Disney World store in Florida in 2002. The character was incorporated into the Disney mythology when its popularity grew in Japan.

25497 ■ "Diving Into Internet Marketing" in American Agent and Broker (Vol. 81, December 2009, No. 12, pp. 24)
Pub: Summit Business Media
Ed: Steve Anderson. **Description:** Internet marketing is becoming an essential tool for most businesses; advice is provided regarding the social networking opportunities available for marketing one's product or service on the Internet.

25498 ■ "Downtown Evens Tenant Ledger" in The Business Journal-Serving Metropolitan Kansas City (Vol. 26, July 11, 2008, No. 44, pp. 1)
Pub: American City Business Journals, Inc.
Ed: Rob Roberts. **Description:** Financial services company PricewaterhouseCoopers will relocate its office from the Broadway Square building, but it will not leave downtown as it signs a long-term lease for a 27,000 square feet of space in Town Pavilion. Town Pavilion is the biggest multitenant office building in downtown. Downtown's market competitiveness is also examined.

25499 ■ "Efficient Cash Management Essential To Be Competitive" in Crain's Cleveland Business (Vol. 28, November 12, 2007, No. 45, pp. 25)
Pub: Crain Communications, Inc.
Ed: Ken Moultrie. **Description:** In order to sustain a business it is important to organize cash-management efforts around three core areas: cash in, static cash and cash out. Tips for the successful management of these areas are provided.

25500 ■ "Elanco Challenges Bayer's Advantage, K9 Advantix Ad Claims" in Pet Product News (Vol. 64, November 2010, No. 11, pp. 11)
Pub: BowTie Inc.
Description: Elanco Animal Health has disputed Bayer Animal Health's print and Web advertising claims involving its flea, tick, and mosquito control products Advantage and K9 Advantix. The National Advertising Division of the Council of Better Business Bureaus recommended the discontinuation of ads, while Bayer Animal Health reiterated its commitment to self-regulation.

25501 ■ "Election Could Undo Renewable Energy Quotas" in The Business Journal - Serving Phoenix and the Valley of the Sun (Vol. 28, July 11, 2008, No. 45, pp. 1)
Pub: American City Business Journals, Inc.
Ed: Patrick O'Grady. **Description:** Competition for the three open seats in the Arizona Corporation Commission is intense, with 12 candidates contesting for the three slots. The commission's mandates for renewable energy and infrastructure investment will also be at stake.

25502 ■ The Emerging Markets Century: How a New Breed of World-Class Companies is Overtaking the World
Pub: Free Press/Simon & Schuster Inc.
Ed: Antoine van Agtmael. **Released:** 2007. **Price:** $29.00. **Description:** An exploration of how companies like Lenovo and Haier who are presently in emerging economies are already competing with household name brands like Ford and Sony, thus proving globalization is here to stay.

25503 ■ "Engine of Growth: U.S. Industry Funk hasn't Hurt Cummins or Its Investors" in Barron's (Vol. 88, July 14, 2008, No. 28, pp. 43)
Pub: Dow Jones & Co., Inc.
Ed: Shirley A. Lazo. **Description:** Engine maker Cummins increased its quarterly common dividend by 40 percent to 17.5 cents per share from 12.5 cents. CVS Caremark's dividend saw a hike of 18.4 percent from 9.5 cents to 11.25 cents per share while its competitor Walgreen is continuing its 75th straight year of dividend distribution and its 33rd straight year of dividend hikes.

25504 ■ Entrepreneurship and Economic Growth
Pub: Edward Elgar Publishing, Incorporated
Ed: Carree. **Released:** October 2006. **Price:** $195.00. **Description:** Historic and country-specific studies and articles regarding entrepreneurship and innovation, growth models, competition and productivity, and empirical evidence.

25505 ■ "An Equity Fund of Their Own" in Entrepreneur (Vol. 35, October 2007, No. 10, pp. 68)
Pub: Entrepreneur Media Inc.
Ed: Lee Gimpel. **Description:** About 100 new private equity funds have formed since 2002, proof that private equity investing is becoming popular among companies. There is also an increase in competition to close deals owing to the large number of investors that companies can choose; advantages of smaller funds over the larger one is explained.

25506 ■ "Evaluate Your Process and Do It Better" in Modern Machine Shop (Vol. 84, October 2011, No. 5, pp. 34)
Pub: Gardner Business Media, Inc.
Contact: Richard G. Kline, President
E-mail: rkline@gardnerweb.com
Ed: Wayne S. Chaneski. **Description:** In order to be more competitive, many machine shops owners are continually looking at their processes and procedures in order to be more competitive.

25507 ■ "Family Firm Performance: Further Evidence" in Family Business Review (Vol. 19, June 2006, No. 2, pp. 103)
Pub: Family Firm Institute
Contact: Judy L. Green, President
Ed: Jim Lee. **Description:** Empirical results of regression analysis, which is used to examine the competitiveness of family owned businesses and non-family firms are presented.

25508 ■ Faster Cheaper Better
Pub: Crown Business Books
Ed: Michael Hammer. **Released:** December 28, 2010. **Price:** $27.50. **Description:** Nine levels for transforming work in order to achieve business growth are outlined. The book helps small business compete against the low-wage countries.

25509 ■ "Film Incentives: A Hit or a Flop?" in Michigan Vue (Vol. 13, July-August 2008, No. 4, pp. 10)
Pub: Entrepreneur Media Inc.
Description: Michigan's new film incentive legislation is fulfilling its core purpose, according to Lisa Dancsok of the Michigan Economic Development Corp. (MEDC), by kickstarting the state's entry into the multi-billion dollar industry; the initiative is considered to be very competitive with other states and countries and is thought to be a way in which to help revitalize Michigan's struggling economy.

25510 ■ "Find Your Marketing Mojo" in Business Owner (Vol. 35, July-August 2011, No. 4, pp. 14)
Pub: DL Perkins Company
Description: Marketing and branding a small business can be learned and implemented by following a process that begins with setting and creating the vision that every successful venture requires: a crystal-clear vision for who you are, what you stand for, and why customers will come to you rather than competitors.

25511 ■ "Finding Competitive Advantage in Adversity" in Harvard Business Review (Vol. 88, November 2010, No. 11, pp. 102)
Pub: Harvard Business School Publishing
Ed: Bhaskar Chakravorti. **Description:** Four opportunities in adversity are identified and applied to business scenarios. These are matching unmet needs with unneeded resources, seeking collaboration from unlikely partners, developing small/appropriate solutions to large/complex issues, and focusing on the platform as well as the product.

25512 ■ *"Finding a Way to Continue Growing"* in *Green Industry Pro (Vol. 23, March 2011, No. 3, pp. 31)*
Pub: Cygnus Business Media
Description: Profile of Brett Lemcke, VP of R.M. Landscape located in Rochester, New York. Lemcke tells how his Landscape Industry Certified credentials helped him to grow his business and beat out his competition.

25513 ■ *"Five Reasons Why the Gap Fell Out of Fashion"* in *Globe & Mail (January 27, 2007, pp. B4)*
Pub: CTVglobemedia Publishing Inc.
Ed: Keith McArthur. **Description:** The five major market trends that have caused the decline of fashion clothing retailer Gap Inc.'s sales are discussed. The shift in brand, workplace fashion culture, competition, demographics, and consumer preferences have lead to the Gap's brand identity.

25514 ■ *"Flights of Fancy"* in *Crain's Chicago Business (Vol. 31, April 21, 2008, No. 16, pp. 27)*
Pub: Crain Communications, Inc.
Ed: Sarah A. Klein. **Description:** Due to the competition for business travelers, who account for 30 percent of airline revenue, airlines are offering a number of luxury amenities, especially on long-haul routes.

25515 ■ *"Food Fight"* in *Canadian Business (Vol. 79, November 6, 2006, No. 22, pp. 18)*
Pub: Rogers Media
Ed: Zena Olijnyk. **Description:** The war between Canadian grocers and Wal-Mart due to its plans for opening new stores is analyzed.

25516 ■ *"For Bombardier, a Case of Deja Vu"* in *Canadian Business (Vol. 83, August 17, 2010, No. 13-14, pp. 28)*
Pub: Rogers Media Ltd.
Ed: Laura Cameron. **Description:** Foreign competitors have accused the Quebec government and the Societe de transport de Montreal of giving Bombardier preferential treatment when it bids for contract to replace Montreal metro's rail cars. Bombardier was in a similar situation in 1974 when it won the contract to build the metro's second generation rail cars.

25517 ■ *"Ford, Chrysler Dinged as Little Cars Rule Road"* in *Globe & Mail (March 2, 2007, pp. B3)*
Pub: CTVglobemedia Publishing Inc.
Ed: Greg Keenan. **Description:** The Ford Motor Co. and the Chrysler Group posted a decline in automobile sales in the first two months of 2007. The sales statistics of other automobile companies in Canada are also presented.

25518 ■ *"Forward Motion"* in *Green Industry Pro (July 2011)*
Pub: Cygnus Business Media
Ed: Gregg Wartgow. **Description:** Several landscape contractors have joined this publication's Working Smarter Training Challenge over the last year. This process is helping them develop ways to improve work processes, boost morale, drive out waste, reduce costs, improve customer service, and be more competitive.

25519 ■ *"Fox"* in *Brandweek (Vol. 49, April 21, 2008, No. 16, pp. SR3)*
Pub: VNU Business Media, Inc.
Ed: John Consoli. **Description:** Provides contact information for sales and marketing personnel for the Fox network as well as a listing of the station's top programming and an analysis of the current season and the target audience for those programs running in the current season. In terms of upfront advertising dollars, it looks as if Fox will be competing against NBC for third place due to its success at courting the 18-49-year-old male demographic.

25520 ■ *"Franchisees Lose Battle Against BK"* in *Advertising Age (Vol. 79, June 2, 2008, No. 22, pp. 46)*
Pub: Crain Communications, Inc.
Ed: Emily Bryson York. **Description:** Burger King has had continuing litigation with former franchisees from New York, Luan and Elizabeth Sadik, who claim

that Burger King's double cheeseburger, along with additional problems, created the environment for their eventual insolvency. Burger King has since terminated its test of selling the double cheeseburger for $1, although the company declined to comment on the reason for this decision.

25521 ■ *"From Concept To Consumer: How to Turn Ideas Into Money"*
Pub: Pearson Education Inc.
Ed: Phil Baker. **Released:** 2009. **Price:** $24.99. **Description:** Renowned product developer Phil Baker explains how a great idea accounts for only 5 percent of all the factors of success and why the majority of success is dependent upon a myriad of other factors, including the time it takes to get to market, price, marketing and distribution. By being their own best competition, a small company can stay one step ahead of competitors.

25522 ■ *"The Future of Private Equity"* in *Canadian Business (Vol. 80, March 26, 2007, No. 7, pp. 19)*
Pub: Rogers Media
Ed: Jack Mintz. **Description:** The impact growing Canadian economy and competition in global business on the performance of private equity funds is analyzed.

25523 ■ *"Game On: The Hunt Is On for Nation's Top Keeper"* in *Farmer's Weekly (March 28, 2008, No. 320)*
Pub: Reed Business Information
Contact: Jeff Greisch, President
Description: Gamekeepers must strike the natural balance that encourages wildlife and protects game. CLA Game Fair and Farmer's Weekly are holding a competition for Gamekeeper of the Year 2008.

25524 ■ *"Gatorade Loses Its Competitive Edge; Upstart Rivals Undercut Its Domination of Game"* in *Crain's Chicago Business (April 28, 2008)*
Pub: Crain Communications, Inc.
Ed: Natalie Zmuda. **Description:** According to beverage-marketing experts, Gatorade is losing some of its market share to aggressive new rivals who are appealing to younger consumers.

25525 ■ *"Getting to Scale: Growing Your Business Without Selling Out"*
Pub: Berrett-Koehler Publishers, Incorporated
Ed: Jill Bamburg. **Released:** July 2006. **Price:** $14.95. **Description:** Ways for entrepreneurs to preserve the value of their company while maintaining growth and competitiveness.

25526 ■ *"Give It Your All, and Don't Worry About the Rest"* in *Inc. (Vol. 33, November 2011, No. 9, pp. 37)*
Pub: Inc. Magazine
Ed: Norm Brodsky. **Description:** In the early stage of a service company, the owners sell themselves to the customers.

25527 ■ *"Gordon Nixon"* in *Canadian Business (Vol. 80, November 5, 2007, No. 22, pp. 9)*
Pub: Rogers Media
Ed: Rachel Pulfer. **Description:** Royal Bank of Canada (RBC) CEO, Gordon Nixon, believes the Canadian financial services segment is heavily regulated. Nixon also feels that it has become difficult for local banks to enter the market since foreign banks can easily come in and compete with them. His views on RBC's success are provided.

25528 ■ *"Gordon Nixon Q&A"* in *Canadian Business (Vol. 80, November 5, 2007, No. 22, pp. 9)*
Pub: Rogers Media
Ed: Rachel Pulfer. **Description:** Royal Bank of Canada (RBC) chief executive officer Gordon Nixon believes that the Canadian financial services segment is heavily regulated. Nixon also feels that it has become difficult for local banks to enter the market since foreign banks can easily come in and compete with Canadian banks. His views on RBC's success are provided.

25529 ■ *Green to Gold*
Pub: Yale University Press
Contact: John Donatich, Director
Ed: Daniel C. Esty; Andrew S. Winston. **Released:** January 2009. **Price:** $19.95. **Description:** Examples are given for small businesses to beat competition while tackling sustainability, engage stakeholders, develop NGO partnerships, and work environmental stewardship into corporate culture.

25530 ■ *Greening Your Small Business: How to Improve Your Bottom Line, Grow Your Brand, Satisfy Your Customers and Save the Planet*
Pub: Prentice Hall Press
Contact: Dame Marjorie M. Scardino, Chief Executive Officer
Ed: Jennifer Kaplan. **Released:** November 3, 2009. **Price:** $19.95. **Description:** A definitive resource for anyone who wants their small business to be cutting-edge, competitive, profitable, and eco-conscious. Stories from small business owners address every aspect of going green, from basics such as recycling waste, energy efficiency, and reducing information technology footprint, to more in-depth concerns such as green marketing and communications, green business travel, and green employee benefits.

25531 ■ *"Greg Stringham"* in *Canadian Business (Vol. 81, March 3, 2008, No. 3, pp. 8)*
Pub: Rogers Media
Ed: Michelle Magnan. **Description:** Canadian Association of Petroleum Producers' Greg Stringham thinks that the new royalty plan will result in companies pulling out their investments for Alberta's conventional oil and gas sector. Stringham adds that Alberta is losing its competitive advantage and companies must study their cost profiles to retrieve that advantage. The effects of the royalty system on Alberta's economy are examined further.

25532 ■ *"Guts Not Included"* in *Canadian Business (Vol. 81, March 31, 2008, No. 5, pp. 46)*
Pub: Rogers Media
Ed: Andrew Wahl. **Description:** Executives need the vision to create a strategy that prepares for an uncertain future in light of growing global competition. Canadian business leaders have the right skills and education but do not have enough tolerance for risk.

25533 ■ *"Hit the Books"* in *Entrepreneur (Vol. 36, April 2008, No. 4, pp. 74)*
Pub: Entrepreneur Media, Inc.
Ed: Nichole L. Torres. **Description:** Lists of the top business schools in different U.S. universities are presented. These lists are categorized according to best professors, best classroom experience, most competitive students, greatest opportunity for women, and greatest opportunity for minority students. The lists, compiled by the Princeton Review, are based on student opinion.

25534 ■ *"Hola and Aloha"* in *Hawaii Business (Vol. 53, December 2007, No. 6, pp. 131)*
Pub: Hawaii Business Publishing
Ed: Jason Ubay. **Description:** Juan Carlos Bianchetti is the trilingual owner of Ole Tours Hawaii, a travel wholesaler that targets Portuguese and Spanish-speaking visitors. The competition for American and Japanese tourists is already tight, which is why Bianchetti opted to target a different segment of the Hawaii tourism market. Plans for the company's expansion in Kauai, Brazil, and Argentina, are mentioned.

25535 ■ *"Hoover's Mobile, MobileSP Now Available"* in *Information Today (Vol. 26, February 2009, No. 2, pp. 29)*
Pub: Information Today, Inc.
Description: Hoover's Inc. introduced its Hoover's Mobile for iPhone, BlackBerry and Windows Mobile smartphones along with Hoover's MobileSP for Black-Berry and Windows Mobile. Both products allow users to access customer, prospect, and partner information; analyze competitors; prepare for meetings; and find new opportunities. In addition, MobileSP adds one-click calling to executives, GPS-

enabled location searches, advanced search and list building, and a custom call queue and a 'save to contacts' capabilities.

25536 ■ *"Hopkins, UMd Worry Reduced NIH Budget Will Impact Research" in Boston Business Journal (Vol. 29, August 19, 2011, No. 15, pp. 1)*
Pub: American City Business Journals Inc.

Ed: Scott Dance. **Description:** The budget for the National Institutes of Health (NIH) is slated to be cut by at least 7.9 percent to $2.5 billion in 2013. This will have a big negative effect on medical and biotech research in Maryland, especially Johns Hopkins University and University of Maryland, Baltimore which could face stiffer completion for grants from the NIH.

25537 ■ *"Hostess Reveals Grand Prize Winner of 'CupCake Jackpot' Promotion" in Entertainment Close-Up (August 19, 2011)*
Pub: Close-Up Media

Description: Tricia Botbyl was the grand prize winner of the Hostess 'CupCake Jackpot promotion that asked consumers to 'spin' online to win $10,000. Consumers were asked to vote for their favorite Hostess Brand cupcake flavor.

25538 ■ *Housecleaning Business: Organize Your Business - Get Clients and Referrals - Set Rates and Services*
Pub: Globe Pequot Press

Ed: Laura Jorstad, Melinda Morse. **Released:** June 1, 2009. **Price:** $18.95. **Description:** This book shares insight into starting a housecleaning businesses. It shows how to develop a service manual, screen clients, serve customers, select cleaning products, competition, how to up a home office, using the Internet to grow the business and offering green cleaning options to clients.

25539 ■ *How to Become a Great Boss: The Rules for Getting and Keeping the Best Employees*
Pub: Hyperion Special Markets

Ed: Jeffrey J. Fox. **Released:** May 15, 2002. **Price:** $16.95. **Description:** The book offers valuable advice to any manager or entrepreneur to improve leadership and management skills. Topics covered include: hiring, managing, firing, partnership and competition, self and organization, employee performance, attitude, and priorities.

25540 ■ *"How Dell Will Dial for Dollars" in Austin Business JournalInc. (Vol. 29, December 4, 2009, No. 39, pp. 1)*
Pub: American City Business Journals

Ed: Christopher Calnan. **Description:** Dell Inc. revealed plans to launch a Mini3i smartphone in China which could enable revenue sharing by bundling with wireless service subscription. Dell's smartphone plan is similar to the netbook business, which Dell sold with service provided by AT&T Inc.

25541 ■ *How to Get Rich*
Pub: Ebury Press

Ed: Felix Dennis. **Released:** 2008. **Price:** $25.95. **Description:** Publisher of Maxim, The Week, and Stuff magazines, discusses the mistakes he made running his companies. He didn't understand that people who buy computer gaming magazines wanted a free game with each copy, as one of his rivals was offering. And he laments not diversifying into television and exploiting the Internet.

25542 ■ *How to Make Big Money*
Pub: Hyperion Books

Ed: Jeffrey J. Fox. **Released:** May 19, 2004. **Price:** $16.95. **Description:** Entrepreneur and consultant offers advice to help others create successful startups and prosper. Fox directs new business owners with a counterintuitive style and describes essential methods that beat the competition. Tips include: setting priorities, getting a personal driver, creating a contingency plan for employees, pricing to value, saving money, and getting an office outside of the home.

25543 ■ *How to Write a Business Plan*
Pub: Kogan Page, Limited
Contact: Ben Glover, Director of Marketing

Ed: Brian Finch. **Released:** February 10, 2010. **Price:** $17.95. **Description:** Starting with the premise that there's only one chance to make a good impression, this book covers all the issues involved in producing a successful business plan, from profiling competitors to forecasting marketing development.

25544 ■ *How You Do..What You Do: Create Service Excellence That Wins Clients For Life*
Pub: McGraw-Hill

Ed: Bob Livingston. **Released:** June 6, 2008. **Price:** $27.95. **Description:** Today's marketplace has become a tougher place to do business because of new challenges such as escalating competition, well-informed clients, and dismal customer service. Clients now have more influence and choices than ever. Tips for achieving service excellence are provided.

25545 ■ *"HP Eats Into Rival Dell Sales as Profits Soar" in Globe & Mail (February 21, 2007, pp. B15)*
Pub: CTVglobemedia Publishing Inc.

Ed: Connie Guglielmo. **Description:** The world's largest personal computer maker Hewlett Packard Co. has reported increased profits by 26 percent to $1.55 billion during the first quarter. The company has outpaced its competitor Dell Inc. by offering low priced personal computers during this period.

25546 ■ *If You Have to Cry, Go Outside: And Other Things Your Mother Never Told You*
Pub: HarperOne

Ed: Kelly Cutrone. **Released:** February 2, 2010. **Price:** $22.99. **Description:** Women's mentor advices on how to make it in one of the most competitive industries in the world, fashion. She has kicked people out of fashion shows, forced some of reality television's shiny start to fire their friends, and built her own company which is one of the most powerful public relations firms in the fashion business.

25547 ■ *"Inco's Takeover Offer Extended Four Months" in Globe & Mail (February 22, 2006, pp. B1)*
Pub: CTVglobemedia Publishing Inc.

Ed: Wendy Stueck. **Description:** United States and Europe competition authorities wanted more time to investigate Inco Ltd.'s takeover of Falconbridge Ltd. and compelling Inco to extend its $12.5 billion offer for the third time.

25548 ■ *"Increased Competition Prompts Detroit Hotels to Make Upgrades" in Crain's Detroit Business (Vol. 24, March 31, 2008, No. 13, pp. 1)*
Pub: Crain Communications, Inc.

Ed: Daniel Duggan. **Description:** Five Detroit hotels have recently undergone upgrades or are preparing for major construction projects due to a more competitive hospitality market in the city.

25549 ■ *"Inland Snaps Up Rival REITs" in Crain's Chicago Business (Vol. 31, November 17, 2008, No. 46, pp. 3)*
Pub: Crain Communications, Inc.

Ed: Alby Gallun. **Description:** Discusses Inland American Real Estate Trust Inc., a real estate investment trust that is napping up depressed shares of publicly traded competitors, a possible first step toward taking over these companies; however, with hotel and retail properties accounting for approximately 70 percent of its portfolio, the company could soon face its own difficulties.

25550 ■ *Innovation and Its Discontents*
Pub: Princeton University Press

Ed: Josh Lerner, Adam B. Jaffe. **Released:** 2006. **Price:** $21.95 paperback. **Description:** According to the authors, America's patent system does not effectively serve as a generator and protector of patents and intellectual property.

25551 ■ *Innovation Nation: How America Is Losing Its Innovation Edge, Why It Matters, and How We Can Get It Back*
Pub: Free Press/Simon & Schuster

Ed: John Kao. **Released:** October 2, 2007. **Price:** $26.00. **Description:** Diagnoses of the lack of innovation being seen in the United States today is

examined by a former Harvard Business School professor. He explains how innovation works and puts forth a strategy proposal in an attempt to help America regain its edge on innovation.

25552 ■ *"Insurers No Longer Paying Premium for Advertising" in Brandweek (Vol. 49, April 21, 2008, No. 16, pp. SR3)*
Pub: VNU Business Media, Inc.

Ed: Eric Newman. **Description:** Insurance companies are cutting their advertising budgets after years of accelerated double-digit growth in spending due to the economic downturn, five years of record-breaking ad spend and a need to cut expenditures as claims costs rise and a competitive market keeps premiums in place. Statistical data included.

25553 ■ *International Entrepreneurship in Small and Medium Size Enterprises: Orientation, Environment and Strategy*
Pub: Edward Elgar Publishing, Incorporated

Ed: Hamid Etemad. **Released:** October 2004. **Price:** $130.00. **Description:** Issues involved in internationalizing small and medium sized (SME) businesses. Topics include an investigation into the emerging patterns of SME growth and international expansion in response to the changing competitive environment, dynamics of competitive behavior, entrepreneurial processes and a formulation of strategy.

25554 ■ *"International Growth" in Black Enterprise (Vol. 38, July 2008, No. 12, pp. 64)*
Pub: Earl G. Graves Publishing Co. Inc.

Ed: Marcia A. Reed-Woodard. **Description:** Becoming an increasingly smaller portion of the global business environment is the U.S. economy. Christopher Catlin, an associate with Booz Allen Hamilton, a technology management and strategy-consulting firm, shares what he has learned about the global market.

25555 ■ *"Into the Light: Making Our Way Through the Economic Tunnel" in Agency Sales Magazine (Vol. 39, August 2009, No. 8, pp. 26)*
Pub: MANA

Ed: Michael Dotson. **Description:** Ways in which to avoid business stagnation brought about by the economic downturn, is presented. Being different, being a puzzle solver, and knowing the competition are among the things marketing personnel should do in order to wade through the economic downturn. Marketing via direct mail and the Internet also recommended.

25556 ■ *"Investing in the IT that Makes a Competitive Difference" in Harvard Business Review (Vol. 86, July-August 2008, No. 8, pp. 98)*
Pub: Harvard Business School Press

Ed: Andrew McAfee; Erik Brynjolfsson. **Description:** Components of a successful information technology management strategy are examined. These techniques are broad in spectrum, produce immediate results, are consistent and precise, facilitate monitoring, and promote enforceability.

25557 ■ *"The iPhone Gets Some Competition" in Inc. (Vol. 31, January-February 2009, No. 1, pp. 42)*
Pub: Mansueto Ventures LLC

Ed: Mark Spoonauer. **Description:** RIM's BlackBerry Storm and T-Mobile's G1 are competing with the iPhone 3G technology; the three systems are profiled.

25558 ■ *"It's Not About the G1; Google Just Wants You to Use the Mobile Web" in Advertising Age (Vol. 79, September 29, 2008, No. 36, pp. 32)*
Pub: Crain Communications, Inc.

Ed: Abbey Klaassen. **Description:** Google's Android is the first serious competitor to Apple's iPhone; the company says that its goal is to simplify the mobile market and get wireless subscribers to use the mobile Internet and purchase smartphones.

25559 ■ *"Jack Be Nimble" in Business Courier (Vol. 24, October 26, 2008, No. 28, pp. 1)*
Pub: American City Business Journals, Inc.

Ed: Laura Baverman. **Description:** Cincinnati Bell is losing around 47,000 phone lines a year due to the advent of wireless technology and increased competition from cable companies.

25560 ■ *"Job Seeker's Readiness Guide: Unemployment's High and Competition is Tough" in Black Enterprise (Vol. 40, July 2010, No. 12, pp. 83)*
Pub: Earl G. Graves Publishing Co. Inc.

Description: Five key areas to help someone seeking employment gain the competitive edge are listed.

25561 ■ *"Joe Wikert, General Manager, O'Reilly Technology Exchange" in Information Today (Vol. 26, February 2009, No. 2, pp. 21)*
Pub: Information Today, Inc.

Ed: Jamie Babbitt. **Description:** Joe Wikert, general manager of O'Reilly Technology Exchange discusses his plans to develop a free content model that will evolve with future needs. O'Reilly's major competitor is Google. Wikert plans to expand the firm's publishing program to include print, online, and in-person products and services.

25562 ■ *"Just Hang Up" in Barron's (Vol. 88, March 10, 2008, No. 10, pp. 45)*
Pub: Dow Jones & Company, Inc.

Ed: Tiernan Ray. **Description:** Sprint's shares are expected to continue falling while the company attempts to attract subscribers by cutting prices, cutting earnings in the process. The company faces tougher competition from better-financed AT&T and Verizon Communications.

25563 ■ *"Kari Leong" in Hawaii Business (Vol. 53, October 2007, No. 4, pp. 39)*
Pub: Hawaii Business Publishing

Ed: Cathy S. Cruz-George. **Description:** Greater Good Inc. president Kari Leong is the number 1 fittest female executive in Hawaii for 2007. Leong exercises at the gym and at her home, and carries her two children for strength training. The physical activities she had undergone during her college life at the Gonzaga University are discussed.

25564 ■ *"Keep Customers Out of the Yellow Pages" in Contractor (Vol. 56, November 2009, No. 11, pp. 47)*
Pub: Penton Media, Inc.

Ed: Matt Michel. **Description:** Mechanical contractors should keep customers away from the Yellow Pages where they could find their competition by putting stickers on the water heater or the front of the directory. Giving out magnets to customers and putting the company name on sink rings and invoices are other suggestions.

25565 ■ *"Keeping the Faith in Fuel-Tech" in Barron's (Vol. 88, March 24, 2008, No. 12, pp. 20)*
Pub: Dow Jones & Company, Inc.

Ed: Christopher C. Williams. **Description:** Shares of air pollution control company Fuel-Tech remain on track to reach $40 each from their $19 level due to a continued influx of contracts. The stock has suffered from lower-than-expected quarterly earnings and tougher competition but stand to benefit from increased orders.

25566 ■ *"Kerkorian Shakes Up Chrysler Race" in Globe & Mail (April 6, 2007, pp. B1)*
Pub: CTVglobemedia Publishing Inc.

Ed: Greg Keenan. **Description:** The bid of Kirk Kerkorian's Tracinda Corp. to acquire Daimler-Chrysler AG for $4.5 billion is discussed.

25567 ■ *"King of the Crib: How Good Samaritan Became Ohio's Baby HQ" in Business Courier (Vol. 27, June 18, 2010, No. 7, pp. 1)*
Pub: Business Courier

Ed: James Ritchie. **Description:** Cincinnati's Good Samaritan hospital had 6,875 live births in 2009, which is more than any other hospital in Ohio. They specialize in the highest-risk pregnancies and deliveries and other hospitals are trying to grab Good Samaritan's share in this niche.

25568 ■ *"Knock Your Socks Off Selling"*
Pub: Amacom

Ed: Jeffrey Gitomer. **Released:** May 1999. **Price:** $17.95. **Description:** Tips for salespeople to succeed in a competitive sales environment.

25569 ■ *"Kraft Taps Cheese Head; Jordan Charged With Fixing Foodmaker's Signature Product" in Crain's Chicago Business (April 14, 2008)*
Pub: Crain Communications, Inc.

Ed: David Sterrett. **Description:** Kraft Foods Inc. has assigned Rhonda Jordan, a company veteran, to take charge of the cheese and dairy division which has been losing market shares to cheaper store-brand cheese among cost-sensitive shoppers as Kraft and its competitors raise prices to offset soaring dairy costs.

25570 ■ *"Kroger Girds for Invasion of U.K. Chain" in Business Courier (Vol. 24, November 2, 2008, No. 29, pp. 1)*
Pub: American City Business Journals, Inc.

Ed: Jon Newberry. **Description:** Tesco PLC will be opening its first Fresh & Easy Neighborhood Markets in Southern California. The company has committed $500 million per year to get a share of the $500 billion US food retailing market and will be opening more stores in quick succession. Tesco's arrival can be difficult for Kroger because Kroger had obtained much of its success by using Tesco's UK model.

25571 ■ *"Leapin' Lizards, Does SoBe Have Some Work To Do On Life Water" in Brandweek (Vol. 49, April 21, 2008, No. 16, pp. 32)*
Pub: VNU Business Media, Inc.

Ed: Amy Shea. **Description:** Discusses the competing marketing campaigns of both Vitaminwater, now owned by Coca-Cola, and SoBe Life Water which is owned by Pepsi; also looks at the repositioning of Life Water as a thirst-quencher, rather than a green product as well as the company's newest advertising campaign.

25572 ■ *"Lessons from Turnaround Leaders" in Strategy and Leadership (Vol. 39, May-June 2011, No. 3, pp. 36-43)*
Pub: Emerald Group Publishing Inc.

Ed: David P. Boyd. **Description:** A study analyzes the cases of some successful turnaround leaders to present a strategic model to help firms tackle challenges such as employee inertia, competition and slow organizational renewal. It describes a change model consisting of five major steps to be followed by firms with environmental uncertainty for the purpose.

25573 ■ *"Let the Big Fish Eat" in Canadian Business (Vol. 80, March 12, 2007, No. 6, pp. 4)*
Pub: Rogers Media

Ed: Joe Chidley. **Description:** The need for profitable Canadian banks to go for mergers to enjoy the benefits of globalization and compete with global banks is discussed.

25574 ■ *"Life After Cod" in Globe & Mail (March 18, 2006, pp. B1)*
Pub: CTVglobemedia Publishing Inc.

Ed: Gordon Pitts. **Description:** Canadian fishing industry is under threat because of Chinese processing competition, high energy costs, rise of powerful retailers and the rise of Canadian dollar value. Fishing industry of Canada is analyzed.

25575 ■ *"Lights, Camera, Action: Tools for Creating Video Blogs" in Inc. (Volume 32, December 2010, No. 10, pp. 57)*
Pub: Inc. Magazine

Ed: John Brandon. **Description:** A video blog is a good way to spread company news, talk about products, and stand out among traditional company blogs. New editing software can create two- to four-minute blogs using a webcam and either Windows Live Essentials, Apple iLife 2011, Powerdirector 9 Ultra, or Adobe Visual Communicator 3.

25576 ■ *"Linking Human Capital to Competitive Advantages" in Human Resource Management (Vol. 49, September-October 2010, No. 5)*
Pub: John Wiley

Ed: Yan Jin, Margaret M. Hopkins, Jenell L.S. Wittmer. **Description:** A study was conducted to confirm the links among human capital, firm flexibility, and firm performance. The study also examines the emerging role of flexibility for a company's performance. A total of 201 senior supply chain management professionals from several manufacturing companies were included in the study.

25577 ■ *"A Look At Three Gas-Less Cars" in Hispanic Business (Vol. 30, September 2008, No. 9, pp. 90)*
Pub: Hispanic Business, Inc.

Ed: Daniel Soussa. **Description:** Three major car manufacturers, Chevrolet, BMW, and Honda, are giving market leader Toyota competition for the next generation of eco-friendly car. The latest and most advanced of the gasoline-less cars designed by the three firms, namely the Chevrolet Volt, BMW's Hydrogen 7, and the Honda FCX Clarity, are reviewed.

25578 ■ *"Look Who's Eating Loblaw's Lunch" in Canadian Business (Vol. 80, February 26, 2007, No. 5, pp. 44)*
Pub: Rogers Media

Ed: Zena Olijnyk. **Description:** Loblaw Cos. Ltd. and Shoppers Drug Mart Corp. of Canada are finding increased competition from the global retail giant Wal-Mart Inc. The financial performance of the companies is analyzed.

25579 ■ *"Lotus Starts Slowly, Dodges Subprime Woes" in Crain's Detroit Business (Vol. 24, April 14, 2008, No. 15, pp. 3)*
Pub: Crain Communications, Inc.

Ed: Tom Henderson. **Description:** Discusses Lotus Bancorp Inc. and their business plan, which although is not right on target due to the subprime mortgage meltdown, is in a much better position than its competitors due to the quality of their loans.

25580 ■ *Macrowikinomics: Rebooting Business and the World*
Pub: Portfolio Hardcover

Ed: Don Tapscott, Anthony D. Williams. **Released:** September 28, 2010. **Price:** $27.95. **Description:** Wikinomics Don Tapscott and Anthony Williams showed how mass collaboration was changing the way businesses communicate, create value,, and compete in the new global marketplace in 2007. Now, in the wake of the global financial crisis, the principles of wikinomics have become more powerful than ever.

25581 ■ *"The Main Event" in Canadian Business (Vol. 80, November 19, 2007, No. 23, pp. 28)*
Pub: Rogers Media

Ed: Zena Olijnyk. **Description:** U.S.-based Lowe's Companies, Inc. will be opening three stores in Canada in December 2007 and another three in 2008. The housing market crisis in the U.S. is the reason behind the home improvement store's Canadian expansion. The impacts of the expansion on Canadian home care stores and on the market competition are evaluated.

25582 ■ *Making People Your Competitive Advantage*
Pub: Jossey Bass

Ed: Edward E. Lawler III. **Released:** 2008. **Price:** $29.95. **Description:** Competitive advantage in most organizations has shifted from reliability to innovation and flexibility. Organizations must combine the right structure with the right people to make it work.

25583 ■ *Marketing in a Web 2.0 World - Using Social Media, Webinars, Blogs, and More to Boost Your Small Business on a Budget*
Pub: Atlantic Publishing Company

Ed: Peter VanRysdam. **Released:** June 1, 2010. **Price:** $24.95. **Description:** Web 2.0 technologies have leveled the playing field for small companies trying to boost their presence by giving them an equal voice against larger competitors. Advice is given to help target your audience using social networking hubs.

25584 ■ *"Marriott Checks Out Hotel Prospect"* in The Business Journal-Serving Metropolitan Kansas City (Vol. 27, November 14, 2008, No. 10)

Pub: American City Business Journals, Inc.

Description: Marriott International Inc. is planning to operate a hotel in Kansas City, Missouri and may take over the Kansas City Marriot Downtown although other hotel operators are interested in bidding on the project.

25585 ■ *Mastering the Complex Sales: How to Compete and Win When the Stakes Are High!*

Pub: John Wiley & Sons, Incorporated

Ed: Jeff Thull. **Released:** May 2003. **Price:** $24.95. **Description:** Guide to compete for and win in complex selling, the business-to-business transactions involving multiple decisions by multiple people from multiple perspectives.

25586 ■ *"McD's Picks a Soda Fight; Takes on 7-Eleven With $1 Pop as Economy Softens"* in Crain's Chicago Business (April 14, 2008)

Pub: Crain Communications, Inc.

Ed: David Sterrett. **Description:** McDonald's Corp. is urging franchise owners to slash prices on large soft drinks to one dollar this summer to win customers from convenience store chains like 7-Eleven.

25587 ■ *"McD's Tries to Slake Consumer Thirst for Wider Choice of Drinks"* in Advertising Age (Vol. 79, June 9, 2008, No. 23, pp. 1)

Pub: Crain Communications, Inc.

Ed: Natalie Zmuda; Emily Bryson York. **Description:** McDonald's is testing the sale of canned and bottled drinks in about 150 locations in an attempt to offer more options to consumers who are going elsewhere for their beverage choices.

25588 ■ *"Media Giant Remakes Itself: Job Cuts Signal Journal Sentinel's Focus on New Products"* in Business Journal-Milwaukee (Oct. 12, 2007)

Pub: American City Business Journals, Inc.

Ed: Rich Kirchen. **Description:** Milwaukee Journal Sentinel is reducing its workforce by offering separation pay, and is willing to consider layoffs if the separation program fails. The downsizing is a result of lowered revenue, which was caused by the decline in printed news demand and increase in online competition. Strategies that the Journal Sentinel are employing, such as developing new products, to increase revenue are presented.

25589 ■ *"Medicare Inc."* in Canadian Business (Vol. 80, October 8, 2007, No. 20, pp. 160)

Pub: Rogers Media

Ed: Erin Pooley. **Description:** State of Canada's health care system is discussed. A report by the Fraser Institute in Vancouver predicts that public health spending in six of ten provinces in the country will use more than half the revenues from all sources by 2020. Experts believe competition in the health care industry will help solve the current problems in the sector.

25590 ■ *"The Middle Ages"* in Hawaii Business (Vol. 53, October 2007, No. 4, pp. 42)

Pub: Hawaii Business Publishing

Ed: Cathy S. Cruz-George. **Description:** Starcom Builders Inc.'s Theodore 'Ted' Taketa, School Kine Cookies' Steven Gold And Sharon Serene of Sharon Serene Creative are among the participants in Hawaii's Fittest CEO competition for executives over 50 years old. Taketa takes yoga classes, and also goes to the gym while Serne has Mike Hann as her professional trainer. Eating habits of the aforementioned executives are also described.

25591 ■ *"Miller's Crossroad"* in Canadian Business (Vol. 83, September 14, 2010, No. 15, pp. 58)

Pub: Rogers Media Ltd.

Ed: Joe Castaldo. **Description:** Future Electronics founder and billionaire Robert Miller shares the secret of Future's unique operating model, which is based on inventory and market research. Miller attributes much of the company's success to its privately held status that enables quick movement against competitors.

25592 ■ *Million Dollar Website: Simple Steps to Help You Compete with the Big Boys-Even on a Small Business Budget*

Pub: Prentice Hall Press

Ed: Lori Culwell. **Released:** May 9, 2010. **Price:** $19.95. **Description:** Resource for any small business owner wishing to build a successful Website in order to compete with big box stores.

25593 ■ *"More Pain"* in Canadian Business (Vol. 81, December 24, 2007, No. 1, pp. 12)

Pub: Rogers Media

Ed: Lauren McKeon. **Description:** Manufacturing sector in Canada is sinking with a forecast by as much as 23 percent for 2008, which can be offset as manufacturers say they plan to increase productivity by 25 percent. Details on the sector's competitiveness, workforce, importing of machinery from the U.S. and financial needs for research and development are examined.

25594 ■ *"Most States Have High-Risk Health Insurance Pools"* in Crain's Detroit Business (Vol. 24, March 24, 2008, No. 12, pp. 31)

Pub: Crain Communications, Inc.

Ed: Jay Greene. **Description:** High-risk health insurance pools, designed to cover individuals with medical conditions that essentially make them otherwise uninsurable, are being debated by the Senate Health Policy Committee; the pool concept is supported by Blue Cross Blue Shield of Michigan and contested by a number of consumer groups and competing health insurers.

25595 ■ *"NBC"* in Brandweek (Vol. 49, April 21, 2008, No. 16, pp. SR6)

Pub: VNU Business Media, Inc.

Ed: John Consoli. **Description:** Provides contact information for sales and marketing personnel for the NBC network as well as a listing of the station's top programming and an analysis of the current season and the target audience for those programs running in the current season. NBC also devised a new strategy of announcing its prime-time schedule 52 weeks in advance which was a hit for advertisers who felt this gave them a better opportunity to plan for product placement. Even with the station's creative sales programs, they could face a challenge from Fox in terms of upfront advertisement purchases.

25596 ■ *"Needed: A Strategy; Banking In China"* in The Economist (Vol. 390, January 3, 2009, No. 8612, pp. 54)

Pub: The Economist Newspaper Inc.

Description: International banks are competing for a role in China but are finding obstacles in their paths such as a reduction in the credit their operations may receive from Chinese banks and the role they can play in the public capital markets which remain limited.

25597 ■ *"New Battle of Alberta: Pipelines"* in Globe & Mail (February 3, 2006, pp. B1)

Pub: CTVglobemedia Publishing Inc.

Ed: Dave Ebner. **Description:** The details on stiffening competition between Enbridge Inc. and TransCanada Corp., to build petroleum pipeline from Alberta to Wisconsin, are presented.

25598 ■ *"The Next Great Canadian Idea?"* in Canadian Business (Vol. 81, July 21, 2008, No. 11, pp. 45)

Pub: Rogers Media Ltd.

Ed: Sharda Prashad. **Description:** Thane Heins has invented a generator that produces energy in an isolated system which contradicts the law of conser-

vation of energy. Perepiteia generator is referred to as a 'perpetual motion machine.' Other inventions slated for the Canadian invention competition include Rob Matthies' batteries and Frank Naumann's Smart Trap.

25599 ■ *Niche and Grow Rich*

Pub: Entrepreneur Press

Ed: Jennifer Basye Sander; Peter Sander. **Released:** 2003. **Description:** Consultants share insight to entrepreneurs wishing to find a profitable niche market. Authors write that good niche businesses are easy to start and easy to defend from competitors. They also report that finding a successful niche can attract and maintain good customers who are willing to pay more for unique goods and services.

25600 ■ *"A Novel Approach to the Market"* in Agency Sales Magazine (Vol. 39, December 2009, No. 11, pp. 10)

Pub: MANA

Ed: Jack Foster. **Description:** R/B Sales created a 'merchandising specialist' position that travels their territory and works with distributor counter sales teams. This puts them ahead of their competition as it increases their visibility, appeal and mix of products in their area.

25601 ■ *"Office Supplier Won't Wait for Opportunity to Knock"* in Business Courier (Vol. 24, December 28, 2008, No. 37, pp. 2)

Pub: American City Business Journals, Inc.

Ed: Lucy May. **Description:** Ace Products, an office supplier, stays competitive through its customer service and pricing.

25602 ■ *"Omniplex on the Case"* in Black Enterprise (Vol. 37, December 2006, No. 5, pp. 38)

Pub: Earl G. Graves Publishing Co. Inc.

Ed: Glenn Townes. **Description:** Office of Personnel Management in Washington D.C. recently awarded a service contract to Omniplex World Services Corp. Virginia-based, The Chantilly, will perform security investigations and background checks on current and prospective federal employees and military personnel and contractors.

25603 ■ *"On tap: More Could Get MEGA Credits; Need to Look Outside State May Be Cut"* in Crain's Detroit Business (April 7, 2008)

Pub: Crain Communications, Inc.

Ed: Amy Lane. **Description:** In order to qualify for Michigan Economic Growth Authority tax credits Michigan businesses may no longer have to shop outside the state due to a new bill which has already passed the state Senate and will move on to the House; the bill, along with further changes to the MEGA program, is designed to provide incentives for investments that would add relevance and make Michigan more competitive.

25604 ■ *"Open Skies: Opportunity, Challenge for Airlines"* in Crain's Chicago Business (April 21, 2008)

Pub: Crain Communications, Inc.

Ed: Paul Merrion. **Description:** Discusses the new aviation agreement between Europe and the United States known as Open Skies; the pact creates opportunities for U.S. carriers to fly to new destinations in Europe from more U.S. cities; it also allows carriers to fly between European cities, something they have not been able to do until now.

25605 ■ *"An Opportunity for Patience"* in Barron's (Vol. 88, June 30, 2008, No. 26, pp. M5)

Pub: Dow Jones & Co., Inc.

Ed: Fleming Meeks. **Description:** Shares of Louisiana-Pacific are near their 52-week low at $8.95 per share making them look like a better buy than they were at $11.51 in May, 2008. The company is a to player in a cyclical business and its balance sheet is sound compared to its peers with net debt at just $84 million or 20 percent of total capital.

25606 ■ Outsmart! How to Do What Your Competitors Can't
Pub: FT Press
Ed: Jim Champy. Released: March 7, 2008. Price: $22.99. Description: Small business growth can be achieved through outsmarting your competition. The author identifies eight powerful ways to compete in the toughest marketplace.

25607 ■ "Ownership Preferences, Competitive Heterogeneity, and Family-Controlled Businesses" in Family Business Review (June 2006)
Pub: Family Firm Institute
Contact: Judy L. Green, President
Ed: David G. Hoopes, Danny Miller. Description: Impact of ownership structure and corporate governance choices on competition among family-owned businesses is explored.

25608 ■ "P&G's Iams Finds Itself in a Pet-Food Dogfight" in Advertising Age (Vol. 78, March 5, 2007, No. 10, pp. 6)
Pub: Crain Communications, Inc.
Ed: Jack Neff. Description: Proctor & Gamble Co.'s Iams has been slow to embrace the trend toward foods for pets that appear fit for human consumption. Competitors such as Nestle Purina have made big gains with its colorful premium Beneful brand and dry nuggets that look like chunks of vegetables and meat. Statistical data included.

25609 ■ "Pavilions Poised for Image Overhaul" in The Business Journal - Serving Phoenix and the Valley of the Sun (Vol. 28, August 22, 2008)
Pub: American City Business Journals, Inc.
Ed: Jan Buchholz. Description: DeRitto Partners Inc. is expected to push through with plans for a major renovation of the 1.1 million-square foot Scottsdale Pavilions in Scottsdale, Arizona. An aggressive marketing campaign is planned to be included in the renovation, which aims to address high vacancy rates and competition. Views and information on the planned renovation are presented.

25610 ■ "Play By Play: These Video Products Can Add New Life to a Stagnant Website" in Black Enterprise (Vol. 41, December 2010, No. 5)
Pub: Earl G. Graves Publishing Co. Inc.
Ed: Marcia Wade Talbert. Description: Web Visible, provider of online marketing products and services, cites video capability as the fastest-growing Website feature for small business advertisers. Profiles of various devices for adding video to a Website are included.

25611 ■ Playing Bigger Than You Are: How to Sell Big Accounts Even If You're David in a World of Goliaths
Pub: John Wiley & Sons, Inc.
Ed: William T. Brooks, William P.G. Brooks. Released: November 1, 2009. Price: $18.99. Description: Small and mid-size companies are shown how to compete with larger firms and sell big accounts.

25612 ■ "Please Pass the Mayo" in Crain's Chicago Business (Vol. 31, April 28, 2008, No. 17, pp. 32)
Pub: Crain Communications, Inc.
Ed: Samantha Stainburn. Description: Fort Dearborn Co. has come a long way since it started as on one-press print shop; the family-owned company was struggling to keep up with the technology of making consumer product labels for curvy bottles of products like V8 V-Fusion juice and in 2006 sold off to Genstar Capital LLC which has pushed for acquisitions; last year, Fort Derborn bought its biggest competitor, Renaissance Mark Inc., doubling its size and adding spirit and wine makers to its client roster.

25613 ■ "Port in the Storm" in Canadian Business (Vol. 81, October 13, 2008, No. 17, pp. 101)
Pub: Rogers Media Ltd.
Ed: Calvin Leung. Description: Interport Inc.'s state-of-the-art studio complex in Toronto is discussed. The strong Canadian dollar, along with disputes within the movie industry, are creating challenges for the studio to secure Hollywood projects. Interport plans to compete for Hollywood projects based on quality.

25614 ■ "Pre-K Pressure" in Hawaii Business (Vol. 53, October 2007, No. 4, pp. 32)
Pub: Hawaii Business Publishing
Ed: David K. Choo. Description: Kindergarten admission in Hawaii is becoming more competitive. Parents, for example, prepare their children for the kindergarten admissions process by bringing them to the schools before the interview or by paying for tutorial services. The impacts of increased competition in school admissions on the life of Hawaiian children are discussed.

25615 ■ "Prepaid Phones Surge in Bad Economy" in Advertising Age (Vol. 79, November 17, 2008, No. 43, pp. 6)
Pub: Crain Communications, Inc.
Ed: Rita Chang. Description: Prepay cell phone offerings are becoming increasingly competitive amid a greater choice of plans and handsets. In an economic environment in which many consumers are unable to pass the credit checks required for traditional cell phone plans, the prepay market is surging.

25616 ■ "The Price of Profitability" in Green Industry Pro (Vol. 23, March 2011, No. 3, pp. 18)
Pub: Cygnus Business Media
Ed: Tony Bass. Description: Profit Builder Process is used to help landscaping companies be more competitive. Landscape contractors report pricing among their largest challenges and although the economy is improving, homeowners are paying closer attention to quality and service.

25617 ■ "Price War: Managerial Salaries Are Beating the National Average, But Maybe Not for Long" in Canadian Business (March 31, 2008)
Pub: Rogers Media
Ed: Megan Harman. Description: Real average hourly earnings of managers increase by 20 percent in ten years as companies increase wages to avoid the risk of losing key managers to the competition and in preparation for the retirement of baby boomers. Tough market conditions affect management more since their incentives are tied to individual and corporate performance.

25618 ■ "Procter & Gamble Boosts Bet on Exclusive Brands" in Business Courier (Vol. 27, July 9, 2010, No. 10, pp. 1)
Pub: Business Courier
Ed: Jon Newberry. Description: Procter & Gamble is creating more special versions of its brands such as Pringles and Pampers exclusively for retail partners such as Tesco in the U.K. The greater push towards this direction is seen as a way to regain market share.

25619 ■ "Putting 'Great' Back Into A&P" in Crain's New York Business (Vol. 24, January 7, 2008, No. 1, pp. 3)
Pub: Crain Communications, Inc.
Description: After five straight years ending in 2005, A&P Grocery lost revenue; due to a sweeping plan to freshen up its supermarkets the company returned to growth mode and was able to acquire longtime competitor Pathmark Stores.

25620 ■ "Q&A: Joseph Ribkoff" in Canadian Business (Vol. 81, March 31, 2008, No. 5, pp. 4)
Pub: Rogers Media
Ed: Zena Olijnyk. Description: Joseph Ribkoff started his career in the garment trade by sweeping floors and running deliveries for a dress manufacturer called Town & Country and earned $16 a week. Ribkoff says that the key to controlling costs in Canada is to invest in the latest equipment and technology to stay competitive.

25621 ■ "Queen Bees: All Sting, No Honey" in Business Horizons (September-October 2007, pp. 348)
Pub: Elsevier Technology Publications
Ed: Catherine M. Dalton. Description: Female rivalry or competition in the workplace and other domains are explained and compared to the behavior of honeybees. Novels and other works on the topic of competition among women are discussed.

25622 ■ "Quiznos Franchisees Walloped by Recession" in Advertising Age (Vol. 79, October 20, 2008, No. 39, pp. 3)
Pub: Crain Communications, Inc.
Ed: Emily Bryson York. Description: While the recession has taken a toll on the entire restaurant industry, a number of Quiznos franchisees claim to have been disproportionately affected due to lackluster marketing, higher-than-average commodity costs, competition with Subway and a premium-pricing structure that is incompatible with a tight economy.

25623 ■ The Race for a New Game Machine: Creating the Chips Inside the Xbox 360 and the PlayStation 3
Pub: Citadel Press
Contact: Steven Zacharius, President
E-mail: szacharius@kensingtonbooks.com
Ed: David Shippy, Mickie Phipps. Released: 2009. Price: $21.95. Description: The story of Microsoft and Sony's race to deliver the goods for the Xbox 360 and Playstation 3 is explored.

25624 ■ "R&R Launches Upscale Spoony's and Low Fat Dragon's Den" in Ice Cream Reporter (Vol. 23, August 20, 2010, No. 9, pp. 3)
Pub: Ice Cream Reporter
Description: European ice cream manufacturer R&R has acquired French ice cream maker Rolland and will position itself as an upscale challenger to brands like Ben & Jerry's.

25625 ■ "Ready To Take Your Business Global?" in Black Enterprise (Vol. 41, August 2010, No. 1, pp. 89)
Pub: Earl G. Graves Publishing Co. Inc.
Ed: Alan Hughes. Description: The 2010 Black Enterprise Entrepreneurs Conference held in May stressed the need for all small firms to promote a global agenda in order to stay competitive.

25626 ■ Reality Check: The Irreverent Guide to Outsmarting, Outmanaging, and Outmarketing Your Competition
Pub: Penguin Group USA Inc.
Ed: Guy Kawasaki. Price: $29.95. Description: Marketing guru and entrepreneur, Guy Kawasaki, provides a compilation of his blog posts on all aspects of starting and operating a business.

25627 ■ "Research and Markets Adds Report: Ghana: Convergence, Broadband and Internet Market" in Wireless News (September 4, 2009)
Pub: Close-Up Media
Description: Overview of a new report by Research and Markets entitled, 'Ghana Convergence, Broadband and Internet Market - Overview, Statistics and Forecasts.' Ghana was among the first countries in Africa connected to the Internet and to introduce ADSL broadband services; however, only 30 of the 140 licensed ISP's are operational making the sector highly competitive.

25628 ■ Researching Company Financial Information
Pub: MarketResearch.com
Contact: Charlie Terry, President
E-mail: cterry@marketresearch.com
URL(s): www.marketresearch.com/vendors/viewvendor.asp?g=1&VendorID=708. Released: Edition V. Price: $59, Individuals. Description: Helps readers learn how to research and understand financial data from companies, as well as compile in-depth financial data on competitors in order to get a better picture of the competition. Publication includes: A directory of corporate financial info sources.

25629 ■ "Retail Health Clinics Sprout in Area; Doctors Feel Threat, Have Concerns" in Crain's Detroit Business (April 7, 2008)
Pub: Crain Communications, Inc.
Ed: Mike Scott. Description: Competing with doctors' offices for routine patient visits are the retail health clinics which have made their way into the metro Detroit area. Physicians are concerned about the limited doctor supervision on site.

25630 ■ *"Rich or Poor, Hospitals Must Work Together"* in *Crain's Chicago Business (Vol. 31, April 28, 2008, No. 17, pp. 22)*
Pub: Crain Communications, Inc.
Description: Chicago-area safety-net hospitals that serve the poor, uninsured and underinsured are struggling to stay open while wealthier areas compete to build advanced facilities for the expensive surgical procedures their privately insured patients can afford. If these safety-net hospitals close, their patients, many of them in ambulances, will show up at the remaining hospitals resulting in a strain that will test the ability of hospitals across the region to care for all of their patients. Hospitals need to address the threats to the local health care system before it slips into crisis since the current every-hospital-for-itself approach that pays off big for some will eventually will make losers of everyone.

25631 ■ *"RIM's Test of Faith"* in *Canadian Business (Vol. 80, April 9, 2007, No. 8, pp. 29)*
Pub: Rogers Media
Ed: Joe Castaldo. Description: The growth of Research In Motion Ltd. in terms of its sales and profits despite a patent suit on it and competition of rivals is discussed.

25632 ■ *"Rivals Blow In"* in *Crain's Cleveland Business (Vol. 30, June 1, 2009, No. 21, pp. 1)*
Pub: Crain Communications, Inc.
Ed: Chuck Soder. Description: U.S. and Canadian competitors are hoping to start construction of offshore wind farm project proposed by Cuyahoga County's Great Lakes Energy Development Task Force. Details of the project are included.

25633 ■ *"Safeway"* in *Ice Cream Reporter (Vol. 23, September 20, 2010, No. 10, pp. 8)*
Pub: Ice Cream Reporter
Description: Safeway supermarkets have upsized their private label ice cream to a full half gallon, thus reversing the trend where most brands were shrinking their containers.

25634 ■ *"St. Elizabeth Fights for Share at St. Lukes"* in *Business Courier (Vol. 27, November 12, 2010, No. 28, pp. 1)*
Pub: Business Courier
Ed: James Ritchie. Description: Key information on how St. Elizabeth Healthcare helps partner St. Luke's Hospitals increase market share in the healthcare industry are presented. Some of St. Luke's hospitals, such as the St. Elizabeth Fort Thomas in Kentucky, are struggling with low occupancy rates, prompting St. Elizabeth to invest about $24 million to help St. Luke's increase its market share.

25635 ■ *"Sales and the Absolute Power of Information"* in *Agency Sales Magazine (Vol. 39, July 2009, No. 7, pp. 16)*
Pub: MANA
Ed: Dave Kahle. Description: Having good information can help a sales representative deliver effective sales performance. A process for collecting information about customers, prospects, and competitors is discussed.

25636 ■ *"Sales Force Expertise: A Competitive Advantage"* in *Agency Sales Magazine (Vol. 39, November 2009, No. 10, pp. 10)*
Pub: MANA
Ed: Ken Valla. Description: Maintaining an expert sales force is a competitive advantage that sales leaders can count on. The skills that the sales force need to have include 'consultative selling' or the ability to understand and link to a customer's business priorities, conducting a process conversation, and asking discovery questions.

25637 ■ *"Satellite Wars"* in *Canadian Business (Vol. 79, October 23, 2006, No. 21, pp. 35)*
Pub: Rogers Media
Ed: Andy Holloway. Description: The strategies used by Sirius Canada Inc. and XM Canada, two major satellite radio companies to acquire more number of suscribers, are discussed.

25638 ■ *The Secret Language of Competitive Intelligence: How to See Through and Stay Ahead of Business Disruptions, Distortions, Rumors, and Smoke*
Pub: Crown Publishing Group
Ed: Leonard M. Fuld. Released: May 2006. Price: $24.95.

25639 ■ *"Service With a Smile..And Comfy Chairs"* in *Crain's Chicago Business (Vol. 31, April 28, 2008, No. 17, pp. 46)*
Pub: Crain Communications, Inc.
Ed: Phuong Ly. Description: O'Hare Auto Group has improved the experience of waiting for service on one's vehicle by offering wireless Internet, comfortable chairs and plasma TVs. The company also has long service hours, running from 6 a.m. to midnight Monday through Thursday so customers don't have to take time off work.

25640 ■ *"Shaw, Telus Take Up Battle Positions"* in *Globe & Mail (January 1, 2006, pp. B1)*
Pub: CTVglobemedia Publishing Inc.
Ed: Catherine McKLean. Description: The competition between Shaw Communications Inc. and Telus Corp. over voice over Internet protocol offer for customers is presented.

25641 ■ *"Shipbuilding & Defence"* in *Canadian Sailings (July 7, 2008)*
Pub: UBM Global Trade
Contact: Leonard J. Corallo, President
Ed: Sharon Hobson. Description: Overview of the Joint Support Ship Project whose initial budget was set at $2.1 billion for the acquisition of the ships required for the Canadian navy; another $800 million was allotted for 20 years of in-service support. Four teams of competitors bid for the contract and the Department of National Defence decided to fund two teams for the project definition phase of the competition.

25642 ■ *"Shout and Devour"* in *Tulsa World (November 7, 2009)*
Pub: Tulsa World
Ed: Kyle Arnold. Description: Profile of convenience store Shout and Sack whose owners have distanced themselves from the corporate fray of the chain stores by offering homemade lunches served at a counter; the store recently gained national exposure that highlighted the popularity despite a market share heavily dominated by franchises and chains.

25643 ■ *Silos, Politics and Turf Wars: A Leadership Fable about Destroying the Barriers That Turn Colleagues Into Competitors*
Pub: Jossey Bass
Ed: Patrick M. Lencioni. Released: February 17, 2006. Price: $24.95. Description: The author addresses management problems through a fable that revolves around a self-employed consultant who has to dismantle silos at an upscale hotel, a technology company and a hospital. The story explains how organizations can use a collective operational vision in order to overcome pride, greed, and tribalism and work as a team with the same goal in mind.

25644 ■ *"Sinai Doctor Seeks FDA OK for Drug"* in *Baltimore Business Journal (Vol. 28, July 16, 2010, No. 10, pp. 1)*
Pub: Baltimore Business Journal
Ed: Emily Mullin. Description: Paul Gurbel, Sinai Hospital Center for Thrombosis Research director, is seeking an FDA approval of Brilinta, a drug which he helped create and test. Gurbel says that the approval could bring the drug to market as early as December 2010. The drug is expected to rival Bristol-Myers' Plavix, which generated almost $6.2 billion in 2009.

25645 ■ *"Six Leading Economists on What to Expect in the Year Ahead: David Wolf"* in *Canadian Business (Dec. 24, 2007)*
Pub: Rogers Media
Ed: David Wolf. Description: The Canadian dollar recently hit parity with the U.S. dollar, and the exchange rate is going fast and overvaluation of the Canadian dollar could bring in competition from U.S. products. Details on the impact of the slowdown of the U.S. economy on the exchange rate speed are discussed.

25646 ■ *"Size Does Matter"* in *International Journal of Globalisation and Small Business (Vol. 4, September 21, 2010, No. 1, pp. 61)*
Pub: Publishers Communication Group
Ed: Julia Cornnell, Ranjit Voola. Description: Examination of how members of an Australian-based manufacturing and engineering cluster share knowledge through networking as a means to improve competitive advantage.

25647 ■ *"Slow but Steady into the Future"* in *Barron's (Vol. 88, July 7, 2008, No. 27, pp. M)*
Pub: Dow Jones & Co., Inc.
Ed: Mark Veverka. Description: Investors are advised to maintain their watch on the shares of business software company NetSuite. The company's chief executive officer, Zach Nelson, claims that the company has a 10-year lead on its competitors with the development of software-as-a service.

25648 ■ *Small Business Survival Guide: Starting, Protecting, and Securing Your Business for Long-Term Success*
Pub: Adams Media Corporation
Ed: Cliff Ennico. Released: September 2005. Price: $12.95 (US), $17.95 (Canadian). Description: Entrepreneurship in the new millennium. Topics include creditors, taxes, competition, business law, and accounting.

25649 ■ *"Small Businesses Get Creative to Retain Workers"* in *Crain's Detroit Business (Vol. 24, March 17, 2008, No. 11, pp. 21)*
Pub: Crain Communications, Inc.
Ed: Nancy Kaffer. Description: Small businesses are often unable to compete with larger firms when it comes to offering employees fringe benefits and such perks as a company gym or an in-house chef; however, many smaller companies have found that the key to gaining employee loyalty lies in creating an atmosphere in which employees feel job satisfaction. Also provides tips on how to keep employees.

25650 ■ *"Small Dutch Islands Saba, Statia Content With Low-Key Niche"* in *Travel Weekly (Vol. 69, August 16, 2010, No. 33, pp. 22)*
Pub: NorthStar Travel Media LLC
Ed: Gay Nagle Myers. Description: Small Caribbean islands market and promote their region for tourism by never competing with the bigger destinations. Saba and Statia are the two smallest islands in the Caribbean and rely on repeat guests, word-of-mouth recommendations and travel agents willing to promote them.

25651 ■ *The Small-Mart Revolution: How Local Businesses Are Beating the Global Competition*
Pub: Berrett-Koehler Publishers, Incorporated
Ed: Michael H. Shuman. Released: July 2007. Price: $16.95. Description: Advice is given to help small businesses compete in a global environment.

25652 ■ *"Smart Car Sales Take Big Hit in Recession"* in *Business Journal-Milwaukee (Vol. 28, December 10, 2010, No. 10, pp. A1)*
Pub: Milwaukee Business Journal
Ed: Stacey Vogel Davis. Description: Sales of smart cars in Milwaukee declined in 2010. Smart Center Milwaukee sold only 52 new cars through October 2010. Increased competition is seen as a reason for the decline in sales.

25653 ■ *"Snatching Talent: Local Law Firms Quietly Boost Poaching"* in *Boston Business Journal (Vol. 31, July 29, 2011, No. 27, pp. 3)*
Pub: Boston Business Journal
Ed: Lisa van der Pool. Description: National law firms Jones Day and Latham & Watkins LLP set up offices in Boston, Massachusetts. Their move also created an upswing on confidential conversation as both firms are aggressively poaching lawyers from Boston's other top firms.

25654 ■ *The Social Media Bible: Tactics, Tools, and Strategies for Business Success*
Pub: John Wiley & Sons, Inc.
Ed: Lon Safko, David Brake. **Released:** June 17, 2009. **Price:** $29.95. **Description:** Information is given to build or transform a business into social media, where customers, employees, and prospects connect, collaborate, and champion products and services in order to increase sales and to beat the competition.

25655 ■ *"Some Relief Possible Following Painful Week" in Barron's (Vol. 88, July 14, 2008, No. 28, pp. M3)*
Pub: Dow Jones & Co., Inc.
Ed: Kopin Tan. **Description:** Dow Chemical is offering a 74 percent premium to acquire Rohm & Haas' coatings and electronics materials operations. Frontline amassed a 5.6 percent stake in rival Overseas Shipholding Group and a merger between the two would create a giant global fleet with pricing power. Highlights of the U.S. stock market during the week that ended in July 11, 2008 are discussed. Statistical data included.

25656 ■ *"Special Sector" in Crain's Cleveland Business (Vol. 28, November 5, 2007, No. 44, pp. 3)*
Pub: Crain Communications, Inc.
Ed: David Bennett. **Description:** Specialty Metals Processing Inc. is investing more than $6 million to amp up productions; the company believes this big investment will pay off due to the company's ability to process complex metal alloys, such as titanium, in a region where there is a small number of competitors.

25657 ■ *"Staging a Martini-and-GQ Lifestyle; Faux Possessions Play to Buyer's Aspirations" in Crain's Chicago Business (April 21, 2008)*
Pub: Crain Communications, Inc.
Ed: Kevin Davis. **Description:** Due to the competition of the slumping housing market, home stagers are becoming more prominent and are using creative ways to make an impression beyond de-cluttering, painting and cleaning by using accents such as casually placed magazines, candles and table settings.

25658 ■ *The Starfish and the Spider: The Unstoppable Power of Leaderless Organizations*
Pub: Portfolio Publishing
Ed: Ori Brafman; Rod A. Beckstrom. **Released:** 2008. **Price:** $15.00 paperback. **Description:** Through their experiences promoting peace and economic development through decentralizing networking, the authors offer insight into ways that decentralizing can change organizations. Three techniques for combating a decentralized competitor are examined.

25659 ■ *Starting Green: An Ecopreneur's Guide to Starting a Green Business from Business Plans to Profits*
Pub: Entrepreneur Press
Contact: Perlman Neil, President
Ed: Glenn E. Croston. **Released:** September 9, 2010. **Price:** $21.95. **Description:** Entrepreneur and scientist outlines green business essentials and helps uncover eco-friendly business opportunities, build a sustainable business plan, and gain the competitive advantage.

25660 ■ *"State Lawmakers Should Try Raising Jobs, Not Taxes" in Crain's Chicago Business (Vol. 31, March 24, 2008, No. 12, pp. 20)*
Pub: Crain Communications, Inc.
Ed: Diug Whitley. **Description:** According to U.S. Department of Labor figures through December 2007, Illinois has ranked 45th in the nation in job growth for seven straight months. Many feel that the state would not need to raise taxes if they spent more time working to keep and attract employers that create jobs.

25661 ■ *"State Wants to Add Escape Clause to Leases" in Sacramento Business Journal*

(Vol. 28, October 14, 2011, No. 33, pp. 1)
Pub: Sacramento Business Journal
Ed: Michael Shaw. **Description:** California Governor Jerry Brown's administration has decided to add escape clauses to new lease agreements, which created new worry for building owners and brokers in Sacramento, California. Real estate brokers believe the appropriation of funds clauses have been making the lenders nervous and would result in less competition.

25662 ■ *"Stepping Up" in Baltimore Business Journal (Vol. 28, October 22, 2010, No. 24, pp. 1)*
Pub: Baltimore Business Journal
Ed: Erik Siemers. **Description:** Uner Armour Inc. will release its Micro G line of four basketball sneakers on October 23, 2010. The company's executives mentioned that Under Armour's goal is to appeal to customers, and not to chip away at Nike Inc.'s supremacy in basketball shoes. The new sneakers will range from $80 to $110.

25663 ■ *"Stikemans' Ascent, Its Legacy, and Its Future" in Globe & Mail (January 29, 2007, pp. B2)*
Pub: CTVglobemedia Publishing Inc.
Ed: Jacquie McNish. **Description:** Pierre Raymond, chairman of legal firm Stikeman Elliott LLP, talks about his strategies to handle competition, his challenges, and about Canada's present mergers and acquisition scenario. Stikeman achieved the first place in 2006 M&A legal rankings.

25664 ■ *"Stuck With Two Mortgages; The Nightmare When Buyers Upgrade" in Crain's Chicago Business (Vol. 31, April 21, 2008, No. 16)*
Pub: Crain Communications, Inc.
Ed: Darci Smith. **Description:** Discusses the problem a number of people are facing due to the slump in the housing market: being stuck with two mortgages when they move because their former homes have not sold. Many thought they could afford to move to a larger home, anticipating significant equity appreciation that did not occur; now they are left with lowering their price and competing with the host of new developments.

25665 ■ *"Suited for Success" in Retail Merchandiser (Vol. 51, July-August 2011, No. 4, pp. 6)*
Pub: Phoenix Media Corporation
Description: MyBestFit is a size-matching body scanner that helps consumers find the perfect size clothing for themselves, giving brick and mortar retailers an edge on ecommerce competitors.

25666 ■ *"Summit, Lions Gate are in Talks to Merge Studios" in Wall Street Journal Eastern Edition (November 29, 2011, pp. B2)*
Pub: Dow Jones & Company Inc. Enterprise Media Group
Contact: Clare Hart, President
Ed: Erica Orden, Michelle Kung. **Description:** Movie studio Summit Entertainment LLC is in talks with television producer Lions Gate Entertainment Corporation about a possible merger. Previous talks have taken place, but no deal was ever reached. Such a deal would create a large, independent studio able to compete in the market with the big Hollywood giants.

25667 ■ *"The Superpower Dilemma" in Canadian Business (Vol. 83, August 17, 2010, No. 13-14, pp. 42)*
Pub: Rogers Media Ltd.
Description: Canada has been an energy superpower partly because it controls the energy source and the production means, particularly of fossil fuels. However, Canada's status as superpower could diminish if it replaces petroleum exports with renewable technology for using sources of energy available globally.

25668 ■ *"Supply Chain Visibility A Two-Way Street" in Canadian Sailings (July 7, 2008)*
Pub: UBM Global Trade
Contact: Leonard J. Corallo, President
Ed: Jack Kohane. **Description:** Canada is experiencing unprecedented market pressures due to globalization. Competition from foreign countries, demand

for better and faster service from customers and shorter innovation cycles are some of the problems the country is facing regarding trade and the importing and exporting industry.

25669 ■ *"Surprise Offer for Dofasco Puts Heat on Arcelor" in Globe & Mail (January 16, 2006, pp. B1)*
Pub: CTVglobemedia Publishing Inc.
Ed: Greg Keenan. **Description:** The details of competition between ThyssenKrupp AG and Arcelor SA to bid Dofasco Inc. are presented.

25670 ■ *"Swift Shift" in Crain's Cleveland Business (Vol. 28, November 12, 2007, No. 45, pp. 1)*
Pub: Crain Communications, Inc.
Ed: Shannon Mortland. **Description:** Discusses the ways in which Southwest General Health Center is working to stay competitive in a region that is highly saturated with health care providers.

25671 ■ *"Tale of the Tape: IPhone Vs. G1" in Advertising Age (Vol. 79, October 27, 2008, No. 40, pp. 6)*
Pub: Crain Communications, Inc.
Ed: Rita Chang. **Description:** T-Mobile's G1 has been positioned as the first serious competitor to Apple's iPhone. G1 is the first mobile phone to run on the Google-backed, open-source platform Android.

25672 ■ *"Tamara Vrooman" in Canadian Business (Vol. 80, November 19, 2007, No. 23, pp. 9)*
Pub: Rogers Media
Ed: Regan Ray. **Description:** Profile of Tamara Vrooman, newly appointed CEO of Canada's largest credit union, Vancity. Vrooman believes that Vancity has an advantage over big bank when it comes to the flexibility of products the company offers. The role of Vancity and credit unions in the banking sector of Canada is discussed.

25673 ■ *"Team Bonding for Fun and Profit" in Women Entrepreneur (December 3, 2008)*
Pub: Entrepreneur Media Inc.
Ed: Eve Gumpel. **Description:** Discusses the benefits that competitions such as the 2008 BG U.S. Challenge in Lake Placid, New York, can offer in terms of team building and employee motivation as well as networking and the development of a positive working relationship with partners and competitors alike.

25674 ■ *"That Vision Thing" in Canadian Business (Vol. 80, December 25, 2006, No. 1, pp. 78)*
Pub: Rogers Media
Description: Suggestions for better Canadian tax policy and making airspace competitive among other things, to improve the economy in 2007, are presented.

25675 ■ *"Thomas Morley; President, The Lube Stop Inc., 37' in Crain's Cleveland Business (Vol. 28, November 19, 2007, No. 46, pp. F-12)*
Pub: Crain Communications, Inc.
Ed: David Bennett. **Description:** Profile of Thomas Morley, president of The Lube Stop Inc., who is dedicated to promoting the company's strong environmental record as an effective way to differentiate Lube Stop from its competition. Since Mr. Morley came to the company in 2004, Lube Stop has increased sales by 10 percent and has boosted its operating profits by 30 percent.

25676 ■ *"Tiny Telecom Big Prize in Bell Aliant Bid Battle" in Globe & Mail (April 4, 2007, pp. B1)*
Pub: CTVglobemedia Publishing Inc.
Ed: Catherine McLean. **Description:** The competition between Bell Aliant Regional Communications Income Fund of BCE Inc. and Bragg Communications Inc. to bid for acquiring Amtelecom Income Fund is discussed.

25677 ■ *"To Be Seen Is to Be Successful" in Pet Product News (Vol. 64, December 2010, No. 12, pp. 12)*
Pub: BowTie Inc.
Ed: David Arvin. **Description:** Guidelines on how pet business retailers can boost customer visibility are described considering that complacency could hamper retailers' efforts to effectively market their businesses. To enhance customer base and stand out from competing businesses, being different, strategic, creative, and differentiated is emphasized.

25678 ■ *"To Keep Freight Rolling, Springfield Must Grease the Hub" in Crain's Chicago Business (Vol. 31, April 21, 2008, No. 16, pp. 22)*
Pub: Crain Communications, Inc.
Ed: Paul O'Connor. **Description:** Discusses the importance of upgrading Chicago's continental-hub freight rail system which is integral to moving international products as well as domestic ones. Global tonnage is expected to double by 2020 and unless more money is designated to upgrade the infrastructure the local and national economy will suffer.

25679 ■ *"Tom Gaglardi" in Canadian Business (Vol. 82, April 27, 2009, No. 7, pp. 56)*
Pub: Rogers Media
Ed: Calvin Leung. **Description:** Northland Properties Corporation president Tom Gaglardi believes that their business model of keeping much of operations in-house allows the firm to crate assets at a lesser price while commanding higher margins than their competitors. He believes that it is an ideal time to invest in the hospitality industry because of opportunities to purchase properties at low prices.

25680 ■ *"Too Much too Soon" in Barron's (Vol. 89, July 27, 2009, No. 30, pp. 33)*
Pub: Dow Jones & Co., Inc.
Ed: Leslie P. Norton. **Description:** Shares of hhgregg have risen 85 percent in the year leading up to July 2009 and analysts believe the stock could hit 25. However, their 113 outlets are concentrated in states where unemployment is above 10 percent and expanding into areas already overstored. Competition is also rife and credit availability is still tight.

25681 ■ *"Top Design Award for Massey Ferguson 7624 Dyna-VT" in Farm Industry News (November 14, 2011)*
Pub: Penton Business Media Inc.
Description: Massey Ferguson won top honors for its MF 7624 Dyna-VT as the Golden Tractor for Design award in the 2012 Tractor of the Year competition. The award is presented annually by journalists from 22 leading farming magazines in Europe and manufacturers have to be nominated to enter.

25682 ■ *"A Torch in the Darkness" in Canadian Business (Vol. 83, August 17, 2010, No. 13-14, pp. 66)*
Pub: Rogers Media Ltd.
Ed: Joe Castaldo. **Description:** Research In Motion (RIM) unveiled the BlackBerry Touch, featuring a touch screen as well as a physical keyboard, in an attempt to repel competitors and expand share in the consumer smart phone market. RIM shares have fallen 43 percent from its peak in 2009.

25683 ■ *"Tourism Bureau Seeks Hotel Tax Hike" in Baltimore Business Journal (Vol. 27, December 18, 2009, No. 32, pp. 1)*
Pub: American City Business Journals
Ed: Rachel Bernstein. **Description:** Baltimore, Maryland's tourism agency, Visit Baltimore, has proposed a new hotel tax that could produce $2 million annually for its marketing budget, fund improvements to the city's 30-year-old convention center and help it compete for World Cup soccer games. Baltimore hotel leaders discuss the new tax.

25684 ■ *"Train Now to Get the Competitive Edge" in Contractor (Vol. 56, October 2009, No. 10, pp. 58)*
Pub: Penton Media, Inc.
Ed: Merry Beth Hall. **Description:** Due to the harsh economic climate, mechanical contractors would be well-served to train their employees while they have time to take them out of the field. This will help ensure that they are not behind when the economic recovery happens. Suggestions on how to choose the best type of training are presented.

25685 ■ *"Travel Rewards Take Off" in Inc. (Vol. 33, October 2011, No. 8, pp. 46)*
Pub: Inc. Magazine
Ed: Matthew DeLuca. **Description:** Credit card companies are offering travel reward cards with special perks, including sign-up bonuses; three such cards are described.

25686 ■ *"TSX Linkup Sets Stage for Battle" in Globe & Mail (March 6, 2007, pp. B1)*
Pub: CTVglobemedia Publishing Inc.
Ed: Boyd Erman; Sinclair Stewart. **Description:** The strategic alliance between TSX Group Inc and International Securities Exchange Holdings Inc. for the establishment of a derivatives exchange in Canada is discussed. The prospects of competition between the new exchange and the Montreal Exchange are discussed.

25687 ■ *"Turfway Slowing its Gait" in Business Courier (Vol. 26, November 6, 2009, No. 28, pp. 1)*
Pub: American City Business Journals, Inc.
Ed: Jon Newberry. **Description:** Kentucky's Turfway Park will be decreasing its weekly race schedule from five days to three days in the first two months of 2010, and to four days in March 2010. The decision to make reductions in the schedule is attributed to the relocation of thoroughbred racing to states that allow casino gambling. As a result, Turfway Park's resources and purse money would be focused on less days.

25688 ■ *"Two Local Bakers Winners of TV's 'Cupcake Wars'" in Toledo Blade (July 6, 2011)*
Pub: Toledo Times
Description: Winners of cable network Food Channel's Cupcake Wars, Lori Jacobs and Dana Iliev own Cake in a Cup in Toledo, Ohio. The partners shop features creative cupcakes with names such as Monkey Business, Pretty in Pink, and Tropical Getaway.

25689 ■ *The Ultimate Competitive Advantage*
Pub: Berrett-Koehler Publishers
Ed: Donald Mitchell; Carol Coles; B. Thomas Golisano. **Released:** March 12, 2003. **Price:** $36.95. **Description:** Results of a ten year study of companies that experienced fast growth over a three year period shows that while unsuccessful companies apply outdated business models, the successful ones improve their business models every two to four years.

25690 ■ *"Unfilled Hotels Go All Out for Business Meetings" in Crain's Detroit Business (Vol. 25, June 8, 2009, No. 23, pp. 9)*
Pub: Crain Communications Inc. - Detroit
Ed: Daniel Duggan. **Description:** Hotels in Michigan are offering discounts to companies holding business meetings at their properties. Details of competition and plans are included.

25691 ■ *"U.S. Attorney Post the Latest Twist" in The Business Journal-Serving Greater Tampa Bay (Vol. 28, July 25, 2008, No. 31, pp. 1)*
Pub: American City Business Journals, Inc.
Ed: Jane Meinhardt. **Description:** Tampa, Florida-based lawyer A. Brian Albritton has been nominated to be the U.S. Attorney for the Middle District of Florida. He is an expert in cases involving white-collar crime, secret theft, noncompete agreements, and other agreements.

25692 ■ *"U.S. Widens Rocket Field" in Wall Street Journal Eastern Edition (October 17, 2011, pp. B4)*
Pub: Dow Jones & Company Inc. Enterprise Media Group
Contact: Clare Hart, President
Ed: Andy Pasztor. **Description:** An agreement has been reached between National Aeronautics and Space Administration, the Department of Defense and the Air Force that will assist small commercial space ventures in bidding for profitable contracts for government launching. The program will give those companies a chance to compete against larger corporations.

25693 ■ *"Warning Lights Flashing for Air Canada: Carty's Back" in Globe & Mail (February 22, 2006, pp. B1)*
Pub: CTVglobemedia Publishing Inc.
Ed: Brent Jang. **Description:** Air Canada's rival, Donald Carty, former chief executive officer at American Airlines and new chairman of Toronto based Regco Holdings Inc., launches Porter Airlines Inc. out of Toronto City Center Airport this fall.

25694 ■ *"Way More Than Mowing" in Green Industry Pro (Vol. 23, September 2011)*
Pub: Cygnus Business Media
Ed: Rod Dickens. **Description:** Shipp Shape Lawn Services located in Sylvester, Georgia now offers aeration, fertilizing and weed control, mulching, yard renovation, flowerbed maintenance, landscaping, as well as irrigation repairs and installation in order to diversify the business and stay competitive.

25695 ■ *The Well-Timed Strategy: Managing Business Cycle for Competitive Advantage*
Pub: Wharton School Publishing
Ed: Peter Navarro. **Released:** January 23, 2006. **Price:** $34.99. **Description:** An overview of business cycles and risks is presented. Recession is a good time to find key personnel for a small business. Other issues addressed include investment, production, and marketing in order to maintain a competitive edge.

25696 ■ *"Wells Fargo Will Soon Lead Local Banks in Deposits" in Austin Business JournalInc. (Vol. 28, December 5, 2008, No. 38, pp. A1)*
Pub: American City Business Journals
Ed: Christopher Calnan. **Description:** Acquisition of Wachovia Corporation by Wells Fargo and Company will leave the latter as the top bank for deposits in Austin, Texas. The merged bank will have deposits of more than $ billion, more than the $3.9 billion deposits Bank of America maintains in the area.

25697 ■ *"WestJet Gears Up for Domestic Dogfight" in Globe & Mail (May 1, 2007, pp. B6)*
Pub: CTVglobemedia Publishing Inc.
Ed: Brent Jang. **Description:** The effort of WestJet Airlines Ltd. to compete with Air Canada for greater market share of passengers is discussed.

25698 ■ *"What Makes for an Effective, Production-Oriented VMC?" in Modern Machine Shop (Vol. 84, November 2011, No. 6, pp. 24)*
Pub: Gardner Business Media, Inc.
Contact: Richard G. Kline, President
E-mail: rkline@gardnerweb.com
Ed: Derek Korn. **Description:** When a machine shop's existing VMC only offers a modest spindle performance and slow, non-cutting functions, the latest VMC technology for high-volume production that minimizes cycle times and maximizes competitiveness could be helpful. Makino's new Production Standard (PS) series of VMCs provides not only a number of standard features to shrink cycle times, but also design elements that can effectively support a shops production elements are defined.

25699 ■ *What Men Don't Tell Woman about Business: Opening Up the Heavily Guarded Alpha Male Playbook*
Pub: John Wiley and Sons, Inc.
Ed: Christopher V. Fleet. **Released:** October 26, 2007. **Description:** Valuable guide for any woman in business, this book helps reveal everything a woman needs to know in order to understand, communicate, and compete with men in business.

25700 ■ *"While Competitors Shut Doors, Subway Is Still Growing" in Advertising Age*

(Vol. 79, July 21, 2008, No. 28, pp. 4)
Pub: Crain Communications, Inc.
Ed: Emily Bryson York. **Description:** Subway, the largest fast-food chain, with 22,000 U.S. locations, is adding 800 this year, despite the economic downturn that has caused competitors such as Starbucks to close stores and McDonald's to focus its expansion abroad.

25701 ■ *"Why LinkedIn is the Social Network that Will Never Die" in Advertising Age (Vol. 81, December 6, 2010, No. 43, pp. 2)*
Pub: Crain Communications, Inc.
Ed: Irina Slutsky. **Description:** Despite the popularity of Facebook, LinkIn in will always be a source for professionals who wish to network.

25702 ■ *"Why-Max?" in Canadian Business (Vol. 81, July 22, 2008, No. 12-13, pp. 19)*
Pub: Rogers Media Ltd.
Ed: Andrew Wahl. **Description:** Nascent technology known as LTE (Long Term Evolution) is expected to challenge Intel's WiMax wireless technology as the wireless broadband standard. LTE , which is believed to be at least two years behind WiMax in development, is likely to be supported by wireless and mobile-phone carriers. Views and information on WiMax and LTE are presented.

25703 ■ *"Why Nestle Should Sell Alcon" in Barron's (Vol. 88, March 17, 2008, No. 11, pp. M12)*
Pub: Dow Jones & Company, Inc.
Ed: Sean Walters. **Description:** Nestle should sell Alcon because Nestle can't afford to be complacent as its peers have made changes to their portfolios to boost competitiveness. Nestle's stake in Alcon and L'Oreal have been ignored by investors and Nestle could realize better value by strengthening its nutrition division through acquisitions.

25704 ■ *"Will Focus on Business Continue?" in Baltimore Business Journal (Vol. 28, November 5, 2010, No. 26, pp. 1)*
Pub: Baltimore Business Journal
Ed: Scott Dance. **Description:** The 2010 election may call for new efforts to teach new lawmakers to assure that the viewpoints of businesses are considered and accurately delivered. The Greater Baltimore Committee and similar groups have gathered reports on the competitiveness of Maryland and are planning to use them to make a case of keeping business a top priority.

25705 ■ *"Will the Force Be With Salesforce?" in Barron's (Vol. 88, March 24, 2008, No. 12, pp. 20)*
Pub: Dow Jones & Company, Inc.
Ed: Mark Veverka. **Description:** Shares of Salesforce.com are likely to drop from the $44.83-a-share level in the face of a deteriorating economy and financial sector and thus lower demand for business software. The company is unlikely to deliver on its ambitious earnings forecasts for 2008 especially with strengthening competition from Oracle.

25706 ■ *"Winburn's Big Idea" in Business Courier (Vol. 27, October 8, 2010, No. 23, pp. 1)*
Pub: Business Courier
Ed: Dan Monk, Lucy May. **Description:** Cincinnati Councilman Charlie Winburn proposed the creation of Cincinnati Competitive Edge Division and to remake a small-business division of the city in order to start a job-creation program. The new division will monitor compliance to the city's small business inclusion regulations, as well as to help small business owners grow.

25707 ■ *Winner Take All: How Competitiveness Shapes the Fate of Nations*
Pub: Basic Books
Ed: Richard J. Elkus Jr. **Released:** 2009. **Price:** $27.00. **Description:** American government and misguided business practices has allowed the U.S. to fall behind other countries in various market sectors such as cameras and televisions, as well as information technologies. It will take a national strategy to for America to regain its lead in crucial industries.

25708 ■ *Winner Takes All: Steve Wynn, Kirk Kerkorian, Gary Loveman, and the Race to Own Vegas*
Pub: Hyperion
Ed: Christina Binkley. **Released:** 2009. **Price:** $25.95. **Description:** The story of three men, Steve Wynn, Kirk Kerkorian, and Gary Loveman, each with different backgrounds are reinventing Las Vegas.

25709 ■ *"A Woman's Advantage" in Black Enterprise (Vol. 38, December 2007, No. 5, pp. 86)*
Pub: Earl G. Graves Publishing Co. Inc.
Ed: Marcia Reed-Woodard. **Description:** Leadership development is essential for any small business. Simmons College's Strategic Leadership for Women educational course offers a five-day program for professional women teaching powerful strategies to perform, compete, and win in the workplace.

25710 ■ *"Xerox's Former CEO On Why Succession Shouldn't Be a Horse Race" in Harvard Business Review (Vol. 88, October 2010, No. 10, pp. 47)*
Pub: Harvard Business School Publishing
Ed: Anne Mulcahy. **Description:** The importance of beginning talks between chief executive officers and boards of directors as early as possible to ensure a smooth transition is stressed. This can also prevent turning successions into competitions, with the resultant loss of talent when other candidates 'lose'.

25711 ■ *"XM Mulls Betting the Bank in Competitive Game of Subscriber Growth" in Globe & Mail (March 18, 2006, pp. B3)*
Pub: CTVglobemedia Publishing Inc.
Ed: Grant Robertson. **Description:** Canadian Satellite Radio Inc., XM Canada, president and Chief Operating Officer Stephen Tapp feel that establishing a profile in satellite radio to attract subscribers is a very big challenge. His views on the Canadian radio market are detailed.

25712 ■ *"Young-Kee Kim; Deputy Director, Fermi National Accelerator Laboratory" in Crain's Chicago Business (Vol. 31, May 5, 2008, No. 18)*
Pub: Crain Communications, Inc.
Ed: Phuong Ly. **Description:** Profile of Young-Kee Kim who is the deputy director of Fermilab, a physics lab where scientists study the smallest particles in the universe; Ms. Kim was a researcher at Fermilab before becoming deputy director two years ago; Fermilab is currently home to the most powerful particle accelerator in the world and is struggling to compete with other countries despite cuts in federal funding.

25713 ■ *Your First Year in Real Estate: Making the Transition from Total Novice to Successful Professional*
Pub: Crown Business Books
Ed: Dirk Zeller. **Released:** $August 3, 2010. **Price:** $20.00. **Description:** Zeller helps new realtors to select the right company, develop mentor and client relationships, using the Internet and social networking to stay ahead of competition, to 'set and reach career goals, to stay current in the market, and more.

VIDEOCASSETTES/ AUDIOCASSETTES

25714 ■ *Concerns Quarterly with Footage from CBS News: General Business*
Harcourt Brace College Publishers
301 Commerce, Ste. 3700
Fort Worth, TX 76102
Ph: (817)334-7500
Free: 800-237-2665
Fax: (817)334-0947
Co. E-mail: info@harcourt.com
URL: http://www.hmhco.com
Released: 1995. **Price:** $80.00. **Description:** Video newsletter containing footage from such CBS programs as CBS Evening News, 48 Hours, Street Stories, and CBS This Morning. Provides information on such topics as ethical responsibilities in business,

people in business, competition, manufacturing, and marketing. Comes with instructor's guide. Available at an annual subscription rate of $300.00. **Availability:** VHS.

25715 ■ *Michael Porter on Competitive Strategy*
Harvard Business School (HBS)
Soldiers Field Rd.
Boston, MA 02163
Ph: (617)495-1003
Fax: (617)495-0594
Co. E-mail: wfriedman@hbs.edu
URL: http://www.hbs.edu
Contact: Brian Kenny, Chief Marketing Officer
E-mail: bkenny@hbs.edu
Released: 1989. **Price:** $1000.00. **Description:** The professor at Harvard Business School gives a few tips that will keep your business on top of its competition. **Availability:** VHS.

25716 ■ *Swim with the Sharks without Being Eaten Alive*
Instructional Video
2219 C St.
Lincoln, NE 68502
Ph: (402)475-6570
Free: 800-228-0164
Fax: (402)475-6500
Co. E-mail: feedback@insvideo.com
URL: http://www.insvideo.com
Released: 19??. **Price:** $595.00. **Description:** Based on Harvey Mackay's best-selling book of the same name. Offers training advice on how to beat your competition, make the crucial sale, open the closed door, and swing the million-dollar deal at the last minute. **Availability:** VHS.

CONSULTANTS

25717 ■ **ARDITO Information & Research Inc.**
1019 Sedwick Dr., Ste. G
Wilmington, DE 19803
Ph: (302)479-5373
Free: 800-836-9068
Fax: (302)479-5375
Co. E-mail: sardito@ardito.com
Contact: Stephanie C. Ardito, President
E-mail: sardito@ardito.com
Scope: A full-service information and research firm. Provides information in areas of financial data, published research, demographic data, industry-specific publications, competitor data, marketing and sales trends, new product developments, government relations, bibliographies. Industries served are pharmaceutical, health, publishing, and environment, and business. **Founded:** 1990. **Publications:** "The Swine flu pandemic: Authoritative information versus community gossip," Searcher, Oct, 2009; "The Medical blogosphere: How social networking platforms are changing medical searching," Searcher, May, 2009; "Social Networking and Video Web Sites: MySpace and YouTube Meet the Copyright Cops," Searcher, May, 2007; "Copyright Clearance Center raises transactional fees," Information Today, Jul, 2004.

25718 ■ **Conor Environmental Services Inc.**
4 Shoppers Ln.
Turnersville, NJ 08012-1400
Ph: (609)589-5475
Fax: (609)589-6037
Co. E-mail: consultces@usa.net
Scope: Firm provides a full range of environmental and engineering consulting services for both public and private organizations. Environmental company provides assessment, engineering, and remediation services, specializing in industrial and hazardous waste management. The integrated approach-combining scientific, engineering, and management services-provides cost-effective solutions to the complex scope of environmental problems, risk assessment and audit programs; and spill response management and planning services. Industries served: manufacturing, petroleum, power plants, utilities, wastewater treatment facilities, pipelines, landfills, banks, financial institutions, real estate

developers, law firms, insurance companies, and government. **Founded:** 1995. **Seminars:** Beating the Competition: Winning with Better Information.

25719 ■ Queens Business Consulting (QBC)
Queens School of Business, Goodes Hall, 143
  Union St.
Kingston, ON, Canada K7L 3N6
Ph: (613)533-2309
Fax: (613)533-2370
Co. E-mail: qbc@business.queensu.ca
URL: http://www.qsbc.com
Contact: Michelle Miatello, Director
E-mail: mmiatello@business.queensu.ca

Scope: Provides business plans, feasibility studies, financial planning, competitor analysis, market research, marketing strategies, production planning and systems implementation. **Founded:** 1973. **Publications:** "Information technology, network structure and competitive action. Information Systems Research," 2010; "The role of dominance in the appeal of violent media depictions. Journal of Advertising," 2010; "Great expectations and broken promises: Misleading claims, product failure, expectancy disconfirmation and consumer distrust. Journal of the

Academy of Marketing Science," 2010; "Development and psychometric properties of the Transformational Teaching Questionnaire. Journal of Health Psychology," 2010; ". Predicting workplace aggression: myths, realities, and remaining questions," 2009; "The Inconvenient Truth about Improving Vehicle Fuel Efficiency: An MultiAttribute Analysis of the Efficient Frontier of the U.S. Automobile Industry, Transportation Research-Part," 2009; "Fraud in Canadian Nonprofit Organizations as Seen through the Eyes of Canadian Newspapers," 2009; "Disentangling the Indirect Links between SES and Health: The Dynamic Roles of Work Stressors and Personal Contro," 2009; "The strong situation hypothesis. Personality and Social Psychology Review," 2009; " Planning Your Next Crisis Decisively and Effectively. Ivey Business Journal," 2009. **Seminars:** Enabling Innovation Discussion Highlights, 2011; Intellectual Capital, 2010; On the diffusion of knowledge inside the organization, 2010; A model of the tacit knowledge lifecycle for decision-making: From creation to utilization, 2010; Individual, group, and organizational learning; A knowledge management perspective, 2009; Political economies of knowledge, with an example, 2009; The alignment of business and knowledge strategies and structures. 2009; Using IT To Support

the Discovery of Novel Knowledge in Organizations, 2008; Leadership: Knowledge Management by a New Name?, 2007; Every User Tells a Story, 2007.

RESEARCH CENTERS

25720 ■ University of California, Los Angeles - Research Program in Takeovers and Corporate Restructuring
258 Tavistock Ave.
Los Angeles, CA 90049-3229
Ph: (310)472-5110
Fax: (310)472-9471
Co. E-mail: jweston@anderson.ucla.edu
URL: http://www.anderson.ucla.edu/faculty/john.
  weston
Contact: Prof. J. Fred Weston, Director

Founded: 1968. **Publications:** *Research Program in Takeovers and Corporate Restructuring Journal articles*; *Research Program in Takeovers and Corporate Restructuring Working papers*. **Educational Activities:** Presentations to congressional committees. **Awards:** Fellowships for doctoral students; Research Program in Takeovers and Corporate Restructuring Paid internships (Occasionally).

EDUCATIONAL PROGRAMS

25721 ■ **How to Bargain & Negotiate with Vendors and Suppliers (Onsite)**
Fred Pryor Seminars & CareerTrack
5700 Broadmoor St., Ste. 300
Mission, KS 66202
Free: 800-780-8476
Fax: (913)967-8849
Co. E-mail: customerservice@pryor.com
URL: http://www.pryor.com
Price: $179.00; $169.00 for groups of 5 or more.
Description: Learn how to get lower prices, quicker delivery, higher quality and better service through negotiation. **Dates and Locations:** Cities throughout the United States.

REFERENCE WORKS

25722 ■ *"The 490 Made Chevy a Bargain Player" in Automotive News (Vol. 86, October 31, 2011, No. 6488, pp. S22)*
Pub: Crain Communications Inc.
Ed: David Phillips. **Description:** The first Chevrolet with the 490 engine was sold in 1913, but it was too expensive for masses. In 1914 the carmaker launched a lower-priced H-series of cars competitively priced. Nameplates such as Corvette, Bel Air, Camaro and Silverado have defined Chevrolet through the years.

25723 ■ *"Advances in Pump Technology - Part Two" in Contractor (Vol. 57, February 2010, No. 2, pp. 22)*
Pub: Penton Media, Inc.
Ed: Mark Eatherton. **Description:** Chinese and Japanese companies have come up with refrigerant based heat pump products that are air based which will significantly lower the installed cost of heat pump based systems. Some of these newer models have variable speed, soft start compressors and have the ability to perform high-efficiency heat pump operation on a modulating basis.

25724 ■ *"After Price Cuts, Competition GPS Makers Lose Direction" in Brandweek (Vol. 49, April 21, 2008, No. 16, pp. 16)*
Pub: VNU Business Media, Inc.
Ed: Steve Miller. **Description:** Garmin and TomTom, two of the leaders in portable navigation devices, have seen lowering revenues due to dramatic price cuts and unexpected competition from the broadening availability of personal navigation on mobile phones. TomTom has trimmed its sales outlook for its first quarter while Garmin's stock dropped 40 percent since February.

25725 ■ *"Auctions and Bidding: a Guide for Computer Scientists" in ACM Computing Surveys (Vol. 43, Summer 2011, No. 2, pp. 10)*
Pub: Association for Computing Machinery
Ed: Simon Parsons, Juan A. Rodriguez-Aguilar, Mark Klein. **Description:** There are various actions: single dimensional, multi-dimensional, single-sided, double-sided, first-price, second-price, English, Dutch, Japanese, sealed-bid, and these have been extensively discussed and analyzed in economics literature. This literature is surveyed from a computer science perspective, primarily from the viewpoint of computer scientists who are interested in learning about auction theory, and to provide pointers into the economics literature for those who want a deeper technical understanding. In addition, since auctions are an increasingly important topic in computer science, the article also looks at work on auctions from the computer science literature. The aim is to identify what both bodies of work tell us about creating electronic auctions.

25726 ■ *"BK Menu Gives Casual Dining Reason to Worry" in Advertising Age (Vol. 79, November 17, 2008, No. 43, pp. 12)*
Pub: Crain Communications, Inc.
Ed: Emily Bryson York. **Description:** Burger King is beginning to compete with such casual dining restaurants as Applebees and the Cheesecake Factory with new premium menu items, including thicker burgers and ribs; statistical data regarding the casual dining segment which continues to fall and Burger King, whose sales continue to rise is included.

25727 ■ *"Blues Asking Price Out of Their League" in Saint Louis Business Journal (Vol. 32, September 23, 2011, No. 4, pp. 1)*
Pub: Saint Louis Business Journal
Ed: Amy Kurtovic. **Description:** St. Louis Blues owner Dave Checketts wanted the hockey team sold before the start of the season and he believed the team could fetch $200 million or more. However, Hockey insiders believe the price was too high when considering the team's high debt ratio and several other National Hockey League teams on the market.

25728 ■ *"Buick Prices Verano Below Rival Luxury Compacts" in Automotive News (Vol. 86, October 31, 2011, No. 6488, pp. 10)*
Pub: Crain Communications Inc.
Ed: Mike Colias. **Description:** General Motors's Verano will compete with other luxury compacts such as the Lexus IS 250 and the Acura TSX, but will be prices significantly lower coming in with a starting price of $23,470, about $6,000 to $10,000 less than those competitors.

25729 ■ *"Builders, Unions Aim to Cut Costs; Pushing Changes to Regain Share of Residential Market; Seek Council's Help" in Crain's New York Business*
Pub: Crain Communications, Inc.
Ed: Erik Engquist. **Description:** Union contractors and workers are worried about a decline in their market share for housing so they intend to ask the City Council to impose new safety and benefit standards on all contractors to avoid being undercut by nonunion competitors.

25730 ■ *"Businesses Keep a Watchful Eye on Worker's Comp" in The Business Journal-Serving Greater Tampa Bay*
(September 5, 2008)
Pub: American City Business Journals, Inc.
Ed: Jane Meinhardt. **Description:** Pending a ruling from the Florida Supreme Court that could uphold the 2003 changes on workers' compensation law, the outcome would include restrictions on claimant attorneys' fees and allow the competitive workers' compensation insurance rates to remain low. However, insurance rates are expected to go up if the court overturns the changes.

25731 ■ *"Cash Rents Reach Sky-High Levels" in Farm Industry News (November 23, 2011)*
Pub: Penton Business Media Inc.
Ed: Karen McMahon. **Description:** Strong commodity prices are driving land values creating a hot rental market for farm land. Highest rents occur when farmers compete head-to-head for land.

25732 ■ *Cheap: The High Cost of Discount Culture*
Pub: Penguin Group USA Inc.
Ed: Ellen Ruppel Shell. **Released:** July 2, 2009. **Price:** $25.95. **Description:** The American drive toward bargain-hunting and low-price goods has hidden costs in lower wages for workers and reduced quality of goods for consumers.

25733 ■ *"Choice Bits" in Crain's Cleveland Business (Vol. 30, June 29, 2009, No. 25, pp. 19)*
Pub: Crain Communications, Inc.
Description: Ross Farro, Cleveland area restaurateur who was featured in the New York Times story about casual dining chains competing over lunch traffic through pricing.

25734 ■ *Complete Idiot's Guide to Starting an Ebay Business*
Pub: Penguin Books USA Inc.
Ed: Barbara Weltman, Malcolm Katt. **Released:** February 2008. **Price:** $19.95 (US), $29.00 (Canadian). **Description:** Guide for starting an eBay business includes information on products to sell, how to price merchandise, and details for working with services like PayPal, and how to organize fulfillment services.

25735 ■ *The Complete Idiot's Guide to Starting and Running a Thrift Store*
Pub: Alpha Publishing House
Ed: Ravel Buckley, Carol Costa. **Released:** January 5, 2010. **Price:** $18.95. **Description:** Thrift stores saw a 35 percent increase in sales during the falling economy in 2008. Despite the low startup costs, launching and running a thrift store is complicated. Two experts cover the entire process, including setting up a store on a nonprofit basis, choosing a location, funding, donations for saleable items, recruiting and managing staff, sorting items, pricing, and recycling donations.

25736 ■ *"Construction Companies Think Smaller, Find Niches as Projects Become*

Fewer" in Crain's Detroit Business (March 10, 2008)

Pub: Crain Communications, Inc.

Ed: Daniel Duggan. **Description:** Due to the decline in development projects, construction firms are facing stronger competition for bids and are relying on their good track records or developing expertise in specific niches to get the job.

25737 ■ *"Consumers Seek to Redo Rate Structure: Smaller Biz Paid Big Rates" in Crain's Detroit Business (Vol. 25, June 22, 2009)*

Pub: Crain Communications Inc. - Detroit

Ed: Amy Lane. **Description:** Consumers Energy Company charged small business customers disproportionately higher rates on June 2009 electric bills than other consumers.

25738 ■ *"Contractors Should Expand Their Services" in Contractor (Vol. 56, July 2009, No. 7, pp. 34)*

Pub: Penton Media, Inc.

Ed: Steven Scandaliato. **Description:** All single family homes will be required to have fire sprinkler systems installed when the 2009 International Residential Code arrives. This presents an opportunity for plumbing contractors and they can be competitively priced against a fire protection contractor if they train their workforce to install sprinklers.

25739 ■ *"Corn Belt Farmland Prices Hit Record Levels" in Farm Industry News (December 1, 2011)*

Pub: Penton Business Media Inc.

Ed: David Hest. **Description:** Farmland prices have set records over the last six months in Iowa. Farmland broker and auction company owner, Murray Wise, believes this is not a bubble, that the economics of this market are solid.

25740 ■ *"COSE Turns On To Electricity Market" in Crain's Cleveland Business (Vol. 30, June 22, 2009, No. 24, pp. 4)*

Pub: Crain Communications, Inc.

Ed: Jay Miller. **Description:** Council of Smaller Enterprises is working to offer small businesses and their employees electricity at discount prices set at auction by the Public Utilities Commission of Ohio and even lower prices from the Northern Ohio Public Energy Council. Details of the program are offered.

25741 ■ *"Cost of Md. Health Plan Not Known" in Baltimore Business Journal (Vol. 28, September 3, 2010, No. 17, pp. 1)*

Pub: Baltimore Business Journal

Ed: Emily Mullin. **Description:** United States health reform is seen to result in increased health insurance prices in Maryland. However, health care reform advocates claim a new marketplace and increased competition will help keep costs down.

25742 ■ *"Crouser Offers UV Coating Price Report" in American Printer (Vol. 128, June 1, 2011, No. 6)*

Pub: Penton Media Inc.

Description: Crouser and Associates will offer the 'Pricing Off-Line UV Coating' report that provides background information on all three types of protective printing coatings and price guidance. The report will also offer comparisons of four popular types of offline equipment.

25743 ■ *"The Data Drivers" in Canadian Business (Vol. 81, September 15, 2008, No. 14-15, pp. 1)*

Pub: Rogers Media Ltd.

Ed: Andrew Wahl. **Description:** Canadian regulators hope that an auction of telecommunications companies will inject more competition into the industry; however, newcomers may not be able to rely on lower prices in order to gain market share from the three major telecommunications companies that already have a stronghold on the market. Analysts feel that providing additional data service is the key to surviving market disruptions.

25744 ■ *"Dean Foods" in Ice Cream Reporter (Vol. 23, November 20, 2010, No. 12, pp. 8)*

Pub: Ice Cream Reporter

Description: The impact of higher commodity prices can be seen in the recent news from Dean Foods, the largest U.S. dairy company, which reported that rising butterfat and other dairy commodity costs have led to lower-than-expected quarterly profits after it cut prices to compete with private-label brands.

25745 ■ *The Designer's Guide to Marketing and Pricing: How to Win Clients and What to Charge Them*

Pub: F and W Publications, Inc.

Ed: Ilise Benun. **Released:** March 2008. **Price:** $19.99. **Description:** Guide to running a creative services business teaches designers how to be more effective, attract new clients, wages, and how to accurately estimate a project.

25746 ■ *"Drop in the Bucket Makes a lot of Waves" in Globe & Mail (March 22, 2007, pp. B1)*

Pub: CTVglobemedia Publishing Inc.

Ed: Greg Keenan. **Description:** The concern of several auto makers in Canada over the impact of providing heavy rebates to customers buying energy-efficient cars is discussed.

25747 ■ *"Dropped Calls" in Canadian Business (Vol. 80, November 5, 2007, No. 22, pp. 34)*

Pub: Rogers Media

Ed: Andrew Wahl. **Description:** Control over Canada's telecommunications market by Telus, Rogers and Bell Canada has resulted in a small number of innovations. The pricing regimes of these carriers have also stifled innovations in the telecommunications industry. The status of Canada's telecommunications industry is further analyzed.

25748 ■ *EBay Income: How ANYONE of Any Age, Location, and/or Background Can Build a Highly Profitable Online Business with eBay*

Pub: Atlantic Publishing Company

Released: December 1, 2010. **Price:** $24.95. **Description:** A complete overview of eBay is given and guides any small company through the entire process of creating the auction and auction strategies, photography, writing copy, text and formatting, multiple sales, programming tricks, PayPal, accounting, creating marketing, merchandising, managing email lists, advertising plans, taxes and sales tax, best time to list items and for how long, sniping programs, international customers, opening a storefront, electronic commerce, buy-it now pricing, keywords, Google marketing and eBay secrets.

25749 ■ *"The Ethics of Price Discrimination" in Business Ethics Quarterly (Vol. 21, October 2011, No. 4, pp. 633)*

Pub: Society for Business Ethics

Ed: Juan M. Elegido. **Description:** Price discrimination is the practice of charging different customers different prices for the same product. Many people consider price discrimination unfair, but economists argue that in many cases price discrimination is more likely to lead to greater welfare than is the uniform pricing alternative, sometimes even for every party in the transaction.

25750 ■ *Faster Cheaper Better*

Pub: Crown Business Books

Ed: Michael Hammer. **Released:** December 28, 2010. **Price:** $27.50. **Description:** Nine levels for transforming work in order to achieve business growth are outlined. The book helps small business compete against the low-wage countries.

25751 ■ *"Flint Group Raises Prices" in American Printer (Vol. 128, August 1, 2011, No. 8)*

Pub: Penton Media Inc.

Description: Due to the rising cost of raw materials, Flint Group is raising their prices for inks and coatings in North American.

25752 ■ *"For His Bigness of Heart: Larry C'Toole: Gentle Giant Moving, Somerville, Massachusetts" in Inc. (Volume 32, December 2010)*

Pub: Inc. Magazine

Description: Profile of Larry O'Toole, owners of Gentle Giant Moving Company, where his company charges more, but in return consumers receive a higher quality service.

25753 ■ *"Fossil Fuel, Renewable Fuel Shares Expected to Flip Flop" in Farm Industry News (April 29, 2011)*

Pub: Penton Business Media Inc.

Description: Total energy use of fossil fuels is predicted to fall 5 percent by the year 2035, with renewable fuel picking it up.

25754 ■ *"Franchisees Lose Battle Against BK" in Advertising Age (Vol. 79, June 2, 2008, No. 22, pp. 46)*

Pub: Crain Communications, Inc.

Ed: Emily Bryson York. **Description:** Burger King has had continuing litigation with former franchisees from New York, Luan and Elizabeth Sadik, who claim that Burger King's double cheeseburger, along with additional problems, created the environment for their eventual insolvency. Burger King has since terminated its test of selling the double cheeseburger for $1, although the company declined to comment on the reason for this decision.

25755 ■ *Free: The Future of a Radical Price*

Pub: Hyperion

Ed: Chris Anderson. **Released:** 2009. **Price:** $26.99. **Description:** A new trend shows companies using giveaways as a means to attract business and increase profits.

25756 ■ *From Concept To Consumer: How to Turn Ideas Into Money*

Pub: Pearson Education Inc.

Ed: Phil Baker. **Released:** 2009. **Price:** $24.99. **Description:** Renowned product developer Phil Baker explains how a great idea accounts for only 5 percent of all the factors of success and why the majority of success is dependent upon a myriad of other factors, including the time it takes to get to market, price, marketing and distribution. By being their own best competition, a small company can stay one step ahead of competitors.

25757 ■ *"Get Sold On eBay" in Entrepreneur (Vol. 36, March 2008, No. 3, pp. 94)*

Pub: Entrepreneur Media Inc.

Ed: Marcia Layton Turner. **Description:** Entrepreneurs are increasingly using eBay to sell products. Some tips to start selling products through eBay include: starting with used items, developing a niche to sell specific products, and researching product pricing. Other tips with regard to starting an eBay business are covered.

25758 ■ *"Getting a Grip on the Saddle: Chasms or Cycles?" in Journal of Marketing (Vol. 75, July 2011, No. 4, pp. 21)*

Pub: American Marketing Association

Ed: Deepa Chandrasekaran, Gerald J. Tellis. **Description:** A study of the saddle's generality across products and countries is presented. The saddle is fairly pervasive based on empirical analysis of historical sales data from ten products across 19 countries. The results indicate chasms and technological cycles for information/entertainment products while business cycles and technological cycles affect kitchen/laundry products.

25759 ■ *"H&M Offers a Dress for Less" in Canadian Business (Vol. 83, September 14, 2010, No. 15, pp. 20)*

Pub: Rogers Media Ltd.

Ed: Laura Cameron. **Description:** Swedish clothing company H&M has implemented loss leader strategy by pricing some dresses at extremely low prices. The economy has forced retailers to keep prices down despite the increasing cost of manufacturing, partly due to Chinese labor becoming more expensive. How the trend will affect apparel companies is discussed.

25760 ■ *"High Anxiety" in Canadian Business (Vol. 80, November 19, 2007, No. 23, pp. 11)*
Pub: Rogers Media
Ed: Zena Olijnyk. **Description:** Value of Canadian dollar continues to rise, and consumers are asking for lower prices of goods. Retailers, on the other hand, are facing concerns over losing sales. The impacts of the rising Canadian dollar on the business sector and consumer behavior are examined.

25761 ■ *"Hospitals Face Big Whammy From State Fees" in Business Courier (Vol. 26, October 2, 2009, No. 23, pp. 1)*
Pub: American City Business Journals, Inc.
Ed: James Ritchie. **Description:** Ohio hospitals are facing losses of nearly $145 million in franchise fees which are set to be levied by the state. Ohio hospitals will be responsible for a total of $718 million franchise fees as required by 2010-2011 state budget but will recover only 80 percent of the amount in increased Medicaid fees. Possible effects of anticipated losses to Ohio hospitals are examined.

25762 ■ *How to Get Rich*
Pub: Ebury Press
Ed: Felix Dennis. **Released:** 2008. **Price:** $25.95. **Description:** Publisher of Maxim, The Week, and Stuff magazines, discusses the mistakes he made running his companies. He didn't understand that people who buy computer gaming magazines wanted a free game with each copy, as one of his rivals was offering. And he laments not diversifying into television and exploiting the Internet.

25763 ■ *"How Has City Golf Privatization Played?" in Business Courier (Vol. 27, September 10, 2010, No. 19, pp. 1)*
Pub: Business Courier
Ed: Dan Monk. **Description:** It was reported that private contractors are getting more revenue from fewer golfers on city-owned courses in Cincinnati, Ohio. In 1998, the city handed over seven municipal courses to private management. However, some believe that the city has escalated a price war among the region's golf courses.

25764 ■ *How to Make Big Money*
Pub: Hyperion Books
Ed: Jeffrey J. Fox. **Released:** May 19, 2004. **Price:** $16.95. **Description:** Entrepreneur and consultant offers advice to help others create successful startups and prosper. Fox directs new business owners with a counterintuitive style and describes essential methods that beat the competition. Tips include: setting priorities, getting a personal driver, creating a contingency plan for employees, pricing to value, saving money, and getting an office outside of the home.

25765 ■ *"How Much Profit is Enough?" in Automotive News (Vol. 86, October 31, 2011, No. 6488, pp. 12)*
Pub: Crain Communications Inc.
Ed: Keith Crain. **Description:** Workers at the big three automobile companies are unhappy about the issues of class wealth, like the high compensations offered to CEOs.

25766 ■ *How to Start a Home-Based Senior Care Business: Develop a Winning Business Plan*
Pub: Globe Pequot Press
Ed: James L. Ferry. **Released:** January 10, 2010. **Price:** $18.95. **Description:** Everything needed to know in order to start and run a profitable, ethical, and satisfying senior care business from your home. Information covers writing a good business plan, marketing services to families, creating a fee structure, and developing a network of trusted caregivers and service providers.

25767 ■ *How to Start and Run a Small Book Publishing Company: A Small Business Guide to Self-Publishing and Independent Publishing*
Pub: HCM Publishing
Ed: Peter I. Hupalo. **Released:** August 30, 2002. **Price:** $18.95. **Description:** The book teaches all aspects of starting and running a small book publishing company. Topics covered include: inventory ac-

counting in the book trade, just-in-time inventory management, turnkey fulfillment solutions, tax deductible costs, basics of sales and use tax, book pricing, standards in terms of the book industry, working with distributors and wholesalers, cover design and book layout, book promotion and marketing, how to select profitable authors to publish, printing process, printing on demand, the power of a strong backlist, and how to value copyright.

25768 ■ *"Innovating Low-Cost Business Models" in Strategy and Leadership (Vol. 39, March-April 2011, No. 2, pp. 43)*
Pub: Emerald Group Publishing Inc.
Ed: Nicholas Kachaner, Zhenya Lindgardt, David Michael. **Description:** A process that can be used to implement low-cost innovation is presented. The process can be used to address the competitive challenges presented by multinationals' practice of presenting applications and price points that are intended for developing markets into developed markets. The process involves targeting large, and low-income segments of the market.

25769 ■ *"Insurers No Longer Paying Premium for Advertising" in Brandweek (Vol. 49, April 21, 2008, No. 16, pp. SR3)*
Pub: VNU Business Media, Inc.
Ed: Eric Newman. **Description:** Insurance companies are cutting their advertising budgets after years of accelerated double-digit growth in spending due to the economic downturn, five years of record-breaking ad spend and a need to cut expenditures as claims costs rise and a competitive market keeps premiums in place. Statistical data included.

25770 ■ *"Is That the Best You Can Do?" in Entrepreneur (Vol. 37, October 2009, No. 10, pp. 85)*
Pub: Entrepreneur Media, Inc.
Ed: Jennifer Wang. **Description:** Small business owners can deal with hagglers better by setting parameters in advance. They should convince hagglers by offering the best value and separating this from price.

25771 ■ *"Just Hang Up" in Barron's (Vol. 88, March 10, 2008, No. 10, pp. 45)*
Pub: Dow Jones & Company, Inc.
Ed: Tiernan Ray. **Description:** Sprint's shares are expected to continue falling while the company attempts to attract subscribers by cutting prices, cutting earnings in the process. The company faces tougher competition from better-financed AT&T and Verizon Communications.

25772 ■ *"Law Firms Plan Rate Bumps" in Houston Business Journal (Vol. 40, December 25, 2009, No. 33, pp. 1)*
Pub: American City Business Journals
Ed: Ford Gunter. **Description:** Survey shows that Houston, Texas-based law firms were in line with a 3.2 percent average rate hike projected for 2010. The big firms were ready to offset some losses with a rate bump of 4 percent while smaller firms have been expecting an increase of about 3 percent.

25773 ■ *"Local Startup Hits Big Leagues" in Austin Business JournalInc. (Vol. 28, December 19, 2008, No. 40, pp. 1)*
Pub: American City Business Journals
Ed: Christopher Calnan. **Description:** Qcue LLC, an Austin, Texas-based company founded in 2007 is developing a software system that can be used by Major League Baseball teams to change the prices of their single-game tickets based on variables affecting demand. The company recently completed a trial with the San Francisco Giants in 2008.

25774 ■ *"Market Share" in Business Journal-Milwaukee (Vol. 28, December 3, 2010, No. 9, pp. A1)*
Pub: Milwaukee Business Journal
Ed: Stacy Vogel Davis. **Description:** Roundy's Supermarkets' market share has decreased with the expansion of low-price grocery chains in Milwaukee, Wisconsin. Wal-Mart stores Inc., Aldi Inc., and Target Corporation have all opened new stores in the area.

25775 ■ *"Medicaid Insurers See Growth in Small Business Market" in Boston Business Journal (Vol. 31, July 15, 2011, No. 25, pp. 1)*
Pub: Boston Business Journal
Ed: Julie M. Donnelly. **Description:** BMC HealthNet Plan announced plans to launch small business products to serve small businesses that are priced out of rising premium rates at large Massachusetts insurers. BMC joined competitors CeltiCare Health Plan and Neighborhood Health Plan in augmenting its core business.

25776 ■ *"Netflix vs. Blockbuster" in Inc. (October 2007, pp. 32)*
Pub: Gruner & Jahr USA Publishing
Description: Nexflix, the mail-order DVD rental service, is losing market share to Blockbuster, even after matching prices to that of its competitors. Entrepreneurs are asked how they would run Netflix to gain back market share.

25777 ■ *"Notes on Current Labor Statistics" in Montly Labor Review (Vol. 133, September 2010, No. 9, pp. 75)*
Pub: Bureau of Labor Statistics
Description: Principal statistics and calculated by the Bureau of Labor Statistics are presented. The series includes statistics on labor force; employment; unemployment; labor compensation; consumer, producer, and international prices; productivity; international comparisons; and injury and illness statistics.

25778 ■ *"Office Supplier Won't Wait for Opportunity to Knock" in Business Courier (Vol. 24, December 28, 2008, No. 37, pp. 2)*
Pub: American City Business Journals, Inc.
Ed: Lucy May. **Description:** Ace Products, an office supplier, stays competitive through its customer service and pricing.

25779 ■ *"Open Skies: Opportunity, Challenge for Airlines" in Crain's Chicago Business (April 21, 2008)*
Pub: Crain Communications, Inc.
Ed: Paul Merrion. **Description:** Discusses the new aviation agreement between Europe and the United States known as Open Skies; the pact creates opportunities for U.S. carriers to fly to new destinations in Europe from more U.S. cities; it also allows carriers to fly between European cities, something they have not been able to do until now.

25780 ■ *"Ownership Form, Managerial Incentives, and the Intensity of Rivalry" in Academy of Management Journal (Vol. 50, No. 4, August 2007)*
Pub: Academy of Management
Contact: Ming-Jer Chen, President
Ed: Govert Vroom, Javier Gimeno. **Description:** Ways in which differences in ownership form between franchised and company-owned units alter managerial incentives and competitive pricing in different oligopolistic contexts, or following competitors into foreign markets, is presented.

25781 ■ *"Paying the Price" in Baltimore Business Journal (Vol. 28, July 9, 2010, No. 9, pp. 1)*
Pub: Baltimore Business Journal
Ed: Emily Mullin. **Description:** Crab prices have never been higher in Baltimore, Maryland and businesses have been led to count on strengthening demand for seafood. For instance, the average price for a dozen large crabs has increased by 5 percent to $58.90. How restaurants have responded to the increase in prices is discussed, along with factors that might have caused the harvest of smaller crabs.

25782 ■ *"Peter Gilgan" in Canadian Business (Vol. 82, April 27, 2009, No. 7, pp. 58)*
Pub: Rogers Media
Ed: Calvin Leung. **Description:** Mattamy Homes Ltd. president and chief executive officer Peter Gilgan believes that their business model of building communities in an organized way brings advantages to the firm and for their customers. He also believes in

adopting their product prices to new market realities. Gilgan considers the approvals regime in Ontario his biggest challenge in the last 20 years.

25783 ■ "Point, Click, Buy" in Barron's (Vol. 90, September 6, 2010, No. 36, pp. 11)
Pub: Barron's Editorial & Corporate Headquarters
Ed: Vito J. Racanelli. **Description:** Non-travel online retail sales from January to July 2010 increased nine percent which indicates that online shopping for the coming holidays will be good. Online sales are outpacing traditional shopping, but pricing is still critical.

25784 ■ "Prepaid Phones Surge in Bad Economy" in Advertising Age (Vol. 79, November 17, 2008, No. 43, pp. 6)
Pub: Crain Communications, Inc.
Ed: Rita Chang. **Description:** Prepay cell phone offerings are becoming increasingly competitive amid a greater choice of plans and handsets. In an economic environment in which many consumers are unable to pass the credit checks required for traditional cell phone plans, the prepay market is surging.

25785 ■ "Price Data" in Montly Labor Review (Vol. 133, September 2010, No. 9, pp. 128)
Pub: Bureau of Labor Statistics
Description: Consumer price indexes for all urban consumers and for urban wage earners and clerical workers is presented with U.S. city average, by expenditure category and commodity or service group.

25786 ■ "The Price of Profitability" in Green Industry Pro (Vol. 23, March 2011, No. 3, pp. 18)
Pub: Cygnus Business Media
Ed: Tony Bass. **Description:** Profit Builder Process is used to help landscaping companies be more competitive. Landscape contractors report pricing among their largest challenges and although the economy is improving, homeowners are paying closer attention to quality and service.

25787 ■ "Q&A: Joseph Ribkoff" in Canadian Business (Vol. 81, March 31, 2008, No. 5, pp. 4)
Pub: Rogers Media
Ed: Zena Olijnyk. **Description:** Joseph Ribkoff started his career in the garment trade by sweeping floors and running deliveries for a dress manufacturer called Town & Country and earned $16 a week. Ribkoff says that the key to controlling costs in Canada is to invest in the latest equipment and technology to stay competitive.

25788 ■ "Quiznos Franchisees Walloped by Recession" in Advertising Age (Vol. 79, October 20, 2008, No. 39, pp. 3)
Pub: Crain Communications, Inc.
Ed: Emily Bryson York. **Description:** While the recession has taken a toll on the entire restaurant industry, a number of Quiznos franchisees claim to have been disproportionately affected due to lackluster marketing, higher-than-average commodity costs, competition with Subway and a premium-pricing structure that is incompatible with a tight economy.

25789 ■ "Rough Q1 Begs Question: Is the Crocs Craze Over?" in Brandweek (Vol. 49, April 21, 2008, No. 16, pp. 16)
Pub: VNU Business Media, Inc.
Ed: Eric Newman. **Description:** Crocs, a rubber shoemaker, announced last week that it missed its expected first quarter revenues by 15 percent. The popular rubber sandals are suffering in sales due to a number of factors including a tougher economic environment, less expensive, knock-off brands, the cold weather delay of the spring season and fading consumer interest in plastic shoes.

25790 ■ "Rumors Kill Algoma Takeover Talks" in Globe & Mail (March 14, 2007, pp. B14)
Pub: CTVglobemedia Publishing Inc.
Ed: Tara Perkins. **Description:** Canada-based steel manufacturing giant Salzgitter AG has dropped its acquisition negotiations with Algoma Steel Inc. The decision comes after the secret price quotation was leaked to competitors.

25791 ■ "Small Business Compensation" in Small Business Economic Trends (September 2010, pp. 10)
Pub: National Federation of Independent Business
Ed: William C. Dunkelberg, Holly Wade. **Description:** A graph from a survey of small businesses in the U.S. is given, representing small business compensation from January 1986 to August 2010. Tables showing actual compensation changes and compensation plans are also presented. A graph comparing small business prices and labor compensation is supplied.

25792 ■ "Small Business Prices" in Small Business Economic Trends (April 2008, pp. 8)
Pub: National Federation of Independent Business
Ed: William C. Dunkelberg, Holly Wade. **Description:** Two tables and a graph presenting the price changes and price plans of small businesses in the U.S. are provided. The net percentage of planned and actual prices includes data from 1968 to 2008.

25793 ■ "Small Business Prices" in Small Business Economic Trends (March 2008, pp. 8)
Pub: National Federation of Independent Business
Ed: William C. Dunkelberg. **Description:** Two tables and a graph presenting the price changes and price plans of small businesses in the U.S. are provided. The net percentage of planned and actual prices includes data from 1986 to 2008.

25794 ■ "Small Business Prices" in Small Business Economic Trends (February 2008, pp. 8)
Pub: National Federation of Independent Business
Ed: William C. Dunkelberg. **Description:** Two tables and a graph presenting the price changes and price plans of small businesses in the U.S. are provided. The net percentage of planned and actual prices includes data from 1974 to 2008.

25795 ■ "Small Business Prices" in Small Business Economic Trends (January 2008, pp. 8)
Pub: National Federation of Independent Business
Description: Graph from a survey of small businesses in the U.S. is given representing business prices from January 1986 to December 2007. Actual prices (last three months) and planned prices (next three months) were compared in the graph. Tables of actual price changes and price plans from January 2002 to December 2007 are also supplied.

25796 ■ "Small Business Prices" in Small Business Economic Trends (September 2010, pp. 8)
Pub: National Federation of Independent Business
Ed: William C. Dunkelberg, Holly Wade. **Description:** A graph from a survey of small businesses in the U.S. is given, representing business prices from January 1986 to August 2010. Actual prices (last three months) and planned prices (next three months) were compared in the graph. Tables of actual price changes and price plans from January 2005 to August 2010 are also supplied.

25797 ■ "Small Business Prices" in Small Business Economic Trends (July 2010, pp. 8)
Pub: National Federation of Independent Business
Description: A graph from a survey of small businesses in the U.S. is given representing business prices from January 1986 to June 2010. Actual prices (last three months) and planned prices (next three months) were compared in the graph. Tables of actual price changes and price plans from January 2005 to June 2010 are also supplied.

25798 ■ "Stepping Up" in Baltimore Business Journal (Vol. 28, October 22, 2010, No. 24, pp. 1)
Pub: Baltimore Business Journal
Ed: Erik Siemers. **Description:** Uner Armour Inc. will release its Micro G line of four basketball sneakers on October 23, 2010. The company's executives mentioned that Under Armour's goal is to appeal to customers, and not to chip away at Nike Inc.'s supremacy in basketball shoes. The new sneakers will range from $80 to $110.

25799 ■ "The Superpower Dilemma" in Canadian Business (Vol. 83, August 17, 2010, No. 13-14, pp. 42)
Pub: Rogers Media Ltd.
Description: Canada has been an energy superpower partly because it controls the energy source and the production means, particularly of fossil fuels. However, Canada's status as superpower could diminish if it replaces petroleum exports with renewable technology for using sources of energy available globally.

25800 ■ "Title Creep: The Chief Revenue Officer" in Inc. (March 2008, pp. 28)
Pub: Gruner & Jahr USA Publishing
Ed: The title, Chief Revenue Officer, is growing. The marketing function of the CRO is to oversee sales, new product development, and pricing.

25801 ■ "Unfilled Hotels Go All Out for Business Meetings" in Crain's Detroit Business (Vol. 25, June 8, 2009, No. 23, pp. 9)
Pub: Crain Communications Inc. - Detroit
Ed: Daniel Duggan. **Description:** Hotels in Michigan are offering discounts to companies holding business meetings at their properties. Details of competition and plans are included.

25802 ■ "Velvet Ice Cream" in Ice Cream Reporter (Vol. 21, July 20, 2008, No. 8, pp. 7)
Pub: Ice Cream Reporter
Description: Velvet Ice Cream is adding a $7 surcharge on deliveries of its products in order to offset rising fuel costs.

25803 ■ "'Wal-Mart Effect' Feeds Grocer Price Wars" in Globe & Mail (March 15, 2007, pp. B14)
Pub: CTVglobemedia Publishing Inc.
Ed: Marina Strauss. **Description:** The decrease in profit reports by Canadian grocery giants amidst high expansion plans by Wal-Mart Stores Inc. are discussed. This industry is witnessing the most severe pricing competitions in recent times.

25804 ■ "While Competitors Shut Doors, Subway Is Still Growing" in Advertising Age (Vol. 79, July 21, 2008, No. 28, pp. 4)
Pub: Crain Communications, Inc.
Ed: Emily Bryson York. **Description:** Subway, the largest fast-food chain, with 22,000 U.S. locations, is adding 800 this year, despite the economic downturn that has caused competitors such as Starbucks to close stores and McDonald's to focus its expansion abroad.

25805 ■ "With New Listings, Business Brokers See Hope" in Business Courier (Vol. 27, September 3, 2010, No. 18, pp. 1)
Pub: Business Courier
Ed: Lucy May. **Description:** Business brokers in Cincinnati, Ohio are expecting better prices in view of the strengthening economy.

VIDEOCASSETTES/ AUDIOCASSETTES

25806 ■ Product Costs: What's In Them
Phoenix Learning Group
2349 Chaffee Dr.
Saint Louis, MO 63146-3306
Ph: (314)569-0211
Free: 800-221-1274
Fax: (314)569-2834
URL: http://www.phoenixlearninggroup.com
Released: 1979. **Description:** This show presents the factors that effect the final price of a product. **Availability:** VHS; 3/4 U.

25807 ■ Swim with the Sharks without Being Eaten Alive
Instructional Video
2219 C St.
Lincoln, NE 68502
Ph: (402)475-6570
Free: 800-228-0164

Fax: (402)475-6500
Co. E-mail: feedback@insvideo.com
URL: http://www.insvideo.com
Released: 19??. **Price:** $595.00. **Description:** Based on Harvey Mackay's best-selling book of the same name. Offers training advice on how to beat your competition, make the crucial sale, open the closed door, and swing the million-dollar deal at the last minute. **Availability:** VHS.

CONSULTANTS

25808 ■ Mark Vanderstelt
9831 Gulfstream Ct.
Fishers, IN 46037
Ph: (317)576-9328

Fax: (317)576-9328
Contact: Mark Vanderstelt, Owner
Scope: Consulting services include financial planning and analysis, inventory control, cash management, return on investment, budgeting, pricing, system design and analysis, mergers and acquisitions, feasibility studies, data processing, cost systems and controls, and performance measurement. Also performs operational and financial reviews. **Founded:** 1985.

RESEARCH CENTERS

25809 ■ Weber State University - Center for Business and Economic Development
3815 University Cir.
Ogden, UT 84408-3815

Ph: (801)626-7232
Fax: (801)626-7423
Co. E-mail: bking1@weber.edu
URL: http://weber.edu/sbdc
Contact: Beverly King, Director

Services: Provides consulting and technical assistance for small businesses and contractual work for government and large businesses. **Founded:** 1972. **Educational Activities:** Courses on business planning and entrepreneurship and 40 annual training events; Center for Business and Economic Development Scholarship (Semiannual), for successful completion of entrepreneurship courses.

START-UP INFORMATION

25810 ■ *Going Solo: Developing a Home-Based Consulting Business from the Ground Up*
Pub: McGraw-Hill Companies Inc.
Contact: Deven Sharma, President
Ed: William J. Bond. **Released:** January 1997. **Description:** Ways to turn specialized knowledge into a home-based successful consulting firm, focusing on targeting client needs, business plans, and growth.

25811 ■ *How to Start a Home-Based Consulting Business: Define Your Specialty Build a Client Base Make Yourself Indispensable*
Pub: Globe Pequot Press
Ed: Bert Holtje. **Released:** January 10, 2010. **Price:** $18.95. **Description:** Everything needed for starting and running a successful consulting business from home.

25812 ■ *Small Business Desk Reference*
Pub: Penguin Books USA Inc.
Ed: Gene Marks. **Released:** December 2004. **Description:** Comprehensive guide for starting or running a successful small business, focusing on buying a business or franchise, writing a business plan, financial management, accounting, legal issues, human resources management, operations, marketing, sales, customer service, taxes, insurance, and ethics. Information for launching a restaurant, property management firm, retail outlet, consulting firm, and service business is included.

25813 ■ *Starting and Running a Coaching Business*
Pub: How To Books
Ed: Aryanne Oade. **Released:** August 9, 2010. **Price:** $26.00. **Description:** Guide for the comprehensive, practical and personalized process of starting and running a coaching business is presented.

25814 ■ *Starting Up On Your Own: How to Succeed as an Independent Consultant or Freelance*
Pub: FT Press
Ed: Mike Johnson. **Released:** February 1, 2010. **Price:** $24.99. **Description:** Concise guide for anyone wanting to start their own consulting firm is provided.

ASSOCIATIONS AND OTHER ORGANIZATIONS

25815 ■ Association of Independent Consultants (AIC)
15 Wilson St.
Markham, ON, Canada L3P 1M9
Ph: (416)410-8163
Fax: (905)669-5233
Co. E-mail: info1@aiconsult.ca
URL: http://www.aiconsult.ca/en
Contact: Lawrence Fox, President
Description: Independent consultants. Promotes professional advancement of members. Facilitates communication and cooperation among members; makes available volume discounts to members. Conducts business education courses; maintains speakers' bureau. **Founded:** 1989. **Publications:** *Thrive-on-Line.* **Educational Activities:** Association of Independent Consultants Meeting (Monthly). **Telecommunication Services:** president1@aiconsult.ca.

25816 ■ Association of Management Consulting Firms (AMCF)
370 Lexington Ave., Ste. 2209
New York, NY 10017
Ph: (212)262-3055
Fax: (212)262-3054
Co. E-mail: info@amcf.org
URL: http://www.amcf.org
Contact: Elizabeth A. Kovacs, President
E-mail: bkovacs@amcf.org
Description: Trade association for consulting organizations that provide a broad range of managerial services to commercial, industrial, governmental, and other organizations and individuals. Seeks to unite management-consulting firms in order to develop and improve professional standards and practice n the field. Offers information and referral services on management consultants; administers public relations program. Conducts research. Monitors regulatory environment. **Scope:** Offers consulting services to management. Assists its members cope with the rapid changes affecting their practices today. Serves as a resource for information on the management of a consulting practice. Provides a forum for the exchange of ideas, helping consultants to better understand developments within the profession and to capitalize on new opportunities. Promotes knowledge exchange and professional standards for the community of management consulting firms from around the world. Serves as the voice of the industry on major issues, representing the profession before government and regulatory bodies, working to improve standards and practices and enabling firms to work smarter. **Founded:** 1929. **Publications:** *15th Annual Operating Ratios for Management Consulting Firms: A Resource for Benchmarking* (Annual). **Educational Activities:** Affinity Groups (Quarterly); Association of Management Consulting Firms Meeting (Annual); Association of Management Consulting Firms Roundtable (Quarterly). **Awards:** AMCF Richard Metzler (Annual).

25817 ■ Association of Professional Computer Consultants (APCC)
2323 Yonge St., Ste. 400
Toronto, ON, Canada M4P 2C9
Ph: (416)545-5275
Free: 888-487-2722
Co. E-mail: information@apcconline.com
URL: http://www.apcconline.com
Description: Promotes the interests of Independent Computer Consultants. **Founded:** 1985. **Subscriptions:** articles. **Publications:** *Gateway* (Periodic).

25818 ■ Association of Proposal Management Professionals (APMP)
PO Box 77272
Washington, DC 20013-8272
Ph: (202)450-2549
URL: http://www.apmp.org
Contact: Rick Harris, Executive Director
Description: Proposal managers, proposal planners, proposal writers, consultants, desktop publishers and marketing managers. Encourages unity and cooperation among industry professionals. Seeks to broaden member knowledge and skills through developmental, educational and social activities. Maintains speakers' bureau. Provides current information and developments in the field. **Founded:** 1989. **Awards:** APMP Fellows Award (Annual).

25819 ■ Canadian Association of International Development Consultants (CAIDC)—Regroupement des consultants canadiens en developpement internationale
260 St. Patrick St., Ste. 101
Ottawa, ON, Canada K1N 5K5
Ph: (613)244-1050
Fax: (613)244-8315
Co. E-mail: caidcrccdi@gmail.com
URL: http://www.caidc-rccdi.ca
Contact: Richard Beattie, President
Description: Aims to provide services for, and to represent the interests of, Canadian international development consultants. **Founded:** 1993.

25820 ■ *Gateway*
2323 Yonge St., Ste. 400
Toronto, ON, Canada M4P 2C9
Ph: (416)545-5275
Free: 888-487-2722
Co. E-mail: information@apcconline.com
URL: http://www.apcconline.com
Released: Periodic **Price:** free.

25821 ■ *Thrive-on-Line*
15 Wilson St.
Markham, ON, Canada L3P 1M9
Ph: (416)410-8163
Fax: (905)669-5233
Co. E-mail: info1@aiconsult.ca
URL: http://www.aiconsult.ca/en
Contact: Lawrence Fox, President
Price: free for members.

REFERENCE WORKS

25822 ■ *10 Make-or-Break Career Moments: Navigate, Negotiate, and Communicate for Success*
Pub: Crown Business Books
Ed: Casey Hawley. **Released:** May 4, 2010. **Price:** $13.99. **Description:** Communication consultant, Casey Hawley, provides a guide to smart communication for any business setting.

25323 ■ *"Achieving Greatness" in Black Enterprise (Vol. 38, January 2008, No. 6, pp. 50)*
Pub: Earl G. Graves Publishing Co. Inc.
Description: Randall Pinkett, winner of a reality show on television and chairman of BCT Partners, insists that a business cannot survive by doing just enough

or more of the same. Pinkett's New Jersey company provides management, technology and consulting to other firms.

25824 ■ "AF Expands in New Green Building in Gothenburg" in Ecology,Environment & Conservation Business (September 24, 2011, pp. 2)
Pub: HighBeam Research

Description: AF signed a ten-year tenancy contract with Skanska for the premises of its new green building in Gothenburg, Sweden. AF offers qualified services and solutions for industrial processes, infrastructure projects and the development of products and IT systems.

25825 ■ "Altegrity Acquires John D. Cohen, Inc." in (November 19, 2009, pp. 14)
Pub: Investment Weekly News

Description: John D. Cohen, Inc., a contract provider of national security policy guidance and counsel to the federal government, was acquired by Altegrity, Inc., a global screening and security solutions provider; the company will become part of US Investigations Services, LLC and operate under the auspices of Altegrity's new business, Altegrity Security Consulting.

25826 ■ "Alto Ventures Retains Investor Relations Professional" in Canadian Corporate News (May 16, 2007)
Pub: Comtex News Network Inc.

Description: Alto Ventures Ltd., a gold exploration and development company with a portfolio of eleven properties in the Canadian Shield, announced that it has engaged the consulting services of Mark Prosser in order to focus on increasing investor awareness and exposure to the investment community through the dissemination of corporate information to a network of North American and European institutions, retail brokerage firms, and private investors.

25827 ■ "The Americans Are Coming" in The Economist (Vol. 390, January 3, 2009, No. 8612, pp. 44)
Pub: The Economist Newspaper Inc.

Description: Student recruitment consultancies, which help place international students at universities in other countries and offer services such as interpreting or translating guidelines, are discussed; American universities who have shunned these agencies in the past; the result has been that America underperforms in relation to its size with a mere 3.5 percent of students on its campuses that are from abroad.

25828 ■ "Applying to Colleges? Consultants Can Demystify the Process" in Palm Beach Post (September 3, 2011)
Pub: Palm Beach Post

Ed: Susan Salisbury. **Description:** More parents are turning to college consultants to help guide them through the process of applying to and choosing the right college or university. These specialized consultants assist with every detail for several years and students can reach them 24/7; costs can vary from several hundred dollars to $10,000 depending on services.

25829 ■ "Ask Inc" in Inc. (February 2008, pp. 52)
Pub: Gruner & Jahr USA Publishing

Ed: James Dyson. **Description:** Owner of a consulting firm seeks advice to help his sales staff become more successful.

25830 ■ "Back Talk With Terrie M. Williams" in Black Enterprise (Vol. 38, December 2007, No. 5, pp. 204)
Pub: Earl G. Graves Publishing Co. Inc.

Ed: Tennille M. Robinson. **Description:** Profile of Terrie M. Williams, president of a public relations agency as well as founder of a youth empowerment organization called Stay Strong Foundation. Williams reflects on her bouts with depression and how the disease impacts sufferers and talks about her book that will inspire others dealing with depression.

25831 ■ "BDC Launches New Online Business Advice Centre" in Internet Wire (July 13, 2010)
Pub: Comtex

Description: The Business Development Bank of Canada (BDC) offers entrepreneurs the chance to use their new online BDC Advice Centre in order to seek advice regarding the challenges of entrepreneurship. Free online business tools and information to help both startups and established firms are also provided.

25832 ■ "Best Foot Forward" in Canadian Business (Vol. 80, October 22, 2007, No. 21, pp. 115)
Pub: Rogers Media

Ed: Jeremy Shinewald. **Description:** Jeremy Shinewald's mbaMission admissions consulting business helps prospective MBA students with essay writing, mock interview preparation and school selection. The consulting fee for application to one school is $2,250. Details of the business schools' MBA programs and tuition fees are explored.

25833 ■ Big Vision, Small Business
Pub: Ivy Sea, Inc.

Ed: Jamie S. Walters. **Released:** October 10, 2002. **Price:** $17.95. **Description:** The power of the small enterprise is examined. The author shares her expertise as an entrepreneur and founder of a business consulting firm to help small business owners successfully run their companies. Interviews with more than seventy small business owners provide insight into visioning, planning, and establishing a small company, as well as strategies for good employee and customer relationships.

25834 ■ Birthing the Elephant: A Woman's Go-For-It Guide to Overcoming the Big Challenges of Launching a Business
Pub: Celestial Arts Publishing Co.
Contact: Patricia Kelly, Manager

Ed: Karin Abarbanel; Bruce Freeman. **Released:** 2008. **Price:** $15.95. **Description:** Consultants help women think like an entrepreneur in order to successfully launch any new business.

25835 ■ Bond's Franchise Guide 2009
Pub: Source Book Publications
Contact: Stephanie Woo, Editor

Ed: Robert E. Bond, Michelle Yang. **Released:** April 7, 2009. **Description:** Comprehensive directory offering prospective franchise owners a current and detailed profile of 1,000 franchises, as well as supplemental profiles of franchise attorneys and consultants; companies are divided into 45 categories for easy comparison.

25836 ■ Business Black Belt: Develop the Strength, Flexibility and Agility to Run Your Company
Pub: Career Press, Inc.

Ed: Burke Franklin. **Released:** November 1, 2010. **Price:** $15.99. **Description:** Manual offering insights that will enable anyone to become successful in small business. Seventy short chapters included topics such as attitude, management, marketing, selling, employees, money, MBAs, lawyers, consultants, and investors.

25837 ■ Business as Usual
Pub: HarperBusiness

Ed: Anita Roddick. **Released:** 2005. **Price:** $12.95. **Description:** Founder of The Body Shop shares her story and gives her opinion on everything from cynical cosmetic companies to destructive consultants.

25838 ■ "Cannabis Science Signs Exclusive and Non-Exclusive Agreement with Prescription Vending Machines" in Benzinga.com (October 29, 2011)
Pub: Benzinga.com

Ed: Benzinga Staff. **Description:** Cannabis Science Inc., a biotech company developing pharmaceutical cannabis products has partnered with Prescription Vending Machines Inc. and its principal Vincent Meddizadeh to provide industry specific consulting and advisory services to Cannabis Science.

25839 ■ "CarBiz Inc. Speaking At NABD" in Canadian Corporate News (May 14, 2007)
Pub: Comtex News Network Inc.

Description: CarBiz Inc., a leading provider of software, consulting, and training solutions to the United States' automotive industry, had two of its executive officers speak at the National Alliance of Buy Here - Pay Here Dealers (NABD), a conference that draws over 2,000 dealers, service providers, and experts from across the United States.

25840 ■ "Certification Experts Germanischer Lloyd Wind Energy Assist NaiKun's Offshore Wind Project" in Canadian Corporate News (May 14, 2007)
Pub: Comtex News Network Inc.

Description: Germanischer Lloyd Wind Energy (GL Wind) will examine, inspect, and provide quality management services for the engineering, design, and construction of the offshore wind project planned by NaiKun Wind Development Inc. in northwest British Columbia.

25841 ■ Chief Culture Officer: How to Create a Living, Breathing Corporation
Pub: Basic Books

Ed: Grant McCracken. **Price:** $26.95. **Description:** Business consultant argues that corporations need to focus on 'reading' what's happening in the culture around them. Otherwise, companies will suffer the consequences, as Levi Strauss did when it missed out on the rise of hip-hop (and the baggy pants that are part of that lifestyle).

25842 ■ "Clean Wind Energy Tower Transitions from R&D Stage Company" in Professional Services Close-Up (September 30, 2011)
Pub: Close-Up Media

Description: Clean Wind Energy designed and is developing large downdraft towers that use benevolent, non-toxic natural elements to generate electricity and clean water. The firm is closing its internally staffed engineering office in Warrenton, Virginia and transitioning a development team to oversee and coordinate industry consultants and advisors to construct their first dual renewable energy tower.

25843 ■ Consultants and Consulting Organizations Directory
Pub: Cengage Learning Inc.
Contact: Ronald Dunn, President

URL(s): www.gale.cengage.com. **Released:** Annual; New edition expected 37th; February, 2012. **Price:** $1392, Individuals. **Covers:** Over 26,000 firms, individuals, and organizations active in consulting. **Entries include:** Individual or organization name, address, phone, fax, e-mail, URL, specialties, founding date, branch offices, names and titles of key personnel, number of employees, financial data, publications, seminars and workshops. **Arrangement:** By broad subject categories. **Indexes:** Subject, geographical, organization name.

25844 ■ "Consulting Firm Goes Shopping" in Crain's Chicago Business (Vol. 31, April 28, 2008, No. 17, pp. 45)
Pub: Crain Communications, Inc.

Ed: Phuong Ly. **Description:** Clark & Wamberg LLC was created last year after the merger of Clark Inc. to a Dutch insurance conglomerate. Clark Inc. was a life insurance and benefits consultancy which had been on a downslide, returning just 5.6 percent a year to shareholders. In contrast Clark & Wamberg posted first-year revenue of $106.8 million, fueled by business from its executive compensation and health care clients.

25845 ■ "A Conversation With; Ron Gatner, Jones Lang LaSalle" in Crain's Detroit Business (Vol. 24, October 6, 2008, No. 40, pp. 9)
Pub: Crain Communications, Inc.

Description: Interview with Ron Gatner who is a corporate real estate adviser with the real estate company Jones Lang LaSalle as well as the company's executive vice president and part of the tenant advisory team; Gatner speaks about the impact that the Wall Street crisis is having on the commercial real estate market in Detroit.

25846 ■ "Cost Remains Top Factor In Considering Green Technology" in Canadian Sailings (June 30, 2008)
Pub: UBM Global Trade
Contact: Leonard J. Corallo, President
Ed: Julie Gedeon. **Description:** Improving its environmental performance remains a priority in the shipping industry; however, testing new technologies can prove difficult due to the harsh conditions that ships endure as well as installation which usually requires a dry dock.

25847 ■ "Counting on Engagement at Ernst and Young" in Workforce Management (Vol. 88, November 16, 2009, No. 12, pp. 25)
Pub: Crain Communications Inc.
Ed: Ed Frauenheim. **Description:** Employee engagement has been difficult to maintain through the recession but firms such as Ernst & Young have found that the effort to keep their employees loyal has paid off.

25848 ■ "Electronic Design and a Greener Environment" in Canadian Electronics (Vol. 23, June-July 2008, No. 4, pp. 6)
Pub: Action Communication Inc.
Ed: Nicholas Deeble. **Description:** Companies seeking to minimize their environmental impact are using Design methodologies of Cadence Design Systems Ltd. The company's Low Power Format and Low Power Design Flow help reduce carbon dioxide emissions.

25849 ■ "Engineering Services Supplier Launches 'Robotic Renaissance'" in Modern Machine Shop (Vol. 84, September 2011, No. 4, pp. 46)
Pub: Gardner Business Media, Inc.
Contact: Richard G. Kline, President
E-mail: rkline@gardnerweb.com
Description: Profile of Applied Manufacturing Technologies (AMT) new hiring initiative that supports continuing growth in the robotics industry. AMT is located in Orion, Michigan and supplies factory automation design, engineering and process consulting services.

25850 ■ The Entrepreneur's Guide to Managing Growth and Handling Crisis
Pub: Greenwood Publishing Group, Inc.
Ed: Theo J. Van Dijk. **Released:** December 2007. **Price:** $39.95. **Description:** The author explains how entrepreneurs can overcome crisis by changing the way they handle customers, by putting new processes and procedures in place, and managing employees in a professional manner. The book includes appendices with tips for hiring consultants, creating job descriptions, and setting up systems to chart cash flow as well as worksheets, tables and figures and a listing of resources.

25851 ■ "Finalist: Private Company, Less Than $100M" in Crain's Detroit Business (Vol. 25, June 22, 2009, No. 25)
Pub: Crain Communications Inc. - Detroit
Ed: Nancy Kaffer. **Description:** Profile of W3R Consulting and CFO Patrick Tomina. The company offers information technology consulting. Tomina discusses the company's 505 strategy: to grow its annual revenue to $50 million in five years.

25852 ■ "For Kenwood, Cavalry Could Be Close" in Business Courier (Vol. 26, October 2, 2009, No. 23, pp. 1)
Pub: American City Business Journals, Inc.
Ed: Dan Monk. **Description:** New York-based Black-Rock Inc. is believed to be participating in the settlement liens at Kenwood Towne Place, a mixed-use development site in Cincinnati, Ohio. BlackRock may play a key role as an advisor or investor representative to an unnamed investors.

25853 ■ Franchise: Freedom or Fantasy
Pub: iUniverse
Ed: Mitchell York. **Released:** June 22, 2009. **Price:** $13.95. **Description:** Successful franchisee and professional certified coach guides individuals through the many steps involved in deciding whether or not to buy a franchise and how to do it correctly.

25854 ■ "Gail Lissner; Vice-President, Appraisal Research Counselors" in Crain's Chicago Business (Vol. 31, May 5, 2008, No. 18, pp. 28)
Pub: Crain Communications, Inc.
Ed: Phuong Ly. **Description:** Profile of Gail Lissner who is the vice-president of the Appraisal Research Counselors, a company that puts out the quarterly 'Residential Benchmark Report,' in which Ms. Lissner co-authors and is considered a must-read in the industry. Ms. Lissner has risen to become one of the most sought-after experts on the Chicago market considering real estate.

25855 ■ Get Clients Now!, 2nd Edition: A 28-Day Marketing Program for Professionals, Consultants, and Coaches
Pub: American Management Association
Contact: Charles R. Craig, Chairman
Ed: C.J. Hayden. **Released:** 2006. **Price:** $19.95.

25856 ■ "Grave Concerns" in Canadian Business (Vol. 81, July 21 2008, No. 11, pp. 25)
Pub: Rogers Media Ltd.
Ed: Andrew Nikiforuk. **Description:** Air pollution control regulations to reduce greenhouse gasses have been implemented by the Canadian government. The federal government is planning to construct a carbon funeral industry that will store the global warming gases, however the expenditure for the project will be shifted to the taxpayers. Details of the Bruce Peachy's initiative on how to reduce GHGs are presented.

25857 ■ "The Green Conversation" in Harvard Business Review (Vol. 86, September 2008, No. 9, pp. 58)
Pub: Harvard Business School Press
Description: Six guidelines are presented for addressing and benefiting from environmentally conscious corporate decision making and practices. Topics covered include marketing, supply chain, and leadership.

25858 ■ "Greg Lueck: Glass Blowing" in Inc. (Volume 32, December 2010, No. 10, pp. 36)
Pub: Inc. Magazine
Ed: April Joyner. **Description:** Profile of Greg Lueck, partner and COO of Centerstance, a tech consulting firm in Portland, Oregon. Lueck opened Firehouse Glass, a studio that provides workspace and equipment for glass blowers. He says glass blowing serves as a welcome counterbalance to the cerebral work he does at the office.

25859 ■ "Hire Power" in Entrepreneur (Vol. 35, November 2007, No. 11, pp. 105)
Pub: Entrepreneur Media Inc.
Ed: Mark Henricks. **Description:** Companies with big resources may hire human resource (HR) consultants to help with writing manuals, drafting policies and designing benefits for employees. HR consultants may also be hired to assist with specific functions or other strategic aspects.

25860 ■ "Housing Slide Picks Up Speed" in Crain's Chicago Business (Vol. 31, April 21, 2008, No. 16, pp. 2)
Pub: Crain Communications, Inc.
Ed: Eddie Baeb. **Description:** According to Tracy Cross & Associates Inc., a real estate consultancy, sales of new homes in the Chicago area dropped 61 percent from the year-earlier period which is more bad news for homebuilders, contractors and real estate agents who are eager for an indication that market conditions are improving.

25861 ■ How to Make Big Money
Pub: Hyperion Books
Ed: Jeffrey J. Fox. **Released:** May 19, 2004. **Price:** $16.95. **Description:** Entrepreneur and consultant offers advice to help others create successful startups and prosper. Fox directs new business owners with a counterintuitive style and describes essential methods that beat the competition. Tips include: setting priorities, getting a personal driver, creating a contingency plan for employees, pricing to value, saving money, and getting an office outside of the home.

25862 ■ "How Much is Too Much?" in Canadian Business (Vol. 79, July 17, 2006, No. 14-15, pp. 55)
Pub: Rogers Media
Ed: John Gray. **Description:** Elucidates the emphasis on the need for companies to analyze the executive pay packages designed by compensation consultants.

25863 ■ "Insider" in Canadian Business (Vol. 81, Summer 2008, No. 9, pp. 170)
Pub: Rogers Media Ltd.
Ed: Thomas Watson; Jeff Sanford. **Description:** Oil peak theory posits that the world has consumed half of the non-renewable resources is indicated by the surging oil prices. However, critics argued that the high oil prices are effects of market speculation and not the depletion of the supply. Ten reasons on why to buy and not buy peak oil are presented.

25864 ■ "Interbrand's Creative Recruiting" in Business Courier (Vol. 27, November 12, 2010, No. 28, pp. 1)
Pub: Business Courier
Ed: Dan Monk. **Description:** Global brand consulting firm Interbrand uses a creative recruitment agency to attract new employees into the company. Interbrand uses themed parties to attract prospective employees. The 'Alice In Wonderland' tea party for example, allowed the company to hire five new employees.

25865 ■ "Into the Groove: Fine-Tune Your Biz By Getting Into the Good Habit Groove" in Small Business Opportunities (Spring 2008)
Pub: Harris Publications Inc.
Description: Profile of Ty Freyvogel and his consulting firm Freyvogel Communications. Freyvogel serves the telecommunications need of Fortune 500 and mid-sized businesses.

25866 ■ Kiss Theory Good Bye: Five Proven Ways to Get Extraordinary Results in Any Company
Pub: Gold Pen Publishing
Ed: Bob Prosen. **Released:** August 2006. **Price:** $21.95. **Description:** Author provides wisdom from his career as a high-level executive at AT&T Global Information Solutions, Sabre, and Hitachi, as well as his consulting firm. The book focuses on business execution rather than processes or theory of business management and provides step-by-step instructions allowing organizations to maximize profitability and results.

25867 ■ "Knowing Is Growing: Five Strategies To Develop You and Your Business" in Black Enterprise (Vol. 38, November 2007, No. 4, pp. 106)
Pub: Earl G. Graves Publishing Co. Inc.
Ed: Erinn R. Johnson. **Description:** Five strategies for growing a small business are listed by Andrew Morrison, founder of the Small Business Camp. The camp provides training, coaching, and marketing services to entrepreneurs.

25868 ■ "Lifebank Grants Stock Options" in Canadian Corporate News (May 16, 2007)
Pub: Comtex News Network Inc.
Description: Lifebank, a biomedical service company that provides processing cryogenic storage of umbilical cord blood stem cells, announced that, under its stock option plan, it has granted incentive stock options to directors, officers, and consultants of the company.

25869 ■ "Making Your Mark: Five Steps To Brand Your Success" in Black Enterprise (Vol. 38, November 2007, No. 4, pp. 106)
Pub: Earl G. Graves Publishing Co. Inc.
Ed: Erinn R. Johnson. **Description:** Founder of Velvet Suite Marketing Consulting Group, Melissa D. Johnson, assists clients in building brands. Johnson offers tips to develop and build a sold brand in her new book, 'Brand Me! Make Your Mark: Turn Passion Into Profit'.

25870 ■ *The Management Myth: Why the "Experts" Keep Getting It Wrong*
Pub: W.W. Norton & Company
Ed: Matthew Stewart. **Released:** August 10, 2009. **Price:** $27.95. **Description:** An insider's perspective on the management consulting industry, which reveals the high fees and incompetent consultants.

25871 ■ *"Managing the Facebookers; Business"* in *The Economist (Vol. 390, January 3, 2009, No. 8612, pp. 10)*
Pub: Economist Newspaper Ltd.
Description: According to a report from PricewaterhouseCoopers, a business consultancy, workers from Generation Y, also known as the Net Generation, are more difficult to recruit and integrate into companies that practice traditional business acumen. 61 percent of chief executive managers say that they have trouble with younger employees who tend to be more narcissistic and more interested in personal fulfillment with a need for frequent feedback and an over-precise set of objectives on the path to promotion which can be hard for managers who are used to a different relationship with their subordinates. Older bosses should prepare to make some concessions to their younger talent since some of the issues that make them happy include cheaper online ways to communicate and additional coaching, both of which are good for business.

25872 ■ *Managing India's Small Industrial Economy: The Catalytic Role of Industrial Counselors and Policy Makers*
Pub: SAGE Publications USA
Contact: Blaise R. Simqu, President
Ed: V. Padmanand, V.G. Patel. **Released:** June 2004. **Price:** $35.95. **Description:** Case studies and methodology are used to discuss the areas where industrial consultants are influencing sustainability and growth of small businesses in India's industrial economy.

25873 ■ *Marketing for Dummies*
Pub: John Wiley & Sons Inc.
Contact: Stephen M. Smith, President
URL(s): www.wiley.com/WileyCDA/WileyTitle/productCd-047050210X.html. **Ed:** Alexander Hiam. **Released:** latest edition 3rd; Published October, 2009. **Price:** $21.99, Individuals paperback. **Publication includes:** Marketing web sites, marketing consultants, trade associations, market researchers, and other experts. **Entries include:** Individual or company name, address, phone number, web site address (where applicable). Principal content of publication is articles on marketing strategies.

25874 ■ *"Meet Rebecca. She's Here to Fire You"* in *Inc. (November 2007, pp. 25-26)*
Pub: Gruner & Jahr USA Publishing
Ed: Max Chafkin. **Description:** Amid liability concerns as well as CEO guilt, more and more firms are using consulting companies to fire workers. These outsourced firms help small companies structure severance and document information in order to limit legal liability when firing an employee.

25875 ■ *The Mirror Test: How to Breathe New Life Into Your Business*
Pub: Grand Central Publishing
Ed: Jeffrey W. Hayzlett. **Released:** May 10, 2010. **Price:** $24.99. **Description:** Consultant and author, Jeffrey Hayzlett, explains why a business is not doing well and asks the questions that most business managers are afraid to ask.

25876 ■ *"More Sales Leads, Please: Or, What Happened When Frontline Selling Started Practicing What It Preaches"* in *Inc. (November 2007)*
Pub: Gruner & Jahr USA Publishing
Description: Frontline Selling located in Oakland, New Jersey helps train sales teams to generate and convert sales leads. The consulting firm doubled their marketing budget to increase their own sales.

25877 ■ *My So-Called Freelance Life: How to Survive and Thrive as a Creative Professional for Hire*
Pub: Seal Press
Contact: Charlie Winton, Manager
Ed: Michelle Goodman. **Released:** October 1, 2008. **Price:** $15.95. **Description:** Guidebook for women wishing to start a freelancing business; tips, advice, how-to's and all the information needed to survive working from home are included.

25878 ■ *"Nampa Police Department: Electronic Systems Just One Tool in Business Security Toolbox"* in *Idaho Business Review (October 29, 2010)*
Pub: Dolan Media Newswires
Ed: Brad Carlson. **Description:** Police departments and private security firms can help small businesses with hard security and business consultants can assist with internal audit security and fraud prevention.

25879 ■ *"New Database Brings Doctors Out of the Dark"* in *Business Courier (Vol. 26, October 23, 2009, No. 26, pp. 1)*
Pub: American City Business Journals, Inc.
Ed: James Ritchie. **Description:** A database created by managed care consulting firm Praesentia allows doctors in Cincinnati to compare average reimbursements from health insurance companies to doctors in different areas. Specialist doctors in the city are paid an average of $172.25 for every office consultation.

25880 ■ *Niche and Grow Rich*
Pub: Entrepreneur Press
Ed: Jennifer Basye Sander; Peter Sander. **Released:** 2003. **Description:** Consultants share insight to entrepreneurs wishing to find a profitable niche market. Authors write that good niche businesses are easy to start and easy to defend from competitors. They also report that finding a successful niche can attract and maintain good customers who are willing to pay more for unique goods and services.

25881 ■ *"Nothing But Net: Fran Harris Offers Advice On Winning the Game of Business"* in *Black Enterprise (Vol. 38, March 2008, No. 8, pp. 50)*
Pub: Earl G. Graves Publishing Co. Inc.
Ed: Chana Garcia. **Description:** Fran Harris, certified life coach, business consultant, and CEO of her business, a multimedia development company, reveals five tips to ensure entrepreneurial success.

25882 ■ *"On Hire Ground"* in *Entrepreneur (Vol. 36, February 2008, No. 2, pp. 19)*
Pub: Entrepreneur Media Inc.
Description: ADP Small Business Services, an economic consulting firm, showed that small businesses had increased employment rates in 2007 and added 77,000 jobs in November 2007. Entrepreneurial employment and data showing the contribution of small businesses to job growth are presented.

25883 ■ *"Outplacement Services"* in *Black Enterprise (Vol. 38, March 2008, No. 8, pp. 60)*
Pub: Earl G. Graves Publishing Co. Inc.
Ed: Marcia Reed Woodard. **Description:** Tips to use while in career-transition are offered. Many times outplacement services are provided as part of a severance package to employees.

25884 ■ *PPC's Guide to Small Business Consulting Engagements*
Pub: Practitioners Publishing Company
Released: March 2004. **Price:** $226.00. **Description:** Technical guide for conducting consulting engagements for small business.

25885 ■ *PPC's Guide to Small Business Consulting Engagements, Vol. 2*
Pub: Practitioners Publishing Company
Released: March 2004. **Description:** Second volume of the technical guide for conducting consulting engagements for small business.

25886 ■ *PPC's Guide to Small Business Consulting Engagements, Vol. 3*
Pub: Practitioners Publishing Company
Released: March 2004. **Description:** Third volume of the technical guide for conducting consulting engagements for small business.

25887 ■ *Professional Services Marketing: How the Best Firms Build Premier Brands*
Pub: John Wiley & Sons, Inc.
Ed: Mike Schultz, John Doerr. **Released:** July 27, 2009. **Price:** $27.95. **Description:** Research based on best practices and processes for the professional services industry is presented. The book covers five key areas: creating a custom marketing and growth strategy, establishing a brand, implementing a marketing communications program, developing a lead strategy, and winning new clients.

25888 ■ *"Provinces Tackle E-Waste Problem"* in *Canadian Electronics (Vol. 23, June-July 2008, No. 4, pp. 1)*
Pub: Action Communication Inc.
Ed: Ken Manchen. **Description:** Canadian provinces are implementing measures concerning the safe and environmentally friendly disposal of electronic waste. Alberta, British Columbia, Nova Scotia, and Saskatchewan impose an e-waste recycling fee on electronic equipment purchases.

25889 ■ *"Putting Vets to Work"* in *Business Week (September 22, 2008, No. 4100, pp. 18)*
Pub: McGraw-Hill Companies, Inc.
Ed: Deborah Stead. **Description:** Advice is provided by former Marine Sal Cepeda, a consultant who advises employers on hiring veterans, for former military personnel coming back into the workforce.

25890 ■ *Raising Capital*
Pub: Greenwood Publishing Group, Inc.
Ed: David Nour. **Released:** March 1, 2009. **Price:** $39.95. **Description:** An overview to help entrepreneurs find capital for starting and maintaining a small business is presented. The author shows how to develop long-term relationships with financial partners and ways to attract financing to fund the startup and growth phases of any business. Entrepreneurs tell how they raised money from friends, family, angel investors, banks and venture capitalists and private equity firms.

25891 ■ *"Raptor Opens Consultancy"* in *Austin Business Journal (Vol. 31, July 8, 2011, No. 18, pp. 1)*
Pub: American City Business Journals Inc.
Ed: Christopher Calnan. **Description:** Boston hedge fund operator Raptor Group launched Raptor Accelerator, a consulting business providing sales and advisory services to early-stage companies in Central Texas. Aside from getting involved with the startups in which the Raptor Group invests, Raptor Accelerator will target firms operating in the sports, media, entertainment, and content technology sectors.

25892 ■ *"Reduce the Risk of Failed Financial Judgments"* in *Harvard Business Review (Vol. 86, July-August 2008, No. 8, pp. 24)*
Pub: Harvard Business School Press
Ed: Robert G. Eccles; Edward J. Fiedl. **Description:** Utilization of business consultants, evaluators, appraisers, and actuaries to decrease financial management risks is discussed.

25893 ■ *"Restoring Grandeur"* in *Business Courier (Vol. 26, December 4, 2009, No. 32, pp. 1)*
Pub: American City Business Journals, Inc.
Ed: Dan Monk. **Description:** Eagle Realty Group intends to spend more than $10 to restore the historic 12-story Phelps apartment building in Lytle Park in Cincinnati. Its president, Mario San Marco, expressed the need to invest in the building in order to maintain operations. The building could be restored into a hotel catering to executives and consultants.

25894 ■ *"Retail in Austin Strong, Will Continue to Be"* in *Austin Business JournalInc. (Vol. 29, January 22, 2010, No. 46, pp. 1)*
Pub: American City Business Journals
Ed: Jacob Dirr. **Description:** Retail sector in Austin, Texas has outpaced the national average in value, mid-tier, high-end and drugs retail sectors, according to a report by Pitney Bowes. The national consulting firm's report has projected growth in every sector until the end of fiscal 2012. Data regarding other sectors is also included.

25895 ■ *"The Right Remedy: Entrepreneur's Success Is a Matter of Life and Death"* in

Black Enterprise (Vol. 38, February 2008, No. 7, pp. 46)
Pub: Earl G. Graves Publishing Co. Inc.
Ed: Tamara E. Holmes. **Description:** Profile of Leah Brown, whose company conducts clinical trials to determine if specific drugs will relieve particular symptoms. Her company will also visit physician's offices to make certain doctors are following proper protocol for a clinical trial or will collect data from patients.

25896 ■ *"The Rise of Pompei" in Retail Merchandiser (Vol. 51, September-October 2011, No. 5, pp. 13)*
Pub: Phoenix Media Corporation
Description: Soho creative consulting group follows its C3 philosophy to create an invigorated brand experience that transforms customers from consumers to empowered buyers. Pompei AD is a leading creative consultancy that specializes in design and branding for retail, museum, hospitality, and other sectors.

25897 ■ *"The Secret Life of a Serial CEO" in Inc. (January 2008, pp. 80-88)*
Pub: Gruner & Jahr USA Publishing
Ed: David H. Freedman. **Description:** Profile of Bob Cramer, who has lead six successful companies and is now searching for a new business venture and thinks he's found it. Cramer shares his journey from wooing venture capital, handling founders and his hunt for his newest venture.

25898 ■ *"Security Alert: Data Server" in Entrepreneur (Vol. 36, February 2008, No. 2, pp. 28)*
Pub: Entrepreneur Media Inc.
Ed: Amanda C. Kooser. **Description:** Michael Kogon is the founder of Definition 6, a technology consulting and interactive marking firm. He believes in the philosophy that the best way to keep sensitive data safe is not to store it. Details on the security policies of his firm are discussed.

25899 ■ *"Selling Your Company" in Inc. (March 2008, pp. 78)*
Pub: Gruner & Jahr USA Publishing
Ed: Myra Goodman. **Description:** Owner of a safety consulting company seeks advice for selling the firm.

25900 ■ *"Sick of Trends? You Should Be" in Brandweek (Vol. 49, April 21, 2008, No. 16, pp. 22)*
Pub: VNU Business Media, Inc.
Ed: Eric Zeitoun. **Description:** Eric Zeitoun, the president of Dragon Rouge, a global brand consultancy, discusses the importance of macrotrends as opposed to microtrends which he feels are often irrelevant, create confusion and cause marketers to lose site of the larger picture of their industry. Macrotrends, on the other hand, create a fundamental, societal shift that influences consumer attitudes over a long period of time.

25901 ■ *Silos, Politics and Turf Wars: A Leadership Fable about Destroying the Barriers That Turn Colleagues Into Competitors*
Pub: Jossey Bass
Ed: Patrick M. Lencioni. **Released:** February 17, 2006. **Price:** $24.95. **Description:** The author addresses management problems through a fable that revolves around a self-employed consultant who has to dismantle silos at an upscale hotel, a technology company and a hospital. The story explains how organizations can use a collective operational vision in order to overcome pride, greed, and tribalism and work as a team with the same goal in mind.

25902 ■ *"Small, But Mighty" in Employee Benefit News (Vol. 25, November 1, 2011, No. 14, pp. 32)*
Pub: SourceMedia Inc.
Ed: Andrea Davis. **Description:** Three consulting firms are facing the challenge of helping clients understand the new health care reform in a tight economy.

25903 ■ *The Sticking Point Solution: 9 Ways to Move Your Business from Stagnation to Stunning Growth in Tough Economic Times*
Pub: Vanguard Press
Contact: Bill Smith, Director
E-mail: bill.smith@perseusbooks.com
Ed: Jay Abraham. **Released:** May 10, 2010. **Price:** $25.95. **Description:** Renowned business consultant, Jay Abraham. reveals the nine ways even successful businesses get stuck, hit plateaus, and fail to achieve their dreams and he explains how to get unstuck and create exponential growth.

25904 ■ *"Survey Finds State Execs Cool On Climate Change" in The Business Journal-Milwaukee (Vol. 25, August 8, 2008, No. 46, pp. A1)*
Pub: American City Business Journals, Inc.
Ed: David Doege. **Description:** According to a survey of business executives in Wisconsin, business leaders do not see climate change as a pressing concern, but businesses are moving toward more energy-efficient operations. The survey also revealed that executives believe that financial incentives can promote energy conservation. Other survey results are provided.

25905 ■ *"Tauri Group Partner Joining Homeland Security and Defense" in Wireless News (December 15, 2009)*
Pub: Close-Up Media
Description: Managing partner Cosmo DiMaggio III of the Tauri Group, a provider of analytic consulting for homeland security, defense and space clients, has been elected to the Board of Directors at Homeland Security and Defense Business Council.

25906 ■ *"Tech Deal Couples Homegrown Firms" in The Business Journal-Serving Greater Tampa Bay (Vol. 28, July 4, 2008, No. 28, pp. 1)*
Pub: American City Business Journals, Inc.
Ed: Michael Hinman. **Description:** Tampa Bay, Florida-based Administrative Partners Inc. was acquired by Tribridge Inc. resulting in the strengthening of the delivery of Microsoft products to clients. Other details of the merger of the management consulting services companies are presented.

25907 ■ *"Think Disruptive! How to Manage In a New Era of Innovation" in Strategy & Leadership (Vol. 38, July-August 2010, No. 4, pp. 5-10)*
Pub: Emerald Inc.
Ed: Brian Leavy, John Sterling. **Description:** The views expressed by Scott Anthony, president of an innovation consultancy Innosight, on the need for corporate leaders to apply disruptive innovation in a recessionary environment are presented. His suggestion that disruptive innovation is the only way to survive during the economic crisis is discussed.

25908 ■ *"Thomas Industrial Network Unveils Custom SPEC" in Entertainment Close-Up (March 3, 2011)*
Pub: Close-Up Media
Description: Thomas Industrial Network assists custom manufacturers and industrial service providers a complete online program called Custom SPEC which includes Website development and Internet exposure.

25909 ■ *The Toilet Paper Entrepreneur: The Tell-It-Like-It-Is Guide to Cleaning Up In Business, Even If You Are At the End of Your Roll*
Pub: Obsidian Launch LLC
Ed: Mike Michalowicz. **Price:** $24.95. **Description:** The founder of three multimillion-dollar companies, including Obsidian Launch, a company that partners with first-time entrepreneurs to grow their concepts into industry leaders.

25910 ■ *"Tool Time" in Entrepreneur (Vol. 36, March 2008, No. 3, pp. 90)*
Pub: Entrepreneur Media Inc.
Ed: Nichole A. Torres. **Description:** DaVinci Institute holds an annual event in Colorado to display new products and inventions. Innovative Design Engineering Animation is a consulting company that helps inventors develop product through various stages. NineSigma Inc. has an online marketplace where inventors can post ideas for clients needing new products.

25911 ■ *"Tough Sell" in Black Enterprise (Vol. 37, October 2006, No. 3, pp. 92)*
Pub: Earl G. Graves Publishing Co. Inc.
Ed: Sonia Alleyne. **Description:** Career coaches can evaluate your talents and skills. In an era where more companies are downsizing a coach can help you decide if you are suited for your industry or should try switching careers.

25912 ■ *"Trend: Tutors to Help You Pump Up the Staff" in Business Week (September 22, 2008, No. 4100, pp. 45)*
Pub: McGraw-Hill Companies, Inc.
Ed: Reena Janaj. **Description:** High-level managers are turning to innovation coaches in an attempt to obtain advice on how to better sell new concepts within their companies. Individuals as well as consulting firms are now offering this service.

25913 ■ *"Tweaking On-Board Activities, Equipment Saves Fuel, Reduces CO2" in Canadian Sailings (June 30, 2008)*
Pub: UBM Global Trade
Contact: Leonard J. Corallo, President
Description: Optimizing ship activities and equipment uses less fuel and therefore reduces greenhouse gas emissions. Ways in which companies are implementing research and development techniques in order to monitor ship performance and analyze data in an attempt to become more efficient are examined.

25914 ■ *"Up Against the Ropes: A Professional Coach May Help" in Black Enterprise (Vol. 37, December 2006, No. 5, pp. 72)*
Pub: Earl G. Graves Publishing Co. Inc.
Description: Executive coaching is now a $1 billion industry. The coaching process itself and traits to look for in a coach are discussed.

25915 ■ *"VeriFone Announces Global Security Solutions Business" in Marketing Weekly News (October 3, 2009)*
Pub: Investment Weekly News
Description: Focused on delivering innovative security solutions, VeriFone Holdings, Inc. announced the formation of its Global Security Solutions Business Unit, including VeriShield Protect, an end-to-end encryption to protect cardholder data throughout the merchant and processor systems. The business will focus on consulting, sales and implementation of these new products in order to help retailers and processors protect customer data.

25916 ■ *"Water Works Spinoff Could Make Big Splash" in Business Courier (Vol. 24, October 19, 2008, No. 27, pp. 1)*
Pub: American City Business Journals, Inc.
Ed: Dan Monk. **Description:** Cincinnati, Ohio city manager Milton Dohoney proposed to spin off the city-owned Greater Cincinnati Water Works into a regionally focused water district that could allow the city to receive millions of dollars in annual dividends. A feasibility study is to be conducted by a team of outside consultants and city staffers and is expected to be finished by summer of 2008.

25917 ■ *A Whack on the Side of the Head*
Pub: Business Plus
Ed: Roger von Oech. **Released:** May 2008. **Price:** $16.99. **Description:** The author, a consultant, shares insight into increasing entrepreneurial creativity.

25918 ■ *"The Whole Package" in Entrepreneur (Vol. 36, February 2008, No. 2, pp. 24)*
Pub: Entrepreneur Media Inc.
Description: Holy Bohn, owner of The Honest Statute, developed an environmentally-friendly packaging for her pet food products. The company hired a packaging consultant and spent $175,000.

Big corporations also spend money and plunge into the latest trends in packaging ranging from lighter and flexible to temperature-sensitive labels.

25919 ■ *"Winner: Private Company, Less Than $100M' in Crain's Detroit Business (Vol. 25, June 22, 2009, No. 25)*
Pub: Crain Communications Inc. - Detroit
Ed: Tom Henderson. **Description:** Profile of ForeSee Results, an Ann Arbor, Michigan-based firm that uses the University of Michigan American Consumer Satisfaction Index to help businesses measure satisfaction with their Websites.

25920 ■ *"Winning Gold' in The Business Journal-Milwaukee (Vol. 25, August 8, 2008, No. 46, pp. A1)*
Pub: American City Business Journals, Inc.
Ed: Rich Rovito. **Description:** Johnson Controls Inc. of Milwaukee, Wisconsin is taking part in the 2008 Beijing Olympics with the installation of its sustainable control equipment and technology that monitor over 58,000 points in 18 Olympic venues. Details of Johnson Controls' green products and sustainable operations in China are discussed.

25921 ■ *Working for Yourself: Law and Taxes for Independent Contractors, Freelancers and Consultants*
Pub: NOLO Publications
Ed: Stephen Fishman. **Released:** March 2008. **Price:** $39.99 paperback. **Description:** In-depth information is shared for contractors, freelancers and consultants involving business law and small business taxes.

25922 ■ *"Your Booming Business: How You Can Align Sales and Marketing for Dynamic Growth' in Small Business Opportunities (Spring 2008)*
Pub: Harris Publications Inc.
Ed: Voss W. Graham. **Description:** Voss Graham, founder and CEO of Inneractive Consulting Group Inc., works with companies to develop and hire successful sales teams. A checklist from the American Bankers Association to help write a business plan is included.

TRADE PERIODICALS

25923 ■ *California Special Education Alert*
Pub: LRP Publications
Contact: Steve Bevilacquar, Director, Editorial
Released: Monthly. **Price:** $260 plus $27 s/h. **Description:** Assists California special education administrators comply with changing special education laws, regulations, and policies on the state and federal level to avoid litigation. Recurring features include letters to the editor, interviews, and reports of meetings.

25924 ■ *SoloDining.com*
Pub: SoloDining.com
Ed: Marya Charles Alexander, Editor. **Released:** Quarterly. **Price:** $25; $25, Canada plus $5 postage. **Description:** Provides strategies and tips on how to increase one's comfort and options when dining alone. Presents information on notable solo-friendly restaurants in the US and other countries. Describes solo-dining amenities to look for or suggest to restaurants. Now includes tips on solo travel.

VIDEOCASSETTES/ AUDIOCASSETTES

25925 ■ *How to Build a Profitable Consulting Practice 1 & 2*
Chesney Communications
2302 Martin St., Ste. 125
Irvine, CA 92612
Ph: (949)263-5500
Free: 800-223-8878
Fax: (949)263-5506
Co. E-mail: videocc@aol.com
URL: http://www.videocc.com
Released: 1987. **Price:** $59.95. **Description:** An entire Howard Shenson seminar about setting up a consulting practice, condensed into two hours. **Availability:** VHS; 3/4 U.

CONSULTANTS

25926 ■ 2010 Fund 5
24351 Spartan St.
Mission Viejo, CA 92691-3920
Ph: (949)583-1992
Fax: (949)583-0474
Contact: Wally Eater, Principal
Scope: Funds in formation that will invest in technologies licensed from 30 universities. **Founded:** 1982.

25927 ■ ADG Group
4261 Northside Dr., Ste. 200
Atlanta, GA 30327
Ph: (404)264-9301
Fax: (404)261-3439
Contact: Cameron Adair, Chairman of the Board
E-mail: camadair@aol.com
Scope: Corporate finance advisory firm specializing in arranging venture capital financing for emerging companies. Assists with mergers, acquisitions, and divestitures. Offers balance sheet restructuring services for bankrupt and financially troubled companies. Also offers independent due diligence investigations. **Founded:** 1986.

25928 ■ Advanced Benefits & Human Resources
9350-F Snowden River Pkwy., Ste. 222
Columbia, MD 21045
Ph: (410)290-9037
Fax: (410)740-2568
Co. E-mail: hrb@abhr.com
Contact: Linda Polacek, President
Scope: Provides human resource consulting to high technology businesses. Offers services in the areas of human resources, benefits, and training. Creates, maintains, or updates current human resource functions. **Founded:** 1996.

25929 ■ The Advantage Group Inc.
20 Toronto St. 6th Fl.
Toronto, ON, Canada M5C 2B8
Ph: (416)863-0685
Free: 800-671-1048
Fax: (416)863-0787
Co. E-mail: answers@advantagegroup.com
URL: http://www.advantagegroup.com
Contact: Ron Pirie, President
E-mail: ronpirie@advantagegroup.com
Scope: Specializes in two key areas: performance benchmarking and pricing strategy. Each stream has developed a wide variety of customizable proprietary research tools to meet the needs of the clients. **Founded:** 1988. **Publications:** "7 Steps to building better customer relationships"; "How to Add Value to Customer Relationships"; "Top 10 Key Benefits of Building Business Relationships"; "Tips for Creating Better Relationships"; "Building Trust in Personal and Business Relationships"; "The Advantage Report Canadian Grocer"; "Customer Relationships"; "Customer Relationship Management: What it is and What it's not"; "The Advantage Report - Measuring the supplier-retailer relationship".

25930 ■ Advisory Management Services Inc.
9600 E 129th St., Ste. B
Kansas City, MO 64149-1025
Ph: (816)765-9611
Fax: (816)765-7447
Contact: Hal Wood, President
Scope: A management consulting and training firm specializing in employee relations, management and staff training, organizational development, strategic planning, and continuous quality improvement. **Founded:** 1979.

25931 ■ Aegis Communications Inc.
2 Greenwich Plz., Ste. 100
Greenwich, CT 06830-6353
Ph: (203)622-4944
Contact: David Bushko, President
Scope: Marketing firm specializing in using visualization tools to help clients define communication needs and develop communication strategies and plans. **Founded:** 1993.

25932 ■ The Alliance Management Group Inc.
38 Old Chester Rd., Ste. 300
Gladstone, NJ 07934
Ph: (908)234-2344
Fax: (908)234-0638
Co. E-mail: kathy@strategicalliance.com
URL: http://www.strategicalliance.com
Contact: Gene Slowinski, Director
E-mail: gene@strategicalliance.com
Scope: The firm enables leading companies to maximize the value of their strategic alliances, mergers and acquisitions. Offers services in partner evaluation process, a planning and negotiating program, mergers and acquisition integration, management issues, the turnaround or termination of poorly performing alliances, and a competitive strategic analysis program. **Publications:** "Effective Practices For Sourcing Innovation," Jan-Feb, 2009; "Intellectual Property Issues in Collaborative Research Agreements," Nov-Dec, 2008; "Building University Relationships in China," Sep-Oct, 2008; "Reinventing Corporate Growth: Implementing the Transformational Growth Model"; "The Strongest Link"; "Allocating Patent Rights in Collaborative Research Agreements"; "Protecting Know-how and Trade Secrets in Collaborative Research Agreements," Aug, 2006; "Sourcing External Technology for Innovation," Jun, 2006. **Special Services:** "Want, Find, Get, Manage" Model®; "Want, Find, Get, Manage" Framework®; WFGM Framework®; The Alliance Implementation Program®; WFGM Paradigm®; WFGM Model®; "Want, Find, Get, Manage" Paradigm®, Transformational Growth®; T-growth®.

25933 ■ Alliance Management International Ltd.
PO Box 470691
Cleveland, OH 44147-0691
Ph: (440)838-1922
Co. E-mail: bob@bgruss.com
Contact: Ashok Vasudevan, Director
Scope: A consulting company that helps to form national and international strategic alliances. Handles alliances between companies forming joint ventures. Staff specialized in small company-large company alliance, alliance assessment and analysis, and alliance strategic planning. **Seminars:** Joint Business Planning; Developing a Shared Vision; Current and New/Prospective Partner Assessment; Customer Service; Sales Training; Leader and Management Skills.

25934 ■ Alternative Services Inc.
32625 7 Mile Rd., Ste. 10
Livonia, MI 48152
Ph: (248)471-4880
Fax: (248)471-5230
URL: http://www.asi-mi.org
Contact: Arthur Mack, President
Scope: Provider of social services management support to group homes for the mentally disabled. Also offers marketing, training, and financial services to businesses and nonprofit organizations. **Founded:** 1978.

25935 ■ Ambler Growth Strategy Consultants Inc.
3432 Reading Ave.
Hammonton, NJ 08037-8008
Ph: (609)567-9669
Free: 888-253-6662
Fax: (609)567-3810
Co. E-mail: thegrowthstrategist@ambler.com
URL: http://www.ambler.com
Contact: Aldonna R. Ambler, Chief Executive Officer
E-mail: aldonna@ambler.com
Scope: Growth strategies, strategic assessments, CEO coaching. **Founded:** 1979. **Publications:** "A joint venture can deliver more than growth"; "Achieving competitive advantage"; "Achieving resilience for your business during difficult times"; "Achieving resilient growth during challenging times"; "Acquisitions: A growth strategy to consider"; "Attracting and retaining longterm corporate sponsors"; "Celebrate Selling: The Consultative Relationship Way"; "A Joint Venture Can Deliver More Than Growth"; "Achieving Competitive Advantage"; "Achieving Resilience for Your Business During Difficult Times"; "Balancing

Revenue Growth with Growth of a Business"; "Capture Your Competitive Advantage"; "Ease Succession Planning"; "Games Employees Play"; "How to Spark Innovation in an Existing Company"; "Managers demands must change with growth"; "Motivating Generation employees"; "Knowing when to hire ratios provide answers"; "Better customer service can bring black ink". **Seminars:** Strategic Leadership; Managing Innovation; Breaking Through Classic Barriers to Growth; Energize Your Enterprise; Capture Your Competitive Advantage; Four Entrepreneurial Styles: Perservance and Resilience; Real-Time Strategic Planning/RO1. **Special Services:** The Growth Strategist™.

25936 ■ American English Academy (AEA)—American English College

111 N Atlantic Blvd., Ste. 112
Monterey Park, CA 91754
Ph: (626)457-2800
Fax: (626)457-2808
Co. E-mail: admission@aea-usa.com
URL: http://www.aea-usa.com
Contact: Charles Policky, President
Scope: Specializes in providing on-site English language and communication development for corporations and individuals. Also develops and delivers training in speaking, writing, pronunciation, grammar, and idioms with an emphasis on business communication. Offers individual, small group, intensive, and long-distance learning. Programs tailor-made for each client. **Founded:** 1983. **Telecommunication Services:** info@aec.edu.

25937 ■ Anderson/Roethle Inc.

700 N Water St., Ste. 325
Milwaukee, WI 53202-4221
Ph: (414)276-0070
Fax: (414)276-4364
Co. E-mail: info@anderson-roethle.com
URL: http://www.anderson-roethle.com
Contact: Stanley C. Johnson, President
E-mail: scj@anderson-roethle.com
Scope: Provider of merger, acquisition and divestiture advisory services. Offers strategic planning, valuations and specialized M and A advisory services. **Founded:** 1963.

25938 ■ Apex Innovations Inc.

19951 W 162nd St.
Olathe, KS 66062
Ph: (913)254-0250
Fax: (913)254-0320
Co. E-mail: sales@apex-innovations.com
URL: http://www.apex-innovations.com
Contact: Wayne Abrams, President
E-mail: wayne.abrams@apex-innovations.com
Scope: A firm of business operations and technology professionals providing solutions nationwide for business needs. Provides a bridge between operations and technology for clients in manufacturing, insurance, banking and government. Offers services in business planning, assessment, education, business performance improvement, change management and the planning, and implementation management of solutions. **Founded:** 2002. **Special Services:** i-INFO. EPR™; i-INFO.WORKS™; i-INFO Classes™.

25939 ■ Association of Home-Based Women Entrepreneurs (HBWE)

PO Box 31561
Saint Louis, MO 63131-1561
Ph: (314)805-9519
Fax: (314)909-8179
Co. E-mail: aschaefer@advbizsol.com
URL: http://www.hbwe.org
Contact: Louise Wiedermann, President
E-mail: lw@projektek.com
Scope: Organization dedicated to women working from home-based offices. Focuses on the needs and interests of women doing their own business. It also focuses on business-related programs and issues, networking, leads and mentoring for professional growth in a dynamic and friendly atmosphere. **Founded:** 1998. **Publications:** "Taking Your Business International"; "Dressing For Success"; "Web 2.0 The Future of the Internet"; "Assertiveness Skills for Women in Business". **Seminars:** Making Connections, Jul, 2008; One Inch Wide, One Mile Deep, Jun,

2008; Accelerating Your Business, May, 2008; Change is Good, Apr, 2008; Pyro Marketing, Jan, 2007; Twenty Five Key Steps To Maintaining A Successful Home-Based Business, Nov, 2006.

25940 ■ Aurora Management Partners Inc.

4485 Tench Rd., Ste. 340
Suwanee, GA 30024
Ph: (770)904-5209
Fax: (770)904-5226
Co. E-mail: rturcotte@auroramp.com
URL: http://www.auroramp.com
Contact: William A. Barbee, Director
E-mail: abarbee@auroramp.com
Scope: Specializes in turnaround management and reorganization consulting. Firm develop strategic initiatives, organize and analyze solutions, deal with creditor issues, review organizational structure and develop time frames for decision making. Turnaround services offered include Recovery plans and their implementation, Viability analysis, Crisis management, Financial restructuring, Corporate and organizational restructuring, Facilities rationalization, Liquidation management, Loan workout, Litigation support and Expert testimony, Contract renegotiation, Sourcing loan refinancing and Sourcing equity investment. **Founded:** 2005. **Publications:** "TMA Turnaround of the Year Award, Small Company, Honorable Mention," Nov, 2005; "Back From The Brink - Bland Farms," Progressive Farmer, Oct, 2004; "New Breed of Turnaround Managers," Catalyst Magazine, Aug, 2004; "Key Performance Drivers - Bland Farms," The Produce News, Apr, 2004; "Corporate Governance: Averting Crisis's Before They Happen," ABJ journal, Feb, 2004.

25941 ■ Bahr International Inc.

PO Box 795
Gainesville, TX 76241
Ph: (940)665-2344
Fax: (940)665-2359
Co. E-mail: info@bahrintl.com
URL: http://www.bahrintl.com
Contact: C. Charles Bahr, III, Chairman of the Board
Scope: Offers consulting in general management, corporate polices and culture, and strategic and long-range planning. Provides management audits and reports and profit improvement programs. High level strategic marketing, advertising strategy/tactics, turnaround consulting and management. **Founded:** 1978.

25942 ■ Beacon Management - Management Consultants

1000 W McNab Rd.
Pompano Beach, FL 33069
Ph: (954)782-1119
Free: 800-771-8721
Fax: (954)969-2566
Co. E-mail: md@beaconmgmt.com
URL: http://www.beaconmgmt.com
Contact: Joyce Slencak, Manager
Scope: Specializes in change management, organized workplaces, multicultural negotiations and dispute resolutions and internet based decision making. **Founded:** 1985. **Publications:** "Sun-Sentinel Article," Oct, 2012.

25943 ■ Beeline Learning Solutions (BLS)

14911 Quorum Dr., Ste. 120
Dallas, TX 75254
Ph: (972)813-0465
Fax: (972)386-8667
Co. E-mail: info@consultingpartners.com
URL: http://www.beeline.com
Contact: Dominic Nagy, Manager
E-mail: dominic.nagy@consultingpartners.com
Scope: Consulting firm offering technology, content, and services addressing recruitment and sourcing, talent management, and learning and performance optimization. Solutions offered include contingent workforce solutions, vendor management software, talent management solutions, recruitment process outsourcing, performance management, applicant tracking, learning management and eLearning. **Founded:** 1990. **Special Services:** Beeline®.

25944 ■ Benchmark Consulting Group Inc.—Benchmark Advisors

283 Franklin St., Ste. 400
Boston, MA 02110-3100
Ph: (617)482-7661
Fax: (617)423-2158
Contact: Walter E. Robb, III, President
E-mail: werobb35@aol.com
Scope: Provides financial and management services to companies. Helps companies grow through debt, equity sourcing and restructuring, business valuation, acquisition and divestiture, computer information systems and improved operation profitability. **Founded:** 1978.

25945 ■ Bio-Technical Resources L.P. (BTR)

1035 S 7th St.
Manitowoc, WI 54220-5301
Ph: (920)684-5518
Fax: (920)684-5519
Co. E-mail: info@biotechresources.com
URL: http://www.biotechresources.com
Contact: Tom Jerrell, President
Scope: Services include strain improvement, process development and metabolic engineering. Solutions are also offered for the development of biotechnology products and processes through contract services in research and development, bio process scale-up, pilot scale manufacturing, technology and economic assessments. Target audience: pharmaceutical, biotechnology, chemical and food and feed industries. Client base may be global leaders as well as small companies and startups. **Founded:** 1962. **Publications:** "A Novel Fungus for the Production of Efficient Cellulases and Hemi-Cellulases," Jun, 2009; "Linoleic Acid Isomerase from Propionibacterium acnes: Purification, Characterization, Molecular Cloning, and Heterologous Expression," 2007; "Purification and Characterization of a Membrane-Bound Linoleic Acid Isomerase from Clostridium sporogenes," 2007; "Metabolic Engineering of Sesquiterpene Metabolism in Yeast," 2007; "Purification and Characterization of a Membrane-Bound Linoleic AcidIsomerase from Clostridium sporogenes," 2007; "Reduction of Background Interference in the Spectrophotometric Assay of Mevalonate Kinase," 2006; "A Soluble Form of Phosphatase in Saccharomyces cerevisiae Capable of Converting Farnesyl Diphosphate to E, E-Farnesol," 2006; "Ascorbate Biosynthesis: A Diversity of Pathways," BIOS Scientific Publishers, 2004; "The Biotechnology of Ascorbic Acid Manufacture," BIOS Scientific Publishers, 2004; "Detection of Farnesyl Diphosphate Accumulation in YeastERG9 Mutants," 2003; "Reverse Two-Hybrid System: Detecting Critical Interaction Domains and Screening for Inhibitors," Eaton Publishing, 2000. **Seminars:** Metabolic Engineering for Industrial Production of Glucosamine and N-Acetylglucosamine, Aug, 2003; Metabolic Engineering of E. coli for the Industrial Production of Glucosamine, Apr, 2003.

25946 ■ BioChem Technology Inc.

3620 Horizon Dr., Ste. 200
King of Prussia, PA 19406
Ph: (610)768-9360
Fax: (610)768-9363
Co. E-mail: sales@biochemtech.com
URL: http://www.biochemtech.com
Contact: George Lee, President
Scope: A process consultation firm specializing in the monitoring, optimization and control of wastewater treatment processes. The technological optimization services include assessment of treatment capacities, facility re-rating, optimization services, de-bottlenecking services, flow dynamics/mixing pattern analysis. **Founded:** 1979. **Publications:** "Process Evaluation Provides Optimization and Energy Reduction"; "Effect of Ionic Strength on Ion Selective Electrodes in the Activated Sludge Process"; "DO Control Based on On-line Ammonia Measurement"; "Energy Savings at Phoenix 23rd Avenue Wastewater Treatment Plant Using Feed-Forward Process Control"; "A Novel Approach for Monitoring and Control of Denitrification in a Biological Nutrient Removal Facility," Oct, 1999; "A Unique Approach for Assessing the Capacity of a Biological Nutrient Removal Facility," Oct, 1999; "Enhancing Competitiveness of an Operations Staff: Five Years Experience with a BNR

Wastewater Treatment Facility," Oct, 1998; "Optimization of Nitrification Process By On-Line Monitoring of Nitrification Time," Jun, 1997; "Monitoring and Control of the Nitrification Process Marine Park Water Reclamation Facility, City of Vancouver, WA," Oct, 1997; "Operational Improvements in a Biological Nutrient Removal Facility Using an Innovative Biological Activity Meter," May, 1996; "Operator Education and an Innovative Monitoring Technology Improve Performance of a Biological Nutrient Removal Facility," Oct, 1996; "Performance Enhancement of a BNR Wastewater Treatment Facility Utilizing a Microcosm Reactor Equipped With a Biological Activity Meter," Oct, 1996; "Optimization of Biological Denitrification Through Biological Activity Monitoring: System Development," Jun, 1995. **Seminars:** A Five Year Case Study of a Feed Forward Nitrogen Reduction Process Control System, Jun, 2009; Alternate DO Control Based on On-line Ammonia Measurement, Jun, 2009.

25947 ■ BioSciCon Inc.
14905 Forest Landing Cir.
Rockville, MD 20850
Ph: (301)610-9130
Fax: (301)610-7662
Co. E-mail: info@bioscicon.com
URL: http://www.bioscicon.com
Contact: Nenad Markovic, President
Scope: Sponsoring development of the technology of the Pap test accuracy via introduction of a new bio-marker that enhances visibility of abnormal cells on Pap smears or mono-layers of cervical cells obtained in solution. Conducts clinical trials for assessment of the test efficacy and safety, manufactures research tools for conduct of trials, and markets IP to license manufacturing, marketing, sales and distribution rights of the new technology line of products. **Founded:** 1996. **Publications:** "Cervical Acid Phosphates: A Biomarker of Cervical Dysplasia and Potential Surrogate Endpoint for Colposcopy," 2004; "Enhancing Pap test with a new biological marker of cervical dysplasia," 2004; "A cytoplasmic biomarker for liquid-based Pap," The FACEB Journal Experimental Biology, 2004; "Pap test and new biomarker-based technology for enhancing visibility of abnormal cells," 2004. **Special Services:** Mark-Pap®; PreservCyt®.

25948 ■ Birchfield Jacobs Foodsystems Inc.
519 N Charles St., Ste. 350A
Baltimore, MD 21201-5022
Ph: (410)528-8700
Fax: (410)528-6060
URL: http://www.birchfieldjacobs.com
Contact: Robert Jacobs, Owner Principal
E-mail: rjacobs@birchfieldJacobs.com
Scope: Food facilities design consultants for colleges; universities; schools; healthcare facilities; government; military; correctional; country clubs and restaurants. Services include facilities design; feasibility studies; operations analysis and master planning. **Founded:** 1979.

25949 ■ Blankinship & Associates Inc.
322 C St.
Davis, CA 95616
Ph: (530)757-0941
Fax: (530)757-0940
Co. E-mail: blankinship@envtox.com
URL: http://www.h2osci.com
Contact: Michael Blankinship, President
E-mail: mike@envtox.com
Scope: Specializes in assisting water resource and conveyance, golf and production, protection and enhancement of natural resources. **Founded:** 2000. **Publications:** "Air Blast Sprayer Calibration and Chlorpyrifos Irrigation Study," Oct, 2007; "How Green is your golf course," Prosper Magazine, 2007. **Seminars:** CDFG Wildlands IPM Seminar, Oct, 2009.

25950 ■ C. Clint Bolte & Associates
809 Philadelphia Ave.
Chambersburg, PA 17201
Ph: (717)263-5768
Fax: (717)263-8954
Co. E-mail: clint@clintbolte.com
URL: http://www.clintbolte.com
Contact: C. Clint Bolte, Principal
E-mail: cbolte3@comcast.net
Scope: Provider of management consulting services to firms involved with the printing industry. Services include outsourcing studies, graphics supply chain management studies, company and equipment valuations, plant layout services, litigation support, fulfillment warehouse consulting and product development services. **Founded:** 1989. **Seminars:** How to compete with the majors.

25951 ■ BPT Consulting Associates Ltd.
12 Parmenter Rd., Ste. B-6
Londonderry, NH 03053
Ph: (603)437-8484
Free: 888-278-0030
Fax: (603)434-5388
Contact: John Kuczynski, Managing Director
Scope: Provides management consulting expertise and resources to cross-industry clients with services for: Business Management consulting, People/Human Resources Transition and Training programs, and a full cadre of multi-disciplined Technology Computer experts. Virtual consultants with expertise in e-commerce, supply chain management, organizational development, and business application development consulting. **Founded:** 1991.

25952 ■ Business Consulting Services (BCS)
207 Dickinson Ave.
Swarthmore, PA 19081-1630
Ph: (610)328-9806
Contact: Thomas K. Casey, President
Scope: Management consulting organization dedicated to providing high quality, professional services to the business, government and non-profit communities. Specializes in the two key areas of business performance improvement and information technology consulting. Specifically for small business owners. **Founded:** 1991. **Publications:** "If You Fail To Plan"; "The True Cost Of Technology"; "Why Projects Fail"; "Planning For A Business Disruption". **Seminars:** How To Select, Manage and Contract Consultants, and Other Resources; How To Market Professional Services; Introduction To Management Consulting.

25953 ■ Business Education Associates (BEA)—Ashford Group Inc.
4 Long Hill Rd.
Bethel, CT 06801
Ph: (203)798-6035
Contact: Robert J. Popp, President
E-mail: bob@ashfordgrp.com
Scope: Offers tailored management education programs. Has been designed to meet the business education needs of companies implementing new systems and companies to re-educate users of existing systems. **Founded:** 1984. **Publications:** "The Ashford Group and TQuist Partner to Provide High Impact Manufacturing Solutions"; "The Future of ERP"; "Winning the Implementation Game". **Special Services:** Building Manufacturing Excellence.

25954 ■ Business Improvement Architects (BIA)
33 Riderwood Dr.
Toronto, ON, Canada M2L 2X4
Ph: (416)444-8225
Free: 866-346-3242
Fax: (416)444-6743
Co. E-mail: info@bia.ca
URL: http://www.bia.ca
Contact: Michael Stanleigh, Chief Executive Officer
E-mail: mstanleigh@bia.ca
Scope: Provider of the following services: strategic planning, leadership development, innovation and project and quality management. Specialize in strategic planning, change management, leadership assessment, and development of skills. **Founded:** 1989. **Publications:** "Avoiding Pit falls to Innovation"; "Create a New Dimension of Performance with Innovation"; "The Power of Appreciation in Leadership"; "Why It Makes Sense To Have a Strategic Enterprise Office"; "Burning Rubber at the Start of Your Project"; "Accounting for Quality"; "How Pareto Charts Can

Help You Improve the Quality of Business Processes"; "Managing Resistance to Change". **Seminars:** The Innovation Process. . .From Vision to Reality, San Diego, Oct, 2007; Critical Thinking, Kuala Lump or, Sep, 2007; Critical Thinking, Brunei, Sep, 2007; Delivering Project Assurance, Auckland, Jun, 2007; From Crisis to Control: A New Era in Strategic Project Management, Prague, May, 2007; What Project Leaders Need to Know to Help Them Sleep Better At Night, London, May, 2007; Innovation Process. . .From Vision To Reality, Orlando, Apr, 2007. **Special Services:** Project Planning Tool™.

25955 ■ ByrneMRG Corp.
22 Isle of Pines Dr.
Hilton Head Island, SC 29928
Ph: (215)630-7411
Free: 888-816-8080
Co. E-mail: info@byrnemrg.com
URL: http://www.byrnemrg.com
Contact: Patrick J. Boyle, President
E-mail: pjboyle@byrnemrg.com
Scope: Specializes in management consulting, including department management, equipment evaluation and selection, project management, research and development planning; and database design and management. **Founded:** 1972. **Publications:** "Implementing Solutions to Everyday Issues". **Telecommunication Services:** pjboyle@byrnemrg.com.

25956 ■ Capell & Associates—Capell's Circulation Report
601 Central Ave.
Barnegat Light, NJ 08006
Ph: (202)572-8774
Fax: (609)494-7369
Co. E-mail: contact@capellandassociates.com
URL: http://www.capellandassociates.com
Contact: E. Daniel Capell, President
E-mail: dan_capell@att.net
Scope: Specialized consulting firm focused on direct marketing, magazine publishing and circulation. Consulting services include due diligence, circulation audits, benchmarking and list rental analysis. **Founded:** 1982. **Seminars:** Circulation for the Non-Circulator.

25957 ■ Casino, Hotel & Resort Consultants L.L.C.
4825 Quality Ct., Ste. B
Las Vegas, NV 89103
Ph: (702)528-9537
Co. E-mail: info@hraba.com
URL: http://www.hraba.com
Contact: John S. Hraba, President
E-mail: jshraba@aol.com
Scope: Casino and hospitality industry consultants. Firm specializes in developing and implementing customized forecast and labor management control systems that deliver immediate, positive impact to the company's bottom line. Involved in production planning, employ surveys and communication, inventory management, business process reviews, audits, development and implementation of key management reports. **Founded:** 1989. **Seminars:** Payroll Cost Control; Effective Staff Scheduling. **Telecommunication Services:** john.hraba@hraba.com.

25958 ■ Jim Castello Marketing Communications Consultants
711 Red Wing Dr.
Lake Mary, FL 32746
Ph: (407)321-6322
Fax: (407)321-8460
Contact: James E. Castello, Jr., President
Scope: Consultant develops creative ideas and marketing strategies, including collateral programs, public relations, advertising, and brochures. Industries served: All golf related industry/business, golf manufacturers, golf resorts, golf residential developments, golf professionals, golf clothing, golf accessories, golf associations, and golf travel. **Founded:** 1989. **Seminars:** How To Seminar for Family Fun Center Entrepreneurs; How To Seminar for Creativity in Golf Marketing; The Golf Business on the Internet.

25959 ■ CBIZ Inc.
6050 Oak Tree Blvd. S, Ste. 500
Cleveland, OH 44131-6951

Ph: (216)447-9000
Fax: (216)447-9007
URL: http://www.cbizinc.com
Contact: Jerome P. Grisko, President
URL(s): www.cbiz.com. **Scope:** A business consulting and tax services firm providing financial, consulting, tax and business services through seven groups: Financial management, tax advisory, construction and real estate, health-care, litigation support, capital resource and CEO outsource. **Founded:** 1996. **Publications:** "FAS 154: Changes in the Way We Report Changes," 2006; "Equity-Based Compensation: How Much Does it Really Cost Your Business," 2006; "Preventing Fraud - Tips for Nonprofit Organizations"; "Today's Workforce and Nonprofit Organizations: Meeting a Critical Need"; "IRS Highlights Top Seven Form 990 Errors". **Seminars:** Health Care - What the Future Holds; Consumer Driven Health Plans; Executive Plans; Health Savings Accounts Healthy Wealthy and Wise; Legislative Update; Medicare Part D; Retirement Plans.

25960 ■ C.C. Comfort Consulting
3370 N Hayden Rd., Ste. 123-127
Scottsdale, AZ 85251
Ph: (480)483-8364
Contact: Clifton C. Comfort, Jr., Principal
Scope: Evaluates, develops and implements financial, operational and compliance management systems strategies, programs and practices. Has professional recognition as certified public accountant, internal auditor, cost analyst and fraud examiner plus investigator, law enforcement, and court experience ensure confidential handling of sensitive and legal matters. Works with management, audit, legal, security and outside personnel to evaluate and improve compliance, efficiency and effectiveness. **Founded:** 1983.

25961 ■ Center for Lifestyle Enhancement - Columbia Medical Center of Plano
3901 W 15th St.
Plano, TX 75075
Ph: (972)596-6800
Fax: (972)519-1299
Co. E-mail: mcp.cle@hcahealthcare.com
URL: http://www.medicalcenterofplano.com
Contact: Harvey Fishero, President
Scope: Provides professional health counseling in the areas of general nutrition for weight management, eating disorders, diabetic education, cholesterol reduction and adolescent weight management. Offers work site health promotion and preventive services. Also coordinates speaker's bureau, cooking classes and physician referrals. Industries served: education, insurance, healthcare, retail or wholesale, data processing and manufacturing throughout Texas. **Founded:** 1975. **Seminars:** Rx Diet and Exercise; Smoking Cessation; Stress Management; Health Fairs; Fitness Screenings; Body Composition; Nutrition Analysis; Exercise Classes; Prenatal Nutrition; SHAPEDOWN; Successfully Managing Diabetes; Gourmet Foods for Your Heart; The Aging Heart; Heart Smart Saturday featuring Day of Dance; Weight-Loss Management Seminars; The Right Stroke for Men; Peripheral Artery Disease Screening; Menstruation: The Cycle Begins; Boot Camp for New Dads; Grand parenting 101: Caring for Kids Today; Teddy Bear Camp; New Baby Day Camp; Safe Sitter Baby-Sitting Class.

25962 ■ The Center for Organizational Excellence Inc.
15204 Omega Dr., Ste. 300
Rockville, MD 20850
Ph: (301)948-1922
Free: 877-674-3923
Fax: (301)948-2158
Co. E-mail: results@center4oe.com
URL: http://www.center4oe.com
Contact: Stephen Goodrich, President
E-mail: sgoodrich@center4oe.com
Scope: An organizational effectiveness consulting firm specializing in helping organizations achieve results through people, process, and performance. Service areas include organizational performance systems, leadership systems, customer systems, and learning systems. **Founded:** 1984.

25963 ■ Center for Personal Empowerment
102 N Main St., Ste. 1
Columbia, IL 62236-1702
Ph: (618)281-3565
Free: 888-657-1550
Fax: (618)476-7083
Co. E-mail: personalempowerment@wholenet.net
Contact: Cherri Hendrix, Owner
Scope: Private consultations and trainings to educate on how to determine which emotions, events, beliefs from the past prevent you from achieving success. Methods used include time line therapy, news linguistic programming and hypnosis. Behavior modification through NLP trainings. **Founded:** 1996. **Seminars:** NLP Practitioner Training; Hypnosis Certification Training; Lifemap Seminars.

25964 ■ CEO Advisors
848 Brickell Ave., Ste. 603
Miami, FL 33131
Ph: (305)371-8560
Fax: (305)371-8563
Co. E-mail: ciaizpurua@ceoadvisors.us
URL: http://www.ceoadvisors.us
Contact: Roberto J. Arguello, President
E-mail: rjarguello@ceoadvisors.us
Scope: Business consulting firm offering clients services in strategy, mergers and acquisitions, corporate finance, corporate advisory, supply chain management, government relations and public affairs. Specializes in strategic planning, profit enhancement, start-up businesses, venture capital, appraisals and valuations. **Founded:** 1989.

25965 ■ CFI Group USA L.L.C.—Claes Fornell International
625 Avis Dr.
Ann Arbor, MI 48108-9649
Ph: (734)930-9090
Free: 800-930-0933
Fax: (734)930-0911
Co. E-mail: askcfi@cfigroup.com
URL: http://www.cfigroup.com
Contact: Sheri Teodoru, Chief Executive Officer
E-mail: steodoru@mail.cfigroup.com
Scope: Management consulting firm that helps its clients worldwide to maximize shareholder value by optimizing customer and employee satisfaction. Clients span a variety of industries, including manufacturing, telecommunications, retail and government. **Founded:** 1988. **Publications:** "Customer Satisfaction and Stock Prices: High Returns, Low Risk," American Marketing Association, Jan, 2006; "Customer Satisfaction Index Climbs," The Wall Street Journal, Feb, 2004; "What's Next? Customer Service is Key to Post-Boom Success," The Bottom Line, Mar, 2003; "Boost Stock Performance, Nation's Economy," Quality Progress, Feb, 2003.

25966 ■ Chamberlain & Cansler Inc.
2251 Perimeter Park Dr.
Atlanta, GA 30341
Ph: (770)457-5699
Contact: Charles L. Cansler, Owner
Scope: Firm specializes in strategic planning; profit enhancement; small business management; interim management; crisis management; turnarounds. **Founded:** 1986.

25967 ■ Charismedia
610 W End Ave., Ste. B1
New York, NY 10001
Ph: (212)362-6808
Fax: (212)362-6809
Co. E-mail: charismedia@earthlink.net
URL: http://www.charismedia.net
Contact: Dr. Doe Lang, President
E-mail: charismedia@earthlink.net
Scope: Offers speech and image training as well as speech writing services for effective presentation skills. Conducts workshops like anti-stage fright breathing, psychophysical exercises, transformational success imagery, face reading and body language, EMDR (Eye Movement Desensitization Re-Processing) for Permanent Trauma and Fear Removal, Bach Flower remedies, thought field therapy, cross-cultural communication, speech, voice and diction; regional and foreign accent elimination and acquisition, Posi-

tive Perception Management (P.P.M.), Ad-libbing, humor and spontaneity training, fast creative speech preparation, Neuro-Linguistic Programming and Hypnosis. **Founded:** 1974. **Publications:** "Flaunt It"; "Improve Your Sex Life"; "Phone Power"; "Train Your Voice"; "Turning Tinny, Tiny Tones To Gold"; "The New Secrets of Charisma: How to Discover and Unleash your Hidden Powers," McGraw-Hill, Jul, 1999. **Seminars:** Services for Comfortable Effective Speaking.

25968 ■ Chartered Management Co.
10 S Riverside Plz., Ste. 1800
Chicago, IL 60606
Ph: (312)214-2575
Contact: William B. Avellone, President
Scope: Operations improvement consultants. Specializes in strategic planning; feasibility studies; management audits and reports; profit enhancement; start-up businesses; mergers and acquisitions; joint ventures; divestitures; interim management; crisis management; turnarounds; business process re-engineering; venture capital; and due diligence. **Founded:** 1985.

25969 ■ The Children's Psychological Trauma Center
2105 Divisadero St.
San Francisco, CA 94115
Ph: (415)292-7119
Fax: (415)749-2802
Co. E-mail: gil.kliman@cphc-sf.org
URL: http://www.cphc-sf.org
Contact: Gilbert Kliman, Director
Scope: Treats those with psychological trauma claimed from stressors including institutional negligence, vehicular and aviation accidents, wrongful death in the family, rape, molestation, fire, explosion, flood, earthquake, loss of parents, terrorism, kidnapping, disfiguring events, emotional damage from social work, medical malpractice or defective products. Provides evaluation and reports to referring professionals. Experienced in forensic consultation and testimony. **Founded:** 1992. **Publications:** "My Personal Story About Tropical Storm Stan," Feb, 2006; "My Personal Story About Hurricanes Katrina and Rita: A guided activity workbook to help coping, learning and Healthy expression," Sep, 2005; "Helping Patients and their Families Cope in a National Disaster," Jan, 2002; "The practice of behavioral treatment in the acute rehabilitation setting".

25970 ■ Claremont Consulting Group
4525 Castle Ln.
La Canada, CA 91011-1436
Ph: (818)249-0584
Fax: (818)249-5811
Contact: Donald S. Remer, Partner
Scope: Consulting, coaching, training, and litigation support in project management, engineering management, system engineering and cost estimating. **Founded:** 1979. **Publications:** "What Every Engineer Should Know About Project Management"; "100% product-oriented work breakdown structures and their importance to system engineering". **Seminars:** Project Management, System Engineering and Cost Estimating.

25971 ■ Clayton/Curtis/Cottrell
1722 Madison Ct.
Louisville, CO 80027-1121
Ph: (303)665-2005
Contact: Robert Cottrell, President
Scope: Market research firm specializes in providing consultations for packaged goods, telecommunications, direct marketing and printing, and packaging industries. Services include strategic planning; profit enhancement; startup businesses; mergers and acquisitions; joint ventures; divestitures; interim management; crisis management; turnarounds; market size, segmentation and rates of growth; competitor intelligence; image and reputation, and competitive analysis. **Founded:** 1981. **Publications:** "Turn an attitude into a purchase," Jul, 1995; "Mixed results for private label: price assaults by the national brands are getting heavy, but there's still a place for private label," Jun, 1995; "In-store promotion goes high-tech: is the conventional coupon destined for obsolescence?," Jun, 1995.

25972 ■ Colmen Menard Company Inc. (CMCI)
The Woods, 994 Old Eagle School Rd., Ste. 1000
Wayne, PA 19087
Ph: (484)367-0300
Fax: (484)367-0305
Co. E-mail: cmci@colmenmenard.com
URL: http://www.colmenmenard.com
Contact: David W. Menard, President
E-mail: dmenard@colmenmenard.com
Scope: Merger and acquisition corporate finance and business advisory services for public and private companies located in North America. **Founded:** 1982. **Publications:** "Success in Selling a Troubled Company," Nov, 2002; "Savvy Dealmakers," May, 2001; "Success in Selling a Troubled Company feature article from The Technology Times bimonthly newspaper," Apr, 2002; "Truisms," M&A Today, Nov, 2000.

25973 ■ Columbia Consultants Ltd.—Columbia Consultants.Net L.L.C.
8950 State Route 108, Ste. 226
Columbia, MD 21045
Ph: (410)992-4700
Free: 800-783-7574
Fax: (410)992-4518
Contact: Carol Price, President
Scope: A complete personnel service offering placement of both permanent and temporary employees. Provides professional services and integrated solutions. **Founded:** 1969.

25974 ■ Comer & Associates L.L.C.—Energy Alliance Group
5255 Holmes Pl.
Boulder, CO 80303
Ph: (303)786-7986
Free: 888-950-3190
Fax: (303)895-2347
Co. E-mail: jerry@comerassociates.com
URL: http://www.comerassociates.com
Contact: Jerry C. Comer, President
E-mail: jerry@comerassociates.com
URL(s): www.energyalliance.biz. **Scope:** Specialize in developing markets and businesses. Marketing support includes: Developing and writing strategic and tactical business plans; developing and writing focused, effective market plans; researching market potential and competition; implementing targeted marketing tactics to achieve company objectives; conducting customer surveys to determine satisfaction and attitudes toward client. Organization development support includes: Executive management training programs; executive coaching; team building; developing effective organization structures; and management of change in dynamic and competitive environments; individual coaching for management and leadership effectiveness. **Founded:** 1993. **Seminars:** Developing a Strategic Market Plan; Market Research: Defining Your Opportunity; Management and Leadership Effectiveness; Team Building; Developing a Business Plan; How to Close; Using Questions to Sell; Sales System Elements and Checklist; Working With Independent Reps; Features vs. Benefits; Overcoming Objections; Sales Force Automation.

25975 ■ Consultants National Resource Center (CNRC)—National Association of Business Coaches
27-A Big Spring Rd.
Clear Spring, MD 21722
Ph: (301)791-9332
Free: 800-290-3196
Fax: (301)582-3639
Co. E-mail: cnrc@erols.com
Contact: Lewis Williams, Director
Scope: Provider of marketing and strategic planning services for consultants. Also serves as membership center for the professional management institute. Industries served: all consulting disciplines. **Founded:** 1981. **Publications:** "Consulting Opportunities Journal"; "How to Master Continuous Learning". **Seminars:** How to Series on Starting and Building a Consulting Practice; Introduction to the Professional Management Institute; Consulting Boot camp; Planagement®.

25976 ■ Consulting & Conciliation Service (CCS)
2219 H St., Ste. 1
Sacramento, CA 95816
Ph: (916)396-0480
Free: 888-898-9780
Fax: (916)441-2828
Co. E-mail: service@azurewings.net
Contact: Jane A. McCluskey, Principal
E-mail: service@azurewings.net
Scope: Offers consulting and conciliation services. Provides pre-mediation counseling, training and research on preparing for a peaceful society, mediation and facilitation, and preparation for shifts in structure, policy and personnel. Offers sliding scale business rates and free individual consultation. **Publications:** "Native America and Tracking Shifts in US Policy"; "Biogenesis: A Discussion of Basic Social Needs and the Significance of Hope". **Seminars:** Positive Approaches to Violence Prevention: Peace building in Schools and Communities.

25977 ■ The Consulting Exchange
1770 Mass Ave., Ste. 288
Cambridge, MA 02140
Ph: (617)576-2100
Free: 800-824-4828
Co. E-mail: gday@consultingexchange.com
Contact: Geoffrey Day, President
E-mail: gday@consultingexchange.com
Scope: A consultant referral service for management and technical consultants. Serves a local, regional and international client base. **Founded:** 1982. **Publications:** "Looking for a Consultant? Success Points for Finding the Right One," Boston Business Journal, Jun, 2001; "Getting Full Value From Consulting is in Your Hands," Mass High Tech, May, 1998; "Developing Knowledge-Based Client Relationships, The Future of Professional Services"; "The Consultant's Legal Guide"; "The Business of Consulting: The Basics and Beyond".

25978 ■ The Consulting Source Inc.
1403 S Addison Ct.
Aurora, CO 80018-6003
Ph: (303)366-4800
Free: 800-520-1998
Fax: (303)366-4801
Co. E-mail: info@consultingsource.com
URL: http://www.consultingsource.com
Contact: Margaret A. Sobey, Owner
E-mail: msobey@consultingsource.com
Scope: Provides customized information technology services to IBM and IBM-compatible computer users. **Founded:** 1990.

25979 ■ The Corlund Group L.L.C. (CG)
101 Federal St., Ste. 310
Boston, MA 02110
Ph: (617)423-9364
Fax: (617)423-9371
Co. E-mail: info@corlundgroup.com
URL: http://www.corlundgroup.com
Contact: Wilmot J. Gravenslund, Director
E-mail: wgravenslund@corlundgroup.com
Scope: Boutique firm offering services in the areas of leadership, governance, and change with a particular focus on CEO and senior executive succession planning, including assessment, development, and orchestrating succession processes with management and Boards of Directors. Also Board governance effectiveness. **Founded:** 1996. **Publications:** "Are You Rolling the Dice on CEO Succession?" Center for Healthcare Governance, 2006; "Leadership Due Diligence: The Neglected Governance Frontier," Directorship, Sep, 2001; "Leadership Due Diligence: Managing the Risks," The Corporate Board, Aug, 2001; "Succession: The need for detailed insight," Directors and Boards, 2001; "CEO Succession: Who's Doing Due Diligence?," 2001. **Telecommunication Services:** corlund@corlundgroup.com.

25980 ■ Corporate Consulting Inc.
3333 Belcaro Dr.
Denver, CO 80209-4912
Ph: (303)698-9292

Fax: (303)698-9292
Co. E-mail: corpcons@compuserve.com
Contact: Devereux C. Josephs, President
Scope: Specializes in feasibility studies, organizational development, small business management, mergers and acquisitions, joint ventures, divestitures, interim management, crisis management, turnarounds, financing, appraisals valuations and due diligence studies. **Founded:** 1983.

25981 ■ COTC Technologies Inc.—COTC-TrenzSoft
172 E Industrial Blvd.
Pueblo, CO 81007-4406
Ph: (719)547-0938
Free: 888-547-0938
Fax: (719)547-1105
Contact: Tom Renz, Chief Executive Officer
E-mail: tom@cotc-consulting.com
Scope: Provides software consulting services to organizations that require assistance with their HP3000 computer system. Provides systems analysis, programming, operations support, and system management. Also provides PC software and hardware support and consulting. Additionally provides various training for the HP3000 computer system. Industries served: healthcare, aerospace procurement, aerospace proposal activities, and HP3000 computer systems. **Founded:** 2006.

25982 ■ Coyne Associates
4010 E Lake St.
Minneapolis, MN 55406-2201
Ph: (612)724-1188
Fax: (612)722-1379
Contact: John T. Coyne, Chief Executive Officer
Scope: A marketing and public relations consulting firm that specializes in assisting architectural, engineering, and contractor/developer firms. Services include: marketing plains and audits, strategic planning, corporate identity, turnarounds, and sales training. **Founded:** 2008.

25983 ■ Creative Computer Resources Inc.
5001 Horizons Dr., Ste. 200
Columbus, OH 43220-5291
Ph: (614)384-7557
Free: 866-720-0209
Fax: (614)573-6331
Co. E-mail: team@planet-ccr.com
URL: http://www.planet-ccr.com
Contact: M. Erik Mueller, President
E-mail: merikm@planet-ccr.com
Scope: Offers information systems support, custom software development, website design, development and implementation. Provides information technology support and management services to small and mid-size businesses. **Founded:** 1996.

25984 ■ Crystal Clear Communications Inc.
1633 W Winslow Dr., Ste. 210
Mequon, WI 53092
Ph: (262)240-0072
Fax: (262)240-0073
Co. E-mail: contact@crystalclear1.com
URL: http://www.crystalclear1.com
Contact: Barry J. Moze, Partner
E-mail: barrymoze@crystalclearl.com
Scope: Specialize in helping executives identify impediments to success, and then develop strategies to surmount them. Serves to identify core problems, suggest appropriate business changes, work with the organization to support these changes, and help executives articulate the behavior that will uphold these changes. Specializes in strategic planning; organizational development; small business management; executive coaching. **Founded:** 1986. **Publications:** "Weakest Link"; "Aware Leadership"; "Integrity"; "When Your Plate is Full"; "Problem Solving"; "Strategic Thinking".

25985 ■ Development Resource Consultants (DRC)
PO Box 118
Rancho Cucamonga, CA 91729
Ph: (909)902-7655

Fax: (909)476-6942
Co. E-mail: drc@gotodrc.com
URL: http://www.gotodrc.com
Contact: Jerry R. Frey, Business Manager
E-mail: jfrey@gotodrc.com

Scope: Specializes in office re-organization, employee training in office organization, communication skills, sales training and career counseling. **Founded:** 1985. **Publications:** "Institute of Management Consultants Southern California Chapter," Jan, 2006.

25986 ■ The Devine Group Inc.
7755 Montgomery Rd., Ste. 180
Cincinnati, OH 45236
Ph: (513)792-7500
Free: 866-792-7500
Fax: (513)793-8535
Co. E-mail: sales@devinegroup.com
URL: http://www.devinegroup.com
Contact: David C. Devine, Chief Executive Officer
E-mail: david@devinegroup.com

Scope: A human resource consulting company devoted to providing reliable and responsive information focusing on performance issues and answers. Dedicated to analyzing and enhancing job performance. Custom design and implement programs and workshops that will result in demonstrable behavior change on the job. Assist clients enhance their productivity via behavior analysis. **Founded:** 1970. **Publications:** "Leveraging Assessments for Enterprise Improvement," Oct, 2006; "Evaluation of Assessment Tools: The Five Criteria," Oct, 2006; "People Improvement Using Behavior Assessment," Aug, 2005; "Measuring Personality: The Good, the Bad and the Ugly". **Special Services:** The Devine Inventory®.

25987 ■ Dimond Hospitality Consulting Group Inc.
5710 Stoneway Trl.
Nashville, TN 37209
Ph: (615)353-0033
Fax: (615)352-5290
Co. E-mail: drew@dimondhotelconsulting.com
URL: http://www.dimondhotelconsulting.com
Contact: Drew W. Dimond, President
E-mail: drew@dimondhotelconsulting.com

Scope: Specializes in strategic planning; start-up businesses; business process re-engineering; team building; competitive analysis; venture capital; competitive intelligence; and due diligence. Offers litigation support. Comprehensive hospitality consulting firm that serves as an adviser to leading hotel companies, independent hotels, lending institutions, trustees, law firms, investment companies and municipalities in the areas of: Asset management, Acquisition due diligence, Arbitration, Disposition advisory services, Exit strategies, Financial review and analysis, Impact studies, Mediation. **Founded:** 1985. **Publications:** "The distressed debt conundrum," Jul, 2009; "How to buy distressed assets," Apr, 2009; "Cmbs Loans: A History and the Future," Apr, 2009; "Opportunity Knocks," Apr, 2009; "Another Reality Check," Mar, 2009; "An Inkling of Hope," Mar, 2009; "Strong World Tourism Growth in 2007," 2007; "Les U.S. Construction Pipeline Sets Another Record at 5011 Hotels with 654503 Rooms"; "Hotel Capitalization Rates Hold for Now"; "Winning Cornell Hotel and Restaurant Administration Quarterly Article Provides Hotel Brand Analysis"; "Breaking News for Lifestyle Hotels. Ian Schrager and Bill Marriott Announce Their Marriage Will the Schrager-Marriott Marriage Lead to Eternal Bliss Or End in Divorce What Will the M Hotels Children Be Named"; "Brands Vs Independents"; "Nyu Conf Takes Industry Temp"; "Economy Hotel Performance Indication of Travel Trends"; "Hotel Sales Continue at Brisk Pace"; "Fundamentals Strong, Weakening Undercurrent"; "Hotel Investments: Where Do We Go From Here"; "On the Road: Aahoa Panel Commits to Change"; "Cuba Not Ready, But Expecting U.S. Tourists".

25988 ■ Diversified Health Resources Inc.
875 N Michigan Ave., Ste. 3250
Chicago, IL 60611-1901
Ph: (312)266-0466

Fax: (312)266-0715
Contact: Andrea R. Rozran, President
Scope: Offers health care consulting for hospitals, nursing homes including homes for the aged, and other health related facilities and companies. Specializes in planning and marketing. Also conducts executive searches for top level health care administrative positions. Serves private industries as well as government agencies. **Founded:** 1979. **Publications:** "City Finance".

25989 ■ Donna Cornell Enterprises Inc.—Cornell Career Center
68 N Plank Rd., Ste. 204
Newburgh, NY 12550-2122
Ph: (845)565-0088
Free: 888-769-3792
Fax: (845)565-0084
Co. E-mail: rc@cornellcareercenter.com
Contact: Donna Cornell, President
E-mail: rc@cornellcareercenter.com

Scope: Offers services in career consultant, professional search, job placement and national professional search. **Founded:** 1996. **Publications:** "The Power of the Woman Within"; "Juggling it All!"; "Journey: A Woman's Guide to Success"; "Shatter the Traditions".

25990 ■ DRI Consulting (DRIC)
2 Otter Ln.
Saint Paul, MN 55127-6436
Ph: (651)415-1400
Free: 866-276-4600
Fax: (651)415-9968
Co. E-mail: dric@dric.com
URL: http://www.dric.com
Contact: Megan Brogger, Principal
E-mail: meganbrogger@dric.com

Scope: Provides high-quality, research-based services and training in leadership, team processes, supervision, and management, and organizational development, clients with direct and substantial impact on individual and team performance and on organizational success through proven processes for selecting, developing and deploying leaders. **Founded:** 1991.

25991 ■ Dubuc Lucke & Company Inc.—Adventa Global Intermediaries
120 W 5th St.
Cincinnati, OH 45202-2713
Ph: (513)579-8330
Fax: (513)241-6669
Contact: Kenneth E. Dubuc, President
Scope: Provides consulting services in the areas of profit enhancement; small business management; mergers and acquisitions; joint ventures; divestitures; interim management; crisis management; turnarounds; appraisals; valuations; due diligence; and international trade. **Founded:** 1999.

25992 ■ The DuMond Group
5282 Princeton Ave.
Westminster, CA 92683-2753
Ph: (714)373-0610
Contact: Adrianne H. Geiger-Dumond, President
Scope: Human resources and executive search consulting firm that specializes in organizational development; small business management; employee surveys and communication; performance appraisals; and team building. **Founded:** 1992.

25993 ■ Dunelm International
437 Colebrook Ln.
Bryn Mawr, PA 19010-3216
Ph: (610)989-0144
Fax: (610)964-9524
Co. E-mail: jecdunelm@worldnet.att.net
Contact: John E. Crowther, President
E-mail: Jecdunelm@dunelm.org.uk

Scope: Firm specializes in feasibility studies; start-up businesses; interim management; crisis management; turnarounds; business process re-engineering; sales forecasting; supply chain solution and project management. **Founded:** 1988.

25994 ■ Eastern Point Consulting Group Inc.
36 Glen Ave.
Newton, MA 02464

Ph: (617)965-4141
Fax: (617)965-4172
Co. E-mail: info@eastpt.com
URL: http://www.eastpt.com
Contact: Katherine A. Herzog, President
E-mail: kherzog@eastpt.com

Scope: Specializes in bringing practical solutions to complex challenges. Provides consulting and training in managing diversity; comprehensive sexual-harassment policies and programs; organizational development; benchmarks 360 skills assessment; executive coaching; strategic human resource planning team building; leadership development for women; mentoring programs; and gender issues in the workplace. **Founded:** 1995. **Seminars:** Leadership Development for Women.

25995 ■ Education Development Center Inc. (EDC)
43 Foundry Ave.
Waltham, MA 02453-8313
Ph: (617)969-7100
Free: 800-225-4276
Fax: (617)969-5979
Co. E-mail: comment@edc.org
URL: http://www.edc.org
Contact: Luther Luedtke, President

Description: Seeks to build bridges among research, policy and practice; programs and products, developed in collaboration with partners worldwide, consistently advance learning and health development for individuals of all ages; manages 335 projects in 50 countries; works to strengthen nearly every facet of society, including early child development, K-12 education, health promotion, workforce preparation, community development, learning technologies, basic and adult education, institutional reform, and social justice. **Scope:** Services include research, training, educational materials and strategy, with activities ranging from seed projects to large-scale national and international initiatives. Specialize in program and fiscal management. Serves to design, deliver and evaluate innovative programs to address some of the world's most urgent challenges in education, health, and economic opportunity. Renders services to U.S. and foreign government agencies, private foundations, healthcare sectors, educational institutions, nonprofit organizations, universities, and corporations. **Founded:** 1958. **Publications:** "A Call to Action: HIV/AIDS, Health, Safety, and the Youth Employment Summit"; "A Case Against "Binge" as the Term of Choice: How to Get College Students to Personalize Messages about Dangerous Drinking"; "A Description of Foundation Skills Interventions for Struggling Middle-Grade Readers in Four Urban Northeast and Islands Region School Districts"; "A Guide to Facilitating Cases in Education"; "A Look at Social, Emotional, and Behavioral Screening Tools for Head Start and Early Head Start"; "A Multifaceted Social Norms Approach to Reduce High-Risk Drinking: Lessons from Hobart and William Smith Colleges"; "The New Media Literacy Handbook"; "Helping Children Outgrow War"; "Worms, Shadows, and Whirlpools: Science in the Early Childhood Classroom"; "Teacher Leadership in Mathematics and Science Casebook and Facilitator's Guide"; "Teachers' Professional Development and the Elementary Mathematics Classroom: Bringing Understandings to Light" **Seminars:** Designed to Introduce the Materials; To Guide Schools Through the Issues. **Telecommunication Services:** contact@edc.org; lluedtke@edc.org.

25996 ■ Effective Compensation Inc. (ECI)
30792 Southview Dr., Ste. 101
Evergreen, CO 80439
Ph: (303)854-1000
Free: 877-746-4324
Fax: (303)854-1030
Co. E-mail: eci@effectivecompensation.com
URL: http://www.effectivecompensation.com
Contact: Terry L. Isselhardt, Chief Executive Officer
E-mail: tisselhardt@effectivecompensation.com

Scope: Independent compensation consulting firm specializing in working with clients on a collaborative basis to improve their organization's efficiency through competitive, focused total compensation processes. Helps organizations determine how to competitively pay their employees. Provides quality, culture sensitive, compensation consulting assistance to all types of employers. Specializes in surveys like drilling industry compensation surveys, environmental industry compensation surveys, liquid pipeline round table compensation surveys; and oil and gas E and P industry compensation surveys. **Founded:** 1991. **Publications:** "Alternative Job Evaluation Approaches"; "Broad Banding: A Management Overview"; "Job Evaluation: Understanding the Issues"; "Industry Compensation Surveys"; "Skill Based Pay"; "Four Levels of Team Membership"; "Factors in Designing an Incentive Plan"; "Key Stock Allocation Issues"; "Stock Plans Primer". **Seminars:** Alternative Job Evaluation Approaches; Broad Banding: A Management Overview; Skill Based Pay; Job Evaluation: Understanding the Issues; Designing Compensation Programs that Motivate Employees; Master the Compensation Maze; Base Salary Administration Manual.

25997 ■ Effective Resources Inc. (ERI)
118 N Peters Rd., Ste. 171
Knoxville, TN 37923
Ph: (865)622-7138
Free: 800-288-6044
Fax: (800)409-2812
Co. E-mail: customerservice@effectiveresources. com
URL: http://www.effectiveresources.com
Contact: Barry L. Brown, Principal
E-mail: barry@effectiveresources.com
Scope: Human resource consulting firm helping clients in all aspects of planning and implementation, to assure the program meets their objectives and budget considerations. Can work with clients on an interim basis or as consultants on short term assignment. Products and services include salary and benefits surveys, employee satisfaction surveys, performance management, compensation administration, compliance assistance and personality profile testing. Specializes in compensation and incentive plans, performance appraisals, team building and personnel policies and procedures, affirmative action plan preparation. **Founded:** 1988. **Special Services:** DiSC® Personality Profile.

25998 ■ Effectiveness Resource Group Inc.
2529 170th Pl. SE
Bellevue, WA 98008-5520
Ph: (206)949-4171
Fax: (425)957-9186
Co. E-mail: don@consultdon.com
Contact: Donald H. Swartz, President
E-mail: dhsergsri@aol.com
Scope: Provider of problem solving help to client organizations in public and private sectors so they can release and mobilize the full potential of their personnel to achieve productive and satisfying results. Emphasis is on technical or human productivity improvement projects and systems, total human resource systems design and implementation, and a whole systems approach to organizational change design and implementation. Serves private industries as well as government agencies. Consults with both internal and external consultants via e-mail and phone. Also offers executive coaching. **Founded:** 1973. **Seminars:** Life/Work Goals Exploration; Influencing Change Thru Consultation; Designing and Leading Participative Meetings; Designing, Leading and Managing Change; Project Management and Leadership; Performance Management; Productive Management of Differences; Performance Correction.

25999 ■ Environmental Health Science Inc.
418 Wall St.
Princeton, NJ 08540
Ph: (609)924-7616
Free: 800-841-8923
Fax: (609)924-0793
Co. E-mail: healthscience@comcast.net
URL: http://www.speechgeneratingdevices.com
Contact: David Goldberg, President
E-mail: davidg@patmedia.net
Scope: Specialists in rehabilitation technology for speech disorder and physically disabled persons. Offers demonstrations, evaluations and sales of the following types of equipment: augmentative speech communication systems, adaptive switches and specialty controls, and computer access devices. Industries served: hospitals and rehabilitation centers, schools, and special service organizations such as United Cerebral Palsy Association, Department of Human Services, etc. **Founded:** 1984. **Publications:** "Play & Learn"; "Bookworm Literacy Tool"; "Meville to Weville". **Seminars:** Augmentative Communication and Assistive Devices. **Special Services:** Boardmaker®; Dynamically Pro®.

26000 ■ Everest Marketing
957 Ashland Ave.
Saint Paul, MN 55104-7019
Ph: (612)581-1333
Fax: (651)221-1978
Contact: Rebecca Aistrup, President
Scope: Provides business-to-business marketing services including marketing plan development, marketing communications, market research and business intelligence. **Founded:** 1993. **Publications:** "Finding and Using Local Market Research To Improve Your Sales"; "Marketing to the Right People at the Right Time"; "Marketing in a Sales-Driven Environment"; "Money Well Spent! (Eight Steps to a successful consulting project)"; "Does this sound like you?"; "Marketing Quickies". **Seminars:** Market Research Basics for Managers; Profiting from Your Customer Database; Developing Your Strategic Marketing Plan from the Ground Up; A Team Process for Developing Your Marketing Plan; Developing a Commercialization Plan for Your SBIR (Small Business Innovation Research)Proposal; Using Marketing Strategies to Jump-Start Your Sales; Marketing in a Sales-Driven Environment and Marketing in a Technology-Driven Environment.

26001 ■ Everett & Co.
3126 S Franklin St.
Englewood, CO 80113
Ph: (303)761-7999
Fax: (303)781-8296
Contact: Robert W. Everett, Manager
Scope: Provides strategic real estate solutions and project management. **Founded:** 1993.

26002 ■ Facility Directions Inc.
PO Box 761
Manchester, MO 63011
Ph: (636)256-4400
Free: 800-536-0044
Fax: (636)227-2868
Co. E-mail: walty@facilitydirections.com
URL: http://www.facilitydirections.com
Contact: Walter E. Yesberg, President
E-mail: walty@facilitydirections.com
Scope: Specializes in service to financial institutions; strategic planning; feasibility studies; facility and space planning; attitude surveys; site selection. **Founded:** 1990.

26003 ■ Family Resource Center on Disabilities (FRCD)
20 E Jackson Blvd., Ste. 300
Chicago, IL 60604-2265
Ph: (312)939-3519
Free: 800-952-4199
Fax: (312)939-7297
Co. E-mail: contact@frcd.org
URL: http://www.frcd.org
Contact: Michelle Phillips, Executive Director
Description: Parents, professionals, and volunteers seeking to improve services for all children with disabilities. Originally organized as a result of the 1969 Illinois law mandating the education of all children with disabilities and operates as a coalition to inform and activate parents. Provides information and referral services, individualized support services for low-income Chicago families, transition services, and special education rights training. **Scope:** Provider of consulting services to advocacy groups and individuals seeking support for children with disabilities. **Founded:** 1969. **Publications:** "How to Get Services By Being Assertive"; "How to Organize an Effective Parent/Advocacy Group and Move Bureaucracies"; "Main roads Travel to Tomorrow - a Road Map for the Future"; "Does Your Child Have Special Education Needs"; "How to Prepare for a Successful Due Process Hearing"; "How to Participate Effectively in Your Child's IEP Meeting"; "Tax Guide for Parents". **Seminars:** How to Support Parents as Effective Advocates; How to Get Services by Being Assertive; How to Develop an Awareness Program for Nondisabled Children; How to Organize a Parent Support Group; How to Move Bureaucratic Mountains; How to Raise Money Painlessly through Publishing; How to Use Humor in Public Presentations. **Telecommunication Services:** frcdptiil@ameritech.net; info@frcd. org.

26004 ■ FCP Consulting
500 Sutter St., Ste. 507
San Francisco, CA 94102-1114
Ph: (415)956-5558
Fax: (415)956-5722
Contact: Cox Ferrall, President
Scope: Management consulting in Business-To-Business sales. **Founded:** 1986.

26005 ■ First Strike Management Consulting Inc.—FSMC Inc.
4001 Loblolly Ave.
Little River, SC 29566-1188
Ph: (843)385-6338
Fax: (843)390-1004
Co. E-mail: info@fsmc.com
URL: http://www.fsmc.com
Contact: J. D. Lewis, Chief Executive Officer
E-mail: jd.lewis@fsmc.com
Scope: Offers proposal management and program management services. Specializes in enterprise systems, management systems, and staff augmentation. Serves the following industries: Nuclear/Fossil Power, Petro-Chemical, Aerospace and Defense, Telecommunications, Engineering and Construction, Information Technology, Golf Course Construction/Management, Utility Engineering/Construction, Civil Works, and Housing Development. **Founded:** 1991. **Publications:** "Project Management for Executives"; "Project Risk Management"; "Project Communications Management"; "Winning Proposals, Four Computer Based Training (CBT) courses"; "Principles of Program Management". **Seminars:** Preparing Winning Proposals in Response to Government RFPs.

26006 ■ Flett Research Ltd.
440 DeSalaberry Ave.
Winnipeg, MB, Canada R2L 0Y7
Ph: (204)667-2505
Fax: (204)667-2505
Co. E-mail: flett@flettresearch.ca
URL: http://www.flettresearch.ca
Contact: Dr. Robert Flett, President
E-mail: flett@flettresearch.ca
Scope: Provider of environmental audits and assessments. Offers contract research and consultation on environmental topics, specializing in limnology, with emphasis in microbiology, bio-geochemistry and radio-chemistry. Performs dating of sediments via Pb-210 and CS-137 methods, to determine sediment accumulation rates in lakes. One of a handful of labs in the world able to carry out total mercury and methyl mercury analyses at the sub-nanogram and L concentration in water. **Founded:** 1978. **Seminars:** Comparison of Two Methods for the Measurement of Methyl Mercury Concentrations in Penobscot River Sediments.

26007 ■ Freese & Associates Inc.
PO Box 814
Chagrin Falls, OH 44022-0814
Ph: (440)564-9183
Fax: (440)564-7339
Co. E-mail: tfreese@freeseinc.com
URL: http://www.freeseinc.com
Contact: Duane L. Hile, Manager
Scope: A management consulting firm offering advice in all forms of business logistics. Consulting services are in the areas of strategic planning; network analysis, site selection, facility layout and design, outsourcing, warehousing, transportation and customer service. Typical projects include 3PL marketing surveys; third party outsourcing selection; operational audits; competitive analysis; inventory management; due diligence; and implementation project management. **Founded:** 1987. **Publications:** "Building Relationships is Key to Motivation," Distribution Center Management, Apr, 2006; "Getting Maximum

Results from Performance Reviews," WERC Sheet, Oct, 2003; "SCM: Making the Vision a Reality," Supply Chain Management Review, Oct, 2003; "Contents Under Pressure," DC Velocity, Aug, 2003; "When Considering Outsourcing, It's Really a Financial Decision," Inventory Management Report, Mar, 2003. **Seminars:** WERC/CAWS Warehousing in China Conference, Sep, 2008; CSCMP Annual Conference, Denver, Oct, 2008; Keys to Retaining and Motivating Your Associates, Dallas, Mar, 2006; The Value and Challenges of Supply Chain Management, Dubai, Feb, 2006; Best Practices in Logistics in China, Jun, 2005; Keys to Motivating Associates, Dallas, May, 2005; The Goal and the Way of International Cooperation in Logistics, Jenobuk, Apr, 2005.

26008 ■ Full Voice
3217 Broadway Ave., Ste. 300
Kansas City, MO 64111
Ph: (816)941-0011
Free: 800-684-8764
Fax: (816)931-8887
Co. E-mail: info@infullvoice.com
URL: http://www.fullvoice.us
Contact: Michienne Dixon, Principal
Scope: Vocal performance training firm offering consulting services and personal training sessions in the implementation of effective vocal communication techniques for the development of business relationships and career enhancement. Formalizes a program of proven techniques into a practical method of helping individuals improve their ability to better present themselves when speaking in a professional situation. Industries served: All. **Founded:** 1992. **Publications:** "You Can Sound Like You Know What You're Saying". **Seminars:** You Can Sound Like You Know What You're Saying; The Psychology of Vocal Performance; Security. . .the Ability to Accept Change; Knowing. . .the Key to Relaxed Public Communication; The Effective Voice for Customer Service Enhancement; You Can Speak With Conviction; How To Make Yours a Championship Team; Functional English For Foreign Trade. **Special Services:** FULL VOICE™.

26009 ■ GEC Consultants Inc.
4604 Birchwood Ave.
Skokie, IL 60076-3835
Ph: (847)674-6310
Fax: (847)674-3946
Co. E-mail: experts@gecconsultants.com
URL: http://www.gecconsultants.com
Contact: Lloyd M. Gordon, President
E-mail: legal@gecconsultants.com
Scope: Consulting in all areas of bar and restaurant operations. Restaurant manager development appraises existing locations or sites. Studies the feasibility of projects. Develop new concepts. Assist in expanding, existing food operations, marketing, expert witness (legal) for hospitality/restaurant industry. **Founded:** 1963. **Publications:** "How You Can Fight Back to Minimize This Recession!"; "New Thoughts On Leases"; "The Use of Job Analysis to Actually Reduce Payroll Costs"; "Do You Need a Feasibility Study?"; "Combat Negative Hospitality"; "How To Run A Successful Night club"; "Are Capitalists In Your Cabinet?"; "Marketing For The 21st Century"; "Profitability In The Banquet Industry"; "Starting a Restaurant, Bar or Catering Business"; "How To Find And Retain Suitable Employees"; "26 Things To Do To Plan A Restaurant"; "Wall Fabric or Paint: Decor Magic It's Your Call"; "The Art of Cafe Ambiance"; "Why You Need A Consultant". **Telecommunication Services:** legal@gecconsultants.com.

26010 ■ Gerson Goodson Inc. (GGI)
2451 McMullen Booth Rd., Ste. 201
Clearwater, FL 33759
Ph: (727)726-7619
Free: 888-237-7424
Fax: (727)726-2406
Co. E-mail: getrich@richgerson.com
URL: http://www.richgerson.com
Contact: Dr. Richard F. Gerson, President
E-mail: richard.gerson@richgerson.com
Scope: Independent consulting firm provides performance management solutions to improve performance and maximize productivity in organizations. Provides assistance to organizations in talent and

performance management, leadership development, selection and hiring practices, employee and customer retention, and customer service. Conducts a systematic needs analysis of the entire marketing, sales and customer service operations of the company. Identifies hidden, neglected and underutilized marketing, sales and customer service assets. **Founded:** 1979. **Publications:** "Winning The Inner Game Of Selling," 1999; "Marketing Strategies for Small Businesses," 1994; "Measuring Customer Satisfaction," 1993; "Beyond Customer Service," 1992; "Achieving High Performance"; "Guaranteeing Performance Improvement"; "The Executive Athlete"; "Positive Performance Improvement". **Seminars:** Marketing Real Estate Services Management Development, Oct, 2007; Presentation Skills, Oct, 2007; From Member Service to Sales, Sep, 2007; Leadership Development, Sep, 2007; The Marketing Difference That Makes The Difference: How To Position Your Company For Rapid Growth Regardless Of The Economy Or The Competition; Growing Your Business With What You Already Have: How To Identify And Profit From The Hidden Marketing Assets That Are Currently Costing You Money; The R Factor In Customer Service: 5Ways To Grow Your Business For Little Or No Cost.

26011 ■ Global Business Consultants (GBC)
200 Lake Hills Rd.
Pinehurst, NC 28374-0776
Ph: (910)295-5991
Fax: (910)295-5991
Co. E-mail: gbc@pinehurst.net
Contact: Nan S. Leaptrott, President
E-mail: nan@yourculturecoach.com
Scope: Firm specializes in human resources management; project management; software development; and international trade. Offers litigation support. **Founded:** 1987. **Publications:** "Culture to Culture: Mission Trip Do's and Don'ts," Jul, 2005; "Rules of the Game: Global Business Protocol". **Seminars:** Cross-Cultural Training.

26012 ■ Global Technology Transfer L.L.C.
1500 Dixie Hwy.
Park Hills, KY 41011-2819
Ph: (859)431-1262
Fax: (859)431-5148
Contact: Anthony Zembrodt, President
Scope: Firm specializes in product development; quality assurance; new product development; and total quality management focusing on household chemical specialties, especially air fresheners. Utilizes latest technology from global resources. Specializes in enhancement products for home and automobile. **Founded:** 1992.

26013 ■ Arnold S. Goldin & Associates Inc.
5030 Champion Blvd., Ste. G-6231
Boca Raton, FL 33496
Ph: (561)994-5810
Fax: (561)994-5860
Co. E-mail: arnold@goldin.com
URL: http://www.goldin.com
Contact: Arnold S. Goldin, Principal
E-mail: arnold@goldin.com
Scope: An accounting and management consulting firm. Serves clients worldwide. Provides management services. Handles monthly write-ups and tax returns. **Founded:** 1978.

26014 ■ Goldore Consulting Inc.
120-5 St. NW, Ste. 1
Linden, AB, Canada T0M 1J0
Ph: (403)546-4208
Fax: (403)546-4208
Co. E-mail: goldore@leadershipessentials.com
Contact: Robert A. Orr, President
E-mail: orr@leadershipessentials.com
Description: Description: Publishes materials on leadership and management skills for churches and charitable organizations that provide services to developing countries. Also publishes in Spanish and Portuguese. Does not accept unsolicited manuscripts. Reaches market through direct mail and wholesalers and distributors, including Leadership Training Ministry Foundation, Inc. **Scope:** Provides consulting service in leadership and management skills. Indus-

tries served: primarily charities, non-profits; some businesses. **Founded:** 1990. **Seminars:** The Challenge Of Leadership.

26015 ■ Great Lakes Consulting Group Inc.
54722 Little Flower Trl.
Mishawaka, IN 46545
Ph: (574)287-4500
Fax: (574)233-2688
Contact: James E. Schrager, President
Scope: Provides consulting services in the areas of strategic planning; feasibility studies; start-up businesses; small business management; mergers and acquisitions; joint ventures; divestitures; interim management; crisis management; turnarounds; business process re-engineering; venture capital; and international trade. **Founded:** 1989.

26016 ■ Great Western Association Management Inc.
7995 E Prentice Ave., Ste. 100
Greenwood Village, CO 80111
Ph: (303)770-2220
Fax: (303)770-1614
Co E-mail: info83@gwami.com
URL: http://www.gwami.com
Contact: Karen M. Wojdyla, President
E-mail: kwojdyla@gwami.com
Scope: Provider of clients with products and services to effectively manage existing and startup, for- and not-for-profit organizations. Clients select from a menu of services including association development and public relations, conferences and seminars, financial management, membership communications, and governance. Expertise also includes association strategic planning, compliance, lobbying, meeting planning, fundraising, marketing and communications. Serves national, regional and state organizations. **Founded:** 1983. **Seminars:** Site selection; Creative program development; Contract negotiations; On-site conference management; Trade show management; Travel and logistics.

26017 ■ Joel Greenstein & Associates (JGA)
6212 Nethercombe Ct.
McLean, VA 22101
Ph: (703)893-1888
Co. E-mail: jgreenstein@contractmasters.com
Contact: Joel Greenstein, Principal
E-mail: jgreenstein@contractmasters.com
Scope: Provides services to minority and women-owned businesses and government agencies. Specializes in interpreting federal, agency-specific acquisition regulations and contract terms and conditions. Offers assistance with preparing technical, cost proposals and sealed bids.

26018 ■ Grief Counseling & Support Services
8600 W Chester Pke., Ste. 304
Upper Darby, PA 19082
Ph: (610)789-7707
Fax: (610)469-9499
Contact: Jeffrey Kauffman, President
E-mail: jkharry@voicenet.com
Scope: Specializing in consulting and training services for organizations dealing with loss, trauma and grief issues. These services may include management consultations, crisis intervention, educational programming, policy development, program design, group process work, individual counseling or other support services. Training and support services also provided for loss issues for mental retardation service providers. Serves private industries as well as government agencies. **Founded:** 1984.

26019 ■ Grimmick Consulting Services (GCS)
455 Donner Way
San Ramon, CA 94582
Ph: (925)735-1036
Fax: (925)735-1100
Co. E-mail: hank@grimmickconsulting.com
URL: http://www.grimmickconsulting.com
Contact: Henry Grimmick, President
E-mail: hank@grimmickconsulting.com
Scope: Provider of consulting services in the areas of strategic planning; organizational assessment; organizational development; leadership and manage-

ment development Baldridge criteria, process improvement and balanced scorecards and team dynamics. **Founded:** 1993.

26020 ■ Harding & Co.
511 Harvard Ave.
Swarthmore, PA 19081
Ph: (610)544-9005
Fax: (973)763-9347
Co. E-mail: fharding@hardingco.com
URL: http://www.hardingco.com
Contact: Mimi Spangler, President
E-mail: mspangler@hardingco.com
Scope: Specializes in sales management, client development and employee training. **Founded:** 1993. **Publications:** "Cross-Selling Success: A Rainmakers Guide to Professional Account Development," Aug, 2002; "Rain Making: The Professional's Guide to Attracting New Clients"; "Creating Rainmakers: The Managers Guide to Training Professionals to Attract New Clients". **Telecommunication Services:** mspangler@hardingco.com.

26021 ■ Health Strategy Group Inc.
46 River Rd.
Chatham, NY 12037
Ph: (518)392-6770
Contact: Cameron Battley, President
Scope: Provides consulting services in the areas of strategic planning, feasibility studies, start-up businesses, organizational development, market research, customer service audits, new product development, marketing, public relations. **Founded:** 1981. **Publications:** "Online Consumer Surveys as a Methodology for Assessing the Quality of the United States Health Care System," 2004.

26022 ■ Hewitt Development Enterprises (HDE)
1717 N Bayshore Dr., Ste. 2154
Miami, FL 33132
Ph: (305)372-0941
Fax: (305)372-0941
Co. E-mail: info@hewittdevelopment.com
URL: http://www.hewittdevelopment.com
Contact: Robert G. Hewitt, Principal
E-mail: bob@hewittdevelopment.com
Scope: Specializes in strategic planning; profit enhancement; start-up businesses; interim management; crisis management; turnarounds; production planning; just-in-time inventory management; and project management. Serves senior management (CEOs, CFOs, division presidents, etc.) and acquirers of distressed businesses. **Founded:** 1985.

26023 ■ Hickey & Hill Inc.
1009 Oak Hill Rd., Ste. 201
Lafayette, CA 94549-3812
Ph: (925)906-5331
Contact: Edwin L. Hill, Chief Executive Officer
Scope: Firm provides management consulting services to companies in financial distress. Expertise area: Corporate restructuring and turnaround. **Founded:** 1984.

26024 ■ hightechbiz.com—Leahy & Associates Inc.
4209 Santa Monica Blvd., Ste. 201
Los Angeles, CA 90029-3027
Ph: (323)913-3355
Free: 877-648-4753
Fax: (323)913-3355
URL: http://www.hightechbiz.com
Contact: Steven L. Hayes, Principal
Scope: A full service marketing agency specializing in integrated marketing solutions. Services include: marketing surveys; positioning surveys; strategic and tactical plans; implementation plans; management consulting; product brochures; product catalogs; product packaging; product data sheets; direct mail programs; media research; competitive research; complete creative; production and film; media placement; corporate identity; in-house creative; public relations. **Founded:** 1980.

26025 ■ Hills Consulting Group Inc.
6 Partridge Ct.
Novato, CA 94945-1315

Ph: (415)898-3944
Contact: Michael R. Hills, President
Scope: Specializes in strategic planning; marketing surveys; market research; customer service audits; new product development; competitive analysis; and sales forecasting. **Founded:** 1985.

26026 ■ Holt Capital
1916 Pike Pl., Ste. 12-344
Seattle, WA 98101
Ph: (206)484-0403
Fax: (206)789-8034
Co. E-mail: info@holtcapital.com
URL: http://www.holtcapital.com
Contact: Marilyn J. Holt, Chief Executive Officer
E-mail: mjholt@holtcapital.com
Scope: Registered investment advisory firm. Services include: Debt planning, private equity, mergers, divestitures and acquisitions, transaction support services. Connects companies with capital. **Founded:** 1980. **Publications:** "Early Sales Key to Early-Stage Funding"; "Financial Transactions: Who Should Be At Your Table"; "Get the Deal Done: The Four Keys to Successful Mergers and Acquisitions"; "Is Your First Paragraph a Turn-off"; "Bubble Rubble: Bridging the Price Gap for an Early-Stage Business"; "Are You Ready For The new Economy"; "Could I Get Money or Jail Time With That The Sarbanes-Oxley Act Of 2002 gives early-stage companies More Risks". **Seminars:** Attracting Private Investors; Five Proven Ways to Finance Your Company; How to Get VC Financing; Venture Packaging; How to Finance Company Expansion.

26027 ■ Hornberger & Associates (H&A)
1966 Lombard St.
San Francisco, CA 94123
Ph: (415)346-2106
Fax: (415)346-9993
Co. E-mail: info@hornbergerassociates.com
URL: http://www.hornbergerassociates.com
Contact: Deborah Hornberger, President
E-mail: deborah@hornbergerassociates.com
Scope: Specialized services include wealth management, retirement programs, small business banking, personal trust, investment management, brokerage services, mutual funds, relationship management, private banking and employee banking. Help clients by offering strategic marketing plans, market segmentation/niche marketing, website strategies and development; product development and introduction; client communications; product, sales and referral training; client retention programs and project management. **Founded:** 1992. **Publications:** "Establishing a Mini-trust Product," Bank Marketing, Oct, 1997. **Seminars:** Building a Marketing Plan Directed at Emerging Wealth Baby Boomers, Strategy Institute conference, Jun, 1999.

26028 ■ Human Resource Specialties Inc.
3 Monroe Pky., Ste. 900
Lake Oswego, OR 97035
Ph: (503)697-3329
Free: 800-354-3512
Fax: (503)636-1594
Co. E-mail: info@hrspecialties.com
URL: http://www.hrspecialties.com
Contact: Sandy Henderson, President
E-mail: sandyh@hrspecialties.com
Scope: Provider of human resources assistance to organizations. Offers preparation of affirmative action plans, support documents, and adverse impact studies of personnel activities. Also offers customized consultations in small business services, diversity and discrimination, and investigations, complaints and grievances. Provides investigations, including allegations of unfair treatment, equal employment opportunity (EEO) and racial or sexual harassment. Offers customized web-based training (webinars) on a variety of HR, EEO and AAP-related topics. **Founded:** 1984.

26029 ■ I.H.R. Solutions
3333 E Bayaud Ave., Ste. 219
Denver, CO 80209
Ph: (303)588-4243

Fax: (303)978-0473
Co. E-mail: dhollands@ihrsolutions.com
Contact: Deborah Hollands, Owner
E-mail: dhollands@ihrsolutions.com
Scope: Provides joint-venture and start-up human resource consulting services as well as advice on organization development for international human capital. Industries served: high-tech and telecommunications. **Founded:** 1997.

26030 ■ IMC Consulting & Training
901 McHenry Ave., Ste. A
Modesto, CA 95350
Ph: (209)572-2271
Fax: (209)572-2862
Co. E-mail: info@imc-1.net
URL: http://www.imc-1.net
Contact: Michael J. Loschke, President
E-mail: michael@imc-1.net
Scope: Helps businesses and professionals identify, develop and market their selling proposition to increase profits. Services include B-to-B surveys, direct marketing, media relations, planning and strategy, sales management, training and leadership coaching. **Founded:** 1994. **Publications:** "Consultant Earns Advanced Certificate," Hccsc Business Review, Dec, 2004; "Adapting to Change - the New Competitive Advantage," Business Journal, Jul, 2004; "Loyalty Marketing Can Divide New Business," Jun, 2004; "Eleven Major Marketing Mistakes," Jul, 2003; "Planning to Win or Racing to Fail," Jun, 2003. **Seminars:** Negotiating High Profit Sales; How to Write Winning Proposals, Modesto Chamber of Commerce, Oct, 2007; Winning the 2nd Half: A 6-month Plan to Score New Customers and Profits. **Telecommunication Services:** imcinfo@imc-1.net.

26031 ■ In Plain English—R.H. Wohl & Associates Inc.
14501 Antigone Dr.
Gaithersburg, MD 20885-3300
Ph: (301)340-2821
Free: 800-274-9645
Fax: (301)279-0115
Co. E-mail: rwohl@inplainenglish.com
URL: http://www.inplainenglish.com
Contact: Ronald H. Wohl, President
E-mail: rwohl@inplainenglish.com
Scope: Management consultants helping government and businesses research, design, write and produce user oriented management information for human resources, employee benefits, business process, corporate and marketing needs. Services include: GSA mob is schedule for consulting to the government; employee benefit communications, plain English business writing workshops for print and electronic media; communicating strategy and tactics; marketing research, business planning and communications; readability testing; usability testing and monitoring strategy. **Founded:** 1977. **Publications:** "The Benefits Communication"; "The Employee Benefits Communication ToolKit," Commerce Clearinghouse; "Benefits Communication," Business and Legal Reports. **Seminars:** Plain English Writing Training; Summary Plan Description Compliance workshops; Re-Humanizing the Corporation, Human Resources and Employee Benefits Communication Workshop; 21 Writing Tips for the 21st Century; Make the Write Impression; Writing to Inform and Instruct; The Dreaded Nuts and Bolts; Writing to Persuade; Writing Policy and Procedure Manuals In Plain English; Writing for Accountants and Auditors In Plain English. **Special Services:** In Plain English®.

26032 ■ Innovative Scientific Analysis & Computing (ISAac)
6168 Flagstaff Rd.
Boulder, CO 80302
Ph: (303)440-7673
Fax: (303)545-6674
Co. E-mail: ros5e@isaac.com
URL: http://www.ros5e.com
Contact: Charlie E. Rose, President
E-mail: ros5e@isaac.com
Scope: Engineering services includes mathematical analysis specializing in optimal estimation, scientific programming, and database design and development, data encryption and security. **Founded:** 1993.

26033 ■ The Institute for Management Excellence
PO Box 5459
Lacey, WA 98509-5459
Ph: (360)412-0404
Co. E-mail: pwoc@itstime.com
URL: http://www.itstime.com
Contact: Michael Anthony, Director
Scope: Management consulting and training focuses on improving productivity, using practices and creative techniques. Practices based on the company's theme: It's time for new ways of doing business. Industries served: public sector, law enforcement, finance or banking, non profit, computers or high technology, education, human resources, utilities. **Founded:** 1995. **Publications:** "Income Without a Job," 2008; "The Other Side of Midnight, 2000: An Executive Guide to the Year 2000 Problem"; "Concordance to the Michael Teachings"; "Handbook of Small Business Advertising"; "The Personality Game"; "How to Market Yourself for Success". **Seminars:** The Personality Game; Power Path Seminars; Productivity Plus; Sexual Harassment and Discrimination Prevention; Worker's Comp Cost Reduction; Americans with Disabilities Act; In Search of Identify: Clarifying Corporate Culture.

26034 ■ Institute of Public Administration (IPA)
295 Lafayette St., Fl. 2
New York, NY 10003
Ph: (212)992-9898
Free: 800-258-1102
Fax: (212)995-4876
Co. E-mail: p553@nyu.edu
URL: http://www.theipa.org
Contact: David Mammen, President
Scope: Provider of consulting and research services. It serves local, state and federal governments, international aid agencies, and foreign governments. **Founded:** 1906. **Publications:** "Local Governance Approach to Social Reintegration and Economic Recovery in Post Conflict Countries: The Political Context for Programs of UNDP/UNCDF Assistance"; "Local Governance Approach to Social Reintegration and Economic Recovery in Post Conflict Countries: Programming Options for UNDP/UNCDF Assistance"; "Local Governance Approach to Social Reintegration and Economic Recovery in Post Conflict Countries: The View from Mozambique"; "Local Governance Approach to Social Reintegration and Economic Recovery in Post Conflict Countries: Towards a Definition and a Rationale"; "Local Governance Approach to Post Conflict Recovery: Perspective from Cambodia"; "The Sustainable Human Development Strategy: A Proposal for Post Conflict Recovery Societies"; "Local Governance Approach to Post Conflict Recovery: Proceedings Report on the Workshop Organized by the Institute of Public Administration". **Seminars:** A Local Governance Approach to Post Conflict Recovery.

26035 ■ Interminds & Federer Resources Inc.
106 E 6th St., Ste. 310
Austin, TX 78701-3659
Ph: (512)476-8800
Fax: (512)476-8811
Co. E-mail: yesyoucan@interminds.com
URL: http://www.interminds.com
Contact: Frank Federer, President
E-mail: ffederer@integra100.com
Scope: Specializes in feasibility studies, startup businesses; small business management; mergers and acquisitions; joint ventures; divestitures; interim management; crisis management; turnarounds; production planning; team building; appraisals and valuations. **Founded:** 1985. **Publications:** "Yes You Can: How To Be A Success No Matter Who You Are Or Where You're From".

26036 ■ Interpersonal Coaching & Consulting (ICC)
1516 W Lake St., Ste. 2000S
Minneapolis, MN 55408
Ph: (612)381-2494

Fax: (612)381-2494
Co. E-mail: mail@interpersonal-coaching.com
URL: http://www.interpersonal-coaching.com
Contact: Mary Belfry, Partner
Scope: Provider of coaching and consulting to businesses and organizations. Assesses the interpersonal workplace through interviews, assessment instruments and individual group settings. Experienced as a therapist for over a decade. **Publications:** "Sexual Harassment In The Workplace For Newspapers". **Seminars:** More On Relationships; Sexual harassment and discrimination issues.

26037 ■ Invent Resources Inc. (IRI)
PO Box 548
Lexington, MA 02420-0005
Ph: (781)862-0200
Fax: (781)721-2300
Co. E-mail: pavelle@comcast.net
URL: http://www.weinvent.com
Contact: Dr. Richard Pavelle, President
E-mail: pavelle@comcast.net
Scope: Provider of consultancy services to provide support in developing and prototyping new, proprietary products. Offer inventory services on demand. Assist clients who need innovations in product lines, have hit technical bottlenecks, or need improvements in manufacturing processes. Provide assistance to individuals and clients in obtaining, reviewing, and strengthening patents. **Founded:** 1991. **Telecommunication Services:** rp@theworld.com.

26038 ■ Jest for the Health of It Services
PO Box 8484
Santa Cruz, CA 95061-8484
Ph: (831)425-8436
Fax: (831)425-8437
Co. E-mail: pwooten@jesthealth.com
URL: http://www.jesthealth.com
Contact: Shirley Trout, Manager
E-mail: strout@nurseswhostay.com
Scope: Develops and presents seminars, keynotes and skill shops about the power of humor. Provides consulting services for development of humor rooms and comedy carts in hospitals. Conducts training for clowns to make visits in hospitals and nursing homes. Industries served: health professionals and businesses wishing to educate staff about healthy lifestyle choices. **Founded:** 1982. **Publications:** "Heart Humor and Healing"; "Compassionate Laughter: Jest for Your Health"; "The Hospital Clown: A Closer Look"; "Humor: An Antidote for Stress"; "Humor, Laughter and Play: Maintaining Balance in a Serious World"; "You've Got to Be Kidding: Humor Skills for Surviving Managed Care"; "Laughter as Therapy for Patient and Caregiver"; "Patty Wooten: Nurse Healer"; "Humor: An antidote for stress".

26039 ■ Johnston Co.
78 Bedford St.
Lexington, MA 02420
Ph: (781)862-7595
Fax: (781)862-9066
Co. E-mail: info@johnstoncompany.com
URL: http://www.johnstoncompany.com
Contact: Claire Sehringer, Manager
Scope: Specializes in management audits and reports; start-up businesses; small business management; mergers and acquisitions; joint ventures; divestitures; interim management; crisis management; turnarounds; cost controls; financing; venture capital; controller services; financial management, strategic and advisory services. **Founded:** 1987. **Publications:** "Why are board meetings such a waste of time," Boston Business Journal, Apr, 2004.

26040 ■ K & T Training—K & T Consulting
103 Greenville St.
Newnan, GA 30263
Ph: (770)253-5870
Fax: (770)253-8866
Contact: J. R. Tumperi, President
Scope: Specializes in strategic planning; profit enhancement; organizational development; start-up businesses; interim management; crisis management; turnarounds; business process re-engineering; team building; cost controls. **Founded:** 1983.

26041 ■ Keiei Senryaku Corp.
19191 S Vermont Ave., Ste. 530
Torrance, CA 90502-1049
Ph: (310)366-3331
Free: 800-951-8780
Fax: (310)366-3330
Co. E-mail: takenakaes@earthlink.net
Contact: Kurt Miyamoto, President
Scope: Offers consulting services in the areas of strategic planning; feasibility studies; profit enhancement; organizational development; start-up businesses; mergers and acquisitions; joint ventures; divestitures; executive searches; sales management; and competitive analysis. **Founded:** 1989.

26042 ■ Koch Group Inc.
129 Fairfield Way, Ste. 219
Bloomingdale, IL 60108
Ph: (630)941-1100
Free: 800-470-7845
Fax: (630)941-3865
Co. E-mail: info@kochgroup.com
URL: http://www.kochgroup.com
Contact: Peter Koch, Manager
Scope: Provider of industrial marketing consulting services to small to mid-sized manufacturers. Primary assistance includes industrial market research and analysis, identification of potential markets, strategic planning and plan implementation, market planning, sales analysis, competitor analysis. Specializes in assisting manufacturers identify, recruit, and manage agents and reps and developing website for business promotion. **Founded:** 1967. **Seminars:** Niche Marketing; Regional Industrial Association Recruiting; Strategic Marketing for Manufacturers; Strategic Marketing; How To Identify, Screen, Interview and Select High Quality Agents; Basics of Industrial Market Research; Elements of Industrial Marketing; Trade Adjustment Assistance For Firms; Developing New Business; Selecting An Industrial Web Site Developer; Strategic Selling; Pick Your Customer; Strategic and Tactical Marketing.

26043 ■ Kostka & Company Inc.
9 Wild Rose Ct.
Cromwell, CT 06416
Ph: (860)257-1045
Contact: Peter Kostka, Managing Partner
E-mail: peterpk@gmail.com
Scope: Areas of expertise: management consulting, global technology sourcing, complex project management, SKU management and new product introduction, application development, medical point-of-sale, multi-touch user interface, made-to-order management systems and Smartphone ERP connectivity. Clients include global fortune 500 companies as well as small and medium-sized businesses and startups. **Founded:** 1994.

26044 ■ Kubba Consultants Inc.
1255 Montgomery Dr.
Deerfield, IL 60015
Ph: (847)867-0874
URL: http://www.kubbainc.com
Contact: Ed Kubba, President
E-mail: edkubba@aol.com
Scope: Industrial and business-to-business marketing research and consulting. Services include new product research, new market evaluation, competitor analysis and customer value analysis. **Founded:** 1987.

26045 ■ William E. Kuhn & Associates
234 Cook St.
Denver, CO 80206-5305
Ph: (303)322-8233
Fax: (303)331-9032
Co. E-mail: billkuhn1@cs.com
Contact: William E. Kuhn, Owner
E-mail: billkuhn1@cs.com
Scope: Firm specializes in strategic planning; profit enhancement; small business management; mergers and acquisitions; joint ventures; divestitures; human resources management; performance appraisals; team building; sales management; appraisals and valuations. **Founded:** 1980. **Publications:** "Creating a High-Performance Dealership," Office SOLUTIONS & Office DEALER, Jul-Aug, 2006.

26046 ■ L G Anthony Associates
40 Wellington Blvd.
Reading, PA 19610
Ph: (610)670-0477
Contact: Louis G. Anthony, Owner
Scope: Provides food service facility planning, layout and design, including equipment selection and specification. Also offers management systems and operations analysis, such as the development of operating policies and procedures. Firm can design menu planning and recipe development, food selection and specification, work simplification, service, and quality control around current concepts in the field. Industries served: hospital, nursing home, restaurant, group homes; commercial and institutional food service industries. **Founded:** 1986. **Seminars:** Food Service Sanitation; Menu Planning; Work Simplification; Quality Control in Food Service.

26047 ■ Liberty Business Strategies Ltd.
The Times Bldg., Ste. 400, Suburban Sq.
Ardmore, PA 19003
Ph: (610)649-3800
Fax: (610)649-0408
Co. E-mail: info@libertystrategies.com
URL: http://www.libertystrategies.com
Contact: Emmy S. Miller, President
E-mail: emmym@libertystrategies.com
Scope: Management consulting firm working with clients to gain speed and agility in driving their business strategy. The consulting model builds the alignment of strategy, organization commitment, and technology. Provides senior leader coaching and team development coaching. **Founded:** 1980. **Seminars:** Winning with Talent, Morison Annual Conference, Jul, 2009.

26048 ■ Linda Lipsky Restaurant Consultants Inc.
216 Foxcroft Rd.
Broomall, PA 19008-2039
Ph: (610)325-3663
Free: 877-425-3663
Fax: (610)325-3329
Co. E-mail: lipsky@restaurantconsult.com
URL: http://www.restaurantconsult.com
Contact: Linda J. Lipsky, President
E-mail: lipsky@restaurantconsult.com
Scope: Provider of marketing and survey solutions. It offers management training and evaluation programs, recipe documentation, cost analysis, and bridge management services. **Founded:** 1988. **Seminars:** Designing Menus for Maximum Sales and Profits; How to Maximize Your Check Average; Going Beyond Your Customer's Expectations; Seeing Your Restaurant Through a Customer's Eyes; Making the Best First and Last Impression; Basic Training in Kitchen Management Techniques; Basic Training in Bar Management Techniques; Make Every Labor Dollar Count; Back to Basics/More Than Shift Management; Conducting Your Own In-House Inspection; Basics of Sanitation Training for Kitchen Employees; Basics of Sanitation Training for Dining Room Employees.

26049 ■ May Toy Lukens
3226 NE 26th Ct.
Renton, WA 98056
Ph: (425)891-3226
Contact: May T. Lukens, Principal
Scope: Provides training to teach people to think of ways to improve their operations continuously by changing the way they think. Industries served: All, particularly financial. Operational analysis and training. **Founded:** 1996. **Seminars:** Seminars and workshops in maximizing resource utilization and staff potential.

26050 ■ Lupfer & Associates (L&A)
92 Glen St.
Natick, MA 01760-5646
Ph: (508)655-3950
Fax: (508)655-7826
Co. E-mail: donlupfer@aol.com
Contact: Donald Lupfer, Owner
E-mail: don.lupfer@lupferassociates.com
Scope: Assists off shore hi-tech companies in entering United States markets and specializes in channel development for all sorts of products. Perform MARCOM support for hi-tech United States clients.

Founded: 1988. **Publications:** "What's Next For Distribution-Feast or Famine"; "The Changing Global Marketplace"; "Making Global Distribution Work". **Seminars:** How to do Business in the United States.

26051 ■ Management Resource Partners
181 2nd Ave., Ste. 542
San Mateo, CA 94401
Ph: (650)401-5850
Fax: (650)401-5850
Contact: John C. Roberts, Owner
Scope: Firm specializes in strategic planning; small business management; mergers and acquisitions; joint ventures; divestitures; interim management; crisis management; turn around; venture capital; appraisals and valuations. **Founded:** 1981.

26052 ■ Management Strategies
1000 S Old Woodward Ave., Ste. 105
Birmingham, MI 48009
Ph: (248)258-2756
Fax: (248)258-3407
Co. E-mail: bob@hois.com
Contact: Robert E. Hoisington, President
E-mail: bob@hois.com
Scope: Firm specializes in strategic planning; feasibility studies; profit enhancement; organizational studies; start up businesses; turnarounds; business process re engineering; industrial engineering; marketing; ecommerce. **Founded:** 1985.

26053 ■ Marketing Leverage Inc.
2022 Laurel Oak Ln.
Palm City, FL 34990
Ph: (772)878-6495
Free: 800-633-1422
Fax: (772)659-8664
Co. E-mail: lkelly@marketingleverage.com
Contact: Lynn C. Kelly, President
E-mail: lkelly@marketingleverage.com
Scope: Consulting and research firm focusing on the targeting, retention and satisfaction of customers. Consulting is offered for due diligence; marketing and customer retention strategy; program design and implementation. Research services offered help clients determine service improvements that increase customer loyalty; boosting sales through better understanding buyer motivations; increasing the odds of product acceptance through new product concept testing; and improving the effectiveness of advertising, collateral, publications through audience evaluation. Clients include top financial services, insurance, health care, technology and management services organizations. **Founded:** 1987. **Publications:** "Creating Strategic Leverage"; "Exploring Corporate Strategy"; "Competitive Advantage"; "Breakpoint and Beyond "; "Competitive Strategy ". **Seminars:** Best Practices in Brainstorming; Getting Results in the Real World; Finding the Leverage in Your Customer Strategy; The Role of Communications in Building Customer Loyalty; Building a Customer Centered Relationship and Making it Pay. **Special Services:** The Marketing Leverage Win/Loss Tracking System™.

26054 ■ McCreight & Company Inc.
36 Grove St.
New Canaan, CT 06840
Ph: (203)801-5000
Fax: (866)646-8339
Co. E-mail: roc@implementstrategy.com
URL: http://www.implementstrategy.com
Contact: John A. McCreight, President
E-mail: jmc@implementstrategy.com
Scope: Assist the global clients with strategy implementation involving large scale change, including mergers, divestitures, alliances and new business launches. **Founded:** 1983. **Publications:** "The Board's Role in Strengthening M and A Success," Boardroom Briefing, 2008; "Creating the Future," Ask Magazine, 2007; "Strategy Implementation Insights," Mccreight and Company Inc, Oct, 2007; "Sustaining Growth," Deloitte and Ct Technology Council, Jul, 2006; "A Four Phase Approach to Succession Planning," Southern Connecticut Newspapers Inc, 2005. **Seminars:** Successful Mergers and Acquisitions-An Implementation Guide; Global 100One-Face-to-the-Customer; Implementation of Strategic Change.

26055 ■ McDonald Consulting Group Inc.
1900 W Park Dr., Ste. 280
Westborough, MA 01581
Co. E-mail: info@mcdonaldconsultinggroup.com
URL: http://www.mcdonaldconsultinggroup.com
Contact: Ron A. McDonald, President
E-mail: rmcdonald@mcdonaldconsultinggroup.com
Scope: A management consulting firm specializing in assisting insurance companies improve operations. Provides services in the areas of strategic planning; profit enhancement; organizational development; interim management; crisis management; turnarounds; business process re-engineering; benefits and compensation planning and total quality management. **Founded:** 1993. **Publications:** "Improving Customer Focus through Organizational Structure," AASCIF News; "Changing Strategies in Hard Markets," The National Underwriter; "Moving Beyond Management 101: Postgraduate Time Management for Executives," The National Underwriter; "A New Attitude: 3 Clients Improved Results Through Our Fundamental Change Process," Bests Review; "How to Organize Your Company Around Your Customers," Bests Review. **Seminars:** How to establish "expense allowable"; How to design an incentive compensation plan around a units core success measures.

26056 ■ McShane Group Inc.
2345 York Rd., Ste. 102
Timonium, MD 21093
Ph: (410)560-0077
Fax: (410)560-2718
Co. E-mail: tmcshane@mcshanegroup.com
URL: http://www.mcshanegroup.com
Contact: Thomas P. McShane, President
E-mail: tmcshane@mcshanegroup.com
Scope: Turnaround consulting and crisis management firm. Specializes in due diligence services, interim management, strategic business realignments, business sale and asset depositions and debt restructuring. Industries served: technology, financial, retail, distribution, medical, educational, manufacturing, contracting, environmental and health care. **Founded:** 1987.

26057 ■ Medical Imaging Consultants Inc. (MIC)
1037 US Highway 46, Ste. G-2
Clifton, NJ 07013-2445
Ph: (973)574-8000
Free: 800-589-5685
Fax: (973)574-8001
Co. E-mail: info@micinfo.com
URL: http://www.micinfo.com
Contact: Dr. Philip A. Femano, President
E-mail: phil@micinfo.com
Scope: Provider of professional support services for radiology management and comprehensive continuing education programs for radiologic technologists. Management services include resource-critical database logistics; customer registration in educational programs; educational program development and Category A accreditation; national agency notification (e.g., ASRT, SNM-TS) of CE credits earned; meeting planning; manpower assessment; market research; expert witness; think-tank probes and executive summaries of industry issues. **Founded:** 1991. **Seminars:** Sectional Anatomy and Imaging Strategies; CT Cross-Trainer; CT Registry Review Program; MR Cross Trainer; MRI Registry Review Program; Digital Mammography Essentials for Technologists; Radiology Trends for Technologists.

26058 ■ Medical Outcomes Management Inc.
132 Central St., Ste. 215
Foxborough, MA 02035-2422
Ph: (508)543-0050
Fax: (508)543-1919
Co. E-mail: info@mom-inc.com
Contact: Alan F. Kaul, President
E-mail: alan@mom-inc.com
Scope: Management and technology consulting firm providing a specially focused group of services such as disease management programs and pharmacoeconomic studies. Services include clinical and educational projects, medical writing and editing, marketing and sales projects, disease registries,

educational seminars, strategic planning projects, managed care organizations; and pharmaceutical and biotechnology companies. **Founded:** 1991. **Publications:** "Treatment of acute exacerbation's of chronic bronchitis in patients with chronic obstructive pulmonary disease: A retrospective cohort analysis logarithmically extended release vs. Azithromycin," 2003; "A retrospective analysis of cyclooxygenase-II inhibitor response patterns," 2002; "DUE criteria for use of regional urokinase infusion for deep vein thrombosis,"2002; "The formulary management system and decision-making process at Horizon Blue Cross Blue Shield of New Jersey," Pharmaco therapy, 2001. **Seminars:** Economic Modeling as a Disease Management Tool, Academy of Managed Care Pharmacy, Apr, 2005; Integrating Disease State Management and Economics, Academy of Managed Care Pharmacy, Oct, 2004; Clinical and economic outcomes in the treatment of peripheral occlusive diseases, Mar, 2003.

26059 ■ Mefford, Knutson & Associates Inc. (MK)
6437 Lyndale Ave. S, Ste. 103
Richfield, MN 55423-1465
Ph: (612)869-8011
Free: 800-831-0228
Fax: (612)869-8004
Co. E-mail: info@mkaonline.net
URL: http://www.mkaonline.net
Contact: Jeanette Mefford, Director
E-mail: jmefford@mkaonline.com
Scope: A consulting and licensed business brokerage firm specializing in start-up businesses; strategic planning; mergers and acquisitions; joint ventures; divestitures; business process re-engineering; personnel policies and procedures; market research; new product development and cost controls. **Founded:** 1990.

26060 ■ Harvey A. Meier Co. (HAM)
410 W Nevada St.
Ashland, OR 97520-1043
Ph: (509)458-3210
Fax: (541)488-7905
Co. E-mail: harvey@harveymeier.com
URL: http://www.harveymeier.com
Contact: Dr. Harvey A. Meier, President
E-mail: harvey@harveymeier.com
Scope: Provider of service to chief executive officers and board of directors. Specializes in interim management, strategic planning, financial planning and organization governance. **Publications:** "The D'Artagnan Way".

26061 ■ Midwest Computer Group L.L.C. (MCG)
6060 Franks Rd.
House Springs, MO 63051
Ph: (314)954-1222
Co. E-mail: sales@mcgcomputer.com
URL: http://www.mcgcomputer.com
Contact: Leon Sanford, Jr., President
E-mail: leonjr@mcgcomputer.com
Scope: Specializes in helping businesses create accounting, marketing and business information systems; software development and database design and management. **Founded:** 1980.

26062 ■ Midwest Research Institute (MRI)
425 Volker Blvd.
Kansas City, MO 64110-2241
Ph: (816)753-7600
Fax: (816)753-8420
Co. E-mail: info@mriresearch.org
URL: http://www.mriresearch.org
Contact: James L. Spigarelli, President
Scope: Independent not-for-profit research institute offering scientific services in the areas of national defense, health sciences, agriculture and food safety, engineering, energy, and infrastructure. Services include biomedical electronics, remote sensing, automation and control electromagnetic radiation, environmental sampling and analysis programs for industry and government, program management, engineering studies, exposure and risk assessment, waste management strategies, contaminant identification, pollution prevention, and waste minimization. Expertise in highway safety/accident analysis, ch-

emometrics/pattern recognition/neural networks, statistical support, process and product engineering. **Founded:** 1943. **Telecommunication Services:** bduncan@mriresearch.org.

26063 ■ Miller, Hellwig Associates
150 W End Ave.
New York, NY 10023-5713
Ph: (212)799-0471
Fax: (212)877-0186
Co. E-mail: millerhelwig@earthlink.net
Contact: Ernest C. Miller, President
Scope: Consulting services in the areas of start-up businesses; small business management; employee surveys and communication; performance appraisals; executive searches; team building; personnel policies and procedures; market research. Also involved in improving cross-cultural and multi-cultural relationships, particularly with Japanese clients. **Founded:** 1984. **Seminars:** Objectives and standards/recruiting for boards of directors.

26064 ■ R.E. Moulton Inc.
50 Doaks Ln.
Marblehead, MA 01945
Ph: (781)631-1325
Fax: (781)631-2165
Co. E-mail: mike_lee@remoultoninc.com
URL: http://www.oneamerica.com/wps/wcm/connect/REMoulton
Contact: Willard A. Knarr, Jr., President
Scope: Offers underwriting services, marketing solutions, claims administration and adjudication; policy and commission administration; and risk management solutions to clients. Supplementary service s include risk management and employee assistance. Clients include individuals, business men, employers and finance professionals. **Founded:** 1976.

26065 ■ Murray Dropkin & Associates—Dropkin Consulting
390 George St.
New Brunswick, NJ 08901
Ph: (732)828-3211
Fax: (732)828-4118
Co. E-mail: murray@dropkin.com
URL: http://www.dropkin.com
Contact: Murray Dropkin, President
E-mail: murray@dropkin.com
Scope: Specializes in feasibility studies; business management; business process re-engineering; and team building, health care and housing. **Founded:** 1969. **Publications:** "Bookkeeping for Nonprofits," Jossey Bass, 2005; "Guide to Audits of Nonprofit Organizations," PPC; "The Nonprofit Report," Warren, Gorham & Lamont; "The Budget Building Book for Nonprofits," Jossey-Bass; "The Cash Flow Management Book for Nonprofits," Jossey-Bass.

26066 ■ National Center for Public Policy Research (NCPPR)
501 Capitol Ct. NE
Washington, DC 20002
Ph: (202)543-4110
Fax: (202)543-5975
Co. E-mail: info@nationalcenter.org
URL: http://www.nationalcenter.org
Contact: Amy Moritz Ridenour, President
E-mail: aridenour@nationalcenter.org
Description: Educates the public about public policy issues. Conducts research; distributes national policy analysis papers, memorandums, brochures, newsletters, article reprints, and other materials to the public, libraries, and the media. **Scope:** A communications and research nonprofit organization offering advice and information on international affairs and United States domestic affairs. Sponsors Project 21. Gives special emphasis an environmental and regulatory issues and civil rights issues. **Founded:** 1982. **Publications:** "National Policy Analysis"; "Legal Briefs"; "White Paper: National Policy Analysis 523"; "Shattered Dreams: One Hundred Stories of Government Abuse"; "Shattered Lives: 100 Victims of Government Health Care".

26067 ■ Navarro, Kim & Associates
529 N Charles St., Ste. 202
Baltimore, MD 21201-5043
Ph: (410)837-6317

Fax: (410)837-6294
Co. E-mail: bnavarro@sprynet.com
Contact: Beltran Navarro, Director
E-mail: bnavarro@sprynet.com
Scope: Specializes in bridging the gap between firms and non-traditional ethnic communities, especially in community development and institutional building. **Founded:** 1984.

26068 ■ New Commons
545 Pawtucket Ave., Studio 106A
Pawtucket, RI 02860
Ph: (401)351-7110
Fax: (401)351-7158
Co. E-mail: info@newcommons.com
URL: http://www.newcommons.com
Contact: Robert Leaver, Chief Executive Officer
E-mail: rleaver@newcommons.com
Scope: Builder of agile human networks to champion innovation and mobilize change; to pursue business opportunities; to custom design agile organizations and communities, to foster civic engagement. Clients include organizations on-profits, corporations, government agencies, educational institutions; networks-Trade/professional groups, IT services collaborations, service-sharing collectives; and communities- municipalities, states and statewide agencies, regional collaborations. **Founded:** 1982. **Publications:** "Plexus Imperative," Sep, 2005; "Creating 21st Century Capable Innovation Systems," Aug, 2004; "Call to Action: Building Providences Creative and Innovative Economy"; "Getting Results from Meetings"; "The Entrepreneur as Artist," Commonwealth Publications; "Leader and Agent of Change," Commonwealth Publications; "Achieving our Providence: Lessons of City-Building," Commonwealth Publications. **Seminars:** Introduction to Social Computing (Web 2.0), Jan, 2009; Every Company Counts, Jun, 2009; Facilitating for Results; Story-Making and Story-Telling. **Telecommunication Services:** inquiries@newcommons.com.

26069 ■ The New Marketing Network Inc.
300 Park Ave., 17th Fl.
New York, NY 10022
Ph: (212)572-6392
Co. E-mail: info@newmarketingnetwork.com
URL: http://www.newmarketingnetwork.com
Contact: Pamela S. Boynton, Director
Scope: Full service firm assisting companies in marketing, creative, research, branding and communications specialties. The firm assists companies achieve their growth initiatives, increase profits and establish a sustainable competitive advantage through successful new products, accurate trend identification; application; business and brand franchise expansion. Additional services include strategic planning and positioning; qualitative and quantitative research. **Founded:** 1989.

26070 ■ Nightingale Associates
7445 Setting Sun Way
Columbia, MD 21046
Ph: (410)381-4280
Fax: (410)381-4280
Co. E-mail: fredericknightingale@nightingaleassociates.net
URL: http://www.nightingaleassociates.net
Contact: Frederick C. Nightingale, Managing Director
E-mail: fredericknightingale@nightingaleAssociates.net
Scope: Management training and consulting firm offering the following skills: productivity and accomplishment; leadership skills for the experienced manager; management skills for the new manager; leadership and teambuilding; supervisory development; creative problem solving; real strategic planning; providing superior customer service; international purchasing and supply chain management; negotiation skills development and fundamentals of purchasing. **Founded:** 1984. **Seminars:** Productivity and Accomplishment Management Skills for the New Manager; Leadership and Team building; Advanced Management; Business Process Re engineering; Strategic Thinking; Creative Problem Solving; Customer Service; International Purchasing and Materials Management; Fundamentals of Purchasing;

Negotiation Skills Development; Providing superior customer service; Leadership skills for the experienced manager.

26071 ■ North Carolina Fair Share (NCFS)
3824 Barrett Dr., Ste. 312
Raleigh, NC 27609
Ph: (919)786-7474
Fax: (919)786-7475
Co. E-mail: ncfslrw@aol.com
URL: http://www.ncfairshare.org
Scope: Social services firm consults on community organizing and lobbying for health issues. **Founded:** 1987.

26072 ■ Occupational & Environmental Health Consulting Services Inc.
635 Harding Rd.
Hinsdale, IL 60521-4814
Ph: (630)325-2083
Fax: (630)325-2098
Co. E-mail: bobb@safety-epa.com
URL: http://www.oehcs.com
Contact: Robert C. Brandys, President
E-mail: bobb@safety-epa.com
Scope: Provider of consulting to industry on safety program development and implementation, industrial hygiene monitoring programs, occupational health nursing, wellness programs, medical monitoring, accident trending and statistics, emergency response planning, multilingual training, right-to-know compliance and training, hazardous waste management, random monitoring and mitigation, asbestos school inspection, and project management. Also offers indoor air quality, expert witnessing service. **Founded:** 1984. **Publications:** "Worldwide Exposure Standards for Mold and Bacteria"; "Global Occupational Exposure Limits for Over 5000 Specific Chemicals"; "Post-Remediation Verification and Clearance Testing for Mold and Bacteria Risk Based Levels of Cleanliness". **Seminars:** Right-To-Know Compliance; Setting Internal Exposure Standards; Hospital Right-to-Know and Contingency Response; Ethylene Oxide Control; Industrial Hygiene Training; Asbestos Worker Training; Biosafety; Asbestos Operations and Maintenance. **Special Services:** Safety Software Program, Audiogram Analysis, First Report of Injury Form, Human Resources Database; Material Safety Data Sheet (MSDS); NPDES Monthly Reports; Lockout/Tagout (LOTO) Procedure Software; VOC Usage Tracking and Reporting Software, Medical Department Patient Records Database, Pictorial Labels for Chemical Containers, TIER II Hazardous Material Inventory Form & Database.

26073 ■ Organizational Improvement Associates L.L.C. (OIA)—OIAUS L.L.C.
40 Gilbert St.
Ridgefield, CT 06877
Ph: (203)417-4957
Fax: (203)244-5737
Co. E-mail: daveknibbe@oiaus.com
URL: http://www.oiaus.com
Contact: Dr. David S. Knibbe, President
E-mail: daveknibbe@oiaus.com
Scope: Specializes in high-performance team development, executive coaching, employee development programs, performance management and reward systems and dispute mediation. Industries served: Consumer products, telecommunications, finance, health-care, amusement/leisure, hospitality/lodging, retail and pharmaceuticals. **Founded:** 1991.

26074 ■ P2C2 Group Inc.
4101 Denfeld Ave.
Kensington, MD 20895-1514
Ph: (301)942-7985
Fax: (301)942-7986
Co. E-mail: info@p2c2group.com
URL: http://www.p2c2group.com
Contact: James E. Kendrick, President
E-mail: kendrick@p2c2group.com
Scope: Works with clients on the business side of federal program and project management. Services include program/project planning and optimization; acquisition strategy and work statements; IT Capital Planning and Investment Control (CPIC); business cases - new, revisions, critiques; budget analysis - cost benefits- alternatives; CPIC, SELC, and security

documentation; research, metrics, analysis, and case studies. Consulting support helping to: Define or redefine programs; strengthen portfolio management; identify alternatives for lean budgets; improve capital planning and investment; develop better plans and documentation, and evaluate performance of existing program investments. **Founded:** 1994. **Publications:** "OMB 300s Go Online," Federal Sector Report, Mar, 2007; "Using Risk-Adjusted Costs for Projects," Federal Sector Report, Feb, 2007; "Make Better Decisions Using Case Studies," Federal Sector Report, Jan, 2007; "PMO Performance Measurement & Metrics"; "Executive Sponsors for Projects"; "ABCs of the Presidential Transition"; "Financial Systems and Enterprise Portfolio Management"; "The Future of CPIC"; "Critical Factors for Program and Project Success"; "Using Risk-Adjusted Costs for Projects"; "Tactics for a Successful Year of CPIC"; "Operational Analysis Reviews"; "Successful IT Strategic Planning"; "Information Technology Investment Management". **Seminars:** Requests For Information; Pre Solicitation Marketing; Qualifications Statement Support For The Capital Planning And Investment Control (cpic) Process; How To Hire A Management Consultant And Get The Results You Expect.

26075 ■ Papa and Associates Inc.
200 Consumers Rd., Ste. 305
Toronto, ON, Canada M2J 4R4
Ph: (416)512-7272
Fax: (416)512-2016
Co. E-mail: ppapa@papa-associates.com
URL: http://www.papa-associates.com
Contact: Peter Papakostantinu, President
E-mail: ppapa@papa-associates.com
Scope: Provider of broad based management consulting services in the areas of quality assurance, environmental, health and safety and integrated management systems. **Founded:** 1989.

26076 ■ Parker Consultants Inc.
230 Mason St.
Greenwich, CT 06830-6633
Ph: (203)861-6698
Contact: Donald L. Parker, President
Scope: Firm specializes in strategic planning; organizational development; small business management; performance appraisals; executive searches; team building; and customer service audits. **Founded:** 1988.

26077 ■ Partners for Market Leadership L.L.C.
400 Galleria Pky., Ste. 1500
Atlanta, GA 30339
Ph: (770)850-1409
Free: 800-984-1110
Co. E-mail: dcarpenter@market-leadership.com
URL: http://www.market-leadership.com
Contact: Nancy Surdyka, Manager
E-mail: nsurdyka@market-leadership.com
Scope: Boutique consulting firm focused on assisting clients to develop sustainable market leadership in geographic, practice area and/or industry markets. Provides consulting on market leadership, revenue enhancement, strategic development and change facilitation. Additional services are offered to legal, accounting, valuation and financial firms. **Founded:** 1995.

26078 ■ Pathways To Wellness
617 Everhart Rd.
Corpus Christi, TX 78411
Ph: (361)985-9642
Fax: (361)949-4627
Co. E-mail: path2wellness@earthlink.net
URL: http://www.path2wellness.com
Contact: Evy Coppola, Owner
Scope: Offer natural holistic health counseling, yoga and hatha yoga classes, teachers training and cookery classes for individuals and companies. Health counseling includes nutritional guidance, kinesiology, iridology, reflexology, energy healing, massage therapy, herbal and vitamin therapy, creative visualization and meditation. Provides supplements which bring about the same effects as that of natural sunshine. **Founded:** 1988. **Seminars:** Is It You Holding You Back?; The Balancing Act. . .Career. . . Family. . .and Self; Learning the Art of Friendly Persua-

sion; Stop Accepting What You Are Getting and Start Asking for What You Want!; Introduction to Natural Health and Healthy Living; Learn Why One Size Approaches to the Answers on Health Do Not Work; Introduction to Yoga. What is it? Who can do it? What can it do for you.

26079 ■ Performance Consulting Associates Inc. (PCA)
3700 Crestwood Pky., Ste. 100
Duluth, GA 30096
Ph: (770)717-2737
Fax: (770)717-7014
Co. E-mail: info@pcaconsulting.com
URL: http://www.pcaconsulting.com
Contact: Richard A. Defazio, President
E-mail: defazio@pcaconsulting.com
Scope: Maintenance consulting and engineering firm specializing in production planning, project management, team building, and re-engineering maintenance. **Founded:** 1976. **Publications:** "Does Planning Pay," Plant Services, Nov, 2000; "Asset Reliability Coordinator," Maintenance Technology, Oct, 2000; "Know What it is You Have to Maintain," Maintenance Technology, May, 2000; "Does Maintenance Planning Pay," Maintenance Technology, Nov, 2000.; "What is Asset Management?"; "Implementing Best Business Practices".

26080 ■ Performance Consulting Group Inc.
8031 SW 35th Terr.
Miami, FL 33155-3443
Ph: (305)264-5577
Fax: (305)264-9079
Contact: Patrick J. O'Brien, President
Scope: Firm provides consulting services in the areas of strategic planning; profit enhancement; product development; and production planning. **Founded:** 1980.

26081 ■ Performance Dynamics Group L.L.C.
1 Ridge Rd.
Green Brook, NJ 08812
Free: 888-720-7337
Co. E-mail: info@performance-dynamics.net
URL: http://www.performance-dynamics.net
Contact: Mark E. Green, President
E-mail: mark.green@performance-dynamics.net
Scope: An organizational consulting group whose approach to learning and employee empowerment is designed to be both effective and efficient in achieving the specific knowledge and skill goals of a given program, in developing changes in thinking and behavior and also to foster and develop initiative, self confidence, creative problem-solving ability and interpersonal effectiveness of all participants. Brings improvement in areas of revenue growth, profitability, sales, marketing effectiveness, and employee and customer loyalty. **Founded:** 2003. **Seminars:** Accelerated Approach to Change; Commitment to Quality; Managing Cultural Diversity; The Corporate Energizer; The Power Pole Experience; Team Assessment; Self-Directed Work Teams.

26082 ■ Plans and Solutions Inc.
7823 Mistic View Ct.
Derwood, MD 20855
Ph: (301)947-8150
Fax: (240)525-5601
Co. E-mail: info@plansandsolutions.com
URL: http://www.plansandsolutions.com
Contact: Kenneth D. Weiss, President
E-mail: kw@plansandsolutions.com
Scope: Market research and competitive analysis; marketing and promotion planning, and executing promotion plans. Specializes in registration and problem solving services that include food canning establishment and process registration, registration under the terrorism act, assistance in case of detention of shipments, and on-site inspection of processing plants and records. Most clients are minority-owned businesses in the USA and companies overseas that want to begin or increase exports to the United States and Canada. **Founded:** 1996. **Publications:** "Building an Import/Export Business," John Wiley & Sons, 2002; "How to Conquer the U.S. Market"; "Going Global (Getting Started in International Trade)". **Seminars:** U.S. Import Regulations on Food Products.

26083 ■ Practice Development Counsel

60 Sutton Pl. S
New York, NY 10022
Ph: (212)593-1549
Fax: (212)980-7940
Co. E-mail: pwhaserot@pdcounsel.com
URL: http://www.pdcounsel.com
Contact: Phyllis Weiss Haserot, President
E-mail: pwhaserot@pdcounsel.com
Scope: Specializes in business and organizaationdal development, and conflict resolution for professional firms. It serves the law, accounting, real estate, and management consulting organizations. **Founded:** 1982. **Publications:** "The Rainmaking Machine: Marketing Planning, Strategy and Management For Law Firms"; "The Marketer's Handbook of Tips & Checklists"; "Venturesome Questions: The Law Firms Guide to Developing a New Business Venture"; "Navigating the Whitewater of Internal Politics"; "Changing Attitudes on Firm Flexibility"; "Transition Planning: A Looming Challenge"; "Don't You Think the Solution Is to Bring In a Good Rainmaker?"; "Aligning Firm Culture with the Needs of the Times"; "What New Partners Need to Know"; "Dangers of Lack of Diversity"; "Learn to Respect Emotion in Business"; "What New Partners Need to Know"; "Taking Responsibility: Implementing Personal Marketing Plans"; "How to Change Unwritten Rules"; "Mentoring and Networking Converge"; "Integrating a New Practice into the Firm"; "Using Conflict Resolution Skills for Marketing Success"; "Sports Team Models for Law Firm Management". **Seminars:** Managing Work Expectations; Effective Coaching Skills; Service Quality; End-Running the Resistance Professionals Have to Getting Client Input; Ancillary Business Activities; Marketing for Professional Firms; Marketing Ethics; Business Development Training; Trends in Professional Services Marketing; Client Relationship Management; Collaborative Culture; Reaching Consensus; Conflict Resolution; Work life Balance; Generaltional Issues; Preparing New Partners; Becoming the Employer of Choice; A Marketing Approach to Recruiting; Implementing Workplace Flexibility; The Business Case for Flexible Work Arrangements.

26084 ■ Praxis Media Inc.

9 Twilight Pl.
Norwalk, CT 06854
Ph: (203)866-6666
Co. E-mail: aldo@praxismediainc.com
Contact: Christopher Campbell, President
Scope: Media needs analysis and project planning specialists provide services in product introductions, communications planning, technology application, promotion and marketing communications. Also assists with focus groups, research, concept development, creative development, scripting and executive speech coaching/training. Industries served: Financial services, high-tech, travel and leisure, health and pharmaceutical and telecommunications. **Founded:** 1979.

26085 ■ ProActive English

4355 SE 29th Ave.
Portland, OR 97202
Ph: (503)231-2906
Co. E-mail: infopae@proactive-english.com
URL: http://www.proactive-english.com
Contact: Margaret Lyman, Manager
E-mail: mlyman@proactive-english.com
Scope: Offers on-site individual and small group language and communication training. Sets up learning plans tailored to the needs and schedules of managers and executives who are non-native English speakers. Serves all industries. **Founded:** 1997. **Seminars:** Communicating in Business Situations; Presentations and Pronunciation; Tailored Curriculum; One-on-One Programs.

26086 ■ Professional Counseling Centers Inc.

543 Coventry Way
Noblesville, IN 46062-9024
Ph: (317)877-3111
Contact: Jack W. Schinderle, President
Scope: Business counselors offering services in the following areas: employee assistance, managed care, alcohol and drug treatment, labor and union consultation, and industrial mental health.

26087 ■ Public Policy Communications

4163 Dingman Dr.
Sanibel, FL 33957
Ph: (941)395-6773
Fax: (941)395-6779
Contact: Robert Schaeffer, President
E-mail: bobschaeffer@earthlink.net
Scope: Provides strategic communications for progressive causes, candidates and socially-responsible businesses. These include public relations strategies, political campaign planning, organizational development and training. Substantial work in report writing, editing and design as well as production of a full range of media materials. Industries served: nonprofit, social change organizations, foundations, political campaigns, environmentally and consumer-oriented businesses, government agencies. **Founded:** 1985. **Publications:** "Winning Local and State Elections," Free Press MacMillan; "Giving the Media Your Message, and The News Media and the Big Lie". **Seminars:** Giving the Media Your Message; Effective Public Relations Practices; Winning Your Election; Understanding the Government Budget Process; How to Be an Effective Advocate; Strategic Planning for Non-Profits; How to Run a News Conference: Ten Key Steps, 1998.

26088 ■ Public Sector Consultants Inc. (PSC)

600 W St. Joseph St., Ste. 10
Lansing, MI 48933-2267
Ph: (517)484-4954
Fax: (517)484-6549
Co. E-mail: psc@pscinc.com
URL: http://www.pscinc.com
Contact: William R. Rustem, President
E-mail: wrustem@pscinc.com
Scope: Offers policy research expertise, specializing in opinion polling, public relations, conference planning, and legislative and economic analysis. Industries served: Associations, education, environment, health-care, and public finance. **Founded:** 1980. **Publications:** "The New Landscape of Civic Business: How Business Leadership Is Influencing Civic Progress in Our Metropolitan Regions Today," Feb, 2012; "Saginaw Bay Watershed and Area of Concern," Mar, 2012; "Michigan Public School Employees Retirement System: Major Changes in Recent Years and More Changes to Come," May, 2012; "Saginaw River/Bay Area of Concern: Restoration Plan for the Habitat and Populations BUIs," Sep, 2012; "Proposal 3: Key Questions and Answers," Sep, 2012; "Final Report of the Michigan State Park and Recreation Blue Ribbon Panel," Oct, 2012; "The Impact of Reducing PIP Coverage in Michigan," Sep, 2011; "Michigan Sales Tax Collection and the Internet: A Need for Fairness," Sep, 2011; "Ingham Community Voices Final Evaluation Report," Nov, 2008; "First Class Schools Analysis," Aug, 2008; "Opportunities for Achieving Efficiency in the Aging, Community Mental Health, Local Public Health, and Substance Abuse Coordinating Agency Networks," Aug, 2008; "Saginaw River Bay Area of Concern," Jun, 2008; "Portage Lake Water shed Forever Plan," May, 2008; "Smoke Free Workplaces," Apr, 2008; "Protecting and Restoring the Upper Looking Glass River," Feb, 2008; "Market Structures and the 21st Century Energy Plan," Sep, 2007; "The Growing Crisis of Aging Dams," Apr, 2007; "Financing Community Health Workers Why and How," Jan, 2007; "Hastings Area: Inter local Approaches to Growth Management," Jan, 2007; "Michigan's Part 201 Environmental Remediation Program Review," Jan, 2007.

26089 ■ The Purchasing Department (TPD)

34 Claremont Ave.
Maplewood, NJ 07040-2118
Fax: (973)275-0749
Co. E-mail: eostpd@aol.com
Contact: James T. Milway, Principal
E-mail: jtmtpd@aol.com
Scope: Provides state of the art procurement arrangements, process re-engineering and outsourcing assistance to any business wishing to achieve purchasing savings and efficiencies to improve bottom line results. Available to provide contract services to businesses requiring specialized supplemental assistance to back up own personnel on special projects. **Founded:** 1992. **Seminars:** Green Purchasing: Buying Recycled Products; Ethics; Measuring Purchasing Performance; Supplier Teaming and Quality; Preparing for ISO 9000 in the Purchasing Department.

26090 ■ Rental Relocation Inc. (RRI)

281 S Atlanta St.
Roswell, GA 30075
Ph: (770)641-8393
Free: 800-641-7368
Fax: (770)641-8607
Co. E-mail: ahlsinfo@rentalrelocation.com
URL: http://www.rentalrelocation.com
Contact: Christopher Bliss, President
E-mail: cbliss@rentalrelocation.com
Scope: Relocation firm offering services in corporate housing, rentals, free metro Atlanta apartment locating service, property management, house and condo rental relocation tours. **Founded:** 1989.

26091 ■ Rose & Crangle Ltd.

117 N 4th St.
Lincoln, KS 67455
Ph: (785)524-5050
Fax: (785)524-3130
Co. E-mail: rcltd@nckcn.com
URL: http://www.roseandcrangle.com
Contact: Robert D. Crangle, President
E-mail: rcltd@nckcn.com
Scope: Provider of evaluation, planning and policy analyzes for universities, associations, foundations, governmental agencies and private companies engaged in scientific, technological or educational activities. Special expertise in the development of new institutions. Special skills in providing planning and related group facilitation workshops. **Founded:** 1984. **Publications:** "Preface to Bulgarian Integration Into Europe and NATO: Issues of Science Policy And research Evaluation Practice," Ios Press, 2006; "Allocating Limited National Resources for Fundamental Research," 2005.

26092 ■ Rothschild Strategies Unlimited L.L.C.

19 Thistle Rd.
Norwalk, CT 06851-1909
Ph: (203)846-6898
Fax: (203)847-1426
Co. E-mail: bill@strategyleader.com
URL: http://www.strategyleader.com
Contact: Stephen M. Rothschild, President
Scope: Consults with senior management and business level strategy teams to develop overall strategic direction, set priorities and creates sustainable competitive advantages and differentiators. Enables organizations to enhance their own strategic thinking and leadership skills so that they can continue to develop and implement profitable growth strategies. **Founded:** 1983. **Publications:** "Putting It All Together-a guide to strategic thinking"; "Competitive Advantage"; "Ristaker, Caretaker, Surgeon & Undertaker four faces of strategic leadership"; "The Secret to GE's Success"; "Having the Right Strategic Leader and Team".

26093 ■ Sanford Consulting

52 Perry Corners Rd., RR 1
Amenia, NY 12501
Ph: (845)373-8960
Fax: (845)373-8961
Co. E-mail: sanford@mohawk.com
Contact: Anne Sanford, President
E-mail: sanford@mohawk.com
Scope: Helps businesses find, sell, to, and keep customers. Provides management and marketing services, including problem analysis and solution design for new business development, market analysis and segmentation, departmental organization and administrative policies and procedures. Industries served: small business, telecommunications, professional services, health care and nonprofits in the continental United States. **Founded:** 1986. **Seminars:** Trade show success; Finding customers; Business attitudes at not for profit and others.

26094 ■ SBR International—SBR Global

30 Adelaide St. E, Ste. 600
The Graeme Bldg.
Toronto, ON, Canada M5C 3G8

Ph: (416)962-7500
Fax: (416)962-7505
Co. E-mail: bizdev@sbr-global.com
URL: http://www.sbr-global.com
Contact: Kevin Gauci, Managing Director
Scope: Specializes in the leasing of multi-disciplinary, high-performance work teams at customer in-house cost, under a mixed military/general contracting model. Engagements include BPR, IE, SA, market and competitor intelligence, logistics, strategy, audit, workouts/turnarounds, M and A support/targeting, statistics and micro-economic modeling, PMO support. **Founded:** 1979. **Seminars:** Electronic counter measures; Strategic planning; Project management. **Telecommunication Services:** info@optimussbr.com.

26095 ■ David G. Schantz
29 Wood Run Cir.
Rochester, NY 14612-2271
Ph: (716)723-0760
Fax: (716)723-8724
Co. E-mail: daveschantz@yahoo.com
URL: http://www.daveschantz.freeservers.com
Contact: David G. Schantz, Manager
Scope: Provider of industrial engineering services for photofinishing labs, including amateur-wholesale, professional, commercial, school, and package. **Founded:** 1992.

26096 ■ Schneider Consulting Group Inc.
50 S Steele St., Ste. 390
Denver, CO 80209-2834
Ph: (303)320-4413
Fax: (303)320-5795
Contact: Kim Schneider Malek, Vice President
E-mail: kim@scgfambus.com
Scope: Assists family-owned and privately-held business transition to the next generation and/or to a more professionally managed company, turn around consulting for small and medium size companies. **Founded:** 1987.

26097 ■ Scott Ashby Teleselling Inc.
1102 Ben Franklin Dr., Ste. 309
Sarasota, FL 34236
Ph: (941)388-4283
Fax: (941)388-5240
URL: http://www.scottashbyteleselling.com
Contact: R. Scott Ashby, President
E-mail: rscottashby@netscape.net
Scope: Provider of consulting services and customized training programs that emphasize consultative telephone selling techniques. **Founded:** 1979. **Publications:** "How Will the Internet Affect Teleselling Programs?"; "When is Telemarketing Really Not Telemarketing?"; "The Future of Account Management Telesales". **Seminars:** Start-Up Educational, Planning and Strategy Development; Existing Program Audit, Evaluation, State-of-the-Art Best Practices Comparison, Tracking and Measurement Review, Systems and Procedures Analysis, and Optional Selling Skills; Develop New or Revised Consultative Telephone Selling; Helping Clients Build Relationship and Grow Their Business by Phone.

26098 ■ Sklar and Associates Inc.
242 Laurel Bay Dr.
Murrells Inlet, SC 29576
Ph: (843)798-0412
Fax: (843)651-3090
Co. E-mail: sklarincdc@aol.com
URL: http://www.sklarinc.com
Contact: Tim Sklar, President
Scope: Provider of consulting services for business acquisitions, business development and project finance. Provides audit oversight services to listed corporations on Sarbanes-Oxley compliance. Services include: Due diligence analyses and corporate governance. Industries served: transportation sectors, energy sector and commercial real estate industries. **Seminars:** Financial Analysis in MBA; Emerging Company Finance; Due Diligence in Business Acquisition; Business Valuation.

26099 ■ Harvey C. Skoog
7151 E Addis Ave.
Prescott Valley, AZ 86314

Ph: (928)772-1448
Scope: Firm has expertise in taxes, payroll, financial planning, budgeting, buy/sell planning, business start-up, fraud detection, troubled business consulting, acquisition, and marketing. Serves the manufacturing, construction, and retailing industries in Arizona. **Founded:** 1977.

26100 ■ Straightline Services Inc.
11 Centre St., Ste. 10
Salem, CT 06420-3845
Ph: (860)889-7929
Fax: (860)885-1894
Co. E-mail: straitln@aol.com
Contact: Wayne J. S. France, President
Scope: Design and implementation of organizational infrastructure, business plans and troubleshooting. Emphasizes on operations with a central and field or satellite offices. Industries served: Construction, resorts, Indian tribes, academies, small-medium sized business, mostly privately held. **Founded:** 1994.

26101 ■ Technology Management Group Co.—Ratafia Ventures
PO Box 3260
New Haven, CT
Ph: (203)387-1430
Fax: (203)387-1470
Co. E-mail: info@commtechsoftware.com
URL: http://www.ratafia.net
Contact: Manny Ratafia, President
E-mail: manny@commtechsoftware.com
Scope: Consulting services include analysis of market opportunities; product introductions; new ventures; acquisitions analysis; licensing, joint ventures, and OEM arrangements. Emphasis on polymers, medical devices, biotechnology, pharmaceuticals, and chemicals. **Founded:** 1981. **Telecommunication Services:** manny@ratafia.net. **Special Services:** CommTechPowerSearch®.

26102 ■ Trendzitions Inc.
25691 Atlantic Ocean, Ste. B13
Lake Forest, CA 92630-8842
Ph: (949)727-9100
Free: 800-266-2767
Fax: (949)727-3444
Co. E-mail: ctooker@trendzitions.com
URL: http://www.trendzitions.com
Contact: Christian Tooker, President
E-mail: ctooker@trendzitions.com
Scope: Provider of services in the areas of communications consulting, project management, construction management, and furniture procurement. Offers information on spatial uses, building codes, ADA compliance and city ordinances. Also offers budget projections. **Founded:** 1986.

26103 ■ Turnaround Inc.
3415 A St. NW
Gig Harbor, WA 98335
Ph: (253)857-6730
Fax: (253)857-6344
Co. E-mail: info@turnround-inc.com
URL: http://www.turnaround-inc.com
Contact: Miles Stover, President
E-mail: mstover@turnaround-inc.com
Scope: Provider of interim executive management assistance and management advisory to small, medium and family-owned businesses that are not meeting their goals. Services include acting as an interim executive or on-site manager. Extensive practices in arena of bankruptcy management. **Founded:** 1997. **Publications:** "How to Identify Problem and Promising Management"; "How to Tell if Your Company is a Bankruptcy Candidate"; "Signs that Your Company is in Trouble"; "The Turnaround Specialist: How to File a Petition Under 11 USC 11". **Seminars:** Competitive Intelligence Gathering.

26104 ■ ValueNomics Value Specialists
50 W San Fernando St., Ste. 600
San Jose, CA 95113
Fax: (408)200-6401
Co. E-mail: info@amllp.com
Contact: Gary E. Jones, Chief Executive Officer
Scope: Consulting is offered in the areas of financial management, process re-engineering, growth business services; governance, risk/compliance, SOX

readiness and compliance, SAS 70, enterprise risk management, system security, operational and internal audit; business advisory services; valuation services; CORE assessment; contract assurance; transaction advisory services, IT solutions and litigation support services. **Founded:** 1993. **Publications:** "Dueling Appraisers: How Differences in Input and Assumptions May Control the Value," Apr, 2005; "The Business of Business Valuation and the CPA as an expert witness"; "The Business of Business Valuation," McGraw-Hill Professional Publishers Inc.

26105 ■ Via Nova Consulting
1228 Winburn Dr.
Atlanta, GA 30344
Ph: (404)761-7484
Fax: (404)762-7123
Scope: Consulting services in the areas of strategic planning; privatization; executive searches; market research; customer service audits; new product development; competitive intelligence; and Total Quality Management (TQM). **Founded:** 1994.

26106 ■ Vision Management
149 Meadows Rd.
Lafayette, NJ 07848-3120
Ph: (973)702-1116
Fax: (973)702-8311
Contact: Norman L. Naidish, President
Scope: Firm specializes in profit enhancement; strategic planning; business process reengineering; industrial engineering; facilities planning; team building; inventory management; and total quality management (TQM). **Founded:** 1984. **Publications:** "To increase profits, improve quality," Manufacturing Engineering, May, 2000.

26107 ■ The Walk The Talk Co.—Performance Systems Corp.
1100 Parker Sq., Ste. 250
Flower Mound, TX 75028-7458
Ph: (972)899-8300
Free: 800-888-2811
Fax: (972)899-9291
Co. E-mail: info@walkthetalk.com
URL: http://www.walkthetalk.com
Contact: Eric L. Harvey, President
E-mail: ericharvey@walkthetalk.com
Scope: Assists a wide variety of organizations in implementing proprietary performance management system developed by the firm which concentrates on individual responsibility and decision making instead of disciplinary penalties. Helps organizations develop and implement peer review, a proven system that helps solve employee problems in a remarkable way-through employees and an evaluation process software is used whereby feedback is compiled from a full-range of sources, including a self-evaluation, leadership development workshops and keynote presentations and publications. **Founded:** 1977. **Publications:** "Positive Discipline"; "Leadership Secrets of Santa Claus"; "Start Right-Stay Right"; "Walk Awhile in My Shoes"; "Listen Up, Leader!"; "Five Star Teamwork"; "Ethics4Everyone"; "Leadership Courage"; "The Manager's Communication Handbook"; "180 Ways to Walk the Recognition Talk"; "The Manager's Coaching Handbook"; "The Best Leadership Advice I Ever Got"; "Power Exchange". **Seminars:** Walk the Talk; Coaching for Continuous Improvement; Managing Employee Performance; Customized Management Development Forums; Keynote presentations; Leadership Development Workshops; Consulting Services and Publications; Customer service training; Ethics and Values training.

26108 ■ Weich & Bilotti Inc.
600 Worcester Rd., 4th Fl.
Framingham, MA 01702
Ph: (508)663-1600
Fax: (508)663-1682
Co. E-mail: info@weich-bilotti.com
Contact: Mervyn D. Weich, Director
E-mail: mweich@weich-bilotti.com
Scope: Specializes in business plans, venture capital, computer information systems, turnaround/interim management, retail consulting, start-up process, college recruiting and IS and IT personnel. **Founded:** 1995.

26109 ■ Wheeler and Young Inc.
33 Peter St.
Markham, ON, Canada L3P 2A5
Ph: (905)471-5709
Fax: (905)471-9989
Co. E-mail: wheeler@ericwheeler.ca
URL: http://www.ericwheeler.ca
Contact: Eric S. Wheeler, Managing Partner
E-mail: ewheeler@yorku.ca
Scope: Provider of consulting services to high-tech companies on the implementation of software development processes; quality management systems (including ISO 9000 compliance) and business management systems. Offers business management and knowledge-management services to organizations. Industries served: Knowledge-based industries, including software and hardware development, medical and legal professionals, information service providers. **Founded:** 1994.

26110 ■ Zolfo Cooper L.L.C.
Grace Bldg., 1114 Ave. of the Americas, 41st Fl.
New York, NY 10036
Ph: (212)561-4000
Fax: (212)213-1749
Co. E-mail: rrandall@zolfocooper.com
URL: http://www.zolfocoooper.com
Contact: Mark Cervi, Director
Scope: Provider of accounting consulting services to businesses. Specializes in restructuring and turn-around consulting; interim and crisis management; performance improvement; creditor advisory; cross-border restructuring and corporate finance. **Founded:** 1985.

26111 ■ ZS Engineering P.C. (ZSE)
99 Tulip Ave.
Floral Park, NY 11001
Ph: (516)328-3200
Fax: (516)328-6195
Co. E-mail: office@zsengineering.com
URL: http://www.zsengineering.com
Contact: Zygmunt Staszewski, President
E-mail: staszewski@zsengineering.com
Scope: Offers engineering consulting services to building owners, building managers and contractors Specializes in design and inspections of fire alarm systems, sprinkler systems, smoke control systems, building evaluations for fire code compliance, violations removal. **Founded:** 1989. **Seminars:** Fire protection courses for contractors and building management.

FRANCHISES AND BUSINESS OPPORTUNITIES

26112 ■ ABX-Associates Business Xchange
7604 Oak St.
Frisco, TX 75034
Ph: (214)850-6131
Fax: (866)462-7229
Description: Nationwide franchise brokers network.
Founded: 1971..

26113 ■ American Franchise Consultants
520 W Gleneagles Dr.
Phoenix, AZ 85023
Free: 800-424-0749
Description: Business consultants. **Founded:** 1995..

26114 ■ Biga & Associates, Inc.
2415 E Kensington Rd.
Arlington Heights, IL 60004
Ph: (847)870-7521
Fax: (847)870-7553
Description: Franchise consultants. **Founded:** 1989..

26115 ■ Franchise Bancorp
294 Walker Dr., Ste. 2
Brampton, ON, Canada L6T 4Z2
Ph: (905)790-9023
Free: 866-463-4124
Fax: (905)790-7059
Co. E-mail: franchises@franchisebancorp.com
URL: http://www.franchisebancorp.com
Description: With a diverse combination of retail formats, Franchise Bancorp offers several business opportunities to satisfy various interests, lifestyles and investment levels. Living Lighting, Rafters, Panhandler, Rafters Home Stores and Global Ryan's Pet Foods forms the portfolio of franchises available through the Franchise Bancorp organization. **No. of Company-Owned Units:** 180. **Founded:** 1968.. **Franchised:** 1968. **Equity Capital Needed:** $160,000-$470,000. **Franchise Fee:** $30,000.

26116 ■ Franchise Development International, LLC
370 SE 15 Ave.
Pompano Beach, FL 33060
Ph: (954)942-9424
Fax: (954)783-5177
Description: Franchise development and marketing.
Founded: 1991..

26117 ■ Franchise Developments Inc. (FDI)
5001 Baum Blvd., Ste. 660
Pittsburgh, PA 15213
Ph: (412)687-8484
Free: 800-576-5115
Fax: (412)687-0541
Co. E-mail: franchise-dev@earthlink.net
URL: http://www.franchise-dev.com
Contact: Kenneth Franklin, President
Description: Develop, implement and launch franchise programs. **Scope:** Offers clients full development services for the purpose of designing and implementing a total franchise program. **Founded:** 1970. **Publications:** "Franchising Your Business," May/Jun, 2003; "Female Entrepreneur," May/Jun, 2003; "Franchising World," May/Jun, 2003; "Canadian Business Franchise," Jul/Aug, 2000. **Seminars:** Has presented franchising seminars under auspices of American Management Association, Management Center Europe and International Franchise Association. Recent programs include Expanding Your Business by Franchising; Writing Effective Franchise Operations Manuals. Also has franchise seminar on Prodigy.

26118 ■ Franchise Foundations
4157 23rd St.
San Francisco, CA 94114
Free: 800-942-4402
Description: Franchise consulting. **Founded:** 1990..

26119 ■ Franchise Specialists, Inc.
1234 Maple St. Ext.
Moon Twp., PA 15108
Ph: (412)262-5055
Description: Professional franchise development and sales. **Founded:** 1978..

26120 ■ Francorp Inc.
20200 Governors Dr.
Olympia Fields, IL 60461
Ph: (708)481-2900
Free: 800-372-6244
Fax: (708)481-5885
Co. E-mail: info@francorp.com
URL: http://www.francorp.com
Contact: Ramon Vinay, President
Description: Offers consultancy on franchising business. Consultants have provided full development programs, including feasibility studies, business plans, legal documents, operations manuals, and marketing materials for clients since 1976. **Scope:** A management consulting firm specializing in franchise development. Provides full development programs, including feasibility studies, business plans, legal documents, operations manuals and marketing materials. Also provides post-development services for established franchisers including lead generation programs, franchise brochures, videotapes, international brokerage, public relations and expert witness services. **Founded:** 1976. **Training:** Provides post-development services for establishing franchisors, including lead generation programs, brochures, videotapes, international brokerage, PR, and expert witness service. **Seminars:** Franchise Your Business, Sep, 2006; A review of both Federal and State laws which govern franchising; An overview of different franchise strategies available for expansion, as well as guidance in choosing the right one for your business; A comparison of the cost of various growth strategies; An overview of revenue streams through franchising; The estimated costs of franchising your business; Calculating returns on franchise development and support costs.

26121 ■ Jones & Co.
365 Bay St., 2nd Fl.
Toronto, ON, Canada M5H 2V1
Ph: (416)703-5716
Fax: (416)703-6180
Description: Law firm experienced in franchising and distribution. **Founded:** 2004..

26122 ■ Kaufman & Canoles, P.C.
150 W Main St., Ste. 2100
Norfolk, VA 23510
Ph: (757)624-3257
Fax: (757)624-3169
Description: Franchise attorneys. **Founded:** 1974..

26123 ■ L. Michael Schwartz, P.A.
10561 Barkley Pl., Ste. 510
Overland Park, KS 66212-1860
Ph: (913)341-1919
Fax: (913)341-0007
Description: Franchise consulting and full legal services.

26124 ■ Leon Gottlieb USA/Int'l Franchise/ Restaurant Consultants
Leon Gottlieb & Associates
4601 Sendero Pl.
Tarzana, CA 91356-4821
Ph: (818)757-1131
Fax: (818)757-1816
Description: Consultant, expert witness, arbitrator. **Founded:** 1960..

26125 ■ Lite For Life
Lite for Life Franchise Corp., Inc.
398 Main St.
Los Altos, CA 94022
Ph: (650)941-3200
Fax: (650)559-3111
Description: Weight loss and nutritional consulting. **No. of Franchise Units:** 2. **No. of Company-Owned Units:** 4. **Founded:** 1978.. **Franchised:** 2003. **Equity Capital Needed:** $75,000+/-. **Franchise Fee:** $20,000. **Training:** Yes.

26126 ■ Marketing Resources Group
83-26 Lefferts Blvd.
Kew Gardens, NY 11415
Ph: (718)261-8882
Description: Franchise development, marketing, and sales.

26127 ■ McGrow Consulting
30 North St.
Hingham, MA 02043
Ph: (800)358-8011
Description: Franchise consulting firm. **Founded:** 1980..

26128 ■ World Franchise Consultants
15965 Jeanette
Southfield, MI 48075
Ph: (248)559-1415
Description: Franchise consulting and referral. **Founded:** 1973..

START-UP INFORMATION

26129 ■ *How to Start a Bankruptcy Forms Processing Service*
Pub: Graphico Publishing Company
Ed: Victoria Ring. **Released:** September 2004. **Price:** $39.00. **Description:** Due to the increase in bankruptcy filings, attorneys are outsourcing related jobs in order to reduce overhead.

ASSOCIATIONS AND OTHER ORGANIZATIONS

26130 ■ National Association of Credit Management (NACM)
8840 Columbia 100 Pkwy.
Columbia, MD 21045-2158
Ph: (410)740-5560
Free: 800-955-8815
Fax: (410)740-5574
Co. E-mail: nacm_national@nacm.org
URL: http://www.nacm.org
Contact: Susan Delloiacono, Director
Description: Credit and financial executives representing manufacturers, wholesalers, financial institutions, insurance companies, utilities, and other businesses interested in business credit. Promotes sound credit practices and legislation. Conducts Graduate School of Credit and Financial Management at Dartmouth College, Hanover, NH. **Founded:** 1896. **Publications:** *Business Credit* (9/year); *Credit Executives Handbook*; *Manual of Credit and Commercial Laws* (Annual); *Business Credit: The Publication for Credit and Finance Professionals.* **Educational Activities:** Credit Congress and Exposition (Annual); Credit Congress and Exposition (Annual). **Awards:** Certified Credit Executive (Annual); Mentor of the Year (Annual); O. D. Glaus Credit Executive of the Year; Alice M.H. McGregor Award of Exceptional Achievement. **Telecommunication Services:** nacm-info@nacm.org; nacm_info@nacm.org.

REFERENCE WORKS

26131 ■ *"Abroad, Not Overboard"* in Entrepreneur (Vol. 36, April 2008, No. 4, pp. 68)
Pub: Entrepreneur Media, Inc.
Ed: Crystal Detamore-Rodman. **Description:** Export-Import Bank is an agency created by the U.S. government to help exporters get credit insurance and capital loans by providing them with loan guarantees. The bank, being criticized as supporting more the bigger exporters, has allotted to smaller businesses a bigger portion of the annual credit being approved.

26132 ■ *"AIG Fixed; Is Michigan Next?"* in Crain's Detroit Business (Vol. 24, September 22, 2008, No. 38, pp. 1)
Pub: Crain Communications Inc.
Ed: Jay Greene. **Description:** Michigan's economic future is examined as is the mortgage buyout plan and American International Group Inc.'s takeover by the U.S. government.

26133 ■ *All About Credit*
Pub: Kaplan Publishing
Ed: Deborah McNaughton. **Released:** April 1999. **Price:** $15.95. **Description:** Debt solution to specific credit problems for individuals denied credit, trying to mortgage a home, problems with creditors, and bankruptcy.

26134 ■ *"All-Star Advice 2010"* in Black Enterprise (Vol. 41, October 2010, No. 3, pp. 97)
Pub: Earl G. Graves Publishing Co. Inc.
Ed: Renita Burns, Sheiresa Ngo, Marcia Wade Talbert. **Description:** Financial experts share tips on real estate, investing, taxes, insurance and debt management.

26135 ■ *"Apartment Market Down, Not Out"* in Crain's Detroit Business (Vol. 24, October 6, 2008, No. 40, pp. 9)
Pub: Crain Communications, Inc.
Ed: Daniel Duggan. **Description:** Detroit's apartment market is considered to have some of the strongest fundamentals of any apartment market in the country with relatively low vacancy rates and a relatively low supply of new units compared with demand. Investors continue to show interest in the buildings but the national lending market is making it difficult to invest in the city.

26136 ■ *"Are We There Yet?"* in Business Courier (Vol. 24, April 4, 2008, No. 52, pp. 1)
Pub: American City Business Journals, Inc.
Ed: Lucy May; Dan Monk. **Description:** Groundbreaking for The Banks project happened in April 2, 2008, however, the future of the development remains uncertain due to some unresolved issues such as financing. Developers Harold A. Dawson Co. and Carter still have to pass final financing documents to Hamilton County and Cincinnati. The issue of financial commitment for the central riverfront project is examined.

26137 ■ *"Asia Breathes a Sigh of Relief"* in Business Week (September 22, 2008, No. 4100, pp. 32)
Pub: McGraw-Hill Companies, Inc.
Ed: Bruce Einhorn; Theo Francis; Chi-Chu Tschang; Moon Ihlwan; Hiroko Tashiro. **Description:** Foreign bankers, such as those in Asia, that had been investing heavily in the United States began to worry as the housing crisis deepened and the impact on Freddie Mac and Fannie Mae became increasingly clear. Due to the government bailout, however, central banks will most likely continue to buy American debt.

26138 ■ *"Attend To Your Corporate Housekeeping"* in Women Entrepreneur (December 4, 2008)
Pub: Entrepreneur Media Inc.
Ed: Nina Kaufman. **Description:** Business owners can lose all the benefits and privileges of the corporate form if they do not follow proper corporate formalities such as holding an annual meeting, electing officers and directors and adopting or passing corporate resolutions. Creditors are able to take from one's personal assets if such formalities have not been followed.

26139 ■ *"Au Revoir Or Goodbye?"* in Barron's (Vol. 88, July 14, 2008, No. 28, pp. 5)
Pub: Dow Jones & Co., Inc.
Ed: Alan Abelson. **Description:** Former Senator Phil Gramm's opinion that the U.S. is a 'nation of whiners' as they moan about recession is another example of the disconnection between Washington and Wall Street on one hand and the real world on the other. It would be a catastrophe for most of the world if Fannie Mae and Freddie Mac were to go under and take their trillions of mortgage debt with them.

26140 ■ *"B2B Commercial Collection Agency Accounts Fall"* in Managing Credit, Receivables & Collections (November 2010, No. 10-11, pp. 9)
Pub: Institute of Management & Administration
Description: A fall in the number of Business-To-Business collection accounts reflects the pace of the global economic recovery.

26141 ■ *"Back on Track-Or Off the Rails?"* in Business Week (September 22, 2008, No. 4100, pp. 22)
Pub: McGraw-Hill Companies, Inc.
Ed: Peter Coy; Tara Kalwarski. **Description:** Discusses the possible scenarios the American economy may undergo due to the takeover of Fannie Mae and Freddie Mac. Statistical data included.

26142 ■ *"Bad-Loan Bug Bites Mid-Tier Banks; More Pain, Tighter Lending Standards Ahead, CEOs Say"* in Crain's Chicago Business (May 5, 2008)
Pub: Crain Communications, Inc.
Ed: Steve Daniels. **Description:** Mid-sized commercial banks form the bedrock of Chicago's financial-services industry and they are now feeling the results of the credit crisis that has engulfed the nation's largest banks and brokerages. Commercial borrowers are seeing tighter terms on loans and higher interest rates while bank investors are unable to forecast lenders' earnings performance from quarter to quarter. Statistical data included.

26143 ■ *"Bad Loans Start Piling Up"* in Crain's New York Business (Vol. 24, January 7, 2008, No. 1, pp. 2)
Pub: Crain Communications, Inc.
Ed: Tom Fredrickson. **Description:** Problems in the subprime mortgage industry have extended to other lending activities as evidenced by bank charge-offs on bad commercial and industrial loans which have more than doubled in the third quarter.

26144 ■ *"Bailout May Force Cutbacks, Job Losses"* in The Business Journal - Serving Phoenix and the Valley of the Sun (Vol. 29, September 26, 2008, No. 4, pp. 1)
Pub: American City Business Journals, Inc.
Ed: Mike Sunnucks. **Description:** Economists say the proposed $700 billion bank bailout could affect Arizona businesses as banks could be forced to

reduce the amount and number of loans it has thereby forcing businesses to shrink capital expenditures and then jobs. However, the plan could also stimulate the economy by taking bad loans off banks balance sheets according to another economist.

26145 ■ "Bank Forces Brooke Founder To Sell His Holdings" in The Business Journal-Serving Metropolitan Kansas City (October 10, 2008)

Pub: American City Business Journals, Inc.

Ed: James Dornbrook. Description: Robert Orr who is the founder of Brooke Corp., a franchise of insurance agencies, says that he was forced to sell virtually all of his stocks in the company by creditors. First United Bank held the founder's stock as collateral for two loans worth $5 million and $7.9 million, which were declared in default in September 2008. Details of the selling of the company's stocks are provided.

26146 ■ "Bank Sticks to Rate Rise Script but 'Modest' is the Salient Word" in Globe & Mail (January 25, 2006, pp. B5)

Pub: CTVglobemedia Publishing Inc.

Ed: Heather Scoffield. Description: The reasons behind the decision of Bank of Canada to increase interest rate, which is posted at 3.5 percent, are presented.

26147 ■ "Bankruptcies Shoot Up 68 Percent" in Sacramento Business Journal (Vol. 25, July 18, 2008, No. 20, pp. 1)

Pub: American City Business Journals, Inc.

Ed: Kathy Robertson. Description: Personal bankruptcy in the Sacramento area rose by 88 percent for the first half of 2008 while business bankruptcies rose by 50 percent for the same period. The numbers of consumer bankruptcy reflects the effect of high debt, rising mortgage costs, and declining home values on U.S. households.

26148 ■ "Bankruptcies Swell" in The Business Journal-Portland (Vol. 25, July 4, 2008, No. 17, pp. 1)

Pub: American City Business Journals. Inc.

Ed: Andy Giegerich. Description: Individual and business bankruptcy filings in Portland, Oregon had increased. The rising gas and food prices, mortgage crisis and tightening lending standards are seen as causes of bankruptcies. Statistics on bankruptcy filings are also provided.

26149 ■ "Bankruptcy Blowback" in Business Week (September 22, 2008, No. 4100, pp. 36)

Pub: McGraw-Hill Companies, Inc.

Ed: Jessica Silver-Greenberg. Description: Changes to bankruptcy laws which were enacted in 2005 after banks and other financial institutions lobbied hard for them are now suffering the consequences of the laws which force more troubled borrowers to let their homes go into foreclosure; lenders suffer financially every time they have to take on a foreclosure and the laws in which they lobbied so hard to see enacted are now becoming a problem for these lending institutions. Details of the changes in the laws are outlined as are the affects on the consumer, the economy and the lenders.

26150 ■ "Banks, Retailers Squabble Over Fees" in Baltimore Business Journal (Vol. 28, June 18, 2010, No. 6, pp. 1)

Pub: Baltimore Business Journal

Ed: Gary Haber. Description: How an amendment to the financial regulatory reform bill would affect the bankers' and retailers' conflict over interchange fees is discussed. Interchange fees are paid for by retailers every time consumers make purchases through debit cards. Industry estimates indicate that approximately $50 million in such fees are paid by retailers.

26151 ■ "Banks Seeing Demand for Home Equity Loans Slowing" in Crain's Cleveland Business (Vol. 28, December 3, 2007, No. 48, pp. 1)

Pub: Crain Communications, Inc.

Ed: Shawn A. Turner. Description: Discusses the reasons for the decline in demand for home equity loans and lines of credit. Statistical data included.

26152 ■ "Barred Collection Agency Sued by Colorado AG" in Collections & Credit Risk (Vol. 15, August 1, 2010, No. 7, pp. 7)

Pub: SourceMedia Inc.

Description: Collection agency run by Chad Lee received notice that it is barred from collecting in the State of Colorado by Attorney General John Suther's office. A ruling cited that the firm engages in harassment or abuse and/or threats of violence, made false representations as to its legal status of debts, made false and misleading representations of nonpayment of debts that would result in arrest, and that Lee failed to disclose his previous felony conviction.

26153 ■ "The Best Option for All" in American Executive (Vol. 7, September 2009, No. 5, pp. 170)

Pub: RedCoat Publishing, Inc.

Ed: Ashley McGown. Description: Plaza Associates, a collections agency that conducts business primarily in the accounts receivable management sector, is the first in the industry to purchase 100 percent of the company from the founders through the formation of a leveraged Employee Stock Ownership Plan (ESOP).

26154 ■ "Best Turnaround Stocks" in Canadian Business (Vol. 81, Summer 2008, No. 9, pp. 65)

Pub: Rogers Media Ltd.

Ed: Calvin Leung. Description: Share prices of Sierra Wireless Inc. and EXFO Electro Optical Engineering Inc. have fallen over the past year but have good chance at a rebound considering that the companies have free cash flow and no long-term debt. One-year stock performance analysis of the two companies is presented.

26155 ■ "Beware the Ides of March" in Canadian Business (Vol. 81, April 14, 2008, No. 6, pp. 13)

Pub: Rogers Media

Ed: Jeff Sanford. Description: Financial troubles of Bear Stearns in March, 2008 was part of the credit crunch that started in the summer of 2007 in the U.S. when subprime mortgages that were written for people who could barely afford the payments started defaulting. The bankruptcy protection given to 20 asset backed commercial paper trusts is being fought by the investors in these securities who could stand to lose 40 percent of their money under the agreement.

26156 ■ "Big Sell-Off At Sunwest" in The Business Journal-Portland (Vol. 25, July 25, 2008, No. 20, pp. 1)

Pub: American City Business Journals, Inc.

Ed: Robin J. Moody. Description: Oregon's largest operator of assisted living facilities Sunwest Management Inc. is expected to sell 132 of its properties. The planned sale, which is believed to be worth more than $1 billion, will help Sunwest pay creditors and investors. Other views and information on the planned sale, as well as on Sunwest's services which include adult day care, are presented.

26157 ■ "Boosting Your Merchant Management Services With Wireless Technology" in Franchising World (Vol. 42, August 2010, No. 8, pp. 27)

Pub: International Franchise Association

Ed: Michael S. Slominski. Description: Franchises should have the capability to accept credit cards away from their businesses. This technology will increase sales.

26158 ■ "Boring Bonds Gain Pizzazz as Investors Flock to Debt Issues" in Baltimore Business Journal (Vol. 28, June 11, 2010, No. 5, pp. 1)

Pub: Baltimore Business Journal

Ed: Gary Haber. Description: Companies and nonprofit organizations have increased the pace of bond offerings in order to take advantage of the bonds' appeal among willing investors. Companies mostly issued corporate bonds to replace existing debt at lower interest rates and save them money from interest payments.

26159 ■ "Bracing for a Bear of a Week" in Barron's (Vol. 88, March 17, 2008, No. 11, pp. 24)

Pub: Dow Jones & Company, Inc.

Ed: Jacqueline Doherty. Description: JPMorgan Chase and the Federal Reserve Bank of New York's opening of a line of credit to Bear Stearns cut the stock price of Bear Stearns by 47 percent to 30 followed by speculation of an imminent sale. JP Morgan may be the only potential buyer for the firm and some investors say Bears could be sold at $20 to $30. Bears prime assets include its enormous asset base worth $395 billion.

26160 ■ "Branching Out" in Canadian Business (Vol. 79, July 17, 2006, No. 14-15, pp. 41)

Pub: Rogers Media

Description: Visa selected this narrative in an attempt to show the company's usefulness.

26161 ■ "Brooke Agents Claim Mistreatment" in The Business Journal-Serving Metropolitan Kansas City (Vol. 27, October 24, 2008, No. 7, pp. 1)

Pub: American City Business Journals, Inc.

Ed: James Dornbrook. Description: Franchisees of Brooke Corp., an insurance franchise, face uncertainty as their bills remain unpaid and banks threaten to destroy their credit. The company bundled and sold franchisee loans to different banks, but the credit crunch left the company with massive debts and legal disputes.

26162 ■ "Burdened by Debt, Borders Group Suspends Dividends, May Be Sold" in Crain's Detroit Business (Vol. 24, March 24, 2008, No. 12)

Pub: Crain Communications, Inc.

Ed: Nancy Kaffer. Description: Ann Arbor-based Borders Group Inc. is exploring its options and may put itself up for sale due to its declining stock price and mounting debt. The company's fiscal year was capped by poor holiday sales and Borders does not have the cash on hand to meet the 2009 goals set in its strategic plan.

26163 ■ "Can Your Business Still Land a Loan?" in Entrepreneur (Vol. 37, August 2009, No. 8, pp. 62)

Pub: Entrepreneur Media, Inc.

Ed: Carol Tice. Description: Banks are now sticking to the rules before making business loans. A business's existing bank should be the first place they should go to for a loan but if this fails, they should then look to smaller community and regional banks.

26164 ■ Chain of Blame: How Wall Street Caused the Mortgage and Credit Crisis

Pub: John Wiley & Sons, Inc.

Ed: Paul Muolo, Mathew Padilla. Released: 2009. Price: $27.95. Description: The book describes how risky loans given irresponsibly put big investment banks at the center of the subprime crisis.

26165 ■ "Chasing Credit" in Canadian Business (Vol. 81, November 10, 2008, No. 19, pp. 59)

Pub: Rogers Media Ltd.

Ed: Joe Castaldo. Description: Small and medium sized companies are dealing with tightening credit because they appear riskier than usual. Some of these businesses are turning to private investors, but this is not easy since many have invested everything in the stock market. The sector is expected to weaken with the broader Canadian market in the next six months from October 2008.

26166 ■ "China's Dagong Show" in Canadian Business (Vol. 83, August 17, 2010, No. 13-14, pp. 15)

Pub: Rogers Media Ltd.

Ed: Matthew McClearn. Description: Beijing, China-based Dagong Global Credit Rating has downgraded US credit ratings, as well as other developed countries such as Canada, while granting higher ratings to China, Russia and Brazil. However, there is a perceived disconnection between Dagong's ratings and its official pronouncements.

26167 ■ *"Citizens Unveils Mobile App for Business Customers"* in New Hampshire Business Review (Vol. 33, March 25, 2011, No. 6, pp. 27)

Pub: Business Publications Inc.

Description: Citizens Financial Group offers a new mobile banking application that allows business customers to manage cash and payments from a mobile device.

26168 ■ *"Clock Ticks On Columbia Sussex Debt"* in Business Courier (Vol. 27, July 30, 2010, No. 13, pp. 1)

Pub: Business Courier

Ed: Dan Monk. **Description:** Cincinnati, Ohio-based Columbia Sussex Corporation has made plans to restructure a $1 billion loan bundle that was scheduled to mature in October 2010. The privately held hotel has strived in a weak hotel market to keep pace with its $3 billion debt load.

26169 ■ *"Collection Agencies Industry Rankings"* in Collections and Credit Risk (Vol. 14, September 1, 2009, No. 8, pp. 18)

Pub: SourceMedia, Inc.

Description: Ranking of the top collection agencies in the United States in terms of the revenue generated in 2007 and 2088; statistical data included.

26170 ■ *"Collection Agencies Industry Rankings"* in Collections and Credit Risk (Vol. 14, September 1, 2009, No. 8, pp. 18)

Pub: SourceMedia, Inc.

Description: Ranking of the top collection agencies in the United States in terms of the revenue generated in 2007 and 2088; statistical data included.

26171 ■ *"Collection Agency Issues Whitepaper on Legal and Ethical Methods of Collecting on Overdue Accounts"* in Internet Wire (July 20, 2009)

Pub: Comtex News Network, Inc.

Description: American Profit Recovery, a collection agency based in Massachusetts and Michigan, has updated and reissued a whitepaper on what businesses can and cannot do regarding conversing with their customers in an attempt to collect on overdue accounts and payments. A detailed summary on the federal laws associated with collecting on overdue accounts is outlined in such a way that any business owner, manager, or responsible party can easily understand.

26172 ■ *"Collection Industry Fights Stigma, Lagging Payments"* in Crain's Cleveland Business (Vol. 30, June 8, 2009, No. 22, pp. 15)

Pub: Crain Communications, Inc.

Ed: Joel Hammond. **Description:** John Murray, co-owner and president of JP Recovery Services Inc. in Rocky River, Ohio discusses the burden of the collection industry during a financial crisis like a recession. Statistical data included.

26173 ■ *"Coming Soon: Bailouts of Fannie and Freddie"* in Barron's (Vol. 88, July 14, 2008, No. 28, pp. 14)

Pub: Dow Jones & Co., Inc.

Ed: Jonathan R. Laing. **Description:** Assurances from the government that Fannie Mae and Freddie Mac are adequately capitalized and able to carry on their duties as guarantors or owners of over $5 trillion of U.S. home mortgages are designed to keep both entities afloat until they attempt to raise $10 billion in new equity. The government would assume any losses in a bailout and owners of the banks' papers would profit as yields drop.

26174 ■ *"Companies Warned About California Collection Agency"* in Cardline (Vol. 10, June 4, 2010, No. 23, pp. 3)

Pub: SourceMedia Inc.

Description: Maxwell, Turner & Associates has received an F-rating from the Better Business Bureau of Central California, citing 32 unanswered complaints in less than a year.

26175 ■ *"Complete Idiot's Guide to Starting an Ebay Business*

Pub: Penguin Books USA Inc.

Ed: Barbara Weltman, Malcolm Katt. **Released:** February 2008. **Price:** $19.95 (US), $29.00 (Canadian). **Description:** Guide for starting an eBay business includes information on products to sell, how to price merchandise, and details for working with services like PayPal, and how to organize fulfillment services.

26176 ■ *"Condominium Sales Fall to a Seven-Year Low"* in Crain's Chicago Business (Vol. 31, November 10, 2008, No. 45, pp. 2)

Pub: Crain Communications, Inc.

Ed: Alby Gallun. **Description:** Downtown Chicago condominium market is experiencing the lowest number of sales in years due to the tightening of the mortgage lending market, the Wall Street crisis and the downturn in the economy. The supply of new condos is soaring, the result of the building boom of 2005 and 2006; many developers are finding it difficult to pay off construction loans and fear foreclosure on their properties. Additional information and statistical data related to the downtown condominium market is provided.

26177 ■ *"Confidence High, But Lenders More Cautious"* in Farmer's Weekly (March 28, 2008, No. 320)

Pub: Reed Business Information

Contact: Jeff Greisch, President

Description: Discusses the effect of the global credit crunch on farmers as well as recent auctions which were timed to beat changes to capital gains tax.

26178 ■ *"Consumers Finding It Harder to Get and Keep Credit"* in Chicago Tribune (January 10, 2009)

Pub: McClatchy-Tribune Information Services

Ed: Susan Chandler. **Description:** Five tips to maintain a good credit rating in these economic times are outlined and discussed.

26179 ■ *"Contractors Fret Over Credit, People, Government"* in Contractor (Vol. 57, February 2010, No. 2, pp. 7)

Pub: Penton Media, Inc.

Ed: Robert P. Mader. **Description:** Telephone interviews with 22 plumbing and HVAC contractors reveal that only two had sales increases for 2009 and that overall, contractors were down anywhere from seven to 25 percent. In the repair/service market, the residential sector was holding its own but the commercial portion was lagging behind.

26180 ■ *"A Conversation With; Ron Gatner, Jones Lang LaSalle"* in Crain's Detroit Business (Vol. 24, October 6, 2008, No. 40, pp. 9)

Pub: Crain Communications, Inc.

Description: Interview with Ron Gatner who is a corporate real estate adviser with the real estate company Jones Lang LaSalle as well as the company's executive vice president and part of the tenant advisory team; Gatner speaks about the impact that the Wall Street crisis is having on the commercial real estate market in Detroit.

26181 ■ *"Cornered by Credit; As $1 Billion in Loans Come Due, Will Landlords Find Funds?"* in Crain's Detroit Business (October 6, 2008)

Pub: Crain Communications, Inc.

Ed: Daniel Duggan. **Description:** Conduit loans are used by many real estate investors and are normally issued in 7- to 10-year terms with balloon payments due at the end, requiring the full balance to be paid upon maturity. Many building owners may find their properties going into foreclosure as these loans mature next year since these loans cannot be extended like typical loans and the credit crisis along with falling property values is making it more difficult to secure new sources of funding. Possible solutions to this problem are also explored.

26182 ■ *"Cost of Business Banking May Soon Go Up"* in Baltimore Business Journal (Vol. 28, October 29, 2010, No. 25, pp. 1)

Pub: Baltimore Business Journal

Ed: Gary Haber. **Description:** Experts in the financial industry expect banks to charge credit card transactions, especially to small business owners and consumers to recover about $11 million in lost revenue annually. Banks are expected to charge old fees and new ones, including $5 to $10 a month for a checking account.

26183 ■ *"Count Out The Consumer"* in Barron's (Vol. 88, July 7, 2008, No. 27, pp. 10)

Pub: Dow Jones & Co., Inc.

Description: American consumers are not expected to give the US economy its much-needed boost as the rising food and energy prices are taking their toll. US consumers have cut spending on utilities and food and are increasing their use of credit cards.

26184 ■ *"Crash Pads"* in Business Courier (Vol. 24, November 2, 2008, No. 29, pp. 1)

Pub: American City Business Journals, Inc.

Ed: Jon Newberry. **Description:** Francisca Webster accumulated $4 million in mortgage debt in about 2 months. She filed a lawsuit against her tax preparer and her mortgage broker contending that the defendants had breached their fiduciary duties to her and made fraudulent misrepresentations to her. The other details of the case are supplied.

26185 ■ *"Credit Card Crackdown"* in Business Journal-Portland (Vol. 24, November 23, 2007, No. 38, pp. 1)

Pub: American City Business Journals, Inc.

Ed: Andy Giegerich. **Description:** Oregon's U.S. Senator Ron Wyden is sponsoring Credit Card Safety Act of 2007, a bill that requires credit card companies to reduce the jargon of credit card agreements and require the Federal Reserve Board to launch a public education campaign among credit card users. The legislation will also impose a rating system for credit card contracts with five being the safest for consumers to use.

26186 ■ *"The Credit Crisis Continues"* in Barron's (Vol. 88, March 10, 2008, No. 10, pp. M12)

Pub: Dow Jones & Company, Inc.

Ed: Randall W. Forsyth. **Description:** Short-term Treasury yields dropped to new cyclical lows in early March 2008, with the yield for the two-year Treasury note falling to 1.532 percent. Spreads of the mortgage-backed securities of Fannie Mae and Freddie Mac rose on suspicion of collapses in financing.

26187 ■ *"Credit Crisis Puts Market in Unprecedented Territory"* in Crain's New York Business (Vol. 24, January 7, 2008, No. 1, pp. 14)

Pub: Crain Communications, Inc.

Ed: Aaron Elstein. **Description:** Banks are being forced to take enormous losses due to investors who are refusing to buy anything linked to subprime mortgages and associated securities.

26188 ■ *"Credit Crunch Gives, Takes Away"* in The Business Journal-Serving Metropolitan Kansas City (Vol. 27, October 17, 2008, No. 5, pp. 1)

Pub: American City Business Journals, Inc.

Ed: Suzanna Stagemeyer. **Description:** Although many Kansas City business enterprises have been adversely affected by the U.S. credit crunch, others have remained relatively unscathed. Examples of how local businesses are being impacted by the crisis are provided including: American Trailer & Storage Inc., which declared bankruptcy after failing to pay a long-term loan; and NetStandard, a technology firm who, on the other hand, is being pursued by prospective lenders.

26189 ■ *"Credit Crunch Takes Bite Out Of McDonald's"* in Advertising Age (Vol. 79, September 29, 2008, No. 36, pp. 1)

Pub: Crain Communications, Inc.

Ed: Emily Bryson York. **Description:** McDonald's will delay its launch of coffee bars inside its restaurants due to the banking crisis which has prompted Bank of America to halt loans to the franchise chains.

26190 ■ *"Credit-Market Crisis Batters Origen Financial's Bottom Line"* in Crain's Detroit Business (Vol. 24, March 31, 2008, No. 13, pp. 4)

Pub: Crain Communications, Inc.

Description: Overview of the effect the credit-market crisis has had on Origen Financial Inc., a company that underwrites and services loans for manufactured housing. CEO Ronald Klein didn't think Origen would be affected by the collapse due to its sound operations but the company's share price dropped considerably causing its auditors to warn that the company's existence could be in jeopardy.

26191 ■ *"Credit Reporting Myths and Reality"* in Black Enterprise (Vol. 41, December 2010, No. 5, pp. 34)

Pub: Earl G. Graves Publishing Co. Inc.

Ed: Denise Campbell. **Description:** It is critical to understand all the factors affecting credit scores before making any major purchase.

26192 ■ *"Curbing the Debt Collector"* in Business Journal-Portland (Vol. 24, October 5, 2007, No. 32, pp. 1)

Pub: American City Business Journals, Inc.

Ed: Andy Giegerich. **Description:** Republican representative Sal Esquivel, who had a bad personal experience with a Houston collector, is developing legislation that would give the state attorney general's office enforcement powers over debt collecting agencies. The existing Oregon legislation concerning the debt collection industry is also discussed.

26193 ■ *"Cutting Credit Card Processing Costs"* in Hawaii Business (Vol. 53, March 2008, No. 9, pp. 56)

Pub: Hawaii Business Publishing

Ed: Robert K.O. Lum. **Description:** Accepting credit card payments offers businesses with profits from the discount rate. The discount rate includes processing fee, VISA & MasterCard assessment and interchange. Details regarding merchant service cost and discount rate portions are discussed. Statistical data included.

26194 ■ *"Dealers Fight To Steer Course"* in The Business Journal-Serving Metropolitan Kansas City (Vol. 27, November 7, 2008, No. 9, pp. 1)

Pub: American City Business Journals, Inc.

Ed: Steve Vockrodt. **Description:** One local automobile dealer says that their sales are down by 30 to 40 percent and that car financing is now in the low 60 percentile from 85 to 88 percent. The National Automobile Dealers Association says that 700 dealerships are likely to be lost for 2008

26195 ■ *"Death Spiral"* in Business Journal Serving Greater Tampa Bay (Vol. 30, October 29, 2010, No. 45, pp. 1)

Pub: Tampa Bay Business Journal

Ed: Margie Manning. **Description:** Bay Cities Bank has started working on the loan portfolio of its acquisition, Progress Bank of Florida. Regulators closed Progress Bank in October 2010 after capital collapsed due to charge-offs and increases in the provision for future loan losses.

26196 ■ *"Debt Buyers Industry Rankings"* in Collections and Credit Risk (Vol. 14, September 1, 2009, No. 8, pp. 19)

Pub: SourceMedia, Inc.

Description: Ranking of the top debt buyers in the United States in terms of the revenue generated in 2007 and 2088; statistical data included.

26197 ■ *"Debt-Collection Agency to Lay Off 368 in Hampton Center"* in Virginian-Pilot (December 4, 2010)

Pub: Virginian-Pilot

Ed: Tom Shean. **Description:** NCO Financial Systems Inc., provider of debt-collection and outsourcing services will permanently lay off 368 workers at its Hampton call center in 2011.

26198 ■ *"Delinquent Properties on the Rise"* in Business Courier (Vol. 27, June 11, 2010, No. 6, pp. 1)

Pub: Business Courier

Ed: Dan Monk. **Description:** Reports show that Cincinnati now ranks in the U.S. Top 20 for its delinquency rate on securitized commercial real estate loans. In December 2009, the region ranked 28th out of 50 cities studied by Trepp LLC. As of May 30, 2010, more than $378 million in commercial mortgage-backed security loans were more than 60 days past due.

26199 ■ *Design and Launch an Online Travel Business in a Week*

Pub: Entrepreneur Press

Contact: Perlman Neil, President

Ed: Charlene Davis. **Released:** May 1, 2009. **Price:** $17.95. **Description:** Guide providing techniques and professional advice for starting an online travel business. Tips are given to build a Website, find qualified providers and to set up a payment system.

26200 ■ *"Developer Wins Bout with Bank in Roundabout Way"* in Tampa Bay Business Journal (Vol. 30, January 29, 2010, No. 6, pp. 1)

Pub: American City Business Journals

Ed: Janet Leiser. **Description:** Developer Donald E. Phillips of Phillips Development and Realty LLC won against the foreclosure filed by First Horizon National Corporation, which is demanding the company to fully pay its $2.9 million loan. Phillips requested that his company pay monthly mortgage and extend the loan's maturity date.

26201 ■ *"Dick Haskayne"* in Canadian Business (Vol. 81, March 31, 2008, No. 5, pp. 72)

Pub: Rogers Media

Ed: Andy Holloway. **Description:** Dick Haskayne says that he learned a lot about business from his dad who ran a butcher shop where they had to make a decision on buying cattle and getting credit. Haskayne says that family, friends, finances, career, health, and infrastructure are benchmarks that have to be balanced.

26202 ■ *"Direct Recovery Associates Debt Collection Agency Beats Industry Record"* in Internet Wire (June 24, 2010)

Pub: Comtex

Description: Direct Recovery Associates Inc. was named as one of the highest collection records in the industry, which has consistently improved over 18 years. The firm is an international attorney-based debt collection agency.

26203 ■ *"Direct Recovery Associates, Inc. Debt Collection Agency Founder Featured in China Daily"* in Internet Wire (November 9, 2010)

Pub: Comtex

Description: Richard Hart, founder of Direct Recovery Associates, was featured in an article published in the China Daily. The article discussed the increased credit and debt collection demands involving the U.S. and China.

26204 ■ *"Doctors, Health Insurers Squabble Over Who Sends Patients the Bill"* in Baltimore Business Journal (Vol. 27, February 6, 2010)

Pub: American City Business Journals

Ed: Scott Graham. **Description:** Issue of allowing patients to send reimbursement checks to physicians who are not part of their health insurer's provider network is being debated in Maryland. Details on the proposed Maryland bill and the arguments presented by doctors and insurers are outlined.

26205 ■ *"Don't Count Your Millions Yet"* in Business Courier (Vol. 24, January 11, 2008, No. 40, pp. 1)

Pub: American City Business Journals, Inc.

Ed: Steve Watkins. **Description:** Merger and acquisition deals have been difficult to complete since 2007 largely due to a weaker economy and the credit crunch. Buyers have become more cautious because

of the state of the economy and capital has become tougher to obtain because of the credit market crisis. The trends in mergers and acquisitions are analyzed further.

26206 ■ *"Don't Expect Quick Fix"* in The Business Journal-Serving Metropolitan Kansas City (Vol. 27, October 3, 2008, No. 3, pp. 1)

Pub: American City Business Journals, Inc.

Ed: James Dornbrook. **Description:** United States governmental entities cannot provide a quick fix solution to the current financial crisis. The economy requires a systemic change in the way people think about credit. The financial services industry should also focus on core lending principles.

26207 ■ *"Don't Quit When The Road Gets Bumpy"* in Women Entrepreneur (November 25, 2008)

Pub: Entrepreneur Media Inc.

Ed: Bonnie Price. **Description:** Discusses techniques four women entrepreneurs are utilizing to keep their businesses successful despite the credit crunch and the economic downturn.

26208 ■ *"DST Turns to Banks for Credit"* in The Business Journal-Serving Metropolitan Kansas City (Vol. 27, October 3, 2008, No. 3, pp. 1)

Pub: American City Business Journals, Inc.

Ed: Rob Roberts. **Description:** Kansas City, Missouri-based DST Systems Inc., a company that provides sophisticated information processing, computer software services and business solutions, has secured a new five-year, $120 million credit facility from Enterprise Bank and Bank of the West. The deal is seen to reflect that the region and community-banking model remain stable. Comments from executives are also provided.

26209 ■ *EBay Income: How ANYONE of Any Age, Location, and/or Background Can Build a Highly Profitable Online Business with eBay*

Pub: Atlantic Publishing Company

Released: December 1, 2010. **Price:** $24.95. **Description:** A complete overview of eBay is given and guides any small company through the entire process of creating the auction and auction strategies, photography, writing copy, text and formatting, multiple sales, programming tricks, PayPal, accounting, creating marketing, merchandising, managing email lists, advertising plans, taxes and sales tax, best time to list items and for how long, sniping programs, international customers, opening a storefront, electronic commerce, buy-it now pricing, keywords, Google marketing and eBay secrets.

26210 ■ *"eBay Inc. Completes Acquisition of Zong"* in Benzinga.com (October 29, 2011)

Pub: Benzinga.com

Ed: Benzinga Staff. **Description:** eBay Inc. acquired Zong, a provider of payments through mobile carrier billing. Terms of the agreement are outlined.

26211 ■ *"eBay Introduces Open Commerce Ecosystem"* in Entertainment Close-Up (October 24, 2011)

Pub: Close-Up Media

Description: eBay's new X.commerce is an open commerce ecosystem that will arm developers and merchants with the technology tools required to keep pace with the ever-changing industry. X.commerce brings together the technology assets and developer communities of eBay, PayPal, Magento and partners to expand on eBays vision for enabling commerce.

26212 ■ *"Economic Trends for Small Business"* in Small Business Economic Trends (April 2008, pp. 1)

Pub: National Federation of Independent Business

Ed: William C. Dunkelberg, Holly Wade. **Description:** Summary of economic trends for small businesses in the U.S. is presented. Economic indicators such as capital spending, inventories and sales, inflation, and profits are given. Analysis of credit markets is also provided.

26213 ■ *"End of the Beginning" in Canadian Business (Vol. 81, November 10, 2008, No. 19, pp. 17)*
Pub: Rogers Media Ltd.
Ed: David Wolf. **Description:** The freeze in the money markets and historic decline in equity markets around the world finally forced governments into aggressive coordinated action. The asset price inflation brought on by cheap credit will now work in reverse and the tightening of credit will be difficult economically. Canada is exposed to the fallout everywhere, given that the U.S, the U.K. and Japan buy 30 percent of Canada's output.

26214 ■ *"Ethics Commission May Hire Collection Agency" in Tulsa World (August 21, 2010)*
Pub: World Publishing
Ed: Barbara Hoberock. **Description:** Oklahoma Ethics Commission is considering a more to hire a collection agency or law firm in order to collect fees from candidates owing money for filing late financial reports.

26215 ■ *"Experts: Market Shaky But Resilient" in The Business Journal-Serving Metropolitan Kansas City (Vol. 27, September 19, 2008, No. 1)*
Pub: American City Business Journals, Inc.
Ed: Steve Vockrodt. **Description:** Investment advisers believe that the local investors in Kansas City who have a long-term approach towards their portfolios may come out even or even experience gains despite the Wall Street financial crisis. The impacts of the crisis are expected to take time to reach the area of Kansas City. The potential impacts of the Wall Street meltdown are examined further.

26216 ■ *"Fannie and Freddie: How They'll Change" in Business Week (September 22, 2008, No. 4100, pp. 30)*
Pub: McGraw-Hill Companies, Inc.
Ed: Jane Sasseen. **Description:** Three possible outcomes of the fate of struggling mortgage giants Freddie Mac and Fannie Mae after the government bailout are outlined.

26217 ■ *"Fewer Banks Offer Big Gifts to Lure Clients" in Globe & Mail (March 14, 2006, pp. D1)*
Pub: CTVglobemedia Publishing Inc.
Ed: Chris Reidy. **Description:** Fewer banks are offering gifts to lure the customers in this year in the wake of less favorable interest rates in the spring season. The market climate is analyzed.

26218 ■ *"Fifth Third Grapples With Account Snafu" in Business Courier (Vol. 24, December 7, 2008, No. 34, pp. 1)*
Pub: American City Business Journals, Inc.
Ed: Jon Newberry. **Description:** Fifth Third Bank's vendor committed an error which led to a badly damaged credit score for Brett and Karen Reloka. The couple reported the incident to the bank and are still waiting for action to be taken. A major outourced services vendor caused paid-off mortgages to be reported delinquent.

26219 ■ *"Fight Ensues Over Irreplaceable Gowns" in Tampa Bay Business Journal (Vol. 30, January 15, 2010, No. 4, pp. 1)*
Pub: American City Business Journals
Ed: Janet Leiser. **Description:** People's Princess Charitable Foundation Inc. founder Maureen Rorech Dunkel has sought Chapter 11 bankruptcy protection before a state court decides on the fate of the five of 13 Princess Diana Gowns. Dunkel and the nonprofit were sued by Patricia Sullivan of HRH Venture LLC who claimed they defaulted on $1.5 million in loans.

26220 ■ *"Financing for NNSA Plant Is a Work in Progress" in The Business Journal-Serving Metropolitan Kansas City (October 24, 2008)*
Pub: American City Business Journals, Inc.
Ed: Rob Roberts. **Description:** The Kansas City Council approved a development plan for a $500 million nuclear weapons parts plant in south Kansas City. The US Congress approved a $59 million annual lease payment to the plant's developer. Financ-

ing for the construction of the plant remains in question as the plant's developers have to shoulder construction costs.

26221 ■ *"Finger-Pointing Time" in Barron's (Vol. 88, March 10, 2008, No. 10, pp. 9)*
Pub: Dow Jones & Company, Inc.
Ed: Michael Santoli. **Description:** Discusses who is to blame for the financial crisis brought about by the credit crunch in the United States; the country's financial markets will eventually digest this crisis but will bottom out first before the situation improves.

26222 ■ *"Firms Sue Doracon to Recoup More Than $1M in Unpaid Bills" in Baltimore Business Journal (Vol. 28, July 9, 2010, No. 9, pp. 1)*
Pub: Baltimore Business Journal
Ed: Scott Dance. **Description:** Concrete supplier Paul J. Rach Inc., Selective Insurance Company, and equipment leasing firm Colonial Pacific Leasing Corporation intend to sue Baltimore, Maryland-based Doracon Contracting Inc. for $1 million in unpaid bills. Doracon owed Colonial Pacific $794,000 and the equipment is still in Doracon's possession. Selective Insurance and Paul J. Rach respectively seek $132,000 and $88,000.

26223 ■ *"FirstMerit's Top Executive Turns Around Credit Quality" in Crain's Cleveland Business (Vol. 28, October 15, 2007, No. 41, pp. 3)*
Pub: Crain Communications, Inc.
Ed: Shawn A. Turner. **Description:** Discusses the ways in which chairman and CEO Paul Greig has been able to improve FirstMerit Corp.'s credit quality and profit margin. Strategies included selling more than $70 million in bad loans, hiring a new chief credit officer and redirecting its focus on cross-selling its wealth and investment services to its commercial customers. Statistical data included.

26224 ■ *"A Flawed Yardstick for Banks" in Barron's (Vol. 88, July 14, 2008, No. 28, pp. M6)*
Pub: Dow Jones & Co., Inc.
Ed: Arindam Nag. **Description:** Return on equity is no longer the best measure for investors to judge banks by in a post-subprime-crises world. Investors should consider the proportion of a bank's total assets that are considered risky and look out for any write-downs of goodwill when judging a bank's financial health.

26225 ■ *"Florida's Housing Gloom May Add To Woes of National City" in Crain's Cleveland Business (Vol. 28, October 29, 2007, No. 43, pp. 1)*
Pub: Crain Communications, Inc.
Ed: Shawn A. Turner. **Description:** Already suffering by bad loans in the troubled mortgage market, National City Corp. is attempting to diversify its geographic presence beyond the slow-growth industrial Midwest by acquiring two Florida firms. Analysts worry that the acquisitions may end up making National City vulnerable to a takeover if the housing slump continues and credit quality becomes more of an issue for the bank.

26226 ■ *"Florin Car Dealers Drive Plan" in Sacramento Business Journal (Vol. 25, August 22, 2008, No. 25, pp. 1)*
Pub: American City Business Journals, Inc.
Ed: Melanie Turner. **Description:** Automobile dealers in Sacramento, California are working with the city and the business district in planning for future redevelopment in Florin Road. The move stemmed from pressure from the Elk Grove Auto Mall, high fuel prices and the credit crunch. The area has suffered business closures recently.

26227 ■ *"Former Mayor Driving $500 Million Real Estate Equity Fund" in The Business Journal - Serving Phoenix and the Valley of the Sun (Vol. 28, August 15, 2008, No. 50, pp. 1)*
Pub: American City Business Journals, Inc.
Ed: Jan Buchholz. **Description:** Paul John, the former mayor of Phoenix, is establishing a $500 million real estate asset management fund. The fund is

dubbed Southwest Next Capital Management and has attracted three local partners, namely Joseph Meyer, Jay Michalowski, and James Mullany, who all have background in finance and construction.

26228 ■ *"Gateway Delays Start" in The Business Journal-Serving Metropolitan Kansas City (Vol. 27, October 31, 2008, No. 8, pp. 1)*
Pub: American City Business Journals, Inc.
Ed: Rob Roberts. **Description:** Economic problems caused, in part, by the Wall Street crisis has resulted in the setback of a proposed mixed-use redevelopment project, The Gateway. The $307 million project, which includes the Kansas Aquarium, will be delayed due to financing problems. Details of the project are given.

26229 ■ *"Get Paid and Get Moving" in Entrepreneur (Vol. 37, October 2009, No. 10, pp. 38)*
Pub: Entrepreneur Media, Inc.
Description: GoPayments application from Intuit allows mobile telephones to process payments like credit card terminals. The application costs $19.95 a month and can be used on the Internet browsers of mobile telephones.

26230 ■ *Get Your Credit Straight: A Sister's Guide to Ditching Your Debt, Mending Your Credit, and Building a Strong Financial Future*
Pub: Broadway Books
Contact: David Drake, Manager
E-mail: ddrake@randomhouse.com
Ed: Glinda Bridgforth. **Price:** $19.95. **Description:** Third book in the series is aimed primarily at African American women and offers helpful and understandable information for a larger audience. The sidebars on how women in particular tend to get into credit trouble and ways they can increase their financial knowledge and reign in their spending habits are especially notable.

26231 ■ *"A Good Step, But There's a Long Way to Go" in Business Week (September 22, 2008, No. 4100, pp. 10)*
Pub: McGraw-Hill Companies, Inc.
Ed: James C. Cooper. **Description:** Despite the historic action by the U.S. government to nationalize the mortgage giants Freddie Mac and Fannie Mae, rising unemployment rates may prove to be an even bigger roadblock to bringing back the economy from its downward spiral. The takeover is meant to restore confidence in the credit markets and help with the mortgage crisis but the rising rate in unemployment may make many households unable to take advantage of any benefits which arise from the bailout. Statistical data included.

26232 ■ *"Goodwill Haunts Local Companies; Bad Buyouts During Boom Times Producing Big Writedowns" in Crain's Chicago Business (Apr. 28, 2008)*
Pub: Crain Communications, Inc.
Ed: Ann Saphir. **Description:** Many companies are having to face the reality that they overpaid for acquisitions made in better economic times; investors often dismiss such one-time charges as mere accounting adjustments but writeoffs related to past acquisitions can signal future problems because they mean the expected profits that justified the purchase have not materialized. Writeoffs are particularly worrisome for firms with a lot of debt and whose banks require them to have enough assets to back up their borrowings.

26233 ■ *"The Great Deleveraging" in Canadian Business (Vol. 81, October 13, 2008, No. 17, pp. 45)*
Pub: Rogers Media Ltd.
Ed: Jeff Sanford. **Description:** 'Hell Week' of financial crisis on Wall Street is believed to have started with the downgrade of AIG Inc.'s credit rating. AIG is a major player in the credit derivatives market, and its bankruptcy would have affected firms on Wall Street.

26234 ■ *"The Great Fall" in Barron's (Vol. 88, March 10, 2008, No. 10, pp. 5)*
Pub: Dow Jones & Company, Inc.
Ed: Alan Abelson. **Description:** Discusses the US economy is considered to be in a recession, with the effects of the credit crisis expected to intensify as a result. Inflation is estimated at 4.3 percent in January 2008, while 63,000 jobs were lost in February 2008.

26235 ■ *"Grin and Bear It" in Canadian Business (Vol. 81, March 3, 2008, No. 3, pp. 53)*
Pub: Rogers Media
Ed: Jeff Sanford. **Description:** Discusses the United States economic downturn, caused by the credit market crisis, which is expected to affect the Canadian economy, as Canada depend on the U.S. for 80 percent of its exports. Economist David Rosenberg thinks that in 2008, housing prices will decline by 15 percent and gross domestic product growth will slow to 0.8 percent. Other forecasts for Canadian economy are given.

26236 ■ *Grow Your Money: 101 Easy Tips to Plan, Save and Invest*
Pub: HarperBusiness
Ed: Jonathan D. Pond. **Released:** December 2007. **Price:** $26.95. **Description:** In what should be required reading for anyone entering the work world, the author offers helpful investment and financial definitions, debt-management strategies, retirement and home ownerships considerations and more.

26237 ■ *"Hank Paulson On the Housing Bailout and What's Ahead" in Business Week (September 22, 2008, No. 4100, pp. 19)*
Pub: McGraw-Hill Companies, Inc.
Ed: Maria Bartiromo. **Description:** Interview with Treasury Secretary Henry Paulson in which he discusses the bailout of Fannie Mae and Freddie Mac as well as the potential impact on the American economy and foreign interests and investments in the country. Paulson has faith that the government's actions will help to stabilize the housing market.

26238 ■ *"Hard Times for Hard Money" in Sacramento Business Journal (Vol. 25, July 18, 2008, No. 20, pp. 1)*
Pub: American City Business Journals, Inc.
Ed: Michael Shaw. **Description:** Three private lenders who supplied $1 million sued VLD Realty, its associated companies and owners Volodymyr and Leonid Dubinsky accusing them of default after a plan to build two subdivisions fell through. Investigators are finding that borrowers and lenders ignored most rules on private investments on real estate.

26239 ■ *"Hastily Enacted Regulation Will Not Cure Economic Crisis" in Crain's Chicago Business (Vol. 31, May 5, 2008, No. 18, pp. 18)*
Pub: Crain Communications, Inc.
Ed: Stephen P. D'Arcy. **Description:** Policymakers are looking for ways to respond to what is possibly the greatest financial crisis of a generation due to the collapse of the housing market, the credit crisis and the volatility of Wall Street.

26240 ■ *"HBC Sells Credit Card Division" in Globe & Mail (February 8, 2006, pp. B1)*
Pub: CTVglobemedia Publishing Inc.
Ed: Sinclair Stewart; Marina Strauss. **Description:** The details on General Electric Co.'s acquisition of Hudson's Bay Co.'s credit card division, for $370 million, are presented.

26241 ■ *"Headwinds From the New Sod Slow Aer Lingus" in Barron's (Vol. 88, March 10, 2008, No. 10, pp. M6)*
Pub: Dow Jones & Company, Inc.
Ed: Sean Walters; Arindam Nag. **Description:** Aer Lingus faces a drop in its share prices with a falling US market, higher jet fuel prices, and lower long-haul passenger load factors. British media companies Johnston Press and Yell Group are suffering from weaker ad revenue and heavier debt payments due to the credit crunch.

26242 ■ *"Health Providers Throw Lifeline to Clinics" in Sacramento Business Journal (Vol. 25, July 25, 2008, No. 21, pp. 1)*
Pub: American City Business Journals, Inc.
Ed: Kathy Robertson. **Description:** Health Net of California Inc., Catholic Healthcare West and Sutter Health are each providing up to $5 million in no-interest and low-interest loans to clinics in California, while the Sisters of Mercy of the Americas Burlingame Regional Community is offering $300,000. Other details on the short term loans are discussed.

26243 ■ *"High-End Jeweler Loses Street Sparkle" in Houston Business Journal (Vol. 40, November 27, 2009, No. 29, pp. 1)*
Pub: American City Business Journals
Ed: Allison Wollam. **Description:** High-end jeweler Bailey Banks & Biddle's 7,000 square foot prototype store in Houston, Texas' CityCentre will be ceasing operations despite its parent company's filing for Chapter 11 protection from creditors. According to the bankruptcy filing, parent company Finlay Enterprises Inc. of New York intends to auction off its business and assets. Finlay has 67 Bailey Banks locations throughout the US.

26244 ■ *"Hit the Green" in Canadian Business (Vol. 79, August 14, 2006, No. 16-17, pp. 73)*
Pub: Rogers Media
Ed: Andrew Wahl. **Description:** Reorganization of the bankrupt 4everSports golf company in the United States is discussed.

26245 ■ *Home-Based Business for Dummies*
Pub: John Wiley and Sons, Inc.
Ed: Paul Edwards, Sarah Edwards, Peter Economy. **Released:** February 25, 2005. **Price:** $19.99. **Description:** Provides all the information needed to start and run a home-based business. Topics include: selecting the right business; setting up a home office; managing money, credit, and financing; marketing; and ways to avoid distractions while working at home.

26246 ■ *"A Home of Her Own" in Hawaii Business (Vol. 53, October 2007, No. 4, pp. 51)*
Pub: Hawaii Business Publishing
Ed: Maria Torres-Kitamura. **Description:** It was observed that the number of single women in Hawaii purchasing their own home has increased, as that in the whole United States where the percentage has increased from 14 percent in 1995 to 22 percent in 2006. However, First Hawaiian Bank's Wendy Lum thinks that the trend will not continue in Hawaii due to lending restrictions. The factors that women consider in buying a home of their own are presented.

26247 ■ *"Homes Stall As Owners Resist Major Price Cuts" in Crain's Chicago Business (Vol. 31, April 21, 2008, No. 16, pp. 38)*
Pub: Crain Communications, Inc.
Ed: Kevin Davis. **Description:** Discusses the high-end housing market and the owners who are resisting major price cuts as well as the buyers who look at long market times as a sign that something is wrong with the property.

26248 ■ *"Hospitals Feel Pain from Slow Economy" in Business Courier (Vol. 27, September 3, 2010, No. 18, pp. 1)*
Pub: Business Courier
Ed: James Ritchie. **Description:** Hospitals in Cincinnati, Ohio have suffered from decreased revenues owing to the economic crises. Declining patient volumes and bad debt have also adversely impacted hospitals.

26249 ■ *How to Collect Debts*
Pub: Amacom
Ed: David Sher, Martin Sher. **Released:** May 1999. **Description:** Suggestions for collecting as much money as possible, as quickly as possible, while maintaining customer goodwill, along with strategies for eliminating bad debt.

26250 ■ *How to Write a Great Business Plan for Your Small Business in 60 Minutes or Less*
Pub: Atlantic Publishing
Ed: Sharon L. Fullen. **Released:** January 2006. **Price:** $39.95 includes CD-Rom. **Description:** A good business plan outlines goals and works as a company's resume to obtain funding, credit from suppliers, management of the operations and finances, promotion and marketing, and more.

26251 ■ *"If You Go Into the Market Today.." in Canadian Business (Vol. 82, Summer 2009, No. 8, pp. 18)*
Pub: Rogers Media
Ed: Jeff Sanford. **Description:** Opinions of experts and personalities who are known to have bear attitudes towards the economy were presented in the event 'A Night with the Bears' in Toronto in April 2009. Known bears that served as resource persons in the event were Nouriel Roubini, Eric Sprott, Ian Gordon, and Meredith Whitney. The bears were observed to have differences regarding consumer debt.

26252 ■ *"Illinois Regulators Revoke Collection Agency's License" in Collections & Credit Risk (Vol. 15, August 1, 2010, No. 7, pp. 13)*
Pub: SourceMedia Inc.
Description: Creditors Service Bureau of Springfield, Illinois had its license revoked by a state regulatory agency and was fined $55,000 because the owner and president, Craig W. Lewis, did not turn over portions of collected funds to clients.

26253 ■ *"Insider" in Canadian Business (Vol. 81, March 31, 2008, No. 5, pp. 76)*
Pub: Rogers Media
Ed: John Gray. **Description:** Discusses a comparison of an average Canadian family's finances in 1990 with the data from 2007. The average family in 2007 has over $80,000 in debt compared to just under $52,000 in 1990. However, Canadians have also been accumulating solid assets such as homes and stocks. This means that Canadian debt load has fallen from 22 percent in 1990 to 20 percent in 2007 when taken as a percentage of total net worth.

26254 ■ *"Karen Case; President of Commercial Real Estate Lending, Privatebancorp Inc." in Crain's Chicago Business (May 5, 2008)*
Pub: Crain Communications, Inc.
Ed: Dee Gill. **Description:** Profile of Karen Case who was hired by PrivateBancorp Inc. to turn its minor share of the city's commercial real estate lending market into a major one.

26255 ■ *"Kenosha 'Lifestyle Center' Delayed" in The Business Journal-Milwaukee (Vol. 25, August 8, 2008, No. 46, pp. A1)*
Pub: American City Business Journals, Inc.
Ed: Rich Kirchen. **Description:** Quality Centers of Orlando, Florida has postponed construction plans for the Kenosha Town Center in Kenosha County, Wisconsin to 2009 due to the economic downturn and lending concerns. The $200-million, 750,000-square-foot retail and residential center will be located near the corner of Wisconsin Highway 50 and I-94.

26256 ■ *"Kimball Hill Files for Chapter 11" in Crain's Chicago Business (Vol. 31, April 28, 2008, No. 17, pp. 12)*
Pub: Crain Communications, Inc.
Description: Homebuilder Kimball Hill filed for Chapter 11 bankruptcy protection after months of negotiations with lenders. The firm plans to continue operations as it restructures its debt.

26257 ■ *"Laugh or Cry?" in Barron's (Vol. 88, March 24, 2008, No. 12, pp. 7)*
Pub: Dow Jones & Company, Inc.
Ed: Alan Abelson. **Description:** Discusses the American economy which is just starting to feel the effect of the credit and housing crises. JPMorgan Chase purchased Bear Stearns for $2 a share, much

lower than its share price of $60, while quasi-government entities Fannie Mae and Freddie Mac are starting to run into trouble.

26258 ■ "Leaders Weigh In On Fannie Mae, Freddie Mac Failure, Fed Bailout" in The Business Journal - Serving Phoenix and the Valley of the Sun (Vol. 28, September 12, 2008, No. 53, pp. 1)
Pub: American City Business Journals, Inc.
Ed: Chris Casacchia; Mike Sunnucks; Jan Buchholz. **Description:** Fannie Mae and Freddie Mac's federal takeover was a move to help stabilize the financial market and it helped bring down interest rates in the past week. Local executives from Arizona's Phoenix area share their thoughts on the immediate effect of the takeover and its upside and downside.

26259 ■ "Lehman's Hail Mary Pass" in Business Week (September 22, 2008, No. 4100, pp. 28)
Pub: McGraw-Hill Companies, Inc.
Ed: Matthew Goldstein; David Henry; Ben Levison. **Description:** Overview of Lehman Brothers' CEO Richard Fuld's plan to keep the firm afloat and end the stock's plunge downward; Fuld's strategy calls for selling off a piece of the firm's investment management business.

26260 ■ "Lenders" in The Business Journal - Serving Phoenix and the Valley of the Sun (Vol. 28, July 25, 2008, No. 47, pp. 1)
Pub: American City Business Journals, Inc.
Ed: Jan Buchholz. **Description:** Private equity lender Investor Mortgage Holdings Inc. has continued growing despite the crisis surrounding the real estate and financial industries and has accumulated a $700 million loan portfolio. Private lending has become increasingly important in financing real estate deals as commercial credit has dried up.

26261 ■ "Lending Door Slams" in Puget Sound Business Journal (Vol. 29, October 24, 2008, No. 27, pp. 1)
Pub: American City Business Journals
Ed: Jeanne Lang Jones, Kirsten Grind. **Description:** KeyBank's closure of its Puget Sound unit that services single-family homebuilders is part of a nationwide shutdown that includes similar closures in other cities. Bank of America is adopting more conservative terms for homebuilding loans while Union Bank of California is still offering credit for market rate housing.

26262 ■ "The Letter of the Law" in Collections and Credit Risk (Vol. 14, November 1, 2009, No. 9, pp. 40)
Pub: SourceMedia, Inc.
Ed: Michelle Dunn. **Description:** Analyzes the regulatory landscape regarding debt collection and the ways in which those in the field are dealing with a tough economy, unclear laws and the newest regulations.

26263 ■ "A Limited Sphere of Influence" in Mergers & Acquisitions: The Dealmaker's Journal (March 1, 2008)
Pub: SourceMedia, Inc.
Ed: Ken MacFadyen. **Description:** Changes to the interest rate has had little impact on the mergers and acquisitions market since the federal funds rate does not link directly to the liquidity available to the M&A market; lenders are looking at cash flows and are likely to remain cautious due to other factors impacting the market.

26264 ■ "Local Firms Will Feel Impact Of Wall St. Woes" in The Business Journal-Milwaukee (Vol. 25, September 19, 2008, No. 52, pp. A1)
Pub: American City Business Journals, Inc.
Ed: Rich Kirchen. **Description:** Wall Street's crisis is expected to affect businesses in Wisconsin, in terms of decreased demand for services and products and increased financing costs. Businesses in Milwaukee area may face higher interest rates and tougher loan standards. The potential impacts of the Wall Street crisis on local businesses are examined further.

26265 ■ "Local M&A Activity Sputters in 1Q" in Crain's Chicago Business (Vol. 31, April 21, 2008, No. 16, pp. 20)
Pub: Crain Communications, Inc.
Ed: H. Lee Murphy. **Description:** Local mergers-and-acquisitions activity is down by 34 percent in the first quarter compared to the fourth quarter of last year due to the credit crisis making financing harder to obtain.

26266 ■ "Marine Act Amendments Gain Parliamentary Approval" in Canadian Sailings (July 7, 2008)
Pub: UBM Global Trade
Contact: Leonard J. Corallo, President
Ed: Alex Binkley. **Description:** Changes to the Canada Marine Act provides better borrowing deals as well as an ability to tap into federal infrastructure funding for environmental protection measures, security improvements and other site enhancements.

26267 ■ "Mass Mailers Try to Lick Rising Postal Rates" in Crain's Detroit Business (Vol. 24, March 10, 2008, No. 10, pp. 6)
Pub: Crain Communications, Inc.
Ed: Sherri Begin. **Description:** Discusses the ways in which companies are trying to mitigate the effect of rising postal costs.

26268 ■ "Measuring the Impact" in Mergers & Acquisitions: The Dealmaker's Journal (March 1, 2008)
Pub: SourceMedia, Inc.
Ed: Ken MacFadyen. **Description:** Discusses a new study out of Europe which contends that the private equity market does not have as much impact on the overall economy as critics contend.

26269 ■ "Media Industry Collection Agency Completes Acquisition" in Collections & Credit Risk (Vol. 15, December 1, 2010, No. 11, pp. 22)
Pub: SourceMedia Inc.
Description: Media Receivable Management Inc. (MRM) will take over the collection operations at Borden, Jones & Mitchell, in Miami, Florida. MRM clients are basically magazine and electronic media publishers.

26270 ■ "Midwest Seeks Concessions From Creditors" in The Business Journal-Milwaukee (Vol. 25, July 25, 2008, No. 44, pp. A1)
Pub: American City Business Journals, Inc.
Ed: Rich Rovito. **Description:** Midwest Airlines Inc. is turning to creditors and lease holders for the financial aspect of its restructuring, which involves going back to serving popular business destinations. Chief executive officer Timothy believes that the company can survive in a niche market as long as it provides quality service. He discusses Midwest's restructuring plan.

26271 ■ "More Ad Shops Link Payment to Results" in Boston Business Journal (Vol. 30, November 12, 2010, No. 42, pp. 1)
Pub: Boston Business Journal
Ed: Lisa van der Pool. **Description:** A growing number of advertising firms are proposing a 'value-based' payment scheme where they are paid a base fee plus a bonus if certain sales goals or other targets are met. The proposed shift in payment scheme is seen as reminiscent of the dot-com boom about ten years ago. Advertising firms are traditionally paid by the hour.

26272 ■ "Mortgage Securities Drop Hits Home" in The Business Journal-Serving Metropolitan Kansas City (Vol. 27, October 17, 2008, No. 5)
Pub: American City Business Journals, Inc.
Ed: Rob Roberts. **Description:** Sale of commercial mortgage-backed securities (CMBS) in Kansas City, Missouri have declined. The area may avoid layoffs if the United States government succeeds in stabilizing the economy. Major CMBS players in the area include Midland Loan Services Inc. and KeyBank Real Estate Capital.

26273 ■ "Mr. Deeds" in Canadian Business (Vol. 81, March 31, 2008, No. 5, pp. 24)
Pub: Rogers Media
Ed: Thomas Watson. **Description:** Ron Sandler has the right experience to help save Northern Rock PLC get through its liquidity problems. Sandler is known for saving Lloyd's of London in the mid-90's and he is not afraid to make enemies. Ron Sandler's assignment to help Northern Rock comes at a time when the health of the U.K. housing is not great.

26274 ■ "Muddy Portfolio Raises a Question: Just What Is National City Worth?" in Crain's Detroit Business (Vol. 24, April 7, 2008, No. 14)
Pub: Crain Communications, Inc.
Ed: Jay Miller. **Description:** National City Bank is looking at strategies to help it deal with its credit and loan problems which are reflected in its falling stock price. One possible solution is a merger with another bank, however most national banks are facing their own home-loan portfolio issues and may be unable to tackle another company's unresolved problems. Statistical data included.

26275 ■ "Needed: A Strategy; Banking In China" in The Economist (Vol. 390, January 3, 2009, No. 8612, pp. 54)
Pub: The Economist Newspaper Inc.
Description: International banks are competing for a role in China but are finding obstacles in their paths such as a reduction in the credit their operations may receive from Chinese banks and the role they can play in the public capital markets which remain limited.

26276 ■ "A New Kid on the Block" in Barron's (Vol. 88, March 17, 2008, No. 11, pp. 58)
Pub: Dow Jones & Company, Inc.
Ed: Thomas G. Donlan. **Description:** Discusses the Federal Reserve which has offered to lend $100 billion in cash to banks and $200 billion in Treasuries to Wall Street investment banks that have problems with liquidity. The reluctance of the banks to lend money to meet a margin call on securities that could still depreciate is the reason why the agency is going into the direct loan business.

26277 ■ "New Money" in Entrepreneur (Vol. 36, February 2008, No. 2, pp. 62)
Pub: Entrepreneur Media Inc.
Ed: C.J. Prince. **Description:** Tips on how to handle business finance, with regard to the tightened credit standards imposed by leading institutions, are provided. These include: selling receivables, margining blue chips, and selling purchase orders.

26278 ■ "New York Collection Agency's Bribery Case Resolved" in Collections & Credit Risk (Vol. 15, August 1, 2010, No. 7, pp. 19)
Pub: SourceMedia Inc.
Description: Criminal conviction and civil settlement in a bribery case and Medicaid scam involving H.I.S. Holdings Inc. and owner Deborah Kantor is examined.

26279 ■ "The Next Government Bailout?" in Barron's (Vol. 88, March 10, 2008, No. 10, pp. 21)
Pub: Dow Jones & Company, Inc.
Ed: Jonathan Laing. **Description:** Fannie Mae may need a government bailout as it faces huge hits brought about by the effects of the housing crisis. The shares of the government-sponsored enterprise have dropped 65 percent since the housing crisis began.

26280 ■ "No More Debt" in Black Enterprise (Vol. 37, November 2006, No. 4, pp. 159)
Pub: Earl G. Graves Publishing Co. Inc.
Ed: Tanisha A. Sykes. **Description:** Eliminating debt is not necessarily easy and can be overwhelming. Here are some tips for reducing and eventually getting out of debt.

26281 ■ "Not Enough To Go Around" in The Business Journal-Milwaukee (Vol. 25, August 15, 2008, No. 47, pp. A1)
Pub: American City Business Journals, Inc.
Ed: David Doege. **Description:** Most of the creditors of bankrupt real estate developer Scott Fergus are likely to remain unpaid as he only has an estimated

$30,000 available for paying debts. Creditors, as of the 13 August 2008 deadline for filing claims, have filed a total of $79.1 million in claims.

26282 ■ *"A Novel Fix for the Credit Mess"* in *Barron's (Vol. 88, March 31, 2008, No. 13, pp. 10)*
Pub: Dow Jones & Company, Inc.
Ed: Michael Santoli. **Description:** Due to the common bank-leverage factor of 10, the $250 billion of lost bank capital would have supported $2.5 trillion in lending capacity. Jeffrey Lewis suggests onerous regulations on bank-holding companies that own 10 to 25 percent, as they are partly to blame. Statistical data included.

26283 ■ *"Ohio Collection Agency Settles Second Lawsuit"* in *Collections & Credit Risk (Vol. 15, July 1, 2010, No. 6, pp. 9)*
Pub: SourceMedia Inc.
Description: National Enterprise Systems, will pay $75,000 for illegal and abusive collection charged in a lawsuit filed by West Virginia's Attorney General's office. Money will be used to reimburse students and consumers who paid the illegal fees to the company.

26284 ■ *"OK, Bring in the Lawyers"* in *Crain's Chicago Business (Vol. 31, November 17, 2008, No. 46, pp. 26)*
Pub: Crain Communications, Inc.
Ed: Daniel Rome Levine. **Description:** Bankruptcy attorneys are finding the economic and credit crisis a benefit for their businesses due to the high number of business owners and mortgage holders that are need of their services. One Chicago firm is handling ten times the number of cases they did the previous year and of that about 80 percent of their new clients are related to the real estate sector.

26285 ■ *The One Minute Entrepreneur*
Pub: Doubleday
Ed: Ken Blanchard; assisted by Don Hutson and Ethan Willis. **Released:** 2008. **Price:** $19.95. **Description:** Four traditional business ideas are covered including: revenue needs to exceed expenses, bill collection, customer service, and employee motivation in order to be successful.

26286 ■ *"Opportunity Now Lies at Short End of the Market"* in *Barron's (Vol. 88, June 30, 2008, No. 26, pp. M9)*
Pub: Dow Jones & Co., Inc.
Ed: Michael S. Derby. **Description:** Renewed credit concerns and the lesser chance of a Federal Reserve interest rate hike boosted the bond market. Some portfolio managers are more bullish on short-dated securities as they expect the market to adjust to a more appropriate outlook.

26287 ■ *"Pay Me! How to Get the Money You're Owed When No One Seems to Have Any"* in *Entrepreneur (Vol. 37, July 2009, No. 7, pp. 49)*
Pub: Entrepreneur Media, Inc.
Ed: Randy B. Hecht. **Description:** How certain collections scenarios with clients, who have already fallen behind on their payments, should be handled is discussed. During a down economy, business owners should properly manage collection and billing because this can actually strengthen client relationships. Insights on hiring a collections agency are also presented.

26288 ■ *"A Pioneer of Paying With Plastic"* in *Crain's Chicago Business (Vol. 31, April 28, 2008, No. 17, pp. 39)*
Pub: Crain Communications, Inc.
Ed: Phuong Ly. **Description:** Profile of Perfect Plastic Printing Corp., a family-owned company which manufactures credit cards, bank cards and gift cards and whose sales hit $50.1 million last year, a 16 percent jump from 2006.

26289 ■ *"Placer Land Sells for $12 Million"* in *Sacramento Business Journal (Vol. 25, July 25, 2008, No. 21, pp. 1)*
Pub: American City Business Journals, Inc.
Ed: Michael Shaw; Celia Lamb. **Description:** Reynen & Bardis Communities Inc., a Sacramento, California-based homebuilder, has purchased the

Antonio Mountain Ranch in Placer County, California shortly before the property's scheduled foreclosure on June 27, 2008. Placer County Recorder's data show that the purchase price of the 808-acre wetland-rich property is $12 million.

26290 ■ *"Port Authority Taking Heat in Kenwood Mess"* in *Business Courier (Vol. 26, September 18, 2009, No. 21, pp. 1)*
Pub: American City Business Journals, Inc.
Ed: Dan Monk. **Description:** Port of Greater Cincinnati Development Authority is being criticized for not requiring payment and performance bonds to ensure that contractors would be paid. The criticism occurred after the general contractor for the project to build a parking garage at Kenwood Towne Plaza stopped paying its subcontractors.

26291 ■ *"Portfolio Recovery Associates Expands Its Hampton Call Center"* in *Internet Wire (January 20, 2010)*
Pub: Comtex News Network, Inc.
Description: Entering into a lease amendment in order to expand its Hampton, Virginia call center and extend its lease agreement, Portfolio Recovery Associates, Inc., a company that collects, purchases and manages defaulted consumer debt, plans to upgrade the existing space enabling them to draw on local talent.

26292 ■ *Practical Debt Collecting for Small Companies and Traders*
Pub: Meadow Books
Ed: Robin Evelegh. **Released:** December 2006. **Price:** $12.99. **Description:** Credit and collection guide for small companies.

26293 ■ *"Prepaid Phones Surge in Bad Economy"* in *Advertising Age (Vol. 79, November 17, 2008, No. 43, pp. 6)*
Pub: Crain Communications, Inc.
Ed: Rita Chang. **Description:** Prepay cell phone offerings are becoming increasingly competitive amid a greater choice of plans and handsets. In an economic environment in which many consumers are unable to pass the credit checks required for traditional cell phone plans, the prepay market is surging.

26294 ■ *"Private Equity Firms Shopping Valley For Deals"* in *The Business Journal - Serving Phoenix and the Valley of the Sun (Vol. 29, September 19, 2008, No. 3, pp. 1)*
Pub: American City Business Journals, Inc.
Ed: Mike Sunnucks. **Description:** Private equity firms from California, Boston, New York, and overseas are expected to invest in growth-oriented real estate markets that include Phoenix. Real estate experts revealed that privately held investment and acquisition firms are looking to invest in real estate markets hit by the housing crisis. Views and information on private equity firms' real estate investments are presented.

26295 ■ *"Put It on MasterCard"* in *Barron's (Vol. 89, July 27, 2009, No. 30, pp. 16)*
Pub: Dow Jones & Co., Inc.
Ed: Bill Alpert. **Description:** Shares of MasterCard trade at a discount at just 15 times its anticipated earnings and some believe that these shares may be a better play in an economic recovery. The prospects of these shares are compared with those of Visa

26296 ■ *"Que Pasa? A Canadian-Cuban Credit Card Crisis"* in *Canadian Business (Vol. 81, March 31, 2008, No. 5, pp. 10)*
Pub: Rogers Media
Ed: Geoff Kirbyson. **Description:** Discusses the acquisition of CUETS Financial Ltd. by the Bank of America which means that CUETS-issued credit cards in Cuba are worthless since U.S. laws prohibit transactions from Cuba and other sanctioned countries. CUETS members are advised to take multiple payment methods to Cuba.

26297 ■ *"RBC Holds Inside Card With HBC Credit Assets"* in *Globe & Mail (January 25, 2006, pp. B1)*
Pub: CTVglobemedia Publishing Inc.
Ed: Marina Strauss; Sinclair Stewart. **Description:** Hudson's Bay Co. (HBC) signed co-branding credit

card agreement with Royal Bank of Canada are presented. The significance of the deal for HBC is discussed.

26298 ■ *"Ready for a Rally?"* in *The Economist (Vol. 390, January 3, 2009, No. 8612, pp. 54)*
Pub: The Economist Newspaper Inc.
Description: Analysts predict that the recession could end by 2010. The current economic crisis is presented in detail.

26299 ■ *"Recession-Proof Your Startup"* in *Crain's Chicago Business (Vol. 31, November 10, 2008, No. 45, pp. 24)*
Pub: Crain Communications, Inc.
Description: Detailed information concerning ways in which to start a business during an economic crisis is provided. Ways in which to find financing, the importance of a solid business plan, customer service, problem-solving and finding the right niche for the region are also discussed.

26300 ■ *"Refi Requests Soar, But New Rules May Mean Fewer Closings"* in *The Business Review Albany (Vol. 35, April 4, 2008, No. 53, pp. 1)*
Pub: The Business Review
Ed: Barbara Pinckney. **Description:** National refinancing applications grew by 82 percent in the week that ended March 21, 2008, due to the depressed real estate market and lower interest rates. Refinancing applicants, however, may be surprised with new rules on loan applications such as the required credit score of at least 720 in avoiding payment of extra fees. The developments in application standards for home loans are also examined.

26301 ■ *"Regulators Revoke Mann Bracken's Collection Agency Licenses"* in *Collections & Credit Risk (Vol. 15, September 1, 2010, No. 8, pp. 19)*
Pub: SourceMedia Inc.
Description: Maryland regulators have revoked the collections licenses of defunct law firm Mann Bracken LLP.

26302 ■ *"Research and Markets Adds Report: Credit and Collection Practices 2009"* in *Wireless News (August 12, 2009)*
Pub: Close-Up Media
Description: Research and Markets announced the addition of the 'Credit and Collection Practices 2009' report which will highlight credit and collection industry practices and technologies. The report also includes an overview of the best practices in the field.

26303 ■ *"Research Reports"* in *Barron's (Vol. 88, March 24, 2008, No. 12, pp. M10)*
Pub: Dow Jones & Company, Inc.
Description: Investors are recommending purchasing shares of Ampco Pittsburgh due to an expected surge in earnings. Deteriorating credit quality presents problems for the shares of BankAtlantic Bancorp, whose price targets have been lowered from $7 to $5 each. Shares of Helicos Biosciences are expected to move sideways from their $6 level. Statistical data included.

26304 ■ *"Return to Wealth; Bank Strategy"* in *The Economist (Vol. 390, January 3, 2009, No. 8612, pp. 56)*
Pub: The Economist Newspaper Inc.
Description: UBS' strategy to survive these trying economic times is presented. Statistical data included. UBS has a stronger balance-sheet than most of its investment-banking peers and has reduced its portfolio.

26305 ■ *"'Rocket Docket' Leaves Memphis Debtors Behind"* in *Commercial Appeal (November 28, 2009)*
Pub: Commercial Appeal
Ed: Bartholomew Sullivan. **Description:** According to an investigation by the Scripps Howard News Service, Memphians lodged 807 formal complaints about debt-collection practices to the Federal Trade Commission in a 2 1/2 -year period ending in July; Nearly 1/3 of the complaints involved some type of error with the

debt in question. The majority of the complaints were leveled at NCO Group, which also generated the most complaints around the country.

26306 ■ "Running the Numbers" in Entrepreneur (Vol. 37, July 2009, No. 7, pp. 87)

Pub: Entrepreneur Media, Inc.

Ed: Carol Tice. **Description:** Ways in which entrepreneurs can assess if they are ready to be a multi-unit franchisee are presented. Choosing the right locations, knowing how much assistance they can get from the franchisor, and financing are the key considerations when planning additional franchise units. Examples of success in multi-unit operations and multi-unit terms are also presented.

26307 ■ Save Your Small Business: 10 Crucial Strategies to Survive Hard Times or Close Down and Move On

Pub: NOLO

Contact: Ralph Warner, Chief Executive Officer

Ed: Ralph Warner, Bethany Laurence. **Released:** August 1, 2009. **Price:** $29.99. **Description:** According to a study among 500 businesses, 44 percent used credit cards in order to meet their firm's needs in the previous six months. Written by a business owner, this book provides twelve strategies to protect personal assets from creditors and survive the current recession.

26308 ■ "SEC Report On Rating Agencies Falls Short" in Barron's (Vol. 88, July 14, 2008, No. 28, pp. 35)

Pub: Dow Jones & Co., Inc.

Ed: Jack Willoughby. **Description:** The Securities and Exchange Commissions report on credit-rating firms should have drawn attention to the slipshod practices in the offerings of collateralized debt obligations. The report fell short of prescribing correctives for the flawed system of these agencies' relationship with their clients.

26309 ■ "Sentiment Split on Financials" in Barron's (Vol. 88, March 24, 2008, No. 12, pp. M14)

Pub: Dow Jones & Company, Inc.

Ed: Steven M. Sears. **Description:** Experts in the financial sector are split as to whether or not the worst of the financial crisis brought on by the credit crunch is over. Some options traders are trading on are defensive puts, expecting the worst, while investors buying calls are considered as bullish.

26310 ■ "Shopped Out; Retailing Gloom" in The Economist (Vol. 390, January 3, 2009, No. 8612, pp. 26)

Pub: The Economist Newspaper Inc.

Description: Economic volatility in the retail sector is having an impact on a number of countries around the globe. Europe is experiencing hard economic times as well and unless businesses have a strong business plan banks feel unable to lend the money necessary to tide the retailers over. The falling pound has increased the cost of imported goods and small to midsize retail chains may not be able to weather such an unforgiving economic climate.

26311 ■ "'Short Sales,' A Sign of Housing Troubles, Start Popping Up" in The Business Review Albany (Vol. 35, April 11, 2008, No. 1, pp. 1)

Pub: The Business Review

Ed: Michael DeMasi. **Description:** Discusses the number of short sales, where homeowners ask banks to forgive part of their mortgages to sell the properties, which is starting to increase in the Albany, New York area. Real estate agents in the area are taking up crash courses in short selling.

26312 ■ "A Slice of Danish; Fixing Finance" in The Economist (Vol. 390, January 3, 2009, No. 8612, pp. 55)

Pub: The Economist Newspaper Inc.

Description: Denmark's mortgage-holders and the county's lending system is presented.

26313 ■ "Small Business Credit Conditions" in Small Business Economic Trends (April 2008, pp. 12)

Pub: National Federation of Independent Business

Ed: William C. Dunkelberg, Holly Wade. **Description:** Graphs and tables that present the credit conditions of small businesses in the U.S. are provided. The tables include figures on availability of loans, interest rates, and expected credit conditions.

26314 ■ "Small Business Credit Conditions" in Small Business Economic Trends (February 2008, pp. 12)

Pub: National Federation of Independent Business

Ed: William C. Dunkelberg, Holly Wade. **Description:** Graphs and tables that present the credit conditions of small businesses in the U.S. are provided. The tables include figures on availability of loans, interest rates, and expected credit conditions.

26315 ■ "Small Business Credit Conditions" in Small Business Economic Trends (January 2008, pp. 12)

Pub: National Federation of Independent Business

Description: Graphs representing loan availability and interest rates among U.S. small businesses surveyed from January 1986 to December 2007 are given. Tables showing regular borrowers, availability of loans, satisfied borrowing needs, expected credit conditions, relative interest rate paid by regular borrowers, and actual interest rate paid on short-term loans by borrowers are also presented.

26316 ■ "Small Business Credit Conditions" in Small Business Economic Trends (September 2010, pp. 12)

Pub: National Federation of Independent Business

Ed: William C. Dunkelberg, Holly Wade. **Description:** Graphs representing loan availability and interest rates among U.S. small businesses surveyed from January 1986 to August 2010 are given. Tables showing regular borrowers, availability of loans, satisfied borrowing needs, expected credit conditions, relative interest rate paid by regular borrowers, and actual interest rate paid on short-term loans by borrowers are also presented.

26317 ■ "Small Business Credit Conditions" in Small Business Economic Trends (July 2010, pp. 12)

Pub: National Federation of Independent Business

Description: Graphs representing loan availability and interest rates among U.S. small businesses surveyed from January 1986 to June 2010 are given. Tables showing regular borrowers, availability of loans, satisfied borrowing needs, expected credit conditions, relative interest rate paid by regular borrowers, and actual interest rate paid on short-term loans by borrowers are also presented.

26318 ■ The Small Business Owner's Manual: Everything You Need to Know to Start Up and Run Your Business

Pub: Career Press, Incorporated

Ed: Joe Kennedy. **Released:** June 2005. **Price:** $19.99 (US), $26.95 (Canadian). **Description:** Comprehensive guide for starting a small business, focusing on twelve ways to obtain financing, business plans, selling and advertising products and services, hiring and firing employees, setting up a Web site, business law, accounting issues, insurance, equipment, computers, banks, financing, customer credit and collection, leasing, and more.

26319 ■ Small Business Survival Guide

Pub: Adams Media Corporation

Contact: Gary Krebs, Director

E-mail: swatrous@adamsmedia.com

Ed: Cliff Ennico. **Price:** $12.95. **Description:** Small business expert provides strategies to start a company and survive in the 21st Century. He shows small business owners how to succeed despite challenges that can defeat any firm. His advice covers suppliers; customers and contractors; competitors and creditors; spouses, family and friends; as well as the ways lawyers, accountants and other can steal an entrepreneur's success. Ennico also describes how startups can comply with local regulations.

26320 ■ Small Business Survival Guide: Starting, Protecting, and Securing Your Business for Long-Term Success

Pub: Adams Media Corporation

Ed: Cliff Ennico. **Released:** September 2005. **Price:** $12.95 (US), $17.95 (Canadian). **Description:** Entrepreneurship in the new millennium. Topics include creditors, taxes, competition, business law, and accounting.

26321 ■ "Startup to Serve Bar Scene" in Austin Business JournalInc. (Vol. 29, December 18, 2009, No. 41, pp. 1)

Pub: American City Business Journals

Ed: Christopher Calnan. **Description:** Startup ATX Innovation Inc. of Austin, Texas has developed a test version of TabbedOut, a Web-based tool that would facilitate mobile phone-based restaurant and bar bill payment. TabbedOut has been tested by six businesses in Austin and will be available to restaurant and bar owners for free. Income would be generated by ATX through a 99-cent convenience charge per transaction.

26322 ■ "State Budget Woes Hurt Many Vendors, Senior Services" in Sacramento Business Journal (Vol. 25, August 15, 2008, No. 24, pp. 1)

Pub: American City Business Journals, Inc.

Ed: Melanie Turner. **Description:** Delays in the passage of the California state budget have adversely affected the health care industry. The Robertson Adult Day Health Care had taken out loans to keep the business afloat. The state Legislature has reduced Medi-Cal reimbursement to health care providers by 10 percent.

26323 ■ "State Targets Credit Fixers" in Business Journal-Portland (Vol. 24, October 12, 2007, No. 33, pp. 1)

Pub: American City Business Journals, Inc.

Ed: Andy Giegerich, Justin Matlick. **Description:** Number of companies that offer quick fix to consumers is growing; the State of Oregon is considering rules to target them. A group working on a study in the state's mortgage lending regulations could craft bills to be examined for legislative session in February 2008.

26324 ■ "Stuck With Two Mortgages; The Nightmare When Buyers Upgrade" in Crain's Chicago Business (Vol. 31, April 21, 2008, No. 16)

Pub: Crain Communications, Inc.

Ed: Darci Smith. **Description:** Discusses the problem a number of people are facing due to the slump in the housing market: being stuck with two mortgages when they move because their former homes have not sold. Many thought they could afford to move to a larger home, anticipating significant equity appreciation that did not occur; now they are left with lowering their price and competing with the host of new developments.

26325 ■ "Summary. Economic Trends for Small Business" in Small Business Economic Trends (March 2008, pp. 1)

Pub: National Federation of Independent Business

Ed: William C. Dunkelberg, Holly Wade. **Description:** Summary of economic trends for small businesses in the U.S. is provided. Economic indicators such as capital spending, inventories and sales, inflation, and profits are given. Analysis of credit markets is also provided.

26326 ■ "Summary. Economic Trends for Small Business" in Small Business Economic Trends (February 2008, pp. 1)

Pub: National Federation of Independent Business

Ed: William C. Dunkelberg, Holly Wade. **Description:** Summary of economic trends for small businesses in the U.S. is provided. Economic indicators such as capital spending, inventories and sales, inflation, and profits are given. Analysis of credit markets is also provided.

26327 ■ "Sunwest Vies To Stave Off Bankruptcy" in The Business Journal-Portland (Vol. 25, August 15, 2008,

No. 23, pp. 1)
Pub: American City Business Journals, Inc.
Ed: Robin J. Moody. **Description:** Sunwest Management Inc. is teetering on the edge of bankruptcy as creditors start foreclosure on nine of their properties. This could potentially displace residents of the assisted living operator. Sunwest is trying to sell smaller packages of properties to get a $100 million bridge loan to maintain operations.

26328 ■ *"The Survey Says" in Collections and Credit Risk (Vol. 14, September 1, 2009, No. 8, pp. 16)*
Pub: SourceMedia, Inc.
Ed: Bill Grabarek; Darren Waggoner. **Description:** Revenue for the top accounts receivable management firms rose nearly 20 percent in 2008 despite lower liquidation rates, a poor economy and riskier, albeit cheaper debt portfolios; the trend may continue this year as collection agencies expect revenue, on average, to increase 5.8 percent. Debt buyers, however, found that their revenue fell nearly 7 percent in 2008 and expect it to fall another 12 percent this year.

26329 ■ *"Survival Guide: There Can Be an Upside to Managing a Downturn" in Canadian Business (Vol. 81, November 10, 2008, No. 19, pp. 54)*
Pub: Rogers Media Ltd.
Ed: Sharda Prashad. **Description:** Canada-based Foxy is already limiting its exposure to retailers who could be a credit problem in case of recession. Retirement Life Communities is entering into fixed-rate and fixed-term loans for them to have sufficient financing to grow. Business owners need to realize that customers want more for less.

26330 ■ *"Taking Collections" in Investment Dealers' Digest (Vol. 75, October 9, 2009, No. 38, pp. 19)*
Pub: SourceMedia, Inc.
Ed: Aleksandrs Rozens. **Description:** Although the nation's debt-collection industry has grown with increased reliance by consumers on credit, valuations of these firms have lessened due to the economy which has hurt some of the success of these firms in obtaining the debt back from consumers who are experiencing trying economic times.

26331 ■ *"Tampa Bay's CMBS Exposure Looms Large" in Tampa Bay Business Journal (Vol. 30, December 4, 2009, No. 50, pp. 1)*
Pub: American City Business Journals
Ed: Margie Manning. **Description:** Tampa, Florida's metropolitan statistical area have listed 50 to 601 commercial mortgage-backed securities loans as delinquent with a total delinquent loan balance of $439 million. The total was 9.7 percent of the $4.5 billion loans outstanding and was higher than the delinquency rate in New York and Los Angeles.

26332 ■ *"Too Much Information?" in Black Enterprise (Vol. 37, December 2006, No. 5, pp. 59)*
Pub: Earl G. Graves Publishing Co. Inc.
Ed: James C. Johnson. **Description:** African American business owners often face the dilemma of whether or not to divulge their minority status when soliciting new customers and financial institutions. The quality of the products or services is always the key factor and race should never define one's business; however, it is appropriate to market oneself as a minority or women-owned business, especially if the company is in an industry where those clients are offered top-tier contracts.

26333 ■ *"Too Much too Soon" in Barron's (Vol. 89, July 27, 2009, No. 30, pp. 33)*
Pub: Dow Jones & Co., Inc.
Ed: Leslie P. Norton. **Description:** Shares of hhgregg have risen 85 percent in the year leading up to July 2009 and analysts believe the stock could hit 25. However, their 113 outlets are concentrated in states where unemployment is above 10 percent and expanding into areas already overstored. Competition is also rife and credit availability is still tight.

26334 ■ *The Trillion Dollar Meltdown: Easy Money, High Rollers, and the Great Credit Crash*
Pub: Public Affairs
Ed: Charles R. Morris. **Released:** 2009. **Price:** $22.95. **Description:** Former banker believes that Wall Street and the financial community have too much power in America. He estimates that writedowns and defaults of residential mortgages, commercial mortgages, junk bonds, leveraged loans, credit cards, and complex securitized bonds could reach $1 trillion.

26335 ■ *"Troubled Project In Court" in The Business Journal-Portland (Vol. 25, July 25, 2008, No. 20, pp. 1)*
Pub: American City Business Journals, Inc.
Ed: Wendy Culverwell. **Description:** Views and information on Salpare Bay's Hayden Island project, as well as on financing problems and cases associated with the project, are presented. Construction of luxurious waterside condominiums stopped last fall, after the discovery of financing problems and subcontractors and other parties started filing claims and counterclaims.

26336 ■ *"Turmoil Means Changes For Retailers" in The Business Journal-Serving Metropolitan Kansas City (Vol. 27, October 10, 2008, No. 4)*
Pub: American City Business Journals, Inc.
Ed: Suzanna Stagemeyer. **Description:** Impacts of the financial crisis on Kansas Metropolitan Area retailers are varied. Rob Dalzell, for instance, found it difficult to secure a loan for his new self-serve yogurt store Yummo. The trends in retailing in the area are examined further as well as ways in which local businesses are changing in an attempt to stay solvent during the economic downturn.

26337 ■ *Ultimate Credit and Collection Handbook*
Pub: Entrepreneur Press
Ed: Michelle Dunn. **Released:** August 2006. **Price:** $36.95. **Description:** Entrepreneurial experts offer advice for successful credit and collection procedures.

26338 ■ *"Unfair Distraction of Employees" in Business Owner (Vol. 35, March-April 2011, No. 2, pp. 8)*
Pub: DL Perkins Company
Description: Fair Credit Collection Practices Act makes it illegal for collectors to contact a debtor at his or her place of employment if the collector is made aware that it is against personnel policy of the employer for the worker to take such a call.

26339 ■ *"U.S. Economy's Underlying Strengths Limit Recession Threat" in Hispanic Business (Vol. 30, April 2008, No. 4, pp. 14)*
Pub: Hispanic Business
Ed: Dr. Juan B. Solana. **Description:** Large and small businesses as well as consumers and policymakers are attempting to identify the areas of risk and loss created by the economic crisis; analysts are now estimating that U.S. mortgage losses could reach the $380 to $400 billion mark. Also discusses the falling of wages and the rising of unemployment. Statistical data included.

26340 ■ *"Unlicensed Utah Collection Agency Settles with Idaho Department of Finance" in Idaho Business Review, Boise (July 15, 2010)*
Pub: Idaho Business Review
Description: Federal Recovery Acceptance Inc., doing business as Paramount Acceptance in Utah, agreed to pay penalties and expenses after the firm was investigated by the state for improprieties. The firm was charged with conducting unlicensed collection activity.

26341 ■ *"Valenti: Roots of Financial Crisis Go Back to 1998" in Crain's Detroit Business (Vol. 24, October 6, 2008, No. 40, pp. 25)*
Pub: Crain Communications, Inc.
Ed: Tom Henderson; Nathan Skid. **Description:** Interview with Sam Valenti III who is the chairman and CEO of Valenti Capital L.L.C., a wealth-management firm; Valenti discusses in detail the history that led up to the current economic crisis as well as his prediction for the future of the country.

26342 ■ *The Visa Approval Backlog and Its Impact on American Small Business: Congressional Hearing*
Pub: DIANE Publishing Company
Ed: Donald A. Manzullo. **Released:** July 2006. **Price:** $30.00. **Description:** Information regarding the Congressional hearing involving the Visa approval backlog is discussed.

26343 ■ *"Welcome Back" in Canadian Business (Vol. 82, April 27, 2009, No. 7, pp. 25)*
Pub: Rogers Media
Ed: Barka Halas. **Description:** Some Canadian companies such as Gennum Corporation have taken advantage of corporate sale-leasebacks to raise money at a time when credit is hard to acquire. Corporate sale-leasebacks allow companies to sell their property assets while remaining as tenants of the building. Sale-leasebacks allow firms to increase capital while avoiding the disruptions that may result with moving.

26344 ■ *"What Are You, A Bank? You Probably Lend Your Customers More Money Than You Realize." in Inc. (November 2007, pp. 81)*
Pub: Gruner & Jahr USA Publishing
Ed: Norm Brodsky. **Description:** Small business owners don't realize when that when customers do not pay on time, it is the same as lending them money. Tips to get customers to pay on time are listed.

26345 ■ *"What the Future Holds for Consumers" in Black Enterprise (Vol. 41, August 2010, No. 1, pp. 47)*
Pub: Earl G. Graves Publishing Co. Inc.
Ed: Sheiresa Ngo. **Description:** The way people purchase goods and service has changed with technology. With an increased focus on security (as well as privacy and fairness) the U.S. Congress began regulating the credit card industry with the Fair Credit Reporting Act of 1970 and the Credit Card Accountability, Responsibility, and Disclosure (CARD) Act of 2009.

26346 ■ *"When Dov Cries" in Canadian Business (Vol. 83, June 15, 2010, No. 10, pp. 71)*
Pub: Rogers Media Ltd.
Ed: Joe Castaldo. **Description:** American Apparel disclosed that they will have problems meeting one of its debt covenants which could trigger a chain reaction that could lead to bankruptcy. The prospects look bleak, but eccentric company founder Dov Charney, has always defied expectations.

26347 ■ *"Where to Stash Your Cash" in Barron's (Vol. 88, March 17, 2008, No. 11, pp. 41)*
Pub: Dow Jones & Company, Inc.
Ed: Mike Hogan. **Description:** Investors are putting their money in money-market mutual funds seeking fractionally better yields and a safe haven from the uncertainties that was brought about by subprime lending. These funds, however, are hovering near 3.20 percent which is less than the 4 percent inflation rate.

26348 ■ *"Wobbling Economy" in The Business Journal-Serving Metropolitan Kansas City (Vol. 27, September 26, 2008, No. 2, pp. 1)*
Pub: American City Business Journals, Inc.
Ed: Rob Roberts. **Description:** Real estate developers in Kansas City Metropolitan Area are worried of the possible impacts of the crisis at Wall Street. They expect tightening of the credit market, which will result in difficulty of financing their projects. The potential effects of the Wall Street crisis are examined further.

26349 ■ *"Woes Portend Consumer Shift" in The Business Journal-Serving Metropolitan Kansas City (Vol. 27, September 26, 2008, No. 2, pp. 1)*

Pub: American City Business Journals, Inc.

Ed: Suzanna Stagemeyer. **Description:** Black Bamboo owner Tim Butt believes that prolonged tightening of the credit market will result in consumer spending becoming more cash-driven that credit card driven. The financial crisis has already constricted spending among consumers. Forecasts for the US economy are provided.

26350 ■ *"The Worst Lies Ahead for Wall Street; More Losses Certain" in Crain's New York Business (Vol. 24, January 21, 2008, No. 3, pp. 1)*

Pub: Crain Communications, Inc.

Ed: Aaron Elstein. **Description:** Due to the weakening economy, many financial institutions will face further massive losses forcing them to borrow more at higher interest rates and dragging down their earnings for years to come. The effects on commercial real estate and credit card loans are also discussed as well as the trend to investing in Asia and the Middle East.

26351 ■ *"The Wrong Tune" in The Business Journal-Portland (Vol. 25, July 25, 2008, No. 20, pp. 1)*

Pub: American City Business Journals, Inc.

Ed: Robin J. Moody. **Description:** Views and information on turnaround management and recovery plans of the Oregon Symphony, are presented. The non-profit organization has lost a total of $5.1 million between 2002 and 2008, and $400,000 annual interest payments for a $7 million bank loan. Increased ticket sales, as well as cost cutting measures, are helping improve the finance of the organization.

26352 ■ *"Your Exposure to Bear Stearns" in Barron's (Vol. 88, March 17, 2008, No. 11, pp. 45)*

Pub: Dow Jones & Company, Inc.

Ed: Tom Sullivan; Jack Willoughby. **Description:** Bear Stearns makes up 5.5 percent of Pioneer Independence's portfolio, 1.4 percent of Vanguard Windsor II's portfolio, 1.2 percent of Legg Mason Value Trust, about 1 percent of Van Kampen Equity & Income, and 0.79 percent of Putnam Fund for Growth & Income. Ginnie Mae securities are now trading at 1.78 percentage points over treasuries due to the mortgage crises.

26353 ■ *"Your Startup may be Worth Less than You Think" in Entrepreneur (Vol. 37, October 2009, No. 10, pp. 96)*

Pub: Entrepreneur Media, Inc.

Ed: Asheesh Advani. **Description:** Valuations of startups at the idea stage are dropping due to the effects of the recession. This drop is due to the decreasing availability of investment capital, the reduction in portfolio values of investors, and the increase in early stage startups.

TRADE PERIODICALS

26354 ■ *Collections & Credit Risk: The Monthly Magazine for Collections and Credit Policy Professionals*

Pub: SourceMedia Inc.

Contact: Douglas J. Manoni, Chief Executive Officer

E-mail: doug.manoni@sourcemedia.com

URL(s): www.collectionscreditrisk.com/. **Released:** Monthly **Price:** $119, Individuals; C$148, Individuals; $213, Two years; $376, Two years in Canada.

26355 ■ *What's Working in Credit & Collections*

Pub: Progressive Business Publications

Contact: Ron McRae, Editor-in-Chief

Ed: Russell Case, Editor. **Released:** Semimonthly. **Price:** $253, individuals. **Description:** Teaches successful credit and collection techniques to build credit sales while avoiding losses. Recurring features include interviews, news of research, a calendar of events, and a column titled Sharpen Your Judgment.

VIDEOCASSETTES/ AUDIOCASSETTES

26356 ■ *It's in the Mail: Techniques for Collecting Debts*

Video Arts, Inc.

c/o Aim Learning Group

8238-40 Lehigh

Morton Grove, IL 60053-2615

Free: 877-444-2230

Fax: (416)252-2155

Co. E-mail: service@aimlearninggroup.com

URL: http://www.aimlearninggroup.com

Released: 1989. **Price:** $755.00. **Description:** A business guide to pressuring and applying legal leans on outstanding debtors. **Availability:** VHS; 3/4 U.

CONSULTANTS

26357 ■ **NetKnowledge Technologies L.L.C. (NKT)—NKSoft Corp.**

6565 N MacArthur Blvd., Ste. 800

Irving, TX 75039

Ph: (214)624-5122

Fax: (972)910-0069

Co. E-mail: aubrey.roberts@nksoft.com

Scope: Works with executives worldwide to solve pressing business problems through the integration of business strategy and operations; information technology; and change management. **Founded:** 1997.

LIBRARIES

26358 ■ **Loan Brokers Association Information Services**

917 S. Park St.

Owosso, MI 48867-4422

Contact: Ben Campbell, Director

Scope: Loan brokers, loan consulting, credit repair, lending, credit cards, venture capital. **Services:** Copying; SDI; library to members or by permission.

ASSOCIATIONS AND OTHER ORGANIZATIONS

26359 ■ Help Desk Institute (HDI)
121 S Tejon, Ste. 1100
Colorado Springs, CO 80903
Ph: (719)268-0174
Free: 800-248-5667
Fax: (719)268-0184
Co. E-mail: support@thinkhdi.com
URL: http://www.thinkhdi.com
Contact: Darien Chimoff, Chairperson
Description: Corporations, organizations, and agencies offering help desks or other customer or user information services. Promotes effective operation of help desks and related services. Facilitates exchange of information among members; evaluates and certifies support centers; conducts research and educational programs. **Founded:** 1989. **Publications:** *HDI Industry Insider* (Biweekly); *Support and Service Suppliers Directory* (Periodic); *SupportWorld*. **Awards:** HDI All Star Award (Monthly); Help Desk Analyst of the Year Award (Annual); Help Desk Hero Award (Quarterly); Team Excellence Award (Annual); All Star Award; Analyst of the Year Award; Help Desk Hero Award; Team Excellence Award.

26360 ■ International Customer Service Association (ICSA)
1110 South Ave., Ste. No. 50
Staten Island, NY 10314
Ph: (374)273-1303
Fax: (347)273-1403
Co. E-mail: info@icsatoday.org
URL: http://www.icsa.com
Contact: Bill Gessert, President
Description: Customer service professionals in public and private sectors united to develop the theory and understanding of customer service and management. Goals are to: promote professional development; standardize terminology and phrases; provide career counseling and placement services; establish hiring guidelines, performance standards and job descriptions. Provides a forum for shared problems and solutions. Compiles statistics. **Founded:** 1981. **Publications:** *ICSA News* (Bimonthly). **Educational Activities:** International Customer Service Association Conference (Annual). **Awards:** Award of Excellence (Annual); Award of Excellence.

EDUCATIONAL PROGRAMS

26361 ■ Achieving Excellence in Customer Service (Onsite)
Learning Tree International Inc.
1805 Library St.
Reston, VA 20190-5660
Ph: (703)709-9119
Free: 800-843-8733
Fax: (703)709-6405
Co. E-mail: uscourses@learningtree.com
URL: http://www.learningtree.com
Contact: Nick Schacht, President
Price: $2,490.00. **Description:** This course provides the tools and techniques to ensure you build and maintain mutually beneficial relationships with customers. **Dates and Locations:** Reston, VA; New York, NY; Washington, DC; and Rockville, MD.

26362 ■ The Conference on Customer Service (Onsite)
Seminar Information Service. Inc.
20 Executive Park, Ste. 120
Irvine, CA 92614
Ph: (949)261-9104
Free: 877-SEM-INFO
Fax: (949)261-1963
Co. E-mail: info@seminarinformation.com
URL: http://www.seminarinformation.com
Price: $149.00; $139.00 for four or more. **Description:** Learn techniques and tips for effectively and successfully dealing with customers, including what customer service representatives need to stay motivated and productive. **Dates and Locations:** Cities throughout the United States.

26363 ■ Customer Satisfaction and Loyalty Research (Onsite)
Seminar Information Service, Inc.
20 Executive Park, Ste. 120
Irvine, CA 92614
Ph: (949)261-9104
Free: 877-SEM-INFO
Fax: (949)261-1963
Co. E-mail: info@seminarinformation.com
URL: http://www.seminarinformation.com
Price: $2,495.00. **Description:** Learn why it is important to assess customer satisfaction and the consequences of ignoring this vital area; how to design a study to measure customer satisfaction, how to structure and administer the survey questionnaire and how to select the sample; and how to implement results from the study to establish performance standards and goals for the future. **Dates and Locations:** Chicago, IL.

26364 ■ Customer Service Excellence: How to Win and Keep Customers (Onsite)
American Management Association
600 AMA Way
Saranac Lake, NY 12983-5534
Ph: (212)586-8100
Free: 877-566-9441
Fax: (518)891-0368
Co. E-mail: customerservice@amanet.org
URL: http://www.amaseminars.org
Price: $1,895.00 for non-members; $1,695.00 for AMA members; and $1,451.00 for General Services Administration (GSA) members. **Description:** Covers the skills needed to communicate professionalism, gain respect, improve customer relationships, and secure competitive advantage. **Dates and Locations:** Atlanta, GA; New York, NY; and San Francisco CA.

26365 ■ Customer Service That Wows! (Onsite)
Seminar Information Service, Inc.
20 Executive Park, Ste. 120
Irvine, CA 92614
Ph: (949)261-9104
Free: 877-SEM-INFO
Fax: (949)261-1963
Co. E-mail: info@seminarinformation.com
URL: http://www.seminarinformation.com
Price: $199.00. **Description:** Learn how to determine what the customer needs before they ask and giving them more than they expect. **Dates and Locations:** Cities throughout the United States.

26366 ■ Exceptional Customer Service Leadership
Canadian Management Centre (CMC)
150 York St., 5th Fl.
Toronto, ON, Canada M5H 3S5
Ph: (416)214-5678
Free: 877-262-2519
Fax: (416)313-4985
Co. E-mail: cmcinfo@cmctraining.org
URL: http://www.cmctraining.org
Contact: John Wright, President
Price: $1,85.00 for members; $1,995.00 for non-members. **Description:** Guides you through proven approaches for excellent customer service leadership. **Dates and Locations:** Toronto, ON.

26367 ■ How to Collect Accounts Receivable (Onsite)
Fred Pryor Seminars & CareerTrack
5700 Broadmoor St., Ste. 300
Mission, KS 66202
Free: 800-780-8476
Fax: (913)967-8849
Co. E-mail: customerservice@pryor.com
URL: http://www.pryor.com
Price: $149.00; $139.00 for groups of 5 or more. **Description:** Learn to collect pastdue accounts without losing your customer. **Dates and Locations:** Cities throughout the United States.

REFERENCE WORKS

26368 ■ *101 Ways to Really Satisfy Your Customers: How to Keep Your Customers and Attract New Ones*
Pub: Allen & Unwin Pty., Limited

Ed: Andrew Griffiths. **Released:** April 2007. **Price:** $14.95. **Description:** Tips for providing excellent customer service that ensure loyalty and interest to a small business are examined.

26369 ■ *"2009: A Call For Vision" in Women Entrepreneur (January 28, 2009)*
Pub: Entrepreneur Media Inc.

Ed: Elinor Robin. **Description:** Providing exemplary customer service, reducing expenses and creating an out-of-the-box niche are three key factors that will help business survive during this economic crisis. Business owners must see potential where others see failure in order to create new opportunities that may not only allow their business to survive during these times but may actually cause some businesses to thrive despite this economic downturn.

26370 ■ "2010 American Business Woman of ABWA" in Women In Business (Vol. 61, October-November 2009, No. 5, pp. 22)
Pub: American Business Women's Association
Ed: Doris Brown. **Description:** Achievements of Doris Brown are presented in light of her being named as the 2010 American Business Woman of American Business Women's Association (ABWA). She specializes in the field of client and customer satisfaction for Avue Technologies. Brown believes that her involvement in the ABWA has helped her to see the importance of being a resource for other people.

26371 ■ Alpha Dogs: How Your Small Business Can Become a Leader of the Pack
Pub: HarperInformation
Ed: Donna Fenn. **Released:** May 2007. **Price:** $14.95. **Description:** Ways for an entrepreneur to outsmart competitors in the marketplace, to generate higher sales, and earn lasting customer and employee loyalty.

26372 ■ Alpha Dogs: How Your Small Business Can Become a Leader of the Pack
Pub: HarperCollins Publishers, Inc.
Ed: Donna Fenn. **Released:** May 2007. **Price:** $14.95. **Description:** Profiles of eight successful entrepreneurs along with information for developing customer service, technology and competition.

26373 ■ "Apparel Apparatchic at Kmart" in Barron's (Vol. 88, March 17, 2008, No. 11, pp. 16)
Pub: Dow Jones & Company, Inc.
Description: Kmart began a nationwide search for women to represent the company in a national advertising campaign. Contestants need to upload their photos to Kmart's website and winners will be chosen by a panel of celebrity judges. The contest aims to reverse preconceived negative notions about the store's quality and service.

26374 ■ "Applying Continuous Process Improvement for Managing Customer Loyalty" in Agency Sales Magazine (Vol. 39, November 2009, No. 10)
Pub: MANA
Ed: Bob Cicerone; Aaron Hekele; Jason Morado. **Description:** Steps in effective process improvement that reveals where opportunities exist to improve management practices and control customer loyalty are discussed. The process consists of thirteen factors grouped into three sets.

26375 ■ "Attention, Shoppers Take a Deep Breath: Why It Pays to Help Customers Relax" in Inc. (Vol. 33, November 2011, No. 9, pp. 26)
Pub: Inc. Magazine
Ed: J.J. McCorvey. **Description:** According to a current study, along with festive music and decorations for holiday shoppers, some merchants are considering back messages and pedicures to keep customers happy.

26376 ■ Authenticity: What Consumers Really Want
Pub: Harvard Business School Press
Ed: James H. Gilmore. **Released:** September 24, 2007. **Price:** $26.95. **Description:** In today's marketplace, consumers tend to buy based on how authentic a company's offer appears. A company's identity is explored through case studies and advertising slogans. The authors write from the theory that most everything is artificial, manmade, and fake.

26377 ■ Awesomely Simple: Essential Business Strategies for Turning Ideas Into Action
Pub: Jossey-Bass
Ed: John Spence. **Released:** September 8, 2009. **Price:** $24.95. **Description:** Six key strategies that create a foundation for achieving business excellence include: vivid vision, best people, a performance-oriented culture, robust communication, a sense of urgency, and extreme customer focus.

26378 ■ "Bad Client? Make Break Cleanly, Swiftly - and Based On Numbers" in Crain's Detroit Business (Vol. 23, November 19, 2007, No. 47)
Pub: Crain Communications Inc. - Detroit
Ed: Sheena Harrison. **Description:** Firing a difficult customer can be hard to do, but the best way to do it is cleanly and amicably.

26379 ■ "Bank Bullish on Austin" in Austin Business JournalInc. (Vol. 29, November 13, 2009, No. 36, pp. A1)
Pub: American City Business Journals
Ed: Kate Harrington. **Description:** American Bank's presence in Austin, Texas has been boosted by new management and a new 20,000 square foot building. This community bank intends to focus on building relationship with commercial banking customers. American Bank also plans to extend investment banking, treasury management, and commercial lending services.

26380 ■ "Banking on Twitter" in Baltimore Business Journal (Vol. 27, February 6, 2010, No. 40, pp. 1)
Pub: American City Business Journals
Ed: Gary Haber. **Description:** Ways that banks are using Twitter, Facebook and other social networking sites to provide customer services is discussed. First Mariner Bank is one of those banks that are finding the social media platform as a great way to reach customers. Privacy issues regarding this marketing trend are examined.

26381 ■ "Banks Deposit Reassurance, Calm Customers" in The Business Journal-Serving Greater Tampa Bay (Vol. 28, August 22, 2008)
Pub: American City Business Journals, Inc.
Ed: Margie Manning. **Description:** Community banks in the Tampa Bay Area are training tellers and other customer care workers to help reassure customers that their deposits are safe. Other measures to reassure depositors include joining a network that allows banks to share deposits. Additional information on moves community banks are making to reassure consumers is presented.

26382 ■ Battling Big Box: How Nimble Niche Companies Can Outmaneuver Giant Companies
Pub: Career Press, Inc.
Ed: Henry Dubroff, Susan J. Marks. **Released:** January 1, 2009. **Price:** $15.99. **Description:** Small companies can compete with larger firms through agility, adaptability, customer service, and credibility. Topics include information to help empower employees, build a powerful brand, manage cash flow, and maintaining a business vision.

26383 ■ "Be Innovative In Other Ways" in Green Industry Pro (Vol. 23, March 2011, No. 3, pp. 4)
Pub: Cygnus Business Media
Ed: Rod Dickens. **Description:** Emphasis is put on the importance of putting the customer first in order to successfully market any product or service. Six marketing ideas are presented to promote a landscaping business.

26384 ■ Behind the Cloud
Pub: Jossey-Bass
Ed: Marc Benioff, Carlye Adler. **Released:** 2010. **Price:** $27.95. **Description:** Salesforce.com is the world's most successful business-to-business cloud-computing company that sells an online service that helps businesses manage sales, customer service, and marketing functions.

26385 ■ "Best In Show" in Pet Product News (Vol. 64, November 2010, No. 11, pp. 20)
Pub: BowTie Inc.
Ed: Lizett Bond. **Description:** Cherrybrook Premium Pet Supplies offers an expanded array of quality holistic products and is staffed by people who possess wide knowledge of these products. Aside from receiving the Outstanding Holistic Approach award, Cherrybrook has opened three stores in New Jersey. How a holistic approach to service kept customers coming back is discussed.

26386 ■ "Best Practices: Just Say No" in Entrepreneur (Vol. 35, October 2007, No. 10, pp. 107)
Pub: Entrepreneur Media Inc.
Ed: Chris Penttila. **Description:** Customer service must have boundaries to prevent abuse by customers. Companies should learn to refuse unreasonable customer demands, set limitations and make customers understand and accept these limitations. Details on customer service policies are given.

26387 ■ "The Best and Worst Economic Times" in Agency Sales Magazine (Vol. 39, December 2009, No. 11, pp. 22)
Pub: MANA
Ed: Mark Young. **Description:** U.S. gross domestic product grew 3.5 percent and the stock market has improved but manufacturers are cutting commissions or dropping sales representatives. Despite these challenges, it can a good time for salespeople because clients need them more than ever. Salesmen should find new ways to do business for their clients during this current challenging environment.

26388 ■ Beyond Booked Solid: Your Business, Your Life, Your Way-It's All Inside
Pub: John Wiley and Sons, Inc.
Ed: Michael Port. **Released:** April 2008. **Price:** $24.95. **Description:** Professional service providers and small business owners will discover tactics and strategies for growing and expanding their companies while allowing them to find time to relax and enjoy their lives. Owners will learn to attract new clients and grow profits.

26389 ■ Big Vision, Small Business
Pub: Ivy Sea, Inc.
Ed: Jamie S. Walters. **Released:** October 10, 2002. **Price:** $17.95. **Description:** The power of the small enterprise is examined. The author shares her expertise as an entrepreneur and founder of a business consulting firm to help small business owners successfully run their companies. Interviews with more than seventy small business owners provide insight into visioning, planning, and establishing a small company, as well as strategies for good employee and customer relationships.

26390 ■ "Blockbuster Launches Internet Movie Downloads to Compete Against Netflix, Others" in Chicago Tribune (December 3, 2008)
Pub: McClatchy-Tribune Information Services
Ed: Eric Benderoff. **Description:** Blockbuster Inc., the DVD rental giant, has launched a new service that delivers movies to their customer's homes via the Internet in an attempt to compete against Netflix and other competitors.

26391 ■ "Boosting Worried Customers' Confidence" in Gallup Management Journal (November 8, 2011)
Pub: Gallup
Ed: Jessica Tyler, Patrick Whiston. **Description:** While customers fear a double-dip recession and US economic confidence is low, leading edge firms have found a timely and creative way to win customers: they are improving their wellbeing.

26392 ■ "Bottoms Up!" in Entrepreneur (Vol. 36, April 2008, No. 4, pp. 128)
Pub: Entrepreneur Media, Inc.
Ed: Amanda C. Kooser. **Description:** Jill Bernheimer launched her online alcohol business Domaine547 in 2007, and encountered challenges as legal issues over the licensing and launching of the business took about seven months to finish. Domain547 features blog and forum areas. Marketing strategy that connects to the social community is one of the ways to reach out to customers.

26393 ■ "Business Forecast: Stormy and Successful" in Women In Business (Vol. 62, June 2010, No. 2, pp. 12)
Pub: American Business Women's Association
Ed: Kathleen Leighton. **Description:** Stormy Simon, vice president of customer service at Overstock.com is a self-made career woman who started out as a temporary employee in the company in 2001. She

was not able to attend college because she had two sons to care for after her divorce. Simon got involved in advertising and media buying and shares her love for business.

26394 ■ *Business Process Mapping Workbook: Improving Customer Satisfaction*
Pub: John Wiley & Sons, Inc.
Ed: J. Mike Jacka, Paulette J. Keller. **Released:** July 7, 2009. **Price:** $50.00. **Description:** The various steps involved in performing a business process map to achieve optimal customer satisfaction are outlined.

26395 ■ *"Buying In" in Harvard Business Review (Vol. 86, September 2008, No. 9, pp. 36)*
Pub: Harvard Business School Press
Ed: Andrew O'Connell. **Description:** Review of the book entitled, 'Buying In: The Secret Dialogue between What We Buy and Who We Are' which offers tips that those in the field of marketing will find useful.

26396 ■ *"Buying Power of Hispanics Growing" in Austin Business JournalInc. (Vol. 29, November 27, 2009, No. 38, pp. 1)*
Pub: American City Business Journals
Ed: Sandra Zaragoza. **Description:** Hispanic Marketing Symposium presented a report stating that the buying power of Hispanics of Austin, Texas has grown by 54 percent in last five years to $9.4 billion in 2009. Details on the projected growth of the Hispanic market in the are is covered.

26397 ■ *"Calming Customers" in The Business Journal-Portland (Vol. 25, August 29, 2008, No. 25, pp. 1)*
Pub: American City Business Journals, nc.
Ed: Kirsten Grind; Rob Smith. **Description:** Credit unions and banks in the Portland area are reaching out to clients in an effort to reassure them on the security of their money and the firms' financial stability. Roy Whitehead of Washington Federal Savings, for instance, wrote 41,000 customers of the bank to reassure them. The strategies of different banks and credit unions to answer their client's worries are discussed.

26398 ■ *"Cashing In: Gleaning an Education from Our Economic State" in Agency Sales Magazine (Vol. 39, August 2009, No. 8, pp. 22)*
Pub: MANA
Ed: John Graham. **Description:** Businesses have learned that cutting price can kill business and being tough is normal. The recession has also taught that getting the right vision and gaining the confidence and trust of consumers are important.

26399 ■ *"Certified Technicians can Increase Bottom Line" in Contractor (Vol. 56, September 2009, No. 9, pp. 37)*
Pub: Penton Media, Inc.
Ed: Ray Isaac. **Description:** Certified technicians increase the value of HVAC firms, a survey by Service Round Table has reported. The increased value has been attributed to fewer callbacks, less warranty work and greater ability to educate consumers. Meanwhile, consumers are willing to pay more for the services of certified technicians.

26400 ■ *"Changing Prescriptions" in Business North Carolina (Vol. 28, March 2008, No. 3, pp. 52)*
Pub: Business North Carolina
Description: Profile of Moose Drug Company, founded by Archibald Walter Moose in 1882. Family owners share how they focus on pharmacoeconomics (cost-benefit analyses of drugs or drug therapy) and customer service.

26401 ■ *Cisco Network Design Solutions for Small-Medium Businesses*
Pub: Cisco Press
Ed: Peter Rybaczyk. **Released:** August 2004. **Price:** $55.00. **Description:** Solutions for computer networking professionals using computer networks within a small to medium-sized business. Topics cover not only core networking issues and solutions, but security, IP telephony, unified communications, customer relations management, wireless LANs, and more.

26402 ■ *Clued In*
Pub: Financial Times/Prentice Hall
Contact: Richard Stagg, Director
Ed: Lewis Carbone. **Released:** May 24, 2004. **Price:** $34.99. **Description:** Tips for providing excellent customer service that keeps clients coming back are shared. Brand management and Experience Value Management are defined.

26403 ■ *"Come Together" in Pet Product News (Vol. 64, December 2010, No. 12, pp. 28)*
Pub: BowTie Inc.
Ed: Lizett Bond. **Description:** Pet supply retailers have posted improved sales and improved customer service by bundling their offerings. Bundling pertains to grouping related items such as collars and leashes into a single unit for marketing purposes. Aside from providing convenience and enhanced product information to customers, bundling has facilitated more efficient purchases.

26404 ■ *Consumer Behavior*
Pub: Prentice Hall Business Publishing
Contact: Jerome Grant, President
Ed: Leon Schiffman, Leslie Kanuk. **Released:** August 7, 2009. **Price:** $180.00. **Description:** Consumer behavior is central to the planning, development and implementation of marketing strategies.

26405 ■ *"Conversations with Customers" in Business Journal Serving Greater Tampa Bay (Vol. 31, December 31, 2010, No. 1, pp. 1)*
Pub: Tampa Bay Business Journal
Description: Tampa Bay, Florida-based businesses have been using social media to interact with customers. Forty percent of businesses have been found to have at least one social media platform to reach customers and prospects.

26406 ■ *"Convert New Customers to Long Term Accounts" in Indoor Comfort Marketing (Vol. 70, February 2011, No. 2, pp. 22)*
Pub: Industry Publications Inc.
Description: Marketing to new customers and suggestions for retaining them is covered.

26407 ■ *"Courier Service Delivers Big Profits and Top-Notch Customer Service" in Small Business Opportunities (November 2007)*
Pub: Harris Publications Inc.
Description: Profile of Relay Express, a courier franchising business started by three friends in 1986. The company focuses on customer service and calls them every 19 minutes to report on progress of a parcel until it is delivered.

26408 ■ *"The Customer Is Right Even If He's Wrong" in Contractor (Vol. 57, February 2010, No. 2, pp. 12)*
Pub: Penton Media, Inc.
Ed: Al Schwarz. **Description:** Mechanical contractors should note that customers who make a judgment based upon the impression that they form on their first meeting. Contractors can maintain a professional image by washing their trucks and having the personnel dress uniformly. Contractors have every right to demand that employees clean up and make a better impression on customers.

26409 ■ *"Customer Loyalty: Making Your Program Excel" in Franchising World (Vol. 42, August 2010, No. 8, pp. 47)*
Pub: International Franchise Association
Ed: Steve Baxter. **Description:** Customer loyalty is key to any franchise operation's growth. Tips for identifying preferred customers are outlined.

26410 ■ *"Customer OKs on Press" in American Printer (Vol. 128, August 1, 2011, No. 8)*
Pub: Penton Media Inc.
Description: Printers discuss the value of having customers meet at the plant in order to okay print colors for projects.

26411 ■ *"Customer Preferences Control Skid Steer Choices" in Rental Product News (Vol. 33, June 2011)*
Pub: Cygnus Business Media
Ed: Jenny Lescohier. **Description:** Understanding the types of controls available on skid steer equipment is essential. The article provides a comprehensive guide to using and maintaining skid steers for rental agencies.

26412 ■ *"Customer Retention is Proportionate to Employee Retention" in Green Industry Pro (Vol. 23, September 2011)*
Pub: Cygnus Business Media
Description: Presented in a question-answer format, information is provided to help retain customers as well as keeping workers happy.

26413 ■ *"Customer Service Center Will Rise in Indian Land" in Charlotte Observer (February 4, 2007)*
Pub: Knight-Ridder/Tribune Business News
Ed: Taylor Bright. **Description:** Kennametal is building a new customer service center in Lancaster County, North Carolina. Kennametal makes metal tools and parts, specializing in metals highly resistant to heat.

26414 ■ *Cute Little Store: Between the Entrepreneurial Dream and Business Reality*
Pub: Outskirts Press, Incorporated
Ed: Adeena Mignogna. **Released:** May 2006. **Price:** $11.95. **Description:** Challenges of starting and growing a retail business are profiled.

26415 ■ *"The Dean of Design" in Canadian Business (Vol. 79, November 6, 2006, No. 22, pp. 42)*
Pub: Rogers Media
Ed: Erin Pooley. **Description:** The need of a good business design to increase the business in saturated markets with relation to customer satisfaction is emphasized.

26416 ■ *Design and Launch Your Online Boutique in a Week*
Pub: Entrepreneur Press
Ed: Melissa Campanelli. **Released:** June 26, 2008. **Price:** $17.95. **Description:** Tips for starting an online boutique in a short amount of time are given. The books shows how to build the online boutique with designer goods or your own product, ways to create eye-catching content, online tools to handle payments and accept orders, marketing and advertising techniques, and customer service.

26417 ■ *"Designing Solutions Around Customer Network Identity Goals" in Journal of Marketing (Vol. 75, March 2011, No. 2, pp. 36)*
Pub: American Marketing Association
Ed: Amber M. Epp, Linda L. Price. **Description:** The role re ational and collective goals in creating customer solutions is investigated using in-depth interviews with 21 families. Findings revealed four integration processes in customer networks, namely, offerings formed around individual coalitions, concurrent participation, alternate participation, and offerings formed around priority goals.

26418 ■ *"Don't' Hate the Cable Guy" in Saint Louis Business Journal (Vol. 31, August 5, 2011, No. 50, pp. 1)*
Pub: Saint Louis Business Journal
Ed: Angela Mueller. **Description:** Charter Communications named John Birrer as senior vice president of customer experience. The company experienced problems with its customer services.

26419 ■ *"Down by the Bay" in Canadian Business (Vol. 81, December 8, 2008, No. 21, pp. 15)*
Pub: Rogers Media Ltd.
Ed: Calvin Leung. **Description:** Hudsons Bay Company chief executive Jeffrey Sherman believes that his vast experience in retail will help him find the company's customer base. Sales are estimated to

increase 3.6 percent in 2009 after posting average annual retail sales increases of 5 percent between 2006 and 2008.

26420 ■ *"The Downside of Self-Management"* in Academy of Management Journal (August 2007)
Pub: Academy of Management
Contact: Ming-Jer Chen, President
Ed: Claus W. Langfred. **Description:** Study reveals that self-managing teams might accidentally restructure themselves inefficiently in response to conflict, thus the possible structure-related effects are analyzed.

26421 ■ *"Dream Big! When the Going Gets Tough, Reps Work Harder and Smarter"* in Agency Sales Magazine (Vol. 39, July 2009, No. 7, pp. 22)
Pub: MANA
Ed: John Chapin. **Description:** Sales representatives should use the tough economy as a warning and motivation to work harder and smarter. Reps should improve their selling by reading books, listening to tapes and CDs. They should also keep a good attitude and build relationships.

26422 ■ *"eBay Business Looking Up"* in Zacks (July 26, 2011)
Pub: Comtex News Network Inc.
Ed: Sejuti Banerjea. **Description:** eBay reported solid revenue growth for 2011 second quarter, keeping in line with the Zacks Consensus Estimate, and third quarter earnings are expected to be higher. eBay's new strategy is to direct traffic to bigger sellers with improved customer service, making this good for eBay businesses.

26423 ■ *"Emack & Bolio"* in Ice Cream Reporter (Vol. 23, October 20, 2010, No. 11, pp. 8)
Pub: Ice Cream Reporter
Description: Emack & Bolio's is engaging in scent marketing using various odors to help boost sales by attracting consumers with scents appropriate to their products.

26424 ■ *"Empowered"* in Harvard Business Review (Vol. 88, July-August 2010, No. 7-8, pp. 94)
Pub: Harvard Business School Publishing
Ed: Josh Bernoff, Ted Schadler. **Description:** HERO concept (highly empowered and resourceful operative) which builds a connection between employees, managers, and IT is outlined. The resultant additional experience and knowledge gained by employees improves customer relationship management.

26425 ■ Exceptional Service, Exceptional Profit: The Secrets of Building a Five-Star Customer Service Organization
Pub: AMACOM
Ed: Leonard Inghilleri, Micah Solomon. **Released:** April 1, 2010. **Price:** $21.95. **Description:** Team of insiders share exclusive knowledge of the loyalty-building techniques pioneered by the world's most successful service leaders, including brick-and-mortar stars such as The Ritz-Carlton and Lexus and online success stories such as Netflix and CD Baby.

26426 ■ *"Experts Strive to Educate on Proper Pet Diets"* in Pet Product News (Vol. 64, November 2010, No. 11, pp. 40)
Pub: BowTie Inc.
Ed: John Hustace Walker. **Description:** Pet supply manufacturers have been bundling small mammal food and treats with educational sources to help retailers avoid customer misinformation. This action has been motivated by the customer's quest to seek proper nutritional advice for their small mammal pets.

26427 ■ *"Fast Fact: Quality of Foods, Cost Top Factors in Determining Where to Grocery Shop"* in Marketing to Women (Vol. 22, August 2009)
Pub: EPM Communications Inc.
Contact: Ira Mayer, President
E-mail: imayer@epmcom.com
Description: Efficient check-outs, customer service and a wide variety of products were all less important

to female shoppers than the quality of food and value, which were seen as the ultimate factors in a woman's decision as to which grocery store they decide to frequent.

26428 ■ *"Feet on the Street: Reps Are Ready to Hit the Ground Running"* in Agency Sales Magazine (Vol. 39, July 2009, No. 7, pp. 12)
Pub: MANA
Ed: Jack Foster. **Description:** One of the major benefits to manufacturers in working with sales representatives is the concept of synergistic selling where the rep shows his mettle. The rep of today is a solution provider that anticipates and meets the customer's needs.

26429 ■ Financial Times Guide to Business Start Up 2007
Pub: Pearson Education, Limited
Contact: Steven A. Dowling, President
Ed: Sara Williams; Jonquil Lowe. **Released:** November 2006. **Price:** $52.50. **Description:** Guide for starting and running a new business is presented. Sections include ways to get started, direct marketing, customer relations, management and accounting.

26430 ■ *"Five Tips for New Managers"* in Hawaii Business (Vol. 53, November 2007, No. 5, pp. 59)
Pub: Hawaii Business Publishing
Ed: Jason Ubay. **Description:** New managers should remember to know what their roles are, learn from others, build an infrastructure according to the customer's needs, communicate professionally and have consideration.

26431 ■ *"Forward Motion"* in Green Industry Pro (July 2011)
Pub: Cygnus Business Media
Ed: Gregg Wartgow. **Description:** Several landscape contractors have joined this publication's Working Smarter Training Challenge over the last year. This process is helping them develop ways to improve work processes, boost morale, drive out waste, reduce costs, improve customer service, and be more competitive.

26432 ■ *"Fresh Direct's Crisis"* in Crain's New York Business (Vol. 24, January 14, 2008, No. 2, pp. 3)
Pub: Crain Communications, Inc.
Ed: Lisa Fickenscher. **Description:** Freshdirect, an Internet grocery delivery service, finds itself under siege from federal immigration authorities, customers and labor organizations due to its employment practice of hiring illegals. At stake is the grocer's reputation as well as its ambitious growth plans, including an initial public offering of its stock.

26433 ■ *"FTC Takes Aim At Foreclosure 'Rescue' Firm"* in The Business Journal-Serving Greater Tampa Bay (Vol. 28, September 19, 2008, No. 39)
Pub: American City Business Journals, Inc.
Ed: Michael Hinman. **Description:** United Home Savers LLP has been ordered to halt its mortgage foreclosure rescue services after the Federal Trade Commission accused it of deceptive advertising. The company is alleged to have charged customers $1,200 in exchange for unfulfilled promises to keep them in their homes.

26434 ■ *"Get Back To Business Planning Fundamentals"* in Entrepreneur (October 24, 2008)
Pub: Entrepreneur Media Inc.
Ed: Tim Berry. **Description:** During a recession it is important to know what adjustment to make to your business plan. Some fundamentals to remember include: watching things more closely by tracking progress on cash, sales, new projects, customer satisfaction, ad spending and expenses; looking for built-in indicators such as what drives sales or expenses; watching what drives cash flow; and do not make mistakes such as laying off experienced employees too soon.

26435 ■ *"Get Personal"* in Entrepreneur (Vol. 36, April 2008, No. 4)
Pub: Entrepreneur Media, Inc.
Ed: Romanus Wolter. **Description:** Customers appreciate personal contact, and communicating with them can help business owners' customer relations. Some ways on how to keep a personal touch with customers and improve business dealings include blending technology with personal interaction and knowing what the customers want. Other tips are provided.

26436 ■ Getting Clients and Keeping Clients for Your Service Business
Pub: Atlantic Publishing Company
Ed: Anne M. Miller; Gail Brett Levine. **Released:** August 28, 2008. **Price:** $24.95 paperback. **Description:** Tips are offered to help any small service business identify customers, brand and grow the business, as well as development of logos, brochures and Websites.

26437 ■ The Girl's Guide to Building a Million-Dollar Business
Pub: AMACOM
Ed: Susan Wilson Solovic. **Released:** 2008. **Price:** $21.95. **Description:** Success plan for women business owners; the book includes tips for determination, managing changing relationships, keeping employees and customers happy, getting and maintaining credit, overcoming gender bias, and creating a good business plan and solid brand.

26438 ■ *"Give It Your All, and Don't Worry About the Rest"* in Inc. (Vol. 33, November 2011, No. 9, pp. 37)
Pub: Inc. Magazine
Ed: Norm Brodsky. **Description:** In the early stage of a service company, the owners sell themselves to the customers.

26439 ■ *"Good Price, Best Brands"* in Retail Merchandiser (Vol. 51, July-August 2011, No. 4, pp. 58)
Pub: Phoenix Media Corporation
Description: Flemington Department Store has been a family-owned and operated retailer for over 50 years. Customer service is key to the store's success.

26440 ■ *"Good Questions and the Basics of Selling"* in Agency Sales Magazine (Vol. 39, September-October 2009, No. 9, pp. 14)
Pub: MANA
Ed: Dave Kahle. **Description:** Six basic elements to enhance the job of a sales person in regards to his relationship to a customer are presented.

26441 ■ Greening Your Small Business: How to Improve Your Bottom Line, Grow Your Brand, Satisfy Your Customers and Save the Planet
Pub: Prentice Hall Press
Contact: Dame Marjorie M. Scardino, Chief Executive Officer
Ed: Jennifer Kaplan. **Released:** November 3, 2009. **Price:** $19.95. **Description:** A definitive resource for anyone who wants their small business to be cutting-edge, competitive, profitable, and eco-conscious. Stories from small business owners address every aspect of going green, from basics such as recycling waste, energy efficiency, and reducing information technology footprint, to more in-depth concerns such as green marketing and communications, green business travel, and green employee benefits.

26442 ■ *"Harnessing the Wisdom of Crowds"* in Entrepreneur (Vol. 37, September 2009, No. 9, pp. 74)
Pub: Entrepreneur Media, Inc.
Ed: Mark Henricks. **Description:** Online customer service business Get Satisfaction has registered growth. The business enables customers to search for answers to common product questions. Customers use the service to post questions, complaints, and even product ideas.

26443 ■ *"Health Care Checkup" in Business Courier (Vol. 24, November 16, 2008, No. 31, pp. 1)*
Pub: American City Business Journals, Inc.
Ed: James Ritchie. **Description:** Discusses a survey of 300 Greater Cincinnati residents about the quality of local health care and access to doctors indicates that there were improvements from five years ago. About 65 percent of those surveyed said the quality of their health care is good or excellent, a 12 percent improvement from a similar survey conducted five years ago. The other findings of the survey are also presented.

26444 ■ *"Help Customers Choose Full Service Over Discount" in Indoor Comfort Marketing (Vol. 70, September 2011, No. 9, pp. 10)*
Pub: Industry Publications Inc.
Ed: Richard Rutigliano. **Description:** Marketing strategies for HVAC/R firms to use in 2011 and 2012 heating seasons are outlined, focusing on oil heat.

26445 ■ *"A Home's Identity in Black and White" in Crain's Chicago Business (Vol. 31, April 21, 2008, No. 16, pp. 35)*
Pub: Crain Communications, Inc.
Ed: Lisa Bertagnoli. **Description:** Real estate agents are finding that showing customers a written floor plan is a trend that is growing since many buyers feel that Online virtual tours distort a room. Although floor plans cost up to $500 to have drawn up, they clearly show potential buyers the exact dimensions of rooms and how they connect.

26446 ■ *"Hometown Value" in Retail Merchandiser (Vol. 51, July-August 2011, No. 4, pp. 50)*
Pub: Phoenix Media Corporation
Ed: Todd Vowell. **Description:** Profile of family-owned Vowell's Marketplace located in Noxapater, Mississippi. The 10-store chain caters to its Southern roots and is run by the third generation of the Vowell family.

26447 ■ *Housecleaning Business: Organize Your Business - Get Clients and Referrals - Set Rates and Services*
Pub: Globe Pequot Press
Ed: Laura Jorstad, Melinda Morse. **Released:** June 1, 2009. **Price:** $18.95. **Description:** This book shares insight into starting a housecleaning businesses. It shows how to develop a service manual, screen clients, serve customers, select cleaning products, competition, how to up a home office, using the Internet to grow the business and offering green cleaning options to clients.

26448 ■ *How to Collect Debts*
Pub: Amacom
Ed: David Sher, Martin Sher. **Released:** May 1999. **Description:** Suggestions for collecting as much money as possible, as quickly as possible, while maintaining customer goodwill, along with strategies for eliminating bad debt.

26449 ■ *How Customers Think*
Pub: Harvard Business School Press
Ed: Gerald Zaltman. **Released:** February 21, 2003. **Price:** $32.95. **Description:** Despite marketing efforts and customer surveys, nearly eighty percent of all new products fail of fall short of prediction within the first six months after introduction. Consumer reactions to products and marketing programs are investigated.

26450 ■ *"How Good Advice 'Online' Can Attract Customers" in Indoor Comfort Marketing (Vol. 70, August 2011, No. 8, pp. 20)*
Pub: Industry Publications Inc.
Ed: Richard Rutigilano. **Description:** Online marketing tips for heating and cooling small businesses are explained.

26451 ■ *"How Growers Buy" in Farm Industry News (Vol. 42, January 1, 2009, No. 1)*
Pub: Penton Media Inc.
Contact: John French, President
Ed: Karen McMahon. **Description:** According to a survey regarding the buying habits among large commercial growers, most prefer to purchase from local retailers, customer service is important concerning their decision on who to buy products from, and price and convenience seem to be more important then brand.

26452 ■ *"How He Thinks" in Canadian Business (Vol. 80, Winter 2007, No. 24, pp. 78)*
Pub: Rogers Media
Ed: Roger Martin. **Description:** Isadore Sharp sought to combine the best of the small hotel with the best of the large hotel so that he could provide his guests with the sense of intimacy and personalized service while also bringing a wide array of amenities. Sharp decreed that there would be no customer service department at his hotel but every member of the staff are in charge of customer service.

26453 ■ *"How to Make Marketing Work" in Agency Sales Magazine (Vol. 39, September-October 2009, No. 9, pp. 30)*
Pub: MANA
Ed: John Graham. **Description:** Marketing's core concept is to focus total attention on the customer. Marketers should stop trying to manipulate customers and recognize that getting people through the door does not make them customers. Customer satisfaction is also important since even the most compelling marketing messages are worthless without this vital relationship.

26454 ■ *"How to Manage Successful Crowdsourcing Projects" in eWeek (September 29, 2010)*
Pub: Ziff Davis Enterprise
Description: The advantages, challenges and pitfalls faced when using crowdsourcing to improve a business are outlined. Crowdsourcing helps to eliminate the need to rely on an internal workforce and the need to forecast task volume.

26455 ■ *"How to Protect Your Job in a Recession" in Harvard Business Review (Vol. 86, September 2008, No. 9, pp. 113)*
Pub: Harvard Business School Press
Ed: Janet Banks; Diane Coutu. **Description:** Strategies are presented for enhancing one's job security. These include being a team player, empathizing with management, preserving optimism, and concentrating on the customer.

26456 ■ *"How Two Flourishing Exporters Did It" in Hispanic Business (Vol. 30, July-August 2008, No. 7-8, pp. 46)*
Pub: Hispanic Business, Inc.
Ed: Richard Kaplan. **Description:** Vigorous growth in export revenues posted by two Hispanic-owned export companies Compasa LLC and Ametza LLC is discussed; both firms have benefited from their closer locations to major Mexican markets, superior quality of their products, market knowledge and the relationships of trust developed with key business partners.

26457 ■ *How You Do..What You Do: Create Service Excellence That Wins Clients For Life*
Pub: McGraw-Hill
Ed: Bob Livingston. **Released:** June 6, 2008. **Price:** $27.95. **Description:** Today's marketplace has become a tougher place to do business because of new challenges such as escalating competition, well-informed clients, and dismal customer service. Clients now have more influence and choices than ever. Tips for achieving service excellence are provided.

26458 ■ *Hug Your Customers*
Pub: Hyperion Books
Ed: Jack Mitchell. **Price:** $19.95. **Description:** The CEO of Mitchells/Roberts, two very successful clothing stores, professes his belief in showering customers with attention. His secrets for long-term business success include advice about attracting a good staff, lowering marketing costs, and maintaining higher gross margins and revenues.

26459 ■ *"The Human Approach" in Entrepreneur (Vol. 37, September 2009, No. 9, pp. 30)*
Pub: Entrepreneur Media, Inc.
Description: Focusing on customer's needs is seen to result in better sales performance. Understanding customer needs is a question of emotional and social intelligence. Such sales competencies are seen as learned capabilities.

26460 ■ *I Love You More Than My Dog*
Pub: Portfolio
Ed: Jeanne Bliss. **Price:** $22.95. **Description:** Ways to win passionate, loyal and vocal customers in order to build a small business is outlined.

26461 ■ *"iMozi Integrates Esprida LiveControl for Advanced DVD Kiosk Hardware" in Wireless News (December 20, 2010)*
Pub: Close-Up Media Inc.
Description: Provider of self-service entertainment technology, iMozi Canada has partnered with Esprida to make its automated DVD Kiosk solutions Esprida-enabled. Esprida develops remote device management solutions and will offer enhanced capabilities and to improve customer experience for users.

26462 ■ *Instant Cashflow: Hundreds of Proven Strategies to Win Customers, Boost Margins and Take More Money Home*
Pub: McGraw-Hill Companies Inc.
Contact: Deven Sharma, President
Ed: Bradley J. Sugars. **Released:** December 2005. **Price:** $17.95 (US), $22.95 (Canadian). **Description:** Nearly 300 proven marketing and sales strategies are shared by the author, a self-made millionaire. Advice on creating the proper mindset, generating new leads, boosting the conversion rate of leads to sales, maximizing the value of the average sale, and measuring results is included.

26463 ■ *"Insurance: Marathon Effort" in Canadian Business (Vol. 80, January 29, 2007, No. 3, pp. 11)*
Pub: Rogers Media
Ed: Jeff Sanford. **Description:** The efforts of the insurance firm ING Canada Inc. to manage its relations with its customers are described. The enhancement of the insurance services provided by the company is discussed.

26464 ■ *"Interchangeable or Irreplaceable?" in American Printer (Vol. 128, August 1, 2011, No. 8)*
Pub: Penton Media Inc.
Description: Creating and maintaining customers is important for all graphic design and printing companies. Tips are shared to help maintain good customer satisfaction and repeat business.

26465 ■ *"Is That the Best You Can Do?" in Entrepreneur (Vol. 37, October 2009, No. 10, pp. 85)*
Pub: Entrepreneur Media, Inc.
Ed: Jennifer Wang. **Description:** Small business owners can deal with hagglers better by setting parameters in advance. They should convince hagglers by offering the best value and separating this from price.

26466 ■ *"It's Not About You" in Entrepreneur (Vol. 35, November 2007, No. 11, pp. 102)*
Pub: Entrepreneur Media Inc.
Ed: Barry Farber. **Description:** Companies should focus on the customers' need and show them that they care about them. Listening to and learning about your customers can make selling easier; tips on how to stay focused on the customers' needs are outlined.

26467 ■ *"Just Be Nice" in Canadian Business (Vol. 79, October 9, 2006, No. 20, pp. 141)*
Pub: Rogers Media
Ed: Joe Castaldo. **Description:** The customer relationship management strategies on customer retention and satisfaction adopted by WestJet are discussed.

26468 ■ *"Keeping Customers Satisfied" in Pet Product News (Vol. 64, December 2010, No. 12, pp. 10)*
Pub: BowTie Inc.
Ed: Devon McPhee. **Description:** Windsor, California-based Debbie's Pet Boutique, recipient of Pet Product News International's Outstanding Customer Service Award, has been dedicated to combin-

ing topnotch grooming services with a robust retail selection. These features might gain return customers for Debbie's Pet Boutique.

26469 ■ The Kindess Revolution: The Company-Wide Culture Shift That Inspires Phenomenal Customer Service
Pub: American Management Association
Contact: Charles R. Craig, Chairman
Ed: Ed Horrell. **Released:** 2006. **Price:** $23.00.

26470 ■ "Kubicki Juggles Lineup at Vianda" in Business Courier (Vol. 26, December 11, 2009, No. 33, pp. 1)
Pub: American City Business Journals, Inc.
Ed: Dan Monk. **Description:** Cincinnati real estate developer Chuck Kubicki replaced the management team of Vianda LLC and cancelled contracts with two vendors that caused a surge of customer complaints. Vianda is a direct-response marketing firm that sells and distributes dietary supplements for wellness and sexual performance.

26471 ■ "Leadership Behavior and Employee Voice: Is the Door Really Open?' in Academy of Management Journal (August 2007)
Pub: Academy of Management
Contact: Ming-Jer Chen, President
Ed: James R. Detert, Ethan R. Burris. **Description:** Relationships between two types of change-oriented leadership and subordinate improvement-oriented voice in a two-phase study are presented.

26472 ■ "Let Emerging Market Customers Be Your Teachers" in Harvard Business Review (Vol. 88, December 2010, No. 12, pp. 115)
Pub: Harvard Business School Publishing
Ed: Guillermo D'Andrea, David Marcotte, Gwen Dixon Morrison. **Description:** Examination of effective strategies for emerging markets is presented. These include helping educate customers as well as selling to them, adapting to customers' habits, and focusing brands appropriately. Magazine Luiza, a chain store in Brazil, is used to illustrate these points.

26473 ■ "Like a Business Militia" in Crain's Detroit Business (Vol. 25,
Pub: Crain Communications Inc. - Detroit
Ed: Daniel Duggan. **Description:** Hotel executives are forming hotel committees and associations in Southeastern Michigan in the hopes of drawing more visitors to the region. Meetings are encouraging the use of promoting specific regions in ways that will secure multi-hotel events.

26474 ■ "Looking Out for the Little Guys" in Black Enterprise (Vol. 38, October 2007, No. 3, pp. 58)
Pub: Earl G. Graves Publishing Co. Inc.
Ed: Kaylyn Kendall Dines. **Description:** Biz TechConnect is a Web portal that offers free online and social networking, along with four modules that help small businesses with marketing and advertising, communications and mobility, financial management, and customer relationship management.

26475 ■ "Loyalty Cards Score Points" in Crain's Cleveland Business (Vol. 30, June 8, 2009, No. 22, pp. 1)
Pub: Crain Communications, Inc.
Ed: Chuck Soder. **Description:** Northeast Ohio retailers are promoting loyalty and rewards programs in order to attract and maintain loyal customers.

26476 ■ "Luxe Men Are In Style" in Brandweek (Vol. 49, April 21, 2008, No. 16, pp. 12)
Pub: VNU Business Media, Inc.
Description: According to a recent survey by Unity Marketing, among 1,300 luxury shoppers found that men spent an average of $2,401 on fashion items over a three-month period which is nearly $1,000 more than women. Men also spring for more luxury items such as vehicles and memberships to exclusive clubs.

26477 ■ "Make Relationships Count: CRM Software That Works" in Black Enterprise (Vol. 38, February 2008, No. 7, pp. 60)
Pub: Earl G. Graves Publishing Co. Inc.
Ed: Fiona Haley. **Description:** Customer relationship management (CRM) software can help any small business keep track of clients. Descriptions of the latest CRM software offered are profiled, including Salesforce.com, Microsoft Dynamics, and Saga Software.

26478 ■ "Making Automated Royalty Payments Work for Your Franchise" in Franchising World (Vol. 42, October 2010, No. 10, pp. 30)
Pub: International Franchise Association
Ed: J.P. O'Brien. **Description:** In the past, royalty payments were sent by franchisees through regular postal mail and accompanied by a single slip of paper with handwritten notes indicating the month's revenue numbers and royalty amounts.

26479 ■ "Making It Click" in Barron's (Vol. 88, March 17, 2008, No. 11, pp. 31)
Pub: Dow Jones & Company, Inc.
Ed: Theresa W. Carey. **Description:** Listing of 23 online brokers that are evaluated based on their trade experience, usability, range of offerings, research amenities, customer service and access, and costs. TradeStation Securities takes the top spot followed by thinkorswim by just a fraction.

26480 ■ "Making It Work" in Pet Product News (Vol. 64, December 2010, No. 12, pp. S8)
Pub: BowTie Inc.
Ed: Kerri Chladnicek. **Description:** How focusing on service and flexibility allowed New Jersey-based pet supply store B.C. Woof to achieve success is discussed. B.C. Woof began as a pet-sitting business which eventually concentrated on natural foods. Aside from conducting a do-it-yourself approach in food formulation for customers, B.C. Woof has also been guiding customers on nutrients they need for their pets.

26481 ■ "Making It Work" in Retail Merchandiser (Vol. 51, July-August 2011, No. 4, pp. 43)
Pub: Phoenix Media Corporation
Ed: Anthony DiPaolo. **Description:** Profile of Anthony DiPaolo and his purchase of the Work 'N Gear retail store in 2002. The brick and mortar shop sells work wear and healthcare apparel and DiPaolo believes customer respect is essential to his success.

26482 ■ Managing a Small Business Made Easy
Pub: Entrepreneur Press
Ed: Martin E. Davis. **Released:** September 2005. **Price:** $19.95 (US), $26.95 (Canadian). **Description:** Examination of the essential elements for an entrepreneur running a business, including advice on leadership, customer service, financials, and more.

26483 ■ Marketing 2.0: Bridging the Gap between Seller and Buyer through Social Media Marketing
Pub: Wheatmark
Ed: Bernie Borges. **Released:** July 14, 2009. **Price:** $22.95. **Description:** Winning strategies to attract people to your company and your employees using social media site on the Internet are outlined.

26484 ■ "McCormick Focuses on Customer, Dealer Service" in Farm Industry News (September 17, 2010)
Pub: Penton Business Media Inc.
Description: McCormick has developed a new plan that focuses on fast and complete service to both customers and dealers.

26485 ■ "McD's Tries to Slake Consumer Thirst for Wider Choice of Drinks" in Advertising Age (Vol. 79, June 9, 2008, No. 23, pp. 1)
Pub: Crain Communications, Inc.
Ed: Natalie Zmuda; Emily Bryson York. **Description:** McDonald's is testing the sale of canned and bottled drinks in about 150 locations in an attempt to offer more options to consumers who are going elsewhere for their beverage choices.

26486 ■ "Mergers Mean Woe for Fliers; Airline Hookups Boost Fares, Diminish Service" in Crain's Chicago Business (April 21, 2008)
Pub: Crain Communications, Inc.
Ed: John Pletz. **Description:** Discusses the impact airline mergers will have on customer service, pricing and business travel, particularly at Chicago's O'Hare International Airport.

26487 ■ "Midwest Seeks Concessions From Creditors" in The Business Journal-Milwaukee (Vol. 25, July 25, 2008, No. 44, pp. A1)
Pub: American City Business Journals, Inc.
Ed: Rich Rovito. **Description:** Midwest Airlines Inc. is turning to creditors and lease holders for the financial aspect of its restructuring, which involves going back to serving popular business destinations. Chief executive officer Timothy believes that the company can survive in a niche market as long as it provides quality service. He discusses Midwest's restructuring plan.

26488 ■ The Mom and Pop Store: How the Unsung Heroes of the American Economy Are Surviving and Thriving
Pub: Walker & Company
Ed: Robert Spector. **Released:** September 1, 2009. **Price:** $26.00. **Description:** The history of small independent retail enterprises and how mom and pop stores in the U.S. continue to thrive through customer service and renewed community support for local businesses.

26489 ■ "Monopoly Money Madness" in Canadian Business (Vol. 81, March 17, 2008, No. 4, pp. 9)
Pub: Rogers Media
Description: Enbridge was given permission by the Ontario Energy Board to collect $22 million it spent on an out-of-court settlement for charging unfair fees from 1994 to 2002. Customers are essentially being gouged twice in this scenario. The monopoly of Enbridge should end and the consumers should not have to pay for the system's faults.

26490 ■ More Than a Pink Cadillac
Pub: McGraw-Hill
Ed: Jim Underwood. **Released:** 2002. **Price:** $23.95. **Description:** Profile of Mary Kay Ash who turned her $5,000 investment into a billion-dollar corporation. Ash's nine principles that form the foundation of her company's global success are outlined. Stories from her sales force leaders share ideas for motivating employees, impressing customers and building a successful company. The book emphasizes the leadership skills required to drive performance in any successful enterprise.

26491 ■ "Muirhead Farmhouse B & B Owners Get Hospitality Right" in Chicago Tribune (July 31, 2008)
Pub: McClatchy-Tribune Information Services
Ed: Glenn Jeffers. **Description:** Profile of the Muirhead Farmhouse, a bed-and-breakfast owned by Mike Petersdorf and Sarah Muirhead Petersdorf; Frank Lloyd Wright designed the historic farmhouse which blends farm life and history into a unique experience that is enhanced by the couple's hospitality.

26492 ■ "Multichannel Marketing: Mindset and Program Development' in Business Horizons (September-October 2007)
Pub: Elsevier Technology Publications
Ed: Bruce D. Weinberg, Salvatore Parise, Patricia J. Guinan. **Description:** Organizations should develop a multichannel mindset and design multichannel marketing programs in order to increase profitability and enhance customer satisfaction. Creating a holistic strategy, crating metrics that measure the impacts and overall performance, and designing organizational structure and incentives are key factors in implementing the marketing program.

26493 ■ "Network Like A Boy Scout" in Women Entrepreneur (January 15, 2009)
Pub: Entrepreneur Media Inc.
Ed: Merrily Orsini. **Description:** Marketing for businesses that provide products or services that people only seek during emergencies or natural disasters

such as hurricanes can be a challenge; tips for branding such businesses, networking and establishing a strong customer base that will refer your business to others are given.

26494 ■ "The Next 20 Years: How Customer and Workforce Attitudes Will Evolve" in Harvard Business Review (Vol. 85, July-August 2007, No. 7-8)
Pub: Harvard Business School Publishing
Ed: Neil Howe, William Strauss. Description: Identification of social categories inhabited by age groups is used to calculate how consumer and employee opinions and behavior will change, and how this will impact economic development and corporate growth.

26495 ■ Niche and Grow Rich
Pub: Entrepreneur Press
Ed: Jennifer Basye Sander; Peter Sander. Released: 2003. Description: Consultants share insight to entrepreneurs wishing to find a profitable niche market. Authors write that good niche businesses are easy to start and easy to defend from competitors. They also report that finding a successful niche can attract and maintain good customers who are willing to pay more for unique goods and services.

26496 ■ "Office Supplier Won't Wait for Opportunity to Knock" in Business Courier (Vol. 24, December 28, 2008, No. 37, pp. 2)
Pub: American City Business Journals, Inc.
Ed: Lucy May. Description: Ace Products, an office supplier, stays competitive through its customer service and pricing.

26497 ■ The One Minute Entrepreneur
Pub: Doubleday
Ed: Ken Blanchard; assisted by Don Hutson and Ethan Willis. Released: 2008. Price: $19.95. Description: Four traditional business ideas are covered including: revenue needs to exceed expenses, bill collection, customer service, and employee motivation in order to be successful.

26498 ■ "The One Thing You Must Get Right When Building a Brand" in Harvard Business Review (Vol. 88, December 2010, No. 12, pp. 80)
Pub: Harvard Business School Publishing
Ed: Patrick Barwise, Sean Meehan. Description: Four uses for new media include: communicating a clearly defined customer promise, creating trust via delivering on the promise, regularly improving on the promise, and innovating past what is familiar.

26499 ■ Organizations Alive!: Six Things That Challenge - Seven That Bring Success
Pub: Yuill & Associates
Ed: Jan Yuill. Released: January 2005. Price: $35.12 for book and guide. Description: New insight into understanding how organizations function as individuals is presented by an international consultant. Customer service, resource management, outsourcing, and management are among the issues covered.

26500 ■ Outfoxing the Small Business Owner
Pub: Adams Media Corporation
Ed: Gene Marks. Released: January 2005. Description: Special skill sets are required to sell, service or deal with small business customers.

26501 ■ Over the Counter
Pub: The Mercier Press, Ltd.
Ed: Keogh. Released: January 1, 2009. Price: $54.95. Description: An overview of the changing landscape of Cork, Ireland's retail stores is presented.

26502 ■ "Pay or Play: Do Nice (Sales) Guys Finish Last?" in Agency Sales Magazine (Vol. 39, August 2009, No. 8, pp. 8)
Pub: MANA
Ed: Julia M. Rahn. Description: How positive interpersonal relationships among salespersons, program coordinators, and other business-related professions will pay in terms of business success is presented. Business people should know the ideal

customers, promise only what they can do, refer out when needed, and follow through with any stated promise. Further insight into these ideas is presented.

26503 ■ "The Perfect Formula to Build Your Brand" in Entrepreneur (Vol. 37, July 2009, No. 7, pp. 70)
Pub: Entrepreneur Media, Inc.
Ed: Susan J. Linder. Description: Combining a product with expertise and a promise is the formula in building a brand for startups. The product will not sell itself, so one must consider what makes the product truly unique. Meanwhile, establishing trust and a foundation for a brand can be achieved by making a promise to the consumer and fulfilling it.

26504 ■ "Perfecting Customer Services" in Pet Product News (Vol. 64, November 2010, No. 11, pp. 18)
Pub: BowTie Inc.
Description: Pet supply retailers are encouraged to emphasize customer experience and sales representatives' knowledge of the store's product offerings to foster repeat business. Employee protocols could be implemented to improve customer interaction. Other guidelines on developing a pet supply retail environment that advances repeat business are presented.

26505 ■ "Perfecting the Process: Creating a Move Efficient Organization On Your Terms" in Black Enterprise (Vol. 41, October 2010, No. 3)
Pub: Earl G. Graves Publishing Co. Inc.
Ed: Tamara E. Holmes. Description: More than ever, entrepreneurs need to identify new ways of doing business in a cost-effective manner in order to expand their companies, while remaining true to their customer demands.

26506 ■ "Peter Gilgan" in Canadian Business (Vol. 82, April 27, 2009, No. 7, pp. 58)
Pub: Rogers Media
Ed: Calvin Leung. Description: Mattamy Homes Ltd. president and chief executive officer Peter Gilgan believes that their business model of building communities in an organized way brings advantages to the firm and for their customers. He also believes in adopting their product prices to new market realities. Gilgan considers the approvals regime in Ontario his biggest challenge in the last 20 years.

26507 ■ "PGA Tour: Course Management" in Retail Merchandiser (Vol. 51, September-October 2011, No. 5, pp. 38)
Pub: Phoenix Media Corporation
Ed: Eric Slack. Description: PGA Tour must reach new customers and solidify relationships with its traditional base in order to continue its success. The PGA brand equity has translated into one of the largest retail licensing operations worldwide.

26508 ■ "The Phone-Service Test" in Canadian Business (Vol. 79, October 9, 2006, No. 20, pp. 137)
Pub: Rogers Media
Ed: Rachel Pulfer. Description: Suggestions to improve the customer services provided by airlines through call centers are discussed.

26509 ■ "The Price of Profitability" in Green Industry Pro (Vol. 23, March 2011, No. 3, pp. 18)
Pub: Cygnus Business Media
Ed: Tony Bass. Description: Profit Builder Process is used to help landscaping companies be more competitive. Landscape contractors report pricing among their largest challenges and although the economy is improving, homeowners are paying closer attention to quality and service.

26510 ■ Principled Profit: Marketing that Puts People First
Pub: Accurate Writing & More
Ed: Shel Horowitz. Price: $17.50. Description: The importance for companies to market ethically and honestly is stressed. Quality marketing will build customer loyalty and that will translate into new customers and repeat business. A customer-retention strategy is outlined along with ideas to increase profits of any small business.

26511 ■ "Putting the Service-Profit Chain to Work" in Harvard Business Review (Vol. 86, July-August 2008, No. 8, pp. 118)
Pub: Harvard Business School Press
Ed: James L. Heskett; Thomas O. Jones; Gary W. Loveman; W. Earl Sasser Jr.; Leonard A. Schlesinger. Description: Advice is given on how to foster profitability in service businesses. Topics include the link between employee satisfaction and customer satisfaction, internal service quality, external service value, and revenue growth.

26512 ■ "Q&A: David Labistour" in Canadian Business (Vol. 81, March 17, 2008, No. 4, pp. 10)
Pub: Rogers Media
Ed: Lauren McKeon. Description: David Labistour says that the difference between being a co-op retailer and a corporate-owned retailer in the case of Mountain Equipment Co-op (MEC) is that the company is owned by their customers and not by shareholders. Labistour also says that MEC works with their factories to ensure that these maintain ethical standards in the manufacturing process.

26513 ■ "The Question: Who Do You Think Is the Most Genuine?" in Advertising Age (Vol. 79, July 7, 2008, No. 26, pp. 4)
Pub: Crain Communications, Inc.
Ed: Ken Wheaton. Description: According to a survey conducted by Harris Interactive Reputation Quotient, Johnson & Johnson was deemed the most genuine brand. Google came in second followed by UPS.

26514 ■ "Rapport Overhaul" in Small Business Opportunities (Winter 2009)
Pub: Entrepreneur Press
Contact: Perlman Neil, President
Ed: Laurie Brown. Description: Advice concerning ways in which to build customer rapport is provided.

26515 ■ Raving Fans: A Revolutionary Approach to Customer Service
Pub: William Morrow
Ed: Ken Blanchard, Sheldon Bowles. Released: May 19, 1993. Price: $22.95. Description: Strategies to improve customer service in any industry are provided.

26516 ■ "Reaping Social-Media Rewards" in Canadian Business (Vol. 83, July 20, 2010, No. 11-12, pp. 19)
Pub: Rogers Media Ltd.
Ed: Lyndsie Bourgon. Description: Foursquare is a social network which provides benefits such as discounts to users who show loyalty to a business or a brand. One marketing executive believes Foursquare is a good platform for loyalty programs and is an inexpensive alternative to Aeroplan.

26517 ■ "Recession-Proof Your Startup" in Crain's Chicago Business (Vol. 31, November 10, 2008, No. 45, pp. 24)
Pub: Crain Communications, Inc.
Description: Detailed information concerning ways in which to start a business during an economic crisis is provided. Ways in which to find financing, the importance of a solid business plan, customer service, problem-solving and finding the right niche for the region are also discussed.

26518 ■ "Renters' Review - Secret Shoppers Strike Again" in Rental Product News (Vol. 33, June 2011)
Pub: Cygnus Business Media
Description: Staff of Rental Product News set out to rent various items from three different rental sources in order to evaluate the rental experience from the eyes of the average customer.

26519 ■ "Reps Have Needs Too!" in Agency Sales Magazine (Vol. 39, December 2009, No. 11, pp. 16)
Pub: MANA
Ed: Bill Heyden. Description: There is common information that a sales representatives needs to know prior to choosing a manufacturer to represent. Both parties must keep promises made to customers

and prospects. Reps also need the support from the manufacturers and to clear matters regarding their commission. Interviewing tips for representatives to get this vital information are presented.

26520 ■ *"Rethinking the Organization" in Strategy & Leadership (Vol. 38, September-October 2010, No. 5, pp. 13-19)*
Pub: Emerald Inc.

Ed: Stephen Denning. **Description:** A study identifies the changes needed to be adopted by top managers to achieve game-changing innovation at an organization-wide level. Findings indicate that CEOs should practice pull management in order to nurture fruitful communication between employees and customers and achieve organizational involvement of customers.

26521 ■ *Rework*
Pub: Crown Business

Ed: Jason Fried, David Heinemeier Hansson. **Released:** March 9, 2010. **Price:** $22.00. **Description:** Works to help entrepreneurs and business owners to rethink strategy, customers, and getting things accomplished.

26522 ■ *"RIM Opts to Be Little Less Open" in Canadian Business (Vol. 83, October 12, 2010, No. 17, pp. 13)*
Pub: Rogers Media Ltd.

Ed: Joe Castaldo. **Description:** RIM is planning to stop releasing quarterly subscriber updates. However, some analysts are skeptical about the change due to the previous drop in company subscribers. The company also decided to stop reporting the average selling price of the BlackBerry, which analysts have also scrutinized.

26523 ■ *"Roger Hickel Contracting: Smoothing the Road for Owners" in Alaska Business Monthly (Vol. 27, October 2011, No. 10, pp. 114)*
Pub: Alaska Business Publishing Company

Ed: Gail West. **Description:** Profile of Roger Hickel and his contracting company that reports nearly $60 million annually in gross revenue. The firm focuses on customer service.

26524 ■ *"Rule of the Masses: Reinventing Fashion Via Crowdsourcing" in WWD (Vol. 200, July 26, 2010, No. 17, pp. 1)*
Pub: Conde Nast Publications

Contact: David Carey, President

Ed: Cate T. Corcoran. **Description:** Large apparel brands and retailers are crowdsourcing as a way to increase customer loyalty and to build their businesses.

26525 ■ *"Sales Force Expertise: A Competitive Advantage" in Agency Sales Magazine (Vol. 39, November 2009, No. 10, pp. 10)*
Pub: MANA

Ed: Ken Valla. **Description:** Maintaining an expert sales force is a competitive advantage that sales leaders can count on. The skills that the sales force need to have include 'consultative selling' or the ability to understand and link to a customer's business priorities, conducting a process conversation, and asking discovery questions.

26526 ■ *"SEC Report On Rating Agencies Falls Short" in Barron's (Vol. 88, July 14, 2008, No. 28, pp. 35)*
Pub: Dow Jones & Co., Inc.

Ed: Jack Willoughby. **Description:** The Securities and Exchange Commissions report on credit-rating firms should have drawn attention to the slipshod practices in the offerings of collateralized debt obligations. The report fell short of prescribing correctives for the flawed system of these agencies' relationship with their clients.

26527 ■ *"Segmenting When It Matters" in Business Strategy Review (Vol. 21, Spring 2010, No. 1, pp. 46)*
Pub: Wiley-Blackwell

Ed: Andreas Birnik, Richard Moat. **Description:** Authors argue that business complexity is directly linked to the degree of segmentation implemented by

a company. They propose an approach to map business activities at the segment level to make sure that complexity is only introduced when it really matters.

26528 ■ *Sell More of Anything to Anyone: Sales Tips for Individuals, Business Owners and Sales Professionals*
Pub: Allen & Unwin

Ed: Andrew Griffiths. **Released:** May 10, 2010. **Price:** $16.95. **Description:** Tips are shared to help anyone improve sales skills while providing strong customer service.

26529 ■ *Serves You Right!*
Pub: Serves You Right!, Incorporated

Ed: Susan Brooks. **Released:** May 2004. **Price:** $15.95. **Description:** Profile of excellence in customer service.

26530 ■ *"Service With a Smile..And Comfy Chairs" in Crain's Chicago Business (Vol. 31, April 28, 2008, No. 17, pp. 46)*
Pub: Crain Communications, Inc.

Ed: Phuong Ly. **Description:** O'Hare Auto Group has improved the experience of waiting for service on one's vehicle by offering wireless Internet, comfortable chairs and plasma TVs. The company also has long service hours, running from 6 a.m. to midnight Monday through Thursday so customers don't have to take time off work.

26531 ■ *"Serving Unfair Customers" in Business Horizons (Vol. 51, January-February 2008, No. 1, pp. 29)*
Pub: Elsevier Advanced Technology Publications

Ed: Leonard L. Berry, Kathleen Seiders. **Description:** Quality service is based on the maxim 'the customer is always right', but customer behavior studies have revealed that customers can be glaringly unjust. These unfair customers exploit the customer service maxim, affecting both the company and other customers. Methods to effectively deal with unfair customers are explored.

26532 ■ *"Show and Tell" in Entrepreneur (Vol. 36, May 2008, No. 5, pp. 54)*
Pub: Entrepreneur Media, Inc.

Ed: Heather Clancy. **Description:** FreshStart Telephone uses recorded video testimonials of customers, by using Pure Digital Flip Video that downloads content directly to the computer, and uploads it in the company's website to promote their wireless phone service.

26533 ■ *"Skinner's No Drive-Thru CEO" in Crain's Chicago Business (Vol. 31, April 28, 2008, No. 17, pp. 1)*
Pub: Crain Communications, Inc.

Ed: David Sterrett. **Description:** Profile of James Skinner who was named CEO for McDonald's Corp. in November 2004 and has proved to be a successful leader despite the number of investors who doubted him when he came to the position. Mr. Skinner has overseen three years of unprecedented sales growth and launched the biggest menu expansion in 30 years.

26534 ■ *Small Business Desk Reference*
Pub: Penguin Books USA Inc.

Ed: Gene Marks. **Released:** December 2004. **Description:** Comprehensive guide for starting or running a successful small business, focusing on buying a business or franchise, writing a business plan, financial management, accounting, legal issues, human resources management, operations, marketing, sales, customer service, taxes, insurance, and ethics. Information for launching a restaurant, property management firm, retail outlet, consulting firm, and service business is included.

26535 ■ *Small Business Survival Guide*
Pub: Adams Media Corporation

Contact: Gary Krebs, Director

E-mail: swatrous@adamsmedia.com

Ed: Cliff Ennico. **Price:** $12.95. **Description:** Small business expert provides strategies to start a company and survive in the 21st Century. He shows small business owners how to succeed despite challenges that can defeat any firm. His advice covers suppliers; customers and contractors; competitors and credi-

tors; spouses, family and friends; as well as the ways lawyers, accountants and other can steal an entrepreneur's success. Ennico also describes how startups can comply with local regulations.

26536 ■ *"Small Fish, Big Box Stores" in Hawaii Business (Vol. 53, November 2007, No. 5, pp. 55)*
Pub: Hawaii Business Publishing

Ed: Jolyn Okimoto Rosa. **Description:** Ohana Seafoods can be found at big-box stores such as Costco, Marukai and Don Quijote. Owner Jeffrey Yee spends his weekend at a farmers market to have direct contact with his customers and get feedback right away. Ohana offers ready-to cook fish products, sauces and fish.

26537 ■ *"Smarts Drive Sales" in Pet Product News (Vol. 64, December 2010, No. 12, pp. 1)*
Pub: BowTie Inc.

Ed: Karen Shugart. **Description:** Retailers could make smart decisions by deciding how to best attract customers into their stores or resolving whether to nurture in-store or buy herps (reptiles) from suppliers. Paying attention to these smart decisions could help boost customer interest in herps and address customer demands.

26538 ■ *The Social Media Bible: Tactics, Tools, and Strategies for Business Success*
Pub: John Wiley & Sons, Inc.

Ed: Lon Safko, David Brake. **Released:** June 17, 2009. **Price:** $29.95. **Description:** Information is given to build or transform a business into social media, where customers, employees, and prospects connect, collaborate, and champion products and services in order to increase sales and to beat the competition.

26539 ■ *"Solutions for the Frustrating Feline" in Pet Product News (Vol. 64, November 2010, No. 11, pp. 46)*
Pub: BowTie Inc.

Ed: Lori Luechtefeld. **Description:** Products that can help customers deal with problematic cat behaviors, such as out-of-the-box urination and scratching are described. Information on such products including litter box deodorants and disposable scratchers is provided. Feline territorial behaviors can also be addressed by pheromone products that can calm hyperactive cats.

26540 ■ *"Sometimes, Second Impressions Count Most" in Canadian Business (Vol. 83, October 12, 2010, No. 17, pp. 11)*
Pub: Rogers Media Ltd.

Ed: Richard Branson. **Description:** Developing a favorable impression at the first point of contact is imperative for businesses. Managers who want their organizations to make positive first and second impressions need to learn to balance the Web's labor-saving efficiencies with human assistants. The importance of considering the customer relations value in company Websites is also explained.

26541 ■ *"Sometimes You Have to Ignore the Rule Book" in Canadian Business (Vol. 83, September 14, 2010, No. 15, pp. 13)*
Pub: Rogers Media Ltd.

Ed: Richard Branson. **Description:** The rule book has provided a clear framework for employees particularly when cash and accounting are at issue. However, sometimes rules were made to be broken and the rule book should not become an excuse for poor customer service or hinder great service. How Virgin Atlantic practices this type of corporate culture is discussed.

26542 ■ *"Sound Check" in Agency Sales Magazine (Vol. 39, August 2009, No. 8, pp. 14)*
Pub: MANA

Ed: Dave Kahle. **Description:** Most customers believe salespersons are unable to do well in terms of listening, which is one of the four fundamental competencies of a sales person. Listening is the primary tool to uncover deeper and more powerful needs and motivations of the customer. A guide on how to listen better and improve listening effectiveness is presented.

26543 ■ *"Speakers Address Authenticity, R&D Evolution"* in *Nation's Restaurant News (Vol. 45, October 24, 2011, No. 32, pp. 32)*
Pub: Penton Media Inc.
Contact: John French, President
Ed: Bret Thorn. Description: Culinary trends are discussed, along with an examination of the food truck trend and how this small sector is creating a great influence on food and communication with customers and delivery expectations

26544 ■ *"Sponsorship, Booths Available for Spring Business Showcase"* in *Bellingham Business Journal (Vol. February 2010, pp. 3)*
Pub: Sound Publishing Inc.
Description: Third Annual Spring Business Showcase still have space available for vendors and sponsors. The event gives local businesses the opportunity to increase their visibility and provides a means to increase sales and build relationships.

26545 ■ *"The Start of a Beautiful Friendship: Partnering with Your Customers on R&D"* in *Inc. (March 2008, pp. 37-38)*
Pub: Gruner & Jahr USA Publishing
Ed: Leigh Buchanan. Description: Joint research and development projects between customers and suppliers are a growing trend in the small business community; these ventures can help keep new product development costs lower. Four tips to maintain a good working relationship in these ventures are outlined.

26546 ■ *"State's Glass Ceiling Gets Higher"* in *Business Journal-Milwaukee (Vol. 25, October 5, 2007, No. 1, pp. A1)*
Pub: American City Business Journals, Inc.
Ed: Jennifer Batog. Description: Report showed that more than a third of Wisconsin's fifty largest companies have no female executive officers, and the number of companies with at least one woman at top departments has also decreased since 2005. Companies lacking women at upper management levels risk jeopardizing their firms' vitality as diversity in executive offices leads to diverse ideas that can help in relating better to customers and clients.

26547 ■ *"Stop Trying to Delight Your Customers"* in *Harvard Business Review (Vol. 88, July-August 2010, No. 7-8, pp. 116)*
Pub: Harvard Business School Publishing
Ed: Matthew Dixon, Karen Freeman, Nicholas Toman. Description: Importance of resolving issues for customers is key to increasing their loyalty, rather than by exceeding customer expectations. Areas to address include decreasing customer need for follow-up calls, switching service channels, and the potential for negative emotional response.

26548 ■ *"Stress-Test Your Strategy: the 7 Questions to Ask"* in *Harvard Business Review (Vol. 88, November 2010, No. 11, pp. 92)*
Pub: Harvard Business School Publishing
Ed: Robert Simons. Description: Seven questions organizations should use to assess crisis management capabilities are: who is the primary customer, how do core values prioritize all parties, what performance variables are being tracked, what strategic boundaries have been set, how is creative tension being produced, how committed are workers to assisting each other, and what uncertainties are causing worry?.

26549 ■ *"Supply Chain Visibility A Two-Way Street"* in *Canadian Sailings (July 7, 2008)*
Pub: UBM Global Trade
Contact: Leonard J. Corallo, President
Ed: Jack Kohane. Description: Canada is experiencing unprecedented market pressures due to globalization. Competition from foreign countries, demand for better and faster service from customers and shorter innovation cycles are some of the problems the country is facing regarding trade and the importing and exporting industry.

26550 ■ *"Take Out the Garbage"* in *Entrepreneur (Vol. 37, August 2009, No. 8, pp. 26)*
Pub: Entrepreneur Media, Inc.
Ed: Michael Port. Description: Canned 1-2-3 sales tactics should be ditched since consumers express their values with the products and services they buy. Sales people should instead work their call list and become a masterful permission marketer, make relevant sales offers proportionate to the trust they have earned, and build credibility with the people they are meant to serve.

26551 ■ *"Take This Job and Love It"* in *Green Industry Pro (Vol. 23, October 2011)*
Pub: Cygnus Business Media
Ed: Gregg Wartgow. Description: Details of the lawsuit filed by the Professional Landcare Network (PLANET) against the U.S. Department of Labor are explained. Challenges faced by landscape firms because of employment costs are outlined. Statistical data included.

26552 ■ *"Taking a Chance"* in *Baltimore Business Journal (Vol. 28, July 16, 2010, No. 10, pp. 1)*
Pub: Baltimore Business Journal
Ed: Scott Dance. Description: North Avenue in Baltimore, Maryland is considered a rough neighborhood due to the dangers of prostitution and drug dealing. However, some entrepreneurs have taken the risk of building their businesses on North Avenue as revitalization efforts grow. One of the challenges for businesses in rough neighborhoods is bringing customers to their stores or offices.

26553 ■ *"Tap the iPad and Mobile Internet Device Market"* in *Franchising World (Vol. 42, September 2010, No. 9, pp. 43)*
Pub: International Franchise Association
Ed: John Thomson. Description: The iPad and other mobile Internet devices will help franchise owners interact with customers. It will be a good marketing tool for these businesses.

26554 ■ *"Tapping the 'Well' in Wellness"* in *Pet Product News (Vol. 64, November 2010, No. 11, pp. 1)*
Pub: BowTie Inc.
Ed: Wendy-Bedwell Wilson. Description: Healthy food and treats are among the leading wellness products being sought by customers from specialty retailers to keep their pets healthy. With this demand for pet wellness products, retailers suggest making sure that staff know key ingredients to emphasize to customers. Other insights into this trend and ways to engage customers are discussed.

26555 ■ *"Teachable Moments: Worth Every Penny"* in *Pet Product News (Vol. 64, December 2010, No. 12, pp. 34)*
Pub: BowTie Inc.
Ed: Cheryl Reeves. Description: Pet bird retailers can attain both outreach to customers and enhanced profitability by staging educational events such as the annual Parrot Palooza event of Burlington, New Jersey-based Bird Paradise. Aside from attracting a global audience, Parrot Palooza features seminars, workshops, classes, and bird-related contests.

26556 ■ *"Technology: What Seems To Be the Problem? Self Service Gets a Tune-Up"* in *Inc. (February 2008, pp. 43-44)*
Pub: Gruner & Jahr USA Publishing
Ed: Darren Dahl. Description: Self-service software can save companies money when responding to customer service phone calls, text or email messages. More companies are relying on alternatives such as automated Web-based self-service systems.

26557 ■ *"Tell Us What You Really Think Collecting Customer Feedback"* in *Inc. (Vol. 30, December 2008, No. 12, pp. 52)*
Pub: Mansueto Ventures LLC
Ed: Ryan Underwood. Description: According to a recent survey, nearly 77 percent of online shoppers review consumer-generated reviews of products before making a purchase.

26558 ■ *Thank God It's Monday! How to Create a Workplace You and Your Customers Love*
Pub: FT Press
Ed: Roxanne Emmerich. Released: April 18, 2009. Price: $19.99. Description: Tips on creating a positive environment for both employees and customers.

26559 ■ *Trade-Off: The Ever-Present Tension Between Quality and Conscience*
Pub: Crown Business Books
Ed: Kevin Maney. Released: August 17, 2010. Price: $15.00. Description: The tension between fidelity (the quality of a consumer's experience) and convenience (the ease of getting and paying for a product) are shown to be the forces that determine the success or failure of new products and services in the marketplace.

26560 ■ *"The Transparent Supply Chain"* in *Harvard Business Review (Vol. 88, October 2010, No. 10, pp. 76)*
Pub: Harvard Business School Publishing
Ed: Steve New. Description: Examination of the use of new technologies to create a transparent supply chain, such as next-generation 2D bar codes in clothing labels that can provide data on a garment's provenance.

26561 ■ *Treasure Hunt*
Pub: Penguin Group Incorporated
Ed: Michael J. Silverstein; John Butman. Released: May 4, 2006. Description: Explanation of people's spending habits and how to capitalize on retail sales.

26562 ■ *"Turning Trust Into Success"* in *Retail Merchandiser (Vol. 51, July-August 2011, No. 4, pp. 52)*
Pub: Phoenix Media Corporation
Ed: Karen Kondilis. Description: Shopko Stores employs tenured and trustworthy pharmacists and believes it is the core to their success.

26563 ■ *Up the Loyalty Ladder*
Pub: HarperCollins Publishers Inc.
Ed: Murray Rephel; Neil Raphel. Released: September 1996. Description: Marketing consultants share insight into growing any retail business and gain customer loyalty.

26564 ■ *"Visionary Riches"* in *Small Business Opportunities (Winter 2009)*
Pub: Entrepreneur Press
Contact: Perlman Neil, President
Description: Profile of Sterling Optical, which was included in a recent listing of 25 franchise high performers in The Wall Street Journal and is poised for mega-growth due to its offerings of professional eye exams, impeccable customer service, convenient locations and a great selection of eyewear.

26565 ■ *We Are Smarter Than Me: How to Unleash the Power of Crowds in Your Business*
Pub: Wharton School Publishing
Ed: Barry Libert; Jon Spector; Don Tapscott. Released: October 5, 2007. Price: $21.99. Description: Ways to use social networking and community in order to make decisions and plan your business, with a focus on product development, manufacturing, marketing, customer service, finance, management, and more.

26566 ■ *"'We Had to Won the Mistakes"* in *Harvard Business Review (Vol. 88, July-August 2010, No. 7-8, pp. 108)*
Pub: Harvard Business School Publishing
Ed: Adi Ignatius. Description: Interview with Howard Schultz, CEO of Starbucks, covers topics that include investment in retraining, the impact of competition, premium quality, authenticity, customer services, strategy development, work-and-life issues, and international presence.

26567 ■ *"A Weak Link Can Break the Chain of Good Service"* in *Canadian Business (Vol. 83, August 17, 2010, No. 13-14, pp. 11)*
Pub: Rogers Media Ltd.
Ed: Richard Branson. Description: Good customer service is a practice that requires the efforts of the

entire chain of coworkers that work as a team from beginning to end. The chain of assistance is only as strong as the weakest link when it comes to helping a customer.

26568 ■ "What Brain Science Tells Us About How to Excel" in Harvard Business Review (Vol. 88, December 2010, No. 12, pp. 123)
Pub: Harvard Business School Publishing

Ed: Edward M. Hallowell. Description: Relevant discoveries in brain research as they apply to boosting employee motivation and organizational effectiveness are explained. Included is a checklist of 15 items for use in assessing the fitness of a person for a particular job, focusing on the intersection of what one likes to do, what one does best, and what increases organizational value.

26569 ■ "What Most Banks Fail to See; New and Complex Financial Regulations Can be Daunting" in Gallup Management Journal (March 10, 2011)
Pub: Gallup

Ed: Sean Williams, Daniel Porcelli. Description: New financial regulations are complicated and politically charged. But banks that move beyond the fear of those regulations will find a new opportunity to engage customers.

26570 ■ "When Dov Cries" in Canadian Business (Vol. 83, June 15, 2010, No. 10, pp. 71)
Pub: Rogers Media Ltd.

Ed: Joe Castaldo. Description: American Apparel disclosed that they will have problems meeting one of its debt covenants which could trigger a chain reaction that could lead to bankruptcy. The prospects look bleak, but eccentric company founder Dov Charney, has always defied expectations.

26571 ■ Who's Your Gladys?: How to Turn Even the Most Difficult Customer into Your Biggest Fan
Pub: AMACOM

Ed: Marilyn Suttle, Lori Jo Vest. Released: September 9, 2009. Price: $22.95. Description: Every customer oriented business has a hard-to-satisfy client. This book shows how to serve customers who require a higher degree of skill to manage.

26572 ■ "Will Call Center Servicing Solve Labor's Customer Satisfaction Problems?" in WorkingUSA (Vol. 11, September 2008, No. 3, pp. 383)
Pub: Blackwell Publishers Ltd.

Ed: Steve Early. Description: Service Employees International Union (SEIU) has launched an ambitious plan to service hundreds of thousands of members through a network of Member Resource Centers (MRCs). This call center servicing strategy draws on the experience of unions in Australia and the customer service centers operated by major corporations. Call center critics fear the role of union stewards and shop floor activity will be undermined by the introduction of this system in SEIU workplaces in the U.S.

26573 ■ "Winner: Private Company, Less Than $100M" in Crain's Detroit Business (Vol. 25, June 22, 2009, No. 25)
Pub: Crain Communications Inc. - Detroit

Ed: Tom Henderson. Description: Profile of ForeSee Results, an Ann Arbor, Michigan-based firm that uses the University of Michigan American Consumer Satisfaction Index to help businesses measure satisfaction with their Websites.

26574 ■ "With a Smile: Customer Service Affects Every Aspect Of Your Business" in Black Enterprise (Vol. 38, January 2008, No. 6, pp. 43)
Pub: Earl G. Graves Publishing Co. Inc.

Ed: Ayana Dixon. Description: A good customer service program is essential for any small business; learning to anticipate what a customer needs before they even know they need it is key.

26575 ■ "You Can Rebuild It" in Entrepreneur (Vol. 37, July 2009, No. 7, pp. 28)
Pub: Entrepreneur Media, Inc.

Ed: Robert Kiyosaki. Description: Entrepreneurs, during tough times, should melt down old business strategies and start rebuilding the business. The business and its customers should be redefined in order to maximize marketing efforts and stay afloat when business slows down. Personal experiences in melting down a business and starting over are also given.

26576 ■ "You Can't Beat Habit" in Entrepreneur (Vol. 37, July 2009, No. 7, pp. 61)
Pub: Entrepreneur Media, Inc.

Ed: Neale Martin. Description: Customers are changing their spending behavior because of the financial meltdown, and this poses an opportunity for businesses to change their marketing practices in order to regain customers. Being flexible is one way to reestablish purchase behavior, along with paying attention to customer feedback.

26577 ■ "You Can't Fix It If You Don't Face It!" in Indoor Comfort Marketing (Vol. 70, June 2011, No. 6, pp. 14)
Pub: Industry Publications Inc.

Ed: John Levey. Description: Tips for avoiding repeat customer calls when installing or servicing HVAC/R equipment are provided.

26578 ■ "Your Guide to Local Style Business" in Hawaii Business (Vol. 53, December 2007, No. 6, pp. 36)
Pub: Hawaii Business Publishing

Ed: David K. Choo. Description: Discusses the importance of studying the Hawaiian culture when doing business locally. It was observed that geographical aspects increase emphasis on culture and lifestyle more than the need to rectify false imaging do. Details of how locals adhere to their culture are supplied.

26579 ■ "Zappo's CEO On Going to Extremes for Customers" in Harvard Business Review (Vol. 88, July-August 2010, No. 7-8, pp. 41)
Pub: Harvard Business School Publishing

Ed: Tony Hsieh. Description: Footwear firm Zappos.com Inc. improved corporate performance through enhanced customer service. Enhancements include highly visible phone numbers, avoidance of scripts, and viewing call centers as marketing departments.

26580 ■ "Zen and the Art of Twitter Maintenance" in Agency Sales Magazine (Vol. 39, September-October 2009, No. 9, pp. 48)
Pub: MANA

Ed: Terry Brock. Description: Online social networks such as Twitter, LinkedIn, and Facebook should be used to stay in touch with business relationships, especially customers. There should be a focus on making customers happy and building the bottom-line when using these tools.

26581 ■ "Zeon Solutions Teams with Endeca for SaaS Version of Endeca InFront" in Entertainment Close-Up (October 25, 2011)
Pub: Close-Up Media

Description: Zeon Solutions, an enterprise e-commerce and Website development firm announced a special licensing partnership with Endeca Technologies. Endeca is an information management software company that provides small and mid-size retailers with high-performance Customer Experience Management technology.

TRADE PERIODICALS

26582 ■ Customer Service Advantage
Pub: Progressive Business Publications

Ed: Michele McGovern, Editor. Released: Semi-monthly. Price: $253, individuals. Description: Presents practical methods for quantifying customer service benefits and motivating employees day in and day out. Recurring features include interviews, news of research, a calendar of events, news of educational opportunities, and a column titled Sharpen Your Judgment.

26583 ■ First-Rate Customer Service
Pub: Briefings Publishing Group

Ed: John McDonnel, Editor, edit@epinc.com. Released: Biweekly. Description: Offers customer contact personnel advice on enthusiasm and a service-oriented attitude on the job. Recurring features include feature titled A Case in Point. Remarks: Also available in Spanish.

26584 ■ Journal of Relationship Marketing
Pub: Routledge Journals Taylor & Francis Group

URL(s): www.tandfonline.com/toc/wjrm20/current. Ed: David Bejou. Released: Quarterly Price: $114, Individuals online only; $123, Individuals print + online; $523, Institutions online only; $581, Institutions print + online.

26585 ■ Smart Customer Service
Pub: Clement Communications Inc.

Contact: Mike Johnson, Senior Editor

Released: Biweekly. Price: $195. Description: Provides managers and supervisors with techniques and strategies to improve customer service and employee satisfaction. Includes information on recruiting higher quality employees.

VIDEOCASSETTES/AUDIOCASSETTES

26586 ■ Competing Through Customer Service
Video Arts, Inc.
c/o Aim Learning Group
8238-40 Lehigh
Morton Grove, IL 60053-2615
Free: 877-444-2230
Fax: (416)252-2155
Co. E-mail: service@aimlearninggroup.com
URL: http://www.aimlearninggroup.com
Released: 1989. Price: $730.00. Description: This video shows sure-fire methods for improving customer service by understanding and responding effectively to customer needs. Availability: VHS; 8 mm; 3/4 U; Special order formats.

26587 ■ Customer Care Classic Moments
Video Arts, Inc.
c/o Aim Learning Group
8238-40 Lehigh
Morton Grove, IL 60053-2615
Free: 877-444-2230
Fax: (416)252-2155
Co. E-mail: service@aimlearninggroup.com
URL: http://www.aimlearninggroup.com
Released: 1991. Price: $200.00. Description: Dealing with difficult customers is the focus of this video. Can be used to inject humor into a meeting, or as a meaningful exercise. Availability: VHS; 8 mm; 3/4 U; Special order formats.

26588 ■ Customer Expectations
1st Financial Training Services
1515 E. Woodfield Rd., Ste. 345
Schaumburg, IL 60173
Ph: (847)969-0900
Free: 800-442-8662
Fax: (847)969-0521
URL: http://www.1stfinancialtraining.com
Released: 1987. Price: $299.00. Description: Companies have to know what customers want before they can give it to them. Availability: VHS; 3/4 U.

26589 ■ Customer Retention/Service Quality
1st Financial Training Services
1515 E. Woodfield Rd., Ste. 345
Schaumburg, IL 60173
Ph: (847)969-0900
Free: 800-442-8662
Fax: (847)969-0521
URL: http://www.1stfinancialtraining.com
Released: 1987. Price: $250.00. Description: Pope tells businesses how to keep their customers coming back. Availability: VHS; 3/4 U.

26590 ■ *Customer Service or Else*
Enterprise Media
91 Harvey St.
Cambridge, MA 02140
Ph: (617)354-0017
Free: 800-423-6021
Fax: (617)354-1637
URL: http://www.enterprisemedia.com
Released: 19??. **Price:** $795.00. **Description:** Peter Glen lectures on customer service issues. Full of funny, entertaining stories about customer service successes and nightmares. Comes with guide. **Availability:** VHS.

26591 ■ *Customer Service: It's Good Business & It's Everybody's Business*
1st Financial Training Services
1515 E. Woodfield Rd., Ste. 345
Schaumburg, IL 60173
Ph: (847)969-0900
Free: 800-442-8662
Fax: (847)969-0521
URL: http://www.1stfinancialtraining.com
Released: 1987. **Price:** $325.00. **Description:** A demonstration of what some good workers have in common-good customer service skills **Availability:** VHS; 3/4 U.

26592 ■ *Dealing with the Irate Customer*
Advantage Media
c/o Kantola Productions
55 Sunnyside Ave.
Mill Valley, CA 94941
Ph: (415)381-9363
Free: 800-280-1180
Fax: (415)381-9801
Co. E-mail: kantola@kantola.com
URL: http://www.kantola.com/d/advantage.htm
Contact: Daniel Amos, Chief Executive Officer
Released: 1988. **Price:** $495.00. **Description:** Features role play as a model for dealing with the three types of anger. Good visual reinforcement. **Availability:** VHS.

26593 ■ *Don't Mind Him—He's Only a Customer*
Video Arts, Inc.
c/o Aim Learning Group
8238-40 Lehigh
Morton Grove, IL 60053-2615
Free: 877-444-2230
Fax: (416)252-2155
Co. E-mail: service@aimlearninggroup.com
URL: http://www.aimlearninggroup.com
Released: 1989. **Price:** $415.00. **Description:** Ideas are given as to how customers can be treated better. **Availability:** VHS; 3/4 U.

26594 ■ *Effective Telephone Calling*
Encyclopedia Britannica
331 N. LaSalle St.
Chicago, IL 60654
Ph: (312)347-7159
Free: 800-323-1229
Fax: (312)294-2104
URL: http://www.britannica.com
Released: 1989. **Description:** This program demonstrates an easy-to-follow procedure for placing outgoing calls to reduce telephone cost, avoid misunderstandings and project a courteous, business-like image. **Availability:** VHS; 3/4 U.

26595 ■ *The End of the Line*
American Media, Inc.
4621 121st St.
Urbandale, IA 50323-2311
Ph: (515)224-0919
Free: 888-776-8268
Fax: (515)327-2555
Co. E-mail: custsvc@ammedia.com
URL: http://www.ammedia.com
Released: 1992. **Price:** $495.00. **Description:** Teaches employees how to effectively deal with angry customers over the telephone. Includes a leader's guide. **Availability:** VHS; 3/4 U; 8 mm.

26596 ■ *The Good Old Days of Quality Service*
American Media, Inc.
4621 121st St.
Urbandale, IA 50323-2311
Ph: (515)224-0919
Free: 888-776-8268
Fax: (515)327-2555
Co. E-mail: custsvc@ammedia.com
URL: http://www.ammedia.com
Released: 1992. **Price:** $350.00. **Description:** A motivational program to teach employees about quality customer service through narrated musical vignettes. **Availability:** VHS; 3/4 U; 8 mm.

26597 ■ *Hot Under the Collar: Dealing with Angry Customers*
American Media, Inc.
4621 121st St.
Urbandale, IA 50323-2311
Ph: (515)224-0919
Free: 888-776-8268
Fax: (515)327-2555
Co. E-mail: custsvc@ammedia.com
URL: http://www.ammedia.com
Released: 1989. **Price:** $495.00. **Description:** Employees are taught how to properly deal with customers who are not happy. A leader's guide and reminder cards are available. **Availability:** VHS; 3/4 U; Special order formats.

26598 ■ *How to Deliver Superior Customer Service*
Instructional Video
2219 C St.
Lincoln, NE 68502
Ph: (402)475-6570
Free: 800-228-0164
Fax: (402)475-6500
Co. E-mail: feedback@insvideo.com
URL: http://www.insvideo.com
Released: 19??. **Price:** $99.00. **Description:** Offers advice from 15 experts on how to improve customer service, including how to perceive what the customer wants and motivating employees. **Availability:** VHS.

26599 ■ *How to Lose Customers without Really Trying: Attack & Defend*
Video Arts, Inc.
c/o Aim Learning Group
8238-40 Lehigh
Morton Grove, IL 60053-2615
Free: 877-444-2230
Fax: (416)252-2155
Co. E-mail: service@aimlearninggroup.com
URL: http://www.aimlearninggroup.com
Released: 1988. **Price:** $790.00. **Description:** A two-pronged approach to customer service that helps to identify and eliminate the most common pitfalls in dealing with customers when things go wrong. **Availability:** VHS; 8 mm; 3/4 U; Special order formats.

26600 ■ *I Love People. . .It's Customers I Can't Stand*
Instructional Video
2219 C St.
Lincoln, NE 68502
Ph: (402)475-6570
Free: 800-228-0164
Fax: (402)475-6500
Co. E-mail: feedback@insvideo.com
URL: http://www.insvideo.com
Released: 19??. **Price:** $98.00. **Description:** Discusses five different types of problem customers and procedures for dealing with them. **Availability:** VHS.

26601 ■ *It's Your Choice*
American Media, Inc.
4621 121st St.
Urbandale, IA 50323-2311
Ph: (515)224-0919
Free: 888-776-8268

Fax: (515)327-2555
Co. E-mail: custsvc@ammedia.com
URL: http://www.ammedia.com
Released: 1988. **Price:** $495.00. **Description:** A service manager is told that he can either change his attitude or find another job. The importance of treating customers politely is stressed. **Availability:** VHS; 3/4 U.

26602 ■ *Managing for Customer Care*
American Media, Inc.
4621 121st St.
Urbandale, IA 50323-2311
Ph: (515)224-0919
Free: 888-776-8268
Fax: (515)327-2555
Co. E-mail: custsvc@ammedia.com
URL: http://www.ammedia.com
Released: 1990. **Price:** $495.00. **Description:** Aimed at managers and supervisors, this video tells how to deal with day-to-day customer service situations. Includes a trainer's guide, six overhead transparencies, and masters for photocopying. **Availability:** VHS; 3/4 U; 8 mm.

26603 ■ *Objection Handling: Overcoming the Hurdles*
Aspen Publishers, Inc.
7201 McKinney Cir.
Frederick, MD 21704
Ph: (301)698-7100
Free: 800-234-1660
Fax: (800)901-9075
Co. E-mail: customerservice@aspenpublisher.com
URL: http://www.aspenpublishers.com
Contact: Robert Becker, President
Released: 19??. **Price:** $495.00. **Description:** Suggests a five-step strategy to overcoming common customer objections. Unfortunately, the stiff actors provide poor examples. **Availability:** VHS.

26604 ■ *Partnering: The Heart of Selling Today*
American Media, Inc.
4621 121st St.
Urbandale, IA 50323-2311
Ph: (515)224-0919
Free: 888-776-8268
Fax: (515)327-2555
Co. E-mail: custsvc@ammedia.com
URL: http://www.ammedia.com
Released: 19??. **Price:** $475.00. **Description:** Focuses on building lasting relationships with customers through partnering, a technique that helps customers solve their problems and questions. **Availability:** VHS; 3/4 U; 8 mm.

26605 ■ *The Power of Customer Service*
Nightingale-Conant Corp.
6245 W. Howard St.
Niles, IL 60714
Ph: (847)647-0300
Free: 800-560-6081
URL: http://www.nightingale.com
Released: 1991. **Price:** $95.00. **Description:** Customer-oriented service can be the greatest asset for any business. This video discusses the training and building of a service-oriented team. Includes an audio cassette and book. **Availability:** VHS.

26606 ■ *Quality Service: Frontline Commitment*
Phoenix Learning Group
2349 Chaffee Dr.
Saint Louis, MO 63146-3306
Ph: (314)569-0211
Free: 800-221-1274
Fax: (314)569-2834
URL: http://www.phoenixlearninggroup.com
Released: 19??. **Price:** $495.00. **Description:** Focuses on customer service breakdowns and the necessary skills to remedy the situation. One in a pair of videos using the same scenarios to illustrate different points. **Availability:** VHS.

26607 ■ Quality Service: The Three R's for Managers
Phoenix Learning Group
2349 Chaffee Dr.
Saint Louis, MO 63146-3306
Ph: (314)569-0211
Free: 800-221-1274
Fax: (314)569-2834
URL: http://www.phoenixlearninggroup.com
Released: 19??. **Price:** $495.00. **Description:** Focuses on customer service breakdowns and the necessary skills to remedy the situation. One of a pair of videos using the same scenarios to illustrate different points. **Availability:** VHS.

26608 ■ Service Excellence
Video Arts, Inc.
c/o Aim Learning Group
8238-40 Lehigh
Morton Grove, IL 60053-2615
Free: 877-444-2230
Fax: (416)252-2155
Co. E-mail: service@aimlearninggroup.com
URL: http://www.aimlearninggroup.com
Released: 1989. **Price:** $730.00. **Description:** This two-part video shows how your company can increase its profits by improving the three principal areas of customer service. At the end of the program is an opportunity to develop a customized strategy for customer service. **Availability:** VHS; 8 mm; 3/4 U; Special order formats.

26609 ■ Service Sells/Phil Wexler
Instructional Video
2219 C St.
Lincoln, NE 68502
Ph: (402)475-6570
Free: 800-228-0164
Fax: (402)475-6500
Co. E-mail: feedback@insvideo.com
URL: http://www.insvideo.com
Released: 19??. **Price:** $395.00. **Description:** Phil Wexler offers tips on customer service and its effects on the success of the business. He covers the difference between operations-based thinking and market-based thinking, how the right choices can have an immediate impact on your business, targeting the needs of the customer, and minimizing customer complaints and objections. **Availability:** VHS.

26610 ■ Service That Sells
International Dairy-Deli-Bakery Association (IDDBA)
PO Box 5528
Madison, WI 53705-0528
Ph: (608)310-5000
Fax: (608)238-6330
Co. E-mail: iddba@iddba.org
URL: http://www.iddba.org
Contact: Steve Beekhuizen, President
Released: 19??. **Price:** $160.00. **Description:** Bakery customer service training video. **Availability:** VHS.

26611 ■ Tony Alessandra, Ph.D.: On Customer-Driven Service
Instructional Video
2219 C St.
Lincoln, NE 68502
Ph: (402)475-6570
Free: 800-228-0164
Fax: (402)475-6500
Co. E-mail: feedback@insvideo.com
URL: http://www.insvideo.com
Released: 19??. **Price:** $95.00. **Description:** Part of the Tony Alessandra, Ph.D. Series. Outlines techniques to identify and exceed customer expectations and build strong, long-term customer relationships. **Availability:** VHS.

26612 ■ Twelve Steps to Superior Customer Service
Aspen Publishers, Inc.
7201 McKinney Cir.
Frederick, MD 21704
Ph: (301)698-7100
Free: 800-234-1660
Fax: (800)901-9075
Co. E-mail: customerservice@aspenpublisher.com
URL: http://www.aspenpublishers.com
Contact: Robert Becker, President
Released: 1986. **Price:** $495.00. **Description:** A manager's step-by-step guide to effective customer service. **Availability:** VHS; 3/4 U; Special order formats.

26613 ■ Who Killed Service?
American Media, Inc.
4621 121st St.
Urbandale, IA 50323-2311
Ph: (515)224-0919
Free: 888-776-8268
Fax: (515)327-2555
Co. E-mail: custsvc@ammedia.com
URL: http://www.ammedia.com
Released: 19??. **Price:** $1495.00. **Description:** Two programs, one for employees of all levels and one for management, discuss ways to provide top-notch customer service through a motivating and humorous video about a detective searching for the person who committed "servicide" at a company. **Availability:** VHS; 3/4 U; 8 mm.

CONSULTANTS

26614 ■ The Advantage Group Inc.
20 Toronto St. 6th Fl.
Toronto, ON, Canada M5C 2B8
Ph: (416)863-0685
Free: 800-671-1048
Fax: (416)863-0787
Co. E-mail: answers@advantagegroup.com
URL: http://www.advantagegroup.com
Contact: Ron Pirie, President
E-mail: ronpirie@advantagegroup.com
Scope: Specializes in two key areas: performance benchmarking and pricing strategy. Each stream has developed a wide variety of customizable proprietary research tools to meet the needs of the clients. **Founded:** 1988. **Publications:** "7 Steps to building better customer relationships"; "How to Add Value to Customer Relationships"; "Top 10 Key Benefits of Building Business Relationships"; "Tips for Creating Better Relationships"; "Building Trust in Personal and Business Relationships"; "The Advantage Report Canadian Grocer"; "Customer Relationships"; "Customer Relationship Management: What it is and What it's not"; "The Advantage Report - Measuring the supplier-retailer relationship".

26615 ■ Ann Arbor Consulting Associates Inc.
5204 Jackson Rd.
Ann Arbor, MI 48103-9625
Ph: (734)995-2404
Fax: (734)930-2018
Co. E-mail: philalexander@b2badvantage.net
URL: http://www.annarborconsulting.b2badvantage.net
Contact: C. Philip Alexander, President
Scope: Offers coaching and consulting to CEOs and top managers of smaller businesses in the areas of human resources development, total quality management, JP and R performance management systems, employee surveys, team building and strategic planning. **Founded:** 1974. **Publications:** "Jp&R System Manuals and Forms". **Special Services:** Beige Bag Software.

26616 ■ Asset Development Two (AD2)
74 Blue Heron Dr.
Toms River, NJ 08753
Ph: (732)255-7855
Fax: (732)864-1816
Co. E-mail: bobsdoyle@comcast.net
URL: http://www.assetdevelopmenttwo.com
Contact: Robert S. Doyle, President
E-mail: bobsdoyle@comcast.net
Scope: A human resource consulting firm whose mission is twofold: to help people and their organizations to achieve their full potential and to help companies expand their strategic and financial perspectives. To this end, ADG develops programs that make significant and measurable improvements in productivity, profitability, customer satisfaction, operations, and in most areas of an organization. Specific areas include: sales and marketing, leadership and management development, customer service, critical thinking, strategic thinking and planning/selecting/assessing human resources, career management, and continuous process (quality) improvement. **Founded:** 1985.

26617 ■ Barker & Associates
1974 Wexford Cir.
Wheaton, IL 60187-6166
Ph: (630)260-9927
Fax: (630)260-9928
Contact: Patricia D. Barker, President
Scope: Consulting, training, and coaching firm specializing in providing human resource assessment, selection and development services focused primarily on people skills. Serves small, mid, and large-size organizations in both private industry and not-for-profit associations. **Founded:** 1982. **Seminars:** Strategic Marketing; Consultative Selling and Customer Service; From Hiring to Appraising - Developing Your Employees; Increased Productivity Through Managed Stress; Producing People Results Through Team building; Conflict Management; Communications, Managing Transition and Change; Creative Problem Solving.

26618 ■ The Benchmarking Network Inc.
4606 FM 1960 W, Ste. 300
Houston, TX 77069-9949
Ph: (281)440-5044
Free: 888-323-6246
Fax: (281)440-6677
Co. E-mail: additional@benchmarkingnetwork.com
URL: http://www.benchmarkingnetwork.com
Contact: Mark T. Czarnecki, President
E-mail: eczarnecki@benchmarkingnetwork.com
Description: Works to promote benchmarking among members. Provides networking services and information. **Scope:** Provider of measures and metrics expertise, training, research, and implementation in support of process improvement, reengineering efforts and six sigma programs. Industries served: service, manufacturing, financial, retail, telecommunications, utilities, insurance, information systems, and healthcare. **Founded:** 1992. **Seminars:** Benchmarking - Introduction; Benchmarking - Advanced Topics; Customer Satisfaction Measurement; Total Quality Management; New Product Development as well as others; Over a dozen annual networking meetings targeting various industries or business processes.

26619 ■ Business Ventures Corp.
1650 Oakbrook Dr., Ste. 405
Norcross, GA 30093-1881
Ph: (770)729-8000
Fax: (770)729-8028
Co. E-mail: info@bventures.com
Contact: Ruth A. King, President
E-mail: ruthking@bventures.com
Scope: Business development consultants specializing in construction industry. Works with HVAC, plumbing, and electrical contraction who need assistance in marketing, sales and promotion, operations management or finance. Also plan, execute, and monitor the marketing, sales, and promotional activities for new product introductions. Firm also writes business plans, monitors financial health of businesses, and performs operations management. **Founded:** 1981. **Publications:** "The Ugly Truth about Managing People," 2007; "The Ugly Truth about Small Business," 2006; "How to Write a Business Plan," Atlanta Business Chronicle; "Ask 10 Questions Before You Begin Your Business," Income Opportunities "HVAC Bookkeeping and Financial Statements"; "Service Manager's Guide to Running a Profitable Service Department"; "HVAC Career Training Manual"; "Technician's Procedures Manual"; "HVAC Residential Pricing Manual"; "21 Ways to Keep the Honest People Honest Manual"; "Keeping Score: Financial Management for Entrepreneurs"; "Keeping Score: Improving Contractor Productivity and Profitability"; "Keeping Score: Financial Management for Contractors". **Seminars:** The Seven Rules for Business Success; The Seven Greatest Lies of Small Business; Understanding the Financial Side of Business; Small Business Marketing; Strategic Business Planning.

26620 ■ Creative Communications International—CCI Publishing
1605 N Germantown Pkwy.
Cordova, TN 38016-5974
Ph: (901)755-2013
Free: 800-989-2013
Fax: (901)755-2228
Contact: Michael W. Hall, President
E-mail: mwhall@cci4pros.com
Scope: A communication consulting, training and publishing company. Trains customer service, teleservice, order fulfillment and reservation call center personnel on "developing a dynamic phone personality". **Publications:** "Becoming An Effective Storyteller".

26621 ■ Creative Concepts International Inc.
108 Eagle Glen Dr.
Woodstock, GA 30189
Ph: (770)926-1395
Fax: (770)926-1806
Co. E-mail: gene@geneswindell.com
URL: http://www.geneswindell.com
Contact: Gene Swindell, President
E-mail: gene@geneswindell.com
Scope: The firm provides companies with motivational keynotes and informative seminars on leadership, customer service, team building and consultative selling. **Founded:** 1979. **Seminars:** Leadership for Mastering Change; Quality Customer Service; Team building That Works; Coach Management; Customer Service is Your Only Business; Consultative Sales; Team Dynamics.

26622 ■ David Herson Associates
524 Baldwin St.
Virginia Beach, VA 23452-7104
Ph: (757)463-7424
Contact: David Champion, Owner
Scope: Provider of programs for organizations to increase understanding in various human resources areas. Specialty is customized training, that is, researching and developing programs with the purpose of meeting the program needs of the client. Industries served: Clients of all sizes in businesses, government agencies and associations. **Founded:** 1985. **Seminars:** Diversity; Sexual Harassment; Stress Management; Self Esteem; Conflict Management.

26623 ■ donphin.com Inc.
1001 B Ave., Ste. 200
Coronado, CA 92118
Ph: (619)550-3533
Free: 800-234-3304
Fax: (619)600-0096
Co. E-mail: inquiry@donphin.com
URL: http://www.donphin.com
Contact: Vito Tanzi, President
Scope: Offers a comprehensive approach to understanding and applying a broad range of business principles: legal compliance issues, management concerns, health and safety, customer service, marketing, information management. Industries served: All developing small businesses. **Publications:** "Doing Business Right!"; "HR That Works!"; "Lawsuit Free! How to Prevent Employee Lawsuits"; "Building Powerful Employment Relationships!"; "Victims, Villains and Heroes: Managing Emotions in The Workplace". **Seminars:** Doing Business Right!; HR That Works!; Building Powerful Employment Relationships; Lawsuit Free!.

26624 ■ Dynamic Development
11 Bel Aire Dr.
Stamford, CT 06905
Ph: (203)329-0695
Fax: (203)329-1062
Contact: Gilda E. Dangot-Simpkin, President
Scope: Offers a wide variety of customized training programs in management/supervisory, communication, interpersonal, customer service, and sales skills. Specializes in design of unique training, team building and other interactive learning solutions to organizational problems. Provides assessment services to diagnose training needs and organizational problems. Clients include major corporations in a wide range of industries, small companies, governmental and educational institutions. **Founded:** 1980. **Publica-**

tions: "The Dangers of Goals Setting," Supervisory Management, 1992; "Are You Stifling Your Employees?" Supervisory Management, 1992; "7 Ways Managers Undermine Teamwork," Supervisory Management, 1992. **Seminars:** Appraising Performance; Communicating Effectively; Cross-cultural Communication; Conducting Productive Meetings; Conflict Resolution; Customer Service Techniques; Decision Making; Delegating; Group Decision-Making; Interviewing Skills; Leadership Styles and Selection; Legal Issues in Human Resources; Listening Skills; Motivating and Rewarding Performance; Managing Change; Negotiation Skills; Networking Skills; Non-Verbal Communication; Problem-Solving; Proposal Writing; Public Speaking and Presentations; Sales Techniques; Supervising Employees; Stress Management; Team Building; Time Management; Training Trainers.

26625 ■ Enterprise Consulting Inc.
151 Fulton St.
Norwood, MA 02062-2334
Ph: (781)762-4680
URL: http://www.eci-soft.com
Contact: Robert Calligan, Principal
E-mail: rcalligan@eci-soft.com
Scope: Provider of telecommunication design and analysis solutions. It serves health care facilities, colleges and universities, utilities, and government agencies. **Founded:** 1975. **Seminars:** Voice Processing Systems Design; Basic Telecommunications for New Managers; Information Transport Network Design. **Special Services:** SMART.

26626 ■ Golden Eagle Business Services Inc.
PO Box 43447
Atlanta, GA 30336-0447
Ph: (404)881-6777
Fax: (770)944-9495
Co. E-mail: ivorydorsey@ivorydorsey.com
URL: http://www.ivorydorsey.com
Contact: Ivory J. Dorsey, President
E-mail: ivorydorsey@att.net
Scope: Provider of sales, management, customer service change management and motivational training and consulting programs. Also public speaking engagements and special business projects. Serves private industries as well as government agencies. **Founded:** 1984. **Publications:** "Universal Appeal: The Bottom Line Benefit of Diversity"; "Winds of Change and the Business of Competition"; "Redefining Success"; "Personally Responding to the Challenge of Change"; "Diversity, Competition, and Your Bottom Line"; "E-Commerce and the Displacement Sales/Service Professional Eliminated or Empowered". **Seminars:** The Art of Delegation; The Winds of Change; Employee Motivation; Managing Diversity: Perception, Performance and Power; Developing a Sales Mentality in Customer Service.

26627 ■ Richard M. Harris Associates—RMHarris Associates
255 Carlton Terr.
Teaneck, NJ 07666
Ph: (201)801-0087
Fax: (201)801-0087
Co. E-mail: rmharrassoc@aol.com
URL: http://www.rmharrisassociates.com
Contact: Dr. Richard M. Harris, President
Scope: Offers small-group, customized workshops as well as one-on-one training in speaking skills and listening skills. Applications include: leadership development, management and sales presentation, meeting management, customer service, coaching and counseling and team building. Industries served: Drug and pharmaceutical, telecommunications, newspaper publishing, chemicals, advertising, printing and the military. **Founded:** 1976. **Publications:** "The Listening Leader: Powerful New Strategies for Becoming an Influential Communicator," Praeger Publishers, Apr, 2006; "Don't Get Emotional: A Crash Course on Listening," Feb, 2005. **Seminars:** Dialogues for Dating, Apr, 2007; The Advanced Persuasive Speaking; Persuasive Speaking Seminar; Selling Communications Skills; Listening to Lead; Executive Presentation Skills; Professional Communications Skills(PCS); A Practical Telephone-Skills Enhancement Workshop.

26628 ■ Health Strategy Group Inc.
46 River Rd.
Chatham, NY 12037
Ph: (518)392-6770
Contact: Cameron Battley, President
Scope: Provides consulting services in the areas of strategic planning, feasibility studies, start-up businesses, organizational development, market research, customer service audits, new product development, marketing, public relations. **Founded:** 1981. **Publications:** "Online Consumer Surveys as a Methodology for Assessing the Quality of the United States Health Care System," 2004.

26629 ■ Hills Consulting Group Inc.
6 Partridge Ct.
Novato, CA 94945-1315
Ph: (415)898-3944
Contact: Michael R. Hills, President
Scope: Specializes in strategic planning; marketing surveys; market research; customer service audits; new product development; competitive analysis; and sales forecasting. **Founded:** 1985.

26630 ■ Hissong Associates Inc.
2335 Riviera Dr.
Vienna, VA 22181-3117
Ph: (703)281-2817
Fax: (703)242-8055
Contact: Jerry B. Hissong, President
E-mail: jerry@hissong-inc.com
Scope: Training consultants offering applied programs for organizational effectiveness, human resources development, and sales. Provides customized programs aimed at improving management, productivity, sales and harmony in the workplace. Primary focus is management and supervisory training, sales training and customer service training, team innovation, as well as consultation and personnel screening. Also offers a full range of videos, audio albums, training manuals, computer software and assessment instruments on many business subjects. Serves private industries, associations and government agencies. **Founded:** 1983. **Seminars:** Reading the Customer: A Differential Approach to Increased Sales; Teambuilding; The Empowered Manager; Presentation Excellence: People-Reading Secrets; Quality Customer Service; Customer Focused Selling; Time Management; Transcending the Recession on the Bridge of Eagles; Managing with Style.

26631 ■ Howick Associates
14 W Mifflin St., Ste. 300
Madison, WI 53703
Ph: (608)233-3377
Free: 800-236-3370
Fax: (608)233-1194
Co. E-mail: info@howickassociates.com
URL: http://www.howickassociates.com
Contact: Drew Howick, President
E-mail: dhowick@showickassociates.com
Scope: Organizational development and training firm committed to helping organizations meet the demand for greater productivity by enhancing individual, team and organizational effectiveness. **Founded:** 1984. **Publications:** "The New Compleat Facilitator: A Handbook for Facilitators". **Seminars:** The Complete Virtual; Enhancing Your Presentation Style; Perceptive Communications; Listening; Effective Meeting Skills; Strategic Thinking and Planning; Performance Measurement; Facilitation Skills. **Telecommunication Services:** lod@patinasolutions.com.

26632 ■ Impact Training Associates Inc.
320 Arden Ave., Ste. 240
Glendale, CA 91203
Ph: (818)241-3537
Fax: (818)241-4416
Scope: Provider of customized training that strengthens both individuals and organizations. This enables clients to better meet the changing requirements in the competitive market place of the 21st century. Focuses on accelerated learning and action-oriented training that can be applied immediately. **Founded:** 1980.

26633 ■ Bill Johnson
1118 E Orangewood Ave.
Phoenix, AZ 85020-5029

Ph: (602)870-3333
Fax: (602)997-1676
Co. E-mail: BJCSP@aol.com
URL: http://www.billjohnson.com
Contact: Bill L. Johnson, President
E-mail: bjcsp@aol.com
Scope: Advises in the areas of sales and sales management, focusing on customer service and telephone courtesy. Presents seminars on team building, management, sales and organization assessments, including retail distributor sales of tangibles, managing priorities, handling stress and time management. Also offers individual consulting. Industries served hospitality, automotive, banking and finance, entertainment, legal, nonprofit and retail and wholesale in public and private sector. **Founded:** 1979. **Publications:** "Managing Different People Differently," 1999; "Your Back Door To More Revenue"; "The Irate Customer: A Big Opportunity"; "Effective Priorities in Management and Life"; "Managing Multiple Priorities". **Seminars:** Managing and Selling Different People Differently; Will you be running with the Tall Dogs?; Customer Service and Telephone Courtesy; Managing Priorities and Stress; Building High Performing Teams; Ways to Keep Customers Coming Back; The Way Pros Sell Today. **Special Services:** FreedomMike®.

26634 ■ Kutler Consultants
1420 Locust St., Ste. 35Q
Philadelphia, PA 19102
Ph: (215)732-2284
Contact: Edwin Kutler, Owner
Scope: Merchandise operations management consultants whose focus is on maximizing customer service and profitability through effective inventory management-assuring that quality merchandise, properly packaged, is in the right place at the right time, and to fill customer orders immediately. Specific areas of consulting include forecasting, inventory control, quality assurance and packaging, transportation and distribution, management information, order processing and fulfillment, statistical analysis, operations research and systems development. Industries served: Catalog, direct mail, television shopping, and home party plan. **Founded:** 1988.

26635 ■ Lieber & Associates
3740 N Lake Shore Dr., Ste. 15B-2
Chicago, IL 60613-4202
Ph: (773)325-9400
Fax: (773)325-0621
Co. E-mail: info@lieberandassociates.com
URL: http://www.lieberandassociates.com
Contact: Mitchell A. Lieber, President
E-mail: m_lieber@lieberandassociates.com
Scope: Provider of telephone marketing (inbound and outbound); database marketing; and telecommunications technology services for sales, customer service, and order departments. Also upgrades existing operations and start-ups. Performs strategic planning, facility design, equipment specification, network (telephone line) design, software recommendations, staff planning, database design, management systems development, program design, scripting, and project management to meet client requirements. Projects800 number call volumes. Industries served: Direct marketing, catalog order, customer service, utilities, cable television, travel and hospitality, advertising, broadcasting, general business and government in the United States and Worldwide. **Founded:** 1977. **Publications:** "BTB, Inbound Regulation on Horizon," DM News, May, 2006; "ATA Summit: Be Proactive on Regulation," DM News, Apr, 2006; "Contact and Call Centers Today," 2005; "Six Ways to Conduct Successful Telemarketing in a Do-Not-Call World," Oct, 2004; "How to Integrate Telephone and Direct Marketing," 1993. **Seminars:** How to Integrate Telephone and Direct Marketing; Outsourcing Nuts and Bolts; How to Measure and Manage Telemarketing: How to Integrate Telephone, Direct and Internet Marketing-30 Ideas; Repackaging Tele services-A Public Image Make-Over; Transforming your Call Center into a Contact Center; Three Paradigm Shifts that are Changing Tele services Today.

26636 ■ Marketing Leverage Inc.
2022 Laurel Oak Ln.
Palm City, FL 34990
Ph: (772)878-6495
Free: 800-633-1422
Fax: (772)659-8664
Co. E-mail: lkelly@marketingleverage.com
Contact: Lynn C. Kelly, President
E-mail: lkelly@marketingleverage.com
Scope: Consulting and research firm focusing on the targeting, retention and satisfaction of customers. Consulting is offered for due diligence; marketing and customer retention strategy; program design and implementation. Research services offered help clients determine service improvements that increase customer loyalty; boosting sales through better understanding buyer motivations; increasing the odds of product acceptance through new product concept testing; and improving the effectiveness of advertising, collateral, publications through audience evaluation. Clients include top financial services, insurance, health care, technology and management services organizations. **Founded:** 1987. **Publications:** "Creating Strategic Leverage"; "Exploring Corporate Strategy"; "Competitive Advantage"; "Breakpoint and Beyond "; "Competitive Strategy ". **Seminars:** Best Practices in Brainstorming; Getting Results in the Real World; Finding the Leverage in Your Customer Strategy; The Role of Communications in Building Customer Loyalty; Building a Customer Centered Relationship and Making it Pay. **Special Services:** The Marketing Leverage Win/Loss Tracking System™.

26637 ■ McDargh Communications
33465 Dosinia Dr.
Dana Point, CA 92629-4488
Ph: (949)496-8640
Free: 877-477-4718
Fax: (949)248-7805
Co. E-mail: eileen@eileenmcdargh.com
URL: http://www.eileenmcdargh.com
Contact: Eileen McDargh, President
E-mail: eileen@eileenmcdargh.com
Scope: Provides management communications consulting for team building, management communication and training in a variety of communication related skills facilitates management retreats. **Founded:** 1980. **Publications:** "The Spirit of Nurse Leadership"; "Burn out, Balance & Bounty"; "Books: Work for a Living and Still Be Free to Live"; "The Resilient Spirit"; "Off the Chart Results"; "A Woman's Way to Incredible Success"; "Meditations for the Road Warrior"; "Talk Ain't Cheap...It's Priceless"; "Gifts from the Mountain". **Seminars:** Work for a Living and Still Be Free to Live; The Energy Connection.

26638 ■ onFocus Healthcare Inc.
5141 Virginia Way, Ste. 440
Brentwood, TN 37027
Ph: (615)871-4321
Free: 800-899-0021
Fax: (615)871-9821
Co. E-mail: info@m21partners.com
URL: http://www.onfocushealthcare.com
Contact: Steven Mason, President
Scope: Training and consulting firm providing tested models for improving organizational and individual performance. Offers an architecture for organizational transformation that can involve a wide scope of dimensions including assessment of organizational effectiveness, strategic planning, assessment and development of leadership and consulting skills, role clarification, continuous improvement and customer satisfaction, and nontraditional selling. **Founded:** 1985. **Seminars:** Breakthrough Leadership Workshops; Organizational Transformation Architecture System; Design Your Future system; The Lifetime Customer process; Creating and Leading High Performance Teams; Role Clarification; Partnership Selling system. **Telecommunication Services:** sales@onfocushealthcare.com.

26639 ■ Parker Consultants Inc.
230 Mason St.
Greenwich, CT 06830-6633

Ph: (203)861-6698
Contact: Donald L. Parker, President
Scope: Firm specializes in strategic planning; organizational development; small business management; performance appraisals; executive searches; team building; and customer service audits. **Founded:** 1988.

26640 ■ Personal Achievement Institute
1 Speaking Success Rd.
Kingman, AZ 86402-6543
Ph: (928)753-5315
Free: 800-793-3316
Fax: (928)753-7554
Co. E-mail: info@speakingbizsuccess.com
URL: http://www.speakingsuccess.com
Contact: Burt Dubin, President
E-mail: burt@speakingsuccess.com
Scope: Consulting firm serves professional speakers, offering expertise in such areas as positioning, packaging, promotion, and presentation. **Founded:** 1978. **Publications:** "Speaking Success System: Professional Speakers Profit Letter"; "Burt Dubin Private Letter"; "Inner Circle Letter"; "Mission Possible"; "Positioning Magic"; "Selling to the Corporate Market"; "Positioning Magic Special Report"; "177 Wow! Wow! Showmanship Stratagems". **Seminars:** Speaking Success Boot Camps; Boot Camps-at-Sea, Inner Circle Retreats.

26641 ■ The Plotkin Group
5650 El Camino Real, Ste. 223
Carlsbad, CA 92008-7146
Ph: (760)603-8791
Free: 800-877-5685
Fax: (760)603-8570
Co. E-mail: info@plotkingroup.com
URL: http://www.plotkingroup.com
Contact: James Plotkin, President
E-mail: jim@plotkingroup.com
Scope: Employee testing and training organization offering pre-employment honesty, altitude, aptitude and skills tests; and past employment, 360degree assessments, behavior, style and communication tests by phone, paper and pencil, computers, the web, employee attitude surveys, customer service, sales, and management training. **Founded:** 1968. **Publications:** "Building a Winning Team"; "Achieving Above and Beyond Service"; "American Businesses Face Mountain of Problems"; "Appreciating the Richness of Cultural Diversity"; "Attitude is Everything"; "Club members spems are Driving Us All Crazy"; "Credibility and Trust"; "Crime Prevention: The Integrity Business"; "Employee Theft: Hidden Enemy"; "Empowering Employees Without Losing Control"; "How to Build Customer Loyalty"; "Hr Issues of the Millennium"; "Just the Facts (Honesty Testing)"; "Nation's Jobless Must Be Retrained, Put to Work"; "Phone Answering Systems: A Blessing Or a Curse?"; "Strive to Convert Poor Service Into Good Service"; "Tests are Best for Picking Best Worker for the Job"; "The Pre-Interview Hiring Process"; "Time Management"; "What Do Members Want"; "Who to Promote"; "You Can't Turn a Frog Into a Prince"; "Club members speak out about their dining room"; "Companies should stress attitudes over skills (SUN)"; "Companies will always need honest and dependable workers (SUN)"; "Dealing with the angry member"; "Employee selection: A key to member retention"; "Good customer service is the best route to profits (SUN)"; "Hiring, the key to profitability (SUN)"; "Honesty tests are legitimate tool for finding good employees (SUN)"; "How not to handle a crisis"; "How not to open a theater"; "How to determine an applicant's attitude"; "How to identify and develop leadership traits in employees"; "How to introduce pre-employment testing into an organization"; "Integrity among youth is on decline (SUN)"; "Issues of concern for owners"; "Issues of concern for golf companies"; "Ownership and empowerment"; "Road to success paved with customer satisfaction (SUN)"; "Screen applicants to weed out thieves (SUN)"; "When the going gets tough". **Seminars:** Building a Winning Team; Above and Beyond Customer Service Training; Taking the Guess Work Out of Hiring and Promoting.

26642 ■ Retail Management Consultants (RMC)—Pilot Whalin Inc.
2382 Camino Vita Roble, Ste. L
Carlsbad, CA 92011-1508

Ph: (760)632-7500
Free: 800-766-1908
Fax: (760)431-2915
Co. E-mail: info@whalinonretail.com
URL: http://www.whalinonretail.com
Contact: George Whalin, President
E-mail: george@whalinonretail.com
Scope: Specializes in helping retail organizations become more efficient, productive, and profitable. Consulting services include advertising and marketing, employee training programs, customer service improvement, and customer research. Industries served: All segments of the retail industry. **Founded:** 1987. **Seminars:** Retail Success!; Great Store Managers Make Great Stores!; Competition: Powerful trends that are changing what people buy, how they buy, and where they buy!; Stop, Look, Touch, and Buy: The Dynamics of Merchandising; Double Your Sales and Triple Your Profits with High-Impact Marketing and Promotions!; Every Customer Every Day; Customer Focused Selling; Competition? What Competition! Standing Out in Today's Competitive Retail Marketplace; How to Find an Eagle in a Flock of Turkeys! Finding, Hiring, and Keeping the BEST Retail Employees; Double Your Sales and Triple Your Profits with High-Impact Marketing and Promotions!; Customer-Direct Marketing: Increase Retail Sales with High-Impact Direct Mail & E-Mail; Power, Punch & Pizzazz! Create Advertising that Grabs Customer Attention and Sells More Merchandise; 12 Powerful Advertising Secrets Every Retailer Should Know; Great Store Managers Make Great Stores!; Into the Future! Powerful Trends Shaping the Future of Retailing.

26643 ■ James P. Schiller
1621 N 50th Pl.
Milwaukee, WI 53208-2206
Ph: (414)771-3372
Fax: (414)771-8224
Contact: James P. Schiller, Owner
Scope: Training consulting firm offers management research and training. Specializes in personal development programs, management and supervisory skills development. Focuses on performance, improvement, time strategies, mastering work skills, team building, leadership and effective communications. Systems used include: Performax Systems programs, profiles and assessment instruments. Serves corporate, nonprofit, and federal, state and local government employee audiences. **Founded:** 1977. **Seminars:** Time Management Strategies; Effective Listening; Improving Group Relationships; Innovation Seminar; Effective Management Strategies.

26644 ■ Service Quality Institute (SQI)
9201 E Bloomington Fwy.
Minneapolis, MN 55420-3437
Ph: (952)884-3311
Free: 800-548-0538
Fax: (952)884-8901
Co. E-mail: quality@servicequality.com
URL: http://www.customer-service.com
Contact: John Tschohl, President
Scope: Offers customer service training. It provides 30 customers service training programs that busi-

nesses can pick and choose from to improve the quality of customer care. **Founded:** 1972. **Publications:** "Achieving Excellence Through Customer Service," Bestsellers Publishers; "Ca$hing In: Get Promoted, Make More Money, Love Your Job," Bestsellers Publishing; "The Spirit of Excellence"; "Servicio Al Cliente". **Seminars:** E-Service; Achieving Excellence Through Customer Service; Cashing In Feelings; Leading Empowered Teams for Service Quality; Exceptional Service; Attaining Excellence by Keeping More Customers; Customer Service Excellence; Five Star Service; Creating a Service Culture Strategy; Leading Empowered Teams.

26645 ■ Joe Turner
3525 Sandybrook Ln.
Napa, CA 94558
Ph: (707)224-6344
Free: 888-754-6900
Fax: (707)224-6392
Co. E-mail: jmturner@joeturner.com
URL: http://www.joeturner.com
Contact: Joe Turner, Owner
Scope: Provider of customer service consulting, materials, software and training for the new home industry. Specializes in construction defect litigation. Specific problem solving, including recruiting, validating employment information, meeting with homeowners and strategic assessment are available. Produces homeowner manuals for builders and developers. **Founded:** 1982. **Seminars:** TeamTraks.

26646 ■ Your Writing Partner
2137 Mount Vernon Rd.
Atlanta, GA 30338
Ph: (770)395-7483
Free: 800-745-0494
Fax: (770)395-1931
Co. E-mail: kay@yourwritingpartner.net
Contact: Jeffrey E. Disend, President
Description: Description: Publishes communication resources. In addition to books, offers audio and video cassettes, training programs, consulting services, games and role plays, speaking engagements, editing and rewriting services and a newsletter. Reaches market through direct mail and trade sales. Does not accept unsolicited manuscripts. **Scope:** Human resource consultants who provide custom-designed and generic programs for clients. Services include customer analysis, instructional design, and training program design. Also provide performance improvement, editing, proofing, and rewriting services; meeting emceeing, planning and facilitation; conflict resolution; executive coaching. Industries served: banking, healthcare, hospitality, utilities, credit unions, insurance, food, and associations. **Founded:** 1980. **Publications:** "Writing for Big Results," Jan, 2008; "Writing Skills for the College-Bound Student "; "Don't Let Your Participles Dangle in Public," 2005; "Business Etiquette and Professionalism"; "Handling Diversity in the Workplace: Communication is the Key"; "How to Provide Excellent Service in Any Organization"; "Loving Mr. Lincoln". **Seminars:** Business Etiquette and Professionalism; Understanding and Communicating With Others; Politically Correct and Profitable Writing

Skills; Setting the Stage for Excellent Service; The Art of Successful Presentations; Friendly Fire: How Being Your Own Sweet Self Can Burn Others; Ideas Into Action: How to Keep All Those Good Conference Ideas From Going to Waste; Management and Supervisory Skills; How to Proofread Like a Pro; How to Excel at Editing; Grammar for Grownups; Writing for Today's Busy Readers (and Writers); Grammar For Youth; Writing Skills For College-Bound Students.

26647 ■ Ziglar Inc.—The Zig Ziglar Corp.Ziglar Training Systems;
5055 W Park Blvd., Ste. 700
Plano, TX 75093
Ph: (972)233-9191
Free: 800-527-0306
Fax: (469)326-7556
Co. E-mail: info@ziglar.com
URL: http://www.ziglar.com
Contact: Michael Norton, President
URL(s): www.zigziglar.com. **Scope:** Offers management planning, strategic planning, team building, skills assessment, and custom training to provide clients with the tools to build their business. **Founded:** 1970. **Publications:** "Better Than Good"; "Embrace the Struggle"; "God's Way Is Still the Best Way"; "Life Lifters"; "Secrets Of Closing The Sale"; "Raising Positive Kids In a Negative World"; "Ziglar on Selling"; "Over the Top"; "Qualities of Success"; "Changing the Picture"; "One Step at a Time". **Seminars:** Get Motivated, Salt Lake City, Jun, 2010; Born to win; Get Motivated; Ziglar Sales System; Essential Presentation Skills: Custom Curricula.

COMPUTER SYSTEMS/ SOFTWARE

26648 ■ *Measuring Customer Satisfaction*
Crisp Learning Thomson Learning
PO Box 25690
Rochester, NY 14625
Ph: (888)534-5556
Free: 800-442-7477
Fax: (888)715-0220
Co. E-mail: customerservice@axzopress.com
URL: http://www.axzopress.com
Price: $13.95. **Description:** Based on the Measuring Customer Satisfaction video and book. Includes book and user's guide.

RESEARCH CENTERS

26649 ■ Purdue University - Center for Customer-Driven Quality (CCDQ)
1262 Matthews Hall, Ste. 118
West Lafayette, IN 47907-1262
Ph: (765)494-9933
Fax: (765)494-0287
Co. E-mail: xdj1@cfs.purdue.edu
Contact: Dr. Richard Feinberg, Director
Founded: 1993. **Educational Activities:** Courses and guest lectures; Quality customer service video training; Call Center Campus (Annual); Call Center Certification Program. **Telecommunication Services:** ccdq@cfs.purdue.edu.

ASSOCIATIONS AND OTHER ORGANIZATIONS

26650 ■ Americans With Disabilities Act (ADA)
9841 SW 100 Ave.
Miami, FL 33176
Ph: (305)271-0012
Fax: (305)273-1221
Co. E-mail: ergobob@consultant.com
URL: http://www.rehabserv.com
Description: Individuals and organizations united to ensure compliance with the Americans With Disabilities Act of 1992. Compiles statistics; sponsors competitions; maintains speakers' bureau; and operates a museum with cones for visually impaired individuals. **Founded:** 1990. **Publications:** *ADA Compliance Kit*; *ADA Compliance Sourcebook*.

26651 ■ Common Destiny Alliance (CODA)
University of Maryland
2110 Benjamin Bldg.
College Park, MD 20742
Ph: (301)405-0639
Fax: (301)405-3573
Co. E-mail: mh267@umail.umd.edu
URL: http://www.education.umd.edu/CODA/index.html
Description: Organizations and scholars interested in working to end prejudice. Fosters the viewpoint that cultural diversity is "a resource that can help the nation attain goals such as improving economic productivity and the academic achievement of all children." Seeks to end racial isolation in schools, neighborhoods, and the work force. Promotes social policies, especially those related to education, that encourage racial and ethnic understanding and cooperation. Conducts research to identify the causes of racism and means to overcome racism. **Scope:** multicultural education, race relations, postsecondary education, professional development. **Founded:** 1991. **Publications:** *Tracking, Diversity, and Educational Equity: What's New in the Research*; *Toward a Common Destiny: Improving Race and Ethnic Relations in America*.

EDUCATIONAL PROGRAMS

26652 ■ Employment Discrimination Law Update (Onsite)
Seminar Information Service, Inc.
20 Executive Park, Ste. 120
Irvine, CA 92614
Ph: (949)261-9104
Free: 877-SEM-INFO
Fax: (949)261-1963
Co. E-mail: info@seminarinformation.com
URL: http://www.seminarinformation.com
Price: $895.00. **Description:** Covers changes in EEO law and enforcement, sexual harassment, resolving claims and implementing ADA, and the FMLA. **Dates and Locations:** San Francisco, CA; Chicago, IL; and Washington, DC.

26653 ■ Harassment Prevention and Appropriate Behaviors in the Workplace (Onsite)
Seminar Information Service, Inc.
20 Executive Park, Ste. 120
Irvine, CA 92614
Ph: (949)261-9104
Free: 877-SEM-INFO
Fax: (949)261-1963
Co. E-mail: info@seminarinformation.com
URL: http://www.seminarinformation.com
Price: $895.00. **Description:** Explore the legal and policy concerns related to this complex workplace issue, including review and explore the guidelines for identifying inappropriate behavior; the laws, agency interpretations and court cases; and the key elements necessary for writing and implementing policies and procedures. **Dates and Locations:** New York, NY.

REFERENCE WORKS

26654 ■ "$3.5 Million Lawsuit Points Finger at Black Firm" in Black Enterprise (Vol. 38, March 2008, No. 8)
Pub: Earl G. Graves Publishing Co. Inc.
Ed: Cliff Hocker. **Description:** World Wide Technology, the world's largest black-owned company is being sued by a former employee for racial discrimination and retaliation. Details of the lawsuit are outlined.

26655 ■ "Barred Collection Agency Sued by Colorado AG" in Collections & Credit Risk (Vol. 15, August 1, 2010, No. 7, pp. 7)
Pub: SourceMedia Inc.
Description: Collection agency run by Chad Lee received notice that it is barred from collecting in the State of Colorado by Attorney General John Suther's office. A ruling cited that the firm engages in harassment or abuse and/or threats of violence, made false representations as to its legal status of debts, made false and misleading representations of nonpayment of debts that would result in arrest, and that Lee failed to disclose his previous felony conviction.

26656 ■ "Crafting Kinship at Home and Work: Women Miners in Wyoming" in WorkingUSA (Vol. 11, December 2008, No. 4, pp. 439)
Pub: Blackwell Publishers Ltd.
Ed: Jessica M. Smith. **Description:** Institutional policies and social dynamics shaping women working in the northeastern Wyoming mining industry are examined. Ethnographic research suggests that the women's successful integration into this nontraditional workplace is predicated on their ability to craft and maintain kin-like social relationships in two spheres. First, women miners have addressed the challenges of managing their home and work responsibilities by cultivating networks of friends and family to care for their children while they are at work. Second, women miners craft close relationships with coworkers in what are called 'crew families'. These relationships make their work more enjoyable and the ways in which they create camaraderie prompt a reconsideration of conventional accounts of sexual harassment in the mining industry.

26657 ■ "EEOC Sues Charlotte-Based Lebo's" in Charlotte Observer (February 7, 2007)
Pub: Knight-Ridder/Tribune Business News
Ed: Mike Drummond. **Description:** The U.S. Equal Employment Opportunity Commission filed a pregnancy discrimination lawsuit against Lebo's Shoe Stores, located in Charlotte, North Carolina. The suit alleges the store withdrew an offer to hire a woman after finding out she was pregnant.

26658 ■ "The Ethics of Price Discrimination" in Business Ethics Quarterly (Vol. 21, October 2011, No. 4, pp. 633)
Pub: Society for Business Ethics
Ed: Juan M. Elegido. **Description:** Price discrimination is the practice of charging different customers different prices for the same product. Many people consider price discrimination unfair, but economists argue that in many cases price discrimination is more likely to lead to greater welfare than is the uniform pricing alternative, sometimes even for every party in the transaction.

26659 ■ "Human Capital: When Change Means Terminating an Employee" in Black Enterprise (Vol. 41, November 2010, No. 4, pp. 40)
Pub: Earl G. Graves Publishing Co. Inc.
Ed: Tamara E. Holmes. **Description:** Covering successful business change strategies, this article focuses on how the law and nondiscrimination policies can affect this aspect of the workplace.

26660 ■ It's Your Ship
Pub: Warner Books Inc.
Ed: Michael Abrashoff. **Released:** May 1, 2002. **Price:** $24.95. **Description:** Naval Captain D. Michael Abrashoff shares management principles he used to shape his ship, the U.S.S. Benfold, into a model of progressive leadership. Abrashoff revolutionized ways to face the challenges of excessive costs, low morale, sexual harassment, and constant turnover.

26661 ■ "Less Than Zero" in Canadian Business (Vol. 80, November 5, 2007, No. 22, pp. 36)
Pub: Rogers Media
Ed: Andy Holloway. **Description:** Zero-tolerance policy with regards to discrimination and harassment at the workplace has been adopted by many companies. However, employers must exercise caution in terminating employees based on zero-tolerance policies since there are laws governing illegal dismissals. Important considerations employers should make in dismissing workers, such as proof of willful misconduct, are discussed.

26662 ■ "Looking To Hire Young? Be Careful" in Boston Business Journal (Vol. 30, November 19, 2010, No. 43, pp. 1)
Pub: Boston Business Journal
Ed: Lisa van der Pool. **Description:** The Massachusetts Commission Against Discrimination (MCAD) has been using undercover job applicants to

expose discrimination. Cabot's ce Cream and Restaurant has been accused of denying older workers equal employment opportunit es. MCAD has discovered unfair hiring practices such as hiring high school and college students.

26663 ■ *"Maryland Ready to Defend Slots Minority Policy" in Boston Business Journal (Vol. 29, July 8, 2011, No. 9, pp. 3)*
Pub: American City Business Journals Inc.
Ed: Scott Dance. **Description:** The legality of Maryland's minority inclusion policy may be put under scrutiny once the lawsuit filed by rejected slots developer Baltimore City Entertainment Group on July 5, 2011 is heard in court. The lawsuit aims to stop the bidding process on a proposed casino in Baltimore because the minority policy amounts to reverse discrimination.

26664 ■ *"Remind Managers to Avoid Talk of Employee Longevity" in HR Specialist (Vol. 8, September 2010, No. 9, pp. 3)*
Pub: Capitol Information Group Inc.
Description: Supervisors need to understand that casual conversations can be used against an organization in law suits.

26665 ■ *"Research: Mind the Gap" in Business Strategy Review (Vol. 21, Summer 2010, No. 2, pp. 84)*
Pub: Wiley-Blackwell
Description: Isabel Fernandez-Mateo's cumulative gender disadvantage in contract employment is presented.

26666 ■ *"Save the Date" in Barron's (Vol. 90, September 13, 2010, No. 37, pp. 35)*
Pub: Barron's Editorial & Corporate Headquarters
Ed: Mark Veverka. **Description:** Mark Hurd is the new Co-President of Oracle after being forced out at Hewlett-Packard where he faced a harassment complaint. HP fired Hurd due to expense account malfeasance. Hurd is also set to speak at an Oracle trade show in San Francisco on September 20, 2010.

26667 ■ *Sexual Harassment: A Reference Handbook*
Pub: ABC-Clio Inc.
Contact: Ron Boehm, President
E-mail: rboehm@abc-clio.com
URL(s): www.abc-clio.com/product.aspx?id=2147520636. **Ed:** Lynn Eisaguirre. **Released:** Latest edition 2nd; December 1997. **Publication includes:** List of agencies and organizations in the U.S. Concerned with sexual harassment. **Entries include:** Organization name, address, phone. Principal content of publication is information on the history, social context, legal precedent, and legislative background of sexual harassment issues. Part of "Contemporary World Issues Series.". **Arrangement:** Directory of organizations, selected print resources, film, Internet resources.

26668 ■ *"Subprime Lenders Under Fire: Does the NAACP Have a Viable Case?" in Black Enterprise (Vol. 38, October 2007, No. 3, pp. 31)*
Pub: Earl G. Graves Publishing Co. Inc.
Ed: Trevor Delaney. **Description:** NAACP filed a lawsuit charging a number of mortgage lenders with 'institutionalized systematic racism'. Lenders named in the suit include Accredited Home Lenders, Ameriquest Mortgage Company, BNC Mortgage, Citigroup, Encore Credit, First Franklin Financial Corporation, Fremont Investment and Loan, HSBC Finance Corporation, Long Beach Mortgage Company, Option One Mortgage Corporation, Washington Mutual Inc., and WMC Mortgage Corporation. Details of the lawsuit are included.

26669 ■ *"'Tone-Deaf' Suitor or True Harasser: How to Tell" in HR Specialist (Vol. 8, September 2010, No. 9, pp. 1)*
Pub: Capitol Information Group Inc.
Description: Details are critical to any harassment charge in the workplace. Courts now list factors employers should consider when trying to determine whether an employee has been sexually harassed at work.

26670 ■ *"Unseen Injustice: Incivility as Modern Discrimination in Organizations" in Academy of Management Review (January 2008, pp. 55)*
Pub: ScholarOne, Inc.
Ed: Lilia M. Cortina. **Description:** Analysis of social psychological research on modern discrimination to explain the theory of incivility used as part of sexism and racism in organizations. The selective incivility observed is discussed, as well as its implications and efforts to eliminate it.

26671 ■ *"Words at Work" in Information Today (Vol. 26, February 2009, No. 2, pp. 25)*
Pub: Information Today, Inc.
Description: Current new buzzwords include the following: digital amnesia, or overload by availability, speed and volume of digital information; maternal profiling, a form a discrimination against women; recipe malpractice, a reminder that just because you can turn on a stove it doesn't make you a chef; ringxiety, the act when everyone reaches for their cell phone when one rings; verbing, the practice of turning good nouns into verbs.

TRADE PERIODICALS

26672 ■ *The Columbus Times*
Pub: Columbus Times
Contact: Ophelia Mitchell, Chief Executive Officer
URL(s): www.columbustimes.com/. **Released:** Weekly (Wed.) **Price:** $65.48, Individuals; $0.50, Single issue.

26673 ■ *Manager's Legal Bulletin*
Pub: Alexander Hamilton Institute Inc.
Ed: Gloria Ju, Editor. **Released:** Semimonthly. **Price:** $72, individuals; $3.00, single issue. **Description:** Shows managers how to handle problems in the workplace without provoking lawsuits for illegal discrimination in hiring, firing, promotions, sexual harassment, or discipline decisions.

26674 ■ *Mealey's Emerging Insurance Disputes*
Pub: LexisNexis
Ed: Steve Berstler, Editor. **Released:** Semimonthly. **Price:** $1,464, U.S. **Description:** Finds and tracks new areas of insurance litigation as they arise. Follows coverage actions involving underlying claims of sexual harassment and discrimination; sexual molestation and assault; attorney liability; patent and trademark infringement; construction defects, directors and officers claims; emotional distress; and intentional acts.

26675 ■ *The Webb Report*
Pub: Pacific Resource Development Group, Inc.
Released: Monthly. **Price:** Free; $10, single issue subscribers; $15, single issue non-subscribers. **Description:** Provides information on court cases and issues involving sexual harassment and guidelines concerning what is and what is not considered to be harassment and what to do about it. Recurring features include news of research and notices of publications available.

VIDEOCASSETTES/ AUDIOCASSETTES

26676 ■ *ADA: Commonsense Compliance*
Audio Graphics Training Systems
301 West Broome St., Suite 100
Lagrange, GA 30240
Ph: (404)507-2487
Free: 800-814-9792
Fax: (706)883-7136
Co. E-mail: customerservice@agts-web.com
URL: http://www.agts-web.com
Released: 19??. **Price:** $695.00. **Description:** Illustrates the legal issues of the ADA through well-acted vignettes. Designed to be viewed in conjunction with "ADA: Understanding the Law.". **Availability:** VHS.

26677 ■ *The ADA Maze: What You Can Do*
Commonwealth Films, Inc.
223 Commonwealth Ave.
Boston, MA 02116
Ph: (617)262-5634
Fax: (617)262-6948
Co. E-mail: info@commonwealthfilms.com
URL: http://www.commonwealthfilms.com
Released: 1991. **Price:** $425.00. **Description:** Defines the legal aspects of hiring according to the ADA through a combination of interviews and graphics. Aimed at managers, topics include the intent of the ADA, writing job descriptions, interviewing guidelines and more. **Availability:** VHS.

26678 ■ *ADA: Understanding the Law*
Audio Graphics Training Systems
301 West Broome St., Suite 100
Lagrange, GA 30240
Ph: (404)507-2487
Free: 800-814-9792
Fax: (706)883-7136
Co. E-mail: customerservice@agts-web.com
URL: http://www.agts-web.com
Released: 19??. **Price:** $695.00. **Description:** Discusses the new ADA laws in a conference room setting. Confronts typical objections from management and gives clear information on legal requirements and ramifications. Designed to be viewed in conjunction with "ADA: Commonsense Compliance.". **Availability:** VHS.

26679 ■ *Adjust Your Set: The Static Is Real*
University of Toronto
Media Commons
Robarts Library
130 St. George St., 3rd Fl.
Toronto, ON, Canada M5S 1A5
Ph: (416)978-6520
Fax: (416)978-8707
Co. E-mail: luke.dellcese@utoronto.ca
URL: http://www.utoronto.ca
Released: 19??. **Price:** $79.95. **Description:** Adcresses the issues that exist between men and women on the subject of sexual harassment. Contains vignettes on emotional manipulation, subtle threats of violence, heterosexism, feminist backlash in the classroom, harassment of disabled women, and battering in heterosexual relationships. Written and presented by students. **Availability:** VHS.

26680 ■ *The Americans with Disabilities Act: New Access to the Workplace*
Phoenix Learning Group
2349 Chaffee Dr.
Saint Louis, MO 63146-3306
Ph: (314)569-0211
Free: 800-221-1274
Fax: (314)569-2834
URL: http://www.phoenixlearninggroup.com
Released: 19??. **Price:** $495.00. **Description:** Covers a broad scope of information through interviews with government officials. Intended mainly for employers. **Availability:** VHS.

26681 ■ *Bridges: Skills to Manage a Diverse Workforce*
Learning Communications L.L.C.
5520 Trabuco Rd.
Irvine, CA 92620-5705
Free: 800-622-3610
Fax: (949)727-4323
Co. E-mail: sales@learncom.com
URL: http://www.learncom.com
Contact: Lloyd W. Singer, President
Released: 1990. **Price:** $175.00. **Description:** An eight-part series designed to train supervisors and managers to deal with a culturally diverse workforce. The tapes are available individually or as a set. Trainer's manuals and participants manuals are included. **Availability:** VHS; 3/4 U.

26682 ■ *Choices*
Learning Communications L.L.C.
5520 Trabuco Rd.
Irvine, CA 92620-5705
Free: 800-622-3610

Fax: (949)727-4323
Co. E-mail: sales@learncom.com
URL: http://www.learncom.com
Contact: Lloyd W. Singer, President
Released: 1990. **Price:** $175.00. **Description:** A 12-part training course, designed to help train managers in EEO and affirmative action. Tapes are available as a set or individually. Trainer and participant manuals are included. **Availability:** VHS; 3/4 U.

26683 ■ Expanding Equal Opportunities—Implementing the Americans with Disabilities Act
National Audiovisual Center
5301 Shawnee Rd.
Alexandria, VA 22312
Ph: (703)605-6000
Free: 800-553-6847
Fax: (703)321-8547
Co. E-mail: customerservice@ntis.gov
URL: http://www.ntis.gov/products/nac.aspx
Released: 1991. **Price:** $35.00. **Description:** Explains aspects of the Americans with Disabilities Act and how it affects the workplace. **Availability:** VHS.

26684 ■ The Fairer Sex?
corVISION Media, Inc.
872 S Milwaukee Ave. Ste. 295
Northbrook, IL 60062
Ph: (877)364-7485
Free: 877-364-7485
Fax: (866)440-2614
Co. E-mail: corvision@aol.com
URL: http://www.corvision.com
Released: 19??. **Price:** $295.00. **Description:** Tests whether women are truly discriminated in job market and in consumer purchasing situations. Intended to modify discriminatory behavior. **Availability:** VHS.

26685 ■ Gateway to Opportunity: Interviewing Job Applicants with Disabilities
Advantage Media
c/o Kantola Productions
55 Sunnyside Ave.
Mill Valley, CA 94941
Ph: (415)381-9363
Free: 800-280-1180
Fax: (415)381-9801
Co. E-mail: kantola@kantola.com
URL: http://www.kantola.com/d/advantage.htm
Contact: Daniel Amos, Chief Executive Officer
Released: 1992. **Price:** $495.00. **Description:** Illustrates detailed guidelines for interviewing according to the ADA through a combination of short scenarios and interviews. Note, however, that the guidelines don't necessarily address the legal issues per se. **Availability:** VHS.

26686 ■ Given the Opportunity: Interacting with Individuals with Disabilities
American Media, Inc.
4621 121st St.
Urbandale, IA 50323-2311
Ph: (515)224-0919
Free: 888-776-8268
Fax: (515)327-2555
Co. E-mail: custsvc@ammedia.com
URL: http://www.ammedia.com
Released: 1992. **Price:** $450.00. **Description:** A guide to interaction with the disabled in the workplace. Focuses primarily on four disabilities: hearing, sight, immobility, and the developmentally challenged, and the means of overcoming awkwardness when confronted with the disabled. **Availability:** VHS.

26687 ■ Handling the Sexual Harassment Complaint
Excellence in Training Corp.
c/o ICON Training
804 Roosevelt St.
Polk City, IA 50226
Free: 800-609-0479
Co. E-mail: info@icontraining.com
URL: http://www.icontraining.com
Released: 1991. **Price:** $495.00. **Description:** A program designed to train managers and supervisors how to avoid problems by the handling sexual harass-

ment complaints correctly and legally. Includes a leader's guide and desk reminder cards. **Availability:** VHS; 3/4 U; Special order formats.

26688 ■ Intent vs. Impact
Learning Communications L.L.C.
5520 Trabuco Rd.
Irvine, CA 92620-5705
Free: 800-622-3610
Fax: (949)727-4323
Co. E-mail: sales@learncom.com
URL: http://www.learncom.com
Contact: Lloyd W. Singer, President
Released: 1991. **Price:** $175.00. **Description:** Two complete video training programs designed to help identify subtle forms of sexual harassment in the workplace. A trainer's manual and participants' manuals are included. **Availability:** VHS; 3/4 U.

26689 ■ It's Not Just Courtesy—It's the Law
Excellence in Training Corp.
c/o ICON Training
804 Roosevelt St.
Polk City, IA 50226
Free: 800-609-0479
Co. E-mail: info@icontraining.com
URL: http://www.icontraining.com
Released: 1991. **Price:** $495.00. **Description:** A training program to raise awareness of sexual harassment among employees and teach them how to handle it. A leader's guide is included. **Availability:** VHS; 3/4 U; Special order formats.

26690 ■ Preventing Sexual Harassment: A Management Responsibility
Learning Communications L.L.C.
5520 Trabuco Rd.
Irvine, CA 92620-5705
Free: 800-622-3610
Fax: (949)727-4323
Co. E-mail: sales@learncom.com
URL: http://www.learncom.com
Contact: Lloyd W. Singer, President
Released: 1992. **Description:** Training program consisting of two videotapes designed to show managers how to identify and prevent sexual harassement in the workplace and minimize liability. Defines sexual harassment, shows managers and supervisors how they can be held personally liable, presents practical steps to prevent harassment, details the elements of effective remedial action, and examines case studies. **Availability:** VHS; 3/4 U.

26691 ■ Preventing Sexual Harassment: A Shared Responsibility
Learning Communications L.L.C.
5520 Trabuco Rd.
Irvine, CA 92620-5705
Free: 800-622-3610
Fax: (949)727-4323
Co. E-mail: sales@learncom.com
URL: http://www.learncom.com
Contact: Lloyd W. Singer, President
Released: 1992. **Description:** Training program designed to prevent sexual harassment by employees and to minimize liability. Demonstrates the employer's prohibition against sexual harassment, highlights the availability of internal procedures for the resolution of complaints, and encourages employees to use internal procedures. **Availability:** VHS; 3/4 U.

26692 ■ Putting the ADA to Work for You
American Occupational Therapy Association (AOTA)
4720 Montgomery Ln., Ste. 200
Bethesda, MD 20824-1220
Ph: (301)652-2682
Free: 800-377-8555
Fax: (301)652-7711
Co. E-mail: members@aota.org
URL: http://www.aota.org
Contact: Frederick P. Somers, Executive Director
Released: 1992. **Price:** $50.00. **Description:** A real bargain for its low price and straight-forward approach. Combines interviews and short vignettes to suggest approaches to "reasonable accommodations.". **Availability:** VHS.

26693 ■ Sexual Harassment: Handling the Complaint
Audio Graphics Training Systems
301 West Broome St., Suite 100
Lagrange, GA 30240
Ph: (404)507-2487
Free: 800-814-9792
Fax: (706)883-7136
Co. E-mail: customerservice@agts-web.com
URL: http://www.agts-web.com
Released: 19??. **Price:** $1295.00. **Description:** Part two in a two-part series addressing the behavioral and legal issues surrounding sexual harassment. Directly confronts sensitive material in a constructive manner through well-acted vignettes. **Availability:** VHS.

26694 ■ Sexual Harassment: Serious Business
American Management Association (AMA)
1601 Broadway
New York, NY 10019-7420
Ph: (212)586-8100
Free: 877-566-9441
Fax: (212)903-8168
Co. E-mail: customerservice@amanet.org
URL: http://www.amanet.org
Contact: Charles R. Craig, Chairman
Released: 19??. **Price:** $495.00. **Description:** Provides information on how to recognize and prevent sexual harassment in the workplace. **Availability:** VHS; CC.

26695 ■ Sexual Harassment in the Workplace. . .Identify. Stop. Prevent.
Excellence in Training Corp.
c/o ICON Training
804 Roosevelt St.
Polk City, IA 50226
Free: 800-609-0479
Co. E-mail: info@icontraining.com
URL: http://www.icontraining.com
Released: 1991. **Price:** $575.00. **Description:** A training program in the prevention and/or eliminating of sexual harassment in the workplace. A leader's guide and desk reminder cards are included. **Availability:** VHS; 3/4 U; Special order formats.

26696 ■ Welcome to the Team: Disability Etiquette in the Workplace
Advantage Media
c/o Kantola Productions
55 Sunnyside Ave.
Mill Valley, CA 94941
Ph: (415)381-9363
Free: 800-280-1180
Fax: (415)381-9801
Co. E-mail: kantola@kantola.com
URL: http://www.kantola.com/d/advantage.htm
Contact: Daniel Amos, Chief Executive Officer
Released: 1992. **Price:** $495.00. **Description:** Illustrates the concept of "reasonable accommodations," through various examples and practical suggestions. Recommended for both managers and employees. Part one of a two part program. **Availability:** VHS.

CONSULTANTS

26697 ■ AIDS Partnership Michigan (APM)
2751 E Jefferson Ave., Ste. 301
Detroit, MI 48207
Ph: (313)446-9800
Free: 800-515-3434
Fax: (313)446-9839
Co. E-mail: info@aidspartnership.org
URL: http://www.aidspartnership.org
Contact: Tom Verwest, President
Description: Services include case management, behavioral health services, AIDS Interfaith Network, Linda's Home Delivered Meals, Project Med-Line, transportation, Michigan AIDS Hotline, Teen link HIV/STD Hotline, speaker's bureau, and HIV counseling and testing. **Scope:** Offers advice to corporations on the effects of HIV and AIDS in the workplace. Focus

is on infected employee rights, co-worker rights, and employer responsibilities. Serves all industries. **Founded:** 1996.

26698 ■ Applied Personnel Research (APR)
62 Candlewood Rd.
Scarsdale, NY 10583
Ph: (617)244-8859
Fax: (617)244-8904
Co. E-mail: information@appliedpersonnelresearch.com
URL: http://www.appliedpersonnelresearch.com
Contact: Dr. Joel P. Wiesen, Director
E-mail: wiesen@appliedpersonnelresearch.com
Scope: Industrial psychology consulting services in the areas of personnel assessment and selection, and solution-oriented applied personnel research involving data collection and data analysis. Customized Consulting solutions can be provided. **Founded:** 1980. **Seminars:** The Recent Judicial Decision Concerning Two NYC Firefighter Exams, 2009; Possible New Approaches to Reduce Adverse Impact, 2007; Thinking Outside the Box in Merit Selection, Princeton, Nov, 2006; Limitations and Flaws in the Research Supporting Field Sobriety Tests, Las Vegas, Oct, 2006.

26699 ■ D.R. Bennett & Associates
11846 Balboa Blvd., Ste. 298
Granada Hills, CA 91344
Ph: (818)360-2375
Fax: (818)366-7593
Contact: Deborah R. Bennett, President
E-mail: dbennett69@aol.com
Scope: Human resources consultant who writes all human resources forms including employee handbooks and job descriptions; sets up employment applications, employee files and procedures to comply with regulations affecting employers; and finds and screens applicants and does the initial interviewing. Also offers management training in the areas of interviewing, employee evaluations, how to handle sexual harassment claims and progressive discipline and documentation. All services are tailored to meet EEOC and INS regulations as well as labor laws, to reduce exposure to worker's compensation stress claims, unemployment claims and wrongful termination suits. Industries served: small businesses with 25-100employees. **Founded:** 1984. **Seminars:** Interviewing Skills Seminar; Performance Appraisal Seminar.

26700 ■ Dr. John A. Berger and Associates
2021 Midwest Rd., Ste. 200
Oak Brook, IL 60523
Ph: (630)953-8638
Fax: (630)953-8687
Contact: Dr. John A. Berger, Owner
Scope: Full service human resources consulting firm specializing in the practice of industrial/organizational psychology. Specializes in the areas of recruitment and selection; management continuity, development and succession planning; capability and performance testing and evaluation; organizational analysis and design, performance management; outplacement and terminations; turnarounds and crisis management; compensation; family owned business counseling - conflict resolution, management succession, and career planning for family members. Has developed structured hiring guides and selection systems; Has designed, developed and implemented a variety of performance appraisal systems both as part of total compensation projects and stand alone systems. Has served as an expert witness in a number of wrongful discharge and EEO discrimination cases. Industries served: manufacturing, financial services, high-tech, insurance, utilities, construction, retail, professional services, government, health care, publishing, leisure and food services. **Founded:** 1982.

26701 ■ Coastal Training Technologies Corp.
500 Studio Dr.
Virginia Beach, VA 23452
Ph: (757)498-9014
Free: 800-861-7668
Fax: (757)498-3657
Co. E-mail: info@coastal.com
URL: http://www.coastalhr.com
Contact: Matt McGonegle, Manager
Scope: Provides consulting services and seminars on all aspects of management, human resources, and business, including customer relations and sexual harassment, works with managers one-on-one, implements programs, and presents seminars for entire departments. Serves private industries as well as government agencies. **Founded:** 1977. **Seminars:** Accounting and Corporate Finance; Americans with Disabilities Act (ADA); Business Meetings; Change Management; Coaching; Communication; Conflict Resolution; Creativity; Customer Service; Diversity; Drug-Free Workplace; Employee Development; Employee Retention; Government Employee; Group Dynamics; Harassment; Homeland Security; Interviewing Skills. **Special Services:** Coastal®.

26702 ■ DiversityWorks
800 Heinz Ave., Ste. 14
Berkeley, CA 94710
Ph: (510)540-7008
Fax: (510)540-6976
Co. E-mail: mail@diversityworks.org
URL: http://www.diversityworks.org
Contact: Moses J. Ceaser, President
Scope: Offers diversity consulting to businesses, schools, youth groups, and a variety of organizations. Designs programs to suit to individual clients' needs. Areas of expertise include: Community-building (and team-building), consciousness-raising, skill building (leadership development, popular education, facilitation) and taking action. **Founded:** 1998. **Publications:** "Diversity Words"; "A Woman's Beauty"; "Youth Violence"; "Modern Day Minstrels"; "Love Makes the World Go Round"; "Glorification of White Supremacy through Movies".

26703 ■ DJT Consulting Group L.L.C.
PO Box 8595
San Jose, CA 95155
Ph: (408)280-1153
Co. E-mail: info@djtconsulting.com
URL: http://www.djtconsulting.com
Contact: Sherry V. Bruning, Principal
Scope: Offers a range of grant management services including contract monitoring, research, grant writing, evaluation and project management. Specializes in grant proposal writing, project management and program development. Assists enhance financial resources, programs and services. **Founded:** 2000. **Seminars:** Finding and Winning Government Grants. **Telecommunication Services:** sherry@djtconsulting.com.

26704 ■ Eastern Point Consulting Group Inc.
36 Glen Ave.
Newton, MA 02464
Ph: (617)965-4141
Fax: (617)965-4172
Co. E-mail: info@eastpt.com
URL: http://www.eastpt.com
Contact: Katherine A. Herzog, President
E-mail: kherzog@eastpt.com
Scope: Specializes in bringing practical solutions to complex challenges. Provides consulting and training in managing diversity; comprehensive sexual-harassment policies and programs; organizational development; benchmarks 360 skills assessment; executive coaching; strategic human resource planning; team building; leadership development for women; mentoring programs; and gender issues in the workplace. **Founded:** 1995. **Seminars:** Leadership Development for Women.

26705 ■ FW Consultants Ltd.
1025 W Glen Oaks Ln., Ste. 105
Mequon, WI 53092-3372
Ph: (262)241-8234
Fax: (262)241-8340
URL: http://www.fwcons.com
Contact: Evelyn F. Walker, President
Scope: Human resources consultants specializing in equal employment opportunity and affirmative action programs, demographic analyses, EEO/AA training, and statistical analyses to defend discrimination charges. Serves private industries as well as government agencies. **Founded:** 1993. **Seminars:** Affirmative Action Program Development; EEO/Affirmative Action Training.

26706 ■ Haight Consulting
1726 Palisades Dr.
Pacific Palisades, CA 90272-9867
Ph: (310)454-2988
Fax: (310)454-4516
Co. E-mail: haightcnsl@yahoo.com
Contact: Marcia K. Haight, President
E-mail: haightcns@aol.com
Scope: Human Resources compliance: helping employers prevent and resolve issues on sexual harassment, disability discrimination, other forms of discrimination and harassment, retaliation, FMLA, and employee safety. Training (management, HR staff and internal investigators); policies and procedures; compliance program audits; expert witness/litigation consulting; and on-call consultation on individual issues and investigations. **Founded:** 1989. **Publications:** "Sexual Harassment Investigations Manual," CCH Inc, 2000; "The Federal Leave Compliance Kit," 1995; "Disability discrimination Reasonable Accommodation Kit," 1995; "Disability discrimination Administration Package"; "The Sexual Harassment Investigator's Kit"; "The California Sexual Harassment Compliance Kit". **Seminars:** Management and HR training on disability discrimination; sexual harassment; discrimination and harassment laws; FMLA; retaliation; recruiting and selection; preventing and resolving performance issues.

26707 ■ Human Resources Group Ltd.
318 Maple St.
Beecher, IL 60401
Ph: (708)946-9652
Fax: (708)946-9653
Co. E-mail: rorr@hrgroupltd.com
URL: http://www.hrgroupltd.com
Contact: Robert C. Orr, Owner
E-mail: rorr@hrgroupltd.com
Scope: Offers human resource consulting to small or medium-sized companies with limited human resource staff. Areas of expertise include sales and management training and development, employee opinion surveys, employee retention programs, customer service, communication strategies, and performance evaluation programs. Development of policies and procedures, employee handbooks, jobs compendium, and turnover reduction strategies. Provides training in legal compliance, i.e. Americans with Disabilities Act, sexual harassment, etc. Industries served: retail, casino gaming(including Indian gaming) and hospitality. **Founded:** 1991. **Publications:** "Employee Surveys: Being a "Mind Reader" Was never So Easy"; "Getting Over The "HR-Marketing Strange Bedfellows"; Underachievers"; "Employee Retention? No Problem!"; "Is Your Company The Employer Of Choice?"; "What is the Role of Your HR Department"; "Managing from A to Almost Z"; "The Top 10 Things HR Should be Doing"; "HR Department Assessment for the GM & HR Executive"; "Evaluating Executives"; "Economic Challenges - 11 Steps". **Seminars:** Effective Sales Management; Basics of Supervisory Management; Human Resource Educational Program; Human Resources and the Small Business; Customer Service. **Telecommunication Services:** hrgltd@aol.com.

26708 ■ The Kaleel Jamison Consulting Group Inc.
5 3rd St.
Troy, NY 12180
Ph: (518)271-7000
Free: 888-552-4662
Fax: (518)271-4400
Co. E-mail: kjcg411@kjcg.com
URL: http://www.kjcg.com
Contact: Corey L. Jamison, President
Scope: The firm creates high performing, worthy organizations through its unique brand of management consulting and strategic culture change, also assists organizations to become places where all people can do their work by shifting focus to business cultures that integrate individual and organizational needs and competencies, which improve productivity, product or service quality and bottom line performance. **Founded:** 1970. **Publications:**

"The Next Leap Forward Diversity and Inclusion An OD Opportunity"; "Inclusion 3.5: Our Vision of the Future," Profiles in Diversity Journal, 2007; "The Next Leap Forward," 2007; "Tapping the Wisdom of the Ages: Ageism and the Need for Multi generational Organizations"; "Developing a Comprehensive Pipeline Strategy"; "White Awareness: Handbook for Anti-Racism Training," University of Oklahoma Press, 2003; "The Inclusion Breakthrough: Unleashing the Real Power of Diversity," Berrett-Koehler, 2002; "Eight Essential Axioms for Rapid Culture Change"; "The Need for Silence, Spontaneity and Thinking Time in 21st Century Organization"; "Road Map for the Path to Strategic Culture Change"; "Thee Path From Exclusive Club to Inclusive Organization". **Seminars:** Multicultural Forum on Workplace Diversity, Mar, 2012; Be BIG: Four Behaviors That Change Everything to Enable You to Step Up, Step Out, Be Bold, May, 2012, Singapore; Be Big: 4 Keys That Change Everything, Singapore, Jul, 2012; Be Big: 4 Keys That Change Everything, Chennai, India, Oct, 2012; OD Network Conference, Nov, 2011; Bring Your Whole Self To Life: Developing The Organizational And Personal Self (D/OPS), Potomac, Aug, 2008; D/Ops: Developing The Organizational And Personal Self; Dealing with Covert Processes.

26709 ■ Litigation Management & Training Services Inc.

301 E Ocean Blvd., Ste. 520
Long Beach, CA 90802-4862
Ph: (562)495-0098
Free: 800-548-6468
Fax: (562)495-1786
Co. E-mail: info@preventlitigation.com
URL: http://www.preventlitigation.com
Contact: Patricia S. Eyres, President
E-mail: patricia@preventlitigation.com
Scope: Consults with private industry employers and government agencies on proactive legal management of the workplace, including sexual harassment prevention, legal aspects of human resources management, how to hire, fire and manage employees legally. Special programs for adopting and enforcing e-mail and internet abuse policies. Also trains on avoiding liabilities for design and delivery of training programs, health and safety regulatory compliance issues and legal aspects of violence prevention and workplace security. Personnel policy development, internal discrimination and misconduct investigations. **Founded:** 1987. **Publications:** "Heading off harassment. Effective training is critical to limiting legal exposure for workplace harassment".

26710 ■ Pacific Resource Development Group Inc.

1651 NE 185th St.
Seattle, WA 98155-3938
Ph: (206)367-1418
Free: 800-767-3062
Fax: (206)367-1418
Co. E-mail: pacres@shadesofgray.com
Contact: Susan L. Webb, President
E-mail: susan@shadesofgray.com
Scope: A consulting firm specializing in sexual harassment. Firm provides consulting and training services for managers, supervisors, general employees and individuals. Services include training, investigations, expert witness, training products and materials such as videos and books. **Founded:** 1981. **Publications:** "Training and Investigator Manuals," 2002; "Step Forward: Sexual Harassment in the Workplace," 1998; "Shockwaves: The Global Impact of Sexual Harassment," Master Media Ltd., Mar, 1994; "Step Forward," Mastermedia, 1991; "25 Things to Do If Sexual Harassment Happens to You"; "Six Simple Steps to Stop Sexual Harassment"; "How to

Handle Sexual Harassment Complaints". **Seminars:** Sexual Harassment; Employee Training; Train-the-Trainer; Investigator Training; One-to-One Training. **Special Services:** Shades of Gray™.

26711 ■ John Smithkey, III, RN

1271 Overland Ave. NE
North Canton, OH 44720-1731
Ph: (330)494-3729
Co. E-mail: schoolnurse007@aol.com
Scope: Specializes in public and occupational health, HIV/AIDS education and prevention programs, grant and proposal writing, and programs for businesses and employees. **Publications:** "The Strange World of Head Lice Information," Jun, 2003. **Seminars:** CPR; Communicable Diseases; Bloodborne Pathogen Training; Delegation of Nursing Tasks and Medication Administration Certification; Anaphylactic Shock and EpiPen Training.

26712 ■ Stier Associates

4 Dunellen
Cromwell, CT 06416-2702
Ph: (860)635-1590
Fax: (860)635-1591
Co. E-mail: sstier7@comcast.net
Contact: Dr. Suzanne Stier, President
Scope: Offers personal development consulting. Services include: succession planning, executive coaching, strategic management, team building, and board development. Consulting services for public companies include: process consulting, team building, executive coaching, diversity management, strategic management and religious institutions. **Founded:** 1981.

26713 ■ The Training Station

5017 Dawnwood Ct.
Arlington, TX 76003
Ph: (817)478-9816
Free: 800-594-8181
Fax: (817)478-9816
Contact: Reginald Ferrell, Vice President
E-mail: reg_ferrell@yahoo.com
Scope: Training, human resource development, and marketing services consultants. Conducts needs analysis, program development, design, writing, execution, follow-up and assessment. Provides speaking engagements and seminars for all personnel. Specialize in sales and marketing, sexual harassment, recruiting, interviewing, selection and management skills. Management assessment tools and programs available. Standard or generic programs are available for immediate tailoring or modification, as well as custom developed materials and programs. Train-the-trainer methodology is also an option. Consulting on human resource issues are available upon request. Industries served: Chemical, food service, manufacturing, banking, medical, pharmaceutical, optical, and hard goods; also serve the electrical utility, retail, and power goods markets. **Founded:** 1981. **Seminars:** R.I.S.K.; S.H.A.M.E. (Sexual Harassment Awareness Managed Effectively); M.U.S.T. (Management Understanding of Sales and Training); Power Sales Management; Stress Management Training; Show Selling Seminar.

26714 ■ Vaccari & Associates Inc.

17 Cypress St. 1
Marblehead, MA 01945-1925
Ph: (781)639-0946
Fax: (781)639-0946
Co. E-mail: rvaccari1@verizon.net
Contact: Ralph J. Vaccari, President
E-mail: rvaccari@rcn.com
Scope: A provider of appraisals for primary and secondary mortgages, mortgage refinancing, em-

ployee relocation, private mortgage insurance removal, estate planning and divorce settlement. **Founded:** 1996.

COMPUTERIZED DATABASES

26715 ■ *Employment Discrimination Report™*

1801 S Bell St.
Arlington, VA 22202
Free: 800-372-1033
Co. E-mail: customercare@bna.com
URL: http://www.bna.com
Availability: Online: Bloomberg LP-Bloomberg BNA; Thomson Reuters - Westlaw. **Type:** Full-text.

LIBRARIES

26716 ■ Tennessee Human Rights Commission - Resource Library

710 James Robertson Pkwy., Ste. 100
Corner of Rosa Parks Blvd.
Nashville, TN 37243-1219
Ph: (615)741-5825
Free: 800-251-3589
Fax: (615)532-2197
URL: http://www.state.tn.us/humanrights/mang_staff.html
Contact: Beverly L. Watts, Executive Director
Scope: Race relations; discrimination in employment, housing, and public accommodations; legislation and decisions rendered in discrimination cases. **Services:** Library open to the public with restrictions. **Holdings:** 75 books; 500 bound periodical volumes; commission-related materials. **Subscriptions:** 10 journals and other serials.

26717 ■ U.S. Equal Employment Opportunity Commission Library—EEOC.

131 M St., NE
Washington, DC 20507
Ph: (202)663-4900
Free: 800-669-6820
URL: http://www.eeoc.gov/
Contact: Susan D. Taylor, Director, Information Services Director, Library Services
Scope: Employment discrimination, minorities, women, aged, persons with disabilities, labor law, civil rights. **Services:** Interlibrary loan; copying; Library open to the public by appointment. **Founded:** 1964. **Holdings:** 25,000 books. **Subscriptions:** 300 journals and other serials; 8 newspapers.

RESEARCH CENTERS

26718 ■ Center for Women Policy Studies (CWPS)

1776 Massachusetts Ave. NW, Ste. 450
Washington, DC 20036
Ph: (202)872-1770
Fax: (202)296-8962
Co. E-mail: cwps@centerwomenpolicy.org
URL: http://www.centerwomenpolicy.org
Contact: Dr. Leslie R. Wolfe, President
Founded: 1972. **Publications:** *E-News* (Monthly). **Educational Activities:** Foreign Policy Institute for State Legislators (Annual), educates U.S. women state legislators on the impact of U.S. foreign policy on women worldwide and the role of state-level officials in influencing foreign policy; GlobalPOWER (Biennial), builds sustainable partnerships, across borders and over time, of women members of parliament/ministers to confront global women's human rights crisis; State policy sessions with legislators, on trafficking of women and girls into the United States and the role of state law and policy. **Telecommunication Services:** lwolfe@centerwomenpolicy.org.

ASSOCIATIONS AND OTHER ORGANIZATIONS

26719 ■ Canadian Association of Chemical Distributors (CACD)—L'Association Canadienne des Distributeurs de Produits Chimiques
349 Davis Rd., Unit A
Oakville, ON, Canada L6J 5Z7
Ph: (905)844-9140
Fax: (905)844-5706
Co. E-mail: ccampbell@cacd.ca
URL: http://www.cacd.ca
Contact: Cathy Campbell, Executive Director
Description: Chemical distributors in Canada. Represents members to governments, allied associations, and the public. **Founded:** 1986. **Publications:** *The Chemunicator* (3/year).

26720 ■ The Chemunicator
349 Davis Rd., Unit A
Oakville, ON, Canada L6J 5Z7
Ph: (905)844-9140
Fax: (905)844-5706
Co. E-mail: ccampbell@cacd.ca
URL: http://www.cacd.ca
Contact: Cathy Campbell, Executive Director
Released: 3/year

26721 ■ Distribution Business Management Association (DBMA)
2938 Columbia Ave., Ste. 1102
Lancaster, PA 17603
Ph: (717)295-0033
Fax: (717)299-2154
Co. E-mail: dbminfo@dbm-assoc.com
URL: http://www.dcenter.com
Contact: Amy Z. Thorn, Executive Director
Description: Management personnel in the wholesale distribution industries. Promotes education and continuing professional development in the materials handling, distribution, and supply chain industries. Conducts educational programs. **Founded:** 1992. **Publications:** *Distribution Business Management Journal* (Semiannual). **Educational Activities:** Distribution Business Management Association Conference (Annual). **Awards:** Circle of Excellence Award (Annual); Distinguished Service Award (Annual).

26722 ■ Global Market Development Center (GMDC)
1275 Lake Plaza Dr.
Colorado Springs, CO 80906-3583
Ph: (719)576-4260
Fax: (719)576-2661
Co. E-mail: info@gmdc.org
URL: http://www.gmdc.org
Contact: David T. McConnell, Jr., President
Description: General merchandise (nonfood) units of wholesale grocers, cooperatives, and voluntaries (110); chain food stores, service merchandisers, drug chains, mass merchandisers, wholesale drug companies, and wholesale clubs; manufacturers or suppliers of general merchandise (540) and health and beauty care products. Works to improve management operations, marketing programs, sales techniques, merchandising, and distribution functions of members; furthers management education and employee training; and promotes understanding and cooperation among members, the public, and government. Conducts research and compiles statistics. **Founded:** 1970. **Educational Activities:** GM Marketing (Annual); HBW Marketing (Annual).

26723 ■ LTD Shippers Association (LTD)
1230 Pottstown Pike, Ste. 6
Glenmoore, PA 19343
Ph: (610)458-3636
Fax: (610)458-8039
Co. E-mail: tomltd@aol.com
URL: http://www.ltdmgmt.com
Contact: Tom Craig, President
Description: Works to leverage the buying power of the members for lower ocean freight prices. Has scope that includes ocean rates from Asia to United States, to Canada, Mexico, Puerto Rico and many other destinations; also rates to the U.S. and Canada from Brazil, the Mediterranean, India and other origins. Aims to design, develop, negotiate, implement and manage logistics or transportation programs for members. **Founded:** 1994.

26724 ■ National Association of Wholesaler-Distributors (NAW)
1325 G St. NW, Ste. 1000
Washington, DC 20005
Ph: (202)872-0885
Fax: (202)785-0586
Co. E-mail: naw@naw.org
URL: http://www.naw.org
Contact: Dirk Van Dongen, President
Description: Federation of national, state, and regional associations, and individual wholesaler-distributor firms. Represents industry's views to the federal government. Analyzes current and proposed legislation and government regulations affecting the industry. Maintains public relations and media programs and a research foundation. Conducts wholesale executive management courses. **Founded:** 1946. **Publications:** *NAW Report*; *NAW Report* (Bimonthly); *SmartBrief*. **Telecommunication Services:** naw@nawd.org.

26725 ■ National Convenience Store Distributors Association (NACDA)—Association nationale des distributeurs aux petites surfaces alimentaires
1695 Laval Blvd., Ste. 410
Laval, QC, Canada H7S 2M2
Ph: (450)967-3858
Free: 888-686-2823
Fax: (450)967-8839
Co. E-mail: nacda@nacda.ca
URL: http://www.nacda.ca
Contact: Raymond Bouchard, Chairman
Description: Assists members in providing dependable distribution of convenience products between suppliers and retailers. Represents member's interests with the government and other industry key players. Conducts educational seminars and programs relevant to member's business needs, thus contributing to the improvement of the convenience supply chain. **Founded:** 1955. **Publications:** *Distribution Management in the New Economy: A Blueprint for Success*; *Electronic-Commerce for Distribution Channels*; *Values Shift*.

26726 ■ NAW Institute for Distribution Excellence
1325 G St. NW, Ste. 1000
Washington, DC 20005
Ph: (202)872-0885
Fax: (202)785-0586
Co. E-mail: naw@naw.org
URL: http://www.naw.org/institute/iindex.php
Contact: Ruth Stadius, President
Description: Firms that are members of the National Association of Wholesaler-Distributors, wholesalers, and trade associations. Seeks to advance knowledge in the field of wholesale distribution by means of long-range research projects. **Founded:** 1967. **Publications:** *Facing the Forces of Change: The Road to Opportunity* (Triennial); *Connect with Your Suppliers: A Wholesaler-Distributor's Guide to Electronic Communications Systems*; *Price for Success: A Practical Guide for Improving Margins in Wholesale Distribution*.

REFERENCE WORKS

26727 ■ "Adapt or Die" in Black Enterprise (Vol. 38, July 2008, No. 12, pp. 27)
Pub: Earl G. Graves Publishing Co. Inc.
Ed: Oguntoyinbo Lekan. **Description:** Turbulence in the domestic auto industry is hitting auto suppliers hard and black suppliers, the majority of whom contract with the Big Three, are just beginning to establish relationships with import car manufacturers. The more savvy CEOs are adopting new technologies in order to weather the downturn in the economy and in the industry as a whole.

26728 ■ "Alliance Unit Signs Movie Distribution Deal' in Globe & Mail (January 24, 2006, pp. B6)
Pub: CTVglobemedia Publishing Inc.
Ed: Grant Robertson. **Description:** The details on the distribution agreement between Movie Distribution Income Fund and Weinstein Co. are presented. Movie Distribution Income Fund is a unit of Alliance Atlantis Communication Inc.

26729 ■ "Amcon Distributing Co." in Arkansas Business (Vol. 26, November 9, 2009, No. 45, pp. 13)
Pub: Journal Publishing Inc.
Description: Amcon Distributing Co., a consumer products company, has bought the convenience store distribution assets of Discount Distributors from its parent, Harps Food Stores Inc., significantly increasing its wholesale distribution presence in the northwest Arkansas market. The acquisition will be funded through Amcon's existing credit facilities.

26730 ■ American Wholesalers and Distributors Directory
Pub: Cengage Learning Inc.
Contact: Ronald Dunn, President
URL(s): www.gale.cengage.com. **Released:** Annual; Latest edition 22nd; April, 2011. **Price:** $410, Individuals. **Covers:** Name and address, fax number, SIC code, principal product lines, total number of employees, estimated annual sales volume and principal officers' information of 27,000 large and small wholesalers and distributors in the U.S. and Puerto Rico. **Arrangement:** By broad subject from principal product line, by Standard Industrial Classification code (SIC index), by state and city (geographical index), and by company name (alphabetic index). **Indexes:** SIC, geographical, alphabetical. **Availability:** Online: Cengage Learning Inc. **Type:** Directory.

26731 ■ "ART Announces New Distribution Arrangement with GE Healthcare for eXplore Optix" in Canadian Corporate News (May 14, 2007)
Pub: Comtex News Network Inc.
Description: ART Advanced Research Technologies Inc., a medical device company and a leader in optical molecular imaging products for the pharmaceutical and healthcare industries, announced that it signed an agreement with GE Healthcare regarding worldwide distribution of its eXplore Optix preclinical optical molecular imaging system.

26732 ■ Associated Equipment Distributors--Membership Directory
Pub: Associated Equipment Distributors Inc.
Contact: Toby Mack, President
URL(s): www.aednet.org/products/productitem.cfm-?recordID=665. **Released:** Annual; Latest edition 2011-2012. **Price:** $75, Members single copy; $150, Nonmembers single copy; $250, Members 5 copies; $500, Nonmembers 5 copies. **Covers:** Fifteen hundred U.S. and Canadian distributors. Available as a special issue of Construction Equipment Distribution magazine. **Entries include:** Information on each company's branches, manufacturer members, banks, finance companies, specialized service firms and trade press, and AED contact person.

26733 ■ "Auto Supplier Stock Battered In Wake Of Wall Street Woes" in Crain's Detroit Business (Vol. 24, September 29, 2008, No. 39, pp. 4)
Pub: Crain Communications Inc.
Ed: Ryan Beene. **Description:** Due to the volatility of the stock market and public perception of the $700 billion banking bailout, auto suppliers are now facing a dramatic drop in their shares. Statistical data included.

26734 ■ "AV Concept Expands Into Green Energy Storage" in Wireless News (January 25, 2010)
Pub: Close-Up Media
Description: Electronics distributor and manufacturer AV Concept Holdings Limited announced a marketing partnership with Boston-Power, a provider of lithium-ion batteries, with a focus in the Chinese and Korean markets.

26735 ■ "avVaa World Health Care Products Rolls Out Internet Marketing Program" in Health and Beauty Close-Up (September 18, 2009)
Pub: Close-Up Media
Description: avVaa World Health Care Products, Inc., a biotechnology company, manufacturer and distributor of nationally branded therapeutic, natural health care and skin products, has signed an agreement with Online Performance Marketing to launch of an Internet marketing campaign in order to broaden its presence online. The impact of advertising on the Internet to generate an increase in sales is explored.

26736 ■ "Beer Sales 'Foament' a Dispute" in Philadelphia Business Journal (Vol. 28, October 9, 2009, No. 34, pp. 1)
Pub: American City Business Journals
Ed: Peter van Allen. **Description:** Malt Beverages Distributors Association of Pennsylvania filed a case against the Liquor Control Board (LCB) at the

Pennsylvania Supreme Court in order to further restrict store sales. The dispute stems from the supermarket chains circumventing the liquor law with the blessings of LCB.

26737 ■ "Black Diamond Holdings Corp. Receives SEC Approval" in Canadian Corporate News (May 16, 2007)
Pub: Comtex News Network Inc.
Description: Black Diamond Holdings, Corp., a British Columbia domiciled company and its two wholly owned subsidiaries are engaged in the bottling, importation, distribution, marketing, and brand creation of premium spirits and wines to worldwide consumers, announced that it has completed the SEC review process and has applied to list for trading in the United States on the OTC.BB.

26738 ■ "Blue Bell Breaks Ground in South Carolina" in Ice Cream Reporter (Vol. 23, August 20, 2010, No. 9, pp. 3)
Pub: Ice Cream Reporter
Description: Texas-based Blue Bell Creameries will open a new 2,000 square foot transfer facility in North Charleston, South Carolina. The facility will expand Blue Bell's distribution efforts in the state.

26739 ■ "Brewed to Succeed; Mokarbia Perks Up Sales for King Coffee" in Crain's Detroit Business (Vol. 24, March 17, 2008, No. 11, pp. 3)
Pub: Crain Communications, Inc.
Ed: Brent Snavely. **Description:** Profile of King Coffee Tea Services, Royal Oak-based company, whose distributing deal with Mokarabia coffee has generated an increase in sales.

26740 ■ "Brewing a Love-Haiti Relationship" in The Business Journal - Serving Phoenix and the Valley of the Sun (Vol. 28, July 4, 2008, No. 44)
Pub: American City Business Journals, Inc.
Ed: Yvonne Zusel. **Description:** Jean and Alicia Marseille have ventured into a coffee distribution company called Ka Bel LLC which markets Marabou brand of coffee imported from Haiti. Part of the proceeds of the business is donated to entrepreneurs from Jean's country, Haiti. Details of the Marseille's startup business and personal mission to help are discussed.

26741 ■ "Cannabis Science Signs Exclusive and Non-Exclusive Agreement with Prescription Vending Machines" in Benzinga.com (October 29, 2011)
Pub: Benzinga.com
Ed: Benzinga Staff. **Description:** Cannabis Science Inc., a biotech company developing pharmaceutical cannabis products has partnered with Prescription Vending Machines Inc. and its principal Vincent Meddizadeh to provide industry specific consulting and advisory services to Cannabis Science.

26742 ■ "CBC Eyes Partners for TV Downloads" in Globe & Mail (February 9, 2006, pp. B1)
Pub: CTVglobemedia Publishing Inc.
Ed: Grant Robertson. **Description:** The details on Canadian Broadcasting Corp.'s distribution agreement with Google Inc. and Apple Computer Inc. are presented.

26743 ■ "Cheese Spread Whips Up a Brand New Bowl" in Brandweek (Vol. 49, April 21, 2008, No. 16, pp. 17)
Pub: VNU Business Media, Inc.
Ed: Mike Beirne. **Description:** Mrs. Kinser's Pimento Cheese Spread is launching a new container for its product in order to attempt stronger brand marketing with a better bowl in order to win over the heads of households as young as in their 30s. The company also intends to begin distribution in Texas and the West Coast. Mrs. Kinser's is hoping that the new packaging will provide a more distinct branding and will help consumers distinguish what flavor they are buying.

26744 ■ "Children's Products Maker Not the New Kid on the Block" in Crain's Cleveland Business (Vol. 28, November 26, 2007, No. 47, pp. 3)
Pub: Crain Communications, Inc.
Ed: David Bennett. **Description:** Discusses the business model employed by Shamrock Industries Inc., a rising star in the competitive world of children's products; the company, which does business as Foundations Quality Children's Products, has expanded into a 63,000-square-foot distribution center which has boosted its local profile significantly.

26745 ■ "Chinese Fund Loans $33.5 Million to Prestolite" in Crain's Detroit Business (Vol. 26, January 18, 2010, No. 3, pp. 1)
Pub: Crain Communications Inc.
Ed: Ryan Beene. **Description:** Prestolite Electric Inc., a distributor of alternators and starter motors for commercial and heavy-duty vehicles, looked to China for fresh capital in order to fund new product launches.

26746 ■ "Datran Media Executives to Lead Industry Debates Across Q1 Conferences" in Internet Wire (January 22, 2010)
Pub: Comtex News Network, Inc.
Description: Datran Media, an industry-leading digital marketing technology company, will be sending members of its management team to several conferences in the early part of the first quarter of 2010; discussions will include Internet marketing innovations, e-commerce and media distribution.

26747 ■ "Deal Braces Cramer for Growth Run" in The Business Journal-Serving Metropolitan Kansas City (Vol. 26, July 4, 2008, No. 43, pp. 1)
Pub: American City Business Journals, Inc.
Ed: James Dornbook. **Description:** Gardner, Kansas-based Cramer Products Inc. bought 100 percent of the stocks of Louisville, Kentucky-based Active Ankle Inc. from 26 private investors increasing its revenue by 20 percent. The latter is the second largest vendor of Cramer. Other details of the merger are presented.

26748 ■ "The Doomsday Scenario" in Conde Nast Portfolio (Vol. 2, June 2008, No. 6, pp. 91)
Pub: Conde Nast Publications
Contact: David Carey, President
Ed: Jeffrey Rothfeder. **Description:** Detroit and the U.S. auto industry are discussed as well as the ramifications of the demise of this manufacturing base. Similarities and differences between the downfall of the U.S. steel business and the impact it had on Pittsburg, Pennsylvania is also discussed.

26749 ■ "Egg Fight: The Yolk's on the Short" in Barron's (Vol. 88, July 7, 2008, No. 27, pp. 20)
Pub: Dow Jones & Co., Inc.
Ed: Christopher C. Williams. **Description:** Shares of Cal-Maine Foods, the largest egg producer and distributor in the US, are due for a huge rise because of the increase in egg prices. Short sellers, however, continue betting that the stock, priced at $31.84 each, will eventually go down.

26750 ■ "Energy Outfitter Wings Into Houston" in Houston Business Journal (Vol. 40, December 4, 2009, No. 30, pp. 2A)
Pub: American City Business Journals
Ed: Ford Gunter. **Description:** Red Wing Shoe Company Inc. has launched its personal protective equipment (PPE) line for oil and gas industry crewmen in North America by opening a 13,000 square foot distribution hub in Houston, Texas. The Houston facility was created to supply directly the oil and gas industry and to carry inventory for select distributors.

26751 ■ "Familiar Face Aims to Rebuild Distributor's Once-Strong Local Ties" in Crain's Cleveland Business (December 3, 2007)
Pub: Crain Communications, Inc.
Ed: David Bennett. **Description:** Phillips Contractors Supply, a tool distributor, has a new president and

co-owner, James Beckett. Beckett was once vice president of operations so he knows the company well and has plans to re-establish the firm's presence in the region.

26752 ■ "Finalist: BlackEagle Partners L.L.C." in Crain's Detroit Business (Vol. 24, March 24, 2008, No. 12, pp. 12)
Pub: Crain Communications, Inc.
Ed: Brent Snavely. **Description:** Overview of private-equity firm, BlackEagle Partners L.L.C., an upstart that acquired Rockford Products Corp. in order to improve the performance of the company who does business with several major tier-one automotive suppliers; Rockford manufactures highly engineered chassis and suspension components for automakers and the automotive aftermarket.

26753 ■ "Fogg Planning Twinsburg Warehouse Project" in Crain's Cleveland Business (Vol. 28, November 26, 2007, No. 47, pp. 6)
Pub: Crain Communications, Inc.
Ed: Stan Bullard. **Description:** Discusses such projects as the proposed 205,000-square-foot distribution center in the works by Ray Fogg Corporate Properties LLC as well as other industrial real estate developments that are looking to target tenants that need larger spaces.

26754 ■ "Fraser and Neave Acquires King's Creameries" in Ice Cream Reporter (Vol. 23, November 20, 2010, No. 12, pp. 1)
Pub: Ice Cream Reporter
Description: Fraser and Neave Ltd., a Singapore-based consumer products marketer, has entered a conditional agreement to acquire all outstanding shares of King's Creameries, the leading manufacturer and distributor of frozen desserts.

26755 ■ From Concept To Consumer: How to Turn Ideas Into Money
Pub: Pearson Education Inc.
Ed: Phil Baker. **Released:** 2009. **Price:** $24.99. **Description:** Renowned product developer Phil Baker explains how a great idea accounts for only 5 percent of all the factors of success and why the majority of success is dependent upon a myriad of other factors, including the time it takes to get to market, price, marketing and distribution. By being their own best competition, a small company can stay one step ahead of competitors.

26756 ■ "Furniture Chain Moving to Harford" in Baltimore Business Journal (Vol. 27, January 22, 2010, No. 38, pp. 1)
Pub: American City Business Journals
Ed: David J. Sernovitz. **Description:** Manchester, Connecticut-based Bob's Discount Furniture signed a lease for 672,000 square feet of space in Harford County, Maryland. The site will become the discount furniture retailer's distribution center in mid-Atlantic US. As many as 200 jobs could be generated when the center opens.

26757 ■ "Gallery Street Launches ArtCandy" in Art Business News (Vol. 34, November 2007, No. 11, pp. 8)
Pub: Pfingsten Publishing, LLC
Description: Fine-art reproduction house Gallery Street recently launched its new division, ArtCandy Editions; the division was created in order to help a network of artists expand the distribution of their work.

26758 ■ "Handleman Liquidation Leaves Questions For Shareholders" in Crain's Detroit Business (Vol. 24, October 6, 2008, No. 40, pp. 4)
Pub: Crain Communications, Inc.
Ed: Nancy Kaffer. **Description:** Discusses Handleman Co., a Troy-based music distribution company, and their plan of liquidation and dissolution as well as how shareholders will be affected by the company's plan. Handleman filed its plan to liquidate and dissolve assets with the Securities and Exchange Commission in mid-August, following several quarters of dismal earnings.

26759 ■ How to Start and Run a Small Book Publishing Company: A Small Business Guide to Self-Publishing and Independent Publishing
Pub: HCM Publishing
Ed: Peter I. Hupalo. **Released:** August 30, 2002. **Price:** $18.95. **Description:** The book teaches all aspects of starting and running a small book publishing company. Topics covered include: inventory accounting in the book trade, just-in-time inventory management, turnkey fulfillment solutions, tax deductible costs, basics of sales and use tax, book pricing, standards in terms of the book industry, working with distributors and wholesalers, cover design and book layout, book promotion and marketing, how to select profitable authors to publish, printing process, printing on demand, the power of a strong backlist, and how to value copyright.

26760 ■ "Industry Escalates Lobbying Efforts For Loan Program" in Crain's Detroit Business (Vol. 24, September 22, 2008, No. 38, pp. 22)
Pub: Crain Communications Inc.
Ed: Jay Greene; Ryan Beene; Harry Stoffer. **Description:** Auto suppliers such as Lear Corp., which is best known for vehicle seating, also supplies high-voltage wiring for Ford hybrids and is developing other hybrid components. These suppliers are joining automakers in lobbying for the loan program which would promote the accelerated development of fuel-efficient vehicles.

26761 ■ "Ingrian and Channel Management International Sign Distribution Agreement" in Canadian Corporate News (May 16, 2007)
Pub: Comtex News Network Inc.
Description: Channel Management International (CMI), a Canadian channel management and distribution company, and Ingrian Networks, Inc., the leading provider of data privacy solutions, announced a Canadian distribution agreement to resell Ingrian encryption solutions to the Canadian market.

26762 ■ "Jacksonville-based Interline Expanding in Janitorial-Sanitation Market" in Florida Times-Union (May 10, 2011)
Pub: Florida Times-Union
Ed: Mark Basch. **Description:** Interline Brands Inc., located in Jacksonville, Florida, aims to grow its business with two recent acquisitions of firms that distribute janitorial and sanitation products. Interline markets and distributes maintenance, repair and operations products.

26763 ■ "Kellog Pores Over KC Sites" in Business Journal-Serving Metropolitan Kansas City (Vol. 26, November 23, 2007, No. 11, pp. 1)
Pub: American City Business Journals, Inc.
Ed: Jim Davis. **Description:** Kellog Company is searching Kansas City for a parcel about 1.3 million square feet to build its product distribution center. According to brokers, a selection might come by end of November 2007. Some of the potential sites are detailed.

26764 ■ "Last Founder Standing" in Conde Nast Portfolio (Vol. 2, June 2008, No. 6, pp. 124)
Pub: Conde Nast Publications
Contact: David Carey, President
Ed: Kevin Maney. **Description:** Interview with Amazon CEO Jeff Bezos in which he discusses the economy, the company's new distribution center and the hiring of employees for it, e-books, and the overall vision for the future of the firm.

26765 ■ "Lightening the Load" in Crain's Cleveland Business (Vol. 28, October 8, 2007, No. 40, pp. 3)
Pub: Crain Communications, Inc.
Ed: Jay Miller. **Description:** Companies reliant on barge deliveries are running well below capacity due to both the building up of silt at the bottom of the Cuyahoga River as well as the lower water levels which are causing a number of problems for the barges and big boats that deliver goods to the region.

26766 ■ "Linens 'N Things, Dyson in Dust-Up" in Crain's Chicago Business (Vol. 31, March 24, 2008, No. 12, pp. 12)
Pub: Crain Communications, Inc.
Description: Linens 'N Things is being sued by vacuum-cleaner manufacturer Dyson who is alleging that it hasn't been paid some of the $1.3 million it says it is owed for merchandise.

26767 ■ "Lynn Johnson, President: Dowland-Bach" in Alaska Business Monthly (Vol. 27, October 2011, No. 10, pp. 11)
Pub: Alaska Business Publishing Company
Ed: Peg Stomierowski. **Description:** Profile of Lynn C. Johnson cofounder of Dowland-Bach Corporation, a manufacturing and distribution company is presented. The firms primary products are wellhead control and chemical injection systems for corrosion control, UL industrial control panels, and specialty stainless steel sheet metal fabrication.

26768 ■ "The Macomb Group: Bigger Can Be Better" in Crain's Detroit Business (Vol. 24, September 29, 2008, No. 39, pp. 34)
Pub: Crain Communications Inc.
Ed: Chad Halcom. **Description:** Overview of the plan of The Macomb Group includes a strategy of growing from a small supplier to a medium-sized regional distributor of valves, pipes and fittings.

26769 ■ Marketing for Entrepreneurs
Pub: FT Press
Ed: Jurgen Wolff. **Released:** December 9, 2010. **Price:** $24.99. **Description:** This text identifies marketing as the entire process of researching, creating, distributing and selling a product or service. It isn't about theory and metrics, rather it is a practical guide that starts with the basics of all marketing aspects.

26770 ■ "Mexican Companies to Rent Space in TechTown, Chinese Negotiating" in Crain's Detroit Business (Vol. 24, September 29, 2008, No. 39)
Pub: Crain Communications Inc.
Ed: Tom Henderson. **Description:** Wayne State University's TechTown, the business incubator and research park, has signed an agreement with the Mexican government that will provide temporary office space to 25 Mexican companies looking to find customers or establish partnerships in Michigan. TechTown's executive director is negotiating with economic development officials from China. To accommodate foreign visitors the incubator is equipping offices with additional equipment and resources.

26771 ■ "Mini Melts" in Ice Cream Reporter (Vol. 23, August 20, 2010, No. 9, pp. 8)
Pub: Ice Cream Reporter
Description: Mini Melts appointed David S. Tade to position of director of sales USA in order to cultivate existing distributors and add new partners to its distribution network.

26772 ■ "Minority Auto Suppliers Get Help Diversifying" in Crain's Detroit Business (Vol. 26, January 11, 2010, No. 2, pp. 3)
Pub: Crain Communications, Inc.
Ed: Sherri Welch. **Description:** Displaced minority auto suppliers are being given assistance by the Kauffman's Foundation Urban Entrepreneur Partnership Detroit program, a three-year effort to assist 150 of the region's suppliers into more diversified businesses.

26773 ■ "A Novel Approach to the Market" in Agency Sales Magazine (Vol. 39, December 2009, No. 11, pp. 10)
Pub: MANA
Ed: Jack Foster. **Description:** R/B Sales created a 'merchandising specialist' position that travels their territory and works with distributor counter sales teams. This puts them ahead of their competition as it increases their visibility, appeal and mix of products in their area.

26774 ■ *"Oakland County Hopes Auto Suppliers Can Drive Medical Industry Growth"* in Crain's Detroit Business (March 10, 2008)
Pub: Crain Communications, Inc.

Ed: Chad Halcom. **Description:** Oakland County officials are hoping to create further economic development for the region by pairing health care companies and medical device makers with automotive suppliers in an attempt to discover additional crossover technology.

26775 ■ *"Old Ford Plant to Sign New Tenants"* in Business Courier (Vol. 27, August 13, 2010, No. 15, pp. 1)
Pub: Business Courier

Ed: Dan Monk. **Description:** Ohio Realty Advisors LLC, a company handling the marketing of the 1.9 million-square-foot former Ford Batavia plant is on the brink of landing one distribution and three manufacturing firms as tenants. These tenants are slated to occupy about 20 percent of the facility and generate as many as 250 jobs in Ohio.

26776 ■ *"On the Itinerary: Your Future"* in Entrepreneur (Vol. 37, October 2009, No. 10, pp. 92)
Pub: Entrepreneur Media, Inc.

Ed: Joel Holland. **Description:** Josh Hackler's Spanish Vines imports and distributes wines from Spain while using Spanish culture to help market the wines. The business was hatched after Hackler signed up for a study-abroad program in Spain.

26777 ■ *"Online Marketing and Promotion of Canadian Films via Social Media Tools"* in CNW Group (January 27, 2010)
Pub: Comtex News Network, Inc.

Description: Telefilm Canada announced the launch of a pilot initiative aimed at encouraging the integration of online marketing and the use of social media tools into means of distribution ahead of a films' theatrical release. During this pilot phase Web-Cine 360 will target French-language feature films.

26778 ■ *"O'Reilly Will Soup Up KC Warehouse"* in The Business Journal-Serving Metropolitan Kansas City (Vol. 26, August 15, 2008, No. 49)
Pub: American City Business Journals, Inc.

Ed: Rob Roberts. **Description:** O'Reilly Automotive Inc. plans to construct a 215,000-square foot warehouse in Kansas City. The move is expected to triple the size of the company's distribution center. Other views and information on the planned warehouse construction, are presented.

26779 ■ *"Poisoning Relationships: Perceived Unfairness in Channels of Distribution"* in Journal of Marketing (Vol. 75, May 2011, No. 3, pp. 99)
Pub: American Marketing Association

Ed: Stephen A. Samaha, Robert W. Palmatier, Rajiv P. Dant. **Description:** The effects of perceived unfairness on the relationships among members of distribution channels are examined. Perceived unfairness is found to directly damage relationships, aggravate the negative effects of conflict and opportunism, and undermine the benefits of the contract.

26780 ■ *"Pop N Go Launching Into Dollar Store Market"* in Internet Wire (July 14, 2009)
Pub: Comtex News Network, Inc.

Description: Pop N Go, Inc. announced that it will test the company's flagship popcorn vending machine in the rapidly growing dollar store distribution channel.

26781 ■ *"Public Media Works to Launch DVD Kiosk Operations in Toronto, Canada"* in Internet Wire (November 15, 2010)
Pub: Comtex

Description: Public Media Works Inc. along with its EntertainmentXpress Inc., have partnered with Spot Venture Distribution Inc. and Signifi Solutions Inc., both headquartered in Toronto, Canada, to manage and expand the Spot DVD movie and game kiosk business in greater Toronto and other Canadian locations.

26782 ■ *"S3 Entertainment Group Partners with WFW International for Film Services in Michigan"* in Michigan Vue (July-August 2008)
Pub: Entrepreneur Media Inc.

Description: William F. White (WFW), one of North America's largest production equipment providers has partnered with S3 Entertainment Group (S3EG), a Michigan-based full-service film production services company due to the new incentives package which currently offers the highest incentives in the United States, up to 42 percent. S3EG will actively store, lease, manage, distribute and sell WFW's equipment to the growing number of production teams that are filming in the state.

26783 ■ *"Shipping 2.0"* in Entrepreneur (Vol. 36, April 2008, No. 4, pp. 54)
Pub: Entrepreneur Media, Inc.

Ed: Heather Clancy. **Description:** Doggypads.com contacted with Web 2.0 service provider Shipwire to handle its warehouse concerns. The service works by paying a rent to Shipwire and they will store the client's items. The client's customers can continue to order from the client's website and Shipwire will take care of delivery. Doggypads was able to save up on costs by using Shipwire.

26784 ■ *"Slimmed-Down Supplier TI Automotive Relaunches"* in Crain's Detroit Business (Vol. 26, January 11, 2010, No. 2, pp. 14)
Pub: Crain Communications Inc.

Ed: Robert Sherefkin. **Description:** TI Automotive Ltd., one of the world's largest suppliers of fuel storage and delivery systems, has reorganized the company by splitting it into five global divisions and is relaunching its brand which is now more focused on new technology.

26785 ■ *"Sources"* in Canadian Electronics (Vol. 23, August 2008, No. 5, pp. 12)
Pub: Action Communication Inc.

Description: Directory of electronic manufacturers, distributors and representatives in Canada is provided. The list presents distributors and representatives under each manufacturer.

26786 ■ *"Speak Better: Five Tips for Polished Presentations"* in Women Entrepreneur (September 19, 2008)
Pub: Entrepreneur Media Inc.

Ed: Suzannah Baum. **Description:** Successful entrepreneurs agree that exemplary public speaking skills are among the core techniques needed to propel their business forward. A well-delivered presentation can result in securing a new distribution channel, gaining new customers, locking into a new referral stream or receiving extra funding.

26787 ■ *"Substantial Deal Expected to Create Jobs, Help Industrial Market"* in Tampa Bay Business Journal (Vol. 30, January 8, 2010, No. 3)
Pub: American City Business Journals

Ed: Janet Leiser. **Description:** Food distribution firm Gordon Food Service (GFS) is on the brink of purchasing Albertson's million-square-foot warehouse along with 158 acres of space. The deal between GFS and Albertson's could expand GFS' presence in west Central Florida. A history of GFS' growth is included.

26788 ■ *"Super Success"* in Small Business Opportunities (November 2008)
Pub: Entrepreneur Press
Contact: Perlman Neil, President

Description: Profile of PromoWorks LLC, a company founded by Michael Kent, that distributes samples of food at grocery stores for clients like Kraft Foods, Inc. and Kellogg Co. and also handles the logistics, provides the employees and tracks the products' sales.

26789 ■ *"Suppliers Look to Rack Up Big Sales to Distributors"* in The Business Journal-Serving Metropolitan Kansas City

(August 15, 2008)
Pub: American City Business Journals, Inc.

Ed: James Dornbrook. **Description:** Suppliers of shelving units, conveyor systems and other equipment used in distribution facilities are expecting new business opportunities along with the planned intermodal projects in the Kansas City area. Suppliers have already observed that small distributors have started to relocate to the city because of the intermodal projects. Demand for shelves and lifts have also increased.

26790 ■ *"Supply Chain Visibility A Two-Way Street"* in Canadian Sailings (July 7, 2008)
Pub: UBM Global Trade
Contact: Leonard J. Corallo, President

Ed: Jack Kohane. **Description:** Canada is experiencing unprecedented market pressures due to globalization. Competition from foreign countries, demand for better and faster service from customers and shorter innovation cycles are some of the problems the country is facing regarding trade and the importing and exporting industry.

26791 ■ *"Sustaining Supply"* in Crain's Cleveland Business (Vol. 28, November 19, 2007, No. 46, pp. 3)
Pub: Crain Communications, Inc.

Ed: David Bennett. **Description:** Local firms are playing key roles in preparing Wal-Mart suppliers to develop sustainable, or ecologically conscious, packaging. New products such as the innovative 'eco-bottle' - a collapsed container made of recyclable plastic that will expand to its traditional size and shape once water is added and would transform to such items as window cleaner when the water mixes with the container's dry contents - are being designed by firms such as Nottingham Spirk.

26792 ■ *"Tech Deal Couples Homegrown Firms"* in The Business Journal-Serving Greater Tampa Bay (Vol. 28, July 4, 2008, No. 28, pp. 1)
Pub: American City Business Journals, Inc.

Ed: Michael Hinman. **Description:** Tampa Bay, Florida-based Administrative Partners Inc. was acquired by Tribridge Inc. resulting in the strengthening of the delivery of Microsoft products to clients. Other details of the merger of the management consulting services companies are presented.

26793 ■ *"Technology Protects Lottery"* in Arkansas Business (Vol. 26, September 28, 2009, No. 39, pp. 1)
Pub: Journal Publishing Inc.

Ed: George Waldon. **Description:** Arkansas Lottery Commission was initially criticized for what was seen as a major breach in security protocol by revealing the exact location of 26 million lottery tickets during a publicity stunt in which the media was invited to the main distribution center; however, due to the high-tech security that has been implemented the tickets are worthless until their status is changed after passing through multiple security scans.

26794 ■ *"Top 50 Exporters"* in Hispanic Business (Vol. 30, July-August 2008, No. 7-8, pp. 42)
Pub: Hispanic Business, Inc.

Ed: Hildy Medina. **Description:** Increases in exports revenues reported by food exporters and green companies in a time of economic slowdown in the U.S are described. Food exporters have benefited from the growth of high-volume grocery stores in underdeveloped countries and the German governments' promotion of solar energy has benefited the U.S. solar heating equipment and solar panel manufactures.

26795 ■ *"The Trouble With $150,000 Wine"* in Barron's (Vol. 88, July 7, 2008, No. 27, pp. 33)
Pub: Dow Jones & Co., Inc.

Ed: Orley Ashenfelter. **Description:** Review of the book, 'The Billionaire's Vinegar: The Mystery of the World's Most Expensive Bottle of Wine,' which discusses vintners along with the marketing and distribution of wine as well as the winemaking industry as a whole.

26796 ■ *"Unilever Acquiring EVGA's Ice Cream Brands in Greece"* in *Ice Cream Reporter (Vol. 23, October 20, 2010, No. 11, pp. 1)*
Pub: Ice Cream Reporter
Description: Unilever will acquire the ice cream brands and distribution network of the Greek frozen dessert manufacturer EVGA.

26797 ■ *"US Cavalry Store"* in *Retail Merchandiser (Vol. 51, September-October 2011, No. 5, pp. 70)*
Pub: Phoenix Media Corporation
Description: US Cavalry Store serves enlisted military members. The store has launched a newly upgraded Website and has expanded its distribution center.

26798 ■ *Values Sell: Transforming Purpose into Profit through Creative Sales and Distribution Strategies*
Pub: Berrett-Koehler Publishers, Incorporated
Ed: Nadine A. Thompson; Angela E. Soper. **Released:** March 28, 2007. **Price:** $16.95. **Description:** Sales and distribution are the lifeblood of any business, socially responsible businesses are no different.

26799 ■ *"Vitabath: Sweet Smell of Success"* in *Retail Merchandiser (Vol. 51, September-October 2011, No. 5, pp. 82)*
Pub: Phoenix Media Corporation
Description: After taking over at Vitabath, Rich Brands developed new scents and products and while discovering new channels to distribute these items.

26800 ■ *"Web-Based Marketing Excites, Challenges Small Business Use"* in *Colorado Springs Business Journal (January 20, 2010)*
Pub: Dolan Media Co.
Ed: Becky Hurley. **Description:** Business-to-business and consumer-direct firms alike are using the fast-changing Web technologies to increase sales, leads and track consumer behavior but once a company commits to an Online marketing plan, experts believe, they must be prepared to consistently tweak and overhaul content and distribution vehicles in order to keep up.

26801 ■ *"The Wine Spectator"* in *Business Courier (Vol. 27, November 26, 2010, No. 30, pp. 1)*
Pub: Business Courier
Ed: Dan Monk. **Description:** Vintner Select, a wine distributor, will introduce an internationally known portfolio of more than 50 German and Austrian wines. The company now distributes about 900 different wine labels from 220 producers in 10 countries to smaller, independent retailers in Indiana, Kentucky and Ohio.

26802 ■ *"Wirtz Partners With California Liquor Wholesaler To Expand Reach"* in *Chicago Tribune (December 17, 2008)*
Pub: McClatchy-Tribune Information Services
Ed: Mike Hughlett. **Description:** Young's Market Co. and Wirtz Beverage Group have tentatively agreed to a joint venture that will give both companies a larger reach in the wine and liquor distribution business.

26803 ■ *"Worldwide Food Services (EREI) Tests Mini Dollar Store Program"* in *Internet Wire (August 6, 2009)*
Pub: Comtex News Network, Inc.
Description: Mini Dollar Stores and Eagle View LLC, wholly-owned subsidiaries of Worldwide Food Services, Inc., recently met with government officials and purchasing agents to lay out a test program which would distribute Mini Dollar Store items into VA hospital gift shops.

TRADE PERIODICALS

26804 ■ *Distribution Center Management*
Pub: Alexander Research & Communications Inc.
Contact: Margaret DeWitt, Publisher
Ed: Troy Reynolds, Editor. **Released:** Monthly. **Price:** $199, individuals. **Description:** The monthly newslet-ter for distribution centers and warehouse managers with ideas and information on how to run their facilities more productively.

26805 ■ *Drop Shipping Marketing Methods*
Pub: Consolidated Marketing Services, Inc.
Ed: Nicholas T. Scheel. Editor, nscheel@drop-shipping-news.com. **Released:** Monthly. **Price:** $18, U.S. $25/year. **Description:** Supplies data on firms that drop ship their products as a means of distribution. Contains information on sources of consumer and industrial products, formulation of marketing policy, and on the pricing, ordering, packaging, and handling of drop shipments. Includes articles on uses of direct mail and direct-response advertising.

26806 ■ *Profiles in PDM*
Pub: Hunt Personnel Ltd.
Ed: Alex Metz, Editor. **Released:** Bimonthly. **Price:** Free. **Description:** Published as a series of bulletins on basic principles of physical distribution management. Carries articles written to highlight trends, provoke ideas or provide general information.

TRADE SHOWS AND CONVENTIONS

26807 ■ **The FMI Show**
International Foodservice Distributors Association
1410 Spring Hill Rd., Ste. 210
McLean, VA 22102
Ph: (703)532-9400
Fax: (703)538-4673
URL: http://www.ifdaonline.org
Contact: Mark Allen, Chief Executive Officer
URL(s): www.fmi.org. **Price:** $745, Pre-registered, members; $795, Onsite registered, members; $1095, Pre-registered, non-members; $1195, Onsite registered, non-members. **Frequency:** Annual. **Audience:** Wholesale grocers, foodservice distributors, food industry executives, retail chains, and grocery manufacturers. **Principal Exhibits:** Material handling equipment, trucks, fork lifts, trailers, trucks, racks and pallets, computers and software, warehouse and fleet consultants and other services and equipment related to warehousing, distribution, human resources, information technology, logistics and transportation.

CONSULTANTS

26808 ■ **Myron I. Blumenfeld & Associates (MIBA)**
500 E 77th St., Ste. 2324
New York, NY 10162
Ph: (212)706-2112
Fax: (212)706-2118
Co. E-mail: mikeblumenfeld@myroniblumenfeld.com
URL: http://www.myroniblumenfeld.com
Contact: Myron I. Blumenfeld, President
E-mail: mike@myroniblumenfeld.com
Scope: Management specialists for consumer goods manufactures, wholesalers and retail in the areas of inventory management, strategic planning, logistics, merchandise planning, merchandise distribution and organization structure and development. **Founded:** 1981. **Seminars:** Starting Your Own Business. Business Planning. Inventory Management. New Innovations in Retail Distribution Technology. Bar Coding and Quick Response. Merchandise Planning for Quick Response. Global Marketing.

26809 ■ **Clear Light Books**
823 Don Diego Ave.
Santa Fe, NM 87505
Ph: (505)989-9590
Free: 800-253-2747
Fax: (505)989-9519
Co. E-mail: service@clearlightbooks.com
URL: http://www.clearlightbooks.com
Contact: Mary Kay, Editor
Description: Description: Publishes art, culture and folklore books on Native American and Southwest topics. **Scope:** Business management consulting specifically in the area of profit planning, as well as warehouse and distribution assistance. Additional expertise in computer system design. Industries served: small, medium-sized businesses and warehouse and distribution. **Founded:** 1980. **Special Services:** Warestudy™; Profit Planning™.

26810 ■ **Compliance Systems Inc.**
Hamilton House, 26 E Bryan St.
Savannah, GA 31401
Ph: (912)233-8181
Fax: (912)231-2938
Co. E-mail: csi@compliancesystemsinc.com
URL: http://www.compliancesystemsinc.com
Contact: William D. Shrader, Manager
Scope: Marine consultants specializing in all areas of shipping and marine safety, including Port State Control Compliance, ISM Code Internal Auditing, and OPA 90 Compliance and Maritime Security. **Founded:** 1988. **Seminars:** Safety Training.

26811 ■ **General Business Consultants Inc.**
1502 Elmwood Ave.
Wilmette, IL 60091-1653
Ph: (847)256-3260
Fax: (847)256-1410
Co. E-mail: dick@genbuscon.com
Contact: Richard Friedman, President
Scope: Specializes in helping wholesalers, distributors supply houses and manufacturers acquire and use information technology more profitably. Firm services help avoid the pitfalls and problems of complex, confusing things such as: long range business or systems planning; system selection, contract negotiation and installation management of complete systems and warehouse management systems; do it yourself warehouse management systems. Business improvement services involve advanced recommendations for improving: profits and customer service; inventory management and warehouse operations; gross margins; business or systems continuity; ecommerce. **Founded:** 1976. **Publications:** "The Butler Did It: Errors That Get Customers Angry"; "Do You Really Need a New System"; "New Warehouse Management Technologies Beat the Old Ones"; "How to Avoid a Warehouse Management System Horror Story"; "Don't Sign That System Contract-Until Its Changed to Include Protections"; "Why Some Systems are Decreasing Customer Service, Margins and Inventory Profitability"; "How to Modify a System to Maximize Inventory-Based Customer Service and Roi"; "What Lists of Software Don't Show Can Kill a Distributor"; "Great Software Does Not Manage Inventory Effectively"; "System Contracts: Add Specific Performance Guarantees to Avoid Problems"; "RF, RFID, WMS, VDP, PTL: A Review of warehouse Technologies". **Seminars:** Tech Trends That Can Hurt Distributors And Wholesalers; Do you really need a new system?; Warehouse Management Systems (WMS): New Technologies, And Tips For A Successful WMS; Avoiding Excess Inventory And Shortages While Keeping Customer Service High; Why Some Systems Are Decreasing Customer Service, Margins And Return On Inventory Investment-And What To Do About It; Don't Sign That System Contract-Until You Change It To Protect Yourself; Talking Chips Replace Printed Bar Codes; Wireless Digital Networks Result in Go-Anywhere Data Communications; Warehouse Management Systems Become Affordable and Practical; Supply Chain Management Dramatically Alters Business Relationships; The Plot to Take Away Distributors Computers; Software Support Moves Overseas-the Pros and Cons.

26812 ■ **Geomatrix Productions**
270 Amity Rd.
Woodbridge, CT 06525-2236
Ph: (203)389-0001
Co. E-mail: info@geomatrixproductions.com
URL: http://geomatrixproductions.com
Contact: Arthur C. Bulger, President
URL(s): www.geomatrixproductions.com. **Scope:** Specializes in facility planning, staffing, and startup activities. It serves the manufacturing and distribution, rubber, plastics, chemical, electrical, and printing industries. **Founded:** 1978.

26813 ■ **Irving Shaw and Associates**
417 C Andover Dr.
Monroe Township, NJ 08831-4304

Ph: (609)860-1122
Contact: Irving Shaw, President
E-mail: isa@nerc.com
Scope: Management consultants specializing in facilities design for factories and distribution centers. Consulting includes, but is not limited to, factory layout, distribution center planning, materials handling improvement, organization, planning, scheduling and controls. Active with a variety of manufacturers and distribution companies. **Founded:** 1961.

26814 ■ Wesley-Kind Associates Inc.
200 Old Country Road, Ste. 364
Mineola, NY 11501-4235
Ph: (516)747-3434
Fax: (516)248-2728
Contact: Daniel A. Kind, Executive Director
Scope: Material handling and distribution consultants offering advice on plant and warehouse layouts and operating systems for the movement, storage and control of materials and products. Expertise includes materials and production management, advanced handling/storage systems, packaging and unitizing systems, capacity, productivity and customer service audits, order filling systems, data processing control systems, transportation systems, site location analysis, facilities planning, and implementation. Industries served: manufacturing, distribution and retail corporations and state and U.S. Government agencies. **Founded:** 1974. **Publications:** "How to Reengineer the Storage Function," Penton Publishing, 1995.

RESEARCH CENTERS

26815 ■ National Association of Wholesaler-Distributors - NAW Institute for Distribution Excellence
1325 G St. NW, Ste. 1000
Washington, DC 20005
Ph: (202)872-0885
Fax: (202)785-0586
Co. E-mail: rschreibman@naw.org
URL: http://www.naw.org/institute/iindex.php
Contact: Ron Schreibman, Executive Director
Founded: 1967. **Telecommunication Services:** naw@naw.org.

26816 ■ Texas A&M University - Thomas and Joan Read Center for Distribution Research and Education
3367 TAMU
College Station, TX 77843-3367
Ph: (979)845-4984
Free: 866-260-2463
Fax: (979)845-4980
Co. E-mail: lawrence@entc.tamu.edu
URL: http://id.tamu.edu/professional-development
Contact: Dr. F. Barry Lawrence, Director

Founded: 1986. **Publications:** *Thomas and Joan Read Center for Distribution Research and Education E-newsletter* (3/year). **Educational Activities:** Certificate in Distribution Management program; Continuing education programs for distributors and manufacturers; Distributor Management Development Seminars. **Telecommunication Services:** read-center@entc.tamu.edu.

START-UP INFORMATION

26817 ■ *How to Start a Home-Based Mail Order Business*
Pub: Globe Pequot Press
Ed: Georganne Fiumara. **Released:** January 2005.
Price: $17.95. **Description:** Step-by-step guide for starting and growing a home-based mail order business. Information about equipment, pricing, online marketing, are included along with worksheets and checklists for planning.

26818 ■ *"Your Startup may be Worth Less than You Think" in Entrepreneur (Vol. 37, October 2009, No. 10, pp. 96)*
Pub: Entrepreneur Media, Inc.
Ed: Asheesh Advani. **Description:** Valuations of startups at the idea stage are dropping due to the effects of the recession. This drop is due to the decreasing availability of investment capital, the reduction in portfolio values of investors, and the increase in early stage startups.

ASSOCIATIONS AND OTHER ORGANIZATIONS

26819 ■ Action for Enterprise (AFE)
4600 North Fairfax Dr., Ste. 304
Arlington, VA 22203
Ph: (703)243-9172
Fax: (703)243-9123
URL: http://www.actionforenterprise.org
Contact: Frank Lusby, Executive Director
Description: Seeks to design and implement small enterprise development programs, based on a comprehensive analysis of business sectors and the interrelationships of enterprises that function with them. Initiates efforts to develop sustainable business development service providers at the local level. **Founded:** 1991.

26820 ■ Asia Pacific Foundation of Canada (APFC)—Fondation Asie Pacifique du Canada
890 W Pender St., Ste. 220
Vancouver, BC, Canada V6C 1J9
Ph: (604)684-5986
Fax: (604)681-1370
Co. E-mail: info@asiapacific.ca
URL: http://www.asiapacific.ca
Contact: Mr. Yuen Pau Woo, President
Description: Seeks to remove barriers to international trade between Canada and Asia. Conducts applied research and policy analysis for issues related to Canada-Asia relations. Maintains network of study and research centers; works to improve access to information on Asian cultures and trade within Canada. **Founded:** 1984. **Telecommunication Services:** president@asiapacific.ca.

26821 ■ Brazil-Canada Chamber of Commerce (BCCC)
401 Bay St., Ste. 1608
Toronto, ON, Canada M5H 2Y4
Ph: (416)646-6770
Fax: (416)363-0406
Co. E-mail: info@brazcanchamber.org
URL: http://brazcanchamber.org
Contact: Raul Papaleo, President
Description: Canadian corporations doing business in Brazil. Promotes increased trade between Canada and Brazil. Provides assistance to companies wishing to trade with Brazil. Represents members before international trade organizations and government agencies and lobbies for removal of statutory barriers to commerce. **Founded:** 1973.

26822 ■ British Canadian Chamber of Trade and Commerce (BCCTC)—La Chambre de Commerce Canada - Grande Bretagne
Trust Tower
77 King St. W, Ste. 2401
Toronto, ON, Canada M5K 1G8
Ph: (416)816-9154
Fax: (647)594-9501
Co. E-mail: idalia@bcctc.ca
URL: http://bcctc.ca
Contact: Idalia Obregon, Executive Director
Description: Canadian corporations doing business in the United Kingdom. Promotes increased trade between Britain and Canada. Represents members' interests; lobbies for removal of statutory impediments to trade. **Publications:** *Connections* (Quarterly).

26823 ■ Canada-Czech Republic Chamber of Commerce (CCRCC)
115 George St., Ste. 709
Oakville, ON, Canada L6J 0A2
Ph: (905)845-9606
Co. E-mail: admin@ccrcc.net
URL: http://www.ccrcc.net
Contact: Miroslav Princ, President
E-mail: miroslav.princ@ccrcc.net
Description: Businesses in Canada and the Czech Republic. Promotes increased trade and investment between Canada and the Czech Republic. Promotes the Czech Republic as a gateway to Central and Eastern Europe, and Canada as a gateway to the North American Free Trade Agreement countries. Conducts educational programs. **Scope:** international trade. **Founded:** 1994. **Subscriptions:** archival material. **Publications:** *CNACC Links Page*; *Chamber Members List--Canada Czech Republic Chamber of Commerce*.

26824 ■ Canada-Finland Chamber of Commerce (CFCC)
c/o Finnish Credit Union
191 Eglinton Ave. E
Toronto, ON, Canada M4P 1K1
Ph: (416)486-1533
Fax: (416)486-1592
Co. E-mail: info@canadafinlandcc.com
URL: http://canadafinlandcc.com
Contact: Peter Auvinen, President
Description: Canadian and Finnish businesses. Promotes increased trade between Canada and Finland. Provides information, assistance, and services to Finnish and Canadian corporations wishing to participate in international trade. **Founded:** 1971.

26825 ■ Canada-India Business Council (C-IBC)—Conseil de Commerce Canada-Inde
1 St. Clair Ave. E, Ste. 302
Toronto, ON, Canada M4T 2V7
Ph: (416)214-5947
Fax: (416)214-9081
Co. E-mail: info@canada-indiabusiness.ca
URL: http://canada-indiabusiness.ca
Contact: Mr. Rana Sarkar, President
Description: Canadian businesses trading with India. Promotes increased trade between Canada and India. Advocates for legislation conducive to trade; represents members before trade and industrial organizations and the public. **Founded:** 1982.

26826 ■ *Canada Pakistan Bulletin*
7825 Bayview Ave., Ste. 1311
Thornhill, ON, Canada L3T 7N2
Ph: (905)763-8281
Co. E-mail: info@cpbcoline.org
URL: http://www.cpbconline.org
Contact: Andy Merchant, President
Released: Quarterly **Price:** free for members and government organizations.

26827 ■ Canada-Pakistan Business Council (CPBC)
7825 Bayview Ave., Ste. 1311
Thornhill, ON, Canada L3T 7N2
Ph: (905)763-8281
Co. E-mail: info@cpbcoline.org
URL: http://www.cpbconline.org
Contact: Andy Merchant, President
Description: Businesses and service providers. Promotes increased trade between Canada and Pakistan. Facilitates mutual economic development through transfer of technology; encourages and assists in the formation of joint ventures involving Canadian and Pakistani companies. Conducts educational programs. **Founded:** 1983. **Publications:** *Canada Pakistan Bulletin* (Quarterly). **Educational Activities:** Service and Infrastructure Mission (Periodic); Telecommunication Mission (Periodic).

26828 ■ Canadian Association of Regulated Importers (CARI)—Association Canadienne des Importateurs Reglementes
2525 St. Laurent Blvd., Ste. 203
Ottawa, ON, Canada K1H 8P5
Ph: (613)738-1729
Fax: (613)733-9501
Co. E-mail: devalk@magma.ca
URL: http://www.cariimport.org
Contact: Lucky Bilkhu, Chairman
Description: Companies engaged in the importation of goods into Canada. Promotes removal of international and domestic barriers to trade. Represents members before government agencies and international trade organizations. **Founded:** 1986.

26829 ■ Canadian Chamber of Commerce—La Chambre de Commerce du Canada
360 Albert St., Ste. 420
Ottawa, ON, Canada K1R 7X7
Ph: (613)238-4000
Fax: (613)238-7643
Co. E-mail: info@chamber.ca
URL: http://www.chamber.ca
Contact: Robert Youden, Chairman
Description: As Canada's largest and most influential business association, the Canadian Chamber of Commerce is the primary and vital connection between business and the federal government. It continually demonstrates impact on public policy and decision-making to the benefit of businesses, communities and families across Canada. Experience the power of a network of over 420 chambers of commerce and boards of trade, representing 192,000 businesses of all sizes in all sectors of the economy and in all regions. **Scope:** internal trade, access to capital, job creation, electronic commerce. **Founded:** 1925. **Subscriptions:** 70 books.

26830 ■ Canadian Council for Aboriginal Business (CCAB)—Conseil Canadien pour le Commerce Autochtone
250 The Esplanade, Ste. 204
Toronto, ON, Canada M5A 1J2
Ph: (416)961-8663
Fax: (416)961-3995
Co. E-mail: info@ccab.com
URL: http://www.ccab.com
Contact: Clint Davis, President
Description: Promotes the full participation of aboriginal people in the Canadian economy. Seeks to connect aboriginal and non-aboriginal people and companies with the opportunities required to achieve personal and business success. Develops and operates the Progressive Aboriginal Relations (PAR) benchmarking and hallmarking program. Administers the Canadian Aboriginal Business Hall of Fame. **Founded:** 1984. **Awards:** Foundation for the Advancement of Aboriginal Youth Bursary Program; Foundation for the Advancement of Aboriginal Youth Scholarships.

26831 ■ Canadian Council of Chief Executives (CCCE)—Conseil Canadien des Chefs d'Enterprise
99 Bank St., Ste. 1001
Ottawa, ON, Canada K1P 6B9
Ph: (613)238-3727
Fax: (613)238-3247
Co. E-mail: info@ceocouncil.ca
URL: http://www.ceocouncil.ca
Contact: John P. Manley, President
Description: Businesses and trade organizations. Promotes a healthy national economy. Conducts research; lobbies for legislation favorable to business; represents members' interests. **Founded:** 1976.

26832 ■ Canadian Federation of Independent Business (CFIB)—Federation Canadienne de l'Entreprise Independante
401-4141 Yonge St., Ste. 401
Toronto, ON, Canada M2P 2A6
Ph: (416)222-8022
Free: 888-234-2232
Fax: (416)222-6103
Co. E-mail: cfib@cfib.ca
URL: http://www.cfib-fcei.ca/english/index.html
Contact: Danny Kelly, President
Description: Independent businesses. Promotes economic well-being of members and seeks to maintain a healthy domestic business climate. Represents members' interests before government agencies, labor and industrial organizations, and the public. **Scope:** entrepreneurship, economic policy, small business, public policy. **Founded:** 1971. **Subscriptions:** 4000 books periodicals reports. **Publications:** *Mandate* (Quarterly); *Quarterly Business Barometer* (3/year). **Awards:** Canada Awards for Excellence.

26833 ■ Canadian German Chamber of Industry and Commerce (CGCIC)—La Chambre Canadienne Allemande de l'Industrie et du Commerce
480 University Ave., Ste. 1500
Toronto, ON, Canada M5G 1V2
Ph: (416)598-3355
Fax: (416)598-1840
Co. E-mail: info.toronto@germanchamber.ca
URL: http://kanada.ahk.de/en/home
Contact: Thomas Beck, President
Description: Canadian and German corporations and trade and industrial organizations. Promotes increased trade between Canada and Germany. Lobbies for removal of barriers to trade; represents the interests of business before government agencies, international trade organizations, and the public. **Founded:** 1968. **Publications:** *Canadian German Headlines* (Monthly).

26834 ■ *Canadian German Headlines*
480 University Ave., Ste. 1500
Toronto, ON, Canada M5G 1V2
Ph: (416)598-3355
Fax: (416)598-1840
Co. E-mail: info.toronto@germanchamber.ca
URL: http://kanada.ahk.de/en/home
Contact: Thomas Beck, President
Released: Monthly

26835 ■ Canadian Labour Congress (CLC)—Congres du travail du Canada
2841 Riverside Dr.
Ottawa, ON, Canada K1V 8X7
Ph: (613)521-3400
Fax: (613)521-4655
URL: http://www.canadianlabour.ca/home
Contact: Ken Georgetti, President
Description: Works to ensure that all Canadians are able to find employment at fair wages, with union representation and the right to collective bargaining, in a safe environment. Seeks to create a just and equitable society. Joins with other organizations for advocacy and action on behalf of working Canadians. Facilitates establishment of grass roots organizations. Conducts research and educational programs; maintains speakers' bureau; compiles statistics. **Founded:** 1956. **Publications:** *C.L.C. Fax-Press* (Weekly); *Sweatshop Alert*; *UI Bulletin* (Periodic).

26836 ■ Canadian Netherlands Business and Professional Association (CNBPA)
Sta. A
Toronto, ON, Canada M5W 1N4
Ph: (416)981-3424
Fax: (416)981-3424
Co. E-mail: info@cnbpa.ca
URL: http://www.cnbpa.ca
Contact: Tom Vandeloo, President
Description: Business people and professionals in Canada and the Netherlands. Promotes increased trade and communication between Canada and the Netherlands. Serves as a forum for the exchange of information among members. **Founded:** 1979.

26837 ■ *C.L.C. Fax-Press*
2841 Riverside Dr.
Ottawa, ON, Canada K1V 8X7
Ph: (613)521-3400
Fax: (613)521-4655
URL: http://www.canadianlabour.ca/home
Contact: Ken Georgetti, President
Released: Weekly

26838 ■ *Commerce News*
No. 700 - 9990 Jasper Ave.
Edmonton, AB, Canada T5J 1P7
Ph: (780)409-4620
Fax: (780)424-7946
Co. E-mail: info@edmontonchamber.com
URL: http://www.edmontonchamber.com
Contact: Mr. Martin Salloum, President
Released: Monthly **Price:** free for members.

26839 ■ Committee for Economic Development (CED)
2000 L St. NW, Ste. 700
Washington, DC 20036-4915

Ph: (202)296-5860
Free: 800-676-7353
Fax: (202)223-0776
Co. E-mail: info@ced.org
URL: http://www.ced.org
Contact: Donald K. Peterson, Co-Chairman
Description: Trustees are heads of major corporations or university presidents. Works with expert advisers. Conducts research and formulates policy recommendations on national and international economic issues, including education, trade policy, U.S.-Japan economic relations, and problems of the inner city. Seeks to contribute to full employment, higher living standards, and increased opportunities for all through its studies and reports; promote economic growth and stability; strengthen the concepts and institutions essential to progress in a free society. **Founded:** 1942. **Publications:** *CED Forum* (Semiannual).

26840 ■ *Connections*
Trust Tower
77 King St. W, Ste. 2401
Toronto, ON, Canada M5K 1G8
Ph: (416)816-9154
Fax: (647)594-9501
Co. E-mail: idalia@bcctc.ca
URL: http://bcctc.ca
Contact: Idalia Obregon, Executive Director
Released: Quarterly

26841 ■ Corporation for Enterprise Development (CFED)
1200 G St. NW, Ste. 400
Washington, DC 20005
Ph: (202)408-9788
Fax: (202)408-9793
Co. E-mail: info@cfed.org
URL: http://www.cfed.org
Contact: Andrea Levere, President
E-mail: alevere@cfed.org
Description: Provides assistance to public and private organizations concerned with increasing economic opportunity of individuals through the encouragement and support of enterprise development; serves as a forum for the exchange of ideas. Strives to research, develop, and disseminate entrepreneurial policy initiatives at the local, state, and federal levels. Conducts consulting services and compiles statistics. **Scope:** Offers expertise in economic research. Offers services as identify promising ideas, test and refine them in communities to find out what works, craft policies and products to help good ideas reach scale, and foster new markets to achieve greater economic impact. **Founded:** 1979. **Publications:** "Children's Savings Accounts and Financial Aid"; "Linking Youth Savings and Entrepreneurship". **Educational Activities:** Assets Learning Conference (Biennial). **Seminars:** Fighting Poverty: The Role of Asset Building in Public Policy; IDAS and Microenterprise; Self-Sustaining IDA Initiatives; Serving Multi-Cultural Markets; Asset Purchase Effective Practices; Policy Proposals, Opportunities, and Barriers for Youth Savings. **Telecommunication Services:** info-dc@cfed.org; alevere@cfed.org.

26842 ■ Council of Development Finance Agencies (CDFA)
85 E Gay St., Ste. 700
Columbus, OH 43215
Ph: (614)224-1300
Fax: (614)224-1343
Co. E-mail: info@cdfa.net
URL: http://www.cdfa.net
Contact: Toby Rittner, President
Description: Works for the advancement of development finance concerns and interests. Represents members of the development finance community from the public, private and non-profit sectors. **Founded:** 1982. **Publications:** *Development Finance Review Weekly* (Weekly). **Educational Activities:** Development Finance Summit (Annual). **Awards:** Practitioners Showcase.

26843 ■ Dialogue on Diversity
1629 K St. NW, Ste. 300
Washington, DC 20006
Ph: (703)631-0650

Fax: (703)631-0617
Co. E-mail: dialog.div@prodigy.net
URL: http://www.dialogueondiversity.org
Contact: Ma. Cristina C. Caballero, President
Description: Promotes social and political advancement of women and men from diverse ethnic and national traditions; fosters increased economic empowerment; aims to promote and develop entrepreneurial excellence, technology, networking, and education. **Founded:** 1989.

26844 ■ Edmonton Chamber of Commerce
No. 700 - 9990 Jasper Ave.
Edmonton, AB, Canada T5J 1P7
Ph: (780)409-4620
Fax: (780)424-7946
Co. E-mail: info@edmontonchamber.com
URL: http://www.edmontonchamber.com
Contact: Mr. Martin Salloum, President
Description: Serves as the official voice of business in the Edmonton area. Provides networking opportunities via special events held during the year. Provides discount and affinity programs, business referrals and business resources. Owns and operates the World Trade Center Edmonton (WTCE), which is a member of the World Trade Centers Organization, a network of 300 centers in almost 100 countries worldwide. Assists businesses, professionals, and interested individuals in developing national and international trade by providing information and advice on new markets and products. Organizes trade missions to World Trade Centers and facilitates contact with government agencies. Offers research and information gathering on trade opportunities, educational programs, and consumer and business assistance. **Scope:** country information and trade. **Publications:** *Commerce News* (Monthly); *Edmonton Commerce Directory* (Annual); *Commerce News: Reaching Edmonton's Entire Business Community* (Monthly). **Awards:** Centennial Scholarship (Annual).

26845 ■ Edmonton Commerce Directory
No. 700 - 9990 Jasper Ave.
Edmonton, AB, Canada T5J 1P7
Ph: (780)409-4620
Fax: (780)424-7946
Co. E-mail: info@edmontonchamber.com
URL: http://www.edmontonchamber.com
Contact: Mr. Martin Salloum, President
Released: Annual **Price:** available to members only.

26846 ■ I.E. Canada—Association canadienne des importateurs et exportateurs
10 Saint Mary St., Ste. 200
Toronto, ON, Canada M4Y 1P9
Ph: (416)595-5333
Fax: (416)595-8226
Co. E-mail: info@iecanada.com
URL: http://www.iecanada.com
Contact: Mary Anderson, President
E-mail: manderson@iecanada.com
Description: Individuals and firms with an interest in Canada's international trade. Promotes increased participation by Canada in the global economy; seeks to maintain a business climate conducive to increased international trade. Represents members' interests before government agencies; prepares model trade programs, regulations, and policies. Provides advice and assistance to members; serves as a clearinghouse on international trade. **Founded:** 1932. **Publications:** *I.E. Global* (Semiannual); *Tradeweek* (Semimonthly); *Canadian Importers Association, Inc.--Membership Directory* (Annual); *Importing into Canada.* **Educational Activities:** I.E. Canada Conference (Annual); Emerging Issues in Customs Conference (Semiannual).

26847 ■ I.E. Global
10 Saint Mary St., Ste. 200
Toronto, ON, Canada M4Y 1P9
Ph: (416)595-5333
Fax: (416)595-8226
Co. E-mail: info@iecanada.com
URL: http://www.iecanada.com
Contact: Mary Anderson, President
E-mail: manderson@iecanada.com
Released: Semiannual

26848 ■ Insight Center for Community Economic Development
2201 Broadway, Ste. 815
Oakland, CA 94612-3024
Ph: (510)251-2600
Fax: (510)251-0600
Co. E-mail: info@insightcced.org
URL: http://insightcced.org
Contact: Roger A. Clay, Jr., President
URL(s): www.insightcced.org. **Description:** Aims to build economic health in vulnerable communities. Develops and promotes innovative solutions that help people and communities become, and remain, economically secure. Collaborates with foundations, nonprofits, educational institutions, government and businesses to develop, strengthen and promote programs and public policy that: lead to good jobs, strengthen early care and education systems, and enable people and communities to build financial and educational assets. **Scope:** A research, consulting, and legal organization dedicated to building economic health in vulnerable communities. Services include maximization of financial resources for community economic development (CED); qualitative and quantitative research; planning, implementation, and evaluation of programs; legal resources to community-based organizations engaged in CED; organizational capacity-building and sustainability planning; strategic support to foundation initiatives; innovative business models such as employee-owned businesses and alternative staffing agencies; applied research in areas such as feasibility, scalability, case studies, and best practices; training and curriculum development; coalition-building; and policy, advocacy, and communications strategies. **Founded:** 1969.

26849 ■ International Economic Development Council (IEDC)
734 15th St. NW, Ste. 900
Washington, DC 20005
Ph: (202)223-7800
Fax: (202)223-4745
Co. E-mail: kbielen@iedconline.org
URL: http://www.iedconline.org
Contact: Jeff Finkle, President
E-mail: cziegler@iedconline.org
URL(s): www.iedc.org. **Description:** Works to help economic development professionals improve the quality of life in their communities. Represents all levels of government, academia, and private industry; provides a broad range of member services including research, advisory services, conferences, professional certification, professional development, publications, legislative tracking and more. **Founded:** 1967. **Publications:** *Economic Development Journal* (Quarterly); *Economic Development Now* (Bimonthly); *Federal Review* (Annual); *Economic Development Review; International Economic Development Council--Membership Directory* (Irregular); *Annual Federal Review and Budget Overview* (Annual). **Educational Activities:** Tech-Link Conference (Biennial); IEDC Annual Conference (Annual). **Awards:** Internet and New Media Awards; Leadership Awards; Partnership Awards; Program Awards; Promotional Awards; Lifetime Achievement Award for Excellence in Economic Development. **Telecommunication Services:** kburns@iedconline.org.

26850 ■ International Finance Corporation (IFC)
2121 Pennsylvania Ave. NW
Washington, DC 20433
Ph: (202)473-1000
Fax: (202)974-4384
Co. E-mail: CShanahan@ifc.org
URL: http://www1.ifc.org/wps/wcm/connect/corp_ext_content/ifc_external_corporate_site/home
Contact: Lars Thunell, Chief Executive Officer
URL(s): www.ifc.org. **Description:** Promotes sustainable private sector investments in developing countries, as a way to reduce poverty and improve people's lives. **Founded:** 1956. **Publications:** *ESTOCK; Emerging Markets Data Base.*

26851 ■ Mandate
401-4141 Yonge St., Ste. 401
Toronto, ON, Canada M2P 2A6
Ph: (416)222-8022

Free: 888-234-2232
Fax: (416)222-6103
Co. E-mail: cfib@cfib.ca
URL: http://www.cfib-fcei.ca/english/index.html
Contact: Danny Kelly, President
Released: Quarterly

26852 ■ National Association of Development Organizations Research Foundation (NADO)
400 N Capitol St. NW, Ste. 390
Washington, DC 20001
Ph: (202)624-7806
Fax: (202)624-8813
Co. E-mail: info@nado.org
URL: http://www.nado.org
Contact: Matthew Chase, Executive Director
Description: Identifies, studies and promotes regional solutions and approaches to improving local prosperity and services through the nationwide network of regional development organizations. Shares best practices and offers professional development training, analyzes the impact of federal policies and programs on regional development organizations, and examines the latest developments and trends in small metro and rural America. Provides federal advocacy, informative research, special reports and training to the nation's rural regional development organizations. **Founded:** 1988. **Educational Activities:** Training Conference (Annual). **Awards:** Congressional Partnership Award (Biennial); Innovations Award (Annual).

26853 ■ National Development Council (NDC)
708 Third Ave., Ste. 710
New York, NY 10017
Ph: (212)682-1106
Fax: (212)573-6118
Co. E-mail: training@nationaldevelopmentcouncil.org
URL: http://www.nationaldevelopmentcouncil.org
Contact: Samuel S. Beard, Chairman
Description: Brings innovative economic development financing programs to urban and rural communities interested in local business and industrial growth, commercial revitalization, and permanent job creation. Finances professionals' work with cities, counties, and states to: build permanent systems for developing financing; train local staff; structure and negotiate financing for development projects, local business development, and industrial expansion. Conducts intensive training program for economic development professionals with courses in business credit analysis, real estate financing, loan packaging, federal financing, and program management and implementation; has provided advice to congress and federal agencies that has helped create lending programs for job creation and small business investment; has initiated and managed presidential programs for Presidents Nixon, Ford, Carter, and Reagan. **Founded:** 1969. **Publications:** *Developments* (Quarterly).

26854 ■ Pacific Basin Economic Council - Canadian Committee (PBECCC)
c/o Asia Pacific Foundation of Canada
890 W Pender St., Ste. 220
Vancouver, BC, Canada V6C 1J9
Ph: (604)684-5986
Fax: (604)681-1370
Co. E-mail: info@asiapacific.ca
URL: http://www.asiapacific.ca
Contact: John H. McArthur, Chairman
Description: Canadian corporations. Promotes increased trade between the countries bordering the Pacific Ocean. Gathers and disseminates information on international trade issues. **Founded:** 1967. **Publications:** *PBEC Report* (Periodic). **Telecommunication Services:** communications@asiapacific.ca.

26855 ■ PBEC Report
c/o Asia Pacific Foundation of Canada
890 W Pender St., Ste. 220
Vancouver, BC, Canada V6C 1J9
Ph: (604)684-5986
Fax: (604)681-1370
Co. E-mail: info@asiapacific.ca
URL: http://www.asiapacific.ca
Contact: John H. McArthur, Chairman
Released: Periodic

26856 ■ *Quarterly Business Barometer*
401-4141 Yonge St., Ste. 401
Toronto, ON, Canada M2P 2A6
Ph: (416)222-8022
Free: 888-234-2232
Fax: (416)222-6103
Co. E-mail: cfib@cfib.ca
URL: http://www.cfib-fcei.ca/english/index.html
Contact: Danny Kelly, President
Released: 3/year

26857 ■ *Sounding Board*
c/o Vancouver Board of Trade
999 Canada Pl., Ste. 400
Vancouver, BC, Canada V6C 3E1
Ph: (604)681-2111
Fax: (604)681-0437
Co. E-mail: wtc@boardoftrade.com
URL: http://www.boardoftrade.com
Contact: Ellen Norris, Director
Released: Monthly **Price:** free.

**26858 ■ Sustainable Development
Technology Canada (SDTC)—Technologies
du Developpement Durable du Canada**
45 O'Connor St., Ste. 1850
Ottawa, ON, Canada K1P 1A4
Ph: (613)234-6313
Fax: (613)234-0303
Co. E-mail: info@sdtc.ca
URL: http://www.sdtc.ca
Contact: Vicky J. Sharpe, President
Description: Seeks to promote a sustainable development technology infrastructure in Canada.
Founded: 2001.

26859 ■ *Sweatshop Alert*
2841 Riverside Dr.
Ottawa, ON, Canada K1V 8X7
Ph: (613)521-3400
Fax: (613)521-4655
URL: http://www.canadianlabour.ca/home
Contact: Ken Georgetti, President

**26860 ■ Swedish-Canadian Chamber of
Commerce (SCCC)**
2 Bloor St. W, Ste. 2109
Toronto, ON, Canada M4W 3E2
Ph: (416)925-8661
Co. E-mail: info@sccc.ca
URL: http://www.sccc.ca
Contact: Erik Thorsrud, Chairman
Description: Facilitates business and cultural development between Sweden and Canada. Provides knowledge about both countries and promotes trade and business opportunities. Serves as a forum allowing Swedes and Canadians with mutual interests to connect at various levels, affords members' business and finds cultural and social opportunities. **Founded:** 1965.

26861 ■ *Tradeweek*
10 Saint Mary St., Ste. 200
Toronto, ON, Canada M4Y 1P9
Ph: (416)595-5333
Fax: (416)595-8226
Co. E-mail: info@iecanada.com
URL: http://www.iecanada.com
Contact: Mary Anderson, President
E-mail: manderson@iecanada.com
Released: Semimonthly

26862 ■ *UI Bulletin*
2841 Riverside Dr.
Ottawa, ON, Canada K1V 8X7
Ph: (613)521-3400
Fax: (613)521-4655
URL: http://www.canadianlabour.ca/home
Contact: Ken Georgetti, President
Released: Periodic

26863 ■ USA Engage
1625 K St. NW, Ste. 200
Washington, DC 20006
Ph: (202)887-0278

Fax: (202)452-8160
Co. E-mail: usaengage@nftc.org
URL: http://www.usaengage.org
Description: Promotes economic strength in America as integral to the nation's security and worldwide leadership. **Founded:** 1997.

**26864 ■ World Trade Centre Montreal
(WTCM)**
c/o Board of Trade of Metropolitan Montreal
380 St. Antoine St. W, Ste. 6000
Montreal, QC, Canada H2Y 3X7
Ph: (514)871-4002
Free: 877-590-4040
Fax: (514)849-3813
Co. E-mail: wtcmontreal@ccmm.qc.ca
URL: http://www.btmm.qc.ca/en/lachambre-World_
Trade_Centre_Montreal
Contact: Mr. Guy Jobin, Executive Director
Description: Businesses, professionals, and interested individuals. Seeks to foster the export of products and services by supporting, training and advising companies, associations and economic development institutions and organizations on certain activities on international markets through an integrated programme of export solutions. **Founded:** 1984. **Telecommunication Services:** info@ccmm.qc.ca.

**26865 ■ World Trade Centre Vancouver (WTC
Vancouver)**
c/o Vancouver Board of Trade
999 Canada Pl., Ste. 400
Vancouver, BC, Canada V6C 3E1
Ph: (604)681-2111
Fax: (604)681-0437
Co. E-mail: wtc@boardoftrade.com
URL: http://www.boardoftrade.com
Contact: Ellen Norris, Director
URL(s): www.wtcaonline.com/cms_wtca/index.
php?option=com_gcontact&view=contact&id=4485:-
norris&group=city&filter=Vancouver&Itemid=105. **Description:** Businesses, professionals, and interested individuals. Facilitates the development of national and international trade by providing traders and investors with information and advice on new markets and products. Organizes trade missions to World Trade Centers and facilitates contact with government agencies. Offers research and information gathering on trade opportunities, educational programs, and consumer and business assistance. **Scope:** international trade. **Founded:** 1897. **Publications:** *Sounding Board* (Monthly). **Awards:** Business and the Arts Awards; Business Hall of Fame; Chairman's Award; Women in the Spotlight; Business and the Arts Awards (Annual); Business Hall of Fame (Annual); Chairman's Award (Periodic); Women in Spotlight (Semiannual).

**26866 ■ World Trade and Convention Centre
Halifax (WTCC)**
1800 Argyle St.
Halifax, NS, Canada B3J 2V9
Ph: (902)421-1302
Fax: (902)422-2922
Co. E-mail: paulc@tclns.com
URL: http://www.wtcchalifax.com
Contact: Mr. Paul A. Cody, Manager, Sales
Description: Represents businesses, professionals, and interested individuals. Facilitates the development of national and international trade by providing traders and investors with information and advice on new markets and products. Organizes trade missions to World Trade Centers and facilitates contact with government agencies. Offers services such as research and information gathering on trade opportunities, educational programs, and consumer and business assistance. **Founded:** 1985.

REFERENCE WORKS

**26867 ■ *"$3 Million in Repairs Prep Cobo for
Auto Show"* in Crain's Detroit Business (Vol.
26, January 4, 2010, No. 1, pp. 1)**
Pub: Crain Communications Inc.
Ed: Nancy Kaffer. **Description:** Overview of the six projects priced roughly at $3 million which were needed in order to host the North American Interna-

tional Auto Show; show organizers stated that the work was absolutely necessary to keep the show in the city of Detroit.

**26868 ■ *"3CDC Investing $8 Million To Put
New Life Into Old Homes"* in Globe & Mail
(February 28, 2006, pp. B1)**
Pub: CTVglobemedia Publishing Inc.
Ed: Lucy May. **Description:** The Cincinnati Center City Development Corp. has bought more than 100 empty buildings and many around Washington Park in Over-the-Rhine. Its new project, called 3CDC, is to revitalize the historic neighborhood in the Washington Park area near Music Hall.

**26869 ■ *The 5 Big Lies About American
Business: Combating Smears Against the
Free-Market Economy***
Pub: Crown Business Books
Ed: Michael Medved. **Released:** November 2, 2010.
Price: $15.00. **Description:** Michael Medved, talk-radio personality and bestselling author, argues for capitalism. He presents popular myths about the free market system and discusses why each myth is instead good for Americans and our economy.

**26870 ■ *"$50 Million Project for West
Chester"* in Business Courier (Vol. 24,
December 14, 2008, No. 35, pp. 1)**
Pub: American City Business Journals, Inc.
Ed: Laura Baverman. **Description:** Commercial developer Scott Street Partners is planning to invest $50 million for the development of a site south of the Streets of West Chester retail center. The 31-acre project will generate 1,200 jobs, and will bring in offices, restaurants and a hotel. The development plans and the features of the site are discussed as well.

**26871 ■ *"217 Homes Planned for Former
Crystal Cream Site"* in Sacramento Business
Journal (Vol. 25, August 8, 2008, No. 23, pp.
1)**
Pub: American City Business Journals, Inc.
Ed: Michael Shaw. **Description:** MetroNova Development LLC plans to develop housing at the former Crystal Cream & Butter Co. site near downtown Sacramento. The developer expects to sell the new loft houses for about $300,000 without public subsidies. Views and other information on the planned development project, is presented.

**26872 ■ *"2009: A Call For Vision"* in Women
Entrepreneur (January 28, 2009)**
Pub: Entrepreneur Media Inc.
Ed: Elinor Robin. **Description:** Providing exemplary customer service, reducing expenses and creating an out-of-the-box niche are three key factors that will help business survive during this economic crisis. Business owners must see potential where others see failure in order to create new opportunities that may not only allow their business to survive during these times but may actually cause some businesses to thrive despite this economic downturn.

**26873 ■ *"2010: Important Year Ahead for
Waterfront"* in Bellingham Business Journal
(Vol. March 2010, pp. 2)**
Pub: Sound Publishing Inc.
Ed: Isaac Bonnell. **Description:** A tentative timeline has been established for the environmental impact statement (EIS) slated for completion in May 2010. The plan for the Waterfront District includes detailed economic and architectural analysis of the feasibility of reusing remaining structures and retaining some industrial icons.

**26874 ■ *"According to the Chinese Zodiac,
2009 is the Year of the Ox"* in Canadian
Business (Vol. 81, December 8, 2008, No. 21,
pp. 74)**
Pub: Rogers Media Ltd.
Ed: Zarka Halas. **Description:** Forecasts for China in 2009 are presented. China is expected to maintain an 8 percent growth rate to keep the current labor market. A total of 68,000 companies have collapsed in China in the first half of 2008, while 2.5 million workers are likely to lose jobs in the Pearl River Delta by the end of 2008.

26875 ■ *"Actions to Implement Three Potent Post-Crisis Strategies"* in *Strategy & Leadership (Vol. 38, September-October 2010, No. 5)*
Pub: Emerald Inc.
Ed: Saul J. Berman, Richard Christner, Ragna Bell. **Description:** The need for organizations to design and implement strategies to cope with the possible situations in the post-economic crisis environment is emphasized. The plans that organizations should implement to successfully manage uncertainty and complexity and to foster their eventual growth are discussed.

26876 ■ *"Active Sales"* in *Green Industry Pro (Vol. 23, September 2011)*
Pub: Cygnus Business Media
Ed: Gregg Wartgow. **Description:** Craig den Hartog, owner of Emerald Magic Lawn Care located in Holtsville, New York, describes the various marketing tactics he has developed to increase sales in the current economic environment. Statistical data included.

26877 ■ *"Adapt or Die"* in *Black Enterprise (Vol. 38, July 2008, No. 12, pp. 27)*
Pub: Earl G. Graves Publishing Co. Inc.
Ed: Oguntoyinbo Lekan. **Description:** Turbulence in the domestic auto industry is hitting auto suppliers hard and black suppliers, the majority of whom contract with the Big Three, are just beginning to establish relationships with import car manufacturers. The more savvy CEOs are adopting new technologies in order to weather the downturn in the economy and in the industry as a whole.

26878 ■ *"Affordable Again"* in *The Business Journal-Serving Greater Tampa Bay (Vol. 28, July 18, 2008, No. 30, pp. 1)*
Pub: American City Business Journals, Inc.
Ed: Janet Leiser. **Description:** Rental rates for office space in the Tampa Bay area has dropped to $21.68 a foot, after demand for the second quarter of 2008 has remained low. Commercial real estate experts say that the industry can easily rebound from what is believed to be the weakest demand in 20 years. Other views, information and statistics on real estate demand and prices in Tampa Bay are, are presented.

26879 ■ *"Affordable Housing on the Rise"* in *Philadelphia Business Journal (Vol. 28, October 23, 2009, No. 36, pp. 1)*
Pub: American City Business Journals
Ed: Natalie Kostelni. **Description:** Philadelphia, Pennsylvania led an affordable housing boom with more than 800 new affordable housing units in the works in spite of the recession. The converging of developers and federal stimulus money has driven the sudden increase with the launching of several projects across the city.

26880 ■ *"Aging Boomers to Slow Growth, Study Says"* in *Globe & Mail (March 15, 2006, pp. B5)*
Pub: CTVglobemedia Publishing Inc.
Ed: Heather Scoffield. **Description:** Acording to a research study by economic forecasters at Global Insight (Canada) Inc., an issue about Canada controlling its economy, as the country's population is aging, is discussed.

26881 ■ *"AIG Fixed; Is Michigan Next?"* in *Crain's Detroit Business (Vol. 24, September 22, 2008, No. 38, pp. 1)*
Pub: Crain Communications Inc.
Ed: Jay Greene. **Description:** Michigan's economic future is examined as is the mortgage buyout plan and American International Group Inc.'s takeover by the U.S. government.

26882 ■ *"Ailing Economy Nibbling at Tech-Sector Jobs"* in *Puget Sound Business Journal (Vol. 29, November 7, 2008, No. 29, pp. 1)*
Pub: American City Business Journals
Ed: Eric Engleman, John Cook. **Description:** Seattle-area tech start-up companies including Redfin, Zillow, WildTangent, Daptiv, Avelle, and Intrepid Learning Solutions have cut staff as the nation's economy staggers. The layoffs are reminiscent of the tech bubble era, but most startups these days have been more prudent about spending and hiring as compared to that period.

26883 ■ *"Akerman Senterfitt Merger Deal Close"* in *The Business Journal-Serving Greater Tampa Bay (Vol. 28, July 18, 2008, No. 30, pp. 1)*
Pub: American City Business Journals, Inc.
Ed: Jeff Blumenthal. **Description:** Sources familiar to the negotiations of Akerman Senterfitt's planned merger with Wolf Block has disclosed that executive committees of both firms have approved the deal. They expect to create an 800-lawyer firm with a significant presence in the U.S. East Coast. Other views and information on the deal and its expected impact on law practice in Florida are presented.

26884 ■ *"Alberta: Help Wanted, Badly"* in *Globe & Mail (March 11, 2006, pp. B5)*
Pub: CTVglobemedia Publishing Inc.
Ed: Patrick Brethour; Dawn Walton. **Description:** The issue of unemployment rate, which fell by 3.1 percent in Alberta, is discussed.

26885 ■ *"Alberta Warns Ottawa On Taxes"* in *Globe & Mail (March 9, 2007, pp. B1)*
Pub: CTVglobemedia Publishing Inc.
Ed: Steven Chase. **Description:** Ottawa's proposal to remove the tax break for oil sands projects has been criticized by Alberta finance minister Lyle Oberg. The cancelling of tax breaks could hamper development in oil sands and thus hit Alberta's economy.

26886 ■ *"Alberta's Runaway Train"* in *Canadian Business (Vol. 80, December 25, 2006, No. 1, pp. 17)*
Pub: Rogers Media
Ed: Andrew Nikiforuk. **Description:** The high revenue brought about by the growth in the number of oil sand plants in Canada and the simultaneous burden on infrastructure and housing is discussed.

26887 ■ *"All Indicators in Michigan Innovation Index Drop in 4Q"* in *Crain's Detroit Business (Vol. 25, June 22, 2009, No. 25, pp. 9)*
Pub: Crain Communications Inc. - Detroit
Ed: Ryan Beene. **Description:** Economic indicators that rate Michigan's innovation fell in the fourth quarter of 2008. The index of trademark applications, SBA loans, venture capital funding, new incorporations and other indicators traced dropped 12.6 points.

26888 ■ *"An Amazing Race"* in *Canadian Business (Vol. 81, March 3, 2008, No. 3, pp. 25)*
Pub: Rogers Media
Ed: Rachel Pulfer. **Description:** U.S. presidential candidates Barack Obama and Hilary Clinton lead the Democratic Part primaries while John McCain is a frontrunner at the Republican Party. These leading candidates have different plans for the U.S. economy which will affect Canada's own economy particularly concerning trade policies. The presidential candidates' proposals and the impacts of U.S. economic downturn on Canada are examined.

26889 ■ *"Amid Recession, Companies Still Value Supplier Diversity Programs"* in *Hispanic Business (July-August 2009, pp. 34)*
Pub: Hispanic Business
Ed: Joshua Molina. **Description:** The decline of traditionally strong industries, from automotive manufacturing to construction, has shaken today's economy and has forced small businesses, especially suppliers and minority-owned firms, turn to diversity programs in order to make changes.

26890 ■ *"And In This Briefcase"* in *Mergers & Acquisitions: The Dealmaker's Journal (March 1, 2008)*
Pub: SourceMedia, Inc.
Description: ACG San Diego decided to address the impact the changes in the economy will have on potential private equity transactions as well as what criteria private equity firms are looking for when assessing a company. At the opening of the chapter's 2008 breakfast meeting, real-world case studies were utilized with the audiences' participation in order to assess pre-deal risk scenarios.

26891 ■ *"And The Winner Is.."* in *Canadian Business (Vol. 81, March 3, 2008, No. 3, pp. 21)*
Pub: Rogers Media
Ed: Joe Castaldo. **Description:** Thirty out of 141 Canadian chief executive officers think that Hilary Clinton would be best for U.S.-Canada relations if elected as U.S. president. Findings also revealed that 60 respondents believe that presidential candidate John McCain would be best on handling issues of international military-security. Views on the candidates' performance and their ability to deal with the declining U.S. economy as well as international trade issues are also given.

26892 ■ *Animal Spirits: How Human Psychology Drives the Economy, and Why it Matters for Global Capitalism*
Pub: Princeton University Press
Ed: George A. Akerlof, Robert J. Shiller. **Released:** 2009. **Price:** $24.95. **Description:** Psychological factors that led to the depressed economy and how it may impede a turnaround.

26893 ■ *"Another Baby Step"* in *Canadian Business (Vol. 81, March 31, 2008, No. 5, pp. 32)*
Pub: Rogers Media
Ed: Andrew Wahl. **Description:** Discusses the Canadian government's federal budget which makes it easier to tap into tax credits for corporate research and development. However, these steps do not really go far enough to boost industrial research levels in Canada. Making these incentives at least partially refundable could help during tough economic times.

26894 ■ *"Another Man's Pain"* in *Canadian Business (Vol. 80, October 22, 2007, No. 21, pp. 33)*
Pub: Rogers Media
Ed: Andy Holloway. **Description:** U.S. financial collapse can have a positive impact on Canadian investors. Graphs on the total number of home foreclosures in the U.S. from January to August 2007, as well as foreclosure market by type, are presented.

26895 ■ *Antitrust Law: Economic Theory and Common Law Evolution*
Pub: Cambridge University Press
Contact: Richard Ziemacki, President
E-mail: rziemacki@cambridge.org
Ed: Keith N. Hylton. **Released:** January 22, 2010. **Price:** $39.99. **Description:** A consolidation of various perspectives on antitrust law and its evolution.

26896 ■ *"Apartment Ambitions"* in *The Business Journal-Portland (Vol. 25, August 8, 2008, No. 22, pp. 1)*
Pub: American City Business Journals, Inc.
Ed: Wendy Culverwell. **Description:** Unico Properties LLC's Asa FlatsLofts is one of the first of eight high-end apartment projects planned for Portland which will add a total of 2,130 new units to the Pearl District, South Waterfront, and downtown Portland. These apartments charge costs more than $1,600 or more per month over the average rent.

26897 ■ *"Apartment Market Down, Not Out"* in *Crain's Detroit Business (Vol. 24, October 6, 2008, No. 40, pp. 9)*
Pub: Crain Communications, Inc.
Ed: Daniel Duggan. **Description:** Detroit's apartment market is considered to have some of the strongest fundamentals of any apartment market in the country with relatively low vacancy rates and a relatively low supply of new units compared with demand. Investors continue to show interest in the buildings but the national lending market is making it difficult to invest in the city.

26898 ■ *"Ardesta Venture-Capital Fund Folds"* in *Crain's Detroit Business (Vol. 24, September 22, 2008, No. 38, pp. 24)*
Pub: Crain Communications Inc.
Ed: Tom Henderson. **Description:** Due to the downturn in the local economy, Ann Arbor-based Ardesta LLC. a venture-capital firm specializing in micro- and

nanotechnology research, has pulled the plug on its planned fund of $100 million and said no to an investment of up to $15 million from the state.

26899 ■ Are the Rich Necessary? Great Economic Arguments and How They Reflect Our Personal Values
Pub: Axios Press
Contact: Stephanie Bosserman, President
Ed: Hunter Lewis. **Released:** 2007. **Price:** $20.00. **Description:** Investment advisor argues whether today's economic system promotes greed. Each chapter of the book poses a question and then he answers.

26900 ■ "Are You Ready for Dow 20,000?" in Barron's (Vol. 88, March 24, 2008, No. 12, pp. 26)
Pub: Dow Jones & Company, Inc.
Ed: Jonathan R. Laing. **Description:** Stock strategist James Finucane forecasts that the Dow Jones Industrial Average will rise from its 12,361 level to as high as 20,000 from 2008 to 2009. He believes that stock liquidation and a buildup of cash provide the perfect conditions for a huge rally.

26901 ■ "Are You Rich?" in Barron's (Vol. 88, March 10, 2008, No. 10, pp. 27)
Pub: Dow Jones & Company, Inc.
Ed: Tom Sullivan. **Description:** Discusses the minimum net worth of people considered as rich in America is now at $25 million. There are about 125,000 households in America that meet this threshold, while 49,000 households have a net worth between $25 million and $ 500 million, and about 1,400 US households have a net worth over $500 million.

26902 ■ "An Artwork in Progress" in Hawaii Business (Vol. 53, March 2008, No. 9, pp. 45)
Pub: Hawaii Business Publishing
Ed: Jolyn Okimoto Rosa. **Description:** Art galleries in Honolulu, Hawaii holds the First Friday Gallery Walk and other special events, which draw crowd to and increase sales activities in the city's downtown. The district also advocates for the reintroduction of Honolulu's Chinatown to the people. Details regarding the art galleries' Chinatown revival and its local economic impact are discussed.

26903 ■ "As Capital Gains Tax Hike Looms, Merger Activity Percolates" in Baltimore Business Journal (Vol. 28, August 27, 2010, No. 16, pp. 1)
Pub: Baltimore Business Journal
Ed: Scott Dance. **Description:** Concerns for higher capital gains taxes in 2011 have been provoking buyers and sellers to engage in mergers and acquisitions activity, which is expected to gain momentum before the end of 2010. Companies that have saved cash during the recession have been taking advantage of the buyer's market. Other trends in local and national mergers and acquisitions activity are presented.

26904 ■ The Ascent of Money: A Financial History of the World
Pub: Penguin Group USA Inc.
Ed: Niall Ferguson. **Released:** 2009. **Price:** $29.95. **Description:** How financial considerations prompted the Crusades and other surprising explanations of famous events are uncovered.

26905 ■ "Asia Breathes a Sigh of Relief" in Business Week (September 22, 2008, No. 4100, pp. 32)
Pub: McGraw-Hill Companies, Inc.
Ed: Bruce Einhorn; Theo Francis; Chi-Chu Tschang; Moon Ihlwan; Hiroko Tashiro. **Description:** Foreign bankers, such as those in Asia, that had been investing heavily in the United States began to worry as the housing crisis deepened and the impact on Freddie Mac and Fannie Mae became increasingly clear. Due to the government bailout, however, central banks will most likely continue to buy American debt.

26906 ■ Asian Godfathers: Money and Power in Hong Kong and Southeast Asia
Pub: Grove/Atlantic Inc.
Contact: Morgan Entrekin, President
E-mail: mentrekin@groveatlantic.com
Ed: Joe Studwell. **Released:** September 2008. **Price:** $15.00 paperback. **Description:** Expose of some of

Southeast Asia's top business moguls is highlighted, along with a look into the region's economic and social cultures.

26907 ■ "Athletes Face Wins and Losses After Pro Sport" in The Business Journal - Serving Phoenix and the Valley of the Sun (Vol. 29, September 19, 2008, No. 3, pp. 1)
Pub: American City Business Journals, Inc.
Ed: Chris Casacchia. **Description:** Professional athletes like hockey star Jeremy Roenick start businesses, while others like Joel Adamson work to boost local communities. Former athletes were found to be particularly interested with real estate businesses. Other views and information on former athletes and their life after sports are presented.

26908 ■ Atiyah's Accidents, Compensation and the Law
Pub: Cambridge University Press
Contact: Richard Ziemacki, President
E-mail: rziemacki@cambridge.org
Ed: Peter Cane, Patrick Atiyah. **Released:** January 22, 2010. **Price:** $56.00. **Description:** Leading authority on the law of personal injuries compensation and the social, political and economic issues surrounding it.

26909 ■ "Au Revoir Or Goodbye?" in Barron's (Vol. 88, July 14, 2008, No. 28, pp. 5)
Pub: Dow Jones & Co., Inc.
Ed: Alan Abelson. **Description:** Former Senator Phil Gramm's opinion that the U.S. is a 'nation of whiners' as they moan about recession is another example of the disconnection between Washington and Wall Street on one hand and the real world on the other. It would be a catastrophe for most of the world if Fannie Mae and Freddie Mac were to go under and take their trillions of mortgage debt with them.

26910 ■ "Auctions and Bidding: a Guide for Computer Scientists" in ACM Computing Surveys (Vol. 43, Summer 2011, No. 2, pp. 10)
Pub: Association for Computing Machinery
Ed: Simon Parsons, Juan A. Rodriguez-Aguilar, Mark Klein. **Description:** There are various actions: single dimensional, multi-dimensional, single-sided, double-sided, first-price, second-price, English, Dutch, Japanese, sealed-bid, and these have been extensively discussed and analyzed in economics literature. This literature is surveyed from a computer science perspective, primarily from the viewpoint of computer scientists who are interested in learning about auction theory, and to provide pointers into the economics literature for those who want a deeper technical understanding. In addition, since auctions are an increasingly important topic in computer science, the article also looks at work on auctions from the computer science literature. The aim is to identify what both bodies of work tell us about creating electronic auctions.

26911 ■ "Austin on Verge of Losing 7,500 Jobs" in Austin Business Journal (Vol. 31, May 6, 2011, No. 9, pp. 1)
Pub: American City Business Journals Inc.
Ed: Jacob Dirr. **Description:** Proposed state budget cuts are seen to result in the loss of as many as 7,500 public and private sector jobs in Austin, Texas, with the private sector losing the majority of workers. Comments from analysts are included.

26912 ■ "Auto Sector's Outlook Dims, Survey Finds" in Globe & Mail (January 4, 2006, pp. B4)
Pub: CTVglobemedia Publishing Inc.
Ed: Greg Keenan. **Description:** The findings of KPMG's survey, on the opinions of chief executives of automotive sector on the impact of higher gas prices, are presented.

26913 ■ "Auto Show Aims to Electrify" in Crain's Detroit Business (Vol. 26, January 11, 2010, No. 2, pp. 1)
Pub: Crain Communications, Inc.
Ed: Ryan Beene. **Description:** Overview of the North American International Auto show include sixteen production and concept vehicles including eight from the Detroit 3. High-tech battery suppliers as well as hybrid and electric vehicles will highlight the show.

26914 ■ "Auto Supplier Stock Battered In Wake Of Wall Street Woes" in Crain's Detroit Business (Vol. 24, September 29, 2008, No. 39, pp. 4)
Pub: Crain Communications Inc.
Ed: Ryan Beene. **Description:** Due to the volatility of the stock market and public perception of the $700 billion banking bailout, auto suppliers are now facing a dramatic drop in their shares. Statistical data included.

26915 ■ "Automotive Trouble" in Canadian Business (Vol. 82, April 27, 2009, No. 7, pp. 11)
Pub: Rogers Media
Ed: Thomas Watson. **Description:** The likely effects of a possible bailout of the U.S. automotive industry are examined. Some experts believe that a bailout will be good for the automotive industry and on the U.S. economy. Others argue however, that the nationalization may have a negative impact on the industry and on the economy.

26916 ■ "B2B Commercial Collection Agency Accounts Fall" in Managing Credit, Receivables & Collections (November 2010, No. 10-11, pp. 9)
Pub: Institute of Management & Administration
Description: A fall in the number of Business-To-Business collection accounts reflects the pace of the global economic recovery.

26917 ■ "BABs in Bond Land" in Barron's (Vol. 89, July 6, 2009, No. 27, pp. 14)
Pub: Dow Jones & Co., Inc.
Ed: Jim McTague. **Description:** American Recovery and Reinvestment Act has created taxable Build America Bonds (BAB) to finance new construction projects. The issuance of the two varieties of taxable BABs is expected to benefit the municipal bond market.

26918 ■ "A Baby Step to the South" in Canadian Business (Vol. 81, July 22, 2008, No. 12-13, pp. 21)
Pub: Rogers Media Ltd.
Ed: Jane Bao. **Description:** Canada's free trade agreement (FTA) with Colombia is seen as Canada's re-engagement with Latin America. Some politicians believe that the FTA is more of a political agreement than a trade agreement with Colombia. Key information on Canada's trade agreements, as well as trade with Colombia and Latin American countries, is presented.

26919 ■ "Back in the Race" in Barron's (Vol. 88, March 17, 2008, No. 11, pp. 43)
Pub: Dow Jones & Company, Inc.
Ed: Leslie P. Norton. **Description:** Katherine Schapiro was able to get Sentinel International Equity's Morningstar classification to blended fund from a value fund rating after joining Sentinel from her former jobs at Strong Overseas Fund. Schapiro aims to benefit from the global rebalancing as the U.S.'s share of the world economy shrinks.

26920 ■ "Back on Track-Or Off the Rails?" in Business Week (September 22, 2008, No. 4100, pp. 22)
Pub: McGraw-Hill Companies, Inc.
Ed: Peter Coy; Tara Kalwarski. **Description:** Discusses the possible scenarios the American economy may undergo due to the takeover of Fannie Mae and Freddie Mac. Statistical data included.

26921 ■ "Bad-Loan Bug Bites Mid-Tier Banks; More Pain, Tighter Lending Standards Ahead, CEOs Say" in Crain's Chicago Business (May 5, 2008)
Pub: Crain Communications, Inc.
Ed: Steve Daniels. **Description:** Mid-sized commercial banks form the bedrock of Chicago's financial-services industry and they are now feeling the results of the credit crisis that has engulfed the nation's largest banks and brokerages. Commercial borrowers are seeing tighter terms on loans and higher interest rates while bank investors are unable to forecast lenders' earnings performance from quarter to quarter. Statistical data included.

26922 ■ *Bad Money*
Pub: Viking Press/Penguin Group
Ed: Kevin Phillips. **Released:** April 15, 2008. **Description:** How the financial sector has hijacked the American economy, aided by Washington's ruinous faith in the efficiency of markets.

26923 ■ *Bad Samaritans: The Myth of Free Trade and the Secret History of Capitalism*
Pub: Bloomsbury USA
Ed: Ha-Joon Chang. **Released:** 2009. **Price:** $26.95. **Description:** Economist challenges open-market proponents and believes that free trade would do more harm than good.

26924 ■ *"Bailout Forgets the 'Little Guys" in The Business Journal-Milwaukee (Vol. 25, September 26, 2008, No. 53, pp. A1)*
Pub: American City Business Journals, Inc.
Ed: Rich Kirchen. **Description:** Community Bankers of Wisconsin and the Wisconsin Bankers Association are urging members to approach congressional representatives and remind them to include local banks in building the $700 billion bailout plan. WBA president and CEO Kurt Bauer thinks that it is only fair to include smaller institutions in the bailout. The initial bailout plan and its benefit for the smaller banks are examined.

26925 ■ *"Bailout May Force Cutbacks, Job Losses" in The Business Journal - Serving Phoenix and the Valley of the Sun (Vol. 29, September 26, 2008, No. 4, pp. 1)*
Pub: American City Business Journals, Inc.
Ed: Mike Sunnucks. **Description:** Economists say the proposed $700 billion bank bailout could affect Arizona businesses as banks could be forced to reduce the amount and number of loans it has thereby forcing businesses to shrink capital expenditures and then jobs. However, the plan could also stimulate the economy by taking bad loans off banks balance sheets according to another economist.

26926 ■ *"Baker Building A Snapshot Of Corridor's Future; Long-Empty Euclid Avenue Site Already Houses Two Tech Tenants" in Crain's Cleveland Business*
Pub: Crain Communications, Inc.
Ed: Stan Bullard. **Description:** Due to a new transit line and the redevelopment of the old Eaker Electric Building, the Euclid Ave. area of Cleveland is transforming from a known drug activity area to a new area for high-tech ventures.

26927 ■ *"Bank Forces Brooke Founder To Sell His Holdings" in The Business Journal-Serving Metropolitan Kansas City (October 10, 2008)*
Pub: American City Business Journals, Inc.
Ed: James Dornbrook. **Description:** Robert Orr who is the founder of Brooke Corp., a franchise of insurance agencies, says that he was forced to sell virtually all of his stocks in the company by creditors. First United Bank held the founder's stock as collateral for two loans worth $5 million and $7.9 million, which were declared in default in September 2008. Details of the selling of the company's stocks are provided.

26928 ■ *"Bank Sticks to Rate Rise Script but 'Modest' is the Salient Word" in Globe & Mail (January 25, 2006, pp. B5)*
Pub: CTVglobemedia Publishing Inc.
Ed: Heather Scoffield. **Description:** The reasons behind the decision of Bank of Canada to increase interest rate, which is posted at 3.5 percent, are presented.

26929 ■ *"Banking Bailout: Boost or Bust?" in Crain's Detroit Business (Vol. 24, September 29, 2008, No. 39, pp. 1)*
Pub: Crain Communications Inc.
Ed: Amy Lane. **Description:** Economic insiders discuss the banking bailout and how it might impact the state of Michigan.

26930 ■ *"Bankruptcies" in Crain's Detroit Business (Vol. 26, January 4, 2010, No. 1, pp. 5)*
Pub: Crain Communications, Inc.
Ed: Dustin Walsh. **Description:** Listing of local businesses that filed for Chapter 7 or 11 protection in U.S. Bankruptcy Court in Detroit December 11-28. Under Chapter 11, a company files for reorganization. Chapter 7 involves total liquidation.

26931 ■ *"Bankruptcies" in Crain's Detroit Business (Vol. 26, January 11, 2010, No. 2, pp. 7)*
Pub: Crain Communications, Inc.
Ed: Dustin Walsh. **Description:** Listing of local businesses that filed for Chapter 7 or 11 protection in U.S. Bankruptcy Court in Detroit December 11-28. Under Chapter 11, a company files for reorganization. Chapter 7 involves total liquidation.

26932 ■ *"Bankruptcies Shoot Up 68 Percent" in Sacramento Business Journal (Vol. 25, July 18, 2008, No. 20, pp. 1)*
Pub: American City Business Journals, Inc.
Ed: Kathy Robertson. **Description:** Personal bankruptcy in the Sacramento area rose by 88 percent for the first half of 2008 while business bankruptcies rose by 50 percent for the same period. The numbers of consumer bankruptcy reflects the effect of high debt, rising mortgage costs, and declining home values on U.S. households.

26933 ■ *"Bankruptcies Soar As Market Takes a Tumble" in The Business Journal - Serving Phoenix and the Valley of the Sun (Vol. 28, August 22, 2008, No. 51, pp. 1)*
Pub: American City Business Journals, Inc.
Ed: Chris Casacchia. **Description:** Chapter 7 and Chapter 13 bankruptcy filings have increased 112 percent in July 2008, for a total of 1,225 filings in Phoenix. Chapter 11 business reorganizations also increased by 86 percent compared to 2007 figures because of the challenging national economy. Other views and information on the rise in bankruptcy filings in Phoenix are presented.

26934 ■ *"Bankruptcies Swell" in The Business Journal-Portland (Vol. 25, July 4, 2008, No. 17, pp. 1)*
Pub: American City Business Journals, Inc.
Ed: Andy Giegerich. **Description:** Individual and business bankruptcy filings in Portland, Oregon had increased. The rising gas and food prices, mortgage crisis and tightening lending standards are seen as causes of bankruptcies. Statistics on bankruptcy filings are also provided.

26935 ■ *"Bankruptcy Blowback" in Business Week (September 22, 2008, No. 4100, pp. 36)*
Pub: McGraw-Hill Companies, Inc.
Ed: Jessica Silver-Greenberg. **Description:** Changes to bankruptcy laws which were enacted in 2005 after banks and other financial institutions lobbied hard for them are now suffering the consequences of the laws which force more troubled borrowers to let their homes go into foreclosure; lenders suffer financially every time they have to take on a foreclosure and the laws in which they lobbied so hard to see enacted are now becoming a problem for these lending institutions. Details of the changes in the laws are outlined as are the affects on the consumer, the economy and the lenders.

26936 ■ *"Banks Fret About Gist Of Bailout" in The Business Journal-Serving Metropolitan Kansas City (Vol. 27, September 26, 2008, No. 2)*
Pub: American City Business Journals, Inc.
Ed: James Dornbrook. **Description:** Banks from the Kansas City area hope that the proposed $700 billion bailout will not send the wrong message. UMB Financial Corp. chairman says that he hopes that the bailout would benefit companies that were more risk restrained and punish those that took outsized risk. Other bank executives' perceptions on the planned bailout are given.

26937 ■ *"Banks Lower Rates on CDs, Deposits" in Baltimore Business Journal (Vol. 27, January 1, 2010, No. 35, pp. 1)*
Pub: American City Business Journals, Inc.
Ed: Gary Haber. **Description:** Greater Baltimore area banks in Maryland have lowered their rates on certificates of deposits (CDs) and money market accounts, which could indicate the incoming trend for the first half of 2010. A banking industry forecast shows that lower Federal Funds rate, low inflation, and a new Federal Deposit Insurance Corporation (FDIC) rule might cause the rates to drop even further. Details on the FDIC rule are given.

26938 ■ *"Bargain Hunting In Vietnam" in Barron's (Vol. 88, July 14, 2008, No. 28, pp. M6)*
Pub: Dow Jones & Co., Inc.
Ed: Elliot Wilson. **Description:** Vietnam's economy grew by just 6.5 percent for the first half of 2008 and its balance of payments ballooned to $14.4 billion. The falling stock prices in the country is a boon for bargain hunters and investing in the numerous domestic funds is one way of investing in the country. Some shares that investors are taking an interest in are also discussed.

26939 ■ *"Bark Up The Right Tree" in Small Business Opportunities (Winter 2009)*
Pub: Entrepreneur Press
Contact: Perlman Neil, President
Description: Profile of Central Bark, a daycare company catering to pets that offers franchise opportunities and is expanding rapidly despite the economic downturn; the company's growth strategy is also discussed.

26940 ■ *"Bartering is Local Club's Stock in Trade" in Pueblo Chieftain (September 6, 2010)*
Pub: The Pueblo Chieftain
Ed: Loretta Sword. **Description:** As the economy waivers, a barter club in Pueblo, Colorado thrives. An examination of the club and the way it operates is included.

26941 ■ *"Bartering Makes a Return in Hard Times" in Atlanta Journal-Constitution (October 2, 2010, pp. A15)*
Pub: Atlanta Journal-Constitution
Ed: Bill York. **Description:** The advantages of bartering are explored.

26942 ■ *"Bartering Trades on Talents" in Reading Eagle (June 20, 2010)*
Pub: Reading Eagle/Reading Times
Ed: Tony Lucia. **Description:** Bartering is not just a way of trading goods and services, it can be an essential tool for small business to survive in a bad economy.

26943 ■ *"Basel3 Quick Fix Actually Neither" in Canadian Business (Vol. 83, October 12, 2010, No. 17, pp. 19)*
Pub: Rogers Media Ltd.
Ed: Thomas Watson. **Description:** Information about the so-called Basel 3 standards, which will require banks to hold top-quality capital totaling at least 7 percent of their risk-bearing assets is provided. The rules' supporters believe that a good balance has been reached between improving the Basel 2 framework and maintaining enough lending capital to stimulate an economic growth.

26944 ■ *"The Bear Arrives - With Bargain Hunters" in Barron's (Vol. 88, July 7, 2008, No. 27, pp. M3)*
Pub: Dow Jones & Co., Inc.
Ed: Kopin Tan. **Description:** US stock markets have dropped 20 percent below their highs, entering the bear market at the end of June 2008. It was also the worst performance of the stock markets during June. Wine maker Constellation Brands, however, reported a 50 percent rise in net income for the first quarter of 2008.

26945 ■ *"Bear Market Tough On Investors" in The Business Journal-Milwaukee (Vol. 25, July 4, 2008, No. 41, pp. A1)*
Pub: American City Business Journals, Inc.
Ed: Rich Kirchen. **Description:** Public companies and their investors in the Milwaukee area suffered as the bear market took hold of the Wisconsin stock market. There were 18 stocks out of the 36 publicly traded stocks that have fallen into the bear market, meaning a 20 percent decline from the market peak in the fall of 2007. The impacts of the bear market on investors are evaluated.

26946 ■ *"The Bear's Back"* in *Barron's (Vol. 88, July 7, 2008, No. 27, pp. 17)*
Pub: Dow Jones & Co., Inc.
Ed: Randall W. Forsyth; Vito Racanelli. **Description:** US stock markets have formally entered the bear market after the Dow Jones Industrial Average dropped 20 percent from its high as of June 2008. Investors remain uncertain as to how long the bear market will persist, especially with the US economy on the edge of recession.

26947 ■ *"The Beauty of Banking's Big Ugly"* in *Barron's (Vol. 89, July 27, 2009, No. 30, pp. 31)*
Pub: Dow Jones & Co., Inc.
Ed: Andrew Bary. **Description:** Appeal of the shares of Citigroup comes from its sharp discount to its tangible book value and the company's positive attributes include a strong capital position, high loan-loss reserves, and their appealing global-consumer. The shares have the potential to generate nice profits and decent stock gains as the economy turns.

26948 ■ *"Bertha's Birth Stirs Juice"* in *Barron's (Vol. 88, July 14, 2008, No. 28, pp. M11)*
Pub: Dow Jones & Co., Inc.
Ed: Tom Sellen. **Description:** Price of frozen concentrated orange juice, which has risen to four-month highs of $1.3620 in July 2008 is due, in part, to the hurricane season that has come earlier than normal in the far eastern Atlantic thereby possibly harming the 2008-2009 Florida orange crop. Future tropical-storm development will affect the prices of this commodity.

26949 ■ *"Best Growth Stocks"* in *Canadian Business (Vol. 81, Summer 2008, No. 9, pp. 61)*
Pub: Rogers Media Ltd.
Ed: Calvin Leung. **Description:** Table showing the one-year performance of growth stocks is presented. Edmonton-based Stantec Inc. expects to advance its sales and profits by 15 percent to 20 percent per year through tapping international markets and acquisitions. Analysts forecast a 17.1 percent growth rate annually over the next 3 to 5 years.

26950 ■ *"Best Turnaround Stocks"* in *Canadian Business (Vol. 81, Summer 2008, No. 9, pp. 65)*
Pub: Rogers Media Ltd.
Ed: Calvin Leung. **Description:** Share prices of Sierra Wireless Inc. and EXFO Electro Optical Engineering Inc. have fallen over the past year but have good chance at a rebound considering that the companies have free cash flow and no long-term debt. One-year stock performance analysis of the two companies is presented.

26951 ■ *"Best Value Stocks"* in *Canadian Business (Vol. 81, Summer 2008, No. 9, pp. 63)*
Pub: Rogers Media Ltd.
Ed: Calvin Leung. **Description:** Table showing the one-year performance of bargain or best-value stocks is presented. These stocks are undervalued compared to their North American peers, but it is projected that their five-year average return on equity is greater.

26952 ■ *"Best Value Stocks"* in *Canadian Business (Vol. 82, Summer 2009, No. 8, pp. 30)*
Pub: Rogers Media
Ed: Calvin Leung. **Description:** Canadian companies that are believed to have the best value stocks are suggested. Suggestions include publishing firm Glacier Media, which has reported a four-fold growth in sales in the last three years. While publishers like Glacier Media face challenges such as declining circulation, the firm's industry diversification is expected to help it weather the economic downturn.

26953 ■ *"The Best and Worst Economic Times"* in *Agency Sales Magazine (Vol. 39, December 2009, No. 11, pp. 22)*
Pub: MANA
Ed: Mark Young. **Description:** U.S. gross domestic product grew 3.5 percent and the stock market has improved but manufacturers are cutting commissions

or dropping sales representatives. Despite these challenges, it can a good time for salespeople because clients need them more than ever. Salesmen should find new ways to do business for their clients during this current challenging environment.

26954 ■ *"Bet on China"* in *Canadian Business (Vol. 80, November 5, 2007, No. 22, pp. 30)*
Pub: Rogers Media
Ed: Thomas Watson. **Description:** Former U.S. Federal Reserve Board head, Alan Greenspan, warns that contraction will happen in the Chinese market. However, the economic success of China does not seem to be at the point of ending, as the country remains the largest market for mobile telecommunications. Forecasts for Chinese trading and investments are provided.

26955 ■ *"Bet on the Subcontinent"* in *Canadian Business (Vol. 81, April 14, 2008, No. 6, pp. 27)*
Pub: Rogers Media
Ed: Calvin Leung. **Description:** Morgan Stanley Capital International India Index is down 28 percent for the first half of 2008 but this index rebounded 6 percent in 2002 then skyrocketed 65 percent in 2003. The economic reforms in the 1990's have created a growing middle class and households that can afford discretionary items will grow from eight million to 94 million by 2025. India's equity market could outperform developed markets if its economy grows at its current rate.

26956 ■ *"Better Made's Better Idea: Diversify Despite Rising Costs"* in *Crain's Detroit Business (Vol. 24, September 22, 2008, No. 38, pp. 18)*
Pub: Crain Communications Inc.
Ed: Nathan Skid. **Description:** Better Made Snack Foods Inc. is planning to expand its product lines and market reach as well as boost manufacturing capability during a time in which the company is being buffeted by rising commodity and fuel costs. The company feels that diversification is the key to maintain sales and growth.

26957 ■ *"Betting On Volatile Materials"* in *Barron's (Vol. 88, July 14, 2008, No. 28, pp. M11)*
Pub: Dow Jones & Co., Inc.
Ed: John Marshall. **Description:** Economic slowdowns in the U.S., Europe and China could cause sharp short-term declines in the materials sector. The S&P Materials sector is vulnerable to shifts in the flow of funds. Statistical data included.

26958 ■ *"Beware of Rotting Money"* in *Barron's (Vol. 89, July 13, 2009, No. 28, pp. 31)*
Pub: Dow Jones & Co., Inc.
Ed: Thomas G. Donlan. **Description:** Inflation can take hold of a country and do it great harm; it is caused by people, most particularly central bankers in charge of the world's reserve currency. Arrogant economists pushed the belief that the government can engineer the economy and it is argued that there is trouble ahead when the government tries to control the economy.

26959 ■ *Big-Box Swindle: The True Cost of Mega-Retailers and the Fight for America's Independent Businesses*
Pub: Beacon Press
Ed: Stacy Mitchell. **Released:** October 2007. **Price:** $15.00. **Description:** Examination of the economic, environmental, and social damage done by big-box retailers like Wal-Mart, Costco, and Home Depot. Labor policies of these retailers, particularly those enforced by Wal-Mart, are discussed at length.

26960 ■ *"Big Losses Mount for Hospitals"* in *Baltimore Business Journal (Vol. 27, October 23, 2009, No. 24, pp. 1)*
Pub: American City Business Journals
Ed: Scott Graham. **Description:** Reported losses by nine of the 22 hospitals in the Greater Baltimore area during fiscal 2009 have proven that the health care

industry is not immune to the recession. The rising costs of doing business and losses in the stock market have strongly affected the financial status of hospitals.

26961 ■ *The Big Squeeze: Tough Times for the American Workers*
Pub: Pantheon Books
Ed: Steven Greenhouse. **Released:** 2009. **Price:** $25.95. **Description:** Labor correspondent for the New York Times reports on the bleak condition of the current workplace environment, citing violations of child labor laws and forced slave labor conditions in third world countries and robber baron era occurring often here in America that are expanding the number of working poor.

26962 ■ *The Big Switch*
Pub: W. W. Norton & Company, Inc.
Ed: Nicholas Carr. **Released:** January 19, 2009. **Price:** $16.95 paperback. **Description:** Today companies are dismantling private computer systems and tapping into services provided via the Internet. This shift is remaking the computer industry, bringing competitors such as Google to the forefront ant threatening traditional companies like Microsoft and Dell. The book weaves together history, economics, and technology to explain why computing is changing and what it means for the future.

26963 ■ *"'Biggest Loser' Adds Bit of Muscle to Local Economy"* in *Crain's Detroit Business (Vol. 26, January 4, 2010, No. 1, pp. 1)*
Pub: Crain Communications Inc.
Ed: Chad Halcom. **Description:** NBC's weight-loss reality show, 'The Biggest Loser' has helped the local economy and generated a new crop of local startup businesses due to past contestants that were from the Detroit area.

26964 ■ *"Bill Kaneko"* in *Hawaii Business (Vol. 53, December 2007, No. 6, pp. 32)*
Pub: Hawaii Business Publishing
Ed: David K. Choo. **Description:** Hawaii Institute for Public Affairs chief executive officer and president Bill Kaneko believes that the Hawaiian economy is booming, however, he also asserts that the economy is too focused on tourism and real estate. Kaneko has also realized the that the will of the people is strong while he was helping with the Hawaiian 2050 Sustainability Plan. The difficulties of making a sustainable Hawaii are discussed.

26965 ■ *"Bill Lee's Auto Repair Business Chugs Along Despite Life's Obstacles"* in *Bradenton Herald (August 22, 2010)*
Pub: Bradenton Herald
Ed: Grace Gagliano. **Description:** Profile of Bill Lee's Professional Automotive Services located in Bradenton, Florida. The auto repair business was opened 26 years ago and provides repair for an assortment of fleet vehicles, including truck repair.

26966 ■ *"Biz Assesses 'Textgate' Fallout; Conventions, Smaller Deals Affected"* in *Crain's Detroit Business (Vol. 24, March 31, 2008)*
Pub: Crain Communications, Inc.
Ed: Tom Henderson. **Description:** Businesspeople who were trying to measure the amount of economic damage is likely to be caused due to Mayor Kwame Kilpatrick's indictment on eight charges and found that: automotive and other large global deals are less likely to be affected than location decisions by smaller companies and convention site decisions. Also being affected are negotiations in which Mexican startup companies were planning a partnership with the TechTown incubator to pursue opportunities in the auto sector; those plans are being put on hold while they look at other sites.

26967 ■ *"A Bleak Earnings View"* in *Barron's (Vol. 88, March 10, 2008, No. 10, pp. 15)*
Pub: Dow Jones & Company, Inc.
Description: Analysts expect consumer discretionary profits in the S&P 500 to drop 8.4 percent in the first quarter of 2008. A less confident consumer is expected to pull profits down, putting forecasts of earnings growth in the S&P 500 at risk. Statistical data included.

26968 ■ *"Block Plans Office Park Along K-10 Corridor"* in *The Business Journal-Serving Metropolitan Kansas City* (Vol. 27, October 3, 2008)
Pub: American City Business Journals, Inc.
Ed: Rob Roberts. **Description:** Kansas City, Missouri-based Block and Co. is planning to build four office buildings at the corner of College Boulevard and Ridgeview Road in Olathe. Features of the planned development are provided. Comments from executives are also presented.

26969 ■ *"Block Pulls Plug On Riverside Deal"* in *The Business Journal-Serving Metropolitan Kansas City* (Vol. 27, October 10, 2008, No. 4)
Pub: American City Business Journals, Inc.
Ed: Rob Roberts. **Description:** Real estate developer Ken Block has backed out from a $300 million Riverside industrial project. Block says he has already invested $1 million of his own money into the deal. Details regarding the project are given.

26970 ■ *"The Board Shorts Executive"* in *Hawaii Business* (Vol. 53, January 2008, No. 7, pp. 33)
Pub: Hawaii Business Publishing
Ed: Mike Markrich. **Description:** Vans Triple Crown of Surfing executive director Randy Rarick believes that the surfing business requires knowledge of the sport and integity to the game's lifestyle and spirit. His organization manages surfing events, and has generated jobs for the locals. Plans for Vans Triple Crown are supplied.

26971 ■ *"Boat Sales Sputter as Cash-Strapped Buyers Drift Away"* in *Puget Sound Business Journal* (Vol. 29, August 15, 2008, No. 17, pp. 1)
Pub: American City Business Journals
Ed: Greg Lamm. **Description:** Boat sales in Washington fell by 44 percent in the second quarter of 2008. The decline is attributed to the soft economy, which has given customers second thoughts on purchasing recreational water vehicles.

26972 ■ *"Bonds v. Stocks: Who's Right About Recession?"* in *Barron's* (Vol 90, August 23, 2010, No. 34, pp. M3)
Pub: Barron's Editorial & Corporate Headquarters
Ed: Kopin Tan. **Description:** The future of treasury securities and stocks should the U.S. enter or avoid a recession are discussed. The back to school business climate and BHP Billiton's bid for Potash Corporation of Saskatchewan are also discussed.

26973 ■ *"Book of Lists 2010"* in *Philadelphia Business Journal* (Vol. 28, December 25, 2009, No. 45, pp. 1)
Pub: American City Business Journals
Description: Rankings of companies and organizations within the banking, biotechnology, economic development, healthcare, hospitality, law and accounting, marketing and media, real estate, and technology industries in the Philadelphia, Pennsylvania area are presented. Rankings are based on sales, business size, and more.

26974 ■ *"Boosting Worried Customers' Confidence"* in *Gallup Management Journal* (November 8, 2011)
Pub: Gallup
Ed: Jessica Tyler, Patrick Whiston. **Description:** While customers fear a double-dip recession and US economic confidence is low, leading edge firms have found a timely and creative way to win customers: they are improving their wellbeing.

26975 ■ *"Borrow For Tomorrow"* in *Canadian Business* (Vol. 80, October 8, 2007, No. 20, pp. 193)
Pub: Rogers Media
Ed: David Wolf. **Description:** The possibility of running deficits in order to finance infrastructures in Canada is discussed. Statistics show that the country's net government debt is below 25 percent of GDP as of 2007, and that the government is spending less on public infrastructure. Based on these figures, it is expected that an increase in government debt could help in making infrastructure investments.

26976 ■ *"Bottom-Fishing and Speed-Dating in India"* in *Barron's* (Vol. 88, March 24, 2008, No. 12, pp. M12)
Pub: Dow Jones & Company, Inc.
Ed: Elliot Wilson. **Description:** Indian stocks have fallen hard in 2008, with Mumbai's Sensex 30 down 30 percent from its January 2008 peak of 21,000 to 14,995 in March. The India Private Equity Fair 2008 attracted 140 of the world's largest private equity firms and about 24 of India's fastest-growing corporations. Statistical data included.

26977 ■ *"Bottom's Up"* in *Barron's* (Vol. 88, July 14, 2008, No. 28, pp. 25)
Pub: Dow Jones & Co., Inc.
Ed: Jonathan R. Laing. **Description:** Economist Chip Case believes that home prices are nearing a bottom based on his analysis of the history of the housing market; surprisingly, in the past the housing market has rebounded after a quarter from a massive housing start drop. The drop in early stage delinquencies is another sign of the housing market's recovery.

26978 ■ *"Bracing for a Bear of a Week"* in *Barron's* (Vol. 88, March 17, 2008, No. 11, pp. 24)
Pub: Dow Jones & Company, Inc.
Ed: Jacqueline Doherty. **Description:** JPMorgan Chase and the Federal Reserve Bank of New York's opening of a line of credit to Bear Stearns cut the stock price of Bear Stearns by 47 percent to 30 followed by speculation of an imminent sale. JP Morgan may be the only potential buyer for the firm and some investors say Bears could be sold at $20 to $30. Bears prime assets include its enormous asset base worth $395 billion.

26979 ■ *"Bracing for More Layoffs"* in *Sacramento Business Journal* (Vol. 28, September 30, 2011, No. 31, pp. 1)
Pub: Sacramento Business Journal
Ed: Melanie Turner. **Description:** Sacramento, California workers are preparing for a fresh wave of layoffs. The weak economy is seen to drive the development.

26980 ■ *"Brad Wall"* in *Canadian Business* (Vol. 82, April 27, 2009, No. 7, pp. 9)
Pub: Rogers Media
Ed: Joe Castaldo. **Description:** Saskatchewan Premier Brad Wall believes that the mood in the province is positive, as its economy is one of the few that is expected to post growth in 2009. Wall actively promotes the province in job fairs, offering $20,000 in tuition for recent college and university graduates that relocate in the province for seven years. Wall's views on the province's economy and challenges are presented.

26981 ■ *"Brazil's New King of Food"* in *Barron's* (Vol. 89, July 13, 2009, No. 28, pp. 28)
Pub: Dow Jones & Co., Inc.
Ed: Kenneth Rapoza. **Description:** Perdigao and Sadia's merger has resulted in the creation of Brasil Foods and the shares of Brasil Foods provides a play on both Brazil's newly energized consumer economy and its role as a major commodities exporter. Brasil Foods shares could climb as much as 36 percent.

26982 ■ *"Breadwinner Tries on Designer Jeans"* in *Houston Business Journal* (Vol. 40, December 18, 2009, No. 32, pp. 1)
Pub: American City Business Journals
Ed: Allison Wollam. **Description:** Chuck Cain, the franchisee who introduced Panera Bread to Houston, Texas has partnered with tax accountant Jim Jacobsen to introduce custom-make Tattu Jeans. As more Tattu Jeans outlets are being planned, Cain is using entrepreneurial lessons learned from Panera Bread in the new venture. Both Panera Bread and Tattu Jeans were opened by Cain during economic downturns.

26983 ■ *"Briarcliff Office Building Fills Up Fast"* in *The Business Journal-Serving Metropolitan Kansas City* (Vol. 26, Sept. 5,

2008, pp. 1)
Pub: American City Business Journals, Inc.
Ed: Rob Roberts. **Description:** Prior to its opening the Hilltop Office Building in Kansas City Missouri has attained 80 percent occupancy. FCStone Group Inc.'s plan to move to the building has boosted the facility's occupancy. Description and dimensions of the office building are also provided.

26984 ■ *"Bridging the Ingenuity Gap"* in *Canadian Business* (Vol. 79, November 6, 2006, No. 22, pp. 12)
Pub: Rogers Media
Ed: Rachel Pulfer. **Description:** The views of Patrick Whitney, director of Illinois Institute of Technology's Institute of design, on globalization and business design methods are presented.

26985 ■ *"BRIEF: Montana Street Pawn Shop Closing Doors"* in *Montana Standard* (November 6, 2010)
Pub: Montana Standard
Ed: John Grant Emeigh. **Description:** First National Pawn located in Butte, Montana will close its doors after losing its lease. Co-owner Pat Evenson reported the lease situation coupled with the economy prompted the decision to close.

26986 ■ *"Bringing Big Guns"* in *Business Courier* (Vol. 24, January 18, 2008, No. 41, pp. 1)
Pub: American City Business Journals, Inc.
Ed: Lucy May. **Description:** Chief executive officer of Nidland Co. John Hayden was assigend as Cincinnati USA Partnership chairman. Hayden will bring his expertise to help the partnership drive economic development in the Greater Cincinnati area. Details of the parntership's plans are suplied.

26987 ■ *"Bryan Berg"* in *Hawaii Business* (Vol. 53, March 2008, No. 9, pp. 28)
Pub: Hawaii Business Publishing
Ed: David K. Choo. **Description:** Bryan Berg, senior vice president at Target Corp.'s Region 1, shares his thoughts about entering the Hawaiian market and Target representatives bringing malasadas when visiting a business in the state. Berg finds the state's aloha spirit interesting and feels that it is important to be respectful of the Hawaiian culture and traditions in doing their business there.

26988 ■ *"Budget Cuts Afflict Health Department"* in *Business Courier* (Vol. 24, November 23, 2008, No. 32, pp. 1)
Pub: American City Business Journals, Inc.
Ed: Lucy May; James Ritchie. **Description:** Cincinnati must cut $25 million to balance its budget for 2008. As a result, the city will be cutting $704,000 from its Health Department's budget of $42 million, and will eliminate 31.6 positions by the end of 2007.

26989 ■ *"Builder's Bankruptcy Fans Fears"* in *Crain's Cleveland Business* (Vol. 28, October 22, 2007, No. 42, pp. 1)
Pub: Crain Communications, Inc.
Ed: Stan Bullard. **Description:** Whitlatch & Co., Northeast Ohio's largest builder by unit volume in the early 1990s, has filed for Chapter 11 bankruptcy. This is causing builders and others in the real estate industry to wonder how long and severe the housing slump will be and which companies will survive.

26990 ■ *"Building Portfolios for a World of 2.5 Percent Gains"* in *Barron's* (Vol. 88, July 7, 2008, No. 27, pp. L9)
Pub: Dow Jones & Co., Inc.
Ed: Karen Hube. **Description:** Interview with Harold Evenski whom is a financial planner running a fee-only planning practice; he continues to caution investors against pursuing short-term gains and focusing on long-term trends. He advises investors against investing in commodity and real estate stocks and is concerned about the possible effects of high inflation.

26991 ■ *"Bumpy Ride Ahead for United"* in *Crain's Chicago Business* (Vol. 31, May 5, 2008, No. 18, pp. 3)
Pub: Crain Communications, Inc.
Ed: John Pletz. **Description:** Continental Airlines Inc. walked away from merger talks with United Airlines last week. Now the choices facing United boil

down to going it alone in an increasingly stormy airline business or a less-desirable merger with US Airways Group Inc. Analysts expect United to lose $977 million this year due, mainly, to the high price of fuel.

26992 ■ *"Business Diary" in Crain's Detroit Business (Vol. 24, October 6, 2008, No. 40, pp. 23)*
Pub: Crain Communications, Inc.
Description: Detailed listing of acquisitions, expansions, new products, new services, business contracts and startups from the Detroit area is provided.

26993 ■ *"Business Diary" in Crain's Detroit Business (Vol. 26, January 11, 2010, No. 2, pp. 16)*
Pub: Crain Communications Inc.
Description: Listing of local businesses involved in acquisitions, contracts, expansions, new products and services as well as startups in the region.

26994 ■ *"Business Must Stand Up And Be Counted" in Crain's Detroit Business (Vol. 24, October 6, 2008, No. 40, pp. 6)*
Pub: Crain Communications, Inc.
Description: Discusses the challenges that the new mayor of Detroit faces concerning business, the state of the economy and the exceptionally tight budget the city is running on, which includes a lot of red ink. It is very likely that the city is going to see tax revenues fall substantially in the next few months and business leaders may find it in their favor to lend their support to the new mayor as well as provide him with the executive talent necessary to overcome some of these crucial issues.

26995 ■ *"Business Plan Refines Focus" in Business Journal Portland (Vol. 27, December 10, 2010, No. 41, pp. 1)*
Pub: Portland Business Journal
Ed: Wendy Culverwell. **Description:** Organizers of the Oregon Business Plan's Leadership Summit 2010 seek the opinions of nearly 1,000 business, education, political, and civic leaders in an effort to address how to rehabilitate Oregon's economy. The opinion-seeking actions recognize the organizers' belief that the economic fate of the state depends on rural Oregon.

26996 ■ *"Business Stands Firm for Reform" in Crain's Detroit Business (Vol. 26, January 4, 2010, No. 1, pp. 3)*
Pub: Crain Communications, Inc.
Ed: Amy Lane. **Description:** As Michigan faces a new year of budgetary problems, many business groups are preparing to hold firm against tax increases and instead push for enacting spending reforms.

26997 ■ *"Business Through Hollywood's Lens" in Harvard Business Review (Vol. 88, October 2010, No. 10, pp. 146)*
Pub: Harvard Business School Publishing
Ed: Batia Wiesnefeld, Gino Cattani. **Description:** The authors contend that businesses are likely to be portrayed as villains in movies because corruption has higher entertainment draw. However, movies also depict popular opinion, which encourages businesses to be accountable and to help build communities.

26998 ■ *"The Business Value of Social Networks" in Agency Sales Magazine (Vol. 39, July 2009, No. 7, pp. 44)*
Pub: MANA
Ed: Daniel Burrus. **Description:** Personal and business uses of several Web 2.0 tools for salespeople are discussed. Leading questions which will guide salespeople in finding out if one particular tool will benefit them are presented.

26999 ■ *"Business Warns Against Tax Hike" in Puget Sound Business Journal (Vol. 29, November 14, 2008, No. 30, pp. 1)*
Pub: American City Business Journals
Ed: Deirdre Gregg. **Description:** Washington-based businesses have warned state lawmakers against imposing new taxes because of the economic decline. They suggest the government should focus on spending cuts to address the $3 billion shortfall.

27000 ■ *"Businesses Band Together in Destin Bartering to Keep Heads Above Water" in Destin Log (July 24, 2010)*
Pub: The Destin Log
Ed: Andrew Metz. **Description:** Profile of The Barter Company located in Destin, Florida, whose owner believes that bartering for goods and services can help small companies in a down economy.

27001 ■ *"Businesses Still on the Mend" in Boston Business Journal (Vol. 29, September 9, 2011, No. 18, pp. 1)*
Pub: American City Business Journals Inc.
Ed: Scott Dance. **Description:** The 9/11 terrorist attacks have caused many companies in the US to dramatically shift course in response to changes in the economy. The concern that the cost of being unprepared for future disasters could be larger has remained among many companies.

27002 ■ *"A Busy Little Parasite" in Hawaii Business (Vol. 53, March 2008, No. 9, pp. 1)*
Pub: Hawaii Business Publishing
Ed: Jason Ubay. **Description:** Bee mites were first sighted in Hawaii by Michael Kliks on April 6, 2007 and have since been a cause of concern for the beekeeping industry and pollinated-dependent crop industry. Hawaii's agricultural industry estimates that the losses due to bee mites may amount to between $42 million and $62 million. Steps taken to address the issue are discussed.

27003 ■ *"But Who's Counting.." in Canadian Business (Vol. 79, Winter 2006, No. 24, pp. 27)*
Pub: Rogers Media
Ed: David Wolf. **Description:** The analysis of the debt management policies of the Canadian government is presented. The plans of the Canadian government to repay all of its debts by the year 2020 are discussed.

27004 ■ *"Buy Now?" in Hawaii Business (Vol. 53, March 2008, No. 9, pp. 32)*
Pub: Hawaii Business Publishing
Ed: David K. Choo. **Description:** Discusses the Honolulu Board of REALTORS which said that the last two months of 2007 saw double-digit housing sales drop, with December figures showing 30.6 percent and 22.9 percent decline in sales of single-family homes and condominiums, respectively. Forecasts on Hawaii's real estate market for 2008 are discussed.

27005 ■ *"Calendar" in Crain's Detroit Business (Vol. 24, March 10, 2008, No. 10, pp. 21)*
Pub: Crain Communications, Inc.
Description: Listing of events in the Detroit area include conferences addressing entrepreneurialism, economic development, and women business ownership.

27006 ■ *"Calendar" in Crain's Detroit Business (Vol. 24, March 17, 2008, No. 11, pp. 20)*
Pub: Crain Communications, Inc.
Description: Listing of events in the Detroit area include conferences addressing entrepreneurialism, economic development, and women business ownership.

27007 ■ *"Calendar" in Crain's Detroit Business (Vol. 24, March 24, 2008, No. 12, pp. 25)*
Pub: Crain Communications, Inc.
Description: Listing of events in the Detroit area include conferences addressing entrepreneurialism, economic development, and women business ownership.

27008 ■ *"Calendar" in Crain's Detroit Business (Vol. 24, March 31, 2008, No. 13, pp. 1)*
Pub: Crain Communications, Inc.
Description: Listing of events in the Detroit area include conferences addressing entrepreneurialism, economic development, and minority business ownership.

27009 ■ *"Calendar" in Crain's Detroit Business (Vol. 24, April 7, 2008, No. 14, pp. 27)*
Pub: Crain Communications, Inc.
Description: Listing of events in the Detroit area include conferences addressing entrepreneurialism, economic development, and minority business ownership.

27010 ■ *"Calendar" in Crain's Detroit Business (Vol. 24, April 14, 2008, No. 15, pp. 25)*
Pub: Crain Communications Inc.
Description: Listing of events in the Detroit area include conferences addressing entrepreneurialism, economic development, and ways in which to develop environmentally friendly buildings.

27011 ■ *"Calendar" in Crain's Detroit Business (Vol. 24, September 22, 2008, No. 38, pp. 17)*
Pub: Crain Communications Inc.
Description: Listing of events in the Detroit area include conferences addressing entrepreneurialism, economic development, and women business ownership.

27012 ■ *"Calendar" in Crain's Detroit Business (Vol. 24, October 6, 2008, No. 40, pp. 22)*
Pub: Crain Communications, Inc.
Description: Listing of events in the Detroit area include conferences addressing entrepreneurialism, economic development, manufacturing, marketing, the housing crisis and women business ownership.

27013 ■ *"Calendar" in Crain's Detroit Business (Vol. 26, January 11, 2010, No. 2, pp. 16)*
Pub: Crain Communications Inc.
Description: Listing of events includes seminars sponsored by the Detroit Economic Club as well as conferences dealing with globalization and graphic design.

27014 ■ *"Calendar" in Crain's Detroit Business (Vol. 26, January 18, 2010, No. 3, pp. 16)*
Pub: Crain Communications Inc.
Description: Listing of events includes seminars sponsored by the Detroit Economic Club as well as conferences dealing with globalization and marketing.

27015 ■ *"Calgary East" in Canadian Business (Vol. 80, January 15, 2007, No. 2, pp. 13)*
Pub: Rogers Media
Ed: Charles Mandel. **Description:** The positive impact on the economy of Saint John city of New Brunswick province of Canada, due to the establishment of oil refineries by Irving Oil Ltd. in the area, is discussed.

27016 ■ *"Call of Prepaid Heard by More" in Chicago Tribune (November 26, 2008)*
Pub: McClatchy-Tribune Information Services
Ed: Wailin Wong. **Description:** Due to the economic downturn, more consumers are switching to no-contract, prepaid cell phone service. Customers find that the cost savings, flexibility and lack of contract are appealing in such uncertain times.

27017 ■ *"Calling All Recruiters: Agent HR Puts Staffing Agents In Charge" in Black Enterprise (Vol. 38, December 2007, No. 5, pp. 72)*
Pub: Earl G. Graves Publishing Co. Inc.
Ed: Chana Garcia. **Description:** Recruiting and staffing agencies are seeing a drop in services due to slow economic growth. AgentHR partners with full-service recruiters who have three to five year's experience-specialists soliciting their own clients, provide staffing services, and manage their own accounts, thus combining the roles of recruiter and salesperson.

27018 ■ *"Calling An Audible" in The Business Journal-Milwaukee (Vol. 25, August 1, 2008, No. 45, pp. A1)*
Pub: American City Business Journals, Inc.
Ed: David Dedge. **Description:** Tough economic conditions are forcing entertainment businesses in Milwaukee, Wisconsin, to try new business strategies to keep attracting customers. These strategies include keeping prices steady despite increasing costs and new sales promotions.

27019 ■ *"Can America Invent Its Way Back?" in Business Week (September 22, 2008, No. 4100, pp. 52)*
Pub: McGraw-Hill Companies, Inc.
Description: Business leaders as well as economists agree that innovative new products, services and ways of doing business may be the only way in which America can survive the downward spiral of the economy; innovation economics may be the answer and may even provide enough growth to enable Americans to prosper in the years to come.

27020 ■ *"Can Avenue be Fashionable Again? Livernois Merchants, City Want Revival" in Crain's Detroit Business (March 10, 2008)*
Pub: Crain Communications, Inc.
Ed: Nancy Kaffer. **Description:** Once a busy retail district, the Avenue of Fashion, a Livernois Avenue strip between Six Mile and Eight Mile roads, is facing a community business effort being backed by city support whose aim is to restore the area to its former glory.

27021 ■ *"Can the State Afford a Big Time College Football Program?" in Hawaii Business (Vol. 53, March 2008, No. 9, pp. 26)*
Pub: Hawaii Business Publishing
Description: Jill Nunokawa, civil rights at University of Hawaii, believes that athletics are extra-curricular and that the state needs to focus on priorities. State representative K. Mark Takai says that a football program brings pride and inspiration and can generate revenue and provide economic opportunities.

27022 ■ *"Canada Nears European Trade Treaty" in Globe & Mail (February 5, 2007, pp. B1)*
Pub: CTVglobemedia Publishing Inc.
Ed: Steven Chase. **Description:** The probable establishment of a treaty by Canada with Norway, Switzerland and Iceland for free-trade is discussed. The treaty will allow an annual business of $11 billion to take place in Canada.

27023 ■ *"Canada, Not China, Is Partner In Our Economic Prosperity" in Crain's Chicago Business (Vol. 31, April 14, 2008, No. 15, pp. 14)*
Pub: Crain Communications, Inc.
Ed: Paul O'Connor. **Description:** In 2005 more than $500 billion in two-way trade crossed the friendly border between the Great Lakes states and Canadian provinces and for decades Canada is every Great Lakes State's number one and growing export market.

27024 ■ *"Canada Tomorrow" in Canadian Business (Vol. 80, October 8, 2007, No. 20, pp. 14)*
Pub: Rogers Media
Ed: Donald J. Johnston. **Description:** An assessment of Canada's future in terms of its educational, social, and economic environment is presented. Concerns regarding the country's educational system such as the declining interest in science and technology and the possible lack of teachers in the future are discussed. In terms of its social and economic aspects, the need to support entrepreneurs and other qualified people is explained.

27025 ■ *"Canada Tops Again in G7: Study" in Globe & Mail (March 22, 2006, pp. B8)*
Pub: CTVglobemedia Publishing Inc.
Ed: Roma Luciw. **Description:** Canada is still the cheapest place to do business among G7 countries, even though the rising dollar has eroded some of its advantages over the United States. The survey is detailed.

27026 ■ *"Canada's Uber-Wealthy" in Canadian Business (Vol. 80, Winter 2007, No. 24, pp. 16)*
Pub: Rogers Media
Description: Statistics of the concentration of millionaire households around the world and the wealth of major cities in Canada are presented. The data reveals that Montreal has the highest concentration of billionaires and that the U.S. has the highest concentration of millionaire households.

27027 ■ *"Canadian Research Generates Innovation and Prosperity" in Canadian Business (Vol. 81, October 27, 2008, No. 18, pp. 87)*
Pub: Rogers Media Ltd.
Description: Universities play a key role in helping Canadians achieve prosperity, competitiveness, and quality of life by conducting more than a third of Canada's research. Research in universities help train graduates to apply sophisticated knowledge to real problems.

27028 ■ *"Canadian Vehicle Sales Accelerate in April, but U.S. Goes on Bumpy Ride" in Globe & Mail (May 2, 2007, pp. B7)*
Pub: CTVglobemedia Publishing Inc.
Ed: Greg Keenan. **Description:** The increase in Canadian vehicle sales to 169,280 in April 2007, but decline in their sales in the United States due to slump in housing sector are discussed.

27029 ■ *"Candidates Differ On State's Green Streak" in Business Journal Portland (Vol. 27, October 22, 2010, No. 34, pp. 1)*
Pub: Portland Business Journal
Ed: Andy Giegerich. **Description:** The views of Oregon gubernatorial candidates Chris Dudley and John Kitzhaber on the state's economy and on environmental policies are presented. Both Dudley, who is a Republican, and his Democratic challenger believe that biomass could help drive the state's economy. Both candidates also pledged changes in Oregon's business energy tax credit (BETC) program.

27030 ■ *"Candidates Won't Bash Fed; Rate Cuts Bash Savers" in Barron's (Vol. 88, March 24, 2008, No. 12, pp. 31)*
Pub: Dow Jones & Company, Inc.
Ed: Jim McTague. **Description:** Candidates in the 2008 US presidential election, like the current administration, do not and will not bash the Federal Reserve. The Federal Reserve's aggressive interest rate cuts hurt the incomes of people depending on their savings accounts.

27031 ■ *"Capital Ideas: Regions to Lansing: Focus on Taxes, Reform, Keeping Talent" in Crain's Detroit Business (Vol. 24, October 6, 2008)*
Pub: Crain Communications, Inc.
Ed: Amy Lane. **Description:** Michigan must make bold and dramatic changes in public policy regarding business legislation. The tax structure, unemployment issues and attracting and retaining talent are among the issues the state must confront, especially in this tough economic climate.

27032 ■ *"The Carbon Equation" in Canadian Business (Vol. 81, October 27, 2008, No. 18, pp. 109)*
Pub: Rogers Media Ltd.
Ed: Jack M. Mintz. **Description:** Economic and environmental impacts of the likely rejection of a carbon tax for the cap-and-trade system in Canada are discussed. The Conservative Party is expected tow in the 2008 elections and would likely pursue the cap-and-trade system.

27033 ■ *"The Case of the Deflated IPO" in Boston Business Journal (Vol. 29, June 24, 2011, No. 7, pp. 1)*
Pub: American City Business Journals Inc.
Ed: Scott Dance. **Description:** IPO market is on the rebound from the recession but for some companies in Maryland, the time is not yet ripe to go public. One of the companies that chooses to wait for better timing is SafeNet Inc. and it is eyeing some possible acquisitions while doing so.

27034 ■ *"Cash for Appliances Targets HVAC Products, Water Heaters" in Contractor (Vol. 56, October 2009, No. 10, pp. 1)*
Pub: Penton Media, Inc.
Ed: Candace Roulo. **Description:** States and territories would need to submit a full application that specifies their implementation plans if they are interested in joining the Cash for Appliances program funded by the American Recovery and Reinvestment Act. The Department of Energy urges states to focus on heating and cooling equipment, appliances and water heaters since these offer the greatest energy savings potential.

27035 ■ *"Cashing In: Gleaning an Education from Our Economic State" in Agency Sales Magazine (Vol. 39, August 2009, No. 8, pp. 22)*
Pub: MANA
Ed: John Graham. **Description:** Businesses have learned that cutting price can kill business and being tough is normal. The recession has also taught that getting the right vision and gaining the confidence and trust of consumers are important.

27036 ■ *"Casinos See College as Job Jackpot" in The Business Journal-Serving Metropolitan Kansas City (Vol. 26, August 1, 2008, No. 47)*
Pub: American City Business Journals, Inc.
Ed: Suzanna Stagemeyer. **Description:** Wyandotte County casino managers revealed plans to develop partnerships with Kansas City Kansas Community College. The planned partnership is expected to include curriculum development and degree programs that would help train employees for the planned casinos. Other views and information on the project are presented.

27037 ■ *The Catalyst Code: The Strategies Behind the World's Most Dynamic Companies*
Pub: Harvard Business School Press
Ed: David S. Evans; Richard Schmalensee. **Released:** May 9, 2007. **Price:** $29.95. **Description:** Economic catalysts businesses can bring consumers and merchants together in order to survive in an economy where markets, consumers and technology are always changing.

27038 ■ *"Catching Creatives; Detroit Group Gets Grant to Attract 1,000 Design Pros" in Crain's Detroit Business (March 24, 2008)*
Pub: Crain Communications, Inc.
Ed: Sherri Begin. **Description:** Design Detroit was given a $200,000 planning grant by the Knight Foundation, an organization that strives to back initiatives that leverage talent and resources in each of the 26 U.S. cities it funds, to inspire strategies to attract up to 1,000 creative professionals to live in Detroit.

27039 ■ *"CBC Chief: Future is Now" in Business Courier (Vol. 27, August 13, 2010, No. 15, pp. 1)*
Pub: Business Courier
Ed: Lucy May. **Description:** Tom Williams, chairman of the Cincinnati Business Committee (CBC), maintains that politicians and business leaders must cooperate to ensure the competitiveness of the city for the 21st Century. Under Williams' leadership, the CBC has put emphasis on initiatives related to government efficiency, economic development, and public education. Williams' views on a proposed inland port are given.

27040 ■ *"CBC and Chrysler Strike Deal" in Black Enterprise (Vol. 37, December 2006, No. 5, pp. 36)*
Pub: Earl G. Graves Publishing Co. Inc.
Ed: Kiara Ashanti. **Description:** Congressional Black Foundation and Chrysler Financial have partnered to provide financial education to students at historically black colleges and universities. The prime objective of the program is to reduce the number of college students that graduate with poor credit scores and high debt.

27041 ■ *"Celebrate Success. Embrace Innovation"* in *Black Enterprise (Vol. 37, February 2007, No. 7, pp. 145)*
Pub: Earl G. Graves Publishing Co. Inc.
Description: 2007 Women of Power Summit provides networking opportunities, empowerment sessions, and nightly entertainment. More than 500 executive women of color are expected to attend this inspiring summit in Phoenix, February 7-10.

27042 ■ *"CEO Forecast"* in *Hispanic Business (January-February 2009, pp. 34, 36)*
Pub: Hispanic Business
Ed: Jessica Haro, Richard Kaplan. **Description:** As economic uncertainty fogs the future, executives turn to government contracts in order to boost business. Revenue sources, health care challenges, environmental consulting and remediation services, as well as technological strides are discussed.

27043 ■ *"C'est Bon"* in *Canadian Business (Vol. 79, September 25, 2006, No. 19, pp. 39)*
Pub: Rogers Media
Ed: Benoit Aubin. **Description:** Economic development of Quebec City are evaluated on the eve of its formation anniversary.

27044 ■ *"Challenges, Responses and Available Resources"* in *Journal of Small Business and Entrepreneurship (Vol. 23, Winter 2010, No. 1)*
Pub: Canadian Council for Small Business and Entrepreneurship
Ed: Lynne Siemens. **Description:** Rural communities and their residents are exploring the potential of small business and entrepreneurship to address the economic changes they are facing. While these rural areas present many opportunities, business people in these areas face challenges which they must navigate to operate successfully.

27045 ■ *"Change Is in the Air"* in *Agency Sales Magazine (Vol. 39, August 2009, No. 8, pp. 30)*
Pub: MANA
Ed: Jack Foster. **Description:** Highlights of the Power-Motion Technology Representatives Association (PTRA) 37th Annual Conference, which projected an economic upturn, are presented. Allan Beaulieu of the Institute for Trend Research gave the positive news while Manufacturer's Agents National Association (MANA) president Brain Shirley emphasized the need to take advantage of a turnaround.

27046 ■ *"Channelside On the Blocks"* in *The Business Journal-Serving Greater Tampa Bay (Vol. 28, August 29, 2008, No. 36, pp. 1)*
Pub: American City Business Journals, Inc.
Ed: Michael Hinman. **Description:** In a bankruptcy auction for The Place, one of the more visible condominium projects at Channelside, the lowest bid is just below $73 a square foot. KeyBank National Association, the Key Developers Group LLC's lender, leads the auction planned for October 15, 2008. The reason behind the low minimum bid required to participate in the said action is discussed.

27047 ■ *"Chasing Credit"* in *Canadian Business (Vol. 81, November 10, 2008, No. 19, pp. 59)*
Pub: Rogers Media Ltd.
Ed: Joe Castaldo. **Description:** Small and medium sized companies are dealing with tightening credit because they appear riskier than usual. Some of these businesses are turning to private investors, but this is not easy since many have invested everything in the stock market. The sector is expected to weaken with the broader Canadian market in the next six months from October 2008.

27048 ■ *"Cheap Deposits Fuel Bank Profits"* in *Boston Business Journal (Vol. 31, July 29, 2011, No. 27, pp. 1)*
Pub: Boston Business Journal
Ed: Tim MacLaughlin. **Description:** Massachusetts-are banks increased profits primarily due to inexpensive deposits. The cheaper deposits have provided profit stability and fuel loan growth in an environment of historically low interest rates and uncertain economic recovery. Details of the banks' move to shed the more expensive certificates of deposit in favor of money market accounts are discussed.

27049 ■ *"Cheap Thrills: Where to Look When You're Craving a Low-Price Wine"* in *Chicago Tribune (January 12, 2009)*
Pub: McClatchy-Tribune Information Services
Ed: Bill Daley. **Description:** Wines priced $15 and above are being hit the hardest by the economic downturn while cheaper wines, specifically those priced between $3 and $6, are seeing a growth in sales.

27050 ■ *"The China Connection"* in *Crain's Chicago Business (Vol. 31, March 24, 2008, No. 12, pp. 26)*
Pub: Crain Communications, Inc.
Ed: Samantha Stainburn. **Description:** Interview with Ben Munoz who studied abroad in Beijing, China for three months to study international economics, e-commerce and global leadership.

27051 ■ *"China Pegs Surplus at $101.9 Billion"* in *Globe & Mail (January 12, 2006, pp. B1)*
Pub: CTVglobemedia Publishing Inc.
Ed: Barrie McKenna. **Description:** The reasons behind the trade surplus of $101.9 billion, in China, are presented.

27052 ■ *"China Trade Deficit Costs California Jobs"* in *Sacramento Business Journal (Vol. 25, August 8, 2008, No. 23, pp. 1)*
Pub: American City Business Journals, Inc.
Ed: Melanie Turner. **Description:** California topped the ranking of states with job losses because of the rising trade deficit with China, losing 325,800 jobs between 2001-2007. The U.S. has lost 2.3 million workers within the period. Other views and information on the job loses because of the trade deficit with China, are presented.

27053 ■ *"China's Dagong Show"* in *Canadian Business (Vol. 83, August 17, 2010, No. 13-14, pp. 15)*
Pub: Rogers Media Ltd.
Ed: Matthew McClearn. **Description:** Beijing, China-based Dagong Global Credit Rating has downgraded US credit ratings, as well as other developed countries such as Canada, while granting higher ratings to China, Russia and Brazil. However, there is a perceived disconnection between Dagong's ratings and its official pronouncements.

27054 ■ *Chinese Ethnic Business: Global and Local Perspectives*
Pub: Routledge
Ed: Eric Fong; Chiu Luk. **Released:** May 2009. **Price:** $39.95 paperback. **Description:** Globalization impacts on the development of Chinese businesses are analyzed, focusing on economic globalization of the United States, Australia, and Canada. Information is focused on economic globalization and Chinese community development, transnational linkages, local urban structures, homogenization and place attachment, as well as methodology such as ethnographic studies, historical analysis, geographic studies and statistical analysis.

27055 ■ *"City a Pawn in Airlines' Chess Game"* in *Business Courier (Vol. 24, January 18, 2008, No. 41, pp. 1)*
Pub: American City Business Journals, Inc.
Ed: Lisa Biank Fasig. **Description:** Delta Air Lines is under negotitaions with Northwest Airlines and UAL Corp. for a proposed merger. The deal will have a negative impact on Cincinnati as a hub regardless whether it goes to UAL or Northwest. The impacts of the planned merger on Cincinnati's labor market and airport traffic are discussed.

27056 ■ *"City Sets Yamhill Makeover"* in *The Business Journal-Portland (Vol. 25, July 4, 2008, No. 17, pp. 1)*
Pub: American City Business Journals, Inc.
Ed: Andy Giegerich. **Description:** City government is scheduled to redevelop Peterson's property on Yamhill Street in Portland. The redevelopment is seen as a way to better developing commercial properties in the area. Problems associated with the project, which include cost and developer selection, are also discussed.

27057 ■ *"City Slickers"* in *Canadian Business (Vol. 81, March 31, 2008, No. 5, pp. 36)*
Pub: Rogers Media
Ed: Joe Castaldo. **Description:** Richard Florida believes that the creative class drives the economy and the prosperity of countries depends on attracting and retaining these people. Florida has brought attention to developing livable and economically vibrant cities thanks in part to his promotional skills. However, he has also drawn critics who see his data on his theories as flimsy and inadequate.

27058 ■ *"Clean-Tech Focus Sparks Growth"* in *Philadelphia Business Journal (Vol. 28, January 15, 2010, No. 48, pp. 1)*
Pub: American City Business Journals
Ed: Peter Key. **Description:** Keystone Redevelopment Group and economic development organization Ben Franklin Technology Partners of Southeastern Pennsylvania have partnered in supporting the growth of new alternative energy and clean technology companies. Keystone has also been developing the Bridge Business Center.

27059 ■ *"Closed Minds and Open Skies"* in *Barron's (Vol. 88, March 10, 2008, No. 10, pp. 50)*
Pub: Dow Jones & Company, Inc.
Ed: Thomas Donlan. **Description:** American politicians have closed minds when it comes to fair trade. The American government must not interfere with the country's manufacturing industries or worry about outsourcing defense contracts to European aerospace company Airbus.

27060 ■ *"Clothier Delays Opening"* in *The Business Journal-Serving Metropolitan Kansas City (Vol. 27, November 14, 2008, No. 10, pp. 1)*
Pub: American City Business Journals, Inc.
Ed: Suzanna Stagemeyer. **Description:** Jos A. Bank Clothiers Inc. has delayed the opening of its store at the Kansas City Power and Light District in Missouri for the first quarter of 2009. The company is still waiting for other tenants to open shop in the district. Comments from officials concerning the retail sector are also presented.

27061 ■ *Code of Federal Regulations: Title 13: Business Credit and Assistance*
Pub: U.S. Government Printing Office
Ed: Department of Commerce Staff. **Released:** May 2007. **Price:** $55.00. **Description:** Title 13 covers regulations governing the activities of the Small Business Administration and the Department of Commerce. Book covers information on business credit, finance, and economic development.

27062 ■ *"Collection Industry Fights Stigma, Lagging Payments"* in *Crain's Cleveland Business (Vol. 30, June 8, 2009, No. 22, pp. 15)*
Pub: Crain Communications, Inc.
Ed: Joel Hammond. **Description:** John Murray, co-owner and president of JP Recovery Services Inc. in Rocky River, Ohio discusses the burden of the collection industry during a financial crisis like a recession. Statistical data included.

27063 ■ *A Colossal Failure of Common Sense: The Inside Story of the Collapse of Lehman Brothers*
Pub: Crown Business
Ed: Lawrence G. McDonald, Patrick Robinson. **Released:** 2009. **Price:** $27.00. **Description:** Former employee of Lehman Brothers details the failure of leadership that led to the demise of the company.

27064 ■ *"The Colt Effect"* in *Hawaii Business (Vol. 53, January 2008, No. 7, pp. 30)*
Pub: Hawaii Business Publishing
Ed: David K. Choo. **Description:** Participation at the Bowl Championship Games can help the University of Hawaii financially. Playing at a prominent sports event could provoke donations from alumni and

increase enrollment at the university. Examples of universities that earned generous income by becoming a part of prestigious sporting events are presented.

27065 ■ *"Coming: Cheaper Oil and a Stronger Buck" in Barron's (Vol. 88, March 24, 2008, No. 12, pp. 53)*
Pub: Dow Jones & Company, Inc.
Ed: Lawrence C. Strauss. **Description:** Carl C. Weinberg, the chief economist of High Frequency Economics, forecasts that Chinese economic growth will slow down and that oil prices will drop to $80 a barrel in 2008. He also believes that the US dollar will start rising the moment the Federal Reserve stops cutting interest rates.

27066 ■ *"Coming Soon: Bailouts of Fannie and Freddie" in Barron's (Vol. 88, July 14, 2008, No. 28, pp. 14)*
Pub: Dow Jones & Co., Inc.
Ed: Jonathan R. Laing. **Description:** Assurances from the government that Fannie Mae and Freddie Mac are adequately capitalized and able to carry on their duties as guarantors or owners of over $5 trillion of U.S. home mortgages are designed to keep both entities afloat until they attempt to raise $10 billion in new equity. The government would assume any losses in a bailout and owners of the banks' papers would profit as yields drop.

27067 ■ *"Commentary" in Small Business Economic Trends (September 2010, pp. 3)*
Pub: National Federation of Independent Business
Ed: William C. Dunkelberg, Holly Wade. **Description:** A commentary on the economic trends for small businesses in the U.S. is presented. An analysis of the unemployment rate and inflation is given. Economic growth is also expected to remain sub-par for some time, unless new policies are introduced.

27068 ■ *"Commentary. Economic Trends for Small Business" in Small Business Economic Trends (April 2008, pp. 3)*
Pub: National Federation of Independent Business
Ed: William C. Dunkelberg, Holly Wade. **Description:** Commentary on the economic trends for small businesses in the U.S. is presented. Analysis of recession possibilities is given. Reports indicate that the number of business owners citing inflation as their number one problem is at its highest point since 1982.

27069 ■ *"Commentary. On Federal Reserve's Cut of Interest Rates" in Small Business Economic Trends (January 2008, pp. 3)*
Pub: National Federation of Independent Business
Description: Federal Reserve cut interest rates and announced its economic outlook on September 18, 2007 to stimulate spending. The cut in interest rates, however, may not help in supporting consumer spending because savers may lose interest income. The expected economic impact of the interest rate cuts and the U.S. economic outlook are also discussed.

27070 ■ *"Commentary. Small Business Economic Trends" in Small Business Economic Trends (March 2008, pp. 3)*
Pub: National Federation of Independent Business
Ed: William C. Dunkelberg, Holly Wade. **Description:** Commentary on the economic trends for small businesses in the U.S. is presented. Analysis of the labor market and low interest rates is given. The effect of the Federal Reserve's policy announcement on small business owner optimism is also discussed.

27071 ■ *"Commentary. Small Business Economic Trends" in Small Business Economic Trends (February 2008, pp. 3)*
Pub: National Federation of Independent Business
Ed: William C. Dunkelberg, Holly Wade. **Description:** Commentary on the economic trends for small businesses in the U.S. is presented. Analysis of the U.S. Federal Reserve Board's efforts to prevent a recession is given. Reduction in business inventories is also discussed.

27072 ■ *"Commentary: US Economic Recovery and Policy" in Small Business Economic Trends (July 2010, pp. 3)*
Pub: National Federation of Independent Business
Description: U.S. Government is making economic recovery difficult, with one of the largest tax increases in history arriving in six months. Meanwhile, Congress is looking into taxing successful businesses, which will potentially hamper growth and real investment. Other insights on the government's role in the country's economic growth are presented.

27073 ■ *"Commitment Issues" in Workforce Management (Vol. 88, November 16, 2009, No. 12, pp. 20)*
Pub: Crain Communications Inc.
Ed: Ed Frauenheim. **Description:** Employee engagement refers to how committed workers are to their company and how much extra effort they are willing to put in on the job; firms could find that they are having a more difficult time coming out of the recession if they lack this important feature in workplace relations.

27074 ■ *Common Sense Business: Starting, Operating, and Growing Your Small Business-In Any Economy!*
Pub: HarperInformation
Ed: Steve Gottry. **Released:** July 2005. **Price:** $19.95 (US), $26.95 (Canadian). **Description:** Strategies for starting, operating and growing a small business in any economy. .

27075 ■ *"Companies Must Innovate, Regardless of Economy" in Crain's Detroit Business (Vol. 25, June 1, 2009, No. 22, pp. M007)*
Pub: Crain Communications Inc. - Detroit
Ed: Sherri Begin Welch. **Description:** Despite the economy, leaders of Michigan's successful companies stress that small businesses must innovate in order to grow.

27076 ■ *"Competition At Last?" in Canadian Business (Vol. 81, July 22, 2008, No. 12-13, pp. 7)*
Pub: Rogers Media Ltd.
Description: Competition Policy Review Panel's 'Compete to Win' report revealed that Canada is being 'hollowed-out' by foreign acquisitions. The panel investigated competition and foreign investment policies in Canada. Key information on the report, as well as views on the Investment Canada Act and the Competition Act, is presented.

27077 ■ *The Complete Idiot's Guide to Starting and Running a Thrift Store*
Pub: Alpha Publishing House
Ed: Ravel Buckley, Carol Costa. **Released:** January 5, 2010. **Price:** $18.95. **Description:** Thrift stores saw a 35 percent increase in sales during the falling economy in 2008. Despite the low startup costs, launching and running a thrift store is complicated. Two experts cover the entire process, including setting up a store on a nonprofit basis, choosing a location, funding, donations for saleable items, recruiting and managing staff, sorting items, pricing, and recycling donations.

27078 ■ *"Concierges Get New Marching Orders" in New York Times (Vol. 158, January 11, 2009, No. 54552, pp. 1)*
Pub: New York Times Co./Globe Newspaper Co.
Ed: Vivian S. Toy. **Description:** Effects of the slowing economy are felt by individuals working as concierges.

27079 ■ *"Condominium Sales Fall to a Seven-Year Low" in Crain's Chicago Business (Vol. 31, November 10, 2008, No. 45, pp. 2)*
Pub: Crain Communications, Inc.
Ed: Alby Gallun. **Description:** Downtown Chicago condominium market is experiencing the lowest number of sales in years due to the tightening of the mortgage lending market, the Wall Street crisis and the downturn in the economy. The supply of new condos is soaring, the result of the building boom of 2005 and 2006; many developers are finding it difficult to pay off construction loans and fear foreclosure

on their properties. Additional information and statistical data related to the downtown condominium market is provided.

27080 ■ *"Confidence High, But Lenders More Cautious" in Farmer's Weekly (March 28, 2008, No. 320)*
Pub: Reed Business Information
Contact: Jeff Greisch, President
Description: Discusses the effect of the global credit crunch on farmers as well as recent auctions which were timed to beat changes to capital gains tax.

27081 ■ *"Consumers Finding It Harder to Get and Keep Credit" in Chicago Tribune (January 10, 2009)*
Pub: McClatchy-Tribune Information Services
Ed: Susan Chandler. **Description:** Five tips to maintain a good credit rating in these economic times are outlined and discussed.

27082 ■ *"Contractors Fret Over Credit, People, Government" in Contractor (Vol. 57, February 2010, No. 2, pp. 7)*
Pub: Fenton Media, Inc.
Ed: Robert P. Mader. **Description:** Telephone interviews with 22 plumbing and HVAC contractors reveal that only two had sales increases for 2009 and that overall contractors were down anywhere from seven to 25 percent. In the repair/service market, the residential sector was holding its own but the commercial portion was lagging behind.

27083 ■ *"Conversation: Historian Geoffrey Jones On Why Knowledge Stays Put" in Harvard Business Review (Vol. 86, July-August 2008, No. 8)*
Pub: Harvard Business School Press
Ed: Gardiner Morse. **Description:** Geoffrey Jones, Harvard Business School's professor of business history, discusses factors that cause knowledge to concentrate in particular regions, rather than disperse, such as the location of wealth.

27084 ■ *"Conversation Starters for the Holiday" in Barron's (Vol. 89, July 6, 2009, No. 27, pp. 7)*
Pub: Dow Jones & Co., Inc.
Ed: Michael Santoli. **Description:** Investors are concerned that the US will experience high inflation due to low interest rates and improved money supply. US consumer spending has increased to 70 percent of gross domestic product, brought by health-care spending increases, while savings rates have risen to 6.9 percent.

27085 ■ *"A Conversation With Money Manager William Vellon" in Crain's Chicago Business (Vol. 31, November 17, 2008, No. 46, pp. 4)*
Pub: Crain Communications, Inc.
Ed: Mike Colias. **Description:** Interview with William Vellon, the executive vice-president of Kingsbury Capital Investment Advisors; Vellon discusses ways in which the government can help the financial sector, his client base and bargains that investors should consider.

27086 ■ *"A Conversation With Steven Hilfinger, Foley & Lardner L.L.P." in Crain's Detroit Business (Vol. 24, March 24, 2008, No. 12, pp. 1)*
Pub: Crain Communications, Inc.
Description: Interview with Steven Hilfinger who is a member of Foley & Lardner L.L.P.'s mergers and acquisitions practice and is co-chair of its automotive industry team. Hilfinger discusses such issues as the role a board of directors can play in the M&A process and the future of the auto market.

27087 ■ *"A Conversation with; Renea Butler, Real Estate One Inc." in Crain's Detroit Business (Vol. 25, June 8, 2009, No. 23, pp. 12)*
Pub: Crain Communications Inc. - Detroit
Ed: Ryan Beene. **Description:** Renea Butler, vice president of administration and human resources for Real Estate One Inc. in Southfield as well as vice

president for public relations for the Human Resource Association of Greater Detroit, talks about how the economy has affected human resource services.

27088 ■ "A Conversation With; Ron Gatner, Jones Lang LaSalle" in Crain's Detroit Business (Vol. 24, October 6, 2008, No. 40, pp. 9)
Pub: Crain Communications, Inc.
Description: Interview with Ron Gatner who is a corporate real estate adviser with the real estate company Jones Lang LaSalle as well as the company's executive vice president and part of the tenant advisory team; Gatner speaks about the impact that the Wall Street crisis is having on the commercial real estate market in Detroit.

27089 ■ "Cool Jobs in Hot Markets" in Canadian Business (Vol. 80, March 26, 2007, No. 7, pp. 66)
Pub: Rogers Media
Ed: Marlene Rego. **Description:** The growth in employment opportunities in various parts of the Canada is analyzed.

27090 ■ "Coping With a Shrinking Planet" in Agency Sales Magazine (Vol. 39, December 2009, No. 11, pp. 46)
Pub: MANA
Ed: Mark Young. **Description:** China and India are forcing big changes in the world and are posing a huge threat to U.S. manufacturers and their sales representatives. Reps may want to consider expanding into these territories. Helping sell American products out of the country presents an opportunity for economic expansion.

27091 ■ "Cornered by Credit; As $1 Billion in Loans Come Due, Will Landlords Find Funds?" in Crain's Detroit Business (October 6, 2008)
Pub: Crain Communications, Inc.
Ed: Daniel Duggan. **Description:** Conduit loans are used by many real estate investors and are normally issued in 7- to 10-year terms with balloon payments due at the end, requiring the full balance to be paid upon maturity. Many building owners may find their properties going into foreclosure as these loans mature next year since these loans cannot be extended like typical loans and the credit crisis along with falling property values is making it more difficult to secure new sources of funding. Possible solutions to this problem are also explored.

27092 ■ "Corporate Elite Show Resilience" in The Business Journal-Serving Greater Tampa Bay (Vol. 28, August 1, 2008, No. 32, pp. 1)
Pub: American City Business Journals, Inc.
Ed: Margie Manning; Alexis Muellner. **Description:** Stocks of the largest public companies in Tampa Bay, Florida, outperformed the S&P 500 index by 28 percent in the first half of 2008. The escalation is attributed to the growth orientation of the companies in the area and the lack of exposure to the real estate and financial services sectors.

27093 ■ "Corporation, Be Good! The Story of Corporate Social Responsibility" in Business and Society (December 2007, pp. 479-485)
Pub: SAGE Publications USA
Contact: Blaise R. Simqu, President
Ed: David M. Wasieleski. **Description:** Review of the book, 'Corporation, Be Good! The Story of Corporate Social Responsibility' is presented. The book examines the importance of corporate responsibility and its economic impact.

27094 ■ "Council Power Shift Could Benefit Business" in Business Courier (Vol. 26, November 6, 2009, No. 28, pp. 1)
Pub: American City Business Journals, Inc.
Ed: Lucy May. **Description:** A majority in the Cincinnati City Council, which is comprised of reelected members, might be created by Charlie Winburn's impending return to the council. It would be empowered to decide on public safety, stock options taxes, and environmental justice. How the presumed majority would affect the city's economic progress is discussed.

27095 ■ "Count Out The Consumer" in Barron's (Vol. 88, July 7, 2008, No. 27, pp. 10)
Pub: Dow Jones & Co., Inc.
Description: American consumers are not expected to give the US economy its much-needed boost as the rising food and energy prices are taking their toll. US consumers have cut spending on utilities and food and are increasing their use of credit cards.

27096 ■ "Countdown" in Canadian Business (Vol. 81, March 3, 2008, No. 3, pp. 27)
Pub: Rogers Media
Ed: Al Rosen. **Description:** According to a recent poll only 42 percent of portfolio managers in Canada are aware that the country is planning to adopt the International Financial Reporting Standards beginning 2011. The shift to the new standards will have significant impacts on investment values and will be the biggest revolution in Canadian financial reporting. The effects of the transition on portfolio managers and investors are analyzed.

27097 ■ "Counting on Engagement at Ernst and Young" in Workforce Management (Vol. 88, November 16, 2009, No. 12, pp. 25)
Pub: Crain Communications Inc.
Ed: Ed Frauenheim. **Description:** Employee engagement has been difficult to maintain through the recession but firms such as Ernst & Young have found that the effort to keep their employees loyal has paid off.

27098 ■ "Courier 250 Companies Hope to Rebound From 2009" in Business Courier (Vol. 27, July 16, 2010, No. 11, pp. 1)
Pub: Business Courier
Ed: Dan Monk, Jon Newberry. **Description:** Private companies that are featured in the Courier 250 publication have lost almost $4 billion in revenue, while combined sales dropped by 11 percent to 32 billion in 2009. Courier 250 is a guide to public companies, large nonprofits, private firms, and other related entities in Ohio's Cincinnati region.

27099 ■ "CPI, Coal Lead Local Stock Decline" in Saint Louis Business Journal (Vol. 32, October 14, 2011, No. 7, pp. 1)
Pub: Saint Louis Business Journal
Ed: Greg Edwards. **Description:** Coal companies and CPI Corporation were among those whose stocks have declined in St. Louis, Missouri. The stocks of local firms have plunged by 28 percent during the first nine months of 2011.

27100 ■ "Craig Muhlhauser" in Canadian Business (Vol. 81, September 15, 2008, No. 14-15, pp. 6)
Pub: Rogers Media Ltd.
Ed: Andrew Wahl. **Description:** Interview with Craig Muhlhauser who is the CEO of Celestica, a manufacturing company that provides services for the electronics sector; Muhlhauser discusses the company's restructuring program, which he feels was the secret to their surprising first-quarter results. Muhlhauser states that the company is operating with more forward visibility and that understanding the opportunities during the current economic situation presents the biggest challenge.

27101 ■ Crash Proof 2.0: How to Profit From the Economic Collapse
Pub: John Wiley & Sons, Inc.
Ed: Peter D. Schiff. **Released:** September 22, 2009. **Price:** $27.95. **Description:** Factors that will affect financial stability in the coming years are explained. A three step plan to battle the current economic downturn is also included.

27102 ■ "'Crazy' Or Not, Restaurateurs Are Finding Ways to Open New Eateries" in Baltimore Business Journal (Vol. 28, October 8, 2010)
Pub: Baltimore Business Journal
Ed: Joanna Sullivan. **Description:** New restaurants have been opening in Maryland. However, 515 restaurants have closed down due to the economic crisis. Comments from restaurateurs are also provided.

27103 ■ "The Credit Crisis Continues" in Barron's (Vol. 88, March 10, 2008, No. 10, pp. M12)
Pub: Dow Jones & Company, Inc.
Ed: Randall W. Forsyth. **Description:** Short-term Treasury yields dropped to new cyclical lows in early March 2008, with the yield for the two-year Treasury note falling to 1.532 percent. Spreads of the mortgage-backed securities of Fannie Mae and Freddie Mac rose on suspicion of collapses in financing.

27104 ■ "Credit Crisis Puts Market in Unprecedented Territory" in Crain's New York Business (Vol. 24, January 7, 2008, No. 1, pp. 14)
Pub: Crain Communications, Inc.
Ed: Aaron Elstein. **Description:** Banks are being forced to take enormous losses due to investors who are refusing to buy anything linked to subprime mortgages and associated securities.

27105 ■ "Credit Crunch Gives, Takes Away" in The Business Journal-Serving Metropolitan Kansas City (Vol. 27, October 17, 2008, No. 5, pp. 1)
Pub: American City Business Journals, Inc.
Ed: Suzanna Stagemeyer. **Description:** Although many Kansas City business enterprises have been adversely affected by the U.S. credit crunch, others have remained relatively unscathed. Examples of how local businesses are being impacted by the crisis are provided including: American Trailer & Storage Inc., which declared bankruptcy after failing to pay a long-term loan; and NetStandard, a technology firm who, on the other hand, is being pursued by prospective lenders.

27106 ■ "Credit Crunch Takes Bite Out Of McDonald's" in Advertising Age (Vol. 79, September 29, 2008, No. 36, pp. 1)
Pub: Crain Communications, Inc.
Ed: Emily Bryson York. **Description:** McDonald's will delay its launch of coffee bars inside its restaurants due to the banking crisis which has prompted Bank of America to halt loans to the franchise chains.

27107 ■ "Critics: Efforts to Fix Loans Won't Stop Foreclosure Wave" in Business First Columbus (Vol. 25, November 14, 2008, No. 12, pp. A1)
Pub: American City Business Journals
Ed: Adrian Burns. **Description:** Efforts by U.S. banks to help homeowners pay mortgages are seen to have little if any impact on foreclosures. Banks have announced plans to identify and aid troubled borrowers. Statistical data included.

27108 ■ "Crouching Tigers Spring to Life" in Globe & Mail (April 14, 2007, pp. B1)
Pub: CTVglobemedia Publishing Inc.
Ed: Grant Robertson. **Description:** The prospects of the acquisition of BCE Inc, by Canadian pension funds are discussed. The effect of the growth of these pension funds on the Canadian economy is described.

27109 ■ "Crude Awakening" in Canadian Business (Vol. 81, October 27, 2008, No. 18, pp. 14)
Pub: Rogers Media Ltd.
Ed: Jeff Sanford. **Description:** Jim Grays believes that a global liquid fuels crisis is coming and hopes the expected transition from oil dependence will be smooth. Charles Maxwell, on the other hand, predicts that a new world economy will arrive in three waves. Views of both experts are examined.

27110 ■ "Cruising In Choppy Water" in The Business Journal-Portland (Vol. 25, August 22, 2008, No. 24, pp. 1)
Pub: American City Business Journals, Inc.
Ed: Erik Siemers. **Description:** Yacht builder Christensen Shipyards Inc. is experiencing robust business despite the slowing US economy, building four yachts a year as of 2008. The company expects revenues to hit $90 million and is opening a 500,000-square-foot plant in Tennessee.

27111 ■ *"The Cudgel of Samson" in Barron's (Vol. 88, March 24, 2008, No. 12. pp. 62)*
Pub: Dow Jones & Company, Inc.
Ed: Thomas G. Donlan. **Description:** Discusses the Federal Reserve is jawboning businesses against inflation while inflation is starting to rise because of the abundance of cheap money. The practice of jawboning has been used by the administrations of past US presidents with limited effect.

27112 ■ *"Daley's Efforts to Ease Traffic Woes Fall Short" in Crain's Chicago Business (Vol. 31, May 5, 2008, No. 18, pp. 18)*
Pub: Crain Communications, Inc.
Description: Discusses some of the inherent problems of Mayor Daley's plan to reduce traffic congestion by creating a tax on drivers who park their cars downtown during peak traffic periods and putting articulated buses on new bus-only lanes on major arterial streets leading into the Loop.

27113 ■ *"Darkness Falling.." in Barron's (Vol. 89, July 20, 2009, No. 29, pp. 13)*
Pub: Dow Jones & Co., Inc.
Description: Newsletter writer Arch Crawford believes that market indicators signal a possible downturn in US stock markets. High risk areas also include China and Japan .

27114 ■ *"Datebook" in Crain's Chicago Business (Vol. 31, March 24, 2008, No. 12, pp. 18)*
Pub: Crain Communications, Inc.
Description: Listing of events in the Detroit area include conferences addressing entrepreneurialism, economic development, secrets of getting hired, and women business ownership.

27115 ■ *"Datebook" in Crain's Chicago Business (Vol. 31, March 31, 2008, No. 13, pp. 1)*
Pub: Crain Communications, Inc.
Description: Listing of events in the Detroit area include conferences addressing entrepreneurialism, economic development, secrets of getting hired, and women business ownership.

27116 ■ *"Datebook" in Crain's Chicago Business (Vol. 31, April 28, 2008, No. 17, pp. 18)*
Pub: Crain Communications, Inc.
Description: Listing of events in the Detroit area include conferences addressing entrepreneurialism, economic development, and women business ownership.

27117 ■ *"David Azrieli" in Canadian Business (Vol. 82, April 27, 2009, No. 7, pp. 54)*
Pub: Rogers Media
Ed: Alex Mlynek. **Description:** David Azrieli wants to take advantage of opportunities, revealing that he has increased his portfolio nearly every recession. Azrieli has recently purchased properties of General Electric near the Toronto airport for about $100 million. He believes the economy will rebound in the second half of 2009.

27118 ■ *"Deal With Tribes Revives Revenue Stream" in Crain's Detroit Business (Vol. 24, March 24, 2008, No. 12, pp. 6)*
Pub: Crain Communications, Inc.
Ed: Amy Lane. **Description:** Michigan Bureau of State Lottery's 2003 launch of its Club Keno game caused the Little River Band of Ottawa Indians and the Little Traverse Bay Bands of Odawa Indians to halt payments of shared casino revenue with the state. The federal lawsuit that resulted has now been settled and tribal revenue-sharing will resume as well as $26 million in previous payments to the state of Michigan that the tribes had put into escrow.

27119 ■ *"Dealers Trying Not to Fold" in Business First Columbus (Vol. 25, December 5, 2008, No. 15, pp. A1)*
Pub: American City Business Journals
Ed: Dan Eaton. **Description:** Increase in the number of automobile dealer closures in Ohio is seen to impact the state's economy. The trend of consolidation is forecasted to adversely affect employment and sales. Statistical data included.

27120 ■ *"Debut Year Brings Success for Bike-Trail Boosters" in Business Courier (Vol. 24, January 4, 2008, No. 39, pp. 4)*
Pub: American City Business Journals, Inc.
Ed: Dan Monk. **Description:** Discusses the first year of Cincinnati's Trail Yeah has brought in success as five local government boards approve the bike-trail enthusiast group's endorsement of a cycling path that would connect the city's downtown to the Loveland Bike Trail. The group is planning to raise $3 million to $5 million for the trails first phase.

27121 ■ *"Decline in Assets Is Costly for Advisers" in The Business Journal-Serving Metropolitan Kansas City (Vol. 27, October 24, 2008)*
Pub: American City Business Journals, Inc.
Ed: James Dornbrook. **Description:** Financial advisers in the Kansas City, Missouri area are forced to cut costs as their assets have decreased sharply due to the huge drop in stock prices. American Century Investments was forced to diversify into foreign assets and cut 90 jobs as its assets dropped to $84 billion. Diversification has softened the impact of the steep decline in stock prices for Waddell & Reed Financial Inc.

27122 ■ *"Dedge Rejects Inflation Concerns" in Globe & Mail (January 26, 2007, pp. B3)*
Pub: CTVglobemedia Publishing Inc.
Ed: Heather Scoffield. **Description:** The rejection of concern over inflation by Governor of the Bank of Canada David Dodge and his views on checking inflation in Alberta are discussed.

27123 ■ *"Defying Gravity?" in Canadian Business (Vol. 81, October 13, 2008, No. 17, pp. 17)*
Pub: Rogers Media Ltd.
Ed: Joe Castaldo. **Description:** Airlines around the world are expected to lose $4.1 billion in 2009, but experts believe Canadian airlines will be able to survive the economic challenges. Lower demand for air travel and uncertainty on oil prices are also expected to make the conditions more challenging. Views and key information on airlines in Canada and around the world are cited.

27124 ■ *"Department of Agriculture" in Ice Cream Reporter (Vol. 23, November 20, 2010, No. 12, pp. 8)*
Pub: Ice Cream Reporter
Description: Department of Agriculture notes that food price inflation for 2010 will be at its lowest since 1992.

27125 ■ *"Despite Economic Upheaval Generation Y is Still Feeling Green: RSA Canada Survey" in CNW Group (October 28, 2010)*
Pub: CNW Group
Contact: Carolyn McGill-Davidson, President
Description: Canadian Generation Y individuals believe it is important for their company to be environmentally-friendly and one-third of those surveyed would quit their job if they found their employer was environmentally irresponsible, despite the economy.

27126 ■ *"Despite Gloom, Auto Sales Saw Gains in 2005" in Globe & Mail (January 5, 2006, pp. B1)*
Pub: CTVglobemedia Publishing Inc.
Ed: Greg Keenan. **Description:** An overview of positve automotive sales in Canada, for 2005, is presented.

27127 ■ *"Detroit 3's Fall Would Be a Big One in Ohio" in Business First Columbus (Vol. 25, November 28, 2008, No. 14, pp. A1)*
Pub: American City Business Journals
Ed: Dan Eaton. **Description:** Ohio's economy will suffer huge negative effects in the event of a failure of one or more of the automotive companies, General Motors Corporation, Ford Motor Company, or Chrysler LLC. The state is home to 97,900 jobs in the automotive industry and is a vital link to the industry's supply network.

27128 ■ *"Detroit Residential Market Slows; Bright Spots Emerge" in Crain's Detroit Business (Vol. 24, October 6, 2008, No. 40, pp. 11)*
Pub: Crain Communications, Inc.
Ed: Daniel Duggan. **Description:** Discusses the state of the residential real estate market in Detroit; although condominium projects receive the most attention, deals for single-family homes are taking place in greater numbers due to financing issues. Buyers can purchase a single family home with a 3.5 percent down payment compared to 20 percent for some condo deals because of the number of first-time homebuyer programs under the Federal Housing Administration.

27129 ■ *"Detroit Scores When Tigers Play; Studies Predict Winning Economy" in Crain's Detroit Business (Vol. 24, March 31, 2008, No. 13)*
Pub: Crain Communications, Inc.
Ed: Bill Shea. **Description:** East Lansing-based Anderson Economic Group and the Detroit Regional Chamber predict that the economic impact of the Detroit Tigers will be very positive for the region due to an unexpected World Series trip two years ago followed by another strong season in 2007, player acquisitions and the popular Jim Leyland again managing the team. Statistical data included.

27130 ■ *"Developer Banks On East Submarket, Slowdown Not a Hinderance" in The Business Journal-Serving Greater Tampa Bay (August 1, 2008)*
Pub: American City Business Journals, Inc.
Ed: Janet Leiser. **Description:** CLW Industrial Group and Cobalt Industrial REIT II have teamed up to develop a 14-acre area in northeast Hillsborough County, Florida. The $15 million industrial park project includes the 175,000-square-foot New Tampa Commerce Center, scheduled for completion in the first quarter of 2009.

27131 ■ *"Developers Await Hotel" in The Business Journal-Portland (Vol. 25, July 11, 2008, No. 18, pp. 1)*
Pub: American City Business Journals, Inc.
Ed: Wendy Culverwell. **Description:** Developers are eager to start the construction of a new hotel at the Oregon Convention Center in Portland, Oregon as hey say that the project will help boost the convention center neighborhood. The project, called The Westin Portland at the Convention Center, is partly handled by Ashforth Pacific Inc.

27132 ■ *Developmental Entrepreneurship: Adversity, Risk, and Isolation*
Pub: Elsevier Science and Technology Books
Ed: Craig Galbraith. **Released:** August 2006. **Price:** $99.95. **Description:** Volume five of the series, this book focuses on the fields of entrepreneurship, sociology, and economics. Fifteen articles related to entrepreneurship and small business development within a global environment are included.

27133 ■ *"Diary of a Short-Seller" in Conde Nast Portfolio (Vol. 2, June 2008, No. 6, pp. 44)*
Pub: Conde Nast Publications
Contact: David Carey, President
Ed: Jesse Eisinger. **Description:** Profile of David Einhorn who is a fund manager that spoke out against finance company Allied Capital whose stock fell nearly 20 percent the day after Einhorn's critique; Einhorn subsequently had to contend with attacks against his credibility as well as investigations by the S.E.C.; Einhorn's experience illuminates our current economic crisis.

27134 ■ *"Dick Evans" in Canadian Business (Vol. 82, April 27, 2009, No. 7, pp. 78)*
Pub: Rogers Media
Ed: Sean Silcoff. **Description:** Former Rio Tinto Alcan chief executive officer Dick Evans believes that the 1982 downturn was worse than the current recession, at least for the mining sector. He also believes that while people are anxious, there is confidence

that the economy will recover in two to three years. Key information on Evans, as well as his other views on being a CEO is presented.

27135 ■ *"Different This Time?'* in Canadian Business (Vol. 81, April 14, 2008, No. 6, pp. 38)
Pub: Rogers Media
Ed: Matthew McClearn. **Description:** Irving Fisher believed that the low interest rates of the 1920's spurred investors to borrow and use the money to speculate with the proceeds thereby increasing the debt to unmanageable levels prior to the stock market crash in Oct. 29, 1929. The U.S. economic conditions in 1929 and U.S. economic conditions in 2008 are discussed.

27136 ■ *"Dirty Work Required'* in Workforce Management (Vol. 88, November 16, 2009, No. 12, pp. 34)
Pub: Crain Communications Inc.
Ed: John Hollon. **Description:** Due to salary freezes, pay cuts, layoffs, buyouts and a number of other stress factors brought about by the recession, employee engagement has been difficult to maintain by managers.

27137 ■ *"Do You Have A Retirement Parachute?'* in Barron's (Vol. 88, July 7, 2008, No. 27, pp. 32)
Pub: Dow Jones & Co., Inc.
Ed: Jane White. **Description:** The idea that American companies should emulate the Australian retirement system which implements a forced contribution rate for all employers regarding an adequate retirement plan for their employees is discussed.

27138 ■ *"Dr. Mark Holder'* in Crain's Cleveland Business (Vol. 30, June 29, 2009, No. 25, pp. 14)
Pub: Crain Communications, Inc.
Ed: Kathy Ames Carr. **Description:** Dr. Mark Holder is the director of the financial engineering program at Kent State University. Dr. Holder discusses his role to help teach his students how to market themselves for finance jobs in a down economy.

27139 ■ *"Dodge Pushes Reform Agenda'* in Globe & Mail (February 6, 2006, pp. B1)
Pub: CTVglobemedia Publishing Inc.
Ed: Heather Scoffield. **Description:** The impact of variations in global economy, on Canadian economy, is discussed. The recommendations of Governor David Dodge of Bank of Canada to resolve the issue are presented.

27140 ■ *"Dodge Slashes Growth Estimate'* in Globe & Mail (January 19, 2007, pp. B3)
Pub: CTVglobemedia Publishing Inc.
Ed: Heather Scoffield. **Description:** Bank of Canada Governor David Dodge decision to keep the interest rate 4.25 percent despite a slowdown in the economy is discussed.

27141 ■ *"Does it Add Up?'* in Canadian Business (Vol. 81, October 13, 2008, No. 17, pp. 18)
Pub: Rogers Media Ltd.
Ed: Jack Mintz. **Description:** Views on Canada's tax policy, as well as on tax reforms planned by major parties and their expected economic impact are discussed. The Tories' proposal to cut federal diesel fuel tax is seen as politically smart, but reforms on other taxes could help generate economic growth. High income tax rates are believed to discourage talented individuals from working in Canada.

27142 ■ *"The Dogs of TSX'* in Canadian Business (Vol. 81, Summer 2008, No. 9, pp. 77)
Pub: Rogers Media Ltd.
Ed: Calvin Leung. **Description:** Table showing the one-year stock performance of the ten highest dividend-yielding stocks on the S&P/TSX 60 Composite Index is presented. This technique is similar to the 'Dogs of the Dow' approach. The idea in this investment strategy is to buy equal amounts of stocks from these companies and selling them a year later, and then repeat the process.

27143 ■ *"Dollar Daze: Canadian Businesses Must Adjust to a New Reality'* in Canadian Business (Vol. 80, Winter 2007, No. 24, pp. 11)
Pub: Rogers Media
Ed: Jeff Sanford. **Description:** Several Canadian businessmen lost massive amounts in the Canadian value of their investments due to the volatility of the U.S. dollar. The factors that weighed down the value of the U.S. dollar include the announcement by China to diversify their currency reserves away from the U.S. dollar and concerns about the price of oil.

27144 ■ *"Dollar Doldrums; How American Companies are Beating the Currency Crunch'* in Inc. (March 2008, pp. 45-46)
Pub: Gruner & Jahr USA Publishing
Ed: Sarah Goldstein. **Description:** Despite the low American dollar, some exporters are seeing a growth in their businesses, while other have had to relocate operations and switch to U.S. supplier. Four business owners tell how they are dealing with the current economic conditions.

27145 ■ *"Don't Bet Against The House'* in Barron's (Vol. 88, July 14, 2008, No. 28, pp. 20)
Pub: Dow Jones & Co., Inc.
Ed: Sandra Ward. **Description:** Shares of Nasdaq OMX have lost more than 50 percent of their value from November 2007 to July 2008 but the value of these shares could climb 50 percent on the strength of world security exchanges. Only 15 percent of the company's revenues come from the U.S. and the shares are trading at 12.5 times the amount expected for 2008.

27146 ■ *"Don't Expect Quick Fix'* in The Business Journal-Serving Metropolitan Kansas City (Vol. 27, October 3, 2008, No. 3, pp. 1)
Pub: American City Business Journals, Inc.
Ed: James Dornbrook. **Description:** United States governmental entities cannot provide a quick solution to the current financial crisis. The economy requires a systemic change in the way people think about credit. The financial services industry should also focus on core lending principles.

27147 ■ *"Don't Get Lulled by the Calm'* in Barron's (Vol. 89, July 27, 2009, No. 30, pp. M13)
Pub: Dow Jones & Co., Inc.
Ed: Steven M. Sears. **Description:** Options traders expect volatility to return in the fall of 2009 and to bring correlation with it. September and October are typically the most volatile months and the trick is to survive earnings season.

27148 ■ *"Don't Quit When The Road Gets Bumpy'* in Women Entrepreneur (November 25, 2008)
Pub: Entrepreneur Media Inc.
Ed: Bonnie Price. **Description:** Discusses techniques four women entrepreneurs are utilizing to keep their businesses successful despite the credit crunch and the economic downturn.

27149 ■ *"The Doomsday Scenario'* in Conde Nast Portfolio (Vol. 2, June 2008, No. 6, pp. 91)
Pub: Conde Nast Publications
Contact: David Carey, President
Ed: Jeffrey Rothfeder. **Description:** Detroit and the U.S. auto industry are discussed as well as the ramifications of the demise of this manufacturing base. Similarities and differences between the downfall of the U.S. steel business and the impact it had on Pittsburg, Pennsylvania is also discussed.

27150 ■ *"Doubtful Donors'* in Canadian Business (Vol. 81, December 8, 2008, No. 21, pp. 8)
Pub: Rogers Media Ltd.
Ed: Dennis Seguin. **Description:** Key information on fundraising consultancy Inspire, as well as views and information on charitable organizations in Canada is presented. Inspire designs the financial architecture

of charitable foundations in Canada, which was affected by the current financial crisis. Inspire advises foundations to keep existing donors.

27151 ■ *"Down Mexico Way'* in Canadian Business (Vol. 79, September 25, 2006, No. 19, pp. 27)
Pub: Rogers Media
Description: Presidential election in Mexico and its effects on its economy is discussed.

27152 ■ *"Down a 'Peg'* in Canadian Business (Vol. 79, September 25, 2006, No. 19, pp. 41)
Pub: Rogers Media
Ed: Bryan Borzykowski. **Description:** Economic development in Canada's Winnipeg city is evaluated.

27153 ■ *"Down the Tracks, a Whistle Is a Blowin'* in Barron's (Vol. 89, July 27, 2009, No. 30, pp. 36)
Pub: Dow Jones & Co., Inc.
Ed: Jim McTague. **Description:** Higher numbers of freight-rail carloads are a sign that the economy is improving and it is no stretch to imagine that this is aided by the American Recovery and Reinvestment Act. It is also predicted that 2009 municipal bond issuance will be above $373 billion with at least $55 billion of it made up of Buy America Bonds that are subsidized by the federal government.

27154 ■ *"Downtown Detroit Needs More Retail'* in Crain's Detroit Business (Vol. 24, March 10, 2008, No. 10, pp. 9)
Pub: Crain Communications, Inc.
Ed: Robin Boyle; James Bieri. **Description:** Although Detroit is doing well with event-driven traffic, the city remains far off the site selection rosters of major national retailers as well as smaller retail outlets.

27155 ■ *"Downturn Tests HCL's Pledge to Employees'* in Workforce Management (Vol. 88, November 16, 2009, No. 12, pp. 23)
Pub: Crain Communications Inc.
Ed: Ed Frauenheim. **Description:** HCL Technologies has kept its promise to keep from laying any employees off during the recession which served as a test for the tech firm's Employee First program, which seeks to give workers greater income security as well as a stronger voice in the firm.

27156 ■ *"Dream Big! When the Going Gets Tough, Reps Work Harder and Smarter'* in Agency Sales Magazine (Vol. 39, July 2009, No. 7, pp. 22)
Pub: MANA
Ed: John Chapin. **Description:** Sales representatives should use the tough economy as a warning and motivation to work harder and smarter. Reps should improve their selling by reading books, listening to tapes and CDs. They should also keep a good attitude and build relationships.

27157 ■ *"Dream On: California's Budget Fix may not Last for Long."* in Barron's (Vol. 89, July 27, 2009, No. 30, pp. 21)
Pub: Dow Jones & Co., Inc.
Ed: Jonathan R. Laing. **Description:** California's budget agreement which purports to eliminate a $26 billion deficit is discussed. The frequent budgetary dustups in the state calls for several reforms including a rainy day fund of 15 percent of any budget and a constitutional convention. Other reform suggestions are discussed.

27158 ■ *"Dreaming in Macau'* in Canadian Business (Vol. 81, December 8, 2008, No. 21, pp. 65)
Pub: Rogers Media Ltd.
Ed: Joe Chidley. **Description:** Key information, as well as views on the economic aspects of Macau are presented. Macau was once monopolized by Stanley Ho's Sociedad de Turismo e Diversoes de Macau, but the government transformed the area into a leisure-and-entertainment spot. Details about Cirque de Soleil are also presented.

27159 ■ "Drug, Seed Firms Offer Antidote For Inflation" in Crain's Chicago Business (Vol. 31, April 21, 2008, No. 16, pp. 4)
Pub: Crain Communications, Inc.

Ed: Daniel Rome Levine. **Description:** Interview with Jerrold Senser, the CEO of Institutional Capital LLC in Chicago, in which he discusses the ways that the company is adjusting to the economic slowdown and rising inflation, his favorite firms for investment and his prediction of an economic turnaround; he also recommends five companies he feels are worth investing in.

27160 ■ "DST Turns to Banks for Credit" in The Business Journal-Serving Metropolitan Kansas City (Vol. 27, October 3, 2008, No. 3, pp. 1)
Pub: American City Business Journals, Inc.

Ed: Rob Roberts. **Description:** Kansas City, Missouri-based DST Systems Inc., a company that provides sophisticated information processing, computer software services and business solutions, has secured a new five-year, $120 million credit facility from Enterprise Bank and Bank of the West. The deal is seen to reflect that the region and community-banking model remain stable. Comments from executives are also provided.

27161 ■ "Dueling Visions" in Barron's (Vol. 89, July 27, 2009, No. 30, pp. 13)
Pub: Dow Jones & Co., Inc.

Ed: Michael Santoli. **Description:** Goldman Sachs' market strategists believe the stock market has entered a 'sustained-rally' mode while Morgan Stanley's strategist believes this is a 'rally to sell into'. What is not known in the stock market is how much of a 'V'-shaped recovery in earning the market rebound has already priced in.

27162 ■ "Early Spring Halts Drilling Season" in Globe & Mail (March 14, 2007, pp. B14)
Pub: CTVglobemedia Publishing Inc.

Ed: Norval Scott. **Description:** Decreased petroleum productivity in Canadian oil drilling rigs due to early spring season in western regions is discussed.

27163 ■ "Easy to be Queasy" in Canadian Business (Vol. 81, December 24, 2007, No. 1, pp. 25)
Pub: Rogers Media

Ed: Jack Mintz. **Description:** Canada could be facing a slowdown in economic growth for 2008 as the country's economy depends on the U.S. economy, which is still facing recession in the subprime market. Details on Canada's economic growth, the impact of the weak U.S. dollar, increase in the unemployment rate, and decline in tax revenue are explored.

27164 ■ "Economic Crises Calls For Better Marketing Plans" in Entrepreneur (October 1, 2008)
Pub: Entrepreneur Media Inc.

Ed: Tim Berry. **Description:** Revising one's business plan is essential, especially during times of economic crisis; sales and marketing plans should be reviewed, analyzed and changed in an attempt to survive the economic downturn.

27165 ■ "Economic Crisis and Accounting Evolution" in Accounting and Business Research (Vol. 41, Summer 2011, No. 3, pp. 2159)
Pub: American Institute of Certified Public Accountants

Contact: Barry C. Melancon, President
E-mail: bmelancon@aicpa.org

Ed: Gregory Waymire, Sudipta Basu. **Description:** Financial reporting changes at the face of economic crises are studied using a punctuated equilibrium evolution. Findings show that financial reporting has a minor impact but may amplify economic crises. Attempts to enhance accounting amid economic crises may not be as beneficial as planned.

27166 ■ "Economic Crisis and Accounting Evolution" in Accounting and Business

Research (Vol. 41, Summer 2011, No. 3, pp. 2159)
Pub: Routledge

Ed: Gregory Waymire, Sudipta Basu. **Description:** Financial reporting changes at the face of economic crises are studied using a punctuated equilibrium evolution. Findings show that financial reporting has a minor impact but may amplify economic crises. Attempts to enhance accounting and economic crises may not be as beneficial as planned.

27167 ■ Economic Development Administration--Annual Report
Pub: U.S. Economic Development Administration

URL(s): http://www.eda.gov/annualReports.htm. **Released:** Annual; Latest edition 2011. **Covers:** Recipients of grants, grant supplements, and loan guarantees from the Economic Development Administration under the Public Works and Economic Development Act of 1965. Projects funded include public works, business development, research, planning, and disaster recovery. **Entries include:** Recipient name, location, date of obligation, funds received by type of assistance, type of project, identification number. **Arrangement:** Geographical.

27168 ■ "Economic Distance and the Survival of Foreign Direct Investments" in Academy of Management Journal (Vol. 50, No. 5, October 2007)
Pub: Academy of Management

Contact: Ming-Jer Chen, President

Ed: Eric W.K. Tsang, Paul S.L. Yip. **Description:** Study was undertaken to assess the relationship between economic disparities of various countries and foreign direct investments, focusing on Singapore. Results revealed that economic distance has a definite impact on foreign direct investment hazard rates.

27169 ■ Economic Freedom and the American Dream
Pub: Palgrave Macmillan

Ed: Joseph Shaanan. **Released:** January 5, 2010. **Price:** $55.00. **Description:** An exploration into the effects of economic freedom on American in several areas such as markets, politics, and opportunities for would-be entrepreneurs.

27170 ■ "Economic Outlook 2009" in Hispanic Business (January-February 2009, pp. 30, 32)
Pub: Hispanic Business

Ed: Dr. Juan Solana. **Description:** Successful business policies of the past no longer work in this economic climate. New tools and initiatives regarding monetary policy, fiscal policy and a higher multiplier are required to survive the crisis.

27171 ■ "Economic Prognosis" in Barron's (Vol. 89, July 13, 2009, No. 28, pp. 11)
Pub: Dow Jones & Co., Inc.

Ed: Karen Hube. **Description:** Loomis Sayles Bond Fund manager Dan Fuss believes that the economy is bottoming and that recovery will be long and drawn out. Fuss guesses that the next peak in 10-year Treasury yields will be about 6.25% in around 4 and a half or five years ahead of 2009.

27172 ■ "Economic Stimulus Plan Needs Scrutiny" in Crain's Detroit Business (Vol. 24, April 7, 2008, No. 14, pp. 8)
Pub: Crain Communications, Inc.

Description: Overview of Mayor Kwame Kilpatrick's economic stimulus package which many believe needs to be scrutinized closely since the true financial status of Detroit is unclear.

27173 ■ "Economic Trends for Small Business" in Small Business Economic Trends (April 2008, pp. 1)
Pub: National Federation of Independent Business

Ed: William C. Dunkelberg, Holly Wade. **Description:** Summary of economic trends for small businesses in the U.S. is presented. Economic indicators such as capital spending, inventories and sales, inflation, and profits are given. Analysis of credit markets is also provided.

27174 ■ The Economics of Entrepreneurship
Pub: Edward Elgar Publishing, Incorporated

Ed: Parker. **Released:** April 2006. **Price:** $240.00. **Description:** Previously published articles influencing research into the economic structure of entrepreneurship are examined.

27175 ■ The Economics and Management of Small Business: An International Perspective
Pub: Routledge

Ed: Graham Bannock. **Released:** May 2005. **Price:** $65.00. **Description:** International perspectives on the economics and management of small business, featuring case studies and empirical research.

27176 ■ The Economics of Self-Employment and Entrepreneurship
Pub: Cambridge University Press

Contact: Richard Ziemacki, President
E-mail: rziemacki@cambridge.org

Ed: Simon C. Parker. **Released:** July 2006. **Price:** $50.00. **Description:** The importance of self-employment and entrepreneurship in a modern economy is explored.

27177 ■ The Economics of Small Firms
Pub: Routledge Inc.

Ed: Johnson. **Released:** December 2006. **Price:** $41.95. **Description:** Introduction to the economics of small business, covering both theoretical and empirical issues.

27178 ■ "Economy Forcing Meeting Planners to Think Fast" in Crain's Cleveland Business (Vol. 30, June 15, 2009, No. 23, pp. 15)
Pub: Crain Communications, Inc.

Ed: Amy Ann Stoessel. **Description:** Meeting planners are working hard to meet lower corporate budgets when planning events.

27179 ■ "Economy Peddles Rent In This Cycle" in The Business Journal-Serving Metropolitan Kansas City (Vol. 26, August 8, 2008, No. 48)
Pub: American City Business Journals, Inc.

Ed: Ashlee Kieler. **Description:** Rental demand for apartment units in downtown Kansas City, Missouri, is increasing due to the housing crisis, lack of real estate development, and increasing popularity of the downtown area. The downtown area has 7,378 multifamily units as of June 2008, of which 4,114 are rentals.

27180 ■ "Economy Should Play Big Role When Presidential Spotlight Returns" in Business First-Columbus (November 9, 2007, pp. A1)
Pub: American City Business Journals, Inc.

Ed: Jeff Bell. **Description:** Ohio leaders, including the president of Columbus Chamber, Ty Marsh, suggests that Ohio has benefited from past campaigns as candidates spend money on advertising along with the media exposure the state received. The significance of Ohio in determining the winner in the 2008 presidential elections is discussed.

27181 ■ "Editor's Note" in Canadian Business (Vol. 81, March 17, 2008, No. 4, pp. 7)
Pub: Rogers Media

Ed: Joe Chidley. **Description:** Canadian Consolidated government expenditures increased by an average of 4.5 percent annually from 2003 to 2007. Health care, housing, and the environment were some of the areas which experienced higher spending. However, government spending in labor, employment, and immigration dropped 6.6 percent.

27182 ■ "Effect of Oil Prices on the Economy" in Canadian Business (Vol. 81, September 15, 2008, No. 14-15, pp. 5)
Pub: Rogers Media Ltd.

Ed: Joe Chidley. **Description:** Rise of oil prices above $100 in February 2008 and $140 in July signals the birth of a 'new economy' according to commentators; this shift is causing uneasiness from oil industry professionals who are unsure of how this trend could be sustained. Oil dropped below $120 in August, which could slow down global economic growth followed by oil demand, then oil prices.

27183 ■ Effect of the Overvalued Dollar on Small Exporters: Congressional Hearing
Pub: DIANE Publishing Company
Ed: Donald Manzullo. Released: September 2002. Price: $30.00. Description: Congressional hearing: Witnesses: Dr. Lawrence Chimerine, Economist; Tony Raimondo, President and CEO, Behlen Manufacturing Company; Robert J. Weskamp, President, Wes-Tech, Inc.; Wayne Dollar, President, Georgia Farm Bureau; and Vargese George, President and CEO, Westex International, Inc. Appendix includes correspondence sent to committee on the overvalued dollar.

27184 ■ "Egg Fight: The Yolk's on the Short" in Barron's (Vol. 88, July 7, 2008, No. 27, pp. 20)
Pub: Dow Jones & Co., Inc.
Ed: Christopher C. Williams. Description: Shares of Cal-Maine Foods, the largest egg producer and distributor in the US, are due for a huge rise because of the increase in egg prices. Short sellers, however, continue betting that the stock, priced at $31.84 each, will eventually go down.

27185 ■ Electronic Commerce
Pub: Course Technology
Ed: Gary Schneider, Bryant Chrzan, Charles McCormick. Released: May 1, 2010. Price: $117.95. Description: E-commerce can open the door to more opportunities than ever before for small business. Packed with real-world examples and cases, the book delivers comprehensive coverage of emerging online technologies and trends and their influence on the electronic marketplace. It details how the landscape of online commerce is evolving, reflecting changes in the economy and how business and society are responding to those changes. Balancing technological issues with the strategic business aspects of successful e-commerce, the new edition includes expanded coverage of international issues, social networking, mobile commerce, Web 2.0 technologies, and updates on spam, phishing, and identity theft.

27186 ■ "Elements For Success" in Small Business Opportunities (November 2008)
Pub: Entrepreneur Press
Contact: Perlman Neil, President
Description: Profile of Elements, a physical fitness club that approach a healthy lifestyle for women, which includes the components of body, beauty and mind; the network of upscale, boutique style health clubs differ from other providers in its 'balanced lifestyle' approach to a healthy lifestyle. This unique niche is gaining in popularity despite the faltering economy.

27187 ■ The Elephant and the Dragon: The Rise of India and China and What It Means to All of Us
Pub: W.W. Norton & Company
Ed: Robyn Meredith. Released: 2008. Price: $15.95. Description: The author illustrates how both China and India have followed their own economic path, and examines the countries' similarities and considers the repercussions of their growing involvement in the world market.

27188 ■ Elsewhere, U.S.A.: How We Got From the Company Man, Family Dinners, and the Affluent Society to the Home Office, Blackberry Moms, and Economic Anxiety
Pub: Pantheon Books
Ed: Dalton Conley. Released: 2009. Price: $24.00. Description: The alienation of the working middle class in America and the downturned economy is examined.

27189 ■ "Embarq Sale Sets New Tone" in The Business Journal-Serving Metropolitan Kansas City (Vol. 27, October 31, 2008, No. 8, pp. 1)
Pub: American City Business Journals, Inc.
Ed: Suzsanna Stagemeyer. Description: CenturyTel Inc. has agreed to acquire Embarq Corp., a large phone company based in Overland Park. The acquisition deal is valued at $11.6 billion. The potential impacts of the deal on Kansas City's economy are analyzed.

27190 ■ The Emerging Digital Economy: Entrepreneurship, Clusters, and Policy
Pub: Springer
Ed: Borje Johansson; Charlie Karlsson; Roger Stough. Released: August 2006. Price: $119.00. Description: The new economy, or digital economy, and its impact on the way industries and firms choose to locate and cluster geographically.

27191 ■ The Emerging Markets Century: How a New Breed of World-Class Companies is Overtaking the World
Pub: Free Press/Simon & Schuster Inc.
Ed: Antoine van Agtmael. Released: 2007. Price: $29.00. Description: An exploration of how companies like Lenovo and Haier who are presently in emerging economies are already competing with household name brands like Ford and Sony, thus proving globalization is here to stay.

27192 ■ "Empathy: An Entrepreneur's Killer App" in Women Entrepreneur (February 3, 2009)
Pub: Entrepreneur Media Inc.
Ed: Kristi Hedges. Description: It is just as important to treat employees with courtesy and respect during bad economic times as it is in a good economy. Employers sometimes take advantage of such bad economic times since they realize that employees are grateful to have a job and cannot just quit and easily find work elsewhere. The importance of empathy in a company's leadership personnel is discussed.

27193 ■ "End of the Beginning" in Canadian Business (Vol. 81, November 10, 2008, No. 19, pp. 17)
Pub: Rogers Media Ltd.
Ed: David Wolf. Description: The freeze in the money markets and historic decline in equity markets around the world finally forced governments into aggressive coordinated action. The asset price inflation brought on by cheap credit will now work in reverse and the tightening of credit will be difficult economically. Canada is exposed to the fallout everywhere, given that the U.S, the U.K. and Japan buy 30 percent of Canada's output.

27194 ■ "End of an Era" in Barron's (Vol. 88, July 7, 2008, No. 27, pp. 3)
Pub: Dow Jones & Co., Inc.
Ed: Alan Abelson. Description: June 2008 was a very bad month for US stocks, with investors losing as much as 41.9 percent in the first half of 2008 signaling an end to the financial environment that prevailed around the world since the 1980's. The US job market lost 62,000 jobs in June 2008.

27195 ■ "Endowments for Colleges Hit Hard in '09" in Milwaukee Business Journal (Vol. 27, February 12, 2010, No. 20, pp. A1)
Pub: American City Business Journals
Ed: Corrinne Hess. Description: Southeast Wisconsin college endowments declined by as much as 35 percent in 2009 due to the economic downturn. A list of 2009 endowments to colleges in southeast Wisconsin and their percent change from 2008 is presented.

27196 ■ "Enforcer In Fantasyland" in Crain's New York Business (Vol. 24, February 25, 2008, No. 8, pp. 10)
Pub: Crain Communications Inc.
Ed: Hilary Potkewitz. Description: Patent law, particularly in the toy and game industry, is recession-proof according to Barry Negrin, partner at Pryor Cashman. Negrin co-founded his patent practice group. Despite massive recalls of toys and the concern over toxic toys, legal measures are in place in this industry.

27197 ■ The Entrepreneurial Imperative: How America's Economic Miracle Will Reshape the World
Pub: HarperCollins Publishers, Inc.
Ed: Carl J. Schramm. Released: October 2006. Price: $24.95. Description: Carl Schramm, president of Kauffman Foundation discusses the secret to America's economy.

27198 ■ "Entrepreneurs Save the World" in Women In Business (Vol. 61, December 2009, No. 6, pp. 12)
Pub: American Business Women's Association
Ed: Leigh Elmore. Description: American economic growth is attributed to small businesses but more than one-third of these businesses have had to cut jobs in 2009, while only five percent have increased workforces. This trend motivated organizations, such as the Ewing Marion Kauffman Foundation, to bring together entrepreneurs and assist them in having greater participation in public dialogues about America's economy.

27199 ■ Entrepreneurship and Economic Growth
Pub: Edward Elgar Publishing, Incorporated
Ed: Carree. Released: October 2006. Price: $195.00. Description: Historic and country-specific studies and articles regarding entrepreneurship and innovation, growth models, competition and productivity, and empirical evidence.

27200 ■ Entrepreneurship and Economic Progress
Pub: Routledge Inc.
Ed: Randall Holcombe. Released: October 2006. Description: Economic models of economic growth and the ways entrepreneurial progress are highlighted.

27201 ■ Entrepreneurship, Geography, and American Economic Growth
Pub: Cambridge University Press
Contact: Richard Ziemacki, President
E-mail: rziemacki@cambridge.org
Ed: Zoltan Acs; Catherine Armington. Released: June 2006. Price: $70.00. Description: Knowledge among college-educated workers was among the key reasons for economic growth throughout the U.S. in the 1990s.

27202 ■ Entrepreneurship, Innovation and Economic Growth
Pub: Edward Elgar Publishing, Incorporated
Ed: David B. Audretsch. Released: July 2006. Price: $145.00. Description: Links between entrepreneurship, innovation and economic growth are examined.

27203 ■ Entrepreneurship, Innovation and the Growth Mechanism of the Free-Enterprise Economies
Pub: Princeton University Press
Ed: Eytan Sheshinski; William J. Baumol. Released: January 2007. Price: $65.00. Description: Scholars address the free-enterprise Western economies.

27204 ■ Entrepreneurship, Investment and Spatial Dynamics Lessons and Implications for an Enlarged EU
Pub: Edward Elgar Publishing, Incorporated
Ed: Nijkamp. Released: September 2006. Price: $100.00. Description: Understanding the impact and interaction between investment, knowledge and entrepreneurship with an expanding European Union.

27205 ■ Entrepreneurship in the U.S.: The 2005 Assessment
Pub: Springer
Ed: Paul Reynolds. Released: March 2007. Price: $79.95. Description: Entrepreneurship and its role in the U.S. economy is discussed, examining new business creation and its impact on job growth, productivity enhancements, innovation, and social mobility.

27206 ■ "Evaluating the 1996-2006 Employment Projections" in Montly Labor Review (Vol. 133, September 2010, No. 9, pp. 33)
Pub: Bureau of Labor Statistics
Description: Bureau of Labor Statistics employment projections outperformed alternative naive models, but not projecting the housing bubble or the rise in oil prices caused some inaccuracies in the projects. These projections are used by policymakers, economists, and students.

27207 ▪ *"Even Gold Gets Tarnished When Everyone Wants Cash"* in *Globe & Mail (February 28, 2007, pp. B1)*
Pub: CTVglobemedia Publishing Inc.
Ed: John Partridge. **Description:** The impact of fall in Chinese equities on the United States stock market and metal prices, including gold, is discussed.

27208 ▪ *"Even Money on Recession"* in *Barron's (Vol. 88, March 10, 2008, No. 10, pp. M9)*
Pub: Dow Jones & Company, Inc.
Ed: Gene Epstein. **Description:** Discusses the US unemployment rate which was steady in February 2008 at 4.8 percent, while nonfarm payroll employment decreased by 63,000 in the same month, with the private sector losing 101,000 jobs. The economic indicators showed mixed signals on whether or not the US economy is in a recession.

27209 ▪ *"Event Stresses Cross-Border Cooperation"* in *Crain's Detroit Business (Vol. 24, March 31, 2008, No. 13, pp. 5)*
Pub: Crain Communications, Inc.
Ed: Chad Halcom. **Description:** According to John Austin, a senior fellow of The Brookings Institution, open immigration policies, better transportation and trade across the border and a cleanup of the Great Lakes will bring economic resurgence to Midwestern states and Canadian provinces with manufacturing economies.

27210 ▪ *"Exit Strategy"* in *Barron's (Vol. 89, July 6, 2009, No. 27, pp. 3)*
Pub: Dow Jones & Co., Inc.
Ed: Alan Abelson. **Description:** US Federal Reserve is not likely to change its easy-money strategy in the short term. States such as California are suffering from spiraling costs and declining revenues and are struggling to balance their budgets. The US unemployment rate climbed to 9.5 percent in June 2009.

27211 ▪ *"Experts: Market Shaky But Resilient"* in *The Business Journal-Serving Metropolitan Kansas City (Vol. 27, September 19, 2008, No. 1)*
Pub: American City Business Journals, Inc.
Ed: Steve Vockrodt. **Description:** Investment advisers believe that the local investors in Kansas City who have a long-term approach towards their portfolios may come out even or even experience gains despite the Wall Street financial crisis. The impacts of the crisis are expected to take time to reach the area of Kansas City. The potential impacts of the Wall Street meltdown are examined further.

27212 ▪ *"Experts Take the Temp of Obama Plan"* in *The Business Journal-Serving Metropolitan Kansas City (Vol. 27, November 14, 2008, No. 10)*
Pub: American City Business Journals, Inc.
Ed: Rob Roberts. **Description:** Kansas City, Missouri-based employee benefits experts say president-elect Barack Obama's health care reform plan is on track. Insurance for children and capitalization for health information technology are seen as priority areas. The plan is aimed at reducing the number of uninsured people in the United States.

27213 ▪ *"Export Opportunity"* in *Business Journal-Portland (Vol. 24, October 12, 2007, No. 33, pp. 1)*
Pub: American City Business Journals, Inc.
Ed: Matthew Kish. **Description:** U.S. dollar is weak, hitting an all-time low against the Euro, while the Canadian dollar is also performing well it hit parity for the first time after more than thirty years. The weak U.S. dollar is making companies that sell overseas benefit as it makes their goods cheaper to buy.

27214 ▪ *"Face Values: Going for Global Growth"* in *Business Strategy Review (Vol. 21, Autumn 2010, No. 3, pp. 60)*
Pub: Wiley-Blackwell
Ed: Laura Tyson. **Description:** Global economic issues are discussed with Laura Tyson, former Dean of the London Business School, professor at University of California Berkeley, and current advisor to President Obama.

27215 ▪ *"Facebook: A Promotional Budget's Best Friend"* in *Women Entrepreneur (February 1, 2009)*
Pub: Entrepreneur Media Inc.
Ed: Tamara Monosoff. **Description:** Facebook began as a social networking website but has become a valuable marketing tool for all types of businesses, organizations and causes. Tips are provided for creating a Facebook account and growing one's network on Facebook.

27216 ▪ *"Facing the Future"* in *Canadian Business (Vol. 81, March 31, 2008, No. 5, pp. 69)*
Pub: Rogers Media
Ed: John Gray. **Description:** Discusses a web poll of 122 Canadian CEOs which shows that these leaders are convinced that the U.S. economy is slowing but are split on the impact that this will have on the Canadian economy. The aging and retiring workforce and the strong Canadian dollar are other concerns by these leaders.

27217 ▪ *"Fair Exchange"* in *Food and Drink (Winter 2010, pp. 84)*
Pub: Schofield Media Group
Ed: Don Mardak. **Description:** Bartering can assist firms in the food and beverage industry to attract new customers, maximize resources, and reduce cash expenses.

27218 ▪ *Falling Behind: How Rising Inequality Harms the Middle Class*
Pub: University of California Press
Contact: Alison Mudditt, Director
Ed: Robert H. Frank. **Released:** July 2007. **Price:** $21.95 paperback. **Description:** Economist argues that though middle-class American families aren't earning much more than they were a few decades ago, they are spending considerably more, a pattern attributed primarily to the context of seeing and emulating the spending habits of the rich.

27219 ▪ *"Falling Markets' Nastiest Habits"* in *Barron's (Vol. 88, July 7, 2008, No. 27, pp. 7)*
Pub: Dow Jones & Co., Inc.
Ed: Michael Santoli. **Description:** US market conditions reflect a bear market, with the S&P 500 index falling 20 percent below its recent high as of June 2008. The bear market is expected to persist in the immediate future, although bear market rallies are likely to occur.

27220 ▪ *False Economy: A Surprising Economic History of the World*
Pub: Riverhead Booksk
Ed: Alan Beattie. **Released:** 2009. **Price:** $26.95. **Description:** History shows that the choices made by countries, not luck, determine its economic fate.

27221 ▪ *Family Business*
Pub: Cengage South-Western
Ed: Ernesto J. Poza. **Released:** January 1, 2009. **Price:** $96.95. **Description:** Family-owned businesses face unique challenges in today's economy. This book provides the next generation of knowledge and skills required for profitable management and leadership in a family enterprise.

27222 ▪ *"Fannie and Freddie: How They'll Change"* in *Business Week (September 22, 2008, No. 4100, pp. 30)*
Pub: McGraw-Hill Companies, Inc.
Ed: Jane Sasseen. **Description:** Three possible outcomes of the fate of struggling mortgage giants Freddie Mac and Fannie Mae after the government bailout are outlined.

27223 ▪ *"The Fed Still Has Ammunition"* in *Barron's (Vol. 90, August 30, 2010, No. 35, pp. M9)*
Pub: Barron's Editorial & Corporate Headquarters
Ed: Randall W. Forsyth. **Description:** Federal Reserve chairman Ben Bernanke said the agency still has tools to combat deflation and a second downturn but these strategies are not needed at this time. The prospects of the Federal Open Market Committee's purchasing of treasuries are also discussed.

27224 ▪ *"Fed Tackles Bear of a Crisis"* in *Barron's (Vol. 88, March 17, 2008, No. 11, pp. M10)*
Pub: Dow Jones & Company, Inc.
Ed: Randall W. Forsyth. **Description:** Emergency funding package for Bear Stearns from the Federal Reserve Bank of New York through JPMorgan Chase is one of the steps taken by the central bank shore up bank liquidity. Prior to the emergency funding, the central bank announced the Term Securities Lending Facility to allow dealers to borrow easily saleable Treasuries in exchange for less-liquid issues.

27225 ▪ *"Federal Bailout, Three Years Later"* in *Business Owner (Vol. 35, September-October 2011, No. 5, pp. 6)*
Pub DL Perkins Company
Description: State of the economy and small business sector three years after the government stimulus and bailout programs were instituted.

27226 ▪ *Female Enterprise in the New Economy*
Pub: University of Toronto Press
Ed: Karen D. Hughes. **Released:** January 2006. **Price:** $67.00, paperback $27.50. **Description:** Examination of whether the increasingly entrepreneurial economy is offering women more opportunity or increases their risk for poverty and economic insecurity.

27227 ▪ *"Festivals Press on Despite Loss of Sponsors"* in *Crain's Detroit Business (Vol. 25, June 22, 2009, No. 25, pp. 3)*
Pub: Crain Communications Inc. - Detroit
Ed: Sherri Began Welch. **Description:** Organizers of local festivals are experiencing a decrease in sponsorship this summer due to the slow economy. These events help keep areas vibrant and stress the importance of community and cultural events.

27228 ▪ *"A Few Points of Contention"* in *Barron's (Vol. 88, July 14, 2008, No. 28, pp. 3)*
Pub: Dow Jones & Co., Inc.
Ed: Michael Santoli. **Description:** Headline inflation tends to revert to the lower core inflation, which excludes food and energy in its calculation over long periods. Prominent private equity figures believe that regulators should allow more than the de facto 10 percent to 25 percent limit of commercial banks to hasten the refunding of the financial sector.

27229 ▪ *"Fewer Banks Offer Big Gifts to Lure Clients"* in *Globe & Mail (March 14, 2006, pp. D1)*
Pub: CTVglobemedia Publishing Inc.
Ed: Chris Reidy. **Description:** Fewer banks are offering gifts to lure the customers in this year in the wake of less favorable interest rates in the spring season. The market climate is analyzed.

27230 ▪ *"Fewer People Dying At Work"* in *Sacramento Business Journal (Vol. 25, August 29, 2008, No. 26, pp. 1)*
Pub: American City Business Journals, Inc.
Ed: Kathy Robertson. **Description:** Statistics show that workplace deaths in California dropped by 24 percent in 2007 compared with the previous year. Much of the decline was observed in the construction industry, where a slowing economy affected employment and dangerous work. The number of workplace deaths in the state also declined in all major categories except fires and explosions.

27231 ▪ *"Fight Over Casino Funds Limits Kitty for MEDC"* in *Crain's Detroit Business (Vol. 24, January 21, 2008, No. 3, pp. 3)*
Pub: Crain Communications Inc. - Detroit
Ed: Amy Lane. **Description:** Michigan Economic Development Corporation is facing uncertainty due to a Michigan American Indian tribe from the southwestern portion of the state withholding its 8 percent casino revenue share.

27232 ▪ *"Filling the Business Gap"* in *Hispanic Business (December 2010)*
Pub: Hispanic Business
Ed: Richard Larsen. **Description:** New York group seeks to increase state diversity supplier spending to help create jobs and boost the economy. According

to a recent study, six out of 10 small business owners will increase capital spending but delay hiring in 2011. However, potential job creation is good among businesses owned by women and minorities.

27233 ■ "Film Incentives: A Hit or a Flop?" in Michigan Vue (Vol. 13, July-August 2008, No. 4, pp. 10)
Pub: Entrepreneur Media Inc.
Description: Michigan's new film incentive legislation is fulfilling its core purpose, according to Lisa Dancsok of the Michigan Economic Development Corp. (MEDC), by kickstarting the state's entry into the multi-billion dollar industry; the initiative is considered to be very competitive with other states and countries and is thought to be a way in which to help revitalize Michigan's struggling economy.

27234 ■ "The Final Frontier" in Canadian Business (Vol. 80, October 8, 2007, No. 20, pp. 127)
Pub: Rogers Media
Ed: Andy Holloway. **Description:** Effects of economic development in Northern Canada's natural environment are discussed. The caribou, which are still a primary source of food and clothing in the region, are dying. It is assumed that mining and petroleum projects are affecting the migration patterns of the animals inhabiting the region. The need to maintain a balance between the needs of resource companies and traditional businesses is also discussed.

27235 ■ "Financing for NNSA Plant Is a Work in Progress" in The Business Journal-Serving Metropolitan Kansas City (October 24, 2008)
Pub: American City Business Journals, Inc.
Ed: Rob Roberts. **Description:** The Kansas City Council approved a development plan for a $500 million nuclear weapons parts plant in south Kansas City. The US Congress approved a $59 million annual lease payment to the plant's developer. Financing for the construction of the plant remains in question as the plant's developers have to shoulder construction costs.

27236 ■ "Find the Upside to a Down Economy" in Women Entrepreneur (September 30, 2008)
Pub: Entrepreneur Media Inc.
Ed: Tamara Monosoff. **Description:** Starting a new business in this economic crisis may not be as daunting of a pursuit as one might think. Aspiring entrepreneurs may find success by looking for opportunities in unusual places and relying on what they do best.

27237 ■ "Finding Competitive Advantage in Adversity" in Harvard Business Review (Vol. 88, November 2010, No. 11, pp. 102)
Pub: Harvard Business School Publishing
Ed: Bhaskar Chakravorti. **Description:** Four opportunities in adversity are identified and applied to business scenarios. These are matching unmet needs with unneeded resources, seeking collaboration from unlikely partners, developing small/appropriate solutions to large/complex issues, and focusing on the platform as well as the product.

27238 ■ "Finding Room for Financing" in The Business Journal-Serving Metropolitan Kansas City (Vol. 26, August 1, 2008, No. 47, pp. 1)
Pub: American City Business Journals, Inc.
Ed: Rob Roberts. **Description:** Kansas City officials are expecting to receive financing recommendations for a new 1,000-room convention headquarters hotel. The $300-million project could be financed either through private ownership with public subsidies, or through public ownership with tax-exempt bond financing. Other views and information on the project and its expected economic impact, are presented.

27239 ■ "Finger-Pointing Time" in Barron's (Vol. 88, March 10, 2008, No. 10, pp. 9)
Pub: Dow Jones & Company, Inc.
Ed: Michael Santoli. **Description:** Discusses who is to blame for the financial crisis brought about by the credit crunch in the United States; the country's financial markets will eventually digest this crisis but will bottom out first before the situation improves.

27240 ■ "First Franchising Census Report Highlights Industry's Economic Role" in Franchising World (Vol. 42, November 2010, No. 11, pp. 41)
Pub: International Franchise Association
Ed: John Reynolds. **Description:** Franchise businesses accounted for 10.5 percent of businesses with paid employees in the year 2007.

27241 ■ "Five Low-Cost Home Based Startups" in Women Entrepreneur (December 16, 2008)
Pub: Entrepreneur Media Inc.
Ed: Lesley Spencer Pyle. **Description:** During tough economic times, small businesses have an advantage over large companies because they can adjust to economic conditions more easily and without having to go through corporate red tape that can slow the implementation process. A budding entrepreneur may find success by taking inventory of his or her skills, experience, expertise and passions and utilizing those qualities to start a business. Five low-cost home-based startups are profiled. These include starting an online store, a virtual assistant service, web designer, sales representative and a home staging counselor.

27242 ■ "A Flawed Yardstick for Banks" in Barron's (Vol. 88, July 14, 2008, No. 28, pp. M6)
Pub: Dow Jones & Co., Inc.
Ed: Arindam Nag. **Description:** Return on equity is no longer the best measure for investors to judge banks by in a post-subprime-crises world. Investors should consider the proportion of a bank's total assets that are considered risky and look out for any write-downs of goodwill when judging a bank's financial health.

27243 ■ "Florin Car Dealers Drive Plan" in Sacramento Business Journal (Vol. 25, August 22, 2008, No. 25, pp. 1)
Pub: American City Business Journals, Inc.
Ed: Melanie Turner. **Description:** Automobile dealers in Sacramento, California are working with the city and the business district in planning for future redevelopment in Florin Road. The move stemmed from pressure from the Elk Grove Auto Mall, high fuel prices and the credit crunch. The area has suffered business closures recently.

27244 ■ "Ford Canada's Edsel of a Year: Revenue Plummets 24 Percent in '05" in Globe & Mail (February 2, 2006, pp. B1)
Pub: CTVglobemedia Publishing Inc.
Ed: Greg Keenan. **Description:** Ford Motor Company of Canada Ltd. posted 24% decline in revenues for 2005. The drop in earnings is attributed to plant shutdown in Oaksville, Canada.

27245 ■ Freakonomics: A Rogue Economist Explores the Hidden Side of Everything
Pub: William Morrow
Ed: Steven D. Levitt; Stephen J. Dubner. **Price:** $25. 95.

27246 ■ "From Buyout to Busted" in Business Week (September 22, 2008, No. 4100, pp. 18)
Pub: McGraw-Hill Companies, Inc.
Ed: Emily Thornton; Deborah Stead. **Description:** Bankruptcy filings by private equity-backed companies are at a record high with 134 American firms taken private (or invested in) by buyout firms that have filed for protection this year under Chapter 11; this is 91 percent higher than the previous year, which had set a record when 70 of such companies filed for protection under Chapter 11.

27247 ■ "Fuel for Thought; Canadian Business Leaders on Energy Policy" in Canadian Business (Vol. 81, September 15, 2008, No. 14-15, pp. 12)
Pub: Rogers Media Ltd.
Ed: Joe Castaldo. **Description:** Most Canadian business leaders worry about the unreliability of the oil supply but feel that Canada is in a better position to

benefit from the energy supply crisis than other countries. Many respondents also highlighted the need to invest in renewable energy sources.

27248 ■ "Funeral Directors Get Creative As Boomers Near Great Beyond" in Advertising Age (Vol. 79, October 13, 2008, No. 38, pp. 30)
Pub: Crain Communications, Inc.
Ed: Lenore Skenazy. **Description:** Despite the downturn in the economy, the funeral business is thriving due to the number of baby boomers who realize the importance of making preparations for their death. Marketers are getting creative in their approach and many companies have taken into consideration the need for a more environmental friendly way to dispose of bodies and thus have created innovative businesses that reflect this need.

27249 ■ "The Future Is Another Country; Higher Education" in The Economist (Vol. 390, January 3, 2009, No. 8612, pp. 43)
Pub: The Economist Newspaper Inc.
Description: Due to the growth of the global corporation, more ambitious students are studying at universities abroad; the impact of this trend is discussed.

27250 ■ "The Future of Private Equity" in Canadian Business (Vol. 80, March 26, 2007, No. 7, pp. 19)
Pub: Rogers Media
Ed: Jack Mintz. **Description:** The impact growing Canadian economy and competition in global business on the performance of private equity funds is analyzed.

27251 ■ "Futures Shock for the CME" in Crain's Chicago Business (Vol. 31, November 10, 2008, No. 45, pp. 8)
Pub: Crain Communications, Inc.
Ed: Ann Saphir. **Description:** Chicago-based CME Group Inc., the largest futures exchange operator in the U.S., is facing a potentially radically altered regulatory landscape as Congress weighs sweeping reform of financial oversight. The possible merger of the CFTC and the Securities and Exchange Commission are among CME's concerns. Other details of possible regulatory measures are provided.

27252 ■ "Game On! African Americans Get a Shot at $17.9 Billion Video Game Industry" in Black Enterprise (Vol. 38, July 2008, No. 12, pp. 56)
Pub: Earl G. Graves Publishing Co. Inc.
Ed: Carolyn M. Brown. **Description:** Despite the economic crisis, consumers are still purchasing the hottest video games and hardware. Tips for African American developers who want to become a part of this industry that lacks content targeting this demographic are offered.

27253 ■ "Gas Supplies Low Heading Into Summer Season" in Globe & Mail (April 13, 2007, pp. B6)
Pub: CTVglobemedia Publishing Inc.
Ed: Shawn McCarthy. **Description:** The decrease in the supply of gas due to maintenance problems at refineries in the United States and Canada is discussed.

27254 ■ "George Cohon" in Canadian Business (Vol. 79, November 20, 2006, No. 23, pp. 70)
Pub: Rogers Media
Ed: Zena Olijnyk. **Description:** George Cohon, the founder of McDonald's in Canada and Russia, speaks about the Canadian market and the experience of starting McDonald's in Canada.

27255 ■ "German Win Through Sharing" in Canadian Business (Vol. 83, September 14, 2010, No. 15, pp. 16)
Pub: Rogers Media Ltd.
Ed: Jordan Timm. **Description:** German economic historian Eckhard Hoffner has a two-volume work showing how German's relaxed attitude toward copyright and intellectual property helped it catch up to industrialized United Kingdom. Hoffner's research

was in response to his interest in the usefulness of software patents. Information on the debate regarding Canada's copyright laws is given.

27256 ■ *"Get Back To Business Planning Fundamentals" in Entrepreneur (October 24, 2008)*
Pub: Entrepreneur Media Inc.
Ed: Tim Berry. **Description:** During a recession it is important to know what adjustment to make to your business plan. Some fundamentals to remember include: watching things more closely by tracking progress on cash, sales, new projects, customer satisfaction, ad spending and expenses; looking for built-in indicators such as what drives sales or expenses; watching what drives cash flow; and do not make mistakes such as laying off experienced employees too soon.

27257 ■ *"Get in Line" in Canadian Business (Vol. 79, September 25, 2006, No. 19, pp. 43)*
Pub: Rogers Media
Ed: Andy Holloway. **Description:** The needs of economically developing Canada's urban regions are discussed.

27258 ■ *"Get Off The Rollercoaster" in Michigan Vue (Vol. 13, July-August 2008, No. 4, pp. 19)*
Pub: Entrepreneur Media Inc.
Ed: Donald N. Hobley Jr. **Description:** Benefits of creating and implementing a solid financial plan during these rocky economic times are examined. Things to keep in mind before meeting with a financial planner include risk assessment, investment goals, the length of time required to meet those goals and the amount of money one has available to invest.

27259 ■ *"Get Over Your Fear of Change" in Canadian Business (Vol. 83, June 15, 2010, No. 10, pp. 38)*
Pub: Rogers Media Ltd.
Ed: Michelle Magnan. **Description:** Organizational behavior professor Chip Heath says that resistance to change is based on the conflict between our analytical, rational side and our emotional side that is in love with comfort. Heath states that businesses tend to focus on the negatives during an economic crisis while they should be focusing on what is working and ways to do more of that.

27260 ■ *"Getting In on the Ground Floor" in Barron's (Vol. 89, July 27, 2009, No. 30, pp. 32)*
Pub: Dow Jones & Co., Inc.
Ed: Jacqueline Doherty. **Description:** Shares of AvalonBay Communities have fallen 61 percent in the past two and a half years to July 2009 but at $56, the stock is trading near the asset value. The shares could rise as the economy improves and if the recovery takes longer, investors will be rewarded with a yield of 3.5 percent.

27261 ■ *"Ghazi Insists Downtown Project Still On" in The Business Journal-Milwaukee (Vol. 25, August 1, 2008, No. 45, pp. A1)*
Pub: American City Business Journals, Inc.
Ed: Rich Kirchen. **Description:** Afshin Ghazi remains confident that his $200 million Catalyst project in downtown Milwaukee, Wisconsin, will push through despite financial disputes delaying his EpiCentre project in Charlotte, North Carolina. He added that the Catalyst is on schedule for groundbreaking in the spring of 2009.

27262 ■ *Global Economic Crisis: Impact on Small Business*
Pub: Cengage South-Western
Ed: Global Economics Crisis Resource Center. **Released:** March 1, 2009. **Price:** $17.95. **Description:** A discussion of the historical context of the global economic crisis is presented, along with a discussion on the impact of this crisis on small businesses. It also provides learning goals, questions, key terms, and digital access to the Global Economic Crisis Resource Center.

27263 ■ *"The Global Economy, the Labor Force and Franchising's Future" in Franchising World (Vol. 42, September 2010,*

No. 9, pp. 35)
Pub: International Franchise Association
Ed: Jeffrey A. Rosensweig. **Description:** Point forecasting and the methodology called scenario analysis are presented looking at the global economy and future of franchising in the U.S. and abroad.

27264 ■ *"Global Market Could Be Silver Lining" in Hispanic Business (January-February 2008, pp. 14, 16, 18)*
Pub: Hispanic Business
Description: Economic slowdown in the U.S. is expected to continue through 2008. However, the export sector should hold steady during the same period.

27265 ■ *"Global Pain: Alberta's Gain" in Canadian Business (Vol. 79, August 14, 2006, No. 16-17, pp. 60)*
Pub: Rogers Media
Ed: Jeff Sanford. **Description:** Political problems and conflicts in oil-rich countries like Iran, Venezuela, and Russia among others, which have benefited the petroleum industry in Alberta, is discussed.

27266 ■ *"The Global Talent Hunt" in Business Strategy Review (Vol. 21, Spring 2010, No. 1, pp. 78)*
Pub: Wiley-Blackwell
Ed: Richard Emerton. **Description:** Richard Emerton explains how the new 'triple context' of economy, environment and society will have profound implications for human resource practices. He suggests that viewing talent as abundant is the right perspective for a manager.

27267 ■ *"Go Green Or Go Home" in Black Enterprise (Vol. 41, August 2010, No. 1, pp. 53)*
Pub: Earl G. Graves Publishing Co. Inc.
Ed: Tennille M. Robinson. **Description:** The green economy has become an essential part of every business, however, small business owners need to learn how to participate, including minority owned entrepreneurs.

27268 ■ *"Going Dutch" in Canadian Business (Vol. 81, October 27, 2008, No. 18, pp. 40)*
Pub: Rogers Media Ltd.
Description: Experts like Philippe Bergevin suggest that current economic conditions in Canada are similar to those of the Netherlands in the 1970s. The Organisation for Economic Co-operation suggested that Canada should instead invest in sovereign wealth funds similar to Norway's policy.

27269 ■ *"A Good Book Is Worth a Thousand Blogs" in Barron's (Vol. 88, July 14, 2008, No. 28, pp. 42)*
Pub: Dow Jones & Co., Inc.
Ed: Gene Epstein. **Description:** Nine summer book suggestions on economics are presented. The list includes 'The Revolution' by Ron Paul, 'The Forgotten Man' by Amity Shales, 'The Commitments of Traders Bible' by Stephen Briese, and 'Economic Facts and Fallacies' by Thomas Sowell.

27270 ■ *"Good for Business: Houston is a Hot Spot for Economic Growth" in Black Enterprise (Vol. 37, October 2006, No. 3, pp. 216)*
Pub: Earl G. Graves Publishing Co. Inc.
Ed: Jeanette Valentine. **Description:** Fast-growing sectors in the biotechnology and healthcare industries are among the driving forces of Houston's economic growth. More than 76,000 small businesses in the area employ about one in four area workers, according to the Small Business Administration. Housing and business costs are 26 and 11 percent below the national average, respectively, garnering the attention of corporate giants.

27271 ■ *Good Capitalism, Bad Capitalism, and the Economics of Growth and Prosperity*
Pub: Yale University Press
Ed: William J. Baumol, Robert E. Litan, Carl J. Schramm. **Released:** October 1, 2009. **Price:** $22.00. **Description:** The book identifies the conditions that characterize good capitalism and discusses capitalist economies.

27272 ■ *"A Good Sign for Commercial Real Estate" in Austin Business JournalInc. (Vol. 29, December 18, 2009, No. 41, pp. 1)*
Pub: American City Business Journals
Ed: Kate Harrington. **Description:** Factors that could contribute to the reemergence of the commercial mortgage-backed securities market in Texas are discussed. These securities can potentially boost the commercial real estate market statewide as well as nationwide. Commercial mortgage-backed securities origination in 2009 is worth less that $1 billion, compared with $238 billion in 2008.

27273 ■ *"A Good Step, But There's a Long Way to Go" in Business Week (September 22, 2008, No. 4100, pp. 10)*
Pub: McGraw-Hill Companies, Inc.
Ed: James C. Cooper. **Description:** Despite the historic action by the U.S. government to nationalize the mortgage giants Freddie Mac and Fannie Mae, rising unemployment rates may prove to be an even bigger roadblock to bringing back the economy from its downward spiral. The takeover is meant to restore confidence in the credit markets and help with the mortgage crisis but the rising rate in unemployment may make many households unable to take advantage of any benefits which arise from the bailout. Statistical data included.

27274 ■ *"Good Things Happen When We Buy Local" in Crain's Detroit Business (Vol. 24, October 6, 2008, No. 40, pp. 7)*
Pub: Crain Communications, Inc.
Description: Michigan is facing incredibly difficult economic times. One way in which each one of us can help the state and the businesses located here is by purchasing our goods and services from local vendors. The state Agriculture Department projected that if Michigan households earmarked $10 per week in their grocery purchases to made-in-Michigan products, this would generate $30 million a week in economic impact.

27275 ■ *"Goodwill Haunts Local Companies; Bad Buyouts During Boom Times Producing Big Writedowns" in Crain's Chicago Business (Apr. 28, 2008)*
Pub: Crain Communications, Inc.
Ed: Ann Saphir. **Description:** Many companies are having to face the reality that they overpaid for accuisitions made in better economic times; investors often dismiss such one-time charges as mere accounting adjustments but writeoffs related to past acquisitions can signal future problems because they mean the expected profits that justified the purchase have not materialized. Writeoffs are particularly worrisome for firms with a lot of debt and whose banks require them to have enough assets to back up their borrowings.

27276 ■ *"Government Intervention" in Canadian Business (Vol. 79, November 6, 2006, No. 22, pp. 116)*
Pub: Rogers Media
Description: The effects of income trust tax on economic conditions and investment of Canada are presented.

27277 ■ *"Grainger Show Highlights Building Green, Economy" in Contractor (Vol. 57, February 2010, No. 2, pp. 3)*
Pub: Penton Media, Inc.
Ed: Candace Roulo. **Description:** chief U.S. economist told attendees of the Grainger's 2010 Total MRO Solutions National Customer Show that the economic recovery would be subdued. Mechanical contractors who attended the event also learned about building sustainable, green products, and technologies, and economic and business challenges.

27278 ■ *"Grand Letdown" in The Business Journal-Milwaukee (Vol. 25, September 12, 2008, No. 51, pp. A1)*
Pub: American City Business Journals, Inc.
Ed: Rich Kirchen. **Description:** Overview of retail trade in Milwaukee, Wisconsin is presented. It has been observed that vacancies in storefronts both east and west of the Milwaukee River have increased,

and the Shops of Grand Avenue has yet to attract new retailers or shoppers. The completion of the Marquette Interchange is also discussed.

27279 ■ *"Gray, Gray, & Gray: a Difficult Year for Oilheat" in Indoor Comfort Marketing (Vol. 70, September 2011, No. 9, pp. 30)*
Pub: Industry Publications Inc.

Description: According to the 20th Annual Oilheat Industry Survey, 2011 will be another dismal year for the industry sector.

27280 ■ *"The Great Cleanup" in Canadian Business (Vol. 81, April 14, 2008, No. 6, pp. 50)*
Pub: Rogers Media

Ed: Graham Silnicki. **Description:** China's rectification program includes the licensing of 100 percent of food producers and monitoring of 100 percent of raw materials for exports between August and December, 2007. There is a lot of money to be made for those who are willing to help China win its quality battle. PharmEng International Inc. is one of the companies that helps Chinese companies meet international quality standards.

27281 ■ *"The Great Deleveraging" in Canadian Business (Vol. 81, October 13, 2008, No. 17, pp. 45)*
Pub: Rogers Media Ltd.

Ed: Jeff Sanford. **Description:** 'Hell Week' of financial crisis on Wall Street is believed to have started with the downgrade of AIG Inc.'s credit rating. AIG is a major player in the credit derivatives market, and its bankruptcy would have affected firms on Wall Street.

27282 ■ *"The Great Fall" in Barron's (Vol. 88, March 10, 2008, No. 10, pp. 5)*
Pub: Dow Jones & Company, Inc.

Ed: Alan Abelson. **Description:** Discusses the US economy is considered to be in a recession, with the effects of the credit crisis expected to intensify as a result. Inflation is estimated at 4.3 percent in January 2008, while 63,000 jobs were lost in February 2008.

27283 ■ *The Great Inflation and Its Aftermath: The Past and Future of American Affluence*
Pub: Random House Inc.

Contact: Richard Sarnoff, President

Ed: Robert J. Samuelson. **Released:** 2009. **Price:** $26.00. **Description:** How inflation has shaped the economics in today's United States is examined.

27284 ■ *"The Great Moderation" in Canadian Business (Vol. 80, February 12, 2007, No. 4, pp. 25)*
Pub: Rogers Media

Ed: David Wolf. **Description:** Caution over the changes to stock inventory levels and their adverse impact on the Canadian economy is discussed.

27285 ■ *The Green Collar Economy: How One Solution Can Fix Our Two Biggest Problems*
Pub: HarperCollins Publishers

Ed: Van Jones. **Released:** November 1, 2009. **Price:** $14.99. **Description:** This book offers insight into rebuilding the nation's infrastructure and creating alternative energy sources that could boost the economy through increased employment and higher wages while decreasing our dependence on fossil fuels.

27286 ■ *"Greg Stringham" in Canadian Business (Vol. 81, March 3, 2008, No. 3, pp. 8)*
Pub: Rogers Media

Ed: Michelle Magnan. **Description:** Canadian Association of Petroleum Producers' Greg Stringham thinks that the new royalty plan will result in companies pulling out their investments for Alberta's conventional oil and gas sector. Stringham adds that Alberta is losing its competitive advantage and companies must study their cost profiles to retrieve that advantage. The effects of the royalty system on Alberta's economy are examined further.

27287 ■ *The Gridlock Economy: How Too Much Ownership Wrecks Markets, Stops Innovation, and Costs Lives*
Pub: Basic Books

Ed: Michael Heller. **Released:** 2009. **Price:** $26.00. **Description:** While private ownership generally creates wealth, the author believes that economic gridlock results when too many people own pieces of one thing, which results in too many people being able to block each other from creating or using a scarce source.

27288 ■ *"Grin and Bear It" in Canadian Business (Vol. 81, March 3, 2008, No. 3, pp. 53)*
Pub: Rogers Media

Ed: Jeff Sanford. **Description:** Discusses the United States economic downturn, caused by the credit market crisis, which is expected to affect the Canadian economy, as Canada depend on the U.S. for 80 percent of its exports. Economist David Rosenberg thinks that in 2008, housing prices will decline by 15 percent and gross domestic product growth will slow to 0.8 percent. Other forecasts for Canadian economy are given.

27289 ■ *"Growing Field" in Crain's Detroit Business (Vol. 26, January 11, 2010, No. 2, pp. 3)*
Pub: Crain Communications Inc.

Description: Detroit's TechTown was awarded a combination loan and grant of $4.1 million from the U.S. Department of Housing and Urban Development to build a 15,000-square-foot stem cell center, a collection of laboratories that will be available to both for-profit companies and university researchers.

27290 ■ *"Growing Pains" in Crain's Cleveland Business (Vol. 30, June 22, 2009, No. 24, pp. 3)*
Pub: Crain Communications, Inc.

Ed: Shannon Mortland. **Description:** Judson's latest retirement community, called South Franklin Circle, is near completion despite a faltering economy and delays. Details of the project are explored.

27291 ■ *"Growth in Fits and Starts" in Canadian Business (Vol. 83, July 20, 2010, No. 11-12, pp. 18)*
Pub: Rogers Media Ltd.

Ed: James Cowan. **Description:** US home sales and manufacturing indicators have dropped and fears of a double-dip recession are widespread. However, a chief economist says that this is endemic to what can be seen after a recession caused by a financial crisis. In Canada, consumer optimism is rising and anxiety over losing one's job is waning.

27292 ■ *"Growth Seen Climbing Out of a Trough" in Globe & Mail (March 3, 2007, pp. B5)*
Pub: CTVglobemedia Publishing Inc.

Ed: Tavia Grant. **Description:** The economic condition of Canada in the fourth quarter 2006 is analyzed. The gross domestic product rose 1.4 percent in the fourth quarter.

27293 ■ *Guerrilla Marketing During Tough Times*
Pub: Morgan James Publishing, LLC

Ed: Jay Conrad Levinson. **Released:** November 2005. **Price:** $14.00. **Description:** Ways to market a small business during slow economic times.

27294 ■ *"H&M Offers a Dress for Less" in Canadian Business (Vol. 83, September 14, 2010, No. 15, pp. 20)*
Pub: Rogers Media Ltd.

Ed: Laura Cameron. **Description:** Swedish clothing company H&M has implemented loss leader strategy by pricing some dresses at extremely low prices. The economy has forced retailers to keep prices down despite the increasing cost of manufacturing, partly due to Chinese labor becoming more expensive. How the trend will affect apparel companies is discussed.

27295 ■ *"Hank and Ben: Hedgies' BFFs" in Barron's (Vol. 88, March 31, 2008, No. 13, pp. 50)*
Pub: Dow Jones & Company, Inc.

Ed: Tom Sullivan. **Description:** David Ballin of Alternative Investment Solutions says that everything in the financial markets is tainted and beaten-up which presents an extraordinary opportunity for hedge funds as long as they back up their decisions with sharp and intensive research. He adds that money managers should short suspect stocks and go long on undeservedly battered stocks in the same sector.

27296 ■ *"Hank Paulson On the Housing Bailout and What's Ahead" in Business Week (September 22, 2008, No. 4100, pp. 19)*
Pub: McGraw-Hill Companies, Inc.

Ed: Maria Bartiromo. **Description:** Interview with Treasury Secretary Henry Paulson in which he discusses the bailout of Fannie Mae and Freddie Mac as well as the potential impact on the American economy and foreign interests and investments in the country. Paulson has faith that the government's actions will help to stabilize the housing market.

27297 ■ *"Has Daylight Savings Time Fuelled Gasoline Consumption" in Globe & Mail (April 14, 2007, pp. B1)*
Pub: CTVglobemedia Publishing Inc.

Ed: Shawn McCarthy. **Description:** The prospects of the acquisition of BCE Inc, by Canadian pension funds are discussed. The effect of the growth of these pension funds on the Canadian economy is described.

27298 ■ *"Hastily Enacted Regulation Will Not Cure Economic Crisis" in Crain's Chicago Business (Vol. 31, May 5, 2008, No. 18, pp. 18)*
Pub: Crain Communications, Inc.

Ed: Stephen P. D'Arcy. **Description:** Policymakers are looking for ways to respond to what is possibly the greatest financial crisis of a generation due to the collapse of the housing market, the credit crisis and the volatility of Wall Street.

27299 ■ *"Have High-Tech Tax Credits Helped or Hurt Hawaii?" in Hawaii Business (Vol. 53, December 2007, No. 6, pp. 28)*
Pub: Hawaii Business Publishing

Description: Presents the opinons of Channel Capital LLC's Walter R. Roth and Hawaii Venture Capital Association's Bill Spencer concerning the impacts of tax credits. Roth thinks that Act 221 appeals to investors who can earn despite business failure while Spencer thinks that the legislation promotes investments in innovative technology firms. The need to support tax credits is also discussed.

27300 ■ *"Hawaii's Identity Crisis" in Hawaii Business (Vol. 53, November 2007, No. 5, pp. 10)*
Pub: Hawaii Business Publishing

Ed: Kelli Abe Trifonovitch. **Description:** Some Hawaiians have shown that the Superferry controversy makes it seem to the rest of the world as if they do not know what they are doing, and intensifies several issues regarding the stability of investing in Hawaii. With or without the Superferry, there is still no evidence that investors are afraid to put their money in Hawaii.

27301 ■ *"Headwinds From the New Sod Slow Aer Lingus" in Barron's (Vol. 88, March 10, 2008, No. 10, pp. M6)*
Pub: Dow Jones & Company, Inc.

Ed: Sean Walters; Arindam Nag. **Description:** Aer Lingus faces a drop in its share prices with a falling US market, higher jet fuel prices, and lower long-haul passenger load factors. British media companies Johnston Press and Yell Group are suffering from weaker ad revenue and heavier debt payments due to the credit crunch.

27302 ■ *"A Heavy Burden" in Crain's Cleveland Business (Vol. 30, June 8, 2009,*

No. 22, pp. 13)
Pub: Crain Communications, Inc.

Ed: Chuck Soder. **Description:** Small business owners are making sacrifices in the tight economy. In a recent survey conducted by American Express, 30 percent of the 727 small business owners questioned said they no longer take salaries from their firms.

27303 ■ *"Help for Job Seekers" in Crain's Detroit Business (Vol. 26, January 4, 2010, No. 1, pp. 14)*
Pub: Crain Communications Inc.

Description: CareerWorks is weekly paper targeting readers who are in a career transition or are looking for new employment.

27304 ■ *"High Anxiety" in Canadian Business (Vol. 80, November 19, 2007, No. 23, pp. 11)*
Pub: Rogers Media

Ed: Zena Olijnyk. **Description:** Value of Canadian dollar continues to rise, and consumers are asking for lower prices of goods. Retailers, on the other hand, are facing concerns over losing sales. The impacts of the rising Canadian dollar on the business sector and consumer behavior are examined.

27305 ■ *"High-End Blunders" in Crain's Chicago Business (Vol. 31, April 21, 2008, No. 16, pp. 54)*
Pub: Crain Communications, Inc.

Ed: Laura Bianchi. **Description:** Discusses some of the biggest errors sellers make that keep their homes from selling including: pricing too high; expecting to recoup the cost of very high-end amenities and decor; avant-garde decorating; owners that hover when the house is being shown; stripping the home of top-quality light fixtures and hardware and replacing them with inferior versions with the assumption that the new buyer will come in with their own decorator and redo it; and poorly maintained properties.

27306 ■ *"The High-Intensity Entrepreneur" in Harvard Business Review (Vol. 88, September 2010, No. 9, pp. 74)*
Pub: Harvard Business School Publishing

Ed: Anne S. Habiby, Deirdre M. Coyle Jr. **Description:** Examination of the role of small companies in promoting global economic growth is presented. Discussion includes identifying entrepreneurial capability.

27307 ■ *High Wire: The Precarious Financial Lives of American Families*
Pub: Basic Books

Ed: Peter Gosselin. **Released:** 2009. **Price:** $26.95. **Description:** Despite the general prosperity in America, household finances are growing more precarious making people more anxious about their economic prospects in the future.

27308 ■ *"High-Yield Turns Into Road Kill" in Barron's (Vol. 88, July 7, 2008, No. 27, pp. M7)*
Pub: Dow Jones & Co., Inc.

Ed: Emily Barrett. **Description:** High-yield bonds have returned to the brink of collapse after profits have recovered from the shock brought about by the collapse of Bear Stearns. The high-yield bond market could decline again due to weakness in the automotive sector, particularly in Ford and General Motors.

27309 ■ *"Hispanic Business 100 Fastest-Growing Companies" in Hispanic Business (July-August 2009, pp. 16-18)*
Pub: Hispanic Business

Ed: Joshua Molina. **Description:** Despite the recession, the 100 fastest growing companies profiled are able to maintain their competitive edge federal contracts are key to their success. Service companies are at the top of the list and Texas and Florida are the states in which the top are located.

27310 ■ *"Hispanic Executives Continue Their Rise to Prominence Amid a Shaky Economy" in Hispanic Business (January-February*

2009, pp. 12-14)
Pub: Hispanic Business

Ed: Michael Bowker. **Description:** Hispanic Business Media's 2009 Corporate Elite winners defied expectations and a tough economy and rose to the top of their industries; innovation being cited as key to growth of Hispanic-owned companies.

27311 ■ *"Hispantelligence Report" in Hispanic Business (January-February 2009, pp. 10)*
Pub: Hispanic Business

Description: U.S. Hispanic purchasing power is expected to reach $958 billion in 2009 and projected to reach $1.25 trillion by 2015, a rate of more than two times the overall national rate. Statistical data included.

27312 ■ *A History of Small Business in America*
Pub: University of North Carolina Press
Contact: Kate Douglas Torrey, Director
E-mail: kate_torrey@unc.edu
Ed: Mansel G. Blackford. **Released:** May 2003. **Price:** $22.95. **Description:** History of American small business from the colonial era to present, showing how it has played a role in the nation's economic, political, and cultural development across manufacturing, sales, services and farming.

27313 ■ *"Hitting Bottom?" in Barron's (Vol. 88, March 24, 2008, No. 12, pp. 21)*
Pub: Dow Jones & Company, Inc.

Ed: Jacqueline Doherty. **Description:** Brokerage houses and banks may stabilize in 2008 as a result of regulatory responses brought about by the near-collapse of Bear Stearns. Some of their shares may rise by as much as 20 percent from 2008 to 2009.

27314 ■ *"Ho, Ho, Ho!" in Retail Merchandiser (Vol. 51, September-October 2011, No. 5, pp. 10)*
Pub: Phoenix Media Corporation

Ed: Ted Vaughan. **Description:** Despite consumer caution and economic woes, retail leaders are expecting a high volume holiday selling season for 2011 Christmas. Statistical data covering holiday sales expectations is included.

27315 ■ *"Hobbies Hold Fast" in Playthings (Vol. 106, November 1, 2008, No. 1, pp. 6)*
Pub: Reed Business Information
Contact: Jeff Greisch, President
Ed: Karyn M. Peterson. **Description:** Profile of the 24th Annual iHobby Expo is presented. The event is a combined trade and consumer show offering a look at the latest releases in die-cast collectibles, model railroads and aircraft, slot cars, remote control vehicles, rocketry, robotics, military toys, wood/plastic model kits, games, etc.

27316 ■ *"Hold the McJobs: Canada's High-End Employment Boom" in Globe & Mail (February 17, 2006, pp. B1)*
Pub: CTVglobemedia Publishing Inc.

Ed: Heather Scoffield. **Description:** A focus the increasing rate of high-end or professional jobs Canada and its negative influence on low-end and middle level jobs is presented.

27317 ■ *"Hold Your Nose, Say 'Da'" in Canadian Business (Vol. 79, September 11, 2006, No. 18, pp. 151)*
Pub: Rogers Media

Ed: Thomas Watson. **Description:** The changing business environment and investment opportunities in Russia despite its instable democracy are discussed. Russia's potential and its ability to attract productive investment are presented.

27318 ■ *"Holiday Parties to Take a Hit in Hard Times" in Philadelphia Business Journal (Vol. 28, November 6, 2009, No. 38, pp. 1)*
Pub: American City Business Journals

Ed: Peter van Allen. **Description:** Companies are cutting expenses in view of the economic downturn and are changing the way holiday parties will be held. Sixty-two percent of firms will still hold parties in 2009, but last minute decisions about reduced-cost parties are being made.

27319 ■ *"Holiday Sales Look Uncertain for Microsoft and PC Sellers" in Puget Sound Business Journal (Vol. 29, November 28, 2008, No. 32)*
Pub: American City Business Journals

Ed: Todd Bishop. **Description:** Personal computer makers face uncertain holiday sales for 2008 as a result of the weak U.S. economy and a shift toward low-cost computers. Personal computer shipments for the fourth quarter 2008 are forecast to drop 1 percent compared to the same quarter 2007.

27320 ■ *"The Hollow Debate" in Canadian Business (Vol. 81, March 3, 2008, No. 3, pp. 26)*
Pub: Rogers Media

Ed: Thomas Watson. **Description:** According to a report conducted by the Conference Board of Canada, the Canadian business community is not being hollowed out by acquisitions made by foreign companies. Findings further showed that local businesses are protected by dual shares and that the economy can benefit more from foreign acquisitions than local mergers. The need to relax foreign ownership restrictions and other recommendations are presented.

27321 ■ *"The Home Game" in Canadian Business (Vol. 80, October 8, 2007, No. 20, pp. 68)*
Pub: Rogers Media

Ed: Rachel Pulfer. **Description:** Analysis of Canada's banking industry is presented. Trends show that Canadian banks avoid risks in their investments, and usually choose to take safer paths. Experts believe these trends affect the country's economy and that Canadian banks do not play a significant role in economic development.

27322 ■ *"A Home of Her Own" in Hawaii Business (Vol. 53, October 2007, No. 4, pp. 51)*
Pub: Hawaii Business Publishing

Ed: Maria Torres-Kitamura. **Description:** It was observed that the number of single women in Hawaii purchasing their own home has increased, as that in the whole United States where the percentage has increased from 14 percent in 1995 to 22 percent in 2006. However, First Hawaiian Bank's Wendy Lum thinks that the trend will not continue in Hawaii due to lending restrictions. The factors that women consider in buying a home of their own are presented.

27323 ■ *"Home Prices Sag" in Crain's Chicago Business (Vol. 31, April 28, 2008, No. 17, pp. 3)*
Pub: Crain Communications, Inc.

Ed: Alby Gallun. **Description:** Since the slump in the housing market is continuing with no sign of recovery, Chicago-area home prices are poised for an even steeper drop this year. In 2007, the region's home prices fell nearly 5 percent and according to a forecast by Fiserv Inc., they will decline 8.1 percent this year and another 2.2 percent in 2009. Statistical data included.

27324 ■ *"Homeownership: Still the American Dream?" in Gallup Management Journal (May 5, 2011)*
Pub: Gallup

Description: The mortgage finance system is broken. Housing prices continue to fall. Foreclosures are expected to increase in the coming months. However, Gallup's chief economist does not believe this is the end of the American dream of owning one's own home.

27325 ■ *"Homes, Not Bars, Stay Well Tended" in Advertising Age (Vol. 79, January 28, 2008, No. 4, pp. 8)*
Pub: Crain Communications, Inc.

Ed: Jeremy Mullman. **Description:** Due to the downturn in the economy, consumers are drinking less at bars and restaurants; however, according to the Distilled Spirits Council of the United States, they are still purchasing expensive liquor to keep in their homes.

27326 ■ "Honest Harry" in Hawaii Business (Vol. 53, November 2007, No. 5, pp. 39)
Pub: Hawaii Business Publishing

Ed: David K. Choo. Description: Mayor Harry Kim testified in support of the Superferry controversial in Hawaii last September 2007. Kim says that the Superferry would allow local business and families to have more opportunities for commerce and recreation. Kim's testimony was not persuasive enough for Maui Circuit Judge Joseph Cardoza who ruled that the Superferry may not operate while an environmental assessment is being completed.

27327 ■ "Hospitals Feel Pain from Slow Economy" in Business Courier (Vol. 27, September 3, 2010, No. 18, pp. 1)
Pub: Business Courier

Ed: James Ritchie. Description: Hospitals in Cincinnati, Ohio have suffered from decreased revenues owing to the economic crises. Declining patient volumes and bad debt have also adversely impacted hospitals.

27328 ■ "Hot-Button Ordinances May Go Up for Review" in Crain's Detroit Business (Vol. 26, January 18, 2010, No. 3, pp. 1)
Pub: Crain Communications Inc.

Ed: Nancy Kaffer. Description: Detroit's economic fate may be tied to the city's anti-privatization ordinance and its policy of giving contract preference to Detroit-based businesses. The new administration feels that it is time to put everything on the table in an attempt to look for ways in which to save the city money.

27329 ■ "Hot For All The Wrong Reasons" in Canadian Business (Vol. 81, March 31, 2008, No. 5, pp. 19)
Pub: Rogers Media

Ed: Andrea Jezovit. Description: Soaring platinum prices are due to South Africa's platinum mining industry's safety issues and power supply disruptions that exacerbate the metal's supply problems. South Africa supplies 80 percent of the world's platinum. South Africa's power utility has said that it cannot guarantee the industry's power needs until 2013.

27330 ■ "Hotel Woes Reflect Area Struggle" in Business Journal Serving Greater Tampa Bay (Vol. 30, December 3, 2010, No. 50, pp. 1)
Pub: Tampa Bay Business Journal

Ed: Mark Holan. Description: Quality Inn and Suites in East Tampa, Florida has struggled against the sluggish economy but remained open to guests despite facing a foreclosure. The hotel project is the center of East Tampa's redevelopment plans and public officials defend the $650,000 investment in public amenities near the building.

27331 ■ "Hotels' Healthy Finish in '07" in Crain's Chicago Business (Vol. 31, March 24, 2008, No. 12, pp. 16)
Pub: Crain Communications, Inc.

Ed: Alby Gallun. Description: Chicago's hotel market saw mostly rising occupancies and room rates in the fourth quarter of 2007, reflecting continued strong demand from leisure and business travelers; however, due to the current state of the economy hoteliers face an increasingly uncertain outlook.

27332 ■ House of Cards
Pub: Doubleday, a Division of Random House

Ed: William D. Cohan. Released: March 10, 2009. Price: $27.95. Description: The fall of Bear Stearns and the beginning of the Wall Street Collapse.

27333 ■ "House Prices Cooling Off, With Alberta Gearing Down" in Globe & Mail (February 9, 2007, pp. B4)
Pub: CTVglobemedia Publishing Inc.

Ed: Tavia Grant. Description: The house prices in Alberta, which are experiencing a torrid pace in price growth, are steady in the first month of 2007. The easing in house prices may show impact on inflation.

27334 ■ "Housing Market Dinged, But Not Done In, By Nationwide Slump" in Business

Review, Albany New York (Vol. 34, December 21, 2007)
Pub: American City Business Journals, Inc.

Ed: Michael DeMasi. Description: Kirsten Keefe, a staff attorney of the Empire Justice Center, is questioning the validity of statistics that represent the number of home foreclosures in New York.

27335 ■ "Housing Markets Still Struggling" in Montana Business Quarterly (Vol. 49, Spring 2011, No. 1, pp. 17)
Pub: Bureau of Business & Economic Research

Ed: Scott Rickard. Description: Montana's economic conditions are a bit better than national averages. Data ranked by state, year-over-year price change, and total price peak is presented, along with statistical data for the entire nation.

27336 ■ "How Bad Is It?" in Hawaii Business (Vol. 54, July 2008, No. 1, pp. 35)
Pub: Hawaii Business Publishing

Ed: Jolyn Okimoto Rosa. Description: Donald G. Horner, chief executive officer of First Hawaiian Bank, says that the current Hawaiian economic situation is a cyclical slowdown. Maurice Kaya, an energy consultant, says the slowdown is due to overdependence on imported fuels. Other local leaders, such as Constance H. Lau, also discuss their view on the current economic situation in Hawaii.

27337 ■ "How to Beat the Pros" in Canadian Business (Vol. 81, Summer 2008, No. 9, pp. 59)
Pub: Rogers Media Ltd.

Ed: Calvin Leung. Description: Table showing the results of the Investor 500 beat the S&P/TSX composite index is presented. The average total return, best performing stocks and total return of the 2007 stock screen are provided.

27338 ■ "How Exports Could Save America" in Barron's (Vol. 89, July 20, 2009, No. 29, pp. 15)
Pub: Dow Jones & Co., Inc.

Ed: Jonathan R. Laing. Description: Increase in US exports should help drive up the nation's economic growth, according to Wells Capital Management strategist Jim Paulsen. He believes US gross domestic product could grow by 3-3.5 percent annually starting in 2010 due to a more favorable trade balance.

27339 ■ How to Make Money in Stocks: A Winning System in Good Times and Bad
Pub: The McGraw-Hill Companies

Ed: William J. O'Neil. Released: June 12. 2009. Price: $16.95. Description: The bestselling guide to buying stocks, from the founder of Investor's Business Daily. The technique is based on a study of the greatest stock market winners dating back to 1953 and includes a seven-step process for minimizing risk, maximizing return, and finding stocks that are ready to perform.

27340 ■ "How Our Picks Beat The Bear" in Barron's (Vol. 88, July 14, 2008, No. 28, pp. 18)
Pub: Dow Jones & Co., Inc.

Ed: Andrew Bary. Description: Performance of the stocks that Barron's covered in the first half of 2008 is discussed; some of the worst picks and most rewarding pans have been in the financial sector while the best plays were in the energy, materials, and the transportation sectors.

27341 ■ "How to Ramp Up Marketing in a Downturn" in Entrepreneur (Vol. 37, July 2009, No. 7, pp. 55)
Pub: Entrepreneur Media, Inc.

Ed: Jeff Wuorio. Description: How businesses can save money while boosting their marketing efforts during a down economy is discussed. Using price-driven marketing, online social networks, and cause-driven marketing are among the suggested ways companies can attract more customers. Guarantees and warranties, as well as contests, can also be used as marketing tools.

27342 ■ How to Start Your Own Business for Entrepreneurs
Pub: FT Press

Ed: Robert Ashton. Released: December 9, 2010. Price: $24.99. Description: More than 300,000 individuals start a business every year. That number will rise over the next year or two if the current economic downturn leads to widespread job losses.

27343 ■ "The HST Hornet's Nest" in Canadian Business (Vol. 83, September 14, 2010, No. 15, pp. 17)
Pub: Rogers Media Ltd.

Ed: Michael McCullough. Description: Canadian Premier Gordon Campbell's Harmonized Sales Tax (HST) initiative has left British Columbia's economic and political future stuck in uncertainty. The petition of a coalition group forced a bill to abolish the HST through legislation or referendum. How the HST's abolition will affect British Columbia's revenues is also discussed.

27344 ■ "The Human Factor" in Canadian Business (Vol. 80, October 8, 2007, No. 20, pp. 22)
Pub: Rogers Media

Ed: Alex Mynek. Description: David Foot, a demographer and an economics professor at the University of Toronto, talks about Canada's future, including economic and demographic trends. He discusses activities that should be done by businessmen in order to prepare for the future. He also addresses the role of the Canadian government in economic development.

27345 ■ "I-5 Bridge Funding Unclear" in The Business Journal-Portland (Vol. 25, July 11, 2008, No. 18, pp. 1)
Pub: American City Business Journals, Inc.

Ed: Andy Giegerich. Description: Financing for a new Interstate 5 bridge is unclear as Washington lawmakers identify two priority projects other than the planned bridge, which is shared with Oregon. An estimate says that the two states could pay between $487.6 million and $1.5 billion for the new bridge. Other details on the financing of the project are discussed.

27346 ■ "Idea Nation" in Canadian Business (Vol. 80, December 25, 2006, No. 1, pp. 57)
Pub: Rogers Media

Ed: Andy Holloway. Description: The potential of manufacturing companies and their innovations in the progress of the Canadian economy is discussed.

27347 ■ "Ideas at Work: Total Communicator" in Business Strategy Review (Vol. 21, Autumn 2010, No. 3, pp. 10)
Pub: Blackwell Publishers Ltd.

Ed: Stuart Crainer. Description: Vittorio Colao has been chief executive of Vodafone Group for two years. He brings to the company special experience as CEO of RCS MediaGroup in Milan, which publishes newspapers, magazines and books in Italy, Spain and France. Prior to RCS, he held other positions within Vodaphone. Colao shares his views on business, the global economy and leading Vodafone.

27348 ■ "Ideas at Work: Total Communicator" in Business Strategy Review (Vol. 21, Autumn 2010, No. 3, pp. 10)
Pub: Wiley-Blackwell

Ed: Stuart Crainer. Description: Vittorio Colao has been chief executive of Vodafone Group for two years. He brings to the company some special experience: from 2004-2006 he was CEO of RCS Media-Group in Milan, which publishes newspapers, magazines and books in Italy, Spain and France. Colao shares his views on business, the global economy and leading Vodafone.

27349 ■ "If You Go Into the Market Today.." in Canadian Business (Vol. 82, Summer 2009, No. 8, pp. 18)
Pub: Rogers Media

Ed: Jeff Sanford. Description: Opinions of experts and personalities who are known to have bear attitudes towards the economy were presented in the event 'A Night with the Bears' in Toronto in April 2009.

Known bears that served as resource persons in the event were Nouriel Roubini, Eric Sprott, Ian Gordon, and Meredith Whitney. The bears were observed to have differences regarding consumer debt.

27350 ■ "IFRS Monopoly: the Pied Piper of Financial Reporting" in Accounting and Business Research (Vol. 41, Summer 2011, No. 3, pp. 291)
Pub: American Institute of Certified Public Accountants
Contact: Barry C. Melancon, President
E-mail: bmelancon@aicpa.org
Ed: Shyam Sunder. **Description:** The disadvantages of granting monopoly to the international financial reporting standards (IFRS) are examined. Results indicate that an IFRS monopoly removes the chances for comparing alternative practices and learning from them. An IFRS monopoly also eliminates customization of financial reporting to fit local differences in governance, business, economic, and legal conditions.

27351 ■ "An Ill Wind: Icelandic Bank Failures Chill Atlantic Canada" in Canadian Business (Vol. 81, November 10, 2008, No. 19, pp. 10)
Pub: Rogers Media Ltd.
Ed: Charles Mandel. **Description:** Bank failures in Iceland have put a stop to flights ferrying Icelanders to Newfoundland to purchase Christmas gifts, thereby threatening Newfoundland's tourism industry. The credit of Newfoundland's fisheries is also being squeezed since most of Atlantic Canadian seafood processors hold lines of credit from Icelandic banks.

27352 ■ "Ill Winds; Cuba's Economy" in The Economist (Vol. 390, January 3, 2009, No. 8612, pp. 20)
Pub: The Economist Newspaper Inc.
Description: Cuba's long-term economic prospects remain poor with the economy forecasted to grow only 4.3 percent for the year, about half of the original forecast, due in part to Hurricane Gustav which caused $10 billion in damage and disrupted the food-supply network and devastated farms across the region; President Raul Castro made raising agricultural production a national priority and the rise in global commodity prices hit the country hard. The only bright spot has been the rise in tourism which is up 9.3 percent over 2007.

27353 ■ Immigrant, Inc.: Why Immigrant Entrepreneurs Are Driving the New Economy
Pub: John Wiley & Sons, Inc.
Ed: Richard T. Herman, Robert L. Smith. **Released:** November 9, 2009. **Price:** $19.77. **Description:** Immigrant entrepreneurs are driving the new economy and will play a role in saving American jobs.

27354 ■ "The Impact of Immigrant Entrepreneurs" in Business Week (February 7, 2007)
Pub: McGraw-Hill Companies
Ed: Kerry Miller. **Description:** Overview of immigrant entrepreneur's impact on economic development and their status as a driving force for the U.S. economy.

27355 ■ "In the Bag?" in Canadian Business (Vol. 81, March 3, 2008, No. 3, pp. 57)
Pub: Rogers Media
Ed: Calvin Leung. **Description:** American stocks are beginning to appear cheap amidst the threat of a worldwide economic slowdown, United States economic crisis and declining stock portfolios. Investors looking for bargain stocks should study the shares of Apple and Oshkosh Corp. Evaluation of other cheap-looking stocks such as the shares of Coach and 3M is also given.

27356 ■ In Fed We Trust: Ben Bernanke's Ware on the Great Panic
Pub: Crown Business
Ed: David Wessel. **Released:** 2009. **Price:** $27.99. **Description:** A look at the central bank's reaction to the crisis and Ben Bernanke has been forced to play the crisis by ear in order to keep the economy from imploding.

27357 ■ "In Search of the Next Big Thing: It's Out There - Just Waiting For You To Find It" in Inc. (Volume 32, December 2010, No. 10, pp. 34)
Pub: Inc. Magazine
Ed: April Joyner. **Description:** Innovation is the future for small business. A new book, Inside Real Innovation: How the Right Approach Can Move Ideas from R&D to Market - And Get the Economy Moving helps to break down the process by which innovation occurs.

27358 ■ "In Surging Oil Industry, Good Fortune Comes In Stages" in Barron's (Vol. 88, July 7, 2008, No. 27, pp. 12)
Pub: Dow Jones & Co. Inc.
Ed: Sandra Ward. **Description:** Shares of US land oil and gas driller Helmerich and Payne, priced at $69 each, are estimated to be at peak levels. The shares are trading at 17 times 2008 earnings and could be in for some profit taking.

27359 ■ "Incentives Debate Rages On Unabated" in The Business Journal-Serving Metropolitan Kansas City (Vol. 26, September 5, 2008, No. 52)
Pub: American City Business Journals, Inc.
Ed: Rob Roberts. **Description:** Debate on the new economic development and incentives policy adopted by the Kansas City Council is still on. The city's Planned Industrial Expansion Authority has rejected a standard property tax abatement proposal. The real estate development community has opposed the rejection of proposed the tax incentives policy.

27360 ■ "Inc. 500: the Class of 2011" in Inc. (Vol. 33, September 2011, No. 7, pp. 71)
Pub: Inc. Magazine
Description: A listing of the Inc. 500 businesses that are rebuilding the economy and changing the world is presented.

27361 ■ "Independence's Day Keeps on Getting Brighter" in Business Courier (Vol. 27, June 11, 2010, No. 6, pp. 1)
Pub: Business Courier
Ed: Lucy May. **Description:** Reports show that residential and commercial development continues in Independence, Kentucky despite the recession, with a 144-unit apartment complex under construction. The city recorded 152 new-home closings in 2009, or 25 percent of all new homes closed in Boone, Campbell, and Kenton counties.

27362 ■ "Indigenous Tourism Operators" in International Journal of Entrepreneurship and Small Business (Vol. 10, July 6, 2010, No. 4)
Pub: Publishers Communication Group
Ed: Andrews Cardow, Peter Wiltshier. **Description:** Emergent enthusiasm for tourism as a savior for economic development in the Chatham Islands of New Zealand is highlighted.

27363 ■ "Indulgent Parsimony: an Enduring Marketing Approach" in Strategy and Leadership (Vol. 39, March-April 2011, No. 2, pp. 36)
Pub: Emerald Group Publishing Inc.
Ed: Kenneth Alan Grossberg. **Description:** Indulgent parsimony (IP), a marketing strategy employed on consumers that are affected by recession, is found to be a relevant and appropriate approach that can help encourage buying. IP involves the selling of cheaper goods and services that allow consumers experience comfort and relief from stress.

27364 ■ "Industrial Vacancies Hit High; Economic Downturn Taking Toll on Area's Demand for Space" in Crain's Chicago Business (Apr. 21, 2008)
Pub: Crain Communications, Inc.
Ed: Alby Gallun. **Description:** Hitting its highest level in four years in the first quarter is the Chicago-area industrial vacancy rate, a sign that the slumping economy is depressing demand for warehouse and manufacturing space.

27365 ■ "The Influencers" in Entrepreneur (Vol. 36, March 2008, No. 3, pp. 66)
Pub: Entrepreneur Media Inc.
Ed: Andrea Cooper. **Description:** Among the 25 people, events, and trends that will influence business in 2008 are: the 2008 U.S. presidential elections, climate change, China, weakening U.S. dollar, mortgage crisis, generational shift, Bill Drayton, and Bill Gates. Other 2008 influencers are presented.

27366 ■ "Inland Snaps Up Rival REITs" in Crain's Chicago Business (Vol. 31, November 17, 2008, No. 46, pp. 3)
Pub: Crain Communications, Inc.
Ed: Alby Gallun. **Description:** Discusses Inland American Real Estate Trust Inc., a real estate investment trust that is napping up depressed shares of publicly traded competitors, a possible first step toward taking over these companies; however, with hotel and retail properties accounting for approximately 70 percent of its portfolio, the company could soon face its own difficulties.

27367 ■ Innovate to Great: Re-Igniting Sustainable Innovation to Win in the Global Economy
Pub: McGraw-Hill
Ed: Judy Estrin. **Released:** September 12, 2008. **Price:** $27.95. **Description:** The author explores innovation and creativity as a means for small companies to survive and expand in the global economy.

27368 ■ Innovation and Entrepreneurship
Pub: HarperInformation
Ed: Peter F. Drucker. **Released:** May 2006. **Price:** $16.99. **Description:** Innovation and entrepreneurship in America's new economy.

27369 ■ "Innovation Station" in Canadian Business (Vol. 80, October 8, 2007, No. 20, pp. 42)
Pub: Rogers Media
Ed: Andrew Wahl. **Description:** Study and teaching of entrepreneurship at the University of Waterloo is discussed. Research projects in the university are expected to be influential in Canada's economic development. In spite of the success of these studies, financing is still a problem for the university, especially in technological innovations.

27370 ■ Innovative Approaches to Global Sustainability
Pub: Palgrave Macmillan
Ed: Charles Wankel, James A.F. Stoner. **Released:** April 13, 2010. **Price:** $30.00. **Description:** Examples are given to help businesses become sustainable as we move towards a sustainable world.

27371 ■ "Innovators Critical in Technical Economy" in Crain's Cleveland Business (Vol. 28, November 5, 2007, No. 44, pp. 10)
Pub: Crain Communications, Inc.
Ed: Peter Rea. **Description:** Discusses the importance to attract, develop and retain talented innovators on Ohio's economy. Also breaks down the four fronts on which the international battle for talent is being waged.

27372 ■ "The Ins and Outs of Unemployment in Canada, 1976-2008" in Canadian Journal of Economics (Vol. 44, November 2011, No. 4, pp. 1331)
Pub: Blackwell Publishers Ltd.
Ed: Michele Campolieti. **Description:** Flows into and out of unemployment in Canada at an aggregate and a number of disaggregated levels are studied.

27373 ■ "Insider" in Canadian Business (Vol. 81, March 31, 2008, No. 5, pp. 76)
Pub: Rogers Media
Ed: John Gray. **Description:** Discusses a comparison of an average Canadian family's finances in 1990 with the data from 2007. The average family in 2007 has over $80,000 in debt compared to just under $52,000 in 1990. However, Canadians have also been accumulating solid assets such as homes and stocks. This means that Canadian debt load has fallen from 22 percent in 1990 to 20 percent in 2007 when taken as a percentage of total net worth.

27374 ■ *"Insider" in Canadian Business (Vol. 81, Summer 2008, No. 9, pp. 170)*
Pub: Rogers Media Ltd.
Ed: Thomas Watson; Jeff Sanford. **Description:** Oil peak theory posits that the world has consumed half of the non-renewable resources is indicated by the surging oil prices. However, critics argued that the high oil prices are effects of market speculation and not the depletion of the supply. Ten reasons on why to buy and not buy peak oil are presented.

27375 ■ *"Insitu Looks to Oregon" in Business Journal Portland (Vol. 27, October 29, 2010, No. 35, pp. 1)*
Pub: Portland Business Journal
Ed: Erik Siemers. **Description:** Bingen, Washington-based Insitu Inc. announced that it has narrowed the search for a new corporate campus into five locations within the Columbia Gorge region. However, state economic development officials are curious whether the company will land in Oregon or Washington. Insights on economic impact of Insitu's decision are also given.

27376 ■ *"Insurers No Longer Paying Premium for Advertising" in Brandweek (Vol. 49, April 21, 2008, No. 16, pp. SR3)*
Pub: VNU Business Media, Inc.
Ed: Eric Newman. **Description:** Insurance companies are cutting their advertising budgets after years of accelerated double-digit growth in spending due to the economic downturn, five years of record-breaking ad spend and a need to cut expenditures as claims costs rise and a competitive market keeps premiums in place. Statistical data included.

27377 ■ **International Economic Development Council--Membership Directory**
Pub: International Economic Development Council
Contact: Jeff Finkle, President
E-mail: cziegler@iedconline.org
URL(s): www.iedconline.org. **Released:** Irregular
Covers: Approximately 2,700 economic development professionals working in local and state governments; private sector professionals and corporations; local and community development corporations; neighborhood and manpower groups. **Entries include:** For individual members--Name, address, phone. For corporations and community groups--Organization name, address, phone, fax, name and title of contact. **Arrangement:** Personal. **Indexes:** Geographical, Organizational.

27378 ■ *"International ETFs: Your Passport to the World" in Barron's (Vol. 89, July 13, 2009, No. 28, pp. L10)*
Pub: Dow Jones & Co., Inc.
Ed: John Hintze. **Description:** International exchange traded funds give investors more choices in terms of investment plays and there are 174 U.S. ETF listings worth $141 billion as of July 2009. Suggestions on how to invest in these funds based on one's conviction on how the global economy will unfold are presented.

27379 ■ *"International Growth" in Black Enterprise (Vol. 38, July 2008, No. 12, pp. 64)*
Pub: Earl G. Graves Publishing Co. Inc.
Ed: Marcia A. Reed-Woodard. **Description:** Becoming an increasingly smaller portion of the global business environment is the U.S. economy. Christopher Catlin, an associate with Booz Allen Hamilton, a technology management and strategy-consulting firm, shares what he has learned about the global market.

27380 ■ *"Into the Light: Making Our Way Through the Economic Tunnel" in Agency Sales Magazine (Vol. 39, August 2009, No. 8, pp. 26)*
Pub: MANA
Ed: Michael Dotson. **Description:** Ways in which to avoid business stagnation brought about by the economic downturn, is presented. Being different, being a puzzle solver, and knowing the competition are among the things marketing personnel should do in order to wade through the economic downturn. Marketing via direct mail and the Internet also recommended.

27381 ■ *"Intrepid Souls: Meet a Few Who've Made the Big Leap" in Crain's Chicago Business (Vol. 31, November 10, 2008, No. 45, pp. 26)*
Pub: Crain Communications, Inc.
Ed: Meredith Landry. **Description:** Advice is given from entrepreneurs who have launched businesses in the last year despite the economic crisis. Among the types of businesses featured are a cooking school, a child day-care center, a children's clothing store and an Internet-based company.

27382 ■ *"Inventory Glut" in Business Courier (Vol. 24, March 28, 2008, No. 51, pp. 1)*
Pub: American City Business Journals, Inc.
Ed: Laura Baverman. **Description:** Indian Hill and the downtown area have the highest monthly absorption rate for housing on a list of 42 Greater Cincinnati and Northern Kentucky neighborhoods. The two neighborhoods have 19 and 27 months of housing inventory respectively, which means home sellers need to either lower their prices or be very patient.

27383 ■ *"Is this a Buying Opportunity?" in Canadian Business (Vol. 82, April 27, 2009, No. 7, pp. 46)*
Pub: Rogers Media
Ed: Andy Holloway. **Description:** Home prices in Canada are down by as much as 14.2 percent in 2009 compared to prices in 2008, making homes more affordable now. Some housing experts believe that homes are still good investments as prices of rent and properties always recover. Meanwhile, a survey found that Canadians under 35 plan to buy a home within two years.

27384 ■ *"Is Hawaii Ready for Universal Health Care?" in Hawaii Business (Vol. 53, February 2008, No. 8, pp. 26)*
Pub: Hawaii Business Publishing
Description: Representative Lyn Finnegan does not believe that a universal health is good for Hawaii as health insurance for everyone will be difficult to achieve. Representative John M. Mizuno says that House Bill 1008 introduced in the state was a landmark for Hawaii as it will provide the people with health care insurance. Other details about their opinion on the topic are presented.

27385 ■ *"Is the VIX in Denial?" in Barron's (Vol. 88, July 7, 2008, No. 27, pp. M12)*
Pub: Dow Jones & Co., Inc.
Ed: Lawrence McMillan. **Description:** Volatility Index (VIX) of the Chicago Board Options Exchange did not rise significantly despite the drop in the US stock markets, rising to near 25. This market decline, however, will eventually result in investor panic and the rise of the VIX.

27386 ■ *"It Could Be Worse" in Barron's (Vol. 89, July 27, 2009, No. 30, pp. 5)*
Pub: Dow Jones & Co., Inc.
Ed: Alan Abelson. **Description:** Media sources are being fooled by corporate America who is peddling an economic recovery rather than reality as shown by the report of a rise in existing home sales which boosted the stock market even if it was a seasonal phenomenon. The phrase 'things could be worse' sums up the reigning investment philosophy in the U.S. and this has been stirring up the market.

27387 ■ *"It's Good to be Goldman" in Barron's (Vol. 89, July 20, 2009, No. 29, pp. 5)*
Pub: Dow Jones & Co., Inc.
Ed: Randall W. Forsyth. **Description:** Profits of Goldman Sachs rose to $3.44 billion in the second quarter of 2009, aided by federal financial stimulus programs. CIT Group is facing bankruptcy and may need up to $6 billion to survive. The federal economic stimulus programs are benefiting Wall Street more than the US economy itself.

27388 ■ *"It's Time To Swim" in Canadian Business (Vol. 81, March 3, 2008, No. 3, pp. 37)*
Pub: Rogers Media
Ed: Megan Harman. **Description:** Canadian manufacturers should consider Asian markets such as India and the United Arab Emirates as the U.S.

economic downturn continues. Canada's shortage in skilled labor is also expected to negatively affect manufacturing industries. Ontario's plans to assist manufacturers are also presented.

27389 ■ *"It's Time to Wise Up: Income Trusts" in Canadian Business (Vol. 79, November 6, 2006, No. 22, pp. 24)*
Pub: Rogers Media
Ed: Mark Rosen. **Description:** The effects bogus financial reporting of income trusts on investors are analyzed.

27390 ■ *"Janson: Duke's Dynamo, Regional President Focuses on Economic Development" in Business Courier (Vol. 27, July 9, 2010, No. 10, pp. 1)*
Pub: Business Courier
Ed: Lucy May. **Description:** Duke Energy President Julie Janson is also chair of the Cincinnati USA Partnership for Economic Development and the co-chair of the Cincinnati Business Committee's Economic Development Task Force. Duke is launching a Site Readiness Pilot Program to help the region prepare for an economic recovery.

27391 ■ *"J.C. Evans Seeks Bankruptcy Protection" in Austin Business Journal (Vol. 31, August 12, 2011, No. 23, pp. A1)*
Pub: American City Business Journals Inc.
Ed: Vicky Garza. **Description:** J.C. Evans Construction Holdings Inc., as well as its affiliated companies, has filed for Chapter 11 bankruptcy following its continued financial breakdown which it blames on the tough economy. Details are included.

27392 ■ *"Job Losses and Budget Shortfall Adding to Economic Woes" in Sacramento Business Journal (Vol. 25, July 11, 2008, No. 19, pp. 1)*
Pub: American City Business Journals, Inc.
Ed: Kathy Robertson. **Description:** Budget cuts in California have been approved amid rising unemployment in a slowing economy. Statistics show that total industry employment in the Sacramento region decreased by 3,700 jobs from May 2007 to May 2008. Governor Arnold Schwarzenegger has ordered a 10 percent budget cut for state departments, but this cut will likely mean few layoffs.

27393 ■ *"Jobless Rate Climbs Unexpectedly in December" in Globe & Mail (January 7, 2006, pp. B5)*
Pub: CTVglobemedia Publishing Inc.
Description: The reasons behind increase in unemployment rate by 6.5 percent, in Canada, are presented.

27394 ■ *"Jobs Boom Ramps Up in March" in Globe & Mail (April 7, 2007, pp. B1)*
Pub: CTVglobemedia Publishing Inc.
Ed: Tara Perkins. **Description:** The increase in the number of jobs by 54,900 in Canada and 180,000 in the United States in March 2007 is discussed.

27395 ■ *"Jobs Data Show A Slow Leak" in Barron's (Vol. 88, July 7, 2008, No. 27, pp. 34)*
Pub: Dow Jones & Co., Inc.
Ed: Gene Epstein. **Description:** In June 2008, the United States manufacturing sector showed an expansion, with the purchasing managers' index rising to 50.2 from 49.6; the unemployment rate in the US, which stayed steady at 5.5 percent in June 2008 is also discussed. Statistical data included.

27396 ■ *"Jobs, Export Surge Confirm Recovery" in Globe & Mail (March 10, 2007, pp. B5)*
Pub: CTVglobemedia Publishing Inc.
Ed: Heather Scoffield. **Description:** The increase in the number of jobs and exports that is forecast to reverse the slowdown in the Canadian economy is discussed.

27397 ■ *"The Judgment Deficit" in Harvard Business Review (Vol. 88, September 2010, No. 9, pp. 44)*
Pub: Harvard Business School Publishing
Ed: Amar Bhide. **Description:** The importance of individual, decentralized initiative and judgment in the capitalist system is outlined. While financial models

have their use, they cannot always account appropriately for the inherent uncertainty in economic decision making.

27398 ■ *"KC Plants Downshift' in The Business Journal-Serving Metropolitan Kansas City (Vol. 27, November 7, 2008, No. 9, pp. 1)*
Pub: American City Business Journals, Inc.
Ed: James Dornbrook. **Description:** Discusses Ford Motor Co. and General Motors' factories in the region; Ford Motor Co. removed the second shift on the F-150 line at the Kansas City Assembly Plant but added a shift to the production of the Ford Escape and Mercury Mariner in an attempt to avoid layoffs. One spokesman for General Motors, however, states that they cannot guarantee that they won't make any production cuts and layoffs in the future.

27399 ■ *"Kenosha 'Lifestyle Center' Delayed' in The Business Journal-Milwaukee (Vol. 25, August 8, 2008, No. 46, pp. A1)*
Pub: American City Business Journals, Inc.
Ed: Rich Kirchen. **Description:** Quality Centers of Orlando, Florida has postponed construction plans for the Kenosha Town Center in Kenosha County, Wisconsin to 2009 due to the economic downturn and lending concerns. The $200-million, 750,000-square-foot retail and residential center will be located near the corner of Wisconsin Highway 50 and I-94.

27400 ■ *"Kent Officials Seek Further KSU, City Unity' in Crain's Cleveland Business (Vol. 28, December 3, 2007, No. 48, pp. 3)*
Pub: Crain Communications, Inc.
Ed: Jay Miller. **Description:** Kent State University and Portage County are searching for a developer who will use a three-acre parcel to bring new life to the city's sagging downtown and create an area that will better link the town and the Kent State campus. The project will include a hotel and conference center as well as retail and restaurant space.

27401 ■ *"Kid Rock" in Canadian Business (Vol. 81, Summer 2008, No. 9, pp. 54)*
Pub: Rogers Media Ltd.
Ed: John Gray. **Description:** Damien Reynolds is the founder, chairman and chief executive officer of Vancouver-based Longview Capital Partners. The investment bank, founded in 2005, is one of the fastest-growing companies in British Columbia. The recent economic downturn has battered the stocks of the company and its portfolio of junior miners.

27402 ■ *"The Kitchen is Closed; Eateries Forced Out by Soaring Rents, Declining Revenues" in Crain's New York Business (January 21, 2008)*
Pub: Crain Communications, Inc.
Ed: Lisa Fickenscher. **Description:** Many restaurants have already closed in the area and experts expect many more will follow due to skyrocketing rents and declining revenues.

27403 ■ *"Kodiak Bucks Bear Market" in Austin Business JournalInc. (Vol. 29, December 18, 2009, No. 41, pp. 1)*
Pub: American City Business Journals
Ed: Kate Harrington. **Description:** Austin, Texas-based Kodiak Assembly Solutions LLC, a company that installs components into printed circuit boards for product or evaluation tool kit prototyping purposes, will expand despite the recession. It will relocate from a 28,000 square foot space to a 42,000 square foot space in North Austin. The firm will also increase its workforce by 20 employees.

27404 ■ *"The Labor Crunch is Coming" in Canadian Business (Vol. 80, December 25, 2006, No. 1, pp. 74)*
Pub: Rogers Media
Description: The need for skilled and educated workforce to meet labor shortage in future in Canada is discussed.

27405 ■ *"Labor Pains" in Canadian Business (Vol. 79, August 14, 2006, No. 16-17, pp. 80)*
Pub: Rogers Media
Description: Canada's employment insurance is analyzed in view of the growing shortage of labor.

27406 ■ *"Laced Up and Ready to Run" in Barron's (Vol. 89, July 6, 2009, No. 27, pp. 12)*
Pub: Dow Jones & Co., Inc.
Ed: Christopher C. Williams. **Description:** Shares of Foot Locker could raise from $10 to about $15 a share with the improvement of the economy. The company has benefited from prudent management and merchandising as well as better cost cutting, allowing it to better survive in a recession.

27407 ■ *"Land on Boardwalk" in Canadian Business (Vol. 82, April 27, 2009, No. 7, pp. 19)*
Pub: Rogers Media
Ed: Calvin Leung. **Description:** Boardwalk REIT remains as one of the most attractive real estate investment trusts in Canada, with 73 percent of analysts rating the firm a Buy. Analyst Neil Dowrey believes that good management, as well as a good business model, makes Boardwalk a good investment. Downey is concerned however, that a worsening of Alberta's economy could significantly impact Boardwalk.

27408 ■ *"LaSalle Street Firms Cherry-Pick Talent As Wall Street Tanks" in Crain's Chicago Business (Vol. 31, November 17, 2008, No. 46)*
Pub: Crain Communications, Inc.
Ed: H. Lee Murphy. **Description:** Many local businesses are taking advantage of the lay offs that many major Wall Street firms are undergoing in their workforces; these companies see the opportunity to woo talent and expand their staff with quality executives.

27409 ■ *"Last Founder Standing" in Conde Nast Portfolio (Vol. 2, June 2008, No. 6, pp. 124)*
Pub: Conde Nast Publications
Contact: David Carey, President
Ed: Kevin Maney. **Description:** Interview with Amazon CEO Jeff Bezos in which he discusses the economy, the company's new distribution center and the hiring of employees for it, e-books, and the overall vision for the future of the firm.

27410 ■ *"The Latin Beat Goes On" in Barron's (Vol. 88, July 7, 2008, No. 27, pp. L5)*
Pub: Dow Jones & Co., Inc.
Ed: Tom Sullivan. **Description:** Latin American stocks have outperformed other regional markets due to rising commodities prices and favorable economic climate. Countries such as Brazil, Mexico, Chile, and Peru provide investment opportunities, while Argentina and Venezuela are tougher places to invest.

27411 ■ *"Laugh or Cry?' in Barron's (Vol. 88, March 24, 2008, No. 12, pp. 7)*
Pub: Dow Jones & Company, Inc.
Ed: Alan Abelson. **Description:** Discusses the American economy which is just starting to feel the effect of the credit and housing crises. JPMorgan Chase purchased Bear Stearns for $2 a share, much lower than its share price of $60, while quasi-government entities Fannie Mae and Freddie Mac are starting to run into trouble.

27412 ■ *"Law Firms See Improvement in Financing Climate" in Sacramento Business Journal (Vol. 28, October 14, 2011, No. 33, pp. 1)*
Pub: Sacramento Business Journal
Ed: Kathy Robertson. **Description:** Sacramento, California-based Weintraub Genshlea Chediak Law Corporation has helped close 26 financing deals worth more than $1.6 billion in 2010, providing indication of improvement in Sacramento's economy. Lawyers have taken advantage of low interest rates to make refinancing agreements and help clients get new funds.

27413 ■ *"Law Firms Troll for Complaints Among Disgruntled Workers" in The Business Journal-Serving Greater Tampa Bay (Vol. 28, July 11, 2008)*
Pub: American City Business Journals, Inc.
Ed: Jane Meinhardt. **Description:** Economic slowdown has affected businesses as they downsize, seeing an increase in wage and hour complaints using

loopholes in the Fair Labor Standards Act, from which several law firms are recently generating revenue. Federal judges notice the increase in lawsuits and ordered that law firms show cause for non-compliance.

27414 ■ *"Layoffs Continue to Be a Drag on Region's Recovery" in Philadelphia Business Journal (Vol. 28, January 22, 2010, No. 49, pp. 1)*
Pub: American City Business Journals
Ed: Athena D. Merritt. **Description:** Mass layoffs continue to hamper Pennsylvania's economic recovery. Job losses are predicted to decline in 2010.

27415 ■ *"Leaders and Lagards" in Barron's (Vol. 89, July 13, 2009, No. 28, pp. 14)*
Pub: Dow Jones & Co., Inc.
Ed: J.R. Brandstrader. **Description:** Statistical table that shows the returns of different mutual funds in different categories that include U.S. stock funds, sector funds, world equity funds, and mixed equity funds is presented. The data presented is for the second quarter of 2009.

27416 ■ *"Leaders and Lagards" in Barron's (Vol. 99, July 13, 2009, No. 28, pp. 14)*
Pub: Dow Jones & Co., Inc.
Ed: J.R. Brandstrader. **Description:** Statistical table that shows the returns of different mutual funds in different categories that include U.S. stock funds, sector funds, world equity funds, and mixed equity funds is presented. The data presented is for the second quarter of 2009.

27417 ■ *"Leaders Weigh In On Fannie Mae, Freddie Mac Failure, Fed Bailout" in The Business Journal - Serving Phoenix and the Valley of the Sun (Vol. 28, September 12, 2008, No. 53, pp. 1)*
Pub: American City Business Journals, Inc.
Ed: Chris Casacchia; Mike Sunnucks; Jan Buchholz. **Description:** Fannie Mae and Freddie Mac's federal takeover was a move to help stabilize the financial market and it helped bring down interest rates in the past week. Local executives from Arizona's Phoenix area share their thoughts on the immediate effect of the takeover and its upside and downside.

27418 ■ *Leadership in the Era of Economic Uncertainty: Managing in a Downturn*
Pub: The McGraw-Hill Companies
Ed: Ram Charan. **Released:** December 2008. **Price:** $22.95. **Description:** Management consultant gives advice on how to weather the economic storm, focusing on cash flow and foregoing expansion.

27419 ■ *"Leading Ohio Internet Marketing Firm Announces Growth in September" in Marketing Weekly News (September 26, 2009, pp. 24)*
Pub: Investment Weekly News
Description: Despite a poor economy, Webbed Marketing, a leading social media marketing and search engine optimization firm in the Midwest, has added five additional professionals to its fast-growing team. The company continues to win new business, provide more services and hire talented employees.

27420 ■ *"Legislators Must Cut Cost of Government" in Crain's Detroit Business (Vol. 24, October 6, 2008, No. 40, pp. 6)*
Pub: Crain Communications, Inc.
Description: Southeast and West Michigan business leaders are setting aside their differences and have proposed clear agendas, ranging from eliminating the Michigan Business Tax to overhauling public employee and retiree benefits and pensions. Lawmakers must also come together to find solutions for the state's economy and discover an entirely new vision for the future of Michigan business.

27421 ■ *"Legislature to Tackle Crisis in Jobless Fund" in Baltimore Business Journal (Vol. 27, December 18, 2009, No. 32, pp. 1)*
Pub: American City Business Journals
Ed: Scott Dance. **Description:** Maryland's General Assembly is set to finalize changes to the state's unemployment insurance system as soon as it

convenes for the 2010 session. The move was aimed to draw $127 million in stimulus money that can support the nearly depleted fund of unemployment benefits within 45 days.

27422 ■ "Legoland Plans Could Tumble After State's Modesa Denial" in Business Journal-Serving Metropolitan Kansas City (November 16, 2007)
Pub: American City Business Journals, Inc.

Ed: Jim Davis. **Description:** RED Development LLC's officials are not giving up after the Missouri Department of Economic Development said RED could not exploit the Missouri Downtown and Rural Economic Stimulus Act (Modesa) for the Legoland theme park development in Lee's Summit. Legoland's proposed site southeast of Interstate 470 and U.S. Highway 50 does not fit the Modesa because it is outside Lee's Summit.

27423 ■ "Lenders" in The Business Journal - Serving Phoenix and the Valley of the Sun (Vol. 28, July 25, 2008, No. 47, pp. 1)
Pub: American City Business Journals, Inc.

Ed: Jan Buchholz. **Description:** Private equity lender Investor Mortgage Holdings Inc. has continued growing despite the crisis surrounding the real estate and financial industries and has accumulated a $700 million loan portfolio. Private lending has become increasingly important in financing real estate deals as commercial credit has dried up.

27424 ■ "Lending Stays Down at Local Banks" in Business Courier (Vol. 27, October 1, 2010, No. 22, pp. 1)
Pub: Business Courier

Ed: Steve Watkins. **Description:** Greater Cincinnati's largest banks have experienced decreases in loans in the past year due to weak economy and sagging loan demands. Analysis of mid-year data has shown that loans drop by a total of $3.6 billion or 4 percent at the ten largest banks as of June 30, 2010 compared to same period in 2009.

27425 ■ "Lessons From My Father" in Crain's Chicago Business (Vol. 31, November 10, 2008, No. 45, pp. 28)
Pub: Crain Communications, Inc.

Ed: Rance Crain. **Description:** Rance Crain discusses his father, G.D. Crain Jr., who founded Crain Communications Inc. during the Great Depression. Advice is given for sustaining a business, even one that seems to be failing, during tough economic times.

27426 ■ "Let Markets Decide?" in Canadian Business (Vol. 80, October 8, 2007, No. 20, pp. 67)
Pub: Rogers Media

Ed: James Gillies. **Description:** Need to protect Canadian companies that could help boost the country's economy is discussed. It is expected that free markets alone will solve economic problems. Suggested policies that will discourage the takeover of major companies in the country, such as the organization of capitalization with multiple voting shares, are also presented.

27427 ■ "Let Us Count the Ways" in Barron's (Vol. 88, July 7, 2008, No. 27, pp. M10)
Pub: Dow Jones & Co., Inc.

Ed: Bennet Sedacca. **Description:** Investors are advised to remain cautious after the drop in stock prices in June 2008. The stock markets remain in the downtrend after reaching a peak in October 2007 and are on the verge of a collapse.

27428 ■ "The Letter of the Law" in Collections and Credit Risk (Vol. 14, November 1, 2009, No. 9, pp. 40)
Pub: SourceMedia, Inc.

Ed: Michelle Dunn. **Description:** Analyzes the regulatory landscape regarding debt collection and the ways in which those in the field are dealing with a tough economy, unclear laws and the newest regulations.

27429 ■ "Little Cheer in Holiday Forecast for Champagne" in Advertising Age (Vol. 88, November 17, 2008, No. 43, pp. 6)
Pub: Crain Communications, Inc.

Ed: Jeremy Mullman. **Description:** Due to a weak economy that has forced consumers to trade down from the most expensive alcoholic beverages as well as a weak U.S. dollar that has driven already lofty Champagne prices higher, makers of the French sparkling wine are anticipating a brutally slow holiday season.

27430 ■ "A Load of Bull?" in Canadian Business (Vol. 82, Summer 2009, No. 8, pp. 12)
Pub: Rogers Media

Ed: Joe Castaldo. **Description:** Some experts and analysts believe that the improvement of some economic indicators in Canada suggest an economic recovery. A survey of Russell Investment in March 2009 found that 60 percent of investment managers are bullish on Canadian stocks. Some experts like Mike Zyblock, however, remain cautious on the economy.

27431 ■ Local Enterprises in the Global Economy: Issues of Governance and Upgrading
Pub: Edward Elgar Publishing, Incorporated
Ed: Hubert Schmitz. **Released:** November 2004. **Price:** $35.00 (soft cover), $110.00 (hard bound). **Description:** Examination of the relationships between globalization, corporate governance, and the economic performance of small businesses and local enterprises.

27432 ■ "Local Firms Will Feel Impact Of Wall St. Woes" in The Business Journal-Milwaukee (Vol. 25, September 19, 2008, No. 52, pp. A1)
Pub: American City Business Journals, Inc.

Ed: Rich Kirchen. **Description:** Wall Street's crisis is expected to affect businesses in Wisconsin, in terms of decreased demand for services and products and increased financing costs. Businesses in Milwaukee area may face higher interest rates and tougher loan standards. The potential impacts of the Wall Street crisis on local businesses are examined further.

27433 ■ "Local Hotels Brace for Downturn" in Crain's Chicago Business (Vol. 31, March 31, 2008, No. 13, pp. 3)
Pub: Crain Communications, Inc.

Ed: Bob Tita. **Description:** Chicago hotels are seeing a noticeable drop in business-related guests so far this year due to a slumping national economy, tighter corporate expense budgets and higher airfares.

27434 ■ "Local Industrial Vacancies Climb" in Crain's Chicago Business (Vol. 31, November 17, 2008, No. 46, pp. 18)
Pub: Crain Communications, Inc.

Ed: Eddie Baeb. **Description:** Demand for local industrial real estate has declined dramatically as companies that use warehouse and factory space struggle to survive in an ailing economy. According to a report by Colliers Bennett & Kahnweiler Inc., a commercial real estate brokerage, the regional vacancy rate has risen to 9.86 percent in the third quarter, the fourth straight increase and the highest in the past 14 years.

27435 ■ "Local Knowledge" in Hawaii Business (Vol. 53, December 2007, No. 6, pp. 40)
Pub: Hawaii Business Publishing

Ed: David K. Choo. **Description:** Rules and facts business professionals need to know about the local life in Hawaii are presented. The important components in island life include knowledge Hawaiian high schools' histories and image, the local sports scene, special events, potluck ethics, and locals' favorite destination, which is Las Vegas.

27436 ■ "Local Lending Tumbles $10 Billion Since '08" in Saint Louis Business Journal (Vol. 31, August 26, 2011, No. 53, pp. 1)
Pub: Saint Louis Business Journal

Ed: Greg Edwards. **Description:** St. Louis, Missouri-based banks lending fell by more than 30 percent in less than three years, from about $30 billion in third

and fourth quarters 2008 to about $20 billion in the most recent quarter. However, community banks revealed that they want to lend but there is no loan demand.

27437 ■ "Local M&A Activity Sputters in 1Q" in Crain's Chicago Business (Vol. 31, April 21, 2008, No. 16, pp. 20)
Pub: Crain Communications, Inc.

Ed: H. Lee Murphy. **Description:** Local mergers-and-acquisitions activity is down by 34 percent in the first quarter compared to the fourth quarter of last year due to the credit crisis making financing harder to obtain.

27438 ■ "Local Outlook: Stronger Growth Ahead" in Montana Business Quarterly (Vol. 49, Spring 2011, No. 1, pp. 10)
Pub: Bureau of Business & Economic Research

Ed: Paul E. Polzin. **Description:** Local economic growth is broken down into three areas: fastest growing in Richland, Gallatin and Flathead Counties; the second growth group consists of Yellowstone, Silver Bow, and Lewis and Clark Counties, which all grew at rates higher than the statewide average; slowest growth was seen in Missoula, Ravalli, Cascade, and Custer Counties. Statistical data included.

27439 ■ "Locally Based Stocks Escape Worst of Market's Turmoil" in Crain's Detroit Business (Vol. 24, September 22, 2008, No. 38, pp. 4)
Pub: Crain Communications Inc.

Ed: Daniel Duggan. **Description:** Locally-based companies did not take as big a hit as might be expected with the shock to the financial markets last week; this is due mainly to the fact that the region does not have heavy exposure to energy or capital markets.

27440 ■ "Lofty Ambitions" in Canadian Business (Vol. 80, October 22, 2007, No. 21, pp. 26)
Pub: Rogers Media

Ed: Thomas Watson. **Description:** Canada has made its first trade deal in six years through the European Free Trade Agreement. This is a boost to the Canadian economy, but focus must be made on taking out internal barriers to inter-provincial trade and from third-party trade liberalization.

27441 ■ The Logic of Life: The Rational Economics of an Irrational World
Pub: Random House

Ed: Tim Harford. **Released:** February 2009. **Price:** $15.00 paperback. **Description:** Harford excels at making economists' studies palatable for discerning but non-expert readers. The uses hard data to show why promiscuous teens are actually health-conscious, divorce hasn't gotten a fair shake, corporate bosses will always be overpaid and job prospects for minorities continue to be grim.

27442 ■ "Long - And Leery" in Barron's (Vol. 88, March 31, 2008, No. 13, pp. 47)
Pub: Dow Jones & Company, Inc.

Ed: Jack Willoughby. **Description:** Tom Claugus' Bay Resource Partners hedge fund has returned 20 percent annually since it started in 1993. Claugus says that he is as aggressively long as he has ever been despite the dangers of the U.S. market. Claugus' stock picks include Canadian Natural Resources, NII Holdings, and Discover Financial.

27443 ■ "A Long Road to Recovery" in Barron's (Vol. 89, July 27, 2009, No. 30, pp. 37)
Pub: Dow Jones & Co., Inc.

Ed: Henry Kaufman. **Description:** United States' economy remains hobbled by some underlying constraint and real recovery remains ephemeral. Much of the financial problems could have been avoided if t he Federal Reserve was effectively guarding the financial system.

27444 ■ "A Look Ahead Into 2007" in Canadian Business (Vol. 80, December 25,

2006, No. 1, pp. 40)
Pub: Rogers Media
Description: The 2007 forecasts for various industrial sectors like telecom, information technology, manufacturing, retail, financial and energy among others is discussed.

27445 ■ *"Looking For Good Buys" in Black Enterprise (Vol. 38, November 2007, No. 4, pp. 39)*
Pub: Earl G. Graves Publishing Co. Inc.
Ed: Steve Garmhausen. **Description:** Lower interest rates mean consumers generally have more money to spend, which could spur economic growth in the retail sector of the U.S.

27446 ■ *"Loonie Tunes: When Will the Dollar Rise Again?" in Canadian Business (Vol. 81, November 10, 2008, No. 19, pp. 62)*
Pub: Rogers Media Ltd.
Ed: Joe Castaldo. **Description:** The Canadian dollar has weakened against the U.S. Dollar as the U.S. financial crisis rocked global markets A currency strategist says that the strength of the U.S. dollar is not based on people's optimism on the U.S. economy but on a structural demand where U.S. non-financial corporations have been repatriating greenbacks from foreign subsidiaries.

27447 ■ *"Loop 360 Offices Planned" in Austin Business JournalInc. (Vol. 28, December 5, 2008, No. 38, pp. A1)*
Pub: American City Business Journals
Ed: Kate Harrington. **Description:** Nearly 356,000 square feet of office space is planned in the South Capital of Texas Highway Corridor, also known as Loop 360 in Austin. Riverside Developers plans to wait until the economy improves before starting construction.

27448 ■ *"Lost in America" in Canadian Business (Vol. 79, October 23, 2006, No. 21, pp. 23)*
Pub: Rogers Media
Ed: David Wolf. **Description:** The impact of a decline in the economy of the United States on global economy is analyzed.

27449 ■ *Macrowikinomics: Rebooting Business and the World*
Pub: Portfolio Hardcover
Ed: Don Tapscott, Anthony D. Williams. **Released:** September 28, 2010. **Price:** $27.95. **Description:** Wikinomics Don Tapscott and Anthony Williams showed how mass collaboration was changing the way businesses communicate, create value,, and compete in the new global marketplace in 2007. Now, in the wake of the global financial crisis, the principles of wikinomics have become more powerful than ever.

27450 ■ *Made in China: Secrets of China's Dynamic Entrepreneurs*
Pub: John Wiley & Sons, Inc.
Ed: Winter Nie, Katherine Xin. **Released:** March 1, 2009. **Price:** $24.95. **Description:** Insight and analysis of the strategies leading to China's rapidly growing economy are profiled.

27451 ■ *"Making It Stick" in Business Courier (Vol. 24, November 9, 2008, No. 30, pp. 1)*
Pub: American City Business Journals, Inc.
Ed: Lucy May. **Description:** Discusses a report by the Brookings Institution which shows the need for the U.S. government to offer greater support to the country's metro areas in order to excel globally. Ohio, which has seven of the country's 100 largest metropolitan areas, does not receive enough funds, due to the need to finance less populated areas. Because of this, Ohio politicians have to spread less funding in order to cover more constituents.

27452 ■ *"Management Matters with Mike Myatt: Are You Creating Growth in a Down Economy?" in Commercial Property News (March 17, 2008)*
Pub: Nielsen Company
Ed: Mike Myatt. **Description:** Senior executives are expected to create growth for their company regardless of recession, economic slowdown, inflation, or tight credit and capital markets.

27453 ■ *Managing Economies, Trade and International Business*
Pub: Palgrave Macmillan
Ed: Aidan O'Connor. **Released:** January 19, 2010. **Price:** $90.00. **Description:** An in-depth look at the areas that affect and influence international business, exploring specific issues businesses face in terms of economic development, trade law, and international marketing and management.

27454 ■ *Managing India's Small Industrial Economy: The Catalytic Role of Industrial Counselors and Policy Makers*
Pub: SAGE Publications USA
Contact: Blaise R. Simqu, President
Ed: V. Padmanand, V.G. Patel. **Released:** June 2004. **Price:** $35.95. **Description:** Case studies and methodology are used to discuss the areas where industrial consultants are influencing sustainability and growth of small businesses in India's industrial economy.

27455 ■ *"Managing in Times of Uncertainty; What Leaders Can Learn From the Tumultuous Past Decade" in Gallup Management Journal (June 1, 2011)*
Pub: Gallup
Description: Executives and managers have been facing a global financial meltdown for the past 10 years along with ongoing wars, an increase in terrorism, and epic natural disasters. The leadership lessons learned over this time are examined.

27456 ■ *"Mandel Site Favored For UWM Hall" in The Business Journal-Milwaukee (Vol. 25, September 19, 2008, No. 52, pp. A1)*
Pub: American City Business Journals, Inc.
Description: University of Wisconsin-Milwaukee student residence hall's leading location is a site pushed by Mandel Group Inc. Real estate sources say that the developer's proposal offers the best opportunity for business development and the least conflict with nearby neighborhoods. Plans for the Mandel site are presented.

27457 ■ *"Manufacturing Jobs Go Begging in Downturn" in Puget Sound Business Journal (Vol. 29, December 26, 2008, No. 36, pp. 1)*
Pub: American City Business Journals
Ed: Steve Wilhelm. **Description:** Trends show that skilled jobs in aerospace and other technology manufacturing industries are in a state of decline as layoffs hit broad sectors of the economy. Too few people are entering the field, prompting companies to try to maintain these skilled workers, thus creating problems that could affect the sector's vitality.

27458 ■ *"Many Retailers Soften Return Policies" in Austin Business JournalInc. (Vol. 28, December 26, 2008, No. 41, pp. 1)*
Pub: American City Business Journals
Ed: Jean Kwon. **Description:** National Retail Federation reported the percentage of retailers saying their holiday return policy in 2008 will slacken compared to last season has increased from 3.4 percent to 11 percent. An increasing percentage of retailers are also getting stingier, as 17.1 percent revealed that their return policies will be stricter.

27459 ■ *"Many Sectors Lost Jobs In Detroit Area" in Crain's Detroit Business (Vol. 24, February 11, 2008, No. 6, pp. 3)*
Pub: Crain Communications Inc. - Detroit
Ed: Amy Lane. **Description:** Southeast Michigan reported its highest jobless rate since 1992 in fourth quarter 2007. Statistical data included.

27460 ■ *"Marathon Money" in Hawaii Business (Vol. 53, December 2007, No. 6, pp. 127)*
Pub: Hawaii Business Publishing
Ed: Jolyn Okimoto Rosa. **Description:** Discusses the effects of the Honolulu Marathon on small businesses' sales. The Running Room, for instance, experience growth in sales starting from the training season up to the end of the race, as a surge of Hawaiian residents and tourists come into the store for items such as running shoes and blister kits. The marathon's impact on Hawaii's tourism is examined as well.

27461 ■ *"Market Recoups Its Losses - And Its Optimism" in Barron's (Vol. 89, July 20, 2009, No. 29, pp. M3)*
Pub: Dow Jones & Co., Inc.
Ed: Kopin Tan. **Description:** US stock markets gained heavily in the third week of July 2009, rising by about 7 percent during the week. The shares of human resource management companies could be overpriced as they are trading at very high price-earnings multiples. Baxter International faces a class-action suit due to its alleged conspiracy with CSL to fix blood-plasma product prices.

27462 ■ *"Market for Retail Space Flat, but Recovery Still Uncertain" in Sacramento Business Journal (Vol. 28, August 26, 2011, No. 26, pp. 1)*
Pub: Sacramento Business Journal
Ed: Kelly Johnson. **Description:** The retail market in the Sacramento, California region remains challenged with the stock market volatility being the latest of its hurdles. The overall vacancy was 13.1 percent as of mid-2011, but retail real estate professionals express hopes that the worst is behind. A list and description of the region's winners and losers in retail vacancies is provided.

27463 ■ *"Market Squeezes Some Lawyers" in Austin Business JournalInc. (Vol. 28, December 12, 2008, No. 39, pp. 1)*
Pub: American City Business Journals
Ed: Jean Kwon. **Description:** Austin, Texas-based lawyers have been adversely affected by the economic downturn. Fewer works for lawyers in mergers and acquisitions and other activities are being offered. Lawyers are refinancing debts and offering other services.

27464 ■ *"Market Watch" in Barron's (Vol. 88, March 24, 2008, No. 12, pp. M18)*
Pub: Dow Jones & Company, Inc.
Ed: Ashraf Laidi; Marc Pado; David Kotok. **Description:** Latest measures implemented by the Federal Reserve to address the credit crisis did not benefit the US dollar, with the Japanese yen and the euro recouping earlier losses against the dollar. Goldman Sachs reported earnings of $3.23 per share, claiming a stronger liquidity position. The US markets bottomed early on 22 January 2007, according to evidence.

27465 ■ *"Market Watch" in Barron's (Vol. 89, July 20, 2009, No. 29, pp. M10)*
Pub: Dow Jones & Co., Inc.
Ed: Peter Greene; Michael Darda; Ian Wyatt; Stephanie Pomboy. **Description:** Concerns about a possible increase in US inflation rates are overblown as the country remains in a deflationary environment. Goldman Sachs's second quarter 2009 earnings have already been priced in as its shares rose. Germany's plans of a possible dollar bond sale are in anticipation of a rise in the euro's value.

27466 ■ *"Markets in Disarray..Fundamentals Still Strong?" in Hispanic Business (October 2007, pp. 14, 16, 18)*
Pub: Hispanic Business
Ed: Dr. Juan B. Solana. **Description:** Quarterly economic forecast is presented, covering credit, interest rates, home prices, stock market, and what lies ahead.

27467 ■ *"Marriott Checks Out Hotel Prospect" in The Business Journal-Serving Metropolitan Kansas City (Vol. 27, November 14, 2008, No. 10)*
Pub: American City Business Journals, Inc.
Description: Marriott International Inc. is planning to operate a hotel in Kansas City, Missouri and may take over the Kansas City Marriot Downtown although other hotel operators are interested in bidding on the project.

27468 ■ "Mason Fashions Its Future" in Business Courier (Vol. 24, December 7, 2008, No. 34, pp. 1)
Pub: American City Business Journals, Inc.
Ed: Laura Baverman. Description: Economic Development Director Michele Blair contracted Cincinnati-based Jack Rouse & Associates to tap the remaining undeveloped land in Mason. The real estate firm is set to develop the 2,000 acres of undeveloped land.

27469 ■ "The Massachusetts Mess: Good Health Care Is Expensive" in Barron's (Vol. 89, July 27, 2009, No. 30, pp. 39)
Pub: Dow Jones & Co., Inc.
Ed: Thomas G. Donlan. Description: Massachusetts' mandatory health insurance has produced the highest rate of insurance coverage among the states but the state is now unable to afford its dream of universal coverage just three years after they enacted it. This supposed model for federal health-care reform is turning out to be a joke.

27470 ■ "Massive Ford Restructuring to Cut 1,200 More Canadian Jobs" in Globe & Mail (January 24, 2006, pp. B1)
Pub: CTVglobemedia Publishing Inc.
Ed: Greg Keenan. Description: The details on streamlining of operations of Ford Motor Co., in Canada, are presented.

27471 ■ "Maximize Your Marketing Results In a Down Economy" in Franchising World (Vol. 42, November 2010, No. 11, pp. 45)
Pub: International Franchise Association
Ed: Loren Rakich. Description: Strategies to help any franchisee to maximize their marketing efforts in a slow economy are outlined.

27472 ■ "Mayor Unveils Business Plan" in Boston Business Journal (Vol. 29, September 16, 2011, No. 19, pp. 1)
Pub: American City Business Journals Inc.
Ed: Gary Haber. Description: Mayor Stephanie Rawlings-Blake of Baltimore, Maryland unveiled her plan to push the economy forward. Her key objectives include giving more support for the city's technology companies and refocusing the Baltimore Development Corporation on job creation and retention.

27473 ■ "MBA Guide 2008" in Canadian Business (Vol. 81, November 10, 2008, No. 19, pp. 92)
Pub: Rogers Media Ltd.
Ed: Sharda Prashad. Description: Escalating tuition costs for an MBA degree means that the return on investment could take longer. One study found that MBA degree holders who graduated during recessionary times earned less than those who graduated during good economic times.

27474 ■ MBA In a Day
Pub: John Wiley and Sons, Inc.
Ed: Steven Stralser, PhD. Released: 2004. Price: $34.95. Description: Management professor presents important concepts, business topics and strategies that can be used by anyone to manage a small business or professional practice. Topics covered include: human resources and personal interaction, ethics and leadership skills, fair negotiation tactics, basic business accounting practices, project management, and the fundamentals of economics and marketing.

27475 ■ "MBT Add On: Gone by 2012?" in Crain's Detroit Business (Vol. 24, October 6, 2008, No. 40, pp. 1)
Pub: Crain Communications, Inc.
Ed: Amy Lane. Description: Discusses the Michigan Business Tax (MBT), which has angered many businesses in the state due to the addition of a 21.99 percent surcharge. Although the tax policy will cut taxes on 63 percent of businesses in the state and represent no tax liability change for another nine percent of firms, other businesses will see increases of 100 percent or more. This increase means that many business owners will be forced to relocate or

close their establishment and others will have to eliminate jobs. Lawmakers are attempting to find a solution to this problem.

27476 ■ "McD's Dollar-Menu Fixation Sparks Revolt" in Advertising Age (Vol. 79, June 2, 2008, No. 22, pp. 1)
Pub: Crain Communications, Inc.
Ed: Emily Bryson York. Description: McDonald's franchisees say that low-cost dollar-menu offerings are impacting their bottom line and many have discontinued the dollar-menu altogether due to rising commodity costs, an increase in minimum wage and consumers trading down to the lower-price items.

27477 ■ "Measuring the Impact" in Mergers & Acquisitions: The Dealmaker's Journal (March 1, 2008)
Pub: SourceMedia, Inc.
Ed: Ken MacFadyen. Description: Discusses a new study out of Europe which contends that the private equity market does not have as much impact on the overall economy as critics contend.

27478 ■ The Mechanics of Modernity in Europe and East Asia: Institutional Origins of Social Change and Stagnation
Pub: Routledge
Ed: Erik Ringmar. Released: April 1, 2009. Price: $44.95. Description: Discussion of reasons why certain countries embarked on a path of sustained economic growth while others declined in Europe and East Asia.

27479 ■ "Medicare Inc." in Canadian Business (Vol. 80, October 8, 2007, No. 20, pp. 160)
Pub: Rogers Media
Ed: Erin Pooley. Description: State of Canada's health care system is discussed. A report by the Fraser Institute in Vancouver predicts that public health spending in six of ten provinces in the country will use more than half the revenues from all sources by 2020. Experts believe competition in the health care industry will help solve the current problems in the sector.

27480 ■ Medium Sized Firms and Economics Growth
Pub: Nova Science Publishers, Incorporated
Ed: Janez Prasniker. Released: April 2005. Price: $130.00. Description: Medium sized companies should have a more definitive presence in modern microeconomic theory, the theory of entrepreneurship, and the theory of financial markets.

27481 ■ "Members Make Sacrifices for a World-Class Course" in Crain's Detroit Business (Vol. 24, April 7, 2008, No. 14, pp. 21)
Pub: Crain Communications, Inc.
Ed: Jason Deegan. Description: Rees Jones Inc. completed a $1.8 million redesign of the Oakland Hills Country Club golf course last year. By all indications, the redesign has been a success since it is among the handful of courses good enough to host future majors which is beneficial for the local economy.

27482 ■ Memos to the Prime Minister: What Canada Could Be in the 21st Century
Pub: John Wiley & Sons, Incorporated
Ed: Harvey Schacter. Released: April 11, 2003. Price: $16.95. Description: A look into the business future of Canada. Topics include business, healthcare, think tanks, policy groups, education, the arts, economy, and social issues.

27483 ■ "Mequon Plan On Tracks, Bucks Housing Trend" in The Business Journal-Milwaukee (Vol. 25, September 26, 2008, No. 53, pp. A1)
Pub: American City Business Journals, Inc.
Ed: Pete Millard. Description: Insight Development Group plans to build condominium units and single-family homes despite the residential market downturn. The Orchard Glen project, a planned development in Mequon, is a $22 million project which will include 38 condos and 12 single-family homes. Details of the project are provided.

27484 ■ "Mexican Companies to Rent Space in TechTown, Chinese Negotiating" in Crain's Detroit Business (Vol. 24, September 29, 2008, No. 39)
Pub: Crain Communications Inc.
Ed: Tom Henderson. Description: Wayne State University's TechTown, the business incubator and research park, has signed an agreement with the Mexican government that will provide temporary office space to 25 Mexican companies looking to find customers or establish partnerships in Michigan. TechTown's executive director is negotiating with economic development officials from China. To accommodate foreign visitors the incubator is equipping offices with additional equipment and resources.

27485 ■ "Michael Doesn't Live Here Anymore" in Canadian Business (Vol. 80, October 8, 2007, No. 20, pp. 52)
Pub: Rogers Media
Ed: Andrew Wahl. Description: Michael Treacy's career in the U.S. is discussed. Treacy, a Canadian entrepreneur, believes that Canada has few comparative advantages aside from its natural resources. Because of this, he also believes that it would not be feasible to do business in the country. Economic factors influenced him to do business in the U.S. instead.

27486 ■ "Micro-Finance Agencies and SMEs" in International Journal of Entrepreneurship and Small Business (Vol. 11, August 3, 2010)
Pub: Publishers Communication Group
Ed: Patricia A. Rowe, Michael J. Christie, Frank Hoy. Description: Institutional preparedness of economic development agencies for developing small and medium-sized enterprises (SMEs) is discussed. The cases presented illustrate variations in the micro-finance lender agency-enterprise development of processes for sharing vision and interdependence.

27487 ■ Microtrends: The Small Forces Behind Tomorrow's Big Changes
Pub: Business Plus
Ed: Mark J. Penn. Released: 2007. Price: $25.99. Description: Political pollster and lead presidential campaign strategist for Hillary Clinton, identifies seventy-five microtrends he believes are changing the social and cultural landscape in the U.S. and globally. The book covers the areas of health and wellness, technology, education and more.

27488 ■ "Midwest Seeks Concessions From Creditors" in The Business Journal-Milwaukee (Vol. 25, July 25, 2008, No. 44, pp. A1)
Pub: American City Business Journals, Inc.
Ed: Rich Rovito. Description: Midwest Airlines Inc. is turning to creditors and lease holders for the financial aspect of its restructuring, which involves going back to serving popular business destinations. Chief executive officer Timothy believes that the company can survive in a niche market as long as it provides quality service. He discusses Midwest's restructuring plan.

27489 ■ "Millions Needed To Finish First Place" in The Business Journal-Milwaukee (Vol. 25, August 15, 2008, No. 47, pp. A1)
Pub: American City Business Journals, Inc.
Ed: Rich Kirchen. Description: First Place on the River condominium project in Milwaukee, Wisconsin, needs $18.2 million before it can be completed. A total of $6.8 million have already been spent since the project went into receivership on 31 January 2008.

27490 ■ "Mine Woes Could Rouse Zinc" in Barron's (Vol. 88, July 7, 2008, No. 27, pp. M12)
Pub: Dow Jones & Co., Inc.
Ed: Andrea Hotter. Description: Prices of zinc could increase due to supply problems in producing countries such as Australia and China. London Metal Exchange prices for the metal have dropped about 36 percent in 2008.

27491 ■ The Missing Class: Portraits of the Near Poor in America
Pub: Houghton Mifflin
Ed: Katherine S. Newman; Victor Tan Chen. Released: 2007. Description: Information regarding

the 57 million Americans existing on the razor-thin margin between poverty and middle class.

27492 ■ *"Mitch D'Olier"* in *Hawaii Business (Vol. 53, November 2007, No. 5, pp. 27)*
Pub: Hawaii Business Publishing
Ed: Cathy S. Cruz-George. **Description:** Mitch D'Olier chief executive officer of Kaneohe Ranch/ Harold K.L. Castle Foundation thinks that achievement gaps are a nationwide problem and that the Knowledge is Power Program is one of the programs that focuses on achievement gaps in some communities across the US. He also provides his insights on education in Hawaii and the current shortage of teachers.

27493 ■ *"A Mixed-Bag Quarter"* in *Barron's (Vol. 88, July 7, 2008, No. 27, pp. 19)*
Pub: Dow Jones & Co., Inc.
Ed: Shirley A. Lazo. **Description:** Seven component companies of the Dow Jones Industrial Average increased their dividend payouts in the second quarter of 2008 despite the weak performance of the index. Five companies in the Dow Jones Transportation index and three in the Dow Jones Utilities also increased their dividends.

27494 ■ *"Mom Insight on Family, Current Affairs, and the Economy"* in *Marketing to Women (Vol. 23, November 2010, No. 11, pp. 5)*
Pub: EPM Communications Inc.
Contact: Ira Mayer, President
E-mail: imayer@epmcom.com
Description: Statistics regarding the way moms feel about current events, family and the economy are shared.

27495 ■ *The Mom and Pop Store: How the Unsung Heroes of the American Economy Are Surviving and Thriving*
Pub: Walker & Company
Ed: Robert Spector. **Released:** September 1, 2009. **Price:** $26.00. **Description:** The history of small independent retail enterprises and how mom and pop stores in the U.S. continue to thrive through customer service and renewed community support for local businesses.

27496 ■ *The Mommy Manifesto: How to Use Our Power to Think Big, Break Limitations and Achieve Success*
Pub: John Wiley & Sons, Inc.
Ed: Kim Lavine. **Released:** September 1, 2009. **Price:** $24.95. **Description:** A new women's revolution will help women take control of their careers, their lives, and their economic future. The book shows how mom's control the economy and have the power to become successful entrepreneurs.

27497 ■ *"Moms Are Still Shopping"* in *Marketing to Women (Vol. 21, February 2008, No. 2, pp. 1)*
Pub: EPM Communications Inc.
Contact: Ira Mayer, President
E-mail: imayer@epmcom.com
Description: According to a monthly poll by Parenting Magazine, although the economic signs worsen many moms are still shopping. Statistical data included.

27498 ■ *"Money Ball"* in *Canadian Business (Vol. 80, October 22, 2007, No. 21, pp. 40)*
Pub: Rogers Media
Ed: Andy Holloway. **Description:** Rising Canadian dollar has a positive impact on the sports industry. Canadian team executives earn revenues in Canadian dollar, but pay expensive American dollar. Athletes who play in the Canadian Football Leagues benefit most from the increasing rate.

27499 ■ *"The Money Train: How Public Projects Shape Our Economic Future"* in *Hawaii Business (Vol. 54, September 2008, No. 3, pp. 31)*
Pub: Hawaii Business Publishing
Ed: Jason Ubay. **Description:** Public projects impact the construction industry as such projects create jobs and new infrastructure that can lead to private

developments. Details on the government contracts and construction projects in Hawaii and their rising costs and impact on the state's economy are discussed.

27500 ■ *"Montana Outlook: Stronger Growth Ahead"* in *Montana Business Quarterly (Vol. 49, Spring 2011, No. 1, pp. 7)*
Pub: Bureau of Business & Economic Research
Ed: Patrick M. Barkey. **Description:** A look at Montana's economy and future growth is given. Experts are predicting that the state will experience new growth in 2011, with 2012 showing its best growth since 2006. Statistical data included.

27501 ■ *"The Mood of a Nation"* in *Canadian Business (Vol. 81, April 14, 2008, No. 6, pp. 56)*
Pub: Rogers Media
Ed: Joe Castaldo. **Description:** Independent Fish Harvesters Inc. processes more kilograms a year and has had to hire more workers but its managers worry about how a slowdown in the U.S. economy will affect his business. A planned shopping complex in Mirabel Quebec, the manufacturing industry in Kitchener, Ontario, and a cattle farming business in Sarnia, Ontario are discussed to provide a snapshot of the challenges that business in Canada are facing as recession looms.

27502 ■ *"Moody and Paranoid"* in *Barron's (Vol. 88, March 10, 2008, No. 10, pp. M14)*
Pub: Dow Jones & Company, Inc.
Ed: Steven M. Sears. **Description:** Discusses the options market which remains liquid but is cautious of possible failures, especially for financial companies. Investors are in absolute fear when trading with options involving the financial sector.

27503 ■ *"More Callers Are Cutting Their Landlines"* in *Chicago Tribune (December 30, 2008)*
Pub: McClatchy-Tribune Information Services
Ed: Eric Benderoff. **Description:** Despite sporadic outages for cell phone users, the trend for consumers to cut out the expense of a landline does not appear to be slowing; experts believe that the recession will further increase the number of consumers who decide to go completely wireless.

27504 ■ *"More Manufacturers Scout Military Contracts As Auto Industry Lags"* in *Crain's Detroit Business (Vol. 24, September 29, 2008, No. 39)*
Pub: Crain Communications Inc.
Ed: Chad Halcom. **Description:** Many Michigan manufacturers are looking to grow with new military contracts now that the reality of the auto industry is becoming more clear; these companies see that the government contracts may be the only way in which they will be able to stay in business through these rough economic times.

27505 ■ *"More Offices Planned For Percheron Square"* in *The Business Journal-Milwaukee (Vol. 25, August 22, 2008, No. 48, pp. A1)*
Pub: American City Business Journals, Inc.
Ed: Pete Millard. **Description:** More office projects are under way at Percheron Square. Ryan Cos. US Inc., for example, plans to build nearly 200,000 square feet of office space at the area. Details of new office projects in Wisconsin are presented.

27506 ■ *"More Pain"* in *Canadian Business (Vol. 81, December 24, 2007, No. 1, pp. 12)*
Pub: Rogers Media
Ed: Lauren McKeon. **Description:** Manufacturing sector in Canada is sinking with a forecast by as much as 23 percent for 2008, which can be offset as manufacturers say they plan to increase productivity by 25 percent. Details on the sector's competitiveness, workforce, importing of machinery from the U.S. and financial needs for research and development are examined.

27507 ■ *"Mortgage Securities Drop Hits Home"* in *The Business Journal-Serving Metropolitan Kansas City (Vol. 27, October 17, 2008, No. 5)*
Pub: American City Business Journals, Inc.
Ed: Rob Roberts. **Description:** Sale of commercial mortgage-backed securities (CMBS) in Kansas City, Missouri have declined. The area may avoid layoffs if the United States government succeeds in stabilizing the economy. Major CMBS players in the area include Midland Loan Services Inc. and KeyBank Real Estate Capital.

27508 ■ *"Most See Gloomy Year For Michigan Business"* in *Crain's Detroit Business (Vol. 24, October 6, 2008, No. 40, pp. 4)*
Pub: Crain Communications, Inc.
Ed: Amy Lane. **Description:** Michigan residents are extremely concerned about the economic climate and business conditions in the state. According to the latest quarterly State of the State Survey, conducted by Michigan State University's Institute for Public Policy and Social Research, 63.9 percent of those surveyed anticipate bad times for Michigan businesses over the next year. Additional findings from the survey are also included.

27509 ■ *"Move Over - Or Out"* in *Puget Sound Business Journal (Vol. 29, November 28, 2008, No. 32, pp. 1)*
Pub: American City Business Journals
Ed: Kirsten Grind. **Description:** Real estate agents in the state of Washington are either moving to smaller real estate firms or quitting the industry due to the weak housing market. Lesser-known firms are experiencing an influx of experienced real estate agents, while 2,800 agents in the state have left the industry.

27510 ■ *"Mover and Sheika"* in *Conde Nast Portfolio (Vol. 2, June 2008, No. 6, pp. 104)*
Pub: Conde Nast Publications
Contact: David Carey, President
Ed: John Arlidge. **Description:** Profile of Princess Sheika Lubna who is the first female foreign trade minister in the Middle East, the United Arab Emirates biggest business envoy, paving the way for billions in new investment, and also a manufacturer of her own perfume line.

27511 ■ *"Mr. Deeds"* in *Canadian Business (Vol. 81, March 31, 2008, No. 5, pp. 24)*
Pub: Rogers Media
Ed: Thomas Watson. **Description:** Ron Sandler has the right experience to save Northern Rock PLC get through its liquidity problems. Sandler is known for saving Lloyd's of London in the mid-90's and he is not afraid to make enemies. Ron Sandler's assignment to help Northern Rock comes at a time when the health of the U.K. housing is not great.

27512 ■ *"Mulroney on the Record"* in *Canadian Business (Vol. 79, September 11, 2006, No. 18, pp. 43)*
Pub: Rogers Media
Description: Canada's former prime minister and senior partner at the law firm Ogilvy Renault, Brain Mulroney speaks about the major policies and initiatives of the current government and its impact on the country's economy.

27513 ■ *"Myths of Deleveraging"* in *Barron's (Vol. 90, August 23, 2010, No. 34, pp. M14)*
Pub: Barron's Editorial & Corporate Headquarters
Ed: Gene Epstein. **Description:** The opposite is true against reports about deleveraging or the decrease in credit since inflation-adjusted-investment factories and equipment rose 7.8 percent in the first quarter of 2010. On consumer deleveraging, sales of homes through credit is weak but there is a trend towards more realistic homeownership and consumer spending on durable goods rose 8.8 percent.

27514 ■ *"Native Wisdom"* in *Canadian Business (Vol. 80, October 8, 2007, No. 20, pp. 121)*
Pub: Rogers Media
Ed: Bernd Christmas. **Description:** Roles of Canadian indigenous peoples in the country's economic development are discussed. It is believed that empowering Canadian natives to contribute to the

country's economy will positively affect the country's future. The need for education in preparing natives for the global economy is also tackled.

27515 ■ "New Chief Walking the Talk" in Business Courier (Vol. 27, August 27, 2010, No. 17, pp. 1)
Pub: Business Courier
Ed: Lucy May. **Description:** National Brand & Tag Company president, Eric Haas, has vowed to put his various work experiences when he assumes the presidency of North Kentucky Chamber of Commerce. Haas wants to help the Chamber influence government policies that could help various businesses through the economic depression.

27516 ■ "New Economy Initiative Gains Partners" in Crain's Detroit Business (Vol. 25, June 1, 2009, No. 22, pp. M014)
Pub: Crain Communications Inc. - Detroit
Ed: Sherri Begin Welch. **Description:** New Economy Initiative is a $100 million philanthropic initiative that focuses on regional economic development. Recent grants awarded to Michigan companies are outlined.

27517 ■ The New Innovators: How Canadians are Shaping the Knowledge-Based Economy
Pub: James Lorimer & Company Ltd.
Ed: Roger Voyer; Patti Ryan. **Released:** January 1, 1994. **Price:** $29.95. **Description:** Details are examined showing how the innovation process works and how ideas are successfully translated into marketable products.

27518 ■ "New Jobless Claims Filed in December Soar" in Baltimore Business Journal (Vol. 27, January 29, 2010, No. 39, pp. 1)
Pub: American City Business Journals
Ed: Scott Dance. **Description:** Maryland received 48,693 new claims for unemployment benefits in December 2009, reaching its highest monthly total since 1974. The number of claims was up 49 percent from November and 13 percent from the same period in 2008. Labor officials and economists discuss this trend.

27519 ■ "New King Top the Charts" in The Business Journal-Portland (Vol. 25, August 8, 2008, No. 22, pp. 1)
Pub: American City Business Journals, Inc.
Ed: Andy Giegerich. **Description:** Spanish-language KRYP-FM station's spring 2008 ratings soared to 6.4 from 2.8 for the previous year. The station timing is flawless given the fact that one of every three new Portland-area residents between 2002 and 2007 were Latino.

27520 ■ "New Leadership Panel Has Advice for Collins" in Business First Buffalo (November 23, 2007, pp. 1)
Pub: American City Business Journals, Inc.
Ed: David Bertola. **Description:** Business First and Leadership Buffalo sponsored a meeting that convened business and civic leaders to discuss issues important to the economic growth and development of Western New York. The panel made recommendations to the County Executive-elect Christopher Collins. Details of the forum are included.

27521 ■ "The New Orleans Saints" in Entrepreneur (Vol. 37, August 2009, No. 8, pp. 40)
Pub: Entrepreneur Media, Inc.
Ed: Jason Meyers. **Description:** Idea Village is a nonprofit group that fosters entrepreneurship in New Orleans, Louisiana. Entrepreneurship is indeed growing in the city during a time when the city is still recovering from the damage of hurricane Katrina.

27522 ■ "The New Orleans Saints" in Entrepreneur (Vol. 37, August 2009, No. 8, pp. 40)
Pub: Entrepreneur Media, Inc.
Ed: Jason Meyers. **Description:** Idea Village is a nonprofit group that fosters entrepreneurship in New Orleans, Louisiana. Entrepreneurship is indeed growing in the city during a time when the city is still recovering from the damage of hurricane Katrina.

27523 ■ "A New Reality; There are Some Signs of Hope Amid 2009's Darkness" in Crain's Cleveland Business (Vol. 30, June 29, 2009, No. 25)
Pub: Crain Communications, Inc.
Ed: John Booth. **Description:** Despite all the pessimism, there are some signs that the economy is slowly stabilizing.

27524 ■ "New Thinking for a New Financial Order" in Harvard Business Review (Vol. 86, September 2008, No. 9, pp. 26)
Pub: Harvard Business School Press
Ed: Diana Farell. **Description:** Factors driving the current global economy are analyzed with a focus on the influence of new public and private sectors and the impact of unregulated markets.

27525 ■ "A New World" in Canadian Business (Vol. 80, October 8, 2007, No. 20, pp. 136)
Pub: Rogers Media
Ed: Deborah Harford. **Description:** Effects of climate change in Canada's economy are presented. A report published by Natural Resources Canada's Climate Change Impacts and Adaptation Program shows severe weather events such as droughts and storms will cause severe economic problems. Canada's infrastructure could also be affected by the rise in sea level over the next century.

27526 ■ "Nexstar Super Meeting Breaks Business Barriers" in Contractor (Vol. 56, November 2009, No. 11, pp. 3)
Pub: Penton Media, Inc.
Ed: Candace Roulo. **Description:** Around 400 Nexstar members met to discuss the trends in the HVAC industry and the economic outlook for 2010. Former lead solo pilot John Foley for the Blue Angels made a presentation on how a business can increase overall productivity based on the culture of the Blue Angels. Some breakout sessions tackled how to optimize workflow and marketing.

27527 ■ "The Next 20 Years: How Customer and Workforce Attitudes Will Evolve" in Harvard Business Review (Vol. 85, July-August 2007, No. 7-8)
Pub: Harvard Business School Publishing
Ed: Neil Howe, William Strauss. **Description:** Identification of social categories inhabited by age groups is used to calculate how consumer and employee opinions and behavior will change, and how this will impact economic development and corporate growth.

27528 ■ "The Next Government Bailout?" in Barron's (Vol. 88, March 10, 2008, No. 10, pp. 21)
Pub: Dow Jones & Company, Inc.
Ed: Jonathan Laing. **Description:** Fannie Mae may need a government bailout as it faces huge hits brought about by the effects of the housing crisis. The shares of the government-sponsored enterprise have dropped 65 percent since the housing crisis began.

27529 ■ "The Next Waive" in Hawaii Business (Vol. 53, January 2008, No. 7, pp. 27)
Pub: Hawaii Business Publishing
Ed: Cathy S. Cruz-George. **Description:** Only 40,000 Koreans took a visit to Hawaii in 2007, a decline from the pre-September averages of 123,000 visits. The number of Korean visitors in Hawaii could increase if the visa waiver proposal is passed. Efforts to improve Hawaiian tourism are presented.

27530 ■ "Niche Markets, Green Will Be Okay in 2010" in Contractor (Vol. 57, January 2010, No. 1, pp. 1)
Pub: Penton Media, Inc.
Ed: Robert P. Mader . **Description:** Mechanical contractors will see most of their work stemming from niche markets, such as green work, as well as service work in 2010. It is said that things will turn around for the industry in 2012 and 2013 and one forecast believes that anything outside of the institutional or more public sector work could be down 15 to 30 percent.

27531 ■ "Nightmare on Wall Street" in Canadian Business (Vol. 81, October 13, 2008, No. 17, pp. 9)
Pub: Rogers Media Ltd.
Ed: Rachel Pulfer. **Description:** Information on events that happened on Wall Street on the week that started September 15, 2008, as well as on its effect on financial markets around the world, are presented. Lehman Brothers filed for bankruptcy on September 15, 2008 after negotiations with Barclays Group and Bank of America failed. Details on AIG and Morgan Stanley are also presented.

27532 ■ "Nine Sectors to Watch: Metals" in Canadian Business (Vol. 81, December 24, 2007, No. 1, pp. 46)
Pub: Rogers Media
Ed: John Gray. **Description:** Forecasts on the Canadian metal industries for 2008 are discussed. Details on mine production and the rise in prices are also presented.

27533 ■ "Nine Sectors to Watch: Retail" in Canadian Business (Vol. 81, December 24, 2007, No. 1, pp. 56)
Pub: Rogers Media
Ed: Zena Olijnyk. **Description:** Canadian consumers are expected to spend more in 2008 as the Canadian dollar hit par with the U.S. greenback after the slowdown in the U.S. economy. Forecasts on retail sales growth are presented.

27534 ■ "Nine Sectors to Watch: Telecom" in Canadian Business (Vol. 81, December 24, 2007, No. 1, pp. 44)
Pub: Rogers Media
Ed: Andrew Wahl. **Description:** Forecasts on the Canadian telecommunications industry for 2008 are presented. Details on consumer spending growth, the popularity of broadband, and activities in the wireless sector are also discussed.

27535 ■ "No End to the Nightmare; America's Car Industry" in The Economist (Vol. 390, January 3, 2009, No. 8612, pp. 46)
Pub: The Economist Newspaper Inc.
Description: Detroit's struggling auto industry and the government loan package is discussed as well as the United Auto Worker union, which is loathed by Senate Republicans.

27536 ■ "No Rooms for the Inn In This High-Rise" in Chicago Tribune (October 4, 2008)
Pub: McClatchy-Tribune Information Services
Ed: Ameet Sachdev; Jim Kirk. **Description:** Construction has stalled for several hotel expansion projects due to the economy which has caused a decline in occupancy and little growth in average daily room rates in downtown Chicago because consumers and businesses are becoming more cautious in the amount of money they spend on travel.

27537 ■ "No Shortage of Challenges for Cross-Border Trade" in Canadian Sailings (June 30, 2008)
Pub: UBM Global Trade
Contact: Leonard J. Corallo, President
Ed: Kathlyn Horibe. **Description:** Pros and cons of the North American Free Trade Agreement are examined. The agreement between the U.S. and Canada concerning trade was an essential step toward securing economic growth for Canadian citizens. Two-way trade between the counties has tripled since the agreement and accounts for 7.1 million American and 3 million Canadian jobs.

27538 ■ "No Wild Highs Means No Wild Lows" in Business Courier (Vol. 24, January 18, 2008, No. 41, pp. 1)
Pub: American City Business Journals, Inc.
Ed: Laura Baverman. **Description:** Discusses a PMI Group report which revealed that the Greater Cincinnati area is in the lowest risk category for home value declines. The report forecast that the chance that housing prices in the area will fall below their current status by the year 2010 is less than 5 percent. Housing price forecasts for other areas are also provided.

27539 ■ *"Nonprofits Hope Employees Dig Deep" in Austin Business Journal Inc. (Vol. 28, December 5, 2008, No. 38, pp. A1)*

Pub: American City Business Journals

Ed: Sandra Zaragoza. **Description:** Nonprofit organizations in Austin, Texas are stepping up workplace giving drives in the hope that workers will continue giving donations to them. Corporations are cutting costs due to the recession, reducing donations to nonprofit organizations in the process.

27540 ■ *"Nonprofits Pressured to Rein in Fundraising Events" in Crain's Detroit Business (Vol. 25, June 15, 2009, No. 24, pp. 1)*

Pub: Crain Communications Inc. - Detroit

Ed: Sherri Begin Welch. **Description:** Local corporations have asked nonprofit=s to limit fundraising events in order to cut costs during the recession.

27541 ■ *"Northern Kentucky Adds 1,355 Jobs in '07" in Business Courier (Vol. 24, February 15, 2008, No. 45, pp. 3)*

Pub: American City Business Journals, Inc.

Ed: Lucy May. **Description:** Jobs generated by new and expanding businesses in Northern Kentucky in 2007 totaled to 1,355, which boosted total business sales to $410 million. The ripple effects of the businesses are expected to create 5,432 new jobs and increase business sales to more than $838 million.

27542 ■ *"Northern Overexposure" in Canadian Business (Vol. 79, August 14, 2006, No. 16-17, pp. 36)*

Pub: Rogers Media

Description: Fall in revenue from foreign film productions in Canada due to its overexposure, and incentives offered by other nations to foreign film productions, are discussed.

27543 ■ *"Not In My Backyard" in Entrepreneur (Vol. 36, May 2008, No. 5, pp. 42)*

Pub: Entrepreneur Media, Inc.

Ed: Farnoosh Torabi. **Description:** More investors are turning to overseas real estate investments as the U.S. market sees a slowdown. Analysts say that risk-averse investors opt for funds with record of strong returns and U.S. real estate investment trusts that partner with foreign businesses for transparency purposes. Other details about foreign real estate investments are discussed.

27544 ■ *"A Novel Fix for the Credit Mess" in Barron's (Vol. 88, March 31, 2008, No. 13, pp. 10)*

Pub: Dow Jones & Company, Inc.

Ed: Michael Santoli. **Description:** Due to the common bank-leverage factor of 10, the $250 billion of lost bank capital would have supported $2.5 trillion in lending capacity. Jeffrey Lewis suggests onerous regulations on bank-holding companies that own 10 to 25 percent, as they are partly to blame. Statistical data included.

27545 ■ *"Number of Mechanic's Liens Triple Since 2005" in The Business Journal - Serving Phoenix and the Valley of the Sun (Vol. 28, August 22, 2008, No. 51, pp. 1)*

Pub: American City Business Journals, Inc.

Ed: Jan Buchholtz. **Description:** Experts are blaming the mortgage and banking industries for the tripling of mechanic's liens that were filed in Arizona from 2005 through August 6, 2008. The rise in mechanic's liens is believed to indicate stress in the real estate community. Other views and information on the rise of mechanic's liens filed in Arizona are presented.

27546 ■ *"Numbers Game" in Baltimore Business Journal (Vol. 27, February 6, 2010, No. 40, pp. 1)*

Pub: American City Business Journals

Ed: Scott Dance. **Description:** Doubts are being raised regarding the impact of the federal stimulus spending in addressing unemployment in Maryland, which has experienced 1,800 jobs created so far.

Details on the view of companies and the insufficient amount of contracts that lead to the fewer number of workers being hired are discussed.

27547 ■ *"Nvidia's Picture Brighter Than Stock Price Indicates" in Barron's (Vol. 88, March 24, 2008, No. 12, pp. 46)*

Pub: Dow Jones & Company, Inc.

Ed: Eric J. Savitz. **Description:** Shares of graphics chip maker Nvidia, priced at $18.52 each, do not indicate the company's strong position in the graphics chip market. The company's shares have dropped due to fears of slower demand for PCs, but the company is not as exposed to broader economic forces.

27548 ■ *"Oakland County Hopes Auto Suppliers Can Drive Medical Industry Growth" in Crain's Detroit Business (March 10, 2008)*

Pub: Crain Communications, Inc.

Ed: Chad Halcom. **Description:** Oakland County officials are hoping to create further economic development for the region by pairing health care companies and medical device makers with automotive suppliers in an attempt to discover additional crossover technology.

27549 ■ *"October 2009: Recovery Plods Along" in Hispanic Business (October 2009, pp. 10-11)*

Pub: Hispanic Business

Ed: Dr. Juan Solana. **Description:** Economist reports on a possible economic recovery which will not be allowed to rely on a strong domestic demand in order to sustain it. Consumers, looking to counterbalance years of leverage financing based on unrealistic ever-increasing home and portfolio valuations, are saving rather than spending money.

27550 ■ *"Office Leasing Gains Ground" in Sacramento Business Journal (Vol. 25, July 18, 2008, No. 20, pp. 1)*

Pub: American City Business Journals, Inc.

Ed: Michael Shaw. **Description:** There were at least 84,000 square feet leased to companies in the Sacramento area in the three months prior to August 2008. This development is good news considering that overall vacant leases were around 247,000 square feet for the previous quarter.

27551 ■ *"Office Market May Turn Down" in Crain's New York Business (Vol. 24, January 14, 2008, No. 2, pp. 26)*

Pub: Crain Communications, Inc.

Description: Although still dominated by Wall Street, the downturn in the economy is raising fears that the continuing fallout from the subprime mortgage crisis could result in layoffs that will derail the office market.

27552 ■ *"Ohio's Reputation Lags Its Business Ranking" in Business Courier (Vol. 24, November 23, 2008, No. 32, pp. 1)*

Pub: American City Business Journals, Inc.

Ed: Jon Newberry. **Description:** Site Selection magazine's annual ranking of the top states for new business facilities has ranked Ohio and Kentucky in seventh and eight place respectively, but an opinion survey of real estate executives had placed Ohio much lower at 14. The survey asked 6,000 executives if Ohio's conditions were best for new building projects.

27553 ■ *"Oil Picks and Pans" in Canadian Business (Vol. 79, August 14, 2006, No. 16-17, pp. 67)*

Pub: Rogers Media

Ed: Graham Scott. **Description:** A survey on investments in Canadian energy companies and the inflation caused by oil price hike, are discussed.

27554 ■ *"OK, Bring in the Lawyers" in Crain's Chicago Business (Vol. 31, November 17, 2008, No. 46, pp. 26)*

Pub: Crain Communications, Inc.

Ed: Daniel Rome Levine. **Description:** Bankruptcy attorneys are finding the economic and credit crisis a benefit for their businesses due to the high number of business owners and mortgage holders that are need of their services. One Chicago firm is handling

ten times the number of cases they did the previous year and of that about 80 percent of their new clients are related to the real estate sector.

27555 ■ *"On the Economic Dimensions of Corporate Social Responsibility" in Business and Society (December 2007, pp. 457-478)*

Pub: SAGE Publications USA

Contact: Blaise R. Simqu, President

Ed: Fabienne Fortanier, Ans Kolk. **Description:** Economic impact of Fortune Global 250 firms analyzing concern for corporate social responsibility is discussed, focusing on an illustration of mechanisms by which multinational enterprises affect economic developed.

27556 ■ *"On tap: More Could Get MEGA Credits; Need to Look Outside State May Be Cut" in Crain's Detroit Business (April 7, 2008)*

Pub: Crain Communications, Inc.

Ed: Amy Lane. **Description:** In order to qualify for Michigan Economic Growth Authority tax credits Michigan businesses may no longer have to shop outside the state due to a new bill which has already passed the state Senate and will move on to the House; the bill, along with further changes to the MEGA program, is designed to provide incentives for investments that would add relevance and make Michigan more competitive.

27557 ■ *On the Wealth of Nations: Books That Changed the World*

Pub: Grove/Atlantic Inc.

Contact: Morgan Entrekin, President

E-mail: mentrekin@groveatlantic.com

Ed: P.J. O'Rourke. **Released:** December 21, 2007. **Price:** $21.95. **Description:** Author defends the tenets of freedom of trade, the healthy pursuit of self-interest, and the importance of being a person who 'adheres, on all occasions, steadily and resolutely to his maxims.'.

27558 ■ *"Once More Into the Fray" in Canadian Business (Vol. 80, December 25, 2006, No. 1, pp. 13)*

Pub: Rogers Media

Ed: Jack Mintz. **Description:** A forecast of slow down in the Canadian economy and an election year in 2007 is discussed.

27559 ■ *One Foot Out the Door: How to Combat the Psychological Recession That's Alienating Employees and Hurting American Business*

Pub: AMACOM

Ed: Judith M. Bardwick. **Released:** October 31, 2007. **Price:** $24.95. **Description:** Drawing on research that indicates Generation X and younger baby boomers feel disconnected from their jobs, the author explores the causes (bad management) of that disengagement. Her pragmatic suggestions about how companies can prove their commitment to employees is beneficial.

27560 ■ *"Online All the Time" in Retail Merchandiser (Vol. 51, July-August 2011, No. 4, pp. 18)*

Pub: Phoenix Media Corporation

Description: Ecommerce sales are rising at a steady pace and for cross-channel retailers it is boosting sales in the weak economy. Online sales are expected to reach $188 billion in 2011, boasting a 13.7 rate of growth.

27561 ■ *"OPEC Exposed" in Hawaii Business (Vol. 54, September 2008, No. 3, pp. 2)*

Pub: Hawaii Business Publishing

Ed: Serena Lim. **Description:** Organization of the Petroleum Exporting Countries (OPEC) has said that their effort in developing an alternative energy source has driven prices up. The biofuel sector is criticizing the statement, saying that a research study found that biofuels push petroleum prices down by 15 percent. Details on the effect of rising petroleum prices are discussed.

27562 ■ "Optimism Index" in Black Enterprise (Vol. 41, September 2010, No. 2, pp. 24)
Pub: Earl G. Graves Publishing Co. Inc.
Description: According to a Pew Research Center report, 81 percent of African Americans expect to improve their finances in 2011. Blacks have carried a disproportionate share of job losses and housing foreclosures in the recession that began in 2007.

27563 ■ "Orders Up; Jobs Below Forecast" in Charlotte Observer (February 2, 2007)
Pub: Knight-Ridder/Tribune Business News
Ed: Kerry Hall. **Description:** U.S. Labor Department reported unemployment rates at 4.6 percent, up one-tenth of a percent. Economists had predicted 170,000 new jobs, but only 111,000 were created.

27564 ■ "Others' Economic Woes Bring Business to Bankruptcy Attorney" in The Business Journal - Serving Phoenix and the Valley of the Sun (Vol. 28, July 4, 2008, No. 44, pp. 7)
Pub: American City Business Journals, Inc.
Ed: Mike Sunnucks. **Description:** Economic slowdown has increased the demand for the services offered by law firms and bankruptcy attorneys. The number of small business and consumer bankruptcies has surged in 2005. Attorney Dan Gukeisen of Gukeisen Law Group PC has shifted his focus to handling bankruptcy filings and foreclosure matters.

27565 ■ "Ottawa to Push for Gas Deal Between Petrocan, Gazpron" in Globe & Mail (February 13, 2006, pp. B1)
Pub: CTVglobemedia Publishing Inc.
Ed: Greame Smith. **Description:** Jim Flaherty, finance minister of Canada is negotiating a 1.3 billion dollar deal between state owned Petro-Canada and Russia's OAO Gazprom. This once again highlighted the country's increasing dependence on Russia for its energy requirements.

27566 ■ "Ottawa's Real Estate Targets Exceed Market Appraisals" in Globe & Mail (March 19, 2007, pp. B1)
Pub: CTVglobemedia Publishing Inc.
Ed: Danier Leblanc. **Description:** The growth in the real estate market in Ottawa and the huge revenue the government is expecting from sale of nine buildings as part of its lease back plan is discussed.

27567 ■ "Outlook 2007" in Canadian Business (Vol. 80, December 25, 2006, No. 1, pp.)
Pub: Rogers Media
Ed: David Wolf. **Description:** Economists' 2007 forecast on global economy, particularly about Canada's housing and labor market among other sectors, is discussed.

27568 ■ "Outlook for Montana Agriculture" in Montana Business Quarterly (Vol. 49, Spring 2011, No. 1, pp. 26)
Pub: Bureau of Business & Economic Research
Ed: George Haynes. **Description:** Montana farmers and ranchers are rebounding from lower prices and production to higher prices and record production in 2010. The state has limited dairy and hog production, but farm income is still likely rise between 15 to 25 percent in 2010 over previous year.

27569 ■ "Over A Barrel" in Canadian Business (Vol. 81, July 21, 2008, No. 11, pp. 13)
Pub: Rogers Media Ltd.
Ed: Thomas Watson. **Description:** Analysts predict that the skyrocketing price of fuel will cause a crackdown in the market as purported in the peak oil theory. It is forecasted that the price of oil will reach $200 per barrel. Details of the effect of the increasing oil prices on the market are presented.

27570 ■ "Over a Barrel" in Canadian Business (Vol. 80, February 12, 2007, No. 4, pp. 52)
Pub: Rogers Media
Ed: Andrew Nikoforuk. **Description:** The potential of tar sands of Alberta in becoming the largest source of oil in the world and huge investments of Canadian companies to mine for the oil there are discussed.

27571 ■ Overcoming Barriers to Entrepreneurship in the United States
Pub: Lexington Books
Ed: Diana Furchtgott-Roth. **Released:** March 28, 2008. **Price:** $24.95. **Description:** Real and perceived barriers to the founding and running of small businesses in America are discussed. Each chapter outlines how policy and economic environments can hinder business owners and offers tips to overcome these obstacles. Starting with venture capital access in Silicon Valley during the Internet bubble, the book goes on to question the link between personal wealth and entrepreneurship, examines how federal tax rates affect small business creation and destruction, explains the low rate of self-employment among Mexican immigrants, and suggests ways pension coverage can be increased in small businesses.

27572 ■ "An Overview of Energy Consumption of the Globalized World Economy" in Energy Policy (Vol. 39, October 2011, No. 10, pp. 5920-2928)
Pub: Reed Elsevier Reference Publishing
Ed: Z.M. Chen, G.Q. Chen. **Description:** Energy consumption and its impact on the global world economy is examined.

27573 ■ "Overview - Small Business Optimism" in Small Business Economic Trends (April 2008, pp. 4)
Pub: National Federation of Independent Business
Ed: William C. Dunkelberg, Holly Wade. **Description:** Graph and table representing the optimism index for small businesses in the U.S., based on ten survey indicators, are presented. The index values include data from 1986 to 2008.

27574 ■ "Overview - Small Business Optimism" in Small Business Economic Trends (March 2008, pp. 4)
Pub: National Federation of Independent Business
Ed: William C. Dunkelberg, Holly Wade. **Description:** A graph and a table representing the optimism index for small businesses in the U.S., based on ten survey indicators, are presented. The index values include data from 1986 to 2008.

27575 ■ "Overview - Small Business Optimism" in Small Business Economic Trends (February 2008, pp. 4)
Pub: National Federation of Independent Business
Ed: William C. Dunkelberg, Holly Wade. **Description:** A graph and a table representing the optimism index for small businesses in the U.S., based on ten survey indicators, are presented. The index values include data from 1975 to 2008.

27576 ■ "Overview - Small Business Optimism" in Small Business Economic Trends (January 2008, pp. 4)
Pub: National Federation of Independent Business
Description: Optimism index among small businesses surveyed in the U.S. from 1986 to 1007 is presented in a graph. A small business optimism index from January 2002 to June 2007 is also given in tabular form. The index value was seasonally adjusted at 1986=100.

27577 ■ "Overview - Small Business Optimism" in Small Business Economic Trends (July 2009, pp. 4)
Pub: National Federation of Independent Business
Description: Small businesses surveyed in the United States regarding their optimism index from 1986 to 2009 shows a marked difference as is presented in a graph. A small business optimism index from January 2004 to June 2009 is also given in tabular form. The index value was seasonally adjusted at 1986=100.

27578 ■ "Overview - Small Business Optimism" in Small Business Economic Trends (September 2010, pp. 4)
Pub: National Federation of Independent Business
Ed: William C. Dunkelberg, Holly Wade. **Description:** An optimism index among small businesses surveyed in the U.S. from 1986 to 2010 is presented in a graph. A small business optimism index from 2005 to 2010 is also given in tabular form.

27579 ■ "Pain Ahead as Profit Pressure Increases" in Crain's Chicago Business (Vol. 31, May 5, 2008, No. 18, pp. 4)
Pub: Crain Communications, Inc.
Ed: Daniel Rome Levine. **Description:** Interview with David Klaskin, the chairman and chief investment officer at Oak Ridge Investments LLC, who discusses the outlook for the economy and corporate earnings, particularly in the housing and auto industries, the impact of economic stimulus checks, the weakness of the dollar and recommendations of stocks that individual investors may find helpful.

27580 ■ Panic! The Story of Modern Financial Insanity
Pub: W.W. Norton & Company
Ed: Michael Lewis. **Released:** 2009. **Price:** $27.95. **Description:** Two decades of stock market crashes are outlined.

27581 ■ Paper Fortunes: Modern Wall Street: Where It's Been and Where It's Going
Pub: St. Martin's Press LLC
Ed: Roy C. Smith. **Released:** 2010. **Price:** $35.00. **Description:** Comprehensive history of Wall Street and lessons learned with insight into ways Wall Street will reinvent itself in this new economy.

27582 ■ "Paper Tigers" in Conde Nast Portfolio (Vol. 2, June 2008, No. 6, pp. 84)
Pub: Conde Nast Publications
Contact: David Carey, President
Ed: Roger Lowenstein. **Description:** Newspapers are losing their advertisers and readers and circulation today is equal to that of 1950, a time when the U.S. population was half its present size.

27583 ■ "Past Promises Haunt Project" in The Business Journal-Portland (Vol. 25, August 1, 2008, No. 21, pp. 1)
Pub: American City Business Journals, Inc.
Ed: Aliza Earnshaw. **Description:** Oregon University System and Oregon Health and Science University will face the state Legislature to defend their request for a $250 million in state bonds to fund a life-sciences collaborative research building. The project is meant to help grow the Oregon bioscience industry. Comments from industry observers and legislators are also presented.

27584 ■ "Patchy Oil Profits" in Canadian Business (Vol. 80, February 12, 2007, No. 4, pp. 89)
Pub: Rogers Media
Ed: Michelle Magnan. **Description:** The fall in fourth-quarter earnings of several oil and gas companies in Canada, in view of rise in their expenditure, is discussed.

27585 ■ "Patients to Elect to Cut Care" in The Business Journal-Serving Metropolitan Kansas City (Vol. 27, November 21, 2008, No. 11, pp. 1)
Pub: American City Business Journals, Inc.
Ed: Rob Roberts. **Description:** Patients in Kansas City, Missouri are cutting down on health care services due to the economic crisis. A decline in diagnostic procedures has been observed at Northland Cardiology. Elective reconstructive procedures have also been reduced by 25 percent. Additional information and statistics regarding the healthcare sector is included.

27586 ■ "Paying for the Recession: Rebalancing Economic Growth" in Montana Business Quarterly (Vol. 49, Spring 2011, No. 1, pp. 2)
Pub: Bureau of Business & Economic Research
Ed: Patrick M. Barkey. **Description:** Four key issues required to address in order to rebalance economic growth in America are examined. They include: savings rates, global trade imbalances, government budgets and most importantly, housing price correction.

27587 ■ "PDX Bucks National Trend" in The Business Journal-Portland (Vol. 25, August 1, 2008, No. 21, pp. 1)
Pub: American City Business Journals, Inc.
Ed: Erik Siemers. **Description:** Portland International Airport could face problems as air carriers are planning to reduce capacity at the airport. The airport is

showing signs of growth despite the slowdown in the airline industry. Other airlines that are planning to reduce seating capacity at the airport are also presented.

27588 ■ *"Peak Show" in Canadian Business (Vol. 81, December 24, 2007, No. 1, pp. 28)*
Pub: Rogers Media
Ed: Thomas Watson. **Description:** Factors affecting oil prices could include political instability and economic slowdown, but peak oil is not one of them as it is believed there is still plenty of oil in supply. Details on the oil supply and demand, trend for higher prices, and peak oil expert Matthew Simmons' prediction on the issue are discussed.

27589 ■ *"The People Puzzle; Re-Training America's Workers" in The Economist (Vol. 390, January 3, 2009, No. 8612, pp. 32)*
Pub: The Economist Newspaper Inc.
Description: With thousands of workers losing their jobs, America is now facing the task of getting them back to work. With an overall unemployment rate of 6.7 percent, the federal government has three main ways for leading workers back to employment: training them for new jobs, providing unemployment insurance in order to replace lost wages during the period of job-hunting; and matching employers who desire a skill with workers who have that skill. Specialized staffing agencies provide employers and potential employees with the help necessary to find a job in some of the more niche markets.

27590 ■ *Petty Capitalists and Globalization: Flexibility, Entrepreneurship, and Economic Development*
Pub: State University of New York Press
Ed: Alan Smart, Josephine Smart. **Released:** January 2006. **Price:** $26.95. **Description:** Investigation into ways small businesses in Europe, Asia, and Latin America are required to operate and compete in the fast-growing transnational economy.

27591 ■ *"PGA Tourney Drives Area Economy, Image" in Crain's Detroit Business (Vol. 24, April 7, 2008, No. 14, pp. 22)*
Pub: Crain Communications, Inc.
Ed: Jason Deegan. **Description:** Discusses the major economic impact the 2008 PGA Championship will have when it visits the south course at Oakland Hills Country Club August 4-10.

27592 ■ *"A Place in the Sun" in Canadian Business (Vol. 81, July 22, 2008, No. 12-13, pp. 56)*
Pub: Rogers Media Ltd.
Description: Experts believe that it is the best time for Canadians to own a retirement home in the U.S., where real estate prices are up to 50 percent below their peak. Other views concerning the economic conditions occurring in the United States, as well as on the implications for Canadians planning to invest in the country are presented.

27593 ■ *"Planning Ahead" in Crain's Cleveland Business (Vol. 30, June 15, 2009, No. 23, pp. 12)*
Pub: Crain Communications, Inc.
Ed: Shannon Mortland. **Description:** Cleveland area nonprofit organizations are developing new strategies for raising donations, while keeping costs down in the slow economy.

27594 ■ *"Playing Defense" in Crain's Chicago Business (Vol. 31, November 10, 2008, No. 45, pp. 4)*
Pub: Crain Communications, Inc.
Ed: Monee Fields-White. **Description:** Chicago's money managers are increasingly investing in local companies such as Caterpillar Inc., a maker of construction and mining equipment, Kraft Foods Inc. and Baxter International Inc., a manufacturer of medical products, in an attempt to bolster their portfolios. These companies have a history of surviving tough economic times.

27595 ■ *"Polite Conversation" in Mergers & Acquisitions: The Dealmaker's Journal*

(March 1, 2008)
Pub: SourceMedia, Inc.
Description: In January, industry leaders and dealmakers met at Davos to discuss topics ranging from the possibility of a recession to what lies ahead in the deal market.

27596 ■ *"Poor Economy Inspires Rich Alternatives In a Modern, and Tax-Free, Twist on Bartering" in Houston Chronicle (June 7, 2010)*
Pub: Houston Chronicle Publishing Company
Ed: Michael Rubinkam. **Description:** Time banking helps individuals and firms receive goods or services by depositing time dollars into a bank reserved for receipt of goods and services.

27597 ■ *"Population Growing Faster Than Retail, Service Sector" in Crain's New York Business (Vol. 24, January 14, 2008, No. 2, pp. 30)*
Pub: Crain Communications, Inc.
Ed: Andrew Marks. **Description:** Downtown Manhattan is seeing more residential development; however, as more families call the area home the need for more retail and services is becoming evident.

27598 ■ *"Portfolio: Written in the Polls" in Entrepreneur (Vol. 35, October 2007, No. 10, pp. 74)*
Pub: Entrepreneur Media Inc.
Ed: Scott Bernard Nelson. **Description:** Ibbotsen Associates looked at trends in the U.S. presidential elections to see if the election has something to do with stock market behavior. It was found that election years beat non-election years in the stock market by nearly three percentage points each year. Details of the presidential elections' impact on the stock market are given.

27599 ■ *"Portion of Silver Line Will Run By Year's End" in Crain's Cleveland Business (Vol. 28, November 5, 2007, No. 44, pp. 6)*
Pub: Crain Communications, Inc.
Ed: Jay Miller. **Description:** Cleveland's new Silver Line rapid transit will board its first passengers before the end of the year. The project is expected to spur economic development in the area and will speed transportation along Euclid Avenue.

27600 ■ *The Post-American World*
Pub: W.W. Norton & Company
Ed: Fareed Zakaria. **Released:** 2009. **Price:** $25.95. **Description:** Analysis of the changes taking place as new countries are rising as status players challenging American dominance.

27601 ■ *"The Power of Innovation" in Canadian Business (Vol. 81, March 17, 2008, No. 4, pp. 57)*
Pub: Rogers Media
Ed: Andrew Wahl. **Description:** Canada ranks badly in terms innovation yardsticks that directly translate to economic growth such as business R&D as a percentage of GDP and R&D per capita. Canada's reliance on natural resources does not provide incentives to innovate unlike smaller countries with little natural resources. Canada could spur innovation through regulations that encourage industrial research.

27602 ■ *"Power Partnerships" in Business Courier (Vol. 27, October 22, 2010, No. 25, pp. 1)*
Pub: Business Courier
Ed: Lucy May. **Description:** The $400 million Harrah's casino and the $47 million redevelopment and expansion of Washington Park are project aimed at boosting the economy in downtown Cincinnati, Ohio. These projects will be done in cooperation with the National Association for the Advancement of Colored People. Insights into the role of minority-owned businesses in regional economic development are explored.

27603 ■ *"Practice Problems" in Crain's Cleveland Business (Vol. 30, June 22, 2009, No. 24, pp. 9)*
Pub: Crain Communications, Inc.
Ed: Arielle Kass. **Description:** Many laid off attorneys are finding few options in the down economy and some are setting up their own practices.

27604 ■ *Predictably Irrational: The Hidden Forces That Shape Our Decisions*
Pub: HarperCollins Publishers
Ed: Dan Ariely. **Released:** 2009. **Price:** $25.95. **Description:** Behaviorists are bringing the economics profession around to realizing that human beings are impulsive, shortsighted and procrastinating in behavior. Economists are using this information to market products to consumers.

27605 ■ *"Pricey Oil, High Dollar Wipe Out Jobs" in Globe & Mail (February 11, 2006, pp. B6)*
Pub: CTVglobemedia Publishing Inc.
Ed: Heather Scoffield. **Description:** The impact of higher oil prices and dollar value, on manufacturing jobs in Canada, is discussed.

27606 ■ *"Principles for Creating Growth in Challenging Times" in Agency Sales Magazine (Vol. 39, September-October 2009, No. 9, pp. 35)*
Pub: MANA
Ed: Robert Goshen. **Description:** Creating a productive environment is one vital key for businesses to utilize during the challenging times that arise due to a weak economy; other important factors include maintaining a good relationship with the staff, responding appropriately to challenges and keeping a sense of humor.

27607 ■ *"Priority: Recessionade" in Inc. (February 2008, pp. 19-20)*
Pub: Gruner & Jahr USA Publishing
Ed: Amy Feldman. **Description:** Despite signs of inflation, entrepreneurs see these tough economic times as an opportunity to start or grow their businesses. Five entrepreneurs share insight into ways this economic downturn can work to grow their businesses.

27608 ■ *"Profit Predictions Look Too Plump" in Barron's (Vol. 88, March 31, 2008, No. 13, pp. 37)*
Pub: Dow Jones & Company, Inc.
Ed: Johanna Bennett. **Description:** Full-year forecast points to a 14 percent gain for 2008 but the second-half profit increases would have to grow at a fast rate and peak at 61 percent in the fourth quarter to achieve this. Trends in the U.S. economic conditions are also discussed.

27609 ■ *Profits Aren't Everything. They're the Only Thing: No-Nonsense Rules from the Ultimate Contrarian and Small Business Guru*
Pub: HarperCollins Publishers
Ed: George Cloutier. **Released:** September 9, 2010. **Price:** $24.99. **Description:** In difficult economic times, the only way for small businesses to survive is to maximize profits. Thirteen steps to maximize profits in a slow economy are outlined.

27610 ■ *"Program for Women Entrepreneurs: Tips for Surviving this Economy" in Crain's Detroit Business (Vol. 25, June 22, 2009, No. 25)*
Pub: Crain Communications Inc. - Detroit
Description: Michigan Leadership Institute for Women Entrepreneurs will hold its third and final program, 'Tough Times are Temporary, but Tough People are Permanent' at the Davenport University in Livonia, Michigan.

27611 ■ *"Project Could Forge Path to Jobs, Growth" in Business Courier (Vol. 26, September 11, 2009, No. 20, pp. 1)*
Pub: American City Business Journals, Inc.
Ed: Lucy May. **Description:** The planned 13.5 mile Mill Creek Greenway Trail extension could create 445 jobs and bring $52 million to the economy of Cincinnati, Ohio. The trail extension would cost $24 million and would be used for recreational purposes.

27612 ■ *"PSU Launches $90 Million Project" in The Business Journal-Portland (Vol. 25, July 18, 2008, No. 19, pp. 1)*
Pub: American City Business Journals, Inc.
Ed: Aliza Earnshaw. **Description:** Portland State University (PSU) has launched a $90-million project for a new business school building, which is to be

located at Southwest Market and Southwest Park. The business school is expected to move in to its new 130,000-suqare-foot building by 2013. PSU business school needs to raise $30 million for the project.

27613 ■ "Push Is On To Build Region's Prospects In Film Industry" in Crain's Cleveland Business (Vol. 28, November 19, 2007, No. 46, pp. 1)
Pub: Crain Communications, Inc.
Ed: Jay Miller. **Description:** Overview of a bill that has been introduced by state Representative Thomas Patton that would grant a 25 percent state income tax credit on investments of $300,000 or more in motion picture or television productions filmed in Ohio.

27614 ■ "Put It on MasterCard" in Barron's (Vol. 89, July 27, 2009, No. 30, pp. 16)
Pub: Dow Jones & Co., Inc.
Ed: Bill Alpert. **Description:** Shares of MasterCard trade at a discount at just 15 times its anticipated earnings and some believe that these shares may be a better play in an economic recovery. The prospects of these shares are compared with those of Visa.

27615 ■ "Putting the World at Your Fingertips" in Barron's (Vol. 88, July 7, 2008, No. 27, pp. L13)
Pub: Dow Jones & Co., Inc.
Ed: Neil A. Martin. **Description:** Currency-traded exchange funds allow investors to diversify their assets and take advantage of investment opportunities such as speculation and hedging. Investors can use these funds to build positions in favor of or against the US dollar.

27616 ■ "The Puzzle of Our Productivity" in Canadian Business (Vol. 83, September 14, 2010, No. 15, pp. 22)
Pub: Rogers Media Ltd.
Ed: Rachel Madison. **Description:** Industry Canada economist Annette Ryan revealed in a presentation to the Canadian Association for Business Economics that growth in Canadian labor productivity has steadily declined since the 1980s. Ryan believes that business decisions have played an important role in the poor productivity results. Other details of the findings are presented.

27617 ■ "Q&A" in Canadian Business (Vol. 81, July 22, 2008, No. 12-13, pp. 8)
Pub: Rogers Media Ltd.
Ed: Michelle Magnan. **Description:** Interview with Scott Saxberg who discusses Crescent Point Energy Trust's discovery of resources in Saskatchewan and believes that this is a once-in-a-lifetime type of event. Crescent Point holds 75 percent of its resources in Saskatchewan; this new finding being considered the second-largest pool discovered since the 1950s. Saxberg's other views as well as information on Crescent Point's services are presented.

27618 ■ "Q&A Interview With Perrin Beatty" in Canadian Business (Vol. 80, October 8, 2007, No. 20, pp. 13)
Pub: Rogers Media
Description: Perrin Beatty, president and chief executive officer of the Canadian Chamber of Commerce, talks about his move from the Canadian Manufacturers and Exporters to his current organization. He also discusses the state of Canada's economy, as well as the need for leadership.

27619 ■ "A Questionable Chemical Romance" in Barron's (Vol. 88, July 14, 2008, No. 28, pp. 28)
Pub: Dow Jones & Co., Inc.
Ed: Andrew Bary. **Description:** Dow Chemical paid $78-a-share for the surprise takeover of Rohm & Haas. The acquisition is reducing Dow Chemical's financial flexibility at a time when chemical companies are being affected by high costs and a weak U.S. economy.

27620 ■ "Quick Earnings Revival Unlikely" in Barron's (Vol. 88, June 30, 2008, No. 26, pp. 31)
Pub: Dow Jones & Co., Inc.
Ed: Johanna Bennett. **Description:** Analysts are pushing back their prediction of a U.S. economy

turnaround to 2009. A recession in the first half of 2008 may not have happened but unemployment is rising and house prices continue to fall.

27621 ■ "Quiznos Franchisees Walloped by Recession" in Advertising Age (Vol. 79, October 20, 2008, No. 39, pp. 3)
Pub: Crain Communications, Inc.
Ed: Emily Bryson York. **Description:** While the recession has taken a toll on the entire restaurant industry, a number of Quiznos franchisees claim to have been disproportionately affected due to lackluster marketing, higher-than-average commodity costs, competition with Subway and a premium-pricing structure that is incompatible with a tight economy.

27622 ■ "The Racial Divide and the Class Struggle in the United States" in WorkingUSA (Vol. 11, September 2008, No. 3, pp. 311)
Pub: Blackwell Publishers Ltd.
Ed: Michael Goldfield. **Description:** An examination of questions of race that continue to play such a prominent role in contemporary society is presented, focusing on the undermining of potential solidarity and strength of the working class movement, what sustains racists attitudes, practices and institutions, especially in the face of trends in world economic development.

27623 ■ "Ready for the Back Burner" in Barron's (Vol. 88, March 17, 2008, No. 11, pp. 47)
Pub: Dow Jones & Company, Inc.
Ed: Vito J. Racanelli. **Description:** McDonald's has promised to return $15 billion to $17 billion to shareholders in 2007-2009 but headwinds are rising for the company. December, 2007 same-store sales were flat and the company's traffic growth in the U.S. is slowing. Its shares are likely to trade in tandem with the market until recession fears recede.

27624 ■ "Ready for a Rally?" in The Economist (Vol. 390, January 3, 2009, No. 8612, pp. 54)
Pub: The Economist Newspaper Inc.
Description: Analysts predict that the recession could end by 2010. The current economic crisis is presented in detail.

27625 ■ "Real Estate Market Still in a Slump" in Montana Business Quarterly (Vol. 49, Summer 2011, No. 2, pp. 15)
Pub: Bureau of Business & Economic Research
Ed: Patrick M. Barkey. **Description:** Montana's housing market is still in decline with no sign of improving in the near future. Statistical data included.

27626 ■ "Real Estate Vets Take Times In Stride" in The Business Journal-Serving Metropolitan Kansas City (Vol. 26, July 25, 2008, No. 46)
Pub: American City Business Journals, Inc.
Ed: Rob Roberts. **Description:** Kansas City, Missouri's real estate industry veterans like Allen Block believe that the challenges faced by the industry in the 1980s, when the Federal Reserve Board controlled the money supply to slow down inflation, were worse than the challenges faced today. Other views, trends and information on the real estate industry of the city, are presented.

27627 ■ "Realities May Blur Vision" in The Business Journal-Serving Metropolitan Kansas City (Vol. 27, September 19, 2008, No. 1, pp. 1)
Pub: American City Business Journals, Inc.
Ed: Rob Roberts. **Description:** Vision Metcalf is a study by Kansas City that depicts how Metcalf Avenue could look like if redeveloped. Redevelopment plans for the Metcalf corridor include a 20-story mixed-use building on a vacant car dealership. The challenges that the redevelopment plans will face are also analyzed.

27628 ■ "Realtors Signing Out" in The Business Journal-Serving Metropolitan Kansas City (Vol. 27, November 21, 2008, No. 11, pp. 1)
Pub: American City Business Journals, Inc.
Ed: Rob Roberts. **Description:** The Kansas City Regional Association of Realtors has lost 1,000 of its members due to the downturn in the housing market.

Applications for realtor licenses have dropped by 159 percent. Changes in Missouri's licensing requirements are seen as additional reasons for the declines.

27629 ■ "Recession Fears Power Gold" in Barron's (Vol. 88, March 17, 2008, No. 11, pp. M14)
Pub: Dow Jones & Company, Inc.
Ed: Melanie Burton. **Description:** Gold prices have been more attractive as the U.S. dollar weakens and the Dow Jones Industrial Average has slipped almost 10 percent in 2008. The rate cuts from the Federal Reserve Board has also spurred inflation fears adding upward pressure to the price of the metal.

27630 ■ "Recession Management" in Canadian Business (Vol. 81, March 3, 2008, No. 3, pp. 62)
Pub: Rogers Media
Ed: Joe Castaldo. **Description:** Some companies such as Capital One Financial Corp. are managing their finances as if a recession has already taken place to prepare themselves for the looming economic downturn. Intel Corp., meanwhile shows how increasing its investments during a recession could be advantageous. Tips on how companies can survive a recession are provided.

27631 ■ "The Recession: Problem or Opportunity" in Women In Business (Vol. 61, October-November 2009, No. 5, pp. 34)
Pub: American Business Women's Association
Ed: J. Douglas Bate. **Description:** Business organizations' success during a recession is based on how management views the economic situation. The recession may be deemed as a setback or may be visualized as an opportunity that has to be grabbed for the organization. Suggestions on what management should do in the opportunity-creating or proactive approach are also highlighted.

27632 ■ "Recession-Proof Your Startup" in Crain's Chicago Business (Vol. 31, November 10, 2008, No. 45, pp. 24)
Pub: Crain Communications, Inc.
Description: Detailed information concerning ways in which to start a business during an economic crisis is provided. Ways in which to find financing, the importance of a solid business plan, customer service, problem-solving and finding the right niche for the region are also discussed.

27633 ■ "Recession Survival Tip: Less Is More" in Women Entrepreneur (December 31, 2008)
Pub: Entrepreneur Media Inc.
Ed: Suzy Girard-Ruttenberg. **Description:** These trying economic times can be an opportunity to make bold changes in one's business that may yield lasting results, not just short-term survival; simplification, accountability and shoring up one's margins are things to look at when determining the goals of the company.

27634 ■ "Recipe for Disaster?" in Sacramento Business Journal (Vol. 25, July 4, 2008, No. 18, pp. 1)
Pub: American City Business Journals, Inc.
Ed: Mark Anderson. **Description:** Restaurateurs are challenged with balancing rising operating costs and what customers are willing to pay for their services. Flour prices in 2008 have increased by 46 percent from April 2007. Other views on the situation, as well as trends, forecasts and statistics on sales, outlook on economic conditions, consumer price index, and the typical split of restaurant revenue, are presented.

27635 ■ "Recovery a Ruse?" in Baltimore Business Journal (Vol. 28, August 6, 2010, No. 13, pp. 1)
Pub: Baltimore Business Journal
Ed: Scott Dance. **Description:** Baltimore, Maryland-area businesses have remained cautious as their optimism faded along with the latest indicators on economic recovery. Economists believe they might be justified with their concern since sales were better, but there is no security that they will stay that way.

27636 ■ *"Recovery on Tap for 2010?"* in *Orlando Business Journal (Vol. 26, January 1, 2010, No. 31, pp. 1)*
Pub: American City Business Journals
Ed: Melanie Stawicki Azam, Richard Bilbao, Christopher Boyd, Anjali Fluker. **Description:** Economic forecasts for Central Florida's leading business sectors in 2010 are presented. These sectors include housing, film and TV, sports business, law, restaurants, aviation, tourism and hospitality, banking and finance, commercial real estate, retail, health care, insurance, higher education, and manufacturing. According to some local executives, Central Florida's economy will slowly recover in 2010.

27637 ■ *"Red Tape Ties Detroit Housing Rehab Plan"* in *Crain's Detroit Business (Vol. 24, September 22, 2008, No. 38, pp. 1)*
Pub: Crain Communications Inc.
Ed: Ryan Beene. **Description:** Venture-capital firm Wilherst Oxford LLC is a Florida-based company that has purchased 300 inner-city homes which were in foreclosure in Detroit. Wilherst Oxford is asking the city to forgive the existing tax and utility liens so the firm can utilize the money for home improvements. The city, however, is reluctant but has stated that they are willing to negotiate.

27638 ■ *"Reduce or Repay"* in *Canadian Business (Vol. 80, November 5, 2007, No. 22, pp. 35)*
Pub: Rogers Media
Ed: Regan Ray. **Description:** The new greenhouse gas (GHG) policy of Alberta, Canada requires about 100 industrial facilities that emit over 100,000 tons of GHG per year to reduce emissions by 12 percent by the end of 2007. Facilities that fail to comply will pay $15 per ton of GHG emission beyond target. The economic impacts of the regulation are evaluated.

27639 ■ *"Reform or Perish"* in *Canadian Business (Vol. 82, April 27, 2009, No. 7, pp. 20)*
Pub: Rogers Media
Ed: Al Rosen. **Description:** It is believed that Canada needs to fix its financial regulatory framework in order to provide more oversight on accounting procedures that is often left up to auditors. While the U.S. has constantly rebuilt its regulatory framework, Canada has not instituted reforms on its regulations. Canada entered the recession with a strong system but needs to build more substance into it.

27640 ■ *"Regarding Warren"* in *Canadian Business (Vol. 80, November 5, 2007, No. 22, pp. 29)*
Pub: Rogers Media
Ed: Jeff Sanford. **Description:** Berkshire Hathaway's Warren Buffet believes that investing in energy shares is profitable, however, he warns investors about volatility in prices. Buffet, the second richest man in the world, forecasts that the value of the Canadian dollar will continue to rise. Buffet's investments are also discussed.

27641 ■ *"Region and City Need Influx of Youth"* in *Crain's Detroit Business (Vol. 24, April 14, 2008, No. 15, pp. 8)*
Pub: Crain Communications Inc.
Description: Discusses an upcoming report from Michigan Future Inc. which finds that young professionals, including those with children, are interested in living in an active urban environment. It also states that because many of those young professionals are entrepreneurial in nature, oftentimes businesses follow.

27642 ■ *"Rep Contracts: Simple, Clear, Fair"* in *Agency Sales Magazine (Vol. 39, September-October 2009, No. 9, pp. 3)*
Pub: MANA
Ed: Bryan C. Shirley. **Description:** Things that a manufacturer and a sales representative needs to strive for when creating an Agreement for Representation includes an agreement that is simple and complete, one that covers all the needs of both parties and is fair, equitable, and balanced. Sales representatives need to make more sales calls and find new opportunities during this recession.

27643 ■ *"Reply! Grows at Unprecedented Rate, Rips Beta Off Its Marketplace"* in *Marketing Weekly News (September 19, 2009, pp. 149)*
Pub: Investment Weekly News
Description: Profile of Reply.com, a leader in locally-targeted Internet marketing, announced significant growth in terms of revenue, enhanced features and services and new categories since launching its beta Reply! Marketplace platform. Even in the face of an economic downturn, the company has posted over 50 percent revenue growth in the Real Estate and Automotive categories.

27644 ■ *"Reps Continue to Move to International Trade"* in *Agency Sales Magazine (Vol. 39, September-October 2009, No. 9, pp. 24)*
Pub: MANA
Ed: Jack Foster. **Description:** Sales representatives should get involved and look into international trade if they want to be successful in the future. The weak U.S. dollar, labor costs, and the low cost of transportation are factors that drive the trend towards international trade.

27645 ■ *"Research Highlights Disengaged Workforce"* in *Workforce Management (Vol. 88, November 16, 2009, No. 12, pp. 22)*
Pub: Crain Communications Inc.
Ed: Ed Frauenheim. **Description:** Most researchers have documented a drop in employee engagement during the recession due to such factors as layoffs, restructuring and less job security.

27646 ■ *"Research and Markets Adds Report: Cyprus: Convergence, Broadband and Internet Market"* in *Wireless News (September 4, 2009)*
Pub: Close-Up Media
Description: Overview of a new report by Research and Markets entitled, 'Cyprus Convergence, Broadband and Internet Market - Overview, Statistics and Forecasts.' Highlights include information regarding broadband accounts which now account for the majority of household Internet connections.

27647 ■ *"Research and Markets Adds Report: Ghana: Convergence, Broadband and Internet Market"* in *Wireless News (September 4, 2009)*
Pub: Close-Up Media
Description: Overview of a new report by Research and Markets entitled, 'Ghana Convergence, Broadband and Internet Market - Overview, Statistics and Forecasts.' Ghana was among the first countries in Africa connected to the Internet and to introduce ADSL broadband services; however, only 30 of the 140 licensed ISP's are operational making the sector highly competitive.

27648 ■ *"Research Note"* in *International Journal of Globalisation and Small Business (Vol. 4, September 21, 2010, No. 1, pp. 92)*
Pub: Publishers Communication Group
Ed: Alexander Bode, Tobias B. Talmon l'Armee, Simon Alig. **Description:** The cluster concept has steadily increased its importance during the past years both from practitioners' and reearchers' points of view. Simultaneously, many corporate networks are established. Researchers from different areas (business management, economic social and geographical science) are trying to explain both phenomena.

27649 ■ *"Restaurants Dish Up Meal Deals To Attract Customers"* in *Crain's Detroit Business (Vol. 24, October 6, 2008, No. 40, pp. 1)*
Pub: Crain Communications, Inc.
Ed: Nathan Skid. **Description:** Restaurateurs are devising many creative and rewarding incentives to get customers to frequent their establishments during this economic crisis. Innovative ways in which even higher-end establishments are drawing in business are discussed.

27650 ■ *"Restaurants Slammed by Economy"* in *Business Courier (Vol. 24, April 4, 2008, No. 52, pp. 1)*
Pub: American City Business Journals, Inc.
Ed: Lisa Biank Fasig. **Description:** Restaurants in Cincinnati are closing some of their stores due to growing costs of fuel, eggs and meat. The establishments are also affected by lower consumer spending that was brought on by unemployment, higher grocery prices and foreclosures. The economic problems in Cincinnati are also compared to those in other cities.

27651 ■ *"Restaurants Stewing Over Food Prices"* in *The Business Journal-Milwaukee (Vol. 25, August 22, 2008, No. 48, pp. A1)*
Pub: American City Business Journals, Inc.
Ed: David Doege. **Description:** Many restaurant operators in the Milwaukee area are changing their menus, increasing prices and decreasing workers' hours amid the soaring prices of commodities. The prices of some staples have risen by over 50 percent since 2006. The impacts of the continued rise in food prices are examined further.

27652 ■ *The Retail Revolution: How Wal-Mart Created a Brave New World of Business*
Pub: Metropolitan Books
Ed: Nelson Lichtenstein. **Released:** July 21, 2009. **Price:** $25.00. **Description:** Comprehensive discussion on how Wal-Mart changed retailing, and its place in the changing global economy.

27653 ■ *"Retail Slump Deflates Local Development"* in *Business Courier (Vol. 24, February 29, 2008, No. 47, pp. 1)*
Pub: American City Business Journals, Inc.
Ed: Lisa Biank Fasig. **Description:** 2007 sales of the retail industry are the slowest since the year 2003, driving retail stores to reconsider their expansion plans for 2008. A number of retail projects have been delayed, cancelled or altered, including Newport Pavilion, Rivers Crossing, Wal-Mart Supercenters, Legacy Place and Millworks. The impacts of retail slowdown on development projects are analyzed further.

27654 ■ *"Retailers Dig In For Holiday Shopping Push"* in *Business Review, Albany New York (Vol. 34, November 30, 2007, No. 35, pp. 1)*
Pub: American City Business Journals, Inc.
Ed: Michael DeMasi. **Description:** Tough economic conditions have led to lower consumer spending and retailers in Albany, New York and nationwide experienced mix results during the Black Friday weekend. Local retailers enjoyed higher sales in 2007 compared to 2006 and the National Retail Federation projects that retail sales will climb by four percent. Holiday retail trade forecasts are discussed.

27655 ■ *"Retailers Pull Out All Stops to Combat Poor Projections"* in *Austin Business JournalInc. (Vol. 28, November 21, 2008, No. 36, pp. 1)*
Pub: American City Business Journals
Ed: Jean Kwon. **Description:** Report from Wachovia Economics Group reports that holiday sales for 2008 are expected to decline by 2 percent and local retailers are planning to boost holiday sales through marketing efforts, which include giving freebies to early shoppers. Details on marketing strategies of several retailers are provided.

27656 ■ *The Return of Depression Economics and the Crisis of 2008*
Pub: W.W. Norton & Company, Inc.
Ed: Paul Krugman. **Price:** $16.95. **Description:** The recipient of the 2008 Nobel Memorial Prize in Economics revises his earlier work from 1999 to reflect the current economic crisis of 2008.

27657 ■ *"Return to Wealth; Bank Strategy"* in *The Economist (Vol. 390, January 3, 2009, No. 8612, pp. 56)*
Pub: The Economist Newspaper Inc.
Description: UBS' strategy to survive these trying economic times is presented. Statistical data included. UBS has a stronger balance-sheet than most of its investment-banking peers and has reduced its portfolio.

27658 ■ "Revenue Shortfall Leads to Budget Uncertainty" in Crain's Detroit Business (Vol. 24, March 10, 2008, No. 10, pp. 26)

Pub: Crain Communications, Inc.

Ed: Amy Lane. **Description:** Michigan's current-year budget may face a $134 million shortfall due to such issues as lower-than-anticipated payment from a 1999 national settlement with the U.S. tobacco industry, overestimated growth in property-tax revenue, the impact of the federal stimulus package and the potential settlement of a Midland property-tax dispute. The governor's proposed budget for fiscal year for 2009 may face a $249.6 million shortfall.

27659 ■ "The Right Time for REITs" in Barron's (Vol. 88, July 14, 2008, No. 28, pp. 32)

Pub: Dow Jones & Co., Inc.

Ed: Mike Hogan. **Description:** Discusses the downturn in U.S. real estate investment trusts so these are worth considering for investment. Several Websites that are useful for learning about real estate investment trusts for investment purposes are presented.

27660 ■ "Rising in the East; Research and Development" in The Economist (Vol. 390, January 3, 2009, No. 8612, pp. 47)

Pub: The Economist Newspaper Inc.

Description: Impressive growth of the technological research and development in Asian countries is discussed. Statistical data included.

27661 ■ "Risk and Reward" in Canadian Business (Vol. 81, October 13, 2008, No. 17, pp. 21)

Pub: Rogers Media Ltd.

Ed: Calvin Leung. **Description:** Macro-economist and currency analyst Mark Venezia believes that stable financial institutions, free-market reforms, and the role of central banks in keeping inflation and exchange rates stable could make emerging-market bonds strong performers for better future returns. Venezia's other views on emerging-market bonds are discussed.

27662 ■ The Road from Ruin: How to Revive Capitalism and Put American Back on Top

Pub: Crown Business

Ed: Matthew Bishop, Michael Green. **Released:** January 26, 2010. **Price:** $27.00. **Description:** Authors show why American companies must respond to the economic crisis with long term vision and a renewed emphasis on values.

27663 ■ "Ronald Taketa" in Hawaii Business (Vol. 54, September 2008, No. 3, pp. 28)

Pub: Hawaii Business Publishing

Ed: Shara Enay. **Description:** Interview with Ronald Taketa of the Hawaii Carpenters Union who states that the economic downturn has affected the construction industry as 20 percent of the union's 7,800 members are unemployed. He shares his thoughts about the industry's economic situation, the union's advertisements, and his role as a leader of the union.

27664 ■ "Rough Q1 Begs Question: Is the Crocs Craze Over?" in Brandweek (Vol. 49, April 21, 2008, No. 16, pp. 16)

Pub: VNU Business Media, Inc.

Ed: Eric Newman. **Description:** Crocs, a rubber shoemaker, announced last week that it missed its expected first quarter revenues by 15 percent. The popular rubber sandals are suffering in sales due to a number of factors including a tougher economic environment, less expensive, knock-off brands, the cold weather delay of the spring season and fading consumer interest in plastic shoes.

27665 ■ "Rough Trade" in Canadian Business (Vol. 79, September 11, 2006, No. 18, pp. 31)

Pub: Rogers Media

Ed: Christina Campbell. **Description:** The divergence between trade policy agreements entered into by Chile and the Canadian government are highlighted. Canada-Chile Free Trade Agreement and the myth around the big benefits to be reaped by bilateral trade policy agreements are discussed.

27666 ■ "Roundtable - The Auto Sector Shifts Gears" in Mergers & Acquisitions: The Dealmaker's Journal (March 1, 2008)

Pub: SourceMedia, Inc.

Description: Industry professionals discuss the current state of the automotive sector as well as what they predict for the future of the industry; also provides information for investors about opportunities in the sector.

27667 ■ "Roundy' Pushing Chicago Expansion" in Milwaukee Business Journal (Vol. 27, February 12, 2010, No. 20, pp. A1)

Pub: American City Business Journals

Ed: Rich Kirchen. **Description:** Roundy Supermarkets Inc. is expanding in Chicago, Illinois as the Milwaukee-based company is set to open one store in downtown Chicago and another in the Arlington suburb. The store openings have been pushed back to spring and early summer in 2010 due to the economic downturn.

27668 ■ "Running On Empty" in The Business Journal-Milwaukee (Vol. 25, July 4, 2008, No. 41, pp. A1)

Pub: American City Business Journals, Inc.

Ed: David Doege. **Description:** Employers are more engaged in offering incentives designed to offset commuting costs. Among the incentives offered are gas cards, parking reimbursement and midyear wage increases. The other efforts to help employees with the costs of going to work are discussed.

27669 ■ "Rust Belt No More: The Demise of Manufacturing" in Crain's Chicago Business (Vol. 31, March 31, 2008, No. 13, pp. 52)

Pub: Crain Communications, Inc.

Ed: Sarah A. Klein. **Description:** Discusses the history of manufacturing in the Chicago area as well as the history of manufacturer International Harvester Co.

27670 ■ "A Safety Net in Need of Repair" in The Economist (Vol. 390, January 3, 2009, No. 8612, pp. 33)

Pub: The Economist Newspaper Inc.

Description: America's unemployment-insurance scheme is outdated and skimpy compared to other industrialized countries despite the fact that Americans tend to work harder at returning to the job market; the benefits are lower and available for a smaller amount of time and less unemployed workers are even able to collect these benefits. Statistical data included.

27671 ■ "Sales at Furniture Showrooms Sink" in Puget Sound Business Journal (Vol. 29, October 10, 2008, No. 25, pp. 1)

Pub: American City Business Journals

Ed: Greg Lamm. **Description:** Furniture showrooms are seeing a drop in sales due to the bad economy. Buyer demand has also fallen because of the slumping real estate market.

27672 ■ "Samll Fortunes" in Business Courier (Vol. 27, July 23, 2010, No. 12, pp. 1)

Pub: Business Courier

Ed: Steve Watkins. **Description:** Small banks in Cincinnati, Ohio have been faring well despite the economic crisis, a survey has revealed. Sixty percent of local small banks have capital levels above 15.8 percent median. But regulators are seen to close more banks in 2010 than since the financial crises began.

27673 ■ "Sandi Jackson; Alderman, 7th Ward, City of Chicago" in Crain's Chicago Business (Vol. 31, May 5, 2008, No. 18, pp. 31)

Pub: Crain Communications, Inc.

Ed: Sarah A. Klein. **Description:** Profile of Sandi Jackson who is an alderman of the 7th ward of the city of Chicago and is addressing issues such as poverty and crime as well as counting on a plan to develop the former USX Corp. steel mill to revitalize the area's economic climate.

27674 ■ Saudi Arabia: Moving Towards a Privatized Economy

Pub: Turnaround Associates

Ed: Andrea H. Pampanini. **Released:** April 2005. **Price:** $30.00. **Description:** An overview of how Saudi Arabia took control of its natural resources and created change in the government, education, and culture of the country. Production of oil and natural gas is control entirely by the Saudi Government, however the book discusses the trend towards privatizing particular sectors of the nation in order to compete globally.

27675 ■ "Saudi Overtures" in The Business Journal-Portland (Vol. 25, August 15, 2008, No. 23, pp. 1)

Pub: American City Business Journals, Inc.

Ed: Aliza Earnshaw. **Description:** Saudi Arabia's huge revenue from oil is creating opportunities for Oregon companies as the country develops new cities, industrial zones, and tourism centers. Oregon exported only $46.8 million worth of goods to Saudi Arabia in 2007 but the kingdom is interested in green building materials and methods, renewable energy and water quality control, and nanotechnology all of which Oregon has expertise in.

27676 ■ Save Your Small Business: 10 Crucial Strategies to Survive Hard Times or Close Down and Move On

Pub: NOLO

Contact: Ralph Warner, Chief Executive Officer

Ed: Ralph Warner, Bethany Laurence. **Released:** August 1, 2009. **Price:** $29.99. **Description:** According to a study among 500 businesses, 44 percent used credit cards in order to meet their firm's needs in the previous six months. Written by a business owner, this book provides twelve strategies to protect personal assets from creditors and survive the current recession.

27677 ■ "SBA-Backed Lending Slides; Economy, Close Scrutiny of Applications Cited" in Crain's Detroit Business (March 10, 2008)

Pub: Crain Communications, Inc.

Ed: Nancy Kaffer. **Description:** Due to the state of the economy and a closer scrutiny on applications, Small Business Administration-backed loans are down by a significant margin in one loan program and have decreased slightly across the board. Statistical data included.

27678 ■ "SBA Intervenes to Keep Cash Flowing" in Business First Columbus (Vol. 25, November 21, 2008, No. 14, pp. A1)

Pub: American City Business Journals

Ed: Adrian Burns. **Description:** U.S. Small Business Administration's loan volumes fell as it tried to cushion the impact of the economic crisis on small businesses. Large investors have pulled back buying SBA loans due to declining profits, but demand for SBA loans are seen to resurge due to low risk.

27679 ■ "SEC Report On Rating Agencies Falls Short" in Barron's (Vol. 88, July 14, 2008, No. 28, pp. 35)

Pub: Dow Jones & Co., Inc.

Ed: Jack Willoughby. **Description:** The Securities and Exchange Commissions report on credit-rating firms should have drawn attention to the slipshod practices in the offerings of collateralized debt obligations. The report fell short of prescribing correctives for the flawed system of these agencies' relationship with their clients.

27680 ■ "Selling Pressures Rise in China" in Barron's (Vol. 88, March 10, 2008, No. 10, pp. M9)

Pub: Dow Jones & Company, Inc.

Ed: Mohammed Hadi. **Description:** There are about 1.6 trillion yuan worth of shares up for sale in Chinese stock markets in 2008, adding to the selling pressures in these markets. The Chinese government has imposed restrictions to prevent a rapid rise in selling stocks.

27681 ■ *"Sentiment Split on Financials"* in *Barron's (Vol. 88, March 24, 2008, No. 12, pp. M14)*
Pub: Dow Jones & Company, Inc.
Ed: Steven M. Sears. **Description:** Experts in the financial sector are split as to whether or not the worst of the financial crisis brought on by the credit crunch is over. Some options traders are trading on are defensive puts, expecting the worst, while investors buying calls are considered as bullish

27682 ■ *"Serious Signal Flashing?"* in *Barron's (Vol. 88, July 7, 2008, No. 27, pp. 11)*
Pub: Dow Jones & Co., Inc.
Description: Discusses the Hindenburg Omen, named after the airship disaster of May 1937, which is considered a predictor of market crashes and has appeared twice in June 2008. There is a 25 percent probability that the US stock market will suffer a crash in the July-October 2008 period.

27683 ■ *"A Shallow Pool"* in *Canadian Business (Vol. 81, Summer 2008, No. 9, pp. 44)*
Pub: Rogers Media Ltd.
Ed: Joe Castaldo. **Description:** Bank of Canada projected in its 'Monetary Policy Report' a growth rate of 1.4 percent in 2008 and does not expect the economy to fully recover until mid-2010. The Canadian stock market has been recovering although slowly with just a 1.6 percent gain by April 30. Other details on the Canadian equity market are presented.

27684 ■ *"Shanghai Butterfly"* in *Canadian Business (Vol. 80, March 12, 2007, No. 6, pp. 69)*
Pub: Rogers Media
Ed: Thomas Watson. **Description:** The volatile nature of Shanghai stock markets and its impact on investors and the economy is discussed.

27685 ■ *"Shifting Gears"* in *Business Journal-Serving Phoenix & the Valley of the Sun (Vol. 31, November 12, 2010, No. 10, pp. 1)*
Pub: Phoenix Business Journal
Ed: Patrick O'Grady. **Description:** Automotive parts recyclers in Arizona are benefiting from the challenging national economic conditions as well as from the green movement. Recyclers revealed that customers prefer recycled parts more because they are cheaper and are more environmentally friendly. Other information about the automotive parts recycling industry is presented.

27686 ■ *"Shopped Out; Retailing Gloom"* in *The Economist (Vol. 390, January 3, 2009, No. 8612, pp. 26)*
Pub: The Economist Newspaper Inc.
Description: Economic volatility in the retail sector is having an impact on a number of countries around the globe. Europe is experiencing hard economic times as well and unless businesses have a strong business plan banks feel unable to lend the money necessary to tide the retailers over. The falling pound has increased the cost of imported goods and small to midsize retail chains may not be able to weather such an unforgiving economic climate.

27687 ■ *"'Short Sales,' A Sign of Housing Troubles, Start Popping Up"* in *The Business Review Albany (Vol. 35, April 11, 2008, No. 1, pp. 1)*
Pub: The Business Review
Ed: Michael DeMasi. **Description:** Discusses the number of short sales, where homeowners ask banks to forgive part of their mortgages to sell the properties, which is starting to increase in the Albany, New York area. Real estate agents in the area are taking up crash courses in short selling.

27688 ■ *"Should the Fed Regulate Wall Street?"* in *Barron's (Vol. 88, March 24, 2008, No. 12, pp. M15)*
Pub: Dow Jones & Company, Inc.
Ed: Randall W. Forsyth. **Description:** Greater regulation of the financial sector by the Federal Reserve is essential for it to survive the crisis it is experiencing. The resulting regulation could be in complete contrast with the deregulation the sector previously experienced.

27689 ■ *"Sign Up To Grow Your Business, Generate Jobs"* in *Women Entrepreneur (November 25, 2008)*
Pub: Entrepreneur Media Inc.
Ed: Eve Gumpel. **Description:** Nell Merlino has announced the new Make Mine A Million-Dollar Race, which aims to encourage hundreds of thousands of women entrepreneurs to grow their business to revenue goals of $250,00, $500,000 or $1 million and more as well as create 800,000 new jobs in an attempt to stimulate the nation's economy.

27690 ■ *"Silicon Valley's Economic Recovery Picking Up Pace"* in *Globe & Mail (January 29, 2007, pp. B13)*
Pub: CTVglobemedia Publishing Inc.
Ed: Pui-Wing Tam. **Description:** The addition of 30,000 new jobs, rise in average annual wages and household income, along with other factors that have contributed to Silicon Valley's economic recovery are discussed.

27691 ■ *"Single Most Important Problem"* in *Small Business Economic Trends (April 2008, pp. 18)*
Pub: National Federation of Independent Business
Ed: William C. Dunkelberg, Holly Wade. **Description:** Two graphs and a table presenting the economic problems encountered by small businesses in the U.S. are provided. The figures presented in the graphs include data from 1986 to 2008.

27692 ■ *"Single Most Important Problem"* in *Small Business Economic Trends (March 2008, pp. 18)*
Pub: National Federation of Independent Business
Ed: William C. Dunkelberg, Holly Wade. **Description:** Two graphs and a table representing the economic problems encountered by small businesses in the U.S. are presented. The figures presented in the graphs include data from 1986 to 2008.

27693 ■ *"Single Most Important Problem"* in *Small Business Economic Trends (February 2008, pp. 18)*
Pub: National Federation of Independent Business
Ed: William C. Dunkelberg, Holly Wade. **Description:** Two graphs and a table representing the economic problems encountered by small businesses in the U.S. are presented. The figures presented in the graphs include data from 1974 to 2008.

27694 ■ *"Single Most Important Problem"* in *Small Business Economic Trends (January 2008, pp. 18)*
Pub: National Federation of Independent Business
Description: Table of the single most important problem among small businesses surveyed in the U.S. in December 2007 is presented. Taxes were selected by 21 percent of firms as the single most important problem, followed by cost and availability of insurance at 16 percent. Graphs comparing selected single most important problem from January 1986 to December 2007 are also given.

27695 ■ *"Six Leading Economists on What to Expect in the Year Ahead: David Wolf"* in *Canadian Business (Dec. 24, 2007)*
Pub: Rogers Media
Ed: David Wolf. **Description:** The Canadian dollar recently hit parity with the U.S. dollar, and the exchange rate is going fast and overvaluation of the Canadian dollar could bring in competition from U.S. products. Details on the impact of the slowdown of the U.S. economy on the exchange rate speed are discussed.

27696 ■ *"Six Leading Economists on What to Expect in the Year Ahead: Derek Holt; Housing"* in *Canadian Business (December 24, 2007)*
Pub: Rogers Media
Ed: Derek Holt. **Description:** The Canadian subprime mortgage market could take a different turn from that of the U.S. as laws governing Canada's mortgage market indirectly limit the probability of a slowdown. Details on how Canada avoided the slowdown in the housing market and forecasts of new homes for 2008 are discussed.

27697 ■ *"Six Leading Economists on What to Expect in the Year Ahead: Glen Hodgson; Canada in Depth"* in *Canadian Business (December 24, 2007)*
Pub: Rogers Media
Ed: Glen Hodgson. **Description:** Western Canada is expected to have the best economic performance for 2008 among all of the country's regions with a growth rate of 3.6 percent for Alberta and three percent for British Columbia. Details on the country's growth in real income, trends in the labor market, and the effect of Canadian dollar's parity with the U.S. dollar on exports are discussed.

27698 ■ *"Six Leading Economists on What to Expect in the Year Ahead: Peter Buchanan"* in *Canadian Business (December 24, 2007)*
Pub: Rogers Media
Ed: Peter Buchanan. **Description:** The world economy is expected to grow by five percent in 2008, which is below the pace of the previous two years. Details on the U.S. credit crunch, the U.S. dollar's depreciation, and the economic expansion of developing economies are discussed.

27699 ■ *"Six Things You Can Do To Ride Out a Turbulent Market"* in *Hispanic Business (March 2008, pp. 20-21)*
Pub: Hispanic Business
Ed: Hildy Medina, Michael Bowker. **Description:** Experts in the financial industry suggest shifting portfolios; investing in cash; thinking long-term for market investments; investing in foreign bonds, covered calls and preferred stocks; and to rebalance a portfolio in order to survive the downturn in the stock market.

27700 ■ *"A Slice of Danish; Fixing Finance"* in *The Economist (Vol. 390, January 3, 2009, No. 8612, pp. 55)*
Pub: The Economist Newspaper Inc.
Description: Denmark's mortgage-holders and the county's lending system is presented.

27701 ■ *"Sluggish Market Gives Hospitals the Financial Chills"* in *The Business Journal-Serving Greater Tampa Bay (Vol. 28, August 1, 2008)*
Pub: American City Business Journals, Inc.
Ed: Margie Manning. **Description:** Operating margins for hospitals in the Tampa Bay, Florida area have been reduced from 2 percent in 2006 to 0.8 percent in 2007 due to a weaker US economy. Total margins, on the other hand, rose from 2.9 percent to 3.3 percent in the same period.

27702 ■ *"Small-Business Agenda: Increase Capital, Education, Tax Breaks"* in *Crain's Detroit Business (Vol. 24, March 17, 2008)*
Pub: Crain Communications, Inc.
Ed: Nancy Kaffer. **Description:** Discusses the policy suggestions detailed in the Small Business Association of Michigan's entrepreneurial agenda which include five main categories of focus: making entrepreneurial education a higher state priority; increasing capital available to entrepreneurs; using the state's tax structure as an incentive for entrepreneurial growth; getting university research from the lab to the market; and limiting government regulation that's burdensome to small businesses and getting legislative support of entrepreneurial assistance efforts.

27703 ■ *Small Business Clustering Technology: Applications in Marketing, Management, Finance, and IT*
Pub: Idea Group Publishing
Ed: Robert C. MacGregor; Ann Hodgkinson. **Released:** June 2006. **Description:** An overview of the development and role of small business clusters in disciplines that include economics, marketing, management and information systems.

27704 ■ *"Small Business Earnings"* in *Small Business Economic Trends (April 2008, pp. 6)*
Pub: National Federation of Independent Business
Ed: William C. Dunkelberg, Holly Wade. **Description:** Two tables and a graph presenting the earnings of small businesses in the U.S. are provided. Statistics for actual earnings changes are provided. The figures in the graph include data from 1986 to 2008.

27705 ■ *"Small Business Earnings" in Small Business Economic Trends (March 2008, pp. 6)*
Pub: National Federation of Independent Business
Ed: William C. Dunkelberg, Holly Wade. **Description:** Two tables and a graph representing the earnings of small businesses in the U.S. are presented. Statistics for actual earnings changes are provided. The figures in the graph include data from 1986 to 2008.

27706 ■ *"Small Business Earnings" in Small Business Economic Trends (February 2008, pp. 6)*
Pub: National Federation of Independent Business
Ed: William C. Dunkelberg, Holly Wade. **Description:** Two tables and a graph representing the earnings of small businesses in the U.S. are presented. Statistics for actual earnings changes are provided. The figures in the graph include data from 1974 to 2008.

27707 ■ *"Small Business Earnings" in Small Business Economic Trends (January 2008, pp. 6)*
Pub: National Federation of Independent Business
Description: Graph from a survey of small businesses in the U.S. is given, representing actual small business earnings from January 1986 to December 2007. Tables showing actual earnings changes and most important reason for lower earnings are also presented.

27708 ■ *"Small Business Earnings" in Small Business Economic Trends (September 2010, pp. 6)*
Pub: National Federation of Independent Business
Ed: William C. Dunkelberg, Holly Wade. **Description:** A graph from a survey of small businesses in the U.S. is given, representing actual small business earnings from January 1986 to August 2010. Tables showing actual earnings changes and most important reason for lower earnings are also presented.

27709 ■ *"Small Business Inventories" in Small Business Economic Trends (April 2008, pp. 14)*
Pub: National Federation of Independent Business
Ed: William C. Dunkelberg, Holly Wade. **Description:** Three tables and a graph presenting the inventories of small businesses in the U.S. are provided. The tables include figures on actual inventory changes, inventory satisfaction, and inventory plans.

27710 ■ *"Small Business: Just When Hopes Were High" in Business Week (January 8, 2007)*
Pub: McGraw-Hill Companies
Ed: James Mehring. **Description:** Overview of the reasons for a fall in confidence concerning the economy among small businesses and the affect this could have in the coming year.

27711 ■ *"Small Business Outlook" in Small Business Economic Trends (April 2008, pp. 4)*
Pub: National Federation of Independent Business
Ed: William C. Dunkelberg, Holly Wade. **Description:** Three tables and a graph presenting forecasts in business expansions of small businesses in the U.S. are presented. The figures presented in the graph include data from 1986 to 2008.

27712 ■ *"Small Business Outlook" in Small Business Economic Trends (March 2008, pp. 4)*
Pub: National Federation of Independent Business
Ed: William C. Dunkelberg, Holly Wade. **Description:** Three tables and a graph representing forecasts in business expansions of small businesses in the U.S. are presented. The figures presented in the graph include data from 1986 to 2008.

27713 ■ *"Small Business Outlook" in Small Business Economic Trends (February 2008, pp. 4)*
Pub: National Federation of Independent Business
Ed: William C. Dunkelberg, Holly Wade. **Description:** Three tables and a graph representing forecasts in business expansions of small businesses in the U.S. are presented. The figures presented in the graph include data from 1974 to 2008.

27714 ■ *"Small Business Outlook" in Small Business Economic Trends (January 2008, pp. 4)*
Pub: National Federation of Independent Business
Description: Graph representing outlook among small businesses surveyed in the U.S. from January 1986 to December 2007 is presented. Tables showing small business outlook for expansion and outlook for general business conditions from January 2002 to December 2007 and the most important reasons for expansion outlook are also given.

27715 ■ *"Small Business Outlook" in Small Business Economic Trends (September 2010, pp. 4)*
Pub: National Federation of Independent Business
Ed: William C. Dunkelberg, Holly Wade. **Description:** A graph representing outlook among small businesses surveyed in the U.S. from January 1986 to August 2010 is presented. Tables showing small business outlook for expansion and outlook for general business conditions from January 2005 to August 2010, and most important reasons for expansion outlook are also given.

27716 ■ *"Small Business Prices" in Small Business Economic Trends (September 2010, pp. 8)*
Pub: National Federation of Independent Business
Ed: William C. Dunkelberg, Holly Wade. **Description:** A graph from a survey of small businesses in the U.S. is given, representing business prices from January 1986 to August 2010. Actual prices (last three months) and planned prices (next three months) were compared in the graph. Tables of actual price changes and price plans from January 2005 to August 2010 are also supplied.

27717 ■ *"Small Business Sales" in Small Business Economic Trends (July 2010, pp. 7)*
Pub: National Federation of Independent Business
Description: A graph from a survey of small businesses in the U.S. is given representing sales from January 1986 to June 2010. Actual sales (prior three months) and expected sales (next three months) were compared in the graph. Tables of actual sales changes and sales expectations from January 2005 to June 2010 are also given.

27718 ■ *"Small, But Mighty" in Employee Benefit News (Vol. 25, November 1, 2011, No. 14, pp. 32)*
Pub: SourceMedia Inc.
Ed: Andrea Davis. **Description:** Three consulting firms are facing the challenge of helping clients understand the new health care reform in a tight economy.

27719 ■ *"Smaller Banks Could Face Tough 2008" in Austin Business JournalInc. (Vol. 28, January 2, 2009, No. 1, pp. 3)*
Pub: American City Business Journals
Ed: Christopher Calnan. **Description:** The turbulence in the banking industry is expected to reach Texas in 2009 and industry insiders believe there will be a shift in deposits from small, regional banks to larger banks due to low consumer confidence. One economist says that a large number of banks are going to go out of business in 2009.

27720 ■ *"Smart Year-End Tax Moves" in Business Owner (Vol. 35, November-December 2011, No. 6, pp. 8)*
Pub: DL Perkins Company
Description: Managing small business and individual taxes is more important in a bad economy. It is imperative to seek all tax incentives that apply to your business.

27721 ■ *"Sobering Consequences" in The Business Journal-Milwaukee (Vol. 25, July 11, 2008, No. 42, pp. A1)*
Pub: American City Business Journals, Inc.
Ed: Rich Rovito. **Description:** Milwaukee Mayor Tom Barrett and Wisconsin Governor Jim Doyle met with MillerCoors management in an effort to convince the company to locate its corporate headquarters in the city. The company is expected to announce its deci-

sion by mid-July 2008. It was revealed that the decision-making process is focusing on determining an optimal location for the headquarters.

27722 ■ *Social Enterprise: Developing Sustainable Businesses*
Pub: Palgrave Macmillan
Ed: Frank Martin, Marcus Thompson. **Released:** January 1, 2010. **Price:** $106.00. **Description:** Social enterprises bring people and communities together for economic development and social gain and represent a growing sector of the business community.

27723 ■ *Social Entrepreneurship*
Pub: Palgrave Macmillan
Ed: Johanna Mair; Jeffrey Robinson; Kai Hockerts. **Released:** June 2006. **Price:** $80.00. **Description:** Social entrepreneurship is the process involving innovative approaches to solving social problems while creating economic value.

27724 ■ *"Some More Equal Than Others" in Canadian Business (Vol. 80, April 23, 2007, No. 9, pp. 23)*
Pub: Rogers Media
Ed: Jack Mintz. **Description:** The details of the equalization program to be started by United States to improve economic conditions of Canada are presented.

27725 ■ *"Some Relief Possible Following Painful Week" in Barron's (Vol. 88, July 14, 2008, No. 28, pp. M3)*
Pub: Dow Jones & Co., Inc.
Ed: Kopin Tan. **Description:** Dow Chemical is offering a 74 percent premium to acquire Rohm & Haas' coatings and electronics materials operations. Frontline amassed a 5.6 percent stake in rival Overseas Shipholding Group and a merger between the two would create a giant global fleet with pricing power. Highlights of the U.S. stock market during the week that ended in July 11, 2008 are discussed. Statistical data included.

27726 ■ *"Some Women Warming Up to Economy's Prospects" in Crain's Cleveland Business (Vol. 30, June 1, 2009, No. 21, pp. 9)*
Pub: Crain Communications, Inc.
Ed: Mark Dodosh. **Description:** According to a recent survey conducted by the Center for Women's Business Research and KeyBank focusing on the experience and opinions of women business owners, 48 percent of respondents believe the economy will improve over the next six months. Statistical data included.

27727 ■ *"Souled Out" in Canadian Business (Vol. 81, March 3, 2008, No. 3, pp. 35)*
Pub: Rogers Media
Ed: Calvin Leung. **Description:** According to a survey of over 100 entrepreneurs, 78 percent responded that selling their business was emotionally draining for them. Greig Clark, for example, says that one of the toughest times of his life was selling College Pro Painters, after putting 18 years into that business. The economic impacts of selling out are also examined.

27728 ■ *"Sour Grapes" in Canadian Business (Vol. 79, November 20, 2006, No. 23, pp. 28)*
Pub: Rogers Media
Ed: Michael Mainville. **Description:** The impact of the sanctions imposed by Russia on the Georgian wine exports to Russia is discussed.

27729 ■ *"Spectre of Iran War Spooks Oil Markets" in Globe & Mail (March 28, 2007, pp. B1)*
Pub: CTVglobemedia Publishing Inc.
Ed: Shawn McCarthy. **Description:** The increase in the price of crude oil by $5 a barrel to reach $68 in the United States following speculation over war against Iran, is discussed.

27730 ■ *"Spending on Innovation Down Sharply in State" in Crain's Detroit Business*

(Vol. 24, March 10, 2008, No. 10, pp. 7)
Pub: Crain Communications, Inc.
Ed: Chad Halcom. **Description:** Due to such issues as Michigan's uncertain tax structure, a shaky national economy, the credit crunch and mortgage lending crisis, investments in innovation for the state have sharply declined.

27731 ■ "Spillover Effects" in Crain's Detroit Business (Vol. 24, October 6, 2008, No. 40, pp. 29)
Pub: Crain Communications, Inc.
Description: Earlier this year, the Detroit Regional Chamber estimated that the Detroit Tiger's baseball team's 81 home games would have a $277 million positive economic impact on the region. Due to the poor performance of the team, fewer fans are spending money on tickets, which translates into fewer dollars coming into the region. Lower viewership on television has also been a result of the Tiger's losing season.

27732 ■ "Stadium Developers Seek a Win With the State" in The Business Journal-Serving Metropolitan Kansas City (Vol. 26, August 22, 2008)
Pub: American City Business Journals, Inc.
Ed: Rob Roberts. **Description:** Three Trails Redevelopment LLC is hoping to win $30 million in state tax credits from the Missouri Development Finance Board for the construction of an 18,500-seat Wizards stadium. The project is contingent on state tax incentives and the company remains optimistic about their goal.

27733 ■ "Staffing Firms are Picking Up the Pieces, Seeing Signs of Life" in Milwaukee Business Journal (Vol. 27, February 5, 2010, No. 19)
Pub: American City Business Journals
Ed: Rich Rovito. **Description:** Milwaukee, Wisconsin-based staffing firms are seeing signs of economic rebound as many businesses turned to temporary employees to fill the demands for goods and services. Economic observers believe the growth in temporary staffing is one of the early indicators of economic recovery.

27734 ■ "Standard-of-Living Gap With U.S. Closing" in Globe & Mail (March 27, 2007, pp. B3)
Pub: CTVglobemedia Publishing Inc.
Ed: Heather Scoffield. **Description:** According to latest report released by Statistics Canada, standard-of-living in Canada has increased considerably in last decade to match-up with American economy. Complete analysis in this context is presented.

27735 ■ "Stars Shine Downtown" in The Business Journal-Serving Metropolitan Kansas City (Vol. 26, August 29, 2008, No. 51, pp. 1)
Pub: American City Business Journals, Inc.
Ed: Rob Roberts. **Description:** Movie chain AMC Entertainment Inc. renews its lease for 97,000 square feet of space at Ten Main Center. HNTB Federal Services Corp., meanwhile, is to take up 42,000 square feet at an office building located at 120 W. 12th St. The leases' impacts on downtown office market are examined.

27736 ■ Start-Up Nation
Pub: Twelve/Hatchette Book Group
Ed: Dan Senor, Paul Singer. **Released:** 2009. **Price:** $26.99. **Description:** Amid the turmoil in the Middle East, Israel's economy continues to thrive.

27737 ■ "State Budget Woes Hurt Many Vendors, Senior Services" in Sacramento Business Journal (Vol. 25, August 15, 2008, No. 24, pp. 1)
Pub: American City Business Journals, Inc.
Ed: Melanie Turner. **Description:** Delays in the passage of the California state budget have adversely affected the health care industry. The Robertson Adult Day Health Care had taken out loans to keep the business afloat. The state Legislature has reduced Medi-Cal reimbursement to health care providers by 10 percent.

27738 ■ "State Expects Increase of $50 Million from Film Bills; Come Back, Al Roker" in Crain's Detroit Business (March 24, 2008)
Pub: Crain Communications, Inc.
Ed: Bill Shea. **Description:** Overview of the new film initiative and its incentives designed to entice more film work to Michigan; the measures could bring $50 million to $100 million in movie production work for the rest of this year compared to the $4 million total the state saw last year. Also discusses the show 'DEA' which was filmed in Detroit and stars Al Roker.

27739 ■ "State Lawmakers Should Try Raising Jobs, Not Taxes" in Crain's Chicago Business (Vol. 31, March 24, 2008, No. 12, pp. 20)
Pub: Crain Communications, Inc.
Ed: Diug Whitley. **Description:** According to U.S. Department of Labor figures through December 2007, Illinois has ranked 45th in the nation in job growth for seven straight months. Many feel that the state would not need to raise taxes if they spent more time working to keep and attract employers that create jobs.

27740 ■ "State Shock Prices Take Large Tumble" in The Business Journal-Milwaukee (Vol. 25, September 12, 2008, No. 51, pp. A1)
Pub: American City Business Journals, Inc.
Ed: Rich Rovito. **Description:** Weak economic times have caused the stocks of most publicly traded companies in Wisconsin to dip in 2008. Companies that appeared on the worst performing stocks list also experienced drops in share price to as much as 70 percent. Information about the companies that experienced increases in stock prices is also presented. Statistical data included.

27741 ■ "The State of the Stores" in Playthings (Vol. 106, November 1, 2008, No. 10, pp. 8)
Pub: Reed Business Information
Contact: Jeff Greisch, President
Ed: Dana French. **Description:** Investigation into the top twenty-five toy and game retailers shows that video games and related handheld and console systems as well as computer games were number one with America's children in 2007.

27742 ■ "State Tourism Likely to Decline Two Percent this Year" in Crain's Detroit Business (Vol. 24, April 14, 2008, No. 15, pp. 6)
Pub: Crain Communications Inc.
Ed: Amy Lane. **Description:** Due to such national and state economic conditions such as unemployment, the housing crisis and rising gasoline and food prices, Michigan's tourism industry is likely to decline about 2 percent this year.

27743 ■ "Stay Calm, Bernanke Urges Markets" in Globe & Mail (March 1, 2007, pp. B1)
Pub: CTVglobemedia Publishing Inc.
Ed: Brian McKenna. **Description:** The views of Ben Bernanke, the chief of the United States Federal Reserve Board, on the future trends of the United States' economy are presented. The effect of the global stock market trends on the American stock markets is discussed.

27744 ■ "Stay in School: Economy Got You Down?" in Canadian Business (Vol. 81, November 10, 2008, No. 19, pp. 98)
Pub: Rogers Media Ltd.
Ed: Graham F. Scott, Jane Bao. **Description:** A guide to Canadian MBA programs is presented. The tuition and length of each program is provided along with each school. Details on whether the universities offer part-time options, diversity, and co-op/internships are also given.

27745 ■ "Steady Spending in Retail" in Business Week (September 22, 2008, No. 4100, pp. 13)
Pub: McGraw-Hill Companies, Inc.
Ed: Tara Kalwarski. **Description:** Retail jobs have begun to decline on the national level despite the two percent growth in the industry over the last year; much of the growth has been attributed to the sales of higher-priced oil products.

27746 ■ "Stelco Seeks to Shave Its Fixed Costs" in Globe & Mail (March 8, 2007, pp. B1)
Pub: CTVglobemedia Publishing Inc.
Ed: Greg Keenan. **Description:** The plans of Stelco Inc. to control its fixed costs in order to protect itself from economic downturns are discussed.

27747 ■ "Step Up to Help Regionalism Step Forward" in Crain's Cleveland Business (Vol. 28, November 12, 2007, No. 45, pp. 10)
Pub: Crain Communications, Inc.
Ed: Rob Briggs; William Currin. **Description:** Discusses the importance of regionalism for Northeast Ohio as being a broad, collaborative approach to spur economic development.

27748 ■ The Sticking Point Solution: 9 Ways to Move Your Business from Stagnation to Stunning Growth in Tough Economic Times
Pub: Vanguard Press
Contact: Bill Smith, Director
E-mail: bill.smith@perseusbooks.com
Ed: Jay Abraham. **Released:** May 10, 2010. **Price:** $25.95. **Description:** Renowned business consultant, Jay Abraham, reveals the nine ways even successful businesses get stuck, hit plateaus, and fail to achieve their dreams and he explains how to get unstuck and create exponential growth.

27749 ■ "Stitching the City Together" in Business Courier (Vol. 24, February 8, 2008, No. 44, pp. 1)
Pub: American City Business Journals, Inc.
Ed: Lucy May. **Description:** Nancy Zimpher, University of Cincinnati president, has been given vital leadership posts in regional development organizations in the area. She sees this as part of her job and of the university's mission of serving the community.

27750 ■ Street Fighters: The Last 72 Hours of Bears Stearns, the Toughest Firm on Wall Street
Pub: Portfolio
Ed: Kate Kelly. **Released:** 2009. **Price:** $25.95. **Description:** An account of the investment bank, Bears Stearns fight for survival is documented.

27751 ■ "Stretch Your Advertising Dollars" in Women Entrepreneur (January 27, 2009)
Pub: Entrepreneur Media Inc.
Ed: Rosalind Resnick. **Description:** During such poor economic times, most businesses are having to cut their advertising budgets; tips for targeting your advertising dollars toward the customer base most likely to buy your product are given.

27752 ■ "Struggling Community Banks Find Little Help In Wall Street Bailout" in Crain's Detroit Business (Vol. 24, September 29, 2008)
Pub: Crain Communications Inc.
Ed: Tom Henderson. **Description:** Both public and private Michigan banks have been hit hard by poorly performing loan portfolios and although their problems were not caused by high-risk securities but by a longtime statewide recession and a housing slump, these community banks have little hope of seeing any of the bailout money that has been allotted for the larger institutions.

27753 ■ "Struggling States Slashing Health Care For Poor" in Chicago Tribune (January 15, 2009)
Pub: McClatchy-Tribune Information Services
Ed: Noam N. Levey. **Description:** Health officials warn that even the huge federal rescue plan may not be enough to restore health services being eliminated due to the economic crisis.

27754 ■ "Stuck With Two Mortgages; The Nightmare When Buyers Upgrade" in Crain's Chicago Business (Vol. 31, April 21, 2008, No. 16)
Pub: Crain Communications, Inc.
Ed: Darci Smith. **Description:** Discusses the problem a number of people are facing due to the slump in the housing market: being stuck with two mortgages when they move because their former homes have

not sold. Many thought they could afford to move to a larger home, anticipating significant equity appreciation that did not occur; now they are left with lowering their price and competing with the host of new developments.

27755 ■ Studies of Entrepreneurship, Business and Government in Hong Kong: The Economic Development of a Small Open Economy
Pub: Edwin Mellen Press
Ed: Fu-Lai Tony Yu. **Released:** November 2006. **Price:** $109.95. **Description:** Institutional and Austrian theories are used to analyze the transformation taking place in Hong Kong's economy.

27756 ■ "Studies Mixed on State's 2008 Retail Outlook" in Crain's Detroit Business (Vol. 24, March 24, 2008, No. 12, pp. 28)
Pub: Crain Communications, Inc.
Ed: Nancy Kaffer. **Description:** Marcus and Millichap Real Estate Investment Services and the Michigan Retailers Association have released two separate studies concerning Michigan retailers in 2008. According to its report, MRA is forecasting modest retail growth later this year; however, the study conducted by national commercial real estate brokers Marcus and Millichap predicts increasing vacancy rates, flat employment and decreasing sales for Detroit-area retailers.

27757 ■ "Stung by Recession, Hemmer Regroups with New Strategy" in Business Courier (Vol. 27, June 4, 2010, No. 5, pp. 1)
Pub: Business Courier
Ed: Lucy May. **Description:** Paul Hemmer Companies reduced its work force and outsourced operations such as marketing and architecture, in order for the commercial and construction firm to survive the recession. Hammer's total core revenue in 2009 dropped to less than $30 million forcing the closure of its Chicago office.

27758 ■ "Subprime Problems Loom" in The Business Journal-Portland (Vol. 25, August 29, 2008, No. 25, pp. 1)
Pub: American City Business Journals, Inc.
Ed: Wendy Culverwell. **Description:** Over half of subprime mortgages in Portland are resetting by the end of 2008, which will cause more problems to the local real estate market. The inventory of unsold homes has also been increasing for over a year. Forecasts for the Portland housing market in relation to mortgage resets are supplied.

27759 ■ The Subprime Solution: How Today's Global Financial Crisis Happened, and What to Do About It
Pub: Princeton University Press
Ed: Robert J. Shiller. **Released:** 2009. **Price:** $16.95. **Description:** Yale economist discusses the worldwide financial crisis and offers plans to reform the system.

27760 ■ "Summary. Economic Trends for Small Business" in Small Business Economic Trends (March 2008, pp. 1)
Pub: National Federation of Independent Business
Ed: William C. Dunkelberg, Holly Wade. **Description:** Summary of economic trends for small businesses in the U.S. is provided. Economic indicators such as capital spending, inventories and sales, inflation, and profits are given. Analysis of credit markets is also provided.

27761 ■ "Summary. Economic Trends for Small Business" in Small Business Economic Trends (February 2008, pp. 1)
Pub: National Federation of Independent Business
Ed: William C. Dunkelberg, Holly Wade. **Description:** Summary of economic trends for small businesses in the U.S. is provided. Economic indicators such as capital spending, inventories and sales, inflation, and profits are given. Analysis of credit markets is also provided.

27762 ■ Superfreakonomics
Pub: Morrow/HarperCollins
Ed: Steven D. Levitt, Stephen J. Dubner. **Released:** October 20, 2009. **Price:** $29.99. **Description:** A scholar and a journalist apply economic thinking to everything.

27763 ■ "The Surplus Shell Game" in Canadian Business (Vol. 80, March 12, 2007, No. 6, pp. 72)
Pub: Rogers Media
Description: The effort of successive federal governments in Canada to ensure budget surpluses and its impact on the economy are discussed.

27764 ■ "Survey Distorts Cost of Capitals" in Canadian Business (Vol. 83, October 12, 2010, No. 17, pp. 22)
Pub: Rogers Media Ltd.
Ed: Matthew McClearn. **Description:** Swiss bank UBS publishes a study comparing the costs of goods and services in megalopolises every three years. The study ranked Toronto and Montreal outside the Top 30 in 2009, but the two cities jumped to eighth and ninth in a recent update. This change can be contributed to the conversion of prices into Euros before making comparisons.

27765 ■ "Survey: Don't Expect Big Results From Stimulus" in Crain's Detroit Business (Vol. 25, June 1, 2009, No. 22)
Pub: Crain Communications Inc. - Detroit
Ed: Nancy Kaffer, Chad Halcom. **Description:** In a recent survey, Michigan business owners, operators or managers showed that 48 percent of respondents oppose the President's stimulus package and believe it will have little or no effect on the economy.

27766 ■ "Survey: More Buyers Expect to Spend Less in Most Media" in Advertising Age (Vol. 79, July 7, 2008, No. 26, pp. 3)
Pub: Crain Communications, Inc.
Ed: Megan McIlroy. **Description:** Marketers are decreasing their budgets for advertising in television, radio, newspaper and outdoor due to the economic downturn. Statistical data concerning advertising agencies and marketers included.

27767 ■ "The Survey Says" in Collections and Credit Risk (Vol. 14, September 1, 2009, No. 8, pp. 16)
Pub: SourceMedia, Inc.
Ed: Bill Grabarek; Darren Waggoner. **Description:** Revenue for the top accounts receivable management firms rose nearly 20 percent in 2008 despite lower liquidation rates, a poor economy and riskier, albeit cheaper debt portfolios; the trend may continue this year as collection agencies expect revenue, on average, to increase 5.8 percent. Debt buyers, however, found that their revenue fell nearly 7 percent in 2008 and expect it to fall another 12 percent this year.

27768 ■ "Survey Says Commercial Real Estate Headed for Turbulence" in Commercial Property News (March 17, 2008)
Pub: Nielsen Company
Description: Commercial real estate sector is declining due to the sluggish U.S. economy. According to a recent survey, national office, retail and hospitality markets are also on the decline.

27769 ■ "A Survival Guide for Crazy Times" in Canadian Business (Vol. 81, March 3, 2008, No. 3, pp. 61)
Pub: Rogers Media
Ed: David Wolf. **Description:** Investors should ensure that their portfolios are positioned defensively more than the average as the U.S. and Canadian markets face turbulent times. They should not assume that U.S. residential property is a good place to invest only because prices have dropped and the Canadian dollar is showing strength. Other tips that investors can use during unstable periods are supplied.

27770 ■ "Survival Guide: There Can Be an Upside to Managing a Downturn" in Canadian Business (Vol. 81, November 10, 2008, No. 19, pp. 54)
Pub: Rogers Media Ltd.
Ed: Sharda Prashad. **Description:** Canada-based Foxy is already limiting its exposure to retailers who could be a credit problem in case of recession. Retirement Life Communities is entering into fixed-

rate and fixed-term loans for them to have sufficient financing to grow. Business owners need to realize that customers want more for less.

27771 ■ "Surviving the Storm" in Canadian Business (Vol. 81, July 22, 2008, No. 12-13, pp. 50)
Pub: Rogers Media Ltd.
Ed: Jeff Sanford. **Description:** Investment adviser Harry Dent and finance professor Paul Marsh discuss their views and forecasts on the United States' economic condition. Dent believes advisors should concentrate on wealth preservation rather than on returns. Other views regarding U.S. economic conditions are also presented.

27772 ■ "Suspense Hangs Over Fledging Film Industry" in Crain's Detroit Business (Vol. 26, January 18, 2010, No. 3, pp. 3)
Pub: Crain Communications Inc.
Ed: Bill Shea. **Description:** Overview of the film incentive package which has fostered a growth in the industry with 52 productions completed in 2009, bringing in $223.6 million in gross in-state production expenditures of which the state will refund $87.2 million. Opposition to the incentives has been growing among legislatures who believe that the initiatives cost more than they ultimately bring into the state. Experts believe that the initiatives will remain since they have already fostered economic growth and are good for the state's image.

27773 ■ "Swagelok Boss" in Crain's Cleveland Business (Vol. 30, June 29, 2009, No. 25, pp. 4)
Pub: Crain Communications, Inc.
Ed: Dan Shingler. **Description:** Swagelok Company president and CEO has not laid off an employee in its 65 years of existence and said at a recent convention that he plans to keep his 4,000 employees working and inventories at normal levels despite the recession.

27774 ■ "Swirling Debate" in Business Courier (Vol. 27, August 20, 2010, No. 16, pp. 1)
Pub: Business Courier
Ed: Lucy May. **Description:** The debate on whether to convert Greater Cincinnati Water Works into a public regional district is seen to impact the city's economic recovery. The utility's service area and customer base has significantly grown.

27775 ■ "Taking Collections" in Investment Dealers' Digest (Vol. 75, October 9, 2009, No. 38, pp. 19)
Pub: SourceMedia, Inc.
Ed: Aleksandrs Rozens. **Description:** Although the nation's debt-collection industry has grown with increased reliance by consumers on credit, valuations of these firms have lessened due to the economy which has hurt some of the success of these firms in obtaining the debt back from consumers who are experiencing trying economic times.

27776 ■ "Taking the Over-the-Counter Route to US" in Barron's (Vol. 88, July 7, 2008, No. 27, pp. 24)
Pub: Dow Jones & Co., Inc.
Ed: Eric Uhlfelder. **Description:** Many multinational companies have left the New York Stock Exchange and allowed their shares to trade over-the-counter. The companies have taken advantage of a 2007 SEC rule allowing publicly listed foreign companies to change trading venues if less than 5 percent of global trading volume in the past 12 months occurred in the US.

27777 ■ "Tampa Condo Conversion Sells for $14.8 Million Less" in The Business Journal-Serving Greater Tampa Bay (Vol. 28, September 5, 2008)
Pub: American City Business Journals, Inc.
Ed: Janet Leiser. **Description:** Former apartment complex Village Oaks at Tampa, which was converted to condominiums, has been sold to Tennessee-based real estate investment trust Mid-America Apartment

Communities Inc. for $21.2 million in August 2008. The amount was $14.2 million less than what developer Radco Management LLC paid for in 2005.

27778 ■ *"Tao of Downfall" in International Journal of Entrepreneurship and Small Business (Vol. 11, August 31, 2010, No. 2, pp. 121)*
Pub: Publishers Communication Group
Ed: Wenxian Zhang, Ilan Alon. **Description:** Through historical reviews and case studies, this research seeks to understand why some initially successful entrepreneurs failed in the economic boom of past decades. Among various factors contributing to their downfall are a unique political and business environment, fragile financial systems, traditional cultural influences and personal characteristics.

27779 ■ *"Tech Godfather Steve Walker Winding Down Howard Venture Fund" in Baltimore Business Journal (Vol. 27, December 11, 2009, No. 31)*
Pub: American City Business Journals
Ed: Scott Dance. **Description:** Steve Walker, president of venture capital fund firm Walker Ventures, will be closing the Howard County, Maryland-based firm as the economic situation is finding it difficult to recover investor's money. According to Walker, the economy also constrained investors from financing venture funds. Despite the closure, Walker will continue his work in the local angel investing community.

27780 ■ *"TechLift Strives to Fill in Gaps in Entrepreneurial Support Efforts" in Crain's Cleveland Business (November 12, 2007)*
Pub: Crain Communications, Inc.
Ed: Marsha Powers. **Description:** Profile of the program, TechLift, a new business model launched by NorTech, that is aiming to provide assistance to technology-based companies that may not be a good fit for other entrepreneurial support venues.

27781 ■ *"Tempel Steel To Expand Its Chicago Plant" in Chicago Tribune (August 22, 2008)*
Pub: McClatchy-Tribune Information Services
Ed: James P. Miller. **Description:** Tempel Steel Co. is no longer considering transferring a Libertyville factory's production to Mexico; the company has responded to government incentives and will instead shift that work to its plant on Chicago's North Side.

27782 ■ *"That Empty Feeling" in Crain's Cleveland Business (Vol. 28, October 15, 2007, No. 41, pp. 1)*
Pub: Crain Communications, Inc.
Ed: Stan Bullard. **Description:** Townhouses, cluster homes and condominiums lured both buyers and builders for most of this decade but now that market is suffering to an even greater degree than the single-family home market. Statistical data included.

27783 ■ *"That Vision Thing" in Canadian Business (Vol. 80, December 25, 2006, No. 1, pp. 78)*
Pub: Rogers Media
Description: Suggestions for better Canadian tax policy and making airspace competitive among other things, to improve the economy in 2007, are presented.

27784 ■ *"That's About It for Quantitative Easing" in Barron's (Vol. 89, July 20, 2009, No. 29, pp. M11)*
Pub: Dow Jones & Co., Inc.
Ed: Brian Blackstone. **Description:** US Federal Reserve appears to have decided to halt quantitative easing, causing bond prices to drop and yields to rise. The yield for the 1-year Treasury bond rose more than 0.3 percentage point to about 3.65 percent.

27785 ■ *"There's More Upside in Germany" in Barron's (Vol. 90, September 6, 2010, No. 36, pp. M7)*
Pub: Barron's Editorial & Corporate Headquarters
Ed: Jonathan Buck. **Description:** Germany's stocks have gone up since the beginning of 2010, and investors can still benefit. These stocks will benefit from

Germany's stellar economic performance and the relative weakness of the Euro. The prospects of the shares of Daimler and Hochtief are discussed.

27786 ■ *"Things Fall Apart" in Canadian Business (Vol. 80, October 8, 2007, No. 20, pp. 187)*
Pub: Rogers Media
Ed: Jeff Sanford. **Description:** Infrastructure crisis in Canada and in other countries in North America is examined. Incidents that demonstrate this crisis, such as the collapse of a bridge in Minneapolis and the collapse of an overpass in Quebec, Canada are presented. It is estimated that the reconstruction in the country will cost between C$44 billion and C$200 billion.

27787 ■ *"Things Will Improve, or Not: a Chartered Financial Analyst Explains It All" in Canadian Business (Vol. 81, November 10, 2008)*
Pub: Rogers Media Ltd.
Description: Myles Zyblock expects the global economic slowdown to deepen over the next six to nine months. Zyblock addressed the Toronto CFA Society at their annual dinner in October 2008. He stressed a tight correlation between the credit ratio and asset prices and predicts the S&P 500 to be up by 11 percent by October 2009.

27788 ■ *"Think Disruptive! How to Manage In a New Era of Innovation" in Strategy & Leadership (Vol. 38, July-August 2010, No. 4, pp. 5-10)*
Pub: Emerald Inc.
Ed: Brian Leavy, John Sterling. **Description:** The views expressed by Scott Anthony, president of an innovation consultancy Innosight, on the need for corporate leaders to apply disruptive innovation in a recessionary environment are presented. His suggestion that disruptive innovation is the only way to survive during the economic crisis is discussed.

27789 ■ *"Thomas D'Aquino" in Canadian Business (Vol. 80, November 19, 2007, No. 23, pp. 92)*
Pub: Rogers Media
Ed: Calvin Leung. **Description:** Thomas D'Aquino is the CEO and president of the Canadian Council of Chief Executives since 1981. D'Aquino thinks he has the best job in Canada because he can change the way policies are made and the way people think. Details of his career as a lawyer and CEO and his views on Canada's economy are provided.

27790 ■ *"The Three Amigos" in Canadian Business (Vol. 81, March 17, 2008, No. 4, pp. 19)*
Pub: Rogers Media
Ed: Rachel Pulfer. **Description:** Mexican president Felipe Calderon said that Mexico exported 30 percent more to Europe and 25 percent more to other countries in Latin America in 2006 in light of the downturn in the U.S. economy. Calderon made this announcement in a speech at Harvard University while protestors marched outside protesting against NAFTA.

27791 ■ *"Three Trails Blazes Tax Credit Deal" in The Business Journal-Serving Metropolitan Kansas City (Vol. 27, November 7, 2008, No. 9)*
Pub: American City Business Journals, Inc.
Ed: Rob Roberts. **Description:** Three Trails Redevelopment LLC plans to redevelop the Bannister Mall area. The Missouri Development Finance Board is expected to approve $30 million in tax credits for the project. A verbal agreement on the terms and conditions has already been reached according to the agency's executive director.

27792 ■ *"Tightening Economy Squeezes Business Travel" in HRMagazine (Vol. 53, August 2008, No. 8, pp. 19)*
Pub: Society for Human Resource Management
Contact: Henry G. Jackson, President
E-mail: hjackson@shrm.org
Ed: Kathy Gurchiek. **Description:** New surveys show that some companies are not cutting out business travel, they are using cheaper hotels and cutting back on trade shows and conference travel. Statistical data included.

27793 ■ *"Time for a Leap Of Faith?" in Women Entrepreneur (November 18, 2008)*
Pub: Entrepreneur Media Inc.
Ed: Cynthia McKay. **Description:** Starting a new business, despite the downturn in the economy, can prove to be a successful endeavor if one has the time, energy and most importantly a good idea.

27794 ■ *"Time to Leave the Party?" in Barron's (Vol. 88, March 24, 2008, No. 12, pp. M16)*
Pub: Dow Jones & Company, Inc.
Ed: Andrea Hotter. **Description:** Prices of commodities such as gold, copper, crude oil, sugar, cocoa, and wheat have fallen from their all-time highs set in the middle of March 2008. Analysts, however, caution that this decline in prices may be temporary, and that a banking crisis may trigger new price rises in commodities.

27795 ■ *"Time is Right for Fiscal Authority" in Canadian Business (Vol. 83, July 20, 2010, No. 11-12, pp. 24)*
Pub: Rogers Media Ltd.
Ed: Jacqueline Nelson. **Description:** A survey of Canadian CEOs show that only 5 percent of them believe that the world is in a severe recession. Almost 80 percent of them believe that economic recessions and depressions are caused by failures of the free market and the government.

27796 ■ *"A Timely Matter" in Canadian Business (Vol. 81, March 31, 2008, No. 5, pp. 12)*
Pub: Rogers Media
Description: Discusses the committee responsible for restructuring $33 billion of asset-backed commercial paper which has moved back their implementation plan by a month citing complexities. British Columbia has surpassed the $1 billion mark in fiscal '07-'08 from their oil and gas rights. Biovail Corp. founder Eugene Melnyk said he had lost confidence in the management of the company.

27797 ■ *"Tiptoeing Beyond Treasuries" in Barron's (Vol. 88, March 31, 2008, No. 13, pp. M6)*
Pub: Dow Jones & Company, Inc.
Ed: Michael S. Derby. **Description:** Risk-free assets like treasuries are still a good place for cash even if market conditions have calmed down and Treasury yields are low. Investors looking for yield and safety might want to consider Treasury inflation-indexed securities that are attractive given new inflation pressures.

27798 ■ *"To Keep Freight Rolling, Springfield Must Grease the Hub" in Crain's Chicago Business (Vol. 31, April 21, 2008, No. 16, pp. 22)*
Pub: Crain Communications, Inc.
Ed: Paul O'Connor. **Description:** Discusses the importance of upgrading Chicago's continental-hub freight rail system which is integral to moving international products as well as domestic ones. Global tonnage is expected to double by 2020 and unless more money is designated to upgrade the infrastructure the local and national economy will suffer.

27799 ■ *"Today's Business Sale Climate" in Business Owner (Vol. 35, September-October 2011, No. 5, pp. 10)*
Pub: DL Perkins Company
Description: Despite the weak economy, there is a surplus of individuals wanting to purchase a small business. The Small Business Administration loan guarantees program helps with its loans for purchase/sale of business assistance.

27800 ■ *"Top 50 Exporters" in Hispanic Business (Vol. 30, July-August 2008, No. 7-8, pp. 42)*
Pub: Hispanic Business, Inc.
Ed: Hildy Medina. **Description:** Increases in exports revenues reported by food exporters and green companies in a time of economic slowdown in the U.S are described. Food exporters have benefited from the growth of high-volume grocery stores in

underdeveloped countries and the German governments' promotion of solar energy has benefited the U.S. solar heating equipment and solar panel manufactures.

27801 ■ "Top 50 In Profits" in Canadian Business (Vol. 81, Summer 2008, No. 9, pp. 116)
Pub: Rogers Media Ltd.
Description: Royal Bank of Canada topped the Investor 500 by profits list despite the slower economic growth in Canada and the U.S. The bank was in the runner-up position in the 2007. RBC's growth strategy is through hefty acquisitions in the U.S. A table ranking the top 50 companies in Canada in terms of profits is presented.

27802 ■ "Top 100 Consolidate Gains" in Hispanic Business (Vol. 30, July-August 2008, No. 7-8, pp. 30)
Pub: Hispanic Business, Inc.
Ed: Richard Kaplan. **Description:** Data developed by HispanTelligence on the increase in revenue posted by the top 100 fastest-growing U.S. Hispanic firms over the last five years is reported. Despite the economic downturn, the service sector, IT and health suppliers showed an increase in revenue whereas construction companies showed a marginal slump in revenue growth.

27803 ■ "Top Private Companies" in Baltimore Business Journal (Vol. 28, August 27, 2010, No. 16, pp. 1)
Pub: Baltimore Business Journal
Ed: Gary Haber. **Description:** The combined revenue of the 100 largest private firms in Maryland's Baltimore region dropped from about $22.7 billion in 2008 to $21 billion in 2009, an annual decrease of more than 7 percent. To survive the recession's impact, these firms resorted to strategies such as government contracting and overseas expansion. How these strategies affected the revenue of some firms is described.

27804 ■ "Tory or Liberal, Blue or Red, the Impact of the Election is All in Your Head" in Globe & Mail (January 14, 2006, pp. B19)
Pub: CTVglobemedia Publishing Inc.
Ed: Derek DeCloet. **Description:** The effect of the outcome of 2006 Canadian federal elections on stock markets is discussed.

27805 ■ "Tough Climate for Nurseries" in Crain's Cleveland Business (Vol. 30, June 29, 2009, No. 25, pp. 1)
Pub: Crain Communications, Inc.
Ed: Stan Bullard. **Description:** After 81 years in the business, Sunnybrook Farms & Nursery is closing its doors. The owner sites the bad economy along with cold weather the reason for lack of sales. Other nursery owners discuss the bad economy and weather conditions and how they are affecting their business.

27806 ■ "Tough Sell: Senior Projects Hustle to Keep Buyers" in Puget Sound Business Journal (Vol. 29, November 21, 2008, No. 31, pp.)
Pub: American City Business Journals
Ed: Heidi Dietrich. **Description:** Plans to move to retirement communities are being postponed by seniors in Washington's Puget Sound area due to difficulty selling their current homes in the slow economy. Retirement communities are trying to lure clients by offering new finance programs and sales plans.

27807 ■ "Trade Winds" in Canadian Sailings (June 30, 2008)
Pub: UBM Global Trade
Contact: Leonard J. Corallo, President
Ed: Peter Malkovsky. **Description:** Trade between Canada and the United States is discussed as well as legislation concerning foreign trade and the future of this trade relationship.

27808 ■ Trading Places: SMEs in the Global Economy, A Critical Research Handbook
Pub: Edward Elgar Publishing, Incorporated
Ed: Lloyd-Reason. **Released:** September 2006. **Price:** $110.00. **Description:** An overview of international research for small and medium-sized companies wishing to expand in the global economy.

27809 ■ "Train Now to Get the Competitive Edge" in Contractor (Vol. 56, October 2009, No. 10, pp. 58)
Pub: Penton Media, Inc.
Ed: Merry Beth Hall. **Description:** Due to the harsh economic climate, mechanical contractors would be well-served to train their employees while they have time to take them out of the field. This will help ensure that they are not behind when the economic recovery happens. Suggestions on how to choose the best type of training are presented.

27810 ■ "Travel Leery" in Crain's Chicago Business (Vol. 31, March 31, 2008, No. 13, pp. 3)
Pub: Crain Communications, Inc.
Description: Due to the rise in airline prices and a possible recession, many companies are starting to change their travel policies and limit travel spending.

27811 ■ The Trillion Dollar Meltdown: Easy Money, High Rollers, and the Great Credit Crash
Pub: Public Affairs
Ed: Charles R. Morris. **Released:** 2009. **Price:** $22.95. **Description:** Former banker believes that Wall Street and the financial community have too much power in America. He estimates that writedowns and defaults of residential mortgages, commercial mortgages, junk bonds, leveraged loans, credit cards, and complex securitized bonds could reach $1 trillion.

27812 ■ "Trillium Turmoil" in Canadian Business (Vol. 81, December 8, 2008, No. 21, pp. 16)
Pub: Rogers Media Ltd.
Ed: Jeff Sanford. **Description:** Ontario's manufacturing success in the past was believed to have been built by the 1965 Canada-U.S. automotive pact and by advantages such as low-cost energy. The loss of these advantages along with the challenging economic times has hurt Ontario's manufacturing industry.

27813 ■ "Trimming Costs, But Not Looking It" in Crain's Chicago Business (Vol. 31, November 17, 2008, No. 46, pp. 35)
Pub: Crain Communications, Inc.
Ed: Shia Kapos. **Description:** Advice is given concerning ways in which to keep up appearances of success during these troubled financial times.

27814 ■ "Trust Tax Under Fire as Drain on Revenue" in Globe & Mail (April 9, 2007, pp. B1)
Pub: CTVglobemedia Publishing Inc.
Ed: Steven Chase. **Description:** The economic aspects of the implementation of the trust levy by the Canadian government are discussed. The acquisition of Canadian income trusts by Canadian and international financial institutions is described.

27815 ■ "Turbulent Skies" in The Business Journal-Portland (Vol. 25, August 29, 2008, No. 25, pp. 1)
Pub: American City Business Journals, Inc.
Ed: Erik Siemers. **Description:** Small airlines are struggling to keep their commercial services amid the troubled commercial airline sector. Small communities, for example, were expected to pony up about $650,000 in revenue guarantees each in order to convince SkyWest Airlines to offer two direct flights to Portland daily beginning October 12, 2008. The trends in the commercial airline industry are analyzed.

27816 ■ "Turbulent Times and Golden Opportunity" in Business Strategy Review (Vol. 21, Spring 2010, No. 1, pp. 34)
Pub: Wiley-Blackwell
Ed: Don Sull. **Description:** For those feeling storm-tossed by today's economy, the author believes there's much to learn from Carnival Cruise Lines, a company that discovered that turbulence often has an upside.

27817 ■ "The Turkey Has Landed" in Canadian Business (Vol. 79, November 20, 2006, No. 23, pp. 38)
Pub: Rogers Media
Ed: Erik Heinrich. **Description:** The design and construction of Toronto Pearson International Airport to handle domestic, international and transborder flights in one facility is discussed.

27818 ■ "Turmoil Means Changes For Retailers" in The Business Journal-Serving Metropolitan Kansas City (Vol. 27, October 10, 2008, No. 4)
Pub: American City Business Journals, Inc.
Ed: Suzanna Stagemeyer. **Description:** Impacts of the financial crisis on Kansas Metropolitan Area retailers are varied. Rob Dalzell, for instance, found it difficult to secure a loan for his new self-serve yogurt store Yummo. The trends in retailing in the area are examined further as well as ways in which local businesses are changing in an attempt to stay solvent during the economic downturn.

27819 ■ "A Turn in the South" in The Economist (Vol. 390, January 3, 2009, No. 8612, pp. 34)
Pub: The Economist Newspaper Inc.
Description: Overview of Charleston, South Carolina, a region that lost its navy base in 1996, which had provided work for more than 22,000 people; the city developed a plan called Noisette in order to redevelop the area and today the economy is healthier and more diversified than it was a decade ago. Charleston was described as among the best cities for doing business by Inc. Magazine and seems to be handling the downturn of the economy fairly well. Statistical data regarding growth, business and population is included.

27820 ■ "Twenty Years of Advocacy and Education" in Women Entrepreneur (January 18, 2009)
Pub: Entrepreneur Media Inc.
Ed: Eve Gumpel. **Description:** Profile of Sharon Hadary who served as executive director of the Center for Women's Business Research for two decades; Hadary discusses what she has learned about women business owners, their impact on the economy and what successful business owners share in common.

27821 ■ "Uncle Volodya's Flagging Christmas Spirit; Russia" in The Economist (Vol. 390, January 3, 2009, No. 8612, pp. 22)
Pub: The Economist Newspaper Inc.
Description: Overview of Russia's struggling economy as well as unpopular government decisions such as raising import duties on used foreign vehicles so as to protect Russian carmakers.

27822 ■ "Understanding the Economy: People Worry That a Recession Is Coming" in Inc. (December 2007, pp. 103-104)
Pub: Gruner & Jahr USA Publishing
Ed: Joseph H. Ellis. **Description:** It is suggested that by the time a recession arrives, the worst economic damage has already occurred.

27823 ■ "Unemployment Rates" in The Economist (Vol. 390, January 3, 2009, No. 8612, pp. 75)
Pub: The Economist Newspaper Inc.
Description: Countries that are being impacted the worst by rising unemployment rates are those that have also been suffering from the housing market crisis. Spain has been the hardest hit followed by Ireland. America and Britain are also seeing levels of unemployment that indicate too much slack in the economy.

27824 ■ "Union Questions Patrick Cudahy Layoffs" in Business Journal-Milwaukee (Vol. 28, December 3, 2010, No. 9, pp. A1)
Pub: Milwaukee Business Journal
Ed: Rich Ravito. **Description:** United Food and Commercial Workers Local 1473 is investigating Patrick Cudahy Inc.'s termination of 340 jobs. The union said the company has violated the law for failing to issue proper notice of a mass layoff.

27825 ■ *"The Union of Town and Gown" in Entrepreneur (Vol. 37, October 2009, No. 10, pp. 47)*

Pub: Entrepreneur Media, Inc.

Ed: Jason Daley. **Description:** Ten of the best entrepreneurial initiatives involving cities and local universities in the US are described. Cities and universities are joining up for these efforts to strengthen local economies and stop brain drain.

27826 ■ *"U.S. Economy's Underlying Strengths Limit Recession Threat" in Hispanic Business (Vol. 30, April 2008, No. 4, pp. 14)*

Pub: Hispanic Business

Ed: Dr. Juan B. Solana. **Description:** Large and small businesses as well as consumers and policy-makers are attempting to identify the areas of risk and loss created by the economic crisis; analysts are now estimating that U.S. mortgage losses could reach the $380 to $400 billion mark. Also discusses the falling of wages and the rising of unemployment. Statistical data included.

27827 ■ *"U.S. Recession Officially Over: Is Recovery Ever Going to Arrive?" in Montana Business Quarterly (Vol. 49, Spring 2011, No. 1, pp. 6)*

Pub: Bureau of Business & Economic Research

Ed: Patrick M. Barkey. **Description:** Ten predictions regarding American's economy for 2012 are listed.

27828 ■ *United States Taxes and Tax Policy*

Pub: Cambridge University Press

Contact: Richard Ziemacki, President

E-mail: rziemacki@cambridge.org

Ed: David G. Davies. **Released:** January 22, 2010. **Price:** $34.99. **Description:** This book expands the information on taxes found in public finance texts by using a combination of institutional, factual, theoretical and empirical information. It also stresses the economic effects of taxes and tax policy.

27829 ■ *"Univest Charter Switch Signals Banking Trend" in Philadelphia Business Journal (Vol. 30, September 2, 2011, No. 29, pp. 1)*

Pub: American City Business Journals Inc.

Ed: Jeff Blumenthal. **Description:** Univest Corporation of Pennsylvania changed from a federal to state charter because of cost savings and state agency has greater understanding of the intricacies of the local economy. The Pennsylvania Department of Banking has also received inquiries from seven other banks about doing the same this year.

27830 ■ *"Up In the Air" in The Business Journal-Serving Greater Tampa Bay (Vol. 28, July 18, 2008, No. 30, pp. 1)*

Pub: American City Business Journals, Inc.

Ed: Margie Manning. **Description:** Views and information on Busch Gardens and on its future, are presented. The park's 3,769 employees worry for their future, after tourism industry experts have expressed concerns on possible tax cuts and other cost reductions. The future of the park, which ranks number 19 as the most visited park in the world, is expected to have a major impact on the tourism industry.

27831 ■ *"Up On The Farm" in Canadian Business (Vol. 81, March 31, 2008, No. 5, pp. 23)*

Pub: Rogers Media

Ed: John Gray. **Description:** Agricultural products have outperformed both energy and metal and even the prospect of a global economic slowdown does not seem to hinder its prospects. The Organization for Economic Cooperation and Development sees prices above historic equilibrium levels during the next ten years given that fuel and fertilizers remain high and greater demand from India and China remain steady.

27832 ■ *"An Updated Ranking of Academic Journals in Economics" in Canadian Journal*

of Economics (Vol. 44, November 2011, No. 4, pp. 1525)

Pub: Blackwell Publishers Ltd.

Ed: Pantelis Kalaitzidakis, Theofanis P. Mamuneas, Thanasis Stengos. **Description:** An updated list showing the ranking of economic journals (2003) is presented; however this present study differs methodologically from an earlier study by using a rolling window of years between 2003 and 2008, for each year counting the number of citations of articles published in the previous ten years.

27833 ■ *"The Upside of Fear and Loathing" in Barron's (Vol. 88, March 24, 2008, No. 12, pp. 11)*

Pub: Dow Jones & Company, Inc.

Ed: Michael Santoli. **Description:** Fear and risk aversion prevalent among investors may actually serve to cushion the decline and spark a rally in US stock prices. Surveys of investors indicate rising levels of anxiety and bearishness, indicating a possible positive turnaround.

27834 ■ *"USAmeriBank Deals for Growth" in The Business Journal-Serving Greater Tampa Bay (Vol. 28, September 26, 2008, No. 40, pp. 1)*

Pub: American City Business Journals, Inc.

Ed: Margie Manning. **Description:** It is believed that the pending $14.9 million purchase of Liberty Bank by USAmeriBank could be at the forefront of a trend. Executives of both companies expect the deal to close by the end of 2008. USAmeriBank will have $430 million in assets and five offices in Pinellas, Florida once the deal is completed.

27835 ■ *"Valenti: Roots of Financial Crisis Go Back to 1998" in Crain's Detroit Business (Vol. 24, October 6, 2008, No. 40, pp. 25)*

Pub: Crain Communications, Inc.

Ed: Tom Henderson; Nathan Skid. **Description:** Interview with Sam Valenti III who is the chairman and CEO of Valenti Capital L.L.C., a wealth-management firm; Valenti discusses in detail the history that led up to the current economic crisis as well as his prediction for the future of the country.

27836 ■ *"VC Investing Down 63 Percent" in Austin Business JournalInc. (Vol. 29, January 29, 2010, No. 47, pp. 1)*

Pub: American City Business Journals

Ed: Christopher Calnan. **Description:** Venture capital investments in the Austin, Texas area have declined by about 63 percent from $590.1 million in 2008 to $219.2 million in 2009. Deal volume remained steady at 53 local company fundings, but the median deal value declined from $6.5 million in 2008 to $3 million in 2009. Details on several local deals are presented.

27837 ■ *"Venture Gap" in Canadian Business (Vol. 81, March 17, 2008, No. 4, pp. 82)*

Pub: Rogers Media

Ed: Joe Castaldo. **Description:** Money raised by Canadian venture capitalist firms has been declining since 2001. A strong venture capital market is important if Canada is to build innovative companies. Fixing Canada's tax policy on foreign investments is a start in reviving the industry.

27838 ■ *"The Visitor Rebound" in Canadian Business (Vol. 80, November 5, 2007, No. 22, pp. 23)*

Pub: Rogers Media

Ed: Graham Silnicki. **Description:** Overnight visits to Canada are expected to fall by 5.3 percent in 2008, however spending is expected to drop by only 2 percent. Senior economist Alex Fritsche thinks that tourism from the U.S. will improve in 2009; the reasons for the expected growth in 2009 are examined.

27839 ■ *"Vital Signs: The Big Picture" in Canadian Business (Vol. 81, Summer 2008, No. 9, pp. 153)*

Pub: Rogers Media Ltd.

Description: Results of the Investor 500 showing percentage of companies with positive returns, most actively traded companies over the past six months

and market capitalization by industry are presented. Stock performance and revenues of publicly held corporations in Canada are also provided.

27840 ■ *"Viva Brazil" in Business Strategy Review (Vol. 21, Autumn 2010, No. 3, pp. 24)*

Pub: Wiley-Blackwell

Ed: Georgina Peters. **Description:** Brazil's current status as a major emerging market with a boundless economic horizon is a radical shift from its place in the world in the late 1960s to the mid 1990s. Lessons Brazil can teach other countries are outlined.

27841 ■ *"Viva La Evolucion" in Canadian Business (Vol. 80, February 12, 2007, No. 4, pp. 63)*

Pub: Rogers Media

Ed: Denis Seguin. **Description:** The rise of Cuba as an importance source of oil and its significance for the Canadian economy is discussed.

27842 ■ *"Voices: Breaking the Corruption Habit" in Business Strategy Review (Vol. 21, Autumn 2010, No. 3, pp. 67)*

Pub: Wiley-Blackwell

Ed: David De Cremer. **Description:** In times of crisis, it seems natural that people will work together for the common good. David De Cremer cautions that, on the contrary, both economic and social research prove otherwise. He proposes steps for organizations to take to prevent corrupt behaviors.

27843 ■ *"Wait a Minute!" in Entrepreneur (Vol. 37, September 2009, No. 9, pp. 76)*

Pub: Entrepreneur Media, Inc.

Ed: Jennifer Wang. **Description:** Advice on how entrepreneurs in the United States should secure funding in view of the economic crisis is presented. Enough interest should be stimulated so as to secure a follow-up meeting. Investors should be asked questions that would encourage them to tell stories related to the downturn.

27844 ■ *"Wake-Up Call" in Canadian Business (Vol. 80, October 8, 2007, No. 20, pp. 58)*

Pub: Rogers Media

Ed: Andrea Mandel-Campbell. **Description:** The need for Canadian companies to develop global marketing strategies is discussed. Thomas Caldwell, chairman of Caldwell Securities, believes the country's average performance in global markets should be a cause for alarm. The factors affecting the country's current economic state is also presented.

27845 ■ *"Walker Seeks More Business Participation" in Business Journal-Milwaukee (Vol. 28, December 10, 2010, No. 10, pp. A1)*

Pub: Milwaukee Business Journal

Ed: Rich Kirchen. **Description:** Wisconsin governor Scott Walker is seeking the aid of Milwaukee business leaders to participate in resolving the challenges posed by the economic crisis. Walker is aiming to create 250,000 jobs. He is also planning to call a special session of the legislature to enact strategies to jumpstart the economy.

27846 ■ *"Wannabe Buyers Take Their Own Sweet Time" in Crain's Chicago Business (Vol. 31, April 21, 2008, No. 16, pp. 50)*

Pub: Crain Communications, Inc.

Ed: Lisa Bertagnoli. **Description:** Although all factors are in place for a robust real-estate market in the Chicago area: low interest rates, plenty of inventory and the region's relatively strong employment, buyers are taking their time and doing more research in order to see how bad the economy will get.

27847 ■ *"Want Some of This?" in Canadian Business (Vol. 80, April 9, 2007, No. 8, pp. 71)*

Pub: Rogers Media

Ed: Jeff Sanford. **Description:** The economic impact of growing private equity in Canada is discussed.

27848 ■ *"The War for Good Jobs; The World Will Be Led with Economic Force" in Gallup Management Journal (September 7, 2011)*

Pub: Gallup

Ed: Jim Clifton. **Description:** Gallup's chairman believes the next world war will be for good jobs and the winner will triumph with economic force, driven primarily by job creation and quality GDP growth.

27849 ■ *"Water Works Spinoff Could Make Big Splash"* in Business Courier (Vol. 24, October 19, 2008, No. 27, pp. 1)

Pub: American City Business Journals, Inc.

Ed: Dan Monk. **Description:** Cincinnati, Ohio city manager Milton Dohoney proposed to spin off the city-owned Greater Cincinnati Water Works into a regionally focused water district that could allow the city to receive millions of dollars in annual dividends. A feasibility study is to be conducted by a team of outside consultants and city staffers and is expected to be finished by summer of 2008.

27850 ■ *The Way We'll Be: The Zogby Report on the Transformation of the American Dream*

Pub: Crown Business

Ed: John Zogby. **Released:** 2009. **Price:** $26.00. **Description:** According to a recent poll, the next generation of Americans are not as concerned about making money as they are about making a difference in the world.

27851 ■ *"We May Finally Find the Silver Lining"* in Crain's Detroit Business (Vol. 24, April 7, 2008, No. 14, pp. 8)

Pub: Crain Communications, Inc.

Description: Discusses a possible economic turnaround for Michigan which could be brought forth with such things as the new film initiative incentives which may make filming in the state more appealing than filming in Canada due to the weakened state of the dollar and more exportation from Michigan companies.

27852 ■ *"Weathering the Economic Storm"* in Playthings (Vol. 107, January 1, 2009, No. 1, pp. 10)

Pub: Reed Business Information

Contact: Jeff Greisch, President

Ed: J. Tol Broome Jr. **Description:** Six steps for toy companies to survive the economic turndown are outlined: Outline your business model; seek professional input; meet with your banker; cut your costs; manage your inventory; and use your trade credit.

27853 ■ *"The Weeks Ahead"* in Crain's New York Business (Vol. 24, January 7, 2008, No. 1, pp. 26)

Pub: Crain Communications, Inc.

Description: Listing of events in the Detroit area include conferences addressing entrepreneurialism, economic development, and women business ownership.

27854 ■ *"The Weeks Ahead"* in Crain's New York Business (Vol. 24, January 14, 2008, No. 2, pp. 20)

Pub: Crain Communications, Inc.

Description: Listing of events in the Detroit area include conferences addressing entrepreneurialism, economic development, and women business ownership.

27855 ■ *"Weighing the Write-Off"* in Baltimore Business Journal (Vol. 28, September 10, 2010, No. 18, pp. 1)

Pub: Baltimore Business Journal

Ed: Daniel J. Sernovitz. **Description:** President Barrack Obama has proposed to let business write off their investments in plant and equipment upgrades under a plan aimed at getting the economy going. The plan would allow a company to write off 100 percent of the depreciation for their new investments at one time instead of over several years.

27856 ■ *"What Are You Afraid Of?"* in Entrepreneur (Vol. 37, July 2009, No. 7, pp. 79)

Pub: Entrepreneur Media, Inc.

Ed: Lindsay Holloway. **Description:** According to a survey of entrepreneurs in the US, failure, economic uncertainty, not having enough personal time, being their own boss, and staying afloat are the biggest fears when starting a business. Advice on how to deal with these fears is also given.

27857 ■ *"What Are Your Party's Legislative Priorities for 2008?"* in Hawaii Business (Vol. 53, January 2008, No. 7, pp. 22)

Pub: Hawaii Business Publishing

Description: Discusses the Democratic Party of Hawaii which will prioritize giving more opportunities to earn a living a wage in 2008, according to the party chairwoman Jeani Withington. The Republican Party chairman Willes K. Lee, meanwhile, states that his party will seek to enhance the local business climate. The political parties' plans for Hawaii for the year 2008 are presented in detail.

27858 ■ *"What to Do in an Economic Upswing Before It's too Late"* in Agency Sales Magazine (Vol. 39, November 2009, No. 10, pp. 36)

Pub: MANA

Ed: John Graham. **Description:** Some marketing suggestions for businesses as the economy recovers are presented. These include not waiting for the economy to change and telling your brand's story. Showing people what you can do for them and changing doubters into believers is also advised.

27859 ■ *"What Ever Happened to TGIF?"* in Barron's (Vol. 88, March 10, 2008, No. 10, pp. M3)

Pub: Dow Jones & Company, Inc.

Ed: Kopin Tan. **Description:** US stock markets fell in early March 2008 to their lowest level in 18 months, venturing close to entering a bear market phase. The S&P 500 has dropped an average of 0.78 percent on Fridays for 2008.

27860 ■ *"What Has Sergey Wrought?"* in Barron's (Vol. 89, July 13, 2009, No. 28, pp. 8)

Pub: Dow Jones & Co., Inc.

Ed: Alan Abelson. **Description:** Sergey Aleynikov is a computer expert that once worked for Goldman Sachs but he was arrested after he left the company and charged with theft for bringing with him the code for the company's proprietary software for high-frequency trading. The stock market has been down for four straight weeks as of July 13, 2009 which reflects the reality of how the economy is still struggling.

27861 ■ *"What Recovery?"* in Canadian Business (Vol. 82, April 27, 2009, No. 7, pp. 18)

Pub: Rogers Media

Ed: Rachel Pulfer. **Description:** U.S. markets have rallied on the end of March 2009 but experts and analysts believe that it could be short-lived. Market rallies were found to be common during recessions and are not indicative of economic recovery. Meanwhile, it is believed that employment will be a key factor that will determine the U.S. economic recovery.

27862 ■ *"What's Holding Down Small Business?"* in Business Owner (Vol. 35, November-December 2011, No. 6, pp. 3)

Pub: DL Perkins Company

Description: According to a recent survey conducted by the National Federation of Independent Business, demand is the number one reason for slow growth to any small business in today's economy.

27863 ■ *"What's More Important: Stag or Inflation?"* in Barron's (Vol. 88, July 14, 2008, No. 28, pp. M8)

Pub: Dow Jones & Co., Inc.

Ed: Randall W. Forsyth. **Description:** Economists are divided on which part of stagflation, an economic situation in which inflation and economic stagnation occur simultaneously and remain unchecked for a period of time, is more important. Some economists say that the Federal government is focusing on controlling inflation while others see the central bank as extending its liquidity facilities to the financial sector.

27864 ■ *"When Profit Is Not the Incentive"* in Business North Carolina (Vol. 28, February 2008, No. 2, pp. 42)

Pub: Business North Carolina

Ed: Amanda Parry. **Description:** Novant Health is North Carolina's fifth-largest private-sector employer and one of the largest nonprofit companies. Nonprofits grew 35 percent in North Carolina from 1995 to 2003.

27865 ■ *"Where Are the Vultures?"* in Mergers & Acquisitions: The Dealmaker's Journal (March 1, 2008)

Pub: SourceMedia, Inc.

Ed: Ken MacFadyen. **Description:** Although the real estate market is distressed, not many acquisitions are being made by distress private equity investors; this is due, in part, to the difficulty in assessing real estate industry firms since it is a sector which is so localized.

27866 ■ *"Where Canada Meets the World"* in Canadian Business (Vol. 80, October 8, 2007, No. 20, pp. 86)

Pub: Rogers Media

Ed: Zena Olijnyk. **Description:** An overview of facilities within Canada's borders that contributes to the country's economy is presented. The facilities include fishing vessels and seaports. Agencies that regulate the borders such as the Canada Border Services Agency and the Department of Fisheries and Oceans are also presented.

27867 ■ *"Where Next?"* in Business Strategy Review (Vol. 21, Summer 2010, No. 2, pp. 20)

Pub: Wiley-Blackwell

Description: The emergence of large, vibrant and seemingly unstoppable new markets has been the good news story of the past decade. Brazil, Russia, India and China (BRIC) are among those who have emerged blinking into the new economy.

27868 ■ *"Where Oil-Rich Nations Are Placing Their Bets"* in Harvard Business Review (Vol. 86, September 2008, No. 9, pp. 119)

Pub: Harvard Business School Press

Ed: Rawi Abdelal; Ayesha Khan; Tarun Khanna. **Description:** Investment strategies of the Gulf Cooperation Council nations are examined in addition to how these have impacted the global economy and capitalism.

27869 ■ *"Where's the Lava"* in Hawaii Business (Vol. 53, November 2007, No. 5, pp. 18)

Pub: Hawaii Business Publishing

Ed: Jason Ubay. **Description:** Hawaii Volcanoes National Park used to allow visitors to drive to the end of the paved coastal park road and view flowing lava that came from Kilauea until it reached the sea. On Father's Day morning in June 2007, Kilauea began erupting outside the park and the lava flows inland to Kahaualea and Wao Kele O Puna natural area reserves. In July 2007 321,217 visitors came to the park, a 14 percent increase compared to the same month in 2006.

27870 ■ *"Whiplashed? That's a Bullish Sign"* in Barron's (Vol. 88, March 31, 2008, No. 13, pp. 34)

Pub: Dow Jones & Company, Inc.

Ed: Richard W. Arms. **Description:** Huge volatility often occurs just ahead of a substantial rally, according to an analysis of the volatility in the Dow Jones Index since 2000. The Average Percentage Change based on a 10-day moving average of volatility is a way to measure the level of fear in the market and reveals when buying or selling have been overdone.

27871 ■ *Who's Your City? How the Creative Economy is Making Where to Live the Most Important Decision of Your Life*

Pub: Basic Books

Ed: Richard Florida. **Released:** 2009. **Price:** $26.95. **Description:** Richard Florida disagrees with the notion that under globalization, a leveling has taken away the economic advantages of any place in particular. Florida believes that globalization has also created higher-level economic activities such as innovation, design, finance, and media to cluster in a smaller number of locations.

27872 ■ *"Why Change?"* in Canadian Business (Vol. 80, October 8, 2007, No. 20, pp. 9)

Pub: Rogers Media

Ed: Joe Chidley. **Description:** The need for economic change in Canada is discussed. Despite the country's economic growth and low unemployment rate, economic reform is needed in order to maximize its economic potential in the future. Other reasons for the need to further develop its economy, such as the rise of manufacturing and service industries in Asia and the emergence of regional trade pacts in South America are also tackled.

27873 ■ *"Why the Rally Should Keep Rolling..for Now" in Barron's (Vol. 89, July 27, 2009, No. 30, pp. M3)*
Pub: Dow Jones & Co., Inc.
Ed: Kopin Tan. Description: Stocks rallied for the second straight week as of July 24, 2009 and more companies reported better than expected earnings but the caveat is that companies are beating estimates chiefly by slashing expenses and firing workers. The regulatory risks faced by CME Group and the IntercontinentalExchange are discussed as well as the shares of KKR Private Equity Investors LP.

27874 ■ *"Wikinomics: The Sequel" in Business Strategy Review (Vol. 21, Summer 2010, No. 2, pp. 64)*
Pub: Wiley-Blackwell
Description: Ever-optimistic Don Tapscott and Anthony Williams, coauthors of Wikinomics and individually, of a number of other books that study the Internet and its relation to society, are now working on a new book, one for which they're using the Internet to determine its title.

27875 ■ *"Wild-Goose Chaser" in Entrepreneur (Vol. 37, September 2009, No. 9, pp. 96)*
Pub: Entrepreneur Media, Inc.
Ed: Jason Daley. Description: Geese Police owner David Marcks says he discovered that trained collies could chase geese off golf courses, which started his business. He gives new franchises two dogs to start their business. The company has fared well even during the economic crisis.

27876 ■ *"Will Small Business be Stimulated" in Entrepreneur (Vol. 37, July 2009, No. 7, pp. 18)*
Pub: Entrepreneur Media, Inc.
Ed: Jennifer Wang. Description: Steven Strauss, Alberto G. Alvarado, Jeff Rosenweig, Al Gordon, and Theresa Alfaro Daytner share their views on how the American Recovery and Reinvestment Act of 2009, also known as the economic stimulus, will affect small businesses. Their backgrounds are also provided.

27877 ■ *"Wing and a Prayer" in Canadian Business (Vol. 81, November 10, 2008, No. 19, pp. 70)*
Pub: Rogers Media Ltd.
Ed: Sean Silcoff. Description: The 61st Annual National Business Aviation Association convention in Orlando, Florida saw unabashed display of wealth and privilege, but the U.S. market meltdown and possible economic crash has raised questions on the industry's future. Statistical details included.

27878 ■ *"Winners and Losers" in Crain's Detroit Business (Vol. 25, June 22, 2009, No. 25, pp. 18)*
Pub: Crain Communications Inc. - Detroit
Description: Rankings for Detroit's 50 top-compensated CEOs has changed due to the economic recession. The biggest changes are discussed.

27879 ■ *The Wisdom of Crowds: Why the Many Are Smarter Than the Few and How Collective Wisdom Shapes Business, Economies, Societies and Nations*
Pub: Doubleday Canada, Limited
Ed: James Surrowiecki. Released: May 2004. Description: The premise that the many are smarter than the few and its impact on business, economics, societies and nations is discussed.

27880 ■ *"With the Indian Market, You Take the Good With the Bad" in Globe & Mail (March 23, 2007, pp. B11)*
Pub: CTVglobemedia Publishing Inc.
Ed: David Parkinson. Description: The performance of Bombay Stock Exchange in the month of February 2007 is analyzed. The impact of growing economy on the stock market performance is also analyzed.

27881 ■ *"With New Listings, Business Brokers See Hope" in Business Courier (Vol. 27, September 3, 2010, No. 18, pp. 1)*
Pub: Business Courier
Ed: Lucy May. Description: Business brokers in Cincinnati, Ohio are expecting better prices in view of the strengthening economy.

27882 ■ *"WNY Casing In On Loonie's Climb" in Business First Buffalo (November 23, 2007, pp. 1)*
Pub: American City Business Journals, Inc.
Ed: Scott Thomas. Description: Economy of Western New York has rebounded since the 9/11 recession and the rise of the Canadian dollar, which has contributed to the areas economic growth. Canadian shoppers are frequenting markets in the area due to the parity of the U.S. and Canadian dollar. Details of the cross-border shopping and its impact in WNY are discussed.

27883 ■ *"Wobbling Economy" in The Business Journal-Serving Metropolitan Kansas City (Vol. 27, September 26, 2008, No. 2, pp. 1)*
Pub: American City Business Journals, Inc.
Ed: Rob Roberts. Description: Real estate developers in Kansas City Metropolitan Area are worried of the possible impacts of the crisis at Wall Street. They expect tightening of the credit market, which will result in difficulty of financing their projects. The potential effects of the Wall Street crisis are examined further.

27884 ■ *"Woes Portend Consumer Shift" in The Business Journal-Serving Metropolitan Kansas City (Vol. 27, September 26, 2008, No. 2, pp. 1)*
Pub: American City Business Journals, Inc.
Ed: Suzanna Stagemeyer. Description: Black Bamboo owner Tim Butt believes that prolonged tightening of the credit market will result in consumer spending becoming more cash-driven that credit card driven. The financial crisis has already constricted spending among consumers. Forecasts for the US economy are provided.

27885 ■ *"Work To Do" in Canadian Business (Vol. 81, July 22, 2008, No. 12-13, pp. 22)*
Pub: Rogers Media Ltd.
Ed: Jane Bao. Description: Recruiting firm Manpower revealed that 36 percent of Canadian employers had trouble filling positions in 2007, highlighting the labor shortage and the need to bring in more workers. Underemployment of immigrants costs up to $6 billion to Canada's economy every year. Other views regarding Canada's labor shortage and on its economic impact are presented.

27886 ■ *"The World Is Your Hospital" in Canadian Business (Vol. 81, July 22, 2008, No. 12-13, pp. 62)*
Pub: Rogers Media Ltd.
Ed: Sharda Prashad. Description: Medical tourism is seen as a booming industry around the world and is expected to grow to around $40 billion in 2010. Key information regarding medical tourism and services are presented. Views on the possible impact of medical tourism on Canada's health care industry, as well as medical tourism opportunities in Canada, are also given.

27887 ■ *"A World of Opportunity: Foreign Markets Offer Diversity to Keen Investors" in Canadian Business (Vol. 81, Summer 2008, No. 9)*
Pub: Rogers Media Ltd.
Ed: Andrew Wahl. Description: International Monetary Fund projected in its 'World Economy Outlook' that there is a 25 percent chance that a global recession will occur in 2008 and 2009. Global growth rate is forecasted at 3.7 percent in 2008. Inflation in Asia emerging markets and forecasts on stock price indexes are presented.

27888 ■ *"The World Tomorrow" in Canadian Business (Vol. 81, December 24, 2007, No. 1, pp. 35)*
Pub: Rogers Media
Ed: Zena Olijnyk. Description: Global economy is predicted to be in a difficult period as analysts expect

a slowdown in economic growth. Germany's Deutsche Bank wrote in a report about 'growth recession' that the chances of the world growth falling below two percent being one in three. Forecasts on other global economic aspects are explored.

27889 ■ *"Worry No. 1 at Auto Show" in Crain's Detroit Business (Vol. 24, January 21, 2008, No. 3, pp. 1)*
Pub: Crain Communications Inc. - Detroit
Ed: Brent Snavely. Description: Recession fears clouded activity at the 2008 Annual North American International Auto Show. Automakers are expecting to see a drop in sales due to slow holiday retail spending as well as fallout from the subprime lending crisis.

27890 ■ *The Worst-Case Scenario Business Survival Guide*
Pub: John Wiley & Sons, Inc.
Released: September 28, 2009. Price: $17.95. Description: Since 1999, the Worst-Case Scenario survival handbooks have provided readers with real answers for the most extreme situations. Now, in a time of economic crisis, the series returns with a new, real-world guide to avoiding the worst business cataclysms.

27891 ■ *"The Worst Lies Ahead for Wall Street; More Losses Certain" in Crain's New York Business (Vol. 24, January 21, 2008, No. 3, pp. 1)*
Pub: Crain Communications, Inc.
Ed: Aaron Elstein. Description: Due to the weakening economy, many financial institutions will face further massive losses forcing them to borrow more at higher interest rates and dragging down their earnings for years to come. The effects on commercial real estate and credit card loans are also discussed as well as the trend to investing in Asia and the Middle East.

27892 ■ *"Yamasaki Lays Off Last of U.S. Workers, to Vacate World Headquarters in Troy" in Crain's Detroit Business (Jan. 11, 2010)*
Pub: Crain Communications Inc.
Ed: Chad Halcom. Description: Overview of the impact on the local economy resulting from the closing of Yamasaki Associates, Inc.'s world headquarters located in Troy. The architectural firm notified the last of its employees that they would, indeed be laid off effective December 31.

27893 ■ *"Yamasaki Lays Off Last of U.S. Workers, to Vacate World Headquarters in Troy" in Crain's Detroit Business (Vol. 26, January 11, 2010)*
Pub: Crain Communications, Inc.
Ed: Chad Halcom. Description: Overview of the impact on the local economy resulting from the closing of Yamasaki Associates, Inc.'s world headquarters located in Troy. The architectural firm notified the last of its employees that they would, indeed be laid off effective December 31.

27894 ■ *"Year-End Tax Tips" in Hawaii Business (Vol. 53, December 2007, No. 6, pp. 136)*
Pub: Hawaii Business Publishing
Ed: Kathleen Bryan. Description: Tax planning tips for the end of 2007, in relation to the tax breaks that are scheduled to expire, are presented. Among the tax breaks that will be expiring at the 2007 year-end are sales tax deduction in the state and local level, premiums on mortgage insurance, and deduction on tuition. The impacts of these changes are discussed.

27895 ■ *"You Can Rebuild It" in Entrepreneur (Vol. 37, July 2009, No. 7, pp. 28)*
Pub: Entrepreneur Media, Inc.
Ed: Robert Kiyosaki. Description: Entrepreneurs, during tough times, should melt down old business strategies and start rebuilding the business. The business and its customers should be redefined in order to maximize marketing efforts and stay afloat when business slows down. Personal experiences in melting down a business and starting over are also given.

27896 ■ *"Young Adult, Childless May Help Fuel Post-Recession Rebound" in Pet Product News (Vol. 64, November 2010, No. 11, pp. 4)*
Pub: BowTie Inc.
Description: Pet industry retailers and marketers are encouraged to tap into the young adult and childless couple sectors to boost consumer traffic and sales to pre-recession levels. Among young adult owners, pet ownership increased from 40 percent in 2003 to 49 percent in 2009. Meanwhile, the childless couple sector represented 63 percent of all dog/cat owners in 2009.

27897 ■ *"Your Bottom Line: How To Bring In Dollars When Times Are Tough" in Small Business Opportunities (November 2007)*
Pub: Harris Publications Inc.
Description: Adding a new product or promoting a product in a new way can help any small business during hard economic times.

27898 ■ *"Your Exposure to Bear Stearns" in Barron's (Vol. 88, March 17, 2008, No. 11, pp. 45)*
Pub: Dow Jones & Company, Inc.
Ed: Tom Sullivan; Jack Willoughby. **Description:** Bear Stearns makes up 5.5 percent of Pioneer Independence's portfolio, 1.4 percent of Vanguard Windsor II's portfolio, 1.2 percent of Legg Mason Value Trust, about 1 percent of Van Kampen Equity & Income, and 0.79 percent of Putnam Fund for Growth & Income. Ginnie Mae securities are now trading at 1.78 percentage points over treasuries due to the mortgage crises.

27899 ■ *"Your Guide to Local Style Business" in Hawaii Business (Vol. 53, December 2007, No. 6, pp. 36)*
Pub: Hawaii Business Publishing
Ed: David K. Choo. **Description:** Discusses the importance of studying the Hawaiian culture when doing business locally. It was observed that geographical aspects increase emphasis on culture and lifestyle more than the need to rectify false imaging do. Details of how locals adhere to their culture are supplied.

TRADE PERIODICALS

27900 ■ *ACCRA Research in Review*
Pub: Council for Community and Economic Research
Contact: Tom Tveidt, Chairman
Ed: Dr. Kenneth E. Poole, Editor. **Released:** Quarterly. **Price:** Included in membership. **Description:** Carries information on research methodology specific to the study of community economic development.

27901 ■ *American Institute for Economic Research--Research Reports*
Pub: American Institute for Economic Research
Contact: Stephen Adams, President
Ed: Larry Pratt, Editor. **Released:** Semimonthly. **Price:** $59. **Description:** Presents the results of the institute's research, including analyses of significant economic developments and their implications, especially the statistical indications of business-cycle changes.

27902 ■ *Business Facilities: The Source for Corporate Site Selectors*
Pub: Group C Communications Inc.
Contact: Lyle Connor, Manager
E-mail: lconnor@groupc.com
URL(s): www.businessfacilities.com/. **Released:** Monthly **Price:** Free.

27903 ■ *Economic Development*
Pub: Wakeman/Walworth Inc.
Ed: Keyes Walworth, Editor. **Released:** Weekly, 48/year. **Price:** $245, U.S. and Canada; $265, elsewhere; $435, two years U.S. and Canada;. **Description:** Covers state efforts to attract new industry, jobs, commerce, and tourism, including such factors as environmental requirements, mass transportation policies, highway construction plans, utility rates, changes in labor laws, tax policies, and enterprise

zones. Provides information on urban development programs as affected by growth control legislation, state construction programs, and building codes.

27904 ■ *Economic Development Research Focus*
Pub: Economic Development Institute Georgia Tech
Ed: Lincoln S. Bates, Editor, lincoln.bates@edi.gat-ech.edu. **Released:** 3/year. **Price:** Free. **Description:** Reports on the progress and results of studies and activities undertaken by the Center for Economic Development Services. Covers relevant topics, legislation and resources; and presents success stories. Recurring features include notices of publications available, and departments titled Georgia Text, and What Works.

27905 ■ *Entrepreneurship and Regional Development: An International Journal*
Pub: Routledge, Taylor & Francis Group
Contact: David Smith, Chief Executive Officer
URL(s): www.tandf.co.uk/journals/titles/08985626.asp. **Ed:** Gerald Sweeney, Alistair R. Anderson. **Released:** 10/yr. **Price:** $446, Individuals; $935, Institutions online only; $1039, Institutions print and online.

27906 ■ *Future Economic Trends*
Pub: Conservative Publishing Corp.
Ed: C.J. Jones, Editor. **Released:** Monthly. **Price:** $149 per year; $79 new subscriber. **Description:** Covers economic and political science in an historical perspective. Provides financial survival advice and the destruction of the U.S. economy and the dollar. Recurring features include Feature Article, History Tells Us, Hard Money, and As We Go to Press.

27907 ■ *International Trade Reporter*
Pub: Bureau of National Affairs Inc.
Contact: Linda G. Botsford, Managing Editor
Released: Weekly. **Price:** $1,159. **Description:** Covers current international trade policies of the U.S. and of major U.S. trading partners. Topics include bilateral negotiations, customs, export/import policy, foreign investment, standards, taxation, and other related issues. Recurring features include a calendar of events, reports of meetings, and notices of publications available.

27908 ■ *Journal of Economics and Management Strategy*
Pub: Blackwell Publishing Inc.
Contact: Gordon Tibbitts, President
URL(s): as.wiley.com/WileyCDA/WileyTitle/productCd-JEMS.html. **Ed:** Daniel F. Spulber, Jeffrey L. Coles, Zhiqi Chen, Luis M.B. Cabral, Esther Gal-Or. **Released:** Quarterly **Price:** $62, Individuals print & online; €91, Individuals print & online; £61, Other countries print & online; $59, Individuals online; €87, Individuals online; £57, Other countries online; $466, Institutions print & online; €466, Institutions print & online; $717, Institutions, other countries print & online.

27909 ■ *Quarterly Journal of Finance and Accounting*
Pub: University of Nebraska
URL(s): www.qjbe.unl.edu. **Ed:** Gordon V. Karels. **Released:** Quarterly **Price:** $35, Individuals; $55, Institutions; $47, Other countries; $65, Institutions, other countries.

27910 ■ *Utah Department of Workforce Services Workforce Information*
Pub: Utah Department of Workforce Services
Ed: Kenneth Jensen, Editor. **Released:** Monthly. **Price:** Free. **Description:** Offers economic data and analysis for the state of Utah.

VIDEOCASSETTES/ AUDIOCASSETTES

27911 ■ *Small Business in a Big World*
Instructional Video
2219 C St.
Lincoln, NE 68502
Ph: (402)475-6570
Free: 800-228-0164

Fax: (402)475-6500
Co. E-mail: feedback@insvideo.com
URL: http://www.insvideo.com
Released: 19??. **Price:** $99.00. **Description:** Demonstrates how small business has contributed to the overall economy. Includes profiles of small retail, service, manufacturing, professional, high tech, wholesale, and warehousing operations at work.
Availability: VHS.

TRADE SHOWS AND CONVENTIONS

27912 ■ **National Association Business Economics Annual Meeting**
National Association for Business Economics
1233 20th St., N.W., No. 505
Washington, DC 20036
Ph: (202)463-6223
Co. E-mail: nabe@nabe.com
URL: http://www.nabe.com/
Contact: Tom Beers, Executive Director
E-mail: tbeers@nabe.com
URL(s): www.nabe.com/. **Frequency:** Annual. **Principal Exhibits:** Business economics products and services. **Telecommunication Services:** nabe@nabe.com.

CONSULTANTS

27913 ■ **Consulting, Appraisals & Studies Ltd.**
111 W Jackson Blvd.
Chicago, IL 60604
Ph: (312)939-7775
Contact: Alfred K. Eckersberg, President
Scope: Real estate and planning consultants offering economic market analyses, feasibility studies, appraisals, development and investment evaluations, fiscal impact reviews and counseling for private and public sector clients. Projects have involved housing, retail shopping and services, industrial, office, hotels and motels, recreational, institutional and public facilities. Other services include demographic surveys and social and economic impacts, with specialized expertise in rehab and redevelopment, historical preservation and urban planning and zoning. Industries served: Business, financial, real estate, developers and government agencies in the U.S. and Canada. **Founded:** 1981.

27914 ■ **HyettPalma Inc.**
1600 Prince St., Ste. 110
Alexandria, VA 22314
Ph: (703)683-5126
Fax: (703)836-5887
Contact: Dolores P. Palma, President
Scope: Specializes in economic development in downtown and commercial districts. The firm services feature comprehensive economic enhancement strategies, market analysis, business retention, creation and attraction strategies, business clustering strategies and business district audits. **Founded:** 1985. **Publications:** "Creating the Future Downtown," 2002; "Lure Businesses to Your Downtown--By Making Life Easier for Them," NYCOM, Apr, 2001; "Recruiting Developers: Using Rfps To Package Projects"; "Focus Groups For Downtown"; "Business Clustering: How To Leverage Sales"; "The Arts "Hook" Downtown," 2001; "The Arts Help Revitalize Downtowns," 2001; "Making Downtown Renaissance a Reality," 2000; "Assistance Program Helps Revitalize Conroe, Texas," 2000. **Seminars:** Trends in the Revitalization of Pennsylvania's Downtowns Through the Blueprints for Pennsylvania's Downtowns Program, York, 2005; America Downtown-New Thinking, New Life, Dec, 2005; Americas Downtown Renaissance: Retail Revitalization and More, NYS Tug Hill Commission, 2003; Indiana Downtown; Creating the Future Downtown; How to Revitalize Your Downtown; Trends in the Revitalization of America's Downtowns, Pennsylvania League of Cities and Municipalities, 2003; Indiana Downtown, Indiana Association of Cities and Towns, 2003; Creating the Future Downtown, Indiana Association of Cities and Towns, 2003; How to Revitalize Your Downtown, 2002. **Special Services:** America Downtown®; Indiana Downtown®.

27915 ■ New Commons
545 Pawtucket Ave., Studio 106A
Pawtucket, RI 02860
Ph: (401)351-7110
Fax: (401)351-7158
Co. E-mail: info@newcommons.com
URL: http://www.newcommons.com
Contact: Robert Leaver, Chief Executive Officer
E-mail: rleaver@newcommons.com
Scope: Builder of agile human networks to champion innovation and mobilize change; to pursue business opportunities; to custom design agile organizations and communities, to foster civic engagement. Clients include organizations on-profits, corporations, government agencies, educational institutions; networks- Trade/professional groups, IT services collaborations, service-sharing collectives; and communities- municipalities, states and statewide agencies, regional collaborations. **Founded:** 1982. **Publications:** "Plexus Imperative," Sep, 2005; "Creating 21st Century Capable Innovation Systems," Aug, 2004; "Call to Action: Building Providences Creative and Innovative Economy"; "Getting Results from Meetings"; "The Entrepreneur as Artist," Commonwealth Publications; "Leader and Agent of Change," Commonwealth Publications; "Achieving our Providence: Lessons of City-Building," Commonwealth Publications. **Seminars:** Introduction to Social Computing (Web 2.0), Jan, 2009; Every Company Counts. Jun, 2009; Facilitating for Results; Story-Making and Story-Telling. **Telecommunication Services:** inquiries@newcommons.com.

COMPUTERIZED DATABASES

27916 ■ *ABI/INFORM®*
789 E Eisenhower Pkwy.
Ann Arbor, MI 48106-1346
Ph: (734)761-4700
Free: 800-521-0600
Co. E-mail: info@il.proquest.com
URL: http://www.il.proquest.com
Contact: Matt Dunie, President
Availability: Online: ProQuest Co.; ProQuest LLC- Dialog; ProQuest LLC - Dialog; LexisNexis Group; STN International; Wolters Kluwer Health - Ovid. **Type:** Full-text; Bibliographic; Image.

27917 ■ *Claritas Update Demographics*
770 Broadway
New York, NY 10003-9595
URL: http://www.claritas.com/sitereports/default.jsp
Availability: Online: The Nielsen Co. - Nielsen SiteReports. CD-ROM: The Nielsen Co. - Nielsen SiteReports. **Type:** Statistical.

27918 ■ *County and City Data Book*
4600 Silver Hill Rd.
Washington, DC 20233-0001
Ph: (301)457-4100
Free: 800-923-8282
Fax: (301)457-4714
Co. E-mail: webmaster@census.gov
URL: http://www.census.gov
Availability: Online: U.S. Census Bureau. CD-ROM: U.S. Census Bureau. **Type:** Statistical.

LIBRARIES

27919 ■ LECG, LLC Library
2000 Powell St., Ste. 600
Emeryville, CA 94608
Ph: (510)985-6700
Fax: (510)653-9898
Co. E-mail: nadams@lecg.com
URL: http://www.lecg.com
Contact: Nancy Adams, Librarian
Scope: Economics, business, antitrust. **Services:** Library open to the public by appointment only. **Founded:** 1991. **Holdings:** 2500 books. **Subscriptions:** 50 journals and other serials; 4 newspapers.

27920 ■ Newfoundland and Labrador Business Service Centre
West Block, Confederation Bldg.
St. John's, NL, Canada A1B 4J6
Ph: (709)729-7000

Fax: (709)729-0654
Co. E-mail: mike.howley@acoa-apeca.gc.ca
URL: http://www.intrd.gov.nl.ca/intrd/department/branches/sibd/cnlbsc.html
Contact: Mike Howley, Manager
Scope: Marketing, small business, economic and regional development. **Services:** Copying; SDI; centre open to the public. **Founded:** 1973. **Holdings:** 10,000 books; 20 VF drawers of subject files; Standard Industrial Classification (SIC) files. **Subscriptions:** 300 journals and other serials.

27921 ■ Ontario Ministry of Economic Development and Trade - InfoSource
900 Bay St.
Hearst Block, 8th Fl.
Toronto, ON, Canada M7A 2E1
Ph: (416)325-6666
Fax: (416)325-6688
Co. E-mail: info@edt.gov.on.ca
URL: http://www.ontariocanada.com/ontcan/1medt/en/home_en.jsp
Scope: Trade, industry, small business, management, company information, economic development. **Services:** Copying; scanning. **Founded:** 1994. **Holdings:** 200 books; microfiche; 20 CD-ROMs.

27922 ■ U.S.D.A. National Agricultural Library - Rural Information Center—RIC.
10301 Baltimore Ave., Rm. 132
Beltsville, MD 20705
Ph: (301)504-5547
Free: 800-633-7701
Fax: (301)504-5181
Co. E-mail: ric@nal.usda.gov
URL: http://ric.nal.usda.gov
Contact: William Thomas, Coordinator
Scope: Economic development; small business development; city and county government services; government and private grants and funding sources; rural communities; community leadership; natural resources. **Services:** Copying; center open to the public. **Founded:** 1987. **Holdings:** Figures not available. **Telecommunication Services:** william.thomas@ars.usda.gov.

27923 ■ University of Kentucky - Business & Economics Information Center
B&E Info. Ctr., Rm. 116
335-BA Gatton College of Business & Economics
Lexington, KY 40506-0034
Ph: (859)257-8936
Fax: (859)257-1333
Co. E-mail: mrazeeq@pop.uk.edu
URL: http://www.uky.edu//Provost/academicprograms.html
Contact: Michael A. Razeeq, Librarian, Business
URL(s): gatton.uky.edu/. **Scope:** Business, economics, business management, marketing, finance, accounting. **Services:** Library open to the public for reference use only. **Founded:** 1993. **Telecommunication Services:** cber@uky.edu; klimar@pop.uky.edu; provost@email.uky.edu.

27924 ■ West Virginia University - College of Business and Economics - Bureau of Business and Economic Research
P.O. Box 6527
Morgantown, WV 26506-6025
Ph: (304)293-7831
Fax: (304)293-5652
Co. E-mail: bebureau@mail.wvu.edu
URL: http://be.wvu.edu/bber
Contact: Tom S. Witt, Director
Scope: Economics, West Virginia economy. **Services:** Library not open to the public. **Founded:** 1948. **Holdings:** 300 books; 600 other cataloged items. **Subscriptions:** 12 journals and other serials; 4 newspapers. **Telecommunication Services:** tom.witt@mail.wvu.edu.

RESEARCH CENTERS

27925 ■ Arizona State University - JPMorgan Chase Economic Outlook Center
W.P. Carey School of Business
Tempe, AZ 85287-4011
Ph: (480)965-3963

Fax: (480)965-5458
Co. E-mail: lee.mcpheters@asu.edu
URL: http://wpcarey.asu.edu/seid/EOC
Contact: Lee McPheters, Director
Services: Forecasting newsletters and economic analysis. **Founded:** 1985. **Publications:** *Mexico Consensus Economic Forecast* (Quarterly); *Western Blue Chip Economic Forecast* (10/year).

27926 ■ Atlantic Institute for Market Studies (AIMS)
Cogswell Twr., Ste. 1302
2000 Barrington St.
Halifax, NS, Canada B3J 3K1
Ph: (902)429-1143
Fax: (902)425-1393
Co. E-mail: aims@aims.ca
URL: http://www.aims.ca/
Contact: Charles Cirtwill, President
Founded: 1994. **Publications:** *AIMS On-Line Newsletter*; *AIMS Books*; *AIMS Papers*. **Educational Activities:** Conferences, meetings, seminars; AIMS Lectures; AIMS Training programs. **Telecommunication Services:** charlescirtwill@aims.ca.

27927 ■ Atlantic Provinces Economic Council (APEC)—Conseil Économique Des Provinces De L'Atlantique
5121 Sackville St., Ste. 500
Halifax, NS, Canada B3J 1K1
Ph: (902)422-6516
Fax: (902)429-6803
Co. E-mail: elizabeth.beale@apec-econ.ca
URL: http://www.apec-econ.ca
Contact: Elizabeth Beale, President
Services: Consulting. **Founded:** 1954. **Educational Activities:** Business Outlook Conference (Annual), held each fall; Forums and dinners. **Telecommunication Services:** info@apec-econ.ca.

27928 ■ Ball State University - Bureau of Business Research (BBR)
Whitinger Business Bldg., Rm. 149
2000 W University Ave.
Muncie, IN 47306
Ph: (765)285-5926
Fax: (765)285-8024
Co. E-mail: mhicks@bsu.edu
URL: http://cms.bsu.edu/Academics/CentersandInstitutes/B3R.aspx
Contact: Michael J. Hicks, Director
Services: Publication Services: develop, design, produce hard copy and electronic publications for college and community clients. **Founded:** 1970. **Publications** *Indiana Business Bulletin* (Weekly); *American Journal of Business* (Semiannual). **Educational Activities:** Research Support, editing, data analysis, computer statistical services to faculty; 2 Executive roundtables (Quarterly); Policy Papers for statewide business and law makers (Monthly), published economic impact and analysis of current issues; Staff monograph and paper seminars (Monthly), faculty. **Telecommunication Services:** cber@bsu.edu.

27929 ■ Baylor University - Center for Business and Economic Research
Economics Department
Hankamer School of Business
Waco, TX 76798
Ph: (254)710-4146
Fax: (254)710-6142
Co. E-mail: tom_kelly@baylor.edu
URL: http://www.baylor.edu/business/economic_research
Contact: Dr. Thomas M. Kelly, Director
Founded: 1949.

27930 ■ Center for the Study of Economics (CSE)
413 S 10th St.
Philadelphia, PA 19147
Ph: (215)923-7800
Fax: (215)923-7801
Co. E-mail: barbara@urbantools.org
URL: http://www.urbantoolsconsult.org
Contact: R. Joshua Vincent, Chief Executive Officer
Services: Consulting. **Founded:** 1980. **Publications:** *Incentive Taxation*.

27931 ■ Centre for the Study of Living Standards (CSLS)—Centre d'étude des niveaux de vie (CENV)
151 Slater St., Ste. 710
Ottawa, ON, Canada K1P 5H3
Ph: (613)233-8891
Fax: (613)233-8250
Co. E-mail: info@csls.ca
URL: http://www.csls.ca
Contact: Andrew Sharpe, Executive Director
Services: Database development (Occasionally).
Founded: 1995. **Publications:** *CSLS Research Reports* (10/year); *International Productivity Monitor* (Semiannual). **Telecommunication Services:** andrew.sharpe@csls.ca.

27932 ■ Chapman University - A. Gary Anderson Center for Economic Research (ACER)
1 University Dr.
Orange, CA 92866
Ph: (714)997-6693
Fax: (714)997-6601
Co. E-mail: adibi@chapman.edu
URL: http://www.chapman.edu/argyros/asbecenters/acer/Default.asp
Contact: Esmael Adibi, Director
Services: Consulting. **Founded:** 1979. **Publications:** *Economic & Business Review* (Semiannual); *Local business surveys; ACER Newsletter; ACER Working papers.* **Educational Activities:** Chapman University Economic Forecast Conference (Annual), each December; ACER Workshops, conferences.

27933 ■ East Tennessee State University - Bureau of Business and Economic Research
222 Sam Wilson Hall
College of Business & Technology
Johnson City, TN 37614-1710
Ph: (423)439-5677
Fax: (423)439-8381
Co. E-mail: smitjl01@etsu.edu
URL: http://www.etsu.edu/cbat/bureau
Contact: Jon L. Smith, Director
Services: Business Development Program; Economic feasibility (impact) studies; Global research; Implementation of pay systems; Regional development information. **Founded:** 1967. **Publications:** *East Tennessee Business Indicators; Labor Market Report; Tri-Cities Retail Sales Report* (Quarterly). **Educational Activities:** Economic Development Seminars; Workforce Development Seminars; Business programs. **Telecommunication Services:** bureau@etsu.edu.

27934 ■ Fort Lewis College - Office of Economic Analysis and Business Research
Durango, CO 81301
Ph: (970)247-7624
Fax: (970)247-7623
Co. E-mail: walker_d@fortlewis.edu
URL: http://soba.fortlewis.edu/econoweb/
Contact: Deborah Walker, Director
Services: Conducts contract research and serves as a clearinghouse linking college faculty and the business community. **Founded:** 1990. **Publications:** *Four Corners Economic Quarterly* (Quarterly). **Educational Activities:** Annual Business Conference; Southwest Business Forum, open to the public.

27935 ■ Georgia Southern University - Bureau of Business Research and Economic Development (BBRED)
PO Box 8153-01
Statesboro, GA 30460-8151
Ph: (912)478-0872
Fax: (912)478-5581
Co. E-mail: ehsibbald@georgiasouthern.edu
URL: http://www.bbred.org
Contact: Dr. Edward Sibbald, Director (Acting)
Services: Consulting and assistance for local businesses and communities. **Founded:** 1987. **Awards:** Graduate assistantship.

27936 ■ Georgia State University - Economic Forecasting Center (EFC)
PO Box 3988
Atlanta, GA 30302-3988
Ph: (404)413-7260
Fax: (404)413-7264
Co. E-mail: rdhawan@gsu.edu
URL: http://robinson.gsu.edu/efc/index.html
Contact: Prof. Rajeev Dhawan, Director
Services: Entitles sponsors to all data collected or produced by the Center and to one or two private meetings yearly with the Center director. **Founded:** 1973. **Publications:** *Forecast of the Nation* (Quarterly); *Southeast States Indicators* (Quarterly); *Forecast of Georgia and Atlanta* (Quarterly). **Educational Activities:** Economic Forecasting Conference (Quarterly); Instructs students in applied economics; Sponsors' Seminar (Quarterly); Facilities for research on forecasting and related topics. **Awards:** Four graduate assistantships. **Telecommunication Services:** efc@gsu.edu.

27937 ■ Hawaii Business, Economic Development, and Tourism Department - Research and Economic Analysis Division (READ)
PO Box 2359
Honolulu, HI 96804
Ph: (808)586-2355
Fax: (808)586-2377
Co. E-mail: library@dbedt.hawaii.gov
URL: http://hawaii.gov/dbedt/info/economic
Contact: Richard C. Lim, Director
Services: Statistical and economic information to the public. **Founded:** 1963. **Publications:** *Hawaii's Economy* (Occasionally); *Quarterly Statistical and Economic Report; State of Hawaii Data Book* (Annual). **Educational Activities:** Census data workshops and meetings. **Awards:** University of Hawaii internship position.

27938 ■ Indiana University Bloomington - Indiana Business Research Center (IBRC)
Kelley School of Business
100 S College Ave., Ste. 240
Bloomington, IN 47404
Ph: (812)855-5507
Fax: (812)855-7763
Co. E-mail: conover@indiana.edu
URL: http://www.ibrc.indiana.edu
Contact: Dr. Jerry N. Conover, Director
Founded: 1925. **Publications:** *InContext* (Bimonthly); *Indiana Business Review* (Quarterly). **Educational Activities:** Public presentations and training. **Telecommunication Services:** ibrc@iupui.edu.

27939 ■ Interuniversity Research Centre on Quantitative Economics
3150, rue Jean-Brillant, Bureau C-6084
C.P. 6128, succursale Centre-ville
Montreal, QC, Canada H3C 3J7
Ph: (514)343-6557
Fax: (514)343-5831
Co. E-mail: emanuela.cardia@umontreal.ca
URL: http://www.cireq.umontreal.ca
Contact: Emanuela Cardia, Director
Founded: 1963. **Publications:** *Interuniversity Research Centre on Quantitative Economics Annual report; Interuniversity Research Centre on Quantitative Economics Research papers.* **Educational Activities:** Interuniversity Research Centre on Quantitative Economics Conferences; Interuniversity Research Centre on Quantitative Economics Seminars (Periodic); Special lectures. **Awards:** Interuniversity Research Centre on Quantitative Economics Postdoctoral fellowships. **Telecommunication Services:** cireq@umontreal.ca.

27940 ■ Jacksonville State University - Center for Economic Development (CED)
College of Commerce & Business Administration
Jacksonville, AL 36265-1602
Ph: (256)782-5324
Fax: (256)782-5179
Co. E-mail: pshaddix@jsu.edu
URL: http://www.jsu.edu/depart/ced/
Contact: Pat W. Shaddix, Director
Services: Maintains a small business development center; State Data Center affiliate. **Founded:** 1984. **Publications:** *CED Monographs; JSU Economic Update.* **Educational Activities:** Supervisory training, planning. **Telecommunication Services:** ced@jsu.edu.

27941 ■ North Dakota State University - Institute for Business and Industry Development (IBID)
2718 Gateway Ave., Ste. 104
Bismarck, ND 58503
Ph: (701)328-9718
Fax: (701)328-9721
Co. E-mail: kathleen.tweeten@ndsu.edu
URL: http://www.ag.ndsu.nodak.edu/ibid
Contact: Kathleen Tweeten, Director
Services: Engineering extension services. **Founded:** 1989.

27942 ■ Plattsburgh State University of New York - Technical Assistance Center (TAC)
194 US Oval
Plattsburgh, NY 12903
Ph: (518)564-2214
Fax: (518)564-3220
Co. E-mail: tac@plattsburgh.edu
URL: http://www.plattsburgh.edu/offices/centers/tac/index.php
Contact: Howard Lowe, Director
Founded: 1971. **Publications:** *A Guide to State, Regional, County, and Local Business Financing Programs for Northern New York* (Annual); *NY County demographic profiles* (7/year). **Awards:** Needs assessments, economic impact analyses, competitive intelligence; Telecommunications network planning and development; Tourism marketing conversion analyses. **Telecommunication Services:** loweha@plattsburgh.edu.

27943 ■ Princeton University - Research Program in Development Studies (RPDS)
367 Wallace Hall
Woodrow Wilson School of Public & International Affairs
Princeton, NJ 08544
Ph: (609)258-2177
Fax: (609)258-5974
Co. E-mail: accase@princeton.edu
URL: http://www.princeton.edu/rpds
Contact: Prof. Anne C. Case, Director
Founded: 1967. **Publications:** *Working Paper Series.* **Educational Activities:** Research seminars in economic development for staff and graduate students of the School (Biweekly).

27944 ■ Simon Fraser University - Centre for Sustainable Community Development (CSCD)
TASC2 8900
Faculty of Environment
8888 University Dr.
Burnaby, BC, Canada V5A 1S6
Ph: (778)782-8787
Fax: (778)782-8788
Co. E-mail: roseland@sfu.ca
URL: http://www.sfu.ca/cscd.html
Contact: Prof. Mark Roseland, Director
Services: ced-net: a worldwide discussion group of CED participants. **Founded:** 1989. **Telecommunication Services:** scdadmin@sfu.ca.

27945 ■ State University of New York College at Oneonta - Center for Economic and Community Development (CECD)
Ravine Pky.
Oneonta, NY 13820
Ph: (607)436-2792
Fax: (607)436-2786
Co. E-mail: hayest@oneonta.edu
URL: http://www.oneonta.edu/advancement/cecd
Contact: Timothy Hayes, Director
Founded: 1990. **Educational Activities:** Industry and government conferences (Occasionally); Leadership Otsego (Quadrennial), leadership training for community members. **Telecommunication Services:** cecd@oneonta.edu.

27946 ■ Texas A&M International University - Texas Center for Border Economic and Enterprise Development (TCBEED)
5201 University Blvd.
Laredo, TX 78041-1900
Ph: (956)326-2546

Fax: (956)326-2544
Co. E-mail: baldogarcia@tamiu.edu
URL: http://texascenter.tamiu.edu
Contact: Baldomero Garcia, Program Manager
Services: Data accessible by Internet. **Founded:** 1989. **Publications:** *Border Business Indicators International Trade journal* (Monthly). **Educational Activities:** Internet home pages; Maquila visits; USIA delegations. **Telecommunication Services:** texas-center@tamiu.edu.

27947 ■ University of Alberta - Institute for Public Economics (IPE)
8-26 HM Tory
Department of Economics
Edmonton, AB, Canada T6G 2H4
Ph: (780)492-7198
Fax: (780)492-3300
Co. E-mail: rascah@ualberta.ca
URL: http://www.uofaweb.ualberta.ca/ipe
Contact: Bob Ascah, Director
Founded: 1996. **Publications:** *IPE Working papers.* **Educational Activities:** Lectures, Conferences, Forums. **Telecommunication Services:** ipe@ualberta.ca.

27948 ■ University of Colorado at Boulder - Carl McGuire Center for International Studies
Department of Economics
256 UCB
Boulder, CO 80309-0256
Ph: (303)492-6394
Fax: (303)492-8960
Co. E-mail: wolfgang.keller@colorado.edu
URL: http://www.colorado.edu/Economics/mcguire
Contact: Wolfgang Keller, Director
Founded: 1985. **Educational Activities:** Workshop in international economics for graduate students and faculty of the Economics Department.

27949 ■ University of Connecticut - Connecticut Center for Economic Analysis (CCEA)
341 Mansfield Rd., U-1240
Storrs, CT 06269-1240
Ph: (860)486-0614
Fax: (860)486-4463
Co. E-mail: fred.carstensen@uconn.edu
URL: http://ccea.uconn.edu
Contact: Prof. Fred V. Carstensen, Director
Founded: 1992. **Publications:** *The Connecticut Economy* (Quarterly). **Educational Activities:** CCEA

Outlook (Quarterly), forecast of state employment and gross output; Economic Outlook Conferences (Periodic). **Telecommunication Services:** ccea@uconn.edu.

27950 ■ University of Maryland at College Park - Center for International Economics
3105 Tydings Hall
Department of Economics
College Park, MD 20742
Ph: (301)405-3548
Fax: (301)405-3542
Co. E-mail: mendozae@econ.umd.edu
URL: http://www.econ.umd.edu/about/centers/CIE
Founded: 1993. **Educational Activities:** Center for International Economics Conferences; Graduate Training Program; Professional Training Program in International Economics.

27951 ■ University of North Texas - Center for Economic Development and Research
1155 Union Cir., No. 310469
Denton, TX 76203
Ph: (940)565-4049
Fax: (940)565-4658
Co. E-mail: tclower@unt.edu
URL: http://www.unt.edu/cedr
Contact: Terry L. Clower, Director
Founded: 1989. **Publications:** *Perspectives* (Semi-annual). **Awards:** Graduate student scholarships.

27952 ■ University of Texas at Austin - Bureau of Business Research (BBR)
2815 San Gabriel St.
Austin, TX 78705
Ph: (512)475-7813
Fax: (512)475-8901
Co. E-mail: bkellison@ic2.utexas.edu
URL: http://www.ic2.utexas.edu/bbr
Contact: Dr. Robert A. Peterson, Director
E-mail: rap@mail.utexas.edu
Services: Information services: economic and demographic data for the State of Texas and its metropolitan areas, counties, and places. **Founded:** 1926. **Publications:** *Texas Business Review.* **Educational Activities:** BBR Conferences and workshops, related to the economy of Texas.

27953 ■ University of Texas—Pan American - Center for Entrepreneurship and Economic Development (CEED)
1201 W University Dr.
Edinburg, TX 78539-2999

Ph: (956)381-3361
Fax: (956)381-2322
Co. E-mail: arriola@panam.edu
URL: http://www.coserve.org/ceed
Founded: 1986. **Publications:** *Border Chronicle*; *Red Factbook.* **Educational Activities:** CEED Seminars and workshops; Training in economic development. **Telecommunication Services:** ceed@panam.edu.

27954 ■ University of Utah - Bureau of Economic and Business Research (BEBR)
1645 E Campus Ctr. Dr., Rm. 401
Salt Lake City, UT 84112-9302
Ph: (801)581-6333
Fax: (801)581-3354
Co. E-mail: bureau@business.utah.edu
URL: http://www.bebr.utah.edu
Contact: James A. Wood, Director
Services: Inquiry service for individuals and businesses. **Founded:** 1932. **Publications:** *Utah Construction Report* (Quarterly); *Utah Economic and Business Review* (Quarterly). **Telecommunication Services:** james.wood@business.utah.edu.

27955 ■ University of Wisconsin—Superior - Northern Center for Community and Economic Development (NCCED)
Erlanson Hall 305D
Superior, WI 54880-2898
Ph: (715)394-8208
Fax: (715)394-8592
Co. E-mail: jhembd@uwsuper.edu
URL: http://www.uwsuper.edu/ncced
Contact: Dr. Jerry Hembd, Director
Services: Consulting. **Founded:** 1984. **Educational Activities:** NCCED Training. **Telecommunication Services:** ncced@uwsuper.edu.

27956 ■ Williams College - Center for Development Economics (CDE)
1065 Main St.
Williamstown, MA 01267
Ph: (413)597-2148
Fax: (413)597-4076
Co. E-mail: rachel.louis@williams.edu
URL: http://cde.williams.edu
Contact: Rachel Louis, Assistant Director
Founded: 1960. **Publications:** *Research Memorandum Series.* **Educational Activities:** Public seminars (Occasionally). **Telecommunication Services:** cde@williams.edu.

START-UP INFORMATION

27957 ■ *"218 More Programs"* in *Entrepreneur (Vol. 35, November 2007, No. 11, pp. 96)*

Pub: Entrepreneur Media Inc.

Description: List of 218 colleges and universities in the U.S. offering entrepreneurship programs is presented.

27958 ■ *"Can You Say $1 Million? A Language-Learning Start-Up Is Hoping That Investors Can"* in *Inc. (Vol. 33, November 2011, No. 9, pp. 116)*

Pub: Inc. Magazine

Ed: April Joyner. **Description:** Startup, Verbling is a video platform that links language learners and native speakers around the world. The firm is working to raise money to hire engineers in order to build the product and redesign their Website.

27959 ■ *Entrepreneurship with Online Learning Center Access Card*

Pub: McGraw-Hill Higher Education

Ed: Robert D. Hirich; Michael P. Peters; Dean A. Shepherd. **Released:** October 2006. **Price:** $103.25. **Description:** Book instructs students on entrepreneurial processes that include starting a new business.

27960 ■ *"Franchises with an Eye on Chicago"* in *Crain's Chicago Business (Vol. 34, March 14, 2011, No. 11, pp. 20)*

Pub: Crain Communications Inc.

Description: Profiles of franchise companies seeking franchisees for the Chicago area include: Extreme Pita, a sandwich shop; Hand and Stone, offering massage, facial and waxing services; Molly Maid, home-cleaning service; Primrose Schools, private accredited schools for children 6 months to 6 hears and after-school programs; Protect Painters, residential and light-commercial painting contractor; and Wingstop, a restaurant offering chicken wings in nine flavors, fries and side dishes.

27961 ■ *"Fun And Easy Gold Mines"* in *Small Business Opportunities (Fall 2008)*

Pub: Entrepreneur Media Inc.

Description: Twenty-five businesses that cater to the booming children's market are profiled; day care services, party planning, special events video-making, tutoring, personalized children's toys and products and other services geared toward the kids market are included.

27962 ■ *"Online Fortunes"* in *Small Business Opportunities (Fall 2008)*

Pub: Entrepreneur Media Inc.

Description: Fifty hot, e-commerce enterprises for the aspiring entrepreneur to consider are featured; virtual assistants, marketing services, party planning, travel services, researching, web design and development, importing as well as creating an online store are among the businesses featured.

27963 ■ *"Rehab Will Turn Hospital Into Incubator"* in *The Business Journal-Serving Metropolitan Kansas City (Vol. 26, September 12, 2008)*

Pub: American City Business Journals, Inc.

Ed: Rob Roberts. **Description:** Independence Regional Health Center will be purchased by CEAH Realtors and be converted into the Independence Regional Entrepreneurial Center, a business incubator that will house startups and other tenants. Other details about the planned entrepreneurial center are provided.

27964 ■ *"SBA Streamlines Loans and Ramps Up Web Presence"* in *Hispanic Business (January-February 2008, pp. 64)*

Pub: Hispanic Business

Description: Federal government's Small Business Administration offers informational resources and tools to individuals wishing to start a new company as well as those managing existing firms. The site consists of over 20,000 pages with information, advice and tips on starting, financing and managing any small business. Free online courses are also provided.

27965 ■ *Start Your Own Tutoring and Test Prep Business: Your Step-by-Step Guide to Success*

Pub: Entrepreneur Press

Contact: Perlman Neil, President

Ed: Rich Mintzer. **Released:** September 9, 2010. **Price:** $17.95. **Description:** Are you an advocate of higher learning? Do you enjoy teaching others? Are you interested in starting a business that makes money and a positive impact? Keys for starting a successful tutoring and test preparation small business are presented.

27966 ■ *"Top 25 Graduate Programs"* in *Entrepreneur (Vol. 35, November 2007, No. 11, pp. 92)*

Pub: Entrepreneur Media Inc.

Description: List of the top twenty-five graduate entrepreneurship programs of different colleges and universities in the U.S. for 2007, as ranked by Entrepreneur Magazine and the Princeton Review, is presented.

27967 ■ *"Top 25 Undergrad Programs"* in *Entrepreneur (Vol. 35, November 2007, No. 11, pp. 88)*

Pub: Entrepreneur Media Inc.

Description: List of the top twenty-five undergraduate entrepreneurship programs of different colleges and universities in the U.S. for 2007, as ranked by Entrepreneur Magazine and the Princeton Review, is highlighted.

27968 ■ *"Top of the Class"* in *Entrepreneur (Vol. 35, November 2007, No. 11, pp. 82)*

Pub: Entrepreneur Media Inc.

Ed: Nichole L. Torres. **Description:** Education in entrepreneurship is being pursued by many students and it is important to understand what entrepreneurship program fits you. Aspiring entrepreneurs should also ask about the program's focus. Considerations searched for by students regarding the particular school they chose to study entrepreneurship are discussed.

27969 ■ *"UM-Dearborn to Launch Program for Entrepreneurs"* in *Crain's Detroit Business (Vol. 24, April 14, 2008, No. 15, pp. 7)*

Pub: Crain Communications Inc.

Ed: Chad Halcom. **Description:** Starting this fall the University of Michigan-Dearborn will begin its Product Realization and Technology Commercialization Program for entrepreneurs and innovators with lab-tested, high-technology products. Ultimately, 20 businesses will each work with the university in creating a customer base, commercializing a new high-tech product or process and connecting with venture capitalists who may invest in the new companies.

ASSOCIATIONS AND OTHER ORGANIZATIONS

27970 ■ **AACSB International (AACSB)—Association to Advance Collegiate Schools of Business**
777 S Harbour Island Blvd., Ste. 750
Tampa, FL 33602-5730
Ph: (813)769-6500
Fax: (813)769-6559
Co. E-mail: mediarelations@aacsb.edu
URL: http://www.aacsb.edu
Contact: John J. Fernandes, President
Description: Represents educational institutions, businesses, and other entities devoted to the advancement of management education. Works to advance quality management education worldwide through accreditation. **Founded:** 1916. **Publications:** *eNewsline* (Monthly); *Salary Survey* (Annual); *BizEd: The Leading Voice of Business Education* (Bi-monthly); *International Business Education in the 1990s: A Global Perspective* (Irregular); *Achieving Quality and Continuous Improvement Through Self-Evaluation and Peer Review* (Annual); *AACSB--The International Association for Management Education--Membership Directory* (Annual); *Guide to Doctoral Programs in Business and Management* (Periodic). **Educational Activities:** AACSB International Conference (Annual).

27971 ■ **ASTD—American Society for Training and Development (ASTD)**
1640 King St.
Alexandria, VA 22314-2746
Ph: (703)683-8100
Free: 800-628-2783
Fax: (703)683-1523
Co. E-mail: customercare@astd.org
URL: http://www.astd.org
Contact: Tony Bingham, President
E-mail: tbingham@astd.org
Description: Represents workplace learning and performance professionals. **Scope:** training and development, workplace performance. **Founded:**

1943. **Subscriptions:** 5000. **Publications:** *TD Magazine; ASTD Buyer's Guide* (Annual); *ASTD Buyer's Guide* (Annual); *Info-Line: Tips, Tools, and Intelligence for Trainers* (Monthly); *Learning Circuits* (Monthly); *T and D Magazine; TD Magazine* (Monthly); *Member Information Exchange (MIX); TRAINET; Training Resources: ASTD Buyer's Guide* (Annual); *Buyer's Guide & Consultant Directory; American Society for Training and Development--Training Video Directory; ASTD Buyer's Guide and Consultants Directory; Who's Who in Training and Development* (Annual); *ASTD Buyer's Guide and Consultants Directory; American Society Training and Development Buyer's Guide and Consultant Directory* (Annual); *Technical Training: Learning Technology for Performance Improvement; ASTD Buyer's Guide & Consultant Directory* (Annual); *Infoline Plus* (Monthly). **Educational Activities:** International Exposition (Annual); TechKnowledge Conference & Exposition (Annual); American Society for Training and Development Conference; TechKnowledge Conference and Exposition (Annual). **Awards:** ASTD BEST Award; Awards in the Advancing ASTD's Vision; Awards in the Advancing Workplace Learning and Performance; Excellence in Practice; Dissertation Award; Torch Award; Gordon M. Bliss Memorial Award; Distinguished Contribution to Workplace Learning and Performance Award. **Telecommunication Services:** subscriberservice@astd.org.

27972 ■ *Asynchronous Learning Networks*
260 Dalhousie St., Ste. 204
Ottawa, ON, Canada K1N 7E4
Ph: (613)241-0018
Fax: (613)241-0019
Co. E-mail: cnie-rcie@cnie-rcie.ca
URL: http://www.cnie-rcie.ca
Contact: Lorraine Carter, President
Released: Periodic

27973 ■ Canadian Accredited Independent Schools (CAIS)
PO Box 3013
St. Catharines, ON, Canada L2R 7C3
Ph: (905)684-5658
Fax: (905)684-5057
Co. E-mail: akee@cais.ca
URL: http://www.cais.ca
Contact: Anne-Marie Kee, Executive Director
Description: Private schools. Promotes excellence in independent education. Represents members' interests. **Founded:** 1981.

27974 ■ Canadian Federation of University Women (CFUW)—Federation Canadienne des Femmes Diplomees des Universites
331 Cooper St., Ste. 502
Ottawa, ON, Canada K2P 0G5
Ph: (613)234-8252
Fax: (613)234-8221
Co. E-mail: cfuwgen@rogers.com
URL: http://www.cfuw.org
Contact: Robin Jackson, Executive Director
Description: Women graduates from accredited universities from around the world. Promotes continuing education for women. Fosters communication and fellowship among members. Advocates for status of women and human rights and equality rights. **Founded:** 1919. **Publications:** *The Communicator* (Periodic). **Educational Activities:** Tides of Change (Annual). **Awards:** Beverley Jackson Fellowship; Bourse Georgette LeMoyne; Memorial Fellowship Award; Margaret Dale Philip Award; Beverley Jackson Fellowship (Annual); Bourse Georgette LeMoyne (Annual); CFUW Memorial Fellowship Award (Annual); Dr. Alice E. Wilson Award (Annual); Dr. Marion Elder Grant Award (Annual); Ecole Polytechnique Commemorative Award; Margaret Dale Philip Award; Dr. Alice E. Wilson Award; Dr. Marion Elder Grant Award; Dr. Margaret McWilliams Pre-Doctoral Fellowship; Ecole Polytechnique Commemorative Award; Dr. Margaret McWilliams Pre-Doctoral Fellowship (Annual).

27975 ■ *Canadian Journal of Learning and Technology*
260 Dalhousie St., Ste. 204
Ottawa, ON, Canada K1N 7E4
Ph: (613)241-0018

Fax: (613)241-0019
Co. E-mail: cnie-rcie@cnie-rcie.ca
URL: http://www.cnie-rcie.ca
Contact: Lorraine Carter, President
Released: Semiannual **Price:** $40.

27976 ■ Canadian Network for Innovation in Education (CNIE)—Reseau canadien pour l'innovation en education
260 Dalhousie St., Ste. 204
Ottawa, ON, Canada K1N 7E4
Ph: (613)241-0018
Fax: (613)241-0019
Co. E-mail: cnie-rcie@cnie-rcie.ca
URL: http://www.cnie-rcie.ca
Contact: Lorraine Carter, President
Description: Educators, students, and other individuals with an interest in distance education. Promotes advancement in the field of distance education. Encourages use of new technologies in distance education. **Founded:** 1983. **Publications:** *Asynchronous Learning Networks* (Periodic); *Canadian Journal of Learning and Technology* (Semiannual). **Awards:** Awards of Excellence (Biennial); Graduate Student Stipend Award (Annual); Leadership Award (Annual).

27977 ■ A Commitment to Training and Employment for Women (ACTEW)
215 Spadina Ave., Ste. 350
Toronto, ON, Canada M5T 2C7
Ph: (416)599-3590
Fax: (416)599-2043
Co. E-mail: info@actew.org
URL: http://www.actew.org
Contact: Ursule Critoph, Co-Chairperson
Description: Serves as umbrella organization of agencies, networks, and groups working on the local level to support existing education and training opportunities for women (particularly lower income, refugee, and older women). Encourages the creation of new programs. Conducts research, lobbying, and advocacy. **Founded:** 1987.

27978 ■ *The Communicator*
331 Cooper St., Ste. 502
Ottawa, ON, Canada K2P 0G5
Ph: (613)234-8252
Fax: (613)234-8221
Co. E-mail: cfuwgen@rogers.com
URL: http://www.cfuw.org
Contact: Robin Jackson, Executive Director
Released: Periodic; 7/year. **Price:** C$10, /year.

27979 ■ Community College Business Officers (CCBO)
PO Box 5565
Charlottesville, VA 22905-5565
Ph: (434)293-2825
Fax: (434)245-8453
Co. E-mail: info@ccbo.org
URL: http://www.ccbo.org
Contact: Dr. Bob Hassmiller, Executive Director
Description: Represents business officers. Works to support business officers. **Awards:** Exemplary Practices Award (Annual); Outstanding Business Officers (Annual).

27980 ■ National Black MBA Association (NBMBAA)
180 N Michigan Ave., Ste. 1400
Chicago, IL 60601
Ph: (312)236-2622
Fax: (312)236-0390
Co. E-mail: mail@nbmbaa.org
URL: http://www.nbmbaa.org
Contact: William Wells, Jr., Chairman of the Board
Description: Creates educational opportunities to form professional and economic growth of African-Americans. Develops partnerships to its members and provides educational programs to increase the awareness on business field. **Founded:** 1970. **Publications:** *Black MBA* (Quarterly); *National Black MBA Association--Newsletter* (Monthly); *NBMBAA Program Book* (Annual). **Educational Activities:** National Black Masters of Business Administration Annual Conference and Exposition (Annual). **Awards:** NBMBAA Graduate Scholarships Program; NBMBAA PhD Fellowship Program.

27981 ■ National Business Education Association (NBEA)
1914 Association Dr.
Reston, VA 20191-1596
Ph: (703)860-8300
Fax: (703)620-4483
Co. E-mail: nbea@nbea.org
URL: http://www.nbea.org
Contact: Janet M. Treichel, Executive Director
Description: Teachers of business subjects in secondary and postsecondary schools and colleges; administrators and research workers in business education; businesspersons interested in business education; teachers in educational institutions training business teachers; high school and college students preparing for careers in business. **Founded:** 1892. **Publications:** *Business Education Forum--Professional Leadership Roster Issue; Business Education Forum: Official Journal of the National Business Education Association; National Business Education Yearbook; Business Education Forum; Keying In* (Quarterly); *NBEA Yearbook* (Annual); *Business Education Forum--Professional Leadership Roster Issue* (Quarterly). **Educational Activities:** National Business Education Association Convention (Annual). **Awards:** Distinguished Service Award; Postsecondary Teacher of the Year; Secondary Teacher of the Year; Award of Merit (Annual); Distinguished Service Awards (Annual); Collegiate or University Teacher of the Year; Distinguished Service Award for an Administrator or Supervisor.

EDUCATIONAL PROGRAMS

27982 ■ ACCS - Advanced Cisco Campus Switching (Onsite)
Seminar Information Service, Inc.
20 Executive Park, Ste. 120
Irvine, CA 92614
Ph: (949)261-9104
Free: 877-SEM-INFO
Fax: (949)261-1963
Co E-mail: info@seminarinformation.com
URL: http://www.seminarinformation.com
Price: $3,295.00. **Description:** Covers Catalyst 6000 Series Architecture; Catalyst 2948G-L3 Configuration; Layer 2 and Layer3 Forwarding; Switching Quality of Service Fundamentals and Configuration; Dynamic and Private VLANs; VLAN Access Control Lists; MLS and CEF Operation; High Availability Options for the 6000 Series; FlexWan Configuration and Operation; and Catalyst 6000 Hybrid to Native IOS Conversion.

27983 ■ Adobe Acrobat I (Onsite)
EEI Communications
8945 Guilford Rd., Ste. 145
Columbia, MD 21046
Ph: (410)309-8200
Free: 888-253-2762
Fax: (410)630-3980
Co. E-mail: train@eeicom.com
URL: http://www.eeicom.com/eei-training-services
Price: $797.00. **Description:** Covers creating PDF documents, including using hyperlinks, bookmarks, sound clips, and security. **Dates and Locations:** Silver Spring, MD; Alexandria, VA; and Columbia, MD.

27984 ■ Adobe After Effects I (Onsite)
EEI Communications
8945 Guilford Rd., Ste. 145
Columbia, MD 21046
Ph: (410)309-8200
Free: 888-253-2762
Fax: (410)630-3980
Co. E-mail: train@eeicom.com
URL: http://www.eeicom.com/eei-training-services
Price: $1,097.00. **Description:** Covers using After Effects to create digital composites, smooth 2-D animations, and elaborate special effects. **Dates and Locations:** Columbia, MD; and Silver Spring, MD.

27985 ■ Adobe Director I
EEI Communications
145 Guilford Rd., Ste. 145
Columbia, MD 21046
Ph: (410)309-8200

Free: 888-253-2762
Fax: (410)630-3980
Co. E-mail: train@eeicom.com
URL: http://www.eeicom.com/eei-training-services
Price: $745.00. **Description:** Covers how to create interactive training applications, electronic marketing pieces, and presentations utilizing Macromedia Director. **Dates and Locations:** Silver Spring, MD; Alexandria, VA; Hunt Valley, MD; and Columbia, MD.

27986 ■ Adobe Director II
EEI Communications
8945 Guilford Rd., Ste. 145
Columbia, MD 21046
Ph: (410)306-8200
Free: 888-253-2762
Fax: (410)630-3980
URL: http://www.eeicom.com/eei-training-services
Price: $1,065.00. **Description:** Seminar introduces Lingo, Director's programming language. **Dates and Locations:** Silver Spring, MD; Alexandria, VA; Hunt Valley, MD; and Columbia, MD.

27987 ■ Adobe Flash I (Onsite)
EEI Communications
8945 Guilford Rd.., Ste. 145
Columbia, MD 22314
Ph: (410)309-8200
Free: 888-253-2762
Fax: (410)630-3980
Co. E-mail: train@eeicom.com
URL: http://www.eeicom.com/eei-training-services
Price: $797.00. **Description:** Covers the basics of Flash including creating animation on the Web that downloads fast and takes up less file space. **Dates and Locations:** Silver Spring, MD; Columbia, MD; and Alexandria, VA.

27988 ■ Adobe Flash II (Onsite)
EEI Communications
8945 Guilford Rd., Ste. 145
Columbia, MD 21046
Ph: (410)309-8200
Free: 888-253-2762
Fax: (410)630-3980
Co. E-mail: train@eeicom.com
URL: http://www.eeicom.com/eei-training-services
Price: $797.00 2 days; $1,097.00 3 days. **Description:** Covers advanced techniques including planning, organizing, and creating a Flash project. **Dates and Locations:** Silver Spring, MD; Columbia, MD; and Alexandria, VA.

27989 ■ Adobe FrameMaker I (Onsite)
EEI Communications
8945 Guilford Rd., Ste. 145
Columbia, MD 21046
Ph: (410)683-7453
Free: 888-630-3980
Fax: (410)309-8200
Co. E-mail: train@eeicom.com
URL: http://www.eeicom.com/eei-training-services
Price: $1,097.00. **Description:** Covers paragraph designs, color use, graphics, headers and footers, tables, and advanced editing techniques. **Dates and Locations:** Silver Spring, MD; Alexandria, VA; Hunt Valley, MD; and Columbia, MD.

27990 ■ Adobe FrameMaker II (Onsite)
EEI Communications
8945 Guilford Rd., Ste. 145
Columbia, MD 21046
Ph: (410)309-8200
Free: 888-253-2762
Fax: (410)630-3980
Co. E-mail: train@eeicom.com
URL: http://www.eeicom.com/eei-training-services
Price: $797.00. **Description:** Covers cross-references, footnotes, creating a book file, hyperlinks, and exporting to HTML and PDF. **Dates and Locations:** Silver Spring, MD.

27991 ■ Adobe Illustrator I (Onsite)
EEI Communications
8945 Guilford Rd., Ste. 145
Columbia, MD 21046
Ph: (410)309-8200
Free: 888-253-2762

Fax: (410)630-3980
Co. E-mail: train@eeicom.com
URL: http://www.eeicom.com/eei-training- services
Price: $797.00. **Description:** Covers basic graphic design features, including creating geometric shapes and free forms, using type, creating graphs, and using the manipulation tools. **Dates and Locations:** Silver Spring, MD; Columbia, MD; and Alexandria, VA.

27992 ■ Adobe Illustrator II (Onsite)
EEI Communications
8945 Guilford Rd., Ste. 145
Alexandria, VA 21046
Ph: (410)309-8200
Free: 888-253-2762
Fax: (410)630-3980
Co. E-mail: train@eeicom.com
URL: http://www.eeicom.com/eei-training-services
Price: $797.00. **Description:** Covers some advanced features of Illustrator, including custom brush patterns, blending modes, effects and styles, and image maps. **Dates and Locations:** Silver Spring, MD; Columbia, MD; and Alexandria, VA.

27993 ■ Adobe Illustrator III (Onsite)
EEI Communications
8945 Guilford Rd., Ste. 145
Columbia, MD 21046
Ph: (410)309-8200
Free: 888-253-2762
Fax: (410)630-3980
Co. E-mail: train@eeicom.com
URL: http://www.eeicom.com/eei-trainingservices
Price: $797.00. **Description:** Covers one- and two-point perspective, shadows, geometric depth, and masking and pathfinders. **Dates and Locations:** Silver Spring, MD; and Columbia, MD.

27994 ■ Adobe InDesign CS4 Master Class for Designers Training (Onsite)
EEI Communications
8945 Guilford Rd ., Ste. 145
MD 21046
Ph: (410)309-8200
Free: 888-253-2762
Fax: (410)630-3980
Co. E-mail: train@eeicom.com
URL: http://www.eeicom.com/eei-training-services
Price: $895.00. **Description:** Master Adobe InDesign CS4's styles, text processing capabilities, table-creation tools, automation features, and in-document creativity enhancements to free up countless hours from smaller tasks and concentrate on designing. **Dates and Locations:** Silver Spring, MD; Hunt Valley, MD; Columbia, MD; and Alexandria, VA.

27995 ■ Adobe InDesign I (Onsite)
EEI Communications
8945 Guilford Rd., Ste. 145
Columbia, MD 21046
Ph: (410)309-8200
Free: 888-253-2762
Fax: (410)630-3980
Co. E-mail: train@eeicom.com
URL: http://www.eeicom.com/eei-training-services
Price: $797.00. **Description:** Covers basic techniques for creating graphic-intensive documents including editing master pages, placeholder frames, applying color, and flowing and threading text. **Dates and Locations:** Silver Spring, MD; and Alexandria, VA.

27996 ■ Adobe InDesign II (Onsite)
EEI Communications
66 Canal Center Plz., Ste. 200
Alexandria, VA 22314
Ph: (703)683-7453
Free: 888-253-2762
Fax: (703)683-7310
Co. E-mail: train@eeicom.com
URL: http://www.eeicom.com/training
Price: $745.00. **Description:** Covers techniques for creating graphic-intensive documents including typography, decorative and special font features, exporting documents, importing and linking graphics, drawing straight and curved segments, and advanced frame techniques. **Dates and Locations:** Silver Spring, MD; Alexandria, VA; and Hunt Valley, MD.

27997 ■ Adobe InDesign with InCopy for Workgroups Training (Onsite)
EEI Communications
8945 Guilford Rd., Ste. 145
Columbia, MD 21046
Ph: (410)309-8200
Free: 888-253-2762
Fax: (410)630-3980
Co. E-mail: train@eeicom.com
URL: http://www.eeicom.com/eei-training-services
Price: $425.00. **Description:** Learn a professional writing and editing program that tightly integrates with Adobe InDesign for a complete solution, including assigning editors to work on parts of pages, spreads, or entire documents in parallel with designers, significantly decreasing the production time for projects. **Dates and Locations:** Alexandria, VA.

27998 ■ Adobe Photoshop I (Onsite)
EEI Communications
8945 Guilford Rd., Ste. 145
Columbia, MD 21046
Ph: (410)309-8200
Free: 888-253-2762
Fax: (410)630-3980
Co. E-mail: train@eeicom.com
URL: http://www.eeicom.com/eei-training-services
Price: $797.00. **Description:** Covers the basic photo manipulation features of Photoshop. **Dates and Locations:** Silver Spring, MD; Alexandria, VA; and Columbia, MD.

27999 ■ Adobe Photoshop II (Onsite)
EEI Communications
8945 Guilford Rd., Ste. 145
Columbia, MD 21046
Ph: (410)309-8200
Free: 888-253-2762
Fax: (410)630-3980
Co. E-mail: train@eeicom.com
URL: http://www.eeicom.com/eei-training-services
Price: $1,097.00. **Description:** Covers intermediate techniques including channel and masking, paths, layering, spot techniques, proper file formatting, and gamuts and color transition issues. **Dates and Locations:** Silver Spring, MD; and Alexandria, VA.

28000 ■ Adobe Photoshop III: Tips and Tricks (Onsite)
EEI Communications
8945 Guilford Rd., Ste. 145
Columbia, MD 21046
Ph: (410)309-8200
Free: 888-253-2762
Fax: (410)630-3980
Co. E-mail: train@eeicom.com
URL: http://www.eeicom.com/eei-training-services
Price: $497.00. **Description:** Covers advanced Photoshop techniques and effects. **Dates and Locations:** Silver Spring, MD; and Alexandria, VA.

28001 ■ Adobe Premiere I (Onsite)
EEI Communications
8945 Guilford Rd., Ste. 145
Columbia, MD 21046
Ph: (410)309-8200
Free: 888-253-2762
Fax: (410)630-3980
Co. E-mail: train@eeicom.com
URL: http://www.eeicom.com/eei-training-services
Price: $797.00. **Description:** Covers an introduction to video capture and video editing utilizing Premiere. **Dates and Locations:** Silver Spring, MD.

28002 ■ Advanced Grammar Roundtable (Onsite)
EEI Communications
8945 Guilford Rd., Ste. 145
Columbia, MD 21046
Ph: (410)306-8200
Free: 888-253-2762
Fax: (410)630-3980
URL: http://www.eeicom.com/eei-training-services
Price: $797.00. **Description:** Discuss various philosophies about grammar, the origins of grammar rules and the case against 'rule-based' grammar, diagram sentences, review grammar concepts as

needed, examine particles, determiners and interrupters, examine the difference between an absolute phrase and a descriptive one. **Dates and Locations:** Silver Spring, MD; and Alexandria, VA.

28003 ■ Advanced PC Configuration, Troubleshooting and Data Recovery: Hands-On (Onsite)
Seminar Information Service, Inc.
20 Executive Park, Ste. 120
Irvine, CA 92614
Ph: (949)261-9104
Free: 877-SEM-INFO
Fax: (949)261-1963
Co. E-mail: info@seminarinformation.com
URL: http://www.seminarinformation.com
Price: $2,890.00. **Description:** Learn how to: Recover lost files and directories; Revive non-bootable floppies and hard disks; Create emergency rescue disks to recover crashed Windows systems; Detect, isolate and contain damage from virus programs; Create full disk images for complete backups; Remove unwanted start-up programs from the Registry; Examine system status with Windows XP Computer Management tools; Install and configure a simple TCP/IP network. **Dates and Locations:** New York, NY.

28004 ■ Advertising Research (Onsite)
Seminar Information Service, Inc.
20 Executive Park, Ste. 120
Irvine, CA 92614
Ph: (949)261-9104
Free: 877-SEM-INFO
Fax: (949)261-1963
Co. E-mail: info@seminarinformation.com
URL: http://www.seminarinformation.com
Price: $1,895.00. **Description:** Provides a practical and a comprehensive framework for classifying various advertising research methods based on what they measure, how they measure it and how good they are at it. Participants will be able to evaluate and select among the numerous procedures used in practice to facilitate key advertising decisions.

28005 ■ Air Conditioning & Refrigeration (Onsite)
American Trainco
9785 S Maroon Cir., Ste. 300
Englewood, CO 80112
Ph: (303)531-4560
Free: 877-978-7246
Fax: (303)531-4565
Co. E-mail: Sales@AmericanTrainco.com
URL: http://www.americantrainco.com
Price: $990.00. **Description:** Course designed for anyone who needs to understand basic operation, maintenance, and troubleshooting of air conditioning and refrigeration systems in order to improve efficiencies and uptime at their industrial plants and large building facilities. **Dates and Locations:** Cities throughout the United States.

28006 ■ AMA's PMP Exam Prep Express (Onsite)
American Management Association
600 AMA Way
Saranac Lake, NY 12983-5534
Ph: (212)586-8100
Free: 877-566-9441
Fax: (518)891-0368
Co. E-mail: customerservice@amanet.org
URL: http://www.amaseminars.org
Price: $2,195.00 for non-members; $1,995.00 for AMA members; and $1,708.00 for General Services Administration (GSA) members. **Description:** Three-day seminar to increase the probability of obtaining your PMP. **Dates and Locations:** New York, NY; Washington, DC; and Arlington, VA.

28007 ■ Arc Flash Protection & Electrical Safety 70E
American Trainco
9785 S Maroon Cir., Ste. 300
Englewood, CO 80112
Ph: (303)531-4560
Free: 877-978-7246

Fax: (303)531-4565
Co. E-mail: Sales@AmericanTrainco.com
URL: http://www.americantrainco.com
Price: $990.00. **Description:** Training course designed to save lives, prevent disabling injuries, and prevent damage to plants, buildings and equipment. Participants learn about personal safety for working on or around electrical systems and equipment, how to use proper materials and procedures for doing electrical work, and the potential consequences for themselves and others if they don't. **Dates and Locations:** Cities throughout the United States.

28008 ■ Assertiveness Training (Onsite)
American Management Association
600 AMA Way
Saranac Lake, NY 12983-5534
Ph: (212)586-8100
Free: 877-566-9441
Fax: (518)891-0368
Co. E-mail: customerservice@amanet.org
URL: http://www.amaseminars.org
Price: $2,195.00 for non-members; $1,995.00 for AMA members; and $1,708.00 for General Services Administration (GSA) members. **Description:** Three-day seminar to enhance your assertiveness skills at all levels in the organization. **Dates and Locations:** Chicago, IL; New York, NY; San Francisco, CA; Atlanta, GA; Washington, DC; Dallas, TX; and Arlington, VA.

28009 ■ Basic Electricity for the Non Electrician (Onsite)
American Trainco
9785 S Maroon Cir., Ste. 300
Englewood, CO 80112
Ph: (303)531-4560
Free: 877-978-7246
Fax: (303)531-4565
Co. E-mail: Sales@AmericanTrainco.com
URL: http://www.americantrainco.com
Price: $990.00. **Description:** Understanding and working with industrial electricity. **Dates and Locations:** Cities throughout the United States.

28010 ■ Basic Problem Solving Techniques (Onsite)
Seminar Information Service, Inc.
20 Executive Park, Ste. 120
Irvine, CA 92614
Ph: (949)261-9104
Free: 877-SEM-INFO
Fax: (949)261-1963
Co. E-mail: info@seminarinformation.com
URL: http://www.seminarinformation.com
Price: Contact for fee. **Description:** With the help of several qualitative, quantitative, and creative problem solving methods participants develop their ability to recognize and solve problems through their own efforts. **Dates and Locations:** Waukesha, WI.

28011 ■ Basics of Commercial Contracting (Onsite)
Seminar Information Service, Inc.
20 Executive Park, Ste. 120
Irvine, CA 92614
Ph: (949)261-9104
Free: 877-SEM-INFO
Fax: (949)261-1963
Co. E-mail: info@seminarinformation.com
URL: http://www.seminarinformation.com
Price: $1,025.00. **Description:** Learn the key practical and legal principles applicable to business dealings, as well as a thorough understanding of the Uniform Commercial Code (UCC). **Dates and Locations:** Arlington, VA.

28012 ■ Best Practices in Java Programming: Hands-On (Onsite)
Seminar Information Service, Inc.
20 Executive Park, Ste. 120
Irvine, CA 92614
Ph: (949)261-9104
Free: 877-SEM-INFO

Fax: (949)261-1963
Co. E-mail: info@seminarinformation.com
URL: http://www.seminarinformation.com
Price: $2,890.00. **Description:** Learn how to: Apply Java best practices to increase productivity and build fast, secure and reliable applications; Optimize the compilation, deployment and testing of software applications; Solve architectural problems with proven design patterns and advanced language features; Code securely in Java and authenticate with industry-standard security frameworks; Maximize software performance; Improve the reliability of threaded applications; Extend application functionality non-intrusively. **Dates and Locations:** Reston, VA; Rockville, MD; Ottawa, CN; and New York, NY.

28013 ■ Boiler Operation, Maintenance & Safety (Onsite)
American Trainco
9785 S Maroon Cir., Ste. 300
Englewood, CO 80112
Ph: (303)531-4560
Free: 877-978-7246
Fax: (303)531-4565
Co. E-mail: Sales@AmericanTrainco.com
URL: http://www.americantrainco.com
Price: $990.00. **Description:** Seminar designed to teach building and facility maintenance personnel how to service their own boiler safely reducing the need for outside service contractors, while at the same time increases your confidence and comfort level in operating and maintaining your own broilers. **Dates and Locations:** Cities throughout the United States.

28014 ■ Building Applications with Microsoft Access 2007: Hands-On (Onsite)
Seminar Information Service, Inc.
20 Executive Park, Ste. 120
Irvine, CA 92614
Ph: (949)261-9104
Free: 877-SEM-INFO
Fax: (949)261-1963
Co. E-mail: info@seminarinformation.com
URL: http://www.seminarinformation.com
Price: $2,890.00. **Description:** Learn how to: Develop distributable applications with Microsoft Access 2007; Incorporate user specifications to enhance application functionality; Customize applications by dynamically setting properties and executing methods; Assemble expressions into VBA statements using variables and intrinsic functions; Control program flow with loops and decision-making logic; Apply Data Access Objects (DAO) to incorporate business rules; Centralize the error handling process. **Dates and Locations:** New York, NY; Reston, VA; and Rockville, MD.

28015 ■ Business Process Reengineering for Competitive Advantage (Onsite)
Seminar Information Service, Inc.
20 Executive Park, Ste. 120
Irvine, CA 92614
Ph: (949)261-9104
Free: 877-SEM-INFO
Fax: (949)261-1963
Co. E-mail: info@seminarinformation.com
URL: http://www.seminarinformation.com
Price: $2,890.00. **Description:** Learn how to: Select, organize and implement a business reengineering project using CLAMBRE/UML; Achieve competitive advantage by capitalizing on technology opportunities and the application of UML tools; Maximize customer satisfaction by matching process design to customer needs; Identify typical symptoms of business process dysfunction; Redesign workflow and structure successfully within the business; Ensure best practice through the application of business patterns. **Dates and Locations:** Ottawa, CN; Schaumburg, IL; Toronto, CN; Reston, VA; Irving, TX; and New York, NY.

28016 ■ C++ Programming for Non-C Programmers (Onsite)
Seminar Information Service, Inc.
20 Executive Park, Ste. 120
Irvine, CA 92614
Ph: (949)261-9104
Free: 877-SEM-INFO

Fax: (949)261-1963
Co. E-mail: info@seminarinformation.com
URL: http://www.seminarinformation.com
Price: $2,595.00. **Description:** Provides an accelerated introduction to the most essential components of the C language on the first day, followed by four days focus on object-oriented programming with C. **Dates and Locations:** Cities throughout the United States.

28017 ■ Certified Ethical Hacker (Onsite)
Seminar Information Service, Inc.
20 Executive Park, Ste. 120
Irvine, CA 92614
Ph: (949)261-9104
Free: 877-SEM-INFO
Fax: (949)261-1963
Co. E-mail: info@seminarinformation.com
URL: http://www.seminarinformation.com
Price: $3,395.00. **Description:** Learn to footprint organizations, perform port scanning, and exploit a variety of systems and architectures, including hands-on labs. You'll also receive the CEH study guide, Certified Ethical Hacker Exam Prep, CDs packed with security tools, templates, and white papers, practice exam questions, and an exam voucher.

28018 ■ Chilled Water Systems (Onsite)
American Trainco
9785 S Maroon Cir., Ste. 300
Englewood, CO 80112
Ph: (303)531-4560
Free: 877-978-7246
Fax: (303)531-4565
Co. E-mail: Sales@AmericanTrainco.com
URL: http://www.americantrainco.com
Price: $990.00. **Description:** Learn to control your systems and properly maintain them, getting the most out of them. **Dates and Locations:** Cities throughout the United States.

28019 ■ Creative Problem Solving and Strategic Thinking (Onsite)
Fred Pryor Seminars & CareerTrack
5700 Broadmoor St., Ste. 300
Mission, KS 66202
Free: 800-780-8476
Fax: (913)967-8849
Co. E-mail: customerservice@pryor.com
URL: http://www.pryor.com
Price: $199.00; $189.00 for groups of 5 or more. **Description:** Learn an innovative approach to problem solving. **Dates and Locations:** Cities throughout the United States.

28020 ■ Critical Thinking Skills-Strategic Planning in Action (Onsite)
Seminar Information Service, Inc.
20 Executive Park, Ste. 120
Irvine, CA 92614
Ph: (949)261-9104
Free: 877-SEM-INFO
Fax: (949)261-1963
Co. E-mail: info@seminarinformation.com
URL: http://www.seminarinformation.com
Price: $460.00. **Description:** Seminar provides participants with tools, techniques and the critical thinking skills to identify their critical measures of success, the requirements of internal and external customers, including the strengths and weaknesses of their staff. **Dates and Locations:** Waukesha, WI; and Palatine, IL.

28021 ■ Dealing with Competing Demands (Canada)
Canadian Management Centre (CMC)
150 York St., 5th Fl.
Toronto, ON, Canada M5H 3S5
Ph: (416)214-5678
Free: 877-262-2519
Fax: (416)313-4985
Co. E-mail: cmcinfo@cmctraining.org
URL: http://www.cmctraining.org
Contact: John Wright, President
Price: $2,395.00 Canadian for non-members; $2,195,00 Canadian for CMC members. **Description:** Covers the skills necessary to manage your

objectives with success, including prioritizing, realistic objectives, effective use of communication to meet your goals, and utilize control stress. **Dates and Locations:** Toronto, ON.

28022 ■ Defending Windows Networks (Onsite)
Seminar Information Service, Inc.
20 Executive Park, Ste. 120
Irvine, CA 92614
Ph: (949)261-9104
Free: 877-SEM-INFO
Fax: (949)261-1963
Co. E-mail: info@seminarinformation.com
URL: http://www.seminarinformation.com
Price: $2,995.00. **Description:** Lab-intensive to illustrate defense techniques against real-world threats, instead of simply addressing software security features, including how attacks are performed, how they can compromise a Windows Server Network Infrastructure, and how you can lock down the network.

28023 ■ Deploying Intrusion Detection Systems: Hands-On (Onsite)
Seminar Information Service, Inc.
20 Executive Park, Ste. 120
Irvine, CA 92614
Ph: (949)261-9104
Free: 877-SEM-INFO
Fax: (949)261-1963
Co. E-mail: info@seminarinformation.com
URL: http://www.seminarinformation.com
Price: $2,890.00. **Description:** Learn how to: Detect and respond to network- and host-based intruder attacks; Integrate intrusion detection systems (IDS) into your current network topology; Analyze IDS alerts using the latest tools and techniques; Identify methods hackers use to attack systems; Recognize detection avoidance schemes; Stop attackers with Intrusion Prevention Systems (IPSs). **Dates and Locations:** Rockville, MD.

28024 ■ Deploying Virtual Server and Workstation Technology: Hands-On (Onsite)
Seminar Information Service, Inc.
20 Executive Park, Ste. 120
Irvine, CA 92614
Ph: (949)261-9104
Free: 877-SEM-INFO
Fax: (949)261-1963
Co. E-mail: info@seminarinformation.com
URL: http://www.seminarinformation.com
Price: $2,890.00. **Description:** Learn how to: Implement VMware and Microsoft virtual machine (VM) technologies; Combine Windows and Linux workstations and servers on a single platform; Leverage VMs to build testing, support and training environments; Partition physical servers to decrease operating costs; Migrate from physical to virtual machines; Manage VMs throughout the enterprise. **Dates and Locations:** Reston, VA; Rockville, MD; New York, NY; Toronto, NN; and Ottawa, CN.

28025 ■ Designing and Building Great Web Pages: Hands-On (Onsite)
Seminar Information Service, Inc.
20 Executive Park, Ste. 120
Irvine, CA 92614
Ph: (949)261-9104
Free: 877-SEM-INFO
Fax: (949)261-1963
Co. E-mail: info@seminarinformation.com
URL: http://www.seminarinformation.com
Price: $2,890.00. **Description:** Learn to build powerful Web content that effectively conveys your message; Create graphical content using Photoshop CS2, Fireworks 8 and Flash 8; Develop Web page content with FrontPage and Dreamweaver 8; Generate complex Web pages using Cascading Style Sheets, tables and layers; and Enhance Web pages with special effects and DHTML.

28026 ■ Developing Effective Software Estimation Techniques (Onsite)
Seminar Information Service, Inc.
20 Executive Park, Ste. 120
Irvine, CA 92614
Ph: (949)261-9104

Free: 877-SEM-INFO
Fax: (949)261-1963
Co. E-mail: info@seminarinformation.com
URL: http://www.seminarinformation.com
Price: $2,490.00. **Description:** Learn how to prepare a software project estimate through an iterative process; Develop an initial estimate using the expert judgment method; Apply historical data for greater precision in an estimate; Refine the size or scope estimate using a component-based method; Perform Function Point calculations to determine the magnitude of a project; Translate a size or scope estimate into a time, schedule and cost estimate. **Dates and Locations:** Toronto and Ottawa, CN.

28027 ■ Developing Effective Training
Seminar Information Service, Inc.
20 Executive Park, Ste. 120
Irvine, CA 92614
Ph: (949)261-9104
Free: 877-SEM-INFO
Fax: (949)261-1963
Co. E-mail: info@seminarinformation.com
URL: http://www.seminarinformation.com
Price: $1,495.00. **Description:** Provides less experienced trainers with an overview of the training process and shows them how to make each element yield effective learning results. **Dates and Locations:** New York, NY.

28028 ■ Developing SQL Queries for SQL Server: Hands-On (Onsite)
Seminar Information Service, Inc.
20 Executive Park, Ste. 120
Irvine, CA 92614
Ph: (949)261-9104
Free: 877-SEM-INFO
Fax: (949)261-1963
Co. E-mail: info@seminarinformation.com
URL: http://www.seminarinformation.com
Price: $2,890.00. **Description:** Learn how to develop complex and robust SQL queries for SQL Server 2005 and SQL Server 2000; Query multiple tables with inner joins, outer joins and self joins; Transform data with built-in functions; Summarize data using aggregation and grouping; Execute analytic functions to calculate ranks; Build simple and correlated subqueries. **Dates and Locations:** Cities throughout the United States.

28029 ■ Digital Photography Techniques (Onsite)
EEI Communications
66 Canal Center Plz., Ste. 200
Alexandria, VA 22314
Ph: (703)683-7453
Free: 888-253-2762
Fax: (703)683-7310
Co. E-mail: train@eeicom.com
URL: http://www.eeicom.com/training
Price: $745.00. **Description:** Covers using a digital camera, and manipulating digital pictures with Photoshop. **Dates and Locations:** Silver Spring, MD; Alexandria, VA; Hunt Valley, MD; and Columbia, MD.

28030 ■ Diversity Train-the-Trainer (Onsite)
Seminar Information Service, Inc.
20 Executive Park, Ste. 120
Irvine, CA 92614
Ph: (949)261-9104
Free: 877-SEM-INFO
Fax: (949)261-1963
Co. E-mail: info@seminarinformation.com
URL: http://www.seminarinformation.com
Price: $1,820.00. **Description:** Designed to build the confidence, knowledge, and skills of individuals charged with conducting high impact, relevant, and involved diversity education and training in their organization. **Dates and Locations:** New York, NY.

28031 ■ Effective Training Techniques for Group Leaders (Onsite)
Seminar Information Service, Inc.
20 Executive Park, Ste. 120
Irvine, CA 92614
Ph: (949)261-9104
Free: 877-SEM-INFO

Fax: (949)261-1963
Co. E-mail: info@seminarinformation.com
URL: http://www.seminarinformation.com
Price: $370.00 for non-members; $275.00 for The Management Association, Inc. **Description:** Provides group leaders precise and practical methods to train their employees. Leaders also learn to spot worker training needs and provide effective on-the-job training. **Dates and Locations:** Palatine, IL; and Waukesha, WI.

28032 ■ Electrical Ladder Drawings, Schematics & Design (Onsite)
American Trainco
9785 S Maroon Cir., Ste. 300
Englewood, CO 80112
Ph: (303)531-4560
Free: 877-978-7246
Fax: (303)531-4565
Co. E-mail: Sales@AmericanTrainco.com
URL: http://www.americantrainco.com
Price: $990.00. **Description:** Training will include exercises where participants create schematic diagrams based on circuit descriptions, as well as interpreting schematic drawings so that they can provide verbal or written circuit descriptions and an understanding of several types of drawings and diagrams including Block, Pictorial, One-line, Wiring, Terminal, and Schematic. **Dates and Locations:** Cities throughout the United States.

28033 ■ Electrical Troubleshooting & Preventive Maintenance (Onsite)
American Trainco
9785 S Maroon Cir., Ste. 300
Englewood, CO 80112
Ph: (303)531-4560
Free: 877-978-7246
Fax: (303)531-4565
Co. E-mail: Sales@AmericanTrainco.com
URL: http://www.americantrainco.com
Price: $990.00. **Description:** Two-day seminar designed for anyone who needs to sharpen their electrical troubleshooting skills in order to increase efficiencies and uptime at their industrial plant or building facility. **Dates and Locations:** Cities throughout the United States.

28034 ■ Electronic Editing (Onsite)
EEI Communications
8945 Guilford Rd., Ste. 145
Columbia, MD 21046
Ph: (410)309-8200
Free: 888-253-2762
Fax: (410)630-3980
Co. E-mail: train@eeicom.com
URL: http://www.eeicom.com/eei-training-services
Price: $797.00. **Description:** Seminar that covers marking copy using style sheets, tracking changes and comparing documents, using the 'search and replace' function, analyzing global changes, writing macros to make repetitive tasks simpler, checking references against citations, and develop a systematic approach to electronic manuscripts. **Dates and Locations:** Silver Spring, MD.

28035 ■ Forensic Photoshop (Onsite)
EEI Communications
8945 Guilford Rd., Ste. 145
Columbia, MD 21046
Ph: (410)309-8200
Free: 888-253-2762
Fax: (410)630-3980
Co. E-mail: train@eeicom.com
URL: http://www.eeicom.com/eei-training-services
Price: $745.00. **Description:** Designed for law enforcement and Homeland Security personnel that outlines the processes for using Photoshop in a forensic environment. **Dates and Locations:** Silver Spring, MD; Hunt Valley, MD; Columbia, MD; and Alexandria, VA.

28036 ■ Functional Gage Design (Onsite)
Seminar Information Service, Inc.
20 Executive Park, Ste. 120
Irvine, CA 92614
Ph: (949)261-9104
Free: 877-SEM-INFO

Fax: (949)261-1963
Co. E-mail: info@seminarinformation.com
URL: http://www.seminarinformation.com
Price: $850.00. **Description:** Learn about Gage design principles/tolerances; Ways to avoid commonly used but improper gaging and inspection techniques; Inspection machines; Substitute systems; Surface plate inspection and more. **Dates and Locations:** Schaumburg, IL.

28037 ■ Generators & Emergency Power (Onsite)
American Trainco
9785 S Maroon Cir., Ste. 300
Englewood, CO 80112
Ph: (303)531-4560
Free: 877-978-7246
Fax: (303)531-4565
Co. E-mail: Sales@AmericanTrainco.com
URL: http://www.americantrainco.com
Price: $990.00. **Description:** Learn what you can do, and should do with generators, to make sure your facility will keep running even when the electricity to your facility doesn't. **Dates and Locations:** Cities throughout the United States.

28038 ■ Hands-On UNIX and Linux Tools and Utilities (Onsite)
Seminar Information Service, Inc.
20 Executive Park, Ste. 120
Irvine, CA 92614
Ph: (949)261-9104
Free: 877-SEM-INFO
Fax: (949)261-1963
Co. E-mail: info@seminarinformation.com
URL: http://www.seminarinformation.com
Price: $2,890.00. **Description:** Become an expert builder and user of UNIX/Linux tools and utilities, including how to employ standard, programmable text filters to manipulate text and data, build shell scripts to automate routine tasks, and achieve significant productivity gains by matching the mix of tools to the task at hand. **Dates and Locations:** New York, NY; Rockville, MD; and Reston, VA.

28039 ■ How to Conduct Your Own Energy Audit (Onsite)
American Trainco
9785 S Maroon Cir., Ste. 300
Englewood, CO 80112
Ph: (303)531-4560
Free: 877-978-7246
Fax: (303)531-4565
Co. E-mail: Sales@AmericanTrainco.com
URL: http://www.americantrainco.com
Price: $990.00. **Description:** Two-day hands-on seminar shows you how to find quick and inexpensive ways to immediately cut energy costs at your plant or facility. **Dates and Locations:** Orlando, FL.

28040 ■ HVAC Controls & Air Distribution (Onsite)
American Trainco
9785 S Maroon Cir., Ste. 300
Englewood, CO 80112
Ph: (303)531-4560
Free: 877-978-7246
Fax: (303)531-4565
Co. E-mail: Sales@AmericanTrainco.com
URL: http://www.americantrainco.com
Price: $990.00. **Description:** Learn how to 'control' their controls, and how to use fundamental air distribution principles for achieving consistent HVAC comfort and efficiency in buildings, plants and facilities. **Dates and Locations:** Cities throughout the United States.

28041 ■ Improving Editing Skills (Onsite)
EEI Communications
8945 Guilford Rd., Ste. 145
Columbia, MD 21046
Ph: (410)309-8200
Free: 888-253-2762

Fax: (410)630-3980
Co. E-mail: train@eeicom.com
URL: http://www.eeicom.com/eei-training-services
Price: $497.00. **Description:** Covers the editorial issues such as active and passive voice, lists, redundancy, and sentence construction. **Dates and Locations:** Silver Spring, MD; and Alexandria, VA.

28042 ■ Installing, Configuring, and Troubleshooting Microsoft SQL Server
Seminar Information Service, Inc.
20 Executive Park, Ste. 120
Irvine, CA 92614
Ph: (949)261-9104
Free: 877-SEM-INFO
Fax: (949)261-1963
Co. E-mail: info@seminarinformation.com
URL: http://www.seminarinformation.com
Price: $899.00. **Description:** Learn to manage your database projects efficiently, knowledgeable and effectively. **Dates and Locations:** Cities throughout the United States.

28043 ■ Instrumentation, Process Measurement & Control (Onsite)
American Trainco
9785 S Maroon Cir., Ste. 300
Englewood, CO 80112
Ph: (303)531-4560
Free: 877-978-7246
Fax: (303)531-4565
Co. E-mail: Sales@AmericanTrainco.com
URL: http://www.americantrainco.com
Price: $990.00. **Description:** Learn why it is necessary to measure what is going on with your systems and equipment, how to measure it, and what those measurements may mean in terms of action that should be taken to eliminate future downtime and unnecessary expense. **Dates and Locations:** Phoenix, AZ; Denver, CO; Norcross, GA; Baltimore, MD; Harrisburg, PA; Arlington, TX; Salt Lake City, UT; Richmond, VA; and Everett, WA.

28044 ■ Integrating Forms and Databases on the Web (Onsite)
EEI Communications
66 Canal Center Plz., Ste. 200
Alexandria, VA 22314
Ph: (703)683-7453
Free: 888-253-2762
Fax: (703)683-7310
Co. E-mail: train@eeicom.com
URL: http://www.eeicom.com/training
Price: $1,065.00. **Description:** Covers the basics of integrating a database with the world wide web using a Microsoft Access database, active server pages, or Microsoft's Internet Information Server. **Dates and Locations:** Silver Spring, MD; Alexandria, VA; Hunt Valley, MD and Columbia, MD.

28045 ■ Introduction to OS X
EEI Communications
8945 Guilford Rd., Ste. 145
Columbia, MD 21046
Ph: (410)309-8200
Free: 888-253-2762
Fax: (410)630-3980
Co. E-mail: train@eeicom.com
URL: http://www.eeicom.com/eei-training-services
Price: $425.00. **Description:** Seminar designed for beginning MAC users, which serves as the foundation for all MAC courses. **Dates and Locations:** Silver Spring, MD; Alexandria, VA; Hunt Valley, MD; and Columbia, MD.

28046 ■ Introduction to System and Network Security (Onsite)
Seminar Information Service, Inc.
20 Executive Park, Ste. 120
Irvine, CA 92614
Ph: (949)261-9104
Free: 877-SEM-INFO
Fax: (949)261-1963
Co. E-mail: info@seminarinformation.com
URL: http://www.seminarinformation.com
Price: $2,890.00. **Description:** Learn to analyze your exposure to information assurance threats and protect your organization's systems and data; Reduce

your susceptibility to an attack by deploying firewalls, data encryption and other countermeasures; Manage risks emanating from inside the organization and from the Internet; Protect network users from hostile applications and viruses; Identify the security risks that need to be addressed within your organization. **Dates and Locations:** Reston, VA; Rockville, MD; Alexandria, VA; Ottawa, CN; Toronto, CN; and New York, NY.

28047 ■ Introduction to Windows
EEI Communications
8945 Guilford Rd., Ste. 145
Columbia, MD 21046
Ph: (410)309-8200
Free: 888-253-2762
Fax: (410)630-3980
Co. E-mail: train@eeicom.com
URL: http://www.eeicom.com/eei-training-services
Price: $425.00. **Description:** Covers introduction to the PC and the basics of Windows. **Dates and Locations:** Silver Spring, MD; Alexandria, VA; Hunt Valley, MD; and Columbia, MD.

28048 ■ Inventory Control for Maintenance (Onsite)
American Trainco
9785 S Maroon Cir., Ste. 300
Englewood, CO 80112
Ph: (303)531-4560
Free: 877-978-7246
Fax: (303)531-4565
Co. E-mail: Sales@AmericanTrainco.com
URL: http://www.americantrainco.com
Price: $990.00. **Description:** Focus on building an inventory management system that will lead to better control through optimization of inventory quantities, organization of inventory and access to inventory. **Dates and Locations:** Phoenix, AZ; Salt Lake, UT; Orange County, CA; and Orlando, FL.

28049 ■ Java for Non-Programmers (Onsite)
EEI Communications
66 Canal Center Plz., Ste. 200
Alexandria, VA 22314
Ph: (703)683-7453
Free: 888-253-2762
Fax: (703)683-7310
Co. E-mail: train@eeicom.com
URL: http://www.eeicom.com/training
Price: $1,065.00. **Description:** Covers the basics of Java and how to use it for developing websites. **Dates and Locations:** Silver Spring, MD; Alexandria, VA; Hunt Valley, MD; and Columbia, MD.

28050 ■ Macromedia Authorware I
EEI Communications
8945 Guilford Rd., Ste. 145
Columbia, MD 21046
Ph: (410)309-8200
Free: 888-253-2762
Fax: (410)630-3980
Co. E-mail: train@eeicom.com
URL: http://www.eeicom.com/eei-training-services
Price: $1,695.00. **Description:** Covers how to utilize Authorware to develop presentations, quizzes, interactive hypertext, Help systems, and glossaries. **Dates and Locations:** Silver Spring, MD; Alexandria, VA; Hunt Valley, MD; and Columbia, MD.

28051 ■ Maintenance Welding (Onsite)
American Trainco
9785 S Maroon Cir., Ste. 300
Englewood, CO 80112
Ph: (303)531-4560
Free: 877-978-7246
Fax: (303)531-4565
Co. E-mail: Sales@AmericanTrainco.com
URL: http://www.americantrainco.com
Price: $990.00. **Description:** Learn welding techniques, welding processes, metal and filler selection, cutting processes, new fabrications, troubleshooting defects, welding repair, personal safety, managing costs, record keeping and more. **Dates and Locations:** Cities throughout the United States.

28052 ■ Managing Stress Productively (Onsite)
Seminar Information Service, Inc.
20 Executive Park, Ste. 120
Irvine, CA 92614
Ph: (949)261-9104
Free: 877-SEM-INFO
Fax: (949)261-1963
Co. E-mail: info@seminarinformation.com
URL: http://www.seminarinformation.com
Price: $225.00. **Description:** Learn to deal with the pressures of work and to meet the challenges of stress-related problems. **Dates and Locations:** Waukesha, WI.

28053 ■ Mastering Microsoft Project (Onsite)
Seminar Information Service, Inc.
20 Executive Park, Ste. 120
Irvine, CA 92614
Ph: (949)261-9104
Free: 877-SEM-INFO
Fax: (949)261-1963
Co. E-mail: info@seminarinformation.com
URL: http://www.seminarinformation.com
Price: $499.00; $449.00 each for 4 or more. **Description:** Learn how to import tasks into your project from any source; how to pull resources from Microsoft Outlook Active Directory and other sources; merge multiple projects into a single master project; and take advantage of templates and Wizards that can reduce your project planning time. **Dates and Locations:** Cities throughout the United States.

28054 ■ Mastering QuickBooks Seminars and QuickBooks Classes (Onsite)
Seminar Information Service, Inc.
20 Executive Park, Ste. 120
Irvine, CA 92614
Ph: (949)261-9104
Free: 877-SEM-INFO
Fax: (949)261-1963
Co. E-mail: info@seminarinformation.com
URL: http://www.seminarinformation.com
Price: $449.00. **Description:** Discover how QuickBooks can make you and your business more successful. **Dates and Locations:** Cities throughout the United States.

28055 ■ Microsoft Access 2003: A Comprehensive Hands-On Introduction - Building a Foundation for Client/Server Database Applications (Onsite)
Seminar Information Service, Inc.
20 Executive Park, Ste. 120
Irvine, CA 92614
Ph: (949)261-9104
Free: 877-SEM-INFO
Fax: (949)261-1963
Co. E-mail: info@seminarinformation.com
URL: http://www.seminarinformation.com
Price: $3,190.00. **Description:** Learn how to: Design robust relational database applications using Microsoft Access 2003; Develop client/server database front-ends; Build database applications quickly using Form, Table, Report and Query wizards; Link to ODBC and OLE-DB data sources to leverage enterprise security; Create and integrate macros into your applications; Implement advanced Access reporting features.

28056 ■ Microsoft Access 2007: A Comprehensive Hands-On Introduction (Onsite)
Seminar Information Service, Inc.
20 Executive Park, Ste. 120
Irvine, CA 92614
Ph: (949)261-9104
Free: 877-SEM-INFO
Fax: (949)261-1963
Co. E-mail: info@seminarinformation.com
URL: http://www.seminarinformation.com
Price: $2,890.00. **Description:** Learn how to: Utilize Microsoft Access 2007 to design robust database applications; Apply Form, Table, Report and Query wizards to quickly build database applications; Create and integrate macros into your applications; Quickly modify forms and reports with selective filtering, sorting and grouping; Implement advanced Ac-

cess reporting features; Link to SharePoint and SQL Server data systems. **Dates and Locations:** Alexandria, VA; Reston, VA; New York, NY; Ottawa, CN; and Rockville, MD.

28057 ■ Microsoft Access 2007 - I (Onsite)
EEI Communications
8945 Guilford Rd., Ste. 145
Columbia, MD 21046
Ph: (410)309-8200
Free: 888-253-2762
Fax: (410)630-3980
Co. E-mail: train@eeicom.com
URL: http://www.eeicom.com/eei-training-services
Price: $797.00. **Description:** Covers basic database concepts using Access. **Dates and Locations:** Columbia, MD; and Silver Spring, MD.

28058 ■ Microsoft Access 2007 - II (Onsite)
EEI Communications
8945 Guilford Rd., Ste. 145
Columbia, MD 21046
Ph: (410)309-8200
Free: 888-253-2762
Fax: (410)630-3980
Co. E-mail: train@eeicom.com
URL: http://www.eeicom.com/eei-training-services
Price: $797.00. **Description:** Covers database concepts including table design and relationships, advanced query, functions, and form and report techniques. **Dates and Locations:** Silver Spring, MD.

28059 ■ Microsoft Excel 2007 - I (Onsite)
EEI Communications
8945 Guilford Rd., Ste. 145
Columbia, MD 21046
Ph: (410)309-8200
Free: 888-253-2762
Fax: (410)630-3980
Co. E-mail: train@eeicom.com
URL: http://www.eeicom.com/ee-training-services
Price: $797.00. **Description:** Covers the basics of creating simple spreadsheets, including absolute and relative formulas, formatting cells and cell ranges, control pages, working with multiple sheets, and using templates. **Dates and Locations:** Silver Spring, MD; Columbia, MD; and Alexandria, VA.

28060 ■ Microsoft FrontPage (Onsite)
EEI Communications
8945 Guilford Rd., Ste. 145
Columbia, MD 21046
Ph: (410)309-8200
Free: 888-253-2762
Fax: (410)630-3980
Co. E-mail: train@eeicom.com
URL: http://www.eeicom.com/eei-training-services
Price: $797.00. **Description:** Covers using FrontPage to develop websites. **Dates and Locations:** Silver Spring, MD; Alexandria, VA; and Columbia, MD.

28061 ■ Microsoft Office
Fred Pryor Seminars & CareerTrack
5700 Broadmoor St., Ste. 300
Mission, KS 66202
Ph: (800)780-8476
Free: 800-944-8503
Fax: (913)967-8849
Co. E-mail: customerservice@pryor.com
URL: http://www.careertrack.com
Price: $49.00; $44.00 for groups of 5 or more. **Description:** Covers using Microsoft Office. **Dates and Locations:** Cities throughout the United States.

28062 ■ Microsoft PowerPoint 2007 - I (Onsite)
EEI Communications
8945 Guilford Rd., Ste. 145
Columbia, MD 22314
Ph: (410)309-8200
Free: 888-253-2762
Fax: (410)630-3980
Co. E-mail: train@eeicom.com
URL: http://www.eeicom.com/eei-training-services
Price: $797.00. **Description:** Covers creating slides and electronic presentations utilizing PowerPoint. **Dates and Locations:** Silver Spring, MD; and Columbia, MD.

28063 ■ Microsoft Project 2007 - I (Onsite)
EEI Communications
8945 Guilford Rd., Ste. 145
Columbia, MD 21046
Ph: (410)309-8200
Free: 888-253-2762
Fax: (410)630-3980
Co. E-mail: train@eeicom.com
URL: http://www.eeicom.com/eei-training-services
Price: $797.00. **Description:** Covers using Project to successfully manage projects, including using Gantt charts, resource leveling, and establishing task dependencies. **Dates and Locations:** Silverspring, MD; Columbia, MD; and Alexandria, VA.

28064 ■ Microsoft Project: Managing Multiple and Complex Projects (Onsite)
Seminar Information Service, Inc.
20 Executive Park, Ste. 120
Irvine, CA 92614
Ph: (949)261-9104
Free: 877-SEM-INFO
Fax: (949)261-1963
Co. E-mail: info@seminarinformation.com
URL: http://www.seminarinformation.com
Price: $1,890.00. **Description:** Learn how to: Leverage Microsoft Project Professional tools and techniques in a multi-project environment; Reorganize large or complex projects into master and sub-projects; Optimize resource assignments across projects and resolve over allocations; Track schedule, completeness and budget on complex projects and for distributed teams; Connect project managers, teams and data across the organization; Integrate third-party applications to facilitate data sharing and accessibility.

28065 ■ Microsoft Word 2007 - I (Onsite)
EEI Communications
8945 Guilford Rd., Ste. 145
Columbia, MD 21046
Ph: (410)309-8200
Free: 888-253-2762
Fax: (410)630-3980
Co. E-mail: train@eeicom.com
URL: http://www.eeicom.com/eei-training-training
Price: $497.00. **Description:** Covers how to create basic documents using Word. **Dates and Locations:** Silver Spring, MD.

28066 ■ Microsoft Word 2007 - II (Onsite)
EEI Communications
8945 Guilford Rd., Ste. 145
Columbia, MD 21046
Ph: (410)309-8200
Free: 888-253-2762
Fax: (410)630-3980
Co. E-mail: train@eeicom.com
URL: http://www.eeicom.com/eei-training-services
Price: $497.00. **Description:** Covers techniques including creating styles and sections, newspaper-style layouts, creating charts, and adding clip art. **Dates and Locations:** Silver Spring, MD.

28067 ■ Microsoft Word 2007 - III (Onsite)
EEI Communications
8945 Guilford Rd., Ste. 145
Columbia, MD 21046
Ph: (410)309-8200
Free: 888-253-2762
Fax: (410)630-3980
Co. E-mail: train@eeicom.com
URL: http://www.eeicom.com/eei-training-services
Price: $497.00. **Description:** Covers advanced Word skills including running, recording, and running macros, creating custom toolbars, creating online forms, working with master documents, and creating table of contents and indexes. **Dates and Locations:** Silver Spring, MD.

28068 ■ Motor Selection, Maintenance, Testing & Replacement
American Trainco
9785 S Maroon Cir., Ste. 300
Englewood, CO 80112
Ph: (303)531-4560
Free: 877-978-7246

Fax: (303)531-4565
Co. E-mail: Sales@AmericanTrainco.com
URL: http://www.americantrainco.com
Price: $495.00. **Description:** Seminar designed for anyone whose work is affected by motors at their facility, whether they are mechanics doing the work, a supervisor in charge of fixing problems, or purchasing agents responsible for saving money. **Dates and Locations:** Anchorage, AK; and Honolulu, HI.

28069 ■ Moving Ahead: Breaking Behavior Patterns That Hold You Back (Onsite)
American Management Association
600 AMA Way
Saranac Lake, NY 12983-5534
Ph: (212)586-8100
Free: 877-566-9441
Fax: (518)891-0368
Co. E-mail: customerservice@amanet.org
URL: http://www.amaseminars.org
Price: $2,095.00 for non-members; $1,895.00 for AMA members; and $1,623.00 for General Services Administration (GSA) members. **Description:** Covers resolution techniques for bad workplace behaviors. **Dates and Locations:** New York, NY; San Francisco, CA; Washington, DC; Arlington, VA; and Chicago, IL.

28070 ■ Online Marketing and Search Engine Optimization
EEI Communications
8945 Guilford Rd., Ste. 145
Columbia, MD 21046
Ph: (410)309-8200
Free: 888-253-2762
Fax: (410)630-3980
Co. E-mail: train@eeicom.com
URL: http://www.eeicom.com/eei-training-services
Price: $745.00. **Description:** Covers how to increase traffic to your online site to market your products and services using the Web, including creating and implementation of your plan, setting a budget, redesigning Web site for search engine optimization, tips and tricks, promotion hints, tips, and advice, and how to measure your Internet marketing results. **Dates and Locations:** Alexandria, VA.

28071 ■ Personal Success Strategies (Onsite)
Seminar Information Service, Inc.
20 Executive Park, Ste. 120
Irvine, CA 92614
Ph: (949)261-9104
Free: 877-SEM-INFO
Fax: (949)261-1963
Co. E-mail: info@seminarinformation.com
URL: http://www.seminarinformation.com
Price: $370.00. **Description:** Develop a plan to eliminate weaknesses that inhibit success and replace them with positive actions. **Dates and Locations:** Waukesha, WI.

28072 ■ PLC Programming & Applications (Onsite)
American Trainco
9785 S Maroon Cir., Ste. 300
Englewood, CO 80112
Ph: (303)531-4560
Free: 877-978-7246
Fax: (303)531-4565
Co. E-mail: Sales@AmericanTrainco.com
URL: http://www.americantrainco.com
Price: $990.00. **Description:** Provides skills needed to organize, plan, write, enter, test, and document SLC500 programs using the basic programming instructions and RSLogix software. **Dates and Locations:** Cities throughout the United States.

28073 ■ PLCs for Non-Programmers (Onsite)
American Trainco
9785 S Maroon Cir., Ste. 300
Englewood, CO 80112
Ph: (303)531-4560
Free: 877-978-7246

Fax: (303)531-4565
Co. E-mail: Sales@AmericanTrainco.com
URL: http://www.americantrainco.com
Price: $990.00. **Description:** Seminar designed for maintenance technicians, electricians, or other non-programmers who need a general understanding of automation and Programmable Logic Controllers. **Dates and Locations:** Cities throughout the United States.

28074 ■ Plumbing & Pipefitting for Plants & Buildings (Onsite)
American Trainco
9785 S Maroon Cir., Ste. 300
Englewood, CO 80112
Ph: (303)531-4560
Free: 877-978-7246
Fax: (303)531-4565
Co. E-mail: Sales@AmericanTrainco.com
URL: http://www.americantrainco.com
Price: $990.00. **Description:** Covers the necessary requirements to follow code and safety regulations while providing the student with a practical foundation to quickly identify problems and solve them on their own, whether it's a low-pressure water supply line problem, drippy valve or a clogged drain trap. **Dates and Locations:** Orlando, FL; and Atlanta, GA.

28075 ■ Power Excel: Making Better Decisions (Onsite)
Seminar Information Service, Inc.
20 Executive Park, Ste. 120
Irvine, CA 92614
Ph: (949)261-9104
Free: 877-SEM-INFO
Fax: (949)261-1963
Co. E-mail: info@seminarinformation.com
URL: http://www.seminarinformation.com
Price: $1,890.00. **Description:** Learn how to: Leverage advanced features of Microsoft Excel to facilitate business decisions; Perform 'what-if' analysis for developing budget and project plans; Predict potential business developments using trend analysis; Consolidate and process multidimensional worksheets; Summarize and analyze large amounts of data using PivotTables and Excel features; Automate Excel processes and enhance worksheet models; Generate interactive Web-based worksheet models. **Dates and Locations:** Cities throughout the United States and Ottawa and Toronto, CN.

28076 ■ Predictive Maintenance and Condition Monitoring (Onsite)
American Trainco
9785 S Maroon Cir., Ste. 300
Englewood, CO 80112
Ph: (303)531-4560
Free: 877-978-7246
Fax: (303)531-4565
Co. E-mail: Sales@AmericanTrainco.com
URL: http://www.americantrainco.com
Price: $990.00. **Description:** Provides the fundamentals of PdM and condition monitoring applicable to plants, facilities, and manufacturing lines. **Dates and Locations:** Orange County, CA; Los Angeles, CA; Denver, CO; Hartford, CT; Orlando, FL; Baltimore, MD; Las Vegas, NV; and Norfolk, VA.

28077 ■ Preparing for the Project Management Professional PMP Exam (Onsite)
Seminar Information Service, Inc.
20 Executive Park, Ste. 120
Irvine, CA 92614
Ph: (949)261-9104
Free: 877-SEM-INFO
Fax: (949)261-1963
Co. E-mail: info@seminarinformation.com
URL: http://www.seminarinformation.com
Price: $3,190.00. **Description:** Learn how to: Prepare to pass the PMP(r) exam; Navigate the process groups and knowledge areas of the PMBOK(r) Guide 3rd Edition; Identify and map the inputs and outputs of the PMBOK(r) Guide processes; Align your project management knowledge with PMBOK(r) Guide terminology and definitions; Analyze PMBOK(r) Guide tools and techniques essential for PMP(r) exam success; Improve your exam-taking techniques through PMP(r)-style practice questions; Create a personal-

ized plan for self-study to focus your efforts after the course. **Dates and Locations:** Cities throughout the United States and Toronto and Ottawa, CN.

28078 ■ Programming Boot Camp (Onsite)

EEI Communications
66 Canal Center Plz., Ste. 200
Alexandria, VA 22314
Ph: (703)683-7453
Free: 888-253-2762
Fax: (703)683-7310
Co. E-mail: train@eeicom.com
URL: http://www.eeicom.com/training
Price: $745.00. **Description:** Covers basic concepts of scripting languages and tools, including JavaScript and Visual Basic. **Dates and Locations:** Silver Spring, MD; Alexandria, VA; Hunt Valley, MD; and Columbia, MD.

28079 ■ C Programming: Hands-On (Onsite)

Seminar Information Service, Inc.
20 Executive Park, Ste. 120
Irvine, CA 92614
Ph: (949)261-9104
Free: 877-SEM-INFO
Fax: (949)261-1963
Co. E-mail: info@seminarinformation.com
URL: http://www.seminarinformation.com
Price: $2,890.00. **Description:** Learn how to: Create, compile and run C programs using Visual Studio 2005; Write and understand C language constructs, syntax and classes; Leverage the architecture and namespaces of the .NET Framework library; Manage the Common Language Infrastructure (CLI) to integrate C with Visual Basic 2005 and C; Develop .NET components in C for desktop and distributed multi-tier applications. **Dates and Locations:** Toronto, CN; New York, NY; Los Angeles, CA; Alexandria, VA; Schaumburg, IL; Reston, VA; Ottawa, CN; and Atlanta, GA.

28080 ■ Programming Microsoft Access 2003: Hands-On - Building Database Applications with Access and VBA (Onsite)

Seminar Information Service, Inc.
20 Executive Park, Ste. 120
Irvine, CA 92614
Ph: (949)261-9104
Free: 877-SEM-INFO
Fax: (949)261-1963
Co. E-mail: info@seminarinformation.com
URL: http://www.seminarinformation.com
Price: $2,890.00. **Description:** Learn how to: Develop applications with Microsoft Access 2003 using Visual Basic for Applications (VBA); Identify and populate event properties to satisfy design specifications; Modify object properties and invoke object methods to customize applications; Create VBA statements using variables and built-in functions; Build loops and decision logic; Apply Data Access Objects (DAO) to incorporate business rules; Integrate Access with external applications through automation.

28081 ■ The Project Planning Workshop (Canada)

Canadian Management Centre (CMC)
150 York St., 5th Fl.
Toronto, ON, Canada M5H 3S5
Ph: (416)214-5678
Free: 877-262-2519
Fax: (416)313-4985
Co. E-mail: cmcinfo@cmctraining.org
URL: http://www.cmctraining.org
Contact: John Wright, President
Price: $1,995.00 Canadian for non-members; $1,845.00 Canadian for CMC members. **Description:** Two-day seminar covers the applicable tools, templates and proven practices to plan real life work projects. **Dates and Locations:** Toronto, ON.

28082 ■ Pump Repair & Maintenance (Onsite)

American Trainco
9785 S Maroon Cir., Ste. 300
Englewood, CO 80112
Ph: (303)531-4560
Free: 877-978-7246

Fax: (303)531-4565
Co. E-mail: Sales@AmericanTrainco.com
URL: http://www.americantrainco.com
Price: $990.00. **Description:** Learn common sense pump maintenance and repair techniques to keep facilities and equipment up and running. **Dates and Locations:** Cities throughout the United States.

28083 ■ Pumps & Pump Systems (Onsite)

Seminar Information Service, Inc.
20 Executive Park, Ste. 120
Irvine, CA 92614
Ph: (949)261-9104
Free: 877-SEM-INFO
Fax: (949)261-1963
Co. E-mail: info@seminarinformation.com
URL: http://www.seminarinformation.com
Price: $990.00. **Description:** Learn to identify the real problems causing pump failure, and how to avoid repeating those problems in the future. **Dates and Locations:** Cities throughout the United States.

28084 ■ Pumps & Pump Systems: Specification, Installation & Operation (Onsite)

American Trainco
9785 S Maroon Cir., Ste. 300
Englewood, CO 80112
Ph: (303)531-4560
Free: 877-978-7246
Fax: (303)531-4565
Co. E-mail: Sales@AmericanTrainco.com
URL: http://www.americantrainco.com
Price: $990.00. **Description:** From the pump and pump system, to the people who operate, maintain and design the pump system, this seminar will teach students how to identify the real problems causing pump failure, and how to avoid repeating those problems in the future. **Dates and Locations:** Cities throughout the United States.

28085 ■ QuarkXPress I

EEI Communications
8945 Guilford Rd., Ste. 145
Columbia, MD 21046
Ph: (410)309-8200
Free: 888-253-2762
Fax: (410)630-3980
Co. E-mail: train@eeicom.com
URL: http://www.eeicom.com/eei-training-services
Price: $745.00. **Description:** Covers basic desktop publishing skills including creating and saving documents, formatting text and paragraphs, and manipulating graphics. **Dates and Locations:** Alexandria, VA.

28086 ■ QuarkXPress II

EEI Communications
8945 Guilford Rd., Ste. 145
Columbia, MD 21046
Ph: (410)309-8200
Free: 888-253-2762
Fax: (410)630-3980
Co. E-mail: train@eeicom.com
URL: http://www.eeicom.com/eei-training-services
Price: $745.00. **Description:** Covers desktop publishing skills including paragraph and character style sheets, libraries, master pages, tracking and kerning, and processing colors. **Dates and Locations:** Silver Spring, MD; Alexandria, VA; Hunt Valley, MD; and Columbia, MD.

28087 ■ QuarkXPress III

EEI Communications
8945 Guilford Rd., Ste. 145
Columbia, MD 21046
Ph: (410)309-8200
Free: 888-253-2762
Fax: (703)630-3980
Co. E-mail: train@eeicom.com
URL: http://www.eeicom.com/eei-training-services
Price: $425.00. **Description:** Covers advanced desktop publishing skills including building table of contents and indexes, creating PostScript files, working with books, and synchronizing documents. **Dates and Locations:** Alexandria, VA.

28088 ■ Resume Writing (Onsite)

EEI Communications
8945 Guilford Rd., Ste. 145
Columbia, MD 21046
Ph: (410)309-8200
Free: 888-253-2762
Fax: (410)630-3980
Co. E-mail: train@eeicom.com
URL: http://www.eeicom.com/eei-training-services
Price: $425.00. **Description:** Learn to create an exceptional resume that helps you compete successfully for the job you want, as well as how to customize your resume and cover letter for each targeted employer in just a few strokes. **Dates and Locations:** Alexandria, VA.

28089 ■ Search Engine Optimization Training

EEI Communications
8945 Guilford Rd., Ste. 145
Columbia, MD 21046
Ph: (410)309-8200
Free: 888-253-2762
Fax: (410)630-3980
Co. E-mail: train@eeicom.com
URL: http://www.eeicom.com/eei-training-services
Price: $745.00. **Description:** Learn how to increase traffic to your Web site and get your products and services visible on the Web. **Dates and Locations:** Alexandria, VA.

28090 ■ Speed Reading with Evelyn Wood Reading Dynamics (Onsite)

Fred Pryor Seminars & CareerTrack
5700 Broadmoor St., Ste. 300
Mission, KS 66202
Free: 800-780-8476
Fax: (913)967-8849
Co. E-mail: customerservice@pryor.com
URL: http://www.pryor.com
Price: $99.00; $89.00 for groups of 5 or more. **Description:** Learn Evelyn Wood's basic concepts, how to increase your reading rate, note-taking, studying and listening skills and develop better memory, recall and comprehension. **Dates and Locations:** Cities throughout the United States.

28091 ■ Steam Systems Maintenance, Safety & Optimization (Onsite)

American Trainco
9785 S Maroon Cir., Ste. 300
Englewood, CO 80112
Ph: (303)531-4560
Free: 877-978-7246
Fax: (303)531-4565
Co. E-mail: Sales@AmericanTrainco.com
URL: http://www.americantrainco.com
Price: $990.00. **Description:** This course will teach you how to keep your steam system working efficiently and how to fix common problems and work safely reducing energy loss. **Dates and Locations:** Cities throughout the United States.

28092 ■ Style Summit (Onsite)

EEI Communications
8945 Guilford Rd., Ste. 145
Columbia, MD 21046
Ph: (410)309-8200
Free: 888-253-2762
Fax: (410)630-3980
Co. E-mail: train@eeicom.com
URL: http://www.eeicom.com/eei-training-services
Price: $797.00. **Description:** Covers simplifying the editorial process, including issues such as nouns used as verbs (E-mail me), e-jargon and acronyms, and informal usages that seem to break the rules (like vs. such as; more vs. over). **Dates and Locations:** Silver Spring, MD; and Alexandria, VA.

28093 ■ Technical Writing: A Comprehensive Hands-On Introduction (Onsite)

Seminar Information Service, Inc.
20 Executive Park, Ste. 120
Irvine, CA 92614
Ph: (949)261-9104
Free: 877-SEM-INFO

Fax: (949)261-1963
Co. E-mail: info@seminarinformation.com
URL: http://www.seminarinformation.com
Price: $2,890.00. **Description:** Learn how to: Write clear, effective technical = documents, including user manuals and technical reports; Assess your target audience and develop documents to meet their needs; Choose the appropriate writing style to communicate to specialized audiences; Build effective sentences, paragraphs and sections that explain information clearly; Employ diagrams, tables, charts and other graphical tools effectively; Create informative and interesting content that your readers will comprehend and utilize. **Dates and Locations:** Reston, VA; Toronto, CN; Ottawa, CN; Rockville, MD; New York, NY; and Alexandria, VA.

28094 ■ Troubleshooting Mechanical Drive Systems & Rotating Equipment (Onsite)
American Trainco
9785 S Maroon Cir., Ste. 300
Englewood, CO 80112
Ph: (303)531-4560
Free: 877-978-7246
Fax: (303)531-4565
Co. E-mail: Sales@AmericanTrainco.com
URL: http://www.americantrainco.com
Price: $990.00. **Description:** Provide a new perspective on troubleshooting mechanical and rotating equipment and learn about basic mechanical applications, failures, life expectancy and maintenance shafts, bearings, couplings, chains, sprockets, bushings, gears, belts, sheaves and other mechanical components. You'll learn what data to measure, track and trend so that when equipment fails you can get quick answers to what is wrong, as well as fix the real problems with your equipment and not just the symptoms. **Dates and Locations:** Cities throughout the United States.

28095 ■ Understanding & Troubleshooting Hydraulics (Onsite)
American Trainco
9785 S Maroon Cir., Ste. 300
Englewood, CO 80112
Ph: (303)531-4560
Free: 877-978-7246
Fax: (303)531-4565
Co. E-mail: Sales@AmericanTrainco.com
URL: http://www.americantrainco.com
Price: $990.00. **Description:** Provides the basic building blocks and information you need to become proficient in working with industrial hydraulics and fluid power, whether a small mobile unit or large industrial installation. **Dates and Locations:** Cities throughout the United States.

28096 ■ Uninterruptable Power Supply (UPS) Maintenance and Readiness (Onsite)
American Trainco
9785 S Maroon Cir., Ste. 300
Englewood, CO 80112
Ph: (303)531-4560
Free: 877-978-7246
Fax: (303)531-4565
Co. E-mail: Sales@AmericanTrainco.com
URL: http://www.americantrainco.com
Price: $495.00. **Description:** Seminar designed for personnel responsible for the UPS systems in industrial plants, public facilities, and commercial buildings. **Dates and Locations:** Sacramento, CA.

28097 ■ Variable Frequency Drives (Onsite)
American Trainco
9785 S Maroon Cir., Ste. 300
Englewood, CO 80112
Ph: (303)531-4560
Free: 877-978-7246
Fax: (303)531-4565
Co. E-mail: Sales@AmericanTrainco.com
URL: http://www.americantrainco.com
Price: $990.00. **Description:** Learn how to troubleshoot common VFD problems, take care of your own equipment, and avoid costly repairs or service repairs, including how to identify hazards associated with working on VFDs, an understanding of the importance of safe work practices, recognition of the

main components of a VFD system, and the different methods of controlling a VFD. **Dates and Locations:** Cities throughout the United States.

28098 ■ Visual Design I (Onsite)
EEI Communications
8945 Guilford Rd., Ste. 145
Columbia, MD 21046
Ph: (410)309-8200
Free: 888-253-2762
Fax: (410)630-3980
Co. E-mail: train@eeicom.com
URL: http://www.eeicom.com/eei-training-services
Price: $745.00. **Description:** Covers the history of type, typography's role in visual communication, structural line, space and kinetic lines, the elements of line, shape and space, and typography and type anatomy. **Dates and Locations:** Alexandria, VA.

28099 ■ Visual Design II (Onsite)
EEI Communications
8945 Guilford Rd., Ste. 145
Columbia, MD 21046
Ph: (410)309-8200
Free: 888-253-2762
Fax: (410)630-3980
Co. E-mail: train@eeicom.com
URL: http://www.eeicom.com/eei-training-services
Price: $745.00. **Description:** Covers the principles of texture and the diverse approaches to the element of value. Explore monochromatic, analogous and complementary combinations from Itten's color wheel. **Dates and Locations:** Alexandria, VA.

28100 ■ Visual Design III (Onsite)
EEI Communications
8945 Guilford Rd., Ste. 145
Columbia, MD 21046
Ph: (410)309-8200
Free: 888-253-2762
Fax: (410)630-3980
Co. E-mail: train@eeicom.com
URL: http://www.eeicom.com/eei-training-services
Price: $745.00. **Description:** Covers the compositional elements of line, plane, and form combined with neutral tones, and the Bauhaus and Constructivist theory as it relates to compositional tension and movement created by design. **Dates and Locations:** Alexandria, VA.

28101 ■ Visual Design IV (Onsite)
EEI Communications
8945 Guilford Rd., Ste. 145
Columbia, MD 21046
Ph: (410)309-8200
Free: 888-253-2762
Fax: (410)630-3980
Co. E-mail: train@eeicom.com
URL: http://www.eeicom.com/eei-training-services
Price: $745.00. **Description:** With focus on the works of Malevich and Escher as a foundation, learn the attributes of shape in positive and negative space, organic and geometric differences, metamorphosis, and symbolism. **Dates and Locations:** Alexandria, VA.

28102 ■ Water Treatment for Boilers, Chillers & Cooling Towers (Onsite)
American Trainco
9785 S Maroon Cir., Ste. 300
Englewood, CO 80112
Ph: (303)531-4560
Free: 877-978-7246
Fax: (303)531-4565
Co. E-mail: Sales@AmericanTrainco.com
URL: http://www.americantrainco.com
Price: $495.00. **Description:** One-day seminar to take the mystery out of creating, and stabilizing high water quality for your HVAC systems. **Dates and Locations:** Cities throughout the United States.

28103 ■ Windows Vista: A Hands-On Introduction (Onsite)
Seminar Information Service, Inc.
20 Executive Park, Ste. 120
Irvine, CA 92614
Ph: (949)261-9104
Free: 877-SEM-INFO

Fax: (949)261-1963
Co. E-mail: info@seminarinformation.com
URL: http://www.seminarinformation.com
Price: $2,890.00. **Description:** Learn how to: Install and maintain Windows Vista in a professional environment; Navigate and configure Windows Vista; Create and manage users and groups; Protect resources with rights, access control and encryption; Implement and troubleshoot network and Internet connectivity; Improve application compatibility to maximize user productivity. **Dates and Locations:** Cities throughout the United States; Ottawa, CN; and Toronto, CN.

28104 ■ The Women's Conference (Onsite)
Fred Pryor Seminars & CareerTrack
5700 Broadmoor St., Ste. 300
Mission, KS 66202
Ph: (800)780-8476
Free: 800-944-8503
Fax: (913)967-8849
Co. E-mail: customerservice@pryor.com
URL: http://www.careertrack.com
Price: $149.00; $139.00 for groups of 5 or more. **Description:** Covers the following topics: enhancing your career and professional development; expert communication skills just for women; and the women's professional toolbox. **Dates and Locations:** Cities throughout the United States.

28105 ■ Writing the Perfect Business E-Mail (Onsite)
EEI Communications
66 Canal Ctr. Plz., Ste. 200
Alexandria, VA 22314-5507
Ph: (703)683-7453
Free: 888-253-2762
Fax: (703)683-7310
Co. E-mail: train@eeicom.com
URL: http://www.eeicom.com/training
Price: $425.00. **Description:** Seminar that covers e-mails that get read and are understood, including keeping t short and simple, make it useful, spelling, grammar, and other problems, controlling emotion, writing attachments that get read, progress reports, instructions, and evaluations and recommendations. **Dates and Locations:** Silver Spring, MD; Alexandria, VA; Hunt Valley, MD; and Columbia, MD.

DIRECTORIES OF EDUCATIONAL PROGRAMS

28106 ■ *American Society Training and Development Buyer's Guide and Consultant Directory*
Pub: ASTD
Contact: Tony Bingham, President
E-mail: tbingham@astd.org
URL(s): www.astd.org. **Released:** Annual **Covers:** Over 580 suppliers and consultants in the training and development of employees. **Indexes:** Geographical and by subject.

REFERENCE WORKS

28107 ■ *"2007 Best Schools for Hispanics: Head of the Class" in Hispanic Business (September 2007, pp. 34, 36, 38)*
Pub: Hispanic Business
Ed: Hildy Medina. **Description:** Stanford's business school recruits Hispanic students through the Charles P. Bonini Partnership for Diversity Fellowship program. A listing of the top schools for business, engineering, law, and medicine for Hispanics are included.

28108 ■ *"The 2007 Black Book" in Hawaii Business (Vol. 53, December 2007, No. 6, pp. 43)*
Pub: Hawaii Business Publishing
Description: Brief biographies of 364 top executives in Hawaii are presented. Information on their educational achievement, membership in associations, hobbies, family present position and the company they work for are supplied.

28109 ■ "2010 Book of Lists" in Austin Business JournalInc. (Vol. 29, December 25, 2009, No. 42, pp. 1)
Pub: American City Business Journals
Description: Rankings of companies and organizations within the business services, finance, healthcare, hospitality and travel, insurance, marketing and media, professional services, real estate, education and technology industries in Austin, Texas are presented. Rankings are based on sales, business size, and other statistics.

28110 ■ "2010 Book of Lists" in Business Courier (Vol. 26, December 26, 2009, No. 36, pp. 1)
Pub: American City Business Journals, Inc.
Description: Rankings of companies and organizations within the business services, education, finance, health care, hospitality and tourism, real estate, and technology industries in the Cincinnati, Ohio-Northern Kentucky area are presented. Rankings are based on sales, business size, or other statistics.

28111 ■ "2010 Book of Lists" in Tampa Bay Business Journal (Vol. 30, December 22, 2009, No. 53, pp. 1)
Pub: American City Business Journals
Description: Rankings of companies and organizations within the human resources, banking and finance, business services, healthcare, real estate, technology, hospitality and travel, and education industries in the Greater Tampa Bay area are presented. Rankings are based on sales, business size, and more.

28112 ■ "ACC Game Development Program Opens" in Austin Business JournalInc. (Vol. 28, October 31, 2008, No. 33, pp. 1)
Pub: American City Business Journals
Ed: Sandra Zaragoza. **Description:** Austin, Texas-based Austin Community College has launched its Game Development Institute. The institute was created to meet the gaming industry's demand for skilled workers. One hundred students have enrolled with the institute.

28113 ■ "Active Duty" in Crain's Cleveland Business (Vol. 28, November 26, 2007, No. 47, pp. 3)
Pub: Crain Communications, Inc.
Ed: David Bennett. **Description:** Discusses the Veteran Workforce Training Program, sponsored by the Volunteers of America - Greater Ohio; the program is meant to provide employment training for military veterans and to assist them in transitioning back into the work force.

28114 ■ "Advantage Tutoring Center" in Bellingham Business Journal (Vol. February 2010, pp. 16)
Pub: Sound Publishing Inc.
Ed: Ashley Mitchell. **Description:** Profile of the newly opened Advantage Tutoring, owned by Mary and Peter Morrison. The center offers programs ranging from basic homework help to subject-specific enrichment.

28115 ■ Ahead of the Curve: Two Years at Harvard Business School
Pub: Penguin Group USA Inc.
Ed: Philip Delves Broughton. **Released:** 2009. **Price:** $25.95. **Description:** A behind-the-scenes glimpse at Harvard Business School is given. The author believes Harvard succeeds in transforming students into business leaders but feels they are failing them in every other way.

28116 ■ "All Fired Up!" in Small Business Opportunities (November 2008)
Pub: Entrepreneur Media Inc.
Ed: Stan Roberts. **Description:** Profile of Brixx Wood Fired Pizza, which has launched a franchising program due to the amount of interest the company's founders received over the years; franchisees do not need experience in the food industry or pizza restaurant service business in order to open a franchise of their own because all franchisees receive comprehensive training in which they are educated on all of the necessary tools to effectively run the business.

28117 ■ "The Americans Are Coming" in The Economist (Vol. 390, January 3, 2009, No. 8612, pp. 44)
Pub: The Economist Newspaper Inc.
Description: Student recruitment consultancies, which help place international students at universities in other countries and offer services such as interpreting or translating guidelines, are discussed; American universities who have shunned these agencies in the past; the result has been that America underperforms in relation to its size with a mere 3.5 percent of students on its campuses that are from abroad.

28118 ■ "Angels for the Jobless; Church Volunteer Groups Give Career Guidance" in Crain's Detroit Business (Vol. 24, March 31, 2008, No. 13)
Pub: Crain Communications, Inc.
Ed: Sherri Begin. **Description:** St. Andrew Catholic Church, located in Rochester, offers the St. Andrew Career Mentoring Ministry, a program that brings in professionals who volunteer to aid those seeking jobs or, in numerous cases, new careers.

28119 ■ "Applying to Colleges? Consultants Can Demystify the Process" in Palm Beach Post (September 3, 2011)
Pub: Palm Beach Post
Ed: Susan Salisbury. **Description:** More parents are turning to college consultants to help guide them through the process of applying to and choosing the right college or university. These specialized consultants assist with every detail for several years and students can reach them 24/7; costs can vary from several hundred dollars to $10,000 depending on services.

28120 ■ "Apprenticeship: Earn While You Learn" in Occupational Outlook Quarterly (Vol. 54, Fall 2010, No. 3, pp. 24)
Pub: U.S. Bureau of Labor Statistics
Description: Paid training, or apprenticeships, are examined. Registered apprenticeship programs conform to certain guidelines and industry-established training standards and may be run by businesses, trade or professional associations, or partnerships with business and unions.

28121 ■ "Aquatic Medications Engender Good Health" in Pet Product News (Vol. 64, November 2010, No. 11, pp. 47)
Pub: BowTie Inc.
Ed: Madelaine Heleine. **Description:** Pet supply manufacturers and retailers have been exerting consumer education and preparedness efforts to help aquarium hobbyists in tackling ornamental fish disease problems. Aquarium hobbyists have been also assisted in choosing products that facilitate aquarium maintenance before disease attacks their pet fish.

28122 ■ "Are There Material Benefits To Social Diversity?" in Hispanic Business (Vol. 30, September 2008, No. 9, pp. 10)
Pub: Hispanic Business, Inc.
Ed: Brigida Benitez. **Description:** Diversity in American colleges and universities, where students view and appreciate their peers as individuals and do not judge them on the basis of race, gender, or ethnicity is discussed. The benefits of diversity in higher education are also acknowledged by the U.S. Supreme Court and by leading American corporations.

28123 ■ "Artexpo Celebrates 30th Anniversary" in Art Business News (Vol. 34, November 2007, No. 11, pp. 18)
Pub: Pfingsten Publishing, LLC
Description: In honor of its 30th anniversary Artexpo New York 2008 will be an unforgettable show offering a collection of fine-art education courses for both trade and consumer attendees and featuring a variety of artists working in all mediums.

28124 ■ "Asterand Eyes Jump to Ann Arbor; TechTown Tenant" in Crain's Detroit Business (Vol. 25, June 22, 2009)
Pub: Crain Communications Inc. - Detroit
Ed: Tom Henderson. **Description:** Asterand PLC is considering a move to Ann Arbor from its current location as anchor tenant at TechTown, an incubator and

technology park associated with Wayne State University. The university believes the Ann Arbor location's rent is too expensive for the tissue bank company.

28125 ■ "ASU Explores Russian Partnership" in The Business Journal - Serving Phoenix and the Valley of the Sun (Vol. 28, September 5, 2008)
Pub: American City Business Journals, Inc.
Ed: Mike Sunnucks. **Description:** Arizona State University is planning to partner with Russia-based St. Petersburg State University (SPSU) regarding research, faculty and student exchange, and other joint efforts. SPSU is one of Russia's leading scientific and research institutions. Arizona State's partnerships with other foreign colleges are also mentioned.

28126 ■ "At This Bakery, Interns' Hope Rises Along With the Bread" in Chicago Tribune (October 31, 2008)
Pub: McClatchy-Tribune Information Services
Ed: Mary Schmich. **Description:** Profile of Sweet Miss Givings Bakery and its diverse founder, interns and employees; the bakery was founded by Stan Sloan, an Episcopal priest who started the business to help fund his ministry; Sloan saw a need for jobs for those living with HIV and other disabilities and through the bakery the interns learn the skills needed to eventually find work elsewhere.

28127 ■ "ATI Now Ready to Pounce on Biotech" in Austin Business JournalInc. (Vol. 28, August 22, 2008, No. 23, pp. 1)
Pub: American City Business Journals
Ed: Laura Hipp. **Description:** Austin Technology Incubator has entered the biotechnology sector through a program of the University of Texas incubator. The company's bioscience program was set off by a grant from the City of Austin worth $125,000. The growth of Austin's biotechnology sector is examined.

28128 ■ "The Balancing Act: How Busy Executives Make Their Lives Work" in Black Enterprise (Vol. 37, February 2007, No. 7, pp. 118)
Pub: Earl G. Graves Publishing Co. Inc.
Ed: Marcia A. Reed-Woodard. **Description:** More than 70 percent of women with children work outside the home, according to a 2005 survey conducted by the U.S. Department of Labor Bureau. One of the biggest struggles these women face is balancing family with career aspirations and climbing the corporate ranks.

28129 ■ "Banks Deposit Reassurance, Calm Customers" in The Business Journal-Serving Greater Tampa Bay (Vol. 28, August 22, 2008)
Pub: American City Business Journals, Inc.
Ed: Margie Manning. **Description:** Community banks in the Tampa Bay Area are training tellers and other customer care workers to help reassure customers that their deposits are safe. Other measures to reassure depositors include joining a network that allows banks to share deposits. Additional information on moves community banks are making to reassure consumers is presented.

28130 ■ Barron's Guide to Graduate Business Schools
Pub: Barron's Educational Series Inc.
Contact: Alex Holtz, President
E-mail: aholtz@berronseduc.com

URL(s): barronseduc.stores.yahoo.net/0764137581.html. **Released:** Biennial; latest edition 15th; published August, 2007. **Price:** $18.99, Individuals paperback; list price; $17.09, Individuals web price. **Covers:** More than 600 colleges offering graduate business degrees, including Master of Business Administration. **Entries include:** Institution name, address, phone, fax, e-mail, website, enrollment, description of graduate program, admission requirements, availability of financial aid, library and computer facilities, placement programs. Includes information on applications, selection of school, tests, etc. **Arrangement:** Geographical. **Indexes:** Institution name.

28131 ■ *"BC Forest Safety Council Unveils Supervisor Course to Respond to Industry Demands"* in *Canadian Corporate News (May 14, 2007)*
Pub: Comtex News Network Inc.
Description: BC Forest Safety Council launched the sector's first supervisor training program that will lead to certification of forest supervisors in response to an industry-wide demand for standardized safety training for supervisors.

28132 ■ *"The Bell Tolls for Thee"* in *Canadian Business (Vol. 81, March 3, 2008, No. 3, pp. 36)*
Pub: Rogers Media
Ed: Andrew Wahl. **Description:** Bell Canada has formed the Canadian Coalition for Tomorrow's IT Skills to solve the shortage of technology talent in the country. Canada's total workforce has only around 4%, or 600,000 people employed in information technology-related fields. The aims of the Bell-led coalition, which is supported by different industry associations and 30 corporations, are investigated.

28133 ■ *"Best Foot Forward"* in *Canadian Business (Vol. 80, October 22, 2007, No. 21, pp. 115)*
Pub: Rogers Media
Ed: Jeremy Shinewald. **Description:** Jeremy Shinewald's mbaMission admissions consulting business helps prospective MBA students with essay writing, mock interview preparation and school selection. The consulting fee for application to one school is $2,250. Details of the business schools' MBA programs and tuition fees are explored.

28134 ■ *"Better Card Collecting"* in *Canadian Business (Vol. 80, January 15, 2007, No. 2, pp. 66)*
Pub: Rogers Media
Ed: Sarah B. Hood. **Description:** Tips on how to collect business cards and use them for enhancing one's business performance are presented. Targeting specific people, taking notes and giving follow ups are some suggestions.

28135 ■ *"The BIG Picture"* in *Crain's Cleveland Business (Vol. 30, June 22, 2009, No. 24, pp. 12)*
Pub: Crain Communications, Inc.
Ed: Arielle Kass. **Description:** Entrepreneurs are quick to praise their colleges and universities and attribute both personal and business success to them.

28136 ■ *"Biggest UM Landlords"* in *Crain's Detroit Business (Vol. 25, June 15, 2009, No. 24, pp. 1)*
Pub: Crain Communications Inc. - Detroit
Description: University of Michigan will purchase the two million-square-foot Pfizer campus in June 2009. The university is the largest occupier of commercial real estate off campus in and around Ann Arbor, Michigan.

28137 ■ *"Biz U: Cool for School"* in *Entrepreneur (Vol. 35, October 2007, No. 10, pp. 144)*
Pub: Entrepreneur Media Inc.
Ed: Nichole L. Torres. **Description:** Forming a high technology business while still in college has its advantages such as having information resources nearby and having students from various fields to ask for help and advice. School business competitions are also helpful in building networks with investors. Ways that the college environment can be useful to aspiring entrepreneurs, particularly to those who are into high technology business, are discussed.

28138 ■ *"Bold Goals Will Require Time"* in *Contractor (Vol. 56, October 2009, No. 10, pp. S2)*
Pub: Penton Media, Inc.
Ed: Ted Lower. **Description:** Offering a broad range of courses is the Radiant Panel Association (RPA), an organization that holds education as its top priority. The RPA must lead the industry by raising the educational bar for future installers.

28139 ■ *"Bond Hill Cinema Site To See New Life"* in *Business Courier (Vol. 27, October 29, 2010, No. 26, pp. 1)*
Pub: Business Courier
Ed: Dan Monk. **Description:** Avondale, Ohio's Corinthian Baptist Church will redevelop the 30-acre former Showcase Cinema property to a mixed-use site that could feature a college, senior home, and retail. Corinthian Baptist, which is one of the largest African-American churches in the region, is also planning to relocate the church.

28140 ■ *"Book Smart"* in *Hawaii Business (Vol. 53, December 2007, No. 6, pp. 39)*
Pub: Hawaii Business Publishing
Ed: David K. Choo. **Description:** Different parts of a biography entry in the Black Book are examined in relation to their usage in starting a conversation with an executive. The second part, which is the educational background, is considered the most significant of all, due to the amount of information given. The importance of making connections in Hawaii is discussed.

28141 ■ *"Boosting Corporate Entrepreneurship Through HRM Practices"* in *Human Resource Management (Vol. 49, July-August 2010, No. 4)*
Pub: John Wiley
Ed: Ralf Schmelter, Rene Mauer, Christiane Borsch, Malte Brettel. **Description:** A study was conducted to determine which human resource management (HRM) practices promote corporate entrepreneurship (CE) in small and medium-sized enterprises (SMEs). Findings indicate that staff selection, staff development, training, and staff rewards on CE have a strong impact on SMEs.

28142 ■ *"Brad Wall"* in *Canadian Business (Vol. 82, April 27, 2009, No. 7, pp. 9)*
Pub: Rogers Media
Ed: Joe Castaldo. **Description:** Saskatchewan Premier Brad Wall believes that the mood in the province is positive, as its economy is one of the few that is expected to post growth in 2009. Wall actively promotes the province in job fairs, offering $20,000 in tuition for recent college and university graduates that relocate in the province for seven years. Wall's views on the province's economy and challenges are presented.

28143 ■ *"Bridging the Academic-Practitioner Divide in Marketing Decision Models"* in *Journal of Marketing (Vol. 75, July 2011, No. 4, pp. 196)*
Pub: American Marketing Association
Ed: Gary L. Lilien. **Description:** A study to determine the reason for the relatively low level of practical use of the many marketing models is presented. Changing the incentive and reward systems for marketing academics, practitioners, and intermediaries can bring about adoption and implementation improvements. Those changes could be beneficial by bridging the academic-practitioner divide.

28144 ■ *"Bridging the Talent Gap Through Partnership and Innovation"* in *Canadian Business (Vol. 81, October 27, 2008, No. 18, pp. 88)*
Pub: Rogers Media Ltd.
Description: Research revealed that North America is short by more than 60,000 qualified networking professionals. Businesses, educators and communities are collaborating in order to address the shortfall.

28145 ■ *"Budget Woes Endanger E-Prep Progress"* in *Crain's Cleveland Business (Vol. 30, June 22, 2009, No. 24, pp. 6)*
Pub: Crain Communications, Inc.
Ed: Brian Tucker. **Description:** The future of the Entrepreneurship Preparatory School located in Cleveland is being threatened by State budget concerns. The charter school requires all students to wear uniforms, respect discipline, and attend for longer hours and more weeks.

28146 ■ *Business Black Belt: Develop the Strength, Flexibility and Agility to Run Your Company*
Pub: Career Press, Inc.
Ed: Burke Franklin. **Released:** November 1, 2010. **Price:** $15.99. **Description:** Manual offering insights

that will enable anyone to become successful in small business. Seventy short chapters included topics such as attitude, management, marketing, selling, employees, money, MBAs, lawyers, consultants, and investors.

28147 ■ *"Business Plan Refines Focus"* in *Business Journal Portland (Vol. 27, December 10, 2010, No. 41, pp. 1)*
Pub: Portland Business Journal
Ed: Wendy Culverwell. **Description:** Organizers of the Oregon Business Plan's Leadership Summit 2010 seek the opinions of nearly 1,000 business, education, political, and civic leaders in an effort to address how to rehabilitate Oregon's economy. The opinion-seeking actions recognize the organizers' belief that the economic fate of the state depends on rural Oregon.

28148 ■ *The Campus CEO: The Student Entrepreneur's Guide to Launching a Multi-Million Dollar Business*
Pub: Kaplan Books
Ed: Randal Pinkett. **Released:** February 2007. **Price:** $21.00 (CND). **Description:** Tips for generating income, while attending college is presented to students.

28149 ■ *"Canada Tomorrow"* in *Canadian Business (Vol. 80, October 8, 2007, No. 20, pp. 14)*
Pub: Rogers Media
Ed: Donald J. Johnston. **Description:** An assessment of Canada's future in terms of its educational, social and economic environment is presented. Concerns regarding the country's educational system such as the declining interest in science and technology and the possible lack of teachers in the future are discussed. In terms of its social and economic aspects, the need to support entrepreneurs and other qualified people is explained.

28150 ■ *"Canadian Research Generates Innovation and Prosperity"* in *Canadian Business (Vol. 81, October 27, 2008, No. 18, pp. 87)*
Pub: Rogers Media Ltd.
Description: Universities play a key role in helping Canadians achieve prosperity, competitiveness, and quality of life by conducting more than a third of Canada's research. Research in universities help train graduates to apply sophisticated knowledge to real problems.

28151 ■ *"Cancer-Fighting Entrepreneurs"* in *Austin Business Journal (Vol. 31, August 5, 2011, No. 22, pp. 1)*
Pub: American City Business Journals Inc.
Ed: Sandra Zaragoza. **Description:** Cancer Prevention and Research Institute of Texas has invested $10 million in recruiting known faculty to the University of Texas. The move is seen to bolster Austin's position as a major cancer research market. The institute has awarded grants to researchers Jonghwan Kim, Guangbin Dong and Kyle Miller.

28152 ■ *"A Capitol Opportunity"* in *Hispanic Business (Vol. 30, September 2008, No. 9, pp. 82)*
Pub: Hispanic Business, Inc.
Ed: John Schumacher. **Description:** Launched in 2003, the Polanco fellows program is named after former state Senator Richard Polanco, a founder and chairman of the California Latino Caucus Institute. The program offers young Hispanics a chance to experience public policy and the functioning of the California Capitol through a 12-month, on-the-job Capitol training.

28153 ■ *"Casinos See College as Job Jackpot"* in *The Business Journal-Serving Metropolitan Kansas City (Vol. 26, August 1, 2008, No. 47)*
Pub: American City Business Journals, Inc.
Ed: Suzanna Stagemeyer. **Description:** Wyandotte County casino managers revealed plans to develop partnerships with Kansas City Kansas Community College. The planned partnership is expected to include curriculum development and degree programs

that would help train employees for the planned casinos. Other views and information on the project are presented.

28154 ■ *"CBC Chief: Future is Now" in Business Courier (Vol. 27, August 13, 2010, No. 15, pp. 1)*
Pub: Business Courier
Ed: Lucy May. **Description:** Tom Williams, chairman of the Cincinnati Business Committee (CBC), maintains that politicians and business leaders must cooperate to ensure the competitiveness of the city for the 21st Century. Under Williams' leadership, the CBC has put emphasis on initiatives related to government efficiency, economic development, and public education. Williams' views on a proposed inland port are given.

28155 ■ *"CBC and Chrysler Strike Deal" in Black Enterprise (Vol. 37, December 2006, No. 5, pp. 36)*
Pub: Earl G. Graves Publishing Co. Inc.
Ed: Kiara Ashanti. **Description:** Congressional Black Foundation and Chrysler Financial have partnered to provide financial education to students at historically black colleges and universities. The prime objective of the program is to reduce the number of college students that graduate with poor credit scores and high debt.

28156 ■ *"The China Connection" in Crain's Chicago Business (Vol. 31, March 24, 2008, No. 12, pp. 26)*
Pub: Crain Communications, Inc.
Ed: Samantha Stainburn. **Description:** Interview with Ben Munoz who studied abroad in Beijing, China for three months to study international economics, e-commerce and global leadership.

28157 ■ *"A Class Act" in Hawaii Business (Vol. 53, March 2008, No. 9, pp. 25)*
Pub: Hawaii Business Publishing
Ed: Cathy S. Cruz-George. **Description:** UBoost is a startup company that offers online content for the educational magazine 'Weekly Reader'. The website features quizzes and allows users to accumulate points and redeem rewards afterward. Other details about the company are discussed.

28158 ■ *"Class Management" in Canadian Business (Vol. 80, April 23, 2007, No. 9, pp. 64)*
Pub: Rogers Media
Ed: Erin Pooley. **Description:** The role of executive MBA programs in improving performance of employees is presented.

28159 ■ *"College Opens On St. Luke's Site" in The Business Journal - Serving Phoenix and the Valley of the Sun (Vol. 28, September 5, 2008)*
Pub: American City Business Journals, Inc.
Ed: Angela Gonzales. **Description:** Fortis College is planning to offer classes in Phoenix, Arizona. It has made its home at the St. Luke's Medical Center. Courses to be offered by the college are also provided.

28160 ■ *"The Colt Effect" in Hawaii Business (Vol. 53, January 2008, No. 7, pp. 30)*
Pub: Hawaii Business Publishing
Ed: David K. Choo. **Description:** Participation at the Bowl Championship Games can help the University of Hawaii financially. Playing at a prominent sports event could provoke donations from alumni and increase enrollment at the university. Examples of universities that earned generous income by becoming a part of prestigious sporting events are presented.

28161 ■ *"Companies Urged to Take Steps to Replenish Work Force" in Crain's Cleveland Business (Vol. 28, October 29, 2007, No. 43, pp. 9)*
Pub: Crain Communications, Inc.
Ed: Mike Verespej. **Description:** If America wants to stay competitive in the global marketplace, experts say that the education system will need serious improvements. According to Thomas J. Donahue,

president and CEO of the U.S. Chamber of Commerce, one-third of the K-through-12 students in the United States don't graduate from high school.

28162 ■ *"The Competitive Imperative Of Learning" in Harvard Business Review (Vol. 86, July-August 2008, No. 8, pp. 60)*
Pub: Harvard Business School Press
Ed: Amy C. Edmondson. **Description:** Experimentation and reflection are important components for maintaining success in the business world and are the kind of character traits that can help one keep his or her competitive edge.

28163 ■ *"Contractors Debate Maximizing Green Opportunities, Education" in Contractor (Vol. 56, November 2009, No. 11, pp. 3)*
Pub: Penton Media, Inc.
Ed: Robert P. Mader. **Description:** Attendees at the Mechanical Service Contractors Association convention were urged to get involved with their local U.S. Green Building Council chapter by one presenter. Another presenter says that one green opportunity for contractors is the commissioning of new buildings.

28164 ■ *"Convention Calendar" in Black Enterprise (Vol. 37, December 2006, No. 5, pp. 74)*
Pub: Earl G. Graves Publishing Co. Inc.
Description: Listing of conferences and summits targeting African American business owners and executives.

28165 ■ *"Convention Calendar" in Black Enterprise (Vol. 37, November 2006, No. 4, pp. 76)*
Pub: Earl G. Graves Publishing Co. Inc.
Description: Listing of conferences targeted at African American executives and business owners.

28166 ■ *"Conversation: Historian Geoffrey Jones On Why Knowledge Stays Put" in Harvard Business Review (Vol. 86, July-August 2008, No. 8)*
Pub: Harvard Business School Press
Ed: Gardiner Morse. **Description:** Geoffrey Jones, Harvard Business School's professor of business history, discusses factors that cause knowledge to concentrate in particular regions, rather than disperse, such as the location of wealth.

28167 ■ *"Could UNCC Be Home to Future Med School Here?" in Charlotte Business Journal (Vol. 25, July 23, 2010, No. 18, pp. 1)*
Pub: Charlotte Business Journal
Ed: Jennifer Thomas. **Description:** University of North Carolina, Charlotte chancellor Phil Dubois is proposing that a medical school be established at the campus. The idea began in 2007 and Dubois' plan is for students to spend all four years in Charlotte and train at the Carolinas Medical Center.

28168 ■ *"David Saunders Q&A" in Canadian Business (Vol. 80, October 22, 2007, No. 21, pp. 11)*
Pub: Rogers Media
Ed: Erin Pooley. **Description:** David Saunders, chairman of the Federation of Business School Deans, talks about the changes in business education in Canada. He stresses that a master's degree in business administration is vital and a good investment that would reap rewards in a business career.

28169 ■ *"Day Care for Affluent Drawing a Crowd" in Business First Columbus (Vol. 24, August 15, 2008, No. 52, pp. 1)*
Pub: American City Business Journals
Ed: Carrie Ghose. **Description:** Day care centers for affluent families have grown in popularity in Columbus, Ohio. Primrose Schools Franchising Company has opened three such schools in the area. Statistical data included.

28170 ■ *"Day-Care Center Owner to Argue Against Liquor Store Opening Nearby" in*

Chicago Tribune (March 13, 2008)
Pub: McClatchy-Tribune Information Services
Ed: Matthew Walberg. **Description:** NDLC's owner feels that Greenwood Liquors should not be granted its liquor license due to the claim that the NDLC is not only a day-care center but also a school that employs state-certified teachers.

28171 ■ *"Deal Made for Pontiac Home of Film Studio" in Crain's Detroit Business (Vol. 25, June 1, 2009, No. 22, pp. 3)*
Pub: Crain Communications Inc. - Detroit
Ed: Daniel Duggan. **Description:** Details of the $75 million movie production and training facility in Pontiac, Michigan are revealed.

28172 ■ *"Deep Thoughts: Getting Employees to Think Better Requires a Bit of Creative Thinking Itself" in Canadian Business (March 17, 2008)*
Pub: Rogers Media
Ed: Lauren McKeon. **Description:** Discusses the reason a company needs to make their employees understand that ideas are the stuff of life. For employees to be more creative, they need to cultivate spark moments, play with possibilities, and venture into the unknown.

28173 ■ *"Defensive Training" in Crain's Detroit Business (Vol. 24, September 22, 2008, No. 38, pp. 11)*
Pub: Crain Communications Inc.
Ed: Robert Ankeny. **Description:** Rising retaliation claims in regards to discrimination complaints are creating an atmosphere in which managers must learn how to avoid or deal with these lawsuits as well as the retaliation that often follows. Examples of cases are given as well as advice for dealing with such problems that may arise in the workplace.

28174 ■ *"DePaul To Train Hotel Leaders" in Chicago Tribune (September 22, 2008)*
Pub: McClatchy-Tribune Information Services
Ed: Kathy Bergen. **Description:** With help from a $7.5 million grant from the Conrad N. Hilton Foundation, DePaul University will dramatically expand its role as a training ground for the tourism-industry with the opening of a School of Hospitality.

28175 ■ *"Design program in Athletic Footwear" in Occupational Outlook Quarterly (Vol. 55, Fall 2011, No. 3, pp. 21)*
Pub: U.S. Bureau of Labor Statistics
Description: The Fashion Institute of Technology offers the only certificate program in performance athletic footwear design in the U.S. The program focuses on conceptualizing and sketching shoe designs and covers ergonomic, anatomical, and material considerations for athletic footwear design.

28176 ■ *"Developers Vie for UWM Dorm" in The Business Journal-Milwaukee (Vol. 25, July 11, 2008, No. 42, pp. A1)*
Pub: American City Business Journals, Inc.
Ed: Rich Kirchen. **Description:** Eight developers are competing to build a 500- to 700-student residence hall for the University of Wisconsin-Milwaukee. The residence hall will probably be developed within two miles of the main campus. It was revealed that the university's real estate foundation will select the successful bidder on July 25, 2008, and construction will begin by January 2009.

28177 ■ *"Dick Haskayne" in Canadian Business (Vol. 81, March 31, 2008, No. 5, pp. 72)*
Pub: Rogers Media
Ed: Andy Holloway. **Description:** Dick Haskayne says that he learned a lot about business from his dad who ran a butcher shop where they had to make a decision on buying cattle and getting credit. Haskayne says that family, friends, finances, career, health, and infrastructure are benchmarks that have to be balanced.

28178 ■ *"Dr. Mark Holder" in Crain's Cleveland Business (Vol. 30, June 29, 2009,*

No. 25, pp. 14)
Pub: Communications, Inc.

Ed: Kathy Ames Carr. **Description:** Dr. Mark Holder is the director of the financial engineering program at Kent State University. Dr. Holder discusses his role to help teach his students how to market themselves for finance jobs in a down economy.

28179 ■ *"Don't Shoot the Messenger: A Wake-Up Call For Academics" in Academy of Management Journal (Vol. 50, No. 5, October 2007, pp. 1020)*
Pub: Academy of Management
Contact: Ming-Jer Chen, President

Ed: David E. Guest. **Description:** Author evaluates two well-known publications: HR Magazine and People Management, to emphasize the role of U.S. academics in communicating management practice.

28180 ■ *"Downtowns Must Court Young, CEOs for Cities President Says" in Crain's Detroit Business (Vol. 24, October 6, 2008, No. 40, pp. 18)*
Pub: Crain Communications, Inc.

Ed: Amy Lane. **Description:** It is important to produce more college graduates, and keep them in Michigan, according to CEOs for Cities President Carol Coletta when she spoke to a session at the West Michigan Regional Policy Conference which was held in September in Grand Rapids. Ways in which city leaders can connect students to communities, resulting in employees who have vested interest in the region, are also discussed.

28181 ■ *"Dozens 'Come Alive' in Downtown Chicago" in Green Industry Pro (July 2011)*
Pub: Cygnus Business Media

Ed: Gregg Wartgow. **Description:** Highlights from the Come Alive Outside training event held in Chicago, Illinois July 14-15, 2011 are shared. Nearly 80 people representing 38 landscape companies attended the event that helps contractors review their services and find ways to sell them in new and various ways.

28182 ■ *"The Early Bird Gets the Worm" in Black Enterprise (Vol. 37, January 2007, No. 6, pp. 111)*
Pub: Earl G. Graves Publishing Co. Inc.

Ed: Tykisha N. Lundy. **Description:** General Motors hosts the Black Enterprise Conference And Expo: Where Deals Are Made at Walt Disney World's Swan and Dolphin Resort, May 9-12. The conference will offer great information to entrepreneurs.

28183 ■ *"East Coast Solar" in Contractor (Vol. 57, February 2010, No. 2, pp. 17)*
Pub: Penton Media, Inc.

Ed: Dave Yates. **Description:** U.S. Department of Energy's Solar Decathlon lets 20 college student-led teams from around the world compete to cesign and build a solar-powered home. A mechanical contractor discusses his work as an advisor during the competition.

28184 ■ *"An Educated Play on China" in Barron's (Vol. 88, June 30, 2008, No. 26, pp. M6)*
Pub: Dow Jones & Co., Inc.

Ed: Mohammed Hadi. **Description:** New Oriental Education & Technology Group sells English-language courses to an increasingly competitive Chinese workforce that values education. The shares in this company have been weighed down by worries on the impact of the Beijing Olympics on enrollment and the Sichuan earthquake. These shares could be a great way to get exposure to the long-term growth in China.

28185 ■ *"EMU, Spark Plan Business Incubator for Ypsilanti" in Crain's Detroit Business (Vol. 23, October 15, 2007, No. 42, pp. 3)*
Pub: Crain Communications Inc. - Detroit

Ed: Chad Halcom. **Description:** Eastern Michigan University is seeking federal grants and other funding for a new business incubator program that would be in cooperation with Ann Arbor Spark. The site would

become a part of a network of three Spark incubator programs with a focus on innovation in biotechnology and pharmaceuticals.

28186 ■ *"Encouraging Study in Critical Languages" in Occupational Outlook Quarterly (Vol. 55, Summer 2011, No. 2, pp. 23)*
Pub: U.S. Bureau of Labor Statistics

Description: Proficiency in particular foreign languages is vital to the defense, diplomacy, and security of the United States. Several federal programs provide scholarships and other funding to encourage high school and college students to learn languages of the Middle East, China, and Russia.

28187 ■ *"Endowments for Colleges Hit Hard in '09" in Milwaukee Business Journal (Vol. 27, February 12, 2010, No. 20, pp. A1)*
Pub: American City Business Journals

Ed: Corrinne Hess. **Description:** Southeast Wisconsin college endowments declined by as much as 35 percent in 2009 due to the economic downturn. A list of 2009 endowments to colleges in southeast Wisconsin and their percent change from 2008 is presented.

28188 ■ *"Enlightened Leadership: Best Practice Guidelines and Time Tools for Easily Implementing Learning Organizations*
Pub: Learning House Publishing, Inc.

Ed: Ralph LoVuolo; Alan G. Thomas. **Released:** May 2006. **Price:** $79.99. **Description:** Innovation and creativity are essential for any successful small business. The book provides owners, managers, anc team leaders with the tools necessary to produce 'disciplined innovation'.

28189 ■ *"Enlightened Leadership: Best Practice Guidelines and Timesaving Tools for Easily Implementing Learning Organizations*
Pub: Learning House Publishing, Incorporated

Ed: Alan G. Thomas; Ralph L. LoVuolo; Jeanne C. Hillson. **Released:** September 2006, printable 3 times/year. **Price:** $21.00. **Description:** Book provides the tools required to create a learning organization management model along with a step-by-step guide for team planning and learning. The strategy works as a manager's self-help guide as well as offering continuous learning and improvement for company-wide success.

28190 ■ *"Essentially Organic Vending Takes Healthy Snacks to Ohio High School" in Entertainment Close-Up (September 13, 2011)*
Pub: Close-Up Media

Description: Essentially Organic Vending is offering students a healthy alternative for their snacking. The vending machines will be stocked with nutritious energy options.

28191 ■ *"Etextbook Space Heats Up" in Information Today (Vol. 28, November 2011, No. 10, pp. 10)*
Pub: Information Today, Inc.

Ed: Paula J. Hane. **Description:** The use of etextbooks is expected to grow with the use of mobile devices and tablets. A new group of activists is asking students, faculty members and others to sign a petition urging higher education leaders to prioritize affordable textbooks or free ebooks over the traditional, expensive new books required for classes.

28192 ■ *"Etextbooks: Coming of Age" in Information Today (Vol. 28, September 2011, No. 8, pp. 1)*
Pub: Information Today, Inc.

Ed: Amanda Mulvihill. **Description:** National average for textbooks costs was estimated at $1,137 annually at a 4-year public college for the 2010-2011 school year. Amazon reported selling 105 etextbooks for every 100 print books, while Barnes and Noble announced that their etextbooks were outselling print 3 to 1.

28193 ■ *"EVMS Gets Grant to Train Providers for Elder Care" in Virginian-Pilot (October 29, 2010)*
Pub: Virginian-Pilot

Ed: Elizabeth Simpson. **Description:** Eastern Virginia Medical School received a federal grant to train health providers in elder care. Details of the program are provided.

28194 ■ *"Executive Training" in Black Enterprise (Vol. 37, December 2006, No. 5, pp. 70)*
Pub: Earl G. Graves Publishing Co. Inc.

Ed: Marcia A. Reed-Woodard. **Description:** Roy N. Gundy, Jr. was preparing to introduce a new strategic plan within his division and understood that his plan may fail if not executed properly. He discusses his experience in the Wharton School's executive education workshop Implementing Strategy, at the University of Pennsylvania and gives tips on putting strategy into action.

28195 ■ *"Experts Strive to Educate on Proper Pet Diets" in Pet Product News (Vol. 64, November 2010, No. 11, pp. 40)*
Pub: BowTie Inc.

Ed: John Hustace Walker. **Description:** Pet supply manufacturers have been bundling small mammal food and treats with educational sources to help retailers avoid customer misinformation. This action has been motivated by the customer's quest to seek proper nutritional advice for their small mammal pets.

28196 ■ *"Export Initiative Launched" in Philadelphia Business Journal (Vol. 28, December 11, 2009, No. 43, pp. 1)*
Pub: American City Business Journals

Ed: Athena D. Merritt. **Description:** The first initiative that came out of the partnership between the Export-Import Bank of the US, the city of Philadelphia, and the World Trade Center of Greater Philadelphia is presented. A series of export finance workshops have featured Ex-Im Bank resources that can provide Philadelphia businesses with working capital, insurance protection and buyer financing.

28197 ■ *"Facilitating and Rewarding Creativity During New Product Development" in Journal of Marketing (Vol. 75, July 2011, No. 4, pp. 53)*
Pub: American Marketing Association

Ed: James E. Burroughs, Darren W. Dahl, C. Page Moreau, Amitava Chattopadhay, Gerald J. Gorn. **Description:** A study to determine the effects of rewards to creativity in the process of new product development is presented. The findings show that the effect of rewards can be made positive if combined with appropriate creativity training.

28198 ■ *"Feds to Pay University $20M" in Business Courier (Vol. 27, July 23, 2010, No. 12, pp. 3)*
Pub: Business Courier

Ed: James Ritchie. **Description:** The U.S. government is set to pay University Hospital and medical residents who trained there $20 million as part of a tax dispute settlement. Around 1,000 former residents are to receive tax refunds. But the hospital must provide the U.S. Internal Revenue Service with extensive documentation.

28199 ■ *"Fighting the Good Fight" in Inc. (Vol. 33, October 2011, No. 8, pp. 8)*
Pub: Inc. Magazine

Ed: Eric Markowitz. **Description:** Rob Roy, former Navy SEAL, runs SOT-G a firm that offers an 80-hour leadership training course inspired by military combat preparations. Details of the program are outlined.

28200 ■ *"Finding Life Behind the Numbers" in Crain's Chicago Business (Vol. 31, March 24, 2008, No. 12, pp. 25)*
Pub: Crain Communications, Inc.

Ed: Samantha Stainburn. **Description:** Interview with Phillip Capodice who is a graduate student at DePaul University's Kellstadt Graduate School of Business and studied abroad in Lima, Peru where he visited a number of companies including some who are trade partners with the United States.

28201 ■ *"Finishing High School Leads to Better Employment Prospects" in Occupational Outlook Quarterly (Vol. 55, Summer 2011, No. 2, pp. 36)*
Pub: U.S. Bureau of Labor Statistics

Description: Students who drop out of high school are more likely to face unemployment than those who finish. Statistical data included.

28202 ■ *"Fitness: Dispelling Rocky Mountain Myths Key to Wellness"* in *Employee Benefit News (Vol. 25, November 1, 2011, No. 14, pp. 12)*
Pub: SourceMedia Inc.

Ed: Andrea Davis. **Description:** Andrew Sykes, chairman of Health at Work Wellness Actuaries, states that it is a myth that Colorado is ranked as the healthiest state in America. Sykes helped implement a wellness programs at Brighton School District in the Denver area.

28203 ■ *"Five New Scientists Bring Danforth Center $16 Million"* in *Saint Louis Business Journal (Vol. 32, October 7, 2011, No. 6, pp. 1)*
Pub: Saint Louis Business Journal

Ed: E.B. Solomont. **Description:** Donald Danforth Plant Science Center's appointment of five new lead scientists has increased its federal funding by $16 million. Cornell University scientist Tom Brutnell is one of the five new appointees.

28204 ■ *"Five Steps for Handling Independent Contractors"* in *Hawaii Business (Vol. 53, January 2008, No. 7, pp. 49)*
Pub: Hawaii Business Publishing

Ed: Jason Ubay. **Description:** Small companies should be cautious in dealing with independent contractors. They must understand that they cannot dictate specific operational procedures, job duties, standards of conduct and performance standards to the contractors, and they cannot interfere with the evaluation and training of the contractors' employees. Tips on negotiating with independent contractors are given.

28205 ■ *"Follow the ABCs of Buying a Business"* in *Women Entrepreneur (September 10, 2008)*
Pub: Entrepreneur Media Inc.

Ed: Nina Kaufman. **Description:** Buying a business will likely result in the largest single asset one will ever own. A list of steps one can take in order to educate and protect themselves is provided.

28206 ■ *"Forget the Elaborate Business Plans, Kids With Passion Are Our Next Great Entrepreneurs"* in *Inc. (October 2007, pp. 87-88)*
Pub: Gruner & Jahr USA Publishing

Description: George Gendron, founder and executive director of the Innovation and Entrepreneurship Program at Clark University, stresses the importance of encouraging business students in his entrepreneurial program to follow their passion. The program is dedicated to real-world entrepreneurship by creating businesses rather than business plans.

28207 ■ *"Forward Motion"* in *Green Industry Pro (July 2011)*
Pub: Cygnus Business Media

Ed: Gregg Wartgow. **Description:** Several landscape contractors have joined this publication's Working Smarter Training Challenge over the last year. This process is helping them develop ways to improve work processes, boost morale, drive out waste, reduce costs, improve customer service, and be more competitive.

28208 ■ *"Funbrain Launches Preschool Content"* in *Marketing to Women (Vol. 21, March 2008, No. 3, pp. 3)*
Pub: EPM Communications Inc.
Contact: Ira Mayer, President
E-mail: imayer@epmcom.com

Description: Funbrain.com launches The Moms and Kids Playground, a section of the website devoted to activities and games for moms and kids aged 2 to 6; content aims at building early computer skills and to teach basic concepts such as counting and colors.

28209 ■ *"Future Autoworkers will Need Broader Skills"* in *Crain's Detroit Business (Vol. 25, June 8, 2009, No. 23, pp. 13)*
Pub: Crain Communications Inc. - Detroit

Ed: Ryan Beene. **Description:** Auto industry observers report that new workers in the industry will need advanced skills and educational backgrounds in engineering and technical fields because jobs in the factories will become more technology-based and multidisciplinary.

28210 ■ *"The Future Is Another Country; Higher Education"* in *The Economist (Vol. 390, January 3, 2009, No. 8612, pp. 43)*
Pub: The Economist Newspaper Inc.

Description: Due to the growth of the global corporation, more ambitious students are studying at universities abroad; the impact of this trend is discussed.

28211 ■ *"Get With the Program"* in *Entrepreneur (Vol. 36, April 2008, No. 4, pp. 130)*
Pub: Entrepreneur Media, Inc.

Ed: Nichole L. Torres. **Description:** Entrepreneurship initiatives help college students get connected with other students, teach them about how to start their own business while still in school, and help with funding. Some of these programs are the Harold Grinspoon Charitable Foundation's Entrepreneurship Initiative and the Syracuse Campus-Community Entrepreneurship Initiative.

28212 ■ *"Give 'Em a Break"* in *Entrepreneur (Vol. 35, November 2007, No. 11, pp. 32)*
Pub: Entrepreneur Media Inc.

Ed: J.J. Ramberg. **Description:** Andy Walter and Peer Pedersen founded Blue Orchid Capital, a fund of hedge funds, and Steamboat Foundation a foundation that helps college students find high-profile summer internships. Details on the fund and the foundation are presented.

28213 ■ *"Giving Biotech Startups a Hand"* in *Philadelphia Business Journal (Vol. 28, January 8, 2010, No. 47, pp. 1)*
Pub: American City Business Journals

Ed: John George. **Description:** Elkins Park, Pennsylvania-based BioStrategy Partners is a virtual life sciences incubator that is seeking to improve the dull ranking of Philadelphia in the small business vitality index of life sciences. BioStrategy provides technology and business development services to startup life sciences companies and university-based research projects.

28214 ■ *"Glendale Pumping $29 Million Into Redevelopment"* in *The Business Journal - Serving Phoenix and the Valley of the Sun (Vol. 28, August 1, 2008, No. 48, pp. 1)*
Pub: American City Business Journals, Inc.

Ed: Mike Sunnucks. **Description:** Glendale City is planning to invest $29 million to improve city infrastructure like roadways and water and sewer lines over the next five years. Glendale's city council is also planning to hold a workshop on the redevelopment projects in September 2008. Other views and information on the redevelopment project, are presented.

28215 ■ *"Going for the APEX"* in *Women In Business (Vol. 62, September 2010, No. 3, pp. 28)*
Pub: American Business Women's Association

Description: Information about the American Business Women's Association (ABWA) professional development tools, which keep members focused on personal excellence, is presented. The organization recently launched the APEX (Achieving Personal Excellence) Award to honor women who are making a commitment to themselves.

28216 ■ *"Goodbye, Locker Room: Hello, Boardroom"* in *Inc. (Vol. 33, October 2011, No. 8, pp. 30)*
Pub: Inc. Magazine

Ed: Issie Lapowsky, Kasey Wehrum. **Description:** In 2005, the National Football League started the NFL Business Management and Entrepreneurial Program. Since the onset of the program, 700 players have participated in the program which takes place at the business schools of Harvard, the University of Pennsylvania, Northwestern and Stanford.

28217 ■ *"Groomers Eye Profit Growth Through Services"* in *Pet Product News (Vol. 64, December 2010, No. 12, pp. 26)*
Pub: BowTie Inc.

Ed: Kathleen M. Mangan. **Description:** Pet groomers can successfully offer add-on services by taking into account insider customer knowledge, store image, and financial analysis in the decision-making process. Many pet groomers have decided to add services such as spa treatments and training due to a slump in the bathing and grooming business. How some pet groomers gained profitability through add-on services is explored.

28218 ■ *"Group Learning"* in *Academy of Management Review (October 2007, pp. 1041)*
Pub: ScholarOne, Inc.

Ed: Jeanne M. Wilson, Paul S. Goodman, Matthew A. Cronin. **Description:** The processes that constitute group learning in order to undertake necessary modifications are covered.

28219 ■ *"Growing Your Business Through BPI Certification"* in *Indoor Comfort Marketing (Vol. 70, May 2011, No. 5, pp. 12)*
Pub: Industry Publications Inc.

Ed: Scott Vadino. **Description:** Profile of the Building Performance Institute and the ways BPI certification will help grow a heating, ventilation, cooling firm.

28220 ■ *"Guts Not Included"* in *Canadian Business (Vol. 81, March 31, 2008, No. 5, pp. 46)*
Pub: Rogers Media

Ed: Andrew Wahl. **Description:** Executives need the vision to create a strategy that prepares for an uncertain future in light of growing global competition. Canadian business leaders have the right skills and education but do not have enough tolerance for risk.

28221 ■ *"Head of the Class"* in *Entrepreneur (Vol. 37, October 2009, No. 10, pp. 59)*
Pub: Entrepreneur Media, Inc.

Description: Top 25 graduate and undergraduate entrepreneurship programs in the US for 2009 as ranked by The Princeton Review are listed. Babson College in Wellesley, Massachusetts topped both categories.

28222 ■ *"Henry Mintzberg: Still the Zealous Skeptic and Scold"* in *Strategy and Leadership (Vol. 39, March-April 2011, No. 2, pp. 4)*
Pub: Emerald Group Publishing Inc.

Ed: Robert J. Allio. **Description:** Henry Mintzberg, professor at the McGill University in Montreal, Canada, shares his thoughts on issues such as inappropriate methods in management education and on trends in leadership and management. Mintzberg believes that US businesses are facing serious management and leadership challenges.

28223 ■ *"Higher Education"* in *Canadian Business (Vol. 79, October 23, 2006, No. 21, pp. 129)*
Pub: Rogers Media

Ed: Erin Pooley; Laura Bogomolny; Joe Castaldo; Michelle Magnan. **Description:** Details of some Canadian business schools, where students can simultaneously pursue a master of business administration degree and also be employed on a part time basis, are presented.

28224 ■ *"Hire Education"* in *Canadian Business (Vol. 79, September 11, 2006, No. 18, pp. 114)*
Pub: Rogers Media

Ed: Erin Pooley. **Description:** Study results showing the perceptions of students while considering full-time employment and the attributes they look for in their future employers are presented.

28225 ■ *"His Brother's Keeper: a Mentor Learns the True Meaning of Leadership"* in *Black Enterprise (Vol. 37, December 2006, No. 5, pp. 69)*
Pub: Earl G. Graves Publishing Co. Inc.

Ed: Laura Egodigwe. **Description:** Interview with Keith R. Wyche of Pitney Bowes Management Services which discusses the relationship between a mentor and mentee as well as sponsorship.

28226 ■ *"Hit the Books"* in *Entrepreneur (Vol. 36, April 2008, No. 4, pp. 74)*
Pub: Entrepreneur Media, Inc.
Ed: Nichole L. Torres. **Description:** Lists of the top business schools in different U.S. universities are presented. These lists are categorized according to best professors, best classroom experience, most competitive students, greatest opportunity for women, and greatest opportunity for minority students. The lists, compiled by the Princeton Review, are based on student opinion.

28227 ■ *"Hitting the E-Books"* in *Inc. (Vol. 33, September 2011, No. 7, pp. 36)*
Pub: Inc. Magazine
Ed: Shivani Vora. **Description:** Textbooks may be getting cheaper for college students now that they can use electronic textbooks that can be read on a laptop or tablet. The market is growing about 50 percent annually. Statistical data included.

28228 ■ *"Holy Wasabi! Sushi Not Just For Parents Anymore"* in *Chicago Tribune (March 13, 2008)*
Pub: McClatchy-Tribune Information Services
Ed: Christopher Borrelli. **Description:** Wicker Park cooking school, The Kid's Table, specializes in cooking classes for pre-teens; Elena Marre who owns the school was surprised when she was asked to plan a children's party in which she would teach a course in sushi making. More and more adolescents and small children are eating sushi.

28229 ■ *"Home Grown"* in *Hawaii Business (Vol. 53, November 2007, No. 5, pp. 51)*
Pub: Hawaii Business Publishing
Ed: Jolyn Okimoto Rosa. **Description:** Discusses a program that focuses on Native Hawaiian entrepreneurs and offers business training at the Kapiolani Community College; upon completion of the program, participants may apply for a loan provided by the Office of Hawaiian Affairs (OHA) to help them start their business. OHA plans to present the restructured loan program in November 2007, with aims of shortening the loan process.

28230 ■ *"Hopkins' Security, Reputation Face Challenges in Wake of Slaying"* in *Baltimore Business Journal (Vol. 28, August 6, 2010, No. 13)*
Pub: Baltimore Business Journal
Ed: Gary Haber. **Description:** The slaying of Johns Hopkins University researcher Stephen Pitcairn has not tarnished the reputation of the elite school in Baltimore, Maryland among students. Maintaining Hopkins' reputation is important since it is Baltimore's largest employer with nearly 32,000 workers. Insights on the impact of the slaying among the Hopkins' community are also given.

28231 ■ *How to Hire, Train, and Keep the Best Employees for Your Small Business*
Pub: Atlantic Publishing Company
Ed: Dianna Podmoroff. **Released:** June 2004. **Price:** $29.95. **Description:** Costs of hiring, training, and lost productivity costs related to losing employees.

28232 ■ *"How to Survive This Mess"* in *Crain's Chicago Business (Vol. 31, April 14, 2008, No. 15, pp. 18)*
Pub: Crain Communications, Inc.
Ed: Christina Le Beau. **Description:** Small business owners can make it through a possible recession with preparations such as reviewing their balance sheet and cash flow every week and spotting trends then reacting quickly to them.

28233 ■ *"How Will You Ever Replace Yourself?"* in *Canadian Business (Vol. 83, August 17, 2010, No. 13-14, pp. 77)*
Pub: Rogers Media Ltd.
Ed: Jacqueline Nelson. **Description:** SoftBank founder and CEO masayoshi Son created his very own school called SoftBank Academia in order to pick a successor that will follow his footprint. Son's strategy is extreme but other corporate leaders should pay attention to succession planning.

28234 ■ *"Human Resource Management: Challenges for Graduate Education"* in *Business Horizons (Vol. 51, March-April 2008, No. 2, pp. 151)*
Pub: Elsevier Advanced Technology Publications
Ed: James C. Wimbush. **Description:** Human resource management education at the master's and doctoral degree levels is discussed. There is an ever-increasing need to produce human resource managers who understand the value of human resource management as a strategic business contributor. uman.

28235 ■ *"Innovation Station"* in *Canadian Business (Vol. 80, October 8, 2007, No. 20, pp. 42)*
Pub: Rogers Media
Ed: Andrew Wahl. **Description:** Study and teaching of entrepreneurship at the University of Waterloo is discussed. Research projects in the university are expected to be influential in Canada's economic development. In spite of the success of these studies, financing is still a problem for the university, especially in technological innovations.

28236 ■ *"The Innovator: Rob McEwen's Unique Vision of Philanthropy and Business"* in *Canadian Business (Vol. 81, November 10, 2008, No. 19)*
Pub: Rogers Media Ltd.
Ed: Alex Mlynek. **Description:** Rob McEwen says that his donation to the Schulich School of Business is his first large donation. He went to the University Health Network and was told about their pan for regenerative medicine, helping him make the decision. McEwan wants to be involved in philanthropy in the areas of leadership and education.

28237 ■ *"Innovators Critical in Technical Economy"* in *Crain's Cleveland Business (Vol. 28, November 5, 2007, No. 44, pp. 10)*
Pub: Crain Communications, Inc.
Ed: Peter Rea. **Description:** Discusses the importance to attract, develop and retain talented innovators on Ohio's economy. Also breaks down the four fronts on which the international battle for talent is being waged.

28238 ■ *"Integrating Business Core Knowledge through Upper Division Report Composition"* in *Business Communication Quarterly (December 2007)*
Pub: SAGE Publications USA
Contact: Blaise R. Simqu, President
Ed: Joy Roach, Daniel Tracy Kay Durden. **Description:** An assignment that integrates subjects and encourages the use of business communication report-writing skills is presented. This assignment is designed to complement business school curricula and help develop critical thinking and organizational skills.

28239 ■ *International Entrepreneurship Education Issues and Newness*
Pub: Edward Elgar Publishing, Incorporated
Ed: Fayolle. **Released:** August 2006. **Price:** $120.00. **Description:** Entrepreneurial education, focusing on economic, political and social needs of a changing world; ideas for reassessing, redeveloping, and renewing curricula and methods for teaching entrepreneurship are offered.

28240 ■ *"International Growth"* in *Black Enterprise (Vol. 38, July 2008, No. 12, pp. 64)*
Pub: Earl G. Graves Publishing Co. Inc.
Ed: Marcia A. Reed-Woodard. **Description:** Becoming an increasingly smaller portion of the global business environment is the U.S. economy. Christopher Catlin, an associate with Booz Allen Hamilton, a technology management and strategy-consulting firm, shares what he has learned about the global market.

28241 ■ *Introduction to Business*
Pub: The McGraw-Hill Companies
Ed: Laura Portolese Dias, Amit J. Shah. **Released:** January 1, 2009. **Price:** $70.94. **Description:** Introduction to business course discusses the changing educational environment for teaching business courses in colleges and universities.

28242 ■ *"Is Business Ethics Getting Better? A Historical Perspective"* in *Business Ethics Quarterly (Vol. 21, April 2011, No. 2, pp. 335)*
Pub: Society for Business Ethics
Ed: Joanne B. Ciulla. **Description:** The question 'Is Business Ethics Getting Better?' as a heuristic for discussing the importance of history in understanding business and ethics is answered. The article uses a number of examples to illustrate how the same ethical problems in business have been around for a long time. It describes early attempts at the Harvard School of Business to use business history as a means of teaching students about moral and social values. In the end, the author suggests that history may be another way to teach ethics, enrich business ethics courses, and develop the perspective and vision in future business leaders.

28243 ■ *"It's Not Rocket Science"* in *Hispanic Business (September 2007, pp. 30, 32)*
Pub: Hispanic Business
Ed: Hildy Medina. **Description:** Profile of France Cordova, president of Purdue University. Cordova has established many diversity programs at the school.

28244 ■ *"Jean-Rober's 'oui"* in *Business Courier (Vol. 27, August 6, 2010, No. 14, pp. 1)*
Pub: Business Courier
Ed: Dan Monk. **Description:** Jean-Robert de Cavel will open his new restaurant in Cincinnati, Ohio. The culinary arts program at Cincinnati State Technical and Community College offered him $100,000 to be its 'chef in residence'. He was able to energize students, boost enrollment, and increase the stature of the culinary program.

28245 ■ *"Kids, Computers and the Social Networking Evolution"* in *Canadian Business (Vol. 81, October 27, 2008, No. 18, pp. 93)*
Pub: Rogers Media Ltd.
Ed: Penny Milton. **Description:** Social networking was found to help educate students in countries like the U.S., Canada and Mexico. Schools that embrace social networking teach students how to use computers safely and responsibility in order to counter threats to children on the Internet.

28246 ■ *"Knowing is Growing: Five Strategies To Develop You and Your Business"* in *Black Enterprise (Vol. 38, November 2007, No. 4, pp. 106)*
Pub: Earl G. Graves Publishing Co. Inc.
Ed: Erinn R. Johnson. **Description:** Five strategies for growing a small business are listed by Andrew Morrisor, founder of the Small Business Camp. The camp provides training, coaching, and marketing services to entrepreneurs.

28247 ■ *"Knox County Schools Debate Outsourcing Janitorial Services"* in *(March 29, 2011)*
Pub: Knoxville News Sentinel
Ed: Lola Alapo. **Description:** Custodial services of Knox County Schools in Tennessee may be outsourced in move to save money for the school district. Details of the proposed program are included.

28248 ■ *"The Labor Crunch is Coming"* in *Canadian Business (Vol. 80, December 25, 2006, No. 1, pp. 74)*
Pub: Rogers Media
Description: The need for skilled and educated workforce to meet labor shortage in future in Canada is discussed.

28249 ■ *The Leadership Challenge*
Pub: Jossey-Bass Publishers
Ed: James M. Kouzes, Barry Z. Posner. **Released:** June 30, 1995. **Price:** $22.00. **Description:** According to research by the authors, people can make extraordinary things happen by liberating the leader within everyone around them. This handbook gives practical tips to aspire leaders in retail, manufacturing, government, community, church and school settings.

28250 ■ "Leadership Training" in Black Enterprise (Vol. 37, January 2007, No. 6, pp. 56)

Pub: Earl G. Graves Publishing Co. Inc.

Ed: Sonia Alleyne. **Description:** Profile of Theopolis Holman, Group Vice-President of Duke Energy, who discusses how he prepared for the merger between Duke Energy and Cinergy. Holman oversees a division of 9,000 service contractors and employees.

28251 ■ "Leaks in the Pipeline" in Hispanic Business (September 2007, pp. 18, 20, 22, 24)

Pub: Hispanic Business

Ed: Holly Ocasio Rizzo. **Description:** Graduate schools need to focus on domestic diversity in order to attract Hispanic students in a growing global economy.

28252 ■ "Learning by Doing: Engaging Students through Learner-Centered Activities" in Business Communication Quarterly (Dec. 2007, pp. 451)

Pub: SAGE Publications USA

Contact: Blaise R. Simqu, President

Ed: Karl L. Smart, Nancy Csapo. **Description:** Active learning techniques, such as the Puzzle Brain Spark activity, allow students to engage in learning activities that allow deeper thinking, critical thinking, and problem solving ability that develop business management skills.

28253 ■ "Lessons Learned from Instructional Design Theory" in Business Communication Quarterly (December 2007, pp. 414)

Pub: SAGE Publications USA

Contact: Blaise R. Simqu, President

Ed: Lisa A. Burke. **Description:** Instructors should present course information to business students in a way that enhances understanding and should use presentation techniques that students may eventually use; course materials should be kept relevant and simple.

28254 ■ "The Life Changers" in Canadian Business (Vol. 81, October 27, 2008, No. 18, pp. 86)

Pub: Rogers Media Ltd.

Description: The first season of 'The Life Changers' was produced in September 2007 to feature stories about research and development (R&D) efforts by universities in Atlantic Canada. The program addresses the need to inform the public about university R&D and its outcomes.

28255 ■ "Local Researchers Get Cash Infusion" in Business Courier (Vol. 26, October 9, 2009, No. 24, pp. 1)

Pub: American City Business Journals, Inc.

Ed: James Ritchie. **Description:** Cincinnati's Children's Hospital Medical Center and the University of Cincinnati researchers are set to receive at least $56 million from the stimulus bill. The cash infusion has reenergized research scientists and enhances Cincinnati's national clout as a major research center.

28256 ■ "The Long View: Roberta Bondar on Science and the Need for Education" in Canadian Business (Vol. 81, October 27, 2008, No. 18)

Pub: Rogers Media Ltd.

Ed: Alex Mlynek. **Description:** Roberta Bondar believes that energy and renewable energy is a critical environmental issue faced by Canada today. Bondar is the first Canadian woman and neurologist in space.

28257 ■ "Macomb County, OU Eye Business Incubator" in Crain's Detroit Business (Vol. 24, February 11, 2008, No. 6, pp. 1)

Pub: Crain Communications Inc. - Detroit

Ed: Chad Halcom. **Description:** Officials in Macomb County, Michigan are discussing plans to create a defense-themed business incubator in the county. Macomb County was awarded $282,000 in federal budget appropriation for the project.

28258 ■ "Making the Most of Milk to Revive a Falling Market" in Farmer's Weekly (March 28, 2008, No. 320)

Pub: Reed Business Information

Contact: Jeff Greisch, President

Description: DairyCo, eight of whom are working dairy farmers, aim to promote a feeding campaign for better herd health, provide research into efficient labor use, and sponsor discussion groups to enhance business skills.

28259 ■ "Making Waves" in Business Journal Portland (Vol. 27, November 26, 2010, No. 39, pp. 1)

Pub: Portland Business Journal

Ed: Erik Siemers. **Description:** Corvallis, Oregon-based Columbia Power Technologies LLC is about to close a $2 million Series A round of investment initiated by $750,000 from Oregon Angel Fund. The wave energy startup company was formed to commercialize the wave buoy technology developed by Oregon State University researchers.

28260 ■ "Managing the Facebookers; Business" in The Economist (Vol. 390, January 3, 2009, No. 8612, pp. 10)

Pub: Economist Newspaper Ltd.

Description: According to a report from PricewaterhouseCoopers, a business consultancy, workers from Generation Y, also known as the Net Generation, are more difficult to recruit and integrate into companies that practice traditional business acumen. 61 percent of chief executive managers say that they have trouble with younger employees who tend to be more narcissistic and more interested in personal fulfillment with a need for frequent feedback and an overprecise set of objectives on the path to promotion which can be hard for managers who are used to a different relationship with their subordinates. Older bosses should prepare to make some concessions to their younger talent since some of the issues that make them happy include cheaper online ways to communicate and additional coaching, both of which are good for business.

28261 ■ Managing for Success: The Latest in Management Thought and Practice from Canada's Premier Business School

Pub: Harperaudio

Contact: Catherine MacGregor, Director

E-mail: catherine.macgregor@harpercollins.com

Ed: Monica Fleck. **Released:** December 2000. **Description:** Canadian business school offers insight into the latest management skills of the nation's business leaders.

28262 ■ "Mandel Site Favored For UWM Hall" in The Business Journal-Milwaukee (Vol. 25, September 19, 2008, No. 52, pp. A1)

Pub: American City Business Journals, Inc.

Description: University of Wisconsin-Milwaukee student residence hall's leading location is a site pushed by Mandel Group Inc. Real estate sources say that the developer's proposal offers the best opportunity for business development and the least conflict with nearby neighborhoods. Plans for the Mandel site are presented.

28263 ■ "Manufacturers Urged to Adapt to Defense" in Crain's Cleveland Business (Vol. 30, June 22, 2009, No. 24, pp. 3)

Pub: Crain Communications, Inc.

Ed: Dan Shingler. **Description:** Manufacturers in Northeast Ohio are making products for the military from steel, polymers or composite materials. The U.S. Department of Defense is teaching companies to work with titanium and other advanced metals in order to further manufacture for the military.

28264 ■ "Market Forces" in Canadian Business (Vol. 79, October 23, 2006, No. 21, pp. 93)

Pub: Rogers Media

Ed: Erin Pooley. **Description:** The tremendous rise in the number of business schools offering Master of business administration degree in Canada and the depletion in the quality of education provided in these business schools is discussed.

28265 ■ "Marketing Scholarship 2.0" in Journal of Marketing (Vol. 75, July 2011, No. 4, pp. 225)

Pub: American Marketing Association

Ed: Richard J. Lutz. **Description:** A study of the implications of changing environment and newer collaborative models for marketing knowledge production and dissemination is presented. Crowdsourcing has become a frequently employed strategy in industry. Academic researchers should collaborate more as well as the academe and industry, to make sure that important problems are being investigated.

28266 ■ "MBA Essentials: Real-Life Instruction" in Women In Business (Vol. 61, October-November 2009, No. 5, pp. 28)

Pub: American Business Women's Association

Ed: Leigh Elmore. **Description:** University of Kansas School of Business allied itself with the American Business Women's Association (ABWA) which led to the formation of the ABWA-KU MBA essentials program. With this program, ABWA members are exposed to graduate-level coursework that delves on business topics, such as strategy and operations.

28267 ■ "MBA Guide 2008" in Canadian Business (Vol. 81, November 10, 2008, No. 19, pp. 92)

Pub: Rogers Media Ltd.

Ed: Sharda Prashad. **Description:** Escalating tuition costs for an MBA degree means that the return on investment could take longer. One study found that MBA degree holders who graduated during recessionary times earned less than those who graduated during good economic times.

28268 ■ MBA In a Day

Pub: John Wiley and Sons, Inc.

Ed: Steven Stralser, PhD. **Released:** 2004. **Price:** $34.95. **Description:** Management professor presents important concepts, business topics and strategies that can be used by anyone to manage a small business or professional practice. Topics covered include: human resources and personal interaction, ethics and leadership skills, fair negotiation tactics, basic business accounting practices, project management, and the fundamentals of economics and marketing.

28269 ■ "MBAs Plus Designers Equals New Life for Business" in Globe & Mail (April 24, 2007, pp. B1)

Pub: CTVglobemedia Publishing Inc.

Ed: Gordon Pitts. **Description:** The need for Canadian companies to combine the skills of management graduates and designers to achieve corporate growth is discussed.

28270 ■ "Meet UT's New Business Mind" in Austin Business Journal (Vol. 31, May 13, 2011, No. 10, pp. A1)

Pub: American City Business Journals Inc.

Ed: Sandra Zaragoza. **Description:** University of Texas (UT) chief commercialization officer, Dr. Richard Miller, has opened a satellite office in Silicon Valley, California in the hopes of luring Californian investors to the science and technology at UT. The satellite office is just one of Miller's efforts to reshape and widen the commercialization of UT-Austin. Insights into Miller's long-term view approach to commercialization are also covered.

28271 ■ "Mentoring Support" in Black Enterprise (Vol. 38, July 2008, No. 12, pp. 64)

Pub: Earl G. Graves Publishing Co. Inc.

Description: With his relocation from his multicultural team in New York to the less diverse Scripps Networks' headquarters in Knoxville, Earl Cokley has made it a top priority to push for more diversity and mentoring opportunities within the management of the media and marketing company.

28272 ■ "Mettle Detector" in Canadian Business (Vol. 79, July 17, 2006, No. 14-15, pp. 63)

Pub: Rogers Media

Ed: Calvin Leung. **Description:** The difficulties faced in completing the Certified Financial Analyst course, and the rewards one can expect after its completion, are discussed.

28273 ■ *Microtrends: The Small Forces Behind Tomorrow's Big Changes*
Pub: Business Plus

Ed: Mark J. Penn. **Released:** 2007. **Price:** $25.99. **Description:** Political pollster and lead presidential campaign strategist for Hillary Clinton, identifies seventy-five microtrends he believes are changing the social and cultural landscape in the U.S. and globally. The book covers the areas of health and wellness, technology, education and more.

28274 ■ *"MindLeaders' Online Training Courses Come to ePath Learning" in Information Today (Vol. 26, February 2009, No. 2, pp. 4)*
Pub: Information Today, Inc.

Description: MindLeaders has partnered with ePath Learning to provide clients with over 2,200 new on-line courses. ePath's integrated Learning Management Service (iLMS) allows organizations to create online training programs for employees.

28275 ■ *"Mitch D'Olier" in Hawaii Business (Vol. 53, November 2007, No. 5, pp. 27)*
Pub: Hawaii Business Publishing

Ed: Cathy S. Cruz-George. **Description:** Mitch D'Olier chief executive officer of Kaneohe Ranch/ Harold K.L. Castle Foundation thinks that achievement gaps are a nationwide problem and that the Knowledge is Power Program is one of the programs that focuses on achievement gaps in some communities across the US. He also provides his insights on education in Hawaii and the current shortage of teachers.

28276 ■ *"Moooove Over, Sodas: Okaloosa to Get Dairy Vending Machines for Two Schools" in Northwest Florida Daily News (September 27, 2001)*
Pub: Freedom Communications

Ed: Katie Tammen. **Description:** Two Okaloosa County high schools will be offering more lunch options by installing refrigerated vending machines featuring dairy-related food.

28277 ■ *"More Cuts On the Way At Ag School" in Business First-Columbus (December 14, 2007, pp. A1)*
Pub: American City Business Journals, Inc.

Ed: Carrie Ghose. **Description:** Program cuts at Ohio State University's Agriculture School are discussed. A voluntary retirement incentive to reduce staff was approved by the University's trustees. Since 2000, the College of Food, Agricultural and Environmental Sciences' staff have decreased by 21 percent, while the faculty experienced a 25 percent reduction. According to Bobby Moser, the college's dean, the institution is looking for other ways to generate income.

28278 ■ *"More Sales Leads, Please: Cr, What Happened When Frontline Selling Started Practicing What It Preaches" in Inc. (November 2007)*
Pub: Gruner & Jahr USA Publishing

Description: Frontline Selling located in Oakland, New Jersey helps train sales teams to generate and convert sales leads. The consulting firm doubled their marketing budget to increase their own sales.

28279 ■ *"Natalie Peterson; Corporate Counsel, Steris Corp., 39" in Crain's Cleveland Business (Vol. 28, November 19, 2007, No. 46, pp. F-14)*
Pub: Crain Communications, Inc.

Ed: Chuck Soder. **Description:** Profile of Natalie Peterson, corporate counsel for Steris Corp., a manufacturer of sterilization products; Peterson's blue-collar background did not detour her from her collegiate goals although she hardly knew how to fill out a college application. After graduating from Stanford Law School in 1997, she opted to return to Cleveland in lieu of more lucrative job offers in San Francisco. She has joined the school board and has participated in the 3Rs program, in which lawyers visit public schools in Cleveland to get students thinking about career choices and talk about constitutional law.

28280 ■ *"Native Wisdom" in Canadian Business (Vol. 80, October 8, 2007, No. 20, pp. 121)*
Pub: Rogers Media

Ed: Bernd Christmas. **Description:** Roles of Canadian indigenous peoples in the country's economic development are discussed. It is believed that empowering Canadian natives to contribute to the country's economy will positively affect the country's future. The need for education in preparing natives for the global economy is also tackled.

28281 ■ *"Nat'l Instruments Connects with Lego" in Austin Business JournalInc. (Vol. 28, August 22, 2008, No. 23, pp. 1)*
Pub: American City Business Journals

Ed: Laura Hipp. **Description:** Austin-based National Instruments Corporation has teamed with Lego Group from Denmark to create a robot that can be built by children and can be used to perform tasks. Lego WeDo, their latest product, uses computer connection to power its movements. The educational benefits of the new product are discussed.

28282 ■ *"Negotiating Tips" in Black Enterprise (Vol. 37, December 2006, No. 5, pp. 70)*
Pub: Earl G. Graves Publishing Co. Inc.

Description: Sekou Kaalund, head of strategy, mergers & acquisitions at Citigroup Securities & Fund Services, states that 'Negotiation skills are paramount to success in a business environment because of client, employee, and shareholder relationships'. He discusses how the book by George Kohlrieser, Hostage at the Table: How Leaders Can Overcome Conflict, Influence Others, and Raise Performance, has helped him negotiate more powerfully and enhance his skills at conflict-resolution.

28283 ■ *"Netting Degrees: More Professionals Continuing Their Education Online" in Hispanic Business (September 2007, pp. 62, 64)*
Pub: Hispanic Business

Ed: Hildy Medina. **Description:** Traditional universities and private institutions offer online courses to professionals wishing to further their education.

28284 ■ *"New Approach Could Boost Ivory Tower Innovation" in Business Journal-Portland (Vol. 24, November 16, 2007, No. 37, pp. 1)*
Pub: American City Business Journals, Inc.

Ed: Aliza Earnshaw. **Description:** New approach which aims to help universities move to a corporate structure, secure funds, and find professional managers is being explored. Accelerator Corporation was able to help six companies through its funding. Joe Tanous who is behind Oregon's State University's enhanced commercialization, would like to apply the same approach Accelerator used to help Oregon State University, the University of Oregon, Portland State University and Oregon Health and Science University.

28285 ■ *"New Career Center Opens at Right Time: Laid-Off Freightliner Workers Will Need Help" in Charlotte Observer (February 1, 2007)*
Pub: Knight-Ridder/Tribune Business News

Ed: Gail Smith-Arrants. **Description:** Rowan-Cabarrus Community College announced the opening of its new career development center that will help area workers train for new careers.

28286 ■ *"The New Schools" in Black Enterprise (February 2008)*
Pub: Earl G. Graves Publishing Co. Inc.

Ed: Kinsley Kanu, Jr. **Description:** Ten educational programs to help top executives keep pace with the ever-changing market trends while gaining perspective on innovation and new ideas are examined.

28287 ■ *"No Fast Cash Class" in Black Enterprise (Vol. 37, December 2006, No. 5, pp. 72)*
Pub: Earl G. Graves Publishing Co. Inc.

Description: There are no shortcuts to a obtaining a career as a financial planner. Certified Financial Planner Board of Standards has specific requirements for

certification which include having a bachelor's degree from an accredited U.S. school before candidates are even eligible for taking the certification exam. Other criteria and requirements are discussed.

28288 ■ *"No, Management Is Not a Profession" in Harvard Business Review (Vol. 88, July-August 2010, No. 7-8, pp. 52)*
Pub: Harvard Business School Publishing

Ed: Richard Barker. **Description:** An argument is presented that management is not a profession, as it is less focused on mastering a given body of knowledge than it is on obtaining integration and collaboration skills. Implications for teaching this new approach are also examined.

28289 ■ *"Nonprofit Ready to Get More Girls into 'STEM' Jobs" in Austin Business JournalInc. (Vol. 29, December 25, 2009, No. 42, pp. 1)*
Pub: American City Business Journals

Ed: Sandra Zaragoza. **Description:** Girlstart has completed its $1.5 million capital campaign to buy the building it will care the Girlstart Tech Center. Girlstart is a nonprofit organization that prepares girls for science, technology, engineering and mathematics or STEM careers. Details of the program are highlighted.

28290 ■ *"Nurturing Talent for Tomorrow" in Restaurants and Institutions (Vol. 118, September 15, 2008, No. 14, pp. 90)*
Pub: Reed Business Information
Contact: Jeff Greisch, President

Description: Hormel Foods Corporation and The Culinary Institute of America (CIA) have teamed to develop The Culinary Enrichment and Innovation Program that supports future culinary leaders by providing creative and competitive staff development. Sixteen students attend four three-day sessions at the CIA's campus in Hyde Park, New York; sessions include classroom teaching, one-on-one interaction with leading culinarians, and hands-on kitchen time.

28291 ■ *"Oakland County to Survey Employers on Needed Skills" in Crain's Detroit Business (Vol. 24, April 14, 2008, No. 15, pp. 30)*
Pub: Crain Communications Inc.

Ed: Chad Halcom. **Description:** In an attempt to aid educators and attract talent, Oakland County plans to collect data from 1,000 local employers on workforce skills they need now or will need soon.

28292 ■ *The Official Guide for GMAT Verbal Review, 2nd Edition*
Pub: John Wiley & Sons, Inc.

Ed: Graduate Management Admissions Council. **Released:** August 17, 2009. **Price:** $17.95. **Description:** The only official verbal review for the GMAT from the creators of the test. The guide provides questions, answers, and explanations and targets study and helps improve verbal skills by focusing on the ability to read and comprehend written material, to reason and evaluate arguments, and to correct written material to conform to Standard English.

28293 ■ *"On Beyond Powerpoint: Presentations Get a Wake-Up Call" in Inc. (November 2007, pp. 58-59)*
Pub: Gruner & Jahr USA Publishing

Ed: Michael Fitzgerald. **Description:** New software that allows business presentations to be shared online are profiled, including ProfCast, audio podcasts for sales, marketing, and training; SmartDraw2008, software that creates professional graphics; Dimdim, an open-Web conferencing tool; Empressr, a hosted Web service for creating, managing, and sharing multimedia presentations; Zentation, a free tool that allows users to watch slides and a videos of presenter; Spresent, a Web-based presentation tool for remote offices or conference calls.

28294 ■ *"On the Clock" in Canadian Business (Vol. 82, April 27, 2009, No. 7, pp. 28)*
Pub: Rogers Media

Ed: Sarka Halas. **Description:** Survey of 100 Canadian executives found that senior managers can be out of a job for about nine months before their careers are adversely affected. The nine month mark can be avoided if job seekers build networks even before they lose their jobs. Job seekers should also take volunteer work and training opportunities to increase their changes of landing a job.

28295 ■ "On Their Own: Bronx High School Students Open a Bank Branch" in Black Enterprise (Vol. 38, February 2008, No. 7, pp. 42)

Pub: Earl G. Graves Publishing Co. Inc.

Ed: Jessica Jones. **Description:** Students at Fordham Leadership Academy for Business and Technology in New York City opened a student-run bank branch at their high school. The business paid high school seniors $11 per hour to work as tellers. Students were also taught interviewing basics.

28296 ■ "One Hundred Years of Excellence in Business Education: What Have We Learned?" in Business Horizons (January-February 2008)

Pub: Elsevier Advanced Technology Publications

Ed: Frank Acito, Patricia M. McDougall, Daniel C. Smith. **Description:** Business schools have to be more innovative, efficient and nimble, so that the quality of the next generation of business leaders is improved. The Kelley School of Business, Indiana University ahs long been a leader in business education. The trends that influence the future of business education and useful success principles are discussed.

28297 ■ "One Laptop Per Child Weighs Going For-Profit" in Boston Business Journal (Vol. 31, May 20, 2011, No. 17, pp. 1)

Pub: Boston Business Journal

Ed: Mary Moore. **Description:** Nonprofit organization One Laptop Per Child is thinking of shifting into a for-profit structure in order to raise as much as $10 million in capital to achieve its goal of distributing more XO laptops to poor children worldwide. The organization has distributed 2 million computers since 2008 with Uruguay, Peru and Rwanda as its biggest markets.

28298 ■ "Online Training Requires Tools, Accessories" in Contractor (Vol. 56, September 2009, No. 9, pp. 67)

Pub: Penton Media, Inc.

Ed: Larry Drake. **Description:** Importance of the right equipment and tools to members of the United States plumbing industry undergoing online training is discussed. Portable devices such as Blackberrys and I-phones could be used for online training. The use of headphones makes listening easier for the trainee.

28299 ■ "The Outcome of an Organization Overhaul" in Black Enterprise (Vol. 41, December 2010, No. 5)

Pub: Earl G. Graves Publishing Co. Inc.

Ed: Tamara E. Holmes. **Description:** Savvy business owners understand the need for change in order to stay competitive and be successful. This article examines how to manage change as well as what strategies can help employees to get with the program faster.

28300 ■ "Palace Adds Marketing Arm; College Sponsorships First Step In New Effort" in Crain's Detroit Business (October 1, 2007)

Pub: Crain Communications Inc. - Detroit

Ed: Bill Shea. **Description:** Palace Sports and Entertainment is restructuring itself from operating the Detroit Piston's basketball team and concert venues into a marketing company that also runs sports teams and venues. The firm signed a deal to handle sponsorship sales for colleges and universities.

28301 ■ "Past Promises Haunt Project" in The Business Journal-Portland (Vol. 25, August 1, 2008, No. 21, pp. 1)

Pub: American City Business Journals, Inc.

Ed: Aliza Earnshaw. **Description:** Oregon University System and Oregon Health and Science University will face the state Legislature to defend their request for a $250 million in state bonds to fund a life-sciences collaborative research building. The project

is meant to help grow the Oregon bioscience industry. Comments from industry observers and legislators are also presented.

28302 ■ "The People Puzzle; Re-Training America's Workers" in The Economist (Vol. 390, January 3, 2009, No. 8612, pp. 32)

Pub: The Economist Newspaper Inc.

Description: With thousands of workers losing their jobs, America is now facing the task of getting them back to work. With an overall unemployment rate of 6.7 percent, the federal government has three main ways for leading workers back to employment: training them for new jobs, providing unemployment insurance in order to replace lost wages during the period of job-hunting; and matching employers who desire a skill with workers who have that skill. Specialized staffing agencies provide employers and potential employees with the help necessary to find a job in some of the more niche markets.

28303 ■ "Perfecting Customer Services" in Pet Product News (Vol. 64, November 2010, No. 11, pp. 18)

Pub: BowTie Inc.

Description: Pet supply retailers are encouraged to emphasize customer experience and sales representatives' knowledge of the store's product offerings to foster repeat business. Employee protocols could be implemented to improve customer interaction. Other guidelines on developing a pet supply retail environment that advances repeat business are presented.

28304 ■ "Physics for Females" in Occupational Outlook Quarterly (Vol. 55, Summer 2011, No. 2, pp. 22)

Pub: U.S. Bureau of Labor Statistics

Description: Free resources to help females investigate careers in medical physics and health physics are available from the American Physical Society. The booklet is designed for girls in middle and high school and describes the work of 15 women who use physics to solve medical mysteries, discover planets, research new materials, and more.

28305 ■ Planning Your Future: Resources on Careers and Higher Education

Pub: AMIDEAST Publications

Contact: Theodore H. Kattouf, President

URL(s): www.amideast.org. **Released:** Irregular **Price:** $29.95, Individuals first class mail; $13, Other countries international mail. **Covers:** over 1,000 printed and electronic sources of information on education and training for approximately 150 careers, including accredited programs, nontraditional education, internships, and disabled student services. **Entries include:** Title name, date of publication, order address. **Arrangement:** Alphabetical by Occupation. **Indexes:** Alphabetical by Publisher, subject and title.

28306 ■ "PMA Launches Online Education Program" in Contractor (Vol. 56, October 2009, No. 10, pp. 8)

Pub: Penton Media, Inc.

Description: Plumbing & Mechanical Association of Georgia launched an online program that covers technical and business management that will help contractors run their businesses. Future courses will include math for plumbers, graywater systems, and recession-proofing your business.

28307 ■ The Portable MBA in Entrepreneurship

Pub: John Wiley & Sons, Inc.

Ed: Andrew Zacharakis, William D. Bygrave. **Released:** December 9, 2010. **Price:** $34.95. **Description:** An updated and revised new edition of the comprehensive guide to modern entrepreneurship that tracks the core curriculum of leading business schools.

28308 ■ "Post-Prison Center Idea Rankles OTR" in Business Courier (Vol. 26, November 27, 2009, No. 31, pp. 1)

Pub: American City Business Journals, Inc.

Ed: Lucy May. **Description:** Cincinnati officials and community leaders oppose Firetree Ltd.'s plan to launch a residential program for federal offenders near the School for the Creative and Performing Arts in Over-the-Rhine. Firetree, a Pennsylvania-based

reentry center services firm, proposed a five-year contract with the Federal Bureau of Prisons based on a letter to Cincinnati Police Chief Thomas Streicher.

28309 ■ "The Power of ABWA" in Women In Business (Vol. 62, September 2010, No. 3, pp. 36)

Pub: American Business Women's Association

Ed: Leigh Elmore. **Description:** Information about the internship received by Erica Rockley at American Business Women's Association (ABWA) headquarters is presented. Rockley received heartfelt professional advice the days she spent at the office. She also learned the importance of networking.

28310 ■ "Pre-K Pressure" in Hawaii Business (Vol. 53, October 2007, No. 4, pp. 32)

Pub: Hawaii Business Publishing

Ed: David K. Choo. **Description:** Kindergarten admission in Hawaii is becoming more competitive. Parents, for example, prepare their children for the kindergarten admissions process by bringing them to the schools before the interview or by paying for tutorial services. The impacts of increased competition in school admissions on the life of Hawaiian children are discussed.

28311 ■ "The Preparation Gap" in Hawaii Business (Vol. 53, February 2008, No. 8, pp. 37)

Pub: Hawaii Business Publishing

Ed: Ashley Hamershock. **Description:** Discussion of the educational gap in Hawaii's workforce is being addressed by educational workshops that aim to improve students' knowledge in science, technology, math, and engineering, and prepare them for their entry into the workforce. Education beyond high school is required for jobs to be filled in the coming years.

28312 ■ "Prison Farms are Closing, but the Manure Remains" in Canadian Business (Vol. 83, August 17, 2010, No. 13-14, pp. 9)

Pub: Rogers Media Ltd.

Ed: Steve Maich. **Description:** The explanation given by Canada's government ministers on planned closure of the prison farms and scrapping of the long form census are designed by mixing of spin, argument and transparent justification. The defense should have been plausible but the ministers could not handle the simple questions about statistics and prison job training with pretense.

28313 ■ "Programs Provide Education and Training" in Contractor (Vol. 56, September 2009, No. 9, pp. 56)

Pub: Penton Media, Inc.

Ed: William Feldman; Patti Feldman. **Description:** Opportunity Interactive's Showroom v2 software provides uses computer graphics to provide education and training on HVAC equipment and systems. It can draw heat pump balance points for a specific home. Meanwhile, Simutech's HVAC Training Simulators provide trainees with 'hands-on' HVACR training.

28314 ■ "Promoting Academic Programs Using Online Videos" in Business Communication Quarterly (December 2007, pp. 478)

Pub: SAGE Publications USA

Contact: Blaise R. Simqu, President

Ed: Thomas Clark, Julie Stewart. **Description:** Xavier Entrepreneurial Center successfully used online videos to promote the effectiveness of its academic programs. Online videos are a cost-effective way of publicizing academic programs.

28315 ■ "PSU Launches $90 Million Project" in The Business Journal-Portland (Vol. 25, July 18, 2008, No. 19, pp. 1)

Pub: American City Business Journals, Inc.

Ed: Aliza Earnshaw. **Description:** Portland State University (PSU) has launched a $90-million project for a new business school building, which is to be located at Southwest Market and Southwest Park. The business school is expected to move in to its new 130,000-suqare-foot building by 2013. PSU business school needs to raise $30 million for the project.

28316 ■ *"A Quick Guide to NATE" in Indoor Comfort Marketing (Vol. 70, February 2011, No. 2, pp. 12)*
Pub: Industry Publications Inc.
Description: Guide for training and certification in the North American Technician Excellence award.

28317 ■ *"Reaching Your Potential" in Harvard Business Review (Vol. 86, July-August 2008, No. 8, pp. 45)*
Pub: Harvard Business School Press
Ed: Robert S. Kaplan. **Description:** Being proactive in developing one's career is an important part of entrepreneurship. Keys to successful development include knowing oneself and one's goals, and taking calculated risks.

28318 ■ *"Real Estate Ambitions" in Black Enterprise (Vol. 37, January 2007, No. 6, pp. 101)*
Pub: Earl G. Graves Publishing Co. Inc.
Description: National Real Estate Investors Association is a nonprofit trade association for both advanced as well as novice real estate investors that offers information on builders to contractors to banks. When looking to become a real estate investor utilize this organization, talk to various investors like the president of your local chapter, let people know your aspirations, and see if you can find a partner who has experience in the field. Resources included.

28319 ■ *"Real-Life Coursework for Real-Life Business People" in Women In Business (Vol. 63, Summer 2011, No. 2, pp. 22)*
Pub: American Business Women's Association
Ed: Leigh Elmore. **Description:** American Business Women's Association National Women's Leadership Conference provides members with academic business training courses. Members can take a variety of MBA-level courses that are taught by University of Kansas School of Business professors. Courses include marketing, management, leadership and communication and decision making.

28320 ■ *"Real-Time Computer-Mediated Communication" in Business Communication Quarterly (December 2007, pp. 466)*
Pub: SAGE Publications USA
Contact: Blaise R. Simqu, President
Ed: Amy Newman. **Description:** Technology-based simulation for business students to respond to emails and instant messages is presented. The simulation allows students to handle volume business correspondence at work with organizational context and under real-word business situations.

28321 ■ *"Rebels' Cause: Adult Stem Cell" in Austin Business Journal (Vol. 31, June 3, 2011, No. 13, pp. 1)*
Pub: American City Business Journals Inc.
Ed: Sandra Zaragoza. **Description:** MedRebels Foundation was launched in February 2011 with the goal of providing millions of dollars for research funding, education and advocacy for adult stem cell-focused medicine. The foundation, whose major contributor is SpineSmith LP, is a collaboration of other adult stem cell-related companies and nonprofit partners. It hopes to raise $200,000 by the end of 2011.

28322 ■ *"Recovery on Tap for 2010?" in Orlando Business Journal (Vol. 26, January 1, 2010, No. 31, pp. 1)*
Pub: American City Business Journals
Ed: Melanie Stawicki Azam, Richard Bilbao, Christopher Boyd, Anjali Fluker. **Description:** Economic forecasts for Central Florida's leading business sectors in 2010 are presented. These sectors include housing, film and TV, sports business, law, restaurants, aviation, tourism and hospitality, banking and finance, commercial real estate, retail, health care, insurance, higher education, and manufacturing. According to some local executives, Central Florida's economy will slowly recover in 2010.

28323 ■ *"Red One and The Rain Chronicles" in Michigan Vue (Vol. 13, July-August 2008, No. 4, pp. 30)*
Pub: Entrepreneur Media Inc.
Ed: Evan Cornish. **Description:** Troy-based film school the Motion Picture Institute (MPI) implemented the latest technology by shooting the second of their trilogy, 'The Rain Chronicles', on the Red One camera. This is the first feature film in Michigan to utilize this exciting new camera, which includes proprietary software for rendering and color correction. Brian K. Johnson heads up the visual effects team as visual effects supervisor and lead CG artist. His company, Dream Conduit Studios, had to tackle the task of employing the new work flow through a post-production pipeline that would allow him to attack complex visual effects shots, many of which were shot with a moving camera, a technique rarely seen in films at this budgetary level where the camera is traditionally locked off.

28324 ■ *"Region to Be Named Innovation Hub" in Business Courier (Vol. 27, July 2, 2010, No. 9, pp. 1)*
Pub: Business Courier
Ed: Dan Monk. **Description:** The selection of Cincinnati's consumer-marketing cluster as a 'Hub of Innovation' by the Ohio Department of Development could boost Cincinnati's chances of receiving $100 million in grants from Ohio's Third Frontier program and other funding sources. Implications of the University of Cincinnati's designation as a Center of Excellence in Advanced Transportation and Aerospace are also discussed.

28325 ■ *"Region Ready to Dig Deeper into Tech Fund" in Business Courier (Vol. 26, October 30, 2009, No. 27, pp. 1)*
Pub: American City Business Journals, Inc.
Ed: James Ritchie. **Description:** Southwest Ohio region aims for a bigger share in the planned renewal of Ohio's Third Frontier technology funding program. Meanwhile, University of Cincinnati vice president Sarah Degen will be appointed to the program's advisory board if the renewal proceeds.

28326 ■ *"Regional Talent Network Unveils Jobs Web Site" in Crain's Cleveland Business (Vol. 30, June 1, 2009, No. 21, pp. 11)*
Pub: Crain Communications, Inc.
Description: Regional Talent Network launched WhereToFindHelp.org, a Website designed to act as a directory of all Northeast Ohio resources that can help employers recruit and job seekers look for positions. The site also lists organizations offering employment and training services.

28327 ■ *"Revisiting Rep Coping Strategies" in Agency Sales Magazine (Vol. 39, December 2009, No. 11, pp. 32)*
Pub: MANA
Ed: Jack Foster. **Description:** Independent manufacturers representatives should become a well-rounded and complete businessman with continued education. The new type of representative is a problem solver and the resource for answering questions. Employing the concept of synergistic selling is also important to salespeople.

28328 ■ *"The Right Stuff" in Canadian Business (Vol. 79, October 23, 2006, No. 21, pp. 151)*
Pub: Rogers Media
Ed: Laura Bogomolny. **Description:** The profile of Linda Duxbury, the winner of the Sprott MBA Students Society 2003-04 Best teacher award as well as Carleton University Students' Association 2002-03 award, is presented.

28329 ■ *"The Right Time for REITs" in Barron's (Vol. 88, July 14, 2008, No. 28, pp. 32)*
Pub: Dow Jones & Co., Inc.
Ed: Mike Hogan. **Description:** Discusses the downturn in U.S. real estate investment trusts so these are worth considering for investment. Several Websites that are useful for learning about real estate investment trusts for investment purposes are presented.

28330 ■ *"The Role for Canada's Research Universities" in Canadian Business (Vol. 81, October 27, 2008, No. 18, pp. 84)*
Pub: Rogers Media Ltd.
Description: Great students tend to be the foundation of a great research-intensive university, enabling it to attract great teachers and researchers. Success is likely to attract the brightest graduate students to do research, leading to further success.

28331 ■ *"Rosewood Site Faces Big Cleanup" in Baltimore Business Journal (Vol. 27, February 6, 2010, No. 40, pp. 1)*
Pub: American City Business Journals
Ed: Daniel J. Sernovitz. **Description:** Environmental assessment report states that Maryland's Rosewood Center for the Developmentally Disabled has significant amounts of toxic chemicals, which could impact Stevenson University's decision to purchase the property. Senator Robert A. Zirkin believes that the state should pay for the cleanup, which is expected to cost millions.

28332 ■ *"SAGE Publications Announced a Partnership with Which Medical Device" in Information Today (Vol. 28, November 2011, No. 10, pp. 15)*
Pub: Information Today, Inc.
Description: SAGE Publications has partnered with Which Medical Device to offer insights, tutorials, and reviews of medical devices.

28333 ■ *"St. Rose Professor Builds Contractors and Micro-Doctors" in Business Review, Albany New York (Vol. 34, December 28, 2007, No. 39)*
Pub: American City Business Journals, Inc.
Ed: Robin K. Cooper. **Description:** Mike Mathews is an associate professor at the College of Saint Rose School of Business and one of the founders of the Center for Micro Enterprises Development, which provides training programs on business planning and management. Details of the business school's curricula and foundations are discussed.

28334 ■ *"Scholarships for Minority Students" in Occupational Outlook Quarterly (Vol. 54, Fall 2010, No. 3, pp. 25)*
Pub: U.S. Bureau of Labor Statistics
Description: Gates Millennium Scholars scholarship is awarded to minority students with leadership skills, a good GPA, and college aspirations.

28335 ■ *"Second Chance Counselor" in Business Courier (Vol. 27, July 2, 2010, No. 9, pp. 1)*
Pub: Business Courier
Ed: Lucy May. **Description:** Stephen Tucker, director of workforce development for the Urban League of Greater Cincinnati, is an example of how ex-offenders can be given chances for employment after service jail sentences. How the Urban Leagues' Solid Opportunities for Advancement job training program helped Tucker and other ex-offenders is discussed.

28336 ■ *"Selling With Strengths; Talent Trumps Training" in Gallup Management Journal (March 24, 2011)*
Pub: Gallup
Description: What are the strengths of salespeople, and how can organizations develop them? What do great sales managers do differently? The authors of, 'Strengths Based Selling' answer these questions and others, including: why money is overrated as a motivator.

28337 ■ *"Senate OKs Funds for Promoting Tourism" in Crain's Detroit Business (Vol. 24, March 31, 2008, No. 13, pp. 6)*
Pub: Crain Communications, Inc.
Ed: Amy Lane. **Description:** Discusses the Senate proposal which allocates funds for Michigan tourism and business promotion as well as Michigan's No Worker Left Behind initiative, a program that provides free tuition at community colleges and other venues to train displaced workers for high-demand occupations.

28338 ■ *"Senators Predict Online School Changes" in Puget Sound Business Journal (Vol. 29, September 19, 2008, No. 22, pp. 1)*
Pub: American City Business Journals
Ed: Clay Holtzman. **Description:** State senators promise to create new legislation that would tighten the monitoring and oversight of online public schools. The officials are concerned about the lack of oversight of the programs as well as lack of knowledge about content of the lessons.

28339 ■ *"The Service Imperative"* in *Business Horizons (Vol. 51, January-February 2008, No. 1, pp. 39)*

Pub: Elsevier Advanced Technology Publications

Ed: Mary Jo Bitner, Stephen W. Brown. **Description:** The importance of services is growing in developing countries like India and China, but little attention is given to service research, education and innovation. The 'service imperative' seeks to promote the advancement of services. The scope, objectives and philosophy of the service imperative platform are outlined.

28340 ■ *"Sewing Is a Life Skill; Teaching To Sew Is An Art"* in *Virginia-Pilot (August 31, 2010)*

Pub: Virginian-Pilot

Ed: Jamesetta Walker. **Description:** In conjunction with National Sewing Month, the American Sewing Guild is sponsoring a two-day workshop featuring Stephanie Kimura.

28341 ■ *"Small-Business Agenda: Increase Capital, Education, Tax Breaks"* in *Crain's Detroit Business (Vol. 24, March 17, 2008)*

Pub: Crain Communications, Inc.

Ed: Nancy Kaffer. **Description:** Discusses the policy suggestions detailed in the Small Business Association of Michigan's entrepreneurial agenda which include five main categories of focus: making entrepreneurial education a higher state priority; increasing capital available to entrepreneurs; using the state's tax structure as an incentive for entrepreneurial growth; getting university research from the lab to the market; and limiting government regulation that's burdensome to small businesses and getting legislative support of entrepreneurial assistance efforts.

28342 ■ *"Some Good Earners: Preparing Prison Inmates to Start Businesses Upon Their Release"* in *Inc. (Vol. 31, January-February 2009, No. 1)*

Pub: Mansueto Ventures LLC

Ed: Mike Hoffman. **Description:** Prison Entrepreneurship Program (PEP) is a nonprofit organization that works with the Texas Department of Criminal Justice to teach entrepreneurship to prison inmates. Profiled is Hans Becker, owner of Armadillo Tree and Shrub in Dallas; Becker studied the PEP program while serving five years in prison and started his successful company when released.

28343 ■ *"Spotlight; 'Classroom Focus' at Encyclopaedia Britannica"* in *Crain's Chicago Business (Vol. 34, October 24, 2011, No. 42, pp. 6)*

Pub: Crain Communications Inc.

Ed: Paul Merrion. **Description:** Profile of Gregory Healy, product officer for Encyclopaedia Britannica is presented. Healy took the position in May 2010 and is focused on online offerings of their publication and to make them more useful to teachers.

28344 ■ *"Staples Advantage Receives NJPA National Contract for Janitorial Supplies"* in *Professional Services Close-Up (April 22, 2011)*

Pub: Close-Up Media

Description: Staples Advantage, the business-to-business division of Staples Inc. was awarded a contract for janitorial supplies to members of the National Joint Powers Alliance (NJPA). NJPA is a member-owned buying cooperative serving public and private schools, state and local governments, and nonprofit organizations.

28345 ■ *StartingUp Now Facilitator Guide*

Pub: StartingUp Now

Ed: L. Jenkins. **Released:** September 11, 2011. **Price:** $29.95. **Description:** Guide for those teaching entrepreneurship using StartingUp Now; the guide provides 24 lesson plans for each of the 24 steps/chapters in the book.

28346 ■ *"Stay in School: Economy Got You Down?"* in *Canadian Business (Vol. 81,*

November 10, 2008, No. 19, pp. 98)

Pub: Rogers Media Ltd.

Ed: Graham F. Scott, Jane Bao. **Description:** A guide to Canadian MBA programs is presented. The tuition and length of each program is provided along with each school. Details on whether the universities offer part-time options, diversity, and co-op/internships are also given.

28347 ■ *"Stop the Madness"* in *Hawaii Business (Vol. 53, October 2007, No. 4, pp. 10)*

Pub: Hawaii Business Publishing

Ed: Kelli Abe Trifonovitch. **Description:** Discusses the number of parents paying for kindergarten admissions tutorials for their kids which has increased, as parents want to improve their children's chances of being admitted at a prestigious school. Some schools in Hawaii are not in favor of this trend, and they actually rate an applicant negatively if his or her answers seem to be too rehearsed. Some of the lessons in the admissions tutorials are discussed.

28348 ■ *"Storytelling Star of Show for Scripps"* in *Business Courier (Vol. 26, November 13, 2009, No. 29, pp. 1)*

Pub: American City Business Journals, Inc.

Ed: Dan Monk. **Description:** Rich Boehne, CEO Of the EW Scripps Company in Cincinnati has authorized a new training program in storytelling for employees at Scripps' 10 television stations. He believes that the training will improve the quality of broadcasting content. His plans to improve quality of newspaper content are also discussed.

28349 ■ *"Study Puts Hub On Top of the Tech Heap"* in *Boston Business Journal (Vol. 30, November 26, 2010, No. 44, pp. 1)*

Pub: Boston Business Journal

Ed: Galen Moore. **Description:** The Ewing Marion Kauffman Foundation ranked Massachusetts at the top in its evaluations of states' innovative industries, government leadership, and education. Meanwhile, research blog formDs.com also ranked Massachusetts number one in terms of venture-capital financings per capita.

28350 ■ *"Suddenly, Sewing Is Hip Again for Kids, Moms and Crafters"* in *Atlanta Journal-Constitution (August 29, 2010)*

Pub: Atlanta Journal-Constitution

Ed: Rosalind Bentley. **Description:** Across Atlanta, Georgia, along with the entire nation, sewing classes are increasing in popularity.

28351 ■ *"Survey: Don't Expect Big Results From Stimulus"* in *Crain's Detroit Business (Vol. 25, June 1, 2009, No. 22)*

Pub: Crain Communications Inc. - Detroit

Ed: Nancy Kaffer, Chad Halcom. **Description:** In a recent survey, Michigan business owners, operators or managers showed that 48 percent of respondents oppose the President's stimulus package and believe it will have little or no effect on the economy.

28352 ■ *"Teachable Moments: Worth Every Penny"* in *Pet Product News (Vol. 64, December 2010, No. 12, pp. 34)*

Pub: BowTie Inc.

Ed: Cheryl Reeves. **Description:** Pet bird retailers can attain both outreach to customers and enhanced profitability by staging educational events such as the annual Parrot Palooza event of Burlington, New Jersey-based Bird Paradise. Aside from attracting a global audience, Parrot Palooza features seminars, workshops, classes, and bird-related contests.

28353 ■ *"Ted Stahl: Executive Chairman"* in *Inside Business (Vol. 13, September-October 2011, No. 5, pp. NC6)*

Pub: Great Lakes Publishing Co.

Ed: Miranda S. Miller. **Description:** Profile of Ted Stahl, who started working in his family's business when he was ten years old is presented. The firm makes dies for numbers and letters used on team uniforms. Another of the family firms manufactures stock and custom heat-printing products, equipment and supplies. It also educates customers on ways to

decorate garments with heat printing products and offers graphics and software for customers to create their own artwork.

28354 ■ *"Texas State Poised for Boom"* in *Austin Business JournalInc. (Vol. 29, January 29, 2010, No. 47, pp. 1)*

Pub: American City Business Journals

Ed: Sandra Zaragoza. **Description:** Texas State University, San Marcos has seen its student population grow to 30,800 and the university is set for $633 million in construction projects to address demand for student housing and building expansions and renovations. Details on the buildings and student housing plans for the projects are provided.

28355 ■ *"The Thinker"* in *Canadian Business (Vol. 81, March 31, 2008, No. 5, pp. 52)*

Pub: Rogers Media

Ed: Andrew Wahl. **Description:** Mihnea Moldoveanu provides much of the academic rigor that underpins Roger Martin's theories on how to improve the way business leaders think. Moldoveanu is also a classically trained pianist and founder of Redline Communications and has a mechanical engineering degree from MIT on top of his astounding knowledge on many academic fields.

28356 ■ *"Thinking Aloud: Julian Franks"* in *Business Strategy Review (Vol. 21, Autumn 2010, No. 3, pp. 35)*

Pub: Blackwell Publishers Ltd.

Ed: Stuart Crainer. **Description:** Julian Franks is Academic Director of the Centre for Corporate Governance at London Business School and lead investigator for a 1.4 million (sterling pounds) grand for research into corporate governance.

28357 ■ *"Thinking Aloud: Julian Franks"* in *Business Strategy Review (Vol. 21, Autumn 2010, No. 3, pp. 35)*

Pub: Wiley-Blackwell

Ed: Stuart Crainer. **Description:** Julian Franks is academic director of the Centre for Corporate Governance at London Business School and lead investigator for a (pounds sterling) 1.4 million grant for research into corporate governance.

28358 ■ *"Top Marks"* in *Canadian Business (Vol. 79, October 23, 2006, No. 21, pp. 143)*

Pub: Rogers Media

Ed: Erin Pooley; Laura Bogomolny. **Description:** Profiles of some top grade master of business administration students like Hogan Mullally and Will mercer, belonging to reputed business schools, are presented.

28359 ■ *"Trade Craft: Take Pride in Your Trade, Demand Excellence"* in *Contractor (Vol. 56, October 2009, No. 10, pp. 24)*

Pub: Penton Media, Inc.

Ed: Al Schwartz. **Description:** There is a need for teaching, developing, and encouraging trade craft. An apprentice plumber is not only versed in the mechanical aspects of the trade but he also has a working knowledge of algebra, trigonometry, chemistry, and thermal dynamics. Contractors should be demanding on their personnel regarding their trade craft and should only keep and train the very best people they can hire.

28360 ■ *"Train Now to Get the Competitive Edge"* in *Contractor (Vol. 56, October 2009, No. 10, pp. 58)*

Pub: Penton Media, Inc.

Ed: Merry Beth Hall. **Description:** Due to the harsh economic climate, mechanical contractors would be well-served to train their employees while they have time to take them out of the field. This will help ensure that they are not behind when the economic recovery happens. Suggestions on how to choose the best type of training are presented.

28361 ■ *"Training Center Wants to be College"* in *Austin Business JournalInc. (Vol. 29, November 13, 2009, No. 36, pp. A1)*

Pub: American City Business Journals

Ed: Sandra Zaragoza. **Description:** Texas-based CyberTex Institute, a job training center, has established technical careers in an effort to obtain federal accreditation as a college. A college status would allow CyberTex to extend financial assistance to students. Aside from potentially having an enlarged student body and expanded campus, CyberTex would be allowed to engage in various training programs.

28362 ■ *"Training Essential For Growth; It Doesn't Have To Cost Much"* in *Crain's Detroit Business* (Vol. 24, January 21, 2008, No. 3, pp. 14)

Pub: Crain Communications Inc. - Detroit

Ed: Sheena Harrison. **Description:** Employee training is essential for small companies to achieve growth.

28363 ■ *Training Resources: ASTD Buyer's Guide*

Pub: ASTD

Contact: Tony Bingham, President

E-mail: tbingham@astd.org

URL(s): www.astd.org. **Released:** Annual December. **Entries include:** Company name, contact information and name, profile, list of products and services. **Database covers:** Businesses and individual consultants offering products, services, and equipment for sale to persons in corporate training and human resource development. **Arrangement:** Alphabetical. **Indexes:** Subject, geographical, industry focus.

28364 ■ *"Training the Troops: Battlefield Simulations Bring Growth to UNITECH"* in *Black Enterprise* (Vol. 38, February 2008, No. 7, pp. 30)

Pub: Earl G. Graves Publishing Co. Inc.

Ed: Cliff Hocker. **Description:** Universal Systems and Technology (UNITECH) received a total of over $45 million U.S. Department of Defense orders during September and October 2007. UNITECH designs and manufactures battlefield simulation devices used to train troops in the Army and Marine Corps.

28365 ■ *"Trend: Tutors to Help You Pump Up the Staff"* in *Business Week* (September 22, 2008, No. 4100, pp. 45)

Pub: McGraw-Hill Companies, Inc.

Ed: Reena Janaj. **Description:** High-level managers are turning to innovation coaches in an attempt to obtain advice on how to better sell new concepts within their companies. Individuals as well as consulting firms are now offering this service.

28366 ■ *"Trinity Western University Offers Project Management Course"* in *Bellingham Business Journal* (Vol. February 2010 pp. 4)

Pub: Sound Publishing Inc.

Description: Trinity Western University in Bellinham, Washington is offering a new certification program in project management. Students who take and pass the certification examination of the International Project Management Institutes will lead to positions in many industries. Details of the program are provided.

28367 ■ *Trump University Entrepreneurship 101*

Pub: John Wiley and Sons, Inc.

Ed: Mike Gordon. **Released:** January 2007. **Price:** $21.95. **Description:** Entrepreneurs, past, present or future, will find this book helpful. The book covers three objectives: to energize readers to be courageous when taking steps toward an entrepreneurial goal, works to demystify the entrepreneurial process, and to help individuals improve success.

28368 ■ *"U Overhauling Its Janitorial Program, but Custodians Taking Exception"* in *Saint Paul Pioneer Press* (August 20, 2011)

Pub: McClatchy-Tribune Regional News

Ed: Mila Koumpilova. **Description:** University of Minnesota developed a new team cleaning approach for its campus. The new custodian program will save $3.1 million annually while providing a cleaner campus. The union representing the custodians questions both claims.

28369 ■ *"UA, BP Test Unmanned Aircraft"* in *Alaska Business Monthly* (Vol. 27, October 2011, No. 10, pp. 8)

Pub: Alaska Business Publishing Company

Ed: Nancy Pounds. **Description:** University of Alaska Fairbanks Geophysical Institute and BP Exploration Alaska tested the oil-spill capabilities of an unmanned aircraft. The aircraft will be used to gather 3-D ariel data to aid in oil-spill cleanup.

28370 ■ *"UA Turns Ann Arbor Green"* in *Contractor* (Vol. 56, September 2009, No. 9, pp. 5)

Pub: Penton Media, Inc.

Ed: Robert P. Mader. **Description:** Instructors at the United Association of Plumbers and Steamfitters have studied the latest in green and sustainable construction and service at the Washtenaw Community College in Michigan. Classes included building information modeling, hydronic heating and cooling and advanced HVACR troubleshooting. The UA is currently focusing on green training.

28371 ■ *"UAlbany on the Hunt for New Brand"* in *Business Review, Albany New York* (Vol. 34, October 5, 2007, No. 27, pp. 1)

Pub: American City Business Journals, Inc.

Ed: Richard A. D'Errico. **Description:** State University of New York at Albany is working on a new marketing and branding initiative to help communicate its message better. The initiative is for the school to better understand its target audiences and their perception of the university.

28372 ■ *"UC May Expand into Old Ford Plant"* in *Business Courier* (Vol. 26, December 25, 2009, No. 35, pp. 1)

Pub: American City Business Journals, Inc.

Ed: Dan Monk. **Description:** Developer Stuart Lichter is planning to acquire University of Cincinnati (UC) as a tenant at a two-story office building on a 132-acre site where a vacant Ford transmission plant is located. Details of the transaction are outlined.

28373 ■ *"UMKC, Hospital Drill Down on Deal"* in *The Business Journal-Serving Metropolitan Kansas City* (Vol. 26, July 18, 2008, No. 45, pp. 1)

Pub: American City Business Journals, Inc.

Ed: Rob Roberts. **Description:** University of Missouri Kansas City and Children's Mercy Hospital are negotiating the hospital's potential acquisition of the university's School of Dentistry building. The deal would transfer the 240,000-square foot dental school building to Children's Mercy. Plans for a new dental school building for the UMKC are also presented.

28374 ■ *"University Book Store Inc.: an Act of Independence"* in *Retail Merchandiser* (Vol. 51, September-October 2011, No. 5, pp. 68)

Pub: Phoenix Media Corporation

Ed: Lori Sichtermann. **Description:** University Book Store Inc. is a campus bookstore located at the University of Washington, in Seattle. The book store provides more than $1 million in UW customer rebates and discounts annually and donated more than $800,000 in UW student scholarships.

28375 ■ *"Up Against the Ropes: A Professional Coach May Help"* in *Black Enterprise* (Vol. 37, December 2006, No. 5, pp. 72)

Pub: Earl G. Graves Publishing Co. Inc.

Description: Executive coaching is now a $1 billion industry. The coaching process itself and traits to look for in a coach are discussed.

28376 ■ *"An Updated Ranking of Academic Journals in Economics"* in *Canadian Journal of Economics* (Vol. 44, November 2011, No. 4, pp. 1525)

Pub: Blackwell Publishers Ltd.

Ed: Pantelis Kalaitzidakis, Theofanis P. Mamuneas, Thanasis Stengos. **Description:** An updated list showing the ranking of economic journals (2003) is presented; however this present study differs methodologically from an earlier study by using a rolling window of years between 2003 and 2008, for each year counting the number of citations of articles published in the previous ten years.

28377 ■ *"Using Teaching Teams to Encourage Active Learning"* in *Business Communication Quarterly* (December 2007, pp. 457)

Pub: SAGE Publications USA

Contact: Blaise R. Simqu, President

Ed: Lisa E. Gueldenzoph. **Description:** The practice of dividing classes into teaching teams to encourage active learning is studied. Students in business management courses become more involved in the learning process with this technique and collaborate to enhance better understanding of course content.

28378 ■ *"USM Focuses on Turning Science Into New Companies, Cash"* in *Boston Business Journal* (Vol. 29, July 1, 2011, No. 8, pp. 1)

Pub: American City Business Journals Inc.

Ed: Alexander Jackson. **Description:** University System of Maryland gears up to push for its plan for commercializing its scientific discoveries which by 2020 could create 325 companies and double the $1.4 billion the system's eleven schools garner in yearly research grants. It is talking with University of Utah and University Maryland, Baltimore to explore ways to make this plan a reality.

28379 ■ *"UT Deans Serious about Biz"* in *Austin Business Journal* (Vol. 31, May 20, 2011, No. 11, pp. 1)

Pub: American City Business Journals Inc.

Ed: Sandra Zaragoza. **Description:** Dean Thomas Gilligan of the University of Texas, McCombs School of Business and engineering school Dean Gregory Fenves have partnered to develop a joint engineering and business degree. Their partnership has resulted in an undergraduate course on initiating startups.

28380 ■ *"The Valuation of Players"* in *Canadian Business* (Vol. 80, October 22, 2007, No. 21, pp. 39)

Pub: Rogers Media

Ed: Jeff Sanford. **Description:** Business professionals are supplementing their Masters in Business Administration degrees with CBV or chartered business valuator. CBVs are trained, not only in business tangibles but also in business intangibles such as market position, reputation, intellectual property, and patent. Details of employment opportunities for chartered business valuators are discussed.

28381 ■ *"Verdict: Few Legal Jobs"* in *Boston Business Journal* (Vol. 31, June 17, 2011, No. 21, pp. 1)

Pub: Boston Business Journal

Ed: Lisa van der Pool. **Description:** Law school graduates in Massachusetts are finding it harder to find work as the legal job market remains weak. The national employment rate for the 2010 law school class fell to 87.6 percent, while only 68.4 percent held jobs that require passing the bar examination.

28382 ■ *"Vision for Camden in Better Focus"* in *Philadelphia Business Journal* (Vol. 30, September 30, 2011, No. 33, pp. 1)

Pub: American City Business Journals Inc.

Ed: Natalie Kostelni. **Description:** More than $500 million worth of projects aimed at redeveloping the downtown and waterfront areas of Camden, New Jersey are being planned. These include the construction of residential, commercial, and education buildings.

28383 ■ *"The Way I Work: Kim Kleeman"* in *Inc.* (October 2007, pp. 110-112, 114)

Pub: Gruner & Jahr USA Publishing

Ed: Leigh Buchanan. **Description:** Profile of Kim Kleemna, founder and president of ShakespeareSquared, a firm that develops educational materials, including lesson plans, teacher guides, activity workbooks, and discussion guides for large publishers. Kleeman talks about the challenges she faces running her nearly all-women company while maintaining a balance with her family.

28384 ■ *"What Businesses Can Do: Growing the Supply of Highly Skilled Graduates"* in *Canadian Business* (Vol. 81, October 27,

2008, No. 18)
Pub: Rogers Media Ltd.

Description: Employers in Canada have expressed concerns over the findings of various studies that revealed current and projected labor shortages in the country. A low birthrate and an aging population is contributing to the problem. Ways businesses can increase the supply of highly skilled workers in Canada is presented.

28385 ■ *"What School Did You Attend?" in Hawaii Business (Vol. 53, December 2007, No. 6, pp. 14)*
Pub: Hawaii Business Publishing

Ed: Kelli Abe Trifonovitch. **Description:** Discusses the question 'what school did you attend?' which is observed to be the most important inquiry in Hawaiian business discourse. The principle behind the question is based on establishing connections. The relation between the aforementioned inquiry and Hawaiian culture is explained.

28386 ■ *"What's Working Now: In Providing Jobs for North Carolinians" in Business North Carolina (Vol. 28, February 2008, No. 2, pp. 16)*
Pub: Business North Carolina

Ed: Edward Martin, Frank Maley. **Description:** Individuals previously employed in the furniture, tobacco, or textile manufacturing sectors have gone back to school to be trained in new sectors in the area such as life sciences, finances and other emerging sectors.

28387 ■ *"Wheatfield First Choice for Canadian Manufacturer" in Business First Buffalo (November 23, 2007, pp. 1)*
Pub: American City Business Journals, Inc.

Ed: James Fink. **Description:** Niagara County Industrial Development Agency is preparing an enticement program that would lure automotive parts manufacturer Pop & Lock Corporation to shift manufacturing operations to Wheatfield, Niagara County, New York. The package includes job-training grants and assistance for acquiring new machinery. Details of the plan are included.

28388 ■ *"Where to Buy the Right MBA" in Canadian Business (Vol. 79, October 23, 2006, No. 21, pp. 99)*
Pub: Rogers Media

Ed: Erin Pooley; Laura Bogomolny; Joe Castaldo; Michelle Magnan; Claire Gagne. **Description:** Details of Canadian graduate business schools offering Master of business administration degree are presented.

28389 ■ *"Where New Economy Initiative Grants Have Gone" in Crain's Detroit Business (Vol. 25, June 1, 2009, No. 22, pp. M014)*
Pub: Crain Communications Inc. - Detroit

Description: Listing of grants totaling $20.5 million focusing on talent development, attraction and retention; innovation and entrepreneurship; and shifting to a culture that values learning, work and innovation, is presented.

28390 ■ *"The WIN Library" in Women In Business (Vol. 61, August-September 2009, No. 4, pp. 36)*
Pub: American Business Women's Association

Ed: Leigh Elmore. **Description:** Women's Instructional Network (WIN) offers members of the American Business Women's Association with information about the organization and 15 Team Tools learning modules to help further the learning of business women. Other training programs and services offered by WIN are presented.

28391 ■ *"A Woman's Advantage" in Black Enterprise (Vol. 38, December 2007, No. 5, pp. 86)*
Pub: Earl G. Graves Publishing Co. Inc.

Ed: Marcia Reed-Woodard. **Description:** Leadership development is essential for any small business. Simmons College's Strategic Leadership for Women

educational course offers a five-day program for professional women teaching powerful strategies to perform, compete, and win in the workplace.

28392 ■ *"Women as 21st Century Leaders" in Women In Business (Vol. 63, Summer 2011, No. 2, pp. 26)*
Pub: American Business Women's Association

Ed: Leigh Elmore. **Description:** American Business Women's Association and Park University have partnered to provide a leadership training program to attendees of the 2011 National Women's Leadership Conference. The courses will incorporate introduction to concepts, development of critical thinking skills and direct application through exercises. Comments from executives are also included.

28393 ■ *"Women and Higher Education" in Montly Labor Review (Vol. 133, September 2010, No. 9, pp. 70)*
Pub: Bureau of Labor Statistics

Description: The increase in people going to college has been mostly among women. Statistical data included.

28394 ■ *"Work Force: In the Mix" in Entrepreneur (Vol. 35, October 2007, No. 10, pp. 109)*
Pub: Entrepreneur Media Inc.

Ed: Mark Henricks. **Description:** A study of 708 companies' diversity programs shows that diversity training alone is not the most effective way of increasing diversity in management. It was found that one effective way of putting minorities and women in management teams is to give a team or a person the task of improving diversity in the company. The reason why accountability succeeds in diversifying the workforce is discussed.

28395 ■ *"Work Less, Earn More" in Canadian Business (Vol. 80, March 12, 2007, No. 6, pp. 30)*
Pub: Rogers Media

Ed: Erin Pooley. **Description:** Expert advice on ways to work efficiently to complete the job instead of extending work hours is presented.

28396 ■ *Working Papers, Chapters 1-14 for Needles/Powers/Crosson's Financial and Managerial Accounting*
Pub: Cengage South-Western

Ed: Belverd E. Needles, Marian Powers, Susan V. Crosson. **Released:** May 10, 2010. **Price:** $62.95. **Description:** Appropriate accounting forms for completing all exercises, problems and cases in the text are provided for financial management of a small company.

28397 ■ *"The World Is Your Oyster" in Canadian Business (Vol. 80, October 22, 2007, No. 21, pp. 140)*
Pub: Rogers Media

Ed: Regan Ray. **Description:** Business graduates are not that keen on working abroad. Fortune 500 companies are requiring executives to have a multi-country focus. The skill required for jobs abroad, as well as employment opportunities are discussed.

28398 ■ *"The World is Their Classroom" in Crain's Chicago Business (Vol. 31, March 24, 2008, No. 12, pp. 24)*
Pub: Crain Communications, Inc.

Ed: Samantha Stainburn. **Description:** Due to globalization more business students are studying abroad; 89 percent of eligible students in its executive MBA program went overseas in 2007 compared to 15 percent ten years ago.

28399 ■ *"Young Entrepreneur Gets Some Recognition and Some Help for College" in Philadelphia Inquirer (August 30, 2010)*
Pub: Philadelphia Inquirer

Ed: Susan Snyder. **Description:** Profile of Zachary Gosling, age 18, who launched an online auction Website from his bedroom, using advertising and sponsorship funds rather than charging fees to users.

TRADE PERIODICALS

28400 ■ *AACE Bonus Briefs*
Pub: American Association for Career Education

Ed: Pat Nellor Wickwire, Editor. **Released:** Quarterly. **Price:** Included in membership. **Description:** Contains brief papers by American Association for Career Education members on current issues in careers, education, and employment.

28401 ■ *AACE Distinguished Member Series*
Pub: American Association for Career Education

Ed: Pat Nellor Wickwire, Editor. **Released:** Periodic. **Price:** Included in membership. **Description:** Publication of the American Association for Career Education. Provides information on careers, education, and employment.

28402 ■ *AACSB Newsline*
Pub: AACSB--American Assembly of Collegiate Schools of Business

Ed: Becky Johnson, Editor. **Released:** 4/yr. **Price:** $25 /year; $35 elsewhere. **Description:** Covers issues and events affecting management education, and Association projects and activities. Recurring features include notices of publications available and news of educational opportunities.

28403 ■ *California Special Education Alert*
Pub: LRP Publications

Contact: Steve Bevilacquar, Director, Editorial

Released: Monthly. **Price:** $260 plus $27 s/h. **Description:** Assists California special education administrators comply with changing special education laws, regulations, and policies on the state and federal level to avoid litigation. Recurring features include letters to the editor, interviews, and reports of meetings.

28404 ■ *The Chemical Educator*
Pub: The Chemical Educator

URL(s): chemeducator.org. **Ed:** Hugh Cartwright. **Released:** Bimonthly **Price:** $29.95, Individuals; $149.95, Institutions print archive edition available separately; $10, Single issue + shipping.

28405 ■ *Multimedia Internet@Schools: A Practical Journal of Multimedia, CD-ROM, Online, & Internet in K-12*
Pub: Information Today Inc.

Contact: Thomas H. Hogan, President

E-mail: ctuthill@infotoday.com

URL(s): www.mmischools.com/. **Ed:** David Hoffman. **Released:** Bimonthly **Price:** $45.95, U.S.; $64, Canada and Mexico; $73, Other countries; $94, Two years; $144, Individuals 3 years.

28406 ■ *School Scene*
Pub: Technology Student Association

Contact: Dhruv Pillai, President

Ed: Jane Wright, Editor. **Released:** 3x/yr. **Price:** Included in membership. **Description:** Functions as a member newsletter for the Technology Student Association. Dedicated to preparing membership for the challenges of a dynamic world by promoting personal growth and opportunities. Also provides competitive event news and tips, along with conference news. Recurring features include interviews, a calendar of events, reports of meetings, news of educational opportunities, and notices of publications available.

28407 ■ *Teach Magazine: Education for Today and Tomorrow*
Pub: TEACH Magazine

URL(s): teachmag.com/. **Ed:** Vinicio Scarci, Wili Liberman. **Released:** 5/yr. **Price:** C$21.41, Canada; C$28.95, Other countries.

28408 ■ *Thimband-The Newsletter*
Pub: Continnuus

Ed: A.C. Doyle, Editor. **Released:** Annual. **Price:** $6. **Description:** Provides useful information for homemakers and consumers.

VIDEOCASSETTES/ AUDIOCASSETTES

28409 ■ *Adult Learning Video? You've Got to Be Kidding!*
ASTD
1640 King St.
Alexandria, VA 22314-2746

Ph: (703)683-8100
Free: 800-628-2783
Fax: (703)683-1523
Co. E-mail: customercare@astd.org
URL: http://www.astd.org
Contact: Tony Bingham, President
E-mail: tbingham@astd.org
Released: 1989. **Description:** A look at the seven steps to becoming an all-star trainer in business and industry. Describes how to use the principles of learning theory to improve training sessions. Focuses on the issues of the adult learner, including fear of failure, new technology vs. past experience, and bureaucractic systems. **Availability:** VHS; 3/4 U.

28410 ■ Basic Techniques in Practical Chemistry
TMW Media Group
2321 Abbot Kinney Blvd., Ste. 101
Venice, CA 90291
Ph: (310)577-8581
Free: 800-262-8862
Fax: (310)574-0886
Co. E-mail: general@tmwmedia.com
URL: http://www.tmwmedia.com
Released: 1997. **Price:** $395.00. **Description:** Ten-volume series provide hands on presentations and precise, analytical content that make difficult chemistry understandable for all levels. **Availability:** VHS.

28411 ■ Charley Chapters: Contraction Action
Media, Inc.
PO Box 496
Media, PA 19063
Ph: (610)565-2844
Free: 800-523-0118
Fax: (610)565-3614
URL: http://www.mediaincorporated.com
Released: 1996. **Price:** $225.00. **Description:** Explains the rules for changing two words into one. **Availability:** VHS.

28412 ■ Charley Chapters: Root Words, Prefixes, and Suffixes
Media, Inc.
PO Box 496
Media, PA 19063
Ph: (610)565-2844
Free: 800-523-0118
Fax: (610)565-3614
URL: http://www.mediaincorporated.com
Released: 1996. **Price:** $225.00. **Description:** Provides lessons for making spelling easier. **Availability:** VHS.

28413 ■ Charley Chapters: Suffixes and Their Rule Changes
Media, Inc.
PO Box 496
Media, PA 19063
Ph: (610)565-2844
Free: 800-523-0118
Fax: (610)565-3614
URL: http://www.mediaincorporated.com
Released: 1996. **Price:** $225.00. **Description:** Explains the rules for the ways words change when suffixes are added. **Availability:** VHS.

28414 ■ Charley Chapters: Writing with Synonyms, Antonyms, and the Thesaurus
Media, Inc.
PO Box 496
Media, PA 19063
Ph: (610)565-2844
Free: 800-523-0118
Fax: (610)565-3614
URL: http://www.mediaincorporated.com
Released: 1995. **Price:** $225.00. **Description:** Explains how to expand vocabulary and writing skills. **Availability:** VHS.

28415 ■ Common Miracles: The New American Revolution in Learning
MPI Home Video
16101 S. 108th Ave.
Orland Park, IL 60467
Ph: (708)460-0555

Free: 800-323-0442
Fax: (708)873-3177
URL: http://www.mpihomevideo.com
Released: 1997. **Price:** $19.98. **Description:** Peter Jennings examines the future of education. **Availability:** VHS.

28416 ■ Disney Presents Bill Nye the Science Guy Sampler III
Buena Vista Home Entertainment
500 S Buena Vista St.
Burbank, CA 91521-1120
Ph: (800)723-4763
Fax: (818)845-8728
URL: http://www.bvhe.com
Contact: Bob Chapek, President
Released: 19??. **Price:** $199.00. **Description:** Collection of 10 full-length shows featuring lessons in archeology, volcanoes, inventions, animal locomotion, and more. **Availability:** VHS.

28417 ■ The Eisenhower Era, 1940-1960
Buena Vista Home Entertainment
500 S Buena Vista St.
Burbank, CA 91521-1120
Ph: (800)723-4763
Fax: (818)845-8728
URL: http://www.bvhe.com
Contact: Bob Chapek, President
Released: 19??. **Price:** $699.00. **Description:** Twenty-volume series covers four thematic units: World War II, The Cold War, The Eisenhower Presidency (Domestic Policy), and The Eisenhower Presidency (Foreign Policy). Includes teacher's guide, companion software, and activities. **Availability:** VHS.

28418 ■ Got a Problem? Solve It!
Sunburst Digital Inc.
1550 Executive Dr.
Elgin, IL 60123-9311
Free: 800-321-7511
Fax: (914)747-4109
Co. E-mail: service@sunburst.com
URL: http://www.sunburst.com
Contact: Dan Figurski, President
Released: 1997. **Price:** $59.95. **Description:** Four vignettes present positive strategies for logical thinking and problem solving. On-screen questions promote classroom discussions. **Availability:** VHS.

28419 ■ Helping Your Child Succeed in School
Tapeworm Video Distributors
25876 The Old Road #141
Stevenson Ranch, CA 91381
Ph: (661)257-4904
Fax: (661)257-4820
Co. E-mail: sales@tapeworm.com
URL: http://www.tapeworm.com
Released: 19??. **Price:** $18.95. **Description:** Six part video series discussing aspects of all stages of learning and development. **Availability:** VHS.

28420 ■ Hola Amigos Boxed Set
Monterey Home Video
566 St. Charles Dr.
Thousand Oaks, CA 91360-3953
Ph: (805)494-7199
Free: 800-424-2593
Fax: (805)496-6061
Co. E-mail: customerservice@montereymedia.com
URL: http://www.montereymedia.com
Contact: Scott Mansfield, President
Released: 1997. **Price:** $54.95. **Description:** Three-volume set uses songs and games to provide a gentle introduction to the Spanish language. **Availability:** VHS.

28421 ■ Johnny Tremain
Buena Vista Home Entertainment
500 S Buena Vista St.
Burbank, CA 91521-1120
Ph: (800)723-4763

Fax: (818)845-8728
URL: http://www.bvhe.com
Contact: Bob Chapek, President
Released: 1997. **Price:** $99.00. **Description:** Presents reenactments of historical figures and events such as the Boston Tea Party, Paul Revere, and Samuel Adams. **Availability:** VHS.

28422 ■ Science in Action
TMW Media Group
2321 Abbot Kinney Blvd., Ste. 101
Venice, CA 90291
Ph: (310)577-8581
Free: 800-262-8862
Fax: (310)574-0886
Co. E-mail: general@tmwmedia.com
URL: http://www.tmwmedia.com
Released: 1997. **Price:** $119.00. **Description:** Six-volume series explains basic scientific concepts and principles in an easy-to-understand manner. **Availability:** VHS.

28423 ■ Something Special
Educational Activities, Inc.
PO Box 87
Baldwin, NY 11510
Free: 800-797-3223
Fax: (516)623-9282
URL: http://www.edact.com
Released: 1997. **Price:** $19.95. **Description:** Teaches movement vocabulary skills and promotes self-esteem. **Availability:** VHS.

28424 ■ Table Time for Tots
Tapeworm Video Distributors
25876 The Old Road #141
Stevenson Ranch, CA 91381
Ph: (661)257-4904
Fax: (661)257-4820
Co. E-mail: sales@tapeworm.com
URL: http://www.tapeworm.com
Released: 1997. **Price:** $14.95. **Description:** Introduces children to the basic food groups using poem and song. **Availability:** VHS.

28425 ■ Training 101: Principles, Processes and People Every Trainer Should Know
ASTD
1640 King St.
Alexandria, VA 22314-2746
Ph: (703)683-8100
Free: 800-628-2783
Fax: (703)683-1523
Co. E-mail: customercare@astd.org
URL: http://www.astd.org
Contact: Tony Bingham, President
E-mail: tbingham@astd.org
Released: 1989. **Description:** A video overview of training, designed to give trainers more competence and confidence. Basic processes and concepts are explained and human resource development experts present descriptions of their work. **Availability:** VHS; 3/4 U.

28426 ■ Transformations: Science, Technology, and Society
Karol Media
Hanover Industrial Estates
375 Stewart Rd.
Wilkes Barre, PA 18773-7600
Ph: (570)822-8899
Free: 800-526-4773
Co. E-mail: sales@karolmedia.com
URL: http://www.karolmedia.com
Released: 1997. **Price:** $125.00. **Description:** Eight-volume series designed to motivate learning and enhance science instruction. **Availability:** VHS.

28427 ■ Volcanoes: Cauldrons of Fury
MPI Home Video
16101 S. 108th Ave.
Orland Park, IL 60467
Ph: (708)460-0555
Free: 800-323-0442
Fax: (708)873-3177
URL: http://www.mpihomevideo.com
Released: 19??. **Price:** $19.98. **Description:** Examines the causes, history and future of volcanoes. **Availability:** VHS.

TRADE SHOWS AND CONVENTIONS

28428 ■ Michigan Association for Computer Users in Learning Conference
Michigan Association for Computer Users in Learning
3410 Belle Chase Way, Ste. 100
Lansing, MI 48911
Ph: (517)882-1403
Fax: (517)882-2362
Co. E-mail: macul@macul.org
URL: http://www.macul.org
Contact: Ric Wiltse, Executive Director
URL(s): www.macul.org. **Frequency:** Annual. **Audience:** Educational technology professionals. **Principal Exhibits:** Computer and educational equipment, supplies, and services.

CONSULTANTS

28429 ■ American English Academy (AEA)—American English College
111 N Atlantic Blvd., Ste. 112
Monterey Park, CA 91754
Ph: (626)457-2800
Fax: (626)457-2808
Co. E-mail: admission@aea-usa.com
URL: http://www.aea-usa.com
Contact: Charles Policky, President
Scope: Specializes in providing on-site English language and communication development for corporations and individuals. Also develops and delivers training in speaking, writing, pronunciation, grammar, and idioms with an emphasis on business communication. Offers individual, small group, intensive, and long-distance learning. Programs tailor-made for each client. **Founded:** 1983. **Telecommunication Services:** info@aec.edu.

28430 ■ Beeline Learning Solutions (BLS)
14911 Quorum Dr., Ste. 120
Dallas, TX 75254
Ph: (972)813-0465
Fax: (972)386-8667
Co. E-mail: info@consultingpartners.com
URL: http://www.beeline.com
Contact: Dominic Nagy, Manager
E-mail: dominic.nagy@consultingpartners.com
Scope: Consulting firm offering technology, content, and services addressing recruitment and sourcing, talent management, and learning and performance optimization. Solutions offered include contingent workforce solutions, vendor management software, talent management solutions, recruitment process outsourcing, performance management, applicant tracking, learning management and eLearning. **Founded:** 1990. **Special Services:** Beeline®.

28431 ■ Blackmon Roberts Group Inc.
902 S S Florida Ave., Ste. 205
Lakeland, FL 33803
Ph: (863)802-1280
Free: 877-450-3237
Fax: (863)802-1290
Co. E-mail: dbeinformation@blackmonroberts.com
URL: http://www.blackmonroberts.com
Contact: Sylvia Blackmon Roberts, President
E-mail: sylvia@blackmonroberts.com
Scope: Technical support consultant in technical writing, planning, research, needs analysis, marketing and training, offers training programs from cultural sensitivity issues to effective listening skills. **Founded:** 1992.

28432 ■ Daniel Bloom and Associates Inc. (DBAI)
11517 128th Ave. N
Largo, FL 33778
Ph: (727)581-6216
Fax: (727)216-8532
Co. E-mail: dan@dbaiconsulting.com
URL: http://www.dbaiconsulting.com
Contact: Sharon Megiel, Consultant
Scope: Human resources management consultant with a specialization in corporate relocation. Offers clients a turn key service aimed at meeting the unique relocation needs of their employees. Develops and implements training programs within the relocation industry. **Founded:** 1980. **Publications:** "Where Have All the Elders Gone," Aug, 2002; "Recoup Your Hiring Investment," Brainbuzz.com, Aug, 2000; "Managing Your Lump Sum Program," Brainbuzz.com, Jun, 2000; "Buyer Value Options," Brainbuzz.com, Apr, 2000; "Just Get Me There". **Seminars:** Chaos in the Workplace: Multiple Generational Interactions; Training Effectiveness: Is the Cost Justified?; Human Capital Resource Management: A Six-Sigma Based Approach to Paving Your Way to the Table; Welcome to My World.

28433 ■ Business Education Associates (BEA)—Ashford Group Inc.
4 Long Hill Rd.
Bethel, CT 06801
Ph: (203)798-6035
Contact: Robert J. Popp, President
E-mail: bob@ashfordgrp.com
Scope: Offers tailored management education programs. Has been designed to meet the business education needs of companies implementing new systems and companies to re-educate users of existing systems. **Founded:** 1984. **Publications:** "The Ashford Group and TQuist Partner to Provide High Impact Manufacturing Solutions"; "The Future of ERP"; "Winning the Implementation Game". **Special Services:** Building Manufacturing Excellence.

28434 ■ Business Improvement Architects (BIA)
33 Riderwood Dr.
Toronto, ON, Canada M2L 2X4
Ph: (416)444-8225
Free: 866-346-3242
Fax: (416)444-6743
Co. E-mail: info@bia.ca
URL: http://www.bia.ca
Contact: Michael Stanleigh, Chief Executive Officer
E-mail: mstanleigh@bia.ca
Scope: Provider of the following services: strategic planning, leadership development, innovation and project and quality management. Specialize in strategic planning, change management, leadership assessment, and development of skills. **Founded:** 1989. **Publications:** "Avoiding Pit falls to Innovation"; "Create a New Dimension of Performance with Innovation"; "The Power of Appreciation in Leadership"; "Why It Makes Sense To Have a Strategic Enterprise Office"; "Burning Rubber at the Start of Your Project"; "Accounting for Quality"; "How Pareto Charts Can Help You Improve the Quality of Business Processes"; "Managing Resistance to Change". **Seminars:** The Innovation Process. . .From Vision to Reality, San Diego, Oct, 2007; Critical Thinking, Kuala Lump or, Sep, 2007; Critical Thinking, Brunei, Sep, 2007; Delivering Project Assurance, Auckland, Jun, 2007; From Crisis to Control: A New Era in Strategic Project Management, Prague, May, 2007; What Project Leaders Need to Know to Help Them Sleep Better At Night, London, May, 2007; Innovation Process. . .From Vision To Reality, Orlando, Apr, 2007. **Special Services:** Project Planning Tool™.

28435 ■ Center for Personal Empowerment
102 N Main St., Ste. 1
Columbia, IL 62236-1702
Ph: (618)281-3565
Free: 888-657-1530
Fax: (618)476-7083
Co. E-mail: personalempowerment@wholenet.net
Contact: Cherri Hendrix, Owner
Scope: Private consultations and trainings to educate on how to determine which emotions, events, beliefs from the past prevent you from achieving success. Methods used include time line therapy, news linguistic programming and hypnosis. Behavior modification through NLP trainings. **Founded:** 1996. **Seminars:** NLP Practitioner Training; Hypnosis Certification Training; Lifemap Seminars.

28436 ■ Competitive Edge Inc.
241 E Crestwood Rd.
Peachtree City, GA 30269
Ph: (770)487-6460
Fax: (770)487-2919
Co. E-mail: judy@competitiveedgeinc.com
URL: http://www.competitiveedgeinc.com
Contact: Judy I. Suiter, President
E-mail: judy@competitiveedgeinc.com
Scope: A human resources consulting firm providing customized training and software solutions to assist clients in optimizing their human intellectual capital through effective selection, coaching, and training. Works with a network of consultants that are located throughout the United States, Canada, and Europe. **Founded:** 1981. **Publications:** "Beteenden och drivkrafter"; "Energizing People: Unleashing The Power of DISC"; "The Ripple Effect: How the Global Model of Endorsement Opens Doors to Success"; "The Journey - Quotes to keep your boat afloat"; "The Universal Language DISC Reference Manual"; "Exploring Values: Releasing the Power of Attitudes"; "COMPETITIVE PRODUCTS REVIEW BOOK"; "The Mother Of All Minds"; "The Sea of Change: Solutions for Navigating the Disconnects in the Workplace". **Seminars:** How to Recruit and Retain High Performing Employees; The Importance of Values Matching For Sales Selection; How to Build a High Performance Team; Dynamic Communication Skills; Creating Nurturing Customer Relationships; Your Attitude Is Showing; Sales Strategy Index; Validity Study.

28437 ■ Donna Cornell Enterprises Inc.—Cornell Career Center
68 N Plank Rd., Ste. 204
Newburgh, NY 12550-2122
Ph: (845)565-0088
Free: 888-769-3792
Fax: (845)565-0084
Co. E-mail: rc@cornellcareercenter.com
Contact: Donna Cornell, President
E-mail: rc@cornellcareercenter.com
Scope: Offers services in career consultant, professional search, job placement and national professional search. **Founded:** 1996. **Publications:** "The Power of the Woman Within"; "Juggling it All!"; "Journey: A Woman's Guide to Success"; "Shatter the Traditions".

28438 ■ donphin.com Inc.
1001 B Ave., Ste. 200
Coronado, CA 92118
Ph: (619)550-3533
Free: 800-234-3304
Fax: (619)600-0096
Co. E-mail: inquiry@donphin.com
URL: http://www.donphin.com
Contact: Vito Tanzi, President
Scope: Offers a comprehensive approach to understanding and applying a broad range of business principles: legal compliance issues, management concerns, health and safety, customer service, marketing, information management. Industries served: All developing small businesses. **Publications:** "Doing Business Right!"; "HR That Works!"; "Lawsuit Free! How to Prevent Employee Lawsuits"; "Building Powerful Employment Relationships!"; "Victims, Villains and Heroes: Managing Emotions in The Workplace". **Seminars:** Doing Business Right!; HR That Works!; Building Powerful Employment Relationships; Lawsuit Free!.

28439 ■ Dorn & Associates Inc.
8506 Bass Lake Rd.
Minneapolis, MN 55428-5304
Ph: (763)533-7689
Fax: (763)533-1143
Contact: John L. Dorn, President
Scope: Services include accounting, marketing, employment partnership, new doctor agreements, personnel issues and human resources assessment, practice management, practice merger acquisition sale and liquidation, practice surveys and valuation, staff development and training. **Founded:** 2000.

28440 ■ Full Voice
3217 Broadway Ave., Ste. 300
Kansas City, MO 64111
Ph: (816)941-0011
Free: 800-684-8764

Fax: (816)931-8887
Co. E-mail: info@infullvoice.com
URL: http://www.fullvoice.us
Contact: Michienne Dixon, Principal
Scope: Vocal performance training firm offering consulting services and personal training sessions in the implementation of effective vocal communication techniques for the development of business relationships and career enhancement. Formalizes a program of proven techniques into a practical method of helping individuals improve their ability to better present themselves when speaking in a professional situation. Industries served: All. **Founded:** 1992. **Publications:** "You Can Sound Like You Know What You're Saying". **Seminars:** You Can Sound Like You Know What You're Saying; The Psychology of Vocal Performance; Security. . .the Ability to Accept Change; Knowing. . .the Key to Relaxed Public Communication; The Effective Voice for Customer Service Enhancement; You Can Speak With Conviction; How To Make Yours a Championship Team Functional English For Foreign Trade. **Special Services:** FULL VOICE™.

28441 ■ Harding & Co.
511 Harvard Ave.
Swarthmore, PA 19081
Ph: (610)544-9005
Fax: (973)763-9347
Co. E-mail: fharding@hardingco.com
URL: http://www.hardingco.com
Contact: Mimi Spangler, President
E-mail: mspangler@hardingco.com
Scope: Specializes in sales management, client development and employee training. **Founded:** 1993. **Publications:** "Cross-Selling Success: A Rainmakers Guide to Professional Account Development," Aug, 2002; "Rain Making: The Professional's Guide to Attracting New Clients"; "Creating Rainmakers: The Managers Guide to Training Professionals to Attract New Clients". **Telecommunication Services:** mspangler@hardingco.com

28442 ■ Hills Consulting Group Inc.
6 Partridge Ct.
Novato, CA 94945-1315
Ph: (415)898-3944
Contact: Michael R. Hills, President
Scope: Specializes in strategic planning; marketing surveys; market research; customer service audits; new product development; competitive analysis; and sales forecasting. **Founded:** 1985.

28443 ■ Interpersonal Coaching & Consulting (ICC)
1516 W Lake St., Ste. 2000S
Minneapolis, MN 55408
Ph: (612)381-2494
Fax: (612)381-2494
Co. E-mail: mail@interpersonal-coaching.com
URL: http://www.interpersonal-coaching.com
Contact: Mary Belfry, Partner
Scope: Provider of coaching and consulting to businesses and organizations. Assesses the interpersonal workplace through interviews, assessment instruments and individual group settings. Experienced as a therapist for over a decade. **Publications:** "Sexual Harassment In The Workplace For Newspapers". **Seminars:** More On Relationships; Sexual harassment and discrimination issues.

28444 ■ Mandalay Associates L.L.C.
190 El Cerrito Plz., Ste. 226
El Cerrito, CA 94530-4002
Ph: (510)526-4651
Fax: (510)526-5774
Contact: Kristina Combs, Member
Scope: Business management firm specializes in conflict resolution, employee relations, employment and placement, organizational analysis and development, human resources program development, program and project management, and staff development and training.

28445 ■ Milestone Inc.—Blue SuitMilestone Consulting;
PO Box 630
Dedham, MA 02027
Ph: (781)467-1200

Fax: (781)467-0299
Co. E-mail: bob@milestoneideas.com
URL: http://www.milestoneideas.com
Contact: Robert J. Taraschi, President
E-mail: bob@milestoneideas.com
Scope: Facilitates 100 business creativity and innovation growth sessions per year. Assists to: Discover new growth strategies and planning options; create new ideas, new promises, value propositions, products and programs; identify and integrate customer passions in new and surprising ways; realize higher returns on involvement, interest and investment; refine processes, accelerate innovative growth and build better teams. **Founded:** 1980. **Publications:** "Can your brand tell a bigger story". **Seminars:** Ideas in Action; Double-Gesturing; Growth in a period of no growth; Strike while the iron is cold; Natural Creative Strategies; The Enduring Power of Open Ended Creativity; Ideation Techniques to Drive Brand Value. **Special Services:** Milestone®; IMMERgENT®; SmartAlec.

28446 ■ Art Munin Consulting
c/o Assistant Dean of Students Office
Depaul University, Student Ctr.
Chicago, IL 60614-3673
Ph: (773)316-2276
Co. E-mail: art@artmunin.com
URL: http://www.artmunin.com
Contact: Art Munin, Principal
Scope: Consulting firm committed to advancing multicultural education and imparting advocacy. Expands the opportunities to engage people in conversations about diversity and social justice. Other areas of interest include counseling skills, crisis response, improving the campus climate for bi/multiracial students, sexual assault, GLBT advocacy, team building, and other diversity-related training topics. **Publications:** "Would they still have written if they knew I had to go home and tell my wife?," 2009; "The leadership bookshelf," 2009; "Improving the campus environment for bi/multiracial students," Peter Lang Publishing, 2009; "Empathy: Love the sinner, hate the sin. About Campus," 2007; "Factors influencing the ally development of college students". **Seminars:** White Privilege 101; Locating Justice; Targeting the Majority in Diversity Education; Art of War - Targeting the Majority in Multicultural Education; Higher Education: The Gate-Keeper to the Middle Class; Who Are Our Transgendered Students?; The Basics of Diversity Training; Retreats; Ethics and Leadership: Making Choices for Social Justice; Color by Number.

28447 ■ National Pediculosis Association (NPA)
1005 Boylston St., Ste. 343
Newton, MA 02461
Ph: (781)449-6487
Free: 800-446-4672
Fax: (800)235-1305
Co. E-mail: npa@headlice.org
URL: http://www.headlice.org
Contact: Deborah Z. Altschuler, President
E-mail: dza@headlice.org
Description: Parents, physicians, school nurses, and individuals representing hospitals and county health departments. Works to eliminate the incidence, particularly among children, of pediculosis (head lice). Conducts public education campaign to make pediculosis control a public health priority; acts as consumer advocate to ensure the quality and safety of products for treating pediculosis and scabies; encourages scientific research to discover methods of treatment that minimize the use of pesticides, which may harm pregnant and nursing women as well as infants and children. Disseminates information on identifying, treating, and preventing pediculosis, with emphasis on finding and removing nits (louse eggs) in the hair. Provides consultations to schools, camps, and other organizations. **Scope:** Consultants in head lice and scabies management, treatment, prevention, and education. Specializes in monitoring health policy administration in schools and trends in the treatment of head lice. Emphasis is on educational activities. Industries served: schools, health professionals, medical professionals, child care centers, health departments, hospitals, HMO's,

clinics, libraries, parents, PTA's, camps, military bases, and churches. **Founded:** 1983. **Publications:** "All out Comb out".

28448 ■ ProActive English
4355 SE 29th Ave.
Portland, OR 97202
Ph: (503)231-2906
Co. E-mail: infopae@proactive-english.com
URL: http://www.proactive-english.com
Contact: Margaret Lyman, Manager
E-mail: mlyman@proactive-english.com
Scope: Offers on-site individual and small group language and communication training. Sets up learning plans tailored to the needs and schedules of managers and executives who are non-native English speakers. Serves all industries. **Founded:** 1997. **Seminars:** Communicating in Business Situations; Presentations and Pronunciation; Tailored Curriculum: One-on-One Programs.

28449 ■ Professional Psychological Services (PPS)
4130 Linden Ave., Ste. 309
Dayton, OH 45432-3034
Ph: (937)254-7301
Fax: (937)254-2117
Co. E-mail: ppsdocs@aol.com
Contact: Dr. Michael A. Williams, Partner
Scope: Offers clinical services, human relations training, multicultural and pluralistic training, and staff development and training. **Founded:** 1994.

28450 ■ Sandy Corp.
300 E Big Beaver Rd., Ste. 500
Troy, MI 48084-3526
Ph: (248)649-0800
Free: 800-733-4739
Fax: (248)729-4700
Co. E-mail: info@sandycorp.com
URL: http://www.sandycorp.com
Contact: Dave Gugala, Manager
Scope: It provides the design, development and production of specific consulting, training, communicating and evaluating programs to help clients improve the capabilities of their people to such a level that consistent performance on the job becomes a visible, valued competitive strength. **Founded:** 1911.

28451 ■ Tamayo Consulting Inc.
169 Saxony Rd., Ste. 112
Encinitas, CA 92024-6779
Ph: (760)479-1352
Fax: (760)479-1465
Co. E-mail: info@tamayoconsulting.com
URL: http://www.tamayoconsulting.com
Contact: Jennifer Dreyer, President
E-mail: jcreyer@earthlink.net
Scope: I Provides training and consulting services. And also it specializes in leadership and team development. Industries served: private, non-profit, government, educational. **Founded:** 1986. **Seminars:** Presentation AdvantEdge Program; Lead point Development Program; Supervisor Development Programs.Identify Presentation Objectives; Implement 360-degree presentation assessment; conduct baseline-coaching session; Develop coaching plan; Staying connected.

28452 ■ Training Systems Plus
742 Brent Dr.
Mulvane, KS 67110-1245
Ph: (316)777-1337
Contact: Charles M. Cadwell, Owner
E-mail: chastrain@cox.net
Scope: Provider of management and training systems to businesses to improve operational profitability as well as individual management and employee performance. Activities include consultation, job descriptions, evaluation forms, training seminars, training materials, operations manuals and employee handbooks. **Founded:** 1986. **Seminars:** Effective Classroom Instruction; Training System Design; Interviewing and Selecting; Performance Management, Leadership Skills.

FRANCHISES AND BUSINESS OPPORTUNITIES

28453 ■ Canadian School of Natural Nutrition
10720 Yonge St., Ste. 220
Richmond Hill, ON, Canada L4C 3C9
Ph: (905)737-8729
Free: 800-569-9938
Fax: (905)737-7830
Co. E-mail: hq@csnn.ca
URL: http://www.csnn.ca
Description: private vocational school offering adult education leading to professional designations: RHN-Reg. Holistic Nutritionist, and RECP-Reg, ElderCare Practitioner. Franchisees are licensed to distribute CSNN curriculum material to students through classroom education. CSNN offers two programs: Natural Nutrition and Elder Care. CSNN is privately owned, incorporated as 3393291 Canada Inc. **No. of Franchise Units:** 4. **No. of Company-Owned Units:** 10. **Founded:** 1994.. **Franchised:** 1996. **Equity Capital Needed:** $70,000 Canadian Capital. **Franchise Fee:** $12,000. **Training:** Ongoing.

28454 ■ Club Scientific
636 Steels Bridge Rd.
Canton, GA 30114
Ph: (678)294-9504
Description: Science enrichment program. **No. of Franchise Units:** 5. **No. of Company-Owned Units:** 8. **Founded:** 1987.. **Franchised:** 2007. **Equity Capital Needed:** $56,825-$84,720. **Franchise Fee:** $20,000-$24,500. **Royalty Fee:** 6%. **Financial Assistance:** Third party financing available. **Training:** Provides 4 days training at headquarters, 4 days at franchisee's location and ongoing support.

28455 ■ Cybertary
1217 Pleasant Grove Blvd., Ste. 100
Roseville, CA 95678
Ph: (916)781-7799
Free: 888-292-8279
Fax: (877)292-8279
Co. E-mail: Franchise@Cybertary.com
URL: http://www.CybertaryFranchise.com
Description: Virtual assistant (VA) industry providing on-demand administrative support to businesses, entrepreneurs, and busy people through a nationwide team network to meet the needs of any business. This home-based B2B service offers low overhead and a flexible schedule. **No. of Franchise Units:** 23. **Founded:** 2005.. **Franchised:** 2006. **Equity Capital Needed:** $39,500-$78,500. **Franchise Fee:** $37,500-$56,250. **Royalty Fee:** 5%. **Training:** Receive 4 days of intensive training.

28456 ■ Drama Kids International, Inc.
525-K E Market St., Ste. 250
Leesburg, VA 20176
Free: 866-809-1055
Co. E-mail: dramakids@starpower.net
URL: http://www.dramakids.com
Description: After-school developmental drama program. Curriculum uses fun and creative drama activities so kids ages 5-17 act confidently and speak clearly. **No. of Franchise Units:** 56. **Founded:** 1979. **Franchised:** 1989. **Equity Capital Needed:** $33,550-38,950. **Franchise Fee:** $29,000. **Royalty Fee:** 8-9%. **Financial Assistance:** Third party financing available. **Training:** Available 5 days at headquarters, 5 days at franchisee's location, 1 day of regional training plus annual conference and ongoing support.

28457 ■ E.nopi
50 Passaic St.
Hackensack, NJ 07601
Ph: (201)498-1212
Free: 888-835-1212
Fax: (201)498-1218
Description: Supplemental education. **No. of Franchise Units:** 125. **No. of Company-Owned Units:** 513. **Founded:** 1976. **Franchised:** 1976. **Equity Capital Needed:** $52,000-$91,000. **Franchise Fee:** $12,000. **Royalty Fee:** $15/student. **Training:** Offers 16 hours training at headquarters, at franchisee's location and ongoing.

28458 ■ Estrada Strategies Franchise Inc.
3400 Inland Empire Blvd., Ste. 101
Ontario, CA 91764
Ph: (909)476-3510
Fax: (909)476-3511
URL: http://estradastrategies.com
URL(s): efranchise.estradastrategies.com. **Description:** Executive coaching programs. **No. of Franchise Units:** 2. **No. of Company-Owned Units:** 1. **Founded:** 2000.. **Franchised:** 2006. **Equity Capital Needed:** $43,300-$77,200. **Franchise Fee:** $25,000. **Royalty Fee:** Varies. **Training:** Training at corporate headquarters, onsite and ongoing support provided.

28459 ■ Fastrackids International, Ltd.
6900 E Belleview Ave., Ste. 300
Greenwood Village, CO 80111
Ph: (303)224-0200
Fax: (303)224-0222
Co. E-mail: info@fastrackids.com
URL: http://www.fastrackids.com
Description: An accelerated learning system for children. **No. of Franchise Units:** 150. **Founded:** 1998.. **Franchised:** 1998. **Equity Capital Needed:** $33,800-$183,500. **Franchise Fee:** $22,000. **Financial Assistance:** 30-V, FRA handbook. **Training:** Provides initial training, periodic regional seminars, an annual international conference, sales/telemarketing assistance, and classroom facilitation tips.

28460 ■ Frozen Ropes Training Centers
24 Old Black Meadow Rd.
Chester, NY 10918
Ph: (845)469-7331
Fax: (845)469-6742
Co. E-mail: info@frozenropes.com
Description: Baseball & softball instruction. **No. of Franchise Units:** 8. **No. of Company-Owned Units:** 1. **Founded:** 1994.. **Franchised:** 2003. **Equity Capital Needed:** $219,800-$276,200. **Franchise Fee:** $45,000. **Royalty Fee:** 3-6%.

28461 ■ Ho Math & Chess Learning Centre
2265 W 41st St., Rm. 4
Vancouver, BC, Canada V6M 2A3
Ph: (604)263-4321
Fax: (604)266-0974
Co. E-mail: mathandchess@telus.net
URL: http://www.mathandchess.com
Description: Math & chess learning program. **No. of Franchise Units:** 4. **No. of Company-Owned Units:** 1. **No. of Operating Units:** 8. **Founded:** 1995.. **Franchised:** 2004. **Equity Capital Needed:** $25,150. **Franchise Fee:** $2,100. **Royalty Fee:** None. **Training:** 1 week training provided at headquarters.

28462 ■ KidzArt
KidzArt Texas LLC
1001 Laurence Ave., Ste. E
Jackson, MI 49201
Ph: (888)813-2287
Free: 800-379-8302
Fax: (517)338-5300
Co. E-mail: info@kidzart.com
URL: http://www.kidzart.com
Description: Offers children's products and education services. **No. of Franchise Units:** 65. **Founded:** 1997.. **Franchised:** 2002. **Equity Capital Needed:** $15,045-$38,150, includes working capital and franchise fee. **Franchise Fee:** $9,900-$19,900. **Financial Assistance:** Yes. **Training:** Offers 1 week business/operations training and cutting edge franchisee support; conferences, monthly training calls, one on one quick start coaching and ongoing support.

28463 ■ KnowledgePoints Inc.
5 Centerpoint Dr., Ste. 250
Lake Oswego, OR 97035
Ph: (503)270-5100
Fax: (503)270-5117
Description: Tutoring programs. **No. of Franchise Units:** 46. **No. of Company-Owned Units:** 1. **Founded:** 1999. **Franchised:** 2003. **Equity Capital Needed:** $89,350-$150,250. **Franchise Fee:** $22,500. **Royalty Fee:** 8%. **Training:** Provides 6 days training at headquarters, 3 weeks at franchisee's location, and ongoing support for franchisee & managers.

28464 ■ Kumon North America, Inc.
Glenpointe Centre East
300 Frank W Burr Blvd., Ste. 6
Teaneck, NJ 07666
Ph: (866)633-0740
Fax: (201)692-3130
Co. E-mail: franchise@kumon.com
URL: http://www.kumonfranchise.com
Description: North America provider of supplemental math and learning material. The learning center caters to all ages and abilities from pre-school through high school. **No. of Franchise Units:** 2,000. **No. of Company-Owned Units:** 24. **Founded:** 1958.. **Franchised:** 1980. **Equity Capital Needed:** $70,000 cash, $150,000 net worth; $69,943-$144,050 initial investment. **Franchise Fee:** $1,000. **Training:** Kumon has offices worldwide to provide training, support and onsite consultation to franchisee's.

28465 ■ Language Leaders Franchising LLC
Foreign Language Network, L.L.C.
401 W. State St.
Geneva, IL 60134
Ph: (630)377-8794
Description: Foreign language education and interpreting. **No. of Company-Owned Units:** 1. **Founded:** 1998.. **Franchised:** 2004. **Equity Capital Needed:** $18,700-$107,000. **Franchise Fee:** $10,000-$90,000. **Royalty Fee:** 15%. **Training:** 2 days training at headquarters.

28466 ■ LearningRX Franchise Corp.
LearningRx, Inc.
5085 List Dr., Ste. 200
Colorado Springs, CO 80919
Ph: (719)264-8808
Fax: (719)484-8930
Description: One on one brain skills and reading training. **No. of Franchise Units:** 80. **No. of Company-Owned Units:** 2. **Founded:** 1987.. **Franchised:** 2003. **Equity Capital Needed:** $200,000. **Franchise Fee:** $25,000-$35,000. **Training:** Yes.

28467 ■ The LiceSquad Inc.
Lice Squad Canada Inc.
3A King St.
Cookstown, ON, Canada L0L 1L0
Ph: (705)458-4448
Free: 888-542-3778
Fax: (705)458-8887
Co. E-mail: franchiseinfo@licesquad.com
URL: http://www.licesquad.com
Description: Join Canada's leading head lice removal and Education Company. Low start up costs and proven potential. Perfect for those in the nursing, hairdressing and child care fields. Our clients include schools, families, camps and other child care organizations. Our home-based business model allows flexibility. Enjoy both family and career. 15 successful LiceSquad franchises operating in Ontario with master franchises available. **No. of Franchise Units:** 9. **No. of Company-Owned Units:** 20. **Founded:** 2001. **Franchised:** 2002. **Equity Capital Needed:** $42,000-$85,000 investment required; start-up capital required $25,000-$35,000. **Franchise Fee:** $20,000. **Training:** Provides training (excluding travel/hotel costs).

28468 ■ Little City Kids
10127 Northwestern Ave.
Franksville, WI 53126
Ph: (262)884-4226
Fax: (262)884-4230
Co. E-mail: littlecitykids@tds.net
URL: http://www.littlecitykids.com
Description: Educational playcare for your child. The environment is set into action in an interactive world filled with imagination stations, innovative online curriculum and team teaching methods. We offer two models, the Little City Kids model is for children ages 2-13 years and the Itty Bitty Kids model adds infant and toddler care. **No. of Company-Owned Units:** 1. **Founded:** 1998.. **Franchised:** 2004. **Equity Capital Needed:** $118,000-$189,000. **Franchise Fee:** $35,000. **Royalty Fee:** 7%. **Training:** Available at headquarters 30-60 days, 10 days at franchisee's location and oning support.

28469 ■ The Mad Science Group
8360 Bougainville St., Ste. 201
Montreal, QC, Canada H4P 2G1
Ph: (514)344-4181
Fax: (514)344-6695
Co. E-mail: joel@madscience.org
URL: http://www.madscience.org
Description: Mad Science is a service company specializing in fun hands on educational science for children. We send trained instructors with all required materials and supplies to conduct onsite activities to schools and other organizations dealing with kids. Our franchisees are sales marketing oriented individuals who enjoy a hands-on owner operated business that enriches children and contributes to the community. No. of Franchise Units: 200. Founded: 1985.. Franchised: 1995. Equity Capital Needed: $10,000-$23,500 franchise fee, $25,000 equipment package; $20,000-$30,000 working capital. Franchise Fee: $10,000-$23,500. Financial Assistance: Yes. Training: 6 day training at corporate headquarters followed by 5 day training onsite.

28470 ■ Math Monkey Knowledge Centers
56 Winchester Rd.
Newton, MA 02458
Ph: (954)384-1050
Free: 877-468-6284
Description: After school enrichment program. No. of Franchise Units: 14. No. of Company-Owned Units: 1. Founded: 2006. Franchised: 2006. Equity Capital Needed: $99,000-$164,000. Franchise Fee: $31,500. Royalty Fee: 6%. Training: 2 weeks training at headquarters included, 2 weeks at franchisee's location, 1 week at existing franchise location, online seminars and ongoing support.

28471 ■ Mathnasium Learning Centers
5120 W Goldleaf Cir., Ste. 300
Los Angeles, CA 90056
Ph: (877)531-6284
Fax: (310)943-2111
Co. E-mail: franchise@mathnasium.com
URL: http://www.mathnasium.com
Description: Mathnasium provides the most effective mathematics in education available to grade school children after school, in an attractive neighborhood learning center environment. The Mathnasium Method, developed over 30 years of hands-on experience, is engaging for students and builds confidence as it builds real understanding. Created to address a real need in the market by a team with unparalleled success in the industry, the business model is strong and the opportunity is now. No. of Franchise Units: 389. No. of Company-Owned Units: 2. Founded: 2002.. Franchised: 2003. Equity Capital Needed: $82,250-$136,000 initial investment range. Franchise Fee: $37,000. Training: Initial training 1 week online followed by 1 week in person at corporate headquarters. Support continues with ongoing training, in-the-field regional managers and monthly conference calls.

28472 ■ Motion Golf LLC
55 Lane Rd.
Fairfield, NJ 07004
Free: 866-585-6033
Description: Golf swing analysis, instruction, and club fitting. No. of Company-Owned Units: 3. Founded: 2006. Franchised: 2007. Equity Capital Needed: $250,000 (Express/kiosk option available). Franchise Fee: $79,500. Royalty Fee: 6%. Training: 1 week at franchisee's location.

28473 ■ Online Trading Academy
18004 Sky Park Cir. S, Ste. 140
Irvine, CA 92614
Ph: (949)608-6020
Fax: (949)608-6026
Description: Stock-trading instruction. No. of Franchise Units: 16. Founded: 1998.. Franchised: 2004. Equity Capital Needed: $209,800-$388,000. Franchise Fee: $80,000-$200,000. Royalty Fee: 10%. Training: Offers 2 weeks training at headquarters, 1 week at franchisees location and ongoing support.

28474 ■ Oxford Learning Centers Inc.
747 Hyde Park Rd., Ste. 230
London, ON, Canada N6H 3S3
Ph: (519)473-1207
Free: 888-559-2212
Fax: (519)473-6086
Co. E-mail: franchise@oxfordlearning.com
URL: http://www.oxfordlearning.com
Description: Oxford is an educational franchise in Canada, which provides extensive training in all fields. No. of Franchise Units: 108. No. of Company-Owned Units: 5. Founded: 1984.. Franchised: 1991. Equity Capital Needed: $140,000-$210,000 plus applicable taxes. Franchise Fee: $40,000 plus applicable taxes. Training: Provides 2 weeks training and ongoing support.

28475 ■ Parisi Speed School
291 Franklin Ave.
Wyckoff, NJ 07481
Ph: (201)847-1938
Fax: (201)540-0143
Description: Youth performance training. No. of Franchise Units: 44. No. of Company-Owned Units: 5. Founded: 1992.. Franchised: 2005. Equity Capital Needed: $132,500-$300,100. Franchise Fee: $29,900. Royalty Fee: $1,000/month.

28476 ■ Parmasters Golf Training Centers
29 Evergreen Dr.
Whitby, ON, Canada L1N 6S6
Ph: (905)721-7593
Free: 866-966-0676
Fax: (416)352-1537
Co. E-mail: andre_ferris@parmastersgolf.com
URL: http://www.parmastersfranchise.com
URL(s): www.parmastersgolf.com. Description: Year-round indoor golf training center. No. of Franchise Units: 27. No. of Company-Owned Units: 7. Founded: 2000.. Franchised: 2001. Equity Capital Needed: $300,000-$2,500,000. Franchise Fee: $50,000.

28477 ■ Pathways Education & Training Centers, Inc.
333 S Parkside Cir.
St. George, UT 84770
Ph: (435)674-1331
Fax: (435)674-1831
Description: Brain integration program. No. of Franchise Units: 6. No. of Company-Owned Units: 1. Founded: 2000.. Franchised: 2005. Equity Capital Needed: $20,000. Training: Yes.

28478 ■ Spirit of Math Schools
178 Willowdale Ave.
Toronto, ON, Canada M2N 4Y8
Ph: (416)223-1985
Fax: (416)946-1902
Co. E-mail: franchising@spiritofmath.com
URL: http://www.spiritofmath.com
Description: Offers an after-school classroom program for high performing students. It develops as skill-based understanding of math focusing on problem solving, co-operation and numeric skills and produces some of the top math students in the nation. No. of Franchise Units: 13. No. of Company-Owned Units: 13. Founded: 1992.. Franchised: 2006. Equity Capital Needed: $32,000-$70,000. Franchise Fee: $39,000. Training: A comprehensive training and support program is provided.

28479 ■ Thinkertots
Thinkertots Franchise Inc.
22214 Union Tpke.
Bayside, NY 11364
Ph: (718)740-1616
Description: Educational parent/child classes. No. of Franchise Units: 4. No. of Company-Owned Units: 1. Founded: 1998.. Franchised: 2005. Equity Capital Needed: $42,000-$160,000. Franchise Fee: $15,000-$25,000. Training: Yes.

28480 ■ The Whole Child Learning Co.
2200 Kraft Dr., Ste. 1350
Blacksburg, VA 24060
Ph: (540)443-9252

Fax: (540)242-3214
URL: http://www.wholechild.com
Description: Educational services for children. No. of Franchise Units: 6. No. of Company-Owned Units: 4. Founded: 1996.. Franchised: 1999. Equity Capital Needed: $7,500. Franchise Fee: $15,000. Financial Assistance: Yes. Training: Yes.

28481 ■ Young Rembrandts - The Power Of Drawing
Young Rembrandts Franchise, Inc.
23 N Union St.
Elgin, IL 60123
Ph: (847)742-6999
Free: 866-300-6010
Fax: (847)742-7197
Co. E-mail: yr@youngrembrandts.com
URL: http://www.youngrembrandts.com
Description: Developed a proven method that ensures artistic and academic success for every child. Our unique method and original curriculum teaches drawing, the fundamental skill of visual arts to children ages 3 1/2 to 12. No. of Franchise Units: 80. Founded: 1988.. Franchised: 2001. Equity Capital Needed: Liquid $50,000; $100,000 net. Franchise Fee: $31,500. Training: Provides 1 week initial training program for up to 2 people at corporate office. This covers sales, marketing, the Young & Rembrandts method, classroom training and more. We provide complete operation and training manuals, and continual training and coaching calls and an Annual Conference.

COMPUTERIZED DATABASES

28482 ■ *Health & Wellness InSite*
610 Opperman Dr.
Eagen, MN 55122
Free: 800-477-4300
Co. E-mail: gale.contentlicensing@cengage.com
URL: http://www.insite2.gale.com
Availability: Online: Cengage Learning Inc. - Gale - InSite2. Type: Full-text.

LIBRARIES

28483 ■ American Society for Training and Development - Information Center
1640 King St.
Alexandria, VA 22313-2043
Ph: (703)683-8100
Free: 800-628-2783
Fax: (703)683-1523
Co. E-mail: customercare@astd.org
URL: http://www.astd.org
Scope: Human resource development - general, management, training, career development, Organization development, consulting skills. Services: Library open to national members of the Society. Founded: 1984. Holdings: 3000 bound volumes. Subscriptions: 60 journals and other serials.

RESEARCH CENTERS

28484 ■ Center for Entrepreneurial Studies and Development (CESD)
College of Engineering & Mineral Research, Ste. B
W Virginia University
1062 Maple Dr.
Morgantown, WV 26505
Ph: (304)293-5551
Fax: (304)293-6707
Co. E-mail: chadsell@mail.cesd.wvu.edu
URL: http://www.cesd.wvu.edu
Contact: Carl Hadsell, Managing Director
Services: Competitive and economic development strategies; Market assessment and development; Operational improvements; Performance management; Provides assistance in new product or service development. Founded: 1981. Telecommunication Services: info@cesd.wvu.edu.

28485 ■ Center for Occupational Research and Development (CORD)
PO Box 21689
Waco, TX 76702-1689

Ph: (254)772-8756
Free: 800-972-2766
Fax: (254)772-8972
Co. E-mail: hinckley@cord.org
URL: http://www.cord.org
Contact: Dr. Richard Hinckley, President
Description: Provides innovative changes in education to prepare students for better chances in career and higher education. Assists educators in secondary schools and colleges through new curricula, teaching strategies, professional development and partnerships with community leaders. Initiates developments in curriculum design, learning tools and creating applications in educational technology and conducting educational research and evaluation. **Services:** Consulting and coordination services; Forms networks and partnerships. **Founded:** 1979. **Publications:** *CORD Newsletter* (Monthly); *White papers*; *Teaching Mathematics Contextually*; *Rigor and Relevance: A New Vision for Career and Technical Education*; *Teacher Professional Development: It's Not an Event, It's a Process*; *Technology to Improve Texas Education*; *Tech Prep: The Next Generation*. **Educational Activities:** Curricula development; Teacher workshops.

28486 ■ Illinois State Board of Education - Data Analysis and Progress Reporting Division
100 N 1st St.
Springfield, IL 62777
Ph: (217)782-3950
Fax: (217)524-7784
Co. E-mail: gjohnson@isbe.net
URL: http://www.isbe.net/research/Default.htm
Contact: Gayle Johnson, Administrator

28487 ■ Indiana University Bloomington - Center for Evaluation and Education Policy (CEEP)
1900 E 10th St.
Bloomington, IN 47406-7512
Ph: (812)855-4438
Free: 800-511-6575
Fax: (812)856-5890
Co. E-mail: jplucker@indiana.edu
URL: http://ceep.indiana.edu
Contact: Prof. Jonathan A. Plucker, Director
Founded: 1990. **Publications:** *Policy Bulletins* (Monthly); *Policy Reports*; *Special Reports and Technical Studies*. **Telecommunication Services:** ceep@indiana.edu.

28488 ■ Indiana University Bloomington - Center for Postsecondary Research (CPR)
Eigenmann Hall, Ste. 419
1900 E 10th St.
Bloomington, IN 47406-7512
Ph: (812)856-5824
Free: 866-435-6773
Fax: (812)856-5150
Co. E-mail: vatorres@indiana.edu
URL: http://cpr.iub.edu/index.cfm
Contact: Vasti Torres, Director
Founded: 1986. **Publications:** *National Survey of Student Engagement* (Annual).

28489 ■ Indiana University Bloomington - Center for the Study of Institutions, Population, and Environmental Change (CIPEC)
408 N Indiana Ave.
Bloomington, IN 47408-3799
Ph: (812)855-2230
Fax: (812)855-2634
Co. E-mail: cipec@indiana.edu
URL: http://www.indiana.edu/~cipec
Contact: Prof. Tom Evans, Director
Founded: 1996. **Telecommunication Services:** evans@indiana.edu.

28490 ■ Indiana University-Purdue University at Indianapolis - Center for the Study of Religion and American Culture
425 University Blvd., Rm. 417
Indianapolis, IN 46202-5140
Ph: (317)274-8409

Fax: (317)278-3354
Co. E-mail: pgoff@iupui.edu
URL: http://www.iupui.edu/~raac/
Contact: Dr. Philip K. Goff, Director
Founded: 1989. **Publications:** *News from the Center for the Study of Religion and American Culture* (Semiannual); *Religion and American Culture: A Journal of Interpretation* (Semiannual). **Educational Activities:** Public lectures, conferences, and symposia; Young Scholars in American Religion Program. **Telecommunication Services:** raac@iupui.edu.

28491 ■ Indiana University-Purdue University at Indianapolis - CyberLab
799 W Michigan St., ET 232
Indianapolis, IN 46202
Ph: (317)278-2630
Fax: (317)278-9171
Co. E-mail: cyberlab@iupui.edu
URL: http://www.iupui.edu/~solctr/research/details.
　php?id=247
Contact: Ali Jafari, Director
Founded: 1989.

28492 ■ Indiana University-Purdue University at Indianapolis - Nuclear Magnetic Resonance Laboratory
402 N Blackford St., Rm. 154
Indianapolis, IN 46202
Ph: (317)274-6900
Fax: (317)274-2393
Co. E-mail: bray@iupui.edu
URL: http://www.physics.iupui.edu/NMR.html
Founded: 1992. **Educational Activities:** Nuclear Magnetic Resonance Laboratory Training, for scientists interested in learning or using NMR techniques.

28493 ■ Indiana University-Purdue University at Indianapolis - Peirce Edition Project
0010 Education/Social Work
Indianapolis, IN 46202-5157
Ph: (317)274-3374
Fax: (317)274-2170
Co. E-mail: adetienn@iupui.edu
URL: http://www.iupui.edu/~peirce
Contact: Prof. André De Tienne, Director
Founded: 1976. **Publications:** *Peirce Project News* (Periodic); *Writings of Charles S. Peirce: A Chronological Edition* (Occasionally). **Educational Activities:** Indianapolis Peirce Seminar (Periodic), lecture series where the speakers are scholars or researchers that are Peirce Project visitors willing to share the latest stage of their research with the Project's specialists and philosophy students. **Telecommunication Services:** cpeirce@iupui.edu.

28494 ■ Institute for Forensic Imaging (IFI)
9855 Crosspoint Blvd., Ste. 126
Fishers, IN 46256
Ph: (317)356-0245
Fax: (317)842-6974
Co. E-mail: jward@ifi-indy.org
URL: http://www.ifi-indy.org/
Contact: Joe Ward, Executive Director
Services: Consulting; Research. **Founded:** 1995. **Educational Activities:** College courses, through the School of Informatics at IUPUI (Indiana University Purdue University Indianapolis); Student centered training; IFI Training programs, certified by the Indiana Law Enforcement Academy. **Telecommunication Services:** jdickinson@wolftechnical.com.

28495 ■ Massachusetts Institute of Technology - Center for Technology, Policy and Industrial Development - International Motor Vehicle Program (IMVP)
Bldg. E40-207
1 Amherst St.
Cambridge, MA 02139-4307
Ph: (617)253-8973
Fax: (617)253-7140
Co. E-mail: imvpmail@mit.edu
URL: http://imvp.mit.edu
Contact: John Moavenzadeh, Executive Director
E-mail: moavenza@wharton.upenn.edu
Founded: 1979. **Publications:** *IMVP Working papers*. **Educational Activities:** IMVP Workshops (Periodic); Sponsors' meeting (Annual). **Telecommunication Services:** ctpidcom@mit.edu.

28496 ■ Massachusetts Institute of Technology - Japan Program
MIT Bldg., Rm. E40-455
77 Massachusetts Ave.
Cambridge, MA 02139-4307
Ph: (617)258-2449
Fax: (617)258-7432
Co. E-mail: samuels@mit.edu
URL: http://web.mit.edu/misti/mit-japan
Contact: Dr. Richard J. Samuels, Director
Founded: 1983. **Publications:** *Japan Program Newsletter* (Monthly); *Sponsor Update* (Quarterly); *Working Papers Series*; *MIT Japan Science, Technology & Management Report*. **Educational Activities:** Japan Target Seminars, for technologically sophisticated professionals in business and government; Japan East Asia Networking Initiative. **Telecommunication Services:** japanprogram@mit.edu.

28497 ■ Massachusetts Institute of Technology - Program on the Pharmaceutical Industry (POPI)
77 Massachusetts Ave., E19-611
Cambridge, MA 02139-4307
Ph: (617)253-0257
Fax: (617)253-0687
Co. E-mail: ghirsch@mit.edu
URL: http://cbi.mit.edu/resources/working-papers/
　popi-working-papers/
Contact: Gigi Hirsch, Executive Director
Founded: 1991. **Telecommunication Services:** cbi@mit.edu.

28498 ■ Rice University - Center for Education
6100 Main St., MS-147
Houston, TX 77005-1892
Ph: (713)348-5145
Fax: (713)348-4229
Co. E-mail: lmcneil@rice.edu
URL: http://centerforeducation.rice.edu
Contact: Prof. Linda McSpadden McNeil, Director
Founded: 1988. **Publications:** *CenterPiece*.

28499 ■ Rice University - Center for the Study of Languages (CSL)
6100 Main St., MS 36
Houston, TX 77005
Ph: (713)348-5844
Fax: (713)348-5846
Co. E-mail: wfreeman@rice.edu
URL: http://langcenter.rice.edu
Contact: Prof. Wendy Freeman, Director
Founded: 1997. **Educational Activities:** CSL Seminar, in language methodology; CSL Seminar, in language methodology; CSL Workshops. **Telecommunication Services:** csladmin@rice.edu.

28500 ■ University of Connecticut - Institute for Teaching and Learning (ITL)
Ctr. for Undergraduate Education
386 Fairfield Rd., Unit 2142
Storrs, CT 06269-2142
Ph: (860)486-2686
Fax: (860)486-5724
Co. E-mail: kb@uconn.edu
URL: http://www.itl.uconn.edu/
Contact: Dr. Keith Barker, Director
Services: Consulting; Instructional design. **Founded:** 1996. **Publications:** *TA Handbook*; *The Journal of Graduate Teaching Assistant Development*. **Educational Activities:** ITL Workshops, conferences.

28501 ■ University of Delaware - Delaware Education Research and Development Center (DERDC)
Pearson Hall
College of Education & Human Development
Newark, DE 19716
Ph: (302)831-4433
Fax: (302)831-4438
Co. E-mail: jbuttram@udel.edu
URL: http://www.rdc.udel.edu
Contact: Joan Buttram, Director
Founded: 1992.

28502 ■ University of Toronto - Ontario Institute for Studies in Education - Centre for Teacher Development (CTD)
252 Bloor St. W
Toronto, ON, Canada M5S 1V6
Ph: (416)978-0227
Fax: (416)926-4754
Co. E-mail: ckosnik@oise.utoronto.ca
URL: http://www.oise.utoronto.ca/cted/index.html
Contact: Dr. Clare Kosnik, Director
Founded: 1989. **Publications:** *CTD Newsletter* (Semiannual). **Educational Activities:** CTD Confer-ence (Biennial), in late October/early November, at-tended by educators, holistic practitioners, education officials; Holistic Educators meetings and seminars (Monthly), held on Saturdays, attended by educators who specialize holistic learning and teaching.

28503 ■ University of Toronto - Ontario Institute for Studies in Education - International Centre for Educational Change (ICEC)
252 Bloor St. W
Toronto, ON, Canada M5S 1V6
Fax: (416)926-4741
Co. E-mail: sanderson@oise.utoronto.ca
URL: http://icec.oise.utoronto.ca
Contact: Stephen Anderson, Director (Acting)
Services: Practical field development, professional development activities, and consulting. **Founded:** 1997. **Educational Activities:** Study groups, presen-tations, discussions, and debates. **Telecommunica-tion Services:** icec@oise.utoronto.ca.

START-UP INFORMATION

28504 ■ *101 Internet Businesses You Can Start from Home: How to Choose and Build Your Own Successful E-Business*
Pub: Maximum Press
Ed: Susan Sweeney. **Released:** June 2006. **Price:** $29.95. **Description:** Guide for starting and growing an Internet business; information for developing a business plan, risk levels, and promotional techniques are included.

28505 ■ *202 Things You Can Buy and Sell for Big Profits*
Pub: Entrepreneur Press
Ed: James Stephenson; Jason R. Rich. **Released:** July 2008. **Price:** $19.95. **Description:** Become an entrepreneur at selling new and used products. This handbook will help individuals cash in on the boom in reselling new and used products online. A new section defines ways to set realistic goals while distinguishing between 'get-rich schemes' and long term, viable businesses. A discussion about targeting and reaching the right customer base is included, along with finding and obtaining the service support needed for starting a new business.

28506 ■ *Complete Idiot's Guide to Starting an Ebay Business*
Pub: Penguin Books USA Inc.
Ed: Barbara Weltman, Malcolm Katt. **Released:** February 2008. **Price:** $19.95 (US), $29.00 (Canadian). **Description:** Guide for starting an eBay business includes information on products to sell, how to price merchandise, and details for working with services like PayPal, and how to organize fulfillment services.

28507 ■ *Design and Launch Your eCommerce Business in a Week*
Pub: Entrepreneur Press
Contact: Perlman Neil, President
Ed: Jason R. Rich. **Released:** July 2008. **Price:** $17.95. **Description:** Guide to help anyone start an online business in one week; included tips for Website design.

28508 ■ *Design and Launch Your Online Boutique in a Week*
Pub: Entrepreneur Press
Ed: Melissa Campanelli. **Released:** June 26, 2008. **Price:** $17.95. **Description:** Tips for starting an online boutique in a short amount of time are given. The books shows how to build the online boutique with designer goods or your own product, ways to create eye-catching content, online tools to handle payments and accept orders, marketing and advertising techniques, and customer service.

28509 ■ *E-Preneur*
Pub: Career Press, Inc.
Ed: Richard Goossen. **Released:** April 2008. **Price:** $15.99. **Description:** Entrepreneurs in the new virtual marketplace are examined. The book surveys and explains the field of Web 2.0 and entrepreneurs successfully using the virtual marketplace.

28510 ■ *eBay Business the Smart Way*
Pub: AMACOM
Ed: Joseph T. Sinclair. **Released:** June 6, 2007. **Price:** $17.95. **Description:** eBay commands ninety percent of all online auction business. Computer and software expert and online entrepreneur shares information to help online sellers get started and move merchandise on eBay. Tips include the best ways to build credibility, find products to sell, manage inventory, create a storefront Website, and more.

28511 ■ *EBay Business Start-up Kit: 100s of Live Links to All the Information and Tools You Need*
Pub: NOLO
Ed: Richard Stim. **Released:** July 2008. **Price:** $24.99. **Description:** Interactive kit that connects user directly to EBay is presented.

28512 ■ *Entrepreneurship with Online Learning Center Access Card*
Pub: McGraw-Hill Higher Education
Ed: Robert D. Hirich; Michael P. Peters; Dean A. Shepherd. **Released:** October 2006. **Price:** $103.25. **Description:** Book instructs students on entrepreneurial processes that include starting a new business.

28513 ■ *How to Start a Home-Based Mail Order Business*
Pub: Globe Pequot Press
Ed: Georganne Fiumara. **Released:** January 2005. **Price:** $17.95. **Description:** Step-by-step guide for starting and growing a home-based mail order business. Information about equipment, pricing, online marketing, are included along with worksheets and checklists for planning.

28514 ■ *How to Start a Home-Based Online Retail Business*
Pub: Globe Pequot Press
Ed: Jeremy Shepherd. **Released:** February 2007. **Price:** $18.95. **Description:** Information for starting an online retail, home-based business is shared.

28515 ■ *How to Start an Internet Sales Business*
Pub: Lulu.com
Ed: Dan Davis. **Released:** August 2005. **Price:** $19.95. **Description:** Small business guide for launching an Internet sales company. Topics include business structure, licenses, and taxes.

28516 ■ *"Online Fortunes" in Small Business Opportunities (Fall 2008)*
Pub: Entrepreneur Media Inc.
Description: Fifty hot, e-commerce enterprises for the aspiring entrepreneur to consider are featured; virtual assistants, marketing services, party planning, travel services, researching, web design and development, importing as well as creating an online store are among the businesses featured.

28517 ■ *"Power Up" in Entrepreneur (Vol. 35, November 2007, No. 11, pp. 140)*
Pub: Entrepreneur Media Inc.
Ed: Amanda C. Kooser. **Description:** PowerSeller is a status in the Internet company eBay, wherein sellers average at least $1,000 in sales per month for three consecutive months. There are five tiers in the PowerSeller status, which ranges from Bronze to Titanium. Launching startups at eBay can help entrepreneurs pick up a wide customer base, but getting and maintaining PowerSeller status is a challenge.

28518 ■ *Scrapbooking for Profit: Cashing in on Retail, Home-Based and Internet Opportunities*
Pub: Allworth Press
Ed: Rebecca Pittman. **Released:** June 2005. **Price:** $19.95 (US), $22.95 (Canadian). **Description:** Eleven strategies for starting a scrapbooking business, including brick-and-mortar stores, home-based businesses, and online retail and wholesale outlets.

28519 ■ *Start Your Own Blogging Business, Second Edition*
Pub: Entrepreneur Press
Contact: Perlman Neil, President
Released: July 1, 2010. **Price:** $17.95. **Description:** Interviews with professional bloggers from some of the most popular blogs on the Internet will help anyone interested in starting their own blogging business.

28520 ■ *Start Your Own Business on eBay, 2nd Edition*
Pub: Entrepreneur Press
Ed: Jacquelyn Lynn. **Released:** May 2007. **Price:** $19.95. **Description:** Tips for starring a new online business on eBay are shared.

28521 ■ *Start Your Own Net Services Business*
Pub: Entrepreneur Press
Contact: Perlman Neil, President
Released: February 1, 2009. **Price:** $17.95. **Description:** Web design, search engine marketing, new-media online, and blogging, are currently the four most popular web services available. This book provides information to start a net service business.

28522 ■ *Starting an Ebay Business for Canadians for Dummies*
Pub: John Wiley & Sons, Incorporated
Ed: Marsha Collier; Bill Summers. **Released:** February 2007. **Price:** $35.99. **Description:** Tips for turning a hobby into a successful online eBay company.

28523 ■ *Starting an iPhone Application Business for Dummies*
Pub: Wiley Publishing Inc.
Contact: William J. Pesce, President
Ed: Aaron Nicholson, Joel Elad, Damien Stolarz. **Released:** October 26, 2009. **Price:** $24.99. **Description:** Ways to create a profitable, sustainable business developing and marketing iPhone applications are profiled.

28524 ■ *Starting a Yahoo! Business for Dummies*
Pub: John Wiley & Sons, Incorporated
Ed: Rob Snell. **Released:** June 2006. **Price:** $24.99. **Description:** Rob Snell offers advice for turning online browsers into buyers, increase online traffic, and build an online store from scratch.

28525 ■ *Starting a Yahoo! Business For Dummies*

Pub: John Wiley & Sons, Incorporated

Ed: Rob Snell. **Released:** May 27, 2006. **Price:** $24.99. **Description:** Advice helps turn Web browsers into buyers, boost online traffic, and information to launch a profitable online business.

28526 ■ *"Startup Aims to Cut Out Coupon Clipping" in The Business Journal-Serving Metropolitan Kansas City (Vol. 26, August 15, 2008, No. 49)*

Pub: American City Business Journals, Inc.

Ed: Suzanna Stagemeyer. **Description:** TDP Inc., who started operations 18 months ago, aims to transform stale coupon promotions using technology by digitizing the entire coupon process. The process is expected to enable consumers to hunt coupons online where they will be automatically linked to loyalty cards. Other views and information on TDP and its services are presented.

28527 ■ *"Truthfully Speaking" in Entrepreneur (Vol. 35, November 2007, No. 11, pp. 118)*

Pub: Entrepreneur Media Inc.

Ed: Amanda C. Kooser. **Description:** Internet startup guru Guy Kawasaki talks about his new Web venture Truemors and shares tips on creating a successful Web-based company.

28528 ■ *"Virtual Playground" in Entrepreneur (Vol. 36, March 2008, No. 3, pp. 112)*

Pub: Entrepreneur Media Inc.

Ed: Amanda C. Kooser. **Description:** The growing number of children visiting virtual worlds provides opportunity for entrepreneurs to start online businesses catering to this market. Entrepreneurs need to be aware of the Children's Online Privacy Protection Act with regard to collecting children's information. Details of other things to know about with reference to these businesses are examined.

ASSOCIATIONS AND OTHER ORGANIZATIONS

28529 ■ Internet Alliance (IA)

c/o Tammy Cota, Exec. Dir.
1615 L St. NW, Ste. 1100
Washington, DC 20036-5624
Ph: (202)861-2407
Co. E-mail: tammy@internetalliance.org
URL: http://www.internetalliance.org
Contact: Tammy Cota, Executive Director
Description: Companies offering Internet services. Seeks to "build the confidence and trust necessary for the Internet to become the global mass market medium of the 21st century". Represents members' commercial and regulatory interests; conducts promotional activities; facilitates communication and cooperation among members. **Founded:** 1981. **Holdings:** The Alliance maintains a reference library in its field of interest. **Educational Activities:** Annual Interactive Service Association Conference (Annual). **Telecommunication Services:** info@internetalliance.org.

EDUCATIONAL PROGRAMS

28530 ■ Developing Web E-Commerce Applications

EEI Communications
8945 Guilford Rd., Ste. 145
Columbia, MD 22314
Ph: (410)309-8200
Free: 888-253-2762
Fax: (410)630-3980
Co. E-mail: train@eeicom.com
URL: http://www.eeicom.com/eei-training-services
Price: $1,065.00. **Description:** Experienced Web producers will learn how to build a shopping cart/order management system for secure transaction processing using the scripting languages ColdFusion and PHP. **Dates and Locations:** Silver Spring, MD; Hunt Valley, MD; Columbia, MD; and Alexandria, VA.

REFERENCE WORKS

28531 ■ *"3Par: Storing Up Value" in Barron's (Vol. 90, August 30, 2010, No. 35, pp. 30)*

Pub: Barron's Editorial & Corporate Headquarters

Ed: Mark Veverka. **Description:** Dell and Hewlett Packard are both bidding for data storage company 3Par. The acquisition would help Dell and Hewlett Packard provide customers with a one-stop shop as customers move to a private cloud in the Internet.

28532 ■ *6 Steps to Free Publicity*

Pub: ReadHowYouWant.com, Ltd.

Ed: Marcia Yudkin. **Released:** July 9, 2010. **Price:** $15.99. **Description:** Six steps to help promote a small business are given. The history of the Internet and its use to help provide free publicity to small firms is outlined.

28533 ■ *10 Steps to Successful Social Networking for Business*

Pub: ASTD

Contact: Tony Bingham, President

E-mail: tbingham@astd.org

Ed: Darin Hartley. **Released:** July 1, 2010. **Price:** $19.95. **Description:** Designed for today's fast-paced, need-it-yesterday business environment and for the thousands of workers who find themselves faced with new assignments, responsibilities, and requirements and too little time to learn what they must know.

28534 ■ *"3.4 Million Votes Cast in 2011 eBay Motors People's Pick Poll - Winners Announced at SEMA Show" in Benzinga.com (, 2011)*

Pub: Benzinga.com

Ed: Benzinga Staff. **Description:** eBay Motors sponsored the 2011 People's Picks survey, an annual poll inviting car enthusiasts to vote on their favorite auto thing, ranging from the best camshaft, favorite ignition, to favorite muscle car. More than 3.4 million votes were counted this year. A complete profile of eBay Motors is also provided.

28535 ■ *"55-Alive! Wants To Be MySpace for the Baby Boomer Set. Can It Raise $250,000?" in Inc. (October 2007, pp. 50)*

Pub: Gruner & Jahr USA Publishing

Description: Profile of 55-Alive! The online community created especially for individuals over the age of 50. The Website offers blogs, a dating section, listings for recreational vehicles for sale, movie reviews, advertising and articles of interest to users.

28536 ■ *202 Things You Can Make and Sell for Big Profits*

Pub: Entrepreneur Press

Ed: James Stephenson. **Released:** September 2005. **Price:** $19.95. **Description:** Instructions for 202 products that can be made and sold over the Internet.

28537 ■ *Advanced Selling for Dummies*

Pub: John Wiley and Sons, Inc.

Ed: Ralph R. Roberts; Joe Kraynak (As told to). **Released:** September 2007. **Price:** $21.99. **Description:** This book explores topics such as: visualizing success (includes exercises), investing and reinvesting in your own success, harnessing media and multimedia outlets, calculating risks that stretch your limits, creating lasting relationships, finding balance to avoid burnout and more. This guide is for salespeople who have already read 'Selling for Dummies' and now want forward-thinking, advanced strategies for recharging and reenergizing their careers and their lives. Blogging, Internet leads and virtual assistants are also discussed.

28538 ■ *"AllHipHop.com's Founders Thought a Weeklong Event Would Raise the Company" in Inc. (February 2008, pp. 48-51)*

Pub: Gruner & Jahr USA Publishing

Ed: Kermit Pattison. **Description:** Co-founders Greg Watkins and Chuck Creekmur, planned a weeklong festival to promote their company, AllHipHop.com; the event nearly ruined the firm. The online firm provides news about hip hop artists and the industry and is updated daily.

28539 ■ *"American Chemistry Council Launches Flagship Blog" in Ecology,Environment & Conservation Business (October 29, 2011, pp. 5)*

Pub: HighBeam Research

Description: American Chemistry Council (ACC) launched its blog, American Chemistry Matters, where interactive space allows bloggers to respond to news coverage and to discuss policy issues and their impact on innovation, competitiveness, job creation and safety.

28540 ■ *"Analyzing the Analytics" in Entrepreneur (Vol. 37, October 2009, No. 10, pp. 42)*

Pub: Entrepreneur Media, Inc.

Ed: Mikal E. Belicove. **Description:** Startups can maximize Web analytics by using them to monitor traffic sources and identify obstacles to converting them into targeted behaviors . Startups should set trackable Web site goals and continuously track traffic and conversion rates.

28541 ■ *"Ann Arbor Google's Growth Dips" in Crain's Detroit Business (Vol. 25, June 8, 2009, No. 23, pp. 3)*

Pub: Crain Communications Inc. - Detroit

Ed: Bill Shea. **Description:** Global recession has slowed the growth of Google Inc. Three years ago, when Google moved to Ann Arbor, Michigan it estimated it would provide 1,000 new jobs within five years, so far the firm employs 250.

28542 ■ *"Another California Firm On Way" in Austin Business Journal (Vol. 31, May 6, 2011, No. 9, pp. 1)*

Pub: American City Business Journals Inc.

Ed: Christopher Calnan. **Description:** Main Street Hub Inc. is planning to build a facility in Austin, Texas. The company helps businesses manage their online reputations. Main Street has selected Aquila Commercial LLC as its real estate broker.

28543 ■ *"Anthem Leading the Way in Social Tech Revolution" in Inside Business (Vol. 13, September-October 2011, No. 5, pp. 1B3)*

Pub: Great Lakes Publishing Co.

Ed: Ryan Clark. **Description:** Anthem Blue Cross and Blue Shield is leading the way in social technology. The firm's social media initiatives to promote itself are outlined.

28544 ■ *"Anything Could Happen" in Inc. (March 2008, pp. 116-123)*

Pub: Gruner & Jahr USA Publishing

Ed: Max Chafkin. **Description:** Profile of Evan Williams, founder of Blogger and Twitter, a new type of technology idea; Williams answers ten questions and share insight into growing both of his companies.

28545 ■ *"Aptitudes for Apps" in Boston Business Journal (Vol. 31, July 1, 2011, No. 23, pp. 3)*

Pub: Boston Business Journal

Ed: Kyle Alspach. **Description:** Startups Apperian Inc. and Kinvey Inc. are aiming to accelerate the development and deployment of mobile applications and have received fund pledges from Boston-area venture capital firms.

28546 ■ *"Are Offline Pushes Important to E-Commerce?" in DM News (Vol. 31, September 14, 2009, No. 23, pp. 10)*

Pub: Haymarket Media, Inc.

Description: With the importance of Internet marketing and the popularity of ecommerce increasing experts debate the relevance of more traditional channels of advertising.

28547 ■ *"Are You Ready To Do It Yourself? Discipline and Self-Study Can Help You Profit From Online Trading" in Black Enterprise (Feb. 2008)*

Pub: Earl G. Graves Publishing Co. Inc.

Ed: Steve Garmhausen. **Description:** Steps to help individuals invest in stocks online is given by an expert broker. Discount brokerage houses can save money for online investors.

28548 ■ "Area VCs Take Praise, Lumps, on Web site" in Boston Business Journal (Vol. 27, October 26, 2007, No. 39, pp. 1)
Pub: American City Business Journals Inc.
Ed: Jesse Noyes. Description: TheFunded.com is a social networking site that allows entrepreneurs to rate venture capitalists and post their comments. Information about venture capitalist firms such as size and the partners behind it are also provided.

28549 ■ "Art of the Online Deal" in Farm Industry News (March 25, 2011)
Pub: Penton Business Media Inc.
Description: Farmers share advice for shopping online for machinery; photos, clean equipment, the price, equipment details, and online sources topped their list.

28550 ■ "As Seen On TV" in Canadian Business (Vol. 80, November 5, 2007, No. 22, pp. 93)
Pub: Rogers Media
Ed: Zena Olijnyk. Description: StarBrand Media Inc. is one of the companies providing fans with information on how and where to purchase the items that television characters are using. StarBrand created the style section found on different television shows' Websites, such as that of the Gossip Girl and Smallville. The benefits of using sites like StarBrand are evaluated.

28551 ■ "As Technology Changes, So Must African American Business" in Black Enterprise (Vol. 41, August 2010, No. 1, pp. 61)
Pub: Earl G. Graves Publishing Co. Inc.
Ed: Sonya A. Donaldson. Description: Social media is essential to compete in today's business environment, especially for African American firms.

28552 ■ "Ask Inc." in Inc. (October 2007, pp. 73-74)
Pub: Gruner & Jahr USA Publishing
Description: An online marketing research firm investigates the use of online communities such as MySpace and Second life in order to recruit individuals to answer surveys.

28553 ■ "Ask Inc." in Inc. (January 2008, pp. 60)
Pub: Gruner & Jahr USA Publishing
Description: Ways to manage high volumes of email are examined.

28554 ■ "Atlific Adds Management of 4 Hotels to Its Portfolio in Fort McMurray" in Canadian Corporate News (May 16, 2007)
Pub: Comtex News Network Inc.
Description: Atlific Hotels & Resorts took over management for Merit Inn & Suites, The Merit Hotel, The Nomad Hotel and The Nomad Suites in Fort Mc-Murray. The company feels that they will be able to increase the hotels' abilities to promote their services through their vast network of sales personnel and marketing and e-commerce team.

28555 ■ "Attention, Please" in Entrepreneur (Vol. 36, April 2008, No. 4, pp. 52)
Pub: Entrepreneur Media, Inc.
Ed: Andrea Cooper. Description: Gurbaksh Chahal created his own company ClickAgents at the age of 16, and sold it two years later for $40 million to ValueClick. He then founded BlueLithium, an online advertising network on behavioral targeting, which Yahoo! Inc. bought in 2007 for $300 million. Chahal, now 25, talks about his next plans and describes how BlueLithium caught Yahoo's attention.

28556 ■ "Attract More Online Customers: Make Your Website Work Harder for You" in Black Enterprise (Vol. 37, November 2006, No. 4, pp. 66)
Pub: Earl G. Graves Publishing Co. Inc.
Description: Having an impressive presence on the Internet has become crucial. Detailed advice on making your website serve your business in the best way possible is included.

28557 ■ "Auctions and Bidding: a Guide for Computer Scientists" in ACM Computing Surveys (Vol. 43, Summer 2011, No. 2, pp. 10)
Pub: Association for Computing Machinery
Ed: Simon Parsons, Juan A. Rodriguez-Aguilar, Mark Klein. Description: There are various actions: single dimensional, multi-dimensional, single-sided, double-sided, first-price, second-price, English, Dutch, Japanese, sealed-bid, and these have been extensively discussed and analyzed in economics literature. This literature is surveyed from a computer science perspective, primarily from the viewpoint of computer scientists who are interested in learning about auction theory, and to provide pointers into the economics literature for those who want a deeper technical understanding. In addition, since auctions are an increasingly important topic in computer science, the article also looks at work on auctions from the computer science literature. The aim is to identify what both bodies of work tell us about creating electronic auctions.

28558 ■ "AVG Introduces Security Software Suite for SMBs 551179" in eWeek (October 12, 2010)
Pub: Ziff Davis Enterprise
Description: AVG Technologies is offering its AVG Internet Security 2011 Business Edition and AVG Anti-Virus Business Edition designed to give Internet-active SMB owners protection. The system protects online transactions and email communications as well as sensitive customer data and AVG Anti-Virus 2011 Business edition offers real-time protection against the latest online threats.

28559 ■ "Babynut.com to Shut Down" in Bellingham Business Journal (Vol. February 2010, pp. 3)
Pub: Sound Publishing Inc.
Description: Saralee Sky and Jerry Kilgore, owners of Babynut.com will close their online store. The site offered a free online and email newsletter to help mothers through pregnancy and the first three years of their child's life. Products being sold at clearance prices include organic and natural maternity and nursing clothing, baby and toddler clothes, books on pregnancy, and more.

28560 ■ "Banking on Twitter" in Baltimore Business Journal (Vol. 27, February 6, 2010, No. 40, pp. 1)
Pub: American City Business Journals
Ed: Gary Haber. Description: Ways that banks are using Twitter, Facebook and other social networking sites to provide customer services is discussed. First Mariner Bank is one of those banks that are finding the social media platform as a great way to reach customers. Privacy issues regarding this marketing trend are examined.

28561 ■ "The Bankrate Double Pay" in Barron's (Vol. 88, March 24, 2008, No. 12, pp. 27)
Pub: Dow Jones & Company, Inc.
Ed: Neil A. Martin. Description: Shares of Bankrate may rise as much as 25 percent from their level of $45.08 a share due to a strong cash flow and balance sheet. The company's Internet business remains strong despite weakness in the online advertising industry and is a potential takeover target.

28562 ■ "Banks Fall Short in Online Services for Savvy Traders" in Barron's (Vol. 88, March 17, 2008, No. 11, pp. 35)
Pub: Dow Jones & Company, Inc.
Ed: Theresa W. Carey. Description: Banc of America Investment Services, WellsTrade, and ShareBuilder are at the bottom of the list of online brokerages because they offer less trading technologies and product range. Financial shoppers miss out on a lot of customized tools and analytics when using these services.

28563 ■ "BayTSP, NTT Data Corp. Enter Into Reseller Pact to Market Online IP Monitoring" in Professional Services Close-Up (Sept. 11, 2009)
Pub: Close-Up Media
Description: Due to incredible interest from distributors and content owners across Asia, NTT Data Corp.

will resell BayTSP's online intellectual property monitoring, enforcement, business intelligence and monetization services in Japan.

28564 ■ "BBB Hires Marketing Firm to Attract More Businesses" in Baltimore Business Journal (Vol. 27, January 1, 2010, No. 35, pp. 1)
Pub: American City Business Journals
Ed: Julekha Dash. Description: Better Business Bureau (BBB) of Greater Maryland hired Bystry Carson & Associates Ltd. to assist in its rebranding efforts in order to entice more businesses. Bystry Carson will promote BBB's new mission at lectures, seminars, and networking events, as well as educate businesses about the agency through blogs and Twitter. BBB's services are also outlined.

28565 ■ "BDC Launches New Online Business Advice Centre" in Internet Wire (July 13, 2010)
Pub: Comtex
Description: The Business Development Bank of Canada (BDC) offers entrepreneurs the chance to use their new online BDC Advice Centre in order to seek advice regarding the challenges of entrepreneurship. Free online business tools and information to help both startups and established firms are also provided.

28566 ■ "Before You Hit Send: Crafting Workplace E-Mails to Avoid Mishaps" in Black Enterprise (Vol. 38, January 2008, No. 6, pp. 85)
Pub: Earl G. Graves Publishing Co. Inc.
Ed: Tennille M. Robinson. Description: Tips to use before sending an office email our presented. It is important to keep emails looking professional.

28567 ■ Behind the Cloud
Pub: Jossey-Bass
Ed: Marc Benioff, Carlye Adler. Released: 2010. Price: $27.95. Description: Salesforce.com is the world's most successful business-to-business cloud-computing company that sells an online service that helps businesses manage sales, customer service, and marketing functions.

28568 ■ "Being all a-Twitter" in Canadian Business (Vol. 81, December 8, 2008, No. 21, pp. 22)
Pub: Rogers Media Ltd.
Ed: Andrew Wahl. Description: Marketing experts suggest that advertising strategies have to change along with new online social media. Companies are advised to find ways to incorporate social software because workers and customers are expected to continue its use.

28569 ■ "Best Buy's CEO On Learning to Love Social Media" in Harvard Business Review (Vol. 88, December 2010, No. 12, pp. 43)
Pub: Harvard Business School Publishing
Ed: Brian J. Dunn. Description: Effective utilization of online social networks to enhance brand identity, connect with consumers, and address bad publicity scenarios is examined.

28570 ■ "Beyond YouTube: New Uses for Video, Online and Off" in Inc. (October 2007, pp. 53-54)
Pub: Gruner & Jahr USA Publishing
Ed: Leah Hoffmann. Description: Small companies are using video technology for embedding messages into email, broadcasting live interactive sales and training seminars, as well as marketing campaigns. Experts offer insight into producing and broadcasting business videos.

28571 ■ The Big Switch
Pub: W. W. Norton & Company, Inc.
Ed: Nicholas Carr. Released: January 19, 2009. Price: $16.95 paperback. Description: Today companies are dismantling private computer systems and tapping into services provided via the Internet. This shift is remaking the computer industry, bringing competitors such as Google to the forefront ant threatening traditional companies like Microsoft and

Dell. The book weaves together history, economics, and technology to explain why computing is changing and what it means for the future.

28572 ■ *The Big Switch: Rewiring the World, From Edison to Google*
Pub: W.W. Norton & Company
Ed: Nicholas Carr. **Released:** 2009. **Price:** $25.95. **Description:** Companies such as Google, Microsoft, and Amazon.com are building huge centers in order to create massive data centers. Together these centers form a giant computing grid that will deliver the digital universe to scientific labs, companies and homes in the future. This trend could bring about a new, darker phase for the Internet, one where these networks could operate as a fearsome entity that will dominate the lives of individuals worldwide.

28573 ■ *"Blacks Go Broadband: High Speed Internet Adoption Grows Among African Americans"* in Black Enterprise (Vol. 38, February 2008)
Pub: Earl G. Graves Publishing Co. Inc.
Ed: Cliff Hocker. **Description:** Number of black households using broadband Internet services tripled since 2005 according to a survey conducted by Pew Internet and American Life Project.

28574 ■ *"Bloomberg Law Upgraded Its Online Legal Research Platform"* in Information Today (Vol. 28, September 2011, No. 8, pp. 28)
Pub: Information Today, Inc.
Description: Bloomberg Law upgraded its online legal research platform for law practices. The new services includes a redesigned interface, improved search capabilities, and expanded collaboration and workflow features, while maintaining it comprehensive law resources such as mergers and acquisitions, antitrust, and securities.

28575 ■ *"Boise-based Highway 12 Invests in Crowdsourcing Platform"* in Idaho Business Review (September 24, 2010)
Pub: Dolan Media Newswires
Ed: Simon Shifrin. **Description:** The only venture capital fund in Idaho, Highway 12 Ventures, is funding Kapost a new company that helps news Websites, blogs and other online venues to pull content from a larger network of writers.

28576 ■ *"Boom and Bust in the Book Biz"* in Canadian Business (Vol. 83, August 17, 2010, No. 13-14, pp. 16)
Pub: Rogers Media Ltd.
Ed: Jordan Timm. **Description:** Electronic book marketplace is booming with Amazon.com's e-book sales for the Kindle e-reader exceeding the hardcover sales. Kobo Inc. has registered early success with its Kobo e-reader and has partnered with Hong Kong telecom giant on an e-book store.

28577 ■ *"Boosting Strategy With An Online Community"* in Business Strategy Review (Vol. 21, Spring 2010, No. 1, pp. 40)
Pub: Wiley-Blackwell
Ed: Lynda Gratton, Joel Casse. **Description:** A program that merged online communities with strategic development and implementation at Nokia has provided valuable lessons about new ways employees are able to engage and interact.

28578 ■ *"Boosting Your Merchant Management Services With Wireless Technology"* in Franchising World (Vol. 42, August 2010, No. 8, pp. 27)
Pub: International Franchise Association
Ed: Michael S. Slominski. **Description:** Franchises should have the capability to accept credit cards away from their businesses. This technology will increase sales.

28579 ■ *"Borders Previews New Web Site"* in Crain's Detroit Business (Vol. 23, October 8, 2007, No. 41, pp. 4)
Pub: Crain Communications Inc. - Detroit
Ed: Sheena Harrison. **Description:** Borders Group Inc. previewed its new Website that allows customers to buy items that include the Magic Shelf, a virtual bookcase that displays available recommended books, movies and music.

28580 ■ *"Bottoms Up!"* in Entrepreneur (Vol. 36, April 2008, No. 4, pp. 128)
Pub: Entrepreneur Media, Inc.
Ed: Amanda C. Kooser. **Description:** Jill Bernheimer launched her online alcohol business Domaine547 in 2007, and encountered challenges as legal issues over the licensing and launching of the business took about seven months to finish. Domain547 features blog and forum areas. Marketing strategy that connects to the social community is one of the ways to reach out to customers.

28581 ■ *"Brands' Mass Appeal"* in ADWEEK (Vol. 51, June 14, 2010, No. 24)
Pub: Nielsen Business Media Inc.
Ed: Lisa Thorell, James Sherret. **Description:** Engineering/science crowdsourced projects tend to result from posting and/or publishing interim results as well as from other talents building upon those results to produce even better results. However, the author does not see the same results in the creative world.

28582 ■ *"Brief: US-Business/eBay Earnings Rise 31 Per Cent"* in Denver Post (July 21, 2011)
Pub: The Denver Post
Ed: Andy Goldberg. **Description:** eBay's strong performance in second quarter 2011 is being attributed to Paypal online payments division. eBay's online auction sites reported gross merchandise volume up 34 percent. Statistical data included.

28583 ■ *"Brite-Strike Tactical Launches New Internet Marketing Initiatives"* in Internet Wire (September 15, 2009)
Pub: Comtex News Network, Inc.
Description: Brite-Strike Tactical Illumination Products, Inc. has enlisted the expertise of Internet marketing guru Thomas J. McCarthy to help revamp the company's Internet campaign. An outline of the Internet marketing strategy is provided.

28584 ■ *"Broadband Reaches Access Limits in Europe"* in Information Today (Vol. 26, February 2009, No. 2, pp. 22)
Pub: Information Today, Inc.
Ed: Jim Ashling. **Description:** Eurostat (the Statistical Office of the European communities) reports results from is survey regarding Internet use by businesses throughout its 27-member states. Iceland, Finland and the Netherlands provide the most access at broadband speeds, followed by Belgium, Spain and France.

28585 ■ *"Building a Better Twitter Brand: My Foray Into Social Analytics"* in Inc. (Vol. , pp.)
Pub: Inc. Magazine
Ed: John Brandon. **Description:** A small business using Twitter to research and promote the firm decided to test some Web-based dashboards that allow you to manage and analyze accounts on multiple social media networks including Facebook, Twitter, and LinkedIn.

28586 ■ *"Building Your Business: A Strong Web Presence Is a Must"* in Black Enterprise (Vol. 38, December 2007, No. 5, pp. 74)
Pub: Earl G. Graves Publishing Co. Inc.
Ed: Tennille M. Robinson. **Description:** Building a strong presence on the Internet is crucial to any growing business. Websites can provide information or sell merchandise, but the site must also make sure the customer knows how to use and navigate around within the site. Common mistakes to avoid when designing a small business Website are outlined.

28587 ■ *"The Business Case for Mobile Content Acceleration"* in Streaming Media (November 2011, pp. 78)
Pub: Information Today Inc.
Ed: Dan Rayburn. **Description:** Last holiday season, eBay became a mobile commerce (m-commerce) giant when sales rose by 134 percent, as most online retailers offered customers the ability to purchase items using their mobile devices.

28588 ■ *"Business Forecast: Stormy and Successful"* in Women In Business (Vol. 62, June 2010, No. 2, pp. 12)
Pub: American Business Women's Association
Ed: Kathleen Leighton. **Description:** Stormy Simon, vice president of customer service at Overstock.com is a self-made career woman who started out as a temporary employee in the company in 2001. She was not able to attend college because she had two sons to care for after her divorce. Simon got involved in advertising and media buying and shares her love for business.

28589 ■ *"Buy Local to Land Great Deals"* in Inside Business (Vol. 13, September-October 2011, No. 5, pp. SS8)
Pub: Great Lakes Publishing Co.
Description: Buy Lakewood! Loyalty Program offers residents great bargains for shopping at local retailers. Residents sign up online and the city mails them a letter of appreciations along with a key card. Showing the key card at any participating businesses listed on the Website will provide discounts.

28590 ■ *"Campaigner Survey: 46 Percent of Small Businesses Use Email Marketing"* in Wireless News (November 21, 2009)
Pub: Close-Up Media
Description: Almost half (46 percent) of small businesses surveyed by Campaigner's 2009 State of Small Business Online Marketing, say that they rely on email marketing to help them find new customers, keep existing ones and grow their businesses. The survey also found that 36 percent of small businesses plan to begin using email marketing over the next year. The trend to utilize Internet marketing tools is allowing small businesses to grow faster and generate higher revenues than those that are not using these mediums.

28591 ■ *"Capturing Generation Y: Ready, Set, Transform"* in Credit Union Times (Vol. 21, July 14, 2010, No. 27, pp. 20)
Pub: Summit Business Media
Ed: Senthil Kumar. **Description:** The financial services sector recognizes that Generation Y will have a definite impact on the way business is conducted in the future. The mindset of Generation Y is social and companies need to use networking tools such as Facebook in order to reach this demographic.

28592 ■ *"The China Connection"* in Crain's Chicago Business (Vol. 31, March 24, 2008, No. 12, pp. 26)
Pub: Crain Communications, Inc.
Ed: Samantha Stainburn. **Description:** Interview with Ben Munoz who studied abroad in Beijing, China for three months to study international economics, e-commerce and global leadership.

28593 ■ *"Chris Curtis Preaches the Gospel of Internet Success"* in Black Enterprise (Vol. 38, March 2008, No. 8, pp. 56)
Pub: Earl G. Graves Publishing Co. Inc.
Ed: Anthony Calypso. **Description:** Profile of the Web Business Ownership Series, a collection of 20 free seminars that help small businesses learn about the Web development process.

28594 ■ *"Click Here to Book"* in Caterer & Hotelkeeper (October 28, 2011, No. 288)
Pub: Reed Reference Publishing
Ed: Ross Bentley. **Description:** Customers expectations are determined by the quality of a Website when booking hotel rooms.

28595 ■ *"A Click In the Right Direction: Website Teaches Youth Financial Literacy"* in Black Enterprise (Vol. 38, December 2007, No. 5)
Pub: Earl G. Graves Publishing Co. Inc.
Ed: Nicole Norfleet. **Description:** Profile of Donald Lee Robinson who launched SkillsThatClick, a Website that teaches young individuals ages 12 to 15 about money management. Robinson shares how he used his Navy career as a model for designing the site.

28596 ■ *"ClickFuel Unveils Internet Marketing Tools for Small Businesses" in Internet Wire (October 19, 2009)*
Pub: Comtex News Network, Inc.
Description: ClickFuel, a firm that manages, designs and tracks marketing campaigns has unveiled a full software suite of affordable services and technology solutions designed to empower small business owners and help them promote and grow their businesses through targeted Internet marketing campaigns.

28597 ■ *Clicking Through: A Survival Guide for Bringing Your Company Online*
Pub: Bloomberg Press
Ed: Jonathan I. Ezor. **Released:** October 1999. **Description:** Summary of legal compliance issues faced by small companies doing business on the Internet, including copyright and patent laws.

28598 ■ *"Clicks For Cash: Earning More From Your Website" in Inc. (December 2007, pp. 64-65)*
Pub: Gruner & Jahr USA Publishing
Ed: Michael Fitzgerald. **Description:** Ways to use a company's Website to generate revenue are discussed. Free services for placing ads include Google AdSense, AdBrite, AuctionAds, Chitkia eMiniMalls, Vizu Answers, and Value Click; profiles of each service are presented.

28599 ■ *"Clicks From Round the World: Simplifying International E-Commerce" in Inc. (Volume 32, December 2010, No. 10, pp. 146)*
Pub: Inc. Magazine
Ed: Ryan Underwood. **Description:** By 2014, global e-commerce spending is expected to increase more than 90 percent, with much of that growth coming from Latin America.

28600 ■ *"Cloudy Future for VMware?" in Barron's (Vol. 90, September 13, 2010, No. 37, pp. 21)*
Pub: Barron's Editorial & Corporate Headquarters
Ed: Jonathan R. Laing. **Description:** VMWare dominated the virtualization market for years, but it may be ending as it faces more competition from rivals that offer cloud computing services. The company's stocks are also expensive and are vulnerable to the smallest mishap.

28601 ■ *"Complete Discovery Source, Inc. (CDS) Receives Minority Owned Business Certification" in Internet Wire (December 14, 2010)*
Pub: Comtex
Description: Complete Discovery Source Inc. (CDS) was granted Minority-Owned Business Enterprise status by the New York State Department of Economic Development. The certification provides CDS, an end-to-end eDiscovery services provider, with access to contracting opportunities with 130 government agencies throughout New York state.

28602 ■ *The Complete Guide to Google Adwords: Secrets, Techniques, and Strategies You Can Learn to Make Millions*
Pub: Atlantic Publishing Company
Released: December 1, 2010. **Price:** $24.95. **Description:** Google AdWords, when it launched in 2002 signaled a fundamental shift in what the Internet was for so many individuals and companies. Learning and understanding how Google AdWords operates and how it can be optimized for maximum exposure, boosting click through rates, conversions, placement, and selection of the right keywords, can be the key to a successful online business.

28603 ■ *"Connections: United We Gab" in Entrepreneur (Vol. 35, October 2007, No. 10, pp. 60)*
Pub: Entrepreneur Media Inc.
Ed: Mike Hogan. **Description:** T-Mobile and AT&T introduced dual-mode service to consumers, helping them to switch between cellular and Wi-Fi networks easily. These services, such as Hotspot@Home, reduces the cost of long distance calls by routing them over the Internet with the use of WiFi. Benefits of dual mode service, such as lower hardware price and better call coverage are given.

28604 ■ *"Consumer Electronics: Brick and Mortar Vs. Online" in Retail Merchandiser (Vol. 51, September-October 2011, No. 5, pp. 15)*
Pub: Phoenix Media Corporation
Description: Brick and mortar retailers with Websites are discovering that the Internet is used more for research than purchasing when it comes to electronics products. According to a recent study conducted by The NPD Group shows that 56 percent of consumers research televisions online before purchasing, but only 19 percent actually buy them online.

28605 ■ *"Consumer Trust in E-Commerce Web Sites: a Meta-Study" in ACM Computing Surveys (Vol. 43, Fall 2011, No. 3, pp. 14)*
Pub: Association for Computing Machinery
Ed: Patricia Beatty, Ian Reay, Scott Dick, James Miller. **Description:** Trust is at once an elusive, imprecise concept, and a critical attribute that must be engineered into e-commerce systems. Engineering trust is examined.

28606 ■ *Content Rich: Writing Your Way to Wealth on the Web*
Pub: 124 S Mercedes Rd.
Ed: Jon Wuebben. **Released:** April 2008. **Price:** $19.95. **Description:** A definitive search engine optimization (SEO) copywriting guide for search engine rankings and sales conversion. It includes topics not covered in other books on the subject and targets the small to medium sized business looking for ways to maximize online marketing activities as well as designers and Web developers seeking to incorporate more SEO techniques into design and content.

28607 ■ *"Contest Produce Ad Designs on a Dime" in San Diego Business Journal (Vol. 31, August 23, 2010, No. 31, pp. 1)*
Pub: San Diego Business Journal
Ed: Mike Allen. **Description:** San Diego-based Prova.fm runs design contests for clients such as the U.S. Postal Service. The client then chooses the best entry from the contest. Prova.fm relies on the Internet to deliver a range of possible graphic solutions and allowing the customer to make the right selection for its business through a process called crowdsourcing.

28608 ■ *"Conversations with Customers" in Business Journal Serving Greater Tampa Bay (Vol. 31, December 31, 2010, No. 1, pp. 1)*
Pub: Tampa Bay Business Journal
Description: Tampa Bay, Florida-based businesses have been using social media to interact with customers. Forty percent of businesses have been found to have at least one social media platform to reach customers and prospects.

28609 ■ *"Coping with the Web" in Agency Sales Magazine (Vol. 39, December 2009, No. 11, pp. 52)*
Pub: MANA
Ed: Karen Saunders. **Description:** When branding your company on the Internet, strategy should first be discussed with the website designer and the target and niche audience should also be defined. Describing 'what' and 'how' the product or service is offering is also important. In addition, perception, the logo, and the tag line are some elements that are needed to create a brand.

28610 ■ *"Copyright Clearance Center (CCC) Partnered with cSubs" in Information Today (Vol. 28, November 2011, No. 10, pp. 14)*
Pub: Information Today, Inc.
Description: Copyright Clearance Center (CCC) partnered with cSubs to integrate CCC's point-of-content licensing solution RightsLink Basic directly into cSubs workflow. The partnership will allow cSubs' customers a user-friendly process for obtaining permissions. Csubs is a corporate subscription management service for books, newspapers, and econtent.

28611 ■ *"The Copyright Evolution" in Information Today (Vol. 28, November 2011,*

No. 10, pp. 1)
Pub: Information Today, Inc.
Ed: Nancy Davis Kho. **Description:** For information professionals, issues surrounding copyright compliance have traditionally been on the consumption side. However, today, content consumption is only half the program because blogging, tweeting, and commenting is a vital part of more standard duties for workers as corporations aim to create authentic communications with customers.

28612 ■ *Crossing the Chasm: Marketing and Selling Disruptive Products to Mainstream Customers*
Pub: HarperInformation
Ed: Geoffrey A. Moore. **Released:** September 2002. **Price:** $17.95. **Description:** A guide for marketing in high-technology industries, focusing on the Internet.

28613 ■ *"Crowdsourcing their Way into One Big Mess" in Brandweek (Vol. 51, October 25, 2010, No. 38, pp. 26)*
Pub: Nielsen Business Media, Inc.
Ed: Gregg S. Lipman. **Description:** The Gap, was counting on crowdsourcing to provide feedback for its new logo, but it did not prove positive for the retailer. However, a massive outcry of negative opinion, via crowdsourcing, may not always equal valid, constructive criticism.

28614 ■ *Crowdsourcing: Why the Power of the Crowd is Driving the Future of Business*
Pub: Crown Business
Ed: Jeff Howe. **Released:** 2009. **Price:** $26.95. **Description:** Small businesses are shown how to use social networks online to promote goods and services.

28615 ■ *Crush It!*
Pub: HarperStudio/HarperCollins
Ed: Gary Vaynerchuk. **Released:** 2009. **Price:** $19.99. **Description:** Ways the Internet can help entrepreneurs turn their passions into successful companies.

28616 ■ *"Cyber Thanksgiving Online Shopping a Growing Tradition" in Marketing Weekly News (December 12, 2009, pp. 137)*
Pub: Investment Weekly News
Description: According to e-commerce analysts, Thanksgiving day is becoming increasingly important to retailers in terms of online sales. Internet marketers are realizing that consumers are already searching for Black Friday sales and if they find deals on the products they are looking for, they are highly likely to make their purchase on Thanksgiving day instead of waiting.

28617 ■ *"Cyberwise" in Black Enterprise (Vol. 41, December 2010, No. 5, pp. 50)*
Pub: Earl G. Graves Publishing Co. Inc.
Ed: Marica Wade Talbert. **Description:** Information is given regarding single platforms that can be used to develop applications for iPhone, Android, Blackberry, and Nokia.

28618 ■ *"Cyberwise" in Black Enterprise (Vol. 41, September 2010, No. 2, pp. 49)*
Pub: Earl G. Graves Publishing Co. Inc.
Ed: Marcia Wade Talbert. **Description:** Advice is given to assist in selling an online store called theupscalegaragesale.com. A listing of business brokers specializing in the sale of Internet businesses is included.

28619 ■ *"Datran Media Executives to Lead Industry Debates Across Q1 Conferences" in Internet Wire (January 22, 2010)*
Pub: Comtex News Network, Inc.
Description: Datran Media, an industry-leading digital marketing technology company, will be sending members of its management team to several conferences in the early part of the first quarter of 2010; discussions will include Internet marketing innovations, e-commerce and media distribution.

28620 ■ *"Dear Customer: Managing E-Mail Campaigns" in Inc. (March 2008, pp. 58-59)*
Pub: Gruner & Jahr USA Publishing
Ed: Ryan Underwood. **Description:** Internet services that help firms manage their online business including email marketing, to manage subscriber lists,

comply with spam regulations, monitor bouncebacks, and track potential customers are profiled. Constant Contact, MobileStorm Stun, Campaign Monitor, Pop Commerce, Emma, and StrongMail E-mail Server are among software and services highlighted.

28621 ■ Designing Websites for Every Audience
Pub: F & W Publications, Incorporated
Ed: Ilise Benun. **Released:** January 2003. **Description:** Twenty-five case studies targeting six difference audiences are used to help a business design, or make over, a Website.

28622 ■ "DHS Finalizes Rules Allowing Electronic I-9s" in HR Specialist (Vol. 8, September 2010, No. 9, pp. 5)
Pub: Capitol Information Group Inc.
Description: U.S. Department of Home and Security issued regulations that give employers more flexibility to electronically sing and store I-9 employee verification forms.

28623 ■ Digital Divide: Civic Engagement, Information Poverty, and the Internet Worldwide
Pub: Cambridge University Press
Contact: Richard Ziemacki, President
E-mail: rziemacki@cambridge.org
Ed: Pippa Norris. **Released:** January 22, 2010. **Price:** $28.99. **Description:** The expansive growth of the Internet is intensifying existing inequalities between the information rich and poor. The book examines the evidence for access and use of the Internet in 179 countries and discusses the global divide that is evident between industrialized and developing societies.

28624 ■ "The Digital Revolution is Over. Long Live the Digital Revolution!" in Business Strategy Review (Vol. 21, Spring 2010, No. 1, pp. 74)
Pub: Wiley-Blackwell
Ed: Gianvito Lanzolla, Jamie Anderson. **Description:** Many businesses are now involved in the digital marketplace. The authors argue that the new reality of numerous companies offering overlapping products means that it is critical for managers to understand digital convergence and to observe the imperatives for remaining competitive.

28625 ■ "Do-It-Yourself Portfolio Management" in Barron's (Vol. 89, July 13, 2009, No. 28, pp. 25)
Pub: Dow Jones & Co., Inc.
Ed: Mike Hogan. **Description:** Services of several portfolio management web sites are presented. These web sites include MarketRiders E.Adviser, TD Ameritrade and E.

28626 ■ "Dollar General Selects GSI Commerce to Launch Its eCommerce Business" in Benzinga.com (October 29, 2011)
Pub: Benzinga.com
Ed: Benzinga Staff. **Description:** Dollar General Corporation chose GSI Commerce, a leading provider of ecommerce and interactive marketing solutions, to launch its online initiative. GSI Commerce is an eBay Inc. company.

28627 ■ "Dots Sings To New Tune With Its Radio Station" in Crain's Cleveland Business (Vol. 30, June 15, 2009, No. 23, pp. 7)
Pub: Crain Communications, Inc.
Description: Dots LLC, a women's clothing retailer, has launched an online radio station on its Website. The station plays the in-store music to customers while they are shopping online.

28628 ■ Double or Nothing: How Two Friends Risked It All to Buy One of Las Vegas' Legendary Casinos
Pub: HarperBusiness
Ed: Tom Breitling, with Cal Fussman. **Released:** March 2008. **Price:** $24.95. **Description:** Founders of a successful Internet travel agency share their experience from startup to selling the company.

28629 ■ "Dramatic Results: Making Opera (Yes, Opera) Seem Young and Hip" in Inc. (October 2007, pp. 61-62)
Pub: Gruner & Jahr USA Publishing
Description: Profile of Peter Gelb, who turned New York's Metropolitan Opera into one of the most media-savvy organizations in the country, using a multifaceted marketing strategy through the media. Gelb used streaming audio and simulcasts on satellite radio and movie theaters to promote a message that opera is hip.

28630 ■ "Drive Traffic To Your Blog" in Women Entrepreneur (January 13, 2009)
Pub: Entrepreneur Media Inc.
Ed: Lesley Spencer Pyle. **Description:** Internet social networking has become a vital component to marketing one's business. Tips are provided on how to establish a blog that will attract attention to one's business and keep one's customers coming back for more.

28631 ■ e-Business, e-Government and Small and Medium-Size Enterprises: Opportunities and Challenges
Pub: Idea Group Publishing
Ed: Brian J. Corbitt, Nabeel A.Y. Al-Qirim. **Released:** February 2004. **Price:** $64.95. **Description:** Electronic commerce and information technology research in small and medium-sized enterprises (SMEs). Policymakers, legislators, researchers and professionals address significant issues of importance to the small business sector.

28632 ■ E-Commerce in Regional Small to Medium Enterprises
Pub: Idea Group Publishing
Ed: Robert MacGregor. **Released:** July 2007. **Price:** $99.95. **Description:** Strategies small to medium enterprises (SMEs) need to implement in order to compete with larger, global businesses and the role electronic commerce plays in this process are outlined. Studies of e-commerce in multiple regional areas, focusing on the role of business size, business sector, market focus, gender of CEO, and education level of the CEO are discussed.

28633 ■ e-Riches 2.0: Next-Generation Marketing Strategies for Making Million Online
Pub: AMACOM
Ed: Scott Fox. **Released:** May 27, 2009. **Price:** $25. 00. **Description:** Beginner's guide to using the Internet to help grow business, including the best ways to use email lists and newsletters, RSS feeds, online viral marketing, social networking, microblogging, online video and radio/podcasts, tele-seminars and webinars, search engine keyword advertising and affiliate program advertising.

28634 ■ "eBay Business Looking Up" in Zacks (July 26, 2011)
Pub: Comtex News Network Inc.
Ed: Sejuti Banerjea. **Description:** eBay reported solid revenue growth for 2011 second quarter, keeping in line with the Zacks Consensus Estimate, and third quarter earnings are expected to be higher. eBay's new strategy is to direct traffic to bigger sellers with improved customer service, making this good for eBay businesses.

28635 ■ "EBay Finally Gaining Traction in China" in San Jose Mercury News (October 26, 2011)
Pub: San Jose Mercury News
Ed: John Boudreau. **Description:** eBay has developed a new strategy in China that allows exporters of every type of merchandise to sell directly to eBays 97 million overseas users.

28636 ■ EBay Income: How ANYONE of Any Age, Location, and/or Background Can Build a Highly Profitable Online Business with eBay
Pub: Atlantic Publishing Company
Released: December 1, 2010. **Price:** $24.95. **Description:** A complete overview of eBay is given and guides any small company through the entire process of creating the auction and auction strategies,

photography, writing copy, text and formatting, multiple sales, programming tricks, PayPal, accounting, creating marketing, merchandising, managing email lists, advertising plans, taxes and sales tax, best time to list items and for how long, sniping programs, international customers, opening a storefront, electronic commerce, buy-it now pricing, keywords, Google marketing and eBay secrets.

28637 ■ "eBay Inc. Completes Acquisition of Zong" in Benzinga.com (October 29, 2011)
Pub: Benzinga.com
Ed: Benzinga Staff. **Description:** eBay Inc. acquired Zong, a provider of payments through mobile carrier billing. Terms of the agreement are outlined.

28638 ■ "eBay Introduces Open Commerce Ecosystem" in Entertainment Close-Up (October 24, 2011)
Pub: Close-Up Media
Description: eBay's new X.commerce is an open commerce ecosystem that will arm developers and merchants with the technology tools required to keep pace with the ever-changing industry. X.commerce brings together the technology assets and developer communities of eBay, PayPal, Magento and partners to expand on eBays vision for enabling commerce.

28639 ■ "eBay and Jonathan Adler Team to Launch 'The eBay Inspiration Shop" in Entertainment Close-Up (October 25, 2011)
Pub: Close-Up Media
Description: Designer Jonathan Adler partnered with eBay to create a collection of new must-have merchandise for the fall season. Top trendsetters, including actors, designers, bloggers, stylists, editors, photographers, models and musicians helped curate the items being featured in the windows by sharing their shopping wish lists with users.

28640 ■ The Ebay Seller's Tax and Legal Answer Book
Pub: AMACOM
Ed: Cliff Ennico. **Released:** April 30, 2007. **Price:** $19.95. **Description:** Helps sellers using Ebay to file taxes properly, while saving money.

28641 ■ Ebay the Smart Way: Selling, Burying, and Profiting on the Web's Number One Auction Site
Pub: AMACOM
Ed: Joseph T. Sinclair. **Released:** May 2007. **Price:** $17.95. **Description:** Resource to help individuals sell, buy and profit using the Internet auction site Ebay.

28642 ■ Effective Web Presence Solutions for Small Businesses: Strategies for Successful Implementation
Pub: IGI Global
Ed: Stephen Burgess,, Carmine Sellitto, Stergios Karanasio, Stan Karanasios. **Released:** March 1, 2009. **Price:** $165.00. **Description:** Business strategies to implement a Web presence for any small business, is examined, focusing on website development.

28643 ■ "Elanco Challenges Bayer's Advantage, K9 Advantix Ad Claims" in Pet Product News (Vol. 64, November 2010, No. 11, pp. 11)
Pub: BowTie Inc.
Description: Elanco Animal Health has disputed Bayer Animal Health's print and Web advertising claims involving its flea, tick, and mosquito control products Advantage and K9 Advantix. The National Advertising Division of the Council of Better Business Bureaus recommended the discontinuation of ads, while Bayer Animal Health reiterated its commitment to self-regulation.

28644 ■ Electronic Commerce
Pub: Course Technology
Ed: Gary Schneider, Bryant Chrzan, Charles McCormick. **Released:** May 1, 2010. **Price:** $117.95. **Description:** E-commerce can open the door to more opportunities than ever before for small business. Packed with real-world examples and cases, the book delivers comprehensive coverage of emerging online technologies and trends and their influence on the electronic marketplace. It details how the landscape

of online commerce is evolving, reflecting changes in the economy and how business and society are responding to those changes. Balancing technological issues with the strategic business aspects of successful e-commerce, the new edition includes expanded coverage of international issues, social networking, mobile commerce, Web 2.0 technologies, and updates on spam, phishing, and identity theft.

28645 ■ *Electronic Commerce: Technical, Business, and Legal Issues*

Pub: Prentice Hall PTR

Ed: Oktay Dogramaci; Aryya Gangopadhyay; Yelena Yesha; Nabil R. Adam. **Released:** August 1998. **Description:** Provides insight into the goals of using the Internet to grow a business in the areas of networking and telecommunication, security, and storage and retrieval; business areas such as marketing, procurement and purchasing, billing and payment, and supply chain management; and legal aspects such as privacy, intellectual property, taxation, contractual and legal settlements.

28646 ■ *Email Marketing by the Numbers: How to Use the World's Greatest Marketing Tool to Take Any Organization to the Next Level*

Pub: John Wiley and Sons Inc.

Ed: Chris Baggott. **Released:** April 2007. **Price:** $29.99 (CND). **Description:** Tips for using email to market small business products and services are provided.

28647 ■ *Emerging Business Online: Global Markets and the Power of B2B Internet Marketing*

Pub: FT Press

Ed: Lara Fawzy, Lucas Dworksi. **Released:** October 1, 2010. **Price:** $49.99. **Description:** An introduction into ebocube (emerging business online), a comprehensive proven business model for Internet B2B marketing in emerging markets.

28648 ■ *"Empowered" in Harvard Business Review (Vol. 88, July-August 2010, No. 7-8, pp. 94)*

Pub: Harvard Business School Publishing

Ed: Josh Bernoff, Ted Schadler. **Description:** HERO concept (highly empowered and resourceful operative) which builds a connection between employees, managers, and IT is outlined. The resultant additional experience and knowledge gained by employees improves customer relationship management.

28649 ■ *"Endeca Gears Up for Likely IPO Bid" in Boston Business Journal (Vol. 31, July 1, 2011, No. 23, pp. 1)*

Pub: Boston Business Journal

Ed: Kyle Alspach. **Description:** Endeca Inc. is readying itself for its plans to register as a public company. The search engine technology leader is enjoying continued growth with revenue up by 30 percent in 2010 while its expansion trend makes it an unlikely candidate for an acquisition.

28650 ■ *The Essential Online Solution: The 5-Step Formula for Small Business Success*

Pub: John Wiley & Sons, Incorporated

Ed: Rick Segel; Barbara Callan-Bogia. **Released:** October 2006. **Price:** $22.95. **Description:** Strategies to help any small business increase its online presence and compete with big retail chains. Tips for success Web design are included.

28651 ■ *Essentials of Entrepreneurship and Small Business Management*

Pub: Prentice Hall PTR

Ed: Thomas W. Zimmerer; Norman M. Scarborough; Doug Wilson. **Released:** February 2007. **Price:** $106. 67. **Description:** New venture creation and the knowledge required to start a new business are shared. The challenges of entrepreneurship, business plans, marketing, e-commerce, and financial considerations are explored.

28652 ■ *"Etextbook Space Heats Up" in Information Today (Vol. 28, November 2011,*

No. 10, pp. 10)

Pub: Information Today, Inc.

Ed: Paula J. Hane. **Description:** The use of etextbooks is expected to grow with the use of mobile devices and tablets. A new group of activists is asking students, faculty members and others to sign a petition urging higher education leaders to prioritize affordable textbooks or free ebooks over the traditional, expensive new books required for classes.

28653 ■ *"Etextbooks: Coming of Age" in Information Today (Vol. 28, September 2011, No. 8, pp. 1)*

Pub: Information Today, Inc.

Ed: Amanda Mulvihill. **Description:** National average for textbooks costs was estimated at $1,137 annually at a 4-year public college for the 2010-2011 school year. Amazon reported selling 105 etextbooks for every 100 print books, while Barnes and Noble announced that their etextbooks were outselling print 3 to 1.

28654 ■ *"Etiquette, Common Sense Often Lag Behind Smarter Devices" in Crain's Cleveland Business (Vol. 28, October 22, 2007, No. 42, pp. 21)*

Pub: Crain Communications, Inc.

Ed: Chrissy Kadleck. **Description:** Discusses the importance of good etiquette in regards to electronic communication both within as well as outside the business world.

28655 ■ *"F1 Makes Room(s) for Aspiring Entrepreneur" in Austin Business Journal (Vol. 31, July 1, 2011, No. 17, pp. 1)*

Pub: American City Business Journals Inc.

Ed: Vicky Garza. **Description:** Formula One fan and graphic designer Danielle Crespo cashes in on the June 17, 2012 racing event in Austin, Texas via hosting a Website that allows users to book hotel rooms. She invested less than $100 and long hours on this enterprise which now has 74,000-plus visitors.

28656 ■ *The Facebook Effect: The Inside Story of the Company That Is Connecting the World*

Pub: Simon & Shuster

Ed: David Kirkpatrick. **Released:** June 8, 2010. **Price:** $26.00. **Description:** There's never been a Website like Facebook: more than 350 million people have accounts, and if the growth rate continues, by 2013 every Internet user worldwide will have his or her own page. No one's had more access to the inner workings of the phenomenon than Kirkpatrick, a senior tech writer at Fortune magazine. Written with the full cooperation of founder Mark Zuckerberg, the book follows the company from its genesis in a Harvard dorm room through its successes over Friendster and MySpace, the expansion of the user base, and Zuckerberg's refusal to sell.

28657 ■ *The Facebook Era: Tapping Online Social Networks to Build Better Products, Reach New Audiences, and Sell More Stuff*

Pub: Prentice Hall

Ed: Clara Shih. **Price:** $24.99. **Description:** The '90s were about the World Wide Web of information and the power of linking Web pages. Today it's about the World Wide Web of people and the power of the social graph. Online social networks are fundamentally changing the way we live, work, and interact. They offer businesses immense opportunities to transform customer relationships for profit: opportunities that touch virtually every business function, from sales and marketing to recruiting, collaboration to executive decision-making, product development to innovation.

28658 ■ *Facebook Marketing: Designing Your Next Marketing Campaign*

Pub: Que

Ed: Justin R. Levy. **Released:** May 1, 2010. **Price:** $24.99. **Description:** Detailed steps are given in order to develop, use, and create awareness for any business. The book provides detailed instructions, along with case studies from known brands, for launching marketing campaigns on Facebook.

28659 ■ *"Facebook Purchased Push Pop Press" in Information Today (Vol. 28, October 2011, No. 9, pp. 12)*

Pub: Information Today, Inc.

Description: Facebook purchased Push Pop Press, a digital publishing company that developed a multi-touch interface for ebook publishing on the iPad.

28660 ■ *"Fifty Percent of Global Online Retail Visits Were to Amazon, eBay and Alibaba in June 2011" in Benzinga.com (October 29, 2011)*

Pub: Benzinga.com

Ed: Benzinga Staff. **Description:** Current statistics and future forecasts through the year 2015 for Amazon, eBay and Alibaba are explored.

28661 ■ *"Financo Panel Lauds Product, Online Marketing" in Home Textiles Today (Vol. 31, January 25, 2010, No. 3, pp. 1)*

Pub: Reed Business Information, Inc.

Ed: James Mammarella. **Description:** Overview of the Financo Annual Merchandising Industry Chief Executives Event during which there was much discussion on the merits of e-commerce, online marketing as well as the traditional methods of brand recognition and retailing.

28662 ■ *"Five Low-Cost Home Based Startups" in Women Entrepreneur (December 16, 2008)*

Pub: Entrepreneur Media Inc.

Ed: Lesley Spencer Pyle. **Description:** During tough economic times, small businesses have an advantage over large companies because they can adjust to economic conditions more easily and without having to go through corporate red tape that can slow the implementation process. A budding entrepreneur may find success by taking inventory of his or her skills, experience, expertise and passions and utilizing those qualities to start a business. Five low-cost home-based startups are profiled. These include starting an online store, a virtual assistant service, web designer, sales representative and a home staging counselor.

28663 ■ *"Fly Phishing" in Canadian Business (Vol. 80, October 22, 2007, No. 21, pp. 42)*

Pub: Rogers Media

Ed: Andy Holloway. **Description:** Symantec Corporation's report shows consumers and companies have effectively installed network defenses that prevent unwanted access. Phishing packages are readily available and are widely used. Other details of the Internet Security Threat Report are presented.

28664 ■ *"For Apple, It's Showtime Again" in Barron's (Vol. 90, August 30, 2010, No. 35, pp. 29)*

Pub: Barron's Editorial & Corporate Headquarters

Ed: Eric J. Savitz. **Description:** Speculations on what Apple Inc. will unveil at its product launch event are presented. These products include a possible new iPhone Nano, a new update to its Apple TV, and possibly a deal with the Beatles to distribute their songs over iTunes.

28665 ■ *"For MySpace, A Redesign to Entice Generation Y" in The New York Times (October 27, 2010, pp. B3)*

Pub: The New York Times Company

Ed: Miguel Helft. **Description:** MySpace is redesigning its Website in order to attract individuals from the Generation Y group.

28666 ■ *"ForeSee Finds Satisfaction On Web Sites, Bottom Line" in Crain's Detroit Business (Vol. 24, February 25, 2008, No. 8, pp. 3)*

Pub: Crain Communications Inc. - Detroit

Ed: Tom Henderson. **Description:** Ann Arbor-based ForeSee Results Inc. evaluates user satisfaction on Web sites. The company expects to see an increase of 40 percent in revenue for 2008 with plans to expand to London, Germany, Italy and France by the end of 2009.

28667 ■ *"Free Speech Vs. Privacy in Data Mining" in Information Today (Vol. 28, September 2011, No. 8, pp. 22)*
Pub: Information Today, Inc.
Ed: George H. Pike. Description: The U.S. Constitution does not explicitly guarantee the right of privacy. Organizations and businesses that require obtaining and disseminating information can be caught in the middle of privacy rights. The long-term impact on data mining, Internet marketing, and Internet privacy issues are examined.

28668 ■ *Freelancing for Journalists*
Pub: Routledge
Ed: Diana Harris. Released: January 1, 2010. Price: $110.00. Description: Comprehensive guide showing the specific skills required for those wishing to freelance in newspapers, magazines, radio, television, and as online journalists.

28669 ■ *"Fresh Direct's Crisis" in Crain's New York Business (Vol. 24, January 14, 2008, No. 2, pp. 3)*
Pub: Crain Communications, Inc.
Ed: Lisa Fickenscher. Description: Freshdirect, an Internet grocery delivery service, finds itself under siege from federal immigration authorities, customers and labor organizations due to its employment practice of hiring illegals. At stake is the grocer's reputation as well as its ambitious growth plans, including an initial public offering of its stock.

28670 ■ *"Friendly Ice Cream Corporation" in Ice Cream Reporter (Vol. 23, August 20, 2010, No. 9, pp. 8)*
Pub: Ice Cream Reporter
Description: Friendly Ice Cream Corporation appointed Andrea M. McKenna as vice president of marketing and chief marketing officer.

28671 ■ *From Entrepreneur to Infopreneur: Make Money with Books, E-Books, and Other Information Products*
Pub: John Wiley & Sons, Incorporated
Ed: Stephanie Chandler. Released: November 2006. Price: $19.95. Description: Infopreneurs sell information online in the forms of books, e-books, special reports, audio and video products, seminars, and more.

28672 ■ *"The Future of Work" in Black Enterprise (Vol. 41, August 2010, No. 1, pp. 65)*
Pub: Earl G. Graves Publishing Co. Inc.
Ed: Annya M. Lott. Description: Technology, globalization, and outsourcing will continue to shape the future of work. Social media is a means for small companies to market goods and services.

28673 ■ *"gdgt: The New Online Home for Gadget Fans" in Hispanic Business (July-August 2009, pp. 15)*
Pub: Hispanic Business
Ed: Jeremy Nisen. Description: Profile of the new online Website for gadget lovers. The site combines a leek interface, gadget database, and social networking-type features which highlights devices for the consumer.

28674 ■ *"Generation Y Chooses the Mobile Web" in PR Newswire (November 24, 2010)*
Pub: PR Newswire Association LLC
Description: Generation Y individuals between the ages of 18 - 27 use their mobile phones to browse the Internet more often than a desktop or laptop computer, according to a survey conducted by Opera, a Web browser company.

28675 ■ *"Get Paid and Get Moving" in Entrepreneur (Vol. 37, October 2009, No. 10, pp. 38)*
Pub: Entrepreneur Media, Inc.
Description: GoPayments application from Intuit allows mobile telephones to process payments like credit card terminals. The application costs $19.95 a month and can be used on the Internet browsers of mobile telephones.

28676 ■ *"Get Sold On eBay" in Entrepreneur (Vol. 36, March 2008, No. 3, pp. 94)*
Pub: Entrepreneur Media Inc.
Ed: Marcia Layton Turner. Description: Entrepreneurs are increasingly using eBay to sell products. Some tips to start selling products through eBay include: starting with used items, developing a niche to sell specific products, and researching product pricing. Other tips with regard to starting an eBay business are covered.

28677 ■ *"Get Them Talking" in Entrepreneur (Vol. 36, February 2008, No. 2, pp. 50)*
Pub: Entrepreneur Media Inc.
Ed: Heather Clancy. Description: Yelp.com is an Internet search site that presents businesses across the U.S., sorted according to the number of customer reviews they have received. One to five stars are used by the reviewers, or yelpers, to rate businesses. Details on how the International Orange day spa benefited from Yelp are discussed.

28678 ■ *Getting Clients and Keeping Clients for Your Service Business*
Pub: Atlantic Publishing Company
Ed: Anne M. Miller; Gail Brett Levine. Released: August 28, 2008. Price: $24.95 paperback. Description: Tips are offered to help any small service business identify customers, brand and grow the business, as well as development of logos, brochures and Websites.

28679 ■ *"Ghouls, Goblins, and Harry Potter: Cashing In On Halloween" in Inc. (Vol. 33, October 2011, No. 8, pp. 24)*
Pub: Inc. Magazine
Ed: Darren Dahl. Description: Costume Craze, an online costume retailer reports $13.2 million in sales last year. Originally the family business started out as a software company called StaticAdvantage, but switched gears.

28680 ■ *Global E-Commerce: Impacts of National Environment and Policy*
Pub: Cambridge University Press
Contact: Richard Ziemacki, President
E-mail: rziemacki@cambridge.org
Ed: Kenneth L. Kraemer; Jason Dedrick; Nigel P. Melville; Kevin Zhu. Released: August 2006. Price: $75.00. Description: Global assessment of the impact of e-business on companies as well as countries.

28681 ■ *Global Electronic Business Research: Opportunities and Directions*
Pub: Idea Group Publishing
Ed: Nabeel A.Y. Al-Qirim. Released: December 2005. Price: $ 74.95. Description: Importance electronic commerce research plays in small to medium-sized enterprises in various countries.

28682 ■ *"Global Imagery in Online Advertisements" in Business Communication Quarterly (December 2007, pp. 487)*
Pub: SAGE Publications USA
Contact: Blaise R. Simqu, President
Ed: Geraldine E. Hynes, Marius Janson. Description: Respondents from six countries were interviewed about their reactions to two online ads to determine cultural differences in understanding advertising elements. Universal appeals and cultural values determine the effectiveness of symbols in online advertising.

28683 ■ *"Google Places a Call to Bargain Hunters" in Advertising Age (Vol. 79, September 29, 2008, No. 36, pp. 13)*
Pub: Crain Communications, Inc.
Ed: Abbey Klaassen. Description: Google highlighted application developers who have created tools for its Android mobile phone in the device's unveiling; applications such as ShopSavvy and CompareEverywhere help shoppers to find bargains by allowing them to compare prices in their local areas and across the web.

28684 ■ *The Google Story: Inside the Hottest Business, Media, and Technology Success of Our Time*
Pub: Random Housing Publishing Group
Ed: David A. Vise; Mark Malseed. Price: $26.00.

28685 ■ *"Google's Next Stop: Below 350?" in Barron's (Vol. 88, March 10, 2008, No. 10, pp. 17)*
Pub: Dow Jones & Company, Inc.
Ed: Jacqueline Doherty. Description: Share prices of Google Inc. are expected to drop from their level of $433 each to below $350 per share. The company is expected to miss its earnings forecast for the first quarter of 2008, and its continued aggressive spending on non-core areas will eventually bring down earnings.

28686 ■ *"Googly Eyed" in Entrepreneur (Vol. 36, February 2008, No. 2, pp. 48)*
Pub: Entrepreneur Media Inc.
Ed: Mike Hogan. Description: Linux has developed desktops that boot into the Google toolbar and applications. These desktops include: Zonbu, Everex gPCTC2502, and Asus Eee PC 4G mini laptop. Details on the applications of these desktops are discussed.

28687 ■ *"Government Says Self-Regulation of Online Privacy is Coming Up Short" in Advertising Age (Vol. 81, December 6, 2010, No. 43, pp. 1)*
Pub: Crain Communications, Inc.
Ed: Edmund Lee. Description: U.S. Federal Trade Commission and the Department of Commerce are concerned about the current state of digital privacy and stated that self-regulation has not been sufficient to date.

28688 ■ *"Grand Bohemian Hotel in Orlando, Fla. Takes Lead in Wedding Planning" in Benzinga.com (August 4, 2011)*
Pub: Benzinga.com
Ed: Benzinga Staff. Description: MAD-Marketing launched a newly-designed Website for the Grand Bohemian Hotel in Orlando, Florida. The site features the hotel's wedding vanity site to help target prospective couples planning their weddings.

28689 ■ *"Grooming Your Online Persona" in Women In Business (Vol. 62, June 2010, No. 2, pp. 36)*
Pub: American Business Women's Association
Ed: Diane Stafford. Description: Employees' use of online social networks could become a basis on how their employers, clients, or business partners would judge them. Personal details, pictures and other online data should be filtered to avoid inappropriate or uncomfortable situations and distinguish personal from professional or work life.

28690 ■ *Groundswell: Winning in a World Transformed by Social Technologies*
Pub: Harvard Business School Press
Ed: Charlene Li; Josh Bernoff. Released: April 21, 2008. Price: $29.95. Description: Individuals are using online social technologies such as blogs, social networking sites, YouTube, and podcasts to discuss products and companies, write their own news, and find their own deals. When consumers you've never met are rating your company's products in public forums with which you have no experience or influence, your company is vulnerable. This book teaches the tools and data necessary to turn this treat into an opportunity.

28691 ■ *Groundswell: Winning in a World Transformed by Social Technologies*
Pub: Harvard Business School Press
Ed: Charlene Li, Josh Bernoff. Released: 2008. Price: $29.95. Description: Corporate executives are struggling with a new trend: people using online social technologies (blogs, social networking sites, YouTube, podcasts) to discuss products and companies, write their own news, and find their own deals.

28692 ■ "Group-Buying Site Hones In on Hispanics" in Austin Business Journal (Vol. 31, July 1, 2011, No. 17, pp. 1)

Pub: American City Business Journals Inc.

Ed: Vicky Garza. Description: Descuentl Libre is a new group-buying site from Austin, Texas that targets the Hispanic market, offering discounts of practical items and family-friendly activities. The Hispanic market constitutes 17 percent of the U.S. population and spends $23 billion yearly online.

28693 ■ Grown Up Digital: How the Net Generation Is Changing Your World

Pub: The McGraw-Hill Companies

Ed: Don Tapscott. Released: 2009. Price: $27.95. Description: As baby boomers retire, business needs to understand what makes the Internet work for business.

28694 ■ Guerrilla Marketing for the New Millennium

Pub: Morgan James Publishing, LLC

Ed: Jay Conrad Levinson. Released: September 2005. Price: $14.00. Description: Steps to successfully market a small business on the Internet.

28695 ■ Guerrilla Marketing: Put Your Advertising on Steroids

Pub: Morgan James Publishing, LLC

Ed: Jay Conrad Levinson. Released: December 2005. Price: $14.00. Description: Marketing concepts to successfully advertise any Internet business, featuring the ten most successful advertising campaigns of the 20th Century.

28696 ■ "Haagen-Dazs Recruits Shop Owners through Facebook" in Ice Cream Reporter (Vol. 23, November 20, 2010, No. 12, pp. 1)

Pub: Ice Cream Reporter

Description: Haagen-Dazs Shoppe Company is using Facebook, the leading social media, to recruit new franchises.

28697 ■ "Happy Blogging" in Black Enterprise (Vol. 38, January 2008, No. 6, pp. 47)

Pub: Earl G. Graves Publishing Co. Inc.

Ed: Sonya A. Donaldson. Description: Individual seeks advice for setting up a Website and starting a blog; Squarespace and Weebly both offer Web design.

28698 ■ "Harlequin Leads the Way" in Marketing to Women (Vol. 22, July 2009, No. 7, pp. 1)

Pub: EPM Communications Inc.

Contact: Ira Mayer, President

E-mail: imayer@epmcom.com

Description: Although the publishing industry has been slow to embrace new media options, the Internet is now a primary source for reaching women readers. Harlequin has been eager to court their female consumers over the Internet and often uses women bloggers in their campaigns strategies.

28699 ■ "Harley-Davidson Moves to Unconventional Marketing Plan" in Business Journal-Milwaukee (Vol. 28, November 26, 2010, No. 8, pp. A1)

Pub: Milwaukee Business Journal

Ed: Rich Rovito. Description: Harley Davidson Inc. hired Boulder, Colorado-based Victors & Spoils, an agency that specializes in crowdsourcing, to implement a new creative marketing model. Under the plan, Harley Davidson will draw on the ideas of its brand enthusiasts to help guide the brand's marketing direction.

28700 ■ "Harness the Internet to Boost Equipment Sales" in Indoor Comfort Marketing (Vol. 70, July 2011, No. 7, pp. 24)

Pub: Industry Publications Inc.

Ed: Richard Rutigliano. Description: Advice is given to increase HVAC/R equipment sales using the Internet.

28701 ■ "Health-Care Highway" in Saint Louis Business Journal (Vol. 32, October 14, 2011, No. 7, pp. 1)

Pub: Saint Louis Business Journal

Ed: Angela Mueller. Description: Around $2.6 billion will be invested in health care facilities along the Highway 64/40 corridor in St. Louis, Missouri. Mercy Hospital is planning to invest $19 million in a virtual care center. St. Elizabeth's Hospital on the other hand, will purchase 105 acres in the corridor.

28702 ■ "Helping Customers Fight Pet Waste" in Pet Product News (Vol. 64, November 2010, No. 11, pp. 52)

Pub: BowTie Inc.

Ed: Sandy Robins. Description: Pet cleaning products manufacturers have been enjoying high sales figures by paying attention to changing pet ownership trends and environmental awareness. Meanwhile, the inclusion of user-friendly features in these products has also been boosted by the social role of pets and the media attention to pet waste. How manufacturers have been responding to this demand is explored.

28703 ■ Here Come the Regulars: How to Run a Record Label on a Shoestring Budget

Pub: Faber & Faber, Inc.

Ed: Ian Anderson. Released: October 1, 2009. Price: $15.00. Description: Author, Ian Anderson launched his own successful record label, Afternoon Records when he was 18 years old. Anderson shares insight into starting a record label, focusing on label image, budget, blogging, potential artists, as well as legal aspects.

28704 ■ "HER's: the Future is Free" in Benzinga.com (October 29, 2011)

Pub: Benzinga.com

Ed: Benzinga Staff. Description: In order to create and maintain electronic health records that connects every physician and hospital it is essential to create a reliable, easy-to-use, certified Web-based ambulatory ERH using an ad-supported model. eBay seems to be the company showing the most potential for improving services to physicians and consumers, but requires sellers to pay fees based upon sales price.

28705 ■ "The Hired Guns" in Business Courier (Vol. 26, November 13, 2009, No. 29, pp. 1)

Pub: American City Business Journals, Inc.

Ed: Lisa Biank Fasig. Description: YourForce has nearly 6,000 retired scientists and researchers who work together in helping Procter & Gamble (P&G) and other companies in addressing various project needs. Operating as an online innovation community, YourEncore is a result of P&G's Connect Develop program.

28706 ■ "Hitting the E-Books" in Inc. (Vol. 33, September 2011, No. 7, pp. 36)

Pub: Inc. Magazine

Ed: Shivani Vora. Description: Textbooks may be getting cheaper for college students now that they can use electronic textbooks that can be read on a laptop or tablet. The market is growing about 50 percent annually. Statistical data included.

28707 ■ "Hoover's Mobile, MobileSP Now Available" in Information Today (Vol. 26, February 2009, No. 2, pp. 29)

Pub: Information Today, Inc.

Description: Hoover's Inc. introduced its Hoover's Mobile for iPhone, BlackBerry and Windows Mobile smartphones along with Hoover's MobileSP for Black-Berry and Windows Mobile. Both products allow users to access customer, prospect, and partner information; analyze competitors; prepare for meetings; and find new opportunities. In addition, MobileSP adds one-click calling to executives, GPS-enabled location searches, advanced search and list building, and a custom call queue and a 'save to contacts' capabilities.

28708 ■ Housecleaning Business: Organize Your Business - Get Clients and Referrals - Set Rates and Services

Pub: Globe Pequot Press

Ed: Laura Jorstad, Melinda Morse. Released: June 1, 2009. Price: $18.95. Description: This book shares insight into starting a housecleaning business. It shows how to develop a service manual, screen clients, serve customers, select cleaning products, competition, how to up a home office, using the Internet to grow the business and offering green cleaning options to clients.

28709 ■ "How to Boost Your Super Bowl ROI" in Advertising Age (Vol. 80, December 7, 2009, No. 41, pp. 3)

Pub: Crain's Communications

Ed: Abbey Klaassen. Description: Internet marketing is essential, even for the corporations that can afford to spend $3 million on a 30-second Super Bowl spot; last year, Super Bowl advertising reached an online viewership of 99.5 million while 98.7 million people watched the game on television validating the idea that public relations must go farther than a mere television ad campaign. Social media provides businesses with a longer shelf life for their ad campaigns. Advice is also given regarding ways in which to strategize a smart and well-thought plan for utilizing the online marketing options currently available.

28710 ■ How to Get Rich on the Internet

Pub: Morgan James Publishing, LLC

Ed: Ted Ciuba. Released: August 2004. Price: $19. 95. Description: Interviews with successful Internet entrepreneurs provide insight into marketing products and services online using minimal investment. The importance of a sound marketing ad campaign using the Internet is discussed; maintaining a database and Website will automatically carry out business transactions daily. Suggestions for various types of businesses to run online are given.

28711 ■ "How Good Advice 'Online' Can Attract Customers" in Indoor Comfort Marketing (Vol. 70, August 2011, No. 8, pp. 20)

Pub: Industry Publications Inc.

Ed: Richard Rutigilano. Description: Online marketing tips for heating and cooling small businesses are explained.

28712 ■ "How I Did It: Jack Ma" in Inc. (January 2008, pp. 94-102)

Pub: Gruner & Jahr USA Publishing

Ed: Rebecca Fannin. Description: Profile of Jack Ma, who started as a guide and interpreter for Western tourists in Hangzhou. Ma used the Internet to build Alibaba.com, China's largest business-to-business site and one of the hottest IPOs in years.

28713 ■ How to Make Money with Social Media: Using New and Emerging Media to Grow Your Business

Pub: FT Press

Ed: Jamie Turner, Reshma Shah. Released: October 1, 2010. Price: $24.99. Description: Marketers, executives, entrepreneurs are shown more effective ways to utilize Internet social media to make money. This guide brings together both practical strategies and proven execution techniques for driving maximum value from social media marketing.

28714 ■ "How to Make Your Website Really Sell" in Entrepreneur (Vol. 37, September 2009, No. 9, pp. 79)

Pub: Entrepreneur Media, Inc.

Ed: David Port. Description: Advice on how to succeed in Internet marketing is presented. Offering visitors purchase incentives on the home page is encouraged. Delivery of customized landing pages and content is also recommended.

28715 ■ "How to Manage Successful Crowdsourcing Projects" in eWeek (September 29, 2010)

Pub: Ziff Davis Enterprise

Description: The advantages, challenges and pitfalls faced when using crowdsourcing to improve a business are outlined. Crowdsourcing helps to eliminate the need to rely on an internal workforce and the need to forecast task volume.

28716 ■ How to Market and Sell Your Art, Music, Photographs, and Handmade Crafts Online

Pub: Atlantic Publishing Group, Inc.

Ed: Lee Rowley. Released: May 2008. Price: $24. 95. Description: The book provides all the basics for starting and running an online store selling arts, crafts, photography or music. There are more than 300 Websites listed to help anyone market and promote their arts and/or crafts online.

28717 ■ *How to Open and Operate a Financially Successful Bookstore on Amazon and Other Web Sites: With Companion CD-ROM*

Pub: Atlantic Publishing Company

Released: December 1, 2010. **Price:** $39.95. **Description:** This book was written for every used book aficionado and bookstore owner who currently wants to take advantage of the massive collection of online resources available to start and run your own online bookstore business.

28718 ■ *How to Start and Run a Home-Based Landscaping Business*

Pub: Globe Pequot Press

Ed: Owen E. Dell. **Released:** December 2005. **Price:** $18.95. **Description:** Guide to starting and running a successful home-based landscaping business, including tips for marketing on the Internet.

28719 ■ *"How To Get a Loan the Web 2.0 Way" in Black Enterprise (Vol. 41, December 2010, No. 5, pp. 23)*

Pub: Earl G. Graves Publishing Co. Inc.

Ed: John Simons. **Description:** People are turning to online peer-to-peer network for personal loans as banks are lending less money.

28720 ■ *"How-To Workshops Teach Sewing, Styles" in St. Louis Post-Dispatch (September 14, 2010)*

Pub: St. Louis Post-Dispatch

Ed: Kalen Ponche. **Description:** Profile of DIY Style Workshop in St. Charles, Missouri, where sewing, designing and teaching is offered. The shop is home base for DIY Style, a Website created by mother and daughter to teach younger people how to sew.

28721 ■ *How to Use the Internet to Advertise, Promote, and Market Your Business or Web Site: With Little or No Money*

Pub: Atlantic Publishing Company

Released: December 1, 2010. **Price:** $24.95. **Description:** Information is given to help build, promote, and make money from your Website or brick and mortar store using the Internet, with minimal costs.

28722 ■ *"I Hear You're Interested In a.." in Inc. (January 2008, pp. 40-43)*

Pub: Gruner & Jahr USA Publishing

Ed: Leah Hoffmann. **Description:** Four tips to help any small business generate sales leads online are examined.

28723 ■ *I'm on LinkedIn - Now What? (Second Edition): A Guide to Getting the Most Out of LinkedIn*

Pub: Happy About

Ed: Diane Danielson. **Released:** January 7, 2009. **Price:** $19.95. **Description:** Designed to help get the most out of LinkedIn, the popular business networking site and follows the first edition and includes the latest and great approaches using LinkedIn. With over 32 million members there is a lot of potential to find and develop relationships to help in your business and personal life, but many professionals find themselves wondering what to do once they sign up. This book explains the different benefits of the system and recommends best practices (including LinkedIn Groups) so that you get the most out of LinkedIn.

28724 ■ *Information Technology for the Small Business: How to Make IT Work For Your Company*

Pub: TAB Computer Systems, Incorporated

Ed: T.J. Benoit. **Released:** June 2006. **Price:** $17.95. **Description:** Basics of information technology to help small companies maximize benefits are covered. Topics include pitfalls to avoid, email and Internet use, data backup, recovery and overall IT organization.

28725 ■ *"InnoCentive Announces Next Generation Crowdsourcing Platform" in Internet Wire (June 15, 2010)*

Pub: Comtex

Description: InnoCentive, Inc., a world leader in open innovation, is launching InnoCentive@Work3, a third generation of its @Work enterprise platform for collaborative-driven innovation for companies. The product will help clients solve critical business and technical issues by tapping information both inside and outside of a company.

28726 ■ *Integration Marketing: How Small Businesses Become Big Businesses and Big Businesses Become Empires*

Pub: John Wiley & Sons, Inc.

Ed: Mark Joyner. **Released:** May 1, 2009. **Price:** $22.95. **Description:** Leading Internet marketing expert offers a marketing methodology to grow any business.

28727 ■ *"Internet Marketing and Social Media Knowledge Vital for SMBs" in Internet Wire (November 24, 2009)*

Pub: Comtex News Network, Inc.

Description: Small and medium-size businesses must learn to market themselves over the Internet in order to succeed and grow in today's marketplace. Web Marketing Today offers the largest source of the most important information concerning doing business on the Internet including e-commerce, email marketing and social networking opportunities.

28728 ■ *"Internet and Mobile Media" in MarketingMagazine (Vol. 115, September 27, 2010, No. 13, pp. 60)*

Pub: Rogers Publishing Ltd.

Description: Market data covering the Internet and mobile media in Canada is given.

28729 ■ *"Internet Translation Service Helps Burmese" in News-Sentinel (May 10, 2011)*

Pub: New-Sentinel

Ed: Ellie Bogue. **Description:** Catherine Kasper Place, Parkview Health Community Outreach, Allen County-Fort Wayne Department of Health and Advantage Health have partnered to help the Burmese Community in the area by providing an online service that links doctors' offices with translators in order to provide better healthcare.

28730 ■ *"Israeli Spam Law May Have Global Impact" in Information Today (Vol. 26, February 2009, No. 2, pp. 28)*

Pub: Information Today, Inc.

Ed: David Mirchin. **Description:** Israels new law, called Amendment 40 of the Communications Law, will regulate commercial solicitations including those sent without permission via email, fax, automatic phone dialing systems, or short messaging technologies.

28731 ■ *"iSymmetry's Technological Makeover Or, How a Tech Company Finally Grew Up and Discovered the World Wide Web" in Inc. (October 2007)*

Pub: Gruner & Jahr USA Publishing

Description: Profile of iSymmetry, an Atlanta, Georgia-based IT recruiting firm, covering the issues the company faces keeping its technology equipment up-to-date. The firm has devised a program that will replace its old server-based software systems with on-demand software delivered via the Internet, known as software-as-a-service. Statistical information included.

28732 ■ *"It's Back to Business for the Ravens" in Boston Business Journal (Vol. 29, July 29, 2011, No. 12, pp. 1)*

Pub: American City Business Journals Inc.

Ed: Scott Dance. **Description:** The Baltimore Ravens football team has been marketing open sponsorship packages following the end of the National Football League lockout. Team officials are working to get corporate logos and slogans on radio and television commercials and online advertisements.

28733 ■ *"It's a Hit" in Entrepreneur (Vol. 36, March 2008, No. 3, pp. 110)*

Pub: Entrepreneur Media Inc.

Ed: John Jantsch. **Description:** Entrepreneurs use the Web to market business and keeping relevant content in the Website is important to address questions from customers. Other considerations in marketing businesses online include: interacting with site visitors, using Web applications for project collaboration and file storage, and encouraging customers to post reviews.

28734 ■ *"It's a New Game: Killerspin Pushes Table Tennis to Extreme Heights" in Black Enterprise (Vol. 37, October 2006, No. 3, pp. 73)*

Pub: Earl G. Graves Publishing Co. Inc.

Ed: Bridget McCrea. **Description:** Profile of Robert Blackwell and his company Killerspin L.L.C., which is popularizing the sport of table tennis. Killerspin has hit $1 million in revenues due to product sales primarily generated through the company's website, magazines, DVDs, and event ticket sales.

28735 ■ *"Jo-Ann Fabric and Craft Stores Joins ArtFire.com to Offer Free Online Craft Marketplace" in Internet Wire (January 26, 2010)*

Pub: Comtex News Network, Inc.

Description: Jo-Ann Fabric and Craft Stores has entered into a partnership with ArtFire.com which will provide sewers and crafters all the tools they need in order to make and sell their products from an online venue.

28736 ■ *"Joe Wikert, General Manager, O'Reilly Technology Exchange" in Information Today (Vol. 26, February 2009, No. 2, pp. 21)*

Pub: Information Today, Inc.

Ed: Jamie Babbitt. **Description:** Joe Wikert, general manager of O'Reilly Technology Exchange discusses his plans to develop a free content model that will evolve with future needs. O'Reilly's major competitor is Google. Wikert plans to expand the firm's publishing program to include print, online, and in-person products and services.

28737 ■ *"Johnson Publishing Expands: Moving Into Television and Internet To Extend Brand" in Black Enterprise (October 2007)*

Pub: Earl G. Graves Publishing Co. Inc.

Ed: Tamara E. Holmes. **Description:** Johnson Publishing Company has followed the lives of black families in both Ebony and Jet magazines. The media firm has expanded its coverage by developing entertainment content for television, the Internet and other digital arenas.

28738 ■ *"Keep Them Posted" in Entrepreneur (Vol. 35, October 2007, No. 10, pp. 39)*

Pub: Entrepreneur Media Inc.

Ed: Gwen Moran. **Description:** Survey by the Pew Internet and American Life Project found that 12 million American adults maintain blogs, which are created for personal and business reasons. Blogs are effective in giving a business a personal touch while informing the public about its operations and products. Tips on how to create an effective business blog are presented.

28739 ■ *"Kids, Computers and the Social Networking Evolution" in Canadian Business (Vol. 81. October 27, 2008, No. 18, pp. 93)*

Pub: Rogers Media Ltd.

Ed: Penny Milton. **Description:** Social networking was found to help educate students in countries like the U.S., Canada and Mexico. Schools that embrace social networking teach students how to use computers safely and responsibility in order to counter threats to children on the Internet.

28740 ■ *"Know the Facts About Natural Gas!" in Indoor Comfort Marketing (Vol. 70, August 2011, No. 8, pp. 26)*

Pub: Industry Publications Inc.

Description: AEC Activity Update is presented on the American Energy Coalition's Website.

28741 ■ "Kodak Offers Cloud-Based Operating Option" in American Printer (Vol. 128, June 1, 2011, No. 6)
Pub: Penton Media Inc.
Description: Kodak partnered with VMware to offer its first Virtual Operating Environment option for Kodak Unified Workflow Solutions. The new feature enables cost savings, increased efficiency and failover protection.

28742 ■ "Kuno Creative to Present B2B Social Media Campaign Webinar" in Entertainment Close-Up (August 25, 2011)
Pub: Close-Up Media
Description: Kuno Creative, an inbound marketing agency, will host Three Steps of a Successful B2B Social Media Campaign. The firm is a provider of Website development, branding, marketing strategy, public relations, Internet marketing, and inbound marketing.

28743 ■ "Last Founder Standing" in Conde Nast Portfolio (Vol. 2, June 2008, No. 6, pp. 124)
Pub: Conde Nast Publications
Contact: David Carey, President
Ed: Kevin Maney. **Description:** Interview with Amazon CEO Jeff Bezos in which he discusses the economy, the company's new distribution center and the hiring of employees for it, e-books, and the overall vision for the future of the firm.

28744 ■ "Lavante, Inc. Joins Intersynthesis, Holistic Internet Marketing Company" in Internet Wire (November 5, 2009)
Pub: Comtex News Network, Inc.
Description: Lavante, Inc., the leading provider of on-demand vendor information and profit recovery audit solutions for Fortune 1000 companies has chosen Intersynthesis, a new holistic Internet marketing firm, as a provider of pay for performance services. Lavante believes that Intersynthesis' expertise and knowledge combined with their ability to develop integrated strategies, will help them fuel more growth.

28745 ■ "Legislating the Cloud" in Information Today (Vol. 28, October 2011, No. 9, pp. 1)
Pub: Information Today, Inc.
Description: Internet and telecommunications industry leaders are asking for legislation to address the emerging market in cloud computing. Existing communications laws do not adequately govern the modern Internet.

28746 ■ "Lights, Camera, Action: Tools for Creating Video Blogs" in Inc. (Volume 32, December 2010, No. 10, pp. 57)
Pub: Inc. Magazine
Ed: John Brandon. **Description:** A video blog is a good way to spread company news, talk about products, and stand out among traditional company blogs. New editing software can create two- to four-minute blogs using a webcam and either Windows Live Essentials, Apple iLife 2011, Powerdirector 9 Ultra, or Adobe Visual Communicator 3.

28747 ■ "Looking Out for the Little Guys" in Black Enterprise (Vol. 38, October 2007, No. 3, pp. 58)
Pub: Earl G. Graves Publishing Co. Inc.
Ed: Kaylyn Kendall Dines. **Description:** Biz Tech-Connect is a Web portal that offers free online and social networking, along with four modules that help small businesses with marketing and advertising, communications and mobility, financial management, and customer relationship management.

28748 ■ "Looking To Leap?" in Black Enterprise (Vol. 38, January 2008, No. 6, pp. 64)
Pub: Earl G. Graves Publishing Co. Inc.
Ed: Tennille M. Robinson. **Description:** Websites and organizations providing resources for any young entrepreneur wishing to start a new business are outlined.

28749 ■ "A Love of Likes" in Boston Business Journal (Vol. 31, July 8, 2011, No. 24, pp. 1)
Pub: Boston Business Journal
Ed: Lisa van der Pool. **Description:** An increasing number of companies in Boston, Massachusetts have been keen on getting Facebook 'likes' from people. Business owners realize that Facebook 'likes' could generate sales and based on some studies, equate to specific dollar values.

28750 ■ Low-Budget Online Marketing for Small Business
Pub: International Self-Counsel Press, Limited
Ed: Holly Berkley. **Released:** July 2005. **Price:** $14.95. **Description:** Low-cost, effective online marketing tips for small companies selling products or services over the Internet.

28751 ■ Low-Budget Online Marketing for Small Business
Pub: Self-Counsel Press, Incorporated
Ed: Holley Berkley. **Released:** July 2005. **Price:** $14.95, CD-Rom. **Description:** Low-cost, effective online marketing tips for small companies selling products or services over the Internet.

28752 ■ Low-Budget Online Marketing for Small Business
Pub: Self-Counsel Press Inc.
Ed: Holly Berkley. **Released:** August 2006. **Price:** $14.95, include CD-ROM. **Description:** Low-budget advertising campaigns are presented to help market any small business.

28753 ■ "Luxe Hotels on a Budget" in Inc. (Volume 32, December 2010, No. 10, pp. 60)
Pub: Inc. Magazine
Ed: Adam Baer. **Description:** Off & Away Website allows users to vie for discounted hotel rooms at more than 100 luxury properties. To compete, uses buy $1 bids and each time an individual bids the price of the room goes up by 10 cents.

28754 ■ "MaggieMoo's Ice Cream and Treatery" in Ice Cream Reporter (Vol. 23, September 20, 2010, No. 10, pp. 7)
Pub: Ice Cream Reporter
Description: MaggieMoo's Ice Cream and Treatery has launched a new Website where visitors can learn about the brands newest ice cream innovations.

28755 ■ Mail Order in the Internet Age
Pub: Morgan James Publishing, LLC
Ed: Ted Ciuba. **Released:** May 2004. **Price:** $19.95. **Description:** Direct response market, or mail order, for marketing and selling a product or service is discussed, with emphasis on how direct marketing compares favorably to other methods in terms of speed, ease, profitability, and affordability. Advice is given for writing ads; seminars to attend; and newsletters, mailing lists and magazines in which to subscribe.

28756 ■ "Making It Click" in Barron's (Vol. 88, March 17, 2008, No. 11, pp. 31)
Pub: Dow Jones & Company, Inc.
Ed: Theresa W. Carey. **Description:** Listing of 23 online brokers that are evaluated based on their trade experience, usability, range of offerings, research amenities, customer service and access, and costs. TradeStation Securities takes the top spot followed by thinkorswim by just a fraction.

28757 ■ "Mapping the Social Internet" in Harvard Business Review (Vol. 88, July-August 2010, No. 7-8, pp. 32)
Pub: Harvard Business School Publishing
Description: Chart compares and contrasts online social networks in selected countries.

28758 ■ Marketing 2.0: Bridging the Gap between Seller and Buyer through Social Media Marketing
Pub: Wheatmark
Ed: Bernie Borges. **Released:** July 14, 2009. **Price:** $22.95. **Description:** Winning strategies to attract people to your company and your employees using social media site on the Internet are outlined.

28759 ■ "Marketing in the Digital World: Here's How to Craft a Smart Online Strategy" in Black Enterprise (Vol. 40, July 2010, No. 12, pp. 47)
Pub: Earl G. Graves Publishing Co. Inc.
Ed: Sonya A. Donaldson. **Description:** Social media is an integral part of any small business plan in addressing marketing, sales, and branding strategies.

28760 ■ "Marketing Scholarship 2.0" in Journal of Marketing (Vol. 75, July 2011, No. 4, pp. 225)
Pub: American Marketing Association
Ed: Richard J. Lutz. **Description:** A study of the implications of changing environment and newer collaborative models for marketing knowledge production and dissemination is presented. Crowdsourcing has become a frequently employed strategy in industry. Academic researchers should collaborate more as well as the academe and industry, to make sure that important problems are being investigated.

28761 ■ Marketing in a Web 2.0 World - Using Social Media, Webinars, Blogs, and More to Boost Your Small Business on a Budget
Pub: Atlantic Publishing Company
Ed: Peter VanRysdam. **Released:** June 1, 2010. **Price:** $24.95. **Description:** Web 2.0 technologies have leveled the playing field for small companies trying to boost their presence by giving them an equal voice against larger competitors. Advice is given to help target your audience using social networking hubs.

28762 ■ Marketing Without Money for Small and Midsize Businesses: 300 FREE and Cheap Ways to Increase Your Sales
Pub: Halle House Publishing
Contact: Nicholas E. Bade, Publisher
Ed: Nicholas E. Bade. **Released:** July 2005. **Price:** $16.95. **Description:** Three hundred practical low-cost or no-cost strategies to increase sales, focusing on free advertising, free marketing assistance, and free referrals to the Internet.

28763 ■ Marketing Your Product
Pub: Self-Counsel Press, Incorporated
Ed: Donald Cyr, Douglas Gray. **Released:** September 2009. **Price:** $20.95. **Description:** Tips for marketing any product in today's competitive consumer environment. One chapter focuses on using the Internet as a marketing tool.

28764 ■ "Mattel's Got a Monster Holiday Hit, But Will Franchise Have Staying Power?" in Advertising Age (Vol. 81, December 6, 2010, No. 43)
Pub: Crain Communications, Inc.
Ed: Beth Snyder Bulik. **Description:** Monster High transmedia play expands beyond dolls to merchandise, apparel and entertainment.

28765 ■ Maximum Marketing, Minimum Dollars: The Top 50 Ways to Grow Your Small Business
Pub: Kaplan Books
Ed: Kim Gordon. **Released:** April 2006. **Price:** $24.00. **Description:** Marketing tips to increase sales are presented. Small business owners will learn to maximize marketing with 50 innovative and affordable methods, including online marketing.

28766 ■ "Media Giant Remakes Itself: Job Cuts Signal Journal Sentinel's Focus on New Products" in Business Journal-Milwaukee (Oct. 12, 2007)
Pub: American City Business Journals, Inc.
Ed: Rich Kirchen. **Description:** Milwaukee Journal Sentinel is reducing its workforce by offering separation pay, and is willing to consider layoffs if the separation program fails. The downsizing is a result of lowered revenue, which was caused by the decline in printed news demand and increase in online competition. Strategies that the Journal Sentinel are employing, such as developing new products, to increase revenue are presented.

28767 ■ *"Media Terminology"* in *MarketingMagazine (Vol. 115, September 27, 2010, No. 13, pp. 80)*
Pub: Rogers Publishing Ltd.
Description: Media terminology is provided.

28768 ■ *"Media Wars"* in *Canadian Business (Vol. 83, August 17, 2010, No. 13-14, pp. 32)*
Pub: Rogers Media Ltd.
Ed: Thomas Watson. **Description:** Canada's newspaper industry has changed considerably with The Glove, under Philip Crawley, positioned as corporate Canada's newspaper of record. However, the National Post under Paul Godfrey is making a comeback by re-launching it as the flagship of a national chain of so-called digital first news organizations.

28769 ■ *"Microsoft Releases Office Security Updates"* in *Mac World (Vol. 27, November 2010, No. 11, pp. 66)*
Pub: Mac Publishing
Ed: David Dahlquist. **Description:** Office for Mac and Mac Business Unit are Microsoft's pair of security- and stability-enhancing updates for Office 2008 and Office 2004. The software will improve the stability and compatibility and fixes vulnerabilities that would allow attackers to overwrite Mac's memory with malicious code.

28770 ■ *Million Dollar Website: Simple Steps to Help You Compete with the Big Boys-Even on a Small Business Budget*
Pub: Prentice Hall Press
Ed: Lori Culwell. **Released:** May 9, 2010. **Price:** $19.95. **Description:** Resource for any small business owner wishing to build a successful Website in order to compete with big box stores.

28771 ■ *"MindLeaders' Online Training Courses Come to ePath Learning"* in *Information Today (Vol. 26, February 2009, No. 2, pp. 4)*
Pub: Information Today, Inc.
Description: MindLeaders has partnered with ePath Learning to provide clients with over 2,200 new online courses. ePath's integrated Learning Management Service (iLMS) allows organizations to create online training programs for employees.

28772 ■ *"Mobility: So Happy Together"* in *Entrepreneur (Vol. 35, October 2007, No. 10, pp. 64)*
Pub: Entrepreneur Media Inc.
Ed: Heather Clancy. **Description:** Joshua Burnett, CEO and founder of 9ci, uses index cards to keep track of what he needs to do despite the fact that he has a notebook computer, cell phone and PDA. Kim Hahn, a media entrepreneur, prefers jotting her ideas down in a spiral notebook, has a team that would organize her records for her, and a personal assistant that would keep track of changes to her schedule. Reasons why these entrepreneurs use old-fashioned methods along with new technology are given.

28773 ■ *"More Leading Retailers Using Omniture Conversion Solutions to Boost Sales and Ecommerce Performance"* in *Internet Wire (Sept. 22,2009)*
Pub: Comtex News Network, Inc.
Description: Many retailers are utilizing Omniture conversion solutions to improve the performance of their ecommerce businesses; recent enhancements to Omniture Merchandising and Omniture Recommendations help clients drive increased conversion to their Internet ventures.

28774 ■ *"More Leading Retailers Using Omniture Conversion Solutions to Boost Sales and Ecommerce Performance"* in *Internet Wire (Sept. 22,2009)*
Pub: Comtex News Network, Inc.
Description: Many retailers are utilizing Omniture conversion solutions to improve the performance of their ecommerce businesses; recent enhancements to Omniture Merchandising and Omniture Recommendations help clients drive increased conversion to their Internet ventures.

28775 ■ *"Most Viewed Stories, Videos on farmindustrynews.com in 2010"* in *Farm Industry News (January 4, 2011)*
Pub: Penton Business Media Inc.
Description: The top ten most popularly viewed stories and videos presented on farmindustrynews.com Website are listed.

28776 ■ *"Moving Into the Digital Space: How New Media Create Opportunities for Minorities"* in *Black Enterprise (February 2008)*
Pub: Earl G. Graves Publishing Co. Inc.
Ed: Sonia Alleyne. **Description:** The Internet is becoming an alternative to traditional sources of entertainment; nearly 16 percent of American households who use the Internet watch television online. One such Internet show features a variety of African American lifestyles.

28777 ■ *"My Favorite Tool for Managing Expenses"* in *Inc. (Volume 32, December 2010, No. 10, pp. 60)*
Pub: Inc. Magazine
Ed: J.J. McCorvey. **Description:** Web-based service called Expensify is outlined. The service allows companies to log expenses while away from the office using the service's iPhone application.

28778 ■ *"Nationwide Bank Ready for December Conversion"* in *Business First-Columbus (October 12, 2007, pp. A1)*
Pub: American City Business Journals, Inc.
Ed: Adrian Burns. **Description:** Nationwide Bank will increase marketing to its customers, including the 45,000 that came from the acquisition of Nationwide Federal Credit Union in December 2006. Upgrading its online banking system and Website will bring the company and its services closer to clients. The influence of the insurance industry on the bank's marketing strategy is also examined.

28779 ■ *"Navigate to Better Direct Response Messaging Through Search Marketing"* in *DM News (Vol. 32, January 18, 2010, No. 2, pp. 26)*
Pub: Haymarket Media, Inc.
Ed: Mark Simon. **Description:** Important lessons to apply when utilizing Internet marketing schemes include telling your customers you have what they want to buy, provide them with discounts or ways to save additional money and drive them to a customized destination like an Online store.

28780 ■ *Nerds on Wall Street: Math, Machines and Wired Markets*
Pub: John Wiley & Sons, Inc.
Ed: David J. Leinweber. **Released:** May 27, 2009. **Price:** $39.95. **Description:** The history of technology and how it will transform investing and trading on Wall Street is outlined.

28781 ■ *"Net Profits: Get a Social Life"* in *Entrepreneur (Vol. 35, October 2007, No. 10, pp. 140)*
Pub: Entrepreneur Media Inc.
Ed: Amanda C. Kooser. **Description:** Social networking sites such as Facebook and MySpace have millions of users, a sign that social networking is a growing industry. One way to enter this industry is target marketing, like Med3Q, a site for health-conscious individuals had done. How Med3q is earning through online advertising and sponsors is explained.

28782 ■ *"Netflix Gets No Respect"* in *Barron's (Vol. 89, July 27, 2009, No. 30, pp. 26)*
Pub: Dow Jones & Co., Inc.
Ed: Tiernan Ray. **Description:** Netflix met expectations when they announced their second quarter sales but their shares still fell by almost 10 percent. Analysts say their entry into the 'streaming video' business is a mixed bag since customers are increasingly buying the cheaper monthly plan and this is dragging the economics of the business.

28783 ■ *"Netting Degrees: More Professionals Continuing Their Education Online"* in *Hispanic Business (September 2007, pp. 62, 64)*
Pub: Hispanic Business
Ed: Hildy Medina. **Description:** Traditional universities and private institutions offer online courses to professionals wishing to further their education.

28784 ■ *"The New Basics of Marketing"* in *Inc. (February 2008, pp. 75-81)*
Pub: Gruner & Jahr USA Publishing
Ed: Leigh Buchanan. **Description:** New tools for marketing a business or service include updating or upgrading a Website, using email or texting, or advertising on a social Internet network.

28785 ■ *"The New Face of Social Media"* in *Hispanic Business (December 2010)*
Pub: Hispanic Business
Ed: Gary D. Fackler. **Description:** Latina bloggers carve out a new niche in social media that helps preserve their unique cultural identities.

28786 ■ *"The New Guard"* in *Entrepreneur (Vol. 36, February 2008, No. 2, pp. 46)*
Pub: Entrepreneur Media Inc.
Ed: Amanda C. Kooser. **Description:** A natural language search engine is being developed by Powerset for better online searching. Zannel Inc. offers Instant Media Messaging platform, which allows for social networking using phones. Ning is an online platform that allows users to customize and control their social networks.

28787 ■ *"New Wave of Business Security Products Ushers in the Kaspersky Anti-Malware Protection System"* in *Internet Wire (October 26, 2010)*
Pub: Comtex
Description: Kaspersky Anti-Malware System provides anti-malware protection that requires minimal in-house resources for small businesses. The system offers a full range of tightly integrated end-to-end protection solutions, ensuring unified protection across an entire network, from endpoint and mobile device protection to file server, mail server, network storage and gateway protection. It provides flexible centralized management, immediate threat visibility and a level of responsiveness not seen in other anti-malware approaches.

28788 ■ *"A New Way to Tell When to Fold"* in *Barron's (Vol. 88, July 7, 2008, No. 27, pp. 27)*
Pub: Dow Jones & Co., Inc.
Ed: Theresa W. Carey. **Description:** Overview of the Online trading company SmartStops, a firm that aims to tell investors when to sell the shares of a particular company. The company's Web site categorizes stocks as moving up, down, or sideways, and calculates exit points for individual stocks based on an overall market trend.

28789 ■ *"New Ways to Catch a Thief"* in *Barron's (Vol. 88, March 10, 2008, No. 10, pp. 37)*
Pub: Dow Jones & Company, Inc.
Ed: Theresa W. Carey. **Description:** Online brokerage firms employ different methods to protect the accounts of their customers from theft. These methods include secure Internet connections, momentary passwords, and proprietary algorithms.

28790 ■ *"The Next Dimension"* in *Entrepreneur (Vol. 35, November 2007, No. 11, pp. 62)*
Pub: Entrepreneur Media Inc.
Ed: Heather Clancy. **Description:** Entrepreneurs can make use of virtual worlds like Second Life to promote their products or services. Details and cautions on the use of virtual worlds are discussed.

28791 ■ *"Nobody Knows What To Do"* in *Barron's (Vol. 88, March 17, 2008, No. 11, pp. 40)*
Pub: Dow Jones & Company, Inc.
Ed: Mark Veverka. **Description:** Attendees of the South by Southwest Interactive conference failed to get an insight on how to make money on the Web from former Walt Disney CEO Michael Eisner when Eisner said there's no proven business model for

financing projects. Eisner said he finances his projects with the help of his connections to get product-placement deals.

28792 ■ *"Nowspeed and OneSource to Conduct Webinar" in Internet Wire (December 14, 2009)*
Pub: Comtex News Network, Inc.
Description: OneSource, a leading provider of global business information, and Nowspeed, an Internet marketing agency, will conduct a webinar titled 'How to Develop Social Media Content That Gets Results' in order to provide marketers insight into how to develop and optimize effective social media content to get consumer results that translate into purchases and lead generation.

28793 ■ *"Obama Plan May Boost Maryland Cyber Security" in Boston Business Journal (Vol. 29, May 20, 2011, No. 2, pp. 1)*
Pub: American City Business Journals Inc.
Ed: Scott Dance. **Description:** May 12, 2011 outline of the cyber security policies of President Obama may improve the cyber security industry in Maryland as the state is home to large defense and intelligence activities. Details of the proposed policies are discusses as well as their advantages to companies that deal in developing cyber security plans for other companies.

28794 ■ *"Old Spice Guy (Feb.-July 2010)" in Canadian Business (Vol. 83, August 17, 2010, No. 13-14, pp. 23)*
Pub: Rogers Media Ltd.
Ed: Andrew Potter. **Description:** Old Spice Guy was played by ex-football player and actor Isaiah Mustafa who made the debut in the ad for Old Spice Red Zone body wash that was broadcast during Super Bowl XLIV in February 2010. Old Spice Guy has become one of social marketing success but was cancelled in July when online viewership started to wane.

28795 ■ *"On Beyond Powerpoint: Presentations Get a Wake-Up Call" in Inc. (November 2007, pp. 58-59)*
Pub: Gruner & Jahr USA Publishing
Ed: Michael Fitzgerald. **Description:** New software that allows business presentations to be shared online are profiled, including ProfCast, audio podcasts for sales, marketing, and training; SmartDraw2008, software that creates professional graphics; Dimdim, an open-Web conferencing tool; Empressr, a hosted Web service for creating, managing, and sharing multimedia presentations; Zentation, a free tool that allows users to watch slides and a videos of presenter; Spresent, a Web-based presentation tool for remote offices or conference calls.

28796 ■ *"The One Thing You Must Get Right When Building a Brand" in Harvard Business Review (Vol. 88, December 2010, No. 12, pp. 80)*
Pub: Harvard Business School Publishing
Ed: Patrick Barwise, Sean Meehan. **Description:** Four uses for new media include: communicating a clearly defined customer promise, creating trust via delivering on the promise, regularly improving on the promise, and innovating past what is familiar.

28797 ■ *"Online All the Time" in Retail Merchandiser (Vol. 51, July-August 2011, No. 4, pp. 18)*
Pub: Phoenix Media Corporation
Description: Ecommerce sales are rising at a steady pace and for cross-channel retailers it is boosting sales in the weak economy. Online sales are expected to reach $188 billion in 2011, boasting a 13.7 rate of growth.

28798 ■ *"Online Book Sales Surpass Bookstores" in Information Today (Vol. 28, September 2011, No. 8, pp. 11)*
Pub: Information Today, Inc.
Ed: Cindy Martine. **Description:** Online book sales outpaced bookstore purchases in the United States, signaling a shift in the US book industry. Statistical data included.

28799 ■ *"Online Forex Broker Tadawul FX Intros Arabic Website" in Entertainment Close-Up (June 23, 2011)*
Pub: Close-Up Media
Description: Online forex broker, Tadawul FX, launched its Arabic language Website, noting that the Middle East is a key market for the investment firm.

28800 ■ *"Online Marketing: Puppy Power: Using a New Tool Called a Widget To Boost Your Brand" in Inc. (November 2007, pp. 55-56)*
Pub: Gruner & Jahr USA Publishing
Ed: Dan Brody. **Description:** Widgets look like small television screens posted on Websites, blogs or desktops with a company's brand or logo. It can display any type of information or image, including sports scores, news headlines, weather reports, animated graphics, or a slide show. Profiles of Car-Domain Network, Babystrology, DailyPuppy.com, AnchorBank and more are included.

28801 ■ *"Online Pet Medication Store Supports Free Vaccinations for Cats" in Internet Wire (August 31, 2010)*
Pub: Comtex
Description: Pethealth Inc., The Petango Store will help to support The Humane Society of Tampa Bay's efforts by offering free feline vaccinations for the cat's entire lifetime that is adopted between September 1, 2010 and February 28, 2010. The cat must be one year or older at time of adoption.

28802 ■ *"Online Postings Really Influence Older Women" in Marketing to Women (Vol. 22, July 2009, No. 7, pp. 8)*
Pub: EPM Communications Inc.
Contact: Ira Mayer, President
E-mail: imayer@epmcom.com
Description: Women over the age of 55 are more likely to be swayed to purchase a product by referrals from others, including Online postings by strangers. Another key influence is associated with the brand's ability to address their lifestyle needs.

28803 ■ *"Online Radio That's Cool, Addictive, Free, and Just Maybe A Lasting Business" in Inc. (October 2007, pp. 100-106, 108)*
Pub: Gruner & Jahr USA Publishing
Ed: Stephanie Clifford. **Description:** Profile of the Internet radio company, Pandora, whose founder, Tim Westergren discusses his business plans to fruition. The station has over eight million loyal listeners, advertisers and a database of 500,000 songs.

28804 ■ *"Online Reverse Auctions: Common Myths Versus Evolving Reality" in Business Horizons (September-October 2007, pp. 373)*
Pub: Elsevier Technology Publications
Ed: Tobias Schoenherr, Vincent A. Mabert. **Description:** Common misconceptions about online reverse auctions are examined based on the data obtained from 30 case study companies. Strategies for maintaining a good buyer-supplier relationship and implications for firms and supply managers are presented.

28805 ■ *"Online Security Crackdown: Scanning Service Oversees Site Security at David's Bridal" in (Vol. 84, July 2008, No. 7, pp. 46)*
Pub: Chain Store Age
Ed: Samantha Murphy. **Description:** Online retailers are beefing up security on their Websites. Cyber thieves use retail systems in order to gain entry to consumer data. David's Bridal operates over 275 bridal showrooms in the U.S. and has a one-stop wedding resource for new brides planning weddings.

28806 ■ *"Online Translation Service Aids Battlefield Troops" in Product News Network (August 30, 2011)*
Pub: Thomas Publishing Company
Description: Linquist online service, LinGo Link provides real-time interpreter support to military troops overseas. Interpreters skilled in multiple languages and dialects are used in various areas and in multiple instances without requiring physical presence. The service is available through com-

mercial cellular or WiFi services or tactical communications network. The system accommodates exchange of audio, video, photos, and text during conversations via smartphones and mobile peripheral devices.

28807 ■ *"The Open Mobile Summit Opens in San Francisco Today: John Donahoe CEO eBay to Keynote" in Benzinga.com (November 2, 2011)*
Pub: Benzinga.com
Ed: Benzinga Staff. **Description:** eBay's CEO, John Donahoe was keynote speaker at the 4th Annual Open Mobile Summit held in San Francisco, California. eBay is one of the 130 companies participating as speakers at the event.

28808 ■ *Open Source Solutions for Small Business Problems*
Pub: Charles River Media
Ed: John Locke. **Released:** May 2004. **Price:** $35.95. **Description:** Open source software provides solutions to many small business problems such as tracking electronic documents, scheduling, accounting functions, managing contact lists, and reducing spam.

28809 ■ *"Optimize.ca Supplies Free Online Financial Advice" in Entertainment Close-Up (October 9, 2010)*
Pub: Close-Up Media Inc.
Description: Optimize.ca provides free online financial advice, focusing on instant savings for their mutual funds and other banking products while improving rates of return and overall financial health.

28810 ■ *Outsourcing: Information Technology, Original Equipment Manufacturer, Leo, Oursourcing, Offshoring Research Network, Crowdsourcing*
Pub: General Books LLC
Released: May 1, 2010. **Price:** $14.14. **Description:** Chapters include information for outsourcing firms and how to maintain an outsourcing business.

28811 ■ *"Over and Out" in Entrepreneur (Vol. 36, February 2008, No. 2, pp. 25)*
Pub: Entrepreneur Media Inc.
Ed: Julie Moline. **Description:** Ben Wolin, owner of Waterfront Media that operates wellness and health Websites, had employed the services of human resource consulting firm to advise him in regard to overtime pay. Guidelines on how to avoid overtime pay violations are presented.

28812 ■ *"Pagetender LLC Releases Website Design Package for HubSpot Users" in Internet Wire (September 30, 2009)*
Pub: Comtex News Network, Inc.
Description: Profile of Pagetender LLC, a Certified HubSpot partner, who announced a Website Design Package marketed specifically for HubSpot Owner and Marketer users. This packaged was developed for small to medium sized businesses that want a website designed or their current site redesigned on HubSpot's Content Management System. Companies that would like a more robust site have the option of adding Flash development, ecommerce and photo galleries.

28813 ■ *"P&G to Mine E-Commerce Potential" in Business Courier (Vol. 26, September 18, 2009, No. 21, pp. 1)*
Pub: American City Business Journals, Inc.
Ed: Lisa Biank Fasig. **Description:** Procter & Gamble (P&G) is looking to turn the hits to the company's Websites into increased sales. The program will include a shop now option to track all emerging sales.

28814 ■ *"Paper a la Carte" in American Printer (Vol. 128, June 1, 2011, No. 6)*
Pub: Penton Media Inc.
Description: Blurb, the online publishing platform, launched ProLine which features Mohawk Superfine and Mohawk proPhoto papers. ProLine papers offer two finishes: Pearl Photo and Uncoated.

28815 ■ *"PC Connection Acquires Cloud Software Provider" in New Hampshire Business Review (Vol. 33, March 25, 2011,*

No. 6, pp. 8)
Pub: Business Publications Inc.
Description: Merrimack-based PC Connection Inc. acquired ValCom Technology, a provider of cloud-based IT service management software. Details of the deal are included.

28816 ■ *"PD Targeting Audience Growth with Web Initiatives" in Crain's Cleveland Business (Vol. 30, June 29, 2009, No. 25, pp. 1)*
Pub: Crain Communications, Inc.
Ed: Kathy Ames Carr. **Description:** Plain Dealer's publisher C.Z. Egger has his news organization focusing on online offerings in order to build circulation of its newspaper. The 167-year-old paper boasts 1,305,203 readers in print and online weekly.

28817 ■ *"People; E-Commerce, Online Games, Mobile Apps" in Advertising Age (Vol. 80, October 19, 2009, No. 35, pp. 14)*
Pub: Crain's Communications
Ed: Nat Ives. **Description:** Profile of People Magazine and the ways in which the publisher is moving its magazine forward by exploring new concepts in a time of declining newsstand sales and advertising pages; among the strategies are e-commerce such as the brand People Style Watch in which consumers are able highlight clothing and jewelry and then connect to retailers' sites and a channel on Taxi TV, the network of video-touch screens in New Your City taxis.

28818 ■ *"People; E-Commerce, Online Games, Mobile Apps: This Isn't Your Mom's People" in Advertising Age (Vol. 80, October 19, 2009, No. 35)*
Pub: Crain's Communications
Ed: Nat Ives. **Description:** Profile of People Magazine and the ways in which the publisher is moving its magazine forward by exploring new concepts in a time of declining newsstand sales and advertising pages; among the strategies are e-commerce such as the brand People Style Watch in which consumers are able highlight clothing and jewelry and then connect to retailers' sites and a channel on Taxi TV, the network of video-touch screens in New Your City taxis.

28819 ■ *"The Perfect Fit" in Small Business Opportunities (Fall 2007)*
Pub: Harris Publications Inc.
Description: Launched in 2004, Jigsaw provides an online database of more than 5.5 million business contacts and company information for entrepreneurs.

28820 ■ *"Plan Your Future with My Next Move" in Occupational Outlook Quarterly (Vol. 55, Summer 2011, No. 2, pp. 22)*
Pub: U.S. Bureau of Labor Statistics
Description: My Next Move, an online tool offering a variety of user-friendly ways to browse more than 900 occupations was created by the National Center for O NET Development for the US Department of Labor's Employment and Training Administration. Clicking on an occupation presents a one-page profile summarizing key information for specific careers.

28821 ■ *Planet Google: One Company's Audacious Plan to Organize Everything We Know*
Pub: Free Press
Ed: Randall Stross. **Released:** 2009. **Price:** $26.00. **Description:** The book examines Google, the leader in Internet search engines.

28822 ■ *"Play By Play: These Video Products Can Add New Life to a Stagnant Website" in Black Enterprise (Vol. 41, December 2010, No. 5)*
Pub: Earl G. Graves Publishing Co. Inc.
Ed: Marcia Wade Talbert. **Description:** Web Visible, provider of online marketing products and services, cites video capability as the fastest-growing Website feature for small business advertisers. Profiles of various devices for adding video to a Website are included.

28823 ■ *"Points of Light Sells MissionFish to eBay" in Non-Profit Times (Vol. 25, May 15, 2011, No. 7, pp. May 15, 2011)*
Pub: NPT Publishing Group Inc.
Contact: John McIlquham, President
Description: eBay purchased MissionFish, a subsidiary of Points of Light Institute for $4.5 million. MissionFish allows eBay sellers to give proceeds from sales to their favorite nonprofit organization and helps nonprofits raise funds by selling on eBay.

28824 ■ *"The Power of Negative Thinking" in Inc. (Volume 32, December 2010, No. 10, pp. 43)*
Pub: Inc. Magazine
Ed: Jason Fried. **Description:** A Website is software and most businesses have and need a good Website to generate business. Understanding for building a powerful Website is presented.

28825 ■ *The Power of Social Networking: Using the Whuffie Factor to Build Your Business*
Pub: Crown Business Books
Ed: Tara Hunt. **Released:** May 4, 2010. **Price:** $15.00. **Description:** This book shows how any small business can harness its power by increasing whuffie, the store of social capital that is the currency of the digital world. Blogs and social networks such as Facebook and Twitter are used to help grow any small firm.

28826 ■ *"Pro Livestock Launches Most Comprehensive Virtual Sales Barn for Livestock and Breed Stock" in Benzinga.com (October 29, 2011)*
Pub: Benzinga.com
Ed: Benzinga Staff. **Description:** Pro Livestock Marketing launched the first online sales portal for livestock and breed stock. The firm has designed a virtual sales barn allowing individuals to purchase and sell cattle, swine, sheep, goats, horses, rodeo stock, show animals, specialty animals, semen and embryos globally. It is like an eBay for livestock and will help ranchers and farmers grow.

28827 ■ *"Promote Your Business Through New Media" in Business Week (November 5, 2009)*
Pub: McGraw-Hill Companies
Ed: Karen E. Klein. **Description:** Traditional public relations strategies are becoming more and more outdated due to the rapid shift in Internet marketing opportunities. Ideas for marketing your company online are presented.

28828 ■ *"Promoting Academic Programs Using Online Videos" in Business Communication Quarterly (December 2007, pp. 478)*
Pub: SAGE Publications USA
Contact: Blaise R. Simqu, President
Ed: Thomas Clark, Julie Stewart. **Description:** Xavier Entrepreneurial Center successfully used online videos to promote the effectiveness of its academic programs. Online videos are a cost-effective way of publicizing academic programs.

28829 ■ *"Promotions Create a Path to Better Profit" in Pet Product News (Vol. 64, December 2010, No. 12, pp. 1)*
Pub: BowTie Inc.
Ed: Joan Hustace Walker. **Description:** Pet store retailers can boost small mammal sales by launching creative marketing and promotions such as social networking and adoption days.

28830 ■ *"Providers Ride First Wave of eHealth Dollars" in Boston Business Journal (Vol. 31, June 10, 2011, No. 20, pp. 1)*
Pub: Boston Business Journal
Ed: Julie M. Donnelly. **Description:** Health care providers in Massachusetts implementing electronic medical records technology started receiving federal stimulus funds. Beth Israel Deaconess Medical Center was the first hospital to qualify for the funds.

28831 ■ *"Punta Gorda Interested in Wi-Fi Internet" in Charlotte Observer (February 1, 2007)*
Pub: Knight-Ridder/Tribune Business News
Ed: Steve Reilly. **Description:** Punta Gorda officials are developing plans to provide free wireless Internet services to businesses and residents.

28832 ■ *"Putting the App in Apple" in Inc. (Vol. 30, November 2008, No. 11, pp.)*
Pub: Mansueto Ventures LLC
Ed: Nitasha Tiku. **Description:** Aftermarket companies are scrambling to develop games and widgets for Apple's iPhone. Apple launched a kit for developers interested in creating iPhone-specific software along with the App Store, and an iTunes spinoff. Profiles of various software programs that may be used on the iPhone are given.

28833 ■ *"Putting SogoTrade Through Its Paces" in Barron's (Vol. 89, July 27, 2009, No. 30, pp. 27)*
Pub: Dow Jones & Co., Inc.
Ed: Theresa W. Carey. **Description:** SogoTrade options platform streams options quotes in real time and lets users place a trade in several ways. The site also features notable security tactics and is a reasonable choice for bargain-seekers. OptionsXpress' Xtend platform lets users place trades and get real time quotes.

28834 ■ *"Q&A Patrick Pichette" in Canadian Business (Vol. 81, October 13, 2008, No. 17, pp. 6)*
Pub: Rogers Media Ltd.
Ed: Andrew Wahl. **Description:** Patrick Pichette finds challenge in taking over the finances of an Internet company that has a market cap of about $140 billion. He feels, however, that serving as Google's chief financial officer is nothing compared to running Bell Canada Enterprises (BCE). Pichette's other views on Google and BCE are presented.

28835 ■ *"Quickoffice's MobileFiles Pro App Enables Excel Editing On-the-Go" in Information Today (Vol. 26, February 2009, No. 2, pp. 31)*
Pub: Information Today, Inc.
Description: Quickoffice Inc. introduced MobileFiles Pro, which features editable Microsoft Office functionality for the iPone and iPod touch. The application allows users to edit and save Microsoft Excel files in .xls format, transfer files to and from PC and Mac desktops via Wi-Fi, and access and synchronize with Apple MobileMe accounts.

28836 ■ *"Real-Time Computer-Mediated Communication" in Business Communication Quarterly (December 2007, pp. 466)*
Pub: SAGE Publications USA
Contact: Blaise R. Simqu, President
Ed: Amy Newman. **Description:** Technology-based simulation for business students to respond to emails and instant messages is presented. The simulation allows students to handle volume business correspondence at work with organizational context and under real-word business situations.

28837 ■ *"Reaping Social-Media Rewards" in Canadian Business (Vol. 83, July 20, 2010, No. 11-12, pp. 19)*
Pub: Rogers Media Ltd.
Ed: Lyncsie Bourgon. **Description:** Foursquare is a social network which provides benefits such as discounts to users who show loyalty to a business or a brand. One marketing executive believes Foursquare is a good platform for loyalty programs and is an inexpensive alternative to Aeroplan.

28838 ■ *"Recovery2.0: a Work in Progress" in Tampa Bay Business Journal (Vol. 30, December 18, 2009, No. 52, pp. 3)*
Pub: American City Business Journals
Ed: Margaret Cashill. **Description:** The debut of the Recovery.gov 2.0 version has raised questions regarding the Website's price tag, which will cost nearly $13 million. Tampa, Florida-based GSL Solutions Inc. president Michael Gaines believes the Web-

sites created with existing technologies tend to cost less than custom development. The difference between Recovery.org and Recovery.gov are explained.

28839 ■ "Recruiting 2.0" in Entrepreneur (Vol. 35, November 2007, No. 11, pp. 100)
Pub: Entrepreneur Media Inc.

Ed: Andrea Cooper. **Description:** Technology is becoming a tool to help small companies find the best employees. Firms can look into social networking sites to see recommendations from the applicants' colleagues. Tips on how to select the employees online are listed.

28840 ■ "Regional Talent Network Unveils Jobs Web Site" in Crain's Cleveland Business (Vol. 30, June 1, 2009, No. 21, pp. 11)
Pub: Crain Communications, Inc.

Description: Regional Talent Network launched WhereToFindHelp.org, a Website designed to act as a directory of all Northeast Ohio resources that can help employers recruit and job seekers look for positions. The site also lists organizations offering employment and training services.

28841 ■ "Reinventing Marketing to Manage the Environmental Imperative" in Journal of Marketing (Vol. 75, July 2011, No. 4, pp. 132)
Pub: American Marketing Association

Ed: Philip Kotler. **Description:** Marketers must now examine their theory and practices due to the growing recognition of finite resources and high environmental costs. Companies also need to balance more carefully their growth goals with the need to purse sustainability. Insights on the rise of demarketing and social marketing are also given.

28842 ■ "Remodeled Stores Help Fabric Retailer Stitch Up Profit Growth" in Investor's Business Daily (January 7, 2010, pp. A06)
Pub: Investor's Business Daily

Ed: Marilyn Much. **Description:** Overview of the successful plan implemented by Darrell Webb for Jo-Ann Fabric and Craft stores to stimulate growth and generate revenue; changes include better inventory controls and remodeling; statistical data included.

28843 ■ "Remote Control: Working From Wherever" in Inc. (February 2008, pp. 46-47)
Pub: Gruner & Jahr USA Publishing

Ed: Ryan Underwood. **Description:** New technology allows workers to perform tasks from anywhere via the Internet. Profiles of products to help connect to your office from afar include, LogMein Pro, a Web-based service that allowsaccess to a computer from anywhere; Xdrive, an online service that allows users to store and swap files; Basecamp, a Web-based tools that works like a secure version of MySpace; MojoPac Freedom, is software that allows users to copy their computer's desktop to a removable hard drive and plug into any PC; WatchGuard Firebox X Core e-Series UTM Bundle, hardware that blocks hackers and viruses while allowing employees to work remotely; TightVNC, a free open-source software that lets you control another computer via the Internet.

28844 ■ "Renren Partners With Recruit to Launch Social Wedding Services" in Benzinga.com (June 7, 2011)
Pub: Benzinga.com

Ed: Benzinga Staff. **Description:** Renren Inc. and Recruit Company Ltd. partnered to build a wedding social media catering to engaged couples and newlyweds in China. The platform will integrate online wedding related social content and offline media such as magazine and wedding exhibitions.

28845 ■ "Renren Partnership With Recruit to Launch Social Wedding Services" in Benzinga.com (June 7, 2011)
Pub: Benzinga.com

Ed: Benzinga Staff. **Description:** Renren Inc., the leading real name social networking Internet platform in China has partnered with Recruit Company Limited, Japan's largest human resource and classified media group to form a joint venture to build a wedding social media catering to the needs of engaged couples and newlyweds in China.

28846 ■ "Rep. Loretta Sanchez Holds a Hearing on Small Business Cyber Security" in Political/Congressional Transcript Wire (July 29, 2010)
Pub: CQ Roll Call

Description: U.S. House Committee on Armed Services, Subcommittee on Terrorism, Unconventional Threats and Capabilities held a hearing on small business cyber security innovation.

28847 ■ "Research and Markets Adds Report: Asian - Internet Market" in Health and Beauty Close-Up (January 19, 2010)
Pub: Close-Up Media

Description: Overview of Research and Markets new report regarding Internet marketing and e-commerce in the Asian region; statistical data included.

28848 ■ "Research and Markets Adds Report: USA - Internet Market - Analysis, Statistics and Forecasts" in Wireless News (January 15, 2010)
Pub: Close-Up Media

Description: According to Research and Markets new report concerning the United State's Internet market, e-commerce and Online advertising are expected to recover strongly in 2010.

28849 ■ "The Return of the Infomercial" in Canadian Business (Vol. 83, September 14, 2010, No. 15, pp. 19)
Pub: Rogers Media Ltd.

Ed: James Cowan. **Description:** Infomercials or direct response ads have helped some products succeed in the marketplace. The success of infomercials is due to the cheap advertising rates, expansion into retail stores and the products' oddball appeal. Insights into the popularity of infomercial products on the Internet and on television are given.

28850 ■ "Ric Elis/Dan Feldstein" in Charlotte Business Journal (Vol. 25, December 31, 2010, No. 41, pp. 6)
Pub: Charlotte Business Journal

Ed: Ken Elkins. **Description:** Charlotte, North Carolina-based Internet marketing firm Red Ventures has grown significantly. General Atlantic has purchased stakes in Red Ventures.

28851 ■ "Rise Interactive, Internet Marketing Agency, Now Offers Social Media Training and Advisory Services" in Internet Wire (Nov. 4, 2009)
Pub: Comtex News Network, Inc.

Description: Profile of Rise Interactive, a full-service Internet marketing agency which has recently added social media to its list of offerings; the agency touts that its newest service gives their clients the power to have ongoing communication with current and potential customers on the sites they are most actively visiting.

28852 ■ "Ritchie Bros. Breaks Record for Internet Sales at Fort Worth Site During Multi-Million Dollar Unreserved Auction" in Canadian Corporate News
Pub: Comtex News Network Inc.

Description: Ritchie Bros. Auctioneers, the world's largest auctioneer of trucks and industrial equipment, conducted a large unreserved auction at its permanent auction facility in Fort Worth, Texas, in which the company broke the record for Internet sales with bidders using the company's online bidding service, rbauctionBid-Live. Internet bidders purchased more than 440 lots in the auction.

28853 ■ "ROIonline Announces Streaming Video Products" in Marketing Weekly News (December 5, 2009, pp. 155)
Pub: Investment Weekly News

Description: ROIonline LLC, an Internet marketing firm serving business-to-business and the industrial marketplace, has added streaming video options to the Internet solutions it offers its clients; due to the huge increase of broadband connections, videos are now commonplace on the Internet and can often convey a company's message in a must more ef-

ficient, concise and effective way that will engage a website's visitor thus delivering a high return on a company's investment.

28854 ■ "Rumor Has It" in Entrepreneur (Vol. 35, October 2007, No. 10, pp. 30)
Pub: Entrepreneur Media Inc.

Ed: Chris Penttila. **Description:** Some entrepreneurs like Ren Moulton and Dan Scudder regard rumor sites and product blogs as great sources of market research. However, there are legal issues that must be studied before using these Internet sites in marketing and product development. The use and limitations of rumor sites and product blogs are provided.

28855 ■ Salesforce.com Secrets of Success: Best Practices for Growth and Profitability
Pub: Prentice Hall Business Publishing

Contact: Jerome Grant, President

Ed: David Taber. **Released:** May 15, 2009. **Price:** $34.99. **Description:** Guide for using Salesforce.com; it provides insight into navigating through user groups, management, sales, marketing and IT departments in order to achieve the best results.

28856 ■ The Savvy Gal's Guide to Online Networking
Pub: Booklocker.com Inc.

Ed: Diane K. Daneilson, Lindsey Pollak. **Released:** August 10, 2007. **Price:** $14.95. **Description:** It is a truth universally acknowledged that a woman in search of a fabulous career must be in want of networking opportunities. Or so Jane Austen would say if she were writing, or more likely, blogging today. So begins the must-read guide to networking in the 21st Century. Authors and networking experts share the nuts, bolts and savvy secrets that business-women need in order to use technology to build professional relationships.

28857 ■ The Savvy Girl's Guide to Online Networking
Pub: Booklocker.com Inc.

Ed: Diane K. Danielson; Lindsey Pollak. **Released:** August 10, 2007. **Price:** $14.95. **Description:** The book offers tips, tactics and etiquette for business-women wishing to build professional relationships via email, online networks, blogs, and message boards.

28858 ■ Say Everything: How Blogging Began, What It's Becoming, and Why It Matters
Pub: Crown Business

Ed: Scott Rosenberg. **Released:** 2009. **Price:** $26.00. **Description:** A history of Internet blogs that explains how they started and why they matter to any small business.

28859 ■ "Scientific American Builds Novel Blog Network" in Information Today (Vol. 28, September 2011, No. 8, pp. 12)
Pub: Information Today, Inc.

Ed: Kurt Schiller. **Description:** Scientific American launched a new blog network that joins a diverse lineup of bloggers cover various scientific topics under one banner. The blog network includes 60 bloggers providing insights into the ever-changing world of science and technology.

28860 ■ "Scitable Puts Nature Education on the Map" in Information Today (Vol. 26, February 2009, No. 2, pp. 29)
Pub: Information Today, Inc.

Description: Nature Education, a division of the Nature Publishing Group, released its first product, Scitable, a free online resource for undergraduate biology students and educators. The service includes over 180 overviews of key genetics concepts as well as social networking features, including groups and functionality, that lets students work with classmates and others. Teachers can use the service to set up public or private groups for students.

28861 ■ "Search and Discover New Opportunities" in DM News (Vol. 31, December 14, 2009, No. 29, pp. 13)
Pub: Haymarket Media, Inc.

Ed: Chantal Tode. **Description:** Although other digital strategies are gaining traction in Internet marketing, search marketing continues to dominate this advertising forum. Companies like American Greetings, which markets e-card brands online, are utilizing social networking sites and affiliates to generate a higher demand for their products.

28862 ■ The Search: How Google and Its Rival Rewrote the Rules of Business and Transformed Our Culture
Pub: Penguin Group Incorporated

Ed: John Battelle. **Released:** October 3, 2006. **Price:** $14.95. **Description:** Provides a history of Internet search technology.

28863 ■ Selling Online: Canada's Bestselling Guide to Becoming a Successful E-Commerce Merchant
Pub: John Wiley and Sons Canada Ltd.

Ed: Jim Carroll; Rick Broadhead. **Released:** September 6, 2002. **Description:** Helps individuals build on-line retail enterprises; this updated version includes current tools, information and success strategies, how to launch an online storefront, security, marketing strategies, and mistakes to avoid.

28864 ■ "Senators Predict Online School Changes" in Puget Sound Business Journal (Vol. 29, September 19, 2008, No. 22, pp. 1)
Pub: American City Business Journals

Ed: Clay Holtzman. **Description:** State senators promise to create new legislation that would tighten the monitoring and oversight of online public schools. The officials are concerned about the lack of oversight of the programs as well as lack of knowledge about content of the lessons.

28865 ■ The SEO Manifesto: A Practical and Ethical Guide to Internet Marketing and Search Engine Optimization
Pub: Cape Project Management Inc.

Ed: Dan Tousignant, Pamela Gobiel. **Released:** December 5, 2011. **Price:** $14.99. **Description:** Comprehensive guide for each phase of launching an online business; chapters include checklists, process descriptions, and examples.

28866 ■ "Serials Solutions Launches 360 Resource Manager Consortium Edition" in Information Today (Vol. 26, February 2009, No. 2, pp. 32)
Pub: Information Today, Inc.

Description: Serials Solutions new Serials Solutions 360 Resource Manager Consortium Edition helps consortia, groups and member libraries with their e-resource management services. The products allows users to consolidate e-resource metadata and acquisition information into one place, which enables groups to manage holdings, subscriptions, licensing, contacts, and cost information and to streamline delivery of information to members.

28867 ■ "Sharing the Micro Wealth" in Entrepreneur (Vol. 37, July 2009, No. 7, pp. 46)
Pub: Entrepreneur Media, Inc.

Ed: Jennie Dorris. **Description:** Step-by-step guide is presented on how Kiva.org, a website which allows people to make microloans to entrepreneurs across the world, works. The website, founded by Matt Flannery, raises $1 million weekly and it will add U.S. entrepreneurs to its list of loan recipients in June 2010. Other features of Kiva.org are discussed.

28868 ■ "Shoestring-Budget Marketing" in Women Entrepreneur (January 5, 2009)
Pub: Entrepreneur Media Inc.

Ed: Maria Falconer. **Description:** Pay-per-click search engine advertising is the traditional type of e-marketing that may not only be too expensive for certain kinds of businesses but also may not attract the quality customer base a business looking to grow needs to find. Social networking websites have become a mandatory marketing tool for business owners who want to see growth in their sales; tips are provided for utilizing these networking websites in order to gain more visibility on the Internet which can, in turn, lead to the more sales.

28869 ■ "Silverpop Recognized for Email Marketing Innovations by Econsultancy" in Marketing Weekly News (January 23, 2010, pp. 124)
Pub: Investment Weekly News

Description: Econsultancy, a respected source of insight and advice on digital marketing and e-commerce, recognized Silverpop, the world's only provider of both marketing automation solutions and email marketing specifically tailored to the unique needs of B2C and B2B marketers at Econsultancy's 2009 Innovation Awards.

28870 ■ "Simplifying Social Media for Optimum Results" in Franchising World (Vol. 42, August 2010, No. 8, pp. 12)
Pub: International Franchise Association

Ed: Paul Segreto. **Description:** Keys to effective technology usage requires the development of an integrated plan, choosing the most complementary tools and implementing well-planned strategies.

28871 ■ "Sites Set" in Entrepreneur (Vol. 35, November 2007, No. 11, pp. 112)
Pub: Entrepreneur Media Inc.

Ed: Nichole L. Torres. **Description:** Marketing information online can be a good bui9sness if you know who to target. Partnering with other online companies to provide information services that cater to specific groups of people is also helpful.

28872 ■ "Siteworx Earns 4 Interactive Media Awards in Q1 of 2011" in Entertainment Close-Up (, 2011)
Pub: Close-Up Media

Description: Details of the four awards Siteworx earned for its achievements in Web development and design are outlined.

28873 ■ "Skype Ltd. Acquired GroupMe" in Information Today (Vol. 28, October 2011, No. 9, pp. 12)
Pub: Information Today, Inc.

Description: Skype Ltd. acquired GroupMe, a group messaging company that allows users to form impromptu groups where they can text message, share data, and make conference calls for free and is supported on Android, iPhone, BlackBerry, and Windows phones.

28874 ■ "Small Budget, Big Impact" in Small Business Opportunities (Summer 2010)
Pub: Harris Publications Inc.

Ed: Hilary J.M. Topper. **Description:** Ways to use social media to get in from of a target audience for small businesses are examined.

28875 ■ Small Business Clustering Technology: Applications in Marketing, Management, Finance, and IT
Pub: Idea Group Publishing

Ed: Robert C. MacGregor; Ann Hodgkinson. **Released:** June 2006. **Description:** An overview of the development and role of small business clusters in disciplines that include economics, marketing, management and information systems.

28876 ■ Small Business for Dummies
Pub: John Wiley & Sons, Incorporated

Ed: Eric Tyson, Jim Schell. **Released:** March 2008. **Price:** $21.99. **Description:** Advice for launching and growing a small business; insights into using the Internet as business tool are included.

28877 ■ Small Business Management
Pub: John Wiley & Sons, Incorporated

Ed: Margaret Burlingame. **Released:** March 2007. **Price:** $44.95. **Description:** Advice for starting and running a small business as well as information on the value and appeal of small businesses, is given. Topics include budgets, taxes, inventory, ethics, e-commerce, and current laws.

28878 ■ Small Business Taxes Made Easy: How to Increase Your Deductions, Reduce What You Owe, and Boost Your Profits
Pub: McGraw-Hill Companies Inc.

Contact: Deven Sharma, President

Ed: Eva Rosenberg. **Released:** December 2004. **Price:** $16.95. **Description:** Tax expert gives advice to small business owners regarding tax issues. Tax-Mamma.com, run by Eva Rosenberg, is one of the top seven tax advice Websites on the Internet.

28879 ■ SMEs and New Technologies: Learning E-Business and Development
Pub: Palgrave Macmillan

Ed: Banji Oyelaran-Oyeyinka; Kaushalesh Lal. **Released:** October 2006. **Price:** $85.00. **Description:** Adoption and learning of new information technologies in developing nations is covered. New technologies are opening opportunities for small companies in these countries.

28880 ■ The Social Media Bible: Tactics, Tools, and Strategies for Business Success
Pub: John Wiley & Sons, Inc.

Ed: Lon Safko, David Brake. **Released:** June 17, 2009. **Price:** $29.95. **Description:** Information is given to build or transform a business into social media, where customers, employees, and prospects connect collaborate, and champion products and services in order to increase sales and to beat the competition.

28881 ■ "Social Media By the Numbers: Social-Media Marketing Is All the Rage" in Inc. (Vol. 33, November 2011, No. 9, pp. 70)
Pub: Inc. Magazine

Ed: J.J. McCorvey, Issie Lapowsky. **Description:** Six strategies to help small businesses use social media sites such as Facebook and Twitter to promote their companies are presented.

28882 ■ "Social Media Event Slated for March 25" in Bellingham Business Journal (Vol. February 2010, pp. 3)
Pub: Sound Publishing Inc.

Description: Center for Economic Vitality (CEV) and the Technology Alliance Group (TAG) will host the 2010 Social Media Conference at the McIntyre Hall Performing Arts & Conference Center in Mt. Vernon, Washington. The event will provide networking opportunities for attendees.

28883 ■ "Social Networkers for Hire" in Black Enterprise (Vol. 40, December 2009, No. 5, pp. 56)
Pub: Earl G. Graves Publishing Co., Inc.

Ed: Brittany Hutson. **Description:** Companies are utilizing social networking sites in order to market their brand and personally connect with consumers and are increasingly looking to social media specialists to help with this task. Aliya S. King is one such web strategist, working for ICED Media by managing their Twitter, Facebook, YouTube and Flickr accounts for one of their publicly traded restaurant clients.

28884 ■ "Social Networks in the Workplace" in Strategy & Leadership (Vol. 38, July-August 2010, No. 4, pp. 50-53)
Pub: Emerald Inc.

Ed: Daniel Burrus. **Description:** The opinions of futurist Daniel Burrus on a novel trend called 'Business 2.0', which involves the use of social networking applications as business tools, are presented. His suggestion that personal social networking technology can be used by businesses to improve collaboration, problem solving, and leadership communications to achieve continuous value innovation is discussed.

28885 ■ "Sometimes, Second Impressions Count Most" in Canadian Business (Vol. 83, October 12, 2010, No. 17, pp. 11)
Pub: Rogers Media Ltd.

Ed: Richard Branson. **Description:** Developing a favorable impression at the first point of contact is imperative for businesses. Managers who want their organizations to make positive first and second impressions need to learn to balance the Web's labor-saving efficiencies with human assistants. The importance of considering the customer relations value in company Websites is also explained.

28886 ■ "Sounders Kicking Ball to Fans" in Puget Sound Business Journal (Vol. 29, November 28, 2008, No. 32, pp. 1)
Pub: American City Business Journals

Ed: Greg Lamm. **Description:** Major League Soccer expansion team, Seattle Sounders FC, hopes to build fan support leading to its inaugural season 2009-

2010 by tapping online social networks. The club launched fan clubs with actual powers over its decision making and Websites similar to Facebook.

28887 ■ "Startup on Cusp of Trend" in Austin Business JournalInc. (Vol. 29, January 8, 2010, No. 44, pp. 1)
Pub: American City Business Journals
Ed: Christopher Calnan. **Description:** Austin-based Socialware Inc. introduced a new business called social middleware, which is a software that is layered between the company network and social networking Website used by workers. The software was designed to give employers a measure of control over content while allowing workers to continue using online social networks.

28888 ■ "Startup to Serve Bar Scene" in Austin Business JournalInc. (Vol. 29, December 18, 2009, No. 41, pp. 1)
Pub: American City Business Journals
Ed: Christopher Calnan. **Description:** Startup ATX Innovation Inc. of Austin, Texas has developed a test version of TabbedOut, a Web-based tool that would facilitate mobile phone-based restaurant and bar bill payment. TabbedOut has been tested by six businesses in Austin and will be available to restaurant and bar owners for free. Income would be generated by ATX through a 99-cent convenience charge per transaction.

28889 ■ Stealing MySpace: The Battle to Control the Most Popular Website in America
Pub: Random House Inc.
Contact: Richard Sarnoff, President
Ed: Julia Angwin. **Released:** 2009. **Price:** $27.00.
Description: Information regarding Rupert Murdoch's outwitting Viacom's Tom Freston and details of the deal are presented.

28890 ■ Success Secrets of Social Media Marketing Superstars
Pub: Entrepreneur Press
Contact: Perlman Neil, President
Ed: Mitch Meyerson. **Released:** June 1, 2010. **Price:** $21.95. **Description:** Provides access to the playbooks of social media marketers who reveal their most valuable strategies and tactics for standing out in the new online media environment.

28891 ■ "Sunbrella Engages Consumers Via Social Media" in Home Textiles Today (Vol. 31, May 24, 2011, No. 13, pp. 4)
Pub: Reed Business Information
Contact: Jeff Greisch, President
Description: Performance fabric brand Sunbrella is marketing to social media, such as Facebook and Twitter, in order to boost consumer interest and retailer support.

28892 ■ "Sylvie Collection Offers a Feminine Perspective and Voice in Male Dominated Bridal Industry" in Benzinga.com (October 29, 2011)
Pub: Benzinga.com
Ed: Benzinga Staff. **Description:** Bridal jewelry designer Sylvie Levine has created over 1,000 customizable styles of engagement rings and wedding bands and is reaching out to prospective new brides through a new Website, interactive social media campaign and monthly trunk show appearances.

28893 ■ "Taking the Steps Into the Clouds" in New Hampshire Business Review (Vol. 33, March 25, 2011, No. 6, pp. 19)
Pub: Business Publications Inc.
Ed: Tim Wessels. **Description:** Cloud services include Internet and Web security, spam filtering, message archiving, work group collaboration, IT asset management, help desk and disaster recovery backup.

28894 ■ "Tap the iPad and Mobile Internet Device Market" in Franchising World (Vol. 42, September 2010, No. 9, pp. 43)
Pub: International Franchise Association
Ed: John Thomson. **Description:** The iPad and other mobile Internet devices will help franchise owners interact with customers. It will be a good marketing tool for these businesses.

28895 ■ "Technology Drivers to Boost Your Bottom Line" in Franchising World (Vol. 42, August 2010, No. 8, pp. 15)
Pub: International Franchise Association
Ed: Dan Dugal. **Description:** Technological capabilities are expanding quickly and smart franchises should stay updated on all the new developments, including smart phones, global positioning systems, and social media networks.

28896 ■ "Technology: What Seems To Be the Problem? Self Service Gets a Tune-Up" in Inc. (February 2008, pp. 43-44)
Pub: Gruner & Jahr USA Publishing
Ed: Darren Dahl. **Description:** Self-service software can save companies money when responding to customer service phone calls, text or email messages. More companies are relying on alternatives such as automated Web-based self-service systems.

28897 ■ "Tee Off Online" in Black Enterprise (Vol. 37, January 2007, No. 6, pp. 52)
Pub: Earl G. Graves Publishing Co. Inc.
Ed: James C. Johnson. **Description:** The E-Com Resource Center is one of many resources that are available for those interested in starting an e-commerce business. One of the first steps is to create a business plan, of which there are free samples available at BPlans.com.

28898 ■ "Tell Us What You Really Think Collecting Customer Feedback" in Inc. (Vol. 30, December 2008, No. 12, pp. 52)
Pub: Mansueto Ventures LLC
Ed: Ryan Underwood. **Description:** According to a recent survey, nearly 77 percent of online shoppers review consumer-generated reviews of products before making a purchase.

28899 ■ "Things Really Clicking for Macy's Online" in Business Courier (Vol. 24, November 30, 2008, No. 33, pp. 1)
Pub: American City Business Journals, Inc.
Ed: Lisa Biank Fasig. **Description:** Retailer Macy's online division Macys.com are projecting sales at $1billion in 2007, compared to $620 million in 2006. Macy's new online features and products and the growth of online retail sector are also discussed.

28900 ■ "Thomas Industrial Network Unveils Custom SPEC" in Entertainment Close-Up (March 3, 2011)
Pub: Close-Up Media
Description: Thomas Industrial Network assists custom manufacturers and industrial service providers a complete online program called Custom SPEC which includes Website development and Internet exposure.

28901 ■ "Tim Tebow Foundation to Hold Pink 'Cleats for a Cure' Auction" in Travel & Leisure Close-Up (October 20, 2011)
Pub: Close-Up Media
Description: Tim Tebow Foundation partnered with XV Enterprises to hold the 'Cleats for a Cure' auction on eBay. Tebow is auctioning off a pair of pink cleans he wore during the Denver Broncos vs. Tennessee Titans game October 3, 2010. All funds will go toward finding a cure for breast cancer.

28902 ■ Titanium EBay: A Tactical Guide to Becoming a Millionaire PowerSeller
Pub: Penguin Group Incorporated
Ed: Skip McGrath. **Released:** June 2006. **Price:** $24.95. **Description:** Advice is given to help anyone selling items on eBay to become a Power Seller, an award presented based on monthly gross merchandise sales.

28903 ■ "Tool-o-Rama" in Barron's (Vol. 90, September 6, 2010, No. 36)
Pub: Barron's Editorial & Corporate Headquarters
Description: New trading tool features from several online brokers are discussed. The new features from Fidelity, ChoiceTrade, JunoTrade and TradeKing are examined. Investors can now screen exchanged traded funds in the same way as stocks with Fidelity, while ChoiceTrade can run in any browser without the need to install additional plug-ins.

28904 ■ "Tool Time" in Entrepreneur (Vol. 36, March 2008, No. 3, pp. 90)
Pub: Entrepreneur Media Inc.
Ed: Nichole A. Torres. **Description:** DaVinci Institute holds an annual event in Colorado to display new products and inventions. Innovative Design Engineering Animation is a consulting company that helps inventors develop product through various stages. NineSigma Inc. has an online marketplace where inventors can post ideas for clients needing new products.

28905 ■ "Traffic's Up: Website's Down Preventing Costly Crashes" in Inc. (March 2008, pp. 55-56)
Pub: Gruner & Jahr USA Publishing
Ed: Darren Dahl. **Description:** Grid Web hosting protects a small company's Website when a sudden burst of Internet traffic hits enabling it to continue rather than be crippled. Options can vary in cost from $4 to $1,000 monthly and include using a shared server, grid server, virtual private server, or a dedicated server. The article explains each option.

28906 ■ "Try a Little Social Media" in American Printer (Vol. 128, June 1, 2011, No. 6)
Pub: Penton Media Inc.
Description: Social media helps keep Ussery Printing on customers radar. Jim David, VP of marketing for the firm, states that 350 people following them on Facebook are from the local area.

28907 ■ "TW Trade Shows to Offer Seminars On Niche Selling, Social Media" in Travel Weekly (Vol. 69, October 4, 2010, No. 40, pp. 9)
Pub: NorthStar Travel Media LLC
Description: Travel Weekly's Leisure World 2010 and Fall Home Based Travel Agent Show focused on niche selling, with emphasis on all-inclusives, young consumers, groups, incentives, culinary vacations, and honeymoon or romance travel.

28908 ■ "Twitter Hack: Made in Japan? User Says Attack Showed Security Flaw" in Houston Chronicle (September 24, 2010, pp. 3)
Pub: Houston Chronicle
Ed: Tomoko A. Hosaka. **Description:** Details of the attack on Twitter caused by a Japanese computer hacker are revealed.

28909 ■ Twitterville: How Businesses Can Thrive in the New Global Neighborhoods
Pub: Portfolio Hardcover
Ed: Shel Israel. **Price:** $23.95. **Description:** Twitter is the most rapidly adopted communication tool in history, going from zero to ten million users in just over two years. On Twitter, word can spread faster than wildfire. Companies no longer have the option of ignoring the conversation. Unlike other hot social media spaces, Twitterville is dominated by professionals, not students. And despite its size, it still feels like a small town. Twitter allows people to interact much the way they do face-to-face, honestly and authentically.

28910 ■ "Two Ways to Find New Customers" in Inc. (Vol. 31, January-February 2009, No. 1, pp. 41)
Pub: Mansueto Ventures LLC
Description: Latest software programs that help sales staff connect to new leads are profiled. Salesconx provides online leads while Demandbase reports users on a particular Website.

28911 ■ The Ultimate Guide to Electronic Marketing for Small Business: Low-Cost/High Return Tools and Techniques That Really Work
Pub: John Wiley & Sons, Incorporated
Ed: Tom Antion. **Released:** June 2005. **Price:** $19.95 (US), $25.99 (Canadian). **Description:** Online marketing techniques for small business to grow and increase sales.

28912 ■ *"Understanding Persuasive Online Sales Messages from eBay Auctions"* in *Business Communication Quarterly (December 2007, pp. 482)*
Pub: SAGE Publications USA
Contact: Blaise R. Simqu, President
Ed: Barbara Jo White, Daniel Clapper, Rita Noel, Jenny Fortier, Pierre Grabolosa. **Description:** eBay product listings were studied to determine the requirements of persuasive sales writing. Potential sellers should use the proper keywords and make an authentic description with authentic photographs of the item being auctioned.

28913 ■ *"U.S. Enters BlackBerry Dispute Compromise Sought Over Security Issues"* in *Houston Chronicle (August 6, 2010)*
Pub: Houston Chronicle
Ed: Matthew Lee. **Description:** U.S. State Department is working for a compromise with Research in Motion, manufacturer of the BlackBerry, over security issues. The Canadian company makes the smartphones and foreign governments believe they pose a security risk.

28914 ■ *"Universal Music Sues Grooveshark's Parent"* in *Wall Street Journal Eastern Edition (November 22, 2011, pp. B5)*
Pub: Dow Jones & Company Inc.
Ed: Ethan Smith. **Description:** Escape Media Group Inc., the parent company of online-music service Grooveshark, and seven of its executives have been sued by Universal Music Group, which alleges patent infringement involving its sound recordings. The executives are alleged to have uploaded thousands of songs onto Grooveshark.

28915 ■ *"Unlimited Priorities Strengthens Executive Team"* in *Entertainment Close-Up (November 1, 2011)*
Pub: Close-Up Media
Description: Founder and president of Unlimited Priorities Corporation, Iris L. Hanney, added two executive level professionals to her team. The new employees will help increase the firm's capabilities in social media and information technology.

28916 ■ *"Up To Code? Website Eases Compliance Burden for Entrepreneurs"* in *Black Enterprise (Vol. 38, March 2008, No. 8, pp. 48)*
Pub: Earl G. Graves Publishing Co. Inc.
Ed: Robin White-Goode. **Description:** Business.gov is a presidential E-government project created to help small businesses easily find, understand, and comply with laws and regulations pertaining to a particular industry.

28917 ■ *"Uptick in Clicks: Nordstrom's Online Sales Surging"* in *Puget Sound Business Journal (Vol. 29, August 22, 2008, No. 18, pp. 1)*
Pub: American City Business Journals
Ed: Gregg Lamm. **Description:** Nordstrom Inc.'s online division grew its sales by 15 percent in the second quarter of 2008, compared to 2007's 4.3 percent in overall decline. The company expects their online net sales to reach $700 million in 2008 capturing eight percent of overall sales.

28918 ■ *"Utah Technology Council: Social Media Is Here to Stay; Embrace It"* in *Wireless News (December 14, 2009)*
Pub: Close-Up Media
Description: Social media outlets such as Facebook and Twitter are blurring the lines between advertising, public relations, branding and marketing; businesses must stop thinking in terms of traditional marketing versus Internet marketing if they want to succeed in today's marketing climate.

28919 ■ *"A View to a Killer Business Model"* in *Black Enterprise (Vol. 40, December 2009, No. 5, pp. 50)*
Pub: Earl G. Graves Publishing Co., Inc.
Ed: Sonya A. Donaldson. **Description:** Profile of Gen2Media Corp., a production, technology and Internet marketing firm based in Florida with offices in New York; Gen2Media is utilizing the advances in technology to now include video in its online marketing offerings.

28920 ■ *"Virgin America Flies with V&S on Web"* in *ADWEEK (Vol. 51, July 12 2010, No. 27, pp. 31)*
Pub: Nielsen Business Media Inc.
Description: Victors & Spoils, a crowdsourcing agency is examined.

28921 ■ *"Vistaprint Survey Indicates that Online Marketing Taking Hold Among Small Businesses"* in *Internet Wire (December 10, 2009)*
Pub: Comtex News Network, Inc.
Description: According to a comprehensive survey from Vistaprint N.V., small businesses are very likey to increase their use of Internet marketing strategies such as paid and organic search, email marketing, social media networking and custom websites over the next year. Trends continue to show that more small businesses are indeed adapting to the changing marketplace and are more willing to diversify their marketing strategies than ever before.

28922 ■ *"The Way I Work"* in *Inc. (March 2008, pp. 102-104, 106)*
Pub: Gruner & Jahr USA Publishing
Ed: Hannah Clark Steiman. **Description:** Profile of Howard Lefkowitz, CEO of Vegas.com, a Website that allows visitors to book flights, reserve hotel rooms, buy show tickets, make spa appointments, and coordinate any and all aspects of a trip to Las Vegas. The firm also runs brick-and-mortar box offices and concierge desks at various cities.

28923 ■ *"Web-Based Marketing Excites, Challenges Small Business Use"* in *Colorado Springs Business Journal (January 20, 2010)*
Pub: Dolan Media Co.
Ed: Becky Hurley. **Description:** Business-to-business and consumer-direct firms alike are using the fast-changing Web technologies to increase sales, leads and track consumer behavior but once a company commits to an Online marketing plan, experts believe, they must be prepared to consistently tweak and overhaul content and distribution vehicles in order to keep up.

28924 ■ *"Web-Preneuring"* in *Small Business Opportunities (May 2008)*
Pub: Harris Publications Inc.
Description: 1&1 Internet provides known servers with more than 6.84 million customers through contracts with both consumer and business users. It operates five secure data centers housing 40,000 servers that process more than 5 billion monthly emails.

28925 ■ *"Web to Print"* in *American Printer (Vol. 128, August 1, 2011, No. 8)*
Pub: Penton Media Inc.
Description: Jerry Kennelly, CEO and founder of Tweak.com believes that Web-to-Design is middleware with no content. His firm offers an easy to use interface that flows right into the printer's workflow with no additional costs.

28926 ■ *"Web Sight: Do You See What I See?"* in *Entrepreneur (Vol. 35, October 2007, No. 10, pp. 58)*
Pub: Entrepreneur Media Inc.
Ed: Heather Clancy. **Description:** Owners of Trunkt, a boutique in New York that showcases independent designs, have created a new style of Website called Trunkt.org. The Website allows buyers to select the products they want to see and designers can choose anytime which of their items will be displayed on the site. An explanation of the strategy that helped bring Trunkt closer to its clients is presented.

28927 ■ *"Web Traffic Numbers Facing Scrutiny"* in *Boston Business Journal (Vol. 27, November 2, 2007, No. 40, pp. 1)*
Pub: American City Business Journals Inc.
Ed: Jesse Noyes. **Description:** Interactive Advertising Bureau (IAB) held a summit meeting with major industry players in an effort to create more transparent standards for measuring Internet traffic. The terms at issue were registered users, unique visitors, time spent and retention.

28928 ■ *"Web Translation Made Simple"* in *Inc. (Vol. 33, October 2011, No. 8, pp. 44)*
Pub: Inc. Magazine
Ed: Adam Baer. **Description:** Smartling is a Web-based service that translates sites into more than 50 foreign languages. The software will begin translation right after setting up the account.

28929 ■ *"Webadvertising"* in *MarketingMagazine (Vol. 115, September 27, 2010, No. 13, pp. 70)*
Pub: Rogers Publishing Ltd.
Description: Website advertising in Canada is examined.

28930 ■ *"Web.Preneuring: How Local TV Ads and Online Marketing Can Help You Win Big"* in *Small Business Opportunities (January 2008)*
Pub: Harris Publications Inc.
Ed: David Waxman. **Description:** Spot Runner, an Internet-based advertising agency offers low-cost local business television ads. The company secures the ad buy, places and tracks the ads, and analyzes viewership and demographics for clients.

28931 ■ *"What the Future Holds for Consumers"* in *Black Enterprise (Vol. 41, August 2010, No. 1, pp. 47)*
Pub: Earl G. Graves Publishing Co. Inc.
Ed: Sheiresa Ngo. **Description:** The way people purchase goods and service has changed with technology. With an increased focus on security (as well as privacy and fairness) the U.S. Congress began regulating the credit card industry with the Fair Credit Reporting Act of 1970 and the Credit Card Accountability, Responsibility, and Disclosure (CARD) Act of 2009.

28932 ■ *"What's Your Personal Social Media Strategy?"* in *Harvard Business Review (Vol. 88, November 2010, No. 11, pp. 127)*
Pub: Harvard Business School Publishing
Ed: Soumitra Dutta. **Description:** Identification of four distinct sectors and how they interrelate to social media is given. The sectors are personal and private; professional and private; personal and public; and professional and public. Appropriate topics and types of social media are discussed for each.

28933 ■ *"What's Your Social Media Strategy?"* in *Black Enterprise (Vol. 41, November 2010, No. 4, pp. 75)*
Pub: Earl G. Graves Publishing Co. Inc.
Ed: Denise Campbell. **Description:** Advice for using social media sites such as Twitter, Facebook and LinkedIn as a professional networking tool is given.

28934 ■ *"White Cat Media Tells You Where to Get a Bargain. Now It's Shopping for $1.5 Million"* in *Inc. (March 2008, pp. 48)*
Pub: Gruner & Jahr USA Publishing
Ed: Athena Schindelheim. **Description:** Profile of White Cat Media which runs two shopping Websites: SheFinds.com for fashion and beauty items, and MomFinds.com for mothers. The New York City firm reported revenues for 2007 at $400,000 and is looking for funding capital in the amount of $1.7 million.

28935 ■ *"Why LinkedIn is the Social Network that Will Never Die"* in *Advertising Age (Vol. 81, December 6, 2010, No. 43, pp. 2)*
Pub: Crain Communications, Inc.
Ed: Irina Slutsky. **Description:** Despite the popularity of Facebook, LinkedIn will always be a source for professionals who wish to network.

28936 ■ *"Why Some Get Shaften By Google Pricing"* in *Advertising Age (Vol. 79, July 14, 2008, No. 7, pp. 3)*
Pub: Crain Communications, Inc.
Ed: Abbey Klaassen. **Description:** Google's search advertising is discussed as well as the company's pricing structure for these ads.

28937 ■ *"Why We'll Never Escape Facebook"* in *Canadian Business (Vol. 83, June 15, 2010, No. 10, pp. 28)*
Pub: Rogers Media Ltd.
Ed: James Cowan, Tamara Shopsin, Jason Fulford. **Description:** Facebook users are growing in numbers despite criticism of the site's privacy policies that

have put the onus of keeping anonymous to the user. Facebook's business model and its growing influence on the Internet are discussed.

28938 ■ *"Why You Need a New-Media 'Ringmaster" in Harvard Business Review (Vol. 88, December 2010, No. 12, pp. 78)*
Pub: Harvard Business School Publishing

Ed: Patrick Spenner. **Description:** The concept of ringmaster is applied to brand marketing. This concept includes integrative thinking, lean collaboration skills, and high-speed decision cycles.

28939 ■ *"Wi-Fi On Steroids: Will WiMAX Provide the Juice For Souped-Up Connections?" in Black Enterprise (November 2007)*
Pub: Earl G. Graves Publishing Co. Inc.

Ed: Fiona Haley. **Description:** WiMAX, Worldwide Interoperability for Microwave Access in the U.S. WiMax is technology that moves data and connects faster and at greater distances than before.

28940 ■ *Wikinomics: How Mass Collaboration Changes Everything*
Pub: Penguin Group Incorporated

Ed: Don Tapscott; Anthony D. Williams. **Released:** April 2008. **Price:** $27.95. **Description:** Research and information about the every changing world of the Internet is provided to help small businesses.

28941 ■ *"Wikinomics: The Sequel" in Business Strategy Review (Vol. 21, Summer 2010, No. 2, pp. 64)*
Pub: Blackwell Publishers Ltd.

Description: Ever optimistic Don Tapscott and Anthony Willis, co-authors of Wikinomics (Atlantic Books 2008) as well as various other books that study the Internet and its relationship to society are now working on a new book, one for which they are using the Internet to determine its title.

28942 ■ *"Wikinomics: The Sequel" in Business Strategy Review (Vol. 21, Summer 2010, No. 2, pp. 64)*
Pub: Wiley-Blackwell

Description: Ever-optimistic Don Tapscott and Anthony Williams, coauthors of Wikinomics and individually, of a number of other books that study the Internet and its relation to society, are now working on a new book, one for which they're using the Internet to determine its title.

28943 ■ *"Will mCommerce Make Black Friday Green?" in Retail Merchandiser (Vol. 51, September-October 2011, No. 5, pp. 8)*
Pub: Phoenix Media Corporation

Ed: Scott Miller. **Description:** Retailers speculate the possibilities of mobile commerce and are implementing strategies at their stores. Consumers using mobile devices accounted for only 0.1 percent of visits to retail Websites on Black Friday 2009 and rose to 5.6 percent in 2010; numbers are expected to rise for 2011.

28944 ■ *"Winner: Private Company, Less Than $100M" in Crain's Detroit Business (Vol. 25, June 22, 2009, No. 25)*
Pub: Crain Communications Inc. - Detroit

Ed: Tom Henderson. **Description:** Profile of ForeSee Results, an Ann Arbor, Michigan-based firm that uses the University of Michigan American Consumer Satisfaction Index to help businesses measure satisfaction with their Websites.

28945 ■ *Winner Take All: How Competitiveness Shapes the Fate of Nations*
Pub: Basic Books

Ed: Richard J. Elkus Jr. **Released:** 2009. **Price:** $27.00. **Description:** American government and misguided business practices has allowed the U.S. to fall behind other countries in various market sectors such as cameras and televisions, as well as information technologies. It will take a national strategy to for America to regain its lead in crucial industries.

28946 ■ *"Wireless: Full Service" in Entrepreneur (Vol. 35, October 2007, No. 10, pp. 60)*
Pub: Entrepreneur Media Inc.

Ed: Amanda C. Kooser. **Description:** Palm Foleo, the $599 smart phone enables users to access and compose email, browse the Internet, view documents and play Powerpoint files. It weighs 2.5 pounds and has a 10-inch screen. Other features, such as built-in WiFi are described.

28947 ■ *"Women Clicking to Earn Virtual Dollars" in Sales and Marketing Management (November 11, 2009)*
Pub: Nielsen Business Media, Inc.

Ed: Stacy Straczynski. **Description:** According to a new report from Internet marketing firm Q Interactive, women are increasingly playing social media games where they are able to click on an ad or sign up for a promotion to earn virtual currency. Research is showing that this kind of marketing may be a potent tool, especially for e-commerce and online stores.

28948 ■ *"Women Workers Spend Lunchtime on Fridays Shopping Online" in Marketing to Women (Vol. 23, November 2010, No. 11, pp. 8)*
Pub: EPM Communications Inc.
Contact: Ira Mayer, President
E-mail: imayer@epmcom.com

Description: Forty percent of women shop online during work hours, particularly on Fridays. The largest number of women make these purchases during their lunch break. Demographics are included.

28949 ■ *"WordStream Announces a Pair of Firsts for SEO and PPC Keyword Research Tools" in Internet Wire (November 10, 2009)*
Pub: Comtex News Network, Inc.

Description: WordSteam, Inc., a provider of pay-per-click (PPC) and search engine optimization (SEO) solutions for continuously expanding and optimizing search marketing efforts has released two new features in their flagship Keyword Management solution; these tools will allow marketers to analyze data from paid search, organic search and estimated totals from keyword suggestion tools side-by-side.

28950 ■ *Work at Home Now*
Pub: Career Press, Inc.

Ed: Christine Durst, Michael Haaren. **Released:** October 9, 2010. **Price:** $14.99. **Description:** There are legitimate home-based jobs and projects that can be found on the Internet, but trustworthy guidance is scarce. There is a 58 to 1 scam ratio in work at-home advertising filled with fraud.

28951 ■ *"Xtium Has Its Head in the Clouds" in Philadelphia Business Journal (Vol. 30, September 23, 2011, No. 32, pp. 1)*
Pub: American City Business Journals Inc.

Ed: Peter Key. **Description:** Philadelphia-based cloud computing firm Xtium LLC received an $11.5 million first-round investment from Boston-Massachusetts-based OpenView Venture Partners. Catering to midsize businesses and unit of bigger firms, Xtium offers disaster-recovery, hosting, and managed-information-technology-infrastructure services.

28952 ■ *"The Yahoo Family Tree" in Conde Nast Portfolio (Vol. 2, June 2008, No. 6, pp. 34)*
Pub: Conde Nast Publications
Contact: David Carey, President

Ed: Blaise Zerega. **Description:** Yahoo, founded in 1994 by Stanford students Jerry Yang and David Filo, is still an Internet powerhouse. The company's history is also outlined as well as the reasons in which Microsoft desperately wants to acquire the firm.

28953 ■ *"Yahoo! - Microsoft Pact: Alive Again?" in Barron's (Vol. 89, July 27, 2009, No. 30, pp. 8)*
Pub: Dow Jones & Co., Inc.

Ed: Mark Veverka. **Description:** Yahoo! reported higher than expected earnings in the second quarter of 2009 under CEO Carol Bartz who has yet to articulate her long-term vision and strategy for turn-

ing around the company. The media reported that Yahoo! and Microsoft are discussing an advertising-search partnership which should benefit both companies.

28954 ■ *"Yammer Gets Serious" in Inc. (Volume 32, December 2010, No. 10, pp. 58)*
Pub: Inc. Magazine

Ed: Eric Markowitz. **Description:** Yammer, an internal social network for companies, allows coworkers to share ideas and documents in real-time. Details of this service are included.

28955 ■ *"You Are What They Click" in Entrepreneur (Vol. 37, July 2009, No. 7, pp. 43)*
Pub: Entrepreneur Media, Inc.

Ed: Mikal Belicove. **Description:** Hiring the right website design firm is the first stage in building an online business, and this involves various factors such as price, technical expertise, and talent. Writing a request for proposal (RFP) detailing the website's details, which include purpose, budget and audience, is the first step the process. Other tips in finding the right web designer are given.

28956 ■ *Your First Year in Real Estate: Making the Transition from Total Novice to Successful Professional*
Pub: Crown Business Books

Ed: Dirk Zeller. **Released:** $August 3, 2010. **Price:** $20.00. **Description:** Zeller helps new realtors to select the right company, develop mentor and client relationships, using the Internet and social networking to stay ahead of competition, to set and reach career goals, to stay current in the market, and more.

28957 ■ *"Your Turn in the Spotlight" in Inc. (Volume 32, December 2010, No. 10, pp. 57)*
Pub: Inc. Magazine

Ed: John Brandon. **Description:** Examples of three video blogs created by entrepreneurs to promote their businesses and products are used to show successful strategies. Wine Library TV promotes a family's wine business; SHAMA.TV offers marketing tips and company news; and Will It Blend? promotes sales of a household blender.

28958 ■ *YouTube and Video Marketing: An Hour a Day*
Pub: Sybex

Ed: Greg Jarboe. **Released:** August 10, 2009. **Price:** $29.99. **Description:** The importance of online video marketing for businesses is stressed. Tips for developing and implementing video marketing are outlined.

28959 ■ *"Zeon Solutions Teams with Endeca for SaaS Version of Endeca InFront" in Entertainment Close-Up (October 25, 2011)*
Pub: Close-Up Media

Description: Zeon Solutions, an enterprise e-commerce and Website development firm announced a special licensing partnership with Endecca Technologies. Endeca is an information management software company that provides small and mid-size retailers with high-performance Customer Experience Management technology.

CONSULTANTS

28960 ■ BIA/Kelsey
15120 Enterprise Ct.
Chantilly, VA 20151
Ph: (703)818-2425
Free: 800-331-5086
Fax: (703)803-3299
Co. E-mail: info@bia.com
URL: http://www.bia.com
Contact: Neal Polachek, President
E-mail: npolachek@kelseygroup.com

URL(s): www.kelseygroup.com. **Scope:** A provider of research and fact-based analysis focusing on local advertising and electronic commerce. **Founded:** 1983. **Publications:** "Penetration of Online Media Surpasses Traditional Media for First Time Among Small-Business Advertisers," Aug, 2009; "Rapid Adoption of Advanced Mobile Devices Driving Increased Mobile Local Search Activity, According to

The Kelsey Group," Nov, 2008; "Online Consumer Generated Reviews Have Significant Impact on Offline Purchase Behavior," Nov, 2007. **Seminars:** Drilling Down on Local: Marketplaces, The Westin Seattle, Seattle, Washington, Apr, 2008 The Future of Local Search in Europe, London, Jun, 2007; DDC2006?Directory Driven Commerce Conference, Hyatt Century Plaza, LA, Sep, 2006; Drilling Down on Local: Targeting the On-Demand Marketplace, 2005. **Telecommunication Services:** tkg@kelseygroup.com.

28961 ■ Digital Deli Inc.
3145 Geary Blvd., Ste. 532
San Francisco, CA 94118-3316
Ph: (415)387-7653
Free: 800-557-3354
Fax: (415)387-7656
Co. E-mail: sales@thedeli.com
Contact: Antonio White, President
E-mail: white@theDeli.com
Scope: Specializes in interactive marketing development. Provides strategic and tactical planning for interactive media. Specializes in marketing communications. **Founded:** 1995.

28962 ■ Digitas L.L.C.
33 Arch St.
Boston, MA 02110-1424
Ph: (617)867-1000
Fax: (617)867-1111
Co. E-mail: contact@digitas.com
URL: http://www.digitas.com
Contact: Glenn Engler, President
Scope: Helps clients determine how to use the Internet and emerging technologies to create new business models and enterprise-wide customer value propositions to gain competitive advantages, improved market share, and enhanced profitability. Technology, architecture, and infrastructure service marketing and creative services were focused on enabling brands to connect with the right customer at the right time through the right channels in the most effective way possible. Performance measurement provides the ultimate yardstick and continuous feedback mechanisms. **Founded:** 1980. **Telecommunication Services:** newbusiness@digitas.com.

28963 ■ Organic Inc.
555 Market St., 4th Fl.
San Francisco, CA 94105-2873
Ph: (415)581-5300
Fax: (415)581-5400
Co. E-mail: pressroom@organic.com
URL: http://www.organic.com
Contact: Mark Kingdon, Chief Executive Officer
Scope: Strategic consulting, e-business, marketing solutions, e-commerce website creation, customer service and fulfillment. **Founded:** 1993.

28964 ■ Sapient Corp.
131 Dartmouth St., 3rd Fl.
Cambridge, MA 02116
Ph: (617)621-0200
Fax: (617)621-1300
Co. E-mail: info@sapient.com
URL: http://www.sapient.com
Contact: Alan Herrick, President
Scope: The company offers its services in the areas of business and information technology (IT) strategy business applications, business intelligence, marketing, and outsourcing. Its business and IT strategy services include business-process consulting, business applications and enterprise architecture planning, e-business and Web strategy, IT governance and advisory services, and program management office. **Founded:** 1990. **Publications:** "Here Today, Gone Tomorrow: How to Get the Most Out of Your Ads," Mar, 2009; "New Media Age," Dec, 2005.

28965 ■ Spherix Inc.
6430 Rockledge Dr., Ste. 503
Bethesda, MD 20817-1836
Ph: (301)897-2540
Fax: (301)897-2567
Co. E-mail: info@spherix.com
URL: http://www.spherix.com
Contact: Robert Lodder, President
URL(s): www.biospherics.com. **Scope:** Provides health sciences consulting services that provides scientific and strategic support for suppliers, manufacturers, distributors and retailers of: Conventional foods, biotechnology-derived foods, medical foods, infant formulas, food ingredients, dietary supplements, food contact substances, pharmaceuticals, medical devices, consumer products and industrial chemicals and pesticides. Provides teleservices, ebusinesses, and IT solutions for the health and information industries. **Founded:** 1967. **Publications:** "Viking found no life on Mars, and, just as important, it found why there can be no life". **Special Services:** Naturlose®.

28966 ■ Stratamar Inc.
5661 Seapine Rd.
Hlliard, OH 43026
Ph: (614)946-4614
Fax: (614)529-2945
Co. E-mail: info@stratamar.com
URL: http://www.stratamar.com
Contact: Nancy Brown, Owner
Scope: A full-spectrum strategic marketing consulting company. Areas of concentration include product development, product management, strategic planning, development and implementation of tactical marketing plans, and Internet marketing. The primary focus is upon maximizing the benefit, cost ratio of promotions through the use of direct marketing, low cost media, and the like. **Founded:** 1998. **Publications:** "Business Plans," Feb, 2006.

COMPUTERIZED DATABASES

28967 ■ BtoB
1155 Gratiot Ave.
Detroit, MI 48207
Ph: (313)446-6000
Free: 800-678-2427
Fax: (313)446-1616
Co. E-mail: info@crain.com
URL: http://www.crain.com
Availability: Online: Crain Communications Inc.
Type: Full-text.

EDUCATIONAL PROGRAMS

28968 ■ Administrative Professionals Retreat
Padgett-Thompson Seminars
Rockhurst University CEC
14502 W. 105th St.
Lenexa, KS 66215
Free: 800-349-1935
URL: http://www.findaseminar.com/tpd/Padgett-Thompson-Seminars.asp
Price: $348.00. **Description:** A two-day seminar for administrative professionals. **Dates and Locations:** Charlotte, NC; Boston, MA; Farmington, CT.

28969 ■ Advanced Issues in Employee Relations
Seminar Information Service, Inc.
20 Executive Park, Ste. 120
Irvine, CA 92614
Ph: (949)261-9104
Free: 877-SEM-INFO
Fax: (949)261-1963
Co. E-mail: info@seminarinformation.com
URL: http://www.seminarinformation.com
Price: $1,495.00. **Description:** Key topics include coaching managers to more effectively manage high performing employees who consistently demonstrate one serious performance failing, collaborating with managers to assist them in focusing on performance issues without being influenced by employees' personal circumstances, working with managers on dealing more effectively with strong negative employee reactions to direction or feedback, and addressing managers' behavior that is inappropriate and potentially high risk. **Dates and Locations:** New York, NY.

28970 ■ AMA's Myers-Briggs Type Indicator (MBTI) Certification Program
American Management Association
600 AMA Way
Saranac Lake, NY 12983-5534
Ph: (212)586-8100
Free: 877-566-9441
Fax: (518)891-0368
Co. E-mail: customerservice@amanet.org
URL: http://www.amaseminars.org
Price: $1,795.00 for non-members; $1,595.00 for AMA members; and $1,366.00 for General Services Administration (GSA) members. **Description:** Updated MBTI program that focuses on team building, leadership, and individual development. **Dates and Locations:** Cities throughout the United States.

28971 ■ The Art of Coaching: Enabling Employees to Achieve Their Potential (Onsite)
Seminar Information Service, Inc.
20 Executive Park, Ste. 120
Irvine, CA 92614
Ph: (949)261-9104
Free: 877-SEM-INFO
Fax: (949)261-1963
Co. E-mail: info@seminarinformation.com
URL: http://www.seminarinformation.com
Price: $1,890.00. **Description:** Learn how to: Apply coaching techniques to unlock employee potential and maximize performance; Harness the art of coaching to forge collaborative relationships; Structure a framework for mutually effective learning and development; Develop the coaching skills, attitudes and behaviors to foster success at all levels; Recognize and adapt to individual and situational differences; Create a positive, supportive environment that generates commitment and enthusiasm. **Dates and Locations:** Reston, VA.

28972 ■ Assertive Management (Onsite)
Seminar Information Service, Inc.
20 Executive Park, Ste. 120
Irvine, CA 92614
Ph: (949)261-9104
Free: 877-SEM-INFO
Fax: (949)261-1963
Co. E-mail: info@seminarinformation.com
URL: http://www.seminarinformation.com
Price: Contact for fees. **Description:** Develop the qualities necessary for successful, assertive management. Participants gain confidence and skill in being 'pro-active' in communicating with others, including how to use positive, win-win approaches and to defuse emotionally charged situations in order to work more effectively with their fellow workers, supervisors and subordinates.

28973 ■ Basic Problem Solving Techniques (Onsite)
Seminar Information Service, Inc.
20 Executive Park, Ste. 120
Irvine, CA 92614
Ph: (949)261-9104
Free: 877-SEM-INFO
Fax: (949)261-1963
Co. E-mail: info@seminarinformation.com
URL: http://www.seminarinformation.com
Price: Contact for fee. **Description:** With the help of several qualitative, quantitative, and creative problem solving methods participants develop their ability to recognize and solve problems through their own efforts. **Dates and Locations:** Waukesha, WI.

28974 ■ Building Better Work Relationships: New Techniques for Results-oriented Communication (Onsite)
American Management Association
600 AMA Way
Saranac Lake, NY 12983-5534
Ph: (212)586-8100
Free: 877-566-9441
Fax: (518)891-0368
Co. E-mail: customerservice@amanet.org
URL: http://www.amaseminars.org
Price: $2,345.00 for non-members; $2,095.00 for AMA members; and $1,794.00 for General Services Administration (GSA) members. **Description:** Covers effective work relationships, communication and perceptions, investigating emotions and emotional intelligence, relationship building, relational communication and listening and more. **Dates and Locations:** Cities throughout the United States.

28975 ■ Business Conversation for Sales and Service (Onsite)
Seminar Information Service, Inc.
20 Executive Park, Ste. 120
Irvine, CA 92614
Ph: (949)261-9104
Free: 877-SEM-INFO
Fax: (949)261-1963
Co. E-mail: info@seminarinformation.com
URL: http://www.seminarinformation.com
Price: $225.00 for non-members; $165.00 for The Management Association, Inc. **Description:** Participants will learn practical tips and practice conversation. Build common ground with colleagues, customers, and senior managers, including methods to develop a repertoire of topics, make skillful transitions, develop confidence and draw people to you. **Dates and Locations:** Waukesha, WI.

28976 ■ Coaching and Teambuilding Skills for Managers and Supervisors (Onsite)
Seminar Information Service, Inc.
20 Executive Park, Ste. 120
Irvine, CA 92614
Ph: (949)261-9104
Free: 877-SEM-INFO
Fax: (949)261-1963
Co. E-mail: info@seminarinformation.com
URL: http://www.seminarinformation.com
Price: $199.00; $189.00 for four or more. **Description:** Gain team building expertise guaranteed to make your team more cohesive, motivated, and productive. **Dates and Locations:** Cities throughout the United States.

28977 ■ Creativity and Innovation (Onsite)
Seminar Information Service, Inc.
20 Executive Park, Ste. 120
Irvine, CA 92614
Ph: (949)261-9104
Free: 877-SEM-INFO
Fax: (949)261-1963
Co. E-mail: info@seminarinformation.com
URL: http://www.seminarinformation.com
Price: $2,095.00. **Description:** Develop creative thinking methods to generate ideas and solutions and learn how to align your ideas with corporate needs to add value and increase recognition. **Dates and Locations:** New York, NY; and Arlington, VA.

28978 ■ Criticism & Discipline Skills for Managers and Supervisors (Onsite)
Fred Pryor Seminars & CareerTrack
5700 Broadmoor St., Ste. 300
Mission, KS 66202
Free: 800-780-8476
Fax: (913)967-8849
Co. E-mail: customerservice@pryor.com
URL: http://www.pryor.com
Price: $249.00; $229.00 for groups of 5 or more. **Description:** Learn proven techniques for managing difficult employees without incurring resentment, mak-

ing enemies, or destroying relationships, including how to discipline employees who have a bad attitude, are chronically tardy, miss work often, refuse to take responsibility and challenge your authority. **Dates and Locations:** Cities throughout the United States.

28979 ■ Effective Communication and Motivation (Onsite)
Seminar Information Service, Inc.
20 Executive Park, Ste. 120
Irvine, CA 92614
Ph: (949)261-9104
Free: 877-SEM-INFO
Fax: (949)261-1963
Co. E-mail: info@seminarinformation.com
URL: http://www.seminarinformation.com
Price: $580.00 for non-members; $435.00 for MRA members. **Description:** Gives managerial personnel a sound understanding of the principles of effective communication and the skill to recognize and to resolve communication breakdowns in the workplace. Participants learn to apply communication skills to problem solving, employee relations and performance appraisal. **Dates and Locations:** Waukesha, WI; and Palatine, IL.

28980 ■ The Effective Facilitator (Canada)
Canadian Management Centre (CMC)
150 York St., 5th Fl.
Toronto, ON, Canada M5H 3S5
Ph: (416)214-5678
Free: 877-262-2519
Fax: (416)313-4985
Co. E-mail: cmcinfo@cmctraining.org
URL: http://www.cmctraining.org
Contact: John Wright, President
Price: $2,395.00 Canadian for non-members; $2,195.00 Canadian for CMC members. **Description:** Covers achieving positive results in group settings such as meetings, project teams, and group work projects. **Dates and Locations:** Toronto, ON.

28981 ■ The Effective Facilitator: Maximizing Involvement and Results (Onsite)
American Management Association
600 AMA Way
Saranac Lake, NY 12983-5534
Ph: (212)586-8100
Free: 877-566-9441
Fax: (518)891-0368
Co. E-mail: customerservice@amanet.org
URL: http://www.amaseminars.org
Price: $2,345.00 for non-members; $2,095.00 for AMA members; and $1,794.00 for General Services Administration (GSA) members. **Description:** Covers achieving positive results in group settings such as meetings, project teams, and group work projects. **Dates and Locations:** Chicago, IL; Atlanta, GA; Arlington, VA; and Washington, DC.

28982 ■ Effective Project Communications, Negotiations and Conflict (Onsite)
EEI Communications
8945 Guilford ., Ste. 145
Columbia, MD 21046
Ph: (410)309-8200
Free: 888-253-2762
Fax: (410)630-3980
Co. E-mail: train@eeicom.com
URL: http://www.eeicom.com/eei-training-services
Price: $1,065.00. **Description:** Learn what you need to know to lead projects through their initiation, planning, execution, and control phases, including the skills needed to find common ground, overcome resistance, resolve disputes, and gain commitment to project management efforts. **Dates and Locations:** Silver Spring, MD; Hunt Valley, MD; Columbia, MD; and Alexandria, VA.

28983 ■ Enhancing Your Management Skills (Onsite)
Seminar Information Service, Inc.
20 Executive Park, Ste. 120
Irvine, CA 92614
Ph: (949)261-9104
Free: 877-SEM-INFO

Fax: (949)261-1963
Co. E-mail: info@seminarinformation.com
URL: http://www.seminarinformation.com
Price: $1,995.00. **Description:** Learn the critical success factors for driving results through goal alignment, coaching for performance, building trust, and driving committed action through stronger leadership. Receive practical, state-of-the-art tools and techniques for holding conversations that set clear expectations, provide focused feedback, create a motivational environment, and build commitment for needed change.

28984 ■ Enhancing Your People Skills
Seminar Information Service, Inc.
20 Executive Park, Ste. 120
Irvine, CA 92614
Ph: (949)261-9104
Free: 877-SEM-INFO
Fax: (949)261-1963
Co. E-mail: info@seminarinformation.com
URL: http://www.seminarinformation.com
Price: $1,495.00. **Description:** Build awareness and skill in the areas of team dynamics, group problem solving, and group decision making. The critical structural and behavioral dimensions of building and leading an effective work team or task force are fully explored. You will develop leadership skills applicable to many areas, but especially suited to self-directed work teams, employee participation teams, interdepartmental task groups, and other group situations where combined efforts are needed to reach optimal performance levels. **Dates and Locations:** New York, NY.

28985 ■ Essential Skills for the First-Time Manager or Supervisor (Onsite)
Fred Pryor Seminars & CareerTrack
5700 Broadmoor St., Ste. 300
Mission, KS 66202
Free: 800-780-8476
Fax: (913)967-8849
Co. E-mail: customerservice@pryor.com
URL: http://www.pryor.com
Price: $179.00; $169.00 for groups of 5 or more. **Description:** Gain all the skills and insights you need to lead with confidence and conviction, including how to start producing results right away, what it takes to get productivity from people who aren't used to you being the boss. **Dates and Locations:** Cities throughout the United States.

28986 ■ The Exceptional Assistant (Onsite)
Fred Pryor Seminars & CareerTrack
5700 Broadmoor St., Ste. 300
Mission, KS 66202
Free: 800-780-8476
Fax: (913)967-8849
Co. E-mail: customerservice@pryor.com
URL: http://www.pryor.com
Price: $99.00; $89.00 for groups of 5 or more. **Description:** Covers the necessary skills for success including prioritizing, problem solving, political and people skills, managing time and resources, crises and decision making. **Dates and Locations:** Cities throughout the United States.

28987 ■ Greater Productivity Through Improved Work Processes: A Guide for Administrative Professionals (Onsite)
American Management Association
600 AMA Way
Saranac Lake, NY 12983-5534
Ph: (212)586-8100
Free: 877-566-9441
Fax: (518)891-0368
Co. E-mail: customerservice@amanet.org
URL: http://www.amaseminars.org
Description: Two-day seminar for administrative professionals with three or more years of experience; covers increasing productivity and efficiency, dealing with change, improving your work, and assisting in improving various aspects of the organization.

28988 ■ How to Be a Dynamic Trainer (Onsite)
Seminar Information Service, Inc.
20 Executive Park, Ste. 120
Irvine, CA 92614

Ph: (949)261-9104
Free: 877-SEM-INFO
Fax: (949)261-1963
Co. E-mail: info@seminarinformation.com
URL: http://www.seminarinformation.com
Price: $249.00. **Description:** Learn how to motivate reluctant learners and how to engage learners to get them to participate. **Dates and Locations:** Denver, CO; Albuquerque, NM; Phoenix, AZ; Las Vegas, NV; and Salt Lake City, UT.

28989 ■ How to Be a Highly Successful Team Leader (Onsite)
Seminar Information Service, Inc.
20 Executive Park, Ste. 120
Irvine, CA 92614
Ph: (949)261-9104
Free: 877-SEM-INFO
Fax: (949)261-1963
Co. E-mail: info@seminarinformation.com
URL: http://www.seminarinformation.com
Price: $299.00. **Description:** Intensive two-day workshop that teaches the many dimensions of effective leadership and develop the skills needed to lead your team to maximum performance.

28990 ■ Leadership Skills: Building Success Through Teamwork (Onsite)
Seminar Information Service, Inc.
20 Executive Park, Ste. 120
Irvine, CA 92614
Ph: (949)261-9104
Free: 877-SEM-INFO
Fax: (949)261-1963
Co. E-mail: info@seminarinformation.com
URL: http://www.seminarinformation.com
Price: $2,490.00. **Description:** Learn how to: Develop your teams to maximize their strengths and enhance productivity; Optimize organization and work design for success in service delivery teams; Motivate your team with effective performance measurement; Integrate your role as a leader into your management style; Leverage the complementary skills and styles of your team; Eliminate barriers and chokepoints that block teamwork; Apply a diverse and multilevel approach to minimize communication breakdowns. **Dates and Locations:** Toronto, CN.

28991 ■ Leadership and Team Development for Managerial Success (Onsite) (Canada)
Canadian Management Centre (CMC)
150 York St., 5th Fl.
Toronto, ON, Canada M5H 3S5
Ph: (416)214-5678
Free: 877-262-2519
Fax: (416)313-4985
Co. E-mail: cmcinfo@cmctraining.org
URL: http://www.cmctraining.org
Contact: John Wright, President
Price: $1,845.00 Canadian for non-members; $1,995.00 Canadian for CMC members. **Description:** Covers how to work in a horizontal mode of operation, including when to manage and when to lead your team, distinguishing the three team types, principles that make teams work, differentiating team content and process, and diagnosing work teams. **Dates and Locations:** Toronto, ON.

28992 ■ Leading Effective Teams II - Communicating with Your Teammates (Onsite)
Seminar Information Service, Inc.
20 Executive Park, Ste. 120
Irvine, CA 92614
Ph: (949)261-9104
Free: 877-SEM-INFO
Fax: (949)261-1963
Co. E-mail: info@seminarinformation.com
URL: http://www.seminarinformation.com
Price: $350.00 for non-members; $275.00 for MRA members. **Description:** Leaders learn their communication style and how it relates to their team members, as well as how to motivate through communication. **Dates and Locations:** Waukesha, WI.

28993 ■ Leading High Performance Teams
Seminar Information Service, Inc.
20 Executive Park, Ste. 120
Irvine, CA 92614
Ph: (949)261-9104
Free: 877-SEM-INFO
Fax: (949)261-1963
Co. E-mail: info@seminarinformation.com
URL: http://www.seminarinformation.com
Price: $1,495.00. **Description:** Builds awareness and skill in the areas of team dynamics, group problem solving, and group decision making. You will develop leadership skills applicable to many areas, but especially suited to self-directed work teams, employee participation teams, interdepartmental task groups, and other group situations where combined efforts are needed to reach optimal performance levels. **Dates and Locations:** New York, NY.

28994 ■ Making Successful Business Decisions: Getting it Right the First Time (Onsite)
Seminar Information Service, Inc.
20 Executive Park, Ste. 120
Irvine, CA 92614
Ph: (949)261-9104
Free: 877-SEM-INFO
Fax: (949)261-1963
Co. E-mail: info@seminarinformation.com
URL: http://www.seminarinformation.com
Price: $2,490.00. **Description:** Learn how to make intelligent decisions with limited time and information, how to convert conflicting opinions into useful insights, foster efficient and effective group decision making, and ensure decisions are implemented by the organization.

28995 ■ Management Skills for an IT Environment (Onsite)
Seminar Information Service, Inc.
20 Executive Park, Ste. 120
Irvine, CA 92614
Ph: (949)261-9104
Free: 877-SEM-INFO
Fax: (949)261-1963
Co. E-mail: info@seminarinformation.com
URL: http://www.seminarinformation.com
Price: $2,890.00. **Description:** Learn how to apply a proven management model for leading technical staff to excellence; identify key success criteria for leadership in an IT environment; leverage emotion to optimize communication and performance; motivate and empower technical professionals to achieve results; delegate proactively to focus on strengths of IT teams and build accountability. **Dates and Locations:** Reston, VA; Ottawa, CN; Schaumburg, IL; Los Angeles, CA; Philadelphia, PA; Toronto, CN; New York, NY; Alexandria, VA; and Rockville, MD.

28996 ■ Managing Today's IT and Technical Professionals (Onsite)
Seminar Information Service, Inc.
20 Executive Park, Ste. 120
Irvine, CA 92614
Ph: (949)261-9104
Free: 877-SEM-INFO
Fax: (949)261-1963
Co. E-mail: info@seminarinformation.com
URL: http://www.seminarinformation.com
Price: $2,345.00. **Description:** Learn how to strengthen, motivate and inspire any group or team. **Dates and Locations:** San Francisco, CA.

28997 ■ Managing in Tough Times (Onsite)
Seminar Information Service, Inc.
20 Executive Park, Ste. 120
Irvine, CA 92614
Ph: (949)261-9104
Free: 877-SEM-INFO
Fax: (949)261-1963
Co. E-mail: info@seminarinformation.com
URL: http://www.seminarinformation.com
Price: $2,490.00. **Description:** Learn how to demonstrate authentic and strong leadership to create an atmosphere of confidence and trust in tough times, share your vision and display confidence that the problems your team currently faces will be solved, and minimize stress and maximize productivity and performance during difficult times.

28998 ■ Partnering with Your Boss: Strategic Skills for Administrative Professionals (Onsite)
American Management Association
600 AMA Way
Saranac Lake, NY 12983-5534
Ph: (212)586-8100
Free: 877-566-9441
Fax: (518)891-0368
Co. E-mail: customerservice@amanet.org
URL: http://www.amaseminars.org
Price: $1,645.00 for non-members; $1,495.00 for AMA members; and $1,280.00 for General Services Administration (GSA) members,. **Description:** Covers skills for setting goals, prioritizing, making decisions, building relationships, and communicating in such a way as to represent your boss authoritatively and gain respect in the workplace. **Dates and Locations:** Washington, DC; New York, NY; Arlington, VA; Chicago, IL; San Francisco, CA; and Dallas, TX.

28999 ■ Project Leadership: Building High-Performance Teams (Onsite)
Seminar Information Service, Inc.
20 Executive Park, Ste. 120
Irvine, CA 92614
Ph: (949)261-9104
Free: 877-SEM-INFO
Fax: (949)261-1963
Co. E-mail: info@seminarinformation.com
URL: http://www.seminarinformation.com
Price: $2,890.00. **Description:** Learn how to: Develop the leadership skills to build and sustain high-performing project teams; Develop effective team performance through the Leadership Services Model; Build a strong team identity through vision, purpose and commitment; Foster positive and productive team communication and define ground rules; Protect the team and convert conflicts into advantages that promote high performance; Maximize your leadership abilities when you return to your organization. **Dates and Locations:** Cities throughout the United States and Toronto and Ottawa, CN.

29000 ■ Projecting a Positive Professional Image
American Management Association
600 AMA Way
Saranac Lake, NY 12983-5534
Ph: (212)586-8100
Free: 877-566-9441
Fax: (518)891-0368
Co. E-mail: customerservice@amanet.org
URL: http://www.amaseminars.org
Price: $1,895.00 for non-members; $1,795.00 for AMA members; and $1,537.00 for. **Description:** Covers creating a self-image, including look, dress, and behavior, to project a positive image in your current position and to advance to new positions. **Dates and Locations:** Washington, DC; San Francisco, CA; Atlanta, GA; Chicago, IL; and New York, NY.

29001 ■ Responding to Conflict: Creating Resolution and Cooperation (Onsite)
Seminar Information Service, Inc.
20 Executive Park, Ste. 120
Irvine, CA 92614
Ph: (949)261-9104
Free: 877-SEM-INFO
Fax: (949)261-1963
Co. E-mail: info@seminarinformation.com
URL: http://www.seminarinformation.com
Price: $2,490.00. **Description:** Learn how to: Effectively handle conflict using a powerful conflict resolution method; Anticipate the causes of conflict and respond proactively; Manage strong emotions in a conflict situation; Remove barriers to cooperation; Create productive outcomes and reach a final agreement; Embrace conflict as an opportunity for team and organizational growth. **Dates and Locations:** Toronto, CN.

29002 ■ Sparking Innovation and Creativity (Onsite)
Seminar Information Service, Inc.
20 Executive Park, Ste. 120
Irvine, CA 92614
Ph: (949)261-9104
Free: 877-SEM-INFO
Fax: (949)261-1963
Co. E-mail: info@seminarinformation.com
URL: http://www.seminarinformation.com
Price: $199.00; $189.00 for four or more. **Description:** Innovative problem-solving skills to overcome negative thinking habits within the organization to reach the company's goals and objectives. **Dates and Locations:** Cities throughout the United States.

29003 ■ Strategic Planning (Onsite) (Canada)
Canadian Management Centre (CMC)
150 York St., 5th Fl.
Toronto, ON, Canada M5H 3S5
Ph: (416)214-5678
Free: 877-262-2519
Fax: (416)313-4985
Co. E-mail: cmcinfo@cmctraining.org
URL: http://www.cmctraining.org
Contact: John Wright, President
Price: $2,395.00 Canadian for non-members; $2,195.00 Canadian for CMC members. **Description:** Covers the strategic planning process, identifying threats and opportunities for your company, and developing strategies and action plans. **Dates and Locations:** Toronto, ON.

29004 ■ Total Productive Maintenance (TPM) & 5S (Onsite)
American Trainco
9785 S Maroon Cir., Ste. 300
Englewood, CO 80112
Ph: (303)531-4560
Free: 877-978-7246
Fax: (303)531-4565
Co. E-mail: Sales@AmericanTrainco.com
URL: http://www.americantrainco.com
Price: $990.00. **Description:** Two-day seminar that focuses on getting managers, maintenance personnel and equipment users all working together to prevent equipment problems and reduce expenditures. **Dates and Locations:** Cities throughout the United States.

REFERENCE WORKS

29005 ■ "16 Creative and Cheap Ways to Say 'Thank You'" in HR Specialist (Vol. 8, September 2010, No. 9, pp. 8)
Pub: Capitol Information Group Inc.
Description: Tips for starting an employee appreciation program for a small company are presented.

29006 ■ 30 Reasons Employees Hate their Managers
Pub: AMACOM
Ed: Bruce L. Katcher. **Released:** March 2007. **Price:** $21.95. **Description:** Issues involved in employee negative feelings towards managers are discussed; a survey of more than 50,000 employees in 65 organizations of all types and sizes cited 30 main causes for ill will.

29007 ■ 30 Reasons Employees Hate Their Managers: What Your People May Be Thinking and What You Can Do About It
Pub: AMACOM
Ed: Bruce L. Katcher, with Adam Snyder. **Released:** March 7, 2007. **Price:** $21.95. **Description:** Thirty reasons why American employees are unhappy in their jobs are outlined. Each chapter is opened with a reason, an examination of how it creates work difficulties, and makes suggestions to managers on how to best address each issue.

29008 ■ "Albert Schultz" in Canadian Business (Vol. 83, August 17, 2010, No. 13-14, pp. 71)
Pub: Rogers Media Ltd.
Ed: Steve Maich. **Description:** Soulpepper Theater Company founder and actor/director Albert Schultz shares the key ingredient to his success both artisti-

cally and commercially. Schultz believes his success was a combination of passion and persistence, as well as team building. He believes his entrepreneurial impulse came when he began thinking of making opportunities instead of taking them.

29009 ■ *"All In Good Fun" in Entrepreneur (Vol. 36, May 2008, No. 5, pp. 22)*
Pub: Entrepreneur Media, Inc.
Ed: Christopher Percy Collier. **Description:** According to a study conducted in 2007, humor in the workplace helps people communicate effectively and improves camaraderie. Company leaders and entrepreneurs can also tell humorous stories about themselves, but must also set lines that should not be crossed. The humorous atmosphere in the company YouSendIt is presented.

29010 ■ *Alpha Dogs: How Your Small Business Can Become a Leader of the Pack*
Pub: HarperInformation
Ed: Donna Fenn. **Released:** May 2007. **Price:** $14.95. **Description:** Ways for an entrepreneur to outsmart competitors in the marketplace, to generate higher sales, and earn lasting customer and employee loyalty.

29011 ■ *"The Anatomy of a High Potential" in Business Strategy Review (Vol. 21, Autumn 2010, No. 3, pp. 52)*
Pub: Blackwell Publishers Ltd.
Ed: Doug Ready, Jay Conger, Linda Hill, Emily Stecker. **Description:** Companies have long been interested in identifying high potential employees, but few firms know how to convert top talent into game changers, or people who can shape the future of the business. The authors have found the 'x factors' that can make a high-potential list into a strong competitive advantage.

29012 ■ *"The Anatomy of a High Potential" in Business Strategy Review (Vol. 21, Autumn 2010, No. 3, pp. 52)*
Pub: Wiley-Blackwell
Ed: Doug Ready, Jay Conger, Linda Hill, Emily Stecker. **Description:** Companies have long been interested in identifying high-potential employees, but few firms know how to convert top talent into game changers - people who can shape the future of the business. The authors have found the x-factors that can make the high-potential list into a strong competitive advantage.

29013 ■ *"Anatomy of a Rumor" in Entrepreneur (Vol. 37, September 2009, No. 9, pp. 18)*
Pub: Entrepreneur Media, Inc.
Ed: Jason Daley. **Description:** Progression and adverse effect of office rumors on businesses are discussed. The quality of someone's work, tenure and personnel changes are the most prevalent categories of rumors. Workers can lose trust in management and one another as a result of rumors.

29014 ■ *"The Art of Appreciation" in Business Horizons (November-December 2007, pp. 441)*
Pub: Elsevier Technology Publications
Ed: Catherine M. Dalton. **Description:** The art of appreciation is an art less and less practices by employees. Employers should lead by example and practice this art to inspire employees to do the same.

29015 ■ *"The Art of the Huddle: How To Run a Prompt, Productive, and Painless Morning Meeting" in Inc. (November 2007, pp. 40, 42-43)*
Pub: Gruner & Jahr USA Publishing
Ed: Leigh Buchanan. **Description:** Five CEOs describe the ways they use meetings to improve their companies: team building, coordinating, efficiency, motivation, and strategic planning.

29016 ■ *"At Your Career Crossroads" in Women In Business (Vol. 61, December 2009, No. 6, pp. 26)*
Pub: American Business Women's Association
Ed: Diane Stafford. **Description:** Guidelines for employees who are considering a job or career change are presented. Among the reasons for lead

employees to make these changes are downsizing, job loss, environments that are not conducive to work or unfavorable work relationships with bosses.

29017 ■ *Battling Big Box: How Nimble Niche Companies Can Outmaneuver Giant Companies*
Pub: Career Press, Inc.
Ed: Henry Dubroff, Susan J. Marks. **Released:** January 1, 2009. **Price:** $15.99. **Description:** Small companies can compete with larger firms through agility, adaptability, customer service, and credibility. Topics include information to help empower employees, build a powerful brand, manage cash flow, and maintaining a business vision.

29018 ■ *Be a Brilliant Business Writer: Write Well, Write Fast, and Whip the Competition*
Pub: Crown Business Books
Ed: Jane Curry, Diana Young. **Released:** October 5, 2010. **Price:** $13.99. **Description:** Tools for mastering the art of persuasive writing in every document created, from email and client letters to reports and presentations, this book will help any writer convey their message with clarity and power, increase productivity by reducing rewrites, and provide the correct tone for navigating office politics.

29019 ■ *Big Vision, Small Business*
Pub: Ivy Sea, Inc.
Ed: Jamie S. Walters. **Released:** October 10, 2002. **Price:** $17.95. **Description:** The power of the small enterprise is examined. The author shares her expertise as an entrepreneur and founder of a business consulting firm to help small business owners successfully run their companies. Interviews with more than seventy small business owners provide insight into visioning, planning, and establishing a small company, as well as strategies for good employee and customer relationships.

29020 ■ *"Blast from the Past" in Entrepreneur (Vol. 35, November 2007, No. 11, pp. 48)*
Pub: Entrepreneur Media Inc.
Ed: Robert Kiyosaki. **Description:** Entrepreneurs of today face the challenge of creating new ideas. Collaborating with younger employees provides new perspective, but it also has to be a partnership with old ideas and sharing experiences between the older and the younger to forecast the future.

29021 ■ *"Boosting Corporate Entrepreneurship Through HRM Practices" in Human Resource Management (Vol. 49, July-August 2010, No. 4)*
Pub: John Wiley
Ed: Ralf Schmelter, Rene Mauer, Christiane Borsch, Malte Brettel. **Description:** A study was conducted to determine which human resource management (HRM) practices promote corporate entrepreneurship (CE) in small and medium-sized enterprises (SMEs). Findings indicate that staff selection, staff development, training, and staff rewards on CE have a strong impact on SMEs.

29022 ■ *"Boosting Strategy With An Online Community" in Business Strategy Review (Vol. 21, Spring 2010, No. 1, pp. 40)*
Pub: Wiley-Blackwell
Ed: Lynda Gratton, Joel Casse. **Description:** A program that merged online communities with strategic development and implementation at Nokia has provided valuable lessons about new ways employees are able to engage and interact.

29023 ■ *Bottom-Line Training: Performance-Based Results*
Pub: Training Education Management
Ed: Donald J. Ford. **Released:** June 2005. **Price:** $29.99. **Description:** Training is critical to any successful enterprise. The key to any successful training program involves defining and constantly focusing on the desired results of the program. The author provides a training model based on five phases, known as ADDIE: analysis, design, development, implementation and evaluation.

29024 ■ *"Breaking Bad: Rid Yourself of Negative Habits" in Black Enterprise (Vol. 40, July 2010, No. 12, pp. 104)*
Pub: Earl G. Graves Publishing Co. Inc.
Ed: Renita Burns. **Description:** Tardiness, procrastination, chronic complaining are among the bad habits that can make people bad employees; tips for breaking these habits are outlined.

29025 ■ *"Brief: Janitorial Company Must Pay Back Wages" in Buffalo News (September 24, 2011)*
Pub: The Buffalo News
Ed: Jonathan D. Epstein. **Description:** Knights Facilities Management, located in Michigan, provides grounds maintenance and janitorial services at the Ralph Wilson Stadium in Buffalo, New York. The US Department of Labor ordered the firm to pay $22,000 in back wages and damages to 26 employees for overtime and minimum wage compensation. Details of the company's violation of the Fair Labor Standards Act are included.

29026 ■ *"Build a Better Bonus" in Canadian Business (Vol. 80, January 15, 2007, No. 2, pp. 65)*
Pub: Rogers Media
Ed: John Gray. **Description:** The use of employee performance incentives to enhance employee productivity is discussed. Tips for employers, on how to creative an effective bonus plan, are presented.

29027 ■ *Business Upgrade: 21 Days to Reignite the Entrepreneurial Spirit in You and Your Team*
Pub: John Wiley and Sons, Inc.
Ed: Richard P. Cordock. **Released:** January 2007. **Price:** $18.95. **Description:** Business consultant works to inspire and guide entrepreneurs to spark growth in their companies while motivating workers.

29028 ■ *"Can You Hear Me Now?" in Harvard Business Review (Vol. 86, July-August 2008, No. 8, pp. 23)*
Pub: Harvard Business School Press
Ed: Katharina Pick. **Description:** Tips for improving communication among boardroom members are presented. These include encouraging frankness via in-meeting leaders, and the ability of directors to meet without managers.

29029 ■ *The Carrot Principle: How the Best Managers Use Recognition to Engage Their Employees*
Pub: Free Press
Ed: Adrian Gostick; Chester Elton. **Released:** April 2009. **Price:** $22.95. **Description:** Book show ways that managers can fail to acknowledge special achievements of employees thereby risking alienating the best workers or losing them to competing firms.

29030 ■ *"Celebrate Success. Embrace Innovation" in Black Enterprise (Vol. 37, February 2007, No. 7, pp. 145)*
Pub: Earl G. Graves Publishing Co. Inc.
Description: 2007 Women of Power Summit provides networking opportunities, empowerment sessions, and nightly entertainment. More than 500 executive women of color are expected to attend this inspiring summit in Phoenix, February 7-10.

29031 ■ *"Class Management" in Canadian Business (Vol. 80, April 23, 2007, No. 9, pp. 64)*
Pub: Rogers Media
Ed: Erin Pooley. **Description:** The role of executive MBA programs in improving performance of employees is presented.

29032 ■ *"Commitment Issues" in Workforce Management (Vol. 88, November 16, 2009, No. 12, pp. 20)*
Pub: Crain Communications Inc.
Ed: Ed Frauenheim. **Description:** Employee engagement refers to how committed workers are to their company and how much extra effort they are willing

to put in on the job; firms could find that they are having a more difficult time coming out of the recession if they lack this important feature in workplace relations.

29033 ■ "Complaints, Workforce Composition, Productivity, Organizational Values" in HRMagazine (Vol. 54, January 2009, No. 1, pp. 29)
Pub: Society for Human Resource Management
Contact: Henry G. Jackson, President
E-mail: hjackson@shrm.org
Ed: Amy Maingault, Regan Halvorsen, Rue Dooley, Liz Petersen. **Description:** Workforce composition trends that management should monitor are outlined. A goal-development process is discussed.

29034 ■ "The Consequences of Tardiness" in Modern Machine Shop (Vol. 84, August 2011, No. 3, pp. 34)
Pub: Gardner Business Media, Inc.
Contact: Richard G. Kline, President
E-mail: rkline@gardnerweb.com
Ed: Wayne S. Chaneski. **Description:** Five point addressing motivating factors behind employees who are tardy and those who choose to be on time in the workplace are shared.

29035 ■ Coolhunting
Pub: AMACOM
Ed: Peter A. Gloor; Scott W. Cooper. **Released:** June 1, 2007. **Price:** $24.95. **Description:** Lessons for unlocking and applying swarm creativity in organizations to increase creativity, productivity, and efficiency.

29036 ■ "Corporate Etiquette: The Art of Apology" in Canadian Business (Vol. 80, January 29, 2007, No. 3, pp. 62)
Pub: Rogers Media
Ed: John Gray. **Description:** The methods of nurturing professional relationships, by apologizing for the mistakes committed by individuals and institutions, are described.

29037 ■ "Corporate Responsibility" in Professional Services Close-Up (July 2, 2010)
Pub: Close-Up Media
Description: List of firms awarded the inaugural Best Corporate Citizens in Government Contracting by the Corporate Responsibility Magazine is presented. The list is based on the methodology of the Magazine's Best Corporate Citizen's List, with 324 data points of publicly-available information in seven categories which include: environment, climate change, human rights, philanthropy, employee relations, financial performance, and governance.

29038 ■ "Counting on Engagement at Ernst and Young" in Workforce Management (Vol. 88, November 16, 2009, No. 12, pp. 25)
Pub: Crain Communications Inc.
Ed: Ed Frauenheim. **Description:** Employee engagement has been difficult to maintain through the recession but firms such as Ernst & Young have found that the effort to keep their employees loyal has paid off.

29039 ■ "Crafting Kinship at Home and Work: Women Miners in Wyoming" in WorkingUSA (Vol. 11, December 2008, No. 4, pp. 439)
Pub: Blackwell Publishers Ltd.
Ed: Jessica M. Smith. **Description:** Institutional policies and social dynamics shaping women working in the northeastern Wyoming mining industry are examined. Ethnographic research suggests that the women's successful integration into this nontraditional workplace is predicated on their ability to craft and maintain kin-like social relationships in two spheres. First, women miners have addressed the challenges of managing their home and work responsibilities by cultivating networks of friends and family to care for their children while they are at work. Second, women miners craft close relationships with coworkers in what are called 'crew families'. These relationships make their work more enjoyable and the ways in which they create camaraderie prompt a reconsideration of conventional accounts of sexual harassment in the mining industry.

29040 ■ "A Crowd for the Cloud" in CIO (Vol. 24, October 2, 2010, No. 1, pp. 16)
Pub: CIO
Ed: Stephanie Overby. **Description:** Information about a project which aimed to implement a cloud-based crowdsourcing platform and innovation-management process is provided. Chubb Group of Insurance Companies wanted to mine revenue-generating ideas from its 10,400 employees and hundreds of thousands of external agents. The company hosted its first innovation event using its new system in October 2008.

29041 ■ "Cultural Due Diligence" in Canadian Business (Vol. 80, April 23, 2007, No. 9, pp. 60)
Pub: Rogers Media
Ed: Graham Lowe. **Description:** The factors to be considered by job seekers during judging good workplace with relation to corporate culture are presented.

29042 ■ "Culture Club" in Canadian Business (Vol. 79, October 9, 2006, No. 20, pp. 115)
Pub: Rogers Media
Ed: Calvin Leung. **Description:** Positive impacts of an effective corporate culture on the employees' productivity and the performance of the business are discussed.

29043 ■ "Customer Retention is Proportionate to Employee Retention" in Green Industry Pro (Vol. 23, September 2011)
Pub: Cygnus Business Media
Description: Presented in a question-answer format, information is provided to help retain customers as well as keeping workers happy.

29044 ■ Cute Little Store: Between the Entrepreneurial Dream and Business Reality
Pub: Outskirts Press, Incorporated
Ed: Adeena Mignogna. **Released:** May 2006. **Price:** $11.95. **Description:** Challenges of starting and growing a retail business are profiled.

29045 ■ "Deep Thoughts: Getting Employees to Think Better Requires a Bit of Creative Thinking Itself" in Canadian Business (March 17, 2008)
Pub: Rogers Media
Ed: Lauren McKeon. **Description:** Discusses the reason a company needs to make their employees understand that ideas are the stuff of life. For employees to be more creative, they need to cultivate spark moments, play with possibilities, and venture into the unknown.

29046 ■ "Demystifying Demotion" in Business Horizons (November-December 2007, pp. 455)
Pub: Elsevier Technology Publications
Ed: Paula Phillips Carson, Kerry David Carson. **Description:** A model of employee demotion is developed after conducting personal interviews with more than 20 demotees. The effects of demotion, such as economic harm, lower well-being, underemployment, and grief reactions and identity crises are studied.

29047 ■ Design Your Own Effective Employee Handbook: How to Make the Most of Your Staff with Companion CD-ROM
Pub: Atlantic Publishing Company
Ed: Michelle Devon. **Released:** June 2006. **Price:** $39.95. **Description:** An employee handbook should include clearly written policies covering the rights and responsibilities of workers.

29048 ■ "Desk-Bound No More" in Charlotte Business Journal (Vol. 25, August 13, 2010, No. 21, pp. 1)
Pub: Charlotte Business Journal
Ed: Adam O' Daniel. **Description:** Bank of America has launched a program that encourages employees to work on their own schedules. The program encourages productivity and health work-life balance. A survey has also revealed that employees feel more productive under the program.

29049 ■ "Dirty Work Required" in Workforce Management (Vol. 88, November 16, 2009, No. 12, pp. 34)
Pub: Crain Communications Inc.
Ed: John Hollon. **Description:** Due to salary freezes, pay cuts, layoffs, buyouts and a number of other stress factors brought about by the recession, employee engagement has been difficult to maintain by managers.

29050 ■ "Discount Shopping: Holiday Shopping Meets Social Media" in Employee Benefit News (Vol. 25, December 1, 2011, No. 15)
Pub: SourceMedia Inc.
Ed: Rob J. Thurston. **Description:** Offering employees access to discount shopping using social media sites for Christmas bonuses, could be the gift that keeps on giving.

29051 ■ "Do Something!" in Entrepreneur (Vol. 36, March 2008, No. 3, pp. 79)
Pub: Entrepreneur Media Inc.
Ed: Chris Penttila. **Description:** Employers are addressing the cause of employee stress by adjusting work structure. Some of the actions taken to tackle the concern include examples such as the eCast executive having quick one-on-one talks with employees and GlaxoSmithKlline employees taking online stress assessment. Other details on reducing job/employee stress are discussed.

29052 ■ "Does Rudeness Really Matter?" in Academy of Management Journal (October 2007, pp. 1181)
Pub: Academy of Management
Contact: Ming-Jer Chen, President
Ed: Christine L. Porath, Amir Erez. **Description:** Study assessing the effect of impoliteness on performance and helpfulness showed rude behavior lowered performance levels and also decreased attitude of helpfulness.

29053 ■ "The Don't Do Lists" in Inc. (Vol. 33, October 2011, No. 8, pp. 65)
Pub: Inc. Magazine
Ed: Jennifer Alsever, Adam Bluestein. **Description:** Ten business leaders and experts share their don't do lists, the things that should be avoided when going on sales calls, planning business lunches, motivating employees and more are presented.

29054 ■ "Don't Leave Employees on the Outside Looking In" in Canadian Business (Vol. 83, July 20, 2010, No. 11-12, pp. 13)
Pub: Rogers Media Ltd.
Ed: Richard Branson. **Description:** Managers should be careful with employee's tendencies to use the word 'they' when problems occur since this shows that employees are not associating themselves with their company. Employees should be involved in the development of the company and improving the flow of information is important in overcoming this communication challenge.

29055 ■ "Downturn Tests HCL's Pledge to Employees" in Workforce Management (Vol. 88, November 16, 2009, No. 12, pp. 23)
Pub: Crain Communications Inc.
Ed: Ed Frauenheim. **Description:** HCL Technologies has kept its promise to keep from laying any employees off during the recession which served as a test for the tech firm's Employee First program, which seeks to give workers greater income security as well as a stronger voice in the firm.

29056 ■ The Dream Manager
Pub: Hyperion
Ed: Matthew Kelly. **Price:** $19.95. **Description:** A business fable about the virtues of helping those working for and with you to achieve their dreams. Managers can boost morale and control turnover by adopting this policy.

29057 ■ "The Dynamic DUO" in Canadian Electronics (Vol. 23, February 2008, No. 1, pp. 24)
Pub: CLB Media Inc.
Description: Citronics Corporation not only aims to proved a good working environment for its employees, it also values the opinions of its personnel. Cit-

ronics had its employees test different workbenches before finally purchasing thirty-five of Lista's Align adjustable height workstation, which combines flexibility with aesthetics. The design of the Alin workbench is described.

29058 ■ *"The Employee Brand: Is Yours an All-Star?" in Business Horizons (September-October 2007, pp. 423)*
Pub: Elsevier Technology Publications
Ed: W. Glynn Mangold, Sandra Jeanquart Miles. **Description:** Employees can influence the brand image either positively or negatively. The typology presented provides guidelines on how employees can reflect a company's brand image. Classifications of organizations into all-star rookies, injured reserves, or strike-out kings are also discussed.

29059 ■ *"Employee Motivation: A Powerful New Model" in Harvard Business Review (Vol. 86, July-August 2008, No. 8, pp. 78)*
Pub: Harvard Business School Press
Ed: Nitin Nohria; Boris Groysbert; Linda Eling Lee. **Description:** Four drives underlying employee motivation are discussed as well as processes for leveraging these drives through corporate culture, job design, reward systems, and resource-allocation priorities.

29060 ■ *"Empowered" in Harvard Business Review (Vol. 88, July-August 2010, No. 7-8, pp. 94)*
Pub: Harvard Business School Publishing
Ed: Josh Bernoff, Ted Schadler. **Description:** HERO concept (highly empowered and resourceful operative) which builds a connection between employees, managers, and IT is outlined. The resultant additional experience and knowledge gained by employees improves customer relationship management.

29061 ■ *"The End of Clock-Punching" in Canadian Business (Vol. 83, September 14, 2010, No. 15, pp. 96)*
Pub: Rogers Media Ltd.
Ed: Lyndsie Bourgon. **Description:** Workplace consultant Peter Hadwen is pushing for the transformation of Canada's government departments into results-only work environments (ROWE). ROWE does not require employees to show up to work at a certain time as long as they are meeting goals and achieving results in their jobs. Details of studies regarding ROWE in US companies are examined.

29062 ■ *Enlightened Leadership: Best Practice Guidelines and Timesaving Tools for Easily Implementing Learning Organizations*
Pub: Learning House Publishing, Incorporated
Ed: Alan G. Thomas; Ralph L. LoVuolo; Jeanne C. Hillson. **Released:** September 2006, printable 3 times/year. **Price:** $21.00. **Description:** Book provides the tools required to create a learning organization management model along with a step-by-step guide for team planning and learning. The strategy works as a manager's self-help guide as well as offering continuous learning and improvement for company-wide success.

29063 ■ *"Entrepreneurial Human Resource Leadership" in Human Resource Management (Vol. 49, July-August 2010, No. 4, pp. 793-804)*
Pub: John Wiley
Ed: David C. Strubler, Benjamin W. Redekop. **Description:** Dwight Carlson, a visionary entrepreneur, talks about his main role as a leader. He believes that experience can help in making choices between difficult alternatives. He also thinks that leaders do not really motivate people, they actually create an environment where they motivate themselves.

29064 ■ *"Facilitating and Rewarding Creativity During New Product Development" in Journal of Marketing (Vol. 75, July 2011, No. 4, pp. 53)*
Pub: American Marketing Association
Ed: James E. Burroughs, Darren W. Dahl, C. Page Moreau, Amitava Chattopadhay, Gerald J. Gorn. **Description:** A study to determine the effects of rewards to creativity in the process of new product develop-

ment is presented. The findings show that the effect of rewards can be made positive if combined with appropriate creativity training.

29065 ■ *"Feeling the Heat: Effects of Stress, Commitment, and Job Experience On Job Performance" in Academy of Management Journal (Aug. 2007)*
Pub: Academy of Management
Contact: Ming-Jer Chen, President
Ed: Larry W. Hunter, Sherry M.B. Thatcher. **Description:** Links between bank branch employees' felt job stress, organizational commitment, job experience, and performance is analyzed. Results found are uniform with the attention view of stress.

29066 ■ *The Five Dysfunctions of a Team: A Leadership Fable*
Pub: John Wiley & Sons, Incorporated
Ed: Patrick M. Lencioni. **Released:** April 2002. **Price:** $22.95. **Description:** Analysis of a hypothetical tale of the CEO of a struggling, high-profile firm with a dysfunctional executive team.

29067 ■ *"Five Steps to an Effective Meeting" in Hawaii Business (Vol. 53, March 2008, No. 9, pp. 55)*
Pub: Hawaii Business Publishing
Ed: Jason Ubay. **Description:** Identifying goals and writing them down can help in knowing what needs get done. Engaging everyone is a way to get cooperation in reaching the goals set. Other tips on how to have an effective meeting are discussed.

29068 ■ *"Forward Motion" in Green Industry Pro (July 2011)*
Pub: Cygnus Business Media
Ed: Gregg Wartgow. **Description:** Several landscape contractors have joined this publication's Working Smarter Training Challenge over the last year. This process is helping them develop ways to improve work processes, boost morale, drive out waste, reduce costs, improve customer service, and be more competitive.

29069 ■ *"Gain the 'Come Alive Outside' Selling Edge" in Green Industry Pro (July 2011)*
Pub: Cygnus Business Media
Ed: Jim Paluch. **Description:** Marketing the 'Come Alive Outside' slogan can help landscapers to increase their market share by identifying and applying these elements to each customer as well as their workers.

29070 ■ *The Game-Changer: How Every Leader Can Drive Everyday Innovation*
Pub: Crown Business
Ed: A.G. Lafley, Ram Charan. **Price:** $27.50. **Description:** Management guru Charan and Proctor & Gamble CEO Lafley provide lessons to encourage innovation at all levels, including how to hire for and encourage an environment of communication and tangible work processes.

29071 ■ *"Get Your Mojo Working" in Small Business Opportunities (March 2011)*
Pub: Harris Publications Inc.
Ed: Holly G. Green. **Description:** Ways to keep employees engaged and productive are discussed.

29072 ■ *"Getting Drowned Out by the Brainstorm" in Canadian Business (Vol. 83, June 15, 2010, No. 10, pp. 91)*
Pub: Rogers Media Ltd.
Ed: Joe Castaldo. **Description:** A study reveals that people generate more ideas when they do it alone rather than as part of a brainstorming group. The limited range of ideas is due to the fixation of group members on the first idea that gets offered.

29073 ■ *The Girl's Guide to Building a Million-Dollar Business*
Pub: AMACOM
Ed: Susan Wilson Solovic. **Released:** 2008. **Price:** $21.95. **Description:** Success plan for women business owners; the book includes tips for determination, managing changing relationships, keeping

employees and customers happy, getting and maintaining credit, overcoming gender bias, and creating a good business plan and solid brand.

29074 ■ *Go Put Your Strengths to Work*
Pub: Free Press/Simon & Schuster
Ed: Marcus Buckingham. **Price:** $30.00. **Description:** A guide to being more productive, focused and creative at work.

29075 ■ *"Go Team? Why Building a Cohesive Organization Is a Necessary Exercise" in Black Enterprise (Vol. 38, February 2008, No. 7, pp. 56)*
Pub: Earl G. Graves Publishing Co. Inc.
Ed: Angeli Rasbury. **Description:** Tips to help manage successful as well as productive teams are outlined for small business managers.

29076 ■ *"Good Decisions. Bad Outcomes" in Harvard Business Review (Vol. 88, December 2010, No. 12, pp. 40)*
Pub: Harvard Business School Publishing
Ed: Dan Ariely. **Description:** Suggestions are provided for developing and implementing improved reward systems that in turn produce better decision-making processes. These include documenting critical assumptions and changing mind sets.

29077 ■ *Group Genius: The Creative Power of Collaboration*
Pub: Basic Books/Perseus Books Group
Ed: Keith Sawyer. **Released:** March 2008. **Price:** $16.95 paperback. **Description:** Organizations can foster creativity and innovation through discussion, argumentation and group activities.

29078 ■ *"Group Learning" in Academy of Management Review (October 2007, pp. 1041)*
Pub: ScholarOne, Inc.
Ed: Jeanne M. Wilson, Paul S. Goodman, Matthew A. Cronin. **Description:** The processes that constitute group learning in order to undertake necessary modifications are covered.

29079 ■ *"Growing Pains" in Canadian Business (Vol. 80, November 19, 2007, No. 23, pp. 41)*
Pub: Rogers Media
Ed: Lauren McKeon. **Description:** Employee promotions must be done with consideration to the effects of ill-prepared leadership, which include high worker turnover, low morale, and ineffective management. Organizations must handle the transition period involved in promotion by setting clear expectations, providing guidelines on approaching different situations, and by welcoming the promoted employees; impacts are further analyzed.

29080 ■ *"He Said, She Said: Stay Clear of Gossip in the Workplace With a Mature Attitude" in Black Enterprise (February 2008)*
Pub: Earl G. Graves Publishing Co. Inc.
Ed: Akotc Ofori-Atta. **Description:** It is important for employees to avoid gossip in the workplace because of the negative impact; it is recommended focusing on conversations that will help an individual's professional goals.

29081 ■ *"Health Nuts and Bolts" in Entrepreneur (Vol. 36, April 2008, No. 4, pp. 24)*
Pub: Entrepreneur Media, Inc.
Ed: Jacquelyn Lynn. **Description:** Encouraging employees to develop good eating habits can promote productivity at work. Ways on how to improve employee eating habits include employers setting a good example themselves and offering employees healthy options. Other details about the topic are discussed.

29082 ■ *"Help Employees Give Away Some Of That Bonus" in Harvard Business Review (Vol. 86, July-August 2008, No. 8, pp. 1)*
Pub: Harvard Business School Press
Ed: Michael I. Norton; Elizabeth W. Dunn. **Description:** Research indicates that how employees spend their bonuses is key to their resultant happiness,

rather than simply receiving the bonus itself. Firms that offer donation options can thereby increase employee satisfaction.

29083 ■ "The Hidden Advantages of Quiet Bosses" in Harvard Business Review (Vol. 88, December 2010, No. 12, pp. 28)
Pub: Harvard Business School Publishing

Ed: Adam M. Grant, Francesca Gino, David A. Hofmann. **Description:** Research on organizations behavior indicates that, while extroverts most often become managers, introvert managers paired with proactive employees make a highly efficient and effective combination.

29084 ■ "High Octane Team Building: Adventure Spas for Office Retreats" in Inc. (Vol. 33, September 2011, No. 7, pp. 54)
Pub: Inc. Magazine

Ed: Adam Baer. **Description:** Adventure spas offer plush accommodations for hosting team-building activities. The Resort at PAWS UP, Topnotch Resort and Spa, Dunton Hot Springs and Miraval Resort and Spa are among the retreats revealed.

29085 ■ "HireDiversity: Some Companies Developing Affinity for Employee Groups" in Hispanic Business (October 2007, pp. 86-87)
Pub: Hispanic Business

Ed: Hildy Medina. **Description:** Affinity groups, also known as employee resource networks, help companies identify and recruit candidates.

29086 ■ "Holidays Should Foster Mutual Respect" in Women In Business (Vol. 61, October-November 2009, No. 5, pp. 33)
Pub: American Business Women's Association

Ed: Diane Stafford. **Description:** Workplaces have modified the way year-end holiday celebrations are held in an effort to promote mutual respect. The workers' varying religious beliefs, political affiliations, and other differences have brought about the modifications. The importance of developing mutual understanding is emphasized as a mechanism to stimulate successful business ties.

29087 ■ How to Become a Great Boss: The Rules for Getting and Keeping the Best Employees
Pub: Hyperion Special Markets

Ed: Jeffrey J. Fox. **Released:** May 15, 2002. **Price:** $16.95. **Description:** The book offers valuable advice to any manager or entrepreneur to improve leadership and management skills. Topics covered include: hiring, managing, firing, partnership and competition, self and organization, employee performance, attitude, and priorities.

29088 ■ "How to Divorce Your Office Spouse" in Canadian Business (Vol. 83, June 15, 2010, No. 10, pp. 74)
Pub: Rogers Media Ltd.

Ed: Jacqueline Nelson. **Description:** A work spouse or the platonic relationship between male and female coworkers can increase productivity in some cases, but these friendships can become complicated due to power struggles and sexual tension. When this type of relationship goes sour, it is advised to tell the spouse honestly how you feel.

29089 ■ "How the Generation Gap Can Hurt Your Business" in Agency Sales Magazine (Vol. 39, November 2009, No. 10, pp. 16)
Pub: MANA

Ed: Jack Foster. **Description:** Now that there are four generations of people in the workplace, there is a need to add flexibility to communications for independent manufacturers representatives. Managers can encourage the younger generations to do the research and the boomers to process information and let each side report to the other.

29090 ■ "How Pixar Fosters Collective Creativity" in Harvard Business Review (Vol. 86, September 2008, No. 9, pp. 64)
Pub: Harvard Business School Press

Ed: Ed Catmull. **Description:** Pixar Animation Studios illustrates peer-culture methods for fostering product development. These include allowing any

employee to communicate with any other employee, providing a safe environment for new ideas, and watching the academic community closely for innovations.

29091 ■ "How to Protect Your Job in a Recession" in Harvard Business Review (Vol. 86, September 2008, No. 9, pp. 113)
Pub: Harvard Business School Press

Ed: Janet Banks; Diane Coutu. **Description:** Strategies are presented for enhancing one's job security. These include being a team player, empathizing with management, preserving optimism, and concentrating on the customer.

29092 ■ How to Recognize and Reward Employees: 150 Ways to Inspire Peak Performance
Pub: American Management Association

Contact: Charles R. Craig, Chairman

Ed: Donna Deeprose. **Released:** 2006. **Price:** $13.95.

29093 ■ "How To Turn Your Efforts Into Results" in Green Industry Pro (Vol. 23, September 2011)
Pub: Cygnus Business Media

Ed: Bob Coulter. **Description:** Working Smarter Training Challenge teaches that leaders are able to carry out solutions directly into their organization, develop skills and drive business results in key areas by creating a culture of energized workers who are able to take ownership of their performance as well as the performance of the company as a whole.

29094 ■ "How to Turn Employee Conflict Into a Positive, Productive Force" in HR Specialist (Vol. 8, September 2010, No. 9, pp. 6)
Pub: Capitol Information Group Inc.

Description: Ways to help manage a team of workers are presented, focusing on ways to avoid conflict within the group are discussed.

29095 ■ "Hunter and the Hunted" in Canadian Business (Vol. 81, Summer 2008, No. 9, pp. 12)
Pub: Rogers Media Ltd.

Ed: Thomas Watson. **Description:** Brian Hunter, a partner in oil and gas engineering firm Montane Resources, invested his life savings in Vancouver-based Canacord Capital Corp. Details of the asset-backed commercial paper fiasco and Hunter's use of Facebook to encourage other investors to participate in his claim against the mortgage company are presented.

29096 ■ "Inside the Googleplex" in Canadian Business (Vol. 79, November 6, 2006, No. 22, pp. 59)
Pub: Rogers Media

Ed: Christina Campbell. **Description:** The views of Clive Wilkinson, a designer, on relationship between interior design and employee's productivity are presented.

29097 ■ "Into the Wild" in Inc. (October 2007, pp. 116-120, 122, 124, 126)
Pub: Gruner & Jahr USA Publishing

Ed: Alison Stein Wellner. **Description:** Perry Klebahn, CEO of Timbuk2, manufacturer of messenger bags, tells how he took his top executives into the deep Wyoming wilderness in order to build employee team work skills. Other options for this type of team-building include cooking courses, changing a tire together, solving a kidnapping, or discussing ways to survive a nuclear winter.

29098 ■ "Is the Generation Gap Gone?" in Agency Sales Magazine (Vol. 39, November 2009, No. 10, pp. 3)
Pub: MANA

Ed: Bryan C. Shirley. **Description:** Four generations are working side-by-side in the workplace for the first time in history and this is a big opportunity to get different perspectives and views on life. In the sales representatives business, there is a need to better understand the upcoming generations and understand their specific abilities to their risk/reward business.

29099 ■ "It's Not 'Unprofessional' To Gossip At Work" in Harvard Business Review (Vol. 88, September 2010, No. 9, pp. 28)
Pub: Harvard Business School Publishing

Ed: Joe Labianca. **Description:** Gossip can be of value to a company as an exchange of information and its use as a diagnostic tool can enable managers to address problems promptly and even head them off.

29100 ■ It's Your Ship
Pub: Warner Books Inc.

Ed: Michael Abrashoff. **Released:** May 1, 2002. **Price:** $24.95. **Description:** Naval Captain D. Michael Abrashoff shares management principles he used to shape his ship, the U.S.S. Benfold, into a model of progressive leadership. Abrashoff revolutionized ways to face the challenges of excessive costs, low morale, sexual harassment, and constant turnover.

29101 ■ "Junior Executives Need Hugs Too" in Canadian Business (Vol. 83, October 12, 2010, No. 17, pp. 87)
Pub: Rogers Media Ltd.

Ed: James Cowan. **Description:** Psychology professor Mark Frame believes that sensitive men fail to meet perceptions of how a chief executive officer (CEO) should act. The results of a study show that communal qualities are highly valued in first-line and middle managers, but these qualities become less important when employees move closer to senior executive roles.

29102 ■ "Just Shut The Hell Up" in Canadian Business (Vol. 81, July 22, 2008, No. 12-13, pp. 33)
Pub: Rogers Media Ltd.

Ed: Jane Bao. **Description:** Employees desire better communication as opposed to more communication from their managers. Advice regarding managing communication in the workplace is given including ways in which speakers can say more with fewer words.

29103 ■ "Labor and Management: Working Together for a Stable Future" in Alaska Business Monthly (Vol. 27, October 2011, No. 10, pp. 130)
Pub: Alaska Business Publishing Company

Ed: Nicole A. Bonham Colby. **Description:** Alaska unions and employers are working to ensure a consistent flow of skilled Alaska workers as current the current workforce reaches retirement age.

29104 ■ "Leadership in Flight" in Women In Business (Vol. 63, Fall 2011, No. 3, pp. 24)
Pub: American Business Women's Association

Ed: Leigh Elmore. **Description:** Flight attendants in major airlines are trained to keep passengers comfortable and to calmly deal with emergencies. They also have a significant role in brand image and customer loyalty as they interact with the customers directly. Examples of teamwork leadership for flight attendants are given.

29105 ■ "Leadership Training" in Black Enterprise (Vol. 37, January 2007, No. 6, pp. 56)
Pub: Earl G. Graves Publishing Co. Inc.

Ed: Sonia Alleyne. **Description:** Profile of Theopolis Holman, Group Vice-President of Duke Energy, who discusses how he prepared for the merger between Duke Energy and Cinergy. Holman oversees a division of 9,000 service contractors and employees.

29106 ■ Leading at a Higher Level
Pub: FT Press

Ed: Ken Blanchard. **Released:** November 2006. **Price:** $26.99. **Description:** Tips, advice and techniques from a management consultant to help entrepreneurs create a vision for their company; includes information on manager-employee relationships.

29107 ■ "Lessons from Turnaround Leaders" in Strategy and Leadership (Vol. 39, May-June 2011, No. 3, pp. 36-43)
Pub: Emerald Group Publishing Inc.

Ed: David P. Boyd. **Description:** A study analyzes the cases of some successful turnaround leaders to present a strategic model to help firms tackle challenges such as employee inertia, competition and slow organizational renewal. It describes a change model consisting of five major steps to be followed by firms with environmental uncertainty for the purpose.

29108 ■ "Let the Insults Fly: Want to Learn What Your Employees Really Think?" in Inc. (Vol. 33, October 2011, No. 8, pp. 36)
Pub: Inc. Magazine
Ed: Jason Fried. **Description:** A company that hosts a Comedy Central-style celebrity roast of its top-selling product was able to improve their business.

29109 ■ "Let's Go Team: When a Retail Professional Leads by Example, Everyone Benefits" in Black Enterprise (Vol. 41, November 2010, No. 4)
Pub: Earl G. Graves Publishing Co. Inc.
Ed: Aisha I. Jefferson. **Description:** Profile of Derek Jenkins, senior vice president of Target Stores Northeast Region is presented. Jenkins oversees the management of 450 retail stores with nearly 75,000 workers. He shares insight into managing by making sure every interaction with his team counts.

29110 ■ "Life's Work: Ben Bradlee" in Harvard Business Review (Vol. 88, September 2010, No. 9, pp. 128)
Pub: Harvard Business School Publishing
Ed: Alison Beard. **Description:** Newspaper publisher Ben Bradlee discusses factors that lead to success, including visible supervisors, enthusiasm, appropriate expansion, and the importance in truth in reporting.

29111 ■ "Making Diverse Teams Click" in Harvard Business Review (Vol. 86, July-August 2008, No. 8, pp. 20)
Pub: Harvard Business School Press
Ed: Jeffrey T. Polzer. **Description:** 360-degree feedback to increase the efficacy of diverse-member workplace teams, which involves each member providing feedback to the others on the team is discussed.

29112 ■ Management Rewired: Why Feedback Doesn't Work and Other Surprising Lessons from the Latest Brain Science
Pub: Portfolio
Ed: Charles S. Jacobs. **Released:** 2009. **Price:** $25.95. **Description:** According to the author, human psychology works better than feedback, praise or criticism when managing employees.

29113 ■ "Managerial Rudeness: Bad Attitudes Can Demoralize Your Staff" in Black Enterprise (Vol. 37, January 2007, No. 6, pp. 58)
Pub: Earl G. Graves Publishing Co. Inc.
Ed: Chauntelle Folds. **Description:** Positive leadership in the managerial realm leads to a more productive workplace. Managers who are negative, hostile, arrogant, rude or fail to accept any responsibility for their own mistakes find that employees will not give their all on the job.

29114 ■ The Manager's Guide to Rewards: What You Need to Know to Get the Best of-and-from-Your Employees
Pub: American Management Association
Contact: Charles R. Craig, Chairman
Ed: Doug Jensen; Tom McMullen; Mel Stark. **Released:** 2006. **Price:** $24.95.

29115 ■ "Managing Corporate Social Networks" in Harvard Business Review (Vol. 86, July-August 2008, No. 8, pp. 26)
Pub: Harvard Business School Press
Ed: Adam M. Kleinbaum; Michael L. Tushman. **Description:** Tips on how to promote business creativity and foster knowledge building through business social networks are given.

29116 ■ Managing the Older Worker: How to Prepare for the New Organizational Order
Pub: Harvard Business Press
Ed: Peter Cappelli, Bill Novelli. **Price:** $29.95. **Description:** Your organization needs older workers more than ever: They transfer knowledge between

generations, transmit your company's values to new hires, make excellent mentors for younger employees, and provide a 'just in time' workforce for special projects.

29117 ■ "The Mobile Workforce Revolution" in Canadian Business (Vol. 81, March 31, 2008, No. 5, pp. 28)
Pub: Rogers Media
Ed: Diane Horton. **Description:** Diane Horton explains how a mobile workforce helps companies cut costs, increase productivity, and boost employee motivation. Horton says that employees believe they usually become more productive by 15 to 30 percent after their companies go mobile.

29118 ■ "Monitor Work Productivity" in Business Owner (Vol. 35, July-August 2011, No. 4, pp. 4)
Pub: DL Perkins Company
Description: Tips for tracking employee productivity are explained.

29119 ■ "The Moody Blues" in Entrepreneur (Vol. 36, April 2008, No. 4, pp. 87)
Pub: Entrepreneur Media, Inc.
Ed: Mark Henricks. **Description:** Depression among employees can affect their productivity and cost the company. Businesses with a workforce that is likely to have depression should inform their employees about the health benefits covered by insurance. Other details on how to address depression concerns among employees are discussed.

29120 ■ "More Important than Results" in Business Strategy Review (Vol. 21, Summer 2010, No. 2, pp. 81)
Pub: Blackwell Publishers Ltd.
Ed: Bert De Reyck, Zeger Degraeve. **Description:** Managing only for results leads to crises. It is important to reward people for the decisions they make, not just for the results they create.

29121 ■ "More Important than Results" in Business Strategy Review (Vol. 21, Summer 2010, No. 2, pp. 81)
Pub: Wiley-Blackwell
Ed: Bert De Reyck, Zeger Degraeve. **Description:** Managing only for results leads to crises. Reward people for decisions they make, not just for the results they create.

29122 ■ More Than a Pink Cadillac
Pub: McGraw-Hill
Ed: Jim Underwood. **Released:** 2002. **Price:** $23.95. **Description:** Profile of Mary Kay Ash who turned her $5,000 investment into a billion-dollar corporation. Ash's nine principles that form the foundation of her company's global success are outlined. Stories from her sales force leaders share ideas for motivating employees, impressing customers and building a successful company. The book emphasizes the leadership skills required to drive performance in any successful enterprise.

29123 ■ "Negotiating Tips" in Black Enterprise (Vol. 37, December 2006, No. 5, pp. 70)
Pub: Earl G. Graves Publishing Co. Inc.
Description: Sekou Kaalund, head of strategy, mergers & acquisitions at Citigroup Securities & Fund Services, states that 'Negotiation skills are paramount to success in a business environment because of client, employee, and shareholder relationships'. He discusses how the book by George Kohlrieser, Hostage at the Table: How Leaders Can Overcome Conflict, Influence Others, and Raise Performance, has helped him negotiate more powerfully and enhance his skills at conflict-resolution.

29124 ■ "A New Challenge Facing Reps: The Generation Gap!" in Agency Sales Magazine (Vol. 39, November 2009, No. 10, pp. 9)
Pub: MANA
Ed: Roger Ralston. **Description:** Different generations in the workplace is one of the many drivers of change that reps are facing today. Pre-boomers and boomers historically put work first while Gen-Xers

and Millennials think lifestyle before work. A sales rep should listen and learn, while providing a strong sense of flexibility in this environment.

29125 ■ "The Next 20 Years: How Customer and Workforce Attitudes Will Evolve" in Harvard Business Review (Vol. 85, July-August 2007, No. 7-8)
Pub: Harvard Business School Publishing
Ed: Neil Howe, William Strauss. **Description:** Identification of social categories inhabited by age groups is used to calculate how consumer and employee opinions and behavior will change, and how this will impact economic development and corporate growth.

29126 ■ "Nine Paradoxes of Problem Solving" in Strategy and Leadership (Vol. 39, May-June 2011, No. 3, pp. 25-31)
Pub: Emerald Group Publishing Inc.
Ed: Alex Lowy. **Description:** Nine frequently-occurring inherent paradoxes in corporate decision making for solving complex problems are identified. The methods with which these paradoxes and their influence can be recognized and dealt with for firm leaders and management team members to better understand and solve the problems are discussed.

29127 ■ The No Asshole Rule
Pub: Warner Books Inc.
Ed: Robert I. Sutton PhD. **Released:** February 22, 2007. **Price:** $22.99. **Description:** Problem employees are more than just a nuisance they are a serious and costly threat to corporate success and employee health.

29128 ■ "No Secrets; Businesses Find It Pays to Open Books to Employees" in Crain's Detroit Business (Vol. 26, January 18, 2010, No. 3)
Pub: Crain Communications Inc.
Ed: Dustin Walsh. **Description:** Many businesses are finding that practicing an open-book management wherein employees share financial and decision-making duties that are usually left up to executives of firms creates a transparency within a company that eliminates the us versus them mentality between management and employees. Another benefit to this business model is that employees get to really participate in the business, learning to manage money and run a business entity.

29129 ■ "Not Just for Kids: ADHD can be Debilitating for an Employee, and Frustrating for Bosses" in Canadian Business (April 14, 2008)
Pub: Rogers Media
Ed: Andy Holloway. **Description:** Up to four percent of North American adults continue to feel the effects of Attention Deficit Hyperactivity Disorder or Attention Deficit Disorder. Explaining the value of the task at hand to people who are afflicted with these conditions is one way to keep them engaged in the workplace. Giving them opportunities to create their own working structure is another strategy to manage these people.

29130 ■ Now, Discover Your Strengths
Pub: Free Press/Simon & Schuster
Ed: Marcus Buckingham; Donald O. Clifton. **Price:** $30.00. **Description:** How to identify and develop your talents and those of your employees.

29131 ■ "The Office: Good to Great" in Inc. (October 2007, pp. 140)
Pub: Gruner & Jahr USA Publishing
Ed: Leigh Buchanan. **Description:** Qualities that make a good manager great are explored. Great bosses make their employees feel smart, they know who performs what job, know when to step back, and remember things about each employee such as their families' names.

29132 ■ One Foot Out the Door: How to Combat the Psychological Recession That's Alienating Employees and Hurting American Business
Pub: AMACOM
Ed: Judith M. Bardwick. **Released:** October 31, 2007. **Price:** $24.95. **Description:** Drawing on research that indicates Generation X and younger baby

boomers feel disconnected from their jobs, the author explores the causes (bad management) of that disengagement. Her pragmatic suggestions about how companies can prove their commitment to employees is beneficial.

29133 ■ The One Minute Entrepreneur
Pub: Doubleday

Ed: Ken Blanchard; assisted by Don Hutson and Ethan Willis. **Released:** 2008. **Price:** $19.95. **Description:** Four traditional business ideas are covered including: revenue needs to exceed expenses, bill collection, customer service, and employee motivation in order to be successful.

29134 ■ The Orange Revolution
Pub: Free Press

Ed: Adrian Gostick, Chester Elton. **Released:** September 21, 2010. **Price:** $25.00. **Description:** Based on a 350,000-person study by the Best Companies Group, as well as research into exceptional teams at leading companies, including Zappos.com, Pepsi Beverages Company, and Madison Square Garden, the authors have determined a key set of characteristics displayed by members of breakthrough teams, and have identified a set of rules great teams live by, which generate a culture of positive teamwork and led to extraordinary results. Using specific stories from the teams they studied, they reveal in detail how these teams operate and how managers can transform their own teams into such high performers by fostering: stronger clarity of goals, greater trust among team members, more open and honest dialogue, stronger accountability for all team members, and purpose-based recognition of team member contributions.

29135 ■ Our Iceberg is Melting
Pub: St. Martin's Press

Contact: Sally Richardson, President

E-mail: sally.richardson@stmartins.com

Ed: John Kotter; Holger Rathgeber. **Released:** September 2006. **Price:** $19.95. **Description:** A fable about how to bring about change in a group.

29136 ■ "The Outcome of an Organization Overhaul" in Black Enterprise (Vol. 41, December 2010, No. 5)
Pub: Earl G. Graves Publishing Co. Inc.

Ed: Tamara E. Holmes. **Description:** Savvy business owners understand the need for change in order to stay competitive and be successful. This article examines how to manage change as well as what strategies can help employees to get with the program faster.

29137 ■ Overcoming the Five Dysfunctions of a Team: A Field Guide for Leaders, Manager, and Facilitators
Pub: John Wiley and Sons, Inc.

Ed: Patrick M. Lencioni. **Released:** March 2005. **Price:** $26.95. **Description:** Tools, exercises, assessment, and real-world examples for overcoming the five dysfunctions of a team.

29138 ■ "Pay or Play: Do Nice (Sales) Guys Finish Last?" in Agency Sales Magazine (Vol. 39, August 2009, No. 8, pp. 8)
Pub: MANA

Ed: Julia M. Rahn. **Description:** How positive interpersonal relationships among salespersons, program coordinators, and other business-related professions will pay in terms of business success is presented. Business people should know the ideal customers, promise only what they can do, refer out when needed, and follow through with any stated promise. Further insight into these ideas is presented.

29139 ■ "Pep Talk" in Black Enterprise (Vol. 40, July 2010, No. 12, pp. 104)
Pub: Earl G. Graves Publishing Co. Inc.

Ed: Tennille M. Robinson. **Description:** Advice for maintaining motivation in any small business is given.

29140 ■ "Positive Social Interactions and the Human Body at Work" in Academy of Management Review (January 2008, pp. 137)
Pub: ScholarOne, Inc.

Ed: Emily D. Heaphy, Jane E. Dutton. **Description:** Research is recommended for the manner in which positive social interactions in organizational contexts can influence employees' health and physiological resourcefulness.

29141 ■ "Power Play" in Harvard Business Review (Vol. 88, July-August 2010, No. 7-8, pp. 84)
Pub: Harvard Business School Publishing

Ed: Jeffrey Pfeffer. **Description:** Guidelines include in-depth understanding of resources at one's disposal, relentlessness that still provides opponents with opportunities to save face, and a determination not to be put off by the processes of politics.

29142 ■ "Powerlessness Corrupts" in Harvard Business Review (Vol. 88, July-August 2010, No. 7-8, pp. 36)
Pub: Harvard Business School Publishing

Ed: Rosabeth Moss Kanter. **Description:** Studies show that individuals who perceive that they are being treated poorly and denied sufficient freedom for a certain level of autonomy are more likely to act negatively.

29143 ■ "Principles for Creating Growth in Challenging Times" in Agency Sales Magazine (Vol. 39, September-October 2009, No. 9, pp. 35)
Pub: MANA

Ed: Robert Goshen. **Description:** Creating a productive environment is one vital key for businesses to utilize during the challenging times that arise due to a weak economy; other important factors include maintaining a good relationship with the staff, responding appropriately to challenges and keeping a sense of humor.

29144 ■ "A Proper Welcome" in Canadian Business (Vol. 79, July 17, 2006, No. 14-15, pp. 67)
Pub: Rogers Media

Ed: Graham Lowe. **Description:** New-employee orientation programs of various companies are highlighted. Useful practices to create a comfortable ambiance for new recruits are elucidated as well.

29145 ■ "Proud Out Loud" in Canadian Business (Vol. 80, April 23, 2007, No. 9, pp. 52)
Pub: Rogers Media

Description: The role of accomplishments of employees in improving workplace conditions is presented.

29146 ■ "Putting the Service-Profit Chain to Work" in Harvard Business Review (Vol. 86, July-August 2008, No. 8, pp. 118)
Pub: Harvard Business School Press

Ed: James L. Heskett; Thomas O. Jones; Gary W. Loveman; W. Earl Sasser Jr.; Leonard A. Schlesinger. **Description:** Advice is given on how to foster profitability in service businesses. Topics include the link between employee satisfaction and customer satisfaction, internal service quality, external service value, and revenue growth.

29147 ■ "QuikTrip Makes Fortune 'Best' List" in Tulsa World (January 22, 2010)
Pub: Tulsa World

Ed: Kyle Arnold. **Description:** According to a list released by Fortune Magazine, QuikTrip Corp. is once again ranked among the best companies in the country to work for due to the core values and culture held by the company's management.

29148 ■ Reality-Based Leadership: Ditch the Drama, Restore Sanity to the Workplace
Pub: Jossey-Bass

Ed: Cy Wakeman. **Price:** $27.95. **Description:** Recent polls show that 71 percent of workers think about quitting their jobs every day. That number would be shocking if people actually were quitting. Worse, they go to work, punching time clocks and collecting pay checks, while checked out emotionally. Cy Wakeman reveals how to be the kind of leader who changes the way people think about and perceive their circumstances, one who deals with the facts, clarifies roles, gives clean and direct feedback, and insists that everyone do the same without drama or defensiveness.

29149 ■ "Reinventing Your Rep Training Program" in Agency Sales Magazine (Vol. 39, August 2009, No. 8, pp. 40)
Pub: MANA

Description: Tips on how to encourage manufacturer's representatives to attend scheduled training sessions are given. Manufacturers should learn the value of keeping the training program up-to-date and communicate with the sales team to know what needs to be revamped. Problems faced by representatives with inside sales staff should also be addressed by the manufacturer.

29150 ■ "Research Highlights Disengaged Workforce" in Workforce Management (Vol. 88, November 16, 2009, No. 12, pp. 22)
Pub: Crain Communications Inc.

Ed: Ed Frauenheim. **Description:** Most researchers have documented a drop in employee engagement during the recession due to such factors as layoffs, restructuring and less job security.

29151 ■ "Retiring Baby Boomers and Dissatisfied Gen-Xers Cause..Brain Drain" in Agency Sales Magazine (Vol. 39, November 2009, No. 10)
Pub: MANA

Ed: Denise Kelly. **Description:** Due to the impending retirement of the baby boomers a critical loss of knowledge and experience in businesses will result. Creating a plan to address this loss of talent centered on the development of the younger generation is discussed.

29152 ■ "RIM Rocks Out: Billionaire Bosses Sponsor a Free Concert for Deserving Staff" in Canadian Business (Vol. 80, Winter 2007, No. 24)
Pub: Rogers Media

Ed: Joe Castaldo. **Description:** Jim Balsillie and Mike Lazaridis of Research in Motion Ltd. (RIM) rented out the Air Canada Centre in Toronto to give their employees a free concert that features performances by the Tragically Hip and Van Halen on November 15, 2007. RIM has sponsored concerts by Aerosmith, Tom Cochrane, and the Barenaked Ladies in past parties that only shows how far the company goes in terms of employee appreciation.

29153 ■ "Say No to Slackers" in Canadian Business (Vol. 79, November 6, 2006, No. 22, pp. 105)
Pub: Rogers Media

Ed: Erin Pooley. **Description:** The effects of underperformers on performance of other colleagues with relation to company productivity are analyzed.

29154 ■ "Scouting and Keeping Good Talent in the Workplace" in Hawaii Business (Vol. 53, January 2008, No. 7, pp. 50)
Pub: Hawaii Business Publishing

Ed: Christie Dermegian. **Description:** Tips on improving employee selection and retention are presented. The strategies in choosing and keeping the right employees include identifying which type of people the company needs and improving the workplace environment.

29155 ■ "The Secret Strategy for Meaningful Sales Meetings" in Agency Sales Magazine (Vol. 39, December 2009, No. 11, pp. 40)
Pub: MANA

Ed: Dave Kahle. **Description:** Sales meetings can be made more meaningful by focusing on the end results that the meeting seeks to achieve. Describing the changed behavior that is sought from the sales force and working backwards from there also help make a sales meeting more meaningful.

29156 ■ "Shared Leadership In Teams: An Investigation of Antecedent Conditions and Performance" in Academy of Management Journal (Oct. 2007)
Pub: Academy of Management

Contact: Ming-Jer Chen, President

Ed: Jay B. Carson, Paul E. Tesluk, Jennifer A. Marrone. **Description:** Study assessed the advantages of distribution of leadership among team members rather than on a single person revealed advantages that ranged from support and shared functions along with higher ratings from clients on their performance.

29157 ■ Shop Class as Soulcraft
Pub: Penguin Group USA Inc.
Ed: Matthew B. Crawford. **Released:** May 28, 2009. **Price:** $25.95. **Description:** A philosopher and mechanic argues for the satisfaction and challenges of manual work.

29158 ■ Silos, Politics and Turf Wars: A Leadership Fable about Destroying the Barriers That Turn Colleagues Into Competitors
Pub: Jossey Bass
Ed: Patrick M. Lencioni. **Released:** February 17, 2006. **Price:** $24.95. **Description:** The author addresses management problems through a fable that revolves around a self-employed consultant who has to dismantle silos at an upscale hotel, a technology company and a hospital. The story explains how organizations can use a collective operational vision in order to overcome pride, greed, and tribalism and work as a team with the same goal in mind.

29159 ■ "Size Does Matter" in International Journal of Globalisation and Small Business (Vol. 4, September 21, 2010, No. 1, pp. 61)
Pub: Publishers Communication Group
Ed: Julia Cornnell, Ranjit Voola. **Description:** Examination of how members of an Australian-based manufacturing and engineering cluster share knowledge through networking as a means to improve competitive advantage.

29160 ■ Small Business, Big Life: Five Steps to Creating a Great Life with Your Own Small Business
Pub: Thomas Nelson Inc.
Ed: Louis Barajas. **Price:** $22.99. **Description:** Barajas describes his and his father's independent entrepreneurial paths and suggests an inspirational approach to business that relies on four personal greatness cornerstones: truth, responsibility, awareness, and courage, and on keeping in mind your vision and your team's needs. The book provides a new look at achieving a work/life balance

29161 ■ "Small Businesses Get Creative to Retain Workers" in Crain's Detroit Business (Vol. 24, March 17, 2008, No. 11, pp. 21)
Pub: Crain Communications, Inc.
Ed: Nancy Kaffer. **Description:** Small businesses are often unable to compete with larger firms when it comes to offering employees fringe benefits and such perks as a company gym or an in-house chef; however, many smaller companies have found that the key to gaining employee loyalty lies in creating an atmosphere in which employees feel job satisfaction. Also provides tips on how to keep employees.

29162 ■ "Social Intelligence and the Biology of Leadership" in Harvard Business Review (Vol. 86, September 2008, No. 9, pp. 74)
Pub: Harvard Business School Press
Ed: Daniel Goleman; Richard Boyatzis. **Description:** Social intelligence within the framework of corporate leadership is defined and described. Guidelines for assessing one's own capabilities as a socially intelligent leader include empathy, teamwork, inspiration, and influence.

29163 ■ The Social Media Bible: Tactics, Tools, and Strategies for Business Success
Pub: John Wiley & Sons, Inc.
Ed: Lon Safko, David Drake. **Released:** June 17, 2009. **Price:** $29.95. **Description:** Information is given to build or transform a business into social media, where customers, employees, and prospects connect, collaborate, and champion products and services in order to increase sales and to beat the competition.

29164 ■ "A Stalled Culture Change?" in Workforce Management (Vol. 88, December 14, 2009, No. 13, pp. 1)
Pub: Crain Communications Inc.
Ed: Jeremy Smerd. **Description:** General Motors CEO Fritz Henderson's abrupt resignation shocked

employees and signaled that Henderson had not done enough to change the company's culture, especially in dealing with its top management.

29165 ■ The Starbucks Experience
Pub: McGraw-Hill
Ed: Joseph A. Michelli. **Released:** September 14, 2006. **Price:** $24.95. **Description:** Boardroom strategies, employee motivation tips, community involvement, and customer satisfaction are issues addressed, using Starbucks as a model.

29166 ■ "Start Filling Your Talent Gap - Now" in Business Strategy Review (Vol. 21, Spring 2010, No. 1, pp. 56)
Pub: Wiley-Blackwell
Ed: Alan Bird, Lori Flees, Paul Di Paola. **Description:** As businesses steer their way out of turbulence, they have a unique opportunity to identify their leadership supply and demand and then to close the talent gap in their organization. Authors explain how to take immediate steps to build the right team now and lay the groundwork for a long-term approach for nurturing talent within the organization.

29167 ■ "Storytelling Star of Show for Scripps" in Business Courier (Vol. 26, November 13, 2009, No. 29, pp. 1)
Pub: American City Business Journals, Inc.
Ed: Dan Monk. **Description:** Rich Boehne, CEO of the EW Scripps Company in Cincinnati has authorized a new training program in storytelling for employees at Scripps' 10 television stations. He believes that the training will improve the quality of broadcasting content. His plans to improve quality of newspaper content are also discussed.

29168 ■ Streetwise Motivating and Rewarding Employees: New and Better Ways to Inspire Your People
Pub: Adams Media Corporation
Contact: Gary Krebs, Director
E-mail: swatrous@adamsmedia.com
Ed: Alexander Hiam. **Released:** March 1999. **Description:** Ways for employers and business managers to motivate difficult employees.

29169 ■ "Stress-Test Your Strategy: the 7 Questions to Ask" in Harvard Business Review (Vol. 88, November 2010, No. 11, pp. 92)
Pub: Harvard Business School Publishing
Ed: Robert Simons. **Description:** Seven questions organizations should use to assess crisis management capabilities are: who is the primary customer, how do core values prioritize all parties, what performance variables are being tracked, what strategic boundaries have been set, how is creative tension being produced, how committed are workers to assisting each other, and what uncertainties are causing worry?.

29170 ■ "Stylish Successes" in Women In Business (Vol. 61, October-November 2009, No. 5, pp. 12)
Pub: American Business Women's Association
Ed: Leigh Elmore; Megan L. Reese. **Description:** Amanda Horan Kennedy, Angela Samuels, Barbara Nast Saletan, and Patty Nast Canton are career women who ventured into entrepreneurship. They are deemed to possess networking and teamwork skills that ensured their success in the garment industry.

29171 ■ "The Superfluous Position" in Entrepreneur (Vol. 37, July 2009, No. 7, pp. 62)
Pub: Entrepreneur Media, Inc.
Description: Profile of an anonymous editor at a multimedia company that publishes tourism guides who shares his experiences in dealing with an officemate who was promoted as creative manager of content. Everyone was irritated by this person, who would constantly do something to justify his new title. The biggest problem was the fact that this person didn't have a clear job description.

29172 ■ "The Sustainable Supply Chain" in Harvard Business Review (Vol. 88, October 2010, No. 10, pp. 70)
Pub: Harvard Business School Publishing
Ed: Steven Prokesch. **Description:** Peter Senge, founder of the Society for Organizational Learning, emphasizes the importance of assessing the system as a whole under which one is operating, and learning how to work with individuals with which one has not worked previously. He also points to nongovernmental organizations to provide assistance and legitimacy.

29173 ■ Switch: How to Change Things When Change Is Hard
Pub: Broadway Books
Contact: David Drake, Manager
E-mail: ddrake@randomhouse.com
Ed: Chip Heath, Dan Heath. **Released:** February 16, 2010. **Price:** $26.00. **Description:** Change is difficult for everyone. This book helps business leaders to motivate employees as well as to help everybody motive themselves and others.

29174 ■ "Team Bonding for Fun and Profit" in Women Entrepreneur (December 3, 2008)
Pub: Entrepreneur Media Inc.
Ed: Eve Gumpel. **Description:** Discusses the benefits that competitions such as the 2008 BG U.S. Challenge in Lake Placid, New York, can offer in terms of team building and employee motivation as well as networking and the development of a positive working relationship with partners and competitors alike.

29175 ■ "Team Implicit Coordination Processes: A Team Knowledge-based Approach" in Academy of Management Review (January 2008, pp. 163)
Pub: ScholarOne, Inc.
Ed: Ramon Rico, Miriam Sanchez-Manzanares, Francisco Gil, Cristina Gibson. **Description:** An integrated theoretical framework is developed to enhance understanding of the functioning of work teams and implicit coordination behaviors; the implications for team coordination theory and effective management of work teams is discussed.

29176 ■ Thank God It's Monday! How to Create a Workplace You and Your Customers Love
Pub: FT Press
Ed: Roxanne Emmerich. **Released:** April 18, 2009. **Price:** $19.99. **Description:** Tips on creating a positive environment for both employees and customers.

29177 ■ The Thin Book of Naming Elephants: How to Surface Undiscussables for Greater Organizational Success
Pub: Thin Book Publishing Co.
Contact: Sue Annis Hammond, Owner
E-mail: sue@thinbook.com
Ed: Sue Annis Hammond; Andrea B. Mayfield. **Released:** January 2004. **Price:** $10.95. **Description:** Organizational success is of upmost importance to today's entrepreneurs and organizations. The hierarchal system in which people are afraid to speak up in organizations is discussed. The points of view and inability to see things from an overall perspective can cause insecurity among employees. The three elephants present in every organization include: arrogance, hubris, and screamers and the damage caused by these elephants in any organization is examined.

29178 ■ Ubuntu!: An Aspiring Story About an African Tradition of Teamwork and Collaboration
Pub: Broadway Books
Contact: David Drake, Manager
E-mail: ddrake@randomhouse.com
Ed: Bob Nelson, Stephen Lundin. **Released:** March 30, 2010. **Price:** $19.99. **Description:** The African tradition of teamwork and collaboration is used to demonstrate these skills to small business leaders.

29179 ■ *"The Uncompromising Leader" in Harvard Business Review (Vol. 86, July-August 2008, No. 8, pp. 50)*
Pub: Harvard Business School Press
Ed: Russell A. Eisenstat; Michael Beer; Nathaniel Foote; Tobias Fredburg; Flemming Norrgren. **Description:** Advice regarding how to drive performance without sacrificing commitment to people is given. Topics include development of shared purpose, organizational engagement, the fostering of collective leadership capability, and maintaining perspective.

29180 ■ *"The Value of Conversations With Employees; Talk Isn't Cheap" in Gallup Management Journal (June 30, 2011)*
Pub: Gallup
Ed: Jessica Tyler. **Description:** When managers have meaningful exchanges with their employees, they don't only show they care, they also add value to their organization's bottom line.

29181 ■ *"We Move Forward as a Team" in Women In Business (Vol. 61, December 2009, No. 6, pp. 6)*
Pub: American Business Women's Association
Ed: Rene Street. **Description:** Based on her experiences in ABWA's National Board of Directors retreat, an executive director of the American Business Women's Association, shares her belief that interaction is necessary for a successful business enterprise. She believes that the problems presented in the retreat's team-building exercises are similar to challenges which are faced in ABWA, in the workplace, and in the marketplace.

29182 ■ *"We Were Strutting Our Stuff" in Women In Business (Vol. 63, Summer 2011, No. 2, pp. 10)*
Pub: American Business Women's Association
Ed: Rene Street, Leigh Elmore. **Description:** American Business Women's Association's STRUT relay race event helped raise awareness of the group in the United States. The event also provided excellent team-building exercises for ABWA chapters. It also helped participants boost their leadership and business skills.

29183 ■ *"A Weak Link Can Break the Chain of Good Service" in Canadian Business (Vol. 83, August 17, 2010, No. 13-14, pp. 11)*
Pub: Rogers Media Ltd.
Ed: Richard Branson. **Description:** Good customer service is a practice that requires the efforts of the entire chain of coworkers that work as a team from beginning to end. The chain of assistance is only as strong as the weakest link when it comes to helping a customer.

29184 ■ *"What Employees Worldwide Have in Common" in Gallup Management Journal (September 22, 2011)*
Pub: Gallup
Ed: Steve Crabtree. **Description:** According to a Gallup study, workplace conditions are strongly tied to personal wellbeing, regardless of geographic region. The employee study covered 116 countries.

29185 ■ *"What Your Employees Need to Know; They Probably Don't Know How They're Performing" in Gallup Management Journal (April 13, 2011)*
Pub: Gallup
Ed: Steve Crabtree. **Description:** Personalized feedback and recognition aren't just extras that make workers feel good about themselves they are critical predictors of positive performance.

29186 ■ *"When Emotional Reasoning Trumps IQ" in Harvard Business Review (Vol. 88, September 2010, No. 9, pp. 27)*
Pub: Harvard Business School Publishing
Ed: Roderick Gilkey, Ricardo Caceda, Clinton Kilts. **Description:** Strategic reasoning was found to be linked more closely to areas of the brain associated with intuition and emotion, rather than the prefrontal cortex, which is typically thought to be the center of such activity. Implications for management skills are discussed.

29187 ■ *"When the Longtime Star Fades" in Harvard Business Review (Vol. 88, September 2010, No. 9, pp. 117)*
Pub: Harvard Business School Publishing
Ed: Jimmy Guterman. **Description:** A fictitious aging employee scenario is presented, with contributors offering advice. The scenarios focuses on an older employee's match with a rapidly changing industry; suggestions include consolidating a niche business around the employee, and also engaging the older employee in solving the productivity issue.

29188 ■ *"When R&D Spending Is Not Enough" in Human Resource Management (Vol. 49, July-August 2010, No. 4, pp. 767-792)*
Pub: John Wiley
Ed: Sheng Wang, Rebecca M. Guidice, Judith W. Tansky, Zhong-Ming Wang. **Description:** A study was conducted to examine the effect of contextual contingencies on innovation. Findings indicate that Chinese manufacturers with cultures emphasizing innovation and teamwork more effectively utilize financial resources in the innovation process. Results also show that a culture emphasizing outcomes and stability leads to lower levels innovation irrespective of investments.

29189 ■ *"Why Did We Ever Go Into HR?" in Harvard Business Review (Vol. 86, July-August 2008, No. 8, pp. 39)*
Pub: Harvard Business School Press
Ed: Matthew D. Breitfelder; Daisy Wademan Dowling. **Description:** Examines the role of human resource directors and how their jobs foster new ideas and generate optimism.

29190 ■ *Why Work Sucks and How To Fix It*
Pub: Portfolio Publishing
Ed: Cali Ressler; Jody Thompson. **Released:** May 1, 2008. **Price:** $23.95. **Description:** Results-Only Work Environments (ROWE) not only make employees happier, it also delivers better results. ROWE allows employees to do whatever they want, whenever they want as long as business objectives are met. No more pointless meetings, fighting traffic to be to work on time, or asking for permission for time off.

29191 ■ *"Work Buds" in Canadian Business (Vol. 80, April 23, 2007, No. 9, pp. 56)*
Pub: Rogers Media
Ed: Andrew Wahl. **Description:** The role of team work and cooperation in improving workplace environment is presented.

29192 ■ *"Work Pray Love" in Harvard Business Review (Vol. 88, December 2010, No. 12, pp. 38)*
Pub: Harvard Business School Publishing
Ed: Rosabeth Moss Kanter. **Description:** It is recommended to reinvest in values in order to promote better employee-company engagement and performance.

29193 ■ *"Working It Out! How a Young Executive Overcomes Obstacles on the Job" in Black Enterprise (Vol. 37, January 2007, No. 6, pp. 55)*
Pub: Earl G. Graves Publishing Co. Inc.
Ed: Laura Egodigwe. **Description:** Interview with Susan Chapman, Global Head of Operations for Citigroup Realty Services, in which she discusses issues such as the important skills necessary for overcoming obstacles in the workplace.

29194 ■ *Ya Gotta Wanna*
Pub: Creative Book Publishers
Ed: Malcolm Paice. **Released:** July 2005. **Price:** $12.95. **Description:** Three phases of teamwork are outlined: identifying the people and creating the team, analyzing the components of the team, and implementing the project. The author compares a soccer team to a management team and that a successful soccer team has three main area attributes: a solid defense, a creative midfield, and a potent strike force.

29195 ■ *"Your First 100 Days on Your New Job" in Women In Business (Vol. 63, Spring 2011, No. 1, pp. 28)*
Pub: American Business Women's Association
Ed: Diane Stafford. **Description:** The first 100 days on the job are crucial if the person's permanent hiring is conditional on surviving a probationary period. The new hire must do more than just master the job's technical details to maximize the chance of success. Details of some basic tips to fit into the corporate culture and get along with coworkers are also discussed.

TRADE PERIODICALS

29196 ■ *The Journal for Quality and Participation*
Pub: American Society for Quality
Contact: Paul E. Borawski, Chief Executive Officer
URL(s): www.asq.org/pub/jqp/. **Released:** 4/yr. **Price:** $52, Members domestic, individuals; $82, Members international, individuals; $75, Members includes GST individual, Canada; $87, Nonmembers domestic, individuals; $98, Nonmembers international, individuals; $98, Nonmembers Canadian, includes GST individual.

29197 ■ *Teamwork*
Pub: Dartnell Publications
Released: Biweekly. **Price:** $197. **Description:** Focuses on successful teamwork in manufacturing and corporate businesses. Recurring features include columns titled What Would You Do?, Test Yourself and See, and Teamwork in Action.

VIDEOCASSETTES/ AUDIOCASSETTES

29198 ■ *Better Productivity Is Not By Chance—Dr. Robert Lorher*
Instructional Video
2219 C St.
Lincoln, NE 68502
Ph: (402)475-6570
Free: 800-228-0164
Fax: (402)475-6500
Co. E-mail: feedback@insvideo.com
URL: http://www.insvideo.com
Released: 19??. **Price:** $169.00. **Description:** Dr. Robert Lorher offers five factors that will improve motivational skills and productivity, and support the importance of setting reachable goals. **Availability:** VHS.

29199 ■ *Building Blocks for Team Performance*
Instructional Video
2219 C St.
Lincoln, NE 68502
Ph: (402)475-6570
Free: 800-228-0164
Fax: (402)475-6500
Co. E-mail: feedback@insvideo.com
URL: http://www.insvideo.com
Released: 19??. **Price:** $295.00. **Description:** Teaches the importance of teamwork and offers concepts to be used to build successful teams within your organization, including effective listening, developing top performers, and time management. Includes workbook. **Availability:** VHS.

29200 ■ *Building High Performing Teams*
Excellence in Training Corp.
c/o ICON Training
804 Roosevelt St.
Polk City, IA 50226
Free: 800-609-0479
Co. E-mail: info@icontraining.com
URL: http://www.icontraining.com
Released: 1991. **Price:** $995.00. **Description:** A presentation on the four steps of building an effective management team. **Availability:** VHS; 3/4 U; Special order formats.

29201 ■ *Coaching Skills: Developing a Better Employee*
American Media, Inc.
4621 121st St.
Urbandale, IA 50323-2311
Ph: (515)224-0919
Free: 888-776-8268

Fax: (515)327-2555
Co. E-mail: custsvc@ammedia.com
URL: http://www.ammedia.com
Released: 19??. **Price:** $495.00. **Description:** Focuses on ways to coach employees with training, motivation, and delegation to help employees grow in their positions. Two videos discuss coaching methods and show examples of good and bad coaching. A trainer's guide is included. **Availability:** VHS; 3/4 U; 8 mm.

29202 ■ Coaching for Top Performance
Cambridge Educational
c/o Films Media Group
132 West 31st Street, 17th Floor
Ste. 124
New York, NY 10001
Free: 800-257-5126
Fax: (609)671-0266
Co. E-mail: custserve@films.com
URL: http://www.cambridgeol.com
Released: 1992. **Description:** Get the best work possible out of your team by using these coaching strategies. **Availability:** VHS.

29203 ■ Dealing with Difficult People Volume Two
RMI Media
1365 N. Winchester St.
Olathe, KS 66061-5880
Ph: (913)768-1696
Free: 800-745-5480
Fax: (800)755-6910
Co. E-mail: actmedia@act.org
URL: http://www.actmedia.com
Released: 1993. **Price:** $99.00. **Description:** Ed Greif explains how to handle very difficult problems with people. **Availability:** VHS.

29204 ■ Developing Strategies for Teamwork
Aspen Publishers, Inc.
7201 McKinney Cir.
Frederick, MD 21704
Ph: (301)698-7100
Free: 800-234-1660
Fax: (800)901-9075
Co. E-mail: customerservice@aspenpublisher.com
URL: http://www.aspenpublishers.com
Contact: Robert Becker, President
Released: 1986. **Price:** $495.00. **Description:** Strategy tips to teach your supervisors how to get their employees working together and working harder are shown. **Availability:** VHS; 3/4 U; Special order formats.

29205 ■ Discipline: A Matter of Judgment
Encyclopedia Britannica
331 N. LaSalle St.
Chicago, IL 60654
Ph: (312)347-7159
Free: 800-323-1229
Fax: (312)294-2104
URL: http://www.britannica.com
Released: 1989. **Description:** This video teaches that discipline must educate, not humiliate, and urges fair, prompt, and consistent disciplinary action. **Availability:** VHS; 3/4 U.

29206 ■ Empowering Employees to Claim Their Autonomy
ASTD
1640 King St.
Alexandria, VA 22314-2746
Ph: (703)683-8100
Free: 800-628-2783
Fax: (703)683-1523
Co. E-mail: customercare@astd.org
URL: http://www.astd.org
Contact: Tony Bingham, President
E-mail: tbingham@astd.org
Released: 1989. **Description:** Peter Block shows how to get past the passivity inherent in large organizations and help employees take charge of their individual needs, creating more creativity and energy in the workplace. **Availability:** VHS; 3/4 U.

29207 ■ Empowerment: Communicating with Others
International Training Consultants, Inc.
1838 Park Oaks
Kemah, TX 77565
Free: 800-998-8764
Co. E-mail: itc@trainingitc.com
URL: http://www.trainingitc.com
Released: 19??. **Price:** $495.00. **Description:** Part of the "Empowerment: The Employee Development Series." Provides instructional material for employees which helps them becoming better communicators. Covers both speaking and listening techniques. **Availability:** VHS.

29208 ■ Empowerment: Meeting Change Creatively
International Training Consultants, Inc.
1838 Park Oaks
Kemah, TX 77565
Free: 800-998-8764
Co. E-mail: itc@trainingitc.com
URL: http://www.trainingitc.com
Released: 19??. **Price:** $495.00. **Description:** Part of the "Empowerment: The Employee Development Series." Helps employees learn to cope with change by showing them how to increase their tolerance to change and benefit from it. **Availability:** VHS.

29209 ■ Empowerment: Solving Problems Together
International Training Consultants, Inc.
1838 Park Oaks
Kemah, TX 77565
Free: 800-998-8764
Co. E-mail: itc@trainingitc.com
URL: http://www.trainingitc.com
Released: 19??. **Price:** $495.00. **Description:** Part of the "Empowerment: The Employee Development Series." Illustrates skills which will help employees become better problem solvers. **Availability:** VHS.

29210 ■ Empowerment: Team Skills for Meeting Together
International Training Consultants, Inc.
1838 Park Oaks
Kemah, TX 77565
Free: 800-998-8764
Co. E-mail: itc@trainingitc.com
URL: http://www.trainingitc.com
Released: 19??. **Price:** $495.00. **Description:** Part of the "Empowerment: The Employee Development Series." Teaches employees skills which help them become better meeting and team participants, including those of the group leader, recorder, facilitator, observer, and group member. **Availability:** VHS.

29211 ■ Empowerment: Working Effectively with Others
International Training Consultants, Inc.
1838 Park Oaks
Kemah, TX 77565
Free: 800-998-8764
Co. E-mail: itc@trainingitc.com
URL: http://www.trainingitc.com
Released: 19??. **Price:** $495.00. **Description:** Part of the "Empowerment: The Employee Development Series." Examines methods which help employees work together more effectively. Covers two important areas which affect teamwork: individual behaviors and interaction. **Availability:** VHS.

29212 ■ Everything You Always Wanted to Know about Management
American Media, Inc.
4621 121st St.
Urbandale, IA 50323-2311
Ph: (515)224-0919
Free: 888-776-8268
Fax: (515)327-2555
Co. E-mail: custsvc@ammedia.com
URL: http://www.ammedia.com
Released: 1995. **Price:** $595. **Description:** Outlines the essentials of good management, including the six steps of delegation, employee empowerment, communication, feedback, and goal achievement. Includes course guide with participant exercises and case studies. **Availability:** VHS; CC.

29213 ■ How to Motivate Your People
1st Financial Training Services
1515 E. Woodfield Rd., Ste. 345
Schaumburg, IL 60173
Ph: (847)969-0900
Free: 800-442-8662
Fax: (847)969-0521
URL: http://www.1stfinancialtraining.com
Released: 1987. **Price:** $250.00. **Description:** The program answers questions about how to motivate people and why some people are harder to motivate than others. **Availability:** VHS; 3/4 U.

29214 ■ How to Supervise People
Nightingale-Conant Corp.
6245 W. Howard St.
Niles, IL 60714
Ph: (847)647-0300
Free: 800-560-6081
URL: http://www.nightingale.com
Released: 19??. **Price:** $95.00. **Description:** Eileen Parkinson presents techniques for building a winning team by leading people, as opposed to managing them. Includes an audio cassette and book. **Availability:** VHS.

29215 ■ Motivating/Directing/Leading—The Basics of Winning with People
RMI Media
1365 N. Winchester St.
Olathe, KS 66061-5880
Ph: (913)768-1696
Free: 800-745-5480
Fax: (800)755-6910
Co. E-mail: actmedia@act.org
URL: http://www.actmedia.com
Released: 1989. **Price:** $129.00. **Description:** Find out how to get other people to do what you want them to do. **Availability:** VHS; 3/4 U.

29216 ■ Motivating Others
American Management Association (AMA)
1601 Broadway
New York, NY 10019-7420
Ph: (212)586-8100
Free: 877-566-9441
Fax: (212)903-8168
Co. E-mail: customerservice@amanet.org
URL: http://www.amanet.org
Contact: Charles R. Craig, Chairman
Released: 1993. **Price:** $215.00. **Description:** Provides tips on how to motivate employees to perform better. Contains information on proven, top-rated employee motivators and how to use them. **Availability:** VHS.

29217 ■ Motivating People Toward Peak Performance
Nightingale-Conant Corp.
6245 W. Howard St.
Niles, IL 60714
Ph: (847)647-0300
Free: 800-560-6081
URL: http://www.nightingale.com
Released: 19??. **Price:** $95.00. **Description:** A look at motivational strategies for encouraging top-notch performance from ordinary people. Includes two audio cassettes and two workbooks. **Availability:** VHS.

29218 ■ Motivation & a Positive Attitude
University of Wisconsin-Madison Center on Education & Work
1025 W. Johnson St., Rm. 964
Madison, WI 53706-1796
Ph: (608)265-6700
Free: 800-862-1071
Co. E-mail: cewmail@education.wisc.edu
URL: http://www.cew.wisc.edu
Released: 1997. **Price:** $79.00. **Description:** Looks at how to develop motivational behavior and a positive attitude. **Availability:** VHS.

29219 ■ Muppet Sales: Make-a-Buck
Video Arts, Inc.
c/o Aim Learning Group
8238-40 Lehigh
Morton Grove, IL 60053-2615
Free: 877-444-2230

Fax: (416)252-2155
Co. E-mail: service@aimlearninggroup.com
URL: http://www.aimlearninggroup.com
Released: 19??. **Price:** $795.00. **Description:** Topic-specific selections from "The Muppets Show" provide motivation and humor to meetings and work related obligations. **Availability:** VHS.

29220 ■ *Planning a Project and Building Your Project Team*
ISA -The International Society of Automation (ISA)
67 Alexander Dr.
Research Triangle Park, NC 27709
Ph: (919)549-8411
Fax: (919)549-8288
Co. E-mail: info@isa.org
URL: http://www.isa.org
Contact: Robert Renner, Director
Released: 199?. **Price:** $95.00. **Description:** An instrument technology training program on planning a project and building your project team. Includes a manual. **Availability:** VHS.

29221 ■ *Team Building*
Excellence in Training Corp.
c/o ICON Training
804 Roosevelt St.
Polk City, IA 50226
Free: 800-609-0479
Co. E-mail: info@icontraining.com
URL: http://www.icontraining.com
Released: 1991. **Price:** $495.00. **Description:** A detailed discussion of the ingredients of building an effective work team. A detailed leader's guide is included. **Availability:** VHS; 3/4 U; Special order formats.

29222 ■ *Team of Champions*
Excellence in Training Corp.
c/o ICON Training
804 Roosevelt St.
Polk City, IA 50226
Free: 800-609-0479
Co. E-mail: info@icontraining.com
URL: http://www.icontraining.com
Released: 1991. **Price:** $595.00. **Description:** John Parker Stewart discusses how to combine empowerment, teamwork, and quality improvement to build a more effective working environment. A leader's guide is included. **Availability:** VHS; 3/4 U; Special order formats.

29223 ■ *Team Excellence*
Home Vision Cinema
c/o Image Entertainment
20525 Nordhoff St., Ste. 200
Chatsworth, CA 91311
Co. E-mail: inquiries@image-entertainment.com
URL: http://www.homevision.com
Released: 1987. **Price:** $995.00. **Description:** Walter Cronkite emphasizes the importance of teamwork in the workplace. **Availability:** VHS; 3/4 U.

29224 ■ *Team Player*
American Media, Inc.
4621 121st St.
Urbandale, IA 50323-2311
Ph: (515)224-0919
Free: 888-776-8268
Fax: (515)327-2555
Co. E-mail: custsvc@ammedia.com
URL: http://www.ammedia.com
Released: 1993. **Price:** $650.00. **Description:** Features a scene in which the main character develops a team approach to problem-solving in a very realistic way. **Availability:** VHS.

29225 ■ *Together!*
American Media, Inc.
4621 121st St.
Urbandale, IA 50323-2311
Ph: (515)224-0919
Free: 888-776-8268

Fax: (515)327-2555
Co. E-mail: custsvc@ammedia.com
URL: http://www.ammedia.com
Released: 1990. **Price:** $325.00. **Description:** Focuses on the importance of teamwork in business using a story about a group of boys and girls working together to perform a complicated task. **Availability:** VHS; 3/4 U; 8 mm.

29226 ■ *Together We Can!*
American Media, Inc.
4621 121st St.
Urbandale, IA 50323-2311
Ph: (515)224-0919
Free: 888-776-8268
Fax: (515)327-2555
Co. E-mail: custsvc@ammedia.com
URL: http://www.ammedia.com
Released: 1991. **Price:** $545.00. **Description:** Discusses actions individuals can take to ensure good teamwork. Includes a discussion guide. **Availability:** VHS; 3/4 U; 8 mm; CC.

29227 ■ *Trust Your Team*
Excellence in Training Corp.
c/o ICON Training
804 Roosevelt St.
Polk City, IA 50226
Free: 800-609-0479
Co. E-mail: info@icontraining.com
URL: http://www.icontraining.com
Released: 1987. **Price:** $595.00. **Description:** This video is designed to help managers open up their management styles, to allow all employees to function better, and take on more responsibility. **Availability:** VHS; 3/4 U.

29228 ■ *Where There's a Will. . .: Leadership and Motivation*
Video Arts, Inc.
c/o Aim Learning Group
8238-40 Lehigh
Morton Grove, IL 60053-2615
Free: 877-444-2230
Fax: (416)252-2155
Co. E-mail: service@aimlearninggroup.com
URL: http://www.aimlearninggroup.com
Released: 1988. **Price:** $790.00. **Description:** Find out how you can motivate your workers to a higher productivity level. **Availability:** VHS; 8 mm; 3/4 U; Special order formats.

29229 ■ *Working Teams: Helping Your Team Succeed*
American Management Association (AMA)
1601 Broadway
New York, NY 10019-7420
Ph: (212)586-8100
Free: 877-566-9441
Fax: (212)903-8168
Co. E-mail: customerservice@amanet.org
URL: http://www.amanet.org
Contact: Charles R. Craig, Chairman
Released: 19??. **Price:** $645.00. **Description:** Outlines the principles of being a contributing team member and not just a team player. **Availability:** VHS; CC.

29230 ■ *Workplace Readiness: Teamwork*
Agency for Instructional Technology (AIT)
1800 N Stonelake Dr., Box A
Bloomington, IN 47404-1517
Ph: (812)339-2203
Free: 800-457-4509
Fax: (812)333-4218
Co. E-mail: info@ait.net
URL: http://www.ait.net
Contact: Sandra L. McBrayer, Chief Executive Officer
Released: 1992. **Price:** $395.00. **Description:** Series of seven programs introducing students to the idea of teamwork in culturally diverse work forces. Programs deal with specific examples. Comes with guide. **Availability:** VHS; CC.

29231 ■ *Workplace Teams*
American Management Association (AMA)
1601 Broadway
New York, NY 10019-7420

Ph: (212)586-8100
Free: 877-566-9441
Fax: (212)903-8168
Co. E-mail: customerservice@amanet.org
URL: http://www.amanet.org
Contact: Charles R. Craig, Chairman
Released: 19??. **Price:** $975.00. **Description:** Contains information on the concept of building productive teams and the use of teamwork. **Availability:** VHS; CC.

CONSULTANTS

29232 ■ Adventure Learning Associates Inc.
567 Hale Rd.
Brattleboro, VT 05302
Ph: (802)254-6160
Free: 800-551-3210
Fax: (802)254-3852
Co. E-mail: info@alrna.com
URL: http://www.alrna.com
Contact: Paul A. Kidder, Owner Founder
E-mail: paul@alrna.com
Scope: Provider of consulting services and training in experiential training and development. Specifically provides team building, communications skills and empowerment skill sessions. Also focuses on needs analysis, strategic planning and visioning for newly developing groups. Firm specializes in training trainers in experiential outdoor programming. Industries served: all including government and can work with intact groups at all levels from line staff to boards and executive committees. **Founded:** 1990. **Seminars:** Train the Adventure Trainer.

29233 ■ Advisory Management Services Inc.
9600 E 129th St., Ste. B
Kansas City, MO 64149-1025
Ph: (816)765-9611
Fax: (816)765-7447
Contact: Hal Wood, President
Scope: A management consulting and training firm specializing in employee relations, management and staff training, organizational development, strategic planning, and continuous quality improvement. **Founded:** 1979.

29234 ■ Arete Ventures Administration L.L.C.
3 Bethesda Metro Ctr., Ste. 770
Bethesda, MD 20814-5330
Ph: (301)657-6268
Fax: (301)770-2877
Contact: Robert W. Shaw, Jr., President
Scope: Provider of team based management consulting services to organizations of all types. Provides management consulting services by bridging traditional strategic consulting that focuses on the numbers and largely ignores the human side of organizations, and typical organization consulting that stresses team development but avoids the pragmatic realities of running an organization. Focuses on strategic planning, organization design and effectiveness, managing human resources, and teambuilding or group dynamics. **Founded:** 1983.

29235 ■ The Axelrod Group Inc.
723 Laurel Ave.
Wilmette, IL 60091
Ph: (847)251-7361
Fax: (847)251-7370
Co. E-mail: info@axelrodgroup.com
URL: http://www.axelrodgroup.com
Contact: Thava Govender, Manager
Scope: Provider of organizational development consulting services in the following areas: conference Model approach to redesign, strategic planning, organization assessment, self directed work teams, cultural change and team development, and management. Clients include major corporations and nonprofit organizations. **Founded:** 1981. **Publications:** "Large Group Interventions"; "Future Search"; "Real Time Strategic Change"; "The Path of Least Resistance for Managers"; "Open Space Technology"; "Flawless Consulting"; "Leadership and the New Science"; "The Birth of the Chaordic Age"; "Beyond the Wall of Resistance"; "Beat the Odds and Succeed in Organizational Change," Consulting to Management Magazine, Jun, 2006; "You Don't Have to Do it Alone," Oct,

2004; "Terms of Engagement," Barrett-Koehler Publishers; "The Conference Model"; "Harnessing Complexity"; "The Philosophy Behind Our Systems"; "Considerations Before You Build a Collaborative Process"; "Making Teams Work"; "Purpose is the Cornerstone"; "How to Build Relationships"; "How to Maximize Information Sharing"; "How to Promote Equity and Fairness"; "How to Create Freedom and Autonomy"; "The Handbook of Large Group Methods"; "The Change Handbook"; "The Intelligence Advantage: Organizing for Complexity"; "Investors Business Daily Leaders and Success: Top 10 Secrets to Success"; "Terms of Engagement: An Interview with Dick Axelrod," Per dido Magazine; "The Beauty of the Beast". **Seminars:** Conference Model Professional Skills; Team Development; Creating Team Based Organizations; Conflict Management for Managers; Working Together; Communications Skills for Improving Productivity and Relationships; Designing for Engagement; Terms of Engagement.

29236 ■ Bloch Consulting Group
2033 Wild Cherry Ln.
Kalamazoo, MI 49009-9168
Ph: (616)375-6849
Fax: (616)375-6849
Contact: Raleigh Bloch, President
E-mail: rbloch@compuserve.com
Scope: Managing creative processes to develop new ideas and products. Firm offers expertise in high performance work systems, teamwork, self-regulated teams, total quality management, employee involvement, and creativity session facilitation **Founded:** 1993.

29237 ■ Business Development Group Inc. (BDG)
29255 Laurel Woods Dr., Ste. 202
Southfield, MI 48034
Ph: (248)358-0121
Fax: (248)350-3025
Co. E-mail: info@busdevgroup.com
URL: http://www.busdevgroup.com
Contact: Neil J. Simon, President
E-mail: njsimon@aol.com
Scope: Consulting firm expertise in leadership development; strategic thinking; organizational transformation; team-based work systems; organizational learning; rapid change; knowledge management; competitive intelligence; crisis management; merger and acquisition integration; product integration and new product development. **Founded:** 1985. **Publications:** "Navigating in the Sea of Change," Competitive Intelligence Review Journal; "The Influence of Cultural Aspects of Strategic Information, Analysis and Delivery"; "What Leadership Needs From Competitive Intelligence Professionals," Journal of Association for Global and Strategic Information. **Seminars:** Process of Self-Design for the Evolving Organization; Large System Change Intervention; Self Assessment and the Transformational Process; The Knowledge Exchange - Shared Practices Workshop.

29238 ■ CFI Group USA L.L.C.—Claes Fornell International
625 Avis Dr.
Ann Arbor, MI 48108-9649
Ph: (734)930-9090
Free: 800-930-0933
Fax: (734)930-0911
Co. E-mail: askcfi@cfigroup.com
URL: http://www.cfigroup.com
Contact: Sheri Teodoru, Chief Executive Officer
E-mail: steodoru@mail.cfigroup.com
Scope: Management consulting firm that helps its clients worldwide to maximize shareholder value by optimizing customer and employee satisfaction. Clients span a variety of industries, including manufacturing, telecommunications, retail and government. **Founded:** 1988. **Publications:** "Customer Satisfaction and Stock Prices: High Returns, Low Risk," American Marketing Association, Jan, 2006; "Customer Satisfaction Index Climbs," The Wall Street Journal, Feb, 2004; "What's Next? Customer Service is Key to Post-Boom Success," The Bottom Line, Mar, 2003; "Boost Stock Performance, Nation's Economy," Quality Progress, Feb, 2003.

29239 ■ Charismedia
610 W End Ave., Ste. 31
New York, NY 10001
Ph: (212)362-6808
Fax: (212)362-6809
Co. E-mail: charismedia@earthlink.net
URL: http://www.charismedia.net
Contact: Dr. Doe Lang, President
E-mail: charismedia@earthlink.net
Scope: Offers speech and image training as well as speech writing services for effective presentation skills. Conducts workshops like anti-stage fright breathing, psychophysical exercises, transformational success imagery, face reading and body language, EMDR (Eye Movement Desensitization Re-Processing) for Permanent Trauma and Fear Removal, Bach Flower remedies, thought field therapy, cross-cultural communication, speech, voice and diction; regional and foreign accent elimination and acquisition, Positive Perception Management (P.P.M.), Ad-libbing, humor and spontaneity training, fast creative speech preparation, Neuro-Linguistic Programming and Hypnosis. **Founded:** 1974. **Publications:** "Flaunt It"; "Improve Your Sex Life"; "Phone Power"; "Train Your Voice"; "Turning Tinny, Tiny Tones To Gold"; "The New Secrets of Charisma: How to Discover and Unleash your Hidden Powers," McGraw-Hill, Jul, 1999. **Seminars:** Services for Comfortable Effective Speaking.

29240 ■ Cole Financial Service Inc.
3170 E, Lafayette Blvd.
Detroit, MI 48207-4378
Ph: (313)962-7055
Free: 877-972-7055
Fax: (313)962-7815
Co. E-mail: jason.a.cole@colefinancial1.net
URL: http://www.colefinancial1.net
Contact: Patricia Allen Cole, President
E-mail: Patricia.a.cole@colefinancial1.net
Scope: A full service human capital development firm providing services in recruiting, coaching, retaining, developing and retiring. Works with front line staff, managers and executive level decision makers that set strategy. Industries served: Engineering, construction, government and other business entities. **Founded:** 1983. **Seminars:** How to Run Your Own Business; 25Ways to stay in Business 25Years; How to Tap Your Potential and Discover Your GENIUS; The Job Ladder Steps to SUCCESS; Making and Keeping a Budget; Records Retention and Disposal; Take Control of Your Life; Time and Priority Management; TQM - Total Quality Management; Leadership 101; Leadership 201; Diversity Agent or Opponent A Personal Development Workshop; Coaching in a Diverse Workplace.

29241 ■ Competitive Edge Inc.
241 E Crestwood Rd.
Peachtree City, GA 30269
Ph: (770)487-6460
Fax: (770)487-2919
Co. E-mail: judy@competitiveedgeinc.com
URL: http://www.competitiveedgeinc.com
Contact: Judy I. Suiter, President
E-mail: judy@competitiveedgenc.com
Scope: A human resources consulting firm providing customized training and software solutions to assist clients in optimizing their human intellectual capital through effective selection, coaching, and training. Works with a network of consultants that are located throughout the United States, Canada, and Europe. **Founded:** 1981. **Publications:** "Beteenden och drivkrafter"; "Energizing People: Unleashing The Power of DISC"; "The Ripple Effect: How the Global Model of Endorsement Opens Doors to Success"; "The Journey - Quotes to keep your boat afloat"; "The Universal Language DISC Reference Manual"; "Exploring Values: Releasing the Power of Attitudes"; "COMPETITIVE PRODUCTS REVIEW BOOK"; "The Mother Of All Minds"; "The Sea of Change: Solutions for Navigating the Disconnects in the Workplace". **Seminars:** How to Recruit and Retain High Performing Employees; The Importance of Values Matching For Sales Selection; How to Build a High Performance Team; Dynamic Communication Skills; Creating Nurturing Customer Relationships; Your Attitude Is Showing; Sales Strategy Index; Validity Study.

29242 ■ The Corlund Group L.L.C. (CG)
101 Federal St., Ste. 310
Boston, MA 02110
Ph: (617)423-9364
Fax: (617)423-9371
Co. E-mail: info@corlundgroup.com
URL: http://www.corlundgroup.com
Contact: Wilmot J. Gravenslund, Director
E-mail: wgravenslund@corlundgroup.com
Scope: Boutique firm offering services in the areas of leadership, governance, and change with a particular focus on CEO and senior executive succession planning, including assessment, development, and orchestrating succession processes with management and Boards of Directors. Also Board governance effectiveness. **Founded:** 1996. **Publications:** "Are You Rolling the Dice on CEO Succession?" Center for Healthcare Governance, 2006; "Leadership Due Diligence: The Neglected Governance Frontier," Directorship, Sep, 2001; "Leadership Due Diligence: Managing the Risks," The Corporate Board, Aug, 2001; "Succession: The need for detailed insight," Directors and Boards, 2001; "CEO Succession: Who's Doing Due Diligence?," 2001. **Telecommunication Services:** corlund@corlundgroup.com.

29243 ■ The Cradlerock Group
65 High Ridge Rd., Ste. 229
Stamford, CT 06905
Ph: (203)324-0088
Fax: (203)547-7778
Co. E-mail: info@cradlerock.com
URL: http://www.cradlerock.com
Contact: Scott Conley, President
Scope: Provider of teambuilding and personal challenge programs for both corporate and nonprofit groups. Utilizing both team-challenge and personal initiative courses, along with a variety of other outdoor-based adventure activities, participants being encouraged to explore group dynamics and personal abilities. Cradle rock facilitators then help the participants tolerate the outdoor experience to the business, education and social worlds. Industries served: large corporations, school districts, nonprofit organizations, and government agencies. **Founded:** 1984. **Seminars:** Team Start; Who Are We?; Who's On First?; Getting Past Stuck; Team Skills; Group Skills; Effective Team Leadership; Leading Global Teams; 360Coaching; The Other Diversity; Harnessing Change; The Art of Sale.

29244 ■ Delta Systems
5621 Somerset Dr.
Brooklyn, MI 49230
Ph: (517)592-5463
Fax: (517)592-5463
Co. E-mail: renee@4deltasystems.com
URL: http://www.4deltasystems.com
Contact: Renee R. Merchant, Owner
E-mail: renee@4deltasystems.com
Scope: Organizational development consultant specializing in team-building training and keynote speeches. Industries served: manufacturing, automotive suppliers, and nuclear power plants. **Founded:** 1982. **Publications:** "Teamwork Case"; "Changes, Choices, and Commitment"; "Make Teamwork a Way of Life"; "Checkered Flag Teams: Driving Your Workplace Into the Winners Circle"; "Success is a Team Effort"; "CARStyles™ - A Communication Style Model"; "Face Posters"; "CAR Styles Communication Model and Assessment". **Seminars:** Team Leader Training; Fast Cycle Time and Process Improvement; Change Leadership; Revitalizing Mature Teams; Fast Problem Solving; Pit Crew Challenge; Leadership Skills for Non-Supervisory People; Fast Start Teamwork; The Pit Crew Challenge.

29245 ■ Dimond Hospitality Consulting Group Inc.
5710 Stoneway Trl.
Nashville, TN 37209
Ph: (615)933-0033
Fax: (615)352-5290
Co. E-mail: drew@dimondhotelconsulting.com
URL: http://www.dimondhotelconsulting.com
Contact: Drew W. Dimond, President
E-mail: drew@dimondhotelconsulting.com
Scope: Specializes in strategic planning; start-up businesses; business process re-engineering; team

building; competitive analysis; venture capital; competitive intelligence; and due diligence. Offers litigation support. Comprehensive hospitality consulting firm that serves as an adviser to leading hotel companies, independent hotels, lending institutions, trustees, law firms, investment companies and municipalities in the areas of: Asset management, Acquisition due diligence, Arbitration, Disposition advisory services, Exit strategies, Financial review and analysis, Impact studies, Mediation. **Founded:** 1985. **Publications:** "The distressed debt conundrum," Jul, 2009; "How to buy distressed assets," Apr, 2009; "Cmbs Loans: A History and the Future," Apr, 2009; "Opportunity Knocks," Apr, 2009; "Another Reality Check," Mar, 2009; "An Inkling of Hope," Mar, 2009; "Strong World Tourism Growth in 2007," 2007; "Les U.S. Construction Pipeline Sets Another Record at 5011 Hotels with 654503 Rooms"; "Hotel Capitalization Rates Hold for Now"; "Winning Cornell Hotel and Restaurant Administration Quarterly Article Provides Hotel Brand Analysis"; "Breaking News for Lifestyle Hotels. Ian Schrager and Bill Marriott Announce Their Marriage Will the Schrager-Marriott Marriage Lead to Eternal Bliss Or End in Divorce What Will the M Hotels Children Be Named"; "Brands Vs Independents"; "Nyu Conf Takes Industry Temp"; "Economy Hotel Performance Indication of Travel Trends"; "Hotel Sales Continue at Brisk Pace"; "Fundamentals Strong, Weakening Undercurrent"; "Hotel Investments: Where Do We Go From Here"; "On the Road: Aahoa Panel Commits to Change"; "Cuba Not Ready, But Expecting U.S. Tourists".

29246 ■ The DuMond Group
5282 Princeton Ave.
Westminster, CA 92683-2753
Ph: (714)373-0610
Contact: Adrianne H. Geiger-Dumond, President
Scope: Human resources and executive search consulting firm that specializes in organizational development; small business management; employee surveys and communication; performance appraisals; and team building. **Founded:** 1992.

29247 ■ Dynamic Firm Management Inc.
4570 Campus Dr., Ste. 60
Newport Beach, CA 92660
Ph: (949)640-2220
Co. E-mail: info@dynamicfirm.com
URL: http://www.dynamicfirm.com
Contact: Dennis McCue, Principal
E-mail: mccue@dynamicfirm.com
Scope: Management consulting to law firms, accounting firms and other professional service providers. Emphasis on partnership relations, compensation, strategic planning, increasing revenues, profitable firm operations and effective management and team building. Initial work includes the determination of client's objectives; quantifying measurable accomplishments and outlining the consulting requirements. Industries served: law firms, attorneys, professional service. **Founded:** 1987. **Publications:** "Workflow Management," C2M: Consulting to Management - The Journal of Management Consulting, Jun, 2006; "Why Good Partnerships Go Bad," The Journal of Law Office Economics and Management, Feb, 2006; "The Wisdom of Ambulance Chasers," LACBA Update, Feb, 2005; "7 Components to Building A Successful Firm," LACBA Update, Nov, 2004; "Maximize the Productivity of Your Support Team," LACBA Update, Mar, 2004; "Perfect Union," Daily Journal, Mar, 2004; "Future Perfect," Daily Journal, Dec, 2003.

29248 ■ Eastern Point Consulting Group Inc.
36 Glen Ave.
Newton, MA 02464
Ph: (617)965-4141
Fax: (617)965-4172
Co. E-mail: info@eastpt.com
URL: http://www.eastpt.com
Contact: Katherine A. Herzog, President
E-mail: kherzog@eastpt.com
Scope: Specializes in bringing practical solutions to complex challenges. Provides consulting and training in managing diversity; comprehensive sexual-harassment policies and programs; organizational development; benchmarks 360 skills assessment; executive coaching; strategic human resource plan-

ning; team building; leadership development for women; mentoring programs; and gender issues in the workplace. **Founded:** 1995. **Seminars:** Leadership Development for Women.

29249 ■ Effective Resources Inc. (ERI)
118 N Peters Rd., Ste. 171
Knoxville, TN 37923
Ph: (865)622-7138
Free: 800-288-6044
Fax: (800)409-2812
Co. E-mail: customerservice@effectiveresources.com
URL: http://www.effectiveresources.com
Contact: Barry L. Brown, Principal
E-mail: barry@effectiveresources.com
Scope: Human resource consulting firm helping clients in all aspects of planning and implementation, to assure the program meets their objectives and budget considerations. Can work with clients on an interim basis or as consultants on short term assignment. Products and services include salary and benefits surveys, employee satisfaction surveys, performance management, compensation administration, compliance assistance and personality profile testing. Specializes in compensation and incentive plans, performance appraisals, team building and personnel policies and procedures, affirmative action plan preparation. **Founded:** 1988. **Special Services:** DiSC® Personality Profile.

29250 ■ Employee Development Systems Inc. (EDSI)
7308 S Alton Way, Ste. 2J
Centennial, CO 80112
Ph: (303)221-0710
Free: 800-282-3374
Fax: (303)221-0704
Co. E-mail: info@edsiusa.com
URL: http://www.employeedevelopmentsystems.com
Contact: Suzanne Updegraff, President
Scope: Produces training systems that increase employee productivity by motivating employees to take responsibility for their own performance and by showing employees and managers how to improve communications and create productive team relationships. **Founded:** 1979. **Publications:** "Company Connection Life Changing Lessons"; "Why People Skills are Still Being Taught at Work"; "Leading With Credibility Manage Up"; "Words of Peter Drucker"; "Coaching for Results". **Seminars:** Increasing Personal Effectiveness; Communicating to Manage Performance; ProAction: Responding to Change; Just-in-Time Training: Working Successfully in a Changing Environment, Challenging the Status Quo for Continuous Improvement, Assertive Communication and Reaching Agreement; Learning in the 21st Century, Apr, 2007.

29251 ■ Goldore Consulting Inc.
120-5 St. NW, Ste. 1
Linden, AB, Canada T0M 1J0
Ph: (403)546-4208
Fax: (403)546-4208
Co. E-mail: goldore@leadershipessentials.com
Contact: Robert A. Orr, President
E-mail: orr@leadershipessentials.com
Description: Description: Publishes materials on leadership and management skills for churches and charitable organizations that provide services to developing countries. Also publishes in Spanish and Portuguese. Does not accept unsolicited manuscripts. Reaches market through direct mail and wholesalers and distributors, including Leadership Training Ministry Foundation, Inc. **Scope:** Provides consulting service in leadership and management skills. Industries served: primarily charities, non-profits; some businesses. **Founded:** 1990. **Seminars:** The Challenge Of Leadership.

29252 ■ Grimmick Consulting Services (GCS)
455 Donner Way
San Ramon, CA 94582
Ph: (925)735-1036

Fax: (925)735-1100
Co. E-mail: hank@grimmickconsulting.com
URL: http://www.grimmickconsulting.com
Contact: Henry Grimmick, President
E-mail: hank@grimmickconsulting.com
Scope: Provider of consulting services in the areas of strategic planning; organizational assessment; organizational development; leadership and management development Baldridge criteria, process improvement and balanced scorecards and team dynamics. **Founded:** 1993.

29253 ■ Interminds & Federer Resources Inc.
106 E 6th St., Ste. 310
Austin, TX 78701-3659
Ph: (512)476-8800
Fax: (512)476-8811
Co. E-mail: yesyoucan@interminds.com
URL: http://www.interminds.com
Contact: Frank Federer, President
E-mail: ffederer@integra100.com
Scope: Specializes in feasibility studies; startup businesses; small business management; mergers and acquisitions; joint ventures; divestitures; interim management; crisis management; turnarounds; production planning; team building; appraisals and valuations. **Founded:** 1985. **Publications:** "Yes You Can: How To Be A Success No Matter Who You Are Or Where You're From".

29254 ■ Interpersonal Communication Programs Inc. (ICP)—Couple Communication
30772 Southview Dr., Ste. 200
Evergreen, CO 80439
Ph: (303)674-2051
Free: 800-328-5099
Fax: (303)674-4283
Co. E-mail: icp@comskills.com
URL: http://www.couplecommunication.com
Contact: Phyllis A. Miller, President
E-mail: phyllis@comskills.com
Description: Description: Publishes works dealing with communications. Offers instructor and participant materials plus training. Reaches market through direct mail and trade sales. Does not accept unsolicited manuscripts. **Scope:** Provider of team building and interpersonal communication training in small and large corporations. Serves private industries as well as government agencies. **Founded:** 1972. **Publications:** "CC I & II texts"; "Collaborative Marriage Skills and Thriving Together in the Skills Zone"; "Core communication"; "Alive and Aware"; "Straight Talk," Connecting With Self and Others. **Seminars:** Collaborative Team Skills for Intact Work Groups; Core Communication: Skills and Processes for Managers, Supervisors and Employees; Couple communication I and II. **Special Services:** Awareness Wheel®; Styles of Communication® ; Listening Cycle®; Styles of Communication®.

29255 ■ K & T Training—K & T Consulting
103 Greenville St.
Newnan, GA 30263
Ph: (770)253-5870
Fax: (770)253-8866
Contact: J. R. Tumperi, President
Scope: Specializes in strategic planning; profit enhancement; organizational development; start-up businesses; interim management; crisis management; turnarounds; business process re-engineering; team building; cost controls. **Founded:** 1983.

29256 ■ Ken Blanchard Co.
125 State Pl.
Escondido, CA 92029-1323
Ph: (760)489-5005
Free: 800-728-6000
Fax: (760)489-8407
Co. E-mail: contact@kenblanchard.com
URL: http://www.kenblanchard.com
Contact: Howard Farfel, President
Scope: Full service management development-training company known for development of the one minute manager concept. Develops and sells quality products and services that enhance management and leadership skills. Offers seminars, workshops, in house consulting, videos, audio tapes, slides, books, instruments and games. Areas of expertise include management training, team building, attitude and

needs assessment, productivity improvement, motivation, and corporate development. Industries served: health, hospitality, financial, food service, telecommunications, retail, utilities, associations, aerospace, automotive, military, education, manufacturing, and government agencies. **Founded:** 1979. **Publications:** "Who Killed Change? Solving the Mystery of Leading People Through Change," 2009; "Helping People Win at Work: A Business Philosophy Called Don't Mark My Paper, Help Me Get An A," 2009; "Leading at a Higher Level," 2009; "The One Minute Entrepreneur," 2008; "Coaching in Organizations," 2008; "Know Can Do! Put Your Know-How Into Action," Oct, 2007; "Hamster Revolution, The: Stop Info Glut-Reclaim Your Life!"; "Leading at a Higher Level: Blanchard on Leadership and Creating High Performing Organizations"; "The Simple Truths of Service"; "Building High Performing Teams"; "Leadership Training for Supervisors"; "Legendary Service"; "The One Minute Manager"; "Whale Done!"; "The Power of Ethical Management"; "Managing By Values"; "The Leader Within"; "Leverage Your Best, Ditch the Rest"; "High Five". **Seminars:** Situational Leadership II®; Situational Team Leadership; The One Minute Manager; Leadership and The One Minute Manager; Putting The One Minute Manager to Work; Ethical Management; Situational Frontline Leadership; The Magic of Situational Self Leadership; DISCovering Self and Others; Coaching Essentials for Leaders; Legendary Service; Whale Done!®; GungHo!®.

29257 ■ William E. Kuhn & Associates
234 Cook St.
Denver, CO 80206-5305
Ph: (303)322-8233
Fax: (303)331-9032
Co. E-mail: billkuhn1@cs.com
Contact: William E. Kuhn, Owner
E-mail: billkuhn1@cs.com

Scope: Firm specializes in strategic planning; profit enhancement; small business management; mergers and acquisitions; joint ventures; divestitures; human resources management; performance appraisals; team building; sales management; appraisals and valuations. **Founded:** 1980. **Publications:** "Creating a High-Performance Dealership," Office SOLUTIONS & Office DEALER, Jul-Aug, 2006.

29258 ■ LDG Associates
8094 Mission Vista Dr.
San Diego, CA 92120-1537
Ph: (619)583-0261
Fax: (619)583-4608
Co. E-mail: doug144@carolina.rr.com
Contact: Larry D. Gable, Manager

Scope: Consultants in leadership training and development, coaching, 360 degree feedback, and team building. Specialize in helping leaders build effective teams. Leaders learn specific skills to help them achieve individual and organizational objectives. Industries served medical manufacturing, aerospace, electrical manufacturing, manufacturing, petroleum, and government agencies. **Founded:** 1988. **Seminars:** Leadership Styles and Strategies; Influencing Styles and Strategies; Organizing Yourself and Others; Team Building; 360 Degree Feedback; Executive Coaching; Stress Management; Leadership 2000; Team Building 2000. **Telecommunication Services:** doug144@earthlink.net.

29259 ■ May Toy Lukens
3226 NE 26th Ct.
Renton, WA 98056
Ph: (425)891-3226
Contact: May T. Lukens, Principal

Scope: Provides training to teach people to think of ways to improve their operations continuously by changing the way they think. Industries served: All, particularly financial. Operational analysis and training. **Founded:** 1996. **Seminars:** Seminars and workshops in maximizing resource utilization and staff potential.

29260 ■ Lupfer & Associates (L&A)
92 Glen St.
Natick, MA 01760-5646
Ph: (508)655-3950

Fax: (508)655-7826
Co. E-mail: donlupfer@aol.com
Contact: Donald Lupfer, Owner
E-mail: don.lupfer@lupferassociates.com

Scope: Assists off shore hi-tech companies in entering United States markets and specializes in channel development for all sorts of products. Perform MARCOM support for hi-tech United States clients. **Founded:** 1988. **Publications:** "What's Next For Distribution-Feast or Famine"; "The Changing Global Marketplace"; "Making Global Distribution Work". **Seminars:** How to do Business in the United States.

29261 ■ MAA Consulting Inc.
546 Hillcrest Dr.
Bowling Green, OH 43402
Ph: (419)352-7782
Fax: (419)354-8781
Co. E-mail: maa@wcnet.org
Contact: Ruth P. Varney, President

Scope: Offers counsel in organizational diagnosis, development and change, as well as management development, manpower planning and forecasting, performance appraisal, management by objectives, team building, related industrial and human relations areas, and a strong emphasis on self directed work teams. Industries served: energy, health care, auto parts manufacturers, chemical, financial, petroleum, and government agencies. **Founded:** 1967. **Publications:** "Caribbean Island Survival II"; "Alaskan Adventure"; "Task Force"; "Group Process Questionnaire"; "Acceleration"; "Contracting for Change"; "The Discipline of Change Management," 2005; "An Operational Definition of Odc," 2004; "Cases in Organization Development," 1999; "Measuring and Improving Teamwork," 1998; "Name Recognition of Master Level Graduate Programs in Organization Development and Change," 1998; "A Critical Examination of a Failed Attempt to Implement Self-Directed Work Teams," 1996; "Organization Development," 1996; "Rethinking the Knowledge Worker: Where Have All the Workers Gone," 1995; "The Primary Determinant of Successful Application of Self-Directed Work Teams," 1994; "Helping a Team Find All the Answers," 1991; "The Caster Case," 1990; "Teamwork Survey and Planning Guide," 1990. **Seminars:** Implementing Self-Directed Work Teams; SDWT Simulation; Managing Team Productivity; Navigating the Mine Fields of Change.

29262 ■ Mandalay Associates L.L.C.
190 El Cerrito Plz., Ste. 226
El Cerrito, CA 94530-4002
Ph: (510)526-4651
Fax: (510)526-5774
Contact: Kristina Combs, Member

Scope: Business management firm specializes in conflict resolution, employee relations, employment and placement, organizational analysis and development, human resources program development, program and project management, and staff development and training.

29263 ■ Miller, Hellwig Associates
150 W End Ave.
New York, NY 10023-5713
Ph: (212)799-0471
Fax: (212)877-0186
Co. E-mail: millerhelwig@earthlink.net
Contact: Ernest C. Miller, President

Scope: Consulting services in the areas of start-up businesses; small business management; employee surveys and communication; performance appraisals; executive searches; team building; personnel policies and procedures; market research. Also involved in improving cross-cultural and multi-cultural relationships, particularly with Japanese clients. **Founded:** 1984. **Seminars:** Objectives and standards/recruiting for boards of directors.

29264 ■ Jane Moosbruker, Organization Development Consultant
72 Coventry Wood Rd.
Bolton, MA 01740-1123
Ph: (978)779-5423

Fax: (978)779-6036
Co. E-mail: jamoos@ziplink.net
Contact: Jane Moosbruker, Owner

Scope: Offers process-oriented consultation to organizations, in the areas of organizational change, team building, management development, and conflict utilization. Industries served include biotechnology, information services, computer technology, aerospace, education, healthcare, and environmental. **Founded:** 1970. **Publications:** "Transitioning Work Groups Into High Performing Teams," 1993; "Group Dynamics- History and Future," Vienna: Wuv-Verlag, 1993; "Business Process Redesign and Organization Development-Applied Behavioral Science," 1998; "Forgotten Elements: Including Structure and Process in Recovery Efforts". **Seminars:** Managing Organizational Change; Facilitating and Managing Complex Systems Change; Team Leadership for Developing a High Productivity Team; Building a Team-based Organization; Conflict Utilization; Team Skills.

29265 ■ Murray Dropkin & Associates—Dropkin Consulting
390 George St.
New Brunswick, NJ 08901
Ph: (732)828-3211
Fax: (732)828-4118
Co. E-mail: murray@dropkin.com
URL: http://www.dropkin.com
Contact: Murray Dropkin, President
E-mail: murray@dropkin.com

Scope: Specializes in feasibility studies; business management; business process re-engineering; and team building, health care and housing. **Founded:** 1969. **Publications:** "Bookkeeping for Nonprofits," Jossey Bass, 2005; "Guide to Audits of Nonprofit Organizations," PPC; "The Nonprofit Report," Warren, Gorham & Lamont; "The Budget Building Book for Nonprofits," Jossey-Bass; "The Cash Flow Management Book for Nonprofits," Jossey-Bass.

29266 ■ MW Corp.
2538 Crompond Rd.
Yorktown Heights, NY 10598
Ph: (914)528-0888
Contact: Ann Harper, Owner

Scope: Training firm provides training materials books and videos and conducts public workshops and custom-designed on-site training and development in the areas of management development, supervisor technical leader training and development, team development, facilitator training, self-directed work teams, quality customer service workshops, and employee involvement programs. Serves all types of organizations. **Founded:** 1983. **Publications:** "Leading a Service Team"; "A Team Leader's Day"; "The Changing Workplace"; "Self-Directed Work Teams"; "Supervisor in Transition". **Seminars:** Self-Directed Work Teams; The Management Workshop; First-line Supervisor/Technical Leader Workshop.

29267 ■ New Commons
545 Pawtucket Ave., Studio 106A
Pawtucket, RI 02860
Ph: (401)351-7110
Fax: (401)351-7158
Co. E-mail: info@newcommons.com
URL: http://www.newcommons.com
Contact: Robert Leaver, Chief Executive Officer
E-mail: rleaver@newcommons.com

Scope: Builder of agile human networks to champion innovation and mobilize change; to pursue business opportunities; to custom design agile organizations and communities, to foster civic engagement. Clients include organizations on-profits, corporations, government agencies, educational institutions; networks-Trade/professional groups, IT services collaborations; service-sharing collectives; and communities- municipalities, states and statewide agencies, regional collaborations. **Founded:** 1982. **Publications:** "Plexus Imperative," Sep, 2005; "Creating 21st Century Capable Innovation Systems," Aug, 2004; "Call to Action: Building Providences Creative and Innovative Economy" "Getting Results from Meetings"; "The Entrepreneur as Artist," Commonwealth Publications; "Leader and Agent of Change," Commonwealth Publications; "Achieving our Providence: Lessons of City-Building," Commonwealth Publications. **Seminars:** Introduction to Social Computing (Web 2.0),

Jan, 2009; Every Company Counts, Jun, 2009; Facilitating for Results; Story-Making and Story-Telling. **Telecommunication Services:** inquiries@new-commons.com.

29268 ■ Organizational Transformations
PO Box 2553
Aptos, CA 95001-2553
Ph: (831)688-1344
Fax: (831)688-8091
URL: http://www.orgtrans.com
Contact: Rochelle Sjolseth, Owner
E-mail: rochelle@orgtrans.com
Scope: A management and organizational consulting firm that provides customized strategies to help companies increase productivity and profit. Specializes in organizational development, executive coaching, team building, conflict resolution and work comp reduction.

29269 ■ P2C2 Group Inc.
4101 Denfeld Ave.
Kensington, MD 20895-1514
Ph: (301)942-7985
Fax: (301)942-7986
Co. E-mail: info@p2c2group.com
URL: http://www.p2c2group.com
Contact: James E. Kendrick, President
E-mail: kendrick@p2c2group.com
Scope: Works with clients on the business side of federal program and project management. Services include program/project planning and optimization; acquisition strategy and work statements; IT Capital Planning and Investment Control (CPIC); business cases - new, revisions, critiques; budget analysis - cost benefits- alternatives; CPIC, SELC, and security documentation; research, metrics, analysis, and case studies. Consulting support helping to: Define or redefine programs; strengthen portfolio management; identify alternatives for lean budgets; improve capital planning and investment; develop better plans and documentation, and evaluate performance of existing program investments. **Founded:** 1994. **Publications:** "OMB 300s Go Online," Federal Sector Report, Mar, 2007; "Using Risk-Adjusted Costs for Projects," Federal Sector Report, Feb, 2007; "Make Better Decisions Using Case Studies," Federal Sector Report, Jan, 2007; "PMO Performance Measurement & Metrics"; "Executive Sponsors for Projects"; "ABCs of the Presidential Transition"; "Financial Systems and Enterprise Portfolio Management"; "The Future of CPIC"; "Critical Factors for Program and Project Success"; "Using Risk-Adjusted Costs for Projects"; "Tactics for a Successful Year of CPIC"; "Operational Analysis Reviews"; "Successful IT Strategic Planning"; "Information Technology Investment Management". **Seminars:** Requests For Information; Pre Solicitation Marketing; Qualifications Statement Support For The Capital Planning And Investment Control (cpic) Process; How To Hire A Management Consultant And Get The Results You Expect.

29270 ■ Glenn M. Parker Associates Inc.—Glenn Parker Team Building Consultant
36 Otter Creek Rd.
Skillman, NJ 08558
Ph: (609)333-0203
Fax: (609)333-0204
Co. E-mail: glenn@glennparker.com
URL: http://www.glennparker.com
Contact: Glenn M. Parker, President
E-mail: gparker@glennparker.com
Scope: Provider of the following services: teambuilding without business teams, training workshops in team effectiveness, facilitation skills and meeting management, consulting to help organizations transition to a team-based operation, speaking at professional conferences and corporate meeting and diagnostic services to assess the effectiveness of teams and organizations. **Founded:** 1971. **Publications:** "Women Love Team Players"; "Meeting Excellence: 33 Tools to Lead Meetings That Get Results," Jossey Bass/Wiley, 2006; "Cross Functional Teams: Working with Allies, Enemies and Other Strangers, Completely Revised and Updates," 2003; "Team Depot: A Warehouse of 585 Tools to Reassess, Rehabilitate and Rejuvenate Your Team," Jossey-Bass/Pfeiffer/Wiley, 2002; "Team Workout: A Trainer's Source book of 50 Team Building Games and Activi-

ties," Hrd Press, 2001; "Rewarding Teams: Lessons From the Trenches," Jossey-Bass/Wiley, 2000; "Teamwork and Team play: Games and Activities for Building and Training Teams," Jossey-Bass/Pfeiffer, 1999; "25 Instruments for Team Building," Hrd Press, 1998; "Video: Team Building: What Makes a Good Team Player," Crm Learning, 1996; "Cross-Functional Teams Tool Kit," Pfeiffer/Jossey Bass, 1997; "Best Practices for Teams," Hrd Press, 1996; "50 Activities for Self-Directed Teams," Hrd Press, 1994; "50 Activities for Team Building," Hrd Press, 1992; "Instruments: Parker Team Player Survey," Consulting Psychologists Press, 1992; "Team Development Survey," Consulting Psychologists Press, 1992; "Team Players and Teamwork," Jossey-Bass, 1990. **Seminars:** Effective Conflict Resolution; How to Build Strong Teams and Develop Team Players; Effective Meetings; Skills and Techniques for Successful Cross-Functional Teamwork; Boundary Management; How to Plan and Conduct a Successful Team Meeting; Building A Facilitator's Tool Kit.

29271 ■ Parker Consultants Inc.
230 Mason St.
Greenwich, CT 06830-6633
Ph: (203)861-6698
Contact: Donald L. Parker, President
Scope: Firm specializes in strategic planning; organizational development; small business management; performance appraisals; executive searches; team building; and customer service audits. **Founded:** 1988.

29272 ■ Partnerwerks Inc.
PO Box 1046
Comfort, TX 78013
Ph: (830)995-4853
Fax: (830)995-4854
Co. E-mail: info@partnerwerks.com
URL: http://www.christopheravery.com
Contact: Christopher M. Avery, President
E-mail: cavery@partnerwerks.com
Scope: Specializes in development of leadership skills for managing relationships with a client company's customers, suppliers and employees. **Founded:** 1991. **Publications:** "Teamwork Is An Individual Skill: Getting Your Work Done When Sharing Responsibility," Berrett-Kohler, 2001; "The Leaders Guide". **Seminars:** Leadership: Simply Solve the Real Problem, Jun, 2010; Project Team Leadership; Managing Teams; Team Planning.

29273 ■ Performance Consulting Associates Inc. (PCA)
3700 Crestwood Pky., Ste. 100
Duluth, GA 30096
Ph: (770)717-2737
Fax: (770)717-7014
Co. E-mail: info@pcaconsulting.com
URL: http://www.pcaconsulting.com
Contact: Richard A. Defazio, President
E-mail: defazio@pcaconsulting.com
Scope: Maintenance consulting and engineering firm specializing in production planning, project management, team building, and re-engineering maintenance. **Founded:** 1976. **Publications:** "Does Planning Pay," Plant Services, Nov, 2000; "Asset Reliability Coordinator," Maintenance Technology, Oct, 2000; "Know What it is You Have to Maintain," Maintenance Technology, May, 2000; "Does Maintenance Planning Pay," Maintenance Technology, Nov, 2000.; "What is Asset Management?"; "Implementing Best Business Practices".

29274 ■ Performance Technologies Inc.
137 N main St., Ste. 1016
Dayton, OH 45414
Ph: (937)296-5060
Fax: (937)890-7853
Co. E-mail: info@performancetec.com
Contact: Norm Evans, Sr., Principal
Scope: A consulting/training firm that designs and instills sales, leadership and management skills, processes, and tools that strengthens overall organizational effectiveness. Services include: organizational transformation, creation of vision, values and operating philosophy, business analysis, impact analysis, innovation technology, succession planning, and process mapping. Training services include:

Advanced sales strategies, sales coaching and management, training processes, management effectiveness, leadership development, performance management, measurement and assessment. **Founded:** 1982. **Publications:** "Get- Real Selling".

29275 ■ Pilot Consulting Corp.
29 Wildhorse Trl.
Crested Butte, CO 81224-1249
Ph: (970)349-1250
Fax: (970)349-1251
Co. E-mail: info@pilotconsulting.com
URL: http://www.pilotconsulting.com
Contact: Christopher A. Cappy, President
E-mail: ccappy@pilotconsulting.com
Scope: Specializes in the implementation of strategy, management of transition and development of leadership in companies. **Founded:** 1995. **Publications:** "Leading Beyond the Walls". **Seminars:** Facilitative Leadership Training. **Telecommunication Services:** ccappy@pilotconsulting.com.

29276 ■ Pioneering Management Possibilities (PMP)—Personal Mastery Programs
31000 Telegraph Rd., Ste. 260
Bingham Farms, MI 48025
Ph: (248)647-9290
Fax: (248)647-1537
Co. E-mail: bzimmerman@pmpcoach.com
URL: http://www.pioneeringmanagement.com
Contact: Mark B. Stein, President
E-mail: mstein@pmpcoach.com
Scope: A team of management consultants and business coaches specializing in the application of management principles. Areas include team building, strategic planning, personal development, leadership development and management training. **Founded:** 1987. **Publications:** "Accountability - Compliance or Commitment"; "Leadership - The Missing Link"; "Succession Planning: An Imperative for Personal Growth"; "The Soft Stuff Yields Hard Results". **Seminars:** Fomenting Innovation; The Practice of Leadership; Leadership, Culture and Corporate Performance; Transforming Behavioral Health care Through Innovation and Collaboration; Leadership Succession.

29277 ■ Positive Impact Consulting
9845 Horn Rd., Ste. 120
Sacramento, CA 95827
Ph: (916)366-3000
Free: 800-376-7484
Fax: (916)364-9860
Co. E-mail: info@positiveimpact.com
URL: http://www.positiveimpact.com
Contact: Michele Mansfield, President
Scope: Management services in executive development, strategic planning, team building, organization-wide surveys, customer surveys, systems and process redesigns, skills assessments, TQM overview training, TQM tools training, positive impact facilitator training, the coaching experience (TQM leadership training), customized course designing. **Founded:** 1985. **Seminars:** The Coaching Experience, Jul, 2007; Facilitator Boot Camp, May, 2007; On-The-Spot Communicating, May, 2007; Cafe de la Facilitation, Apr, 2007; Becoming a Great Recorder, Mar, 2007.

29278 ■ Profit Associates Inc.
26 Hunters Forest Dr.
Charleston, SC 29414
Ph: (843)763-5718
Free: 800-688-6304
Fax: (843)763-5719
Co. E-mail: bobrog@profit-associates.com
URL: http://www.profit-associates.com
Contact: Bob Rogers, Managing Director
E-mail: bobrog@awod.com
Scope: A team of management and turnaround specialists providing consulting services. Focuses on the problems of small to medium-sized businesses in the manufacturing, distribution, construction, software. Specializes in employee productivity and incentives, management reengineering, profit and expense controls, production planning, strategic business planning, marketing and public relations, or ISO 9000 support. **Founded:** 1993. **Seminars:** Essential Ele-

ments of a Good Incentive Program; Why Look at Management Re-engineering; The Profit & Expense Control Process; The Executive Coaching Alternative.

29279 ■ Renaissance Leadership
2500 Olde King Cir.
Midlothian, VA 23113-9685
Ph: (804)423-4266
Fax: (804)423-4267
Co. E-mail: tomnewton@renlead.com
URL: http://www.renlead.com
Contact: Thomas W. Newton, President
E-mail: tomnewton@renlead.com
Scope: Specializes in the strategic building of high performance organizations and culture. Offer strategic consulting, executive coaching, team development and cultural transformation seminars which combine contemporary learning theory, leadership practice, and work-related outdoor adventures. Serves all industries in the United States, Europe, Central America and Asia. **Founded:** 1978. **Seminars:** Culture Change Leadership; Creating High Performance Learning Organizations; Life Planning; Thriving on Change; Team Building and Alignment; Creativity, Risk Taking, and Innovation; Creating a High Performance Culture; Servant Leadership; Capitalizing on Diversity; Coaching for Optimal Performance.

29280 ■ Soul Works
3809 County Road E
Swanton, OH 43558-9276
Ph: (419)825-2444
Contact: Robert Anderson, Owner
Scope: Organizational development consulting and training firm that specializes in leadership development and creating high performance work systems. Focuses on organizational system change and work redesign efforts. Also supports system change with an integrated curriculum of leadership development workshops. Provides workshops and consulting services including empowered entrepreneurial leadership, personal and organizational vision, teamwork and involvement and a whole systems perspective when implementing change. Industries served: private industries including healthcare organizations, manufacturing, service and nonprofit. **Founded:** 1986. **Seminars:** Organizational Control and Dependency; Aligned Teams; Mastering Leadership!.

29281 ■ Stier Associates
4 Dunellen
Cromwell, CT 06416-2702
Ph: (860)635-1590
Fax: (860)635-1591
Co. E-mail: sstier7@comcast.net
Contact: Dr. Suzanne Stier, President
Scope: Offers personal development consulting. Services include: succession planning, executive coaching, strategic management, team building, and board development. Consulting services for public companies include: process consulting, team building, executive coaching, diversity management, strategic management and religious institutions. **Founded:** 1981.

29282 ■ Tamayo Consulting Inc.
169 Saxony Rd., Ste. 112
Encinitas, CA 92024-6779
Ph: (760)479-1352
Fax: (760)479-1465
Co. E-mail: info@tamayoconsulting.com
URL: http://www.tamayoconsulting.com
Contact: Jennifer Dreyer, President
E-mail: jdreyer@earthlink.net
Scope: It Provides training and consulting services. And also it specializes in leadership and team development. Industries served: private, non-profit, government, educational. **Founded:** 1996. **Seminars:** Presentation AdvantEdge Program; Lead point Development Program; Supervisor Development Programs.Identify Presentation Objectives; Implement 360-degree presentation assessment; conduct baseline-coaching session; Develop coaching plan; Staying connected.

29283 ■ Vision Management
149 Meadows Rd.
Lafayette, NJ 07848-3120
Ph: (973)702-1116
Fax: (973)702-8311
Contact: Norman L. Naidish, President
Scope: Firm specializes in profit enhancement; strategic planning; business process reengineering; industrial engineering; facilities planning; team building; inventory management; and total quality management (TQM). **Founded:** 1984. **Publications:** "To increase profits, improve quality," Manufacturing Engineering, May, 2000.

29284 ■ Steve Wilson and Co.
1159 S Creekway Ct.
Columbus, OH 43230
Ph: (614)855-4733
Free: 800-669-5233
Fax: (614)855-4889
Co. E-mail: steve@stevewilson.com
URL: http://www.stevewilson.com
Contact: Steve Wilson, President
E-mail: steve@stevewilson.com
Scope: Specializing in team building, staff development and personal growth, consultant presents the way humor works and awakens new ways of relating to ourselves and others. Consultant carries designation of Certified Speaking Professional (CSP) and is one of seven persons worldwide certified in I Power program instruction. The topics that consultant specializes in are: health and humor, funny business, motivation and productivity, human relations, stress management, team building, communication, and creativity. Industries served: Education, medical, telecommunications, service, allied medical, sales, training, real estate, associations, universities and colleges, temporary services, state and federal government, churches, and manufacturing worldwide. **Founded:** 1985. **Publications:** "Good Hearted Living"; "Birthrights: Your Essence, Purpose & Self-Esteem"; "Toilet Paper, Toothpaste, and Tuna Noodle Casserole"; "The Steve Wilson Report"; "The Art of Mixing Work and Play," Sep, 1992; "Super Humor Power," Oct, 1992; "Remarried with Children," May, 1992; "Eat Dessert First," May, 1990; "CHILL!". **Seminars:** Creating Positive Working Environments@su1TM@su2; Putting Humor to Work at Work; Pulling Together Instead of Falling Apart; Winning over Customers from Hell; The Play shop Lab@su1TM@su2; Humor For the Health of It; I-Power; Don't Postpone Joy@su1TM@su2; Laughing Matters in the Classroom; The Art of Mixing Work and Play@su1TM@su2; and Managing Stress Through Humor.

FRANCHISES AND BUSINESS OPPORTUNITIES

29285 ■ Turbo Leadership Systems Ltd.
36280 NE Wilsonville Rd.
Newberg, OR 97132
Ph: (503)625-1867
Fax: (503)625-2699
Description: Management training and team building training. **No. of Company-Owned Units:** 1. **Founded:** 1985.. **Franchised:** 1995. **Equity Capital Needed:** $49,000. **Franchise Fee:** $39,000. **Training:** Yes.

COMPUTER SYSTEMS/ SOFTWARE

29286 ■ *Facilitation Skills for Team Leaders*
Chris Learning
PO Box 25690
Rochester, NY 14625
Ph: (888)534-5556
Free: 800-442-7477
Fax: (888)715-0220
Co. E-mail: customerservice@axzopress.com
URL: http://www.axzopress.com
Price: $13.95. **Description:** Bring out the collaborative voices of your team members. Get started with

this simple six-step plan. Increase participation and team efficiency. Develop feedback and clarification skills. Shortcut the path to team consensus.

29287 ■ *Team Problem Solving*
Chris Learning
PO Box 25690
Rochester, NY 14625
Ph: (888)534-5556
Free: 800-442-7477
Fax: (888)715-0220
Co. E-mail: customerservice@axzopress.com
URL: http://www.axzopress.com
Price: $13.95 (VCI CD-ROM). **Description:** Based on the Team Problem-Solving and Decision-Making video and book. Includes book and user's guide.

LIBRARIES

29288 ■ Employment Support Center Library
1556 Wisconsin Ave., NW
Washington, DC 20007
Ph: (202)628-2919
Fax: (703)790-1469
Co. E-mail: escjobclubs@yahoo.com
URL: http://jobclubs.angelfire.com/
Contact: Ellie Wegener, Executive Director
Scope: Employment networking, self-esteem, starting your own business, setting up job clubs, training facilitators, maintaining a large job bank, providing job-searching skills. **Services:** Library open to the public. **Founded:** 1984. **Holdings:** 150 articles; books; periodicals; videos on job search; interviews; reports; manuscripts. **Subscriptions:** 4 journals and other serials; 2 newspapers.

RESEARCH CENTERS

29289 ■ Riegel and Emory Human Resource Research Center
Darla-Moore School of Business
University of S Carolina at Columbia
1705 College St.
Columbia, SC 29208
Ph: (803)777-4901
Fax: (803)777-6876
Co. E-mail: klaasb@moore.sc.edu
URL: http://www.moore.sc.edu/facultyandresearch/researchcenters/riegelemoryhrcenter.asp x
Contact: Prof. Brian S. Klaas, Director
Founded: 1982. **Publications:** *Values Research Project Reprint Series.*

29290 ■ University of North Carolina at Chapel Hill - Frank Hawkins Kenan Institute of Private Enterprise
Kenan Ctr., CB 3440
Chapel Hill, NC 27599-3440
Ph: (919)962-8201
Fax: (919)962-8202
Co. E-mail: john_kasarda@kenan-flagler.unc.edu
URL: http://www.kenan-flagler.unc.edu/KI
Contact: Raymond Farrow, Executive Director
E-mail: raymond_farrow@unc.edu
Founded: 1985. **Educational Activities:** Carolina Challenge Star Program; Carolina Entrepreneurial Initiative; International Executive Series and MBA Enterprise Corps. **Awards:** Citibank International Fellows Program. **Telecommunication Services:** kenan_institute@unc.edu.

29291 ■ University of Southern California - Center for Effective Organizations (CEO)
Davidson Conference Ctr., Ste. 200
Marshall School of Business
3415 S Figueroa St.
Los Angeles, CA 90089-0871
Ph: (213)740-9814
Fax: (213)740-4354
Co. E-mail: elawler@marshall.usc.edu
URL: http://ceo.usc.edu
Contact: Prof. Edward E. Lawler, III, Director
Founded: 1979. **Educational Activities:** HCEO Certificate Program; Organization Design Workshop and Organization Design Certificate. **Telecommunication Services:** ceo@usc.edu.

ASSOCIATIONS AND OTHER ORGANIZATIONS

29292 ■ **International Association of Professional Security Consultants (IAPSC)**
575 Market St., Ste. 2125
San Francisco, CA 94105
Ph: (415)536-0288
Fax: (415)764-4915
Co. E-mail: iapsc@iapsc.org
URL: http://www.iapsc.org
Contact: Richard Grassie, President

Description: Security management, technical, training and forensic consultants. Promotes understanding and cooperation among members and industries or individuals requiring such services. Seeks to enhance members' knowledge through seminars, training programs and educational materials. Works to foster public awareness of the security consulting industry; serves as a clearinghouse for consultants' requirements. Maintains code of conduct, ethics and professional standards. Offers consultant referral service; operates speakers' bureau. **Founded:** 1984. **Publications:** *IAPSC News* (Quarterly); *IAPSC Consultants Directory* (Annual). **Educational Activities:** International Association of Professional Security Consultants Convention (Annual); How to Succeed as a Professional Security Consultant. **Awards:** Charles A. Sennewald Distinguished Service Accolade (Annual).

REFERENCE WORKS

29293 ■ *"How to Detect and Prevent Employee Fraud" in Contractor (Vol. 56, October 2009, No. 10, pp. 57)*
Pub: Penton Media, Inc.

Ed: James R. Leichter. **Description:** Mechanical contractors can prevent employee fraud by handing out a detailed employment policy manual to their employees and making sure that their invoices are numbered. It is also highly advised to have bank statements reconciled by a third party.

29294 ■ *"Retailers Report 'Shrinkage' of Inventory on the Rise" in Arkansas Business (Vol. 26, September 28, 2009, No. 39, pp. 17)*
Pub: Journal Publishing Inc.

Ed: Mark Friedman. **Description:** According to a National Retail Security Survey report released last June, retailers across the country have lost about $36.5 billion in shrinkage, most of it at the hands of employees and shoplifters alike. Statistical data included.

29295 ■ *"What Has Sergey Wrought?" in Barron's (Vol. 89, July 13, 2009, No. 28, pp. 8)*
Pub: Dow Jones & Co., Inc.

Ed: Alan Abelson. **Description:** Sergey Aleynikov is a computer expert that once worked for Goldman Sachs but he was arrested after he left the company and charged with theft for bringing with him the code for the company's proprietary software for high-frequency trading. The stock market has been down for four straight weeks as of July 13, 2009 which reflects the reality of how the economy is still struggling.

TRADE PERIODICALS

29296 ■ *Security Letter*
Pub: Security Letter Inc.
Contact: Maria Madia, Manager
Ed: Robert D. McCrie, Editor, rmccrie@mindspring.com. **Released:** 22/year. **Price:** $217, U.S. and Canada. **Description:** Contains solution-oriented information on security and protection of assets from loss, particularly for executives concerned about the following: internal checks and controls, personnel practices, management of change, fraud and embezzlement, business crime trends, security, and urban terrorism. Recurring features include news of research, a calendar of events, semiannual FBI crime data, quarterly financial news of major companies in the security industry, book reviews, security and safety pointers, and a question-and-answer feature.

VIDEOCASSETTES/AUDIOCASSETTES

29297 ■ *Choices: How to Control Internal Shrink*
Excellence in Training Corp.
c/o ICON Training
804 Roosevelt St.
Polk City, IA 50226
Free: 800-609-0479
Co. E-mail: info@icontraining.com
URL: http://www.icontraining.com
Released: 1987. **Price:** $550.00. **Description:** Offers tips for retail stores to cut down employee theft through a look at two new employees: one conscientious, one not. **Availability:** VHS; 3/4 U.

29298 ■ *Stop Business Crime: Shoplifting & Employee Theft*
Instructional Video
2219 C St.
Lincoln, NE 68502
Ph: (402)475-6570
Free: 800-228-0164
Fax: (402)475-6500
Co. E-mail: feedback@insvideo.com
URL: http://www.insvideo.com
Released: 19??. **Price:** $79.95. **Description:** Offers solutions the problems of shoplifting and employee theft. Includes examples of how each is done followed by several alternatives that could be used to prevent them. **Availability:** VHS.

CONSULTANTS

29299 ■ **AlixPartners**
2000 Town Ctr., Ste. 2400
Southfield, MI 48075-1250
Ph: (248)358-4420
Fax: (248)358-1969
Co. E-mail: info@alixpartners.com
URL: http://www.alixpartners.com
Contact: Jay Alix, Chief Executive Officer
E-mail: jalix@alixpartners.com
Scope: Corporate turnaround and crisis management consultants specialize in debt restructuring, chapter 11 reorganizations, workout negotiations, refinancing, litigation support, forensic accounting, fraud investigations, valuation and expert testimony and information technology outsourcing management and realignment. **Founded:** 1981. **Publications:** "Managing Along the Cutting Edge," Newsweek, Feb, 2009; "Mitigating Fcpa Risks When Doing Business in China," Bloomberg Corporate Law Journal, Feb, 2009; "Crisis Management Alix partners," Consulting Magazine, 2008; "Getting The Most Out Of IT C Suite Survey"; "Vestar Minority Deal Turns Into Turnaround"; "The Impact of US Style Regulation in Europe"; "The Corporate Superheroes Who Support Strapped Businesses in Their Hour of Need," the Daily Telegraph, Dec, 2008; "Changes to Claim Objection Rules Go Effective," Dec, 2007; "Squeeze Makes Life Harder," Financial Times, Oct, 2007; "Dialing for Dollars and Other Tactics for Finding Cash for the Estate," Abi Journal, Oct, 2007; "Don't Blame the Tool," Sep, 2007; "Claims Chats Guide to Claims Settlement Letters," Abi Journal, Aug, 2007; "Managing it Through Tough Times," Architecture and Governance, Jul, 2007; "Marketers Must Learn New Brand Imperatives," Cpg Matters, Jun, 2007. **Seminars:** A Business Perspective on Bankruptcy and Insolvency; How to Avoid Corporate Bankruptcy; The Accountant's Role in Bankruptcy and Insolvency.

29300 ■ **Assets Protection Inc. (API)**
421 Eastern Blvd.
Essex, MD 21221-6715
Ph: (410)780-0010
Fax: (410)327-3025
URL: http://www.sasi1968.com/api
Contact: Roger B. Copinger, Jr., President
Scope: Security consultants providing professional loss prevention assistance, development and maintenance of security programs for both small and large businesses in retail and manufacturing. Loss prevention security surveys conducted and cost effective strategies designed to reduce and eliminate security hazards, risks and exposures. **Founded:** 1968.

29301 ■ **Beall Investigation Bureau Inc.**
318 Country Ln.
San Antonio, TX 78209-2319
Ph: (210)822-7197
Contact: Lynne O. Beall, President
Scope: Specializes in investigation and loss control prevention. Assists with criminal, civil, domestic trial preparation. Assignments accepted on worldwide basis. Serves all industries including government. General practice and private investigation. **Founded:** 1954.

29302 ■ **Frederick A. Bornhofen & Associates—Bornhofen & Associates**
220 Isabella Rd.
Elverson, PA 19520-9141

Ph: (610)942-9140
Fax: (610)942-9576
Contact: Frederick A. Bornhofen, President
E-mail: fborn@comcast.net
Scope: Offers commercial and industrial security services, specializes in areas of robbery and violence prevention, business ethics, cargo security, commercial loss prevention techniques, and security management. Industries served: retail, convenience store, transportation, manufacturing, and energy. **Founded:** 1989. **Publications:** "Everything Changes Sometime". **Seminars:** Business Ethics; Fraud in the Business World.

29303 ■ Dale System Inc.
1101 Stewart Ave., Ste. 300
Garden City, NY 11530-4826
Ph: (516)794-2800
Free: 800-645-6366
Fax: (516)542-1063
Contact: Harvey M. Yaffe, President
Scope: Provider of advice, guidance and services covering internal security to industrial firms, retail stores and theater owners. Loss prevention services include undercover operations, shopping services, polygraph, and recreation or entertainment checking. Also surveys retail operations for price maintenance and product presentation. Additionally provides background investigations for business purposes. Serves private industries as well as government agencies. **Founded:** 1933.

29304 ■ Executive Management Services Inc.
307 4th Ave.
Pittsburgh, PA 15222
Ph: (412)471-8858
Fax: (412)221-5780
Contact: Robert H. Ralicki, President
Scope: Security management loss prevention consulting and service company providing planning services and security awareness programs to its clients. Expertise focuses on providing solutions to internal theft issues, and loss prevention contingency planning. **Founded:** 1987.

29305 ■ Fidelity Polygraph & Investigation Consultants Inc.
2163 Pelham Pkwy., Ste. 218
Pelham, AL 35124
Ph: (205)988-8644
Fax: (205)663-1489
Contact: Albert J. Silvani, President
Scope: Offers pre-employment screening as well as polygraph examinations and specific issue polygraph examinations; in-depth interviewing; loss prevention consulting; lectures on loss prevention; and shopping services interrogation, interviewing, and investigations. Serves retail businesses including clothing, hardware, auto, materials, and attorneys. **Founded:** 1985.

29306 ■ Greene Group
500 Market St.
Portsmouth, NH 03801
Contact: Ben W. Greene, Jr., President
Scope: Firm specializes in business research and risk assessment: handles discreet, time-sensitive as-

signments, including site security systems and controls for clients in the United States, Latin America and Southeast Asia. **Founded:** 1977.

29307 ■ Richard Haynes & Associates L.L.C.
1021 Temple St.
Charleston, WV 25312-2153
Ph: (304)346-6228
Fax: (304)346-9135
Co. E-mail: captrah@citynet.net
Contact: Capt. Richard A. Haynes, President
E-mail: captrah@citynet.net
Scope: Security management consultant. Offers the following services: security surveys and audits; security readiness for labor disputes; investigations; security training and awareness programs; special projects. Industries served: mining, petroleum, law enforcement, private security companies and government agencies. **Founded:** 1980. **Publications:** "Let's Talk Security," Kanawha Valley Business Monthly; "The SWAT Cyclopedia" Aug, 1999. **Seminars:** Personal Protection Workshop: Workplace Violence.

29308 ■ Hub Kelsh Inc.
5312 Claridge Sq.
Atlanta, GA 30338
Ph: (770)730-8575
Fax: (770)730-8575
Contact: Hubert G. Kelsh, President
E-mail: hubkelsh@dscga.com
Scope: Investigations, and loss prevention consulting for business (theft, harassment, drug activity, fraud, sabotage, hostile work environment and other inappropriate workplace conduct). Employee involvement programs for loss prevention and a drug-free workplace. Conducts physical security surveys. Inventory shrinkage a specialty. **Founded:** 1985. **Seminars:** Theft By Employees & Outsiders; Substance Abuse in the Workplace; Sexual Harassment; Workplace Violence; Dealing with Diversity Issues. Seminars, keynote speaker on integrity, workplace substance abuse, and employee misconduct.

29309 ■ Kies Intelligence Agency (KIA)
13630 Eldridge Ave.
Sylmar, CA 91342
Ph: (818)367-8416
Fax: (818)367-4983
Co. E-mail: kies@intelligence.org
URL: http://www.intelligence.org
Contact: Rudolf Kies, President
E-mail: kies@intelligence.org
Scope: Offers expertise in civil and criminal investigations, fingerprint analysis, missing persons and embezzlement investigations, employee background investigations and asset searches. Also specializes in messenger services, all kinds of investigative work and undercover assignments. Industries served: insurance companies, corporations and attorneys in United States branch office in Europe. **Founded:** 1976.

29310 ■ Navigator Research Group Inc.
310 Blount St., Ste. 221
Tallahassee, FL 32317
Ph: (850)878-5437
Free: 866-620-4636

Fax: (850)878-1131
Co. E-mail: info@navigatorresearchgroup.com
URL: http://www.navigatorresearchgroup.com
Contact: Lorena N. Ratcliff, Manager
Scope: Licensed company that conducts person and background checks. Industries served include private investigators, insurance companies and adjustors, law firms and other corporations. The firm serves the state of Florida, but has a network of correspondents nationwide and access to various databases which provides coverage across the country, private investigation agency specializing in locating missing. **Founded:** 1986. **Telecommunication Services:** support@navigatorresearchgroup.com; orders@navigatorresearchgroup.com.

29311 ■ Security & Loss Prevention Associates Inc.
4718 Sylvia Ln.
Manvel, TX 77578
Fax: (281)489-8636
Contact: Jack R. Barbour, Director
Scope: Security and loss control consultants in physical security, operating systems and procedures and personnel practices, investigations of internal and external fraud, and offers expert witness testimony in negligence litigation. Serve the convenience store industry, chain restaurants and health food industry. **Founded:** 1979.

RESEARCH CENTERS

29312 ■ University of Montreal - International Centre for Comparative Criminology (ICCC)—University of Montreal - Centre International de Criminologie Comparée (CICC)
Downtown Station
Montreal, QC, Canada H3C 3J7
Ph: (514)343-7065
Fax: (514)343-2269
Co. E-mail: cicc@umontreal.ca
URL: http://www.cicc.umontreal.ca
Contact: Prof. Benoît Dupont, Director
Founded: 1969. **Publications:** *ICCC Annual report* (Annual); *CICC-Hebdo* (Weekly); *CICC-Info* (Semiannual); *Proceedings Collaborates in the publication of four specialized reviews: Criminologie* (Semiannual); *ICCC Research Reports.* **Educational Activities:** ICCC Conferences (Weekly); International congresses (3/year); ICCC Research seminars (Occasionally). **Awards:** ICCC Grants (Periodic); Postdoctoral fellowship (Annual).

29313 ■ Vera Institute of Justice, Inc. - Research Department
233 Broadway, 12th Fl.
New York, NY 10279
Ph: (212)334-1300
Fax: (212)941-9407
Co. E-mail: mjacobson@vera.org
URL: http://www.vera.org/content/research
Contact: Michael P. Jacobson, President
Founded: 1961. **Publications:** *Research Department Monographs*; *Research Department Reports.* **Awards:** Research Department Scholarships. **Telecommunication Services:** contactvera@vera.org.

START-UP INFORMATION

29314 ■ *The 100 Best Businesses to Start When You Don't Want To Work Hard Anymore*
Pub: Career Press Inc.
Ed: Lisa Rogak. **Price:** $16.99. **Description:** Author helps burned-out workers envision a new future as a small business owner. Systems analysis, adventure travel outfitting, bookkeeping, food delivery, furniture making, and software development are among the industries examined.

29315 ■ *The 100 Best Businesses to Start When You Don't Want to Work Hard Anymore*
Pub: Career Press
Ed: Lisa Rogak. **Price:** $14.99.

29316 ■ *101 Businesses You Can Satrt at with Less Thank One Thousand Dollars: For Retirees*
Pub: Atlantic Publishing Company
Ed: Christina Bultinck. **Released:** December 2006. **Price:** $21.95. **Description:** Business ideas to help retirees start a home-based business on a low budget.

29317 ■ *101 Businesses You Can Start at with Less Than One Thousand Dollars: For Stay-At-Home Moms and Dads*
Pub: Atlantic Publishing Company
Ed: Christina Bultinck. **Released:** December 2006. **Price:** $21.95. **Description:** Business ideas to help stay-at-home moms and dads start a home-based business on a low budget.

29318 ■ *101 Small Business Ideas for Under $5000*
Pub: John Wiley & Sons, Incorporated
Ed: Corey Sandler, Janice Keefe. **Released:** April 2005. **Price:** $21.95. **Description:** Entrepreneurial ideas for starting companies that can be run part-time or full-time, and some as an absentee owner.

29319 ■ *202 Things You Can Buy and Sell for Big Profits*
Pub: Entrepreneur Press
Ed: James Stephenson; Jason R. Rich. **Released:** July 2008. **Price:** $19.95. **Description:** Become an entrepreneur at selling new and used products. This handbook will help individuals cash in on the boom in reselling new and used products online. A new section defines ways to set realistic goals while distinguishing between 'get-rich schemes' and long term, viable businesses. A discussion about targeting and reaching the right customer base is included, along with finding and obtaining the service support needed for starting a new business.

29320 ■ *"218 More Programs" in Entrepreneur (Vol. 35, November 2007, No. 11, pp. 96)*
Pub: Entrepreneur Media Inc.
Description: List of 218 colleges and universities in the U.S. offering entrepreneurship programs is presented.

29321 ■ *250 Questions Every Self-Employed Person Should Ask*
Pub: Adams Media Corporation
Contact: Gary Krebs, Director
E-mail: swatrous@adamsmedia.com
Ed: Mary Mihaly. **Released:** January 1, 2010. **Price:** $10.95. **Description:** Comprehensive information is given for anyone wishing to start their own business.

29322 ■ *The Accidental Entrepreneur: Practical Wisdom for People Who Never Expected to Work for Themselves*
Pub: Career Steps
Ed: Susan Urquhart-Brown. **Released:** October 20, 2005. **Description:** Steps for launching, growing and running a successful small company.

29323 ■ *The Accidental Entrepreneur: The 50 Things I Wish Someone Had Told Me About Starting a Business*
Pub: AMACOM
Ed: Susan Urquhart-Brown. **Released:** March 2008. **Price:** $17.95. **Description:** Advice is offered to any would-be entrepreneur, including eight questions to ask before launching a new business, ten traits of a successful entrepreneur, how to obtain licenses and selling permits, best way to create a business plan, ten ways to get referrals, six secrets of marketing, investment and financial information, ways to avoid burnout, and the seven biggest pitfalls to avoid.

29324 ■ *The Accidental Startup: How to Realize Your True Potential by Becoming Your Own Boss*
Pub: Penguin Group USA Inc.
Ed: Danielle Babb. **Released:** May 1, 2009. **Price:** $18.95. **Description:** Advice is given to help would-be entrepreneurs realize their goals for starting and running a successful small business.

29325 ■ *Advancing Research on Minority Entrepreneurship*
Pub: SAGE Publications USA
Contact: Blaise R. Simqu, President
Ed: James H. Johnson Jr.; Timothy Bates; William E. Jackson III; James H. Johnson; William E. Jackson. **Released:** September 2007. **Price:** $34.00. **Description:** Although minorities are more likely to engage in start-up businesses than others, minority entrepreneurs are less likely to get their enterprises off the ground or succeed in growing their businesses. The higher failure rates, lower sales and profits and less employment are among topics discussed.

29326 ■ *Angel Financing: How to Find and Invest in Private Equity*
Pub: John Wiley and Sons, Inc.
Ed: Gerald A. Benjamin; Joel B. Margulis. **Price:** $65.00. **Description:** The book provides a proven strategy to help entrepreneurs find angel investors. Interviews with angel investors as well as information about investors' hedging strategies, risk assessments, syndication orientation, financial return expectations, deal structuring preferences, monitoring investments, harvesting returns, and realist exit strategies are covered.

29327 ■ *The Art of the Start*
Pub: Portfolio Publishing
Ed: Guy Kawasaki. **Price:** $26.95. **Description:** Apple's Guy Kawasaki offers information to help would-be entrepreneurs create new enterprises. As founder and CEO of Garage Technology Ventures, he has field-tested his ideas with newly hatched companies and he takes readers through every phase of creating a business, from the very basics of raising money and designing a business model through the many stages that eventually lead to success and thus giving back to society.

29328 ■ *The Art of the Start: The Time-Tested, Battle-Hardened Guide for Anyone Starting Anything*
Pub: Penguin Books USA Inc.
Ed: Guy Kawasaki. **Released:** September 2004. **Price:** $26.95. **Description:** Advice for someone starting a new business covering topics such as hiring employees, building a brand, business competition, and management.

29329 ■ *Awakening the Entrepreneur Within: How Ordinary People Can Create Extraordinary Companies*
Pub: HarperCollins Publishers
Ed: Michael E. Gerber. **Released:** December 1, 2009. **Price:** $15.99. **Description:** Four dimensions of the entrepreneurial personality are explored: dreamer, thinker, performer and leader.

29330 ■ *Be Your Own Boss*
Pub: Wet Feet, Incorporated
Ed: Marcia Passos. **Released:** November 2006. **Price:** $24.95. **Description:** Tips for starting a freelance business in any career or industry are covered.

29331 ■ *The Beermat Entrepreneur: Turn Your Good Idea Into a Great Business*
Pub: Pearson Education Ltd.
Contact: Rod Bristow, President
Ed: Mike Southon, Andrew Leigh, Chris West. **Released:** March 1, 2009. **Price:** $39.50. **Description:** Information to help start, maintain and grow a small business is given, along with suggestions for working with a bank.

29332 ■ *Birthing the Elephant: The Woman's Go-for-It! Guide to Overcoming the Big Challenges of Launching a Business*
Pub: Celestial Arts Publishing Co.
Contact: Patricia Kelly, Manager
Ed: Karin Abarbanel; Bruce Freeman. **Released:** March 2008. **Price:** $15.95. **Description:** Advice for women entrepreneurs is given. The book explores the emotional challenges faced by women starting businesses, along with advice for reshaping image. This handbook helps women survive and succeed in business.

29333 ■ *Breaking Free: How to Quit Your Job and Start Your Own Business*
Pub: Greenwood Publishing Group, Inc.
Ed: Chris Lauer. **Released:** March 1, 2009. **Price:** $34.95. **Description:** This books helps individuals transition from working for others to starting their own business.

29334 ■ *Brewing Up a Business: Adventures in Entrepreneurship from the Founder of Dogfish Head Craft*
Pub: John Wiley and Sons, Inc.
Ed: Sam Calagione. **Released:** October 2006. **Price:** $16.95. **Description:** Author shares nontraditional success secrets. Calgione began his business with a home brewing kit and grew it into Dogfish Head Craft Beer, the leading craft brewery in the U.S.

29335 ■ *The Campus CEO: The Student Entrepreneur's Guide to Launching a Multi-Million Dollar Business*
Pub: Kaplan Books
Ed: Randal Pinkett. **Released:** February 2007. **Price:** $21.00 (CND). **Description:** Tips for generating income, while attending college is presented to students.

29336 ■ *Canadian Small Business Kit for Dummies*
Pub: CDG Books Canada, Incorporated
Ed: Margaret Kerr, JoAnn Kurtz. **Released:** March 2007. **Price:** $37.99 (Canadian). **Description:** Entrepreneurial guide to starting and running a small business in Canada.

29337 ■ *Careers for Self-Starters and Other Entrepreneurial Types*
Pub: McGraw-Hill Companies Inc.
Contact: Deven Sharma, President
Ed: Blythe Camenson. **Released:** September 2004. **Price:** $9.99 (US). **Description:** Advice to entrepreneurs wishing to start their own small company. Tips for turning hobbies into job skills are included.

29338 ■ *Cash In On Cash Flow*
Pub: Simon and Schuster Inc.
Contact: Carolyn Reidy, President
E-mail: carolyn.reidy@simonandschuster.com
Ed: Lawrence J. Pino. **Released:** July 2005. **Price:** $19.95. **Description:** Guide to assist entrepreneurs with starting a new business as a cash flow specialist.

29339 ■ *The Complete Startup Guide for the Black Entrepreneur*
Pub: Career Press
Ed: Bill Bourdreaux. **Price:** $15.99.

29340 ■ *"Confessions Of Serial Entrepreneurs" in Entrepreneur (January 8, 2009)*
Pub: Entrepreneur Media Inc.
Ed: Jennifer Wang. **Description:** Serial entrepreneurs are those individuals that are able to start business after business. These individuals enjoy the process of starting a company then handing off the finished product and starting over with a new endeavor. Several serial entrepreneurs are profiled.

29341 ■ *Crush It!*
Pub: HarperStudio/HarperCollins
Ed: Gary Vaynerchuk. **Released:** 2009. **Price:** $19.99. **Description:** Ways the Internet can help entrepreneurs turn their passions into successful companies.

29342 ■ *Cute Little Store: Between the Entrepreneurial Dream and Business Reality*
Pub: Outskirts Press, Incorporated
Ed: Adeena Mignogna. **Released:** May 2006. **Price:** $11.95. **Description:** Challenges of starting and growing a retail business are profiled.

29343 ■ *E-Myth Enterprise: How to Turn a Great Idea into a Thriving Business*
Pub: HarperCollins Publishers
Ed: Michael E. Gerber. **Released:** July 1, 2009. **Price:** $21.99. **Description:** This book explores the requirement needed to start and run a successful small business.

29344 ■ *E-Preneur*
Pub: Career Press, Inc.
Ed: Richard Goossen. **Released:** April 2008. **Price:** $15.99. **Description:** Entrepreneurs in the new virtual marketplace are examined. The book surveys and explains the field of Web 2.0 and entrepreneurs successfully using the virtual marketplace.

29345 ■ *Effective Small Business Management: An Entrepreneurial Approach*
Pub: Prentice Hall Higher Education
Ed: Norman M. Scarborough; Thomas W. Zimmerer; Douglas L. Wilson. **Released:** March 2006. **Price:** $178.33. **Description:** Provides undergraduate and graduate entrepreneurship and/or small business management courses with information to successfully launch a new company. The books offers entrepreneurs the tools required to develop staying power to succeed and grow their new business.

29346 ■ *Enterprise Planning and Development: Small Business and Enterprise Start-Up Survival and Growth*
Pub: Elsevier Science and Technology Books
Ed: David Butler. **Released:** August 2006. **Price:** $42.95. **Description:** Innovation, intellectual property, and exit strategies are among the issues discussed in this book involving current entrepreneurship.

29347 ■ *Entrepreneurial Itch: What No One Tells You About Starting Your Own Business*
Pub: Self-Counsel Press Inc.
Ed: David Trahair. **Released:** December 2006. **Price:** $13.95. **Description:** Small business accountant shares a plan for starting a business.

29348 ■ *Entrepreneurial Management*
Pub: McGraw-Hill
Ed: Robert J. Calvin. **Description:** Starting a new business takes careful consideration, determined preparation and a well-developed plan president of an international company that helps startups offers strategies, tools, techniques, models and methodologies for starting a new business. This guidebook covers all aspects of launching a new company as well as hands-on business skills and the motivation to keep new business owners moving towards success while conquering the entrepreneurial challenges along with way.

29349 ■ *"Entrepreneurs: Search Party" in Business Strategy Review (Vol. 21, Autumn 2010, No. 3, pp. 30)*
Pub: Wiley-Blackwell
Ed: Georgina Peters. **Description:** Entrepreneurs tend to be fixated on coming up with a foolproof idea for a new business and then raising money to start it. Raising startup funds is difficult, but it doesn't have to be that way. Search funds offers an innovative alternative, and the results are often impressive.

29350 ■ *Entrepreneurship*
Pub: John Wiley and Sons Inc.
Ed: William D. Bygrave; Andrew Zacharakis. **Released:** March 2007. **Price:** $115.95. **Description:** Information for starting a new business is shared, focusing on marketing and financing a product or service.

29351 ■ *Entrepreneurship and the Creation of Small Firms Empirical Studies of New Ventures*
Pub: Edward Elgar Publishing, Inc.
Ed: C. Holmquist Wiklund. **Released:** February 10, 2010. **Price:** $110.00. **Description:** Study focuses on the important issue of new venture creation. Using a variety of data sources, methods and theories, the authors demonstrate the factors that aid or hinder new venture creation in a number of settings.

29352 ■ *Entrepreneurship and the Financial Community Starting Up and Growing New Businesses*
Pub: Edward Elgar Publishing, Incorporated
Ed: Clarysse. **Released:** November 2006. **Price:** $75.00. **Description:** Understanding the role of private equity providers in the development and growth processes of small business.

29353 ■ *Entrepreneurship with Online Learning Center Access Card*
Pub: McGraw-Hill Higher Education
Ed: Robert D. Hirich; Michael P. Peters; Dean A. Shepherd. **Released:** October 2006. **Price:** $103.25. **Description:** Book instructs students on entrepreneurial processes that include starting a new business.

29354 ■ *Entrepreneurship Strategy: Changing Patterns in New Venture Creation, Growth, and Reinvention*
Pub: SAGE Publications USA
Contact: Blaise R. Simqu, President
Ed: Lisa K. Gundry; Jill R. Kickul. **Released:** August 2006. **Price:** $69.95. **Description:** Entrepreneurial strategies that incorporate new venture emergence, early growth, and reinvention and innovation are examined.

29355 ■ *Entrepreneurship: Successfully Launching New Ventures*
Pub: Pearson Education Canada
Ed: Bruce Barringer; Duane Ireland. **Released:** January 2007. **Price:** $139.95 (CND). **Description:** Guide to help any entrepreneur successfully launch a new venture.

29356 ■ *Escape from Corporate America: A Practical Guide to Creating the Career of Your Dreams*
Pub: Ballantine/Random House
Ed: Pamela Skillings. **Released:** 2008. **Price:** $15.00. **Description:** How to quit your job and start your own business.

29357 ■ *Escape from Cubicle Nation: From Corporate Prisoner to Thriving Entrepreneur*
Pub: Penguin Group USA Inc.
Ed: Pamela Slim. **Released:** April 1, 2009. **Price:** $25.95. **Description:** Insight if offered to help anyone wishing to leave their corporate position and start their own small business is offered.

29358 ■ *Essentials of Entrepreneurship and Small Business Management*
Pub: Prentice Hall PTR
Ed: Thomas W. Zimmerer; Norman M. Scarborough; Doug Wilson. **Released:** February 2007. **Price:** $106.67. **Description:** New venture creation and the knowledge required to start a new business are shared. The challenges of entrepreneurship, business plans, marketing, e-commerce, and financial considerations are explored.

29359 ■ *Extraordinary Entrepreneurship: The Professional's Guide to Starting an Exceptional Enterprise*
Pub: John Wiley and Sons, Inc.
Ed: Stephen C. Harper. **Released:** October 2006. **Price:** $45.00. **Description:** New rules to assist entrepreneurs in the 21st Century. The book focuses on thinking outside the box.

29360 ■ *Fast-Track Business Start-Up Kit: California*
Pub: DP Group, Incorporated
Ed: Carolyn Usinger. **Released:** September 2006. **Price:** $29.00. **Description:** Step-by-step guide for starting and running a business in California, including information on sole proprietors, partnerships, limited liability companies, S and C corporations, as well as details concerning business entities, sales taxes, environmental issues, human resources, and more.

29361 ■ *Financial Times Guide to Business Start Up 2007*
Pub: Pearson Education, Limited
Contact: Steven A. Dowling, President
Ed: Sara Williams; Jonquil Lowe. **Released:** November 2006. **Price:** $52.50. **Description:** Guide for starting and running a new business is presented. Sections include ways to get started, direct marketing, customer relations, management and accounting.

29362 ■ *"Find the Upside to a Down Economy" in Women Entrepreneur (September 30, 2008)*
Pub: Entrepreneur Media Inc.
Ed: Tamara Monosoff. **Description:** Starting a new business in this economic crisis may not be as daunting of a pursuit as one might think. Aspiring entrepreneurs may find success by looking for opportunities in unusual places and relying on what they do best.

29363 ■ *"Former Boxer Fits Into New Business Role" in Houston Business Journal (Vol. 40, January 8, 2010, No. 35, pp. 1)*
Pub: American City Business Journals
Ed: Greg Barr. **Description:** Lou Savarese explains how the lessons he learned as a professional boxer help him to manage his new business venture, a gym called Savarese Fight Gym. Customers who desire to learn boxing and to stay fit like a boxer comprise the fitness center's target market.

29364 ■ *Franchising for Dummies*
Pub: John Wiley & Sons, Incorporated
Ed: Dave Thomas, Michael Seid. **Released:** October 2006. **Price:** $24.99. **Description:** Advice to help entrepreneurs choose the right franchise, as well as financing, managing and expanding the business.

29365 ■ *Getting Rich In Your Underwear: How To Start and Run a Profitable Home-Based Business*
Pub: HCM Publishing
Ed: Peter I. Hupalo. **Released:** April 1, 2005. **Price:** $17.95. **Description:** Book offers insight into starting a home-based business. Entrepreneurs will learn about business models and the home business; distribution and fulfillment of product or service; marketing and sales; how to overcome the fear of starting a business; personal success characteristics; naming a business; zoning and insurance; intellectual capital; copyrights, trademarks, and patents; limited liability companies and S-corporations; business expenses and accounting; taxes; fifteen basic steps for starting a home-based business, state resources for starting a home company; and seven home-based business ideas.

29366 ■ *The Girl's Guide to Starting Your Own Business: Candid Advice, Frank Talk, and True Stories*
Pub: Collins Publications
Contact: Rachel Anderson, Director
Ed: Caitlin Friedman; Kimberly Yorio. **Released:** January 1, 2005. **Price:** $14.95. **Description:** Advice is given to help any woman start her own company. Every chapter includes interviews, charts, quizzes and witty directives about self-employment. Topics include, choosing a name and logo, business law, communication and information about business associations.

29367 ■ *"Gordon Stollery" in Canadian Business (Vol. 81, December 24, 2007, No. 1, pp. 76)*
Pub: Rogers Media
Ed: Michelle Magnan. **Description:** Gordon Stollery of Highpine Oil and Gas Ltd. talks about being a hard-rock geologist and his move to start his oil and gas business. Other aspects of his business career are discussed.

29368 ■ *Harmonic Wealth*
Pub: Hyperion Books
Ed: Linda Sivertsen; James Arthur Ray. **Released:** May 6, 2008. **Price:** $24.95. **Description:** Secrets for attracting the life you want through entrepreneurship; tips for timing a startup are included.

29369 ■ *How I Made It: 40 Successful Entrepreneurs Reveal How They Made Millions*
Pub: Kogan Page, Limited
Contact: Ben Glover, Director of Marketing
Ed: Rachel Bridge. **Released:** May 10, 2010. **Price:** $19.95. **Description:** Inspiration is given to anyone wishing to become a successful entrepreneur.

29370 ■ *How to Make Big Money*
Pub: Hyperion Books
Ed: Jeffrey J. Fox. **Released:** May 19, 2004. **Price:** $16.95. **Description:** Entrepreneur and consultant offers advice to help others create successful startups and prosper. Fox directs new business owners with a counterintuitive style and describes essential methods that beat the competition. Tips include: setting priorities, getting a personal driver, creating a contingency plan for employees, pricing to value, saving money, and getting an office outside of the home.

29371 ■ *How to Start and Run a Small Book Publishing Company: A Small Business Guide to Self-Publishing and Independent Publishing*
Pub: HCM Publishing
Ed: Peter I. Hupalo. **Released:** August 30, 2002. **Price:** $18.95. **Description:** The book teaches all aspects of starting and running a small book publishing company. Topics covered include: inventory accounting in the book trade, just-in-time inventory management, turnkey fulfillment solutions, tax deductible costs, basics of sales and use tax, book pricing, standards in terms of the book industry, working with distributors and wholesalers, cover design and book layout, book promotion and marketing, how to select profitable authors to publish, printing process, printing on demand, the power of a strong backlist, and how to value copyright.

29372 ■ *How to Start Your Own Business for Entrepreneurs*
Pub: FT Press
Ed: Robert Ashton. **Released:** December 9, 2010. **Price:** $24.99. **Description:** More than 300,000 individuals start a business every year. That number will rise over the next year or two if the current economic downturn leads to widespread job losses.

29373 ■ *How to Succeed As a Lifestyle Entrepreneur*
Pub: Dearborn Trade Publishing Inc.
Contact: Roy Lipner, President
Ed: Gary Schine. **Released:** May 12, 2003. **Description:** Consultant helps entrepreneurs start a new business on their own terms and create flexibility in their lifestyles. Shine offers various ways to create a business around your passions while utilizing the same business tools used by more traditional businesses.

29374 ■ *"I Have A Business Idea. What Now?" in Women Entrepreneur (October 15, 2008)*
Pub: Entrepreneur Media Inc.
Ed: Cheryl Isaac. **Description:** Four pre-planning steps to take before launching a new business are discussed in detail.

29375 ■ *International Entrepreneurship: Starting, Developing, and Managing a Global Venture*
Pub: SAGE Publications USA
Contact: Blaise R. Simqu, President
Ed: Robert D. Hisrich. **Released:** February 1, 2009. **Price:** $53.95. **Description:** International entrepreneurship combines the aspects of domestic entrepreneurship along with other disciplines, including anthropology, economics, geography, history, jurisprudence, and language.

29376 ■ *Legal Guide for Starting and Running a Small Business*
Pub: NOLO
Ed: Fred S. Steingold. **Released:** August 2006. **Price:** $34.99. **Description:** Legal issues any small business owner needs to know for starting and running a successful business are outlined.

29377 ■ *Life Entrepreneurs*
Pub: Jossey Bass
Ed: Christopher Gergen; Gregg Vanourek. **Released:** 2008. **Price:** $24.95. **Description:** Consultants Christopher Gergen and Gregg Vanourek present the basic principles for becoming a successful entrepreneur: recognizing opportunity, taking risks, and innovation.

29378 ■ *"Looking To Leap?" in Black Enterprise (Vol. 38, January 2008, No. 6, pp. 64)*
Pub: Earl G. Graves Publishing Co. Inc.
Ed: Tennille M. Robinson. **Description:** Websites and organizations providing resources for any young entrepreneur wishing to start a new business are outlined.

29379 ■ *Low Risk, High Reward*
Pub: R & R Publishing
Ed: Bob Reiss with Jeffrey L. Cruikshank. **Released:** 2000. **Price:** $19.95. **Description:** Successful entrepreneur teaches others about creating, growing and maintaining a successful business venture. The book offers a step-by-step approach to helping entrepreneurs minimize the risk involved in a new business while examining the skills and resources needed to succeed.

29380 ■ *Making a Living Without a Job: Winning Ways for Creating Work That You Love*
Pub: Random House Publishing Group
Ed: Barbara Winter. **Released:** August 9, 2010. **Price:** $16.00. **Description:** For all Americans who are out of work, soon to be out of work, or wishing to be freed from unrewarding work: here is the must-have book that shows how to make a living by working when, where, and how you want to work.

29381 ■ *Mommy Millionaire: How I Turned My Kitchen Table Idea Into a Million Dollars and How You Can, Too!*
Pub: St. Martin's Press LLC
Ed: Kim Lavine. **Released:** February 19, 2008. **Price:** $14.95. **Description:** Advice, secrets and lessons for making a million dollars from a mom who turned her kitchen into a successful business; tools cover developing and patenting an idea, cold calling, trade shows, QVC, big retailers, manufacturing, and raising venture capital.

29382 ■ *"Mount Laurel Woman Launches Venture Into Children's Used Clothing" in Philadelphia Inquirer (September 17, 2010)*
Pub: Philadelphia Media Network
Ed: Maria Panaritis. **Description:** Profile of Jennifer Frisch, stay-at-home mom turned entrepreneur. Frisch started a used-clothing store Once Upon a Child after opening her franchised Plato's Closet, selling unwanted and used baby clothing and accessories at her new shop, while offering used merchandise to teens at Plato's Closet.

29383 ■ *The Mousedriver Chronicles*
Pub: Perseus Books Group
Ed: John Lusk; Kyle Harrison. **Released:** 2003. **Price:** $16.95. **Description:** Entrepreneurial voyage through the startup business of two ivy-league business school graduates and the lessons they learned while developing their idea of a computer mouse that looks like a golf driver into the marketplace. The book is an inspiration for those looking to turn an idea into a company.

29384 ■ *"New Program for Entrepreneurs" in Austin Business JournalInc. (Vol. 29, February 12, 2010, No. 29, pp. 1)*
Pub: American City Business Journals
Ed: Christopher Calnan. **Description:** Nonprofit group Economic Development Catalyst Organization (ECDO) is formalizing its BizLaunch mentoring program, which was stated in 2009. The program aims to offer support networks to entrepreneurs and assistance regarding early-stage venture capital.

29385 ■ *New Venture Creation: Entrepreneurship for the 21st Century with Online Learning Center Access Card*
Pub: McGraw-Hill
Ed: Jeffrey A. Timmons; Stephen Spinelli. **Released:** November 1, 2008. **Price:** $71.97. **Description:** A handbook for students that explores all the concepts necessary for successfully launching a new enterprise.

29386 ■ *"The Next Generation: African Americans Are Successfully Launching Businesses Earlier In Life" in Black Enterprise (January 2008)*
Pub: Earl G. Graves Publishing Co. Inc.
Ed: Tennille M. Robinson. **Description:** According to a survey conducted by OPEN, a team dedicated small business at American Express, Generation Y individuals are three times more likely to start their own company. Three African American individuals who did just that are profiled.

29387 ■ Niche and Grow Rich

Pub: Entrepreneur Press

Ed: Jennifer Basye Sander; Peter Sander. Released: 2003. Description: Consultants share insight to entrepreneurs wishing to find a profitable niche market. Authors write that good niche businesses are easy to start and easy to defend from competitors. They also report that finding a successful niche can attract and maintain good customers who are willing to pay more for unique goods and services

29388 ■ "Oh, Grow Up!" in Entrepreneur (Vol. 35, October 2007, No. 10, pp. 120)

Pub: Entrepreneur Media Inc.

Ed: Mark Henricks. Description: Most entrepreneurs are overwhelmed with the idea of expanding their business, forgetting to strategically plan the process of business growth. However, there are certain steps entrepreneurs must take in turning a startup business into a bigger venture. Eight steps to growing a business, such as asking for advice and deciding on a focus are presented.

29389 ■ Overcoming Barriers to Entrepreneurship in the United States

Pub: Lexington Books

Ed: Diana Furchtgott-Roth. Released: March 28, 2008. Price: $24.95. Description: Real and perceived barriers to the founding and running of small businesses in America are discussed. Each chapter outlines how policy and economic environments can hinder business owners and offers tips to overcome these obstacles. Starting with venture capital access in Silicon Valley during the Internet bubble, the book goes on to question the link between personal wealth and entrepreneurship, examines how federal tax rates affect small business creation and destruction, explains the low rate of self-employment among Mexican immigrants, and suggests ways pension coverage can be increased in small businesses.

29390 ■ Prepare to Be a Teen Millionaire

Pub: Health Communications, Inc.

Contact: Peter Vegso, President

Ed: Robyn Collins; Kimberly Spinks Burleson. Released: April 1, 2008. Price: $16.95. Description: Business reference for any teenager wishing to become a successful entrepreneur; advice is given from successful teenage millionaires. Topics covered include: choosing a business name, type, and location; use of the Internet; legal issues; branding, sales, and marketing; funding and financial management; return on investment; retirement; development of a sound business plan; and certification for minority or women-owned companies.

29391 ■ The Professional Chef: The Business of Doing Business As a Personal Chef

Pub: John Wiley and Sons Inc.

Ed: Candy Wallace; Greg Forte. Released: February 2007. Price: $50.00. Description: Resources for starting a personal chef business are covered; CD-ROM included.

29392 ■ Seed-Stage Venture Investing: The Ins and Outs for Entrepreneurs, Start-Ups, and Investors on Successfully Starting a New Business

Pub: Aspatore Books, Incorporated

Ed: William J. Robbins. Released: July 2006. Price: $199.95. Description: Ideas for starting, funding, and managing technology-based firms, also known as, venture capitalists, are featured.

29393 ■ "Slow-Down Startups Hot" in Austin Business JournalInc. (Vol. 28, September 12, 2008, No. 26, pp. 1)

Pub: American City Business Journals

Ed: Sandra Zaragoza. Description: A number of entrepreneurs from Austin, Texas are starting their own small business despite the economic slowdown. The Small Business Development Program in Austin has seen a 50 percent increase in the demand for its services in 2008 as compared to demand in 2007. Other details about the entrepreneurship trend are discussed.

29394 ■ Small Business, Big Life: Five Steps to Creating a Great Life with Your Own Small Business

Pub: Thomas Nelson Inc.

Ed: Louis Barajas. Price: $22.99. Description: Barajas describes his and his father's independent entrepreneurial paths and suggests an inspirational approach to business that relies on four personal greatness cornerstones: truth, responsibility, awareness, and courage, and on keeping in mind your vision and your team's needs. The book provides a new look at achieving a work/life balance.

29395 ■ Small Business for Dummies, 3rd Ed.

Pub: John Wiley and Sons, Inc.

Ed: Eric Tyson; Jim Schell. Released: March 2008. Price: $21.99. Description: Guidebook for anyone wanting to start or grow a small business; topics include information financing, budgeting, marketing, management and more.

29396 ■ Small Business Entrepreneur: Launching a New Venture and Managing a Business on a Day-to-Day Basis

Pub: Austin & Company, Incorporated

Ed: Rory Burke. Released: February 2006. Price: $19.95. Description: Comprehensive guide examining the management skills required to launch and run a small business.

29397 ■ Small Business Management

Pub: John Wiley & Sons, Incorporated

Ed: Margaret Burlingame. Released: March 2007. Price: $44.95. Description: Advice for starting and running a small business as well as information on the value and appeal of small businesses, is given. Topics include budgets, taxes, inventory, ethics, e-commerce, and current laws.

29398 ■ Small Business Savvy

Pub: Adams Media Corporation

Contact: Gary Krebs, Director

E-mail: swatrous@adamsmedia.com

Ed: Norma J. Rist; Katina Z. Jones. Released: 2002. Description: Advice is given to women wishing to start their own companies using guidance and real-world examples to help position themselves for future growth. Tips to survive through a bad economic environment, breaking into a market, working with less money, accepting change, and ways to balance success with personal life are explored.

29399 ■ The Small Business Start-Up Kit

Pub: NOLO

Ed: Peri Pakroo. Released: January 2008. Price: $29.99. Description: Entrepreneurial advice for launching a new business. Topics include compliance with state regulations, sole proprietorships, partnerships, corporations, limited liability companies, as well as accounting and tax information.

29400 ■ Small Business Start-Up Workbook: A Step-by-Step Guide to Starting the Business You've Dreamed Of

Pub: How To Books

Ed: Cheryl D. Rickman. Released: February 2006. Price: $24.75. Description: Book provides practical exercises for starting a small business, including marketing and management strategies.

29401 ■ Small Business Survival Guide

Pub: Adams Media Corporation

Contact: Gary Krebs, Director

E-mail: swatrous@adamsmedia.com

Ed: Cliff Ennico. Price: $12.95. Description: Small business expert provides strategies to start a company and survive in the 21st Century. He shows small business owners how to succeed despite challenges that can defeat any firm. His advice covers suppliers; customers and contractors; competitors and creditors; spouses, family and friends; as well as the ways lawyers, accountants and other can steal an entrepreneur's success. Ennico also describes how startups can comply with local regulations.

29402 ■ Small Business Tool Kit

Pub: Lessons Professional Publishing

Ed: Linda M. Magoon. Released: April 10, 2010. Price: $40.00. Description: When starting a business, new managers and entrepreneurs require many resources to get the company up and running successfully. This book covers a wide range of topics that are critical for any new business owner.

29403 ■ So You Want to Start a Business?

Pub: Pearson Education, Limited

Contact: Steven A. Dowling, President

Ed: Edward D. Hess; Charles Goetz. Released: August 30, 2008. Price: $18.99. Description: Over sixty percent of Americans say they would like to own their own business and more than five million business startups are launched annually. However, fifty to seventy percent of new businesses fail. This book identifies the eight mistakes that cause these business failures and offers entrepreneurs the knowledge, tools, templates, strategies, and hands-on how-to advice needed to avoid these errors and succeed.

29404 ■ "Some Good Earners: Preparing Prison Inmates to Start Businesses Upon Their Release" in Inc. (Vol. 31, January-February 2009, No. 1)

Pub: Mansueto Ventures LLC

Ed: Mike Hoffman. Description: Prison Entrepreneurship Program (PEP) is a nonprofit organization that works with the Texas Department of Criminal Justice to teach entrepreneurship to prison inmates. Profiled is Hans Becker, owner of Armadillo Tree and Shrub in Dallas; Becker studied the PEP program while serving five years in prison and started his successful company when released.

29405 ■ Soul Proprietor: 101 Lessons from a Lifestyle Entrepreneur

Pub: Crossing Press, Incorporated

Ed: Jane Pollak. Released: September 2004. Description: More than 100 tips and stores to inspire and guide any would-be entrepreneur to earn a living from a favorite hobby or passion.

29406 ■ The Spiritual Entrepreneur

Pub: New Paradigm Media

Ed: Robert Morgen. Released: January 1, 2010. Price: $16.95. Description: Step-by-step guide to start a small business and then use that business to create various streams of passive income to support yourself and charities is presented.

29407 ■ Start Business in California, 3E

Pub: Sourcebooks, Inc.

Contact: Len Vlahos, President

E-mail: dominique@sourcebooks.com

Ed: John J. Talamo. Released: July 2006. Price: $24.95. Description: Information required for starting any business in California.

29408 ■ "Start-Up Pointers" in Inside Business (Vol. 13, September-October 2011, No. 5, pp. Y3)

Pub: Great Lakes Publishing Co.

Description: Four tips to help entrepreneurs with startup firms are provided by Youngstown Business Incubator.

29409 ■ Start-ups That Work: Surprise Research on What Makes or Breaks a New Company

Pub: Penguin Group

Ed: Joel Kurtzman; Glenn Rifkin. Released: October 2005. Price: $25.95.

29410 ■ Start Your Own Business, Fifth Edition

Pub: Entrepreneur Press

Contact: Perlman Neil, President

Ed: Rieva Lesonsky. Released: October 1, 2010. Price: $24.95. Description: Author and the staff of Entrepreneur Magazine provide business resources and information for starting a successful business. The book guides you through the first three years of ownership and provides work sheets and checklists.

29411 ■ *Starting Green: An Ecopreneur's Guide to Starting a Green Business from Business Plans to Profits*
Pub: Entrepreneur Press
Contact: Perlman Neil, President
Ed: Glenn E. Croston. **Released:** September 9, 2010. **Price:** $21.95. **Description:** Entrepreneur and scientist outlines green business essentials and helps uncover eco-friendly business opportunities, build a sustainable business plan, and gain the competitive advantage.

29412 ■ *Starting an iPhone Application Business for Dummies*
Pub: Wiley Publishing Inc.
Contact: William J. Pesce, President
Ed: Aaron Nicholson, Joel Elad, Damien Stolarz. **Released:** October 26, 2009. **Price:** $24.99. **Description:** Ways to create a profitable, sustainable business developing and marketing iPhone applications are profiled.

29413 ■ *Starting a Successful Business in Canada*
Pub: Self-Counsel Press Inc.
Ed: Jack D. James. **Released:** 2000. **Description:** Provides a framework for entrepreneurs launching a new business in Canada.

29414 ■ *StartingUp Now Facilitator Guide*
Pub: StartingUp Now
Ed: L. Jenkins. **Released:** September 11, 2011. **Price:** $29.95. **Description:** Guide for those teaching entrepreneurship using StartingUp Now; the guide provides 24 lesson plans for each of the 24 steps/chapters in the book.

29415 ■ *Steps to Small Business Start-Up*
Pub: Kaplan Books
Ed: Linda Pinson; Jerry Jinnett. **Released:** July 2006. **Price:** $29.00. **Description:** Tips for starting and running a new company are presented.

29416 ■ *Structuring Your Business*
Pub: Adams Media Corporation
Contact: Gary Krebs, Director
E-mail: swatrous@adamsmedia.com
Ed: Michele Cagan. **Released:** 2004. **Price:** $19.95. **Description:** Accountant and author shares insight into starting a new company. The guide assists entrepreneurs through the process, whether it is a corporation, an LLC, a sole proprietorship, or a partnership. Tax codes, accounting practices and legislation affecting every business as well as tips on managing finances are among the topics covered.

29417 ■ *"Survival of the Fittest" in Black Enterprise (November 2007)*
Pub: Earl G. Graves Publishing Co. Inc.
Ed: Tennille M. Robinson. **Description:** Black Enterprise has developed the Small Business Success Guide for prospective and current entrepreneurs.

29418 ■ *Swimming Against the Stream: Launching Your Business and Making Your Life*
Pub: Macmillan Publishers Limited
Ed: Tim Waterstone. **Released:** March 2007. **Price:** $17.99. **Description:** Ten rules for launching a new business are outlined using real-life experiences.

29419 ■ *Technology Ventures: From Idea to Enterprise*
Pub: McGraw-Hill Higher Education
Ed: Thomas Byers, Richard Dorf, Andrew Nelson. **Released:** January 10, 2010. **Description:** An action-approached through the use of examples, exercises, cases, sample business plans, and recommended sources helps entrepreneurs start and run a technology-base small business.

29420 ■ *Technology Ventures: From Idea to Enterprise with Student DVD*
Pub: McGraw-Hill Higher Education
Ed: Richard C. Dorf; Thomas H. Byers. **Released:** October 2006. **Price:** $100.68. **Description:** Textbook examining technology entrepreneurship on a global basis; technology management theories are explored.

29421 ■ *There's a Business In Every Woman: A 7-Step Guide to Discovering, Starting, and Building the Business of Your Dreams*
Pub: Ballantine/Random House
Ed: Ann M. Holmes. **Released:** 2008. **Price:** $15.00 paperback. **Description:** Economist and workplace expert provides a no-nonsense guide detailing seven steps to creating a successful business, based on her own experiences and on those of her employees. She highlights the importance of understanding and using your core competencies, building an organized infrastructure from the start, and planning for and managing your growth.

29422 ■ *"Time for a Leap Of Faith?" in Women Entrepreneur (November 18, 2008)*
Pub: Entrepreneur Media Inc.
Ed: Cynthia McKay. **Description:** Starting a new business, despite the downturn in the economy, can prove to be a successful endeavor if one has the time, energy and most importantly a good idea.

29423 ■ *The Toilet Paper Entrepreneur: The Tell-It-Like-It-Is Guide to Cleaning Up In Business, Even If You Are At the End of Your Roll*
Pub: Obsidian Launch LLC
Ed: Mike Michalowicz. **Price:** $24.95. **Description:** The founder of three multimillion-dollar companies, including Obsidian Launch, a company that partners with first-time entrepreneurs to grow their concepts into industry leaders.

29424 ■ *"Top 25 Graduate Programs" in Entrepreneur (Vol. 35, November 2007, No. 11, pp. 92)*
Pub: Entrepreneur Media Inc.
Description: List of the top twenty-five graduate entrepreneurship programs of different colleges and universities in the U.S. for 2007, as ranked by Entrepreneur Magazine and the Princeton Review, is presented.

29425 ■ *"Top 25 Undergrad Programs" in Entrepreneur (Vol. 35, November 2007, No. 11, pp. 88)*
Pub: Entrepreneur Media Inc.
Description: List of the top twenty-five undergraduate entrepreneurship programs of different colleges and universities in the U.S. for 2007, as ranked by Entrepreneur Magazine and the Princeton Review, is highlighted.

29426 ■ *"Top of the Class" in Entrepreneur (Vol. 35, November 2007, No. 11, pp. 82)*
Pub: Entrepreneur Media Inc.
Ed: Nichole L. Torres. **Description:** Education in entrepreneurship is being pursued by many students and it is important to understand what entrepreneurship program fits you. Aspiring entrepreneurs should also ask about the program's focus. Considerations searched for by students regarding the particular school they chose to study entrepreneurship are discussed.

29427 ■ *"Troy Patent Law Firm Launches Rent-Free Tech Incubator" in Crain's Detroit Business (Vol. 25, June 8, 2009, No. 23, pp. 4)*
Pub: Crain Communications Inc. - Detroit
Ed: Tom Henderson. **Description:** Young Basile Hanlon MacFarlane & Helmholdt PC, a patent law firm located in Troy, Michigan has created a small, rent-free technology incubator on site. The incubator will be called North Woodward Tech Incubator and has room for four or five startups. The incubator is for the earliest or pre-seed stage for entrepreneurs who have not yet gotten significant investment capital.

29428 ■ *Trump University Entrepreneurship 101: How to Turn Your Idea Into a Money Machine*
Pub: John Wiley & Sons, Inc.
Ed: Michael E. Gordon. **Released:** September 1, 2009. **Price:** $24.95. **Description:** Current and expanded edition to the Trump guide to starting a business where Trump teams with Professor Michael Gordon to show how to take a dream and turn it into a successful enterprise.

29429 ■ *Ultimate Startup Directory: Expert Advice and 1,500 Great Startup Ideas*
Pub: Entrepreneur Press
Ed: James Stephenson. **Released:** February 2007. **Price:** $30.95 (CND). **Description:** Startup opportunities in over 30 industries are given, along with information on investment, earning potential, skills, legal requirements and more.

29430 ■ *"UM-Dearborn to Launch Program for Entrepreneurs" in Crain's Detroit Business (Vol. 24, April 14, 2008, No. 15, pp. 7)*
Pub: Crain Communications Inc.
Ed: Chad Halcom. **Description:** Starting this fall the University of Michigan-Dearborn will begin its Product Realization and Technology Commercialization Program for entrepreneurs and innovators with lab-tested, high-technology products. Ultimately, 20 businesses will each work with the university in creating a customer base, commercializing a new high-tech product or process and connecting with venture capitalists who may invest in the new companies.

29431 ■ *Upstarts! How GenY Entrepreneurs Are Rocking the World of Business and 8 Ways You Can Profit from Their Success*
Pub: The McGraw-Hill Companies
Ed: Donna Fenn. **Released:** September 1, 2009. **Price:** $25.95. **Description:** An inside glance at the GenY startup companies that are changing the way the world conducts business.

29432 ■ *Weekend Small Business Start*
Pub: Sourcebooks, Inc.
Contact: Len Vlahos, President
E-mail: dominique@sourcebooks.com
Ed: Mark Warda. **Released:** June 2007. **Price:** $19.95. **Description:** Information for starting a new business is presented.

29433 ■ *What No One Ever Tells You About Starting Your Own Business: Real-Life Start-Up Advice from 101 Successful Entrepreneurs*
Pub: Kaplan Publishing
Ed: Jan Norman. **Released:** July 2004. **Price:** $18.95 (US), $28.95 (Canadian). **Description:** From planning to marketing, advice is given to entrepreneurs starting new companies. s.

29434 ■ *Working for Yourself: An Entrepreneur's Guide to the Basics*
Pub: Kogan Page, Limited
Contact: Ben Glover, Director of Marketing
Ed: Jonathan Reuvid. **Released:** September 2006. **Description:** Guide for starting a new business venture, focusing on raising financing, legal and tax issues, marketing, information technology, and site location.

29435 ■ *You Can Do It Too: The 20 Essential Things Every Budding Entrepreneur Should Know*
Pub: Kogan Page, Limited
Contact: Ben Glover, Director of Marketing
Ed: Rachel Bridge. **Released:** May 10, 2010. **Price:** $29.95. **Description:** Collective wisdom of successful entrepreneurs in the form of twenty essential elements to focus on when starting a new company is illustrated by real-life entrepreneurial stories.

29436 ■ *You Need to be a Little Bit Crazy: The Truth about Starting and Growing Your Business*
Pub: Dearborn Trade Publishing Inc.
Contact: Roy Lipner, President
Ed: Barry J. Moltz. **Description:** Offers entrepreneurs and small business owners insight into the ups and downs of running a business.

29437 ■ *You Need To Be a Little Crazy*
Pub: Dearborn Trade Publishing Inc.
Contact: Roy Lipner, President
Ed: Barry J. Moltz. **Released:** December 2008. **Price:** $14.95. **Description:** Entrepreneur and investor who has founded several successful startups provides a guide using personal experience to help anyone start a new business.

29438 ■ *Your Million-Dollar Idea: From Concept to Marketplace*
Pub: Adams Media Corporation
Ed: Sandy Abrams. **Released:** March 1, 2010. **Price:** $14.95. **Description:** Self-taught entrepreneur provides a 12-step plan to make a new product or service a profitable reality.

ASSOCIATIONS AND OTHER ORGANIZATIONS

29439 ■ **Advancing Canadian Entrepreneurship (ACE)**
266 King St. W, Ste. 403
Toronto, ON, Canada M5V 1H8
Ph: (416)304-1566
Free: 800-766-8169
Fax: (416)864-0514
Co. E-mail: amy@acecanada.ca
URL: http://www.acecanada.ca
Contact: Ian Aitken, Chairman
Description: Young people, business owners, or engaged in entrepreneurial activities. Promotes growth and development of members' business interests. Provides support and services to businesses owned by young people; encourages communication and mutual support among collegiate entrepreneurs. **Awards:** Alumnus or Alumna of the Year (Annual); Most Improved Award (Annual); Alumnus/Alumna of the Year Award; Most Improved Award; Student Leader of the Year Award; Student Leader of the Year (Annual); Most Supportive Business Advisory Board Member of the Year (Annual); Most Supportive Dean or Department Chair of the Year (Annual); Most Supportive Business Advisory Board Member of the Year Award; Most Supportive Dean or Department Chair of the Year Award.

29440 ■ **Canadian Association of Family Enterprise (CAFE)—Association Canadienne des Entreprises Familiales**
465 Morden Rd., Ste. 112
Oakville, ON, Canada L6K 3W6
Ph: (905)337-8375
Free: 866-849-0099
Fax: (905)337-0572
Co. E-mail: office@cafenational.org
URL: http://www.cafecanada.ca
Contact: Peter G. White, Director
Description: Family-owned businesses. Seeks to "encourage, educate, and inform members in disciplines unique to the family business." Fosters increased understanding of the importance of family-owned enterprises in the national economy among government agencies and the public. Gathers and disseminates information of interest to members. Conducts educational and lobbying activities. Provides technical support and advisory services to small businesses in areas including succession planning, taxation, family law, and arbitration and mediation. Maintains network of Family Councils, which serve as a forum for discussion of family and business matters. **Scope:** business, personal wellness, family business. **Founded:** 1983. **Subscriptions:** books. **Publications:** *Family Business Magazine* (Quarterly); *Family Enterpriser* (Quarterly); *International Magazine for Family Businesses* (Bimonthly); *Canadian Association of Family Enterprise--Annual Membership Directory*. **Educational Activities:** National Symposium for Families in Business (Semiannual). **Awards:** Family Enterprise of the Year Award.

29441 ■ **Canadian Innovation Centre**
Waterloo Research and Technology Park
Accelerator Centre
295 Hagey Blvd., Ste. 15
Waterloo, ON, Canada N2L 6R5
Ph: (519)885-5870
Fax: (519)513-2421
Co. E-mail: info@innovationcentre.ca
URL: http://innovationcentre.ca
Contact: Ted Cross, Chief Executive Officer
Description: Investors, entrepreneurs, and innovative companies. Promotes innovation in economic activity; seeks to ensure that developers of inventions or innovations receive full credit for their discoveries. Provides support and assistance to members. Conducts research and educational programs. **Scope:** innovation, patent law. **Founded:** 1981. **Subscriptions:** books business records clippings periodicals. **Publications:** *Eureka!* (Quarterly).

29442 ■ **Eureka!**
Waterloo Research and Technology Park
Accelerator Centre
295 Hagey Blvd., Ste. 15
Waterloo, ON, Canada N2L 6R5
Ph: (519)885-5870
Fax: (519)513-2421
Co. E-mail: info@innovationcentre.ca
URL: http://innovationcentre.ca
Contact: Ted Cross, Chief Executive Officer
Released: Quarterly

29443 ■ **Family Business Magazine**
465 Morden Rd., Ste. 112
Oakville, ON, Canada L6K 3W6
Ph: (905)337-8375
Free: 866-849-0099
Fax: (905)337-0572
Co. E-mail: office@cafenational.org
URL: http://www.cafecanada.ca
Contact: Peter G. White, Director
Released: Quarterly

29444 ■ **Family Enterpriser**
465 Morden Rd., Ste. 112
Oakville, ON, Canada L6K 3W6
Ph: (905)337-8375
Free: 866-849-0099
Fax: (905)337-0572
Co. E-mail: office@cafenational.org
URL: http://www.cafecanada.ca
Contact: Peter G. White, Director
Released: Quarterly

29445 ■ **International Magazine for Family Businesses**
465 Morden Rd., Ste. 112
Oakville, ON, Canada L6K 3W6
Ph: (905)337-8375
Free: 866-849-0099
Fax: (905)337-0572
Co. E-mail: office@cafenational.org
URL: http://www.cafecanada.ca
Contact: Peter G. White, Director
Released: Bimonthly

29446 ■ **National Federation of Filipino American Associations (NaFFAA)**
1322 18th St. NW
Washington, DC 20036-1803
Ph: (202)361-0296
Fax: (202)478-5109
Co. E-mail: naffaanational@gmail.com
URL: http://www.naffaausa.org
Contact: Eduardo Navarra, Chairperson
Description: Filipino American individuals and organizations. Seeks to promote the interests and well-being of the 3 million Filipinos and Filipino Americans residing in the United States by getting them involved as leaders and participants in United States society. Major programs include citizenship and leadership development, voter education, entrepreneurial training, and community development. **Founded:** 1997. **Awards:** Azores Fellowship Award (Annual).

29447 ■ **National Foundation for Teaching Entrepreneurship (NFTE)**
120 Wall St., 18th Fl.
New York, NY 10005
URL: http://www.nfte.com
Contact: Steve Mariotti, Founder
Description: Devoted to teaching entrepreneurship education to low-income young people, ages 11 through 18. **Founded:** 1987. **Publications:** *NFTE News* (Quarterly).

REFERENCE WORKS

29448 ■ *The 4 Routes to Entrepreneurial Success*
Pub: Berrett-Koehler Publishers
Ed: John B. Miner. **Price:** $18.95. **Description:** After researching one hundred successful entrepreneurs, the author discovered there are basically four personality types of entrepreneurs: the personal achiever, the super salesperson, the real manager, and the expert idea generator.

29449 ■ *The 30-Second Commute*
Pub: McGraw-Hill
Ed: Beverley Williams; Don Cooper. **Released:** 2004. **Price:** $19.95. **Description:** Home-based business owners explain how entrepreneurs can avoid long commutes and high costs of working outside the home by starting a home-based company. Essential steps for launching a successful home-based business are covered, including type of business, legal issues, and writing a business plan.

29450 ■ *32 Ways to Be a Champion in Business*
Pub: Three Rivers Press
Ed: Earvin Magic Johnson. **Released:** December 29, 2009. **Price:** $18.94. **Description:** Earvin Johnson discusses his transition from athlete to entrepreneur and discusses the importance of hard work in order to pursue your dreams of starting and running a successful business.

29451 ■ *"75 Most Powerful Blacks on Wall Street" in Black Enterprise (Vol. 37, October 2006, No. 3, pp. 136)*
Pub: Earl G. Graves Publishing Co. Inc.
Ed: Carolyn M. Brown. **Description:** Profiles of seventy-five African American top executives. The listing is a compilation of the brightest and best venture capitalists, asset managers, CEOs, traders, and investment bankers.

29452 ■ *"The 100 Fastest-Growing Companies" in Hispanic Business (Vol. 30, July-August 2008, No. 7-8, pp. 22)*
Pub: Hispanic Business, Inc.
Ed: Michael Bowker. **Description:** CEO's of the five fastest growing Hispanic-owned companies discuss the success of their companies; most of them attribute their success to proper investment and diversification, effective innovations and seeing growth opportunities where others see roadblocks.

29453 ■ *201 Great Tips for Your Small Business: Increase Your Profit and Joy in Your Work*
Pub: Dundren Press Limited
Ed: Julie V. Watson. **Released:** April 2006. **Price:** $24.99. **Description:** Tips and hints for home-based, micro, and small businesses are presented.

29454 ■ *401 Questions Every Entrepreneur Should Ask*
Pub: Career Press, Incorporated
Ed: James L. Silvester. **Released:** October 2006. **Price:** $17.99. **Description:** Review of 25 functional areas of running a small business are covered along with questions entrepreneurs should ask in order to correct and avoid unwanted issues.

29455 ■ *"The 2007 Black Book" in Hawaii Business (Vol. 53, December 2007, No. 6, pp. 43)*
Pub: Hawaii Business Publishing
Description: Brief biographies of 364 top executives in Hawaii are presented. Information on their educational achievement, membership in associations, hobbies, family, present position and the company they work for are supplied.

29456 ■ *"2008 Woman of the Year Gala" in Hispanic Business (Vol. 30, July-August 2008, No. 7-8, pp. 58)*
Pub: Hispanic Business, Inc.
Ed: Brynne Chappell. **Description:** Brief report on the sixth annual Women of the Year Awards gala which was held at JW Marriott Desert Ridge Resort and Spa is given; 20 women were honored with these

awards for their professional contribution, commitment to the advancement of the Hispanic community and involvement with charitable organizations.

29457 ■ "2009: A Call For Vision" in Women Entrepreneur (January 28, 2009)
Pub: Entrepreneur Media Inc.
Ed: Elinor Robin. **Description:** Providing exemplary customer service, reducing expenses and creating an out-of-the-box niche are three key factors that will help business survive during this economic crisis. Business owners must see potential where others see failure in order to create new opportunities that may not only allow their business to survive during these times but may actually cause some businesses to thrive despite this economic downturn.

29458 ■ "2009 Corporate Elite: Our Top 25 Executives" in Hispanic Business (January-February 2009, pp. 16, 18, 20, 22)
Pub: Hispanic Business
Description: Profiles of Hispanic Business Media's 2009 Corporate Elite are presented.

29459 ■ "2010 American Business Woman of ABWA" in Women In Business (Vol. 61, October-November 2009, No. 5, pp. 22)
Pub: American Business Women's Association
Ed: Doris Brown. **Description:** Achievements of Doris Brown are presented in light of her being named as the 2010 American Business Woman of American Business Women's Association (ABWA). She specializes in the field of client and customer satisfaction for Avue Technologies. Brown believes that her involvement in the ABWA has helped her to see the importance of being a resource for other people.

29460 ■ The Accidental Millionaire: How to Succeed in Life Without Really Trying
Pub: BenBella Books
Contact: Glen Yeffeth, President
Ed: Gary Fong. **Released:** January 1, 2010. **Price:** $11.99 (GBP). **Description:** Gary Fong shares his memoirs about growing up in poverty in Los Angeles. Fong discusses how he revolutionized wedding photography and invented photography aids.

29461 ■ "Adapt or Die" in Black Enterprise (Vol. 38, July 2008, No. 12, pp. 27)
Pub: Earl G. Graves Publishing Co. Inc.
Ed: Oguntoyinbo Lekan. **Description:** Turbulence in the domestic auto industry is hitting auto suppliers hard and black suppliers, the majority of whom contract with the Big Three, are just beginning to establish relationships with import car manufacturers. The more savvy CEOs are adopting new technologies in order to weather the downturn in the economy and in the industry as a whole.

29462 ■ "Albert Schultz" in Canadian Business (Vol. 83, August 17, 2010, No. 13-14, pp. 71)
Pub: Rogers Media Ltd.
Ed: Steve Maich. **Description:** Soulpepper Theater Company founder and actor/director Albert Schultz shares the key ingredient to his success both artistically and commercially. Schultz believes his success was a combination of passion and persistence, as well as team building. He believes his entrepreneurial impulse came when he began thinking of making opportunities instead of taking them.

29463 ■ "All In Good Fun" in Entrepreneur (Vol. 36, May 2008, No. 5, pp. 22)
Pub: Entrepreneur Media, Inc.
Ed: Christopher Percy Collier. **Description:** According to a study conducted in 2007, humor in the workplace helps people communicate effectively and improves camaraderie. Company leaders and entrepreneurs can also tell humorous stories about themselves, but must also set lines that should not be crossed. The humorous atmosphere in the company YouSendIt is presented.

29464 ■ Alpha Dogs: How Your Small Business Can Become a Leader of the Pack
Pub: HarperInformation
Ed: Donna Fenn. **Released:** May 2007. **Price:** $14.95. **Description:** Ways for an entrepreneur to outsmart competitors in the marketplace, to generate higher sales, and earn lasting customer and employee loyalty.

29465 ■ Alpha Dogs: How Your Small Business Can Become a Leader of the Pack
Pub: HarperCollins Publishers, Inc.
Ed: Donna Fenn. **Released:** May 2007. **Price:** $14.95. **Description:** Profiles of eight successful entrepreneurs along with information for developing customer service, technology and competition.

29466 ■ "Always Striving" in Women In Business (Vol. 61, December 2009, No. 6, pp. 28)
Pub: American Business Women's Association
Ed: Kathleen Leighton. **Description:** Jennifer Mull discusses her responsibilities and how she attained success as CEO of Backwoods, a gear and clothing store founded by her father in 1973. She places importance on being true to one's words and beliefs, while emphasizing the capacity to tolerate risks in business. Mull defines success as an evolving concept and believes there must always be something to strive for.

29467 ■ The AMA Handbook of Project Management
Pub: AMACOM
Ed: Paul C Dinsmore, Jeannette Cabanis-Brewin. **Released:** September 15, 2010. **Price:** $79.95. **Description:** A comprehensive reference presenting the critical concepts and theories all project managers must master using essays and advice from the field's top professionals.

29468 ■ "Amit Wadhwaney" in Canadian Business (Vol. 80, March 12, 2007, No. 6, pp. 22)
Pub: Rogers Media
Ed: Rachel Pulfer. **Description:** Manager of Third Avenue International Value Fund, Amit Wadhwaney, shares his views on buying Canadian agricultural and forestry stocks.

29469 ■ "ANATURALCONCEPT" in Crain's Cleveland Business (Vol. 30, June 22, 2009, No. 24, pp. 1)
Pub: Crain Communications, Inc.
Ed: Dan Shingler. **Description:** Cleveland-based Biomimicry Institute, led by Cleveland's Entrepreneurs for Sustainability and the Cuyahoga County Planning Commission, are using biomimicry to incorporate eco-friendliness with industry. Biomimicry studies nature's best ideas then imitates these designs and processes to solve human problems.

29470 ■ "And the Money Comes Rolling In" in Inc. (Vol. 31, January-February 2009, No. 1, pp. 62)
Pub: Mansueto Ventures LLC
Ed: Max Chafkin. **Description:** Profile of Markus Frind, founder of the online dating service in British Columbia called Plenty of Fish. Frind works one hour a day and earns $10 million a year by keeping things simple.

29471 ■ "Anja Carroll; Media Director-McDonald's USA" in Advertising Age (Vol. 79, November 17, 2008, No. 34, pp. 6)
Pub: Crain Communications, Inc.
Ed: Emily Bryson York. **Description:** Profile of Anja Carroll who is the media director for McDonald's USA and has the challenge of choosing the right mix of media for the corporation.

29472 ■ "Another Determinant of Entrepreneurship" in International Journal of Entrepreneurship and Small Business (Vol. 10, July 6, 2010)
Pub: Publishers Communication Group
Ed: Felix Pauligard Ntep, Wilton Wilton. **Description:** Interviews were carried out with entrepreneurs of Douala, Cameroon. These entrepreneurs believe that witchcraft existed and could bring harm to them or their enterprises.

29473 ■ "Anything Could Happen" in Inc. (March 2008, pp. 116-123)
Pub: Gruner & Jahr USA Publishing
Ed: Max Chafkin. **Description:** Profile of Evan Williams, founder of Blogger and Twitter, a new type of technology idea; Williams answers ten questions and share insight into growing both of his companies.

29474 ■ "The Art of Persuasion: How You Can Get the Edge You Need To Reach Every Goal" in Small Business Opportunities (November 2007)
Pub: Harris Publications Inc.
Ed: Paul Endress. **Description:** Expert in the field of psychology to business in the areas of communication, hiring and retention discusses a unique approach to solving business problems.

29475 ■ "The Art of War for Women" in Hawaii Business (Vol. 54, July 2008, No. 1, pp. 23)
Pub: Hawaii Business Publishing
Description: Business consultant Chi-Ning Chu talks about her new book 'The Art of War for Women: Sun Tzu's Ancient Strategies and Wisdom for Winning at Work', which discusses how women can more effectively win in business. She also shares her thoughts about the advantages that women have, which they can use in businesses decisions.

29476 ■ "Attending to the Needs of the Too Busy" in New York Times (Vol. 158, October 1, 2008, No. 54450, pp. 7)
Pub: New York Times Co./Globe Newspaper Co.
Ed: Ken Belson. **Description:** Profiles of individuals working as concierges to meet the needs of their clients are presented.

29477 ■ "Attention, Please" in Entrepreneur (Vol. 36, April 2008, No. 4, pp. 52)
Pub: Entrepreneur Media, Inc.
Ed: Andrea Cooper. **Description:** Gurbaksh Chahal created his own company ClickAgents at the age of 16, and sold it two years later for $40 million to ValueClick. He then founded BlueLithium, an online advertising network on behavioral targeting, which Yahoo! Inc. bought in 2007 for $300 million. Chahal, now 25, talks about his next plans and describes how BlueLithium caught Yahoo's attention.

29478 ■ Attracting Investors: A Marketing Approach to Finding Funds for Your Business
Pub: John Wiley and Sons, Inc.
Ed: Philip Kotler, Hermawan Kartajaya, S. David Young. **Released:** August 2004. **Price:** $29.95 (US), $42.99 (Canadian). **Description:** Marketing experts advise entrepreneurs in ways to find investors in order to raise capital for their companies.

29479 ■ Awesomely Simple: Essential Business Strategies for Turning Ideas Into Action
Pub: Jossey-Bass
Ed: John Spence. **Released:** September 8, 2009. **Price:** $24.95. **Description:** Six key strategies that create a foundation for achieving business excellence include: vivid vision, best people, a performance-oriented culture, robust communication, a sense of urgency, and extreme customer focus.

29480 ■ "Back Talk with Chris Gardner" in Black Enterprise (Vol. 37, January 2007, No. 6, pp. 112)
Pub: Earl G. Graves Publishing Co. Inc.
Ed: Kenneth Meeks. **Description:** Profile of with Chris Gardner and his Chicago company, Gardner Rich L.L.C., a multimillion-dollar investment firm. During an interview, Gardner discusses his rise from homelessness. His story became a book, The Pursuit of Happyness and was recently released as a film starring Will Smith.

29481 ■ "Back Talk With Terrie M. Williams" in Black Enterprise (Vol. 38, December 2007, No. 5, pp. 204)
Pub: Earl G. Graves Publishing Co. Inc.
Ed: Tennille M. Robinson. **Description:** Profile of Terrie M. Williams, president of a public relations agency as well as founder of a youth empowerment organization called Stay Strong Foundation. Williams reflects on her bouts with depression and how the disease impacts sufferers and talks about her book that will inspire others dealing with depression.

29482 ■ Balls!: 6 Rules for Winning Today's Business Game

Pub: John Wiley & Sons, Incorporated

Ed: Alexi Venneri. Released: January 2005. Price: $29.95. Description: In order to be successful business leaders must be brave, authentic, loud, lovable, and spunky and they need to lead their competition.

29483 ■ "Barriers to Small Business Creations in Canada" in International Journal of Entrepreneurship and Small Business (Vol. , pp.)

Pub: Publishers Communication Group

Ed: Amarjit Gill, Nahum Biger, Vivek Nacpal. Description: Studies of Hatala (2005) and Choo and Wong (2006) related to the barriers to new venture creations in Canada are examined.

29484 ■ Battling Big Box: How Nimble Niche Companies Can Outmaneuver Giant Companies

Pub: Career Press, Inc.

Ed: Henry Dubroff, Susan J. Marks. Released: January 1, 2009. Price: $15.99. Description: Small companies can compete with larger firms through agility, adaptability, customer service, and credibility. Topics include information to help empower employees, build a powerful brand, manage cash flow, and maintaining a business vision.

29485 ■ "BDC Launches New Online Business Advice Centre" in Internet Wire (July 13, 2010)

Pub: Comtex

Description: The Business Development Bank of Canada (BDC) offers entrepreneurs the chance to use their new online BDC Advice Centre in order to seek advice regarding the challenges of entrepreneurship. Free online business tools and information to help both startups and established firms are also provided.

29486 ■ "Be a Better Manager: Live Abroad" in Harvard Business Review (Vol. 88, September 2010, No. 9, pp. 24)

Pub: Harvard Business School Publishing

Ed: William W. Maddux, Adam D. Galinsky, Carmit T. Tadmor. Description: Interrelationship between international experience and entrepreneurship is discussed. Individuals with international experience are likelier to be promoted and to develop new products and businesses.

29487 ■ Be the Elephant: Build a Bigger, Better Business

Pub: Workman Publishing Company

Ed: Steve Kaplan. Price: $19.95. Description: Entrepreneur and author sets out an accessible, no-frills plan for business owners, managers, and other industrialists to grow their businesses into elephants: big and strong but also smart. Advice is given on fostering a growth mind-set, assessing risk, and creating unique selling propositions.

29488 ■ Be the Hero: Three Powerful Ways to Overcome Challenges in Work and In Life

Pub: Berrett-Koehler Publishers, Inc.

Ed: Noah Blumenthal. Released: August 1, 2009. Price: $19.95. Description: Details are given to help individuals perform at their best when challenges are the greatest. It shows how to turn self-defeating thoughts and behavior into heroic actions.

29489 ■ "Because 10 Million Zumba Lovers Can't Be Wrong" in Inc. (Volume 32, December 2010, No. 10, pp. 106)

Pub: Inc. Magazine

Ed: Christine Lagorio. Description: Profile of partners, Alberto Perez, Alberto Perlman, and Alberto Aghion, founders of Zumba, a form of dance used for fitness.

29490 ■ "Because He Is Still Growing: Horst Rechelbacher: Intelligent Nutrients Minneapolis" in Inc. (Volume 32, December 2010, No. 10)

Pub: Inc. Magazine

Ed: Mike Hoffman. Description: Horst Rechelbacher, founder of hair care company Aveda, and after selling Aveda to Estee Lauder, he is expanding into a nutraceuticals company offering hair care products that are organically grown.

29491 ■ "Become A Brand" in Women Entrepreneur (September 14, 2008)

Pub: Entrepreneur Media Inc.

Ed: Suzy Girard-Ruttenberg. Description: Powerful brands are effective, innovative, exclusive or even socially conscious; it is important for small businesses to understand the power of becoming a brand since it is one of the best ways in which to position one's company and drive its growth.

29492 ■ "Beer Drinkers Wanted More. The Brewer Had No Room to Expand. How Could It Keep the Taps Flowing?" in Inc. (October 2007, pp. 65-66)

Pub: Gruner & Jahr USA Publishing

Ed: Alex Salkever. Description: Profile of John McDonald, founder of Boulevard, the second-largest beer company located in Kansas City, Missouri. McDonald tells how he was able to expand his turn-of-the-century brick building he had imported from Bavaria by developing a 70,000-square-foot building on four acres adjacent to his existing location rather move to a suburb.

29493 ■ "Being Emotional During Decision Making-Good or Bad?" in Academy of Management Journal (Vol. 50, No. 4, August 2007)

Pub: Academy of Management

Contact: Ming-Jer Chen, President

Ed: Myeong-Gu Seo, Lisa Feldman Barrett. Description: Relationship between affective experience and decision-making performance is studied.

29494 ■ Ben Franklin: America's Original Entrepreneur, Franklin's Autobiography Adapted for Modern Times

Pub: McGraw-Hill

Ed: Blaine McCormick; Benjamin Franklin. Released: September 2005.

29495 ■ "The Best Advice I Ever Got" in Harvard Business Review (Vol. 86, September 2008, No. 9, pp. 29)

Pub: Harvard Business School Press

Ed: Daisy Wademan Dowling. Description: Bright Horizons Family Solutions founder and chair Linda Mason illustrates how letting one's life passion direct entrepreneurship and business success. She describes how her humanitarian interests and efforts gave her the drive to launch a childcare service.

29496 ■ "The Best Execs in Canada" in Canadian Business (Vol. 79, October 9, 2006, No. 20, pp. 68)

Pub: Rogers Media

Description: The annual list of the most outstanding and innovative business executives of Canada is presented.

29497 ■ "Better Card Collecting" in Canadian Business (Vol. 80, January 15, 2007, No. 2, pp. 66)

Pub: Rogers Media

Ed: Sarah B. Hood. Description: Tips on how to collect business cards and use them for enhancing one's business performance are presented. Targeting specific people, taking notes and giving follow ups are some suggestions.

29498 ■ "Beverage Brand Vies To Be the Latest Purple Prince" in Brandweek (Vol. 49, April 21, 2008, No. 16, pp. 20)

Pub: VNU Business Media, Inc.

Ed: Becky Ebenkamp. Description: Profile on the new beverage product Purple and its founder, Ted Farnsworth; Purple is a drink that blends seven antioxidant-rich juices to create what Mr. Farnsworth calls a 'Cascade Effect' that boosts antioxidants' ef-

fectiveness. Mr. Farnsworth is marketing the brand's Oxygen Radical Absorbance Capability (ORAC) which is a value of 7,600 compared with orange juice's 1,200.

29499 ■ The Big Book of Small Business: You Don't Have to Run Your Business by the Seat of Your Pants

Pub: HarperCollins Publishers, Inc.

Ed: Tom Gegax; Phil Bolsta. Released: February 2007. Price: $29.95. Description: Entrepreneur shares his experiences starting and running his small business.

29500 ■ The Big Payback: The History of the Business of Hip-Hop

Pub: New American Library/Penguin Group

Ed: Dan Charnas. Price: $24.95. Description: The complete history of hip-hop music is presented, by following the money and the relationship between artist and merchant. In its promise of economic security and creative control for black artist-entrepreneurs, it is the culmination of dreams of black nationalists and civil rights leaders.

29501 ■ "The BIG Picture" in Crain's Cleveland Business (Vol. 30, June 22, 2009, No. 24, pp. 12)

Pub: Crain Communications, Inc.

Ed: Arielle Kass. Description: Entrepreneurs are quick to praise their colleges and universities and attribute both personal and business success to them.

29502 ■ The Big Rich: The Rise and Fall of the Greatest Texas Oil Fortunes

Pub: Penguin Group USA Inc.

Ed: Bryan Burrough. Released: 2009. Price: $29.95. Description: The story of the great 20th Century oilmen offers lessons on the value of confidence, grit and guile.

29503 ■ Big Vision, Small Business

Pub: Ivy Sea, Inc.

Ed: Jamie S. Walters. Released: October 10, 2002. Price: $17.95. Description: The power of the small enterprise is examined. The author shares her expertise as an entrepreneur and founder of a business consulting firm to help small business owners successfully run their companies. Interviews with more than seventy small business owners provide insight into visioning, planning, and establishing a small company, as well as strategies for good employee and customer relationships.

29504 ■ "Bill Lee's Auto Repair Business Chugs Along Despite Life's Obstacles" in Bradenton Herald (August 22, 2010)

Pub: Bradenton Herald

Ed: Grace Gagliano. Description: Profile of Bill Lee's Professional Automotive Services located in Bradenton, Florida. The auto repair business was opened 26 years ago and provides repair for an assortment of fleet vehicles, including truck repair.

29505 ■ Billions of Entrepreneurs: How China and India Are Reshaping Their Futures and Yours

Pub: Harvard Business School Press

Ed: Tarun Khanna. Released: 2009. Price: $29.95. Description: Various success strategies for success in both China and India are examined. Implications of the concurrent economic booms in both countries are cited.

29506 ■ "Black Lotus Brewing Co." in Crain's Detroit Business (Vol. 23, October 1, 2007, No. 40, pp. 13)

Pub: Crain Communications Inc. - Detroit

Ed: Leah Boyd. Description: Profile of Black Lotus Brewing Company and owner, Mike Allan who converted a drug store location into a brewery while restoring the building's original architecture.

29507 ■ The Black Swan

Pub: Random House

Description: A black swan is a highly improbably event with three principle characteristics: it is unpredictable, it carries a massive impact, and after the fact, we concoct an explanation that makes it appear less random and more predictable than it really was.

The success of Google was a black swan; so was 9/11. According to the author, black swans underlie almost everything about the world, from the rise of religions to events in personal lives.

29508 ■ *"Blast from the Past" in Entrepreneur (Vol. 35, November 2007, No. 11, pp. 48)*
Pub: Entrepreneur Media Inc.
Ed: Robert Kiyosaki. **Description:** Entrepreneurs of today face the challenge of creating new ideas. Collaborating with younger employees provides new perspective, but it also has to be a partnership with old ideas and sharing experiences between the older and the younger to forecast the future.

29509 ■ *"Boar Market: Penny-Wise Consumers Favoring Pork" in Crain's Chicago Business (Vol. 31, April 14, 2008, No. 15, pp. 4)*
Pub: Crain Communications, Inc.
Ed: Bruce Blythe. **Description:** Interview with Alan Cole who is the president of Cedar Hill Associates Inc. and who discusses ways in which his company is taking advantage of the record highs of oil and natural gas as well as his overall outlook on the market.

29510 ■ *The Book of Entrepreneurs' Wisdom*
Pub: John Wiley and Sons Inc.
Ed: Peter Krass. **Price:** $26.95.

29511 ■ *The Book of Hard Choices: Making the Right Decisions at Work without Losing Your Self-Respect*
Pub: Broadway Books
Contact: David Drake, Manager
E-mail: ddrake@randomhouse.com
Ed: Peter Roy; James A. Autry. **Released:** December 2006. **Price:** $23.95.

29512 ■ *"Boosting Corporate Entrepreneurship Through HRM Practices" in Human Resource Management (Vol. 49, July-August 2010, No. 4)*
Pub: John Wiley
Ed: Ralf Schmelter, Rene Mauer, Christiane Borsch, Malte Brettel. **Description:** A study was conducted to determine which human resource management (HRM) practices promote corporate entrepreneurship (CE) in small and medium-sized enterprises (SMEs). Findings indicate that staff selection, staff development, training, and staff rewards on CE have a strong impact on SMEs.

29513 ■ *Bo's Lasting Lessons*
Pub: Business Plus
Ed: Bo Schembechler; John U. Bacon. **Price:** $13.99. **Description:** Leadership skills are taught.

29514 ■ *Bottom-Line Training: Performance-Based Results*
Pub: Training Education Management
Ed: Donald J. Ford. **Released:** June 2005. **Price:** $29.99. **Description:** Training is critical to any successful enterprise. The key to any successful training program involves defining and constantly focusing on the desired results of the program. The author provides a training model based on five phases, known as ADDIE: analysis, design, development, implementation and evaluation.

29515 ■ *"Bottoms Up!" in Entrepreneur (Vol. 36, April 2008, No. 4, pp. 128)*
Pub: Entrepreneur Media, Inc.
Ed: Amanda C. Kooser. **Description:** Jill Bernheimer launched her online alcohol business Domaine547 in 2007, and encountered challenges as legal issues over the licensing and launching of the business took about seven months to finish. Domain547 features blog and forum areas. Marketing strategy that connects to the social community is one of the ways to reach out to customers.

29516 ■ *Brag!: The Art of Tooting Your Own Horn Without Blowing It*
Pub: Warner Books, Incorporated
Ed: Peggy Klaus. **Released:** May 2004. **Price:** $13.95. **Description:** A plan to promote a small business by effectively selling one's self.

29517 ■ *"Branding Specialist" in Black Enterprise (Vol. 38, July 2008, No. 12, pp. 1)*
Pub: Earl G. Graves Publishing Co. Inc.
Ed: Faith Chukwudi. **Description:** Interview with Wonya Lucas who is the chief marketing officer for Discovery Communications and is known for building strong brands by understanding her audience and generating buy-in throughout the organization; Lucas discusses her role in the corporation, guerilla marketing techniques, and what companies tend to overlook in marketing their products or services.

29518 ■ *"Breadwinner Tries on Designer Jeans" in Houston Business Journal (Vol. 40, December 18, 2009, No. 32, pp. 1)*
Pub: American City Business Journals
Ed: Allison Wollam. **Description:** Chuck Cain, the franchisee who introduced Panera Bread to Houston, Texas has partnered with tax accountant Jim Jacobsen to introduce custom-make Tattu Jeans. As more Tattu Jeans outlets are being planned, Cain is using entrepreneurial lessons learned from Panera Bread in the new venture. Both Panera Bread and Tattu Jeans were opened by Cain during economic downturns.

29519 ■ *"Breaking Through" in Inc. (January 2008, pp. 90-93)*
Pub: Gruner & Jahr USA Publishing
Ed: Mike Hofman. **Description:** Entrepreneur Keith R. McFarland, shares insight into why most successful companies eventually plateau, while others keep on growing.

29520 ■ *The Breakthrough Company*
Pub: Crown Publishing/Random House
Ed: Keith McFarland. **Released:** September 1, 2009. **Price:** $16.00 paperback. **Description:** Traits of high-growth players that actually make it in business.

29521 ■ *The Breakthrough Company: How Everyday Companies Become Extraordinary Performers*
Pub: Crown Publishing Company
Ed: Keith R. McFarland. **Released:** September 2009. **Price:** $16.00 paperback. **Description:** Author shares five years of building and analyzing the world's largest growth companies performance database and interviews with over 1,500 growth-company executives to help identify the secrets of breakthrough. This book will help any small business learn ways to avoid potential hazards along with way.

29522 ■ *"Brett Wilson" in Canadian Business (Vol. 81, July 22, 2008, No. 12-13, pp. 80)*
Pub: Rogers Media Ltd.
Ed: Michelle Magnan. **Description:** Interview with Brett Wilson who believes he became a 'capitalist with a heart' because he had a father who sold cars and a mother who was a social worker. He feels that being accelerated a grade was one of the biggest opportunities and challenges in his life. Brett Wilson's other views on business and on his family are presented.

29523 ■ *"Bring It On" in Entrepreneur (Vol. 35, November 2007, No. 11, pp. 52)*
Pub: Entrepreneur Media Inc.
Ed: Guy Kawasaki. **Description:** Tips on managing corporate competition in order to drive a company to success are presented.

29524 ■ *"Bringing Manufacturing Concerns to Springfield" in Crain's Chicago Business (Vol. 31, March 31, 2008, No. 13, pp. 6)*
Pub: Crain Communications, Inc.
Ed: Paul Merrion. **Description:** Profile of the new executive vice-president of Tooling & Manufacturing Assn., Paul Merrion, a man who plans to grow TMA's membership with an aggressive legislative agenda in Springfield.

29525 ■ *"The Buck Stops Here" in Canadian Business (Vol. 81, November 10, 2008, No. 19, pp. 25)*
Pub: Rogers Media Ltd.
Ed: Sarka Halas. **Description:** Reputation strategist Leslie Gaines-Ross says that minimizing the damage followed by the identification of what went wrong are the first steps that companies need to take when try-

ing to salvage their reputation. Gaines-Ross states that it is up to the CEO to ensure the company's speedy recovery and they need to be at the forefront of the process.

29526 ■ *"Budget Woes Endanger E-Prep Progress" in Crain's Cleveland Business (Vol. 30, June 22, 2009, No. 24, pp. 6)*
Pub: Crain Communications, Inc.
Ed: Brian Tucker. **Description:** The future of the Entrepreneurship Preparatory School located in Cleveland is being threatened by State budget concerns. The charter school requires all students to wear uniforms, respect discipline, and attend for longer hours and more weeks.

29527 ■ *"Building Alexian Brothers' Clinical Reputation" in Crain's Chicago Business (Vol. 31, May 5, 2008, No. 18, pp. 6)*
Pub: Crain Communications, Inc.
Ed: Mike Colias. **Description:** Profile of the CEO of Alexian Brothers Medical Center in Elk Grove Village who plans to stabilize Alexian Brothers' financial performance in part by eliminating $20 million in annual costs.

29528 ■ *Building a Business the Buddhist Way*
Pub: Celestial Arts Publishing Company
Ed: Geri Larkin. **Released:** September 2004. **Price:** $11.67 (Canadian). **Description:** Principles of entrepreneurship for starting and growing a business while maintaining a balance between business goals and spiritual goals.

29529 ■ *"Building His Dream" in Business Courier (Vol. 24, January 25, 2008, No. 42, pp. 1)*
Pub: American City Business Journals, Inc.
Ed: Laura Baverman. **Description:** Technology entrepreneur Mahendra Vora plans to build a more than $100 million local IT headquarters for VTech Holdings Ltd by 2010. Acquisition of four $5 million companies within 2008 are part of the owner's plan to expand the office equipment company. Other plans for the IT company are discussed.

29530 ■ *Building Wealth in China: 36 True Stories of Chinese Millionaires and How They Made Their Fortunes*
Pub: Crown Business Books
Ed: Ling, Zhu. **Released:** April 27, 2010. **Price:** $15.00. **Description:** Thirty-six of China's most successful and innovative entrepreneurs discuss valuable lessons for growing a business in China.

29531 ■ *Built to Last: Successful Habits of Visionary Companies*
Pub: HarperCollins Publishers Inc.
Ed: James C. Collins; Jerry I. Porras. **Released:** January 2002. **Price:** $17.95 paperback.

29532 ■ *Business for Beginners, Canadian Edition: A Simple Step-By-Step Guide to Starting a Small Business*
Pub: Sourcebooks Mediafusion
Ed: Frances McGuckin. **Released:** March 15, 2005. **Price:** $16.95. **Description:** Small business advice is shared by seven successful entrepreneurs.

29533 ■ *Business Black Belt: Develop the Strength, Flexibility and Agility to Run Your Company*
Pub: Career Press, Inc.
Ed: Burke Franklin. **Released:** November 1, 2010. **Price:** $15.99. **Description:** Manual offering insights that will enable anyone to become successful in small business. Seventy short chapters included topics such as attitude, management, marketing, selling, employees, money, MBAs, lawyers, consultants, and investors.

29534 ■ *Business Fairy Tales*
Pub: Thomson South-Western
Ed: Cecil W. Jackson. **Released:** July 2006. **Price:** $39.95. **Description:** The seven most-common business schemes are uncovered.

29535 ■ *Business Management for Entrepreneurs*
Pub: Double Storey Books
Ed: Cecile Nieuwenhuizen. **Released:** March 1, 2009. **Price:** $35.95. **Description:** Lack of good management skills are usually the reason for any small company to fail. This book introduces entrepreneurs and managers of small to medium-sized firms to all functions required to manage successfully.

29536 ■ *Business Plans to Game Plans*
Pub: John Wiley and Sons, Inc.
Ed: Jan B. King. **Released:** 2003. **Price:** $27.50. **Description:** Information for running a small business are examined, focusing on action plans and ways to avoid the pitfalls of strategic planning. The book describes how entrepreneurs should set standards, lead by example, look to the future, focus on important details, face reality, grow profitability, and take action.

29537 ■ *The Business of Small Business: Succeeding and Prospering in Business for Reasonably Intelligent Entrepreneurs*
Pub: Allen-Reed Publishing Company
Released: August 2006. **Price:** $27.95. **Description:** Tips for running a successful company are presented to entrepreneurs.

29538 ■ *Business Stripped Bare: Adventures of a Global Entrepreneur*
Pub: Virgin Books/Random House
Ed: Sir Richard Branson. **Released:** January 22, 2010. **Price:** $26.95. **Description:** Successful entrepreneur, Sir Richard Branson, shares the inside track on some of his greatest achievements in business and the lessons learned from setbacks.

29539 ■ *Business Unusual*
Pub: Thorsons
Ed: Anita Roddick. **Price:** $24.95.

29540 ■ *Business Upgrade: 21 Days to Reignite the Entrepreneurial Spirit in You and Your Team*
Pub: John Wiley and Sons, Inc.
Ed: Richard P. Cordock. **Released:** January 2007. **Price:** $18.95. **Description:** Business consultant works to inspire and guide entrepreneurs to spark growth in their companies while motivating workers.

29541 ■ *Business as Usual*
Pub: HarperBusiness
Ed: Anita Roddick. **Released:** 2005. **Price:** $12.95. **Description:** Founder of The Body Shop shares her story and gives her opinion on everything from cynical cosmetic companies to destructive consultants.

29542 ■ *Business Vision: Beyond the Horizon, 2nd Ed.*
Pub: Business Vision Group
Ed: Dennis Wengert. **Released:** January 2009. **Description:** Challenges small business owners face when running their companies are addressed in order to position themselves for the future. The book teaches how to envision future direction and measure personal and business activities that provide an indication of personal progress in achieving visionary business leadership.

29543 ■ *Business Warrior: Strategy for Entrepreneurs*
Pub: Clearbridge Publishing
Ed: Sun Tzu. **Released:** September 2006. **Price:** $19.95. **Description:** Advice to help entrepreneurs understand competitive strategies in order to succeed, focusing on sales, marketing, and personnel management.

29544 ■ *"Businessman Legend Passes: Charles H. James II Credited With Transforming Family Business" in Black Enterprise (December 2007)*
Pub: Earl G. Graves Publishing Co. Inc.
Ed: Tara C. Walker. **Description:** Profile of Charles H. James II, president and chairman of The James Corporation, a family-owned multigenerational food distribution company that started as a produce firm.

29545 ■ *Busting the Myth of the Heroic CEO*
Pub: Cornell University Press
Contact: John G. Ackerman, Director
E-mail: jga4@cornell.edu
Ed: Michel Villette, Catherine Vuillermot. **Released:** 2010. **Price:** $24.95. **Description:** According to the authors, corporate leaders do not get ahead through productive risk-taking and innovation, but through ruthless exploitation of market imperfections and rivals.

29546 ■ *BUZZ: How to Create It and Win With It*
Pub: AMACOM
Ed: Edward I. Koch; Christy Heady. **Released:** June 2007. **Price:** $21.95. **Description:** Former New York City Mayor, Edward Koch demonstrates buss to define a small business image, how to create buzz with honesty, engage the media, withstand public scrutiny, turn mistakes into opportunities, and create loyal followers.

29547 ■ *"Bye-Bye, Ol' Boys" in Canadian Business (Vol. 80, January 15, 2007, No. 2, pp. 16)*
Pub: Rogers Media
Ed: Michelle Magnan. **Description:** A profile of Kathy Sendall, senior vice-president of Petro-Canada of the North American division and chairperson of the Canadian Association of Petroleum Producers, is presented.

29548 ■ *"C. Andrew McCartney; President, Owner, Bowden Manufacturing Corp., 37" in Crain's Cleveland Business (November 19, 2007)*
Pub: Crain Communications, Inc.
Ed: David Bennett. **Description:** Profile of C. Andrew McCartney who was named president of Bowden Manufacturing Corp., a company that machines and fabricates metal and plastic parts for products ranging from airplanes to medical equipment; Mr. McCartney has since purchased the company, which posted $8 million in sales last year. He feels that part of his success is due to adherence to such policies such as gaining the employees trust and to avoid making promises to customers that Bowden cannot keep.

29549 ■ *"Calendar" in Crain's Detroit Business (Vol. 24, March 10, 2008, No. 10, pp. 21)*
Pub: Crain Communications, Inc.
Description: Listing of events in the Detroit area include conferences addressing entrepreneurialism, economic development, and women business ownership.

29550 ■ *"Calendar" in Crain's Detroit Business (Vol. 24, March 17, 2008, No. 11, pp. 20)*
Pub: Crain Communications, Inc.
Description: Listing of events in the Detroit area include conferences addressing entrepreneurialism, economic development, and women business ownership.

29551 ■ *"Calendar" in Crain's Detroit Business (Vol. 24, March 24, 2008, No. 12, pp. 25)*
Pub: Crain Communications, Inc.
Description: Listing of events in the Detroit area include conferences addressing entrepreneurialism, economic development, and women business ownership.

29552 ■ *"Calendar" in Crain's Detroit Business (Vol. 24, March 31, 2008, No. 13, pp. 1)*
Pub: Crain Communications, Inc.
Description: Listing of events in the Detroit area include conferences addressing entrepreneurialism, economic development, and minority business ownership.

29553 ■ *"Calendar" in Crain's Detroit Business (Vol. 24, April 7, 2008, No. 14, pp. 27)*
Pub: Crain Communications, Inc.
Description: Listing of events in the Detroit area include conferences addressing entrepreneurialism, economic development, and minority business ownership.

29554 ■ *"Calendar" in Crain's Detroit Business (Vol. 24, April 14, 2008, No. 15, pp. 25)*
Pub: Crain Communications Inc.
Description: Listing of events in the Detroit area include conferences addressing entrepreneurialism, economic development, and ways in which to develop environmentally friendly buildings.

29555 ■ *"Calendar" in Crain's Detroit Business (Vol. 24, September 22, 2008, No. 38, pp. 17)*
Pub: Crain Communications Inc.
Description: Listing of events in the Detroit area include conferences addressing entrepreneurialism, economic development, and women business ownership.

29556 ■ *"Calendar" in Crain's Detroit Business (Vol. 24, October 6, 2008, No. 40, pp. 22)*
Pub: Crain Communications, Inc.
Description: Listing of events in the Detroit area include conferences addressing entrepreneurialism, economic development, manufacturing, marketing, the housing crisis and women business ownership.

29557 ■ *Call Me Ted*
Pub: Grand Central Publishing
Ed: Ted Turner. **Released:** 2008. **Price:** $30.00. **Description:** Media mogul, Ted Turner's biography is full of personal and business details from his careers in advertising and broadcasting.

29558 ■ *"Can He Win the Patent Game?" in Globe & Mail (February 20, 2006, pp. B1)*
Pub: CTVglobemedia Publishing Inc.
Ed: Simon Avery; Paul Waldie. **Description:** A profile on managerial abilities of chief executive officer Jim Balsillie of Research In Motion Ltd., who will face the patent case with NTP Inc., is presented.

29559 ■ *"Canada Tomorrow" in Canadian Business (Vol. 80, October 8, 2007, No. 20, pp. 14)*
Pub: Rogers Media
Ed: Donald J. Johnston. **Description:** An assessment of Canada's future in terms of its educational, social, and economic environment is presented. Concerns regarding the country's educational system such as the declining interest in science and technology and the possible lack of teachers in the future are discussed. In terms of its social and economic aspects, the need to support entrepreneurs and other qualified people is explained.

29560 ■ *"Canada's Uber-Wealthy" in Canadian Business (Vol. 80, Winter 2007, No. 24, pp. 16)*
Pub: Rogers Media
Description: Statistics of the concentration of millionaire households around the world and the wealth of major cities in Canada are presented. The data reveals that Montreal has the highest concentration of billionaires and that the U.S. has the highest concentration of millionaire households.

29561 ■ *Canadian Entrepreneurship and Small Business Management*
Pub: McGraw-Hill Ryerson, Limited
Ed: D. Wesley Balderson. **Released:** February 2005. **Description:** Successful entrepreneurship and small business management is shown through the use of individual Canadian small business experiences.

29562 ■ *Canadian Small Business Kit for Dummies*
Pub: John Wiley & Sons, Incorporated
Ed: Margaret Kerr; JoAnn Kurtz. **Released:** May 2006. **Price:** $28.99. **Description:** Resources include information on changes to laws and taxes for small businesses in Canada.

29563 ■ *"Career Transition" in Crain's Detroit Business (Vol. 26, January 4, 2010, No. 1, pp. 14)*
Pub: Crain Communications Inc.
Description: Profile of Nicole Longhini-McElroy who has opted to radically change her career path from working in the manufacturing sector to becoming a self-published author of 'Charmed Adventures', a book series created to engage children in creative thought.

29564 ■ *Careers for Homebodies and Other Independent Souls*
Pub: McGraw-Hill
Ed: Jan Goldberg. **Released:** March 2007. **Price:** $13.95. **Description:** The books offers insight into choosing the right career for individuals. Jobs range from office to outdoors, job markets, and levels of education requirements.

29565 ■ *"Carving a Niche" in Hawaii Business (Vol. 53, November 2007, No. 5, pp. 58)*
Pub: Hawaii Business Publishing
Ed: Kyle Galdeira. **Description:** Stephanie Lay created Extreme Surf Fitness which is a program that promotes natural performance enhancement and rehabilitation of surfers using core and balance exercises. Lay's goal is to become a full time coach for a big surf brand and tour the world with the team.

29566 ■ *"Carving Passion, Talent Help Couple Craft Business on Wood-Rich Land" in Crain's Cleveland Business (October 8, 2007)*
Pub: Crain Communications, Inc.
Ed: Sharon Schnall. **Description:** Profile of Wood-carved Art Gallery & Studio, a family-owned business which includes several ventures of the husband-and-wife team, Jim Stadtlander and Diane Harto.

29567 ■ *Cash In a Flash*
Pub: Crown Business Books
Ed: Robert G. Allen, Mark Victor Hansen. **Released:** December 28, 2010. **Price:** $15.00. **Description:** Proven, practical advice and techniques are given to help entrepreneurs make money quickly using skills and resources known to generate permanent and recurring income.

29568 ■ *"The Caterer and Hotelkeeper Interview Patrick Harbour and Nathan Jones" in Caterer & Hotelkeeper (October 28, 2011, No. 288)*
Pub: Reed Reference Publishing
Description: Profiles of Patrick Harbour and Nathan Jones who quit their jobs to start their own catering business. The partners discuss their business strategy when launching their boutique catering firm and ways they are adapting to the slow economy in order to remain successful.

29569 ■ *"A Cautionary Tale for Emerging Market Giants" in Harvard Business Review (Vol. 88, September 2010, No. 9, pp. 99)*
Pub: Harvard Business School Publishing
Ed: J. Stewart Black, Allen J. Morrison. **Description:** Key factors that negatively affected Japan corporate growth and organizational effectiveness include: devotion to established path, isolated domestic markets, homogenous executive teams, and a non-contentious labor force. Solutions include leadership development programs, multicultural input, and cross-cultural training.

29570 ■ *"Celebrate Success. Embrace Innovation" in Black Enterprise (Vol. 37, February 2007, No. 7, pp. 145)*
Pub: Earl G. Graves Publishing Co. Inc.
Description: 2007 Women of Power Summit provides networking opportunities, empowerment sessions, and nightly entertainment. More than 500 executive women of color are expected to attend this inspiring summit in Phoenix, February 7-10.

29571 ■ *"The Center of Success: Author Explores How Confidence Can Take You Further" in Black Enterprise (Vol. 38, March 2008, No. 8)*
Pub: Earl G. Graves Publishing Co. Inc.
Ed: Ayana Dixon. **Description:** Motivational speaker and author, Valorie Burton, provides a 50-question confidence quotient assessment to help business owners and managers develop confidence in order to obtain goals.

29572 ■ *"CEO Forecast" in Hispanic Business (January-February 2009, pp. 34, 36)*
Pub: Hispanic Business
Ed: Jessica Haro, Richard Kaplan. **Description:** As economic uncertainty fogs the future, executives turn to government contracts in order to boost business.

Revenue sources, health care challenges, environmental consulting and remediation services, as well as technological strides are discussed.

29573 ■ *"Challenges, Responses and Available Resources" in Journal of Small Business and Entrepreneurship (Vol. 23, Winter 2010, No. 1)*
Pub: Canadian Council for Small Business and Entrepreneurship
Ed: Lynne Siemens. **Description:** Rural communities and their residents are exploring the potential of small business and entrepreneurship to address the economic changes they are facing. While these rural areas present many opportunities, business people in these areas face challenges which they must navigate to operate successfully.

29574 ■ *"Changing Society One Organization at a Time" in Hispanic Business (January-February 2008, pp. 55-56)*
Pub: Hispanic Business
Ed: Hildy Median. **Description:** Profile of Jerry Porras, Stanford professor, whose mission is to create a healthier society. Porras discusses what makes any business successful.

29575 ■ *The Checklist Manifesto: How to Get Things Right*
Pub: Metropolitan Books
Ed: Dr. Atul Gawande. **Price:** $24.50. **Description:** How tragic errors can be sharply reduced with a piece of paper, hand-drawn boxes, and a pencil.

29576 ■ *China's Rational Entrepreneurs: The Development of the New Private Business Sector*
Pub: Routledge
Ed: Barbara Krug. **Released:** March 2004. **Price:** $195.00 (US). **Description:** Difficulties faced by entrepreneurs in China are discussed, including analysis for understanding their behavior and relations with local governments in order to secure long-term business success.

29577 ■ *"Choice Bits" in Crain's Cleveland Business (Vol. 30, June 29, 2009, No. 25, pp. 19)*
Pub: Crain Communications, Inc.
Description: Ross Farro, Cleveland area restaurateur who was featured in the New York Times story about casual dining chains competing over lunch traffic through pricing.

29578 ■ *"City Slickers" in Canadian Business (Vol. 81, March 31, 2008, No. 5, pp. 36)*
Pub: Rogers Media
Ed: Joe Castaldo. **Description:** Richard Florida believes that the creative class drives the economy and the prosperity of countries depends on attracting and retaining these people. Florida has brought attention to developing livable and economically vibrant cities thanks in part to his promotional skills. However, he has also drawn critics who see his data on his theories as flimsy and inadequate.

29579 ■ *"The Classless Workplace: The Digerati and the New Spirit of Technocapitalism" in WorkingUSA (Vol. 11, June 2008, No. 2, pp. 181)*
Pub: Blackwell Publishers Ltd.
Ed: Eran Fisher. **Description:** Article argues the formation of a new type of economic actor at the intersection of a new capitalism and a new technology: The Dierati. The discourse in based on the analysis of the popular magazine Wired, which registers the culture of contemporary technocapitalism. The suggestion that the new persona of the digerati is constructed as a rejection of the ethics, which dominated the Fordist workplace and Fordist society: Hierarchy and differentiation between workers, on the one hand and capitalists and managers, on the other hand. The transformation of these two categories, workers and capitalists into the digerati worker and the digerati entrepreneur, is described. Set within the context of the structural transformations of capitalism from Fordism to post-Fordism, the article shows the ideological fit of the new ethics of

the digerati to the new working arrangements of post-Fordist capitalism, characterized by more privatizes, flexible, and precarious working arrangements.

29580 ■ *"Clay Riddell" in Canadian Business (Vol. 80, February 12, 2007, No. 4, pp. 86)*
Pub: Rogers Media
Ed: Michelle Magnan. **Description:** Chief executive officer of Paramount Resources Clay Riddell shares his passion for oil and gas business.

29581 ■ *"Code Name: Investors: Go From Golden Idea to Agent of Invention" in Black Enterprise (Vol. 41, November 2010, No. 4, pp. 78)*
Pub: Earl G. Graves Publishing Co. Inc.
Ed: Renita Burns. **Description:** Profile of Andre Woolery, inventor of a magnetic wristband that holds small nails, screws, drill bits, and small tools, allowing handymen to keep essential tools at hand while working.

29582 ■ *Common Problems; Common Sense Solutions: Practical Advice for Small Business Owners*
Pub: iUniverse, Incorporated
Ed: Greg Hadley. **Released:** September 2004. **Price:** $14.95. **Description:** Common sense advice for entrepreneurs running a small business.

29583 ■ *Common Sense Business: Starting, Operating, and Growing Your Small Business-In Any Economy!*
Pub: HarperInformation
Ed: Steve Gottry. **Released:** July 2005. **Price:** $19.95 (US), $26.95 (Canadian). **Description:** Strategies for starting, operating and growing a small business in any economy. .

29584 ■ *The Commonsense Way to Build Wealth: One Entrepreneur Shares His Secrets*
Pub: Griffin Publishing Group
Ed: Jack Chou. **Released:** September 2004. **Price:** $19.95. **Description:** Entrepreneurial tips to accumulate wealth, select the proper business or franchise, choose and manage rental property, and how to negotiate a good lease.

29585 ■ *The Company We Keep: Reinventing Small Business for People, Community, and Place*
Pub: Chelsea Green Publishing
Ed: John Abrams, William Grieder. **Released:** June 2006. **Price:** $18.00. **Description:** The new business trend in social entrepreneurship as a business plan enables small business owners to meet the triple bottom line of profits for people (employees and owners), community, and the environment.

29586 ■ *"The Competitive Imperative Of Learning" in Harvard Business Review (Vol. 86, July-August 2008, No. 8, pp. 60)*
Pub: Harvard Business School Press
Ed: Amy C. Edmondson. **Description:** Experimentation and reflection are important components for maintaining success in the business world and are the kind of character traits that can help one keep his or her competitive edge.

29587 ■ *The Complete Idiot's Guide to Finance for Small Business*
Pub: Penguin Group Incorporated
Ed: Kenneth E. Little. **Released:** April 2006. **Price:** $19.95. **Description:** Financial experts helps small business owners through strategies for long-term financial success.

29588 ■ *The Complete Small Business Guide: A Sourcebook for New and Small Businesses*
Pub: John Wiley & Sons, Incorporated
Ed: Colin Barrow. **Released:** March 2006. **Price:** $27.95. **Description:** Sourcebook for creating new small companies and running established small businesses.

29589 ■ *"Conference Calendar" in Marketing to Women (Vol. 21, March 2008, No. 3, pp. 7)*
Pub: EPM Communications Inc.
Contact: Ira Mayer, President
E-mail: imayer@epmcom.com
Description: Listing of current conferences and events aimed at women entrepreneurs and leaders.

29590 ■ *"Conference Calendar" in Marketing to Women (Vol. 22, July 2009, No. 7, pp. 7)*
Pub: EPM Communications Inc.
Contact: Ira Mayer, President
E-mail: imayer@epmcom.com
Description: Listing of conferences and seminars targeting female entrepreneurs.

29591 ■ *"Conference Calendar" in Marketing to Women (Vol. 22, August 2009, No. 8, pp. 7)*
Pub: EPM Communications Inc.
Contact: Ira Mayer, President
E-mail: imayer@epmcom.com
Description: Listing of conferences and seminars targeting female entrepreneurs.

29592 ■ *Confessions of a Serial Entrepreneur: Why I Can't Stop Starting Over*
Pub: John Wiley and Sons Inc.
Ed: Stuart Skorman. **Released:** February 2007. **Price:** $27.99. **Description:** Profile of Stuart Skorman who was raised in a retail family; Skorman shares his business success.

29593 ■ *"Congratulations to the 2010 Top Ten Business Women of ABWA" in Women In Business (Vol. 61, August-September 2009, No. 4, pp. 12)*
Pub: American Business Women's Association
Description: Listing of the top 10 members of the American Business Women's Association (ABWA) for 2010 is presented. The lists of the top ten 2010 members selected by each of the six ABWA chapters are also provided.

29594 ■ *The Connection Key: Seven Ways the World's Most Successful Entrepreneurs Trounce the Competition and How You Can, Too*
Pub: John Wiley & Sons, Inc.
Ed: Maribeth Kuzmeski. **Released:** September 22, 2009. **Price:** $22.95. **Description:** The book is written under the premise that getting ahead in business does not come down to smarts, guts, rare talent, or plain old luck. While those things are helpful, the real missing ingredient is the ability to meaningfully connect with others.

29595 ■ *"Connie Ozan; Founder, Design Director, Twist Creative, 37" in Crain's Cleveland Business (Vol. 28, November 19, 2007, No. 46)*
Pub: Crain Communications, Inc.
Ed: John Booth. **Description:** Profile of Connie Ozan, design director and founder of Twist Creative, an advertising agency that she runs with her husband, Michael; Ms. Ozan credits her husband's business sense in bringing a more strategic side to the company in which to complement her art direction.

29596 ■ *"Convention Calendar" in Black Enterprise (Vol. 37, December 2006, No. 5, pp. 74)*
Pub: Earl G. Graves Publishing Co. Inc.
Description: Listing of conferences and summits targeting African American business owners and executives.

29597 ■ *"Convention Calendar" in Black Enterprise (Vol. 37, November 2006, No. 4, pp. 76)*
Pub: Earl G. Graves Publishing Co. Inc.
Description: Listing of conferences targeted at African American executives and business owners.

29598 ■ *"Conversation" in Harvard Business Review (Vol. 86, September 2008, No. 9, pp. 32)*
Pub: Harvard Business School Press
Ed: Susan Donovan. **Description:** Danish software entrepreneur Thorkil Sonne has helped improve employment for individuals with autism after discovering the perception of detail and remarkable memory skills in his own son, who has autism. His company, Specialisterne, was built via focusing on these strengths.

29599 ■ *"Conversation: Historian Geoffrey Jones On Why Knowledge Stays Put" in Harvard Business Review (Vol. 86, July-August 2008, No. 8)*
Pub: Harvard Business School Press
Ed: Gardiner Morse. **Description:** Geoffrey Jones, Harvard Business School's professor of business history, discusses factors that cause knowledge to concentrate in particular regions, rather than disperse, such as the location of wealth.

29600 ■ *"A Conversation With Steven Hilfinger, Foley & Lardner L.L.P." in Crain's Detroit Business (Vol. 24, March 24, 2008, No. 12, pp. 1)*
Pub: Crain Communications, Inc.
Description: Interview with Steven Hilfinger who is a member of Foley & Lardner L.L.P.'s mergers and acquisitions practice and is co-chair of its automotive industry team. Hilfinger discusses such issues as the role a board of directors can play in the M&A process and the future of the auto market.

29601 ■ *Coolhunting*
Pub: AMACOM
Ed: Peter A. Gloor; Scott W. Cooper. **Released:** June 1, 2007. **Price:** $24.95. **Description:** Lessons for unlocking and applying swarm creativity in organizations to increase creativity, productivity, and efficiency.

29602 ■ *Corporate Crisis and Risk Management: Modeling, Strategies and SME Application*
Pub: Elsevier Science and Technology Books
Ed: M. Aba-Bulgu; S.M.N. Islam. **Released:** December 2006. **Price:** $115.00. **Description:** Methods and tools for handling corporate risk and crisis management are profiled for small to medium-sized businesses.

29603 ■ *Corporate Entrepreneurship & Innovation*
Pub: Thomson South-Western
Ed: Michael H. Morris; Donald F. Kuratko. **Released:** January 2007. **Price:** $104.95. **Description:** Innovation is the key to running a successful small business. The book helps entrepreneurs to develop the skills and business savvy to sustain a competitive edge.

29604 ■ *Corporate Entrepreneurship: Top Managers and New Business Creation*
Pub: Cambridge University Press
Contact: Richard Ziemacki, President
E-mail: rziemacki@cambridge.org
Ed: Vijay Sathe. **Released:** February 2007. **Price:** $35.00. **Description:** Studies covering entrepreneurship and business growth are examined.

29605 ■ *"Corporate Etiquette: The Art of Apology" in Canadian Business (Vol. 80, January 29, 2007, No. 3, pp. 62)*
Pub: Rogers Media
Ed: John Gray. **Description:** The methods of nurturing professional relationships, by apologizing for the mistakes committed by individuals and institutions, are described.

29606 ■ *"Corporate Responsibility" in Professional Services Close-Up (July 2, 2010)*
Pub: Close-Up Media
Description: List of firms awarded the inaugural Best Corporate Citizens in Government Contracting by the Corporate Responsibility Magazine is presented. The list is based on the methodology of the Magazine's Best Corporate Citizen's List, with 324 data points of publicly-available information in seven categories which include: environment, climate change, human rights, philanthropy, employee relations, financial performance, and governance.

29607 ■ *Country Studies in Entrepreneurship: A Historical Perspective*
Pub: Palgrave Macmillan
Ed: Ioanna Minoglou; Cassis Youssef. **Released:** July 2006. **Price:** $80.00. **Description:** Comparison of eight national entrepreneurial ventures, covering three continents, is discussed.

29608 ■ *Creating Success from the Inside Out: Develop the Focus and Strategy to Uncover the Life You Want*
Pub: John Wiley and Sons, Inc.
Ed: Ephren W. Taylor. **Released:** November 16, 2007. **Price:** $24.95. **Description:** Ephren Taylor founded his first business at age 12 and was a multimillionaire CEO ten years later. Taylor explains how he and other successful young entrepreneurs think about success and achievement.

29609 ■ *Creativity and Innovation: Breaking New Ground..Without Breaking the Bank*
Pub: A. & C. Black
Ed: Janice Armstrong. **Released:** March 1, 2009. **Price:** $12.95. **Description:** Advice is given to help small business owners be creative in order to compete in their sector.

29610 ■ *"Crisis Management" in Black Enterprise (Vol. 38, October 2007, No. 3, pp. 69)*
Pub: Earl G. Graves Publishing Co. Inc.
Ed: Faith Chukwudi. **Description:** Shirley W. Bridges, chief information officer for Delta Air Lines, discusses leadership skills that establish trust within an organization.

29611 ■ *Crunch Point: The Secret to Succeeding When it Matters Most*
Pub: American Management Association
Contact: Charles R. Craig, Chairman
Ed: Brian Tracy. **Released:** 2006. **Price:** $17.95.

29612 ■ *"Customized Before Custom Was Cool" in Green Industry Pro (July 2011)*
Pub: Cygnus Business Media
Ed: Gregg Wartgow. **Description:** Profile of Turf Care Enterprises and owner Kevin Vogeler, who discusses his desire to use more natural programs using little or no chemicals in 1986. At that time, that sector represented 20 percent of his business, today it shares 80 percent.

29613 ■ *Dare to Prepare - How to Win Before You Begin*
Pub: Crown Publishing/Random House
Ed: Ronald M. Shapiro; Gregory Jordan. **Released:** February 24, 2009. **Price:** $14.95 paperback. **Description:** Shapiro uses his experience as one of America's top negotiators and lawyers to show how meticulous planning can raise the odds of success in business as well as in life.

29614 ■ *"Datebook" in Crain's Chicago Business (Vol. 31, March 24, 2008, No. 12, pp. 18)*
Pub: Crain Communications, Inc.
Description: Listing of events in the Detroit area include conferences addressing entrepreneurialism, economic development, secrets of getting hired, and women business ownership.

29615 ■ *"Datebook" in Crain's Chicago Business (Vol. 31, March 31, 2008, No. 13, pp. 1)*
Pub: Crain Communications, Inc.
Description: Listing of events in the Detroit area include conferences addressing entrepreneurialism, economic development, secrets of getting hired, and women business ownership.

29616 ■ *"Datebook" in Crain's Chicago Business (Vol. 31, April 28, 2008, No. 17, pp. 18)*
Pub: Crain Communications, Inc.
Description: Listing of events in the Detroit area include conferences addressing entrepreneurialism, economic development, and women business ownership.

29617 ■ *"David Low" in Hawaii Business (Vol. 53, October 2007, No. 4, pp. 38)*
Pub: Hawaii Business Publishing
Ed: Cathy S. Cruz-George. **Description:** Hawaii Capital Management managing director David Low ranked first in the 2007 competition for fittest male executives in Hawaii. This 5-foot-9 executive, who weighed 225 lbs. in 2003, weighs 150 lbs. in 2007. The activities that improved Low's fitness, such as weight training, swimming, biking, and running, are discussed.

29618 ■ *Dead on Arrival: How the Anti-Business Backlash is Destroying Entrepreneurship in America and What We Can Still Do About It!*
Pub: HarperCollins Publishers, Inc.
Ed: Bernie Marcus; Steve Gottry. **Released:** November 2006. **Price:** $23.95. **Description:** Bernie Marcus, Home Depot leader, addresses regulations hurting small businesses in America.

29619 ■ *Dealing with the Tough Stuff: Practical Wisdom for Running a Values-Driven Business*
Pub: Berrett-Koehler Publishers, Inc.
Ed: Margot Fraser, Lisa Lorimer. **Released:** November 1, 2009. **Price:** $16.95. **Description:** Advice is given to help small firms run a value-driven business.

29620 ■ *The Definitive Drucker: The Final Word from the Father of Modern Management*
Pub: McGraw-Hill
Ed: Elizabeth Haas Edersheim; A.G. Lafley. **Released:** December 2006. **Price:** $27.95.

29621 ■ *"Deja Vu" in Canadian Business (Vol. 81, July 22, 2008, No. 12-13, pp. 38)*
Pub: Rogers Media Ltd.
Ed: Joe Castaldo. **Description:** Laurent Beaudoin has retired as chief executive officer for Bombardier Inc.'s, a manufacturer of regional and business aircraft, but kept a role in the firm as a non-executive chairman. Beaudoin first resigned from the company in 1999, but had to return in 2004 to address challenging situations faced by the company. Beaudoin's views on management and the company are presented.

29622 ■ *"Describing the Entrepreneurial Profile" in International Journal of Entrepreneurship and Small Business (Vol. 11, November 1, 2010)*
Pub: Publishers Communication Group
Ed: Serena Cubico, Elisa Bortolani, Giuseppe Favretto, Riccardo Sartori. **Description:** An illustration of metric characteristics and selected research applications of an instrument that can be used to define aptitude for an entrepreneurial profile (created in the 1990s) is examined. The entrepreneurial aptitude test (TAI) describes entrepreneurial potential with regard to eight factors.

29623 ■ *"The Design of Things to Come" in Business Horizons (Vol. 51, January-February 2008, No. 1, pp. 74)*
Pub: Elsevier Advanced Technology Publications
Ed: Mimi Dollinger. **Description:** Review of the book that helps entrepreneurs develop and market new products, 'The Design of Things to Come: How Ordinary People Create Extraordinary Products'.

29624 ■ *Developmental Entrepreneurship: Adversity, Risk, and Isolation*
Pub: Elsevier Science and Technology Books
Ed: Craig Galbraith. **Released:** August 2006. **Price:** $99.95. **Description:** Volume five of the series, this book focuses on the fields of entrepreneurship, sociology, and economics. Fifteen articles related to entrepreneurship and small business development within a global environment are included.

29625 ■ *"Diana Sands; Vice-President of Investor Relations, Boeing Co." in Crain's Chicago Business (Vol. 31, May 5, 2008, No. 18, pp. 32)*
Pub: Crain Communications, Inc.
Ed: John Rosenthal. **Description:** Profile of Diana Sands who is the vice-president of investor relations at Boeing Co. which entails explaining the company's performance to securities analysts and institutional investors.

29626 ■ *"Diary of a Short-Seller" in Conde Nast Portfolio (Vol. 2, June 2008, No. 6, pp. 44)*
Pub: Conde Nast Publications
Contact: David Carey, President
Ed: Jesse Eisinger. **Description:** Profile of David Einhorn who is a fund manager that spoke out against finance company Allied Capital whose stock fell nearly 20 percent the day after Einhorn's critique; Einhorn subsequently had to contend with attacks against his credibility as well as investigations by the S.E.C.; Einhorn's experience illuminates our current economic crisis.

29627 ■ *"Dick Haskayne" in Canadian Business (Vol. 81, March 31, 2008, No. 5, pp. 72)*
Pub: Rogers Media
Ed: Andy Holloway. **Description:** Dick Haskayne says that he learned a lot about business from his dad who ran a butcher shop where they had to make a decision on buying cattle and getting credit. Haskayne says that family, friends, finances, career, health, and infrastructure are benchmarks that have to be balanced.

29628 ■ *"Did I Do That?" in Entrepreneur (Vol. 35, November 2007, No. 11, pp. 144)*
Pub: Entrepreneur Media Inc.
Ed: Romanus Wolter. **Description:** Entrepreneurs need to watch habits as some bad habits can affect business operations. Tips on ways to identify bad habits and how to address them are presented.

29629 ■ *"A Different Breed of Deal Maker is Emerging" in Globe & Mail (January 14, 2006, pp. B2)*
Pub: CTVglobemedia Publishing Inc.
Ed: Eric Reguly. **Description:** The managerial strategies of chief executive officers in business acquisitions of companies, such as Dofasco Inc., are presented.

29630 ■ *"Digging Deep for Gold" in Barron's (Vol. 88, March 24, 2008, No. 12, pp. 49)*
Pub: Dow Jones & Company, Inc.
Ed: Suzanne McGee. **Description:** David Iben, manager of the Nuveen Tradewinds Value Opportunities Fund, looks for value in companies and industries where the consensus of analysts is negative. He started investing in gold stocks well before gold prices started to rise.

29631 ■ *Divas Doing Business: What the Guidebooks Don't Tell You About Being A Woman Entrepreneur*
Pub: Nouveau Connoisseurs Corporation
Ed: Monique Hayward. **Released:** February 14, 2009. **Price:** $19.95. **Description:** A must-read for any woman who's currently running a business or is thinking of starting one.

29632 ■ *Divine Wisdom at Work: 10 Universal Principles for Enlightened Entrepreneurs*
Pub: Aha! House
Ed: Tricia Molloy. **Released:** July 2006. **Price:** $20.00. **Description:** Entrepreneurial advice for managing a small enterprise is given using inspiration, anecdotes and exercises.

29633 ■ *Do You! 12 Laws to Access the Power in You to Achieve Happiness and Success*
Pub: Gotham/Penguin Group Incorporated
Ed: Russell Simmons; Chris Morrow. **Released:** April 2008. **Price:** $15.00. **Description:** Hip-Hop mogul describes his successful visions and ventures.

29634 ■ *"Do Your Really Know Your Problem: Entrepreneurs Have a Tendency To See What They Want To See" in Inc. (December 2007, pp. 95-96)*
Pub: Gruner & Jahr USA Publishing
Ed: Norm Brodsky. **Description:** Information is offered to help entrepreneurs diagnose and resolve company issues.

29635 ■ *Doing Business with Beauty: Black Women, Hair Salons, and the Racial Enclave Economy*
Pub: Rowman & Littlefield Publishers Inc.
Contact: Jason Aronson, President
Ed: Adia Harvey Wingfield. **Released:** June 28, 2008. **Price:** $19.95. **Description:** Factors that draw black women into the hair industry are examined. Interviews with hair salon owners explore aspects of owning a salon, owner-employee relationships, and the black female owner's struggle for autonomy and success in entrepreneurship.

29636 ■ *"Doing It Right" in Black Enterprise (Vol. 38, October 2007, No. 3, pp. 53)*
Pub: Earl G. Graves Publishing Co. Inc.
Ed: Sheiresa McRae. **Description:** One of the hardest things for every entrepreneur to do is delegate responsibility to employees; Anthony Samuels offers tips on the art of delegating.

29637 ■ *"Don Bell" in Canadian Business (Vol. 80, November 5, 2007, No. 22, pp. 164)*
Pub: Rogers Media
Ed: Michelle Magnan. **Description:** Don Bell was not able to finish his degree at University of Calgary, however, he managed to build companies such as WestJet. Bell hates bureaucracy and believes in the importance of a good corporate culture. Details on his life as a father and a pilot along with his advice for entrepreneurs are given.

29638 ■ *"Donald Tarlton" in Canadian Business (Vol. 80, March 26, 2007, No. 7, pp. 70)*
Pub: Rogers Media
Ed: Andy Holloway. **Description:** Donald Tarlton, owner of Donald K Donald Entertainment Group, shares few things about his childhood and career.

29639 ■ *"Don's Pomeroy House a Strongsville Staple" in Crain's Cleveland Business (Vol. 30, June 1, 2009, No. 21, pp. 12)*
Pub: Crain Communications, Inc.
Ed: Kathy Ames Carr. **Description:** Profile of Don's Pomeroy House, an upscale restaurant inside a 162-year-old brick mansion. The building is listed on the National Register of Historic Places and features a main restaurant, pub and outdoor patio.

29640 ■ *Don't Bitch, Just Get Rich*
Pub: Simon and Schuster Inc.
Contact: Carolyn Reidy, President
E-mail: carolyn.reidy@simonandschuster.com
Ed: Toney Fitzgerald. **Released:** June 2006. **Price:** $16.00. **Description:** Advice is given to business leaders to help them shift from the position whereby money has power over you to taking responsibility for life choices in order to meet new challenges.

29641 ■ *"The Don't Do Lists" in Inc. (Vol. 33, October 2011, No. 8, pp. 65)*
Pub: Inc. Magazine
Ed: Jennifer Alsever, Adam Bluestein. **Description:** Ten business leaders and experts share their don't do lists, the things that should be avoided when going on sales calls, planning business lunches, motivating employees and more are presented.

29642 ■ *"Don't Quit When The Road Gets Bumpy" in Women Entrepreneur (November 25, 2008)*
Pub: Entrepreneur Media Inc.
Ed: Bonnie Price. **Description:** Discusses techniques four women entrepreneurs are utilizing to keep their businesses successful despite the credit crunch and the economic downturn.

29643 ■ *Double or Nothing: How Two Friends Risked It All to Buy One of Las Vegas' Legendary Casinos*
Pub: HarperBusiness
Ed: Tom Breitling, with Cal Fussman. **Released:** March 2008. **Price:** $24.95. **Description:** Founders of a successful Internet travel agency share their experience from startup to selling the company.

29644 ■ The Dream Manager
Pub: Hyperion
Ed: Matthew Kelly. Price: $19.95. Description: A business fable about the virtues of helping those working for and with you to achieve their dreams. Managers can boost morale and control turnover by adopting this policy.

29645 ■ Dreams with a Deadline: How to Turn a Strategy for Tomorrow Into a Plan for Today
Pub: Pearson Education, Limited
Contact: Steven A. Dowling, President
Ed: Jacques Horovitz; Anne-Valerie Ohlsson-Corboz. Released: November 2006. Price: $54.00. Description: Tips for successful entrepreneurship are covered.

29646 ■ "Driving Passion" in Small Business Opportunities (Spring 2008)
Pub: Harris Publications Inc.
Ed: Chuck Green. Description: Profile of Joe Assell, founder of Golftec, a company offering golf instruction that uses the latest technology with professional teachers.

29647 ■ Driving With No Brakes: How a Bunch of Hooligans Built the Best Travel Company in the World
Pub: Grand Circle Corporation
Ed: Alan and Harriet Lewis. Price: $19.95. Description: Inspirational book about how two courageous leaders built a remarkable company that can thrive in change and succeed in an unpredictable world. Important lessons for any business leader trying to create value in the 21st Century are included.

29648 ■ "The Duty of Wealth: Canadian Business Leaders on Nepotism and Philanthropy" in Canadian Business (Vol. 80, Winter 2007, No. 24)
Pub: Rogers Media
Ed: Joe Castaldo. Description: Fifty-one percent of the respondents in a survey of business leaders say that the decision to allow adult children to join a family firm should be based on the circumstances at the time. He CEOs that were surveyed also believed that billionaires should donate an average of forty percent of their estates and keep the rest for their family.

29649 ■ E-Myth Mastery: The Seven Essential Disciplines for Building a World Class Company
Pub: HarperCollins Publishers Inc.
Ed: Michael E. Gerber. Released: March 2007. Price: $16.95. Description: Leadership, marketing, money, management, lead conversion, lead generation, client fulfillment are the seven keys to successful entrepreneurship.

29650 ■ The E Myth Revisited: Why Most Small Businesses Don't Work and What to Do
Pub: HarperCollins Publishers
Ed: Michael E. Gerber. Released: January 18, 2010. Price: $11.10. Description: The book dispels the myths surrounding starting a business and shows how traditional assumptions can get in the way of running a small company. Topics cover entrepreneurship from infancy to growth and covers franchising.

29651 ■ "The Early Bird Gets the Worm" in Black Enterprise (Vol. 37, January 2007, No. 6, pp. 111)
Pub: Earl G. Graves Publishing Co. Inc.
Ed: Tykisha N. Lundy. Description: General Motors hosts the Black Enterprise Conference And Expo: Where Deals Are Made at Walt Disney World's Swan and Dolphin Resort, May 9-12. The conference will offer great information to entrepreneurs.

29652 ■ "The Early Bird Really Does Get the Worm" in Harvard Business Review (Vol. 88, July-August 2010, No. 7-8, pp. 30)
Pub: Harvard Business School Publishing
Ed: Christoph Randler. Description: Research indicates that those who identify themselves as 'morning people' tend to be more proactive and thus have a career-development advantage over those who identify themselves as 'night people'. Implications of the research are also discussed.

29653 ■ "Eat, Drink and Be a Success" in Entrepreneur (Vol. 37, August 2009, No. 8, pp. 70)
Pub: Entrepreneur Media, Inc.
Ed: Joel Holland. Description: Profile of Fritz Brogan, who is a full time student but also runs a successful bar and restaurant named Gin & Tonic and Kitchen. The bar was built with their target audience in mind which happens to be Brogan's college friends.

29654 ■ Eco Barons: The New Heroes of Environmental Activism
Pub: Ecco/HarperCollins
Ed: Edward Humes. Released: January 19, 2010. Price: $14.99. Description: Profiles of business leaders who have dedicated their lives to saving the planet from ecological devastation.

29655 ■ Economic Freedom and the American Dream
Pub: Palgrave Macmillan
Ed: Joseph Shaanan. Released: January 5, 2010. Price: $55.00. Description: An exploration into the effects of economic freedom on American in several areas such as markets, politics, and opportunities for would-be entrepreneurs.

29656 ■ The Economics of Entrepreneurship
Pub: Edward Elgar Publishing, Incorporated
Ed: Parker. Released: April 2006. Price: $240.00. Description: Previously published articles influencing research into the economic structure of entrepreneurship are examined.

29657 ■ The Economics of Self-Employment and Entrepreneurship
Pub: Cambridge University Press
Contact: Richard Ziemacki, President
E-mail: rziemacki@cambridge.org
Ed: Simon C. Parker. Released: July 2006. Price: $50.00. Description: The importance of self-employment and entrepreneurship in a modern economy is explored.

29658 ■ Ecopreneuring: Putting Purpose and the Planet Before Profits
Pub: New Society Publishers
Ed: John Ivanko; Lisa Kivirist. Released: July 1, 2008. Price: $17.95 paperback. Description: Ecopreneurs in America are shifting profits and market share towards green living. The book provides a guideline for ecopreneurs in the areas of eco-business basics, purposeful management, marketing in the green economy, and running a lifestyle business.

29659 ■ "Ed Otto, Director of Biotechnology at RCCC" in Charlotte Observer (February 8, 2007)
Pub: Knight-Ridder/Tribune Business News
Ed: Gail Smith-Arrants. Description: Profile of Ed Otto, director of biotechnology at Rowan-Cabarrus Community College. Before taking the position at RCCC, Otto directed the Food and Drug Administration office responsible for regulating cellular, tissue and gene therapies products.

29660 ■ Edgewalkers: People and Organizations That Take Risks, Build Bridges, and Break New Ground
Pub: Greenwood Publishing Group Inc.
Contact: Janann Sherman, Manager
Ed: Judi Neal. Released: October 2006. Price: $39. 95. Description: Profiles of entrepreneurs who thrive on change and challenge in order to create successful companies in today's complex business climate.

29661 ■ Effective Operations and Controls for the Small Privately Held Business
Pub: John Wiley and Sons, Inc.
Ed: Rob Reider. Released: January 2008. Price: $75.00. Description: Guide for implementing effective operations and controls for non-regulated small businesses with the least cost possible is presented.

29662 ■ Effectuation
Pub: Edward Elgar Publishing, Incorporated
Ed: Sarasvathy. Released: October 2006. Price: $85.00. Description: Effectuation is the idea that the future is unpredictable while being controllable. A study of 27 entrepreneurs shows effective effectuators.

29663 ■ Embedded Entrepreneurship: The Institutional Dynamics of Innovation
Pub: Routledge
Ed: Alexander Ebner. Released: April 10, 2010. Price: $150.00. Description: In this book, Alexander Ebner reconstructs the theory of entrepreneurship from an institutional perspective.

29664 ■ The Emerging Digital Economy: Entrepreneurship, Clusters, and Policy
Pub: Springer
Ed: Borje Johansson; Charlie Karlsson; Roger Stough. Released: August 2006. Price: $119.00. Description: The new economy, or digital economy, and its impact on the way industries and firms choose to locate and cluster geographically.

29665 ■ "Empathy: An Entrepreneur's Killer App" in Women Entrepreneur (February 3, 2009)
Pub: Entrepreneur Media Inc.
Ed: Kristi Hedges. Description: It is just as important to treat employees with courtesy and respect during bad economic times as it is in a good economy. Employers sometimes take advantage of such bad economic times since they realize that employees are grateful to have a job and cannot just quit and easily find work elsewhere. The importance of empathy in a company's leadership personnel is discussed.

29666 ■ "Empire of Pixels" in Entrepreneur (Vol. 37, September 2009, No. 9, pp. 50)
Pub: Entrepreneur Media, Inc.
Ed: Jason Daley. Description: Entrepreneur Jack Levin has successfully grown Imageshack, an image-hosting Web service. The Website currently gets 50 million unique visitors a month. Levin has launched Y-Frog, an application that uses Imageshack to allow Twitter users to add images to their posts.

29667 ■ Employee Management for Small Business
Pub: Self-Counsel Press, Incorporated
Ed: Lin Grensing-Pophal. Released: November 2009. Price: $20.95. Description: Management tools to help entrepreneurs maintain an effective human resources plan for a small company.

29668 ■ "Employee Motivation: A Powerful New Model" in Harvard Business Review (Vol. 86, July-August 2008, No. 8, pp. 78)
Pub: Harvard Business School Press
Ed: Nitin Nohria; Boris Groysbert; Linda Eling Lee. Description: Four drives underlying employee motivation are discussed as well as processes for leveraging these drives through corporate culture, job design, reward systems, and resource-allocation priorities.

29669 ■ Encyclopedia of Small Business
Pub: Cengage Gale
Ed: Arsen Darnay; Monique D. Magee; Kevin Hillstrom. Released: November 2010. Description: Concise encyclopedia of small business information.

29670 ■ "The Endless Flow of Russell Simmons" in Entrepreneur (Vol. 37, September 2009, No. 9, pp. 24)
Pub: Entrepreneur Media, Inc.
Ed: Josh Dean. Description: Entrepreneur Russell Simmons has successfully grown his businesses by focusing on underserved markets. Simons has never given up on any business strategy. He has also entered the music, clothing and television industries.

29671 ■ The Engine of America: The Secrets to Small Business Success from Entrepreneurs Who Have Made It!
Pub: John Wiley and Sons, Inc.
Ed: Hector Barreto; Robert J. Wagman (As told to). Released: September 2007. Price: $24.95. Description: Successful business strategies from CEOs of

fifty small businesses (some of which are now large corporations) are shared to help entrepreneurs start or grow an existing company.

29672 ■ Enlightened Leadership: Best Practice Guidelines and Time Tools for Easily Implementing Learning Organizations
Pub: Learning House Publishing, Inc.

Ed: Ralph LoVuolo; Alan G. Thomas. **Released:** May 2006. **Price:** $79.99. **Description:** Innovation and creativity are essential for any successful small business. The book provides owners, managers, and team leaders with the tools necessary to produce 'disciplined innovation'.

29673 ■ Enlightened Leadership: Best Practice Guidelines and Timesaving Tools for Easily Implementing Learning Organizations
Pub: Learning House Publishing, Incorporated

Ed: Alan G. Thomas; Ralph L. LoVuolo; Jeanne C. Hillson. **Released:** September 2006, printable 3 times/year. **Price:** $21.00. **Description:** Book provides the tools required to create a learning organization management model along with a step-by-step guide for team planning and learning. The strategy works as a manager's self-help guide as well as offering continuous learning and improvement for company-wide success.

29674 ■ Enterprise, Entrepreneurship and Innovation: Concepts, Context and Commercialization
Pub: Elsevier Science and Technology Books

Ed: Robin Lowe, Sue Marriott. **Released:** June 2006. **Price:** $39.95. **Description:** Application of enterprise, innovation and entrepreneurship are discussed to help companies grow.

29675 ■ Enterprise and Small Business: Principles, Practice and Policy
Pub: Pearson Education, Limited
Contact: Steven A. Dowling, President

Ed: Sara Carter; Dylan Jones-Evans. **Released:** September 2006. **Price:** $79.50. **Description:** Introduction to small business, challenges of a changing environment, and the nature of entrepreneurship are among the issues covered.

29676 ■ Enterprising Women in Urban Zimbabwe: Gender, Microbusiness, and Globalization
Pub: Indiana University Press
Contact: Janet Rabinowitch, Director
E-mail: jrabinow@indiana.edu

Ed: Mary Johnson Osirim. **Released:** April 1, 2009. **Price:** $39.95. **Description:** An investigation into the business and personal experiences of women entrepreneurs in the microenterprise sector in Zimbabwe. Many of these women work as market traders, crocheters, seamstresses, and hairdressers.

29677 ■ The Entrepreneur Next Door: Discover the Secrets to Financial Independence
Pub: Entrepreneur Press

Ed: William F. Wagner. **Released:** May 2006. **Price:** $19.95. **Description:** Traits required to become a successful entrepreneur are highlighted.

29678 ■ "Entrepreneur Says Spirituality Has Been a Key to Her Success" in Business First Columbus (Vol. 25, October 17, 2008, No. 8, pp. 1)
Pub: American City Business Journals

Ed: Scott Rawdon. **Description:** Profile of Carolyn Williams Francis, CEO of Williams Interior Designs Inc. She outlines her mantra for success in her furniture design business, but emphasizes that faith has taken her business to greater heights.

29679 ■ The Entrepreneur and Small Business Problem Solver
Pub: John Wiley & Sons, Incorporated

Ed: William A. Cohen. **Released:** December 2005. **Price:** $24.95 (US), $31.99 (Canadian). **Description:** Revised edition of the resource for entrepreneurs and small business owners that covers everything from start-up financing and loans to new product promotion and more.

29680 ■ The Entrepreneurial Author
Pub: Morgan James Publishing, LLC

Ed: David L. Hancock. **Released:** October 2009. **Price:** $17.95. **Description:** Handbook to help entrepreneurs author and publish a book based on their expertise in their chosen field.

29681 ■ The Entrepreneurial Culture Network Advantage Within Chinese and Irish Software Firms
Pub: Edward Elgar Publishing, Incorporated

Ed: Tsang. **Released:** October 2006. **Price:** $95.00. **Description:** Ways national cultural heritage influences entrepreneurial ventures are discussed.

29682 ■ Entrepreneurial Decision-Making Individuals, Tasks and Cognitions
Pub: Edward Elgar Publishing, Incorporated

Ed: Gusfasson. **Released:** December 2006. **Price:** $85.00. **Description:** Entrepreneurial decision-making is examined by comparing various individuals with differing levels of expertise and potential.

29683 ■ Entrepreneurial Finance
Pub: Pearson Education, Limited
Contact: Steven A. Dowling, President

Ed: Philip J. Adelman; Alan M. Marks. **Released:** July 2006. **Price:** $87.35. **Description:** Financial aspects of running a small business are covered; topics include sole proprietorships, partnerships, limited liability companies, and private corporations.

29684 ■ Entrepreneurial Finance: A Casebook
Pub: John Wiley and Sons Inc.

Ed: Paul A. Gompers; William Sahlman. **Released:** September 2006. **Price:** $63.00. **Description:** Investment analysis, entrepreneurial financing, harvesting, and renewal in the entrepreneurial firm are among the topics discussed.

29685 ■ "Entrepreneurial Human Resource Leadership" in Human Resource Management (Vol. 49, July-August 2010, No. 4, pp. 793-804)
Pub: John Wiley

Ed: David C. Strubler, Benjamin W. Redekop. **Description:** Dwight Carlson, a visionary entrepreneur, talks about his main role as a leader. He believes that experience can help in making choices between difficult alternatives. He also thinks that leaders do not really motivate people, they actually create an environment where they motivate themselves.

29686 ■ The Entrepreneurial Imperative: How America's Economic Miracle Will Reshape the World
Pub: HarperCollins Publishers, Inc.

Ed: Carl J. Schramm. **Released:** October 2006. **Price:** $24.95. **Description:** Carl Schramm, president of Kauffman Foundation discusses the secret to America's economy.

29687 ■ "Entrepreneurial Orientation and Firm Performance" in Journal of Small Business and Entrepreneurship (Vol. 23, Winter 2010, No. 1)
Pub: Canadian Council for Small Business and Entrepreneurship

Description: The article develops a theoretical model of the relationship between firm-level entrepreneurship and firm performance. This model is intended to further clarify the consequences of an 'entrepreneurial orientation', paying particular attention to the differential relationship that exists between the three sub-dimensions of entrepreneurial orientation and firm performance. Included in the theoretical model are other important variables (such as organizational structure and environmental characteristics) that may impact the EO-performance relationship. Propositions are developed regarding the various configurations of the sub-dimensions of EO and organizational structure that would be most appropriate in a given environmental context. Future research may also benefit from considering the important role that organizational strategy and life cycle stage play in this model. The implications of this model for both researchers and managers are discussed.

29688 ■ Entrepreneurial Skills: 2nd Edition
Pub: Double Storey Books

Ed: Cecile Nieuwenhuizen. **Released:** March 1, 2009. **Price:** $32.00. **Description:** Entrepreneurial skills are examined, showing how entrepreneurship differs from management mostly in attitude and approach.

29689 ■ Entrepreneurial Small Business
Pub: McGraw-Hill Higher Education

Ed: Richard P. Green; Jerome A. Katz. **Released:** January 2008. **Price:** $139.43. **Description:** Students are able to get a clear vision of small enterprise in today's business climate. The textbook helps focus on the goal of having personal independence with financial security as an entrepreneur.

29690 ■ Entrepreneurial Strategies: New Technologies and Emerging Markets
Pub: Blackwell Publishing Inc.
Contact: Gordon Tibbitts, President

Ed: Arnold Cooper; Sharon Alvarez; Alejandro Carrera; Luiz Mesquita; Robert Vassolo. **Released:** August 2006. **Price:** $69.95. **Description:** Ideas to help a small business expand into emerging market economies (EMEs) are discussed. Despite the high failure rate, this book helps a small firm develop a successful plan.

29691 ■ Entrepreneurial Strategy Emerging Businesses in Declining Industries
Pub: Edward Elgar Publishing, Incorporated

Ed: Cassia. **Released:** July 2006. **Price:** $110.00. **Description:** Role of entrepreneurship in context of older and declining industries is explored. The book offers insight into entrepreneurial dynamics behind emerging businesses in declining industries, especially the roles of resources processes and people.

29692 ■ The Entrepreneur's Almanac: Fascinating Figures, Fundamentals and Facts You Need to Run and Grow Your Business
Pub: Entrepreneur Press

Ed: Jacquelyn Lynn. **Released:** October 2007. **Price:** $24.95. **Description:** Reference containing a collection of tips, ideas and wisdom required to run and grow a successful business. Short articles, anecdotes, powerful lists and checklists, charts, and profiles of successful entrepreneurs are included.

29693 ■ "Entrepreneurs Conference" in Black Enterprise (Vol. 38, February 2008, No. 7, pp. 163)
Pub: Earl G. Graves Publishing Co. Inc.

Description: Black Enterprise Entrepreneurs Conference and Expo will be held May 14-17, 2008 at the Charlotte Westin Hotel and Charlotte Convention Center in North Carolina. Entrepreneurs are given the opportunity to present their business ideas in the Bevator Pitch Competition for a chance to win products and services.

29694 ■ The Entrepreneur's Edge: Finding Money, Making Money, Keeping Money
Pub: Silver Lake Publishing

Ed: Daniel Hogan. **Released:** October 2006. **Price:** $24.95. **Description:** Advice for starting, running and growing a new business is given.

29695 ■ The Entrepreneur's Guide to Managing Growth and Handling Crisis
Pub: Greenwood Publishing Group, Inc.

Ed: Theo J. Van Dijk. **Released:** December 2007. **Price:** $39.95. **Description:** The author explains how entrepreneurs can overcome crisis by changing the way they handle customers, by putting new processes and procedures in place, and managing employees in a professional manner. The book includes appendices with tips for hiring consultants, creating job descriptions, and setting up systems to chart cash flow as well as worksheets, tables and figures and a listing of resources.

29696 ■ Entrepreneurs in the Southern Upcountry: Commercial Culture in

Spartanburg, South Carolina, 1845-1880
Pub: University of Georgia Press
Contact: Stacey Hayes, Manager
E-mail: shayes@ugapress.uga.edu
Ed: Bruce W. Eelman. **Released:** February 2008.
Price: $42.95. **Description:** Historical account of the
entrepreneurial culture in a nineteenth-century
southern community outside the plantation belt is
given.

29697 ■ *The Entrepreneur's Strategy Guide:*
Ten Keys for Achieving Marketplace
Leadership
Pub: Greenwood Publishing Group Inc.
Contact: Janann Sherman, Manager
Ed: Tom Cannon. **Released:** September 2006. **Price:**
$44.95. **Description:** Ten principles of marketplace
leadership are explored. The book provides a plan
for small businesses, including diagnostics, check-
lists, and other interactive exercises to study both
external and internal principles.

29698 ■ *The Entrepreneur's Strategy Guide:*
Ten Keys for Achieving Marketplace
Leadership and Operational Excellence
Pub: Greenwood Publishing Group Inc.
Contact: Janann Sherman, Manager
Ed: Tom Cannon. **Released:** June 2006. **Price:** $38.
45. **Description:** Business plan for entrepreneurs is
offered from a fifty-year business veteran. The book
is divided into tow parts: the marketplace and the
internal environment.

29699 ■ *Entrepreneurship*
Pub: McGraw-Hill Higher Education
Ed: Robert D. Hisrich; Michael P. Peters; Dean A.
Shepherd. **Released:** October 2006. **Price:** $106.50.
Description: Advice is offered to entrepreneurs in
formulating, planning, and implementing a business
plan.

29700 ■ *Entrepreneurship*
Pub: Blackwell Publishing Inc.
Contact: Gordon Tibbitts, President
Ed: R. Duane Ireland; Michael A. Hitt. **Released:**
June 2006. **Price:** $99.95. **Description:** Overview of
entrepreneurship through the use of dictionary defini-
tions as well as entries of 2,500 words explaining
advanced issues and debates.

29701 ■ *Entrepreneurship*
Pub: Thomson South-Western
Ed: Donald F. Kuratko; Richard M. Hodgetts. **Re-**
leased: April 2006. **Price:** $125.95. **Description:**
Understanding the process of entrepreneurship.

29702 ■ *Entrepreneurship*
Pub: Greenwood Publishing Group Inc.
Contact: Janann Sherman, Manager
Ed: Alan L. Carsrud; Malin E. Brannback. **Released:**
March 2007. **Price:** $55.00. **Description:** Entrepre-
neurial process is profiles, examining how these
individuals identify opportunity and ways they address the personal, social, and financial risks involved
in starting a new business venture.

29703 ■ *Entrepreneurship*
Pub: John Wiley and Sons Inc.
Ed: William D. Bygrave; Andrew Zacharakis. **Re-**
leased: March 2007. **Price:** $109.95. **Description:**
Process for starting a new business is shared, focus-
ing on marketing and financing a product or service.

29704 ■ *Entrepreneurship: A Process*
Perspective
Pub: Thomson South-Western
Ed: Robert A. Baron; Scott A. Shane. **Released:**
February 2007. **Price:** $137.95. **Description:** Entre-
preneurial process covering team building, finances,
business plan, legal issues, marketing, growth and
exit strategies.

29705 ■ *Entrepreneurship: A Small Business*
Approach
Pub: McGraw-Hill Higher Education
Ed: Charles E. Bamford, Garry D. Bruton. **Released:**
January 10, 2010. **Price:** $83.44. **Description:** This
text takes a hands-on, problem-based learning ap-
proach that works through real problems faced by
entrepreneurs and small business owners.

29706 ■ *"Entrepreneurship: As Cool As It*
Gets" in Canadian Business (Vol. 80, January
29, 2007, No. 3, pp. 10)
Pub: Rogers Media
Ed: Norman de Bono. **Description:** The proposed
construction of a restaurant with ice in Dubai by the
Canadian firm Iceculture Inc. for the Sharaf Group is
discussed. The growth of the clientele of Iceculture
Inc. is described.

29707 ■ *Entrepreneurship As Social Change:*
A Third New Movements in Entrepreneurship
Book
Pub: Edward Elgar Publishing, Incorporated
Ed: Steyaert. **Released:** February 2007. **Price:** $120.
00. **Description:** Third book in a series, the edition
examines entrepreneurship as a societal phenom-
enon.

29708 ■ *Entrepreneurship and Economic*
Growth
Pub: Edward Elgar Publishing, Incorporated
Ed: Carree. **Released:** October 2006. **Price:** $195.
00. **Description:** Historic and country-specific studies and articles regarding entrepreneurship and innovation, growth models, competition and productivity, and empirical evidence.

29709 ■ *Entrepreneurship and Economic*
Progress
Pub: Routledge Inc.
Ed: Randall Holcombe. **Released:** October 2006.
Description: Economic models of economic growth
and the ways entrepreneurial progress are high-
lighted.

29710 ■ *Entrepreneurship: Frameworks and*
Empirical Investigations from Forthcoming
Leaders of European Research
Pub: Elsevier Science and Technology Books
Ed: Johan Wiklund; Dimc Dimov; Jerome A. Katz;
Dean Shepherd. **Released:** July 2006. **Price:** $99.
95. **Description:** Entrepreneurial research and theory
cover the early growth of research-based startups
and the role of learning in international entrepreneur-
ship, focusing on Europe.

29711 ■ *Entrepreneurship: From Opportunity*
to Action
Pub: Palgrave Macmillan
Ed: David Rae. **Released:** March 2007. **Price:**
$63.95 (CND). **Description:** Learning enterprise
theory is discussed, focusing on the individual as an
entrepreneur and ways to create and take advantage
of opportunities.

29712 ■ *Entrepreneurship, Geography, and*
American Economic Growth
Pub: Cambridge University Press
Contact: Richard Ziemacki, President
E-mail: rziemacki@cambridge.org
Ed: Zoltan Acs; Catherine Armington. **Released:**
June 2006. **Price:** $70.00. **Description:** Knowledge
among college-educated workers was among the key
reasons for economic growth throughout the U.S. in
the 1990s.

29713 ■ *Entrepreneurship and the Growth of*
Firms
Pub: Edward Elgar Publishing, Incorporated
Ed: Davidsson. **Released:** December 2006. **Price:**
$100.00. **Description:** Relationships between entre-
preneurial skills and business growth are explored.

29714 ■ *Entrepreneurship and How to*
Establish Your Own Business
Pub: Double Storey Books
Ed: Johan Strydon. **Released:** March 1, 2009. **Price:**
$37.95. **Description:** Guidelines are given to help
develop a small business idea and to establish a suc-
cessful enterprise. .

29715 ■ *Entrepreneurship, Innovation and*
Economic Growth
Pub: Edward Elgar Publishing, Incorporated
Ed: David B. Audretsch. **Released:** July 2006. **Price:**
$145.00. **Description:** Links between entrepreneur-
ship, innovation and economic growth are examined.

29716 ■ *Entrepreneurship, Innovation and*
the Growth Mechanism of the Free-Enterprise
Economies
Pub: Princeton University Press
Ed: Eytan Sheshinski; William J. Baumol. **Released:**
January 2007. **Price:** $65.00. **Description:** Scholars
address the free-enterprise Western economies.

29717 ■ *Entrepreneurship, Investment and*
Spatial Dynamics Lessons and Implications
for an Enlarged EU
Pub: Edward Elgar Publishing, Incorporated
Ed: Nijkamp. **Released:** September 2006. **Price:**
$100.00. **Description:** Understanding the impact and
interaction between investment, knowledge and
entrepreneurship with an expanding European Union.

29718 ■ *Entrepreneurship and Small*
Business
Pub: Palgrave Macmillan
Ed: Paul Burns. **Released:** January 2007. **Price:**
$74.95. **Description:** Entrepreneurial skills, focusing
on good management practices are discussed. Topics include family businesses, corporate, international
and social entrepreneurship.

29719 ■ *Entrepreneurship and Small*
Business Development in the Former Soviet
Bloc
Pub: Routledge
Ed: David Smallbone, Friederike Welter. **Released:**
January 10, 2010. **Price:** $140.00. **Description:**
Examination of entrepreneurship and small business
in Russia and other key countries of Eastern Europe,
showing how far small businesses have developed in
the region.

29720 ■ *Entrepreneurship and SMEs in the*
Euro-Zone
Pub: Imperial College Press
Ed: Dana. **Released:** May 2006. **Price:** $48.00. **De-**
scription: Information regarding entrepreneurship
and SMEs in Europe is presented.

29721 ■ *Entrepreneurship and Technology*
Policy
Pub: Edward Elgar Publishing, Incorporated
Ed: Link. **Released:** August 2006. **Price:** $190.00.
Description: Journal articles focusing how and the
ways small businesses' technical contributions are
affecting business. The book is divided into four parts:
Government's Direct Support of R&D, Government's
Leveraging of R&D, Government's Infrastructure Poli-
cies; and Knowledge Flows from Universities and
Laboratories.

29722 ■ *Entrepreneurship: The Engine of*
Growth
Pub: Greenwood Publishing Group Inc.
Contact: Janann Sherman, Manager
Ed: Maria Minniti; Andrew Zacharakis; Stephen
Spinelli; Mark P. Rice; Timothy G. Habbershon. **Re-**
leased: November 2006. **Price:** $300.00. **Descrip-**
tion: Dynamics of entrepreneurship are examined.

29723 ■ *Entrepreneurship in the U.S.: The*
2005 Assessment
Pub: Springer
Ed: Paul Reynolds. **Released:** March 2007. **Price:**
$79.95. **Description:** Entrepreneurship and its role in
the U.S. economy is discussed, examining new business creation and its impact on job growth, productivity enhancements, innovation, and social mobility.

29724 ■ *Ethnic Solidarity for Economic*
Survival: Korean Greengrocers in New York
City
Pub: Russell Sage Foundation Publications
Ed: Pyong Gap Min. **Released:** August 2008. **Price:**
$32.50. **Description:** Investigations into the entrepre-
neurial traditions of Korean immigrant families in New
York City running ethnic businesses, particularly small
grocery stores and produce markets. Social, cultural
and economic issues facing these retailers are
discussed.

29725 ■ "Everett Dowling" in Hawaii Business (Vol. 54, August 2008, No. 2, pp. 32)
Pub: Hawaii Business Publishing

Ed: Jason Ubay. Description: Real estate developer Everett Dowling, president of Dowling Company Inc., talks about the company's sustainable management and services. The company's office has been retrofitted to earn a Leadership in Energy and Environmental Design (LEED) certification. Dowling believes that real estate development can be part of the sustainable solution.

29726 ■ Everything I Know About Business I Learned from My Mama: A Down-Home Approach to Business and Personal Success
Pub: John Wiley & Sons, Incorporated

Ed: Tim Knox. Released: June 22, 2007. Price: $22.95. Description: Part memoir, part self-help, and part business how-to manual designed to help any small business owner/entrepreneur.

29727 ■ Everything is Possible: Life and Business Lessons from a Self-Made Billionaire and the Founder of Slim-Fast
Pub: Newmarket Press

Ed: S. Daniel Abraham. Released: February 10, 2010. Price: $24.95. Description: A profile of the founder of Slim-Fast nutritional diet drink used to help people lose weight.

29728 ■ "The Evolution of Corporate Social Responsibility" in Business Horizons (November-December 2007, pp. 449)
Pub: Elsevier Technology Publications

Ed: Philip L. Cochran. Description: Corporate social responsibility is now perceived as vital in enhancing the profitability of businesses while improving their reputation. It has changed business practices such as philanthropy, investment, and entrepreneurship.

29729 ■ Execution: The Discipline of Getting Things Done
Pub: Crown Publishing/Random House

Ed: Larry Bossidy, Ram Charan, Charles Burck. Released: June 15, 2002. Price: $27.50. Description: The book shows how to get things done and deliver results whether you are running an entire company or in your first management position.

29730 ■ "The Executive Brain" in Canadian Business (Vol. 80, October 22, 2007, No. 21, pp. 41)
Pub: Rogers Media

Ed: Rachel Pulfer. Description: Studies by Jordan Petersen, Frank Schmidt, and John Hunter show that leaders have highly evolved capacities to think using the prefrontal cortex of the brain. Inspirational leadership ability is located in the parietal lobe. Other details of the research are discussed.

29731 ■ "Expanding Middleby's Food Processing Biz" in Crain's Chicago Business (Vol. 31, April 21, 2008, No. 16, pp. 6)
Pub: Crain Communications, Inc.

Ed: David Sterrett. Description: Profile of the executive vice-president of the food processing company, Middleby Corp, whose business plan is to develop new products, begin looking for acquisitions and simplify operations in order to expand the firm.

29732 ■ The Facebook Effect: The Inside Story of the Company That Is Connecting the World
Pub: Simon & Shuster

Ed: David Kirkpatrick. Released: June 8, 2010. Price: $26.00. Description: There's never been a Website like Facebook: more than 350 million people have accounts, and if the growth rate continues, by 2013 every Internet user worldwide will have his or her own page. No one's had more access to the inner workings of the phenomenon than Kirkpatrick, a senior tech writer at Fortune magazine. Written with the full cooperation of founder Mark Zuckerberg, the book follows the company from its genesis in a Harvard dorm room through its successes over Friendster and MySpace, the expansion of the user base, and Zuckerberg's refusal to sell.

29733 ■ "Facing the Future" in Canadian Business (Vol. 81, March 31, 2008, No. 5, pp. 69)
Pub: Rogers Media

Ed: John Gray. Description: Discusses a web poll of 122 Canadian CEOs which shows that these leaders are convinced that the U.S. economy is slowing but are split on the impact that this will have on the Canadian economy. The aging and retiring workforce and the strong Canadian dollar are other concerns by these leaders.

29734 ■ "A Failed Promise: A Dream Job Gone..or Just Delayed?" in Restaurant Business (Vol. 107, September 2008, No. 9, pp. 34)
Pub: Ideal Media

Ed: Patricia Cobe, Joan M. Lang, Dana Tanyeri. Description: Profile of Jeremy Lycanwas, executive chef who taught at the California Culinary Academy. Lycanwas tells of accepting a position as executive chef from his mentor, and later started his own restaurant.

29735 ■ "The Family Tools" in Canadian Business (Vol. 80, March 26, 2007, No. 7, pp. 14)
Pub: Rogers Media

Description: A few strategies for running family businesses successfully are presented.

29736 ■ "Fashion Forward - Frugally" in Entrepreneur (Vol. 37, July 2009, No. 7, pp. 18)
Pub: Entrepreneur Media, Inc.

Ed: Jason Daley. Description: Staci Deal, a Fayetteville-based franchisee of fashion brand Plato's Closet, shares her experiences on the company's growth. Deal believes that the economy, and the fact that Fayetteville is a college town, played a vital role in boosting the used clothing store's popularity. Her thoughts on being a young business owner, and the advantages of running a franchise are also given.

29737 ■ Fast Company's Greatest Hits: Ten Years of the Most Innovative Ideas in Business
Pub: Penguin Group Incorporated

Ed: John Byrne; David Lidsky; Mark N. Vamos. Released: July 2006. Price: $24.95. Description: Offering of Fast Company's best articles covering business ideas and profiles of successful firms and their leaders.

29738 ■ Fast-Track Employer's Kit: California
Pub: Kaplan Books

Ed: Carolyn Usinger. Released: May 2006. Price: $29.95. Description: Requirements for running a small business in California re outlined.

29739 ■ Female Entrepreneurship in East and South-East Asia: Opportunities and Challenges
Pub: Woodhead Publishing Ltd.

Ed: Philippe Debroux. Released: February 10, 2010. Description: A detailed study of female entrepreneurship in Asia, where public authorities are slowly realizing the importance of women as workers and entrepreneurs.

29740 ■ Fierce Conversations
Pub: Berkley Trade

Ed: Susan Scott. Released: January 6, 2004. Price: $15.00. Description: Seven Principles of Fierce Conversations are addressed to help readers become effective conversationalists in both business and social settings.

29741 ■ Fierce Leadership
Pub: Crown Business Books

Ed: Susan Scott. Released: January 11, 2011. Price: $15.00. Description: A bold alternative to the worst 'best' practices of business in the 21st Century.

29742 ■ "The File On..Skoda Minotti" in Crain's Cleveland Business (Vol. 28, October 8, 2007, No. 40, pp. 26)
Pub: Crain Communications, Inc.

Ed: Kimberly Bonvissuto. Description: Overview of Skoda Minotti, the accounting and financial services firm located in Mayfield Village; the company has 140 employees and an expanded slate of services.

29743 ■ "Filling the Gap" in Canadian Business (Vol. 80, March 12, 2007, No. 6, pp. 62)
Pub: Rogers Media

Ed: Andrew Wahl. Description: The chief executive officer of GAP, Bruce Poon Tip, shares his experience and efforts in the growth of the company to a leading position in Canada.

29744 ■ "Finding A Higher Gear" in Harvard Business Review (Vol. 86, July-August 2008, No. 8, pp. 68)
Pub: Harvard Business School Press

Ed: Thomas A. Stewart; Anand P. Raman. Description: Anand G. Mahindra, the chief executive officer of Mahindra and Mahindra Ltd., discusses how his company fosters innovation, drawn from customer centricity, and how this will grow the company beyond India's domestic market.

29745 ■ "Finding Good Bets Down on the Farm" in Crain's Chicago Business (Vol. 31, March 24, 2008, No. 12, pp. 4)
Pub: Crain Communications, Inc.

Ed: Daniel Rome Levine. Description: Interview with money manager Jeff James, the portfolio manager for Driehaus Capital Management LLC, who discusses the Federal Reserve and recommends several companies in which to make investments.

29746 ■ "Finishing Touches: the Fashion Statement is in the Detail" in Black Enterprise (Vol. 37, January 2007, No. 6, pp. 106)
Pub: Earl G. Graves Publishing Co. Inc.

Ed: Sonia Alleyne. Description: Men are discovering the importance of dressing for success. Paying attention to the details such as shoes, socks, cuffs, and collars are just as important as finding the right suit.

29747 ■ "Fiscally Fit" in Entrepreneur (Vol. 37, October 2009, No. 10, pp. 130)
Pub: Entrepreneur Media, Inc.

Ed: Jason Daley. Description: Landrie Peterman, owner of an Anytime Fitness franchise in Oregon, describes how she turned her business around. The franchise, located in an industrial park, saw growth after six months with the help of corporate clients.

29748 ■ "Five Low-Cost Home Based Startups" in Women Entrepreneur (December 16, 2008)
Pub: Entrepreneur Media Inc.

Ed: Lesley Spencer Pyle. Description: During tough economic times, small businesses have an advantage over large companies because they can adjust to economic conditions more easily and without having to go through corporate red tape that can slow the implementation process. A budding entrepreneur may find success by taking inventory of his or her skills, experience, expertise and passions and utilizing those qualities to start a business. Five low-cost home-based startups are profiled. These include starting an online store, a virtual assistant service, web designer, sales representative and a home staging counselor.

29749 ■ "Five More Great Books on Entrepreneurship" in Entrepreneur (Vol. 37, July 2009, No. 7, pp. 19)
Pub: Entrepreneur Media, Inc.

Description: 800-CEO-Read founder, Jack Covert, and president, Todd Sattersten, share five books that would have been included in the book, 'The 100 Business Books of All Time' if space was not an issue. 'You Need to Be a Little Crazy,' 'Oh, the Places You'll Go!,' 'Founders at Work,' 'The Innovator's Dilemma,' and 'Purple Cow' are highly recommended for entrepreneurs.

29750 ■ "Five Steps to the Corner Office" in Canadian Business (Vol. 80, March 12, 2007, No. 6, pp. 36)
Pub: Rogers Media

Ed: Marlene Rego. Description: Chief executive of Rona Retail Canada Inc., Robert Dutton, and chief executive of Sysco Food Services Winnipeg, Kim Doherty explain the way they reached the top of their careers.

29751 ■ *"Floral-Design Kiosk Business in Colorado Springs Blossoming" in Colorado Springs Business Journal (September 24, 2010)*
Pub: Dolan Media Newswires
Ed: Monica Mendoza. **Description:** Profile of Shellie Greto and her mother Jackie Martin who started a wholesale flower business in their garage. The do-it-yourself floral arrangement firm started a kiosk business in supermarkets called Complete Design.

29752 ■ *"For Developer, a Boulevard of Golden Dreams" in Globe & Mail (February 10, 2007, pp. B3)*
Pub: CTVglobemedia Publishing Inc.
Ed: Elizabeth Church. **Description:** A profile of Ian Gillespie, president of Westbank Projects Corp., including his achievements in the real estate industry which are presented.

29753 ■ *"For Giving Us a Way To Say Yes To Solar: Lynn Jurich and Edward Fenster" in Inc. (Volume 32, December 2010, No 10, pp. 110)*
Pub: Inc. Magazine
Description: Profile of entrepreneurs Lynn Jurich and Edward Fenster, cofounders of SunRun. The firm installs solar panels at little or no cost and homeowners sign 20-year contracts to buy power at a fixed price.

29754 ■ *"For His Bigness of Heart: Larry O'Toole: Gentle Giant Moving, Somerville, Massachusetts" in Inc. (Volume 32, December 2010)*
Pub: Inc. Magazine
Description: Profile of Larry O'Toole, owners of Gentle Giant Moving Company, where his company charges more, but in return consumers receive a higher quality service.

29755 ■ *"For Staying True: Bobby Flam: Jumbo's Restaurant, Miami" in Inc. (Volume 32, December 2010, No. 10, pp. 102)*
Pub: Inc. Magazine
Ed: Leigh Buchanan. **Description:** Profile of Bobby Flam, owner of Jumbo's Restaurant in Miami, Florida.

29756 ■ *Forces of Fortune: The Rise of the New Muslim Middle Class and What It Will Mean for Our World*
Pub: Free Press Media Group Inc.
Ed: Vali Nasr. **Released:** September 10, 2009. **Price:** $26.00. **Description:** The author argues that entrepreneurial, religiously conservative contingents in such countries as Turkey, Pakistan, and Iran can propel the Middle East into democratic and prosperous times.

29757 ■ *"Forget the Elaborate Business Plans, Kids With Passion Are Our Next Great Entrepreneurs" in Inc. (October 2007, pp. 87-88)*
Pub: Gruner & Jahr USA Publishing
Description: George Gendron, founder and executive director of the Innovation and Entrepreneurship Program at Clark University, stresses the importance of encouraging business students in his entrepreneurial program to follow their passion. The program is dedicated to real-world entrepreneurship by creating businesses rather than business plans.

29758 ■ *"Former Apprentice Candidate Launches Jewelry Line" in Black Enterprise (Vol. 37, October 2006, No. 3, pp. 36)*
Pub: Earl G. Graves Publishing Co. Inc.
Ed: Philana Patterson. **Description:** Star of the second season of NBC's The Apprentice, Stacie J, has launched a line of jewelry and accessories which will be sold at Claire's stores nationwide.

29759 ■ *"Former Chrysler Dealers Build New Business Model" in Crain's Detroit Business (Vol. 25, June 22, 2009, No. 25, pp. 3)*
Pub: Crain Communications Inc. - Detroit
Ed: Daniel Duggan. **Description:** Joe Ricci is one of 14 Detroit area dealerships whose franchises have been terminated. Ricci and other Chrysler dealers in

the area are starting new businesses or switching to new franchises.= Ricci's All American Buyer's Service will be located in Dearborn and will sell only used cars.

29760 ■ *"Formula for Success: Dispelling the Age-Old Myths" in Agency Sales Magazine (Vol. 39, July 2009, No. 7, pp. 26)*
Pub: MANA
Ed: Douglas Smith. **Description:** Common misperceptions about selling and salespeople include the idea that anyone can be successful in selling if they work hard enough and that successful salespeople are born that way. In fact, top performers take risks and they invest in themselves.

29761 ■ *The Foundations of Female Entrepreneurship: Women in Business in Mid-Victorian London*
Pub: Routledge
Ed: Alison Kay. **Released:** April 1, 2009. **Price:** $130.00. **Description:** This book argues that active business did not exclude women from 1747 to 1880, although careful representation was necessary and this has obscured the similarities of women's businesses to those of many male business owners.

29762 ■ *Foundations of Small Business Enterprise*
Pub: Routledge Inc.
Ed: G. Reid. **Released:** December 2006. **Price:** $120.00. **Description:** Insight is given into the life cycle of entrepreneurial ventures; 150 new firms are tracked through early years.

29763 ■ *Founders at Work*
Pub: Apress
Ed: Jessica Livingston. **Description:** Through interviews with founders of companies such as Apple, Flickr and PayPal, the book shows the qualities required to be a successful entrepreneur.

29764 ■ *"Four Lessons in Adaptive Leadership" in Harvard Business Review (Vol. 88, November 2010, No. 11, pp. 86)*
Pub: Harvard Business School Publishing
Ed: Michael Useem. **Description:** Four key factors to effective leadership are presented. These are establishing a personal link, making sound and timely decisions, developing a common purpose while avoiding personal gain, and ensuring that objectives are clear without micromanaging those implementing them.

29765 ■ *The Four Routes to Entrepreneurial Success*
Pub: Berrett-Koehler Publishers, Incorporated
Ed: John B. Miner. **Released:** January 1, 1996. **Price:** $18.95. **Description:** Insight is provided to help entrepreneurs run their business successfully.

29766 ■ *"Francois Coutu" in Canadian Business (Vol. 80, March 12, 2007, No. 6, pp. 66)*
Pub: Rogers Media
Ed: Erin Pooley. **Description:** Pharmacist Francois Coutu shares his passion for the work of a pharmacist and sports.

29767 ■ *"Francois Joly" in Canadian Business (Vol. 79, September 11, 2006, No. 18, pp. 146)*
Pub: Rogers Media
Ed: Andy Holloway. **Description:** President and chief operating officer of Desjardins Financial Security, Francois Joly speaks about his interests and emphasizes the need to be passionate about work.

29768 ■ *"From the Battlefield to the Boardroom" in Business Horizons (Vol. 51, March-April 2008, No. 2, pp. 79)*
Pub: Elsevier Advanced Technology Publications
Ed: Catherine M. Dalton. **Description:** Effective intelligence gathering, a thorough understanding of the mission, efficient use of resources, and strategic leadership are vital to achieving success in business as well as in the battlefield. Examples of effective leadership in the battle of Gettysburg are cited.

29769 ■ *From Entrepreneur to Infopreneur: Make Money with Books, E-Books, and Other Information Products*
Pub: John Wiley & Sons, Incorporated
Ed: Stephanie Chandler. **Released:** November 2006. **Price:** $19.95. **Description:** Infopreneurs sell information online in the forms of books, e-books, special reports, audio and video products, seminars, and more.

29770 ■ *"From Lone Hero to a Culture of Leadership" in Harvard Business Review (Vol. 88, November 2010, No. 11, pp. 146)*
Pub: Harvard Business School Publishing
Ed: Charles J. Palus, John B. McGuire. **Description:** Review of the book, 'Working Together: Why Great Partnerships Succeed', is given.

29771 ■ *"The Frugal Billionaire" in Canadian Business (Vol. 79, Winter 2006, No. 24, pp. 63)*
Pub: Rogers Media
Ed: Joe Castaldo. **Description:** The achievements of David Cheriton are described, along with his investments in various firms, including Google Inc.

29772 ■ *"Fueling Change" in Entrepreneur (Vol. 35, November 2007, No. 11, pp. 46)*
Pub: Entrepreneur Media Inc.
Ed: Carol Tice. **Description:** Creativity guru John Kao says the United States is complacent when it comes to business. He talks about how entrepreneurs should think innovatively in terms of big changes.

29773 ■ *The Future Arrived Yesterday: The Rise of the Protean Corporation and What It Means for You*
Pub: Crown Business
Ed: Michael S. Malone. **Released:** 2009. **Price:** $27.50. **Description:** Reasons why dominant companies of the next decade will behave like perpetual entrepreneurial startups are investigated.

29774 ■ *"Gail Lissner; Vice-President, Appraisal Research Counselors" in Crain's Chicago Business (Vol. 31, May 5, 2008, No. 18, pp. 28)*
Pub: Crain Communications, Inc.
Ed: Phuong Ly. **Description:** Profile of Gail Lissner who is the vice-president of the Appraisal Research Counselors, a company that puts out the quarterly 'Residential Benchmark Report,' in which Ms. Lissner co-authors and is considered a must-read in the industry. Ms. Lissner has risen to become one of the most sought-after experts on the Chicago market considering real estate.

29775 ■ *"Galvanizing the Scientific Community" in Information Today (Vol. 26, February 2009, No. 2, pp. 20)*
Pub: Information Today, Inc.
Ed: Barbara Brynko. **Description:** Profile of John Haynes, newly appointed vice president of publishing for the American Institute of Physics; the Institute consists of ten organizations specializing in STM publishing as well as providing publishing services for over 170 science and engineering journals.

29776 ■ *"A Gambling Man: Career Transitions that Put a Vegas Hotshot on Top" in Black Enterprise (Vol. 37, October 2006, No. 3, pp. 89)*
Pub: Earl G. Graves Publishing Co. Inc.
Ed: Laura Egodigwe. **Description:** Interview with Lorenzo Creighton, president and chief operating officer of MGM Mirage's New York-New York Hotel and Casino. Creighton talks about his history and the challenges he faced since he didn't come from the casino industry.

29777 ■ *"Game On at Jordan's New Spot" in Crain's Chicago Business (Vol. 34, October 24, 2011, No. 42, pp. 34)*
Pub: Crain Communications Inc.
Ed: Laura Bianchi. **Description:** Michael Jordan partnered with Cornerstone Restaurant Group to launch Michael Jordan's Steakhouse in Chicago. Details are included.

29778 ■ *"A General's Pep Talk Taught Me That a Leader Can't Lose Sight of What It Means To Be a Grunt"* in Inc. *(March 2008, pp. 85-86)*
Pub: Gruner & Jahr USA Publishing
Ed: Joel Spolsky. **Description:** An Israeli general offers leadership advice to entrepreneurs.

29779 ■ *"George Cohon"* in Canadian Business *(Vol. 79, November 20, 2006, No. 23, pp. 70)*
Pub: Rogers Media
Ed: Zena Olijnyk. **Description:** George Cohon, the founder of McDonald's in Canada and Russia, speaks about the Canadian market and the experience of starting McDonald's in Canada.

29780 ■ *Get in the Game: 8 Elements of Perseverance that Make the Difference*
Pub: Gotham/Penguin Group Incorporated
Ed: Cal Ripken, Jr.; Donald T. Phillips. **Released:** April 10, 2008. **Price:** $15.00. **Description:** Guidebook written by superstar athlete Cal Ripkin to help managers and entrepreneurs achieve success.

29781 ■ *"Get With the Program"* in Entrepreneur *(Vol. 36, April 2008, No. 4, pp. 130)*
Pub: Entrepreneur Media, Inc.
Ed: Nichole L. Torres. **Description:** Entrepreneurship initiatives help college students get connected with other students, teach them about how to start their own business while still in school, and help with funding. Some of these programs are the Harold Grinspoon Charitable Foundation's Entrepreneurship Initiative and the Syracuse Campus-Community Entrepreneurship Initiative.

29782 ■ *Get Your Business to Work!: 7 Steps to Earning More, Working Less and Living the Life You Want*
Pub: BenBella Books
Contact: Glen Yeffeth, President
Ed: George Hedley. **Released:** June 9, 2010. **Price:** $24.95. **Description:** Complete step-by-step guide for the small business owner to realize profits, wealth and freedom.

29783 ■ *Getting to Innovation: How Asking the Right Questions Generates the Great Ideas Your Company Needs*
Pub: AMACOM
Ed: Arthur B. VanGundy. **Released:** July 2007. **Price:** $29.95. **Description:** Guide to achieving the critical first step in formulating creative and useful ideas that lead to results for any small company.

29784 ■ *"Getting Inventive With..Ed Spellman"* in Crain's Cleveland Business *(Vol. 28, October 22, 2007, No. 42, pp. 18)*
Pub: Crain Communications, Inc.
Ed: Kimberly Bonvissuto. **Description:** Profile featuring Ed Spellman, a mechanical engineer who decided to quit his job at Invacare Corp., a medical equipment manufacturer and distributor, in order to devote his full attention to promoting his numerous inventions, including the DV-Grip, a vehicle mount for portable DVD players.

29785 ■ *"Getting Inventive With..John Nottingham and John Spirk"* in Crain's Cleveland Business *(Vol. 28, October 22, 2007, No. 42, pp. 19)*
Pub: Crain Communications, Inc.
Ed: Kimberly Bonvissuto. **Description:** Profile featuring John Spirk and John Nottingham of the Cleveland-based firm, Nottingham-Spirk Design Associates; the company holds 486 issued and commercialized patents and has reported over $30 billion in new product sales.

29786 ■ *"Getting Inventive With..Richard Brindisi and Gregory Vittardi"* in Crain's Cleveland Business *(Vol. 28, October 22, 2007, No. 42)*
Pub: Crain Communications, Inc.
Ed: Kimberly Bonvissuto. **Description:** Profile of the SmartShopper, a handheld, voice-recognition device for dictating shopping and errand lists, and its creators, Richard G. Brindisi and Gregory Vittardi.

29787 ■ *"Getting It Sold"* in Black Enterprise *(Vol. 38, November 2007, No. 4, pp. 54)*
Pub: Earl G. Graves Publishing Co. Inc.
Ed: Tennille M. Robinson. **Description:** Artist is given advice for marketing and selling paintings, as well as getting artwork published.

29788 ■ *"Getting Others To Take Your Startup Seriously"* in Women Entrepreneur *(August 1, 2008)*
Pub: Entrepreneur Media Inc.
Ed: Tamara Monosoff. **Description:** Writing a serious business plan is essential if you want others to take your startup endeavor seriously. As friends, family and acquaintances see you taking positive steps toward your goal they will begin to lend their support and may even help get the business off the ground.

29789 ■ *Getting to Scale: Growing Your Business Without Selling Out*
Pub: Berrett-Koehler Publishers, Incorporated
Ed: Jill Bamburg. **Released:** July 2006. **Price:** $14.95. **Description:** Ways for entrepreneurs to preserve the value of their company while maintaining growth and competitiveness.

29790 ■ *Getting Things Done*
Pub: Warner Books Inc.
Ed: David Allen. **Released:** December 2002. **Price:** $16.00. **Description:** Methods for reducing stress and increasing performance are described.

29791 ■ *"Gillette Creamery"* in Ice Cream Reporter *(Vol. 23, September 20, 2010, No. 10, pp. 8)*
Pub: Ice Cream Reporter
Description: Gillette family of Gillette Creamery in Ellenville have been Entrepreneurs of the Year in Ulster County, New York. Gillette is the largest supplier of ice cream products in Eastern New York.

29792 ■ *The Girl's Guide to Being a Boss (Without Being a Bitch): Valuable Lessons, Smart Suggestions, and True Stories for Succeeding*
Pub: Random Housing Publishing Group
Ed: Caitlin Friedman; Kimberly Yorio. **Released:** April 2006.

29793 ■ *"Give 'Em a Boost"* in Entrepreneur *(Vol. 36, April 2008, No. 4, pp. 120)*
Pub: Entrepreneur Media, Inc.
Ed: Kristen Henning. **Description:** Amir Levin of Kaboost Corp. markets a plastic booster system that attaches to the bottom of a regular chair and raises it. He thought of the idea of creating the product after seeing his young cousins refusing to sit in their booster seats. Levin started his company in 2006.

29794 ■ *"Gloria Christiansen: Tennessee's Unselfish Citizen"* in Women In Business *(Vol. 61, December 2009, No. 6, pp. 10)*
Pub: American Business Women's Association
Description: Gloria Christiansen, a Colombian-born secretary of the Knoxville Area American Business Women's Association (ABWA) Council, shares her experiences as an immigrant in Tennessee who has been provided with the opportunity to grow professionally through ABWA. Aside from participating in community development projects, she deems her American citizenship as an inspiring and honorable experience.

29795 ■ *"Go East"* in Canadian Business *(Vol. 80, February 26, 2007, No. 5, pp. 21)*
Pub: Rogers Media
Ed: Claire Gagne. **Description:** The managerial strategies followed by Doug Doust, who left Wal-Mart to take over the position of senior vice-president of supply chain at the struggling Seiyu of Japan are presented.

29796 ■ *The Go-Giver: A Little Story About a Powerful Business Idea*
Pub: Penguin Group
Ed: Bob Burg; John David Mann. **Released:** December 27, 2007. **Price:** $19.95. **Description:** Story of an ambitious young man named Joe who years for success. The book is a heartwarming tale that brings new relevance to the old proverb, 'Give and you shall receive'.

29797 ■ *"Go Green Or Go Home"* in Black Enterprise *(Vol. 41, August 2010, No. 1, pp. 53)*
Pub: Earl G. Graves Publishing Co. Inc.
Ed: Tennille M. Robinson. **Description:** The green economy has become an essential part of every business, however, small business owners need to learn how to participate, including minority owned entrepreneurs.

29798 ■ *Going to Extremes: How Like Minds Unite and Divide*
Pub: Oxford University Press
Ed: Cass R. Sunstein. **Released:** 2009. **Price:** $21.95. **Description:** Solutions to marketplace problems are examined.

29799 ■ *"Gold Medal"* in Canadian Business *(Vol. 79, October 9, 2006, No. 20, pp. 57)*
Pub: Rogers Media
Ed: Andrew Wahl. **Description:** Creativity skills and management strategies of Rob McEwen, founder and chief executive officer of Goldcorp Inc., are presented.

29800 ■ *"A Good Book Is Worth a Thousand Blogs"* in Barron's *(Vol. 88, July 14, 2008, No. 28, pp. 42)*
Pub: Dow Jones & Co., Inc.
Ed: Gene Epstein. **Description:** Nine summer book suggestions on economics are presented. The list includes 'The Revolution' by Ron Paul, 'The Forgotten Man' by Amity Shales, 'The Commitments of Traders Bible' by Stephen Briese, and 'Economic Facts and Fallacies' by Thomas Sowell.

29801 ■ *Good to Great*
Pub: Harper Business
Ed: Jim Collins. **Price:** $27.50.

29802 ■ *"Goodbye, Locker Room: Hello, Boardroom"* in Inc. *(Vol. 33, October 2011, No. 8, pp. 30)*
Pub: Inc. Magazine
Ed: Issie Lapowsky, Kasey Wehrum. **Description:** In 2005, the National Football League started the NFL Business Management and Entrepreneurial Program. Since the onset of the program, 700 players have participated in the program which takes place at the business schools of Harvard, the University of Pennsylvania, Northwestern and Stanford.

29803 ■ *"Got Skills? (Entrepreneurs' Adeptness In Other Fields)"* in Entrepreneur *(Vol. 35, October 2007, No. 10, pp. 31)*
Pub: Entrepreneur Media Inc.
Ed: Laura Tifanny. **Description:** Entrepreneurs such as Jim Mousner, Hugh Briathwaite, and Joi Ito, has been known to apply their skills and interests in other fields on their business operations. Knowing something outside the realm of their industry helps entrepreneurs think of fresh ideas that are beneficial not only to them but also to their clients. Details of how having a different kind of interest helped Mousner, Braithwaite and Ito are presented.

29804 ■ *Goventure: Live the Life of an Entrepreneur*
Pub: Houghton Mifflin College Division
Ed: Hatten. **Released:** May 2006. **Price:** $28.47. **Description:** Challenges of operating a small business are presented with more than 6,000 graphics, audio, and interactive video.

29805 ■ *"A Graceful (and Lucrative) Exit"* in Black Enterprise *(Vol. 38, November 2007, No. 4, pp. 108)*
Pub: Earl G. Graves Publishing Co. Inc.
Ed: Tamara E. Holmes. **Description:** BlueKey Business Brokerage helps clients buy, grow or sell a business. Four key points are examined in order to successfully exit a business.

29806 ■ *Great Big Book of Business Lists: All the Info You Need to Run a Small Business*
Pub: Entrepreneur Press
Ed: Courtney Thurman; Ashlee Gardner. **Released:** April 2006. **Price:** $45.95. **Description:** Reference guide for small business that includes information for

starting and running a small business; lists are organized for easy access and cover every aspect of small business.

29807 ■ *Green to Gold*
Pub: Yale University Press
Contact: John Donatich, Director

Ed: Daniel C. Esty; Andrew S. Winston. **Released:** January 2009. **Price:** $19.95. **Description:** Examples are given for small businesses to beat competition while tackling sustainability, engage stakeholders, develop NGO partnerships, and work environmental stewardship into corporate culture.

29808 ■ *"Ground Floor Opportunity" in Small Business Opportunities (July 2008)*
Pub: Entrepreneur Press
Contact: Perlman Neil, President

Description: Profile of Doug Disney, the founder of the booming franchise Tile Outlet Always in Stock, which sells ceramic and porcelain tile and stone products at wholesale prices; Disney found inspiration in a book he read in two days and that motivated him to expand his venture into a huge franchise opportunity.

29809 ■ *Groups in Context: Leadership and Participation in Small Groups*
Pub: McGraw-Hill Companies Inc.
Contact: Deven Sharma, President

Ed: Gerald L. Wilson. **Released:** June 2004. **Price:** $62.98. **Description:** Small group communication skills for the workplace, in churches, social groups, or civic organizations.

29810 ■ *Growing Business Handbook: Inspirational Advice from Successful Entrepreneurs and Fast-Growing UK Companies*
Pub: Kogan Page, Limited
Contact: Ben Glover, Director of Marketing

Ed: Adam Jolly. **Released:** February 2007. **Price:** $49.95. **Description:** Tips for growing and running a successful business are covered, focusing on senior managers in middle market and SME companies.

29811 ■ *Growing Local Value: How to Build Business Partnerships That Strengthen Your Community*
Pub: Berrett-Koehler Publishers, Incorporated

Ed: Laury Hammel; Gun Denhart. **Released:** December 2006. **Price:** $15.00. **Description:** Advice and examples are provided for building socially responsible entrepreneurship.

29812 ■ *Growing and Managing a Small Business: An Entrepreneurial Perspective*
Pub: Houghton Mifflin College Division

Ed: Kathleen R. Allen. **Released:** July 2006. **Price:** $105.27. **Description:** Introduction to business ownership and management from startup through growth.

29813 ■ *Growing Your Business*
Pub: Routledge Inc.

Ed: Burke. **Released:** December 2006. **Price:** $150.00. **Description:** Growth strategies for small businesses are presented.

29814 ■ *Growth Oriented Women Entrepreneurs and Their Businesses: A Global Research Perspective*
Pub: Edward Elgar Publishing, Incorporated

Ed: Candida G. Brush. **Released:** June 2006. **Price:** $135.00. **Description:** Roles women play in entrepreneurship globally and their economic impact are examined.

29815 ■ *Habitual Entrepreneurs*
Pub: Edward Elgar Publishing, Incorporated

Ed: Ucbasaran. **Released:** December 2006. **Price:** $100.00. **Description:** Habitual entrepreneurship is explored. Tools for developing a plan for successful leadership are offered.

29816 ■ *"Halls Give Hospital Drive $11 Million Infusion" in The Business Journal-Serving Metropolitan Kansas City (Vol. 26, July 18, 2008)*
Pub: American City Business Journals, Inc.

Ed: Rob Roberts. **Description:** Don Hall, chairman of Hallmark Cards Inc., and eight family members have announced that they will give $11 million to Children's Mercy Hospitals and Clinics for its $800 million expansion plan. Hall Family Foundation president Bill Hall that contributions such as that for Children's Mercy reflect the charitable interests of the foundation's board and founders. The possible impacts of the Hall's donation are analyzed.

29817 ■ *The Halo Effect: And the Eight Other Business Delusions That Deceive Managers*
Pub: Free Press/Simon & Schuster Inc.

Ed: Phil Rosenzweig. **Released:** January 6, 2009. **Price:** $16.00 paperback. **Description:** Nine common business delusions, including the halo effect (which the author describes as the need to attribute positive qualities to successful individuals and companies), are illustrated using case studies of Lego, Cisco, and Nokia to show how adhering to myths can be bad for any business.

29818 ■ *Handbook of Quality Research in Entrepreneurship*
Pub: Edward Elgar Publishing, Incorporated

Ed: Neergaard. **Released:** March 2007. **Price:** $215.00. **Description:** Advice for researchers to make informed choices and to design more stringent and sophisticated studies in the field of entrepreneurship.

29819 ■ *Happy About Joint Venturing: The 8 Critical Factors of Success*
Pub: Happy About

Ed: Valerie Orsoni-Vauthey. **Released:** June 2006. **Price:** $23.95. **Description:** An overview of joint venturing is presented.

29820 ■ *"Having Words with Matt Maroni: Chef-Owner, Gaztro-Wagon, Chicago" in Nation's Restaurant News (Vol. 45, April 4, 2011, No. 7, pp. 62)*
Pub: Penton Media, Inc.

Ed: Mike Dempsey. **Description:** Profile of Matt Maroni, chef and owner of Gaztro-Wagon in Chicago, Illinois is presented. Maroni tells how he found his niche in the food truck industry.

29821 ■ *"Hawaii Business 2008 SB Success Awards" in Hawaii Business (Vol. 53, February 2008, No. 8, pp. 43)*
Pub: Hawaii Business Publishing

Description: Winners in the Hawaii Business 2008 SB Success Awards are presented; the awards give recognition for Hawaii small businesses with less than 100 employees and are based on four criteria, namely: unique service or product; rapid expansion or sales growth; longevity; and competency in overcoming challenges.

29822 ■ *"He Has a Sky-High Outlook on His Business" in Charlotte Observer (February 4, 2007)*
Pub: Knight-Ridder/Tribune Business News

Ed: Stella M. Hopkins. **Description:** Profile of Chuck Boyle, former Army pilot; Boyle patrols over construction sites in the Charlotte, North Carolina area. The firm's team of engineers and geologists specialize in services such as: rock blasting, roads, testing concrete and other construction materials, and more.

29823 ■ *"Head of the Class" in Entrepreneur (Vol. 37, October 2009, No. 10, pp. 59)*
Pub: Entrepreneur Media, Inc.

Description: Top 25 graduate and undergraduate entrepreneurship programs in the US for 2009 as ranked by The Princeton Review are listed. Babson College in Wellesley, Massachusetts topped both categories.

29824 ■ *"A Heavy Burden" in Crain's Cleveland Business (Vol. 30, June 8, 2009,*

No. 22, pp. 13)
Pub: Crain Communications, Inc.

Ed: Chuck Soder. **Description:** Small business owners are making sacrifices in the tight economy. In a recent survey conducted by American Express, 30 percent of the 727 small business owners questioned said they no longer take salaries from their firms.

29825 ■ *Here Come the Regulars: How to Run a Record Label on a Shoestring Budget*
Pub: Faber & Faber, Inc.

Ed: Ian Anderson. **Released:** October 1, 2009. **Price:** $15.00. **Description:** Author, Ian Anderson launched his own successful record label, Afternoon Records when he was 18 years old. Anderson shares insight into starting a record label, focusing on label image, budget, blogging, potential artists, as well as legal aspects.

29826 ■ *"Here's How Buffett Spent 2007" in Barron's (Vol. 88, March 10, 2008, No. 10, pp. 48)*
Pub: Dow Jones & Company, Inc.

Ed: Andrew Bary. **Description:** Earnings of Berkshire Hathaway may decline in 2008 due to a tighter insurance market, but its portfolio is expected to continue growing. Warren Buffett purchased $19.1 billion worth of stocks in 2007.

29827 ■ *"The High-Intensity Entrepreneur" in Harvard Business Review (Vol. 88, September 2010, No 9, pp. 74)*
Pub: Harvard Business School Publishing

Ed: Anne S. Habiby, Deirdre M. Coyle Jr. **Description:** Examination of the role of small companies in promoting global economic growth is presented. Discussion includes identifying entrepreneurial capability.

29828 ■ *High Performance with High Integrity*
Pub: Harvard Business School Press

Ed: Ben W. Heineman Jr. **Released:** May 28, 2008. **Price:** $18.00. **Description:** The dark side of today's free-market capitalist system is examined. Under intense pressure to make the numbers, executives and employees are tempted to cut corners, falsify accounts, or worse. In today's unforgiving environment that can lead to catastrophe for a small company.

29829 ■ *High-Tech Entrepreneurship: Managing Innovation in a World of Uncertainty*
Pub: Routledge Inc.

Ed: Michel Bernasconi; Simon Harris. **Released:** September 2006. **Price:** $42.95. **Description:** Profiles of successful high tech companies is included; high tech companies are driving innovation globally.

29830 ■ *"His Banking Industry Software Never Caught On, so Bill Randle is Now Targeting the Health Care Market" in Inc. (March 2008)*
Pub: Gruner & Jahr USA Publishing

Ed: Alex Salkever. **Description:** Profile of Bill Randle, bank executive turned entrepreneur; Randle tells how he changed his focus for his company from banking software to healthcare software. The firm employs ten people who secure online billing and recordkeeping systems for hospitals and insurers. Randle discusses critical decisions that will impact his firm in the coming year. Three experts offer advice.

29831 ■ *"His Brother's Keeper: a Mentor Learns the True Meaning of Leadership" in Black Enterprise (Vol. 37, December 2006, No. 5, pp. 69)*
Pub: Earl G. Graves Publishing Co. Inc.

Ed: Laura Egodigwe. **Description:** Interview with Keith R. Wyche of Pitney Bowes Management Services which discusses the relationship between a mentor and mentee as well as sponsorship.

29832 ■ *"His Way" in Inc. (February 2008, pp. 90-97)*
Pub: Gruner & Jahr USA Publishing

Ed: Stephanie Clifford. **Description:** Profile of Chris Reed, founder of a natural soda company, who undertook an initial public offering (IPO). Reed discusses the challenges he faced mediating with the Securities Exchange Commission regarding his firm's IPO.

29833 ■ "The Hispanic Business 100 Most Influential Hispanics" in Hispanic Business (October 2007, pp. 30)
Pub: Hispanic Business

Description: Profiles of the one hundred Hispanic business leaders are presented.

29834 ■ "Hispanic Executives Continue Their Rise to Prominence Amid a Shaky Economy" in Hispanic Business (January-February 2009, pp. 12-14)
Pub: Hispanic Business

Ed: Michael Bowker. **Description:** Hispanic Business Media's 2009 Corporate Elite winners defied expectations and a tough economy and rose to the top of their industries; innovation being cited as key to growth of Hispanic-owned companies.

29835 ■ "Hispanics Take Seats in America's Boardrooms" in Hispanic Business (January-February 2009, pp. 24, 28)
Pub: Hispanic Business

Ed: Joshua Molina. **Description:** Three percent of those serving as directors of Fortune 500 companies in America are Hispanic. A listing of forty of these directors is included.

29836 ■ "Home Grown" in Hawaii Business (Vol. 53, November 2007, No. 5, pp. 51)
Pub: Hawaii Business Publishing

Ed: Jolyn Okimoto Rosa. **Description:** Discusses a program that focuses on Native Hawaiian entrepreneurs and offers business training at the Kapiolani Community College; upon completion of the program, participants may apply for a loan provided by the Office of Hawaiian Affairs (OHA) to help them start their business. OHA plans to present the restructured loan program in November 2007, with aims of shortening the loan process.

29837 ■ "Homelessness, Hair Care and 12,000 Bottles of Tequila" in Entrepreneur (Vol. 37, July 2009, No. 7, pp. 5)
Pub: Entrepreneur Media, Inc.

Ed: Dennis Romero. **Description:** John Paul DeJoria believes that the biggest hurdle he has faced in business is rejection, and that the successful people will do whatever is required in order to succeed. DeJoria is the man behind Paul Mitchell Systems and Patron Tequila. He was recently included in Forbes magazine's list of global billionaires.

29838 ■ "Honcoop Honored as BIAWC's Builder of the Year" in Bellingham Business Journal (Vol. February 2010, pp. 17)
Pub: Sound Publishing Inc.

Description: Gary Honcoop, co-owner and president of Roosendaal-Honcoop Construction Inc. was honored by the Building Industry Association of Whatcom County as Builder of the Year. The construction company was founded in 1979.

29839 ■ "Honoring Creativity" in Playthings (Vol. 107, January 1, 2009, No. 1, pp. 28)
Pub: Reed Business Information

Contact: Jeff Greisch, President

Ed: Cliff Annicelli. **Description:** Toy & Game Inventors Expo is held annually in conjunction with the Chicago Toy & Game Fair. The event honors toy inventors in the categories of Game Design, Toy Design and Rising Stars, plus a lifetime achievement award. Profile of the company, Toying With Games, founded by Joyce Johnson and Colleen McCarthy-Evans are included in the article.

29840 ■ Hoover's Vision
Pub: Cengage Learning Inc.

Contact: Michael Hansen, Chief Executive Officer

Ed: Gary Hoover. **Description:** Founder of Bookstop Inc. and Hoover's Inc. provides a plan to turn an enterprise into a success by showing entrepreneurs how to address inputs with an open mind in order to see more than what other's envision. Hoover pushes business owners to create and feed a clear and

consistent vision by recognizing the importance of history and trends, then helps them find the essential qualities of entrepreneurial leadership.

29841 ■ Hoover's Vision: Original Thinking for Business Success
Pub: Thomson South-Western/Texere

Ed: Gary Hoover. **Released:** October 15, 2001. **Description:** Three keys to business success are to observe and understand other people, serve others while making their lives better, and develop a business style that expresses your5 own passions while serving others.

29842 ■ How to Be an Entrepreneur and Keep Your Sanity: The African-American Guide to Owning, Building and Maintaining Successfully Your Own Small Business
Pub: Amber Books

Ed: Paula McCoy Pinderhughes. **Released:** June 2003. **Price:** $14.95. **Description:** Ten easy steps to becoming a successful African-American entrepreneur.

29843 ■ How to Be an Entrepreneur: The Six Secrets of Self-Made Success
Pub: Pearson Education, Limited

Ed: Steve Parks. **Released:** August 2006. **Price:** $37.50. **Description:** Entrepreneurial creativity is examined. Statistical data covering failure rates of small businesses is included.

29844 ■ How to Become a Great Boss: The Rules for Getting and Keeping the Best Employees
Pub: Hyperion Special Markets

Ed: Jeffrey J. Fox. **Released:** May 15, 2002. **Price:** $16.95. **Description:** The book offers valuable advice to any manager or entrepreneur to improve leadership and management skills. Topics covered include: hiring, managing, firing, partnership and competition, self and organization, employee performance, attitude, and priorities.

29845 ■ "How Fast Can This Thing Go Anyway?" in Inc. (March 2008, pp. 94-101)
Pub: Gruner & Jahr USA Publishing

Ed: Stephanie Clifford. **Description:** Founder of Zipcar, an auto rental company, tell how he brought a new CEO into the company to boost revenue. The new CEO instituted a seven-step strategy to increase business.

29846 ■ How to Get Rich
Pub: Ebury Press

Ed: Felix Dennis. **Released:** 2008. **Price:** $25.95. **Description:** Publisher of Maxim, The Week, and Stuff magazines, discusses the mistakes he made running his companies. He didn't understand that people who buy computer gaming magazines wanted a free game with each copy, as one of his rivals was offering. And he laments not diversifying into television and exploiting the Internet.

29847 ■ How to Get Rich on the Internet
Pub: Morgan James Publishing, LLC

Ed: Ted Ciuba. **Released:** August 2004. **Price:** $19.95. **Description:** Interviews with successful Internet entrepreneurs provide insight into marketing products and services online using minimal investment. The importance of a sound marketing ad campaign using the Internet is discussed; maintaining a database and Website will automatically carry out business transactions daily. Suggestions for various types of businesses to run online are given.

29848 ■ "How Hard Could It Be? Why the Most Important Innovations Are Often Those That Appear To Be Fatally Flawed" in Inc. (February 2008)
Pub: Gruner & Jahr USA Publishing

Ed: Joel Spolsky. **Description:** Many times, things that seemed silly or impossible have become great innovations.

29849 ■ "How I Did It: George Naddaff: From Spit 'n' Shine Boy To Boston Chicken and Beyond" in Inc. (February 2008, pp. 98-101)
Pub: Gruner & Jahr USA Publishing

Ed: Leigh Buchanan. **Description:** Profile of George Naddaff, founder of Boston Chicken as well as numerous other business ventures.

29850 ■ "How I Did It: Jack Ma" in Inc. (January 2008, pp. 94-102)
Pub: Gruner & Jahr USA Publishing

Ed: Rebecca Fannin. **Description:** Profile of Jack Ma, who started as a guide and interpreter for Western tourists in Hangzhou. Ma used the Internet to build Alibaba.com, China's largest business-to-business site and one of the hottest IPOs in years.

29851 ■ "How I Did It: Mel Zuckerman" in Inc. (December 2007, pp. 140-142)
Pub: Gruner & Jahr USA Publishing

Ed: Daniel McGinn. **Description:** Profile of Mel Zuckerman, who tells how transformed his life as a middle-aged, overweight homebuilder to a healthy addition to the fitness and spa industry with his posh Canyon Ranch retreats.

29852 ■ How to Make Money with Social Media: Using New and Emerging Media to Grow Your Business
Pub: FT Press

Ed: Jamie Turner, Reshma Shah. **Released:** October 1, 2010. **Price:** $24.99. **Description:** Marketers, executives, entrepreneurs are shown more effective ways to utilize Internet social media to make money. This guide brings together both practical strategies and proven execution techniques for driving maximum value from social media marketing.

29853 ■ How the Mighty Fall: And Why Some Companies Never Give In
Pub: HarperCollins Publishers

Ed: Jim Collins. **Released:** May 19, 2008. **Price:** $23.99. **Description:** Companies fail in stages and their decline can be detected and reversed.

29854 ■ How Remarkable Women Lead: A Breakthrough Model for Work and Life
Pub: Crown Business

Ed: Joanna Barsh, Susie Cranston. **Released:** September 24, 2009. **Price:** $27.50. **Description:** An introduction to remarkable women, from Time Inc.'s Ann Moore to Xerox's Anne Mulcahy, who recount their inspiring struggles.

29855 ■ How to Run Your Business Like a Girl: Successful Strategies from Entrepreneurial Women Who Made It Happen
Pub: Adams Media Corporation

Contact: Gary Krebs, Director

E-mail: swatrous@adamsmedia.com

Ed: Elizabeth Cogswell Baskin. **Released:** September 2005. **Description:** Tour of three women entrepreneurs and their successful companies.

29856 ■ How to Salvage More Millions from Your Small Business
Pub: Mike French Publishing

Ed: Ron Sturgeon. **Released:** April 1, 2009. **Price:** $14.95. **Description:** Entrepreneurs in any industry will learn how strong work ethics and sound business principles will make any small business successful.

29857 ■ How to Start and Run Your Own Corporation: S-Corporations For Small Business Owners
Pub: HCM Publishing

Ed: Peter I. Hupalo. **Released:** March 6, 2003. **Price:** $22.95. **Description:** Basics of corporate business structure are explained. Topics include discovering the best business structure for your company; how to decided between an S-Corporation and LLC; choosing the state in which to incorporate, how to form a corporation, angel investing, special issues for one-person corporations, the role of bylaws and corporate minutes, board of directors, taxes, workers' compensation issues, retirement plans, and more.

29858 ■ How to Succeed As a Lifestyle Entrepreneur
Pub: Dearborn Trade Publishing Inc.

Contact: Roy Lipner, President

Ed: Gary Schine. **Price:** $18.95.

29859 ■ *"How to Survive This Mess" in Crain's Chicago Business (Vol. 31, April 14, 2008, No. 15, pp. 18)*
Pub: Crain Communications, Inc.
Ed: Christina Le Beau. **Description:** Small business owners can make it through a possible recession with preparations such as reviewing their balance sheet and cash flow every week and spotting trends then reacting quickly to them.

29860 ■ *How To Change the World*
Pub: Oxford University Press
Ed: David Bornstein. **Released:** September 2007. **Price:** $15.95. **Description:** Social entrepreneurs are individuals with powerful ideas that improve other people's lives and have implemented these ideas across cities, countries and in some cases, around the world. These are doctors, lawyers, engineers, teachers, journalists and parents who solve social problems on a large scale and have a profound effect on society.

29861 ■ *How We Decide*
Pub: Houghton Mifflin Harcourt
Contact: Barry O'Callaghan, President
Ed: Jonah Lehrer. **Released:** February 2009. **Price:** $25.00. **Description:** Insights for entrepreneurs to help with decision making; the book describes potential traps such as negative information and how it carries more weight than positive information.

29862 ■ *How: Why How We Do Anything Means Everything..in Business*
Pub: John Wiley and Sons, Inc.
Ed: Dov L. Seidman. **Released:** June 4, 2007. **Price:** $27.95. **Description:** Author shares his unique approach to building successful companies using case studies, anecdotes, research, and interviews to help entrepreneurs succeed in the 21st Century.

29863 ■ *"How Will You Ever Replace Yourself?" in Canadian Business (Vol. 83, August 17, 2010, No. 13-14, pp. 77)*
Pub: Rogers Media Ltd.
Ed: Jacqueline Nelson. **Description** SoftBank founder and CEO masayoshi Son created his very own school called SoftBank Academia in order to pick a successor that will follow his footprint. Son's strategy is extreme but other corporate leaders should pay attention to succession planning.

29864 ■ *How to Win Friends and Influence People*
Pub: Simon and Schuster Inc.
Contact: Carolyn Reidy, President
E-mail: carolyn.reidy@simonandschuster.com
Ed: Dale Carnegie. **Released:** February 15, 1990. **Price:** $7.99. **Description:** First published in 1937, this book helps people to understand human nature. The book teaches skills through underlying principles of dealing with people so that they feel important and appreciated.

29865 ■ *How Women Make Money: Inspirational Stories and Practical Advice from Successful Canadian Entrepreneurs*
Pub: Dundurn Press
Ed: Julie V. Watson. **Released:** April 1, 2004. **Price:** $24.99. **Description:** Collection of profiles, anecdotes, and practical advice and guides to help women take control of their lives, start a new business, and reach financial goals.

29866 ■ *I Can't Believe I Get Paid to Do This*
Pub: Gold Leaf Publishing
Ed: Stacey Mayo. **Released:** October 2004. **Description:** This book is targeted to anyone unhappy in their current position. It is designed to help everyone feel good about their job.

29867 ■ *I Fought the Law: a Brewery Comes Out on Top" in Inc. (Vol. 33, November 2011, No. 9, pp. 28)*
Pub: Inc. Magazine
Ed: Darren Dahl. **Description:** Profile of Omar Ansari, founder of Surly Brewing is presented. Ansari credits fans on Facebook and Twitter for contacting legislators with phone calls and emails to allow him to sell his beer to customers on site.

29868 ■ *"Ian Delaney" in Canadian Business (Vol. 81, Summer 2008, No. 9, pp. 168)*
Pub: Rogers Media Ltd.
Ed: Joe Castaldo. **Description:** Interview with Ian Delaney who is the executive chairman of chemical company Sherritt International Corp.; Delaney previously worked as chief executive for a holding company owned by Peter Munk. Details of his beliefs, profession and family life are discussed.

29869 ■ *If Harry Potter Ran General Electric*
Pub: Doubleday Broadway Publishing Group
Ed: Tom Morris PhD. **Released:** May 16, 2006. **Price:** $26.00. **Description:** The values and timeless truths that underlie J.K. Rowling's popular Harry Potter books are discussed showing the lessons they offer to all individuals in their careers and daily lives.

29870 ■ *"I'll Be Back: For Entrepreneurs, Retirement Doesn't Mean Forever" in Inc. (February 2008, pp. 35-36)*
Pub: Gruner & Jahr USA Publishing
Ed: Leigh Buchanan. **Description:** Many entrepreneurs return to business after selling their companies and retiring. Advice is given to company owners for retirement planning.

29871 ■ *Immigrant, Inc.: Why Immigrant Entrepreneurs Are Driving the New Economy*
Pub: John Wiley & Sons, Inc.
Ed: Richard T. Herman, Robert L. Smith. **Released:** November 9, 2009. **Price:** $19.77. **Description:** Immigrant entrepreneurs are driving the new economy and will play a role in saving American jobs.

29872 ■ *"The Impact of Immigrant Entrepreneurs" in Business Week (February 7, 2007)*
Pub: McGraw-Hill Companies
Ed: Kerry Miller. **Description:** Overview of immigrant entrepreneur's impact on economic development and their status as a driving force for the U.S. economy.

29873 ■ *In the Company of Women: Canadian Women Talk About What It Takes to Start and Manage a Successful Business*
Pub: HarperCollins Publishers Inc.
Ed: Katherine Gay. **Released:** 1998. **Description:** Information to help women start and run a small business in Canada.

29874 ■ *"In the Know?" in Entrepreneur (Vol. 37, July 2009, No. 7, pp. 30)*
Pub: Entrepreneur Media, Inc.
Ed: Brad Feld. **Description:** Tips on what entrepreneurs should and should not share with their venture capitalists (VCs) are given. Entrepreneurs must be transparent with their VCs, but they should not bombard VCs with too many details. The aspect of a business that a VC is concerned with varies from one VC to another, and it is important that entrepreneurs understand the best way to communicate with their VC.

29875 ■ *Influence without Authority*
Pub: John Wiley and Sons Inc.
Ed: Allan R. Cohen; David L. Bradford. **Released:** March 2005. **Price:** $29.95.

29876 ■ *"Info Junkie" in Crain's Chicago Business (Vol. 34, October 24, 2011, No. 42, pp. 35)*
Pub: Crain Communications Inc.
Ed: Christina Le Beau. **Description:** Greg Colando president of Flor Inc., an eco-friendly carpet company located I Chicago discusses his marketing program to increase sales.

29877 ■ *Innov and Entrepren in Biotech*
Pub: Edward Elgar Publishing, Incorporated
Ed: Hine. **Released:** April 2006. **Price:** $100.00. **Description:** Innovation processes underlying successful entrepreneurship in the biotechnology sector are explored.

29878 ■ *Innovation and Entrepreneurship*
Pub: Elsevier Science & Technology Books
Ed: Peter F. Drucker. **Released:** May 2007. **Price:** $27.95. **Description:** Profile of entrepreneurial innovation.

29879 ■ *Innovation and Entrepreneurship*
Pub: HarperInformation
Ed: Peter F. Drucker. **Released:** May 2006. **Price:** $16.99. **Description:** Innovation and entrepreneurship in America's new economy.

29880 ■ *Innovation and Entrepreneurship*
Pub: HarperCollins Publishers, Inc.
Ed: Peter F. Drucker. **Released:** May 2006. **Price:** $16.95. **Description:** Presentation of entrepreneurship and innovation and a purposeful and systematic discipline and the challenges and opportunities of the American entrepreneurial economy.

29881 ■ *Innovation Nation: Canadian Leadership from Java to Jurassic Park*
Pub: John Wiley & Sons, Incorporated
Ed: Leonard Brody; Wendy Cukier; Ken Grant; Matt Holland; Catherine Middleton; Denise Shortt. **Released:** January 30, 2003. **Price:** $28.95. **Description:** Canadian's have risen to the top of the largest technology firms, from development of the Java and the Blackberry to defining specifications for XML.

29882 ■ *"Innovation Station" in Canadian Business (Vol. 80, October 8, 2007, No. 20, pp. 42)*
Pub: Rogers Media
Ed: Andrew Wahl. **Description:** Study and teaching of entrepreneurship at the University of Waterloo is discussed. Research projects in the university are expected to be influential in Canada's economic development. In spite of the success of these studies, financing is still a problem for the university, especially in technological innovations.

29883 ■ *"The Innovator: Rob McEwen's Unique Vision of Philanthropy and Business" in Canadian Business (Vol. 81, November 10, 2008, No. 19)*
Pub: Rogers Media Ltd.
Ed: Alex Mlynek. **Description:** Rob McEwen says that his donation to the Schulich School of Business is his first large donation. He went to the University Health Network and was told about their pan for regenerative medicine, helping him make the decision. McEwan wants to be involved in philanthropy in the areas of leadership and education.

29884 ■ *"The Inside and Outside Scoop on CEO Succession" in Globe & Mail (January 2, 2006, pp. B8)*
Pub: CTVglobemedia Publishing Inc.
Ed: Shirley Won. **Description:** The career profile of Randy Eresman as the chief executive officer of Encana Corp. is presented.

29885 ■ *Instant Income*
Pub: McGraw-Hill Inc.
Ed: Janet Switzer. **Released:** February 2007. **Price:** $30.95 (CND). **Description:** Book covers small business advertising techniques, marketing, joint ventures, and sales.

29886 ■ *Instinct: Tapping Your Entrepreneurial DNA to Achieve Your Business Goals*
Pub: Warner Books, Incorporated
Ed: Mary H. Frakes; Thomas L. Harrison. **Released:** September 2006. **Price:** $15.99. **Description:** Research shows that entrepreneurs may attribute their success to genetics.

29887 ■ *International Entrepreneurship*
Pub: Edward Elgar Publishing, Incorporated
Ed: Oviatt. **Released:** March 2007. **Price:** $295.00. **Description:** Universities are focusing research efforts on international entrepreneurship. The book features critical articles on the topic.

29888 ■ *International Entrepreneurship Education Issues and Newness*
Pub: Edward Elgar Publishing, Incorporated
Ed: Fayolle. **Released:** August 2006. **Price:** $120.00. **Description:** Entrepreneurial education, focusing on economic, political and social needs of a changing world; ideas for reassessing, redeveloping, and renewing curricula and methods for teaching entrepreneurship are offered.

29889 ■ *International Entrepreneurship in Small and Medium Size Enterprises: Orientation, Environment and Strategy*
Pub: Edward Elgar Publishing, Incorporated
Ed: Hamid Etemad. **Released:** October 2004. **Price:** $130.00. **Description:** Issues involved in internationalizing small and medium sized (SME) businesses. Topics include an investigation into the emerging patterns of SME growth and international expansion in response to the changing competitive environment, dynamics of competitive behavior, entrepreneurial processes and a formulation of strategy.

29890 ■ *"International Growth" in Black Enterprise (Vol. 38, July 2008, No. 12, pp. 64)*
Pub: Earl G. Graves Publishing Co. Inc.
Ed: Marcia A. Reed-Woodard. **Description:** Becoming an increasingly smaller portion of the global business environment is the U.S. economy. Christopher Catlin, an associate with Booz Allen Hamilton, a technology management and strategy-consulting firm, shares what he has learned about the global market.

29891 ■ *International Handbook of Entrepreneurship and HRM*
Pub: Edward Elgar Publishing, Inc.
Ed: Rowena Barrett, Susan Mayson. **Released:** March 10, 2010. **Price:** $235.00. **Description:** Conceived on the basis that there is a growing recognition of the interplay between human resource management and entrepreneurship, this volume offers insights into the role of HRM and entrepreneurial firms.

29892 ■ *International Handbook of Women and Small Business Entrepreneurship*
Pub: Edward Elgar Publishing, Incorporated
Ed: Fielden. **Released:** December 2006. **Price:** $50.00. **Description:** Practical initiatives and strategies for women entering small business entrepreneurial ventures are examined.

29893 ■ *"Internationalization of Australian Family Businesses" in Family Business Review (Vol. 19, September 2006)*
Pub: Family Firm Institute
Contact: Judy L. Green, President
Ed: Chris Graves, Jill Thomas. **Description:** Concept that managerial capabilities of family firms lag behind those of non-family counterparts as they expand is discussed.

29894 ■ *"Into the Groove: Fine-Tune Your Biz By Getting Into the Good Habit Groove" in Small Business Opportunities (Spring 2008)*
Pub: Harris Publications Inc.
Description: Profile of Ty Freyvogel and his consulting firm Freyvogel Communications. Freyvogel serves the telecommunications need of Fortune 500 and mid-sized businesses.

29895 ■ *"Into the Wild" in Inc. (October 2007, pp. 116-120, 122, 124, 126)*
Pub: Gruner & Jahr USA Publishing
Ed: Alison Stein Wellner. **Description:** Perry Klebahn, CEO of Timbuk2, manufacturer of messenger bags, tells how he took his top executives into the deep Wyoming wilderness in order to build employee team work skills. Other options for this type of team-building include cooking courses, changing a tire together, solving a kidnapping, or discussing ways to survive a nuclear winter.

29896 ■ *"Intrepid Souls: Meet a Few Who've Made the Big Leap" in Crain's Chicago Business (Vol. 31, November 10, 2008, No. 45, pp. 26)*
Pub: Crain Communications, Inc.
Ed: Meredith Landry. **Description:** Advice is given from entrepreneurs who have launched businesses in the last year despite the economic crisis. Among the types of businesses featured are a cooking school, a child day-care center, a children's clothing store and an Internet-based company.

29897 ■ *"Irene Rosenfeld; Chairman and CEO, Kraft Foods Inc." in Crain's Chicago*

Business (Vol. 31, May 5, 2008, No. 18, pp. 31)
Pub: Crain Communications, Inc.
Ed: David Sterrett. **Description:** Profile of Irene Rosenfeld who is the chairman and CEO of Kraft Foods Inc. and is entering the second year of a three-year plan to boost sales of well-known brands such as Oreo, Velveeta and Oscar Mayer while facing soaring commodity costs and a declining market-share. Ms. Rosenfeld's turnaround strategy also entails spending more on advertising and giving managers more control over their budgets and product development.

29898 ■ *"Is Entrepreneurship Right For You?" in Women Entrepreneur (July 25, 2008)*
Pub: Entrepreneur Media Inc.
Ed: Bonnie Price. **Description:** Assessing the marketplace, evaluating your skills and sizing up your passions are three necessary elements to examine before starting a business.

29899 ■ *"It Takes More Than One" in Black Enterprise (Vol. 38, July 2008, No. 12, pp. 38)*
Pub: Earl G. Graves Publishing Co. Inc.
Ed: James A. Anderson. **Description:** Interview with Eric Small, the CEO of SBK-Brooks Investment Corp., whom discusses the importance of versatility when trying to find the best investment choices; the primary factors investors should be mindful of; his current stock picks; and recommendations for investing in an uncertain and volatile market.

29900 ■ *"It Was a Very Good Year..To Be Ted Rogers" in Canadian Business (Vol. 80, Winter 2007, No. 24, pp. 121)*
Pub: Rogers Media
Ed: Andrew Wahl. **Description:** Ted Rogers had a banner year in 2007 as Rogers Communications Inc. (RCI) took in huge profits from its phone and wireless business and his personal wealth grew sixty-seven percent to $7.6 billion. Rogers has record of betting on technologies that get the best returns relative to the investment in the marketplace such as its use of the GSM network and its cable hybrid fiber coaxial network.

29901 ■ *"It's In the Bag" in Entrepreneur (Vol. 36, April 2008, No. 4, pp. 122)*
Pub: Entrepreneur Media, Inc.
Ed: Celeste Hoang. **Description:** Sandy Stein launched Alexx Inc in 2004, which markets keychains, called Finders Key Purse, with unique designs to help find keys easier inside the purse. Some of the key ring designs are hearts, sandals, and crowns. The company has approximately $6 million worth of sales in 2007.

29902 ■ *"It's a New Game: Killerspin Pushes Table Tennis to Extreme Heights" in Black Enterprise (Vol. 37, October 2006, No. 3, pp. 73)*
Pub: Earl G. Graves Publishing Co. Inc.
Ed: Bridget McCrea. **Description:** Profile of Robert Blackwell and his company Killerspin L.L.C., which is popularizing the sport of table tennis. Killerspin has hit $1 million in revenues due to product sales primarily generated through the company's website, magazines, DVDs, and event ticket sales.

29903 ■ *It's Not Who You Know - It's Who Knows You!: The Small Business Guide to Raising Your Profits by Raising Your Profile*
Pub: John Wiley & Sons, Inc.
Ed: David Avrin. **Released:** November 9, 2010. **Price:** $24.95. **Description:** When it comes to promoting a small business or a brand, it is essential to know how valuable high-profile attention can be. But for most small companies, the cost of hiring an outside firm to increase attention can be too expensive.

29904 ■ *It's Your Ship*
Pub: Warner Books Inc.
Ed: Michael Abrashoff. **Released:** May 1, 2002. **Price:** $24.95. **Description:** Naval Captain D. Michael Abrashoff shares management principles he used to shape his ship, the U.S.S. Benfold, into a

model of progressive leadership. Abrashoff revolutionized ways to face the challenges of excessive costs, low morale, sexual harassment, and constant turnover.

29905 ■ *"Janet Froetscher, CEO, United Way of Metropolitan Chicago" in Crain's Chicago Business (Vol. 31, May 5, 2008, No. 18, pp. 26)*
Pub: Crain Communications, Inc.
Ed: Emily Stone. **Description:** Profile of Janet Froetscher who is the CEO of United Way of Metropolitan Chicago who organized the country's largest-ever merger of non-profits with 53 smaller suburban chapters consolidating with the Chicago one. The consolidation saves $4 million a year with departments such as finance, information technology and communications which allows that money be spent funding job training, after-school programs and aid for 7,000 Hurricane Katrina evacuees living in the Chicago area.

29906 ■ *"J.C. Watts First Black John Deere Dealer" in Black Enterprise (Vol. 37, November 2006, No. 4, pp. 36)*
Pub: Earl G. Graves Publishing Co. Inc.
Ed: Kiara Ashanti. **Description:** Profile of former Congressman J.C. Watts Jr., a man who grew up in rural America and is the first African American to own a John Deere Dealership.

29907 ■ *"Jennifer Hernandez Helps Developers Transform Contaminated Properties" in Hispanic Business (Vol. 30, April 2008, No. 4, pp. 32)*
Pub: Hispanic Business
Ed: Hildy Medina. **Description:** Jennifer Hernandez is a partner and head of the law firm of Holland & Knight's environmental practice which specializes in the restoration of polluted land where former industrial and commercial buildings once stood, known as brownfields. Brownfield redevelopment can be lucrative but costly due to the cleaning up of contaminated land and challenging because of federal and state environmental laws.

29908 ■ *The Jewish Century*
Pub: Princeton University Press
Ed: Yuri Slezkins. **Released:** August 2006. **Price:** $18.95. **Description:** Success and vulnerability of individuals of Jewish descent is discussed, uncovering the 'Jewish Revolution' within the Russian Revolution.

29909 ■ *"The Jobs Man" in Business Courier (Vol. 26, December 25, 2009, No. 35, pp. 1)*
Pub: American City Business Journals, Inc.
Ed: Lucy May. **Description:** Entrepreneur Bob Messer, a volunteer for Jobs Plus Employment Network in Cincinnati's Over-the-Rhine neighborhood, regularly conducts a seminar that aims to help attendees prepare for employment. Jobs Plus founder Burr Robinson asked Messer to create the seminar in order to help unemployed jobseekers. So far, the program has helped 144 individuals with full time jobs in 2009.

29910 ■ *John F. Kennedy on Leadership: The Lessons and Legacy of a President*
Pub: AMACOM
Ed: John A. Barnes. **Released:** May 30, 2007. **Price:** $16.00 paperback. **Description:** The author provides concept-based chapters on the life and presidency of John F. Kennedy and his visions. Using his inaugural address, Barnes reflects on JFKs vision and his relationship with his staff.

29911 ■ *"John Risley" in Canadian Business (Vol. 80, February 26, 2007, No. 5, pp. 70)*
Pub: Rogers Media
Ed: Calvin Leung. **Description:** John Risley, co-founder of Clearwater Fine Foods, shares few managerial strategies that helped him to achieve success in various businesses.

29912 ■ *"Julie Holzrichter; Managing Director of Operations, CME Group Inc." in Crain's*

Chicago Business (Vol. 31, May 5, 2008, No. 18)
Pub: Crain Communications, Inc.
Ed: Ann Saphir. **Description:** Profile of Julie Holzrichter who works as the managing director of operations for CME Group Inc. and is known as a decisive leader able to intercept and solve problems.

29913 ■ *"Karen Case; President of Commercial Real Estate Lending, Privatebancorp Inc." in Crain's Chicago Business (May 5, 2008)*
Pub: Crain Communications, Inc.
Ed: Dee Gill. **Description:** Profile of Karen Case who was hired by PrivateBancorp Inc. to turn its minor share of the city's commercial real estate lending market into a major one.

29914 ■ *"Kid-Friendly Business Sources" in Black Enterprise (Vol. 37, January 2007, No. 6, pp. 40)*
Pub: Earl G. Graves Publishing Co. Inc.
Ed: Carolyn M. Brown. **Description:** Financial or business camps are a great way to encourage a child who interested in starting his or her own business. A number of these camps are available each year including Kidpreneurs Conference and Bull and Bear Investment Camp. Other resources are available online. Resources included.

29915 ■ *"Kid Rock" in Canadian Business (Vol. 81, Summer 2008, No. 9, pp. 54)*
Pub: Rogers Media Ltd.
Ed: John Gray. **Description:** Damien Reynolds is the founder, chairman and chief executive officer of Vancouver-based Longview Capital Partners. The investment bank, founded in 2005, is one of the fastest-growing companies in British Columbia. The recent economic downturn has battered the stocks of the company and its portfolio of junior miners.

29916 ■ *King of Capital*
Pub: John Wiley and Sons, Inc.
Ed: Amey Stone; Mike Brewster. **Released:** 2004. **Price:** $16.95. **Description:** Biography of Sandy Weill describes how he became a billionaire business giant by creating successful companies from smaller, sometimes failing firms; creating successful new products where none previously existed; and making deals no one thought possible. He is also responsible for changing the landscape of the banking industry and insurance business when he created Citigroup in 1998, the world's largest financial services firm.

29917 ■ *The King of Vodka: The Story of Pyotr Smirnov and the Upheaval of an Empire*
Pub: HarperCollins Publishers
Ed: Linda Himelstein. **Released:** 2009. **Price:** $29.99. **Description:** Biography of Pyotr Smirnov and how his determination took him from serf to the head of Smirnov Vodka. Smirnov's marketing techniques are defined and show how he expanded the drink worldwide.

29918 ■ *Kitchen Table Entrepreneurs: How Eleven Women Escaped Poverty and Became Their Own Bosses*
Pub: Westview Press
Ed: Martha Shirk, Anna S. Wadia. **Released:** October 2008. **Price:** $16.95. **Description:** Profile of eleven successful women entrepreneurs.

29919 ■ *"A Knack for Entrepreneurship" in Hispanic Business (January-February 2008, pp. 42, 44-45)*
Pub: Hispanic Business
Ed: Hildy Medina. **Description:** Profile of Carlos Antonio Garcia, CEO of Kira, is investing in young companies.

29920 ■ *Knockout Entrepreneur: My Ten Count Strategy for Winning at Business*
Pub: Thomas Nelson Inc.
Ed: George Foreman. **Released:** September 1, 2009. **Price:** $22.99. **Description:** George Foreman offers ten key strategies for running a successful small business.

29921 ■ *Know-How: The 8 Skills That Separate People Who Perform from Those Who Don't*
Pub: Crown Publishing Group
Ed: Ram Charan. **Released:** January 2, 2007. **Price:** $27.50. **Description:** Know-how is what separates leaders who perform and deliver good results from those who don't.

29922 ■ *Know-Who Based Entrepreneurship from Knowledge Creation to Business Implementation*
Pub: Edward Elgar Publishing, Incorporated
Ed: Harryson. **Released:** August 2006. **Price:** $130.00. **Description:** Analysis of the knowledge and interconnected areas of entrepreneurship and networking across various levels is presented. Best practice companies are profiled.

29923 ■ *"Knowing Is Growing: Five Strategies To Develop You and Your Business" in Black Enterprise (Vol. 38, November 2007, No. 4, pp. 106)*
Pub: Earl G. Graves Publishing Co. Inc.
Ed: Erinn R. Johnson. **Description:** Five strategies for growing a small business are listed by Andrew Morrison, founder of the Small Business Camp. The camp provides training, coaching, and marketing services to entrepreneurs.

29924 ■ *"Labor of Love" in Green Industry Pro (Vol. 23, March 2011, No. 3, pp. 14)*
Pub: Cygnus Business Media
Ed: Gregg Wartgow. **Description:** Profile of CLS Landscape Management in Chino, California and its owner who started the company when he was 21 years old. Kevin Davis built his landscape firm into a $20 million a year business without using any dedicated salesperson.

29925 ■ *"Lafley Gives Look At His Game Plan" in Business Courier (Vol. 24, March 21, 2008, No. 50, pp. 1)*
Pub: American City Business Journals, Inc.
Ed: Lisa Biank Fasig. **Description:** Overview of A.G. Lafley's book entitled 'The Game-Changer', is presented. Lafley, Procter & Gamble Co.'s chief executive officer, documented his philosophy and strategy in his book. His work also includes Procter & Gamble's hands-on initiatives such as mock-up grocery stores and personal interviews with homeowners.

29926 ■ *"Last Founder Standing" in Conde Nast Portfolio (Vol. 2, June 2008, No. 6, pp. 124)*
Pub: Conde Nast Publications
Contact: David Carey, President
Ed: Kevin Maney. **Description:** Interview with Amazon CEO Jeff Bezos in which he discusses the economy, the company's new distribution center and the hiring of employees for it, e-books, and the overall vision for the future of the firm.

29927 ■ *"Laurent Beaudoin" in Canadian Business (Vol. 80, April 9, 2007, No. 8, pp. 68)*
Pub: Rogers Media
Ed: Thomas Watson. **Description:** Chief executive officer of Bombardier Inc., Laurent Beaudoin, talks about his personal life and career.

29928 ■ *The Leader of the Future 2*
Pub: Jossey Bass
Ed: Frances Hesselbein; Marshall Goldsmith. **Released:** September 18, 2006. **Price:** $27.95. **Description:** Wisdom is lent to any small business owner or leader of a nonprofit organization.

29929 ■ *"Leaders in Denial" in Harvard Business Review (Vol. 86, July-August 2008, No. 8, pp. 18)*
Pub: Harvard Business School Press
Ed: Richard S. Tedlow. **Description:** Identifying denial in the corporate arena is discussed, along with its impact on business and how to prevent it from occurring.

29930 ■ *Leadership 101: What Every Leader Needs to Know*
Pub: Nelson Business
Ed: John C. Maxwell. **Released:** September 2002. **Price:** $9.99. **Description:** Ways to enhance leadership skills focusing on following a vision and bringing others along.

29931 ■ *The Leadership Challenge*
Pub: Jossey-Bass Publishers
Ed: James M. Kouzes, Barry Z. Posner. **Released:** June 30, 1995. **Price:** $22.00. **Description:** According to research by the authors, people can make extraordinary things happen by liberating the leader within everyone around them. This handbook gives practical tips to aspire leaders in retail, manufacturing, government, community, church and school settings.

29932 ■ *Leadership in the Era of Economic Uncertainty: Managing in a Downturn*
Pub: The McGraw-Hill Companies
Ed: Ram Charan. **Released:** December 2008. **Price:** $22.95. **Description:** Management consultant gives advice on how to weather the economic storm, focusing on cash flow and foregoing expansion.

29933 ■ *The Leadership Secrets of Colin Powell*
Pub: McGraw-Hill Companies Inc.
Contact: Deven Sharma, President
Ed: Oren Harari. **Released:** July 2003. **Price:** $18.95. **Description:** Profile of Colin Powell, stressing his abilities as a world leader.

29934 ■ *"Leadership Training" in Black Enterprise (Vol. 37, January 2007, No. 6, pp. 56)*
Pub: Earl G. Graves Publishing Co. Inc.
Ed: Sonia Alleyne. **Description:** Profile of Theopolis Holman, Group Vice-President of Duke Energy, who discusses how he prepared for the merger between Duke Energy and Cinergy. Holman oversees a division of 9,000 service contractors and employees.

29935 ■ *Leading with Character: Stories of Valor and Virtue and the Principles They Teach*
Pub: Information Age Publishing
Ed: John J. Sosik. **Released:** July 24, 2006. **Price:** $39.99. **Description:** Examination of the kind of character that leaders develop in themselves and others in order to create and sustain extraordinary organizational growth and performance.

29936 ■ *Leading the Charge*
Pub: Palgrave Macmillan
Ed: Tony Zinni, Tony Koltz. **Released:** July 16, 2009. **Price:** $25.00. **Description:** General Anthony Zinni recalls a lifetime of competition on the battlefield and in corporate boardrooms and is leading the call to action to restore American leadership and greatness.

29937 ■ *Leading at a Higher Level*
Pub: FT Press
Ed: Ken Blanchard. **Released:** November 2006. **Price:** $26.99. **Description:** Tips, advice and techniques from a management consultant to help entrepreneurs create a vision for their company; includes information on manager-employee relationships.

29938 ■ *"Leaving a Legacy: Patricia Latimore and Bourdi Apreala Build a Comprehensive Estate Plan" in Black Enterprise (January 2008)*
Pub: Earl G. Graves Publishing Co. Inc.
Ed: Cliff Hocker. **Description:** Estate planning is critical for anyone, especially small business owners.

29939 ■ *Lessons of a Lipstick Queen: Finding and Developing the Great Idea That Can Change Your Life*
Pub: Simon and Schuster Inc.
Contact: Carolyn Reidy, President
E-mail: carolyn.reidy@simonandschuster.com
Ed: Poppy King. **Released:** May 1, 2009. **Price:** $14.00. **Description:** Poppy King tells how she started her lipstick brand at age eighteen. She reveals how

she managed to launch her business using a good idea and finding financing, marketing the product and how she became successful.

29940 ■ "Lessons from Turnaround Leaders" in Strategy and Leadership (Vol. 39, May-June 2011, No. 3, pp. 36-43)
Pub: Emerald Group Publishing Inc.
Ed: David P. Boyd. **Description:** A study analyzes the cases of some successful turnaround leaders to present a strategic model to help firms tackle challenges such as employee inertia, competition and slow organizational renewal. It describes a change model consisting of five major steps to be followed by firms with environmental uncertainty for the purpose.

29941 ■ "Let It Shine: Organization Helps Disadvantaged Girls See Their Worth" in Black Enterprise (Vol. 38, February 2008, No. 7, pp. 142)
Pub: Earl G. Graves Publishing Co. Inc.
Ed: George Alexander. **Description:** Wilson Mourning, founder of the clothing label Honey Child, attributes her success to her mother and other positive women who helped her through her adolescence. Mourning created a mentoring organization that helps young girls in the Miami, Florida area to develop life skills.

29942 ■ Liespotting: Proven Techniques to Detect Deception
Pub: St. Martins Press/Macmillan
Ed: Pamela Meyer. **Released:** July 20, 2010. **Price:** $24.99. **Description:** Liespotting links three disciplines: facial recognition training, interrogation training, and a comprehensive survey of research in the field - into a specialized body of information developed specifically to help business leaders detect deception and get the information they need to successfully conduct their most important interactions and transactions.

29943 ■ The Life Cycle of Entrepreneurial Ventures
Pub: Springer
Ed: Simon Parker. **Released:** October 2006. **Price:** $199.00. **Description:** Issues involved in creating a new business are explored, including venture creation, development and performance.

29944 ■ Life's a Game So Fix the Odds: How to Be More Persuasive and Influential in Your Personal and Business
Pub: John Wiley & Sons, Incorporated
Ed: Philip Hesketh. **Released:** September 2005. **Price:** $24.95 (US), $31.00 (Canadian). **Description:** Seven psychological reasons behind why and how people are persuaded and how to use these reasons to your advantage in both your personal and business life.

29945 ■ "Life's Work" in Harvard Business Review (Vol. 88, July-August 2010, No. 7-8, pp. 172)
Pub: Harvard Business School Publishing
Ed: Alison Beard. **Description:** The founder of appliance company Dyson Ltd. discusses the role of making mistakes in learning and innovation, and emphasizes the importance of hands-on involvement to make a company successful.

29946 ■ "Life's Work: Ben Bradlee" in Harvard Business Review (Vol. 88, September 2010, No. 9, pp. 128)
Pub: Harvard Business School Publishing
Ed: Alison Beard. **Description:** Newspaper publisher Ben Bradlee discusses factors that lead to success, including visible supervisors, enthusiasm, appropriate expansion, and the importance in truth in reporting.

29947 ■ "Life's Work: Manolo Blahnik" in Harvard Business Review (Vol. 88, December 2010, No. 12, pp. 144)
Pub: Harvard Business School Publishing
Ed: Alison Beard. **Description:** Shoe designer Manolo Blahnik recounts his beginnings in the shoe industry and the influence art has had on his work, as well as balancing art and commerce. He also

discusses the importance of quality materials and craftsmanship and the benefits of managing an independent, family-owned business.

29948 ■ "Life's Work: Oliver Sacks" in Harvard Business Review (Vol. 88, November 2010, No. 11, pp. 152)
Pub: Harvard Business School Publishing
Ed: Lisa Burrell. **Description:** Neurologist and author Oliver Sacks discusses whether different types of minds tend toward certain skills, physician-patient communication, and his own perspectives from being a patient himself.

29949 ■ "A Lifetime of Giving: Food Bank CEO Fights Hunger One Mouth At a Time" in Black Enterprise (Vol. 41, November 2010, No. 4, pp. 86)
Pub: Earl G. Graves Publishing Co. Inc.
Ed: Tamara E. Holmes. **Description:** Profile of Valerie Traore, CEO of Food Bank of South Jersey. Traore stresses the importance of volunteerism that she learned from her grandparents. Hunger relief became her passion when she served as a temp office worker for the Maryland Food Bank in Baltimore. She earned her Bachelor's of Science in management and has dedicated herself to a career in nonprofit service.

29950 ■ "A Lifetime of Making Deals" in Crain's Detroit Business (Vol. 24, March 24, 2008, No. 12, pp. 11)
Pub: Crain Communications, Inc.
Ed: Tom Henderson. **Description:** Profile of Walter 'Bud' Aspatore who received Crain's Lifetime Achievement Award for mergers and acquisitions; Aspatore is chairman and co-founder of Amherst Partners L.L.C., an investment banking firm that does evaluations and financings, specializes in turnarounds and advises private and public companies on mergers and acquisitions.

29951 ■ "A Light Bulb Came On, and It Was Energy Efficient" in Globe & Mail (January 27, 2007, pp. B3)
Pub: CTVglobemedia Publishing Inc.
Ed: Shawn McCarthy. **Description:** A brief profile of Edward Weinstein, chief executive officer of the Montreal-based family-run lighting firm Globe Electric Co., is presented The firm's management strategies are described.

29952 ■ "Like All Great Visionaries, Steve Jobs has a Dark Side" in Canadian Business (Vol. 83, July 20, 2010, No. 11-12, pp. 11)
Pub: Rogers Media Ltd.
Ed: Steve Maich. **Description:** All the adoration piled onto Apple can go to a man's head, especially its CEO Steve Jobs. Jobs is a true visionary but his leadership comes with an autocratic side that is worth watching out for; this is shown by his condescending response to the reported reception problems of the iPhone 4.

29953 ■ "Like Father?" in Canadian Business (Vol. 79, Winter 2006, No. 24, pp. 38)
Pub: Rogers Media
Ed: Zena Olijnyk. **Description:** The achievements of the chairman of Thomson Corp., David Thomson, are discussed. The plans of David Thomson to diversify into different areas of business are discussed.

29954 ■ Linchpin: Are you Indispensable?
Pub: Portfolio
Ed: Seth Godin. **Released:** January 26, 2010. **Price:** $25.95. **Description:** The best way to get what you're worth, according to the author, is to exert emotional labor, to be seen as indispensable, and to produce interactions that organizations and people care about.

29955 ■ Lincoln on Leadership: Executive Strategies for Tough Times
Pub: Grand Central Publishing
Ed: Donald T. Phillips. **Released:** February 1, 1993. **Price:** $14.99 (paperback). **Description:** Using President Abraham Lincoln's example of leadership, the author sets out to help business leaders adopt winning strategies.

29956 ■ "Lines of Communication" in Entrepreneur (Vol. 37, October 2009, No. 10, pp. 80)
Pub: Entrepreneur Media, Inc.
Ed: Brad Feld. **Description:** Entrepreneurial companies should establish a clear and open communication culture between their management teams and their venture capital backers. Chief executive officers should trust their leadership teams when it comes to communicating with venture capitalists.

29957 ■ "Live and Learn" in Canadian Business (Vol. 80, April 23, 2007, No. 9, pp. 76)
Pub: Rogers Media
Ed: Chris Buck. **Description:** Paul Anka, a musician, feels that ground work is essential before establishing a company.

29958 ■ "Live and Learn" in Canadian Business (Vol. 79, October 23, 2006, No. 21, pp. 160)
Pub: Rogers Media
Ed: Joe Castaldo. **Description:** Philip Kives, founder and chief executive officer of K-Tel International Inc. discusses his professional achievements.

29959 ■ "Live and Learn: Lionel Hurtubise" in Canadian Business (Vol. 80, January 29, 2007, No. 3, pp. 64)
Pub: Rogers Media
Ed: Andy Holloway. **Description:** The views of Lionel Hurtubise, the chairman of SR Telecom, PolarSat, and STP, on his life and the growth of the Canadian telecommunications industry are presented.

29960 ■ Living Above the Store: Building a Business That Creates Value, Inspires Change, and Restores Land and Community
Pub: Chelsea Green Publishing
Ed: Martin Melaver. **Released:** May 1, 2009. **Price:** $27.95. **Description:** Martin Melaver shares insight into building a business plan that utilizes diversity, shared values, common purpose and land-community ethics that are restorative for humankind and nature.

29961 ■ "The Long Game" in Business Strategy Review (Vol. 21, Summer 2010, No. 2, pp. 36)
Pub: Wiley-Blackwell
Ed: Stuart Crainer. **Description:** Profile of Alibab. com and its CEO David Wei.

29962 ■ Longaberger
Pub: HarperBusiness
Ed: Dave Longaberger. **Description:** J.W. Longaberger, founder of the J.W. Longaberger Handwoven Basket Company offers his personal story of business challenges, mistakes and successes, dreams and accomplishments.

29963 ■ "Looking Back" in Entrepreneur (Vol. 36, March 2008, No. 3, pp. 118)
Pub: Entrepreneur Media Inc.
Ed: Romanus Wolter. **Description:** Entrepreneurs can learn from their mistakes and improve current operations by documenting new strategies and ideas from them, evaluating information and its possible effects, and integrating what has been learned with future plans.

29964 ■ "Looking Like a Million Bucks" in Entrepreneur (Vol. 37, August 2009, No. 8, pp. 102)
Pub: Entrepreneur Media, Inc.
Ed: Jason Daley. **Description:** Sunset Tan's Jeff Bozz says he and Devin Haman are executive producers of the show and that they want to stretch the truth a bit and make fun of it. Haman says the business is all about VIP service for everyone and that they want all their clients to feel like celebrities.

29965 ■ "The Lords of Ideas" in Business Strategy Review (Vol. 21, Autumn 2010, No. 3, pp. 57)
Pub: Wiley-Blackwell
Ed: Stuart Crainer. **Description:** True originators of modern business strategy are interviewed.

29966 ■ *"Losing the Top Job - And Winning It Back"* in Harvard Business Review (Vol. 88, October 2010, No. 10, pp. 136)
Pub: Harvard Business School Publishing
Ed: Alison Beard. **Description:** Michael Mack chronicles the changes in perspectives that occurred when he was fired from Garden Fresh, a restaurant firm he co-owned. Once again at the company helm, he is now more receptive to outside input and acknowledges the importance of work-life balance.

29967 ■ *"Lots More Mr. Nice Guy"* in Canadian Business (Vol. 80, October 22, 2007, No. 21, pp. 58)
Pub: Rogers Media
Ed: Zena Olijnyk. **Description:** Galen Weston Jr., executive chairman of Loblaw and heir to the Weston family business, has his hands full running the company. Details of his turnaround strategies and ambitious plans to increase profitability of the business are discussed.

29968 ■ *"Lynn Johnson, President: Dowland-Bach"* in Alaska Business Monthly (Vol. 27, October 2011, No. 10, pp. 11)
Pub: Alaska Business Publishing Company
Ed: Peg Stomierowski. **Description:** Profile of Lynn C. Johnson cofounder of Dowland-Bach Corporation, a manufacturing and distribution company is presented. The firms primary products are wellhead control and chemical injection systems for corrosion control, UL industrial control panels, and specialty stainless steel sheet metal fabrication.

29969 ■ *Made in China: Secrets of China's Dynamic Entrepreneurs*
Pub: John Wiley & Sons, Inc.
Ed: Winter Nie, Katherine Xin. **Released:** March 1, 2009. **Price:** $24.95. **Description:** Insight and analysis of the strategies leading to China's rapidly growing economy are profiled.

29970 ■ *Made to Stick: Why Some Ideas Survive and Others Die*
Pub: Doubleday Broadway Publishing Group
Ed: Chip Heath; Dan Heath. **Released:** January 2, 2007. **Price:** $26.00. **Description:** Entertaining, practical guide to effective business communication; information is derived form psychosocial studies on memory, emotion and motivation.

29971 ■ *"Madeleine Paquin"* in Canadian Business (Vol. 81, March 3, 2008, No. 3, pp. 92)
Pub: Rogers Media
Ed: Regan Ray. **Description:** Madeleine Paquin, chief executive officer and president of Logistec Corp., talks about how she balanced her career and her life as a mother to two girls. Paquin thinks that working mothers need to focus on some things instead of trying to do everything. Her career in the marine cargo handling industry is also discussed.

29972 ■ *"Magnus Carlsen"* in Canadian Business (Vol. 83, October 12, 2010, No. 17, pp. 79)
Pub: Rogers Media Ltd.
Description: Magnus Carlsen, chess prodigy, talks about the importance of having a good feel for the game. He thinks that there are some similarities between chess and business, as both are about making good decisions in a limited amount of time. His views about motivation are also discussed.

29973 ■ *"The Mailman"* in Canadian Business (Vol. 80, April 9, 2007, No. 8, pp. 14)
Pub: Rogers Media
Ed: Zena Olijnyk. **Description:** Chief executive officer of Pitney Bowes Inc. Murray Martin's entrepreneurial skills in managing the company and his personal career are discussed.

29974 ■ *Make It Big With Yuvi: How to Achieve Poolside Living by Growing Your Small Business*
Pub: AuthorHouse
Ed: Ron Peltier. **Released:** March 2006. **Price:** $17.00. **Description:** Successful entrepreneurship is profiled.

29975 ■ *Make Your Business Survive and Thrive! 100+ Proven Marketing Methods to Help You Beat the Odds*
Pub: John Wiley & Sons, Incorporated
Ed: Priscilla Y. Huff. **Released:** December 2006. **Price:** $19.95. **Description:** Small business and entrepreneurial expert gives information to help small and home-based businesses grow.

29976 ■ *"Making the Cut; Osprey Takes Undervalued Courses to the Leader Board"* in Crain's Detroit Business (Vol. 24, April 7, 2008, No. 14)
Pub: Crain Communications, Inc.
Ed: Jason Deegan. **Description:** Profile of Osprey Management Co., a diverse real estate company that continues to expand its golf portfolio through the company's recreation division; although many developers are getting out of the field due to Michigan's sluggish golf industry, Osprey has found success by purchasing properties in turmoil for more affordable prices.

29977 ■ *Making Difficult Decisions: How to Be Decisive and Get the Business Done*
Pub: John Wiley and Sons, Inc.
Ed: Peter Shaw. **Released:** August 2008. **Price:** $29.95. **Description:** Experience of others can help entrepreneurs and managers make difficult business decisions. The strategies set forth in this book have been used successfully in public, private and voluntary sectors.

29978 ■ *Making a Living Without a Job: Winning Ways For Creating Work That You Love, Revised Ed.*
Pub: Bantam Books
Ed: Barbara Winter. **Released:** August 25, 2009. **Price:** $16.00 paperback. **Description:** Winter gives advice to help anyone turn an interest or hobby into a lucrative business.

29979 ■ *"The Man Behind Brascan"* in Canadian Business (Vol. 79, Winter 2006, No. 24, pp. 64)
Pub: Rogers Media
Ed: Andy Holloway. **Description:** The role of Jack Cockwell in the growth of Brookfield Asset Management Inc., is described.

29980 ■ *Management Rewired: Why Feedback Doesn't Work and Other Surprising Lessons from the Latest Brain Science*
Pub: Portfolio
Ed: Charles S. Jacobs. **Released:** 2009. **Price:** $25.95. **Description:** According to the author, human psychology works better than feedback, praise or criticism when managing employees.

29981 ■ *The Management of Small and Medium Enterprises*
Pub: Routledge
Ed: Matthias Fink. **Released:** April 1, 2009. **Price:** $140.00. **Description:** Investigation into the underlying mechanisms and practices of management within small and medium enterprises is provided.

29982 ■ *Managing for Results*
Pub: HarperCollins Publishers, Inc.
Ed: Peter F. Drucker. **Released:** October 2006. **Price:** $16.95. **Description:** Entrepreneurs running successful small companies focus on opportunity rather than problems.

29983 ■ *Managing a Small Business Made Easy*
Pub: Entrepreneur Press
Ed: Martin E. Davis. **Released:** September 2005. **Price:** $19.95 (US), $26.95 (Canadian). **Description:** Examination of the essential elements for an entrepreneur running a business, including advice on leadership, customer service, financials, and more.

29984 ■ *Managing for Success: The Latest in Management Thought and Practice from Canada's Premier Business School*
Pub: Harperaudio
Contact: Catherine MacGregor, Director
E-mail: catherine.macgregor@harpercollins.com
Ed: Monica Fleck. **Released:** December 2000. **Description:** Canadian business school offers insight into the latest management skills of the nation's business leaders.

29985 ■ *"The Marathon Club: Building a Bridge to Wealth"* in Hispanic Business (March 2008, pp. 24)
Pub: Hispanic Business
Ed: Hildy Median. **Description:** Minority businesses find it more difficult to secure venture capital for entrepreneurial pursuits. Joe Watson, CEO of Without Excuses and Strategic Hire, suggests Hispanics and African Americans collaborate on issues of importance to minority entrepreneurs.

29986 ■ *"Market Forces"* in Canadian Business (Vol. 79, October 23, 2006, No. 21, pp. 93)
Pub: Rogers Media
Ed: Erin Pooley. **Description:** The tremendous rise in the number of business schools offering Master of business administration degree in Canada and the depletion in the quality of education provided in these business schools is discussed.

29987 ■ *Marketing for Entrepreneurs*
Pub: FT Press
Ed: Jurgen Wolff. **Released:** December 9, 2010. **Price:** $24.99. **Description:** This text identifies marketing as the entire process of researching, creating, distributing and selling a product or service. It isn't about theory and metrics, rather it is a practical guide that starts with the basics of all marketing aspects.

29988 ■ *"Marketing: 'Twill Be the Season"* in Entrepreneur (Vol. 35, October 2007, No. 10, pp. 108)
Pub: Entrepreneur Media Inc.
Ed: Kim T. Gordon. **Description:** Entrepreneurs should plan ahead in order to promote products for the holiday season, since it is peak sales time. They can unify their business theme, use customer incentives, advertise early using TV or radio, and reorganize the company Website. Other ways to market for the holiday season are provided.

29989 ■ *Marketing that Works: How Entrepreneurial Marketing Can Add Sustainable Value to Any Sized Company*
Pub: Wharton School Publishing
Ed: Leonard M. Lodish; Howard Morgan; Shellye Archambeau. **Released:** March 2007. **Price:** $36.99 (CND). **Description:** Entrepreneurial marketing techniques are shared in order to help a new company position and target products and services.

29990 ■ *"Marketing: You Are On the Air: Radio and TV Producers Are Looking For Shows Starring Smart CEOs"* in Inc. (December 2007, pp. 67-69)
Pub: Gruner & Jahr USA Publishing
Ed: Sarah Goldstein. **Description:** Many successful entrepreneurs are being hired to host television and radio shows in order to share business expertise.

29991 ■ *Martha, Inc.*
Pub: John Wiley and Sons, Inc.
Ed: Christopher Byron. **Released:** 2002. **Price:** $28.00. **Description:** Profile of Martha Stewart's rise from working class to a billionaire businesswoman is presented. The book covers Stewart's power struggles and personal conflicts as well as her triumphs.

29992 ■ *The Martha Rules: 10 Essentials for Achieving Success as You Start, Build, or Manage a Business*
Pub: Rodale Inc.
Contact: Maria Rodale, Chief Executive Officer
Ed: Martha Stewart. **Released:** October 2006. **Price:** $15.95. **Description:** Martha Stewart offers insight into starting, building and managing a successful business.

29993 ■ *The Martha Rules: 10 Essentials for Achieving Success as You Start, Grow, or Manage a Business*
Pub: Rodale Press, Inc.
Ed: Martha Stewart. **Released:** October 2005.

29994 ■ *"Massage the Message" in Canadian Business (Vol. 79, Winter 2006, No. 24, pp. 137)*
Pub: Rogers Media
Ed: Erin Pooley. **Description:** The methods adopted by Canadian billionaires to manage their public images are described.

29995 ■ *"Master of His Domain" in Canadian Business (Vol. 81, December 8, 2008, No. 21, pp. S17)*
Pub: Rogers Media Ltd.
Ed: Andy Holloway. **Description:** L'Oreal Canada chief executive Javier San Juan believes in being close to consumers and travels to one of his company's fifteen locations in Canada about once a month. San Juan's job is to build the L'Oreal brand in Canada.

29996 ■ *Mastering Business Negotiation*
Pub: Jossey Bass
Ed: Roy J. Lewicki; Alexander Hiam. **Released:** July 21, 2006. **Price:** $24.95. **Description:** Resource guide for any manager requiring practical strategies and ideas for negotiating in business; the book shows how to understand the game to better control the situation, predict the sequence of negotiations, identify tactics of others, and to apply the rules of the game.

29997 ■ *Mastering Business Negotiation: A Working Guide to Making Deals and Resolving Conflict*
Pub: Jossey-Bass Publishers
Ed: Roy J. Lewicki; Alexander Hiam. **Released:** July 21, 2006. **Price:** $24.95. **Description:** Provides extensive insight into practical strategies and ideas for conducting business negotiations.

29998 ■ *"MBA Essentials: Real-Life Instruction" in Women In Business (Vol. 61, October-November 2009, No. 5, pp. 28)*
Pub: American Business Women's Association
Ed: Leigh Elmore. **Description:** University of Kansas School of Business allied itself with the American Business Women's Association (ABWA) which led to the formation of the ABWA-KU MBA essentials program. With this program, ABWA members are exposed to graduate-level coursework that delves on business topics, such as strategy and operations.

29999 ■ *MBA In a Day*
Pub: John Wiley and Sons, Inc.
Ed: Steven Stralser, PhD. **Released:** 2004. **Price:** $34.95. **Description:** Management professor presents important concepts, business topics and strategies that can be used by anyone to manage a small business or professional practice. Topics covered include: human resources and personal interaction, ethics and leadership skills, fair negotiation tactics, basic business accounting practices, project management, and the fundamentals of economics and marketing.

30000 ■ *"Me First!" in Black Enterprise (Vol. 38, December 2007, No. 5, pp. 107)*
Pub: Earl G. Graves Publishing Co. Inc.
Ed: Tamara E. Holmes. **Description:** Profile of Andrew J. Milisits Jr., entrepreneur and operating manager of an information technology firm; Milisits shares his experiences when taking on increasing responsibilities and his inability to balance the conflicting demands of career and family.

30001 ■ *Medici Effect*
Pub: Harvard Business School Press
Ed: Frans Johansson. **Released:** October 30. 2006. **Price:** $16.00. **Description:** Examples of how ideas can be turned into path-breaking innovations.

30002 ■ *Medium Sized Firms and Economics Growth*
Pub: Nova Science Publishers, Incorporated
Ed: Janez Prasniker. **Released:** April 2005. **Price:** $130.00. **Description:** Medium sized companies should have a more definitive presence in modern microeconomic theory, the theory of entrepreneurship, and the theory of financial markets.

30003 ■ *"Michael Doesn't Live Here Anymore" in Canadian Business (Vol. 80, October 8, 2007, No. 20, pp. 52)*
Pub: Rogers Media
Ed: Andrew Wahl. **Description:** Michael Treacy's career in the U.S. is discussed. Treacy, a Canadian entrepreneur, believes that Canada has few comparative advantages aside from its natural resources. Because of this, he also believes that it would not be feasible to do business in the country. Economic factors influenced him to do business in the U.S. instead.

30004 ■ *Microfranchising: Creating Wealth at the Bottom of the Pyramid*
Pub: Edward Elgar Publishing, Incorporated
Ed: W. Gibb Dyer; Jason Fairbourne; Stephen W. Gibson. **Released:** July 2008. **Price:** $35.00. **Description:** Ideas from researchers and social entrepreneurs discusses the movement that moves microfranchising into a mechanism for sustainable poverty reduction on a scale to match microfinance.

30005 ■ *"Midas Touch" in Entrepreneur (Vol. 36, April 2008, No. 4, pp. 160)*
Pub: Entrepreneur Media, Inc.
Ed: Sara Wilson. **Description:** Lana Fertelmeister is a model-turned-jewelry designer. Her company, Lana Jewelry, designs fine jewelry for women. Her jewelry line is available in more than 100 stores worldwide and has been worn by celebrities like Cameron Diaz and Sandra Bullock.

30006 ■ *The Middle Class Millionaire: The Rise of the New Rich and How They Are Changing America*
Pub: Currency/Doubleday Broadway Publishing Group
Ed: Russ Alan Prince; Lewis Schiff. **Released:** February 26, 2008. **Price:** $23.95. **Description:** Examination of the far-reaching impact of the middle class millionaires with net worth ranging from one million to ten million dollars and have earned rather than inherited their wealth.

30007 ■ *Millionaire Upgrade: Lessons in Success from Those Who Travel at the Sharp End of the Plane*
Pub: John Wiley & Sons, Incorporated
Ed: Richard Parkes Cordock. **Released:** September 2006. **Price:** $17.99. **Description:** Interviews with fifty successful millionaire entrepreneurs are used to help a frustrated employee understand the science and secrets behind their successful business ventures.

30008 ■ *"Minority Entrepreneurs, Business Advocate of the Year Named" in Daily News (November 1, 2010)*
Pub: Daily News
Ed: Aniesa Holmes. **Description:** Jacksonville-Onslow Chamber of Commerce Minority Enterprise Development Day honored outstanding entrepreneurs from the region. Candidates were chosen based on criteria such as business accomplishments, chamber involvement and dedication as well as their commitment to serving people in the community.

30009 ■ *"Mobility: So Happy Together" in Entrepreneur (Vol. 35, October 2007, No. 10, pp. 64)*
Pub: Entrepreneur Media Inc.
Ed: Heather Clancy. **Description:** Joshua Burnett, CEO and founder of 9ci, uses index cards to keep track of what he needs to do despite the fact that he has a notebook computer, cell phone and PDA. Kim Hahn, a media entrepreneur, prefers jotting her ideas down in a spiral notebook, has a team that would organize her records for her, and a personal assistant that would keep track of changes to her schedule. Reasons why these entrepreneurs use old-fashioned methods along with new technology are given.

30010 ■ *"Model Citizen" in Entrepreneur (Vol. 36, February 2008, No. 2, pp. 42)*
Pub: Entrepreneur Media Inc.
Ed: Guy Kawasaki. **Description:** A mensch is a person of noble character, as defined by Leo Rosten. Tips on how to be a mensch and a better person, in relation to being an entrepreneur, are given. These

include: helping others without expecting something in return, giving back to society, and knowing the line between right and wrong.

30011 ■ *The Mommy Manifesto: How to Use Our Power to Think Big, Break Limitations and Achieve Success*
Pub: John Wiley & Sons, Inc.
Ed: Kim Lavine. **Released:** September 1, 2009. **Price:** $24.95. **Description:** A new women's revolution will help women take control of their careers, their lives, and their economic future. The book shows how mom's control the economy and have the power to become successful entrepreneurs.

30012 ■ *"Money Man" in Canadian Business (Vol. 80, January 15, 2007, No. 2, pp. 67)*
Pub: Rogers Media
Ed: Jeff Sanford. **Description:** A profile of Donald A. Guloien, chief investment officer of Manulife Financial and chief executive officer of Global Investment Management, is presented.

30013 ■ *"More Power to Your Presentation" in Business Strategy Review (Vol. 21, Spring 2010, No. 1, pp. 50)*
Pub: Wiley-Blackwell
Ed: Roly Grimshaw. **Description:** You might wonder what similarities there can be between a Russian oligarch and an entrepreneur. When it comes to persuading people to invest, there are plenty.

30014 ■ *"More Than a Feeling" in Entrepreneur (Vol. 36, April 2008, No. 4, pp. 10)*
Pub: Entrepreneur Media, Inc.
Ed: Rieva Lesonsky. **Description:** It is said that emotion has no place when it comes to business matters, but it may not be the case as entrepreneurs and other people in business feel passionate about what they do. Emotions can help bring out a positive outlook in them. Other details on the topic are discussed.

30015 ■ *More Than a Pink Cadillac*
Pub: McGraw-Hill
Ed: Jim Underwood. **Released:** 2002. **Price:** $23.95. **Description:** Profile of Mary Kay Ash who turned her $5,000 investment into a billion-dollar corporation. Ash's nine principles that form the foundation of her company's global success are outlined. Stories from her sales force leaders share ideas for motivating employees, impressing customers and building a successful company. The book emphasizes the leadership skills required to drive performance in any successful enterprise.

30016 ■ *"Mover and Sheika" in Conde Nast Portfolio (Vol. 2, June 2008, No. 6, pp. 104)*
Pub: Conde Nast Publications
Contact: David Carey, President

Ed: John Arlidge. **Description:** Profile of Princess Sheika Lubna who is the first female foreign trade minister in the Middle East, the United Arab Emirates biggest business envoy, paving the way for billions in new investment, and also a manufacturer of her own perfume line.

30017 ■ *"Murdock Lifer Mans Main Street Journal" in Advertising Age (Vol. 79, July 7, 2008, No. 26, pp. 1)*
Pub: Crain Communications, Inc.
Ed: Nat Ives. **Description:** Profile of Les Hinton, the U.K. executive who was chosen by Rupert Murdoch to run Dow Jones and The Wall Street Journal; Hinton discusses The Wall Street Journal's unique spot in American business which has helped it survive a dwindling newspaper industry.

30018 ■ *"My Bad: Sometimes, Even CEOs Have to Say They're Sorry" in Inc. (October 2007, pp. 37-38)*
Pub: Gruner & Jahr USA Publishing
Ed: Donna Fenn. **Description:** A leader's stature with his employees can be elevated if he can admit a mistake simply with sincerity. Unfortunately for large companies these blunders make the news.

30019 ■ My Big Idea: 30 Successful Entrepreneurs Reveal How They Found Inspiration
Pub: Kogan Page, Limited
Contact: Ben Glover, Director of Marketing
Ed: Rachel Bridge. **Released:** November 2006. **Price:** $29.95. **Description:** Thirty successful entrepreneurs share insight into starting and running a small business.

30020 ■ "My Day" in Business Strategy Review (Vol. 21, Autumn 2010, No. 3, pp. 77)
Pub: Blackwell Publishers Ltd.
Ed: Julie Meyer. **Description:** Profile of Julie Meyer, who rose to prominence as cofounder of the entrepreneurial network, First Tuesday; Meyer sold the firm for $50 million in 2000.

30021 ■ "My Day" in Business Strategy Review (Vol. 21, Autumn 2010, No. 3, pp. 77)
Pub: Wiley-Blackwell
Ed: Julie Meyer. **Description:** Julie Meyer shot to prominence as cofounder of the entrepreneurial network, First Tuesday. The firm was sold for $50 million in 2000.

30022 ■ "My Inglorious Road to Success" in Harvard Business Review (Vol. 88, July-August 2010, No. 7-8, pp. 38)
Pub: Harvard Business School Publishing
Ed: Warren Bennis. **Description:** The author discusses the intersection of fortune and opportunity in his career success, and emphasizes the important role of awareness when taking advantage of both.

30023 ■ My So-Called Freelance Life: How to Survive and Thrive as a Creative Professional for Hire
Pub: Seal Press
Contact: Charlie Winton, Manager
Ed: Michelle Goodman. **Released:** October 1, 2008. **Price:** $15.95. **Description:** Guidebook for women wishing to start a freelancing business; tips, advice, how-to's and all the information needed to survive working from home are included.

30024 ■ My Start-Up Life: What a (Very) Young C.E.O. Learned on His Journey Through Silicon Valley
Pub: Jossey-Bass Publishers
Ed: Ben Casnocha. **Released:** May 25, 2007. **Price:** $24.95. **Description:** Profile of Ben Casnocha, a young entrepreneur who shares insight into starting a running a new business.

30025 ■ "A Nasty Russian Tale" in Canadian Business (Vol. 81, March 3, 2008, No. 3, pp. 85)
Pub: Rogers Media
Ed: Andrew Nikiforuk. **Description:** Billionaires Alex Shnaider and Michael Shtaif entered a partnership for an oil venture which ended in a slew of litigations. Cases of breach of contract, injurious falsehood and other related lawsuits were filed against Shnaider. Details of the lawsuits and the other parties involved in the disputes are presented.

30026 ■ "Natalie Peterson; Corporate Counsel, Steris Corp., 39" in Crain's Cleveland Business (Vol. 28, November 19, 2007, No. 46, pp. F-14)
Pub: Crain Communications, Inc.
Ed: Chuck Soder. **Description:** Profile of Natalie Peterson, corporate counsel for Steris Corp., a manufacturer of sterilization products; Peterson's blue-collar background did not detour her from her collegiate goals although she hardly knew how to fill out a college application. After graduating from Stanford Law School in 1997, she opted to return to Cleveland in lieu of more lucrative job offers in San Francisco. She has joined the school board and has participated in the 3Rs program, in which lawyers visit public schools in Cleveland to get students thinking about career choices and talk about constitutional law.

30027 ■ "Nation of Islam Businessman Who Became Manager for Muhammnad Ali Dies" in Chicago Tribune (August 28, 2008)
Pub: McClatchy-Tribune Information Services
Ed: Trevor Jensen. **Description:** Profile of Jabir Herbert Muhammad who died on August 25, after heart surgery; Muhammad lived nearly all his life on Chicago's South Side and ran a number of small businesses including a bakery and a dry cleaners before becoming the manager to famed boxer Mohammad Ali.

30028 ■ Navigating Your Way to Business Success: An Entrepreneur's Journey
Pub: FreeBridge Publishing, Inc.
Ed: Kathryn B. Freeland. **Released:** January 10, 2010. **Price:** $24.95. **Description:** Learn first-hand from a successful entrepreneur about assessing skills and talent, envisioning your company, planning a path to success, and then tapping into available government agencies to make your business become a reality.

30029 ■ "A Network of One: Local Writer Adds Web Interviews to Creative Output" in La Crosse Tribune (September 14, 2009)
Pub: La Crosse Tribune
Ed: Geri Parlin. **Description:** Profile of Andrew Revels, a freelance and aspiring writer, who has created a website in order to help gain attention for his own writing as well as for other local artists, musicians and comedians. His latest endeavor includes interviewing local talent and broadcasting the interviews on his site each week.

30030 ■ Never Bet the Farm: How Entrepreneurs Take Risks, Make Decisions and How You Can, Too
Pub: Jossey Bass
Ed: Anthony Iaquinto; Stephen Spinelli Jr. **Released:** March 17, 2006. **Price:** $19.95. **Description:** Two successful entrepreneurs offer advice for others launching new businesses. The authors show that preparing for setbacks and using a framework to reduce risks and simplify decision making can increase chances for success.

30031 ■ Never Eat Alone: And Other Secrets to Success, One Relationship at a Time
Pub: Doubleday Broadway Publishing Group
Ed: Keith Ferrazzi, Tahl Raz. **Released:** February 2005. **Description:** Business networking strategies are offered.

30032 ■ "New Beginnings for VIBE" in Black Enterprise (Vol. 37, November 2006, No. 4, pp. 34)
Pub: Earl G. Graves Publishing Co. Inc.
Ed: Mashaun D. Simon. **Description:** Danyel Smith replaced Mimi Valdes as editor-in-chief of VIBE magazine after the Wicks Group, private equity firm focused on selected segments of the media, communications, and information industries, purchased the magazine.

30033 ■ "A New Breed of Entrepreneurs" in Black Enterprise (Vol. 37, November 2006, No. 4, pp. 16)
Pub: Earl G. Graves Publishing Co. Inc.
Description: Black entrepreneurs are an important part of the chain for providing economic opportunities within the community. Many black business owners are more likely to hire black employees and apply innovative strategies in building their businesses rather than taking the traditional route.

30034 ■ "The New Orleans Saints" in Entrepreneur (Vol. 37, August 2009, No. 8, pp. 40)
Pub: Entrepreneur Media, Inc.
Ed: Jason Meyers. **Description:** Idea Village is a nonprofit group that fosters entrepreneurship in New Orleans, Louisiana. Entrepreneurship is indeed growing in the city during a time when the city is still recovering from the damage of hurricane Katrina.

30035 ■ "The New Orleans Saints" in Entrepreneur (Vol. 37, August 2009, No. 8, pp. 40)
Pub: Entrepreneur Media, Inc.
Ed: Jason Meyers. **Description:** Idea Village is a nonprofit group that fosters entrepreneurship in New Orleans, Louisiana. Entrepreneurship is indeed growing in the city during a time when the city is still recovering from the damage of hurricane Katrina.

30036 ■ The New Social Entrepreneurship What Awaits Social Entrepreneurship Ventures?
Pub: Edward Elgar Publishing, Incorporated
Ed: Perrini. **Released:** October 2006. **Price:** $120.00. **Description:** Social entrepreneurship seeks to improve societal well-being within entrepreneurial organizations.

30037 ■ "New Work Order" in Black Enterprise (Vol. 38, March 2008, No. 8, pp. 60)
Pub: Earl G. Graves Publishing Co. Inc.
Description: Today's management challenges includes issues of more competition, globalization, outsourcing and technological advances. Suggestions to help create progressive leadership in small business that sustains a competitive edge are listed.

30038 ■ Nirvana in a Cup: The Founding of Oregon Chai
Pub: Moby Press
Ed: Tedde McMillen; Heather Hale. **Released:** July 2006. **Price:** $12.99. **Description:** Profile of a mother-daughter team who founded Oregon Chai, a tea company.

30039 ■ Non-Standard Employment under Globalization
Pub: Palgrave Macmillan
Ed: Koich Usami. **Released:** January 19, 2010. **Price:** $100.00. **Description:** Expansion of nonstandard employment under globalization is being recognized in all of the newly industrialized countries. The book examines deregulation of labor markets, social protection for nonstandard workers, and social security reforms in accordance with the transformation of employment.

30040 ■ "Nothing But Net: Fran Harris Offers Advice On Winning the Game of Business" in Black Enterprise (Vol. 38, March 2008, No. 8, pp. 50)
Pub: Earl G. Graves Publishing Co. Inc.
Ed: Chana Garcia. **Description:** Fran Harris, certified life coach, business consultant, and CEO of her business, a multimedia development company, reveals five tips to ensure entrepreneurial success.

30041 ■ "Now Entering A Secure Area" in Women Entrepreneur (January 14, 2009)
Pub: Entrepreneur Media Inc.
Ed: Aliza Sherman. **Description:** Despite the fact that the field of government intelligence and security is dominated by males, many women entrepreneurs are finding opportunities for their products and services in homeland security. Profiles of several women who have found such opportunities are included.

30042 ■ Nudge
Pub: Penguin Group USA Inc.
Ed: Richard H. Thaler, Cass R. Sunstein. **Description:** Advice is given to help improve the decision-making process in order to become a successful entrepreneur.

30043 ■ "Off the Wall: Keith Collins' Larger-Than-Life Designs" in Black Enterprise (Vol. 37, February 2007, No. 7, pp. 138)
Pub: Earl G. Graves Publishing Co. Inc.
Description: Profile of Keith Collins, an entrepreneur who makes carpets for the likes of Jay Leno, Nicolas Cage, Arnold Schwartzenegger, Janet Jackson, and Will Smith. Collins is passionate about this ancient art form and saw a future in it despite the negative feedback from those around him.

30044 ■ "The Office: Do Not Disturb" in Inc. (November 2007, pp. 144)
Pub: Gruner & Jahr USA Publishing
Ed: Leigh Buchanan. Description: The importance for any CEO to be accessible to his employees is stressed.

30045 ■ "The Office: Good to Great" in Inc. (October 2007, pp. 140)
Pub: Gruner & Jahr USA Publishing
Ed: Leigh Buchanan. Description: Qualities that make a good manager great are explored. Great bosses make their employees feel smart, they know who performs what job, know when to step back, and remember things about each employee such as their families' names.

30046 ■ "The Oilman" in Canadian Business (Vol. 79, Winter 2006, No. 24, pp. 64)
Pub: Rogers Media
Ed: Michelle Magnan. Description: The achievements of David Werklund, the chairman of the CCS Income Trust, are described.

30047 ■ "On Their Own" in Crain's Cleveland Business (Vol. 28, November 12, 2007, No. 45, pp. 19)
Pub: Crain Communications, Inc.
Ed: Eileen Beal. Description: Discusses the reasons more physicians with entrepreneurial spirit are opening their own practices as well the added challenges and responsibilities that comes with owning one's own practice.

30048 ■ The One Minute Entrepreneur
Pub: Doubleday
Ed: Ken Blanchard; assisted by Don Hutson and Ethan Willis. Released: 2008. Price: $19.95. Description: Four traditional business ideas are covered including: revenue needs to exceed expenses, bill collection, customer service, and employee motivation in order to be successful.

30049 ■ The One Minute Manager
Pub: William Morrow
Ed: Kenneth H. Blanchard, Spencer Johnson. Released: September 1, 1982. Price: $21.95. Description: Managers of small businesses as well as Fortune 500 companies have been following the management techniques described in this book. Results have shown increased productivity, job satisfaction, and personal prosperity.

30050 ■ "Online Self-Publishing Services" in Black Enterprise (Vol. 37, November 2006, No. 4, pp. 90)
Pub: Earl G. Graves Publishing Co. Inc.
Description: Profiles of five online self-publishing services.

30051 ■ "Operation Fusion" in Black Enterprise (Vol. 38, November 2007, No. 4, pp. 30)
Pub: Earl G. Graves Publishing Co. Inc.
Ed: Tara C. Walker. Description: Entrepreneur Albert H. Frazier tells how he combined three separate acquisitions in order to create Goods Movement Inc.:-W&H Systems Inc., a systems integrator and material handler supplier and North American Conveyor Inc. which fabricates and installs conveyor and sort equipment systems for the U.S. Postal Service and Total Transportation Services, a third-party logistics provider.

30052 ■ The Opposable Mind: How Successful Leaders Win Through Integrative Thinking
Pub: Harvard Business School Press
Ed: Roger Martin. Released: December 2007. Description: The importance of integrative thinking for successful management is discussed.

30053 ■ Other Essentials of Business Ownership
Pub: PublishAmerica, Incorporated
Ed: Charles Shaw. Released: May 2006. Price: $19.95. Description: Things a business owner, entrepreneur, or manager must be aware of in order to successfully manage a small business.

30054 ■ Out of the Comfort Zone: Learning to Expect the Unexpected
Pub: Morgan & Claypool Publishers
Ed: Lisbeth Borbye. Released: May 10, 2010. Price: $35.00. Description: A collection of lectures covering technology, management and entrepreneurship.

30055 ■ "Out of This World: Noah Samara and WorldSpace" in Black Enterprise (November 2007)
Pub: Earl G. Graves Publishing Co. Inc.
Ed: Anthony Calypso. Description: Profile of Noah Samara, CEO of WorldSpace Inc. who raised $1 billion to help create the technological architecture for satellite radio.

30056 ■ Outliers
Pub: Little, Brown and Company
Ed: Malcolm Gladwell. Released: 2008. Description: The book explores reasons for individual success.

30057 ■ Own Your Own Corporation: Why the Rich Own Their Own Companies and Everyone Else Works for Them
Pub: Business Plus
Ed: Garrett Sutton; Robert T. Kiyosaki; Ann Blackman. Released: June 2008. Price: $17.99 paperback. Description: Part of the Rich Dad Advisor's Series, this edition shows how individuals can incorporate themselves and their businesses to save thousands of dollars in taxes and protect against financial disaster.

30058 ■ "Ownership Form, Managerial Incentives, and the Intensity of Rivalry" in Academy of Management Journal (Vol. 50, No. 4, August 2007)
Pub: Academy of Management
Contact: Ming-Jer Chen, President
Ed: Govert Vroom, Javier Gimeno. Description: Ways in which differences in ownership form between franchised and company-owned units alter managerial incentives and competitive pricing in different oligopolistic contexts, or following competitors into foreign markets, is presented.

30059 ■ The Oxford Handbook of Entrepreneurship
Pub: Oxford University Press, Incorporated
Ed: Mark Casson; Bernard Young; Anuradha Basu. Released: October 2006. Price: $155.00. Description: Research covering entrepreneurship is presented by an international team of leading scholars.

30060 ■ The Oz Principle
Pub: Prentice Hall Press
Contact: Dame Marjorie M. Scardino, Chief Executive Officer
Ed: Roger Connors. Released: 1994. Price: $24.95. Description: The role of personal and organizational accountability in getting business results is profiled.

30061 ■ The Pampered Chef
Pub: Doubleday Broadway Publishing Group
Ed: Doris Christopher. Description: The Pampered Chef has been selling high quality kitchen tools through in-home cooking demonstration for twenty-five years. CEO and founder explains how she turned her one woman company into a business with sales approaching $1 billion. Christopher shares her story by providing the foundation, strategies for entrepreneurs, setting priorities, knowing when to expand and when to slow growth, and dealing with adversity.

30062 ■ "A Panel Study of Copreneurs In Business" in Family Business Review (Vol. 19, September 2006, No. 3, pp. 193)
Pub: Family Firm Institute
Contact: Judy L. Green, President
Ed: Glenn Muske, Margaret A. Fitzgerald. Description: Analysis of three groups of copreneurs of family businesses, and their entrepreneurial impact on business success is presented.

30063 ■ "The Paper Shredder" in Business Courier (Vol. 26, September 11, 2009, No. 20, pp. 1)
Pub: American City Business Journals, Inc.
Ed: Dan Monk. Description: DotLoop Company, owned by entrepreneur Austin Allison, is developing the DotLoop software, which eliminates paperwork in the processing of real estate contracts. The software allows realtors to take control of the negotiation process and is adaptable to the rules of different US states.

30064 ■ "Paradise Lost" in Inc. (February 2008, pp. 102-109)
Pub: Gruner & Jahr USA Publishing
Ed: Bo Burlingham. Description: Profile of Bo Burlingham, founder of Precision Manufacturing, a firm cited in books, magazines and newspaper articles for its people-centered culture and success.

30065 ■ "Patricia Hemingway Hall; President, Chief Operating Officer, Health Care Service Corp." in Crain's Chicago Business (May 5, 2008)
Pub: Crain Communications, Inc.
Ed: Mike Colias. Description: Profile of Patricia Hemingway Hall who is the president and chief operating officer of Health Care Service Corp., a new strategy launched by Blue Cross & Blue Shield of Illinois; the new endeavor will emphasize wellness rather than just treatment across its four health plans.

30066 ■ Payback: Reaping the Rewards of Innovation
Pub: Harvard Business School Publishing
Ed: James P. Andrew; Harold L. Sirkin; John Butman. Released: January 9, 2007. Price: $29.95. Description: Three different business innovation models are presented: integration, orchestration, and serving as licensor.

30067 ■ The Peebles Principles: Insights from an Entrepreneur's Life of Business Success, Making Deals, and Creating a Fortune from Scratch
Pub: John Wiley and Sons Inc.
Ed: R. Donahue Peebles. Released: April 2007. Price: $29.99. Description: Successful entrepreneur shares his business experience. Peebles went from CEO of the nation's largest Black-owned real estate development firm to founding his own firm.

30068 ■ "Penny Chapman" in Canadian Business (Vol. 79, July 17, 2006, No. 14-15, pp. 75)
Pub: Rogers Media
Ed: Erin Pooley. Description: Interview with Penny Chapman, president of Chapman's Ice Cream, who speaks about her journey from rags to riches.

30069 ■ "Penny Chief Shops For Shares" in Barron's (Vol. 88, July 7, 2008, No. 27, pp. 29)
Pub: Dow Jones & Co., Inc.
Ed: Teresa Rivas. Description: Myron Ullman III, chairman and chief executive officer of J.C. Penney, purchased $1 million worth of shares of the company. He now owns 393,140 shares of the company and an additional 1,282 on his 401(k) plan.

30070 ■ "The Perfect Fit" in Small Business Opportunities (Fall 2007)
Pub: Harris Publications Inc.
Description: Launched in 2004, Jigsaw provides an online database of more than 5.5 million business contacts and company information for entrepreneurs.

30071 ■ "Perfecting the Process: Creating a Move Efficient Organization On Your Terms" in Black Enterprise (Vol. 41, October 2010, No. 3)
Pub: Earl G. Graves Publishing Co. Inc.
Ed: Tamara E. Holmes. Description: More than ever, entrepreneurs need to identify new ways of doing business in a cost-effective manner in order to expand their companies, while remaining true to their customer demands.

30072 ■ *"Personal File: Dean Williams" in Canadian Business (Vol. 80, April 23, 2007, No. 9, pp. 55)*
Pub: Rogers Media
Description: A brief profile of Dean Williams, architect at Softchoice Corp., including his services to the company, is presented.

30073 ■ *"Personal File: Esther Colwill" in Canadian Business (Vol. 80, April 23, 2007, No. 9, pp. 48)*
Pub: Rogers Media
Description: A brief profile of Esther Colwill, senior manager at Deloitte & Touche LLP, including her achievements which are also presented.

30074 ■ *"Personal File: Laura Laing" in Canadian Business (Vol. 80, April 23, 2007, No. 9, pp. 58)*
Pub: Rogers Media
Description: A brief profile of Laura Laing, director of public relations at AdFarm, including her services, is presented.

30075 ■ *"Personal File: Malcolm Smillie" in Canadian Business (Vol. 80, April 23, 2007, No. 9, pp. 44)*
Pub: Rogers Media
Description: A brief profile of Malcolm Smillie, marketing manager of 1-800-Got-Junk?, including his achievements which are also presented.

30076 ■ *Personal Success and the Bottom Line*
Pub: Successful Publishing
Ed: Mark C. Middleton. **Released:** March 2006. **Price:** $24.95. **Description:** Retired certified public accountant provides a primer for those wishing to achieve a balance between career and their personal life.

30077 ■ *"Peter Bynoe Trades Up" in Black Enterprise (Vol. 38, July 2008, No. 12, pp. 30)*
Pub: Earl G. Graves Publishing Co. Inc.
Ed: Alexis McCombs. **Description:** Chicago-based Loop Capital Markets L.L.C. has named Peter Bynoe managing director of corporate finance. Bynoe was previously a senior partner at the law firm DLA Piper U.S. L.L.P., where he worked on stadium deals.

30078 ■ *"Peter Gilgan" in Canadian Business (Vol. 82, April 27, 2009, No. 7, pp. 58)*
Pub: Rogers Media
Ed: Calvin Leung. **Description:** Mattamy Homes Ltd. president and chief executive officer Peter Gilgan believes that their business model of building communities in an organized way brings advantages to the firm and for their customers. He also believes in adopting their product prices to new market realities. Gilgan considers the approvals regime in Ontario his biggest challenge in the last 20 years.

30079 ■ *Petty Capitalists and Globalization: Flexibility, Entrepreneurship, and Economic Development*
Pub: State University of New York Press
Ed: Alan Smart, Josephine Smart. **Released:** January 2006. **Price:** $26.95. **Description:** Investigation into ways small businesses in Europe, Asia and Latin America are required to operate and compete in the fast-growing transnational economy.

30080 ■ *"Philanthropy Good For Business" in Crain's Detroit Business (Vol. 24, February 18, 2008, No. 7, pp. 14)*
Pub: Crain Communications Inc. - Detroit
Ed: Sheena Harrison. **Description:** Profile of Burce McCully, founder of Dynamic Edge Inc., and his views on philanthropy as a key to any small company's success. The Ann Arbor, Michigan information technology firm has volunteered and raised funds for many causes since 1999 when the company was founded.

30081 ■ *"Picture of Success" in Black Enterprise (Vol. 38, December 2007, No. 5, pp. 71)*
Pub: Earl G. Graves Publishing Co. Inc.
Ed: Sheiresa McRae. **Description:** Profile of Kenya Cagle, president and CEO of Caglevision Inc., an independent motion picture production company.

Cagle, former off-Broadway child actor, kept his company afloat with financial backing and support from friends, employees, and business colleagues.

30082 ■ *"A Piece of the Action" in Black Enterprise (Vol. 38, January 2008, No. 6, pp. 42)*
Pub: Earl G. Graves Publishing Co. Inc.
Ed: Alan Hughes. **Description:** Andre Williams, owner of Kaze Sushi restaurant, offered generous incentive plan-equity in the business in order to acquire Chef Kaze Chan and Chef Hari Chan. Williams' entrepreneurial pursuits are discussed.

30083 ■ *"Pioneering Strategies for Entrepreneurial Success" in Business Horizons (Vol. 51, January-February 2008, No. 1, pp. 21)*
Pub: Elsevier Advanced Technology Publications
Ed: Candida G. Brush. **Description:** Entrepreneurs are known for new products, services, processes, markets and industries. In order to achieve success, they have to develop a clear vision, creatively manage finances, and use social skills to persuade others to commit to the venture. Pioneering strategies and their implementation are examined.

30084 ■ *The Pixar Touch: The Making of a Company*
Pub: Pantheon Books
Ed: David A. Price. **Released:** 2009. **Price:** $27.95. **Description:** Profile of how Pixar's founders turned their computer-animated films into a successful movie studio.

30085 ■ *The Platinum Rule for Small Business Success*
Pub: Morgan James Publishing, LLC
Ed: Scott Zimmerman; Tony Allesandra; Ron Finklestein. **Released:** August 2006. **Description:** Rules for running a successful and profitable small business are shared.

30086 ■ *"Playing to Win" in Entrepreneur (Vol. 36, May 2008, No. 5, pp. 40)*
Pub: Entrepreneur Media, Inc.
Ed: Robert Kiyosaki. **Description:** Four personality types needed by entrepreneurs to drive their leadership in business are given. 'I must be liked' are social directors and go-betweens; 'I must be comfortable' are those who seek job security and are not at ease with deadlines; I must be right are those strong in opinion; and 'I must win' are people in charge.

30087 ■ *Poker Winners are Different*
Pub: Kensington Publishing Corporation
Ed: Alan N. Schoonmaker. **Released:** 2009. **Description:** Poker success requires reading the context and reading people, two skills every entrepreneur needs to possess.

30088 ■ *The Portable MBA in Entrepreneurship*
Pub: John Wiley & Sons, Inc.
Ed: Andrew Zacharakis, William D. Bygrave. **Released:** December 9, 2010. **Price:** $34.95. **Description:** An updated and revised new edition of the comprehensive guide to modern entrepreneurship that tracks the core curriculum of leading business schools.

30089 ■ *Power Ambition Glory*
Pub: Crown Business
Ed: Steve Forbes, John Prevas. **Released:** June 16, 2009. **Price:** $26.00. **Description:** An examination into the lives of the ancient world's greatest leaders and the lessons they have for today's business leaders.

30090 ■ *The Power of Body Language*
Pub: Simon and Schuster Inc.
Contact: Carolyn Reidy, President
E-mail: carolyn.reidy@simonandschuster.com
Ed: Tonya Reiman. **Released:** 2008. **Price:** $15.00. **Description:** Body language expert describes the hidden meaning behind specific gestures, facial cues, stances, and body movements to help anyone communicate in business.

30091 ■ *"The Power of Commitment: Mere Motivation Is Often Not Enough To Achieve Your Goals" in Black Enterprise (November 2007)*
Pub: Earl G. Graves Publishing Co. Inc.
Ed: Tamara E. Holmes. **Description:** Profile of Michelle Tucker Kirk who opened her bridal shop in 2006. Kirk explains how her commitment and determination were keys to the company's success. Five signs to help any would-be entrepreneur discover if they are truly committed to a business idea are listed.

30092 ■ *The Power of Full Engagement: Managing Energy, Not Time, is the Key to High Performance and Personal Renewal*
Pub: Free Press/Simon & Schuster
Ed: Jim Loehr; Tony Schwartz. **Released:** December 21, 2004. **Price:** $15.95 paperback. **Description:** The book presents a program to help stressed individuals find more purpose in their work and ways to better handle overburdened relationships.

30093 ■ *"The Power of Fun" in Canadian Business (Vol. 79, November 6, 2006, No. 22, pp. 58)*
Pub: Rogers Media
Ed: Zena Olijnyk. **Description:** The creative efforts of Phillippe Starck in designing condos are analyzed.

30094 ■ *The Power of Many: Values for Success in Business and in Life*
Pub: Crown Business
Ed: Meg Whitman, Joan O'C Hamilton. **Released:** January 26, 2010. **Price:** $26.00. **Description:** Meg Whitman discusses the important values for success in business and in life: integrity, accountability, authenticity and courage.

30095 ■ *The Power of Nice: How to Conquer the Business World with Kindness*
Pub: Doubleday
Ed: Linda Kaplan Thaler; Robin Koval. **Released:** September 19, 2006. **Price:** $17.95. **Description:** The key principles to running a business through thoughtfulness and kindness are exhibited with the use of success stories.

30096 ■ *The Power of a Positive No: How to Say No and Still Get to Yes*
Pub: Random Housing Publishing Group
Ed: William Ury. **Released:** December 2007. **Price:** $16.00. **Description:** According to the author, a positive no begins with yes and ends with yes.

30097 ■ *The Power of Pull: How Small Moves, Smartly Made, Can Set Big Things in Motion*
Pub: Basic Books
Ed: John Hagel III, Seely Brown, Lang Divison. **Released:** April 13, 2010. **Description:** Examination of how we can effectively address the most pressing challenges in a rapidly changing and increasingly interdependent world is addressed. New ways in which passionate thinking, creative solutions, and committed action can and will make it possible for small businesses owners to seize opportunities and remain in step with change.

30098 ■ *The Power of Social Innovation: How Civic Entrepreneurs Ignite Community Networks for Good*
Pub: John Wiley & Sons, Inc.
Ed: Stephen Goldsmith, Tim Burke, Gigi Georges. **Released:** March 10, 2010. **Price:** $35.00. **Description:** This seminal book provides tools for civic entrepreneurs to create healthier communities and promote innovative solutions to public and social problems. It shows how to effectively tackle the intractable issues facing the country.

30099 ■ *Predictable Results in Unpredictable Times*
Pub: RosettaBooks LLC
Ed: Stephen R. Covey, Bob Whitman, Breck England. **Released:** August 7, 2009. **Price:** $9.99. **Description:** Four essentials for getting great performance in good times and bad are outlined for any small business.

30100 ■ *"Preparing for Weed Control" in Farmer's Weekly (March 28, 2008, No. 320)*
Pub: Reed Business Information
Contact: Jeff Greisch, President
Description: Profile of Richard Beachell who farms in a joint venture with his neighbor. Beachell discusses nitrogen applications, fungicides and the reduction of pesticides.

30101 ■ *Prescriptive Entrepreneurship*
Pub: Edward Elgar Publishing, Inc.
Ed: James O. Fiet. **Released:** March 10, 2010. **Price:** $130.00. **Description:** In the only known program of prescriptive entrepreneurship, the author provides a marked contract to the standard descriptive focus of entrepreneurship studies.

30102 ■ *"Priority: In Memoriam" in Inc. (December 2007, pp. 25-26, 28, 30)*
Pub: Gruner & Jahr USA Publishing
Ed: Ryan McCarthy. **Description:** Profiles of entrepreneurs who died in 2007; these individuals helped to create some major business trends in the last fifty years, from the advent of socially responsible business to development of quality manufacturing.

30103 ■ *"Priority: Recessionade" in Inc. (February 2008, pp. 19-20)*
Pub: Gruner & Jahr USA Publishing
Ed: Amy Feldman. **Description:** Despite signs of inflation, entrepreneurs see these tough economic times as an opportunity to start or grow their businesses. Five entrepreneurs share insight into ways this economic downturn can work to grow their businesses.

30104 ■ *"Profile" in Business Strategy Review (Vol. 21, Summer 2010, No. 2, pp. 86)*
Pub: Blackwell Publishers Ltd.
Description: In a new series, profiles of a major thinker who has made a significant difference in how organizations are managed and how business careers are shaped are presented.

30105 ■ *"Program for Women Entrepreneurs: Tips for Surviving this Economy" in Crain's Detroit Business (Vol. 25, June 22, 2009, No. 25)*
Pub: Crain Communications Inc. - Detroit
Description: Michigan Leadership Institute for Women Entrepreneurs will hold its third and final program, 'Tough Times are Temporary, but Tough People are Permanent' at the Davenport University in Livonia, Michigan.

30106 ■ *Progress-Driven Entrepreneurs, Private Equity Finance and Regulatory Issues*
Pub: Palgrave Macmillan
Ed: Zuhayr Mikdashi. **Released:** October 1, 2009. **Price:** $90.00. **Description:** Durable business performance is critically dependent on a stakeholders strategy along with accessible entrepreneurial financing availability within macro-economic and economic regulatory environments.

30107 ■ *"Proof That Good Entrepreneurs Can Make Bad Investors" in Inc. (October 2007, pp. 77-78)*
Pub: Gruner & Jahr USA Publishing
Ed: Norm Brodsky. **Description:** Information for small business owners is offered to help decide which investments are right for them.

30108 ■ *"Protect Your Trade Secrets" in Business Owner (Vol. 35, July-August 2011, No. 4, pp. 11)*
Pub: DL Perkins Company
Description: Every business has secret information which can include customer lists and contracts or secret formulas and methods used in production of goods vital to the operation. A list of things every small business owner should do to protect these secrets is outlined.

30109 ■ *The Psychology of Entrepreneurship*
Pub: Lawrence Erlbaum Associates Inc.
Contact: Paul Dukes, Manager
E-mail: paul.dukes@taylorandfrancis.com
Ed: J. Robert Baum; Michael Frese. **Released:** July 2006. **Price:** $99.95. **Description:** Psychology as the basis for understanding successful entrepreneur-

ship is used to discuss how these small firms impact international social and economic well-being and how they are the main source of job creation, market innovation, and economic growth in most societies.

30110 ■ *Purple Cow*
Pub: Penguin Group USA Inc.
Ed: Seth Godin. **Description:** Being a purple cow means you are exciting, phenomenal and unforgettable, the traits required to be a successful entrepreneur.

30111 ■ *The Pursuit of Happyness*
Pub: HarperCollins Publishers Inc.
Ed: Chris Gardner. **Released:** May 2006. **Price:** $25.95. **Description:** Rags-to-riches saga of a homeless father who raised and cared for his son on the streets of San Francisco and worked to become a powerful leader on Wall Street.

30112 ■ *Put Your Business on Autopilot: The 7-Step System to Create a Business That Works So Well That You Don't Have To*
Pub: Morgan James Publishing LLC
Ed: Greg Roworth. **Released:** April 1, 2009. **Price:** $16.95. **Description:** Failure rates still remain as high as 80 percent within five years of starting a small business despite the hard work by their owners. The author suggests that working harder doesn't necessarily equate to a successful enterprise.

30113 ■ *"Q&A" in Canadian Business (Vol. 81, July 22, 2008, No. 12-13, pp. 8)*
Pub: Rogers Media Ltd.
Ed: Michelle Magnan. **Description:** Interview with Scott Saxberg who discusses Crescent Point Energy Trust's discovery of resources in Saskatchewan and believes that this is a once-in-a-lifetime type of event. Crescent Point holds 75 percent of its resources in Saskatchewan; this new finding being considered the second-largest pool discovered since the 1950s. Saxberg's other views as well as information on Crescent Point's services are presented.

30114 ■ *"Q&A: David Labistour" in Canadian Business (Vol. 81, March 17, 2008, No. 4, pp. 10)*
Pub: Rogers Media
Ed: Lauren McKeon. **Description:** David Labistour says that the difference between being a co-op retailer and a corporate-owned retailer in the case of Mountain Equipment Co-op (MEC) is that the company is owned by their customers and not by shareholders. Labistour also says that MEC works with their factories to ensure that these maintain ethical standards in the manufacturing process.

30115 ■ *"Q&A: Joseph Ribkoff" in Canadian Business (Vol. 81, March 31, 2008, No. 5, pp. 4)*
Pub: Rogers Media
Ed: Zena Olijnyk. **Description:** Joseph Ribkoff started his career in the garment trade by sweeping floors and running deliveries for a dress manufacturer called Town & Country and earned $16 a week. Ribkoff says that the key to controlling costs in Canada is to invest in the latest equipment and technology to stay competitive.

30116 ■ *Race and Entrepreneurial Success: Black-, Asian-, and White-Owned Businesses in the United States*
Pub: The MIT Press
Contact: Ellen W. Faran, Director
E-mail: ewfaran@mit.edu
Ed: Robert W. Fairlie. **Released:** September 30, 2008. **Price:** $35.00. **Description:** Trends in minority small business ownership are explored, focusing on the importance of human capital, financial capital, and family business background in successful business ownership.

30117 ■ *"Radio Roots Run Deep" in The Business Journal-Milwaukee (Vol. 25, July 4, 2008, No. 41, pp. A1)*
Pub: American City Business Journals, Inc.
Ed: Rich Kirchen. **Description:** Profile of Steve Palec, a real estate broker at CB Richard Ellis, also works as a radio host for shows 'Rock & Roll Roots'

and 'Legends of Rock'. Palec shares that real estate is still his top priority, even with his radio gig. Palec's career as a broker and as a radio host is discussed.

30118 ■ *"Reaching Your Potential" in Harvard Business Review (Vol. 86, July-August 2008, No. 8, pp. 45)*
Pub: Harvard Business School Press
Ed: Robert S. Kaplan. **Description:** Being proactive in developing one's career is an important part of entrepreneurship. Keys to successful development include knowing oneself and one's goals, and taking calculated risks.

30119 ■ *"Ready To Take Your Business Global?" in Black Enterprise (Vol. 41, August 2010, No. 1, pp. 89)*
Pub: Earl G. Graves Publishing Co. Inc.
Ed: Alan Hughes. **Description:** The 2010 Black Enterprise Entrepreneurs Conference held in May stressed the need for all small firms to promote a global agenda in order to stay competitive.

30120 ■ *"Real Estate Ambitions" in Black Enterprise (Vol. 37, January 2007, No. 6, pp. 101)*
Pub: Earl G. Graves Publishing Co. Inc.
Description: National Real Estate Investors Association is a nonprofit trade association for both advanced as well as novice real estate investors that offers information on builders to contractors to banks. When looking to become a real estate investor utilize this organization, talk to various investors like the president of your local chapter, let people know your aspirations, and see if you can find a partner who has experience in the field. Resources included.

30121 ■ *Reality-Based Leadership: Ditch the Drama, Restore Sanity to the Workplace*
Pub: Jossey-Bass
Ed: Cy Wakeman. **Price:** $27.95. **Description:** Recent polls show that 71 percent of workers think about quitting their jobs every day. That number would be shocking if people actually were quitting. Worse, they go to work, punching time clocks and collecting pay checks, while checked out emotionally. Cy Wakeman reveals how to be the kind of leader who changes the way people think about and perceive their circumstances, one who deals with the facts, clarifies roles, gives clean and direct feedback, and insists that everyone do the same without drama or defensiveness.

30122 ■ *"Recent Deals Signal an M&A Resurgence" in Austin Business JournalInc. (Vol. 29, January 22, 2010, No. 46, pp. 1)*
Pub: American City Business Journals
Ed: Jacob Dirr. **Description:** The acquisition of at least six Austin, Texas technology companies reflects the growing acquisition activity in the US. Corporations have bought 86 companies and spent $7.3 billion during the fourth quarter of 2009. Insights into the impact of the acquisition activity to Austin's entrepreneurial energy are also given.

30123 ■ *"Recession-Proof Your Startup" in Crain's Chicago Business (Vol. 31, November 10, 2008, No. 45, pp. 24)*
Pub: Crain Communications, Inc.
Description: Detailed information concerning ways in which to start a business during an economic crisis is provided. Ways in which to find financing, the importance of a solid business plan, customer service, problem-solving and finding the right niche for the region are also discussed.

30124 ■ *"Reinventing the Cheeseburger" in Inc. (November 2007, pp. 124-125)*
Pub: Gruner & Jahr USA Publishing
Ed: Chris Lydgate. **Description:** Profile of Burgerville's Tom Mears, who turned his drive-through burger restaurant green.

30125 ■ *"Reinventing Management" in Harvard Business Review (Vol. 88, July-August 2010, No. 7-8, pp. 167)*
Pub: Harvard Business School Publishing
Ed: Roberta Fusaro. **Description:** Review of the book, 'Reinventing Management' is presented.

30126 ■ *"The Reinvention of Management" in Strategy and Leadership (Vol. 39, March-April 2011, No. 2, pp. 9)*
Pub: Emerald Group Publishing Inc.
Ed: Stephen Denning. **Description:** An examination found that critical changes in management practice involves five shifts. These shifts involve the firm's goals, model of coordination, the role of managers and values practiced. Other findings of the study are discussed.

30127 ■ *Remarkable Leadership*
Pub: Jossey Bass
Ed: Kevin Eikenberry. **Released:** August 30, 2007. **Price:** $27.95. **Description:** Handbook for anyone wishing to be an outstanding business leader; the framework and a mechanism for learning new things and applying current knowledge in a practical to any business situation is outlined.

30128 ■ *Renovate Before You Innovate: Why Doing the New Thing Might Not Be the Right Thing*
Pub: Portfolio Publishing
Ed: Sergio Zyman, with Armin A Brott. **Released:** Octobr 4, 2004. **Description:** The author uses his experience as the manager behind the introduction to the New Coke as an example of a lazy business growth strategy. He offers insight into successful growth strategies for any small business owner.

30129 ■ *"Resource Line" in Black Enterprise (Vol. 37, January 2007, No. 6, pp. 6)*
Pub: Earl G. Graves Publishing Co. Inc.
Description: Interactive Media Editor, Philara Patterson, writes a column for blackenterprise.com that offers advice and provides resources for entrepreneurs, corporate executives, business owners, and budding investors.

30130 ■ *Rework*
Pub: Crown Business
Ed: Jason Fried, David Heinemeier Hansson. **Released:** March 9, 2010. **Price:** $22.00. **Description:** Works to help entrepreneurs and business owners to rethink strategy, customers, and getting things accomplished.

30131 ■ *The Rhythm of Success: How an Immigrant Produced His Own American Dream*
Pub: Penguin Group USA Inc.
Ed: Emilio Estefan. **Released:** January 10, 2010. **Price:** $24.95. **Description:** Emilio Estafan, husband to singer Gloria Estefan and founder of the Latin pop legend Miami Sound Machine, is the classic example of the American dream. He shares his guiding principles that entrepreneurs need to start and grow a business.

30132 ■ *"The Rich 100" in Canadian Business (Vol. 79, Winter 2006, No. 24, pp. 78)*
Pub: Rogers Media
Description: The rankings of the 100 richest billionaires in Canada are presented, along with the description of their achievements and their net worth.

30133 ■ *"Riding High" in Small Business Opportunities (November 2008)*
Pub: Entrepreneur Press
Contact: Perlman Neil, President
Ed: Stan Roberts. **Description:** Profile of David Sanborn who found a way to turn his passion for biking into a moneymaking opportunity by opening his own bicycle shops; Sanborn's goal is to become the largest independent bike retailer in the United States.

30134 ■ *"The Right Remedy: Entrepreneur's Success Is a Matter of Life and Death" in Black Enterprise (Vol. 38, February 2008, No. 7, pp. 46)*
Pub: Earl G. Graves Publishing Co. Inc.
Ed: Tamara E. Holmes. **Description:** Profile of Leah Brown, whose company conducts clinical trials to determine if specific drugs will relieve particular symptoms. Her company will also visit physician's offices to make certain doctors are following proper protocol for a clinical trial or will collect data from patients.

30135 ■ *"The Right Stuff" in Canadian Business (Vol. 79, October 23, 2006, No. 21, pp. 151)*
Pub: Rogers Media
Ed: Laura Bogomolny. **Description:** The profile of Linda Duxbury, the winner of the Sprott MBA Students Society 2003-04 Best teacher award as well as Carleton University Students' Association 2002-03 award, is presented.

30136 ■ *Risk-Free Entrepreneur*
Pub: Adams Media Corporation
Ed: Don Debelak. **Released:** June 2006. **Price:** $14.95. **Description:** Information is offered to help entrepreneurs to develop an idea for a product or service and have other companies provide the marketing, manufacturing and staff.

30137 ■ *Risk Takers and Innovators, Great Canadian Business Ventures Since 1950*
Pub: Altitude Publishing
Ed: Sandra Phinney. **Released:** June 15, 2004. **Price:** $7.95. **Description:** Successful business leaders share their creativity, technology skills, and entrepreneurship.

30138 ■ *"Road Warriors: How To Survive Business Travel" in Crain's Detroit Business (Vol. 24, February 4, 2008, No. 5, pp. 11)*
Pub: Crain Communications Inc. - Detroit
Description: Entrepreneurs share tips that help save time and energy at airports when traveling for business.

30139 ■ *"Rob McEwen" in Canadian Business (Vol. 80, Winter 2007, No. 24, pp. 138)*
Pub: Rogers Media
Ed: John Gray. **Description:** Rob McEwen's interest in gold started with his father who was in the investment industry and was always talking about the value of gold. McEwen believes that there is a lot of room to innovate in mining and that Canada should be a leader in this field.

30140 ■ *"Rob Ritchie" in Canadian Business (Vol. 80, January 15, 2007, No. 2, pp. 70)*
Pub: Rogers Media
Ed: Michelle Magnan. **Description:** The former president of the Canadian Pacific Railway, Rob Ritchie, reveals facts about his personal and professional life.

30141 ■ *"Robert S. McNamara and the Evolution of Modern Management" in Harvard Business Review (Vol. 88, December 2010, No. 12, pp. 86)*
Pub: Harvard Business School Publishing
Ed: Phil Rosenzweig. **Description:** A chronicle of the emergence and development of Robert S. McNamara's management skills and perspectives, focusing on the role of his idealism. Lessons learned during the course of the Vietnam Ware are also delineated.

30142 ■ *"Roger Hickel Contracting: Smoothing the Road for Owners" in Alaska Business Monthly (Vol. 27, October 2011, No. 10, pp. 114)*
Pub: Alaska Business Publishing Company
Ed: Gail West. **Description:** Profile of Roger Hickel and his contracting company that reports nearly $60 million annually in gross revenue. The firm focuses on customer service.

30143 ■ *"Roger Rechler Played Major Role in Long Island's Evolution" in Commercial Property News (March 17, 2008)*
Pub: Nielsen Company
Description: Profile of Roger Rechler, real estate developer on Long Island, New York, is presented. Rechler, who died in March 2008, was instrumental in the development, ownership and operations of the largest commercial real estate portfolio on Long Island.

30144 ■ *The Role of the Non-Executive Director in the Small to Medium-Sized Business*
Pub: Palgrave Macmillan
Ed: John Smithson. **Released:** March 2004. **Price:** $95.00. **Description:** The role of the non-executive director in a small to medium-sized business is examined.

30145 ■ *"The Romance of Good Deeds: a Business With a Cause Can Do Good in the World" in Inc. (Volume 32, December 2010, No. 10, pp. 47)*
Pub: Inc. Magazine
Ed: Meg Cadoux Hirshberg. **Description:** Entrepreneurship and family relationships are discussed. When a small business has a passion for philanthropy it can help any marriage by creating even greater passion for each other.

30146 ■ *"Running the Numbers" in Entrepreneur (Vol. 37, July 2009, No. 7, pp. 87)*
Pub: Entrepreneur Media, Inc.
Ed: Carol Tice. **Description:** Ways in which entrepreneurs can assess if they are ready to be a multi-unit franchisee are presented. Choosing the right locations, knowing how much assistance they can get from the franchisor, and financing are the key considerations when planning additional franchise units. Examples of success in multi-unit operations and multi-unit terms are also presented.

30147 ■ *"Sage Advice" in Canadian Business (Vol. 80, October 22, 2007, No. 21, pp. 70)*
Pub: Rogers Media
Ed: John Gray. **Description:** Seymour Schulich, one of Canada's richest men and generous philanthropist, wrote the book, 'Get Smarter: Life and Business Lessons'. The business book sold more than 50,000 copies and now sits on Canada's bestseller's list. Its popularity s attributed to the marketing efforts of the entrepreneur and author.

30148 ■ *"Savvas Chamberlain" in Canadian Business (Vol. 81, March 17, 2008, No. 4, pp. 92)*
Pub: Rogers Media
Ed: Andrew Wahl. **Description:** Savvas Chamberlain says he feels cheated during his teenage years because life was not normal for him growing up in Cyprus with all the uprisings against Britain. Chamberlain says he runs Dalsa like he plays chess because all his positions are shown all the time but he keeps his strategy to himself.

30149 ■ *Science Lessons: What the Business of Biotech Taught Me About Management*
Pub: Harvard Business School Press
Ed: Gordon Binder, Philip Bashe. **Released:** 2009. **Price:** $29.95. **Description:** Former CFO of biotechnology startup Amgen and veteran of Ford Motor Company provides a universal guide to management based on some of the same scientific principles used to create new drugs.

30150 ■ *"Scoring Music" in Canadian Business (Vol. 81, December 8, 2008, No. 21, pp. S3)*
Pub: Rogers Media Ltd.
Ed: Jay Somerset. **Description:** Boyd Devereaux, who plays with the Toronto Maple Leafs, collaborates with musicians through his record label Elevation Records. Devereaux won a Stanley Cup with the Detroit Red Wings in 2002 and has released five limited edition discs through Elevation records.

30151 ■ *"Screen Time" in Canadian Business (Vol. 81, October 13, 2008, No. 17, pp. 93)*
Pub: Rogers Media Ltd.
Ed: Calvin Leung. **Description:** Young Canadian entertainment business up-and-comers like Ari Lantos and Brian Mossof plan to produce movies that cold earn and entertain audiences rather than focusing on winning awards. English movies continue to struggle in Canada, while French-language films continue to thrive. Details on Canada's movie industry are furnished.

30152 ■ *"Second Cup?" in Canadian Business (Vol. 81, July 21, 2008, No. 11, pp. 50)*
Pub: Rogers Media Ltd.
Ed: Calvin Leung. **Description:** Profile of James Gosling who is credited as the inventor of the Java programming language; however, the 53-year-old software developer feels ambivalent for being credited

as inventor since many people contributed to the language. Netscape and Sun Microsystems incorporation of the programming language into Java is presented.

30153 ■ *The Secret Language of Competitive Intelligence: How to See Through and Stay Ahead of Business Disruptions, Distortions, Rumors, and Smoke*
Pub: Crown Publishing Group

Ed: Leonard M. Fuld. **Released:** May 2006. **Price:** $24.95.

30154 ■ *"The Secret Life of a Serial CEO" in Inc. (January 2008, pp. 80-88)*
Pub: Gruner & Jahr USA Publishing

Ed: David H. Freedman. **Description:** Profile of Bob Cramer, who has lead six successful companies and is now searching for a new business venture and thinks he's found it. Cramer shares his journey from wooing venture capital, handling founders and his hunt for his newest venture.

30155 ■ *Secrets of Millionaire Moms*
Pub: McGraw-Hill

Ed: Tamara Monosoff. **Released:** March 2007. **Price:** $16.95. **Description:** Profiles of successful women/mother entrepreneurs are presented, including Julie Clark, Lane Nemeth, Lillian Vernon, Victoria Knight, Rachel Ashwell and other powerful businesswomen.

30156 ■ *"SEEing an Opportunity; Golden's Eyewear Chain Has a National Vision" in Crain's Detroit Business (Vol. 24, January 7, 2008, No. 1)*
Pub: Crain Communications Inc. - Detroit

Ed: Sheena Harrison. **Description:** Richard Golden, who recently sold D.O.C. Optics Corporation is planning to build a new national eyewear chain called SEE Inc., which stands for Selective Eyewear Elements. SEE will sell expensive-looking glasses at lower prices than designer styles.

30157 ■ *"The Self-Destructive Habits of Good Companies, and How to Break Them" in Harvard Business Review (Vol. 85, July-August 2007, No. 7-8)*
Pub: Harvard Business School Publishing

Ed: John T. Landry. **Description:** Review of the book that helps companies break bad habits and develop new ones for growth and success.

30158 ■ *Sell Your Business Your Way: Getting Out, Getting Rich, and Getting on with Your Life*
Pub: American Management Association

Contact: Charles R. Craig, Chairman

Ed: Rick Rickertsen; Robert Gunther. **Released:** 2006. **Price:** $27.95.

30159 ■ *"Sellers Shift Gears" in Crain's Detroit Business (Vol. 25, June 22, 2009, No. 25, pp. 3)*
Pub: Crain Communications Inc. - Detroit

Description: Of the 14 new car Chrysler dealerships in the Detroit area who had franchises terminated, Joe Ricci of Dearborn will sell used cars at his new business called All American Buyer's Service; Lochmoor Automotive Group in Detroit will focus on Mahindra & Mahindra trucks; Mt. Clemens Dodge, Clinton Township is also selling Mahindra & Mahindra trucks; and Monicatti Chrysler Jeep, Sterling Heights, will offer service along with selling used cars.

30160 ■ *"Serial Starter" in Entrepreneur (Vol. 36, April 2008, No. 4, pp. 17)*
Pub: Entrepreneur Media, Inc.

Ed: Andrea Cooper. **Description:** Some entrepreneurs are engaged in serial entrepreneurship as they feel that they are no longer satisfied with their business and they decide to sell it. Others start out new businesses because they believe they can try out and be successful in different kinds of businesses. Details on how to identify and handle new entrepreneurial opportunities are discussed.

30161 ■ *Setting the Table*
Pub: HarperCollins Publishers Inc.

Ed: Danny Meyer. **Price:** $29.95. **Description:** Renowned restauranteur profiles his success in the hospitality business.

30162 ■ *Setting the Table: The Transforming Power of Hospitality in Business*
Pub: HarperCollins Publishers Inc.

Released: October 2006.

30163 ■ *"Seymour Schulich" in Canadian Business (Vol. 79, Winter 2006, No. 24, pp. 144)*
Pub: Rogers Media

Ed: John Gray. **Description:** The views of the Canadian billionaire Seymour Schulich, on the evaluation of donations and gifts, are presented.

30164 ■ *"Shape Up! Jamal Williams Develops KIDFIT App to Combat Childhood Obesity" in Black Enterprise (Vol. 41, August 2010, No. 1, pp. 62)*
Pub: Earl G. Graves Publishing Co. Inc.

Ed: Sonya A. Donaldson. **Description:** Profile of Jamal Williams who developed KIDFIT, an app that helps to combat childhood obesity by offering 150 various exercises for children, with an emphasis on training, conditioning, coordination, and flexibility.

30165 ■ *"Shared Leadership In Teams: An Investigation of Antecedent Conditions and Performance" in Academy of Management Journal (Oct. 2007)*
Pub: Academy of Management

Contact: Ming-Jer Chen, President

Ed: Jay B. Carson, Paul E. Tesluk, Jennifer A. Marrone. **Description:** Study assessed the advantages of distribution of leadership among team members rather than on a single person revealed advantages that ranged from support and shared functions along with higher ratings from clients on their performance.

30166 ■ *"Shoe's On Other Foot" in Business Courier (Vol. 24, November 30, 2008, No. 33, pp. 1)*
Pub: American City Business Journals, Inc.

Description: Ronald Hummons was fresh out of prison for felony in 2000, and through the help of spiritual non-profit group the Lord's Gym he was able to turn his life around and start his own company Grapevine Ltd. LLC, which makes C-town athletic shoes.

30167 ■ *"Siemens Boss on Big Scandals, Bullet-Proof Limos" in Globe & Mail (March 5, 2007, pp. B11)*
Pub: CTVglobemedia Publishing Inc.

Description: Interview with Klaus Kleinfeld, the chief executive officer of Siemens AG, in which he shares his views on the job challenges faced by him.

30168 ■ *"Sign, Sign, Everywhere a Sign: How I Did It: Richard Schaps" in Inc. (October 2007, pp. 128)*
Pub: Gruner & Jahr USA Publishing

Ed: Stephanie Clifford. **Description:** Richard Schaps shares the story of selling his outdoor-advertising firm, Van Wagner for $170 million and sharing the wealth with his employees. Schaps then started another outdoor-sign company.

30169 ■ *"Sign Up To Grow Your Business, Generate Jobs" in Women Entrepreneur (November 25, 2008)*
Pub: Entrepreneur Media Inc.

Ed: Eve Gumpel. **Description:** Nell Merlino has announced the new Make Mine A Million-Dollar Race, which aims to encourage hundreds of thousands of women entrepreneurs to grow their business to revenue goals of $250,00, $500,000 or $1 million and more as well as create 800,000 new jobs in an attempt to stimulate the nation's economy.

30170 ■ *Silos, Politics and Turf Wars: A Leadership Fable about Destroying the Barriers That Turn Colleagues Into*

Competitors
Pub: Jossey Bass

Ed: Patrick M. Lencioni. **Released:** February 17, 2006. **Price:** $24.95. **Description:** The author addresses management problems through a fable that revolves around a self-employed consultant who has to dismantle silos at an upscale hotel, a technology company and a hospital. The story explains how organizations can use a collective operational vision in order to overcome pride, greed, and tribalism and work as a team with the same goal in mind.

30171 ■ *The Six Sigma for Small and Medium Businesses: What You Need to Know Explained Simply*
Pub: Atlantic Publishing Company

Ed: Marsha R. Ford. **Released:** January 1, 2009. **Price:** $24.95. **Description:** The Six Sigma set of practices used to systematically improve business practices by eliminating defects. To be Six Sigma compliant, a company must produce no more than 3.4 defects per one million products, and if achieved will save the firm millions of dollars. The two main methodologies of Six Sigma are outlined.

30172 ■ *"Size Matters" in Entrepreneur (Vol. 36, April 2008, No. 4, pp. 44)*
Pub: Entrepreneur Media, Inc.

Ed: Robert Kiyosaki. **Description:** Entrepreneurs planning to expand their business face challenges when it comes to employing more people and addressing internal relationships, communications and procedures. People skills, organizational skills and leadership skills are some of the things to consider before adding employees.

30173 ■ *"Skinner's No Drive-Thru CEO" in Crain's Chicago Business (Vol. 31, April 28, 2008, No. 17, pp. 1)*
Pub: Crain Communications, Inc.

Ed: David Sterrett. **Description:** Profile of James Skinner who was named CEO for McDonald's Corp. in November 2004 and has proved to be a successful leader despite the number of investors who doubted him when he came to the position. Mr. Skinner has overseen three years of unprecedented sales growth and launched the biggest menu expansion in 30 years.

30174 ■ *Small Business: An Entrepreneur's Business Plan*
Pub: South-Western

Ed: J.D Ryan, Gail P. Hiduke. **Released:** October 2008. **Price:** $119.95. **Description:** Assistance in preparing a business plan that identifies opportunities and ways to target a customer market.

30175 ■ *Small Business: An Entrepreneur's Plan*
Pub: Nelson Thomson Learning

Ed: Ronald A. Knowles. **Released:** December 2006. **Description:** Entrepreneur's guide to planning a small business.

30176 ■ *Small Business, Big Life: Five Steps to Creating a Great Life with Your Own Small Business*
Pub: Rutledge Books Inc.

Ed: Louis Barajas. **Released:** May 2007. **Price:** $22.99. **Description:** Five steps for planning, starting and running a small business, while maintaining a good life, are presented.

30177 ■ *Small Business and Entrepreneurship*
Pub: SAGE Publications USA

Contact: Blaise R. Simqu, President

Ed: Robert Blackburn. **Released:** January 2008. **Price:** $1,275.00. **Description:** Research covering small business and entrepreneurship.

30178 ■ *Small Business Management*
Pub: John Wiley and Sons Inc.

Ed: Margaret Burlingame; Don Gulbrandsen; Richard M. Hodgetts; Donald F. Kuratko. **Released:** March 2007. **Price:** $44.95. **Description:** Tips for starting and running a successful small business are given, including advice on writing a business plan, financing, and the law.

30179 ■ Small Business Management in Canada
Pub: McGraw-Hill Companies Inc.
Contact: Deven Sharma, President
Ed: Robert M. Knight. **Released:** June 1981. **Description:** Small business management in Canada.

30180 ■ Small-Business Management Guide: Advice from the Brass-Tacks Entrepreneur
Pub: Henry Holt & Company
Ed: Jim Schell. **Released:** October 1995. **Description:** Entrepreneurs offer advice for managing a small business.

30181 ■ Small-Business Management Guide: Advice from the Brass-Tacks Entrepreneur
Pub: BookSurge LLC
Ed: Jim Schell. **Released:** 1995. **Description:** Collection of stories, tales and snippets from the perspective of a small business owner.

30182 ■ Small Business Survival Guide: Starting, Protecting, and Securing Your Business for Long-Term Success
Pub: Adams Media Corporation
Ed: Cliff Ennico. **Released:** September 2005. **Price:** $12.95 (US), $17.95 (Canadian). **Description:** Entrepreneurship in the new millennium. Topics include creditors, taxes, competition, business law, and accounting.

30183 ■ "Smart Investor's Shopping List: Coke, Walgreen, Drill Bits; A Conversation with Money Manager Paula Dorion-Gray" in Crain's Chicago Business
Pub: Crain Communications, Inc.
Ed: Bruce Blythe. **Description:** Interview with Paula Dorion-Gray, president of Dorion-Gray Retirement Planning Inc., discusses the state of the investing environment, favored industries, industries to avoid, and her approach towards investing.

30184 ■ "Smoke Signals: Johnny Drake On What To Expect In a Fine Cigar" in Black Enterprise (Vol. 38, December 2007, No. 5, pp. 195)
Pub: Earl G. Graves Publishing Co. Inc.
Ed: Alan Hughes. **Description:** Profile of Johnny Drake, co-owner of the retail tobacco company Renaissance Cigar Emporium. According to the Retail Tobacco Dealers of America, 320 million handmade cigars are sold in the U.S. annually.

30185 ■ The Snowball: Warren Buffett and the Business of Life
Pub: Bantam Books
Ed: Alice Schroeder. **Released:** 2009. **Price:** $35.00. **Description:** The first authorized biography of Warren Buffett provides deep and timely insight into the psyche of the billionaire investor.

30186 ■ Social Enterprise in Europe
Pub: Routledge Inc.
Ed: Marthe Nyssens. **Released:** August 2006. **Price:** $145.00 hardcopy; $46.95 paperback. **Description:** Social enterprises in Europe are examined through three ideas: that they have a complex mixture of goals, that they mobilize various kinds of markets and non-market resources, and that they are embedded in the political context.

30187 ■ Social Entrepreneurship
Pub: Palgrave Macmillan
Ed: Johanna Mair; Jeffrey Robinson; Kai Hockerts. **Released:** June 2006. **Price:** $80.00. **Description:** Social entrepreneurship is the process involving innovative approaches to solving social problems while creating economic value.

30188 ■ Social Entrepreneurship For Dummies
Pub: John Wiley & Sons
Ed: Mark Derieux, Robert Stebbins. **Released:** April 10, 2010. **Price:** $24.99. **Description:** Discover ways to bring social entrepreneurship to a small company in today's business environment. Today, a company is not measured by financial performance alone, but also on social entrepreneurship.

30189 ■ Social Entrepreneurship: What Everyone Needs to Know
Pub: Oxford University Press, Inc.
Ed: David Bornstein, Susan Davis. **Released:** April 10, 2010. **Price:** $16.95. **Description:** In development circles, there is now a widespread consensus that social entrepreneurs represent a far better mechanism to respond to needs than we have ever had before, a decentralized and emergent force that remains the best hope for solutions.

30190 ■ "Social Intelligence and the Biology of Leadership" in Harvard Business Review (Vol. 86, September 2008, No. 9, pp. 74)
Pub: Harvard Business School Press
Ed: Daniel Goleman; Richard Boyatzis. **Description:** Social intelligence within the framework of corporate leadership is defined and described. Guidelines for assessing one's own capabilities as a socially intelligent leader include empathy, teamwork, inspiration, and influence.

30191 ■ "Social Networking Butterfly" in Entrepreneur (Vol. 37, September 2009, No. 9, pp. 48)
Pub: Entrepreneur Media, Inc.
Ed: Jason Daley. **Description:** Entrepreneur Ashley Qualls has successfully grown Whateverlife.com. The site was originally created to share Qualls' custom MySpace.com templates with friends and family. Qualls is planning to redesign the site as a social network focused on Web design.

30192 ■ "Souled Out" in Canadian Business (Vol. 81, March 3, 2008, No. 3, pp. 35)
Pub: Rogers Media
Ed: Calvin Leung. **Description:** According to a survey of over 100 entrepreneurs, 78 percent responded that selling their business was emotionally draining for them. Greig Clark, for example, says that one of the toughest times of his life was selling College Pro Painters, after putting 18 years into that business. The economic impacts of selling out are also examined.

30193 ■ "A Sound Setup" in Black Enterprise (Vol. 38, November 2007, No. 4, pp. 100)
Pub: Earl G. Graves Publishing Co. Inc.
Ed: Anthony Calypso. **Description:** Choosing the right corporate identity can ensure that a business has the right foundation on which to build and grow.

30194 ■ "Speak Better: Five Tips for Polished Presentations" in Women Entrepreneur (September 19, 2008)
Pub: Entrepreneur Media Inc.
Ed: Suzannah Baum. **Description:** Successful entrepreneurs agree that exemplary public speaking skills are among the core techniques needed to propel their business forward. A well-delivered presentation can result in securing a new distribution channel, gaining new customers, locking into a new referral stream or receiving extra funding.

30195 ■ "Speed Reader" in Crain's Chicago Business (Vol. 30, February 2007, No. 6, pp. 58)
Pub: Crain Communications, Inc.
Ed: Laura Bianchi. **Description:** Interview with Paul Tamraz, president and CEO of Motor Werkes, which carries luxury vehicle lines like BMW, Porsche, and Mercedes-Benz. Tamraz discusses the importance of keeping up to speed with not only U.S. business but what is happening around the world.

30196 ■ The Speed of Trust
Pub: Simon and Schuster Inc.
Contact: Carolyn Reidy, President
E-mail: carolyn.reidy@simonandschuster.com
Ed: Stephen M.R. Covey with Rebecca R. Merrill. **Description:** Advice is given to help cultivate trust in business, politics and personal relationships.

30197 ■ The SPEED of Trust: The One Thing That Changes Everything
Pub: Free Press/Simon & Schuster Inc.
Ed: Stephen M.R. Covey. **Released:** February 5, 2008. **Price:** $15.95. **Description:** Because of recent business scandals, trust and a desire for accountability is addressed by the author.

30198 ■ The Spirit of Entrepreneurship: Exploring the Essence of Entrepreneurship Through Personal Stories
Pub: Springer
Ed: Sharda S. Nandram; Karel J. Samson. **Released:** October 2006. **Price:** $79.95. **Description:** Case studies involving 60 entrepreneurs and executives explores the fundamentals in starting a new business, techniques and mindsets.

30199 ■ "The Spirit of a Man: Kedar Massenburg's Intoxicating Style of Conducting Business" in Black Enterprise (Vol. 38, March 2008)
Pub: Earl G. Graves Publishing Co. Inc.
Ed: Sonia Alleyne. **Description:** Profile of Kedar Massenburg, personal trainer at The Gym in Montvale, New Jersey. Massenburg also operates an independent record label and management company as well as Kedar Beverages LLC founded in 2005. His latest venture is winemaking.

30200 ■ "Spread Your Wings" in Canadian Business (Vol. 81, March 17, 2008, No. 4, pp. 31)
Pub: Rogers Media
Ed: Megan Harman. **Description:** Financing from angel investors is one avenue that should be explored by startups. Angel investors are typically affluent individuals who invest their own money. Angel investors usually want at least 10 times their initial investment within eight years but they benefit the businesses through their help in decision-making and the industry expertise they provide.

30201 ■ The Starfish and the Spider
Pub: Portfolio
Ed: Ori Brafman; Rod A. Beckstrom. **Released:** 2007. **Price:** $24.95.

30202 ■ The Starfish and the Spider: The Unstoppable Power of Leaderless Organizations
Pub: Portfolio Publishing
Ed: Ori Brafman; Rod A. Beckstrom. **Released:** 2008. **Price:** $15.00 paperback. **Description:** Through their experiences promoting peace and economic development through decentralizing networking, the authors offer insight into ways that decentralizing can change organizations. Three techniques for combating a decentralized competitor are examined.

30203 ■ "The Stars Align: Trail Blazers, Headline Makers on 2007 List Set Example for Others" in Hispanic Business (October 2007, pp. 22)
Pub: Hispanic Business
Description: Top one hundred most influential Hispanic business leaders comprise of 66 percent men and 34 percent women, distributed by 27 percent in government, 42 percent corporate, 11 percent education, five percent art and entertainment, and 15 percent in other sectors. Statistical data included.

30204 ■ "Start or Buy? It's a Tough Question for Eager Entrepreneurs" in Crain's Cleveland Business (Vol. 28, October 8, 2007, No. 40)
Pub: Crain Communications, Inc.
Ed: David Prizinsky. **Description:** Discusses different approaches to becoming a small business owner.

30205 ■ Start, Run, and Grow a Successful Small Business, 2nd Edition
Pub: CCH Inc.
Contact: Mike Sabbatis, President
Ed: Susan M. Jacksack. **Price:** $24.95.

30206 ■ Start Small, Finish Big
Pub: Business Plus/Warner Business Books
Ed: Fred DeLuca with John P. Hayes. **Released:** April 2009. **Price:** $16.95. **Description:** Fred DeLuca is profiled; after founding the multi-billion dollar chain of Subway sandwich restaurants, DeLuca is committed to helping microentrepreneurs, people who start successful small businesses with less than $1,000.

30207 ■ *"Staying Engaged" in Black Enterprise (Vol. 38, February 2008, No. 7, pp. 64)*
Pub: Earl G. Graves Publishing Co. Inc.
Ed: Sonia Alleyne. **Description:** Rules to help business leaders construct networking contacts in order to maximize professional success are outlined.

30208 ■ *"Steve Meginniss Helped Reinvent the Toothbrush. Can He Do the Same Thing for Wheels?" in Inc. (February 2008, pp. 32)*
Pub: Gruner & Jahr USA Publishing
Ed: Dalia Fahmy. **Description:** Profile of Steve Meginniss, co-inventor of Sonicare Toothbrush and inventor of a two-gear wheel for wheelchairs. Mgeinniss discusses his need to raid $1 million to promote and cut manufacturing costs for this new product that helps reduce pain for users.

30209 ■ *"Still on the Block" in Entrepreneur (Vol. 35, November 2007, No. 11, pp. 22)*
Pub: Entrepreneur Media Inc.
Ed: Laura Tiffany. **Description:** Neighborhoods where business enterprises are located sometimes go into decline, particularly in low-income communities with high crime rates. Some entrepreneurs share stories about getting involved to help revive the community and keep their businesses thriving.

30210 ■ *"Stitching the City Together" in Business Courier (Vol. 24, February 8, 2008, No. 44, pp. 1)*
Pub: American City Business Journals, Inc.
Ed: Lucy May. **Description:** Nancy Zimpher, University of Cincinnati president, has been given vital leadership posts in regional development organizations in the area. She sees this as part of her job and of the university's mission of serving the community.

30211 ■ *Stop Working: Start a Business, Globalize It, and Generate Enough Cash Flow to Get Out of the Rat Race*
Pub: Eye Contact Media
Ed: Rohan Hall. **Released:** November 2004. **Price:** $15.99. **Description:** Advice is given to small companies to compete in the global marketplace by entrepreneur using the same strategy for his own business.

30212 ■ *Strategic Entrepreneurship*
Pub: Prentice Hall PTR
Ed: Philip A. Wickham. **Released:** September 2006. **Price:** $90.00. **Description:** Conceptual and practical ideas for managing a small business are explored.

30213 ■ *Strategic Partnerships: An Entrepreneur's Guide to Joint Ventures and Alliances*
Pub: Kaplan Publishing
Ed: Robert Wallace. **Released:** September 2004. **Description:** Ways to develop and execute joint venture relationships with larger business entities for small company owners.

30214 ■ *Strengths Based Leadership*
Pub: Gallup Press
Ed: Tom Rath, Barry Conchie. **Description:** Three keys to being a more effective leader.

30215 ■ *Strengthsfinder 2.0*
Pub: Gallup Press
Ed: Tom Rath. **Released:** 2007. **Price:** $22.95. **Description:** Author helps people uncover their talents in order to achieve their best each day.

30216 ■ *"Stress-Test Your Strategy: the 7 Questions to Ask" in Harvard Business Review (Vol. 88, November 2010, No. 11, pp. 92)*
Pub: Harvard Business School Publishing
Ed: Robert Simons. **Description:** Seven questions organizations should use to assess crisis management capabilities are: who is the primary customer, how do core values prioritize all parties, what performance variables are being tracked, what strategic boundaries have been set, how is creative tension being produced, how committed are workers to assisting each other, and what uncertainties are causing worry?.

30217 ■ *Studies of Entrepreneurship, Business and Government in Hong Kong: The Economic Development of a Small Open Economy*
Pub: Edwin Mellen Press
Ed: Fu-Lai Tony Yu. **Released:** November 2006. **Price:** $109.95. **Description:** Institutional and Austrian theories are used to analyze the transformation taking place in Hong Kong's economy.

30218 ■ *Success Built to Last: Creating a Life That Matters*
Pub: Penguin Group Incorporated
Ed: Jerry Porras; Stewart Emery; Mark Thompson. **Released:** August 28, 2007. **Price:** $15.00. **Description:** Interviews with successful individuals are presented to help any entrepreneur or manager.

30219 ■ *"Success Products" in Black Enterprise (Vol. 37, February 2007, No. 7, pp. 135)*
Pub: Earl G. Graves Publishing Co. Inc.
Ed: Tanisha A. Sykes. **Description:** Using innovative resources that are already at your fingertips instead of trying to reach out to companies first is a great way to discover whether you have a viable idea or product. Be motivated to start an e-newsletter letting people know about your products and attend conferences like The Motivation Show, the world's largest exhibition of motivational products and services related to performance in business.

30220 ■ *The Successful Entrepreneur's Guidebook: Where You Are Now, Where You Want to Be and How to Get There*
Pub: Kogan Page, Limited
Contact: Ben Glover, Director of Marketing
Ed: Colin Barrow; Robert Brown. **Released:** January 2007. **Price:** $35.00. **Description:** Characteristics of successful entrepreneurship are examined. The book helps new business owners to develop and grow a business.

30221 ■ *"Sullivan Led Bucyrus through Unforgettable Year" in Business Journal-Milwaukee (Vol. 28, December 17, 2010, No. 11, pp. A1)*
Pub: Milwaukee Business Journal
Ed: Rich Rovito. **Description:** Bucyrus International's president and CEO, Tim Sullivan, was chosen as Milwaukee, Wisconsin's Executive of the Year for 2010. Sullivan led Bucyrus through a year of dramatic change which started with the acquisition of the mining business of Terex Corporation and culminating with a deal to sell Caterpillar Inc.

30222 ■ *"Survive the Small-to-Big Transition" in Entrepreneur (November 4, 2008)*
Pub: Entrepreneur Media Inc.
Ed: Elizabeth Wilson. **Description:** Transitioning a small company to a large company can be a challenge, especially during the time when it is too big to be considered small and too small to be considered big. Common pitfalls during this time are discussed as well as techniques business owners should implement when dealing with this transitional period.

30223 ■ *"The Sweet Spot: A Sugar-Coated Pitch Paid Off Big Time" in Black Enterprise (Vol. 37, November 2006, No. 4, pp. 71)*
Pub: Earl G. Graves Publishing Co. Inc.
Ed: Laura Egodigwe. **Description:** In an interview with Debra Sandler, president of McNeil Nutritionals L.L.C., Sandler talks about the challenges of bringing a new product to the marketplace, how her personal experiences effect her business decisions, and the difficulties of re-entering the workforce.

30224 ■ *Swimming Against the Tide*
Pub: Macmillan Publishers Limited
Ed: Tim Waterstone. **Released:** October 2006. **Price:** $29.95. **Description:** Tim Waterstone shares ten rules for creating successful small businesses.

30225 ■ *Switch: How to Change Things When Change Is Hard*
Pub: Broadway Books
Contact: David Drake, Manager
E-mail: ddrake@randomhouse.com
Ed: Chip Heath, Dan Heath. **Released:** February 16, 2010. **Price:** $26.00. **Description:** Change is difficult

for everyone. This book helps business leaders to motivate employees as well as to help everybody motive themselves and others.

30226 ■ *"Sykes Shift from GunnAllen to New Venture" in Tampa Bay Business Journal (Vol. 30, December 18, 2009, No. 52, pp. 1)*
Pub: American City Business Journals
Ed: Margie Manning. **Description:** Tampa, Florida's entrepreneur John H. Sykes acquired Pointe Capital Inc., a GunnAllen Holdings Inc. subsidiary, through his JHS Capital Holdings Inc. and changed the name to JHS Capital Advisors Inc. Sykes will become president and CEO of JHS Capital Advisors and will relocate its corporate headquarters to Tampa, Florida.

30227 ■ *Tactical Entrepreneur: The Entrepreneur's Game Plan*
Pub: Sortis Publishing
Ed: Brian J. Hazelgren. **Released:** September 2005. **Price:** $14.95. **Description:** A smart, realistic business plan is essential for any successful entrepreneur. Besides offering products or services, small business owners must possess skills in accounting, planning, human resources management, marketing, and information technology.

30228 ■ *"Take the Plunge" in Small Business Opportunities (July 2008)*
Pub: Entrepreneur Press
Contact: Perlman Neil, President
Description: Resources are provided for starting a new business venture for under $500 as well as fifteen different suggestions for different kinds of businesses that can be created with minimal expense.

30229 ■ *"Taking a Chance" in Baltimore Business Journal (Vol. 28, July 16, 2010, No. 10, pp. 1)*
Pub: Baltimore Business Journal
Ed: Scott Dance. **Description:** North Avenue in Baltimore, Maryland is considered a rough neighborhood due to the dangers of prostitution and drug dealing. However, some entrepreneurs have taken the risk of building their businesses on North Avenue as revitalization efforts grow. One of the challenges for businesses in rough neighborhoods is bringing customers to their stores or offices.

30230 ■ *"Taking the Right Road" in Entrepreneur (Vol. 37, October 2009, No. 10, pp. 104)*
Pub: Entrepreneur Media, Inc.
Ed: Jason Daley. **Description:** Joe Grubb's franchise of BrightStar Healthcare, a home health care provider, in Knoxville, Tennessee has grown into a $1 million business. Grubb, a former sales agent, experienced slow growth for his franchise and had to deal with cash flow issues during its first few months.

30231 ■ *"Taking on the World" in Canadian Business (Vol. 79, November 20, 2006, No. 23, pp. 43)*
Pub: Rogers Media
Description: The rankings of the top Canadian business executives are presented.

30232 ■ *"A Tale of Two Brothers" in Canadian Business (Vol. 80, March 26, 2007, No. 7, pp. 18)*
Pub: Rogers Media
Description: The successful business strategies followed by Tyler Gompf and Kirby Gompf, owners of Tell Us About Us Inc., are presented.

30233 ■ *The Talent Masters: Why Smart Leaders Put People Before Numbers*
Pub: Crown Business Books
Ed: Bill Conaty, Ram Charan. **Released:** November 9, 2010. **Price:** $27.50. **Description:** This book helps leaders recognize talent in their employees, and to put that talent to work to help achieve business success.

30234 ■ *"Tao of Downfall" in International Journal of Entrepreneurship and Small Business (Vol. 11, August 31, 2010, No. 2, pp. 121)*
Pub: Publishers Communication Group
Ed: Wenxian Zhang, Ilan Alon. **Description:** Through historical reviews and case studies, this research seeks to understand why some initially successful

entrepreneurs failed in the economic boom of past decades. Among various factors contributing to their downfall are a unique political and business environment, fragile financial systems, traditional cultural influences and personal characteristics.

30235 ■ *"Tap Into Food Truck Trend to Rev Up Sales, Build Buzz" in Nation's Restaurant News (Vol. 45, February 7, 2011, No. 3, pp. 18)*
Pub: Penton Media, Inc.
Ed: Brian Sacks. **Description:** Food truck trend is growing, particularly in New York City, Philadelphia, Washington DC, and Los Angeles, California. Man entrepreneurs are using a mobile food component to market their food before opening a restaurant.

30236 ■ *"The Tapestry of Life" in Women In Business (Vol. 61, December 2009, No. 6, pp. 8)*
Pub: American Business Women's Association
Ed: Kathleen Leighton. **Description:** Suzanne Fanch, co-owner of the Devil's Thumb Ranch, discusses the family and career-related influences that helped her to achieve success as a small business proprietor. She advises that opportunities should be treated as building blocks towards success. Fanch's involvement in advocacies that take care of the welfare of community, children, and environment is also discussed.

30237 ■ *"Tastee-Freez Celebrates 60th Anniversary" in Ice Cream Reporter (Vol. 23, July 20, 2010, No. 8, pp. 2)*
Pub: Ice Cream Reporter
Description: Tastee-Freez founders, Leo Moranz (inventor) and Harry Axene, an inventor partnered to market the soft-serve pump and freezer for serving frozen treats back in 1950.

30238 ■ *"The Tea Bag Test" in Canadian Business (Vol. 79, October 23, 2006, No. 21, pp. 83)*
Pub: Rogers Media
Ed: Clive Mather. **Description:** Tips for business executives, on how to manage leadership skills to attain optimal business growth, are presented.

30239 ■ *"Tech Giving 2.0" in Boston Business Journal (Vol. 31, August 5, 2011, No. 28, pp. 1)*
Pub: Boston Business Journal
Ed: Mary Moore. **Description:** Entrepreneurs and venture capitalists in Boston have launched Technology Underwriting Greater Good, the tech industry's answer to the criticism that they are not charitable. The foundation finances nonprofits that aid young people through entrepreneurship, education and life experience. Other tech firms in Boston doing charitable works are discussed.

30240 ■ *"TechLift Strives to Fill in Gaps in Entrepreneurial Support Efforts" in Crain's Cleveland Business (November 12, 2007)*
Pub: Crain Communications, Inc.
Ed: Marsha Powers. **Description:** Profile of the program, TechLift, a new business model launched by NorTech, that is aiming to provide assistance to technology-based companies that may not be a good fit for other entrepreneurial support venues.

30241 ■ *Technological Entrepreneurship*
Pub: Edward Elgar Publishing, Incorporated
Ed: Donald Siegel. **Released:** October 2006. **Price:** $230.00. **Description:** Technological entrepreneurship at universities is discussed. The book covers four related topics: university licensing and patenting; science parks and incubators; university-based startups; and the role of academic science in entrepreneurship.

30242 ■ *"Ted Stahl: Executive Chairman" in Inside Business (Vol. 13, September-October 2011, No. 5, pp. NC6)*
Pub: Great Lakes Publishing Co.
Ed: Miranda S. Miller. **Description:** Profile of Ted Stahl, who started working in his family's business when he was ten years old is presented. The firm makes dies for numbers and letters used on team uniforms. Another of the family firms manufactures stock and custom heat-printing products, equipment

and supplies. It also educates customers on ways to decorate garments with heat printing products and offers graphics and software for customers to create their own artwork.

30243 ■ *"Teeling and Gallagher: A Textbook for Success" in Agency Sales Magazine (Vol. 39, September-October 2009, No. 9, pp. 20)*
Pub: MANA
Ed: Jack Foster. **Description:** Profile of Teeling & Gallagher, a manufacturing firm that was founded in 1946 as the D.G. Teeling Company and continued as a one-person agency until 1960 when Tom Gallagher joined the company. Tom Gallagher talks about how things have changed and his work with his son Bob in the agency.

30244 ■ *The Ten Faces of Innovation*
Pub: Doubleday Broadway Publishing Group
Ed: Tom Kelley. **Price:** $29.95.

30245 ■ *The Ten Laws of Enduring Success*
Pub: Crown Business Books
Ed: Maria Bartiromo, Catherine Whitney. **Released:** March 1, 2011. **Price:** $15.00. **Description:** A new meaning for success is described by financial expert, Maria Bartiromo, with advice on how to adapt with the changing times.

30246 ■ *"The Ten Worst Leadership Habits" in Canadian Business (Vol. 81, March 31, 2008, No. 5, pp. 63)*
Pub: Rogers Media
Ed: Michael Stern. **Description:** Ten leadership behaviors that aspiring leaders need to avoid are presented. These include expecting colleagues and subordinates to be like themselves, attending too many meetings, being miserly when it comes to recognition and praise, and giving an opinion often.

30247 ■ *"Tenacious Trailblazer" in Hispanic Business (Vol. 30, April 2008, No. 4, pp. 26)*
Pub: Hispanic Business
Ed: Melinda Burns. **Description:** Dr. Sandra Hernandez has been named as Hispanic Business Woman of the Year for her pioneering work in health care reform. Dr. Hernandez is the first Hispanic and the first woman to serve as public health director for the city and county of San Francisco.

30248 ■ *They Made America*
Pub: Little Brown Company/Time Warner Book Group
Ed: Harold Evans, Gail Buckland, David Lefer. **Released:** 2006. **Price:** $18.95. **Description:** Coffee table book highlighting entrepreneurship; this book is filled with interesting illustrated portraits of entrepreneurs and innovators like Thomas Edison, George Doriot (a venture capital pioneer), and Ida Rosenthal (inventor of the Maidenform bra).

30249 ■ *The Thin Book of Naming Elephants: How to Surface Undiscussables for Greater Organizational Success*
Pub: Thin Book Publishing Co.
Contact: Sue Annis Hammond, Owner
E-mail: sue@thinbook.com
Ed: Sue Annis Hammond; Andrea B. Mayfield. **Released:** January 2004. **Price:** $10.95. **Description:** Organizational success is of upmost importance to today's entrepreneurs and organizations. The hierarchal system in which people are afraid to speak up in organizations is discussed. The points of view and inability to see things from an overall perspective can cause insecurity among employees. The three elephants present in every organization include: arrogance, hubris, and screamers and the damage caused by these elephants in any organization is examined.

30250 ■ *"Think Again: What Makes a Leader?" in Business Strategy Review (Vol. 21, Autumn 2010, No. 3, pp. 64)*
Pub: Wiley-Blackwell
Ed: Rob Goffee, Gareth Jones. **Description:** Leadership cannot be faked and all the self-help books in the world won't make you a leader - but there are four characteristics any leader must possess and they are outlined.

30251 ■ *Think Big and Kick Ass in Business and Life*
Pub: HarperBusiness
Ed: Donald J. Trump; Bill Zanker. **Price:** $26.95.
Description: The philosophy of thinking big and acting aggressively on the path to prosperity is examined.

30252 ■ *"The Thinker" in Canadian Business (Vol. 81, March 31, 2008, No. 5, pp. 52)*
Pub: Rogers Media
Ed: Andrew Wahl. **Description:** Mihnea Moldoveanu provides much of the academic rigor that underpins Roger Martin's theories on how to improve the way business leaders think. Moldoveanu is also a classically trained pianist and founder of Redline Communications and has a mechanical engineering degree from MIT on top of his astounding knowledge on many academic fields.

30253 ■ *"This CEO's Mom Taught Him Everything He Needs to Know" in Globe & Mail (February 19, 2007, pp. B9)*
Pub: CTVglobemedia Publishing Inc.
Ed: Gordon Pitts. **Description:** Interview with Paul House, chairman and chief executive officer of Tim Hortons Inc., who shares a few things about his entrepreneurial life and career.

30254 ■ *"Thomas D'Aquino" in Canadian Business (Vol. 80, November 19, 2007, No. 23, pp. 92)*
Pub: Rogers Media
Ed: Calvin Leung. **Description:** Thomas D'Aquino is the CEO and president of the Canadian Council of Chief Executives since 1981. D'Aquino thinks he has the best job in Canada because he can change the way policies are made and the way people think. Details of his career as a lawyer and CEO and his views on Canada's economy are provided.

30255 ■ *"Thomas Morley; President, The Lube Stop Inc., 37" in Crain's Cleveland Business (Vol. 28, November 19, 2007, No. 46, pp. F-12)*
Pub: Crain Communications, Inc.
Ed: David Bennett. **Description:** Profile of Thomas Morley, president of The Lube Stop Inc., who is dedicated to promoting the company's strong environmental record as an effective way to differentiate Lube Stop from its competition. Since Mr. Morley came to the company in 2004, Lube Stop has increased sales by 10 percent and has boosted its operating profits by 30 percent.

30256 ■ *Three Moves Ahead*
Pub: John Wiley and Sons, Inc.
Ed: Bob Rice. **Released:** March 30, 2008. **Price:** $24.95. **Description:** Things the game of chess can teach about business are explored.

30257 ■ *"Three Weeks To Startup" in Entrepreneur (December 19, 2008)*
Pub: Entrepreneur Media Inc.
Ed: Tim Berry; Sabrina Parsons. **Description:** Breakdown for realistically starting a business in three weeks is provided in detail.

30258 ■ *"Tim Armstrong" in Canadian Business (Vol. 81, July 21, 2008, No. 11, pp. 10)*
Pub: Rogers Media Ltd.
Ed: Calvin Leung. **Description:** Interview with Tim Armstrong who is the president of advertising and commerce department of Google Inc. for North America; the information technology company executive talked about the emerging trends and changes to YouTube made by the company since its acquisition in 2006.

30259 ■ *"Times are Tough, I Figure I'm Tougher" in Inc. (Vol. 33, September 2011, No. 7, pp. 92)*
Pub: Inc. Magazine
Ed: April Joyner. **Description:** Profile of Frank Campanaro and his company, Trillacorpe Construction located in Bingham Farms, Michigan. Campanaro has partnered with other companies that have bonding in reserve and lets them take the lion's share.

30260 ■ *"Tips From a Turnaround Expert" in Business Owner (Vol. 35, July-August 2011, No. 4, pp. 8)*
Pub: DL Perkins Company
Description: The book, 'The Six Month Fix: Adventures in Rescuing Failing Companies' by Gary Sutton is summarized. It provides lessons for finding and building profits in failing firms.

30261 ■ *"To Build for the Future, Reach Beyond the Skies" in Canadian Business (Vol. 83, June 15, 2010, No. 10, pp. 11)*
Pub: Rogers Media Ltd.
Ed: Richard Branson. **Description:** Richard Branson says that tackling an engineering challenge or a scientific venture is a real adventure for an entrepreneur. Branson discusses Virgin's foray into the aviation business and states that at Virgin, they build for the future.

30262 ■ *"To Live and Thrive in L.A." in Canadian Business (Vol. 81, October 13, 2008, No. 17, pp. 78)*
Pub: Rogers Media Ltd.
Ed: Rachel Pulfer. **Description:** Toronto entrepreneur Shereen Arazm thrived in Los Angeles, California as the queen of nightlife. Arazm holds or has held ownership stakes in bars, nightspots and restaurants that include the Geisha House, Concorde, Shag, Parc and Central, and Terroni L.A.

30263 ■ *"Tom Gaglardi" in Canadian Business (Vol. 82, April 27, 2009, No. 7, pp. 56)*
Pub: Rogers Media
Ed: Calvin Leung. **Description:** Northland Properties Corporation president Tom Gaglardi believes that their business model of keeping much of operations in-house allows the firm to crate assets at a lesser price while commanding higher margins than their competitors. He believes that it is an ideal time to invest in the hospitality industry because of opportunities to purchase properties at low prices.

30264 ■ *"Tony Hawk Carves a New Niche" in Entrepreneur (Vol. 37, October 2009, No. 10, pp. 26)*
Pub: Entrepreneur Media, Inc.
Ed: Gary Cohn. **Description:** Professional skateboarder Tony Hawk discusses the growth of Birdhouse, the skateboard company he founded. He is excited about the release of Tony Hawk Ride, a videogame with a skateboard controller.

30265 ■ *"Too Much Information?" in Black Enterprise (Vol. 37, December 2006, No. 5, pp. 59)*
Pub: Earl G. Graves Publishing Co. Inc.
Ed: James C. Johnson. **Description:** African American business owners often face the dilemma of whether or not to divulge their minority status when soliciting new customers and financial institutions. The quality of the products or services is always the key factor and race should never define one's business; however, it is appropriate to market oneself as a minority or women-owned business, especially if the company is in an industry where those clients are offered top-tier contracts.

30266 ■ *"Top Marks" in Canadian Business (Vol. 79, October 23, 2006, No. 21, pp. 143)*
Pub: Rogers Media
Ed: Erin Pooley; Laura Bogomolny. **Description:** Profiles of some top grade master of business administration students like Hogan Mullally and Will mercer, belonging to reputed business schools, are presented.

30267 ■ *Tough Choices: A Memoir*
Pub: Penguin Group
Ed: Carly Florina. **Released:** October 2006. **Price:** $24.95. **Description:** Former woman CEO at Hewlett-Packard is profiled.

30268 ■ *"Tough Times for the Irving Clan" in Canadian Business (Vol. 83, August 17, 2010, No. 13-14, pp. 14)*
Pub: Rogers Media Ltd.
Ed: Dean Jobb. **Description:** The death of John E. Irving and reported health problems of his nephew Kenneth Irving was a double blow to the billionaire

Irving clan. Kenneth suddenly left his job as CEO of Fort Reliance, holding company for Irving Oil and new energy ventures, wherein the explanation was for personal reasons.

30269 ■ *The Towering World of Jimmy Choo: A Story of Power, Profits, and the Pursuit of the Perfect Shoe*
Pub: Bloomsbury USA
Ed: Lauren Goldstein Crowe, Sagra Maceira de Rosen. **Released:** 2009. **Description:** Profile of Jimmy Choo and his pursuit to manufacture the perfect shoe.

30270 ■ *"Transcendent Leadership" in Business Horizons (Vol. 51, March-April 2008, No. 2, pp. 131)*
Pub: Elsevier Advanced Technology Publications
Ed: Mary Crossan, Daina Mazutis. **Description:** Transcendent leadership is framework integrating the leadership of self, others, and organizations. Much of the discourse regarding leadership has focused on leadership of others and the organization, while leadership of self is rarely tackled. Successful leaders are able to integrate these three levels of leadership.

30271 ■ *"Transform Your Life" in Black Enterprise (Vol. 37, January 2007, No. 6, pp. 14)*
Pub: Earl G. Graves Publishing Co. Inc.
Description: Through the magazine, television and radio programs, events, and the website, the various platforms of Black Enterprise will provide the tools necessary to achieve success in business ventures, career aspirations, and personal goals.

30272 ■ *"Transportation Enterprise" in Advertising Age (Vol. 79, June 9, 2008, No. 23, pp. S10)*
Pub: Crain Communications, Inc.
Ed: Jean Halliday. **Description:** Overview of Enterprise rent-a-car's plan to become a more environmentally-friendly company. The family-owned business has spent $1 million a year to plant trees since 2006 and has added more fuel-efficient cars, hybrids and flex-fuel models.

30273 ■ *True to Yourself: Leading a Values-Based Business*
Pub: Berrett-Koehler Publishers, Incorporated
Ed: Mark S. Albion. **Released:** June 2006. **Price:** $14.95. **Description:** Pressures faced by entrepreneurs running small companies are discussed. Advice is offered to help grow and maintain a profitable business.

30274 ■ *The Trump Card: Playing to Win in Work and Life*
Pub: Touchstone/Simon & Schuster Inc.
Ed: Ivanka Trump. **Released:** October 12, 2009. **Price:** $24.99. **Description:** Profile of Ivanka Trump, the daughter of Donald and Ivana Trump; she shares the life lessons and hard-won insights that have made her successful in the business world.

30275 ■ *Trump University Entrepreneurship 101*
Pub: John Wiley and Sons, Inc.
Ed: Mike Gordon. **Released:** January 2007. **Price:** $21.95. **Description:** Entrepreneurs, past, present or future, will find this book helpful. The book covers three objectives: to energize readers to be courageous when taking steps toward an entrepreneurial goal, works to demystify the entrepreneurial process, and to help individuals improve success.

30276 ■ *"Truthfully Speaking" in Entrepreneur (Vol. 35, November 2007, No. 11, pp. 118)*
Pub: Entrepreneur Media Inc.
Ed: Amanda C. Kooser. **Description:** Internet startup guru Guy Kawasaki talks about his new Web venture Truemors and shares tips on creating a successful Web-based company.

30277 ■ *"Turning Bright Ideas Into Profitable Businesses" in Inside Business (Vol. 13, September-October 2011, No. 5, pp. SS6)*
Pub: Great Lakes Publishing Co.
Ed: Susan Keen Flynn. **Description:** Startup Lakewood was launched by Mickie Rinehart. She provides free resources to entrepreneurs in the city in order to help them turn their small business vision into reality.

30278 ■ *"Twenty Years of Advocacy and Education" in Women Entrepreneur (January 18, 2009)*
Pub: Entrepreneur Media Inc.
Ed: Eve Gumpel. **Description:** Profile of Sharon Hadary who served as executive director of the Center for Women's Business Research•for two decades; Hadary discusses what she has learned about women business owners, their impact on the economy and what successful business owners share in common.

30279 ■ *"Two of a Kind" in Entrepreneur (Vol. 35, November 2007, No. 11, pp. 103)*
Pub: Entrepreneur Media Inc.
Ed: Chris Penttila. **Description:** Entrepreneurs need support and advice once in a while as pressure from work gets to them. It is good to have people from the same industry to give advice on particular topics when needed.

30280 ■ *Ubuntu!: An Aspiring Story About an African Tradition of Teamwork and Collaboration*
Pub: Broadway Books
Contact: David Drake, Manager
E-mail: ddrake@randomhouse.com
Ed: Bob Nelson, Stephen Lundin. **Released:** March 30, 2010. **Price:** $19.99. **Description:** The African tradition of teamwork and collaboration is used to demonstrate these skills to small business leaders.

30281 ■ *"The Ultimate Business Tune-Up: For Times Like These" in Inc. (Vol. 31, January-February 2009, No. 1, pp. 70)*
Pub: Mansueto Ventures LLC
Description: Twenty-three things do energize a small business in tough economic times are outlined with insight from successful entrepreneurs.

30282 ■ *The Ultimate Competitive Advantage*
Pub: Berrett-Koehler Publishers
Ed: Donald Mitchell; Carol Coles; B. Thomas Golisano. **Released:** March 12, 2003. **Price:** $36.95. **Description:** Results of a ten year study of companies that experienced fast growth over a three year period shows that while unsuccessful companies apply outdated business models, the successful ones improve their business models every two to four years.

30283 ■ *Ultimate Small Business Advisor*
Pub: Entrepreneur Press
Ed: Andi Axman. **Released:** May 2007. **Price:** $30.95. **Description:** Tip for starting and running a small business, including new tax rulings and laws affecting small business, are shared.

30284 ■ *Understanding Small Business*
Pub: Tate Publishing and Enterprises, LLC
Ed: Edward McMahon. **Released:** May 2006. **Price:** $20.95. **Description:** Three step process to help an entrepreneur build a basic business plan and an effective cash flow statement to minimize risk.

30285 ■ *"U.S. Attorney Post the Latest Twist" in The Business Journal-Serving Greater Tampa Bay (Vol. 28, July 25, 2008, No. 31, pp. 1)*
Pub: American City Business Journals, Inc.
Ed: Jane Meinhardt. **Description:** Tampa, Florida-based lawyer A. Brian Albritton has been nominated to be the U.S. Attorney for the Middle District of Florida. He is an expert in cases involving white-collar crime, secret theft, noncompete agreements, and other agreements.

30286 ■ *"Up To Code? Website Eases Compliance Burden for Entrepreneurs" in Black Enterprise (Vol. 38, March 2008, No. 8, pp. 48)*
Pub: Earl G. Graves Publishing Co. Inc.

Ed: Robin White-Goode. **Description:** Business.gov is a presidential E-government project created to help small businesses easily find, understand, and comply with laws and regulations pertaining to a particular industry.

30287 ■ *Use What You've Got*
Pub: Portfolio Publishing

Ed: Barbara Corcoran, Bruce Littlefield. **Released:** 2003. **Price:** $24.95. **Description:** Founder and chairman of New York's premier real estate company, the Corcoran Group, shares her successes in the real estate industry. The book offers tips and pointers to salespeople, entrepreneurs and business people alike. Corcoran explains how she went from waiting tables and borrowed $1,000 from a boyfriend to build her real estate company into the industry's powerhouse.

30288 ■ *"Used to Being Courted" in Business Courier (Vol. 24, March 14, 2008, No. 49, pp. 1)*
Pub: American City Business Journals, Inc.

Ed: Dan Monk. **Description:** College basketball coach Sean Miller is reported to be earning up to $900,000 a year. A look into the contract at regional universities show Thad Matta makes over $2 million in a year and that UK's Billy Gillispie makes over $2.7 million.

30289 ■ *"Valuation: Confusing and Misunderstood" in Business Owner (Vol. 35, July-August 2011, No. 4, pp. 10)*
Pub: DL Perkins Company

Description: Business valuation is explained to help small business owners realize the value of their company.

30290 ■ *Values-Centered Entrepreneurship*
Pub: Routledge

Ed: David Y. Choi, Edmund Gray. **Released:** August 10, 2010. **Price:** $39.95. **Description:** A new brand of entrepreneurs has arrived on the business scene, carrying with them a new set of values. They possess a sense of social responsibility, the need to protect the planet, and to do the right thing for all stakeholders.

30291 ■ *Values and Opportunities in Social Entrepreneurship*
Pub: Palgrave Macmillan

Ed: Kai Hockerts. **Released:** November 1, 2009. **Price:** $90.00. **Description:** Social entrepreneurship has grown as a research field. This book discusses social entrepreneurship as well as the identification and exploitation of social venturing opportunities.

30292 ■ *The Venture Cafe*
Pub: Business Plus

Ed: Teresa Esser. **Released:** 2002. **Description:** Research covering the types of entrepreneurs who build new, high-technology ventures from the ground up. Author interviewed over 150 high-tech professionals in order to gather information to help others start high-tech companies.

30293 ■ *"Victoria Colligan; Co-Founder, Ladies Who Launch Inc., 38" in Crain's Cleveland Business (Vol. 28, November 19, 2007, No. 46)*
Pub: Crain Communications, Inc.

Ed: Jay Miller. **Description:** Profile of Victoria Colligan who is the co-founder of Ladies Who Launch Inc., an organization with franchises in nearly 50 cities; the company offers women entrepreneurs workshops and a newsletter to help women balance their businesses with other aspects of their lives. Ms. Colligan found that women were learning about being business owners differently than men and she felt that there was a need to create opportunities for networking for women launching businesses that had more of a lifestyle purpose.

30294 ■ *Wake Up and Smell the Zeitgeist*
Pub: Basic Books

Ed: Grand McCracken. **Released:** 2010. **Price:** $26.95. **Description:** Insight is given into an element of corporate success that's often overlooked and valuable suggestions are offered for any small business to pursue.

30295 ■ *The Wall Street Journal. Complete Small Business Guidebook*
Pub: Three Rivers Press

Ed: Colleen DeBaise. **Released:** December 29, 2009. **Price:** $15.00. **Description:** The mechanics of building, running and growing a profitable business are outlined, teaching how to write a business plan, ways to finding money during lean years, how to keep stress in check, time management, investment in technology, hiring, marketing, management basics, angel investing and venture capital, as well as an exit strategy.

30296 ■ *"Watchful Eye: Entrepreneur Protects Clients and His Bottom Line" in Black Enterprise (Vol. 38, March 2008, No. 8, pp. 46)*
Pub: Earl G. Graves Publishing Co. Inc.

Ed: Tennille M. Robinson. **Description:** Profile of Elijah Shaw, founder of Icon Services Corporation, a full service security and investigative service; Shaw shares his plans to protect clients while growing his business.

30297 ■ *"Wattles Plugs Back Into State" in Business Journal Portland (Vol. 27, November 19, 2010, No. 38, pp. 1)*
Pub: Portland Business Journal

Ed: Wendy Culverwell. **Description:** Denver, Colorado-based Ultimate Electronics Inc.'s first store in Oregon was opened in Portland and the 46th store in the chain of electronic superstores is expected to employ 70-80 workers. The venture is the latest for Mark Wattles, one of Oregon's most successful entrepreneurs, who acquired Ultimate from bankruptcy.

30298 ■ *We Are Smarter Than Me: How to Unleash the Power of Crowds in Your Business*
Pub: Wharton School Publishing

Ed: Barry Libert; Jon Spector; Don Tapscott. **Released:** October 5, 2007. **Price:** $21.99. **Description:** Ways to use social networking and community in order to make decisions and plan your business, with a focus on product development, manufacturing, marketing, customer service, finance, management, and more.

30299 ■ *"Wealth and Jobs: the Broken Link" in Harvard Business Review (Vol. 88, November 2010, No. 11, pp. 44)*
Pub: Harvard Business School Publishing

Ed: Nitin Nohria. **Description:** Rebuilding the link between business and job creation to shore up the middle class is advocated. A blend of government policies and business strategies that foster entrepreneurship and innovation are essential.

30300 ■ *Wealth Without a Job: The Entrepreneur's Guide to Freedom and Security Beyond the 9 to 5 Lifestyle*
Pub: John Wiley & Sons, Incorporated

Ed: Phil Laut; Andy Fuehl. **Released:** May 2006. **Price:** $16.95. **Description:** Strategies for successful business ownership and job security are explored.

30301 ■ *"Wear More Hats" in Canadian Business (Vol. 80, March 12, 2007, No. 6, pp. 39)*
Pub: Rogers Media

Ed: Michael Stern. **Description:** The need on the part of managers to volunteer to accept more responsibilities for their growth as well as that of company's is discussed.

30302 ■ *The Weather Channel*
Pub: Harvard Business School Press

Ed: Frank Batten with Jeffrey L. Cruikshank. **Released:** 2002. **Price:** $29.95. **Description:** Frank Batten illustrates the power of a resourceful growth strategy along with details the journey he successfully took his small, private newspaper into the cable industry.

30303 ■ *A Weekend with Warren Buffett: And Other Shareholder Meeting Adventures*
Pub: Basic Books/Perseus Books Group

Ed: Randy Cepuch. **Released:** February 23, 2007. **Price:** $23.95. **Description:** Financial writer and personal investor relates his experiences attending various shareholder meetings, reviewing each meeting and grading its educational value. The book is essential for those hoping to learn more about the way companies invest and do business.

30304 ■ *"The Weeks Ahead" in Crain's New York Business (Vol. 24, January 7, 2008, No. 1, pp. 26)*
Pub: Crain Communications, Inc.

Description: Listing of events in the Detroit area include conferences addressing entrepreneurialism, economic development, and women business ownership.

30305 ■ *"The Weeks Ahead" in Crain's New York Business (Vol. 24, January 14, 2008, No. 2, pp. 20)*
Pub: Crain Communications, Inc.

Description: Listing of events in the Detroit area include conferences addressing entrepreneurialism, economic development, and women business ownership.

30306 ■ *"Welcome to a New Kind of Cubicle Culture" in Boston Business Journal (Vol. 29, August 19, 2011, No. 15, pp. 1)*
Pub: American City Business Journals Inc.

Ed: Alexander Jackson. **Description:** Beehive Baltimore offers a co-working space where independent freelancers and entrepreneurs can work. There are two other companies that provide the same service and the value of these services to these professional is that it provides them with an office that is both convenient and affordable aside from letting them network with peers.

30307 ■ *The Well-Timed Strategy: Managing Business Cycle for Competitive Advantage*
Pub: Wharton School Publishing

Ed: Peter Navarro. **Released:** January 23, 2006. **Price:** $34.99. **Description:** An overview of business cycles and risks is presented. Recession is a good time to find key personnel for a small business. Other issues addressed include investment, production, and marketing in order to maintain a competitive edge.

30308 ■ *"Wendy Turner; Vice-President and General Manager, Vocalo.org" in Crain's Chicago Business (Vol. 31, May 5, 2008, No. 18, pp. 22)*
Pub: Crain Communications, Inc.

Ed: Kevin McKeough. **Description:** Profile of Wendy Turner who is a leader at Vocalo, a combination of talk radio and Web site, where listeners can set up profile pages similar to those on Facebook.

30309 ■ *A Whack on the Side of the Head*
Pub: Business Plus

Ed: Roger von Oech. **Released:** May 2008. **Price:** $16.99. **Description:** The author, a consultant, shares insight into increasing entrepreneurial creativity.

30310 ■ *"Wham-O's Wisdom" in Playthings (Vol. 107, January 1, 2009, No. 1, pp. 13)*
Pub: Reed Business Information
Contact: Jeff Greisch, President

Ed: Tim Walsh. **Description:** Toy historian Tim Walsh discusses the history of the toy industry and shares secrets to his success. Walsh is the creator of toys and board games.

30311 ■ *"What Are You Afraid Of?" in Entrepreneur (Vol. 37, July 2009, No. 7, pp. 79)*
Pub: Entrepreneur Media, Inc.

Ed: Lindsay Holloway. **Description:** According to a survey of entrepreneurs in the US, failure, economic uncertainty, not having enough personal time, being their own boss, and staying afloat are the biggest fears when starting a business. Advice on how to deal with these fears is also given.

30312 ■ *"What CEOs Will Admit Out of the Office"* in Inc. (November 2007, pp. 30)
Pub: Gruner & Jahr USA Publishing
Ed: Sarah Goldstein. **Description:** Thirty CEOs from the fastest growing companies in the U.S. answer questions about their firms.

30313 ■ *"What Dead Zone?"* in Entrepreneur (Vol. 37, October 2009, No. 10, pp. 128)
Pub: Entrepreneur Media, Inc.
Ed: Jason Daley. **Description:** Joe Purifico, Halloween Adventure franchises co-owner and chief executive officer, discusses the Halloween superstore phenomenon. Malls allow seasonal leasing for Halloween stores due to the high number of customers these stores attract.

30314 ■ *What Got You Here Won't Get You There*
Pub: Hyperion Books
Ed: Marshall Goldsmith; Mark Reiter. **Released:** January 9, 2007. **Price:** $24.95. **Description:** Executive coach teaches how to climb the ladder to upper levels of management.

30315 ■ *What Losing Taught Me about Winning: The Ultimate Guide for Success in Small and Home-Based Business*
Pub: Fireside Publishing
Ed: Fran Tarkenton; Wes Smith. **Released:** April 7, 1999. **Price:** $17.95. **Description:** Provides insight into running a successful small business.

30316 ■ *What Men Don't Tell Woman about Business: Opening Up the Heavily Guarded Alpha Male Playbook*
Pub: John Wiley and Sons, Inc.
Ed: Christopher V. Fleet. **Released:** October 26, 2007. **Description:** Valuable guide for any woman in business, this book helps reveal everything a woman needs to know in order to understand, communicate, and compete with men in business.

30317 ■ *What Self-Made Millionaires Really Think, Know and Do: A Straight-Talking Guide to Business Success and Personal Riches*
Pub: John Wiley & Sons, Incorporated
Ed: Richard Dobbins; Barrie Pettman. **Released:** September 2006. **Price:** $24.95. **Description:** Guide for understanding the concepts of entrepreneurial success; the book offers insight into bringing an idea into reality, marketing, time management, leadership skills, and setting clear goals.

30318 ■ *What Works: Success in Stressful Times*
Pub: Harper Press
Ed: Hamish McRae. **Released:** January 21, 2010. **Price:** $30.12. **Description:** Exploration of success stories from across the glove, and what Michelle Obama referred to as 'the flimsy difference between success and failure.' Why do some initiatives take off while others flounder? How have communities managed to achieve so much while others struggle? What distinguishes the good companies from the bad? What lessons can be learned from the well-ordered Mumbai community made famous by 'Slumdog Millionaire'? Why have Canadian manners helped Whistler become the most popular ski resort in North America?.

30319 ■ *When Growth Stalls: How It Happens, Why You're Stuck, and what To Do About It*
Pub: John Wiley & Sons, Inc.
Ed: Steve McKee. **Released:** March 1, 2009. **Price:** $27.95. **Description:** Marketing expert presents evidence that demonstrates that slow growth experienced by a firm is usually not the cause of mismanagement or blundering, but by natural market forces and destructive internal dynamics that are often unrecognized.

30320 ■ *"Where Are They Now?"* in Canadian Business (Vol. 79, October 9, 2006, No. 20, pp. 71)
Pub: Rogers Media
Description: The profile of the top chief executive officers of Canada for the year 2005 is discussed.

30321 ■ *"Where to be an Entrepreneur: Ten Startup-Friendly Cities"* in Entrepreneur (Vol. 37, August 2009, No. 8, pp. 49)
Pub: Entrepreneur Media, Inc.
Ed: Jason Daley. **Description:** Ten U.S. cities that embody the entrepreneurial spirit are presented. These cities are ideal for startup companies and profiles of businesses that are making it in these cities are discussed.

30322 ■ *Where Have All the Leaders Gone?*
Pub: Scribner Educational Publishers
Contact: Jack Romanos, President
Ed: Lee Iacocca. **Released:** April 2007. **Description:** Lee Iacocca discusses the principles of great leadership.

30323 ■ *"A Whiff of TV Reality"* in Houston Business Journal (Vol. 40, January 22, 2010, No. 37, pp. A1)
Pub: American City Business Journals
Ed: Christine Hall. **Description:** Houston, Texas-based Waste Management Inc.'s president and chief operation officer, Larry O'Donnell shares some of his experience as CBS Television Network reality show 'Undercover Boss' participant. O'Donnell believes the show was a great way to show the customers how tough their jobs are and reveals that the most difficult job was being a sorter at the recycling center.

30324 ■ *Who's Got Your Back*
Pub: Broadway Books, a Division of Random House
Ed: Keith Ferrazzi. **Price:** $25.00. **Description:** Achieving goals by building close relationships with a small circle of trusted individuals.

30325 ■ *"Why Entrepreneurs Matter More Than Innovators"* in Gallup Management Journal (November 22, 2011)
Pub: Gallup
Ed: Jim Clifton. **Description:** In the race to create good jobs, leaders are not paying enough attention to cultivating talented entrepreneurs, rather they invest too much attention on innovation.

30326 ■ *"Why Is It So Hard To Find Good People? The Problem Might Be You"* in Inc. (Vol. 33, November 2011, No. 9, pp. 100)
Pub: Inc. Magazine
Ed: April Joyner. **Description:** Entrepreneurs sometimes struggle to find good workers. A recent survey shows hiring as their top concern. Four common mistakes that can occur during the hiring process our outlined.

30327 ■ *Why We Want You to be Rich: Two Men - One Message*
Pub: Rich Publishing LLC
Ed: Donald J. Trump; Robert T. Kiyosaki; Meredith McIver; Sharon Lechter. **Released:** October 9, 2006. **Price:** $24.95. **Description:** Authors explain why some people get rich while others don't.

30328 ■ *"William Barr III; President, Co-Founder, Universal Windows Direct, 33"* in Crain's Cleveland Business (November 19, 2007)
Pub: Crain Communications, Inc.
Ed: David Bennett. **Description:** Profile of William Barr III, the president and co-founder of Universal Windows Direct, a manufacturer of vinyl windows and siding, whose successful salesmanship and leadership has propelled his company forward.

30329 ■ *Winner Takes All: Steve Wynn, Kirk Kerkorian, Gary Loveman, and the Race to Own Vegas*
Pub: Hyperion
Ed: Christina Binkley. **Released:** 2009. **Price:** $25. 95. **Description:** The story of three men, Steve Wynn, Kirk Kerkorian, and Gary Loveman, each with different backgrounds are reinventing Las Vegas.

30330 ■ *Winning!*
Pub: HarperCollins Publishers Inc.
Ed: Jack and Suzy Welch. **Price:** $27.95.

30331 ■ *"Wise Guy: Get In Good"* in Entrepreneur (Vol. 35, October 2007, No. 10, pp. 46)
Pub: Entrepreneur Media Inc.
Ed: Guy Kawasaki. **Description:** Good public relations are a requirement for business entrepreneurs, and it can be achieved through proper communication. Giving of and asking for favors are some of the ways to build relationships in the business world. Other tips on how to build good business relationships are provided.

30332 ■ *"Women as 21st Century Leaders"* in Women In Business (Vol. 63, Summer 2011, No. 2, pp. 26)
Pub: American Business Women's Association
Ed: Leigh Elmore. **Description:** American Business Women's Association and Park University have partnered to provide a leadership training program to attendees of the 2011 National Women's Leadership Conference. The courses will incorporate introduction to concepts, development of critical thinking skills and direct application through exercises. Comments from executives are also included.

30333 ■ *"Women: the Alpha Advantage"* in Entrepreneur (Vol. 36, February 2008, No. 2, pp. 34)
Pub: Entrepreneur Media Inc.
Ed: Aliza Sherman. **Description:** Women entrepreneurs are said to be mistaken with the belief that they need to display aggression and compete with other women to gain power. Workshops and books address this issue and discuss how women could be alpha entrepreneurs. Recommendations with regard to the topic are explored.

30334 ■ *Women Entrepreneurs*
Pub: Edward Elgar Publishing, Incorporated
Ed: Andrea Smith-Hunter. **Released:** October 2006. **Price:** $120.00. **Description:** Focus is on women entrepreneurs; information includes human capital, network structures and financial capital, with comparative analysis across racial lines.

30335 ■ *"Work Is An Action Word"* in Black Enterprise (Vol. 38, December 2007, No. 5, pp. 86)
Pub: Earl G. Graves Publishing Co. Inc.
Ed: Marcia Reed-Woodard. **Description:** Understanding your company's culture, knowing the importance of networking, and connecting with the right mentors to guide you are the ingredients required for any entrepreneur.

30336 ■ *"Work Naked"* in Canadian Business (Vol. 80, March 12, 2007, No. 6, pp. 33)
Pub: Rogers Media
Ed: Andrew Wahl. **Description:** The disadvantages of teleworking for both employees and the company, in view of lack of an office environment and self-discipline on the part of workers, are discussed.

30337 ■ *"Work Together"* in Entrepreneur (Vol. 35, November 2007, No. 11, pp. 34)
Pub: Entrepreneur Media Inc.
Ed: Aliza Sherman. **Description:** Marsha Firestone founded Women Presidents' Organization, creating small groups of women who head their own businesses. The idea was for each chapter of the organization to have businesswomen share experiences to help others learn from running their own business.

30338 ■ *"Working It Out! How a Young Executive Overcomes Obstacles on the Job"* in Black Enterprise (Vol. 37, January 2007, No. 6, pp. 55)
Pub: Earl G. Graves Publishing Co. Inc.
Ed: Laura Egodigwe. **Description:** Interview with Susan Chapman, Global Head of Operations for Citigroup Realty Services, in which she discusses issues such as the important skills necessary for overcoming obstacles in the workplace.

30339 ■ *Working for Yourself: Law and Taxes for Independent Contractors, Freelancers and*

Consultants
Pub: NOLO Publications
Ed: Stephen Fishman. **Released:** March 2008. **Price:** $39.99 paperback. **Description:** In-depth information is shared for contractors, freelancers and consultants involving business law and small business taxes.

30340 ■ "World's Best CEOs" in Barron's (Vol. 88, March 24, 2008, No. 12, pp. 33)
Pub: Dow Jones & Company, Inc.
Ed: Andrew Bary. **Description:** Listing of the 30 best chief executive officers worldwide which was compiled through interviews with investors and analysts, analysis of financial and stock market performance, and leadership and industry stature.

30341 ■ "The Worm Lady" in Hawaii Business (Vol. 53, October 2007, No. 4, pp. 57)
Pub: Hawaii Business Publishing
Ed: Jolyn Okimoto Rosa. **Description:** Mindy Jaffe, also known as the worm lady, founded the Waikiki Worm Company in 2004 and sells composting worms. The company, which received much attention from the media, has earned $54,000 in revenue in 2004, and $92,000 and $120,000 in 2005 and 2006, respectively. Jaffe's past ventures and the challenges she is facing with her new company are discussed.

30342 ■ "Worth His Salt" in Hawaii Business (Vol. 53, January 2008, No. 7, pp. 45)
Pub: Hawaii Business Publishing
Ed: Jolyn Okimoto Rosa. **Description:** Bryan Zada owns three PretzelMaker franchises, whose total loss amounted to $40,000 in 2003. Zada believes that listening to employees was one of the key steps in turning the business around. The efforts made to improve the franchises' products are also given.

30343 ■ "Wowing Her Customers" in Women In Business (Vol. 61, August-September 2009, No. 4, pp. 34)
Pub: American Business Women's Association
Ed: Kathleen Leighton. **Description:** Gail Worth, together with her brother, bought her parents' Harley-Davidson motorcycle dealership in Grandview, Missouri. She eventually had the dealership to herself when her brother broke out of the partnership. Gail says she is comfortable in a man's world kind of business and has expanded the business with a 10-acre site.

30344 ■ "Wrap It Up" in Entrepreneur (Vol. 36, April 2008, No. 4, pp. 84)
Pub: Entrepreneur Media, Inc.
Ed: Barry Farber. **Description:** Tips on how to manage and get through the closing of a business sale are presented. Focus on what solutions you can bring and not on emotional attachments that can show your eagerness for the sale. Having a track of positive accomplishments can also help.

30345 ■ Ya Gotta Wanna
Pub: Creative Book Publishers
Ed: Malcolm Paice. **Released:** July 2005. **Price:** $12.95. **Description:** Three phases of teamwork are outlined: identifying the people and creating the team, analyzing the components of the team, and implementing the project. The author compares a soccer team to a management team and that a successful soccer team has three main area attributes: a solid defense, a creative midfield, and a potent strike force.

30346 ■ "Yamana's Golden Boy" in Canadian Business (Vol. 80, November 19, 2007, No. 23, pp. 49)
Pub: Rogers Media
Ed: John Gray. **Description:** Profile of Peter Marrone, founder of the gold-producing company Yamana Gold Inc. in 2003. Yamana has grown since its 2003 launch, with $110 million reported earnings for the first three quarters in 2007. Marrone's career and how he built Yamana are discussed.

30347 ■ "You Can Rebuild It" in Entrepreneur (Vol. 37, July 2009, No. 7, pp. 28)
Pub: Entrepreneur Media, Inc.
Ed: Robert Kiyosaki. **Description:** Entrepreneurs, during tough times, should melt down old business strategies and start rebuilding the business. The business and its customers should be redefined in order to maximize marketing efforts and stay afloat when business slows down. Personal experiences in melting down a business and starting over are also given.

30348 ■ Young Bucks: How to Raise a Future Millionaire
Pub: Thomas Nelson Inc.
Ed: Troy Dunn. **Released:** November 2007. **Price:** $17.99. **Description:** Advice is given to parents to teach their children how to save money, invest wisely and even start their own business.

30349 ■ "Young Giants" in Canadian Business (Vol. 79, August 14, 2006, No. 16-17, pp. 47)
Pub: Rogers Media
Ed: Brad Purdy. **Description:** New generations of young chiefs of oil and gas companies in Canada, are featured.

30350 ■ "Young-Kee Kim; Deputy Director, Fermi National Accelerator Laboratory" in Crain's Chicago Business (Vol. 31, May 5, 2008, No. 18)
Pub: Crain Communications, Inc.
Ed: Phuong Ly. **Description:** Profile of Young-Kee Kim who is the deputy director of Fermilab, a physics lab where scientists study the smallest particles in the universe; Ms. Kim was a researcher at Fermilab before becoming deputy director two years ago; Fermilab is currently home to the most powerful particle accelerator in the world and is struggling to compete with other countries despite cuts in federal funding.

30351 ■ "Young Millionaires" in Entrepreneur (Vol. 35, October 2007, No. 10, pp. 76)
Pub: Entrepreneur Media Inc.
Ed: Jessica Chen, Lindsay Hollway, Amanda C. Kooser, Kim Orr, James Park, Nichole L. Torres, and Sarah Wilson. **Description:** Young successful entrepreneurs of 2007 were chosen to talk about their success story and their business strategies in the past and those for the future. Among those featured are Kelly Flatley, Brendan Synnott, Herman Flores, Myles Kovacs, Haythem Haddad, Jim Wetzel, Lance Lawson, Jacob DeHart, Jake Nickell, Tim Vanderhook, Chris Vanderhook, Russell Vanderhook, Megan Duckett, Brad Sugars, John Vechey, Brian Fiete, Jason Kapalka, Nathan Jones, Devon Rifkin, Ryan Black, Ed Nichols, Jeremy Black, Amy Smilovic, Bob Shallenberger, and John Cavanagh.

30352 ■ "Your Annual Business Tune-Up" in Business Week (December 28, 2006)
Pub: McGraw-Hill Companies
Ed: Karen E. Klein. **Description:** Interview with entrepreneurial expert, Ty Freyvogel, founder of EntrpreneursLab.com. Freyvogel gives tips on how a thorough review of existing systems, vendors, customers, and employees could help keep an entrepreneur's business not only safe but highly successful in the upcoming year.

30353 ■ Your Business, Your Future: How to Predict and Harness Growth
Pub: Allen and Unwin Pty., Limited
Ed: Linda Hailey. **Released:** January 2007. **Price:** $16.95. **Description:** Four distinct phases every small companies faces during growth are profiled.

30354 ■ "Your Turn in the Spotlight" in Inc. (Volume 32, December 2010, No. 10, pp. 57)
Pub: Inc. Magazine
Ed: John Brandon. **Description:** Examples of three video blogs created by entrepreneurs to promote their businesses and products are used to show successful strategies. Wine Library TV promotes a family's wine business; SHAMA.TV offers marketing tips and company news; and Will It Blend? promotes sales of a household blender.

TRADE PERIODICALS

30355 ■ The Small Business Advisor
Pub: Small Business Advisors Inc.
Contact: Joseph Gelb, Publisher
Ed: Ann Liss, Editor. **Released:** Monthly. **Price:** $35.
Description: Seeks to help emerging growth companies increase profits. Considers small business issues, including marketing sales, finance, taxes, organizing, competition, management, and human resources. Recurring features include letters to the editor, interviews, and columns titled Info Bank, In the Mail Box, Taxes, Human Resources, Marketing, Insurance and Law. **Remarks:** Publication suspended in 1980; resumed publication Fall 1993.

VIDEOCASSETTES/ AUDIOCASSETTES

30356 ■ The Achievement Challenge
4th Generation Systems
113 N. Grant St.
Barrington, IL 60010-3001
Ph: (847)381-7797
Free: 800-227-4332
Fax: (847)381-7301
Co. E-mail: info@4thgenerationsystems.com
URL: http://www.4thgenerationsystems.com
Released: 1988. **Price:** $995.00. **Description:** A series of programs that explain things to be done and attitudes to be taken to do better in business. **Availability:** VHS.

30357 ■ The American Entrepreneur Today
GPN Educational Media
1550 Executive Drive
Elgin, IL 60123
Ph: (402)472-2007
Free: 800-228-4630
Fax: (800 306-2330
Co. E-mail: askgpn@smarterville.com
URL: http://www.shopgpn.com
Released: 1991. **Price:** $785.00. **Description:** A 14-part course focuses on the creativity and dedication needed to making a good idea work. Six successful entrepreneurs offer insight into their business success. Course text is "New Venture Creation: Entrepreneurship in the 1990s" by Jeffry A. Timmons. **Availability:** VHS.

30358 ■ The Applied Management Series
SkillSoft
107 Northeastern Blvd.
Nashua, NH 03062
Ph: (603)324-3000
Free: 877-545-5763
Fax: (603 324-3009
Co. E-mail: information@skillsoft.com
URL: http://www.skillsoft.com
Contact: Chuck Moran, President
Released: 1984. **Description:** This series of four six hour programs will train people in current effective management techniques. **Availability:** 3/4 U.

30359 ■ Business, Careers, and Lifestyle Series
RMI Media
1365 N. Winchester St.
Olathe, KS 66061-5880
Ph: (913)768-1696
Free: 800-745-5480
Fax: (800 755-6910
Co. E-mail: actmedia@act.org
URL: http://www.actmedia.com
Released: 1984. **Description:** In this series of 56 half-hour programs, host Dick Goldberg interviews top business leaders in various fields to find out what it takes to be successful in business. **Availability:** VHS; 3/4 U.

30360 ■ Creativity in Business
Advantage Media
c/o Kantola Productions
55 Sunnyside Ave.
Mill Valley, CA 94941
Ph: (415)381-9363
Free: 800-280-1180
Fax: (415)381-9801
Co. E-mail: kantola@kantola.com
URL: http://www.kantola.com/d/advantage.htm
Contact: Daniel Amos, Chief Executive Officer
Released: 1998. **Price:** $95.00. **Description:** Dr. Michael Ray demonstrates how to apply the principles of consciousness expansion, intuition and creativity to business ventures. **Availability:** VHS.

30361 ■ Decision Making: How to Make Better, Faster, Smarter Decisions
Instructional Video
2219 C St.
Lincoln, NE 68502
Ph: (402)475-6570
Free: 800-228-0164
Fax: (402)475-6500
Co. E-mail: feedback@insvideo.com
URL: http://www.insvideo.com
Released: 19??. **Price:** $59.95. **Description:** Profiles effective decision-making techniques. Includes interactive guidebook. **Availability:** VHS.

30362 ■ Empowerment: How to Receive Work Assignments
International Training Consultants, Inc.
1838 Park Oaks
Kemah, TX 77565
Free: 800-998-8764
Co. E-mail: itc@trainingitc.com
URL: http://www.trainingitc.com
Released: 19??. **Price:** $495.00. **Description:** Part of the "Empowerment: The Employee Development Series." Teaches employees proper procedures in receiving work assignments from their superiors. Includes instruction on how to obtain task objectives, ask for needed details, determine resources available, analyze contraints, ask for training, offer suggestions, and establish performance measures. Emphasis is placed on the employee's knowledge that it is their responsibility to finish the assignment correctly and on time. **Availability:** VHS.

30363 ■ Empowerment: Moving from Criticism to Feedback
International Training Consultants, Inc.
1838 Park Oaks
Kemah, TX 77565
Free: 800-998-8764
Co. E-mail: itc@trainingitc.com
URL: http://www.trainingitc.com
Released: 19??. **Price:** $495.00. **Description:** Part of the "Empowerment: The Employee Development Series." Illustrates proper ways of giving and receiving criticism. Teaches a six-step method which helps turn criticism into constructive feedback. Also discusses methods which help an individual receive criticism without becoming defensive. Comes with leader's guide, self-study instructions, and five participant booklets. **Availability:** VHS.

30364 ■ Empowerment: The Employee Development Series
International Training Consultants, Inc.
1838 Park Oaks
Kemah, TX 77565
Free: 800-998-8764
Co. E-mail: itc@trainingitc.com
URL: http://www.trainingitc.com
Released: 19??. **Price:** $10350.00. **Description:** Employee development series which prepares employees to meet the demands of today's workplace with skill and confidence. Covers such topics as time management, team work, communication, career advancement, working together, and problem solving. Comes with leader's guide, overhead transparencies, five participant booklets, and a complete participant's manual. **Availability:** VHS.

30365 ■ Everything You Always Wanted to Know about Management
American Media, Inc.
4621 121st St.
Urbandale, IA 50323-2311
Ph: (515)224-0919
Free: 888-776-8268
Fax: (515)327-2555
Co. E-mail: custsvc@ammedia.com
URL: http://www.ammedia.com
Released: 1995. **Price:** $595. **Description:** Outlines the essentials of good management, including the six steps of delegation, employee empowerment, communication, feedback, and goal achievement. Includes course guide with participant exercises and case studies. **Availability:** VHS; CC.

30366 ■ The Good Business Basics Series: The Basics of Entrepreneuring
Cambridge Educational
c/o Films Media Group
132 West 31st Street, 17th Floor
Ste. 124
New York, NY 10001
Free: 800-257-5126
Fax: (609)671-0266
Co. E-mail: custserve@films.com
URL: http://www.cambridgeol.com
Released: 1992. **Price:** $98.00. **Description:** So you think you have a good idea. How do you get started in business? This program overviews the basics of getting a business off the ground, from finding a niche in the marketplace, building a staff, learning from others' mistakes, and much more. **Availability:** VHS.

30367 ■ How You Can Start, Build, Manage, or Turn Around Any Business
Nightingale-Conant Corp.
6245 W. Howard St.
Niles, IL 60714
Ph: (847)647-0300
Free: 800-560-6081
URL: http://www.nightingale.com
Released: 19??. **Price:** $395.00. **Description:** Brian Tracy presents a mini-course in business management. **Availability:** VHS.

30368 ■ I Can Do It! Ed Lewis
Direct Cinema Ltd.
PO Box 10003
Santa Monica, CA 90410-1003
Ph: (310)636-8200
Free: 800-525-0000
Fax: (310)636-8228
Co. E-mail: orders@directcinemalimited.com
URL: http://www.directcinema.com
Released: 1984. **Description:** The creator of GMS explains the art, drive and knowledge necessary for successful entrepreneurism. **Availability:** VHS; 3/4 U; Special order formats.

30369 ■ Leadership: Building Rainbows
Eastern Kentucky University
Div. of Media Resources
521 Lancaster Ave.
Richmond, KY 40475-3102
Ph: (859)622-1000
URL: http://www.mediaresources.eku.edu
Released: 1984. **Description:** Professionals in leadership positions looking to gain personal and organizational goals are acquainted with effective persuasive communication skills. **Availability:** VHS.

30370 ■ Product Strategy: All the Right Moves
RMI Media
1365 N. Winchester St.
Olathe, KS 66061-5880
Ph: (913)768-1696
Free: 800-745-5480
Fax: (800)755-6910
Co. E-mail: actmedia@act.org
URL: http://www.actmedia.com
Released: 1991. **Price:** $89.95. **Description:** Presents a case study of Carushka, a dance and exercise wear manufacturer, to demonstrate successful methods for increasing product use and customers; finding new uses for existing products; and broadening the product appeal to old and new markets. **Availability:** VHS.

30371 ■ Speaking of Success
RMI Media
1365 N. Winchester St.
Olathe, KS 66061-5880
Ph: (913)768-1696
Free: 800-745-5480
Fax: (800)755-6910
Co. E-mail: actmedia@act.org
URL: http://www.actmedia.com
Released: 1988. **Price:** $69.95. **Description:** A series of business-oriented programs endeavoring to help the viewer improve his or her self, relations with others, and various manipulative techniques useful in business transactions. **Availability:** VHS; 3/4 U.

30372 ■ Why Study Business?: Skills For the 21st Century
Cambridge Educational
c/o Films Media Group
132 West 31st Street, 17th Floor
Ste. 124
New York, NY 10001
Free: 800-257-5126
Fax: (609)671-0266
Co. E-mail: custserve@films.com
URL: http://www.cambridgeol.com
Released: 1990. **Price:** $98.00. **Description:** Introduces the various facets of the business world, and profiles careers in business which utilize several different skills. **Availability:** VHS.

CONSULTANTS

30373 ■ Association of Home-Based Women Entrepreneurs (HBWE)
PO Box 31561
Saint Louis, MO 63131-1561
Ph: (314)805-9519
Fax: (314)909-8179
Co. E-mail: aschaefer@advbizsol.com
URL: http://www.hbwe.org
Contact: Louise Wiedermann, President
E-mail: lw@projektek.com
Scope: Organization dedicated to women working from home-based offices. Focuses on the needs and interests of women doing their own business. It also focuses on business-related programs and issues, networking, leads and mentoring for professional growth in a dynamic and friendly atmosphere. **Founded:** 1998. **Publications:** "Taking Your Business International"; "Dressing For Success"; "Web 2.0 The Future of the Internet"; "Assertiveness Skills for Women in Business". **Seminars:** Making Connections, Jul, 2008; One Inch Wide, One Mile Deep, Jun, 2008; Accelerating Your Business, May, 2008; Change is Good, Apr, 2008; Pyro Marketing, Jan, 2007; Twenty Five Key Steps To Maintaining A Successful Home-Based Business, Nov, 2006.

30374 ■ Beacon Management - Management Consultants
1000 W McNab Rd.
Pompano Beach, FL 33069
Ph: (954)782-1119
Free: 800-771-8721
Fax: (954)969-2566
Co. E-mail: md@beaconmgmt.com
URL: http://www.beaconmgmt.com
Contact: Joyce Slencak, Manager
Scope: Specializes in change management, organized workplaces, multicultural negotiations and dispute resolutions and internet based decision making. **Founded:** 1985. **Publications:** "Sun-Sentinel Article," Oct, 2012.

30375 ■ Donna Cornell Enterprises Inc.—Cornell Career Center
68 N Plank Rd., Ste. 204
Newburgh, NY 12550-2122
Ph: (845)565-0088
Free: 888-769-3792
Fax: (845)565-0084
Co. E-mail: rc@cornellcareercenter.com
Contact: Donna Cornell, President
E-mail: rc@cornellcareercenter.com
Scope: Offers services in career consultant, professional search, job placement and national professional search. **Founded:** 1996. **Publications:** "The Power of the Woman Within"; "Juggling it All!"; "Journey: A Woman's Guide to Success"; "Shatter the Traditions".

30376 ■ Entrepreneurial Strategies
107 S Yellowstone Ave., Ste. C
Bozeman, MT 59715
Ph: (406)587-5664
Fax: (406)586-0396
Co. E-mail: nfkrueger@rocketmail.com
Contact: Norris F. Krueger, Jr., Principal
E-mail: nfkrueger@hotmail.com
Scope: Academic consultants helping organizations become more entrepreneurial; helping communities

become more entrepreneurial; providing market assessments for 'really new' products and technologies; offering strategic planning and marketing planning.

30377 ■ Third Sector New England Inc. (TSNE)
89 South St., Ste. 700
Boston, MA 02111
Ph: (617)523-6565
Fax: (617)523-2070
Co. E-mail: info@tsne.org
URL: http://www.tsne.org
Contact: Jonathan Spack, Executive Director

Scope: A team of faculty, consultants, project managers, researchers and a variety of strategic alliances provide leadership training, consulting seminars, educational programs, research and conferences. **Founded:** 1959. **Publications:** "Executive Directors Guide"; "Creative Disruption: Sabbaticals for Capacity Building and Leadership Development in the Nonprofit Sector"; "A Step-by-Step Guide to Achieving Diversity in the Workplace"; "Valuing Our Nonprofit Workforce 2010: A Compensation Survey of and for Nonprofits in Massachusetts and Adjoining Communities"; "Shared Services: A Guide to Collaborative Solutions for Nonprofits"; "TSNe-Bulletin". **Seminars:** Supporting Nonprofits and Communities Through the Rough Times.

LIBRARIES

30378 ■ Canadian Federation of Independent Business Research Library
401-4141 Yonge St.
Toronto, ON, Canada M2P 2A6
Ph: (416)222-8022
Free: 888-234-2232
Fax: (416)222-6103
Co. E-mail: cfib@cfib.ca
URL: http://www.cfib-fcei.ca/english/index.html
Contact: Katalin Coorsh, Librarian

Scope: Small business, entrepreneurship, economic policy, politics and government. **Services:** Interlibrary loan; copying; Library open to the public by appointment. **Founded:** 1980. **Holdings:** 4000 volumes; 32 VF drawers of subject files; Annual reports. **Subscriptions:** 100 journals and other serials; 4 newspapers. **Telecommunication Services:** msont@cfib.ca.

RESEARCH CENTERS

30379 ■ Baylor University - Center for Private Enterprise
1 Bear Pl.
Waco, TX 76798
Ph: (254)710-6898
Fax: (254)710-6142
Co. E-mail: kimberly_mencken@baylor.edu
URL: http://www.baylor.edu/business/enterprise
Contact: Kimberly Mencken, Director
Founded: 1978. **Educational Activities:** Economic Forecast Conference; Leaderships programs, for high school seniors; Seminars, in-service workshops, and programs to teach economics, personal finance, and consumer economics, for elementary and secondary teachers.

30380 ■ Boston University - Institute for Technology Entrepreneurship and Commercialization (ITEC)
595 Commonwealth Ave.
Boston, MA 02215
Ph: (617)353-9391
Fax: (617)353-1695
Co. E-mail: pmcmanus@bu.edu
URL: http://www.bu.edu/itec
Contact: Paul McManus, Managing Director
Founded: 2006. **Publications:** *ITEC Newsletter* (Monthly). **Educational Activities:** Annual Business Plan Competition; Business Plan Boot Camp; Entrepreneurial Research Lab (Annual). **Telecommunication Services:** itec@bu.edu.

30381 ■ Lehigh University - Small Business Development Center (SBDC)
125 Goodman Dr.
Bethlehem, PA 18015
Ph: (610)758-3980
Fax: (610)758-5205
Co. E-mail: insbdc@lehigh.edu
URL: http://www.lehigh.edu/~insbdc/index.html
Contact: Sandra F. Holsonback, Executive Director
Services: Administers various loan pools for lending to small businesses; Consulting and research in management assistance, international trade, government marketing, and financing assistance; Lehigh University Management Assistance Counseling (LUMAC) Program: a field studies course for senior students. **Founded:** 1978. **Publications:** *Financing Your Business*; *Market Planning Guide*; *Export Plan-*

ning Guide; *Financing Guide for Northampton*; *Lehigh and Berks County*; *Lehigh Valley Business Support Services*. **Educational Activities:** SBDC Seminars. **Awards:** Business analyst positions with tuition and stipend. **Telecommunication Services:** shl2@lehigh.edu.

30382 ■ New York University - Berkley Center for Entrepreneurial Studies (BCES)
NYU Stern School of Business, Ste. 7-150, KMC
44 W 4th St.
New York, NY 10012
Ph: (212)998-0070
Fax: (212)995-4211
Co. E-mail: jeffrey.carr@stern.nyu.edu
URL: http://w4.stern.nyu.edu/berkley
Contact: Jeffrey A. Carr, Executive Director
Founded: 1984. **Publications:** *Case series*; *BCES Working papers*. **Educational Activities:** Business Plan Competition; BCES Conferences; Entrepreneur in Residence Program; Forums and workshops. **Awards:** Harold Price Entrepreneurship Award; Rennert Entrepreneurial Prize; Gloria Appel Fellowship; Price Institute for Entrepreneurial Studies Fellowship.

30383 ■ Southern Methodist University - Caruth Institute of Entrepreneurship
Fincher Bldg., Rm. 143
Cox School of Business
Dallas, TX 75275-0333
Ph: (214)768-3689
Fax: (214)768-3604
Co. E-mail: jwhite@cox.smu.edu
URL: http://www.cox.smu.edu/web/caruth-institute
Contact: Prof. Jerry F. White, Director
Founded: 1970. **Publications:** *Caruth Institute of Entrepreneurship Newsletter*. **Educational Activities:** Southwest Venture Forum; Bimonthly Breakfast Meeting. **Awards:** Dallas 100 Award, recognizing the 100 fastest growing private companies in Dallas.

30384 ■ University of British Columbia - W. Maurice Young Entrepreneurship and Venture Capital Research Centre
Sauder School of Business
2053 Main Mall
Vancouver, BC, Canada V6T 1Z2
Ph: (604)822-8476
Fax: (604)822-8477
Co. E-mail: hellmann@sauder.ubc.ca
URL: http://evc.sauder.ubc.ca
Contact: Thomas F. Hellman, Director
Founded: 1992. **Publications:** *Industry reports*. **Educational Activities:** Entrepreneurship Luncheon (Annual).

ASSOCIATIONS AND OTHER ORGANIZATIONS

30385 ■ The Entrepreneurship Institute (TEI)
3700 Corporate Dr., Ste. 145
Columbus, OH 43231
Ph: (614)895-1153
Co. E-mail: info@tei.net
URL: http://www.tei.net
Contact: Dr. Jan W. Zupnick, President
Description: Provides encouragement and assistance to entrepreneurs who operate companies with revenue in excess of $1 million. Unites financial, legal, and community resources to help foster the success of companies. Promotes sharing of information and interaction between members. Operates President's forums and projects which are designed to improve communication between businesses, develop one-to-one business relationships between small and mid-size businesses and local resources, provide networking, and stimulate the growth of existing companies. **Scope:** growth strategies, accounting, finance, investments 401K. **Founded:** 1976. **Subscriptions:** audiovisuals books software. **Publications:** *The President's Forum* (Monthly). **Educational Activities:** The Entrepreneurship Institute Meeting (Periodic).

EDUCATIONAL PROGRAMS

30386 ■ Building XML Web Services with Java- Hands-On (Onsite)
Seminar Information Service, Inc.
20 Executive Park, Ste. 120
Irvine, CA 92614
Ph: (949)261-9104
Free: 877-SEM-INFO
Fax: (949)261-1963
Co. E-mail: info@seminarinformation.com
URL: http://www.seminarinformation.com
Price: $2,890.00. **Description:** Learn how to: Develop and deploy Web services with Java and XML; Describe the functionality of Web services using WSDL; Write interoperable SOAP-based services and clients using JAX-RPC; Generate Java source files for services from WSDL and XML schemas; Customize SOAP messages using SAAJ; Implement strategies to secure your Web services; Locate Web services in XML registries using JAXR. **Dates and Locations:** New York, NY; Reston, VA; Rockville, MD; and Toronto, CN.

30387 ■ Building XML Web Services with .NET: Hands-On (Onsite)
Seminar Information Service, Inc.
20 Executive Park, Ste. 120
Irvine, CA 92614
Ph: (949)261-9104
Free: 877-SEM-INFO
Fax: (949)261-1963
Co. E-mail: info@seminarinformation.com
URL: http://www.seminarinformation.com
Price: $2,890.00. **Description:** Learn how to: Develop highly scalable distributed applications with XML Web services; Process XML documents with System.Xml library classes; Describe and publish Web services using standard protocols (SOAP, WSDL); Leverage ASP.NET for rapid development and monitoring of Web services; Build high-performance multithreaded and Web clients; Secure XML Web services using encryption and authentication. **Dates and Locations:** Toronto, CN; and New York, NY.

30388 ■ Cascading Style Sheets CSS for Web Page Development (Onsite)
Seminar Information Service, Inc.
20 Executive Park, Ste. 120
Irvine, CA 92614
Ph: (949)261-9104
Free: 877-SEM-INFO
Fax: (949)261-1963
Co. E-mail: info@seminarinformation.com
URL: http://www.seminarinformation.com
Price: $2,490.00. **Description:** Learn how to: Develop fast, efficient, accessible and attractive Web pages using CSS; Generate tableless page layouts with pure CSS; Structure site layout and content to make your site faster and more maintainable; Apply best practices to develop cross-browser compatible Web pages and avoid pitfalls; Implement menu designs for effective site navigation; Create Web sites that meet Section 508 and W3C accessibility standards. **Dates and Locations:** New York, NY; Reston, VA; and Rockville, MD.

30389 ■ Cisco Networking Introduction: Hands-On (Onsite)
Seminar Information Service, Inc.
20 Executive Park, Ste. 120
Irvine, CA 92614
Ph: (949)261-9104
Free: 877-SEM-INFO
Fax: (949)261-1963
Co. E-mail: info@seminarinformation.com
URL: http://www.seminarinformation.com
Price: $2,890.00. **Description:** Learn how to: Successfully install and configure Cisco routers and switches to build internetworks; Create Cisco device configurations from scratch; Configure IP routing protocols; Troubleshoot complex IP routing problems; Perform software and hardware upgrades; Effectively manage and maintain Cisco routers with SNMP. **Dates and Locations:** New York, NY; El Segundo, CA; Atlanta, GA; Reston, VA; and Rockville, MD.

30390 ■ Database Design for Web Development
EEI Communications
8945 Guilford Rd., Ste. 145
Columbia, MD 21046
Ph: (410)309-8200
Free: 888-253-2762
Fax: (410)630-3980
Co. E-mail: train@eeicom.com
URL: http://www.eeicom.com/eei-training-services
Price: $745.00. **Description:** Web designers learn how to design and structure a database efficiently. **Dates and Locations:** Silver Spring, MD; Hunt Valley, MD; Columbia, MD; and Alexandria, VA.

30391 ■ Developing AJAX Web Applications: Hands-On - Enhancing the Web User Experience (Onsite)
Seminar Information Service, Inc.
20 Executive Park, Ste. 120
Irvine, CA 92614
Ph: (949)261-9104
Free: 877-SEM-INFO
Fax: (949)261-1963
Co. E-mail: info@seminarinformation.com
URL: http://www.seminarinformation.com
Price: $2,890.00. **Description:** Learn how to: Develop AJAX-powered interactive and dynamic Web sites; Design accessible interfaces for cross-browser compatibility; Integrate frameworks for data exchange on multiple server environments; Leverage toolkits to rapidly create rich user-friendly interfaces; Optimize and strengthen code to build stable applications; Protect vital information from interception. **Dates and Locations:** Ottawa, CN; Reston, VA; and New York, NY.

30392 ■ Developing a Web Site: Hands-On (Onsite)
Seminar Information Service, Inc.
20 Executive Park, Ste. 120
Irvine, CA 92614
Ph: (949)261-9104
Free: 877-SEM-INFO
Fax: (949)261-1963
Co. E-mail: info@seminarinformation.com
URL: http://www.seminarinformation.com
Price: $2,890.00. **Description:** Learn how to: Establish, configure and maintain an intranet or Internet Web site; Develop and publish Web pages using HyperText Markup Language (HTML); Create image maps to allow easy navigation of your Web site; Configure a Web server; Capture, retrieve and display information via a database; Produce dynamic Web pages using server-side and client-side scripts. **Dates and Locations:** Reston, VA; Alexandria, VA; Rockville, MD; New York, NY; Toronto, CN; and Ottawa, CN.

30393 ■ Internet Marketing
EEI Communications
8945 Guilford Rd., Ste. 145
Columbia, MD 21046
Ph: (410)309-8200
Free: 888-253-2762
Fax: (410)630-3980
Co. E-mail: train@eeicom.com
URL: http://www.eeicom.com/eei-training-services
Price: $745.00. **Description:** Covers how businesses can use the Internet to market products, including increasing traffic to your site, and measuring results. **Dates and Locations:** Alexandria, VA.

30394 ■ .NET Best Practices and Design Patterns: Hands-On - Building Successful Applications with Proven Techniques (Onsite)
Seminar Information Service, Inc.
20 Executive Park, Ste. 120
Irvine, CA 92614
Ph: (949)261-9104

Free: 877-SEM-INFO
Fax: (949)261-1963
Co. E-mail: info\@seminarinformation.com
URL: http://www.seminarinformation.com
Price: $2,890.00. **Description:** Learn to apply proven methods to build adaptable, secure and efficient .NET Web and smart client applications; Solve complex programming problems with industry-standard design patterns; Deliver bug-free code using test-driven development, NUnit and Visual Studio 2005; Increase team productivity by building a scalable business application framework; Protect applications and data with code-based and role-based security and encryption; Simplify complex and repetitive tasks using .NET reflection and custom attributes. **Dates and Locations:** Cities throughout the United States and Ottawa and Toronto, CN.

30395 ■ SharePoint I (Onsite)
EEI Communications
8945 Guilford Rd., Ste. 145
Columbia, MD 21046
Ph: (410)309-8200
Free: 888-253-2762
Fax: (410)630-3980
Co. E-mail: train\@eeicom.com
URL: http://www.eeicom.com/eei-training-services
Price: $797.00. **Description:** Learn how to simplify team collaboration using Windows SharePoint Services. **Dates and Locations:** Silver Spring, MD; Columbia, MD; and Alexandria, VA.

30396 ■ SharePoint II (Onsite)
EEI Communications
8945 Guilford Rd., Ste. 145
Columbia, MD 21046
Ph: (410)309-8200
Free: 888-253-2762
Fax: (410)630-3980
Co. E-mail: train\@eeicom.com
URL: http://www.eeicom.com/eei-training-services
Price: $1,097.00. **Description:** Learn skills to design, maintain, and publish a custom SharePoint site. **Dates and Locations:** Columbia, MD; Silver Spring, MD; and Alexandria, VA.

30397 ■ SharePoint III (Onsite)
EEI Communications
8945 Guilford Rd., Ste. 145
Columbia, MD 22314
Ph: (410)309-8200
Free: 888-253-2762
Fax: (410)630-3980
Co. E-mail: train\@eeicom.com
URL: http://www.eeicom.com/eei-training-services
Price: $1,097.00. **Description:** Learn how to create and make modifications that can be applied to all users on the site or to individual users using Microsoft SharePoint controls, as well as how to apply personalization to Web pages so that when users modify pages and controls, the settings can be saved to retain a user's personal preferences. **Dates and Locations:** Alexandria, VA.

30398 ■ Web Design
EEI Communications
8945 Guilford Rd., Ste. 145
Columbia, MD 21046
Ph: (410)309-8200
Free: 888-253-2762
Fax: (410)630-3980
Co. E-mail: train\@eeicom.com
URL: http://www.eeicom.com/eei-training-services
Price: $745.00. **Description:** Covers various aspects of graphic interface design for World Wide Web sites, including site conception; navigational and schematic design; processes from delivery of content to page layout for HTML; editorial, informational, and navigational graphics; and related topics. **Dates and Locations:** Silver Spring, MD; Alexandria, VA; Hunt Valley, MD; and Columbia, MD.

30399 ■ Webinars with a WOW Factor: Creating Memorable Meeting Across the Globe (Onsite)
Seminar Information Service, Inc.
20 Executive Park, Ste. 120
Irvine, CA 92614
Ph: (949)261-9104

Free: 877-SEM-INFO
Fax: (949)261-1963
Co. E-mail: info\@seminarinformation.com
URL: http://www.seminarinformation.com
Price: $1,595.00. **Description:** Discover techniques that will make your material come to life on the screen and over the phone. **Dates and Locations:** Minneapolis, MN.

30400 ■ Writing for the Web I (Onsite)
EEI Communications
8945 Guilford Rd., Ste. 145
Columbia, MD 21046
Ph: (410)309-8200
Free: 888-253-2762
Fax: (410)630-3980
Co. E-mail: train\@eeicom.com
URL: http://www.eeicom.com/eei-training-services
Price: $797.00. **Description:** Covers how to write and edit for sites on the World Wide Web, including understanding the Web's strengths and limitations, providing your audience the information it needs, organizing information with flowcharts and site maps, and using techniques of multimedia writing. **Dates and Locations:** Columbia, MD; and Silver Spring.

30401 ■ (X)HTML and CSS I (Onsite)
EEI Communications
8945 Guilford Rd., Ste. 145
Columbia, MD 21046
Ph: (410)309-8200
Free: 888-253-2762
Fax: (410)630-3980
Co. E-mail: train\@eeicom.com
URL: http://www.eeicom.com/eei-training-services
Price: $497.00. **Description:** Covers the fundamentals of Web page design, including formatting text, using graphics in a Web page, creating links, making simple tables in HTML, and avoiding common page design flaws. **Dates and Locations:** Columbia, MD; Silver Spring, MD; and Alexandria, VA.

30402 ■ (X)HTML and CSS II (Onsite)
EEI Communications
8945 Guilford Rd., Ste. 145
Columbia, MD 21046
Ph: (410)309-8200
Free: 888-253-2762
Fax: (410)630-3980
Co. E-mail: train\@eeicom.com
URL: http://www.eeicom.com/eei-training-services
Price: $497.00. **Description:** Covers intermediate Web page design techniques, including creating forms, including radio buttons and check boxes, creating transparent and interlaced GIFs, using tables for page layout, and creating client-side image maps. **Dates and Locations:** Columbia, MD; Silver Spring, MD; and Alexandria, VA.

30403 ■ (X)HTML and CSS III (Onsite)
EEI Communications
8945 Guilford Rd., Ste. 145
Columbia, MD 21046
Ph: (410)309-8200
Free: 888-253-2762
Fax: (410)630-3980
Co. E-mail: train\@eeicom.com
URL: http://www.eeicom.com/eei-training-services
Price: $497.00. **Description:** Covers advanced Web page development techniques, including using frames, animated GIFs, cascading style sheets, and javascript. **Dates and Locations:** Columbia, MD; Silver Spring, MD; and Alexandria, VA.

CONSULTANTS

30404 ■ Creative Computer Resources Inc.
5001 Horizons Dr., Ste. 200
Columbus, OH 43220-5291
Ph: (614)384-7557
Free: 866-720-0209

Fax: (614)573-6331
Co. E-mail: team\@planet-ccr.com
URL: http://www.planet-ccr.com
Contact: M. Erik Mueller, President
E-mail: merikm\@planet-ccr.com
Scope: Offers information systems support, custom software development, website design, development and implementation. Provides information technology support and management services to small and mid-size businesses. **Founded:** 1996.

RESEARCH CENTERS

30405 ■ Corporation for Enterprise Development (CFED)
1200 G St. NW, Ste. 400
Washington, DC 20005
Ph: (202)408-9788
Fax: (202)408-9793
Co. E-mail: info\@cfed.org
URL: http://www.cfed.org
Contact: Andrea Levere, President
E-mail: a.evere\@cfed.org
Description: Provides assistance to public and private organizations concerned with increasing economic opportunity of individuals through the encouragement and support of enterprise development; serves as a forum for the exchange of ideas. Strives to research, develop, and disseminate entrepreneurial policy initiatives at the local, state, and federal levels. Conducts consulting services and compiles statistics. **Scope:** Offers expertise in economic research. Offers services as identify promising ideas, test and refine them in communities to find out what works, craft policies and products to help good ideas reach scale, and foster new markets to achieve greater economic impact. **Founded:** 1979. **Publications:** "Children's Savings Accounts and Financial Aid"; "Linking Youth Savings and Entrepreneurship". **Educational Activities:** Assets Learning Conference (Biennial). **Seminars:** Fighting Poverty: The Role of Asset Building in Public Policy; IDAS and Microenterprise; Self-Sustaining IDA Initiatives; Serving Multi-Cultural Markets; Asset Purchase Effective Practices; Policy Proposals, Opportunities, and Barriers for Youth Savings. **Telecommunication Services:** info-dc\@cfed.org; alevere\@cfed.org.

30406 ■ University of California, Los Angeles - Harold and Pauline Price Center for Entrepreneurial Studies
Anderson Graduate School of Management
110 Westwood Plz., Rm. C305
Los Angeles, CA 90095-1481
Ph: (310)825-2985
Fax: (310)206-9102
Co. E-mail: esctr\@anderson.ucla.edu
URL: http://www.anderson.ucla.edu/price.xml
Contact: Elaine K. Hagan, Executive Director
E-mail: elaine.hagan\@anderson.ucla.edu
Founded: 1987. **Educational Activities:** Annual entrepreneurship conference for business people and students, in the spring; Research grants for selected faculty members for entrepreneurially related work; Roundtable sessions, entrepreneur-in-residence series, mentor programs, speaker series, venture proposal competitions, and student investment fund; Sponsors certificate programs in management development for entrepreneurs in various industries, including telecommunications and directors of early child care programs; Venture Fellows Program.

30407 ■ University of South Florida - Small Business Development Center (SBDC)
1101 Channelside Dr., Ste. 210
Tampa, FL 33602
Ph: (813)905-5800
Fax: (813)905-5801
Co. E-mail: sbdc\@coba.usf.edu
URL: http://www.sbdctampabay.com
Contact: Eileen Rodriguez, Director
Services: Counseling. **Founded:** 1980. **Publications:** *Entrepreneurial Training Schedule* (Monthly); *Minding Your Own Business* (3/year). **Educational Activities:** Entrepreneurship seminars; Government contracting trade fair; Seminars on Small Business

Management (Monthly); Small Business Trade Conference; SBDC Training; Women Executive Forum.
Awards: Two graduate paid internships.

CPSIA information can be obtained
at www.ICGtesting.com
Printed in the USA
FFOW051026250313
1030FF